SCRABBLE®
BRAND Crossword Game

LISTS

HarperCollins Publishers
Westerhill Road
Bishopbriggs
Glasgow
G64 2QT
Great Britain

Revised first edition 2006

© HarperCollins Publishers 2005, 2006

ISBN-13 978-0-00-720648-3
ISBN-10 0-00-720648-8

www.collins.co.uk

A catalogue record for this book is available
from the British Library

This book is set in CollinsFedra,
a typeface specially created for Collins
dictionaries by Peter Bil'ak.

Typeset by ISL, Gloucester, UK

Printed in Germany by Bercker

FOR THE PUBLISHER
Morven Dooner
Elaine Higgleton
Elspeth Summers

COMPUTING SUPPORT
Thomas Callan

Contents

Introduction

Collins Scrabble Lists is the companion volume to *Collins Scrabble Words*, the official wordlist for Scrabble. While *Words* contains the complete list of words that are valid in Scrabble, *Lists* provides strategies for memorising the most useful of these words.

With over 260,000 words eligible for play in Scrabble, it is virtually impossible for anyone to learn them all. What this book does is to provide the best of the words – those that are most useful in the game – in a manner in which they can be easily learned and remembered for Scrabble situations. Essentially, *Collins Scrabble Lists* is a manual of tactics for learning different groups of words and spotting opportunities to play them during a game.

The lists in this book bring to the fore a great many words that will be unfamiliar to most people, and even to most Scrabble players. By adding these words to their vocabulary, players are equipping themselves with a powerful arsenal that they can deploy on the Scrabble board. These words, and the varied approaches to word-learning in this book, should enable any player to improve his or her game, no matter what level he or she plays at.

Foreword – My Top 100 Words

Philip Nelkon, Manager — Scrabble Promotions and Licensing, Mattel Inc.

Picking 100 words from the many thousands that feature in *Collins Scrabble Lists* is rather like being shown the wonders of the whole world and then being asked to live on a rock in the Pacific. I've tried, however, even with this small sample, to give a flavour of all of the words in the book.

My main principle in selecting such words has been usefulness for playing Scrabble. If you learn just a few of them, I'm sure they'll increase the scores you get. I've included a lot of words that will not be in most people's general vocabulary, although, having said that, it's amazing how often a word that you have learnt for Scrabble crops up in 'real life'. I well remember watching a play about an unsuccessful expedition to Africa in the nineteenth century, where one of the characters staggered about the stage shouting 'Atebrin, atebrin!' and thinking, somewhat smugly, to myself that I must have been one of the few people in the audience who knew that ATEBRIN was a medicine used against malaria – a fact I had learnt when adding the word to my Scrabble vocabulary.

I did indulge myself slightly by picking ten words that just sounded good, the reason why you'll find BORSCHT and SQUAMAE in the list and surely one of the most unbelievable – KGOTLAS.

Whether you're looking to become the next World Scrabble Champion or just to learn a few words to enable you to turn the tables on that friend or relation who always seems to beat you. I'm sure you'll find that *Collins Scrabble Lists* is an invaluable addition to your armoury.

ACOEMETI:	Byzantine monks
AEGIRINE:	green mineral
AIA:	maidservant or nursemaid
AINEE:	elder
AL:	Chaucerian spelling of all
ALA:	wing or winglike structure
ALEURONE:	protein found in the oute
ANESTRA:	periods of sexual inacti
ATEBRIN:	drug formerly used to t
AZO:	consisting of, or cont:
BAGH:	garden
BOHO:	bohemian
BORSHCHT:	Russian and Polish soup based

GN

GRE

IDEE:

INDUCIA

ISATINE:

ITA:

IZARD:

JAFA:

JIAO:

JINN:

de

wig

CH: dialect word for I

CHOG: core of a piece of fruit

DEBE: tin

DEF: very good

EAU: water

EGOITIES: personalities

ENTERATE: possessing an alimentary canal

EQUID: equine

ERIONITE: white crystalline mineral

ET: and

ETAERIO: aggregate fruit such as the raspberry

ETESIAN: recurring annually in the summer

ETOURDIE: foolish

EUOI: cry of Dionysian frenzy

EUOUAE: Gregorian cadence

FAQIR: Muslim ascetic

FY: fie

AUJE: Scots word for a fellow

OW: ground-dwelling bird

: group of plants from the same hybrid parent group

idea or concept

E: time by which a defendant must appear in court

yellowish-red crystalline compound

type of palm tree

sure-footed goat antelope

offensive name for a person from Auckland

unit of Chinese currency

mon in Muslim belief

JO:	Scots word for sweetheart
KEX:	hollow-stemmed plant
KGOTLAS:	assemblies of Botswanan elders
KOMITAJI:	Balkan guerilla
KY:	cattle
LAIRISE:	dress flashily
METANOIA:	repentance
MYXO:	myxomatosis
NABK:	edible berries of the Zizyphys Lotus tree
NARQUOIS:	malicious
NIDI:	nests of small animals
NODI:	problematic situation
ODEA:	buildings for musical performances
OESTRAL:	of the period of sexual receptivity in female mammals
OXO:	containing oxygen
PHIZ:	face or facial expression
QADI:	Muslim judge
QAID:	Muslim leader
QANAT:	ancient water-supply system
QAT:	evergreen shrub
QI:	vital energy in Chinese medicine
QIBLA:	direction of the Kaaba in Mecca
QOPH:	letter of the Hebrew alphabet
QUAT:	evergreen shrub
QUENA:	Andean flute
REORIENT:	adjust or align in a new or different way
RESIDUA:	residues
SAOUARI:	butternut tree
SEROTINE:	insectivorous bat

SHEQEL:	currency of Israel
SIPE:	ooze
SOHO:	exclamation announcing the sighting of a hare
SQUAMAE:	scales or scalelike structures
SQUEG:	oscillate irregularly
SWARAJ:	self-government
TAENIAE:	headbands
TAI:	member of the Tai-speaking tribes of Southeast Asia
TALA:	standard monetary unit of Samoa
TALAQ:	Muslim divorce
TANH:	hyperbolic tangent
TRANQ:	tranquilizer
TWAL:	Scots variant of twelve
UINTAITE:	natural bitumen
URINOSE:	of urine
VATU:	standard monetary unit of Vanuatu
VEGO:	vegetarian
WAQF:	charitable donation of land
WILI:	ghost of a betrothed girl who died before her wedding
WUD:	Scots word for wood
VUDU:	Islamic practice of ritual washing before daily prayer
JLL:	will
:	casual term of address
λ	fourteenth letter of the Greek alphabet
ZED.	Vietnamese unit of currency
ZERDA:	the letter Z
ZITI:	fennec fox
ZO:	pasta tubes
	Tibetan animal bred from cows and yaks

Chapter 1: Forming Words

The key to successful Scrabble is constant awareness of the various opportunities for forming words on the board. At the end of a game, the Scrabble board looks like a completed crossword – but always remember that it looks like an American crossword, with blocks of letters in which many short words are contained, rather than a British crossword where words intersect each other without overlap. Indeed, Scrabble was invented by a crossword enthusiast, Alfred Butts; as Mr Butts was American, the US type of crossword was the model for the game.

	U_1	R_1	I_1	N_1		M_3	I_1	A_1					P_3	
						O_1		N_1					I_1	
						V_4		Y_4					L_1	
				D_2	E_1								E_1	
				J_8	E_1	E_1	R_1			L_1	A_1	C_3	E_1	D_2
	Z_{10}			T_1	O_1	M_3	B_3			F_4	U_1	G_2		
	E_1			I_1		T_1			Q_{10}	A_1	T_1			
O_1	A_1	K_5		N_1		S_1	H_4	I_1	N_1	E_1	S_1			
F_4		O_1	A_1	T_1							O_1			
	O_1		B_3								S_1			
	T_1		L_1			V_4	I_1	R_1	G_2	E_1	S_1			
	R_1	U_1	E_1			D_2								
N_1	Y_4		R_1	I_1	D_2	G_2	E_1			C_3	H_4	E_1	E_1	R_1
I_1						A_1	W_4	A_1	I_1	T_1				
X_8	O_1	A_1	N_1	A_1		P_3	L_1	O_1	W_4					

The board looks like this because Scrabble words can be formed in seve[n] other than by simply playing the new word so that it intersects a word a[lrea]rd. the board through a common letter, or adding letters to an exis[ting] ame, Scrabble veterans know this already, of course; if you are new t[o] nto the however, you might want to read the rest of this chapter before mo[v] lists themselves.

When words are formed in ways other than simple intersectio[n] expansion, more than one new word will be created in the process, giving a h[igh]er score. The two main ways of doing this are 'hooking' and 'tagging'.

Hooking

Hooking is a Scrabble term for the act of 'hanging' one word on another – the word already on the board acts as a 'hook' on which the other word can be hung – changing the first word in the process. When you form a word by hooking, you add a letter to the beginning or end of a word already on the board in the process, transforming it into a longer word as you do so, as in the following example:

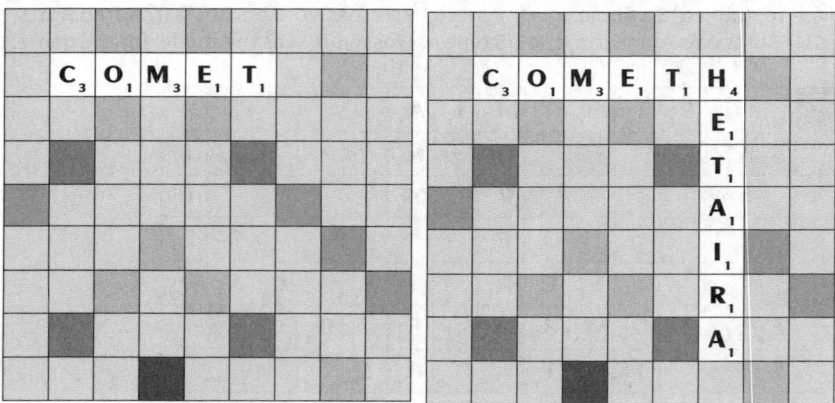

In this situation, you get the points for COMETH (13) as well as for HETAIRA. COMET is thus an 'end-hook', allowing any word with an H or S to be 'hung' on it. S is a particularly useful letter when hooking, as most nouns have a plural formed by adding an S to the end of the singular form.

Here you g... he 13 points for FOX as well as those for FICKLE. So you can see that hooking is gen... ally a much more profitable method of word-formation than

Collins Scrabble Lis...

simply playing a word through, or adjacent to, one that is already on the board. In particular, hooking allows you to benefit from high-scoring 'power tiles' that your opponent has played, as with the X in FOX in the above example.

Obviously, only certain words can act as hooks. Those that cannot form other words by having a letter added to their front or back are known as blockers, as they prevent other players from adding words by hooking.

Tagging

Playing a word parallel to one already on the board, so that one or more tiles are in contact, is known as tagging. Tagging is more difficult than hooking because you need to form one additional word for each tile in contact with the word already on the board. In most circumstances, these will be two-letter words, which is why these short words are so vital to the game. The more two-letter words you know, the greater your opportunities for fitting words onto the board through tagging – and of running up some impressive scores!

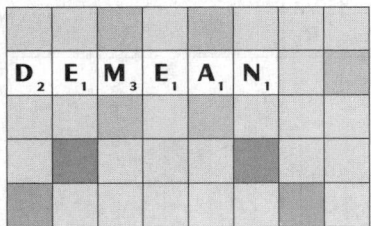 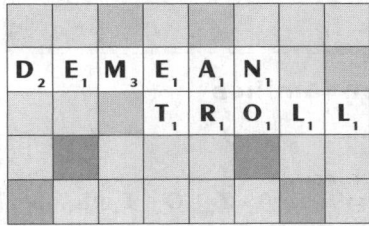

In the example above, playing TROLL thus forms ET, AR and NO (all valid two-letter words), adding the scores for these three words to the points you make from TROLL.

In theory, you could form eight words at once by tagging (though this is unlikely to happen very often!). Consider the following situation:

If you had the letters AEINRST, you could play RETINAS as shown above, earning the points for RETINAS, the 50-point bonus for using all your tiles, plus the points for RE, EX, TI, IT, NA and SCREED, giving you a very decent score indeed!

Short words are obviously very handy for tagging, as in the following examples:

```
A N A                        A N A
N O M A D I C                N O M A D I C
      N O T            S O         N O T
                       A M
                       T A R
                       L O
                       Y A
                       R
```

Word families

```
    A Z O T E      Z O D I A C
A Z O N     D Z O       O U Z O
    A Z O      Z O A
V I Z O R      Z O      Z O E A
      Z O O         Z O O T
Z O N E      Z O O M
O Z O N E      Z O N O I D
```

While hooking and tagging are lucrative ways of forming words, the bread and butter of Scrabble is still expanding words already on the board by adding letters to the beginning, end or both. The Word Families diagrams in Chapter 2 show how 30 of the most interesting short words in Scrabble can be expanded by successive additions of letters. This is useful not only when one of these short words is on the board, but also when you spot it on your rack – there may be a longer, and thus higher-scoring, word there as well.

Learning some of the word families allows you a degree of lateral thinking during games, as you will be able to think of words other than by length, frequency or meaning. This fresh approach can be particularly helpful when you find yourself frustrated by your tiles and the situation on the board; recalling some of the word families may enable you to spot 'building blocks' for high-scoring words.

Short words

Two-letter words are essential for tagging: generally, you need one two-letter word for every 'point of contact'. Three-letter words are also very useful in Scrabble, as a crowded board will often prevent you from playing longer words late in the game. Moreover, some very respectable scores can be generated by tagging with three-letter words – creating more two-letter words in the process. Chapter 3 lists all the two- and three-letter words that are valid for Scrabble.

				D_2	U_1	G_2								
			S_1	O_1		I_1	C_3	E_1						
			I_1	N_1			V_4	E_1	E_1					
		Q_{10}	A_1	T_1		T_1	I_1	E_1						
L_1	E_1	I_1						I_1	W_4	I_1				
O_1						A_1	L_1	F_4						
O_1	R_1			R_1	I_1	D_2								
E_1	L_1		J_8	A_1	Y_4		O_1	A_1	K_5					
	E_1		I_1	R_1	E_1			A_1	M_3		T_1			
	A_1	D_2	Z_{10}					E_1	X_8	O_1				
		A_1							I_1					
								S_1	U_1	N_1				

While many of these words will be familiar, it's a good idea to equip yourself with some of the less common ones, as knowing whether a given combination of two or three letters is a valid word can be vital when you are trying to get a high-scoring set of tiles onto the board through tagging or hooking.

Power tiles

It's important to use the 'power tiles' – J, Q, X and Z – wisely when they land on your rack. Chapter 4 gives lists of words that use these letters. Learning some of these words will help you to employ the power tiles judiciously when they appear on your rack. Of especial interest here are words that use Q but not U, as these allow you to avoid the problem of needing to find a U to play your high-scoring Q tile.

In the average two-player Scrabble game, you are likely to have two of the power tiles on your rack at some point during play. It's a very good idea, therefore, to give some thought to how best to use these tiles, as they are easily wasted on fairly mediocre plays. Learning 'power tile' words will help you to manoeuvre your power tiles onto premium squares for high scores.

Bonus words

Always remember that no matter how many words you form, you are likely to achieve a higher score by playing all seven of your letters in one go, as this earns you a 50-point bonus. It takes a lot of power tiles or bonus squares to achieve 50 points, so playing a bonus word – or 'bingo', as they are known in the US – is the most reliable method of getting an impressive score, which is why much of this book concentrates on ways of achieving bonus words (Chapter 7).

A bonus play generally involves a word of seven or eight letters – either by tagging or hooking a complete seven-letter word onto a word already on the board, or by forming an eight-letter word intersecting an existing word by playing all seven tiles.

The various lists in this section will help you to remember bonus words in a variety of ways, including devising mnemonic sentences or phrases to help you to remember which groups of tiles form either seven- or eight-letter words.

Variants

A resourceful Scrabble player will always remember that many words can be spelt in different ways. Chapter 8 provides useful lists of these variants, which give you options when trying to fit your letters onto a crowded Scrabble board.

Collins Scrabble Lists 2005 includes many old-fashioned or archaic spellings, which are not usually part of a player's general vocabulary. Studying some of these unusual variants can enable you to spring a few surprises on your opponents – and there is a particular satisfaction to be had when your opponent challenges a word that you know to be valid!

This section of the book also includes a list of verbs that *don't* have both -ISE and -IZE forms, as the list of those that do would take up too much space. Learning the exceptions to the -ISE/-IZE rule can help you to avoid tempting but invalid letter combinations – and thus stop you squandering a turn by playing a word that your opponent can successfully challenge.

							M_3	E_1	T_1	R_1	E_1			
							E_1							
							T_1							
						C_3	E_1	N_1	T_1	R_1	E_1			
		V_4	E_1	N_1	D_2	E_1	R_1							
		E_1				N_1			W_4	I_1	N_1	Y_4		
		N_1				T_1			I_1					
		D_2		D_2	A_1	E_1	M_3	O_1	N_1					
		O_1		E_1		R_1			E_1					
		R_1		M_3					Y_4					
				O_1										
		B_3	O_1	N_1	I_1	E_1								
		O_1												
		N_1												
		Y_4												

Hooks and blockers

You are unlikely to be able to play bonus words every turn, however many seven- and eight-letter combinations you know. It's therefore equally important to be able to make best use of your tiles when there is no opportunity for a bonus play. That's where tagging and two-letter words come in so useful, and why the second chapter of this book is devoted to short words. Hooking can be equally handy, and Chapter 9 lists both hooks and blockers – words that can't be hooked onto. Hooks also often represent the best chance of playing a bonus word, particularly if you can form a full word with the tiles on your rack.

Blockers are useful for preventing your opponent from capitalizing on words that you have played, and for blocking off sections of the board. If you are ahead on the scoreboard in the latter part of a game, you may wish to concentrate on blockers to prevent your opponent from getting further opportunities to play high-scoring words.

S_1								M_3	Y_4		B_3			
C_3	H_4	O_1	O_1	K_5	S_1						E_1			
R_1					H_4		T_1	H_4	A_1	T_1	Z_{10}			
U_1					E_1									
M_3					A_1		M_3		P_3	A_1	X_8			R_1
		A_1	T_1		A_1									E_1
		S_1	P_3	E_1	N_1	T_1				G_2				S_1
		S_1			T_1					A_1				O_1
E_1	H_4	E_1			E_1					S_1				L_1
	O_1	N_1			R_1					H_4				D_2
	A_1	T_1	A_1											
	R_1	A_1	S_1	P_3	Y_4			F_4	O_1	E_1	T_1	I_1	D_2	
		E_1												

Anagrams

Perhaps the most essential Scrabble skill is the ability to find anagrams for any given word – or set of letters. Chapter 10 lists all the valid anagrams for each combination of seven or eight letters.

It's well worth committing some of these sets of anagrams to memory, as it's exceptionally frustrating to have a good bonus word sitting on your rack but to be unable to play it because of the positioning of words on the board. If you know that a given bonus word on your rack has one or more valid anagrams, then you immediately have another option, should the first word prove unplayable. In this regard, it's a good idea to start by learning the words that have three or more anagrams, as these are obviously the most versatile.

This section is also useful after a game, when you are wondering whether you could have achieved a better score. This can be painful, but is a good way of honing your Scrabble skills and learning from your mistakes!

Chapter 10 also contains a list of 'transposals' – words made of two shorter words that form another valid word when transposed. This subset of anagrams is particularly useful because it's very easy to memorize these words. Learning the transposal list will also help you to spot opportunities for adding letters to existing words, other than obvious inflections. This can be handy in a tight game, and can help you to open up areas of the board that were previously inaccessible.

SIMILES
MISSILE
MARGINAL
IDOLATRY
ALARMING
STRING
DILATORY
TRYINGS

Chapter 2: Word Families

by Allan Simmons

You wouldn't be reading this book if you weren't interested in learning some useful word for Scrabble. But not everyone has the patience to memorize tedious lists of words. I have always found it best to learn words in small, manageable sets that have a high yield on the Scrabble board. To be manageable, a list has to be fairly short – no more than a single page. To have a high yield, the list must focus on words that are likely to crop up during play.

It was with these criteria in mind that I first created the concept of word families – a sort of mind-map of words centred around a short root word. Two- and three-letter words regularly appear on the board, so showing how they can be developed is very relevant to the game. And because all the words in the 'family' contain the embedded root word, clumps of words with similar patterns naturally occur, which can be grouped together for convenient learning. Through careful arrangement of family members, with shorter words near the centre and longer words further away, it is possible to also reflect the natural extension of the shorter words into longer words. Generally, I try to show the words that start with the root word flowing to the right of each diagram and those that contain the root word flowing to the left, but this will always depend on the number of words in the family that start or end with the root word.

In selecting the root words, I have analysed the two- and three-letter words to ascertain those that produce the most useful families. For example, there's little point in using the word IT because it will generate far too many words, and the IT within longer words will not be a significant component of most of those words. On the other hand, a root word with a higher-scoring tile or an unusual combination of two-letters (eg KO, ZO, IO) generates a shorter list, in which the two-letter sequence remains a key component of the family members.

The maximum word-length for each family is generally five or six, depending on the volume of words generated in each case. In some cases, words of seven letters have been included to provide a useful group (eg the LEX family).

For clarity, all -S plurals of words have been excluded. To show -S extension an asterisk follows every word that **cannot** be extended by -S. This does not mean that such words cannot be pluralized, because the plural may be something other than an -S. Inflections that take the form -ES have been included, providing they are within the length criteria.

I trust you find the word families of use and interest in improving your Scrabble vocabulary. They've been fun to compile and I'm sure I've learned one or two new words in the process.

Happy families!

Allan Simmons

This is an original idea by Allan Simmons, reproduced here with his kind permission. These word families first appeared in Onwords Scrabble Magazine in 1995 and have featured regularly since then.

		MAAING *	
		CAAING *	MAAED *
		FAAING *	CAAED *
		BAAING	FAAED *
			BAAED *
	ALAAP		
BAALIM *	PRAAM		
BAASES *	PLAAS *		
LAAGER			
	DWAAL	JAAP	
	CRAAL	WAAC	
OUBAAS *	GRAAL		
	KRAAL	BAAS *	
BRAATA		KAAS *	
	BRAAI	HAAF	
SALAAM	KIAAT	HAAR	
SAMAAN		MAAR	
	LAARI *		
BAZAAR	MAARE *	NAAM	
		NAAN	
KAAMA			
TAATA			

MAA
CAA
FAA   AAHING *
BAA   AAHED *

                        AH

AA   AAL   AALII

BAAL
KAAL *   KAALER *
PAAL   KAALLY *
TAAL *

                AARGH *
                AARRGH *

* = The word cannot take an –S extension

KABAKA
KABALA
LABARA *   KABAYA
RABATO

RABAT

KABAB
KABAR
BABACO   BABA

CABA   **ABA**

WABAIN   CABAL

SEABAG   CABALA   CASABA
CABANA
TABARD

DAGABA

INDABA

ANABUS *
ATABAL

ABAYA   ABASIA
ARABA

ABAKA   ABAFT *
ABACA   ABAMP   ABACUS *
                 ABAND
ABAC   ABACI * ABASH *
                 ABASK *
        ABACK *

                 ABASE
                 ABATE
        ABATTU *   ABASED *
                                   ABATED *
                                   ABASER
                                   ABATER
                                   ABATOR
        ABATIS *

* = The word does NOT take an –S extension

```
                    ANSAE *
PSOAE *             ANTAE *              RIMAE *
STOAE *                                  MINAE *          LAEVO *
                                         VITAE *
                ISNAE *
                ULNAE *
                ULSAE *
    TUBAE *
    PUPAE *
                                     NAEVE
                         AQUAE *     NAEVI
                SETAE *  ZOEAE *
                TELAE *
                VENAE *
                                                          NAE *
                         ZONAE                            MAE *
AREAE *                  COMAE
AURAE *         CYMAE *  COXAE
               GYNAE    NOVAE                    SAE *
URAEI *                  VOLAE

KOAEA          ALGAE *                            KAE
ZOAEA          BIGAE *            KAED *          TAE
               NUGAE *           TAED *           DAE
               RUGAE *           DAED *           GAE
               TOGAE *           GAED *
                        GAEN *   HAED *
                        HAEN *
                        HAEM
                        HAET
OLPAE *                                  BAEL
               POTAE                     TAEL
               PORAE *
               MORAE                     LAER
               MARAE
```

CAESE °

PAEAN
PAEON

CAECA °
FAENA

UVAE °
VIAE °

AEON

AESIR °
AESC °

AERO
AERY

VAE
FAE °

ALAE °

FAERY °

SPAE
SLAE
BLAE
BRAE
FRAE °

CLAES °

BLAER °
SPAER
SPAED °

AECIA °
AERIE

AE °

AEDES °
AEGIS °

HAE
WAE
YAE

THAE °
TWAE
WHAE °

SCRAE
STRAE
THRAE °

BAAED °
CAAED °
FAAED °
MAAED °

HOAED °
TEAED °

° = The word does NOT take an –S extension

SUBAH

BAHUT   EPHAH   KAHAL
           NAHAL
BAHT   LAHAR

        SHAH

DONAH BAH *
MYNAH   HAH
MINAH

    NAH *   FAH

    NOAH

ALMAH   PAH   **AH**
BIMAH OPAH

        LAH

MAHOE   DAH
MAHUA BELAH
MAHWA SELAH   RAH
     SOLAH
CAHOW GALAH RAHED *
     MILAH   PRAHU
        RAHUI

           ARRAH *

SAHIB OMLAH OMRAH
SAHEB   GERAH
           MARAH
           SURAH

```
                                          AHEAD *
        TAHR                              AHEAP *
        TAHA                              AHENT *
        HAHA                              AHINT *
                                          AHIND *
                          AAHED *         AHING *
                                          AHIGH *
  AHA *                   AHED *          AHOLD *
                          AHEM *          AHULL *
    AAH                   AHOY
```

```
      YAH *              YEAH *
                                                    OBEAH
              AYAH
                                  YAHOO
    DAHL                          WAHOO
        DADAH *          RAYAH
                         RAJAH             SAWAH
                         PUJAH             TAVAH

                         BEKAH             LATAH *
    HORAH                SOKAH             LOTAH
    TORAH
```

* = The word does NOT take an –S extension

CAMAIL
HAMAUL   HAMAL
                         RAMAL *
HAMADA   TAMAL
KAMALA
SAMARA

TAMALE   CAMAS   CAMASH *
TAMANU   GAMASH *
          JICAMA

                    GAMAY
                         AGAMA
ASRAMA
TARAMA   KAAMA
RETAMA   KAMA

                    LLAMA   LAMA
     PALAMA *   ULAMA
PYJAMA   PAJAMA
          PANAMA
                    ZAMAN   DRAMA
                                  GRAMA
          ZAMANG
SQUAMA *

                    HAMATE
     UJAAMA   RAMATE *

DAMAGE
DAMASK

SEAMAN *
DAMAR   ATAMAN
SHAMAN

DAMAN
CAMAN   SHAMA
SAMAN

SAMAAN

CAMA   AMADOU

        SAMA

GAMA   AMATOL

AMAH

AMA

AMATE   AMATED *
AMAZE   AMAZED *

MAMA

AMAZON

AMAIN *
AMAUT

AMARNA *

TAMARA
TAMARI

KAMAHI

* = The word does NOT take an –S extension

GAVAGE

LAVAGE

NAVAID

SAVANT SAVAGE

SAVATE

RAVAGE NAVAL *

NAVAR

PAVAGE

PAVAN

PAVANE

FAVA

CAVASS *

BHAVAN

CASAVA JAVA

CRAVAT KAVA

LAVA

LAVABO

TAVA

TAVAH

OTTAVA

AVAILE

AVAIL

AVALED *

AVALE

AVAL *

AVA

AVATAR

AVAST *

AVANT *

BRAVA

AVANTI *

GUAVA

AVAUNT

* = The word does NOT take an –S extension

```
                        FAXED *                              COAX *
                        RAXED *                              HOAX •
                        TAXED *
                        WAXED *              FAXES *
                                             RAXES *
                                             TAXES *              FAX *
              WAXEN *                        WAXES *              RAX *
                              WAXY *                              TAX *
                  JAXIE       JAXY *                              WAX *
CAXON
      TAXON
      TAXOL           TAXA *              TAXER
      TAXOR           TAXI               WAXER
                      MAXI               LAXER *

TAXUS *

              MAXIM           RETAX *
                              REWAX *              LAXES *              LAX *
                              RELAX *              MAXES *              MAX *
                  UNTAX *                          PAXES *              PAX *
                  DEWAX *                           SAXES *             SAX *
                              LAXLY *              ZAXES *              ZAX *
```

ADDAX *

ATAXY *

GALAX *
MALAX *
BRAXY *   HAPAX *
FLAXY *   PANAX *
FLAX *   LIMAX *
                 BORAX *
                 HYRAX *

AXING
AXED

AXAL *   AXIAL *
AX   AXEL   AXILE *
        AXIL   AXITE
        AXLE   AXLED *
        AXIS *
AXE   AXON

AXOID
AXONE

AXMAN *   AXIOM
AXMEN *   AXION

* = The word does NOT take an –S extension

DRACHM
RHYTHM   PASHM

MEGOHM   ABOHM

ASTHMA   OMH
BRAHMA

                                    FEHM °
                                    VEHM °
FEHME °
VEHME °

FEHMIC °
VEHMIC °
                                    ISTHMI °
                                    MISHMI

ASHMAN *
ASHMEN *

OHMAGE

OHMIC *

MAHMAL

HMM *

HM *

SHMEK
SHMEAR

SHMO *
SCHMO
SCHMOE

SHMOCK
SHMUCK

* = The word does NOT take an –S extension

```
                                                       ENRICH *
                                               WHICH * UNLICH *
                               CHICHA          CHICH *
        SEICHE                 CHICHI          STICH


        CLICHE                                 QUICH *
        ELICHE                                 LAICH *
                       QUICHE


                       QUAICH
                                                       LICHES *
                                                       RICHES *
                                                       TICHES *
                               DREICH *                WICHES *
                               DROICH

                                                               TICH *
                       STRICH         FETICH *                 WICH *


                                               TICHY *
                                               VICHY *
```

```
                                        LICHEE
                          LICHI
                                        LICHEN
                                        RICHEN
LICH °        LICHT
RICH °        RICHT
SICH °        SICHT
DICH °        DICHT         BRICHT       RICHLY °
MICH °        MICHT °       FRICHT
              NICHT

                                        RICHED °
                                        MICHED °
                          MICHE         NICHED °
                          NICHE
                          FICHE         RICHER °
              ICHES °                   MICHER
              ICHED °     FICHU         NICHER
              ICHOR


ICH


              ICHING°
```

```
          FIORD
          KIOSK
          RIOJA        KIORE


          PIOUS *
                       PIONY
                       PIOYE
          AIOLI


                       ARIOT *
                       GRIOT


          DANIO        BIOME
                       BIONT
          RADIO
          RATIO                      BIO
          PATIO                      GIO


                  AGIO
                  OLIO
          FOLIO                      BRIO
          POLIO                      SKIO
          HELIO                      THIO *
                  FUGIO              TRIO
                  CURIO
                  AUDIO


          ADDIO
          AMNIO        NGAIO
```

```
                  DIODE
DIOL
VIOL
                  VIOLA
CION              VIOLD *
LION


PION
PIOY                             BIOTA
                                DIOTA
RIOT


BIOG          IOTA                      IODIC *
                                        IODID
                                        IODIN
                                        IONIC
                          ION
```

IO

```
                                ANION
                                INION
                                ONION
ADIOS *                         UNION
APIOL
AVION
AXIOM
AXION
                        CRIOS *
                        SCION
                        PSION
                        PRION
              IDIOM     PRIOR
              IDIOT     TRIOR
                        TRIOL
                        THIOL
```

JOVIAL

    JOYFUL
    ✻

POPJOY

    JOYOUS ✻   ENJOY   JOY
    JOYPOP

          JOYED✻   JOB
    JOYING ✻ JOBED ✻ JOG
    JOBING ✻ JOKED ✻
HOBJOB   JOKING ✻ JOLED ✻ JOL
    JOLING ✻ JOWED ✻ JOW
CAJOLE   JOWING ✻
FRIJOL ✻

    JOWARI   JOWAR
    AJOWAN   JOEY
PAJOCK
                   JOE
  FEIJOA   BANJO
               DOJO
  BIJOUX ✻ BIJOU GAJO **JO** ✻
  ACAJOU   SAJOU SIJO
               MOJO

  MOJOES ✻

        CAJON ✻ FJORD
DONJON   REJON ✻
GOUJON   MAJOR JOR
    ADJOIN   JOT
    COJOIN
    ENJOIN JOINT
    REJOIN JOIST
          JOUST   JOTA

JONTY *   JOBBED *   JOBBER   JOBBIE
JOTTY *   JOGGED *   JOGGER   JOGGLE
JOBE   JOTTED *   JOTTER
JOLE   JOLTY *   JOLTED *   JOLTER
JOLT   JOLLY *   JOLLED *
JOLL   JOWLY *   JOWLED *   JOWLER   JOLLEY
JOWL   JOLLOP

JOOK   JOCK   JOCKO   JOCKEY
JOUK   JOCO *   JOKOL *   JOKILY *
         JOKE   JOKER   JOKIER *
JOUR   JOKY *   JOKEY *

               JOULE   JOOKED *
               JOUAL   JOUKED *   JOCOSE *
               JOUGS *   JOULED *   JOCUND *
JOMO   JONES *   JOSHED *
JOIN   JOSHER
JOHN   JOSH *   JOSSER   JOJOBA
JONG *   JOSS *
                                 JOSTLE
                                 JOSKIN
                        JOINER
JORAM   JOHNNY *   JOINED *
JORUM   JOANNA
               JOSEPH
               JORDAN
                                    JOUNCE
                                    JOUNCY *
JOTUN   JOURNO
     JOTUNN

* = The word does NOT take an –S extension

```
                                    MAIKO

                                    BERKO *
                ALKO                MILKO
                                    SHAKO
                BOKO
                TOKO                            NKOSI
IROKO           MOKO        PEKOE
CHOKO           MAKO                    SEKOS *
SMOKO           YUKO                    ASKOS *
                                        ASKOI *
                HIKOI
                KIKOI


        DONKO                                       KOS
        BUNKO                       KOINE
        PINKO
        SANKO       YAKOW                    KOI *
                                KOW


                KOFTA
                                    KOFF        KOP
            SKOFF
            SKOSH *                     KOPH

                                    KOPJE
                                    KOPPA
                BUCKO *
        DEKKO   DECKO
                GECKO
                JOCKO
                SOCKO *                 KOHA
                SICKO                   KOHL
                WACKO
                YUCKO *
```

JOKOL *
SOKOL

SKOAL
SKOOL

SKOL *

KOAEA

KOSES *

KOALA

KOEL

KOSS *

KOLA

KOAN

KOLO
KOTO

KOA

KOTOW

KOBO *

KOB

KORO

KOBAN

KO

KOOKY *

KOOK

KON

KOKER

KOR

KOKRA

IKON

KOND *

KOKUM

KONK

KORA
KORE
KORU

EIKON

KOPEK

KONDO
KONDU

KORAI *
KORAT

KOORI
KOURA

KOMBU

KORMA
KORUN *

* = The word does NOT take an –S extension

OUTLAW   PILAW
BYELAW
BYRLAW

       UNLAW
       BYLAW

     BLAWN *
FLAWY *   FLAWN   BLAW
               FLAW

BLAWED *
FLAWED *
CLAWED *   CLAW

CLAWER
                             SLAW
DECLAW

LAWNY *

LAWFUL *

LAWN

LAW

LAWED *
LAWER *
LAWIN

LAWEST *

LAWING
LAWINE

LAWK

LAWYER

LAWMAN *
LAWMEN *

* = The word does NOT take an –S extension

SILEXES *

POLLEX *
SCOLEX *
ISOLEX *

SILEX *

ILEXES *   ILEX *

ULEXES *   ULEX *

ULEXITE

CULEX *

TELEXES *
TELEXED *   TELEX *

BIFLEX *
DFLEX *
REFLEX *

APOPLEX *
COMPLEX *
PERPLEX *   FLEXES *
TRIPLEX *   FLEXED *
SIMPLEX *

IMPLEX *   FLEXOR
DIPLEX *   PLEXAL *   PLEXOR
DUPLEX *   PLEXUS *
SUPLEX *

ALEXIA

ALEXIC *

ALEXIN   ALEXINE

                                    LEXEME
                        LEXEX *

LEX *   LEXEMIC *
                        LEXIS *

FLEX *   LEXISES *

FLEXO *   LEXICA *

        FLEXING *   LEXICAL *
        FLEXION   LEXICON
        FLEXILE *

        FLEXURE
        PLEXURE

* = The word does NOT take an -S extension

CLOGGY *

BECLOG
UNCLOG

LOGGY *

GLOGG

CLOG

ANALOG
APOLOG   COLOG   FLOG   **LOG**
DIALOG   LOLOG
DUOLOG
EPILOG   SLOG
ISOLOG
PROLOG   LOGLOG

MOBLOG *
PUTLOG   EULOGY *
SAWLOG
WEBLOG

```
                                              LOGOFF
                                              LOGOUT
ALOGIA
                    LOGOI *                    LOGJAM
                                              LOGWAY

       LOGIA *              LOGGIA
       LOGIE               LOGGIE *
                                    LOGGAT
              LOGO                  LOGGED *
                                    LOGGER
              LOGE
                           LOGAN            SLOGAN
ELOGE        LOGY *        LOGIN
ELOGY *                    LOGON
                                    LOGILY *

     OLOGY *      LOGIC
        OOLOGY *                     LOGIER *
                                    LOGION
```

* = The word does NOT take an –S extension

HALLOO   AGLOO   LOOKUP
HOLLOO   IGLOO

MOOLOO   BALOO   RELOOK
                                         UPLOOK

ABLOOM *

                                          PLOOKY *

GALOOT   PLOOK
SALOON   BLOOMY *
SALOOP   SLOOMY *   BLOOM
             GLOOMY *   SLOOM
                        GLOOM   LOOM

    GLOOPY *   LOOP

                                             LOOR *
FLOOSY *   GLOOP
FLOOZY *   CLOOP   FLOOR
                   BLOOP   LOORD
                   SLOOP
    BLOODY *

              BLOOD   LOOKED *   LOOKER
             FLOOD   LOOMED *
                       LOOPED *   LOOPER
                       LOOSED *   LOOSER *
                       LOOTED *   LOOTER

LOOVES *

ALOOF *   LOOFAH
KLOOF   BLOOEY *
          LOOFA   FLOOEY *
                      BLOOIE *
                      FLOOIE *
     LOOF   LOOEY
LOOK   LOOIE
                      LOONEY
                      LOONIE

LOO

        LOOED *
              LOOING *

LOOT   LOON   LOONY *
                      LOOBY *
   CLOOT   LOOPY *
   SLOOT

                      KLOOCH *

      LOOSE

                      SLOOSH *

LOOSEN
LOOTEN *

GOBONY *

GOBOES *
HOBOES *   GOBO

HOBOED *   HOBO

                                              KOBO *

            KOBOLD

                                              LOBO
LOBOLA   LOBOSE *
LOBOLO   ZOBO

            ADOBO

BONOBO
            DSOBO

BOOBOO

NOBODY *

ROBOT

OBOIST

OBOE

OBO

SOBOLE

OBOL

OBOLE
OBOLI *

BOBOL

DIOBOL

OBOLUS *

* = The word does NOT take an –S extension

			POFFLE
		FEOFF	COFFLE
SHROFF			
	CLOFF		BOFF
	SKOFF		COFF
	SCOFF		KOFF
	SPOFFY *		DOFF
			GOFF
	TOFFY *		TOFF

CUTOFF	
FLYOFF	RIPOFF
LAYOFF	RUBOFF
LOGOFF	RUNOFF
PAYOFF	SETOFF
PUTOFF	TIPOFF

SOFFIT

BOFFIN
COFFIN

	BOFFED °	
	COFFED °	COFFER
	DOFFED °	DOFFER
BOFFO °	GOFFED °	GOFFER

COFFEE
TOFFEE

	OFFED °	OFFING
OFF	OFFAL	OFFISH °
	OFFER	

MOFFIE

		OFFCUT
	OFFEND	OFFKEY °
	OFFICE	OFFPUT
		OFFSET

° = The word does NOT take an –S extension

COHOE
COHOG

COHAB

ALOHA
AROHA *

OOHED *

EVOHE *

BOOH
POOH

OOH

BOHEA

BOH

DOHYO

DOH

LOHAN

SOH

KOHL
MOHR

FOH

MOHEL
MOHUR

FOHN
JOHN

PHOH

BOHO *
COHO
SOHO *
TOHO

OHONE *

OHIA

OHO

OHING *

OHED *

OH

OHM   OHMIC *

ABOHM

NOH *

POH *

NOHOW *

HOH

HOHED *

HOHA
KOHA

* = The word does NOT take an –S extension

CHOKE

SMOKE		BOKE
SNOKE		COKE
SPOKE		HOKE
STOKE	BLOKE	LOKE
	CLOKE	MOKE

OKE

WROKE *		
TROKE		
PROKE		
BROKE		
	JOKER	JOKE
	POKER	POKE
	ROKER	ROKE
	TOKER	TOKE
ATOKE		SOKE
AWOKE *	KOKER	WOKE
EVOKE		YOKE

BOKED *
COKED *
HOKED *

HOKEY *
JOKEY *
POKEY *

OKEH

JOKED *
POKED *
ROKED *
TOKED *

YOKED *   TOKEN
            SOKEN
            WOKEN *

YOKER
YOKEL

* = The word does NOT take an –S extension

```
AGORA
  IXORA
        FLORA                              JORAM
                                           CORAM *
                      BORAL                FORAM
                      CORAL
                      GORAL
                      MORAL          FORAY              FORA *
HORAH                 RORAL          MORAY
TORAH                                                   MORA
                      HORAL *
TORAN                 LORAL *              HORA
LORAN                 PORAL *
                      SORAL *              TORA
                                                 KORA


                                           KORAT
                      KORAI *              MORAT


              MORAE *
              PORAE *
```

BORAK
BORAX *

    BORA

                DORAD

                          ORATE

              ORAD *

ORA *

                          ORANG
             ORAL   ORANT

    SORA

                          ORACH *
PSORA   ORACY *

* = The word does NOT take an –S extension

```
                              COXAE *
                              COXAL *
                              DOXIE          COXA *
            LUMMOX *          MOXIE          MOXA
                              FOXIE


HATBOX *                                                    BOXY *
HAYBOX *        EMBOX *         BOXIER *                     COXY *
HOTBOX *        UNBOX *         COXIER *                     DOXY *
ICEBOX *                       FOXIER *                     FOXY *
JAWBOX *                       POXIER *                     POXY *
OUTBOX *
PEGBOX *                          EPOXY *
SKYBOX *       ANOXIA
TEABOX *       ANOXIC *      MAGNOX *


                  BOLLOX *          PHLOX *


               CARFOX *        DETOX *
COWPOX *       DOGFOX *        REDOX *
               OUTFOX *        XEROX *


CARFOX *
DOGFOX *                     VOLVOX *              OXO *
OUTFOX *

            DIOXAN
            DIOXID              TOXINE    TOXIC
            DIOXIN              TOXOID    TOXIN
                                                  OXY *

         ALKOXY *
         DESOXY *     DEOXY *
         ETHOXY *
         PEROXY *
```

	WOXEN *	**BOXCAR**	
WOX *	BOXEN *	**BOXFUL**	
	BOXER		

BOX *	BOXES *	BOXING	
COX *	COXES *	COXING *	
LOX *	LOXES *	LOXING	
HOX *	HOXES *	HOXING *	
POX *	POXES *	POXING *	
FOX *	FOXES *	FOXING *	
			FOXILY *
NOX *	NOXES *		
GOX *	GOXES *		
	NOXAL *		

OX *

	OXID	OXIDE	OXIDIC *
	OXIM	OXIME	OXALIC *
	OXEN *		OXALIS *
	OXER	OXBOW	
	OXES *	OXEYE	
SOX *		OXLIP	
VOX *		OXTER	OXCART
			OXFORD
	VOXEL		OXGANG
			OXGATE
			OXHEAD
OXYGEN			OXHIDE
OXYMEL			OXLAND
			OXSLIP
			OXTAIL

* = The word does NOT take an –S extension

```
                                             QUANT
                                             QUART
                          EQUANT              QUARE *
SQUARE                    EQUATE              QUATE *
                                             QUALE *
SQUAIL                    EQUALI *            QUAIL
SQUALL                                        QUAIR
                           EQUAL              QUALM

SQUAMA *
SQUAME


                          AQUA                         QUA *

                          AQUAE *

ASQUAT *

DIQUAT
LOQUAT                            SQUAB
                                  SQUAD
                                  SQUAT
                                  SQUAW
            SQUASH *
            SQUAWK
```

QUANTA *
QUARRY *
QUAERE
QUARER *

QUARTE
QUARTO
QUARTZ *

QUALIA *
QUALMY *

QUASH *   QUARK   QUAKED *
QUASI *   QUAKE   QUAKER
QUASS *   QUAKY *   QUAVER
                 QUACK
QUAFF
                                QUASAR

QUAT   QUAZZY *
QUAD   QUADDY *
QUAG   QUAGGY *   QUAINT *
                          QUATCH *
                          QUAICH
QUAI   QUAGGA   QUAIGH
QUAY   QUAHOG

QUAYD *   QUANGO

* = The word does NOT take an –S extension

QUIPPU

SQUIFF *
SQUILL

QUIFF

QUIPU
QUIPO

QUILL
QUILT

EQUID
EQUIP

YANQUI

EQUIPE

QUIP

MAQUI

SEQUIN
REQUIN
REQUIT

QUID

SQUIER

SQUIRE
FAQUIR   SQUIRR
SQUIRM

LIQUID

QUIDAM

SQUID
SQUIB
SQUIT
SQUIZ *

SQUIRT   SQUINT
SQUISH *   SQUINY *

QUINIC *
QUININ
QUINOA
QUINOL

QUICHE

QUICH *   EQUINE   QUINIE
QUICK
                QUINE   QUINSY *
                QUINA   QUINCE
                                                    QUINZE

QUIM
        QUIN   QUINT

QUI *   QUINTA
                    QUIST   QUINTE

                QUIRT
NB – QUI is not a word itself   QUIRK
                QUIRE   QUIRKY *
QUIZ *   QUIT
                                QUIRED *   QUITCH *
                                QUITED *

                QUITE
                QUIET
EQUITY *
                                        QUIVER
ACQUIT   QUIGHT

* = The word does NOT take an –S extension

AERIAL
OORIAL
SERIAL   NARIAL *
STRIAE *   GARIAL
        STRIA *   PARIAL

LARIAT   PARIAH
                                       PARIAN
                    AGRIA
                    ATRIA *   DURIAN
        LATRIA
        NUTRIA
        YTTRIA
                    VARIA *   ARIA
                    MARIA *

KERRIA   FERIAL *   FERIA   MORIA
            FERIAE *   CERIA   NORIA
                                       CORIA *
                     CURIA
        CURIAE *
                     CURIAL *   URIAL
MYRIAD   BURIAL   PRIAL
                                         TRIAL
                ATRIAL *
                                              TRIAC
                                              TRIAD
                          TRIACT *
        ERIACH   TRIAGE

PRIAPI *

BRIARD

BRIARY *   FRIAND
FRIARY *

BRIAR
FRIAR   CRIANT *

RIANCY *

RIANT *

RIA

RIATA

RIAL

RIALTO

APORIA
CHORIA *
GLORIA
SCORIA *
THORIA   ORARIA *   HYDRIA *
ZOARIA *

SHARIA
SHERIA   ANURIA
PYURIA

PTERIA *

* = The word does NOT take an –S extension

*

BEWEEP

AWEEL *

PEWEE

SWEEPO

SWEED *

WOWEE *

SWEEPY * SWEEL
SWEENY * SWEEP   AWEE *
SWEETY * SWEER
SWEET   SWEE

SWEERT *

ETWEE   TWEE *

TWEED
TWEEDY * TWEEL
TWEELY * TWEEN *   TWEEST *
TWEENY * TWEER
TWEET

ATWEEL *   NGWEE
ATWEEN *

DWEEB

TWEEZE

DWEEBY *

DRAWEE

WEENSY *

PEEWEE
WEEWEE

WEEPIE
WEENIE

WEEING *

WEED
WEEP

WEEDY *

WEEPY *

WEEVIL

WEEL
WEEM
WEEN

WEENY *

WEE

WEEDED *
WEENED *
WEETED *

WEEVER
WEEDER
WEEPER

WEER *
WEET
WEEK

WEETER *

WEEST *

WEETE*
WEEKE

WEETEN *

WEEKLY *

* = The word does NOT take an –S extension

CYANO *

SPYAL

GAYAL

CYAN   EYAS *   LYARD *   LOYAL *
DRYAD   DYAD   NYAS *   LYART *   ROYAL
                                          LYASE   RIYAL

KYAK
BOYAR   KYAR
BOYAU *   KYAT   AYAH
NOYAU   PYAT   YAR *

                            YAY   YAE *

GYAL   PYA
MYALL   MYAL *   YA *
RYAL   RYA

GEYAN *   LYAM   YAM
DAYAN
MAYAN *   YAD

              HIYA *   YAMEN
MAYA   HOYA   YAMUN
RAYA   MOYA
              SOYA
RAYAH
KAYAK

                            SHAYA   BUNYA
                            CHAYA   PLAYA
                            KHAYA   THUJA

```
                YAIRD
YAGER           YAULD *

                                        YARFA
YAGI                    YALD *           YARTA
                       YARD              YARTO
            YALE       YARK *            YARER *
            YARE *     YARN
            YATE
                                        YACHT
                       YANK                             YABBA
YAHOO                  YANG      KYANG                  YACCA
                                 KYACK                  YAKKA
YAH                    YACK
                                        YACKA
      YAK                                              YAKOW

                                 NYALA
   YAP                 YAFF      NYAFF
                       YAPP
                       YARR
YAW                                     YAPOK
                                        YAPON
      YAWY *

                       YAUD            YAPPY *
                       YAUP            YABBY *
                       YAWP
ALIYA                  YAWL                      YAMPY *
ABAYA                  YAWN
                                        YAWED *
                                        YAWEY *
                                        YAWNY *
```

YONKS *
DOHYO   YONIC *

HYOID
PYOID *   YOND *
MYOID *   YONT *
PSYOP   AYONT *   YONI

MYOMA
MYOPE   GUYOT
GYOZA   MYOPS *   YON
MYOPY *

EYOT
PYOT
BOYO   RYOT
TOYON   TOYO   YOM *
RAYON   YOMP
SAYON   KAYO   YOU
MAYO   YOMIM *

KARYO *
YOUR
YOUK
MAYOR   YOUS *   YOOF
PAYOR   YOOP

YOURN *
YOURT

BAYOU   YOUNG
POYOU   YOUTH
YOUSE *

YOWED °
YOWIE

YOBBO   YOWE
               YOWL

YOB
                                                  YOGEE

     YOW   YOGA   YOGIC °
                      YOGI   YOGIN
                      YOGH
                                                            YOJAN
YO   YOD

                      YODE °   YODEL
                      YODH   YODLE

     YOK

                                    YOKED °
YORE   YOKE   YOKER
YORK   YOCK   YOKEL
YORP °   YOLK   YOKUL °
              YOLD °

                      YOLKY °

                      YOICK

° = The word does NOT take an –S extension

SOZINE

DAZING *
FAZING *
GAZING *
PIZING *　　　　HAZING　　　　AZINE
SIZING　　　　LAZING *
　　　　　　MAZING *
FUZING *　　　　RAZING
　*

SOZIN

ZIN

COZING *
DOZING
MOZING *
　　　OOZING

　*

TOZING *

BENZIN

DIAZIN

SEIZIN

```
                    ZINEB                              ZINKE
        ZINE

                                                ZINCO              ZINCIC *
        ZINC                  ZINKY *
                              ZINCY *
                                       ZINCKY *         ZINCED *

DEZINC               ZINGY *                            ZINKED *

        ZING                                           ZINGED *
                                                       ZINGER
                                                       ZINGEL

              ZINNIA
```

* = The word does NOT take an –S extension

REBOZO
ABRAZO
COROZO
SCHIZO
SLEAZO *
STANZO

GONZO *
PIEZO *
DIAZO

BIZZO
LAZOED *   LAZZO *
LAZOES *   MEZZO

BOZO
LAZO
MATZOH *   MOZO
MATZOT *   OUZO
                  MATZO

MAZOUT

AZOLE
AZOLLA   AZOIC *
                  AZOTIC *   AZOTH   DZO
                  AZOTED *   AZOTE

EPIZOA *

                                    ZOA *
                         AZO *

MAHZOR *
RIZZOR   RAZOR   ZO
SEIZOR   VIZOR

                         AZON   ZOO

BEZOAR
HUZOOR

GAZOON   GAZON
          GAZOO
          KAZOO
AMAZON   RAZOO
BLAZON
SCAZON
TENZON   AZONAL
          AZONIC
          OZONIC

                              OZONE

PHIZOG
BORZOI
BENZOL   BIZONE
PODZOL   ENZONE
                    EVZONE
                    REZONE

```
                                              ZOMBIE
                    ZOMBI                     ZOFTIG *
                    ZOWIE *                   ZOYSIA


                              ZOPPA *
                              ZOPPO *         ZODIAC
                              ZORRO           ZOSTER
                                              ZOUNDS *
           ZOBO
           ZOBU               ZORBS *
                                              ZORBED *


           ZOUK
                              ZOISM           ZOARIA *
                              ZOIST           ZOECIA *
                                              ZOETIC *
           ZOIC *             ZOEAL *
                              ZOEAE *
                              ZOAEA
                              ZOOEA           ZOAEAE *
           ZOEA                               ZOOEAE *
                                              ZOOEAL *

                              ZORIL           ZORINO

                              ZOOID           ZOOMED *
           ZOOM                               ZOONAL *
           ZOON               ZOOKS *         ZOONIC *
           ZOOT               ZOOTY *


                                              ZONARY *
    ZONA *            ZONAE *                  ZONATE *
                      ZONAL *

    ZONE              ZONED *         ZONING
                      ZONER           ZONOID *
                      ZONDA           ZONULA
                                      ZONULE
    ZONK                              ZONURE



                      ZONKED *
```

* = The word does NOT take an –S extension

Chapter 3: Short words

While long words may yield spectacular scores in Scrabble–and words of up to 15 letters in length can be formed–the chances to achieve such coups are few and far between. A Scrabble player's best chance of consistently high scores comes not from long words but from remembering the short, useful words that can ensure a good play in even the most difficult situations.

By definition, short words are easy to squeeze onto the board when there is little or no room for longer words. Not only can they be fitted in to a cramped board; they can also open up sections of the board that were previously unavailable for play.

Short words are also useful as building blocks for longer words that can be formed by adding letters to the front or end–see Chapter 2: Word Families.

Finally, short words are very handy for clearing unwanted letters from your rack. This is especially true when you are lumbered with multiple vowels. Words like AA, EE and OO are ideal for this purpose.

Two-letter words

Two-letter words are vital to the serious Scrabble player. While very few two-letter words afford big scores in their own right, they are crucial linking elements in the game. Essentially, two-letter words are the nuts and bolts of the game, allowing longer words to be joined to each other. To play one word parallel and adjacent to another already on the board ('tagging'), you will need to know a valid two-letter word for each point of contact between the two words.

There are 122 valid two-letter words in Scrabble, all of which are listed in this section.

Three-letter words

Three-letter words aren't quite as important as two-letter words, but they are still an essential weapon in every Scrabble player's armoury. It's especially worth noting those three-letter words that are plurals of two-letter ones, as these provide you with opportunities for 'hooking' with an S tile. Three-letter words are also useful for tagging because they are easier to fit in than longer words: obviously, if your new word has only three letters, you may well be able to find a spot on the board where you can tag onto a word and form two or three two-letter words in the process.

There are 1,264 valid three-letter words in Scrabble, all of which are listed in this section.

Two-letter words

AA	DO	IF	NY	SO
AB	EA	IN	OB	ST
AD	ED	IO	OD	TA
AE	EE	IS	OE	TE
AG	EF	IT	OF	TI
AH	EH	JA	OH	TO
AI	EL	JO	OI	UG
AL	EM	KA	OM	UH
AM	EN	KI	ON	UM
AN	ER	KO	OO	UN
AR	ES	KY	OP	UP
AS	ET	LA	OR	UR
AT	EX	LI	OS	US
AW	FA	LO	OU	UT
AX	FE	MA	OW	WE
AY	FY	ME	OX	WO
BA	GI	MI	OY	XI
BE	GO	MM	PA	XU
BI	GU	MO	PE	YA
BO	HA	MU	PI	YE
BY	HE	MY	PO	YO
CH	HI	NA	QI	YU
DA	HM	NE	RE	ZA
DE	HO	NO	SH	ZO
DI	ID	NU	SI	

Three-letter words

AAH	AIR	ARC	AYU	BIS
AAL	AIS	ARD	AZO	BIT
AAS	AIT	ARE	BAA	BIZ
ABA	AKA	ARF	BAC	BOA
ABB	AKE	ARK	BAD	BOB
ABO	ALA	ARM	BAG	BOD
ABS	ALB	ARS	BAH	BOG
ABY	ALE	ART	BAL	BOH
ACE	ALF	ARY	BAM	BOI
ACH	ALL	ASH	BAN	BOK
ACT	ALP	ASK	BAP	BON
ADD	ALS	ASP	BAR	BOO
ADO	ALT	ASS	BAS	BOP
ADS	AMA	ATE	BAT	BOR
ADZ	AMI	ATT	BAY	BOS
AFF	AMP	AUA	BED	BOT
AFT	AMU	AUE	BEE	BOW
AGA	ANA	AUF	BEG	BOX
AGE	AND	AUK	BEL	BOY
AGO	ANE	AVA	BEN	BRA
AGS	ANI	AVE	BES	BRO
AHA	ANN	AVO	BET	BRR
AHI	ANT	AWA	BEY	BRU
AHS	ANY	AWE	BEZ	BUB
AIA	APE	AWL	BIB	BUD
AID	APO	AWN	BID	BUG
AIL	APP	AXE	BIG	BUM
AIM	APT	AYE	BIN	BUN
AIN	ARB	AYS	BIO	BUR

BUS	DAM	EAR	FAE	GAM
BUT	DAN	EAS	FAG	GAN
BUY	DAP	EAT	FAH	GAP
BYE	DAS	EAU	FAN	GAR
BYS	DAW	EBB	FAP	GAS
CAA	DAY	ECH	FAR	GAT
CAB	DEB	ECO	FAS	GAU
CAD	DEE	ECU	FAT	GAY
CAG	DEF	EDH	FAW	GED
CAM	DEG	EDS	FAX	GEE
CAN	DEI	EEK	FAY	GEL
CAP	DEL	EEL	FED	GEM
CAR	DEN	EEN	FEE	GEN
CAT	DEV	EFF	FEG	GEO
CAW	DEW	EFS	FEH	GET
CAY	DEX	EFT	FEM	GEY
CAZ	DEY	EGG	FEN	GHI
CEE	DIB	EGO	FER	GIB
CEL	DID	EHS	FES	GID
CEP	DIE	EIK	FET	GIE
CHA	DIF	EKE	FEU	GIF
CHE	DIG	ELD	FEW	GIG
CHI	DIM	ELF	FEY	GIN
CID	DIN	ELK	FEZ	GIO
CIG	DIP	ELL	FIB	GIP
CIS	DIS	ELM	FID	GIS
CIT	DIT	ELS	FIE	GIT
CLY	DIV	ELT	FIG	GJU
COB	DOB	EME	FIL	GNU
COD	DOC	EMO	FIN	GOA
COG	DOD	EMS	FIR	GOB
COL	DOE	EMU	FIT	GOD
CON	DOF	END	FIX	GOE
COO	DOG	ENE	FIZ	GON
COP	DOH	ENG	FLU	GOO
COR	DOL	ENS	FLY	GOR
COS	DOM	EON	FOB	GOS
COT	DON	ERA	FOE	GOT
COW	DOO	ERE	FOG	GOV
COX	DOP	ERF	FOH	GOX
COY	DOR	ERG	FON	GOY
COZ	DOS	ERK	FOP	GUB
CRU	DOT	ERN	FOR	GUE
CRY	DOW	ERR	FOU	GUL
CUB	DOY	ERS	FOX	GUM
CUD	DRY	ESS	FOY	GUN
CUE	DSO	EST	FRA	GUP
CUM	DUB	ETA	FRO	GUR
CUP	DUD	ETH	FRY	GUS
CUR	DUE	EUK	FUB	GUT
CUT	DUG	EVE	FUD	GUV
CUZ	DUH	EVO	FUG	GUY
CWM	DUI	EWE	FUM	GYM
DAB	DUN	EWK	FUN	GYP
DAD	DUO	EWT	FUR	HAD
DAE	DUP	EXO	GAB	HAE
DAG	DUX	EYE	GAD	HAG
DAH	DYE	FAA	GAE	HAH
DAK	DZO	FAB	GAG	HAJ
DAL	EAN	FAD	GAL	HAM

HAN	IFF	KAY	LID	MIM
HAO	IFS	KEA	LIE	MIR
HAP	IGG	KEB	LIG	MIS
HAS	ILK	KED	LIN	MIX
HAT	ILL	KEF	LIP	MIZ
HAW	IMP	KEG	LIS	MNA
HAY	INK	KEN	LIT	MOA
HEH	INN	KEP	LOB	MOB
HEM	INS	KET	LOD	MOC
HEN	ION	KEX	LOG	MOD
HEP	IOS	KEY	LOO	MOE
HER	IRE	KHI	LOP	MOG
HES	IRK	KID	LOR	MOI
HET	ISH	KIF	LOS	MOL
HEW	ISM	KIN	LOT	MOM
HEX	ISO	KIP	LOU	MON
HEY	ITA	KIR	LOW	MOO
HIC	ITS	KIS	LOX	MOP
HID	IVY	KIT	LOY	MOR
HIE	IWI	KOA	LUD	MOS
HIM	JAB	KOB	LUG	MOT
HIN	JAG	KOI	LUM	MOU
HIP	JAI	KON	LUR	MOW
HIS	JAK	KOP	LUV	MOY
HIT	JAL	KOR	LUX	MOZ
HMM	JAM	KOS	LUZ	MUD
HOA	JAP	KOW	LYE	MUG
HOB	JAR	KUE	LYM	MUM
HOC	JAW	KYE	MAA	MUN
HOD	JAY	KYU	MAC	MUS
HOE	JEE	LAB	MAD	MUT
HOG	JET	LAC	MAE	MUX
HOH	JEU	LAD	MAG	MYC
HOI	JEW	LAG	MAK	NAB
HOM	JIB	LAH	MAL	NAE
HON	JIG	LAM	MAM	NAG
HOO	JIN	LAP	MAN	NAH
HOP	JIZ	LAR	MAP	NAM
HOS	JOB	LAS	MAR	NAN
HOT	JOE	LAT	MAS	NAP
HOW	JOG	LAV	MAT	NAS
HOX	JOL	LAW	MAW	NAT
HOY	JOR	LAX	MAX	NAW
HUB	JOT	LAY	MAY	NAY
HUE	JOW	LEA	MED	NEB
HUG	JOY	LED	MEE	NED
HUH	JUD	LEE	MEG	NEE
HUI	JUG	LEG	MEL	NEF
HUM	JUN	LEI	MEM	NEG
HUN	JUS	LEK	MEN	NEK
HUP	JUT	LEP	MES	NEP
HUT	KAB	LES	MET	NET
HYE	KAE	LET	MEU	NEW
HYP	KAF	LEU	MEW	NIB
ICE	KAI	LEV	MHO	NID
ICH	KAK	LEW	MIB	NIE
ICK	KAM	LEX	MIC	NIL
ICY	KAS	LEY	MID	NIM
IDE	KAT	LEZ	MIG	NIP
IDS	KAW	LIB	MIL	NIS

NIT	OOP	PIC	REB	SAT
NIX	OOR	PIE	REC	SAU
NOB	OOS	PIG	RED	SAV
NOD	OOT	PIN	REE	SAW
NOG	OPE	PIP	REF	SAX
NOH	OPS	PIR	REG	SAY
NOM	OPT	PIS	REH	SAZ
NON	ORA	PIT	REI	SEA
NOO	ORB	PIU	REM	SEC
NOR	ORC	PIX	REN	SED
NOS	ORD	PLU	REO	SEE
NOT	ORE	PLY	REP	SEG
NOW	ORF	POA	RES	SEI
NOX	ORS	POD	RET	SEL
NOY	ORT	POH	REV	SEN
NTH	OSE	POI	REW	SER
NUB	OUD	POL	REX	SET
NUN	OUK	POM	REZ	SEW
NUR	OUP	POO	RHO	SEX
NUS	OUR	POP	RHY	SEY
NUT	OUT	POS	RIA	SEZ
NYE	OVA	POT	RIB	SHA
NYS	OWE	POW	RID	SHE
OAF	OWL	POX	RIF	SHH
OAK	OWN	POZ	RIG	SHY
OAR	OWT	PRE	RIM	SIB
OAT	OXO	PRO	RIN	SIC
OBA	OXY	PRY	RIP	SIF
OBE	OYE	PSI	RIT	SIK
OBI	OYS	PST	RIZ	SIM
OBO	PAC	PUB	ROB	SIN
OBS	PAD	PUD	ROC	SIP
OCA	PAH	PUG	ROD	SIR
OCH	PAL	PUH	ROE	SIS
ODA	PAM	PUL	ROK	SIT
ODD	PAN	PUN	ROM	SIX
ODE	PAP	PUP	ROO	SKA
ODS	PAR	PUR	ROT	SKI
OES	PAS	PUS	ROW	SKY
OFF	PAT	PUT	RUB	SLY
OFT	PAV	PUY	RUC	SMA
OHM	PAW	PYA	RUD	SNY
OHO	PAX	PYE	RUE	SOB
OHS	PAY	PYX	RUG	SOC
OIK	PEA	QAT	RUM	SOD
OIL	PEC	QIS	RUN	SOG
OKA	PED	QUA	RUT	SOH
OKE	PEE	RAD	RYA	SOL
OLD	PEG	RAG	RYE	SOM
OLE	PEH	RAH	SAB	SON
OLM	PEN	RAI	SAC	SOP
OMS	PEP	RAJ	SAD	SOS
ONE	PER	RAM	SAE	SOT
ONO	PES	RAN	SAG	SOU
ONS	PET	RAP	SAI	SOV
ONY	PEW	RAS	SAL	SOW
OOF	PHI	RAT	SAM	SOX
OOH	PHO	RAW	SAN	SOY
OOM	PHT	RAX	SAP	SPA
OON	PIA	RAY	SAR	SPY

SRI	TIC	UNS	WAR	YEH
STY	TID	UPO	WAS	YEN
SUB	TIE	UPS	WAT	YEP
SUD	TIG	URB	WAW	YES
SUE	TIL	URD	WAX	YET
SUI	TIN	URE	WAY	YEW
SUK	TIP	URN	WEB	YEX
SUM	TIS	URP	WED	YGO
SUN	TIT	USE	WEE	YID
SUP	TIX	UTA	WEM	YIN
SUQ	TOC	UTE	WEN	YIP
SUR	TOD	UTS	WET	YOB
SUS	TOE	UTU	WEX	YOD
SWY	TOG	UVA	WEY	YOK
SYE	TOM	VAC	WHA	YOM
SYN	TON	VAE	WHO	YON
TAB	TOO	VAG	WHY	YOS
TAD	TOP	VAN	WIG	YOU
TAE	TOR	VAR	WIN	YOW
TAG	TOT	VAS	WIS	YUG
TAI	TOW	VAT	WIT	YUK
TAJ	TOY	VAU	WIZ	YUM
TAK	TRY	VAV	WOE	YUP
TAM	TSK	VAW	WOF	YUS
TAN	TUB	VEE	WOG	ZAG
TAO	TUG	VEG	WOK	ZAP
TAP	TUI	VET	WON	ZAS
TAR	TUM	VEX	WOO	ZAX
TAS	TUN	VIA	WOP	ZEA
TAT	TUP	VID	WOS	ZED
TAU	TUT	VIE	WOT	ZEE
TAV	TUX	VIG	WOW	ZEK
TAW	TWA	VIM	WOX	ZEL
TAX	TWO	VIN	WRY	ZEP
TAY	TWP	VIS	WUD	ZEX
TEA	TYE	VLY	WUS	ZHO
TEC	TYG	VOE	WYE	ZIG
TED	UDO	VOL	WYN	ZIN
TEE	UDS	VOR	XIS	ZIP
TEF	UEY	VOW	YAD	ZIT
TEG	UFO	VOX	YAE	ZIZ
TEL	UGH	VUG	YAG	ZOA
TEN	UGS	VUM	YAH	ZOL
TES	UKE	WAB	YAK	ZOO
TET	ULE	WAD	YAM	ZOS
TEW	ULU	WAE	YAP	ZUZ
TEX	UMM	WAG	YAR	ZZZ
THE	UMP	WAI	YAW	
THO	UMU	WAN	YAY	
THY	UNI	WAP	YEA	

Chapter 4: Power Tiles

The highest-scoring tiles in the game are J, Q, X and Z, with J and X scoring eight points each, while Q and Z are worth ten. These 'power tiles' are the most potent weapons in the Scrabble player's arsenal, but need to be carefully deployed. This isn't always a matter of using them in a long word – a carefully positioned short word can be just as good a move.

This section lists all of the power-tile words of two and three letters, with a brief definition for each. It's worth learning all of these words as they can be tremendously useful, combining the assets of all short words with the high scores afforded by the power tiles. Knowing the definitions of these words will help you commit them to memory.

The subsequent lists include all of the power-tile words from four to eight letters. While there may be too many of these to remember, studying the list will provide you with a range of useful options for game situations where you have one of these valuable tiles on your rack.

J

There is only one J tile in Scrabble, so for any word with two Js (e.g. **hajj** or **hajjah**) a blank is required. When you are trying to use a word with J for tagging, remember that there are only two two-letter words with J **ja** and **jo**. Bearing this in mind will prevent you from wasting time looking for options that aren't there. If there is a Z on the board or on your rack when you have a J, remember that there are quite a few words that use both J and Z (**jiz** and **jazy**, for example, though you will need a blank tile to take advantage of the **jazz** family of words). Don't forget unusual combinations like the FJ in **fjeld** and **fjord**, or the DJ in **djin**, **djinn** and their plurals, or the JH in words like **jhala** and **jhakta**. An examination of the following lists will also reveal a number of words that contain a JR combination, including **bajra**, **bajiri**, **hijra**, and **bajree**. Learning some of these words can help you use potentially awkward racks to your advantage.

Two-letter words

JA	yes
JO	Scots word for sweetheart

Three-letter words

GJU	type of violin used in Shetland
HAJ	pilgrimage a Muslim makes to Mecca
JAB	poke sharply
JAG	period of uncontrolled indulgence in an activity
JAI	victory (to)
JAK	tree of the East Indies
JAL	as in 'Ganja jal' sacred water from the Ganges
JAM	pack tightly into a place
JAP	splash

JAR	wide-mouthed container, usu round and made of glass
JAW	one of the bones in which the teeth are set
JAY	bird with a pinkish body and blue-and-black wings
JEE	mild exclamation of surprise, admiration, etc
JET	aircraft driven by jet propulsion
JEU	game
JEW	obsolete offensive word for haggle
JIB	taunt or jeer
JIG	type of lively dance
JIN	Chinese unit of weight
JIZ	wig
JOB	occupation or paid employment
JOE	Scots word for sweetheart
JOG	run at a gentle pace, esp for exercise
JOL	party
JOR	movement in Indian music
JOT	write briefly
JOW	ring (a bell)
JOY	feeling of great delight or pleasure
JUD	large block of coal
JUG	container for liquids, with a handle and small spout
JUN	North and South Korean monetary unit worth one hundredth of a won
JUS	right, power, or authority
JUT	project or stick out
RAJ	(in India) government
TAJ	tall conical cap worn as a mark of distinction by Muslims

Four-letter words

AJAR	JAPS	JELL	JOCK	JUDO
AJEE	JARK	JEON	JOCO	JUDS
BAJU	JARL	JERK	JOES	JUDY
BENJ	JARP	JESS	JOEY	JUGA
DJIN	JARS	JEST	JOGS	JUGS
DOJO	JASP	JETE	JOHN	JUJU
FUJI	JASS	JETS	JOIN	JUKE
GAJO	JASY	JEUX	JOKE	JUKU
GJUS	JATO	JEWS	JOKY	JUMP
HADJ	JAUK	JIAO	JOLE	JUNK
HAJI	JAUP	JIBB	JOLL	JUPE
HAJJ	JAVA	JIBE	JOLS	JURA
JAAP	JAWS	JIBS	JOLT	JURE
JABS	JAXY	JIFF	JOMO	JURY
JACK	JAYS	JIGS	JONG	JUST
JADE	JAZY	JILL	JOOK	JUTE
JAFA	JAZZ	JILT	JORS	JUTS
JAGA	JEAN	JIMP	JOSH	JUVE
JAGG	JEAT	JINK	JOSS	JYNX
JAGS	JEDI	JINN	JOTA	KOJI
JAIL	JEED	JINS	JOTS	MOJO
JAIS	JEEL	JINX	JOUK	PUJA
JAKE	JEEP	JIRD	JOUR	RAJA
JAKS	JEER	JISM	JOWL	ROJI
JAMB	JEES	JIVE	JOWS	SIJO
JAMS	JEEZ	JIVY	JOYS	SJOE
JANE	JEFE	JIZZ	JUBA	SOJA
JANN	JEFF	JOBE	JUBE	
JAPE	JEHU	JOBS	JUCO	

Five-letter words

AFLAJ	JAKES	JENNY	JOKED	JUNKY
AJIVA	JAKEY	JERID	JOKER	JUNTA
AJUGA	JALAP	JERKS	JOKES	JUNTO
AJWAN	JALOP	JERKY	JOKEY	JUPES
BAJAN	JAMBE	JERRY	JOKOL	JUPON
BAJRA	JAMBO	JESSE	JOLED	JURAL
BAJRI	JAMBS	JESTS	JOLES	JURAT
BAJUS	JAMBU	JESUS	JOLLS	JUREL
BANJO	JAMES	JETES	JOLLY	JUROR
BHAJI	JAMMY	JETON	JOLTS	JUSTS
BIJOU	JANES	JETTY	JOLTY	JUTES
BUNJE	JANNS	JEUNE	JOMON	JUTTY
BUNJY	JANNY	JEWED	JOMOS	JUVES
CAJON	JANTY	JEWEL	JONES	KANJI
CAJUN	JAPAN	JEWIE	JONTY	KHOJA
DJINN	JAPED	JHALA	JOOKS	KOJIS
DJINS	JAPER	JIAOS	JORAM	KOPJE
DOJOS	JAPES	JIBBS	JORUM	LAPJE
EEJIT	JARKS	JIBED	JOTAS	MAJOR
EJECT	JARLS	JIBER	JOTTY	MOJOS
ENJOY	JARPS	JIBES	JOTUN	MUJIK
FALAJ	JARTA	JIFFS	JOUAL	NINJA
FJELD	JARUL	JIFFY	JOUGS	OBJET
FJORD	JASEY	JIGGY	JOUKS	OJIME
FUJIS	JASPE	JIGOT	JOULE	OUIJA
GADJE	JASPS	JIHAD	JOURS	POLJE
GADJO	JATOS	JILLS	JOUST	POOJA
GAJOS	JAUKS	JILTS	JOWAR	PUJAH
GANJA	JAUNT	JIMMY	JOWED	PUJAS
GAUJE	JAUPS	JIMPY	JOWLS	PUNJI
HADJI	JAVAS	JINGO	JOWLY	RAJAH
HAJES	JAVEL	JINKS	JOYED	RAJAS
HAJIS	JAWAN	JINNE	JUBAS	RAJES
HAJJI	JAWED	JINNI	JUBES	REJIG
HEJAB	JAXIE	JINNS	JUCOS	REJON
HEJRA	JAZZY	JIRDS	JUDAS	RIOJA
HIJAB	JEANS	JIRGA	JUDGE	ROJAK
HIJRA	JEATS	JIRRE	JUDOS	ROJIS
HODJA	JEBEL	JISMS	JUGAL	SAJOU
JAAPS	JEDIS	JIVED	JUGUM	SHOJI
JABOT	JEELS	JIVER	JUICE	SIJOS
JACAL	JEELY	JIVES	JUICY	SLOJD
JACKS	JEEPS	JIVEY	JUJUS	SOJAS
JACKY	JEERS	JNANA	JUKED	SUJEE
JADED	JEFES	JOBED	JUKES	TAJES
JADES	JEFFS	JOBES	JUKUS	THUJA
JAFAS	JEHAD	JOCKO	JULEP	UNJAM
JAGAS	JEHUS	JOCKS	JUMAR	UPJET
JAGER	JELAB	JODEL	JUMBO	WILJA
JAGGS	JELLO	JOEYS	JUMBY	YOJAN
JAGGY	JELLS	JOHNS	JUMPS	ZANJA
JAGIR	JELLY	JOINS	JUMPY	
JAGRA	JEMBE	JOINT	JUNCO	
JAILS	JEMMY	JOIST	JUNKS	

Six-letter words

ABJECT	GAIJIN	JAILER	JAWARI	JEZAIL
ABJURE	GANJAH	JAILOR	JAWBOX	JHALAS
ACAJOU	GANJAS	JAKEYS	JAWING	JHATKA
ADJIGO	GARJAN	JALAPS	JAXIES	JIBBAH
ADJOIN	GAUJES	JALOPS	JAYGEE	JIBBED
ADJURE	GIDJEE	JALOPY	JAYVEE	JIBBER
ADJUST	GOUJON	JAMBED	JAZIES	JIBERS
AJIVAS	GURJUN	JAMBEE	JAZZBO	JIBING
AJOWAN	GYTTJA	JAMBER	JAZZED	JICAMA
AJUGAS	HADJEE	JAMBES	JAZZER	JIGGED
AJWANS	HADJES	JAMBOK	JAZZES	JIGGER
BAJADA	HADJIS	JAMBOS	JEANED	JIGGLE
BAJANS	HAJJAH	JAMBUL	JEBELS	JIGGLY
BAJRAS	HAJJES	JAMBUS	JEEING	JIGJIG
BAJREE	HAJJIS	JAMJAR	JEELED	JIGOTS
BAJRIS	HANJAR	JAMMED	JEELIE	JIGSAW
BANJAX	HEJABS	JAMMER	JEEPED	JIHADI
BANJOS	HEJIRA	JAMPAN	JEERED	JIHADS
BEJADE	HEJRAS	JAMPOT	JEERER	JILBAB
BEJANT	HIJABS	JANDAL	JEFFED	JILGIE
BENJES	HIJACK	JANGLE	JEHADI	JILLET
BHAJAN	HIJRAH	JANGLY	JEHADS	JILTED
BHAJEE	HIJRAS	JANKER	JEJUNA	JILTER
BHAJIS	HOBJOB	JANSKY	JEJUNE	JIMINY
BIJOUS	HODJAS	JANTEE	JELABS	JIMJAM
BIJOUX	INJECT	JAPANS	JELLED	JIMMIE
BOOJUM	INJERA	JAPERS	JELLOS	JIMPER
BUNJEE	INJURE	JAPERY	JEMBES	JIMPLY
BUNJES	INJURY	JAPING	JEMIMA	JIMSON
BUNJIE	INKJET	JAPPED	JENNET	JINGAL
CAJOLE	JABBED	JARFUL	JERBIL	JINGKO
COJOIN	JABBER	JARGON	JERBOA	JINGLE
CONJEE	JABBLE	JARINA	JEREED	JINGLY
CROJIK	JABERS	JAROOL	JERIDS	JINKED
DEEJAY	JABIRU	JARPED	JERKED	JINKER
DEJECT	JABOTS	JARRAH	JERKER	JINNEE
DJEBEL	JACALS	JARRED	JERKIN	JINNIS
DJEMBE	JACANA	JARTAS	JERQUE	JINXED
DJINNI	JACARE	JARULS	JERRID	JINXES
DJINNS	JACENT	JARVEY	JERSEY	JIRBLE
DJINNY	JACKAL	JARVIE	JESSED	JIRGAS
DONJON	JACKED	JASEYS	JESSES	JISSOM
EEJITS	JACKER	JASIES	JESSIE	JITNEY
EJECTA	JACKET	JASMIN	JESTED	JITTER
EJECTS	JACKSY	JASPER	JESTEE	JIVERS
ENJAMB	JADERY	JASPES	JESTER	JIVIER
ENJOIN	JADING	JASPIS	JESUIT	JIVING
ENJOYS	JADISH	JASSES	JETLAG	JIZZES
EVEJAR	JAEGER	JASSID	JETONS	JNANAS
FAJITA	JAGAED	JATAKA	JETSAM	JOANNA
FANJET	JAGERS	JAUKED	JETSOM	JOBBED
FEIJOA	JAGGED	JAUNCE	JETSON	JOBBER
FIGJAM	JAGGER	JAUNSE	JETTED	JOBBIE
FINJAN	JAGHIR	JAUNTS	JETTON	JOBING
FJELDS	JAGIRS	JAUNTY	JETWAY	JOCKEY
FJORDS	JAGRAS	JAUPED	JEWELS	JOCKOS
FRIJOL	JAGUAR	JAVELS	JEWIES	JOCOSE
GADJES	JAILED	JAWANS	JEWING	JOCUND

JODELS	JOUKED	JUICER	JUSTLE	PUJAHS
JOGGED	JOULED	JUICES	JUSTLY	PUNJIS
JOGGER	JOULES	JUJUBE	JUTTED	PYJAMA
JOGGLE	JOUNCE	JUKING	JYMOLD	RAJAHS
JOHNNY	JOUNCY	JULEPS	JYNXES	RAMJET
JOINED	JOURNO	JUMARS	KANJIS	REJECT
JOINER	JOUSTS	JUMART	KHODJA	REJIGS
JOINTS	JOVIAL	JUMBAL	KHOJAS	REJOIN
JOISTS	JOWARI	JUMBIE	KOPJES	RHANJA
JOJOBA	JOWARS	JUMBLE	LAPJES	RIOJAS
JOKERS	JOWING	JUMBLY	LOGJAM	ROJAKS
JOKIER	JOWLED	JUMBOS	MAJLIS	ROMAJI
JOKILY	JOWLER	JUMPED	MAJORS	SAJOUS
JOKING	JOYFUL	JUMPER	MASJID	SANJAK
JOLING	JOYING	JUNCOS	MATJES	SEJANT
JOLLED	JOYOUS	JUNCUS	MEJLIS	SHINJU
JOLLEY	JOYPOP	JUNGLE	MOJOES	SHOJIS
JOLLOP	JUBATE	JUNGLI	MOUJIK	SLOJDS
JOLTED	JUBBAH	JUNGLY	MUJIKS	SOOJEY
JOLTER	JUBHAH	JUNIOR	MUSJID	SUJEES
JOOKED	JUBILE	JUNKED	MUZJIK	SVARAJ
JORAMS	JUDDER	JUNKER	NINJAS	SWARAJ
JORDAN	JUDGED	JUNKET	OBJECT	TAJINE
JORUMS	JUDGER	JUNKIE	OBJETS	THUJAS
JOSEPH	JUDGES	JUNTAS	OBJURE	TINAJA
JOSHED	JUDIES	JUNTOS	OJIMES	TRIJET
JOSHER	JUDOGI	JUPATI	OUIJAS	UJAMAA
JOSHES	JUDOKA	JUPONS	OUTJET	UNJAMS
JOSKIN	JUGALS	JURANT	OUTJUT	UNJUST
JOSSER	JUGATE	JURATS	PAJAMA	UPJETS
JOSSES	JUGFUL	JURELS	PAJOCK	VEEJAY
JOSTLE	JUGGED	JURIED	POLJES	WILJAS
JOTTED	JUGGLE	JURIES	POOJAH	WILTJA
JOTTER	JUGLET	JURIST	POOJAS	YOJANA
JOTUNN	JUGULA	JURORS	POPJOY	YOJANS
JOTUNS	JUGUMS	JUSTED	PRAJNA	ZANJAS
JOUALS	JUICED	JUSTER	PROJET	

Seven-letter words

ABJECTS	ANTIJAM	BUNJIES	DEJECTA	FIGJAMS
ABJOINT	APAREJO	CAJAPUT	DEJECTS	FINJANS
ABJURED	AZULEJO	CAJEPUT	DEJEUNE	FJORDIC
ABJURER	BAJADAS	CAJOLED	DISJECT	FRIJOLE
ABJURES	BAJREES	CAJOLER	DISJOIN	GANJAHS
ACAJOUS	BANJOES	CAJOLES	DISJUNE	GARJANS
ADJIGOS	BASENJI	CAJONES	DJEBELS	GIDJEES
ADJOINS	BEJADED	CAJUPUT	DJEMBES	GJETOST
ADJOINT	BEJADES	CARJACK	DJIBBAH	GOUJONS
ADJOURN	BEJANTS	CATJANG	DONJONS	GURJUNS
ADJUDGE	BEJESUS	COJOINS	EJECTED	GYTTJAS
ADJUNCT	BEJEWEL	COJONES	EJECTOR	HADJEES
ADJURED	BHAJANS	CONJECT	ENJAMBS	HAJJAHS
ADJURER	BHAJEES	CONJEED	ENJOINS	HANDJAR
ADJURES	BLOWJOB	CONJEES	ENJOYED	HANJARS
ADJUROR	BLUEJAY	CONJOIN	ENJOYER	HARIJAN
ADJUSTS	BONJOUR	CONJURE	EVEJARS	HEJIRAS
AJOWANS	BOOJUMS	CONJURY	FAJITAS	HIJACKS
AJUTAGE	BRINJAL	CROJIKS	FANJETS	HIJINKS
ALFORJA	BUNJEES	DEEJAYS	FEIJOAS	HIJRAHS

HOBJOBS	JALOUSE	JATAKAS	JEREEDS	JIGJIGS
IJTIHAD	JAMADAR	JAUKING	JERKERS	JIGLIKE
INJECTS	JAMBART	JAUNCED	JERKIER	JIGSAWN
INJELLY	JAMBEAU	JAUNCES	JERKIES	JIGSAWS
INJERAS	JAMBEES	JAUNSED	JERKILY	JIHADIS
INJOINT	JAMBERS	JAUNSES	JERKING	JILBABS
INJUNCT	JAMBEUX	JAUNTED	JERKINS	JILGIES
INJURED	JAMBIER	JAUNTEE	JERQUED	JILLETS
INJURER	JAMBING	JAUNTIE	JERQUER	JILLION
INJURES	JAMBIYA	JAUPING	JERQUES	JILTERS
JABBERS	JAMBOKS	JAVELIN	JERREED	JILTING
JABBING	JAMBONE	JAWARIS	JERRIDS	JIMJAMS
JABBLED	JAMBOOL	JAWBONE	JERRIES	JIMMIED
JABBLES	JAMBULS	JAWFALL	JERSEYS	JIMMIES
JABIRUS	JAMDANI	JAWHOLE	JESSAMY	JIMMINY
JACALES	JAMESES	JAWINGS	JESSANT	JIMPEST
JACAMAR	JAMJARS	JAWLESS	JESSIES	JIMPIER
JACANAS	JAMLIKE	JAWLIKE	JESSING	JINGALL
JACARES	JAMMERS	JAWLINE	JESTEES	JINGALS
JACCHUS	JAMMIER	JAYBIRD	JESTERS	JINGLED
JACINTH	JAMMIES	JAYGEES	JESTFUL	JINGLER
JACKALS	JAMMING	JAYVEES	JESTING	JINGLES
JACKASS	JAMPANI	JAYWALK	JESUITS	JINGLET
JACKDAW	JAMPANS	JAZZBOS	JETBEAD	JINGOES
JACKEEN	JAMPOTS	JAZZERS	JETFOIL	JINJILI
JACKERS	JANDALS	JAZZIER	JETLAGS	JINKERS
JACKETS	JANGLED	JAZZILY	JETLIKE	JINKING
JACKIES	JANGLER	JAZZING	JETPORT	JINXING
JACKING	JANGLES	JAZZMAN	JETSAMS	JIPYAPA
JACKLEG	JANITOR	JAZZMEN	JETSOMS	JIRBLED
JACKMAN	JANIZAR	JEALOUS	JETSONS	JIRBLES
JACKMEN	JANKERS	JEELIED	JETTIED	JISSOMS
JACKPOT	JANNIES	JEELIES	JETTIER	JITNEYS
JACKSIE	JANNOCK	JEELING	JETTIES	JITTERS
JACOBIN	JANSKYS	JEEPERS	JETTING	JITTERY
JACOBUS	JANTIER	JEEPING	JETTONS	JIVEASS
JACONET	JANTIES	JEEPNEY	JETWAYS	JIVIEST
JACUZZI	JAPINGS	JEERERS	JEWELED	JOANNAS
JADEDLY	JAPPING	JEERING	JEWELER	JOANNES
JADEITE	JARFULS	JEFFING	JEWELRY	JOBBERS
JADITIC	JARGONS	JEHADIS	JEWFISH	JOBBERY
JAEGERS	JARGONY	JEJUNAL	JEZAILS	JOBBIES
JAGAING	JARGOON	JEJUNUM	JEZEBEL	JOBBING
JAGGARY	JARHEAD	JELLABA	JHATKAS	JOBLESS
JAGGERS	JARINAS	JELLIED	JIBBAHS	JOBNAME
JAGGERY	JARKMAN	JELLIES	JIBBERS	JOCKEYS
JAGGIER	JARKMEN	JELLIFY	JIBBING	JOCKNEY
JAGGIES	JARLDOM	JELLING	JIBBONS	JOCULAR
JAGGING	JAROOLS	JEMADAR	JIBBOOM	JODHPUR
JAGHIRE	JARPING	JEMIDAR	JICAMAS	JOGGERS
JAGHIRS	JARRAHS	JEMIMAS	JIFFIES	JOGGING
JAGLESS	JARRING	JEMMIED	JIGABOO	JOGGLED
JAGUARS	JARSFUL	JEMMIER	JIGAJIG	JOGGLER
JAILERS	JARVEYS	JEMMIES	JIGAJOG	JOGGLES
JAILING	JARVIES	JENNETS	JIGGERS	JOGTROT
JAILORS	JASMINE	JENNIES	JIGGIER	JOHNNIE
JAKESES	JASMINS	JEOFAIL	JIGGING	JOHNSON
JALAPIC	JASPERS	JEOPARD	JIGGISH	JOINDER
JALAPIN	JASPERY	JERBILS	JIGGLED	JOINERS
JALOPPY	JASSIDS	JERBOAS	JIGGLES	JOINERY

JOINING	JOURNEY	JUMARED	JUTTING	PIROJKI
JOINTED	JOURNOS	JUMARTS	JUVENAL	POOJAHS
JOINTER	JOUSTED	JUMBALS	JYMOLDS	POPJOYS
JOINTLY	JOUSTER	JUMBIES	KAJAWAH	PRAJNAS
JOISTED	JOWARIS	JUMBLED	KAJEPUT	PREJINK
JOJOBAS	JOWLERS	JUMBLER	KHANJAR	PROJECT
JOKIEST	JOWLIER	JUMBLES	KHODJAS	PROJETS
JOLLEYS	JOWLING	JUMBUCK	KILLJOY	PROPJET
JOLLIED	JOYANCE	JUMELLE	KUNJOOS	PYJAMAS
JOLLIER	JOYLESS	JUMPERS	LOCKJAW	RAMJETS
JOLLIES	JOYPOPS	JUMPIER	LOGJAMS	REEJECT
JOLLIFY	JOYRIDE	JUMPILY	MAATJES	REENJOY
JOLLILY	JOYRODE	JUMPING	MAHJONG	REJECTS
JOLLING	JUBBAHS	JUMPOFF	MAJAGUA	REJOICE
JOLLITY	JUBHAHS	JUNCATE	MAJESTY	REJOINS
JOLLOPS	JUBILEE	JUNCOES	MAJORAT	REJONEO
JOLLYER	JUBILES	JUNGLED	MAJORED	REJONES
JOLTERS	JUDASES	JUNGLES	MAJORLY	REJOURN
JOLTIER	JUDDERS	JUNGLIS	MANJACK	REJUDGE
JOLTILY	JUDGERS	JUNIORS	MASJIDS	RESOJET
JOLTING	JUDGING	JUNIPER	MISJOIN	RHANJAS
JONESED	JUDOGIS	JUNKERS	MOJARRA	ROMAJIS
JONESES	JUDOIST	JUNKETS	MOUJIKS	SANJAKS
JONNOCK	JUDOKAS	JUNKIER	MUDEJAR	SAPAJOU
JONQUIL	JUGFULS	JUNKIES	MUNTJAC	SEJEANT
JONTIES	JUGGING	JUNKING	MUNTJAK	SHINJUS
JOOKERY	JUGGINS	JUNKMAN	MUSJIDS	SJAMBOK
JOOKING	JUGGLED	JUNKMEN	MUZJIKS	SKYJACK
JORDANS	JUGGLER	JUPATIS	NAARTJE	SOJOURN
JOSEPHS	JUGGLES	JURALLY	NARTJIE	SOOJEYS
JOSHERS	JUGHEAD	JURANTS	NONJURY	SUBJECT
JOSHING	JUGLETS	JURIDIC	OBJECTS	SUBJOIN
JOSKINS	JUGSFUL	JURISTS	OBJURED	TAJINES
JOSSERS	JUGULAR	JURYING	OBJURES	TINAJAS
JOSTLED	JUGULUM	JURYMAN	OUTJEST	TOLARJI
JOSTLER	JUICERS	JURYMEN	OUTJETS	TRAJECT
JOSTLES	JUICIER	JUSSIVE	OUTJINX	TRIJETS
JOTTERS	JUICILY	JUSTERS	OUTJUMP	TWINJET
JOTTING	JUICING	JUSTEST	OUTJUTS	UJAMAAS
JOTUNNS	JUJITSU	JUSTICE	OVERJOY	UNJADED
JOUKERY	JUJUBES	JUSTIFY	PAJAMAS	UNJOINT
JOUKING	JUJUISM	JUSTING	PAJOCKE	VEEJAYS
JOULING	JUJUIST	JUSTLED	PAJOCKS	WILTJAS
JOUNCED	JUJUTSU	JUSTLES	PERJINK	WUDJULA
JOUNCES	JUKEBOX	JUTTIED	PERJURE	YOJANAS
JOURNAL	JUKSKEI	JUTTIES	PERJURY	ZANJERO

Eight-letter words

ABJECTED	ADJUNCTS	ALFORJAS	BEJEWELS	BRINJALS
ABJECTLY	ADJURERS	APAREJOS	BEJUMBLE	CAJAPUTS
ABJOINTS	ADJURING	AZULEJOS	BENJAMIN	CAJEPUTS
ABJURERS	ADJURORS	BANJAXED	BIJUGATE	CAJOLERS
ABJURING	ADJUSTED	BANJAXES	BIJUGOUS	CAJOLERY
ADJACENT	ADJUSTER	BANJOIST	BIJWONER	CAJOLING
ADJOINED	ADJUSTOR	BASENJIS	BLOWJOBS	CAJUPUTS
ADJOINTS	ADJUTAGE	BEJABERS	BLUEJACK	CARCAJOU
ADJOURNS	ADJUTANT	BEJADING	BLUEJAYS	CARJACKS
ADJUDGED	ADJUVANT	BEJEEZUS	BOERTJIE	CARJACOU
ADJUDGES	AJUTAGES	BEJESUIT	BOOTJACK	CATJANGS

COJOINED	JACKAROO	JANIZARS	JEMIDARS	JINGLETS
CONJECTS	JACKBOOT	JANIZARY	JEMMIEST	JINGLIER
CONJOINS	JACKDAWS	JANNOCKS	JEMMYING	JINGLING
CONJOINT	JACKEENS	JANTIEST	JEOFAILS	JINGOISH
CONJUGAL	JACKEROO	JAPANISE	JEOPARDS	JINGOISM
CONJUNCT	JACKETED	JAPANIZE	JEOPARDY	JINGOIST
CONJUNTO	JACKFISH	JAPANNED	JEREMIAD	JINJILIS
CONJURED	JACKINGS	JAPANNER	JEREPIGO	JIPIJAPA
CONJURER	JACKLEGS	JAPERIES	JERKIEST	JIPYAPAS
CONJURES	JACKPOTS	JAPINGLY	JERKINGS	JIRBLING
CONJUROR	JACKROLL	JAPONICA	JEROBOAM	JIRKINET
CRACKJAW	JACKSIES	JARARACA	JERQUERS	JITTERED
CUNJEVOI	JACKSTAY	JARARAKA	JERQUING	JIUJITSU
DEEJAYED	JACOBINS	JARGONED	JERREEDS	JIUJUTSU
DEJECTED	JACONETS	JARGONEL	JERRICAN	JOBATION
DEJEUNER	JACQUARD	JARGOONS	JERRYCAN	JOBBINGS
DEJEUNES	JACULATE	JARHEADS	JERSEYED	JOBNAMES
DEMIJOHN	JACUZZIS	JARLDOMS	JESTBOOK	JOBSHARE
DISJECTS	JADEITES	JAROSITE	JESTINGS	JOCKETTE
DISJOINS	JADELIKE	JAROVISE	JESUITIC	JOCKEYED
DISJOINT	JADERIES	JAROVIZE	JESUITRY	JOCKNEYS
DISJUNCT	JADISHLY	JARRINGS	JETBEADS	JOCOSELY
DISJUNES	JAGGEDER	JASMINES	JETFOILS	JOCOSITY
DJELLABA	JAGGEDLY	JASPISES	JETLINER	JOCUNDLY
DJIBBAHS	JAGGHERY	JAUNCING	JETPLANE	JODELLED
DOORJAMB	JAGGIEST	JAUNDICE	JETPORTS	JODHPURS
EJECTING	JAGHIRES	JAUNSING	JETTIEST	JOGGINGS
EJECTION	JAILABLE	JAUNTIER	JETTISON	JOGGLERS
EJECTIVE	JAILBAIT	JAUNTIES	JETTYING	JOGGLING
EJECTORS	JAILBIRD	JAUNTILY	JEWELERS	JOGPANTS
ENJAMBED	JAILLESS	JAUNTING	JEWELING	JOGTROTS
ENJOINED	JAKFRUIT	JAVELINA	JEWELLED	JOHANNES
ENJOINER	JALAPENO	JAVELINS	JEWELLER	JOHNBOAT
ENJOYERS	JALAPINS	JAWBONED	JEZEBELS	JOHNNIES
ENJOYING	JALOPIES	JAWBONER	JIBBERED	JOHNSONS
FLAPJACK	JALOUSED	JAWBONES	JIBBINGS	JOINABLE
FORJUDGE	JALOUSES	JAWBOXES	JIBBOOMS	JOINDERS
FRABJOUS	JALOUSIE	JAWFALLS	JIBINGLY	JOININGS
FRIJOLES	JAMADARS	JAWHOLES	JICKAJOG	JOINTERS
GJETOSTS	JAMBARTS	JAWLINES	JIGABOOS	JOINTING
GOUJEERS	JAMBEAUX	JAYBIRDS	JIGAJIGS	JOINTURE
HANDJARS	JAMBIERS	JAYWALKS	JIGAJOGS	JOISTING
HARIJANS	JAMBIYAH	JAZERANT	JIGGERED	JOKESOME
HIGHJACK	JAMBIYAS	JAZZIEST	JIGGIEST	JOKESTER
HIJACKED	JAMBOLAN	JAZZLIKE	JIGGINGS	JOKINESS
HIJACKER	JAMBONES	JEALOUSE	JIGGLIER	JOKINGLY
IJTIHADS	JAMBOOLS	JEALOUSY	JIGGLING	JOLLEYER
INJECTED	JAMBOREE	JEANETTE	JIGSAWED	JOLLIERS
INJECTOR	JAMDANIS	JEELYING	JIHADISM	JOLLIEST
INJOINTS	JAMMABLE	JEEPNEYS	JIHADIST	JOLLYERS
INJUNCTS	JAMMIEST	JEERINGS	JILLAROO	JOLLYING
INJURERS	JAMPANEE	JEHADISM	JILLIONS	JOLTHEAD
INJURIES	JAMPANIS	JEHADIST	JIMCRACK	JOLTIEST
INJURING	JANGLERS	JEJUNELY	JIMMYING	JONCANOE
JABBERED	JANGLIER	JEJUNITY	JIMPIEST	JONESING
JABBERER	JANGLING	JELLABAH	JIMPNESS	JONGLEUR
JABBLING	JANIFORM	JELLABAS	JINGALLS	JONQUILS
JACAMARS	JANISARY	JELLYING	JINGBANG	JORDELOO
JACINTHE	JANITORS	JELUTONG	JINGKOES	JOSTLERS
JACINTHS	JANITRIX	JEMADARS	JINGLERS	JOSTLING

JOTTINGS	JUMBLING	KINKAJOU	OVERJOYS	REOBJECT
JOUNCIER	JUMBOISE	KNEEJERK	OVERJUMP	RESOJETS
JOUNCING	JUMBOIZE	KOMITAJI	OVERJUST	SAPAJOUS
JOURNALS	JUMBUCKS	LOCKJAWS	PAJAMAED	SCRAMJET
JOURNEYS	JUMELLES	LOGJUICE	PAJOCKES	SERJEANT
JOUSTERS	JUMPABLE	LONGJUMP	PEJORATE	SJAMBOKS
JOUSTING	JUMPIEST	MAHARAJA	PERJURED	SKIJORER
JOVIALLY	JUMPINGS	MAHJONGG	PERJURER	SKIPJACK
JOVIALTY	JUMPOFFS	MAHJONGS	PERJURES	SKYJACKS
JOWLIEST	JUMPSUIT	MAJAGUAS	POPINJAY	SLAPJACK
JOYANCES	JUNCATES	MAJESTIC	POPJOYED	SOJOURNS
JOYFULLY	JUNCTION	MAJLISES	PREJUDGE	STICKJAW
JOYOUSLY	JUNCTURE	MAJOLICA	PROJECTS	SUBJECTS
JOYRIDER	JUNCUSES	MAJORATS	PROPJETS	SUBJOINS
JOYRIDES	JUNGLIER	MAJORING	PULSEJET	SUCURUJU
JOYSTICK	JUNGLIST	MAJORITY	PULSOJET	SUPERJET
JUBILANT	JUNIPERS	MANJACKS	PYJAMAED	SVARAJES
JUBILATE	JUNKANOO	MARJORAM	QUILLAJA	SWARAJES
JUBILEES	JUNKETED	MARYJANE	RAJASHIP	TJANTING
JUDDERED	JUNKETER	MEJLISES	READJUST	TOLARJEV
JUDGMENT	JUNKIEST	MICROJET	REEJECTS	TRAJECTS
JUDICIAL	JUNKYARD	MIJNHEER	REENJOYS	TURBOJET
JUDOISTS	JURASSIC	MISJOINS	REINJECT	TWINJETS
JUGGINGS	JURATORY	MISJUDGE	REINJURE	UNDERJAW
JUGGLERS	JURISTIC	MOJARRAS	REINJURY	UNJAMMED
JUGGLERY	JURYLESS	MULTIJET	REJACKET	UNJOINED
JUGGLING	JURYMAST	MUNTJACS	REJACKED	UNJOINTS
JUGHEADS	JUSSIVES	MUNTJAKS	REJECTED	UNJOYFUL
JUGULARS	JUSTICER	NAARTJES	REJECTEE	UNJOYOUS
JUGULATE	JUSTICES	NAARTJIE	REJECTER	UNJUDGED
JUICIEST	JUSTLING	NARTJIES	REJECTOR	UNJUSTER
JUJITSUS	JUSTNESS	NIGHTJAR	REJIGGED	UNJUSTLY
JUJUISMS	JUTELIKE	NINJITSU	REJIGGER	UPJETTED
JUJUISTS	JUTTYING	NINJUTSU	REJOICED	VERJUICE
JUJUTSUS	JUVENALS	NONJUROR	REJOICER	WATERJET
JUKSKEIS	JUVENILE	NONMAJOR	REJOICES	WHIPJACK
JULIENNE	KABELJOU	OBJECTED	REJOINED	WUDJULAS
JUMARING	KAJAWAHS	OBJECTOR	REJONEOS	ZABAJONE
JUMARRED	KAJEPUTS	OBJURING	REJOURNS	ZANJEROS
JUMBLERS	KHANJARS	OUTJESTS	REJUDGED	
JUMBLIER	KILLJOYS	OUTJUMPS	REJUDGES	
			REJUGGLE	

Q

Along with Z, Q is the highest-scoring letter in Scrabble. Unlike Z, Q can be tricky to use because the majority of words that contain Q also require a U. There are, however, a number of words that contain Q but no U; a complete list of these follows in this section. It's easy enough to learn all of these. There's only one two-letter word with Q, **qi**, which is very useful as it allows you to tag onto one of the most common tiles in the game. It's also worth committing all of the three-letter words that use Q to memory. If you are lucky enough to draw a Q when you also have a U on your rack, or there is a U available on the board, remember that the four-letter words that can be formed with one vowel and one consonant (**quad**, **quey**, **quiz** and **quod**, for example). Learning the four-letter Q words will give you a good range of options for when you get the chance to play Q and U together.

Two-letter words

QI	vital energy believed to circulate round the body

Three-letter words

QAT	white-flowered evergreen shrub of Africa and Asia whose leaves have narcotic properties
QIS	plural of qi
QUA	in the capacity of
SUQ	open-air marketplace

Four-letter words

AQUA	QUAD	QUEP	QUIP	SUQS
QADI	QUAG	QUEY	QUIT	WAQF
QAID	QUAI	QUID	QUIZ	
QATS	QUAT	QUIM	QUOD	
QOPH	QUAY	QUIN	QUOP	

Five-letter words

AQUAE	QUAIL	QUEER	QUINS	QUOTH
AQUAS	QUAIR	QUELL	QUINT	QURSH
BURQA	QUAIS	QUEME	QUIPO	QUYTE
EQUAL	QUAKE	QUENA	QUIPS	ROQUE
EQUID	QUAKY	QUERN	QUIPU	SQUAB
EQUIP	QUALE	QUERY	QUIRE	SQUAD
FAQIR	QUALM	QUEST	QUIRK	SQUAT
FIQUE	QUANT	QUEUE	QUIRT	SQUAW
MAQUI	QUARE	QUEYN	QUIST	SQUEG
NIQAB	QUARK	QUEYS	QUITE	SQUIB
PIQUE	QUART	QUICH	QUITS	SQUID
QADIS	QUASH	QUICK	QUOAD	SQUIT
QAIDS	QUASI	QUIDS	QUODS	SQUIZ
QANAT	QUASS	QUIET	QUOIF	TALAQ
QIBLA	QUATE	QUIFF	QUOIN	TOQUE
QOPHS	QUATS	QUILL	QUOIT	TRANQ
QORMA	QUAYD	QUILT	QUOLL	TUQUE
QUACK	QUAYS	QUIMS	QUONK	UMIAQ
QUADS	QUBIT	QUINA	QUOPS	USQUE
QUAFF	QUEAN	QUINE	QUOTA	WAQFS
QUAGS	QUEEN	QUINO	QUOTE	

Six-letter words

ACQUIT	BURQAS	CIRQUE	EQUALI	EQUIPS
ASQUAT	CAIQUE	CLAQUE	EQUALS	EQUITY
BARQUE	CALQUE	CLIQUE	EQUANT	EXEQUY
BASQUE	CASQUE	CLIQUY	EQUATE	FAQIRS
BISQUE	CHEQUE	CLOQUE	EQUIDS	FAQUIR
BOSQUE	CHEQUY	COQUET	EQUINE	FIQUES
BUQSHA	CINQUE	DIQUAT	EQUIPE	HAIQUE

JERQUE	QUAKED	QUERNS	QUIRTS	SQUALL
LASQUE	QUAKER	QUESTS	QUISTS	SQUAMA
LIQUID	QUAKES	QUETCH	QUITCH	SQUAME
LIQUOR	QUALIA	QUETHE	QUITED	SQUARE
LOQUAT	QUALMS	QUEUED	QUITES	SQUARK
MANQUE	QUALMY	QUEUER	QUIVER	SQUASH
MAQUIS	QUANGO	QUEUES	QUOHOG	SQUATS
MARQUE	QUANTA	QUEYNS	QUOIFS	SQUAWK
MASQUE	QUANTS	QUEZAL	QUOINS	SQUAWS
MOSQUE	QUARER	QUICHE	QUOIST	SQUEAK
NIQABS	QUARKS	QUICKS	QUOITS	SQUEAL
OPAQUE	QUARRY	QUIDAM	QUOKKA	SQUEGS
PIQUED	QUARTE	QUIETS	QUOLLS	SQUIBS
PIQUES	QUARTO	QUIFFS	QUONKS	SQUIDS
PIQUET	QUARTS	QUIGHT	QUOOKE	SQUIER
PLAQUE	QUARTZ	QUILLS	QUORUM	SQUIFF
PULQUE	QUASAR	QUILTS	QUOTAS	SQUILL
QABALA	QUATCH	QUINAS	QUOTED	SQUINT
QANATS	QUATRE	QUINCE	QUOTER	SQUINY
QASIDA	QUAVER	QUINES	QUOTES	SQUIRE
QAWWAL	QUAZZY	QUINIC	QUOTHA	SQUIRM
QIBLAS	QUBITS	QUINIE	QUOTUM	SQUIRR
QIGONG	QUBYTE	QUININ	QURUSH	SQUIRT
QINDAR	QUEACH	QUINOA	QUYTED	SQUISH
QINTAR	QUEANS	QUINOL	QUYTES	SQUITS
QIVIUT	QUEASY	QUINOS	QWERTY	SQUUSH
QORMAS	QUEAZY	QUINSY	REQUIN	TALAQS
QUACKS	QUEENS	QUINTA	REQUIT	TOQUES
QUACKY	QUEENY	QUINTE	RISQUE	TOQUET
QUAERE	QUEERS	QUINTS	ROQUES	TORQUE
QUAFFS	QUEEST	QUINZE	ROQUET	TRANQS
QUAGGA	QUEINT	QUIPOS	SACQUE	TUQUES
QUAGGY	QUELCH	QUIPPU	SAIQUE	UBIQUE
QUAHOG	QUELEA	QUIPPY	SEQUEL	UMIAQS
QUAICH	QUELLS	QUIPUS	SEQUIN	UNIQUE
QUAIGH	QUEMED	QUIRED	SHEQEL	USQUES
QUAILS	QUEMES	QUIRES	SQUABS	YANQUI
QUAINT	QUENAS	QUIRKS	SQUADS	YAQONA
QUAIRS	QUENCH	QUIRKY	SQUAIL	

Seven-letter words

ACEQUIA	BANQUET	CASQUED	COQUINA	EQUATOR
ACQUEST	BAROQUE	CASQUES	COQUITO	EQUERRY
ACQUIRE	BARQUES	CAZIQUE	CROQUET	EQUINAL
ACQUIST	BASQUED	CHARQUI	CROQUIS	EQUINES
ACQUITE	BASQUES	CHEQUER	CUMQUAT	EQUINIA
ACQUITS	BEQUEST	CHEQUES	DAQUIRI	EQUINOX
ALFAQUI	BEZIQUE	CINQUES	DIQUARK	EQUIPES
ALIQUOT	BISQUES	CIRQUES	DIQUATS	EQUITES
ANTIQUE	BOSQUES	CLAQUER	DOCQUET	ESQUIRE
AQUAFER	BOSQUET	CLAQUES	ENQUIRE	FAQUIRS
AQUARIA	BOUQUET	CLIQUED	ENQUIRY	GRECQUE
AQUATIC	BRIQUET	CLIQUES	EQUABLE	HAIQUES
AQUAVIT	BRUSQUE	CLIQUEY	EQUABLY	INQILAB
AQUEOUS	BUQSHAS	CLOQUES	EQUALED	INQUERE
AQUIFER	CACIQUE	COEQUAL	EQUALLY	INQUEST
AQUILON	CAIQUES	COMIQUE	EQUANTS	INQUIET
AQUIVER	CALQUED	CONQUER	EQUATED	INQUIRE
ASQUINT	CALQUES	COQUETS	EQUATES	INQUIRY

JERQUED	QUADRAT	QUEMING	QUINTIC	SEQUELS
JERQUER	QUADRIC	QUERIDA	QUINTIN	SEQUENT
JERQUES	QUAERED	QUERIED	QUINZES	SEQUINS
JONQUIL	QUAERES	QUERIER	QUIPPED	SEQUOIA
KUMQUAT	QUAFFED	QUERIES	QUIPPER	SHEQELS
LACQUER	QUAFFER	QUERIST	QUIPPUS	SILIQUA
LACQUEY	QUAGGAS	QUESTED	QUIRING	SILIQUE
LALIQUE	QUAHAUG	QUESTER	QUIRKED	SQUABBY
LASQUES	QUAHOGS	QUESTOR	QUIRTED	SQUACCO
LEQUEAR	QUAICHS	QUETHES	QUITING	SQUADDY
LIQUATE	QUAIGHS	QUETSCH	QUITTAL	SQUAILS
LIQUEFY	QUAILED	QUETZAL	QUITTED	SQUALID
LIQUEUR	QUAKERS	QUEUERS	QUITTER	SQUALLS
LIQUIDS	QUAKIER	QUEUING	QUITTOR	SQUALLY
LIQUIFY	QUAKILY	QUEYNIE	QUIVERS	SQUALOR
LIQUORS	QUAKING	QUEZALS	QUIVERY	SQUAMAE
LOQUATS	QUALIFY	QUIBBLE	QUIXOTE	SQUAMES
MACAQUE	QUALITY	QUIBLIN	QUIZZED	SQUARED
MADOQUA	QUAMASH	QUICHED	QUIZZER	SQUARER
MAQUILA	QUANGOS	QUICHES	QUIZZES	SQUARES
MARQUEE	QUANNET	QUICKEN	QUODDED	SQUARKS
MARQUES	QUANTAL	QUICKER	QUODLIN	SQUASHY
MARQUIS	QUANTED	QUICKIE	QUOHOGS	SQUATLY
MASQUER	QUANTIC	QUICKLY	QUOIFED	SQUATTY
MASQUES	QUANTUM	QUIDAMS	QUOINED	SQUAWKS
MESQUIN	QUAREST	QUIDDIT	QUOISTS	SQUAWKY
MESQUIT	QUARREL	QUIDDLE	QUOITED	SQUEAKS
MEZQUIT	QUARTAN	QUIESCE	QUOITER	SQUEAKY
MOSQUES	QUARTER	QUIETED	QUOKKAS	SQUEALS
OBLIQUE	QUARTES	QUIETEN	QUOMODO	SQUEEZE
OBLOQUY	QUARTET	QUIETER	QUONDAM	SQUEEZY
OBSEQUY	QUARTIC	QUIETLY	QUONKED	SQUELCH
OPAQUED	QUARTOS	QUIETUS	QUOPPED	SQUIDGE
OPAQUER	QUARTZY	QUIGHTS	QUORATE	SQUIDGY
OPAQUES	QUASARS	QUILLAI	QUORUMS	SQUIERS
OQUASSA	QUASHED	QUILLED	QUOTERS	SQUIFFY
PARQUET	QUASHEE	QUILLET	QUOTING	SQUILLA
PASQUIL	QUASHER	QUILLON	QUOTUMS	SQUILLS
PERIQUE	QUASHES	QUILTED	QURSHES	SQUINCH
PICQUET	QUASHIE	QUILTER	QUYTING	SQUINNY
PIQUANT	QUASSES	QUINARY	QWERTYS	SQUINTS
PIQUETS	QUASSIA	QUINATE	RACQUET	SQUINTY
PIQUING	QUASSIN	QUINCES	REEQUIP	SQUIRED
PIROQUE	QUATRES	QUINCHE	RELIQUE	SQUIRES
PLAQUES	QUAVERS	QUINELA	REPIQUE	SQUIRMS
PREQUEL	QUAVERY	QUINIES	REQUERE	SQUIRMY
PULQUES	QUAYAGE	QUININA	REQUEST	SQUIRRS
QABALAH	QUBYTES	QUININE	REQUIEM	SQUIRTS
QABALAS	QUEACHY	QUININS	REQUINS	SQUISHY
QASIDAS	QUEECHY	QUINNAT	REQUIRE	SQUITCH
QAWWALI	QUEENED	QUINOAS	REQUITE	SQUOOSH
QAWWALS	QUEENIE	QUINOID	REQUITS	SUBAQUA
QIGONGS	QUEENLY	QUINOLS	REQUOTE	TEQUILA
QINDARS	QUEERED	QUINONE	RISQUES	TOQUETS
QINTARS	QUEERER	QUINTAL	ROCQUET	TORQUED
QIVIUTS	QUEERLY	QUINTAN	ROQUETS	TORQUER
QUACKED	QUEESTS	QUINTAR	RORQUAL	TORQUES
QUACKER	QUELEAS	QUINTAS	SACQUES	TSADDIQ
QUACKLE	QUELLED	QUINTES	SAIQUES	TZADDIQ
QUADDED	QUELLER	QUINTET	SEQUELA	UNEQUAL

UNIQUER	UNQUEEN	UNQUOTE	YANQUIS	
UNIQUES	UNQUIET	VAQUERO	YAQONAS	

Eight-letter words

ACEQUIAS	BOUTIQUE	EQUATION	LOQUITUR	PIROQUES
ACQUAINT	BRELOQUE	EQUATORS	LUSTIQUE	POSTIQUE
ACQUESTS	BRIQUETS	EQUINELY	MACAQUES	PRATIQUE
ACQUIGHT	BRUSQUER	EQUINIAS	MADOQUAS	PREQUELS
ACQUIRAL	CACIQUES	EQUINITY	MAQUETTE	QABALAHS
ACQUIRED	CALQUING	EQUIPAGE	MAQUILAS	QABALISM
ACQUIREE	CAZIQUES	EQUIPPED	MAROQUIN	QABALIST
ACQUIRER	CHAQUETA	EQUIPPER	MARQUEES	QAIMAQAM
ACQUIRES	CHARQUID	EQUISETA	MARQUESS	QALAMDAN
ACQUISTS	CHARQUIS	EQUITANT	MARQUISE	QAWWALIS
ACQUITES	CHEQUERS	EQUITIES	MASQUERS	QINDARKA
ADEQUACY	CHEQUING	EQUIVOKE	MBAQANGA	QUAALUDE
ADEQUATE	CINQUAIN	ESQUIRED	MESQUINE	QUACKERS
AEQUORIN	CLAQUERS	ESQUIRES	MESQUITE	QUACKERY
ALFAQUIN	CLAQUEUR	ESQUISSE	MESQUITS	QUACKIER
ALFAQUIS	CLINIQUE	EXEQUIAL	MEZQUITE	QUACKING
ALIQUANT	CLIQUIER	EXEQUIES	MEZQUITS	QUACKISH
ALIQUOTS	CLIQUING	FILIOQUE	MIQUELET	QUACKISM
ANTIQUED	CLIQUISH	FREQUENT	MISQUOTE	QUACKLED
ANTIQUER	CLIQUISM	GODSQUAD	MOQUETTE	QUACKLES
ANTIQUES	COEQUALS	GRECQUES	MORESQUE	QUADDING
ANTIQUEY	COEQUATE	HAQUETON	MOSQUITO	QUADPLEX
APPLIQUE	COLLOQUE	HENEQUEN	MUQADDAM	QUADRANS
AQUACADE	COLLOQUY	HENEQUIN	MUSQUASH	QUADRANT
AQUAFARM	COMIQUES	HENIQUEN	MYSTIQUE	QUADRATE
AQUAFERS	CONQUERS	HENIQUIN	NARQUOIS	QUADRATS
AQUALUNG	CONQUEST	HUAQUERO	NONEQUAL	QUADRICS
AQUANAUT	CONQUIAN	ILLIQUID	NONQUOTA	QUADRIGA
AQUARIAL	COQUETRY	INEQUITY	OBLIQUED	QUADROON
AQUARIAN	COQUETTE	INIQUITY	OBLIQUER	QUAESTOR
AQUARIST	COQUILLA	INQILABS	OBLIQUES	QUAFFERS
AQUARIUM	COQUILLE	INQUERED	OBLIQUID	QUAFFING
AQUASHOW	COQUINAS	INQUERES	OBSEQUIE	QUAGGIER
AQUATICS	COQUITOS	INQUESTS	ODALIQUE	QUAGMIRE
AQUATINT	COTQUEAN	INQUIETS	OLDSQUAW	QUAGMIRY
AQUATONE	CRITIQUE	INQUIRED	OPAQUELY	QUAHAUGS
AQUAVITS	CROQUETS	INQUIRER	OPAQUEST	QUAICHES
AQUEDUCT	CUMQUATS	INQUIRES	OPAQUING	QUAILING
AQUIFERS	DAIQUIRI	JACQUARD	OQUASSAS	QUAINTER
AQUILINE	DAQUIRIS	JERQUERS	OUTQUOTE	QUAINTLY
AQUILONS	DETRAQUE	JERQUING	PARAQUAT	QUAKIEST
ARQUEBUS	DIQUARKS	JONQUILS	PARAQUET	QUAKINGS
BANQUETS	DISQUIET	KUMQUATS	PAROQUET	QUALMIER
BARBEQUE	DOCQUETS	LACQUERS	PARQUETS	QUALMING
BAROQUES	ELOQUENT	LACQUEYS	PASQUILS	QUALMISH
BASQUINE	EMBUSQUE	LALIQUES	PEQUISTE	QUANDANG
BEDQUILT	ENQUIRED	LEQUEARS	PERIQUES	QUANDARY
BELIQUOR	ENQUIRER	LIQUABLE	PERRUQUE	QUANDONG
BEQUEATH	ENQUIRES	LIQUATED	PETANQUE	QUANNETS
BEQUESTS	EQUALING	LIQUATES	PHYSIQUE	QUANTICS
BEZIQUES	EQUALISE	LIQUESCE	PICQUETS	QUANTIFY
BIUNIQUE	EQUALITY	LIQUEURS	PIQUANCE	QUANTILE
BLANQUET	EQUALIZE	LIQUIDLY	PIQUANCY	QUANTING
BOSQUETS	EQUALLED	LIQUIDUS	PIQUETED	QUANTISE
BOUQUETS	EQUATING	LIQUORED	PIQUILLO	QUANTITY

QUANTIZE	QUERYING	QUINOIDS	REPIQUED	SQUARING
QUANTONG	QUESTANT	QUINOLIN	REPIQUES	SQUARISH
QUARRELS	QUESTERS	QUINONES	REQUERED	SQUARSON
QUARRIAN	QUESTING	QUINSIED	REQUERES	SQUASHED
QUARRIED	QUESTION	QUINSIES	REQUESTS	SQUASHER
QUARRIER	QUESTORS	QUINTAIN	REQUIEMS	SQUASHES
QUARRIES	QUETCHED	QUINTALS	REQUIGHT	SQUATTED
QUARRION	QUETCHES	QUINTANS	REQUIRED	SQUATTER
QUARTANS	QUETHING	QUINTARS	REQUIRER	SQUATTLE
QUARTERN	QUETZALS	QUINTETS	REQUIRES	SQUAWKED
QUARTERS	QUEUEING	QUINTETT	REQUITAL	SQUAWKER
QUARTETS	QUEUINGS	QUINTICS	REQUITED	SQUAWMAN
QUARTETT	QUEYNIES	QUINTILE	REQUITER	SQUAWMEN
QUARTICS	QUEZALES	QUINTINS	REQUITES	SQUEAKED
QUARTIER	QUIBBLED	QUIPPERS	REQUOTED	SQUEAKER
QUARTILE	QUIBBLER	QUIPPIER	REQUOTES	SQUEALED
QUARTZES	QUIBBLES	QUIPPING	REQUOYLE	SQUEALER
QUASHEES	QUIBLINS	QUIPPISH	ROCQUETS	SQUEEGEE
QUASHERS	QUICHING	QUIPSTER	ROQUETED	SQUEEZED
QUASHIES	QUICKENS	QUIRKIER	ROQUETTE	SQUEEZER
QUASHING	QUICKEST	QUIRKILY	RORQUALS	SQUEEZES
QUASSIAS	QUICKIES	QUIRKING	SEAQUAKE	SQUEGGED
QUASSINS	QUICKSET	QUIRKISH	SEQUELAE	SQUEGGER
QUATCHED	QUIDDANY	QUIRTING	SEQUENCE	SQUELCHY
QUATCHES	QUIDDITS	QUISLING	SEQUENCY	SQUIBBED
QUATORZE	QUIDDITY	QUITCHED	SEQUENTS	SQUIDDED
QUATRAIN	QUIDDLED	QUITCHES	SEQUINED	SQUIDGED
QUAVERED	QUIDDLER	QUITRENT	SEQUITUR	SQUIDGES
QUAVERER	QUIDDLES	QUITTALS	SEQUOIAS	SQUIFFED
QUAYAGES	QUIDNUNC	QUITTERS	SERVQUAL	SQUIFFER
QUAYLIKE	QUIESCED	QUITTING	SHEQALIM	SQUIGGLE
QUAYSIDE	QUIESCES	QUITTORS	SILIQUAE	SQUIGGLY
QUAZZIER	QUIETENS	QUIVERED	SILIQUAS	SQUILGEE
QUEACHES	QUIETERS	QUIVERER	SILIQUES	SQUILLAE
QUEASIER	QUIETEST	QUIXOTES	SOLIQUID	SQUILLAS
QUEASILY	QUIETING	QUIXOTIC	SQUABASH	SQUINIED
QUEAZIER	QUIETISM	QUIXOTRY	SQUABBED	SQUINIES
QUEENDOM	QUIETIST	QUIZZERS	SQUABBER	SQUINTED
QUEENIER	QUIETIVE	QUIZZERY	SQUABBLE	SQUINTER
QUEENIES	QUIETUDE	QUIZZIFY	SQUACCOS	SQUIRAGE
QUEENING	QUIGHTED	QUIZZING	SQUADDED	SQUIREEN
QUEENITE	QUILLAIA	QUODDING	SQUADDIE	SQUIRELY
QUEENLET	QUILLAIS	QUODLINS	SQUADRON	SQUIRESS
QUEERDOM	QUILLAJA	QUOIFING	SQUAILED	SQUIRING
QUEEREST	QUILLETS	QUOINING	SQUAILER	SQUIRISH
QUEERING	QUILLING	QUOITERS	SQUALENE	SQUIRMED
QUEERISH	QUILLMAN	QUOITING	SQUALLED	SQUIRMER
QUEERITY	QUILLMEN	QUOMODOS	SQUALLER	SQUIRRED
QUELCHED	QUILLONS	QUONKING	SQUALOID	SQUIRREL
QUELCHES	QUILTERS	QUOPPING	SQUALORS	SQUIRTED
QUELLERS	QUILTING	QUOTABLE	SQUAMATE	SQUIRTER
QUELLING	QUINCHED	QUOTABLY	SQUAMOSE	SQUISHED
QUENCHED	QUINCHES	QUOTIENT	SQUAMOUS	SQUISHES
QUENCHER	QUINCUNX	QURUSHES	SQUAMULA	SQUIZZES
QUENCHES	QUINELAS	QWERTIES	SQUAMULE	SQUOOSHY
QUENELLE	QUINELLA	RACQUETS	SQUANDER	SQUUSHED
QUERCINE	QUINIELA	RAMEQUIN	SQUARELY	SQUUSHES
QUERIDAS	QUININAS	REEQUIPS	SQUARERS	SUBEQUAL
QUERIERS	QUININES	RELIQUES	SQUAREST	SURQUEDY
QUERISTS	QUINNATS	REMARQUE	SQUARIAL	TAQUERIA

TEQUILAS	TRANQUIL	UBIQUITY	UNQUIETS	VAQUEROS
TEQUILLA	TRUQUAGE	UMQUHILE	UNQUOTED	VEHMIQUE
TOQUILLA	TRUQUEUR	UNEQUALS	UNQUOTES	VERQUERE
TORQUATE	TSADDIQS	UNIQUELY	USQUABAE	VERQUIRE
TORQUERS	TURQUOIS	UNIQUEST	USQUEBAE	
TORQUING	TZADDIQS	UNQUEENS	VANQUISH	

Q but not U

There are few things more infuriating than having a Q on your rack but no U with which to play it! But this situation needn't be disastrous: there is a surprisingly high number of words that have a Q but not U. A complete list of these words is included here. These have short definitions to help you remember them; it is well worth learning them all, as they can be extremely useful.

FAQIR	FAQIRS	
INQILAB	INQILABS	
MBAQANGA	MBAQANGAS	
NIQAB	NIQABS	
QABALA		
QABALAH	QABALAHS	QABALAS
QABALISM	QABALISMS	
QABALIST	QABALISTS	
QADI	QADIS	
QAID	QAIDS	
QAIMAQAM	QAIMAQAMS	
QALAMDAN	QALAMDANS	
QANAT	QANATS	
QASIDA	QASIDAS	
QAT	QATS	
QAWWAL	QAWWALI	
QAWWALIS	QAWWALS	
QI		
QIBLA	QIBLAS	
QIGONG	QIGONGS	
QINDAR	QINDARKA	QINDARS
QINTAR	QINTARS	
QIS		
QOPH	QOPHS	
QORMA	QORMAS	
QWERTIES	QWERTY	QWERTYS
SHEQALIM	SHEQEL	SHEQELS
TALAQ	TALAQS	
TRANQ	TRANQS	
TSADDIQ	TSADDIQIM	TSADDIQS
TZADDIQ	TZADDIQIM	TZADDIQS
WAQF	WAQFS	
YAQONA	YAQONAS	

Q and K

Looking at the words that contain Q but not U, you may well notice that many are of Arabic or Hebrew origin. Of course, these languages aren't written using the Roman alphabet, so these words are transliterations from a different script. It's an interesting – and helpful – fact that the Arabic consonant that is represented as a Q in Roman script can also be transliterated as a K, which means that many of the Q-but-no-U words can also be spelt with a K. This is useful for two reasons. Firstly, looking at the list of K alternatives will help you remember the Q-only words. Secondly, K is a sort of 'semi-power' tile, scoring five points and being the most valuable letter after the power tiles. Thus it's quite useful to know these unusual words using K for their own sake.

FAQIR	FAKIR	QALAMDAN	KALAMDAN	SHEQELS	SHEKELS
FAQIRS	FAKIRS	QALAMDANS	KALAMDANS	TALAQ	TALAK
QABALA	KABALA	QAT	KAT	TALAQS	TALAKS
QABALAS	KABALAS	QATS	KATS	TRANQ	TRANK
QABALISM	KABALISM	QI	KI	TRANQS	TRANKS
QABALISMS	KABALISMS	QIBLA	KIBLA	TSADDIQ	TSADDIK
QABALIST	KABALIST	QIBLAS	KIBLAS	TSADDIQIM	TSADDIKIM
QABALISTS	KABALISTS	QIS	KIS	TSADDIQS	TSADDIKS
QADI	KADI	QOPH	KOPH	TZADDIQ	TZADDIK
QADIS	KADIS	QOPHS	KOPHS	TZADDIQIM	TZADDIKIM
QAID	KAID	QORMA	KORMA	TZADDIQS	TZADDIKS
QAIDS	KAIDS	QORMAS	KORMAS	WAQF	WAKF
QAIMAQAM	KAIMAKAM	SHEQALIM	SHEKALIM	WAQFS	WAKFS
QAIMAQAMS	KAIMAKAMS	SHEQEL	SHEKEL		

X

X is perhaps the most versatile of the power tiles. It's useful for tagging as it forms a two-letter word with every vowel. This means that when you have X on your rack, you should look out for opportunities to tag your new word on to a word on the board so that you can harvest the eight points for X twice. Towards the end of a game, when the board is filling up, it's worth considering tagging with a two-letter word containing X; words like **ax, ex** and **xi** are very easy to tag onto others to form four words, two of which will contain the eight-point power-tile. X also forms more three-letter words than J, Q or Z. It's well worth learning all of them, along with the two-letter words, so that you can make full use of the X tile, whether it's on your rack or on the board.

Two-letter words

AX	tool with a sharp blade for felling trees or chopping wood
EX	not including
OX	castrated bull
XI	14th letter in the Greek alphabet
XU	Vietnamese currency unit

Three-letter words

AXE	tool with a sharp blade for felling trees or chopping wood
BOX	container with a firm flat base and sides
COX	coxswain
DEX	dextroamphetamine
DUX	(in Scottish and certain other schools) the top pupil in a class or school
EXO	informal word for excellent

FAX	electronic system for sending facsimiles of documents by telephone
FIX	make or become firm, stable, or secure
FOX	reddish-brown bushy-tailed animal of the dog family
GOX	gaseous oxygen
HEX	of or relating to hexadecimal notation
HOX	hamstring
KEX	any of several large hollow-stemmed umbelliferous plants, such as cow parsnip and chervil
LAX	not strict
LEX	system or body of laws
LOX	load fuel tanks of spacecraft with liquid oxygen
LUX	unit of illumination
MAX	reach the full extent
MIX	combine or blend into one mass
MUX	spoil
NIX	be careful! watch out!
NOX	nitrogen oxide
OXO	as in 'oxo acid' acid that contains oxygen
OXY	containing oxygen
PAX	kiss of peace
PIX	any receptacle for the Eucharistic Host
POX	disease in which skin pustules form
PYX	any receptacle for the Eucharistic Host
RAX	stretch or extend
REX	king
SAX	saxophone
SEX	state of being male or female
SIX	one more than five
SOX	informal spelling of 'socks'
TAX	compulsory payment levied by a government on income, property, etc to raise revenue
TEX	unit of weight used to measure yarn density
TIX	tickets
TUX	dinner jacket
VEX	frustrate, annoy
VOX	voice or sound
WAX	solid shiny fatty or oily substance used for sealing, making candles, etc
WEX	obsolete form of wax
WOX	obsolete form of wax
XIS	plural of xi
YEX	hiccup
ZAX	tool for cutting roofing slate
ZEX	tool for cutting roofing slate

Four-letter words

APEX	COAX	EXED	FLIX	LANX
AXAL	COXA	EXES	FLUX	LUXE
AXED	COXY	EXIT	FOXY	LYNX
AXEL	CRUX	EXON	GREX	MAXI
AXES	DEXY	EXPO	HOAX	MINX
AXIL	DIXI	EXUL	IBEX	MIXT
AXIS	DIXY	FAIX	ILEX	MIXY
AXLE	DOUX	FALX	IXIA	MOXA
AXON	DOXY	FAUX	JAXY	MYXO
BOXY	EAUX	FIXT	JEUX	NEXT
BRUX	EXAM	FLAX	JINX	NIXE
CALX	EXEC	FLEX	JYNX	NIXY

ONYX	OXID	PREX	TAXA	WAXY
ORYX	OXIM	ROUX	TAXI	WEXE
OXEN	PIXY	SAXE	TEXT	XYST
OXER	PLEX	SEXT	ULEX	YUNX
OXES	POXY	SEXY	VEXT	

Five-letter words

ADDAX	DIXIT	HEXER	NOXES	SIXTY
ADMIX	DOXIE	HEXES	ORIXA	SOREX
AFFIX	DRUXY	HEXYL	OXBOW	TAXED
ANNEX	DUXES	HOXED	OXERS	TAXER
ATAXY	EMBOX	HOXES	OXEYE	TAXES
AUXIN	ENFIX	HYRAX	OXIDE	TAXIS
AXELS	EPOXY	IMMIX	OXIDS	TAXOL
AXIAL	EXACT	INDEX	OXIME	TAXON
AXILE	EXALT	INFIX	OXIMS	TAXOR
AXILS	EXAMS	IXIAS	OXLIP	TAXUS
AXING	EXCEL	IXORA	OXTER	TELEX
AXIOM	EXEAT	IXTLE	PANAX	TEXAS
AXION	EXECS	JAXIE	PAXES	TEXES
AXITE	EXEEM	KEXES	PHLOX	TEXTS
AXLED	EXEME	KYLIX	PIXEL	TOXIC
AXLES	EXERT	LATEX	PIXES	TOXIN
AXMAN	EXIES	LAXER	PIXIE	TUXES
AXMEN	EXILE	LAXES	PODEX	TWIXT
AXOID	EXINE	LAXLY	POXED	UNBOX
AXONE	EXING	LEXES	POXES	UNFIX
AXONS	EXIST	LEXIS	PREXY	UNMIX
BEAUX	EXITS	LIMAX	PROXY	UNSEX
BEMIX	EXODE	LINUX	PYREX	UNTAX
BOLIX	EXONS	LOXED	PYXED	VARIX
BORAX	EXPAT	LOXES	PYXES	VEXED
BOXED	EXPEL	LUREX	PYXIE	VEXER
BOXEN	EXPOS	LUXES	PYXIS	VEXES
BOXER	EXTOL	MALAX	RADIX	VEXIL
BOXES	EXTRA	MAXED	RAXED	VIBEX
BRAXY	EXUDE	MAXES	RAXES	VITEX
BUXOM	EXULS	MAXIM	REDOX	VIXEN
CALIX	EXULT	MAXIS	REDUX	VOXEL
CALYX	EXURB	MIREX	REFIX	WAXED
CAREX	FAXED	MIXED	RELAX	WAXEN
CAXON	FAXES	MIXEN	REMEX	WAXER
CHOUX	FEDEX	MIXER	REMIX	WAXES
CIMEX	FIXED	MIXES	RETAX	WEXED
CODEX	FIXER	MIXTE	REWAX	WEXES
COMIX	FIXES	MIXUP	REXES	WOXEN
COXAE	FIXIT	MOXAS	SALIX	WUXIA
COXAL	FLAXY	MOXIE	SAXES	XEBEC
COXED	FLEXO	MUREX	SEXED	XENIA
COXES	FOREX	MUXED	SEXER	XENIC
CULEX	FOXED	MUXES	SEXES	XENON
CYLIX	FOXES	MYXOS	SEXTO	XERIC
DEOXY	FOXIE	NEXTS	SEXTS	XEROX
DESEX	GALAX	NEXUS	SILEX	XERUS
DETOX	GOXES	NIXED	SIXER	XOANA
DEWAX	HAPAX	NIXER	SIXES	XYLAN
DEXES	HELIX	NIXES	SIXMO	XYLEM
DEXIE	HEXAD	NIXIE	SIXTE	XYLIC
DIXIE	HEXED	NOXAL	SIXTH	XYLOL

XYLYL	XYSTS	YEXES	ZEXES	
XYSTI	YEXED	ZAXES		

Six-letter words

ADIEUX	CARFAX	EXCESS	EXTOLD	HOXING
ADMIXT	CARFOX	EXCIDE	EXTOLL	IBEXES
ADNEXA	CAUDEX	EXCISE	EXTOLS	ICEBOX
AFFLUX	CAXONS	EXCITE	EXTORT	ILEXES
ALEXIA	CERVIX	EXCUSE	EXTRAS	IMBREX
ALEXIC	CHENIX	EXEATS	EXUDED	IMPLEX
ALEXIN	CLAXON	EXEDRA	EXUDES	INFLUX
ALKOXY	CLIMAX	EXEEMS	EXULTS	ISOLEX
ANNEXE	COAXAL	EXEMED	EXURBS	IXODID
ANOXIA	COAXED	EXEMES	EXUVIA	IXORAS
ANOXIC	COAXER	EXEMPT	FAXING	IXTLES
APEXES	COAXES	EXEQUY	FIXATE	JAWBOX
ATAXIA	COCCYX	EXERTS	FIXERS	JAXIES
ATAXIC	COMMIX	EXEUNT	FIXING	JINXED
ATWIXT	CONFIX	EXHALE	FIXITY	JINXES
AUSPEX	CONVEX	EXHORT	FIXIVE	JYNXES
AUXINS	CORTEX	EXHUME	FIXURE	KLAXON
AXEMAN	COWPOX	EXILED	FLAXEN	LARNAX
AXEMEN	COXIER	EXILER	FLAXES	LARYNX
AXENIC	COXING	EXILES	FLEXED	LAXEST
AXILLA	CRUXES	EXILIC	FLEXES	LAXISM
AXIOMS	DEFLEX	EXINES	FLEXOR	LAXIST
AXIONS	DEIXES	EXISTS	FLEXOS	LAXITY
AXISED	DEIXIS	EXITED	FLIXED	LEXEME
AXISES	DELUXE	EXODES	FLIXES	LEXICA
AXITES	DENTEX	EXODIC	FLUXED	LOXING
AXLIKE	DEXIES	EXODOI	FLUXES	LUMMOX
AXOIDS	DEXTER	EXODOS	FORFEX	LUXATE
AXONAL	DEXTRO	EXODUS	FORNIX	LUXURY
AXONES	DIAXON	EXOGEN	FOXIER	LYNXES
AXONIC	DIOXAN	EXOMIS	FOXIES	MAGNOX
AXSEED	DIOXID	EXONIC	FOXILY	MASTIX
BANJAX	DIOXIN	EXONYM	FOXING	MATRIX
BAXTER	DIPLEX	EXOPOD	FRUTEX	MAXIMA
BEMBEX	DIXIES	EXOTIC	GALAXY	MAXIMS
BEMBIX	DIXITS	EXPAND	GREXES	MAXING
BEMIXT	DOGFOX	EXPATS	GUANXI	MAXIXE
BIAXAL	DOXIES	EXPECT	HALLUX	MENINX
BIFLEX	DUPLEX	EXPELS	HANDAX	MINXES
BIJOUX	EARWAX	EXPEND	HATBOX	MIXENS
BOLLIX	EFFLUX	EXPERT	HAYBOX	MIXERS
BOLLOX	ELIXIR	EXPIRE	HEXACT	MIXIER
BOMBAX	ETHOXY	EXPIRY	HEXADE	MIXING
BOMBYX	EUTAXY	EXPORT	HEXADS	MIXUPS
BONXIE	EXACTA	EXPOSE	HEXANE	MOXIES
BOXCAR	EXACTS	EXPUGN	HEXENE	MUSKOX
BOXERS	EXACUM	EXSECT	HEXERS	MUXING
BOXFUL	EXALTS	EXSERT	HEXING	MYXOID
BOXIER	EXAMEN	EXTANT	HEXONE	MYXOMA
BOXILY	EXARCH	EXTASY	HEXOSE	NEXTLY
BOXING	EXCAMB	EXTEND	HEXYLS	NIXERS
BOYAUX	EXCEED	EXTENT	HOAXED	NIXIES
BRUXED	EXCELS	EXTERN	HOAXER	NIXING
BRUXES	EXCEPT	EXTINE	HOAXES	NONTAX
CALXES	EXCESS	EXTIRP	HOTBOX	ONYXES

OREXIS	PIXELS	SEXIER	TAXIES	VORTEX
ORIFEX	PIXIES	SEXILY	TAXING	VOXELS
ORIXAS	PLEXAL	SEXING	TAXITE	WAXERS
ORYXES	PLEXES	SEXISM	TAXMAN	WAXEYE
OUTBOX	PLEXOR	SEXIST	TAXMEN	WAXIER
OUTFOX	PLEXUS	SEXPOT	TAXOLS	WAXILY
OXALIC	POLEAX	SEXTAN	TAXONS	WAXING
OXALIS	POLLEX	SEXTET	TAXORS	WEXING
OXBOWS	POXIER	SEXTON	TEABOX	WRAXLE
OXCART	POXING	SEXTOS	TETTIX	WUXIAS
OXEYES	PRAXES	SEXUAL	TEXTER	XEBECS
OXFORD	PRAXIS	SILVEX	THORAX	XENIAL
OXGANG	PREFIX	SIXAIN	TOXICS	XENIAS
OXGATE	PREMIX	SIXERS	TOXINE	XENIUM
OXHEAD	PRETAX	SIXMOS	TOXINS	XENONS
OXHIDE	PREXES	SIXTES	TOXOID	XEROMA
OXIDES	PROLIX	SIXTHS	TUTRIX	XOANON
OXIDIC	PTYXES	SKYBOX	TUXEDO	XYLANS
OXIMES	PTYXIS	SMILAX	ULEXES	XYLEMS
OXLAND	PYXIES	SPADIX	UNAXED	XYLENE
OXLIKE	PYXING	SPHINX	UNFIXT	XYLOID
OXLIPS	RAXING	SPHYNX	UNISEX	XYLOLS
OXSLIP	REFLEX	STORAX	UNMIXT	XYLOMA
OXTAIL	REFLUX	STYRAX	UNSEXY	XYLOSE
OXTERS	REMIXT	SUBFIX	UNVEXT	XYLYLS
OXYGEN	REXINE	SUFFIX	URTEXT	XYSTER
OXYMEL	RHEXES	SUPLEX	VERNIX	XYSTOI
PAXWAX	RHEXIS	SURTAX	VERTEX	XYSTOS
PEGBOX	SAXAUL	SYNTAX	VEXERS	XYSTUS
PEROXY	SAXONY	SYRINX	VEXILS	YEXING
PHENIX	SCOLEX	TAXEME	VEXING	YUNXES
PICKAX	SEXERS	TAXERS	VIXENS	
PINXIT	SEXFID	TAXIED	VOLVOX	

Seven-letter words

ABAXIAL	ANTISEX	AXINITE	BOXFULS	COANNEX
ABAXILE	ANTITAX	AXOLOTL	BOXHAUL	COAXERS
ABRASAX	ANXIETY	AXONEME	BOXIEST	COAXIAL
ABRAXAS	ANXIOUS	AXSEEDS	BOXINGS	COAXING
ADAXIAL	APOPLEX	BANDBOX	BOXLIKE	COEXERT
ADDAXES	APRAXIA	BATEAUX	BOXROOM	COEXIST
ADMIXED	APRAXIC	BAUXITE	BOXWOOD	COMMIXT
ADMIXES	APTERYX	BAXTERS	BRAXIES	COMPLEX
ADNEXAL	ARUSPEX	BEATBOX	BROADAX	CONFLUX
AFFIXAL	ASEXUAL	BEESWAX	BRUXING	CONTEXT
AFFIXED	ASPHYXY	BEMIXED	BRUXISM	CORIXID
AFFIXER	ATARAXY	BEMIXES	BUREAUX	COTEAUX
AFFIXES	ATAXIAS	BETAXED	BUXOMER	COXALGY
ALEXIAS	ATAXICS	BETWIXT	BUXOMLY	COXCOMB
ALEXINE	ATAXIES	BIAXIAL	CACHEXY	COXIEST
ALEXINS	AUXESES	BOLIXED	CADEAUX	COXITIS
ALLOXAN	AUXESIS	BOLIXES	CALYXES	COXLESS
ANAXIAL	AUXETIC	BONXIES	CARAPAX	CULEXES
ANNEXED	AUXINIC	BOOMBOX	CASHBOX	CURTAXE
ANNEXES	AXEBIRD	BORAXES	CELOTEX	DEINDEX
ANOREXY	AXIALLY	BOSTRYX	CHAMOIX	DESEXED
ANOXIAS	AXILLAE	BOXBALL	CHOENIX	DESEXES
ANTEFIX	AXILLAR	BOXCARS	CLAXONS	DETOXED
ANTHRAX	AXILLAS	BOXFISH	COALBOX	DETOXES

DEWAXED	EXCITES	EXPIRED	FIXTURE	INDEXAL
DEWAXES	EXCITON	EXPIRER	FIXURES	INDEXED
DEXTERS	EXCITOR	EXPIRES	FLAXIER	INDEXER
DEXTRAL	EXCLAIM	EXPLAIN	FLEXILE	INDEXES
DEXTRAN	EXCLAVE	EXPLANT	FLEXING	INDOXYL
DEXTRIN	EXCLUDE	EXPLODE	FLEXION	INEXACT
DIAXONS	EXCRETA	EXPLOIT	FLEXORS	INFIXED
DIGOXIN	EXCRETE	EXPLORE	FLEXURE	INFIXES
DIOXANE	EXCUDIT	EXPORTS	FLIXING	INVEXED
DIOXANS	EXCURSE	EXPOSAL	FLUMMOX	IXODIDS
DIOXIDE	EXCUSAL	EXPOSED	FLUXING	JAMBEUX
DIOXIDS	EXCUSED	EXPOSER	FLUXION	JINXING
DIOXINS	EXCUSER	EXPOSES	FLUXIVE	JUKEBOX
DISTRIX	EXCUSES	EXPOSIT	FOREXES	KICKBOX
DRUXIER	EXECUTE	EXPOUND	FOWLPOX	KLAXONS
EDITRIX	EXEDRAE	EXPRESS	FOXFIRE	KLEENEX
ELIXIRS	EXEEMED	EXPUGNS	FOXFISH	LATEXES
EMBOXED	EXEGETE	EXPULSE	FOXHOLE	LAXATOR
EMBOXES	EXEMING	EXPUNCT	FOXHUNT	LAXISMS
ENFIXED	EXEMPLA	EXPUNGE	FOXIEST	LAXISTS
ENFIXES	EXEMPLE	EXPURGE	FOXINGS	LAXNESS
EPAXIAL	EXEMPTS	EXSCIND	FOXLIKE	LEXEMES
EPITAXY	EXERGUE	EXSECTS	FOXSHIP	LEXEMIC
EPOXIDE	EXERTED	EXSERTS	FOXSKIN	LEXICAL
EPOXIED	EXHALED	EXTATIC	FOXTAIL	LEXICON
EPOXIES	EXHALES	EXTENDS	FOXTROT	LEXISES
EPOXYED	EXHAUST	EXTENSE	FUNPLEX	LINUXES
EQUINOX	EXHEDRA	EXTENTS	GALAXES	LIXIVIA
ETHOXYL	EXHIBIT	EXTERNE	GATEAUX	LOCKBOX
EUTAXIA	EXHORTS	EXTERNS	GEARBOX	LOXYGEN
EUTEXIA	EXHUMED	EXTINCT	GRAVLAX	LUREXES
EXABYTE	EXHUMER	EXTINES	GUANXIS	LUXATED
EXACTAS	EXHUMES	EXTIRPS	HAPAXES	LUXATES
EXACTED	EXIGENT	EXTOLLS	HELIXES	MAILBOX
EXACTER	EXILERS	EXTORTS	HELLBOX	MALAXED
EXACTLY	EXILIAN	EXTRACT	HEXACTS	MALAXES
EXACTOR	EXILING	EXTRAIT	HEXADES	MARTEXT
EXACUMS	EXILITY	EXTREAT	HEXADIC	MAXILLA
EXALTED	EXISTED	EXTREMA	HEXAGON	MAXIMAL
EXALTER	EXITING	EXTREME	HEXANES	MAXIMIN
EXAMENS	EXOCARP	EXTRUDE	HEXAPLA	MAXIMUM
EXAMINE	EXODERM	EXUDATE	HEXAPOD	MAXIMUS
EXAMPLE	EXODIST	EXUDING	HEXARCH	MAXIXES
EXAPTED	EXOGAMY	EXULTED	HEXENES	MAXWELL
EXARATE	EXOGENS	EXURBAN	HEXEREI	MEATAXE
EXARCHS	EXOMION	EXURBIA	HEXINGS	METHOXY
EXARCHY	EXONYMS	EXUVIAE	HEXONES	MILIEUX
EXCAMBS	EXOPODS	EXUVIAL	HEXOSAN	MINIMAX
EXCEEDS	EXORDIA	EXUVIUM	HEXOSES	MINXISH
EXCEPTS	EXOSMIC	FAREBOX	HEXYLIC	MIREXES
EXCERPT	EXOTICA	FEDEXED	HOAXERS	MIXABLE
EXCHEAT	EXOTICS	FEDEXES	HOAXING	MIXDOWN
EXCIDED	EXOTISM	FEEDBOX	HOMOSEX	MIXEDLY
EXCIDES	EXPANDS	FIREBOX	HUMIDEX	MIXIBLE
EXCIMER	EXPANSE	FIXABLE	HYDROXY	MIXIEST
EXCIPLE	EXPECTS	FIXATED	HYPOXIA	MIXTION
EXCISED	EXPENDS	FIXATES	HYPOXIC	MIXTURE
EXCISES	EXPENSE	FIXATIF	HYRAXES	MONAXON
EXCITED	EXPERTS	FIXEDLY	IMMIXED	MUREXES
EXCITER	EXPIATE	FIXINGS	IMMIXES	MYXOMAS

NARTHEX	PHLOXES	SAXAULS	TAXITIC	VITEXES
NEXUSES	PHOENIX	SAXHORN	TAXIWAY	VITRAUX
NOXIOUS	PICKAXE	SAXTUBA	TAXLESS	VIXENLY
ORATRIX	PILLBOX	SEALWAX	TAXPAID	WAXABLE
OUTJINX	PIXYISH	SEEDBOX	TAXWISE	WAXBILL
OVERLAX	PLANXTY	SEXFOIL	TAXYING	WAXEYES
OVERMIX	PLEXORS	SEXIEST	TECTRIX	WAXIEST
OVERTAX	PLEXURE	SEXISMS	TELEFAX	WAXINGS
OXALATE	PODEXES	SEXISTS	TELETEX	WAXLIKE
OXAZINE	POLEAXE	SEXLESS	TELEXED	WAXWEED
OXBLOOD	POSTBOX	SEXPERT	TELEXES	WAXWING
OXCARTS	POSTFIX	SEXPOTS	TEXASES	WAXWORK
OXFORDS	POSTTAX	SEXTAIN	TEXTERS	WAXWORM
OXGANGS	POXIEST	SEXTANS	TEXTILE	WOADWAX
OXGATES	PRETEXT	SEXTANT	TEXTUAL	WOODBOX
OXHEADS	PREXIES	SEXTETS	TEXTURE	WOODWAX
OXHEART	PRINCOX	SEXTETT	TOOLBOX	WORKBOX
OXHIDES	PROXIES	SEXTILE	TORTRIX	WRAXLED
OXIDANT	PROXIMO	SEXTONS	TOXEMIA	WRAXLES
OXIDASE	PYREXES	SEXTUOR	TOXEMIC	XANTHAM
OXIDATE	PYREXIA	SHOEBOX	TOXICAL	XANTHAN
OXIDISE	PYREXIC	SHOWBOX	TOXINES	XANTHIC
OXIDIZE	PYXIDES	SILEXES	TOXOIDS	XANTHIN
OXLANDS	PYXIDIA	SIMPLEX	TREEWAX	XENOPUS
OXONIUM	QUIXOTE	SIXAINE	TRIAXON	XERAFIN
OXSLIPS	RADIXES	SIXAINS	TRIOXID	XERARCH
OXTAILS	REAFFIX	SIXFOLD	TRIPLEX	XERASIA
OXTERED	REANNEX	SIXTEEN	TUBIFEX	XEROMAS
OXYACID	RECTRIX	SIXTHLY	TUXEDOS	XEROSES
OXYGENS	REDOXES	SIXTIES	ULEXITE	XEROSIS
OXYMELS	REEXPEL	SOAPBOX	UNBOXED	XEROTES
OXYMORA	REFIXED	SONOVOX	UNBOXES	XEROTIC
OXYNTIC	REFIXES	SOREXES	UNFIXED	XEROXED
OXYPHIL	REINDEX	SPANDEX	UNFIXES	XEROXES
OXYSALT	RELAXED	SUBTAXA	UNMIXED	XERUSES
OXYSOME	RELAXER	SUBTEXT	UNMIXES	XIPHOID
OXYTONE	RELAXES	SYNAXES	UNSEXED	XYLENES
PACKWAX	RELAXIN	SYNAXIS	UNSEXES	XYLENOL
PANAXES	REMIXED	TALKBOX	UNTAXED	XYLIDIN
PANCHAX	REMIXES	TAXABLE	UNTAXES	XYLITOL
PARADOX	RESEAUX	TAXABLY	UNVEXED	XYLOGEN
PAXIUBA	RETAXED	TAXEMES	UNWAXED	XYLOMAS
PEMPHIX	RETAXES	TAXEMIC	URTEXTS	XYLONIC
PEROXID	REWAXED	TAXICAB	UXORIAL	XYLOSES
PERPLEX	REWAXES	TAXIING	VAUDOUX	XYSTERS
PERSPEX	REXINES	TAXIMAN	VEXEDLY	ZEUXITE
PHALANX	SALPINX	TAXIMEN	VEXILLA	ZOOTAXY
PHARYNX	SALTBOX	TAXINGS	VEXINGS	
PHENOXY	SANDBOX	TAXITES	VICTRIX	

Eight-letter words

ACETOXYL	ALEXINES	ANNEXION	APOMIXES	ATARAXIC
ADMIXING	ALEXINIC	ANNEXURE	APOMIXIS	AUXETICS
AFFIXERS	ALKOXIDE	ANOREXIA	APOPLEXY	AUXILIAR
AFFIXIAL	ALLOXANS	ANOREXIC	APPENDIX	AUXOCYTE
AFFIXING	AMPHIOXI	ANOXEMIA	APRAXIAS	AVIATRIX
AFFLUXES	AMPLEXUS	ANOXEMIC	APYREXIA	AXEBIRDS
AFTERTAX	ANATOXIN	ANTEFIXA	ASPHYXIA	AXIALITY
ALDOXIME	ANNEXING	ANTHELIX	ATARAXIA	AXILEMMA

AXILLARS	CHAPEAUX	DUPLEXED	EXCESSED	EXHIBITS
AXILLARY	CHATEAUX	DUPLEXER	EXCESSES	EXHORTED
AXINITES	CHENIXES	DUPLEXES	EXCHANGE	EXHORTER
AXIOLOGY	CHRONAXY	DUXELLES	EXCHEATS	EXHUMATE
AXLETREE	CICATRIX	DYSLEXIA	EXCIDING	EXHUMERS
AXOLEMMA	CINEPLEX	DYSLEXIC	EXCIMERS	EXHUMING
AXOLOTLS	CLACKBOX	DYSTAXIA	EXCIPLES	EXIGEANT
AXONEMAL	CLANGBOX	EARTHWAX	EXCISING	EXIGENCE
AXONEMES	CLIMAXED	EARWAXES	EXCISION	EXIGENCY
AXOPLASM	CLIMAXES	ECONOBOX	EXCITANT	EXIGENTS
BANDEAUX	COCCYXES	ECOTOXIC	EXCITERS	EXIGIBLE
BANJAXED	COEXERTS	EFFLUXES	EXCITING	EXIGUITY
BANJAXES	COEXISTS	EKTEXINE	EXCITONS	EXIGUOUS
BANXRING	COEXTEND	EMBOXING	EXCITORS	EXILABLE
BATTEAUX	COMMIXED	ENDEIXES	EXCLAIMS	EXIMIOUS
BAUXITES	COMMIXES	ENDEIXIS	EXCLAVES	EXISTENT
BAUXITIC	CONFIXED	ENDEXINE	EXCLUDED	EXISTING
BEAUXITE	CONFIXES	ENFIXING	EXCLUDEE	EXITANCE
BEMBEXES	CONTEXTS	EPICALYX	EXCLUDER	EXITLESS
BEMBIXES	CONVEXED	EPITAXES	EXCLUDES	EXOCARPS
BEMIXING	CONVEXES	EPITAXIC	EXCRETAL	EXOCRINE
BERCEAUX	CONVEXLY	EPITAXIS	EXCRETED	EXOCYTIC
BICONVEX	CORIXIDS	EPOXIDES	EXCRETER	EXODERMS
BIOTOXIN	CORTEXES	EPOXYING	EXCRETES	EXODISTS
BISEXUAL	COTURNIX	ETHOXIDE	EXCUBANT	EXODUSES
BOBBYSOX	COUTEAUX	ETHOXIES	EXCURSED	EXOERGIC
BOLIXING	COWPOXES	ETHOXYLS	EXCURSES	EXOGAMIC
BOLLIXED	COXALGIA	EUTAXIAS	EXCURSUS	EXOMIONS
BOLLIXES	COXALGIC	EUTAXIES	EXCUSALS	EXOMISES
BOLLOXED	COXCOMBS	EUTAXITE	EXCUSERS	EXONUMIA
BOLLOXES	COXINESS	EUTEXIAS	EXCUSING	EXOPHAGY
BOMBAXES	COXSWAIN	EUXENITE	EXCUSIVE	EXOPLASM
BOMBYXES	CREATRIX	EXABYTES	EXECRATE	EXORABLE
BORDEAUX	CRUCIFIX	EXACTERS	EXECUTED	EXORCISE
BOXBALLS	CURATRIX	EXACTEST	EXECUTER	EXORCISM
BOXBERRY	CURTALAX	EXACTING	EXECUTES	EXORCIST
BOXBOARD	CURTAXES	EXACTION	EXECUTOR	EXORCIZE
BOXHAULS	CYBERSEX	EXACTORS	EXECUTRY	EXORDIAL
BOXINESS	DEFLEXED	EXAHERTZ	EXEEMING	EXORDIUM
BOXROOMS	DEFLEXES	EXALTERS	EXEGESES	EXOSMOSE
BOXTHORN	DEIXISES	EXALTING	EXEGESIS	EXOSPORE
BOXWOODS	DENTEXES	EXAMINED	EXEGETES	EXOTERIC
BRAINBOX	DESEXING	EXAMINEE	EXEGETIC	EXOTISMS
BREADBOX	DETOXIFY	EXAMINER	EXEMPLAR	EXOTOXIC
BROADAXE	DETOXING	EXAMINES	EXEMPLES	EXOTOXIN
BRUXISMS	DEWAXING	EXAMPLAR	EXEMPLUM	EXPANDED
BUXOMEST	DEXTRANS	EXAMPLED	EXEQUIAL	EXPANDER
CACHEXIA	DEXTRINE	EXAMPLES	EXEQUIES	EXPANDOR
CACHEXIC	DEXTRINS	EXANTHEM	EXERCISE	EXPANSES
CACODOXY	DEXTROSE	EXAPTIVE	EXERGUAL	EXPECTED
CACOMIXL	DEXTROUS	EXARCHAL	EXERGUES	EXPECTER
CAMAIEUX	DIGOXINS	EXCAMBED	EXERTING	EXPEDITE
CARBOXYL	DIOXANES	EXCAVATE	EXERTION	EXPELLED
CARFAXES	DIOXIDES	EXCEEDED	EXERTIVE	EXPELLEE
CARFOXES	DIPLEXER	EXCEEDER	EXHALANT	EXPELLER
CARNIFEX	DISANNEX	EXCELLED	EXHALENT	EXPENDED
CATHEXES	DOGFOXES	EXCEPTED	EXHALING	EXPENDER
CATHEXIS	DOXASTIC	EXCEPTOR	EXHAUSTS	EXPENSED
CAUDEXES	DOXOLOGY	EXCERPTA	EXHEDRAE	EXPENSES
CERVIXES	DRUXIEST	EXCERPTS		EXPERTED

EXPERTLY	EXTREATS	HATBOXES	LUXURIES	OUTBOXES
EXPIABLE	EXTREMAL	HAYBOXES	LUXURIST	OUTFOXED
EXPIATED	EXTREMER	HERETRIX	LYNXLIKE	OUTFOXES
EXPIATES	EXTREMES	HERITRIX	MAGNOXES	OXALATED
EXPIATOR	EXTREMUM	HEXAFOIL	MALAXAGE	OXALATES
EXPIRANT	EXTRORSE	HEXAGLOT	MALAXATE	OXALISES
EXPIRERS	EXTRUDED	HEXAGONS	MALAXING	OXAZEPAM
EXPIRIES	EXTRUDER	HEXAGRAM	MANTEAUX	OXAZINES
EXPIRING	EXTRUDES	HEXAMINE	MARTEXTS	OXBLOODS
EXPLAINS	EXTUBATE	HEXANOIC	MASTIXES	OXHEARTS
EXPLANTS	EXUDATES	HEXAPLAR	MATCHBOX	OXIDABLE
EXPLICIT	EXULTANT	HEXAPLAS	MATRIXES	OXIDANTS
EXPLODED	EXULTING	HEXAPODS	MAXICOAT	OXIDASES
EXPLODER	EXURBIAS	HEXAPODY	MAXILLAE	OXIDASIC
EXPLODES	EXUVIATE	HEXARCHY	MAXILLAR	OXIDATED
EXPLOITS	FABLIAUX	HEXEREIS	MAXILLAS	OXIDATES
EXPLORED	FEDEXING	HEXOSANS	MAXIMALS	OXIDISED
EXPLORER	FIXATIFS	HEXYLENE	MAXIMINS	OXIDISER
EXPLORES	FIXATING	HOMEOBOX	MAXIMISE	OXIDISES
EXPONENT	FIXATION	HORSEBOX	MAXIMIST	OXIDIZED
EXPORTED	FIXATIVE	HORSEPOX	MAXIMITE	OXIDIZER
EXPORTER	FIXATURE	HOTBOXES	MAXIMIZE	OXIDIZES
EXPOSALS	FIXITIES	HYDROXYL	MAXIMUMS	OXIMETER
EXPOSERS	FIXTURES	HYPOXIAS	MAXWELLS	OXIMETRY
EXPOSING	FLAXIEST	ICEBOXES	MEATAXES	OXONIUMS
EXPOSITS	FLAXSEED	IMMIXING	MEGAPLEX	OXPECKER
EXPOSURE	FLEXAGON	IMPLEXES	METHOXYL	OXTERING
EXPOUNDS	FLEXIBLE	INDEXERS	MICROLUX	OXTONGUE
EXPRESSO	FLEXIBLY	INDEXING	MILLILUX	OXYACIDS
EXPUGNED	FLEXIONS	INDOXYLS	MIREPOIX	OXYGENIC
EXPULSED	FLEXTIME	INEXPERT	MIXDOWNS	OXYMORON
EXPULSES	FLEXUOSE	INFIXING	MIXOLOGY	OXYPHILE
EXPUNCTS	FLEXUOUS	INFIXION	MIXTIONS	OXYPHILS
EXPUNGED	FLEXURAL	INFLEXED	MIXTURES	OXYSALTS
EXPUNGER	FLEXURES	INFLUXES	MONAXIAL	OXYSOMES
EXPUNGES	FLUXGATE	INTERMIX	MONAXONS	OXYTOCIC
EXPURGED	FLUXIONS	INTERREX	MONOXIDE	OXYTOCIN
EXPURGES	FORFEXES	INTERSEX	MORCEAUX	OXYTONES
EXSCINDS	FOURPLEX	ISOLEXES	MUSKOXEN	PAINTBOX
EXSECANT	FOXBERRY	JAMBEAUX	MYXAMEBA	PANMIXES
EXSECTED	FOXFIRES	JANITRIX	MYXEDEMA	PANMIXIA
EXSERTED	FOXGLOVE	JAWBOXES	MYXOCYTE	PANMIXIS
EXTASIES	FOXHOLES	KETOXIME	MYXOMATA	PARADOXY
EXTENDED	FOXHOUND	KLAXONED	NALOXONE	PARALLAX
EXTENDER	FOXHUNTS	LARYNXES	NAPROXEN	PARAXIAL
EXTENSOR	FOXINESS	LAXATION	NEOTOXIN	PAROXYSM
EXTERIOR	FOXSHARK	LAXATIVE	NEURAXON	PAXIUBAS
EXTERNAL	FOXSHIPS	LAXATORS	NEXTDOOR	PAXWAXES
EXTERNAT	FOXSKINS	LAXITIES	NEXTNESS	PEGBOXES
EXTERNES	FOXTAILS	LEXICONS	NITROXYL	PEROXIDE
EXTINCTS	FOXTROTS	LEXIGRAM	NONTAXES	PEROXIDS
EXTIRPED	GALAXIES	LIXIVIAL	NONTOXIC	PHENIXES
EXTOLLED	GENETRIX	LIXIVIUM	NOUVEAUX	PHORMINX
EXTOLLER	GENITRIX	LOOSEBOX	OCTUPLEX	PHYLAXIS
EXTORTED	GEOTAXES	LOXYGENS	OPOPANAX	PICKAXED
EXTORTER	GEOTAXIS	LUMMOXES	OREXISES	PICKAXES
EXTRACTS	GIAMBEUX	LUNCHBOX	ORIFEXES	PIXIEISH
EXTRADOS	GLOXINIA	LUXATING	ORTHODOX	PIXINESS
EXTRAITS	HANDAXES	LUXATION	OTOTOXIC	PLATEAUX
EXTRANET	HARUSPEX	LUXMETER	OUTBOXED	PLEXURES

PLEXUSES	SARDONYX	SUBINDEX	TOXAEMIC	WAXPLANT
POLEAXED	SAUCEBOX	SUBOXIDE	TOXEMIAS	WAXWEEDS
POLEAXES	SAXATILE	SUBTAXON	TOXICANT	WAXWINGS
POLYAXON	SAXHORNS	SUBTEXTS	TOXICITY	WAXWORKS
PONTIFEX	SAXICOLE	SUFFIXAL	TOXOCARA	WAXWORMS
POXVIRUS	SAXONIES	SUFFIXED	TRACTRIX	WRAXLING
PRAXISES	SAXONITE	SUFFIXES	TRANSFIX	XANTHAMS
PREAXIAL	SAXTUBAS	SUPERFIX	TRIAXIAL	XANTHANS
PREEXIST	SCRUMPOX	SUPERMAX	TRIAXONS	XANTHATE
PREFIXAL	SEXFOILS	SUPERSEX	TRIOXIDE	XANTHEIN
PREFIXED	SEXINESS	SUPERTAX	TRIOXIDS	XANTHENE
PREFIXES	SEXOLOGY	SUPLEXES	TRUMEAUX	XANTHINE
PREMIXED	SEXPERTS	SURTAXED	TUTRIXES	XANTHINS
PREMIXES	SEXTAINS	SURTAXES	TUXEDOED	XANTHISM
PRETEXTS	SEXTANTS	SWEATBOX	TUXEDOES	XANTHOMA
PROLIXLY	SEXTARII	SWINEPOX	ULEXITES	XANTHONE
PROTOXID	SEXTETTE	SYNTAXES	UNBOXING	XANTHOUS
PROXEMIC	SEXTETTS	SYNTEXIS	UNDERTAX	XENOGAMY
PROXIMAL	SEXTILES	SYRINXES	UNEXOTIC	XENOGENY
PYREXIAL	SEXTOLET	TABLEAUX	UNEXPERT	XENOLITH
PYREXIAS	SEXTUORS	TAXABLES	UNFIXING	XENOPHYA
PYROXENE	SEXTUPLE	TAXATION	UNFIXITY	XENOTIME
PYROXYLE	SEXTUPLY	TAXATIVE	UNFLEXED	XENURINE
PYXIDIUM	SEXUALLY	TAXIARCH	UNIAXIAL	XERAFINS
QUADPLEX	SILOXANE	TAXICABS	UNISEXES	XERANSES
QUINCUNX	SILVEXES	TAXINGLY	UNMIXING	XERANSIS
QUIXOTES	SIXAINES	TAXIWAYS	UNSEXING	XERANTIC
QUIXOTIC	SIXPENCE	TAXONOMY	UNSEXIST	XERAPHIM
QUIXOTRY	SIXPENNY	TAXPAYER	UNSEXUAL	XERASIAS
REEXPELS	SIXSCORE	TEABOXES	UNTAXING	XEROMATA
REEXPORT	SIXTEENS	TEGUEXIN	UXORIOUS	XEROSERE
REEXPOSE	SIXTIETH	TELETEXT	VERNIXES	XEROXING
REFIXING	SIXTYISH	TELEXING	VERTEXES	XIPHOIDS
REFLEXED	SKYBOXES	TETRAXON	VEXATION	XYLENOLS
REFLEXES	SMALLPOX	TETROXID	VEXATORY	XYLIDINE
REFLEXLY	SMILAXES	TETTIXES	VEXILLAR	XYLIDINS
REFLUXED	SNUFFBOX	TEXTBOOK	VEXILLUM	XYLITOLS
REFLUXES	SOUNDBOX	TEXTILES	VEXINGLY	XYLOCARP
RELAXANT	SPADIXES	TEXTLESS	VIDEOTEX	XYLOGENS
RELAXERS	SPARAXIS	TEXTUARY	VIXENISH	XYLOIDIN
RELAXING	SPHINXES	TEXTURAL	VOLVOXES	XYLOLOGY
RELAXINS	SPHYNXES	TEXTURED	VORTEXES	XYLOMATA
REMIXING	SPINIFEX	TEXTURES	WATCHBOX	XYLONITE
RETAXING	SPINTEXT	THORAXES	WATERPOX	XYLOTOMY
REWAXING	STORAXES	THYROXIN	WAXBERRY	ZELATRIX
RHEXISES	STYRAXES	TOADFLAX	WAXBILLS	ZEUXITES
RONDEAUX	SUBAXIAL	TONNEAUX	WAXCLOTH	ZOOTOXIC
ROULEAUX	SUBFIXES	TOXAEMIA	WAXINESS	ZOOTOXIN

Z

Z scores the same as Q ten points but is an easier letter to use, as there is no need for a U as there is in the majority of Q words. The only two-letter word containing Z, **zo**, is useful as it allows you to tag onto one of the most common tiles in the game. It's a good idea to learn the short Z words that use other power tiles, such as **jiz, jazy, zax** and **zex**, as these can provide high scores, especially if you can deploy them on bonus squares. There are also quite a few words with a double Z (**buzz** and **fuzz**, for example); while these may appear useless for Scrabble, as there is only one Z in the game, remember the blank tiles, which may allow you to play a word with two Zs such as the high-scoring **jazz** and its inflections.

Two-letter words

ZA	pizza
ZO	Tibetan breed of cattle, developed by crossing the yak with common cattle

Three-letter words

ADZ	tool with an arched blade at right angles to the handle
AZO	of, consisting of, or containing the divalent group -N-
BEZ	part of deer's horn
BIZ	business
CAZ	short for casual
COZ	archaic word for cousin
CUZ	cousin
DZO	Tibetan breed of cattle, developed by crossing the yak with common cattle
FEZ	brimless tasselled cap, orig. from Turkey
FIZ	fizz
JIZ	wig
LEZ	short form of lesbian
LUZ	supposedly indestructible bone of the human body
MIZ	shortened form of misery
MOZ	hex
POZ	positive
REZ	informal word for an instance of reserving; reservation
RIZ	(in some dialects) past form of rise
SAZ	Middle Eastern stringed instrument
SEZ	informal spelling of 'says'
WIZ	shortened form of wizard
ZAG	change direction sharply
ZAP	kill (by shooting)
ZAS	pizzas
ZAX	tool for cutting roofing slate
ZEA	corn silk
ZED	British and New Zealand spoken form of the letter 'z'
ZEE	US spoken form of the letter 'z'
ZEK	Soviet prisoner
ZEL	Turkish cymbal
ZEP	type of long sandwich
ZEX	tool for cutting roofing slate
ZHO	Tibetan breed of cattle, developed by crossing the yak with common cattle

ZIG	change direction sharply
ZIN	short form of zinfandel, a type of Californian wine
ZIP	fastening device with metal or plastic teeth that are interlocked by a sliding tab
ZIT	spot or pimple
ZIZ	short sleep
ZOA	independent animal bodies, such as the individuals of a coral colony
ZOL	South African slang for a cannabis cigarette
ZOO	place where live animals are kept for show
ZOS	plural of zo
ZUZ	ancient Hebrew silver coin
ZZZ	informal word for sleep

Four-letter words

ADZE	GIZZ	OOZE	YUZU	ZINE
AZAN	HAZE	OOZY	ZACK	ZING
AZON	HAZY	ORZO	ZAGS	ZINS
AZYM	HIZZ	OUZO	ZANY	ZIPS
BIZE	IZAR	OYEZ	ZAPS	ZITE
BOZO	JAZY	PHIZ	ZARF	ZITI
BUZZ	JAZZ	PIZE	ZATI	ZITS
CHEZ	JEEZ	POZZ	ZEAL	ZIZZ
CHIZ	JIZZ	PREZ	ZEAS	ZOBO
COZE	KAZI	PUTZ	ZEBU	ZOBU
COZY	KUZU	QUIZ	ZEDS	ZOEA
CZAR	LAZE	RAZE	ZEIN	ZOIC
DAZE	LAZO	RAZZ	ZEKS	ZOLS
DITZ	LAZY	RITZ	ZELS	ZONA
DOZE	LEZZ	RIZA	ZEPS	ZONE
DOZY	LUTZ	SITZ	ZERK	ZONK
DZHO	MAZE	SIZE	ZERO	ZOOM
DZOS	MAZY	SIZY	ZEST	ZOON
FAZE	MEZE	SPAZ	ZETA	ZOOS
FIZZ	MEZZ	SWIZ	ZEZE	ZOOT
FOZY	MIZZ	TIZZ	ZHOS	ZORI
FRIZ	MOZE	TOZE	ZIFF	ZOUK
FUTZ	MOZO	TREZ	ZIGS	ZULU
FUZE	MOZZ	TUZZ	ZILA	ZUPA
FUZZ	MUZZ	TZAR	ZILL	ZURF
GAZE	NAZE	VIZY	ZIMB	ZYGA
GAZY	NAZI	WHIZ	ZINC	ZYME
GEEZ		YUTZ		ZZZS

Five-letter words

ABUZZ	AZIDO	AZYGY	BIZZY	BUAZE
ADOZE	AZINE	AZYME	BLAZE	BUZZY
ADZED	AZLON	AZYMS	BLITZ	BWAZI
ADZES	AZOIC	BAIZA	BONZA	CAPIZ
AGAZE	AZOLE	BAIZE	BONZE	CEAZE
AIZLE	AZONS	BAZAR	BOOZE	CHIZZ
AMAZE	AZOTE	BAZOO	BOOZY	CLOZE
ASSEZ	AZOTH	BEZEL	BORTZ	COBZA
AVIZE	AZUKI	BEZES	BOZOS	COLZA
AVYZE	AZURE	BEZIL	BRAZA	COOZE
AZANS	AZURN	BIZES	BRAZE	COZED
AZIDE	AZURY	BIZZO	BRIZE	COZEN

COZES	GRENZ	MZEES	TIZZY	ZEXES
COZEY	GRIZE	NAZES	TOAZE	ZEZES
COZIE	GROSZ	NAZIR	TOPAZ	ZHOMO
CRAZE	GYOZA	NAZIS	TOUZE	ZIBET
CRAZY	HAFIZ	NEEZE	TOUZY	ZIFFS
CROZE	HAMZA	NERTZ	TOWZE	ZIGAN
CZARS	HAZAN	NIZAM	TOWZY	ZILAS
DARZI	HAZED	NUDZH	TOZED	ZILCH
DAZED	HAZEL	OOZED	TOZES	ZILLA
DAZER	HAZER	OOZES	TOZIE	ZILLS
DAZES	HAZES	ORZOS	TROOZ	ZIMBI
DIAZO	HEEZE	OUZEL	TZARS	ZIMBS
DITZY	HERTZ	OUZOS	ULZIE	ZINCO
DIZEN	HIZEN	OZEKI	UNZIP	ZINCS
DIZZY	HUZZA	OZONE	VEZIR	ZINCY
DOOZY	HUZZY	OZZIE	VIZIR	ZINEB
DOZED	IZARD	PEAZE	VIZOR	ZINES
DOZEN	IZARS	PEIZE	VOZHD	ZINGS
DOZER	IZZAT	PIEZO	WALTZ	ZINGY
DOZES	JAZZY	PIZED	WANZE	ZINKE
DURZI	KANZU	PIZES	WAREZ	ZINKY
DZHOS	KARZY	PIZZA	WAZIR	ZIPPO
ENZYM	KAZIS	PLAZA	WAZOO	ZIPPY
FAZED	KAZOO	PLOTZ	WEIZE	ZIRAM
FAZES	KHAZI	PONZU	WHIZZ	ZITIS
FEAZE	KLUTZ	POZZY	WINZE	ZIZEL
FEEZE	KRANZ	PRIZE	WIZEN	ZIZIT
FEZES	KUDZU	PZAZZ	WIZES	ZLOTE
FEZZY	KUZUS	RAZED	WOOTZ	ZLOTY
FIZZY	LAZAR	RAZEE	WOOZY	ZOAEA
FORZA	LAZED	RAZER	YUZUS	ZOBOS
FRITZ	LAZES	RAZES	ZABRA	ZOBUS
FRIZE	LAZOS	RAZOO	ZACKS	ZOCCO
FRIZZ	LAZZI	RAZOR	ZAIRE	ZOEAE
FROZE	LAZZO	RITZY	ZAKAT	ZOEAL
FURZE	LEAZE	RIZAS	ZAMAN	ZOEAS
FURZY	LEZES	ROZET	ZAMBO	ZOISM
FUZED	LEZZA	ROZIT	ZAMIA	ZOIST
FUZEE	LEZZY	SADZA	ZANJA	ZOMBI
FUZES	LOZEN	SAZES	ZANTE	ZONAE
FUZIL	MAIZE	SCUZZ	ZANZA	ZONAL
FUZZY	MATZA	SEAZE	ZANZE	ZONDA
GAUZE	MATZO	SEIZE	ZAPPY	ZONED
GAUZY	MAZED	SENZA	ZARFS	ZONER
GAZAL	MAZER	SIZAR	ZATIS	ZONES
GAZAR	MAZES	SIZED	ZAXES	ZONKS
GAZED	MAZEY	SIZEL	ZAYIN	ZOOEA
GAZER	MAZUT	SIZER	ZAZEN	ZOOEY
GAZES	MEZES	SIZES	ZEALS	ZOOID
GAZON	MEZZE	SMAZE	ZEBEC	ZOOKS
GAZOO	MEZZO	SOYUZ	ZEBRA	ZOOMS
GHAZI	MILTZ	SOZIN	ZEBUB	ZOONS
GINZO	MIRZA	SPAZA	ZEBUS	ZOOTY
GIZMO	MIZEN	SPAZZ	ZEINS	ZOPPA
GLAZE	MIZZY	SPITZ	ZERDA	ZOPPO
GLAZY	MOTZA	SQUIZ	ZERKS	ZORIL
GLITZ	MOZED	SWIZZ	ZEROS	ZORIS
GLOZE	MOZES	TAZZA	ZESTS	ZORRO
GONZO	MOZOS	TAZZE	ZESTY	ZOUKS
GRAZE	MUZZY	TEAZE	ZETAS	ZOWIE

ZULUS	ZUPAS	ZUZIM	ZYGON	ZYMIC
ZUPAN	ZURFS	ZYGAL	ZYMES	

Six-letter words

ABLAZE	BEZANT	CORYZA	FEZZES	GLAZES
ABRAZO	BEZAZZ	COUZIN	FIZGIG	GLITZY
ADZING	BEZELS	COZENS	FIZZED	GLOZED
ADZUKI	BEZILS	COZEYS	FIZZEN	GLOZES
AGAZED	BEZOAR	COZIED	FIZZER	GOZZAN
AGNIZE	BEZZLE	COZIER	FIZZES	GRAZED
AGRIZE	BIZAZZ	COZIES	FIZZLE	GRAZER
AGRYZE	BIZONE	COZILY	FLOOZY	GRAZES
AGUIZE	BIZZES	COZING	FOOZLE	GRIZES
AIZLES	BIZZOS	COZZES	FORZAS	GROSZE
ALTEZA	BLAIZE	CRAZED	FOZIER	GROSZY
AMAZED	BLAZED	CRAZES	FRANZY	GUIZER
AMAZES	BLAZER	CROZER	FRAZIL	GUTZER
AMAZON	BLAZES	CROZES	FREEZE	GUZZLE
APOZEM	BLAZON	CRUZIE	FRENZY	GYOZAS
ASSIZE	BLINTZ	CUZZES	FRIEZE	HALUTZ
AVIZED	BLOWZE	CZAPKA	FRIZED	HAMZAH
AVIZES	BLOWZY	DARZIS	FRIZER	HAMZAS
AVYZED	BONZER	DAZERS	FRIZES	HAZANS
AVYZES	BONZES	DAZING	FRIZZY	HAZARD
AZALEA	BOOZED	DAZZLE	FROUZY	HAZELS
AZERTY	BOOZER	DEFUZE	FROWZY	HAZERS
AZIDES	BOOZES	DEZINC	FROZEN	HAZIER
AZINES	BOOZEY	DIAZIN	FURZES	HAZILY
AZIONE	BORZOI	DIAZOS	FUTZED	HAZING
AZLONS	BRAIZE	DITZES	FUTZES	HAZMAT
AZOLES	BRAZAS	DIZAIN	FUZEES	HAZZAN
AZOLLA	BRAZED	DIZENS	FUZILS	HEEZED
AZONAL	BRAZEN	DONZEL	FUZING	HEEZES
AZONIC	BRAZER	DOOZER	FUZZED	HEEZIE
AZOTED	BRAZES	DOOZIE	FUZZES	HIZENS
AZOTES	BRAZIL	DORIZE	FUZZLE	HIZZED
AZOTHS	BREEZE	DOZENS	GAUZES	HIZZES
AZOTIC	BREEZY	DOZERS	GAZABO	HOWZAT
AZUKIS	BRIZES	DOZIER	GAZALS	HOWZIT
AZURES	BRONZE	DOZILY	GAZARS	HUTZPA
AZYGOS	BRONZY	DOZING	GAZEBO	HUZOOR
AZYMES	BROUZE	DRAZEL	GAZERS	HUZZAH
BAIZAS	BUAZES	DURZIS	GAZIER	HUZZAS
BAIZED	BUZUKI	DZEREN	GAZING	IMBIZO
BAIZES	BUZZED	ECZEMA	GAZONS	IODIZE
BANZAI	BUZZER	ENTREZ	GAZOON	IONIZE
BARAZA	BUZZES	ENZIAN	GAZOOS	IZARDS
BAZAAR	BWAZIS	ENZONE	GAZUMP	IZZARD
BAZARS	BYZANT	ENZYME	GEEZAH	IZZATS
BAZAZZ	CEAZED	ENZYMS	GEEZER	JAZIES
BAZOOS	CEAZES	EPIZOA	GHAZAL	JAZZBO
BEDAZE	CHAZAN	ERSATZ	GHAZEL	JAZZED
BEEZER	CHINTZ	EVZONE	GHAZIS	JAZZER
BEGAZE	CIZERS	FAZING	GIZMOS	JAZZES
BENZAL	CLOZES	FEAZED	GIZZEN	JEZAIL
BENZIL	COBZAS	FEAZES	GIZZES	JIZZES
BENZIN	COLZAS	FEEZED	GLAZED	KAIZEN
BENZOL	COOZES	FEEZES	GLAZEN	KAMEEZ
BENZYL	COROZO	FEZZED	GLAZER	KANZUS

KAZOOS	MIZZLY	PRIZES	SIZISM	VIZORS
KHAZEN	MOMZER	PUTZED	SIZIST	VIZSLA
KHAZIS	MOTZAS	PUTZES	SIZZLE	VIZZIE
KIBITZ	MOZING	PUZZEL	SLEAZE	VOZHDS
KLUTZY	MOZZES	PUZZLE	SLEAZO	WANZED
KOLHOZ	MOZZIE	QUARTZ	SLEAZY	WANZES
KOLKOZ	MOZZLE	QUAZZY	SLEEZY	WAZIRS
KRANTZ	MUZAKY	QUEAZY	SMAZES	WAZOOS
KUDZUS	MUZHIK	QUEZAL	SNAZZY	WEAZEN
KUVASZ	MUZJIK	QUINZE	SNEEZE	WEIZED
KWANZA	MUZZED	RANZEL	SNEEZY	WEIZES
LAZARS	MUZZES	RAZEED	SNOOZE	WEZAND
LAZIED	MUZZLE	RAZEES	SNOOZY	WHEEZE
LAZIER	MZUNGU	RAZERS	SOZINE	WHEEZY
LAZIES	NAZIFY	RAZING	SOZINS	WHIZZY
LAZILY	NAZIRS	RAZOOS	SOZZLE	WINZES
LAZING	NEEZED	RAZORS	SOZZLY	WIZARD
LAZOED	NEEZES	RAZURE	SPELTZ	WIZENS
LAZOES	NIZAMS	RAZZED	SPRITZ	WIZIER
LAZULI	NOZZER	RAZZES	STANZA	WIZZEN
LEAZES	NOZZLE	RAZZIA	STANZE	WIZZES
LEZZAS	NUZZER	RAZZLE	STANZO	WURZEL
LEZZES	NUZZLE	REBOZO	SUIVEZ	WUZZLE
LEZZIE	NYANZA	RESIZE	SYZYGY	YAKUZA
LIZARD	OOZIER	REZERO	TARZAN	YUTZES
LIZZIE	OOZILY	REZONE	TAZZAS	ZABETA
LOZELL	OOZING	REZZES	TEAZED	ZABRAS
LOZENS	OUZELS	RHIZIC	TEAZEL	ZADDIK
LUTZES	OYEZES	RITZES	TEAZES	ZAFFAR
LUZERN	OZAENA	RIZARD	TEAZLE	ZAFFER
LUZZES	OZALID	RIZZAR	TENZON	ZAFFIR
MAHZOR	OZEKIS	RIZZER	TIZWAS	ZAFFRE
MAIZES	OZONES	RIZZOR	TIZZES	ZAFTIG
MAMZER	OZONIC	RONZER	TOAZED	ZAGGED
MATZAH	OZZIES	ROZETS	TOAZES	ZAIKAI
MATZAS	PANZER	ROZITS	TOLZEY	ZAIRES
MATZOH	PATZER	ROZZER	TOUZED	ZAKATS
MATZOS	PAZAZZ	SADZAS	TOUZES	ZAMANG
MATZOT	PEAZED	SAZHEN	TOUZLE	ZAMANS
MAZARD	PEAZES	SAZZES	TOWZED	ZAMBOS
MAZERS	PEIZED	SCAZON	TOWZES	ZAMBUK
MAZHBI	PEIZES	SCHIZO	TOZIES	ZAMIAS
MAZIER	PEZANT	SCHIZY	TOZING	ZANANA
MAZILY	PHEEZE	SCHNOZ	TREZES	ZANDER
MAZING	PHIZES	SCOZZA	TUZZES	ZANIED
MAZOUT	PHIZOG	SCRUZE	TWEEZE	ZANIER
MAZUMA	PIAZZA	SCUZZY	TZETSE	ZANIES
MAZUTS	PIAZZE	SEAZED	TZETZE	ZANILY
MEAZEL	PIZAZZ	SEAZES	TZURIS	ZANJAS
MEZAIL	PIZING	SEIZED	ULZIES	ZANTES
MEZCAL	PIZZAS	SEIZER	UMFAZI	ZANZAS
MEZUZA	PIZZAZ	SEIZES	UNZIPS	ZANZES
MEZZES	PIZZLE	SEIZIN	UPGAZE	ZAPATA
MEZZOS	PLAZAS	SEIZOR	UPSIZE	ZAPPED
MIRZAS	PODZOL	SHAZAM	VEZIRS	ZAPPER
MIZENS	PONZUS	SIZARS	VIZARD	ZARAPE
MIZUNA	POTZER	SIZELS	VIZIED	ZAREBA
MIZZEN	POZOLE	SIZERS	VIZIER	ZARIBA
MIZZES	PRIZED	SIZIER	VIZIES	ZARNEC
MIZZLE	PRIZER	SIZING	VIZIRS	ZAYINS

ZAZENS	ZEUGMA	ZIPPED	ZOISMS	ZOONIC
ZEALOT	ZHOMOS	ZIPPER	ZOISTS	ZOOZOO
ZEATIN	ZIBETH	ZIPPOS	ZOMBIE	ZORILS
ZEBECK	ZIBETS	ZIPTOP	ZOMBIS	ZORINO
ZEBECS	ZIGANS	ZIRAMS	ZONARY	ZORROS
ZEBRAS	ZIGGED	ZIRCON	ZONATE	ZOSTER
ZEBUBS	ZIGZAG	ZITHER	ZONDAS	ZOUAVE
ZECHIN	ZILLAH	ZIZELS	ZONERS	ZOUNDS
ZELANT	ZILLAS	ZIZITH	ZONING	ZOYSIA
ZELOSO	ZIMBIS	ZIZZED	ZONKED	ZUFOLI
ZENANA	ZIMMER	ZIZZES	ZONOID	ZUFOLO
ZENDIK	ZINCED	ZIZZLE	ZONULA	ZUPANS
ZENITH	ZINCIC	ZLOTYS	ZONULE	ZYDECO
ZEPHYR	ZINCKY	ZOAEAE	ZONURE	ZYGOID
ZERDAS	ZINCOS	ZOAEAS	ZOOEAE	ZYGOMA
ZEREBA	ZINEBS	ZOARIA	ZOOEAL	ZYGOSE
ZERIBA	ZINGED	ZOCALO	ZOOEAS	ZYGOTE
ZEROED	ZINGEL	ZOCCOS	ZOOIDS	ZYMASE
ZEROES	ZINGER	ZODIAC	ZOOIER	ZYMITE
ZEROTH	ZINKED	ZOECIA	ZOOMED	ZYMOID
ZESTED	ZINKES	ZOETIC	ZOONAL	ZYMOME
ZESTER	ZINNIA	ZOFTIG	ZOONED	ZYTHUM

Seven-letter words

ABRAZOS	AVYZING	BENZINS	BORZOIS	CAPSIZE
ADONIZE	AZALEAS	BENZOIC	BRAIZES	CAZIQUE
ADZUKIS	AZIMUTH	BENZOIN	BRAZENS	CEAZING
AGATIZE	AZIONES	BENZOLE	BRAZERS	CERVEZA
AGENIZE	AZOLLAS	BENZOLS	BRAZIER	CHALAZA
AGNIZED	AZOTISE	BENZOYL	BRAZILS	CHALUTZ
AGNIZES	AZOTIZE	BENZYLS	BRAZING	CHAMETZ
AGONIZE	AZOTOUS	BEZANTS	BREEZED	CHAZANS
AGRIZED	AZULEJO	BEZIQUE	BREEZES	CHAZZAN
AGRIZES	AZUREAN	BEZOARS	BRITZKA	CHAZZEN
AGRYZED	AZURINE	BEZZANT	BROMIZE	CHINTZY
AGRYZES	AZURITE	BEZZLED	BRONZED	CHIZZED
AGUIZED	AZYGIES	BEZZLES	BRONZEN	CHIZZES
AGUIZES	AZYGOUS	BIZARRE	BRONZER	CHOMETZ
ALBIZIA	AZYMITE	BIZARRO	BRONZES	CHORIZO
ALCAZAR	AZYMOUS	BIZNAGA	BROUZES	CHUTZPA
ALCORZA	BAIZING	BIZONAL	BRULZIE	CITIZEN
ALFEREZ	BANZAIS	BIZONES	BUMBAZE	COALIZE
ALIZARI	BAPTIZE	BIZZIES	BUZUKIA	COGNIZE
ALTEZAS	BARAZAS	BLAZERS	BUZUKIS	COROZOS
ALTEZZA	BAZAARS	BLAZING	BUZZARD	CORYZAL
AMAZING	BAZOOKA	BLAZONS	BUZZCUT	CORYZAS
AMAZONS	BAZOOMS	BLINTZE	BUZZERS	COUZINS
ANALYZE	BAZOUKI	BLITZED	BUZZIER	COZENED
ANODIZE	BEDAZED	BLITZER	BUZZING	COZENER
ANZIANI	BEDAZES	BLITZES	BUZZWIG	COZIERS
APOZEMS	BEDIZEN	BLOWZED	BYZANTS	COZIEST
APPRIZE	BEEZERS	BLOWZES	CABEZON	COZYING
ARABIZE	BEGAZED	BONANZA	CADENZA	CRAZIER
ASSIZED	BEGAZES	BOOZERS	CALZONE	CRAZIES
ASSIZER	BEMAZED	BOOZIER	CALZONI	CRAZILY
ASSIZES	BENZALS	BOOZILY	CANZONA	CRAZING
ATHEIZE	BENZENE	BOOZING	CANZONE	CROZERS
ATOMIZE	BENZILS	BORAZON	CANZONI	CROZIER
AVIZING	BENZINE	BORTZES	CAPIZES	CRUIZIE

CRUZADO	EMPRIZE	GAUZILY	HUTZPAS	LOZENGE
CRUZIES	ENDOZOA	GAZABOS	HUZOORS	LOZENGY
CYANIZE	ENFROZE	GAZANIA	HUZZAED	LUZERNS
CYCLIZE	ENTOZOA	GAZEBOS	HUZZAHS	MACHZOR
CZAPKAS	ENZIANS	GAZEFUL	HUZZIES	MADZOON
CZARDAS	ENZONED	GAZELLE	ICONIZE	MAHZORS
CZARDOM	ENZONES	GAZETTE	IDOLIZE	MAMZERS
CZARINA	ENZYMES	GAZIEST	IMBIZOS	MATZAHS
CZARISM	ENZYMIC	GAZINGS	IMBLAZE	MATZOHS
CZARIST	EPAZOTE	GAZOOKA	IODIZED	MATZOON
DAMOZEL	EPIZOAN	GAZOONS	IODIZER	MATZOTH
DANAZOL	EPIZOIC	GAZUMPS	IODIZES	MAZARDS
DAZEDLY	EPIZOON	GEEZAHS	IONIZED	MAZEDLY
DAZZLED	EROTIZE	GEEZERS	IONIZER	MAZEFUL
DAZZLER	EVZONES	GENIZAH	IONIZES	MAZHBIS
DAZZLES	FAHLERZ	GHAZALS	IRIDIZE	MAZIEST
DEFROZE	FANZINE	GHAZELS	IRONIZE	MAZOUTS
DEFUZED	FAZENDA	GHAZIES	ISOZYME	MAZUMAS
DEFUZES	FEAZING	GINZOES	ITEMIZE	MAZURKA
DEGLAZE	FEEZING	GIZZARD	IZZARDS	MAZZARD
DENIZEN	FILAZER	GIZZENS	JACUZZI	MEAZELS
DEUTZIA	FIZGIGS	GLAZERS	JANIZAR	MENAZON
DEZINCS	FIZZENS	GLAZIER	JAZZBOS	MESTIZA
DIALYZE	FIZZERS	GLAZILY	JAZZERS	MESTIZO
DIARIZE	FIZZGIG	GLAZING	JAZZIER	METAZOA
DIAZINE	FIZZIER	GLITZED	JAZZILY	MEZAILS
DIAZINS	FIZZING	GLITZES	JAZZING	MEZCALS
DIAZOES	FIZZLED	GLOZING	JAZZMAN	MEZQUIT
DIAZOLE	FIZZLES	GOZZANS	JAZZMEN	MEZUZAH
DITZIER	FLOOZIE	GRAZERS	JEZAILS	MEZUZAS
DIZAINS	FOOZLED	GRAZIER	JEZEBEL	MEZUZOT
DIZENED	FOOZLER	GRAZING	KAIZENS	MIDSIZE
DIZZARD	FOOZLES	GRECIZE	KARZIES	MILTZES
DIZZIED	FORZATI	GRIZZLE	KHAZENS	MITZVAH
DIZZIER	FORZATO	GRIZZLY	KIBBITZ	MIZMAZE
DIZZIES	FOZIEST	GROZING	KIBBUTZ	MIZUNAS
DIZZILY	FRAWZEY	GUEREZA	KLEZMER	MIZZENS
DOCKIZE	FRAZILS	GUIZERS	KLUTZES	MIZZLED
DONZELS	FRAZZLE	GUTZERS	KOLHOZY	MIZZLES
DOOZERS	FREEZER	GUZZLED	KOLKHOZ	MOMZERS
DOOZIES	FREEZES	GUZZLER	KOLKOZY	MOZETTA
DOPIAZA	FRIEZED	GUZZLES	KRANZES	MOZETTE
DORIZED	FRIEZES	HAFIZES	KREUZER	MOZZIES
DORIZES	FRITZES	HAMZAHS	KUNZITE	MOZZLES
DOZENED	FRIZERS	HAZANIM	KWANZAS	MUEZZIN
DOZENTH	FRIZING	HAZARDS	KYANIZE	MUZHIKS
DOZIEST	FRIZZED	HAZELLY	LAICIZE	MUZJIKS
DOZINGS	FRIZZER	HAZIEST	LAIRIZE	MUZZIER
DRAZELS	FRIZZES	HAZINGS	LAYDEEZ	MUZZILY
DRIZZLE	FRIZZLE	HAZMATS	LAZARET	MUZZING
DRIZZLY	FRIZZLY	HAZZANS	LAZIEST	MUZZLED
DUALIZE	FURZIER	HEEZIES	LAZOING	MUZZLER
DZERENS	FUTZING	HEEZING	LAZULIS	MUZZLES
EBONIZE	FUZZIER	HEROIZE	LAZYING	MYTHIZE
ECHOIZE	FUZZILY	HERTZES	LAZYISH	MZUNGUS
ECTOZOA	FUZZING	HIZZING	LEZZIES	NEEZING
ECZEMAS	FUZZLED	HOATZIN	LIONIZE	NETIZEN
EGOTIZE	FUZZLES	HORIZON	LIZARDS	NONZERO
ELEGIZE	GALLIZE	HUMBUZZ	LIZZIES	NOZZERS
EMBLAZE	GAUZIER	HUTZPAH	LOZELLS	NOZZLES

NUDZHED	PUZZLER	SCRUZES	SWOZZLE	VIZSLAS
NUDZHES	PUZZLES	SCUZZES	SYZYGAL	VIZYING
NUZZERS	PZAZZES	SEAZING	TAILZIE	VIZZIED
NUZZLED	QUARTZY	SEIZERS	TARZANS	VIZZIES
NUZZLER	QUETZAL	SEIZING	TEAZELS	WALTZED
NUZZLES	QUEZALS	SEIZINS	TEAZING	WALTZER
NYANZAS	QUINZES	SEIZORS	TEAZLED	WALTZES
OBELIZE	QUIZZED	SEIZURE	TEAZLES	WANZING
ODORIZE	QUIZZER	SELTZER	TENDENZ	WARZONE
ODZOOKS	QUIZZES	SHEGETZ	TENZONS	WAZZOCK
OOZIEST	RANZELS	SHIATZU	THIAZIN	WEAZAND
ORGANZA	RAZORED	SHMALTZ	THIAZOL	WEAZENS
OUTGAZE	RAZURES	SHMOOZE	TIZZIES	WEIZING
OUTSIZE	RAZZIAS	SHOWBIZ	TOAZING	WEZANDS
OXAZINE	RAZZING	SIAMEZE	TOLZEYS	WHAIZLE
OXIDIZE	RAZZLES	SIZABLE	TOPAZES	WHEEZED
OZAENAS	REALIZE	SIZABLY	TOUZIER	WHEEZER
OZALIDS	REBOZOS	SIZEISM	TOUZING	WHEEZES
OZONATE	REFROZE	SIZEIST	TOUZLED	WHEEZLE
OZONIDE	REGLAZE	SIZIEST	TOUZLES	WHIZZED
OZONISE	REPRIZE	SIZINGS	TOWZIER	WHIZZER
OZONIZE	RESEIZE	SIZISMS	TOWZING	WHIZZES
OZONOUS	RESIZED	SIZISTS	TRAPEZE	WIZARDS
PALAZZI	RESIZES	SIZZLED	TRIAZIN	WIZENED
PALAZZO	REZEROS	SIZZLER	TRIZONE	WIZIERS
PANZERS	REZONED	SIZZLES	TUILZIE	WIZZENS
PARAZOA	REZONES	SLEAZES	TWEEZED	WOOTZES
PATZERS	RHIZINE	SNEEZED	TWEEZER	WOOZIER
PAZZAZZ	RHIZOID	SNEEZER	TWEEZES	WOOZILY
PEAZING	RHIZOMA	SNEEZES	TWIZZLE	WRIZLED
PECTIZE	RHIZOME	SNOOZED	TZADDIK	WURZELS
PEIZING	RHIZOPI	SNOOZER	TZADDIQ	WUZZLED
PEPTIZE	RIOTIZE	SNOOZES	TZARDOM	WUZZLES
PEZANTS	RITZIER	SNOOZLE	TZARINA	ZABETAS
PHEAZAR	RITZILY	SNUZZLE	TZARISM	ZABTIEH
PHEEZED	RIZARDS	SOVKHOZ	TZARIST	ZACATON
PHEEZES	RIZZARS	SOYUZES	TZETSES	ZADDICK
PHIZOGS	RIZZART	SOZINES	TZETZES	ZADDIKS
PHIZZES	RIZZERS	SOZZLED	TZIGANE	ZAFFARS
PIAZZAS	RIZZORS	SOZZLES	TZIGANY	ZAFFERS
PIZAZZY	ROMANZA	SPATZLE	TZIMMES	ZAFFIRS
PIZZAZZ	RONZERS	SPAZZED	TZITZIS	ZAFFRES
PIZZLES	ROZELLE	SPAZZES	TZITZIT	ZAGGING
PLOTZED	ROZETED	SPITZES	UMFAZIS	ZAIKAIS
PLOTZES	ROZITED	SPREAZE	UNCRAZY	ZAITECH
PODZOLS	ROZZERS	SPREEZE	UNFAZED	ZAKUSKA
POETIZE	SAZERAC	SPULZIE	UNFROZE	ZAKUSKI
POLYZOA	SAZHENS	SQUEEZE	UNISIZE	ZAMANGS
POTZERS	SCAZONS	SQUEEZY	UNITIZE	ZAMARRA
POZOLES	SCHANZE	STANZAS	UNRAZED	ZAMARRO
POZZIES	SCHERZI	STANZES	UNSIZED	ZAMBUCK
PRENZIE	SCHERZO	STANZOS	UNZONED	ZAMBUKS
PRETZEL	SCHIZOS	STARETZ	UPGAZED	ZAMOUSE
PREZZES	SCHIZZY	STYLIZE	UPGAZES	ZAMPONE
PREZZIE	SCHMALZ	SUBZERO	UPSIZED	ZAMPONI
PRIZERS	SCHMELZ	SUBZONE	UPSIZES	ZANANAS
PRIZING	SCHMOOZ	SWAZZLE	UTILIZE	ZANDERS
PUTZING	SCHNOZZ	SWIZZED	VIZARDS	ZANELLA
PUZZELS	SCOZZAS	SWIZZES	VIZIERS	ZANIEST
PUZZLED	SCRUZED	SWIZZLE	VIZORED	ZANJERO

ZANYING	ZEMSTVA	ZINCING	ZOARIUM	ZOOTIER
ZANYISH	ZEMSTVO	ZINCITE	ZOCALOS	ZOOTOMY
ZANYISM	ZENAIDA	ZINCKED	ZOCCOLO	ZOOTYPE
ZAPATEO	ZENANAS	ZINCODE	ZODIACS	ZOOZOOS
ZAPPERS	ZENDIKS	ZINCOID	ZOECIUM	ZORBING
ZAPPIER	ZENITHS	ZINCOUS	ZOEFORM	ZORGITE
ZAPPING	ZEOLITE	ZINGANI	ZOISITE	ZORILLA
ZAPTIAH	ZEPHYRS	ZINGANO	ZOMBIES	ZORILLE
ZAPTIEH	ZEPPOLE	ZINGARA	ZOMBIFY	ZORILLO
ZARAPES	ZEPPOLI	ZINGARE	ZONALLY	ZORINOS
ZAREBAS	ZEREBAS	ZINGARI	ZONATED	ZOSTERS
ZAREEBA	ZERIBAS	ZINGARO	ZONINGS	ZOUAVES
ZARIBAS	ZEROING	ZINGELS	ZONKING	ZOYSIAS
ZARNECS	ZESTERS	ZINGERS	ZONULAE	ZUFFOLI
ZARNICH	ZESTFUL	ZINGIER	ZONULAR	ZUFFOLO
ZEALANT	ZESTIER	ZINGING	ZONULAS	ZYDECOS
ZEALFUL	ZESTILY	ZINKIER	ZONULES	ZYGOMAS
ZEALOTS	ZESTING	ZINKIFY	ZONULET	ZYGOSES
ZEALOUS	ZETETIC	ZINKING	ZONURES	ZYGOSIS
ZEATINS	ZEUGMAS	ZINNIAS	ZOOECIA	ZYGOTES
ZEBECKS	ZEUXITE	ZIPLESS	ZOOGAMY	ZYGOTIC
ZEBRAIC	ZIBETHS	ZIPLOCK	ZOOGENY	ZYMASES
ZEBRANO	ZIFFIUS	ZIPPERS	ZOOGLEA	ZYMITES
ZEBRASS	ZIGANKA	ZIPPIER	ZOOGONY	ZYMOGEN
ZEBRINA	ZIGGING	ZIPPING	ZOOIDAL	ZYMOMES
ZEBRINE	ZIGZAGS	ZIRCONS	ZOOIEST	ZYMOSAN
ZEBROID	ZIKURAT	ZITHERN	ZOOLITE	ZYMOSES
ZEBRULA	ZILCHES	ZITHERS	ZOOLITH	ZYMOSIS
ZEBRULE	ZILLAHS	ZIZANIA	ZOOLOGY	ZYMOTIC
ZECCHIN	ZILLION	ZIZZING	ZOOMING	ZYMURGY
ZECHINS	ZIMMERS	ZIZZLED	ZOONING	ZYTHUMS
ZEDOARY	ZIMOCCA	ZIZZLES	ZOONITE	ZYZZYVA
ZELANTS	ZINCATE	ZLOTIES	ZOONOMY	
ZELATOR	ZINCIER	ZLOTYCH	ZOOPERY	
ZELKOVA	ZINCIFY	ZOARIAL	ZOOTAXY	

Eight-letter words

ACTIVIZE	ALLOZYME	ARMOZINE	AZOTURIA	BENZIDIN
ADONIZED	ALTEZZAS	ARRHIZAL	AZULEJOS	BENZINES
ADONIZES	AMAZEDLY	ASSIZERS	AZURINES	BENZOATE
AGATIZED	AMORTIZE	ASSIZING	AZURITES	BENZOINS
AGATIZES	ANALYZED	ATHEIZED	AZYGOSES	BENZOLES
AGENIZED	ANALYZER	ATHEIZES	AZYMITES	BENZOYLS
AGENIZES	ANALYZES	ATHETIZE	BANALIZE	BENZYLIC
AGNIZING	ANNALIZE	ATMOLYZE	BAPTIZED	BEZAZZES
AGONIZED	ANODIZED	ATOMIZED	BAPTIZER	BEZIQUES
AGONIZES	ANODIZES	ATOMIZER	BAPTIZES	BEZONIAN
AGRIZING	ANTICIZE	ATOMIZES	BAROMETZ	BEZZANTS
AGRYZING	APHETIZE	ATRAZINE	BARTIZAN	BEZZLING
AGUIZING	APHORIZE	ATTICIZE	BAZAZZES	BITESIZE
ALBITIZE	APPETIZE	AUTOLYZE	BAZOOKAS	BIZARRES
ALBIZIAS	APPRIZED	AVIANIZE	BAZOUKIS	BIZARROS
ALBIZZIA	APPRIZER	AZIMUTHS	BEDAZING	BIZAZZES
ALCAZARS	APPRIZES	AZOTEMIA	BEDAZZLE	BIZCACHA
ALCORZAS	ARABIZED	AZOTEMIC	BEDIZENS	BIZNAGAS
ALGUAZIL	ARABIZES	AZOTISED	BEGAZING	BLAZERED
ALIZARIN	ARBORIZE	AZOTISES	BEJEEZUS	BLAZONED
ALIZARIS	ARCHAIZE	AZOTIZED	BEMUZZLE	BLAZONER
ALKALIZE	ARMOZEEN	AZOTIZES	BENZENES	BLAZONRY

BLINTZES	CAPSIZES	DEFREEZE	ELEGIZES	FRANCIZE
BLITZERS	CATALYZE	DEFROZEN	EMBEZZLE	FRANZIER
BLITZING	CAZIQUES	DEFUZING	EMBLAZED	FRAWZEYS
BLIZZARD	CENOZOIC	DEGLAZED	EMBLAZER	FRAZZLED
BLOWZIER	CERVEZAS	DEGLAZES	EMBLAZES	FRAZZLES
BLOWZILY	CHALAZAE	DEIONIZE	EMBLAZON	FREEZERS
BONANZAS	CHALAZAL	DEMONIZE	EMBOLIZE	FREEZING
BOOZIEST	CHALAZAS	DENAZIFY	EMPERIZE	FRENZIED
BORAZONS	CHALAZIA	DENIZENS	EMPRIZES	FRENZIES
BOTANIZE	CHAZANIM	DEPUTIZE	ENDOZOIC	FRENZILY
BOUZOUKI	CHAZZANS	DEUTZIAS	ENDOZOON	FRIEZING
BOZZETTI	CHAZZENS	DEZINCED	ENERGIZE	FRIZETTE
BOZZETTO	CHINTZES	DIALYZED	ENFREEZE	FRIZZERS
BRAZENED	CHIZZING	DIALYZER	ENFROZEN	FRIZZIER
BRAZENLY	CHORIZOS	DIALYZES	ENTOZOAL	FRIZZIES
BRAZENRY	CHROMIZE	DIARIZED	ENTOZOAN	FRIZZILY
BRAZIERS	CHUTZPAH	DIARIZES	ENTOZOIC	FRIZZING
BRAZIERY	CHUTZPAS	DIAZEPAM	ENTOZOON	FRIZZLED
BRAZILIN	CITIZENS	DIAZINES	ENZONING	FRIZZLER
BREEZIER	CIVILIZE	DIAZINON	ENZOOTIC	FRIZZLES
BREEZILY	COALIZED	DIAZOLES	EPAZOTES	FROUZIER
BREEZING	COALIZES	DIGITIZE	EPIZOANS	FROUZILY
BRITZKAS	COENZYME	DIMERIZE	EPIZOISM	FROWZIER
BRITZSKA	COGNIZED	DIPLOZOA	EPIZOITE	FROWZILY
BROMIZED	COGNIZER	DISPRIZE	EPIZOOTY	FROZENLY
BROMIZES	COGNIZES	DISSEIZE	EQUALIZE	FURZIEST
BRONZERS	COLONIZE	DITZIEST	ERGOTIZE	FUZZIEST
BRONZIER	COLORIZE	DIVINIZE	EROTIZED	FUZZLING
BRONZIFY	COMPRIZE	DIZENING	EROTIZES	FUZZTONE
BRONZING	COZENAGE	DIZYGOUS	ERSATZES	GADZOOKS
BRONZITE	COZENERS	DIZZARDS	ETERNIZE	GALLIZED
BRUILZIE	COZENING	DIZZIEST	ETHERIZE	GALLIZES
BRULZIES	COZINESS	DIZZYING	ETHICIZE	GARBANZO
BRUNIZEM	CRAZIEST	DOCKIZED	EULOGIZE	GAUZIEST
BRYOZOAN	CREDENZA	DOCKIZES	EUPHUIZE	GAZABOES
BULLDOZE	CREOLIZE	DOPIAZAS	EVENTIZE	GAZANIAS
BUMBAZED	CREUTZER	DORIZING	EXAHERTZ	GAZEBOES
BUMBAZES	CROZIERS	DOUZEPER	EXORCIZE	GAZELLES
BURDIZZO	CROZZLED	DOWNSIZE	FABULIZE	GAZEMENT
BUZKASHI	CRUIZIES	DOWNZONE	FANZINES	GAZETTED
BUZZARDS	CRUZADOS	DOZENING	FARADIZE	GAZETTES
BUZZCUTS	CRUZEIRO	DOZENTHS	FAZENDAS	GAZOGENE
BUZZIEST	CURARIZE	DOZINESS	FEMINAZI	GAZOOKAS
BUZZINGS	CUTINIZE	DRIZZLED	FEMINIZE	GAZPACHO
BUZZWIGS	CYANIZED	DRIZZLES	FIBERIZE	GAZUMPED
BUZZWORD	CYANIZES	DUALIZED	FILAZERS	GAZUMPER
CABEZONE	CYCLIZED	DUALIZES	FINALIZE	GAZUNDER
CABEZONS	CYCLIZES	DYNAMIZE	FIZZGIGS	GENIZAHS
CADENZAS	CZARDOMS	EBENEZER	FIZZIEST	GIZZARDS
CALABAZA	CZAREVNA	EBIONIZE	FIZZINGS	GIZZENED
CALORIZE	CZARINAS	EBONIZED	FIZZLING	GLAZIERS
CALZONES	CZARISMS	EBONIZES	FLOOZIES	GLAZIERY
CANALIZE	CZARISTS	ECHOIZED	FLUIDIZE	GLAZIEST
CANONIZE	CZARITSA	ECHOIZES	FOCALIZE	GLAZINGS
CANZONAS	CZARITZA	ECTOZOAN	FOOZLERS	GLITZIER
CANZONES	DAIDZEIN	ECTOZOIC	FOOZLING	GLITZILY
CANZONET	DAMOZELS	ECTOZOON	FORZANDI	GLITZING
CAPONIZE	DANAZOLS	EGOTIZED	FORZANDO	GLOZINGS
CAPSIZAL	DAZZLERS	EGOTIZES	FORZATOS	GOHONZON
CAPSIZED	DAZZLING	ELEGIZED	FOZINESS	GOLDSIZE

GRAECIZE	ITEMIZED	MADZOONS	MYTHIZED	PEPTIZER
GRAZABLE	ITEMIZER	MAGAZINE	MYTHIZES	PEPTIZES
GRAZIERS	ITEMIZES	MAHZORIM	NASALIZE	PETUNTZE
GRAZINGS	IZVESTIA	MAMZERIM	NAZIFIED	PEZIZOID
GRAZIOSO	JACUZZIS	MANZELLO	NAZIFIES	PHEAZARS
GRECIZED	JANIZARS	MARZIPAN	NEBULIZE	PHEEZING
GRECIZES	JANIZARY	MATZOONS	NETIZENS	PHENAZIN
GRIZZLED	JAPANIZE	MAXIMIZE	NIZAMATE	PIAZZIAN
GRIZZLER	JAROVIZE	MAZAEDIA	NODALIZE	PINTSIZE
GRIZZLES	JAZERANT	MAZARINE	NOMADIZE	PIROZHKI
GUEREZAS	JAZZIEST	MAZELIKE	NOTARIZE	PIROZHOK
GUZZLERS	JAZZLIKE	MAZELTOV	NOVELIZE	PIZZAZES
GUZZLING	JEZEBELS	MAZEMENT	NUDZHING	PIZZAZZES
HALAZONE	JUMBOIZE	MAZINESS	NUZZLERS	PIZZAZZY
HALUTZIM	KAMEEZES	MAZOURKA	NUZZLING	PIZZELLE
HAZARDED	KAMIKAZE	MAZURKAS	OBELIZED	PIZZERIA
HAZARDER	KAZACHKI	MAZZARDS	OBELIZES	PLOTZING
HAZARDRY	KAZACHOK	MECHITZA	ODORIZED	PODZOLIC
HAZELHEN	KAZATSKI	MELANIZE	ODORIZES	POETIZED
HAZELNUT	KAZATSKY	MELODIZE	OOZINESS	POETIZER
HAZINESS	KAZATZKA	MEMORIZE	OPALIZED	POETIZES
HAZZANIM	KHAZENIM	MENAZONS	OPSONIZE	POLARIZE
HEBRAIZE	KIBITZED	MESOZOAN	OPTIMIZE	POLEMIZE
HEMOLYZE	KIBITZER	MESOZOIC	ORGANIZE	POLONIZE
HEPATIZE	KIBITZES	MESPRIZE	ORGANZAS	POLYZOAN
HEROIZED	KLEZMERS	MESTIZAS	OUTBLAZE	POLYZOIC
HEROIZES	KLUTZIER	MESTIZOS	OUTGAZED	POLYZOON
HIZZONER	KOLHOZES	METALIZE	OUTGAZES	POZZOLAN
HOACTZIN	KOLKHOZY	METAZOAL	OUTPRIZE	PREFROZE
HOATZINS	KOLKOZES	METAZOAN	OUTSIZED	PRETZELS
HOLOZOIC	KRANTZES	METAZOIC	OUTSIZES	PREZZIES
HOMINIZE	KREUTZER	METAZOON	OVERSIZE	PRIZABLE
HORIZONS	KREUZERS	METRAZOL	OVERZEAL	PRIZEMAN
HOWITZER	KUNZITES	MEZEREON	OXAZEPAM	PRIZEMEN
HUMANIZE	KUVASZOK	MEZEREUM	OXAZINES	PROTOZOA
HUTZPAHS	KYANIZED	MEZQUITE	OXIDIZED	PTYALIZE
HUZZAHED	KYANIZES	MEZQUITS	OXIDIZER	PUZZLERS
HUZZAING	LAICIZED	MEZUZAHS	OXIDIZES	PUZZLING
HYDROZOA	LAICIZES	MEZUZOTH	OZONATED	PYRAZOLE
HYLOZOIC	LAIRIZED	MIDSIZED	OZONATES	PYRITIZE
ICONIZED	LAIRIZES	MINIMIZE	OZONIDES	PYROLIZE
ICONIZES	LATERIZE	MISPRIZE	OZONISED	PYROLYZE
IDEALIZE	LATINIZE	MITZVAHS	OZONISER	QUANTIZE
IDOLIZED	LAZARETS	MITZVOTH	OZONISES	QUARTZES
IDOLIZER	LAZINESS	MIZMAZES	OZONIZED	QUATORZE
IDOLIZES	LAZULITE	MIZZLIER	OZONIZER	QUAZZIER
IMBLAZED	LAZURITE	MIZZLING	OZONIZES	QUEAZIER
IMBLAZES	LEGALIZE	MOBILIZE	PAGANIZE	QUETZALS
IMMUNIZE	LIONIZED	MOMZERIM	PALAZZOS	QUEZALES
INFAMIZE	LIONIZER	MONAZITE	PAPALIZE	QUIZZERS
IODIZERS	LIONIZES	MONETIZE	PARALYZE	QUIZZERY
IODIZING	LOCALIZE	MORALIZE	PARAZOAN	QUIZZIFY
IONIZERS	LOGICIZE	MOTORIZE	PARAZOON	QUIZZING
IONIZING	LOZENGED	MOZETTAS	PARTIZAN	RACEMIZE
IRIDIZED	LOZENGES	MOZZETTA	PATINIZE	RAZEEING
IRIDIZES	LYRICIZE	MOZZETTE	PAZAZZES	RAZMATAZ
IRONIZED	LYSOZYME	MUEZZINS	PECTIZED	RAZORING
IRONIZES	MACARIZE	MUZZIEST	PECTIZES	REALIZED
ISOZYMES	MACHZORS	MUZZLERS	PENALIZE	REALIZER
ISOZYMIC	MADERIZE	MUZZLING	PEPTIZED	REALIZES

REFREEZE	SEIZINGS	SPOROZOA	TRAPEZES	VIZIRIAL
REFROZEN	SEIZURES	SPREAZED	TRAPEZIA	VIZORING
REGLAZED	SELTZERS	SPREAZES	TRAPEZII	VOCALIZE
REGLAZES	SFORZATI	SPREEZED	TRIAZINE	VOLUMIZE
REGULIZE	SFORZATO	SPREEZES	TRIAZINS	VOWELIZE
RENDZINA	SHIATZUS	SPRITZED	TRIAZOLE	VUVUZELA
REPRIZED	SHKOTZIM	SPRITZER	TRISTEZA	WALTZERS
REPRIZES	SHMALTZY	SPRITZES	TRIZONAL	WALTZING
RESEIZED	SHMOOZED	SPRITZIG	TRIZONES	WARZONES
RESEIZES	SHMOOZES	SPUILZIE	TSARITZA	WAZZOCKS
RESINIZE	SHVARTZE	SPULZIED	TUILZIED	WEAZANDS
RESIZING	SIAMEZED	SPULZIES	TUILZIES	WEAZENED
REZEROED	SIAMEZES	SQUEEZED	TUTORIZE	WHAIZLED
REZEROES	SIEROZEM	SQUEEZER	TWEEZERS	WHAIZLES
REZONING	SIMAZINE	SQUEEZES	TWEEZING	WHEEZERS
RHIZINES	SIMILIZE	SQUIZZES	TWIZZLED	WHEEZIER
RHIZOBIA	SIMONIZE	STANZAED	TWIZZLES	WHEEZILY
RHIZOIDS	SINICIZE	STANZAIC	TZADDIKS	WHEEZING
RHIZOMES	SIRENIZE	STANZOES	TZADDIQS	WHEEZLED
RHIZOMIC	SIRONIZE	STARGAZE	TZARDOMS	WHEEZLES
RHIZOPOD	SITZMARK	STRELITZ	TZAREVNA	WHIZBANG
RHIZOPUS	SIZEABLE	STYLIZED	TZARINAS	WHIZZERS
RIBOZYME	SIZEABLY	STYLIZER	TZARISMS	WHIZZIER
RIGIDIZE	SIZEISMS	STYLIZES	TZARISTS	WHIZZING
RIOTIZES	SIZEISTS	SUBERIZE	TZARITZA	WIZARDLY
RITZIEST	SIZINESS	SUBITIZE	TZATZIKI	WIZARDRY
RIVALIZE	SIZZLERS	SUBSIZAR	TZIGANES	WIZENING
RIZZARED	SIZZLING	SUBZONAL	TZITZITH	WOMANIZE
RIZZARTS	SLEAZIER	SUBZONES	UNAMAZED	WOOZIEST
RIZZERED	SLEAZILY	SURPRIZE	UNDAZZLE	WURTZITE
RIZZORED	SLEAZOID	SUZERAIN	UNFREEZE	WUZZLING
ROBOTIZE	SLEEZIER	SWAZZLES	UNFROZEN	YAHRZEIT
ROMANIZE	SMORZATO	SWIZZING	UNGAZING	YOKOZUNA
ROMANZAS	SNAZZIER	SWIZZLED	UNGLAZED	ZABAIONE
ROYALIZE	SNAZZILY	SWIZZLER	UNGRAZED	ZABAJONE
ROZELLES	SNEEZERS	SWIZZLES	UNIONIZE	ZABTIEHS
ROZETING	SNEEZIER	SWOZZLES	UNITIZED	ZACATONS
ROZITING	SNEEZING	SYZYGIAL	UNITIZER	ZADDIKIM
RURALIZE	SNOOZERS	SYZYGIES	UNITIZES	ZAIBATSU
SALINIZE	SNOOZIER	TAILZIES	UNMUZZLE	ZAITECHS
SAMIZDAT	SNOOZING	TEAZELED	UNPRIZED	ZAKOUSKA
SANITIZE	SNOOZLED	TEAZLING	UNPUZZLE	ZAKOUSKI
SARRAZIN	SNOOZLES	TERRAZZO	UNSEIZED	ZAMARRAS
SATIRIZE	SNUZZLED	TERZETTA	UNVIZARD	ZAMARROS
SAZERACS	SNUZZLES	TERZETTI	UNZIPPED	ZAMBOMBA
SCHANTZE	SOBERIZE	TERZETTO	UPGAZING	ZAMBUCKS
SCHANZES	SODOMIZE	TETANIZE	UPSIZING	ZAMINDAR
SCHERZOS	SOLARIZE	THEORIZE	URBANIZE	ZAMOUSES
SCHIZIER	SOLECIZE	THIAZIDE	UTILIZED	ZAMPOGNA
SCHIZOID	SOLONETZ	THIAZINE	UTILIZER	ZAMZAWED
SCHIZONT	SORORIZE	THIAZINS	UTILIZES	ZANELLAS
SCHMALTZ	SOVKHOZY	THIAZOLE	VALORIZE	ZANINESS
SCHMALZY	SOZZLIER	THIAZOLS	VAPORIZE	ZANJEROS
SCHMELZE	SOZZLING	TIZWASES	VELARIZE	ZANYISMS
SCHMOOZE	SPAETZLE	TOPAZINE	VIRILIZE	ZAPATEOS
SCHMOOZY	SPATZLES	TOTALIZE	VITALIZE	ZAPPIEST
SCHNOZES	SPAZZING	TOUZIEST	VIZAMENT	ZAPTIAHS
SCRUZING	SPELTZES	TOUZLING	VIZARDED	ZAPTIEHS
SCUZZIER	SPETSNAZ	TOWZIEST	VIZCACHA	ZARATITE
SEIZABLE	SPETZNAZ	TRAPEZED	VIZIRATE	ZAREEBAS

ZARNICHS	ZESTIEST	ZIZANIAS	ZOOLITIC	ZOOTROPE
ZARZUELA	ZESTLESS	ZIZYPHUS	ZOOLOGIC	ZOOTYPES
ZASTRUGA	ZETETICS	ZIZZLING	ZOOMANCY	ZOOTYPIC
ZASTRUGI	ZEUXITES	ZOCCOLOS	ZOOMANIA	ZOPILOTE
ZEALANTS	ZIBELINE	ZODIACAL	ZOOMETRY	ZORBINGS
ZEALLESS	ZIGANKAS	ZOETROPE	ZOOMORPH	ZORGITES
ZEALOTRY	ZIGGURAT	ZOIATRIA	ZOONITES	ZORILLAS
ZEBRANOS	ZIGZAGGY	ZOISITES	ZOONITIC	ZORILLES
ZEBRINAS	ZIKKURAT	ZOMBIISM	ZOONOMIA	ZORILLOS
ZEBRINES	ZIKURATS	ZOMBORUK	ZOONOMIC	ZUCCHINI
ZEBRINNY	ZILLIONS	ZONATION	ZOONOSES	ZUCHETTA
ZEBRULAS	ZIMOCCAS	ZONELESS	ZOONOSIS	ZUCHETTO
ZEBRULES	ZINCATES	ZONETIME	ZOONOTIC	ZUGZWANG
ZECCHINE	ZINCIEST	ZONULETS	ZOOPATHY	ZWIEBACK
ZECCHINI	ZINCITES	ZOOBLAST	ZOOPERAL	ZYGAENID
ZECCHINO	ZINCKIER	ZOOCHORE	ZOOPHAGY	ZYGANTRA
ZECCHINS	ZINCKIFY	ZOOCHORY	ZOOPHILE	ZYGODONT
ZELATORS	ZINCKING	ZOOCYTIA	ZOOPHILY	ZYGOMATA
ZELATRIX	ZINCODES	ZOOECIUM	ZOOPHOBE	ZYGOSITY
ZELKOVAS	ZINDABAD	ZOOGENIC	ZOOPHORI	ZYGOTENE
ZEMINDAR	ZINGIBER	ZOOGLEAE	ZOOPHYTE	ZYLONITE
ZEMSTVOS	ZINGIEST	ZOOGLEAL	ZOOSCOPY	ZYMOGENE
ZENAIDAS	ZINKIEST	ZOOGLEAS	ZOOSPERM	ZYMOGENS
ZENITHAL	ZIPPERED	ZOOGLOEA	ZOOSPORE	ZYMOGRAM
ZEOLITES	ZIPPIEST	ZOOGRAFT	ZOOTHOME	ZYMOLOGY
ZEOLITIC	ZIRCALOY	ZOOLATER	ZOOTIEST	ZYMOSANS
ZEPPELIN	ZIRCONIA	ZOOLATRY	ZOOTOMIC	ZYMOTICS
ZEPPOLES	ZIRCONIC	ZOOLITES	ZOOTOXIC	ZYZZYVAS
ZERUMBET	ZITHERNS	ZOOLITHS	ZOOTOXIN	

Chapter 5: Beginnings and Endings

Prefixes

It's very useful to be aware of the common prefixes in English, as these provide a wealth of opportunities for building on words that are already on the board. The following lists show the most common prefixes in English, along with the valid words of seven and eight letters that they form from other existing words. Only those words which can be formed from a word already on the board are shown.

In some cases, the words shown are not strictly examples of the prefix in question: ABALONE (AB - ALONE), for instance. These are still included, however, because they work in the same way on the Scrabble board, and are useful in encouraging a little lateral thinking when trying to build on words already in play.

Of especial interest here are the words beginning with EX-, as these provide a very useful means of using X to form some high-scoring extensions of words.

Words that begin with AB-

Seven-letter words

-ACTOR	-FARAD	-OUGHT	-ROADS	-USAGE
-ALONE	-HENRY	-RAIDS	-SEILS	-USERS
-ASHED	-JOINT	-RAYED	-SENTS	-USING
-ASHES	-LATED	-REACT	-SOLVE	-UTTER
-AXIAL	-LINGS	-REAST	-SORBS	-VOLTS
-AXILE	-LUTED	-REGES	-STAIN	-WATTS
-DUCES	-OLLAS	-RIDGE	-SURDS	
-DUCTS	-OMASA	-ROACH	-THANE	

Eight-letter words

-ACTORS	-ESSIVE	-OMASUM	-RIDGES	-SONANT
-AMPERE	-FARADS	-ORALLY	-ROOKED	-SORBED
-APICAL	-HENRYS	-ORIGIN	-SEILED	-STAINS
-ASHING	-JOINTS	-RAIDED	-SENTED	-STRICT
-DUCTED	-LEGATE	-RAYING	-SOLUTE	-THANES
-EARING	-NEGATE	-REACTS	-SOLVED	-USABLE
-EGGING	-NORMAL	-RIDGED	-SOLVER	-USAGES
-ERRANT	-OMASAL	-RIDGER	-SOLVES	-UTTERS

Words that begin with AD-

Seven-letter words

-AGIOS	-DEEMS	-DUCES	-JUDGE	-MIRES
-APTED	-DICTS	-DUCTS	-JUROR	-MIXED
-APTER	-DOOMS	-HERES	-JUSTS	-MIXES
-AWING	-DRESS	-JOINS	-LANDS	-NOUNS
-AXIAL	-DREST	-JOINT	-MIRED	-OPTED

-OPTER	-SORBS	-VERTS	-VISOR	-WOMEN
-PRESS	-VENTS	-VICES	-WARDS	
-READS	-VERBS	-VISED	-WARES	
-RENAL	-VERSE	-VISES	-WOMAN	

Eight-letter words

-APTING	-ENOSIS	-JUDGES	-MONISH	-UMBRAL
-DEBTED	-EQUATE	-JURORS	-NATION	-UNCATE
-DEEMED	-ESSIVE	-JUSTED	-OPTERS	-VERSER
-DICTED	-JACENT	-JUSTER	-OPTING	-VERTED
-DOOMED	-JOINED	-MASSES	-OPTION	-VISING
-DUCTED	-JOINTS	-MIRING	-SCRIPT	-VISORS
-ENOSES	-JUDGED	-MIXING	-SORBED	-WARDED

Words that begin with AIR-

Seven-letter words

-BAGS	-FOIL	-LINE	-SHIP	-WARD
-BASE	-GAPS	-LOCK	-SHOT	-WAVE
-BOAT	-GLOW	-MAIL	-SHOW	-WAYS
-CREW	-HEAD	-PARK	-SICK	-WISE
-DATE	-HOLE	-PLAY	-SIDE	
-DROP	-LESS	-PORT	-STOP	
-FARE	-LIFT	-POST	-TIME	
-FLOW	-LIKE	-SHED	-TING	

Eight-letter words

-BASES	-DATES	-HOLES	-PROOF	-STRIP
-BOATS	-DRAWN	-LIFTS	-SCAPE	-THING
-BORNE	-DROME	-LINER	-SCREW	-TIGHT
-BOUND	-DROPS	-LINES	-SHAFT	-TIMES
-BRICK	-FARES	-LOCKS	-SHEDS	-WARDS
-BRUSH	-FIELD	-MAILS	-SHIPS	-WAVES
-BURST	-FLOWS	-PARKS	-SHOTS	-WOMAN
-BUSES	-FOILS	-PLANE	-SHOWS	-WOMEN
-CHECK	-FRAME	-PLAYS	-SIDES	
-COACH	-GLOWS	-PORTS	-SPACE	
-CRAFT	-GRAPH	-POSTS	-SPEED	
-CREWS	-HEADS	-POWER	-STOPS	

Words that begin with BE-

Seven-letter words

-ACHED	-CALMS	-COMES	-DAUBS	-DIRTY
-ACHES	-CAUSE	-CRAWL	-DAZED	-DIZEN
-ADMAN	-CHALK	-CRIME	-DAZES	-DRAIL
-ADMEN	-CHARM	-CROWD	-DECKS	-DRAPE
-ARISH	-CLASP	-CRUST	-DELLS	-DROLL
-AVERS	-CLOAK	-CURLS	-DEMAN	-DROPS
-BLOOD	-CLOGS	-CURSE	-DEVIL	-DROPT
-BUNGS	-CLOUD	-CURST	-DEWED	-DRUGS
-CALLS	-CLOWN	-DAMNS	-DIGHT	-DUCKS

-DUMBS	-HOOFS	-MIRES	-SHOUT	-TAKEN
-DUNCE	-HOOVE	-MISTS	-SHREW	-TAKES
-DUNGS	-HOVED	-MIXED	-SIDES	-TAXED
-DUSTS	-HOVES	-MIXES	-SIEGE	-TEEMS
-DWARF	-HOWLS	-MOANS	-SIGHS	-THANK
-ECHES	-INKED	-MOCKS	-SINGS	-THINK
-FALLS	-JADED	-MOILS	-SLAVE	-THORN
-FLAGS	-JADES	-MOUTH	-SLIME	-THUMB
-FLEAS	-JESUS	-MUSED	-SMEAR	-THUMP
-FLECK	-JEWEL	-MUSES	-SMILE	-TIDED
-FOAMS	-KNAVE	-NAMED	-SMOKE	-TIDES
-FOOLS	-KNOTS	-NAMES	-SMUTS	-TIGHT
-FOULS	-KNOWN	-NEATH	-SNOWS	-TIMED
-FRETS	-LABOR	-NEMPT	-SORTS	-TIMES
-GALLS	-LACED	-NIGHT	-SPAKE	-TITLE
-GAZED	-LACES	-NUMBS	-SPATE	-TOILS
-GAZES	-LATED	-PAINT	-SPEAK	-TOKEN
-GIFTS	-LAUDS	-PEARL	-SPEED	-TRAYS
-GILDS	-LAYED	-PELTS	-SPICE	-TREAD
-GIRDS	-LAYER	-PROSE	-SPITS	-TRIMS
-GLADS	-LEAPS	-PUFFS	-SPOKE	-TROTH
-GLOOM	-LEAPT	-QUEST	-SPORT	-TWEEN
-GNAWS	-LIEFS	-RAKED	-SPOTS	-TWIXT
-GOING	-LIERS	-RAKES	-SPOUT	-VOMIT
-GONIA	-LIEVE	-RATED	-STAIN	-WAILS
-GORED	-LONGS	-RATES	-STARS	-WARED
-GRIME	-LOVED	-RAYED	-STEAD	-WARES
-GROAN	-LOVES	-REAVE	-STICK	-WEARY
-GUILE	-LYING	-RHYME	-STILL	-WEEPS
-GULFS	-MADAM	-RIMED	-STING	-WHORE
-GUNKS	-MAULS	-RIMES	-STIRS	-WITCH
-HAVER	-MAZED	-ROBED	-STORM	-WORMS
-HAVES	-MEANS	-SAINT	-STOWS	-WORRY
-HEADS	-MEANT	-SCOUR	-STREW	-WRAPS
-HESTS	-MEDAL	-SEEMS	-STROW	-WRAPT
-HIGHT	-METED	-SHAME	-STUCK	
-HINDS	-METES	-SHINE	-STUDS	
-HOLDS	-MIRED	-SHONE	-SWARM	

Eight-letter words

-ACHIER	-COMING	-DAZZLE	-DUMBED	-FUDDLE
-ACHING	-COWARD	-DEAFEN	-DUNCES	-GALLED
-ARABLE	-CRAWLS	-DECKED	-DUNGED	-GAZING
-BLOODS	-CRIMED	-DESMAN	-DUSTED	-GEMMED
-BOPPED	-CRIMES	-DEVILS	-DWARFS	-GETTER
-BOPPER	-CROWDS	-DEWING	-DYEING	-GIFTED
-CALLED	-CRUSTS	-DIAPER	-FALLEN	-GILDED
-CALMED	-CUDGEL	-DIGHTS	-FINGER	-GINNER
-CAPPED	-CURLED	-DIMMED	-FINNED	-GIRDED
-CARPET	-CURSED	-DIMPLE	-FITTED	-GIRDLE
-CHALKS	-CURSES	-DIZENS	-FLECKS	-GLAMOR
-CHANCE	-DABBLE	-DOTTED	-FLOWER	-GLOOMS
-CHARMS	-DAGGLE	-DRAILS	-FOAMED	-GNAWED
-CLAMOR	-DAMNED	-DRAPED	-FOGGED	-GOTTEN
-CLASPS	-DARKEN	-DRAPES	-FOOLED	-GRIMED
-CLOAKS	-DASHED	-DRENCH	-FOULED	-GRIMES
-CLOTHE	-DASHES	-DRIVEL	-FOULER	-GROANS
-CLOUDS	-DAUBED	-DROLLS	-FRIEND	-GRUDGE
-CLOWNS	-DAZING	-DUCKED	-FRINGE	-GUILED

-GUILER	-LONGER	-PRAISE	-SLAVER	-STRODE
-GUILES	-LOVING	-PROSED	-SLAVES	-STROWN
-GULFED	-MADAMS	-PROSES	-SLIMED	-STROWS
-HALVES	-MADDED	-PUFFED	-SLIMES	-SUITED
-HAPPEN	-MADDEN	-QUESTS	-SMEARS	-SWARMS
-HATTED	-MAULED	-RAKING	-SMILED	-TAKING
-HAVERS	-MEANED	-RASCAL	-SMILES	-TATTER
-HAVING	-MEDALS	-RATING	-SMIRCH	-TEEMED
-HAVIOR	-METING	-RAYING	-SMOKED	-THANKS
-HEADED	-MINGLE	-REAVED	-SMOKES	-THINKS
-HEADER	-MIRING	-REAVER	-SMOOTH	-THORNS
-HIGHTS	-MISTED	-REAVES	-SMUDGE	-THRALL
-HOLDEN	-MIXING	-RHYMED	-SMUTCH	-THUMBS
-HOLDER	-MOANED	-RHYMES	-SNOWED	-THUMPS
-HOOVED	-MOANER	-RIMING	-SOOTHE	-THWACK
-HOOVES	-MOCKED	-RINGED	-SORTED	-TIDING
-HOVING	-MOILED	-ROBBED	-SOTTED	-TIMING
-HOWLED	-MOUTHS	-ROUGED	-SOUGHT	-TITLED
-JABERS	-MUDDED	-SAINTS	-SOULED	-TITLES
-JADING	-MUDDLE	-SCORCH	-SPEAKS	-TOILED
-JESUIT	-MUFFLE	-SCOURS	-SPEEDS	-TOKENS
-JEWELS	-MURMUR	-SCRAWL	-SPICED	-TONIES
-JUMBLE	-MUSING	-SCREEN	-SPICES	-TOSSED
-KISSED	-MUZZLE	-SEEING	-SPOKEN	-TOSSES
-KISSES	-NAMING	-SEEMED	-SPORTS	-TREADS
-KNAVES	-NETTED	-SEEMLY	-SPOUSE	-TROTHS
-KNIGHT	-NIGHTS	-SETTER	-SPOUTS	-TWEENS
-LABORS	-NUMBED	-SHADOW	-SPREAD	-UNCLED
-LABOUR	-PAINTS	-SHAMED	-SPRENT	-VOMITS
-LACING	-PATTED	-SHAMES	-STAINS	-WAILED
-LADIES	-PEARLS	-SHINES	-STEADS	-WAILER
-LAUDED	-PELTED	-SHIVER	-STICKS	-WARING
-LAYERS	-PEPPER	-SHOUTS	-STILLS	-WETTED
-LAYING	-PESTER	-SHREWS	-STORMS	-WHORED
-LEAPED	-PIMPLE	-SHROUD	-STOWED	-WHORES
-LEEING	-PITIED	-SIEGED	-STOWER	-WIGGED
-LIEVER	-PITIES	-SIEGER	-STREAK	-WILDER
-LIQUOR	-PLUMED	-SIEGES	-STREWN	-WINGED
-LITTLE	-POMMEL	-SIGHED	-STREWS	-WORMED
-LONGED	-POWDER	-SLAVED	-STRIDE	

Words that begin with BI-

Seven-letter words

-ASSED	-CORNS	-LEVEL	-OPTIC	-STATE
-ASSES	-CYCLE	-LIMBI	-PACKS	-TABLE
-AXIAL	-DENTS	-LOBAR	-PARTY	-TINGS
-BASIC	-DINGS	-LOBED	-PEDAL	-TONAL
-BLESS	-FACES	-METAL	-PLANE	-VALVE
-BLIST	-FILAR	-MODAL	-POLAR	-VINYL
-CARBS	-FOCAL	-MORPH	-PRISM	-ZONAL
-CHORD	-KINGS	-OLOGY	-SECTS	-ZONES
-COLOR	-LAYER	-ONTIC	-SHOPS	

Eight-letter words

-ACETYL	-DENTAL	-LINEAR	-PARTED	-STABLE
-ANNUAL	-ELDING	-LOBATE	-PHASIC	-STOURY
-CAUDAL	-FACIAL	-MANUAL	-PHENYL	-TEWING
-CHROME	-FORKED	-MENSAL	-PLANES	-TINGLY
-COLORS	-FORMED	-MESTER	-PRISMS	-UNIQUE
-COLOUR	-GEMINY	-METALS	-RACIAL	-VALVED
-CONVEX	-HOURLY	-METHYL	-RADIAL	-VALVES
-CUSPID	-JUGATE	-MORPHS	-RAMOSE	-VINYLS
-CYCLED	-LABIAL	-OBLAST	-RAMOUS	-WEEKLY
-CYCLER	-LANDER	-OTITIC	-SECTOR	-YEARLY
-CYCLES	-LAYERS	-OVULAR	-SERIAL	
-CYCLIC	-LEVELS	-PAROUS	-SEXUAL	

Words that begin with COM-

Seven-letter words

-AKES	-FIER	-MONS	-PASS	-PONE
-ARBS	-FITS	-MOTE	-PAST	-PONY
-ARTS	-FORT	-MOTS	-PEAR	-PORT
-ATES	-ICES	-MOVE	-PEER	-POSE
-BATS	-MAND	-MUTE	-PEND	-POST
-BIER	-MEND	-PACT	-PERE	-POTE
-BINE	-MENT	-PAGE	-PILE	-POTS
-BING	-MERE	-PAND	-PING	-RADE
-BUST	-MIXT	-PARE	-PLEX	-USES
-ETIC	-MODE	-PART	-PLOT	

Eight-letter words

-AKING	-MENDS	-MUTER	-PENDS	-PORTS
-BATED	-MERES	-MUTES	-PERES	-POSED
-BINER	-MERGE	-PACTS	-PILED	-POSER
-BINES	-MIXED	-PADRE	-PILER	-POSES
-BINGS	-MIXES	-PAGES	-PILES	-POSTS
-BLESS	-MODES	-PANDS	-PINGS	-POTES
-BUSTS	-MONER	-PARED	-PLAIN	-POUND
-EMBER	-MONEY	-PARER	-PLEAT	-PRESS
-ETHER	-MOTES	-PARES	-PLIED	-PRINT
-FIEST	-MOVED	-PARTS	-PLIER	-PRISE
-FORTS	-MOVES	-PEARS	-PLIES	-PRIZE
-INGLE	-MUTED	-PEERS	-PLOTS	-PULSE

Words that begin with CON-

Seven-letter words

-ACRE	-CORD	-DONE	-FINE	-GEED
-ARIA	-CREW	-DORS	-FIRM	-GEES
-CAVE	-CURS	-DUCE	-FITS	-GEST
-CEDE	-CUSS	-DUCT	-FLUX	-GOES
-CENT	-DIES	-DUIT	-FORM	-GREE
-CERT	-DOES	-FABS	-FUSE	-GRUE
-CHAL	-DOLE	-FESS	-GAED	-JEED
-CHAS	-DOMS	-FEST	-GEAL	-JEES

-JOIN	-SEIL	-SORT	-TEXT	-VENT
-JURE	-SENT	-TACT	-TORT	-VERT
-JURY	-SIGN	-TAIN	-TOUR	-VIVE
-KIER	-SIST	-TEND	-TRAT	
-KING	-SOLE	-TENT	-TUND	
-NOTE	-SOLS	-TEST	-URES	

Eight-letter words

-ACRED	-DUCES	-GLOBE	-SISTS	-TRAIL
-ACRES	-DUCTS	-GREED	-SOLED	-TRATS
-CAUSE	-DUITS	-GREES	-SOLER	-TRIST
-CAVED	-FINED	-GREET	-SOLES	-TRITE
-CAVES	-FINER	-GRUED	-SORTS	-TUNDS
-CEDED	-FINES	-GRUES	-SPIRE	-URBAN
-CEDER	-FIRMS	-JOINS	-STATE	-URBIA
-CEDES	-FIXED	-JOINT	-TACTS	-VENTS
-CENTS	-FIXES	-JUGAL	-TAINS	-VERGE
-CERTS	-FOCAL	-JUNTO	-TANGO	-VERSE
-CLAVE	-FORMS	-JUROR	-TEMPO	-VERSO
-COLOR	-FOUND	-NOTED	-TEMPT	-VERTS
-CORDS	-FRERE	-NOTES	-TENDS	-VEXED
-COURS	-FRONT	-QUEST	-TENTS	-VEXES
-CREWS	-FUSED	-SEILS	-TESTS	-VIVES
-DENSE	-FUSES	-SENTS	-TEXTS	-VOLVE
-DOLED	-GEALS	-SERVE	-TORTS	
-DOLES	-GENIC	-SIDER	-TOURS	
-DONER	-GESTS	-SIGNS	-TRACT	

Words that begin with DE-

Seven-letter words

-ADMAN	-CAMPS	-CRIED	-FINES	-GRADE
-ADMEN	-CANAL	-CRIER	-FLEAS	-GREED
-AIRED	-CANES	-CRIES	-FOAMS	-GREES
-ALATE	-CANTS	-CROWN	-FOCUS	-GUSTS
-ASHED	-CARBS	-CRYPT	-FORCE	-HORNS
-ASHES	-CARES	-CURIA	-FORMS	-ICERS
-BARKS	-CEASE	-CURVE	-FOULS	-ICING
-BASED	-CIDED	-DUCES	-FRAGS	-ICTIC
-BASER	-CIDER	-DUCTS	-FRAUD	-INDEX
-BASES	-CIDES	-FACED	-FRAYS	-JEUNE
-BATED	-CLAIM	-FACER	-FROCK	-LAPSE
-BATES	-CLASS	-FACES	-FROST	-LATED
-BEAKS	-CLAWS	-FAMED	-FROZE	-LAYED
-BEARD	-CLINE	-FAMES	-FUELS	-LAYER
-BONED	-CODED	-FANGS	-FUNDS	-LEADS
-BONER	-CODER	-FAULT	-FUSED	-LEAVE
-BONES	-CODES	-FEATS	-FUSES	-LIGHT
-BRIDE	-COKED	-FENCE	-FUZED	-LIMED
-BRIEF	-COKES	-FENDS	-FUZES	-LIMES
-BUNKS	-COLOR	-FIERS	-GAMES	-LIMIT
-BURRS	-COYED	-FILED	-GASES	-LISTS
-BUSED	-COYER	-FILER	-GAUSS	-LIVER
-BUSES	-CREED	-FILES	-GERMS	-LOPED
-CADES	-CREES	-FINED	-GLAZE	-LOPES
-CAFFS	-CREWS	-FINER	-GOUTS	-LOUSE

-LUDES	-NUDER	-RATES	-SKILL	-TUNED
-LUGED	-NUDES	-RAYED	-SNOOD	-TUNES
-LUGES	-NYING	-RIDER	-SORBS	-VALUE
-MAINS	-ONTIC	-RIDES	-SPITE	-VEINS
-MARKS	-ORBIT	-RIVED	-SPOIL	-VESTS
-MASTS	-PAINT	-RIVER	-SPOTS	-VICES
-MEANE	-PARTS	-RIVES	-STAIN	-VISED
-MEANS	-PENDS	-SALTS	-STOCK	-VISES
-MERGE	-PERMS	-SANDS	-STROY	-VISOR
-MERIT	-PLANE	-SCALE	-SUGAR	-VOICE
-MERSE	-PLOYS	-SCANT	-SYNED	-VOLVE
-MESNE	-PLUME	-SCEND	-SYNES	-VOTED
-MISES	-PONES	-SCENT	-TAILS	-VOTES
-MISTS	-PORTS	-SERVE	-TAINS	-WATER
-MOSES	-POSED	-SEXED	-TENTS	-WAXED
-MOTED	-POSER	-SEXES	-TENUE	-WAXES
-MOTES	-POSES	-SIGNS	-TESTS	-WOOLS
-MOUNT	-POSIT	-SINED	-TICKS	-WORMS
-MURED	-PRESS	-SINES	-TORTS	-ZINCS
-MURES	-RAILS	-SIRED	-TOURS	
-NOTED	-RANGE	-SIRES	-TRACT	
-NOTES	-RATED	-SISTS	-TRAIN	

Eight-letter words

-AERATE	-CADENT	-CURVED	-FOULED	-LEGACY
-AIRING	-CALLED	-CURVES	-FRAUDS	-LEGATE
-ALATED	-CAMPED	-DUCTED	-FRAYED	-LIBATE
-ALATES	-CANTED	-FACERS	-FREEZE	-LIGHTS
-ARLING	-CANTER	-FACING	-FROCKS	-LIMING
-ASHING	-CEASED	-FAMING	-FROSTS	-LIMITS
-BAGGED	-CEASES	-FANGED	-FROZEN	-LISTED
-BARKED	-CENTER	-FATTED	-FUELED	-LIVERS
-BARKER	-CENTRE	-FAULTS	-FUNDED	-LIVERY
-BARRED	-CERNED	-FEATED	-FUSING	-LOPING
-BASING	-CIDERS	-FEATER	-FUZING	-LOUSED
-BATING	-CIDING	-FENCED	-GASSED	-LOUSER
-BEAKED	-CIPHER	-FENCES	-GASSER	-LOUSES
-BEARDS	-CLAIMS	-FENDED	-GASSES	-LUGING
-BELLED	-CLAWED	-FENDER	-GENDER	-LUSTER
-BITING	-CLINAL	-FIANCE	-GERMED	-MANNED
-BONERS	-CLINES	-FILERS	-GLAZED	-MARKED
-BONING	-CLUTCH	-FILING	-GLAZES	-MARKET
-BOSHES	-CODERS	-FINERS	-GRADED	-MASTED
-BOSSED	-CODING	-FINING	-GRADER	-MEANED
-BOSSES	-COKING	-FINITE	-GRADES	-MEANES
-BOUCHE	-COLORS	-FLEXED	-GREASE	-MERGED
-BRIDED	-COLOUR	-FLEXES	-GUMMED	-MERGER
-BRIDES	-COMMIT	-FLOWER	-GUSTED	-MERGES
-BRIEFS	-COUPLE	-FLUENT	-HORNED	-MERITS
-BRUISE	-COYING	-FOAMED	-HORNER	-MERSES
-BUDDED	-CREASE	-FOAMER	-IONISE	-MESNES
-BUGGED	-CREWED	-FOGGED	-IONIZE	-MISTED
-BUGGER	-CRIERS	-FOGGER	-LAPSED	-MISTER
-BUNKED	-CROWNS	-FORCED	-LAPSES	-MOBBED
-BUNKER	-CRYING	-FORCER	-LAYERS	-MONISM
-BURRED	-CRYPTS	-FORCES	-LAYING	-MONIST
-BUSING	-CUBITI	-FOREST	-LEADED	-MOTION
-BUSSED	-CURIAS	-FORMED	-LEAVED	-MOUNTS
-BUSSES	-CURIES	-FORMER	-LEAVES	-MURING

-NATURE	-POSING	-SCANTS	-SORBED	-TRACTS
-NAZIFY	-POSITS	-SCENDS	-SPIGHT	-TRAINS
-NETTED	-RAILED	-SCENTS	-SPITED	-TUNING
-NOTATE	-RAILER	-SCHOOL	-SPITES	-VALUED
-NOTING	-RANGED	-SCRIBE	-SPOILS	-VALUES
-ORBITS	-RANGER	-SCRIED	-STAINS	-VEINED
-PAINTS	-RANGES	-SCRIES	-STOCKS	-VERBAL
-PARTED	-RATING	-SCRIVE	-STROYS	-VESTED
-PARTER	-RATION	-SELECT	-SUGARS	-VIATOR
-PEINCT	-RATTED	-SERVED	-SULFUR	-VISING
-PENDED	-RAYING	-SERVER	-SYNING	-VISORS
-PEOPLE	-RELICT	-SERVES	-TACHES	-VOICED
-PERMED	-RIDERS	-SEXING	-TAILED	-VOICES
-PLANED	-RIDING	-SIGNED	-TAILER	-VOLVED
-PLANES	-RIGGED	-SIGNEE	-TASSEL	-VOLVES
-PLOYED	-RINGER	-SIGNER	-TENUES	-VOTING
-PLUMED	-RIVERS	-SILVER	-TESTED	-WATERS
-PLUMES	-RIVING	-SINING	-TESTER	-WAXING
-POLISH	-SALTED	-SIRING	-THATCH	-WITTED
-PONENT	-SALTER	-SISTED	-THRONE	-WOOLED
-PORTED	-SANDED	-SKILLS	-TICKED	-WORMED
-PORTER	-SCALED	-SNOODS	-TICKER	-WORMER
-POSERS	-SCALES	-SOLATE	-TOURED	-ZINCED

Words that begin with DIS-

Seven-letter words

-ABLE	-CUSS	-LIKE	-PART	-SENT
-ALLY	-EASE	-LIMB	-PEND	-SING
-ARMS	-EDGE	-LIMN	-PLAY	-TAIN
-AVOW	-FAME	-LINK	-PLED	-TEND
-BAND	-FORM	-LOAD	-PONE	-TENT
-BARK	-GEST	-MALS	-PORT	-TICH
-BARS	-GOWN	-MANS	-POSE	-TILL
-BUDS	-GUST	-MASK	-POST	-TILS
-CAGE	-HELM	-MAST	-PRAD	-TOME
-CANT	-HING	-MAYS	-RANK	-TORT
-CARD	-HOME	-MISS	-RATE	-TUNE
-CASE	-HORN	-NEST	-ROBE	-USED
-CIDE	-JOIN	-OBEY	-ROOT	-USES
-COED	-KING	-OWNS	-SAVE	-YOKE
-CORD	-LEAF	-PACE	-SEAT	
-CURE	-LEAL	-PARK	-SECT	

Eight-letter words

-ABLED	-ARMER	-CAGED	-CLOSE	-EDGED
-ABLER	-ARRAY	-CAGES	-COLOR	-EDGES
-ABLES	-ASTER	-CANDY	-CORDS	-ENDOW
-ABUSE	-AVOWS	-CANTS	-COUNT	-ENROL
-ADORN	-BANDS	-CARDS	-COURE	-FAMES
-AGREE	-BARKS	-CASED	-COVER	-FAVOR
-ALLOW	-BENCH	-CASES	-CROWN	-FLESH
-ANNEX	-BOSOM	-CIDED	-CURED	-FORMS
-ANNUL	-BOUND	-CIDES	-CURES	-FROCK
-APPLY	-BOWEL	-CINCT	-EASED	-GAVEL
-ARMED	-BURSE	-CLAIM	-EASES	-GESTS

-GORGE	-LIKED	-PARKS	-QUIET	-TILLS
-GOWNS	-LIKEN	-PARTS	-RANKS	-TINCT
-GRACE	-LIKER	-PATCH	-RATED	-TOMES
-GRADE	-LIKES	-PEACE	-RATES	-TORTS
-GUISE	-LIMBS	-PENCE	-ROBED	-TRACT
-GUSTS	-LIMNS	-PENDS	-ROBES	-TRAIL
-HABIT	-LINKS	-PERSE	-ROOTS	-TRAIN
-HABLE	-LOADS	-PLACE	-SAVED	-TRAIT
-HELMS	-LODGE	-PLANT	-SAVES	-TRESS
-HINGS	-LOYAL	-PLAYS	-SEATS	-TRUST
-HOMED	-MASKS	-PLING	-SECTS	-TUNED
-HOMES	-MASTS	-PLUME	-SEISE	-TUNES
-HONOR	-MAYED	-PONES	-SEIZE	-UNION
-HORNS	-MOUNT	-PORTS	-SENTS	-UNITE
-HORSE	-NESTS	-POSED	-SERVE	-UNITY
-HOUSE	-OBEYS	-POSER	-SEVER	-USAGE
-INTER	-ORBED	-POSES	-SIGHT	-USING
-INURE	-ORDER	-POSTS	-SOLVE	-VALUE
-JOINS	-OWNED	-PRIZE	-TAINS	-VOUCH
-JOINT	-OWNER	-PROOF	-TALLY	-YOKED
-LEAFS	-PACED	-PROVE	-TASTE	-YOKES
-LEAVE	-PACES	-PURSE	-TENDS	

Words that begin with EM-

Seven-letter words

-AILED	-BAYED	-BRACE	-MOVED	-PLACE
-BAILS	-BLAZE	-BRAID	-MOVES	-PLANE
-BALED	-BLOOM	-BRAVE	-PAIRE	-PLOYS
-BALES	-BOILS	-BREAD	-PALED	-PLUME
-BALLS	-BOLUS	-BROIL	-PALER	-POWER
-BALMS	-BOSKS	-BROWN	-PALES	-PRESS
-BANKS	-BOSOM	-BRUTE	-PANEL	-PRISE
-BARKS	-BOUND	-BUSED	-PARED	-PRIZE
-BASED	-BOWED	-BUSES	-PARES	-PUSES
-BASES	-BOWEL	-ENDED	-PARTS	
-BASSY	-BOWER	-ENDER	-PEACH	
-BASTE	-BOXED	-IRATE	-PERCE	
-BATHE	-BOXES	-MEWED	-PIGHT	

Eight-letter words

-AILING	-BEZZLE	-BOSSER	-BROWNS	-MOVING
-BAILED	-BITTER	-BOSSES	-BRUTED	-PACKET
-BALING	-BLAZED	-BOUNDS	-BRUTES	-PAIRED
-BALLED	-BLAZER	-BOWELS	-BUSIED	-PAIRES
-BALMED	-BLAZES	-BOWERS	-BUSIES	-PALING
-BANKED	-BLAZON	-BOWING	-BUSING	-PANADA
-BANKER	-BLOOMS	-BOXING	-BUSSED	-PANELS
-BARKED	-BODIED	-BRACED	-BUSSES	-PARING
-BARRED	-BODIES	-BRACER	-DASHES	-PARLED
-BASING	-BOGGED	-BRACES	-ENDERS	-PARTED
-BATHED	-BOILED	-BRAIDS	-ENDING	-PATHIC
-BATHES	-BOLDEN	-BRAVED	-MARBLE	-PATRON
-BATTLE	-BORDER	-BRAVES	-MESHED	-PEOPLE
-BAYING	-BOSOMS	-BREADS	-MESHES	-PERCED
-BEDDED	-BOSSED	-BROILS	-MEWING	-PERCES

-PERISH	-PLACED	-PLONGE	-POLDER	-PYEMIC
-PHASES	-PLACES	-PLOYED	-POWERS	
-PHASIS	-PLANED	-PLUMED	-PRISES	
-PHATIC	-PLANES	-PLUMES	-PRIZES	
-PIERCE	-PLEACH	-POISON	-PURPLE	

Words that begin with EN-

Seven-letter words

-ABLED	-DITED	-GORES	-RACED	-SWEPT
-ABLER	-DITES	-GORGE	-RACES	-TAILS
-ABLES	-DIVES	-GRACE	-RAGED	-TAMED
-ACTED	-DORSE	-GRAFF	-RAGES	-TAMES
-ACTOR	-DOWED	-GRAFT	-RANGE	-TICED
-AMINE	-DOWER	-GRAIL	-RANKS	-TICES
-AMOUR	-DUING	-GRAIN	-RHEUM	-TIRES
-ARMED	-DURED	-GRAMS	-RINGS	-TITLE
-CAGED	-DURES	-GRASP	-RIVEN	-TOILS
-CAGES	-DUROS	-GRAVE	-ROBED	-TOMBS
-CALMS	-FACED	-GROSS	-ROBES	-TOPIC
-CAMPS	-FACES	-GUARD	-ROLLS	-TRAIL
-CASED	-FELON	-GULFS	-ROOTS	-TRAIN
-CASES	-FEOFF	-GULPH	-ROUGH	-TRANT
-CAVED	-FEVER	-HALOS	-ROUND	-TRAPS
-CAVES	-FILED	-HANCE	-SEALS	-TREAT
-CHAFE	-FIRED	-ISLED	-SEAMS	-TREES
-CHAIN	-FIRES	-ISLES	-SEARS	-TRIES
-CHANT	-FIXED	-JAMBS	-SERFS	-TRIST
-CHARM	-FIXES	-JOINS	-SEWED	-TRUST
-CHASE	-FLAME	-JOYED	-SHELL	-TWINE
-CHEER	-FLESH	-LACED	-SIGNS	-TWIST
-CLASP	-FOLDS	-LACES	-SILED	-VAULT
-CLAVE	-FORCE	-LARDS	-SILES	-VENOM
-CLOSE	-FORMS	-LARGE	-SKIED	-VIERS
-CLOUD	-FRAME	-LIGHT	-SKIES	-VYING
-CODED	-FREED	-LINKS	-SKYED	-WALLS
-CODER	-FREES	-LISTS	-SLAVE	-WHEEL
-CODES	-FROZE	-LIVEN	-SNARE	-WINDS
-CORED	-GAGED	-LOCKS	-SNARL	-WOMBS
-CORES	-GAGER	-MEWED	-SOULS	-WOUND
-CRUST	-GAGES	-MOVED	-STAMP	-WRAPS
-CRYPT	-GAOLS	-MOVES	-STEEP	-ZONED
-CYSTS	-GILDS	-NOBLE	-STYLE	-ZONES
-DARTS	-GIRDS	-OLOGY	-SUING	-ZYMES
-DEARS	-GLOBE	-OUNCE	-SURED	-ZYMIC
-DEMIC	-GLOOM	-PLANE	-SURER	
-DEWED	-GLUTS	-PRINT	-SURES	
-DINGS	-GORED	-QUIRE	-SWEEP	

Eight-letter words

-ABLING	-AMINES	-CAGING	-CASING	-CHARGE
-ACTING	-AMOURS	-CALMED	-CAVING	-CHARMS
-ACTION	-ARCHED	-CAMPED	-CHAFED	-CHASED
-ACTIVE	-ARCHES	-CARPUS	-CHAFES	-CHASER
-ACTORS	-ARMING	-CASHED	-CHAINS	-CHASES
-ACTURE	-AUNTER	-CASHES	-CHANTS	-CHEERS

-CHORIC	-FIERCE	-GULFED	-RAUNGE	-SWEEPS
-CIPHER	-FIRING	-GULPHS	-RAVISH	-TAILED
-CIRCLE	-FIXING	-HALOED	-RHEUMS	-TAILER
-CLASPS	-FLAMED	-HALOES	-RICHED	-TAMING
-CLAVES	-FLAMES	-HANCES	-RICHER	-TANGLE
-CLITIC	-FLOWER	-HEARSE	-RICHES	-TELLUS
-CLOSED	-FOLDED	-HUNGER	-RIDGED	-TENDER
-CLOSER	-FOLDER	-HYDROS	-RINGED	-THETIC
-CLOSES	-FORCED	-ISLING	-ROBING	-THRALL
-CLOTHE	-FORCER	-JAMBED	-ROLLED	-THRONE
-CLOUDS	-FORCES	-JOINED	-ROLLER	-THUSES
-CODERS	-FOREST	-JOINER	-ROOTED	-TICING
-CODING	-FORMED	-JOYING	-ROUGHS	-TITLED
-COLOUR	-FRAMED	-KERNEL	-ROUNDS	-TITLES
-COLURE	-FRAMES	-KINDLE	-SAMPLE	-TOILED
-CORING	-FREEZE	-LACING	-SCONCE	-TOMBED
-CRADLE	-FROZEN	-LARDED	-SCROLL	-TRAILS
-CREASE	-GAGERS	-LARGEN	-SEALED	-TRAINS
-CRINAL	-GAGING	-LARGER	-SEAMED	-TRANCE
-CRUSTS	-GAOLED	-LARGES	-SEARED	-TRANTS
-CRYPTS	-GENDER	-LIGHTS	-SEMBLE	-TREATS
-CUMBER	-GILDED	-LINKED	-SEWING	-TREATY
-CYCLIC	-GIRDED	-LISTED	-SHEATH	-TRENCH
-DAMAGE	-GIRDLE	-LISTEE	-SHELLS	-TROPIC
-DANGER	-GLOBED	-LISTER	-SHIELD	-TRUSTS
-DARTED	-GLOBES	-LIVENS	-SHRINE	-TWINED
-DASHES	-GLOOMS	-LOCKED	-SHROUD	-TWINES
-DEARED	-GORGED	-LUMINE	-SIGNED	-TWISTS
-DEIXES	-GORGES	-MESHED	-SILAGE	-URESES
-DEIXIS	-GORING	-MESHES	-SILING	-URESIS
-DERMIC	-GRACED	-MEWING	-SKYING	-URETIC
-DEWING	-GRACES	-MOSSED	-SLAVED	-VASSAL
-DITING	-GRAFFS	-MOVING	-SLAVER	-VAULTS
-DORSER	-GRAFTS	-NOBLER	-SLAVES	-VENOMS
-DORSES	-GRAILS	-NOBLES	-SNARED	-VIABLE
-DOSSED	-GRAINS	-OUNCES	-SNARER	-VIABLY
-DOSSES	-GRAMMA	-PLANED	-SNARES	-VISAGE
-DOWERS	-GRAMME	-PLANES	-SNARLS	-VISION
-DOWING	-GRASPS	-PRINTS	-SOULED	-WALLED
-DURING	-GRAVED	-QUIRED	-SPHERE	-WALLOW
-FACING	-GRAVEN	-QUIRES	-STAMPS	-WHEELS
-FEEBLE	-GRAVER	-RACING	-STEEPS	-WOMBED
-FELONS	-GRAVES	-RAGING	-STYLED	-WREATH
-FEOFFS	-GRIEVE	-RANGED	-STYLES	-ZONING
-FETTER	-GROOVE	-RANGES	-SURING	
-FEVERS	-GUARDS	-RANKED	-SWATHE	

Words that begin with EX-

Seven-letter words

-ACTED	-CIDED	-EMPTS	-PLAIN	-PRESS
-ACTOR	-CIDES	-HALED	-PLANT	-PULSE
-ALTER	-CITED	-HALES	-PORTS	-PURGE
-AMENS	-CITER	-ODIST	-POSED	-SECTS
-AMINE	-CITES	-OSMIC	-POSER	-TENDS
-AMPLE	-CLAIM	-PANDS	-POSES	-TENSE
-APTED	-CLAVE	-PENDS	-POSIT	-TENTS
-CHEAT	-CURSE	-PERTS	-POUND	-TERNE

-TERNS	-TOLLS	-TRAIT	-URBAN
-TINCT	-TORTS	-TREAT	-URBIA
-TINES	-TRACT	-TREMA	

Eight-letter words

-ACTING	-CITERS	-OSMOSE	-POSITS	-TINCTS
-ACTION	-CITING	-PANDER	-POUNDS	-TOLLED
-ACTORS	-CLAIMS	-PELLED	-PULSED	-TOLLER
-ALTERS	-CLAVES	-PENDED	-PULSES	-TRACTS
-AMINES	-CURSED	-PERTLY	-PURGED	-TRAITS
-ANTHEM	-CURSES	-PLAINS	-PURGES	-TREATS
-CELLED	-CURSUS	-PLANTS	-SECANT	-TUBATE
-CESSED	-EMPTED	-PONENT	-TENDED	-URBIAS
-CESSES	-HALING	-PORTED	-TENDER	
-CHANGE	-HUMATE	-PORTER	-TENSOR	
-CHEATS	-ODISTS	-POSERS	-TERNAL	
-CIDING	-OGAMIC	-POSING	-TERNES	

Words that begin with FOOT-

Seven-letter words

-AGE	-BOY	-LES	-PAD	-WAY
-BAG	-ERS	-MAN	-RAS	
-BAR	-LED	-MEN	-ROT	

Eight-letter words

-AGES	-GEAR	-NOTE	-ROPE	-WAYS
-BAGS	-HILL	-PACE	-ROTS	-WEAR
-BALL	-HOLD	-PADS	-RULE	-WELL
-BARS	-LESS	-PAGE	-SIES	-WORK
-BATH	-LIKE	-PATH	-SLOG	-WORN
-BOYS	-LING	-POST	-SORE	
-ERED	-MARK	-RACE	-STEP	
-FALL	-MUFF	-REST	-WALL	

Words that begin with FOR-

Seven-letter words

-AGED	-DING	-GOER	-MALS	-SAYS
-AGER	-DOES	-GOES	-MATE	-SLOE
-AGES	-DONE	-GONE	-MATS	-SLOW
-AMEN	-ESTS	-HENT	-MICA	-SOOK
-BADE	-EVER	-HOWS	-MING	-TIES
-BARE	-EXES	-KIER	-MOLS	-TING
-BEAR	-FAIR	-KING	-PETS	-TUNE
-BIDS	-FEND	-LANA	-PINE	-WARD
-BODE	-GAVE	-LEND	-PITS	-WARN
-BORE	-GETS	-LENT	-RAYS	-WENT
-CATS	-GING	-LORE	-SAID	-WORN
-CEPS	-GIVE	-LORN	-SAKE	-ZATI

Eight-letter words

-AGERS	-ESTER	-JUDGE	-SAKER	-SWINK
-AGING	-FAIRS	-LANAS	-SAKES	-SWORE
-AMENS	-FAULT	-LENDS	-SLACK	-SWORN
-BEARS	-FENDS	-LESES	-SLOES	-THINK
-BODED	-GINGS	-MATED	-SLOWS	-TRESS
-BODES	-GIVEN	-MATES	-SOOTH	-TUNED
-BORNE	-GIVER	-MICAS	-SPEAK	-TUNES
-DOING	-GIVES	-MINGS	-SPEND	-WARDS
-EKING	-GOERS	-PINED	-SPENT	-WARNS
-ELAIN	-GOING	-PINES	-SPOKE	-WASTE
-ELAND	-HENTS	-RAYED	-SWEAR	-WEARY

Words that begin with IM-

Seven-letter words

-AGERS	-BRAST	-PAINT	-PEACH	-POSED
-AGING	-BROWN	-PAIRS	-PEARL	-POSER
-AGISM	-BRUTE	-PALAS	-PEDES	-POSES
-AGIST	-BURSE	-PALED	-PENDS	-POSTS
-AMATE	-MASKS	-PALER	-PERIL	-POUND
-ARETS	-MENSE	-PALES	-PIETY	-POWER
-BALMS	-MERGE	-PANEL	-PINGS	-PRESA
-BARKS	-MERSE	-PARKS	-PIOUS	-PRESE
-BASED	-MEWED	-PARTS	-PLANT	-PRESS
-BASES	-MIXED	-PASSE	-PLATE	-PREST
-BATHE	-MIXES	-PASTE	-PLEAD	-PRINT
-BLAZE	-MORAL	-PAVED	-PLIED	-PROVE
-BOSKS	-MURED	-PAVES	-PLIES	-PULSE
-BOSOM	-MURES	-PAVID	-PONES	-PURER
-BOWER	-PACTS	-PAWNS	-PORTS	

Eight-letter words

-AGINGS	-BOWERS	-MORTAL	-PERILS	-POSING
-AGISMS	-BROWNS	-MOTILE	-PINGED	-POSTED
-AGISTS	-BRUTED	-MURING	-PINGER	-POSTER
-AMATES	-BRUTES	-PAINTS	-PLANTS	-POTENT
-BALMED	-BURSES	-PAIRED	-PLATED	-POUNDS
-BARKED	-MANENT	-PAIRER	-PLATES	-POWERS
-BARRED	-MANTLE	-PALING	-PLEACH	-PRESES
-BASING	-MASKED	-PANELS	-PLEADS	-PRESTS
-BATHED	-MATURE	-PARITY	-PLEDGE	-PRINTS
-BATHES	-MERGED	-PARKED	-PLEXES	-PRISON
-BEDDED	-MERGES	-PARLED	-PLUNGE	-PROPER
-BITTER	-MERSES	-PARTED	-PLYING	-PROVED
-BLAZED	-MESHED	-PARTER	-POCKET	-PROVER
-BLAZES	-MESHES	-PASSES	-POLDER	-PROVES
-BODIED	-MEWING	-PASTED	-POLICY	-PUDENT
-BODIES	-MINGLE	-PASTES	-POLITE	-PULSED
-BOLDEN	-MINUTE	-PAVING	-PONENT	-PULSES
-BORDER	-MIXING	-PAWNED	-POROUS	-PURELY
-BOSOMS	-MOBILE	-PEARLS	-PORTED	-PUREST
-BOSSED	-MODEST	-PELLED	-PORTER	-PURITY
-BOSSES	-MOMENT	-PENDED	-POSERS	-PURPLE

Words that begin with IN-

Seven-letter words

-ANGAS	-DEXES	-GATES	-QUIRE	-TINES
-APTLY	-DICES	-GENUS	-ROADS	-TITLE
-ARMED	-DICTS	-GESTS	-SANER	-TOMBS
-BEING	-DITED	-GLOBE	-SCAPE	-TONED
-BOARD	-DITES	-GOING	-SCULP	-TONER
-BOUND	-DOLES	-GRAFT	-SEAMS	-TONES
-BREAK	-DOORS	-GRAIN	-SECTS	-TORTS
-BREED	-DORSE	-GRATE	-SEEMS	-TRANT
-BRING	-DOWED	-GROSS	-SHELL	-TREAT
-BUILT	-DRAFT	-GROUP	-SHIPS	-TRONS
-BURST	-DRAWN	-GROWN	-SHORE	-TRUST
-CAGED	-DUCES	-GULFS	-SIDER	-TURNS
-CAGES	-DUCTS	-GULPH	-SIDES	-TWINE
-CANTS	-DUING	-HABIT	-SIGHT	-TWIST
-CASED	-DWELL	-HALED	-SINEW	-URNED
-CASES	-DWELT	-HALER	-SISTS	-UTILE
-CAVED	-EARTH	-HALES	-SNARE	-VADED
-CAVES	-EXACT	-HAULS	-SOFAR	-VADES
-CEDED	-FALLS	-HERES	-SOLES	-VALID
-CEDES	-FAMED	-HOOPS	-SOOTH	-VENTS
-CENSE	-FAMES	-HUMAN	-SOULS	-VERSE
-CENTS	-FANCY	-ISLED	-SPANS	-VERTS
-CHASE	-FARES	-ISLES	-SPIRE	-VESTS
-CITED	-FAUNA	-JELLY	-STALL	-VEXED
-CITER	-FEOFF	-JOINT	-STARS	-VITAL
-CITES	-FESTS	-LACED	-STATE	-VOICE
-CIVIL	-FIELD	-LACES	-STEAD	-VOLVE
-CLASP	-FIGHT	-LANDS	-STEPS	-WALLS
-CLINE	-FILLS	-LAYER	-STILL	-WARDS
-CLIPS	-FIRMS	-LIERS	-SURED	-WEAVE
-CLOSE	-FIXED	-LOCKS	-SURER	-WICKS
-COMER	-FIXES	-LYING	-SURES	-WINDS
-COMES	-FLAME	-MATES	-SWEPT	-WORKS
-CROSS	-FLOWS	-NARDS	-SWING	-WOUND
-CRUST	-FOLDS	-NERVE	-TAKES	-WOVEN
-CURVE	-FORCE	-ORBED	-TENDS	-WRAPS
-DARTS	-FORMS	-PHASE	-TENSE	
-DENES	-FRACT	-POURS	-TENTS	
-DENTS	-FUSED	-QUEST	-TERNE	
-DEWED	-FUSES	-QUIET	-TERNS	

Eight-letter words

-ACTION	-BRINGS	-CENTRE	-COMING	-DENTED
-ACTIVE	-BURSTS	-CHASED	-CORPSE	-DEVOUT
-ARABLE	-CAGING	-CHASES	-CREASE	-DEWING
-ARCHED	-CANTED	-CITERS	-CREATE	-DICTED
-ARCHES	-CASING	-CITING	-CRUSTS	-DIGEST
-ARMING	-CAVING	-CIVISM	-CUMBER	-DIRECT
-AURATE	-CEDING	-CLASPS	-CURRED	-DITING
-BEINGS	-CENSED	-CLINES	-CURVED	-DOCILE
-BOARDS	-CENSER	-CLOSED	-CURVES	-DOLENT
-BOUNDS	-CENSES	-CLOSER	-DARTED	-DORSER
-BREAKS	-CENSOR	-CLOSES	-DEBTED	-DORSES
-BREEDS	-CENTER	-COMERS	-DECENT	-DOWING

-DRAFTS	-FORCES	-LOCKED	-SISTER	-TREATS
-DRENCH	-FORMAL	-MESHED	-SNARED	-TRENCH
-DUCTED	-FORMED	-MESHES	-SNARER	-TREPID
-DWELLS	-FORMER	-NATIVE	-SNARES	-TRUSTS
-EARTHS	-FOUGHT	-NERVED	-SOLATE	-TUBATE
-EDIBLE	-FRACTS	-NERVES	-SOULED	-TURNED
-EDITED	-FRINGE	-NOCENT	-SPHERE	-TWINED
-EQUITY	-FRUGAL	-ORBING	-SPIRED	-TWINES
-ERRANT	-FUSING	-ORNATE	-SPIRES	-TWISTS
-ESSIVE	-FUSION	-POURED	-SPIRIT	-UNDATE
-EXPERT	-GATHER	-PUTTED	-STABLE	-URBANE
-FAMING	-GLOBED	-PUTTER	-STALLS	-URNING
-FAMOUS	-GLOBES	-QUESTS	-STANCE	-USTION
-FAUNAE	-GOINGS	-QUIETS	-STATED	-VADING
-FAUNAL	-GRAFTS	-QUIRED	-STATES	-VENTED
-FAUNAS	-GRAINS	-QUIRES	-STILLS	-VENTER
-FECUND	-GRATES	-RUSHES	-STRESS	-VERITY
-FEOFFS	-GROOVE	-SANELY	-STROKE	-VERSED
-FERIAE	-GROUND	-SANEST	-SUCKEN	-VERSES
-FESTER	-GROUPS	-SANIES	-SURING	-VERTED
-FIELDS	-GROWTH	-SANITY	-SWATHE	-VESTED
-FIGHTS	-GULFED	-SCAPES	-SWINGS	-VIABLE
-FILLED	-GULPHS	-SCIENT	-TARSIA	-VIABLY
-FINITE	-HABITS	-SCONCE	-TENDED	-VIRILE
-FIRMED	-HALERS	-SCRIBE	-TENDER	-VISCID
-FIRMER	-HALING	-SCROLL	-TENSER	-VOICED
-FIRMLY	-HAULER	-SCULPS	-TERNAL	-VOICES
-FIXING	-HEARSE	-SCULPT	-TERNED	-VOLUTE
-FLAMED	-HOLDER	-SEAMED	-TERNES	-VOLVED
-FLAMER	-HOOPED	-SECURE	-THRALL	-VOLVES
-FLAMES	-HUMANE	-SEEMED	-THRONE	-WALLED
-FLATUS	-HUMATE	-SETTER	-TIMIST	-WEAVED
-FLEXED	-ISLING	-SHEATH	-TITLED	-WEAVES
-FLIGHT	-JOINTS	-SHELLS	-TITLES	-WICKED
-FLUENT	-JURIES	-SHRINE	-TITULE	-WORKED
-FLUXES	-LACING	-SIDERS	-TOMBED	
-FOLDED	-LANDER	-SIGHTS	-TONERS	
-FOLDER	-LAYERS	-SINEWS	-TONING	
-FORCED	-LAYING	-SISTED	-TRANTS	

Words that begin with ISO-

Seven-letter words

-AMYL	-DOSE	-GRAM	-MERE	-TONE
-BARE	-FORM	-LATE	-NOME	-TOPE
-BARS	-GAMY	-LEAD	-PODS	-TRON
-BASE	-GONE	-LINE	-SPIN	-TYPE
-BATH	-GONS	-LOGS	-TACH	-ZYME

Eight-letter words

-AMYLS	-CHASM	-GAMIC	-LATED	-NOMES
-BARES	-CHIME	-GENIC	-LEADS	-NOMIC
-BARIC	-CHORE	-GLOSS	-LEXES	-PHONE
-BASES	-CLINE	-GRAFT	-LINES	-SPINS
-BATHS	-DOSES	-GRAMS	-MERES	-TACHS
-BUTYL	-FORMS	-GRAPH	-MORPH	-THERE

-THERM	-TONIC	-TOPIC	-TYPES	-ZYMES
-TONES	-TOPES	-TRONS	-TYPIC	-ZYMIC

Words that begin with MAN-

Seven-letter words

-AGED	-GELS	-KIER	-NITE	-TIDS
-AGER	-GING	-KIND	-NOSE	-TIES
-AGES	-GLED	-LESS	-PACK	-TOES
-AKIN	-GOES	-LIER	-REDS	-TRAM
-ANAS	-GOLD	-LIKE	-RENT	-TRAP
-DATE	-HOLE	-LILY	-ROPE	-URES
-DOMS	-HOOD	-MADE	-SARD	-WARD
-GABY	-HUNT	-NANS	-TEEL	-WISE
-GALS	-JACK	-NISH	-TELS	

Eight-letter words

-AGERS	-FULLY	-JACKS	-RENTS	-TEELS
-AGING	-GOLDS	-KINDS	-RIDER	-TRAMS
-DATED	-GROVE	-NITES	-ROPES	-TRAPS
-DATES	-HOLES	-NOSES	-SARDS	-URIAL
-DRAKE	-HOODS	-PACKS	-SHIFT	-WARDS
-DRILL	-HUNTS	-POWER	-SWORN	

Words that begin with MIS-

Seven-letter words

-ACTS	-DOER	-HITS	-PAGE	-SORT
-ADDS	-DOES	-JOIN	-PART	-SOUT
-AIMS	-DONE	-KEEP	-PENS	-STEP
-ALLY	-DRAW	-KENS	-PLAN	-STOP
-AVER	-DREW	-KENT	-PLAY	-SUIT
-BIAS	-EASE	-KEPT	-PLED	-TAKE
-BILL	-EATS	-KEYS	-RATE	-TELL
-BIND	-EDIT	-KICK	-READ	-TEND
-BORN	-ERES	-KNEW	-RELY	-TERM
-CALL	-FALL	-KNOW	-RULE	-TIER
-CAST	-FARE	-LAID	-SAID	-TIME
-CITE	-FEED	-LAIN	-SALS	-TING
-CODE	-FELL	-LAYS	-SAYS	-TOLD
-COIN	-FILE	-LEAD	-SEAT	-TOOK
-COOK	-FIRE	-LIES	-SEEM	-TUNE
-COPY	-FITS	-LIKE	-SEEN	-TYPE
-CUED	-FORM	-LIVE	-SEES	-USED
-CUES	-GAVE	-LUCK	-SELS	-USER
-CUTS	-GIVE	-MADE	-SEND	-USES
-DATE	-GOES	-MAKE	-SENT	-WEEN
-DEAL	-GONE	-MARK	-SETS	-WEND
-DEED	-GREW	-MATE	-SHOD	-WENT
-DEEM	-GROW	-MEET	-SIES	-WORD
-DIAL	-HAPS	-MOVE	-SILE	-WRIT
-DIET	-HEAR	-NAME	-SING	-YOKE

Eight-letter words

-ACTED	-DEEDS	-GUIDE	-PLACE	-SUITS
-ADAPT	-DEEMS	-HEARD	-PLANS	-SUSES
-ADDED	-DEMPT	-HEARS	-PLANT	-TAKEN
-AGENT	-DIALS	-INFER	-PLAYS	-TAKER
-AIMED	-DIETS	-INTER	-PLEAD	-TAKES
-ALIGN	-DIGHT	-JOINS	-POINT	-TEACH
-ALLOT	-DOERS	-JUDGE	-POISE	-TELLS
-ALTER	-DOING	-KEEPS	-PRICE	-TENDS
-APPLY	-DONNE	-KEYED	-PRINT	-TERMS
-ARRAY	-DOUBT	-KICKS	-PRISE	-THINK
-ASSAY	-DRAWN	-KNOWN	-PRIZE	-THREW
-ATONE	-DRAWS	-KNOWS	-PROUD	-THROW
-AVERS	-DREAD	-LABEL	-QUOTE	-TIMED
-AWARD	-DRIVE	-LABOR	-RAISE	-TIMES
-BEGAN	-DROVE	-LAYER	-RATED	-TINGS
-BEGIN	-EASES	-LEADS	-RATES	-TITLE
-BEGOT	-EATEN	-LEARN	-READS	-TOUCH
-BEGUN	-EDITS	-LIGHT	-REFER	-TRACE
-BILLS	-ENROL	-LIKED	-ROUTE	-TRAIN
-BINDS	-ENTER	-LIKER	-RULED	-TREAT
-BIRTH	-ENTRY	-LIKES	-RULES	-TRESS
-BOUND	-EVENT	-LIVED	-SABLE	-TRIAL
-BRAND	-FAITH	-LIVES	-SEATS	-TRUST
-BUILD	-FALLS	-LODGE	-SEEMS	-TRUTH
-BUILT	-FARED	-LUCKS	-SENDS	-TRYST
-CALLS	-FARES	-LYING	-SENSE	-TUNED
-CARRY	-FEEDS	-MAKES	-SHAPE	-TUNES
-CASTS	-FEIGN	-MARKS	-SILES	-TUTOR
-CHIEF	-FIELD	-MARRY	-SISES	-TYPED
-CHOSE	-FILED	-MATCH	-SORTS	-TYPES
-CITED	-FILES	-MATED	-SOUND	-UNION
-CITES	-FIRED	-MATES	-SOUTS	-USAGE
-CLAIM	-FIRES	-MEETS	-SPACE	-USERS
-CLASS	-FOCUS	-METRE	-SPEAK	-USING
-CODED	-FORMS	-MOVED	-SPELL	-VALUE
-CODES	-FRAME	-MOVES	-SPELT	-WEENS
-COINS	-GAUGE	-NAMED	-SPEND	-WENDS
-COLOR	-GIVEN	-NAMES	-SPENT	-WORDS
-COOKS	-GIVES	-OLOGY	-SPOKE	-WRITE
-COUNT	-GOING	-ORDER	-STAMP	-WROTE
-CREED	-GRADE	-PAGED	-START	-YOKED
-CUING	-GRAFF	-PAGES	-STATE	-YOKES
-DATED	-GRAFT	-PAINT	-STEER	
-DATES	-GROWN	-PARSE	-STEPS	
-DEALS	-GROWS	-PARTS	-STOPS	
-DEALT	-GUESS	-PATCH	-STYLE	

Words that begin with OUT-

Seven-letter words

-ACTS	-BARK	-BRAG	-CAST	-CROW
-ADDS	-BARS	-BRED	-CHID	-DARE
-AGES	-BAWL	-BULK	-CITY	-DATE
-ASKS	-BEAM	-BURN	-COME	-DOER
-BACK	-BEGS	-BUYS	-COOK	-DOES
-BAKE	-BIDS	-CALL	-CROP	-DONE

-DOOR	-GROW	-MODE	-ROLL	-TASK
-DRAG	-GUNS	-MOST	-ROOP	-TELL
-DRAW	-GUSH	-MOVE	-ROOT	-TOLD
-DREW	-HAUL	-NAME	-ROPE	-TOOK
-DROP	-HEAR	-NESS	-ROWS	-TOPS
-DUEL	-HIRE	-PACE	-RUNG	-TROT
-DURE	-HITS	-PART	-RUNS	-TURN
-EARN	-HOWL	-PASS	-RUSH	-VIED
-EATS	-HUNT	-PEEP	-SAID	-VIES
-ECHO	-JEST	-PEER	-SAIL	-VOTE
-EDGE	-JETS	-PITY	-SANG	-WAIT
-FACE	-JINX	-PLAN	-SAYS	-WALK
-FALL	-JUMP	-PLAY	-SEEN	-WARD
-FAST	-JUTS	-PLOD	-SEES	-WARS
-FAWN	-KEEP	-PLOT	-SELL	-WASH
-FEEL	-KEPT	-POLL	-SETS	-WEAR
-FELT	-KICK	-PORT	-SHOT	-WEED
-FIND	-KILL	-POST	-SIDE	-WEEP
-FIRE	-KISS	-POUR	-SING	-WELL
-FISH	-LAID	-PRAY	-SINS	-WENT
-FITS	-LAIN	-PULL	-SITS	-WEPT
-FLEW	-LAND	-PUSH	-SIZE	-WICK
-FLOW	-LASH	-PUTS	-SOAR	-WILE
-FOOL	-LAST	-RACE	-SOLD	-WILL
-FOOT	-LAWS	-RAGE	-SOLE	-WIND
-GAIN	-LAYS	-RANG	-SPAN	-WING
-GATE	-LEAD	-RANK	-SPED	-WINS
-GAVE	-LEAP	-RATE	-STAY	-WISH
-GAZE	-LETS	-RAVE	-STEP	-WITH
-GIVE	-LIED	-READ	-SULK	-WITS
-GLOW	-LIER	-REDS	-SUMS	-WORE
-GNAW	-LIES	-RIDE	-SUNG	-WORK
-GOER	-LINE	-RIGS	-SWAM	-WORN
-GOES	-LIVE	-RING	-SWIM	-WRIT
-GONE	-LOOK	-ROAR	-SWUM	-YELL
-GREW	-LOVE	-ROCK	-TAKE	-YELP
-GRIN	-MANS	-RODE	-TALK	

Eight-letter words

-ACTED	-BOUND	-CAPER	-CROSS	-DRESS
-ADDED	-BOXED	-CASTE	-CROWD	-DRINK
-ARGUE	-BOXES	-CASTS	-CROWS	-DRIVE
-ASKED	-BRAGS	-CATCH	-CURSE	-DROPS
-BACKS	-BRAVE	-CAVIL	-CURVE	-DROVE
-BAKED	-BRAWL	-CHARM	-DANCE	-DRUNK
-BAKES	-BREAK	-CHEAT	-DARED	-DUELS
-BARKS	-BREED	-CHIDE	-DARES	-DURED
-BAWLS	-BRIBE	-CLASS	-DATED	-DURES
-BEAMS	-BROKE	-CLIMB	-DATES	-DWELL
-BITCH	-BUILD	-CLOMB	-DODGE	-DWELT
-BLAZE	-BUILT	-COACH	-DOERS	-EARNS
-BLEAT	-BULGE	-COMES	-DOING	-EATEN
-BLESS	-BULKS	-COOKS	-DOORS	-EDGES
-BLOOM	-BULLY	-COUNT	-DRAGS	-FABLE
-BLUFF	-BURNS	-CRAWL	-DRANK	-FACED
-BLUSH	-BURNT	-CRIED	-DRAWN	-FACES
-BOARD	-BURST	-CRIES	-DRAWS	-FALLS
-BOAST	-CALLS	-CROPS	-DREAM	-FASTS

-FAWNS	-HOWLS	-POWER	-SIDER	-TALKS
-FEAST	-HUMOR	-PRAYS	-SIDES	-TASKS
-FEELS	-HUNTS	-PREEN	-SIGHT	-TELLS
-FENCE	-JESTS	-PRESS	-SINGS	-THANK
-FIELD	-JUMPS	-PRICE	-SIZED	-THINK
-FIGHT	-KEEPS	-PRIZE	-SIZES	-THREW
-FINDS	-KICKS	-PULLS	-SKATE	-THROB
-FIRED	-KILLS	-PUNCH	-SKIRT	-THROW
-FIRES	-LANDS	-PUPIL	-SLEEP	-TOWER
-FLANK	-LASTS	-QUOTE	-SLEPT	-TRADE
-FLASH	-LAUGH	-RACED	-SLICK	-TRICK
-FLIES	-LAWED	-RACES	-SMART	-TROTS
-FLING	-LEADS	-RAGED	-SMELL	-TRUMP
-FLOAT	-LEAPS	-RAGES	-SMELT	-TURNS
-FLOWN	-LEAPT	-RAISE	-SMILE	-VALUE
-FLOWS	-LEARN	-RANCE	-SMOKE	-VAUNT
-FLUSH	-LIERS	-RANGE	-SNORE	-VENOM
-FOOLS	-LINED	-RANKS	-SOARS	-VOICE
-FOOTS	-LINER	-RATED	-SOLES	-VOTED
-FOUND	-LINES	-RATES	-SPANS	-VOTER
-FOXED	-LIVED	-RAVED	-SPEAK	-VOTES
-FOXES	-LIVER	-RAVES	-SPEED	-VYING
-FROWN	-LIVES	-REACH	-SPELL	-WAITS
-GAINS	-LOOKS	-READS	-SPELT	-WALKS
-GASES	-LOVED	-REIGN	-SPEND	-WARDS
-GATES	-LOVES	-RIDER	-SPENT	-WASTE
-GAZED	-LYING	-RIDES	-SPOKE	-WATCH
-GAZES	-MARCH	-RIGHT	-SPORT	-WEARS
-GIVEN	-MATCH	-RINGS	-STAND	-WEARY
-GIVES	-MODES	-RIVAL	-STARE	-WEEDS
-GLARE	-MOVED	-ROARS	-START	-WEEPS
-GLEAM	-MOVES	-ROCKS	-STATE	-WEIGH
-GLOWS	-NAMED	-ROLLS	-STAYS	-WELLS
-GNAWN	-NAMES	-ROOPS	-STEER	-WHIRL
-GNAWS	-NIGHT	-ROOTS	-STEPS	-WICKS
-GOERS	-PACED	-ROPER	-STOOD	-WILED
-GOING	-PACES	-ROPES	-STRIP	-WILES
-GRINS	-PAINT	-ROWED	-STUDY	-WILLS
-GROSS	-PARTS	-SAILS	-STUNT	-WINDS
-GROUP	-PEEPS	-SAVOR	-SULKS	-WINGS
-GROWN	-PEERS	-SCOLD	-SWARE	-WORKS
-GROWS	-PITCH	-SCOOP	-SWEAR	-WORTH
-GUARD	-PLACE	-SCORE	-SWEEP	-WOUND
-GUESS	-PLANS	-SCORN	-SWELL	-WREST
-GUIDE	-PLAYS	-SELLS	-SWEPT	-WRITE
-HAULS	-PLODS	-SERVE	-SWIMS	-WROTE
-HEARD	-PLOTS	-SHAME	-SWING	-YELLS
-HEARS	-POINT	-SHINE	-SWORE	-YELPS
-HIRED	-POLLS	-SHONE	-SWORN	-YIELD
-HIRES	-PORTS	-SHOOT	-SWUNG	
-HOMER	-POSTS	-SHOTS	-TAKEN	
-HOUSE	-POURS	-SHOUT	-TAKES	

Words that begin with OVER-

Seven-letter words

-ACT	-ALL	-ARM	-AWE	-BET
-AGE	-APT	-ATE	-BED	-BID

-BIG	-EGG	-JOY	-NEW	-SET
-BUY	-EYE	-LAP	-PAY	-SEW
-COY	-FAR	-LAX	-PLY	-SOW
-CUT	-FAT	-LAY	-RAN	-SUP
-DID	-FED	-LET	-RED	-TAX
-DOG	-FIT	-LIE	-REN	-TIP
-DRY	-FLY	-LIT	-RUN	-TOP
-DUB	-GET	-MAN	-SAD	-USE
-DUE	-GOT	-MEN	-SAW	-WET
-DYE	-HIT	-MIX	-SEA	
-EAT	-HOT	-NET	-SEE	

Eight-letter words

-ABLE	-CUTS	-GIRT	-LARD	-PLUS
-ACTS	-DARE	-GIVE	-LATE	-POST
-AGED	-DEAR	-GLAD	-LAYS	-PUMP
-AGES	-DECK	-GOAD	-LEAF	-RACK
-ALLS	-DOER	-GOES	-LEAP	-RAKE
-ARCH	-DOES	-GONE	-LEND	-RANK
-ARMS	-DOGS	-GREW	-LENT	-RASH
-AWED	-DONE	-GROW	-LETS	-RATE
-AWES	-DOSE	-HAIR	-LEWD	-READ
-BAKE	-DRAW	-HALE	-LIER	-REDS
-BEAR	-DREW	-HAND	-LIES	-RENS
-BEAT	-DUBS	-HANG	-LIVE	-RICH
-BETS	-DUST	-HARD	-LOAD	-RIDE
-BIDS	-DYED	-HATE	-LOCK	-RIFE
-BILL	-DYER	-HAUL	-LONG	-RIPE
-BITE	-DYES	-HEAD	-LOOK	-RODE
-BLEW	-EASY	-HEAP	-LORD	-RUDE
-BLOW	-EATS	-HEAR	-LOUD	-RUFF
-BOIL	-EDIT	-HEAT	-LOVE	-RULE
-BOLD	-EGGS	-HELD	-LUSH	-RUNS
-BOOK	-EYED	-HENT	-MANS	-SAIL
-BOOT	-EYES	-HIGH	-MANY	-SALE
-BORE	-FALL	-HITS	-MAST	-SALT
-BORN	-FAST	-HOLD	-MEEK	-SAVE
-BRED	-FEAR	-HOLY	-MELT	-SEAS
-BRIM	-FEED	-HOPE	-MILD	-SEED
-BROW	-FELL	-HUNG	-MILK	-SEEN
-BULK	-FILL	-HUNT	-MINE	-SEER
-BURN	-FINE	-HYPE	-MUCH	-SEES
-BUSY	-FISH	-IDLE	-NAME	-SELL
-BUYS	-FLEW	-JOYS	-NEAR	-SETS
-CALL	-FLOW	-JUMP	-NEAT	-SEWN
-CAME	-FOLD	-JUST	-NETS	-SEWS
-CAST	-FOND	-KEEN	-NICE	-SHOE
-CLAD	-FOUL	-KEEP	-PACK	-SHOT
-CLOY	-FREE	-KEPT	-PAGE	-SICK
-COAT	-FULL	-KEST	-PAID	-SIDE
-COLD	-FUND	-KILL	-PART	-SIZE
-COME	-GALL	-KIND	-PASS	-SKIP
-COOK	-GANG	-KING	-PAST	-SLIP
-COOL	-GAVE	-KNEE	-PAYS	-SLOW
-CRAM	-GEAR	-LADE	-PEER	-SOAK
-CRAW	-GETS	-LAID	-PERT	-SOFT
-CROP	-GILD	-LAIN	-PLAN	-SOLD
-CROW	-GILT	-LAND	-PLAY	-SOON
-CURE	-GIRD	-LAPS	-PLOT	-SOUL

-SOWN	-SWUM	-TONE	-VOTE	-WING
-SOWS	-TAKE	-TOOK	-WARM	-WISE
-SPIN	-TALK	-TOPS	-WARY	-WORD
-STAY	-TAME	-TRIM	-WASH	-WORE
-STEP	-TART	-TRIP	-WEAK	-WORK
-STIR	-TASK	-TURN	-WEAR	-WORN
-SUDS	-TEEM	-TYPE	-WEEN	-YEAR
-SUPS	-THIN	-URGE	-WENT	-ZEAL
-SURE	-TIME	-USED	-WETS	
-SWAM	-TIPS	-USES	-WIDE	
-SWAY	-TIRE	-VEIL	-WILY	
-SWIM	-TOIL	-VIEW	-WIND	

Words that begin with PER-

Seven-letter words

-ACID	-FINS	-KING	-PEND	-TAKE
-AEON	-FORM	-KINS	-PENT	-TEST
-CASE	-FUME	-KISH	-PLEX	-TOOK
-CENT	-FUMY	-LITE	-SALT	-UKES
-CHER	-FUSE	-LOUS	-SANT	-USED
-CINE	-HAPS	-MING	-SING	-USER
-CUSS	-ICON	-MUTE	-SIST	-USES
-DUES	-JINK	-NODS	-SONS	-VADE
-DURE	-JURE	-ONES	-SUED	-VERT
-EGAL	-JURY	-ORAL	-SUES	
-EONS	-KIER	-OXID	-TAIN	

Eight-letter words

-ACIDS	-FUMED	-MEANT	-PENTS	-TAINS
-ACUTE	-FUMER	-MEASE	-RADII	-TAKEN
-AEONS	-FUMES	-MUTED	-SALTS	-TAKES
-CENTS	-FUSED	-MUTES	-SAUNT	-USERS
-COLIN	-FUSES	-NANCY	-SEITY	-USING
-DURED	-IODIC	-ORATE	-SISTS	-VADED
-DURES	-IODID	-OXIDE	-SPIRE	-VADES
-FORCE	-ISHES	-OXIDS	-SPIRY	-VERSE
-FORMS	-LITES	-PENDS	-SUING	-VERTS

Words that begin with PRE-

Seven-letter words

-ACED	-BEND	-CENT	-DIVE	-FILL
-ACES	-BIDS	-CESS	-DOOM	-FIRE
-ACHY	-BILL	-CODE	-DUSK	-FORM
-ACTS	-BIND	-COOK	-DYED	-FUND
-AGED	-BOIL	-COOL	-DYES	-GAME
-AMPS	-BOOK	-COUP	-EDIT	-HEAT
-ANAL	-BOOM	-CURE	-EMPT	-HEND
-ARMS	-BORN	-CUTS	-EVES	-JINK
-AVER	-BUYS	-DATE	-FABS	-LACY
-BADE	-CAST	-DAWN	-FACE	-LATE
-BAKE	-CAVA	-DIAL	-FADE	-LIFE
-BASE	-CEDE	-DICT	-FILE	-LOAD

-LUDE	-PACK	-ROCK	-SORT	-VAIL
-MADE	-PAID	-SAGE	-STED	-VENT
-MEAL	-PARE	-SALE	-TAPE	-VERB
-MEDS	-PAVE	-SELL	-TEEN	-VIEW
-MEET	-PAYS	-SENT	-TELL	-VISE
-MISE	-PILL	-SETS	-TEND	-WARM
-MISS	-PLAN	-SHIP	-TERM	-WARN
-MOLD	-PONE	-SHOW	-TEST	-WASH
-MOLT	-POSE	-SIDE	-TEXT	-WIRE
-MOVE	-PUCE	-SIFT	-TOLD	-WORK
-NAME	-PUPA	-SOAK	-TORS	-WORN
-NOON	-RACE	-SOLD	-TRIM	-WRAP
-ORAL	-RIOT	-SONG	-TYPE	-WYNS

Eight-letter words

-ACHED	-CLEAR	-FOCUS	-PAVES	-SPLIT
-ACHES	-CODED	-FORMS	-PLACE	-STAMP
-ACING	-CODES	-FRANK	-PLANS	-STING
-ACTED	-COOKS	-FROZE	-PLANT	-STORE
-ADAPT	-COOLS	-FUNDS	-PONES	-TAPED
-ADMIT	-CRASH	-GAMES	-POSED	-TAPES
-ADULT	-CURED	-GUIDE	-POSES	-TASTE
-ALLOT	-CURES	-HEATS	-PRESS	-TEENS
-ALTER	-CURSE	-HENDS	-PRICE	-TELLS
-AMBLE	-DATED	-HUMAN	-PRINT	-TENDS
-APPLY	-DATES	-JUDGE	-PUBES	-TENSE
-ARMED	-DAWNS	-LEGAL	-PUBIS	-TERMS
-ASSED	-DEATH	-LIMIT	-PUCES	-TESTS
-ASSES	-DICTS	-LOADS	-PUNCH	-TEXTS
-AUDIT	-DIVES	-LOVED	-PUPAE	-TONIC
-AVERS	-DOOMS	-LUDES	-PUPAL	-TRAIN
-AXIAL	-DRAFT	-LUNCH	-PUPAS	-TREAT
-BAKED	-DRIED	-MEDIC	-RADIO	-TRIAL
-BAKES	-DRIES	-MEETS	-RENAL	-TRIMS
-BASAL	-DRILL	-MISES	-RINSE	-TYPED
-BENDS	-DUSKS	-MIXED	-SAGER	-TYPES
-BILLS	-EDITS	-MIXES	-SAGES	-UNION
-BINDS	-ELECT	-MOLAR	-SALES	-UNITE
-BIRTH	-EMPTS	-MOLDS	-SCORE	-VAILS
-BLESS	-ENACT	-MOLTS	-SCUTA	-VALUE
-BOARD	-ERECT	-MORAL	-SELLS	-VENTS
-BOILS	-EXIST	-MORSE	-SENTS	-VERBS
-BOOKS	-FACED	-MOVED	-SERVE	-VIEWS
-BOUND	-FACER	-MOVES	-SHAPE	-VISED
-BUILD	-FACES	-NAMES	-SHIPS	-VISES
-BUILT	-FADED	-NASAL	-SHOWN	-VISIT
-CASTS	-FADES	-NATAL	-SHOWS	-VISOR
-CEDED	-FIGHT	-NOMEN	-SIDED	-WARMS
-CEDES	-FILED	-ORDER	-SIDER	-WARNS
-CENTS	-FILES	-OWNED	-SIDES	-WEIGH
-CHECK	-FILLS	-PACKS	-SIFTS	-WIRED
-CHILL	-FIRED	-PARED	-SLEEP	-WIRES
-CHOSE	-FIRES	-PARER	-SLICE	-WORKS
-CINCT	-FIXED	-PARES	-SOAKS	-WRAPS
-CITED	-FIXES	-PASTE	-SOLVE	
-CLEAN	-FLAME	-PAVED	-SORTS	

Words that begin with PRO-

Seven-letter words

-BALL	-FANE	-LONG	-PEND	-TEST
-BAND	-FESS	-MINE	-PENE	-TONS
-BANG	-FILE	-MISE	-PONE	-TORE
-BATE	-FITS	-MOTE	-POSE	-VANT
-BING	-FUSE	-NAOI	-RATE	-VEND
-BITS	-GRAM	-NAOS	-SAIC	-VERB
-CARP	-JETS	-NEST	-SECT	-VERS
-CESS	-KING	-NOTA	-SERS	-VIDE
-CURE	-LATE	-NOUN	-SING	-VINE
-DRUG	-LEGS	-OTIC	-SOMA	-WEST
-DUCE	-LINE	-PAGE	-STIE	
-DUCT	-LING	-PALE	-TEAS	
-FACE	-LOGS	-PANE	-TEND	

Eight-letter words

-BANDS	-FILER	-MOTOR	-POSER	-TEASE
-BANGS	-FILES	-NATES	-POSES	-TENDS
-BATED	-FOUND	-NOTAL	-POUND	-TENSE
-BATES	-GRADE	-NOTUM	-PYLON	-TESTS
-CARPS	-GRAMS	-NOUNS	-RATED	-TONIC
-CHAIN	-LABOR	-PAGED	-RATES	-TORES
-CINCT	-LAPSE	-PAGES	-ROGUE	-TRACT
-CLAIM	-LATED	-PALED	-SAIST	-TRADE
-CURED	-LINES	-PALES	-SECTS	-UNION
-CURER	-LONGE	-PANES	-SEMEN	-VANTS
-CURES	-LONGS	-PENDS	-SINGS	-VENDS
-DROME	-METAL	-PENES	-SODIC	-VERBS
-DRUGS	-MINES	-PHAGE	-SOMAS	-VINED
-DUCES	-MISER	-PHASE	-STATE	-VINES
-DUCTS	-MISES	-POLIS	-STIES	-VIRAL
-FANES	-MOTED	-PONES	-STYLE	-VIRUS
-FILED	-MOTES	-POSED	-TAMIN	-VISOR

Words that begin with RE-

Seven-letter words

-ACHED	-AMEND	-BAITS	-BOOKS	-CANES
-ACHES	-ANNEX	-BATED	-BOOTS	-CANTS
-ACTED	-APERS	-BATES	-BORED	-CARRY
-ACTOR	-APING	-BECKS	-BORES	-CASTS
-ADAPT	-APPLY	-BEGAN	-BOUND	-CATCH
-ADDED	-ARGUE	-BEGIN	-BOZOS	-CEDED
-ADMIT	-ARISE	-BEGUN	-BRACE	-CEDES
-ADOPT	-ARMED	-BILLS	-BRAND	-CENSE
-ADORN	-AROSE	-BINDS	-BREED	-CHART
-AFFIX	-AVAIL	-BIRTH	-BUFFS	-CHEAT
-AGENT	-AVERS	-BITES	-BUILD	-CHECK
-AKING	-AVOWS	-BLEND	-BUILT	-CHEWS
-ALIGN	-AWAKE	-BLENT	-BUKES	-CHOSE
-ALIST	-AWOKE	-BLOOM	-BUSES	-CITAL
-ALLOT	-BACKS	-BOARD	-CALLS	-CITED
-ALTER	-BADGE	-BOILS	-CANED	-CITER

-CITES	-EDITS	-GAUGE	-LIERS	-PAIRS
-CLAIM	-EJECT	-GEARS	-LIEVE	-PANEL
-CLAME	-EKING	-GENTS	-LIGHT	-PAPER
-CLASP	-ELECT	-GESTS	-LINED	-PARKS
-CLEAN	-ELMEN	-GILDS	-LINES	-PASTS
-CLIMB	-EMITS	-GIVEN	-LINKS	-PATCH
-CLINE	-ENACT	-GIVES	-LISTS	-PAVED
-CLOSE	-ENDOW	-GLAZE	-LIVED	-PAVES
-COALS	-ENJOY	-GLOSS	-LIVER	-PEALS
-COATS	-ENTER	-GLOWS	-LIVES	-PEATS
-COCKS	-ENTRY	-GLUED	-LOADS	-PENTS
-CODED	-EQUIP	-GLUES	-LOANS	-PERKS
-CODES	-ERECT	-GORGE	-LOCKS	-PINED
-COILS	-EVOKE	-GRADE	-LOOKS	-PINES
-COINS	-EXPEL	-GRAFT	-LYING	-PIQUE
-COLOR	-FACED	-GRANT	-MAILS	-PLACE
-COMBS	-FACES	-GRATE	-MAINS	-PLANS
-COOKS	-FALLS	-GREEN	-MAKER	-PLANT
-CORDS	-FEEDS	-GREET	-MAKES	-PLATE
-CORKS	-FEELS	-GRIND	-MANET	-PLAYS
-COUNT	-FENCE	-GROOM	-MARKS	-PLEAD
-COUPE	-FIGHT	-GROUP	-MARRY	-PLICA
-COUPS	-FILED	-GROWN	-MATCH	-PLIED
-COURE	-FILES	-GROWS	-MATED	-PLIER
-COVER	-FILLS	-GULAR	-MATES	-PLIES
-COWER	-FILMS	-HANGS	-MEADS	-PLOTS
-CRATE	-FINDS	-HEARD	-MEETS	-PLOWS
-CROSS	-FINED	-HEARS	-MELTS	-PLUMB
-CROWN	-FINER	-HEATS	-MENDS	-POINT
-CURED	-FINES	-HEELS	-MERCY	-POLLS
-CURES	-FIRED	-HINGE	-MERGE	-PONES
-CURVE	-FIRES	-HIRED	-MINDS	-PORTS
-CYCLE	-FIXED	-HIRES	-MINTS	-POSED
-DATED	-FIXES	-HOUSE	-MISES	-POSER
-DATES	-FLAGS	-IMAGE	-MIXED	-POSES
-DEALS	-FLIES	-INCUR	-MIXES	-POSIT
-DEALT	-FLOAT	-INDEX	-MODEL	-POSTS
-DEARS	-FLOOD	-INKED	-MOLDS	-POURS
-DEEMS	-FLOWN	-INTER	-MORAS	-POWER
-DIALS	-FLOWS	-ISSUE	-MORSE	-PRESS
-DOCKS	-FOCUS	-JOINS	-MOTES	-PRICE
-DOING	-FOLDS	-JONES	-MOULD	-PRIME
-DOUBT	-FOOTS	-JUDGE	-MOUNT	-PRINT
-DOUTS	-FORGE	-KEYED	-MOVED	-PRISE
-DRAFT	-FORMS	-KNITS	-MOVER	-PRIZE
-DRAWN	-FOUND	-KNOTS	-MOVES	-PROBE
-DRAWS	-FRACT	-LABEL	-NAILS	-PROOF
-DREAM	-FRAME	-LACED	-NAMED	-PROVE
-DRESS	-FRESH	-LACES	-NAMES	-PULPS
-DRIED	-FRIED	-LANDS	-NESTS	-PULSE
-DRIES	-FRIES	-LAPSE	-NEWED	-PUMPS
-DRILL	-FRONT	-LATED	-NEWER	-PURED
-DRIVE	-FROZE	-LATER	-NYING	-PURES
-DROVE	-FUELS	-LAXER	-OCCUR	-QUEST
-DUCES	-FUNDS	-LAXES	-OFFER	-QUINS
-DUITS	-FUSED	-LAYED	-OILED	-QUIRE
-EARNS	-FUSES	-LEARN	-OPENS	-QUITE
-ECHED	-GAINS	-LEASE	-ORDER	-QUITS
-ECHES	-GALES	-LENDS	-PACKS	-QUOTE
-EDIFY	-GALLY	-LIEFS	-PAINT	-RACKS

-RAILS	-SIGNS	-STING	-TOTAL	-VIEWS
-RAISE	-SILED	-STIVE	-TOUCH	-VILER
-READS	-SILES	-STOCK	-TOURS	-VISED
-REDOS	-SINED	-STOKE	-TRACE	-VISES
-RENTS	-SISTS	-STORE	-TRACK	-VISIT
-RISEN	-SITED	-STUDY	-TRACT	-VISOR
-RISES	-SITES	-STUFF	-TRAIN	-VIVER
-ROLLS	-SIZED	-STUMP	-TRAIT	-VIVES
-ROOFS	-SIZES	-STYLE	-TREAD	-VOICE
-ROUTE	-SKEWS	-SURGE	-TREAT	-VOLTS
-SAILS	-SKILL	-TABLE	-TREES	-VOLVE
-SALES	-SLATE	-TACKS	-TRIAL	-VOTED
-SAWED	-SMELT	-TAILS	-TRIED	-VOTES
-SCALE	-SOAKS	-TAINS	-TRIES	-VYING
-SCORE	-SOLED	-TAKEN	-TRIMS	-WAKED
-SEALS	-SOLES	-TAKER	-TUNDS	-WAKEN
-SEATS	-SOLVE	-TAKES	-TUNED	-WAKES
-SECTS	-SORBS	-TALLY	-TUNES	-WARDS
-SEEDS	-SORTS	-TAPED	-TURFS	-WARMS
-SEEKS	-SOUND	-TAPES	-TURNS	-WAXED
-SEIZE	-SOWED	-TASTE	-TWIST	-WAXES
-SELLS	-SPACE	-TAXED	-TYING	-WEARS
-SENDS	-SPADE	-TAXES	-TYPED	-WEAVE
-SENTS	-SPEAK	-TEACH	-TYPES	-WEIGH
-SERVE	-SPELL	-TEAMS	-UNIFY	-WELDS
-SEWED	-SPELT	-TEARS	-UNION	-WIDEN
-SHAPE	-SPIRE	-TELLS	-UNITE	-WINDS
-SHAVE	-SPITE	-TENES	-URGED	-WIRED
-SHINE	-SPLIT	-TESTS	-URGES	-WIRES
-SHIPS	-SPOKE	-THINK	-USING	-WOKEN
-SHOED	-SPOOL	-TILED	-UTTER	-WORDS
-SHOES	-SPOTS	-TILES	-VALUE	-WORKS
-SHONE	-SPRAY	-TIMED	-VAMPS	-WOUND
-SHOOT	-STACK	-TIMES	-VEALS	-WOVEN
-SHOWN	-STAFF	-TINES	-VENGE	-WRAPS
-SHOWS	-STAGE	-TINTS	-VENUE	-WRAPT
-SIDED	-STAMP	-TIRED	-VERBS	-WRITE
-SIDER	-START	-TIRES	-VERSE	-WROTE
-SIDES	-STATE	-TITLE	-VERSO	-ZEROS
-SIFTS	-STEMS	-TOOLS	-VERTS	-ZONED
-SIGHT	-STIFF	-TORTS	-VESTS	-ZONES

Eight-letter words

-ABSORB	-ADOPTS	-ARGUES	-ATTACK	-BIDDEN
-ACCEDE	-ADORNS	-ARISEN	-ATTAIN	-BILLED
-ACCENT	-ADVISE	-ARISES	-AVAILS	-BIRTHS
-ACCEPT	-AFFIRM	-ARMING	-AVOWED	-BITING
-ACCUSE	-AGENCY	-AROUSE	-AWAKED	-BITTEN
-ACHING	-AGENTS	-ARREST	-AWAKEN	-BLENDS
-ACTANT	-ALIGNS	-ASCEND	-AWAKES	-BLOOMS
-ACTING	-ALLIED	-ASCENT	-AWOKEN	-BOARDS
-ACTION	-ALLIES	-ASSAIL	-BACKED	-BODIED
-ACTIVE	-ALLOTS	-ASSERT	-BADGED	-BODIES
-ACTORS	-ALTERS	-ASSESS	-BADGES	-BOILED
-ADAPTS	-AMENDS	-ASSIGN	-BAITED	-BOOKED
-ADDICT	-ANOINT	-ASSORT	-BATING	-BOOTED
-ADDING	-ANSWER	-ASSUME	-BEGINS	-BORING
-ADJUST	-APPEAR	-ASSURE	-BELLED	-BORROW
-ADMITS	-ARGUED	-ATTACH	-BELLOW	-BOTTLE

-BOUGHT	-COILER	-DRAFTS	-FLUENT	-HARDEN
-BOUNDS	-COINED	-DRAWER	-FLUXED	-HASHED
-BRACED	-COLLET	-DREAMS	-FLUXES	-HASHES
-BRACES	-COLORS	-DREAMT	-FLYING	-HEARSE
-BRANCH	-COMBED	-DRILLS	-FOLDED	-HEATED
-BREEDS	-COMMIT	-DRIVEN	-FOOTED	-HEATER
-BUFFED	-CONFER	-DRIVES	-FOREST	-HEELED
-BUILDS	-CONNED	-DRYING	-FORGED	-HEMMED
-BURIAL	-CONVEY	-DUBBED	-FORGES	-HINGED
-BURIED	-COOKED	-DYEING	-FORMAT	-HINGES
-BURIES	-COPIED	-EARNED	-FORMED	-HIRING
-BUTTED	-COPIES	-ECHING	-FORMER	-HOUSED
-BUTTER	-CORDED	-ECHOED	-FOUGHT	-HOUSES
-BUTTON	-CORDER	-ECHOES	-FOUNDS	-IGNITE
-BUYING	-CORKED	-EDITED	-FRACTS	-ILLUME
-CALLED	-COUNTS	-EJECTS	-FRAMED	-IMAGED
-CALLER	-COUPED	-ELECTS	-FRAMES	-IMAGES
-CANING	-COUPLE	-EMBARK	-FREEZE	-IMPORT
-CANTED	-COURED	-EMBODY	-FRINGE	-IMPOSE
-CANTER	-COURES	-EMERGE	-FRONTS	-INCITE
-CAPPED	-COURSE	-EMPLOY	-FROZEN	-INCURS
-CAPTOR	-COVERS	-ENACTS	-FRYING	-INDICT
-CARPET	-COWERS	-ENDOWS	-FUELED	-INDUCE
-CAUGHT	-CRATED	-ENGAGE	-FUNDED	-INDUCT
-CEDING	-CRATES	-ENJOYS	-FUNDER	-INFECT
-CEMENT	-CREANT	-ENLIST	-FUSING	-INFORM
-CENSED	-CREATE	-ENROLL	-FUSION	-INFUSE
-CENSES	-CROWNS	-ENTERS	-GAINED	-INJECT
-CENSOR	-CURING	-EQUIPS	-GAINER	-INJURE
-CENTER	-CURRED	-ERECTS	-GATHER	-INJURY
-CENTRE	-CURVED	-EVOKED	-GAUGED	-INKING
-CESSED	-CURVES	-EVOKES	-GAUGES	-INSERT
-CESSES	-CYCLED	-EXPELS	-GEARED	-INSTAL
-CHANGE	-CYCLER	-EXPORT	-GELATE	-INSURE
-CHARGE	-CYCLES	-EXPOSE	-GILDED	-INTERS
-CHARTS	-DAMAGE	-FACING	-GIVING	-INVADE
-CHEATS	-DATING	-FALLEN	-GLAZED	-INVENT
-CHECKS	-DECIDE	-FASTEN	-GLAZES	-INVEST
-CHEWED	-DEEMED	-FELLED	-GLOWED	-INVITE
-CHOOSE	-DEFEAT	-FENCED	-GLUING	-INVOKE
-CHOSEN	-DEFECT	-FENCES	-GORGED	-ISSUED
-CIRCLE	-DEFIED	-FIGHTS	-GORGES	-ISSUER
-CITALS	-DEFIES	-FIGURE	-GRADED	-ISSUES
-CITERS	-DEFINE	-FILING	-GRADES	-JACKET
-CITING	-DEMAND	-FILLED	-GRAFTS	-JIGGED
-CLAIMS	-DENIED	-FILMED	-GRANTS	-JIGGER
-CLAMES	-DENIES	-FILTER	-GRATED	-JOINED
-CLASPS	-DEPLOY	-FINERS	-GRATER	-JUDGED
-CLEANS	-DESIGN	-FINERY	-GRATES	-JUDGES
-CLIMBS	-DIALED	-FINING	-GREENS	-JUGGLE
-CLINES	-DIGEST	-FINISH	-GREETS	-KEYING
-CLOSED	-DIPPED	-FIRING	-GRINDS	-KINDLE
-CLOSES	-DIRECT	-FITTED	-GROOMS	-LABELS
-CLOTHE	-DISTIL	-FIXING	-GROOVE	-LACHES
-COALED	-DIVIDE	-FLEXED	-GROUND	-LACING
-COATED	-DOCKED	-FLEXES	-GROUPS	-LANDED
-COCKED	-DOLENT	-FLOATS	-GROWTH	-LAPSED
-CODIFY	-DONNED	-FLOODS	-HAMMER	-LAPSER
-CODING	-DOUBLE	-FLOWED	-HANDLE	-LAPSES
-COILED	-DOUBTS	-FLOWER	-HANGED	-LAUNCH

-LAYING	-NAMING	-POLISH	-ROLLED	-SITING
-LEARNS	-NATURE	-POLLED	-ROLLER	-SIZING
-LEARNT	-NEGATE	-PORTED	-ROOFED	-SKETCH
-LEASED	-NESTED	-PORTER	-ROUTED	-SKEWED
-LEASER	-NEWING	-POSERS	-ROUTES	-SKILLS
-LEASES	-NOTIFY	-POSING	-SADDLE	-SLATED
-LEGATE	-NUMBER	-POSITS	-SAILED	-SLATES
-LETTER	-OBJECT	-POSTED	-SALUTE	-SMELTS
-LEVANT	-OBTAIN	-POTTED	-SAMPLE	-SMOOTH
-LIABLE	-OCCUPY	-POURED	-SAWING	-SOAKED
-LIEVER	-OCCURS	-POUSSE	-SAYING	-SODDED
-LIGHTS	-OFFEND	-POWERS	-SCALED	-SOFTEN
-LINING	-OFFERS	-PREEVE	-SCALES	-SOLDER
-LINKED	-OILING	-PRICED	-SCHOOL	-SOLING
-LISTED	-OPENED	-PRICES	-SCORED	-SOLUTE
-LIVERS	-OPENER	-PRIEFE	-SCORES	-SOLVED
-LIVING	-OPPOSE	-PRIEVE	-SCREEN	-SOLVER
-LOADED	-ORDAIN	-PRIMED	-SCRIPT	-SOLVES
-LOADER	-ORDERS	-PRIMES	-SCULPT	-SONANT
-LOANED	-ORIENT	-PRINTS	-SEALED	-SORBED
-LOCATE	-OUTFIT	-PRISED	-SEARCH	-SORTED
-LOCKED	-PACIFY	-PRISES	-SEASON	-SORTER
-LOOKED	-PACKED	-PRIZED	-SEATED	-SOUGHT
-LUCENT	-PAINTS	-PRIZES	-SECURE	-SOUNDS
-LUMINE	-PAIRED	-PROBED	-SEEDED	-SOURCE
-MAILED	-PAIRER	-PROBES	-SEEING	-SOWING
-MAINED	-PANELS	-PROOFS	-SEIZED	-SPACED
-MAKERS	-PAPERS	-PROVED	-SEIZES	-SPACES
-MAKING	-PARKED	-PROVER	-SELECT	-SPADED
-MANENT	-PASSED	-PROVES	-SELLER	-SPADES
-MANIES	-PASSES	-PUBLIC	-SEMBLE	-SPEAKS
-MANNED	-PASTED	-PULPED	-SENTED	-SPELLS
-MAPPED	-PAVING	-PULSED	-SERVED	-SPIRED
-MARKED	-PAYING	-PULSER	-SERVER	-SPIRES
-MARKER	-PEALED	-PULSES	-SERVES	-SPITED
-MARKET	-PEGGED	-PUMPED	-SETTER	-SPITES
-MARQUE	-PELLED	-PURIFY	-SETTLE	-SPLICE
-MASTER	-PEOPLE	-PURING	-SEWING	-SPLITS
-MATING	-PERKED	-PURSUE	-SHAPED	-SPOKEN
-MEDIAL	-PERUSE	-QUESTS	-SHAPER	-SPOOLS
-MELTED	-PHRASE	-QUIGHT	-SHAPES	-SPRANG
-MEMBER	-PINING	-QUIRED	-SHAVED	-SPRAYS
-MENDED	-PINNED	-QUIRES	-SHAVEN	-SPREAD
-MERGED	-PIQUED	-QUITED	-SHAVES	-SPRING
-MERGES	-PIQUES	-QUITES	-SHINED	-SPROUT
-MINDED	-PLACED	-QUOTED	-SHINES	-SPRUNG
-MINDER	-PLACER	-QUOTES	-SHOOTS	-STABLE
-MINTED	-PLACES	-RACKED	-SHOWED	-STACKS
-MIXING	-PLANTS	-RAILED	-SHOWER	-STAFFS
-MODELS	-PLATED	-RAISED	-SIDERS	-STAGED
-MODIFY	-PLATES	-RAISES	-SIDING	-STAGES
-MOLDED	-PLAYED	-RECORD	-SIFTED	-STAMPS
-MORSES	-PLEADS	-REMIND	-SIGHTS	-STARTS
-MOTION	-PLEDGE	-RENTED	-SIGNED	-STATED
-MOULDS	-PLIERS	-REPEAT	-SIGNER	-STATES
-MOUNTS	-PLOWED	-REVIEW	-SILING	-STINGS
-MOVERS	-PLUMBS	-REVISE	-SILVER	-STITCH
-MOVING	-PLUNGE	-REWARD	-SINING	-STOCKS
-MURMUR	-PLYING	-RIGGED	-SISTED	-STOKED
-NAILED	-POINTS	-RISING	-SISTER	-STOKES

-STORED	-TAILOR	-TRACTS	-VENGED	-WAKENS
-STORER	-TAKERS	-TRAINS	-VENGER	-WAKING
-STORES	-TAKING	-TRAITS	-VENGES	-WARDED
-STRAIN	-TAPING	-TREADS	-VENUES	-WARDER
-STRESS	-TARGET	-TREATS	-VERIFY	-WARMED
-STRICT	-TASTED	-TRENCH	-VERIST	-WASHED
-STRIKE	-TASTES	-TRIALS	-VERSAL	-WASHES
-STRING	-TAUGHT	-TRYING	-VERSED	-WAXING
-STRIVE	-TAXING	-TUNDED	-VERSER	-WEAVED
-STROVE	-TEAMED	-TUNING	-VERSES	-WEAVES
-STRUCK	-TELLER	-TURFED	-VERSOS	-WEDDED
-STRUNG	-TEMPER	-TURNED	-VERTED	-WEIGHS
-STUFFS	-TESTED	-TURNER	-VESTED	-WELDED
-STUMPS	-THINKS	-TWISTS	-VESTRY	-WETTED
-STYLED	-THREAD	-TYPING	-VETTED	-WIDENS
-STYLES	-TIEING	-UNIONS	-VIEWED	-WINDED
-SUBMIT	-TILING	-UNITED	-VIEWER	-WINDER
-SUMMON	-TIMING	-UNITER	-VISING	-WIRING
-SUPINE	-TINTED	-UNITES	-VISION	-WORDED
-SUPPLY	-TIRING	-UPTAKE	-VISITS	-WORKED
-SURGED	-TITLED	-URGING	-VISORS	-WRITER
-SURGES	-TITLES	-USABLE	-VIVERS	-WRITES
-SURVEY	-TOOLED	-UTTERS	-VIVIFY	-ZEROED
-TABLES	-TOTALS	-VALUED	-VOICED	-ZEROES
-TACKED	-TOURED	-VALUES	-VOICES	-ZONING
-TACKLE	-TRACED	-VAMPED	-VOLUTE	
-TAGGED	-TRACER	-VAMPER	-VOLVED	
-TAILED	-TRACES	-VEALED	-VOLVES	
-TAILER	-TRACKS	-VEALER	-VOTING	

Words that begin with RED-

Seven-letter words

-ACTS	-CAPS	-FOOT	-RAFT	-SKIN
-ATES	-COAT	-HEAD	-RAWN	-TAIL
-BACK	-DENS	-LEGS	-RAWS	-TOPS
-BAIT	-DING	-LINE	-REAM	-WARE
-BAYS	-DISH	-NECK	-RILL	-WING
-BIRD	-EARS	-NESS	-RIVE	-WOOD
-BONE	-EYES	-OUTS	-ROOT	
-BUDS	-FINS	-OXES	-ROVE	
-BUGS	-FISH	-POLL	-SEAR	

Eight-letter words

-ACTED	-COATS	-OLENT	-ROOTS	-TAILS
-ACTOR	-DINGS	-ONNED	-SHANK	-WARES
-ARGUE	-FOOTS	-POLLS	-SHARE	-WATER
-BACKS	-HEADS	-RAFTS	-SHIFT	-WINGS
-BAITS	-HORSE	-RAWER	-SHIRE	-WOODS
-BELLY	-LINED	-REAMS	-SHIRT	
-BIRDS	-LINER	-RILLS	-SHORT	
-BONES	-LINES	-RIVEN	-SKINS	
-BRICK	-NECKS	-RIVES	-START	

Words that begin with SEA-

Seven-letter words

-BAGS	-FOWL	-LING	-SIDE	-WARE
-BANK	-GIRT	-MAID	-SING	-WAYS
-BEDS	-GULL	-MARK	-SONS	-WEED
-BIRD	-HAWK	-MING	-SURE	-WIFE
-BOOT	-HOGS	-PORT	-TING	-WORM
-COCK	-KALE	-RATS	-WALL	-ZING
-DOGS	-LANT	-REST	-WANS	
-FOLK	-LIFT	-RING	-WANT	
-FOOD	-LINE	-SICK	-WARD	

Eight-letter words

-BANKS	-FLOOR	-LIFTS	-ROBIN	-WANTS
-BEACH	-FOLKS	-LINES	-SCAPE	-WARDS
-BIRDS	-FOODS	-LINGS	-SCOUT	-WARES
-BLITE	-FOWLS	-MAIDS	-SHELL	-WATER
-BOARD	-FRONT	-MANLY	-SHORE	-WEEDS
-BOOTS	-GOING	-MARKS	-SIDES	-WIVES
-BORNE	-GULLS	-MOUNT	-SPEAK	-WOMAN
-COAST	-HAWKS	-PIECE	-SURES	-WOMEN
-COCKS	-HORSE	-PLANE	-TINGS	-WORMS
-CRAFT	-HOUND	-PORTS	-TRAIN	
-DROME	-KALES	-QUAKE	-TROUT	
-FARER	-LANTS	-RINGS	-WALLS	

Words that begin with SUB-

Seven-letter words

-ACID	-DEBS	-IDEA	-RENT	-TEND
-ACTS	-DEWS	-ITEM	-RING	-TEST
-ALAR	-DUAL	-JOIN	-RULE	-TEXT
-AQUA	-DUCE	-LATE	-SALE	-TILE
-AREA	-DUCT	-LETS	-SECT	-TONE
-ARID	-DUED	-LIME	-SERE	-TYPE
-ATOM	-DUES	-LINE	-SETS	-UNIT
-BASE	-ECHO	-LOTS	-SIDE	-URBS
-BASS	-EDIT	-MENU	-SIST	-VERT
-BING	-ERIC	-MISS	-SITE	-WAYS
-CELL	-FEUS	-NETS	-SOIL	-ZERO
-CLAN	-FILE	-ORAL	-SONG	-ZONE
-CODE	-FUSC	-OVAL	-TACK	
-COOL	-GOAL	-PART	-TASK	
-CULT	-GUMS	-PLOT	-TAXA	
-DEAN	-HEAD	-RACE	-TEEN	

Eight-letter words

-ABBOT	-AGENT	-AXIAL	-BLOCK	-CHIEF
-ACRID	-AREAS	-BASAL	-BREED	-CHORD
-ACTED	-ATOMS	-BASES	-CASTE	-CLAIM
-ACUTE	-AUDIO	-BASIN	-CAUSE	-CLANS
-ADULT	-AURAL	-BINGS	-CELLS	-CLASS

-CLERK	-FLOOR	-MERSE	-SHELL	-TITLE
-CODES	-FLUID	-NASAL	-SHRUB	-TONES
-COOLS	-FRAME	-NICHE	-SIDED	-TONIC
-COSTA	-GENRE	-NODAL	-SIDER	-TOPIC
-CRUST	-GENUS	-OCEAN	-SIDES	-TOTAL
-CULTS	-GOALS	-OPTIC	-SISTS	-TRACT
-CUTES	-GRADE	-ORDER	-SITES	-TREND
-CUTIS	-GRAPH	-OVATE	-SIZAR	-TRIBE
-DEANS	-GROUP	-OXIDE	-SKILL	-TRIST
-DEPOT	-HEADS	-PANEL	-SOILS	-TUNIC
-DEWED	-HUMAN	-PARTS	-SOLAR	-TYPES
-DUALS	-HUMID	-PHASE	-SONGS	-UNITS
-DUCES	-IDEAS	-PHYLA	-SONIC	-URBAN
-DUCTS	-IMAGO	-PLOTS	-SPACE	-URBIA
-DUING	-INDEX	-POLAR	-STAGE	-VERSE
-DUPLE	-ITEMS	-PRIOR	-STATE	-VERST
-DURAL	-JOINS	-PUBIC	-STYLE	-VERTS
-DWARF	-LATED	-RACES	-TACKS	-VICAR
-EDITS	-LEASE	-RENTS	-TASKS	-VIRAL
-ENTRY	-LEVEL	-RINGS	-TAXON	-VIRUS
-EPOCH	-LIMED	-RULES	-TEENS	-VOCAL
-EQUAL	-LIMES	-SALES	-TENDS	-WAYED
-ERECT	-LIMIT	-SCALE	-TENSE	-WORLD
-EROSE	-LINES	-SECTS	-TESTS	-ZONAL
-FEUED	-LUNAR	-SENSE	-TEXTS	-ZONES
-FIELD	-MENTA	-SERES	-THEME	
-FILES	-MENUS	-SERVE	-TIDAL	
-FIXES	-MERGE	-SHAFT	-TILER	

Words that begin with SUN-

Seven-letter words

-BACK	-BOWS	-DOWN	-LAND	-SETS
-BAKE	-BURN	-FAST	-LESS	-SPOT
-BATH	-DAES	-FISH	-LIKE	-STAR
-BEAM	-DARI	-GARS	-NIES	-SUIT
-BEAT	-DECK	-GLOW	-RAYS	-TANS
-BEDS	-DEWS	-HATS	-RISE	-TRAP
-BELT	-DIAL	-KETS	-ROOF	-WARD
-BIRD	-DOGS	-LAMP	-ROOM	-WISE

Eight-letter words

-BAKED	-BLIND	-DIALS	-LAMPS	-SHADE
-BAKES	-BLOCK	-DOWNS	-LANDS	-SHINE
-BATHE	-BURNS	-DRESS	-LIGHT	-SHINY
-BATHS	-BURNT	-DRIES	-PORCH	-SPOTS
-BEAMS	-BURST	-DRILY	-PROOF	-STARS
-BEAMY	-CHOKE	-DROPS	-RISES	-STONE
-BELTS	-DARIS	-GLASS	-ROOFS	-SUITS
-BERRY	-DECKS	-GLOWS	-ROOMS	-TRAPS
-BIRDS	-DERED	-GREBE	-SCALD	-WARDS

Words that begin with TRI-

Seven-letter words

-ABLE	-CEPS	-GAMY	-OXID	-SOME
-ACID	-CLAD	-GONS	-PACK	-SOMY
-AGED	-CORN	-GRAM	-PART	-TEST
-AGES	-COTS	-JETS	-PIER	-TIDE
-ARCH	-DARN	-LITH	-PLED	-TONE
-AXON	-DENT	-LOBE	-PLEX	-TONS
-BADE	-DUAN	-LOGY	-PODS	-UMPH
-BALS	-ENES	-NARY	-PSIS	-VETS
-BLET	-FLED	-ODES	-SECT	-VIAL
-BUTE	-FOLD	-ONES	-SEME	-ZONE
-CARS	-FORM	-OSES	-SHAW	

Eight-letter words

-ACIDS	-CHINA	-GRAPH	-PEDAL	-STICH
-AGING	-CHORD	-LEMMA	-PHASE	-THING
-ALIST	-CLADS	-LITHS	-PHONE	-TICAL
-ANGLE	-COLOR	-LOBED	-PLANE	-TIDES
-AXIAL	-CORNS	-LOBES	-PLIED	-TONES
-AXONS	-CYCLE	-METER	-PLIES	-UNITY
-AZINE	-DARNS	-MORPH	-PLING	-VALVE
-AZOLE	-DENTS	-MOTOR	-POLIS	-ZONAL
-BALLY	-ETHYL	-NODAL	-POSES	-ZONES
-BASIC	-FLING	-OLEIN	-SECTS	
-BLETS	-FOCAL	-OXIDE	-SEMES	
-BRACH	-GLYPH	-OXIDS	-SHAWS	
-BUTES	-GRAMS	-PACKS	-STATE	

Words that begin with UN-

Seven-letter words

-ACTED	-BARES	-BOOTS	-CARTS	-CLOAK
-ADDED	-BARKS	-BORNE	-CASED	-CLOGS
-ADEPT	-BASED	-BOSOM	-CASES	-CLOSE
-ADULT	-BATED	-BOUND	-CEDED	-CLOUD
-AGILE	-BEARS	-BOWED	-CHAIN	-COCKS
-AGING	-BEGET	-BOXED	-CHAIR	-CODED
-AIDED	-BEGOT	-BOXES	-CHARM	-COILS
-AIMED	-BEGUN	-BRACE	-CHARY	-COLTS
-AIRED	-BEING	-BRAID	-CHECK	-COMIC
-AKING	-BELTS	-BRAKE	-CHILD	-COPED
-ALIKE	-BENDS	-BROKE	-CHOKE	-COPES
-ALIST	-BINDS	-BUILD	-CITED	-CORDS
-ALIVE	-BITTS	-BUILT	-CIVIL	-CORKS
-APTLY	-BLENT	-BULKY	-CLAMP	-COUTH
-ARMED	-BLESS	-BURNT	-CLASP	-COVER
-ASKED	-BLEST	-CAGED	-CLEAN	-COWLS
-AWAKE	-BLIND	-CAGES	-CLEAR	-CRATE
-AWARE	-BLOCK	-CAKED	-CLEFT	-CRAZY
-BAKED	-BLOWN	-CAKES	-CLEWS	-CROSS
-BALED	-BOLTS	-CANNY	-CLING	-CROWN
-BALES	-BONED	-CAPED	-CLIPS	-CUFFS
-BARED	-BONES	-CAPES	-CLIPT	-CURBS

-CURED	-GATED	-LADES	-PAGED	-SAWED
-CURLS	-GEARS	-LATCH	-PAINT	-SCALE
-CURSE	-GILDS	-LAWED	-PANEL	-SCARY
-DATED	-GIRDS	-LEADS	-PAPER	-SCREW
-DEALT	-GIRTH	-LEARN	-PARED	-SEALS
-DECKS	-GLOVE	-LEASH	-PAVED	-SEAMS
-DEIFY	-GLUED	-LEVEL	-PERCH	-SEATS
-DERNS	-GLUES	-LIKED	-PICKS	-SEELS
-DIGHT	-GODLY	-LIKES	-PILED	-SELFS
-DINES	-GORED	-LIMED	-PILES	-SELLS
-DOCKS	-GOWNS	-LIMES	-PLACE	-SENSE
-DOERS	-GROWN	-LINED	-PLAIT	-SEWED
-DOING	-GUARD	-LINES	-PLUGS	-SEXED
-DRAPE	-GULAR	-LINKS	-PLUMB	-SEXES
-DRAWN	-GYVED	-LIVED	-PLUME	-SHALE
-DRAWS	-GYVES	-LIVES	-POPES	-SHAPE
-DRESS	-HABLE	-LOADS	-POSED	-SHARP
-DREST	-HAIRS	-LOBED	-PRAYS	-SHELL
-DRIED	-HANDS	-LOCKS	-PROPS	-SHENT
-DRUNK	-HANDY	-LOOSE	-PURSE	-SHEWN
-DYING	-HANGS	-LORDS	-QUEEN	-SHIFT
-EAGER	-HAPPY	-LOVED	-QUIET	-SHIPS
-EARED	-HARDY	-LOVES	-QUOTE	-SHOED
-EARTH	-HASPS	-LUCKY	-RACED	-SHOES
-EASES	-HASTY	-MACHO	-RAKED	-SHOOT
-EATEN	-HEADS	-MAKER	-RAKES	-SHORN
-EDGED	-HEALS	-MAKES	-RATED	-SHOUT
-EDGES	-HEARD	-MANLY	-RAVEL	-SHOWN
-ENDED	-HEART	-MARRY	-RAZED	-SHOWY
-EQUAL	-HEEDY	-MASKS	-READY	-SHUTS
-FACTS	-HELED	-MATED	-REAVE	-SIGHT
-FADED	-HELES	-MEANT	-REELS	-SINEW
-FAIRS	-HELMS	-MERRY	-REEVE	-SIZED
-FAITH	-HINGE	-METED	-REINS	-SLAIN
-FAKED	-HIRED	-MEWED	-RESTS	-SLICK
-FAMED	-HITCH	-MINED	-RIGHT	-SLING
-FANCY	-HIVED	-MITER	-RIMED	-SLUNG
-FAZED	-HIVES	-MITRE	-RIPER	-SMART
-FENCE	-HOARD	-MIXED	-RISEN	-SMOTE
-FEUED	-HOODS	-MIXES	-RIVEN	-SNAGS
-FILED	-HOOKS	-MOLDS	-RIVET	-SNAPS
-FIRED	-HOOPS	-MOORS	-ROBED	-SNARL
-FITLY	-HOPED	-MORAL	-ROBES	-SNECK
-FIXED	-HORSE	-MOULD	-ROLLS	-SOBER
-FIXES	-HOUSE	-MOUNT	-ROOFS	-SOLID
-FLESH	-HUMAN	-MOVED	-ROOST	-SONSY
-FLUSH	-HUSKS	-NAILS	-ROOTS	-SOOTE
-FOLDS	-IDEAL	-NAMED	-ROPED	-SOULS
-FOOLS	-JADED	-NEATH	-ROPES	-SOUND
-FORMS	-JOINT	-NERVE	-ROUGH	-SOWED
-FOUND	-KEMPT	-NESTS	-ROUND	-SPARS
-FREED	-KINGS	-NOBLE	-ROVEN	-SPEAK
-FREES	-KINKS	-NOISY	-ROYAL	-SPELL
-FROCK	-KNITS	-NOTED	-RUFFE	-SPENT
-FROZE	-KNOTS	-OFTEN	-RULED	-SPIDE
-FUMED	-KNOWN	-OILED	-RULES	-SPIED
-FUNNY	-LACED	-ORDER	-SAFER	-SPILT
-FURLS	-LACES	-OWNED	-SAINT	-SPLIT
-FUSED	-LADED	-PACED	-SATED	-SPOKE
-FUSSY	-LADEN	-PACKS	-SAVED	-SPOOL

-STACK	-SWORN	-TREAD	-VEXED	-WISER
-STAID	-TACKS	-TRIDE	-VISOR	-WITCH
-STATE	-TAKEN	-TRIED	-VITAL	-WITTY
-STEEL	-TAMED	-TRIMS	-VOCAL	-WIVED
-STEPS	-TAMES	-TRUER	-VOICE	-WIVES
-STICK	-TAXED	-TRULY	-WAGED	-WOMAN
-STOCK	-TAXES	-TRUSS	-WAKED	-WOOED
-STOPS	-TEACH	-TRUST	-WARES	-WORKS
-STOWS	-TEAMS	-TRUTH	-WATER	-WORTH
-STRAP	-TENTS	-TUCKS	-WAXED	-WOUND
-STRIP	-TENTY	-TUNED	-WAYED	-WOVEN
-STUCK	-THAWS	-TUNES	-WEALS	-WRAPS
-STUNG	-THINK	-TURFS	-WEARY	-WRITE
-SUITS	-TILED	-TURNS	-WEAVE	-WROTE
-SUNNY	-TILES	-TWINE	-WHIPT	-WRUNG
-SURED	-TIMED	-TWIST	-WHITE	-YOKED
-SURER	-TIRED	-TYING	-WILLS	-YOKES
-SWEAR	-TOMBS	-URGED	-WINDS	-YOUNG
-SWEET	-TONED	-USUAL	-WIPED	-ZONED
-SWEPT	-TRACE	-VAILS	-WIRED	
-SWORE	-TRACK	-VEILS	-WIRES	

Eight-letter words

-ABATED	-BEATEN	-BOUGHT	-CASING	-COATED
-ABUSED	-BEDDED	-BOUNCY	-CASKED	-COCKED
-ACHING	-BEGETS	-BOWING	-CATCHY	-COFFIN
-ACIDIC	-BEGGED	-BOXING	-CAUGHT	-COILED
-ACTIVE	-BEINGS	-BRACED	-CAUSED	-COINED
-ADORED	-BELIEF	-BRACES	-CHAINS	-COLTED
-AFRAID	-BELTED	-BRAIDS	-CHAIRS	-COMBED
-AGEING	-BENDED	-BRAKED	-CHANCY	-COMELY
-AGREED	-BENIGN	-BRAKES	-CHARGE	-COMMON
-ALLIED	-BEREFT	-BREECH	-CHARMS	-COOKED
-AMAZED	-BESEEM	-BRIDLE	-CHASTE	-COOLED
-AMUSED	-BIASED	-BRIGHT	-CHECKS	-COPING
-ANCHOR	-BIASES	-BROKEN	-CHEWED	-CORDED
-ANELED	-BIDDEN	-BUCKLE	-CHICLY	-CORKED
-ARCHED	-BILLED	-BUDDED	-CHILDS	-COSTLY
-ARGUED	-BISHOP	-BUILDS	-CHOKED	-COUPLE
-ARISEN	-BITTED	-BUNDLE	-CHOKES	-COVERS
-ARMING	-BITTEN	-BURDEN	-CHOSEN	-COWLED
-ARTFUL	-BITTER	-BURIED	-CHURCH	-CRATED
-ATONED	-BLAMED	-BURIES	-CIPHER	-CRATES
-AVOWED	-BLINDS	-BURNED	-CLAMPS	-CREATE
-AWAKED	-BLOCKS	-BURROW	-CLASPS	-CREWED
-BACKED	-BLOODY	-BUSTED	-CLASSY	-CROWNS
-BAGGED	-BLOWED	-BUTTON	-CLAWED	-CUFFED
-BAITED	-BOBBED	-CAGING	-CLENCH	-CULLED
-BALING	-BODIED	-CAKING	-CLEWED	-CURBED
-BANDED	-BODING	-CALLED	-CLINCH	-CURLED
-BANKED	-BOILED	-CANDID	-CLOAKS	-CURSED
-BANNED	-BOLTED	-CANNED	-CLOSED	-CURSES
-BARBED	-BONDED	-CAPING	-CLOSES	-CURVED
-BARING	-BONING	-CAPPED	-CLOTHE	-DAMMED
-BARKED	-BONNET	-CARDED	-CLOUDS	-DAMNED
-BARRED	-BOOKED	-CARDING	-CLOUDY	-DAMPED
-BASTED	-BOOTED	-CARTED	-CLOVEN	-DARING
-BATHED	-BOSOMS	-CARVED	-CLOYED	-DASHED
-BEARED	-BOTTLE	-CASHED	-CLUTCH	-DAZZLE

-DECENT	-FELLED	-GORGED	-IONIZE	-LORDLY
-DECKED	-FELTED	-GOTTEN	-IRONED	-LOVELY
-DEEDED	-FENCED	-GOWNED	-IRONIC	-LOVING
-DEFIED	-FENCES	-GRACED	-ISSUED	-MAILED
-DENIED	-FETTER	-GRADED	-JAMMED	-MAIMED
-DENTED	-FEUDAL	-GRAZED	-JOINED	-MAKERS
-DERATE	-FILIAL	-GREEDY	-JOINTS	-MAKING
-DESERT	-FILLED	-GROUND	-JOYFUL	-MANFUL
-DEVOUT	-FILMED	-GUARDS	-JOYOUS	-MANNED
-DIGHTS	-FISHED	-GUIDED	-JUDGED	-MANTLE
-DIMMED	-FITTED	-GUILTY	-JUSTER	-MAPPED
-DINTED	-FITTER	-GUMMED	-JUSTLY	-MARKED
-DIPPED	-FIXING	-GYVING	-KEELED	-MARRED
-DIVINE	-FIXITY	-HACKED	-KENNED	-MASKED
-DOABLE	-FLASHY	-HAILED	-KENNEL	-MASKER
-DOCILE	-FLAWED	-HAIRED	-KINDER	-MATTED
-DOCKED	-FLEXED	-HALLOW	-KINDLY	-MEETLY
-DOINGS	-FLUTED	-HALSED	-KINGED	-MELLOW
-DOOMED	-FOILED	-HALVED	-KINGLY	-MELTED
-DOTTED	-FOLDED	-HANDED	-KINKED	-MENDED
-DOUBLE	-FOLDER	-HANGED	-KISSED	-MESHED
-DRAPED	-FOOLED	-HARMED	-KISSES	-MESHES
-DRAPES	-FOOTED	-HASPED	-KNIGHT	-MEWING
-DREAMT	-FORBID	-HATTED	-KNOWNS	-MILKED
-DRIVEN	-FORCED	-HEADED	-KOSHER	-MILLED
-DROSSY	-FORGED	-HEALED	-LACING	-MINDED
-DUBBED	-FORGOT	-HEALTH	-LADING	-MINGLE
-DULLED	-FORKED	-HEARSE	-LASHED	-MISSED
-EARNED	-FORMAL	-HEARTS	-LASHES	-MITERS
-EARTHS	-FORMED	-HEATED	-LAWFUL	-MITRED
-EASIER	-FOUGHT	-HEDGED	-LAWING	-MITRES
-EASILY	-FRAMED	-HEEDED	-LAYING	-MIXING
-EDGING	-FREEZE	-HELING	-LEADED	-MOANED
-EDIBLE	-FRIEND	-HELMED	-LEARNS	-MODISH
-EDITED	-FROCKS	-HELPED	-LEARNT	-MOLDED
-ELATED	-FROZEN	-HEROIC	-LEASED	-MOLTEN
-ENDING	-FUNDED	-HIDDEN	-LETHAL	-MONIED
-ENVIED	-FURLED	-HINGED	-LETTED	-MOORED
-EQUALS	-FURRED	-HINGES	-LEVELS	-MOULDS
-ERASED	-GAGGED	-HIPPER	-LEVIED	-MOUNTS
-EROTIC	-GAINLY	-HIVING	-LICKED	-MOVING
-ERRING	-GALLED	-HOARDS	-LIDDED	-MUFFLE
-ESPIED	-GARBED	-HOLIER	-LIKELY	-MUZZLE
-EVADED	-GAUGED	-HOLILY	-LIMBER	-NAILED
-EVENER	-GAZING	-HOLPEN	-LIMING	-NATIVE
-EVENLY	-GEARED	-HOMELY	-LINEAL	-NEEDED
-EXOTIC	-GELDED	-HONEST	-LINING	-NERVED
-EXPERT	-GENIAL	-HOODED	-LINKED	-NERVES
-FABLED	-GENTLE	-HOOKED	-LISTED	-NESTED
-FADING	-GENTLY	-HOOPED	-LIVELY	-NETTED
-FAIRED	-GIFTED	-HORSED	-LIVING	-NOBLES
-FAIRER	-GILDED	-HORSES	-LOADED	-OBEYED
-FAIRLY	-GIRDED	-HOUSED	-LOADER	-OPENED
-FAITHS	-GIRTHS	-HOUSES	-LOCKED	-ORDERS
-FALLEN	-GIVING	-HUNTED	-LOOKED	-ORNATE
-FAMOUS	-GLAZED	-HUSKED	-LOOSED	-PACKED
-FANNED	-GLOVED	-IDEAED	-LOOSEN	-PACKER
-FASTEN	-GLOVES	-IMBUED	-LOOSES	-PADDED
-FAULTY	-GLUING	-INURED	-LOPPED	-PAINED
-FEARED	-GODDED	-IONISE	-LORDED	-PAINTS

-PAIRED	-QUOTES	-SASHED	-SMOKED	-TACKED
-PANELS	-RACKED	-SATING	-SMOOTH	-TACKLE
-PANGED	-RAISED	-SAVORY	-SNARLS	-TAGGED
-PAPERS	-RAKING	-SAYING	-SNECKS	-TAILED
-PARTED	-RANKED	-SCALED	-SOAKED	-TAMING
-PATHED	-RAVELS	-SCALES	-SOAPED	-TANGLE
-PAYING	-REALLY	-SCREWS	-SOCIAL	-TANNED
-PEELED	-REAPED	-SEALED	-SOCKET	-TAPPED
-PEERED	-REASON	-SEAMED	-SODDEN	-TARRED
-PEGGED	-REAVED	-SEARED	-SOILED	-TASTED
-PENNED	-REAVES	-SEASON	-SOLDER	-TAUGHT
-PEOPLE	-RECKED	-SEATED	-SOLEMN	-TAXING
-PERSON	-SECRET	-SECRET	-SOLVED	-TEAMED
-PICKED	-REELED	-SEEDED	-SONSIE	-TEMPER
-PILING	-REELER	-SEEING	-SORTED	-TENANT
-PINKED	-REEVED	-SEELED	-SOUGHT	-TENDED
-PINNED	-REEVES	-SEELIE	-SOULED	-TENDER
-PITIED	-REINED	-SEEMLY	-SOURED	-TENTED
-PITTED	-RENTED	-SEIZED	-SPARED	-TESTED
-PLACED	-REPAID	-SELDOM	-SPEAKS	-TETHER
-PLACES	-REPAIR	-SELFED	-SPELLS	-THATCH
-PLAITS	-RESTED	-SELVES	-SPHERE	-THAWED
-PLAYED	-RETIRE	-SENSED	-SPOILT	-THINKS
-PLIANT	-RHYMED	-SENSES	-SPOKEN	-THREAD
-PLOWED	-RIBBED	-SERVED	-SPOOLS	-THRIFT
-PLUMBS	-RIDDEN	-SETTLE	-SPRUNG	-THRONE
-PLUMED	-RIDDLE	-SEWING	-STABLE	-TIDIED
-PLUMES	-RIFLED	-SEXING	-STABLY	-TIDIER
-POETIC	-RIGGED	-SEXIST	-STACKS	-TIDIES
-POISED	-RIGHTS	-SEXUAL	-STARCH	-TIDILY
-POISON	-RINGED	-SHADED	-STARRY	-TIEING
-POLISH	-RINSED	-SHADOW	-STATED	-TILING
-POLITE	-RIPELY	-SHAKED	-STATES	-TILLED
-POLLED	-RIPEST	-SHAKEN	-STAYED	-TILTED
-POSTED	-RIPPED	-SHALED	-STEADY	-TIMELY
-POTTED	-RIVETS	-SHALES	-STEELS	-TINGED
-PRAISE	-ROBING	-SHAMED	-STICKS	-TINNED
-PRAYED	-ROLLED	-SHAPED	-STITCH	-TIPPED
-PREACH	-ROOFED	-SHAPEN	-STOCKS	-TIRING
-PRETTY	-ROOSTS	-SHAPES	-STONED	-TITLED
-PRICED	-ROOTED	-SHARED	-STOWED	-TOMBED
-PRIEST	-ROPING	-SHAVED	-STRAPS	-TOWARD
-PRIMED	-ROTTED	-SHAVEN	-STRESS	-TRACED
-PRISON	-ROTTEN	-SHELLS	-STRING	-TRACES
-PRIZED	-ROUGED	-SHIFTS	-STRIPS	-TRACKS
-PROBED	-ROUNDS	-SHOOTS	-STRUCK	-TRADED
-PROPER	-ROUSED	-SHOUTS	-STRUNG	-TREADS
-PROVED	-RUBBED	-SHROUD	-STUFFY	-TRENDY
-PROVEN	-RUFFLE	-SHRUNK	-SUBTLE	-TRUEST
-PRUNED	-RULIER	-SICKER	-SUBTLY	-TRUISM
-PUCKER	-RUSHED	-SIFTED	-SUCKED	-TRUSTS
-PULLED	-RUSTED	-SIGHTS	-SUITED	-TRUSTY
-PURELY	-SADDLE	-SIGNED	-SUMMED	-TRUTHS
-PURGED	-SAFELY	-SILENT	-SUNNED	-TUCKED
-PURSED	-SAFEST	-SINEWS	-SUPPLE	-TUFTED
-PURSES	-SAFETY	-SINFUL	-SURELY	-TUNING
-PUZZLE	-SAILED	-SLAKED	-SUREST	-TURBID
-QUEENS	-SAINED	-SLICED	-SWATHE	-TURFED
-QUIETS	-SAINTS	-SLINGS	-SWAYED	-TURNED
-QUOTED	-SALTED	-SLUICE	-SWEARS	-TWINED

-TWINES	-VETTED	-WARMED	-WEIGHT	-WISHES
-TWISTS	-VIABLE	-WARNED	-WELDED	-WITTED
-UNITED	-VIEWED	-WARPED	-WETTED	-WIVING
-USABLE	-VIRTUE	-WASHED	-WIELDY	-WOMANS
-USABLY	-VISORS	-WASHEN	-WIFELY	-WONTED
-USEFUL	-VIZARD	-WASTED	-WIGGED	-WOODED
-VAILED	-VOICED	-WATERS	-WILFUL	-WORDED
-VALUED	-VOICES	-WATERY	-WILLED	-WORKED
-VARIED	-VULGAR	-WEANED	-WINDER	-WORMED
-VEILED	-WALLED	-WEAPON	-WINGED	-WORTHS
-VEILER	-WANING	-WEAVES	-WIRING	-WORTHY
-VEINED	-WANTED	-WEBBED	-WISDOM	-WRITES
-VENTED	-WARDED	-WEDDED	-WISELY	-YEANED
-VERSED	-WARIER	-WEEDED	-WISEST	-YOKING
-VESTED	-WARILY	-WEENED	-WISHED	-ZIPPED

Words that begin with UP-

Seven-letter words

-BEARS	-DIVED	-HOORD	-RIVER	-SWEEP
-BEATS	-DIVES	-HURLS	-ROARS	-SWELL
-BINDS	-DRAFT	-KEEPS	-ROLLS	-SWEPT
-BLOWN	-DRAGS	-KNITS	-ROOTS	-SWING
-BLOWS	-DRAWN	-LANDS	-ROUSE	-SWUNG
-BOILS	-DRAWS	-LEADS	-SCALE	-TAKEN
-BORNE	-DRIED	-LEANS	-SENDS	-TAKES
-BOUND	-DRIES	-LEANT	-SHIFT	-TALKS
-BRAID	-ENDED	-LEAPS	-SHOOT	-TEARS
-BRAST	-FIELD	-LEAPT	-SHOTS	-TEMPO
-BRAYS	-FILLS	-LIFTS	-SIDES	-THREW
-BREAK	-FLING	-LIGHT	-SIZED	-THROW
-BRING	-FLOWS	-LINKS	-SIZES	-TICKS
-BROKE	-FLUNG	-LOADS	-SKILL	-TIGHT
-BUILD	-FOLDS	-LOCKS	-SLOPE	-TILTS
-BUILT	-FRONT	-LOOKS	-SOARS	-TIMES
-BURST	-FURLS	-LYING	-SPAKE	-TOWNS
-CASTS	-GANGS	-MAKER	-SPEAK	-TRAIN
-CATCH	-GAZED	-MAKES	-SPEAR	-TREND
-CHEER	-GAZES	-PILED	-SPOKE	-TURNS
-CHUCK	-GIRDS	-PILES	-STAGE	-TYING
-CLIMB	-GOING	-PINGS	-STAIR	-VALUE
-CLOSE	-GRADE	-PROPS	-STAND	-WAFTS
-COAST	-GROWN	-RAISE	-STARE	-WARDS
-COILS	-GROWS	-RATED	-START	-WELLS
-COMES	-HANGS	-RATES	-STATE	-WHIRL
-COURT	-HAUDS	-REACH	-STAYS	-WINDS
-CURLS	-HEAPS	-REARS	-STEPS	-WOUND
-CURVE	-HEAVE	-RESTS	-STIRS	-WRAPS
-DARTS	-HILLS	-RIGHT	-STOOD	
-DATED	-HOARD	-RISEN	-SURGE	
-DATER	-HOIST	-RISER	-SWARM	
-DATES	-HOLDS	-RISES	-SWAYS	

Eight-letter words

-BEARER	-BRAIDS	-BREAKS	-BROKEN	-BURSTS
-BOILED	-BRAYED	-BRINGS	-BUILDS	-CAUGHT

-CHEERS	-GOINGS	-LOADED	-SETTER	-SURGES
-CHUCKS	-GRADED	-LOCKED	-SHIFTS	-SWARMS
-CLIMBS	-GRADER	-LOOKED	-SHOOTS	-SWAYED
-CLOSED	-GRADES	-MAKERS	-SIZING	-SWEEPS
-CLOSES	-GROWTH	-MAKING	-SKILLS	-SWELLS
-COILED	-GUSHED	-MARKET	-SOARED	-SWINGS
-COMING	-GUSHES	-PILING	-SPEAKS	-TAKING
-CURLED	-HEAPED	-RAISED	-SPEARS	-TALKED
-CURVED	-HEAVED	-RAISER	-SPOKEN	-TEMPOS
-CURVES	-HEAVER	-RAISES	-SPRANG	-THROWN
-DARTED	-HEAVES	-RATING	-SPRING	-THROWS
-DATERS	-HOARDS	-REARED	-SPRUNG	-THRUST
-DATING	-HOISTS	-RIGHTS	-STAGED	-TILTED
-DIVING	-HOLDER	-RISERS	-STAGER	-TOSSED
-DRAFTS	-HOORDS	-RISING	-STAGES	-TOSSES
-DRYING	-HUDDEN	-RIVERS	-STAIRS	-TRAINS
-ENDING	-HURLED	-ROARED	-STANDS	-TRENDS
-FILLED	-JETTED	-ROLLED	-STARED	-TURNED
-FLINGS	-LANDER	-ROOTED	-STARES	-VALUED
-FLOWED	-LAYING	-ROOTER	-STARTS	-VALUES
-FOLDED	-LEANED	-ROUSED	-STATER	-WAFTED
-FOLLOW	-LEAPED	-ROUSES	-STATES	-WELLED
-FURLED	-LIFTED	-RUSHED	-STAYED	-WHIRLS
-GATHER	-LIFTER	-RUSHES	-STREAM	
-GAZING	-LIGHTS	-SCALED	-STROKE	
-GIRDED	-LINKED	-SCALES	-SURGED	

Words that begin with WAR-

Seven-letter words

-BIER	-HEAD	-MING	-RENS	-WOLF
-BLED	-KING	-PAGE	-RING	-WORK
-DENS	-LESS	-PATH	-SAWS	-WORN
-DING	-LIKE	-PING	-SHIP	-ZONE
-DOGS	-LING	-RAND	-SLED	
-DROP	-LOCK	-RANT	-TIER	
-FARE	-LORD	-RAYS	-TIME	

Eight-letter words

-BLING	-FARER	-LORDS	-PLANE	-TIMES
-CRAFT	-FARES	-MAKER	-POWER	-TWEED
-DERED	-HABLE	-MINGS	-RANDS	-WORKS
-DINGS	-HEADS	-MOUTH	-RANTS	-ZONES
-DRESS	-HORSE	-PAGES	-RAYED	
-DROPS	-LINGS	-PATHS	-SHIPS	
-FARED	-LOCKS	-PINGS	-SLING	

Suffixes

Suffixes are just as useful as prefixes, but it can be less easy to spot opportunities to employ them. Therefore, it's a good idea to study the lists of the most commonly available suffixes to ensure that you keep your end-hooking options open.

This list is also useful for remembering which adjective stems also form adverbs, as a glance at the –LY list demonstrates.

As with the prefixes list, words which end in the suffix letters by coincidence rather than etymology are included, as they are useful in exactly the same way, and may be less obvious.

It's well worth learning one of the shorter lists, the –EAUX endings, as these are an excellent way of using X and of clearing a vowel-heavy rack.

Words that end with -ABLE

Seven-letter words

ACC-	DYE-	LIK-	POK-	TAM-
ACT-	EAT-	LIN-	POS-	TAX-
ADD-	EFF-	LIV-	POT-	TEN-
AFF-	EQU-	LOS-	RAT-	TOT-
AMI-	ERR-	LOV-	RET-	TOW-
AST-	EYE-	MAK-	RID-	TRI-
BAT-	FAD-	MIN-	ROP-	TUN-
BIT-	FIN-	MIR-	ROW-	TYP-
BUY-	FIX-	MIX-	RUL-	UNH-
CAP-	FLY-	MOV-	SAL-	USE-
CIT-	FRI-	MUT-	SAV-	VAT-
COD-	FRY-	NAM-	SAY-	VOC-
CUR-	GEL-	NOT-	SEE-	VOL-
DAT-	GET-	OWN-	SEW-	VOT-
DIS-	GIV-	PAC-	SIZ-	WAD-
DOW-	HAT-	PAP-	SKI-	WAX-
DRY-	HEW-	PAR-	SOW-	WIR-
DUP-	HID-	PAY-	SUE-	
DUR-	HIR-	PLI-	TAK-	

Eight-letter words

ABAT-	BIST-	COIN-	EVAD-	FORM-
ABUS-	BITE-	COOK-	EVIT-	FRAM-
ADOR-	BLAM-	COPY-	EVOC-	FUND-
AGIT-	BOAT-	CULP-	EXIL-	FURL-
ALLI-	BOIL-	CURB-	EXOR-	GAGE-
AMEN-	BOMB-	CUTT-	EXPI-	GAIN-
AMIC-	BOND-	DAMN-	FACE-	GETT-
AMUS-	BOOK-	DATE-	FARM-	GIFT-
ARGU-	BOOT-	DENI-	FEED-	GIVE-
ATON-	BRIB-	DIGG-	FELL-	GNAW-
AVOW-	BUFF-	DIMM-	FILE-	GRAD-
BAIL-	BURN-	DIPP-	FILL-	GRAZ-
BANK-	CALL-	DISH-	FILM-	GROW-
BANN-	CART-	DRAP-	FIND-	GUID-
BARR-	CASC-	DRAW-	FINE-	GULL-
BEAR-	CASH-	DRIV-	FIRE-	GUST-
BEAT-	CAST-	DUTI-	FISH-	HACK-
BEDD-	CAUS-	EDIT-	FITT-	HANG-
BEND-	CHEW-	EDUC-	FOAM-	HATE-
BIDD-	CITE-	ENVI-	FOIL-	HEAL-
BILL-	CLOS-	ERAS-	FOLD-	HEAR-
BIND-	CLUB-	EROD-	FORD-	HEAT-

HELP-	MAKE-	POSE-	SHAK-	TILL-
HIRE-	MAPP-	POUR-	SHAM-	TILT-
HITT-	MASK-	PRIZ-	SHAP-	TIPP-
HOLD-	MELT-	PROB-	SHAR-	TITH-
HUGG-	MEND-	PROV-	SHAV-	TITR-
HUMM-	MILL-	PRUN-	SHED-	TOLL-
HUNT-	MINE-	QUOT-	SHOW-	TOTE-
IMIT-	MISS-	RADI-	SIGN-	TRAD-
INAR-	MOCK-	RAIS-	SING-	TUBB-
INST-	MOLD-	RATE-	SINK-	TUNE-
INVI-	MOOT-	READ-	SIZE-	TURN-
ISOL-	MOVE-	REAP-	SLAK-	TYPE-
ISSU-	NAME-	REEF-	SLAY-	UNDO-
JAIL-	NEST-	REEL-	SLID-	UNST-
JAMM-	NETT-	RELI-	SMOK-	UNUS-
JOIN-	OATH-	RENT-	SOCI-	UNVI-
JUMP-	OBEY-	REST-	SOLV-	VALU-
KEEP-	OBVI-	REUS-	SORB-	VARI-
KICK-	OPEN-	RIDE-	SORT-	VEND-
KILL-	OPER-	RINS-	SPAR-	VIEW-
KISS-	OPIN-	RIPP-	STAT-	VIOL-
KNOW-	OUTF-	ROCK-	STEW-	VITI-
LAPS-	OVEN-	ROLL-	STON-	VOID-
LAUD-	OVER-	ROPE-	STOR-	VOTE-
LEAS-	OXID-	RUIN-	STOW-	WADE-
LEND-	PACK-	RUNN-	SUIT-	WALK-
LETT-	PALP-	RUST-	SUMM-	WARH-
LEVI-	PANT-	SACK-	SURF-	WASH-
LIEN-	PARS-	SAIL-	SWAY-	WAST-
LIFT-	PASS-	SALE-	SYLL-	WEAR-
LIKE-	PAWN-	SALV-	TAKE-	WELD-
LINE-	PECC-	SAND-	TALK-	WETT-
LINK-	PEEL-	SATI-	TAME-	WILL-
LIQU-	PETT-	SAVE-	TANN-	WIND-
LIST-	PICK-	SCAL-	TAPE-	WINN-
LIVE-	PINT-	SEAL-	TAPP-	WORK-
LOAN-	PITI-	SEIS-	TAST-	WRIT-
LOCK-	PLAC-	SEIZ-	TEAR-	
LOVE-	PLAY-	SELL-	TEAS-	
LUGG-	PLOW-	SEND-	TELL-	
MAIL-	PORT-	SERV-	TEST-	

Words that end with -AGE

Seven-letter words

ABUS-	BEER-	CENT-	DISC-	FOOT-
ACRE-	BOND-	COIN-	DOCK-	FROM-
AJUT-	BOSC-	COLL-	DRAY-	FULL-
AMEN-	BOSK-	COMP-	DUNN-	GARB-
APAN-	BREW-	CORD-	ECOT-	GUID-
ARRI-	BROC-	CORK-	ESCU-	GUNN-
ASSU-	BROK-	CORN-	ETAL-	HAUL-
ASSW-	BULK-	CORS-	FALD-	HAYL-
AULN-	BUOY-	COTT-	FARD-	HEAD-
AVER-	BURG-	COUR-	FLOT-	HERB-
BAGG-	CABB-	COWH-	FLOW-	HIRE-
BAND-	CARN-	CRAN-	FOGG-	HOST-
BARR-	CART-	CUTT-	FOLI-	KEEL-

KIPP-	OUTR-	PROP-	SOCC-	VEND-
LAIR-	OUVR-	QUAY-	SOIL-	VENT-
LAST-	OVER-	RAMP-	SOND-	VIDU-
LEAF-	PACK-	REIM-	SPIN-	VILL-
LEAK-	PANN-	REMU-	STOR-	VINT-
LIGN-	PASS-	REST-	STOW-	VITR-
LINE-	PAWN-	RIBC-	SULL-	VOLT-
LINK-	PAYS-	RIFF-	TALL-	VORL-
LOCK-	PEER-	ROOT-	TANK-	WAFT-
LUGG-	PEON-	RUMM-	TANN-	WAIN-
MASS-	PIER-	SACK-	TEEN-	WANT-
MELT-	PILL-	SALV-	TENT-	WARP-
MESS-	PIPE-	SAUS-	THAN-	WAST-
MILE-	PLUM-	SCAL-	THEN-	WATT-
MILL-	PLUS-	SCAV-	TILL-	WEBP-
MINT-	POND-	SCUT-	TOLL-	WEFT-
MISP-	PONT-	SEEP-	TONN-	WIND-
MOCK-	PORT-	SELV-	TRUC-	WORD-
MONT-	POST-	SEPT-	TUNN-	YARD-
MOOR-	POTT-	SERF-	UMBR-	
MOUL-	PRES-	SIGN-	UNIT-	
NONW-	PRIM-	SINK-	UPST-	
ONST-	PRIS-	SOAK-	VANT-	

Eight-letter words

ACCOR-	COMAN-	GRAMM-	PLANT-	STOPP-
ACIER-	COVER-	GRILL-	PLOTT-	STRAV-
ADJUT-	COZEN-	GROUP-	PLUSS-	STREW-
AGIOT-	CREEP-	GUARD-	POUND-	STUMP-
ALIEN-	CRIBB-	HELOT-	PROPH-	SUBST-
ALTAR-	DIALL-	HERIT-	PUCEL-	SUFFR-
AMPER-	DISUS-	HOMEP-	PUPIL-	TASSW-
APPAN-	DRAIN-	INTER-	REDAM-	THIRL-
BADIN-	DRESS-	LANGR-	REENG-	TRACK-
BARON-	DRIFT-	LANGU-	ROUGH-	TRUCK-
BERTH-	ENALL-	LAYER-	SABOT-	TRUQU-
BEVER-	ENDAM-	LEVER-	SEWER-	TUTEL-
BIRDC-	ENSIL-	MALAX-	SHORT-	TUTOR-
BLIND-	ENVIS-	MARIT-	SLIPP-	UMPIR-
BLOCK-	EQUIP-	MARRI-	SMALL-	UNDER-
BRAKE-	FERRI-	MESSU-	SPILL-	VAULT-
BRASS-	FLOAT-	METAY-	SPOIL-	VAUNT-
BREAK-	FLOOR-	METER-	SPOUS-	VERBI-
BROCK-	FOOTP-	MISUS-	SQUIR-	VICAR-
CABOT-	FRAUT-	MORTG-	STAFF-	VICIN-
CARRI-	FROND-	MUCIL-	STALL-	WAGON-
CARUC-	FRONT-	MULTI-	STEAL-	WATER-
CHANT-	FROTT-	NONIM-	STEAR-	WEIGH-
CHUMM-	FRUIT-	OFFST-	STEER-	WHARF-
CLEAR-	FUSEL-	OVERP-	STERN-	WRAPP-
CLEAV-	GRAFT-	PILOT-	STILL-	WRECK-
CLOUD-	GRAIN-	PINOT-	STOCK-	

Words that end with -ANCE

Seven-letter words

ADV-	CRE-	JOY-	SON-
AID-	DUR-	NOY-	SUR-
ASK-	ENH-	PEN-	VAC-
BAL-	FIN-	ROM-	VAL-

Eight-letter words

ABEY-	BRIS-	FEAS-	OUTD-	RESI-
ABID-	BUOY-	GUID-	OUTR-	RIDD-
ACUT-	CREP-	INST-	PARL-	SORT-
ADAM-	DEFI-	ISSU-	PAST-	TADV-
AFFI-	DEVI-	ITER-	PIQU-	TEND-
ALLI-	DIST-	LAIT-	PITT-	VALI-
AMBI-	ELEG-	NOND-	PORT-	VARI-
AMOR-	ENTR-	NUIS-	RADI-	VIBR-
BECH-	EXIT-	ORDN-	RELI-	VOID-

Words that end with -ANCY

Seven-letter words

ERR-	PLI-	TEN-	UNF-
INF-	SON-	TRU-	VAC-

Eight-letter words

ABEY-	DEVI-	INST-	PIQU-	VAGR-
ADAM-	DORM-	MORD-	RADI-	VALI-
BLAT-	ELEG-	MYOM-	RAMP-	VERD-
BUOY-	GEOM-	PECC-	REGN-	VIBR-
CLAM-	IMIT-	PERN-	UNCH-	ZOOM-

Words that end with -ARCH

Seven-letter words

AUT-	HEX-	MON-	NOM-	TRI-
END-	MES-	NAV-	TOP-	XER-

Eight-letter words

ETHN-	HIPP-	OUTM-	PHYL-	TAXI-
HEPT-	OLIG-	OVER-	POLY-	TETR-
HIER-	OMNI-	PENT-	RESE-	UNST-

Words that end with -BACK

Seven-letter words

BUY-	FIN-	OUT-	SET-	TOM-
CUT-	FLY-	PAY-	SOW-	WET-
DIE-	HOG-	RED-	SUN-	
FAT-	LAY-	RUN-	TIE-	

Eight-letter words

BARE-	FEED-	HOLD-	PULL-	SWAY-
BLOW-	FIRE-	HOWL-	ROLL-	TAIL-
BLUE-	FLAT-	HUMP-	ROOR-	TALK-
CALL-	FOLD-	KICK-	SCAT-	TURN-
CASH-	FULL-	LIFT-	SEAT-	WING-
CLAW-	GIVE-	LOAN-	SKEW-	ZWIE-
COME-	GRAY-	MOSS-	SLOT-	
DRAW-	GREY-	PICK-	SLOW-	
FALL-	HALF-	PLAY-	SNAP-	
FAST-	HARD-	PLOW-	SOFT-	

Words that end with -BALL

Seven-letter words

BOX-	GUM-	NET-	PIN-
EAR-	ICE-	ODD-	PRO-
EYE-	LOW-	PAT-	

Eight-letter words

BASE-	FIRE-	GOOF-	KORF-	SOFT-
BEAN-	FISH-	HAIR-	MEAT-	SOUR-
BLOW-	FOOS-	HAND-	MOTH-	SPIT-
BLUE-	FOOT-	HARD-	PITH-	TRAP-
COAL-	FORK-	HEEL-	PUFF-	WASH-
CORN-	FOUR-	HIGH-	PUSH-	
FAST-	GOAL-	KICK-	SNOW-	

Words that end with -BAND

Seven-letter words

ARM-	HAT-	HUS-	RIB-	TUR-
DIS-	HAY-	PRO-	SAL-	

Eight-letter words

BACK-	FAHL-	NECK-	PLAT-	SIDE-
BASE-	HAIR-	NOSE-	RAIN-	WAVE-
BROW-	HEAD-	PASS-	SARA-	WIDE-

Words that end with -BIRD

Seven-letter words

ANT-	BOO-	FAT-	OIL-	SUN-
AWL-	CAT-	JAY-	RED-	WOS-
AXE-	COW-	MAY-	SEA-	

Eight-letter words

BELL-	FIRE-	LADY-	RAIL-	SONG-
BLUE-	GAOL-	LOVE-	RAIN-	SURF-
CAGE-	HANG-	LYRE-	REED-	WHIP-
COCK-	JAIL-	OVEN-	RICE-	YARD-
FERN-	KING-	PUFF-	SNOW-	

Words that end with -DOM

Seven-letter words

BABU-	DOLL-	FREE-	JARL-	SERF-
BORE-	DUKE-	GEEK-	KING-	SHAH-
BOSS-	EARL-	GURU-	PAPA-	STAR-
CHEF-	FIEF-	HALI-	POPE-	TSAR-
CZAR-	FILM-	HEIR-	RHAB-	TZAR-
DOGE-	FOGY-	HOBO-	SELF-	WIFE-

Eight-letter words

BABEL-	FOGEY-	MOVIE-	QUEEN-	UNSEL-
BIRTH-	GIPSY-	NOVEL-	QUEER-	UNWIS-
BLOKE-	GYPSY-	PACHA-	REBEL-	VILLA-
CHIEF-	HIPPY-	PAGAN-	SAINT-	WHORE-
CLERK-	HOTEL-	PAPPA-	SHEIK-	
DEVIL-	LEECH-	PASHA-	SWELL-	
DUNCE-	LIEGE-	POPPA-	THANE-	
FAIRY-	MOTOR-	PUPPY-	THRAL-	

Words that end with -EAUX

Seven-letter words

BAT-	CAD-	GAT-	RES-
BUR-	COT-		

Eight-letter words

BAND-	CHAP-	MANT-	ROND-	TRUM-
BATT-	CHAT-	MORC-	ROUL-	
BERC-	COUT-	NOUV-	TABL-	
BORD-	JAMB-	PLAT-	TONN-	

Words that end with -ENCE

Seven-letter words

ABS-	ESS-	LAT-	POT-	SIL-
CAD-	FAI-	LIC-	REF-	UNF-
COG-	FAY-	LUC-	REG-	URG-
DEF-	FLU-	OFF-	SCI-	VAL-

Eight-letter words

AMBI-	EXIG-	OUTF-	SENT-	TUPP-
AUDI-	FIPP-	PATI-	SEQU-	TWOP-
CLAR-	FLOR-	PRES-	SITH-	VERG-
COMM-	LENI-	PRET-	SIXP-	VIOL-
CRED-	MERG-	PRUD-	SUSP-	
DISP-	NASC-	PUNG-	TANG-	
EMIN-	NOWH-	SALI-	TEND-	
EVID-	OPUL-	SAPI-	TENP-	

Words that end with -ENCY

Seven-letter words

ARD-	FLU-	PAT-	REG-
CAD-	LAT-	POT-	URG-
COG-	LUC-	PUD-	VAL-
DEC-	ORI-	REC-	VIV-

Eight-letter words

CLEM-	FERV-	OPUL-	SAPI-	TURG-
COAG-	FULG-	PEND-	SEQU-	VERG-
CURR-	LAMB-	PUNG-	SOLV-	
EMIN-	LENI-	REAG-	TANG-	
EXIG-	NASC-	SALI-	TEND-	

Words that end with -EST

Seven-letter words

ACHI-	ARTI-	BLUI-	CANI-	CRUD-
ACID-	ASHI-	BOLD-	CANT-	CURT-
ACQU-	AULD-	BONI-	CHIC-	DAFT-
ACUT-	AVID-	BOSS-	CLOS-	DAMP-
ADDR-	AWAR-	BOXI-	COKI-	DANK-
AERI-	AWNI-	BRAV-	COLD-	DARK-
AGIL-	BABI-	BRAW-	CONF-	DEAD-
AIRI-	BADD-	BUFF-	CONG-	DEAF-
AMPL-	BALD-	BUMM-	CONT-	DEAR-
ANAP-	BARG-	BUSI-	COOL-	DEED-
ARCH-	BASS-	CAGI-	COSI-	DEEP-
ARID-	BEQU-	CAKI-	COWI-	DEFF-
ARMR-	BIGG-	CALM-	COXI-	DEFT-
ARSI-	BLAT-	CAMP-	COZI-	DEID-

DEIF-	GASH-	LOWS-	POOR-	STEY-
DENS-	GAZI-	LUNI-	PORI-	SUAV-
DEWI-	GLUI-	LUSH-	POSH-	SUBT-
DICI-	GOLD-	MADD-	POSI-	SUGG-
DIKI-	GOOI-	MAIN-	POXI-	TAKI-
DIMM-	GORI-	MATI-	PRET-	TALL-
DINK-	GOWD-	MAUV-	PRON-	TANN-
DISG-	GRAV-	MAZI-	PROT-	TART-
DISN-	GRAY-	MEAN-	PROW-	TAUT-
DOMI-	GREY-	MEEK-	PUIR-	TAWI-
DOPI-	HADD-	MEET-	PULI-	TEDI-
DOTI-	HARD-	MIDD-	PUNI-	TEMP-
DOUC-	HARV-	MILD-	PUNK-	TENS-
DOUR-	HAZI-	MIMM-	QUAR-	TERS-
DOVI-	HEPP-	MINI-	RACI-	TIDI-
DOWI-	HIGH-	MIRI-	RADD-	TINI-
DOZI-	HIPP-	MIRK-	RADG-	TOEI-
DROL-	HOKI-	MITI-	RANK-	TONI-
DUFF-	HOLI-	MIXI-	RASH-	TOOM-
DULL-	HOMI-	MOOT-	RATH-	TOWI-
DUMB-	HOTT-	MOPI-	REAL-	TRIT-
DUNN-	ICKI-	MOST-	REDD-	TUNI-
DUSK-	ICKL-	MOTI-	RENK-	TYPI-
DYKI-	IFFI-	MURK-	REQU-	UGLI-
EARN-	IMPR-	NAFF-	RICH-	UNBL-
EASI-	INAN-	NAIF-	RICI-	UNCO-
EDGI-	INKI-	NAIV-	RILI-	UNDR-
EELI-	INQU-	NEAR-	RIMI-	VAGU-
EERI-	IRAT-	NEAT-	ROKI-	VAIN-
EGGI-	JIMP-	NESH-	ROPI-	VAST-
ELMI-	JIVI-	NIGH-	RORI-	VERI-
EVEN-	JOKI-	NOBL-	ROSI-	VIBI-
EVIL-	JUST-	NOSI-	RUBI-	VINI-
FABB-	KEEN-	NUMB-	RULI-	VOGI-
FADI-	KEWL-	OAKI-	RUMM-	WACK-
FAIN-	KIND-	OARI-	SADD-	WALI-
FAIR-	LACI-	OBES-	SAFT-	WANI-
FALS-	LAKI-	OILI-	SAGI-	WANN-
FAST-	LANG-	ONLI-	SAID-	WARI-
FATT-	LANK-	OOFI-	SAIR-	WARM-
FAUR-	LARG-	OORI-	SALT-	WATT-
FEAT-	LAZI-	OOSI-	SAMI-	WAVI-
FELL-	LEAL-	OOZI-	SEAR-	WAXI-
FIKI-	LEAN-	OPEN-	SEIK-	WEAK-
FIRM-	LEFT-	ORBI-	SEXI-	WEET-
FITT-	LENG-	OULD-	SICK-	WETT-
FLUI-	LEWD-	OURI-	SIZI-	WHIT-
FOND-	LIEF-	OUTJ-	SKEW-	WILD-
FOUL-	LIEV-	OWLI-	SKYI-	WILI-
FOXI-	LIMI-	OWRI-	SLOW-	WILL-
FOZI-	LIMP-	PACI-	SNID-	WINI-
FULL-	LINI-	PAIR-	SOFT-	WIRI-
FUMI-	LITH-	PALI-	SOON-	WOTT-
FUNF-	LOGI-	PERT-	SOUR-	WOWF-
FUNN-	LONG-	PINI-	SPAR-	YUKI-
GABF-	LOOS-	PINK-	SPRI-	ZANI-
GAIN-	LOTH-	PIPI-	SPRY-	ZOOI-
GAMI-	LOUD-	POKI-	STAL-	

Eight-letter words

ACERB-	BLUFF-	CHIRK-	DILLI-	FEINT-
ACIDI-	BLUNT-	CHOIC-	DINGI-	FELTI-
ACRID-	BODGI-	CHOKI-	DINKI-	FEMMI-
ADEPT-	BOGGI-	CHUFF-	DIPPI-	FENDI-
AFFOR-	BONEY-	CISSI-	DIRTI-	FENNI-
ALCAH-	BONNI-	CLAYI-	DISHI-	FERLI-
ALERT-	BOOFI-	CLEAN-	DITSI-	FERNI-
ALKAH-	BOOKI-	CLEAR-	DITZI-	FESTI-
ALMAG-	BOOKR-	COALI-	DIVIN-	FETID-
ANAPA-	BOOMI-	COARS-	DIZZI-	FICKL-
ANGRI-	BOOZI-	COATT-	DOCIL-	FIERC-
ANTSI-	BORTI-	COBBI-	DODDI-	FIERI-
ARBAL-	BOSKI-	COCKI-	DODGI-	FILMI-
ARBEL-	BOSSI-	COMBI-	DOGGI-	FINNI-
ARTSI-	BOUSI-	COMFI-	DOILT-	FIRRI-
ASTUT-	BOYSI-	CONKI-	DONSI-	FISHI-
BACKR-	BRAGG-	CONQU-	DOOMI-	FISTI-
BAGGI-	BRAID-	COOMI-	DORKI-	FITLI-
BALDI-	BRAKI-	COPSI-	DORTI-	FIZZI-
BALKI-	BRASH-	CORKI-	DOTTI-	FLAKI-
BALMI-	BRENT-	CORNI-	DOTTL-	FLAMI-
BANAL-	BRIEF-	COULD-	DOWDI-	FLARI-
BANDI-	BRILL-	COUTH-	DOWLI-	FLASH-
BARDI-	BRINI-	CRANK-	DOWNI-	FLATT-
BARGH-	BRISK-	CRAPI-	DRABB-	FLAWI-
BARGU-	BROAD-	CRASS-	DREAR-	FLAXI-
BARKI-	BROWN-	CRAZI-	DROLL-	FLEET-
BARMI-	BRUSK-	CREPI-	DRONI-	FLIPP-
BARNI-	BUDDI-	CRISP-	DRUNK-	FLORI-
BARRI-	BUFFI-	CRONK-	DRUSI-	FLUKI-
BASSI-	BUGGI-	CROOK-	DRUXI-	FLUSH-
BATTI-	BULGI-	CROSS-	DUCKI-	FLUTI-
BAWDI-	BULKI-	CRUEL-	DUDDI-	FOAMI-
BEADI-	BULLI-	CRUMP-	DULLI-	FOGGI-
BEAKI-	BUMPI-	CULTI-	DUMMI-	FOLKI-
BEAMI-	BUNTI-	CUPPI-	DUMPI-	FOOTI-
BEATI-	BURLI-	CURDI-	DUNGI-	FOOTR-
BEEFI-	BURRI-	CURLI-	DUNNI-	FORKI-
BEERI-	BUSHI-	CURNI-	DURGI-	FRAIL-
BENDI-	BUSTI-	CURVI-	DURND-	FRANK-
BENTI-	BUTCH-	CUSHI-	DUSKI-	FRESH-
BILGI-	BUXOM-	CUTTI-	DUSTI-	FROWI-
BIRKI-	BUZZI-	DAFFI-	DWARF-	FUBBI-
BIRSI-	CACKI-	DAGGI-	EAGER-	FUBSI-
BITSI-	CADGI-	DAMND-	EARLI-	FUFFI-
BITTI-	CALMI-	DAMPI-	EMONG-	FUGGI-
BLACK-	CAMPI-	DANCI-	EMPTI-	FUGLI-
BLAND-	CANNI-	DANDI-	ENFOR-	FUNKI-
BLANK-	CANTI-	DARND-	EVILL-	FUNNI-
BLEAK-	CARNI-	DASHI-	EXACT-	FURRI-
BLEAR-	CATTI-	DAUBI-	FADDI-	FURTH-
BLIND-	CAULD-	DEBBI-	FAGGI-	FURZI-
BLING-	CHARI-	DEEDI-	FAINT-	FUSSI-
BLITH-	CHAST-	DEFOR-	FANCI-	FUSTI-
BLOKI-	CHEAP-	DEMUR-	FARTH-	FUTIL-
BLOND-	CHEWI-	DICKI-	FATTI-	FUZZI-
BLOWI-	CHIEF-	DICTI-	FAWNI-	GABBI-
BLUDI-	CHILL-	DIDDI-	FEEBL-	GAMMI-

GAPPI-	GUNGI-	ITCHI-	LOUSI-	MUGGI-
GASPI-	GUNKI-	JAGGI-	LOVEF-	MUMSI-
GASSI-	GURLI-	JAMMI-	LOWLI-	MURKI-
GAUCH-	GUSHI-	JANTI-	LOYAL-	MURLI-
GAUCI-	GUSTI-	JAZZI-	LUCID-	MUSHI-
GAUDI-	GUTSI-	JEMMI-	LUCKI-	MUSKI-
GAUMI-	GUTTI-	JERKI-	LUMMI-	MUSSI-
GAUNT-	HAILI-	JETTI-	LUMPI-	MUSTI-
GAUZI-	HAIRI-	JIGGI-	LURID-	MUZZI-
GAWCI-	HAMMI-	JIMPI-	LUSHI-	MYTHI-
GAWKI-	HANDI-	JOLLI-	LUSTI-	NAGGI-
GAWSI-	HANGN-	JOLTI-	MALMI-	NAKED-
GEEKI-	HAPPI-	JOWLI-	MALTI-	NAPPI-
GELID-	HARDI-	JUICI-	MANGI-	NARKI-
GEMMI-	HARSH-	JUMPI-	MANIF-	NASTI-
GENTI-	HASHI-	JUNKI-	MANKI-	NATTI-
GENTL-	HASTI-	KEDGI-	MANLI-	NEDDI-
GERMI-	HEADI-	KEMPI-	MARDI-	NEEDI-
GIDDI-	HEADR-	KERKI-	MARLI-	NERDI-
GIMPI-	HEAPI-	KICKI-	MASHI-	NERVI-
GINNI-	HEAVI-	KIDGI-	MASSI-	NETTI-
GIRLI-	HEDGI-	KINKI-	MASTI-	NEWSI-
GIRNI-	HEFTI-	KITTL-	MATUR-	NIFFI-
GLADD-	HEMPI-	KOOKI-	MAWKI-	NIFTI-
GLADI-	HENNI-	LAIGH-	MEAGR-	NIMBL-
GLARI-	HERBI-	LAIRI-	MEALI-	NIPPI-
GLAZI-	HILLI-	LAMBI-	MEATI-	NIRLI-
GLEGG-	HINKI-	LANKI-	MELTI-	NITTI-
GLIBB-	HIPPI-	LARDI-	MERRI-	NOBBI-
GLIDD-	HISSI-	LARKI-	MESHI-	NOISI-
GLUMM-	HOARI-	LARNI-	MESSI-	NONGU-
GOATI-	HOARS-	LATHI-	MICKL-	NOOKI-
GOBBI-	HOLEY-	LAWNI-	MIFFI-	NOUNI-
GODLI-	HOODI-	LEADI-	MIGHT-	NOWTI-
GOLDI-	HOOKI-	LEAFI-	MILKI-	NUBBI-
GOODI-	HOOLI-	LEAKI-	MILTI-	NURDI-
GOOFI-	HOOTI-	LEARI-	MIMSI-	NUTSI-
GOONI-	HOPPI-	LEAVI-	MINCI-	NUTTI-
GOOPI-	HORNI-	LEDGI-	MINGI-	OBTUS-
GOOSI-	HORSI-	LEERI-	MINTI-	OFTEN-
GORMI-	HOUSI-	LEGGI-	MINUT-	ONERI-
GORSI-	HUFFI-	LEISH-	MIRKI-	OPAQU-
GOUTI-	HUGGI-	LICHT-	MIRLI-	ORANG-
GRAND-	HULKI-	LIGHT-	MISSI-	ORNAT-
GRAPI-	HULLI-	LIMBI-	MISTI-	OUTWR-
GREAT-	HUMAN-	LINGI-	MOCHI-	OVERK-
GREEN-	HUMBL-	LINTI-	MOIST-	PALLI-
GRIMI-	HUMID-	LIPPI-	MOLDI-	PALMI-
GRIMM-	HUMPI-	LITTL-	MOODI-	PALSI-
GRIPI-	HUNKI-	LIVID-	MOONI-	PAPPI-
GRITT-	HUSHI-	LOAMI-	MOORI-	PARKI-
GRODI-	HUSKI-	LOATH-	MOPPI-	PASTI-
GROSS-	IMMOD-	LOFTI-	MOROS-	PAWKI-
GROUS-	IMPUR-	LOGGI-	MOSSI-	PEAKI-
GRUFF-	INDIG-	LOOBI-	MOTHI-	PEART-
GRUMM-	INEPT-	LOONI-	MOTLI-	PEATI-
GUCKI-	INERT-	LOOPI-	MOTTI-	PECKI-
GULFI-	INSAN-	LOPPI-	MOUSI-	PEERI-
GULPI-	INTER-	LOSSI-	MUCKI-	PEPPI-
GUMMI-	IRONI-	LOURI-	MUDDI-	PERKI-

PESKI-	READI-	SEEDI-	SPARS-	TEENI-
PESTI-	REAMI-	SEELI-	SPEWI-	TENTI-
PETTI-	REARR-	SEEPI-	SPICI-	TEPID-
PHATT-	REDDI-	SEMPL-	SPICK-	TESTI-
PHONI-	REDIG-	SEREN-	SPIKI-	TEUCH-
PICKI-	REEDI-	SEVER-	SPINI-	TEUGH-
PIGGI-	REEFI-	SHADI-	SPIRI-	THAWI-
PIPPI-	REEKI-	SHAKI-	SPRUC-	THEWI-
PITHI-	REFOR-	SHALI-	SPUMI-	THICK-
PLAIN-	REINV-	SHARP-	SQUAR-	THINN-
PLATI-	REMOT-	SHEER-	STABL-	THYMI-
PLUMI-	RESTI-	SHINI-	STAGI-	TICHI-
PLUMM-	RIBBI-	SHOAL-	STAID-	TIDDI-
PLUMP-	RICHT-	SHORT-	STARK-	TIGHT-
PLUSH-	RIDGI-	SHOWI-	STEEP-	TILLI-
POCKI-	RIFTI-	SILKI-	STEEV-	TIMID-
PODGI-	RIGHT-	SILLI-	STERN-	TINNI-
POLIT-	RIGID-	SILTI-	STEWI-	TINTI-
PONCI-	RINDI-	SIMPL-	STIEV-	TIPPI-
PONGI-	RISKI-	SINKI-	STIFF-	TIPSI-
POOFI-	RITZI-	SISSI-	STILL-	TIRED-
POOVI-	ROARI-	SKIEY-	STIVI-	TOCKI-
POPPI-	ROCKI-	SKINT-	STONI-	TOFFI-
PORKI-	ROILI-	SKIVI-	STOUT-	TOSHI-
PORNI-	ROOFI-	SLACK-	STYLI-	TOSSI-
PORTI-	ROOKI-	SLATI-	SUBTL-	TOTTI-
POSTT-	ROOMI-	SLEEK-	SUCKI-	TOUGH-
POTTI-	ROOPI-	SLICK-	SUDSI-	TOUSI-
POUTI-	ROOTI-	SLIMI-	SUETI-	TOUTI-
PRICI-	RORTI-	SLIMM-	SULKI-	TOUZI-
PRIMM-	ROUGH-	SLOPI-	SUNNI-	TOWNI-
PRIVI-	ROUND-	SLUGF-	SUPPL-	TOWSI-
PROSI-	ROUPI-	SMALL-	SURFI-	TOWZI-
PROUD-	ROWDI-	SMART-	SURGI-	TRAPN-
PUDGI-	RUDDI-	SMOKI-	SURLI-	TRIFF-
PUDSI-	RUGGI-	SMUGG-	SVELT-	TRIGG-
PUFFI-	RUMMI-	SNAKI-	SWALI-	TRIMM-
PUGGI-	RUNNI-	SNARI-	SWANK-	TRIPI-
PULPI-	RUNTI-	SNELL-	SWEER-	TUBBI-
PUNKI-	RUSHI-	SNIDI-	SWEET-	TUFTI-
PUNNI-	RUSTI-	SNIPI-	SWEIR-	TUMPI-
PURPL-	RUTTI-	SNODD-	SWELL-	TURFI-
PURSI-	SAGGI-	SNOWI-	SWIFT-	TUSKI-
PURTI-	SALTI-	SNUGG-	SWIPI-	TWINI-
PUSHI-	SANDI-	SOAPI-	SWISH-	UNHON-
PUSSI-	SAPPI-	SOBER-	TACKI-	UNIQU-
QUAKI-	SARKI-	SODDI-	TAGGI-	UNPRI-
QUEER-	SASSI-	SOGGI-	TALCI-	UNRIP-
QUICK-	SAUCI-	SOILI-	TALKF-	UNSAF-
QUIET-	SAVAG-	SOLID-	TALKI-	UNSUR-
RABID-	SAVVI-	SOMBR-	TANGI-	UNTRU-
RAGGI-	SCALI-	SONGF-	TARDI-	UNWIS-
RAINI-	SCANT-	SONSI-	TARRI-	URBAN-
RAMMI-	SCARC-	SOOTH-	TARTI-	UTTER-
RANDI-	SCARI-	SOOTI-	TASTI-	VAIRI-
RANGI-	SCODI-	SOPPI-	TATTI-	VALID-
RAPID-	SEAMI-	SORRI-	TAWNI-	VAMPI-
RASPI-	SECUR-	SOUND-	TAWTI-	VAPID-
RATTI-	SEDAT-	SOUPI-	TEARI-	VASTI-
RAUCL-	SEDGI-	SPACI-	TECHI-	VEALI-

VEILI-	WARTI-	WHEYI-	WOODI-	YUCKI-
VEINI-	WASHI-	WHINI-	WOOFI-	YUKKI-
VIEWI-	WASPI-	WHITI-	WOOLI-	YUMMI-
VIVID-	WASPN-	WIFTI-	WOOZI-	ZAPPI-
VOGUI-	WEARI-	WIGGI-	WORDI-	ZESTI-
VUGGI-	WEBBI-	WIMPI-	WORMI-	ZINCI-
VUGHI-	WEDGI-	WINDI-	WOULD-	ZINGI-
VUTTI-	WEEDI-	WINGI-	WRONG-	ZINKI-
WACKI-	WEENI-	WISPI-	WUSSI-	ZIPPI-
WALLI-	WEEPI-	WITHI-	YAPPI-	ZOOTI-
WALTI-	WEIRD-	WITTI-	YAWNI-	
WANKI-	WENNI-	WOMBI-	YOLKI-	
WARBI-	WERSH-	WONKI-	YOUNG-	

Words that end with -ETTE

Seven-letter words

AIL-	CUR-	LAD-	NAV-	ROS-
ARI-	CUV-	LAY-	NED-	STR-
AVI-	DIN-	LOR-	NON-	SYR-
BLU-	FOU-	LUN-	OCT-	TON-
BUR-	FUM-	MIN-	PAL-	VED-
BUV-	GAL-	MOF-	PIP-	VID-
CAS-	GAZ-	MOZ-	POP-	
CUN-	GEN-	MUS-	PRO-	

Eight-letter words

AIGR-	COQU-	GRIS-	PALM-	SEXT-
AMUS-	CORV-	HACK-	PARK-	SOCK-
ANIS-	CREV-	JEAN-	PIAN-	SPIN-
BAGN-	DANC-	JOCK-	POCH-	SUED-
BAGU-	DISK-	MAQU-	RACL-	TOIL-
BARB-	DRAB-	MOFF-	REIN-	UMBR-
BARR-	FAUV-	MOQU-	ROOM-	VIGN-
BIMB-	FLAT-	MOZZ-	ROQU-	
BRUN-	FOSS-	NOIS-	ROUL-	
CASS-	FRIS-	OMEL-	SEPT-	
CHAV-	FRIZ-	PALL-	SEST-	

Words that end with -EUR

Seven-letter words

AMAT-	FLAN-	MASS-	REMU-
DANS-	FRIS-	MINC-	SABR-
DOUC-	HAUT-	PRIM-	SIGN-
FARC-	LIQU-	PRON-	TRAC-

Eight-letter words

BATEL-	COIFF-	GRAND-	SECAT-	TROUV-
BLAGU-	ECRAS-	JONGL-	SEIGN-	TRUQU-
CHASS-	FROID-	LONGU-	SIFFL-	VOYAG-
CISEL-	FROND-	MONSI-	SIGNI-	
CLAQU-	FROTT-	SABOT-	TAILL-	

Words that end with -FISH

Seven-letter words

BAT-	FIN-	JEW-	PIG-	SEL-
BOX-	FOX-	LUB-	PIN-	SER-
CAT-	GAR-	MUD-	PUP-	SUN-
COD-	GEM-	MUF-	RAF-	TOF-
COW-	HAG-	OAR-	RAT-	TUB-
DEA-	HOG-	OUT-	RED-	WAI-
DOG-	HUF-	PAN-	SAW-	WOL-

Eight-letter words

BAIT-	DRUM-	JACK-	ROCK-	STUD-
BILL-	DWAR-	KING-	ROSE-	SUCK-
BLOW-	FALL-	LADY-	SAIL-	SURF-
BLUE-	FILE-	LION-	SALT-	TILE-
BOAR-	FLAT-	LUMP-	SAND-	TOAD-
BONE-	FOOL-	LUNG-	SCAR-	WALL-
CAVE-	FROG-	MILK-	SCOM-	WEAK-
COAL-	GOAT-	MONK-	SCUM-	WOLF-
CRAW-	GOLD-	MOON-	SNIF-	
CRAY-	GRAY-	NUMB-	SPOF-	
DEAL-	GRUF-	OVER-	STAR-	
DRAF-	HEAD-	PIPE-	STIF-	

Words that end with -FORM

Seven-letter words

ACI-	CON-	ISO-	PRE-
ALI-	DEI-	MIS-	TRI-
AUS-	DIF-	OVI-	UNI-
AVI-	DIS-	PER-	ZOE-

Eight-letter words

AERI-	FUSI-	NAPI-	PISI-	ROTI-
ARCI-	GASI-	NATI-	PLAN-	SETI-
AURI-	GRUI-	NUBI-	PLAT-	SLIP-
COLI-	IODO-	OMNI-	POST-	TUBI-
CONI-	JANI-	PALI-	PYRI-	UNCI-
CUBI-	LAND-	PARA-	RAMI-	URSI-
CUNI-	LAVA-	PEDI-	RANI-	VARI-
ENSI-	LYRI-	PICI-	REIN-	VASI-
FILI-	MANI-	PILI-	RENI-	WAVE-
FREE-	MURI-	PIRI-	RETI-	

Words that end with -FUL

Seven-letter words

ARMS-	BALE-	BASH-	BODE-	BOWL-
BAGS-	BANE-	BOAT-	BOOK-	BRIM-

CAGE-	FORM-	KIST-	PITI-	SWAY-
CANS-	FRET-	LIFE-	PLAY-	TACT-
CARE-	GAIN-	LIST-	PLOT-	TALE-
CART-	GASH-	LOCK-	POKE-	TANK-
CROP-	GAZE-	LOOF-	POUT-	TEAR-
CUPS-	GLAD-	LUNG-	PREY-	TEEM-
DARE-	GLEE-	LUST-	PUSH-	TEEN-
DEED-	GUST-	MAST-	RACK-	TENT-
DERN-	GUTS-	MAZE-	RAGE-	TOIL-
DIRE-	HAND-	MIND-	REST-	TRAY-
DISH-	HARM-	MIST-	RISK-	TUBE-
DOLE-	HATE-	MOAN-	ROOM-	TUNE-
DOOM-	HATS-	MUSE-	RUTH-	VIAL-
DURE-	HEAD-	NEED-	SACK-	WAIL-
DUTI-	HEED-	NEST-	SHED-	WAKE-
EASE-	HELP-	ODOR-	SHIP-	WAME-
FACT-	HOPE-	PAGE-	SHOP-	WILE-
FATE-	HORN-	PAIL-	SIGH-	WILL-
FEAR-	HURT-	PAIN-	SKEP-	WISH-
FISH-	HUSH-	PALM-	SKIL-	WIST-
FIST-	JARS-	PEST-	SKIN-	WORK-
FOOD-	JEST-	PIPE-	SONG-	ZEAL-
FORK-	JUGS-	PITH-	SOUL-	ZEST-

Eight-letter words

APRON-	FORKS-	MOURN-	SLOTH-	TRUST-
AVAIL-	FOUNT-	MOUTH-	SMILE-	TRUTH-
BASIN-	FRAUD-	NIEVE-	SNEER-	UDDER-
BELLY-	FREAK-	NOISE-	SNOOT-	UNART-
BLAME-	FRISK-	ODOUR-	SOOTH-	UNJOY-
BLISS-	FRUIT-	PAILS-	SPADE-	UNLAW-
BLUSH-	GHAST-	PAUSE-	SPEED-	UNMAN-
BOAST-	GLASS-	PEACE-	SPELL-	UNSIN-
CHARM-	GLOOM-	PLAIN-	SPITE-	UNUSE-
CHEEK-	GRACE-	PLATE-	SPOIL-	UNWIL-
CHEER-	GRATE-	POUCH-	SPOON-	VAUNT-
CHEST-	GRIEF-	POWER-	SPORT-	VENGE-
CHOCK-	GROAN-	PRANK-	STAGE-	VOICE-
COLOR-	GUILE-	PRESS-	START-	WAGON-
CRATE-	HANDS-	PRIDE-	STICK-	WASTE-
CRIME-	HASTE-	PROUD-	STORM-	WATCH-
DEARN-	HONEY-	PURSE-	SURGE-	WEARI-
DEATH-	HOUSE-	RIGHT-	TABLE-	WORTH-
DIRGE-	HUMOR-	SACKS-	TASTE-	WRACK-
DOUBT-	LADLE-	SCENT-	THANK-	WRATH-
DREAD-	LAUGH-	SCOOP-	TOOTH-	WREAK-
DREAM-	LIGHT-	SCORN-	TRADE-	WRECK-
EVENT-	LOATH-	SENSE-	TRAIN-	WRONG-
FAITH-	MENSE-	SHAME-	TRIST-	WROTH-
FANCI-	MERCI-	SHEEN-	TROTH-	YOUTH-
FAULT-	MIGHT-	SHELF-	TROUT-	
FEAST-	MIRTH-	SHELL-	TRUCK-	
FORCE-	MOIST-	SKILL-	TRUNK-	

Words that end with -GEN

Seven-letter words

ACRO-	HALO-	LOXY-	MUTA-	SMID-
ANLA-	HUMO-	LUCI-	ONCO-	TRUD-
ANTI-	INDI-	LYSO-	PIRO-	TWIG-
CRYO-	IONO-	MITO-	PYRO-	XYLO-
ENDO-	KERO-	MUCI-	RONT-	ZYMO-

Eight-letter words

ABORI-	COLLA-	ESTRO-	HYDRO-	PHOTO-
ALLER-	CULTI-	FLORI-	MISCE-	ROENT-
AMIDO-	CYANO-	GLYCO-	NITRO-	STARA-
AMYLO-	DIPLO-	HISTO-	OSTEO-	
ANDRO-	ENLAR-	HYALO-	PATHO-	

Words that end with -GRAM

Seven-letter words

ANA-	EPI-	ISO-	PAN-	TAN-
DIA-	GRO-	MYO-	PRO-	TRI-

Eight-letter words

AERO-	ETHO-	KYMO-	NANO-	SONO-
BARO-	GENO-	LEXI-	NOMO-	TELE-
DECA-	HEXA-	LIPO-	ONDO-	TOMO-
DECI-	HOLO-	LOGO-	PARA-	VENO-
DEKA-	IDEO-	MAIL-	PICO-	ZYMO-
ECHO-	IDIO-	MARI-	RENO-	
ERGO-	KILO-	MONO-	SKIA-	

Words that end with -HOLE

Seven-letter words

AIR-	CAT-	JAW-	MUD-	POT-
ARM-	DOG-	KEY-	OIL-	RAT-
ASS-	EYE-	LUG-	PIE-	SPY-
BOT-	FOX-	MAN-	PIN-	TAP-

Eight-letter words

ANET-	COAL-	KNEE-	PLUG-	WEEP-
ARSE-	DOWN-	KNOT-	PORT-	WELL-
BLOW-	FEED-	LAMP-	POST-	WOOD-
BOLT-	FUNK-	LOOP-	SHIT-	WORM-
BORE-	GUNK-	PEEP-	SHOT-	
BUNG-	HELL-	PEST-	SINK-	

Words that end with -HOOD

Seven-letter words

APE-	CUB-	HOG-	NUN-	
BOY-	ELF-	LAD-	SON-	
CAT-	GOD-	MAN-		

Eight-letter words

AUNT-	IDLE-	MISS-	PUMP-	WIVE-
BABY-	KING-	MONK-	SELF-	
DOLL-	LADY-	PAGE-	SERF-	
GIRL-	MAID-	POPE-	WIFE-	

Words that end with -HORN

Seven-letter words

ALP-	BIG-	FOG-	SAX-
ALT-	COE-	INK-	TIN-
BET-	DIS-	LEG-	UNS-

Eight-letter words

BOXT-	CRUM-	HAWT-	LONG-	SLUG-
BUCK-	DEER-	KRUM-	RAMS-	STAG-
BULL-	GEMS-	LANT-	SHOE-	WALD-

Words that end with -IBLE

Seven-letter words

ADD-	DOC-	MIX-	RIS-
AUD-	FUS-	PAT-	VIS-
DEL-	LEG-	RIB-	

Eight-letter words

CRED-	EVAD-	FUNG-	PASS-	TENS-
CRUC-	EVAS-	GULL-	POSS-	TERR-
EDUC-	EXIG-	HORR-	REND-	THUR-
ELID-	FALL-	INED-	RINS-	UNED-
ELIG-	FEAS-	LAPS-	RUNC-	VEND-
ELUD-	FENC-	MAND-	SENS-	VINC-
EROD-	FLEX-	MISC-	SUAS-	
EROS-	FORC-	PART-	TANG-	

Words that end with -IFY

Seven-letter words

ACET-	DAND-	LIGN-	PETR-	TERR-
ACID-	DENS-	LIQU-	PLEB-	TEST-
AMPL-	DIGN-	LITH-	PONT-	THUR-
ANGL-	DULC-	MAGN-	PROS-	TIPS-
BEAT-	FALS-	MATT-	PULP-	TORR-
BRUT-	FANC-	MERC-	QUAL-	UNDE-
CALC-	FARC-	METR-	RECT-	VERB-
CAPR-	FISH-	MICR-	REED-	VERS-
CARN-	FORT-	MOLL-	REUN-	VITR-
CERT-	FRUT-	MORT-	RUSS-	YUPP-
CHYL-	GLOR-	MUMM-	SACR-	ZINC-
CHYM-	GRAT-	MUND-	SALS-	ZINK-
CLAR-	HORR-	MYST-	SCAR-	ZOMB-
COAL-	ICON-	NIGR-	SCOR-	
CORN-	JELL-	NITR-	SIGN-	
CRUC-	JOLL-	NULL-	SPEC-	
DAMN-	JUST-	OPAC-	TACK-	

Eight-letter words

ALKAL-	EMULS-	KARST-	RENOT-	SILIC-
AMMON-	ESTER-	LAPID-	REPAC-	SIMPL-
BEAUT-	ETHER-	MOIST-	REPUR-	SOLID-
BRONZ-	FLINT-	OPSON-	RESIN-	STELL-
CLASS-	FLUID-	PRETT-	REVER-	STRAT-
COCKN-	FRUCT-	QUANT-	REVIV-	STULT-
COPUR-	GENTR-	QUIZZ-	RIGID-	TREND-
DENAZ-	GLASS-	REAED-	SANCT-	ZINCK-
DETOX-	HUMID-	RECOD-	SANGU-	
DIVIN-	IDENT-	REMOD-	SAPON-	

Words that end with -INGS

Seven-letter words

ABL-	BON-	DIV-	FIR-	HOL-
ACH-	BOR-	DON-	FIX-	HOM-
ACT-	BOW-	DOP-	FLY-	IMP-
AGE-	BOX-	DOT-	FOX-	INN-
AIR-	BUS-	DOZ-	FRO-	JAP-
ANT-	CAK-	DRY-	FRY-	JAW-
ARC-	CAN-	DYE-	GAM-	KEY-
ARM-	CAS-	EAR-	GAP-	KIT-
ASK-	CAV-	EAT-	GAT-	LAC-
AUD-	CAW-	EDG-	GAZ-	LAD-
AWN-	COD-	EFF-	GIV-	LAK-
BAA-	COM-	ELD-	GOR-	LAS-
BAK-	COO-	END-	HAV-	LAW-
BES-	COP-	ENR-	HAY-	LAY-
BID-	COV-	ERR-	HAZ-	LIK-
BIK-	CRY-	FAC-	HEW-	LIM-
BIT-	DAR-	FAD-	HEX-	LIN-
BLU-	DAT-	FIL-	HID-	LIV-
BOD-	DIC-	FIN-	HIR-	LOB-

LOR-	PAG-	ROB-	STR-	UPP-
LOS-	PAL-	ROD-	TAK-	URG-
LOV-	PAR-	ROP-	TAM-	URN-
LOW-	PAV-	ROV-	TAR-	VEX-
LUG-	PAY-	ROW-	TAW-	VIK-
LUT-	PIK-	RUE-	TAX-	VOT-
MAK-	PIL-	RUL-	TID-	WAD-
MAT-	PIP-	SAV-	TIL-	WAK-
MAY-	POL-	SAW-	TIM-	WAN-
MER-	POS-	SAY-	TIR-	WAV-
MIN-	PRY-	SEE-	TOL-	WAX-
MOW-	PUL-	SEW-	TON-	WIP-
MUS-	RAC-	SID-	TOW-	WIR-
NAM-	RAG-	SIZ-	TOY-	WON-
NID-	RAK-	SKI-	TRY-	WOO-
NOS-	RAT-	SOR-	TUB-	YOK-
OFF-	RAV-	SOW-	TUN-	ZON-
OGL-	RAW-	SPA-	TYP-	
OND-	RID-	SPR-	ULL-	
OUT-	RIS-	SPY-	UNK-	

Eight-letter words

ABID-	BIRL-	CANT-	CYCL-	EAST-
AISL-	BITT-	CAPP-	CYML-	EBAY-
AMBL-	BLAD-	CARD-	DAFF-	EDIT-
ANGL-	BLUE-	CARL-	DAGG-	EEVN-
ARCH-	BOAT-	CARP-	DAMP-	EILD-
ARCK-	BOIL-	CARV-	DANC-	EMPT-
AWAK-	BOLT-	CAST-	DARL-	ENVY-
BACK-	BOMB-	CATL-	DARN-	ERLK-
BAGG-	BOND-	CEAS-	DAUB-	ETCH-
BAIT-	BONK-	CEIL-	DAWN-	EVEN-
BALK-	BOOK-	CHAS-	DEAL-	FABL-
BALL-	BOOM-	CHID-	DECK-	FAGG-
BAND-	BOWL-	CIEL-	DEVL-	FAIL-
BANG-	BRAC-	CISS-	DIAL-	FAIR-
BANK-	BREW-	CLON-	DIET-	FALL-
BANT-	BRIM-	CLOS-	DIGG-	FANN-
BARR-	BROK-	COAM-	DILL-	FARC-
BASH-	BRUT-	COAT-	DIPP-	FARD-
BAST-	BUCK-	CODL-	DISH-	FARM-
BATT-	BUDD-	COGG-	DOAT-	FAST-
BAWL-	BUFF-	COIN-	DOCK-	FATL-
BEAD-	BUGG-	COLL-	DODG-	FAWN-
BEAM-	BULL-	COMB-	DOGG-	FEED-
BEAR-	BUMP-	COMP-	DOPP-	FEEL-
BEAT-	BUNT-	CONN-	DRAW-	FEER-
BEDD-	BURN-	COOK-	DRIV-	FELT-
BEGG-	BUSH-	CORD-	DROV-	FENC-
BELL-	BUSK-	COWL-	DUBB-	FERN-
BELT-	BUSS-	CRAV-	DUCK-	FEUD-
BEND-	BUST-	CUBB-	DUCT-	FILL-
BETT-	BUZZ-	CULL-	DUFF-	FIND-
BIAS-	CABL-	CUNN-	DUMP-	FIRR-
BIDD-	CALK-	CUPP-	DUNN-	FISH-
BIGG-	CALL-	CURB-	DUST-	FITT-
BILL-	CALM-	CURL-	EANL-	FIZZ-
BIND-	CAMP-	CURS-	EARN-	FLUT-
BIRD-	CANN-	CUTT-	EARR-	FLYT-

FOAM-	HEAL-	KEMP-	MARK-	PAST-
FOIL-	HEAR-	KENN-	MARL-	PAUS-
FOLD-	HEAT-	KERB-	MASH-	PECK-
FOOL-	HEAV-	KERN-	MASK-	PEEL-
FOOT-	HEDG-	KIDL-	MATT-	PEGG-
FOPL-	HEEL-	KILL-	MEAN-	PELT-
FORG-	HELP-	KILT-	MEET-	PETT-
FORM-	HERL-	KIRK-	MELT-	PHAS-
FOUL-	HERR-	KITL-	MEND-	PICK-
FOWL-	HIDL-	KNIF-	MERG-	PIEC-
FRAM-	HILD-	KNOW-	MERL-	PIGG-
FRAY-	HINT-	LAGG-	MESH-	PIGL-
FUCK-	HIPP-	LALL-	MICH-	PILL-
FUND-	HIRL-	LAMB-	MILK-	PINK-
FURR-	HISS-	LAMM-	MILL-	PINN-
GADL-	HOGG-	LAMP-	MINC-	PION-
GAFF-	HOLD-	LAND-	MIND-	PITT-
GAIN-	HOPP-	LAPP-	MIST-	PLAC-
GANG-	HORN-	LAPW-	MOBB-	PLAT-
GASK-	HORS-	LASH-	MOCK-	POLL-
GASP-	HOST-	LAST-	MOLD-	POST-
GASS-	HOTT-	LATH-	MOOR-	POUR-
GAUG-	HOUS-	LEAD-	MOOT-	POUT-
GAYW-	HOUT-	LEAN-	MORL-	PRAT-
GEAR-	HOWL-	LEAS-	MORN-	PRAY-
GELD-	HUFF-	LEAV-	MOSH-	PRIC-
GETT-	HUMM-	LEER-	MOSL-	PRIM-
GILD-	HUNT-	LEGG-	MOUS-	PROS-
GINN-	HURL-	LEKK-	MUGG-	PROV-
GIRD-	HUSK-	LEMM-	MUMM-	PRUN-
GLAZ-	HUST-	LEND-	MUNT-	PUDD-
GLEY-	HUTT-	LETT-	NAIL-	PUFF-
GLID-	HYLD-	LICK-	NECK-	PUGG-
GLOV-	IMAG-	LIGG-	NERV-	PUNN-
GLOZ-	INBE-	LIMP-	NEST-	PURG-
GNAW-	INBR-	LIPP-	NETT-	PURL-
GODL-	INGO-	LISP-	NITH-	PURR-
GOLF-	INKL-	LIST-	NODD-	PUTT-
GOSL-	INSW-	LOAD-	NOGG-	QUAK-
GRAT-	IRON-	LOAF-	NOON-	QUEU-
GRAV-	ITCH-	LOAN-	NOTH-	RACK-
GRAZ-	JACK-	LOCK-	NULL-	RAFT-
GREY-	JARR-	LODG-	NURS-	RAGG-
GRIC-	JEER-	LOGG-	NUTT-	RAID-
GROW-	JERK-	LONG-	OAKL-	RAIL-
GUID-	JEST-	LOON-	ONGO-	RAIS-
GUIS-	JIBB-	LOOP-	OPEN-	RAMP-
GUMM-	JIGG-	LOOS-	OUTR-	RANG-
GUNN-	JOBB-	LOOT-	OUTS-	RANK-
HACK-	JOGG-	LOPP-	OUTW-	RANT-
HAIN-	JOIN-	LORD-	PACK-	RAPP-
HALL-	JOTT-	LOUR-	PADD-	RASP-
HALT-	JUGG-	LUGE-	PAIR-	RATL-
HANG-	JUMP-	LURK-	PANN-	RATT-
HARL-	KART-	MADL-	PANT-	READ-
HARP-	KAYO-	MAIL-	PARG-	REDD-
HAST-	KEEL-	MAIM-	PARK-	REDW-
HATT-	KEEN-	MALL-	PARS-	REED-
HAWK-	KEEP-	MALT-	PART-	REEF-
HEAD-	KEGL-	MAPP-	PASS-	REEL-

RENN-	SEIN-	SPAE-	TOLL-	WARM-
RENT-	SEIS-	SPIL-	TOOL-	WARN-
REPP-	SEIZ-	STAG-	TOPP-	WARP-
REST-	SELF-	STAR-	TOSS-	WASH-
RIBB-	SEND-	STEW-	TOTT-	WAST-
RIDG-	SENS-	STON-	TOUR-	WAUL-
RIFL-	SERG-	STOP-	TOUS-	WAWL-
RIGG-	SERV-	STOV-	TRAC-	WAXW-
RIGL-	SETT-	STOW-	TRAD-	WEAR-
RIMM-	SHAD-	STYL-	TUBB-	WEAV-
RING-	SHAK-	SUBB-	TUFT-	WEBB-
RINS-	SHAP-	SUBR-	TUGG-	WEDD-
RIOT-	SHAR-	SUCK-	TUNN-	WEDG-
RISP-	SHAV-	SUGG-	TURF-	WEED-
ROAD-	SHOE-	SUIT-	TURN-	WEEP-
ROAM-	SHOR-	SUMM-	TUSK-	WELD-
ROAR-	SHOV-	SURF-	TUTT-	WELL-
ROCK-	SHOW-	SURG-	TWIN-	WELT-
RODD-	SIBL-	SWAL-	UNBE-	WEST-
ROLF-	SIFT-	SWAY-	UNDO-	WETT-
ROLL-	SIGN-	SYND-	UNIT-	WHAL-
ROOF-	SIND-	TABL-	UNSL-	WHIN-
ROOT-	SING-	TACK-	UNTY-	WHIT-
ROUM-	SINK-	TAGG-	UPBR-	WICK-
ROUT-	SITT-	TAIL-	UPFL-	WIGG-
RUBB-	SKAT-	TALK-	UPGO-	WILD-
RUCH-	SKIV-	TAMP-	UPSW-	WINC-
RUGG-	SLAT-	TANK-	VAMP-	WIND-
RUIN-	SLIC-	TANL-	VANN-	WINK-
RUNN-	SLID-	TANN-	VARY-	WINN-
RUSH-	SLOW-	TAPP-	VEER-	WISH-
RUST-	SMIL-	TARR-	VEIL-	WITL-
RUTT-	SMOK-	TASK-	VEIN-	WITT-
SACK-	SNAR-	TAST-	VEND-	WOLF-
SACR-	SNIP-	TATT-	VENT-	WOLV-
SAGG-	SNOR-	TEAM-	VERB-	WONN-
SAIL-	SOAK-	TEAS-	VERS-	WORD-
SALT-	SOAR-	TELL-	VEST-	WORK-
SALV-	SOBB-	TENT-	VIEW-	WRIT-
SAND-	SOGG-	TEST-	VOGU-	YARD-
SAPL-	SOIL-	THAW-	VOIC-	YAWN-
SARK-	SOOP-	TICK-	VOID-	YAWP-
SCAL-	SOPP-	TIFF-	WADD-	YEAL-
SCOR-	SORN-	TILL-	WAFT-	YELL-
SCRY-	SORT-	TILT-	WAIL-	YELP-
SEAL-	SOSS-	TINN-	WAIT-	YOWL-
SEAR-	SOTT-	TINT-	WALK-	ZORB-
SEAT-	SOUM-	TIPP-	WALL-	
SEED-	SOUR-	TITH-	WANT-	
SEEL-	SOUS-	TITL-	WARD-	
SEEM-	SPAC-	TOIL-	WARL-	

Words that end with -ISE

Seven-letter words

ABSC-	AGEN-	ANOD-	ARAB-	AZOT-
ADON-	AGON-	ANYW-	ATHE-	BAPT-
AGAT-	AIRW-	APPR-	ATOM-	BROM-

CHAM-	EGOT-	IRON-	OXID-	RERA-
CHEM-	ELEG-	ITEM-	OZON-	RIOT-
COAL-	EMPR-	KYAN-	PARV-	SOUB-
COGN-	ENDW-	LAIC-	PECT-	STYL-
CONC-	EROT-	LAIR-	PENT-	SUCC-
COTT-	FADA-	LION-	PEPT-	SUNR-
CYAN-	FANW-	MALA-	POET-	SUNW-
CYCL-	GALL-	MANW-	PREC-	SURM-
DESP-	GENO-	MAPW-	PREM-	TAXW-
DIAR-	GREC-	MORT-	PREV-	TREN-
DOCK-	HERO-	MYTH-	PROM-	UNIT-
DUAL-	ICON-	NICO-	REAL-	UPRA-
EBON-	IDOL-	OBEL-	REAR-	UTIL-
ECHO-	IRID-	ODOR-	REPR-	

Eight-letter words

ACTIV-	DEPUT-	HUMAN-	OPSON-	SINIC-
ALBIT-	DIGIT-	IDEAL-	OPTIM-	SIREN-
ALKAL-	DIMER-	IMMUN-	ORGAN-	SIRON-
AMORT-	DISGU-	INFAM-	OUTRA-	SOBER-
ANNAL-	DISSE-	JAPAN-	OVERW-	SODOM-
ANTIC-	DIVIN-	JAROV-	PAGAN-	SOLAR-
APHET-	DROPW-	JUMBO-	PAIRW-	SOLEC-
APHOR-	DYNAM-	LATER-	PALEW-	SOMEW-
APPET-	EBION-	LATIN-	PAPAL-	SOROR-
APPRA-	EDGEW-	LEGAL-	PARAD-	STEPW-
ARBOR-	EGLOM-	LIKEW-	PATIN-	SUBER-
ARCHA-	ELSEW-	LOCAL-	PENAL-	SUBIT-
ARCHW-	EMBOL-	LOGIC-	POLAR-	SUCHW-
ATHET-	EMPER-	LONGW-	POLEM-	SURPR-
ATTIC-	ENERG-	LYRIC-	POLON-	TEAMW-
AVIAN-	EQUAL-	MACAR-	PORPO-	TELEV-
BANAL-	ERGOT-	MADER-	PORTO-	TENTW-
BENDW-	ETERN-	MARQU-	PRACT-	TETAN-
BEPRA-	ETHER-	MAUVA-	PTYAL-	THEOR-
BOTAN-	ETHIC-	MAXIM-	PYRIT-	THUSW-
BRAND-	EULOG-	MELAN-	PYROL-	TORTO-
CALOR-	EUPHU-	MELOD-	QUANT-	TOTAL-
CANAL-	EVENT-	MEMOR-	RACEM-	TRAVO-
CANON-	EXERC-	MESPR-	READV-	TREAT-
CAPON-	EXORC-	METAL-	REGUL-	TUTOR-
CHAST-	FABUL-	MINIM-	REREV-	UNION-
CHROM-	FARAD-	MISPO-	RESIN-	UNPRA-
CIVIL-	FEMIN-	MISPR-	RIGID-	URBAN-
COLON-	FESSW-	MISRA-	RINGW-	VALOR-
COLOR-	FIBER-	MOBIL-	RIVAL-	VAPOR-
COMBW-	FINAL-	MONET-	ROBOT-	VELAR-
COMPR-	FLATW-	MOONR-	ROMAN-	VIRIL-
COVET-	FLUID-	MORAL-	ROYAL-	VITAL-
CRABW-	FOCAL-	MOTOR-	RURAL-	VOCAL-
CREOL-	FRANC-	NASAL-	SALIN-	VOLUM-
CURAR-	GRAEC-	NEBUL-	SANIT-	VOWEL-
CUTIN-	HEBRA-	NODAL-	SATIR-	WARPW-
DEBRU-	HEPAT-	NOMAD-	SIDEW-	WEFTW-
DEION-	HIGHR-	NOTAR-	SIMIL-	WOMAN-
DEMON-	HOMIN-	NOVEL-	SIMON-	

Words that end with -ISH

Seven-letter words

ABOL-	DONN-	HIPP-	OOFT-	SNAK-
ALUM-	DOVE-	HOBB-	OUTF-	SNOW-
ANGU-	DRON-	HOGF-	OUTW-	SOFT-
BABY-	DULL-	HOGG-	PANF-	SOTT-
BADD-	DUMP-	HORN-	PARK-	SOUR-
BALD-	DUNC-	HOTT-	PEAK-	STON-
BATF-	DUNN-	HUFF-	PECK-	STYL-
BEAM-	DUSK-	JEWF-	PEEV-	SUNF-
BEAR-	ENGL-	JIGG-	PERK-	SWIN-
BEAU-	EVAN-	KADD-	PETT-	TALL-
BIGG-	FADD-	KERN-	PIED-	TANN-
BLEM-	FAIR-	KIDD-	PIGF-	TARN-
BLOK-	FALS-	KNAV-	PIGG-	TART-
BLUE-	FAST-	LADD-	PINF-	TIGR-
BOAR-	FATT-	LADY-	PINK-	TITT-
BOBB-	FENN-	LARG-	PIXY-	TOAD-
BOGG-	FILM-	LARK-	PLAN-	TOFF-
BOOB-	FINE-	LAZY-	PLEN-	TONN-
BOOK-	FINF-	LEFT-	POOR-	TOWN-
BOOR-	FLEM-	LOGG-	POPP-	TUBB-
BOXF-	FOGY-	LOMP-	PRUD-	TUBF-
BRIN-	FOLK-	LONG-	PUBL-	TUND-
BRUT-	FOOL-	LOUD-	PUCK-	VAMP-
BUCK-	FOPP-	LOUT-	PUGG-	VARN-
BULL-	FOXF-	LUBF-	PUNK-	VOGU-
BURN-	FULL-	LUMP-	PUPF-	WAGG-
CADD-	FURB-	LUSK-	RAFF-	WAIF-
CARL-	FURN-	MADD-	RAMM-	WAMP-
CATF-	GAMP-	MAID-	RANK-	WANN-
CATT-	GARF-	MANN-	RASP-	WARM-
CHAV-	GARN-	MAWK-	RATF-	WASP-
CHER-	GAWK-	MINX-	RATT-	WEAK-
CLAY-	GEMF-	MISS-	REDD-	WEAR-
COCK-	GIRL-	MOBB-	REDF-	WEBL-
CODF-	GNOM-	MONK-	RELL-	WENN-
COLD-	GOAT-	MOON-	RIGG-	WETT-
COLT-	GOLD-	MOOR-	ROGU-	WHEY-
COOL-	GOOD-	MORE-	ROIN-	WHIT-
COWF-	GRAY-	MUDF-	ROMP-	WHOR-
CRON-	GREY-	MUFF-	ROOK-	WILD-
CUBB-	GUAR-	MUGG-	ROYN-	WIMP-
CULT-	GULL-	MUMP-	RUBB-	WISP-
CURR-	HAGF-	MURK-	RUMM-	WOGG-
DAMP-	HAGG-	NEBB-	RUNT-	WOLF-
DANK-	HAIM-	NEDD-	RUTT-	WOLV-
DARK-	HARD-	NERD-	SADD-	WORD-
DEAF-	HASH-	NICE-	SALT-	WORM-
DERV-	HAWK-	NOIR-	SAWF-	YOBB-
DIMM-	HEIM-	NOUR-	SELF-	ZANY-
DOGF-	HELL-	NUNN-	SERF-	
DOGG-	HENN-	NURD-	SICK-	
DOLL-	HICK-	OARF-	SLAV-	
DOLT-	HIGH-	OGRE-	SLOW-	

Eight-letter words

ACTOR-	CRAWF-	GRUMP-	RAWMA-	STEEP-
ADMON-	CRAYF-	GYPSY-	REFIN-	STIFF-
ASTON-	CROSS-	HEADF-	REPOL-	STILT-
BABEL-	DANDY-	IDIOT-	RIGHT-	STOCK-
BAIRN-	DEALF-	JACKF-	ROCKF-	STOUT-
BAITF-	DEMOL-	JINGO-	ROSEF-	STUDF-
BAKSH-	DEPOL-	KINGF-	ROUGH-	SUCKF-
BILLF-	DEVIL-	KNACK-	ROUND-	SUMPH-
BLACK-	DIMIN-	LADYF-	ROWDY-	SURFF-
BLAND-	DOWDY-	LANGU-	SAILF-	SWAIN-
BLEAK-	DRABB-	LEMON-	SAINT-	SWAMP-
BLIMP-	DRAFF-	LIGHT-	SALTF-	SWEET-
BLOCK-	DREGG-	LIONF-	SANDF-	SWELL-
BLOKE-	DROLL-	LITTL-	SCAMP-	SYLPH-
BLOND-	DROOG-	LIVER-	SCARF-	THICK-
BLOWF-	DRUMF-	LUMPF-	SCOMF-	THIEV-
BLUEF-	DWARF-	LUNGF-	SCUMF-	THINN-
BLUNT-	DWEEB-	MILKF-	SHARP-	THUGG-
BOARF-	EMPER-	MINID-	SHEEP-	TICKL-
BONEF-	ENRAV-	MONKF-	SHORT-	TIGER-
BOOBY-	ESSAY-	MOONF-	SHREW-	TIGHT-
BRACK-	ETHER-	NABOB-	SISSY-	TILEF-
BRAIN-	FAINT-	NANNY-	SIXTY-	TINGL-
BRAND-	FALLF-	NINNY-	SKIRM-	TOADF-
BRASS-	FEEBL-	NOHOW-	SKITT-	TOADY-
BRATT-	FEVER-	NOVEL-	SLANG-	TOLLD-
BRISK-	FIEND-	NUMBF-	SLIMM-	TOUGH-
BROAD-	FIFTY-	NYMPH-	SLOBB-	TOVAR-
BROGU-	FILEF-	ORANG-	SLUGG-	TRAMP-
BROWN-	FLATF-	OVERF-	SLUTT-	TRICK-
CAMEL-	FLATT-	PAGAN-	SMALL-	UNMOD-
CAVEF-	FLIRT-	PIPEF-	SMART-	UNPOL-
CEORL-	FLOUR-	PIXIE-	SNAPP-	VAGAR-
CHEAP-	FOGEY-	PLAIN-	SNEAK-	VANQU-
CHILD-	FOOLF-	PLUMP-	SNIFF-	VAPOR-
CHURL-	FORTY-	POKER-	SNOBB-	VIGOR-
CLANN-	FRAIL-	POSER-	SNOUT-	VIPER-
CLAPD-	FREAK-	PRANK-	SNUBB-	VIXEN-
CLERK-	FRESH-	PRIGG-	SOLID-	WALLF-
CLIQU-	FROGF-	PROUD-	SORRY-	WATER-
CLODD-	FRUMP-	PSEUD-	SPARK-	WEAKF-
CLOTT-	GHOUL-	PUPPY-	SPOFF-	WOLFF-
CLOWN-	GIPSY-	PURPL-	SPOOK-	WOMAN-
CLUBB-	GLUMP-	PYGMY-	SQUAR-	YOKEL-
CLUMP-	GOATF-	QUACK-	SQUIR-	YOUNG-
COALF-	GOLDF-	QUALM-	STABL-	
COARS-	GRAYF-	QUEER-	STAND-	
COMPL-	GREEN-	QUIPP-	STARF-	
CRANK-	GRUFF-	QUIRK-	START-	

Words that end with -ISM

Seven-letter words

ABLE-	ASTE-	ATOM-	BAPT-	BOGY-
AMOR-	ATAV-	BAAL-	BARD-	BOSS-
ANIM-	ATHE-	BABU-	BIPR-	BROM-

BRUT-	EGOT-	HEUR-	NEUR-	SLUM-
BRUX-	ELIT-	HOBO-	OBEL-	SOPH-
CAMB-	ENTR-	IDOL-	ODYL-	STAT-
CHAR-	EPIC-	IMAG-	OGRE-	TACH-
CHEM-	EROT-	ITAC-	ONAN-	TACT-
CHOR-	ETAC-	JUJU-	ORAL-	TOUR-
CLAD-	ETAT-	KARA-	ORPH-	TROP-
CLON-	EXOT-	LADY-	PEON-	TSAR-
COPY-	FADD-	LAIC-	PHAE-	TYCH-
COSM-	FALS-	LEFT-	PHOB-	TZAR-
CRET-	FASC-	LEGG-	PHOT-	URAN-
CULT-	FATT-	LION-	PIAN-	UTOP-
CZAR-	FAUV-	LOCO-	PIET-	WHOL-
DADA-	FIDE-	LOOK-	PLEN-	YOBB-
DIOR-	FOGY-	MAID-	RANK-	ZANY-
DODO-	FOOD-	MOBB-	REAL-	
DONN-	GURU-	MYAL-	SELF-	
DUAL-	HAND-	MYTH-	SENS-	
ECHO-	HERO-	NARC-	SIZE-	

Eight-letter words

ACOSM-	CRONY-	FOGEY-	NABOB-	PTYAL-
ACROT-	CULLY-	FUTUR-	NASAL-	PUGIL-
ACTIN-	CYNIC-	GIANT-	NATIV-	PUPPY-
ACTIV-	DANDY-	GYPSY-	NATUR-	PYGMY-
ALARM-	DEMON-	HEDON-	NAVAL-	QABAL-
ALBIN-	DEVIL-	HELOT-	NEGRO-	QUACK-
ALGOR-	DIMER-	HOBBY-	NEPHR-	QUIET-
ALIEN-	DIOEC-	HUMAN-	NEPOT-	RACEM-
ALLEL-	DIRIG-	HYLIC-	NIHIL-	REGAL-
ALPIN-	DITHE-	IDEAL-	NIMBY-	RIGHT-
ALTRU-	DONAT-	IDIOT-	NOMAD-	RIGOR-
ANEUR-	DOWDY-	INCIV-	NOVEL-	ROBOT-
APHOR-	DRUDG-	INTIM-	OBEAH-	ROWDY-
APTER-	DRUID-	IOTAC-	OCKER-	ROYAL-
ARCHA-	DWARF-	JEHAD-	OPIUM-	RURAL-
ASTER-	DYNAM-	JIHAD-	OPTIM-	SAINT-
ATROP-	EBION-	JINGO-	ORGAN-	SAPPH-
ATTIC-	EMBOL-	KABAL-	PACIF-	SATAN-
AUTEC-	ENDEM-	LABOR-	PAEAN-	SAVAG-
BABEL-	ENTRY-	LACON-	PAGAN-	SCIOL-
BATHM-	EPIZO-	LEGAL-	PALUD-	SCRIB-
BETAC-	ERETH-	LOBBY-	PAPAL-	SEISM-
BINAR-	ERGOT-	LOCAL-	PAREC-	SIMPL-
BOGEY-	ESCAP-	LOGIC-	PARTY-	SINAP-
BOOBY-	ETHER-	LOOKS-	PELOR-	SNOBB-
BOTUL-	ETHIC-	LOYAL-	PETAL-	SOLAR-
BOYAR-	EUGEN-	LUMIN-	PEYOT-	SOLEC-
BULLY-	EUMER-	LYRIC-	PHALL-	SOLID-
CABAL-	EUPHU-	MACAR-	PHREN-	SOMAT-
CAFFE-	EXORC-	MACHO-	PLUMB-	STOIC-
CASTE-	FAIRY-	MELAN-	POLON-	STRAB-
CENTR-	FAKIR-	MERYC-	POPUL-	SWING-
CHART-	FAMIL-	METOP-	PRIAP-	SYBOT-
CIVIC-	FARAD-	MINIM-	PRIGG-	TANTR-
CLASS-	FATAL-	MODAL-	PROSA-	TERAT-
CLIQU-	FEMIN-	MONAD-	PSELL-	THUGG-
CLUBB-	FINAL-	MORAL-	PSEPH-	TIGER-
COLOR-	FINIT-	MORON-	PSYCH-	TITAN-

TOADY-	TRIAL-	UNION-	VITAL-	YAHOO-
TOKEN-	TROIL-	UNTRU-	VOCAL-	ZOMBI-
TOTAL-	TUTOR-	URBAN-	VOLTA-	
TOTEM-	ULTRA-	VEGAN-	WOMAN-	
TRIAD-	UNDIN-	VIRIL-	XANTH-	

Words that end with -IST

Seven-letter words

ABLE-	CORN-	FATT-	MAPP-	RHYM-
ACQU-	COSM-	FAUN-	METR-	SACR-
AGON-	CULT-	FAUV-	MIDL-	SELF-
ALTO-	CYCL-	FEUD-	MYAL-	SENS-
AMOR-	CZAR-	FIDE-	MYTH-	SIZE-
ANGL-	DADA-	FLOR-	NAIV-	SOLO-
ANIM-	DENT-	FLUT-	NARC-	SOPH-
ATAV-	DIAL-	FUGU-	OCUL-	STAT-
ATHE-	DIAR-	GAMB-	OLIG-	STYL-
ATOM-	DIET-	GNOM-	OLOG-	SUBS-
ATTR-	DUAL-	HARP-	ONAN-	SUMM-
BAPT-	DUEL-	HERB-	ORAL-	SUMO-
BASS-	DUMA-	HORN-	PALM-	TACH-
BIBL-	EBON-	HYGE-	PERS-	TENN-
BUND-	ECHO-	HYLO-	PHOB-	TITL-
CAMB-	EGOT-	HYMN-	PIAN-	TOUR-
CASU-	ELEG-	IAMB-	PIAR-	TROP-
CELL-	ELIT-	IDOL-	PIET-	TSAR-
CHEK-	ELOG-	IDYL-	PLEN-	TUBA-
CHEM-	ENTR-	IMAG-	PLUM-	TZAR-
CHOR-	ENTW-	INTW-	POLL-	UNAL-
CHUT-	EPEE-	IRON-	POLO-	UNTW-
CHYM-	EPIC-	IVOR-	PROT-	UPHO-
CLAD-	ETAT-	JUDO-	QUER-	UTOP-
COEX-	EXOD-	JUJU-	REAL-	VACU-
CONS-	FADD-	LEFT-	RETW-	VIOL-
COPY-	FASC-	LOOK-	REVU-	WHOL-

Eight-letter words

ACOSM-	AVIAR-	CLUBB-	ESSAY-	HAGAD-
ACTIV-	BACKL-	COASS-	ETHER-	HALAK-
ALARM-	BANJO-	COLON-	ETHIC-	HANDL-
ALIEN-	BIGAM-	COLOR-	EUGEN-	HEDON-
ALPIN-	BLURB-	CONTR-	EULOG-	HOBBY-
ALTRU-	BONGO-	CREOL-	EUPHU-	HOMIL-
ANNAL-	BOTAN-	DEMON-	EXORC-	HUMAN-
APHOR-	BURIN-	DEMOT-	FABUL-	HUMOR-
APIAR-	CABAL-	DIALL-	FATAL-	HYGIE-
AQUAR-	CALOR-	DIGAM-	FEMIN-	HYLIC-
ARBAL-	CANOE-	DITHE-	FIGUR-	HYPOC-
ARBOR-	CANON-	DRUGG-	FINAL-	IDEAL-
ARCAN-	CENTO-	DUELL-	FLAUT-	IDYLL-
ARCHA-	CENTR-	DUETT-	FUTUR-	INTIM-
ARMOR-	CERAM-	DYNAM-	GARAG-	JEHAD-
ARSON-	CHART-	ENTRY-	GLOSS-	JIHAD-
ATTIC-	CIVIL-	ERROR-	GREYL-	JINGO-
AVANT-	CLASS-	ESCAP-	GROUP-	JUNGL-

KABAL-	MODAL-	PAROD-	SAFAR-	TENOR-
LABOR-	MODEL-	PEYOT-	SAPPH-	THEOR-
LAPID-	MONOD-	PHALL-	SAROD-	TOTAL-
LEGAL-	MORAL-	PLAYL-	SATAN-	TOTEM-
LIBEL-	MOTOR-	POLEM-	SATIR-	TRIAD-
LINGU-	MURAL-	POPUL-	SCIOL-	TRIAL-
LOBBY-	NATIV-	PREEX-	SEMIT-	TROIL-
LOCAL-	NATUR-	PROSA-	SHITL-	ULTRA-
LOGIC-	NEPOT-	PSALM-	SHOOT-	UNION-
LOYAL-	NIELL-	PSYCH-	SILUR-	UNSEX-
LUMIN-	NIHIL-	PUCKF-	SIMON-	URBAN-
LUNAR-	NOVEL-	PUGIL-	SIMPL-	VEGET-
LUTAN-	ODONT-	QABAL-	SITAR-	VISAG-
LUTEN-	OGHAM-	QUIET-	SODAL-	VITAL-
LUXUR-	OOLOG-	RALLY-	SODOM-	VOCAL-
LYRIC-	OPTIC-	REENL-	SOLAR-	VOLUM-
MAXIM-	OPTIM-	REGAL-	SOLEC-	VOTAR-
MEDAL-	ORGAN-	REVER-	SOLID-	WAITL-
MELAN-	PACIF-	RIGHT-	SOMAT-	WOMAN-
MELOD-	PAGAN-	RIGOR-	STOCK-	
METAL-	PANEL-	ROYAL-	SUBTR-	
MINIM-	PAPAL-	RURAL-	TANGO-	

Words that end with -ITY

Seven-letter words

ABIL-	CLAR-	FURM-	PANE-	SURD-
ACID-	CRUD-	GASE-	PAUC-	TENS-
AGIL-	CURV-	GRAV-	PIOS-	TENU-
AMEN-	DABB-	INAN-	PRAV-	TRIN-
AMIN-	DACO-	JOLL-	PRIV-	UNIC-
ANAL-	DAKO-	LAIC-	PROB-	UTIL-
ANIL-	DENS-	NULL-	QUAL-	VACU-
ANNU-	DIGN-	OBES-	RABB-	VARS-
ARID-	DUAL-	OMNE-	RAUC-	VAST-
AURE-	EDAC-	OPAC-	REAL-	VIDU-
AVID-	EGAL-	ORAL-	RUBB-	
BIGG-	EXIL-	OUTC-	SICC-	
BREV-	FALS-	OUTP-	SPIR-	
CHAR-	FATU-	OVAL-	SUAV-	

Eight-letter words

ACERB-	AXIAL-	CIVIL-	ETERN-	FORTU-
ACRID-	BANAL-	CONCE-	EXIGU-	FUGAC-
ACTIV-	BASIC-	CONIC-	FACIL-	FUMOS-
ADUNC-	BIFID-	CUBIC-	FATAL-	FURAC-
AFFIN-	BISCU-	CUPID-	FELIC-	FUTIL-
ALACR-	BOVIN-	DEBIL-	FELIN-	FUTUR-
ALGID-	CADUC-	DICAC-	FEMAL-	GELID-
ALTER-	CALAM-	DISUN-	FEMIN-	GRATU-
ANTIC-	CALID-	DIVIN-	FERAC-	GULOS-
ASPER-	CANIN-	DOCIL-	FEROC-	HELIC-
ASTUC-	CAPAC-	DUMOS-	FETID-	HERED-
ATROC-	CELER-	ENORM-	FIDEL-	HILAR-
AUDAC-	CHAST-	EQUAL-	FINAL-	HUMAN-
AURAL-	CIRCU-	EQUIN-	FLUID-	HUMID-

HUMIL-	MAJOR-	ORGAN-	SAPID-	TRIAL-
IDEAL-	MATUR-	OTIOS-	SATAN-	TRIUN-
IDENT-	MEGAC-	PENAL-	SCANT-	TUMID-
IDONE-	MINAC-	PERSE-	SCARC-	UBIQU-
IMMAN-	MINOR-	PILOS-	SECUR-	UNFIX-
IMMUN-	MOBIL-	POLAR-	SEDUL-	URBAN-
IMPAR-	MODAL-	POROS-	SENIL-	VAGIL-
IMPUN-	MOLAL-	PRIOR-	SEREN-	VALID-
IMPUR-	MOLAR-	PUDIC-	SEROS-	VAPID-
INEQU-	MORAL-	QUANT-	SEVER-	VELLE-
INFIN-	MORON-	QUEER-	SODAL-	VELOC-
INIQU-	MOROS-	QUIDD-	SODIC-	VENAL-
INSAN-	MOTIL-	RABID-	SOLIC-	VENOS-
INTIM-	MOTIV-	RAMOS-	SOLID-	VERAC-
INVER-	MUCID-	RAPAC-	SONOR-	VICIN-
IONIC-	MUCOS-	RAPID-	SOROR-	VINOS-
JEJUN-	MULTE-	REGAL-	SPARS-	VIRID-
JOCOS-	NASAL-	RIGID-	TEMER-	VIRIL-
LABIL-	NATAL-	RIMOS-	TENAC-	VITAL-
LANOS-	NATIV-	RIVAL-	TEPID-	VIVAC-
LATIN-	NIHIL-	RUGOS-	TIMID-	VIVID-
LEGAL-	NOBIL-	RURAL-	TONAL-	VOCAL-
LEGER-	NODAL-	SAGAC-	TONIC-	VORAC-
LIVID-	NODOS-	SALAC-	TOROS-	ZYGOS-
LOCAL-	NUBIL-	SALIN-	TOTAL-	
LUCID-	OBTUS-	SANCT-	TOXIC-	

Words that end with -IUM

Seven-letter words

ALOD-	ELUV-	LITH-	RHEN-	TRIT-
ALUM-	EROD-	MUON-	RHOD-	TRIV-
BALL-	EXUV-	NATR-	SPOD-	URAN-
BOHR-	FERM-	NIOB-	STAD-	URED-
CADM-	GALL-	ORAR-	STIB-	YTTR-
CAES-	HAFN-	OXON-	STOM-	ZOAR-
CALC-	HAHN-	PALL-	TAED-	ZOEC-
CAMB-	HASS-	PLAG-	TERB-	
CRAN-	HOLM-	PREM-	TERT-	
DUBN-	IRID-	PROT-	THOR-	
ELOG-	ISCH-	PYTH-	THUL-	

Eight-letter words

ACHEN-	BIENN-	DIDYM-	GONID-	LUTET-
ACTIN-	BOTHR-	DILUV-	GRAPH-	MASUR-
AECID-	BRACH-	DOMAT-	GYNEC-	MECON-
AEROB-	CALAD-	DOMIN-	HELEN-	MOTOR-
ALLOD-	CHROM-	EMPOR-	HYMEN-	MYCEL-
ALLUV-	CIBOR-	ENCOM-	ILLIN-	NEBUL-
AMMON-	CONAR-	ERYNG-	ILLUV-	NOBEL-
APTER-	CONID-	EULOG-	IMPER-	ONCID-
AQUAR-	COREM-	EUROP-	INDIC-	ONYCH-
ASCID-	CORON-	EXORD-	INDUS-	OOGON-
ASPID-	CYATH-	FRANC-	INGEN-	OPSON-
BASID-	CYMAT-	FUSAR-	LIXIV-	ORDAL-
BDELL-	DELIR-	GERAN-	LUTEC-	OSSAR-

PATAG-	PUPAR-	SCAND-	SOLAT-	UNUNB-
PECUL-	PYGID-	SCHOL-	SORED-	VANAD-
PEPON-	PYXID-	SEDIL-	SPLEN-	VELAR-
PERID-	RANAR-	SELEN-	SUDAR-	VENID-
PHORM-	REFUG-	SILIC-	SYCON-	VIVAR-
POLON-	ROSAR-	SILPH-	THALL-	ZOOEC-
PROPR-	RUBID-	SIMUL-	TITAN-	
PSYLL-	SAMAR-	SOLAR-	TRILL-	

Words that end with -KIN

Seven-letter words

BARM-	CATS-	GHER-	LORD-	RAMA-
BAWD-	COWS-	GRIS-	LUMP-	RAME-
BODI-	CUTI-	HUFF-	MANA-	REDS-
BOOM-	DOES-	KIDS-	MANI-	SHIN-
BROD-	DOGS-	KIPS-	MINI-	SIMP-
BUMP-	DOIT-	LADY-	OILS-	WOLF-
CANA-	FINI-	LAMB-	PIGS-	
CANI-	FOXS-	LIMP-	PUMP-	

Eight-letter words

BAUDE-	CAPES-	DUNNA-	MOLES-	SWANS-
BEARS-	CIDER-	FINIC-	MOUSE-	THUMB-
BOOTI-	COONS-	FISHS-	MUNCH-	TURNS-
BRODE-	COOTI-	FORES-	MUTCH-	WINES-
BUCKS-	CUITI-	GOATS-	PANNI-	WOLFS-
BYRLA-	DAMAS-	LAMBS-	PONYS-	WOODS-
CALFS-	DEERS-	LARRI-	SEALS-	WOOLS-
CANNI-	DEVIL-	MANNI-	SPILI-	

Words that end with -LAND

Seven-letter words

BAD-	FEN-	HOL-	NOR-	WET-
BOG-	GAR-	LAL-	OUT-	
COT-	GOL-	LAW-	RIM-	
DRY-	GOW-	LOW-	SUN-	
ELF-	HIE-	MID-	TRO-	

Eight-letter words

BACK-	EAST-	HOME-	PINE-	TIDE-
BOOK-	FARM-	LACK-	PLAY-	TOWN-
BUSH-	FILM-	LAKE-	PLOW-	WASH-
CLUB-	FLAT-	MAIN-	PORT-	WILD-
CORN-	FOLK-	MOOR-	SCAB-	WOOD-
CROP-	FORE-	MOSS-	SHET-	YARD-
DOCK-	GANG-	OVER-	SLOB-	
DOWN-	HEAD-	PARK-	SNOW-	
DUNE-	HIGH-	PEAT-	SOAP-	

Words that end with -LESS

Seven-letter words

AGE-	CUB-	HAP-	MAP-	TAX-
AID-	DEW-	HAT-	MAT-	TIE-
AIM-	EAR-	HIP-	NAP-	TIP-
AIR-	EBB-	HIT-	NET-	TOE-
ARM-	EGG-	HUE-	OAR-	TOP-
ART-	EGO-	ICE-	ORB-	TOY-
ASH-	END-	INK-	PEG-	TUG-
AWE-	EYE-	INN-	PIP-	UNB-
AWN-	FAT-	IRE-	RAY-	USE-
BAG-	FEE-	JAG-	RIB-	VOW-
BAR-	FIN-	JAW-	RIM-	WAR-
BED-	FLY-	JOB-	ROD-	WAY-
BIB-	FOG-	JOY-	RUN-	WEB-
BIT-	FUR-	KEY-	SAC-	WIG-
BOW-	GAP-	KIN-	SAP-	WIN-
BRA-	GAS-	LAW-	SEX-	WIT-
BUD-	GOD-	LEG-	SIN-	ZIP-
CAP-	GUM-	LID-	SON-	
CAR-	GUN-	LIP-	SUM-	
COX-	GUT-	MAN-	SUN-	

Eight-letter words

BACK-	COAL-	FEAR-	GRIT-	JAIL-
BARB-	COAT-	FECK-	GUST-	JURY-
BARK-	CODE-	FEET-	HAIR-	KEEL-
BASE-	COMB-	FERN-	HALT-	KIND-
BASH-	COOK-	FILM-	HAND-	KING-
BATE-	CORD-	FINE-	HARM-	KNOT-
BATH-	CORE-	FIRE-	HATE-	LACE-
BEAK-	COST-	FIRM-	HEAD-	LAND-
BEAM-	CREW-	FISH-	HEAT-	LEAD-
BEAT-	CROP-	FLAG-	HEED-	LEAF-
BEEF-	CUFF-	FLAP-	HEEL-	LEAK-
BELT-	CURB-	FLAW-	HEIR-	LENS-
BLOT-	CURE-	FOAM-	HELM-	LIFE-
BODI-	DATE-	FOOD-	HELP-	LIMB-
BOLT-	DEBT-	FOOT-	HERB-	LIME-
BOND-	DEED-	FORD-	HIDE-	LINT-
BONE-	DEVI-	FORK-	HILT-	LIST-
BOOK-	DINT-	FORM-	HIVE-	LOAM-
BOON-	DISK-	FRET-	HOLE-	LOFT-
BOOT-	DOOR-	FUME-	HOME-	LORD-
BRIM-	DOWN-	FUND-	HOOD-	LOSS-
BROW-	DRIP-	FUSE-	HOOF-	LOVE-
BUSH-	DUCT-	GAIN-	HOOK-	LUCK-
CALF-	DUST-	GAOL-	HOOP-	LUST-
CARE-	EASE-	GARB-	HOPE-	MAID-
CASH-	ECHO-	GATE-	HORN-	MAIL-
CHAD-	EDGE-	GAUM-	HUMP-	MAKE-
CHAP-	EXIT-	GEAR-	HURT-	MANE-
CHIN-	FACE-	GIFT-	HYMN-	MASS-
CLAW-	FADE-	GOAL-	IDEA-	MAST-
CLOY-	FAME-	GOLD-	IRON-	MATE-
CLUE-	FANG-	GORM-	ISLE-	MEAL-

MEAT-	PORT-	SEAM-	SUDS-	VENT-
MILK-	PREB-	SEAT-	TACK-	VERB-
MIND-	PULP-	SEED-	TACT-	VEST-
MOON-	PUMP-	SEEM-	TAIL-	VETO-
MOVE-	RAIL-	SELF-	TAME-	VICE-
NAIL-	RAIN-	SHIP-	TANK-	VIEW-
NAME-	RANK-	SHIT-	TAPE-	VINE-
NATH-	RECK-	SHOE-	TASK-	VOTE-
NECK-	REDE-	SHUN-	TEAR-	WAGE-
NEED-	REIN-	SIGH-	TEEM-	WAKE-
NEWS-	REST-	SIGN-	TENT-	WARD-
NORM-	RIFT-	SKIL-	TERM-	WARE-
NOSE-	RIME-	SKIN-	TEXT-	WART-
NOTE-	RIND-	SLIP-	THAW-	WATT-
NOUN-	RING-	SLIT-	THEW-	WAVE-
ODOR-	RISK-	SMOG-	THOW-	WEED-
OUTB-	RITE-	SNAP-	TIDE-	WEET-
PAIN-	RIVA-	SNOW-	TIME-	WELD-
PANE-	ROAD-	SOAP-	TINT-	WICK-
PANG-	ROCK-	SOCK-	TIRE-	WIFE-
PASS-	ROOF-	SODA-	TOAD-	WIND-
PAST-	ROOT-	SOIL-	TOIL-	WINE-
PATH-	ROSE-	SOLE-	TOMB-	WING-
PEAK-	RULE-	SONG-	TONE-	WIRE-
PEER-	RUMP-	SOOT-	TOOL-	WISH-
PELT-	RUNG-	SOUL-	TOWN-	WITE-
PILE-	RUST-	SOUP-	TRAM-	WONT-
PIPE-	RUTH-	SPAN-	TREE-	WOOD-
PITH-	SACK-	SPIN-	TUBE-	WORD-
PITI-	SAIK-	SPOT-	TUNE-	WORK-
PLAN-	SAIL-	SPUR-	TURF-	YOKE-
PLAY-	SALT-	STAR-	TUSK-	YOLK-
PLOT-	SAND-	STAY-	TWIG-	ZEAL-
PLUG-	SASH-	STEM-	TYRE-	ZEST-
POET-	SATE-	STIR-	VANE-	ZONE-
POLE-	SCAR-	STOP-	VEIL-	
POPE-	SCUM-	SUCK-	VEIN-	

Words that end with -LET

Seven-letter words

ANNU-	COVE-	HARS-	OVER-	STAR-
ARCH-	CUMU-	HERB-	PART-	STEM-
BEAM-	DEER-	HOOK-	PIKE-	STER-
BEND-	DEVI-	HORN-	PLAY-	SWAL-
BOMB-	DOUB-	JING-	QUIL-	TART-
BOOK-	DOVE-	KING-	RING-	TEMP-
BOOM-	DRIB-	LAKE-	RIPP-	TOWN-
BULB-	DROP-	LEAF-	RIVU-	TRIB-
CACO-	EPAU-	LOBE-	ROOT-	TRIO-
CANT-	FLAT-	MANT-	ROYA-	TRIP-
CAPE-	FONT-	MART-	RUND-	VEIN-
CHAM-	FORT-	MEDA-	SCAR-	WAVE-
CHAP-	FROG-	MOON-	SERV-	WING-
CIRC-	GANT-	NECK-	SING-	ZONU-
CORS-	GURG-	NOTE-	SKIL-	
COUP-	HACK-	OSSE-	SNIG-	

Eight-letter words

BANDE-	CROSS-	HEART-	PLANT-	STATE-
BARRU-	CROWN-	HERBE-	PLATE-	SWIFT-
BRACE-	DRIBB-	LANCE-	PLUME-	TERCE-
BRACT-	DRUPE-	MANTE-	QUEEN-	TRICK-
BROOK-	FLAME-	MIQUE-	RECOL-	TROUT-
CAPEL-	FOVEO-	MURRE-	RONDE-	UMBEL-
CHAIN-	FRONT-	NERVE-	ROUND-	UNDER-
CHEVA-	FRUIT-	NONUP-	SEXTO-	VALVE-
CLOUD-	GAUNT-	OCTUP-	SPANG-	VEINU-
CORSE-	GLOBU-	PAMPH-	SPARK-	VERSE-
COURT-	GREEN-	PANTA-	SPIKE-	WRIST-
COVER-	GROUP-	PISTO-	SPIRE-	

Words that end with -LIKE

Seven-letter words

AIR-	EEL-	HOG-	NUN-	SAW-
ANT-	ELF-	HUT-	NUT-	SIC-
APE-	EYE-	ICE-	OAK-	SKY-
ARM-	FAD-	INK-	OAR-	SON-
ASS-	FAN-	IVY-	OAT-	SUN-
BAG-	FAT-	JAM-	OWL-	TAG-
BAT-	FIN-	JAW-	PEA-	TEA-
BED-	FOX-	JET-	PEG-	TIN-
BEE-	GEM-	JIG-	PIG-	TOE-
BIB-	GOD-	KID-	POD-	TOY-
BOW-	GUM-	LAW-	POT-	TUB-
BOX-	GUT-	LEG-	PUS-	UNA-
BUD-	HAG-	LIP-	RAT-	URN-
CAT-	HAT-	MAN-	RAY-	WAR-
CUP-	HEN-	MAP-	RIB-	WAX-
DIS-	HIP-	MIS-	ROD-	WEB-
DOG-	HOB-	NET-	RUG-	WIG-
EAR-	HOE-	NIB-	SAC-	

Eight-letter words

AGUE-	CLAW-	DRUM-	GAME-	HERD-
AUNT-	CLAY-	DUNE-	GATE-	HIVE-
BALM-	COCK-	DUST-	GERM-	HOME-
BARN-	COKE-	EPIC-	GLEN-	HOOD-
BEAD-	COMB-	FANG-	GLUE-	HOOF-
BEAK-	CORD-	FAUN-	GNAT-	HOOK-
BEAM-	CORK-	FAWN-	GOAD-	HOOP-
BEAN-	CORM-	FELT-	GOAT-	HORN-
BEAR-	CRAB-	FERN-	GONG-	HOSE-
BIRD-	CULT-	FILM-	GULF-	HUMP-
BOAT-	DAWN-	FISH-	HAIR-	HUSK-
BOLT-	DEER-	FOAM-	HALO-	HYMN-
BOWL-	DISC-	FOLK-	HAND-	IRON-
BUSH-	DISH-	FOOT-	HARE-	JADE-
CAGE-	DISK-	FORK-	HAWK-	JAZZ-
CALF-	DOME-	FROG-	HEAD-	JUTE-
CAVE-	DOVE-	FUME-	HEMP-	KILT-
CLAM-	DOWN-	FUSE-	HERB-	KING-

KITE-	MOTH-	ROOT-	SONG-	VASE-
KNOB-	NECK-	ROPE-	SOUL-	VEIL-
KNOT-	NEST-	ROSE-	SOUP-	VEIN-
LACE-	NOOK-	RUBY-	SPAR-	VEST-
LADY-	NOSE-	RUFF-	STAR-	VICE-
LAKE-	NOVA-	RUNE-	STEM-	VINE-
LAMB-	OVEN-	RUSH-	STEP-	VISE-
LARD-	PALM-	SACK-	SUCH-	WAIF-
LATH-	PARK-	SALT-	SUIT-	WAND-
LAVA-	PEAK-	SAND-	SURF-	WART-
LEAF-	PINE-	SCAB-	SWAN-	WASP-
LIFE-	PIPE-	SCUM-	TAIL-	WAVE-
LILY-	PITH-	SEAL-	TANK-	WEED-
LINE-	PLAY-	SEAM-	TAPE-	WHEY-
LION-	PLUM-	SEED-	TENT-	WHIP-
LOFT-	POET-	SERF-	TIDE-	WIFE-
LORD-	POPE-	SHED-	TILE-	WING-
LYNX-	PUMP-	SIGH-	TOAD-	WIRE-
MASK-	PUSS-	SILK-	TOMB-	WISP-
MAST-	QUAY-	SKIN-	TRAP-	WOLF-
MAZE-	RASH-	SLAB-	TREE-	WOMB-
MILK-	REED-	SLIT-	TUBE-	WOOL-
MOAT-	RING-	SNAG-	TURF-	WORM-
MOON-	ROCK-	SNOW-	TUSK-	
MOSS-	ROOF-	SOAP-	TWIG-	

Words that end with -LOGY

Seven-letter words

ANA-	ECO-	NEO-	TRI-
APO-	ENO-	NOO-	UFO-
BIO-	GEO-	ORO-	URO-
DYS-	MYO-	OTO-	ZOO-

Eight-letter words

AERO-	CHAO-	IDEO-	OPTO-	SINO-
AGRO-	CODO-	KIDO-	OREO-	SITO-
ALGO-	CYTO-	MENO-	OURO-	THEO-
ANTI-	DEKA-	MISO-	PARA-	TOCO-
APIO-	DEMO-	MIXO-	PEDO-	TOKO-
ARCO-	DOSO-	MONO-	PELO-	TOPO-
AREO-	DOXO-	MYCO-	PENO-	TYPO-
ATMO-	ETHO-	NOMO-	PODO-	VENO-
AUTO-	ETIO-	NOSO-	POMO-	VINO-
AXIO-	FETO-	OECO-	POSO-	VIRO-
BATO-	GEMO-	OENO-	PYRO-	XYLO-
BRYO-	HOMO-	OINO-	RHEO-	ZYMO-
CACO-	HORO-	ONCO-	SERO-	
CETO-	IDEA-	ONTO-	SEXO-	

Words that end with -LY

Seven-letter words

ACRID-	BRIST-	DEATH-	FOCAL-	GUTSI-
ACTOR-	BRITT-	DEEDI-	FOGGI-	GYRAL-
ACUTE-	BROAD-	DEERF-	FRAIL-	HAMMI-
ADDED-	BRUTE-	DENSE-	FRANK-	HANDI-
ADEPT-	BUIRD-	DICYC-	FRECK-	HAPPI-
ADULT-	BULKI-	DINGI-	FRESH-	HARDI-
AFFAB-	BUMPI-	DIRTI-	FRIAR-	HARSH-
AGILE-	BURLI-	DISAL-	FRITF-	HARTE-
ALERT-	BUSHF-	DIZZI-	FRIZZ-	HASTI-
ALIEN-	BUSHI-	DOOMI-	FUGAL-	HAZEL-
ALONE-	BUXOM-	DOTTI-	FUGGI-	HEADI-
ALOOF-	CAMPI-	DOUCE-	FUNKI-	HEART-
AMIAB-	CANNI-	DOWDI-	FUNNI-	HEAVI-
ANGER-	CANTI-	DREAD-	FURRI-	HEFTI-
ANGRI-	CAPAB-	DRIBB-	FUSIB-	HOARI-
ANOMA-	CATTI-	DRIZZ-	FUSSI-	HORNI-
ANTIC-	CAVAL-	DROPF-	FUSTI-	HORSI-
APETA-	CECAL-	DUCAL-	FUZZI-	HUFFI-
APHYL-	CHARI-	DUMPI-	GALLF-	HUMAN-
APISH-	CHEAP-	DUOPO-	GASSI-	HUMID-
AREAL-	CHEER-	DURAB-	GAUDI-	HUSKI-
AUDIB-	CHIEF-	DUSKI-	GAUNT-	IDEAL-
AURAL-	CHILD-	DUSTI-	GAUZI-	IGNOB-
AWFUL-	CHIMB-	DYING-	GAWKI-	INANE-
AXIAL-	CIVIL-	EAGER-	GELID-	INAPT-
BAGGI-	CLEAN-	EARTH-	GEMMI-	INEPT-
BAIRN-	CLEAR-	ELDER-	GHAST-	INERT-
BALKI-	CLERK-	EMPTI-	GHOST-	INJEL-
BALMI-	CLOSE-	EPIBO-	GIANT-	INNER-
BANAL-	COCKI-	EQUAB-	GIDDI-	IRATE-
BASAL-	CORNF-	EQUAL-	GINGE-	ITCHI-
BAWDI-	CORNI-	ERECT-	GLAZI-	JADED-
BEADI-	COURT-	EROSE-	GLOWF-	JAZZI-
BEAMI-	COWED-	EXACT-	GODLI-	JERKI-
BEAST-	CRACK-	FADED-	GOOFI-	JOINT-
BEEFI-	CRANK-	FAINT-	GOUTF-	JOLLI-
BEERI-	CRASS-	FAIRI-	GOUTI-	JOLTI-
BEETF-	CRAZI-	FALSE-	GRADE-	JUICI-
BIFID-	CRINK-	FANCI-	GRAND-	JUMPI-
BLACK-	CRISP-	FATAL-	GRAVE-	JURAL-
BLAND-	CROSS-	FATTI-	GRAYF-	KINKI-
BLANK-	CRUDE-	FETID-	GREAT-	KNOBB-
BLEAK-	CRUEL-	FIERI-	GREEN-	KNUBB-
BLIND-	CRUMB-	FIFTH-	GREIS-	KNUCK-
BLOWF-	CRUMP-	FILMI-	GRIES-	LADYF-
BLUFF-	CRUSI-	FINAL-	GRIMI-	LAIRD-
BLUNT-	CUBIC-	FIREF-	GRISE-	LAITH-
BOGUS-	CURAB-	FIRST-	GRIST-	LANKI-
BONNI-	CURLI-	FISHI-	GRIZZ-	LARGE-
BOOZI-	CUSHI-	FIXED-	GROSS-	LEAKI-
BOSSI-	DAFFI-	FLAKI-	GRUFF-	LEERI-
BRAMB-	DANDI-	FLEET-	GRUMB-	LEGAL-
BRASH-	DATED-	FLESH-	GRYSE-	LEGIB-
BRAVE-	DAYLI-	FLUID-	GUMMI-	LEVEL-
BRIEF-	DAZED-	FLUKI-	GUSHI-	LICHT-
BRISK-	DEARN-	FOAMI-	GUSTI-	LICIT-

LIGHT-	NARGI-	PUSHI-	SHOOG-	SWITH-
LITHE-	NASAL-	QUAKI-	SHORT-	TACIT-
LIVID-	NASTI-	QUEEN-	SHOWI-	TACKI-
LOATH-	NATTI-	QUEER-	SHRIL-	TAILF-
LOCAL-	NAVAL-	QUICK-	SIGHT-	TARDI-
LOFTI-	NEEDI-	QUIET-	SILKI-	TARTI-
LOOBI-	NERVI-	RABID-	SILLI-	TASTI-
LOONI-	NIFTI-	RAINI-	SIXTH-	TATTI-
LOOPI-	NIGHT-	RANDI-	SIZAB-	TAWNI-
LOOSE-	NINTH-	RANGI-	SLACK-	TAXAB-
LOUSI-	NIPPI-	RAPID-	SLANT-	TEARI-
LOVAB-	NOBBI-	RATAB-	SLEEK-	TECHI-
LOVER-	NODAL-	RATTI-	SLICK-	TENAB-
LOWLI-	NOISI-	RAVEL-	SLIMI-	TENSE-
LOYAL-	NONOI-	READI-	SMART-	TENTH-
LUCID-	NOTAB-	REAPP-	SMICK-	TEPID-
LUCKI-	NOTED-	REEDI-	SMOKI-	TERSE-
LUMPI-	NOVEL-	REGAL-	SNAKI-	TESTI-
LURID-	NUTTI-	RETAL-	SNIDE-	TEUGH-
LUSTI-	NYMPH-	RIANT-	SNIFF-	THEGN-
LYING-	OBESE-	RIGHT-	SNOWI-	THICK-
MAJOR-	OCTUP-	RIGID-	SNUFF-	THIRD-
MANGI-	ORDER-	RISIB-	SOAPI-	THIST-
MANLI-	OVATE-	RISKI-	SOBER-	THRIL-
MASCU-	OVERF-	RITZI-	SOGGI-	TIDAL-
MAZED-	OVERP-	ROCKI-	SOLID-	TIGER-
MEATI-	OVERT-	ROOMI-	SOLUB-	TIGHT-
MERRI-	PANOP-	ROUGH-	SOOTH-	TIMID-
MESAL-	PAPAL-	ROUND-	SOOTI-	TINNI-
MESSI-	PASTI-	ROUPI-	SOPPI-	TIPSI-
METAL-	PAWKI-	ROWDI-	SORRI-	TIRED-
MIFFI-	PAYAB-	ROYAL-	SOUND-	TONAL-
MILKI-	PEART-	RUDDI-	SPANG-	TOSSI-
MIRKI-	PENAL-	RUMMI-	SPARE-	TOTAL-
MISAL-	PEPPI-	RURAL-	SPARK-	TOUGH-
MISER-	PERKI-	RUSTI-	SPICI-	TREAC-
MISRE-	PESKI-	RUTTI-	SPIKI-	TREMB-
MISTI-	PETTI-	SAINT-	SPIND-	TRICK-
MIXED-	PHONI-	SALAB-	SPRAW-	TRIFO-
MODAL-	PICKI-	SALTI-	SQUAL-	TRITE-
MOIST-	PIOUS-	SANDF-	SQUAT-	TUFTI-
MONTH-	PITHI-	SAPPI-	STAGI-	TUMID-
MOODI-	PLAIN-	SASSI-	STAID-	TUNAB-
MOONI-	PLIAB-	SAUCI-	STALE-	TWADD-
MORAL-	PLUMP-	SAVVI-	STARK-	TWIDD-
MOUSI-	PLUSH-	SCANT-	START-	TWINK-
MOVAB-	POCKI-	SCARI-	STATE-	UNAPT-
MUCKI-	PODGI-	SCRAW-	STEEP-	UNFIT-
MUDDI-	PRICI-	SEEDI-	STERN-	UNGOD-
MUGGI-	PRICK-	SHADF-	STIFF-	UNMAN-
MURKI-	PRIME-	SHADI-	STONI-	UNTRU-
MUSHI-	PRIOR-	SHAKI-	STOUT-	USEAB-
MUSKI-	PRIVI-	SHAMB-	STUBB-	USUAL-
MUSSI-	PRONE-	SHAPE-	STUMB-	UTTER-
MUSTI-	PROSI-	SHARP-	SUAVE-	VAGAL-
MUTAB-	PROUD-	SHEER-	SULKI-	VAGUE-
MUTED-	PUDGI-	SHING-	SUNNI-	VALID-
MUZZI-	PUFFI-	SHINI-	SURLI-	VAPID-
NAIVE-	PULPI-	SHOGG-	SWEET-	VENAL-
NAKED-	PURSI-	SHOOF-	SWIFT-	VERMI-

VEXED-	VOCAL-	WEASE-	WISPI-	WRIGG-
VICAR-	VOLUB-	WEEDI-	WITTI-	WRINK-
VIRAL-	VOWEL-	WEEPI-	WOFUL-	WRONG-
VISIB-	VYING-	WEEVI-	WOMAN-	YOUNG-
VITAL-	WACKI-	WEIRD-	WOOZI-	YOUTH-
VIVID-	WASHI-	WHITE-	WORDI-	ZESTI-
VIXEN-	WASPI-	WIGHT-	WORLD-	ZONAL-
VOCAB-	WEARI-	WINDI-	WORMF-	

Eight-letter words

ABASED-	BESEEM-	CHEERI-	CRYING-	ENTIRE-
ABJECT-	BIASED-	CHEESI-	CULPAB-	ENVIAB-
ABORAL-	BIDDAB-	CHESTI-	CURSED-	EPICAL-
ABRUPT-	BIHOUR-	CHILLI-	CURVED-	EQUINE-
ABSENT-	BINATE-	CHIRPI-	CUSSED-	ERRANT-
ABSURD-	BITCHI-	CHOICE-	CYCLIC-	ERRING-
ACHING-	BITING-	CHOPPI-	CYMOSE-	EVANGE-
ACTIVE-	BITTER-	CHORAL-	DAINTI-	EXPERT-
ACTUAL-	BIWEEK-	CHUBBI-	DAMNAB-	FACETE-
ADORAB-	BIYEAR-	CHUMMI-	DAPPER-	FACIAL-
ADROIT-	BLACKF-	CHUNKI-	DARING-	FACILE-
AERIAL-	BLAMAB-	CHURCH-	DATIVE-	FALLIB-
AFFINE-	BLEARI-	CLAMMI-	DECENT-	FAMOUS-
AGUISH-	BLITHE-	CLASSI-	DEMISS-	FATHER-
AIMFUL-	BLOODI-	CLEVER-	DEMURE-	FAULTI-
ALDERF-	BLOUSI-	CLINAL-	DENIAB-	FAUNAL-
ALPINE-	BLOWSI-	CLOGGI-	DENTAL-	FEASIB-
AMAZED-	BLOWZI-	CLONAL-	DEUCED-	FEISTI-
AMENAB-	BLURRI-	CLOUDI-	DEVOUT-	FELINE-
AMICAB-	BODING-	CLUBBI-	DIRECT-	FELLOW-
AMORAL-	BORING-	CLUMSI-	DISAPP-	FERVID-
AMUSED-	BOTCHI-	COARSE-	DISMAL-	FESTAL-
ANIMAL-	BOUNCI-	COEVAL-	DISTAL-	FEUDAL-
ANNUAL-	BOVINE-	COGENT-	DIVERS-	FIERCE-
ANODAL-	BOWING-	COITAL-	DIVINE-	FILIAL-
APICAL-	BOYISH-	COMELI-	DOCILE-	FILTHI-
ARCANE-	BRAINI-	COMMON-	DOCTOR-	FINITE-
ARDENT-	BRASSI-	CONVEX-	DOGGED-	FISCAL-
ARGUAB-	BRAWNI-	COOING-	DOOLAL-	FITFUL-
ARGUTE-	BRAZEN-	COSTAL-	DORSAL-	FLABBI-
ARRANT-	BREEZI-	COUSIN-	DOTARD-	FLASHI-
ARTFUL-	BRIDAL-	COVERT-	DOTING-	FLEECI-
ASSEMB-	BRIGHT-	COWARD-	DRAFTI-	FLESHI-
ASTRAL-	BROKEN-	COYISH-	DREAMI-	FLEXIB-
ASTUTE-	BROODI-	CRABBI-	DREARI-	FLIMSI-
ATONAL-	BRUTAL-	CRAFTI-	DRESSI-	FLINTI-
AUGUST-	BUCCAL-	CRAGGI-	DRIPPI-	FLOPPI-
AVERSE-	BUNCHI-	CRANEF-	DROOPI-	FLORAL-
AVOWAB-	CAECAL-	CRANKI-	DROWSI-	FLORID-
AVOWED-	CANDID-	CRAVEN-	DUDISH-	FLOSSI-
BADGER-	CARNAL-	CREAKI-	DULCET-	FLUENT-
BANKER-	CASUAL-	CREAMI-	EARTHI-	FLUFFI-
BARREN-	CATCHF-	CREDIB-	EASTER-	FOETID-
BAULKI-	CAUDAL-	CREEPI-	EFFETE-	FOLKSI-
BEARAB-	CAUSAL-	CRISPI-	EIGHTH-	FORCED-
BEASTI-	CHANCI-	CROAKI-	ELATED-	FORCIB-
BEGGAR-	CHASTE-	CROUPI-	ELFISH-	FORKED-
BEHOVE-	CHATTI-	CROUSE-	ELIGIB-	FORMAB-
BENIGN-	CHEEKI-	CRUSTI-	ELVISH-	FORMAL-

FORMER-	HOARSE-	LINEAR-	MULISH-	POROUS-
FOURTH-	HOLLOW-	LIQUID-	MULTIP-	PORTAB-
FREAKI-	HOMELI-	LISSOM-	MUSING-	PORTER-
FRENZI-	HONEST-	LITHER-	MUTUAL-	POSING-
FRIEND-	HONIED-	LIVELI-	MYOPHI-	POSSIB-
FRIGID-	HOPING-	LIVING-	MYSTIC-	POSTAL-
FRISKI-	HORRIB-	LOBATE-	NARGHI-	POTBEL-
FRIZZI-	HORRID-	LOBLOL-	NARROW-	POTENT-
FROSTI-	HORSEF-	LONELI-	NATANT-	PREAPP-
FROTHI-	HOUSEF-	LOSING-	NATIVE-	PREPPI-
FROUZI-	HOVERF-	LOUCHE-	NEURAL-	PRETTI-
FROWZI-	HUMANE-	LOVEAB-	NEWISH-	PRIEST-
FROZEN-	HUNGER-	LOVELI-	NOCENT-	PRIMAL-
FRUGAL-	HUNGRI-	LOVING-	NORMAL-	PRINCE-
FRUITI-	HUNTED-	LUBBER-	NOUNAL-	PRISSI-
FRUMPI-	HUSHED-	LUCENT-	OAFISH-	PROBAB-
FUMING-	IMMANE-	LUMBER-	OBLATE-	PROLIX-
FUTILE-	IMPISH-	LUMPEN-	OBLONG-	PROMPT-
GAGEAB-	IMPURE-	LUNATE-	OBTUSE-	PROPER-
GAPING-	INDIGN-	LURING-	OCCULT-	PROVAB-
GARISH-	INEDIB-	LYRATE-	OCULAR-	PROVEN-
GAUCHE-	INFIRM-	MAIDEN-	ODIOUS-	PRYING-
GENIAL-	INNATE-	MALIGN-	OFFISH-	PUBLIC-
GIBING-	INSANE-	MANFUL-	OGRISH-	PULING-
GIFTED-	INTACT-	MANNER-	ONWARD-	PULPAL-
GINGEL-	INTENT-	MANUAL-	OPAQUE-	PUNCHI-
GINGER-	INVIAB-	MARKED-	OPERAB-	PUTRID-
GLASSI-	INWARD-	MARTYR-	ORNATE-	QUAINT-
GLITZI-	IREFUL-	MASSED-	OTIOSE-	QUEASI-
GLOBAL-	ISSUAB-	MASTER-	OUTBUL-	QUIRKI-
GLOOMI-	JADISH-	MATRON-	OVERHO-	QUOTAB-
GLOSSI-	JAGGED-	MATTED-	OVERWI-	RACIAL-
GLUMPI-	JAPING-	MATURE-	OWLISH-	RADIAL-
GOLDEN-	JAUNTI-	MEAGER-	PALLID-	RAGGED-
GORBEL-	JEJUNE-	MEAGRE-	PALPAB-	RAGING-
GORGED-	JIBING-	MEDIAL-	PALTRI-	RAKISH-
GOSPEL-	JOCOSE-	MEDIAN-	PANDER-	RAMOSE-
GRAITH-	JOCUND-	MELLOW-	PASSAB-	RAMOUS-
GRASSI-	JOKING-	MENIAL-	PASSIB-	RANCID-
GRAVEL-	JOVIAL-	MENTAL-	PASTOR-	RANDOM-
GRAVID-	JOYFUL-	MESIAL-	PATCHI-	RASCAL-
GREASI-	JOYOUS-	METABO-	PATENT-	RATEAB-
GREEDI-	KERNEL-	MIGHTI-	PATRON-	RAVING-
GREENF-	KINDLI-	MINUTE-	PEACHI-	READAB-
GRITTI-	KISSAB-	MISAPP-	PEDATE-	READER-
GROGGI-	KNIGHT-	MODERN-	PETTED-	RECENT-
GRUBBI-	KNOTTI-	MODEST-	PIPING-	RECTAL-
GRUFFI-	LABIAL-	MODISH-	PITCHI-	REDBEL-
GRUMPI-	LAICAL-	MOLTEN-	PITIAB-	REFLEX-
GUILTI-	LATENT-	MOMENT-	PLACAB-	RELIAB-
GULLAB-	LATTER-	MONOPO-	PLACID-	REMISS-
GULLIB-	LAUDAB-	MOPING-	PLAGUI-	REMOTE-
HEARTI-	LAVISH-	MOPISH-	PLIANT-	REPAND-
HEATED-	LAWFUL-	MORBID-	PLUCKI-	RESUPP-
HEAVEN-	LAWYER-	MOROSE-	PLUGUG-	RETRAL-
HECTIC-	LEADEN-	MORTAL-	PLURAL-	RIBALD-
HECTOR-	LETHAL-	MOTHER-	PLUSHI-	RIMOSE-
HEROIC-	LIMBER-	MOUTHI-	PLYING-	RITUAL-
HIDDEN-	LIMPID-	MOVEAB-	POLITE-	ROBUST-
HITCHI-	LINEAL-	MOVING-	POPISH-	ROOTED-

ROTTEN-	SILVER-	SPUNKI-	TONISH-	URGENT-
ROTUND-	SINFUL-	SQUARE-	TOOTHI-	URGING-
ROVING-	SISTER-	SQUIGG-	TORPID-	USEFUL-
RUEFUL-	SIZEAB-	SQUIRE-	TORRID-	UVULAR-
RUGGED-	SKIMPI-	STALKI-	TOUCHI-	VACANT-
RUGOSE-	SLANGI-	STANCH-	TOWARD-	VALUAB-
RUSTIC-	SLEAZI-	STARRI-	TOYISH-	VARIAB-
SACRED-	SLEEPI-	STATED-	TRASHI-	VARIED-
SAILOR-	SLIGHT-	STEADI-	TRENDI-	VEILED-
SALEAB-	SLINKI-	STEAMI-	TREVAL-	VENDIB-
SALLOW-	SLIPPI-	STEEVE-	TRIBAL-	VENIAL-
SALVAB-	SLOPPI-	STICKI-	TRICKI-	VENOUS-
SATIAB-	SLOVEN-	STIEVE-	TRUANT-	VERBAL-
SAVAGE-	SLUSHI-	STINGI-	TRUSTI-	VERNAL-
SAVING-	SMALMI-	STOCKI-	TRYING-	VESTAL-
SAVORI-	SMARMI-	STODGI-	TUNBEL-	VEXING-
SAVOUR-	SMEARI-	STOLID-	TUNEAB-	VINCIB-
SCABBI-	SMIRKI-	STONEF-	TURBID-	VINOUS-
SCALAB-	SMOOTH-	STORMI-	TURGID-	VIOLAB-
SCANTI-	SMUDGI-	STRAGG-	UNCHIC-	VIRGIN-
SCARCE-	SMUTTI-	STRAIT-	UNCIAL-	VIRILE-
SCATTI-	SNAPPI-	STRICT-	UNCOME-	VISCID-
SCRABB-	SNARKI-	STRONG-	UNCOST-	VISUAL-
SCRAGG-	SNAZZI-	STUBBI-	UNEASI-	VOTIVE-
SCRIBB-	SNEAKI-	STUFFI-	UNEVEN-	VULGAR-
SCRIGG-	SNIFFI-	STUMPI-	UNFAIR-	WANTON-
SCRIMP-	SNIPPI-	STUPID-	UNGAIN-	WATERI-
SCUMMI-	SNIVEL-	STURDI-	UNGENT-	WEASEL-
SCURVI-	SNOBBI-	SUDDEN-	UNHOLI-	WEEVIL-
SEAMAN-	SNOOPI-	SUITAB-	UNHOME-	WESTER-
SECANT-	SNOOTI-	SULLEN-	UNIQUE-	WHEEZI-
SECOND-	SNOTTI-	SULTRI-	UNITED-	WHIMSI-
SECRET-	SNUFFI-	SUMMER-	UNJUST-	WHITEF-
SECUND-	SOCIAB-	SUNDRI-	UNKIND-	WICKED-
SECURE-	SOCIAL-	SUPERB-	UNKING-	WILFUL-
SEDATE-	SODDEN-	SUPINE-	UNLIKE-	WINGED-
SELDOM-	SOLEMN-	SUPPLE-	UNLIVE-	WINTER-
SELECT-	SOMBER-	SVELTE-	UNLORD-	WINTRI-
SENILE-	SOMBRE-	SWANKI-	UNLOVE-	WITTOL-
SENSIB-	SORDID-	SWEATI-	UNMEET-	WIZARD-
SERENE-	SORTAB-	SWIMMI-	UNPURE-	WOEFUL-
SERIAL-	SOTTED-	SYMPHI-	UNREAL-	WONTED-
SEVERE-	SOUTER-	TAKING-	UNRIPE-	WOODEN-
SEXTUP-	SOVRAN-	TANGIB-	UNSAFE-	WOOING-
SEXUAL-	SOWBEL-	TARNAL-	UNSEEM-	WOOLLI-
SHABBI-	SPARKI-	TARTAR-	UNSTAB-	WORKAB-
SHAGGI-	SPARSE-	TASSEL-	UNSUBT-	WORTHI-
SHAMAB-	SPEEDI-	TAWDRI-	UNSURE-	WOUNDI-
SHAUCH-	SPIFFI-	TAXING-	UNTIDI-	WRATHI-
SHIFTI-	SPINAL-	TENDER-	UNTIME-	WRITER-
SHIRTI-	SPIRAL-	TENSIB-	UNUSAB-	YEASTI-
SHITTI-	SPONGI-	TERRIB-	UNWARE-	YELLOW-
SHODDI-	SPOOKI-	TETCHI-	UNWARI-	YEOMAN-
SHREWD-	SPOONI-	THORNI-	UNWIFE-	YONDER-
SICKER-	SPORTI-	THRAWN-	UNWISE-	ZOOPHI-
SICKLI-	SPOTTI-	THWART-	UPPISH-	
SIGNAL-	SPRITE-	TIMOUS-	UPWARD-	
SILENT-	SPRUCE-	TINSEL-	URBANE-	

Words that end with -MAN

Seven-letter words

ADWO-	DESK-	ISLE-	ODDS-	SNOW-
ALMS-	DOOR-	JACK-	ORRA-	SOCK-
ANAT-	DRAY-	JARK-	OTTO-	SOKE-
ANTI-	DUST-	JAZZ-	OVER-	SONG-
ARTS-	FACE-	JUNK-	PACK-	SPAE-
AUTO-	FIRE-	JURY-	PASS-	SURF-
BASE-	FLAG-	KEEL-	PEAT-	SWAG-
BATS-	FOOT-	KINS-	PIKE-	TAPS-
BEAD-	FORE-	KIRK-	PLOW-	TAXI-
BEDE-	FREE-	LAND-	POLL-	TELE-
BELL-	FROG-	LEAD-	PORT-	TOLL-
BELT-	GADS-	LENS-	POST-	TONG-
BILL-	GATE-	LIFT-	PROP-	TOOL-
BIRD-	GLEE-	LINE-	PULL-	TOPS-
BOAT-	GOOD-	LINK-	RAFT-	TRUE-
BOGY-	GOWN-	LOCK-	RAIL-	TURF-
BOND-	GRIP-	LOCO-	REED-	UNHU-
BOOK-	GUDE-	MAGS-	REEL-	UNWO-
BRAH-	HACK-	MAIL-	REPO-	WAKE-
BUSH-	HANG-	MALT-	RING-	WING-
BYRE-	HANU-	MARK-	ROAD-	WIRE-
CASE-	HARD-	MASH-	RODS-	WOOD-
CAVE-	HEAD-	MEAT-	RUCK-	WOOL-
CHAP-	HELI-	MESS-	SAGA-	WORK-
CLUB-	HERD-	MILK-	SAND-	YARD-
COAL-	HIGH-	MOBS-	SEED-	YEGG-
CREW-	HOOD-	MOOR-	SHIP-	
DAYS-	HOSE-	MOOT-	SHOP-	
DEAD-	INHU-	NEWS-	SHOW-	
DECU-	IRON-	OARS-	SIDE-	

Eight-letter words

AIRWO-	CHAIR-	FORGE-	HOTEL-	NONHU-
ALDER-	CHESS-	FREED-	HOUSE-	OVERS-
BAILS-	CHINA-	FRESH-	HUNTS-	PANHU-
BANDS-	CHOIR-	FRONT-	ISLES-	PENWO-
BANDY-	CHORE-	FUGLE-	KNIFE-	PETER-
BANKS-	CLANS-	FUNNY-	LANDS-	PILOT-
BARGE-	CLASS-	GAMES-	LAYWO-	PITCH-
BATWO-	COACH-	GANGS-	LEADS-	PIVOT-
BEADS-	COLOR-	GAVEL-	LIEGE-	PLACE-
BEDES-	CORPS-	GILDS-	LINES-	PLAID-
BLUES-	CRAGS-	GLASS-	LINKS-	PLATE-
BOARD-	DAIRY-	GOADS-	LOCKS-	POINT-
BOATS-	DALES-	GOWNS-	LODES-	PREHU-
BOGEY-	DOOMS-	HANDY-	LOFTS-	PRESS-
BONDS-	DOORS-	HEADS-	MADWO-	PRIZE-
BOOGY-	DRAGO-	HELMS-	MARCH-	PROSE-
BOTHY-	DRAGS-	HENCH-	MARKS-	PUNTS-
BRAKE-	DUTCH-	HERDS-	MERES-	QUILL-
BRIDE-	EARTH-	HIELA-	MERRY-	RADIO-
BRINK-	EVERY-	HOAST-	MONEY-	RAFTS-
BUTTY-	FERRY-	HOIST-	MOTOR-	RAMPS-
CHAIN-	FOILS-	HORSE-	NOBLE-	RANCH-

REINS- SHORE- STOCK- TIDES- WEALS-
RIFLE- SIDES- STORE- TOWNS- WEIGH-
RIVER- SONAR- STUNT- TOYWO- WHALE-
ROADS- SOUND- SUBHU- TRACK- WHEEL-
ROUTE- SPACE- SUPER- TRAIN- WIDOW-
SALES- SPADE- SWAGS- TRASH- WINCH-
SCENE- SPEAR- SWEET- TREWS- WOODS-
SEAWO- SQUAW- SWING- TRUCH- YACHT-
SEEDS- STAFF- SWORD- TRUCK- YARRA-
SHARE- STALL- TACKS- UNDER-
SHEAR- STEEL- TALES- VERSE-
SHEEP- STICK- TALIS- WATCH-
SHIRE- STILL- TALLY- WATER-

Words that end with -MEN

Seven-letter words

ABDO- DEAD- HOOD- MOOT- SHOW-
ADWO- DESK- HOSE- NEWS- SIDE-
AGNO- DOOR- IRON- OARS- SNOW-
ALBU- DRAY- ISLE- ODDS- SOCK-
ALMS- DURA- JACK- ORRA- SOKE-
ARTS- DUST- JARK- OVER- SONG-
AUTO- FACE- JAZZ- PACK- SPAE-
BASE- FIRE- JUNK- PASS- SUDA-
BATS- FLAG- JURY- PEAT- SURF-
BEAD- FLEH- KEEL- PIKE- SWAG-
BEDE- FOOT- KINS- PLOW- TAPS-
BELL- FORA- KIRK- POLL- TAXI-
BELT- FORE- LAND- PORT- TEGU-
BILL- FREE- LEAD- POST- TELE-
BIRD- FROG- LENS- PROP- TOLL-
BITU- GADS- LIFT- PUTA- TONG-
BOAT- GATE- LINE- RAFT- TOOL-
BOGY- GLEE- LINK- RAIL- TOPS-
BOND- GOOD- LOCK- REED- TRUE-
BOOK- GOWN- LOCO- REEL- TURF-
BUSH- GRIP- MAGS- REGI- VELA-
BYRE- GUDE- MAIL- REPO- WAKE-
CACU- HACK- MALT- RING- WING-
CASE- HANG- MARK- ROAD- WIRE-
CAVE- HARD- MASH- RODS- WOOD-
CERU- HEAD- MEAT- RUCK- WOOL-
CHAP- HEGU- MESS- SAGA- WORK-
CLUB- HELI- MILK- SAND- YARD-
COAL- HERD- MOBS- SEED- YEGG-
CREW- HIGH- MOLI- SHIP-
DAYS- HILL- MOOR- SHOP-

Eight-letter words

AIRWO- BARGE- BOATS- BRIDE- CHINA-
ALDER- BATWO- BOGEY- BRINK- CHOIR-
BAILS- BEADS- BONDS- BUTTY- CHORE-
BANDS- BEDES- BOOGY- CHAIN- CLANS-
BANDY- BLUES- BOTHY- CHAIR- CLASS-
BANKS- BOARD- BRAKE- CHESS- CLINA-

COACH-	GOWNS-	MONEY-	SCENE-	TACKS-
COGNO-	GRAVA-	MOTOR-	SEAWO-	TALES-
COLOR-	HANDY-	NOBLE-	SEEDS-	TALLY-
CORPS-	HEADS-	OVERS-	SHARE-	TIDES-
CRAGS-	HELMS-	PENWO-	SHEAR-	TOWNS-
CYCLA-	HENCH-	PETER-	SHEEP-	TOYWO-
DAIRY-	HERDS-	PILOT-	SHIRE-	TRACK-
DALES-	HOAST-	PITCH-	SHORE-	TRAIN-
DOOMS-	HOIST-	PIVOT-	SIDES-	TRASH-
DOORS-	HORSE-	PLACE-	SONAR-	TREWS-
DRAGO-	HOTEL-	PLAID-	SOUND-	TRUCH-
DRAGS-	HOUSE-	PLATE-	SPACE-	TRUCK-
DUTCH-	HUNTS-	POINT-	SPADE-	UNDER-
EARTH-	ISLES-	PRENO-	SPEAR-	VERSE-
EVERY-	KNIFE-	PRESS-	SPECI-	WATCH-
FERRY-	LANDS-	PRIZE-	SQUAW-	WATER-
FOILS-	LAYWO-	PROSE-	STAFF-	WEALS-
FORGE-	LEADS-	PUNTS-	STALL-	WEIGH-
FREED-	LIEGE-	QUILL-	STEEL-	WHALE-
FRESH-	LINES-	RADIO-	STICK-	WHEEL-
FRONT-	LINKS-	RAFTS-	STILL-	WIDOW-
FUGLE-	LOCKS-	RAMPS-	STOCK-	WINCH-
FUNNY-	LODES-	RANCH-	STORE-	WOODS-
GAMES-	LOFTS-	REINS-	STUNT-	YACHT-
GANGS-	MADWO-	RIFLE-	SUPER-	YARRA-
GAVEL-	MARCH-	RIVER-	SWAGS-	
GILDS-	MARKS-	ROADS-	SWEET-	
GLASS-	MERES-	ROUTE-	SWING-	
GOADS-	MERRY-	SALES-	SWORD-	

Words that end with -NESS

Seven-letter words

ALL-	FAR-	ICI-	ONE-	SLY-
APT-	FAT-	ILL-	OUT-	TWO-
BAD-	FEW-	LAX-	PAT-	WAE-
BIG-	FEY-	LIO-	RAW-	WAN-
COY-	FIT-	LOW-	RED-	WET-
DIM-	FUL-	MAD-	RUM-	WIT-
DRY-	GAY-	NEW-	SAD-	WOE-
DUE-	HAR-	NOW-	SET-	WRY-
DUL-	HIP-	ODD-	SHI-	
DUN-	HOT-	OLD-	SHY-	

Eight-letter words

ACHI-	BALD-	BUSI-	COSI-	DEAR-
ACID-	BARE-	BUSY-	COXI-	DEEP-
AGED-	BARO-	CAGI-	COZI-	DEFT-
AIRI-	BASE-	CAGY-	CURT-	DEMO-
ALBI-	BASS-	CAKI-	CUTE-	DEWI-
ARCH-	BEIN-	CALM-	DAFT-	DIRE-
ARID-	BIAS-	CAMP-	DAMP-	DONE-
ARTI-	BLUE-	CANO-	DANK-	DOPI-
ASHI-	BOLD-	CHIC-	DARK-	DOUR-
AVID-	BONI-	COLD-	DEAD-	DOWF-
AWAY-	BOXI-	COOL-	DEAF-	DOZI-

DRAB-	HALF-	MALE-	POSH-	SURE-
DULL-	HARD-	MATI-	PRIM-	TALL-
DUMB-	HAZI-	MAZI-	PUNI-	TAME-
DUSK-	HERE-	MEAN-	PURE-	TART-
EASI-	HIGH-	MEEK-	RACI-	TAUT-
EDGI-	HOKI-	MEET-	RANK-	THAT-
EERI-	HOLI-	MILD-	RAPT-	THIN-
EVEN-	HOMI-	MIRI-	RARE-	THIS-
EVIL-	HUGE-	MOOT-	RASH-	THUS-
EYED-	ICKI-	MOPI-	REAL-	TIDI-
FAIN-	IDLE-	MORE-	RICH-	TINI-
FAIR-	IFFI-	MUCH-	RIFE-	TITA-
FAST-	INKI-	MUTE-	RIMI-	TRIG-
FELL-	IRON-	NAFF-	RIPE-	TRIM-
FINE-	JIMP-	NAIF-	ROPI-	TRUE-
FIRM-	JOKI-	NEAR-	ROSI-	TWEE-
FLAT-	JUST-	NEAT-	RUDE-	UGLI-
FOND-	KEEN-	NESH-	SAFE-	VAIN-
FOUL-	KIND-	NEXT-	SAGE-	VAST-
FOXI-	LACI-	NICE-	SALT-	VILD-
FOZI-	LAME-	NIGH-	SAME-	VILE-
FREE-	LANK-	NOSI-	SANE-	VOID-
FULL-	LATE-	NUDE-	SEAR-	WARI-
GAME-	LAZI-	NULL-	SEED-	WARM-
GAMI-	LEAN-	NUMB-	SELF-	WAST-
GAMY-	LEWD-	OILI-	SEXI-	WAVI-
GAST-	LIKE-	OOZI-	SICK-	WAXI-
GLAD-	LIMI-	OPEN-	SIZI-	WEAK-
GLEG-	LIMP-	OVAL-	SKEW-	WELL-
GLIB-	LITE-	PACK-	SLIM-	WHAT-
GLUI-	LIVE-	PALE-	SLOW-	WIDE-
GLUM-	LOGI-	PAST-	SMUG-	WILD-
GONE-	LONE-	PERT-	SNUB-	WILI-
GOOD-	LONG-	PIED-	SNUG-	WIRI-
GORI-	LORN-	PINK-	SOFT-	WISE-
GRAY-	LOST-	PIPI-	SOLE-	WOOD-
GREY-	LOTH-	PIXI-	SORE-	WORN-
GRIM-	LOUD-	POKI-	SOUR-	ZANI-
GRUM-	LUNI-	POOR-	SPRY-	
HALE-	LUSH-	PORI-	SUCH-	

Words that end with -OID

Seven-letter words

ACAR-	CEST-	CYST-	GLEN-	LITH-
ADEN-	CHEL-	DELT-	GLOB-	MAST-
AGAM-	CHOR-	DENT-	GOBI-	MATT-
AGAT-	CIRS-	DERM-	HAEM-	MUSC-
AMBR-	CISS-	DESM-	HAPL-	MYEL-
AMEB-	COCC-	DIPL-	HELC-	NAEV-
AMYL-	COLL-	DISC-	HIST-	NEGR-
ANDR-	CORM-	EMER-	HYAL-	NEUR-
ANER-	COSM-	ERIC-	HYDR-	OBOV-
ANTH-	COTT-	ETHM-	HYEN-	OCEL-
ARCT-	CRIC-	EUPL-	HYPN-	OCHR-
ASTR-	CRIN-	FACT-	LABR-	OIDI-
BYSS-	CTEN-	FIBR-	LENT-	OSTE-
CACT-	CYCL-	FUNG-	LIAN-	PERC-

PHAC-	RHIZ-	SPAR-	TENI-	VALG-
PHYT-	SARC-	SPIR-	THER-	VESP-
PIGM-	SAUR-	SPOR-	THYR-	VISC-
PLAC-	SIAL-	STER-	TIGR-	XIPH-
PYGM-	SIGM-	STYL-	TURD-	ZEBR-
QUIN-	SIMI-	TABL-	TYPH-	ZINC-

Eight-letter words

ACTIN-	CORAC-	LAMBD-	PINAK-	SPHEN-
ALKAL-	CORON-	LEMUR-	PITYR-	SPHER-
AMBER-	COTYL-	LIGUL-	PLASM-	SPONG-
AMMON-	DENDR-	LIMUL-	POLYP-	SQUAL-
AMOEB-	DORID-	LYMPH-	PRISM-	STURN-
ANCON-	ECHIN-	MANAT-	PSYCH-	TAENI-
ARILL-	ELYTR-	MEDUS-	PYRAN-	TAPIR-
ASTER-	EMBRY-	MELAN-	PYREN-	TARSI-
ATHET-	EMULS-	MUCIN-	RACEM-	TERAT-
AUTAC-	ERGAT-	MYCEL-	RESIN-	TETAN-
AUTOC-	GABBR-	MYTIL-	RETIN-	THALL-
BEAST-	GALEN-	NEMAT-	RHABD-	THYRE-
BLAST-	GEOMY-	NEPHR-	RHOMB-	THYRS-
BOTRY-	GROUP-	NOCTU-	SCAPH-	TREND-
CALYC-	GYNEC-	NUCLE-	SCHIZ-	TRICH-
CAMEL-	HELIC-	ODONT-	SCINC-	TRIPL-
CANCR-	HEMAT-	OMOHY-	SCIUR-	TROCH-
CARDI-	HISTI-	ONISC-	SCLER-	TUBER-
CATEN-	HOMAL-	PARAN-	SEPAL-	VARIC-
CENTR-	HOMIN-	PAROT-	SESAM-	VIBRI-
CERAT-	HUMAN-	PETAL-	SILUR-	VIRUS-
CHORE-	HYDAT-	PEZIZ-	SINUS-	VOLUT-
CHORI-	HYRAC-	PHALL-	SISTR-	YPSIL-
CICHL-	INDIG-	PHELL-	SLEAZ-	
CLUPE-	ISTHM-	PHYLL-	SOLEN-	
CONCH-	KERAT-	PINAC-	SORIC-	

Words that end with -OR

Seven-letter words

ABACT-	CAMPH-	EJECT-	IGNIT-	NEGAT-
ABETT-	CHADD-	ELECT-	IMPED-	NONPO-
ABLAT-	CHANT-	EMPER-	INCIS-	OBLIG-
ADAPT-	CHIKH-	EMULS-	ISOCH-	OFFER-
ADJUR-	CITAT-	ENACT-	JANIT-	OUTDO-
ADVIS-	CLANG-	EQUAT-	LANGU-	PANDO-
AERAT-	COACT-	ERECT-	LAXAT-	PARAD-
AGIST-	CREAT-	EVERT-	LEGAT-	PARIT-
ALAST-	CURAT-	EVICT-	LEVAT-	PICAD-
ALIEN-	DEBIT-	EXACT-	LOCAT-	PLEDG-
ANAPH-	DECOL-	EXCIT-	MACHZ-	PLESS-
ASSUR-	DELAT-	FEOFF-	MALOD-	PRAET-
ATHAN-	DEVIS-	FUNCT-	MAORM-	PRESS-
AUDIT-	DILAT-	GENIT-	MARKH-	PROCT-
AVIAT-	DILUT-	GRANT-	MATAD-	QUEST-
BELAB-	DIVIS-	GYRAT-	MIRAD-	QUITT-
BICOL-	DONAT-	HERIT-	MONIT-	REACT-
BIOPH-	EDUCT-	HUMID-	MORMA-	REALT-

RECOL-	SCISS-	SIMIL-	TANDO-	UNVIS-
RELAT-	SENAT-	SPONS-	TEMBL-	VAVAS-
REVIS-	SEPTU-	SQUAL-	TRACT-	VENAT-
REVIV-	SETTL-	STENT-	TRAIT-	VISIT-
ROTAT-	SEXTU-	STERT-	TRUST-	WARRI-
SANTO-	SIGNI-	STRID-	TWIST-	ZELAT-

Eight-letter words

ABDUCT-	CONCOL-	GOVERN-	NONACT-	REMITT-
ACCENT-	CONJUR-	HELIOD-	NONCOL-	RESIST-
ACCEPT-	CONVEN-	HYDRAT-	NONJUR-	RETAIL-
ACTUAT-	CONVEY-	IDOLAT-	NONLAB-	RONCAD-
ADDUCT-	COPAST-	IMITAT-	NONMAJ-	SCULPT-
ADJUST-	CORRID-	IMPACT-	OBJECT-	SEAFLO-
ADULAT-	CREDIT-	IMPELL-	OBSESS-	SECRET-
AGITAT-	CREMAT-	IMPOST-	OBVIAT-	SECTAT-
ALACHL-	CURSIT-	INCENS-	OCCLUS-	SEDUCT-
ANCEST-	CUSPID-	INCEPT-	OPERAT-	SEIGNI-
ANIMAT-	DEFECT-	INDENT-	OUTHUM-	SELECT-
ANTERI-	DEFLAT-	INDICT-	OUTSAV-	SERVIT-
APPELL-	DEMEAN-	INDORS-	PALPAT-	SPLEND-
ARREST-	DEPICT-	INDUCT-	PARACH-	STRESS-
ASPERS-	DETECT-	INFECT-	PATENT-	SUBFLO-
ASSENT-	DEVIAT-	INFERI-	PHOSPH-	SUBPRI-
ASSERT-	DICTAT-	INFLAT-	PISCAT-	SUPERI-
ASSESS-	DIFFUS-	INJECT-	PLEDGE-	SURVEY-
ASSIGN-	DIGEST-	INTERI-	PREDAT-	SURVIV-
ASSIST-	DIRECT-	INVENT-	PREVIS-	TESTAT-
ATTEST-	DISCOL-	INVERT-	PRODIT-	THEREF-
AVIGAT-	DISFAV-	INVEST-	PROLAB-	THRUST-
BACHEL-	DISHON-	IODOPH-	PROMIS-	TITRAT-
BACKDO-	EDUCAT-	ISOLAT-	PROMOT-	TOREAD-
BARRAT-	EFFECT-	KOMOND-	PRONAT-	TRADIT-
BARRET-	ELEVAT-	KURVEY-	PROVED-	TRAPDO-
BECLAM-	ELICIT-	LABRAD-	PROVID-	TRICOL-
BEGLAM-	EMANAT-	LAUDAT-	PROVIS-	TRIMOT-
BEHAVI-	EMBRAS-	LICENS-	PULMOT-	ULTERI-
BELIQU-	EMULAT-	MAINDO-	PULSAT-	UNANCH-
BISECT-	ENDEAV-	MANDAT-	PUNDON-	UNICOL-
CANEPH-	ENDORS-	MARKHO-	PURVEY-	URINAT-
CAVEAT-	EPILAT-	MEDIAT-	QUAEST-	UTILID-
CHELAT-	EVOCAT-	METAPH-	RADIAT-	VALUAT-
COANCH-	EXCEPT-	MIGRAT-	RECAPT-	VARACT-
COAUTH-	EXECUT-	MISCOL-	RECENS-	VARIST-
CODEBT-	EXPAND-	MISLAB-	RECEPT-	VAVASS-
COEDIT-	EXPIAT-	MISTUT-	REDACT-	VERDER-
COENAM-	EXTENS-	NARRAT-	REDUCT-	VIBRAT-
COFACT-	EXTERI-	NEIGHB-	REGRAT-	VIOLAT-
COLESS-	FELLAT-	NEXTDO-	REJECT-	VITIAT-
COLLAT-	GILLYV-	NITRAT-	RELEAS-	WHEREF-

Words that end with -OUS

Seven-letter words

ACAJ-	ACET-	ADIP-	AGAM-	AMOR-
ACER-	ACIN-	AENE-	AMAD-	ANUR-

ANXI-	COCC-	GRUM-	ONER-	SIMI-
APOD-	CONG-	GUMM-	ONYM-	SINU-
AQUE-	COPI-	HEIN-	OPAC-	SOUK-
ARDU-	CORI-	HERB-	OSMI-	SPIN-
AREN-	CORM-	HIDE-	OSSE-	SPUM-
ATHE-	COYP-	HOUM-	OZON-	SUCC-
ATOK-	CUPR-	HUGE-	PAPP-	TALC-
AZOT-	CURI-	HYDR-	PARL-	TEDI-
AZYG-	DEVI-	IGNE-	PERL-	TENU-
AZYM-	DUBI-	IMPI-	PETR-	TIME-
BADI-	DUTE-	INVI-	PICE-	TYPH-
BILI-	EMUL-	JEAL-	PILE-	UBER-
BINI-	ENVI-	LENT-	PIST-	UMBR-
BIVI-	ESTR-	LEPR-	PITE-	URAN-
BOUB-	FATU-	LIMB-	PLUM-	URIN-
BRUM-	FEAT-	LUTE-	POMP-	USUR-
BULB-	FERR-	MEVR-	PORT-	VACU-
BULL-	FIBR-	NACR-	PULP-	VALG-
BURN-	FOLI-	NERV-	RAME-	VARI-
CACH-	FULV-	NIMI-	RAUC-	VEIN-
CALL-	FUNG-	NIOB-	RHOD-	VICI-
CARI-	FURI-	NITR-	RIOT-	VIDU-
CASE-	FUSC-	NIVE-	ROUC-	VILL-
CERE-	GALL-	NOCU-	ROUT-	VISC-
CESI-	GASE-	NOXI-	RUBI-	VOUD-
CHYL-	GEAL-	OBVI-	RUIN-	ZEAL-
CHYM-	GIBB-	OCHR-	SANI-	ZINC-
CIRR-	GLEB-	ODOR-	SARC-	
CITR-	GLOB-	OMIN-	SERI-	

Eight-letter words

ACARP-	CADUC-	DIGAM-	FRABJ-	LIBEL-
ACAUL-	CAESI-	DIGYN-	FROND-	LIGNE-
ACOEL-	CANOR-	DIMER-	GEMIN-	LUMIN-
ADUNC-	CAPTI-	DIOIC-	GEMME-	LUSCI-
AMBER-	CARIB-	DIPNO-	GENER-	LUSTR-
ANGIN-	CARNE-	DITOK-	GLABR-	MANIT-
ANGUL-	CAUTI-	DIZYG-	GLARE-	MARAB-
ANOUR-	CERNU-	DOLOR-	GLAUC-	MELAN-
ANSER-	CHLOR-	EDACI-	GLORI-	MIASM-
ANTIC-	CHROM-	ELYTR-	GOITR-	MUCIN-
APHON-	CITRE-	ENGIN-	GORGE-	MUTIC-
APHTH-	CORNE-	ENORM-	GRACI-	MUTIN-
APTER-	COUSC-	EPIGE-	GRIEV-	NACRE-
ARACE-	COVET-	EUROK-	GRISE-	NAUSE-
ARANE-	COVIN-	EXIGU-	GYPSE-	NEBUL-
ARBOR-	CRANK-	EXIMI-	HALIT-	NEMOR-
ARSEN-	CRIBR-	FABUL-	HAMUL-	NIDOR-
ARSON-	CROCE-	FACTI-	HUMOR-	NITRE-
ASPER-	CROUP-	FASHI-	ICHOR-	NODUL-
ASTOM-	CUMBR-	FASTU-	IDONE-	NUBIL-
ATROP-	CUMUL-	FEATE-	IMPOR-	NUMER-
BIBUL-	CUPRE-	FEATU-	INCUB-	NUMIN-
BIGAM-	DARTR-	FELON-	INERM-	OCHER-
BIJUG-	DECOR-	FERRE-	INFAM-	OCHRE-
BIMAN-	DESIR-	FEVER-	KOUSK-	OESTR-
BIPAR-	DEXTR-	FIDDI-	LACTE-	OOGAM-
BIRAM-	DIDYM-	FLATU-	LAMIN-	ORAGI-
BUTYR-	DIECI-	FLEXU-	LEAPR-	ORDUR-

ORGUL-	RAMUL-	SEPAL-	TENUI-	VALOR-
OVARI-	RAVEN-	SETUL-	THALL-	VANAD-
PABUL-	RESIN-	SIBIL-	TIMOR-	VAPOR-
PALUD-	RIGOR-	SOMBR-	TINAM-	VENOM-
PAPUL-	ROSIN-	SONOR-	TITAN-	VENTR-
PATUL-	RUCTI-	SOPOR-	TORTI-	VENUL-
PERIL-	RUMOR-	SPACI-	TORTU-	VERTU-
PERVI-	SABUL-	SPECI-	TRAPP-	VIGOR-
PETAL-	SAPAJ-	SPERM-	TUBER-	VIPER-
PLUMB-	SAPOR-	SPURI-	TUBUL-	VIRTU-
PLUVI-	SAVOR-	SQUAM-	TUMOR-	VITRE-
POACE-	SCABI-	STANN-	TUMUL-	VOMIT-
POLYP-	SCABR-	STOCI-	TURAC-	WAMEF-
POPUL-	SCARI-	STOTI-	ULCER-	WAVER-
PORTE-	SCIOL-	STRAT-	UNCTU-	WONDR-
PRECI-	SCLER-	STRUM-	UNDUL-	WRONG-
PREVI-	SCORI-	STUDI-	UNFAM-	XANTH-
PYRIT-	SEDUL-	SUBER-	UNJOY-	YTTRI-
PYRRH-	SELEN-	SUDOR-	USURI-	
RACEM-	SENSU-	TEMER-	UXORI-	

Words that end with -OUT

Seven-letter words

ASPR-	COOK-	HIDE-	ROLL-	TURN-
BACK-	DROP-	HOLD-	SELL-	UNSH-
BAIL-	EELP-	LOCK-	SHUT-	WALK-
BESH-	FADE-	LOOK-	SICK-	WASH-
BESP-	FALL-	MISS-	SLIP-	WIDE-
BLOW-	FOLD-	PASS-	SPIN-	WIPE-
BURG-	GRAY-	PULL-	SURT-	WITH-
BURN-	HAND-	RAIN-	TAKE-	WORK-
CAMP-	HANG-	READ-	TIME-	

Eight-letter words

BLACK-	FREAK-	PHASE-	SHAKE-	THERE-
BREAK-	GADAB-	PITCH-	SHOOT-	UNDEV-
BROWN-	HORNP-	PRINT-	SLEEP-	WATCH-
BULLP-	INDEV-	RACAH-	SPEAK-	WHERE-
CARRY-	KNOCK-	RESPR-	STAKE-	WHITE-
CHECK-	LAYAB-	RUNAB-	STAND-	
CLOSE-	MARAB-	SEASC-	STICK-	
FLAME-	OUTSH-	SEATR-	TACAH-	

Words that end with -SET

Seven-letter words

BACK-	FILM-	KNES-	OVER-	TYPE-
BONE-	HAND-	LOCK-	SEAM-	
BRAS-	HARD-	MIND-	SIRO-	
CHIP-	HARO-	MOON-	TOOL-	
CRES-	HEAD-	NAIL-	TWIN-	

Eight-letter words

CHARO-	HEAVY-	PHOTO-	SOMER-	THORN-
EARTH-	MARMO-	QUICK-	THICK-	UNDER-

Words that end with -SHIP

Seven-letter words

AIR-	FOX-	KIN-	PAL-	WAR-
DOG-	GOD-	LUD-	PRE-	WOR-
DON-	GUN-	MID-	SIB-	
END-	HER-	NUN-	SON-	

Eight-letter words

AMID-	DUKE-	HEIR-	PEAT-	TRAN-
ANTI-	EARL-	HERO-	POET-	TREE-
BARD-	FIRE-	KING-	POPE-	TWIN-
CHUM-	FLAG-	LADY-	RAJA-	WARD-
CLAN-	FORE-	LONG-	SERF-	WIND-
DEAN-	GURU-	LORD-	STAR-	
DEMY-	HARD-	MAGE-	TANK-	
DOGE-	HEAD-	MATE-	TOWN-	

Words that end with -SKIN

Seven-letter words

CAT-	DOG-	KID-	PIG-
COW-	FOX-	KIP-	RED-
DOE-	GRI-	OIL-	

Eight-letter words

BEAR-	COON-	FORE-	PONY-	WINE-
BUCK-	DAMA-	GOAT-	SEAL-	WOLF-
CALF-	DEER-	LAMB-	SWAN-	WOOD-
CAPE-	FISH-	MOLE-	TURN-	WOOL-

Words that end with -SMAN

Seven-letter words

ALM-	GAD-	MES-	ODD-	TOP-
ART-	KIN-	MOB-	PAS-	
BAT-	LEN-	NEW-	ROD-	
DAY-	MAG-	OAR-	TAP-	

Eight-letter words

BAIL-	BANK-	BEDE-	BOAT-	CHES-
BAND-	BEAD-	BLUE-	BOND-	CLAN-

CLAS-	GILD-	LEAD-	PUNT-	TALE-
CORP-	GLAS-	LINE-	RAFT-	TALI-
CRAG-	GOAD-	LINK-	RAMP-	TIDE-
DALE-	GOWN-	LOCK-	REIN-	TOWN-
DOOM-	HEAD-	LODE-	ROAD-	TREW-
DOOR-	HELM-	LOFT-	SALE-	WEAL-
DRAG-	HERD-	MARK-	SEED-	WOOD-
FOIL-	HUNT-	MERE-	SIDE-	
GAME-	ISLE-	OVER-	SWAG-	
GANG-	LAND-	PRES-	TACK-	

Words that end with -SMEN

Seven-letter words

ALM-	GAD-	MES-	ODD-	TOP-
ART-	KIN-	MOB-	PAS-	
BAT-	LEN-	NEW-	ROD-	
DAY-	MAG-	OAR-	TAP-	

Eight-letter words

BAIL-	CRAG-	HEAD-	MARK-	SWAG-
BAND-	DALE-	HELM-	MERE-	TACK-
BANK-	DOOM-	HERD-	OVER-	TALE-
BEAD-	DOOR-	HUNT-	PRES-	TIDE-
BEDE-	DRAG-	ISLE-	PUNT-	TOWN-
BLUE-	FOIL-	LAND-	RAFT-	TREW-
BOAT-	GAME-	LEAD-	RAMP-	WEAL-
BOND-	GANG-	LINE-	REIN-	WOOD-
CHES-	GILD-	LINK-	ROAD-	
CLAN-	GLAS-	LOCK-	SALE-	
CLAS-	GOAD-	LODE-	SEED-	
CORP-	GOWN-	LOFT-	SIDE-	

Words that end with -SOME

Seven-letter words

AWE-	FUL-	NOI-	TRI-	WAE-
BEE-	GAY-	NOY-	TWA-	WAG-
EPI-	IRK-	OXY-	TWO-	WIN-
EYE-	LIS-	TOY-	URO-	WOE-

Eight-letter words

ACRO-	FLAY-	HAND-	LOVE-	ROOM-
AUTO-	FLEA-	HEAL-	LYSO-	TEDI-
BORE-	FOUR-	HOLE-	MERO-	TIRE-
CLOY-	FRET-	JOKE-	MESO-	TOIL-
CYTO-	GAME-	LARK-	MONO-	TWIG-
DARK-	GLAD-	LIFE-	MURK-	WAIL-
DOLE-	GLEE-	LIPO-	PLAY-	WORK-
DUEL-	GONO-	LONE-	POLY-	
ENDO-	GREW-	LONG-	PYRO-	
FEAR-	GRUE-	LOTH-	RIBO-	

Words that end with -TIME

Seven-letter words

AIR-	BIG-	LAY-	PAS-	TEA-
ANY-	CEN-	MIS-	RAG-	WAR-
BED-	DAY-	ONE-	SEP-	

Eight-letter words

CHOW-	HALF-	MEAN-	SEED-	ZONE-
DOWN-	LIFE-	NOON-	SHOW-	
FLEX-	LONG-	OVER-	SOME-	
FORE-	MARI-	PLAY-	TERM-	
GOOD-	MEAL-	REAL-	XENO-	

Words that end with -TION

Seven-letter words

ALA-	COC-	ENA-	OVA-	TAC-
AMA-	COI-	FAC-	PAC-	TUI-
AMO-	DIC-	FIC-	POR-	UNC-
AUC-	EDI-	LEC-	REC-	UNI-
BAS-	ELA-	MEN-	RUC-	
CAN-	ELU-	MIC-	SEC-	
CAP-	EMO-	MIX-	STA-	
CAU-	EMP-	ORA-	SUC-	

Eight-letter words

ABLA-	DILA-	FUNC-	LUNA-	RELA-
ABLU-	DILU-	GELA-	LUXA-	REMO-
ABOR-	DONA-	GUMP-	MONI-	ROGA-
ADAP-	DOTA-	GYRA-	MUNI-	ROTA-
ADDI-	DURA-	HALA-	MUTA-	SANC-
ADNA-	EDUC-	HIMA-	NATA-	SCON-
ADOP-	EGES-	IDEA-	NEGA-	SEDA-
AERA-	EJEC-	IGNI-	NIDA-	SEDI-
AGNA-	ELEC-	ILLA-	NIVA-	SOLA-
AMBI-	EMIC-	INAC-	NODA-	SOLU-
AUDI-	ENAC-	INUS-	NOLI-	SORP-
AVIA-	EQUA-	IODA-	NOTA-	STIC-
BIBA-	EREC-	JOBA-	NOVA-	SUDA-
CIBA-	ERUP-	JUNC-	NUDA-	SWAP-
CITA-	EVEC-	LAVA-	NUTA-	TAXA-
COAC-	EVIC-	LAXA-	OBLA-	TRAC-
CONA-	EXAC-	LEGA-	PACA-	VACA-
COOP-	EXER-	LENI-	PETI-	VENA-
CREA-	FETA-	LIBA-	POSI-	VEXA-
DELA-	FIXA-	LIGA-	POTA-	VOCA-
DELE-	FLEC-	LIMA-	PUNI-	VOLI-
DEMO-	FRAC-	LOBA-	PUPA-	VOLU-
DERA-	FRIC-	LOCA-	QUES-	ZONA-
DEVO-	FRUI-	LOCU-	REAC-	

Words that end with -URE

Seven-letter words

ABAT-	DISC-	GYPL-	PAST-	SEIS-
BORD-	EPIC-	HACH-	PERD-	SEIZ-
BRAV-	ERAS-	LEAS-	PERJ-	SEYS-
BRIS-	FACT-	LECT-	PICT-	SOIL-
CAPT-	FAIL-	LEIS-	PLEX-	STAT-
CENS-	FEAT-	MEAS-	POST-	TEXT-
CLOS-	FISS-	MIXT-	PREC-	TONS-
CLOT-	FIXT-	MONT-	PROC-	TORT-
COEN-	FLEX-	MORS-	PULT-	VENT-
CONJ-	FRIS-	MULT-	PURP-	VERD-
COUP-	FRIT-	NERV-	RAPT-	VEST-
COUT-	GARB-	NURT-	RECO-	VOIT-
CULT-	GEST-	OBSC-	ROND-	VULT-
DASY-	GRAV-	OUTD-	RUPT-	WAFT-
DENT-	GUIP-	PART-	SEAS-	

Eight-letter words

ANNEX-	CREAT-	GENIT-	OVERS-	RESEC-
APERT-	CUBAT-	HUMIT-	OVERT-	ROUND-
ARCAT-	CYNOS-	IMMAT-	PAINT-	SCISS-
ARMAT-	DENAT-	INCIS-	PEDIC-	SCRIM-
AVENT-	DISCO-	INSEC-	PLEAS-	SINEC-
BROCH-	DISIN-	JOINT-	PRESS-	TAINT-
CEINT-	DOUBL-	JUNCT-	PUNCT-	TINCT-
CINCT-	ENACT-	LIGAT-	REASS-	TOURN-
CISEL-	ENCOL-	LINCT-	REFIG-	TREAS-
COCKS-	EXPOS-	MANIC-	REINJ-	TRESS-
COEND-	FILAT-	MOIST-	REINS-	TUBUL-
COIFF-	FIXAT-	OSSAT-	RENAT-	
COINS-	FRACT-	OVERC-	REPOS-	

Words that end with -WARD

Seven-letter words

AIR-	FRO-	LEE-	OUT-	SUN-
AWK-	GOD-	MAN-	SEA-	VAN-
BED-	HAY-	NAY-	SKY-	WAY-
FOR-	HOG-	NOR-	STE-	WEY-

Eight-letter words

BACK-	FORE-	HOME-	PARK-	THRA-
BEAR-	GOAL-	KIRK-	POLE-	UNTO-
BECO-	HEAD-	LAND-	REAR-	WEST-
CITY-	HELL-	LEFT-	RERE-	WIND-
DOWN-	HIND-	MISA-	SELF-	WOOD-
EAST-	HIVE-	MOON-	SIDE-	WOOL-

Words that end with -WARDS

Seven-letter words

AD-	IN-	RE-	UP-	VA-
CO-	ON-	TO-	US-	

Eight-letter words

AIR-	GOD-	MAN-	SEA-
BED-	HAY-	NAY-	SKY-
FOR-	HOG-	NOR-	STE-
FRO-	LEE-	OUT-	SUN-

Words that end with -WAY

Seven-letter words

ARCH-	FOLK-	LAYA-	RODE-	TIDE-
AREA-	FOOT-	LICH-	ROLL-	TOLL-
BELT-	FREE-	LIFE-	ROPE-	TOWA-
BIKE-	GANG-	PACE-	RUNA-	TRAM-
CARA-	GATE-	PACK-	SHIP-	WALK-
CART-	GETA-	PARK-	SIDE-	WELA-
CUTA-	HADA-	PART-	SKID-	WIND-
DOOR-	HALF-	PATH-	SLIP-	WIRE-
FAIR-	HALL-	RACE-	SOME-	
FARA-	HEAD-	RAIL-	SPUR-	
FISH-	HIGH-	RING-	TAXI-	
FLYA-	LANE-	ROAD-	THRU-	

Eight-letter words

AISLE-	DRANG-	HEREA-	ROLLA-	TEARA-
ALLEY-	DRIVE-	HIDEA-	ROUTE-	THATA-
BROAD-	ENTRY-	HOIST-	SLIDE-	THISA-
CABLE-	EVERY-	HORSE-	SOAKA-	TRACK-
CARRA-	FADEA-	HUNTA-	SOARA-	TRAIN-
CASTA-	FALLA-	LOCKA-	SPEED-	UNDER-
CAUSE-	FLOOD-	MOTOR-	SPILL-	WALKA-
CLEAR-	FOLDA-	MULLO-	STAIR-	WASHA-
COLOR-	GIVEA-	OVERS-	STAYA-	WASTE-
CRAWL-	GREEN-	RIDGE-	STERN-	WATER-
CROSS-	GUIDE-	RIVER-	STOWA-	WELLA-
CYCLE-	HATCH-	ROCKA-	TAKEA-	WIDTH-

Words that end with -WISE

Seven-letter words

AIR-	END-	MAN-	SUN-
ANY-	FAN-	MAP-	TAX-

Eight-letter words

ARCH-	EDGE-	LONG-	SIDE-	TENT-
BEND-	ELSE-	OVER-	SOME-	THUS-
COMB-	FESS-	PAIR-	STEP-	WARP-
CRAB-	FLAT-	PALE-	SUCH-	WEFT-
DROP-	LIKE-	RING-	TEAM-	

Words that end with -WOOD

Seven-letter words

BAR-	CAM-	ELM-	LOG-	SAP-
BAY-	DAG-	FAT-	NUT-	
BOG-	DOG-	GUM-	PLY-	
BOX-	DYE-	INK-	RED-	

Eight-letter words

AGAL-	COLT-	GILT-	MILK-	SASS-
BACK-	CORD-	HARD-	OVEN-	SOFT-
BASS-	CORK-	HARE-	PEAR-	SOUR-
BEAR-	CRAB-	IRON-	PINE-	TEAK-
BEEF-	DEAD-	KING-	PORK-	WILD-
BENT-	FIRE-	LACE-	PULP-	WORM-
BLUE-	FUEL-	LATE-	ROSE-	

Words that end with -WORK

Seven-letter words

ART-	LEG-	PIN-	TIN-	WAX-
CUT-	NET-	PRE-	TOP-	WEB-
DAY-	NON-	RAG-	TUT-	
LAP-	OUT-	RIB-	WAR-	

Eight-letter words

BACK-	FIRE-	IRON-	PART-	STUD-
BEAD-	FLAT-	KNOT-	PILE-	TASK-
BODY-	FLUE-	KOFT-	PIPE-	TEAM-
BOOK-	FOOT-	LACE-	RACK-	TIME-
BUHL-	FORM-	LATH-	RING-	TUBE-
BUSY-	FRET-	LEAD-	ROAD-	WIRE-
CAGE-	HACK-	LIFE-	ROCK-	WOOD-
CAPE-	HAIR-	LINK-	ROPE-	WOOL-
CASE-	HAND-	MESH-	SALT-	YARD-
CRIB-	HEAD-	MILL-	SCUT-	
DUCT-	HOME-	OPEN-	SEAT-	
FARM-	HORN-	OVER-	SLOP-	

Words that end with -WORM

Seven-letter words

BAG-	CUT-	LOB-	RAG-	WEB-
BUD-	EAR-	LUG-	SEA-	
CAT-	EEL-	PIN-	WAX-	

Eight-letter words

ARMY-	FISH-	HORN-	MUCK-	SLOW-
BOLL-	FLAT-	INCH-	PILL-	SPAN-
BOOK-	GAPE-	LEAF-	RING-	TAPE-
CASE-	GLOW-	LIND-	ROOT-	TUBE-
CLAM-	GRUB-	LUNG-	SAND-	WHIP-
CORN-	HAIR-	MALT-	SHIP-	WIRE-
FIRE-	HOOK-	MEAL-	SILK-	WOOD-

Words that end with -WORT

Seven-letter words

AWL-	FAN-	MAD-	RAG-
BLA-	FEL-	MUD-	RIB-
BUG-	FIG-	MUG-	

Eight-letter words

BELL-	FLEA-	LUNG-	PILE-	SOAP-
COLE-	GOUT-	MILK-	PILL-	STAR-
DAME-	HONE-	MODI-	PIPE-	WALL-
DANE-	HORN-	MOON-	SALT-	WART-
DROP-	LEAD-	MOOR-	SAND-	

Words that end with -YARD

Seven-letter words

BEE-	HAL-	INN-	LAN-	TAN-

Eight-letter words

BACK-	DEER-	HAUL-	METE-	TILT-
BALL-	DOCK-	JUNK-	RICK-	VINE-
BARN-	DOOR-	KAIL-	SALE-	WHIN-
BOAT-	FARM-	KALE-	SAVO-	WILL-
BONE-	FEED-	KIRK-	SHIP-	WOOD-
COAL-	FORE-	MAIN-	SHOW-	

Vowel endings

E aside, it can be difficult to think of words that end in the vowels. But these words can be very useful. A, I, O and U represent almost a third of the tiles in the game, and there are a great many two-letter words that begin or end with vowels other than E. Words that end in vowels give you great opportunities for tagging onto words already on the board, creating one or more two-letter words in the process. Thus, if you have a promising rack, vowel endings help you to employ your tiles to good effect; it's no use having a great set of letters if you can't get them onto the board!

The lists in this section detail all words from two letters to eight in length, ending in A, I, O or U. Definitions are provided for the two-letter and three-letter words.

Words that end with -A

Two-letter words

AA	volcanic rock consisting of angular blocks of lava with a very rough surface
BA	symbol for the soul in Ancient Egyptian religion
DA	Burmese knife
EA	river
FA	(in tonic sol-fa) fourth degree of any major scale
HA	exclamation expressing triumph, surprise, or scorn
JA	yes
KA	(in ancient Egypt) attendant spirit supposedly dwelling as a vital force in a man or statue
LA	exclamation of surprise or emphasis
MA	mother
NA	Scots word for no
PA	(formerly) fortified Maori settlement
TA	thank you
YA	you
ZA	pizza

Three-letter words

ABA	type of cloth from Syria, made of goat hair or camel hair
AGA	title of respect, often used with the title of a senior position
AHA	exclamation expressing triumph, surprise, etc, according to the intonation of the speaker
AIA	female servant in East
AKA	vine, Metrosideros scandens, found in New Zealand
ALA	wing or flat winglike process or structure, such as a part of some bones and cartilages
AMA	vessel for water
ANA	(of ingredients in a prescription) in equal quantities
AUA	yellow-eye mullet
AVA	at all
AWA	away
BAA	make the characteristic bleating sound of a sheep
BOA	large nonvenomous snake

BRA	brassiere
CAA	Scots word for call
CHA	tea
ERA	period of time considered as distinctive
ETA	seventh letter in the Greek alphabet, a long vowel sound
FAA	(in tonic sol-fa) fourth degree of any major scale
FRA	brother: a title given to an Italian monk or friar
GOA	gazelle, Procapra picticaudata, inhabiting the plains of the Tibetan plateau, having a brownish-grey coat and backward-curving horns
HOA	imitation or representation of the sound of a deep laugh
ITA	type of palm
KEA	large brownish-green parrot of NZ
KOA	Hawaiian leguminous tree
LEA	meadow
MAA	(of goats) bleat
MNA	ancient unit of weight and money, used in Asia Minor, equal to one sixtieth of a talent
MOA	large extinct flightless New Zealand bird
OBA	(in W Africa) a Yoruba chief or ruler
OCA	any of various South American herbaceous plants
ODA	room in a harem
OKA	unit of weight used in Turkey
ORA	mouths or mouthlike parts or openings
OVA	unfertilized egg cells
PEA	climbing plant with seeds growing in pods
PIA	innermost of the three membranes that cover the brain and the spinal cord
POA	type of grass
PYA	monetary unit of Myanmar worth one hundredth of a kyat
QUA	in the capacity of
RIA	long narrow inlet of the seacoast, being a former valley that was submerged by a rise in the level of the sea. Rias are found esp on the coasts of SW Ireland and NW Spain
RYA	type of rug originating in Scandinavia
SEA	mass of salt water covering three quarters of the earth's surface
SHA	be quiet
SKA	type of West Indian pop music of the 1960s
SMA	Scots word for small
SPA	resort with a mineral-water spring
TEA	drink made from infusing the dried leaves of an Asian bush in boiling water
TWA	Scots word for two
UTA	side-blotched lizard
UVA	grape or fruit resembling this
VIA	by way of
WHA	Scots word for who
YEA	yes
ZEA	corn silk
ZOA	independent animal bodi es, such as the individuals of a coral colony

Four-letter words

ABBA	AIGA	AMIA	ANSA	ARIA
ACCA	ALBA	AMLA	ANTA	ARNA
ACTA	ALFA	ANGA	AQUA	ASEA
AGHA	ALGA	ANNA	ARBA	ATMA
AGMA	ALMA	ANOA	AREA	ATUA

AULA	GENA	LEVA	PAUA	SURA
AURA	GETA	LIMA	PAWA	TAHA
BABA	GIGA	LIPA	PEBA	TAKA
BEMA	GILA	LIRA	PELA	TALA
BETA	GLIA	LOCA	PICA	TANA
BIGA	GORA	LOMA	PIKA	TAPA
BIMA	GUGA	LOTA	PILA	TARA
BOBA	GULA	LUMA	PIMA	TAVA
BOLA	HAHA	LUNA	PINA	TAWA
BOMA	HAKA	LYRA	PIPA	TAXA
BONA	HILA	MALA	PITA	TELA
BORA	HIYA	MAMA	PLEA	TEPA
BOTA	HOHA	MANA	PROA	TIKA
BUBA	HOKA	MARA	PUHA	TOEA
BUDA	HOMA	MASA	PUJA	TOGA
BUNA	HORA	MAYA	PUKA	TOLA
BURA	HOYA	MEGA	PULA	TORA
CABA	HUIA	MELA	PUMA	TOSA
CACA	HULA	MESA	PUNA	TUBA
CAMA	HUMA	META	PUPA	TUFA
CAPA	HYLA	MICA	RACA	TUNA
CASA	IDEA	MIHA	RAGA	ULNA
CAVA	ILEA	MINA	RAIA	ULVA
CECA	ILIA	MOLA	RAJA	UPTA
CHIA	ILKA	MONA	RANA	UREA
COCA	INIA	MORA	RATA	URSA
CODA	IOTA	MOWA	RAYA	URVA
COLA	ISBA	MOXA	RHEA	UVEA
COMA	ISNA	MOYA	RIBA	VARA
COXA	IXIA	MURA	RIMA	VASA
CYMA	JAFA	MYNA	RIVA	VEGA
DADA	JAGA	NADA	RIZA	VELA
DATA	JAVA	NAGA	ROMA	VENA
DEVA	JOTA	NALA	ROTA	VERA
DIKA	JUBA	NANA	RUGA	VIGA
DISA	JUGA	NAPA	RUSA	VINA
DITA	JURA	NEMA	SAGA	VISA
DIVA	KAKA	NIPA	SAMA	VITA
DONA	KAMA	NOMA	SENA	VIVA
DOPA	KANA	NONA	SERA	VOLA
DUKA	KAPA	NOTA	SETA	WAKA
DUMA	KARA	NOVA	SHEA	WAWA
DURA	KATA	OBIA	SHWA	WEKA
EGMA	KAVA	OCTA	SIDA	WENA
EINA	KAWA	ODEA	SIKA	WETA
EKKA	KETA	OHIA	SIMA	WHOA
EMMA	KINA	OKRA	SKUA	YABA
EPHA	KIVA	OKTA	SOBA	YOGA
ETNA	KOHA	OLEA	SOCA	YUCA
EYRA	KOLA	OLLA	SODA	YUGA
FAVA	KORA	ORCA	SOFA	ZETA
FETA	KUIA	ORRA	SOJA	ZILA
FILA	KULA	OSSA	SOLA	ZOEA
FLEA	KUNA	OUMA	SOMA	ZONA
FORA	KUTA	OUPA	SORA	ZUPA
GAGA	LAMA	PACA	SOYA	ZYGA
GALA	LANA	PAPA	STOA	
GAMA	LAVA	PARA	SUBA	

Five-letter words

ABACA	BETTA	CRENA	FOVEA	INTRA
ABAKA	BHUNA	CRURA	FRENA	INULA
ABAYA	BIGHA	CULPA	FURCA	IXORA
ABOMA	BIOTA	CUPPA	GALEA	JAGRA
ABUNA	BIVIA	CURIA	GAMBA	JARTA
ACETA	BOCCA	DABBA	GAMMA	JHALA
ADYTA	BOHEA	DACHA	GANJA	JIRGA
AECIA	BONZA	DAGGA	GARDA	JNANA
AFARA	BORNA	DARGA	GEMMA	JUNTA
AGAMA	BOYLA	DELTA	GENOA	KAAMA
AGILA	BRAVA	DERMA	GENUA	KACHA
AGITA	BRAZA	DICTA	GLEBA	KAIKA
AGORA	BUBBA	DINNA	GOGGA	KALPA
AGRIA	BUFFA	DIOTA	GOMPA	KANGA
AINGA	BULLA	DOBLA	GONIA	KAPPA
AJIVA	BUNIA	DOBRA	GONNA	KARMA
AJUGA	BUNYA	DOGMA	GOTTA	KASHA
AKELA	BURKA	DOLIA	GOURA	KEHUA
AKITA	BURQA	DOLMA	GRAMA	KERMA
ALAPA	BURSA	DONGA	GRANA	KHAYA
ALDEA	BWANA	DONNA	GROMA	KHEDA
ALIYA	CAECA	DOONA	GUANA	KHOJA
ALOHA	CALLA	DORBA	GUAVA	KIBLA
ALPHA	CALPA	DORSA	GUMMA	KINDA
ALULA	CANNA	DOULA	GUSLA	KIPPA
AMEBA	CARTA	DOUMA	GUTTA	KOALA
AMIGA	CAUDA	DOURA	GYOZA	KOFTA
AMNIA	CAUSA	DOWNA	HAIKA	KOKRA
ANANA	CEIBA	DRAMA	HAKEA	KOPPA
ANATA	CELLA	DUKKA	HALFA	KORMA
ANIMA	CERIA	DULIA	HALMA	KOURA
ANTRA	CESTA	DUMKA	HALVA	KRONA
AORTA	CHARA	DURRA	HAMBA	KURTA
APNEA	CHAYA	EDEMA	HAMZA	KWELA
ARABA	CHEKA	ENEMA	HANSA	LABDA
ARECA	CHELA	ENTIA	HAOMA	LABIA
ARENA	CHICA	ERBIA	HASTA	LABRA
AREPA	CHINA	ERICA	HATHA	LAIKA
AROBA	CHOLA	ETYMA	HEJRA	LAKSA
AROHA	CHOMA	EXTRA	HENNA	LAMIA
AROMA	CHOTA	FACIA	HERMA	LARVA
ASANA	CHUFA	FAENA	HEVEA	LAURA
ASYLA	CILIA	FANGA	HIJRA	LAVRA
ATRIA	CIRCA	FATWA	HODJA	LEHUA
BABKA	CNIDA	FAUNA	HOLLA	LEMMA
BACCA	COALA	FELLA	HONDA	LEPRA
BACHA	COBIA	FERIA	HOOKA	LEPTA
BAIZA	COBRA	FESTA	HOSTA	LEZZA
BAJRA	COBZA	FETTA	HOVEA	LIANA
BAKRA	COCOA	FETWA	HUDNA	LIBRA
BALSA	COLZA	FINCA	HURRA	LIMBA
BANDA	COMMA	FITNA	HUTIA	LIMMA
BANIA	CONGA	FLORA	HUZZA	LIMPA
BARCA	CONIA	FLOTA	HYDRA	LINGA
BARRA	COPRA	FOLIA	HYENA	LLAMA
BASTA	CORIA	FONDA	HYPHA	LOGIA
BATTA	COSTA	FORZA	IDOLA	LONGA
BELGA	COTTA	FOSSA	INFRA	LOOFA

LOUMA	NALLA	POLKA	SCUTA	TAYRA
LUBRA	NAMMA	PONGA	SELLA	TAZZA
LUFFA	NANNA	POOJA	SELVA	TECTA
LUTEA	NANUA	POOKA	SENNA	TEGUA
LYCEA	NAPPA	POPPA	SENSA	TELIA
LYCRA	NERKA	PORTA	SENZA	TENIA
LYSSA	NGANA	PRANA	SEPIA	TERGA
LYTTA	NGOMA	PRESA	SEPTA	TERRA
MAFIA	NINJA	PRIMA	SERRA	TESLA
MAGMA	NORIA	PRUTA	SESSA	TESTA
MAHUA	NORMA	PSORA	SHAMA	TETRA
MAHWA	NUBIA	PUCKA	SHAYA	THANA
MALVA	NUCHA	PUKKA	SHEVA	THECA
MALWA	NULLA	PULKA	SHIVA	THEMA
MAMBA	NYALA	PUNGA	SHOLA	THETA
MAMMA	NYSSA	PUNKA	SHURA	THUJA
MANGA	OCREA	PURDA	SIDHA	THUYA
MANIA	OIDIA	QIBLA	SIGLA	TIARA
MANNA	OMASA	QORMA	SIGMA	TIBIA
MANTA	OMEGA	QUENA	SIGNA	TICCA
MARIA	OPERA	QUINA	SILVA	TIKKA
MARKA	ORGIA	QUOTA	SIMBA	TINEA
MASSA	ORIXA	RAGGA	SIRRA	TOMIA
MATZA	OSSIA	RAITA	SITKA	TONGA
MBIRA	OSTIA	RASTA	SOFTA	TONKA
MECCA	OUIJA	RATHA	SOPRA	TORTA
MEDIA	PACHA	REATA	SORDA	TREFA
MEKKA	PACTA	RECTA	SORRA	TREMA
MENSA	PADMA	REDIA	SORTA	TRONA
MENTA	PAISA	REGMA	SPAZA	TRYMA
MICRA	PAKKA	REGNA	SPICA	TSUBA
MIKRA	PALEA	RENGA	SPINA	TUGRA
MILIA	PALLA	REPLA	SPUTA	TUINA
MILPA	PAMPA	RETIA	STELA	TULPA
MIRZA	PANDA	RHYTA	STIPA	ULAMA
MISSA	PANGA	RIATA	STOMA	ULEMA
MOCHA	PARKA	RIOJA	STRIA	ULTRA
MOHUA	PARRA	ROOSA	STUPA	UMBRA
MOIRA	PASHA	RUANA	SUBHA	UNCIA
MOLLA	PASTA	RUMBA	SULFA	URBIA
MOMMA	PELMA	RUPIA	SUMMA	URENA
MOOLA	PELTA	RUSMA	SUNNA	USNEA
MORIA	PENNA	SABRA	SUPRA	UVULA
MORRA	PEPLA	SACRA	SURRA	VACUA
MOTZA	PEREA	SADZA	SUTRA	VANDA
MOWRA	PHOCA	SAIGA	SUTTA	VARIA
MUDRA	PHYLA	SAKIA	SYLVA	VARNA
MUGGA	PICRA	SALPA	TAATA	VEENA
MULGA	PIETA	SALSA	TABLA	VERRA
MULLA	PILEA	SAMBA	TAFIA	VESPA
MUNGA	PINNA	SANGA	TAGMA	VESTA
MURRA	PINTA	SANSA	TAIGA	VIFDA
MURVA	PITTA	SAUBA	TAIRA	VIGIA
MUSCA	PIZZA	SAUNA	TALEA	VILLA
MUSHA	PLAYA	SCALA	TALMA	VINCA
MUTHA	PLAZA	SCAPA	TALPA	VIOLA
MYOMA	PLENA	SCENA	TANGA	VIRGA
NABLA	PLICA	SCHWA	TANKA	VISTA
NAIRA	POAKA	SCOPA	TANNA	VITTA
NAKFA	PODIA	SCUBA	TAPPA	VIVDA

VODKA	WHATA	WONGA	YARTA	ZEBRA
VOEMA	WICCA	WUXIA	YENTA	ZERDA
VOILA	WIGGA	XENIA	YERBA	ZILLA
VOLTA	WILGA	XOANA	YUCCA	ZOAEA
VOLVA	WILJA	YABBA	YURTA	ZONDA
VULVA	WINNA	YACCA	ZABRA	ZOOEA
WAGGA	WIRRA	YACKA	ZAMIA	ZOPPA
WALLA	WISHA	YAKKA	ZANJA	
WANNA	WOKKA	YARFA	ZANZA	

Six-letter words

ABASIA	ARAARA	BRAHMA	CHIMLA	CZAPKA
ABELIA	ARALIA	BREGMA	CHOANA	DAGABA
ABOLLA	ARCANA	BROLGA	CHOKRA	DAGOBA
ABULIA	AREOLA	BUCKRA	CHOLLA	DAHLIA
ACACIA	ARGALA	BUDDHA	CHORDA	DATCHA
ACEDIA	ARISTA	BUGSHA	CHOREA	DATURA
ADNEXA	ARMADA	BUNNIA	CHORIA	DEFLEA
AFTOSA	ARNICA	BUQSHA	CHROMA	DHAMMA
AGENDA	AROLLA	BUSERA	CHUKKA	DHARMA
AGGADA	ARRIBA	BUSHWA	CHUPPA	DHARNA
AGOUTA	ARROBA	CABALA	CICADA	DHOORA
AHIMSA	ASRAMA	CABANA	CICALA	DHURNA
AIKONA	ASTHMA	CADAGA	CICUTA	DHURRA
AKATEA	ATAATA	CAEOMA	CINEMA	DOLINA
AKHARA	ATAXIA	CAFILA	CITOLA	DOOSRA
ALALIA	ATOCIA	CALESA	CLIVIA	DUENNA
ALASKA	ATONIA	CALIMA	CLOACA	DUHKHA
ALBATA	AUCUBA	CALTHA	CLUSIA	DUKKHA
ALEXIA	AURORA	CAMBIA	COAITA	DUMELA
ALISMA	AVRUGA	CAMERA	COBAEA	ECZEMA
ALODIA	AXILLA	CAMISA	CODEIA	EGESTA
ALOGIA	AZALEA	CANADA	CONCHA	EIDOLA
ALPACA	AZOLLA	CANCHA	CONIMA	EJECTA
ALTEZA	BACKRA	CANOLA	CONTRA	ELODEA
ALTHEA	BACULA	CANULA	COPITA	ELUVIA
ALUMNA	BAHADA	CAPITA	COPPRA	ELYTRA
AMARNA	BAJADA	CARDIA	COPULA	EMPUSA
AMELIA	BALATA	CARINA	CORNEA	ENCINA
AMENTA	BALBOA	CASABA	CORNUA	ENIGMA
AMOEBA	BANANA	CASAVA	CORONA	ENTERA
AMRITA	BARAZA	CASITA	CORREA	EPEIRA
AMUSIA	BARYTA	CASSIA	CORYZA	EPIZOA
ANATTA	BATATA	CATENA	COSMEA	EPOCHA
ANCORA	BAUERA	CEDULA	COWPEA	ERRATA
ANEMIA	BEFANA	CEMBRA	CRACKA	ESPADA
ANGINA	BEFLEA	CENTRA	CRANIA	EUPNEA
ANGOLA	BELUGA	CESURA	CRESTA	EUREKA
ANGORA	BEMATA	CHACMA	CRISSA	EXACTA
ANICCA	BERTHA	CHAETA	CRISTA	EXEDRA
ANNONA	BHAKTA	CHAKRA	CROWEA	EXUVIA
ANOPIA	BILBOA	CHALLA	CRUSTA	FACULA
ANOXIA	BOCCIA	CHANGA	CUBICA	FAJITA
ANTARA	BODEGA	CHAPKA	CUESTA	FANEGA
ANTLIA	BONITA	CHARKA	CUMBIA	FARINA
ANURIA	BOONGA	CHARTA	CUPOLA	FASCIA
APHTHA	BOORKA	CHATTA	CUPULA	FATSIA
APNOEA	BOSHTA	CHICHA	CURARA	FAVELA
APORIA	BRAATA	CHIGGA	CUTCHA	FECULA

FEDORA	HUTZPA	KORORA	MEGARA	PALAPA
FEIJOA	HYAENA	KORUNA	MELENA	PALLIA
FEMORA	HYDRIA	KUMARA	MESETA	PANADA
FERULA	IDEATA	KUMERA	METEPA	PANAMA
FIBULA	IGUANA	KUTCHA	MEZUZA	PAPAYA
FIESTA	IMPALA	KWACHA	MGANGA	PAPULA
FLAUTA	INANGA	KWANZA	MIASMA	PARERA
FOOTRA	INDABA	LABARA	MIMOSA	PARURA
FOUSSA	INDUNA	LACUNA	MINIMA	PASHKA
FOUTRA	INFIMA	LAGENA	MIZUNA	PATACA
FRAENA	INFULA	LAGUNA	MODENA	PATAKA
FRISKA	INJERA	LAMBDA	MODICA	PATELA
FRUSTA	INSULA	LAMINA	MOKSHA	PATERA
FULCRA	INTIMA	LATERA	MONERA	PATINA
FUNKIA	INYALA	LATINA	MOORVA	PAYOLA
FUSUMA	ISCHIA	LATRIA	MORCHA	PELOTA
GALENA	ISTANA	LEIPOA	MORULA	PENNIA
GAMBIA	JACANA	LEXICA	MOTUCA	PERAEA
GARRYA	JARINA	LIGULA	MUCOSA	PEREIA
GARUDA	JATAKA	LIKUTA	MULETA	PESETA
GEISHA	JEJUNA	LIMINA	MUMMIA	PESEWA
GELADA	JEMIMA	LINGUA	MURENA	PESHWA
GENERA	JERBOA	LIPOMA	MURRHA	PETARA
GENEVA	JHATKA	LITHIA	MUTUCA	PHARMA
GITANA	JICAMA	LOBOLA	MYOPIA	PHOBIA
GLIOMA	JOANNA	LOCHIA	MYRICA	PIAZZA
GLORIA	JOJOBA	LOGGIA	MYXOMA	PICARA
GLOSSA	JUDOKA	LOMATA	NAGANA	PILULA
GNAMMA	JUGULA	LORCHA	NATURA	PINATA
GOANNA	KABAKA	LORICA	NAUSEA	PINETA
GOONDA	KABALA	LUCUMA	NEBULA	PIRANA
GOPURA	KABAYA	LUMINA	NEPETA	PIRAYA
GORGIA	KACCHA	LUNULA	NOCTUA	PITARA
GOTCHA	KAFILA	LUSTRA	NOMINA	PITAYA
GRAMMA	KAHUNA	MABELA	NOVENA	PLANTA
GRAMPA	KAINGA	MACOYA	NUMINA	PLASMA
GRAPPA	KALMIA	MACULA	NUTRIA	PLEURA
GRINGA	KAMALA	MAFFIA	NYANZA	PNEUMA
GUINEA	KAMELA	MAKUTA	NYMPHA	POISHA
GYTTJA	KAMILA	MALTHA	OBELIA	POPERA
HALALA	KANAKA	MANAIA	OCHREA	PORINA
HALLOA	KANGHA	MANANA	OEDEMA	POSADA
HAMADA	KANTHA	MANAWA	OMENTA	PRAJNA
HANIWA	KANUKA	MANILA	OMERTA	PREMIA
HAPUKA	KAPUKA	MANTRA	ONYCHA	PROTEA
HARIRA	KARAKA	MANTUA	OPTIMA	PRUINA
HAWALA	KATANA	MANUKA	ORARIA	PSYLLA
HEBONA	KEMBLA	MARACA	ORBITA	PTERIA
HEDERA	KENTIA	MARINA	ORGANA	PULKHA
HEGIRA	KERRIA	MARKKA	ORISHA	PUNCTA
HEJIRA	KETMIA	MASALA	OSCULA	PURANA
HEMINA	KGOTLA	MASHUA	OSETRA	PYEMIA
HERNIA	KHANDA	MASULA	OTTAVA	PYJAMA
HILLOA	KHANGA	MATATA	OZAENA	PYROLA
HOLLOA	KHODJA	MAUNNA	PAELLA	PYURIA
HOLMIA	KHURTA	MAXIMA	PAGODA	QABALA
HOODIA	KINARA	MAZUMA	PAJAMA	QASIDA
HOOPLA	KINEMA	MEDAKA	PAKEHA	QUAGGA
HRYVNA	KISHKA	MEDINA	PAKORA	QUALIA
HULLOA	KOCHIA	MEDUSA	PALAMA	QUANTA

QUELEA	SAMOSA	SMEGMA	TEGULA	VELETA
QUINOA	SANCTA	SOLERA	TELEGA	VESICA
QUINTA	SAPOTA	SOMATA	TEPHRA	VICUNA
QUOKKA	SASTRA	SONATA	TERATA	VIHARA
QUOTHA	SATARA	SPIREA	TERBIA	VIMANA
RADULA	SATYRA	SQUAMA	TEREFA	VIMINA
RAFFIA	SCARPA	SRADHA	TERTIA	VIZSLA
RAMADA	SCHEMA	STADDA	THANNA	VOMICA
RAMBLA	SCILLA	STADIA	THORIA	WAIATA
RAMONA	SCLERA	STANZA	THULIA	WAIRUA
RANULA	SCOLIA	STATUA	TINAJA	WHATNA
RAPHIA	SCORIA	STELLA	TIPULA	WHENUA
RAZZIA	SCOTIA	STEMMA	TIPUNA	WILTJA
REALIA	SCOZZA	STERNA	TORANA	WOMERA
REDOWA	SCROTA	STIGMA	TORULA	XEROMA
REGINA	SEMEIA	STIRRA	TOTARA	XYLOMA
REGULA	SEMINA	STOMIA	TRAUMA	YAKUZA
RELATA	SENECA	STRATA	TREIFA	YANTRA
REMORA	SENEGA	STRIGA	TRIVIA	YAQONA
REMUDA	SENORA	STROMA	TROIKA	YARPHA
RESEDA	SEROSA	STRUMA	TSAMBA	YAUTIA
RETAMA	SHAMBA	SUBSEA	TUATUA	YOJANA
RETINA	SHARIA	SULPHA	TUGHRA	YTTRIA
RHANJA	SHEILA	SUNDRA	TUNDRA	YUKATA
RHUMBA	SHELTA	SYLVIA	TUNICA	ZABETA
RISTRA	SHERIA	SYNURA	TUPUNA	ZANANA
ROSTRA	SHERPA	TABULA	UJAMAA	ZAPATA
ROSULA	SHIKSA	TAENIA	ULTIMA	ZAREBA
ROTULA	SHIRRA	TAFFIA	UNGULA	ZARIBA
RUCOLA	SHISHA	TAHINA	URANIA	ZENANA
RUGOLA	SHOORA	TAIAHA	UREDIA	ZEREBA
RUGOSA	SIDDHA	TAIHOA	UREMIA	ZERIBA
RUMINA	SIENNA	TALUKA	URTICA	ZEUGMA
RUSSIA	SIERRA	TAMARA	UTOPIA	ZINNIA
SABKHA	SIESTA	TANKIA	VAGINA	ZOARIA
SAHIBA	SIFAKA	TANTRA	VAHANA	ZOECIA
SALINA	SILICA	TAONGA	VALETA	ZONULA
SALIVA	SISTRA	TAPETA	VALUTA	ZOYSIA
SALVIA	SITULA	TARAMA	VARROA	ZYGOMA
SAMARA	SKOLIA	TARSIA	VEDUTA	

Seven-letter words

ABOMASA	ADENOMA	ALLODIA	AMPULLA	ANTENNA
ABOULIA	ADHARMA	ALLUVIA	AMREETA	APADANA
ABROSIA	ADIPSIA	ALPACCA	ANAEMIA	APEPSIA
ACANTHA	AECIDIA	ALTEZZA	ANALGIA	APHAGIA
ACAPNIA	AEROBIA	ALTHAEA	ANALOGA	APHAKIA
ACCIDIA	AGEUSIA	ALUMINA	ANCHUSA	APHASIA
ACEQUIA	AGNOSIA	AMADODA	ANCILIA	APHELIA
ACEROLA	AGRAPHA	AMANDLA	ANCILLA	APHONIA
ACHARYA	AKRASIA	AMANITA	ANERGIA	APLASIA
ACHENIA	ALAMEDA	AMBOINA	ANESTRA	APRAXIA
ACHOLIA	ALBIZIA	AMBOYNA	ANGARIA	APTERIA
ACICULA	ALCHERA	AMENTIA	ANGIOMA	AQUARIA
ACRASIA	ALCORZA	AMMONIA	ANHINGA	ARABICA
ACROMIA	ALFALFA	AMNESIA	ANNATTA	ARAROBA
ACTINIA	ALFORJA	AMOKURA	ANONYMA	ARCADIA
ACUSHLA	ALGEBRA	AMOROSA	ANOPSIA	ARCHAEA
ADDENDA	ALGESIA	AMPHORA	ANOSMIA	ARGYRIA

ARIETTA	BRACCIA	CHALUPA	DELENDA	EXOTICA
ARMILLA	BRACHIA	CHAMISA	DELIRIA	EXTREMA
ARUGOLA	BRAVURA	CHARKHA	DEODARA	EXURBIA
ARUGULA	BRECCIA	CHECHIA	DEUTZIA	FALBALA
ASCIDIA	BRITSKA	CHIASMA	DHOURRA	FALCULA
ASHRAMA	BRITZKA	CHICANA	DIANOIA	FARINHA
ASPIDIA	BRUHAHA	CHIKARA	DICAMBA	FARRUCA
ASTASIA	BUBINGA	CHIMERA	DIGAMMA	FAUNULA
ASTERIA	BUCCINA	CHOLERA	DIHEDRA	FAVELLA
ATALAYA	BULIMIA	CHRISMA	DILEMMA	FAZENDA
ATEMOYA	BULLOSA	CHUTZPA	DILUVIA	FELICIA
ATHLETA	BUMELIA	CIBORIA	DIORAMA	FELUCCA
ATRESIA	BURSERA	CIMELIA	DIPLOMA	FERMATA
ATROPIA	BUZUKIA	CINEREA	DIPTERA	FIBROMA
AURELIA	CABBALA	CINGULA	DIPTYCA	FILARIA
AUREOLA	CABOMBA	CITHARA	DOGMATA	FIMBRIA
BABESIA	CADENZA	CLARKIA	DOMATIA	FISTULA
BACCARA	CAESURA	COAGULA	DONGOLA	FLORULA
BACHCHA	CAFFILA	COCHLEA	DOPATTA	FLUTINA
BACLAVA	CALDERA	CODEINA	DOPIAZA	FONTINA
BAKLAVA	CALLUNA	CODETTA	DOULEIA	FORLANA
BAKLAWA	CALUMBA	CODILLA	DRACENA	FORMICA
BALISTA	CAMELIA	COMITIA	DRACHMA	FORMULA
BANDANA	CAMISIA	COMMATA	DROSERA	FOSSULA
BANDORA	CAMORRA	CONARIA	DUODENA	FOVEOLA
BANDURA	CAMPANA	CONIDIA	DUPATTA	FREESIA
BANKSIA	CANASTA	COPAIBA	DVANDVA	FRENULA
BANSELA	CANDELA	COPAIVA	DYSPNEA	FUCHSIA
BARBOLA	CANDIDA	COQUINA	DYSURIA	FURCULA
BARILLA	CANELLA	CORALLA	ECHIDNA	FURLANA
BARISTA	CANNULA	CORBINA	ECTASIA	FUSARIA
BARTSIA	CANTALA	CORDOBA	ECTHYMA	GALABEA
BASIDIA	CANTATA	CORELLA	ECTOPIA	GALABIA
BATAVIA	CANTINA	COREMIA	ECTOZOA	GALANGA
BATTUTA	CANZONA	COROLLA	EDEMATA	GALATEA
BAZOOKA	CAPUERA	CORPORA	EMBLEMA	GALLETA
BEFFANA	CARAMBA	CORRIDA	EMERITA	GALLICA
BEGONIA	CARANNA	CORTINA	EMPORIA	GANGLIA
BEGORRA	CARAUNA	CORVINA	EMPYEMA	GANGSTA
BERETTA	CARBORA	COTINGA	ENCOMIA	GAROUPA
BERGAMA	CARIAMA	CRAPOLA	ENDOZOA	GASTREA
BHANGRA	CARIOCA	CREMONA	ENEMATA	GAZANIA
BIDARKA	CASCARA	CRIMINA	ENTASIA	GAZOOKA
BIENNIA	CASSABA	CROTALA	ENTOZOA	GENISTA
BIODATA	CASSATA	CURACOA	EPHEDRA	GERBERA
BIRETTA	CASSAVA	CURCUMA	EPISCIA	GERMINA
BISNAGA	CASSENA	CURIOSA	EPYLLIA	GERTCHA
BIZNAGA	CASSINA	CURTANA	EQUINIA	GIARDIA
BOFFOLA	CATALPA	CYATHIA	EROTEMA	GINGIVA
BOHEMIA	CATASTA	CYMATIA	EROTICA	GLOMERA
BOLIVIA	CATAWBA	CYPSELA	EUGENIA	GLUCINA
BOLOGNA	CAVALLA	CZARINA	EUGLENA	GOBURRA
BOMBORA	CEDILLA	DAMIANA	EULOGIA	GODETIA
BONAMIA	CELESTA	DAPHNIA	EUPNOEA	GONDOLA
BONANZA	CELOSIA	DAROGHA	EUTAXIA	GONIDIA
BONSELA	CEMENTA	DATARIA	EUTEXIA	GORDITA
BORONIA	CEREBRA	DAVIDIA	EXCRETA	GORILLA
BOTHRIA	CERVEZA	DECIDUA	EXEMPLA	GOSPODA
BOTTEGA	CHACHKA	DECURIA	EXHEDRA	GRANDMA
BOURKHA	CHALAZA	DEJECTA	EXORDIA	GRANDPA

GRANITA	KALIMBA	MAMPARA	NARCOMA	PARGANA
GRANOLA	KANTELA	MANCALA	NEMESIA	PARTITA
GRAVIDA	KARAKIA	MANDALA	NEUROMA	PASSATA
GUARANA	KARANGA	MANDIRA	NEURULA	PASTINA
GUEREZA	KATCINA	MANDOLA	NGARARA	PATAGIA
GUMMATA	KATORGA	MANDORA	NIGELLA	PATELLA
GUNNERA	KATSURA	MANILLA	NIHONGA	PAVLOVA
GYNECIA	KAUPAPA	MANIOCA	NIRVANA	PAXIUBA
HAFTARA	KEITLOA	MANUMEA	NONCOLA	PECULIA
HAGGADA	KERBAYA	MANYATA	NORTENA	PEISHWA
HALACHA	KERYGMA	MAQUILA	NOTANDA	PELORIA
HALAKHA	KHALIFA	MARANTA	NOTITIA	PEMBINA
HAMMADA	KHEDIVA	MARASCA	NOUMENA	PENTHIA
HARAMDA	KIBITKA	MAREMMA	NOVALIA	PEREIRA
HARIANA	KITHARA	MARGOSA	NOVELLA	PERGOLA
HARISSA	KOEKOEA	MARIMBA	OCARINA	PERIDIA
HARMALA	KOPIYKA	MARKKAA	OCTAPLA	PERILLA
HELLOVA	KUCHCHA	MARSALA	OLEARIA	PERINEA
HELLUVA	LABELLA	MASCARA	OLESTRA	PERSONA
HEMIOLA	LACINIA	MASTABA	OMMATEA	PESSIMA
HETAERA	LAMBADA	MATILDA	OMNIANA	PETUNIA
HETAIRA	LAMELLA	MAXILLA	ONDATRA	PHILTRA
HEUREKA	LAMPUKA	MAZURKA	ONYCHIA	PIASABA
HEXAPLA	LANGAHA	MEDACCA	OOGONIA	PIASAVA
HIDALGA	LANTANA	MEDULLA	OOTHECA	PICCATA
HIMATIA	LASAGNA	MEGILLA	OPHIURA	PIGNORA
HOROEKA	LATAKIA	MELISMA	OPUNTIA	PINNULA
HOSANNA	LATILLA	MELODIA	OQUASSA	PINTADA
HRYVNIA	LAVOLTA	MEROPIA	ORGANZA	PIRAGUA
HRYVNYA	LEMMATA	MESHUGA	OROPESA	PIRANHA
HYDROMA	LEMPIRA	MESTIZA	OSMUNDA	PISCINA
HYGROMA	LEUCOMA	METAZOA	OSSETRA	PITUITA
HYMENIA	LEUKOMA	MICELLA	OSTEOMA	PLACITA
HYPOGEA	LEWISIA	MILITIA	OSTRACA	PLANULA
HYPONEA	LINGULA	MINEOLA	OSTRAKA	PLATINA
HYPOXIA	LIPEMIA	MINORCA	OTALGIA	PLECTRA
IGNATIA	LIPURIA	MINUTIA	OUGUIYA	PLEROMA
IKEBANA	LIXIVIA	MITUMBA	OVERSEA	PLUGOLA
ILLUVIA	LOBELIA	MOCHILA	OVIPARA	PLUMULA
IMPERIA	LOCUSTA	MOJARRA	OXYMORA	PODAGRA
IMPRESA	LOGANIA	MOMENTA	PADELLA	PODESTA
INDICIA	LOMENTA	MONARDA	PAENULA	POGONIA
INDUSIA	LORDOMA	MONILIA	PAISANA	POLACCA
INEDITA	MACCHIA	MORPHIA	PALABRA	POLENTA
INERTIA	MACUMBA	MORRHUA	PALINKA	POLYNIA
INFANTA	MADEIRA	MOUSAKA	PALMYRA	POLYNYA
INFAUNA	MADONNA	MOVIOLA	PALOOKA	POLYOMA
INGESTA	MADOQUA	MOZETTA	PANACEA	POLYZOA
INOCULA	MADRASA	MUDIRIA	PANDORA	POTASSA
INTRADA	MADRONA	MULATTA	PANDURA	PRECAVA
IPOMOEA	MAGENTA	MURAENA	PANOCHA	PREPUPA
ISODICA	MAGMATA	MUTANDA	PAPAUMA	PRIMULA
ISODOMA	MAHATMA	MYALGIA	PAPILLA	PRONOTA
JAMBIYA	MAHONIA	MYCELIA	PAPRICA	PROPRIA
JELLABA	MAJAGUA	MYCELLA	PAPRIKA	PROPYLA
JIPYAPA	MALACCA	MYELOMA	PARATHA	PROSOMA
KABBALA	MALACIA	MYOMATA	PARAZOA	PTERYLA
KACHCHA	MALANGA	MYRINGA	PAREIRA	PUDENDA
KACHERA	MALARIA	NANDINA	PARELLA	PUKATEA
KACHINA	MAMILLA	NAPHTHA	PARERGA	PUNALUA

PUPARIA	SABURRA	SOKAIYA	TEMPERA	VERRUCA
PUPUNHA	SACELLA	SOLARIA	TEMPURA	VERRUGA
PURPURA	SADHANA	SOLATIA	TEQUILA	VETTURA
PYAEMIA	SAGITTA	SOREDIA	TEREBRA	VEXILLA
PYGIDIA	SAGRADA	SPATULA	TESSERA	VIATICA
PYREXIA	SAMBUCA	SPECTRA	THANGKA	VICUGNA
PYXIDIA	SAMSARA	SPECULA	THEMATA	VIDENDA
QUASSIA	SANGOMA	SPICULA	THRIMSA	VIHUELA
QUERIDA	SANGRIA	SPINULA	THRYMSA	VINCULA
QUINELA	SANTERA	SPIRAEA	TIKANGA	VIRANDA
QUININA	SAPHENA	SPIRULA	TILAPIA	VIREMIA
RABANNA	SARCINA	SPLENIA	TIMPANA	VISCERA
RADIATA	SARCOMA	SQUILLA	TITANIA	VIVARIA
RAMENTA	SARDANA	SRADDHA	TOCCATA	VIVERRA
RAOULIA	SATSUMA	STAMINA	TOHEROA	VOLUSPA
RASBORA	SAVANNA	STASIMA	TOHUNGA	WAKANDA
RATAFIA	SAXTUBA	STHENIA	TOMBOLA	WALLABA
REFUGIA	SCAGLIA	STOMATA	TOMENTA	WANKSTA
REGALIA	SCANDIA	STRETTA	TORMINA	WEIGELA
REGATTA	SCAPULA	STRIATA	TOSTADA	WHOOPLA
REGMATA	SCHISMA	SUBAQUA	TOXEMIA	WIRILDA
REPLICA	SCHOLIA	SUBAREA	TRACHEA	WOMMERA
RESIDUA	SCOPULA	SUBIDEA	TREHALA	WOODSIA
RETSINA	SCOTOMA	SUBPENA	TRIELLA	WOOMERA
RHIZOMA	SCYBALA	SUBTAXA	TRISULA	WOORARA
RHODORA	SECRETA	SUCCUBA	TRITOMA	WUDJULA
RHYTINA	SEDILIA	SUDARIA	TRYMATA	XERASIA
RICKSHA	SELECTA	SULTANA	TSANTSA	YAMALKA
RICOTTA	SENHORA	SUMATRA	TSARINA	YAMULKA
RIFFOLA	SENOPIA	SYCONIA	TUATARA	YESHIVA
RIKISHA	SEQUELA	SYNOVIA	TUATERA	ZAKUSKA
RIVIERA	SEQUOIA	SYRINGA	TURISTA	ZAMARRA
ROBINIA	SERIEMA	TACHINA	TUTANIA	ZANELLA
ROBUSTA	SERINGA	TAFFETA	TYMPANA	ZAREEBA
ROMAIKA	SERPULA	TAGMATA	TZARINA	ZEBRINA
ROMANZA	SESTINA	TALARIA	ULNARIA	ZEBRULA
ROMNEYA	SEVRUGA	TALOOKA	URAEMIA	ZELKOVA
ROSACEA	SHAHADA	TAMASHA	URETHRA	ZEMSTVA
ROSALIA	SHAMINA	TAMBALA	VACCINA	ZENAIDA
ROSARIA	SHASTRA	TAMBURA	VALONEA	ZIGANKA
ROSELLA	SHEHITA	TAMPALA	VALONIA	ZIMOCCA
ROSEOLA	SHEIKHA	TANAGRA	VALVULA	ZINGARA
ROTUNDA	SHICKSA	TANIWHA	VANESSA	ZIZANIA
RUBELLA	SHORTIA	TANTARA	VANILLA	ZOOECIA
RUBEOLA	SIGNORA	TAPIOCA	VARIOLA	ZOOGLEA
RUELLIA	SILESIA	TARAMEA	VASCULA	ZORILLA
RUFIYAA	SILIQUA	TARTANA	VEDALIA	ZYZZYVA
RUNANGA	SILPHIA	TAUPATA	VELARIA	
RUSALKA	SINOPIA	TAVERNA	VENTANA	
RUSSULA	SITELLA	TEDESCA	VERANDA	
SABELLA	SKIMMIA	TEGMINA	VERBENA	

Eight-letter words

ABDOMINA	ACHILLEA	AGENESIA	ALBIZZIA	AMBERINA
ABRACHIA	ACIDEMIA	AGLOSSIA	ALGAROBA	AMBROSIA
ABSCISSA	ACIDURIA	AGNOMINA	ALIGARTA	AMPHIBIA
ACADEMIA	ADESPOTA	AGRAPHIA	ALLELUIA	AMYGDALA
ACELDAMA	ADULARIA	AGRYPNIA	ALOCASIA	ANABAENA
ACHAENIA	ADYNAMIA	AKINESIA	ALOPECIA	ANACONDA

ANALECTA	BEDSONIA	CAVATINA	CZARITZA	FALDETTA
ANALEMMA	BERGENIA	CECROPIA	DAHABIYA	FANEGADA
ANAPHORA	BERRETTA	CELOMATA	DECENNIA	FANTASIA
ANASARCA	BERYLLIA	CERCARIA	DEMENTIA	FASCIOLA
ANATHEMA	BETHESDA	CHALAZIA	DEMERARA	FASCISTA
ANECDOTA	BIGNONIA	CHAMPACA	DENTALIA	FENESTRA
ANGELICA	BIRRETTA	CHAQUETA	DENTARIA	FETERITA
ANOESTRA	BISCACHA	CHARANGA	DIARRHEA	FIBRILLA
ANOOPSIA	BIZCACHA	CHARISMA	DIASPORA	FISTIANA
ANOREXIA	BLASTEMA	CHATCHKA	DIASTEMA	FLABELLA
ANOXEMIA	BLASTOMA	CHICKPEA	DICENTRA	FLAGELLA
ANTEFIXA	BLASTULA	CHILLADA	DICHASIA	FLOTILLA
ANTHELIA	BOLTONIA	CHIMAERA	DIELYTRA	FOCACCIA
ANTHEMIA	BONSELLA	CHINAMPA	DIPLEGIA	FORAMINA
ANTHODIA	BORRELIA	CHINKARA	DIPLOPIA	FRITTATA
ANTIDORA	BOTANICA	CHIRAGRA	DIPLOZOA	FUGHETTA
ANTISERA	BRACIOLA	CHLOASMA	DJELLABA	FURCRAEA
APIMANIA	BRANCHIA	CHOLEMIA	DRACAENA	GALABIYA
APOLOGIA	BRASSICA	CHURINGA	DULCIANA	GALLABEA
APOSITIA	BREGMATA	CHYLURIA	DULCINEA	GALLABIA
APYREXIA	BRITZSKA	CIABATTA	DYSCHROA	GALLERIA
ARAPAIMA	BROMELIA	CINCHONA	DYSLALIA	GALTONIA
ARAPONGA	BRONCHIA	CISTERNA	DYSLEXIA	GAMBETTA
ARAPUNGA	BROUGHTA	CLAUSTRA	DYSMELIA	GAMBUSIA
ARBORETA	BROUHAHA	CLAUSULA	DYSPNOEA	GAMMADIA
ARETHUSA	BRUCELLA	CLITELLA	DYSTAXIA	GAMMATIA
ARMONICA	BUDDLEIA	COCCIDIA	DYSTOCIA	GARCINIA
ARYTHMIA	BURLETTA	COCINERA	DYSTONIA	GARDENIA
ASPERMIA	CAATINGA	COCOBOLA	DYSTOPIA	GASTRAEA
ASPHYXIA	CABRESTA	COENOBIA	EARTHPEA	GASTRULA
ASPIRATA	CABRETTA	COLCHICA	ECCLESIA	GELSEMIA
ASTHENIA	CABRILLA	COLLEGIA	EFFLUVIA	GEMATRIA
ASTIGMIA	CACHEXIA	COLLUVIA	EGOMANIA	GERARDIA
ASYNDETA	CACHUCHA	COLLYRIA	EMPANADA	GEROPIGA
ATARAXIA	CACUMINA	COLOBOMA	ENCAENIA	GESNERIA
ATHEROMA	CALABAZA	COLUMNEA	ENDAMEBA	GLABELLA
ATROPHIA	CALAMATA	COMATULA	ENDOSTEA	GLADIOLA
AUBRETIA	CALATHEA	CONFERVA	ENGRAMMA	GLAUCOMA
AUBRIETA	CALCANEA	CONSULTA	ENIGMATA	GLIOMATA
AURICULA	CALCARIA	CONTAGIA	ENTAMEBA	GLORIOSA
AUTOMATA	CALCTUFA	CONTESSA	EPENDYMA	GLOSSINA
AUTOPSIA	CALDARIA	CONTINUA	EPHEMERA	GLOXINIA
AVIFAUNA	CALISAYA	CONURBIA	EPICEDIA	GLUMELLA
AXILEMMA	CALVARIA	COPREMIA	EPIFAUNA	GLYCEMIA
AXOLEMMA	CALYPTRA	COPROSMA	EPIMYSIA	GLYCERIA
AYURVEDA	CAMBOGIA	COQUILLA	EPITHECA	GOLCONDA
AZOTEMIA	CAMELLIA	CORMIDIA	EPITHEMA	GOLFIANA
AZOTURIA	CAMPAGNA	COXALGIA	EPOPOEIA	GOLGOTHA
BABIRUSA	CAPITULA	CREDENDA	EQUISETA	GUERILLA
BABUSHKA	CAPOEIRA	CREDENZA	ERYTHEMA	GURDWARA
BACTERIA	CAPONATA	CRIBELLA	ESTANCIA	GYMKHANA
BAIDARKA	CAPYBARA	CRITERIA	ESTHESIA	GYMNASIA
BALLISTA	CARACARA	CROMORNA	ETCETERA	GYNAECEA
BANDANNA	CARAGANA	CTENIDIA	EUPEPSIA	GYNAECIA
BAPTISIA	CARNAUBA	CUBICULA	EUPHOBIA	GYNOECIA
BARATHEA	CARPALIA	CUNABULA	EUPHONIA	HABANERA
BARRANCA	CASTELLA	CUTICULA	EUPHORIA	HACIENDA
BASILICA	CATHEDRA	CYMBIDIA	EUTHYMIA	HAMARTIA
BATTALIA	CATHISMA	CZAREVNA	EXCERPTA	HAPHTARA
BAUHINIA	CATTLEYA	CZARITSA	EXONUMIA	HAPLOPIA

HATTERIA	LEKGOTLA	MOUSSAKA	PHYSALIA	SANTERIA
HEARTPEA	LEUCEMIA	MOVIEOLA	PIASSABA	SAPREMIA
HEKETARA	LEUKEMIA	MOZZETTA	PIASSAVA	SAPUCAIA
HEMATOMA	LEVODOPA	MRIDANGA	PIGNOLIA	SARMENTA
HEMIOLIA	LINGUICA	MYCETOMA	PITAHAYA	SASARARA
HEMIOPIA	LINGUISA	MYOTONIA	PIZZERIA	SASTRUGA
HEPATICA	LIPAEMIA	MYXAMEBA	PLACENTA	SAYONARA
HEPATOMA	LIPOMATA	MYXEDEMA	PLANARIA	SCABIOSA
HERBARIA	LISTERIA	MYXOMATA	PLANURIA	SCHAPSKA
HETAIRIA	LITHEMIA	NASSELLA	PLATANNA	SCHEMATA
HEUCHERA	LODICULA	NAVICULA	PLATYSMA	SCIATICA
HINAHINA	LONICERA	NOCTURIA	PLETHORA	SCLEREMA
HIRAGANA	LYMPHOMA	NONQUOTA	PLUMERIA	SCLEROMA
HORDEOLA	MACAHUBA	NUBECULA	POLLINIA	SCOLIOMA
HOROKAKA	MADRASSA	NYMPHAEA	POLYGALA	SCOTOMIA
HOSPITIA	MAGNESIA	OCCIPITA	POLYPNEA	SCOTOPIA
HYDREMIA	MAGNOLIA	ODONTOMA	POLYURIA	SCROFULA
HYDRILLA	MAHARAJA	OEDEMATA	POSTCAVA	SCUTELLA
HYDROZOA	MAIOLICA	OITICICA	PREDELLA	SEMANTRA
HYPALGIA	MAJOLICA	OLIGEMIA	PRESCUTA	SEMICOMA
HYPHEMIA	MALAROMA	OLIGURIA	PRESIDIA	SEMIGALA
HYPOGAEA	MALVASIA	OMBRELLA	PRIMITIA	SEMINOMA
HYPONOIA	MAMALIGA	OMNIVORA	PROFORMA	SEMOLINA
HYPOPNEA	MAMMILLA	ONGAONGA	PROGERIA	SEMUNCIA
HYSTERIA	MANDIOCA	OPERCULA	PROTOZOA	SENORITA
ICEKHANA	MANDORLA	OPERETTA	PRUNELLA	SENSILLA
IMPLUVIA	MANTILLA	OPUSCULA	PRYTANEA	SENSORIA
INSIGNIA	MANTISSA	ORCHELLA	PSORALEA	SEPARATA
INSOMNIA	MANUBRIA	ORCHILLA	PTERYGIA	SEPTARIA
INTARSIA	MANYATTA	PAHAUTEA	PUERPERA	SEPTLEVA
INTIFADA	MARCELLA	PALESTRA	PUTAMINA	SERENATA
ISABELLA	MARCHESA	PALLADIA	PYCNIDIA	SHAMIANA
ISCHEMIA	MARINARA	PALPEBRA	PYODERMA	SHECHITA
ISCHURIA	MARINERA	PANATELA	PYORRHEA	SHIGELLA
IZVESTIA	MARIPOSA	PANCETTA	QINDARKA	SHILLALA
JAPONICA	MARSUPIA	PANDEMIA	QUADRIGA	SHRADDHA
JARARACA	MARTYRIA	PANETELA	QUILLAIA	SIDALCEA
JARARAKA	MASSOOLA	PANMIXIA	QUILLAJA	SIGNORIA
JAVELINA	MATADORA	PANORAMA	QUINELLA	SILICULA
JIPIJAPA	MATAMATA	PARABEMA	QUINIELA	SIMARUBA
KALAMATA	MAUSOLEA	PARABOLA	RACHILLA	SINFONIA
KALYPTRA	MAZAEDIA	PARANOEA	RADIALIA	SITTELLA
KAMAAINA	MAZOURKA	PARANOIA	RAKSHASA	SONATINA
KARATEKA	MBAQANGA	PARAPARA	RAMTILLA	SORBARIA
KAREAREA	MECHITZA	PARHELIA	RANGIORA	SPARTINA
KATAKANA	MELANOMA	PAROEMIA	RAPHANIA	SPIRILLA
KATCHINA	MELODICA	PAROSMIA	REDDENDA	SPORIDIA
KAUMATUA	MENSTRUA	PAROUSIA	RENDZINA	SPOROZOA
KAVAKAVA	MESHUGGA	PASHMINA	REPTILIA	SQUAMULA
KAWAKAWA	MESOGLEA	PELLAGRA	RESINATA	STAPELIA
KAZATZKA	METANOIA	PENUMBRA	RESPONSA	STAROSTA
KERATOMA	METASOMA	PEPONIDA	RETICULA	STEATOMA
KHANSAMA	MIASMATA	PERFECTA	RETINULA	STEMMATA
KIELBASA	MILIARIA	PERIAGUA	REWAREWA	STERIGMA
KINAKINA	MILTONIA	PETECHIA	RHIZOBIA	STICHERA
KRAMERIA	MINNEOLA	PHACELIA	ROSTELLA	STIGMATA
LABRUSCA	MOKOPUNA	PHELONIA	RUTABAGA	STOCCATA
LAVALAVA	MOLLUSCA	PHOTINIA	SACRARIA	STOKESIA
LAVATERA	MONSTERA	PHOTOPIA	SALICETA	STOMODEA
LECANORA	MONTARIA	PHRYGANA	SALSILLA	STOTINKA

STROBILA	TAMANDUA	TOXOCARA	URINEMIA	VUVUZELA
STROMATA	TAMBOURA	TRACHOMA	UROPYGIA	WAHCONDA
STRONTIA	TAPADERA	TRAPEZIA	VACCINIA	WEIGELIA
SUBCOSTA	TAQUERIA	TRAUMATA	VAGINULA	WISTARIA
SUBMENTA	TEGMENTA	TRICHINA	VALENCIA	WISTERIA
SUBPHYLA	TEGUMINA	TRIDACNA	VALLONIA	XANTHOMA
SUBPOENA	TENACULA	TRIENNIA	VELAMINA	XENOPHYA
SUBTOPIA	TENTORIA	TRIFECTA	VELATURA	XEROMATA
SUBUCULA	TEQUILLA	TRIFORIA	VENDETTA	XYLOMATA
SUBURBIA	TERATOMA	TRIHEDRA	VERATRIA	YARMULKA
SUDAMINA	TERRARIA	TRILEMMA	VERONICA	YERSINIA
SVASTIKA	TERRELLA	TRIPTYCA	VERTEBRA	YOKOZUNA
SWASTICA	TERZETTA	TRIPUDIA	VESICULA	YTTERBIA
SWASTIKA	TESSELLA	TRISTEZA	VESTIGIA	ZAKOUSKA
SWEETPEA	TETRAPLA	TRITONIA	VIBRISSA	ZAMBOMBA
SYMPODIA	THERIACA	TROCHLEA	VICTORIA	ZAMPOGNA
SYMPOSIA	THIOTEPA	TROPARIA	VIEWDATA	ZARZUELA
SYNANGIA	THIOUREA	TSAREVNA	VINIFERA	ZASTRUGA
SYNAPHEA	TIGRIDIA	TSARITSA	VIRAEMIA	ZIRCONIA
SYNCYTIA	TITHONIA	TSARITZA	VIRGINIA	ZOIATRIA
SYNECHIA	TOKONOMA	TZAREVNA	VIRTUOSA	ZOOCYTIA
SYNEDRIA	TOPALGIA	TZARITZA	VISCACHA	ZOOGLOEA
SYNERGIA	TOQUILLA	ULTIMATA	VISCARIA	ZOOMANIA
SYNKARYA	TORMENTA	UMBRELLA	VITICETA	ZOONOMIA
SYNTAGMA	TORTILLA	UNDERSEA	VIVIPARA	ZUCHETTA
SYSSITIA	TOURISTA	UNGUENTA	VIZCACHA	ZYGANTRA
TAKAMAKA	TOXAEMIA	UREDINIA	VULSELLA	ZYGOMATA

Words that end with -I

Two-letter words

AI	shaggy-coated slow-moving animal of South America
BI	bisexual
DI	gods
GI	loose-fitting white suit worn in judo, karate, and other martial arts
HI	hello
KI	Japanese martial art
LI	Chinese measurement of distance
MI	(in tonic sol-fa) third degree of any major scale
OI	shout to attract attention
PI	sixteenth letter in the Greek alphabet
QI	vital energy believed to circulate round the body in currents
SI	(in tonic sol-fa) seventh degree of any major scale
TI	(in tonic sol-fa) seventh degree of any major scale
XI	14th letter in the Greek alphabet

Three-letter words

AHI	yellowfin tuna
AMI	male friend
ANI	any of several gregarious tropical American birds of the genus Crotophaga: family Cuculidae (cuckoos). They have a black plumage, long square-tipped tail, and heavily hooked bill
BOI	lesbian who dresses like a boy
CHI	22nd letter of the Greek alphabet, a consonant, transliterated as ch or rarely kh

DEI	god
DUI	duos
GHI	(in Indian cookery) clarified butter
HOI	cry used to attract someone's attention
HUI	meeting of Maori people
IWI	Maori tribe
JAI	victory (to)
KAI	food
KHI	letter of the Greek alphabet
KOI	any of various ornamental forms of the common carp
LEI	standard monetary unit of Romania and Moldova, divided into 100 bani
MOI	me
OBI	broad sash tied in a large flat bow at the back, worn by Japanese women and children
PHI	21st letter in the Greek alphabet
POI	ball of woven flax swung rhythmically by Maori women during poi dances
PSI	23rd letter of the Greek alphabet
RAI	type of Algerian popular music based on traditional Algerian music influenced by modern Western pop
REI	name for a former Portuguese coin, more properly called a real
SAI	South American monkey
SEI	type of rorqual
SKI	one of a pair of long runners fastened to boots for gliding over snow or water
SRI	title of respect used when addressing a Hindu
SUI	of itself
TAI	as in tai chi chuan Chinese system of callisthenics characterized by coordinated and rhythmic movements
TUI	New Zealand honeyeater that mimics human speech and the songs of other birds
UNI	(in informal English) university
WAI	in New Zealand, water

Four-letter words

ABRI	DUCI	KADI	MAXI	PENI
ACAI	ELHI	KAKI	MERI	PERI
ANTI	ETUI	KALI	MIDI	PFUI
ARTI	EUOI	KAMI	MIHI	PIKI
ASCI	FENI	KATI	MINI	PILI
BANI	FIFI	KAZI	MIRI	PIPI
BENI	FINI	KEPI	MOAI	PTUI
BIDI	FOCI	KIWI	MODI	PULI
BREI	FUCI	KOJI	MOKI	PURI
BUDI	FUJI	KUFI	MOMI	QADI
CADI	GADI	KURI	MOOI	QUAI
CAPI	GARI	KUTI	MOTI	RABI
CEDI	GLEI	LARI	MUNI	RAGI
CHAI	GORI	LATI	MUTI	RAKI
CONI	GYRI	LIRI	NAOI	RAMI
DALI	HAJI	LOBI	NAZI	RANI
DARI	HILI	LOCI	NEVI	ROJI
DEFI	HIOI	LOTI	NIDI	ROTI
DELI	HOKI	LWEI	NISI	SADI
DENI	HORI	MAGI	NODI	SAKI
DESI	IMPI	MAKI	NONI	SARI
DIVI	INTI	MALI	NORI	SATI
DIXI	JEDI	MANI	PADI	SEMI

SHRI	TABI	TITI	VALI	YETI
SIMI	TAKI	TOPI	VLEI	YOGI
SIRI	TALI	TORI	WADI	YONI
SOLI	TAXI	UNAI	WALI	ZATI
SORI	TIKI	UNCI	WILI	ZITI
SYLI	TIPI	VAGI	YAGI	ZORI

Five-letter words

AALII	CHOLI	HOURI	NGATI	SENTI
AARTI	CIPPI	IAMBI	NIMBI	SERAI
ABACI	CIRRI	IMARI	NISEI	SHCHI
ACARI	CLAVI	IMSHI	NKOSI	SHIAI
ACINI	COATI	INDRI	NOMOI	SHOGI
ADUKI	COCCI	ISSEI	OBELI	SHOJI
AGAMI	COMBI	JINNI	OBOLI	SOLDI
AGGRI	CORGI	KANJI	OCULI	SOLEI
AGUTI	CORNI	KARRI	OKAPI	SPAHI
AIDOI	CROCI	KATTI	ORIBI	STOAI
AIOLI	CULTI	KAURI	OVOLI	STYLI
ALIBI	CUNEI	KHADI	OZEKI	SUCCI
AMICI	CURLI	KHAKI	PADRI	SULCI
ANIMI	CURSI	KHAZI	PAGRI	SUSHI
APPUI	DARZI	KIBBI	PALKI	SWAMI
ARDRI	DASHI	KIBEI	PALPI	TAKHI
ARIKI	DESHI	KIKOI	PAOLI	TANGI
ASKOI	DHOBI	KIRRI	PAPPI	TANTI
ASSAI	DHOTI	KOORI	PARDI	TARSI
ATIGI	DHUTI	KORAI	PARKI	TAWAI
AULOI	DILLI	KRUBI	PARTI	TELOI
AUREI	DISCI	KUKRI	PENNI	TEMPI
AZUKI	DOLCI	KULFI	PERAI	TERAI
BAJRI	DUOMI	LAARI	PETTI	TETRI
BALTI	DURZI	LANAI	PILEI	THAGI
BAMBI	ELCHI	LASSI	PIRAI	THALI
BASSI	ELEMI	LATHI	POORI	THOLI
BASTI	ENNUI	LAZZI	PRIMI	THYMI
BEEDI	ENOKI	LENTI	PSOAI	TONDI
BENNI	ENVOI	LIBRI	PULLI	TOPHI
BESTI	FARCI	LICHI	PUNJI	TOPOI
BHAJI	FASCI	LIMBI	PUTTI	TORII
BIALI	FASTI	LITAI	QUASI	TORSI
BINDI	FERMI	LOGOI	RABBI	TRAGI
BLINI	FILMI	LUNGI	RADII	TSADI
BOCCI	FRATI	LURGI	RAHUI	TUTTI
BRAAI	FUNDI	MACHI	RANGI	UGALI
BRAVI	FUNGI	MANDI	RECTI	UMAMI
BUFFI	GADDI	MAQUI	REIKI	URAEI
BUSTI	GARNI	MARRI	RISHI	URALI
BWAZI	GENII	MATAI	ROSHI	URARI
BYSSI	GHAZI	MAURI	ROSTI	UTERI
CACTI	GIBLI	MEDII	RUBAI	VILLI
CAMPI	GLOBI	MODII	SAKAI	VOLTI
CARDI	GOBBI	MOOLI	SALMI	WONGI
CARPI	GUSLI	MUFTI	SAMPI	XYSTI
CEILI	HADJI	MURRI	SATAI	ZIMBI
CELLI	HAJJI	MURTI	SCAPI	ZOMBI
CERCI	HANGI	MYTHI	SCUDI	
CESTI	HIKOI	NAEVI	SEGNI	
CHILI	HONGI	NASHI	SENGI	

Six-letter words

ACULEI	CYATHI	KAIKAI	OUREBI	SILENI
ADSUKI	CYTISI	KAMAHI	PAKAHI	SIMPAI
ADZUKI	DALASI	KIMCHI	PAKIHI	SMALTI
AGAPAI	DECANI	KOKIRI	PALAGI	SMRITI
AGOUTI	DEGAMI	KONAKI	PANINI	SOLIDI
ALFAKI	DENARI	KONINI	PAPYRI	SOMONI
ALKALI	DEWANI	KORARI	PATIKI	SONERI
ALUMNI	DHOOTI	KOUROI	PERITI	SOUARI
AMBARI	DJINNI	KOWHAI	PETSAI	STELAI
ANNULI	DROMOI	KROONI	PHALLI	STRATI
ARCHEI	DUELLI	KULAKI	PILOTI	SUNDRI
ARGALI	DUETTI	KUMARI	PIROGI	SURIMI
ARGULI	ECHINI	LAOGAI	PITHOI	TABULI
ARILLI	ELTCHI	LAZULI	PITURI	TAHINI
ARIOSI	EMBOLI	LIMULI	PLUTEI	TAMARI
ASKARI	EPHEBI	LITCHI	POHIRI	TANUKI
AVANTI	EPHORI	LOBULI	POLYPI	TAPETI
BAILLI	EQUALI	LOCULI	PRIAPI	TATAMI
BANZAI	EURIPI	LUNGYI	PROTEI	TATSOI
BHAKTI	EXODOI	MALLEI	PURIRI	TAUIWI
BHINDI	FAMULI	MALOTI	PUTELI	TAWHAI
BHISTI	FLOCCI	MANATI	PYLORI	TENUTI
BIKINI	FRACTI	MARABI	RAGINI	THALLI
BINDHI	FUMULI	MARARI	RAMULI	THOLOI
BINGHI	GARDAI	MAULVI	RAPINI	THYRSI
BOLETI	GELATI	MAZHBI	REGULI	TIFOSI
BONACI	GEMINI	MEHNDI	RENVOI	TIRITI
BONSAI	GHARRI	MEISHI	RHOMBI	TITOKI
BOOHAI	GHIBLI	MILADI	ROMAJI	TITULI
BORZOI	GILGAI	MIRCHI	RUBATI	TOITOI
BUIBUI	GLUTEI	MIRITI	RUMAKI	TORULI
BUKSHI	GOMUTI	MISHMI	SACCOI	TROCHI
BURITI	GRIGRI	MODULI	SAFARI	TROPHI
BUZUKI	GUANXI	MOIRAI	SAIKEI	TSOTSI
CADAGI	GURAMI	MOKIHI	SAKKOI	TUFOLI
CALAMI	HAIKAI	MOOLVI	SALAMI	TULADI
CANTHI	HAKARI	MOPANI	SALUKI	TUMULI
CAROLI	HAMULI	MUESLI	SAMITI	UAKARI
CASINI	HEGARI	MUNSHI	SANCAI	UMFAZI
CENTAI	HEISHI	MYTHOI	SANDHI	UNCINI
CESTOI	HERMAI	NAGARI	SANSEI	URACHI
CESTUI	HUMERI	NEINEI	SATORI	WAKIKI
CHADRI	ILLUPI	NEROLI	SBIRRI	WAPITI
CHATTI	INCAVI	NIELLI	SCAMPI	WARAGI
CHICHI	INCUBI	NIGIRI	SCYPHI	WASABI
CHILLI	ISTHMI	NILGAI	SENITI	XYSTOI
CHOKRI	JAWARI	NOSTOI	SENSEI	YANQUI
CHOWRI	JEHADI	NUCLEI	SESELI	YIDAKI
CLYPEI	JIHADI	OCELLI	SHALLI	YOGINI
COLOBI	JOWARI	OCTOPI	SHANTI	ZAIKAI
COLONI	JUDOGI	OCTROI	SHTCHI	ZUFOLI
CONGII	JUNGLI	ONAGRI	SHUFTI	
CUBITI	JUPATI	OORALI	SIDDHI	
CUMULI	KABIKI	OURALI	SIFREI	
CURARI	KABUKI	OURARI	SIGLOI	

Seven-letter words

ABOMASI	CHOREGI	INTAGLI	PALAZZI	SERKALI
ACANTHI	CHUPATI	JACUZZI	PANDANI	SERRATI
ACOUCHI	CLARINI	JAMDANI	PARODOI	SHIKARI
AFGHANI	COENURI	JAMPANI	PECCAVI	SHIVITI
ALFAQUI	COLIBRI	JINJILI	PENTITI	SIGNORI
ALIZARI	COLOSSI	JUKSKEI	PENUCHI	SKYPHOI
ALVEOLI	CORTILI	KABADDI	PIEROGI	SONDELI
AMORINI	CREMINI	KACHERI	PIGNOLI	SOPRANI
ANESTRI	CRIMINI	KAHAWAI	PINDARI	SORDINI
ANZIANI	DACTYLI	KAMICHI	PIROGHI	SPINONI
APICULI	DAKOITI	KAROSHI	PIROJKI	SPLENII
APPALTI	DAQUIRI	KOKOWAI	PLATYPI	SPUMONI
ARCHAEI	DASHEKI	KOLBASI	POLYNYI	STAMNOI
ASSAGAI	DASHIKI	KONGONI	PORANGI	STICHOI
ASSEGAI	DEMENTI	KOROWAI	PORCINI	STIMULI
ASTATKI	DENARII	LAMPUKI	POWHIRI	STRETTI
BACCHII	DIDAKAI	LAPILLI	PRELUDI	SUCCUBI
BACILLI	DIDAKEI	LECYTHI	PRONAOI	SUFFARI
BAMBINI	DIDICOI	LEKYTHI	PULVINI	SUNDARI
BANDARI	DOCHMII	MACRAMI	QAWWALI	SURCULI
BANOFFI	EFFENDI	MAESTRI	QUILLAI	SYLLABI
BASENJI	ELENCHI	MAFIOSI	RABBONI	TABOULI
BASMATI	EMERITI	MAMMATI	RANGOLI	TANKINI
BAZOUKI	EPHEBOI	MARCONI	RAPPINI	TAWHIRI
BHISHTI	EPIGONI	MARTINI	RAURIKI	TERMINI
BILIMBI	EPINAOI	MATSURI	RAVIOLI	THALAMI
BIRIANI	EREMURI	MELTEMI	REMBLAI	THROMBI
BIRYANI	ETOURDI	MENISCI	REREMAI	TIMPANI
BOUILLI	FAGOTTI	MERANTI	REVERSI	TOFUTTI
BREWSKI	FIASCHI	MINISKI	RHIZOPI	TOLARJI
BROCOLI	FLOKATI	MODELLI	RHOMBOI	TONDINI
BRONCHI	FORZATI	MODIOLI	RHONCHI	TORTONI
BUSUUTI	FUMETTI	MOLOSSI	RHYTHMI	TRIPOLI
CADUCEI	FUSILLI	MONOSKI	RIKISHI	TSUNAMI
CALATHI	GHILGAI	NAUPLII	RILIEVI	TURFSKI
CALCULI	GINGELI	NAUTILI	RIPIENI	TYMPANI
CALZONI	GINGILI	NEGRONI	SACCULI	URCEOLI
CAMOODI	GLUTAEI	NILGHAI	SAIMIRI	VENTURI
CANNOLI	GNOCCHI	NONETTI	SAMADHI	VIRELAI
CANZONI	GOURAMI	NUCELLI	SAMITHI	VITELLI
CAVETTI	GRADINI	NURAGHI	SAMURAI	VOLVULI
CEMBALI	GUARANI	NYLGHAI	SANTIMI	WISTITI
CHAPATI	HALLALI	OBLASTI	SANYASI	WOORALI
CHARPAI	HALOUMI	OMPHALI	SAOUARI	WOORARI
CHARQUI	HARAMDI	ORIGAMI	SARANGI	WOURALI
CHIANTI	HAVARTI	OUAKARI	SASHIMI	ZAKUSKI
CHIASMI	HEITIKI	OUSTITI	SCALENI	ZAMPONI
CHILIOI	HELLERI	PACHISI	SCHERZI	ZEPPOLI
CHIVARI	HEXEREI	PADRONI	SCIRRHI	ZINGANI
CHONDRI	HIBACHI	PAESANI	SECONDI	ZINGARI
CHORAGI	HOKONUI	PAHLAVI	SENARII	ZUFFOLI

Eight-letter words

ACERVULI	AMARETTI	ANOESTRI	BANDITTI	BIRIYANI
ACOEMETI	AMORETTI	ANTENATI	BERIBERI	BISCOTTI
ALBERGHI	AMPHIOXI	ASSEGAAI	BIMBASHI	BONAMANI

BORLOTTI	DAISHIKI	KIRIGAMI	PACHOULI	SIGNIORI
BOSTANGI	DECUBITI	KOFTGARI	PARCHESI	SOFFIONI
BOUSOUKI	DIADOCHI	KOHLRABI	PARCHISI	SOLFEGGI
BOUZOUKI	DIGERATI	KOLBASSI	PASTICCI	SOUVLAKI
BOZZETTI	DIPTEROI	KOLINSKI	PASTRAMI	STACCATI
BRAHMANI	DIVIDIVI	KOMITAJI	PASTROMI	STAPEDII
BRINDISI	DOUPIONI	KUMBALOI	PATUTUKI	STOTINKI
BROCCOLI	DRACHMAI	KUMIKUMI	PECORINI	STROBILI
BUMALOTI	DUPONDII	LEKYTHOI	PEDICULI	SUKIYAKI
BUZKASHI	DURUKULI	LEMNISCI	PEPERONI	SUMOTORI
CALAMARI	DUUMVIRI	LEYLANDI	PERFECTI	TABBOULI
CALCANEI	ESOPHAGI	LIBRETTI	PERRADII	TAGLIONI
CALYCULI	FASCISMI	LINGUINI	PIHOIHOI	TANDOORI
CANCELLI	FASCISTI	LITERATI	PIROSHKI	TARAKIHI
CANTHARI	FEDELINI	LUMBRICI	PIROZHKI	TEDESCHI
CAPITANI	FEMINAZI	MACARONI	POPLITEI	TEOCALLI
CAPRICCI	FLOCCULI	MAHARANI	POSTNATI	TERAKIHI
CASTRATI	FORZANDI	MAHIMAHI	PRINCIPI	TERIYAKI
CHAPATTI	FRASCATI	MALIHINI	PRODROMI	TERZETTI
CHAPPATI	FUNICULI	MALLEOLI	PULVILLI	THESAURI
CHIGETAI	GINGELLI	MANUHIRI	RASMALAI	TRAPEZII
CHUPATTI	GINGILLI	MARAVEDI	RENMINBI	TROCHILI
CICERONI	GINGLYMI	MARCHESI	RETIARII	TZATZIKI
CICISBEI	GLADIOLI	MARIACHI	RIGATONI	UMBILICI
CLAFOUTI	GRAFFITI	MENOMINI	RISPETTI	URANISCI
CONCEPTI	GRISSINI	MONOKINI	RYOTWARI	UTRICULI
CONCERTI	HAEREMAI	MORBILLI	SANNYASI	VIRTUOSI
CONCETTI	HALLOUMI	NANNYGAI	SARTORII	WATERSKI
CONDUCTI	HETAIRAI	NARCISSI	SASTRUGI	WHARENUI
CONFETTI	HYDROSKI	NENNIGAI	SCALDINI	YAKITORI
CORNETTI	IGNORAMI	NIRAMIAI	SEXTARII	ZAKOUSKI
COTHURNI	KACHAHRI	NOTTURNI	SFORZATI	ZASTRUGI
CROSTINI	KAKARIKI	NUCLEOLI	SHANGHAI	ZECCHINI
CUMBUNGI	KAZACHKI	OBLIGATI	SHERWANI	ZOOPHORI
CUNJEVOI	KAZATSKI	OSTINATI	SHILINGI	ZUCCHINI
DAIQUIRI	KIELBASI	OUISTITI	SIGISBEI	

Words that end with -O

Two-letter words

BO	exclamation uttered to startle or surprise someone, esp a child in a game
DO	perform or complete (a deed or action)
GO	move to or from a place
HO	derogatory term for a woman
IO	type of moth
JO	Scots word for sweetheart
KO	(in New Zealand) traditional digging tool
LO	look!
MO	moment
NO	expresses denial, disagreement, or refusal
OO	Scots word for wool
PO	chamber pot
SO	such an extent
TO	indicating movement towards, equality or comparison, etc
WO	archaic spelling of woe

| YO | expression used as a greeting or to attract someone's attention |
| ZO | Tibetan breed of cattle, developed by crossing the yak with common cattle |

Three-letter words

ABO	offensive name for aborigine
ADO	fuss, trouble
AGO	in the past
APO	type of protein
AVO	Macao currency unit
AZO	of, consisting of, or containing the divalent group -N-
BIO	biography
BOO	shout of disapproval
BRO	family member
COO	(of a dove or pigeon) make a soft murmuring sound
DOO	Scots word for dove
DSO	Tibetan breed of cattle, developed by crossing the yak with common cattle
DUO	duet
DZO	Tibetan breed of cattle, developed by crossing the yak with common cattle
ECO	ecology activist
EGO	conscious mind of an individual
EMO	type of music combining hard rock with emotional lyrics
EVO	evening
EXO	excellent
FRO	away
GEO	(esp in Shetland) a small fjord or gully
GIO	(esp in Shetland) a small fjord or gully
GOO	sticky substance
HAO	monetary unit of Vietnam, worth one tenth of a dong
HOO	she
ISO	short segment of film that can be replayed easily
LOO	informal word meaning lavatory
MHO	former name for the SI unit of electrical conductance
MOO	long deep cry of a cow
NOO	type of Japanese musical drama
OBO	ship carrying oil and ore
OHO	exclamation expressing surprise, exultation, or derision
ONO	Hawaiian fish
OXO	as in 'oxo acid' acid that contains oxygen
PHO	Vietnamese noodle soup
POO	defecate
PRO	in favour of
REO	language
RHO	17th letter in the Greek alphabet, a consonant transliterated as r or rh
ROO	kangaroo
TAO	(in Confucian philosophy) the correct course of action
THO	though
TOO	also, as well
TWO	one more than one
UDO	stout perennial plant of Japan and China with berry-like black fruits and young shoots that are edible when blanched
UFO	flying saucer
UPO	upon
WHO	which person
WOO	seek the love or affection of (a woman)

YGO	archaic past participle of go
ZHO	Tibetan breed of cattle, developed by crossing the yak with common cattle
ZOO	place where live animals are kept for show

Four-letter words

AERO	DERO	JOCO	MOJO	SKIO
AFRO	DIDO	JOMO	MOKO	SOHO
AGIO	DINO	JUCO	MONO	SOLO
ALCO	DOCO	JUDO	MOZO	SUMO
ALKO	DODO	KAGO	MUSO	SYBO
ALSO	DOJO	KARO	MYXO	TACO
ALTO	DURO	KAYO	NOLO	TARO
AMBO	DZHO	KENO	ODSO	THIO
AMMO	ECCO	KERO	OLEO	THRO
ANNO	ECHO	KETO	OLIO	TIRO
APSO	EDDO	KILO	ONTO	TOCO
ARCO	ERGO	KINO	OPPO	TOHO
ARVO	EURO	KOBO	ORDO	TOKO
AUTO	EXPO	KOLO	ORZO	TOMO
BEGO	FADO	KORO	OTTO	TOPO
BIRO	FANO	KOTO	OUZO	TORO
BITO	FARO	KUDO	PACO	TOYO
BOHO	FICO	KYBO	PEPO	TRIO
BOKO	FIDO	LAZO	PESO	TYPO
BOLO	FIGO	LENO	PISO	TYRO
BOYO	FILO	LEVO	POCO	UMBO
BOZO	FINO	LIDO	POGO	UNCO
BRIO	GAJO	LILO	POLO	UNDO
BROO	GAPO	LIMO	POMO	UNTO
BUBO	GIRO	LINO	PRAO	UPDO
BUDO	GOBO	LIPO	PROO	UPGO
BUFO	GOGO	LOBO	PYRO	URAO
CALO	GYRO	LOCO	RATO	VEGO
CAMO	HALO	LOGO	REDO	VETO
CAPO	HARO	LOTO	REGO	VINO
CERO	HELO	LUDO	REPO	VIVO
CHAO	HERO	MAKO	RIVO	WERO
CIAO	HOBO	MANO	ROTO	WHIO
CITO	HOMO	MAYO	SADO	WINO
COCO	HUSO	MEMO	SAGO	YEBO
COHO	HYPO	MENO	SECO	YUKO
DADO	INFO	MICO	SEGO	ZERO
DAGO	INGO	MILO	SHMO	ZOBO
DATO	INRO	MINO	SHOO	
DECO	INTO	MIRO	SIJO	
DELO	JATO	MISO	SILO	
DEMO	JIAO	MOFO	SKEO	

Five-letter words

ABMHO	ALTHO	ANGLO	AZIDO	BARRO
ACHOO	AMIDO	APPRO	BABOO	BASHO
ADDIO	AMIGO	ASPRO	BACCO	BASSO
ADOBO	AMINO	AUDIO	BALOO	BASTO
AGGRO	AMNIO	AVISO	BANCO	BAZOO
AGLOO	ANCHO	AWATO	BANJO	BEANO
ALAMO	ANDRO	AWETO	BARDO	BENTO

BERKO	DANIO	HALLO	MIMEO	RATIO
BIFFO	DATTO	HELIO	MISDO	RATOO
BILBO	DECKO	HELLO	MISGO	RAUPO
BIMBO	DEFFO	HILLO	MOLTO	RAZOO
BINGO	DEKKO	HIMBO	MONDO	REALO
BIZZO	DERRO	HIPPO	MONGO	RECCO
BOFFO	DIAZO	HOLLO	MORRO	RECTO
BOMBO	DILDO	HOWSO	MOSSO	REFFO
BONGO	DINGO	HULLO	MOTTO	REGGO
BORGO	DIPSO	HYDRO	MUCHO	REPRO
BRAVO	DISCO	IGAPO	MUCRO	RESTO
BROMO	DITTO	IGLOO	MUNGO	RETRO
BUCKO	DOBRO	IMAGO	NACHO	RHINO
BUFFO	DOGGO	IMIDO	NAPOO	RODEO
BUMBO	DOHYO	IMINO	NARCO	ROMEO
BUNCO	DONKO	INTRO	NEGRO	RONDO
BUNKO	DRACO	IROKO	NGAIO	RONEO
BUROO	DSOBO	JAMBO	NITRO	RUMBO
BURRO	DSOMO	JELLO	NUTSO	RUMPO
BUTEO	DUBBO	JINGO	ORTHO	SADDO
CACAO	DUMBO	JOCKO	OUTDO	SALTO
CAMEO	DUNNO	JUMBO	OUTGO	SALVO
CAMPO	DUOMO	JUNCO	OUTRO	SAMBO
CANSO	ERUGO	JUNTO	OVOLO	SANGO
CANTO	ESTRO	KAROO	PANTO	SANKO
CARBO	FANGO	KAZOO	PAOLO	SANTO
CARGO	FATSO	KEENO	PAREO	SARGO
CASCO	FIBRO	KEMBO	PARGO	SCHMO
CELLO	FILLO	KENDO	PARVO	SCUDO
CENTO	FLEXO	KIDDO	PASEO	SECCO
CHACO	FOLIO	KIMBO	PATIO	SEGNO
CHADO	FORDO	KONDO	PEDRO	SERVO
CHEMO	FORGO	KUSSO	PENGO	SEXTO
CHIAO	FUERO	LAEVO	PESTO	SHAKO
CHICO	FUGIO	LARGO	PETTO	SHISO
CHIMO	FUNGO	LASSO	PHONO	SICKO
CHINO	GADJO	LAZZO	PHOTO	SIXMO
CHIRO	GADSO	LENTO	PIANO	SKIMO
CHOCO	GALVO	LESBO	PIEZO	SMOKO
CHOKO	GAMBO	LEUCO	PILAO	SOCKO
CHOLO	GARBO	LIMBO	PINGO	SOLDO
CISCO	GAZOO	LINGO	PINKO	SORBO
CLARO	GECKO	LITHO	PINTO	SORDO
COCCO	GENRO	LLANO	PISCO	SORGO
COMBO	GESSO	LOTTO	POLIO	SPADO
COMMO	GINZO	MACHO	PONGO	STENO
COMPO	GIPPO	MACRO	PORNO	STYLO
CONDO	GISMO	MAIKO	POSHO	SULFO
CONGO	GIZMO	MAMBO	POTOO	TABOO
CONTO	GOBBO	MANGO	POTTO	TACHO
CONVO	GODSO	MANTO	PRIMO	TANGO
CORNO	GOMBO	MATLO	PROMO	TANTO
CORSO	GONZO	MATZO	PROSO	TARDO
CREDO	GREGO	MENTO	PULAO	TELCO
CUFFO	GUACO	MESTO	PULMO	TEMPO
CURIO	GUANO	METHO	PUNTO	TENNO
CUSSO	GUIRO	METRO	PUTTO	THORO
CUTTO	GUMBO	MEZZO	QUINO	TIMBO
CYANO	GUSTO	MICRO	QUIPO	TONDO
CYCLO	GYPPO	MILKO	RADIO	TORSO

TRIGO	VIDEO	WALDO	YARCO	ZHOMO
TRUGO	VIREO	WAZOO	YARTO	ZINCO
TURBO	VISTO	WHAMO	YOBBO	ZIPPO
TYPTO	VULGO	WHOSO	YUCKO	ZOCCO
UREDO	WACKO	WILCO	YUMMO	ZOPPO
VERSO	WAHOO	YAHOO	ZAMBO	ZORRO

Six-letter words

ABRAZO	CABRIO	FOREDO	KATIPO	OVERGO
ADAGIO	CALICO	FOREGO	KEKENO	PAKOKO
ADJIGO	CALIGO	FORHOO	KIMONO	PALOLO
AERUGO	CAMSHO	FRANCO	KLEPTO	PANINO
AHCHOO	CARDIO	FRESCO	KOKAKO	PARAMO
AIKIDO	CASHOO	FUGATO	KOODOO	PEDALO
AKIMBO	CASINO	FUMADO	KORERO	PEPINO
ALBEDO	CATALO	GABBRO	KOUSSO	PERNIO
ALBINO	CHARRO	GALAGO	KWAITO	PHYLLO
ALBUGO	CHEAPO	GAUCHO	LADINO	PHYSIO
ALNICO	CHEERO	GAZABO	LANUGO	PICARO
AMMINO	CHOCHO	GAZEBO	LATIGO	PIOPIO
AMMONO	CHOCKO	GELATO	LATINO	PLONKO
ANATTO	CHROMO	GENTOO	LAVABO	POMATO
ANGICO	CHURRO	GHERAO	LEGATO	POMELO
APOLLO	CICERO	GHETTO	LIBERO	PONCHO
ARIOSO	COGITO	GIGOLO	LIBIDO	POTATO
ARISTO	COLUGO	GINGKO	LIVEDO	PRESTO
ARROYO	COMEDO	GINKGO	LOBOLO	PRONTO
ARSENO	COMODO	GITANO	LOLIGO	PSEUDO
ARSINO	CONCHO	GIUSTO	LUCUMO	PSYCHO
ASIAGO	COOCOO	GOMBRO	MACACO	PUEBLO
AUSUBO	COROZO	GOMUTO	MADURO	PUKEKO
AWHATO	CRAMBO	GONGYO	MAMAKO	PUMELO
AWHETO	CRYPTO	GOOROO	MANITO	PUNCTO
BABACO	CUATRO	GORGIO	MANOAO	QUANGO
BAGNIO	CUCKOO	GREEBO	MAOMAO	QUARTO
BAGUIO	DAIMIO	GRINGO	MATICO	RABATO
BAMBOO	DAIMYO	GROTTO	MATIPO	RANCHO
BAROLO	DAYGLO	GUANGO	MEDICO	REBATO
BARRIO	DEXTRO	HAIRDO	MELANO	REBOZO
BASUCO	DINERO	HALLOO	MENUDO	REECHO
BAYAMO	DOMINO	HERETO	MERINO	REGULO
BEENTO	DOODOO	HETERO	MIKADO	REZERO
BILLYO	DOPPIO	HOLLOO	MIOMBO	RIALTO
BISTRO	DORADO	HONCHO	MODULO	RIGHTO
BLANCO	DRONGO	HOODOO	MOKORO	ROADEO
BLOTTO	DUELLO	HOOPOO	MONOAO	ROBALO
BOLERO	DUETTO	HOOROO	MOOLOO	ROCOCO
BONITO	DYNAMO	HULLOO	MORPHO	ROMANO
BONOBO	EMBRYO	HUPIRO	NANDOO	ROTOLO
BOOBOO	ENDURO	IGNARO	NARDOO	RUBATO
BOOCOO	ENHALO	IMBIZO	NIELLO	RUBIGO
BOOHOO	ENVIRO	INCAVO	NONEGO	SAMFOO
BOOKOO	ERINGO	INDIGO	NOSTRO	SANCHO
BRASCO	ERYNGO	JAZZBO	NUNCIO	SANPRO
BRILLO	ESCUDO	JINGKO	NYMPHO	SAPEGO
BROCHO	FASCIO	JOURNO	OBENTO	SBIRRO
BRONCO	FIASCO	KAKAPO	OCTAVO	SCAMTO
BUMALO	FINITO	KARORO	OLINGO	SCHIZO
BURGOO	FINSKO	KARROO	OVERDO	SCRUTO

SHACKO	SPINTO	TERCIO	TUXEDO	WEIRDO
SHEEPO	STALKO	TEREDO	ULTIMO	WHACKO
SHIPPO	STANZO	THICKO	VAUDOO	WHAMMO
SHIVOO	STEREO	THUGGO	VELCRO	WHATSO
SHYPOO	STINGO	TIFOSO	VIBRIO	WHOMSO
SISSOO	STINKO	TOLEDO	VIGORO	ZELOSO
SKIDOO	STUCCO	TOMATO	VIRAGO	ZOCALO
SLEAZO	STUDIO	TORERO	VIRINO	ZOOZOO
SMALTO	SUBITO	TRILLO	VOMITO	ZORINO
SOLANO	TAPALO	TROPPO	VOODOO	ZUFOLO
SOLITO	TATTOO	TUKTOO	VORAGO	ZYDECO
SORGHO	TECHNO	TUPELO	VOSTRO	
SPEEDO	TENUTO	TURACO	WANDOO	

Seven-letter words

AGITATO	CALYPSO	HAPKIDO	NORTENO	REJONEO
AILANTO	CANTICO	HIDALGO	OKIMONO	RELIEVO
AKIRAHO	CARABAO	HISTRIO	OLOROSO	RELLENO
ALBERGO	CASSINO	HORNITO	OREGANO	REVERSO
ALFREDO	CATTALO	HUANACO	OUTECHO	RIDOTTO
ALLEGRO	CAVETTO	IMPASTO	PACHUCO	RILIEVO
AMORINO	CEMBALO	INFERNO	PAESANO	RIPIENO
AMOROSO	CENTAVO	JIGABOO	PAISANO	RISOTTO
ANIMATO	CENTIMO	KARENGO	PAKAPOO	ROGALLO
ANNATTO	CHAMISO	KERCHOO	PALAZZO	RONDINO
APAREJO	CHANOYO	LENTIGO	PAMPERO	ROSOLIO
APPALTO	CHEERIO	LLANERO	PAPILIO	RUBABOO
ARBORIO	CHICANO	LUMBAGO	PASSADO	SAGUARO
ARNATTO	CHORIZO	MADRONO	PATRICO	SAHUARO
ARNOTTO	CLARINO	MAESTRO	PEDRERO	SALTATO
ARRIERO	COMMODO	MAFIOSO	PEKEPOO	SAMSHOO
ASINICO	CONCEDO	MAGNETO	PENTITO	SANTERO
ATISHOO	COQUITO	MALICHO	PERSICO	SAPSAGO
AVOCADO	CORANTO	MANGEAO	PETITIO	SCALADO
AZULEJO	CORNUTO	MARCATO	PIANINO	SCHERZO
BACALAO	CRIOLLO	MARENGO	PICACHO	SCIOLTO
BAMBINO	CRUSADO	MARRANO	PICCOLO	SECONDO
BANDITO	CRUZADO	MEMENTO	PIFFERO	SEMIPRO
BAROCCO	CURACAO	MENDIGO	PIMENTO	SENECIO
BARRICO	CYMBALO	MESTESO	PINTADO	SENTIMO
BATTERO	DIABOLO	MESTINO	PINTANO	SERPIGO
BEEFALO	DINITRO	MESTIZO	PLACEBO	SERRANO
BIZARRO	EIGHTVO	MISTICO	PLENIPO	SFUMATO
BONIATO	ELECTRO	MOCKADO	POBLANO	SHAKUDO
BOTARGO	EMBARGO	MODELLO	POINADO	SHAMPOO
BRACCIO	ESPARTO	MOMENTO	POMPANO	SIROCCO
BRACERO	ETAERIO	MONTERO	POMPELO	SKIDDOO
BRASERO	FAGOTTO	MORELLO	PORCINO	SMOKEHO
BRAVADO	FARRAGO	MORENDO	PORRIGO	SOLDADO
BRONCHO	FERRUGO	MORISCO	PORTICO	SOPRANO
BUDGERO	FINNSKO	MOROCCO	POTOROO	SORDINO
BUFFALO	FORZATO	MULATTO	PRIMERO	SQUACCO
BUGABOO	FUMETTO	NATHEMO	PRIVADO	STRETTO
BUMMALO	FURIOSO	NAVARHO	PROVISO	SUBECHO
BURRITO	GAMBADO	NELUMBO	PROXIMO	SUBZERO
BUSHIDO	GESTAPO	NITROSO	PRURIGO	SUPREMO
CABILDO	GIOCOSO	NONETTO	PUMMELO	SYNCHRO
CALALOO	GRADINO	NONHERO	QUOMODO	TALLYHO
CALANDO	GUANACO	NONZERO	RABBITO	TAMARAO

TANGELO	TONDINO	UNDERDO	VILIAGO	ZANJERO
TEDESCO	TORNADO	UNDERGO	VIRANDO	ZAPATEO
TENTIGO	TORPEDO	UNMACHO	VOLCANO	ZEBRANO
TESTUDO	TOSTADO	UPTEMPO	VOLPINO	ZEMSTVO
THEORBO	TOURACO	VAQUERO	WENDIGO	ZINGANO
THERETO	TREMOLO	VERISMO	WHERESO	ZINGARO
TIMPANO	TROMINO	VERTIGO	WHERETO	ZOCCOLO
TOBACCO	TWIGLOO	VIBRATO	WINDIGO	ZORILLO
TOMBOLO	TYMPANO	VILIACO	ZAMARRO	ZUFFOLO

Eight-letter words

ALFRESCO	CONCERTO	HABANERO	MODERATO	RISOLUTO
AMARETTO	CONCETTO	HALLALOO	MOKOMOKO	RISPETTO
AMORETTO	CONFETTO	HEREINTO	MONTANTO	RITENUTO
ANTIHERO	CONJUNTO	HEREUNTO	MOSQUITO	ROSOGLIO
ARMIGERO	CONTANGO	HITHERTO	MUCHACHO	RUBBABOO
ARPEGGIO	CONTEMPO	HOROPITO	MUNDUNGO	SALTANDO
ASSIENTO	CONTINUO	HUAQUERO	NEUTRINO	SARGASSO
ATAMASCO	CONTORNO	HUARACHO	NOCTILIO	SCALDINO
AUTOGIRO	CONVERSO	HUBBUBOO	NONMETRO	SCENARIO
AUTOGYRO	CORAGGIO	IMPETIGO	NONPALITO	SCIROCCO
BALLYHOO	CORNETTO	INNUENDO	NOTTURNO	SCORDATO
BARBASCO	COROCORO	INTAGLIO	OBLIGATO	SEICENTO
BARGELLO	COURANTO	INTONACO	OCOTILLO	SEMIHOBO
BARRANCO	CROSTINO	JACKAROO	ORATORIO	SERAGLIO
BESOGNIO	CRUZEIRO	JACKEROO	OSTINATO	SESTETTO
BISCOTTO	CURCULIO	JALAPENO	OTTAVINO	SFORZATO
BOCACCIO	DOLCETTO	JEREPIGO	PACHINKO	SIGISBEO
BONAMANO	DOLOROSO	JILLAROO	PADERERO	SMORZATO
BORACHIO	DUECENTO	JORDELOO	PALAMINO	SOLIDAGO
BORDELLO	DUETTINO	JUNKANOO	PALISADO	SOMBRERO
BOZZETTO	ELDORADO	KAKEMONO	PALMETTO	SPADILLO
BUCKAROO	ENCIERRO	KAMOKAMO	PALOMINO	SPICCATO
BUCKAYRO	ESCALADO	KANGAROO	PARLANDO	STACCATO
BUCKEROO	ESCAPADO	KORIMAKO	PASTITSO	STAMPEDO
BURDIZZO	ESPRESSO	KOROMIKO	PATERERO	STICCADO
CABESTRO	ESPUMOSO	LARGANDO	PECORINO	STICCATO
CABRESTO	EXPRESSO	LEGGIERO	PEDERERO	STILETTO
CACAFOGO	FALSETTO	LENTANDO	PEEKABOO	STOCCADO
CALLALOO	FANDANGO	LIBECCIO	PEEKAPOO	SUBAUDIO
CAMISADO	FAROLITO	LIBRETTO	PEPERINO	SUBIMAGO
CAPITANO	FASCISMO	LITERATO	PERDENDO	SUPEREGO
CAPUCCIO	FELLATIO	LOCOFOCO	PERFECTO	SUPERLOO
CASTRATO	FINNESKO	LOTHARIO	PIMIENTO	SUPERPRO
CAUDILLO	FINOCHIO	MACHISMO	PIQUILLO	SUPPEAGO
CAVALERO	FLAMENCO	MAESTOSO	PLUMBAGO	TALEGGIO
CHARANGO	FLAMINGO	MAKIMONO	POIGNADO	TAPACOLO
CHARNECO	FORZANDO	MALGRADO	POLITICO	TAPACULO
CHECHAKO	FRICANDO	MALLECHO	PRELUDIO	TAPADERO
CHUBASCO	GALAPAGO	MAMELUCO	PRERADIO	TENEBRIO
CICISBEO	GARBANZO	MANCANDO	PRESIDIO	TERRAZZO
CILANTRO	GARDYLOO	MANZELLO	PRUNELLO	TERZETTO
CIOPPINO	GAZPACHO	MARTELLO	PULVILIO	TOKOTOKO
CLASSICO	GERONIMO	MERCAPTO	PULVILLO	TORNILLO
COCKAPOO	GILLAROO	MICROMHO	PYINKADO	TRAPUNTO
COCKATOO	GRACIOSO	MILESIMO	RANCHERO	TRECENTO
COCOBOLO	GRAFFITO	MILLIMHO	REDDENDO	TUCOTUCO
COLORADO	GRAZIOSO	MINIMOTO	RENEGADO	TUCUTUCO
COMMANDO	GUACHARO	MIROMIRO	RIRORIRO	TWELVEMO

UMBRELLO	VIGOROSO	VIRTUOSO	WATERLOO	ZECCHINO
VARGUENO	VILLAGIO	VITILIGO	WAYLEGGO	ZUCHETTO
VARLETTO	VILLIAGO	WALLAROO	WHAKAIRO	
VERDELHO	VINDALOO	WANDEROO	YAKIMONO	

Words that end with -U

Two-letter words

GU	type of violin used in Shetland
MU	12th letter in the Greek alphabet, a consonant, transliterated as m
NU	13th letter in the Greek alphabet
OU	man, bloke, or chap
XU	Vietnamese currency unit
YU	jade

Three-letter words

MU	unit of mass
AYU	small Japanese fish
BRU	friend
CRU	(in France) a vineyard, group of vineyards, or wine-producing region
EAU	water
ECU	any of various former French gold or silver coins
EMU	large Australian flightless bird with long legs
FEU	(in Scotland) right of use of land in return for a fixed annual payment
FLU	any of various viral infections, esp a respiratory or intestinal infection
FOU	full
GAU	district set up by the Nazi Party during the Third Reich
GJU	type of violin used in Shetland
GNU	ox-like S African antelope
JEU	game
KYU	(in judo) one of the five student grades for inexperienced competitors
LEU	standard monetary unit of Romania and Moldova, divided into 100 bani
LOU	Scots word for love
MEU	European umbelliferous plant
MOU	Scots word for mouth
PIU	more (quickly, softly, etc)
PLU	beaver skin used as a standard unit of value in the fur trade
SAU	archaic past tense of see
SOU	former French coin
TAU	19th letter in the Greek alphabet
ULU	type of knife
UMU	type of oven
UTU	reward
VAU	sixth letter of the Hebrew alphabet
YOU	person or people addressed

Four-letter words

AGLU	GENU	KUTU	PATU	TEGU
AITU	GURU	KUZU	PRAU	THOU
BABU	HABU	LATU	PUDU	THRU
BAJU	HAKU	LEKU	PUKU	TOFU
BALU	HAPU	LIEU	PULU	TOLU
BAPU	HUHU	LITU	PUPU	TUTU
BEAU	IGLU	LUAU	RAKU	UNAU
BEDU	JEHU	LULU	RATU	VATU
BUBU	JUJU	MASU	RIMU	VROU
CHOU	JUKU	MENU	RURU	WUDU
CLOU	KAGU	MEOU	SULU	YUZU
ECRU	KORU	MOTU	SUSU	ZEBU
EMEU	KUDU	MUMU	TABU	ZOBU
FRAU	KUKU	NAMU	TAPU	ZULU
FUGU	KURU	OMBU	TATU	

Five-letter words

ADIEU	CHIRU	KONBU	PERDU	TAHOU
AHURU	CORNU	KUDZU	PIKAU	TATOU
BANTU	COYPU	LASSU	PILAU	TENDU
BATTU	FICHU	MAPAU	POILU	TUKTU
BAYOU	FONDU	MIAOU	PONZU	UHURU
BIJOU	HAIKU	MUNTU	POYOU	URUBU
BITOU	HINAU	NAIRU	PRAHU	VERTU
BOYAU	HOKKU	NANDU	QUIPU	VIRTU
BUCHU	JAMBU	NIKAU	SADHU	VODOU
BUCKU	KANZU	NOYAU	SAJOU	VOULU
BUNDU	KAURU	OTAKU	SAMFU	WUSHU
BUSSU	KAWAU	PAREU	SHOYU	
CENTU	KOMBU	PENDU	SNAFU	

Six-letter words

ABATTU	COTEAU	KIKUYU	MZUNGU	SAMSHU
ACAJOU	COYPOU	KOKOPU	NHANDU	SENRYU
ALLYOU	DETENU	KOTUKU	NILGAU	SHINJU
AMADOU	EPERDU	LANDAU	NOGAKU	SUBFEU
APERCU	GAGAKU	MADAFU	ORIHOU	TAMANU
BATEAU	GATEAU	MAHEWU	ORMOLU	TAUHOU
BHIKHU	GOMOKU	MAKUTU	PILLAU	TELEDU
BINIOU	GRUGRU	MALIBU	PISTOU	VOUDOU
BOUBOU	HALERU	MAMAKU	PIUPIU	WHANAU
BUREAU	HAPUKU	MANATU	QUIPPU	YNAMBU
CACHOU	INGENU	MANITU	RAWARU	
CADEAU	JABIRU	MEVROU	RESEAU	
CALALU	KARAMU	MILIEU	ROUCOU	
CONGOU	KERERU	MUUMUU	SADDHU	

Seven-letter words

ANTIFLU	BERCEAU	CATECHU	CORBEAU	JAMBEAU
BABASSU	BUNRAKU	CATTABU	COUTEAU	JUJITSU
BANDEAU	CAMAIEU	CHANOYU	DAIMOKU	JUJUTSU
BATTEAU	CARDECU	CHAPEAU	FABLIAU	MAMAKAU
BEBEERU	CARIBOU	CHATEAU	INCONNU	MANITOU

MANTEAU	NYLGHAU	RONDEAU	SUBMENU	TONNEAU
MARABOU	PARVENU	ROULEAU	TABLEAU	TRUMEAU
MOINEAU	PLATEAU	SANTIMU	TAMANDU	TURACOU
MORCEAU	PONCEAU	SAPAJOU	TAMARAU	UMLUNGU
MWALIMU	PURLIEU	SEPPUKU	TAUHINU	WAMEFOU
NILGHAU	RAUPATU	SHIATSU	TIMARAU	WAREHOU
NOUVEAU	ROKKAKU	SHIATZU	TINAMOU	

Eight-letter words

ABOIDEAU	FELDGRAU	KEIRETSU	PIRARUCU	TIRAMISU
ABOITEAU	FLAMBEAU	KINKAJOU	PRIEDIEU	TSUTSUMU
BERIMBAU	FROUFROU	MAIREHAU	PYENGADU	TUCUTUCU
CARCAJOU	HAUSFRAU	MINSHUKU	ROUSSEAU	VERMOULU
CARIACOU	JIUJITSU	NINJITSU	SUCURUJU	WILLIWAU
CARJACOU	JIUJUTSU	NINJUTSU	SURUCUCU	ZAIBATSU
COUMAROU	KABELJOU	NUNCHAKU	THANKYOU	

Chapter 6: Unusual Letter Combinations

A challenge that every Scrabble player faces at some point in almost every game is dealing with an unpromising combination of letters on their rack. Having too many of the same letter, too many vowels or too many consonants can put you in a situation where it is very difficult to come up with a viable word, let alone a high-scoring one.

This section contains various lists that may prove useful in dealing with an awkward combination of tiles, because they consist of words with unusual letter combinations.

Words from World English

One method of dealing with the awkward tile combinations that inevitably appear on your rack at some point in a game is to memorize a wide selection of words outside the core vocabulary of English. As the most widely spoken language in the world, English is rich in loan-words from other languages, and the versatility of the Roman alphabet and of English pronunciation means that these words tend to be assimilated without much corruption of their original sound. This means that there are many words in English that use 'foreign' letter combinations, which are ideal for Scrabble players. The following lists contain words from Australia, Canada, New Zealand and South Africa, as well as words from the main languages of the Indian Subcontinent – Hindi and Urdu – which have entered British English.

Australian words

Australian English is distinguished not only by the numerous Aboriginal terms for Australia's flora and fauna, but also by a great many shortened forms of commonplace English words. The Australian propensity to slang and short informal words is extremely useful to Scrabble players, especially as many of these words end in O, one of the most common tiles in the game. If you spot an O on the board when you have a difficult set of letters on your rack, there's a good chance that you'll be able to form an informal Aussie word. Native Australian words provide a range of unusual letter combinations, as well as a tendency to include double Os – ideal for rack balancing. Double Rs are also common in Australian English, as are Ks and Ys, so it's well worth acquiring some Antipodean vocabulary.

ADJIGO	yam plant
ALF	an uncultivated Australian
ARVO	afternoon
ASPRO	associate professor
BARRO	embarrassing
BAUERA	small evergreen shrub
BEAUT	outstanding person or thing
BELAH	casuarina tree
BERKO	berserk
BIFFO	fighting or aggressive behaviour

BILBY	burrowing marsupial
BIZZO	empty and irrelevant talk
BOAB	baobab tree
BODGIE	unruly or uncouth man
BOGAN	fool
BOOBOOK	small spotted brown owl
BOOFY	strong but stupid
BOONG	offensive word for a Black person
BOOSHIT	very good
BORA	native Australian coming-of-age ceremony
BORAK	rubbish or nonsense
BRASCO	lavatory
BROLGA	large grey crane with red-and-green head
BRUMBY	wild horse
BUNYA	tall dome-shaped coniferous tree
BUNYIP	legendary monster
CADAGI	tropical eucalyptus tree
CARBY	carburettor
CHEWIE	chewing gum
CHIACK	tease or banter
CHOCO	conscript or militiaman
CHOOK	hen or chicken
CHOOM	Englishman
COMMO	communist
COMPO	compensation
CORREA	evergreen shrub
COUCAL	long-legged bird
COUGAN	rowdy person
CRONK	unfit or unsound
CROOL	spoil
CROWEA	pink-flowered shrub
DACK	forcibly remove someone's trousers
DADAH	illegal drugs
DAGGY	untidy or dishevelled
DASYURE	small carnivorous marsupial
DELO	delegate
DERRO	vagrant
DINGO	wild dog
DINKUM	genuine or right
DOCO	documentary
DONGA	steep-sided gully
DORBA	stupid, inept, or clumsy person
DRACK	unattractive
DRONGO	slow-witted person
DROOB	pathetic person
DUBBO	stupid
DUGITE	venomous snake
DURRY	cigarette
EARBASH	talk incessantly
EMU	large flightless bird
EUMUNG	type of acacia
EVO	evening
EXO	excellent
FASTIE	deceitful act
FESTY	dirty or smelly
FIBRO	house built of fibrocement
FIGJAM	very conceited person
FIZGIG	frivolous or flirtatious girl
FOULIE	bad mood
FRIB	short heavy-conditioned piece of wool

FUNDIE	fundamentalist Christian
FURPHY	rumour or fictitious story
GALAH	grey-and-pink cockatoo
GARBO	dustman
GEEBUNG	tree with edible but tasteless fruit
GIDGEE	small acacia tree that sometimes emits an unpleasant smell
GILGAI	natural water hole
GING	child's catapult
GNOW	ground-dwelling bird
GOANNA	monitor lizard
GOOG	egg
GOOLIE	stone or pebble
GUNYAH	bush hut or shelter
GYMPIE	tall tree with stinging hairs on its leaves
HAKEA	type of shrub or tree
HOSTIE	air hostess
HOVEA	plant with purple flowers
HUTCHIE	groundsheet draped over an upright stick as a temporary shelter
JARRAH	type of eucalyptus tree
JEFF	downsize or close down an organization
JUMBUCK	sheep
KARRI	type of eucalyptus tree
KOALA	slow-moving arboreal marsupial
KOORI	native Australian
KYBO	temporary lavatory
KYLIE	boomerang that is flat on one side and convex on the other
LOPPY	man employed to do maintenance work on a ranch
LOWAN	ground-dwelling bird
LUBRA	Aboriginal woman
MALLEE	low shrubby eucalyptus tree
MARRI	type of eucalyptus
MIDDY	middle-sized glass of beer
MILKO	milkman
MOLOCH	spiny lizard
MOPOKE	small spotted owl
MOZ	hoodoo or hex
MUGGA	eucalyptus tree with pink flowers and dark bark
MULGA	acacia shrub
MULLOCK	waste material from a mine
MURREE	native Australian
MURRI	native Australian
MUSO	musician
MYALL	native Australian living independently of society
MYXO	myxomatosis
NANA	head
NARDOO	cloverlike fern
NEDDY	horse
NOAH	shark
NONG	stupid or incompetent person
NORK	female breast
NUDDY	in the nude
NUMBAT	small marsupial with long snout
OCKER	uncultivated or boorish Australian
PIKER	wild bullock
PINDAN	desert region of Western Australia
PITURI	shrub with narcotic leaves
PLONKO	alcoholic, especially one who drinks wine
PLURRY	euphemism for bloody
PODDY	handfed calf or lamb

POKIE	poker machine
POON	stupid or ineffectual person
POONCE	male homosexual
POSSIE	position
PRELOVED	second-hand
QUOKKA	small wallaby
QUOLL	native cat
RAZOO	imaginary coin
REFFO	offensive term for a European refugee after World War Two
REGO	registration of a motor vehicle
RESTO	restored antique, vintage car, etc
ROO	kangaroo
ROUGHIE	something unfair, especially a trick
SANGER	sandwich
SANGO	sandwich
SCOZZA	rowdy person
SCUNGY	miserable, sordid or dirty
SHARPIE	a member of a teenage group with short hair and distinctive clothes
SHERANG	boss
SHYPOO	liquor of poor quality
SITELLA	small black-and-white bird
SKEG	rear fin on the underside of a surfboard
SKITE	boast
SMOKO	cigarette break
SMOODGE	smooch
SPAG	offensive term for an Italian
SPRUIK	speak in public
SWAGGIE	vagrant worker
SWAGMAN	vagrant worker
SWY	a gambling game
TONK	effeminate man
TOOSHIE	angry or upset
TRIELLA	three horse races nominated for a bet
TROPPO	mentally affected by a tropical climate
TRUCKIE	truck driver
TRUGO	game similar to croquet
TUAN	flying phalanger
TUART	type of eucalyptus tree
UMPIE	umpire
UNCO	awkward or clumsy
UPTA	of poor quality
UPTER	of poor quality
UTE	utility
VAG	vagrant
VEGO	vegetarian
VIGORO	women's game similar to cricket
WADDY	heavy wooden club used by native Australians
WAGGA	blanket made of sacks stitched together
WALLABY	marsupial resembling a small kangaroo
WANDOO	eucalyptus tree with white bark
WARATAH	shrub with dark green leaves and crimson flowers
WARB	dirty or insignificant person
WHARFIE	wharf labourer
WIDGIE	female bodgie
WILGA	small drought-resistant tree
WIRILDA	acacia tree with edible seeds
WIRRAH	saltwater fish with bright blue spots
WOF	fool or idiot
WOMBAT	burrowing marsupial

WOOMERA	spear-throwing stick
WURLEY	Aboriginal hut
YABBER	talk or jabber
YABBY	small freshwater crayfish
YACCA	grass tree
YACKA	grass tree
YARRAN	small hardy tree
YATE	small eucalyptus tree
YIKE	argument, squabble or fight
YUCKO	disgusting
YUMMO	delicious
ZAMBUCK	St John ambulance attendant
ZIFF	beard

Canadian words

Canadian English combines a broad range of British and US terms with words derived from Inuit, as well as from other Native American languages such as Algonquin. Canadian English incorporates many Canadian French words from Quebec, and there are also a number of recently coined Canadian terms. Inuit words can be helpful to Scrabble players because they tend to be quite vowel-heavy. K occurs frequently in Inuit terms, and sometimes appears twice. Such words require a blank tile for the second K if they are to be played during a game.

AGLOO	breathing hole made in ice by a seal
AGLU	breathing hole made in ice by a seal
AMAUT	hood on an Inuit woman's parka for carrying a child
AMOWT	hood on an Inuit woman's parka for carrying a child
ATIGI	Inuit parka
BABICHE	thongs or lacings of rawhide
BARACHOIS	shallow lagoon formed by a sand bar
BATEAU	light flat-bottomed boat
BEIGNET	deep-fried pastry
BOGAN	sluggish side stream
BREWIS	Newfoundland cod stew
BUTTE	isolated steep-sided flat-topped hill
CABOOSE	mobile bunkhouse used by lumbermen
CANOLA	cooking oil extracted from a variety of rapeseed developed in Canada
CAYUSE	small Native American pony used by cowboys
COULEE	dry stream valley
CUSK	gadoid food fish
DEKE	act or instance of feinting in ice hockey
GROWLER	small iceberg that has broken off from a larger iceberg or glacier
HONKER	Canada goose
HOSER	unsophisticated rural person
ICEWINE	dessert wine made from frozen grapes
JIGGER	device used when setting a gill net beneath ice
JOUAL	nonstandard Canadian French dialect
KAMIK	Inuit boot made of caribou hide or sealskin
KLOOCH	North American Indian woman
KLOOTCH	North American Indian woman
KUDLIK	Inuit soapstone seal-oil lamp
LOGAN	backwater
LOONIE	Canadian dollar coin with loon bird on one face
MUCKAMUCK	food

MUKTUK	beluga skin used as food
NANOOK	polar bear
PARFLECHE	dried rawhide
PARKADE	building used as a car park
PARKETTE	small public park
PLEW	beaver skin used as standard unit in fur trading
POGEY	financial relief for the unemployed
POGY	financial relief for the unemployed
POKELOGAN	backwater
POUTINE	chipped potatoes topped with curd cheese and tomato sauce
PUNG	horse-drawn sleigh
REDEYE	drink incorporating beer and tomato juice
RUBABOO	soup made by boiling pemmican
RUBBY	rubbing alcohol mixed with cheap wine for drinking
SKOOKUM	strong or brave
SNYE	side channel of a river
SPLAKE	hybrid trout bred by Canadian zoologists
SWILER	seal hunter
TILLICUM	friend
TOONIE	Canadian two-dollar coin
TULLIBEE	whitefish found in the Great Lakes
TUPEK	Inuit tent of animal skins
TUPIK	Inuit tent of animal skins
TWONIE	Canadian two-dollar coin
WAWA	speech or language
WENDIGO	evil spirit or cannibal

Hindi words

After Chinese, Hindi, the dominant language of India, is the most widely spoken language in the world. Many Hindi words entered British English during the Raj, and some have become everyday terms – **bungalow** and **pundit,** for example. Others are less common, but are useful to Scrabble players because they provide unusual letter combinations and thus solutions to difficult racks. Combinations such as BH, DH and KH are common in Hindi-derived words, and the preponderance of As, Is and Us can be very helpful in trying to balance a vowel-heavy rack. Above all, Hindi words are useful because they are quite unusual, and so provide a range of options for Scrabble players that aren't immediately obvious – front-hooking onto **hang** with a B, for example, or end-hooking onto **punk** with an A. Committing some Hindi-derived words to memory will help to keep your opponents on their toes.

AKHARA	gymnasium
ALAP	vocal music without words
AMBARY	tropical plant
ANKUS	elephant goad
ANNA	old copper coin
ARTI	Hindu ritual
AYAH	maidservant or nursemaid
BABU	Mr
BAEL	spiny tree
BAHADUR	title for distinguished Indians during the Raj
BANDH	general strike
BANYAN	tree with aerial roots
BHAJI	deep-fried vegetable savoury
BHANG	psychoactive drug made of hemp

BHANGRA	music combining traditional Punjabi music with Western pop
BHAVAN	large house or building
BHEESTY	water-carrier
BHINDI	okra used in cooking
BHISHTI	water-carrier
BINDI	decorative dot in middle of forehead
BOBBERY	mixed pack of hunting dogs
BUND	embankment
CHAI	tea, especially with added spices
CHAMPAC	tree with fragrant yellow flowers
CHAPATI	flat coarse unleavened bread
CHAPPAL	sandal
CHARAS	hashish
CHARKHA	spinning wheel
CHEETAH	large swift feline mammal
CHETAH	large swift feline mammal
CHELA	disciple of a religious teacher
CHICHI	person of mixed British and Indian descent
CHILLUM	pipe for smoking cannabis
CHINTZ	printed cotton with glazed finish
CHITAL	the axis deer
CHOKEY	prison
CHOLI	short-sleeved bodice
CHOWK	marketplace
CHUDDAR	large shawl or veil
CHUDDIES	underpants
CHUKAR	Indian partridge
CHUKKA	period of play in polo
CHUTNEY	Indian pickle
COOLIE	cheaply hired unskilled labourer
COOLY	cheaply hired unskilled labourer
COWAGE	tropical climbing plant with stinging pods
COWHAGE	tropical climbing plant with stinging pods
CRORE	ten million
CUSHY	comfortable
DACOIT	a member of a gang of armed robbers
DACOITY	robbery by an armed gang
DAK	system of mail delivery
DAL	split grain
DATURA	plant with trumpet-shaped flowers
DEKKO	look or glance
DEODAR	Himalayan cedar
DEWAN	chief minister of an Indian princedom
DHAK	tropical tree with red flowers
DHAL	curry made from lentils
DHARNA	method of obtaining justice by fasting
DHOBI	washerman
DHOTI	loincloth
DUPATTA	scarf
DURBAR	court of an Indian ruler
DURRIE	cotton carpet
DURZI	Indian tailor
GANJA	potent form of cannabis
GAUR	large wild cow
GARIAL	fish-eating crocodilian with long slender snout
GAVIAL	fish-eating crocodilian with long slender snout
GHARIAL	fish-eating crocodilian with long slender snout
GHARRI	horse-drawn vehicle for hire
GHARRY	horse-drawn vehicle for hire
GHAT	stairs or passage leading down to a river

GHEE	clarified butter
GHERAO	industrial action in which workers imprison their employers
GINGILI	oil obtained from sesame seeds
GORAL	small goat antelope
GUAR	plant that produces gum
GUNNY	coarse fabric used for sacks
GURU	Hindu or Sikh religious teacher
HARTAL	act of closing shop or stopping work as a political protest
HOWDAH	seat for riding on an elephant's back
JAGGERY	coarse brown sugar
JAI	victory
KHADDAR	cotton cloth
KHEDA	enclosure for captured elephants
KHEDAH	enclosure for captured elephants
KHEDDAH	enclosure for captured elephants
KOEL	parasitic cuckoo
KOS	Indian unit of distance
KRAIT	brightly coloured venomous snake
KUKRI	Ghurka knife
KULFI	Indian dessert
KURTA	long loose garment like a shirt without a collar
LAC	resinous substance secreted by insects
LAKH	100,000
LANGUR	arboreal monkey
LASSI	yoghurt drink
LATHI	long heavy stick used as a weapon
LUNGI	long piece of cloth worn as loincloth or turban
MACHAN	platform used in tiger hunting
MAHOUT	elephant driver
MAHSEER	large freshwater fish
MANDI	big market
MANDIR	Hindu or Jain temple
MAUND	unit of weight
MEHNDI	practice of painting designs on the hands and feet using henna
MELA	cultural or religious festival
MOHUR	old gold coin
MONAL	Asian pheasant
MORCHA	hostile demonstration against the government
MRIDANG	drum used in Indian music
MYNAH	tropical starling
NAUCH	intricate Indian dance
NAUTCH	intricate Indian dance
NAWAB	Muslim prince in India
NEEM	large tree
NILGAI	large Indian antelope
NULLAH	stream or drain
NUMDAH	coarse felt
OONT	camel
PACHISI	game resembling backgammon
PAISA	one hundredth of a rupee
PAKORA	dish of deep-fried chicken or vegetables
PANEER	soft white cheese
PARATHA	flat unleavened bread
PEEPUL	tree similar to the banyan
PUNKA	fan made of palm leaves
PUNKAH	fan made of palm leaves
PURDA	custom of keeping women secluded
PURDAH	custom of keeping women secluded
PURI	unleavened flaky bread

PUTTEE	strip of cloth wound around the leg
RAGGEE	cereal grass
RAGI	cereal grass
RAITA	yoghurt-and-vegetable dish served with curry
RAJ	government
RAJAH	ruler or landlord
RAMTIL	African plant grown in India
RANEE	queen or princess
RANI	queen or princess
RATHA	four-wheeled carriage drawn by horses or bullocks
ROTI	type of unleavened bread
RUPEE	standard monetary unit of India
RUPIAH	standard monetary unit of Indonesia
RYOT	peasant or tenant farmer
SAMBAR	deer with three-tined antlers
SAMITI	political association
SAMOSA	triangular pastry containing spiced vegetables or meat
SARANGI	stringed instrument played with a bow
SARDAR	Sikh title
SARI	traditional dress of Indian women
SAROD	Indian stringed instrument
SWAMI	title for a Hindu saint or religious teacher
TABLA	pair of drums whose pitches can be varied
THALI	meal consisting of several small dishes
TIL	sesame
TOLA	unit of weight
TONGA	light two-wheeled vehicle
TOPEE	pith helmet
TOPI	pith helmet
URD	bean plant
VAHANA	vehicle in Indian myth
VANDA	type of orchid
VINA	stringed musical instrument
WALLAH	person in charge of a specific thing
ZENANA	part of a house reserved for women and girls
ZILA	administrative district in India
ZILLA	administrative district in India
ZILLAH	administrative district in India

New Zealand

While New Zealand and Australian English have many words in common, the Kiwi lexicon is greatly enriched by New Zealand's Maori heritage. Maori-derived words are a marvellous resource for the Scrabble player, providing a wealth of unusual vowel combinations, and frequently using consonants that are rarer in European words, such as K, W and H. Maori words are especially good for balancing vowel-heavy racks, as many words use several As, Us or Is – sometimes with three vowels in a row. Relatively high-scoring consonants are also very common, especially K and H. Unfortunately, there is only one K in Scrabble, so many Maori words with two Ks are less useful than they might initially appear. Don't forget blank tiles, however: if you have a blank, a K and a couple of vowels on your rack, there's a good chance that you can find a New Zealand word to play profitably. There are also some unusual words that have entered the vocabulary of New Zealanders from European or Asian languages.

ATUA	spirit or demon
BOOHAI	thoroughly lost
COOTIE	body louse
GOORIE	mongrel dog
GRAUNCH	crush or destroy
HAKA	war dance
HANGI	open-air cooking pit
HAPU	subtribe
HAPUKA	large fish
HAPUKU	large fish
HEITIKI	neck ornament
HIKOI	protest march
HOKONUI	illicit whisky
HONGI	nose-touching greeting
HUHU	hairy beetle
HUI	conference or meeting
HUIA	extinct New Zealand bird
JAFA	offensive term for someone from Auckland
JANOLA	household bleach
KAHAWAI	large fish
KAI	food
KAIK	village
KAINGA	village
KAKA	long-billed parrot
KAKAPO	ground-dwelling parrot
KARAKIA	prayer
KARANGA	call or chant of welcome
KATIPO	small venomous spider
KAUPAPA	strategy, policy or cause
KAURI	coniferous tree
KAWA	protocol or etiquette
KIEKIE	climbing bush plant
KIWI	flightless bird with long beak and no tail
KOHA	gift or donation
KOKAKO	long-tailed crow
KONEKE	farm vehicle
KORU	curved pattern
KOWHAI	small tree
KUIA	female elder
KURI	mongrel dog
KUTU	body louse
MANUKA	myrtaceous tree
MATAI	evergreen tree
MIHI	ceremonial greeting
MOA	extinct large flightless bird
MOKI	edible sea fish
MOKO	Maori tattoo or tattoo pattern
MOOLOO	person from Waikato
MOPOKE	small spotted owl
MUNGA	army canteen
NGAIO	small tree
NGATI	tribe or clan
NIKAU	palm tree
PAKAHI	acid soil or land
PAKAPOO	Chinese lottery
PAKOKO	small freshwater fish
PAUA	edible abalone
PERFING	early retirement from the police force with financial compensation
PIKAU	rucksack

PIPI	shellfish
PIUPIU	leaf skirt
POI	ball of woven flax
PONGA	tall tree fern
PORAE	edible sea fish
PORANGI	crazy
PORINA	moth larva
POTAE	hat
POWHIRI	welcoming ceremony
PUGGY	sticky
PUHA	sow thistle
PUKEKO	wading bird
PURIRI	forest tree
RAHUI	Maori prohibition
RATA	myrtaceous forest tree
RAUPATU	seizure of land
RAURIKI	sow thistle
SHEEPO	person who brings sheep to the catching pen for shearing
TAIAHA	ceremonial fighting staff
TAIHOA	hold on!
TAKAHE	rare flightless bird
TANGI	Maori funeral ceremony
TANIWHA	legendary monster
TAONGA	treasure
TAPU	sacred or forbidden
TARSEAL	bitumen surface of a road
TAUIWI	non-Maori people of New Zealand
TIKANGA	Maori customs
TOETOE	type of tall grass
TOITOI	type of tall grass
TWINK	white correction fluid
WAKA	Maori canoe
WEKA	flightless bird
WERO	warrior's challenge
WETA	long-legged wingless insect
WHANAU	family
WHENAU	native land

South Africa

South African English includes words from Nguni languages such as Xhosa and Zulu, as well as Afrikaans, amongst other languages. For Scrabble players, South African English offers a host of useful words for balancing vowel-heavy racks. Many Afrikaans-derived words contain a double A, while Nguni words often contain two or three As. It's a good idea, therefore, to have some South African words up your sleeve for when you find yourself with two or more As on your rack. There are also a lot of K words in South African English. As K can be an awkward letter to use effectively, these can come in very handy, as can the Afrikaans-derived words containing V, which are most helpful in trying to use a difficult tile.

AMADODA	grown men
AMANDLA	political slogan calling for power to the Black population
BAAS	boss
BABALAS	drunk or hungover
BAKKIE	small truck
BRAAI	grill or roast meat

BRAAIVLEIS	barbecue
BUNDU	wild, remote region
DAGGA	marijuana
DWAAL	state of befuddlement
GEELBEK	yellow-jawed fish
HAMBA	go away
JA	yes
JAAP	simpleton
JEREPIGO	heavy dessert wine
JONG	friend
KAAL	naked
KEREL	chap or fellow
KRAAL	stockaded village
KWAITO	type of pop music
LEGUAAN	large monitor lizard
MEERKAT	sociable mongoose
MENEER	Mr or Sir
MEVROU	Mrs or Madam
MOOI	pleasing
MUTI	herbal medicine
NAARTJIE	tangerine
NEK	mountain pass
NKOSI	master or chief
OKE	man
OOM	title of respect
OUBAAS	person senior in rank or years
PADKOS	snacks for a long journey
PLAAS	farm
ROOIKAT	lynx
SCAMTO	argot of urban South African Blacks
SKOLLY	hooligan
SNOEK	edible marine fish
SPEK	bacon, fat or fatty pork
STEEN	variety of white grape
STOKVEL	savings pool or syndicate
VLEI	area of marshy ground
VOEMA	vigour or energy
VOETSEK	expression of dismissal or rejection
VROU	woman or wife
YEBO	yes

Urdu words

Urdu, the official language of Pakistan and one of the official languages of India, is closely related to Hindi. Urdu, however, contains many more words derived from Arabic and Persian, and also uses a different system of writing from Hindi, lending a different character to the words that have entered English. Many Urdu culinary terms will be familiar to British Scrabble players from Indian restaurants, while most Anglo-Indian military vocabulary also derives from Urdu rather than Hindi. As with Hindi, the variant spellings of many Urdu words provide opportunities for Scrabble players, as does the frequency of the letter K.

BAGH	garden
BALTI	spicy Indian dish stewed until most liquid has evaporated
BASTI	slum
BEGUM	woman of high rank
BIRIANI	Indian dish of highly flavoured rice mixed with meat or fish
BIRYANI	Indian dish of highly flavoured rice mixed with meat or fish

BUSTEE	slum
BUSTI	slum
CHARPAI	bedstead of woven webbing on a wooden frame
CHARPOY	bedstead of woven webbing on a wooden frame
DAROGHA	manager
DHANSAK	Indian dish of meat or vegetables braised with lentils
INQILAB	revolution
IZZAT	honour or prestige
JACONET	light cotton fabric
JEMADAR	officer in the Indian police
KAMEEZ	long tunic
KEBAB	dish of meat, onions, etc, grilled on skewers
KHAKI	dull yellowish-brown colour
KHARIF	crop harvested at beginning of winter
KHAYAL	kind of Indian classical vocal music
KINCOB	fine silk fabric embroidered with gold or silver threads
KOFTA	Indian dish of seasoned minced meat shaped into balls
KOFTGAR	person skilled in inlaying steel with gold
KOFTGARI	art of inlaying steel with gold
KORMA	Indian dish of meat or vegetables braised with yoghurt or cream
LASCAR	sailor from the East Indies
MAIDAN	open space used for meetings and sports
MASALA	mixed spices ground into a paste
MOOLVI	Muslim doctor of the law
MOOLVIE	Muslim doctor of the law
MURDABAD	down with; death to
MUSTH	frenzied sexual excitement in male elephants
NUMDAH	coarse felt
QORMA	Indian dish of meat or vegetables braised with yoghurt or cream
RABI	crop harvested at the end of winter
SAHIB	title placed after a man's name
SAICE	servant who looks after horses
SARPANCH	head of a village council
SEPOY	Indian soldier in the service of the British
SHALWAR	loose-fitting trousers
SHIKAR	hunting
SHIKAREE	hunter
SHIKARI	hunter
SICE	servant who looks after horses
SUBADAH	chief native office in a company of sepoys
SUBADAR	chief native office in a company of sepoys
SUBAH	chief native office in a company of sepoys
SYCE	servant who looks after horses
TAHSIL	administrative division
TALOOKA	subdivision of a district
TALUK	subdivision of a district
TALUKA	subdivision of a district
TAMASHA	show or entertainment
TANDOORI	method of cooking on a spit in a clay oven

Awkward vowel combinations

The problem every Scrabble player faces is an unpromising combination of letters. With the exception of E, drawing duplicates of any vowel can be awkward, as it is often difficult to think of words that use the same vowel twice and are of a length easily playable in Scrabble. In this respect duplicate As and Os are bad enough, but Is and Us are even worse. And because I is one of the most common letters in the game, if you don't get rid of both Is in a single turn, you are highly likely to end up with the same problem in the next round. It's a very good idea, therefore, to have a cache of words that use duplicate vowels so that you can deal with the problem as soon as it arises, allowing you to clear out your rack without falling behind on the scoreboard while missing a turn to play letters.

The lists in this section provide three- and four-letter words with two of each vowel (except E), and five and six-letter words with three or more Us.

As

Three-letter words with two As

AAH	AGA	ALA	AVA	FAA
AAL	AHA	AMA	AWA	MAA
AAS	AIA	ANA	BAA	
ABA	AKA	AUA	CAA	

Four-letter words with two As

AAHS	AMLA	BAAL	KANA	RACA
AALS	ANAL	BAAS	KAPA	RAGA
ABAC	ANAN	BABA	KARA	RAIA
ABAS	ANAS	CAAS	KATA	RAJA
ABBA	ANGA	CABA	KAVA	RANA
ACAI	ANNA	CACA	KAWA	RATA
ACCA	ANOA	CAMA	LAMA	RAYA
ACTA	ANSA	CAPA	LANA	SAGA
ADAW	ANTA	CASA	LAVA	SAMA
AFAR	APAY	CAVA	MAAR	TAAL
AGAR	AQUA	DADA	MAAS	TAHA
AGAS	ARAK	DATA	MALA	TAKA
AGHA	ARAR	FAAN	MAMA	TALA
AGMA	ARBA	FAAS	MANA	TANA
AIAS	AREA	FAVA	MARA	TAPA
AIGA	ARIA	GAGA	MASA	TARA
AJAR	ARNA	GALA	MAYA	TAVA
ALAE	ASAR	GAMA	NAAM	TAWA
ALAN	ASEA	HAAF	NAAN	TAXA
ALAP	ATAP	HAAR	NADA	VARA
ALAR	ATMA	HAHA	NAGA	VASA
ALAS	ATUA	HAKA	NALA	WAAC
ALAY	AULA	JAAP	NANA	WAKA
ALBA	AURA	JAFA	NAPA	WAWA
ALFA	AVAL	JAGA	PAAL	YAAR
ALGA	AVAS	JAVA	PACA	YABA
ALMA	AWAY	KAAL	PAPA	
AMAH	AXAL	KAAS	PARA	
AMAS	AYAH	KAKA	PAUA	
AMIA	AZAN	KAMA	PAWA	

Five-letter words with three As

ABACA	AFARA	ALAPA	ARABA	TAATA
ABAKA	AGAMA	ANANA	ASANA	
ABAYA	ALAAP	ANATA	KAAMA	

Six-letter words with three As

ABACAS	ANABAS	BALATA	KABAKA	PANAMA
ABAKAS	ANANAS	BANANA	KABALA	PAPAYA
ABASIA	ANATAS	BARAZA	KABAYA	PATACA
ABAYAS	ANATTA	BATATA	KAMALA	PATAKA
ACACIA	ANTARA	BAZAAR	KANAKA	QABALA
AFARAS	ARABAS	BRAATA	KARAKA	RAMADA
AGAMAS	ARALIA	CABALA	KATANA	SALAAM
AGAPAE	ARCANA	CABANA	LABARA	SAMAAN
AGAPAI	ARGALA	CADAGA	MANAIA	SAMARA
AGGADA	ARMADA	CANADA	MANANA	SATARA
AKATEA	ASANAS	CASABA	MANAWA	TAATAS
AKHARA	ASRAMA	CASAVA	MARACA	TAIAHA
ALAAPS	ATABAL	DAGABA	MASALA	TAMARA
ALALIA	ATAMAN	HALALA	MATATA	TARAMA
ALAPAS	ATAXIA	HAMADA	NAGANA	UJAMAA
ALASKA	AVATAR	HAWALA	PAJAMA	VAHANA
ALBATA	AZALEA	JACANA	PALAMA	WAIATA
ALPACA	BAHADA	JATAKA	PALAPA	ZANANA
AMARNA	BAJADA	KAAMAS	PANADA	ZAPATA

Es

Four-letter words with three Es

EPEE

Five-letter words with three Es

BELEE	EMEER	GELEE	NEEZE	SEMEE
BESEE	EPEES	HEEZE	PEECE	TEENE
DEERE	ETWEE	KEEVE	PEEPE	TEPEE
DEEVE	EXEEM	LEESE	PEEVE	WEEKE
EERIE	EXEME	LEVEE	PEWEE	WEETE
EEVEN	FEESE	MELEE	REEDE	
ELPEE	FEEZE	NEELE	REEVE	
EMCEE	GEESE	NEESE	RESEE	

Six-letter words with four Es

BEEBEE	PEEWEE	TEEPEE	VEEPEE	WEEWEE

Is

Four-letter words with two Is

BIDI	ILIA	IWIS	NIDI	TIPI
DIVI	IMID	IXIA	NISI	TITI
DIXI	IMPI	KIWI	PIKI	WILI
FIFI	INIA	LIRI	PILI	ZITI
FINI	INTI	MIDI	PIPI	
HILI	IRID	MIHI	SIMI	
HIOI	IRIS	MINI	SIRI	
IBIS	ISIT	MIRI	TIKI	

Five-letter words with two Is

AALII	DIXIT	INDRI	LIPIN	RICIN
ACINI	FICIN	INFIX	LITAI	RIGID
AIDOI	FILMI	INION	LIVID	RISHI
AIOLI	FINIS	INTIL	MEDII	SHIAI
ALIBI	FIRIE	INTIS	MIDIS	SIGIL
AMICI	FIXIT	INWIT	MIHIS	SIMIS
ANIMI	GENII	IODIC	MILIA	SIRIH
ARIKI	GIBLI	IODID	MIMIC	SIRIS
ATIGI	HIKOI	IODIN	MINIM	TEIID
BIALI	HIOIS	IONIC	MINIS	TIBIA
BIDIS	IAMBI	IRIDS	MIRIN	TIKIS
BIFID	ICIER	IRING	MITIS	TIMID
BIKIE	ICILY	ISSEI	MODII	TIPIS
BINDI	ICING	IVIED	NIHIL	TITIS
BINIT	ICTIC	IVIES	NIMBI	TORII
BIVIA	IDIOM	IXIAS	NISEI	VIGIA
BLINI	IDIOT	JINNI	NITID	VIGIL
CEILI	ILIAC	KIBBI	NIXIE	VILLI
CHILI	ILIAD	KIBEI	OBIIT	VINIC
CILIA	ILIAL	KIKOI	OIDIA	VIRID
CIPPI	ILIUM	KILIM	ORIBI	VISIE
CIRRI	IMARI	KININ	PIING	VISIT
CIVIC	IMIDE	KIRRI	PIKIS	VIVID
CIVIE	IMIDO	KIWIS	PILEI	VIZIR
CIVIL	IMIDS	LIBRI	PILIS	WIFIE
DIDIE	IMINE	LICHI	PIPIS	WILIS
DIGIT	IMINO	LICIT	PIPIT	YITIE
DILLI	IMMIT	LIKIN	PIRAI	ZIMBI
DINIC	IMMIX	LIMBI	PIXIE	ZITIS
DISCI	IMPIS	LIMIT	PRIMI	ZIZIT
DIVIS	IMSHI	LININ	RADII	
DIXIE	INDIE	LIPID	REIKI	

Six-letter words with three Is

BIKINI	IRIDIC	IRITIS	NIGIRI	
IMIDIC	IRITIC	MIRITI	TIRITI	

Os

Five-letter words with three Os

OVOLO	POTOO

Six-letter words with three or more Os

BONOBO	COOCOO	GOOROO	LOBOLO	POTOOS
BOOBOO	COROZO	HOLLOO	MOKORO	ROCOCO
BOOCOO	DOOCOT	HOODOO	MONOAO	ROTOLO
BOOHOO	DOODOO	HOOPOE	MOOLOO	VOODOO
BOOKOO	DOOWOP	HOOPOO	OOLOGY	ZOOZOO
COCOON	FORHOO	HOOROO	OOLONG	
COMODO	GOOGOL	KOODOO	OVOLOS	

Us

Three-letter words with two Us

ULU	UMU	UTU

Four-letter words with two Us

BUBU	KUDU	LULU	RURU	URUS
FUGU	KUKU	MUMU	SULU	UTUS
GURU	KURU	PUDU	SUSU	WUDU
HUHU	KUTU	PUKU	TUTU	YUZU
JUJU	KUZU	PULU	ULUS	ZULU
JUKU	LUAU	PUPU	UNAU	

Five-letter words with two or more Us

AHURU	FUGUS	KUZUS	RUBUS	UNGUM
AUGUR	GURUS	LUAUS	RURUS	UPRUN
AURUM	HUDUD	LULUS	SULUS	URUBU
BUBUS	HUHUS	LUPUS	SUNUP	USQUE
BUCHU	HUMUS	LUSUS	SUSUS	USUAL
BUCKU	JUGUM	MUCUS	TUKTU	USURE
BUNDU	JUJUS	MUMUS	TUQUE	USURP
BUSSU	JUKUS	MUNTU	TUTUS	USURY
BUTUT	KAURU	PUDUS	UHURU	UVULA
CUTUP	KUDUS	PUKUS	UNAUS	VOULU
DUFUS	KUDZU	PULUS	UNCUS	WUDUS
DURUM	KUKUS	PUPUS	UNCUT	WUSHU
FUCUS	KURUS	QUEUE	UNDUE	YUZUS
FUGUE	KUTUS	QUIPU	UNDUG	ZULUS

Six-letter words with three Us

MUTUUM	URUBUS
UHURUS	

Light words

While duplicate vowels on your rack can be a real pain, having too many vowels in general can be frustrating. For this reason, it's helpful to have a number of 'light' words up your sleeve – words that contain a high proportion of vowels. The lists of light words include words from two to eight letters, of which more than half are vowels. Words of four or more letters are listed alphabetically according to the vowels they contain.

Two-letter words (two vowels)

AA	AI	EE	OE	OO
AE	EA	IO	OI	OU

Three-letter words (three vowels)

AIA AUA AUE EAU

Four-letter words (three vowels or more)

AAE ALAE AREA ASEA
AAI ACAI AIAS AIGA AMIA ARIA RAIA
AAO ANOA
AAU AQUA ATUA AULA AURA PAUA
AEE AGEE AJEE AKEE ALEE AWEE EALE EASE EAVE
AEI AIDE AINE EINA IDEA ILEA KAIE VIAE
AEO AEON AERO ALOE EOAN ODEA OLEA TOEA ZOEA
AEU AGUE AUNE BEAU EAUS EAUX UREA UVAE UVEA
AII ILIA INIA IXIA
AIO AGIO CIAO IOTA JIAO MOAI NAOI OBIA OHIA
AIU AITU HUIA KUIA QUAI UNAI
AOU AUTO OUMA OUPA URAO
AUU LUAU UNAU
EEE EPEE
EEI EIDE EINE IDEE
EEO EVOE OGEE
EEU EMEU EUGE
EIO ONIE
EIOU EUOI
EIU ETUI IURE LIEU
EOO OBOE OLEO OOSE OOZE
EOU EURO MEOU MOUE ROUE
IIO HIOI
IOO MOOI OLIO
OOU OUZO

Five-letter words (four vowels)

AAEE AREAE
AAEI AECIA
AAEO ZOAEA
AAEU AQUAE AURAE
AAII AALII
AEEI AERIE AINEE
AEEO ZOEAE
AEIU ADIEU AUREI URAEI
AEOO ZOOEA
AIIO AIDOI AIOLI OIDIA
AIOU AUDIO AULOI MIAOU OUIJA
EEEI EERIE
EEOO COOEE
EEUU QUEUE
EIOO LOOIE OORIE
EIOU LOUIE OURIE

Six-letter words (four vowels or more)

AAAA ARAARA ATAATA
AAAE AGAPAE AKATEA AZALEA
AAAI ABASIA ACACIA AGAPAI ALALIA ARALIA ATAXIA MANAIA TAIAHA WAIATA
AAAU UJAMAA
AAEE AERATE AKEAKE AMEBAE EATAGE GALEAE PALEAE PERAEA TALEAE
AAEEO ZOAEAE
AAEI ABELIA ACEDIA AECIAL AERIAL ALEXIA AMELIA ANEMIA ARAISE AVAILE AVIATE FACIAE IDEATA LAMIAE REALIA TAENIA
AAEO AGORAE AMOEBA AORTAE APNOEA AREOLA CAEOMA COBAEA OARAGE OZAENA ZOAEAS
AAEU ACUATE ALULAE AUBADE AURATE BATEAU BAUERA CADEAU CAUDAE CAUSAE FAUNAE GATEAU LAURAE NAUSEA
AAII AALIIS HAIKAI KAIKAI ZAIKAI
AAIO ADAGIO AIKONA ALODIA ALOGIA ANOPIA ANOXIA APORIA ASIAGO ATOCIA ATONIA COAITA LAOGAI ORARIA TAIHOA ZOARIA
AAIU ABULIA AMUSIA ANURIA AUDIAL AUMAIL GUAIAC IGUANA QUALIA UAKARI URANIA WAIRUA YAUTIA
AAOO MANOAO MAOMAO
AAOU ACAJOU AGOUTA AMADOU AOUDAD AURORA OUBAAS
AAUU AUCUBA TUATUA
AEEE HEALEE
AEEI AEDILE

AEDINE	SAIKEI	DOUANE	EPOPEE	COORIE
AERIED	TIBIAE	OPAQUE	**EEEU** EKUELE	COOTIE
AERIER	**AEIO** AEONIC	OUTAGE	EMEUTE	DOOBIE
AERIES	ANOMIE	OUTATE	**EEII** FEIRIE	DOOLIE
APIECE	ARIOSE	OUTEAT	HEINIE	DOOZIE
BAILEE	AZIONE	ZOUAVE	KIEKIE	EXODOI
BEANIE	BOATIE	**AEUU** AUREUS	KIERIE	FLOOIE
DEARIE	CODEIA	AUTEUR	MEINIE	FOODIE
DEAWIE	EIDOLA	BUREAU	MIELIE	FOOTIE
EASIED	EOLIAN	URAEUS	NEINEI	GOODIE
EASIER	EONIAN	UVULAE	WIENIE	GOOIER
EASIES	EPIZOA	**AIIO** AIKIDO	**EEIO** EOSINE	GOOLIE
EPEIRA	FEIJOA	AIOLIS	ETOILE	GOONIE
FAERIE	GOALIE	ARIOSI	LOERIE	GOORIE
FERIAE	HOAGIE	DAIMIO	OLEINE	HOODIE
HEARIE	IODATE	MOIRAI	OREIDE	HOOLIE
IDEAED	LEIPOA	**AIIU** TAUIWI	SOIREE	IONONE
IDEATE	OAKIER	**AIOO** ARIOSO	TOEBIE	KOOKIE
KEAVIE	OAKIES	BOOHAI	TOEIER	LOOIES
LAESIE	OARIER	HOODIA	VOIDEE	LOONIE
MEALIE	OBELIA	OOIDAL	**EEIU** ECURIE	LOOSIE
MEANIE	OPIATE	OOMIAC	EPUISE	NOOGIE
MEDIAE	ROADIE	OOMIAK	EQUINE	NOOKIE
PEREIA	ROARIE	OORALI	EQUIPE	OOFIER
REDIAE	SOAPIE	OORIAL	UREIDE	OOLITE
SEMEIA	ZOECIA	**AIOU** AGOUTI	**EEOO** BOOTEE	OORIER
TENIAE	**AEIU** ACULEI	AUDIOS	COOEED	OOSIER
AEEO AEROBE	ADIEUS	BAGUIO	COOEES	OOZIER
APOGEE	ADIEUX	GIAOUR	DOOLEE	ORIOLE
AREOLE	AECIUM	MIAOUS	SOOGEE	OROIDE
COATEE	AGUISE	OUIJAS	TOETOE	OTIOSE
ELODEA	AGUIZE	OURALI	**EEOU** COULEE	ROOFIE
EVOVAE	AUDILE	OURARI	COUPEE	ROOKIE
FOVEAE	AUGITE	QUINOA	EVOLUE	ROOMIE
GOATEE	AUNTIE	SOUARI	MEOUED	SOOGIE
OCREAE	CAIQUE	UTOPIA	OEUVRE	TOONIE
OEDEMA	CURIAE	**AOOO** MONOAO	OUTSEE	TOORIE
OLEATE	DAUTIE	**AOOU** VAUDOO	TOUPEE	WOODIE
AEEOO ZOOEAE	ELUVIA	**AOUU** AUROUS	**EEUU** QUEUED	WOOLIE
AEEOUU EUOUAE	EQUALI	AUSUBO	QUEUER	WOOPIE
AEEU AEMULE	EUCAIN	TAUHOU	QUEUES	ZOOIER
AENEUS	EXUVIA	**EEEE** BEEBEE	**EIIO** IODIDE	**EIOU** BOUGIE
AVENUE	GAUCIE	PEEWEE	IODINE	COURIE
BAUBEE	GUINEA	TEEPEE	IODISE	FOULIE
ELUATE	HAIQUE	VEEPEE	IODIZE	LOUIES
EPAULE	SAIQUE	WEEWEE	IOLITE	LOURIE
EQUATE	SAULIE	**EEEI** DEEPIE	IONISE	MOUSIE
EUPNEA	TAUPIE	EELIER	IONIZE	OUGLIE
EUREKA	UNCIAE	EERIER	OILIER	OUREBI
FEAGUE	UREDIA	FEERIE	**EIIU** EURIPI	OURIER
HEAUME	UREMIA	HEEZIE	MILIEU	OUTLIE
LEAGUE	**AEOO** AMOOVE	JEELIE	QUINIE	OUTVIE
QUAERE	ROADEO	KEELIE	**EIOO** BLOOIE	POURIE
QUELEA	ZOOEAL	MEEMIE	BOOBIE	SOUTIE
RESEAU	ZOOEAS	PEERIE	BOODIE	TOURIE
UNEASE	**AEOU** AERUGO	REEKIE	BOOGIE	TOUTIE
UREASE	AROUSE	SEELIE	BOOKIE	**EIUU** UBIQUE
AEII AIRIER	AUTOED	WEENIE	BOOTIE	UNIQUE
BAILIE	AVOURE	WEEPIE	COOKIE	**EOOO** HOOPOE
LIAISE	COTEAU	**EEEO** EOCENE	COOLIE	**EOOU** QUOOKE

EOUU	UVEOUS	**IIUU**	BUIBUI		BOOCOO		HOOPOO		ROUCOU

EOUU UVEOUS	**IIUU** BUIBUI	BOOCOO	HOOPOO	ROUCOU
IIOO OPIOID	PIUPIU	BOOHOO	HOOROO	VOUDOU
PIOPIO	**IOOU** IODOUS	BOOKOO	KOODOO	**UUUU** MUUMUU
TOITOI	KOUROI	COOCOO	MOOLOO	
IIOU BINIOU	ODIOUS	DOODOO	VOODOO	
IONIUM	ORIHOU	GOOROO	ZOOZOO	
OIDIUM	**OOOO** BOOBOO	HOODOO	**OOUU** BOUBOU	

Seven-letter words (five vowels or more)

AAAEI ANAEMIA		EUTAXIA	**AEEIU** AUDITEE	**AEIOU** DOULEIA
AAAIU AQUARIA		URAEMIA	EUCAINE	EULOGIA
AAEEI TAENIAE	**AAEOU** AUREOLA	EUGARIE	MIAOUED
AAEEO AMOEBAE	AURORAE	EUGENIA	MOINEAU
AREOLAE	**AAIIO** DIANOIA	EUTEXIA	SEQUOIA
AAEEU AUREATE	**AAIOU** ABOULIA	EXUVIAE	**AEOUU** AQUEOUS
AAEII AECIDIA	OUABAIN	**AEEOO** KOEKOEA	AUTOCUE
AAEIO AEOLIAN	OUAKARI	**AEEOU** AENEOUS	COUTEAU
AEONIAN	RAOULIA	AUREOLE	NOUVEAU
AEROBIA	SAOUARI	EUPNOEA	ROULEAU
OLEARIA	**AEEEI** ALIENEE	**AEEOUU** EUOUAES	**AIOOO** OOGONIA
AAEIU ACEQUIA	EATERIE	**AEIIO** EPINAOI	**AIOUU** OUGUIYA
AGEUSIA	**AEEEU** EVACUEE	**AEIIU** EQUINIA	**EEEIU** EPUISEE
AURELIA	**AEEII** AIERIES	**AEIOO** IPOMOEA	QUEENIE
CAMAIEU	**AEEIO** ETAERIO	ZOOECIA	**IIIOO** OIDIOID

Eight-letter words (five vowels or more)

AAAAE ANABAENA		DEAERATE		SEAQUAKE		ABOITEAU
AAAAI ARAPAIMA		HETAERAE	**AAEII** ACIDEMIA	**AAEIU** ACAULINE
ATARAXIA	**AAEEI** ACIERAGE	ACTINIAE	ACEQUIAS
KAMAAINA	ACIERATE	AECIDIAL	ACICULAE
AAAEE KAREAREA	AGACERIE	AKINESIA	AGEUSIAS
AAAEI ACADEMIA	AGENESIA	APIARIES	ALLELUIA
ACHAENIA	ALIENAGE	AVIANISE	AUBRETIA
ANAEMIAS	ALIENATE	AVIANIZE	AUBRIETA
ASSEGAAI	AWEARIED	AVIARIES	AUMAILED
MAZAEDIA	EMACIATE	CAVIARIE	AURELIAN
AAAEO PARANOEA	ENCAENIA	FILARIAE	AURELIAS
AAAEU ACAUDATE	EPIGAEAL	HETAIRAI	CAMAIEUX
AGUACATE	EPIGAEAN	HETAIRIA	DIAPAUSE
AQUACADE	ERADIATE	LACINIAE	EPIFAUNA
PAHAUTEA	FACETIAE	LIPAEMIA	EUTAXIAS
AAAII APIARIAN	HAEREMAI	VIRAEMIA	INAURATE
APIMANIA	TAENIATE	**AAEIO** AERATION	INFAUNAE
RADIALIA	**AAEEO** AMOEBEAN	AGIOTAGE	MAIREHAU
AAAIO ALOCASIA	ANAEROBE	ALOPECIA	MAUVAISE
PARANOIA	AREOLATE	ANOREXIA	PERIAGUA
AAAIU ADULARIA	OEDEMATA	ANOXEMIA	TAQUERIA
AQUARIAL	**AAEEOU** AUREOLAE	APOGAEIC	URAEMIAS
AQUARIAN	**AAEEU** ACULEATE	AZOTEMIA	**AAEOU** ACAULOSE
AULARIAN	ADEQUATE	CAPOEIRA	AERONAUT
AVIFAUNA	CAESURAE	EGOMANIA	ANALOGUE
MAIASAUR	ECAUDATE	METANOIA	AQUATONE
SAPUCAIA	EVACUATE	OLEARIAS	ARACEOUS
AAAOU AUTOMATA	EVALUATE	PAROEMIA	ARANEOUS
AAAUU AQUANAUT	LAUREATE	TOXAEMIA	AUREOLAS
KAUMATUA	NAUSEATE	ZABAIONE	AUROREAN
AAEEE AMEERATE	PAENULAE	**AAEIOU** ABOIDEAU	AUTOCADE

	AUTOMATE		IDEATIVE
	MAUSOLEA		INERTIAE
	OCEANAUT		INFERIAE
	OUBAASES		METAIRIE
AAEUU	FAUNULAE		WEIGELIA
	QUAALUDE	**AEEIO**	ACOEMETI
	USQUABAE		AEROLITE
AAIII	MILIARIA		AMEIOSES
	NIRAMIAI		ETAERIOS
AAIIO	APOSITIA		ETIOLATE
	AVIATION		FOEDARIE
	DIANOIAS		OEDIPEAN
	MAIOLICA		OEILLADE
	ZOIATRIA		PAEONIES
AAIIU	ACIDURIA	**AEEIOO**	EPOPOEIA
	AUXILIAR	**AEEIOU**	EULOGIAE
	BAUHINIA	**AEEIU**	ACQUIREE
	IGUANIAN		AEDICULE
	QUILLAIA		AGUELIKE
	UNIAXIAL		AUDIENCE
AAIOO	ANOOPSIA		AUDITEES
	APOLOGIA		BANLIEUE
	ZOOMANIA		BEAUTIED
AAIOU	ABOULIAS		BEAUTIES
	AUTACOID		BEAUXITE
	AUTOPSIA		CAUSERIE
	AZOTURIA		DECIDUAE
	CARIACOU		ELUVIATE
	GUAIACOL		EQUALISE
	OUABAINS		EQUALIZE
	OUAKARIS		EQUIPAGE
	PAROUSIA		EQUISETA
	RAOULIAS		EUCAINES
	SAOUARIS		EUGARIES
AAIUU	AQUARIUM		EUGENIAS
	AURICULA		EUPEPSIA
	GUAIACUM		EUTAXIES
AAOUU	ACAULOUS		EUTAXITE
AEEEE	EMEERATE		EUTEXIAS
	RELEASEE		EXEQUIAL
AEEEI	ALIENEES		EXUVIATE
	DETAINEE		LEUCEMIA
	EARPIECE		LEUKEMIA
	EATERIES		MAUVEINE
	EMERITAE		QUEASIER
	EXAMINEE		QUEAZIER
	SEAPIECE		UNEASIER
AEEEU	AGUEWEED		UNIDEAED
	EMERAUDE	**AEEOO**	AEROTONE
	EVACUEES		FOVEOLAE
	SEQUELAE		OOGAMETE
AEEII	AEGIRINE		OOTHECAE
	AEGIRITE		PAHOEHOE
	AERIFIED		PEEKABOO
	AERIFIES		PEEKAPOO
	ASEITIES		ZOOGLEAE
	EPICEDIA	**AEEOU**	AEGLOGUE
	GAIETIES		ALEHOUSE
	IDEALISE		ALEURONE
	IDEALIZE		AUREOLED

	AUREOLES		EUPHONIA
	COEQUATE		EUPHORIA
	EUDAEMON		EUSOCIAL
	EUPNOEAS		EXONUMIA
	FEATEOUS		JALOUSIE
	JEALOUSE		MOINEAUS
	OUTEATEN		ODALIQUE
	REAROUSE		OUTRAISE
	TEAHOUSE		POULAINE
AEEUU	NEURULAE		SAUTOIRE
	URAEUSES		SEQUOIAS
	USQUEBAE		THIOUREA
AEIII	INITIATE	**AEIUU**	AUGURIES
	RETIARII		AUTUNITE
AEIIO	AMEIOSIS		FAUTEUIL
	HEMIOLIA	**AEOOO**	ZOOGLOEA
	HEMIOPIA	**AEOOU**	ACOELOUS
	IBOGAINE		APOLOGUE
	IDEATION		AUTOSOME
	IODINATE		POACEOUS
	NOTITIAE	**AEOUU**	AUTOCUES
	OLIGEMIA		AUTOTUNE
	TAENIOID		BEAUCOUP
AEIIU	ACUITIES		COUTEAUX
	AECIDIUM		FEATUOUS
	AIGUILLE		HUAQUERO
	AQUILINE		NAUSEOUS
	AUDITIVE		NOUVEAUX
	AURIFIED		OUTARGUE
	AURIFIES		OUTVALUE
	EQUINIAS		ROULEAUS
	INDUCIAE		ROULEAUX
	INDUVIAE		ROUSSEAU
	MAIEUTIC	**AIIIO**	OITICICA
	MINUTIAE	**AIIIU**	DAIQUIRI
	QUINIELA	**AIIOO**	AVOISION
	SILIQUAE		IODATION
	UINTAITE	**AIIOU**	AUDITION
	UREDINIA		MIAOUING
	URINEMIA		OLIGURIA
AEIOO	AEROFOIL	**AIOOO**	OOGONIAL
	AMOEBOID		ORATORIO
	COENOBIA		ZOONOMIA
	IPOMOEAS	**AIOOU**	AUTOCOID
	MOVIEOLA		AUTOGIRO
	OOGAMIES		ORACIOUS
	OVARIOLE		OVARIOUS
	PATOOTIE	**AIOUU**	CAUTIOUS
AEIOU	AEQUORIN		GUAIOCUM
	AEROBIUM		OUGUIYAS
	AGOUTIES		SUBAUDIO
	CAESIOUS	**AOOOU**	OOGAMOUS
	DIALOGUE	**AOOUU**	ANOUROUS
	DOUANIER		COUMAROU
	DOULEIAS	**EEEEI**	EYEPIECE
	EDACIOUS	**EEEEU**	SQUEEGEE
	EQUATION	**EEEIO**	EOLIENNE
	EUDAIMON		TOEPIECE
	EULOGIAS	**EEEIU**	EUXENITE
	EUPHOBIA		EXEQUIES

	MEUNIERE		PRIEDIEU	**EEIUU** EUPHUISE		EUROPIUM
	QUEENIER		QUIETIVE	EUPHUIZE		EXIGUOUS
	QUEENIES		UBIETIES	QUEUEING		OUTGUIDE
	QUEENITE	**EEIOO** COOEEING	QUIETUDE		TENUIOUS
	UNSEELIE		EOLIPILE	**EEOOU** EURONOTE	**E0000** BOOHOOED
EEEOU	ETOUFFEE		MOVIEOKE	**EIIIO** IDIOCIES		HOODOOED
EEIIO	BOISERIE		OOGENIES	**EIIOO** ONIONIER		VOODOOED
	DEIONISE		OPTIONEE	**EIIOU** DIECIOUS	**EOOUU** DUOLOGUE
	DEIONIZE	**EEIOU** BOUDERIE	EXIMIOUS		EUROKOUS
	DIOECIES		EPIGEOUS	FILIOQUE		OUTHOUSE
	EBIONISE		EPILOGUE	UNIONISE		OUTQUOTE
	EBIONIZE		EQUIVOKE	UNIONIZE		VOUDOUED
	EGOITIES		ETOURDIE	**EIIUU** BIUNIQUE	**IIIOO** PIHOIHOI
	EOLIPILE		EULOGIES	**EI000** FORHOOIE	**IIIOU** OUISTITI
	EPIZOITE		EULOGISE	OOLOGIES	**IIOOU** DIOICOUS
	ERIONITE		EULOGIZE	**EIOOU** IDONEOUS		DOUPIONI
	MEIONITE		EUPNOEIC	ISOLOGUE	**IOOOU** OOGONIUM
	MOIETIES		EUROKIES	OUTVOICE	**IOOUU** BOUSOUKI
	OILERIES		ICEHOUSE	ZOOECIUM		BOUZOUKI
	OSIERIES		OBSEQUIE	**EIOUU** BOUTIQUE		UXORIOUS
EEIIU	EQUITIES		OUVRIERE	EULOGIUM	**IOUUU** USURIOUS

Awkward consonant combinations

Certain consonants can be just as awkward as vowels when they show up more than one at a time on your rack. The following lists provide words of three to five letters with doubles of B, C, F, H, V, W and Y (where such words exist: there are no three-letter words with two Cs, Vs or Ys).

Bs

Three-letter words with two Bs

ABB	BIB	BOB	BUB	EBB

Four-letter words with two Bs

ABBA	BABY	BLUB	BUBA	COBB
ABBE	BARB	BOAB	BUBO	EBBS
ABBS	BIBS	BOBA	BUBS	JIBB
BABA	BLAB	BOBS	BUBU	SIBB
BABE	BLEB	BOMB	BULB	
BABU	BLOB	BOOB	BURB	

Five-letter words with two or more Bs

ABBAS	BABOO	BIBBS	BLURB	BOMBS
ABBED	BABUL	BIBLE	BOABS	BOOBS
ABBES	BABUS	BILBO	BOBAC	BOOBY
ABBEY	BAMBI	BILBY	BOBAK	BRIBE
ABBOT	BARBE	BIMBO	BOBAS	BUBAL
BABAS	BARBS	BLABS	BOBBY	BUBAS
BABEL	BARBY	BLEBS	BOBOL	BUBBA
BABES	BEBOP	BLOBS	BOMBE	BUBBY
BABKA	BEROB	BLUBS	BOMBO	BUBUS

BULBS	DEBBY	HOBBY	NABOB	TABBY
BUMBO	DIBBS	HUBBY	NOBBY	TUBBY
BURBS	DOBBY	JIBBS	NUBBY	WEBBY
BUSBY	DUBBO	KABAB	RABBI	YABBA
CABBY	EBBED	KABOB	REBBE	YABBY
CABOB	EBBET	KEBAB	RIBBY	YOBBO
COBBS	FUBBY	KEBOB	RUBBY	ZEBUB
COBBY	GABBY	KIBBE	SIBBS	
CUBBY	GOBBI	KIBBI	SLUBB	
CUBEB	GOBBO	LOBBY	SUBBY	
DABBA	GOBBY	MOBBY	SYBBE	

Cs

Four-letter words with two Cs

ACCA	CHIC	COCH	CROC	OCCY
CACA	CHOC	COCK	ECCE	
CECA	COCA	COCO	ECCO	

Five-letter words with two or more Cs

ACCAS	CECUM	CIVIC	COOCH	CYNIC
ACCOY	CERCI	CLACH	COSEC	ICTIC
ACMIC	CERIC	CLACK	COUCH	LECCY
ACOCK	CHACE	CLECK	CRACK	MECCA
BACCA	CHACK	CLICK	CRAIC	MUCIC
BACCO	CHACO	CLOCK	CRICK	OCCAM
BACCY	CHECK	CLUCK	CROCI	OCCUR
BICCY	CHICA	COACH	CROCK	PICCY
BOCCA	CHICH	COACT	CROCS	RECCE
BOCCE	CHICK	COCAS	CRUCK	RECCO
BOCCI	CHICO	COCCI	CUBIC	RECCY
CABOC	CHICS	COCCO	CULCH	SECCO
CACAO	CHOCK	COCKS	CUMEC	SUCCI
CACAS	CHOCO	COCKY	CURCH	TICCA
CACHE	CHOCS	COCOA	CUSEC	WICCA
CACKY	CHUCK	COCOS	CUTCH	YACCA
CACTI	CINCH	CODEC	CWTCH	YECCH
CAECA	CINCT	COLIC	CYCAD	YUCCA
CASCO	CIRCA	COMIC	CYCAS	YUCCH
CATCH	CIRCS	CONCH	CYCLE	ZOCCO
CECAL	CISCO	CONIC	CYCLO	

Fs

Three-letter words with two Fs

AFF	EFF	IFF	OFF

Four-letter words with two or more Fs

AFFY	CAFF	DOFF	FIFE	GUFF
BAFF	COFF	DUFF	FIFI	HAFF
BIFF	CUFF	EFFS	FUFF	HUFF
BOFF	DAFF	FAFF	GAFF	IFFY
BUFF	DIFF	FIEF	GOFF	JEFF

JIFF	MIFF	OFFS	RUFF	WAFF
KIFF	MUFF	PFFT	TEFF	YAFF
KOFF	NAFF	PUFF	TIFF	ZIFF
LUFF	NIFF	RAFF	TOFF	
MEFF	NUFF	RIFF	TUFF	

Five-letter words with two or more Fs

AFFIX	CUFFS	GLIFF	NIFFY	SNUFF
BAFFS	DAFFS	GOFFS	NUFFS	SOWFF
BAFFY	DAFFY	GRAFF	NYAFF	SPIFF
BIFFO	DEFFO	GRIFF	OFFAL	STAFF
BIFFS	DIFFS	GRUFF	OFFED	STIFF
BIFFY	DOFFS	GUFFS	OFFER	STUFF
BLAFF	DRAFF	HAFFS	PLUFF	TAFFY
BLUFF	DUFFS	HOWFF	PUFFS	TEFFS
BOFFO	EFFED	HUFFS	PUFFY	TIFFS
BOFFS	FAFFS	HUFFY	QUAFF	TOFFS
BUFFA	FEOFF	JEFFS	QUIFF	TOFFY
BUFFE	FIEFS	JIFFS	RAFFS	TRIFF
BUFFI	FIFED	JIFFY	REFFO	TUFFE
BUFFO	FIFER	KOFFS	RIFFS	TUFFS
BUFFS	FIFES	LUFFA	RUFFE	WAFFS
BUFFY	FIFTH	LUFFS	RUFFS	WAUFF
CAFFS	FIFTY	MEFFS	SCAFF	WHIFF
CHAFF	FLAFF	MIFFS	SCOFF	YAFFS
CHUFF	FLUFF	MIFFY	SCUFF	ZIFFS
CLIFF	FUFFS	MUFFS	SKIFF	
CLOFF	FUFFY	NAFFS	SKOFF	
COFFS	GAFFE	NIFFS	SLUFF	
CUFFO	GAFFS		SNIFF	

Hs

Three-letter words with two Hs

| HAH | HEH | HOH | HUH | SHH |

Four-letter words with two Hs

HAHA	HECH	HISH	HUHU	SHAH
HAHS	HEHS	HOGH	HUNH	
HASH	HETH	HOHA	HUSH	
HATH	HIGH	HOHS	PHOH	

Five-letter words with two Hs

AHIGH	HATHA	HIGHT	HOUGH	PHOHS
CHETH	HAUGH	HILCH	HUHUS	PHPHT
CHICH	HEATH	HITCH	HUMPH	SHAHS
EPHAH	HECHT	HITHE	HUNCH	SHASH
HAHAS	HEIGH	HOGHS	HUSHY	SHCHI
HAITH	HETHS	HOHED	HUTCH	SHISH
HANCH	HEUCH	HOOCH	HYPHA	SHUSH
HARSH	HEUGH	HOOSH	HYTHE	THIGH
HASHY	HEWGH	HORAH	KHAPH	WHICH
HATCH	HIGHS	HOTCH	KHETH	WHISH

Vs

Four-letter words with two Vs

VAVS	VIVA	VIVE	VIVO

Five-letter words with two Vs

BEVVY	LUVVY	VARVE	VIVDA	VOLVA
BIVVY	NAVVY	VERVE	VIVER	VOLVE
CIVVY	SAVVY	VIVAS	VIVES	VULVA
DIVVY	VALVE	VIVAT	VIVID	

Ws

Three-letter words with two Ws

WAW	WOW

Four-letter words with two Ws

WAWA	WAWL	WHEW	WOWF
WAWE	WAWS	WHOW	WOWS

Five-letter words with two Ws

EWHOW	WAWAS	WAWLS	WIDOW	WOWEE
PAWAW	WAWES	WHEWS	WOWED	WRAWL

Ys

Four-letter words with two Ys

EYRY	TYPY	YAYS	YUKY
GYNY	YAWY		

Five-letter words with two Ys

AZYGY	FLYBY	PYGMY	WRYLY	YESTY
BOYSY	GAYLY	SHYLY	XYLYL	YEUKY
BYWAY	GYNNY	SKYEY	YABBY	YIPPY
COYLY	GYPPY	SLYLY	YAMPY	YOLKY
DOYLY	GYPSY	STYMY	YAPPY	YUCKY
DRYLY	HAYEY	THYMY	YAWEY	YUKKY
DYKEY	MYOPY	TYIYN	YAWNY	YUMMY
FEYLY	MYTHY	TYPEY	YECHY	YUPPY

Heavy words

In contrast to light words, 'heavy' words have a high proportion of consonants (Y is used as a vowel in many of these words, but counts as a consonant for our purposes). These lists contain words with no vowels (apart from Y), of two to five letters, and words of six letters that contain either no vowels or only one. Noun plurals ending in S have not been included in these lists.

Two-letter words (no vowels except Y)

BY	FY	KY	MY	SH
CH	HM	MM	NY	ST

Three-letter words (no vowels except Y)

BRR	GYP	PRY	SNY	TWP
CLY	HMM	PST	SPY	TYG
CRY	HYP	PYX	STY	VLY
CWM	LYM	RHY	SWY	WHY
DRY	MYC	SHH	SYN	WRY
FLY	NTH	SHY	THY	WYN
FRY	PHT	SKY	TRY	ZZZ
GYM	PLY	SLY	TSK	

Four-letter words (no vowels except Y)

BRRR	HYMN	PRYS	SPRY	TYPP
BYRL	JYNX	PSST	SYNC	TYPY
CYST	KYND	RYND	SYND	WYCH
FYRD	LYCH	SCRY	SYPH	WYND
GYMP	LYNX	SKRY	TRYP	WYNN
GYNY	MYTH	SKYF	TYMP	XYST
HWYL	PFFT	SKYR	TYND	YMPT

Five-letter words (no vowels except Y)

CHYND	GLYPH	LYNCH	SHYLY	TRYST
CRWTH	GRYPT	MYRRH	SLYLY	WRYLY
CRYPT	GYNNY	MYTHY	STYMY	XYLYL
CWTCH	GYPPY	NYMPH	SYLPH	
DRYLY	GYPSY	PHPHT	SYNCH	
FLYBY	KYDST	PSYCH	SYNTH	
GHYLL	LYMPH	PYGMY	THYMY	

Six-letter words (one vowel)

BLANCH	BRICHT	CHURCH	CRATCH	FLANCH
BLENCH	BRIGHT	CLASPT	CROTCH	FLENCH
BLIGHT	BROWST	CLATCH	CRUNCH	FLETCH
BLINTZ	BRUNCH	CLENCH	CRUTCH	FLIGHT
BLOTCH	CATCHT	CLINCH	CULTCH	FLINCH
BORSCH	CHINCH	CLUNCH	DIRNDL	FLITCH
BORSHT	CHINTS	CLUTCH	DRACHM	FLYSCH
BRANCH	CHINTZ	CRANCH	DRENCH	FRATCH
BRANKS	CHRISM	CRANTS	DROWND	FRENCH

FRICHT	SCHLEP	SHRIMP	SPRACK	STRUNG
FRIGHT	SCHLUB	SHRINK	SPRANG	STRUNT
FROWST	SCHNOZ	SHROFF	SPRAWL	SWARTH
GLITCH	SCHORL	SHROWD	SPREDD	SWATCH
GLUMPS	SCHRIK	SHRUNK	SPRENT	SWITCH
GLUNCH	SCHROD	SHTCHI	SPRING	SWOWND
GRINCH	SCHTIK	SHTETL	SPRINT	TCHICK
GROWTH	SCHULN	SHTICK	SPRITZ	THATCH
GRUMPH	SCHUSS	SHTUCK	SPRONG	THETCH
GRUTCH	SCLAFF	SHTUMM	SPRUNG	THIRST
HIGHTH	SCLIFF	SKARTH	SPRUSH	THRALL
KIRSCH	SCORCH	SKETCH	STANCH	THRANG
KITSCH	SCOTCH	SKITCH	STANCK	THRASH
KLATCH	SCOWTH	SKLENT	STARCH	THRAWN
KLEPHT	SCRAMB	SKLIFF	STENCH	THRESH
KNICKS	SCRAWL	SKRIMP	STIRPS	THRIFT
KNIGHT	SCRAWM	SKRUMP	STITCH	THRILL
KNITCH	SCRAWP	SLATCH	STOWND	THRIST
KRANTZ	SCRIMP	SLIGHT	STRAFF	THRONG
KVETCH	SCRIPT	SLUTCH	STRAMP	THROWN
LENGTH	SCROLL	SMATCH	STRAND	THRUSH
MENSCH	SCRORP	SMIGHT	STRANG	THRUST
MONGST	SCROWL	SMIRCH	STRASS	THWACK
PHLEGM	SCRUFF	SMUTCH	STRATH	THWART
PLANCH	SCRUMP	SNATCH	STRAWN	TIGHTS
PLENCH	SCRUNT	SNITCH	STRESS	TRENCH
PLIGHT	SCULCH	SPARTH	STREWN	TROGGS
PLINTH	SCULPT	SPELTZ	STRICH	TROWTH
PLONGD	SCUTCH	SPERST	STRICK	TSKING
PRANCK	SHLEPP	SPETCH	STRICT	TSKTSK
PROMPT	SHLOCK	SPHINX	STRIFT	TWIGHT
PUTSCH	SHLUMP	SPHYNX	STRING	TWITCH
RHYTHM	SHMOCK	SPIGHT	STRIPT	WARMTH
SCARPH	SHMUCK	SPILTH	STROLL	WHILST
SCARTH	SHNAPS	SPLASH	STROMB	WHISHT
SCATCH	SHRANK	SPLENT	STROND	WRENCH
SCHELM	SHREWD	SPLIFF	STRONG	WRETCH
SCHISM	SHRIFT	SPLINT	STROWN	WRIGHT
SCHIST	SHRILL	SPLOSH	STRUCK	

Chapter 7: Bonus Words

No matter what letters you have on your rack, using all of them in a single turn is usually the best way to score points. The 50-point bonus that you get for using all the letters on your rack is likely to exceed any other score except that from an exceptionally high-scoring word that lands on a triple-word square. For this reason, any serious Scrabble player should devote some effort to mastering 'bonus words' – words of seven or eight letters that will allow you to empty your rack in one go.

This section contains a number of different methods of memorizing words that will help you to scoop up those 50-point bonuses.

Stems and Mnemonics

Knowing whether the letters on your rack can be used to form a word that will use up all your tiles gives you a great advantage in a game. If you know that there is a seven or eight-letter word that fits your letters, then it's simply a matter of decoding the letters. If, on the other hand, you know that there isn't a viable word that you can fit on the board, you won't waste time looking for one. One invaluable way of working out whether your rack can furnish you with a bonus word is to learn with which letters a given rack will combine.

The best method for this is to learn which letters combine with which six-letter and seven-letter 'stems' to form a valid word. This can be a daunting task, but it's made much easier if you concentrate only on the stems that are both likely and rewarding (ie those that are most common, and which will combine with many letters). In the following lists, the best stems have been determined for you, based on an algorithm of likelihood and fruitfulness applied to **Collins Scrabble Words 2005**.

The next step is to devise some mnemonics that will help you to remember this information. To create a mnemonic, simply work the letters that combine with a given stem into a phrase, and then arrange the letters of the stem into a word or words with some connection to the phrase. For example:

AEGINRS goes with A B D C E G H K L M N O P R S T V W Y

So you might come up with:

regains: Polly gets her money back – very well done

Similarly:

EINORST goes with A B C D E G H I J K L N O P R S T U V Y Z

In store: Lazy Jane helps buy good stock every time

Alternatively, form a mnemonic from the stem letters and the letters that **don't** work with it. For example:

AEINST goes with A B C D E F G H I J K L M N O P R S T U V W X Z

So, with reference to James Bond, you could ask:

Y Q **is neat**

Collins Scrabble Lists

This is easy to remember, and it's obvious that Y and Q are the letters in question, and that **IS NEAT** is the stem.

Many veteran Scrabble players will have their own mnemonics, but if you are new to the game, try devising some for yourself from the stems and combining sets listed here. The key is getting a memorable phrase with a strong association with the stem word. This is a great test of your skill with anagrams, and your creativity generally; if you can come up with some good mnemonics, you will be honing your Scrabble skills in the process!

Six-letter stems

The 250 stems given here are listed in alphabetical order, and ranked according to their placing in the algorithm for frequency and fruitfulness.

AAEINT 167

TAENIA	L ANTLIAE	ANIMATE	S ENTASIA
E TAENIAE	M AMENTIA	P PATINAE	TAENIAS

AAELOR 212

AREOLA	E AREOLAE	R AREOLAR	U AUREOLA
C ACEROLA	I OLEARIA	S AREOLAS	

AAENST 204

ANSATE	G AGNATES	M NAMASTE	R ANESTRA
A ANATASE	I ENTASIA	N ANNATES	SANTERA
C CATENAS	TAENIAS	P ANAPEST	V SAVANTE
D ANSATED	L SEALANT	PEASANT	W SEAWANT

AAERST 111

SEARAT	E AERATES	ASTERIA	RETAMAS	R ERRATAS
B ABATERS	G AGRASTE	ATRESIA	N ANESTRA	S SEARATS
ABREAST	GASTREA	K KARATES	SANTERA	U AURATES
C ACATERS	TEARGAS	L TARSEAL	O AEROSAT	W AWAREST
CARATES	I ARISTAE	M AMEARST	P PETARAS	

ABDEIR 227

BRAIDE	BRIGADE	N BANDIER	BARDIES	U DAUBIER
A BRAAIED	L BALDIER	BRAINED	BRAISED	W BAWDIER
C CARBIDE	BEDRAIL	R BARDIER	DARBIES	X AXEBIRD
D BRAIDED	BRAILED	BRAIDER	SEABIRD	
E BEADIER	RAILBED	BRIARED	SIDEBAR	
BEARDIE	RIDABLE	RABIDER	T REDBAIT	
G ABRIDGE	M EMBRAID	S ABIDERS	TRIBADE	

ABEINT 127

BINATE	G BEATING	M AMBIENT	R ATEBRIN	BESAINT
C CABINET	I BAINITE	O NIOBATE	S BANTIES	BESTAIN
E BETAINE	K BEATNIK	P BEPAINT	BASINET	T TABINET

ABEIRT 195

TERBIA	EBRIATE	TRIABLE	S BAITERS	T BATTIER
D REDBAIT	F BAREFIT	N ATEBRIN	BARITES	BIRETTA
TRIBADE	L LIBRATE	R ARBITER	REBAITS	RATBITE
E BEATIER	TABLIER	RAREBIT	TERBIAS	V VIBRATE

ABEORT 169

REBATO	E ABORTEE	P PROBATE	BOATERS	BATTERO
A AEROBAT	L BLOATER	R ABORTER	BORATES	TABORET
D ABORTED	M BROMATE	ARBORET	REBATOS	
BORATED	N BARONET	TABORER	SORBATE	
TABORED	REBOANT	S BOASTER	T ABETTOR	

ACDEIR 226

CARIED	G CADGIER	RADICLE	PERACID	RADICES
A CARDIAE	H CHAIRED	N CAIRNED	R ACRIDER	SIDECAR
B CARBIDE	I ACIDIER	CARNIED	CARRIED	U DECURIA
E DECIARE	L DECRIAL	DANCIER	S CARDIES	
F FARCIED	RADICEL	P EPACRID	DARCIES	

ACEINR 97

CARNIE	DANCIER	L CARLINE	S ARCSINE	CERTAIN
A ACARINE	E CINEREA	M CARMINE	ARSENIC	CREATIN
CARINAE	F FANCIER	N CANNIER	CARNIES	CRINATE
B CARBINE	G ANERGIC	NARCEIN	CERASIN	NACRITE
D CAIRNED	GRECIAN	P CAPRINE	T CANTIER	TACRINE
CARNIED	H ARCHINE	R CARNIER	CERATIN	

ACEINT 161

ENATIC	N ANCIENT	CERTAIN	CANIEST	X INEXACT
B CABINET	O ACONITE	CREATIN	CINEAST	Y CYANITE
H CHANTIE	ANOETIC	CRINATE	T NICTATE	Z ZINCATE
K ANTICKE	P PICANTE	NACRITE	TETANIC	
M EMICANT	R CANTIER	TACRINE	TUNICAE	U TUNICAE
NEMATIC	CERATIN	S ACETINS	V VENATIC	

ACENOT 133

OCTANE	G COAGENT	J JACONET	R ENACTOR	V CENTAVO
C COENACT	COGNATE	L LACTONE	S COSTEAN	
D TACNODE	I ACONITE	N CONNATE	OCTANES	
E ACETONE	ANOETIC	P PATONCE	T ATTONCE	

ACENRT 192

TRANCE	F CANTREF	CRINATE	CARNETS	U CENTAUR
A CATERAN	H CHANTER	NACRITE	NECTARS	UNCRATE
D CANTRED	TRANCHE	TACRINE	RECANTS	UNTRACE
TRANCED	I CANTIER	L CENTRAL	SCANTER	Y ENCRATY
E CENTARE	CERATIN	M CREMANT	TANRECS	NECTARY
CRENATE	CERTAIN	O ENACTOR	TRANCES	
REENACT	CREATIN	S CANTERS	T TRANECT	

ACEORS 202

ROSACE	H CHOREAS	ESCOLAR	CORNEAS	RECOATS
A ROSACEA	ORACHES	ORACLES	EARCONS	U ACEROUS
B BORACES	ROACHES	RECOALS	NARCOSE	CAROUSE
D SARCODE	I CARIOSE	SOLACER	R COARSER	W CROWEAS
E ACEROSE	ORACIES	M AMORCES	CORREAS	X COAXERS
G CARGOES	SCORIAE	N CANOERS	S ROSACES	
CORSAGE	L CLAROES	CARNOSE	T COASTER	
SOCAGER	COALERS	COARSEN	COATERS	

ACEORT 175

RECOAT	I EROTICA	CREATOR	RECOATS
D CORDATE	L LOCATER	REACTOR	U OUTRACE
REDCOAT	N ENACTOR	S COASTER	V OVERACT
E OCREATE	R ACROTER	COATERS	X EXACTOR

ADEEIR 156

REDIAE	C DECIARE	F AREFIED	L LEADIER	READIES
B BEADIER	D DEAIRED	FEDARIE	R READIER	W WEARIED
BEARDIE	READIED	H HEADIER	S DEARIES	

ADEELT 242

ELATED	F DEFLATE	N EDENTAL	REDEALT	V VALETED
A DEALATE	G GELATED	LATENED	RELATED	VELATED
B BELATED	LEGATED	P PETALED	TREADLE	X EXALTED
BLEATED	TEAGLED	PLEATED	S DELATES	Z TEAZLED
C CLEATED	M MEDALET	R ALERTED	STEALED	
D DELATED	METALED	ALTERED	T LADETTE	

ADEERS 136

SEARED	H ADHERES	LEADERS	SPEARED	REASTED
B BEADERS	HEADERS	REDEALS	R DREARES	REDATES
DEBASER	HEARSED	M REMADES	READERS	SEDATER
SABERED	HEDERAS	REMEADS	REDEARS	STEARED
C CREASED	SHEARED	SMEARED	REDSEAR	TASERED
DECARES	I DEARIES	N DEANERS	REREADS	V ADVERSE
SEARCED	READIES	ENDEARS	S RESEDAS	EVADERS
D DEADERS	K DEKARES	O OREADES	T DEAREST	W DRAWEES
G DRAGEES	SKEARED	P PREASED	DERATES	RESAWED
GREASED	L DEALERS	RESPADE	ESTRADE	

ADEERT 115

TEARED	CEDRATE	H EARTHED	P ADEPTER	ESTRADE
A AERATED	CERATED	HEARTED	PREDATE	REASTED
B BERATED	CREATED	L ALERTED	RETAPED	REDATES
BETREAD	REACTED	ALTERED	TAPERED	SEDATER
DEBATER	D DERATED	REDEALT	R RETREAD	STEARED
REBATED	REDATED	RELATED	TREADER	TASERED
TABERED	TREADED	TREADLE	S DEAREST	T ARETTED
C CATERED	F DRAFTEE	M REMATED	DERATES	TREATED

| V AVERTED | W DEWATER | WATERED | X RETAXED |
| TAVERED | TARWEED | | |

ADEEST 179

TEASED	F DEAFEST	STEALED	REASTED	U SAUTEED
B BESTEAD	DEFASTE	M STEAMED	REDATES	W SWEATED
DEBATES	DEFEATS	N STANDEE	SEDATER	Y YEASTED
C TEDESCA	FEASTED	STEANED	STEARED	
D DEADEST	H HEADSET	R DEAREST	TASERED	
SEDATED	I IDEATES	DERATES	S SEDATES	
STEADED	L DELATES	ESTRADE	T ESTATED	

ADEGOT 209

TOGAED	F FAGOTED	N TANGOED	DOTAGES	
E DOGEATE	I GODETIA	R GAROTED	T TOGATED	
GOATEED	L GLOATED	S DOGATES		

ADEILN 144

NAILED	G ALIGNED	INHALED	P PLAINED	UNIDEAL
C INLACED	DEALING	K KNAIDEL	S DENIALS	V ANDVILE
E ALIENED	LEADING	N ANNELID	SNAILED	ANVILED
DELAINE	H HIELAND	LINDANE	U ALIUNDE	X INDEXAL

ADEILR 23

RELAID	RADICEL	IRIDEAL	R LARDIER	U UREDIAL
A RADIALE	RADICLE	L DALLIER	S DERAILS	V RIVALED
B BALDIER	D DIEDRAL	DIALLER	DIALERS	VALIDER
BEDRAIL	DRAILED	RALLIED	REDIALS	Y READILY
BRAILED	E LEADIER	O DARIOLE	SIDERAL	
RAILBED	G GLADIER	P LIPREAD	T DILATER	
RIDABLE	GLAIRED	PEDRAIL	REDTAIL	
C DECRIAL	I DELIRIA	PREDIAL	TRAILED	

ADEILS 62

SAILED	G SILAGED	M MAELIDS	LAIPSED	DEASILS
B BALDIES	H HALIDES	MEDIALS	LAPIDES	T DETAILS
DIABLES	I DAILIES	MISDEAL	PAIDLES	DILATES
DISABLE	LIAISED	MISLEAD	PALSIED	U AUDILES
C SCAILED	SEDILIA	N DENIALS	PLEIADS	DEASIUL
D DAIDLES	K SKAILED	SNAILED	R DERAILS	DUALISE
LADDIES	L DALLIES	O DEASOIL	DIALERS	V DEVISAL
E AEDILES	DISLEAL	ISOLEAD	REDIALS	Y DIALYSE
DEISEAL	LALDIES	P ALIPEDS	SIDERAL	EYLIADS
F DISLEAF	SALLIED	ELAPIDS	S AIDLESS	

ADEINR 5

RANDIE		DRAINED		READING	R	DRAINER	U	UNAIRED
A	ARANEID	F	FRIANDE	H	HANDIER		RANDIER		URANIDE
B	BANDIER	G	AREDING	I	DENARII	S	RANDIES	V	INVADER
	BRAINED		DEARING	M	ADERMIN		SANDIER		RAVINED
C	CAIRNED		DERAIGN		INARMED		SARDINE		
	CARNIED		EARDING	N	NARDINE	T	ANTIRED		
	DANCIER		GRADINE	O	ANEROID		DETRAIN		
D	DANDIER		GRAINED	P	PARDINE		TRAINED		

ADEINS 27

SDAINE		E	ANISEED		MEDIANS		PANSIED		INSTEAD
A	NAIADES	F	FADEINS		MEDINAS		SPAINED		NIDATES
B	BANDIES	G	AGNISED		SIDEMAN	R	RANDIES		SAINTED
	BASINED	K	KANDIES	N	DANNIES		SANDIER		SATINED
C	CANDIES	L	DENIALS	O	ADONISE		SARDINE		STAINED
	INCASED		SNAILED		ANODISE	S	SDAINES	V	INVADES
D	DANDIES	M	DEMAINS		SODAINE	T	DESTAIN	W	DEWANIS
	SDAINED		MAIDENS	P	PANDIES		DETAINS		

ADEINT 45

NIDATE		M	MEDIANT		DETRAIN		NIDATES	U	AUDIENT
D	NIDATED	P	DEPAINT		TRAINED		SAINTED	V	DEVIANT
F	DEFIANT		PAINTED	S	DESTAIN		SATINED		
	FAINTED		PATINED		DETAINS		STAINED		
I	INEDITA	R	ANTIRED		INSTEAD	T	TAINTED		

ADEIOR 121

ROADIE		L	DARIOLE	S	ROADIES	V	AVODIRE	X	EXORDIA
D	RADIOED	N	ANEROID		SOREDIA		AVOIDER		

ADEIRS 18

SAIRED		E	DEARIES		DIARISE	N	RANDIES		ASTERID
A	ARAISED		READIES	K	DAIKERS		SANDIER		ASTRIDE
B	ABIDERS	F	FARSIDE		DARKIES		SARDINE		DIASTER
	BARDIES		FRAISED	L	DERAILS	O	ROADIES		DISRATE
	BRAISED	G	AGRISED		DIALERS		SOREDIA		STAIDER
	DARBIES	H	AIRSHED		REDIALS	P	ASPIRED		STAIRED
	SEABIRD		DASHIER		SIDERAL		DESPAIR		TARDIES
	SIDEBAR		HARDIES	M	ADMIRES		DIAPERS		TIRADES
C	CARDIES	I	AIRSIDE		MARDIES		PRAISED	U	RESIDUA
	DARCIES		DAIRIES		MISREAD	R	ARRIDES	V	ADVISER
	RADICES		DIARIES		SEDARIM		RAIDERS		VARDIES
	SIDECAR		DIARIES		SIDEARM	T	ARIDEST	X	RADIXES

ADEIRT 19

TIRADE		B	REDBAIT	H	AIRTHED		TRAILED		TRAINED
A	AIRDATE		TRIBADE	K	TRAIKED	M	READMIT	P	DIPTERA
	RADIATE	D	TARDIED	L	DILATER	N	ANTIRED		PARTIED
	TIARAED	G	TRIAGED		REDTAIL		DETRAIN		PIRATED

Bonus Words | 266

R TARDIER	ASTERID	DISRATE	TARDIES	V TARDIVE
TARRIED	ASTRIDE	STAIDER	TIRADES	Y DIETARY
S ARIDEST	DIASTER	STAIRED	T ATTIRED	

ADELNR 148

RELAND	E LEARNED	L LANDLER	LANDERS	LURDANE
A ADRENAL	G DANGLER	M MANDREL	RELANDS	RUNDALE
B BLANDER	GNARLED	O LADRONE	SLANDER	Y DEARNLY
C CANDLER	H HANDLER	S DARNELS	SNARLED	
D DANDLER	K RANKLED	ENLARDS	U LAUNDER	

ADELNT 217

DENTAL	E EDENTAL	M MANTLED	S DENTALS	UNDEALT
A LANATED	LATENED	O TALONED	SLANTED	W WETLAND
C CANTLED	G TANGLED	P PLANTED	U LUNATED	

ADELOR 142

RELOAD	F ALFREDO	N LADRONE	S LOADERS	LEOTARD
B LABORED	I DARIOLE	P LEOPARD	ORDEALS	U ROULADE
C CAROLED	L ODALLER	PAROLED	RELOADS	
ORACLED	M EARLDOM	PRELOAD	T DELATOR	

ADELOS 176

ALDOSE	H SHOALED	N LOADENS	RELOADS	V SALVOED
B ALBEDOS	I DEASOIL	P DEPOSAL	S ALDOSES	W WALDOES
C COLEADS	ISOLEAD	PEDALOS	LASSOED	
SOLACED	K SKOALED	R LOADERS	T SALTOED	
E ELODEAS	M DAMOSEL	ORDEALS	SOLATED	

ADELRS 168

SARDEL	E DEALERS	DIALERS	LANDERS	R LARDERS
B BEDRALS	LEADERS	REDIALS	RELANDS	S RASSLED
BLADERS	REDEALS	SIDERAL	SLANDER	SARDELS
C CRADLES	F FARDELS	K DARKLES	SNARLED	T DARTLES
SCALDER	G DARGLES	L LADLERS	O LOADERS	SLARTED
D LADDERS	H HARELDS	M MEDLARS	ORDEALS	U LAUDERS
RADDLES	HERALDS	N DARNELS	RELOADS	W WARSLED
SADDLER	I DERAILS	ENLARDS	P PEDLARS	Z DRAZELS

ADELRT 132

DARTLE	E ALERTED	I DILATER	S DARTLES	Y LYRATED
A LATERAD	ALTERED	REDTAIL	SLARTED	
B BLARTED	REDEALT	TRAILED	T RATTLED	
C CLARTED	RELATED	O DELATOR	W TRAWLED	
D DARTLED	TREADLE	LEOTARD	X DEXTRAL	

ADELST 221

STALED	D	STADDLE	K	SKLATED	O	SALTOED	S	DESALTS
B BALDEST	E	DELATES		STALKED		SOLATED	T	SLATTED
BLASTED		STEALED	L	STALLED	P	SPALTED	U	AULDEST
STABLED	H	DALETHS	M	MALTEDS		STAPLED		SALUTED
C CASTLED	I	DETAILS	N	DENTALS	R	DARTLES		
SCLATED		DILATES		SLANTED		SLARTED		

ADENOS 232

ANODES	I ADONISE	M DAEMONS		NOMADES		ONSTEAD
C ACNODES	ANODISE	MASONED	P	DAPSONE	U	DOUANES
DEACONS	SODAINE	MODENAS	T	ASTONED	Y	NOYADES
G SONDAGE	L LOADENS	MONADES		DONATES		

ADENOT 51

DONATE	NODATED	P NOTEPAD	DONATES	Z ZONATED
B BATONED	G TANGOED	TONEPAD	ONSTEAD	
C TACNODE	L TALONED	R TORNADE	T NOTATED	
D DONATED	O ODONATE	S ASTONED	V NOVATED	

ADENRS 112

SNARED	GANDERS	ENLARDS	P PANDERS	U ASUNDER
B BANDERS	GARDENS	LANDERS	R DARNERS	DANSEUR
C DANCERS	H HANDERS	RELANDS	ERRANDS	DAUNERS
D DANDERS	HARDENS	SLANDER	SNARRED	W DAWNERS
E DEANERS	I RANDIES	SNARLED	S SANDERS	WANDERS
ENDEARS	SANDIER	M DAMNERS	SARSDEN	WARDENS
F FARDENS	SARDINE	MANREDS	T ENDARTS	Z ZANDERS
SNARFED	K DARKENS	RANDEMS	STANDER	
G DANGERS	L DARNELS	REMANDS	STARNED	

ADENRT 98

RANTED	G DRAGNET	O TORNADE	U DAUNTER	X DEXTRAN
B BARTEND	GRANTED	S ENDARTS	NATURED	Y DENTARY
C CANTRED	I ANTIRED	STANDER	UNRATED	TRAYNED
TRANCED	DETRAIN	STARNED	UNTREAD	TYRANED
D DRANTED	TRAINED	T TRANTED	V VERDANT	

ADENRU 117

UNREAD	RAUNGED	RUNDALE	UNPARED	UNTREAD
B UNBARED	H UNHEARD	M DURAMEN	S ASUNDER	Y UNREADY
C DURANCE	I UNAIRED	MANURED	DANSEUR	Z UNRAZED
UNRACED	URANIDE	MAUNDER	DAUNERS	
D DAUNDER	K UNRAKED	UNARMED	T DAUNTER	
E UNEARED	L LAUNDER	O RONDEAU	NATURED	
G ENGUARD	LURDANE	P UNDRAPE	UNRATED	

ADENST 72

	STANED	G	STANGED		SATINED	N	STANDEN		STANDER
A	ANSATED	H	HANDSET		STAINED	O	ASTONED		STARNED
C	DECANTS	I	DESTAIN	K	DANKEST		DONATES	T	ATTENDS
	DESCANT		DETAINS		STANKED		ONSTEAD	U	SAUNTED
	SCANTED		INSTEAD	L	DENTALS	P	PEDANTS		UNSATED
E	STANDEE		NIDATES		SLANTED		PENTADS	V	ADVENTS
	STEANED		SAINTED	M	TANDEMS	R	ENDARTS	Y	STAYNED

ADENTU 188

	UNDATE		UNGATED	M	UNMATED		UNRATED		TAUNTED
B	UNBATED	H	HAUNTED		UNTAMED		UNTREAD	V	VAUNTED
C	UNACTED	I	AUDIENT	P	UNADEPT	S	SAUNTED	X	UNTAXED
D	DAUNTED	J	JAUNTED	Q	QUANTED		UNSATED		
	UNDATED	L	LUNATED	R	DAUNTER	T	ATTUNED		
G	GAUNTED		UNDEALT		NATURED		NUTATED		

ADEORS 43

	SOARED	G	DOGEARS		RELOADS	S	SARODES	U	AROUSED
C	SARCODE	I	ROADIES	M	RADOMES	T	DOATERS	V	OVERSAD
D	DEODARS		SOREDIA	O	ROADEOS		ROASTED		SAVORED
E	OREADES	L	LOADERS	R	ADORERS		TORSADE	W	REDOWAS
F	FEDORAS		ORDEALS		DROSERA		TROADES		

ADEORT 55

	TROADE		REDCOAT	N	TORNADE		ROASTED	U	OUTDARE
B	ABORTED	G	GAROTED	O	ODORATE		TORSADE		OUTREAD
	BORATED	K	TROAKED	P	ADOPTER		TROADES		READOUT
	TABORED	L	DELATOR		READOPT	T	ROTATED		
C	CORDATE		LEOTARD	S	DOATERS		TROATED		

ADERST 78

	TREADS		STEARED		DIASTER		STANDER		TRADERS
B	DABSTER		TASERED		DISRATE		STARNED	T	STARTED
	TABERDS	F	STRAFED		STAIDER	O	DOATERS		TETRADS
C	REDACTS	G	RADGEST		STAIRED		ROASTED	V	ADVERTS
	SCARTED	H	DEARTHS		TARDIES		TORSADE		STARVED
D	ADDREST		HARDEST		TIRADES		TROADES	W	STEWARD
	RADDEST		HARDSET	K	DARKEST	P	DEPARTS		STRAWED
E	DEAREST		HATREDS		STARKED		DRAPETS		WRASTED
	DERATES		THREADS		STRAKED		PETARDS	Y	STRAYED
	ESTRADE		TRASHED	L	DARTLES	R	DARTERS		
	REASTED	I	ARIDEST		SLARTED		DARTRES		
	REDATES		ASTERID	M	SMARTED		RETARDS		
	SEDATER		ASTRIDE	N	ENDARTS		STARRED		

ADINOR 83

	ORDAIN	G	ADORING	N	ANDIRON	S	INROADS	V	VIRANDO
B	INBOARD		GRADINO	P	PADRONI		ORDAINS		
D	ANDROID		ROADING		PONIARD		SADIRON		
E	ANEROID	L	ORDINAL	R	ORDINAR	T	DIATRON		

ADINRS 236

RANIDS	SARDINE	L ALDRINS	SADIRON	W INWARDS
A RADIANS	F FRIANDS	M MANDIRS	Q QINDARS	
B RIBANDS	G DARINGS	N INNARDS	T INDARTS	
E RANDIES	GRADINS	O INROADS	U DURIANS	
SANDIER	K DISRANK	ORDAINS	SUNDARI	

ADINRT 155

INDART	B ANTBIRD	TRAINED	TRADING	S INDARTS
A INTRADA	E ANTIRED	F INDRAFT	O DIATRON	U TRIDUAN
RADIANT	DETRAIN	G DARTING	R TRIDARN	UNITARD

AEEGNR 182

GENERA	ENRAGED	I REGINAE	N ENRANGE	REAGENT
B REBEGAN	GRANDEE	L ENLARGE	S ENRAGES	U RENAGUE
C ENGRACE	GRENADE	GENERAL	T GRANTEE	UNEAGER
D ANGERED	F FREEGAN	GLEANER	GREATEN	V AVENGER
DERANGE	G ENGAGER	M GERMANE	NEGATER	ENGRAVE

AEEGNT 246

NEGATE	E TEENAGE	M GATEMEN	REAGENT	
C CENTAGE	F FANTEEG	R GRANTEE	S NEGATES	
D AGENTED	H THENAGE	GREATEN	T TENTAGE	
NEGATED	L ELEGANT	NEGATER	V VENTAGE	

AEEINT 44

TENIAE	L LINEATE	R ARENITE	S ETESIAN	
A TAENIAE	M ETAMINE	RETINAE	V NAIVETE	
B BETAINE	MATINEE	TRAINEE		

AEEIRS 81

EASIER	FAERIES	REALISE	EPEIRAS	SERIATE
D DEARIES	FREESIA	M SEAMIER	R REARISE	W WEARIES
READIES	I AIERIES	SERIEMA	RERAISE	
F AREFIES	L EARLIES	P APERIES	T AERIEST	

AEELNR 114

LEANER	D LEARNED	I ALIENER	R LEARNER	ENTERAL
B ENABLER	G ENLARGE	M REELMAN	RELEARN	ETERNAL
C CLEANER	GENERAL	N LERNEAN	S LEANERS	TELERAN
RECLEAN	GLEANER	P REPANEL	T ALTERNE	W RENEWAL

AEELNS 243

ENSEAL	ENLACES	M ENAMELS	R LEANERS	V ENSLAVE
B BALEENS	SCALENE	MELENAS	S ENSEALS	LEAVENS
ENABLES	D LEADENS	O ENOLASE	T ELANETS	W WEANELS
C CLEANSE	I SEALINE	P ALPEENS	LATEENS	
ELANCES	K ALKENES	SPELEAN	LEANEST	

AEELNT 170

LATEEN	LATENED	K KANTELE	ENTERAL	LATEENS
B TENABLE	G ELEGANT	M MANTEEL	ETERNAL	LEANEST
C LATENCE	H LETHEAN	TELEMAN	TELERAN	Y ENTAYLE
D EDENTAL	I LINEATE	R ALTERNE	S ELANETS	

AEELRS 118

SEALER	E RELEASE	O AREOLES	RESEALS	LEAVERS
C ALERCES	G GALERES	P LEAPERS	SEALERS	REVEALS
CEREALS	REGALES	PLEASER	T ELATERS	SEVERAL
RELACES	H HEALERS	PRESALE	REALEST	VEALERS
RESCALE	I EARLIES	RELAPSE	RELATES	X RELAXES
SCLERAE	REALISE	REPEALS	RESLATE	Y SEALERY
D DEALERS	K LEAKERS	S EARLESS	STEALER	
LEADERS	M MEALERS	LEASERS	U LEASURE	
REDEALS	N LEANERS	RESALES	V LAVEERS	

AEELRT 102

RELATE	REDEALT	REALTIE	PLEATER	S ELATERS
A LAETARE	RELATED	M LAMETER	PRELATE	REALEST
B BLEATER	TREADLE	N ALTERNE	REPLATE	RELATES
RETABLE	F REFLATE	ENTERAL	R ALERTER	RESLATE
C TREACLE	H HALTERE	ETERNAL	ALTERER	STEALER
D ALERTED	LEATHER	TELERAN	REALTER	X EXALTER
ALTERED	I ATELIER	P PETRALE	RELATER	

AEELST 240

TEASEL	GELATES	N ELANETS	RESLATE	V SALVETE
B BELATES	LEGATES	LATEENS	STEALER	VALETES
C CELESTA	SEGETAL	LEANEST	S ALTESSE	VELETAS
SELECTA	TEAGLES	O OLEATES	STEALES	X LATEXES
D DELATES	TELEGAS	R ELATERS	TEASELS	Y EYALETS
STEALED	H LATHEES	REALEST	U ELUATES	Z TEAZELS
G EAGLETS	L LEALEST	RELATES	SETUALE	TEAZLES

AEENRS 101

RANEES	D DEANERS	L LEANERS	O ARENOSE	T EARNEST
C CAREENS	ENDEARS	M MEANERS	P PANEERS	EASTERN
CASERNE	G ENRAGES	RENAMES	R EARNERS	NEAREST
ENRACES	H ARSHEEN	N ENSNARE	REEARNS	RATEENS
RECANES	K SNEAKER	RENNASE	S ENSEARS	W WEANERS

AEENRT 54

RATEEN	NEGATER	TRAINEE	M REMANET	T ENTREAT
C CENTARE	REAGENT	K RETAKEN	R TERRANE	RATTEEN
CRENATE	H EARTHEN	L ALTERNE	S EARNEST	TERNATE
REENACT	HEARTEN	ENTERAL	EASTERN	V AVENTRE
G GRANTEE	I ARENITE	ETERNAL	NEAREST	NERVATE
GREATEN	RETINAE	TELERAN	RATEENS	VETERAN

AEENST 106

	STEANE	H	ETHANES	M	ENTAMES	R	EARNEST		SENATES
C	CETANES	I	ETESIAN		MEANEST		EASTERN		SENSATE
	TENACES	J	SEJEANT	N	NEATENS		NEAREST		STEANES
D	STANDEE	L	ELANETS	P	NEPETAS		RATEENS	T	NEATEST
	STEANED		LATEENS		PENATES	S	ENTASES		
G	NEGATES		LEANEST		PESANTE		SATEENS		

AEERST 30

	TEASER		REDATES	K	RETAKES		NEAREST		STEARES
A	AERATES		SEDATER		SAKERET		RATEENS		TEASERS
B	BEATERS		STEARED	L	ELATERS	O	ROSEATE		TESSERA
	BERATES		TASERED		REALEST	P	REPEATS	T	ESTREAT
	REBATES	F	AFREETS		RELATES		RETAPES		RESTATE
C	CERATES		FEASTER		RESLATE	R	RETEARS		RETASTE
	CREATES	G	ERGATES		STEALER		SERRATE	U	AUSTERE
	ECARTES		RESTAGE	M	REMATES		TEARERS	W	SWEATER
	SECRETA	H	AETHERS		RETEAMS	S	EASTERS	X	RETAXES
D	DEAREST		HEATERS		STEAMER		RESEATS		
	DERATES		REHEATS		TEAMERS		SAETERS		
	ESTRADE	I	AERIEST	N	EARNEST		SEAREST		
	REASTED		SERIATE		EASTERN		SEATERS		

AEGILN 100

	LINAGE		LEAFING		LEAMING		ENGRAIL		ELATING
C	ANGELIC	G	EAGLING		MEALING		LAERING		GELATIN
	ANGLICE		GEALING	N	ANELING		LEARING		GENITAL
	GALENIC		LIGNAGE		EANLING		NARGILE		TAGLINE
D	ALIGNED	H	HEALING		LEANING		REALIGN	U	LINGUAE
	DEALING	K	LEAKING		NEALING		REGINAL		UNAGILE
	LEADING		LINKAGE	P	LEAPING	S	LEASING	V	LEAVING
E	LINEAGE	L	GALLEIN		PEALING		LINAGES		VEALING
F	FEALING		NIGELLA		PLEAING		SEALING	Y	ALEYING
	FINAGLE	M	GEMINAL	R	ALIGNER	T	ATINGLE		YEALING

AEGINR 16

	REGINA	F	FEARING		GERMINA		GRAINER	T	GRANITE
A	ANERGIA	G	GEARING		MANGIER		RANGIER		GRATINE
B	BEARING		NAGGIER		MEARING		REARING		INGRATE
C	ANERGIC	H	HEARING		REAMING	S	ANGRIES		TANGIER
	GRECIAN	K	REAKING	N	AGINNER		EARINGS		TEARING
D	AREDING	L	ALIGNER		EARNING		ERASING	V	REAVING
	DEARING		ENGRAIL		ENGRAIN		GAINERS		VINEGAR
	DERAIGN		LAERING		GRANNIE		GRAINES	W	WEARING
	EARDING		LEARING		NEARING		REAGINS	Z	ZINGARE
	GRADINE		NARGILE	O	ORIGANE		REGAINS		
	GRAINED		REALIGN	P	REAPING		REGINAS		
	READING		REGINAL	R	ANGRIER		SEARING		
E	REGINAE	M	GERMAIN		EARRING		SERINGA		

AEGINS 74

EASING	LINAGES	SPAEING	SERINGA	TANGIES
B SABEING	SEALING	SPINAGE	S AGNISES	TEASING
C CEASING	M ENIGMAS	R ANGRIES	SEASING	TSIGANE
INCAGES	GAMINES	EARINGS	T EASTING	U GUINEAS
D AGNISED	MEASING	ERASING	EATINGS	Y EASYING
E AGENISE	SEAMING	GAINERS	GAINEST	Z AGNIZES
F FEASING	N INNAGES	GRAINES	GENISTA	SEAZING
G AGEINGS	SEANING	REAGINS	INGATES	
SIGNAGE	O AGONIES	REGAINS	INGESTA	
K SINKAGE	AGONISE	REGINAS	SEATING	
L LEASING	P PEASING	SEARING	TAGINES	

AEGINT 129

TEAING	GENITAL	R GRANITE	GENISTA	U UNITAGE
B BEATING	TAGLINE	GRATINE	INGATES	V VINTAGE
F FEATING	M MINTAGE	INGRATE	INGESTA	Z TEAZING
H GAHNITE	TEAMING	TANGIER	SEATING	TZIGANE
HEATING	TEGMINA	TEARING	TAGINES	
L ATINGLE	N ANTEING	S EASTING	TANGIES	
ELATING	ANTIGEN	EATINGS	TEASING	
GELATIN	GENTIAN	GAINEST	TSIGANE	

AEGIRT 151

TRIAGE	M MIGRATE	TANGIER	GAITERS	TRIAGES
C CIGARET	RAGTIME	TEARING	SEAGIRT	V VIRGATE
D TRIAGED	N GRANITE	O GOATIER	STAGIER	VITRAGE
F FRIGATE	GRATINE	S AGISTER	STRIGAE	
G TAGGIER	INGRATE	AIGRETS	TIRAGES	

AEGIST 184

AGEIST	LIGATES	INGATES	AIGRETS	SAGIEST
A AGATISE	TAIGLES	INGESTA	GAITERS	U AUGITES
C CAGIEST	M GAMIEST	SEATING	SEAGIRT	Y GASEITY
D AGISTED	SIGMATE	TAGINES	STAGIER	Z GAZIEST
G STAGGIE	N EASTING	TANGIES	STRIGAE	
L AGILEST	EATINGS	TEASING	TIRAGES	
AIGLETS	GAINEST	TSIGANE	TRIAGES	
GELATIS	GENISTA	R AGISTER	S AGEISTS	

AEGLNR 178

REGNAL	E ENLARGE	LAERING	M MANGLER	T TANGLER
A ALNAGER	GENERAL	LEARING	P GRAPNEL	TRANGLE
B BRANGLE	GLEANER	NARGILE	S ANGLERS	U GRANULE
C CLANGER	F FLANGER	REALIGN	ERLANGS	W WANGLER
GLANCER	G GANGREL	REGINAL	LANGERS	WRANGLE
D DANGLER	I ALIGNER	J JANGLER	LARGENS	Y ANGERLY
GNARLED	ENGRAIL	L LANGREL	SLANGER	

AEGNOR 90

ORANGE	D	GROANED		MEGARON	S	ONAGERS	Y	ORANGEY
B BEGROAN	I	ORIGANE	O	OREGANO		ORANGES		
C ACROGEN	K	KARENGO	R	GROANER	T	NEGATOR		
CORNAGE	M	MARENGO		ORANGER	W	WAGONER		

AEGNRS 171

SERANG	H GNASHER		REGAINS	M	ENGRAMS	T	ARGENTS
B BANGERS	HANGERS		REGINAS		GERMANS		GARNETS
GRABENS	REHANGS		SEARING		MANGERS		STRANGE
D DANGERS	SHERANG		SERINGA	O	ONAGERS	U	RAUNGES
GANDERS	I ANGRIES	K	SKANGER		ORANGES		UNGEARS
GARDENS	EARINGS	L	ANGLERS	P	ENGRASP	W	GNAWERS
E ENRAGES	ERASING		ERLANGS	R	GARNERS		
G GANGERS	GAINERS		LANGERS		RANGERS		
GRANGES	GRAINES		LARGENS	S	SANGERS		
NAGGERS	REAGINS		SLANGER		SERANGS		

AEGNRT 52

GARNET	NEGATER		TANGIER		RAGMENT	S	ARGENTS
A TANAGER	REAGENT		TEARING	N	REGNANT		GARNETS
D DRAGNET	F ENGRAFT	L	TANGLER	O	NEGATOR		STRANGE
GRANTED	I GRANITE		TRANGLE	P	TREPANG	U	GAUNTER
E GRANTEE	GRATINE	M	GARMENT	R	GRANTER	W	TWANGER
GREATEN	INGRATE		MARGENT		REGRANT	Y	AGENTRY

AEGNST 200

AGENTS	EATINGS	TAGINES		TANGLES		GARNETS
A AGNATES	GAINEST	TANGIES	M	MAGNETS		STRANGE
D STANGED	GENISTA	TEASING	N	GANNETS	T	GESTANT
E NEGATES	INGATES	TSIGANE	O	ONSTAGE		
H STENGAH	INGESTA	L GELANTS		TANGOES		
I EASTING	SEATING	LANGEST	R	ARGENTS		

AEGORS 238

SORAGE	CORSAGE	L	GALORES	S	SORAGES	U	AERUGOS
A AGAROSE	SOCAGER		GAOLERS	T	GAROTES		
OARAGES	D DOGEARS	M	ROMAGES		ORGEATS		
B BORAGES	F FORAGES	N	ONAGERS		STORAGE		
C CARGOES	H GHERAOS		ORANGES		TOERAGS		

AEGORT 63

TOERAG	L GLOATER	P	PORTAGE		ORGEATS	U	OUTRAGE
D GAROTED	LEGATOR		POTAGER		STORAGE		
F FAGOTER	N NEGATOR	R	GARROTE		TOERAGS		
I GOATIER	O ROOTAGE	S	GAROTES	T	GAROTTE		

AEGRST 139

TARGES	G GAGSTER	SEAGIRT	STRANGE	GRATERS
A AGRASTE	GARGETS	STAGIER	O GAROTES	S GASTERS
GASTREA	STAGGER	STRIGAE	ORGEATS	STAGERS
TEARGAS	TAGGERS	TIRAGES	STORAGE	T TARGETS
B BARGEST	H GATHERS	TRIAGES	TOERAGS	V GRAVEST
D RADGEST	I AGISTER	L LARGEST	P PARGETS	Y GRAYEST
E ERGATES	AIGRETS	N ARGENTS	R GARRETS	GYRATES
RESTAGE	GAITERS	GARNETS	GARTERS	STAGERY

AEILMN 247

MENIAL	INFLAME	L MANILLE	MANIPLE	MALINES
A LAMINAE	G GEMINAL	M MAILMEN	R MANLIER	MENIALS
B MINABLE	LEAMING	N LINEMAN	MARLINE	SEMINAL
C CNEMIAL	MEALING	MELANIN	MINERAL	T AILMENT
MELANIC	H HELIMAN	O MINEOLA	RAILMEN	ALIMENT
F FEMINAL	K MANLIKE	P IMPANEL	S ISLEMAN	U ALUMINE

AEILMR 224

REMAIL	MIRACLE	K ARMLIKE	P IMPALER	REALISM
B BALMIER	RECLAIM	M MALMIER	IMPEARL	REMAILS
LAMBIER	E MEALIER	N MANLIER	LEMPIRA	T LAMITER
MIRABLE	F FLAMIER	MARLINE	PALMIER	MALTIER
REMBLAI	G GREMIAL	MINERAL	R LARMIER	MARLITE
C CALMIER	LAMIGER	RAILMEN	MARLIER	
CLAIMER	I RAMILIE	O LOAMIER	S MAILERS	

AEILNO 42

EOLIAN	M MINEOLA	ALERION	T ELATION	
A AEOLIAN	P OPALINE	ALIENOR	TOENAIL	
K KAOLINE	R AILERON	S ANISOLE		

AEILNR 6

RENAIL	REALIGN	MARLINE	PRALINE	RELIANT
C CARLINE	REGINAL	MINERAL	R LARNIER	RETINAL
E ALIENER	H HERNIAL	RAILMEN	S ALINERS	TRENAIL
G ALIGNER	INHALER	O AILERON	NAILERS	V RAVELIN
ENGRAIL	I AIRLINE	ALERION	RENAILS	W LAWNIER
LAERING	K LANKIER	ALIENOR	T ENTRAIL	X RELAXIN
LEARING	L RALLINE	P PEARLIN	LATRINE	Y INLAYER
NARGILE	M MANLIER	PLAINER	RATLINE	NAILERY

AEILNS 32

SILANE	E SEALINE	L AINSELL	PINEALS	SILANES
B LESBIAN	F FINALES	M ISLEMAN	SPANIEL	T EASTLIN
C INLACES	G LEASING	MALINES	SPLENIA	ELASTIN
SANICLE	LINAGES	MENIALS	R ALINERS	ENTAILS
SCALENI	SEALING	SEMINAL	NAILERS	NAILSET
D DENIALS	H INHALES	O ANISOLE	RENAILS	SALIENT
SNAILED	K ALKINES	P ALPINES	S SALINES	SALTINE

SLAINTE	TENAILS	INULASE	VALINES	X ALEXINS
STANIEL	U INSULAE	V ALEVINS	W LAWINES	Y ELYSIAN

AEILNT 17

TINEAL	GENITAL	P PANTILE	S EASTLIN	STANIEL
A ANTLIAE	TAGLINE	R ENTRAIL	ELASTIN	TENAILS
E LINEATE	K ANTLIKE	LATRINE	ENTAILS	U ALUNITE
F INFLATE	M AILMENT	RATLINE	NAILSET	V VENTAIL
G ATINGLE	ALIMENT	RELIANT	SALIENT	
ELATING	O ELATION	RETINAL	SALTINE	
GELATIN	TOENAIL	TRENAIL	SLAINTE	

AEILRR 190

RERAIL	LEARIER	I LAIRIER	MARLIER	T RETIRAL
C CERRIAL	F FLARIER	K LARKIER	N LARNIER	RETRIAL
D LARDIER	FRAILER	L RALLIER	S RAILERS	TRAILER
E EARLIER	G GLARIER	M LARMIER	RERAILS	

AEILRS 22

SERIAL	E EARLIES	L RALLIES	R RAILERS	SALTIRE
A AERIALS	REALISE	SALLIER	RERAILS	SLATIER
B BAILERS	G GLAIRES	M MAILERS	S AIRLESS	TAILERS
C CLARIES	GRAILES	REALISM	RESAILS	V REVISAL
ECLAIRS	H HAILERS	REMAILS	SAILERS	W SWALIER
SCALIER	SHALIER	N ALINERS	SERAILS	WAILERS
D DERAILS	I LAIRISE	NAILERS	SERIALS	
DIALERS	J JAILERS	RENAILS	T REALIST	
REDIALS	K LAIKERS	P PALSIER	RETAILS	
SIDERAL	SERKALI	PARLIES	SALTIER	

AEILRT 15

TAILER	TRAILED	M LAMITER	P PLAITER	SLATIER
B LIBRATE	E ATELIER	MALTIER	PLATIER	TAILERS
TABLIER	REALTIE	MARLITE	R RETIRAL	T TERTIAL
TRIABLE	H LATHIER	N ENTRAIL	RETRIAL	U URALITE
C ARTICLE	K RATLIKE	LATRINE	TRAILER	W WALTIER
RECITAL	TALKIER	RATLINE	S REALIST	Y IRATELY
TALCIER	L LITERAL	RELIANT	RETAILS	REALITY
D DILATER	TALLIER	RETINAL	SALTIER	TEARILY
REDTAIL	TRIELLA	TRENAIL	SALTIRE	

AEILST 37

STELAI	ELASTIC	GELATIS	TALLIES	O ISOLATE
B ABLEIST	LACIEST	LIGATES	N EASTLIN	P APLITES
ALBITES	LATICES	TAIGLES	ELASTIN	PALIEST
ASTILBE	SALICET	H HALITES	ENTAILS	PLATIES
BASTILE	D DETAILS	HELIAST	NAILSET	TALIPES
BESTIAL	DILATES	I LAITIES	SALIENT	R REALIST
BLASTIE	F FETIALS	K LAKIEST	SALTINE	RETAILS
LIBATES	SEALIFT	TALKIES	SLAINTE	SALTIER
STABILE	G AGILEST	L SITELLA	STANIEL	SALTIRE
C ASTELIC	AIGLETS	TAILLES	TENAILS	SLATIER

TAILERS	U	SITULAE	W	WALIEST	Z	LAZIEST
S SALTIES	V	ESTIVAL	Y	TAILYES		

AEIMNO 239

ANOMIE	D	AMIDONE	L	MINEOLA		ROMAINE	T	AMNIOTE
C ENCOMIA		DOMAINE	R	MORAINE	S	ANOMIES	U	MOINEAU

AEIMNR 99

REMAIN	G GERMAIN	RAMEKIN	P PERMIAN	MINARET
B MIRBANE	GERMINA	L MANLIER	R MARINER	RAIMENT
C CARMINE	MANGIER	MARLINE	S MARINES	V VERMIAN
D ADERMIN	MEARING	MINERAL	REMAINS	W WIREMAN
INARMED	REAMING	RAILMEN	SEMINAR	
E REMANIE	H HARMINE	O MORAINE	SIRNAME	
F FIREMAN	K MANKIER	ROMAINE	T MERANTI	

AEIMNS 201

SEMINA	SIDEMAN	H HAEMINS	MISNAME	INMATES
A AMNESIA	E MEANIES	HEMINAS	O ANOMIES	MAINEST
ANEMIAS	NEMESIA	J JASMINE	R MARINES	MANTIES
C AMNESIC	F FAMINES	K KINEMAS	REMAINS	TAMEINS
CINEMAS	INFAMES	L ISLEMAN	SEMINAR	TAMINES
D DEMAINS	G ENIGMAS	MALINES	SIRNAME	W MANWISE
MAIDENS	GAMINES	MENIALS	S INSEAMS	
MEDIANS	MEASING	SEMINAL	SAMISEN	
MEDINAS	SEAMING	M AMMINES	T ETAMINS	

AEIMNT 59

TAMINE	E ETAMINE	MINIATE	RAIMENT	X TAXIMEN
A AMENTIA	MATINEE	L AILMENT	S ETAMINS	Y AMENITY
ANIMATE	G MINTAGE	ALIMENT	INMATES	ANYTIME
B AMBIENT	TEAMING	N MANNITE	MAINEST	
C EMICANT	TEGMINA	O AMNIOTE	MANTIES	
NEMATIC	H HEMATIN	R MERANTI	TAMEINS	
D MEDIANT	I INTIMAE	MINARET	TAMINES	

AEIMRS 228

SARMIE	F MISFARE	REMAILS	R MARRIES	SEMITAR
B AMBRIES	G GISARME	M MAIMERS	SIMARRE	SMARTIE
D ADMIRES	IMAGERS	RAMMIES	S MASSIER	U UREMIAS
MARDIES	MAIGRES	N MARINES	SARMIES	V MISAVER
MISREAD	MIRAGES	REMAINS	T IMARETS	W AWMRIES
SEDARIM	H MASHIER	SEMINAR	MAESTRI	SEMIRAW
SIDEARM	MISHEAR	SIRNAME	MAISTER	Y RIMAYES
E SEAMIER	L MAILERS	P IMPRESA	MASTIER	
SERIEMA	REALISM	SAMPIRE	MISRATE	

AEIMRT 91

MATIER	C MATRICE	E EMERITA	MEATIER	RAGTIME
A AMIRATE	D READMIT	EMIRATE	G MIGRATE	I AIRTIME

		P PRIMATE	MASTIER	U MURIATE
L LAMITER	TRAMMIE	S IMARETS	MISRATE	V VITAMER
MALTIER	N MERANTI	MAESTRI	SEMITAR	W WARTIME
MARLITE	MINARET	MAISTER	SMARTIE	
M MARMITE	RAIMENT			

AEIMST 208

		MAINEST	R IMARETS	SAMIEST
TAMISE	H ATHEISM	MANTIES	MAESTRI	SAMITES
C ACMITES	I AMITIES	TAMEINS	MAISTER	TAMISES
ETACISM	ATIMIES	TAMINES	MASTIER	T ETATISM
MICATES	K KETMIAS	O AMOSITE	MISRATE	MATIEST
SEMATIC	MISTAKE	ATOMIES	SEMITAR	MATTIES
D DIASTEM	M MISMATE	ATOMISE	SMARTIE	Z MAZIEST
MISDATE	SEMIMAT	OSMIATE	S ASTEISM	MESTIZA
E STEAMIE	TAMMIES	P IMPASTE	MISEATS	
G GAMIEST	N ETAMINS	PASTIME	MISSEAT	
SIGMATE	INMATES			

AEINNT 186

		O ENATION	TRANNIE	T ANTIENT
TANNIE	ANTIGEN	P PANTINE	S INANEST	
C ANCIENT	GENTIAN	PINNATE	STANINE	
F INFANTE	K NEATNIK	R ENTRAIN	TANNIES	
G ANTEING	M MANNITE			

AEINPR 160

RAPINE	F FIREPAN	L PEARLIN	N PANNIER	T PAINTER
C CAPRINE	G REAPING	PLAINER	P NAPPIER	PERTAIN
D PARDINE	H HEPARIN	PRALINE	S PANIERS	REPAINT
E PERINEA	K RANPIKE	M PERMIAN	RAPINES	

AEINPT 152

PINETA	PAINTED	PINNATE	PATINES	Y PANEITY
A PATINAE	PATINED	R PAINTER	SAPIENT	
B BEPAINT	H PENTHIA	PERTAIN	SPINATE	
C PICANTE	L PANTILE	REPAINT	T PATIENT	
D DEPAINT	N PANTINE	S PANTIES	U PETUNIA	

AEINRS 10

SARNIE	EARINGS	I SENARII	INSNARE	RATINES
C ARCSINE	ERASING	J INJERAS	O ERASION	RESIANT
ARSENIC	GAINERS	K SNAKIER	P PANIERS	RETAINS
CARNIES	GRAINES	L ALINERS	RAPINES	RETINAS
CERASIN	REAGINS	NAILERS	R SIERRAN	RETSINA
D RANDIES	REGAINS	RENAILS	SNARIER	STAINER
SANDIER	REGINAS	M MARINES	S ARSINES	STARNIE
SARDINE	SEARING	REMAINS	SARNIES	STEARIN
F INFARES	SERINGA	SEMINAR	T ANESTRI	V AVENIRS
SERAFIN	H ARSHINE	SIRNAME	ANTSIER	RAVINES
G ANGRIES	HERNIAS	N INSANER	NASTIER	

AEINRT 1

RETINA	TRAINEE	K KERATIN	PERTAIN	STARNIE
B ATEBRIN	F FAINTER	L ENTRAIL	REPAINT	STEARIN
C CANTIER	FENITAR	LATRINE	R RETRAIN	T INTREAT
CERATIN	G GRANITE	RATLINE	TERRAIN	ITERANT
CERTAIN	GRATINE	RELIANT	TRAINER	NATTIER
CREATIN	INGRATE	RETINAL	S ANESTRI	NITRATE
CRINATE	TANGIER	TRENAIL	ANTSIER	TARTINE
NACRITE	TEARING	M MERANTI	NASTIER	TERTIAN
TACRINE	H HAIRNET	MINARET	RATINES	U RUINATE
D ANTIRED	INEARTH	RAIMENT	RESIANT	TAURINE
DETRAIN	THERIAN	N ENTRAIN	RETAINS	URANITE
TRAINED	I INERTIA	TRANNIE	RETINAS	URINATE
E ARENITE	J JANTIER	O OTARINE	RETSINA	W TAWNIER
RETINAE	NARTJIE	P PAINTER	STAINER	TINWARE

AEINST 2

TISANE	NAIFEST	TANKIES	O ATONIES	SESTINA
A ENTASIA	G EASTING	L EASTLIN	P PANTIES	TANSIES
TAENIAS	EATINGS	ELASTIN	PATINES	TISANES
B BANTIES	GAINEST	ENTAILS	SAPIENT	T INSTATE
BASINET	GENISTA	NAILSET	SPINATE	SATINET
BESAINT	INGATES	SALIENT	R ANESTRI	U AUNTIES
BESTAIN	INGESTA	SALTINE	ANTSIER	SINUATE
C ACETINS	SEATING	SLAINTE	NASTIER	V NAIVEST
CANIEST	TAGINES	STANIEL	RATINES	NATIVES
CINEAST	TANGIES	TENAILS	RESIANT	VAINEST
D DESTAIN	TEASING	M ETAMINS	RETAINS	W AWNIEST
DETAINS	TSIGANE	INMATES	RETINAS	TAWNIES
INSTEAD	H SHEITAN	MAINEST	RETSINA	WANIEST
NIDATES	STHENIA	MANTIES	STAINER	WANTIES
SAINTED	I ISATINE	TAMEINS	STARNIE	X ANTISEX
SATINED	J JANTIES	TAMINES	STEARIN	SEXTAIN
STAINED	TAJINES	N INANEST	S ENTASIS	Z ZANIEST
E ETESIAN	K INTAKES	STANINE	NASTIES	ZEATINS
F FAINEST	KENTIAS	TANNIES	SEITANS	

AEINTU 96

AUNTIE	J JAUNTIE	Q ANTIQUE	URANITE	V VAUNTIE
C TUNICAE	K UNAKITE	QUINATE	URINATE	
D AUDIENT	L ALUNITE	R RUINATE	S AUNTIES	
G UNITAGE	P PETUNIA	TAURINE	SINUATE	

AEIORS 84

ARIOSE	ORACIES	SOREDIA	T OARIEST
B ISOBARE	SCORIAE	N ERASION	OTARIES
C CARIOSE	D ROADIES	P SOAPIER	V OVARIES

AEIPRS 143

SPIREA	SCRAPIE	DESPAIR	E APERIES	PRISAGE
A SPIRAEA	SPACIER	DIAPERS	EPEIRAS	SPAIRGE
C EPACRIS	D ASPIRED	PRAISED	G GASPIER	H HARPIES

```
  SHARPIE         RAPINES         RASPIER         PARTIES       UPRAISE
K PARKIES       O SOAPIER         REPAIRS         PASTIER     V PARVISE
  SPARKIE       P APPRISE       S ASPIRES         PIASTER       PAVISER
L PALSIER         SAPPIER         PARESIS         PIASTRE     W WASPIER
  PARLIES       R ASPIRER         PARISES         PIRATES
M IMPRESA         PARRIES         PRAISES         PRATIES
  SAMPIRE         PRAISER         SPIREAS         TRAIPSE
N PANIERS         RAPIERS       T PAIREST       U SPURIAE
```

AEIPRT 116

```
  PTERIA          PIRATED         PERTAIN         PASTIER     T PARTITE
A APTERIA       E PEATIER         REPAINT         PIASTER     V PRIVATE
C PARETIC       L PLAITER       P PERIAPT         PIASTRE     W WIRETAP
  PICRATE         PLATIER       R PARTIER         PIRATES
D DIPTERA       M PRIMATE       S PAIREST         PRATIES
  PARTIED       N PAINTER         PARTIES         TRAIPSE
```

AEIRRS 250

```
  SIERRA        E REARISE       M MARRIES         RAPIERS         SERRATI
B BARRIES         RERAISE         SIMARRE         RASPIER         TARRIES
  BRASIER       H HARRIES       N SIERRAN         REPAIRS         TARSIER
C CARRIES       K KERRIAS         SNARIER       S ARRISES       V ARRIVES
  SCARIER         SARKIER       P ASPIRER         RAISERS         VARIERS
D ARRIDES       L RAILERS         PARRIES         SIERRAS
  RAIDERS         RERAILS         PRAISER       T ARTSIER
```

AEIRRT 58

```
  IRATER        D TARDIER       N RETRAIN         SERRATI       W WARTIER
A TARAIRE         TARRIED         TERRAIN         TARRIES       Y RETIARY
B ARBITER       E TEARIER         TRAINER         TARSIER
  RAREBIT       L RETIRAL       P PARTIER       T RATTIER
C CIRRATE         RETRIAL       R TARRIER         RETRAIT
  ERRATIC         TRAILER       S ARTSIER         TARTIER
```

AEIRST 3

```
  TERAIS          STAIRED       K ARKITES         RATINES       R ARTSIER
A ARISTAE         TARDIES         KARITES         RESIANT         SERRATI
  ASTERIA         TIRADES       L REALIST         RETAINS         TARRIES
  ATRESIA       E AERIEST         RETAILS         RETINAS         TARSIER
B BAITERS         SERIATE         SALTIER         RETSINA       S ARSIEST
  BARITES       F FAIREST         SALTIRE         STAINER         ARTSIES
  REBAITS       G AGISTER         SLATIER         STARNIE         SAIREST
  TERBIAS         AIGRETS         TAILERS         STEARIN         SATIRES
C ATRESIC         GAITERS       M IMARETS       O OARIEST         TIRASSE
  CRISTAE         SEAGIRT         MAESTRI         OTARIES       T ARTIEST
  RACIEST         STAGIER         MAISTER       P PAIREST         ARTISTE
  STEARIC         STRIGAE         MASTIER         PARTIES         ATTIRES
D ARIDEST         TIRAGES         MISRATE         PASTIER         IRATEST
  ASTERID         TRIAGES         SEMITAR         PIASTER         RATITES
  ASTRIDE       H HASTIER         SMARTIE         PIASTRE         STRIATE
  DIASTER         SHERIAT       N ANESTRI         PIRATES         TASTIER
  DISRATE       I AIRIEST         ANTSIER         PRATIES         TERTIAS
  STAIDER         IRISATE         NASTIER         TRAIPSE       V TAIVERS
```

| VASTIER | W WAISTER | WARIEST | WASTRIE |
| VERITAS | WAITERS | | |

AEIRTT 49

TERTIA	D ATTIRED	NITRATE	ARTISTE	TATTIER
A ARIETTA	E ARIETTE	TARTINE	ATTIRES	TITRATE
B BATTIER	ITERATE	TERTIAN	IRATEST	V TAIVERT
BIRETTA	F FATTIER	P PARTITE	RATITES	W TAWTIER
RATBITE	L TERTIAL	R RATTIER	STRIATE	X EXTRAIT
C ATRETIC	N INTREAT	RETRAIT	TASTIER	
CATTIER	ITERANT	TARTIER	TERTIAS	
CITRATE	NATTIER	S ARTIEST	T ATTRITE	

AEIRTV 196

TAIVER	D TARDIVE	VITRAGE	S TAIVERS	T TAIVERT
A VARIATE	E EVIRATE	M VITAMER	VASTIER	Y VARIETY
B VIBRATE	G VIRGATE	P PRIVATE	VERITAS	

AEISTT 163

TATIES	H ATHEIST	O OSTIATE	RATITES	W TAWIEST
A SATIATE	STAITHE	TOASTIE	STRIATE	TWAITES
B BATISTE	K TAKIEST	P PATTIES	TASTIER	X TAXITES
BISTATE	M ETATISM	TAPETIS	TERTIAS	Y SATIETY
C CATTIES	MATIEST	R ARTIEST	T ETATIST	
STATICE	MATTIES	ARTISTE	TATTIES	
TIETACS	N INSTATE	ATTIRES	U SITUATE	
F FATTIES	SATINET	IRATEST	V STATIVE	

AELNOR 120

RELOAN	I AILERON	L LLANERO	S LOANERS	U ALEURON
C CORNEAL	ALERION	M ALMONER	ORLEANS	V VERONAL
D LADRONE	ALIENOR	NEMORAL	RELOANS	

AELNOS 76

LANOSE	E ENOLASE	M MELANOS	R LOANERS	TOLANES
B BONSELA	G ENGAOLS	O ALSOONE	ORLEANS	
C SECONAL	H ENHALOS	P ESPANOL	RELOANS	
D LOADENS	I ANISOLE	NOPALES	T ETALONS	

AELNOT 93

TOLANE	G TANGELO	TOENAIL	P POLENTA	Y ANOLYTE
B NOTABLE	H ANETHOL	M LOMENTA	S ETALONS	
C LACTONE	ETHANOL	OMENTAL	TOLANES	
D TALONED	I ELATION	TELAMON	V VOLANTE	

AELNRS 64

RANSEL	RELANDS	SLANGER	ORLEANS	SLANTER
A ARSENAL	SLANDER	I ALINERS	RELOANS	STERNAL
B BRANLES	SNARLED	NAILERS	P PLANERS	V VERLANS
BRANSLE	E LEANERS	RENAILS	REPLANS	Y LARNEYS
C LANCERS	F SALFERN	K RANKLES	R SNARLER	Z RANZELS
RANCELS	G ANGLERS	M ALMNERS	S RANSELS	
D DARNELS	ERLANGS	N ENSNARL	T ANTLERS	
ENLARDS	LANGERS	LANNERS	RENTALS	
LANDERS	LARGENS	O LOANERS	SALTERN	

AELNRT 53

TERNAL	TELERAN	RATLINE	P PANTLER	SLANTER
B BRANTLE	G TANGLER	RELIANT	PLANTER	STERNAL
C CENTRAL	TRANGLE	RETINAL	REPLANT	T TRENTAL
E ALTERNE	H ENTHRAL	TRENAIL	S ANTLERS	U NEUTRAL
ENTERAL	I ENTRAIL	L ENTRALL	RENTALS	V VENTRAL
ETERNAL	LATRINE	N LANTERN	SALTERN	

AELNST 66

LATENS	LEANEST	SALTINE	N STANNEL	T LATENTS
A SEALANT	G GELANTS	SLAINTE	O ETALONS	LATTENS
C CANTLES	LANGEST	STANIEL	TOLANES	TALENTS
CENTALS	TANGLES	TENAILS	P PLANETS	U ELUANTS
LANCETS	H HANTLES	K ANKLETS	PLATENS	LUNATES
SCANTLE	I EASTLIN	ASKLENT	R ANTLERS	UNLASTE
D DENTALS	ELASTIN	LANKEST	RENTALS	V LEVANTS
SLANTED	ENTAILS	M LAMENTS	SALTERN	Y STANYEL
E ELANETS	NAILSET	MANTELS	SLANTER	Z ZELANTS
LATEENS	SALIENT	MANTLES	STERNAL	

AELORS 46

SOLERA	RECOALS	SAFROLE	ORLEANS	OARLESS
A AREOLAS	SOLACER	G GALORES	RELOANS	SEROSAL
B LABROSE	D LOADERS	GAOLERS	O AEROSOL	SOLERAS
C CLAROES	ORDEALS	H SHOALER	ROSEOLA	T OESTRAL
COALERS	RELOADS	L ROSELLA	P PAROLES	OLESTRA
ESCOLAR	E AREOLES	M MORALES	REPOSAL	
ORACLES	F LOAFERS	N LOANERS	S LASSOER	

AELORT 40

LORATE	F FLOATER	H LOATHER	R REALTOR	U ROTULAE
B BLOATER	FLOREAT	RATHOLE	RELATOR	TORULAE
C LOCATER	REFLOAT	L REALLOT	S OESTRAL	V LEVATOR
D DELATOR	G GLOATER	M MOLERAT	OLESTRA	Y ROYALET
LEOTARD	LEGATOR	P PROLATE	T RETOTAL	Z ZELATOR

AELOST 65

SOLATE	OBLATES	LACTOSE	SCATOLE	D SALTOED
B BOATELS	C ALECOST	LOCATES	TALCOSE	SOLATED

E OLEATES	H LOATHES	N ETALONS	R OESTRAL	Z ZEALOTS
F FOLATES	I ISOLATE	TOLANES	OLESTRA	
G GELATOS	K SKATOLE	P APOSTLE	S SOLATES	
LEGATOS	M MALTOSE	PELOTAS	V SOLVATE	

AELRST 48

TARSEL	REALEST	SLATIER	O OESTRAL	STARLET
A TARSEAL	RELATES	TAILERS	OLESTRA	STARTLE
B ALBERTS	RESLATE	K STALKER	P PALTERS	TATLERS
BATLERS	STEALER	TALKERS	PERSALT	U ESTRUAL
BLASTER	F FALTERS	L STELLAR	PLASTER	SALUTER
LABRETS	G LARGEST	TELLARS	PLATERS	V TRAVELS
STABLER	H HALTERS	M ARMLETS	PSALTER	VARLETS
C CARTELS	HARSLET	LAMSTER	STAPLER	VESTRAL
CLARETS	LATHERS	MARTELS	S ARTLESS	W WARSTLE
CRESTAL	SLATHER	TRAMELS	LASTERS	WASTREL
SCARLET	THALERS	N ANTLERS	SALTERS	WRASTLE
TARCELS	I REALIST	RENTALS	SLATERS	Y RAYLETS
D DARTLES	RETAILS	SALTERN	TARSELS	
SLARTED	SALTIER	SLANTER	T RATTLES	
E ELATERS	SALTIRE	STERNAL	SLATTER	

AEMNOR 110

MONERA	F FORAMEN	ROMAINE	R ORRAMEN	NEUROMA
A AMARONE	FOREMAN	L ALMONER	S ENAMORS	V OVERMAN
C CREMONA	G MARENGO	NEMORAL	MOANERS	Y ANYMORE
ROMANCE	MEGARON	N MONERAN	OARSMEN	ROMNEYA
D MADRONE	H MENORAH	P MANROPE	T TONEARM	
ROADMEN	I MORAINE	REPOMAN	U ENAMOUR	

AEMNOT 235

OMENTA	MEGATON	L LOMENTA	N MONTANE	T TOMENTA
B BOATMEN	MONTAGE	OMENTAL	NONMEAT	U AUTOMEN
G GEOMANT	H NATHEMO	TELAMON	R TONEARM	NOTAEUM
MAGNETO	I AMNIOTE	M MOMENTA	S MANTOES	OUTNAME

AENORS 21

SENORA	EARCONS	SENHORA	MOANERS	T ATONERS
B BORANES	NARCOSE	I ERASION	OARSMEN	SANTERO
C CANOERS	E ARENOSE	L LOANERS	P PERSONA	SENATOR
CARNOSE	G ONAGERS	ORLEANS	R SERRANO	TREASON
COARSEN	ORANGES	RELOANS	S REASONS	U ARENOUS
CORNEAS	H HOARSEN	M ENAMORS	SENORAS	

AENORT 8

ORNATE	D TORNADE	M TONEARM	PROTEAN	SENATOR
B BARONET	G NEGATOR	N NORTENA	R ORNATER	TREASON
REBOANT	H ANOTHER	P OPERANT	S ATONERS	U OUTEARN
C ENACTOR	I OTARINE	PRONATE	SANTERO	V VENATOR

AENOST 38

ATONES	DONATES	L ETALONS	SANTERO	NOTATES
B ONBEATS	ONSTEAD	TOLANES	SENATOR	U SOUTANE
C COSTEAN	G ONSTAGE	M MANTOES	TREASON	
OCTANES	TANGOES	P TEOPANS	S ASTONES	
D ASTONED	I ATONIES	R ATONERS	T ATTONES	

AENRRT 191

RANTER	G GRANTER	TERRAIN	P PARTNER	T TRANTER
A NARRATE	REGRANT	TRAINER	S ERRANTS	Y TERNARY
E TERRANE	I RETRAIN	O ORNATER	RANTERS	

AENRST 14

TRANSE	E EARNEST	RETAINS	MARTENS	R ERRANTS
A ANESTRA	EASTERN	RETINAS	SARMENT	RANTERS
SANTERA	NEAREST	RETSINA	SMARTEN	S SARSNET
B BANTERS	RATEENS	STAINER	N TANNERS	TRANSES
BARNETS	G ARGENTS	STARNIE	O ATONERS	T NATTERS
C CANTERS	GARNETS	STEARIN	SANTERO	RATTENS
CARNETS	STRANGE	K RANKEST	SENATOR	U AUNTERS
NECTARS	H ANTHERS	STARKEN	TREASON	NATURES
RECANTS	HARTENS	TANKERS	P ARPENTS	SAUNTER
SCANTER	THENARS	L ANTLERS	ENTRAPS	V SERVANT
TANRECS	I ANESTRI	RENTALS	PANTERS	TAVERNS
TRANCES	ANTSIER	SALTERN	PARENTS	VERSANT
D ENDARTS	NASTIER	SLANTER	PASTERN	W STRAWEN
STANDER	RATINES	STERNAL	PERSANT	WANTERS
STARNED	RESIANT	M ARTSMEN	TREPANS	Y TRAYNES

AENRTT 140

RATTEN	RATTEEN	NITRATE	P PATTERN	U TAUNTER
A TARTANE	TERNATE	TARTINE	REPTANT	Y NATTERY
C TRANECT	I INTREAT	TERTIAN	R TRANTER	
D TRANTED	ITERANT	L TRENTAL	S NATTERS	
E ENTREAT	NATTIER	N ENTRANT	RATTENS	

AENRTU 50

NATURE	D DAUNTER	UNEARTH	URINATE	SAUNTER
A NATURAE	NATURED	UNHEART	L NEUTRAL	T TAUNTER
TAUREAN	UNRATED	URETHAN	M TRUEMAN	V VAUNTER
C CENTAUR	UNTREAD	I RUINATE	O OUTEARN	W UNWATER
UNCRATE	G GAUNTER	TAURINE	S AUNTERS	
UNTRACE	H HAUNTER	URANITE	NATURES	

AENSTU 187

UNSEAT	I AUNTIES	UNTEAMS	NATURES	TAUTENS
B BUTANES	SINUATE	O SOUTANE	SAUNTER	TETANUS
SUNBEAT	L ELUANTS	P PEANUTS	S NASUTES	UNSTATE
C NUTCASE	LUNATES	PESAUNT	UNSEATS	X UNTAXES
D SAUNTED	UNLASTE	Q EQUANTS	T ATTUNES	
UNSATED	M UNTAMES	R AUNTERS	NUTATES	

AEOPRT 199

PROTEA		E	OPERATE	L	PROLATE	R	PRAETOR	SEAPORT
B	PROBATE	G	PORTAGE	N	OPERANT		PRORATE	T	PORTATE
D	ADOPTER		POTAGER		PRONATE	S	ESPARTO	V	OVERAPT
	READOPT	H	PHORATE		PROTEAN		PROTEAS	

AEORST 9

ROATES			RECOATS		TOERAGS		MAESTRO	R	ROASTER
A	AEROSAT	D	DOATERS	H	ASTHORE		OMERTAS	S	OSETRAS
B	BOASTER		ROASTED		EARSHOT	N	ATONERS		OSSETRA
	BOATERS		TORSADE		HAROSET		SANTERO	T	ROTATES
	BORATES		TROADES	I	OARIEST		SENATOR		TOASTER
	REBATOS	E	ROSEATE		OTARIES		TREASON	
	SORBATE	G	GAROTES	L	OESTRAL	P	ESPARTO	
C	COASTER		ORGEATS		OLESTRA		PROTEAS	
	COATERS		STORAGE	M	AMORETS		SEAPORT	

AERRST 215

TERRAS			RETARDS	G	GARRETS		KRATERS	S	ARRESTS
A	ERRATAS		STARRED		GARTERS		STARKER		RASTERS
B	BARRETS		TRADERS		GRATERS	M	ARMREST		STARERS
	BARTERS	E	RETEARS	H	TRASHER		SMARTER	T	RATTERS
C	CARTERS		SERRATE	I	ARTSIER	N	ERRANTS		RESTART
	CRATERS		TEARERS		SERRATI		RANTERS		STARTER
	TRACERS	F	FRATERS		TARRIES	O	ROASTER	V	STARVER
D	DARTERS		RAFTERS		TARSIER	P	PARTERS	Y	STRAYER
	DARTRES		STRAFER	K	KARTERS		PRATERS	

AERSTT 193

TREATS			RATHEST	L	RATTLES	P	PATTERS		TARTEST
B	BATTERS		SHATTER		SLATTER		SPATTER		TATTERS
	TABRETS		THREATS		STARLET		TAPSTER	U	ASTUTER
C	SCATTER	I	ARTIEST		STARTLE	R	RATTERS		STATURE
D	STARTED		ARTISTE		TATLERS		RESTART	V	VATTERS
	TETRADS		ATTIRES	M	MATTERS		STARTER	W	SWATTER
E	ESTREAT		IRATEST		SMATTER	S	ASTERTS		TEWARTS
	RESTATE		RATITES	N	NATTERS		STARETS	Y	YATTERS
	RETASTE		STRIATE		RATTENS		STATERS	Z	STARETZ
G	TARGETS		TASTIER	O	ROTATES		TASTERS	
H	HATTERS		TERTIAS		TOASTER	T	STRETTA	

AERSTU 173

URATES			CAUTERS		SALUTER	P	PASTURE		QUATRES
A	AURATES		CRUSTAE	M	MATURES		UPRATES	T	ASTUTER
B	ARBUTES		CURATES		STRUMAE		UPSTARE		STATURE
	BURSATE	E	AUSTERE	N	AUNTERS		UPTEARS	U	AUTEURS
	SURBATE	F	FAUREST		NATURES	Q	QUAREST	Y	ESTUARY
C	ACTURES	L	ESTRUAL		SAUNTER		QUARTES	

AGINOR 183

ORIGAN	ROADING	M ROAMING	S IGNAROS	T ORATING
C ORGANIC	E ORIGANE	P PIGNORA	ORIGANS	ROATING
D ADORING	H HOARING	PORANGI	SIGNORA	Z ZINGARO
GRADINO	L RANGOLI	R ROARING	SOARING	

AGINOT 234

GITANO	D DOATING	M MOATING	S AGONIST	V OVATING
B BOATING	F ANTIFOG	N ATONING	GITANOS	Z TOAZING
C COATING	G GIGATON	R ORATING	U AUTOING	
COTINGA	L ANTILOG	ROATING	OUTGAIN	

AGINRT 107

TARING	GRATINE	TARGING	O ORATING	RATINGS
A GRANITA	INGRATE	I AIRTING	ROATING	STARING
C CARTING	TANGIER	RAITING	P PARTING	TARINGS
CRATING	TEARING	K KARTING	PRATING	T RATTING
TRACING	F FARTING	L RATLING	TRAPING	TARTING
D DARTING	INGRAFT	M MARTING	R TARRING	W RINGTAW
TRADING	RAFTING	MIGRANT	S GASTRIN	Y GIANTRY
E GRANITE	G GRATING	N RANTING	GRATINS	

AILNOS 233

SIALON	D DOLINAS	K KAOLINS	N SOLANIN	TALIONS
B ALBINOS	LADINOS	M MALISON	S ALISONS	
C ALNICOS	E ANISOLE	MONIALS	SIALONS	
OILCANS	I LIAISON	SOMNIAL	T LATINOS	

AILNOT 131

TALION	B BITONAL	G ANTILOG	TALIONS	
A AILANTO	E ELATION	N ANTLION	U OUTLAIN	
ALATION	TOENAIL	S LATINOS		

AILNST 214

INSTAL	ELASTIN	STANIEL	STALING	S INSTALS
A LATINAS	ENTAILS	TENAILS	L INSTALL	T LATTINS
C CATLINS	NAILSET	G ANGLIST	O LATINOS	U UNALIST
TINCALS	SALIENT	LASTING	TALIONS	Y NASTILY
D TINDALS	SLAINTE	SALTING	P PLAINTS	SAINTLY
E EASTLIN		SLATING	R RATLINS	

AILOST 159

OSTIAL	E ISOLATE	N LATINOS	RIALTOS	X OXTAILS
A SOLATIA	G GALIOTS	TALIONS	SLIOTAR	
B OBLASTI	LATIGOS	P APOSTIL	TAILORS	
C CITOLAS	SALIGOT	TOPSAIL	T ALTOIST	
STOICAL	M SOMITAL	R ORALIST	U OUTSAIL	

AILRST 248

	TRIALS	E	REALIST		TAILERS	O	ORALIST	U	RITUALS
A	LARIATS		RETAILS	I	LIATRIS		RIALTOS		TRISULA
	LATRIAS		SALTIER	M	MISTRAL		SLIOTAR	Y	TRYSAIL
B	TRIBALS		SALTIRE		RAMTILS		TAILORS		
C	CITRALS		SLATIER	N	RATLINS	T	STARLIT		

AINORS 162

	NORIAS		SADIRON		ORIGANS	P	PARISON		RATIONS
C	SARONIC	E	ERASION		SIGNORA		PORINAS	W	WARISON
D	INROADS	F	INSOFAR		SOARING		SOPRANI		
	ORDAINS	G	IGNAROS	M	MAINORS	T	AROINTS		

AINORT 26

	RATION	D	DIATRON	H	ORTHIAN	P	ATROPIN	W	WAITRON
B	TABORIN	E	OTARINE	J	JANITOR	S	AROINTS	X	TRIAXON
C	CAROTIN	G	ORATING	M	TORMINA		RATIONS		
	CORTINA		ROATING	O	ORATION	U	RAINOUT		

AINRST 86

	TRAINS		ANTSIER		STARNIE	K	KIRTANS	S	INSTARS
A	ANTIARS		NASTIER		STEARIN	L	RATLINS		SANTIRS
	ARTISAN		RATINES	G	GASTRIN	M	MARTINS		STRAINS
	TSARINA		RESIANT		GRATINS	O	AROINTS	T	STRAINT
B	BRISANT		RETAINS		RATINGS		RATIONS		TRANSIT
C	NARCIST		RETINAS		STARING	P	SPIRANT	U	NUTRIAS
D	INDARTS		RETSINA		TARINGS		SPRAINT		
E	ANESTRI		STAINER	H	TARNISH	Q	QINTARS		

AINRTU 181

	NUTRIA		UNITARD		URINATE	O	RAINOUT	S	NUTRIAS
C	CURTAIN	E	RUINATE	F	ANTIFUR	P	PURITAN	Y	UNITARY
	TURACIN		TAURINE	M	NATRIUM		UPTRAIN		
D	TRIDUAN		URANITE	N	URINANT	Q	QUINTAR		

AIORST 68

	SATORI	G	AGISTOR	L	ORALIST		RATIONS		SATORIS
B	ORBITAS		ORGIAST		RIALTOS	P	AIRPOST	U	SAUTOIR
D	ASTROID	H	AIRSHOT		SLIOTAR		AIRSTOP	V	TRAVOIS
E	OARIEST		SHORTIA		TAILORS		PAROTIS		VIATORS
	OTARIES		THORIAS	M	AMORIST	S	AORISTS	Y	OSTIARY
F	FAITORS	K	TROIKAS	N	AROINTS		ARISTOS		

ANORST 109

	TRONAS		CRATONS		RATIONS	O	RATOONS		RATTONS
A	TORANAS	E	ATONERS	L	LATRONS		SANTOOR		ROTTANS
B	BARTONS		SANTERO	M	MATRONS	P	PARTONS	U	ROUSANT
C	CANTORS		SENATOR		TRANSOM		PATRONS		SANTOUR
	CARTONS		TREASON	N	NATRONS		TARPONS	Y	AROYNTS
	CONTRAS	I	AROINTS		NONARTS	T	ATTORNS		

CEINOR 220

RECOIN	INFORCE	PONCIER	ORCINES	NOURICE
B BICORNE	G COREIGN	PORCINE	RECOINS	V CORVINE
C CORNICE	H CHORINE	R CORNIER	SERICON	Y ORIENCY
CROCEIN	I ONEIRIC	S COINERS	T COINTER	
CROCINE	K CONKIER	CRINOSE	NOTICER	
F COINFER	M INCOMER	CRONIES	RECTION	
CONIFER	P PERICON	ORCEINS	U COENURI	

CEINOT 198

NOTICE	DEONTIC	L LECTION	P ENTOPIC	S NOTICES
A ACONITE	NOTICED	M CENTIMO	NEPOTIC	SECTION
ANOETIC	H HENOTIC	ENTOMIC	R COINTER	T ENTOTIC
C CONCEIT	K KENOTIC	TONEMIC	NOTICER	TONETIC
D CTENOID	KETONIC	O COONTIE	RECTION	X EXCITON

CEIORT 134

TERCIO	E COTERIE	L CORTILE	S EROTICS	X EXCITOR
A EROTICA	G ERGOTIC	M MORTICE	TERCIOS	XEROTIC
C CEROTIC	H ROTCHIE	N COINTER	T COTTIER	
ORECTIC	THEORIC	NOTICER	V EVICTOR	
D CORDITE	K TOCKIER	RECTION	W COWRITE	

CEIOST 231

OECIST	H ECHOIST	O COOTIES	OECISTS	COXIEST
A SOCIATE	TOISECH	P POETICS	T COTTISE	EXOTICS
D CESTOID	K COKIEST	R EROTICS	SCOTTIE	Y SOCIETY
COEDITS	L CITOLES	TERCIOS	V COSTIVE	Z COZIEST
COTISED	N NOTICES	S COSIEST	W COWIEST	
E COESITE	SECTION	COTISES	X COEXIST	

DEEILR 241

RELIED	FIELDER	N REDLINE	S RESILED	REVILED
A LEADIER	REFILED	RELINED	T RETILED	W WIELDER
D DREIDEL	G GELIDER	O REOILED	V DELIVER	Y REEDILY
F DEFILER	LEDGIER	P PERILED	LIVERED	YIELDER
FERLIED	LEIDGER	REPLIED	RELIVED	

DEEINR 61

RENIED	ENFIRED	REIGNED	P REPINED	U UREDINE
B BENDIER	FENDIER	H INHERED	RIPENED	W REWIDEN
INBREED	REFINED	K REINKED	R DERNIER	WIDENER
C CEDRINE	G DREEING	L REDLINE	NERDIER	X INDEXER
D NEDDIER	ENERGID	RELINED	S DENIERS	REINDEX
E NEEDIER	GREINED	M ERMINED	NEREIDS	
F DEFINER	REEDING	O ORDINEE	RESINED	

DEEINS 210

	SEINED	F	DEFINES		ENSILED		NEREIDS	V	DEVEINS
A	ANISEED	G	SDEIGNE		LINSEED		RESINED		ENDIVES
C	INCEDES		SEEDING	M	DESMINE	S	DESINES	W	ENDWISE
D	DESINED	K	ENSKIED		SIDEMEN	T	DESTINE		SINEWED
	NEDDIES		SKEINED	N	INDENES		ENDITES	X	INDEXES
	SDEINED	L	ENISLED	R	DENIERS		STEINED		

DEEINT 137

	ENDITE		TEINDED	L	LENITED	S	DESTINE	T	DINETTE
C	ENTICED	F	FEINTED	M	DEMENTI		ENDITES	U	DETINUE
D	ENDITED	I	DIETINE	N	DENTINE		STEINED	V	EVIDENT

DEEIRS 87

	RESIDE		RESIDED		RESINED		SERRIED	V	DERIVES
A	DEARIES	E	SEEDIER	O	OREIDES	S	DESIRES		DEVISER
	READIES	F	DEFIERS		OSIERED		RESIDES		DIVERSE
B	BREDIES		SERIFED	P	PRESIDE	T	DIESTER		REVISED
	DERBIES	G	SEDGIER		SPEIRED		DIETERS	W	SWEIRED
C	DECRIES	L	RESILED		SPIERED		REEDITS	Z	RESIZED
	DEICERS	M	REMEIDS	R	DERRIES		REISTED		
D	DERIDES		REMISED		DESIRER		RESISTED		
	DESIRED	N	DENIERS		REDRIES	U	RESIDUE		
	DIEDRES		NEREIDS		RESIDER		UREIDES		

DEENOR 147

	REDONE	C	ENCODER	M	MODERNE	S	ENDORSE	Z	REZONED
B	DEBONER		ENCORED	N	ENDERON	T	ERODENT		
	ENROBED	G	ENGORED	O	RONEOED	W	ENDOWER		
	REDBONE	I	ORDINEE	P	REPONED		REENDOW		

DEENRS 197

	SENDER	E	NEEDERS		NEREIDS	O	ENDORSE		TENDERS
A	DEANERS		SERENED		RESINED	P	SPENDER		TENDRES
	ENDEARS		SNEERED	L	LENDERS	R	RENDERS	U	ENDURES
B	BENDERS	F	FENDERS		RELENDS	S	REDNESS		ENSURED
C	DECERNS	G	GENDERS		SLENDER		RESENDS	V	VENDERS
	SCERNED	H	HERDENS	M	MENDERS		SENDERS	Z	DZERENS
D	REDDENS	I	DENIERS		REMENDS	T	STERNED		

DEGINR 166

	RINGED		READING		GREINED		RENDING		REGRIND
A	AREDING	B	BREDING		REEDING	O	ERODING	S	DINGERS
	DEARING	C	CRINGED		REIGNED		GROINED		ENGIRDS
	DERAIGN	D	GRINDED	F	FRINGED		IGNORED	U	DUNGIER
	EARDING		REDDING	H	HERDING		NEGROID	W	REDWING
	GRADINE	E	DREEING	I	DINGIER		REDOING		WRINGED
	GRAINED		ENERGID	N	GRINNED	R	GRINDER	Y	YERDING

DEIINT 205

TINEID	D INDITED	IGNITED	NITRIDE
A INEDITA	E DIETINE	O EDITION	S INDITES
C IDENTIC	G DIETING	TENIOID	TINEIDS
INCITED	EDITING	R INDITER	V INVITED

DEILNO 213

INDOLE	G GLENOID	S DOLINES	SONDELI	U UNOILED
E ELOINED	O EIDOLON	INDOLES	T LENTOID	

DEILOR 105

ROILED	D DROILED	GOLDIER	P LEPORID	W DOWLIER
A DARIOLE	E REOILED	K RODLIKE	S SOLDIER	
B BROILED	G GLORIED	L DOLLIER	SOLIDER	
C DOCILER	GODLIER	M MOLDIER	T DOILTER	

DEILOS 123

SOILED	E OILSEED	MIDSOLE	P DESPOIL	R SOLDIER
A DEASOIL	I DOILIES	SMOILED	DIPLOES	SOLIDER
ISOLEAD	IDOLISE	N DOLINES	DIPOLES	V LIVEDOS
B BOLIDES	K KELOIDS	INDOLES	PELOIDS	Y DOYLIES
C COLDIES	L DOLLIES	SONDELI	SOLIPED	
D DILDOES	M MELOIDS	O DOOLIES	SPOILED	

DEILRT 130

TIRLED	B DRIBLET	TRIFLED	N TENDRIL	U DILUTER
A DILATER	D TIDDLER	H THIRLED	TRINDLE	W TWIRLED
REDTAIL	E RETILED	K KIRTLED	O DOILTER	Y TIREDLY
TRAILED	F FLIRTED	L TRILLED	P TRIPLED	

DEINOR 29

ROINED	IGNORED	N ENDIRON	INDORSE	W DOWNIER
A ANEROID	NEGROID	P POINDER	ORDINES	WINDORE
B INORBED	REDOING	PROINED	ROSINED	
E ORDINEE	H HORDEIN	R DRONIER	SORDINE	
G ERODING	J JOINDER	S DINEROS	U DOURINE	
GROINED	M MINORED	DONSIER	NEUROID	

DEINOS 75

ONSIDE	D NODDIES	INDOLES	P DISPONE	SORDINE
A ADONISE	G DINGOES	SONDELI	SPINODE	S ONSIDES
ANODISE	H HOIDENS	M DOMINES	R DINEROS	T DITONES
SODAINE	I IODINES	EMODINS	DONSIER	STONIED
C CODEINS	IONISED	MISDONE	INDORSE	
CONDIES	K DOESKIN	N DONNIES	ORDINES	
SECONDI	L DOLINES	ONDINES	ROSINED	

DEINOT 113

OINTED	NOTICED	I EDITION	L LENTOID	P POINTED
C CTENOID	D DENTOID	TENIOID	N INTONED	S DITONES
DEONTIC	G INGOTED	J JOINTED	NOINTED	STONIED

DEINRS 85

SNIDER	RESCIND	ENGIRDS	M MINDERS	SORDINE
A RANDIES	E DENIERS	H HINDERS	REMINDS	P PINDERS
SANDIER	NEREIDS	NERDISH	N DINNERS	T TINDERS
SARDINE	RESINED	SHRINED	ENDRINS	U INSURED
B BINDERS	F FINDERS	I INSIDER	O DINEROS	V VERDINS
INBREDS	FRIENDS	SNIDIER	DONSIER	W REWINDS
REBINDS	REDFINS	K KINDERS	INDORSE	WINDERS
C CINDERS	REFINDS	KINREDS	ORDINES	
DISCERN	G DINGERS	REDSKIN	ROSINED	

DEINRT 126

TRINED	I INDITER	P PRINTED	TURDINE	X DEXTRIN
A ANTIRED	NITRIDE	S TINDERS	UNTIRED	Y TINDERY
DETRAIN	L TENDRIL	T TRIDENT	UNTRIDE	
TRAINED	TRINDLE	U INTRUDE	UNTRIED	

DEINRU 79

URINED	E UREDINE	J INJURED	NEUROID	UNTIRED
A UNAIRED	F UNFIRED	M UNRIMED	R NURDIER	UNTRIDE
URANIDE	G DUNGIER	N DUNNIER	S INSURED	UNTRIED
C INDUCER	H UNHIRED	INURNED	T INTRUDE	W UNWIRED
D UNDRIED	I URIDINE	O DOURINE	TURDINE	

DEINST 56

TEINDS	D DISTEND	TINEIDS	O DITONES	DISTENT
A DESTAIN	E DESTINE	K DINKEST	STONIED	STINTED
DETAINS	ENDITES	KINDEST	P DIPNETS	U DISTUNE
INSTEAD	STEINED	L DENTILS	STIPEND	DUNITES
NIDATES	F SNIFTED	M MINDSET	R TINDERS	Y DENSITY
SAINTED	G NIDGETS	MISTEND	S DISNEST	DESTINY
SATINED	STEDING	N DENTINS	DISSENT	
STAINED	STINGED	INDENTS	SNIDEST	
B BIDENTS	I INDITES	INTENDS	T DENTIST	

DEINTU 218

UNTIED	G DUETING	MUNITED	R INTRUDE	UNTRIED
A AUDIENT	L DILUENT	MUTINED	TURDINE	S DISTUNE
C UNCITED	UNTILED	UNTIMED	UNTIRED	DUNITES
E DETINUE	M MINUTED	N DUNNITE	UNTRIDE	

DEIORS 36

ROSIED	SOREDIA	DISROBE	SCODIER	SODDIER
A ROADIES	B BORIDES	C DISCOER	D DORISED	E OREIDES

OSIERED	N DINEROS	OROIDES	SORTIED	VISORED
H RHODIES	DONSIER	P PERIODS	STEROID	VOIDERS
I IODISER	INDORSE	S DORISES	STORIED	W DOWRIES
L SOLDIER	ORDINES	DOSSIER	TIERODS	ROWDIES
SOLIDER	ROSINED	T EDITORS	TRIODES	WEIRDOS
M MISDOER	SORDINE	ROISTED	V DEVISOR	Z DORIZES
MOIDERS	O ODORISE	ROSITED	DEVOIRS	

DEIORT 47

TRIODE	H THEROID	PROTEID	STEROID	IODURET
B DEBITOR	I DIORITE	R DORTIER	STORIED	OUTRIDE
DEORBIT	L DOILTER	S EDITORS	TIERODS	Z ROZITED
ORBITED	P DIOPTER	ROISTED	TRIODES	
C CORDITE	DIOPTRE	ROSITED	T DOTTIER	
G GOITRED	PERIDOT	SORTIED	U ETOURDI	

DEIOST 70

TODIES	H HOISTED	O OSTEOID	ROISTED	STOITED
A IODATES	J JOISTED	P DEPOSIT	ROSITED	U OUTSIDE
TOADIES	M DISTOME	DOPIEST	SORTIED	TEDIOUS
C CESTOID	DOMIEST	PODITES	STEROID	V DOVIEST
COEDITS	MODISTE	POSITED	STORIED	W DOWIEST
COTISED	MOISTED	SOPITED	TIERODS	X EXODIST
D TODDIES	N DITONES	TOPSIDE	TRIODES	Z DOZIEST
F FOISTED	STONIED	R EDITORS	T DOTIEST	

DEIRST 104

STRIDE	B BESTRID	H DITHERS	SORTIED	STRIDES
A ARIDEST	BISTRED	SHIRTED	STEROID	U DUSTIER
ASTERID	C CREDITS	I DIRTIES	STORIED	REDUITS
ASTRIDE	DIRECTS	DITSIER	TIERODS	STUDIER
DIASTER	E DIESTER	TIDIERS	TRIODES	V DIVERTS
DISRATE	DIETERS	K SKIRTED	P SPIRTED	STRIVED
STAIDER	REEDITS	N TINDERS	STRIPED	VERDITS
STAIRED	REISTED	O EDITORS	R STIRRED	
TARDIES	RESITED	ROISTED	STRIDER	
TIRADES	F FRISTED	ROSITED	S DISSERT	

DELORT 203

RETOLD	F TELFORD	O ROOTLED	OLDSTER	U TROULED
A DELATOR	I DOILTER	P DROPLET	STRODLE	
LEOTARD	L TROLLED	PRETOLD	T DOTTLER	
D TODDLER	N ENTROLD	S DROLEST	DOTTREL	

DENORS 150

SORNED	SNODDER	ROSINED	RESPOND	SOUNDER
B BONDERS	E ENDORSE	SORDINE	R DRONERS	UNDOERS
C CONDERS	H DEHORNS	L RONDELS	S SONDERS	V VENDORS
CORSNED	I DINEROS	M MODERNS	T RODENTS	W DOWNERS
SCORNED	DONSIER	RODENTS	SNORTED	WONDERS
D DONDERS	INDORSE	RODSMEN	U ENDUROS	Y YONDERS
NODDERS	ORDINES	P PERNODS	RESOUND	
		PONDERS		

DENORT 124

RODENT	F FRONTED	THRONED	TENDRON	SNORTED
A TORNADE	H NORTHED	L ENTROLD	P PORTEND	
D TRODDEN	THONDER	M MORDENT	PROTEND	
E ERODENT	THORNED	N DONNERT	S RODENTS	

DENORU 177

UNDOER	ROUNDED	H HOUNDER	N ENROUND	RESOUND
A RONDEAU	UNDERDO	I DOURINE	P POUNDER	SOUNDER
B BOUNDER	F FOUNDER	NEUROID	UNROPED	UNDOERS
REBOUND	REFOUND	L LOUNDER	R RONDURE	W REWOUND
UNROBED	G GUERDON	ROUNDEL	ROUNDER	WOUNDER
C CRUNODE	UNDERGO	ROUNDLE	UNORDER	
D REDOUND	UNGORED	M MOURNED	S ENDUROS	

DENOST 128

STONED	C DOCENTS	K STONKED	STOODEN	SNOUTED
A ASTONED	E DENOTES	M ENDMOST	R RODENTS	
DONATES	F FONDEST	N STONNED	SNORTED	
ONSTEAD	I DITONES	TENDONS	T SNOTTED	
B OBTENDS	STONIED	O SNOOTED	U DEUTONS	

DEORST 89

TRODES	F DEFROST	STORIED	O ROOSTED	DOUTERS
A DOATERS	FROSTED	TIERODS	P DEPORTS	OUTREDS
ROASTED	G STODGER	TRIODES	REDTOPS	REDOUTS
TORSADE	H DEHORTS	K STROKED	SPORTED	ROUSTED
TROADES	SHORTED	L DROLEST	R DORTERS	W STROWED
B DEBTORS	I EDITORS	OLDSTER	RODSTER	WORSTED
STROBED	ROISTED	STRODLE	T DETORTS	Y DESTROY
E OERSTED	ROSITED	M STORMED	DOTTERS	ROYSTED
ROSETED	SORTIED	N RODENTS	U DETOURS	STROYED
TEREDOS	STEROID	SNORTED	DOUREST	

DEORTU 189

TOURED	OUTBRED	GROUTED	OUTRODE	OUTREDS
A OUTDARE	REDOUBT	I ETOURDI	P TROUPED	REDOUTS
OUTREAD	C COURTED	IODURET	Q TORQUED	ROUSTED
READOUT	EDUCTOR	OUTRIDE	S DETOURS	T TUTORED
B DOUBTER	F FOUTRED	L TROULED	DOUREST	U OUTDURE
OBTRUDE	G DROGUET	O OUTDOER	DOUTERS	W OUTDREW

EEILNR 180

RELINE	C RECLINE	G LEERING	O ELOINER	V LIVENER
A ALIENER	D REDLINE	REELING	S LIERNES	
B BERLINE	RELINED	M ERMELIN	RELINES	

EEILNS 207

SILENE	ENSILED	M ISLEMEN	ENSILES	SETLINE
A SEALINE	LINSEED	O OLEINES	SENILES	TENSILE
C LICENSE	F FELINES	P PENSILE	SENSILE	Y YEELINS
SELENIC	G LEESING	R LIERNES	SILENES	
SILENCE	SEELING	RELINES	T LENITES	
D ENISLED	L NELLIES	S ENISLES	LISENTE	

EEILNT 157

LENITE	D LENITED	N LENIENT	SETLINE	
A LINEATE	G GENTILE	P PENLITE	TENSILE	
C CENTILE	H THEELIN	S LENITES	T ENTITLE	
LICENTE	K NETLIKE	LISENTE	V VEINLET	

EEILRS 95

RESILE	F FERLIES	L LEISLER	R RELIERS	V LEVIERS
A EARLIES	REFILES	RELLIES	S IRELESS	RELIVES
REALISE	REFLIES	N LIERNES	RESILES	REVILES
B BELIERS	RELIEFS	RELINES	T LEISTER	SERVILE
C CEILERS	G LEIGERS	O LOERIES	RETILES	VEILERS
D RESILED	LIEGERS	P REPLIES	STERILE	X EXILERS
E SEELIER	H LEISHER	SPIELER	U LEISURE	

EEILRT 138

RETILE	TIERCEL	L TREILLE	REPTILE	T RETITLE
A ATELIER	D RETILED	M MELTIER	S LEISTER	
REALTIE	F FELTIER	O TROELIE	RETILES	
C RETICLE	FERTILE	P PERLITE	STERILE	

EEILST 164

LISTEE	LIEFEST	M ELMIEST	P EPISTLE	TIELESS
C SECTILE	G ELEGIST	N LENITES	PELITES	V EVILEST
D ISLETED	ELEGITS	LISENTE	R LEISTER	LEVITES
E EELIEST	H SHELTIE	SETLINE	RETILES	LIEVEST
STEELIE	K KELTIES	TENSILE	STERILE	VELITES
F FELSITE	SLEEKIT	O ESTOILE	S LISTEES	X SEXTILE
LEFTIES	L TELLIES	ETOILES	TELESIS	

EEINRS 73

SERINE	FEERINS	M ERMINES	T ENTIRES	VENIRES
C CERESIN	FINEERS	N NERINES	ENTRIES	VERSINE
SCRIENE	REFINES	P EREPSIN	NERITES	W NEWSIER
SINCERE	REPINES	REPINES	RETINES	WEINERS
D DENIERS	G GREISEN	R RERISEN	TRENISE	WIENERS
NEREIDS	H HENRIES	RESINER	TRIENES	X REXINES
RESINED	INHERES	S SEINERS	V ENVIERS	
E ESERINE	L LIERNES	SEREINS	INVERSE	
F ENFIRES	RELINES	SERINES	VEINERS	

EEINRT 12

TRIENE	F FEINTER	NITERIE	S ENTIRES	U NEURITE
A ARENITE	G GENTIER	K KERNITE	ENTRIES	RETINUE
RETINAE	INTEGER	N INTERNE	NERITES	REUNITE
TRAINEE	TEERING	P INEPTER	RETINES	UTERINE
B BENTIER	TREEING	R INERTER	TRENISE	
C ENTERIC	H NEITHER	REINTER	TRIENES	
ENTICER	THEREIN	RENTIER	T NETTIER	
E TEENIER	I ERINITE	TERRINE	TENTIER	

EEINST 60

SEITEN	H THEINES	M EMETINS	NERITES	T NETTIES
A ETESIAN	I SIENITE	N INTENSE	RETINES	V TENSIVE
C ENTICES	L LENITES	TENNIES	TRENISE	VENITES
D DESTINE	LISENTE	P PENTISE	TRIENES	X EXTINES
ENDITES	SETLINE	R ENTIRES	S SEITENS	SIXTEEN
STEINED	TENSILE	ENTRIES	SESTINE	Y SYENITE

EEIORS 146

SOIREE	OSIERED	M ISOMERE	T EROTISE
B EBRIOSE	H HEROISE	R ROSIERE	V EROSIVE
D OREIDES	L LOERIES	S SOIREES	

EEIORT 145

TOEIER	C COTERIE	S EROTISE	Z EROTIZE
A ETAERIO	L TROELIE		

EEIRST 28

RETIES	RESITED	REEMITS	P PESTIER	V RESTIVE
A AERIEST	E EERIEST	RETIMES	RESPITE	SIEVERT
SERIATE	F FESTIER	TREMIES	R ETRIERS	STIEVER
B REBITES	H HEISTER	TRISEME	REITERS	VERIEST
C CERITES	K KEISTER	N ENTIRES	RESTIER	VERITES
RECITES	KIESTER	ENTRIES	RETIRES	W STEWIER
TIERCES	L LEISTER	NERITES	RETRIES	Z ZESTIER
D DIESTER	RETILES	RETINES	TERRIES	
DIETERS	STERILE	TRENISE	S RESITES	
REEDITS	M MEISTER	TRIENES	T TESTIER	
REISTED	METIERS	O EROTISE	U SUETIER	

EENRST 69

TREENS	E ENTREES	TRIENES	SERPENT	U NEUTERS
A EARNEST	RETENES	K RENKEST	R RENTERS	RETUNES
EASTERN	TEENERS	L NESTLER	RERENTS	TENURES
NEAREST	G GERENTS	RELENTS	STERNER	TUREENS
RATEENS	REGENTS	SLENTER	S NESTERS	V VENTERS
C CENTERS	H THRENES	N RENNETS	RENESTS	VENTRES
CENTRES	I ENTIRES	TENNERS	RESENTS	W WESTERN
TENRECS	ENTRIES	O ESTRONE	STRENES	X EXTERNS
D STERNED	NERITES	P PENSTER	T NETTERS	Y STYRENE
TENDERS	RETINES	PRESENT	TENTERS	YESTERN
TENDRES	TRENISE	REPENTS	TESTERN	

EEORST 92

STEREO	H HETEROS	M EMOTERS	S OSSETER	REVOTES
A ROSEATE	I EROTISE	METEORS	STEREOS	VETOERS
D OERSTED	J RESOJET	REMOTES	T ROSETTE	X XEROTES
ROSETED	K RESTOKE	N ESTRONE	V ESTOVER	Y ESOTERY
TEREDOS	L SOLERET	R RESTORE	OVERSET	

EGILNT 135

TINGLE	D GLINTED	J JINGLET	R RINGLET	TINGLES
A ATINGLE	TINGLED	K KINGLET	TINGLER	T ETTLING
ELATING	E GENTILE	L GILLNET	TRINGLE	LETTING
GELATIN	F FELTING	TELLING	S GLISTEN	U ELUTING
GENITAL	H ENLIGHT	M MELTING	LESTING	W WELTING
TAGLINE	LIGHTEN	O LENTIGO	SINGLET	WINGLET
B BELTING	I LIGNITE	P PELTING	SNIGLET	

EGINOR 67

REGION	IGNORED	N NEGRONI	R IGNORER	T GENITOR
A ORIGANE	NEGROID	O GOONIER	S ERINGOS	V OVERING
C COREIGN	REDOING	P PERIGON	IGNORES	Z ZEROING
D ERODING	F FOREIGN	PIROGEN	REGIONS	
GROINED	M MOERING	PONGIER	SIGNORE	

EGINOS 119

SOIGNE	D DINGOES	LEGIONS	NOOGIES	SIGNORE
A AGONIES	E GENOISE	LIGNOSE	P EPIGONS	U IGNEOUS
AGONISE	SOIGNEE	LINGOES	PIGEONS	W WIGEONS
B BINGOES	H HONGIES	LONGIES	PINGOES	Y ISOGENY
BIOGENS	SHOEING	M MISGONE	R ERINGOS	Z GINZOES
C COGNISE	J JINGOES	O GOONIES	IGNORES	
COIGNES	L ELOIGNS	ISOGONE	REGIONS	

EGINRS 122

SINGER	C CRINGES	LINGERS	PINGERS	U REUSING
A ANGRIES	D DINGERS	SLINGER	SPRINGE	RUEINGS
EARINGS	ENGIRDS	M GERMINS	R ERRINGS	SIGNEUR
ERASING	E GREISEN	MERINGS	GIRNERS	V SERVING
GAINERS	F FINGERS	MINGERS	RINGERS	VERSING
GRAINES	FRINGES	N ENRINGS	SERRING	W SWINGER
REAGINS	G GINGERS	GINNERS	S INGRESS	WINGERS
REGAINS	NIGGERS	O ERINGOS	RESIGNS	Y SYRINGE
REGINAS	SERGING	IGNORES	SIGNERS	Z ZINGERS
SEARING	SNIGGER	REGIONS	SINGERS	
SERINGA	H HINGERS	SIGNORE	T RESTING	
B BINGERS	L GIRNELS	P PERSING	STINGER	

EGINRT 77

ENGIRT	INGRATE	E GENTIER	TREEING	TIERING
A GRANITE	TANGIER	INTEGER	H RIGHTEN	TIGRINE
GRATINE	TEARING	TEERING	I IGNITER	L RINGLET

TINGLER	TERMING	TERNING	STINGER	U TRUEING
TRINGLE	N RENTING	O GENITOR	T GITTERN	V VERTING
M METRING	RINGENT	S RESTING	RETTING	Y RETYING

EGINST 225

TINGES	TANGIES	J JESTING	N NESTING	U GUNITES
A EASTING	TEASING	K KESTING	SENTING	V VESTING
EATINGS	TSIGANE	L GLISTEN	TENSING	W STEWING
GAINEST	B BESTING	LESTING	R RESTING	TWINGES
GENISTA	D NIDGETS	SINGLET	STINGER	WESTING
INGATES	STEDING	SNIGLET	S INGESTS	Z ZESTING
INGESTA	STINGED	TINGLES	SIGNETS	
SEATING	H NIGHEST	M STEMING	T SETTING	
TAGINES	I IGNITES	TEMSING	TESTING	

EGIORT 206

GOITRE	D GOITRED	GOITRES	V VERTIGO
A GOATIER	N GENITOR	GORIEST	Z ZORGITE
C ERGOTIC	S GOITERS	U GOUTIER	

EIINRT 57

TINIER	D INDITER	TIERING	MINTIER	V INVITER
A INERTIA	NITRIDE	TIGRINE	TERMINI	VITRINE
C CITRINE	E ERINITE	H INHERIT	N TINNIER	W TWINIER
CRINITE	NITERIE	L LINTIER	T NITRITE	
INCITER	F NIFTIER	NITRILE	NITTIER	
NERITIC	G IGNITER	M INTERIM	TINTIER	

EIINST 94

TINIES	E SIENITE	LINTIES	PINITES	V INVITES
A ISATINE	F FINITES	M MINIEST	TIEPINS	VINIEST
B STIBINE	NIFTIES	N INTINES	T SITTINE	W WINIEST
C INCITES	G IGNITES	TINNIES	TINIEST	
D INDITES	K INKIEST	O INOSITE	U UNITIES	
TINEIDS	L LINIEST	P PINIEST	UNITISE	

EILNOR 35

NEROLI	ALIENOR	O LOONIER	R LORINER
A AILERON	E ELOINER	P PLERION	S NEROLIS
ALERION	N ONLINER	PROLINE	T RETINOL

EILNOS 33

SOLEIN	SONDELI	I ELISION	O LOONIES	T ENTOILS
A ANISOLE	E OLEINES	ISOLINE	P EPSILON	LIONETS
B BOLINES	F OLEFINS	LIONISE	PINOLES	ONLIEST
C CINEOLS	G ELOIGNS	K SONLIKE	R NEROLIS	U ELUSION
CONSEIL	LEGIONS	L LIONELS	S ESLOINS	
INCLOSE	LIGNOSE	NIELLOS	INSOLES	
D DOLINES	LINGOES	M LOMEINS	LESIONS	
INDOLES	LONGIES	MOLINES	LIONESS	

EILNOT 34

LIONET	G LENTIGO	P POINTEL	S ENTOILS	V VIOLENT
A ELATION	H HOTLINE	PONTILE	LIONETS	W TOWLINE
TOENAIL	NEOLITH	POTLINE	ONLIEST	
C LECTION	I ETIOLIN	TOPLINE	U ELUTION	
D LENTOID	M MOLINET	R RETINOL	OUTLINE	

EILNRS 154

LINERS	E LIERNES	I INLIERS	M LIMNERS	SLINTER
A ALINERS	RELINES	RESILIN	MERLINS	SNIRTLE
NAILERS	G GIRNELS	K LINKERS	O NEROLIS	V SILVERN
RENAILS	LINGERS	RELINKS	P PILSNER	
B BERLINS	SLINGER	SLINKER	T LINTERS	

EILNRT 125

LINTER	RELIANT	TRINDLE	I LINTIER	S LINTERS
A ENTRAIL	RETINAL	G RINGLET	NITRILE	SLINTER
LATRINE	TRENAIL	TINGLER	K TINKLER	SNIRTLE
RATLINE	D TENDRIL	TRINGLE	O RETINOL	Y INERTLY

EILNST 80

TINSEL	LECTINS	TINGLES	ONLIEST	U LUNIEST
A EASTLIN	STENCIL	I LINIEST	P LEPTINS	LUTEINS
ELASTIN	D DENTILS	LINTIES	PINTLES	UNTILES
ENTAILS	E LENITES	K LENTISK	PLENIST	UTENSIL
NAILSET	LISENTE	TINKLES	R LINTERS	V VENTILS
SALIENT	SETLINE	L LENTILS	SLINTER	W WESTLIN
SALTINE	TENSILE	LINTELS	SNIRTLE	WINTLES
SLAINTE	G GLISTEN	TELLINS	S ENLISTS	
STANIEL	LESTING	N LINNETS	LISTENS	
TENAILS	SINGLET	O ENTOILS	SILENTS	
C CLIENTS	SNIGLET	LIONETS	TINSELS	

EILORS 39

REOILS	D SOLDIER	M MOILERS	S LORISES	U LOURIES
B BOILERS	SOLIDER	N NEROLIS	LOSSIER	LOUSIER
LIBEROS	E LOERIES	O ORIOLES	RISSOLE	SOILURE
REBOILS	G GLOIRES	P SLOPIER	T ESTRIOL	V OLIVERS
C COILERS	GLORIES	SPOILER	LOITERS	VIOLERS
RECOILS	I SOILIER	R LORRIES	TOILERS	W LOWRIES

EILORT 25

TOILER	E TROELIE	M MOTLIER	POLITER	T TORTILE
B TRILOBE	F LOFTIER	N RETINOL	S ESTRIOL	TRIOLET
C CORTILE	TREFOIL	O TROOLIE	LOITERS	U OUTLIER
D DOILTER	J JOLTIER	P POITREL	TOILERS	V OVERLIT

EILOST 31

	TOILES		LOGIEST		TOLLIES		STOOLIE		TOILETS
A	ISOLATE	H	EOLITHS	M	MOTILES	P	PIOLETS	U	OUTLIES
B	BETOILS		HOLIEST	N	ENTOILS		PISTOLE	V	OLIVETS
C	CITOLES		HOSTILE		LIONETS	R	ESTRIOL		VIOLETS
E	ESTOILE	I	IOLITES		ONLIEST		LOITERS	W	OWLIEST
	ETOILES		OILIEST	O	OOLITES		TOILERS	Z	ZLOTIES
G	ELOGIST	L	OILLETS		OSTIOLE	T	LITOTES		

EILRST 71

	TILERS	E	LEISTER		SILTIER		SLINTER		SLITTER
A	REALIST		RETILES	J	JILTERS		SNIRTLE		STILTER
	RETAILS		STERILE	K	KILTERS	O	ESTRIOL		TESTRIL
	SALTIER	F	FILTERS		KIRTLES		LOITERS		TILTERS
	SALTIRE		LIFTERS		KLISTER		TOILERS		TITLERS
	SLATIER		STIFLER	L	RILLETS	P	RESPLIT	U	LUSTIER
	TAILERS		TRIFLES		STILLER		SPIRTLE		RULIEST
B	BLISTER	G	GLISTER		TILLERS		TRIPLES		RUTILES
	BRISTLE		GRISTLE		TRELLIS	S	LISTERS	Y	STYLIER
	RIBLETS	H	SLITHER	M	MILTERS		RELISTS		
C	RELICTS	I	RILIEST	N	LINTERS	T	LITTERS		

EINNRT 223

	TINNER	G	RENTING	I	TINNIER	P	ENPRINT
A	ENTRAIN		RINGENT	O	INTONER	S	INTERNS
	TRANNIE		TERNING		NOINTER		TINNERS
E	INTERNE	H	THINNER		TERNION	V	VINTNER

EINNST 245

	TENNIS		INDENTS		TENSING	P	PINNETS		SINNETS
A	INANEST		INTENDS	I	INTINES		SPINNET	T	INTENTS
	STANINE	E	INTENSE		TINNIES		TENPINS		TENNIST
	TANNIES		TENNIES	L	LINNETS	R	INTERNS	U	TUNNIES
C	INCENTS	G	NESTING	O	INTONES		TINNERS	V	INVENTS
D	DENTINS		SENTING		TENSION	S	SENNITS		

EINOPR 141

	PROINE	E	PEREION	H	PHONIER	R	PORNIER		PTERION
C	PERICON		PIONEER	I	RIPIENO	S	ORPINES		REPOINT
	PONCIER	F	FORPINE	L	PLERION		PIONERS		TROPINE
	PORCINE	G	PERIGON		PROLINE		PROINES	V	PROVINE
D	POINDER		PIROGEN	M	PROMINE	T	POINTER		
	PROINED		PONGIER	P	POPERIN		PROTEIN		

EINOPS 219

	PONIES	E	PEONIES	I	PIONIES	M	IMPONES	P	PEPINOS
A	EPINAOS	G	EPIGONS		SINOPIE		PEONISM	R	ORPINES
	SENOPIA		PIGEONS	K	PINKOES	N	PENSION		PIONERS
D	DISPONE		PINGOES	L	EPSILON		PINONES		PROINES
	SPINODE	H	PHONIES		PINOLES		SPINONE	S	SPINOSE

| T PINTOES | PONTIES | WINESOP | Y PIONEYS |
| POINTES | W POWNIES | | |

EINORR 174

IRONER	E ONERIER	I IRONIER	S IRONERS
C CORNIER	G IGNORER	L LORINER	ROSINER
D DRONIER	H HORNIER	P PORNIER	

EINORS 7

SONERI	INDORSE	IRONIES	PIONERS	STONIER
A ERASION	ORDINES	IRONISE	PROINES	TERSION
C COINERS	ROSINED	NOISIER	R IRONERS	TRIONES
CRINOSE	SORDINE	J JOINERS	ROSINER	U URINOSE
CRONIES	G ERINGOS	REJOINS	S ORNISES	V ENVIROS
ORCEINS	IGNORES	L NEROLIS	SENIORS	RENVOIS
ORCINES	REGIONS	M MERINOS	SONERIS	VERSION
RECOINS	SIGNORE	MERSION	SONSIER	W SNOWIER
SERICON	H HEROINS	N RONNIES	T NORITES	
D DINEROS	INSHORE	O EROSION	OESTRIN	
DONSIER	I IONISER	P ORPINES	ORIENTS	

EINORT 11

TONIER	G GENITOR	P POINTER	OESTRIN	U ROUTINE
A OTARINE	J JOINTER	PROTEIN	ORIENTS	W NOWTIER
B BORNITE	L RETINOL	PTERION	STONIER	TOWNIER
C COINTER	N INTONER	REPOINT	TERSION	Z TRIZONE
NOTICER	NOINTER	TROPINE	TRIONES	
RECTION	TERNION	S NORITES	T TRITONE	

EINOST 13

TONIES	HISTONE	SENTIMO	OESTRIN	TONIEST
A ATONIES	I INOSITE	N INTONES	ORIENTS	TONITES
B BONIEST	J JONTIES	TENSION	STONIER	W TOWNIES
EBONIST	L ENTOILS	O ISOTONE	TERSION	TWONIES
C NOTICES	LIONETS	TOONIES	TRIONES	X TOXINES
SECTION	ONLIEST	P PINTOES	S NOSIEST	
D DITONES	M MESTINO	POINTES	SONTIES	
STONIED	MOISTEN	PONTIES	STONIES	
H ETHIONS	MONTIES	R NORITES	T SNOTTIE	

EINRST 24

TRINES	CRETINS	K REKNITS	O NORITES	STINTER
A ANESTRI	D TINDERS	SKINTER	OESTRIN	TINTERS
ANTSIER	E ENTIRES	STINKER	ORIENTS	U NUTSIER
NASTIER	ENTRIES	TINKERS	STONIER	TRIUNES
RATINES	NERITES	L LINTERS	TERSION	UNITERS
RESIANT	RETINES	SLINTER	TRIONES	V INVERTS
RETAINS	TRENISE	SNIRTLE	P NIPTERS	STRIVEN
RETINAS	TRIENES	M ENTRISM	PTERINS	W TWINERS
RETSINA	F SNIFTER	MINSTER	S ESTRINS	WINTERS
STAINER	G RESTING	MINTERS	INSERTS	Y SINTERY
STARNIE	STINGER	REMINTS	SINTERS	
STEARIN	H HINTERS	N INTERNS	T ENTRIST	
C CISTERN	NITHERS	TINNERS	RETINTS	

EINRSU 222

URSINE	G REUSING	NEURISM	PURINES	SUNRISE
B BURNIES	RUEINGS	N SUNNIER	UPRISEN	T NUTSIER
RUBINES	SIGNEUR	UNREINS	Q REQUINS	TRIUNES
SUBERIN	J INJURES	UNRISEN	R INSURER	UNITERS
D INSURED	M MUREINS	O URINOSE	RUINERS	W UNWIRES
F INFUSER	MURINES	P PRUINES	S INSURES	UNWISER

EINRTT 149

TINTER	TERTIAN	G GITTERN	TRINKET	U NUTTIER
A INTREAT	B BITTERN	RETTING	O TRITONE	W TWINTER
ITERANT	C CITTERN	I NITRITE	S ENTRIST	WRITTEN
NATTIER	D TRIDENT	NITTIER	RETINTS	
NITRATE	E NETTIER	TINTIER	STINTER	
TARTINE	TENTIER	K KNITTER	TINTERS	

EINRTU 41

UNITER	TURBINE	RETINUE	UNMITRE	T NUTTIER
A RUINATE	D INTRUDE	REUNITE	O ROUTINE	V UNRIVET
TAURINE	TURDINE	UTERINE	P REPUNIT	VENTURI
URANITE	UNTIRED	G TRUEING	R RUNTIER	W UNWRITE
URINATE	UNTRIDE	M MINUTER	S NUTSIER	
B BUNTIER	UNTRIED	MUNTRIE	TRIUNES	
TRIBUNE	E NEURITE	UNMITER	UNITERS	

EINSTU 153

UNTIES	G GUNITES	UTENSIL	N TUNNIES	TRIUNES
A AUNTIES	I UNITIES	M MINUETS	P PUNIEST	UNITERS
SINUATE	UNITISE	MINUTES	PUNTIES	S INTUSES
C NEUSTIC	L LUNIEST	MISTUNE	Q INQUEST	T TUNIEST
D DISTUNE	LUTEINS	MUNITES	QUINTES	
DUNITES	UNTILES	MUTINES	R NUTSIER	

EIOOST 172

OTIOSE	FOOTSIE	L OOLITES	P ISOTOPE	S OOSIEST
B BOOTIES	OOFIEST	OSTIOLE	R OORIEST	T TOOTSIE
C COOTIES	G GOOIEST	STOOLIE	ROOTIES	Z OOZIEST
D OSTEOID	H TOOSHIE	N ISOTONE	SOOTIER	ZOOIEST
F FOOTIES	K STOOKIE	TOONIES	TOORIES	

EIOPST 211

SOPITE	TOPSIDE	STOMPIE	REPOSIT	SPOTTIE
A ATOPIES	E POETISE	N PINTOES	RIPOSTE	TIPTOES
OPIATES	H ETHIOPS	POINTES	ROPIEST	U PITEOUS
C POETICS	OPHITES	PONTIES	S POSIEST	X EXPOSIT
D DEPOSIT	K POKIEST	O ISOTOPE	POSTIES	POXIEST
DOPIEST	L PIOLETS	P POTPIES	POTSIES	Y ISOTYPE
PODITES	PISTOLE	R PERIOST	SEPIOST	
POSITED	M MOPIEST	PORIEST	SOPITES	
SOPITED	OPTIMES	PROSTIE	T POTTIES	

EIORST 4

TRIOSE	TRIODES	LOITERS	SOOTIER	SORTIES
A OARIEST	E EROTISE	TOILERS	TOORIES	STORIES
OTARIES	F FOISTER	M EROTISM	P PERIOST	TOSSIER
B ORBIEST	FORTIES	MOISTER	PORIEST	TRIOSES
SORBITE	G GOITERS	MORTISE	PROSTIE	T STOITER
C EROTICS	GOITRES	TRISOME	REPOSIT	U OURIEST
TERCIOS	GORIEST	N NORITES	RIPOSTE	STOURIE
D EDITORS	H HERIOTS	OESTRIN	ROPIEST	TOURIES
ROISTED	HOISTER	ORIENTS	R RIOTERS	TOUSIER
ROSITED	SHORTIE	STONIER	ROISTER	V TORSIVE
SORTIED	TOSHIER	TERSION	RORIEST	W OWRIEST
STEROID	I RIOTISE	TRIONES	S ROSIEST	TOWSIER
STORIED	K ROKIEST	O OORIEST	SIROSET	
TIERODS	L ESTRIOL	ROOTIES	SORITES	

EIORTU 82

TOURIE	F OUTFIRE	L OUTLIER	S OURIEST	T TOUTIER
D ETOURDI	G GOUTIER	N ROUTINE	STOURIE	V VOITURE
IODURET	H OUTHIRE	P POUTIER	TOURIES	Z TOUZIER
OUTRIDE	ROUTHIE	Q QUOITER	TOUSIER	

EIRSTT 237

TRITES	B BITTERS	K SKITTER	RETINTS	S SITTERS
A ARTIEST	C TRISECT	L LITTERS	STINTER	T STRETTI
ARTISTE	E TESTIER	SLITTER	TINTERS	TITTERS
ATTIRES	F FITTERS	STILTER	O STOITER	TRITEST
IRATEST	TITFERS	TESTRIL	P PITTERS	U TERTIUS
RATITES	H HITTERS	TILTERS	SPITTER	V TRIVETS
STRIATE	TITHERS	TITLERS	TIPSTER	W RETWIST
TASTIER	J JITTERS	M METRIST	R RITTERS	TWISTER
TERTIAS	TRIJETS	N ENTRIST	TERRITS	WITTERS

EIRSTU 108

URITES	REDUITS	K TURKIES	UNITERS	REQUITS
B BUSTIER	STUDIER	TUSKIER	O OURIEST	R RUSTIER
RUBIEST	E SUETIER	L LUSTIER	STOURIE	S SUITERS
C CUITERS	F FUSTIER	RULIEST	TOURIES	T TERTIUS
CURIETS	SURFEIT	RUTILES	TOUSIER	V REVUIST
CURITES	G GUSTIER	M MUSTIER	P PERITUS	STUIVER
ICTERUS	GUTSIER	N NUTSIER	PUIREST	VIRTUES
D DUSTIER	H HIRSUTE	TRIUNES	Q QUERIST	

ELNORS 230

NORSEL	C CLONERS	I NEROLIS	N RONNELS
A LOANERS	CORNELS	K SNORKEL	S NORSELS
ORLEANS	D RONDELS	L ENROLLS	T LENTORS
RELOANS	G LONGERS	M MERLONS	U NOURSLE

ELNOST 216

TELSON	F	TEFLONS	ONLIEST	P	LEPTONS	U	LENTOUS
A ETALONS	G	LONGEST	L STOLLEN	R	LENTORS	V	SOLVENT
TOLANES	I	ENTOILS	M LOMENTS	S	TELSONS		
B NOBLEST		LIONETS	MELTONS	T	TONLETS		

ELORST 88

TORSEL	D DROLEST	TOILERS	TOOLERS	U ELUTORS
A OESTRAL	OLDSTER	J JOLTERS	P PETROLS	OUTLERS
OLESTRA	STRODLE	JOSTLER	REPLOTS	TROULES
B BOLSTER	E SOLERET	L TOLLERS	S OSTLERS	V REVOLTS
BOLTERS	F FLORETS	M MERLOTS	STEROLS	W TROWELS
LOBSTER	LOFTERS	MOLTERS	TORSELS	WORTLES
C COLTERS	H HOLSTER	N LENTORS	T LOTTERS	
CORSLET	HOSTLER	O LOOTERS	SETTLOR	
COSTREL	I ESTRIOL	RETOOLS	SLOTTER	
LECTORS	LOITERS	ROOTLES	TOLTERS	

ENNORT 249

TONNER	TENDRON	F FORNENT	NOINTER	S STONERN
A NORTENA	E ENTERON	G RONTGEN	TERNION	TONNERS
D DONNERT	TENONER	I INTONER	O NORTENO	U NEUTRON

ENORST 20

TRONES	CRONETS	I NORITES	L LENTORS	S NESTORS
A ATONERS	D RODENTS	OESTRIN	M MENTORS	STONERS
SANTERO	SNORTED	ORIENTS	MONSTER	TENSORS
SENATOR	E ESTRONE	STONIER	MONTRES	T ROTTENS
TREASON	F FRONTES	TERSION	N STONERN	SNOTTER
B BRETONS	G TONGERS	TRIONES	TONNERS	STENTOR
SORBENT	H HORNETS	K REKNOTS	O ENROOTS	U TENOURS
C CONSTER	SHORTEN	STONKER	P POSTERN	TONSURE
CORNETS	THRENOS	STROKEN	PRONEST	Y TYRONES
CRESTON	THRONES	TONKERS	R SNORTER	

ENORSU 158

ROUENS	C CONURES	UNDOERS	N NEURONS	TONSURE
A ARENOUS	ROUNCES	G SURGEON	NONUSER	V NERVOUS
B BOURNES	D ENDUROS	H UNHORSE	O ONEROUS	W UNSWORE
UNROBES	RESOUND	I URINOSE	P UNROPES	Z ZONURES
UNSOBER	SOUNDER	L NOURSLE	T TENOURS	

ENORTU 185

TENOUR	RECOUNT	M MONTURE	S TENOURS
A OUTEARN	TROUNCE	MOUNTER	TONSURE
C CORNUTE	F FORTUNE	REMOUNT	W UNWROTE
COUNTER	I ROUTINE	N NEUTRON	Y TOURNEY

ENRSTU 165

UNREST	C	ENCRUST		GURNETS	M	MUNSTER	R	RETURNS
A AUNTERS	D	RETUNDS		SURGENT		MUNTERS		TURNERS
NATURES		UNDREST	H	HUNTERS		STERNUM	S	UNRESTS
SAUNTER	E	NEUTERS		SHUNTER	N	RUNNETS	T	ENTRUST
B BRUNETS		RETUNES		UNHERST		STUNNER		NUTTERS
BUNTERS		TENURES	I	NUTSIER	O	TENOURS		
BURNETS		TUREENS		TRIUNES		TONSURE		
BURSTEN	F	FUNSTER		UNITERS	P	PUNSTER		
SUBRENT	G	GUNTERS	L	RUNLETS		PUNTERS		

EORRST 244

STORER		SHORTER	O	ROOSTER		TERRORS	U	RETOURS
A ROASTER	I	RIOTERS		ROOTERS	S	RESORTS		ROUSTER
C RECTORS		ROISTER		TOREROS		ROSTERS		ROUTERS
D DORTERS		RORIEST	P	PORTERS		SORTERS		TOURERS
RODSTER	K	STROKER		PRESORT		STORERS		TROUSER
E RESTORE	M	STORMER		PRETORS	T	RETORTS	V	TROVERS
G GROSERT		TERMORS		REPORTS		ROTTERS	W	STROWER
H RHETORS		TREMORS		SPORTER		STERTOR	Y	ROYSTER
ROTHERS	N	SNORTER	R	RORTERS		TORRETS		STROYER

EORSTU 229

TROUSE		FOUTRES		OESTRUM		ROQUETS		STOURES
B OBTUSER	H	SHOUTER	N	TENOURS		TORQUES		TOUSERS
C COUTERS		SOUTHER		TONSURE	R	RETOURS		TROUSES
CROUTES	I	OURIEST	P	PETROUS		ROUSTER		TUSSORE
SCOUTER		STOURIE		POSTURE		ROUTERS	T	OUTSERT
D DETOURS		TOURIES		POUTERS		TOURERS		STOUTER
DOUREST		TOUSIER		PROTEUS		TROUSER		TOUTERS
DOUTERS	J	JOUSTER		SEPTUOR	S	ESTROUS	X	SEXTUOR
OUTREDS	L	ELUTORS		SPOUTER		OESTRUS		
REDOUTS		OUTLERS		TROUPES		OUSTERS		
ROUSTED		TROULES	Q	QUESTOR		SOUREST		
F FOUTERS	M	MOUTERS		QUOTERS		SOUTERS		

GINORT 194

TRIGON	F	FORTING	P	PORTING		STORING		ROUTING
A ORATING	I	IGNITOR		TROPING		TRIGONS		TOURING
ROATING		RIOTING	R	RORTING	T	ROTTING	W	ROWTING
D DORTING	K	TROKING	S	ROSTING	U	OUTGRIN		TROWING
E GENITOR	O	ROOTING		SORTING		OUTRING		

INORST 103

NITROS		CORTINS	F	FORINTS	L	NOSTRIL		TRITONS
A AROINTS	E	NORITES	G	ROSTING	N	INTRONS	U	NITROUS
RATIONS		OESTRIN		SORTING	O	ISOTRON		TURIONS
B RIBSTON		ORIENTS		STORING		NITROSO		
C CISTRON		STONIER		TRIGONS		TORSION		
CITRONS		TERSION	H	HORNIST	P	TROPINS		
CORNIST		TRIONES	I	IRONIST	T	INTORTS		

Seven-letter stems

As with the six-letter stems, the seven-letter stems are listed alphabetically and numbered according to their placing for frequency and fruitfulness.

AADEIRT 127

TIARAED	E ERADIATE	RAINDATE	RADIATES
C RADICATE	L LARIATED	S AIRDATES	V VARIATED
D RADIATED	N DENTARIA	DATARIES	

AAEILNT 86

ANTLIAE	E ALIENATE	K ANTILEAK	LAMINATE
C ANALCITE	G AGENTIAL	L ALLANITE	P PALATINE
LAITANCE	ALGINATE	M ALAIMENT	T ANTLIATE
D DENTALIA	H ANTHELIA	ANTIMALE	V AVENTAIL

AAEINST 154

TAENIAS	G SAGINATE	R ANTISERA	SANTERIA	SANITATE
B BASANITE	H ASTHENIA	ARTESIAN	SEATRAIN	TANAISTE
C ESTANCIA	M AMENTIAS	RATANIES	S ENTASIAS	V SANATIVE
F FANTASIE	ANIMATES	RESINATA	T ASTATINE	

AAEIRST 170

ATRESIA	M AMIRATES	SANTERIA	S ASTERIAS	W AWAITERS
D AIRDATES	N ANTISERA	SEATRAIN	ATRESIAS	
DATARIES	ARTESIAN	P ASPIRATE	T ARIETTAS	
RADIATES	RATANIES	PARASITE	ARISTATE	
H HETAIRAS	RESINATA	SEPTARIA	V VARIATES	

AAENRST 79

SANTERA	E ARSENATE	ARTESIAN	J NAARTJES	R NARRATES
B ANTBEARS	SERENATA	RATANIES	L ASTERNAL	S SANTERAS
RATSBANE	G STARAGEN	RESINATA	M SARMENTA	T TARTANES
C CANASTER	TANAGERS	SANTERIA	SEMANTRA	V TAVERNAS
CATERANS	I ANTISERA	SEATRAIN	O ANOESTRA	TSAREVNA

ABEINST 106

BESTAIN	G BEATINGS	M AMBIENTS	R ATEBRINS	BESTAINS
A BASANITE	H ABSINTHE	O BOTANIES	BANISTER	T TABINETS
C BASCINET	I BAINITES	BOTANISE	BARNIEST	
CABINETS	K BEATNIKS	NIOBATES	S BASINETS	
D BANDIEST	SNAKEBIT	OBEISANT	BASSINET	
E BETAINES	L INSTABLE	P BEPAINTS	BESAINTS	

ABEORST 149

SORBATE	D BROADEST	L BLOATERS	P PROBATES	SORBATES
A AEROBATS	E ABORTEES	SORTABLE	R ABORTERS	T ABETTORS
RABATOES	REBATOES	STORABLE	ARBORETS	BATTEROS
C CABESTRO	H BATHORSE	M BROMATES	TABORERS	TABORETS
CABRESTO	I SABOTIER	N BARONETS	S BOASTERS	U SABOTEUR

ACDEINR 243

DANCIER	D CANDIDER	H INARCHED	R RANCIDER
A CANARIED	RIDDANCE	I ACRIDINE	T CRINATED
RADIANCE	E DERACINE	N CRANNIED	DICENTRA

ACEILRT 196

TALCIER	M METRICAL	PRELATIC	SELICTAR	Y LITERACY
A TAILRACE	N CLARINET	R CLARTIER	STERICAL	
D ARTICLED	O EROTICAL	S ALTRICES	T TRACTILE	
LACERTID	LORICATE	ARTICLES	U RETICULA	
K TALCKIER	P PARTICLE	RECITALS	V VERTICAL	

ACEINOT 125

ANOETIC	H ETHANOIC	R ACTIONER	S ACONITES	V CONATIVE
C ACETONIC	INCHOATE	ANORETIC	CANOEIST	INVOCATE
D ACTIONED	M COINMATE	CREATION	SONICATE	X EXACTION
CATENOID	N ENACTION	REACTION	T TACONITE	

ACEINRS 120

CERASIN	INCREASE	INARCHES	NARCEINS	CERATINS
A ACARINES	RESIANCE	I RIANCIES	O SCENARIO	CISTERNA
CANARIES	F FANCIERS	K SKINCARE	S ARCSINES	CREATINS
CESARIAN	FRANCISE	L CARLINES	ARSENICS	NACRITES
SARCINAE	G CREASING	LANCIERS	CERASINS	SCANTIER
B BRISANCE	GRECIANS	M CARMINES	RACINESS	TACRINES
CARBINES	SEARCHING	CREMAINS	T CANISTER	
E CINEREAS	H ARCHINES	N CRANNIES	CARNIEST	

ACEINRT 43

TACRINE	E CENTIARE	CREATING	REACTION	SCANTIER
A CARINATE	CREATINE	REACTING	S CANISTER	TACRINES
CRANIATE	INCREATE	I ARENITIC	CARNIEST	T INTERACT
B BACTERIN	ITERANCE	L CLARINET	CERATINS	U ANURETIC
C ACENTRIC	G ARGENTIC	O ACTIONER	CISTERNA	V NAVICERT
D CRINATED	CATERING	ANORETIC	CREATINS	X XERANTIC
DICENTRA	CITRANGE	CREATION	NACRITES	

ACEINST 83

CINEAST	D DANCIEST	H ASTHENIC	L CANISTEL	CANNIEST
A ESTANCIA	DISTANCE	CHANTIES	M AMNESTIC	INSECTAN
B BASCINET	E CINEASTE	I ANTICISE	SEMANTIC	INSTANCE
CABINETS	F FANCIEST	CANITIES	N ANCIENTS	O ACONITES

CANOEIST	CERATINS	SCANTIER	T CANTIEST	V CISTVAEN
SONICATE	CISTERNA	TACRINES	ENTASTIC	VESICANT
R CANISTER	CREATINS	S CINEASTS	NICTATES	Y CYANITES
CARNIEST	NACRITES	SCANTIES	TETANICS	Z ZINCATES

ACENORT 110

ENACTOR	H ANCHORET	O CORONATE	SARCONET	Y ENACTORY
C ACCENTOR	I ACTIONER	P COPARENT	SORTANCE	
D CARTONED	ANORETIC	PORTANCE	T CONTRATE	
NOTECARD	CREATION	S ANCESTOR	U COURANTE	
E CAROTENE	REACTION	ENACTORS	OUTRANCE	

ACEORST 220

RECOATS	F FORECAST	N ANCESTOR	CREATORS	V OVERACTS
B CABESTRO	G ESCARGOT	ENACTORS	REACTORS	OVERCAST
CABRESTO	H CHAROSET	SARCONET	S COARSEST	X EXACTORS
C ECTOSARC	THORACES	SORTANCE	COASTERS	
D REDCOATS	L LOCATERS	P POSTRACE	T SECTOR	
E CREASOTE	SECTORAL	R ACROTERS	U OUTRACES	

ACINORT 169

CORTINA	E ACTIONER	H ANORTHIC	R CARROTIN	T TRACTION
A RAINCOAT	ANORETIC	K ANTIROCK	CONTRAIR	U NOCTURIA
C CRATONIC	CREATION	L CILANTRO	S CANTORIS	Y CARYOTIN
NARCOTIC	REACTION	CONTRAIL	CAROTINS	
D TORNADIC	F FRACTION	M ROMANTIC	CORTINAS	

ADEEGNR 132

GRENADE	GARDENED	LARGENED	GARDENER	RENAGUED
A GADARENE	E RENEGADE	M GENDARME	GARNERED	UNAGREED
C ENGRACED	H REHANGED	N ENDANGER	S DERANGES	UNDERAGE
D DANGERED	I REGAINED	ENRANGED	GRANDEES	UNGEARED
DERANGED	L ENLARGED	O RENEGADO	GRENADES	V ENGRAVED
GANDERED	LANGERED	R DERANGER	U DUNGAREE	

ADEEILN 231

DELAINE	F ENFILADE	R RENAILED	ENTAILED
B DENIABLE	H HEADLINE	S DELAINES	LINEATED
D DEADLINE	M ENDEMIAL	T DATELINE	

ADEEILR 130

LEADIER	REDIALED	N RENAILED	S REALISED	ELATERID
B RIDEABLE	L REALLIED	P PEDALIER	RESAILED	RETAILED
D DEADLIER	M REMAILED	R DERAILER	SIDEREAL	Z REALIZED
DERAILED	REMEDIAL	RERAILED	T DETAILER	

ADEEILS 211

DEISEAL	I IDEALISE	P PLEIADES	S DEISEALS	Y EYELIADS
B ABSEILED	K LAKESIDE	R REALISED	IDEALESS	
BELADIES	M LIMEADES	RESAILED	T LEADIEST	
H DEISHEAL	N DELAINES	SIDEREAL	V DISLEAVE	

ADEEINS 194

ANISEED	M DEMAINES	ANDESINE	DRAISENE	T ANDESITE
G AGENISED	INSEAMED	R ARSENIDE	NEARSIDE	
L DELAINES	N ADENINES	DENARIES	S ANISEEDS	

ADEEIRS 113

READIES	J JADERIES	N ARSENIDE	R DREARIES	STEADIER
B BEARDIES	L REALISED	DENARIES	RERAISED	V READVISE
C DECIARES	RESAILED	DRAISENE	T READIEST	
F FEDARIES	SIDEREAL	NEARSIDE	SERIATED	
G DISAGREE	M MADERISE	P AIRSPEED	SIDERATE	

ADEEIST 112

IDEATES	F SAFETIED	L LEADIEST	SERIATED	U AUDITEES
B BEADIEST	H ATHEISED	M MEDIATES	SIDERATE	V DEVIATES
DIABETES	HEADIEST	N ANDESITE	STEADIER	SEDATIVE
D STEADIED	J JADEITES	R READIEST	S STEADIES	

ADEELNT 250

LATENED	G DANEGELT	LINEATED	R ANTLERED	V LEVANTED
B BANDELET	I DATELINE	M LAMENTED	T TALENTED	Y ENTAYLED
C LANCETED	ENTAILED	P ENDPLATE	U UNELATED	

ADEELRT 209

TREADLE	F DEFLATER	I DETAILER	N ANTLERED	RESLATED
C CLARETED	FALTERED	ELATERID	P PALTERED	TREADLES
DECRETAL	REFLATED	RETAILED	REPLATED	V TRAVELED
TREACLED	H HALTERED	L TELLARED	R TREADLER	
D TREADLED	LATHERED	M TRAMELED	S DESALTER	

ADEELST 200

STEALED	F DEFLATES	P PEDESTAL	S DATELESS	U ADULTESE
A DEALATES	I LEADIEST	R DESALTER	DETASSEL	Y SEDATELY
D DESALTED	M MEDALETS	RESLATED	TASSELED	
E TEASELED	O DESOLATE	TREADLES	T LADETTES	

ADEENRS 131

ENDEARS	G DERANGES	DRAISENE	REAMENDS	UNERASED
C ASCENDER	GRANDEES	NEARSIDE	N ENSNARED	UNSEARED
REASCEND	GRENADES	K KNEADERS	O REASONED	W ANSWERED
E ENSEARED	I ARSENIDE	M AMENDERS	S DEARNESS	Y YEARENDS
SERENADE	DENARIES	MEANDERS	U UNDERSEA	

ADEERST 108

TASERED	H HEADREST	TREADLES	DREAREST	RESTATED
B BETREADS	I READIEST	M MASTERED	RASTERED	RETASTED
BREASTED	SERIATED	STREAMED	RETREADS	W DEWATERS
DEBATERS	SIDERATE	P PEDERAST	SERRATED	TARWEEDS
C CEDRATES	STEADIER	PREDATES	TREADERS	WASTERED
E RESEATED	K STREAKED	REPASTED	S ASSERTED	Y ESTRAYED
F DRAFTEES	L DESALTER	TRAPESED	ESTRADES	
G RESTAGED	RESLATED	R ARRESTED	T ASTERTED	

ADEGILN 214

LEADING	H HEALDING	N LADENING	R DANGLIER	LEADINGS
B BLINDAGE	I GLIADINE	O GALENOID	DEARLING	SIGNALED
C DECALING	M MALIGNED	P PEDALING	DRAGLINE	T DELATING
F FINAGLED	MEDALING	PLEADING	S DEALINGS	Y DELAYING

ADEGINR 34

READING	READDING	DEARLING	R DREARING	TREADING
A AREADING	E REGAINED	DRAGLINE	S DERAIGNS	Y DERAYING
DRAINAGE	H ADHERING	M DREAMING	GRADINES	READYING
GARDENIA	HEADRING	MARGINED	READINGS	YEARDING
B BEARDING	I DEAIRING	MIDRANGE	T DERATING	
BREADING	K DAKERING	N GRANNIED	GRADIENT	
D DREADING	L DANGLIER	O ORGANDIE	REDATING	

ADEGNOR 185

GROANED	F FRONDAGE	M DRAGOMEN	P DOGNAPER
B BONDAGER	I ORGANDIE	N ANDROGEN	T DRAGONET
E RENEGADO	J JARGONED	DRAGONNE	

ADEGORT 105

GAROTED	H GOATHERD	P PORTAGED	T GAROTTED	W WATERDOG
B BOGARTED	I ERGATOID	R GARROTED	U OUTRAGED	
E DEROGATE	N DRAGONET	S GOADSTER	RAGOUTED	

ADEIINT 181

INEDITA	DIACTINE	M MINIATED	TAENIOID	DAINTIES
C ACTINIDE	INDICATE	O IDEATION	R DAINTIER	V VANITIED
CTENIDIA	G IDEATING	IODINATE	S ADENITIS	

ADEILNS 146

SNAILED	E DELAINES	SIGNALED	LINDANES	R ISLANDER
D ISLANDED	G DEALINGS	K SANDLIKE	O NODALISE	U UNSAILED
LANDSIDE	LEADINGS	N ANNELIDS	P SANDPILE	V ANDVILES

ADEILOR 166

DARIOLE	L ARILLODE	SOREDIAL	V OVERLAID
F FORELAID	S DARIOLES	T IDOLATER	X EXORDIAL
G DIALOGER	SOLIDARE	TAILORED	

ADEILOS 134

ISOLEAD	N NODALISE	SOLIDARE	T DIASTOLE	Z DIAZOLES
C COALISED	P EPISODAL	SOREDIAL	ISOLATED	SLEAZOID
G GOLIASED	OPALISED	S ASSOILED	SODALITE	
M DAMOISEL	SEPALOID	DEASOILS	SOLIDATE	
MELODIAS	R DARIOLES	ISOLEADS	U DOULEIAS	

ADEILRS 52

SIDERAL	RADICELS	G SLAIRGED	O DARIOLES	SPIRALED
A SALARIED	RADICLES	I LAIRISED	SOLIDARE	T DILATERS
B BEDRAILS	D DIEDRALS	L DALLIERS	SOREDIAL	LARDIEST
DISABLER	E REALISED	DIALLERS	P LIPREADS	REDTAILS
RAILBEDS	RESAILED	M DISMALER	PARSLIED	U RESIDUAL
C DECRIALS	SIDEREAL	N ISLANDER	PEDRAILS	Y DIALYSER

ADEILRT 48

TRAILED	LACERTID	L TRIALLED	TRIPEDAL	T DETRITAL
A LARIATED	E DETAILER	O IDOLATER	S DILATERS	Y DIELYTRA
B LIBRATED	ELATERID	TAILORED	LARDIEST	
C ARTICLED	RETAILED	P DIPTERAL	REDTAILS	

ADEILST 126

DILATES	E LEADIEST	MISDEALT	SOLIDATE	REDTAILS
B BALDIEST	G GLADIEST	O DIASTOLE	P TALIPEDS	V VALIDEST
C CITADELS	I IDEALIST	ISOLATED	R DILATERS	Y DIASTYLE
DIALECTS	M MEDALIST	SODALITE	LARDIEST	STEADILY

ADEIMNO 235

DOMAINE	G AMIDOGEN	P DOPAMINE	DOMAINES	NEMATOID
C COMEDIAN	L MELANOID	R RADIOMEN	NOMADIES	U EUDAIMON
DAEMONIC	N DEMONIAN	S AMIDONES	NOMADISE	Z NOMADIZE
DEMONIAC	MONDAINE	DAIMONES	T DOMINATE	

ADEIMNR 168

INARMED	E REMAINED	MIDRANGE	R MANRIDER	U MURAENID
A MARINADE	G DREAMING	I MERIDIAN	S ADERMINS	Y DAIRYMEN
B BRIDEMAN	MARGINED	O RADIOMEN	SIRNAMED	Z ZEMINDAR

ADEINOR 26

ANEROID	G ORGANDIE	REORDAIN	T AROINTED	RATIONED
B DEBONAIR	M RADIOMEN	S ANEROIDS	DERATION	U DOUANIER
D ORDAINED	R ORDAINER	DONARIES	ORDINATE	

ADEINOS 51

SODAINE	ADONISED	M AMIDONES	DONARIES	X DIOXANES
B BEDSONIA	ANODISED	DAIMONES	S ADENOSIS	Z ADONIZES
C CODEINAS	G AGONISED	DOMAINES	ADONISES	ANODIZES
DIOCESAN	DIAGNOSE	NOMADIES	ANODISES	
OCEANIDS	H ADHESION	NOMADISE	T ASTONIED	
D ADENOIDS	L NODALISE	R ANEROIDS	SEDATION	

ADEINPT 247

PATINED	C PEDANTIC	E DIAPENTE	N PINNATED	R DIPTERAN
A PATINAED	PENTADIC	L PANTILED	O ANTIPODE	S DEPAINTS

ADEINRS 8

SARDINE	DRAISENE	L ISLANDER	R DRAINERS	U DENARIUS
A ARANEIDS	NEARSIDE	M ADERMINS	SERRANID	UNRAISED
B BRANDIES	F FRIANDES	SIRNAMED	S ARIDNESS	URANIDES
BRANDISE	G DERAIGNS	N INSNARED	SARDINES	V INVADERS
D SARDINED	GRADINES	O ANEROIDS	T DETRAINS	SANDIVER
E ARSENIDE	READINGS	DONARIES	RANDIEST	Y SYNEDRIA
DENARIES	I DRAISINE	P SPRAINED	STRAINED	

ADEINRT 7

TRAINED	E DETAINER	H ANTHERID	P DIPTERAN	INDURATE
A DENTARIA	RETAINED	I DAINTIER	S DETRAINS	RUINATED
RAINDATE	G DERATING	O AROINTED	RANDIEST	URINATED
C CRINATED	GRADIENT	DERATION	STRAINED	
DICENTRA	REDATING	ORDINATE	T NITRATED	
D INDARTED	TREADING	RATIONED	U DATURINE	

ADEINRU 96

URANIDE	M MURAENID	S DENARIUS	INDURATE	
F UNFAIRED	O DOUANIER	UNRAISED	RUINATED	
H UNHAIRED	P UNPAIRED	URANIDES	URINATED	
I UREDINIA	UNREPAID	T DATURINE	V UNVARIED	

ADEINST 19

STAINED	G SEDATING	TIDESMAN	STRAINED	V DEVIANTS
B BANDIEST	STEADING	O ASTONIED	S DESTAINS	Y DESYATIN
C DANCIEST	H HANDIEST	SEDATION	SANDIEST	
DISTANCE	I ADENITIS	P DEPAINTS	T INSTATED	
D DANDIEST	DAINTIES	R DETRAINS	U AUDIENTS	
E ANDESITE	M MEDIANTS	RANDIEST	SINUATED	

ADEINTU 246

AUDIENT	L UNTAILED	Q ANTIQUED	RUINATED	SINUATED
B UNBAITED	N ANTIDUNE	R DATURINE	URINATED	
C INCUDATE	INUNDATE	INDURATE	S AUDIENTS	

ADEIORS 91

SOREDIA	SIDEROAD	SOLIDARE	DONARIES	T ASTEROID
C IDOCRASE	F FORESAID	SOREDIAL	P DIASPORE	V AVODIRES
D ROADSIDE	L DARIOLES	N ANEROIDS	PARODIES	AVOIDERS

ADEIOST 95

TOADIES	L DIASTOLE	SOLIDATE	SEDATION	X OXIDATES
B BEASTOID	ISOLATED	M ATOMISED	P DIOPTASE	Z AZOTISED
G GODETIAS	SODALITE	N ASTONIED	R ASTEROID	

ADEIPRS 218

PRAISED	G SPAIRGED	SPIRALED	R DRAPIERS	TRAIPSED
A PARADISE	H RAPHIDES	N SPRAINED	S DESPAIRS	U UPRAISED
C EPACRIDS	I PRESIDIA	O DIASPORE	T DIPTERAS	W RIPSAWED
PERACIDS	L LIPREADS	PARODIES	RAPIDEST	
D DISPREAD	PARSLIED	P APPRISED	SPIRATED	
E AIRSPEED	PEDRAILS	DRAPPIES	TARSIPED	

ADEIRST 14

TIRADES	C ACRIDEST	K STRAIKED	STRAINED	DISASTER
A AIRDATES	D DISRATED	L DILATERS	O ASTEROID	DISRATES
DATARIES	E READIEST	LARDIEST	P DIPTERAS	T STRAITED
RADIATES	SERIATED	REDTAILS	RAPIDEST	STRIATED
B BARDIEST	SIDERATE	M MARDIEST	SPIRATED	TARDIEST
BRAIDEST	STEADIER	MISRATED	TARSIPED	W TAWDRIES
RABIDEST	H HAIRSTED	READMITS	TRAIPSED	
REDBAITS	HARDIEST	N DETRAINS	S ASTERIDS	
TRIBADES	I IRISATED	RANDIEST	DIASTERS	

ADEIRTT 212

ATTIRED	TETRADIC	M ADMITTER	S STRAITED	T ATTRITED
C CITRATED	E ITERATED	N NITRATED	STRIATED	TITRATED
TETRACID	L DETRITAL	O TERATOID	TARDIEST	

ADELNOR 208

LADRONE	CONELRAD	F FORELAND	SOLANDER	V OVERLAND
B BANDEROL	E OLEANDER	P PONDERAL	U UNLOADER	RONDAVEL
C COLANDER	RELOANED	S LADRONES	URODELAN	

ADENORT 32

TORNADE	I AROINTED	N NONRATED	T ATTORNED	
C CARTONED	DERATION	O RATOONED	W DANEWORT	
NOTECARD	ORDINATE	P PRONATED	TEARDOWN	
G DRAGONET	RATIONED	S TORNADES	Y AROYNTED	

ADENOST 98

ONSTEAD	E ENDOSTEA	O ODONATES	R TORNADES
C ENDOCAST	I ASTONIED	P NOTEPADS	S ONSTEADS
TACNODES	SEDATION	TONEPADS	

ADENRST 190

STARNED	D DARNDEST	I DETRAINS	R STRANDER	UNTREADS
B BANDSTER	STRANDED	RANDIEST	S STANDERS	X DEXTRANS
BARTENDS	G DRAGNETS	STRAINED	U DAUNTERS	
C CANTREDS	GRANDEST	O TORNADES	TRANSUDE	

ADENRTU 104

UNTREAD	UNTRACED	H UNTHREAD	M UNDREAMT	UNTREADS
B BREADNUT	D DRAUNTED	I DATURINE	P DEPURANT	T TRUANTED
TURBANED	UNTRADED	INDURATE	UNPARTED	X UNDERTAX
C UNCARTED	E DENATURE	RUINATED	R UNTARRED	
UNCRATED	UNDERATE	URINATED	S DAUNTERS	
UNDERACT	UNDEREAT	L DENTURAL	TRANSUDE	

ADEORST 77

TROADES	L DELATORS	P ADOPTERS	S ASSORTED	X EXTRADOS
B BROADEST	LEOTARDS	ASPORTED	TORSADES	
C REDCOATS	LODESTAR	PASTORED	U OUTDARES	
G GOADSTER	M STROAMED	READOPTS	OUTREADS	
I ASTEROID	N TORNADES	R ROADSTER	READOUTS	

ADINORS 99

SADIRON	DISADORN	L ORDINALS	S SADIRONS	V VIRANDOS
B INBOARDS	E ANEROIDS	N ANDIRONS	T DIATRONS	
C SARDONIC	DONARIES	P PONIARDS	INTRADOS	
D ANDROIDS	G ROADINGS	R ORDINARS	U DINOSAUR	

ADINORT 54

DIATRON	E AROINTED	RATIONED	O TANDOORI	U DURATION
A ANTIDORA	DERATION	L TRINODAL	S DIATRONS	
C TORNADIC	ORDINATE	N ORDINANT	INTRADOS	

ADINRST 195

INDARTS	B ANTBIRDS	STRAINED	I DISTRAIN	INTRADOS
A INTRADAS	E DETRAINS	F INDRAFTS	K STINKARD	R TRIDARNS
RADIANTS	RANDIEST	G TRADINGS	O DIATRONS	U UNITARDS

ADIORST 118

ASTROID	G GORDITAS	N DIATRONS	PAROTIDS	T STRADIOT
C CAROTIDS	I TARSIOID	INTRADOS	S ASTROIDS	U AUDITORS
E ASTEROID	L DILATORS	P PARODIST	SARODIST	

AEEGINR 64

REGINAE	D REGAINED	L ALGERINE	R REGAINER	T GRATINEE
B BAREGINE	G AGREEING	M GERMAINE	S ANERGIES	INTERAGE
BERGENIA	I AEGIRINE	P PERIGEAN	GESNERIA	Z RAZEEING

AEEGINS 178

AGENISE	D AGENISED	R ANERGIES	AGENISES	U EUGENIAS
A AGENESIA	L ENSILAGE	GESNERIA	ASSIGNEE	V ENVISAGE
C AGENCIES	LINEAGES	S AGENESIS	T SAGENITE	Z AGENIZES

AEEGNRT 100

REAGENT	TEENAGER	M AGREMENT	GRANTEES	SEGREANT
A TAGAREEN	I GRATINEE	N GENERANT	GREATENS	SERGEANT
E GENERATE	INTERAGE	R ETRANGER	NEGATERS	STERNAGE
RENEGATE	L REGENTAL	S ESTRANGE	REAGENTS	U GAUNTREE

AEEILNR 73

ALIENER	RELIANCE	G ALGERINE	S ALIENERS	TREENAIL
C CARELINE	D RENAILED	P PERINEAL	T ELATERIN	
CINEREAL	F FLANERIE	R NEARLIER	ENTAILER	

AEEILNS 74

SEALINE	E ALIENEES	N SELENIAN	R ALIENERS	
B BASELINE	G ENSILAGE	P ALEPINES	S SEALINES	
C SALIENCE	LINEAGES	PENALISE	V VASELINE	
D DELAINES	M MELANISE	SEPALINE	X ALEXINES	

AEEILNT 63

LINEATE	LINEATED	L TENAILLE	R ELATERIN	VENTAILE
A ALIENATE	G GALENITE	M MELANITE	ENTAILER	
D DATELINE	GELATINE	P PETALINE	TREENAIL	
ENTAILED	LEGATINE	TAPELINE	V ELVANITE	

AEEILRS 61

REALISE	SERAFILE	N ALIENERS	EARLIEST	Z REALIZES
C ESCALIER	G GASELIER	P ESPALIER	LATERISE	SLEAZIER
D REALISED	H SHIRALEE	PEARLIES	LEARIEST	
RESAILED	L REALLIES	R REALISER	REALTIES	
SIDEREAL	M ALMERIES	S REALISES	V VELARISE	
F FILAREES	MEASLIER	T ATELIERS	Y YEARLIES	

AEEILRT 17

REALTIE	FRAILTEE	N ELATERIN	S ATELIERS	LITERATE
B LIBERATE	H ETHERIAL	ENTAILER	EARLIEST	V LEVIRATE
D DETAILER	L LAETRILE	TREENAIL	LATERISE	RELATIVE
ELATERID	M EREMITAL	O AEROLITE	LEARIEST	Z LATERIZE
RETAILED	MATERIEL	P PEARLITE	REALTIES	
F FEATLIER	REALTIME	R RETAILER	T LATERITE	

AEEIMRT 137

MEATIER	REMEDIAT	I METAIRIE	N ANTIMERE	STEAMIER
B AMBERITE	E EMERITAE	L EREMITAL	S EMERITAS	V VIAMETER
C CEMITARE	G EMIGRATE	MATERIEL	EMIRATES	
D DIAMETER	REMIGATE	REALTIME	REAMIEST	

AEEINRT 10

TRAINEE	D DETAINER	HERNIATE	ENTAILER	S ARENITES
C CENTIARE	RETAINED	I INERTIAE	TREENAIL	ARSENITE
CREATINE	G GRATINEE	K ANKERITE	M ANTIMERE	RESINATE
INCREATE	INTERAGE	KREATINE	P APERIENT	STEARINE
ITERANCE	H ATHERINE	L ELATERIN	R RETAINER	TRAINEES

AEEINST 66

ETESIAN	G SAGENITE	SEMINATE	STEARINE	T ANISETTE
B BETAINES	M ETAMINES	R ARENITES	TRAINEES	TETANIES
C CINEASTE	MATINEES	ARSENITE	S ETESIANS	TETANISE
D ANDESITE	MISEATEN	RESINATE	TENIASES	V NAIVETES

AEEIRST 9

SERIATE	EARLIEST	N ARENITES	R ARTERIES	V EVIRATES
D READIEST	LATERISE	ARSENITE	REASTIER	W SWEATIER
SERIATED	LEARIEST	RESINATE	S SERIATES	TAWERIES
SIDERATE	REALTIES	STEARINE	T ARIETTES	WASTERIE
STEADIER	M EMERITAS	TRAINEES	ITERATES	WEARIEST
E EATERIES	EMIRATES	O ETAERIOS	TEARIEST	Y YEASTIER
H HEARTIES	REAMIEST	P PARIETES	TREATIES	
L ATELIERS	STEAMIER	PETARIES	TREATISE	

AEELNRT 50

TELERAN	G REGENTAL	TREENAIL	S ALTERNES	RELEVANT
B RENTABLE	H LEATHERN	M LAMENTER	ETERNALS	W TREELAWN
D ANTLERED	I ELATERIN	N LANNERET	TELERANS	X EXTERNAL
E LATEENER	ENTAILER	R RELEARNT	V LEVANTER	

AEELRST 47

STEALER	TREACLES	EARLIEST	P PETRALES	TEARLESS
A LAETARES	D DESALTER	LATERISE	PLEATERS	TESSERAL
B ARBELEST	RESLATED	LEARIEST	PRELATES	T ALERTEST
BLEAREST	TREADLES	REALTIES	REPLATES	U RESALUTE
BLEATERS	E TEASELER	M LAMETERS	R ALTERERS	X EXALTERS
RESTABLE	F REFLATES	N ALTERNES	REALTERS	Y EASTERLY
RETABLES	H HALTERES	ETERNALS	RELATERS	
C CLEAREST	LEATHERS	TELERANS	S RESLATES	
SCELERAT	I ATELIERS	O OLEASTER	STEALERS	

AEENORS 184

ARENOSE	D REASONED	PERSONAE	S RESEASON	T EARSTONE
B SEABORNE	P PERAEONS	R REASONER	SEASONER	RESONATE

AEENRST 18

RATEENS	E SERENATE	SEGREANT	TRAINEES	S ASSENTER
A ARSENATE	F FASTENER	SERGEANT	J SERJEANT	EARNESTS
SERENATA	FENESTRA	STERNAGE	L ALTERNES	SARSENET
B ABSENTER	REFASTEN	H HASTENER	ETERNALS	T ENTREATS
C CENTARES	G ESTRANGE	HEARTENS	TELERANS	RATTEENS
ENCASTRE	GRANTEES	I ARENITES	M REMANETS	U SAUTERNE
REASCENT	GREATENS	ARSENITE	O EARSTONE	V AVENTRES
REENACTS	NEGATERS	RESINATE	RESONATE	VETERANS
SARCENET	REAGENTS	STEARINE	R TERRANES	

AEENRTT 240

TERNATE	NATTERED	H HATERENT	S ENTREATS	EXTRANET
A ANTEATER	RATTENED	THREATEN	RATTEENS	Y ENTREATY
B BATTENER	E ENTERATE	R NATTERER	V ANTEVERT	
D ATTENDER	F FATTENER	RATTENER	X EXTERNAT	

AEEORST 89

ROSEATE	C CREASOTE	KREASOTE	N EARSTONE	PROTEASE
B ABORTEES	I ETAERIOS	L OLEASTER	RESONATE	V OVEREATS
REBATOES	K KERATOSE	M EROTEMAS	P OPERATES	

AEERRST 213

TEARERS	DREAREST	REASTIER	P TAPERERS	TREATERS
B REBATERS	RASTERED	K RETAKERS	R ARRESTER	U AUSTERER
TABRERES	RETREADS	STREAKER	REARREST	TREASURE
TEREBRAS	SERRATED	L ALTERERS	S ASSERTER	V AVERTERS
C CATERERS	TREADERS	REALTERS	REASSERT	TRAVERSE
RECRATES	E ARRESTEE	RELATERS	SERRATES	W WATERERS
RETRACES	F FERRATES	M REMASTER	TERRASES	
TERRACES	G REGRATES	STREAMER	T RETRATES	
D ARRESTED	I ARTERIES	N TERRANES	RETREATS	

AEGILNR 21

REGINAL	F FINAGLER	MALIGNER	NARGILES	TANGLIER
A GERANIAL	G GANGLIER	MALINGER	REALIGNS	TERAGLIN
REGALIAN	LAGERING	N LEARNING	SALERING	TRIANGLE
B BLEARING	REGALING	O GERANIOL	SANGLIER	V RAVELING
C CLEARING	H NARGHILE	REGIONAL	SIGNALER	X RELAXING
RELACING	NARGILEH	P GRAPLINE	SLANGIER	Y LAYERING
D DANGLIER	I GAINLIER	PEARLING	T ALERTING	RELAYING
DEARLING	J JANGLIER	R GNARLIER	ALTERING	YEARLING
DRAGLINE	L ALLERGIN	S ALIGNERS	INTEGRAL	
E ALGERINE	M GERMINAL	ENGRAILS	RELATING	

AEGILNS 119

SEALING	LEADINGS	F FINAGLES	SHEALING	NIGELLAS
B SIGNABLE	SIGNALED	G LIGNAGES	K LINKAGES	M MEASLING
SINGABLE	E ENSILAGE	H HEALINGS	SNAGLIKE	N EANLINGS
D DEALINGS	LINEAGES	LEASHING	L GALLEINS	LEANINGS

O GASOLINE	NARGILES	SLANGIER	T EASTLING	V LEAVINGS
P ELAPSING	REALIGNS	S GAINLESS	GELATINS	SLEAVING
PLEASING	SALERING	GLASSINE	GENITALS	W SWEALING
R ALIGNERS	SANGLIER	LEASINGS	STEALING	Y YEALINGS
ENGRAILS	SIGNALER	SEALINGS	TAGLINES	

AEGILNT 46

TAGLINE	E GALENITE	M LIGAMENT	R ALERTING	GELATINS
A AGENTIAL	GELATINE	METALING	ALTERING	GENITALS
ALGINATE	LEGATINE	TEGMINAL	INTEGRAL	STEALING
B BELATING	G GELATING	N GANTLINE	RELATING	TAGLINES
BLEATING	LEGATING	LATENING	TANGLIER	V VALETING
TANGIBLE	TEAGLING	O GELATION	TERAGLIN	X EXALTING
C CLEATING	H ATHELING	LEGATION	TRIANGLE	Z TEAZLING
D DELATING	K GNATLIKE	P PLEATING	S EASTLING	

AEGILRS 177

GRAILES	D SLAIRGED	N ALIGNERS	SIGNALER	T GLARIEST
A GASALIER	E GASELIER	ENGRAILS	SLANGIER	REGALIST
LAIRAGES	G SLAGGIER	NARGILES	O GASOLIER	Y GREASILY
REGALIAS	M GREMIALS	REALIGNS	GIRASOLE	Z GLAZIERS
C GLACIERS	LAMIGERS	SALERING	SERAGLIO	
GRACILES	REGALISM	SANGLIER	S GLASSIER	

AEGINOR 147

ORIGANE	D ORGANDIE	REGIONAL	S IGNAROES	ORIGANES
B ABORIGEN	L GERANIOL	R ORANGIER	ORGANISE	Z ORGANIZE

AEGINOS 155

AGONISE	D AGONISED	L GASOLINE	R IGNAROES	S AGONISES
B BEGONIAS	DIAGNOSE	N ANGINOSE	ORGANISE	Z AGONIZES
C COINAGES	G SEAGOING	GANOINES	ORIGANES	

AEGINRS 31

SERINGA	GESNERIA	SANGLIER	SPEARING	INGRATES
A ANERGIAS	G GEARINGS	SIGNALER	R EARRINGS	RANGIEST
ANGARIES	GREASING	SLANGIER	GRAINERS	REASTING
ARGINASE	SNAGGIER	M GERMAINS	S ASSIGNER	STEARING
B BEARINGS	H HEARINGS	SMEARING	REASSIGN	TASERING
SABERING	HEARSING	N AGINNERS	SEARINGS	V VINEGARS
C CREASING	SHEARING	EARNINGS	SERINGAS	W RESAWING
GRECIANS	K SKEARING	ENGRAINS	T ANGRIEST	SWEARING
SEARCING	L ALIGNERS	GRANNIES	ANGSTIER	WEARINGS
D DERAIGNS	ENGRAILS	O IGNAROES	ASTRINGE	Y RESAYING
GRADINES	NARGILES	ORGANISE	GANISTER	SYNERGIA
READINGS	REALIGNS	ORIGANES	GANTRIES	
E ANERGIES	SALERING	P PREASING	GRANITES	

AEGINRT 25

TEARING	GRADIENT	INTEGRAL	ASTRINGE	TREATING
A AERATING	REDATING	RELATING	GANISTER	V AVERTING
B BERATING	TREADING	TANGLIER	GANTRIES	GRIEVANT
REBATING	E GRATINEE	TERAGLIN	GRANITES	TAVERING
TABERING	INTERAGE	TRIANGLE	INGRATES	VINTAGER
C ARGENTIC	H EARTHING	M EMIGRANT	RANGIEST	W TWANGIER
CATERING	HEARTING	REMATING	REASTING	WATERING
CITRANGE	INGATHER	P RETAPING	STEARING	X RETAXING
CREATING	K RETAKING	TAPERING	TASERING	
REACTING	L ALERTING	S ANGRIEST	T ARETTING	
D DERATING	ALTERING	ANGSTIER	GNATTIER	

AEGINST 39

TSIGANE	L EASTLING	N ANTIGENS	RANGIEST	T ESTATING
A SAGINATE	GELATINS	GENTIANS	REASTING	TANGIEST
B BEATINGS	GENITALS	STEANING	STEARING	U SAUTEING
D SEDATING	STEALING	R ANGRIEST	TASERING	UNITAGES
STEADING	TAGLINES	ANGSTIER	S EASTINGS	V VINTAGES
E SAGENITE	M MANGIEST	ASTRINGE	GENISTAS	W SWEATING
F FEASTING	MINTAGES	GANISTER	GIANTESS	Y YEASTING
G NAGGIEST	MISAGENT	GANTRIES	SEATINGS	Z TZIGANES
H GAHNITES	STEAMING	GRANITES	TEASINGS	
HEATINGS	TEAMINGS	INGRATES	TSIGANES	

AEGNORS 245

ORANGES	I IGNAROES	M MEGARONS	NEGATORS	W WAGONERS
B BEGROANS	ORGANISE	O OREGANOS	ORANGEST	
C ACROGENS	ORIGANES	R GROANERS	RAGSTONE	
CORNAGES	K KARENGOS	T ESTRAGON	STONERAG	

AEGNORT 203

NEGATOR	N NEGATRON	ORANGEST	T TETRAGON
D DRAGONET	S ESTRAGON	RAGSTONE	U OUTRANGE
F FRONTAGE	NEGATORS	STONERAG	Y NEGATORY

AEGNRST 111

STRANGE	NEGATERS	ASTRINGE	L STRANGLE	RAGSTONE
A STARAGEN	REAGENTS	GANISTER	TANGLERS	STONERAG
TANAGERS	SEGREANT	GANTRIES	TRANGLES	P TREPANGS
B BANGSTER	SERGEANT	GRANITES	M GARMENTS	R GRANTERS
D DRAGNETS	STERNAGE	INGRATES	MARGENTS	REGRANTS
GRANDEST	F ENGRAFTS	RANGIEST	RAGMENTS	STRANGER
E ESTRANGE	G GANGSTER	REASTING	O ESTRAGON	S STRANGES
GRANTEES	I ANGRIEST	STEARING	NEGATORS	U STRAUNGE
GREATENS	ANGSTIER	TASERING	ORANGEST	W TWANGERS

AEGORST 140

TOERAGS	D GOADSTER	H SHORTAGE	LEGATORS	NEGATORS
C ESCARGOT	F FAGOTERS	L GLOATERS	N ESTRAGON	ORANGEST

RAGSTONE	O ROOTAGES	POTAGERS	S STORAGES	U OUTRAGES
STONERAG	P PORTAGES	R GARROTES	T GAROTTES	

AEHINRT 161

THERIAN	HERNIATE	INGATHER	S HAIRNETS	U HAURIENT
D ANTHERID	G EARTHING	O ANTIHERO	INEARTHS	W TARWHINE
E ATHERINE	HEARTING	P PERIANTH	THERIANS	

AEHIRST 116

SHERIAT	D HAIRSTED	N HAIRNETS	R TRASHIER	Y HYSTERIA
A HETAIRAS	HARDIEST	INEARTHS	S SHERIATS	
C CHARIEST	E HEARTIES	THERIANS	U THESAURI	
STICHERA	F FAITHERS	O HOARIEST	W SWATHIER	
THERIACS	I HAIRIEST	P TRIPHASE	WATERISH	

AEIILNR 244

AIRLINE	C IRENICAL	H HAIRLINE	S AIRLINES	T INERTIAL
B BILINEAR	G GAINLIER	R AIRLINER	SNAILIER	

AEIINRS 157

SENARII	D DRAISINE	SNAILIER	T INERTIAS	
B BINARIES	K KAISERIN	N SIRENIAN	RAINIEST	
C RIANCIES	L AIRLINES	S AIRINESS	Y YERSINIA	

AEIINRT 35

INERTIA	E INERTIAE	N TRIENNIA	RAINIEST	
C ARENITIC	F FAINTIER	P PAINTIER	Z TRIAZINE	
D DAINTIER	L INERTIAL	S INERTIAS		

AEIINST 124

ISATINE	DAINTIES	LITANIES	RAINIEST	V VANITIES
B BAINITES	F FAINITES	M MINIATES	S ISATINES	X AXINITES
C ANTICISE	K KAINITES	P PATINISE	SANITIES	Z SANITIZE
CANITIES	L ALIENIST	PIANISTE	SANITISE	
D ADENITIS	LATINISE	R INERTIAS	TENIASIS	

AEIIRST 94

IRISATE	L LAIRIEST	N INERTIAS	S IRISATES	X SEXTARII
D IRISATED	LISTERIA	RAINIEST	SATIRISE	Z SATIRIZE
F RATIFIES	M AIRTIMES	P PARITIES	V VAIRIEST	
H HAIRIEST	SERIATIM	R RARITIES	W WISTERIA	

AEILNOR 44

ALIENOR	LONICERA	L ALLERION	ALIENORS	TAILERON
C ACROLEIN	F FORELAIN	P PELORIAN	T ORIENTAL	V OVERLAIN
COLINEAR	G GERANIOL	S AILERONS	RELATION	
CREOLIAN	REGIONAL	ALERIONS		

AEILNOS 57

ANISOLE	M LAMINOSE	P OPALINES	S ANISOLES	X SILOXANE
D NODALISE	MINEOLAS	R AILERONS	T ELATIONS	
G GASOLINE	SEMOLINA	ALERIONS	INSOLATE	
K KAOLINES	N SOLANINE	ALIENORS	TOENAILS	

AEILNOT 29

TOENAIL	F OLEFIANT	P ANTIPOLE	TAILERON	TOENAILS
B TAILBONE	G GELATION	R ORIENTAL	S ELATIONS	T TONALITE
D DELATION	LEGATION	RELATION	INSOLATE	

AEILNPT 167

PANTILE	PLANETIC	G PLEATING	TRAPLINE	PLAINEST
A PALATINE	D PANTILED	O ANTIPOLE	TRIPLANE	T TINPLATE
B PINTABLE	E PETALINE	P PIEPLANT	S PANELIST	Y PENALITY
C PECTINAL	TAPELINE	R INTERLAP	PANTILES	

AEILNRS 15

RENAILS	NARGILES	SNAILIER	PRALINES	RETINALS
B RINSABLE	REALIGNS	M MARLINES	R SNARLIER	TRENAILS
C CARLINES	SALERING	MINERALS	S RAINLESS	U LUNARIES
LANCIERS	SANGLIER	MISLEARN	T ENTRAILS	V RAVELINS
D ISLANDER	SIGNALER	O AILERONS	LARNIEST	X RELAXINS
E ALIENERS	SLANGIER	ALERIONS	LATRINES	Y INLAYERS
G ALIGNERS	H INHALERS	ALIENORS	RATLINES	SNAILERY
ENGRAILS	I AIRLINES	P PEARLINS	REINSTAL	

AEILNRT 6

TRENAIL	INTEGRAL	N INTERNAL	LARNIEST	RETINULA
C CLARINET	RELATING	O ORIENTAL	LATRINES	TENURIAL
E ELATERIN	TANGLIER	RELATION	RATLINES	V INTERVAL
ENTAILER	TERAGLIN	TAILERON	REINSTAL	Y INTERLAY
TREENAIL	TRIANGLE	P INTERLAP	RETINALS	
F INFLATER	I INERTIAL	TRAPLINE	TRENAILS	
G ALERTING	M TERMINAL	TRIPLANE	T RATTLINE	
ALTERING	TRAMLINE	S ENTRAILS	U AUNTLIER	

AEILNST 49

TENAILS	I ALIENIST	O ELATIONS	RATLINES	STANIELS
B INSTABLE	LATINISE	INSOLATE	REINSTAL	U ALUNITES
C CANISTEL	LITANIES	TOENAILS	RETINALS	INSULATE
F INFLATES	K LANKIEST	P PANELIST	TRENAILS	V VENTAILS
G EASTLING	M AILMENTS	PANTILES	S EASTLINS	W LAWNIEST
GELATINS	ALIMENTS	PLAINEST	ELASTINS	
GENITALS	MANLIEST	R ENTRAILS	NAILSETS	
STEALING	MELANIST	LARNIEST	SALIENTS	
TAGLINES	SMALTINE	LATRINES	SALTINES	

AEILOST 38

ISOLATE	ISOLATED	OTALGIES	TOENAILS	V VIOLATES
C ALOETICS	SODALITE	K KEITLOAS	P SPOLIATE	
COALIEST	SOLIDATE	M LOAMIEST	R SOTERIAL	
SOCIETAL	F FOLIATES	N ELATIONS	S ISOLATES	
D DIASTOLE	G LATIGOES	INSOLATE	T TOTALISE	

AEILPRT 142

PLATIER	D DIPTERAL	K TRAPLIKE	PETIOLAR	PLAITERS
A PARIETAL	TRIPEDAL	N INTERLAP	R PALTRIER	V LIVETRAP
B PARTIBLE	E PEARLITE	TRAPLINE	PRETRIAL	
C PARTICLE	I LIPARITE	TRIPLANE	S PILASTER	
PRELATIC	REPTILIA	O EPILATOR	PLAISTER	

AEILRRT 160

TRAILER	E RETAILER	PRETRIAL	TRAILERS	Y LITERARY
A ARTERIAL	O RETAILOR	S RETIRALS	T RATTLIER	
C CLARTIER	P PALTRIER	RETRIALS	U RURALITE	

AEILRST 12

TAILERS	REDTAILS	LISTERIA	MISALTER	PLAITERS
B BLASTIER	E ATELIERS	K LARKIEST	N ENTRAILS	R RETIRALS
LIBRATES	EARLIEST	STALKIER	LARNIEST	RETRIALS
TABLIERS	LATERISE	STARLIKE	LATRINES	TRAILERS
C ALTRICES	LEARIEST	L LITERALS	RATLINES	S REALISTS
ARTICLES	REALTIES	TALLIERS	REINSTAL	SALTIERS
RECITALS	F FLARIEST	TRIELLAS	RETINALS	SALTIRES
SELICTAR	FRAILEST	M LAMISTER	TRENAILS	SLAISTER
STERICAL	G GLARIEST	LAMITERS	O SOTERIAL	T TERTIALS
D DILATERS	REGALIST	MARLIEST	P PILASTER	U URALITES
LARDIEST	I LAIRIEST	MARLITES	PLAISTER	

AEILRTT 88

TERTIAL	D DETRITAL	F FILTRATE	M REMITTAL	R RATTLIER
B TITRABLE	E LATERITE	G AGLITTER	N RATTLINE	S TERTIALS
C TRACTILE	LITERATE	I LITERATI	O LITERATO	Y ALTERITY

AEILRTU 156

URALITE	FILATURE	N AUNTLIER	Q QUARTILE	S URALITES
C RETICULA	G LIGATURE	RETINULA	REQUITAL	V VAULTIER
F FAULTIER	L TAILLEUR	TENURIAL	R RURALITE	Z LAZURITE

AEIMNOT 182

AMNIOTE	D DOMINATE	N ANTINOME	S AMNIOTES	SOMNIATE
A METANOIA	NEMATOID	NOMINATE	MASONITE	Z MONAZITE
C COINMATE	M AMMONITE	P PTOMAINE	MISATONE	

AEIMNRS 135

	SIRNAME	E	REMANIES	L	MARLINES		ROMANISE		RAIMENTS
B	MIRBANES	G	GERMAINS		MINERALS	R	MARINERS	U	ANEURISM
C	CARMINES		SMEARING		MISLEARN	S	SEMINARS	Y	SEMINARY
	CREMAINS	H	HARMINES	N	REINSMAN		SIRNAMES		
D	ADERMINS		SHIREMAN	O	MORAINES	T	MERANTIS		
	SIRNAMED	K	RAMEKINS		ROMAINES		MINARETS		

AEIMNRT 93

	RAIMENT	G	EMIGRANT	N	TRAINMEN	T	INTERMAT	Y	TYRAMINE
A	ANIMATER		REMATING	S	MERANTIS		MARTINET		
	MARINATE	L	TERMINAL		MINARETS	U	RUMINATE		
E	ANTIMERE		TRAMLINE		RAIMENTS	W	WARIMENT		

AEIMNST 107

	TAMINES	E	ETAMINES		STEAMING		MANLIEST	R	MERANTIS
A	AMENTIAS		MATINEES		TEAMINGS		MELANIST		MINARETS
	ANIMATES		MISEATEN	H	HEMATINS		SMALTINE		RAIMENTS
B	AMBIENTS		SEMINATE	I	MINIATES	N	MANNITES	S	MANTISES
C	AMNESTIC	F	MANIFEST	K	MANKIEST	O	AMNIOTES		MATINESS
	SEMANTIC	G	MANGIEST		MISTAKEN		MASONITE		
D	MEDIANTS		MINTAGES	L	AILMENTS		MISATONE		
	TIDESMAN		MISAGENT		ALIMENTS		SOMNIATE		

AEIMRST 68

	SMARTIE	E	EMERITAS	K	MISTAKER	N	MERANTIS		SEMITARS
A	AMIRATES		EMIRATES		SITKAMER		MINARETS		SMARTIES
B	BARMIEST		REAMIEST	L	LAMISTER		RAIMENTS	T	MISTREAT
C	CERAMIST		STEAMIER		LAMITERS	O	AMORTISE		TERATISM
	MATRICES	G	MAGISTER		MARLIEST		ATOMISER	U	MURIATES
	MISTRACE		MIGRATES		MARLITES	P	APTERISM		SEMITAUR
	SCIMETAR		RAGTIMES		MISALTER		PRIMATES	V	VITAMERS
D	MARDIEST		STERIGMA	M	MARMITES	S	ASTERISM	W	WARTIMES
	MISRATED	I	AIRTIMES		RAMMIEST		MAISTERS	X	MATRIXES
	READMITS		SERIATIM		TRAMMIES		MISRATES	Y	SYMITARE

AEINNOT 101

	ENATION		ANTINODE		NOMINATE		REANOINT	T	INTONATE
C	ENACTION	G	NEGATION	R	ANOINTER	S	ENATIONS	V	INNOVATE
D	ANOINTED	M	ANTINOME		INORNATE		SONATINE		VENATION

AEINNRS 82

	INSNARE	E	ANSERINE		GRANNIES	P	PANNIERS		TRANNIES
C	CRANNIES	G	AGINNERS	I	SIRENIAN	R	INSNARER	U	ANEURINS
	NARCEINS		EARNINGS	M	REINSMAN	S	INSNARES		UNARISEN
D	INSNARED		ENGRAINS	O	RAISONNE	T	ENTRAINS	W	SWANNIER

AEINNRT 115

TRANNIE	M TRAINMEN	REANOINT	TRANNIES
I TRIENNIA	O ANOINTER	R INERRANT	T INTRANET
L INTERNAL	INORNATE	S ENTRAINS	

AEINORS 13

ERASION	F FARINOSE	ALIENORS	SENSORIA	SENORITA
B BARONIES	G IGNAROES	M MORAINES	T ANOESTRI	V AVERSION
SEAROBIN	ORGANISE	ROMAINES	ARSONITE	
C SCENARIO	ORIGANES	ROMANISE	NOTARIES	
D ANEROIDS	L AILERONS	N RAISONNE	NOTARISE	
DONARIES	ALERIONS	S ERASIONS	ROSINATE	

AEINORT 1

OTARINE	ANORETIC	H ANTIHERO	P ATROPINE	SENORITA
A AERATION	CREATION	L ORIENTAL	R ANTERIOR	T TENTORIA
B BARITONE	REACTION	RELATION	S ANOESTRI	Z NOTARIZE
OBTAINER	D AROINTED	TAILERON	ARSONITE	
REOBTAIN	DERATION	N ANOINTER	NOTARIES	
TABORINE	ORDINATE	INORNATE	NOTARISE	
C ACTIONER	RATIONED	REANOINT	ROSINATE	

AEINOST 16

ATONIES	CANOEIST	TOENAILS	SONATINE	ROSINATE
B BOTANIES	SONICATE	M AMNIOTES	P SAPONITE	SENORITA
BOTANISE	D ASTONIED	MASONITE	R ANOESTRI	S ASSIENTO
NIOBATES	SEDATION	MISATONE	ARSONITE	ASTONIES
OBEISANT	L ELATIONS	SOMNIATE	NOTARIES	V STOVAINE
C ACONITES	INSOLATE	N ENATIONS	NOTARISE	X SAXONITE

AEINPRS 197

RAPINES	PANFRIES	SERAPHIN	P SNAPPIER	PRISTANE
A PANARIES	G PREASING	K RANPIKES	T PAINTERS	REPAINTS
D SPRAINED	SPEARING	L PEARLINS	PANTRIES	U UNPRAISE
E NAPERIES	H HEPARINS	PRALINES	PERTAINS	W SPAWNIER
F FIREPANS	PARISHEN	N PANNIERS	PINASTER	

AEINPRT 40

REPAINT	TAPERING	TRIPLANE	PANTRIES	T TRIPTANE
A ANTIRAPE	H PERIANTH	O ATROPINE	PERTAINS	U PAINTURE
D DIPTERAN	I PAINTIER	R PRETRAIN	PINASTER	X EXPIRANT
E APERIENT	L INTERLAP	TERRAPIN	PRISTANE	
G RETAPING	TRAPLINE	S PAINTERS	REPAINTS	

AEINPST 175

SPINATE	THESPIAN	L PANELIST	O SAPONITE	PERTAINS
B BEPAINTS	I PATINISE	PANTILES	P NAPPIEST	PINASTER
D DEPAINTS	PIANISTE	PLAINEST	R PAINTERS	PRISTANE
H PENTHIAS	K SNAKEPIT	N PANTINES	PANTRIES	REPAINTS

S SAPIENTS   T PATIENTS   SUPINATE   Y EPINASTY
  STEAPSIN   U PETUNIAS

AEINRRS 224

SNARIER	F REFRAINS	K SNARKIER	T RESTRAIN	TRAINERS
D DRAINERS	G EARRINGS	L SNARLIER	RETRAINS	TRANSIRE
SERRANID	GRAINERS	M MARINERS	STRAINER	
E REARISEN	H SHARNIER	N INSNARER	TERRAINS	

AEINRRT 90

TRAINER	O ANTERIOR	S RESTRAIN	TERRAINS	T RETIRANT
E RETAINER	P PRETRAIN	RETRAINS	TRAINERS	V VERATRIN
N INERRANT	TERRAPIN	STRAINER	TRANSIRE	W INTERWAR

AEINRSS 242

SARNIES	E SENARIES	SERINGAS	O ERASIONS	STARNIES
C ARCSINES	F FAIRNESS	H ARSHINES	SENSORIA	STEARINS
ARSENICS	SANSERIF	I AIRINESS	T ARTINESS	U ANURESIS
CERASINS	SERAFINS	L RAINLESS	RESIANTS	SENARIUS
RACINESS	G ASSIGNER	M SEMINARS	RETSINAS	W WARINESS
D ARIDNESS	REASSIGN	SIRNAMES	SNARIEST	X XERANSIS
SARDINES	SEARINGS	N INSNARES	STAINERS	

AEINRST 2

STEARIN	RANDIEST	TASERING	N ENTRAINS	TRANSIRE
A ANTISERA	STRAINED	H HAIRNETS	TRANNIES	S ARTINESS
ARTESIAN	E ARENITES	INEARTHS	O ANOESTRI	RESIANTS
RATANIES	ARSENITE	THERIANS	ARSONITE	RETSINAS
RESINATA	RESINATE	I INERTIAS	NOTARIES	SNARIEST
SANTERIA	STEARINE	RAINIEST	NOTARISE	STAINERS
SEATRAIN	TRAINEES	J NARTJIES	ROSINATE	STARNIES
B ATEBRINS	F FAINTERS	K KERATINS	SENORITA	STEARINS
BANISTER	FENITARS	NARKIEST	P PAINTERS	T INTREATS
BARNIEST	G ANGRIEST	L ENTRAILS	PANTRIES	NITRATES
C CANISTER	ANGSTIER	LARNIEST	PERTAINS	STRAITEN
CARNIEST	ASTRINGE	LATRINES	PINASTER	TARTINES
CERATINS	GANISTER	RATLINES	PRISTANE	TERTIANS
CISTERNA	GANTRIES	REINSTAL	REPAINTS	U RUINATES
CREATINS	GRANITES	RETINALS	R RESTRAIN	TAURINES
NACRITES	INGRATES	TRENAILS	RETRAINS	URANITES
SCANTIER	RANGIEST	M MERANTIS	STRAINER	URINATES
TACRINES	REASTING	MINARETS	TERRAINS	W TINWARES
D DETRAINS	STEARING	RAIMENTS	TRAINERS	

AEINRTT 45

TERTIAN	G ARETTING	MARTINET	S INTREATS	U TAINTURE
A ATTAINER	GNATTIER	N INTRANET	NITRATES	
REATTAIN	TREATING	O TENTORIA	STRAITEN	
C INTERACT	L RATTLINE	P TRIPTANE	TARTINES	
D NITRATED	M INTERMAT	R RETIRANT	TERTIANS	

AEINRTU 24

	URINATE	D	DATURINE	J	JAUNTIER	P	PAINTURE		URANITES
A	INAURATE		INDURATE	L	AUNTLIER	Q	ANTIQUER		URINATES
B	BRAUNITE		RUINATED		RETINULA		QUAINTER	T	TAINTURE
	URBANITE		URINATED		TENURIAL	S	RUINATES	V	VAUNTIER
C	ANURETIC	H	HAURIENT	M	RUMINATE		TAURINES		

AEINSST 144

	TISANES	G	EASTINGS		SANITISE		STANINES	S	SAINTESS
A	ENTASIAS		GENISTAS		TENIASIS	O	ASSIENTO		SESTINAS
B	BASINETS		GIANTESS	K	SNAKIEST		ASTONIES	T	ANTSIEST
	BASSINET		SEATINGS	L	EASTLINS	P	SAPIENTS		INSTATES
	BESAINTS		TEASINGS		ELASTINS		STEAPSIN		NASTIEST
	BESTAINS		TSIGANES		NAILSETS	R	ARTINESS		SATINETS
C	CINEASTS	H	ANTHESIS		SALIENTS		RESIANTS		TITANESS
	SCANTIES		SHANTIES		SALTINES		RETSINAS	U	SINUATES
D	DESTAINS		SHEITANS		STANIELS		SNARIEST	X	SEXTAINS
	SANDIEST		STHENIAS	M	MANTISES		STAINERS		
E	ETESIANS	I	ISATINES		MATINESS		STARNIES		
	TENIASES		SANITIES	N	INSANEST		STEARINS		

AEINSTT 87

	SATINET		NICTATES	G	ESTATING	R	INTREATS		NASTIEST
A	ASTATINE		TETANICS		TANGIEST		NITRATES		SATINETS
	SANITATE	D	INSTATED	H	HESITANT		STRAITEN		TITANESS
	TANAISTE	E	ANISETTE	J	JANTIEST		TARTINES	T	NATTIEST
B	TABINETS		TETANIES	N	ANTIENTS		TERTIANS	V	TASTEVIN
C	CANTIEST		TETANISE		STANNITE	S	ANTSIEST	W	TAWNIEST
	ENTASTIC	F	FAINTEST	P	PATIENTS		INSTATES		

AEINSTU 183

	SINUATE		UNITAGES		INSULATE		QUANTISE		URINATES
D	AUDIENTS	J	JAUNTIES	P	PETUNIAS	R	RUINATES	S	SINUATES
	SINUATED	K	UNAKITES		SUPINATE		TAURINES	V	SUIVANTE
G	SAUTEING	L	ALUNITES	Q	ANTIQUES		URANITES		

AEINSTV 153

	VAINEST		VESICANT	G	VINTAGES	L	VENTAILS	U	SUIVANTE
A	SANATIVE	D	DEVIANTS	I	VANITIES	O	STOVAINE		
C	CISTVAEN	E	NAIVETES	K	KISTVAEN	T	TASTEVIN		

AEIORST 4

	OTARIES	J	JAROSITE		ARSONITE	R	ROARIEST	V	TRAVOISE
B	SABOTIER	L	SOTERIAL		NOTARIES		ROTARIES		VIATORES
D	ASTEROID	M	AMORTISE		NOTARISE	T	TOASTIER		VOTARIES
E	ETAERIOS		ATOMISER		ROSINATE	U	OUTRAISE		
H	HOARIEST	N	ANOESTRI		SENORITA		SAUTOIRE		

AEIORSV 217

OVARIES		AVOIDERS		VALORISE	P VAPORISE		VIATORES
C COVARIES		G VIRAGOES		VARIOLES	R SAVORIER		VOTARIES
VARICOSE		J JAROVISE		VOLARIES	S SAVORIES	W AVOWRIES
D AVODIRES		L OVERSAIL	N AVERSION	T TRAVOISE	

AEIPRST 109

TRAIPSE		PRACTISE	H TRIPHASE		PANTRIES		PIASTRES
A ASPIRATE		D DIPTERAS	I PARITIES		PERTAINS		RASPIEST
PARASITE		RAPIDEST	K PARKIEST		PINASTER		TRAIPSES
SEPTARIA		SPIRATED	L PILASTER		PRISTANE	V PRIVATES
B BAPTISER		TARSIPED		PLAISTER		REPAINTS	W WIRETAPS
C CRAPIEST		TRAIPSED		PLAITERS	P PERIAPTS	Y ASPERITY
CRISPATE	E PARIETES	M APTERISM	R PARTIERS	
PARETICS		PETARIES		PRIMATES	S PASTRIES	
PICRATES	G GRAPIEST	N PAINTERS		PIASTERS	

AEIRRST 78

TARSIER		REASTIER		TRAILERS		TRANSIRE	S TARSIERS
B ARBITERS	F FRATRIES	N RESTRAIN	O ROARIEST	T RETRAITS
BARRIEST	H TRASHIER		RETRAINS		ROTARIES		STRAITER
RAREBITS	I RARITIES		STRAINER	P PARTIERS		TARRIEST
C ERRATICS	L RETIRALS		TERRAINS	R STARRIER	W STRAWIER
E ARTERIES		RETRIALS		TRAINERS		TARRIERS	

AEIRSST 205

TIRASSE	H SHERIATS		MAISTERS		STEARINS		ARTSIEST
A ASTERIAS	I IRISATES		MISRATES	P PASTRIES		STRIATES
ATRESIAS		SATIRISE		SEMITARS		PIASTERS	V TRAVISES
C SCARIEST	K ASTERISK		SMARTIES		PIASTRES	W WAISTERS
D ASTERIDS		SARKIEST	N ARTINESS		RASPIEST		WAITRESS
DIASTERS	L REALISTS		RESIANTS		TRAIPSES		WASTRIES
DISASTER		SALTIERS		RETSINAS	R TARSIERS	
DISRATES		SALTIRES		SNARIEST	S ASSISTER	
E SERIATES		SLAISTER		STAINERS		TIRASSES	
G AGISTERS	M ASTERISM		STARNIES	T ARTISTES	

AEIRSTT 62

TERTIAS		STRIATED	L TERTIALS	O TOASTIER		RATTIEST
A ARIETTAS		TARDIEST	M MISTREAT	R RETRAITS		TARTIEST
ARISTATE	E ARIETTES		TERATISM		STRAITER		TITRATES
B BIRETTAS		ITERATES	N INTREATS		TARRIEST		TRISTATE
C CITRATES		TEARIEST		NITRATES	S ARTISTES	W WARTIEST
CRISTATE		TREATIES		STRAITEN		ARTSIEST	X EXTRAITS
SCATTIER		TREATISE		TARTINES		STRIATES	Z TRISTEZA
D STRAITED	G STRIGATE		TERTIANS	T ATTRITES	

AEIRSTV 238

VERITAS	E EVIRATES	I VAIRIEST		VIATORES	S TRAVISES
A VARIATES	G VIRGATES	M VITAMERS		VOTARIES	Y VESTIARY
B VIBRATES		VITRAGES	O TRAVOISE	P PRIVATES	

AEIRSTW 141

	WASTRIE		TAWERIES		WATERISH	P	WIRETAPS	T	WARTIEST
A	AWAITERS		WASTERIE	I	WISTERIA	R	STRAWIER		
B	WARBIEST		WEARIEST	K	WATERSKI	S	WAISTERS		
D	TAWDRIES	F	WASTRIFE	M	WARTIMES		WAITRESS		
E	SWEATIER	H	SWATHIER	N	TINWARES		WASTRIES		

AELNORS 229

	RELOANS	F	FARNESOL		ALIENORS	P	PERSONAL		NEUROSAL
D	LADRONES	I	AILERONS	L	LLANEROS		PSORALEN	V	VERONALS
	SOLANDER		ALERIONS	M	ALMONERS	U	ALEURONS		

AELNORU 191

	ALEURON		URODELAN	N	NEURONAL		NEUROSAL
D	UNLOADER	E	ALEURONE	S	ALEURONS	T	OUTLEARN

AELNRST 72

	STERNAL		TELERANS		LARNIEST	N	LANTERNS	T	SLATTERN
A	ASTERNAL	G	STRANGLE		LATRINES	P	PANTLERS		TRENTALS
B	BRANTLES		TANGLERS		RATLINES		PLANTERS	U	NEUTRALS
C	CENTRALS		TRANGLES		REINSTAL		REPLANTS	V	VENTRALS
E	ALTERNES	H	ENTHRALS		RETINALS	S	SALTERNS		
	ETERNALS	I	ENTRAILS		TRENAILS		SLANTERS		

AELORST 27

	OLESTRA		LEOTARDS		LEGATORS	P	PETROSAL	T	RETOTALS
B	BLOATERS		LODESTAR	H	LOATHERS		POLESTAR	U	ROSULATE
	SORTABLE	E	OLEASTER		RATHOLES		PROLATES	V	LEVATORS
	STORABLE	F	FLOATERS	I	SOTERIAL	R	REALTORS		OVERSALT
C	LOCATERS		FORESTAL	L	REALLOTS		RELATORS	Y	ROYALETS
	SECTORAL		REFLOATS		ROSTELLA		RESTORAL	Z	ZELATORS
D	DELATORS	G	GLOATERS	M	MOLERATS	S	OLESTRAS		

AELRSTU 221

	SALUTER	E	RESALUTE		TRAGULES	O	ROSULATE		TUTELARS
B	BALUSTER	F	REFUTALS	I	URALITES	P	APLUSTRE	V	VAULTERS
	RUSTABLE	G	GAULTERS	M	STAUMREL	S	SALUTERS		VESTURAL
C	RAUCLEST		GESTURAL	N	NEUTRALS	T	LUSTRATE		

AEMNORS 189

	OARSMEN	F	FORAMENS		ROMAINES	R	RANSOMER	V	OVERMANS
A	AMARONES	G	MEGARONS		ROMANISE	T	MONSTERA		OVERSMAN
C	CREMONAS	H	HORSEMAN	L	ALMONERS		ONSTREAM	Y	ROMNEYAS
	ROMANCES		MENORAHS	N	MONERANS		STOREMAN		
D	MADRONES		RHAMNOSE		SONARMEN		TONEARMS		
	RANSOMED		SHOREMAN	P	MANROPES	U	ENAMOURS		
	ROADSMEN	I	MORAINES		PROSEMAN		NEUROMAS		

AEMNORT 232

TONEARM	O ANTEROOM	ONSTREAM	T TORMENTA
A EMANATOR	P EMPATRON	STOREMAN	U ROUTEMAN
N ORNAMENT	S MONSTERA	TONEARMS	Y MONETARY

AEMORST 206

OMERTAS	F FOREMAST	I AMORTISE	N MONSTERA	O TEAROOMS
B BROMATES	FORMATES	ATOMISER	ONSTREAM	R REARMOST
D STROAMED	MORTSAFE	L MOLERATS	STOREMAN	S MAESTROS
E EROTEMAS	H TERAOHMS	M MARMOSET	TONEARMS	V OVERMAST

AENNORT 223

NORTENA	I ANOINTER	M ORNAMENT	RESONANT
D NONRATED	INORNATE	P PATRONNE	U UNORNATE
G NEGATRON	REANOINT	S NORTENAS	W WANTONER

AENORST 5

TREASON	RESONATE	NOTARIES	RESONANT	TREASONS
A ANOESTRA	F SEAFRONT	NOTARISE	P OPERANTS	T ORNATEST
B BARONETS	G ESTRAGON	ROSINATE	PRONATES	U OUTEARNS
C ANCESTOR	NEGATORS	SENORITA	PROTEANS	V VENATORS
ENACTORS	ORANGEST	M MONSTERA	R ANTRORSE	W STONERAW
SARCONET	RAGSTONE	ONSTREAM	S ASSENTOR	
SORTANCE	STONERAG	STOREMAN	SANTEROS	
D TORNADES	I ANOESTRI	TONEARMS	SENATORS	
E EARSTONE	ARSONITE	N NORTENAS	STARNOSE	

AENORSU 143

ARENOUS	NACREOUS	NEUROSAL	N UNREASON	T OUTEARNS
A ARANEOUS	F FURANOSE	M ENAMOURS	S ANSEROUS	V RAVENOUS
C CARNEOUS	L ALEURONS	NEUROMAS	ARSENOUS	

AENORTU 84

OUTEARN	C COURANTE	G OUTRANGE	M ROUTEMAN	S OUTEARNS
A AERONAUT	OUTRANCE	L OUTLEARN	N UNORNATE	

AENRSTT 215

RATTENS	RATTEENS	TERTIANS	P PATTERNS	U TAUNTERS
A TARTANES	I INTREATS	L SLATTERN	TRANSEPT	
C TRANECTS	NITRATES	TRENTALS	TRAPNEST	
TRANSECT	STRAITEN	N ENTRANTS	R TRANTERS	
E ENTREATS	TARTINES	O ORNATEST	S TARTNESS	

AENRSTU 60

SAUNTER	C CENTAURS	UNTRACES	UNTREADS	G STRAUNGE
B UNBRASTE	RECUSANT	D DAUNTERS	E SAUTERNE	H HAUNTERS
URBANEST	UNCRATES	TRANSUDE	F AFTERSUN	UNEARTHS

UNHEARTS	URANITES	MENSTRUA	S ANESTRUS	W UNWATERS
URETHANS	URINATES	TRANSUME	SAUNTERS	
I RUINATES	L NEUTRALS	O OUTEARNS	T TAUNTERS	
TAURINES	M ANESTRUM	P PERSAUNT	V VAUNTERS	

AEOPRST 226

SEAPORT	READOPTS	H PHORATES	PRONATES	PORTASES
B PROBATES	E OPERATES	POTSHARE	PROTEANS	PROTASES
C POSTRACE	PROTEASE	L PETROSAL	P TRAPPOSE	SEAPORTS
D ADOPTERS	F FOREPAST	POLESTAR	R PRAETORS	T PROSTATE
ASPORTED	G PORTAGES	PROLATES	PRORATES	U APTEROUS
PASTORED	POTAGERS	N OPERANTS	S ESPARTOS	V OVERPAST

AEORRST 114

ROASTER	CREATORS	L REALTORS	P PRAETORS	REASSORT
A AERATORS	REACTORS	RELATORS	PRORATES	ROASTERS
B ABORTERS	D ROADSTER	RESTORAL	R ARRESTOR	T ROSTRATE
ARBORETS	G GARROTES	M REARMOST	S ASSERTOR	
TABORERS	I ROARIEST	N ANTRORSE	ASSORTER	
C ACROTERS	ROTARIES	O SORORATE	ORATRESS	

AEORSTT 145

TOASTER	TABORETS	I TOASTIER	R ROSTRATE	TESTATOR
A AEROSTAT	C SECTATOR	L RETOTALS	S STRATOSE	U OUTRATES
B ABETTORS	G GAROTTES	N ORNATEST	TOASTERS	OUTSTARE
BATTEROS	H RHEOSTAT	P PROSTATE	T ATTESTOR	SEATROUT

AGILNOT 162

ANTILOG	E GELATION	H LOATHING	R TRIGONAL	Y ANTILOGY
A GALTONIA	LEGATION	I INTAGLIO	S ANTILOGS	
B BLOATING	F FLOATING	LIGATION	SALTOING	
OBLIGANT	G GLOATING	TAGLIONI	SOLATING	
C LOCATING	GOATLING	P PLOATING	T TOTALING	

AGINORS 180

SOARING	ORGANISE	L RANGOLIS	ROARINGS	T ORGANIST
C ORGANICS	ORIGANES	M ORGANISM	S ASSIGNOR	ROASTING
D ROADINGS	H ORANGISH	ROAMINGS	SIGNORAS	U AROUSING
E IGNAROES	I SIGNORIA	R GARRISON	SOARINGS	V SAVORING

AGINORT 129

ROATING	G GAROTING	N IGNORANT	T ROTATING	ORGANITY
B ABORTING	I RIGATONI	O ROGATION	TROATING	
BORATING	K TROAKING	S ORGANIST	V GRAVITON	
TABORING	L TRIGONAL	ROASTING	Y GYRATION	

AGINRST 164

TARINGS	GANTRIES	G GRATINGS	STARNING	STARTING
A GRANITAS	GRANITES	H TRASHING	O ORGANIST	V STARVING
B BRASTING	INGRATES	K KARTINGS	ROASTING	W RINGTAWS
C SCARTING	RANGIEST	STARKING	P PARTINGS	STRAWING
TRACINGS	REASTING	L RATLINGS	PRATINGS	WRASTING
D TRADINGS	STEARING	SLARTING	R STARRING	Y STINGRAY
E ANGRIEST	TASERING	STARLING	TARRINGS	STRAYING
ANGSTIER	F INGRAFTS	M MIGRANTS	S GASTRINS	
ASTRINGE	RAFTINGS	SMARTING	STARINGS	
GANISTER	STRAFING	N RANTINGS	T RATTINGS	

AILNOST 139

TALIONS	E ELATIONS	G ANTILOGS	L STALLION	R TONSILAR
A AILANTOS	INSOLATE	SALTOING	N ANTLIONS	Y LANOSITY
ALATIONS	TOENAILS	SOLATING	O SOLATION	

AILORST 150

TAILORS	C CALORIST	N TONSILAR	SLIOTARS	SOLITARY
B LABORIST	D DILATORS	O ISOLATOR	SOLARIST	
ORBITALS	E SOTERIAL	OSTIOLAR	U SUTORIAL	
STROBILA	M MORALIST	S ORALISTS	Y ROYALIST	

AINORST 30

RATIONS	INTRADOS	SENORITA	L TONSILAR	SUTORIAN
B TABORINS	E ANOESTRI	G ORGANIST	O ORATIONS	W WAITRONS
C CANTORIS	ARSONITE	ROASTING	P ATROPINS	X TRIAXONS
CAROTINS	NOTARIES	H TRAHISON	S ARSONIST	
CORTINAS	NOTARISE	J JANITORS	T STRONTIA	
D DIATRONS	ROSINATE	K SKIATRON	U RAINOUTS	

AIORSTU 219

SAUTOIR	SAUTOIRE	N RAINOUTS	T TOURISTA
D AUDITORS	F FAITOURS	SUTORIAN	V VIRTUOSA
E OUTRAISE	L SUTORIAL	S SAUTOIRS	

BEINOST 187

EBONIST	OBEISANT	I NIOBITES	EOBIONTS	T BOTTINES
A BOTANIES	B NOBBIEST	K STEINBOK	R BORNITES	U BOUNTIES
BOTANISE	E BETONIES	N BONNIEST	RIBSTONE	
NIOBATES	EBONITES	O BONITOES	S EBONISTS	

BEIORST 228

SORBITE	DEORBITS	TRILOBES	R ORBITERS
A SABOTIER	I ORBITIES	N BORNITES	S SORBITES
C BISECTOR	K REITBOKS	RIBSTONE	T BORTIEST
D DEBITORS	L STROBILE	O ROBOTISE	Y SOBRIETY

CEINORS 172

SERICON	CONIFERS	H CHORINES	N INCENSOR	NOTICERS
A SCENARIO	FORENSIC	I RECISION	P CONSPIRE	RECTIONS
B BICORNES	FORINSEC	SORICINE	INCORPSE	U COINSURE
C CONCISER	FORNICES	L INCLOSER	R RESORCIN	NOURICES
CORNICES	INFORCES	LICENSOR	S NECROSIS	ROUNCIES
CROCEINS	G COGNISER	M CREMOSIN	SERICONS	
D CONSIDER	COREIGNS	INCOMERS	T COINTERS	
F COINFERS	COSIGNER	SERMONIC	CORNIEST	

CEINORT 80

RECTION	NECROTIC	G GERONTIC	PRETONIC	T CONTRITE
A ACTIONER	D CENTROID	H NOTCHIER	R TRICORNE	CORNETTI
ANORETIC	DOCTRINE	J INJECTOR	S COINTERS	U NEUROTIC
CREATION	E ERECTION	M INTERCOM	CORNIEST	UNEROTIC
REACTION	NEOTERIC	P ENTROPIC	NOTICERS	V CONTRIVE
C CONCERTI	F INFECTOR	INCEPTOR	RECTIONS	

CEINOST 158

SECTION	E ICESTONE	M CENTIMOS	RECTIONS	X EXCITONS
A ACONITES	SEICENTO	O COONTIES	S SECTIONS	Y CYTOSINE
CANOEIST	G ESCOTING	P PONCIEST	T CENTOIST	
SONICATE	K CONKIEST	R COINTERS	STENOTIC	
C CONCEITS	L LECTIONS	CORNIEST	TONETICS	
D DEONTICS	TELSONIC	NOTICERS	U COUNTIES	

DEEILNR 198

RELINED	C DECLINER	G ENGIRDLE	RELINKED	
A RENAILED	RECLINED	LINGERED	R REDLINER	
B LINEBRED	D REDLINED	REEDLING	S REDLINES	
RENDIBLE	E NEEDLIER	K REKINDLE	U UNDERLIE	

DEEILNS 222

LINSEED	E SELENIDE	O ESLOINED	T ENLISTED	Y DYELINES
A DELAINES	G SEEDLING	LESIONED	LINTSEED	
C DECLINES	H ENSHIELD	R REDLINES	LISTENED	
LICENSED	I SIDELINE	S IDLENESS	TINSELED	
SILENCED	K SILKENED	LINSEEDS	V SNIVELED	

DEEINRS 65

RESINED	REDENIES	H DRISHEEN	P SPENDIER	U UREDINES
A ARSENIDE	F DEFINERS	RESHINED	S DIRENESS	V INVERSED
DENARIES	G DESIGNER	K DEERSKIN	T INSERTED	W REWIDENS
DRAISENE	ENERGIDS	L REDLINES	NERDIEST	WIDENERS
NEARSIDE	REDESIGN	N SINNERED	RESIDENT	X INDEXERS
B INBREEDS	REEDINGS	O INDORSEE	SINTERED	
E NEREIDES	RESIGNED	ORDINEES	TRENDIES	

DEEINST 42

STEINED	INFESTED	LINTSEED	DESINENT	TRENDIES
A ANDESITE	G INGESTED	LISTENED	O SIDENOTE	S DESTINES
B BENDIEST	SIGNETED	TINSELED	P PENTISED	T DINETTES
D DESTINED	STEEDING	M DEMENTIS	R INSERTED	INSETTED
NEDDIEST	H DISTHENE	SEDIMENT	NERDIEST	U DETINUES
E NEEDIEST	I DIETINES	TIDESMEN	RESIDENT	V EVIDENTS
F FENDIEST	L ENLISTED	N DENTINES	SINTERED	INVESTED

DEEIRST 37

RESITED	DISCRETE	L RELISTED	TRENDIES	SISTERED
A READIEST	D REDDIEST	M DEMERITS	O EROTISED	T TIREDEST
SERIATED	E REEDIEST	DEMISTER	P PREEDITS	U ERUDITES
SIDERATE	F RESIFTED	DIMETERS	PRIESTED	SURETIED
STEADIER	G DIGESTER	MISTERED	RESPITED	V VERDITES
B BESTRIDE	ESTRIDGE	N INSERTED	R DESTRIER	W WEIRDEST
BISTERED	REDIGEST	NERDIEST	S DIESTERS	
C DESERTIC	H DIETHERS	RESIDENT	EDITRESS	
DISCREET	I SIDERITE	SINTERED	RESISTED	

DEENORS 128

ENDORSE	ENCODERS	I INDORSEE	R ENDORSER	WORSENED
A REASONED	NECROSED	ORDINEES	S ENDORSES	
B DEBONERS	SECONDER	M MODERNES	T ERODENTS	
REDBONES	D ENDORSED	SERMONED	W ENDOWERS	
C CENSORED	E ENDORSEE	N ENDERONS	REENDOWS	

DEENORT 171

ERODENT	THRENODE	RONDELET	O ENROOTED
C CENTRODE	I ORIENTED	M ENTODERM	S ERODENTS
H DETHRONE	L REDOLENT	MENTORED	U DEUTERON

DEENRTU 241

TENURED	D RETUNDED	L UNDERLET	R RETURNED	UNDESERT
A DENATURE	E NEUTERED	N UNRENTED	S DENTURES	UNRESTED
UNDERATE	I RETINUED	UNTENDER	SEDERUNT	V VENTURED
UNDEREAT	REUNITED	O DEUTERON	UNDERSET	

DEEORST 148

TEREDOS	E STEREOED	K RESTOKED	REPOSTED	T ROSETTED
B BESORTED	F DEFOREST	M MODESTER	R RESORTED	TETRODES
BESTRODE	FORESTED	N ERODENTS	RESTORED	X DEXTROSE
C CORSETED	FOSTERED	P DOPESTER	ROSTERED	Y OYSTERED
ESCORTED	G GOSTERED	POSTERED	S DOSSERET	STOREYED
SECTORED	I EROTISED	REEDSTOP	OERSTEDS	

DEGINOR 234

REDOING	O RODEOING	S NEGROIDS	RINGDOVE
A ORGANDIE	P PROIGNED	U GUERIDON	W DOWERING
C RECODING	R ORDERING	V DOVERING	

DEIINOT 248

TENIOID	IODINATE	F NOTIFIED	R RETINOID	SEDITION
A IDEATION	TAENIOID	L TOLIDINE	S EDITIONS	Y IDONEITY

DEIINRT 236

NITRIDE	INDIRECT	G DIRIGENT	P INTREPID	NITRIDES
A DAINTIER	REINDICT	M DIRIMENT	S DISINTER	RINDIEST
C INDICTER	D NITRIDED	O RETINOID	INDITERS	U UNTIDIER

DEILNOS 102

SONDELI	LESIONED	O EIDOLONS	T LENTOIDS	
A NODALISE	G GLENOIDS	SOLENOID	U DELUSION	
C INCLOSED	SIDELONG	R DISENROL	INSOULED	
E ESLOINED	I LIONISED	S SONDELIS	UNSOILED	

DEILNOT 76

LENTOID	E DELETION	I TOLIDINE	P TOPLINED	U OUTLINED
A DELATION	ENTOILED	N INDOLENT	S LENTOIDS	

DEILORS 188

SOLIDER	SOREDIAL	L DOLLIERS	S SOLDIERS	Y SOLDIERY
A DARIOLES	C SCLEROID	N DISENROL	T STOLIDER	
SOLIDARE	I IDOLISER	P LEPORIDS	U SOULDIER	

DEILORT 173

DOILTER	TAILORED	E DOLERITE	L TROLLIED	Y ELYTROID
A IDOLATER	B TRILOBED	LOITERED	S STOLIDER	

DEINORS 20

SORDINE	ORDINEES	RESINOID	PRISONED	SOURDINE
A ANEROIDS	G NEGROIDS	J JOINDERS	R INDORSER	W DISOWNER
DONARIES	H HORDEINS	L DISENROL	S INDORSES	WINDORES
C CONSIDER	I DERISION	N ENDIRONS	SORDINES	WINDROSE
D INDORSED	IRONISED	P DISPONER	T DRONIEST	
E INDORSEE	IRONSIDE	POINDERS	U DOURINES	

DEINOST 58

STONIED	C DEONTICS	I EDITIONS	M DEMONIST	W DOWNIEST
A ASTONIED	E SIDENOTE	SEDITION	R DRONIEST	
SEDATION	H HEDONIST	L LENTOIDS	S DONSIEST	

DEINRST 71

TINDERS	STRAINED	NERDIEST	TRENDIES	INDITERS
A DETRAINS	D STRIDDEN	RESIDENT	G STRINGED	NITRIDES
RANDIEST	E INSERTED	SINTERED	I DISINTER	RINDIEST

L SNIRTLED	TRINDLES	P SPRINTED	TRIDENTS	NURDIEST
TENDRILS	O DRONIEST	T STRIDENT	U INTRUDES	X DEXTRINS

DEINRSU 216

INSURED	B BURNSIDE	I DISINURE	SOURDINE	NURDIEST
A DENARIUS	C INDUCERS	URIDINES	S INSUREDS	
UNRAISED	E UREDINES	N UNRINSED	SUNDRIES	
URANIDES	G GRUNDIES	O DOURINES	T INTRUDES	

DEINRTU 69

UNTRIED	B TURBINED	REUNITED	N INTURNED	W UNDERWIT
A DATURINE	UNDERBIT	I UNTIDIER	P TURNIPED	
INDURATE	C REINDUCT	L UNDERLIT	R INTRUDER	
RUINATED	D INTRUDED	M RUDIMENT	S INTRUDES	
URINATED	E RETINUED	UNMITRED	NURDIEST	

DEINSTU 193

DUNITES	F UNSIFTED	UNTIDIES	N DUNNIEST	S DISTUNES
A AUDIENTS	G DUNGIEST	L DILUENTS	DUNNITES	U UNSUITED
SINUATED	I DISUNITE	INSULTED	Q SQUINTED	
D DISTUNED	NUDITIES	UNLISTED	R INTRUDES	
E DETINUES	UNITISED	M MISTUNED	NURDIEST	

DEIORST 28

TRIODES	G DIGESTOR	M MORTISED	PORTSIDE	U IODURETS
A ASTEROID	GRODIEST	N DRONIEST	PROTEIDS	OUTRIDES
B DEBITORS	STODGIER	P DIOPTERS	RIPOSTED	OUTSIDER
DEORBITS	I DIORITES	DIOPTRES	TOPSIDER	SUITORED
C CORDITES	K DORKIEST	DIPTEROS	S STEROIDS	W ROWDIEST
E EROTISED	L STOLIDER	PERIDOTS	T DORTIEST	WORDIEST

DEIORTU 186

OUTRIDE	E ETOURDIE	R OUTRIDER	OUTSIDER	
B TUBEROID	F OUTFIRED	S IODURETS	SUITORED	
C OUTCRIED	H OUTHIRED	OUTRIDES	V OUTDRIVE	

DEIRSTU 227

STUDIER	E ERUDITES	M DIESTRUM	SUITORED	DRUSIEST
C CRUDITES	SURETIED	N INTRUDES	P DISPUTER	STUDIERS
CURDIEST	G DURGIEST	NURDIEST	STUPIDER	STURDIES
CURTSIED	L DILUTERS	O IODURETS	Q SQUIRTED	T DETRITUS
D RUDDIEST	LURIDEST	OUTRIDES	R STURDIER	X DRUXIEST
STURDIED	STUDLIER	OUTSIDER	S DIESTRUS	

DENORST 201

SNORTED	I DRONIEST	P PORTENDS	TONSURED	
A TORNADES	M MORDENTS	PROTENDS	UNSORTED	
E ERODENTS	N TENDRONS	U ROUNDEST	Y DRYSTONE	

EEGILNR 210

REELING	LINGERED	I LINGERIE	REELINGS	REVELING
A ALGERINE	REEDLING	O ELOIGNER	T GREENLIT	
C CREELING	F FLEERING	R LINGERER	U REGULINE	
D ENGIRDLE	G LEGERING	S LEERINGS	V LEVERING	

EEGINRS 97

GREISEN	REDESIGN	G GREESING	N ENGINERS	INTEGERS
A ANERGIES	REEDINGS	H GREENISH	INGENERS	REESTING
GESNERIA	RESIGNED	REHINGES	SERENING	STEERING
B BIGENERS	E ENERGIES	SHEERING	SNEERING	STREIGNE
BREINGES	ENERGISE	J JEERINGS	O ERINGOES	U SEIGNEUR
REBEGINS	GREENIES	K KREESING	P SPEERING	V SEVERING
C CREESING	RESEEING	SKEERING	SPREEING	VEERINGS
GENERICS	F FEERINGS	L LEERINGS	R RESIGNER	W RESEWING
D DESIGNER	FEIGNERS	REELINGS	S GREISENS	SEWERING
ENERGIDS	REEFINGS	M REGIMENS	T GENTRIES	SWEERING

EEGINRT 121

TREEING	G GREETING	REGIMENT	REESTING	W TWEERING
A GRATINEE	I REIGNITE	N ENTERING	STEERING	X EXERTING
INTERAGE	RETIEING	P PETERING	STREIGNE	GENETRIX
C ERECTING	L GREENLIT	S GENTRIES	U GENITURE	
GENTRICE	M METERING	INTEGERS	V EVERTING	

EEIINRT 123

NITERIE	C ICTERINE	RETIEING	NITERIES	V REINVITE
A INERTIAE	REINCITE	O ERIONITE	T INTERTIE	
B BENITIER	G REIGNITE	S ERINITES	RETINITE	

EEILNRS 199

RELINES	RECLINES	REELINGS	S REINLESS	SILENTER
A ALIENERS	SILENCER	M ERMELINS	T ENLISTER	V LIVENERS
B BERLINES	D REDLINES	O ELOINERS	LISTENER	SNIVELER
C LICENSER	G LEERINGS	P PILSENER	REENLIST	

EEILNST 75

TENSILE	LISTENED	STEELING	O NOSELITE	SILENTER
B STILBENE	TINSELED	H THEELINS	P PENLITES	S LITENESS
TENSIBLE	E ENLISTEE	I LENITIES	PLENTIES	SETLINES
C CENTILES	SELENITE	K NESTLIKE	R ENLISTER	T ENTITLES
D ENLISTED	G GENTILES	N LENIENTS	LISTENER	V VEINLETS
LINTSEED	SLEETING	SENTINEL	REENLIST	

EEILORS 151

LOERIES	F FORELIES	L ORSEILLE	T LITEROSE	RELIEVOS
B EROSIBLE	I OILERIES	N ELOINERS	TROELIES	VOLERIES
C CREOLISE	K ROSELIKE	P PELORIES	V OVERLIES	W OWLERIES

EEILORT 117

TROELIE	D DOLERITE	H HOTELIER	M MOTELIER	S LITEROSE
A AEROLITE	LOITERED	K LORIKEET	R LOITERER	TROELIES

EEILRST 67

STERILE	SCLERITE	F FERLIEST	REENLIST	REPTILES
A ATELIERS	TIERCELS	I TILERIES	SILENTER	SPIRELET
EARLIEST	TRISCELE	K TRISKELE	O LITEROSE	S LEISTERS
LATERISE	D RELISTED	L TREILLES	TROELIES	RITELESS
LEARIEST	E LEERIEST	M TERMLIES	P EPISTLER	TIRELESS
REALTIES	SLEETIER	N ENLISTER	PELTRIES	T RETITLES
C RETICLES	STEELIER	LISTENER	PERLITES	

EEINRST 11

TRIENES	NERDIEST	STREIGNE	SEROTINE	STERNITE
A ARENITES	RESIDENT	I ERINITES	R INSERTER	TRIENTES
ARSENITE	SINTERED	NITERIES	REINSERT	U ESURIENT
RESINATE	TRENDIES	K KERNITES	REINTERS	NEURITES
STEARINE	E ETERNISE	L ENLISTER	RENTIERS	RETINUES
TRAINEES	TEENSIER	LISTENER	TERRINES	REUNITES
C CENTRIES	F FERNIEST	REENLIST	S INTERESS	V NERVIEST
ENTERICS	INFESTER	SILENTER	SENTRIES	REINVEST
ENTICERS	G GENTRIES	M MISENTER	TRENISES	SERVIENT
SCIENTER	INTEGERS	N INTENSER	TRENISES	SIRVENTE
SECRETIN	REESTING	INTERNES	INSETTER	X INTERSEX
D INSERTED	STEERING	O ONERIEST	INTEREST	Y SERENITY

EEINRTT 152

TENTIER	E REINETTE	RETINITE	O TENORITE	STERNITE
B REBITTEN	TEENTIER	L NETTLIER	S INERTEST	TRIENTES
C RETICENT	H THIRTEEN	N INTERNET	INSETTER	Y ENTIRETY
D RETINTED	I INTERTIE	RENITENT	INTEREST	ETERNITY

EEINSTT 176

NETTIES	INSETTED	M MINETTES	R INERTEST	TENTIEST
A ANISETTE	E TEENIEST	N SENTIENT	INSETTER	W TENTWISE
TETANIES	F FEINTEST	O NOISETTE	INTEREST	TWENTIES
TETANISE	G GENTIEST	TEOSINTE	STERNITE	X EXISTENT
B BENTIEST	I ENTITIES	P INEPTEST	TRIENTES	
D DINETTES	L ENTITLES	SPINETTE	T NETTIEST	

EEIORST 53

EROTISE	D EROTISED	THEORISE	N ONERIEST	S EROTESIS
A ETAERIOS	G ERGOTISE	L LITEROSE	SEROTINE	EROTISES
C COTERIES	H ISOTHERE	TROELIES	P POETISER	Z EROTIZES
ESOTERIC	THEORIES	M TIRESOME	POETRIES	

EELORST 136

SOLERET		ELECTROS	I	LITEROSE	N	ENTRESOL	V OVERLETS
A OLEASTER		SELECTOR		TROELIES	S	SOLERETS	
C CORSELET	E	SLOETREE	L	SOLLERET	T	LORETTES	
ELECTORS	H	HOSTELER	M	MOLESTER	U	RESOLUTE	

EENORST 41

ESTRONE		RESOFTEN		SEROTINE		TENONERS	T ONSETTER
A EARSTONE		SOFTENER	L	ENTRESOL	O	OESTRONE	V OVERNETS
RESONATE	G	ESTROGEN	M	SERMONET		ROESTONE	X EXTENSOR
D ERODENTS	H	HONESTER		STOREMEN	P	PROTENSE	
F ENFOREST	I	ONERIEST	N	ENTERONS	S	ESTRONES	

EGINORS 55

SIGNORE	C	COGNISER	I	SEIGNIOR		REPOSING	T GENITORS
A IGNAROES		COREIGNS	L	RESOLING		SPONGIER	ROSETING
ORGANISE		COSIGNER	M	NEGROISM	R	IGNORERS	W RESOWING
ORIGANES	D	NEGROIDS	N	NEGRONIS	S	GORINESS	Y SEIGNORY
B SOBERING	E	ERINGOES	P	PERIGONS		SIGNORES	

EGINORT 165

GENITOR	N	NITROGEN		ROSETING	ROUTEING	X OXTERING
C GERONTIC		RINGTONE	T	OTTERING	V REVOTING	Z ROZETING
H THROEING	S	GENITORS	U	OUTREIGN	W TOWERING	

EGINRST 92

STINGER		STEARING	I GIRNIEST		TRINGLES	STINGERS
A ANGRIEST		TASERING	IGNITERS	N	RENTINGS	TRESSING
ANGSTIER	C	CRESTING	REISTING		STERNING	TRIGNESS
ASTRINGE	D	STRINGED	RESITING	O	GENITORS	T GITTERS
GANISTER	E	GENTRIES	STINGIER		ROSETING	V STERVING
GANTRIES		INTEGERS	STRIGINE	P	PRESTING	W STREWING
GRANITES		REESTING	L LINGSTER	R	RESTRING	WRESTING
INGRATES		STEERING	RINGLETS		RINGSTER	
RANGIEST		STREIGNE	STERLING		STRINGER	
REASTING	H	RIGHTENS	TINGLERS	S	RESTINGS	

EGIORST 233

GORIEST	E	ERGOTISE	N	GENITORS	U	GOUSTIER
D DIGESTOR	H	GHOSTIER		ROSETING	V	VERTIGOS
GRODIEST	M	ERGOTISM	S	GORSIEST	Y	OYSTRIGE
STODGIER		GORMIEST		STRIGOSE	Z	ZORGITES

EGNORST 239

TONGERS		RAGSTONE	I	GENITORS	S	SONGSTER
A ESTRAGON		STONERAG		ROSETING	T	TONGSTER
NEGATORS	E	ESTROGEN	N	RONTGENS	U	STURGEON
ORANGEST	G	GONGSTER	R	STRONGER	W	WRONGEST

EHIORST 225

TOSHIER	THEORIES	N HORNIEST	HORSIEST	U OUTHIRES
A HOARIEST	THEORISE	ORNITHES	HOSTRIES	SHOUTIER
C ROTCHIES	G GHOSTIER	P TROPHIES	SHORTIES	V OVERHITS
THEORICS	M ISOTHERM	R HERITORS	T THEORIST	W WORTHIES
E ISOTHERE	MOITHERS	S HOISTERS	THORITES	

EIILRST 179

SILTIER	D REDISTIL	L STILLIER	NITRILES	STILTIER
A LAIRIEST	E TILERIES	M LIMITERS	O ROILIEST	U UTILISER
LISTERIA	F FILISTER	MIRLIEST	P TRIPLIES	
B TRILBIES	G GIRLIEST	N NIRLIEST	T SLITTIER	

EIINORS 207

NOISIER	D DERISION	G SEIGNIOR	IRONISES	VISIONER
B BRIONIES	IRONISED	L LIONISER	SIRONISE	Z IONIZERS
C RECISION	IRONSIDE	P RIPIENOS	T IRONIEST	IRONIZES
SORICINE	RESINOID	S IONISERS	V REVISION	SIRONIZE

EILNORS 33

NEROLIS	C INCLOSER	G RESOLING	P PLERIONS	T RETINOLS
A AILERONS	LICENSOR	I LIONISER	PROLINES	
ALERIONS	D DISENROL	M MISENROL	R LORINERS	
ALIENORS	E ELOINERS	N ONLINERS	S IRONLESS	

EILNORT 36

RETINOL	TAILERON	TOPLINER	T TROTLINE	
A ORIENTAL	I TRIOLEIN	R RITORNEL	U OUTLINER	
RELATION	P TERPINOL	S RETINOLS	W TOWNLIER	

EILNOST 22

ONLIEST	D LENTOIDS	L STELLION	POTLINES	VIOLENTS
A ELATIONS	E NOSELITE	M MOLINETS	TOPLINES	W TOWLINES
INSOLATE	H HOLSTEIN	N INSOLENT	R RETINOLS	
TOENAILS	HOTLINES	O LOONIEST	U ELUTIONS	
C LECTIONS	NEOLITHS	OILSTONE	OUTLINES	
TELSONIC	I ETIOLINS	P POINTELS	V NOVELIST	

EILNRST 81

SNIRTLE	TRENAILS	SILENTER	NITRILES	S SLINTERS
A ENTRAILS	D SNIRTLED	G LINGSTER	K LINKSTER	SNIRTLES
LARNIEST	TENDRILS	RINGLETS	STRINKLE	U INSULTER
LATRINES	TRINDLES	STERLING	TINKLERS	LUSTRINE
RATLINES	E ENLISTER	TINGLERS	M MINSTREL	Y TINSELRY
REINSTAL	LISTENER	TRINGLES	O RETINOLS	
RETINALS	REENLIST	I NIRLIEST	P SPLINTER	

EILORST 23

TOILERS	COISTREL	TROELIES	TROLLIES	S ESTRIOLS
A SOTERIAL	COSTLIER	F FLORIEST	N RETINOLS	T TRIOLETS
B STROBILE	CREOLIST	TREFOILS	O OESTRIOL	U LOURIEST
TRILOBES	D STOLIDER	I ROILIEST	TROOLIES	OUTLIERS
C CLOISTER	E LITEROSE	L TRILLOES	P POITRELS	

EILRSTU 174

RUTILES	UTRICLES	H LUTHIERS	O LOURIEST	T SLUTTIER
A URALITES	D DILUTERS	I UTILISER	OUTLIERS	SURTITLE
B BURLIEST	LURIDEST	M MURLIEST	Q QUILTERS	V RIVULETS
SUBTILER	STUDLIER	N INSULTER	R SULTRIER	
C CURLIEST	G GURLIEST	LUSTRINE	S SURLIEST	

EIMORST 159

TRISOME	F SETIFORM	MOTORISE	MORTISES	W MISWROTE
A AMORTISE	G ERGOTISM	ROOMIEST	TRISOMES	WORMIEST
ATOMISER	GORMIEST	P IMPOSTER	T OMITTERS	Y ISOMETRY
C MORTICES	H ISOTHERM	R MORTISER	U MISROUTE	
D MORTISED	MOITHERS	STORMIER	MOISTURE	
E TIRESOME	O MOORIEST	S EROTISMS	V VOMITERS	

EINNORT 138

TERNION	D INDENTOR	N NONINERT	T TONTINER	
A ANOINTER	G NITROGEN	S INTONERS	U NEUTRINO	
INORNATE	RINGTONE	NOINTERS	V INVENTOR	
REANOINT	H INTHRONE	TERNIONS	NOVERINT	

EINOPRS 163

PROINES	PEREIONS	L PLERIONS	R PRISONER	REPOINTS
C CONSPIRE	PIONEERS	PROLINES	S PORINESS	TROPINES
INCORPSE	F FORPINES	M PROMINES	PRESSION	U PRUINOSE
D DISPONER	G PERIGONS	O POISONER	ROPINESS	V OVERSPIN
POINDERS	REPOSING	SNOOPIER	T POINTERS	PROVINES
PRISONED	SPONGIER	SPOONIER	PORNIEST	
E ISOPRENE	I RIPIENOS	P POPERINS	PROTEINS	

EINOPRT 204

TROPINE	PRETONIC	POITRINE	S POINTERS	TROPINES
A ATROPINE	D DIPTERON	L TERPINOL	PORNIEST	U ERUPTION
C ENTROPIC	H TRIPHONE	TOPLINER	PROTEINS	
INCEPTOR	I POINTIER	M ORPIMENT	REPOINTS	

EINORSS 202

SONSIER	SORDINES	IRONISES	P PORINESS	TERSIONS
A ERASIONS	E ESSOINER	SIRONISE	PRESSION	U NEUROSIS
SENSORIA	G GORINESS	L IRONLESS	ROPINESS	RESINOUS
C NECROSIS	SIGNORES	M MERSIONS	R ROSINERS	V VERSIONS
SERICONS	H HERISSON	N IRONNESS	S ROSINESS	
D INDORSES	I IONISERS	O EROSIONS	T OESTRINS	

EINORST 3

TRIONES	CORNIEST	I IRONIEST	PROTEINS	U NITREOUS
A ANOESTRI	NOTICERS	J JOINTERS	REPOINTS	ROUTINES
ARSONITE	RECTIONS	K INSTROKE	TROPINES	SNOUTIER
NOTARIES	D DRONIEST	L RETINOLS	R INTRORSE	V INVESTOR
NOTARISE	E ONERIEST	N INTONERS	SNORTIER	Y SEROTINY
ROSINATE	SEROTINE	NOINTERS	S OESTRINS	TYROSINE
SENORITA	G GENITORS	TERNIONS	TERSIONS	Z TRIZONES
B BORNITES	ROSETING	O SNOOTIER	T SNOTTIER	
RIBSTONE	H HORNIEST	P POINTERS	TENORIST	
C COINTERS	ORNITHES	PORNIEST	TRITONES	

EINORSU 230

URINOSE	D DOURINES	MONSIEUR	RESINOUS	V SOUVENIR
C COINSURE	SOURDINE	N REUNIONS	T NITREOUS	
NOURICES	F REFUSION	P PRUINOSE	ROUTINES	
ROUNCIES	M INERMOUS	S NEUROSIS	SNOUTIER	

EINORTT 70

TRITONE	CORNETTI	G OTTERING	N TONTINER	TRITONES
A TENTORIA	D INTORTED	K KNOTTIER	S SNOTTIER	U RITENUTO
C CONTRITE	E TENORITE	L TROTLINE	TENORIST	

EINORTU 103

ROUTINE	G OUTREIGN	L OUTLINER	S NITREOUS	T RITENUTO
C NEUROTIC	ROUTEING	N NEUTRINO	ROUTINES	
UNEROTIC	J JOINTURE	P ERUPTION	SNOUTIER	

EINOSTT 249

TONITES	E NOISETTE	N TINSTONE	TRITONES	TOWNIEST
B BOTTINES	TEOSINTE	TONTINES	S SNOTTIES	
C CENTOIST	F FISTNOTE	P NEPOTIST	STONIEST	
STENOTIC	G TENTIGOS	R SNOTTIER	T TOTIENTS	
TONETICS	J JETTISON	TENORIST	W NOWTIEST	

EINRSTT 237

TINTERS	B BITTERNS	INSETTER	STINTIER	S ENTRISTS
A INTREATS	C CENTRIST	INTEREST	K KNITTERS	STINTERS
NITRATES	CITTERNS	STERNITE	TRINKETS	U RUNTIEST
STRAITEN	D STRIDENT	TRIENTES	O SNOTTIER	W TWINTERS
TARTINES	TRIDENTS	G GITTERNS	TENORIST	Y ENTRYIST
TERTIANS	E INERTEST	I NITRITES	TRITONES	

EINRSTU 56

UNITERS	B TRIBUNES	E ESURIENT	UNITISER	UNMITERS
A RUINATES	TURBINES	NEURITES	L INSULTER	UNMITRES
TAURINES	C CURNIEST	RETINUES	LUSTRINE	N RUNNIEST
URANITES	D INTRUDES	REUNITES	M MUNTRIES	STURNINE
URINATES	NURDIEST	I NEURITIS	TERMINUS	O NITREOUS

ROUTINES	P REPUNITS	UNRIPEST	T RUNTIEST	VENTURIS
SNOUTIER	UNPRIEST	Q SQUINTER	V UNRIVETS	W UNWRITES

EIOPRST 192

ROPIEST	TOPSIDER	M IMPOSTER	SPORTIER	RISPETTO
C PERSICOT	E POETISER	N POINTERS	S PERIOSTS	SPOTTIER
D DIOPTERS	POETRIES	PORNIEST	PROSIEST	U ROUPIEST
DIOPTRES	F FIREPOTS	PROTEINS	PROSTIES	SPOUTIER
DIPTEROS	PIEFORTS	REPOINTS	REPOSITS	V OVERTIPS
PERIDOTS	POSTFIRE	TROPINES	RIPOSTES	PIVOTERS
PORTSIDE	H TROPHIES	O PORTOISE	SPORTIES	SORPTIVE
PROTEIDS	K PORKIEST	ROOPIEST	TRIPOSES	SPORTIVE
RIPOSTED	L POITRELS	R PIERROTS	T PORTIEST	

EIORRST 122

RORIEST	ROTIFERS	N INTRORSE	R ERRORIST	T RORTIEST
A ROARIEST	H HERITORS	SNORTIER	TERROIRS	U STOURIER
ROTARIES	I RIOTRIES	O ROOTSIER	S RESISTOR	V OVERSTIR
B ORBITERS	M MORTISER	P PIERROTS	ROISTERS	SERVITOR
F FROSTIER	STORMIER	SPORTIER	SORRIEST	

EIORSTT 133

STOITER	H THEORIST	TENORIST	RISPETTO	TUTORISE
A TOASTIER	THORITES	TRITONES	SPOTTIER	V VIRETOTS
B BORTIEST	L TRIOLETS	O ROOTIEST	R RORTIEST	W SWOTTIER
C COTTIERS	M OMITTERS	TORTOISE	S STOITERS	
D DORTIEST	N SNOTTIER	P PORTIEST	U TOUSTIER	

EIORSTU 59

TOUSIER	OUTRIDES	H OUTHIRES	N NITREOUS	R STOURIER
A OUTRAISE	OUTSIDER	SHOUTIER	ROUTINES	T TOUSTIER
SAUTOIRE	SUITORED	L LOURIEST	SNOUTIER	TUTORISE
C CITREOUS	F FOUSTIER	OUTLIERS	P ROUPIEST	V VIRTUOSE
OUTCRIES	OUTFIRES	M MISROUTE	SPOUTIER	VITREOUS
D IODURETS	G GOUSTIER	MOISTURE	Q QUOITERS	VOITURES

ENORSTU 85

TONSURE	COUNTERS	F FORTUNES	L TURNSOLE	S TONSURES
A OUTEARNS	RECOUNTS	G STURGEON	M MONTURES	T STENTOUR
B BURSTONE	TROUNCES	H SOUTHERN	MOUNTERS	V VENTROUS
RUBSTONE	D ROUNDEST	I NITREOUS	REMOUNTS	Y TOURNEYS
C CONSTRUE	TONSURED	ROUTINES	N NEUTRONS	
CORNUTES	UNSORTED	SNOUTIER	O OUTSNORE	

AEIOU bonus words

These two short lists contain the very few seven and eight-letter words to contain one each of all five vowels. It's worth learning these words for occasions when you find yourself with an exceptionally vowel-heavy rack. Definitions are provided for these words as an aide-memoire.

Seven-letter words

DOULEIA	veneration accorded to saints in Roman Catholic and Eastern Churches
EULOGIA	blessed bread distributed to members of the congregation after the liturgy, esp to those who have not communed
MIAOUED	made a crying sound characteristic of a cat
MOINEAU	small fortification
SEQUOIA	giant Californian coniferous tree

Eight-letter words

AEQUORIN	type of protein
AEROBIUM	organism that requires oxygen to survive
AGOUTIES	agile long-legged rodents of South and Central America
CAESIOUS	having a waxy bluish-grey coating
DIALOGUE	conversation between two people, esp in a book, film, or play
DOUANIER	customs officer
DOULEIAS	plural of douleia: veneration accorded to saints in Roman Catholic and Eastern Churches
EDACIOUS	devoted to eating
EQUATION	mathematical statement that two expressions are equal
EUDAIMON	benevolent demon or spirit
EULOGIAS	plural of eulogia: blessed bread distributed to members of the congregation after the liturgy, esp to those who have not communed
EUPHOBIA	fear of good news
EUPHONIA	pleasing sound
EUPHORIA	sense of elation
EUSOCIAL	using division of labour
EXONUMIA	objects of interest to numismatists that are not coins, such as medals and tokens
JALOUSIE	window blind or shutter constructed from angled slats of wood, plastic, etc
MOINEAUS	plural of moineau: small fortification
ODALIQUE	female slave in a harem
OUTRAISE	raise more money than
POULAINE	tapering toe of shoe
SAUTOIRE	necklace
SEQUOIAS	plural of sequoia: giant Californian coniferous tree
THIOUREA	white water-soluble crystalline substance with a bitter taste

Non-words

In addition to remembering some of the bonus-word sets listed in this chapter, it's a good idea to remember that sometimes you will draw a rack which cannot form a seven-letter bonus word. If you can recognize such combinations early on, it will save you valuable time, and allow you to look for other options. The following lists contain six- and seven-letter stems that are words in themselves, but which cannot form any valid word with the addition of another letter. If you can form one of the six-letter words with the letters on your rack, you can tell straight away that there is no valid seven-letter word to be formed from it; if you can form one of the seven-letter words, you know to look for opportunities to play it by tagging or hooking, as there is no other way to get a 50-point bonus with that combination.

Six-letter words that do not combine with another letter

AALIIS	AVOUCH	BEKISS	BLUIDS	BRUMBY
ABAMPS	AVOWRY	BEMBEX	BLUNKS	BRUXED
ABLAZE	AVYZED	BEMBIX	BLURRY	BRUXES
ABUNAS	AVYZES	BEMIXT	BLYPES	BRYONY
ACKNEW	AWATCH	BENCHY	BOAKED	BUAZES
ACRAWL	AWEIGH	BEWEPT	BOBAKS	BUBBAS
ADAPTS	AWHATO	BEWIGS	BOBBLY	BUBBLY
ADIEUX	AWHIRL	BEZAZZ	BODGED	BUBOED
ADIPIC	AWRACK	BIBBED	BODILY	BUBOES
ADMIXT	AXEMAN	BIFFED	BOFFED	BUCHUS
ADOBOS	AXIOMS	BIFOLD	BOFFOS	BUGGED
ADYTUM	AZERTY	BIGAMY	BOLDLY	BUILDS
AERIFY	AZOTIC	BIGGED	BOLLEN	BUMBOS
AFFLUX	BABBLY	BIGOTS	BOLLOX	BUMPHS
AFLAME	BABKAS	BIJOUX	BOLSHY	BUNCHY
AFLOAT	BACCAS	BIMBLE	BOMBAX	BUOYED
AGAZED	BADASS	BINMAN	BOMBYX	BUPKES
AHCHOO	BADGED	BINMEN	BOOHED	BUPKUS
AIKONA	BAIZED	BIOPSY	BOOKSY	BURBLY
AIMFUL	BAJRAS	BIPODS	BOOZED	BURPED
AJIVAS	BANJAX	BITCHY	BOOZEY	BUSSUS
AKATEA	BASANS	BITTED	BOPPED	BUTUTS
AKIMBO	BASIFY	BIVIUM	BOUNCY	BUZZED
ALKOXY	BASSOS	BIZAZZ	BOVIDS	BWAZIS
ALLYLS	BAULKS	BIZZOS	BOWMAN	BYKING
ALLYOU	BAULKY	BLABBY	BOXILY	BYLIVE
ALULAE	BAVINS	BLACKS	BOYAUX	BYPASS
AMAZED	BAWDRY	BLANCH	BRAGLY	BYSSUS
AMAZES	BAYOUS	BLANKS	BRANDY	BYWAYS
AMBARY	BAZAZZ	BLAZED	BRANKY	CABMAN
ANBURY	BEACHY	BLEBBY	BRANNY	CABMEN
ANYHOW	BEAUTY	BLENCH	BRASSY	CADGED
APPAID	BEBOPS	BLENNY	BRAVAS	CADMIC
APPAYD	BEDDED	BLIMPS	BRAWNS	CALEFY
ARGUFY	BEDEWS	BLOBBY	BRAWNY	CANNAE
ARILLI	BEDYDE	BLOCKS	BRAZED	CARFAX
ARIOSI	BEDYED	BLOCKY	BREEZY	CARFOX
ARRIBA	BEDYES	BLOKEY	BREKKY	CASEFY
ASQUAT	BEECHY	BLOODY	BRICHT	CAUDAD
ASTOOP	BEEVES	BLOOMY	BRICKY	CEAZED
ASWARM	BEFELL	BLOOPS	BRINNY	CECITY
ATWIXT	BEFOGS	BLOTTO	BRISKS	CERVIX
AUDIAL	BEGEMS	BLOTTY	BROLLY	CHAFFY
AUGURY	BEGETS	BLOWZY	BRONZY	CHALKY
AVIARY	BEGGED	BLUELY	BROODY	CHALLY
AVIZED	BEGUMS	BLUFFS	BROTHY	CHAMMY
AVIZES	BEHALF	BLUGGY	BROWNS	CHAMPS

CHAMPY	COHOGS	DEFOGS	DYSURY	FENMAN
CHAPPY	COLBYS	DEKKOS	EARWAX	FENMEN
CHECKY	COLDLY	DEPUTY	EBBETS	FEOFFS
CHEEKY	COLONY	DESCRY	ECHOEY	FERVID
CHEMMY	COMEDY	DESOXY	EFFETE	FESSES
CHEVAL	COMELY	DHOOLY	EFFIGY	FEVERS
CHICLY	COMMAS	DICKED	EFFLUX	FEYEST
CHIMBS	COMPLY	DICKTY	EGGERY	FEZZED
CHIMPS	CONCHY	DIGAMY	EGOITY	FEZZES
CHINKS	CONFIX	DIGGED	EIKING	FIBBED
CHINKY	CONVEX	DIMPSY	EMBODY	FICINS
CHIPPY	COOCOO	DIPLEX	EMBUSY	FICKLY
CHIVVY	COOEES	DIPODY	EMCEED	FIKERY
CHOCCY	COOLLY	DITTIT	EMCEES	FIKIER
CHOMPS	COOZES	DJINNI	EMMEWS	FIKISH
CHOOFS	CORVUS	DJINNS	ENJOYS	FILIAL
CHOPPY	COSILY	DJINNY	ENTREZ	FILMIC
CHOTTS	COUTHY	DOBBED	EOCENE	FINKED
CHOWRY	COVARY	DODDED	ERUCIC	FIQUES
CHUBBY	COWMAN	DODGED	ETYMIC	FIRMLY
CHUCKY	COWPOX	DOFFED	EULOGY	FISTIC
CHUDDY	COZENS	DOGFOX	EURIPI	FITCHY
CHUFFY	COZILY	DOGGED	EUTAXY	FIXITY
CHUMMY	COZZES	DOHYOS	EVENLY	FIXIVE
CHUNKY	CRAZED	DOITIT	EVILLY	FJELDS
CITIFY	CROUPY	DOOCED	EXEQUY	FJORDS
CITYFY	CROWDY	DOOFUS	EXEUNT	FLABBY
CIVICS	CROWNS	DOUBLY	EXILED	FLAFFS
CLACHS	CRUCKS	DOZILY	EXILIC	FLAGGY
CLAGGY	CRUDDY	DRABBY	EXODIC	FLAKEY
CLAMMY	CRUTCH	DRAFFY	EXODOI	FLAMMS
CLAYEY	CRWTHS	DRAFTY	EXPATS	FLAPPY
CLECKY	CUDDLY	DRAPPY	EXTASY	FLASKS
CLEFTS	CUMECS	DRIFTY	EXTOLD	FLAWNS
CLERGY	CUMULI	DRILLS	EXUDED	FLAXEN
CLICKS	CUPMEN	DRIPPY	EXURBS	FLAXES
CLIFFY	CUPPED	DROOKS	FACEUP	FLEDGY
CLIFTS	CUPRIC	DROOLY	FADGED	FLEECY
CLIFTY	CURACY	DROSSY	FAKERY	FLENCH
CLINCH	CURSUS	DROUKS	FAMISH	FLEWED
CLODDY	CURVEY	DRUGGY	FAMULI	FLEXED
CLODLY	CUVEES	DRUMLY	FANALS	FLEXES
CLOGGY	CYCADS	DRUMMY	FASCES	FLIMPS
CLONAL	CYCLED	DUBBOS	FAULDS	FLIMSY
CLOTTY	CYCLUS	DUCKED	FAUNAE	FLINCH
CLOVEN	CYDERS	DUFFED	FAUNAS	FLISKY
CLOVIS	CYMOID	DUMBED	FAVEST	FLITCH
CLOZES	CYMOLS	DUMBLY	FAVOSE	FLOCCI
CLUBBY	DACKED	DUMBOS	FAWNED	FLOCKS
CLUCKS	DADGUM	DUNKED	FAXING	FLOCKY
CLUCKY	DAFFED	DUOMOS	FAYEST	FLOODS
CLUNCH	DAFTLY	DUPLEX	FAYNES	FLOOZY
CLYPEI	DARCYS	DUPPED	FEALTY	FLOPPY
COAXED	DARKLY	DURZIS	FEASES	FLOURY
COBZAS	DAWNED	DUSKED	FEATLY	FLUFFS
COCCAL	DAWBRY	DUVETS	FEAZED	FLUFFY
COCCIC	DEBYES	DWAUMS	FEAZES	FLUMPS
COCCYX	DEEDED	DWEEBS	FEEZED	FLUTEY
CODIFY	DEFFLY	DWEEBY	FEHMIC	FLUXED
COGGLY	DEFLEX	DYKIER	FEMMES	FLUXES

FLYMAN	FUNDIC	GOURDY	HEXERS	JACKED
FLYMEN	FUNNED	GOWFED	HEXYLS	JADERY
FLYPED	FURPHY	GRABBY	HIGHLY	JADING
FLYPES	FURZES	GRAFTS	HIKOIS	JAGAED
FLYSCH	FUTONS	GREEDY	HOBOED	JAGGED
FOBBED	FUTZED	GREXES	HOHING	JAILED
FOEHNS	FUZILS	GREYED	HOKILY	JAKEYS
FOGASH	FYNBOS	GRIMED	HOKUMS	JALAPS
FOGEYS	GADFLY	GRIPPY	HOLONS	JALOPS
FOGIES	GADJES	GRITTY	HOMILY	JAMBED
FOLEYS	GALAXY	GROGGY	HOMINY	JAMMED
FOLKSY	GAMMED	GROOVY	HONKED	JANGLY
FONDLY	GANGLY	GROSZE	HOODED	JAPPED
FONNED	GAPPED	GROSZY	HOOROO	JARTAS
FOOTSY	GASIFY	GROTTY	HOOTCH	JASPIS
FORGOT	GAUJES	GROUPY	HOOVED	JASSES
FORNIX	GAUPUS	GRUBBY	HOOVEN	JAUKED
FORTHY	GAVOTS	GRUFFS	HORARY	JAUNTY
FORWHY	GAWKED	GRUNGY	HORRID	JAUPED
FORZAS	GAWPED	GRYCES	HOSEYS	JAVELS
FOUNTS	GAWPUS	GRYDES	HOTBOX	JAWBOX
FOUSTY	GAYETY	GRYKES	HOUSEY	JAXIES
FOVEAS	GAZARS	GUIDED	HOVEAS	JAZZED
FOWTHS	GEMMED	GULAGS	HOWKED	JEANED
FOXILY	GEMMEN	GULFED	HOWZAT	JEEPED
FOYLES	GHARRY	GUMBOS	HOWZIT	JEFFED
FOYNED	GHOSTS	GUMMED	HUBBLY	JEJUNE
FOYNES	GHYLLS	GUNMAN	HUDDUP	JERKED
FOZIER	GIGGLY	GUNMEN	HUDUDS	JESSED
FRANCO	GIZMOS	GUNNEN	HUGEST	JEWELS
FRANKS	GLADLY	GYBING	HULKED	JEWIES
FRANZY	GLAURY	GYELDS	HUMBLY	JEWING
FREAKY	GLAZEN	GYLDEN	HUMEFY	JHALAS
FRENCH	GLEGLY	GYMPED	HUMFED	JIBBED
FRENZY	GLIFFS	GYPPED	HUMIFY	JIGGLY
FRETTY	GLISKS	GYPPOS	HUMPHS	JIGOTS
FRIARS	GLITZY	GYVING	HUMUSY	JILTED
FRIGID	GLOBAL	HACKLY	HYLEGS	JINGLY
FRISKY	GLOBBY	HAIKAI	HYMNED	JINKED
FROCKS	GLOPPY	HAINCH	HYOIDS	JINNIS
FROGGY	GLOVED	HAJJES	HYPHAE	JINXED
FRONDS	GLOZED	HAJJIS	HYPHAL	JINXES
FROTHY	GLOZES	HALFEN	HYPOED	JIVIER
FROUZY	GLUILY	HALLUX	HYPPED	JIVING
FROWNS	GLUMLY	HALVED	IBISES	JIZZES
FROWZY	GLUMPS	HANDAX	ICEBOX	JOBBED
FRUMPS	GLUMPY	HAOMAS	IMBODY	JOCKOS
FRUSTS	GLUNCH	HATBOX	IMBREX	JOHNNY
FRYERS	GLYPHS	HAUNCH	IMIDIC	JOISTS
FUCKED	GNATTY	HAVOCS	INBENT	JOKERS
FUDGED	GODDED	HAYBOX	INCONY	JOKIER
FUDGES	GOFFED	HAZERS	INCUBI	JOOKED
FUGIOS	GOGGAS	HAZIER	INFIMA	JORUMS
FUGLED	GOGGLY	HEDGED	INKJET	JOSHED
FUGUED	GOMPAS	HEEDED	IODOUS	JOTTED
FUGUES	GONOFS	HEMMED	IRIDIC	JOUKED
FULGID	GOODLY	HENGES	IRITIC	JOULED
FULVID	GOOFED	HENNAS	IXORAS	JOUSTS
FUMOUS	GOPAKS	HEPPER	IZZATS	JOVIAL
FUMULI	GOSHTS	HERYED	JABOTS	JOWLED

JOYFUL	KLOOFS	LIKUTA	MIGHTY	NUDITY
JOYING	KLUTZY	LIMNIC	MIHIED	NULLED
JOYOUS	KNACKS	LIMULI	MIKVOS	NUMBLY
JUBATE	KNACKY	LIVELY	MILDLY	NUMPTY
JUGALS	KNAGGY	LOLLED	MILIUM	NUTANT
JUGUMS	KNARRY	LONGLY	MILKED	NYAFFS
JUICED	KNAVES	LOOKED	MIMMER	NYLONS
JULEPS	KNELLS	LOOVES	MINIFY	NYSSAS
JUMBLY	KNICKS	LOUCHE	MIRCHI	OBTECT
JUMPED	KNIFED	LOUDLY	MIRVED	ODDITY
JUNCUS	KNOCKS	LOXING	MIXIER	ODIOUS
JUNGLY	KNOLLS	LUBRIC	MIXING	OFFKEY
JUNKED	KNOLLY	LUFFAS	MIXUPS	OIDIUM
JUPONS	KNOSPS	LULLED	MNEMIC	OILILY
JURELS	KNOTTY	LUXURY	MOATED	OJIMES
JURORS	KNOWNS	LYFULL	MODEMS	OKAYED
JUSTLY	KNURLY	MACAWS	MODIFY	OMNIFY
JYNXES	KNURRS	MADDED	MOJOES	ORIHOU
KABABS	KOALAS	MADEFY	MOKIHI	ORIXAS
KABOBS	KOFTAS	MAFTED	MONACT	ORRERY
KAMAHI	KOKERS	MAGICS	MONOAO	ORYXES
KAMEEZ	KOKIRI	MAGNOX	MOSHAV	OSSIFY
KAMIKS	KOKOPU	MAHWAS	MOTORY	OTALGY
KANJIS	KOKRAS	MAJLIS	MOULDY	OUBAAS
KANUKA	KONAKI	MAKUTA	MOULTS	OUIJAS
KANZUS	KOOKED	MALVAS	MOUPED	OUTBOX
KAONIC	KOPJES	MAMAKO	MOUTHY	OUTFOX
KAPPAS	KOPPAS	MAMBAS	MOYITY	OVOIDS
KAPUKA	KORARI	MANQUE	MUCKED	OVOLOS
KAPUTT	KOTUKU	MAOMAO	MUMBLY	OWELTY
KARKED	KOUROI	MAPPED	MUMPED	OXEYES
KAVASS	KRAFTS	MASTIX	MURVAS	OYEZES
KAYAKS	KRANTZ	MATRIX	MUSKED	OZEKIS
KAYOED	KRONOR	MAUNDY	MUSKOX	OZONIC
KAYOES	KRONUR	MAUNGY	MUTINY	PACKED
KAZOOS	KRUBIS	MAUVER	MUXING	PACKLY
KEBABS	KUDZUS	MAVENS	MUZAKY	PAIKED
KEBBED	KUKRIS	MAWGER	MYSELF	PALLID
KECKSY	KULAKI	MAXING	MYXOID	PAMPAS
KEDGED	KULAKS	MAYFLY	NABBED	PANTRY
KEEKED	KUVASZ	MAYHAP	NAFFLY	PAPACY
KEEVES	KVELLS	MAZIER	NAZIFY	PARODY
KEGGED	KYANGS	MAZILY	NAZIRS	PATAKA
KEIGHT	KYBOSH	MECCAS	NEBULY	PATCHY
KEMPED	KYLOES	MEDFLY	NEMNED	PATIKI
KEPPEN	KYNDED	MEEKER	NEXTLY	PAXWAX
KEWLER	KYTHED	MEEKLY	NIMBLY	PEAZED
KHAPHS	LAPJES	MEETLY	NIMMED	PEBBLY
KHAZIS	LARNAX	MEJLIS	NINETY	PEEKED
KHETHS	LARVAS	MEKKAS	NIQABS	PEEPED
KHOUMS	LARYNX	MENINX	NOBBUT	PEGBOX
KIBBIS	LASSUS	MERELY	NOGAKU	PEGGED
KICKED	LAVRAS	MERMEN	NONMAN	PEGHED
KIKOIS	LAWMAN	MEWSES	NONMEN	PEIZED
KINGLY	LAWMEN	MEZZES	NONTAX	PEIZES
KIOSKS	LAXITY	MHORRS	NONYLS	PELVES
KIPPAS	LAZARS	MIAOUS	NOUNAL	PENURY
KISSED	LEETLE	MIAOWS	NOVITY	PEROXY
KITTLY	LEGACY	MIDCAP	NOVUMS	PEYSES
KLICKS	LEKKER	MIEVES	NOWAYS	PIAZZE

PIBALS	PUJAHS	RHEXIS	SHOGIS	SMUDGY
PIDDLY	PULLED	RHIZIC	SHOJIS	SMUGLY
PIKAUS	PULPAL	RHYMED	SHOPPY	SMUTTY
PIMPLY	PUNCTA	RIPPLY	SHOYUS	SNACKS
PINKLY	PUNJIS	RIVERY	SHTUMM	SNAPPY
PINXIT	PURIFY	ROJAKS	SHUFTY	SNAZZY
PINYIN	PURITY	ROOTSY	SHUGGY	SNELLY
PIOPIO	PURPLY	ROZITS	SHYISH	SNIFFS
PIVOTS	PUSHED	RUBATI	SILVEX	SNIFTY
PIXIES	PUTSCH	RUBBLY	SIXMOS	SNIPPY
PLAGAL	PUTZED	RUCKUS	SIXTHS	SNOBBY
PLANKS	PUTZES	RUSCUS	SKALDS	SNOOZY
PLAZAS	PYXING	RYMMED	SKANKS	SNOTTY
PLEBBY	QANATS	SADDOS	SKANKY	SNOUTY
PLEXAL	QIBLAS	SADZAS	SKEGGS	SNOWKS
PLONKY	QORMAS	SAFETY	SKELFS	SNUBBY
PLOOKY	QUACKS	SAJOUS	SKELLS	SNUFFS
PLOTTY	QUACKY	SAKKOI	SKEWED	SODOMY
PLOUKY	QUAFFS	SAKKOS	SKIDDY	SOKOLS
PLUCKY	QUAGGY	SAMFUS	SKILLS	SOWFFS
PLUFFS	QUALMS	SANIFY	SKIMPY	SOZZLY
PLUMMY	QUALMY	SANKOS	SKINKS	SPADIX
PLUNKY	QUARRY	SAVOYS	SKINNY	SPAMMY
PLURRY	QUATCH	SAXONY	SKIPPY	SPASMS
POCKED	QUAZZY	SAYONS	SKIRLS	SPAWNY
POGGES	QUBITS	SCABBY	SKIVVY	SPECCY
POKALS	QUEAZY	SCARFS	SKOFFS	SPECKS
POKEYS	QUELLS	SCAUDS	SKOLLY	SPEWED
POLITY	QUEMED	SCHAVS	SKOOLS	SPHINX
POLJES	QUEMES	SCHUSS	SKULKS	SPHYNX
POLKAS	QUEUED	SCLIMS	SKULLS	SPIFFY
POLLEX	QUEYNS	SCOFFS	SKUNKS	SPIVVY
POMBES	QUICKS	SCOLDS	SKUNKY	SPOKES
PONZUS	QUILTS	SCOOGS	SKURRY	SPOOFS
POOKIT	QUIPOS	SCOUGS	SKYBOX	SPOOFY
POORLY	QUIPPY	SCOUPS	SKYFED	SPOOKS
POOVES	QUIRKS	SCOWPS	SKYISH	SPOOKY
POPPLY	QUIRKY	SCRAGS	SKYLIT	SPOTTY
POTOOS	QUOIFS	SCREWY	SKYMAN	SPRITZ
POUCHY	QUOLLS	SCROGS	SLABBY	SPRODS
POUFFY	QUONKS	SCRUBS	SLAGGY	SPROGS
POUKED	QUOOKE	SCRYDE	SLEAZY	SPRYLY
POUKIT	QUOTHA	SCUNGY	SLEEZY	SPUDDY
POWNDS	QURUSH	SCURVY	SLOJDS	SPUGGY
POXING	QUYTED	SCUZZY	SLOSHY	SPUNKS
PRANKY	RAGULY	SESSES	SLOYDS	SPUTUM
PRAXIS	RAKERY	SEXFID	SLUBBS	SQUADS
PREFIX	RAMIFY	SEXILY	SLUDGY	SQUATS
PREMIX	RARELY	SHAGGY	SLUFFS	SQUEGS
PRIMPS	RAWARU	SHANNY	SLURBS	SQUIDS
PRIZED	RAXING	SHAWLS	SLURRY	SQUUSH
PROLIX	RAZEED	SHAWMS	SLUSHY	STAGGY
PRONKS	RAZOOS	SHEEPY	SMACKS	STEDDY
PRUTAH	RAZORS	SHEESH	SMARMS	STEMMY
PSYOPS	REARLY	SHELLS	SMELLS	STINKS
PTYXES	REMEDY	SHELVY	SMIRKY	STOCKY
PTYXIS	RENKER	SHIFTY	SMIRRS	STODGY
PUBBED	RHEUMY	SHISOS	SMIRRY	STONKS
PUDDLY	RHEXES	SHOALY	SMOGGY	STOTTS
PUDGES		SHODDY	SMOWTS	STOWPS

STROWN	TAUTLY	TWISTY	VALVED	WANNEL
STUFFS	TAVAHS	TYPIFY	VANMAN	WANNER
STUFFY	TAWDRY	TYPTOS	VANMEN	WARMLY
STUGGY	TAXONS	TYTHED	VANNED	WAURED
STULLS	TAZZAS	TYTHES	VARSAL	WAVERY
STULMS	TEPEFY	TZURIS	VARVED	WAVEYS
STUMPY	TETCHY	UBIQUE	VASTLY	WAVILY
STYLUS	TETTIX	UGLILY	VATMAN	WAXIER
STYRAX	THEFTS	UHURUS	VATTED	WAXILY
SUBFIX	THEMED	UMBERY	VAULTY	WAZOOS
SUETTY	THOFTS	UNBEEN	VAUNTY	WEAKLY
SUFFIX	THRAWN	UNBURY	VAWTED	WEBBED
SUGARY	THRUMS	UNBUSY	VEDUTE	WEBFED
SUIVEZ	THRUSH	UNCUTE	VEGETE	WEDDED
SUKKOS	THUJAS	UNDULY	VEGGED	WEDGED
SULCUS	THUMBY	UNDYED	VEHMIC	WEEKES
SUNDRY	THUMPS	UNFIXT	VELDTS	WEEKLY
SUNUPS	THUNKS	UNHOLY	VENERY	WEFTED
SURTAX	THYMEY	UNHUNG	VERNIX	WEIZES
SUSSES	TIGLIC	UNIFIC	VERTEX	WEXING
SVARAJ	TINCTS	UNJAMS	VEXERS	WHACKY
SWABBY	TIZWAS	UNJUST	VEXILS	WHAMMY
SWADDY	TODAYS	UNMEEK	VIABLY	WHARFS
SWAMPS	TOMBED	UNMEWS	VIBIER	WHAURS
SWAMPY	TOMBIC	UNMIRY	VIFDAS	WHEELY
SWANKS	TOOTHY	UNMIXT	VILELY	WHEEZY
SWANNY	TOROTH	UNSEXY	VILIFY	WHEFTS
SWARFS	TOUCHY	UNSOFT	VINIFY	WHELKS
SWASHY	TOWERY	UNSPUN	VINTRY	WHELKY
SWEEPY	TOWNLY	UNSUNK	VIOLAS	WHELMS
SWERFS	TOWZED	UNTIDY	VISTAS	WHELPS
SWEYED	TRAMPY	UNVEXT	VIVARY	WHERRY
SWIFTS	TRIPLY	UNWELL	VIVATS	WHEWED
SWILLS	TRIPPY	UNWISH	VIVELY	WHEYEY
SWIMMY	TROPPO	UNWONT	VIVIFY	WHIFFS
SWINKS	TRUNKS	UNZIPS	VIZORS	WHIFFY
SWIPED	TRUTHY	UPBLEW	VOCABS	WHIFTS
SWIPEY	TRYPAN	UPDOVE	VODKAS	WHILLY
SWIRLY	TUATHS	UPDREW	VOGUED	WHIMMY
SWISHY	TUFTED	UPGOES	VOGUEY	WHINEY
SWIVED	TUKTUS	UPGONE	VOLVAS	WHINNY
SWOONS	TURGID	UPGREW	VOLVOX	WHIPPY
SWOONY	TUTRIX	UPGUSH	VORAGO	WHIRLS
SWOOPY	TUTTED	UPHELD	VOXELS	WHIRLY
SWOTTY	TUTUED	UPHOVE	VOZHDS	WHIRRY
SYBBES	TUZZES	UPHUNG	VROUWS	WHISKS
SYLPHY	TWANGY	UPJETS	VULGUS	WHIZZY
SYNCHS	TWEAKY	UPPITY	VULVAR	WHOLLY
SYNODS	TWEEDY	UPRYST	VULVAS	WHOMPS
SYNTAX	TWEENY	UPTOOK	VUMMED	WHOOPS
SYNTHS	TWENTY	URUBUS	WABBIT	WHOOSH
SYRAHS	TWERPY	USQUES	WABBLY	WHUMPS
SYRINX	TWIGGY	UVEOUS	WAFFLY	WICOPY
SYRUPS	TWILLY	VACANT	WAGGAS	WIFEYS
SYRUPY	TWINKS	VACKED	WAGGLY	WILDLY
SYZYGY	TWIRLS	VAGARY	WAHOOS	WILIER
TAIHOA	TWIRLY	VAGGED	WAIFED	WILILY
TALAQS	TWIRPS	VAKASS	WAIFTS	WIMMIN
TAPPAS	TWIRPY	VAKILS	WAILED	WIRIER
TAUGHT	TWISTS	VALVAR	WAMBLY	WIRILY

WISPED	XYLOLS	YIRKED	ZAMIAS	ZOFTIG
WOADED	XYLYLS	YIRRED	ZANJAS	ZOISTS
WOODSY	XYSTOI	YITIES	ZANZES	ZONARY
WOOLLY	XYSTOS	YOICKS	ZAPATA	ZONDAS
WOUNDY	XYSTUS	YOKELS	ZAPPED	ZONKED
WRAWLS	YACCAS	YOKKED	ZAZENS	ZOOEAE
WRISTS	YAKKAS	YOLKED	ZEBUBS	ZOOEAS
WRISTY	YAKUZA	YOMPED	ZEROTH	ZOOMED
WUDDED	YARELY	YOUNGS	ZESTED	ZOONAL
WUKKAS	YAWPED	YOWIES	ZIGGED	ZOONIC
WURSTS	YBRENT	YUCCAS	ZINCIC	ZORILS
WUSHUS	YEARLY	YUKKED	ZINCKY	ZORROS
WUXIAS	YEASTY	YUMPED	ZIPPED	ZOUNDS
WYCHES	YECCHS	YUNXES	ZIPPOS	ZUPANS
WYTING	YEUKED	YUTZES	ZIPTOP	ZYGOID
XEBECS	YEXING	ZAFTIG	ZIZITH	ZYMOID
XENONS	YIPPED	ZAGGED	ZOAEAE	
XYLANS	YIPPEE	ZAKATS	ZOCCOS	

Seven-letter words that do not combine with another letter

AARRGHH	ADJIGOS	AGUIZED	ANAGOGY	APSARAS
ABASHED	ADJURED	AHEIGHT	ANALOGA	AQUEOUS
ABASHES	ADJUSTS	AHUNGRY	ANALOGY	AQUIVER
ABAXIAL	ADMIXED	AIRSICK	ANANKES	ARBORIO
ABAXILE	ADMIXES	AJOWANS	ANATOMY	ARBUTUS
ABBOTCY	ADNEXAL	AKEAKES	ANAXIAL	ARCADED
ABEYANT	ADOPTED	AKEDAHS	ANCHOVY	ARCHERY
ABIOSIS	ADSORBS	ALALIAS	ANGLIFY	ARDUOUS
ABJECTS	ADSUKIS	ALANYLS	ANLAGEN	ARGYLLS
ABJURED	ADULTLY	ALASKAS	ANNEXED	ARIOSOS
ABRASAX	ADVECTS	ALBINIC	ANNEXES	ARMLIKE
ABRAXAS	ADVERBS	ALCHYMY	ANNUITY	ARRIVED
ABRAZOS	ADVEWED	ALFEREZ	ANNULUS	ARROYOS
ABROACH	ADZUKIS	ALIBIED	ANORAKS	ASEXUAL
ABSORBS	AEFAULD	ALIYOTH	ANOREXY	ASKESES
ABUSIVE	AEOLIAN	ALKALIC	ANOXIAS	ASLAKED
ABVOLTS	AEONIAN	ALLUDED	ANTHRAX	ASPHYXY
ABWATTS	AEROBIA	ALONELY	ANTIFAT	ASPICKS
ACACIAS	AFFABLE	ALOOFLY	ANTIGAY	ASPRAWL
ACADEMY	AFFABLY	ALPHYLS	ANTIJAM	ASSIZED
ACAJOUS	AFFECTS	ALSOONE	ANXIETY	ATAATAS
ACAROID	AFFINAL	ALUMNAE	ANXIOUS	ATARAXY
ACAUDAL	AFFINED	ALUMNUS	ANYBODY	ATAXIAS
ACCEPTS	AFFIXED	ALVEARY	ANYWAYS	ATLATLS
ACIDIFY	AFFRAPS	AMADODA	ANYWHEN	ATOKOUS
ACMATIC	AFFRAYS	AMATIVE	ANZIANI	ATTABOY
ACOUCHY	AFTMOST	AMATORY	AOUDADS	ATTACKS
ACTORLY	AFTOSAS	AMBASSY	APHTHAE	ATTASKT
ADAGIAL	AGAMOUS	AMBATCH	APICULI	ATTUENT
ADAPTED	AGARICS	AMBITTY	APOGAMY	AUCUBAS
ADAXIAL	AGATOID	AMOEBAS	APOZEMS	AUDIBLY
ADDAXES	AGELONG	AMOEBIC	APPALLS	AUDITED
ADDEDLY	AGOROTH	AMOMUMS	APPEACH	AUGITIC
ADDENDA	AGOUTAS	AMOROUS	APPOSED	AURALLY
ADDICTS	AGRIZED	AMPASSY	APPUIED	AUREITY
ADDUCTS	AGRYZED	AMPLIFY	APPUYED	AUTARKY
ADIPOUS	AGRYZES	AMYLUMS	APRAXIC	AUTOBUS

AUTOMAN	BARHOPS	BEKNOWN	BILGIER	BODGING
AUTUMNS	BAROCKS	BELAYED	BILLMEN	BOFFING
AUTUMNY	BASHAWS	BELLMAN	BILOBAR	BOGGIER
AUXESES	BASHFUL	BELLMEN	BILOBED	BOGGISH
AUXESIS	BASQUES	BELTMEN	BINDERY	BOGGLED
AUXINIC	BATATAS	BEMIXED	BINDHIS	BOGOAKS
AVATARS	BATCHED	BEMOCKS	BINGHIS	BOGONGS
AVAUNTS	BATHMIC	BENEMPT	BIODATA	BOGUSLY
AVIZING	BATHYAL	BENNETS	BIODOTS	BOHUNKS
AVOIDED	BATIKED	BENTHIC	BIOLOGY	BOILERY
AVOWALS	BATTIKS	BENUMBS	BIOMASS	BOMBERS
AVOWING	BAUBEES	BENZALS	BIONICS	BONBONS
AVRUGAS	BAWBEES	BENZOIC	BIONOMY	BONDUCS
AVYZING	BAWDILY	BEPELTS	BIPARTY	BONEYER
AWAKENS	BAWSUNT	BEPUFFS	BIRDIED	BONJOUR
AWHAPED	BAXTERS	BERBICE	BIRDIES	BONNILY
AWHAPES	BAYYANS	BESIGHS	BIRRING	BONOBOS
AWKWARD	BAZAARS	BESPATE	BIRSIER	BOOBING
AWNLESS	BAZOOMS	BETAKEN	BISQUES	BOOCOOS
AXSEEDS	BEAMILY	BETAXED	BITCHED	BOOFIER
AZALEAS	BEATBOX	BETIGHT	BITCHEN	BOOGIED
AZOLLAS	BEAVERY	BETWIXT	BIVIOUS	BOOHAIS
AZOTOUS	BECKETS	BEVVIED	BIVVIED	BOOHING
AZUREAN	BECKING	BEVVIES	BIVVIES	BOOHOOS
AZYGIES	BECKONS	BEWEEPS	BIZONAL	BOOJUMS
AZYGOUS	BECLOGS	BEWITCH	BIZZIES	BOOKISH
AZYMOUS	BECOMES	BEWRAPS	BLADDED	BOOKMAN
BABLAHS	BEDAZED	BEWRAPT	BLANDLY	BOOKMEN
BABOOLS	BEDAZES	BEWRAYS	BLANKED	BOOMBOX
BABOONS	BEDBUGS	BEYONDS	BLANKLY	BOOSHIT
BABOOSH	BEDECKS	BEZZLES	BLAZING	BOOSTED
BABYSAT	BEDELLS	BHAJANS	BLEAKLY	BOOZERS
BACCHII	BEDEWED	BHAJEES	BLIGHTS	BOOZILY
BACCOES	BEDIRTY	BHAVANS	BLINDLY	BOOZING
BACKUPS	BEDPANS	BHAWANS	BLINKED	BOPEEPS
BADDISH	BEDUCKS	BHIKHUS	BLISSES	BOPPERS
BADGING	BEDUMBS	BHINDIS	BLITZED	BOPPING
BADMASH	BEEBEES	BIAXIAL	BLOBBED	BORAXES
BAFFIES	BEECHEN	BIBASIC	BLOOPED	BORNYLS
BAFFLED	BEEFILY	BIBBERS	BLOTTED	BORONIC
BAGFULS	BEELIKE	BIBBERY	BLOWBYS	BORRELL
BAGGILY	BEESOME	BIBBING	BLOWUPS	BORROWS
BAGLIKE	BEESWAX	BIBLIKE	BLOWZED	BORSHCH
BAGSFUL	BEETFLY	BICHORD	BLOWZES	BORTZES
BAGWASH	BEEZERS	BIDDIES	BLUBBED	BORZOIS
BAGWIGS	BEFALLS	BIFACES	BLUDGED	BOSONIC
BAHADAS	BEFOAMS	BIFFERS	BLUFFED	BOSTONS
BAININS	BEFOOLS	BIFFIES	BLUFFLY	BOSTRYX
BAIZING	BEGAZED	BIFFING	BLURRED	BOTHANS
BAJADAS	BEGIFTS	BIFFINS	BOAKING	BOTTLED
BAKKIES	BEGILDS	BIFIDLY	BOBBERS	BOTTOMS
BALMILY	BEGNAWS	BIGEYES	BOBBERY	BOTTONY
BAMBINI	BEGULFS	BIGGIES	BOBBIES	BOUBOUS
BAMMERS	BEGUNKS	BIGGISH	BOBBINS	BOUFFES
BANALLY	BEHAVED	BIGGITY	BOBBISH	BOUGHED
BANDBOX	BEHOLDS	BIGGONS	BOBBLED	BOUGIES
BANYANS	BEHOOFS	BIGOTRY	BOBBLES	BOUGING
BAOBABS	BEJADED	BIGWIGS	BOBCATS	BOUTONS
BARAZAS	BEJANTS	BIKINIS	BOCKEDY	BOVINES
BARBUTS	BEJESUS	BIKKIES	BODGIER	BOVVERS

BOWBENT	BUGEYES	CADAGIS	CHIACKS	CLIFFED
BOWFINS	BUGGERY	CADDISH	CHIBBED	CLIMBED
BOWGETS	BUGONGS	CADDYSS	CHICHIS	CLIQUED
BOWLEGS	BUGSHAS	CADEAUX	CHIDDEN	CLIQUEY
BOWPOTS	BUIBUIS	CADENCY	CHIEFLY	CLOACAL
BOWSAWS	BUKSHIS	CADGING	CHIGGAS	CLOCKED
BOWSIES	BULIMUS	CADUACS	CHIGOES	CLODDED
BOWWOWS	BULLIER	CAEOMAS	CHILDLY	CLOGGED
BOXCARS	BULLOUS	CAFARDS	CHILLED	CLOPPED
BOXFISH	BUMBAGS	CAGMAGS	CHINCHY	CLOUGHS
BOXFULS	BUMMEST	CAJOLED	CHINKED	CLOVERS
BOXIEST	BUMMLED	CALCIFY	CHINTZY	CLUBBED
BOXINGS	BUMPIER	CALUMNY	CHIPPED	CLUBMAN
BOXLIKE	BUMPILY	CALVARY	CHIRKER	CLUBMEN
BRAATAS	BUNDLED	CALYXES	CHIVARI	CLUTCHY
BRACTED	BUNGEYS	CALZONI	CHIZZED	CLYPING
BRADDED	BUNJEES	CAMPILY	CHIZZES	COALBOX
BRAMBLY	BUNJIES	CANDLED	CHOCHOS	COALIFY
BRANCHY	BUNKUMS	CANFULS	CHOCKED	COANNEX
BRASHLY	BUNNETS	CANNONS	CHOKEYS	COAXING
BRAUNCH	BUNNIAS	CANOLAS	CHOKIER	COBBIER
BRAVERS	BUNYIPS	CANOPIC	CHOMETZ	COBBLED
BRAVOED	BUOYANT	CANSFUL	CHOMPED	COBLOAF
BRAYERS	BUOYING	CAPFULS	CHOOFED	COBURGS
BRAZILS	BUREAUX	CARAMBA	CHOOKED	COBWEBS
BRAZING	BURGESS	CARAPAX	CHOOSEY	COCCOUS
BREEZED	BURGHAL	CARBOYS	CHOPPED	COCKILY
BREEZES	BURRERS	CARDUUS	CHORDED	COCKISH
BRENNES	BURROWS	CARNIFY	CHOUGHS	COCKLED
BREVITY	BUSBARS	CARROCH	CHUGGED	COCOONS
BRICKEN	BUSBOYS	CARSICK	CHUMASH	COCTILE
BRIDIES	BUSHFLY	CARVERY	CHUMMED	CODDLED
BRIEFLY	BUSHILY	CASBAHS	CHUMPED	CODFISH
BRIGHTS	BUSHMEN	CASHBOX	CHURRED	COFFLED
BRIGUED	BUSYING	CASHOOS	CHURROS	COFFLES
BRIMMED	BUTTLED	CASQUED	CHURRUS	COGGLED
BRISKER	BUTTONS	CATFISH	CHYLIFY	COGNACS
BRISKLY	BUTTONY	CAUSEYS	CHYLOUS	COGWAYS
BROCKIT	BUTYRIC	CAVALLY	CHYMICS	COJONES
BROGGED	BUXOMER	CAVALRY	CHYMIFY	COLICKY
BROKERS	BUXOMLY	CAVEMAN	CHYMOUS	COLOBID
BROKERY	BUYOFFS	CAVEMEN	CIGGIES	COLONUS
BRONZED	BUZUKIA	CAYMANS	CILIARY	COLUGOS
BRONZEN	BUZUKIS	CAYUSES	CIRCARS	COLUMNS
BROUZES	BUZZERS	CEAZING	CIRCLED	COMATIC
BRUTIFY	BUZZIER	CELLING	CIVILLY	COMEDIC
BRUXING	BYCATCH	CELOTEX	CIVISMS	COMFIER
BUBBLED	BYGONES	CHALUTZ	CLADDED	COMMATA
BUBONIC	BYNEMPT	CHAMOIX	CLAGGED	COMMITS
BUCKIES	BYPATHS	CHAMPED	CLAMMED	COMMIXT
BUCKLED	BYREMEN	CHARGED	CLAXONS	COMMODO
BUDDERS	BYRLADY	CHAUFFS	CLEANLY	COMPANY
BUDDHAS	BYRLAWS	CHAVISH	CLECKED	COMPASS
BUDDIED	BYROOMS	CHEBECS	CLEEKED	COMPLEX
BUDDLED	BYTALKS	CHECKED	CLEEKIT	COMPONY
BUDDLES	BYWORDS	CHEEKED	CLEEVES	CONCHED
BUDGETS	BYZANTS	CHEFFED	CLEMENT	CONCHOS
BUDLESS	CABOVER	CHEGOES	CLEMMED	CONCUPY
BUDLIKE	CACHEXY	CHEVENS	CLERKLY	CONCUSS
BUFFIER	CADAGAS	CHEVINS	CLICKED	CONDOMS

CONFABS	CUDDENS	DAYLILY	DIKDIKS	DORADOS
CONFLUX	CULTISH	DAYSMAN	DIKKOPS	DORKIER
CONJEED	CUMBENT	DAZZLED	DIKTATS	DOSSILS
CONJEES	CUPFULS	DECAYED	DILLIER	DOTARDS
CONJURY	CUPPIER	DECENCY	DILUTED	DOTCOMS
CONVOYS	CUPRUMS	DECIDED	DIMMING	DOTTILY
COOEYED	CUPSFUL	DECKLED	DIMWITS	DOTTLED
COOKEYS	CUPULAR	DECODED	DINKUMS	DOUBLED
COOLTHS	CURABLY	DECOYED	DINNLED	DOUCHED
COOMIER	CURFEWS	DEDUCTS	DIPODIC	DOVEISH
COOPERY	CURIUMS	DEEDILY	DIQUATS	DOVENED
COPIOUS	CURLEWS	DEEJAYS	DIRNDLS	DOWDIER
COPPINS	CURLILY	DEERFLY	DIRTILY	DOWDILY
CORNIFY	CURSORY	DEFACED	DISMISS	DOZENED
COROZOS	CURVING	DEFANGS	DITHIOL	DOZINGS
CORYMBS	CURVITY	DEFFEST	DITTANY	DRAFTED
CORYZAS	CUSHATS	DEFRAYS	DITTAYS	DRAMMED
COSYING	CUSHILY	DEFUNDS	DITTOED	DRAPERY
COTTOID	CUSTODY	DEFUSED	DITZIER	DRIBBLY
COTTONY	CUTOFFS	DEFUZED	DIVISIM	DRIFTED
COTWALS	CUTOUTS	DEFUZES	DIVVIED	DRILLED
COUPEES	CWTCHED	DEIFIED	DIZZIED	DRIZZLY
COUZINS	CWTCHES	DEINDEX	DIZZIER	DROOKED
COWARDS	CYATHIA	DEJECTS	DIZZILY	DROOKIT
COWBOYS	CYATHUS	DEKEING	DJEBELS	DROOPED
COWEDLY	CYBORGS	DEKKOED	DJEMBES	DROPFLY
COWFISH	CYBRIDS	DELUDED	DOBBIES	DROPPED
COWITCH	CYCLERY	DELUGES	DOBBING	DROUKED
COWPATS	CYGNETS	DEMIVEG	DOBBINS	DROWNDS
COWPEAS	CYMENES	DEMODED	DOBHASH	DRUDGED
COXALGY	CYTODES	DEMOTED	DOBSONS	DRUGGED
COXITIS	CZAPKAS	DENSIFY	DOCIBLE	DRUIDIC
COXLESS	CZARDAS	DEPUTED	DODDARD	DRUIDRY
COYDOGS	DABBITY	DESEXED	DODDERY	DRUMMED
COZENED	DACKING	DESKMEN	DODDING	DRUNKER
COZIEST	DADDLED	DESYNED	DODDLES	DRUXIER
COZYING	DADOING	DEVALLS	DODGERY	DRYLOTS
CRACKLY	DAFFILY	DEVESTS	DODGIER	DRYNESS
CRAYERS	DAFTARS	DEVIOUS	DODKINS	DUALLED
CRAZING	DAGABAS	DEVOTED	DOFFING	DUARCHY
CREWMAN	DAIDLED	DEWANNY	DOGDAYS	DUBIETY
CRICKED	DAIKONS	DEWAXED	DOGGESS	DUCDAME
CRICKEY	DAIMIOS	DEWFULL	DOGGISH	DUDDERS
CRIMINY	DAKOITY	DEWITTS	DOGMATA	DUDDERY
CRISSUM	DALLIED	DEWLAPT	DOLEFUL	DUDISMS
CROGGED	DAMAGED	DEXTRAL	DOLLOPS	DUELLED
CROJIKS	DAMASKS	DIACIDS	DONJONS	DUETTED
CROQUIS	DAMFOOL	DIALLED	DONKEYS	DUGOUTS
CRUCIFY	DAMMARS	DIALLEL	DONNING	DUHKHAS
CRUDITY	DAMNIFY	DIANDRY	DONNISH	DUKKAHS
CRUMBLY	DANDIFY	DIARIAN	DOODADS	DUKKHAS
CRUMPLY	DANDLED	DIBBUKS	DOODLED	DULCIFY
CRYBABY	DAPPLED	DICKING	DOODOOS	DULLISH
CRYPTIC	DARKISH	DICLINY	DOOKETS	DUMBING
CUBAGES	DARKLED	DICYCLY	DOOMFUL	DUMDUMS
CUBBIES	DATABUS	DIDACTS	DOOMILY	DUMPILY
CUBICLY	DATEDLY	DIDDIER	DOOSRAS	DUMPISH
CUBISMS	DATURIC	DIDDLED	DOOWOPS	DUNCERY
CUBOIDS	DAWTING	DIFFORM	DOPPIES	DUNCHED
CUCKOOS	DAYCHES	DIGHTED	DOPPIOS	DUOLOGS

DUOPOLY	ENJOYED	EXEMPTS	FANCIFY	FINALLY
DUPABLE	ENMEWED	EXHALED	FANCILY	FINICAL
DUPPING	ENMOVED	EXHALES	FANDOMS	FINJANS
DURDUMS	ENNUYEE	EXHUMED	FANEGAS	FINNING
DUSKILY	ENSKYED	EXILERS	FANJETS	FIREBOX
DUSKISH	ENSWEPT	EXILING	FANKLED	FIREFLY
DUSTUPS	ENTETEE	EXILITY	FANNERS	FIRMING
DUTIFUL	ENTROPY	EXISTED	FANTASY	FIRRIER
DWALMED	ENWINDS	EXOGENS	FARCIFY	FISHERY
DWAMMED	ENZONED	EXONYMS	FAREBOX	FISHFUL
DWARFED	ENZONES	EXOPODS	FARFALS	FISSIVE
DWARVES	ENZYMES	EXPANDS	FARRAND	FIXABLE
DWAUMED	ENZYMIC	EXPORTS	FARRING	FIXATED
DYARCHY	EPHEBES	EXSECTS	FARTHER	FIXEDLY
DYBBUKS	EPHEBIC	EXTOLLS	FASHERY	FIXINGS
DYEABLE	EPHEBOI	EXTORTS	FATALLY	FIZZENS
DYINGLY	EPHEBOS	EXUDING	FATHOMS	FJORDIC
DYKIEST	EPHEBUS	EXULTED	FATIDIC	FLACCID
DYNAMOS	EPIBOLY	EXURBAN	FATSOES	FLACKED
DYNASTY	EPIGENE	EXUVIAL	FATUITY	FLAFFED
DYSLOGY	EPINAOI	EXUVIUM	FAUCIAL	FLAGGED
DYSURIC	EPITAXY	EYEABLE	FAVUSES	FLAGMAN
DYVOURS	EPIZOIC	EYECUPS	FEAGUED	FLAILED
DYVOURY	EPONYMS	EYEFULS	FEATEST	FLAMERS
DZERENS	EPONYMY	EYELASH	FEAZING	FLAMMED
EBBLESS	EPOXYED	EYELESS	FEEDBOX	FLANKED
EBRIETY	EPUISEE	EYELIKE	FELLOES	FLANKEN
ECDEMIC	EQUABLE	EYESOME	FEMMIER	FLAPPED
ECDYSES	EQUABLY	EYEWASH	FENNIER	FLAUNCH
ECDYSIS	EQUALLY	FABBEST	FENNISH	FLAYING
ECZEMAS	EQUERRY	FABRICS	FEOFFED	FLEDGED
EDDYING	EQUINOX	FABULAR	FERRUMS	FLEDGES
EDIFIED	ESCHEWS	FACEMAN	FERVENT	FLEETLY
EELLIKE	ETHENES	FACEMEN	FESCUES	FLEGGED
EFFABLE	ETHYNES	FACTIVE	FESTIVE	FLEMING
EFFECTS	EUMUNGS	FACTORY	FETTLED	FLEXING
EFFRAYS	EUNUCHS	FACTUMS	FEUDARY	FLEXORS
EGGCUPS	EUOUAES	FACULAR	FEWMETS	FLICKED
EGGMASS	EUPEPSY	FACULTY	FEWNESS	FLIGHTS
EGGNOGS	EUPHONY	FADABLE	FEWTERS	FLIGHTY
EGGWASH	EURYOKY	FADDIER	FEYNESS	FLIMPED
ELIXIRS	EUSTACY	FADDISH	FIASCHI	FLIPPED
EMANANT	EUSTASY	FADDLED	FIBBERY	FLITTED
EMBARKS	EVEJARS	FADDLES	FIBBING	FLIXING
EMBAYED	EVINCES	FADGING	FIBRILS	FLOCCED
EMBAYLD	EVZONES	FADLIKE	FIBROUS	FLOCCUS
EMBLEMS	EXACTAS	FAGGERY	FIBULAR	FLOCKED
EMBOXED	EXACTED	FAGGOTS	FICKLED	FLOGGED
EMBOXES	EXACUMS	FAGOTTI	FICTIVE	FLOODED
EMEUTES	EXALTED	FAGOTTO	FICTORS	FLOPPED
EMINENT	EXARATE	FAHLERZ	FIDDLED	FLORALS
EMMEWED	EXARCHS	FAIKING	FIDIBUS	FLOUNCY
EMMOVED	EXCAMBS	FAIRILY	FIERCER	FLOWERY
EMMOVES	EXCIDED	FAITHED	FIERILY	FLUBBED
EMPATHY	EXCIDES	FAJITAS	FIFTHLY	FLUFFED
EMPIGHT	EXCISED	FALLALS	FIGGERY	FLUIDAL
EMULGED	EXCISES	FALLERS	FIGJAMS	FLUIDLY
ENFIXES	EXCITED	FALSIFY	FIKIEST	FLUKILY
ENGAGED	EXCUDIT	FALSITY	FILLIPS	FLUMMOX
ENGULFS	EXEEMED	FAMULUS	FIMBLES	FLUNKED

FLUORIC	FRAPPEE	FUSSILY	GELIDLY	GOADING
FLUXING	FRASSES	FUSTICS	GEMFISH	GOANNAS
FLUXIVE	FRATCHY	FUSTOCS	GEMMERY	GOBANGS
FLYABLE	FRATERY	FUTZING	GEMMING	GOBBLED
FLYBLEW	FREAKED	FUZZIER	GENNELS	GODWITS
FLYBOYS	FRIARLY	FUZZILY	GEOGENY	GOFFERS
FLYLEAF	FRICHTS	FUZZLED	GERMIER	GOFFING
FLYLESS	FRIDGED	FUZZLES	GESSOED	GOGGLED
FLYOFFS	FRIGGED	FYLFOTS	GEWGAWS	GOLLOPS
FLYPING	FRISKAS	GABBROS	GHASTED	GOMBROS
FOAMILY	FRISKED	GADOIDS	GHASTLY	GOMOKUS
FOBBING	FRITFLY	GAGAKUS	GHAZALS	GONADIC
FOCALLY	FRIVOLS	GAGGERS	GHAZELS	GONOPHS
FODDERS	FROLICS	GAGGERY	GHESSED	GOODMEN
FOGBOWS	FRONDED	GAGGLED	GHESSES	GOOFIER
FOGDOGS	FROUGHY	GALAGES	GHIBLIS	GOOFILY
FOGGILY	FROWSTS	GALANTY	GHOSTED	GOOGLED
FOINING	FROWSTY	GALLFLY	GHOSTLY	GOOGOLS
FOISONS	FRUGGED	GALLOCK	GIBBOUS	GOOROOS
FOISTED	FRUSHED	GALLOWS	GIBUSES	GOOSEYS
FOLDUPS	FRYABLE	GALYACS	GIDDIED	GOPHERS
FOLIOED	FRYPANS	GALYAKS	GIDDILY	GORGIAS
FOLIOUS	FUBBERY	GAMMATS	GIDDYAP	GORGIOS
FOLKISH	FUBBIER	GAMMING	GIDGEES	GORGONS
FOLLOWS	FUCKERS	GAMMONS	GIDJEES	GOSSANS
FONNING	FUCKUPS	GANJAHS	GIFTEES	GOSSIBS
FOODIES	FUCOIDS	GANNING	GIGGITS	GOSSIPS
FOOLERY	FUCUSED	GAPOSIS	GIMMIES	GOTCHAS
FOOTMAN	FUCUSES	GAPPING	GIMMORS	GOTHICS
FOOTMEN	FUDDLED	GARJANS	GIOCOSO	GOUGING
FOOZLED	FUDGING	GASBAGS	GIPPIES	GOUJONS
FOPPERY	FUGATOS	GASCONS	GIPPOES	GOUTFLY
FOPPISH	FUGGILY	GASKETS	GIPSIED	GOVERNS
FOREBYE	FUGLING	GATEAUX	GIRONNY	GOWDEST
FOREDID	FUGUING	GATELEG	GIVINGS	GOWFERS
FORGAVE	FULGENT	GAUCIER	GIZZENS	GOWFING
FORMFUL	FULLANS	GAUDERY	GLADDED	GOWPENS
FORMYLS	FULLEST	GAUDILY	GLADFUL	GOYISCH
FORSOOK	FULLISH	GAUZIER	GLADIUS	GOZZANS
FORTIFY	FULVOUS	GAUZILY	GLAIKIT	GRAFFED
FOSSATE	FUMAGES	GAVAGES	GLAZILY	GRAHAMS
FOSSORS	FUMBLED	GAVIALS	GLEDGED	GRAMASH
FOUGHTY	FUMETTI	GAWCIER	GLEDGES	GRAPERY
FOUNDRY	FUMETTO	GAWKERS	GLEEKED	GRAPHED
FOUSSAS	FUMULUS	GAWKILY	GLEGGER	GRAPPAS
FOWLPOX	FUNGOES	GAWKING	GLIBBED	GRATIFY
FOXFISH	FUNGOUS	GAWPING	GLITCHY	GRAVITY
FOXIEST	FUNKIAS	GAYSOME	GLITZED	GRAVLAX
FOXINGS	FUNKILY	GAZEFUL	GLOBOUS	GRAYFLY
FOXLIKE	FUNNELS	GAZOONS	GLOMMED	GREYEST
FOYNING	FUNNILY	GAZUMPS	GLORIFY	GREYISH
FOZIEST	FUNNING	GEARBOX	GLOSSAS	GRIESIE
FRABBED	FUNPLEX	GECKING	GLOUTED	GRIGGED
FRABBIT	FURIOUS	GECKOES	GLOWFLY	GRIMILY
FRAGGED	FURKIDS	GEEBAGS	GLUGGED	GRIMING
FRAILLY	FURRILY	GEEGAWS	GLUMMER	GRIMMER
FRAMPAL	FURROWS	GEEKIER	GLUTTED	GRIPPED
FRANKED	FURROWY	GEEZAHS	GLYPHIC	GRITTED
FRANKLY	FUSCOUS	GEEZERS	GNATHAL	GRIZZLY
FRAPPED	FUSIBLY	GEGGIES	GNOMONS	GROCERY

GROGGED	GYPPERS	HAZELLY	HOBBISH	HOUHERE
GROKKED	GYPPIES	HAZMATS	HOBBLED	HOWDAHS
GROUCHY	GYPPING	HEALEES	HOBDAYS	HOWFFED
GROUGHS	GYPSIED	HEALTHY	HOBJOBS	HOWKING
GROUPED	GYRALLY	HEAUMES	HOBNOBS	HUBBIES
GROWTHY	GYRONNY	HEAVILY	HOBOING	HUBBUBS
GROZING	GYRUSES	HEBETIC	HOCKEYS	HUBCAPS
GRUDGED	GYTRASH	HEDDLED	HODADDY	HUCKERY
GRUFFED	GYTTJAS	HEDGERS	HODDENS	HUDDLED
GRUFTED	HABDABS	HEEDFUL	HODDINS	HUELESS
GRUGRUS	HABOOBS	HEEHAWS	HODDLED	HUFFILY
GRUMBLY	HACKERY	HEEZIES	HOGFISH	HUFFISH
GRUMPHY	HACKMAN	HEINIES	HOGGERS	HUGGIER
GRYDING	HACKMEN	HELIUMS	HOGGERY	HULKING
GRYFONS	HADAWAY	HELIXES	HOGGETS	HULLERS
GRYSELY	HADDEST	HELLBOX	HOGGISH	HULLIER
GUAIACS	HADDING	HELLERY	HOGLIKE	HULLOOS
GUANAYS	HADJEES	HELLISH	HOGTIED	HUMBLED
GUANGOS	HAFFETS	HELLOVA	HOGWASH	HUMBUGS
GUANXIS	HAFIZES	HELLUVA	HOISINS	HUMBUZZ
GUARISH	HAGBUSH	HELPFUL	HOLDUPS	HUMERUS
GUBBAHS	HAGFISH	HEMMERS	HOLEYER	HUMFING
GUCKIER	HAGGISH	HEMMING	HOLLOOS	HUMHUMS
GUDDLED	HAGGLED	HENLEYS	HOLLOWS	HUMIDEX
GUDDLES	HAGLIKE	HENLIKE	HOMAGED	HUMIDLY
GUFFAWS	HAIDUKS	HENNERY	HOMOSEX	HUMLIES
GUGGLED	HAIMISH	HENNINS	HONCHOS	HUMMERS
GUILING	HAJJAHS	HENNISH	HONDLED	HUMORAL
GUIMPES	HALFWAY	HERBIER	HONDLES	HUMPHED
GUIZERS	HALLOAS	HERTZES	HONGIED	HUMVEES
GULFING	HALLOES	HEXADES	HONKEYS	HUNKEYS
GULLERS	HALVING	HEXADIC	HONKING	HURLEYS
GULLERY	HAMMAMS	HEXANES	HOODIAS	HURRAHS
GULLETS	HAMMIER	HEXENES	HOODOOS	HURRAYS
GULLEYS	HAMMILY	HEXINGS	HOOKAHS	HURTLED
GULLIES	HAMULAR	HEXONES	HOOKERS	HUSHABY
GULLISH	HAMZAHS	HEXOSES	HOOKIER	HUSHFUL
GUMLIKE	HANDILY	HEXYLIC	HOOKUPS	HUSHIER
GUMMATA	HANGMAN	HEYDAYS	HOOLEYS	HUSKILY
GUMMIER	HANGMEN	HEYDEYS	HOOPOES	HUSSARS
GUMMOUS	HANSOMS	HICCUPS	HOOPOOS	HUSSIFS
GUMNUTS	HAPPENS	HICCUPY	HOORAHS	HUTCHED
GUNNELS	HAPPIED	HICKEYS	HOORAYS	HUZOORS
GUNNERY	HAPPILY	HIGGLED	HOOVING	HUZZAHS
GUPPIES	HAPUKAS	HIGHISH	HOPDOGS	HUZZIES
GURJUNS	HAPUKUS	HIGHMAN	HOPPLED	HYBRIDS
GURSHES	HARIRAS	HIGHMEN	HORKEYS	HYDROUS
GUSHERS	HARSHLY	HIGHTED	HORNISH	HYDYNES
GUSLARS	HASHIER	HIJINKS	HORRIFY	HYENINE
GUTLIKE	HASHISH	HIJRAHS	HORRORS	HYLISMS
GUTROTS	HATPEGS	HIKOIED	HOSEYED	HYMNALS
GUTTERY	HAUDING	HILCHED	HOSIERY	HYMNARY
GUTTLED	HAUGHTY	HILCHES	HOTBEDS	HYMNING
GUTZERS	HAUYNES	HILLMEN	HOTCHED	HYMNODY
GUZZLED	HAVENED	HIMATIA	HOTDOGS	HYPHENS
GYMBALS	HAWALAS	HIPPISH	HOTTEST	HYPNUMS
GYMMALS	HAWKEYS	HITCHED	HOTTISH	HYPOXIC
GYMPIES	HAWKISH	HOARILY	HOUDAHS	HYPURAL
GYMPING	HAYMOWS	HOAXING	HOUFFED	HYRAXES
GYNNEYS	HAZARDS	HOBBIES	HOUGHED	HYSSOPS

MAYVINS	MIRVING	MOUSERY	MUZZILY	NONNIES
MAZEFUL	MISDREW	MOUTHED	MUZZLED	NONOILY
MAZHBIS	MISFITS	MOZZIES	MYCELES	NONPEAK
MAZOUTS	MISGREW	MOZZLES	MYCETES	NONPOOR
MAZUMAS	MISKALS	MUCKILY	MYCOSES	NONSKID
MEADOWS	MISKENS	MUCKING	MYCOTIC	NONSLIP
MEADOWY	MISKNEW	MUCLUCS	MYGALES	NONWAGE
MEDDLED	MISTOOK	MUDBUGS	MYIASIS	NONWOOL
MEDIACY	MISWENT	MUDDIED	MYOPSES	NONWORK
MEDLEYS	MIXABLE	MUDDIER	MYRRHIC	NONZERO
MEEKEST	MIXEDLY	MUDDILY	MYSOSTS	NOTABLY
MEEMIES	MIXIBLE	MUDDLED	MYSTIFY	NOTCHED
MEETEST	MIXIEST	MUDEYES	MYXOMAS	NOVELTY
MEGOHMS	MIZUNAS	MUFFINS	MZUNGUS	NOVENAE
MEMBERS	MIZZLED	MUFFISH	NABBING	NOVENAS
MERCIFY	MIZZLES	MUFFLED	NAGANAS	NOZZERS
MERCURY	MNEMONS	MUGFULS	NAKEDLY	NOZZLES
MERRIER	MOBBERS	MUGGARS	NANKINS	NUBUCKS
MERRILY	MOBCAPS	MUGGIER	NAPRONS	NUDZHED
MESSMEN	MOBSMAN	MUGGILY	NARTHEX	NUDZHES
METHYLS	MOBSMEN	MUGGURS	NASALLY	NULLAHS
METRIFY	MOCKERY	MUHLIES	NAUGHTY	NULLITY
METTLED	MOCKUPS	MUKLUKS	NAUPLII	NUMBERS
MEZCALS	MOCOCKS	MUKTUKS	NAVALLY	NUMBING
MIAOWED	MOCUCKS	MULCHED	NAVVIED	NUMMARY
MIASMAS	MODALLY	MULCTED	NAYSAID	NUNNERY
MICKEYS	MODELLI	MULLAHS	NAYSAYS	NURHAGS
MICRIFY	MODEMED	MULLERS	NEAFFES	NUTTILY
MIDDLED	MODGING	MULLEYS	NEOGENE	NYAFFED
MIDGUTS	MODIOLI	MULTUMS	NEOTENY	NYANZAS
MIDRIBS	MOGGANS	MUMBLED	NEPHEWS	NYBBLES
MIDWAYS	MOGGING	MUMMERS	NERVILY	NYMPHAL
MIFFIER	MOGHULS	MUMMERY	NEWMOWN	NYMPHIC
MIFFILY	MOGULED	MUMMIED	NEWNESS	NYMPHLY
MIFFING	MOHALIM	MUMMIES	NEWSMAN	OAKLEAF
MIHIING	MOHAWKS	MUMMIFY	NEWSMEN	OAKLIKE
MIKVAHS	MOHELIM	MUMPING	NICKUMS	OAKMOSS
MIKVEHS	MOKOROS	MUMPISH	NILLING	OARLIKE
MIKVOTH	MOKSHAS	MUNDIFY	NIMMING	OBCONIC
MILCHIG	MOLLAHS	MURKIER	NINTHLY	OBELION
MILCHIK	MOLLIFY	MURKILY	NIOBOUS	OBIISMS
MILDEWY	MOLOCHS	MURKISH	NITRIFY	OBJECTS
MILIEUX	MOMISMS	MURMURS	NOCAKES	OBJURED
MILKILY	MOMMETS	MURRAMS	NOCUOUS	OBJURES
MILKMAN	MOMMIES	MURREYS	NODDLED	OBLOQUY
MILKMEN	MOMZERS	MUSCIDS	NOISILY	OBOISTS
MILORDS	MONKERY	MUSEFUL	NONANES	OBOVATE
MILTZES	MONTHLY	MUSJIDS	NONBODY	OBOVOID
MILVINE	MOODIED	MUSKEGS	NONCOMS	OBSEQUY
MIMETIC	MOODILY	MUSKILY	NONDRIP	OBVIOUS
MIMICRY	MOOLOOS	MUSKING	NONFANS	OCCULTS
MIMMEST	MOONILY	MUSSILY	NONFOOD	OCTAVAL
MINNIES	MOORVAS	MUTABLY	NONFUEL	OCTAVOS
MINXISH	MOPPING	MUTEDLY	NONGAYS	OCTOFID
MINYANS	MORROWS	MUTTONS	NONHEME	OCTUPLY
MIOCENE	MOSEYED	MUTUUMS	NONHERO	ODOURED
MIRIFIC	MOTIVIC	MUUMUUS	NONHOME	ODZOOKS
MIRITIS	MOTMOTS	MUZHIKS	NONIRON	OFFCUTS
MIRLIER	MOTTLED	MUZJIKS	NONJURY	OFFLINE
MIRRORS	MOUJIKS	MUZZIER	NONNEWS	OFFPEAK

OFFPUTS	OXGANGS	PAYABLY	PHYLLOS	PLOPPED
OFFSETS	OXHIDES	PAYNIMS	PHYLONS	PLOTFUL
OGHAMIC	OXLANDS	PAZZAZZ	PHYSEDS	PLOTTED
OIDIOID	OXSLIPS	PEAKIER	PHYTINS	PLOTZED
OIKISTS	OXYMELS	PEAKISH	PIAFFED	PLOTZES
OILWAYS	OXYMORA	PEAPODS	PIAZZAS	PLOUGHS
OLDWIFE	OZAENAS	PEAVEYS	PICKERY	PLOWMAN
OLITORY	OZONOUS	PEAVIES	PICKILY	PLOWMEN
OLLAMHS	PABULAR	PEBBLED	PICKUPS	PLUFFED
ONFLOWS	PACIFIC	PEBBLES	PIDDLED	PLUGGED
ONYMOUS	PACKMEN	PECCANT	PIFFLED	PLUMPLY
OOFTISH	PACKWAX	PECCARY	PIGFISH	PLUNGED
OPACIFY	PADAUKS	PECKISH	PIGGIER	POACHED
OPAQUED	PADDLED	PEDDLED	PIGLIKE	POCKIER
OPGEFOK	PADOUKS	PEENGED	PIGMOID	POCKILY
OPPUGNS	PADSAWS	PEEPING	PIGWASH	POCKING
ORATRIX	PAIDLED	PEEVISH	PIKAKES	PODDLED
ORGANDY	PAIKING	PEGGIES	PIKEMAN	PODGILY
ORIENCY	PAJAMAS	PEGHING	PIKEMEN	PODLIKE
OSMIOUS	PAKEHAS	PEGLIKE	PILAFFS	PODZOLS
OSMOLAL	PAKIHIS	PEIZING	PILFERY	POFFLES
OSMOSIS	PAKOKOS	PELAGES	PILLBOX	POGROMS
OSPREYS	PALAGIS	PELVICS	PILLOWS	POKABLE
OSSEOUS	PALAPAS	PEMPHIX	PILULAE	POLKAED
OSSIFIC	PALAZZI	PENFULS	PILULES	POLLICY
OSSUARY	PALLAHS	PENNERS	PIMPLES	POLLMAN
OTTAVAS	PALLIAL	PENNILL	PINCHED	POLLMEN
OUGHTED	PALUDAL	PENNONS	PINFISH	POLYNYI
OULONGS	PANAXES	PENSIVE	PINKIES	POLYOLS
OUTADDS	PANCHAX	PENTYLS	PIOUSLY	POMADED
OUTCITY	PANDANI	PEPPERY	PIPPIER	POMPEYS
OUTECHO	PANFISH	PERENTY	PIPPING	POMPOMS
OUTFELT	PANFULS	PERFIDY	PIPPINS	POMPOUS
OUTFISH	PANICKY	PERFUMY	PIQUANT	PONDOKS
OUTFLEW	PANZERS	PERJINK	PIROGHI	PONTIFY
OUTGAVE	PAPAUMA	PERJURY	PIROJKI	POOFIER
OUTGREW	PAPAYAN	PERKILY	PITAYAS	POOGYES
OUTJINX	PAPAYAS	PERKING	PITCHED	POOJAHS
OUTJUTS	PAPPIER	PERPLEX	PITHFUL	POOVERY
OUTKEPT	PAPPOUS	PERSPEX	PITIFUL	POOVIER
OUTLAID	PAPYRAL	PERUKES	PITYING	POPGUNS
OUTMOST	PAPYRUS	PESEWAS	PIUPIUS	POPJOYS
OUTPITY	PARAPHS	PESKILY	PIXYISH	POPPERS
OUTRUNG	PARRALS	PEWTERS	PIZZLES	POPPIED
OUTRUSH	PARTOOK	PHALANX	PLAGUEY	POPPLED
OUTSWAM	PARTWAY	PHANGED	PLAIDED	POPPLES
OUTSWUM	PARURAS	PHARYNX	PLANURY	PORKIER
OUTTOLD	PASSMAN	PHEEZED	PLANXTY	POSSESS
OUTTOOK	PATENCY	PHEEZES	PLAQUES	POSTBOX
OUTWENT	PAUCITY	PHIZOGS	PLATYPI	POSTFIX
OUTPITY	PAUGHTY	PHIZZES	PLAYFUL	POSTTAX
OVARIAN	PAUNCHY	PHLEGMY	PLEBIFY	POTCHED
OVATELY	PAVAGES	PHLOXES	PLEDGED	POTENCY
OVERBIG	PAVANES	PHOEBES	PLIANCY	POTZERS
OVERGOT	PAVONES	PHOENIX	PLIMMED	POUCHED
OVERLAX	PAWAWED	PHONONS	PLINTHS	POUFFED
OVERMIX	PAWKIER	PHOTOGS	PLODDED	POUFFES
OVIFORM	PAWKILY	PHRATRY	PLODGED	POUKING
OVIPARA	PAWNCES	PHREAKS	PLONGES	POULTRY
OVISACS	PAWPAWS	PHUTTED	PLONKED	POUNCED
OXFORDS			PLONKOS	

POUNDED	PUBBING	QASIDAS	REBECKS	ROKKAKU
POUTFUL	PUBERTY	QIGONGS	REBOZOS	ROMAJIS
POWDERY	PUBLISH	QINDARS	RECARRY	ROMCOMS
POWNEYS	PUCKERY	QIVIUTS	RECENCY	RONNING
POWWAWS	PUCKISH	QUAFFED	REDBUDS	ROOIBOS
POWWOWS	PUDDENS	QUAGGAS	REENTRY	ROOKIER
POYNTED	PUDDLED	QUAHOGS	REFALLS	ROOKISH
POZOLES	PUDENCY	QUALIFY	REFUGED	ROOMILY
POZZIES	PUEBLOS	QUAMASH	REKEYED	RORTING
PRAJNAS	PUFFERS	QUANGOS	RELAXED	ROTGUTS
PREBOOM	PUFFERY	QUANTUM	RELOOKS	ROTOLOS
PREBORN	PUFFILY	QUARTZY	RELUMES	ROUGHLY
PREFABS	PUGGERY	QUASARS	REMARRY	ROYALLY
PREJINK	PUGGISH	QUAVERY	RENEWED	ROYALTY
PREPAYS	PUGGLED	QUBYTES	RENEYED	ROYNING
PREROCK	PUKEKOS	QUEACHY	REPERKS	ROYNISH
PRERUPT	PULKHAS	QUEECHY	REPLEVY	ROZZERS
PREVUES	PULLERS	QUEENED	RESEAUX	RUBBERY
PREWORN	PULLUPS	QUEMING	RESKEWS	RUBBIDY
PREWYNS	PULPIFY	QUESTED	RESKUES	RUBBITY
PREYFUL	PULPILY	QUEUERS	RESTUDY	RUBIDIC
PRIAPIC	PULQUES	QUICKLY	RETAXED	RUBIOUS
PRIAPUS	PULTUNS	QUIDAMS	RETTERY	RUDDILY
PRICKLY	PULVINI	QUIGHTS	REUNIFY	RUDESBY
PRIMACY	PULWARS	QUILLED	REVELRY	RUINOUS
PRIMARY	PUMICED	QUINARY	REVIVED	RUMAKIS
PRIMMED	PUNCTUM	QUINZES	REWAXED	RUMMILY
PRIMPED	PUNDITS	QUIPPUS	REWRAPT	RUMMISH
PRINCOX	PUNGENT	QUIRKED	RHACHIS	RUNANGA
PRIVACY	PUNGLED	QUITTED	RHAPHAE	RUNNERS
PRIVIER	PUNKAHS	QUIVERS	RHAPHES	RURALLY
PRIVILY	PUNKEYS	QUIVERY	RHATANY	RUSSIAS
PRIVITY	PUPFISH	QUIZZED	RHEBOKS	RUSSIFY
PRIZING	PUPPETS	QUODDED	RHEUMED	RYMMING
PROBALL	PUPPIED	QUOHOGS	RHOMBOS	RYOKANS
PROBING	PUPPIES	QUOIFED	RHONCHI	SACRUMS
PROBITY	PURANIC	QUOINED	RHYMERS	SADDHUS
PRODDED	PURVEYS	QUOISTS	RHYMING	SADDISH
PROFACE	PUSHFUL	QUOITED	RHYTONS	SAGATHY
PROGGED	PUSHUPS	QUOKKAS	RIBIERS	SAGRADA
PROMPTS	PUTOFFS	QUONDAM	RICRACS	SALLADS
PRONKED	PUTREFY	QUONKED	RIDGILS	SALOONS
PROOFED	PUTZING	QUOPPED	RIFFLED	SALOOPS
PROPMAN	PUZZLED	QUORUMS	RIFLERY	SALTBOX
PROPMEN	PYAEMIC	QUOTUMS	RIFLIPS	SALUKIS
PROPPED	PYCNONS	QUYTING	RIKISHI	SALVORS
PROPRIA	PYGARGS	QWERTYS	RILIEVO	SAMAANS
PROPYLS	PYGMIES	RADULAR	RINDIER	SAMEKHS
PROSIFY	PYJAMAS	RAFFLED	RIPIENI	SAMOSAS
PROSODY	PYKNICS	RAGGERY	RISIBLY	SAMPANS
PROUDLY	PYRENES	RALPHED	RITZIER	SANDBOX
PROXIMO	PYREXES	RAMMISH	RITZILY	SANJAKS
PRUDERY	PYREXIC	RANDANS	RIVALRY	SANSARS
PRUSIKS	PYRITIC	RANZELS	RIVLINS	SAPPANS
PRUSSIC	PYROPUS	RAPPINI	RIZARDS	SARSARS
PRUTOTH	PYROSES	RAUCLER	RIZZORS	SASHAYS
PSOCIDS	PYRUVIC	RAZORED	ROBBING	SASSABY
PSYCHED	PYURIAS	RAZURES	ROBOTRY	SATARAS
PSYCHES	PYXIDES	RAZZIAS	RODEOED	SATIETY
PSYCHOS	PYXIDIA	RAZZING	ROILIER	SATISFY

SAUCILY	SEALWAX	SHOWBOX	SKRYING	SORDORS
SAVVEYS	SEBIFIC	SHRILLS	SKUGGED	SORGHOS
SAVVILY	SEBUNDY	SHRILLY	SKULKED	SOROSIS
SAXAULS	SEEABLE	SHRIMPY	SKULLED	SORRELS
SAYYIDS	SEEDBOX	SHRINKS	SKYCLAD	SORRILY
SCANDIC	SEESAWS	SHROFFS	SKYFING	SORROWS
SCARPAS	SEIZORS	SHROOMS	SKYLIKE	SOUKING
SCARPHS	SEKOSES	SHROUDY	SKYRING	SOULFUL
SCAZONS	SELSYNS	SHROVED	SKYTING	SOUNDLY
SCENERY	SENSORY	SHROVES	SKYWAYS	SOURISH
SCHELMS	SEPHENS	SHTCHIS	SLANTLY	SOVIETS
SCHISTS	SEQUELS	SHTICKY	SLEDDED	SOVRANS
SCHIZOS	SETOFFS	SHUNNED	SLEDGED	SOWARRY
SCHIZZY	SEVENTY	SHUSHED	SLEEKLY	SOWFFED
SCHLOSS	SEXISMS	SHYNESS	SLOUCHY	SOWSSED
SCHLUBS	SEXISTS	SIALOID	SLOUGHS	SOWSSES
SCHMICK	SEXLESS	SICCING	SLOUGHY	SOYUZES
SCHNELL	SEXTONS	SICCITY	SLUDGED	SOZZLED
SCHNOZZ	SFERICS	SICKISH	SLUDGES	SPAMMED
SCHOUTS	SHADOWS	SIDDHAS	SLUMMED	SPANDEX
SCHRODS	SHADUFS	SIDDHIS	SLYNESS	SPAULDS
SCHTOOM	SHALOMS	SIFAKAS	SMACKED	SPAVINS
SCHUYTS	SHAMOYS	SIGNIFY	SMEEKED	SPAYADS
SCIRRHI	SHAPELY	SILICIC	SMEGMAS	SPAZZED
SCLAFFS	SHARPLY	SILLILY	SMELLED	SPAZZES
SCLAVES	SHASHED	SILVICS	SMERKED	SPECCED
SCLIFFS	SHASHES	SIMIOUS	SMICKLY	SPECIFY
SCOFFED	SHAUGHS	SINUOUS	SMIGHTS	SPEEDED
SCOGGED	SHEAFED	SIRDARS	SMOCKED	SPHENES
SCORIFY	SHEATHY	SIRKARS	SMOKERS	SPIKERY
SCOUTHS	SHEEVES	SISKINS	SMUDGED	SPINDLY
SCOWPED	SHEGETZ	SISSOOS	SMUSHED	SPLIFFS
SCOWTHS	SHEKELS	SIXFOLD	SMUTCHY	SPLODGY
SCOZZAS	SHELLED	SIXTHLY	SMUTTED	SPOOKED
SCRAMBS	SHEQELS	SIXTIES	SNAFUED	SPRAWLS
SCRANNY	SHEUGHS	SKANKED	SNAGGED	SPRAWLY
SCRAPPY	SHINDYS	SKENNED	SNEBBED	SPRAYED
SCRAWLS	SHINILY	SKEPPED	SNEBBES	SPRAYEY
SCRAWLY	SHINJUS	SKEPSIS	SNEEZED	SPRIGGY
SCRAWMS	SHIPPED	SKERRED	SNELLED	SPRUIKS
SCRAWNY	SHISHAS	SKETCHY	SNIBBED	SPUDDED
SCRAWPS	SHIURIM	SKEWERS	SNIPPED	SPUMOUS
SCRIMPS	SHIVAHS	SKEWEST	SNODDIT	SPUNGES
SCRITCH	SHIVERY	SKEWING	SNOTTED	SPUNKED
SCROGGY	SHIVOOS	SKIBOBS	SNOWKED	SQUABBY
SCRUBBY	SHIVVED	SKIDDED	SNUBBED	SQUADDY
SCRUFFY	SHODDEN	SKIEYER	SOAPBOX	SQUALLY
SCRUMMY	SHOFARS	SKINKED	SOFFITS	SQUARKS
SCRUMPS	SHOGGLY	SKIPPED	SOFTISH	SQUASHY
SCRUMPY	SHOLOMS	SKIVERS	SOGGILY	SQUATLY
SCRUZED	SHOOFLY	SKIVIER	SOKAIYA	SQUATTY
SCRUZES	SHOOGLY	SKLATED	SOKEMAN	SQUAWKS
SCRYERS	SHOORAS	SKOALED	SOKEMEN	SQUAWKY
SCRYNES	SHOPPED	SKOFFED	SOLANOS	SQUEAKS
SCUGGED	SHORERS	SKOLLED	SOMEHOW	SQUEAKY
SCUNGES	SHOTTED	SKOOKUM	SOMEWHY	SQUEALS
SCUZZES	SHOUGHS	SKRIKED	SONOVOX	SQUEEZY
SCYPHUS	SHOVELS	SKRIMPS	SOOGEED	SQUIDGY
SCYTHED	SHOVERS	SKRUMPS	SOOGEES	SQUIFFY
SDAYNED	SHOWBIZ	SKRYERS	SOOJEYS	SQUINNY

SQUINTY	SWABBED	TALUKAS	THROATY	TOWZING
SQUIRMS	SWACKED	TAMBACS	THRUMMY	TOXICAL
SQUIRMY	SWAGGED	TAMBAKS	THRUTCH	TOXOIDS
SQUIRRS	SWAMIES	TATTERY	THUDDED	TOYTOWN
SQUISHY	SWAMPED	TATTOOS	THUGGOS	TRAIKIT
STACHYS	SWANKED	TATTOWS	THUMBED	TRAMMED
STAGILY	SWAPPED	TAUIWIS	THUMPED	TREEWAX
STALKED	SWARVED	TAUPATA	THUNKED	TREKKED
STALLED	SWARVES	TAWHIRI	THURIFY	TREMBLY
STANZAS	SWAYFUL	TAWNILY	THWACKS	TREVETS
STARKLY	SWERFED	TAXABLY	THYRSUS	TRICKSY
STATUAS	SWEVENS	TAXIMAN	TIDBITS	TRIFFER
STELLED	SWEYING	TAXIMEN	TIGHTLY	TRIFFIC
STEMMED	SWIFTED	TAXINGS	TIKIING	TRIFOLD
STICKIT	SWIFTLY	TAXITIC	TIMBRAL	TRIGAMY
STIFLED	SWINERY	TAXLESS	TIMOTHY	TRIJETS
STOBBED	SWINKED	TAXPAID	TINAJAS	TRIPLEX
STOGEYS	SWISSES	TAXWISE	TINNILY	TROTYLS
STOOKED	SWITCHY	TEAPOYS	TIPTOED	TROWTHS
STOSSES	SWITHLY	TECTRIX	TIPTOPS	TRUDGED
STOUTLY	SWIVETS	TECTUMS	TIRITIS	TRYMATA
STOVIES	SWOBBED	TEEMFUL	TIRRITS	TRYSTED
STOWNDS	SWOOPED	TEENTSY	TISSUEY	TSKTSKS
STRIFTS	SWOPPED	TEEPEES	TITTLED	TUBBISH
STRONDS	SWOTTED	TELEFAX	TITTUPS	TUBFISH
STROPPY	SWOUNES	TELEXED	TITULUS	TUBIFEX
STUMBLY	SWOWNDS	TELEXES	TOAZING	TUBULAR
STUPEFY	SWOWNES	TEMPTED	TOCCATE	TUCHUNS
STYPSIS	SYBOTIC	TENDENZ	TODDLED	TUCKETS
SUASIVE	SYCOSES	TENTHLY	TOETOES	TUFFETS
SUASORY	SYCOSIS	TENUITY	TOFFEES	TUKTOOS
SUAVEST	SYLVANS	TENZONS	TOFFISH	TULWARS
SUAVITY	SYLVIAS	TEPIDLY	TOGGERY	TUMULTS
SUBDEBS	SYNAXIS	TESTIFY	TOGGLED	TUNEUPS
SUBDEWS	SYNCHED	TEUGHER	TOILFUL	TURBARY
SUBFEUS	SYNCOMS	TEUGHLY	TOLARJI	TURDOID
SUBGUMS	SYNDETS	THANKED	TOLLMAN	TURFMAN
SUBMISS	SYNDICS	THANKEE	TOLZEYS	TURNERY
SUBSIDY	SYNGAMY	THATCHT	TOMBING	TURTLED
SUBWAYS	SYNTANS	THEEKED	TOMBOCS	TUSSURS
SUBZERO	SYNTENY	THEGNLY	TOMBOYS	TUTOYED
SUCCORY	SYNTONY	THELVES	TOMCODS	TUYERES
SUCCUBI	SYPHERS	THEMATA	TOOLBOX	TWADDLY
SUDARIA	SYSTEMS	THEMING	TOOTHED	TWEAKED
SUDATES	TABULAR	THEREBY	TOOTSED	TWEEZED
SUDDENS	TACKETY	THETHER	TOPFULL	TWIDDLY
SUKKAHS	TACKIFY	THICKLY	TOPMOST	TWIFOLD
SUKKOTH	TACKILY	THIEVED	TOQUETS	TWIGGED
SULFURS	TACKLED	THIGGIT	TORPEFY	TWIGGEN
SULKILY	TAFFETY	THIGHED	TORRIFY	TWIGHTS
SULPHAS	TAGGEES	THINNED	TORTRIX	TWILLED
SUMMARY	TAGMATA	THIRDLY	TOTALLY	TWINGED
SUNDEWS	TAGUANS	THIRSTY	TOTEMIC	TWINKLY
SUNDOGS	TAIAHAS	THIVELS	TOTTERY	TWISTED
SUNNAHS	TAKKIES	THRALLS	TOUGHED	TWITCHY
SUNNILY	TALCKED	THRETTY	TOUGHLY	TWITTED
SUNRAYS	TALKBOX	THRIFTS	TOUZLED	TWYFOLD
SURIMIS	TALLATS	THRIFTY	TOWHEES	TYCOONS
SURPASS	TALLOLS	THRISTY	TOWKAYS	TYMPANY
SURVEYS	TALLOTS	THRIVED	TOWNEES	TYPHOUS

TYPINGS	UNGYVES	UNWHIPT	UXORIAL	VICTRIX
TYPTOED	UNHANDY	UNWILLS	VACANCY	VIDENDA
TYRANNY	UNHAPPY	UNWIPED	VACKING	VIDIMUS
TYTHING	UNHARDY	UNWITCH	VACUITY	VIDUITY
TZETZES	UNHASTY	UNWITTY	VACUOUS	VIDUOUS
TZIGANY	UNHEEDY	UNWIVES	VAGALLY	VIEWIER
TZIMMES	UNHELMS	UNWOUND	VAGGING	VILLOUS
TZITZIS	UNHIVED	UNWOVEN	VAGITUS	VIMINAL
UFOLOGY	UNHIVES	UNWRAPS	VAGROMS	VIRALLY
ULIKONS	UNHUMAN	UNWRUNG	VAGUELY	VISAGES
UMBONIC	UNHUSKS	UNYOKED	VAGUING	VISCINS
UMFAZIS	UNIBODY	UNYOUNG	VALGOID	VISCOUS
UMWELTS	UNICITY	UNZONED	VALGOUS	VISCUMS
UMWHILE	UNIQUER	UPBEATS	VALIDLY	VISIONS
UNAPTLY	UNJADED	UPBLOWN	VALKYRS	VISNOMY
UNBEGUN	UNKEMPT	UPBLOWS	VALLARY	VISUALS
UNBENDS	UNKNOTS	UPBOILS	VALLUMS	VITALLY
UNBLOWN	UNLINKS	UPBOUND	VALVATE	VITEXES
UNBOOTS	UNLUCKY	UPBRAYS	VALVING	VITRAUX
UNBOUND	UNMACHO	UPBUILT	VAMPISH	VITRIFY
UNBOXED	UNMANLY	UPCOURT	VANNERS	VITTLED
UNBOXES	UNMEWED	UPCURLS	VANWARD	VITTLES
UNBULKY	UNMIXED	UPDIVED	VAPIDLY	VIVACES
UNCANNY	UNMIXES	UPDIVES	VAPOURY	VIVAING
UNCINUS	UNMOVED	UPDRAWS	VAROOMS	VIVENCY
UNCIVIL	UNNEATH	UPENDED	VARROAS	VIVIDLY
UNCLEWS	UNNOISY	UPFLOWS	VASTITY	VIVIFIC
UNCOCKS	UNOFTEN	UPFLUNG	VATFULS	VIZARDS
UNCOMIC	UNPACKS	UPFOLDS	VATTING	VIZIERS
UNCOPED	UNPAVED	UPFRONT	VAUDOOS	VIZORED
UNCOWLS	UNPINKT	UPGANGS	VAUDOUX	VIZSLAS
UNCRAZY	UNPLUGS	UPGAZES	VAUNCES	VIZYING
UNCUFFS	UNPROPS	UPHAUDS	VAWARDS	VIZZIED
UNCURBS	UNROUGH	UPHOLDS	VAWNTIE	VIZZIES
UNCURLS	UNROYAL	UPKEEPS	VAWTING	VOCABLY
UNDEAFS	UNSEWED	UPLOOKS	VEEJAYS	VOGUISH
UNDEIFY	UNSEXED	UPPROPS	VEEPEES	VOLOSTS
UNDRUNK	UNSHARP	UPROLLS	VEGGIES	VOLUBIL
UNDULAR	UNSHORN	UPSWEPT	VEGGING	VOLUBLE
UNDYING	UNSHOWN	UPSWUNG	VELCROS	VOLUBLY
UNFAKED	UNSHOWY	UPTAKEN	VELLUMS	VOLUMED
UNFANCY	UNSLUNG	UPTALKS	VELVETS	VOLVATE
UNFAZED	UNSNAGS	UPTHREW	VELVETY	VOLVULI
UNFEUED	UNSONCY	UPTILTS	VENEFIC	VOMICAE
UNFITLY	UNSONSY	UPWAFTS	VENEWES	VOODOOS
UNFIXED	UNSOULS	UPWARDS	VENOMED	VORRING
UNFLUSH	UNSTUFT	UPWINDS	VERBIFY	VOTIVES
UNFOLDS	UNSUNNY	UPWOUND	VERMILY	VOWELLY
UNFOUND	UNSWEET	UPWRAPS	VERMINY	VOWLESS
UNFUMED	UNSWEPT	URACHUS	VERSIFY	VOYAGED
UNFUNNY	UNTAXES	URANYLS	VERVENS	VUGGIER
UNFURLS	UNTENTY	URINARY	VESPIDS	VUGHIER
UNFUSED	UNTOMBS	URINOUS	VESPINE	VULCANS
UNFUSSY	UNTRULY	URNFULS	VETTERS	VULGARS
UNGLUED	UNTURFS	USEFULS	VEXEDLY	VULPINE
UNGLUES	UNUSUAL	USUALLY	VEXINGS	VULVATE
UNGODLY	UNVEXED	UTMOSTS	VIBICES	VUMMING
UNGROWN	UNWAGED	UVEITIC	VIBIEST	VUTTIER
UNGULED	UNWAXED	UVEITIS	VIBISTS	VYINGLY
UNGYVED		UVULARS	VICIOUS	WABAINS

WABBLED	WEALTHY	WICKEDS	WOUBITS	YIKKERS
WABOOMS	WEAZENS	WICKIES	WOWFEST	YIPPIES
WACKILY	WEBBIER	WIDDIES	WOWSERS	YIRKING
WADDIED	WEBCAMS	WIDGIES	WRACKED	YIRRING
WADMELS	WEBFEET	WIFTIER	WRAWLED	YOBBERY
WAFERED	WEBFOOT	WIGHTLY	WRAXLED	YOBBOES
WAFFIES	WEBLESS	WIGWAGS	WRAXLES	YOJANAS
WAFFLED	WEBLISH	WIGWAMS	WREATHY	YOKKING
WAGGISH	WEBLOGS	WILDISH	WRIGGLY	YONNIES
WAGGLED	WEEDERY	WILEFUL	WRIGHTS	YORKERS
WAGGONS	WEEPILY	WILLEYS	WRINKLY	YORKIES
WAGSOME	WEEWEED	WILLOWS	WRIZLED	YORKING
WAIATAS	WEEWEES	WILLOWY	WRONGLY	YOUNGLY
WAIFING	WEIGHTS	WILTJAS	WRYNESS	YOUTHLY
WAIFISH	WEIGHTY	WIMBLED	WRYTHEN	YOWLEYS
WAILFUL	WEIRDLY	WIMPIER	WUDDING	YSHENDS
WAIRING	WELCHED	WIMPISH	WUNNERS	YSLAKED
WAIRUAS	WETTEST	WINCEYS	WURLEYS	YUCKERS
WAIVING	WEYWARD	WINCHED	WURLIES	YUCKIER
WAKAMES	WHALERS	WINDILY	WURZELS	YUCKING
WAKANES	WHALERY	WINDOWY	WUTHERS	YUKATAS
WAKEMAN	WHAMMED	WINDUPS	WUZZLED	YUKKIER
WAKEMEN	WHAMMOS	WINNOWS	WUZZLES	YUKKING
WAKIKIS	WHANAUS	WIPPENS	WYSIWYG	YUMMIER
WALKUPS	WHANGED	WIREMEN	WYVERNS	YUMPIES
WALLABY	WHAPPED	WISHFUL	XANTHIC	YUMPING
WALLOPS	WHARFED	WISPILY	XERARCH	YUPPIES
WALNUTS	WHATTEN	WISPISH	XEROMAS	YUPPIFY
WALTZED	WHEECHS	WISTFUL	XEROXED	ZABETAS
WAMBLED	WHELKED	WITTILY	XEROXES	ZADDICK
WAMPEES	WHENWES	WITTOLS	XYLENES	ZAFFARS
WAMPUMS	WHEREBY	WIZARDS	XYLOMAS	ZAFFERS
WANGUNS	WHETTED	WIZENED	XYLONIC	ZAFFIRS
WANIONS	WHEUGHS	WIZIERS	XYLOSES	ZAFFRES
WANNEST	WHEWING	WIZZENS	YABBIED	ZAGGING
WANNISH	WHEYIER	WOADWAX	YABBIES	ZAIKAIS
WANZING	WHEYISH	WOBBLED	YACHTED	ZAMANGS
WAPITIS	WHIDAHS	WOENESS	YACKING	ZAMPONE
WAPPEND	WHIDDED	WOESOME	YAFFLES	ZAMPONI
WARAGIS	WHIGGED	WOGGISH	YAMMERS	ZANANAS
WAREHOU	WHIMMED	WOGGLES	YANKERS	ZANDERS
WARRAYS	WHINGED	WOLVISH	YANKING	ZANYING
WARREYS	WHIPPED	WOMBATS	YANQUIS	ZANYISH
WARSAWS	WHISHTS	WOMMITS	YAPOCKS	ZAPPING
WARWOLF	WHISKED	WONTONS	YAPPERS	ZARNECS
WARWORN	WHITISH	WOODWAX	YAQONAS	ZEALFUL
WASABIS	WHIZZED	WOOLMEN	YARKING	ZEBECKS
WASHUPS	WHOMPED	WOOPSED	YARPHAS	ZEBRAIC
WAUCHTS	WHOOPED	WOOZIER	YARROWS	ZEBRASS
WAUGHTS	WHOOSIS	WOOZILY	YAUPONS	ZEDOARY
WAULKED	WHOOTED	WORKBOX	YAUTIAS	ZEMSTVA
WAURING	WHOPPED	WORKMEN	YEALMED	ZENANAS
WAVIEST	WHORISH	WORKSHY	YEGGMAN	ZENDIKS
WAXABLE	WHORLED	WORKUPS	YEGGMEN	ZEPHYRS
WAXEYES	WHUMPED	WORLDED	YELLERS	ZEPPOLI
WAXIEST	WHUPPED	WORLDLY	YETTIES	ZESTFUL
WAXLIKE	WHYDAHS	WORMERY	YEUKING	ZEUGMAS
WAYGONE	WHYEVER	WORMFLY	YIBBLES	ZIFFIUS
WAYLAID	WIBBLED	WOTTEST	YIDAKIS	ZIGGING
WAYWARD	WICCANS	WOTTETH	YIELDED	ZIGZAGS

ZILCHES	ZIPPING	ZONALLY	ZOONOMY	ZYGOMAS
ZILLAHS	ZIRCONS	ZONKING	ZOOPERY	ZYGOSIS
ZIMMERS	ZIZZLED	ZONULAE	ZOOTAXY	ZYGOTES
ZINCKED	ZIZZLES	ZONULAR	ZOOTOMY	ZYGOTIC
ZINCOUS	ZLOTYCH	ZONURES	ZOOZOOS	ZYMASES
ZINGANO	ZOARIAL	ZOOECIA	ZOSTERS	ZYMOMES
ZINGARA	ZOARIUM	ZOOGAMY	ZOUAVES	ZYMURGY
ZINGELS	ZOCALOS	ZOOGENY	ZOYSIAS	ZYTHUMS
ZINNIAS	ZODIACS	ZOOGONY	ZUFFOLI	
ZIPLOCK	ZOEFORM	ZOOLOGY	ZUFFOLO	
ZIPPIER	ZOMBIFY	ZOOMING	ZYDECOS	

Special eights

If you are landed with a 'non-word' rack, you needn't abandon all hope of playing a bonus word. Some racks that don't form seven-letter words will form eight-letter words with letters on the board. This is where 'special eights' come in handy. Special eights are eight-letter words that have no other eight-letter anagrams, and contain no seven-letter words. These are great words to know, as each of them is a solution to eight different problem racks. The complete list of special eights is presented below, in alphabetical order.

AARDVARK	ACIDHEAD	AEQUORIN	AIRTIGHT	AMANDINE
AARDWOLF	ACIDURIA	AEROBIUM	AIRWOMAN	AMARELLE
ABACUSES	ACOELOUS	AEROFOIL	AISLEWAY	AMARETTO
ABAMPERE	ACQUIGHT	AEROGRAM	AKARYOTE	AMBIENCE
ABAPICAL	ACQUIRAL	AEROLOGY	AKINESIA	AMBITION
ABATISES	ACTIVIST	AEROTONE	ALBURNUM	AMBULANT
ABBATIAL	ACTIVITY	AFFERENT	ALCOLOCK	AMBUSHES
ABBESSES	ACTUALLY	AFFINELY	ALDERFLY	AMMOCETE
ABDICATE	ACUITIES	AFFIXING	ALDOLASE	AMMONIFY
ABDUCTOR	ACULEATE	AFFLATED	ALEBENCH	AMMONIUM
ABESSIVE	ACUTANCE	AFFLUXES	ALEHOUSE	AMMONOID
ABEYANCE	ADAMANCE	AFFORDED	ALGAROBA	AMPHIBIA
ABEYANCY	ADAMANCY	AFFRAYER	ALGICIDE	AMPHIOXI
ABHORRER	ADDITION	AFFRIGHT	ALGOLOGY	AMPHIPOD
ABJECTLY	ADDITIVE	AFFUSION	ALGUAZIL	AMYLOGEN
ABJURING	ADDITORY	AFTEREYE	ALKALIZE	ANABAENA
ABNEGATE	ADDOOMED	AFTERTAX	ALKANNIN	ANABASES
ABNORMAL	ADDUCTOR	AGALLOCH	ALKOXIDE	ANABATIC
ABOIDEAU	ADEQUACY	AGALWOOD	ALKYLATE	ANACONDA
ABOITEAU	ADIPOSIS	AGGRIEVE	ALLELISM	ANAEROBE
ABOMASUM	ADJACENT	AGIOTAGE	ALLELUIA	ANAGLYPH
ABOMASUS	ADJUSTOR	AGROLOGY	ALLEYWAY	ANAGOGIC
ABSCISIN	ADJUTANT	AGRONOMY	ALLOGAMY	ANALEMMA
ABSENTEE	ADJUVANT	AGUACATE	ALLOPATH	ANALOGON
ABSTRACT	ADMITTED	AGUELIKE	ALLOTTEE	ANANASES
ABUNDANT	ADULARIA	AGUEWEED	ALLOZYME	ANARCHAL
ACADEMIA	ADULATOR	AGUIZING	ALLUSION	ANATHEMA
ACARPOUS	ADUNCITY	AHEMERAL	ALLUVION	ANATOXIN
ACAULOSE	ADUNCOUS	AIMFULLY	ALLUVIUM	ANATROPY
ACAULOUS	ADVECTED	AIRBRICK	ALMIGHTY	ANNEALED
ACCEPTED	ADVOCAAT	AIRBRUSH	ALOPECIA	ANNEXING
ACCEPTEE	ADVOCACY	AIRBURST	ALPHOSIS	ANNEXION
ACCORAGE	AECIDIUM	AIRCRAFT	ALTHOUGH	ANNOUNCE
ACCORDED	AEDICULE	AIRGRAPH	ALUMINIC	ANNOYING
ACCOYING	AEGIRITE	AIRPOWER	ALVEOLUS	ANNUALLY
ACCURACY	AEGLOGUE	AIRPROOF	AMADAVAT	ANNULOSE

ANOREXIA	ARPEGGIO	AVIATION	BACLOFEN	BASIFIED
ANOREXIC	ARRANTLY	AVIATRIX	BADASSED	BASIFIES
ANOVULAR	ARRAUGHT	AVICULAR	BADASSES	BASILISK
ANOXEMIA	ARRHIZAL	AVIFAUNA	BAGHOUSE	BASQUINE
ANTETYPE	ARRIVING	AVOIDANT	BAGUETTE	BASSNESS
ANTHELIX	ARSONOUS	AVOISION	BAILABLE	BASSWOOD
ANTILOCK	ARTIFACT	AVOWABLE	BAILBOND	BATHMISM
ANTIPYIC	ARTIFICE	AVOWABLY	BAKEMEAT	BATHOSES
ANTITANK	ARYTHMIA	AVOWEDLY	BAKESHOP	BATHROBE
ANTITHET	ASCIDIUM	AWFULLER	BALLADIC	BATHROOM
ANTIWEED	ASCOCARP	AWHAPING	BALLADRY	BATTALIA
ANYWHERE	ASPHYXIA	AXIALITY	BALLCLAY	BAUHINIA
AORTITIS	ASPIDIUM	AXIOLOGY	BALLCOCK	BAUXITIC
APAGOGIC	ASSASSIN	AXOLEMMA	BALLGAME	BAYBERRY
APATHIES	ASSESSED	AXONEMAL	BALLHAWK	BAZAZZES
APERITIF	ASSESSES	AXOPLASM	BALLOCKS	BEACHBOY
APHORIZE	ASTOMOUS	AYURVEDA	BALLONNE	BEACHIER
APHTHOUS	ATAMASCO	AZOTURIA	BALLPARK	BEACONED
APIARIAN	ATARAXIA	BABBLING	BALLROOM	BEADWORK
APICALLY	ATARAXIC	BABIRUSA	BALLYARD	BEAKLIKE
APIMANIA	ATENOLOL	BABUSHKA	BALLYHOO	BEAMLIKE
APOAPSIS	ATHANASY	BABYDOLL	BALLYRAG	BEANLIKE
APOCOPIC	ATHETOID	BABYFOOD	BANAUSIC	BEARABLE
APOGAMIC	ATMOLOGY	BABYHOOD	BANDITTI	BEARABLY
APOGRAPH	ATMOLYZE	BACCHANT	BANDYMAN	BEARBINE
APOLOGAL	ATTACKED	BACILLUS	BANDYMEN	BEAUCOUP
APOLOGIA	ATTASKED	BACKACHE	BANGALAY	BEBOPPED
APOLOGUE	ATTENTAT	BACKBAND	BANGALOW	BEBOPPER
APOMIXES	ATTICIST	BACKBEAT	BANJAXED	BECAPPED
APOMIXIS	ATTICIZE	BACKBEND	BANJAXES	BECARPET
APOPHONY	AUDACITY	BACKBOND	BANKABLE	BECHAMEL
APOSITIA	AUDITION	BACKBONE	BANKBOOK	BECHANCE
APOSTACY	AUDITIVE	BACKCAST	BANKCARD	BECKONED
APOTHECE	AUGURIES	BACKCHAT	BANKNOTE	BECKONER
APPEALED	AUGUSTLY	BACKCOMB	BANKROLL	BECLOTHE
APPELLEE	AURALITY	BACKDATE	BANKRUPT	BECUDGEL
APPENDED	AURICULA	BACKDOWN	BANNABLE	BEDAUBED
APPENDIX	AURIFIED	BACKFALL	BANNERET	BEDEAFEN
APPETENT	AUTACOID	BACKFILE	BANOFFEE	BEDECKED
APPLIQUE	AUTOBAHN	BACKFILL	BAPTISIA	BEDIMMED
APPROVAL	AUTOCOID	BACKFIRE	BARATHEA	BEDOTTED
APRONFUL	AUTODYNE	BACKFLIP	BARBARIC	BEDSOCKS
AQUACADE	AUTOGAMY	BACKFLOW	BARBEQUE	BEDUCKED
AQUAFARM	AUTOGENY	BACKHAND	BARBERRY	BEDUMBED
AQUALUNG	AUTOGIRO	BACKHAUL	BARBITAL	BEEBREAD
AQUANAUT	AUTOHARP	BACKLAND	BARDSHIP	BEEFCAKE
AQUARIST	AUTOLOGY	BACKLASH	BAREBONE	BEEFIEST
AQUARIUM	AUTOLYZE	BACKLESS	BAREHAND	BEEFWOOD
AQUASHOW	AUTOTOMY	BACKLOAD	BAREHEAD	BEETROOT
AQUATONE	AUTOTUNE	BACKPACK	BAROGRAM	BEFALLEN
AQUEDUCT	AUTOTYPE	BACKROOM	BARONIAL	BEFINNED
ARAPAIMA	AUTOTYPY	BACKSTAB	BARRATER	BEFITTED
ARBITRAL	AUTUMNAL	BACKSTAY	BARRATOR	BEFLOWER
ARCOLOGY	AUTUNITE	BACKSTOP	BARRATRY	BEFOAMED
AREOLOGY	AUXILIAR	BACKWARD	BARRENER	BEFOGGED
ARGUABLY	AVADAVAT	BACKWOOD	BARRETRY	BEFOOLED
ARILLARY	AVIANISE	BACKWORD	BASEBAND	BEFOULER
ARILLOID	AVIANIZE	BACKWORK	BASENESS	BEGAZING
ARMORIAL	AVIARIES	BACKWRAP	BASICITY	BEGEMMED
ARMOZEEN	AVIARIST	BACKYARD	BASIDIUM	BEGETTER

BEGNAWED	BEVVYING	BIRROTCH	BOATLOAD	BOTHYMEN
BEGRUDGE	BEWAILED	BISCACHA	BOATNECK	BOTRYOID
BEGULFED	BEWIGGED	BISCOTTO	BOATTAIL	BOTTOMER
BEGUNKED	BEZAZZES	BISEXUAL	BOATYARD	BOTTOMRY
BEHAPPEN	BEZZLING	BISHOPED	BOBBINET	BOUDERIE
BEHAVIOR	BIANNUAL	BISTOURY	BOBBLIER	BOUFFANT
BEHEADAL	BIBATION	BITCHERY	BOBBYSOX	BOUGHPOT
BEHEADED	BICAUDAL	BITESIZE	BOBFLOAT	BOUNCILY
BEHEADER	BICKERER	BITEWING	BOBOLINK	BOUNDARY
BEHEMOTH	BICONVEX	BITINGLY	BOBWHEEL	BOUNTREE
BEHOLDEN	BICUSPID	BITTERED	BOCACCIO	BOUSOUKI
BEHOLDER	BICYCLIC	BITTERER	BODYSURF	BOUTONNE
BEHOVELY	BIDDABLY	BIUNIQUE	BODYWORK	BOUZOUKI
BEHOVING	BIELDIER	BIVVYING	BOEHMITE	BOVINELY
BEJEEZUS	BIENNALE	BIZAZZES	BOERTJIE	BOVINITY
BEJESUIT	BIENNIUM	BIZCACHA	BOLLOXED	BOWFRONT
BEJUMBLE	BIFACIAL	BLABBING	BOLLOXES	BOWWOWED
BEKISSES	BIFIDITY	BLACKBOY	BOLTLIKE	BOXBOARD
BELLOWER	BIFORKED	BLACKGUM	BOMBABLE	BOXTHORN
BELLPULL	BIGAMIES	BLACKLEG	BOMBAXES	BOYARISM
BELLPUSH	BIGEMINY	BLAMABLE	BOMBLOAD	BOYISHLY
BELLWORT	BIGHTING	BLAMABLY	BOMBYCID	BOZZETTI
BELLYFUL	BIGMOUTH	BLASTOFF	BOMBYXES	BOZZETTO
BELTLESS	BIGNONIA	BLATANCY	BONAMANO	BRACHIUM
BELTLINE	BIGSTICK	BLAZONED	BONEFISH	BRACIOLA
BEMADDED	BIHOURLY	BLAZONRY	BONELESS	BRAGGART
BEMBEXES	BIJUGATE	BLEBBING	BONEMEAL	BRAINPAN
BEMINGLE	BIJUGOUS	BLIMPISH	BONHOMIE	BRAKEAGE
BEMIXING	BIKINIED	BLINKARD	BONIBELL	BRAKEMAN
BEMOANER	BILABIAL	BLIPVERT	BONIFACE	BRAKEMEN
BEMOILED	BILLABLE	BLISSFUL	BONTEBOK	BRASSISH
BEMUDDED	BILLBOOK	BLITZING	BOOBHEAD	BRAZENED
BEMUFFLE	BILLFISH	BLIZZARD	BOOFHEAD	BRAZENRY
BEMUZZLE	BILLFOLD	BLOBBIER	BOOGYING	BRAZILIN
BENCHING	BILLHOOK	BLONCKET	BOOHOOED	BREADBOX
BENCHTOP	BILLIARD	BLONDISH	BOOKABLE	BREAKAGE
BENEFACT	BILLOWED	BLOODFIN	BOOKLORE	BREGMATE
BENJAMIN	BILLYBOY	BLOWBACK	BOOKMARK	BREKKIES
BENTWOOD	BILLYCAN	BLOWHARD	BOOKRACK	BRELOQUE
BENUMBED	BIMBASHI	BLOWHOLE	BOOKSHOP	BREVETCY
BENZIDIN	BIMBETTE	BLOWLAMP	BOOKWORK	BREWISES
BENZOATE	BIOASSAY	BLOWPIPE	BOOKWORM	BRIERIER
BENZYLIC	BIOGENIC	BLOWTUBE	BOONDOCK	BRIGUING
BEPEPPER	BIOGRAPH	BLUEBACK	BOORTREE	BRINDISI
BEPITIED	BIOLOGIC	BLUEBALL	BOOTABLE	BRINKMEN
BEPUFFED	BIOLYTIC	BLUEBEAT	BOOTHOSE	BRISKISH
BEQUEATH	BIOMETER	BLUEBELL	BOOTIKIN	BROCHURE
BERBERIN	BIONOMIC	BLUEBILL	BOOTJACK	BROCKRAM
BERGFALL	BIOPSIED	BLUEBUSH	BOOTLACE	BROKENLY
BERGMEHL	BIOPSIES	BLUEGILL	BOOTLICK	BROMIDIC
BERIMBAU	BIOSCOPE	BLUEHEAD	BORACHIO	BRONCHUS
BESEEMED	BIOSCOPY	BLUEJACK	BORDEAUX	BRONZIFY
BESEEMLY	BIOTITIC	BLUELINE	BORECOLE	BROODILY
BESIGHED	BIOTOXIN	BLUEWEED	BOREHOLE	BROWBAND
BESMOOTH	BIPAROUS	BLUEWOOD	BORLOTTI	BROWBEAT
BESOTTED	BIPHENYL	BLUNTISH	BORROWER	BROWNISH
BESTOWED	BIRACIAL	BLURBIST	BOSHVARK	BRUNIZEM
BETOILED	BIRDBATH	BLUSHFUL	BOSTHOON	BRYOLOGY
BETTERED	BIRDFARM	BOATHOOK	BOTCHING	BUBALINE
BEVELING	BIRDSHOT	BOATLIFT	BOTHYMAN	BUCCALLY

BUCKAROO	BUTYLENE	CANTICUM	CENSUSES	CHRONAXY
BUCKBEAN	BUXOMEST	CAPEWORK	CENTONEL	CHTHONIC
BUCKETED	BUZKASHI	CAPIASES	CENTUPLE	CHUBBIER
BUCKHORN	BUZZIEST	CAPOEIRA	CERCARIA	CHUBBILY
BUCKRAKE	BUZZWORD	CAPRICCI	CEREBRIC	CHUGALUG
BUCKSHOT	BYPASSED	CAPRIFIG	CEREMENT	CHUMMAGE
BUCKSKIN	BYSSUSES	CAPSICUM	CERVICUM	CHUMMILY
BUDGEREE	CABINING	CAPUCCIO	CESTUSES	CHUMSHIP
BUDGETER	CABLEWAY	CAPUCHIN	CETYWALL	CHUNKILY
BUFFABLE	CABOBBED	CAPYBARA	CHAFFRON	CHUNKING
BUFFERED	CABOCEER	CARACARA	CHAINMAN	CHUPATTY
BUFFETED	CABOCHON	CARAGANA	CHAINSAW	CHURCHED
BUFFETER	CABOTAGE	CARAPACE	CHALKPIT	CHURIDAR
BUGGERED	CABSTAND	CARBAMYL	CHAMBRAY	CHURLISH
BUHLWORK	CACAFOGO	CARBARYL	CHAMMIED	CHYMOSIN
BUILDING	CACHALOT	CARBOXYL	CHAMPART	CIABATTA
BULLDOZE	CACHEPOT	CARCERAL	CHANFRON	CIBORIUM
BULLDUST	CACHEXIA	CARDAMOM	CHAOLOGY	CICATRIX
BULLDYKE	CACHEXIC	CARDAMUM	CHAPBOOK	CICINNUS
BULLETED	CACHOLOT	CARDIOID	CHARANGA	CICUTINE
BULLETIN	CACHUCHA	CAREENER	CHARANGO	CIMBALOM
BULLFROG	CACODOXY	CAREERER	CHATCHKE	CIMINITE
BULLHEAD	CACOLOGY	CAREFREE	CHATROOM	CINNAMIC
BULLHORN	CACUMINA	CARETOOK	CHAYROOT	CINNAMON
BULLNECK	CADDYING	CARNALLY	CHEAPISH	CIOPPINO
BULLSHOT	CADUCEAN	CARPALIA	CHECHAKO	CIRCLING
BULLWEED	CADUCITY	CARRYALL	CHECKOFF	CITESSES
BULLWHIP	CADUCOUS	CARRYING	CHECKOUT	CITIFIES
BULLYBOY	CAFTANED	CARTROAD	CHEEKFUL	CITRININ
BULLYISM	CAILLACH	CARUCAGE	CHEEKILY	CITYFIES
BULNBULN	CAIMACAM	CARYATID	CHEERFUL	CITYWARD
BULWADDY	CAKEWALK	CASEFIES	CHEMURGY	CITYWIDE
BUMFLUFF	CALABAZA	CASHABLE	CHERRIER	CIVICISM
BUMMAREE	CALADIUM	CASHBOOK	CHERUBIC	CIVILISE
BUNCHILY	CALAMATA	CASTAWAY	CHEVEREL	CIVILIST
BUNCOMBE	CALCANEA	CATACOMB	CHEVERYE	CIVILITY
BUNDWALL	CALCEATE	CATAMITE	CHEVYING	CIVILIZE
BUNFIGHT	CALCIFIC	CATARACT	CHIBBING	CLACKBOX
BUNGHOLE	CALCITIC	CATATONY	CHICHIER	CLADDAGH
BUNGWALL	CALCULUS	CATCHCRY	CHIGETAI	CLAFOUTI
BUNKMATE	CALEFIED	CATCHFLY	CHILDISH	CLAMANCY
BUNODONT	CALFLESS	CATEGORY	CHILLADA	CLAMMILY
BUOYANCE	CALFLICK	CATFIGHT	CHILLILY	CLAMWORM
BUOYANCY	CALISAYA	CATHODAL	CHILOPOD	CLANGBOX
BUPLEVER	CALLBACK	CAUSEWAY	CHIMERIC	CLANNISH
BURDIZZO	CALLIOPE	CAUSEYED	CHINAMAN	CLANSMAN
BURGUNDY	CALVARIA	CAUTIOUS	CHIPMUCK	CLASSMAN
BURLEYED	CAMBOGIA	CAVASSES	CHIPMUNK	CLAWBACK
BURROWER	CAMISADO	CAVATINA	CHIRAGRA	CLEARCUT
BUSHBABY	CAMOMILE	CAVEFISH	CHITCHAT	CLEAVAGE
BUSHBUCK	CAMPAGNE	CAVELIKE	CHOCKFUL	CLECKING
BUSHWALK	CAMSHAFT	CAVITARY	CHOICELY	CLEMENCY
BUSULFAN	CAMSHOCH	CELERIAC	CHOIRBOY	CLENCHED
BUSYBODY	CANALIZE	CELLMATE	CHOKIDAR	CLENCHER
BUSYNESS	CANEWARE	CELLULAR	CHOPPILY	CLERKDOM
BUTSUDAN	CANNABIC	CEMENTED	CHOREMEN	CLEVERLY
BUTTONED	CANNABIN	CEMENTER	CHORISIS	CLIENTAL
BUTTONER	CANNIBAL	CEMENTUM	CHOWCHOW	CLIFFIER
BUTTYMAN	CANNONED	CEMETERY	CHOWTIME	CLIMATAL
BUTYLATE	CANTHOOK	CENOZOIC	CHROMENE	CLIMATIC

CLINCHER	COEQUATE	CONJUNCT	COTQUEAN	CULTURAL
CLINGING	COEVOLVE	CONJUNTO	COTTONED	CULTUSES
CLINIQUE	COEXTEND	CONJUROR	COUMAROU	CUMBUNGI
CLIQUIER	COGENTLY	CONODONT	COUSINRY	CUPBOARD
CLIQUING	COGNOVIT	CONOIDIC	COUTILLE	CUPIDITY
CLIQUISH	COHEADED	CONTEMPT	COVETOUS	CURATRIX
CLIQUISM	COHESION	CONTORNO	COWARDRY	CURCULIO
CLODPOLE	COINCIDE	CONURBAN	COWBOYED	CURCUMIN
CLODPOLL	COITALLY	CONVEXED	COWHOUSE	CURLICUE
CLOGGILY	COJOINED	CONVEXES	COWINNER	CURLYCUE
CLOTPOLL	COKELIKE	CONVEXLY	COWPOXES	CURRENCY
CLOWNERY	COLCHICA	CONVEYED	COXALGIC	CURTALAX
CLOWNISH	COLDCOCK	CONVEYER	COXSWAIN	CUSPIDOR
CLUBBILY	COLIFORM	CONVOLVE	COYISHLY	CUSSEDLY
CLUBBISM	COLISEUM	CONVOYED	COZENAGE	CUSSWORD
CLUBBIST	COLLETED	COOEEING	CRABBILY	CUTCHERY
CLUBFEET	COLLOGUE	COOEYING	CRAGFAST	CUTENESS
CLUBFOOT	COLLOQUE	COOKBOOK	CRAGGILY	CUTGRASS
CLUBHAND	COLLOQUY	COOKLESS	CRAWFISH	CUTICULA
CLUBHAUL	COLLUVIA	COOKROOM	CRAWLWAY	CUTTABLE
CLUBLAND	COLOBOMA	COOKSHOP	CRAYTHUR	CWTCHING
CLUMSILY	COLONIAL	COOKWARE	CREDIBLY	CYATHIUM
CLUTCHED	COLONIZE	COOLABAH	CREEPILY	CYBERPET
COACHDOG	COLOPHON	COOLDOWN	CREMORNE	CYBERSEX
COACHMAN	COLORADO	COOLIBAH	CRENELLE	CYBERWAR
COACTIVE	COLORFUL	COONSKIN	CREOLIZE	CYCLAMEN
COAGULUM	COLORIZE	COOPTION	CREUTZER	CYCLECAR
COALBALL	COLORWAY	COOTCHED	CREVETTE	CYCLEWAY
COALESCE	COLOSSUS	COPURIFY	CREWNECK	CYCLICLY
COATRACK	COLOTOMY	COPYBOOK	CRITICAL	CYCLITOL
COATROOM	COLUBRID	COPYDESK	CRITIQUE	CYCLONAL
COBALTIC	COLUMNAL	COPYLEFT	CROCEOUS	CYCLONIC
COBBIEST	COMATULA	COPYREAD	CROCKPOT	CYCLOPIC
COBWEBBY	COMBATED	COQUETTE	CROMORNA	CYCLOSES
COCCIDIA	COMELIER	COQUILLA	CROPSICK	CYCLOSIS
COCCYGES	COMELILY	COQUILLE	CROSSBOW	CYCLUSES
COCCYXES	COMEOVER	CORACOID	CROWBOOT	CYMATICS
COCKAPOO	COMETARY	CORAGGIO	CROWFOOT	CYMATIUM
COCKATOO	COMMENCE	CORBELED	CROZZLED	CYMBIDIA
COCKBILL	COMMIXED	CORDELLE	CRUCIFER	CYMOGENE
COCKBIRD	COMMONLY	CORDWAIN	CRUCIFIX	CYMOSELY
COCKCROW	COMMUNAL	CORDWOOD	CRUMHORN	CYNICISM
COCKLIKE	COMPESCE	COREDEEM	CRUMMACK	CYNODONT
COCKLOFT	COMPLECT	CORKLIKE	CRUMMOCK	CYSTITIS
COCKNIFY	COMPOUND	CORKWOOD	CRUNCHIE	CYTOGENY
COCKTAIL	COMPRINT	CORMIDIA	CRUTCHED	CYTOLOGY
COCOBOLA	CONCEIVE	CORNBALL	CRYINGLY	CZAREVNA
COCOBOLO	CONCHOID	CORNCRIB	CRYOTRON	CZARITZA
COCOPLUM	CONCOLOR	CORNIFIC	CUBATURE	DABCHICK
CODEBOOK	CONFERVA	CORNMILL	CUBICITY	DAFFODIL
CODEBTOR	CONFETTO	CORNRENT	CUBIFORM	DAHABEAH
CODIFIED	CONFIXES	COROCORE	CUCKOOED	DAHABIAH
CODIFIES	CONFLICT	COROCORO	CUCUMBER	DAHABIEH
CODOLOGY	CONFOCAL	CORONOID	CUCURBIT	DAHABIYA
COEDITED	CONGAING	COROTATE	CUDDLING	DAMAGING
COEFFECT	CONGEING	CORRIDOR	CUFFLINK	DAMNABLY
COEMBODY	CONGENIC	CORUNDUM	CULINARY	DANCETTY
COEMPLOY	CONICITY	COSMESES	CULLYISM	DANDRIFF
COENOBIA	CONIDIUM	COSTALLY	CULPABLY	DANDRUFF
COENZYME	CONJUGAL	COTILLON	CULTLIKE	

DANDYISH	DELEADED	DIGITULE	DODDERED	DOWNZONE
DANELAGH	DELICACY	DIHYBRID	DOGBERRY	DOXOLOGY
DARKROOM	DELIRIUM	DIHYDRIC	DOGFIGHT	DOZENING
DATABANK	DEMIJOHN	DILATANT	DOGFOXES	DRABBISH
DATABASE	DEMIURGE	DILATATE	DOGGEDER	DRAMATIC
DATACARD	DEMOBBED	DILATIVE	DOGGEDLY	DRAMMOCK
DAWNERED	DEMYSHIP	DILEMMIC	DOGTEETH	DRAMSHOP
DAYCHING	DENAZIFY	DILUTING	DOGTOOTH	DRAWBACK
DAYLIGHT	DENTALLY	DILUTIVE	DOGWATCH	DRAWDOWN
DAYSHELL	DENTELLE	DILUVION	DOLDRUMS	DRAWTUBE
DAZZLING	DEPENDED	DILUVIUM	DOLLHOOD	DREGGIER
DEADENED	DEPORTED	DIMERIZE	DOLLOPED	DRENCHED
DEADENER	DEPUTIZE	DIMINISH	DOLOMITE	DRENCHER
DEADFALL	DERIGGED	DIMPSIES	DOMATIUM	DRIFTPIN
DEADHEAD	DERISORY	DIOBOLON	DOMELIKE	DRIPPILY
DEADWOOD	DESKFAST	DIOICOUS	DOMINICK	DRIVEWAY
DEAFENED	DETAINEE	DIORAMIC	DOMINIUM	DRONKLAP
DEBAGGED	DETECTED	DIPCHICK	DONDERED	DROOLIER
DEBEAKED	DETERRED	DIPLEGIA	DONUTTED	DROOPILY
DEBILITY	DETERRER	DIPLEGIC	DOODLING	DROPKICK
DEBOSHED	DETICKED	DIPLOPOD	DOOFUSES	DROPWORT
DEBOSHES	DETOXIFY	DIPSTICK	DOOLALLY	DRUGGIST
DEBOSSED	DEUCEDLY	DIRIGISM	DOOMSMEN	DRUGLORD
DEBOSSES	DEVALLED	DISALLOW	DOORJAMB	DRUMFIRE
DEBUDDED	DEVEINED	DISARRAY	DOORKNOB	DRUMHEAD
DEBUGGED	DEVILDOM	DISCOLOR	DOORPOST	DRUMLIKE
DEBUGGER	DEVILISH	DISCROWN	DOORSILL	DRUMMING
DEBUNKED	DEVILKIN	DISFROCK	DOORSTOP	DRUMROLL
DEBURRED	DEVOTION	DISPATHY	DOORYARD	DRUNKARD
DECAMPED	DEWITTED	DISPIRIT	DOPEHEAD	DUCATOON
DECEMVIR	DEWORMER	DISQUIET	DORIDOID	DUCKBILL
DECENTLY	DIACIDIC	DISSEISE	DORIZING	DUCKFOOT
DECKHAND	DIADEMED	DISSEIZE	DOSOLOGY	DUCKMOLE
DECLUTCH	DIADOCHI	DISSIGHT	DOTARDLY	DUCKTAIL
DECOCTED	DIADOCHY	DISTRICT	DOTATION	DUCKWALK
DECUBITI	DIALOGIC	DISTRUST	DOUBLING	DUDISHLY
DEEDLESS	DIANODAL	DISULFID	DOUBLOON	DUETTINO
DEEPENED	DIAPIRIC	DISUNION	DOUBTFUL	DUKESHIP
DEERHORN	DIARCHIC	DISUNITY	DOUGHBOY	DULCETLY
DEERLIKE	DIAZEPAM	DISVOUCH	DOUGHNUT	DUMBHEAD
DEERWEED	DIAZINON	DITOKOUS	DOUPIONI	DUMFOUND
DEFANGED	DIBBUKIM	DIVEBOMB	DOUZEPER	DUMMKOPF
DEFATTED	DICHOTIC	DIVIDANT	DOWDYISH	DUMMYING
DEFEATED	DICKHEAD	DIVIDING	DOWDYISM	DUMPCART
DEFECTED	DICYCLIC	DIVIDIVI	DOWFNESS	DUNCHING
DEFENDED	DIDACTIC	DIVINELY	DOWNHAUL	DUNNAKIN
DEFERRED	DIDYMIUM	DIVINIFY	DOWNHILL	DUOLOGUE
DEFERRER	DIDYMOUS	DIVINING	DOWNLAND	DUPLEXED
DEFLEAED	DIDYNAMY	DIVINITY	DOWNLINK	DUPONDII
DEFOGGED	DIEGESES	DIVINIZE	DOWNLOAD	DURUKULI
DEFRAYER	DIEGESIS	DIVISION	DOWNPIPE	DUTCHMAN
DEFREEZE	DIELDRIN	DIVVYING	DOWNPLAY	DUXELLES
DEGUMMED	DIEMAKER	DIZYGOUS	DOWNPOUR	DWARFISH
DEHORNED	DIFFERED	DIZZYING	DOWNRUSH	DWAUMING
DEHORNER	DIFFUSOR	DOBCHICK	DOWNSIZE	DWEEBISH
DEHORTED	DIGAMOUS	DOCHMIAC	DOWNTOWN	DYBBUKIM
DEHORTER	DIGHTING	DOCKLAND	DOWNTROD	DYNAMISM
DEIXISES	DIGITATE	DOCKYARD	DOWNWARD	DYNAMIZE
DEKALOGY	DIGITISE	DOCTORED	DOWNWASH	DYSLEXIC
DEKKOING	DIGITIZE	DOCTORLY	DOWNWIND	DYSMELIC

DYSPATHY	EMBODIED	EPICEDIA	EVENSONG	EXPIATOR
DYSPEPSY	EMBOGGED	EPICYCLE	EVENTIZE	EXPIRING
DYSPHAGY	EMBOILED	EPIDEMIC	EVERYDAY	EXPONENT
DYSPNEIC	EMBOXING	EPIFAUNA	EVERYMAN	EXPORTER
DYSTAXIA	EMBUSQUE	EPIFOCAL	EVERYMEN	EXTERIOR
DYSTONIA	EMCEEING	EPIGAMIC	EVERYWAY	EXTOLLED
DYSTOPIA	EMEERATE	EPIGEOUS	EVINCIVE	EXTOLLER
DYTISCID	EMERAUDE	EPILEPSY	EVOLVENT	EXTORTER
EARTHWAX	EMERGENT	EPILOGIC	EVONYMUS	EXTREMUM
EBENEZER	EMINENCE	EPILOGUE	EXAHERTZ	EXTUBATE
EBENISTE	EMINENCY	EPIPHANY	EXAMPLAR	EYEBLACK
EBIONISM	EMMESHED	EPIPHYTE	EXCAVATE	EYELETED
EBURNEAN	EMMEWING	EPISODIC	EXCEEDED	EYELEVEL
ECESISES	EMPACKET	EPITAXIC	EXCEEDER	EYELINER
ECLECTIC	EMPANADA	EPITAXIS	EXCELLED	EYEPIECE
ECLOGITE	EMPEOPLE	EPIZOISM	EXCEPTED	EYESTONE
ECOFREAK	EMPLONGE	EPONYMIC	EXCESSES	EYETEETH
ECOLOGIC	EMPTYSES	EPOPOEIA	EXCHANGE	EYETOOTH
ECONOBOX	EMPYEMIC	EPOXYING	EXCISING	FABULOUS
ECOTOXIC	EMPYESES	EPYLLION	EXCUBANT	FACEABLE
ECTODERM	EMPYESIS	EQUALIZE	EXCURSUS	FACEDOWN
ECTOGENY	EMULSIFY	EQUIPAGE	EXCUSING	FACELESS
ECTOZOIC	ENALLAGE	EQUIVOKE	EXCUSIVE	FACEMASK
ECTOZOON	ENCAENIA	ERUPTIVE	EXECUTRY	FACETELY
ECUMENIC	ENCAGING	ESQUISSE	EXEGESES	FACETIAE
EDDISHES	ENCEINTE	ESSAYISH	EXEGESIS	FACTIOUS
EDGEBONE	ENCLITIC	ETCETERA	EXEGETIC	FACTOTUM
EDGEWAYS	ENCYCLIC	ETHERIZE	EXEMPTED	FADEAWAY
EELWRACK	ENDEARED	ETHICIZE	EXEQUIAL	FAHLBAND
EFFECTED	ENDEXINE	ETHNONYM	EXEQUIES	FAIRYDOM
EFFECTER	ENDOGAMY	ETHONONE	EXERCISE	FAIRYISM
EFFERENT	ENDOSSES	ETHOXIDE	EXERTION	FAITHFUL
EFFETELY	ENDOZOON	ETHOXIES	EXERTIVE	FAKEMENT
EFFICACY	ENFEEBLE	ETHYLENE	EXHORTER	FAKIRISM
EFFIERCE	ENFETTER	ETIOLOGY	EXHUMATE	FALDERAL
EFFIGIAL	ENFIXING	ETOUFFEE	EXHUMING	FALLAWAY
EFFIGIES	ENFREEZE	EUCARYON	EXIGENCE	FALLBACK
EFFLUVIA	ENFROSEN	EUCYCLIC	EXIGENCY	FALLFISH
EFFLUXES	ENGROOVE	EUKARYOT	EXIGIBLE	FALLIBLE
EFFUSION	ENHALOED	EULOGIZE	EXIGUITY	FALLIBLY
EFFUSIVE	ENHUNGER	EUONYMIN	EXIGUOUS	FALLOWER
EGGPLANT	ENJOINED	EUONYMUS	EXILABLE	FALTBOAT
EGGSHELL	ENJOINER	EUPEPSIA	EXIMIOUS	FAMILIAL
EGGWHISK	ENJOYING	EUPEPTIC	EXOCRINE	FAMILISM
EGOISTIC	ENNEAGON	EUPHOBIA	EXOCYTIC	FAMOUSES
EIGHTHLY	ENSCONCE	EUPHONIA	EXODUSES	FAMOUSLY
EIGHTIES	ENSEMBLE	EUPHUISE	EXOERGIC	FANCIFUL
EJECTION	ENTHETIC	EUPHUIST	EXORCISE	FANDANGO
EKTEXINE	ENTICING	EUPHUIZE	EXORCIZE	FANEGADA
ELEGANCE	ENTOZOON	EUROKIES	EXOSMOSE	FANFARON
ELEGANCY	ENTRYWAY	EUROKOUS	EXOTOXIC	FANTASIA
ELEVENTH	ENVIABLE	EURONOTE	EXOTOXIN	FANTOOSH
ELKHOUND	ENWALLOW	EUROPIUM	EXPANDED	FARADIZE
ELOINING	ENZONING	EURYTHMY	EXPANDER	FARCICAL
ELVISHLY	EOHIPPUS	EUTECTIC	EXPECTED	FARMABLE
EMBANKER	EOLIPILE	EUTHYMIA	EXPEDITE	FARMLAND
EMBEDDED	EOLOPILE	EUXENITE	EXPELLED	FARMWIFE
EMBEZZLE	EPHEMERA	EVADABLE	EXPELLEE	FARMWORK
EMBLAZON	EPIBOLIC	EVECTION	EXPENDED	FAROLITO
EMBLEMED	EPICALYX	EVENFALL	EXPIABLE	FASHIOUS

FATALISM	FILIOQUE	FLEABANE	FOLDBOAT	FORRADER
FATALIST	FILLABLE	FLEABITE	FOLKLAND	FORSLACK
FATHOMED	FILLIPED	FLEECILY	FOLKLIFE	FORSWATT
FATSTOCK	FILMCARD	FLEISHIG	FOLKLIKE	FORTHINK
FAUBOURG	FILMLAND	FLEISHIK	FOLKLORE	FORTUITY
FAULTFUL	FILMLIKE	FLENCHED	FOLKSILY	FORZANDI
FAUNALLY	FINALIZE	FLENCHER	FOLKSONG	FORZANDO
FAUTEUIL	FINITISM	FLESHPOT	FOLLICLE	FOUNTFUL
FAUVETTE	FINOCHIO	FLEXAGON	FOLLOWER	FOURCHEE
FAVONIAN	FIPPENCE	FLEXIBLY	FOLLOWUP	FOUREYED
FAVORING	FIREBACK	FLEXTIME	FONDNESS	FOURPLEX
FAYALITE	FIREBIRD	FLEXUOSE	FONTANEL	FOURTHLY
FEAGUING	FIREBOMB	FLEXUOUS	FOODWAYS	FOXBERRY
FEBRIFIC	FIREHALL	FLEXURAL	FOOFARAW	FOXGLOVE
FEDERARY	FIREPINK	FLIMFLAM	FOOLSCAP	FOXHOUND
FEEDBACK	FIRMNESS	FLINGING	FOOTBALL	FOXINESS
FEEDHOLE	FISCALLY	FLIPBOOK	FOOTBATH	FOXSHARK
FEELGOOD	FISHBALL	FLIPFLOP	FOOTFALL	FRABJOUS
FEIGNING	FISHBOLT	FLIPPANT	FOOTHILL	FRAMABLE
FEINTING	FISHBONE	FLIRTISH	FOOTHOLD	FRAMPLER
FEISTILY	FISHHOOK	FLOCCING	FOOTLIKE	FRAMPOLD
FELINELY	FISHKILL	FLOCCOSE	FOOTMUFF	FRANKLIN
FELLABLE	FISHLIKE	FLOCCULE	FOOTNOTE	FRAPPANT
FELLOWED	FISHPOLE	FLOCCULI	FOOTPACE	FRAUDFUL
FELLOWLY	FISHSKIN	FLOODLIT	FOOTPOST	FRAUGHAN
FEMERALL	FISHWIFE	FLOODWAY	FOOTRACE	FRAUTAGE
FEMINACY	FISNOMIE	FLOORAGE	FOOTSLOG	FREAKERY
FEMINAZI	FISSIPED	FLOPOVER	FOOTSTEP	FREAKIER
FEMINISM	FISSURAL	FLOPPILY	FOOTWELL	FREAKOUT
FENTANYL	FISTIANA	FLORALLY	FOOTWORK	FREEBASE
FENTHION	FISTIEST	FLORIDLY	FOOTWORN	FREEBOOT
FERNBIRD	FITFULLY	FLOTILLA	FORAMINA	FREEHAND
FERNLIKE	FIVEFOLD	FLOURISH	FORCEDLY	FREEHOLD
FERRETED	FIXATION	FLOWERER	FORCEFUL	FREEWARE
FERRETER	FIXATIVE	FLUELLEN	FORCIBLY	FREEWILL
FERRYING	FIXITIES	FLUELLIN	FOREBITT	FRENCHED
FERVENCY	FLABBILY	FLUENTLY	FOREBOOM	FRENULUM
FESSWISE	FLAGELLA	FLUFFILY	FOREDOOM	FRENZILY
FESTIEST	FLAGLESS	FLUIDIFY	FOREFELT	FREQUENT
FETATION	FLAGPOLE	FLUIDITY	FOREFOOT	FRESHMAN
FETIDITY	FLAGRANT	FLUIDIZE	FOREHAND	FRETWORK
FETOLOGY	FLAGSHIP	FLUIDRAM	FOREHEAD	FRICANDO
FEUDALLY	FLAMBEAU	FLUMMERY	FOREHOOF	FRITTATA
FEVERFEW	FLAMEOUT	FLUXGATE	FOREKNOW	FRIVOLED
FIBERIZE	FLAMMULE	FLYMAKER	FORELOCK	FRIZETTE
FIBRANNE	FLANCARD	FLYPITCH	FORENOON	FROGFISH
FIBROTIC	FLAPJACK	FLYSCHES	FOREPEAK	FROMENTY
FIDDIOUS	FLASHILY	FLYSPECK	FOREREAD	FROUFROU
FIDGETED	FLATBOAT	FLYWHEEL	FORETELL	FROUZILY
FIERCELY	FLATETTE	FOALFOOT	FOREWORD	FROWZILY
FIFTIETH	FLATFEET	FOAMABLE	FORFAULT	FRUITFUL
FIGURING	FLATFOOT	FOAMLIKE	FORHOOED	FRUITILY
FIGURIST	FLATLAND	FOCACCIA	FORHOOIE	FRUITION
FILCHING	FLATLONG	FODDERED	FORJUDGE	FRUMPILY
FILEABLE	FLATMATE	FOGBOUND	FORKBALL	FRUMPISH
FILEFISH	FLATWARE	FOGFRUIT	FORKEDLY	FRYBREAD
FILIALLY	FLATWAYS	FOGGIEST	FORKLIFT	FUCOIDAL
FILICIDE	FLATWORK	FOLDABLE	FORMABLY	FUDDLING
FILIFORM	FLAVANOL	FOLDAWAY	FORMERLY	FUELWOOD
FILIGREE	FLAVONOL	FOLDBACK	FORMWORK	FUFFIEST

FUGACITY	GAMMONED	GLASSFUL	GOSPELLY	GULLIBLY
FUGGIEST	GAMODEME	GLEESOME	GOSSYPOL	GUMLANDS
FUGHETTA	GANGBANG	GLEETIER	GOUJEERS	GUNFIGHT
FUGITIVE	GANGLAND	GLEGGEST	GRACIOSO	GUNKHOLE
FUGLEMEN	GANGPLOW	GLIFFING	GRAFFITI	GUNNYBAG
FULGURAL	GANGSHAG	GLITZIER	GRAFFITO	GURDWARA
FULLBACK	GANGSMEN	GLITZILY	GRAMERCY	GURGOYLE
FULLFACE	GAPEWORM	GLITZING	GRAMMAGE	GURUSHIP
FULMINIC	GARBOARD	GLOBALLY	GRAPHITE	GUSSYING
FUMARASE	GARCINIA	GLOMMING	GRAPHIUM	GUTTURAL
FUMELIKE	GARDYLOO	GLOOMFUL	GRATUITY	GUZZLING
FUMEROLE	GARGANEY	GLOOMILY	GRAVIDLY	GYMKHANA
FUMOSITY	GARLICKY	GLORYING	GRAVITAS	GYNAECEA
FUNBOARD	GASIFIED	GLOSSILY	GRAVLAKS	GYNANDRY
FUNERARY	GASIFIES	GLOSSIST	GRAYBACK	GYNARCHY
FUNGUSES	GASTFULL	GLOWLAMP	GRAZIOSO	GYPSEOUS
FUNICULI	GASTIGHT	GLOWWORM	GREEBOES	GYPSYDOM
FUNKHOLE	GASWORKS	GLOXINIA	GREEGREE	GYPSYING
FUNKIEST	GAUCHELY	GLUCAGON	GREENWAY	GYPSYISH
FUNNYMAN	GAZOGENE	GLUCINIC	GREWSOME	GYPSYISM
FUNNYMEN	GAZPACHO	GLUCOSIC	GREYBACK	GYRODYNE
FURBELOW	GAZUMPER	GLUHWEIN	GRIDLOCK	GYROSTAT
FURFURAL	GEEKIEST	GLUMELLA	GRILLAGE	HABANERA
FURFURAN	GEEPOUND	GLUTAMIC	GRIPSACK	HABANERO
FURFUROL	GELIDITY	GLYCEMIC	GRITTILY	HABDALAH
FURIBUND	GEMSBUCK	GLYCERIC	GROGGERY	HACKWORK
FURROWED	GEOCARPY	GLYCEROL	GROGGIER	HAEREMAI
FURROWER	GEODETIC	GLYCERYL	GROGGILY	HAFTAROT
FURUNCLE	GEOGONIC	GLYCOGEN	GROGSHOP	HAFTORAH
FUSARIUM	GEOLOGER	GLYCOLIC	GROKKING	HAFTOROT
FUSELIKE	GEOLOGIC	GNAWABLE	GROMWELL	HAGADIST
FUSIFORM	GEOMANCY	GOALBALL	GROOLIER	HAILSHOT
FUSILIER	GEOMETRY	GOALWARD	GROOVING	HAIRGRIP
FUSIONAL	GEOMYOID	GODSQUAD	GROUPAGE	HAIRTAIL
FUTILELY	GEOPHONE	GOHONZON	GROUPOID	HAIRWORK
FUTURIST	GEOPHYTE	GOLDENLY	GROVELER	HAIRWORM
FUTURITY	GEOPROBE	GOLDSIZE	GRUBBILY	HALACHIC
FUZZIEST	GEROPIGA	GOLDTONE	GRUBWORM	HALAKHOT
FUZZTONE	GEWGAWED	GOLGOTHA	GRUFFISH	HALAKOTH
FYNBOSES	GHETTOED	GOLLERED	GRUIFORM	HALAZONE
GABBROIC	GHOULISH	GOLLIWOG	GRUMPILY	HALFBACK
GABBROID	GIAMBEUX	GOLLOPER	GUACHARO	HALFBEAK
GADABOUT	GIDDYING	GOLLYING	GUAIACUM	HALFLIFE
GADZOOKS	GIFTSHOP	GOLLYWOG	GUAIOCUM	HALFPIPE
GAFFSAIL	GIFTWRAP	GOMBROON	GUARDDOG	HALFTIME
GAGEABLE	GIGAFLOP	GONFALON	GUCKIEST	HALLALOO
GAGEABLY	GIGAWATT	GONIDIUM	GUDDLING	HALLIARD
GAIETIES	GIGGITED	GONOCYTE	GUDEWIFE	HALLMARK
GAILLARD	GILDHALL	GONODUCT	GUIDEWAY	HALLOWER
GALABIEH	GILLYVOR	GONOPORE	GUILEFUL	HALLUCAL
GALACTIC	GIMCRACK	GOODTIME	GUILTIER	HALOLIKE
GALAPAGO	GIMLETED	GOODWIFE	GUILTILY	HAMARTIA
GALAVANT	GIPSYISH	GOODWILL	GUIMBARD	HAMEWITH
GALLEASS	GIRAFFID	GOODYEAR	GUITGUIT	HAMMERED
GALLIARD	GIRLHOOD	GOOFBALL	GULCHING	HAMMERER
GALLIASS	GIVEAWAY	GOOSEGOB	GULFLIKE	HAMPERER
GALLIVAT	GIVEBACK	GOOSEGOG	GULFWEED	HAMULOSE
GAMBOGIC	GIZZENED	GOPHERED	GULLABLE	HANCHING
GAMEPLAY	GLADIOLI	GORBELLY	GULLEYED	HANDAXES
GAMESOME	GLADWRAP	GORBLIMY	GULLIBLE	HANDBALL

HANDBELL	HAZARDER	HERITRIX	HOLDDOWN	HORNPOUT
HANDBILL	HAZARDRY	HERMAEAN	HOLDFAST	HORNWORK
HANDCLAP	HAZELHEN	HEROICLY	HOLDOVER	HORNWORM
HANDCUFF	HAZELNUT	HEXAFOIL	HOLLOING	HORNWORT
HANDHOLD	HEADACHE	HEXAGLOT	HOLLOWER	HOROKAKA
HANDMAID	HEADACHY	HEXAGRAM	HOLLOWLY	HOROLOGE
HANDOVER	HEADCASE	HEXYLENE	HOLOGAMY	HOROPITO
HANDPICK	HEADLAMP	HIBISCUS	HOLOGRAM	HORRIBLY
HANDPLAY	HEADLIKE	HICCOUGH	HOLOGYNY	HORRIDER
HANDWRIT	HEADSTAY	HICCUPED	HOLOZOIC	HORRIDLY
HANDYMAN	HEADWIND	HICKWALL	HOMEFELT	HORRIFIC
HANDYMEN	HEALABLE	HICKYMAL	HOMELESS	HOSEPIPE
HANGABLE	HEALSOME	HIDDENLY	HOMELIER	HOSPITIA
HANGOVER	HEARABLE	HIDROSIS	HOMELILY	HOTBLOOD
HANUKIAH	HEAVENLY	HIDROTIC	HOMEMADE	HOTCHING
HAPLOPIA	HEBDOMAD	HIERURGY	HOMEOBOX	HOTCHPOT
HAPLOSIS	HEBETATE	HIGHBALL	HOMEOTIC	HOTHOUSE
HAPPENED	HEBETUDE	HIGHBRED	HOMEPAGE	HOUGHING
HAQUETON	HEBRAIZE	HIGHBROW	HOMEROOM	HOURLONG
HARAKEKE	HECATOMB	HIGHBUSH	HOMESTAY	HOUSEBOY
HARAMBEE	HEDGEHOG	HIGHJACK	HOMETOWN	HOUSEFLY
HARBORER	HEDGEHOP	HIGHLAND	HOMEWARE	HOUSEFUL
HARDBACK	HEDGEPIG	HIGHLIFE	HOMEWORK	HOVELLER
HARDBAKE	HEEHAWED	HIGHMOST	HOMILIES	HOWDYING
HARDBALL	HEELBALL	HIGHNESS	HOMILIST	HOWLBACK
HARDBEAM	HEELLESS	HIGHROAD	HOMINIAN	HUAQUERO
HARDBOOT	HEFTIEST	HIGHTAIL	HOMININE	HUARACHO
HARDPACK	HELILIFT	HIGHVELD	HOMINIZE	HUBBUBOO
HARDWOOD	HELLBENT	HIJACKED	HOMODONT	HUDDLING
HAREWOOD	HELLHOLE	HILARITY	HOMOGAMY	HUFFIEST
HARLOTRY	HELLKITE	HILCHING	HOMOGENY	HUGGABLE
HARROWER	HELLWARD	HILLFOLK	HOMOGONY	HUGGIEST
HARRYING	HELMETED	HILLFORT	HOMOTONY	HUISACHE
HASHEESH	HELMINTH	HINAHINA	HOMOTYPY	HUMANISM
HASHHEAD	HELMLESS	HINDFOOT	HOMUNCLE	HUMANITY
HASHMARK	HELMSMEN	HINDHEAD	HONCHOED	HUMANIZE
HATBOXES	HELOTAGE	HINDMOST	HONEWORT	HUMANOID
HATCHECK	HELPABLE	HINDWARD	HONEYBEE	HUMEFIED
HATCHWAY	HELPLINE	HINNYING	HONEYBUN	HUMEFIES
HATMAKER	HELPMEET	HIPPARCH	HONEYFUL	HUMICOLE
HATSTAND	HEMIOLIC	HIPPURIC	HONEYING	HUMIDIFY
HAURIANT	HEMIOPIA	HIPPUSES	HONORAND	HUMIDITY
HAUSFRAU	HEMIOPIC	HIPPYDOM	HONORARY	HUMIFIED
HAVDOLOH	HEMOCYTE	HISTIDIN	HOODLIKE	HUMIFIES
HAVELOCK	HEMOLYSE	HIVELIKE	HOODMOLD	HUMITURE
HAVILDAR	HEMOLYZE	HIZZONER	HOODOOED	HUMMABLE
HAVOCKED	HEMPLIKE	HOARHEAD	HOOFBEAT	HUMORESK
HAVOCKER	HENCHMAN	HOASTMAN	HOOFLIKE	HUMORFUL
HAWFINCH	HENCHMEN	HOBBITRY	HOOKLIKE	HUMPBACK
HAWKBELL	HENEQUEN	HOBNOBBY	HOOKNOSE	HUMPLIKE
HAWKBILL	HENEQUIN	HOCKSHOP	HOOKWORM	HUMSTRUM
HAWKLIKE	HENHOUSE	HOGGEREL	HOORAHED	HUNCHING
HAWKMOTH	HENIQUEN	HOGMANAY	HOORAYED	HUNGERED
HAWKSHAW	HERALDRY	HOGSHEAD	HORDEOLA	HUNGERLY
HAWKWEED	HERBARIA	HOGTYING	HORMONAL	HUNKERED
HAWTHORN	HERBLIKE	HOIDENED	HORNBEAK	HUNTAWAY
HAYBOXES	HERDLIKE	HOISTWAY	HORNBILL	HUNTEDLY
HAYMAKER	HEREAWAY	HOKYPOKY	HORNBOOK	HURCHEON
HAYSTACK	HEREFROM	HOLARCHY	HORNFELS	HURRYING
HAZARDED	HERETRIX	HOLDBACK	HORNLIKE	HUSHEDLY

HUSKLIKE	ILLUSIVE	INFIRMLY	JABBERER	JODELLED
HUSWIVES	ILLUVIUM	INFIXING	JACKAROO	JOGPANTS
HUZZAING	ILMENITE	INFIXION	JACKBOOT	JOHNBOAT
HYACINTH	IMBECILE	INFLUENT	JACKEROO	JOINABLE
HYBRISES	IMBEDDED	INFOBAHN	JACKROLL	JOISTING
HYDRAGOG	IMBIBING	INFUSION	JACKSTAY	JOKESOME
HYDRATOR	IMBODIED	INFUSORY	JACQUARD	JOKINGLY
HYDROGEL	IMBODIES	INHUMING	JACULATE	JONCANOE
HYDROGEN	IMBOLDEN	INIMICAL	JADELIKE	JORDELOO
HYDROMEL	IMMEWING	INIQUITY	JAGGEDER	JOUNCING
HYDROSOL	IMMINENT	INITIATE	JAGGEDLY	JOVIALLY
HYDROZOA	IMMINUTE	INKBERRY	JAILBAIT	JOYFULLY
HYGIENIC	IMMITTED	INKSTAND	JAILBIRD	JOYOUSLY
HYLICISM	IMMIXING	INNOCENT	JAKFRUIT	JOYSTICK
HYLOBATE	IMMOBILE	INOCULUM	JAMBOLAN	JUBILANT
HYLOZOIC	IMMOLATE	INSPIRIT	JAMBOREE	JUBILATE
HYMENEAN	IMMOMENT	INSTINCT	JAMMABLE	JUDGMENT
HYMENIUM	IMMOTILE	INTENTLY	JAMPANEE	JUDICIAL
HYMNBOOK	IMMUNITY	INTIFADA	JANIFORM	JUGULATE
HYMNLESS	IMMUNIZE	INTIMISM	JANITRIX	JULIENNE
HYMNLIKE	IMPARITY	INTIMIST	JAPANIZE	JUMARING
HYOSCINE	IMPAWNED	INTIMITY	JAPANNED	JUMBOIZE
HYPALGIA	IMPELLED	INTOMBED	JAPANNER	JUMPABLE
HYPERGOL	IMPELLER	INTUITED	JAPONICA	JUMPSUIT
HYPERNYM	IMPETIGO	INUKSHUK	JARARACA	JUNCTURE
HYPEROPE	IMPISHLY	INUNDANT	JARARAKA	JUNCUSES
HYPHEMIA	IMPLEDGE	INVASION	JAROVIZE	JUNKANOO
HYPHENED	IMPLICIT	INVERTOR	JAUNCING	JUNKETED
HYPHENIC	IMPLUVIA	INVIABLE	JAUNTILY	JUNKETER
HYPOBOLE	IMPOLICY	INVISCID	JAWBOXES	JUNKYARD
HYPOGENE	IMPOROUS	INWICKED	JAZZIEST	JURATORY
HYPOGEUM	IMPRIMIS	IODATION	JAZZLIKE	JURISTIC
HYPOGYNY	IMPRISON	IODIZING	JEANETTE	JURYLESS
HYPONOIA	IMPUNITY	IODOFORM	JEJUNELY	KABABBED
HYPOPYON	IMPURITY	IODOPHOR	JEJUNITY	KABELJOU
HYPOTHEC	INASMUCH	IONICITY	JELUTONG	KABOBBED
IANTHINE	INCAVING	IONIZING	JEMMYING	KAFFIYAH
IATRICAL	INCHWORM	IRITISES	JEREPIGO	KAFFIYEH
IBERISES	INCISING	IRONBARK	JEROBOAM	KAIAKING
ICEBOXES	INCISION	IRONLIKE	JERQUING	KAIMAKAM
IDEALITY	INCISIVE	IRONWARE	JESTBOOK	KAKARIKI
IDEALIZE	INCITING	IRONWOOD	JESUITRY	KAKEMONO
IDENTIFY	INCIVISM	IRONWORK	JETLINER	KAKIEMON
IDENTITY	INCUSING	IRRIGATE	JETPLANE	KALAMATA
IDEOGRAM	INDAGATE	IRRISION	JIBINGLY	KALLIDIN
IDEOLOGY	INDICIUM	IRRISORY	JICKAJOG	KALOTYPE
IDIOCIES	INDIGOID	IRRITANT	JIGGERED	KAMAAINA
IDIOTYPE	INDUCIAE	ISATINIC	JIGGIEST	KAMACITE
IDLEHOOD	INDUVIAE	ISCHURIA	JIGSAWED	KAMEESES
IDONEOUS	INEDIBLE	ISOBUTYL	JILLAROO	KAMEEZES
IDYLLIAN	INFAMIZE	ISOCRYME	JIMCRACK	KAMIKAZE
IGNIFIED	INFAMOUS	ISODOMUM	JINGLING	KAMOKAMO
IGNIFIES	INFANTRY	ISOGAMIC	JINGOIST	KANGAROO
IGNOMINY	INFECUND	ISOGRAPH	JIPIJAPA	KANTIKOY
IGUANIAN	INFERIAE	ISOSTASY	JIRKINET	KAOLINIC
ILLATION	INFERNAL	ISOTOPIC	JOCKETTE	KARATEKA
ILLINIUM	INFICETE	ISOZYMIC	JOCKEYED	KAREAREA
ILLIQUID	INFINITE	ISSUABLY	JOCOSELY	KARSTIFY
ILLISION	INFINITY	IZVESTIA	JOCOSITY	KARYOTIN
ILLUSION	INFIRMED	JABBERED	JOCUNDLY	KATAKANA

KATHODAL	KINGKLIP	KYPHOTIC	LAZULITE	LISSOMLY
KATHODIC	KINKAJOU	LABIALLY	LEADWORK	LITHEMIA
KAUMATUA	KIPPERED	LABRADOR	LEECHDOM	LITHEMIC
KAVAKAVA	KIRIGAMI	LABURNUM	LEKYTHUS	LITIGATE
KAWAKAWA	KIRKWARD	LACELIKE	LENGTHEN	LITTLISH
KAZACHKI	KIRKYARD	LACEWOOD	LENIENCE	LITURGIC
KAZACHOK	KITELIKE	LACKADAY	LENIENCY	LITUUSES
KAZATSKI	KLAXONED	LACKEYED	LETHALLY	LIVELILY
KAZATSKY	KLEPHTIC	LACKLAND	LETTABLE	LIVIDITY
KAZATZKA	KLONDIKE	LACRYMAL	LETTERER	LIVINGLY
KEBABBED	KLONDYKE	LACTIFIC	LEUCEMIA	LIXIVIUM
KEBOBBED	KLUTZIER	LADIFIED	LEUCEMIC	LOANBACK
KEELBOAT	KLYSTRON	LADLEFUL	LEUKEMIA	LOBBYGOW
KEELHALE	KNACKING	LADYPALM	LEUKEMIA	LOBBYIST
KEELHAUL	KNACKISH	LAGNAPPE	LEUKEMIC	LOBELINE
KEELLESS	KNAPSACK	LAKELAND	LEUKOSES	LOBLOLLY
KEENNESS	KNEEHOLE	LAKELIKE	LEUKOTIC	LOBSTICK
KEEPABLE	KNEEJERK	LALLYGAG	LEVELING	LOCALITY
KEEPSAKE	KNEESOCK	LAMBENCY	LEVERAGE	LOCKAWAY
KEEPSAKY	KNELLING	LAMBKILL	LEVODOPA	LOCKDOWN
KEESHOND	KNIFEMAN	LAMPHOLE	LEVOGYRE	LOCKPICK
KEFFIYAH	KNIFEMEN	LANCEGAY	LICHWAKE	LOCOFOCO
KEFFIYEH	KNOBHEAD	LANDFILL	LICKSPIT	LOCOMOTE
KEFUFFLE	KNOBLIKE	LANDFORM	LICORICE	LOCOWEED
KELOIDAL	KNOCKOFF	LANDLADY	LIEGEDOM	LODGMENT
KENSPECK	KNOCKOUT	LANDLORD	LIFEBELT	LOFTLIKE
KEPHALIC	KNOLLING	LANDMARK	LIFELINE	LOGBOARD
KEPHALIN	KNOTLIKE	LANDSLID	LIFESOME	LOGICISE
KERATOMA	KNOTTILY	LANDSLIP	LIFETIME	LOGICISM
KERNELLY	KNOTWORK	LANDWARD	LIFTABLE	LOGICIZE
KETOXIME	KOFTWORK	LANDWIND	LIGATIVE	LOGJUICE
KEYBOARD	KOHEKOHE	LANGLAUF	LIGHTFUL	LOGOGRAM
KEYBUGLE	KOLHOZES	LANGSHAN	LIGHTISH	LOGOMACH
KEYPUNCH	KOLINSKY	LANKNESS	LIGNITIC	LOGOTYPE
KHANSAMA	KOLKOZES	LAPBOARD	LIGULOID	LOGOTYPY
KHAZENIM	KOMISSAR	LAPIDIFY	LIKELIER	LOLLIPOP
KHUSKHUS	KOMITAJI	LARBOARD	LIKEWAKE	LOLLOPED
KIBITZED	KOMONDOR	LARRIKIN	LIKEWISE	LOLLYGAG
KIBITZER	KOREROED	LARRUPER	LILLIPUT	LONELILY
KIBITZES	KORFBALL	LARYNGAL	LILYLIKE	LONGHAND
KIBOSHED	KORIMAKO	LATEWAKE	LIMBERER	LONGJUMP
KIBOSHES	KOROMIKO	LATEWOOD	LIMBERLY	LONGSPUR
KICKABLE	KOTOWING	LATHWORK	LIMBLESS	LONGWALL
KICKBACK	KOTTABOS	LATHYRUS	LIMBMEAL	LOOKDOWN
KICKBALL	KROMESKY	LAUDABLY	LIMNETIC	LOOKOVER
KICKSHAW	KRUMHORN	LAUDATOR	LIMPIDLY	LOOPHOLE
KIDOLOGY	KRUMKAKE	LAUGHFUL	LIMULOID	LOOSEBOX
KILLADAR	KRYOLITH	LAVAFORM	LINDWORM	LOOSENER
KILLOGIE	KUMBALOI	LAVALAVA	LINELIKE	LOPGRASS
KILOBAUD	KUMIKUMI	LAVALIKE	LINGUINE	LOPSTICK
KILOGRAM	KURVEYED	LAVASHES	LINGUINI	LOQUITUR
KILOGRAY	KURVEYOR	LAVATORY	LINIMENT	LORDOSIS
KILOMOLE	KUVASZOK	LAVISHLY	LINKWORK	LORDOTIC
KILOVOLT	KVELLING	LAVOLTED	LIONFISH	LORDSHIP
KILOWATT	KVETCHED	LAWGIVER	LIONLIKE	LOSINGLY
KILTLIKE	KYANITIC	LAWYERLY	LIPOGRAM	LOSSIEST
KIMBOING	KYBOSHED	LAXATIVE	LIPOIDAL	LOSSLESS
KIMONOED	KYBOSHES	LAYABOUT	LIPSTICK	LOTHARIO
KINAKINA	KYLLOSES	LAYSHAFT	LIQUIDLY	LOTHFULL
KINDLILY	KYLLOSIS	LAYSTALL	LIQUORED	LOVEBITE
			LIRIPOOP	

LOVEFEST	MAGMATIC	MASSLESS	MEZEREON	MINYANIM
LOVELESS	MAGNIFIC	MASSOOLA	MEZEREUM	MIQUELET
LOVELILY	MAHARAJA	MASTODON	MIAOUING	MIREPOIX
LOVELOCK	MAHIMAHI	MASURIUM	MIAOWING	MIRLITON
LOVELORN	MAHOGANY	MATAMATA	MIASMATA	MIROMIRO
LOVESICK	MAIDENLY	MATCHBOX	MICATING	MIRTHFUL
LOVESOME	MAIDHOOD	MATTEDLY	MICAWBER	MISADAPT
LOVINGLY	MAIEUTIC	MAUMETRY	MICKEYED	MISBIRTH
LOWERIER	MAINBOOM	MAUSOLEA	MICROBIC	MISCHIEF
LOWERING	MAIOLICA	MAWBOUND	MICROCAR	MISCUING
LOWLIGHT	MAJOLICA	MAWMETRY	MICROLUX	MISDIGHT
LUBBERLY	MAJORITY	MAXICOAT	MICRURGY	MISDRIVE
LUBRICAL	MAKEBATE	MAXIMIST	MIDMONTH	MISFEIGN
LUCENTLY	MAKEFAST	MAXIMITE	MIDNIGHT	MISFOCUS
LUCIDITY	MAKEOVER	MAXIMIZE	MIDPOINT	MISGOING
LUCULENT	MAKIMONO	MAYAPPLE	MIDWATCH	MISHMASH
LUGGABLE	MAKUTUED	MAYFLIES	MIGHTFUL	MISHMOSH
LUMBERLY	MALAPROP	MAZAEDIA	MIGHTIER	MISJUDGE
LUMINANT	MALAROMA	MAZARINE	MIGHTILY	MISKEYED
LUMMOXES	MALAXAGE	MAZELIKE	MIJNHEER	MISLIGHT
LUMPENLY	MALAXATE	MAZELTOV	MILESIMO	MISMARRY
LUNANAUT	MALAXING	MBAQANGA	MILKLESS	MISOGYNY
LUNATELY	MALEMIUT	MEALYBUG	MILKLIKE	MISOLOGY
LUNCHBOX	MALIHINI	MEDIANLY	MILKMAID	MISSTAMP
LUNGWORT	MALLEOLI	MEEKENED	MILKWOOD	MISTHINK
LUNKHEAD	MALSTICK	MEGABUCK	MILKWORT	MISTOUCH
LURINGLY	MALTWORM	MEGABYTE	MILLABLE	MISTRYST
LUSCIOUS	MALVASIA	MEGAFLOP	MILLEPED	MITICIDE
LUTETIUM	MAMELUKE	MEGALOPS	MILLIARD	MITSVOTH
LUXATING	MAMMATUS	MEIOCYTE	MILLIBAR	MITTIMUS
LUXMETER	MAMMETRY	MEJLISES	MILLIGAL	MITZVOTH
LUXURIES	MAMMIFER	MELANIZE	MILLILUX	MIXOLOGY
LUXURIST	MAMMITIS	MELINITE	MILLIMHO	MIZZLIER
LYCHGATE	MAMZERIM	MELLIFIC	MILLIOHM	MIZZLING
LYKEWAKE	MANDALIC	MELLOWED	MILLPOND	MOBILITY
LYKEWALK	MANFULLY	MELODIZE	MILLRIND	MOBILIZE
LYMPHOID	MANGANIC	MEMBERED	MILLTAIL	MOBOCRAT
LYMPHOMA	MANIFORM	MEMBRANE	MILLWORK	MOCUDDUM
LYNCHING	MANNERLY	MEMORIZE	MIMEOING	MODIFIED
LYNCHPIN	MANNITIC	MENILITE	MIMETITE	MODIWORT
LYNXLIKE	MANSHIFT	MENOMINI	MIMICKED	MOISTIFY
LYOLYSES	MANUALLY	MENOPOME	MIMICKER	MOKADDAM
LYOLYSIS	MANUBRIA	MENSEFUL	MINDFUCK	MOKOMOKO
LYOPHOBE	MANUHIRI	MENTHENE	MINIBIKE	MOKOPUNA
LYRICISM	MANZELLO	MEPHITIC	MINIDISC	MOLDABLE
LYRICIST	MAPMAKER	MERCURIC	MINIDISH	MOLDWARP
LYRICIZE	MAQUETTE	MERIMAKE	MINIFIED	MOLEHILL
LYRIFORM	MARAGING	MERRYMAN	MINIFIES	MOLOSSUS
LYSOZYME	MARAUDED	MERRYMEN	MINIMENT	MOLYBDIC
MACAHUBA	MARCHMAN	MERYCISM	MINIMILL	MOMZERIM
MACALLUM	MARGARIC	MESDAMES	MINIMISE	MONANDRY
MACARIZE	MARINARA	MESEEMED	MINIMISM	MONAXIAL
MACCABAW	MARKEDLY	MESOGLEA	MINIMIST	MONELLIN
MACCABOY	MARTYRED	MESOSOME	MINIMIZE	MONEYMAN
MACKINAW	MARTYRIA	MESOZOAN	MINIMOTO	MONEYMEN
MACROPOD	MARYJANE	MESOZOIC	MINIPARK	MONGCORN
MADERIZE	MARZIPAN	METABOLY	MINIPILL	MONITION
MADHOUSE	MASHGIAH	METALIZE	MINISTRY	MONKHOOD
MAGICIAN	MASHLOCH	METAMICT	MINSHUKU	MONODONT
MAGICKED	MASKLIKE	MEUNIERE	MINUTELY	MONOGAMY

MONOGENY	MOUTHILY	MYRIADTH	NEWSDESK	NONOBESE
MONOGONY	MOVELESS	MYRIOPOD	NEWSHAWK	NONOHMIC
MONOGYNY	MOVIEDOM	MYRMIDON	NEWSREEL	NONOWNER
MONOHULL	MOVIEOKE	MYRRHINE	NEWWAVER	NONPAGAN
MONOKINE	MOYITIES	MYSTICLY	NEXTDOOR	NONPAPAL
MONOKINI	MUCHACHO	MYTHICAL	NGULTRUM	NONPOINT
MONOMIAL	MUCIDITY	MYXAMEBA	NICKELIC	NONPRINT
MONOMODE	MUCILAGE	MYXEDEMA	NICKNACK	NONQUOTA
MONOPOLE	MUCINOID	MYXOCYTE	NICKNAME	NONRIVAL
MONOPOLY	MUCKERED	NABOBERY	NIDIFIED	NONRURAL
MONOSOME	MUCKHEAP	NABOBESS	NIDIFIES	NONSTICK
MONOSOMY	MUCKLUCK	NABOBISH	NIFFNAFF	NONSTYLE
MONOTINT	MUCKRAKE	NAFFNESS	NIGHTJAR	NONTAXES
MONOTONE	MUCKWORM	NAILFILE	NIHILISM	NONTONAL
MONOTONY	MUDGUARD	NAILFOLD	NIHILIST	NONTONIC
MONTEITH	MUDPUPPY	NALOXONE	NIHILITY	NONTOXIC
MOONBEAM	MUGGIEST	NAMASKAR	NIMBYISM	NONTRUMP
MOONFACE	MUIRBURN	NANNYGAI	NINETEEN	NONTRUTH
MOONPORT	MULETEER	NANNYING	NINJITSU	NONUNION
MOONROOF	MULLARKY	NANNYISH	NINJUTSU	NONURBAN
MOONSHOT	MULLOWAY	NAPHTHYL	NINNYISH	NONVALID
MOONWORT	MULTEITY	NAPOLEON	NIRAMIAI	NONVIRAL
MOORBURN	MULTIFID	NAPROXEN	NIRVANIC	NONWHITE
MOORFOWL	MULTIFIL	NARRATOR	NITROXYL	NONWOODY
MOORWORT	MULTIJET	NARROWER	NIVATION	NONWOVEN
MOPBOARD	MULTITON	NARROWLY	NOBILITY	NOOKLIKE
MOPEHAWK	MUNCHING	NASALIZE	NOBLEMAN	NOSEDOVE
MOPSTICK	MUNCHKIN	NASCENCE	NOBLESSE	NOTATION
MOQUETTE	MUNDUNGO	NASCENCY	NOCENTLY	NOTEBOOK
MORBIDLY	MUNGCORN	NATANTLY	NODALITY	NOTTURNI
MORBIFIC	MUNIMENT	NAUMACHY	NODULOUS	NOTTURNO
MORBILLI	MUQADDAM	NAUSEATE	NOHOWISH	NOUMENON
MOREPORK	MURDABAD	NAUSEOUS	NOMOGENY	NOUNALLY
MORESQUE	MURIATIC	NAVVYING	NONANOIC	NOVELDOM
MORIBUND	MURIFORM	NAYSAYER	NONBEING	NOVELISH
MORPHEME	MURMURER	NAZIFIES	NONBRAND	NOVELIZE
MORTGAGE	MURRELET	NEATENED	NONCOLOR	NOWADAYS
MOSHAVIM	MUSICIAN	NEBULIUM	NONDANCE	NOWHENCE
MOSQUITO	MUSKROOT	NEBULIZE	NONELECT	NUBECULA
MOSSBACK	MUSQUASH	NEBULOUS	NONEMPTY	NUBILOUS
MOSTWHAT	MUSTIEST	NECKATEE	NONENTRY	NUDZHING
MOTHBALL	MUTANDUM	NECKBAND	NONEQUAL	NUGGETED
MOTHLIKE	MUTATIVE	NECKBEEF	NONEVENT	NUMBFISH
MOTILITY	MUTATORY	NECKLIKE	NONFATAL	NUMCHUCK
MOTIVATE	MUTCHKIN	NECKLINE	NONFINAL	NUMERACY
MOTIVING	MUTICATE	NEEDMENT	NONFLUID	NUMEROUS
MOTIVITY	MUTICOUS	NENNIGAI	NONGLARE	NUMINOUS
MOTLEYER	MUTILATE	NENUPHAR	NONGREEN	NUMMULAR
MOTORAIL	MUTINOUS	NEONATAL	NONHARDY	NUMSKULL
MOTORBUS	MUTUALLY	NEOPHOBE	NONHUMAN	NUNCHAKU
MOTORCAR	MUZZIEST	NEOPRENE	NONIONIC	NUNCHEON
MOTORDOM	MYCELIUM	NEOTENIC	NONJUROR	NUNDINAL
MOTORIAL	MYCETOMA	NEOTOXIN	NONLEAFY	NURTURAL
MOTORIUM	MYELINIC	NESHNESS	NONLOYAL	NUTATION
MOTORWAY	MYOLOGIC	NEURALLY	NONMAJOR	NUTBROWN
MOUCHARD	MYOMANCY	NEURAXON	NONMODAL	NUTHATCH
MOUCHOIR	MYOPATHY	NEWELLED	NONMONEY	NUZZLING
MOURNFUL	MYOPHILY	NEWISHLY	NONNAVAL	NYMPHISH
MOUTERED	MYOSOTIS	NEWLYWED	NONNOBLE	OAFISHLY
MOUTHFUL	MYOTONIC	NEWSBEAT	NONNOVEL	OANSHAGH

OBDURACY	OMNIVORY	OUTBITCH	OUTWORTH	OVERURGE
OBDURING	OMOHYOID	OUTBLAZE	OVENABLE	OVERVIEW
OBEYABLE	OMOPHAGY	OUTBLUFF	OVENLIKE	OVERVOTE
OBITUARY	OMOPLATE	OUTBLUSH	OVENWOOD	OVERWARY
OBJECTED	ONCIDIUM	OUTBOARD	OVERBAKE	OVERWIDE
OBJECTOR	ONGAONGA	OUTBOAST	OVERBEAR	OVERWILY
OBJURING	ONIONIER	OUTBOUND	OVERBILL	OVERYEAR
OBLIGATI	ONLOOKER	OUTBOXED	OVERBLEW	OVERZEAL
OBLIQUID	ONTOGENY	OUTBOXES	OVERBLOW	OVIBOSES
OBLIVION	ONYCHIUM	OUTBROKE	OVERBOOK	OVIDUCAL
OBLONGLY	OOGAMETE	OUTBUILD	OVERBOOT	OVIPOSIT
OBSEQUIE	OOGAMOUS	OUTBUILT	OVERBORE	OWERLOUP
OBSESSED	OOGONIUM	OUTBULGE	OVERBORN	OWRECOME
OBSESSES	OOLACHAN	OUTBULLY	OVERBRIM	OWREWORD
OBTECTED	OOMYCETE	OUTCATCH	OVERBULK	OXALISES
OBTESTED	OOPHORON	OUTCHARM	OVERCAME	OXAZEPAM
OBTUSITY	OOPHYTIC	OUTCLIMB	OVERCOME	OXIMETER
OBVIABLE	OOSPORIC	OUTCOACH	OVERCOOK	OXIMETRY
OCCIPITA	OPAQUELY	OUTCOUNT	OVERCOOL	OXPECKER
OCCULTLY	OPAQUING	OUTCRAWL	OVERCRAW	OXYGENIC
OCCUPIED	OPENWORK	OUTDODGE	OVERCROP	OXYMORON
OCCUPIER	OPERCELE	OUTDRUNK	OVERFELL	OXYTOCIC
OCEANAUT	OPHIDIAN	OUTDWELT	OVERFILL	PABOUCHE
OCKODOLS	OPHIURID	OUTEATEN	OVERFINE	PABULOUS
OCOTILLO	OPIATING	OUTFIGHT	OVERFISH	PACHADOM
OCTAPODY	OPOPANAX	OUTFLOAT	OVERFLEW	PACHALIC
OCTARCHY	OPPILATE	OUTFLUSH	OVERFLOW	PACHOULI
OCTOROON	OPPONENT	OUTFOUND	OVERFOUL	PACIFIED
ODIOUSLY	OPPUGNER	OUTFOXED	OVERGANG	PACIFIER
ODOGRAPH	OPSONIFY	OUTFOXES	OVERGIVE	PACIFISM
ODONTOID	OPTATIVE	OUTGOING	OVERGONE	PACIFIST
ODONTOMA	OPTICIST	OUTGROSS	OVERGREW	PACKETED
OEDIPEAN	OPTIMATE	OUTGUIDE	OVERHAND	PACKNESS
OEILLADE	OPTIMISM	OUTHOUSE	OVERHANG	PACKSACK
OFFENDED	OPTIMIST	OUTHUMOR	OVERHEAP	PADUASOY
OFFICIAL	OPTIMIZE	OUTLAWRY	OVERHIGH	PAGANDOM
OFFISHLY	OPTIONEE	OUTMARCH	OVERHOLD	PAGEVIEW
OFFSHOOT	OPULENCE	OUTMATCH	OVERHOLY	PAHAUTEA
OFFSTAGE	OPULENCY	OUTPITCH	OVERHOPE	PAHOEHOE
OFFTRACK	ORATORIO	OUTPOINT	OVERHUNT	PAILLARD
OFTENEST	ORCHITIC	OUTPUPIL	OVERHYPE	PAINTBOX
OILCLOTH	ORDUROUS	OUTQUOTE	OVERJUMP	PAJAMAED
OILFIRED	OREODONT	OUTRIGHT	OVERKEPT	PALEFACE
OILPROOF	ORGULOUS	OUTSMOKE	OVERKILL	PALEWAYS
OILTIGHT	ORIBATID	OUTSPOKE	OVERLARD	PALEWISE
OITICICA	ORILLION	OUTSTART	OVERLEAF	PALLADIA
OKEYDOKE	ORONASAL	OUTSTOOD	OVERLOAD	PALLADIC
OLDSQUAW	ORTHODOX	OUTSTUDY	OVERLOCK	PALLIARD
OLDSTYLE	ORTHOPOD	OUTSTUNT	OVERLONG	PALLIDLY
OLEFINIC	ORTHOTIC	OUTTHANK	OVERLOOK	PALSTAFF
OLIGEMIA	OSSIFIES	OUTTHINK	OVERLORD	PALTRILY
OLIGEMIC	OSTEITIS	OUTTHREW	OVERMILK	PAMPASES
OLIGURIA	OTITISES	OUTTHROB	OVERPACK	PAMPHLET
OMADHAUN	OTOSCOPE	OUTTHROW	OVERPUMP	PANDANUS
OMBRELLA	OTOSCOPY	OUTTRICK	OVERRULE	PANDEMIA
OMELETTE	OTOTOXIC	OUTTRUMP	OVERSOAK	PANDERED
OMMATEUM	OUBAASES	OUTVAUNT	OVERSOLD	PANDOWDY
OMNIFIES	OULACHON	OUTVOICE	OVERSOON	PANDYING
OMNIFORM	OUTADDED	OUTVYING	OVERTART	PANEGYRY
OMNIMODE	OUTASKED	OUTWATCH	OVERTOOK	PANICKED

PANMIXES	PAXWAXES	PHILABEG	PINELIKE	PLUNKING
PANMIXIA	PAYCHECK	PHILIBEG	PINEWOOD	PLURALLY
PANNIKEL	PAYNIMRY	PHILOMEL	PINGUEFY	PLURISIE
PANNIKIN	PEABERRY	PHILOMOT	PINNIPED	PLUVIOUS
PANORAMA	PEAKIEST	PHLEGMON	PINPOINT	POCHETTE
PANSOPHY	PEARWOOD	PHORMIUM	PINPRICK	POCKETED
PANTALON	PEBBLING	PHORONID	PINSWELL	POCKETER
PAPALIZE	PECCABLE	PHOSPHID	PINWHEEL	POCKMARK
PAPERBOY	PECCANCY	PHOSPHOR	PIPECLAY	PODOCARP
PAPISTIC	PECULIUM	PHOTINIA	PIPELIKE	PODOLOGY
PAPPUSES	PEEKABOO	PHOTOFIT	PIPELINE	PODSOLIC
PAPYRIAN	PEELABLE	PHOTOGEN	PIPEWORT	PODZOLIC
PARABEMA	PEEPHOLE	PHOTOMAP	PIQUANCE	POECHORE
PARACHOR	PEEPSHOW	PHOTONIC	PIQUANCY	POKEWEED
PARAFFIN	PEETWEET	PHOTOPIA	PIQUILLO	POLEMIZE
PARAFOIL	PEGBOARD	PHOTOPIC	PIRARUCU	POLITELY
PARAFORM	PEGBOXES	PHRATRAL	PIRIFORM	POLLENED
PARAGRAM	PELERINE	PHREAKER	PIRLICUE	POLLICAL
PARALLAX	PELLETAL	PHRYGANA	PIROZHOK	POLLICIE
PARALOGY	PELLICLE	PHTHALIC	PISIFORM	POLLIWIG
PARALYZE	PELLMELL	PHTHALIN	PITAHAYA	POLLIWOG
PARAMOUR	PELOLOGY	PHTHISES	PITCHMAN	POLLYWOG
PARANOEA	PEMBROKE	PHTHISIC	PITCHMEN	POLOIDAL
PARANOIA	PEMOLINE	PHTHISIS	PITCHOUT	POLONIUM
PARAPARA	PENDENCY	PHYLARCH	PITHBALL	POLTFOOT
PARAPHED	PENITENT	PHYLLODE	PIVOTING	POLTROON
PARAQUAT	PENKNIFE	PHYLLODY	PIXIEISH	POLYAXON
PARASHAH	PENNEECH	PHYLLOME	PIXINESS	POLYBRID
PARASHOT	PENNEECK	PHYSICKY	PIZZELLE	POLYGALA
PARAVAIL	PENNONED	PHYSIQUE	PIZZERIA	POLYGENY
PARAVANE	PENNYBOY	PIACULAR	PLACIDLY	POLYGLOT
PARAVANT	PENNYFEE	PIAFFING	PLACITUM	POLYGYNY
PARAZOON	PENONCEL	PICAYUNE	PLAGUILY	POLYMATH
PARKLAND	PENUCKLE	PICCANIN	PLANARIA	POLYONYM
PARKLIKE	PENUMBRA	PICHURIM	PLANFORM	POLYPHON
PARKWARD	PENWOMAN	PICIFORM	PLANGENT	POLYPILL
PAROXYSM	PENWOMEN	PICKABLE	PLANKTON	POLYPITE
PARVOLIN	PEPPERER	PICKADIL	PLASTRAL	POLYPORE
PASHADOM	PEPTIDIC	PICKBACK	PLASTRUM	POLYSOMY
PASPALUM	PEREOPOD	PICKLOCK	PLATBAND	POLYTENY
PASSBAND	PERFORCE	PICKWICK	PLATYPUS	POLYTYPE
PASSBOOK	PERIODED	PICNICKY	PLAUSIVE	POLYZOIC
PASSIBLY	PERIODID	PICOGRAM	PLAYBOOK	POLYZOON
PASSUSES	PERRUQUE	PICOTING	PLAYDOWN	POMMETTY
PASSWORD	PETABYTE	PICOWAVE	PLAYGIRL	POMOLOGY
PATAGIUM	PETANQUE	PICRITIC	PLAYLAND	POMPILID
PATENTEE	PETRONEL	PIFFLING	PLAYWEAR	POMWATER
PATINIZE	PETTIFOG	PIGSTICK	PLECTRON	PONTIFEX
PATOOTIE	PETUNTZE	PIGSWILL	PLEUGHED	POOLHALL
PATRONLY	PEWTERER	PIHOIHOI	PLOUGHED	POOLROOM
PATTYPAN	PEZIZOID	PILCHARD	PLOUGHER	POONTANG
PATULOUS	PHALANGE	PILEWORK	PLOWABLE	POORTITH
PATUTUKI	PHALLISM	PILIFORM	PLOWBACK	POORWILL
PAUROPOD	PHANTAST	PILLOWED	PLOWHEAD	POPEHOOD
PAUSEFUL	PHANTASY	PILLWORM	PLUGLESS	POPELIKE
PAVILION	PHARMACY	PILLWORT	PLUGUGLY	POPINJAY
PAVONIAN	PHATTEST	PINAKOID	PLUMBISM	POPJOYED
PAVONINE	PHENAZIN	PINCHBUG	PLUMBITE	POPLITEI
PAWNABLE	PHENIXES	PINDLING	PLUMELET	POPPADOM
PAWNSHOP	PHENYLIC	PINECONE	PLUMLIKE	POPULISM

PORKWOOD	PRONOTUM	PUMICATE	PYROXYLE	QUOIFING
PORNOMAG	PROPERER	PUMICING	PYRRHOUS	QUOINING
POROGAMY	PROPERTY	PUMICITE	PYRUVATE	QUONKING
PORPHYRY	PROPHYLL	PUMPHOOD	PYXIDIUM	QUOTABLE
PORTABLY	PROPOLIS	PUMPLIKE	QAIMAQAM	QUOTABLY
PORTAPAK	PROPOUND	PUNCHBAG	QINDARKA	RABBINIC
POSITIVE	PROPPANT	PUNCHEON	QUAALUDE	RACECARD
POSOLOGY	PROPRIUM	PUNCHILY	QUADPLEX	RACEGOER
POSSIBLE	PROPYLON	PUNCTUAL	QUADRANS	RACEMIZE
POSTALLY	PROSOPON	PUNCTULE	QUADRIGA	RACEWALK
POSTCAVA	PROTOCOL	PUNCTURE	QUADROON	RACHITIC
POSTDRUG	PROTOPOD	PUNDITRY	QUAFFING	RACKWORK
POSTFORM	PROTOXID	PUNGENCE	QUAGMIRY	RADIANCY
POSTPAID	PROTOZOA	PUNGENCY	QUAILING	RADIATOR
POSTPONE	PROUDFUL	PUNITORY	QUAKIEST	RAILBIRD
POSTPUNK	PROVABLY	PUPARIUM	QUALMIER	RAILROAD
POSTSHOW	PROVEDOR	PUPILAGE	QUANDANG	RAINBIRD
POSTSYNC	PROVIDOR	PUPPETRY	QUANDARY	RAINFALL
POSTTEST	PROVIRAL	PUPPODUM	QUANDONG	RAINWASH
POTBELLY	PROVIRUS	PUPPYDOM	QUANTIFY	RAINWEAR
POTBOUND	PROXIMAL	PUPPYISH	QUANTITY	RAKEHELL
POTCHING	PRUDENCE	PUPPYISM	QUANTONG	RAMEQUIN
POTENTLY	PRUNELLE	PURBLIND	QUARRIAN	RAMIFIED
POTHERED	PRURITIC	PURDAHED	QUARRIER	RAMIFORM
POUCHFUL	PRYINGLY	PURIFIED	QUARRION	RAMPSMAN
POWERFUL	PSALMODY	PURIFIER	QUATCHED	RANARIAN
POWSOWDY	PSEPHISM	PURIFIES	QUAVERER	RANCHMAN
POWWOWED	PSILOSIS	PURPLISH	QUAYSIDE	RANDLORD
POXVIRUS	PSYCHOID	PURPURIC	QUEASILY	RANIFORM
POZZOLAN	PTERYGIA	PURPURIN	QUEAZIER	RAPACITY
PRANKFUL	PTYALIZE	PURTRAID	QUEENLET	RARIFIED
PRATFALL	PUBLICAN	PURVEYOR	QUEERDOM	RASCALLY
PRECEESE	PUBLICLY	PUSHCART	QUELCHED	RATIFIED
PREDELLE	PUCELAGE	PUSHDOWN	QUELLING	RATPROOF
PREGGERS	PUDENDUM	PUTATIVE	QUENCHED	RAZMATAZ
PRIGGISM	PUDIBUND	PUTCHOCK	QUENELLE	REASSESS
PRIMALLY	PUDICITY	PUTRIDLY	QUETCHED	REBELLER
PRIMITIA	PUFFBALL	PUZZLING	QUETHING	REBELLOW
PRIMROSY	PUFFBIRD	PYCNIDIA	QUICHING	REBOOTED
PRINCIPI	PUFFIEST	PYCNOSIS	QUICKEST	REBORROW
PRINCOCK	PUGILISM	PYCNOTIC	QUICKSET	REBUFFED
PRINTOUT	PUGILIST	PYGIDIUM	QUIDDANY	REBUTTON
PRIORITY	PUIRTITH	PYGMYISH	QUIDNUNC	RECEMENT
PRISSILY	PULLBACK	PYGMYISM	QUIETIST	RECODIFY
PRIZABLE	PULLORUM	PYINKADO	QUIETIVE	RECOILER
PROBABLY	PULLOVER	PYJAMAED	QUIGHTED	RECONVEY
PROCINCT	PULMOTOR	PYKNOSES	QUILLAJA	RECORKED
PRODITOR	PULPALLY	PYKNOSIS	QUILLING	REDDENDO
PRODROMI	PULPITAL	PYKNOTIC	QUINCUNX	REDDENED
PROFORMA	PULPITRY	PYODERMA	QUINOLIN	REDEEMER
PROFOUND	PULPITUM	PYRAZOLE	QUIPPISH	REEDLIKE
PROHIBIT	PULPMILL	PYRIDINE	QUIRKIER	REEMBODY
PROLABOR	PULPWOOD	PYRIFORM	QUIRKILY	REEXPORT
PROLIFIC	PULSEJET	PYRITIZE	QUIRKISH	REFALLEN
PROLOGUE	PULSIFIC	PYRITOUS	QUISLING	REFERRAL
PROMISOR	PULVILIO	PYROLIZE	QUIXOTIC	REFERRED
PROMOTOR	PULVILLE	PYROLOGY	QUIXOTRY	REFERRER
PROMPTER	PULVILLI	PYROLYZE	QUIZZIFY	REFIXING
PROMPTLY	PULVILLO	PYRONINE	QUIZZING	REFLEXLY
PROMULGE	PULVINUS	PYROXENE	QUODDING	REFLOWER

REFOLDED	REVIVIFY	ROTAVATE	SASTRUGA	SENTENCE
REFORMER	REWAREWA	ROTOTILL	SATRAPAL	SEPADDED
REFRYING	REWEDDED	ROTOVATE	SAUCEBOX	SEPTETTE
REFUGIUM	REWORKED	ROUGHAGE	SAVAGISM	SEQUENCE
REGULIZE	REZEROED	ROUGHDRY	SAVOYARD	SEQUENCY
REHABBED	RHABDOID	ROUGHHEW	SAVVYING	SERENELY
REHABBER	RHEOLOGY	ROUGHLEG	SAWTEETH	SEWELLEL
REHAMMER	RHEOPHIL	ROVINGLY	SAWTOOTH	SEWERAGE
REHEATER	RHINITIC	ROWDYDOW	SAYONARA	SEXTUPLY
REHEELED	RHINITIS	ROWELING	SCABBARD	SEXUALLY
REHEMMED	RHIZOBIA	ROWNDELL	SCABBILY	SHADBLOW
REHOBOAM	RHIZOMIC	ROYALISE	SCABIOSA	SHADBUSH
REILLUME	RHIZOPOD	ROYALIZE	SCAFFOLD	SHADCHAN
REJACKET	RHIZOPUS	RUBAIYAT	SCALAWAG	SHAGBARK
REJIGGED	RHODAMIN	RUBBOARD	SCALPRUM	SHAGGILY
REJIGGER	RHONCHAL	RUBICUND	SCAMMONY	SHAGROON
RELAXANT	RHONCHUS	RUBIDIUM	SCANTITY	SHAUCHLY
RELETTER	RHYTHMAL	RUBIFIED	SCARABEE	SHEEPDOG
RELOADED	RHYTHMED	RUBRICAL	SCATBACK	SHEEPISH
RELOADER	RIBAUDRY	RUCKSACK	SCENEMEN	SHEEPMEN
RELOOKED	RIBGRASS	RUGALACH	SCHIZOID	SHEKELIM
REMEMBER	RICEBIRD	RUMBAING	SCHNOZES	SHELLFUL
REMOTELY	RICKYARD	RUMBELOW	SCHOLIUM	SHEUCHED
REMURMUR	RIDGEWAY	RUMOURER	SCHUSSES	SHEUGHED
RENDERED	RIFAMPIN	RURALITY	SCINCOID	SHIDDUCH
RENDERER	RIFFRAFF	RURALIZE	SCISSION	SHILINGI
RENMINBI	RIGHTFUL	RUTABAGA	SCOFFLAW	SHIMMING
RENOWNER	RIGIDIFY	RYEFLOUR	SCOMFISH	SHIRTILY
REOCCUPY	RIGIDITY	RYOTWARI	SCOOBIES	SHITLIST
REPARKED	RIGORISM	SABBATIC	SCOOPFUL	SHIVVING
REPEGGED	RIGORIST	SACCOSES	SCORNFUL	SHKOTZIM
REPELLED	RILLMARK	SACCULUS	SCOTOPIC	SHLEMIEL
REPELLER	RIPARIAN	SACKABLE	SCRABBLY	SHLEPPED
REPEREPE	RIRORIRO	SAFENESS	SCRIBBLY	SHOFROTH
REPERKED	RITUALLY	SAGACITY	SCRIBING	SHOPGIRL
REPORTER	RITZIEST	SAGANASH	SCRIBISM	SHOPTALK
REPREEVE	RIVERWAY	SAILORLY	SCRIGGLY	SHOPWORN
REPUBLIC	RIZZARED	SAKKOSES	SCROUNGY	SHORTISH
REPUGNED	RIZZERED	SALACITY	SCRUMPOX	SHOTHOLE
REPUMPED	RIZZORED	SALINIZE	SCULPTOR	SHOULDST
REPURIFY	ROADWORK	SALIVARY	SCUMFISH	SHOWDOWN
REQUIGHT	ROBORANT	SALTBUSH	SCUMMILY	SHOWGIRL
REREMICE	ROBOTISM	SALTWORT	SCUNGING	SHOWROOM
RERIGGED	ROCKAWAY	SAMIZDAT	SCUPPAUG	SHREWDLY
REROLLER	ROCKFALL	SANCTIFY	SEACOAST	SHTUPPED
REROOFED	ROCKLIKE	SANCTITY	SEAQUAKE	SHUGGIES
RESEEDED	ROCKWORK	SANDHILL	SEASPEAK	SHUTDOWN
RESINIFY	ROLLABLE	SANDPUMP	SEATWORK	SHWESHWE
RESINIZE	ROLLBACK	SANENESS	SEAWIVES	SIALIDAN
RESUMMON	ROLLOVER	SANGUIFY	SEAWOMAN	SIDEWISE
RETAGGED	RONGGENG	SANTALOL	SEBESTEN	SIGHLIKE
RETAUGHT	ROOFTREE	SAPIDITY	SECUNDLY	SIGISBEI
RETELLER	ROOMETTE	SAPONIFY	SEEDIEST	SIKORSKY
RETIARII	ROOMSOME	SAPUCAIA	SEEDNESS	SILICIDE
RETORTER	ROORBACH	SARDONYX	SEGUEING	SILICIFY
RETRENCH	ROORBACK	SARGASSO	SELAMLIK	SILICIUM
RETRONYM	ROOTHOLD	SARRASIN	SELECTLY	SILKTAIL
RETURNER	ROOTWORM	SARRAZIN	SELFLESS	SILKWEED
REVANCHE	ROPELIKE	SARTORII	SEMIOVAL	SIMAZINE
REVERIFY	ROSEWOOD	SASSWOOD	SENSUOUS	SIMILIZE

SIMPLIFY	SNAPBACK	SPAGIRIC	SQUUSHES	SUBFLUID
SIMPLISM	SNAPSHOT	SPANGHEW	STAFFAGE	SUBGENUS
SINCIPUT	SNAZZIER	SPANSPEK	STAGNANT	SUBGRAPH
SINICIZE	SNAZZILY	SPARAXIS	STALLMAN	SUBGROUP
SINUITIS	SNEAKSBY	SPATFALL	STANDPAT	SUBHUMID
SINUSOID	SNEESHAN	SPAZZING	STAPEDII	SUBITIZE
SIRENIZE	SNEESHES	SPECCING	STARTFUL	SUBLEVEL
SIRIASIS	SNOBBERY	SPEEDWAY	STATICKY	SUBNASAL
SISSYISH	SNOBBISH	SPELLFUL	STATUARY	SUBOPTIC
SISTROID	SNOWBANK	SPETCHES	STAYAWAY	SUBOXIDE
SIXTIETH	SNOWBOOT	SPHYGMIC	STAYSAIL	SUBPHASE
SIXTYISH	SNOWDROP	SPHYNXES	STEEDIES	SUBPRIOR
SIZZLING	SNOWLAND	SPICULUM	STEMMATA	SUBPUBIC
SKEWBACK	SNOWMOLD	SPIFFIER	STEWPOND	SUBSENSE
SKEWBALD	SNOWPLOW	SPIFFIES	STICKILY	SUBSHAFT
SKEWNESS	SNOWSHED	SPIFFILY	STICKJAW	SUBSIZAR
SKIJORER	SNOWSLIP	SPIFFING	STICTION	SUBSKILL
SKIMMING	SNUBBISH	SPILIKIN	STIFFEST	SUBSPACE
SKINFOOD	SNUFFBOX	SPILITIC	STIFFISH	SUBTAXON
SKIPJACK	SNUGNESS	SPITBALL	STILTISH	SUBTHEME
SKIRMISH	SNUSHING	SPIVVERY	STIMULUS	SUBTILTY
SKITTISH	SOAKAWAY	SPOFFISH	STOCCADO	SUBTOPIC
SKIVVIES	SOAPROOT	SPONDAIC	STOCIOUS	SUBUCULA
SKOKIAAN	SOAPSUDS	SPOOKERY	STOCKAGE	SUBURBIA
SKOLLING	SOARAWAY	SPOOKILY	STOCKILY	SUBVICAR
SKOOSHED	SOCIABLY	SPOOKISH	STOCKIST	SUBVIRUS
SKULLCAP	SOCIALLY	SPOROZOA	STOCKPOT	SUBWAYED
SKYBOXES	SOCKETTE	SPRITZIG	STOLPORT	SUBWORLD
SKYWRITE	SOCKLESS	SPRYNESS	STOPBANK	SUCCINCT
SKYWROTE	SODALIST	SPURIOUS	STOPCOCK	SUCCINIC
SLAPDASH	SOFFIONI	SPYGLASS	STOPWORD	SUCCUBUS
SLEAZILY	SOFTBACK	SQUADDIE	STORMFUL	SUCKFISH
SLIMDOWN	SOFTWOOD	SQUADRON	STOTINOV	SUCURUJU
SLIPFORM	SOILLESS	SQUAILER	STOVETOP	SUDDENLY
SLIPPILY	SOLARIZE	SQUAMOUS	STOWDOWN	SUDOROUS
SLIPSHOD	SOLECIZE	SQUAMULA	STRAGGLY	SUDSLESS
SLIPSLOP	SOLFEGGI	SQUAMULE	STRAVAIG	SUEDETTE
SLIVOVIC	SOLIDARY	SQUARELY	STRENGTH	SUFFIXAL
SLOBBISH	SOLIDIFY	SQUARIAL	STRICTLY	SUFFIXES
SLOMMOCK	SOLIDISH	SQUARING	STRONGLY	SUILLINE
SLOPWORK	SOLPUGID	SQUARISH	STRONGYL	SUKIYAKI
SLOTHFUL	SOMBROUS	SQUARSON	STUDBOOK	SULFITIC
SLOWPOKE	SONANTAL	SQUATTLE	STUDWORK	SULFONYL
SLOWWORM	SONGBOOK	SQUAWKED	STYLITIC	SULLENLY
SLUGGARD	SONOBUOY	SQUAWMAN	SUBABBOT	SUMMITRY
SLUGGISH	SONOROUS	SQUAWMEN	SUBACUTE	SUMMONER
SLUGHORN	SOOCHONG	SQUEAKED	SUBBASIN	SUMPHISH
SLUMLORD	SOOTHFUL	SQUEEGEE	SUBBLOCK	SUMPWEED
SLUMMOCK	SOOTHSAY	SQUEGGED	SUBCAUSE	SUNDRILY
SLUSHILY	SORORITY	SQUEGGER	SUBCHIEF	SUNDROPS
SLYBOOTS	SORORIZE	SQUIBBED	SUBCHORD	SUNGLASS
SMALLAGE	SORROWER	SQUIDDED	SUBCLASS	SUNPORCH
SMALLPOX	SORRYISH	SQUIFFER	SUBCRUST	SUNSHINY
SMALLSAT	SOULLESS	SQUIGGLY	SUBDUING	SUPPEAGO
SMIRRIER	SOUNDBOX	SQUILGEE	SUBDUPLE	SURCULUS
SMORBROD	SOURPUSS	SQUIRAGE	SUBDWARF	SURFBIRD
SMORZATO	SOUVLAKI	SQUIRELY	SUBEQUAL	SURFFISH
SMOULDRY	SOVRANLY	SQUIRISH	SUBFEUED	SURQUEDY
SMUDGILY	SOZZLING	SQUISHED	SUBFIXES	SURROUND
SMUGNESS	SPACIOUS	SQUUSHED	SUBFLOOR	SURROYAL

SURTAXED	TACKSMAN	TENPENNY	THYMUSES	TOUCHPAD
SURTAXES	TAFFAREL	TEPEFIED	THYROXIN	TOUGHISH
SURUCUCU	TAFFRAIL	TEPIDITY	TICKETED	TOWARDLY
SURVEYED	TAGALONG	TERAKIHI	TICKTACK	TOWNFOLK
SURVIVAL	TAGBOARD	TERATOMA	TICKTOCK	TOWNHALL
SURVIVOR	TAGHAIRM	TERAWATT	TIDELIKE	TOWNHOME
SUSURRUS	TAILLAMP	TEREBENE	TIDYTIPS	TOWNLAND
SVARAJES	TAILPIPE	TERIYAKI	TIFFINED	TOWNWEAR
SVASTIKA	TAILWIND	TERRAZZO	TIGEREYE	TOXICITY
SVEDBERG	TAKAMAKA	TERRIBLE	TIGHTEST	TOXOCARA
SWAGSHOP	TAKEAWAY	TERYLENE	TIGHTISH	TOYWOMAN
SWANKEST	TAKEDOWN	TERZETTA	TIGHTWAD	TRACTRIX
SWANKPOT	TALEGGIO	TERZETTI	TIGRIDIA	TRADEOFF
SWANSKIN	TALIONIC	TERZETTO	TILELIKE	TRAGICAL
SWAPTION	TALKBACK	TETANIZE	TILLABLE	TRANSFIX
SWARAJES	TALLIATE	TETRAXON	TILLICUM	TRAPDOOR
SWASTIKA	TALLITIM	TETTERED	TIMEBOMB	TRAPEZII
SWEATBOX	TALLITOT	TEUCHEST	TIMELINE	TREELIKE
SWEETPEA	TALLYMAN	TEUGHEST	TIMEWORK	TREKKING
SWELLEST	TALUKDAR	TEXTBOOK	TIMIDITY	TRENCHER
SWELLISH	TAMMYING	TEXTUARY	TINSNIPS	TRIAXIAL
SWIFTEST	TAMWORTH	THALLIUM	TIPPYTOE	TRIBALLY
SWIMMILY	TANNABLE	THALLOID	TIPSTAFF	TRIBUNAL
SWIMMING	TAPENADE	THANKYOU	TIPSTOCK	TRICHOID
SWIPIEST	TAPEWORM	THATAWAY	TIRRIVIE	TRICHORD
SWIRLIER	TAQUERIA	THEODICY	TITANITE	TRICKISH
SWIZZING	TARBOOSH	THEOGONY	TITTERED	TRICOLOR
SYCOMORE	TARNALLY	THEOSOPH	TITTERER	TRICTRAC
SYLLABLE	TARTANRY	THETCHES	TITUBANT	TRIFOCAL
SYLLABUB	TARTARIC	THIAZIDE	TIZWASES	TRIFORIA
SYLLABUS	TARTARLY	THIEVERY	TJANTING	TRIGGEST
SYLPHISH	TASKWORK	THIEVISH	TOADFLAX	TRIGRAPH
SYLVATIC	TATAHASH	THINCLAD	TOBOGGAN	TRILLION
SYMBOLIC	TATTOOED	THINDOWN	TOILETED	TRILLIUM
SYMPATHY	TATTOOER	THINGAMY	TOILETTE	TRIMERIC
SYMPATRY	TATTOWED	THINNISH	TOILWORN	TRIMORPH
SYMPHILY	TAXATIVE	THIONATE	TOKONOMA	TRIMOTOR
SYMPLAST	TAXONOMY	THIOPHEN	TOKOTOKO	TRIPUDIA
SYNANTHY	TAYBERRY	THIOPHIL	TOLBOOTH	TRISTICH
SYNAPSID	TEABOXES	THIOTEPA	TOLEWARE	TRIZONAL
SYNAPSIS	TEAMMATE	THRALDOM	TOLLABLE	TROILIST
SYNARCHY	TEAMWORK	THRALLED	TOMAHAWK	TROOPIAL
SYNASTRY	TEDDERED	THRAPPLE	TOMATOEY	TROTHFUL
SYNCYTIA	TEETERED	THRAWARD	TOMBLIKE	TROTTOIR
SYNGRAPH	TEETOTAL	THRAWNLY	TOMMYROT	TROUPIAL
SYNKARYA	TEFILLAH	THREEPER	TOMOGRAM	TROUTFUL
SYNOPSES	TEFILLIN	THRESHED	TOMORROW	TROUTLET
SYNOPSIS	TEKTITIC	THRESHER	TONICITY	TROUVEUR
SYNTONIC	TELEGONY	THRESHES	TOOLROOM	TRUANTLY
SYNTONIN	TELESEME	THRIVING	TOOTHFUL	TRUANTRY
SYPHILIS	TELETYPE	THROBBED	TOPLOFTY	TRUCKFUL
SYRINXES	TELEVIEW	THROTTLE	TOPMAKER	TRUDGING
SYSSITIA	TELLABLE	THRUMMED	TOPNOTCH	TRUEBLUE
SYSTEMED	TELLTALE	THUGGISH	TOPOTYPE	TRUEBORN
SYZYGIES	TELLURAL	THUMBING	TORNILLO	TRUEBRED
TABEFIED	TENDENCE	THUMBKIN	TORRIDLY	TRUISTIC
TABOGGAN	TENDENCY	THUMBNUT	TOTALIZE	TRUMPERY
TABOOLEY	TENDERLY	THUMBPOT	TOTEMITE	TRUNKFUL
TABOULEH	TENEBRAE	THWARTER	TOTITIVE	TRUQUAGE
TACAHOUT	TENONING	THWARTLY	TOUCHILY	TRUQUEUR

TRUSTFUL	UMBELLET	UNDERRAN	UNJOINED	UNSPRUNG
TRYINGLY	UMBRATIC	UNDERRUN	UNJOYFUL	UNSTARRY
TRYWORKS	UMBRELLO	UNDEVOUT	UNJOYOUS	UNSTUFFY
TSESSEBE	UMLAUTED	UNDIPPED	UNJUDGED	UNSUBTLY
TSKTSKED	UMPTIETH	UNDIVINE	UNJUSTER	UNSUMMED
TSORRISS	UMQUHILE	UNDOTTED	UNJUSTLY	UNSUNNED
TSUTSUMU	UNACIDIC	UNDROSSY	UNKENNED	UNSUPPLE
TUBEWORK	UNAFRAID	UNDUBBED	UNKENNEL	UNTACKLE
TUBEWORM	UNAMAZED	UNDULLED	UNKINDLY	UNTANNED
TUBIFORM	UNANCHOR	UNDULOUS	UNKINGLY	UNTAUGHT
TUBULATE	UNAVOWED	UNEASIER	UNKINKED	UNTENANT
TUBULOUS	UNBALING	UNEDIBLE	UNLAWFUL	UNTENTED
TUBULURE	UNBANDED	UNEVENLY	UNLAYING	UNTETHER
TUCKSHOP	UNBANNED	UNEXPERT	UNLETHAL	UNTHATCH
TUCOTUCO	UNBESEEM	UNFAIRLY	UNLIKELY	UNTHRIFT
TUCUTUCO	UNBIDDEN	UNFAMOUS	UNLOOKED	UNTIDILY
TUCUTUCU	UNBISHOP	UNFANNED	UNMANFUL	UNTIMELY
TULLIBEE	UNBITTED	UNFETTER	UNMAPPED	UNTIPPED
TUMEFIED	UNBITTEN	UNFILIAL	UNMEETLY	UNTRENDY
TUMIDITY	UNBLOODY	UNFITTED	UNMELLOW	UNTUCKED
TUMULTED	UNBOBBED	UNFIXING	UNMIXING	UNTUFTED
TUNNELED	UNBONNET	UNFIXITY	UNMODISH	UNTURBID
TUPPENCE	UNBOTTLE	UNFLASHY	UNMOVING	UNTURFED
TUPPENNY	UNBOUGHT	UNFORBID	UNMUFFLE	UNUNBIUM
TURBINAL	UNBOUNCY	UNFOUGHT	UNMUZZLE	UNUSABLY
TURBOFAN	UNBUCKLE	UNFREEZE	UNNETTED	UNUSEFUL
TURBOJET	UNBUDDED	UNFUNDED	UNOBEYED	UNVALUED
TURLOUGH	UNBUNDLE	UNFURRED	UNOPENED	UNVENTED
TURNCOCK	UNBURDEN	UNGAGGED	UNPAINED	UNVETTED
TURNHALL	UNBURIED	UNGAINLY	UNPEGGED	UNVIZARD
TURQUOIS	UNBURNED	UNGAUGED	UNPENNED	UNWANTED
TUSKLIKE	UNBURROW	UNGENTLE	UNPEOPLE	UNWARILY
TWEAKING	UNBUTTON	UNGENTLY	UNPINKED	UNWEANED
TWELVEMO	UNCANDID	UNGIVING	UNPITIED	UNWEAPON
TWICHILD	UNCATCHY	UNGOTTEN	UNPLOWED	UNWEBBED
TWILIGHT	UNCAUGHT	UNGREEDY	UNPOLLED	UNWEENED
TWINBORN	UNCHANCY	UNGUIDED	UNPOTTED	UNWELDED
TWOCCING	UNCHICLY	UNGUILTY	UNPRIZED	UNWETTED
TWOPENNY	UNCHURCH	UNGUMMED	UNPRUNED	UNWIFELY
TYMPANUM	UNCIALLY	UNGYVING	UNPUCKER	UNWILFUL
TYPEFACE	UNCLASSY	UNHAIRER	UNPULLED	UNWISDOM
TYPHUSES	UNCLEWED	UNHALLOW	UNPURELY	UNWISHED
TYPIFIED	UNCLINCH	UNHALVED	UNPUZZLE	UNWITTED
TYPOLOGY	UNCLUTCH	UNHANDED	UNREALLY	UNWIVING
TYRANNIC	UNCOFFIN	UNHEALTH	UNREELER	UNZIPPED
TYRANNIS	UNCOMELY	UNHEPPEN	UNRHYMED	UPADAISY
TZARITZA	UNCOMMON	UNHIDDEN	UNRIPPED	UPBEARER
TZATZIKI	UNCOOKED	UNHIPPER	UNRUBBED	UPCAUGHT
UBIETIES	UNCOUPLE	UNHIVING	UNRULIER	UPCURLED
UBIQUITY	UNCOYNED	UNHOLIER	UNSAFETY	UPDRYING
UDOMETER	UNCREWED	UNHOLILY	UNSEELIE	UPFLOWED
UDOMETRY	UNCTUOUS	UNHOOKED	UNSEEMLY	UPFOLDED
UGLIFIED	UNCUFFED	UNHUSKED	UNSEXUAL	UPFOLLOW
UGLIFIES	UNCULLED	UNIAXIAL	UNSHAKEN	UPGATHER
UINTAITE	UNDECENT	UNIFILAR	UNSHAVEN	UPGUSHED
ULTIMACY	UNDERBUD	UNIFYING	UNSHROUD	UPGUSHES
ULTIMATE	UNDERBUY	UNILOBAR	UNSHRUNK	UPHEAPED
ULTRADRY	UNDERFUR	UNIONIZE	UNSINFUL	UPHEAVAL
ULTRAHOT	UNDERJAW	UNIQUELY	UNSOLEMN	UPHUDDEN
ULTRALOW	UNDERMEN	UNJAMMED	UNSPHERE	UPHURLED

UPJETTED	VASSALRY	VIRGINLY	VUGHIEST	WAVEBAND
UPLEAPED	VAUNTFUL	VIRIDITE	VULGARLY	WAVEFORM
UPLOADED	VEGEMITE	VIRIDITY	VULGUSES	WAVELIKE
UPLOOKED	VEGETATE	VIRILELY	VULSELLA	WAXBERRY
UPMAKING	VEGETIVE	VIRILISM	VULVITIS	WAXCLOTH
UPPERCUT	VEHEMENT	VIRILITY	VUVUZELA	WAXINESS
UPROOTAL	VEHMIQUE	VIROLOGY	WAGMOIRE	WAXPLANT
UPSIZING	VEILEDLY	VIRTUOUS	WAGONFUL	WAYGOING
UPSPRANG	VEILLIKE	VISAGIST	WAIFLIKE	WAYGOOSE
UPSPRUNG	VEINLIKE	VISCACHA	WAILSOME	WAYLAYER
UPSWAYED	VELARIUM	VISCIDLY	WAITLIST	WAYLEAVE
UPTAKING	VELLEITY	VISELIKE	WAKERIFE	WAYLEGGO
UPTALKED	VELOCITY	VISNOMIE	WALDHORN	WAYPOINT
UPWAFTED	VELVETED	VISUALLY	WALDRAPP	WEAKSIDE
UPWARDLY	VENENATE	VITALISM	WALKABLE	WEALSMAN
UPWELLED	VENEREAL	VITALIST	WALKMILL	WEAPONED
URANYLIC	VENEREAN	VITALITY	WALKOVER	WEARABLE
URIDYLIC	VENGEFUL	VITIABLE	WALLAROO	WEAZENED
URINEMIA	VENIDIUM	VITIATOR	WALLFISH	WEBWHEEL
UROBILIN	VENOMOUS	VITICIDE	WALLOPER	WEDDERED
UROCHORD	VENOSITY	VITILIGO	WALLOWER	WEEDLIKE
UROPYGIA	VENVILLE	VIVACITY	WALTZING	WEEKLONG
UROSTOMY	VERBIAGE	VIVARIUM	WANDERED	WEEVILED
URSIFORM	VERJUICE	VIVIDITY	WANDEROO	WEFTWISE
URUSHIOL	VERKRAMP	VIVIFIED	WANTONED	WEIGHAGE
USEFULLY	VERMOULU	VIVIFIER	WANTONLY	WEIGHING
USQUEBAE	VERTUOUS	VIVIFIES	WANWORTH	WEIGHMEN
USTULATE	VESTIGIA	VIVIPARY	WARCRAFT	WELDMENT
USUFRUCT	VESTMENT	VIXENISH	WARDENED	WELLBORN
UTRICULI	VEXATION	VIZAMENT	WARDROOM	WELLCURB
UVULARLY	VEXILLUM	VIZARDED	WARFARIN	WELLHEAD
UVULITIS	VIATICUM	VIZCACHA	WARHABLE	WELLHOLE
UXORIOUS	VIBRANCY	VIZIRATE	WARMOUTH	WETTABLE
VACANTLY	VIBRIOID	VIZIRIAL	WARPOWER	WHALEMAN
VACATION	VIBRISSA	VIZORING	WARRAGAL	WHALEMEN
VACUUMED	VIBURNUM	VOCATIVE	WARRAGUL	WHARFAGE
VAGABOND	VICARIAL	VOICEFUL	WARRENER	WHARFING
VAGINANT	VICENARY	VOIDABLE	WARRIGAL	WHEECHED
VAGOTOMY	VICINITY	VOLITANT	WARTWORT	WHEELMAN
VAGRANCY	VICTORIA	VOLITION	WASHABLE	WHEESHED
VALIANCY	VIDEOFIT	VOLITIVE	WASHAWAY	WHEESHES
VALLHUND	VIDEOTEX	VOLLEYED	WASHBOWL	WHEEZILY
VALUABLE	VIEWABLE	VOLUMING	WASHROOM	WHENEVER
VALUABLY	VILIFIED	VOLUMIZE	WASTEWAY	WHEREVER
VALUATOR	VILIFIES	VOLUTOID	WASTFULL	WHEUGHED
VALVELET	VILIPEND	VOLVOXES	WATCHBOX	WHEYFACE
VAMPIRIC	VILLADOM	VOLVULUS	WATCHCRY	WHEYLIKE
VANADATE	VILLATIC	VOMITING	WATCHDOG	WHIDDING
VANADIUM	VINCIBLE	VOMITIVE	WATCHEYE	WHIFFING
VANADOUS	VINCULUM	VOMITORY	WATCHFUL	WHIMMIER
VANGUARD	VINELIKE	VOODOOED	WATCHMAN	WHIMMING
VANITORY	VINIFERA	VOORSKOT	WATCHOUT	WHIMSIED
VANQUISH	VINIFIED	VOTIVELY	WATERJET	WHIMSIER
VAPORIZE	VINIFIES	VOUDOUED	WATERLOO	WHIMSILY
VARACTOR	VINOLOGY	VOUSSOIR	WATERPOX	WHINCHAT
VARIABLY	VINOSITY	VOWELIZE	WATERWAY	WHINIARD
VARICOID	VINOUSLY	VOWESSES	WATTHOUR	WHINYARD
VARLETRY	VIOLATOR	VOYAGING	WAUGHING	WHIPBIRD
VARTABED	VIOMYCIN	VRAICKER	WAUKMILL	WHIPCORD
VASOTOMY	VIRGINIA	VUGGIEST	WAUKRIFE	WHIPJACK

WHIPLASH	WINNABLE	WOOLSACK	XYLOLOGY	ZIGZAGGY
WHIPTAIL	WINNOWED	WOOLWARD	XYLOMATA	ZIPPERED
WHIPWORM	WINNOWER	WOOLWORK	XYLONITE	ZIRCONIA
WHIRLBAT	WINTRILY	WORDBOOK	XYLOTOMY	ZIRCONIC
WHIRLIES	WIREDRAW	WORDPLAY	YACHTMAN	ZIZYPHUS
WHIRRIES	WIRELIKE	WORKABLY	YAHOOISM	ZODIACAL
WHIRRING	WIREWORK	WORKBOOK	YAHRZEIT	ZOETROPE
WHISKIES	WIREWOVE	WORKFARE	YAKIMONO	ZOIATRIA
WHITENED	WIRINESS	WORKFLOW	YAKITORI	ZOMBORUK
WHITEPOT	WIRRICOW	WORKFOLK	YAMMERED	ZONATION
WHITRACK	WISELIER	WORKGIRL	YAMMERER	ZONELESS
WHITRICK	WISHBONE	WORKHOUR	YARDBIRD	ZOOBLAST
WHIZBANG	WISPIEST	WORKLESS	YARMELKE	ZOOCHORE
WHOMPING	WISTARIA	WORKLOAD	YARMULKE	ZOOCHORY
WHOREDOM	WITCHERY	WORKMATE	YARRAMAN	ZOOCYTIA
WHYDUNIT	WITHDRAW	WORKROOM	YARRAMEN	ZOOLATRY
WICKEDLY	WITHHELD	WORKSHOP	YEASAYER	ZOOMANCY
WIDEBODY	WITHHOLD	WORKSOME	YELDROCK	ZOOMANIA
WIDOWMAN	WITHWIND	WORKWEEK	YELLOWED	ZOOMETRY
WIDOWMEN	WITTERED	WORMHOLE	YELLOWER	ZOOMORPH
WIDTHWAY	WITTOLLY	WORMLIKE	YEOMANLY	ZOONOMIA
WIFELIER	WIVEHOOD	WORMROOT	YICKERED	ZOONOMIC
WIFELIKE	WIZARDLY	WORMWOOD	YIKKERED	ZOONOSIS
WIGGIEST	WIZARDRY	WORRICOW	YOICKSES	ZOONOTIC
WILDCARD	WOMANISM	WORRYCOW	YOKELISH	ZOOPATHY
WILDFIRE	WOMANIZE	WORRYING	YOKEMATE	ZOOPERAL
WILDFOWL	WONDROUS	WORTHFUL	YOKOZUNA	ZOOPHAGY
WILDLAND	WOODCHIP	WORTHILY	YOLKLESS	ZOOPHILE
WILDWOOD	WOODCHOP	WOUNDILY	YONDERLY	ZOOPHILY
WILLABLE	WOODCOCK	WRATHFUL	YOUTHFUL	ZOOPHOBE
WILLIWAU	WOODFREE	WRATHILY	ZABAIONE	ZOOPHORI
WILLIWAW	WOODHOLE	WRECKAGE	ZABAJONE	ZOOSCOPY
WILLOWED	WOODLAND	WRECKFUL	ZADDIKIM	ZOOTHOME
WILLYART	WOODLARK	WRONGOUS	ZAIBATSU	ZOOTOMIC
WILLYWAW	WOODMICE	WROTHFUL	ZAMBOMBA	ZOOTOXIC
WINCHMAN	WOODNOTE	WURTZITE	ZAMPOGNA	ZOOTOXIN
WINCHMEN	WOODPILE	WUZZLING	ZAMZAWED	ZOOTROPE
WINDBILL	WOODROOF	XANTHATE	ZAPPIEST	ZOOTYPIC
WINDBLOW	WOODRUFF	XANTHENE	ZARZUELA	ZUCCHINI
WINDBURN	WOODTONE	XANTHISM	ZASTRUGA	ZUCHETTO
WINDFALL	WOODWALE	XANTHONE	ZEBRINNY	ZUGZWANG
WINDFLAW	WOODWARD	XANTHOUS	ZELATRIX	ZWIEBACK
WINDMILL	WOODWIND	XENOGENY	ZENITHAL	ZYGANTRA
WINDPIPE	WOODWORK	XERAPHIM	ZEOLITIC	ZYGODONT
WINDSAIL	WOODWORM	XEROMATA	ZEPPELIN	ZYGOMATA
WINDSHIP	WOODWOSE	XEROSERE	ZESTLESS	ZYGOSITY
WINDSURF	WOOLFELL	XEROXING	ZIBELINE	ZYGOTENE
WINDWARD	WOOLPACK	XYLOCARP	ZIGGURAT	ZYLONITE

Singles, couplets and triplets

The words presented in these lists are unusual anagrams – unusual because the letter sets in question produce only a very limited number of words. The first set, 'singles', are seven-letter words that have no other anagrams. 'Couplets' are sets that form only two seven-letter words, while 'triplets' have three anagrams.

The benefit of studying these words is that if you get the requisite letters on your rack, you don't need to waste any time on looking for bonus words that aren't there. Also, couplets and triplets can serve as mnemonics for each other.

Singles

AARRGHH	ABSCESS	ACCUSAL	ACUSHLA	ADULTLY
ABALONE	ABSCIND	ACCUSES	ACUTELY	ADVANCE
ABANDED	ABSCISS	ACEDIAS	ACYCLIC	ADVECTS
ABANDON	ABSCOND	ACEQUIA	ACYLATE	ADVENES
ABASERS	ABSENCE	ACERATE	ACYLOIN	ADVENTS
ABASHED	ABSINTH	ACEROLA	ADAGIAL	ADVERBS
ABASHES	ABSOLVE	ACEROSE	ADAGIOS	ADVEWED
ABASIAS	ABSORBS	ACETATE	ADAMANT	ADVICES
ABATING	ABSTAIN	ACETIFY	ADAPTED	ADVISED
ABATTIS	ABSURDS	ACETONE	ADAPTOR	ADVISEE
ABATURE	ABTHANE	ACETOUS	ADAWING	ADVISOR
ABAXIAL	ABUBBLE	ACHAGES	ADAXIAL	ADWARDS
ABAXILE	ABULIAS	ACHARNE	ADDABLE	ADWOMAN
ABBOTCY	ABUSAGE	ACHARYA	ADDAXES	ADZUKIS
ABDOMEN	ABUSING	ACHATES	ADDEDLY	AECIDIA
ABDUCED	ABUSION	ACHENIA	ADDEEMS	AEFAULD
ABDUCTS	ABUSIVE	ACHIEVE	ADDENDA	AEMULED
ABELIAN	ABUTTAL	ACHIOTE	ADDENDS	AEMULES
ABELIAS	ABUTTED	ACHKANS	ADDIBLE	AENEOUS
ABETTAL	ABUTTER	ACHOLIA	ADDLING	AEOLIAN
ABETTED	ABVOLTS	ACICULA	ADDOOMS	AEONIAN
ABEYANT	ABWATTS	ACIDIER	ADDRESS	AERATED
ABFARAD	ABYSSAL	ACIDIFY	ADDUCED	AERATES
ABHENRY	ABYSSES	ACIDITY	ADDUCER	AERATOR
ABIDING	ACACIAS	ACINOSE	ADDUCTS	AERIALS
ABIETIC	ACADEME	ACINOUS	ADEEMED	AEROBAT
ABIGAIL	ACADEMY	ACKNOWN	ADENINE	AEROBES
ABILITY	ACAJOUS	ACKNOWS	ADENOID	AEROBIA
ABIOSIS	ACALEPH	ACLINIC	ADENOMA	AEROBIC
ABIOTIC	ACANTHA	ACMATIC	ADENYLS	AEROBUS
ABJECTS	ACANTHS	ACOLYTH	ADEPTLY	AEROGEL
ABJOINT	ACAPNIA	ACOUCHI	ADHIBIT	AEROSAT
ABJURED	ACARIAN	ACOUCHY	ADIPOSE	AERUGOS
ABJURER	ACAROID	ACQUEST	ADIPOUS	AFEARED
ABJURES	ACAUDAL	ACQUIRE	ADJIGOS	AFFABLE
ABLATOR	ACCABLE	ACQUITE	ADJOINS	AFFABLY
ABLAUTS	ACCEDED	ACRASIA	ADJOINT	AFFAIRE
ABLUTED	ACCEDER	ACRATIC	ADJOURN	AFFEARD
ABODING	ACCEDES	ACREAGE	ADJUDGE	AFFEARE
ABOLISH	ACCENDS	ACRIDIN	ADJUNCT	AFFEARS
ABOLLAE	ACCENTS	ACRIDLY	ADJURED	AFFECTS
ABOLLAS	ACCEPTS	ACROMIA	ADJURER	AFFEERS
ABOMASA	ACCIDIA	ACRONIC	ADJURES	AFFIANT
ABOMASI	ACCIDIE	ACRONYM	ADJUROR	AFFICHE
ABORTEE	ACCINGE	ACROTIC	ADJUSTS	AFFINAL
ABOUGHT	ACCITED	ACRYLIC	ADLANDS	AFFINED
ABOULIA	ACCLAIM	ACRYLYL	ADMIXED	AFFINES
ABOULIC	ACCLOYS	ACTABLE	ADMIXES	AFFIRMS
ABRADED	ACCOAST	ACTANTS	ADNEXAL	AFFIXAL
ABRADER	ACCOIED	ACTINIA	ADNOUNS	AFFIXED
ABRADES	ACCORDS	ACTINIC	ADOPTED	AFFIXES
ABRAIDS	ACCOSTS	ACTIVES	ADOPTEE	AFFLICT
ABRAYED	ACCOUNT	ACTORLY	ADORNED	AFFOORD
ABRAZOS	ACCOURT	ACTUALS	ADREADS	AFFORCE
ABROACH	ACCOYED	ACTUARY	ADRENAL	AFFORDS
ABROADS	ACCRETE	ACTUATE	ADSORBS	AFFRAPS
ABROOKE	ACCREWS	ACULEUS	ADSUKIS	AFFRAYS
ABROSIA	ACCURST	ACUMENS	ADULATE	AFFRONT

AFGHANI	AIDANCE	ALBIZIA	ALLEGGE	AMARONE
AFGHANS	AIERIES	ALBUMEN	ALLEGRO	AMASSED
AFTMOST	AIKIDOS	ALBUMIN	ALLELES	AMASSER
AFTOSAS	AILETTE	ALCAIDE	ALLELIC	AMASSES
AGACANT	AINSELL	ALCALDE	ALLEYED	AMATEUR
AGAMIDS	AIRBAGS	ALCAYDE	ALLHEAL	AMATING
AGAMOID	AIRBOAT	ALCAZAR	ALLICIN	AMATIVE
AGAMONT	AIRCREW	ALCHEMY	ALLIUMS	AMATOLS
AGAMOUS	AIRDROP	ALCHERA	ALLNESS	AMATORY
AGAPEIC	AIRFARE	ALCHYMY	ALLOBAR	AMAZING
AGARICS	AIRFLOW	ALCOHOL	ALLONYM	AMAZONS
AGATISE	AIRFOIL	ALCOOLS	ALLOWED	AMBAGES
AGATIZE	AIRGAPS	ALCOPOP	ALLOXAN	AMBASSY
AGATOID	AIRGLOW	ALCORZA	ALLOYED	AMBATCH
AGEISMS	AIRHEAD	ALCOVED	ALLSEED	AMBIENT
AGELONG	AIRHOLE	ALDRINS	ALLURER	AMBITTY
AGENDAS	AIRLIFT	ALEGGED	ALLUVIA	AMBOYNA
AGENISE	AIRLIKE	ALEGGES	ALLYING	AMBRIES
AGENIZE	AIRLINE	ALENCON	ALLYLIC	AMBROID
AGENTRY	AIRLOCK	ALENGTH	ALMEMAR	AMBSACE
AGEUSIA	AIRMAIL	ALEURON	ALMIRAH	AMEBEAN
AGGADAS	AIRPARK	ALEWIFE	ALMNERS	AMEBOID
AGGADIC	AIRPLAY	ALEXIAS	ALMONDY	AMENAGE
AGGADOT	AIRSHIP	ALEXINE	ALMONRY	AMENTAL
AGGRACE	AIRSHOW	ALEXINS	ALMSMAN	AMENTUM
AGGRATE	AIRSICK	ALFALFA	ALMSMEN	AMESACE
AGILELY	AIRTHED	ALFAQUI	ALNAGER	AMIABLY
AGILITY	AIRTIME	ALFEREZ	ALODIUM	AMIDOLS
AGISTED	AIRWARD	ALFORJA	ALOETIC	AMINITY
AGITATE	AIRWAVE	ALFREDO	ALONELY	AMIRATE
AGITATO	AIRWAYS	ALGEBRA	ALONGST	AMMIRAL
AGITPOP	AIRWISE	ALGESIA	ALOOFLY	AMMONAL
AGLYCON	AJOWANS	ALGESIC	ALPACAS	AMMONIA
AGNAILS	AJUTAGE	ALGETIC	ALPACCA	AMMONIC
AGNATES	AKEAKES	ALGINIC	ALPHORN	AMNESTY
AGNATIC	AKEDAHS	ALIASES	ALPHYLS	AMNIOTE
AGNISED	AKENIAL	ALIBIED	ALREADY	AMOEBAE
AGNIZED	AKHARAS	ALIDADE	ALRIGHT	AMOEBAN
AGNOSIA	AKIRAHO	ALIDADS	ALSOONE	AMOEBAS
AGOGICS	AKRASIA	ALIENEE	ALTEZAS	AMOEBIC
AGONIZE	AKRATIC	ALIENER	ALTEZZA	AMOKURA
AGOROTH	AKVAVIT	ALIENLY	ALTHAEA	AMOMUMS
AGOUTAS	ALALIAS	ALIFORM	ALTHEAS	AMONGST
AGOUTIS	ALAMEDA	ALIGHTS	ALTHORN	AMOOVED
AGRAFES	ALAMODE	ALIMONY	ALTOIST	AMORANT
AGRAFFE	ALAMORT	ALIQUOT	ALUMINA	AMORCES
AGRAPHA	ALANINE	ALIYAHS	ALUMINE	AMORINI
AGRAVIC	ALANINS	ALIYOTH	ALUMINS	AMORINO
AGRISED	ALANNAH	ALIZARI	ALUMISH	AMORISM
AGRIZED	ALARMED	ALKALIC	ALUMIUM	AMORIST
AGRIZES	ALARUMS	ALKALIN	ALUMNAE	AMOROSA
AGROUND	ALASKAS	ALKALIS	ALUMNUS	AMOROSO
AGRYZED	ALASTOR	ALKANES	ALUNITE	AMOROUS
AGRYZES	ALAYING	ALKENES	ALVEARY	AMOTION
AGUISES	ALBEDOS	ALKINES	ALVEOLE	AMOVING
AGUIZED	ALBERGO	ALKYLIC	ALVEOLI	AMPASSY
AGUIZES	ALBINAL	ALKYNES	AMADODA	AMPHORA
AHEIGHT	ALBINIC	ALLAYED	AMADOUS	AMPLEST
AHIMSAS	ALBINOS	ALLEGER	AMALGAM	AMPLIFY
AHUNGRY	ALBITIC	ALLEGES	AMANITA	AMPOULE

AMPULES	ANGIOMA	ANTIENT	APOGEAL	ARANEID
AMPULLA	ANGLING	ANTIFAT	APOGEAN	ARAROBA
AMPUTEE	ANGORAS	ANTIFOG	APOGEES	ARBLAST
AMREETA	ANGULAR	ANTIFUR	APOGEIC	ARBORIO
AMTMANS	ANHINGA	ANTIGAY	APOLOGS	ARBOURS
AMTRACK	ANICCAS	ANTIGUN	APOLOGY	ARBUTUS
AMUSIAS	ANILINE	ANTIJAM	APOLUNE	ARCADED
AMUSING	ANILINS	ANTILOG	APOPLEX	ARCADIA
AMUSIVE	ANILITY	ANTIMAN	APORIAS	ARCANAS
AMYGDAL	ANIMACY	ANTIPOT	APOTHEM	ARCANUM
AMYLASE	ANIMISM	ANTITAX	APOZEMS	ARCHAEA
AMYLENE	ANIONIC	ANTIWAR	APPAIRS	ARCHAEI
AMYLOID	ANISEED	ANTLIAE	APPALLS	ARCHAIC
AMYLOSE	ANISOLE	ANTLIKE	APPALTI	ARCHERY
AMYLUMS	ANKLONG	ANTLION	APPALTO	ARCHEUS
AMYTALS	ANKLUNG	ANTONYM	APPARAT	ARCHFOE
ANAEMIA	ANKUSES	ANURANS	APPAREL	ARCHINE
ANAEMIC	ANLACES	ANXIETY	APPEACH	ARCHIVE
ANAGOGE	ANLAGEN	ANXIOUS	APPEALS	ARCHWAY
ANAGOGY	ANLASES	ANYBODY	APPEARS	ARCSECS
ANAGRAM	ANNATES	ANYONES	APPEASE	ARCSINS
ANALGIA	ANNATTA	ANYROAD	APPLAUD	ARCTICS
ANALITY	ANNATTO	ANYWAYS	APPLIED	ARCUATE
ANALOGA	ANNEALS	ANYWHEN	APPOINT	ARDENCY
ANALOGS	ANNEXED	ANYWISE	APPORTS	ARDOURS
ANALOGY	ANNEXES	ANZIANI	APPOSES	ARDRIGH
ANALYSE	ANNICUT	AOUDADS	APPROOF	ARDUOUS
ANALYST	ANNONAS	APACHES	APPROVE	AREAWAY
ANALYTE	ANNOYER	APADANA	APPUIED	ARENOSE
ANALYZE	ANNUALS	APAGOGE	APPUYED	ARENOUS
ANANKES	ANNUITY	APANAGE	APRAXIA	AREOLAE
ANAPHOR	ANNULAR	APAREJO	APRAXIC	AREOLAR
ANARCHS	ANNULET	APATITE	APROPOS	AREOLAS
ANARCHY	ANNULUS	APAYING	APSARAS	AREOLES
ANATASE	ANOBIID	APEHOOD	APSIDAL	ARGALAS
ANATMAN	ANOESES	APEPSIA	APSIDES	ARGANDS
ANATOMY	ANOESIS	APETALY	APTERAL	ARGOTIC
ANATTAS	ANOLYTE	APHAGIA	APTERIA	ARGUING
ANATTOS	ANOMALY	APHAKIA	APTERYX	ARGULUS
ANAXIAL	ANOMIES	APHASIA	APTOTIC	ARGYLLS
ANCHOVY	ANONYMA	APHASIC	APYRASE	ARGYRIA
ANCHUSA	ANONYMS	APHELIA	AQUAFER	ARIDITY
ANCIENT	ANORAKS	APHESIS	AQUARIA	ARIETTA
ANCILLA	ANOREXY	APHONIA	AQUATIC	ARILLUS
ANCOMES	ANOSMIA	APHONIC	AQUAVIT	ARIOSOS
ANCONAL	ANOTHER	APHOTIC	AQUEOUS	ARKOSIC
ANDANTE	ANOXIAS	APHTHAE	AQUIFER	ARMBAND
ANDIRON	ANSATED	APHYLLY	AQUILON	ARMHOLE
ANDROID	ANTACID	APICIAN	AQUIVER	ARMIGER
ANEARED	ANTARAS	APICULI	ARAARAS	ARMILLA
ANELACE	ANTBEAR	APISHLY	ARABESK	ARMLESS
ANEMONE	ANTBIRD	APLANAT	ARABICA	ARMLIKE
ANERGIA	ANTEFIX	APLASIA	ARABINS	ARMLOAD
ANEROID	ANTENNA	APLITIC	ARABIZE	ARMOIRE
ANEURIN	ANTHILL	APLOMBS	ARABLES	ARMORED
ANGAKOK	ANTHOID	APNOEAL	ARACHIS	ARMORER
ANGARIA	ANTHRAX	APOCARP	ARAISED	ARMOURS
ANGEKOK	ANTIAIR	APOCOPE	ARAISES	ARMOURY
ANGERLY	ANTICAR	APODOUS	ARALIAS	ARMURES
ANGINAL	ANTICKE	APOGAMY	ARAMIDS	ARNATTO

AROLLAS	ASPECTS	ATOMIST	AUSFORM	AWARNED
AROUSAL	ASPHYXY	ATOMIZE	AUSPICE	AWAYDAY
AROUSED	ASPICKS	ATONIAS	AUSTERE	AWFULLY
AROUSER	ASPIRIN	ATONIES	AUSTRAL	AWHAPED
AROUSES	ASPRAWL	ATONING	AUSUBOS	AWHAPES
AROYNTS	ASPROUT	ATROPHY	AUTARCH	AWHEELS
ARRACKS	ASSAGAI	ATROPIA	AUTARKY	AWKWARD
ARRAIGN	ASSAILS	ATROPIN	AUTEURS	AWLBIRD
ARRANGE	ASSAULT	ATTABOY	AUTHORS	AWLWORT
ARRASED	ASSAYED	ATTACHE	AUTISMS	AWNLESS
ARRASES	ASSEGAI	ATTACKS	AUTISTS	AXEBIRD
ARRAYAL	ASSEVER	ATTAINS	AUTOBUS	AXIALLY
ARRAYED	ASSHOLE	ATTAINT	AUTOMAN	AXILLAE
ARRAYER	ASSISTS	ATTASKS	AUTOMAT	AXILLAR
ARREARS	ASSIZED	ATTASKT	AUTONYM	AXILLAS
ARREEDE	ASSIZER	ATTEMPT	AUTOPEN	AXINITE
ARRIAGE	ASSIZES	ATTENDS	AUTOPUT	AXOLOTL
ARRIDED	ASSOILS	ATTENTS	AUTOVAC	AXONEME
ARRIERE	ASSORTS	ATTESTS	AUTUMNS	AXSEEDS
ARRIVAL	ASSUMES	ATTIRED	AUTUMNY	AYWORDS
ARRIVED	ASSUROR	ATTONCE	AUXESES	AZALEAS
ARRIVER	ASSWAGE	ATTRACT	AUXESIS	AZIMUTH
ARROWED	ASTASIA	ATTRAPS	AUXETIC	AZIONES
ARROYOS	ASTATIC	ATTUENT	AUXINIC	AZOLLAS
ARSENAL	ASTATKI	ATTUITE	AVAILES	AZOTISE
ARSHEEN	ASTONES	AUBADES	AVATARS	AZOTIZE
ARTWORK	ASTOUND	AUBERGE	AVAUNTS	AZOTOUS
ARUGOLA	ASTRICT	AUBURNS	AVELLAN	AZULEJO
ARUSPEX	ASTROID	AUCUBAS	AVENSES	AZUREAN
ASARUMS	ASUDDEN	AUDIBLE	AVENUES	AZURINE
ASCARIS	ATAATAS	AUDIBLY	AVERAGE	AZURITE
ASCAUNT	ATABEGS	AUDIENT	AVERRED	AZYGIES
ASCENDS	ATABEKS	AUDINGS	AVERTER	AZYGOUS
ASCESES	ATABRIN	AUDITED	AVIATED	AZYMITE
ASCESIS	ATACTIC	AUDITEE	AVIATES	AZYMOUS
ASCIDIA	ATAGHAN	AUDITOR	AVIATOR	BAALISM
ASCONCE	ATALAYA	AUFGABE	AVIDINS	BAASKAP
ASEPSES	ATAMANS	AUGENDS	AVIDITY	BABACOS
ASEXUAL	ATARAXY	AUGITES	AVIFORM	BABALAS
ASHAMED	ATAVISM	AUGITIC	AVIONIC	BABASSU
ASHAMES	ATAVIST	AUGURED	AVIZING	BABBITT
ASHCAKE	ATAXIAS	AUGURER	AVOCADO	BABBLES
ASHCANS	ATAXICS	AUGUSTE	AVOIDED	BABESIA
ASHFALL	ATAXIES	AUGUSTS	AVOSETS	BABICHE
ASHIVER	ATEBRIN	AUKLETS	AVOURES	BABLAHS
ASHKEYS	ATEMOYA	AUMAILS	AVOUTRY	BABOOLS
ASHLARS	ATHANOR	AURALLY	AVOWALS	BABOONS
ASHRAMA	ATHEISE	AURATED	AVOWING	BABUCHE
ASHRAMS	ATHEISM	AURATES	AVOYERS	BABUDOM
ASHTRAY	ATHEIZE	AUREATE	AVRUGAS	BABUISM
ASIAGOS	ATHEOUS	AUREITY	AVULSED	BABYING
ASINICO	ATHLETA	AURELIA	AVULSES	BABYISH
ASKANCE	ATHLETE	AUREOLA	AVYZING	BABYSAT
ASKANTS	ATHODYD	AUREOLE	AWAITED	BABYSIT
ASKARIS	ATHRILL	AURICLE	AWAITER	BACALAO
ASKESES	ATHWART	AURISTS	AWAKING	BACCARA
ASKESIS	ATISHOO	AUROCHS	AWARDED	BACCARE
ASLAKED	ATLASES	AURORAE	AWARDEE	BACCATE
ASLAKES	ATOKOUS	AURORAL	AWARDER	BACCHIC
ASOCIAL	ATOMISM	AURORAS	AWAREST	BACCHII

BACCOES	BAITING	BANDURA	BARONNE	BATHYAL
BACHCHA	BAIZING	BANEFUL	BAROQUE	BATIKED
BACHING	BAJADAS	BANGING	BARQUES	BATLIKE
BACILLI	BAJREES	BANGKOK	BARRACE	BATONED
BACKARE	BAKKIES	BANGLED	BARRACK	BATOONS
BACKBIT	BAKLAVA	BANGLES	BARRATS	BATSMEN
BACKFIT	BAKLAWA	BANIANS	BARREED	BATTEAU
BACKHOE	BALADIN	BANJOES	BARRELS	BATTENS
BACKIES	BALANCE	BANKETS	BARRENS	BATTERY
BACKING	BALASES	BANKING	BARRICO	BATTIKS
BACKLIT	BALBOAS	BANKITS	BARRIER	BATTILL
BACKLOG	BALCONY	BANKSIA	BARRING	BATTING
BACKLOT	BALDISH	BANNERS	BARRIOS	BATTUES
BACKRAS	BALDRIC	BANNETS	BARROOM	BATTUTA
BACKSAW	BALEFUL	BANNING	BARROWS	BATWING
BACKSEY	BALISTA	BANNOCK	BARTEND	BAUBEES
BACKUPS	BALKERS	BANOFFI	BARTONS	BAUCHLE
BACLAVA	BALKIER	BANQUET	BARWARE	BAUDRIC
BACONER	BALKILY	BANSELA	BARWOOD	BAUKING
BACULUM	BALKING	BANSHIE	BARYONS	BAULKED
BADDEST	BALLADE	BANTENG	BARYTAS	BAULKER
BADDIES	BALLADS	BANTING	BARYTIC	BAUXITE
BADDISH	BALLANS	BANYANS	BARYTON	BAWBEES
BADGERS	BALLANT	BANZAIS	BASALTS	BAWCOCK
BADGING	BALLERS	BAOBABS	BASCULE	BAWDIER
BADIOUS	BALLETS	BAPTISE	BASEMAN	BAWDIES
BADLAND	BALLIES	BAPTIST	BASENJI	BAWDILY
BADMASH	BALLING	BAPTIZE	BASHAWS	BAWDKIN
BADNESS	BALLIUM	BARACAN	BASHFUL	BAWDRIC
BAFFIES	BALLONS	BARBATE	BASHING	BAWNEEN
BAFFING	BALLOON	BARBELL	BASHLYK	BAWSUNT
BAFFLED	BALLOTS	BARBERS	BASIDIA	BAWTIES
BAFFLER	BALLOWS	BARBING	BASILAR	BAXTERS
BAFFLES	BALLUPS	BARBOLA	BASILIC	BAYAMOS
BAGGAGE	BALMILY	BARBULE	BASINAL	BAYARDS
BAGGIER	BALNEAL	BARBUTS	BASKETS	BAYONET
BAGGIES	BALONEY	BARCHAN	BASMATI	BAYTING
BAGGILY	BAMBINI	BARDASH	BASOCHE	BAYWOOD
BAGGING	BAMBINO	BARDISM	BASQUED	BAYYANS
BAGGITS	BAMBOOS	BAREFIT	BASQUES	BAZOOKA
BAGLESS	BAMMERS	BARFING	BASSETT	BAZOOMS
BAGLIKE	BAMMING	BARGAIN	BASSING	BAZOUKI
BAGPIPE	BANALER	BARGEST	BASSIST	BEACHED
BAGUIOS	BANALLY	BARGOON	BASSOON	BEACHES
BAGWASH	BANANAS	BARHOPS	BASTIDE	BEACONS
BAGWIGS	BANDAGE	BARILLA	BASTING	BEADILY
BAGWORM	BANDAID	BARIUMS	BASUCOS	BEADING
BAHADAS	BANDANA	BARKANS	BATABLE	BEADLES
BAHADUR	BANDARI	BARKERS	BATATAS	BEADMAN
BAILEES	BANDBOX	BARKHAN	BATAVIA	BEAGLED
BAILERS	BANDEAU	BARLEYS	BATCHED	BEAGLER
BAILEYS	BANDERS	BARLOWS	BATCHES	BEAGLES
BAILIFF	BANDING	BARMAID	BATEAUX	BEAKIER
BAILING	BANDITO	BARMIER	BATFISH	BEAMIER
BAILLIE	BANDITS	BARMKIN	BATFOWL	BEAMILY
BAILLIS	BANDOGS	BARNEYS	BATGIRL	BEAMING
BAILORS	BANDOOK	BARNIER	BATHING	BEAMISH
BAININS	BANDORA	BARNING	BATHMAT	BEAMLET
BAINITE	BANDROL	BAROCCO	BATHMIC	BEANBAG
BAIRNLY	BANDSAW	BAROCKS	BATHTUB	BEANERY

BEANIES	BEDROLL	BEGROAN	BEMAULS	BEROBED
BEANING	BEDROPS	BEGUILE	BEMAZED	BERRETS
BEARHUG	BEDROPT	BEGUINE	BEMEANT	BERRIES
BEARING	BEDSIDE	BEGULFS	BEMETED	BERSEEM
BEARISH	BEDSITS	BEGUNKS	BEMISTS	BERSERK
BEASTIE	BEDTICK	BEHAVED	BEMIXED	BERTHED
BEATBOX	BEDUCKS	BEHAVER	BEMIXES	BESEEKE
BEATHED	BEDUMBS	BEHAVES	BEMOCKS	BESEEMS
BEATIFY	BEDUNCE	BEHEADS	BEMOUTH	BESHAME
BEATING	BEDUNGS	BEHESTS	BENCHED	BESHINE
BEATNIK	BEDWARD	BEHIGHT	BENCHER	BESHONE
BEAUFET	BEDWARF	BEHINDS	BENCHES	BESHOUT
BEAUFIN	BEEBEES	BEHOLDS	BENDAYS	BESHREW
BEAUISH	BEECHEN	BEHOOFS	BENDEES	BESIDES
BEAVERS	BEEDIES	BEHOOVE	BENDERS	BESIEGE
BEAVERY	BEEFALO	BEHOTES	BENDING	BESIGHS
BEBEERU	BEEFILY	BEHOVED	BENDLET	BESLAVE
BEBLOOD	BEEFING	BEHOVES	BENEATH	BESMOKE
BEBUNGS	BEEHIVE	BEHOWLS	BENEFIC	BESMUTS
BECALLS	BEELIKE	BEIGELS	BENEFIT	BESNOWS
BECASSE	BEELINE	BEIGNES	BENEMPT	BESOINS
BECAUSE	BEEPERS	BEINKED	BENIGHT	BESOMED
BECHALK	BEEPING	BEJADED	BENNETS	BESPATE
BECKETS	BEERAGE	BEJADES	BENNIES	BESPEED
BECKING	BEERIER	BEJANTS	BENOMYL	BESPICE
BECKONS	BEERILY	BEJESUS	BENTHAL	BESPITS
BECLASP	BEESOME	BEJEWEL	BENTHON	BESPOKE
BECLOAK	BEESWAX	BEKNAVE	BENTHOS	BESPORT
BECLOGS	BEETFLY	BEKNOTS	BENTIER	BESPOTS
BECLOUD	BEETLED	BEKNOWN	BENUMBS	BESPOUT
BECLOWN	BEETLER	BELABOR	BENZALS	BESTICK
BECOMES	BEETLES	BELACES	BENZENE	BESTING
BECRAWL	BEFALLS	BELATES	BENZILS	BESTOWS
BECRIME	BEFFANA	BELAUDS	BENZINE	BESTROW
BECROWD	BEFLAGS	BELAYER	BENZINS	BESWARM
BECURLS	BEFLEAS	BELCHED	BENZOIC	BETAINE
BECURSE	BEFLECK	BELCHER	BENZOIN	BETAKEN
BEDAMNS	BEFOAMS	BELCHES	BENZOLE	BETAKES
BEDAUBS	BEFOOLS	BELEAPS	BENZOLS	BETAXED
BEDAWIN	BEFOULS	BELEAPT	BENZOYL	BETEEME
BEDAZED	BEFRETS	BELIEFS	BENZYLS	BETHANK
BEDAZES	BEGALLS	BELIERS	BEPAINT	BETHELS
BEDBUGS	BEGAZED	BELIEVE	BEPEARL	BETHINK
BEDDERS	BEGAZES	BELLBOY	BEPELTS	BETHORN
BEDDING	BEGGARY	BELLEEK	BEPROSE	BETHUMB
BEDECKS	BEGGING	BELLHOP	BEPUFFS	BETHUMP
BEDELLS	BEGHARD	BELLIES	BEQUEST	BETIDES
BEDEMEN	BEGIFTS	BELLING	BERAKED	BETIGHT
BEDEVIL	BEGILDS	BELLMAN	BERBERE	BETIMES
BEDEWED	BEGINNE	BELLMEN	BERBICE	BETISES
BEDFAST	BEGLADS	BELLOCK	BERCEAU	BETITLE
BEDGOWN	BEGLOOM	BELLOWS	BEREAVE	BETOILS
BEDIRTY	BEGNAWS	BELONGS	BERGENS	BETOKEN
BEDIZEN	BEGOING	BELOVED	BERGERE	BETROTH
BEDLAMP	BEGONIA	BELOVES	BERGYLT	BETTERS
BEDLIKE	BEGORAH	BELTING	BERHYME	BETTIES
BEDMATE	BEGORED	BELTMEN	BERLEYS	BETTING
BEDOUIN	BEGORRA	BELTWAY	BERLINE	BETTONG
BEDPANS	BEGRIME	BELYING	BERLINS	BETTORS
BEDPOST	BEGRIMS	BEMADAM	BERMING	BETWEEN

BETWIXT	BICORNE	BILLYOH	BIRTHED	BLAWORT
BEURRES	BICYCLE	BILLYOS	BIRYANI	BLAZERS
BEVELED	BIDARKA	BILOBAR	BISCUIT	BLAZING
BEVELER	BIDDERS	BILSTED	BISECTS	BLAZONS
BEVOMIT	BIDDIES	BIMANAL	BISHOPS	BLEAKER
BEVVIED	BIDDING	BIMODAL	BISMARS	BLEAKLY
BEVVIES	BIDENTS	BIMORPH	BISMUTH	BLEEDER
BEWAILS	BIDINGS	BINDERY	BISQUES	BLEEPED
BEWARED	BIELDED	BINDING	BISTROS	BLEEPER
BEWARES	BIENNIA	BINDLES	BITABLE	BLELLUM
BEWEARY	BIFACES	BINGERS	BITCHED	BLEMISH
BEWEEPS	BIFFERS	BINGHIS	BITCHES	BLENDED
BEWHORE	BIFFIES	BINGIES	BITINGS	BLENDES
BEWITCH	BIFFING	BINGING	BITLESS	BLESBOK
BEWORMS	BIFFINS	BINGLED	BITONAL	BLESSER
BEWORRY	BIFIDLY	BINGLES	BITSIER	BLESSES
BEWRAPS	BIFILAR	BINIOUS	BITTERN	BLETTED
BEWRAPT	BIFOCAL	BINNING	BITTERS	BLEWART
BEWRAYS	BIGEYES	BINOCLE	BITTIER	BLEWITS
BEYLICS	BIGFEET	BIOCHIP	BITTIES	BLIGHTS
BEYLIKS	BIGFOOT	BIOCIDE	BITTING	BLIGHTY
BEYONDS	BIGGEST	BIODATA	BITTOCK	BLIKSEM
BEZANTS	BIGGETY	BIODOTS	BITTOUR	BLINDED
BEZIQUE	BIGGIES	BIOFACT	BITUMED	BLINDLY
BEZOARS	BIGGING	BIOFILM	BITUMEN	BLINGER
BEZZANT	BIGGINS	BIOFUEL	BIVALVE	BLINKED
BEZZLED	BIGGISH	BIOHERM	BIVINYL	BLINKER
BEZZLES	BIGGITY	BIOLOGY	BIVIOUS	BLINNED
BHAJANS	BIGGONS	BIOMASS	BIVOUAC	BLINTZE
BHAJEES	BIGHEAD	BIONICS	BIVVIED	BLIPPED
BHAKTIS	BIGHORN	BIONOMY	BIVVIES	BLISSED
BHANGRA	BIGOSES	BIONTIC	BIZARRO	BLISSES
BHARALS	BIGOTED	BIOPHOR	BIZNAGA	BLITHER
BHAVANS	BIGOTRY	BIOPTIC	BIZONAL	BLITZED
BHAWANS	BIGTIME	BIOTECH	BIZONES	BLITZER
BHEESTY	BIGWIGS	BIOTICS	BIZZIES	BLITZES
BHIKHUS	BIKEWAY	BIOTINS	BLACKED	BLOATER
BHISHTI	BIKINGS	BIOTITE	BLACKEN	BLOCKED
BHISTEE	BIKINIS	BIOTOPE	BLACKER	BLOCKER
BHISTIE	BIKKIES	BIOTRON	BLACKLY	BLOCKIE
BHISTIS	BILAYER	BIOTYPE	BLADDED	BLOKIER
BIASING	BILBIES	BIPACKS	BLADDER	BLOKISH
BIASSED	BILBOAS	BIPARTY	BLAGGED	BLONDER
BIASSES	BILEVEL	BIPLANE	BLAGGER	BLOOMED
BIAXIAL	BILGIER	BIPRISM	BLAGUER	BLOOPED
BIBASIC	BILGING	BIRCHED	BLAHING	BLOOPER
BIBBERS	BILIARY	BIRCHEN	BLANCOS	BLOOSME
BIBBERY	BILIMBI	BIRCHES	BLANDER	BLOSSOM
BIBBING	BILIOUS	BIRDDOG	BLANDLY	BLOTCHY
BIBBLES	BILKERS	BIRDERS	BLANKED	BLOUBOK
BIBCOCK	BILKING	BIRDIED	BLANKER	BLOUSON
BIBELOT	BILLBUG	BIRDMAN	BLANKET	BLOWBYS
BIBLESS	BILLIES	BIRDMEN	BLANKLY	BLOWGUN
BIBLIKE	BILLING	BIRIANI	BLARING	BLOWIER
BIBLIST	BILLION	BIRKIER	BLARNEY	BLOWIES
BICARBS	BILLMAN	BIRKIES	BLARTED	BLOWJOB
BICCIES	BILLMEN	BIRLERS	BLASHES	BLOWOFF
BICHORD	BILLONS	BIRLING	BLATANT	BLOWOUT
BICKERS	BILLOWS	BIRLINN	BLAUBOK	BLOWSED
BICKIES	BILLOWY	BIRRING	BLAUDED	BLOWZED

BLOWZES	BODHRAN	BONACIS	BOOMKIN	BOSTRYX
BLUCHER	BODIKIN	BONANZA	BOOMLET	BOTANIC
BLUDGED	BODINGS	BONASUS	BOONERS	BOTARGO
BLUDGES	BODKINS	BONBONS	BOONIES	BOTCHED
BLUECAP	BODRAGS	BONDERS	BOORDES	BOTCHER
BLUEFIN	BODYING	BONDING	BOORISH	BOTCHES
BLUEGUM	BOERBUL	BONDMAN	BOORKAS	BOTHANS
BLUEJAY	BOFFING	BONDMEN	BOOSHIT	BOTHIES
BLUETIT	BOFFINS	BONDUCS	BOOSING	BOTHOLE
BLUETTE	BOFFOLA	BONEYER	BOOSTED	BOTHRIA
BLUFFED	BOGARTS	BONFIRE	BOOTEES	BOTNETS
BLUFFER	BOGBEAN	BONGING	BOOTERY	BOTONEE
BLUFFLY	BOGEYED	BONGOES	BOOTIES	BOTTEGA
BLUINGS	BOGGARD	BONHAMS	BOOTING	BOTTIES
BLUMING	BOGGART	BONIATO	BOOTLEG	BOTTINE
BLUNKED	BOGGERS	BONINGS	BOOZIER	BOTTING
BLUNKER	BOGGIER	BONISMS	BOOZILY	BOTTLES
BLUNTED	BOGGING	BONISTS	BOOZING	BOTTOMS
BLUNTER	BOGGISH	BONITOS	BOPEEPS	BOTTONY
BLUNTLY	BOGGLED	BONJOUR	BOPPERS	BOTULIN
BLURRED	BOGGLES	BONKERS	BOPPING	BOUBOUS
BLURTED	BOGLAND	BONKING	BORACES	BOUCHEE
BLURTER	BOGOAKS	BONNETS	BORAGES	BOUCLEE
BLUSHED	BOGONGS	BONNIER	BORANES	BOUCLES
BLUSHET	BOGUSLY	BONNILY	BORAXES	BOUDINS
BOAKING	BOGWOOD	BONNOCK	BORAZON	BOUDOIR
BOARISH	BOGYISM	BONOBOS	BORDARS	BOUFFES
BOASTED	BOGYMAN	BONSELA	BORDELS	BOUGHED
BOATFUL	BOGYMEN	BONSOIR	BORDERS	BOUGHTS
BOATIES	BOHEMIA	BONUSES	BORMING	BOUGIES
BOATING	BOHRIUM	BONXIES	BORNEOL	BOUGING
BOATMAN	BOHUNKS	BOOBIES	BORNITE	BOUILLI
BOATMEN	BOILERY	BOOBING	BORNYLS	BOUNCER
BOBBERS	BOILING	BOOBIRD	BORONIA	BOUNCES
BOBBERY	BOILOFF	BOOBISH	BORONIC	BOUNDED
BOBBIES	BOINGED	BOOBOOK	BOROUGH	BOUNING
BOBBING	BOINKED	BOOBOOS	BORRELL	BOUQUET
BOBBINS	BOLASES	BOOCOOS	BORROWS	BOURBON
BOBBISH	BOLDEST	BOODIED	BORSHCH	BOURDON
BOBBITT	BOLEROS	BOODLER	BORSHTS	BOURKHA
BOBBLES	BOLETES	BOODLES	BORSICS	BOURLAW
BOBCATS	BOLETUS	BOOFIER	BORSTAL	BOURREE
BOBECHE	BOLIDES	BOOGEYS	BORTZES	BOURSES
BOBLETS	BOLINES	BOOGIED	BORZOIS	BOURSIN
BOBOTIE	BOLIVAR	BOOHAIS	BOSBOKS	BOUSING
BOBSLED	BOLIVIA	BOOHOOS	BOSCHES	BOUTADE
BOBTAIL	BOLIXED	BOOJUMS	BOSHBOK	BOUVIER
BOBWIGS	BOLIXES	BOOKEND	BOSKAGE	BOVATES
BOCCIAS	BOLLARD	BOOKFUL	BOSKETS	BOVINES
BOCCIES	BOLLING	BOOKING	BOSKIER	BOVVERS
BOCKEDY	BOLLOCK	BOOKISH	BOSOMED	BOWBENT
BOCKING	BOLOGNA	BOOKLET	BOSONIC	BOWERED
BODACHS	BOLONEY	BOOKMAN	BOSQUES	BOWFINS
BODDLES	BOLSHIE	BOOKMEN	BOSQUET	BOWGETS
BODEFUL	BOLSONS	BOOKOOS	BOSSBOY	BOWHEAD
BODEGAS	BOMBARD	BOOLING	BOSSDOM	BOWKNOT
BODGERS	BOMBAST	BOOMBOX	BOSSIES	BOWLFUL
BODGIER	BOMBLET	BOOMERS	BOSSILY	BOWLIKE
BODGIES	BOMBORA	BOOMIER	BOSSISM	BOWLINE
BODGING	BOMMIES	BOOMING	BOSTONS	BOWNING

BOWPOTS	BRAVOED	BRINIER	BROUGHS	BUDGETS
BOWSAWS	BRAVOES	BRINIES	BROUGHT	BUDGIES
BOWSEYS	BRAVURA	BRINISH	BROWNED	BUDGING
BOWSHOT	BRAVURE	BRINJAL	BROWNER	BUDLESS
BOWSIES	BRAWNED	BRIOCHE	BROWNIE	BUDLIKE
BOWWOWS	BRAXIES	BRIQUET	BROWSED	BUDMASH
BOWYANG	BRAYERS	BRISANT	BROWSER	BUDWORM
BOWYERS	BRAYING	BRISKED	BROWSTS	BUFFALO
BOXBALL	BRAZENS	BRISKEN	BRUCHID	BUFFIER
BOXCARS	BRAZERS	BRISKER	BRUCINE	BUFFING
BOXFISH	BRAZILS	BRISKET	BRUCINS	BUFFOON
BOXFULS	BRAZING	BRISKLY	BRUCITE	BUGABOO
BOXHAUL	BREADTH	BRISSES	BRUHAHA	BUGBANE
BOXIEST	BREAKER	BRITSKA	BRUISES	BUGBEAR
BOXINGS	BREATHE	BRITTLY	BRUITED	BUGEYES
BOXLIKE	BREATHY	BRITZKA	BRUITER	BUGGANE
BOXROOM	BRECHAN	BROADAX	BRULOTS	BUGGANS
BOYCHIK	BREDING	BROADLY	BRULYIE	BUGGERS
BOYCOTT	BREENGE	BROCADE	BRULZIE	BUGGERY
BOYHOOD	BREESES	BROCAGE	BRUMMER	BUGGIER
BOYSIER	BREESTS	BROCARD	BRUNTED	BUGGIES
BRAAIED	BREEZED	BROCHAN	BRUSHED	BUGGING
BRAATAS	BREHONS	BROCHED	BRUSHER	BUGGINS
BRACCIA	BREIING	BROCHES	BRUSHUP	BUGLETS
BRACERO	BRENNES	BROCHOS	BRUSQUE	BUGLOSS
BRACERS	BRENTER	BROCKET	BRUSSEN	BUGONGS
BRACHAH	BREVETE	BROCKIT	BRUTIFY	BUGOUTS
BRACHES	BREVETS	BRODDED	BRUTING	BUGSEED
BRACHIA	BREVIER	BRODDLE	BRUTISH	BUGSHAS
BRACING	BREVITY	BRODKIN	BRUTISM	BUGWORT
BRACKEN	BREWAGE	BROGGED	BRUXING	BUHUNDS
BRACKET	BREWERS	BROGUES	BRUXISM	BUIBUIS
BRACTED	BREWERY	BROIDER	BUBALIS	BUILDED
BRADAWL	BREWING	BROILED	BUBBIES	BUIRDLY
BRADDED	BREWPUB	BROILER	BUBBLES	BUKKAKE
BRAGGED	BREWSKI	BROKAGE	BUBINGA	BUKSHEE
BRAGGER	BREYING	BROKERS	BUBONIC	BUKSHIS
BRAHMAN	BRIBEES	BROKERY	BUBUKLE	BULBELS
BRAHMIN	BRIBERY	BROLGAS	BUCCINA	BULBILS
BRAIDED	BRICKED	BROMALS	BUCKEEN	BULBING
BRAMBLE	BRICKEN	BROMATE	BUCKERS	BULBLET
BRAMBLY	BRICKIE	BROMIDE	BUCKEYE	BULBOUS
BRANCHY	BRICKLE	BROMIDS	BUCKIES	BULBULS
BRANDED	BRIDGED	BROMINE	BUCKING	BULGIER
BRANGLE	BRIDLED	BROMISE	BUCKISH	BULGURS
BRANKED	BRIDLER	BROMISM	BUCKLED	BULIMIA
BRANNED	BRIDOON	BROMIZE	BUCKLES	BULIMIC
BRANNER	BRIEFER	BROMMER	BUCKOES	BULIMUS
BRANTLE	BRIEFLY	BRONCHI	BUCKRAM	BULKAGE
BRASCOS	BRIGHTS	BRONCHO	BUCKRAS	BULKIER
BRASHLY	BRIGUED	BRONCOS	BUCKSOM	BULKILY
BRASILS	BRILLER	BRONZED	BUCOLIC	BULKING
BRASSES	BRILLOS	BRONZEN	BUDDHAS	BULLACE
BRAUNCH	BRIMFUL	BRONZER	BUDDIED	BULLARY
BRAVADO	BRIMING	BRONZES	BUDDIER	BULLBAR
BRAVELY	BRIMMED	BROODED	BUDDIES	BULLBAT
BRAVERS	BRIMMER	BROODER	BUDDING	BULLDOG
BRAVERY	BRINDED	BROOKED	BUDDLED	BULLERS
BRAVEST	BRINERS	BROTHEL	BUDDLES	BULLETS
BRAVING	BRINGER	BROTHER	BUDGERO	BULLIED

BULLIER	BURDENS	BUSKINS	BYSSOID	CAFFEIN
BULLIES	BURDOCK	BUSLOAD	BYTALKS	CAFFILA
BULLING	BUREAUS	BUSTARD	BYWONER	CAFTANS
BULLION	BUREAUX	BUSTEES	BYWORDS	CAGEFUL
BULLISH	BURETTE	BUSTERS	BYWORKS	CAGIEST
BULLOCK	BURGAGE	BUSTLED	BYZANTS	CAGMAGS
BULLOSA	BURGEES	BUSUUTI	CABALAS	CAGOULE
BULLPEN	BURGEON	BUSYING	CABANAS	CAGOULS
BULRUSH	BURGERS	BUTANOL	CABBAGE	CAHOOTS
BULWARK	BURGESS	BUTCHER	CABBAGY	CAIMACS
BUMBAGS	BURGHAL	BUTCHES	CABBALA	CAIQUES
BUMBAZE	BURGHER	BUTLING	CABBIES	CAITIFF
BUMBLED	BURGLAR	BUTMENT	CABBING	CAJAPUT
BUMBLER	BURGOOS	BUTTALS	CABEZON	CAJEPUT
BUMBLES	BURGOUT	BUTTERS	CABILDO	CAJOLED
BUMBOAT	BURITIS	BUTTERY	CABINED	CAJOLER
BUMELIA	BURKING	BUTTIES	CABINET	CAJOLES
BUMKINS	BURKITE	BUTTING	CABLERS	CAJONES
BUMMALO	BURLAPS	BUTTLED	CABLETS	CAJUPUT
BUMMERS	BURLEYS	BUTTLES	CABLING	CALALOO
BUMMEST	BURLIER	BUTTOCK	CABOMBA	CALAMAR
BUMMING	BURLILY	BUTTONS	CABOOSE	CALATHI
BUMMOCK	BURLING	BUTTONY	CABOVER	CALCARS
BUMPERS	BURNERS	BUTYRAL	CABRIOS	CALCIFY
BUMPIER	BURNING	BUTYRIC	CABRITS	CALCINE
BUMPILY	BURNISH	BUTYRIN	CACHEXY	CALCITE
BUMPING	BURNOUS	BUTYRYL	CACHOUS	CALCIUM
BUMPKIN	BURPEES	BUVETTE	CACIQUE	CALCULI
BUNCHED	BURRELL	BUXOMER	CACKIER	CALDRON
BUNCHES	BURRERS	BUXOMLY	CACKLES	CALECHE
BUNCING	BURRHEL	BUYABLE	CACOEPY	CALESAS
BUNDING	BURRIER	BUYBACK	CACOLET	CALICLE
BUNDLED	BURRING	BUYOFFS	CACONYM	CALIGOS
BUNDLES	BURRITO	BUZUKIA	CACOONS	CALIPEE
BUNDOOK	BURROWS	BUZUKIS	CACUMEN	CALIPHS
BUNGEES	BURSARS	BUZZARD	CADAGAS	CALKINS
BUNGERS	BURSARY	BUZZCUT	CADAGIS	CALLAIS
BUNGEYS	BURSEED	BUZZERS	CADAVER	CALLANS
BUNGING	BURSTED	BUZZIER	CADDICE	CALLANT
BUNIONS	BURTHEN	BUZZING	CADDIED	CALLBOY
BUNJEES	BURTONS	BUZZWIG	CADDIES	CALLEES
BUNJIES	BURWEED	BYCATCH	CADDISH	CALLETS
BUNKERS	BUSBARS	BYCOKET	CADDYSS	CALLING
BUNKING	BUSBOYS	BYGONES	CADEAUX	CALLOUS
BUNKOED	BUSGIRL	BYLANES	CADELLE	CALLOWS
BUNKUMS	BUSHFLY	BYLINED	CADENCE	CALMING
BUNNETS	BUSHIDO	BYLINER	CADENCY	CALOMEL
BUNNIAS	BUSHIER	BYLINES	CADENZA	CALORIC
BUNNIES	BUSHIES	BYNAMES	CADGERS	CALOTTE
BUNRAKU	BUSHILY	BYNEMPT	CADGIER	CALOYER
BUNSENS	BUSHING	BYPATHS	CADGING	CALPACK
BUNTING	BUSHMAN	BYPLACE	CADMIUM	CALPACS
BUNYIPS	BUSHMEN	BYPLAYS	CADUACS	CALPAIN
BUOYAGE	BUSHPIG	BYREMEN	CADUCEI	CALQUED
BUOYANT	BUSHTIT	BYRLADY	CAEOMAS	CALTHAS
BUOYING	BUSHWAH	BYRLAWS	CAERULE	CALTRAP
BUPPIES	BUSHWAS	BYRLING	CAESARS	CALUMBA
BUQSHAS	BUSKERS	BYRNIES	CAESIUM	CALUMET
BURBLER	BUSKETS	BYROOMS	CAESURA	CALUMNY
BURBOTS	BUSKING	BYSSINE	CAFARDS	CALVING

CALYPSO	CANNELS	CARANNA	CARSICK	CATNIPS
CALYXES	CANNERY	CARAPAX	CARTAGE	CATSPAW
CALZONE	CANNILY	CARAUNA	CARTFUL	CATSUIT
CALZONI	CANNING	CARAVAN	CARTWAY	CATTABU
CAMAIEU	CANNOLI	CARAVEL	CARVERY	CATTAIL
CAMASES	CANNONS	CARAWAY	CARWASH	CATTALO
CAMBIAL	CANNULA	CARBARN	CASBAHS	CATTERY
CAMBISM	CANOLAS	CARBIDE	CASCARA	CATTING
CAMBIST	CANONIC	CARBINE	CASEASE	CATWALK
CAMBIUM	CANONRY	CARBORA	CASEATE	CATWORM
CAMBOGE	CANOPIC	CARBOYS	CASEMAN	CAUDATE
CAMBRIC	CANTALA	CARCAKE	CASEOSE	CAUDLED
CAMELIA	CANTALS	CARCASE	CASEOUS	CAUKERS
CAMELOT	CANTATA	CARCASS	CASETTE	CAULDER
CAMELRY	CANTATE	CARCELS	CASHAWS	CAULINE
CAMEOED	CANTDOG	CARDIAC	CASHBOX	CAULKED
CAMERAE	CANTEEN	CARDIAE	CASHEWS	CAULKER
CAMERAS	CANTEST	CARDING	CASHOOS	CAUMING
CAMESES	CANTHAL	CARDOON	CASINGS	CAUTERY
CAMISAS	CANTICO	CARDUUS	CASITAS	CAVALLA
CAMISES	CANTINA	CAREFUL	CASKETS	CAVALLY
CAMISIA	CANTING	CARFARE	CASQUED	CAVEMAN
CAMMIES	CANTLED	CARFULS	CASSATA	CAVEMEN
CAMMING	CANTLET	CARIAMA	CASSENA	CAVETTI
CAMOGIE	CANTONS	CARIBOU	CASSIAS	CAVETTO
CAMOODI	CANTRAP	CARICES	CASSONE	CAVIARS
CAMORRA	CANTREF	CARIERE	CASSPIR	CAVILED
CAMPANA	CANTRIP	CARIOCA	CASTOCK	CAVINGS
CAMPEST	CANVASS	CARITAS	CASTORY	CAVORTS
CAMPHOL	CANZONA	CARJACK	CASTRAL	CAWINGS
CAMPHOR	CANZONE	CARLINE	CASUIST	CAYENNE
CAMPIER	CANZONI	CARLING	CATALOG	CAYMANS
CAMPILY	CAPABLY	CARLINS	CATALPA	CAZIQUE
CAMPING	CAPELAN	CARLOAD	CATAPAN	CEAZING
CAMPION	CAPELET	CARLOCK	CATARRH	CECITIS
CAMPLES	CAPFULS	CARMINE	CATASTA	CEDARED
CAMPONG	CAPLESS	CARNALS	CATAWBA	CEDILLA
CAMPOUT	CAPPERS	CARNIER	CATBIRD	CEDRINE
CAMUSES	CAPPING	CARNIFY	CATBOAT	CEILERS
CAMWOOD	CAPRATE	CAROACH	CATCALL	CEILIDH
CANADAS	CAPRICE	CAROLER	CATCHED	CELADON
CANAKIN	CAPRIDS	CAROMEL	CATCHEN	CELESTE
CANASTA	CAPRIFY	CARPALE	CATCLAW	CELLING
CANBANK	CAPRINE	CARPALS	CATECHU	CELLIST
CANCANS	CAPROCK	CARPARK	CATELOG	CELLOSE
CANCELS	CAPROIC	CARPOOL	CATENAE	CELLULE
CANCERS	CAPSIDS	CARPORT	CATENAS	CELOMIC
CANCHAS	CAPTIVE	CARRACK	CATERAN	CELOTEX
CANDENT	CAPTORS	CARRACT	CATFACE	CEMBALO
CANDIDA	CAPTURE	CARRATS	CATFALL	CEMENTA
CANDIDS	CAPUCHE	CARRECT	CATFISH	CEMENTS
CANDIED	CAPUERA	CARRELL	CATGUTS	CENACLE
CANDLED	CARABAO	CARRELS	CATHEAD	CENOTES
CANDLER	CARABID	CARRICK	CATHECT	CENSORS
CANDOCK	CARABIN	CARRIER	CATHODE	CENSURE
CANELLA	CARACAL	CARRION	CATHOOD	CENTAGE
CANIKIN	CARACOL	CARROCH	CATJANG	CENTAVO
CANINGS	CARACTS	CARROMS	CATLIKE	CENTIME
CANKERY	CARAFES	CARROTY	CATMINT	CENTNER
CANNACH	CARAMBA	CARRYON	CATNEPS	CENTRAL

CENTRIC	CHAMPED	CHAUFFS	CHEWING	CHIRPED
CENTRUM	CHAMPER	CHAUMER	CHEWINK	CHIRPER
CENTUMS	CHANCED	CHAUNCE	CHIACKS	CHIRRED
CENTURY	CHANCEL	CHAUNGE	CHIANTI	CHIRREN
CEPHEID	CHANCES	CHAUVIN	CHIASMI	CHIRRES
CEREOUS	CHANCEY	CHAVISH	CHIBBED	CHIRRUP
CERISES	CHANGER	CHAWERS	CHIBOLS	CHITALS
CERMETS	CHANNEL	CHAYOTE	CHIBOUK	CHITINS
CERNING	CHANNER	CHAZANS	CHICANA	CHITLIN
CEROONS	CHANOYO	CHAZZAN	CHICANE	CHITONS
CERRIAL	CHANOYU	CHAZZEN	CHICANO	CHITTED
CERUMEN	CHANTED	CHEAPEN	CHICHAS	CHITTER
CERVEZA	CHANTEY	CHEAPIE	CHICHES	CHIVARI
CERVINE	CHANTIE	CHEAPLY	CHICHIS	CHIVIED
CESIOUS	CHANTOR	CHEATED	CHICKEE	CHIVING
CESSING	CHANTRY	CHEBECS	CHICKEN	CHIVVED
CESURAE	CHAOSES	CHECHIA	CHICORY	CHIZZED
CEVICHE	CHAOTIC	CHECKED	CHIDDEN	CHIZZES
CHABLIS	CHAPATI	CHECKUP	CHIDING	CHLAMYS
CHABOUK	CHAPEAU	CHEDDAR	CHIEFER	CHLORAL
CHABUKS	CHAPELS	CHEDERS	CHIEFLY	CHLORIC
CHACKED	CHAPESS	CHEDITE	CHIEFRY	CHLORID
CHACMAS	CHAPLET	CHEEKED	CHIFFON	CHLORIN
CHADARS	CHAPMAN	CHEEPER	CHIGGAS	CHOANAE
CHADDAR	CHAPMEN	CHEERER	CHIGGER	CHOBDAR
CHADDOR	CHAPPAL	CHEERIO	CHIGNON	CHOCHOS
CHADORS	CHAPPED	CHEESED	CHIGOES	CHOCKED
CHAEBOL	CHAPPIE	CHEESES	CHIKARA	CHOCKER
CHAETAE	CHARACT	CHEETAH	CHIKHOR	CHOCKOS
CHAETAL	CHARADE	CHEFDOM	CHILDED	CHOCTAW
CHAFERS	CHARGED	CHEFFED	CHILDLY	CHOENIX
CHAFFED	CHARGER	CHEFING	CHILIAD	CHOICES
CHAFFER	CHARIER	CHEGOES	CHILIES	CHOIRED
CHAFING	CHARILY	CHEKIST	CHILIOI	CHOKIER
CHAGANS	CHARITY	CHELATE	CHILLED	CHOKIES
CHAIRED	CHARKED	CHELLUP	CHILLER	CHOKRAS
CHAISES	CHARKHA	CHELPED	CHILLIS	CHOLLAS
CHALAHS	CHARLEY	CHEMICS	CHILLUM	CHOLTRY
CHALANS	CHARLIE	CHEMISM	CHIMBLY	CHOMETZ
CHALAZA	CHARPIE	CHEQUER	CHIMERA	CHOMMIE
CHALCID	CHARPOY	CHEQUES	CHIMERE	CHOMPED
CHALDER	CHARQUI	CHEROOT	CHIMLAS	CHOMPER
CHALEHS	CHARRED	CHERUBS	CHIMLEY	CHONDRE
CHALLAH	CHARROS	CHERUPS	CHIMNEY	CHONDRI
CHALLAN	CHARTAS	CHERVIL	CHINARS	CHOOFED
CHALLAS	CHARVER	CHESNUT	CHINCHY	CHOOKED
CHALLIS	CHASMAL	CHESSEL	CHINDIT	CHOOKIE
CHALLOT	CHASMED	CHESSES	CHINESE	CHOOSES
CHALONE	CHASMIC	CHESTED	CHINKED	CHOOSEY
CHALOTH	CHASSED	CHETRUM	CHINKIE	CHOPPED
CHALUPA	CHASSES	CHEVENS	CHINNED	CHOPPER
CHALUTZ	CHASSIS	CHEVIED	CHINONE	CHORAGI
CHAMADE	CHATBOT	CHEVINS	CHINOOK	CHORDED
CHAMETZ	CHATEAU	CHEVIOT	CHINTZY	CHOREGI
CHAMFER	CHATONS	CHEVRES	CHIPPED	CHORIAL
CHAMISE	CHATTAS	CHEVRET	CHIPPER	CHORINE
CHAMLET	CHATTED	CHEVRON	CHIPPIE	CHORION
CHAMOIX	CHAUFED	CHEWETS	CHIRKED	CHORIZO
CHAMPAC	CHAUFER	CHEWIER	CHIRKER	CHORRIE
CHAMPAK	CHAUFES	CHEWIES	CHIRMED	CHORTLE

CHOUGHS	CICADAE	CLAPPED	CLIPPIE	COALING
CHOWING	CICADAS	CLAPPER	CLIQUED	COALIZE
CHOWRIS	CICEROS	CLARIFY	CLIQUES	COALMAN
CHOWSES	CICHLID	CLARINI	CLIQUEY	COALMEN
CHRISMS	CICOREE	CLARITY	CLITICS	COAMING
CHRISTY	CIGARET	CLARKIA	CLITTER	COANNEX
CHROMED	CIGGIES	CLARTED	CLIVERS	COAPTED
CHROMEL	CILIARY	CLASHED	CLIVIAS	COASTED
CHROMES	CILIATE	CLASSIC	CLOACAE	COAXERS
CHROMIC	CIMELIA	CLASSIS	CLOACAL	COAXIAL
CHROMOS	CIMICES	CLASSON	CLOACAS	COAXING
CHROMYL	CIMIERS	CLASTIC	CLOAKED	COBAEAS
CHRONIC	CINCHED	CLATTED	CLOCHES	COBALTS
CHRONON	CINCHES	CLATTER	CLOGGER	COBBERS
CHUCKED	CINDERY	CLAUCHT	CLOMPED	COBBIER
CHUCKER	CINEOLE	CLAUGHT	CLONING	COBBING
CHUCKIE	CINEREA	CLAUSES	CLONISM	COBBLED
CHUCKLE	CINERIN	CLAUTED	CLONKED	COBBLES
CHUDDAH	CIPHONY	CLAVATE	CLOPPED	COBLOAF
CHUDDAR	CIRCLED	CLAWERS	CLOQUES	COBNUTS
CHUDDER	CIRCLER	CLAWING	CLOSELY	COBURGS
CHUFFED	CIRCLET	CLAXONS	CLOSING	COBWEBS
CHUFFER	CIRCLIP	CLAYIER	CLOTBUR	COCAINS
CHUGGED	CIRCUIT	CLAYING	CLOTHED	COCCIDS
CHUGGER	CIRCUSY	CLAYISH	CLOTHES	COCCOID
CHUKARS	CIRQUES	CLAYPAN	CLOTTED	COCCOUS
CHUKKAR	CIRROUS	CLEANLY	CLOUDED	COCHAIR
CHUKKAS	CIRSOID	CLEARER	CLOUGHS	COCHLEA
CHUKKER	CISCOES	CLEARLY	CLOURED	COCKADE
CHUKORS	CISSIER	CLEATED	CLOUTED	COCKETS
CHUMASH	CISSIES	CLEAVED	CLOVERY	COCKEYE
CHUMLEY	CISSING	CLEAVER	CLOWDER	COCKIER
CHUMMED	CISSOID	CLEAVES	CLOWNED	COCKIES
CHUMPED	CITABLE	CLECKED	CLOYING	COCKING
CHUNKED	CITHARA	CLEEKED	CLUBBED	COCKISH
CHUNNEL	CITOLES	CLEEKIT	CLUBBER	COCKLES
CHUNNER	CITRALS	CLEEPED	CLUBMAN	COCKNEY
CHUNTER	CITRINS	CLEEVES	CLUBMEN	COCKPIT
CHUPATI	CITROUS	CLEMENT	CLUCKED	COCKSHY
CHUPPAH	CITRUSY	CLEMMED	CLUDGIE	COCKUPS
CHUPPAS	CITTERN	CLEOMES	CLUMPED	COCOMAT
CHURCHY	CIVILLY	CLEPING	CLUNKED	COCONUT
CHURNER	CIVISMS	CLERIDS	CLUPEID	COCOONS
CHURRED	CIVVIES	CLERISY	CLUSIAS	COCOPAN
CHURROS	CLABBER	CLERKED	CLUTCHY	COCOTTE
CHURRUS	CLACHAN	CLERKLY	CLUTTER	COCOYAM
CHUSING	CLADDED	CLERUCH	CLYPEAL	COCTILE
CHUTING	CLADDIE	CLEWING	CLYPEUS	COCTION
CHUTIST	CLADISM	CLICHED	CLYPING	CODABLE
CHUTNEE	CLADIST	CLICKED	CLYSTER	CODDERS
CHUTNEY	CLADODE	CLICKER	COACHED	CODDING
CHUTZPA	CLAGGED	CLICKET	COACHEE	CODDLER
CHYACKS	CLAMMED	CLIFFED	COACTED	CODEIAS
CHYLIFY	CLAMMER	CLIFTED	COACTOR	CODEINE
CHYMICS	CLAMORS	CLIMBED	COADMIT	CODETTA
CHYMIFY	CLAMOUR	CLINGED	COAEVAL	CODFISH
CHYMOUS	CLAMPER	CLINICS	COAGULA	CODGERS
CHYTRID	CLANGOR	CLIPART	COALBIN	CODICES
CIBORIA	CLANKED	CLIPING	COALBOX	CODICIL
CIBOULE	CLAPNET	CLIPPED	COALIFY	CODILLA

CODINGS	COLITIC	COMMODO	CONDYLE	CONVOYS
CODISTS	COLLAGE	COMMONS	CONFABS	COOCHES
CODLINS	COLLARD	COMMOTE	CONFECT	COOEYED
COEHORN	COLLARS	COMMOTS	CONFERS	COOINGS
COELIAC	COLLATE	COMMOVE	CONFESS	COOKERY
COELOME	COLLECT	COMMUNE	CONFEST	COOKEYS
COELOMS	COLLEEN	COMMUTE	CONFIDE	COOKIES
COEMPTS	COLLEGE	COMPAGE	CONFINE	COOKING
COENACT	COLLETS	COMPAND	CONFIRM	COOKOFF
COENURE	COLLIER	COMPANY	CONFITS	COOKTOP
COEQUAL	COLLIES	COMPART	CONFLUX	COOLIES
COERCED	COLLING	COMPASS	CONFORM	COOLISH
COERCER	COLLINS	COMPAST	CONFUSE	COOLTHS
COERCES	COLLOID	COMPELS	CONFUTE	COOMBES
COERECT	COLOBID	COMPEND	CONGEAL	COOMIER
COESITE	COLOGNE	COMPERS	CONGEED	COOMING
COEXERT	COLONEL	COMPETE	CONGEES	COONCAN
COFFEES	COLONIC	COMPING	CONGERS	COONDOG
COFFING	COLONUS	COMPLEX	CONGEST	COONTIE
COFFINS	COLOSSI	COMPLIN	CONGOES	COOPERY
COFFLED	COLOURS	COMPLOT	CONGOUS	COOPING
COFFLES	COLOURY	COMPONE	CONGRUE	COOPTED
COFFRET	COLTANS	COMPONY	CONIDIA	COORIED
COFOUND	COLTING	COMPORT	CONINES	COORIES
COGENCE	COLTISH	COMPOSE	CONIUMS	COOSENS
COGENCY	COLUGOS	COMPOTE	CONJECT	COOSINS
COGGERS	COLUMEL	COMPTED	CONJEED	COOTIES
COGGIES	COLUMNS	COMPTER	CONJEES	COPAIBA
COGGING	COMAKER	COMPUTE	CONJOIN	COPAIVA
COGGLES	COMAKES	COMSYMP	CONJURE	COPALMS
COGITOS	COMARTS	CONACRE	CONJURY	COPECKS
COGNACS	COMATIC	CONCAVE	CONKIER	COPEPOD
COGNIZE	COMATIK	CONCEAL	CONNATE	COPIHUE
COGWAYS	COMBIES	CONCEDE	CONNERS	COPILOT
COHABIT	COMBINE	CONCEDO	CONNING	COPIOUS
COHEADS	COMBING	CONCEIT	CONNIVE	COPLOTS
COHERER	COMBLES	CONCEPT	CONNOTE	COPPERS
COHIBIT	COMBUST	CONCERN	CONOIDS	COPPERY
COHORNS	COMEDIC	CONCERT	CONQUER	COPPICE
COHORTS	COMEDOS	CONCHAE	CONSIGN	COPPIES
COHOSTS	COMETIC	CONCHAL	CONSOLS	COPPING
COHUNES	COMFIER	CONCHAS	CONSULS	COPPINS
COIFFED	COMFITS	CONCHED	CONTACT	COPPLES
COIFING	COMFORT	CONCHES	CONTECK	COPPRAS
COIGNED	COMFREY	CONCHIE	CONTEMN	COPSHOP
COILING	COMICAL	CONCHOS	CONTEND	COPULAE
COINAGE	COMINGS	CONCISE	CONTENT	COPYBOY
COINING	COMIQUE	CONCOCT	CONTEST	COPYCAT
COITION	COMITAL	CONCORD	CONTEXT	COPYING
COJOINS	COMITIA	CONCREW	CONTORT	COPYIST
COJONES	COMMAND	CONCUPY	CONTRAT	COQUETS
COKESES	COMMATA	CONCURS	CONTROL	COQUINA
COKIEST	COMMEND	CONCUSS	CONTUND	COQUITO
COLBIES	COMMENT	CONDEMN	CONVECT	CORACLE
COLDEST	COMMERE	CONDIGN	CONVENE	CORALLA
COLDIES	COMMERS	CONDOLE	CONVENT	CORBEAU
COLDISH	COMMIES	CONDOMS	CONVERT	CORBELS
COLETIT	COMMITS	CONDONE	CONVICT	CORBIES
COLIBRI	COMMIXT	CONDUCE	CONVIVE	CORBINA
COLICIN	COMMODE	CONDUCT	CONVOKE	CORDIAL

CORDING	COSMEAS	COURTLY	CRACKED	CRIBBER
CORDITE	COSMIDS	COUSINS	CRACKER	CRIBBLE
CORDOBA	COSMINS	COUTHIE	CRACKET	CRICKED
COREIGN	COSMISM	COUTURE	CRACKLY	CRICKET
COREMIA	COSMOID	COUVADE	CRACKUP	CRICKEY
CORIOUS	COSSETS	COVELET	CRACOWE	CRICOID
CORIUMS	COSSIES	COVENTS	CRADLER	CRIMING
CORIVAL	COSTALS	COVERED	CRAGGED	CRIMINI
CORIXID	COSTARD	COVERUP	CRAMESY	CRIMINY
CORKAGE	COSTATE	COVETED	CRAMMED	CRIMMER
CORKIRS	COSTIVE	COVETER	CRAMMER	CRIMPED
CORMELS	COSTUME	COVINGS	CRAMPED	CRIMPER
CORMOID	COSYING	COWAGES	CRAMPER	CRIMPLE
CORMOUS	COTEAUX	COWARDS	CRAMPET	CRINGED
CORNCOB	COTERIE	COWBANE	CRAMPON	CRINGER
CORNEAE	COTHURN	COWBELL	CRANKED	CRINGES
CORNEAL	COTIDAL	COWBIND	CRANKER	CRINING
CORNETT	COTLAND	COWBIRD	CRANKLE	CRINKLY
CORNFED	COTTAGE	COWBOYS	CRANKLY	CRINOID
CORNFLY	COTTARS	COWEDLY	CRANNOG	CRINUMS
CORNIER	COTTERS	COWERED	CRAPAUD	CRIOLLO
CORNIFY	COTTIDS	COWFISH	CRAPIER	CRISPIN
CORNING	COTTIER	COWFLAP	CRAPPED	CRISPLY
CORNROW	COTTING	COWFLOP	CRAPPER	CRISSAL
COROLLA	COTTOID	COWGIRL	CRASSLY	CRISSUM
CORONAE	COTTONS	COWHAGE	CRATURS	CRITICS
CORONAL	COTTONY	COWHAND	CRAUNCH	CRITTER
CORONEL	COTTOWN	COWHEEL	CRAVATS	CRITTUR
CORONET	COTWALS	COWHERB	CRAWDAD	CRIVENS
CORONIS	COTYLES	COWHIDE	CRAWLED	CROAKED
COROZOS	COTYPES	COWIEST	CRAWLER	CROAKER
CORPORA	COUCALS	COWITCH	CRAYERS	CROCHES
CORPSED	COUCHED	COWKING	CRAYONS	CROCHET
CORRADE	COUCHEE	COWLICK	CRAZIER	CROCKED
CORRALS	COUCHER	COWLING	CRAZIES	CROCKET
CORRECT	COUCHES	COWPATS	CRAZILY	CROFTER
CORRIDA	COUGANS	COWPEAS	CRAZING	CROGGED
CORRODE	COUGARS	COWPIES	CREACHS	CROJIKS
CORRODY	COUGHED	COWPING	CREAKED	CROMACK
CORRUPT	COUGHER	COWPLOP	CREANCE	CROMBEC
CORSAIR	COUGUAR	COWPOKE	CREATIC	CROMBED
CORSEYS	COULDST	COWRITE	CREELED	CROMING
CORTEGE	COULEES	COWROTE	CREEPER	CRONISH
CORTILE	COULOIR	COWSKIN	CREEPIE	CRONKER
CORTILI	COULOMB	COWSLIP	CREESES	CROOKED
CORULER	COUNCIL	COWTREE	CREESHY	CROOKER
CORVEES	COUNTED	COXALGY	CREMANT	CROONED
CORVIDS	COUNTRY	COXCOMB	CREMORS	CROOVES
CORVINA	COUPEES	COXITIS	CRENELS	CROPFUL
CORVINE	COUPING	COXLESS	CREPONS	CROPPED
CORYLUS	COUPLED	COYDOGS	CRESTED	CROPPER
CORYMBS	COUPLER	COYNESS	CRESYLS	CROPPIE
CORYPHE	COUPURE	COYPOUS	CRETICS	CROQUIS
CORYZAL	COURAGE	COZENED	CREVICE	CROSSLY
CORYZAS	COURANT	COZENER	CREWCUT	CROUPON
COSECHS	COURBED	COZIERS	CREWELS	CROWBAR
COSHERS	COURIED	COZIEST	CREWING	CROWDED
COSHERY	COURIER	COZYING	CREWMAN	CROWDER
COSHING	COURING	CRABBED	CREWMEN	CROWDIE
COSIGNS	COURTER	CRABBER	CRIBBED	CROWEAS

CROWING	CUBLESS	CUPULAR	CUTESIE	CZARINA
CROWNET	CUBOIDS	CUPULES	CUTICLE	CZARISM
CROZERS	CUCKING	CURABLE	CUTIKIN	CZARIST
CROZIER	CUCKOLD	CURABLY	CUTLASS	DABBERS
CRUBEEN	CUCKOOS	CURARAS	CUTOUTS	DABBING
CRUCIAL	CUDBEAR	CURARES	CUTTAGE	DABBITY
CRUCIAN	CUDDENS	CURARIS	CUTTIER	DABBLED
CRUCIFY	CUDDIES	CURATOR	CUTTIES	DACKERS
CRUDDED	CUDDINS	CURBERS	CUTTING	DACKING
CRUDELY	CUDDLED	CURBING	CUTTLED	DACOITS
CRUDITY	CUDGELS	CURCHEF	CUTTOES	DACOITY
CRUELER	CUDWEED	CURCHES	CUTWORK	DACTYLI
CRUELLY	CUFFING	CURCUMA	CUTWORM	DACTYLS
CRUISIE	CUFFINS	CURDING	CUVETTE	DADAISM
CRUIZIE	CUFFLED	CURDLER	CWTCHED	DADAIST
CRULLER	CUIRASS	CURETTE	CWTCHES	DADDIES
CRUMBED	CUISINE	CURFEWS	CYANATE	DADDING
CRUMBER	CUISSES	CURIOUS	CYANIDE	DADDLED
CRUMBLY	CUITTLE	CURIUMS	CYANIDS	DADDOCK
CRUMBUM	CULCHIE	CURLERS	CYANINE	DADOING
CRUMENS	CULEXES	CURLEWS	CYANINS	DAFFIER
CRUMMIE	CULICES	CURLIER	CYANISE	DAFFIES
CRUMPED	CULICID	CURLILY	CYANITE	DAFFILY
CRUMPER	CULLAYS	CURLING	CYANIZE	DAFFING
CRUMPET	CULLETS	CURRACH	CYATHIA	DAFTARS
CRUMPLY	CULLIED	CURRAGH	CYATHUS	DAFTEST
CRUNCHY	CULLIES	CURRANS	CYBORGS	DAGABAS
CRUNODE	CULLING	CURRANT	CYBRIDS	DAGGERS
CRUPPER	CULLION	CURRENT	CYCASES	DAGGIER
CRUSADO	CULMING	CURRIER	CYCASIN	DAGGING
CRUSETS	CULOTTE	CURRING	CYCLERS	DAGGLED
CRUSHED	CULPRIT	CURRISH	CYCLERY	DAGLOCK
CRUSHER	CULTISH	CURSERS	CYCLING	DAGOBAS
CRUSHES	CULTISM	CURSING	CYCLINS	DAGWOOD
CRUSIAN	CULTIST	CURSORS	CYCLIST	DAHLIAS
CRUSILY	CULTURE	CURSORY	CYCLIZE	DAHOONS
CRUZADO	CULVERS	CURTANA	CYCLOID	DAIDLED
CRUZIES	CULVERT	CURTATE	CYCLONE	DAIKONS
CRYBABY	CUMARIC	CURTAXE	CYCLOPS	DAIMIOS
CRYOGEN	CUMBENT	CURVATE	CYGNETS	DAIMOKU
CRYONIC	CUMBIAS	CURVETS	CYMATIA	DAIMYOS
CRYPTAL	CUMMINS	CURVIER	CYMBALO	DAINING
CRYPTIC	CUMQUAT	CURVING	CYMBALS	DAISIED
CRYPTON	CUMSHAW	CURVITY	CYMENES	DAISIES
CRYPTOS	CUMULET	CUSHATS	CYMLING	DAKERED
CRYSTAL	CUMULUS	CUSHAWS	CYMLINS	DAKOITI
CSARDAS	CUNDUMS	CUSHIER	CYNICAL	DAKOITS
CUBAGES	CUNEATE	CUSHILY	CYPRESS	DAKOITY
CUBANES	CUNETTE	CUSHION	CYPRIAN	DALAPON
CUBBIES	CUNNING	CUSPIDS	CYPRIDS	DALASIS
CUBBING	CUPCAKE	CUSSERS	CYPRINE	DALEDHS
CUBBISH	CUPELER	CUSTARD	CYPSELA	DALETHS
CUBHOOD	CUPGALL	CUSTOCK	CYSTIDS	DALGYTE
CUBICAL	CUPHEAD	CUSTODY	CYSTOID	DALLOPS
CUBICAS	CUPLIKE	CUSTOMS	CYTISUS	DAMAGED
CUBICLE	CUPPIER	CUTAWAY	CYTODES	DAMAGES
CUBICLY	CUPPING	CUTBACK	CYTOSOL	DAMASKS
CUBISMS	CUPROUS	CUTBANK	CZAPKAS	DAMBROD
CUBITAL	CUPRUMS	CUTCHES	CZARDAS	DAMFOOL
CUBITUS	CUPULAE	CUTDOWN	CZARDOM	DAMIANA

DAMMARS	DATEDLY	DEBASED	DEEPENS	DEJEUNE
DAMMING	DATINGS	DEBATED	DEEPIES	DEKEING
DAMNIFY	DATIVAL	DEBAUCH	DEERFLY	DEKKOED
DAMNING	DATURAS	DEBBIER	DEERLET	DELATED
DAMOSEL	DATURIC	DEBBIES	DEEVING	DELAYED
DAMOZEL	DAUBERY	DEBEAKS	DEEWANS	DELEADS
DAMPENS	DAUBIER	DEBONED	DEFACED	DELEAVE
DAMPERS	DAUBING	DEBONES	DEFACES	DELEBLE
DAMPIER	DAUDING	DEBOUCH	DEFAMED	DELEING
DAMPING	DAUNDER	DEBRIDE	DEFAMER	DELETED
DAMSELS	DAUNTON	DEBTEES	DEFAMES	DELICTS
DAMSONS	DAUPHIN	DEBUNKS	DEFANGS	DELIMED
DANAZOL	DAURING	DEBURRS	DEFECTS	DELIMES
DANCERS	DAUTIES	DEBUSED	DEFENCE	DELISTS
DANCING	DAUTING	DEBUSES	DEFENDS	DELLIES
DANDERS	DAVIDIA	DEBUTED	DEFENSE	DELOPED
DANDIFY	DAWBAKE	DECADAL	DEFFEST	DELOPES
DANDILY	DAWCOCK	DECADES	DEFICIT	DELOUSE
DANDLED	DAWNING	DECAFFS	DEFILES	DELPHIC
DANDLER	DAWTING	DECALED	DEFINED	DELPHIN
DANDLES	DAYANIM	DECALOG	DEFINES	DELTOID
DANELAW	DAYBEDS	DECAPOD	DEFLATE	DELUDED
DANGING	DAYBOOK	DECARBS	DEFLEAS	DELUDER
DANKISH	DAYBOYS	DECAYED	DEFOAMS	DELUDES
DANNIES	DAYCARE	DECAYER	DEFORCE	DELUGED
DANTING	DAYCHED	DECCIES	DEFRAGS	DELUGES
DAPHNES	DAYCHES	DECEASE	DEFRAUD	DELVERS
DAPHNIA	DAYGLOW	DECEITS	DEFRAYS	DEMAGOG
DAPHNID	DAYLILY	DECEIVE	DEFROZE	DEMAINE
DAPPERS	DAYLONG	DECENCY	DEFTEST	DEMARKS
DAPPING	DAYMARE	DECIARE	DEFUELS	DEMASTS
DAPPLED	DAYMARK	DECIBEL	DEFUNCT	DEMAYNE
DAPSONE	DAYROOM	DECIDED	DEFUNDS	DEMEANE
DAQUIRI	DAYSACK	DECIDES	DEFUSED	DEMENTI
DARBARS	DAYSIDE	DECIDUA	DEFUSES	DEMENTS
DAREFUL	DAYSMAN	DECIMES	DEFUZED	DEMETON
DARGAHS	DAYSMEN	DECKERS	DEFUZES	DEMIGOD
DARGLES	DAYSTAR	DECKING	DEFYING	DEMISES
DARIOLE	DAYTALE	DECKLED	DEGAMES	DEMISTS
DARKENS	DAYTIME	DECLAWS	DEGAMIS	DEMIVEG
DARKEYS	DAZEDLY	DECLINE	DEGASES	DEMODED
DARKING	DAZZLED	DECOCTS	DEGAUSS	DEMONIC
DARKISH	DAZZLER	DECODED	DEGERMS	DEMONRY
DARKLED	DAZZLES	DECODES	DEGGING	DEMOSES
DARKLES	DEADBOY	DECOKES	DEGLAZE	DEMOTED
DAROGHA	DEADENS	DECORUM	DEGOUTS	DEMOTES
DARRAIN	DEADERS	DECOYED	DEGRADE	DEMOTIC
DARRAYN	DEADEYE	DECOYER	DEGREED	DEMURED
DARRING	DEADING	DECREER	DEGREES	DEMURER
DARTLED	DEADMAN	DECRIER	DEGUSTS	DENARII
DASHEEN	DEADPAN	DECRYPT	DEHISCE	DENAYED
DASHEKI	DEAFENS	DECUMAN	DEHORNS	DENIMED
DASHIKI	DEAFISH	DECURIA	DEICIDE	DENIZEN
DASHPOT	DEALATE	DECURVE	DEICING	DENNING
DASSIES	DEANING	DEDUCED	DEICTIC	DENOTED
DASTARD	DEARNLY	DEDUCTS	DEIFEST	DENOTES
DASYPOD	DEASHED	DEEDFUL	DEIFORM	DENSELY
DASYURE	DEASHES	DEEDIER	DEITIES	DENSEST
DATABUS	DEATHLY	DEEJAYS	DEJECTA	DENSIFY
DATCHAS	DEBARKS	DEEMING	DEJECTS	DENTATE

DENTILS	DEVISED	DIATRON	DILATED	DIQUATS
DENTINE	DEVISEE	DIAZINE	DILATOR	DIRDAMS
DENTOID	DEVISES	DIAZOES	DILDOES	DIRDUMS
DENUDED	DEVOICE	DIAZOLE	DILEMMA	DIREFUL
DENYING	DEVORES	DIBASIC	DILLIER	DIREMPT
DEODAND	DEVOTED	DIBBERS	DILLIES	DIRHEMS
DEODARA	DEVOTEE	DIBBING	DILLING	DIRIGES
DEODARS	DEVOTES	DIBBLED	DILUTED	DIRKING
DEODATE	DEVOURS	DIBBLES	DILUTEE	DIRLING
DEPENDS	DEVVELS	DIBBUKS	DILUTER	DIRNDLS
DEPLETE	DEWANIS	DIBUTYL	DILUTOR	DIRTBAG
DEPLORE	DEWANNY	DICAMBA	DILUVIA	DIRTIER
DEPLUME	DEWAXED	DICASTS	DIMBLES	DIRTILY
DEPONED	DEWAXES	DICHORD	DIMERIC	DIRTING
DEPSIDE	DEWCLAW	DICKEYS	DIMMERS	DISALLY
DEPUTED	DEWDROP	DICKIER	DIMMEST	DISARMS
DEPUTES	DEWFALL	DICKIES	DIMMING	DISAVOW
DERHAMS	DEWFULL	DICKING	DIMMISH	DISBAND
DERIDED	DEWIEST	DICLINY	DIMORPH	DISBARK
DERIVED	DEWLAPT	DICOTYL	DIMOUTS	DISBARS
DERMOID	DEWLESS	DICTATE	DIMPLED	DISBUDS
DERNFUL	DEWOOLS	DICTING	DIMWITS	DISCAGE
DERRICK	DEWORMS	DICTION	DINDLED	DISCANT
DESALTS	DEXTERS	DICTUMS	DINERIC	DISCARD
DESCALE	DEXTRAL	DICYCLY	DINETTE	DISCASE
DESEXED	DEXTRAN	DIDAKAI	DINGBAT	DISCIDE
DESEXES	DEXTRIN	DIDAKEI	DINGIER	DISCOED
DESINES	DEZINCS	DIDDERS	DINGIES	DISCOID
DESISTS	DHAMMAS	DIDDIER	DINGILY	DISCORD
DESKMAN	DHARMAS	DIDDIES	DINGING	DISCUSS
DESKMEN	DHARMIC	DIDDLED	DINGOED	DISDAIN
DESKTOP	DHOORAS	DIDDLES	DINGOES	DISEDGE
DESMIDS	DHOOTIE	DIDDLEY	DINITRO	DISEUSE
DESMOID	DHOOTIS	DIDICOI	DINKIER	DISFAME
DESORBS	DHOURRA	DIDICOY	DINKUMS	DISFORM
DESPITE	DHURNAS	DIEBACK	DINMONT	DISGUST
DESPOND	DHURRAS	DIETARY	DINNING	DISHELM
DESPOTS	DIABASE	DIETHER	DINNLED	DISHFUL
DESYNED	DIABOLO	DIETHYL	DIOBOLS	DISHIER
DETENUE	DIACIDS	DIETINE	DIOCESE	DISHOME
DETESTS	DIADEMS	DIFFERS	DIORAMA	DISHPAN
DETINUE	DIADROM	DIFFORM	DIORISM	DISHRAG
DETOXED	DIAGRAM	DIFFUSE	DIORITE	DISJECT
DETOXES	DIAGRID	DIGAMMA	DIOXANE	DISJOIN
DETRUDE	DIALIST	DIGGERS	DIOXIDE	DISJUNE
DETUNED	DIALLEL	DIGGING	DIOXINS	DISKING
DEUTZIA	DIALOGS	DIGHTED	DIPLOIC	DISLEAF
DEVALLS	DIALYZE	DIGICAM	DIPLOID	DISLIKE
DEVALUE	DIAMIDE	DIGITAL	DIPLOMA	DISLIMB
DEVELED	DIAMOND	DIGLOTS	DIPLONS	DISLIMN
DEVELOP	DIANDRY	DIGLYPH	DIPLONT	DISLINK
DEVESTS	DIANOIA	DIGNIFY	DIPODIC	DISLOAD
DEVIANT	DIAPASE	DIGOXIN	DIPOLAR	DISMALS
DEVIATE	DIAPIRS	DIGRAPH	DIPPERS	DISMANS
DEVICES	DIAPSID	DIGRESS	DIPPIER	DISMASK
DEVILED	DIARCHY	DIKASTS	DIPPING	DISMAST
DEVILET	DIARIAL	DIKDIKS	DIPSHIT	DISMAYS
DEVILRY	DIARIAN	DIKIEST	DIPTYCA	DISMISS
DEVIOUS	DIARIST	DIKKOPS	DIPTYCH	DISOBEY
DEVISAL	DIARIZE	DIKTATS	DIQUARK	DISOMIC

DISOWNS	DOBBIES	DOITKIN	DORADOS	DOWNBOW
DISPACE	DOBBING	DOLEFUL	DORBUGS	DOWNING
DISPARK	DOBBINS	DOLENTE	DORHAWK	DOWSETS
DISPART	DOBHASH	DOLLARS	DORIZED	DOYENNE
DISPEND	DOBLONS	DOLLDOM	DORIZES	DOYLEYS
DISPLAY	DOBSONS	DOLLIED	DORKIER	DOYLIES
DISPOSE	DOCENTS	DOLLIER	DORMERS	DOZENED
DISPOST	DOCETIC	DOLLIES	DORMICE	DOZENTH
DISPRAD	DOCHMII	DOLLING	DORNECK	DOZIEST
DISPRED	DOCIBLE	DOLLISH	DORNICK	DOZINGS
DISPUTE	DOCILER	DOLLOPS	DORNOCK	DRABBED
DISRANK	DOCKAGE	DOLMENS	DORPERS	DRABBER
DISRUPT	DOCKENS	DOLOSSE	DORRING	DRABBET
DISSECT	DOCKING	DOLOURS	DORSALS	DRABLER
DISTAFF	DOCKISE	DOLPHIN	DORSERS	DRACENA
DISTAIN	DOCKIZE	DOLTISH	DORTIER	DRACHMA
DISTANT	DOCQUET	DOMATIA	DORTING	DRACHMS
DISTEND	DOCTORS	DOMETTS	DORTOUR	DRAFTED
DISTICH	DODDARD	DOMICAL	DOSSALS	DRAFTEE
DISTILL	DODDERS	DOMICIL	DOSSELS	DRAGGED
DISTILS	DODDERY	DOMINEE	DOSSILS	DRAGGER
DISTORT	DODDIER	DOMINIE	DOSSING	DRAGONS
DISTRIX	DODDIES	DOMINOS	DOTANTS	DRAMADY
DISTURB	DODDING	DONGING	DOTARDS	DRAMEDY
DISTYLE	DODDLES	DONJONS	DOTINGS	DRAMMED
DISUSED	DODGEMS	DONKEYS	DOTTIER	DRANTED
DISUSES	DODGERY	DONNARD	DOTTILY	DRAPERY
DISYOKE	DODGIER	DONNART	DOTTING	DRAPPED
DITHERY	DODKINS	DONNEES	DOTTLED	DRASTIC
DITTANY	DODOISM	DONNING	DOUANES	DRATTED
DITTAYS	DOESKIN	DONNISH	DOUBLED	DRAUGHT
DITTIED	DOFFERS	DONNISM	DOUBTED	DRAWBAR
DITTING	DOFFING	DONNOTS	DOUCELY	DRAWLER
DITTOED	DOGBOLT	DONSHIP	DOUCEUR	DRAZELS
DITZIER	DOGCART	DONZELS	DOUCHED	DREADER
DIURNAL	DOGDAYS	DOOCOTS	DOUCINE	DREAMED
DIVESTS	DOGDOMS	DOODADS	DOUGHTY	DREARER
DIVIDED	DOGEARS	DOODAHS	DOUKING	DREDGED
DIVIDER	DOGEDOM	DOODIES	DOULEIA	DREDGER
DIVIDES	DOGFACE	DOODLED	DOURAHS	DREDGES
DIVINED	DOGFISH	DOODLES	DOUSERS	DREIDEL
DIVINER	DOGGERS	DOODOOS	DOUTING	DRESSED
DIVINES	DOGGERY	DOOKING	DOVECOT	DRESSES
DIVINGS	DOGGESS	DOOLEES	DOVEISH	DREVILL
DIVISIM	DOGGIER	DOOLIES	DOVEKEY	DRIBBED
DIVULGE	DOGGIES	DOOMFUL	DOVEKIE	DRIBBER
DIVULSE	DOGGING	DOOMING	DOVELET	DRIBBLY
DIVVIED	DOGGISH	DOORMAT	DOVENED	DRIBLET
DIVVIES	DOGGONE	DOORWAY	DOVERED	DRIFTED
DIZENED	DOGGREL	DOOSRAS	DOVIEST	DRIFTER
DIZZARD	DOGHOLE	DOOWOPS	DOWABLE	DRILLED
DIZZIED	DOGMATA	DOOZERS	DOWDIER	DRINKER
DIZZIER	DOGNAPS	DOOZIES	DOWDIES	DRIPPED
DIZZIES	DOGSKIN	DOPANTS	DOWDILY	DRIPPER
DIZZILY	DOGSLED	DOPATTA	DOWELED	DRIVELS
DJEBELS	DOGTOWN	DOPIAZA	DOWERED	DRIVERS
DJEMBES	DOGTROT	DOPPERS	DOWIEST	DRIVING
DJIBBAH	DOGVANE	DOPPIES	DOWLIER	DRIZZLE
DOATING	DOGWOOD	DOPPING	DOWLNES	DRIZZLY
DOBBERS	DOILTER	DOPPIOS	DOWLNEY	DROGERS

DROGHER	DUBBING	DUNDERS	DWAUMED	ECDYSES
DROICHY	DUBBINS	DUNGEON	DWELLED	ECDYSIS
DROILED	DUBIETY	DUNGIER	DWELLER	ECDYSON
DROLLED	DUBIOUS	DUNITIC	DYADICS	ECHAPPE
DROLLER	DUBNIUM	DUNKERS	DYARCHY	ECHELLE
DROMOND	DUCALLY	DUNKING	DYBBUKS	ECHINUS
DROMONS	DUCDAME	DUNLINS	DYESTER	ECHIUMS
DRONERS	DUCHESS	DUNNAGE	DYEWEED	ECHOING
DRONGOS	DUCHIES	DUNNART	DYEWOOD	ECHOISE
DRONIER	DUCKERS	DUNNESS	DYINGLY	ECHOISM
DRONING	DUCKIER	DUNNING	DYKIEST	ECHOIZE
DROOKED	DUCKIES	DUNNISH	DYNAMIC	ECLIPSE
DROOKIT	DUCKING	DUNNITE	DYNAMOS	ECLOGUE
DROOPED	DUCKPIN	DUNNOCK	DYNASTS	ECLOSED
DROPFLY	DUCTING	DUNSHED	DYNASTY	ECLOSES
DROPPED	DUCTULE	DUODENA	DYNEINS	ECOCIDE
DROPPER	DUDDERS	DUOLOGS	DYNODES	ECOLOGY
DROPPLE	DUDDERY	DUOPOLY	DYSLOGY	ECORCHE
DROSHKY	DUDGEON	DUPABLE	DYSODIL	ECOTAGE
DROSTDY	DUDHEEN	DUPATTA	DYSPNEA	ECOTONE
DROUGHT	DUDISMS	DUPLETS	DYSURIA	ECOTOUR
DROUKED	DUELLED	DUPLIED	DYSURIC	ECOTYPE
DROUKIT	DUELLER	DUPLIES	DYVOURS	ECTASES
DROUTHS	DUELLOS	DUPPIES	DYVOURY	ECTASIA
DROUTHY	DUENESS	DUPPING	DZERENS	ECTATIC
DROVERS	DUENNAS	DURABLE	EAGERER	ECTHYMA
DROVING	DUETING	DURABLY	EAGERLY	ECTOPIA
DROWNDS	DUETTED	DURBARS	EARACHE	ECTOPIC
DROWNER	DUFFERS	DURDUMS	EARBALL	ECTOZOA
DRUBBED	DUFFING	DUREFUL	EARBASH	ECTYPAL
DRUBBER	DUFUSES	DURESSE	EARBOBS	ECTYPES
DRUCKEN	DUGOUTS	DURGAHS	EARDROP	ECUELLE
DRUDGED	DUHKHAS	DURGANS	EARDRUM	ECURIES
DRUDGER	DUKEDOM	DURGIER	EARLAPS	ECZEMAS
DRUDGES	DULCETS	DURNING	EARLDOM	EDACITY
DRUGGET	DULCIFY	DUSHING	EARLOBE	EDAPHIC
DRUGGIE	DULCOSE	DUSKENS	EARLOCK	EDDYING
DRUIDIC	DULLARD	DUSKEST	EARMARK	EDEMATA
DRUIDRY	DULLEST	DUSKILY	EARMUFF	EDGIEST
DRUMLIN	DULLIER	DUSKING	EARPICK	EDIBLES
DRUMMED	DULLING	DUSKISH	EARWORM	EDIFICE
DRUMMER	DULLISH	DUSTILY	EASEFUL	EDITRIX
DRUNKEN	DULNESS	DUSTING	EASELED	EDUCATE
DRUNKER	DULOSES	DUSTMAN	EASIEST	EECHING
DRUXIER	DULOTIC	DUSTMEN	EASYING	EELFARE
DRYABLE	DUMBEST	DUSTOFF	EATABLE	EELLIKE
DRYADES	DUMBING	DUSTRAG	EATAGES	EELPOUT
DRYADIC	DUMDUMS	DUSTUPS	EATERIE	EELWORM
DRYBEAT	DUMMIED	DUTCHES	EBAUCHE	EERIEST
DRYINGS	DUMPBIN	DUTEOUS	EBBLESS	EFFABLE
DRYLAND	DUMPERS	DUTIFUL	EBBTIDE	EFFACED
DRYLOTS	DUMPIES	DUUMVIR	EBONICS	EFFACER
DRYNESS	DUMPILY	DUVETYN	EBONITE	EFFACES
DRYWALL	DUMPING	DUYKERS	EBONIZE	EFFECTS
DRYWELL	DUMPISH	DVANDVA	EBRIETY	EFFEIRS
DUALISM	DUMPLED	DVORNIK	EBRIOSE	EFFENDI
DUALITY	DUNCERY	DWALMED	ECBOLES	EFFERED
DUALIZE	DUNCHED	DWAMMED	ECBOLIC	EFFERES
DUARCHY	DUNCHES	DWARFED	ECCRINE	EFFINGS
DUBBERS	DUNCISH	DWARFER	ECDEMIC	EFFORCE

EFFORTS	ELOGIUM	EMERITI	ENCHEER	ENGRASP
EFFRAYS	ELOINED	EMERODS	ENCINAL	ENGROSS
EFFULGE	ELOINER	EMEROID	ENCLOSE	ENGULFS
EFFUSED	ELOPING	EMETICS	ENCLOUD	ENGULPH
EFFUSES	ELOPSES	EMETINE	ENCODED	ENHALOS
EGALITE	ELSHINS	EMETINS	ENCOMIA	ENHANCE
EGALITY	ELTCHIS	EMEUTES	ENCRUST	ENJAMBS
EGENCES	ELUSION	EMICATE	ENCRYPT	ENJOINS
EGESTED	ELUSIVE	EMINENT	ENCYSTS	ENJOYED
EGGCUPS	ELUSORY	EMITTED	ENDEMIC	ENLINKS
EGGHEAD	ELUTING	EMMEWED	ENDERON	ENLIVEN
EGGIEST	ELUVIAL	EMMOVED	ENDEWED	ENMEWED
EGGLESS	ELUVIUM	EMMOVES	ENDIRON	ENMOVES
EGGMASS	ELYSIAN	EMONGST	ENDLANG	ENNAGES
EGGNOGS	ELYTRON	EMOTION	ENDLEAF	ENNEADS
EGGWASH	ELYTRUM	EMOTIVE	ENDLESS	ENNOBLE
EGOLESS	EMANANT	EMOVING	ENDLONG	ENNUIED
EGOTISM	EMBACED	EMPAIRE	ENDMOST	ENNUYED
EGOTIST	EMBACES	EMPALED	ENDOGEN	ENNUYEE
EGOTIZE	EMBALES	EMPALES	ENDOPOD	ENOLASE
EIDETIC	EMBALLS	EMPATHY	ENDORSE	ENOMOTY
EIDOLIC	EMBALMS	EMPAYRE	ENDOWED	ENOUGHS
EIDOLON	EMBANKS	EMPEACH	ENDOZOA	ENOUNCE
EIGHTVO	EMBARGO	EMPERCE	ENDPLAY	ENPLANE
EIKONES	EMBARKS	EMPEROR	ENDSHIP	ENPRINT
EINKORN	EMBASED	EMPIGHT	ENDUING	ENQUIRY
EIRACKS	EMBASES	EMPIRIC	ENDURER	ENRAGES
EIRENIC	EMBASSY	EMPLACE	ENDWAYS	ENRANGE
EISELLS	EMBASTE	EMPLOYE	ENDYSIS	ENRANKS
EJECTED	EMBATHE	EMPLOYS	ENEMIES	ENRHEUM
EJECTOR	EMBAYED	EMPLUME	ENERVED	ENROBER
EKPWELE	EMBAYLD	EMPOWER	ENFACED	ENROLLS
ELATIVE	EMBLAZE	EMPRESS	ENFACES	ENROOTS
ELDERLY	EMBLEMA	EMPRIZE	ENFANTS	ENROUND
ELDRESS	EMBLEMS	EMPTIED	ENFELON	ENSEALS
ELECTED	EMBLOOM	EMPTIER	ENFEOFF	ENSEAMS
ELECTEE	EMBOGUE	EMPTILY	ENFEVER	ENSEARS
ELEGANT	EMBOLIC	EMPUSAS	ENFILED	ENSERFS
ELEGIAC	EMBOLUS	EMPUSES	ENFIXED	ENSEWED
ELEGIZE	EMBOSKS	EMPYEMA	ENFIXES	ENSHELL
ELENCHI	EMBOSOM	EMULATE	ENFLAME	ENSKYED
ELENCHS	EMBOUND	EMULGED	ENFLESH	ENSURER
ELEVATE	EMBOWED	EMULOUS	ENFORCE	ENSURES
ELEVENS	EMBOWEL	EMULSOR	ENFORMS	ENSWEEP
ELEVONS	EMBOWER	EMUNGES	ENFREED	ENSWEPT
ELFHOOD	EMBOXED	EMURING	ENFREES	ENTAMED
ELFLAND	EMBOXES	ENABLED	ENFROZE	ENTAYLE
ELFLIKE	EMBRACE	ENABLER	ENGAGED	ENTENTE
ELFLOCK	EMBRAID	ENACTED	ENGAGEE	ENTERED
ELICITS	EMBRAVE	ENACTOR	ENGAGER	ENTETEE
ELITIST	EMBROIL	ENAMINE	ENGAGES	ENTHRAL
ELIXIRS	EMBROWN	ENATION	ENGAOLS	ENTHUSE
ELLAGIC	EMBRUES	ENCAGED	ENGLOBE	ENTICED
ELLIPSE	EMBRUTE	ENCAGES	ENGLOOM	ENTICES
ELLWAND	EMBRYON	ENCALMS	ENGOBES	ENTITLE
ELMIEST	EMBRYOS	ENCAMPS	ENGORED	ENTOMBS
ELMWOOD	EMENDED	ENCAVES	ENGORGE	ENTRALL
ELOCUTE	EMERALD	ENCHAFE	ENGRACE	ENTRANT
ELODEAS	EMERIED	ENCHAIN	ENGRAFF	ENTROLD
ELOGIES	EMERIES	ENCHANT	ENGRAFT	ENTROPY

ENTWINE	EPITOPE	ESCAPES	EUPNOEA	EXCITER
ENURING	EPIZOAN	ESCHEWS	EUREKAS	EXCITES
ENVAULT	EPIZOIC	ESCRIBE	EURIPUS	EXCITON
ENVELOP	EPIZOON	ESCROLL	EURYOKY	EXCLAIM
ENVENOM	EPOCHAL	ESCROWS	EUSTACY	EXCLAVE
ENVIRON	EPONYMS	ESCUAGE	EUSTASY	EXCLUDE
ENVYING	EPONYMY	ESCUDOS	EUSTELE	EXCRETE
ENWALLS	EPOPEES	ESERINE	EUSTYLE	EXCUDIT
ENWHEEL	EPOXIES	ESLOYNE	EUTAXIA	EXCUSAL
ENWINDS	EPOXYED	ESOTERY	EUTEXIA	EXCUSED
ENWOMBS	EPUISEE	ESSAYED	EUTROPY	EXCUSES
ENZIANS	EPULARY	ESSAYER	EVACUEE	EXECUTE
ENZONED	EPURATE	ESSENCE	EVANGEL	EXEDRAE
ENZONES	EPYLLIA	ESSIVES	EVASION	EXEEMED
ENZYMES	EQUABLE	ESTATED	EVASIVE	EXEGETE
ENZYMIC	EQUABLY	ESTATES	EVEJARS	EXEMING
EOBIONT	EQUALED	ESTIVAL	EVENEST	EXEMPLE
EONISMS	EQUALLY	ESTRONE	EVENTED	EXEMPTS
EOSINES	EQUANTS	ESTUARY	EVERTED	EXERGUE
EPAGOGE	EQUATED	ETAERIO	EVERTOR	EXERTED
EPATANT	EQUATES	ETAGERE	EVICTED	EXHALED
EPAULES	EQUERRY	ETCHANT	EVICTEE	EXHALES
EPAULET	EQUINES	ETCHING	EVICTOR	EXHAUST
EPAXIAL	EQUINIA	ETESIAN	EVIDENT	EXHEDRA
EPAZOTE	EQUINOX	ETHANAL	EVILLER	EXHIBIT
EPEEIST	EQUIPES	ETHANES	EVINCED	EXHORTS
EPEIRID	EQUITES	ETHENES	EVINCES	EXHUMED
EPERDUE	ERASERS	ETHINYL	EVIRATE	EXHUMER
EPERGNE	ERASION	ETHMOID	EVITING	EXHUMES
EPHEBES	ERASURE	ETHOSES	EVOCATE	EXIGENT
EPHEBIC	ERECTLY	ETHOXYL	EVOKING	EXILERS
EPHEBOI	ERECTOR	ETHYNES	EVOLUES	EXILIAN
EPHEBUS	ERELONG	ETHYNYL	EVOLVES	EXILING
EPHEDRA	EREMITE	ETIOLIN	EVOVAES	EXILITY
EPHELIS	EREMURI	ETRENNE	EVULSED	EXISTED
EPHORAL	ERGODIC	ETYMONS	EVULSES	EXITING
EPIBLEM	ERGOTIC	EUCAINE	EVZONES	EXOCARP
EPIBOLY	ERICOID	EUCAINS	EXABYTE	EXODERM
EPICEDE	ERLKING	EUCHRED	EXACTAS	EXODIST
EPICENE	ERMELIN	EUCHRES	EXACTED	EXOGAMY
EPICISM	ERMINED	EUCLASE	EXACTLY	EXOGENS
EPICIST	ERMINES	EUCRITE	EXACTOR	EXOMION
EPICURE	ERODENT	EUDEMON	EXACUMS	EXONYMS
EPIDOTE	ERODIUM	EUGARIE	EXALTED	EXOPODS
EPIGEAL	EROSELY	EUGENIA	EXALTER	EXORDIA
EPIGEAN	EROSION	EUGENIC	EXAMENS	EXOSMIC
EPIGEIC	EROSIVE	EUGENOL	EXAMINE	EXOTICA
EPIGENE	EROTEMA	EUGLENA	EXAPTED	EXOTISM
EPIGONE	EROTEME	EULOGIA	EXARATE	EXPANSE
EPIGONI	EROTICA	EUMUNGS	EXARCHS	EXPENDS
EPIGYNY	EROTISE	EUNUCHS	EXARCHY	EXPENSE
EPILOGS	EROTIZE	EUOUAES	EXCAMBS	EXPIATE
EPINAOI	ERRANCY	EUPEPSY	EXCEEDS	EXPIRED
EPISCIA	ERRATAS	EUPHONS	EXCERPT	EXPIRER
EPISOME	ERRHINE	EUPHONY	EXCHEAT	EXPLAIN
EPITAPH	ERUCTED	EUPHORY	EXCIDED	EXPLANT
EPITAXY	ERUDITE	EUPHROE	EXCIMER	EXPLODE
EPITHEM	ESCALOP	EUPLOID	EXCIPLE	EXPLOIT
EPITHET	ESCAPED	EUPNEAS	EXCISES	EXPLORE
EPITOME	ESCAPEE	EUPNEIC	EXCITED	EXPORTS

EXPOSAL	EYEWASH	FAINTLY	FAQUIRS	FATUOUS
EXPOSER	EYEWEAR	FAIREST	FARADAY	FATWAED
EXPOSES	EYEWINK	FAIRIES	FARADIC	FATWAHS
EXPOUND	FABBEST	FAIRILY	FARAWAY	FATWOOD
EXPRESS	FABLERS	FAIRING	FARCEUR	FAUCALS
EXPUGNS	FABLIAU	FAIRWAY	FARCIED	FAUCETS
EXPULSE	FABLING	FAITHED	FARCIFY	FAUCHON
EXPUNCT	FABRICS	FAITHER	FARCING	FAUCIAL
EXPUNGE	FABULAR	FAITORS	FARCINS	FAUNULA
EXPURGE	FACADES	FAITOUR	FARDAGE	FAUNULE
EXSCIND	FACEBAR	FAJITAS	FARDELS	FAUREST
EXSECTS	FACEMAN	FAKEERS	FARDING	FAUTING
EXSERTS	FACEMEN	FALAFEL	FAREBOX	FAUVISM
EXTATIC	FACETED	FALBALA	FARFALS	FAUVIST
EXTENDS	FACINGS	FALCADE	FARINAS	FAVELAS
EXTENSE	FACONNE	FALCATE	FARINHA	FAVELLA
EXTENTS	FACTFUL	FALCULA	FARMERY	FAVISMS
EXTERNE	FACTICE	FALDAGE	FARNESS	FAVORED
EXTERNS	FACTION	FALLACY	FARRAGO	FAVOURS
EXTINCT	FACTIVE	FALLALS	FARRAND	FAVRILE
EXTIRPS	FACTOID	FALLING	FARRANT	FAVUSES
EXTOLLS	FACTORY	FALLOFF	FARRENS	FAWNERS
EXTORTS	FACTUAL	FALLOWS	FARRIER	FAWNIER
EXTRACT	FACTUMS	FALSELY	FARRING	FAWNING
EXTRAIT	FACULAE	FALSIFY	FARROWS	FAYENCE
EXTREAT	FACULAR	FALSING	FARRUCA	FAYNING
EXTREMA	FACULTY	FALSISH	FARSING	FAZENDA
EXTREME	FADABLE	FALSISM	FARTHEL	FEAGUED
EXTRUDE	FADAISE	FALSITY	FARTHER	FEAGUES
EXUDATE	FADDIER	FALTERS	FARTLEK	FEARERS
EXUDING	FADDISH	FAMILLE	FASCIAE	FEARFUL
EXULTED	FADDISM	FAMULUS	FASCIAS	FEARING
EXURBAN	FADDIST	FANATIC	FASCISM	FEASING
EXURBIA	FADDLED	FANCIER	FASCIST	FEATEST
EXUVIAE	FADDLES	FANCIFY	FASHERY	FEATING
EXUVIAL	FADEDLY	FANCILY	FASHING	FEATOUS
EXUVIUM	FADEINS	FANDING	FASHION	FEATURE
EYALETS	FADEOUT	FANDOMS	FASTING	FEAZING
EYASSES	FADEURS	FANEGAS	FASTISH	FEBRILE
EYEABLE	FADGING	FANFARE	FATALLY	FECIALS
EYEBALL	FADINGS	FANFICS	FATBACK	FECKING
EYEBANK	FADLIKE	FANFOLD	FATBIRD	FECULAE
EYEBATH	FAFFING	FANGING	FATEFUL	FECULAS
EYEBEAM	FAGGERY	FANIONS	FATHEAD	FEDAYEE
EYEBOLT	FAGGIER	FANJETS	FATHOMS	FEDERAL
EYEBROW	FAGGING	FANKLES	FATIDIC	FEDEXED
EYECUPS	FAGGOTS	FANLIKE	FATIGUE	FEDEXES
EYEFOLD	FAGGOTY	FANNELS	FATLIKE	FEDORAS
EYEFULS	FAGOTED	FANNERS	FATLING	FEEBLED
EYEHOLE	FAGOTER	FANNING	FATSIAS	FEEBLER
EYEHOOK	FAGOTTI	FANTADS	FATTENS	FEEBLES
EYELASH	FAGOTTO	FANTASM	FATTEST	FEEDBAG
EYELESS	FAHLERZ	FANTAST	FATTIER	FEEDBOX
EYELETS	FAHLORE	FANTASY	FATTIES	FEEDLOT
EYELIAD	FAIBLES	FANTEEG	FATTILY	FEELBAD
EYELIFT	FAIKING	FANTODS	FATTING	FEELESS
EYELIKE	FAILING	FANTOMS	FATTISH	FEERIES
EYESHOT	FAILLES	FANWISE	FATTISM	FEESING
EYESOME	FAILURE	FANWORT	FATTIST	FEEZING
EYESORE	FAINING	FANZINE	FATUITY	FEIJOAS

FEINTED	FESCUES	FIGGERY	FINNACS	FIXURES
FEINTER	FESSING	FIGGING	FINNANS	FIZGIGS
FELAFEL	FESTERS	FIGJAMS	FINNERS	FIZZENS
FELICIA	FESTIER	FIGMENT	FINNIER	FIZZGIG
FELINES	FESTIVE	FIGURAL	FINNING	FIZZIER
FELLAHS	FETCHED	FIGURED	FINNOCK	FIZZING
FELLERS	FETCHES	FIGURER	FINNSKO	FIZZLED
FELLEST	FETIDER	FIGURES	FIORINS	FIZZLES
FELLIES	FETIDLY	FIGWORT	FIPPLES	FJORDIC
FELLING	FETLOCK	FIKIEST	FIREARM	FLACCID
FELLOES	FETTERS	FILABEG	FIREBOX	FLACKED
FELLOWS	FETTING	FILACER	FIREBUG	FLACKER
FELONRY	FETTLED	FILARIA	FIREDOG	FLACKET
FELSPAR	FETTLER	FILAZER	FIREFLY	FLAFFED
FELTING	FETUSES	FILBERD	FIREMAN	FLAFFER
FELUCCA	FEUDARY	FILBERT	FIREMEN	FLAGGED
FELWORT	FEUDING	FILCHED	FIREPAN	FLAGGER
FEMALES	FEUDIST	FILCHER	FIRINGS	FLAGMAN
FEMINIE	FEVERED	FILCHES	FIRKING	FLAGMEN
FEMITER	FEWMETS	FILEMOT	FIRKINS	FLAGONS
FEMMIER	FEWNESS	FILETED	FIRMANS	FLAILED
FEMORAL	FEWTERS	FILFOTS	FIRMERS	FLAKERS
FENAGLE	FEYNESS	FILIATE	FIRMING	FLAKIER
FENCERS	FIASCHI	FILIBEG	FIRRIER	FLAKIES
FENCING	FIASCOS	FILINGS	FIRRING	FLAKILY
FENDERS	FIATING	FILLETS	FIRSTLY	FLAKING
FENDING	FIBBERS	FILLIES	FISCALS	FLAMBEE
FENLAND	FIBBERY	FILLING	FISGIGS	FLAMBES
FENNECS	FIBBING	FILLIPS	FISHERY	FLAMENS
FENNELS	FIBRILS	FILMDOM	FISHEYE	FLAMERS
FENNIER	FIBRINS	FILMIER	FISHFUL	FLAMFEW
FENNIES	FIBROID	FILMILY	FISHGIG	FLAMIER
FENNISH	FIBROIN	FILMING	FISHIER	FLAMING
FENURON	FIBROMA	FILMISH	FISHIFY	FLAMMED
FEOFFED	FIBROSE	FIMBLES	FISHILY	FLANGER
FEOFFEE	FIBROUS	FIMBRIA	FISHING	FLANKEN
FEOFFER	FIBULAE	FINABLE	FISHNET	FLANKER
FEOFFOR	FIBULAR	FINALES	FISHWAY	FLANNEN
FERBAMS	FIBULAS	FINALLY	FISKING	FLAPPED
FERLIER	FICKLES	FINANCE	FISSILE	FLAPPER
FERMATA	FICTILE	FINBACK	FISSION	FLAREUP
FERMATE	FICTION	FINCHED	FISSIVE	FLARING
FERMENT	FICTIVE	FINCHES	FISSLED	FLASHED
FERMION	FICTORS	FINDING	FISSLES	FLASHER
FERMIUM	FICUSES	FINDRAM	FISTFUL	FLASHES
FERNERY	FIDDLED	FINEISH	FISTIER	FLASKET
FERNING	FIDDLER	FINESSE	FISTULA	FLATBED
FERRATE	FIDDLES	FINFISH	FITCHES	FLATCAP
FERRELS	FIDDLEY	FINFOOT	FITCHET	FLATLET
FERRETS	FIDEISM	FINGANS	FITCHEW	FLATTED
FERRETY	FIDEIST	FINICAL	FITMENT	FLATTEN
FERRITE	FIDGETS	FINICKY	FITTEST	FLATTER
FERRUGO	FIDGETY	FINIKIN	FIVEPIN	FLATTIE
FERRULE	FIDGING	FININGS	FIXABLE	FLATTOP
FERRUMS	FIDIBUS	FINISES	FIXATED	FLAUGHT
FERULAE	FIEFDOM	FINJANS	FIXATES	FLAUNCH
FERULED	FIERCER	FINLESS	FIXATIF	FLAUNES
FERVENT	FIERILY	FINLIKE	FIXEDLY	FLAUNTS
FERVORS	FIFTEEN	FINMARK	FIXINGS	FLAUNTY
FERVOUR	FIFTHLY	FINNACK	FIXTURE	FLAUTAS

FLAVINE	FLOKATI	FLYABLE	FOLLIED	FORELAY
FLAVINS	FLOODED	FLYAWAY	FOLLIES	FORELEG
FLAVONE	FLOOZIE	FLYBACK	FOLLOWS	FORELIE
FLAVORS	FLOPPED	FLYBANE	FOMENTS	FOREMEN
FLAVORY	FLOPPER	FLYBELT	FOMITES	FOREPAW
FLAVOUR	FLORALS	FLYBLEW	FONDANT	FORERAN
FLAWIER	FLORIER	FLYBOAT	FONDEST	FORERUN
FLAWING	FLORINS	FLYBOOK	FONDING	FORESAW
FLAXIER	FLORUIT	FLYBOYS	FONDLED	FORESAY
FLAYERS	FLORULA	FLYHAND	FONDUES	FORESEE
FLEABAG	FLORULE	FLYINGS	FONNING	FOREVER
FLEAPIT	FLOSHES	FLYLEAF	FONTINA	FOREXES
FLECHES	FLOSSED	FLYLESS	FOODFUL	FORFAIR
FLECKED	FLOSSER	FLYOFFS	FOODIES	FORFEND
FLEDGED	FLOSSES	FLYPAST	FOODISM	FORGAVE
FLEDGES	FLOSSIE	FLYPING	FOOLERY	FORGERS
FLEECED	FLOTAGE	FLYTIER	FOOLING	FORGERY
FLEECER	FLOTANT	FLYTING	FOOLISH	FORGETS
FLEECES	FLOTELS	FLYTRAP	FOOTAGE	FORGING
FLEECIE	FLOTSAM	FLYWAYS	FOOTBAG	FORGIVE
FLEERED	FLOUNCE	FOAMERS	FOOTBAR	FORGOER
FLEERER	FLOUNCY	FOAMIER	FOOTBOY	FORGOES
FLEETED	FLOUSES	FOAMILY	FOOTIER	FORGONE
FLEETER	FLOUTED	FOAMING	FOOTING	FORHENT
FLEETLY	FLOUTER	FOBBING	FOOTLED	FORHOOS
FLEGGED	FLOWAGE	FOCALLY	FOOTLER	FORHOWS
FLEHMEN	FLOWERY	FODDERS	FOOTLES	FORINTS
FLEMING	FLUBBED	FOGBOWS	FOOTMAN	FORKERS
FLENSED	FLUBBER	FOGDOGS	FOOTMEN	FORKFUL
FLENSES	FLUBDUB	FOGGAGE	FOOTPAD	FORKIER
FLESHES	FLUENCE	FOGGERS	FOOTRAS	FORKING
FLESHLY	FLUENCY	FOGGIER	FOOTROT	FORLANA
FLEURET	FLUFFED	FOGGILY	FOOTWAY	FORLENT
FLEURON	FLUFFER	FOGGING	FOOZLED	FORLESE
FLEXILE	FLUGELS	FOGHORN	FOOZLER	FORLORN
FLEXING	FLUIDAL	FOGLESS	FOOZLES	FORMALS
FLEXION	FLUIDIC	FOGRAMS	FOPLING	FORMANT
FLEXORS	FLUIDLY	FOGYDOM	FOPPERY	FORMATE
FLEXURE	FLUKIER	FOGYISH	FOPPING	FORMFUL
FLEYING	FLUKILY	FOGYISM	FOPPISH	FORMING
FLIGHTS	FLUKING	FOIBLES	FORAGED	FORMOLS
FLIGHTY	FLUMING	FOILING	FORAGER	FORMULA
FLIMPED	FLUMMOX	FOINING	FORAGES	FORMYLS
FLINDER	FLUMPED	FOISONS	FORAYER	FORNENT
FLINGER	FLUNKED	FOISTED	FORBADE	FORPETS
FLINTED	FLUNKER	FOLACIN	FORBIDS	FORPINE
FLIPPED	FLUNKEY	FOLATES	FORBODE	FORSAID
FLIPPER	FLUNKIE	FOLDING	FORBORE	FORSAKE
FLISKED	FLUORIC	FOLDOUT	FORCEPS	FORSAYS
FLITTED	FLUORID	FOLIAGE	FORCERS	FORSLOE
FLITTER	FLUORIN	FOLIATE	FORCING	FORSLOW
FLIVVER	FLURRED	FOLIOED	FORDING	FORSOOK
FLIXING	FLUSHER	FOLIOLE	FORDONE	FORTIFY
FLOATED	FLUSHES	FOLIOUS	FOREARM	FORTING
FLOATEL	FLUTING	FOLIUMS	FOREBAY	FORTLET
FLOCCED	FLUTIST	FOLKIER	FOREBYE	FORTUNE
FLOCCUS	FLUTTER	FOLKIES	FORECAR	FORWARN
FLOCKED	FLUXING	FOLKISH	FOREDID	FORWENT
FLOGGED	FLUXION	FOLKMOT	FOREGUT	FORWORN
FLOGGER	FLUXIVE	FOLKWAY	FOREIGN	FORZATI

FORZATO	FRASSES	FRIZING	FUDDLER	FUNNEST
FOSSICK	FRATCHY	FRIZZED	FUDDLES	FUNNIER
FOSSILS	FRATERY	FRIZZER	FUDGING	FUNNIES
FOSSORS	FRAUGHT	FRIZZLE	FUEHRER	FUNNILY
FOSSULA	FRAWZEY	FRIZZLY	FUELING	FUNNING
FOTHERS	FRAYING	FROGBIT	FUELLED	FUNPLEX
FOUDRIE	FRAZILS	FROGEYE	FUELLER	FUNSTER
FOUETTE	FRAZZLE	FROGGED	FUFFIER	FURBISH
FOUGADE	FREAKED	FROGLET	FUFFING	FURCULA
FOUGHTY	FRECKLY	FROGMAN	FUGALLY	FUREURS
FOULARD	FREEBEE	FROGMEN	FUGATOS	FURFAIR
FOULEST	FREEDOM	FROINGS	FUGGIER	FURFURS
FOULIES	FREEGAN	FROISES	FUGGILY	FURIOSO
FOULING	FREEMEN	FROLICS	FUGGING	FURIOUS
FOUMART	FREEWAY	FROMAGE	FUGUING	FURKIDS
FOUNDRY	FREEZER	FRONDED	FUGUIST	FURLANA
FOURGON	FREEZES	FRONTAL	FUHRERS	FURLERS
FOURSES	FRESCOS	FRONTED	FULCRUM	FURLESS
FOURTHS	FRESHED	FRONTES	FULFILL	FURLING
FOUSSAS	FRESHEN	FRONTON	FULFILS	FURLONG
FOUTRED	FRESHES	FROSHES	FULGENT	FURMETY
FOVEATE	FRESHLY	FROTHED	FULGORS	FURMITY
FOVEOLA	FRETTED	FROTHER	FULGOUR	FURNACE
FOVEOLE	FRETTER	FROUGHY	FULHAMS	FURNISH
FOWLPOX	FRIABLE	FROUNCE	FULLAGE	FURRIER
FOXFIRE	FRIANDE	FROWIER	FULLAMS	FURRILY
FOXFISH	FRIANDS	FROWNED	FULLANS	FURRING
FOXHOLE	FRIARLY	FROWNER	FULLERS	FURROWS
FOXHUNT	FRIBBLE	FROWSTS	FULLERY	FURROWY
FOXIEST	FRICHTS	FROWSTY	FULLEST	FURTHER
FOXINGS	FRIDGED	FRUCTAN	FULLING	FURTIVE
FOXLIKE	FRIDGES	FRUCTED	FULLISH	FURZIER
FOXSHIP	FRIEZED	FRUGGED	FULMINE	FUSAINS
FOXSKIN	FRIEZES	FRUICTS	FULSOME	FUSARIA
FOXTAIL	FRIGATE	FRUITED	FULVOUS	FUSAROL
FOXTROT	FRIGGED	FRUMPED	FUMADOS	FUSCOUS
FOYBOAT	FRIGGER	FRUMPLE	FUMAGES	FUSHION
FOYLING	FRIGHTS	FRUSHED	FUMARIC	FUSIBLY
FOYNING	FRIGOTS	FRUSHES	FUMBLED	FUSILLI
FOZIEST	FRIJOLE	FRUSTUM	FUMBLER	FUSIONS
FRABBED	FRILLED	FRUTIFY	FUMETTE	FUSSERS
FRABBIT	FRILLER	FRYABLE	FUMETTI	FUSSILY
FRACTUR	FRINGED	FRYINGS	FUMETTO	FUSSING
FRACTUS	FRIPONS	FRYPANS	FUMIEST	FUSSPOT
FRAENUM	FRIPPER	FUBBERY	FUMULUS	FUSTETS
FRAGGED	FRIPPET	FUBBIER	FUNCTOR	FUSTICS
FRAGILE	FRISBEE	FUBBING	FUNDING	FUSTILY
FRAGORS	FRISEES	FUBSIER	FUNEBRE	FUSTING
FRAILLY	FRISKAS	FUCHSIA	FUNFEST	FUSTOCS
FRAILTY	FRISKED	FUCHSIN	FUNGALS	FUTCHEL
FRAISES	FRISKER	FUCKERS	FUNGOES	FUTHARC
FRAKTUR	FRISKET	FUCKING	FUNGOID	FUTHARK
FRAMPAL	FRISSON	FUCKOFF	FUNGOUS	FUTHORC
FRANION	FRISTED	FUCKUPS	FUNICLE	FUTHORK
FRANKED	FRITFLY	FUCKWIT	FUNKERS	FUTSALS
FRANKER	FRITTED	FUCOIDS	FUNKIAS	FUTTOCK
FRANKLY	FRITTER	FUCUSED	FUNKIER	FUTURAL
FRAPPED	FRITZES	FUCUSES	FUNKILY	FUTURES
FRAPPEE	FRIVOLS	FUDDIES	FUNKING	FUTZING
FRAPPES	FRIZERS	FUDDLED	FUNNELS	FUZZIER

FUZZILY	GALLOUS	GARGLER	GAVOTTE	GENETTE
FUZZING	GALLOWS	GARIGUE	GAWCIER	GENIPAP
FUZZLED	GALOCHE	GARJANS	GAWKERS	GENITOR
FUZZLES	GALOOTS	GARLAND	GAWKIER	GENIZAH
FYLFOTS	GALOPED	GARLICS	GAWKIES	GENLOCK
GABBARD	GALOPIN	GAROTED	GAWKILY	GENNELS
GABBART	GALOSHE	GAROTTE	GAWKING	GENNETS
GABBERS	GALUMPH	GAROUPA	GAWKISH	GENNING
GABBIER	GALUTHS	GARPIKE	GAWPERS	GENOMIC
GABBING	GALYACS	GARRANS	GAWPING	GENSENG
GABBLED	GALYAKS	GARRING	GAYDARS	GENTEEL
GABBLES	GAMBADE	GARRONS	GAYSOME	GENTILE
GABBROS	GAMBADO	GARROTE	GAZABOS	GENTLER
GABFEST	GAMBETS	GARROTS	GAZANIA	GENTOOS
GABLETS	GAMBIAS	GARRYAS	GAZEBOS	GEODESY
GABLING	GAMBIER	GARUDAS	GAZEFUL	GEODUCK
GADDERS	GAMBIRS	GARVEYS	GAZELLE	GEOFACT
GADDING	GAMBLED	GARVOCK	GAZETTE	GEOGENY
GADGETY	GAMBLES	GASAHOL	GAZIEST	GEOGONY
GADGIES	GAMBOGE	GASBAGS	GAZINGS	GEOIDAL
GADLING	GAMBOLS	GASCONS	GAZOOKA	GEOLOGY
GADOIDS	GAMELAN	GASEITY	GAZOONS	GEORGIC
GADSMAN	GAMETAL	GASEOUS	GAZUMPS	GERBERA
GADSMEN	GAMETIC	GASHEST	GEALOUS	GERBILS
GADWALL	GAMINGS	GASHFUL	GEARBOX	GERENUK
GAFFERS	GAMMATS	GASHING	GECKING	GERMANE
GAFFING	GAMMIER	GASKETS	GECKOES	GERMENS
GAGAKUS	GAMMING	GASKING	GEDACTS	GERMIER
GAGGERS	GAMMOCK	GASOHOL	GEDECKT	GERNING
GAGGERY	GAMMONS	GASSILY	GEEBAGS	GERTCHA
GAGGING	GAMPISH	GASSING	GEEBUNG	GESSING
GAGGLED	GANACHE	GASTRAL	GEECHEE	GESSOED
GAGGLES	GANGLIA	GATEAUS	GEEGAWS	GESSOES
GAINFUL	GANGREL	GATEAUX	GEEKDOM	GESTALT
GAINING	GANGSTA	GATELEG	GEEKIER	GESTANT
GAINSAY	GANGUES	GATEMEN	GEELBEK	GESTURE
GAITING	GANGWAY	GATHERS	GEEZAHS	GETABLE
GALABEA	GANJAHS	GAUCHER	GEEZERS	GETTERS
GALABIA	GANNETS	GAUCHOS	GEFILTE	GETTING
GALAGES	GANNING	GAUCIER	GEGGIES	GEWGAWS
GALAGOS	GANOIDS	GAUDERY	GEISHAS	GEYSERS
GALANGA	GANOINE	GAUDIER	GELADAS	GHARIAL
GALANTY	GANOINS	GAUDILY	GELCAPS	GHARRIS
GALATEA	GANTLET	GAUDING	GELIDLY	GHASTED
GALAXES	GAPLESS	GAUFFER	GELLANT	GHASTLY
GALETTE	GAPOSIS	GAUGERS	GELLIES	GHAZALS
GALILEE	GAPPERS	GAUGING	GELLING	GHAZELS
GALIPOT	GAPPIER	GAUMIER	GEMCLIP	GHAZIES
GALLANT	GAPPING	GAUMING	GEMFISH	GHERAOS
GALLETS	GARAGES	GAUNTER	GEMLIKE	GHERKIN
GALLEYS	GARBAGE	GAUNTLY	GEMMERY	GHESSED
GALLFLY	GARBAGY	GAUNTRY	GEMMILY	GHESSES
GALLIED	GARBLER	GAUPERS	GEMMING	GHETTOS
GALLIOT	GARBLES	GAUPING	GEMMULE	GHIBLIS
GALLIUM	GARBOIL	GAUSSES	GEMOTES	GHILGAI
GALLIZE	GARBURE	GAUZIER	GEMSBOK	GHILLIE
GALLOCK	GARCONS	GAUZILY	GENAPPE	GHOSTED
GALLOON	GARDANT	GAVAGES	GENDERS	GHOSTLY
GALLOOT	GARFISH	GAVELED	GENESES	GHOULIE
GALLOPS	GARGETY	GAVIALS	GENETIC	GIANTLY

GIANTRY	GIPPOES	GLITZES	GOBBLER	GOODISH
GIAOURS	GIPSENS	GLOATED	GOBBLES	GOODMAN
GIARDIA	GIPSIED	GLOBATE	GOBIIDS	GOODMEN
GIBBERS	GIPSIES	GLOBING	GOBIOID	GOOFIER
GIBBETS	GIRDLER	GLOBOID	GOBLETS	GOOFILY
GIBBING	GIRLIER	GLOBOSE	GOBONEE	GOOFING
GIBBOSE	GIRLIES	GLOBOUS	GOBURRA	GOOGLED
GIBBOUS	GIRLISH	GLOBULE	GODDAMN	GOOGLES
GIBLETS	GIRNIER	GLOCHID	GODDAMS	GOOGOLS
GIBUSES	GIROLLE	GLOMMED	GODDESS	GOOIEST
GIDDIED	GIRONIC	GLOOMED	GODETIA	GOOLEYS
GIDDIER	GIROSOL	GLOOPED	GODHEAD	GOOMBAH
GIDDIES	GITTING	GLOPPED	GODHOOD	GOOMBAY
GIDDILY	GIVABLE	GLORIFY	GODLILY	GOONDAS
GIDDYAP	GIVINGS	GLOSSAE	GODOWNS	GOONEYS
GIDDYUP	GIZZARD	GLOSSAL	GODROON	GOONIER
GIDGEES	GIZZENS	GLOSSAS	GODSLOT	GOOPIER
GIDJEES	GJETOST	GLOSSES	GODSONS	GOORALS
GIFTEES	GLACEED	GLOTTAL	GODWARD	GOOROOS
GIFTING	GLADDED	GLOTTIC	GODWITS	GOOSERY
GIGABIT	GLADDER	GLOTTIS	GOFFERS	GOOSEYS
GIGATON	GLADDIE	GLOUTED	GOFFING	GOOSING
GIGGING	GLADDON	GLOVING	GOGGLED	GOPHERS
GIGGITS	GLADFUL	GLOWFLY	GOGGLER	GOPURAM
GIGGLED	GLADIUS	GLOZING	GOGGLES	GOPURAS
GIGGLER	GLAIKIT	GLUCANS	GOITRED	GORCOCK
GIGGLES	GLAIVED	GLUCOSE	GOLDARN	GORCROW
GIGLETS	GLAIVES	GLUEPOT	GOLDBUG	GORDITA
GIGLOTS	GLAMORS	GLUMMER	GOLDEST	GORGERS
GIGOLOS	GLAMOUR	GLUTAEI	GOLDEYE	GORGIAS
GILBERT	GLAREAL	GLUTEAL	GOLDISH	GORGING
GILCUPS	GLARIER	GLUTEUS	GOLDURN	GORGIOS
GILGAIS	GLASSED	GLUTTON	GOLFERS	GORGONS
GILGIES	GLASSEN	GLYCANS	GOLFING	GORHENS
GILLETS	GLAUMED	GLYCINE	GOLIARD	GORILLA
GILLIED	GLAZERS	GLYCINS	GOLIATH	GORMAND
GILLIES	GLAZIER	GLYCOLS	GOLLAND	GORMIER
GILLING	GLAZILY	GLYCOSE	GOLLARS	GORMING
GILLION	GLAZING	GLYCYLS	GOLLERS	GORSIER
GILPEYS	GLEAMED	GLYPHIC	GOLLIED	GORSOON
GILPIES	GLEAMER	GLYPTAL	GOLLIES	GOSHAWK
GILTCUP	GLEBOUS	GLYPTIC	GOLLOPS	GOSLETS
GIMBALS	GLEDGED	GNASHES	GOMBEEN	GOSPELS
GIMLETS	GLEDGES	GNATHAL	GOMBROS	GOSPODA
GIMMALS	GLEEFUL	GNATHIC	GOMEREL	GOSPORT
GIMMICK	GLEEKED	GNAWERS	GOMERIL	GOSSANS
GIMMIES	GLEEMEN	GNAWING	GOMOKUS	GOSSIBS
GIMMORS	GLEENIE	GNOCCHI	GOMUTIS	GOSSING
GIMPIER	GLEETED	GNOMIST	GOMUTOS	GOSSIPS
GIMPING	GLEGGER	GNOMONS	GONADAL	GOSSIPY
GINGELI	GLENOID	GOADING	GONADIC	GOSSOON
GINGHAM	GLIBBED	GOANNAS	GONGYOS	GOTCHAS
GINGILI	GLIMING	GOATEES	GONIDIA	GOTHICS
GINGIVA	GLIMMER	GOATIER	GONIDIC	GOTHITE
GINNING	GLIOMAS	GOATISH	GONOPHS	GOUACHE
GINSENG	GLIOSES	GOBANGS	GONOPOD	GOUGERE
GINZOES	GLIOSIS	GOBBETS	GONYSES	GOUGERS
GIOCOSO	GLITCHY	GOBBIER	GOODBYE	GOUGING
GIPPIES	GLITTER	GOBBING	GOODBYS	GOUJONS
GIPPING	GLITZED	GOBBLED	GOODIER	GOULASH

GOURAMI	GRAVEST	GRIPIER	GRUMOUS	GULDENS
GOURMET	GRAVIDA	GRIPING	GRUMPED	GULLERS
GOUTFLY	GRAVING	GRIPPED	GRUMPHS	GULLERY
GOUTIER	GRAVITY	GRIPPER	GRUMPHY	GULLETS
GOUTILY	GRAVLAX	GRIPPLE	GRUNGER	GULLEYS
GOUTTES	GRAYFLY	GRISING	GRUNION	GULLIED
GOVERNS	GRAYING	GRISTER	GRUNTER	GULLING
GOWDEST	GRAYISH	GRISTLY	GRUNTLE	GULLISH
GOWFERS	GRAYLAG	GRITTED	GRUYERE	GULPIER
GOWFING	GRAYOUT	GRITTER	GRYDING	GULPING
GOWLAND	GRAZERS	GRIVETS	GRYFONS	GUMBALL
GOWLANS	GRAZIER	GRIZZLE	GRYPHON	GUMBOIL
GOWNBOY	GRAZING	GRIZZLY	GRYSBOK	GUMBOOT
GOWNING	GREASES	GROANED	GRYSELY	GUMDROP
GOWNMAN	GREATLY	GROCERS	GUAIACS	GUMLESS
GOWNMEN	GREAVED	GROCERY	GUANACO	GUMLIKE
GOWPENS	GREAVES	GROCKLE	GUANASE	GUMMATA
GOYISCH	GRECIZE	GRODIER	GUANAYS	GUMMERS
GOZZANS	GRECQUE	GROGGED	GUANGOS	GUMMIER
GRABBED	GREECES	GROGRAM	GUANINS	GUMMIES
GRABBER	GREEING	GROKKED	GUANXIS	GUMMILY
GRACING	GREEKED	GROMETS	GUARANA	GUMMING
GRACKLE	GREENIE	GROMMET	GUARANI	GUMMITE
GRADATE	GREENLY	GRONING	GUARDED	GUMMOSE
GRADELY	GREENTH	GROOMED	GUARDEE	GUMMOUS
GRADUAL	GREESES	GROOVER	GUARDER	GUMNUTS
GRAFFED	GREETES	GROOVES	GUARISH	GUMPING
GRAFTED	GREGALE	GROPERS	GUAYULE	GUMSHOE
GRAITHS	GREIGES	GROSERT	GUBBAHS	GUMTREE
GRAKLES	GREISEN	GROSSES	GUCKIER	GUMWEED
GRAMARY	GRENNED	GROSSLY	GUDDLED	GUMWOOD
GRAMMAR	GREWING	GROTTOS	GUDGEON	GUNBOAT
GRAMMAS	GREYEST	GROUCHY	GUENONS	GUNFIRE
GRAMPAS	GREYHEN	GROUGHS	GUEREZA	GUNGING
GRAMPUS	GREYISH	GROUNDS	GUERITE	GUNITES
GRANARY	GREYLAG	GROUPED	GUESSED	GUNKIER
GRANDLY	GRICERS	GROUSER	GUESSER	GUNLOCK
GRANDPA	GRICING	GROUSES	GUESSES	GUNNAGE
GRANGER	GRIDDED	GROUTER	GUESTED	GUNNELS
GRANITA	GRIDDER	GROVETS	GUESTEN	GUNNERA
GRANNAM	GRIECED	GROWING	GUFFAWS	GUNNERS
GRANNOM	GRIEFER	GROWLED	GUFFIES	GUNNERY
GRANOLA	GRIESIE	GROWLER	GUGGLES	GUNNING
GRANTOR	GRIEVER	GROWTHS	GUGLETS	GUNPLAY
GRANULE	GRIFFES	GROWTHY	GUICHET	GUNPORT
GRAPERY	GRIFFON	GROZING	GUIDERS	GUNROOM
GRAPHED	GRIFTED	GRUBBED	GUIDING	GUNWALE
GRAPHIC	GRIFTER	GRUBBER	GUILDER	GUNYAHS
GRAPIER	GRIGGED	GRUBBLE	GUILDRY	GUPPIES
GRAPLES	GRIGRIS	GRUDGES	GUILING	GURAMIS
GRAPNEL	GRILLED	GRUELER	GUIMPED	GURGLED
GRAPPAS	GRILLER	GRUFFED	GUIMPES	GURGLET
GRAPPLE	GRILSES	GRUFFER	GUINEAS	GURJUNS
GRASSED	GRIMACE	GRUFFLY	GUIPURE	GURLETS
GRASSER	GRIMIER	GRUFTED	GUISARD	GURLIER
GRASSUM	GRIMILY	GRUGRUS	GUISERS	GURLING
GRATIFY	GRIMING	GRUMBLE	GUISING	GURNARD
GRAUNCH	GRIMMER	GRUMBLY	GUITARS	GURNEYS
GRAVELY	GRINNER	GRUMMER	GUIZERS	GURNING
GRAVERS	GRIPERS	GRUMMET	GULCHED	GURRAHS

GURRIER	HABITUS	HALACHA	HANDILY	HARNESS
GURUDOM	HACHURE	HALAKIC	HANDING	HARPING
GURUISM	HACKBUT	HALALAH	HANDISM	HARPINS
GUSHILY	HACKEES	HALALAS	HANDJAR	HARPIST
GUSLARS	HACKERS	HALAVAH	HANDLED	HARPOON
GUSSETS	HACKERY	HALBERD	HANDLER	HARRIER
GUSSIED	HACKIES	HALCYON	HANDOUT	HARRIES
GUSSIES	HACKING	HALFLIN	HANDSAW	HARROWS
GUSTOES	HACKLER	HALFWAY	HANDSET	HARSHEN
GUTCHER	HACKLET	HALFWIT	HANGDOG	HARSHER
GUTLIKE	HACKMAN	HALIBUT	HANGING	HARSHLY
GUTSERS	HACKMEN	HALIDES	HANGMAN	HARTALS
GUTTATE	HACKNEY	HALIDOM	HANGMEN	HARUMPH
GUTTERS	HADAWAY	HALIMOT	HANGTAG	HASBIAN
GUTTERY	HADDEST	HALLAHS	HANKIES	HASHIER
GUTTIES	HADDIES	HALLALI	HANKING	HASHING
GUTTING	HADDING	HALLALS	HANSELS	HASHISH
GUTTLER	HADDOCK	HALLELS	HANSOMS	HASSARS
GUTTLES	HADEDAH	HALLIAN	HANTLES	HASSIUM
GUTZERS	HADITHS	HALLING	HANUMAN	HASTATE
GUYLERS	HADJEES	HALLION	HAPAXES	HASTILY
GUYLINE	HADROME	HALLOAS	HAPKIDO	HATABLE
GUZZLED	HADRONS	HALLOES	HAPLITE	HATBAND
GUZZLER	HAEMOID	HALLOTH	HAPLOID	HATCHED
GUZZLES	HAEMONY	HALLWAY	HAPPENS	HATCHEL
GWEDUCK	HAFFETS	HALLYON	HAPPIED	HATCHER
GWEDUCS	HAFFITS	HALOGEN	HAPPIER	HATCHET
GWINIAD	HAFFLIN	HALOIDS	HAPPIES	HATEFUL
GWYNIAD	HAFIZES	HALOING	HAPPILY	HATLIKE
GYMBALS	HAFNIUM	HALOUMI	HAPPING	HATPEGS
GYMMALS	HAFTARA	HALVAHS	HAPTENS	HATPINS
GYMPING	HAFTING	HALVERS	HAPUKAS	HATRACK
GYMSLIP	HAGADIC	HALVING	HAPUKUS	HATTOCK
GYNECIA	HAGBOLT	HALYARD	HARBORS	HAUBERK
GYNECIC	HAGBUSH	HAMADAS	HARBOUR	HAUBOIS
GYNNEYS	HAGBUTS	HAMAULS	HARDBAG	HAUDING
GYNNIES	HAGDOWN	HAMBLED	HARDHAT	HAUGHTY
GYPLURE	HAGFISH	HAMBONE	HARDILY	HAULAGE
GYPPERS	HAGGARD	HAMBURG	HARDISH	HAULERS
GYPPIES	HAGGING	HAMLETS	HARDMAN	HAULIER
GYPPING	HAGGISH	HAMMADA	HARDOKE	HAUNTED
GYPSIED	HAGGLED	HAMMAMS	HARDPAN	HAUSENS
GYPSIES	HAGGLER	HAMMIER	HARDTOP	HAUTBOY
GYPSTER	HAGGLES	HAMMILY	HARELIP	HAUTEUR
GYPSUMS	HAGLETS	HAMMING	HARIANA	HAUYNES
GYRALLY	HAGLIKE	HAMMOCK	HARIJAN	HAVARTI
GYRASES	HAGRODE	HAMPERS	HARIRAS	HAVENED
GYRATOR	HAHNIUM	HAMSTER	HARKING	HAVEOUR
GYRENES	HAIDUKS	HAMULAR	HARLING	HAVERED
GYROCAR	HAILIER	HAMULUS	HARLOTS	HAVEREL
GYRONIC	HAIMISH	HAMZAHS	HARMALA	HAVIORS
GYRONNY	HAINING	HANAPER	HARMANS	HAVIOUR
GYRUSES	HAIRCUT	HANCHED	HARMELS	HAWALAS
GYTRASH	HAIRDOS	HANCHES	HARMERS	HAWBUCK
GYTTJAS	HAIRIER	HANDBAG	HARMFUL	HAWKBIT
HABDABS	HAIRING	HANDCAR	HARMINE	HAWKERS
HABITAN	HAIRPIN	HANDFED	HARMING	HAWKEYS
HABITAT	HAIRSTS	HANDFUL	HARMINS	HAWKING
HABITED	HAJJAHS	HANDGUN	HARMONY	HAWKISH
HABITUE	HAKEEMS	HANDIER	HARMOST	HAWMING

HAYBAND	HEDGERS	HENBITS	HEXEREI	HIPPING
HAYCOCK	HEDGIER	HENCOOP	HEXINGS	HIPPINS
HAYFORK	HEDGING	HENDING	HEXONES	HIPPISH
HAYINGS	HEDONIC	HENLEYS	HEXOSAN	HIPSHOT
HAYLAGE	HEEDFUL	HENLIKE	HEXOSES	HIPSTER
HAYLOFT	HEEHAWS	HENNAED	HEXYLIC	HIRABLE
HAYMOWS	HEELING	HENNERS	HEYDAYS	HIRCINE
HAYRACK	HEELTAP	HENNERY	HEYDEYS	HIREAGE
HAYRICK	HEEZIES	HENNIER	HEYDUCK	HIRLING
HAYSEED	HEEZING	HENNIES	HEYDUCK	HIRPLED
HAYSELS	HEFTIER	HENNING	HIBACHI	HIRPLES
HAYWARD	HEFTILY	HENNINS	HICCUPS	HIRSLED
HAYWIRE	HEFTING	HENNISH	HICCUPY	HIRSTIE
HAZANIM	HEGEMON	HENOTIC	HICKEYS	HIRSUTE
HAZARDS	HEGUMEN	HENPECK	HICKIES	HIRUDIN
HAZELLY	HEIGHTH	HENTING	HICKISH	HISHING
HAZIEST	HEILING	HEPARIN	HICKORY	HISSERS
HAZINGS	HEIMISH	HEPPEST	HIDABLE	HISSIER
HAZZANS	HEINIES	HEPTOSE	HIDAGES	HISSIES
HEADAGE	HEINOUS	HERBAGE	HIDALGA	HISSING
HEADEND	HEIRDOM	HERBALS	HIDALGO	HISTOID
HEADFUL	HEIRING	HERBARY	HIDEOUS	HISTORY
HEADIER	HEISTED	HERBIER	HIDEOUT	HISTRIO
HEADILY	HEISTER	HERBIST	HIDLINS	HITCHED
HEADING	HEITIKI	HERBOSE	HIGGLED	HITCHER
HEADMAN	HEJIRAS	HERBOUS	HIGGLER	HITCHES
HEADMEN	HEKTARE	HERDBOY	HIGGLES	HITHERS
HEADSET	HELIMAN	HERDENS	HIGHBOY	HITLESS
HEADWAY	HELIPAD	HERDERS	HIGHERS	HIZZING
HEALDED	HELIXES	HERDESS	HIGHING	HOAGIES
HEALEES	HELLBOX	HERDING	HIGHISH	HOARDED
HEALERS	HELLCAT	HERDMEN	HIGHMAN	HOARDER
HEALING	HELLERY	HERITOR	HIGHMEN	HOARIER
HEALTHS	HELLING	HERLING	HIGHTHS	HOARILY
HEALTHY	HELLION	HERNIAE	HIGHTOP	HOARING
HEAPIER	HELLISH	HEROINE	HIGHWAY	HOARSER
HEAPING	HELLOED	HEROISE	HIJACKS	HOASTED
HEARING	HELLOES	HEROIZE	HIJINKS	HOATZIN
HEARKEN	HELLOVA	HERONRY	HIJRAHS	HOAXERS
HEARSAY	HELLUVA	HERRING	HIKOIED	HOAXING
HEARSES	HELMERS	HERSALL	HILCHED	HOBBERS
HEARTHS	HELMETS	HERSHIP	HILCHES	HOBBIES
HEASTES	HELMING	HERTZES	HILLIER	HOBBING
HEATHEN	HELOTRY	HERYING	HILLING	HOBBISH
HEATHER	HELPERS	HESSIAN	HILLMEN	HOBBITS
HEAUMES	HELPFUL	HESSITE	HILLOAS	HOBBLED
HEAVENS	HELPING	HETAERA	HILLOCK	HOBBLER
HEAVIER	HELVING	HETAIRA	HILLOED	HOBBLES
HEAVIES	HEMAGOG	HETEROS	HILLTOP	HOBDAYS
HEAVILY	HEMATAL	HEUREKA	HIMATIA	HOBJOBS
HEAVING	HEMATIC	HEWABLE	HINDLEG	HOBLIKE
HEBENON	HEMIOLA	HEXACTS	HINGERS	HOBNAIL
HEBETIC	HEMIONE	HEXADES	HINKIER	HOBNOBS
HEBONAS	HEMIPOD	HEXADIC	HINNIED	HOBODOM
HECKLED	HEMLOCK	HEXAGON	HINNIES	HOBOISM
HECKLER	HEMMERS	HEXANES	HIPLESS	HOCKLED
HECKLES	HEMMING	HEXAPLA	HIPLIKE	HOCKLES
HEDDLED	HEMPIER	HEXAPOD	HIPLINE	HODADDY
HEDDLES	HENBANE	HEXARCH	HIPNESS	HODDING
HEDERAL	HENBANE	HEXENES	HIPPEST	HODDINS

HODDLED	HOMINID	HOPHEAD	HOUGHED	HUMATES
HODDLES	HOMMOCK	HOPLITE	HOUHERE	HUMBLED
HOECAKE	HOMOLOG	HOPPIER	HOUMMOS	HUMBLER
HOELIKE	HOMONYM	HOPPING	HOUMOUS	HUMBLES
HOGBACK	HOMOSEX	HOPPLED	HOUNDED	HUMBUGS
HOGFISH	HONCHOS	HOPPLER	HOUNDER	HUMBUZZ
HOGGERS	HONDLED	HOPPLES	HOUNGAN	HUMDRUM
HOGGERY	HONDLES	HOPSACK	HOUSELS	HUMERAL
HOGGETS	HONESTY	HOPTOAD	HOUSERS	HUMERUS
HOGGING	HONEYED	HORDEIN	HOUSIER	HUMFING
HOGGINS	HONGIED	HORDING	HOUSING	HUMHUMS
HOGGISH	HONGING	HORDOCK	HOVELED	HUMIDER
HOGHOOD	HONKERS	HORIZON	HOVERED	HUMIDEX
HOGLIKE	HONKEYS	HORKEYS	HOVERER	HUMIDLY
HOGMANE	HONKIES	HORNBUG	HOWBEIT	HUMINTS
HOGNOSE	HONKING	HORNERS	HOWDAHS	HUMMAUM
HOGTIED	HONORED	HORNFUL	HOWDIED	HUMMELS
HOGTIES	HONOREE	HORNIER	HOWDIES	HUMMERS
HOGWARD	HONORER	HORNILY	HOWFFED	HUMMING
HOGWASH	HONOURS	HORNING	HOWFING	HUMMOCK
HOGWEED	HOOCHES	HORNISH	HOWKERS	HUMMUMS
HOICKED	HOOCHIE	HORNIST	HOWKING	HUMOGEN
HOIDENS	HOODIAS	HORNITO	HOWLERS	HUMORAL
HOIKING	HOODIER	HORNLET	HOWLING	HUMORED
HOISING	HOODIES	HOROEKA	HOYDENS	HUMOURS
HOISINS	HOODING	HORRIFY	HRYVNAS	HUMPENS
HOISTED	HOODLUM	HORRORS	HRYVNIA	HUMPERS
HOKIEST	HOODMEN	HORSIER	HRYVNYA	HUMPHED
HOKONUI	HOODOOS	HORSILY	HUANACO	HUMPIER
HOLARDS	HOOFERS	HORSONS	HUBBIES	HUMPIES
HOLDALL	HOOFING	HOSANNA	HUBBUBS	HUMPING
HOLDERS	HOOFROT	HOSEMAN	HUBCAPS	HUMUSES
HOLDING	HOOKAHS	HOSEMEN	HUCKERY	HUMVEES
HOLDOUT	HOOKERS	HOSEYED	HUCKLES	HUNCHED
HOLESOM	HOOKEYS	HOSIERS	HUDDLED	HUNCHES
HOLEYER	HOOKIER	HOSIERY	HUDDLES	HUNDRED
HOLIBUT	HOOKIES	HOSPICE	HUELESS	HUNGERS
HOLISMS	HOOKING	HOSTAGE	HUFFERS	HUNKERS
HOLISTS	HOOKLET	HOSTELS	HUFFIER	HUNKEYS
HOLKING	HOOKUPS	HOSTESS	HUFFILY	HUNKIER
HOLLAND	HOOLEYS	HOSTIES	HUFFING	HUNKIES
HOLLERS	HOOLIER	HOTBEDS	HUFFISH	HUNKSES
HOLLOED	HOOLIES	HOTCAKE	HUFFKIN	HUNTING
HOLLOES	HOOLOCK	HOTCHED	HUGEOUS	HUPPAHS
HOLLOOS	HOOPERS	HOTDOGS	HUGGERS	HUPPING
HOLLOWS	HOOPLAS	HOTFOOT	HUGGIER	HURDENS
HOLMIAS	HOOPOES	HOTHEAD	HUGGING	HURDIES
HOLMIUM	HOOPOOS	HOTLINK	HUIPILS	HURDLER
HOLONIC	HOORAHS	HOTNESS	HUITAIN	HURDLES
HOLYDAM	HOORAYS	HOTRODS	HULKIER	HURLBAT
HOLYDAY	HOOSGOW	HOTSHOT	HULKING	HURLERS
HOMAGED	HOOSHED	HOTSPUR	HULLERS	HURLEYS
HOMAGER	HOOSHES	HOTTERS	HULLIER	HURLING
HOMBRES	HOOTIER	HOTTEST	HULLING	HURRAED
HOMBURG	HOOTING	HOTTIES	HULLOAS	HURRAHS
HOMEBOY	HOOVERS	HOTTISH	HULLOED	HURRAYS
HOMELYN	HOOVING	HOUDAHS	HULLOES	HURRIER
HOMERED	HOPBIND	HOUDANS	HULLOOS	HURTERS
HOMIEST	HOPDOGS	HOUFFED	HUMANER	HURTLED
HOMINES	HOPEFUL	HOUFING	HUMANLY	HUSBAND

HUSHABY	HYPNONE	ILLUMED	IMPLORE	INDULTS
HUSHFUL	HYPNUMS	ILLUMES	IMPONED	INDUNAS
HUSHIER	HYPOGEA	ILLUPIS	IMPOSED	INDWELL
HUSHING	HYPOING	ILLUVIA	IMPOUND	INEDITA
HUSKERS	HYPONEA	IMAGERY	IMPOWER	INEPTER
HUSKIER	HYPONYM	IMAGINE	IMPRINT	INEPTLY
HUSKIES	HYPOXIA	IMAGING	IMPROVE	INERTIA
HUSKILY	HYPOXIC	IMAGISM	IMPROVS	INERTLY
HUSKING	HYPPING	IMAGIST	IMPULSE	INEXACT
HUSSARS	HYPURAL	IMAGOES	IMPUTED	INFALLS
HUSSIES	HYRACES	IMAMATE	INANELY	INFAMED
HUSSIFS	HYRAXES	IMBALMS	INANITY	INFANCY
HUSTLED	HYSSOPS	IMBARKS	INBEING	INFANTA
HUSWIFE	IAMBICS	IMBASED	INBOARD	INFANTE
HUTCHED	IAMBIST	IMBASES	INBOUND	INFANTS
HUTCHES	ICEBALL	IMBATHE	INBREAK	INFAUNA
HUTCHIE	ICEBERG	IMBIBED	INBUILT	INFECTS
HUTLIKE	ICEBOAT	IMBIBER	INBURST	INFEOFF
HUTMENT	ICEFALL	IMBIBES	INCAGED	INFERNO
HUTTING	ICELIKE	IMBIZOS	INCAVED	INFIGHT
HUTZPAH	ICEPACK	IMBLAZE	INCAVES	INFILLS
HUTZPAS	ICEWINE	IMBOSKS	INCEDED	INFIMUM
HUZOORS	ICHABOD	IMBRAST	INCEDES	INFIRMS
HUZZAED	ICHTHIC	IMBROWN	INCENSE	INFIXED
HUZZAHS	ICHTHYS	IMBRUED	INCENTS	INFIXES
HUZZIES	ICICLED	IMBUING	INCHPIN	INFLATE
HYAENAS	ICONIFY	IMITANT	INCIPIT	INFLECT
HYALINE	ICONIZE	IMITATE	INCISOR	INFLICT
HYALITE	ICTERIC	IMMASKS	INCITES	INFLOWS
HYBRIDS	IDEALLY	IMMENSE	INCIVIL	INFOLDS
HYDATID	IDEATED	IMMERSE	INCLINE	INFORMS
HYDRANT	IDEATES	IMMEWED	INCLIPS	INFULAE
HYDRASE	IDIOTCY	IMMIXED	INCOMER	INFUSER
HYDRIDE	IDIOTIC	IMMIXES	INCONNU	INFUSES
HYDRIDS	IDOLISM	IMMORAL	INCROSS	INGOING
HYDROID	IDOLIST	IMMUNES	INCRUST	INGOTED
HYDROMA	IDOLIZE	IMPACTS	INCUBUS	INGROWN
HYDROPS	IDYLIST	IMPAIRS	INCURVE	INGULFS
HYDROXY	IDYLLIC	IMPALAS	INCUSES	INGULPH
HYDYNES	IGARAPE	IMPARKS	INDABAS	INHABIT
HYENINE	IGNATIA	IMPARLS	INDAMIN	INHALES
HYENOID	IGNEOUS	IMPAVED	INDARTS	INHAULS
HYGEIST	IGNITES	IMPAVES	INDENES	INHAUST
HYGIENE	IGNOBLY	IMPAVID	INDEXAL	INHERCE
HYGROMA	IGNORER	IMPAWNS	INDEXES	INHERED
HYLDING	IGUANAS	IMPEACH	INDICAN	INHERIT
HYLISMS	IGUANID	IMPEDED	INDICIA	INHIBIN
HYLOIST	IJTIHAD	IMPEDOR	INDICTS	INHIBIT
HYMENAL	IKEBANA	IMPENDS	INDIGEN	INHOOPS
HYMENIA	ILEITIS	IMPERIA	INDIGOS	INHUMAN
HYMNALS	ILEUSES	IMPERIL	INDITED	INHUMED
HYMNARY	ILIACUS	IMPIETY	INDIUMS	INHUMES
HYMNING	ILKADAY	IMPINGE	INDOWED	INISLES
HYMNIST	ILLAPSE	IMPINGS	INDOXYL	INITIAL
HYMNODY	ILLEGAL	IMPIOUS	INDRAFT	INJECTS
HYPATES	ILLIADS	IMPLANT	INDUCED	INJELLY
HYPERON	ILLITES	IMPLETE	INDUCER	INJERAS
HYPHENS	ILLNESS	IMPLIED	INDUCTS	INJOINT
HYPNICS	ILLOGIC	IMPLIES	INDUING	INJUNCT
HYPNOID	ILLUDED	IMPLODE	INDULIN	INJURED

INJURER	INTWINE	ISOBATH	JACKLEG	JAPPING
INJURES	INUTILE	ISOCHOR	JACKMEN	JARGONS
INKBLOT	INVADES	ISODICA	JACKPOT	JARGONY
INKHORN	INVALID	ISODOMA	JACOBIN	JARGOON
INKIEST	INVEIGH	ISODONT	JACOBUS	JARHEAD
INKLIKE	INVENIT	ISODOSE	JACONET	JARINAS
INKWELL	INVENTS	ISOETES	JACUZZI	JARKMAN
INKWOOD	INVESTS	ISOFORM	JADEDLY	JARKMEN
INLACED	INVEXED	ISOGAMY	JADEITE	JARLDOM
INLANDS	INVIOUS	ISOGENY	JADITIC	JAROOLS
INLOCKS	INVITAL	ISOGONS	JAEGERS	JARPING
INLYING	INVITED	ISOGONY	JAGAING	JARRAHS
INNARDS	INVITEE	ISOGRAM	JAGGARY	JARRING
INNERLY	INVOICE	ISOGRIV	JAGGERS	JARVEYS
INNLESS	INVOKED	ISOHELS	JAGGERY	JARVIES
INNYARD	INVOKER	ISOHYET	JAGGIER	JASMINE
INOCULA	INVOKES	ISOKONT	JAGGIES	JASMINS
INORBED	INVOLVE	ISOLATE	JAGGING	JASPERS
INOSINE	INWALLS	ISOLOGS	JAGHIRE	JASPERY
INOSITE	INWARDS	ISOMERE	JAGHIRS	JASSIDS
INPHASE	INWEAVE	ISONOMY	JAGLESS	JATAKAS
INPOURS	INWICKS	ISOPACH	JAGUARS	JAUKING
INQILAB	INWINDS	ISOPODS	JAILERS	JAUNCED
INQUIET	INWORKS	ISOTACH	JAILING	JAUNCES
INQUIRE	INWOUND	ISOTOPE	JAILORS	JAUNSED
INQUIRY	INWOVEN	ISOTOPY	JAKESES	JAUNSES
INSHELL	INYALAS	ISOTYPE	JALAPIC	JAUNTED
INSHIPS	IODISER	ISOZYME	JALAPIN	JAUNTEE
INSIDES	IODISES	ISSUING	JALOPPY	JAUNTIE
INSINEW	IODISMS	ISTANAS	JAMADAR	JAUPING
INSIPID	IODIZED	ISTHMIC	JAMBART	JAVELIN
INSISTS	IODIZER	ISTHMUS	JAMBEAU	JAWARIS
INSOFAR	IODIZES	ITALICS	JAMBEES	JAWBONE
INSOOTH	IONISES	ITCHILY	JAMBERS	JAWFALL
INSOULS	IONIZED	ITCHING	JAMBEUX	JAWHOLE
INSPANS	IONIZES	ITEMING	JAMBIER	JAWLESS
INSTALL	IONOGEN	ITEMISE	JAMBING	JAWLIKE
INSTALS	IONONES	ITEMIZE	JAMBIYA	JAWLINE
INSTANT	IPOMOEA	IVORIED	JAMBOOL	JAYBIRD
INSTILL	IRACUND	IVORIES	JAMDANI	JAYGEES
INSTILS	IRIDIAL	IVYLIKE	JAMESES	JAYWALK
INSULAS	IRIDIAN	IZZARDS	JAMJARS	JAZZBOS
INSULTS	IRIDISE	JABBERS	JAMLIKE	JAZZERS
INSURED	IRIDIUM	JABBING	JAMMERS	JAZZIER
INSWEPT	IRIDIZE	JABBLED	JAMMIER	JAZZILY
INSWING	IRONIER	JABBLES	JAMMING	JAZZING
INTERNE	IRONIST	JABIRUS	JAMPANI	JAZZMAN
INTHRAL	IRONMAN	JACALES	JAMPANS	JAZZMEN
INTIMAL	IRONMEN	JACAMAR	JAMPOTS	JEELIED
INTITLE	ISAGOGE	JACANAS	JANDALS	JEELIES
INTOMBS	ISATINE	JACARES	JANGLED	JEELING
INTRANT	ISATINS	JACCHUS	JANGLER	JEEPERS
INTROFY	ISCHIAL	JACINTH	JANGLES	JEEPING
INTROIT	ISCHIUM	JACKALS	JANITOR	JEEPNEY
INTROLD	ISLANDS	JACKASS	JANIZAR	JEERERS
INTRONS	ISLEMEN	JACKDAW	JANKERS	JEERING
INTRUST	ISLETED	JACKEEN	JANNIES	JEFFING
INTUITS	ISOAMYL	JACKERS	JANNOCK	JEHADIS
INTURNS	ISOBARE	JACKETS	JANSKYS	JEJUNAL
INTUSES	ISOBARS	JACKING	JAPINGS	JEJUNUM

JELLABA	JIBBING	JOGGLED	JUBBAHS	JURYMAN
JELLIED	JIBBONS	JOGGLER	JUBHAHS	JURYMEN
JELLIES	JIBBOOM	JOGGLES	JUBILEE	JUSSIVE
JELLIFY	JICAMAS	JOGTROT	JUBILES	JUSTERS
JELLING	JIFFIES	JOHNNIE	JUDASES	JUSTEST
JEMADAR	JIGABOO	JOHNSON	JUDDERS	JUSTICE
JEMIDAR	JIGAJIG	JOINDER	JUDGERS	JUSTIFY
JEMMIED	JIGAJOG	JOINERY	JUDGING	JUSTING
JEMMIER	JIGGERS	JOINING	JUDOGIS	JUSTLED
JEMMIES	JIGGIER	JOINTED	JUDOIST	JUSTLES
JENNETS	JIGGING	JOINTER	JUDOKAS	JUTTIED
JENNIES	JIGGISH	JOINTLY	JUGGING	JUTTIES
JEOFAIL	JIGGLED	JOISTED	JUGGINS	JUTTING
JEOPARD	JIGGLES	JOJOBAS	JUGGLED	JUVENAL
JERBOAS	JIGJIGS	JOKIEST	JUGGLER	JYMOLDS
JEREEDS	JIGLIKE	JOLLEYS	JUGGLES	KABADDI
JERKERS	JIGSAWS	JOLLIED	JUGHEAD	KABAKAS
JERKIER	JIHADIS	JOLLIER	JUGLETS	KABALAS
JERKIES	JILBABS	JOLLIES	JUGULAR	KABAYAS
JERKILY	JILGIES	JOLLIFY	JUGULUM	KABBALA
JERKING	JILLETS	JOLLILY	JUICERS	KABELES
JERQUED	JILLION	JOLLING	JUICIER	KABIKIS
JERQUER	JILTERS	JOLLOPS	JUICILY	KABUKIS
JERQUES	JILTING	JOLLYER	JUICING	KACCHAS
JERREED	JIMJAMS	JOLTIER	JUJUBES	KACHERA
JERRIDS	JIMMIED	JOLTING	JUJUISM	KACHERI
JERRIES	JIMMIES	JONESED	JUJUTSU	KACHINA
JERSEYS	JIMMINY	JONESES	JUKEBOX	KADDISH
JESSAMY	JIMPEST	JONNOCK	JUKSKEI	KAFFIRS
JESSANT	JIMPIER	JONQUIL	JUMARTS	KAFTANS
JESSIES	JINGALL	JONTIES	JUMBIES	KAGOOLS
JESSING	JINGALS	JOOKERY	JUMBLED	KAGOULE
JESTEES	JINGLED	JOOKING	JUMBLER	KAGOULS
JESTERS	JINGLER	JORDANS	JUMBLES	KAHAWAI
JESTFUL	JINGLES	JOSEPHS	JUMBUCK	KAHUNAS
JESTING	JINGLET	JOSHERS	JUMELLE	KAIAKED
JESUITS	JINGOES	JOSHING	JUMPERS	KAIKAIS
JETBEAD	JINJILI	JOSKINS	JUMPIER	KAINGAS
JETFOIL	JINKING	JOSSERS	JUMPILY	KAINITE
JETLAGS	JINXING	JOSTLED	JUMPING	KAINITS
JETLIKE	JIPYAPA	JOSTLES	JUMPOFF	KAIZENS
JETPORT	JIRBLED	JOTTERS	JUNCATE	KAJAWAH
JETSAMS	JISSOMS	JOTTING	JUNGLED	KAJEPUT
JETSOMS	JITNEYS	JOTUNNS	JUNGLES	KAKAPOS
JETSONS	JITTERY	JOUKERY	JUNGLIS	KAKODYL
JETTIED	JIVEASS	JOUKING	JUNIORS	KALENDS
JETTIER	JIVIEST	JOULING	JUNIPER	KALIANS
JETTIES	JOANNAS	JOUNCED	JUNKERS	KALIMBA
JETTING	JOANNES	JOURNAL	JUNKETS	KALIPHS
JETTONS	JOBBERS	JOURNEY	JUNKIER	KALIUMS
JETWAYS	JOBBERY	JOUSTED	JUNKIES	KALONGS
JEWELED	JOBBIES	JOUSTER	JUNKING	KALPACS
JEWELER	JOBBING	JOWARIS	JUNKMAN	KALPAKS
JEWELRY	JOBLESS	JOWLERS	JUNKMEN	KAMALAS
JEWFISH	JOCKEYS	JOWLIER	JUPATIS	KAMELAS
JEZAILS	JOCKNEY	JOWLING	JURALLY	KAMERAD
JEZEBEL	JOCULAR	JOYANCE	JURANTS	KAMICHI
JHATKAS	JODHPUR	JOYLESS	JURIDIC	KAMISES
JIBBAHS	JOGGERS	JOYRIDE	JURISTS	KAMPONG
JIBBERS	JOGGING	JOYRODE	JURYING	KAMSEEN

KAMSINS	KEELAGE	KETOSIS	KIDDUSH	KIRKMEN
KANAKAS	KEELIES	KETOTIC	KIDGIER	KIRKTON
KANBANS	KEELING	KETTLES	KIDLETS	KIRMESS
KANDIES	KEELMAN	KETUBAH	KIDLIKE	KIRTANS
KANTARS	KEELMEN	KETUBOT	KIDLING	KIRTLED
KANTELE	KEELSON	KEWLEST	KIDSKIN	KISHKAS
KANTENS	KEENERS	KEWPIES	KIDULTS	KISHKES
KANTHAS	KEEPERS	KEYCARD	KIDVIDS	KISMATS
KAOLINE	KEEPNET	KEYHOLE	KIEKIES	KISMETS
KAOLINS	KEFFELS	KEYLESS	KIERIES	KISSELS
KARAISM	KEGELER	KEYLINE	KIKUMON	KISSERS
KARAITS	KEGGING	KEYNOTE	KIKUYUS	KITBAGS
KARAKAS	KEGLERS	KEYPADS	KILERGS	KITENGE
KARAKIA	KEGLING	KEYPALS	KILLCOW	KITHARA
KARAKUL	KEKSYES	KEYSETS	KILLDEE	KITHING
KARANGA	KELLAUT	KEYSTER	KILLICK	KITSETS
KARAOKE	KELOIDS	KEYWAYS	KILLIES	KITTENS
KARATES	KELPERS	KEYWORD	KILLING	KITTENY
KARENGO	KELPIES	KGOTLAS	KILLJOY	KITTIES
KARKING	KELPING	KHADDAR	KILLOCK	KITTING
KAROSHI	KELVINS	KHALATS	KILLUTS	KITTLED
KARSEYS	KEMBING	KHALIFA	KILOBAR	KITTLER
KARSTIC	KEMBLAS	KHALIFS	KILOBIT	KITTULS
KARTING	KEMBOED	KHAMSIN	KILORAD	KLAPPED
KARZIES	KEMPERS	KHANATE	KILOTON	KLATSCH
KASHMIR	KEMPIER	KHANJAR	KILTIES	KLAVERN
KASHRUS	KEMPING	KHANUMS	KIMBOED	KLAVIER
KATANAS	KEMPLES	KHARIFS	KIMCHEE	KLAXONS
KATCINA	KENCHES	KHAYALS	KIMCHIS	KLEAGLE
KATHAKS	KENNELS	KHAZENS	KINARAS	KLEENEX
KATHODE	KENNERS	KHEDAHS	KINASES	KLEPHTS
KATIONS	KENNETS	KHEDIVA	KINCHIN	KLEPTOS
KATIPOS	KENNETT	KHEDIVE	KINCOBS	KLEZMER
KATORGA	KENNING	KHILATS	KINDLED	KLINKER
KATSURA	KENOSES	KHILIMS	KINDLER	KLIPDAS
KATYDID	KENOSIS	KHIRKAH	KINDRED	KLOOTCH
KAUPAPA	KENTING	KHODJAS	KINEMAS	KLUDGED
KAURIES	KEPPING	KHOTBAH	KINESIC	KLUDGES
KAYAKED	KERAMIC	KHOTBEH	KINESIS	KLUDGEY
KAYAKER	KERATIN	KHUTBAH	KINETIC	KLUGING
KAYLIED	KERBAYA	KIAUGHS	KINETIN	KLUTZES
KEASARS	KERBING	KIBBEHS	KINFOLK	KNACKED
KEAVIES	KERCHOO	KIBBITZ	KINGDOM	KNACKER
KEBBIES	KERFING	KIBBLED	KINGING	KNAIDEL
KEBBING	KERKIER	KIBBLES	KINGLES	KNAPPED
KEBBOCK	KERMESS	KIBBUTZ	KINGLET	KNAPPER
KEBBUCK	KERNELS	KIBITKA	KINKIER	KNAPPLE
KEBELES	KERNING	KICKBOX	KINKILY	KNARRED
KEBLAHS	KERNISH	KICKERS	KINKING	KNAVERY
KECKING	KERNITE	KICKIER	KINKLES	KNAVISH
KECKLED	KEROGEN	KICKING	KINONES	KNAWELS
KECKLES	KERRIES	KICKOFF	KINSMAN	KNEADED
KECKSES	KERSEYS	KICKUPS	KINSMEN	KNEECAP
KEDDAHS	KERVING	KIDDIED	KIPPAGE	KNEELED
KEDGERS	KERYGMA	KIDDIER	KIPPING	KNEELER
KEDGIER	KESTING	KIDDIES	KIPSKIN	KNEEPAD
KEDGING	KETCHES	KIDDING	KIRBEHS	KNEEPAN
KEECHES	KETCHUP	KIDDISH	KIRIMON	KNELLED
KEEKERS	KETONES	KIDDLES	KIRKING	KNESSET
KEEKING	KETOSES	KIDDOES	KIRKMAN	KNEVELL

KNICKER	KOTOWED	LABROSE	LAMPION	LASHINS
KNIFERS	KOTOWER	LACKEYS	LAMPOON	LASHKAR
KNIGHTS	KOTWALS	LACQUEY	LAMPREY	LASSOCK
KNISHES	KOULANS	LACTAMS	LAMPUKA	LASSOES
KNITTED	KOUMISS	LACTARY	LAMPUKI	LATAKIA
KNITTLE	KOUMYSS	LACTATE	LANATED	LATCHED
KNIVING	KOUPREY	LACTEAL	LANCHED	LATENCE
KNOBBED	KOUSSOS	LACTEAN	LANCHES	LATENCY
KNOBBER	KOWHAIS	LACTONE	LANCING	LATERAD
KNOBBLE	KOWTOWS	LADANUM	LANDAUS	LATERAL
KNOBBLY	KRAALED	LADDISH	LANDING	LATEXES
KNOCKED	KRANSES	LADETTE	LANDLER	LATHEES
KNOCKER	KRANZES	LADHOOD	LANDMAN	LATHIER
KNOLLED	KREMLIN	LADLERS	LANDMEN	LATILLA
KNOLLER	KREUZER	LADLING	LANEWAY	LATINAS
KNOPPED	KRIMMER	LADRONE	LANGAHA	LATITAT
KNOTTED	KRUBUTS	LADYBOY	LANGLEY	LATOSOL
KNOTTER	KRULLER	LADYBUG	LANGREL	LATRANT
KNOUTED	KRYPSES	LADYCOW	LANGUED	LATRONS
KNOWERS	KRYPSIS	LADYFLY	LANGUET	LATTINS
KNOWHOW	KRYPTON	LADYKIN	LANGUOR	LAUDERS
KNOWING	KRYTRON	LAETARE	LANGURS	LAUGHED
KNUBBLE	KUCHCHA	LAGGARD	LANIARY	LAUGHER
KNUBBLY	KUCHENS	LAGGENS	LANITAL	LAUNDRY
KNUCKLE	KUDLIKS	LAGGING	LANKIER	LAURYLS
KNUCKLY	KUDOSES	LAGOONS	LANKILY	LAUWINE
KOBANGS	KUFIYAH	LAGUNAS	LANOLIN	LAVABOS
KOBOLDS	KULTURS	LAICISE	LANTANA	LAVOLTA
KOCHIAS	KUMERAS	LAICISM	LANTERN	LAVOLTS
KOEKOEA	KUMMELS	LAICITY	LANUGOS	LAVROCK
KOFTGAR	KUMQUAT	LAICIZE	LANYARD	LAWBOOK
KOKAKOS	KUMYSES	LAIGHER	LAPDOGS	LAWINES
KOKANEE	KUNJOOS	LAIKING	LAPELED	LAWLAND
KOKOBEH	KUNKARS	LAIRDLY	LAPFULS	LAWLESS
KOKOWAI	KUNKURS	LAIRIER	LAPHELD	LAWLIKE
KOLACKY	KUNZITE	LAIRISE	LAPILLI	LAWNIER
KOLBASI	KURBASH	LAIRIZE	LAPPELS	LAWSUIT
KOLHOZY	KURGANS	LAITHLY	LAPSANG	LAWYERS
KOLKHOS	KURVEYS	LAITIES	LAPSERS	LAXATOR
KOLKHOZ	KUTCHES	LAKEBED	LAPTOPS	LAXISMS
KOLKOZY	KVASSES	LAKELET	LAPTRAY	LAXISTS
KOMATIK	KVELLED	LALANGS	LAPWING	LAXNESS
KONFYTS	KVETCHY	LALIQUE	LAPWORK	LAYAWAY
KONGONI	KWAITOS	LALLAND	LARCENY	LAYBACK
KONKING	KWANZAS	LALLANS	LARDERS	LAYDEEZ
KONNING	KYANITE	LALLING	LARDIER	LAYETTE
KOODOOS	KYANIZE	LAMBADA	LARDOON	LAYLOCK
KOOKIER	KYLICES	LAMBAST	LARGESS	LAYOFFS
KOOKING	KYNDING	LAMBDAS	LARGEST	LAZARET
KOOLAHS	KYOGENS	LAMBERT	LARGISH	LAZIEST
KOPECKS	KYTHING	LAMBKIN	LARKERS	LAZOING
KOPIYKA	LABARUM	LAMBOYS	LARKIER	LAZULIS
KOPPIES	LABELED	LAMEDHS	LARKING	LAZYING
KOREROS	LABELLA	LAMELLA	LARKISH	LAZYISH
KORKIRS	LABIALS	LAMETER	LARNEYS	LEACHED
KOROWAI	LABIATE	LAMINAE	LARNIER	LEACHES
KORUNAS	LABLABS	LAMININ	LARNING	LEADENS
KOSHERS	LABORED	LAMMING	LARRUPS	LEADIER
KOTCHED	LABORER	LAMPADS	LARVATE	LEADMAN
KOTCHES	LABROID	LAMPERN	LASAGNA	LEADMEN

LEADOFF	LEMMATA	LIANOID	LINKBOY	LIVIERS
LEAFAGE	LEMMING	LIATRIS	LINKMAN	LIXIVIA
LEAFBUD	LEMONED	LIBATED	LINKMEN	LIZARDS
LEAFERY	LENDING	LIBBARD	LINNETS	LIZZIES
LEAGUED	LENGING	LIBBERS	LINNEYS	LLANERO
LEAGUES	LENGTHS	LIBBING	LINNIES	LOADENS
LEAKAGE	LENIENT	LIBELEE	LINNING	LOAMIER
LEAKERS	LENITED	LIBELER	LINOCUT	LOAMING
LEAKILY	LENSMAN	LIBERTY	LINTING	LOANING
LEALEST	LENSMEN	LIBIDOS	LINTOLS	LOATHED
LEANERS	LENTIGO	LIBKENS	LINURON	LOATHES
LEARNED	LENTOID	LIBLABS	LINUXES	LOAVING
LEASHES	LENTORS	LIBRARY	LIONCEL	LOBBING
LEASOWE	LENTOUS	LICENCE	LIONISM	LOBBYER
LEASOWS	LENVOYS	LICHTED	LIONIZE	LOBEFIN
LEASURE	LEONINE	LICHTER	LIPEMIA	LOBELET
LEBBEKS	LEPORID	LICHTLY	LIPIDES	LOBELIA
LECCIES	LEPPING	LICHWAY	LIPIDIC	LOBIPED
LECHAIM	LEPROSY	LICITLY	LIPLESS	LOBOLAS
LECHERS	LEPTOME	LICKING	LIPLIKE	LOBOLOS
LECHING	LEPTONS	LICTORS	LIPOIDS	LOBULAR
LECTERN	LEQUEAR	LIDDING	LIPOMAS	LOBWORM
LECTION	LERNEAN	LIDLESS	LIPPIER	LOCALLY
LECTURE	LESBIAN	LIFEFUL	LIPPIES	LOCATED
LECTURN	LESSEES	LIFEWAY	LIPPING	LOCATER
LEDDENS	LESSENS	LIFTBOY	LIPURIA	LOCATOR
LEECHED	LESSORS	LIFTMAN	LIQUEFY	LOCHANS
LEECHEE	LETCHED	LIFTMEN	LIQUEUR	LOCHIAL
LEERIER	LETCHES	LIFTOFF	LIQUIDS	LOCKAGE
LEERILY	LETDOWN	LIGGERS	LIQUIFY	LOCKBOX
LEEWARD	LETHALS	LIGGING	LIQUORS	LOCKFUL
LEFTISH	LETHEAN	LIGHTLY	LIRIOPE	LOCKJAW
LEFTIST	LETHEES	LIGNIFY	LIRKING	LOCKMAN
LEGALLY	LETHIED	LIGNITE	LISPERS	LOCKMEN
LEGATEE	LETTUCE	LIGNUMS	LISPUND	LOCKNUT
LEGENDS	LEUCHEN	LIGULAE	LISTELS	LOCKOUT
LEGGIER	LEUCINE	LIGULAR	LISTFUL	LOCOISM
LEGGING	LEUCINS	LIKABLE	LITCHIS	LOCOMAN
LEGHORN	LEUCITE	LILLING	LITHATE	LOCULAR
LEGIBLE	LEUGHEN	LIMAILS	LITHELY	LOCULUS
LEGIBLY	LEUKOMA	LIMBECK	LITHIAS	LOCUSTS
LEGISTS	LEUKONS	LIMBERS	LITHIFY	LODGERS
LEGITIM	LEVANTS	LIMBIER	LITHITE	LOERIES
LEGLANS	LEVATOR	LIMBING	LITHIUM	LOESSAL
LEGLENS	LEVELED	LIMBOUS	LITHOED	LOESSES
LEGLESS	LEVELER	LIMELIT	LITHOPS	LOFTILY
LEGLETS	LEVELLY	LIMEPIT	LITORAL	LOFTING
LEGLIKE	LEVERET	LIMINAL	LITOTIC	LOGANIA
LEGONGS	LEVITIC	LIMNING	LITTLER	LOGBOOK
LEGROOM	LEVULIN	LIMOSIS	LITTLES	LOGGATS
LEGWEAR	LEVYING	LIMPING	LITTLIN	LOGGIAS
LEGWORK	LEWDSBY	LIMPKIN	LITURGY	LOGGIER
LEHAIMS	LEWISES	LIMPSEY	LIVABLE	LOGGING
LEHAYIM	LEWISIA	LIMULUS	LIVEDOS	LOGGISH
LEIPOAS	LEXEMES	LINABLE	LIVELOD	LOGICAL
LEISHER	LEXEMIC	LINALOL	LIVENED	LOGJAMS
LEISURE	LEXICAL	LINCTUS	LIVENER	LOGLINE
LEKKING	LEXICON	LINEAGE	LIVEYER	LOGLOGS
LEKVARS	LEZZIES	LINEATE	LIVIDER	LOGOFFS
LEKYTHI	LIAISON	LINEMEN	LIVIDLY	LOGOUTS

LOGROLL	LOUSERS	LUMINAL	LYNCHET	MAGICAL
LOGWAYS	LOUSILY	LUMMIER	LYOPHIL	MAGILPS
LOGWOOD	LOUSING	LUMPILY	LYRATED	MAGISMS
LOIDING	LOUTING	LUMPISH	LYRICAL	MAGLEVS
LOKSHEN	LOUTISH	LUMPKIN	LYRISMS	MAGMATA
LOLIGOS	LOUVRED	LUNATIC	LYRISTS	MAGNETS
LOLIUMS	LOVABLY	LUNCHED	LYSATES	MAGNIFY
LOLLERS	LOVAGES	LUNCHER	LYSOGEN	MAGNUMS
LOLLIES	LOVEBUG	LUNCHES	MAATJES	MAGSMAN
LOLLING	LOVERED	LUNETTE	MABELAS	MAGSMEN
LOLLOPS	LOVERLY	LUNGANS	MACACOS	MAGUEYS
LOLLOPY	LOWBALL	LUNGEES	MACADAM	MAHATMA
LONGANS	LOWBORN	LUNGERS	MACAQUE	MAHEWUS
LONGBOW	LOWBOYS	LUNGFUL	MACCHIA	MAHJONG
LONGERS	LOWBROW	LUNGING	MACCHIE	MAHONIA
LONGEST	LOWDOWN	LUNGYIS	MACHAIR	MAHOUTS
LONGING	LOWLAND	LUNTING	MACHANS	MAHSIRS
LOOBIER	LOWLIER	LUNULAE	MACHETE	MAHUANG
LOOBIES	LOWLIFE	LUNULAR	MACHINE	MAHZORS
LOOBILY	LOWLILY	LUNULES	MACHREE	MAIDANS
LOOFAHS	LOWNDED	LUNYIES	MACHZOR	MAIDING
LOOFFUL	LOWNESS	LUPANAR	MACKLED	MAIDISH
LOOKING	LOWNING	LUPULIN	MACKLES	MAIDISM
LOOKISM	LOWRIES	LUPUSES	MACOYAS	MAIHEMS
LOOKIST	LOWTING	LURCHED	MACRAME	MAILBAG
LOONEYS	LOWVELD	LURCHER	MACRAMI	MAILBOX
LOONIER	LOYALER	LURCHES	MACRONS	MAILCAR
LOONIES	LOYALLY	LURDANS	MACULAE	MAILING
LOONILY	LOYALTY	LUREXES	MACULAR	MAILLOT
LOOPIER	LOZELLS	LURIDER	MACULED	MAILMAN
LOOPILY	LOZENGE	LURIDLY	MACUMBA	MAILMEN
LOOSELY	LOZENGY	LURKERS	MADAFUS	MAILVAN
LOOSENS	LUBBARD	LURKING	MADAMED	MAIMING
LOOSIES	LUBFISH	LUSHERS	MADAMES	MAINING
LOPPIER	LUCENCE	LUSKISH	MADCAPS	MAINORS
LOPPIES	LUCENCY	LUSTFUL	MADDERS	MAINOUR
LOPPING	LUCERNE	LUSTICK	MADDEST	MAJAGUA
LOQUATS	LUCERNS	LUSTILY	MADDING	MAJESTY
LORDKIN	LUCHOTH	LUSTRAL	MADDISH	MAJORAT
LORETTE	LUCIDER	LUSTRUM	MADDOCK	MAJORED
LORGNON	LUCIDLY	LUSUSES	MADEIRA	MAJORLY
LORIMER	LUCKIER	LUTEOUS	MADLING	MAKABLE
LORINER	LUCKIES	LUTHERN	MADONNA	MAKUTUS
LORINGS	LUCKILY	LUTHIER	MADOQUA	MALACCA
LORIOTS	LUCKING	LUTISTS	MADTOMS	MALACIA
LORRELL	LUCUMAS	LUVVIES	MADUROS	MALARIA
LORRIES	LUFFING	LUXATED	MADWORT	MALARKY
LOSABLE	LUGGAGE	LUXATES	MADZOON	MALAXED
LOSINGS	LUGGIES	LUZERNS	MAFFIAS	MALAXES
LOSLYFS	LUGGING	LYCEUMS	MAFFICK	MALEATE
LOTTERY	LUGHOLE	LYCHNIS	MAFFLED	MALEFIC
LOTTING	LUGINGS	LYCOPOD	MAFFLIN	MALGRED
LOUDISH	LUGWORM	LYINGLY	MAFIOSI	MALGRES
LOUNGED	LULIBUB	LYMITER	MAFIOSO	MALISMS
LOUNGER	LULLABY	LYMPHAD	MAFTIRS	MALKINS
LOUNGES	LULLERS	LYNAGES	MAGALOG	MALLAMS
LOUNING	LULLING	LYNCEAN	MAGGIES	MALLARD
LOUPING	LUMBAGO	LYNCHED	MAGGING	MALLEES
LOURIER	LUMBANG	LYNCHER	MAGGOTS	MALLETS
LOURING	LUMENAL	LYNCHES	MAGGOTY	MALLEUS

MALLING	MANILLE	MARMOTS	MATTINS	MEATAXE
MALLOWS	MANIOCA	MARPLOT	MATTOCK	MEATHES
MALMAGS	MANKIND	MARQUEE	MATTOID	MEATMAN
MALMIER	MANLESS	MARQUIS	MATURED	MEATMEN
MALMSEY	MANLIKE	MARRAMS	MATWEED	MEAZELS
MALTEDS	MANLILY	MARRELS	MATZOHS	MEBOSES
MALTHAS	MANMADE	MARRERS	MATZOON	MECONIC
MALTING	MANNANS	MARRIER	MATZOTH	MECONIN
MALTMAN	MANNERS	MARRING	MAUBIES	MEDACCA
MALTMEN	MANNING	MARRONS	MAUDLIN	MEDALED
MALTOLS	MANNISH	MARROWS	MAUGRED	MEDDLED
MALTOSE	MANNITE	MARROWY	MAULGRE	MEDDLER
MALWARE	MANNOSE	MARSALA	MAULING	MEDDLES
MAMAGUY	MANOAOS	MARSHAL	MAULVIS	MEDEVAC
MAMAKAU	MANSARD	MARTEXT	MAUNDED	MEDIACY
MAMBOED	MANTEAU	MARTINI	MAUTHER	MEDIANT
MAMBOES	MANTIDS	MARTINS	MAUVAIS	MEDIATE
MAMELON	MANTLED	MARTLET	MAUVEST	MEDICKS
MAMEYES	MANTLET	MARTYRS	MAUVINS	MEDIGAP
MAMILLA	MANTOES	MARTYRY	MAWKIER	MEDIVAC
MAMLUKS	MANTRAM	MARVELS	MAWKINS	MEDLARS
MAMMALS	MANTRIC	MARVERS	MAWKISH	MEDLEYS
MAMMARY	MANUALS	MARYBUD	MAWMETS	MEDULLA
MAMMATE	MANUARY	MASCLED	MAWSEED	MEDUSAE
MAMMATI	MANUKAS	MASCONS	MAWTHER	MEEKENS
MAMMEES	MANUMEA	MASCULY	MAXILLA	MEEKEST
MAMMERS	MANUMIT	MASHLIM	MAXIMAL	MEEMIES
MAMMETS	MANURER	MASHLIN	MAXIMUM	MEERKAT
MAMMEYS	MANWARD	MASHLUM	MAXIMUS	MEETEST
MAMMIES	MANWISE	MASHMAN	MAXIXES	MEGABIT
MAMMOCK	MAPLIKE	MASHMEN	MAXWELL	MEGAFOG
MAMMONS	MAPPERY	MASHUAS	MAYBIRD	MEGAHIT
MAMMOTH	MAPPING	MASJIDS	MAYBUSH	MEGAPOD
MAMPARA	MAPPIST	MASKEGS	MAYDAYS	MEGILPH
MAMPOER	MAPWISE	MASKERS	MAYHEMS	MEGOHMS
MAMZERS	MAQUILA	MASLINS	MAYINGS	MEHNDIS
MANACLE	MARABOU	MASSAGE	MAYORAL	MEINIES
MANAGER	MARARIS	MASSIFS	MAYPOLE	MEINING
MANAKIN	MARAUDS	MASSING	MAYPOPS	MEIOSES
MANANAS	MARCATO	MASTABA	MAYVINS	MEIOSIS
MANAWAS	MARCELS	MASTFUL	MAYWEED	MEIOTIC
MANCHES	MAREMMA	MASTIFF	MAZARDS	MEISHIS
MANCHET	MAREMME	MASULAS	MAZEDLY	MELAMED
MANDATE	MARGAYS	MATADOR	MAZEFUL	MELANOS
MANDIRA	MARGOSA	MATCHED	MAZHBIS	MELDERS
MANDIRS	MARIMBA	MATCHES	MAZOUTS	MELILOT
MANDOMS	MARINAS	MATCHET	MAZUMAS	MELLING
MANDREL	MARINER	MATCHUP	MAZURKA	MELLITE
MANGABY	MARKETS	MATELOT	MAZZARD	MELLOWS
MANGALS	MARKHOR	MATILDA	MEACOCK	MELLOWY
MANGEAO	MARKING	MATINAL	MEADOWS	MELODIA
MANGILY	MARKKAA	MATLOWS	MEADOWY	MELODIC
MANGING	MARKKAS	MATOKES	MEAGRER	MELTAGE
MANGLED	MARKMAN	MATOOKE	MEAGRES	MELTEMI
MANGLER	MARKMEN	MATRASS	MEALERS	MELTIER
MANGOLD	MARKUPS	MATRICE	MEALIER	MELTING
MANHOLE	MARLING	MATRICS	MEALIES	MELTITH
MANHUNT	MARLINS	MATTERY	MEASLED	MEMBERS
MANIHOT	MARMOSE	MATTIFY	MEASLES	MEMBRAL
MANIKIN		MATTING	MEASURE	MEMENTO

MEMOIRS	METCAST	MIDLINE	MILTING	MIRRORS
MENACED	METEPAS	MIDLIST	MILTZES	MIRVING
MENACER	METERED	MIDMOST	MILVINE	MISADDS
MENAZON	METHANE	MIDNOON	MIMBARS	MISAIMS
MENDING	METHINK	MIDRIBS	MIMEOED	MISALLY
MENEERS	METHODS	MIDRIFF	MIMESIS	MISAVER
MENFOLK	METHOXY	MIDSHIP	MIMETIC	MISBIAS
MENGING	METHYLS	MIDSIZE	MIMICAL	MISBILL
MENHIRS	METISSE	MIDTOWN	MIMICRY	MISBIND
MENISCI	METONYM	MIDWAYS	MIMMEST	MISCALL
MENORAH	METOPAE	MIDWEEK	MIMMICK	MISCITE
MENSCHY	METOPES	MIDWIFE	MIMOSAS	MISCOIN
MENSHED	METOPIC	MIDWIVE	MIMSIER	MISCOOK
MENSHEN	METOPON	MIDYEAR	MIMULUS	MISCUED
MENSHES	METRIFY	MIELIES	MINABLE	MISCUTS
MENSING	METRIST	MIEVING	MINBARS	MISDEEM
MENSUAL	METTLED	MIFFIER	MINCING	MISDOES
MENTEES	METUMPS	MIFFILY	MINDFUL	MISDRAW
MENTHOL	MEUSING	MIFFING	MINDING	MISDREW
MENTION	MEVROUS	MIGHTST	MINEOLA	MISFALL
MENUDOS	MEWLERS	MIGNONS	MINETTE	MISFARE
MEOUING	MEWLING	MIHIING	MINEVER	MISFEED
MEOWING	MEWSING	MIHRABS	MINGIER	MISFELL
MERCATS	MEZAILS	MIKADOS	MINGING	MISFILE
MERCERS	MEZCALS	MIKVAHS	MINGLES	MISFIRE
MERCHET	MEZQUIT	MIKVEHS	MINIBAR	MISFITS
MERCIES	MEZUZAH	MIKVOTH	MINIBUS	MISFORM
MERCIFY	MEZUZAS	MILAGES	MINICAB	MISGAVE
MERCURY	MEZUZOT	MILCHIG	MINICAM	MISGIVE
MERFOLK	MGANGAS	MILCHIK	MINICOM	MISGONE
MERGERS	MIAOUED	MILDENS	MINIEST	MISGREW
MERKINS	MIAOWED	MILDEWS	MINIKIN	MISGROW
MERLONS	MIASMAL	MILDEWY	MINILAB	MISHAPT
MERMAID	MIASMAS	MILDING	MINIMAL	MISHITS
MEROMES	MIASMIC	MILEAGE	MINIMUM	MISHMEE
MERONYM	MIAULED	MILFOIL	MININGS	MISHMIS
MEROPIC	MICATED	MILIARY	MINIONS	MISJOIN
MERRIER	MICELLE	MILIEUS	MINISKI	MISKALS
MERRIES	MICELLS	MILIEUX	MINIVAN	MISKEEP
MERRILY	MICKEYS	MILITAR	MINIVER	MISKENS
MESCLUM	MICKIES	MILITIA	MINIVET	MISKENT
MESELED	MICKLER	MILKERS	MINNICK	MISKEPT
MESHIER	MICRIFY	MILKIER	MINNIES	MISKEYS
MESHING	MICROHM	MILKILY	MINNOCK	MISKICK
MESHUGA	MICTION	MILKING	MINNOWS	MISKNEW
MESQUIN	MIDAIRS	MILKMAN	MINORED	MISKNOW
MESQUIT	MIDCULT	MILKMEN	MINTING	MISLAIN
MESSANS	MIDDENS	MILKSOP	MINUSES	MISLAYS
MESSING	MIDDEST	MILLDAM	MINUTIA	MISLIKE
MESSMAN	MIDDIES	MILLERS	MINXISH	MISLIVE
MESSMEN	MIDDLED	MILLIER	MINYANS	MISLUCK
MESTESO	MIDDLER	MILLIES	MIOCENE	MISMADE
MESTIZO	MIDDLES	MILLIME	MIRADOR	MISMAKE
MESTOME	MIDGETS	MILLINE	MIRBANE	MISMARK
MESTOMS	MIDGIES	MILLING	MIRIFIC	MISMEET
METALLY	MIDGUTS	MILLION	MIRITIS	MISMOVE
METATAG	MIDIRON	MILLRUN	MIRKEST	MISPENS
METATES	MIDLAND	MILNEBS	MIRKIER	MISPLAY
METAYER	MIDLEGS	MILORDS	MIRKILY	MISRULE
METAZOA	MIDLIFE	MILTERS	MIRLIER	MISSAID

MISSALS	MOBLING	MOLTING	MOORAGE	MOSSING
MISSAYS	MOBLOGS	MOMENTA	MOORILL	MOSTEST
MISSELS	MOBSMAN	MOMISMS	MOORISH	MOTETTS
MISSENT	MOBSMEN	MOMMETS	MOORLOG	MOTHERY
MISSETS	MOCHELL	MOMMIES	MOORMAN	MOTIFIC
MISSHOD	MOCKADO	MOMSERS	MOOTERS	MOTILES
MISSIES	MOCKAGE	MOMZERS	MOOTMAN	MOTIONS
MISSING	MOCKERS	MONASES	MOOVING	MOTIVES
MISSION	MOCKERY	MONAXON	MOPANES	MOTIVIC
MISSISH	MOCKING	MONDAIN	MOPANIS	MOTLEYS
MISSIVE	MOCKNEY	MONDIAL	MOPHEAD	MOTLIER
MISSORT	MOCKUPS	MONEMES	MOPOKES	MOTMOTS
MISSTEP	MOCOCKS	MONERAN	MOPPERS	MOTORED
MISSUIT	MOCUCKS	MONERON	MOPPETS	MOTORIC
MISTALS	MODALLY	MONETHS	MOPPING	MOTSERS
MISTBOW	MODELED	MONEYED	MOPUSES	MOTTLED
MISTERM	MODELLI	MONEYER	MORALES	MOTTLER
MISTFUL	MODELLO	MONGERY	MORALLS	MOTTLES
MISTILY	MODEMED	MONGOES	MORALLY	MOTTOED
MISTIME	MODERNE	MONGOLS	MORASSY	MOTUCAS
MISTOLD	MODESTY	MONGREL	MORCEAU	MOUCHED
MISTOOK	MODGING	MONIKER	MORDENT	MOUCHER
MISTYPE	MODICUM	MONILIA	MOREENS	MOUCHES
MISUSED	MODIOLI	MONISTS	MORELLE	MOUFLON
MISUSES	MODISTS	MONKERY	MORELLO	MOUILLE
MISWEEN	MODULAR	MONKEYS	MORGANS	MOUJIKS
MISWEND	MODULUS	MONKISH	MORGAYS	MOULAGE
MISWENT	MOELLON	MONOCOT	MORIONS	MOULDED
MISWORD	MOERING	MONODIC	MORISCO	MOULINS
MISWRIT	MOFETTE	MONOFIL	MORLING	MOULTED
MISYOKE	MOFFIES	MONOLOG	MORNING	MOULTEN
MITCHED	MOGGANS	MONONYM	MOROCCO	MOULTER
MITIEST	MOGGIES	MONOPOD	MORPHED	MOUNDED
MITOSIS	MOGGING	MONOSES	MORPHEW	MOUPING
MITOTIC	MOGHULS	MONSOON	MORPHIA	MOURNED
MITRING	MOGULED	MONTANT	MORPHIC	MOURNER
MITSVAH	MOHAIRS	MONTERO	MORPHIN	MOUSAKA
MITUMBA	MOHALIM	MONTHLY	MORPHOS	MOUSERY
MITZVAH	MOHAWKS	MONURON	MORRELL	MOUSIER
MIXABLE	MOHELIM	MOOCHED	MORRHUA	MOUSIES
MIXDOWN	MOILERS	MOOCHER	MORRICE	MOUSILY
MIXEDLY	MOILING	MOOCHES	MORRION	MOUSLES
MIXIBLE	MOINEAU	MOODIED	MORROWS	MOUSMEE
MIXIEST	MOISTLY	MOODIES	MORSELS	MOUTHED
MIXTION	MOJARRA	MOOKTAR	MORSURE	MOUTHER
MIXTURE	MOKOROS	MOOLAHS	MORTARS	MOUTONS
MIZMAZE	MOKSHAS	MOOLEYS	MORTARY	MOVABLE
MIZUNAS	MOLASSE	MOOLIES	MORTICE	MOVABLY
MIZZENS	MOLDIER	MOOLOOS	MORTIFY	MOVIOLA
MIZZLED	MOLDING	MOOLVIE	MORULAE	MOWBURN
MIZZLES	MOLERAT	MOOLVIS	MORULAR	MOWDIES
MNEMONS	MOLESTS	MOONBOW	MORULAS	MOYLING
MOANFUL	MOLIMEN	MOONERS	MORWONG	MOZETTA
MOANING	MOLINET	MOONEYE	MOSAICS	MOZETTE
MOATING	MOLLIES	MOONILY	MOSELLE	MOZZIES
MOBBISH	MOLLIFY	MOONING	MOSEYED	MOZZLES
MOBBISM	MOLLUSC	MOONISH	MOSHERS	MRIDANG
MOBBLED	MOLLUSK	MOONLIT	MOSQUES	MUCATES
MOBBLES	MOLOCHS	MOONSET	MOSSERS	MUCHELL
MOBCAPS	MOLOSSI	MOOPING	MOSSIES	MUCIGEN

MUCKERS	MUGWORT	MURKILY	MUTTONY	MZUNGUS
MUCKIER	MUGWUMP	MURKISH	MUTUCAS	NAARTJE
MUCKILY	MUKHTAR	MURLANS	MUTUUMS	NABBERS
MUCKING	MUKLUKS	MURLIER	MUUMUUS	NABBING
MUCKLES	MUKTUKS	MURLING	MUZHIKS	NACARAT
MUCLUCS	MULATTA	MURLINS	MUZJIKS	NACELLE
MUCOSAE	MULATTO	MURMURS	MUZZIER	NACKETS
MUCOSAL	MULCHED	MURRAGH	MUZZILY	NACROUS
MUCOSAS	MULCTED	MURRAIN	MUZZING	NAEBODY
MUCUSES	MULESED	MURRAYS	MUZZLED	NAEVOID
MUDBATH	MULESES	MURRENS	MUZZLER	NAFFEST
MUDBUGS	MULLAHS	MURREYS	MUZZLES	NAFFING
MUDCAPS	MULLEIN	MURRHAS	MWALIMU	NAGANAS
MUDCATS	MULLENS	MURRIES	MYALGIA	NAGAPIE
MUDDERS	MULLERS	MURRINE	MYALGIC	NAIADES
MUDDIED	MULLETS	MURRINS	MYALISM	NAIVELY
MUDDIER	MULLEYS	MURRION	MYALIST	NAIVETE
MUDDILY	MULLING	MURTHER	MYCELES	NAIVETY
MUDDING	MULLION	MUSANGS	MYCELIA	NAIVIST
MUDDLED	MULLITE	MUSCATS	MYCELLA	NAKEDLY
MUDDLER	MULLOCK	MUSCIDS	MYCETES	NAMABLE
MUDDLES	MULMULL	MUSCLED	MYCOSES	NAMASTE
MUDEYES	MULMULS	MUSCLES	MYCOSIS	NAMINGS
MUDFISH	MULSHED	MUSEFUL	MYCOTIC	NANDINA
MUDFLAP	MULSHES	MUSETTE	MYELINE	NANDINS
MUDFLAT	MULTUMS	MUSEUMS	MYELINS	NANDOOS
MUDFLOW	MULTURE	MUSHERS	MYELOID	NANISMS
MUDGING	MUMBLER	MUSHILY	MYELOMA	NANKEEN
MUDHENS	MUMMERS	MUSHING	MYELONS	NANKINS
MUDHOLE	MUMMERY	MUSICAL	MYGALES	NANNIES
MUDHOOK	MUMMIAS	MUSICKS	MYIASES	NANOBES
MUDIRIA	MUMMIED	MUSJIDS	MYIASIS	NANODOT
MUDLARK	MUMMIES	MUSKEGS	MYLODON	NANOOKS
MUDPACK	MUMMIFY	MUSKETS	MYNHEER	NAPALMS
MUDROCK	MUMMING	MUSKIER	MYOGENS	NAPHTHA
MUDROOM	MUMMOCK	MUSKIES	MYOGRAM	NAPKINS
MUDSCOW	MUMPERS	MUSKILY	MYOLOGY	NAPLESS
MUDSILL	MUMPING	MUSKING	MYOMATA	NAPOOED
MUDWORT	MUMPISH	MUSKITS	MYOPIAS	NAPPIER
MUEDDIN	MUNCHED	MUSKONE	MYOPIES	NAPPING
MUESLIS	MUNCHER	MUSKRAT	MYOPSES	NAPRONS
MUEZZIN	MUNCHES	MUSLINS	MYOSINS	NARASES
MUFFING	MUNDICS	MUSPIKE	MYOTICS	NARCEEN
MUFFINS	MUNDIFY	MUSROLS	MYOTOME	NARCIST
MUFFISH	MUNGING	MUSSILY	MYOTUBE	NARDINE
MUFFLED	MUNNION	MUSTANG	MYRIADS	NARDOOS
MUFFLER	MUNSHIS	MUSTEES	MYRICAS	NARKIER
MUFFLES	MUNTING	MUSTIER	MYRINGA	NARRATE
MUFLONS	MUNTINS	MUSTILY	MYRRHIC	NARROWS
MUGFULS	MUNTJAC	MUSTING	MYRRHOL	NARTHEX
MUGGARS	MUNTJAK	MUTABLE	MYRTLES	NARWALS
MUGGEES	MUONIUM	MUTABLY	MYSOSTS	NARWHAL
MUGGIER	MUPPETS	MUTANTS	MYSTERY	NASARDS
MUGGILY	MURAENA	MUTASES	MYSTICS	NASCENT
MUGGING	MURALED	MUTATED	MYSTIFY	NASIONS
MUGGINS	MUREXES	MUTATES	MYTHISE	NATHEMO
MUGGISH	MURGEON	MUTCHED	MYTHISM	NATRIUM
MUGGURS	MURIATE	MUTEDLY	MYTHIST	NATTERY
MUGHALS	MURKEST	MUTTERS	MYTHIZE	NATTILY
MUGSHOT	MURKIER	MUTTONS	MYXOMAS	NATURAL

NAUCHES	NERINES	NIGHTLY	NONAGON	NORMALS
NAUGHTS	NEROLIS	NIGRIFY	NONANES	NORMANS
NAUGHTY	NERVERS	NIHONGA	NONBANK	NORSELS
NAUPLII	NERVILY	NILLING	NONBODY	NORTENA
NAUSEAS	NERVING	NIMBLER	NONBOOK	NORTENO
NAUTILI	NERVOUS	NIMIETY	NONCOLA	NORWARD
NAVAIDS	NERVULE	NIMMERS	NONCOMS	NOSEANS
NAVALLY	NERVURE	NIMMING	NONCORE	NOSEBAG
NAVARCH	NESHEST	NIMONIC	NONDRIP	NOSEGAY
NAVARHO	NETBALL	NINCOMS	NONDRUG	NOSHERY
NAVETTE	NETHEAD	NINCUMS	NONEGOS	NOSHING
NAVVIED	NETIZEN	NINEPIN	NONETTE	NOSINGS
NAVVIES	NETLIKE	NINNIES	NONETTO	NOSODES
NAYSAID	NETSUKE	NINTHLY	NONFACT	NOSTRIL
NAYSAYS	NETTIES	NIOBATE	NONFANS	NOSTRUM
NAYWARD	NETTLED	NIOBITE	NONFARM	NOTABLE
NAYWORD	NETWORK	NIOBIUM	NONFOOD	NOTABLY
NEAFFES	NEURINE	NIOBOUS	NONFUEL	NOTANDA
NEATENS	NEURONE	NIPPIER	NONGAYS	NOTATED
NEATEST	NEURULA	NIPPILY	NONHEME	NOTCHED
NEATNIK	NEUSTIC	NIPPING	NONHERO	NOTEDLY
NEBBICH	NEUSTON	NIPPLED	NONHOME	NOTELET
NEBBING	NEUTRAL	NIRLIER	NONIRON	NOTHING
NEBBISH	NEUTRON	NIRLING	NONJURY	NOTIONS
NEBBUKS	NEWBIES	NISGULS	NONLIFE	NOTITIA
NEBECKS	NEWBORN	NITINOL	NONNEWS	NOUMENA
NEBULAE	NEWCOME	NITPICK	NONNIES	NOURISH
NEBULAR	NEWELLS	NITRIDS	NONOILY	NOURSLE
NEBULES	NEWMOWN	NITRIFY	NONORAL	NOUSELL
NECKERS	NEWNESS	NITRILS	NONPEAK	NOUVEAU
NECKING	NEWSBOY	NITRYLS	NONPLAY	NOVATED
NECKLET	NEWSIES	NOBBIER	NONPLUS	NOVELLA
NECKTIE	NEWSING	NOBBILY	NONPOOR	NOVELLE
NEDDIER	NEWSMAN	NOBBLED	NONPROS	NOVELLY
NEDDISH	NEWSMEN	NOBBLER	NONSELF	NOVELTY
NEEDFUL	NEWTONS	NOBBLES	NONSKED	NOVENAE
NEEDIER	NGARARA	NOBLEST	NONSKID	NOVENAS
NEEDLED	NIACINS	NOCAKES	NONSLIP	NOVICES
NEEDLER	NIBBING	NOCHELS	NONSUCH	NOWNESS
NEEDLES	NIBBLED	NOCKETS	NONSUIT	NOXIOUS
NEEZING	NIBBLER	NOCTULE	NONUPLE	NOYADES
NEGATES	NIBBLES	NOCTURN	NONUSES	NOYANCE
NEGATOR	NIBLICK	NOCUOUS	NONWAGE	NOYSOME
NEGLECT	NIBLIKE	NODALLY	NONWARS	NOZZERS
NEGRESS	NICEISH	NODDIES	NONWOOL	NOZZLES
NEGRONI	NICKARS	NODDING	NONWORD	NUANCED
NEINEIS	NICKING	NODDLED	NONWORK	NUANCES
NEKTONS	NICKUMS	NODDLES	NONZERO	NUBBIER
NELLIES	NICOTIN	NODICAL	NOODGED	NUBBING
NELSONS	NIDATED	NODULAR	NOODGES	NUBBINS
NELUMBO	NIDDICK	NOGGINS	NOODLED	NUBBLED
NEMESES	NIDUSES	NOISILY	NOOKIES	NUBBLES
NEMNING	NIFFIER	NOISING	NOOLOGY	NUBUCKS
NEOCONS	NIFFING	NOMBLES	NOONDAY	NUCELLI
NEOGENE	NIFTIER	NOMBRIL	NOONERS	NUCHALS
NEONATE	NIFTILY	NOMINAL	NOONING	NUCLEAL
NEOTENY	NIGGLER	NOMINEE	NOOSING	NUCLEIC
NEOTYPE	NIGHEST	NONACID	NOPLACE	NUCLEIN
NEPHEWS	NIGHTED	NONAGED	NORIMON	NUCLEON
NEPHRON	NIGHTIE	NONAGES	NORLAND	NUDDIES

NUDISMS	NYLGHAU	OCCIPUT	OILHOLE	OOFTISH
NUDISTS	NYMPHAE	OCCLUDE	OILSEED	OOGONIA
NUDNICK	NYMPHAL	OCCULTS	OILSKIN	OOLAKAN
NUDNIKS	NYMPHET	OCELOID	OILWAYS	OOLITHS
NUDZHED	NYMPHIC	OCHREAE	OINKING	OOLITIC
NUDZHES	NYMPHLY	OCHROUS	OINOMEL	OOLOGIC
NUFFINS	NYMPHOS	OCICATS	OINTING	OOLONGS
NUGGARS	OAKIEST	OCREATE	OKIMONO	OOMIACK
NUGGETS	OAKLEAF	OCTAGON	OLDENED	OOMIACS
NUGGETY	OAKLIKE	OCTANTS	OLDNESS	OOMIAKS
NULLAHS	OAKLING	OCTAPLA	OLDWIFE	OOPHYTE
NULLIFY	OAKMOSS	OCTAVAL	OLEARIA	OOSIEST
NULLING	OARFISH	OCTAVOS	OLEATES	OOSPERM
NULLITY	OARLIKE	OCTETTE	OLEFINE	OOSPORE
NUMBATS	OARLOCK	OCTETTS	OLEFINS	OOTHECA
NUMBERS	OARWEED	OCTOFID	OLEINES	OPACIFY
NUMBEST	OATCAKE	OCTOPOD	OLFACTS	OPACITY
NUMBING	OATMEAL	OCTROIS	OLICOOK	OPACOUS
NUMBLES	OBCONIC	OCTUORS	OLIGIST	OPALINE
NUMDAHS	OBDURED	OCTUPLY	OLITORY	OPAQUED
NUMERAL	OBEAHED	OCULATE	OLIVARY	OPAQUER
NUMMARY	OBECHES	ODALISK	OLIVINE	OPAQUES
NUMNAHS	OBEISMS	ODALLER	OLOGIST	OPENING
NUNATAK	OBELIAS	ODDBALL	OLOGOAN	OPERATE
NUNCIOS	OBELION	ODDMENT	OLOROSO	OPEROSE
NUNCLES	OBELISE	ODDSMEN	OLYCOOK	OPGEFOK
NUNDINE	OBELISK	ODONATE	OLYKOEK	OPHITIC
NUNHOOD	OBELIZE	ODONTIC	OMENING	OPHIURA
NUNLIKE	OBENTOS	ODORATE	OMENTUM	OPIATED
NUNNERY	OBESELY	ODORFUL	OMIKRON	OPINION
NUNNISH	OBESEST	ODORIZE	OMINOUS	OPIOIDS
NUNSHIP	OBESITY	ODOROUS	OMITTED	OPORICE
NURAGHE	OBEYERS	ODOURED	OMMATEA	OPOSSUM
NURAGHI	OBIISMS	ODYLISM	OMNIANA	OPPIDAN
NURDIER	OBJECTS	ODYSSEY	OMNIBUS	OPPOSED
NURDISH	OBJURED	ODZOOKS	OMNIFIC	OPPOSES
NURHAGS	OBJURES	OEDEMAS	OMPHALI	OPSONIN
NURLING	OBLASTI	OEDIPAL	ONBEATS	OPTANTS
NURSERS	OBLASTS	OENOMEL	ONCOGEN	OPTIMAL
NURSERY	OBLIGED	OFFBEAT	ONCOMES	OPTIMUM
NUTCASE	OBLIGEE	OFFENCE	ONDATRA	OPULENT
NUTLETS	OBLIGER	OFFENSE	ONEFOLD	OQUASSA
NUTLIKE	OBLIGES	OFFERED	ONEIRIC	ORALISM
NUTMEAL	OBLIGOR	OFFEREE	ONENESS	ORALITY
NUTMEAT	OBLIQUE	OFFEROR	ONERIER	ORANGEY
NUTMEGS	OBLONGS	OFFICER	ONEROUS	ORARIAN
NUTPICK	OBLOQUY	OFFLINE	ONESELF	ORARION
NUTRIAS	OBOISTS	OFFLOAD	ONETIME	ORARIUM
NUTTERY	OBOLARY	OFFPEAK	ONFALLS	ORATION
NUTTIER	OBOVATE	OFFRAMP	ONFLOWS	ORATORS
NUTTILY	OBOVOID	OFFSCUM	ONGOING	ORATORY
NUTTING	OBSCENE	OFTENER	ONIONED	ORATRIX
NUTWOOD	OBSEQUY	OGDOADS	ONLINER	ORBITAL
NUZZERS	OBTENDS	OGHAMIC	ONSIDES	ORBITAS
NUZZLED	OBTESTS	OGREISH	ONWARDS	ORBLESS
NUZZLER	OBTUNDS	OGREISM	ONYCHAS	ORCHARD
NYAFFED	OBTUSER	OIDIOID	ONYCHIA	ORCHATS
NYANZAS	OBVERTS	OIKISTS	ONYMOUS	ORCHILS
NYBBLES	OBVIATE	OILBIRD	OOCYSTS	ORCINOL
NYLGHAI	OBVIOUS	OILCAMP	OODLINS	ORDERED

ORDERLY	OTOLITH	OUTGLOW	OUTROOP	OVATELY
ORDINAL	OTOLOGY	OUTGNAW	OUTROOT	OVATING
ORDINAR	OTTAVAS	OUTGOER	OUTROPE	OVATION
ORDINEE	OTTOMAN	OUTGOES	OUTROWS	OVATORS
ORDURES	OUABAIN	OUTGONE	OUTRUNG	OVENING
OREADES	OUAKARI	OUTGREW	OUTRUSH	OVERACT
OREGANO	OUCHING	OUTGROW	OUTSAID	OVERAGE
OREWEED	OUGLIED	OUTGUSH	OUTSAIL	OVERAPT
ORGANDY	OUGLIES	OUTHAUL	OUTSAYS	OVERARM
ORGANIC	OUGUIYA	OUTHEAR	OUTSEEN	OVERAWE
ORGANUM	OULAKAN	OUTHITS	OUTSEES	OVERBED
ORGANZA	OULONGS	OUTHOWL	OUTSHOT	OVERBET
ORGASMS	OURALIS	OUTHUNT	OUTSITS	OVERBID
ORIENCY	OURANGS	OUTHYRE	OUTSIZE	OVERBIG
ORIFICE	OURARIS	OUTJINX	OUTSOAR	OVERBUY
ORIGAMI	OUSTITI	OUTJUMP	OUTSOLD	OVERCOY
ORIGANE	OUTADDS	OUTJUTS	OUTSOLE	OVERDID
ORIOLES	OUTAGES	OUTKEEP	OUTSPAN	OVERDRY
ORISHAS	OUTASKS	OUTKEPT	OUTSTAY	OVERDUB
ORISONS	OUTBAKE	OUTKICK	OUTSULK	OVERDUE
ORMOLUS	OUTBARK	OUTKILL	OUTSUMS	OVERDYE
ORNATER	OUTBAWL	OUTKISS	OUTSWAM	OVEREGG
OROGENY	OUTBEAM	OUTLAID	OUTSWIM	OVEREYE
OROLOGY	OUTBIDS	OUTLAIN	OUTSWUM	OVERFAT
OROPESA	OUTBRAG	OUTLAND	OUTTALK	OVERFED
OROTUND	OUTBULK	OUTLASH	OUTTASK	OVERFIT
ORPHANS	OUTCALL	OUTLAST	OUTTELL	OVERGET
ORPHREY	OUTCHID	OUTLAWS	OUTTOLD	OVERGOT
ORRAMEN	OUTCITY	OUTLEAD	OUTTOOK	OVERHIT
ORTHIAN	OUTCOME	OUTLEAP	OUTTROT	OVERHOT
ORTHROS	OUTCROP	OUTLETS	OUTVIED	OVERING
ORTOLAN	OUTCROW	OUTLIER	OUTVIES	OVERJOY
OSCULES	OUTDATE	OUTLIES	OUTVOTE	OVERLAP
OSMATES	OUTDOES	OUTLIVE	OUTWAIT	OVERLAX
OSMIOUS	OUTDOOR	OUTLOVE	OUTWARS	OVERLET
OSMIUMS	OUTDRAG	OUTMODE	OUTWEAR	OVERLIT
OSMOLAL	OUTDREW	OUTMOST	OUTWEED	OVERMAN
OSMOLAR	OUTDUEL	OUTMOVE	OUTWEEP	OVERMIX
OSMOLES	OUTDURE	OUTPACE	OUTWELL	OVERNET
OSMOSED	OUTEARN	OUTPART	OUTWENT	OVERPAY
OSMOSES	OUTEATS	OUTPEEP	OUTWEPT	OVERRAN
OSMOSIS	OUTECHO	OUTPEER	OUTWICK	OVERREN
OSMOTIC	OUTEDGE	OUTPITY	OUTWILE	OVERSEA
OSMUNDA	OUTFACE	OUTPLAN	OUTWILL	OVERSEE
OSMUNDS	OUTFAST	OUTPLAY	OUTWIND	OVERSEW
OSSEOUS	OUTFAWN	OUTPLOD	OUTWING	OVERSOW
OSSICLE	OUTFEEL	OUTPLOT	OUTWINS	OVERSUP
OSSIFIC	OUTFELT	OUTPOLL	OUTWISH	OVERTAX
OSTEOID	OUTFIND	OUTPORT	OUTWITS	OVERTLY
OSTEOMA	OUTFIRE	OUTPOUR	OUTWORE	OVERTOP
OSTIARY	OUTFISH	OUTPRAY	OUTWORN	OVERWET
OSTMARK	OUTFITS	OUTPUSH	OUTWRIT	OVICIDE
OSTOSES	OUTFLEW	OUTRACE	OUTYELL	OVIDUCT
OSTOSIS	OUTFLOW	OUTRAGE	OUTYELP	OVIFORM
OSTRACA	OUTFOOL	OUTRANG	OUVERTE	OVIPARA
OSTRAKA	OUTFOOT	OUTRANK	OUVRAGE	OVISACS
OTALGIA	OUTGATE	OUTRATE	OUVRIER	OVOIDAL
OTALGIC	OUTGAVE	OUTRAVE	OVALITY	OVONICS
OTARINE	OUTGAZE	OUTROAR	OVARIAN	OVULARY
OTOCYST	OUTGIVE	OUTROCK	OVARIES	OVULATE

OWLIEST	PADELLA	PALLIAL	PAPADAM	PARKIER
OWLLIKE	PADLOCK	PALLING	PAPADOM	PARKING
OWNABLE	PADOUKS	PALLIUM	PAPADUM	PARKISH
OWRELAY	PADSAWS	PALLORS	PAPAINS	PARKOUR
OXALATE	PADSHAH	PALMATE	PAPALLY	PARKWAY
OXAZINE	PAELLAS	PALMFUL	PAPAUMA	PARLAYS
OXBLOOD	PAENULA	PALMIST	PAPAYAN	PARLORS
OXCARTS	PAESANI	PALMTOP	PAPAYAS	PARLOUR
OXFORDS	PAESANS	PALOOKA	PAPERED	PARLOUS
OXGANGS	PAGEANT	PALPATE	PAPHIAN	PARODOI
OXGATES	PAGEBOY	PALUDAL	PAPILIO	PARODOS
OXHEADS	PAGEFUL	PALUDIC	PAPILLA	PAROLEE
OXHEART	PAGINAL	PAMPEAN	PAPISMS	PARONYM
OXHIDES	PAGODAS	PAMPERO	PAPISTS	PAROTID
OXIDANT	PAGURID	PAMPOEN	PAPOOSE	PARPANE
OXIDASE	PAHLAVI	PANACEA	PAPPIER	PARPEND
OXIDATE	PAIGLES	PANACHE	PAPPIES	PARPENT
OXIDISE	PAIKING	PANADAS	PAPPING	PARQUET
OXIDIZE	PAILFUL	PANAMAS	PAPPOSE	PARRALS
OXLANDS	PAILLON	PANAXES	PAPPOUS	PARRELS
OXONIUM	PAINFUL	PANCAKE	PAPRICA	PARRIER
OXSLIPS	PAINING	PANCHAX	PAPRIKA	PARRING
OXTAILS	PAIOCKE	PANDANI	PAPULAE	PARROCK
OXTERED	PAIOCKS	PANDARS	PAPULAR	PARSNIP
OXYACID	PAIRIAL	PANDECT	PAPYRAL	PARTAKE
OXYGENS	PAIRING	PANDERS	PAPYRUS	PARTIER
OXYMELS	PAISANA	PANDIED	PARABLE	PARTITA
OXYMORA	PAISANS	PANDOOR	PARACME	PARTITE
OXYNTIC	PAISLEY	PANDORA	PARADED	PARTNER
OXYPHIL	PAJAMAS	PANDOUR	PARADER	PARTOOK
OXYSALT	PAJOCKE	PANDURA	PARADOR	PARTWAY
OXYSOME	PAJOCKS	PANEERS	PARADOS	PARURAS
OXYTONE	PAKAHIS	PANEITY	PARADOX	PARVENU
OYESSES	PAKAPOO	PANFISH	PARAGES	PASCALS
OZAENAS	PAKEHAS	PANFULS	PARAGON	PASCHAL
OZALIDS	PAKFONG	PANGAMY	PARAMOS	PASHKAS
OZONIDE	PAKIHIS	PANGENE	PARANGS	PASPIES
OZONISE	PAKOKOS	PANGING	PARANYM	PASQUIL
OZONIZE	PAKORAS	PANGRAM	PARAPET	PASSAGE
OZONOUS	PAKTONG	PANICKS	PARAPHS	PASSANT
PABLUMS	PALABRA	PANICKY	PARASOL	PASSATA
PABULAR	PALACED	PANICUM	PARATHA	PASSERS
PABULUM	PALACES	PANISCS	PARAZOA	PASSION
PACEWAY	PALADIN	PANISKS	PARBAKE	PASSKEY
PACHISI	PALAGIS	PANNAGE	PARCHED	PASSMEN
PACIFIC	PALAMAE	PANNICK	PARDAHS	PASTILY
PACKAGE	PALAPAS	PANNIER	PARDALE	PASTING
PACKETS	PALATAL	PANNING	PARDALS	PATACAS
PACKING	PALATED	PANNOSE	PARDINE	PATAGIA
PACKMEN	PALAVER	PANOCHA	PARDNER	PATAMAR
PACKWAX	PALAZZI	PANOCHE	PARDONS	PATBALL
PACKWAY	PALAZZO	PANOPLY	PAREIRA	PATCHED
PADAUKS	PALEATE	PANPIPE	PARELLA	PATELLA
PADDERS	PALETOT	PANTHER	PARELLE	PATENCY
PADDIES	PALFREY	PANTILE	PARERGA	PATERAE
PADDING	PALIKAR	PANTING	PARFAIT	PATHING
PADDLED	PALINKA	PANTOUM	PARGANA	PATHWAY
PADDLER	PALKEES	PANTUNS	PARGETS	PATIBLE
PADDLES	PALLAHS	PANZERS	PARIALS	PATIENT
PADDOCK	PALLETS	PAPABLE	PARKADE	PATINAE

PATONCE	PECCARY	PELLUMS	PEPTALK	PESTFUL
PATRIOT	PECCAVI	PELORIA	PEPTICS	PESTLED
PATTING	PECHANS	PELOTON	PEPTIDS	PESTLES
PATZERS	PECHING	PELTING	PEPTIZE	PETARAS
PAUCITY	PECKERS	PELVICS	PEPTONE	PETASUS
PAUGHTY	PECKING	PEMBINA	PERAEON	PETCOCK
PAUNCHY	PECKISH	PEMICAN	PERCHED	PETERED
PAUSERS	PECTASE	PEMPHIX	PERCHER	PETIOLE
PAUSING	PECTATE	PENALLY	PERCHES	PETITIO
PAVAGES	PECTENS	PENANCE	PERCINE	PETNAPS
PAVANES	PECTISE	PENCELS	PERCOCT	PETRIFY
PAVINGS	PECTIZE	PENDANT	PERCOID	PETTIER
PAVIORS	PECTOSE	PENDENT	PEREGAL	PETTILY
PAVIOUR	PECULIA	PENDING	PEREIRA	PETTING
PAVLOVA	PEDAGOG	PENDULE	PERENTY	PETTISH
PAVONES	PEDDLED	PENFOLD	PERFIDY	PETTLED
PAWAWED	PEDDLER	PENFULS	PERFING	PETTLES
PAWKIER	PEDESES	PENGUIN	PERFINS	PETUNIA
PAWKILY	PEDETIC	PENICIL	PERFUME	PEWTERS
PAWNAGE	PEDICAB	PENISES	PERFUMY	PEYOTLS
PAWNCES	PEDLARS	PENLITE	PERFUSE	PEYTREL
PAWNEES	PEDLARY	PENNALS	PERGOLA	PEZANTS
PAWNING	PEDLERY	PENNAME	PERHAPS	PFENNIG
PAWNORS	PEDOCAL	PENNANT	PERIAPT	PHACOID
PAWPAWS	PEDRERO	PENNERS	PERIDIA	PHAEISM
PAXIUBA	PEEBEEN	PENNIED	PERIGEE	PHALANX
PAYABLE	PEECING	PENNILL	PERINEA	PHALLIC
PAYABLY	PEENGED	PENNINE	PERIODS	PHALLIN
PAYDAYS	PEENGES	PENNING	PERIWIG	PHALLUS
PAYFONE	PEENING	PENNONS	PERJURE	PHANGED
PAYLOAD	PEEPERS	PENOCHE	PERJURY	PHANTOM
PAYMENT	PEEPING	PENSEES	PERKIER	PHARAOH
PAYNIMS	PEEPULS	PENSILE	PERKILY	PHARMAS
PAYOFFS	PEERAGE	PENSUMS	PERKING	PHARYNX
PAYOLAS	PEERESS	PENTACT	PERKINS	PHASEAL
PAYROLL	PEERIER	PENTELS	PERMIAN	PHASORS
PAYSAGE	PEEVING	PENTENE	PERMUTE	PHATTER
PAZZAZZ	PEEVISH	PENTHIA	PERNING	PHEAZAR
PEACHES	PEEWEES	PENTICE	PEROXID	PHEERES
PEACING	PEEWITS	PENTISE	PERPEND	PHEESED
PEACOAT	PEGASUS	PENTITI	PERPENT	PHEESES
PEACOCK	PEGGIES	PENTITO	PERPLEX	PHEEZED
PEAFOWL	PEGGING	PENTODE	PERRIER	PHEEZES
PEAHENS	PEGHING	PENTYLS	PERRONS	PHELLEM
PEAKIER	PEGLESS	PENUCHE	PERSONA	PHENOLS
PEAKING	PEGLIKE	PENUCHI	PERSONS	PHENOXY
PEAKISH	PEINING	PENULTS	PERSPEX	PHENYLS
PEARLER	PEISHWA	PEONAGE	PERTAKE	PHILTRA
PEATARY	PEIZING	PEONIES	PERTOOK	PHIZOGS
PEATERY	PEKEPOO	PEOPLED	PERTURB	PHIZZES
PEATIER	PELAGES	PEOPLER	PERUKED	PHLEGMS
PEATMAN	PELAGIC	PEOPLES	PERUKES	PHLEGMY
PEATMEN	PELHAMS	PEPINOS	PERVERT	PHLOEMS
PEAVEYS	PELISSE	PEPLUMS	PESADES	PHLOXES
PEAVIES	PELITIC	PEPPERS	PESETAS	PHOBIAS
PEAZING	PELLACH	PEPPERY	PESEWAS	PHOBICS
PEBBLED	PELLACK	PEPPILY	PESHWAS	PHOBISM
PEBBLES	PELLETS	PEPPING	PESKIER	PHOBIST
PEBRINE	PELLING	PEPSINE	PESKILY	PHOEBUS
PECCANT	PELLOCK	PEPSINS	PESSARY	PHOENIX

PHONEME	PICQUET	PILLAGE	PIPAGES	PLACARD
PHONERS	PICRITE	PILLARS	PIPEAGE	PLACATE
PHONEYS	PIDDLED	PILLBOX	PIPEFUL	PLACCAT
PHONIER	PIDDLER	PILLING	PIPERIC	PLACEBO
PHONIES	PIDDOCK	PILLION	PIPETTE	PLACING
PHONILY	PIDGEON	PILLOCK	PIPIEST	PLACKET
PHONING	PIDGINS	PILLORY	PIPKINS	PLAFOND
PHONONS	PIECING	PILLOWS	PIPPIER	PLAGIUM
PHORATE	PIEDISH	PILLOWY	PIPPING	PLAGUED
PHORESY	PIEHOLE	PILOTED	PIPPINS	PLAGUEY
PHOTICS	PIENDED	PILOTIS	PIQUANT	PLAINED
PHOTOED	PIERAGE	PILSNER	PIQUETS	PLAINLY
PHOTOGS	PIERCED	PILULAE	PIQUING	PLAINTS
PHOTONS	PIERIDS	PILULAR	PIRAGUA	PLANCHE
PHRASAL	PIEROGI	PILULES	PIRANHA	PLANING
PHRATRY	PIETIES	PIMPING	PIRATIC	PLANISH
PHREAKS	PIETISM	PIMPLED	PIRAYAS	PLANKED
PHRENSY	PIETIST	PIMPLES	PIRLING	PLANNED
PHUTTED	PIFFERO	PINBALL	PIROGHI	PLANNER
PHYLLID	PIFFLED	PINBONE	PIROJKI	PLANTAR
PHYLLOS	PIFFLER	PINCHED	PIROQUE	PLANTED
PHYLONS	PIFFLES	PINDANS	PISCARY	PLANULA
PHYSEDS	PIGBOAT	PINDERS	PISCINA	PLANURY
PHYSICS	PIGFACE	PINDOWN	PISCINE	PLANXTY
PHYSIOS	PIGFEED	PINETUM	PISHING	PLAPPED
PHYTANE	PIGFISH	PINFALL	PISHOGE	PLAQUES
PHYTINS	PIGGERY	PINFISH	PISKIES	PLASHED
PHYTOLS	PIGGIER	PINFOLD	PISSING	PLASHET
PIAFFED	PIGGIES	PINGING	PISSOIR	PLASMAS
PIAFFER	PIGGING	PINGLED	PISTILS	PLASMID
PIAFFES	PIGGINS	PINGLER	PISTOUS	PLASMON
PIANINO	PIGGISH	PINGUID	PITAPAT	PLASTID
PIANIST	PIGHTED	PINGUIN	PITARAH	PLATEAU
PIARIST	PIGHTLE	PINHOLE	PITARAS	PLATINA
PIASABA	PIGLETS	PINITOL	PITAYAS	PLATING
PIASAVA	PIGLIKE	PINKENS	PITCHED	PLATOON
PIAZZAS	PIGLING	PINKEST	PITCHER	PLATTED
PIBROCH	PIGMEAN	PINKEYE	PITEOUS	PLATYPI
PICACHO	PIGMEAT	PINKEYS	PITFALL	PLAUDIT
PICAMAR	PIGMIES	PINKIES	PITHEAD	PLAYACT
PICANTE	PIGMOID	PINKOES	PITHFUL	PLAYBOY
PICARAS	PIGNOLI	PINNACE	PITHIER	PLAYBUS
PICCATA	PIGOUTS	PINNIES	PITHILY	PLAYDAY
PICCIES	PIGPENS	PINNING	PITHING	PLAYFUL
PICCOLO	PIGTAIL	PINNOCK	PITIFUL	PLAYING
PICEOUS	PIGWASH	PINNOED	PITMANS	PLAYLET
PICKAXE	PIGWEED	PINNULA	PITPROP	PLAYOFF
PICKERY	PIKAKES	PINNULE	PITTING	PLAYPEN
PICKIER	PIKELET	PINTADA	PITTITE	PLEBEAN
PICKILY	PIKEMAN	PINTADO	PITUITA	PLEBIFY
PICKING	PIKEMEN	PINTAIL	PITUITE	PLECTRA
PICKINS	PILAFFS	PINTANO	PITURIS	PLEDGED
PICKLED	PILCHER	PINWALE	PITYING	PLEDGEE
PICKLES	PILCHES	PINWEED	PIUPIUS	PLEDGER
PICKMAW	PILCORN	PINWORK	PIVOTAL	PLEDGES
PICKOFF	PILCROW	PINWORM	PIVOTED	PLEDGET
PICKUPS	PILEOUS	PINYONS	PIXYISH	PLEDGOR
PICNICS	PILFERS	PIONEYS	PIZAZZY	PLENARY
PICOTED	PILFERY	PIOSITY	PIZZAZZ	PLENIPO
PICOTEE	PILGRIM	PIOUSLY	PIZZLES	PLENISH

PLENISM	PLUMOUS	POINDED	POMPANO	POPULAR
PLEOPOD	PLUMPED	POINTED	POMPELO	PORCHES
PLEROME	PLUMPEN	POISING	POMPEYS	PORCINI
PLESHES	PLUMPER	POITINS	POMPION	PORCINO
PLEUCHS	PLUMPLY	POKABLE	POMPOMS	PORIFER
PLEUGHS	PLUMULA	POKEFUL	POMPONS	PORISMS
PLEURAE	PLUMULE	POKIEST	POMPOON	PORKIER
PLEURAL	PLUNDER	POLACCA	POMPOUS	PORKIES
PLEURON	PLUNGER	POLACRE	POMROYS	PORKPIE
PLEXORS	PLUNKED	POLARON	PONCEAU	PORNIER
PLEXURE	PLUNKER	POLEAXE	PONCHOS	POROSES
PLIABLE	PLURALS	POLECAT	PONCING	POROSIS
PLIABLY	PLUSHER	POLENTA	PONDAGE	PORRECT
PLIANCY	PLUSHES	POLEYNS	PONDING	PORRIGO
PLICATE	PLUSHLY	POLICED	PONDOKS	PORTATE
PLIGHTS	PLUSSED	POLICES	PONGEES	PORTENT
PLIMMED	PLUTEAL	POLITIC	PONGING	PORTHOS
PLIMSOL	PLUVIAL	POLKAED	PONGOES	PORTION
PLINKED	PLUVIAN	POLKING	PONTAGE	PORTMAN
PLINKER	PLYWOOD	POLLACK	PONTIFF	PORTMEN
PLINTHS	PNEUMAS	POLLANS	PONTIFY	POSABLE
PLISKIE	POACHED	POLLARD	PONTILS	POSAUNE
PLISSES	POACHER	POLLEES	PONTINE	POSHEST
PLODDER	POBLANO	POLLENS	PONTOON	POSITIF
PLODGED	POCHARD	POLLENT	PONYING	POSOLES
PLONGED	POCHAYS	POLLICY	POOCHED	POSSESS
PLONGES	POCHOIR	POLLIES	POOCHES	POSSETS
PLONKED	POCKARD	POLLING	POOFIER	POSSIES
PLONKER	POCKETS	POLLIST	POOFTAH	POSSUMS
PLONKOS	POCKIER	POLLMAN	POOGYES	POSTBAG
PLOOKIE	POCKIES	POLLMEN	POOJAHS	POSTBOX
PLOSION	POCKILY	POLLOCK	POOKING	POSTBUS
PLOSIVE	POCKING	POLLUTE	POONACS	POSTDOC
PLOTTED	POCKPIT	POLONIE	POONCED	POSTFIX
PLOTTER	POCOSON	POLTING	POORISH	POSTOPS
PLOTTIE	PODAGRA	POLYACT	POOTING	POSTTAX
PLOTZED	PODCAST	POLYCOT	POOTLED	POSTWAR
PLOTZES	PODDIES	POLYENE	POOTLES	POTABLE
PLOUGHS	PODDING	POLYGAM	POOVERY	POTBOIL
PLOUKIE	PODDLES	POLYGON	POOVIER	POTCHED
PLOVERS	PODESTA	POLYMER	POPADUM	POTCHER
PLOWBOY	PODGIER	POLYNIA	POPCORN	POTCHES
PLOWMAN	PODGILY	POLYNYA	POPEDOM	POTENCE
PLOWMEN	PODITIC	POLYNYI	POPERIN	POTENCY
PLOWTER	PODLIKE	POLYOLS	POPETTE	POTENTS
PLOYING	PODSOLS	POLYOMA	POPEYED	POTFULS
PLUCKED	PODZOLS	POLYPED	POPLARS	POTGUNS
PLUCKER	POEPOLS	POLYPES	POPLINS	POTHEAD
PLUFFED	POESIES	POLYPOD	POPOVER	POTHEEN
PLUGGER	POETESS	POLYPUS	POPPERS	POTHERB
PLUGOLA	POETICS	POLYZOA	POPPETS	POTHERY
PLUMAGE	POETISE	POMACES	POPPIED	POTHOLE
PLUMATE	POETIZE	POMADED	POPPIER	POTHOOK
PLUMBED	POFFLES	POMATUM	POPPIES	POTICHE
PLUMBUM	POGOERS	POMELOS	POPPING	POTLACH
PLUMCOT	POGOING	POMEROY	POPPISH	POTLIKE
PLUMERY	POGONIA	POMFRET	POPPITS	POTOROO
PLUMIST	POGROMS	POMMELE	POPPLES	POTPIES
PLUMMER	POHIRIS	POMMELS	POPRINS	POTSHOP
PLUMMET	POINADO	POMMIES	POPSIES	POTTAGE

POTTEEN	PRAYING	PREPUCE	PRIMPED	PRONELY
POTTERY	PREAGED	PREPUPA	PRIMULA	PRONEUR
POTTIER	PREANAL	PREQUEL	PRINCED	PRONGED
POTTING	PREAVER	PREROCK	PRINCOX	PRONKED
POTTLES	PREBASE	PRERUPT	PRINKED	PRONOUN
POTZERS	PREBEND	PRESHOW	PRINKER	PROOFED
POUCHED	PREBIDS	PRESIFT	PRINTED	PROPAGE
POUCHES	PREBILL	PRESOAK	PRIORLY	PROPALE
POUFFED	PREBIND	PRESTED	PRISERS	PROPANE
POUFFES	PREBOIL	PRESTER	PRITHEE	PROPEND
POUFING	PREBOOK	PRETAPE	PRIVACY	PROPHET
POUFTAH	PREBOOM	PRETELL	PRIVADO	PROPJET
POUFTER	PREBORN	PRETERM	PRIVATE	PROPMAN
POUKING	PREBUYS	PRETEXT	PRIVETS	PROPMEN
POULARD	PRECAVA	PRETRIM	PRIVIER	PROPONE
POULTRY	PRECESS	PRETYPE	PRIVIES	PROPPED
POUNCER	PRECIPE	PRETZEL	PRIVILY	PROPRIA
POUNCET	PRECOOK	PREVAIL	PRIVITY	PROPYLA
POUNDAL	PRECOOL	PREVENE	PRIZERS	PROPYLS
POUNDED	PRECOUP	PREVENT	PRIZING	PROSIER
POUPING	PRECURE	PREVERB	PROBALL	PROSIFY
POURSEW	PRECUTS	PREVIEW	PROBAND	PROSILY
POUSSIE	PREDICT	PREVUED	PROBANG	PROSODY
POUTFUL	PREDUSK	PREVUES	PROBATE	PROSOMA
POUTHER	PREDYED	PREWARM	PROBERS	PROTECT
POUTIER	PREDYES	PREWASH	PROBING	PROTEGE
POUTINE	PREEMPT	PREWIRE	PROBITS	PROTHYL
POUTING	PREENED	PREWORK	PROBITY	PROTIUM
POVERTY	PREENER	PREWORN	PROBLEM	PROTONS
POWDERS	PREEVED	PREWYNS	PROCARP	PROTYLE
POWDERY	PREFABS	PREYERS	PROCTOR	PROTYLS
POWERED	PREFACE	PREYFUL	PRODDED	PROUDER
POWHIRI	PREFADE	PREYING	PRODDER	PROUDLY
POWNDED	PREFERS	PREZZES	PRODIGY	PROULER
POWNEYS	PREFILL	PREZZIE	PRODRUG	PROVAND
POWRING	PREFIRE	PRIAPIC	PRODUCT	PROVANT
POWWAWS	PREFUND	PRIAPUS	PROFACE	PROVEND
POWWOWS	PREGAME	PRIBBLE	PROFANE	PROVERB
POYNANT	PREHEAT	PRICIER	PROFESS	PROVERS
POYNTED	PREHEND	PRICILY	PROFFER	PROVIDE
POYSING	PRELACY	PRICING	PROFILE	PROVINE
POYSONS	PRELUDE	PRICKED	PROFUSE	PROVING
POZOLES	PRELUDI	PRICKER	PROGGED	PROVISO
POZZIES	PREMEET	PRICKET	PROGGER	PROVOKE
PRABBLE	PREMIUM	PRICKLY	PROGRAM	PROVOST
PRACTIC	PREMOLD	PRIDING	PROJECT	PROWESS
PRAIRIE	PREMOLT	PRIEFED	PROJETS	PROWLED
PRAJNAS	PREMOVE	PRIGGED	PROLANS	PROWLER
PRANCED	PREMUNE	PRIGGER	PROLATE	PROXIES
PRANCER	PRENAME	PRILLED	PROLEGS	PROXIMO
PRANCES	PRENOON	PRIMACY	PROLERS	PRUDERY
PRANCKE	PRENUPS	PRIMARY	PROLING	PRUDISH
PRANCKS	PRENZIE	PRIMATE	PROLOGS	PRUINAS
PRANGED	PREPACK	PRIMELY	PROLONG	PRUNING
PRANKED	PREPAVE	PRIMERO	PROMINE	PRURIGO
PRANKLE	PREPILL	PRIMERS	PROMMER	PRUSSIC
PRAUNCE	PREPLAN	PRIMINE	PROMOTE	PRUTOTH
PRAVITY	PREPOSE	PRIMING	PROMPTS	PRYTHEE
PRAWLES	PREPPED	PRIMMED	PRONAOI	PSALTRY
PRAWLIN	PREPREG	PRIMMER	PRONAOI	PSAMMON

PSCHENT	PULPIER	PURGING	PYGMEAN	QUANGOS
PSIONIC	PULPIFY	PURIRIS	PYGMOID	QUANNET
PSOCIDS	PULPILY	PURISMS	PYJAMAS	QUANTAL
PSYCHED	PULPING	PURLIEU	PYKNICS	QUANTED
PSYCHES	PULPITS	PURLINE	PYLORIC	QUANTIC
PSYCHIC	PULPOUS	PURLING	PYLORUS	QUANTUM
PSYCHOS	PULQUES	PURLINS	PYRALIS	QUARREL
PSYLLAS	PULSARS	PURLOIN	PYRAMID	QUARTAN
PSYLLID	PULSERS	PURPIES	PYRAMIS	QUARTER
PSYWARS	PULTOON	PURPLED	PYRENES	QUARTET
PUBBING	PULTUNS	PURPLER	PYRETIC	QUARTIC
PUBERAL	PULTURE	PURPORT	PYREXES	QUARTOS
PUBERTY	PULVERS	PURPOSE	PYREXIA	QUARTZY
PUBLICS	PULVILS	PURPURA	PYREXIC	QUASARS
PUBLISH	PULVINI	PURPURE	PYRIDIC	QUASHED
PUCCOON	PULWARS	PURRING	PYRITIC	QUASHEE
PUCELLE	PUMICED	PURSERS	PYROLAS	QUASHER
PUCKERS	PUMICER	PURSEWS	PYROPUS	QUASHES
PUCKERY	PUMICES	PURSILY	PYROSIS	QUASSES
PUCKISH	PUMMELO	PURSING	PYRRHIC	QUASSIA
PUCKLES	PUMMELS	PURSUAL	PYRROLE	QUASSIN
PUDDENS	PUMPING	PURSUES	PYRROLS	QUAVERS
PUDDIES	PUMPION	PURSUIT	PYRUVIC	QUAVERY
PUDDING	PUMPKIN	PURTIER	PYTHIUM	QUAYAGE
PUDDLED	PUNALUA	PURTRAY	PYURIAS	QUBYTES
PUDDLER	PUNCHED	PURVEYS	PYXIDES	QUEACHY
PUDDOCK	PUNCHES	PURVIEW	PYXIDIA	QUEECHY
PUDENCY	PUNCING	PUSHERS	PZAZZES	QUEENED
PUDENDA	PUNCTOS	PUSHFUL	QABALAH	QUEENIE
PUDGIER	PUNCTUM	PUSHIER	QABALAS	QUEENLY
PUDGILY	PUNDITS	PUSHILY	QASIDAS	QUEERED
PUEBLOS	PUNGENT	PUSHPIN	QAWWALI	QUEERLY
PUERILE	PUNKAHS	PUSHROD	QAWWALS	QUEESTS
PUERING	PUNKERS	PUSHUPS	QIGONGS	QUELLED
PUFFERS	PUNKEST	PUSLIKE	QINDARS	QUELLER
PUFFERY	PUNKEYS	PUSSERS	QINTARS	QUEMING
PUFFIER	PUNKIER	PUSSIES	QIVIUTS	QUERIDA
PUFFILY	PUNKINS	PUTAMEN	QUACKED	QUERIED
PUFFING	PUNKISH	PUTCHER	QUACKER	QUESTED
PUFFINS	PUNNERS	PUTCHUK	QUACKLE	QUETHES
PUGAREE	PUNNIER	PUTDOWN	QUADDED	QUETSCH
PUGGERY	PUNNING	PUTLOGS	QUADRAT	QUETZAL
PUGGIER	PUNTEES	PUTREFY	QUADRIC	QUEUERS
PUGGIES	PUNTING	PUTTEES	QUAERED	QUEUING
PUGGING	PUPARIA	PUTTIER	QUAERES	QUEYNIE
PUGGISH	PUPATED	PUTTIES	QUAFFED	QUEZALS
PUGGLES	PUPFISH	PUTTING	QUAFFER	QUIBBLE
PUGGREE	PUPILAR	PUTTOCK	QUAGGAS	QUIBLIN
PUGMARK	PUPPETS	PUTURES	QUAHAUG	QUICHED
PUGREES	PUPPIED	PUTZING	QUAHOGS	QUICHES
PUKATEA	PUPPIES	PUZZLED	QUAICHS	QUICKEN
PUKEKOS	PUPPING	PUZZLER	QUAIGHS	QUICKER
PULDRON	PUPUNHA	PYAEMIA	QUAILED	QUICKIE
PULKHAS	PURANAS	PYAEMIC	QUAKERS	QUICKLY
PULLERS	PURANIC	PYCNICS	QUAKIER	QUIDAMS
PULLETS	PURDAHS	PYCNITE	QUAKILY	QUIDDIT
PULLEYS	PURFLED	PYCNONS	QUAKING	QUIDDLE
PULLING	PURFLER	PYEBALD	QUALIFY	QUIESCE
PULLMAN	PURFLES	PYGARGS	QUALITY	QUIETED
PULLUPS	PURGERS	PYGIDIA	QUAMASH	QUIETEN

QUIETLY	QWERTYS	RAISINY	RATABLY	REAWOKE
QUIETUS	RABANNA	RAIYATS	RATAFEE	REBADGE
QUIGHTS	RABBINS	RAKEOFF	RATAFIA	REBECKS
QUILLAI	RABBITO	RAKSHAS	RATATAT	REBEGAN
QUILLED	RABBITS	RALLIER	RATBAGS	REBEGUN
QUILLET	RABBITY	RALLINE	RATFINK	REBIRTH
QUILLON	RABBLER	RALLYES	RATFISH	REBITES
QUILTED	RABBONI	RALPHED	RATLING	REBLENT
QUILTER	RABIDLY	RAMAKIN	RATLINS	REBORED
QUINARY	RACCOON	RAMBLAS	RATPACK	REBUILT
QUINCHE	RACEWAY	RAMENTA	RATTAIL	REBUKED
QUINIES	RACISMS	RAMEOUS	RATTERY	REBUKER
QUININA	RACKETT	RAMILIE	RATTLED	REBUKES
QUININE	RACKETY	RAMJETS	RATTLER	RECARRY
QUININS	RACKFUL	RAMMERS	RATTLIN	RECCEED
QUINOAS	RACLOIR	RAMMIER	RATTRAP	RECCIED
QUINOID	RACQUET	RAMMING	RAUCITY	RECCIES
QUINOLS	RADDING	RAMMISH	RAUCLER	RECEIPT
QUINONE	RADDLED	RAMPAGE	RAUCOUS	RECEIVE
QUINTAL	RADGEST	RAMPART	RAUPATU	RECENCY
QUINTAR	RADIALE	RAMPICK	RAURIKI	RECENSE
QUINTET	RADIALS	RAMPIKE	RAVAGED	RECITER
QUINTIC	RADIANS	RAMPION	RAVAGER	RECKING
QUINTIN	RADICAL	RAMPIRE	RAVELED	RECLAME
QUINZES	RADIOED	RAMRODS	RAVELER	RECLINE
QUIPPED	RADIUMS	RAMULAR	RAVELIN	RECODES
QUIPPER	RADIXES	RAMULUS	RAVELLY	RECOUPE
QUIPPUS	RADOMES	RANCHER	RAVENED	RECOURE
QUIRING	RADULAE	RANCORS	RAVENER	RECOWER
QUIRKED	RADULAR	RANCOUR	RAVINGS	RECOYLE
QUIRTED	RADULAS	RANDANS	RAVIOLI	RECRUIT
QUITING	RAFALES	RANDILY	RAWBONE	RECTORS
QUITTAL	RAFFISH	RANDONS	RAWHIDE	RECTORY
QUITTED	RAFFLED	RANGING	RAWINGS	RECTRIX
QUITTER	RAFFLER	RANGOLI	RAYLETS	RECTUMS
QUITTOR	RAFTMAN	RANKERS	RAYLIKE	RECUILE
QUIVERS	RAFTMEN	RANKISH	RAZORED	RECURVE
QUIVERY	RAGBAGS	RANKISM	RAZURES	RECYCLE
QUIXOTE	RAGBOLT	RANKLED	RAZZIAS	REDBACK
QUIZZED	RAGEFUL	RANKLES	RAZZING	REDBAYS
QUIZZER	RAGGEDY	RANPIKE	RAZZLES	REDBIRD
QUIZZES	RAGGERY	RANSACK	REACHED	REDDENS
QUODDED	RAGGIER	RANSELS	REACHER	REDDERS
QUODLIN	RAGGING	RANTING	REACHES	REDDLED
QUOHOGS	RAGHEAD	RANULAR	READIER	REDEYES
QUOIFED	RAGMANS	RANULAS	READILY	REDFISH
QUOINED	RAGOUTS	RANZELS	READMIT	REDFOOT
QUOISTS	RAGTOPS	RAOULIA	REAKING	REDNECK
QUOITED	RAGULED	RAPHIDE	REALGAR	REDOWAS
QUOITER	RAGWORK	RAPISTS	REALIZE	REDOXES
QUOKKAS	RAGWORM	RAPLOCH	REALLIE	REDRAWN
QUOMODO	RAGWORT	RAPPEES	REALLOT	REDROOT
QUONDAM	RAIKING	RAPPERS	REANNEX	REDUCED
QUONKED	RAILCAR	RAPPINI	REAPING	REDWARE
QUOPPED	RAILWAY	RAPPORT	REAPPLY	REDWOOD
QUORUMS	RAINBOW	RARKING	REARERS	REEBOKS
QUOTING	RAINIER	RASPISH	REARGUE	REECHES
QUOTUMS	RAINILY	RASSLES	REAROSE	REECHIE
QURSHES	RAINOUT	RASTRUM	REAVERS	REEDBED
QUYTING	RAISINS	RATABLE	REAWAKE	REEDERS

REEDIER	REIMAGE	REPLEVY	RETURFS	RHODIES
REEDIFY	REINKED	REPLIER	RETYING	RHODORA
REEFERS	REITBOK	REPOMEN	RETYPED	RHODOUS
REEFIER	REJECTS	REPONED	RETYPES	RHOMBIC
REEJECT	REJOICE	REPOSER	REUNIFY	RHOMBOI
REEKERS	REJONEO	REPOSES	REURGED	RHOMBOS
REEKIER	REJONES	REPOWER	REVALUE	RHOMBUS
REEKING	REJOURN	REPPING	REVELER	RHONCHI
REELECT	REJUDGE	REPRIVE	REVELRY	RHUBARB
REELERS	REKEYED	REPRIZE	REVENGE	RHYMERS
REELMAN	RELATUM	REPROBE	REVERBS	RHYMING
REELMEN	RELAXED	REPROVE	REVERED	RHYMIST
REENTRY	RELAXER	REPRYVE	REVERER	RHYTHMI
REEVOKE	RELAXES	REPUGNS	REVERIE	RHYTHMS
REEXPEL	RELAXIN	REPULSE	REVERSO	RHYTINA
REFACES	RELEASE	REPUNIT	REVERTS	RHYTONS
REFECTS	RELICTS	REQUIEM	REVEURS	RIANTLY
REFENCE	RELIERS	REQUINS	REVEUSE	RIBANDS
REFEREE	RELIEVE	REQUOTE	REVISAL	RIBBAND
REFFING	RELIQUE	REREDOS	REVISOR	RIBBIER
REFIXED	RELLENO	REROUTE	REVIVAL	RIBBONY
REFIXES	RELUMED	RESCORE	REVIVED	RIBCAGE
REFLAGS	RELYING	RESEAUX	REVIVER	RIBIBES
REFLATE	REMAKER	RESEDAS	REVIVES	RIBIBLE
REFLECT	REMAKES	RESEIZE	REVIVOR	RIBLIKE
REFLOWN	REMANET	RESHOED	REVOICE	RIBSTON
REFORGE	REMANIE	RESHOES	REVOKED	RIBWORK
REFRAIN	REMARRY	RESHONE	REVOKER	RIBWORT
REFRAME	REMATED	RESHOWN	REVOLTS	RICHING
REFROZE	REMBLED	RESIDUA	REVOTED	RICHTER
REFUGED	REMBLES	RESILED	REVVING	RICINUS
REFUGEE	REMEDED	RESITES	REVYING	RICKERS
REFUGES	REMERGE	RESIZED	REWAKES	RICKETY
REFUGIA	REMIXED	RESKUED	REWAXED	RICKING
REFUSER	REMORID	RESKUES	REWAXES	RICKSHA
REFUSES	REMOTER	RESOJET	REWEAVE	RIDDERS
REFUTER	REMOVAL	RESOLED	REWOKEN	RIDDING
REGALER	REMOVED	RESOLES	REWRAPT	RIDDLER
REGATTA	REMOVER	RESOLVE	REWRITE	RIDGILS
REGAUGE	REMOVES	RESORBS	REWROTE	RIDINGS
REGENCE	REMUAGE	RESOWED	REXINES	RIDLEYS
REGENCY	REMUDAS	RESPOKE	REYNARD	RIDOTTO
REGESTS	REMUEUR	RESTERS	REZEROS	RIEMPIE
REGINAE	RENDERS	RESTOKE	REZONED	RIFFLED
REGLAZE	RENEGES	RESTORE	REZONES	RIFFLER
REGLETS	RENEGUE	RESTUDY	RHABDOM	RIFFLES
REGLUES	RENEWAL	RESUMES	RHACHIS	RIFFOLA
REGMATA	RENEWED	RETAKEN	RHAMNUS	RIFLERS
REGNANT	RENEWER	RETAKER	RHAPHAE	RIFLERY
REGORGE	RENEYED	RETAXED	RHAPHES	RIFLING
REGOSOL	RENKEST	RETAXES	RHAPHIS	RIFLIPS
REGRADE	RENNING	RETCHED	RHATANY	RIFTIER
REGREDE	RENNINS	RETIARY	RHEBOKS	RIFTING
REGRETS	RENVOYS	RETILED	RHEUMED	RIGGALD
REGULAR	REOCCUR	RETINOL	RHEUMIC	RIGGERS
REGULOS	REOILED	RETIREE	RHIZINE	RIGGING
REGULUS	REPANEL	RETITLE	RHIZOID	RIGGISH
REHINGE	REPAVES	RETOTAL	RHIZOMA	RIGHTEN
REHOUSE	REPERKS	RETRACT	RHIZOME	RIGHTER
REIFIES	REPLETE	RETTERY	RHIZOPI	RIGHTLY

RIGHTOS	RIZARDS	RONNELS	ROUGHED	RUDESBY
RIGIDLY	RIZZARS	RONNIES	ROUGHER	RUELLES
RIGLING	RIZZART	RONNING	ROUGHIE	RUELLIA
RIGLINS	RIZZERS	RONTGEN	ROUGHLY	RUFFING
RIGOLLS	RIZZORS	RONYONS	ROUILLE	RUFFINS
RIGOURS	ROADEOS	RONZERS	ROULADE	RUFFLED
RIKISHI	ROADWAY	ROOFIER	ROULEAU	RUFFLER
RIKSHAW	ROAMING	ROOFIES	ROUMING	RUFFLES
RILIEVI	ROARERS	ROOFING	ROUNDLY	RUFIYAA
RILIEVO	ROARING	ROOFTOP	ROUNDUP	RUGGERS
RILLING	ROASTER	ROOIBOS	ROUPIER	RUGGIER
RIMAYES	ROBANDS	ROOIKAT	ROUPILY	RUGLIKE
RIMFIRE	ROBBERS	ROOKERY	ROUSERS	RUGOLAS
RIMMERS	ROBBERY	ROOKIER	ROUTINE	RUGOSAS
RIMMING	ROBBING	ROOKING	ROUTOUS	RULERED
RIMPLED	ROBINIA	ROOKISH	ROVINGS	RULESSE
RIMROCK	ROBOTIC	ROOMFUL	ROWABLE	RULINGS
RIMSHOT	ROBOTRY	ROOMIES	ROWBOAT	RULLION
RINDIER	ROCKABY	ROOMILY	ROWLOCK	RULLOCK
RINDING	ROCKERY	ROOPIER	ROWOVER	RUMBAED
RINGBIT	ROCKILY	ROOPING	ROYALET	RUMBLER
RINGMAN	ROCKLAY	ROOSERS	ROYALLY	RUMKINS
RINGMEN	ROCKOON	ROOSING	ROYALTY	RUMMAGE
RINGTAW	ROCOCOS	ROOSTED	ROYNISH	RUMMERS
RINGWAY	RODDING	ROOTAGE	ROZELLE	RUMMEST
RINNING	RODEOED	ROOTCAP	ROZETED	RUMMIER
RINSERS	RODEWAY	ROOTIER	ROZITED	RUMMILY
RINSING	RODINGS	ROOTING	ROZZERS	RUMMISH
RIOTISE	RODLIKE	ROOTLED	RUBABOO	RUMNESS
RIOTIZE	ROEBUCK	ROPABLE	RUBBERS	RUMORED
RIOTOUS	ROGALLO	ROPEWAY	RUBBERY	RUMOURS
RIPCORD	ROGERED	RORQUAL	RUBBIDY	RUMPING
RIPIENI	ROGNONS	RORTING	RUBBIES	RUMPLED
RIPIENO	ROGUERY	ROSACEA	RUBBING	RUNANGA
RIPOFFS	ROGUISH	ROSACES	RUBBISH	RUNAWAY
RIPOSTS	ROILIER	ROSAKER	RUBBITY	RUNBACK
RIPPERS	ROKELAY	ROSARIA	RUBDOWN	RUNCHES
RIPPIER	ROKIEST	ROSBIFS	RUBEOLA	RUNDOWN
RIPPING	ROKKAKU	ROSEATE	RUBICON	RUNFLAT
RIPPLED	ROLFERS	ROSEBAY	RUBIDIC	RUNLETS
RIPPLER	ROLFING	ROSEHIP	RUBIGOS	RUNNELS
RIPRAPS	ROLLBAR	ROSELLA	RUBIOUS	RUNNERS
RIPSAWS	ROLLICK	ROSELLE	RUBOFFS	RUNNIER
RIPSTOP	ROLLING	ROSETTE	RUBOUTS	RUNNING
RISIBLE	ROLLMOP	ROSETTY	RUBRICS	RUNNION
RISIBLY	ROLLOCK	ROSIERE	RUCHING	RUNOFFS
RISINGS	ROLLWAY	ROSINOL	RUCKING	RUNRIGS
RISKERS	ROMAGES	ROSOLIO	RUCKLED	RUNTIER
RISKFUL	ROMAIKA	ROSSERS	RUCKMAN	RUNTISH
RISKIER	ROMAJIS	ROSTRAL	RUCKMEN	RUNWAYS
RISKILY	ROMANZA	ROSTRUM	RUCTION	RUPIAHS
RISOTTO	ROMAUNT	ROSULAS	RUDDERS	RUPTURE
RITARDS	ROMCOMS	ROTATOR	RUDDIER	RURALLY
RITTING	ROMPERS	ROTIFER	RUDDIES	RUSHEES
RITZIER	ROMPING	ROTOLOS	RUDDILY	RUSHERS
RITZILY	RONDEAU	ROTTING	RUDDING	RUSHING
RIVALRY	RONDELS	ROTUNDA	RUDDLED	RUSSELS
RIVIERE	RONDINO	ROTUNDS	RUDDLES	RUSSETY
RIVLINS	RONEOED	ROUBLES	RUDDOCK	RUSSIAS
RIVULET	RONIONS	ROUCOUS	RUDERAL	RUSSIFY

RUSSULA	SAIKEIS	SANDBOX	SATISFY	SCALAGE
RUSTICS	SAILORS	SANDBOY	SATRAPS	SCALARE
RUSTIER	SAIMIRI	SANDBUR	SATRAPY	SCALDED
RUSTILY	SAINING	SANDDAB	SATSUMA	SCALDIC
RUSTING	SAIQUES	SANDEKS	SATYRAS	SCALLED
RUSTLER	SAIYIDS	SANDFLY	SATYRIC	SCALPEL
RUSTRED	SAKIEHS	SANDHIS	SATYRID	SCAMMED
RUTTIER	SAKIYEH	SANDING	SAUCILY	SCAMMER
RUTTILY	SAKSAUL	SANDMAN	SAULGES	SCANDAL
RUTTING	SALAMON	SANDMEN	SAULIES	SCANDIA
RUTTISH	SALBAND	SANGARS	SAUNAED	SCANDIC
RYEPECK	SALCHOW	SANGHAT	SAURELS	SCANNED
RYMMING	SALFERN	SANGOMA	SAURIES	SCANTLY
RYPECKS	SALICES	SANJAKS	SAUROID	SCAPAED
SABATON	SALINAS	SANNOPS	SAUTEED	SCAPOSE
SABAYON	SALIVAL	SANPANS	SAUTEES	SCAPPLE
SABBATH	SALLADS	SANSARS	SAUTING	SCARABS
SABBATS	SALLALS	SANTALS	SAUTOIR	SCARCER
SABBING	SALLEES	SANTIMS	SAVABLE	SCARFED
SABEING	SALLOWS	SANYASI	SAVAGED	SCARILY
SABINES	SALLOWY	SAOUARI	SAVANNA	SCARPAS
SABKHAH	SALMONS	SAPAJOU	SAVANTE	SCARPHS
SABRING	SALOOPS	SAPHEAD	SAVANTS	SCARTHS
SABURRA	SALPIAN	SAPHENA	SAVARIN	SCARVES
SACATON	SALPIDS	SAPONIN	SAVATES	SCATHED
SACCATE	SALPINX	SAPPANS	SAVELOY	SCATTED
SACCULE	SALSIFY	SAPPHIC	SAVEYED	SCATTER
SACCULI	SALTATE	SAPPING	SAVINGS	SCAUPED
SACELLA	SALTATO	SAPPLES	SAVIORS	SCAVAGE
SACKAGE	SALTBOX	SAPROBE	SAVOURS	SCAZONS
SACKFUL	SALTCAT	SAPSAGO	SAVOURY	SCENERY
SACLIKE	SALTIES	SAPWOOD	SAVVEYS	SCENICS
SACRUMS	SALTILY	SARAFAN	SAVVIED	SCEPSIS
SADDEST	SALUKIS	SARCASM	SAVVIER	SCEPTIC
SADDHUS	SALVOED	SARCODE	SAVVIES	SCEPTRY
SADDLES	SALVOES	SARCOID	SAVVILY	SCHANSE
SADHANA	SALVORS	SARCOMA	SAWBILL	SCHANZE
SADISMS	SAMAANS	SARDANA	SAWDUST	SCHAPPE
SADISTS	SAMADHI	SARDARS	SAWFISH	SCHELMS
SADNESS	SAMBAED	SARDIUS	SAWINGS	SCHEMED
SAFARIS	SAMBARS	SARNEYS	SAWLIKE	SCHEMES
SAFFIAN	SAMBUCA	SARODES	SAWLOGS	SCHERZI
SAFFRON	SAMBUKE	SARONGS	SAWMILL	SCHERZO
SAFROLS	SAMBURS	SARONIC	SAWNEYS	SCHISMS
SAGAMAN	SAMEKHS	SARSARS	SAXAULS	SCHISTS
SAGATHY	SAMFOOS	SARSENS	SAXHORN	SCHIZOS
SAGBUTS	SAMITHI	SARTORS	SAYABLE	SCHIZZY
SAGGARD	SAMITIS	SASHAYS	SAYINGS	SCHLEPP
SAGGARS	SAMLORS	SASHIMI	SAYYIDS	SCHLEPS
SAGGING	SAMMIES	SASHING	SAZERAC	SCHLICH
SAGITTA	SAMMING	SASSABY	SAZHENS	SCHLOCK
SAGOINS	SAMOSAS	SASSIER	SCABBED	SCHLONG
SAGOUIN	SAMOVAR	SASSIES	SCABBLE	SCHLOSS
SAGRADA	SAMSHOO	SASSILY	SCABRID	SCHLUBS
SAGUARO	SAMSHUS	SATANGS	SCAFFIE	SCHLUMP
SAGUINS	SAMURAI	SATANIC	SCAGGED	SCHMALZ
SAHIBAH	SANCHOS	SATARAS	SCAGLIA	SCHMECK
SAHIBAS	SANCTUM	SATIATE	SCAILED	SCHMELZ
SAHIWAL	SANDALS	SATIETY	SCAITHS	SCHMICK
SAHUARO	SANDBAG	SATIRIC	SCALADO	SCHMOCK

SCHMOES	SCRANCH	SCULPED	SEEABLE	SEPTUMS
SCHMOOS	SCRANNY	SCULPTS	SEEDBED	SEQUELS
SCHMOOZ	SCRAPPY	SCULTCH	SEEDBOX	SEQUENT
SCHMUCK	SCRATCH	SCUMBAG	SEEDIER	SEQUINS
SCHNAPS	SCRAUCH	SCUMBLE	SEELIER	SEQUOIA
SCHNELL	SCRAWLS	SCUMMED	SEEMERS	SERENES
SCHNOOK	SCRAWLY	SCUNGED	SEEMING	SERFAGE
SCHNORR	SCRAWMS	SCUNGES	SEEPAGE	SERIOUS
SCHNOZZ	SCRAWNY	SCURRED	SEEPING	SERMONS
SCHOLIA	SCRAWPS	SCURRIL	SEERESS	SEROSAE
SCHOOLE	SCREAMS	SCUTAGE	SEESAWS	SERRANO
SCHOOLS	SCREEDS	SCUZZES	SEETHES	SERUEWE
SCHORLS	SCREEVE	SCYBALA	SEGHOLS	SERVERY
SCHRIKS	SCREWER	SCYPHUS	SEGMENT	SESAMES
SCHRODS	SCREWUP	SCYTHED	SEICHES	SESTETT
SCHTOOK	SCRIBAL	SCYTHER	SEIKEST	SESTONS
SCHTOOM	SCRIBED	SCYTHES	SEILING	SETNESS
SCHTUCK	SCRIBER	SDAINES	SEISERS	SETTLED
SCHUITS	SCRIBES	SDAYNED	SEISING	SETTLES
SCHUYTS	SCRIKES	SEABANK	SEISINS	SETULES
SCIENCE	SCRIMPS	SEABOOT	SEISMIC	SEVENTH
SCILLAS	SCRIMPY	SEACOCK	SEISORS	SEVENTY
SCIOLTO	SCRINES	SEAFOLK	SEITIES	SEVRUGA
SCIROCS	SCRIPTS	SEAFOOD	SEIZING	SEWABLE
SCIRRHI	SCRITCH	SEAFOWL	SEIZINS	SEWAGES
SCISSEL	SCRIVES	SEAHAWK	SEIZORS	SEXFOIL
SCISSIL	SCROBES	SEAHOGS	SEIZURE	SEXIEST
SCISSOR	SCROGGY	SEAKALE	SEJEANT	SEXISMS
SCIURID	SCROLLS	SEALANT	SEKOSES	SEXISTS
SCLAFFS	SCROMED	SEALERY	SELECTS	SEXLESS
SCLAVES	SCROMES	SEALGHS	SELFDOM	SEXPOTS
SCLERES	SCROOCH	SEALINE	SELFING	SEXTANS
SCLIFFS	SCROOGE	SEALWAX	SELFISM	SEXTANT
SCOFFED	SCROOPS	SEAMARK	SELKIES	SEXTETS
SCOGGED	SCRORPS	SEAMERS	SELLOFF	SEXTETT
SCOLDER	SCROTUM	SEARATS	SELTZER	SEXTILE
SCONCED	SCROWLS	SEASICK	SEMBLED	SEXTONS
SCONCES	SCROYLE	SEASONS	SEMBLES	SEXTUOR
SCOOGED	SCRUBBY	SEAWALL	SEMEION	SEYSURE
SCOOTCH	SCRUFFS	SEAWANS	SEMEMIC	SFERICS
SCOOTED	SCRUFFY	SEAWANT	SEMIDRY	SFUMATO
SCORIAC	SCRUMMY	SEAWARE	SEMIFIT	SHABASH
SCORIFY	SCRUMPS	SEAWAYS	SEMILOG	SHABBLE
SCORING	SCRUMPY	SEAWEED	SEMPLER	SHACKED
SCORPER	SCRUNCH	SEAWIFE	SEMSEMS	SHADFLY
SCOTIAS	SCRUNTS	SEBATES	SENARII	SHADOOF
SCOTOMA	SCRUNTY	SEBIFIC	SENDALS	SHADOWS
SCOTOMY	SCRUTOS	SEBUNDY	SENECIO	SHADOWY
SCOUGED	SCRUZED	SECEDED	SENNETS	SHADUFS
SCOUPED	SCRUZES	SECEDES	SENORES	SHAFTED
SCOUSES	SCRYERS	SECONAL	SENSEIS	SHAGGED
SCOWDER	SCRYNES	SECONDS	SENSISM	SHAHADA
SCOWLED	SCUCHIN	SECRECY	SENSIST	SHAHDOM
SCOWPED	SCUDDED	SECRETE	SENSORS	SHAIKHS
SCOWTHS	SCUDDER	SECTARY	SENSORY	SHAIRDS
SCOZZAS	SCUFFED	SECTILE	SENVIES	SHAKEUP
SCRAGGY	SCUFFER	SECULUM	SEPIUMS	SHAKIER
SCRAICH	SCUGGED	SEDATES	SEPPUKU	SHAKILY
SCRAIGH	SCULLED	SEDGIER	SEPTAGE	SHAKING
SCRAMBS	SCULLES	SEDUCES	SEPTETS	SHAKOES

SHAKUDO	SHEGETZ	SHITTED	SHOWGHE	SICKBAY
SHALLIS	SHEHITA	SHITTIM	SHOWIER	SICKBED
SHALLON	SHEIKHA	SHIURIM	SHOWILY	SICKEES
SHALLOP	SHEILAS	SHIVAHS	SHOWING	SICKENS
SHALLOT	SHEKELS	SHIVERY	SHOWMAN	SICKEST
SHALOMS	SHELLAC	SHIVITI	SHOWMEN	SICKIES
SHALOTS	SHELLED	SHIVOOS	SHOWOFF	SICKING
SHALWAR	SHELTER	SHIVVED	SHREDDY	SICKISH
SHAMANS	SHELTIE	SHLEPPS	SHREEKS	SICKLES
SHAMBAS	SHELVED	SHLOCKS	SHREWED	SICKOUT
SHAMBLY	SHELVER	SHLUMPS	SHRIEKY	SICLIKE
SHAMINA	SHELVES	SHLUMPY	SHRIEVE	SIDDHIS
SHAMMAS	SHEQELS	SHMALTZ	SHRIFTS	SIDDURS
SHAMMED	SHEREEF	SHMATTE	SHRIGHT	SIEGERS
SHAMMES	SHERIFF	SHMOCKS	SHRILLS	SIEGING
SHAMMOS	SHERRIS	SHMOOSE	SHRILLY	SIENITE
SHAMOIS	SHEUCHS	SHMOOZE	SHRIMPS	SIFAKAS
SHAMOYS	SHEUGHS	SHMUCKS	SHRIMPY	SIFFLED
SHANDRY	SHEWERS	SHNAPPS	SHRINAL	SIFFLES
SHANKED	SHIATZU	SHNOOKS	SHRINKS	SIGANID
SHANTIH	SHIBAHS	SHOALED	SHRITCH	SIGHFUL
SHANTIS	SHICKSA	SHOALER	SHRIVEL	SIGHING
SHAPELY	SHIELDS	SHOCKED	SHRIVEN	SIGHTED
SHARDED	SHIELED	SHODERS	SHRIVER	SIGHTLY
SHARIAH	SHIFTED	SHOEBOX	SHROFFS	SIGMOID
SHARIAT	SHIFTER	SHOFARS	SHROOMS	SIGNIFY
SHARIFS	SHIKARS	SHOGGED	SHROUDS	SILAGED
SHARKED	SHIKKER	SHOGGLE	SHROVED	SILICAS
SHARKER	SHIKSAS	SHOGGLY	SHROWED	SILICIC
SHARPEN	SHIKSES	SHOGUNS	SHRUBBY	SILICLE
SHARPLY	SHILLED	SHOLOMS	SHTCHIS	SILICON
SHASHED	SHILPIT	SHONEEN	SHTETEL	SILIQUA
SHASHES	SHIMAAL	SHOOFLY	SHTETLS	SILIQUE
SHASLIK	SHIMMED	SHOOGIE	SHTOOKS	SILKIER
SHASTRA	SHIMMER	SHOOGLY	SHTUCKS	SILKIES
SHAUGHS	SHIMMEY	SHOOING	SHUCKED	SILKILY
SHAULED	SHINDYS	SHOOLED	SHUCKER	SILLERS
SHAVERS	SHINESS	SHOOLES	SHUDDER	SILLIER
SHAVIES	SHINGLY	SHOORAS	SHUFFLE	SILLIES
SHAWLED	SHINIER	SHOPBOY	SHUFTIS	SILLILY
SHAWLEY	SHINIES	SHOPFUL	SHUNNED	SILLOCK
SHEAFED	SHINILY	SHOPHAR	SHUNNER	SILPHIA
SHEATHE	SHINING	SHOPMAN	SHUNTED	SILURID
SHEATHS	SHINJUS	SHOPPED	SHUSHED	SILVANS
SHEATHY	SHINKIN	SHOPPES	SHUSHES	SILVERN
SHEAVED	SHINNED	SHORANS	SHUTEYE	SILVICS
SHEAVES	SHINNES	SHORERS	SHUTOFF	SIMILAR
SHEBANG	SHINNEY	SHORTLY	SHUTOUT	SIMILOR
SHEBEEN	SHIPFUL	SHOTPUT	SHUTTER	SIMIOID
SHEDDED	SHIPMAN	SHOTTED	SHUTTLE	SIMIOUS
SHEDDER	SHIPMEN	SHOTTEN	SHYNESS	SIMITAR
SHEELED	SHIPPED	SHOTTES	SHYPOOS	SIMKINS
SHEENED	SHIPPON	SHOUGHS	SIALIDS	SIMLINS
SHEENEY	SHIPPOS	SHOUSES	SIALOID	SIMNELS
SHEENIE	SHIPWAY	SHOVELS	SIAMEZE	SIMOOMS
SHEEPLE	SHIRKER	SHOVING	SIBLING	SIMPAIS
SHEEPOS	SHIRRED	SHOWBIZ	SIBSHIP	SIMPKIN
SHEERER	SHISHAS	SHOWBOX	SIBYLIC	SIMPLES
SHEERLY	SHITAKE	SHOWDED	SICCING	SIMPLEX
SHEEVES	SHITTAH	SHOWERY	SICCITY	SIMULAR

SIMURGH	SKELPED	SKULLED	SLIPUPS	SMITTLE
SIMURGS	SKELPIT	SKUMMER	SLISHES	SMOCKED
SINDONS	SKENNED	SKUNKED	SLITHER	SMOKEHO
SINGLES	SKEPFUL	SKUTTLE	SLOGANS	SMOKERS
SINKAGE	SKEPPED	SKYBORN	SLOOMED	SMOKIES
SINKERS	SKEPSIS	SKYCAPS	SLOPPED	SMOKING
SINKIER	SKERRED	SKYCLAD	SLOSHED	SMOOCHY
SINKING	SKETCHY	SKYDIVE	SLOSHES	SMOOGES
SINLESS	SKETTED	SKYDOVE	SLOTHED	SMOOTED
SINNERS	SKEWEST	SKYFING	SLOUGHS	SMOOTHS
SINOPIA	SKEWING	SKYHOME	SLOUGHY	SMOOTHY
SINSYNE	SKIABLE	SKYHOOK	SLOVENS	SMORING
SINTERY	SKIBOBS	SKYIEST	SLOWISH	SMOYLED
SINUOSE	SKIDDED	SKYJACK	SLUBBED	SMOYLES
SINUOUS	SKIDDOO	SKYLABS	SLUDGES	SMRITIS
SINUSES	SKIDLID	SKYLARK	SLUGGED	SMUDGED
SIPPERS	SKIDOOS	SKYLINE	SLUICED	SMUDGES
SIPPETS	SKIDWAY	SKYPHOI	SLUICES	SMUGGED
SIRCARS	SKIEYER	SKYPHOS	SLUMBRY	SMUGGLE
SIRDARS	SKIFFED	SKYSAIL	SLUMGUM	SMUSHED
SIRKARS	SKIFFLE	SKYSURF	SLUMISM	SMUSHES
SIRLOIN	SKILFUL	SKYTING	SLUMMED	SMUTCHY
SIROCCO	SKILLET	SKYWALK	SLUMMER	SMUTTED
SIRRING	SKIMMED	SKYWARD	SLURBAN	SNABBLE
SISKINS	SKIMMIA	SKYWAYS	SLURRED	SNACKED
SISSIER	SKIMPED	SLACKED	SLUSHED	SNAFFLE
SISSIES	SKINFUL	SLACKEN	SLUSHES	SNAGGED
SISSOOS	SKINKED	SLACKLY	SLUTCHY	SNAKIER
SISTING	SKINKER	SLADANG	SMACKED	SNAKILY
SITFAST	SKINNED	SLAIRGS	SMACKER	SNAKING
SITHENS	SKINNER	SLAKERS	SMALLED	SNAKISH
SITTERS	SKIPPED	SLALOMS	SMALLER	SNAPTIN
SITTING	SKIPPET	SLANTLY	SMALTOS	SNARING
SITUATE	SKIRLED	SLATTED	SMARAGD	SNARLER
SITULAE	SKIRRED	SLAVERY	SMARTED	SNASHED
SIXAINE	SKIRTED	SLAVEYS	SMARTLY	SNASHES
SIXAINS	SKITTER	SLAVISH	SMASHED	SNATCHY
SIXFOLD	SKIVERS	SLEAVED	SMASHES	SNEAKED
SIXTHLY	SKIVIER	SLEAVES	SMEATHS	SNEAKER
SIXTIES	SKIWEAR	SLEAZES	SMECTIC	SNEBBED
SIZABLE	SKLENTS	SLEDDED	SMEDDUM	SNEBBES
SIZABLY	SKLIFFS	SLEDGED	SMEEKED	SNECKED
SIZEISM	SKOALED	SLEDGES	SMEETHS	SNEDDED
SIZINGS	SKOFFED	SLEEKED	SMEGMAS	SNEEZED
SIZISMS	SKOLION	SLEEKEN	SMELLED	SNEEZER
SIZISTS	SKOLLED	SLEEKLY	SMELTED	SNEEZES
SIZZLED	SKOLLIE	SLEEVED	SMERKED	SNELLED
SIZZLER	SKOOKUM	SLEEVES	SMEUSES	SNELLER
SIZZLES	SKOSHES	SLEIDED	SMICKER	SNIBBED
SKAILED	SKREEGH	SLEIGHS	SMICKET	SNIDELY
SKAITHS	SKREENS	SLEIGHT	SMICKLY	SNIFFED
SKALDIC	SKRIKED	SLICERS	SMIDGEN	SNIFFLE
SKANGER	SKRIKES	SLICING	SMIDGES	SNIFFLY
SKANKED	SKRIMPS	SLICKLY	SMIDGIN	SNIFTED
SKARTHS	SKRUMPS	SLIEVES	SMIGHTS	SNIFTER
SKATOLE	SKRYERS	SLIGHTS	SMIRKED	SNIPERS
SKATOLS	SKUDLER	SLIMILY	SMIRKER	SNIPING
SKEANES	SKUGGED	SLIMMED	SMIRRED	SNIPPED
SKELDER	SKULKED	SLIMPSY	SMITHED	SNIPPET
SKELLUM	SKULKER	SLIPOUT	SMITTED	SNITCHY

SNIVELS	SOFFITS	SOOTILY	SOWSSES	SPENCES
SNODDED	SOFTENS	SOOTING	SOWTHED	SPENDER
SNODDIT	SOFTEST	SOPHIES	SOYBEAN	SPENSES
SNOGGED	SOFTIES	SOPHISM	SOYUZES	SPEOSES
SNOKING	SOFTING	SOPHIST	SOZINES	SPERMIC
SNOOKED	SOFTISH	SOPPIER	SOZZLED	SPERRED
SNOOKER	SOGGIER	SOPPILY	SOZZLES	SPEWERS
SNOOZED	SOGGILY	SOPPING	SPACKLE	SPEWIER
SNOOZER	SOGGING	SORAGES	SPADING	SPEWING
SNOOZES	SOILIER	SORCERY	SPADOES	SPHERED
SNOOZLE	SOIREES	SORDINI	SPAEMAN	SPHERES
SNORKEL	SOKAIYA	SORDORS	SPAEMEN	SPICERS
SNORTER	SOKEMAN	SORGHOS	SPAGGED	SPICERY
SNOTTED	SOKEMEN	SORGHUM	SPALLED	SPICIER
SNOWCAP	SOLACES	SORITIC	SPALLER	SPICILY
SNOWCAT	SOLANIN	SOROBAN	SPALLES	SPICING
SNOWIER	SOLATES	SORORAL	SPAMMED	SPICULA
SNOWILY	SOLATIA	SOROSES	SPAMMER	SPICULE
SNOWISH	SOLDADO	SOROSIS	SPAMMIE	SPIDERY
SNOWKED	SOLERET	SORRELS	SPANGED	SPIEGEL
SNOWMAN	SOLFEGE	SORRIER	SPANGLE	SPIFFED
SNOWMEN	SOLIDLY	SORRILY	SPANGLY	SPIGHTS
SNUBBED	SOLIDUM	SORROWS	SPANKED	SPIGOTS
SNUBBER	SOLIONS	SORTALS	SPANKER	SPIKERS
SNUBBES	SOLIVES	SOSATIE	SPANNED	SPIKERY
SNUDGED	SOLLARS	SOSSING	SPARIDS	SPIKIER
SNUDGES	SOLOIST	SOTTING	SPARKED	SPIKILY
SNUFFED	SOLUBLY	SOTTISH	SPARKES	SPILITE
SNUFFER	SOLUNAR	SOUARIS	SPARKLE	SPILLED
SNUFFLE	SOLVATE	SOUBISE	SPARKLY	SPILLER
SNUFFLY	SOLVENT	SOUDANS	SPAROID	SPILTHS
SNUGGED	SOLVERS	SOUFFLE	SPARRER	SPINACH
SNUGGLE	SOMBRED	SOUGHED	SPARROW	SPINALS
SNUSHES	SOMBRER	SOUKING	SPARTHS	SPINDLY
SOAKAGE	SOMEHOW	SOUKOUS	SPASMED	SPINNEY
SOAKING	SOMEONE	SOULFUL	SPASTIC	SPINOFF
SOAPBOX	SOMEWAY	SOUNDED	SPATHES	SPINOSE
SOAPERS	SOMEWHY	SOUNDLY	SPATIAL	SPINOUT
SOAPIER	SOMITAL	SOUPFIN	SPATTED	SPIRAEA
SOAPIES	SONATAS	SOUPING	SPATULA	SPIRALS
SOAPILY	SONDAGE	SOUPLED	SPATZLE	SPIRICS
SOAPING	SONDERS	SOUPLES	SPAULDS	SPIRIER
SOARERS	SONGFUL	SOURISH	SPAVIET	SPIRITY
SOBBERS	SONGKOK	SOUROCK	SPAVINS	SPIROID
SOBERLY	SONGMEN	SOURSES	SPAWNED	SPITING
SOBOLES	SONHOOD	SOURSOP	SPAYADS	SPITTED
SOCAGES	SONLIKE	SOUSING	SPAZZED	SPITTEN
SOCCAGE	SONNIES	SOUSLIK	SPAZZES	SPITTLE
SOCIALS	SONOVOX	SOUTANE	SPECCED	SPITZES
SOCIATE	SONTAGS	SOUTARS	SPECIES	SPLAKES
SOCIETY	SOOGEED	SOUTIES	SPECIFY	SPLASHY
SOCKETS	SOOGEES	SOVKHOZ	SPECKED	SPLATCH
SOCKEYE	SOOJEYS	SOVRANS	SPECKLE	SPLAYED
SOCKING	SOOKING	SOWABLE	SPEEDED	SPLEENY
SOCKMAN	SOOMING	SOWBACK	SPEEDUP	SPLENII
SOCKMEN	SOONEST	SOWCARS	SPEELED	SPLENTS
SODDIES	SOOPING	SOWFFED	SPEISES	SPLICED
SODDING	SOOTHED	SOWFING	SPELLED	SPLICER
SODIUMS	SOOTHES	SOWNDED	SPELUNK	SPLICES
SOFABED	SOOTHLY	SOWSSED	SPENCER	SPLIFFS

SPLINTS	SPURTLE	STAMENS	STEMSON	STOOKIE
SPLODGY	SPURWAY	STAMMEL	STENCHY	STOOPED
SPLOOSH	SPYHOLE	STAMMER	STENDED	STOOPES
SPLOTCH	SQUABBY	STAMNOS	STENGAH	STOPGAP
SPLURGY	SQUACCO	STANDBY	STENOKY	STOPOFF
SPOKING	SQUADDY	STANDEN	STEPNEY	STOPPED
SPONDYL	SQUAILS	STANGED	STEPPED	STORMED
SPONGED	SQUALID	STANNEL	STEPPER	STOSSES
SPONGES	SQUALLS	STANNUM	STEPPES	STOTINS
SPONGIN	SQUALLY	STANYEL	STERNLY	STOTTED
SPONSAL	SQUALOR	STANZAS	STETTED	STOUNDS
SPONSON	SQUAMAE	STANZES	STEVENS	STOUTHS
SPONSOR	SQUARED	STANZOS	STEWBUM	STOUTLY
SPOOFED	SQUARER	STAPPED	STEWIER	STOWNDS
SPOOFER	SQUARES	STARCHY	STEWPAN	STRAFED
SPOOKED	SQUARKS	STARETZ	STEWPOT	STRAFFS
SPOOMED	SQUASHY	STARKLY	STEYEST	STRAIKS
SPOONEY	SQUATLY	STARLIT	STIBBLE	STRAMPS
SPOORED	SQUATTY	STARTLY	STIBIAL	STRANDS
SPOORER	SQUAWKS	STARTSY	STIBINE	STRAPPY
SPOROID	SQUAWKY	STARVER	STIBIUM	STRATAL
SPORRAN	SQUEAKS	STARVES	STICHIC	STRATHS
SPOSHES	SQUEAKY	STASHED	STICHOI	STRATUM
SPOTLIT	SQUEEZE	STASHES	STICHOS	STRATUS
SPOTTED	SQUEEZY	STASIMA	STICKIT	STRAYED
SPOUSAL	SQUELCH	STATANT	STICKUM	STRAYER
SPRANGS	SQUIDGE	STATICS	STIFFED	STRAYVE
SPRAWLS	SQUIDGY	STATION	STIFFLY	STREAKY
SPRAWLY	SQUIFFY	STATISM	STIFLED	STREEKS
SPRAYED	SQUILLA	STATIST	STIGMAL	STRETCH
SPRAYEY	SQUILLS	STATIVE	STIGMAS	STREWTH
SPREAGH	SQUINCH	STATORS	STIGMES	STRIATA
SPREAZE	SQUINNY	STATUAS	STILETS	STRICKS
SPREDDS	SQUINTS	STATUED	STILLED	STRIDOR
SPREEZE	SQUINTY	STATUES	STIMULI	STRIFTS
SPRIGGY	SQUIRED	STATUSY	STIRRAH	STRIGIL
SPRIGHT	SQUIRMS	STAVING	STIRRER	STRIKES
SPRINGS	SQUIRMY	STAYNED	STIRRES	STRINGS
SPRINTS	SQUIRRS	STAYNES	STISHIE	STRIPER
SPRUCED	SQUIRTS	STEALTH	STIVING	STRIVER
SPRUCER	SQUISHY	STEAMED	STOBBED	STROBIC
SPRYEST	SQUITCH	STEAMIE	STODGED	STROKED
SPUDDED	SQUOOSH	STEDDED	STODGER	STROKER
SPUEING	SRADDHA	STEDDES	STODGES	STROLLS
SPULYED	STACHYS	STEEKED	STOGEYS	STROMBS
SPULYIE	STACKED	STEEKIT	STOITER	STRONDS
SPULZIE	STACKUP	STEEMED	STOKING	STROPPY
SPUMONE	STACTES	STEENED	STOKVEL	STROUDS
SPUMONI	STADDAS	STEEPLE	STOLLEN	STROUTS
SPUMOUS	STADDLE	STEEPLY	STOLONS	STROWER
SPUNGES	STADIAL	STEEPUP	STOMACH	STRUMAS
SPUNKED	STADIAS	STEEVED	STOMACK	STRUNTS
SPURGES	STAFFED	STEEVER	STOMATA	STUBBED
SPURNED	STAGGIE	STELENE	STOMATE	STUBBIE
SPURNES	STAGILY	STELLED	STOMIUM	STUBBLE
SPURRED	STAIDLY	STEMBOK	STOMPED	STUBBLY
SPURRER	STAITHS	STEMMAS	STONISH	STUCCOS
SPURREY	STALAGS	STEMMED	STONKED	STUDDED
SPURTED	STALELY	STEMMER	STOOGED	STUDDEN
SPURTER	STALLED	STEMMES	STOOGES	STUDDLE

STUDIOS	SUBLOTS	SUETIER	SUNLESS	SWAGMEN
STUMBLY	SUBMENU	SUFFARI	SUNNAHS	SWAMIES
STUMMED	SUBMISS	SUFFECT	SUNNIES	SWAMPED
STUMMEL	SUBMITS	SUFFERS	SUNNILY	SWAMPER
STUMPED	SUBNETS	SUFFETE	SUNNING	SWANKED
STUPEFY	SUBORNS	SUFFICE	SUNRAYS	SWANKEY
STUPENT	SUBOVAL	SUFFUSE	SUNSETS	SWANKIE
STUPIDS	SUBPENA	SUGGEST	SUNTANS	SWANNED
STURMER	SUBPLOT	SUGGING	SUNWISE	SWANNIE
STUTTER	SUBRING	SUICIDE	SUPAWNS	SWANPAN
STYLERS	SUBRULE	SUIPLAP	SUPPAWN	SWAPPED
STYLETS	SUBSALE	SUITERS	SUPPERS	SWARFED
STYLIER	SUBSECT	SUITING	SUPPLED	SWARMED
STYLING	SUBSETS	SUKKAHS	SUPPLES	SWARTHS
STYLISE	SUBSIDE	SUKKOTH	SUPPORT	SWARTHY
STYLIST	SUBSIDY	SULDANS	SUPPOSE	SWARVES
STYLOID	SUBSIST	SULFIDE	SUPREMO	SWASHED
STYLOPS	SUBSOIL	SULFIDS	SURANCE	SWASHES
STYMIED	SUBSONG	SULFONE	SURBEDS	SWATHED
STYMIES	SUBSUME	SULFURS	SURCULI	SWATHES
STYMING	SUBTASK	SULFURY	SURDITY	SWAYFUL
STYPSIS	SUBTEND	SULKERS	SURFACE	SWAYING
STYPTIC	SUBTEST	SULKIER	SURFERS	SWAYLED
STYTING	SUBTEXT	SULKIES	SURFING	SWAZZLE
SUASIVE	SUBTONE	SULKILY	SURFMAN	SWEALED
SUAVELY	SUBTYPE	SULLIES	SURGEON	SWEATED
SUAVEST	SUBUNIT	SULPHAS	SURGERS	SWEATER
SUAVITY	SUBURBS	SULTANA	SURGERY	SWEDGER
SUBACID	SUBVENE	SULTANS	SURIMIS	SWEELED
SUBADAR	SUBVERT	SUMACHS	SURLILY	SWEENEY
SUBALAR	SUBWAYS	SUMMAND	SURLOIN	SWEERER
SUBAQUA	SUBZONE	SUMMARY	SURPASS	SWEETED
SUBATOM	SUCCAHS	SUMMATS	SURPLUS	SWEETEN
SUBBASE	SUCCEED	SUMMERS	SURREAL	SWEETER
SUBBASS	SUCCESS	SUMMERY	SURREYS	SWEETIE
SUBCELL	SUCCISE	SUMMING	SURTOUT	SWEETLY
SUBCLAN	SUCCORS	SUMPITS	SURVEIL	SWEIRED
SUBCODE	SUCCORY	SUNBACK	SURVEYS	SWELLED
SUBCULT	SUCCOSE	SUNBAKE	SURVIEW	SWELLER
SUBDEBS	SUCCOTH	SUNBATH	SURVIVE	SWELTRY
SUBDEWS	SUCCOUR	SUNBEAM	SUSLIKS	SWERFED
SUBDUAL	SUCCOUS	SUNBEDS	SUSPECT	SWERVED
SUBDUCE	SUCCUBA	SUNBIRD	SUSPENS	SWERVER
SUBDUCT	SUCCUBI	SUNBOWS	SUSSING	SWERVES
SUBDUED	SUCCUMB	SUNBURN	SUTLERY	SWEVENS
SUBDUER	SUCCUSS	SUNDAES	SUTTEES	SWEYING
SUBDUES	SUCKENS	SUNDEWS	SUTTLED	SWIDDEN
SUBERIC	SUCKERS	SUNDOGS	SUTTLES	SWIFTED
SUBFEUS	SUCKETS	SUNDOWN	SUTURAL	SWIFTER
SUBFUSC	SUCKIER	SUNDRAS	SUTURED	SWIFTIE
SUBFUSK	SUCKING	SUNDRIS	SUTURES	SWIFTLY
SUBGUMS	SUCKLES	SUNFAST	SWABBED	SWIGGED
SUBHEAD	SUCTION	SUNFISH	SWABBER	SWILERS
SUBIDEA	SUDARIA	SUNGARS	SWABBIE	SWILLED
SUBITEM	SUDATES	SUNGLOW	SWACKED	SWIMMER
SUBJECT	SUDDENS	SUNHATS	SWAGERS	SWINERY
SUBJOIN	SUDDERS	SUNKETS	SWAGGED	SWINGBY
SUBLATE	SUDORAL	SUNKIES	SWAGGIE	SWINISH
SUBLIME	SUDSERS	SUNLAMP	SWAGING	SWINKED
SUBLINE	SUDSING	SUNLAND	SWAGMAN	SWINNEY

SWIPERS	SYNDING	TAGUANS	TANGLED	TASSETS
SWIPLES	SYNERGY	TAHINIS	TANGOED	TASTILY
SWIPPLE	SYNESES	TAIAHAS	TANGUNS	TATAMIS
SWISSES	SYNESIS	TAILARD	TANIWHA	TATOUAY
SWITCHY	SYNFUEL	TAILFIN	TANKAGE	TATSOIS
SWITHLY	SYNGAMY	TAILFLY	TANKARD	TATTERY
SWITSES	SYNODAL	TAILLIE	TANKFUL	TATTILY
SWIVELS	SYNODIC	TAILYES	TANKIAS	TATTING
SWIVETS	SYNONYM	TAILZIE	TANKINI	TATTLED
SWIVING	SYNOVIA	TAINTED	TANLING	TATTLES
SWIZZED	SYNROCS	TAIVERT	TANNAGE	TATTOOS
SWIZZES	SYNTANS	TAKABLE	TANNATE	TATTOWS
SWIZZLE	SYNTENY	TAKAHES	TANNERS	TAUHINU
SWOBBED	SYNTHON	TAKIEST	TANNING	TAUIWIS
SWOBBER	SYNTONY	TAKKIES	TANNINS	TAUNTER
SWOFFER	SYNURAE	TALARIA	TANNISH	TAUPATA
SWOLLEN	SYPHERS	TALAUNT	TANNOYS	TAUPIES
SWOONER	SYPHONS	TALAYOT	TANTIVY	TAUTAUG
SWOOPER	SYRINGE	TALBOTS	TANTONY	TAUTOGS
SWOPPED	SYRPHID	TALCUMS	TANTRIC	TAVERNA
SWOPPER	SYRUPED	TALEFUL	TANTRUM	TAWHAIS
SWOTTED	SYSTEMS	TALIPAT	TANUKIS	TAWHIRI
SWOTTER	SYSTYLE	TALIPOT	TANYARD	TAWNEYS
SWOUNDS	SYZYGAL	TALKBOX	TAONGAS	TAWNILY
SWOUNES	TABANID	TALKING	TAPALOS	TAWPIES
SWOWNDS	TABBIED	TALLBOY	TAPETAL	TAWTIER
SWOWNES	TABBING	TALLENT	TAPETUM	TAWTING
SWOZZLE	TABETIC	TALLIED	TAPHOLE	TAXABLE
SYBOTIC	TABINET	TALLISH	TAPIOCA	TAXABLY
SYCONIA	TABLING	TALLITH	TAPISTS	TAXEMES
SYCOSES	TABLOID	TALLITS	TAPPERS	TAXEMIC
SYCOSIS	TABOOED	TALLOLS	TAPPETS	TAXICAB
SYENITE	TABORIN	TALLOTS	TAPPICE	TAXIING
SYLLABI	TABULAR	TALLOWS	TAPPING	TAXIMAN
SYLPHIC	TABULIS	TALMUDS	TAPROOM	TAXIMEN
SYLPHID	TACETED	TALONED	TAPROOT	TAXINGS
SYLVANS	TACHYON	TALOOKA	TAPSTRY	TAXITES
SYLVIAS	TACKETY	TALUKAS	TARAIRE	TAXITIC
SYLVINE	TACKIER	TALWEGS	TARAMEA	TAXIWAY
SYLVINS	TACKIFY	TAMABLE	TARBOYS	TAXLESS
SYLVITE	TACKILY	TAMARAO	TARBUSH	TAXPAID
SYMBION	TACKING	TAMARAU	TARDIED	TAXYING
SYMBIOT	TACKLER	TAMASHA	TARDILY	TEACAKE
SYMBOLE	TACKLES	TAMBACS	TARDIVE	TEACART
SYMBOLS	TACNODE	TAMBAKS	TARDYON	TEALIKE
SYMPTOM	TACTFUL	TAMBALA	TARGETS	TEAPOYS
SYNAGOG	TACTION	TAMBERS	TARIFFS	TEARIER
SYNANON	TACTISM	TAMBOUR	TARNISH	TEAROOM
SYNAPSE	TACTUAL	TAMBURA	TARRIER	TEASHOP
SYNAPTE	TADDIES	TAMBURS	TARRING	TEATIME
SYNAXES	TAENIAE	TAMMIED	TARROCK	TEAWARE
SYNAXIS	TAFFETA	TAMPALA	TARROWS	TEAZLED
SYNCARP	TAFFETY	TAMPING	TARSEAL	TECHIES
SYNCHED	TAFFIAS	TANADAR	TARTANE	TECHNIC
SYNCHRO	TAFFIES	TANAGER	TARTARE	TECKELS
SYNCING	TAGGANT	TANAGRA	TARTARS	TECTITE
SYNCOMS	TAGGEES	TANBARK	TARTUFE	TECTRIX
SYNCOPE	TAGGIER	TANDEMS	TARZANS	TECTUMS
SYNDETS	TAGGING	TANGELO	TASKBAR	TEDDING
SYNDICS	TAGMATA	TANGENT	TASSELS	TEDESCA

TEDIEST	TERCELS	THEMING	THRETTY	TIFFINS
TEEMFUL	TERCETS	THENAGE	THRIFTS	TIGERLY
TEENAGE	TEREBIC	THEOLOG	THRIFTY	TIGGING
TEENDED	TERGITE	THEORBO	THRILLS	TIGHTEN
TEENFUL	TERMERS	THEOREM	THRILLY	TIGHTER
TEENIER	TERNARY	THERAPY	THRIVED	TIGHTLY
TEENING	TERRANE	THEREBY	THRIVEN	TIGRESS
TEENTSY	TERRETS	THEREOF	THRIVER	TIGRISH
TEEPEES	TERRIFY	THEREON	THRIVES	TIGROID
TEETHED	TERTIAL	THERETO	THROATS	TIKANGA
TEETHER	TERTIUM	THERIAC	THROATY	TIKIING
TEFLONS	TERTIUS	THERMAL	THROMBI	TILAPIA
TEGULAE	TESTACY	THERMEL	THRONGS	TILBURY
TEGUMEN	TESTATE	THERMES	THROUGH	TILLAGE
TEKKIES	TESTIER	THERMIC	THROWER	TILLIER
TEKTITE	TESTIFY	THERMIT	THROWES	TIMARAU
TELECOM	TESTOON	THEROID	THRUMMY	TIMBALS
TELEDUS	TETANAL	THETHER	THRUPUT	TIMBERY
TELEFAX	TETCHED	THEURGY	THRUSTS	TIMBRAL
TELEOST	TETHERS	THEWIER	THRUTCH	TIMBREL
TELERGY	TETOTUM	THIAMIN	THRUWAY	TIMEOUS
TELESES	TETRACT	THIAZIN	THRYMSA	TIMEOUT
TELESMS	TETRYLS	THIAZOL	THUDDED	TIMIDER
TELETEX	TEUCHAT	THIBETS	THUGGEE	TIMIDLY
TELEXED	TEUCHER	THIBLES	THUGGOS	TIMISTS
TELEXES	TEUGHER	THICKED	THULITE	TIMOLOL
TELFORD	TEUGHLY	THICKER	THULIUM	TIMOTHY
TELLENS	TEXASES	THICKET	THUMBED	TIMPANA
TELLIES	TEXTERS	THICKIE	THUMPED	TINAJAS
TELOMIC	TEXTILE	THICKLY	THUMPER	TINCTED
TELPHER	TEXTUAL	THICKOS	THUNDER	TINDALS
TELSONS	TEXTURE	THIEVED	THUNKED	TINDERS
TEMBLOR	THACKED	THIEVES	THURIFY	TINDERY
TEMPEHS	THALAMI	THIGGER	THWACKS	TINFOIL
TEMPERA	THALIAN	THIGGIT	THWAITE	TINFULS
TEMPERS	THALLIC	THILLER	THWARTS	TINGING
TEMPEST	THALLUS	THIMBLE	THYLOSE	TINHORN
TEMPLED	THALWEG	THINNED	THYMINE	TINKING
TEMPLET	THANAGE	THINNER	THYMOLS	TINKLED
TEMPORE	THANAHS	THIOLIC	THYROID	TINKLER
TEMPTED	THANGKA	THIONIC	THYRSUS	TINLIKE
TEMPTER	THANKED	THIONIN	THYSELF	TINNIER
TEMPURA	THANKEE	THIONYL	TICCING	TINNILY
TENABLE	THANKER	THIRDED	TICKETS	TINNING
TENABLY	THANNAH	THIRDLY	TICKEYS	TINPOTS
TENANCY	THATCHT	THIRLED	TICKING	TINSEYS
TENDENZ	THATCHY	THISTLY	TICKLED	TINTACK
TENFOLD	THAWIER	THITHER	TICTOCS	TINTING
TENSEST	THAWING	THIVELS	TIDALLY	TINTYPE
TENSITY	THEAVES	THOLING	TIDBITS	TINWORK
TENTAGE	THECATE	THONGED	TIDDLED	TIPCART
TENTFUL	THEEING	THORITE	TIDDLER	TIPCATS
TENTHLY	THEEKED	THORIUM	TIDDLES	TIPOFFS
TENTIGO	THEELIN	THORONS	TIDEWAY	TIPPERS
TENUITY	THEELOL	THOTHER	TIDINGS	TIPPETS
TENUOUS	THEINES	THOUGHT	TIEBACK	TIPPIER
TENZONS	THEISMS	THRALLS	TIERCET	TIPPING
TEOPANS	THEISTS	THRANGS	TIETACK	TIPPLED
TEPIDLY	THELVES	THREAVE	TIFFANY	TIPSIFY
TERAOHM	THEMATA	THRENES	TIFFING	TIPSILY

TIPTOED	TOGGLED	TONSILS	TOTANUS	TRACEUR
TIPTOPS	TOGGLER	TONSORS	TOTARAS	TRACHEA
TIPULAS	TOHEROA	TOOARTS	TOTEMIC	TRACKED
TIPUNAS	TOILFUL	TOOLBAG	TOTIENT	TRACTOR
TIREDLY	TOILING	TOOLBAR	TOTTERY	TRACTUS
TIRITIS	TOISONS	TOOLBOX	TOTTIER	TRAFFIC
TIRLING	TOITING	TOOLKIT	TOTTING	TRAIKED
TIRRING	TOITOIS	TOOLMAN	TOUCHED	TRAIKIT
TIRRITS	TOKAMAK	TOOSHIE	TOUCHES	TRAITOR
TISICKS	TOKENED	TOOTERS	TOUCHUP	TRAJECT
TISSUAL	TOKOMAK	TOOTHED	TOUGHEN	TRAMCAR
TISSUEY	TOLARJI	TOOTING	TOUGHER	TRAMELL
TITANIA	TOLIDIN	TOOTLED	TOUGHIE	TRAMMED
TITANIC	TOLLAGE	TOOTSED	TOUGHLY	TRAMMEL
TITBITS	TOLLBAR	TOOTSES	TOUKING	TRAMPED
TITCHES	TOLLERS	TOOTSIE	TOUPEES	TRAMPER
TITLARK	TOLLING	TOPARCH	TOURACO	TRAMPET
TITLIST	TOLLMAN	TOPAZES	TOURISM	TRAMWAY
TITMICE	TOLLMEN	TOPCOAT	TOURIST	TRANECT
TITOKIS	TOLSELS	TOPIARY	TOURNEY	TRANKUM
TITRANT	TOLUATE	TOPKICK	TOUSTIE	TRANTED
TITTIES	TOLUENE	TOPKNOT	TOUTIER	TRANTER
TITTING	TOLUIDS	TOPLESS	TOUTING	TRAPEZE
TITTISH	TOLUOLE	TOPMAST	TOUZIER	TRAPPED
TITTLED	TOLUOLS	TOPMOST	TOUZING	TRAPPER
TITTLES	TOLUYLS	TOPONYM	TOUZLED	TRASHER
TITTUPS	TOLZEYS	TOPPING	TOUZLES	TRAVAIL
TITTUPY	TOMBACK	TOPPLED	TOWARDS	TRAWLED
TITULAR	TOMBAKS	TOPSPIN	TOWAWAY	TRAWLER
TITULED	TOMBING	TOQUETS	TOWBARS	TRAWLEY
TITULUS	TOMBOCS	TORANAS	TOWBOAT	TRAYBIT
TIZZIES	TOMBOLA	TORCHED	TOWELED	TRAYFUL
TOADISH	TOMBOLO	TORCHER	TOWERED	TRAYNES
TOASTED	TOMBOYS	TORCHON	TOWHEAD	TREACLE
TOAZING	TOMCATS	TORDION	TOWHEES	TREACLY
TOBACCO	TOMENTA	TORGOCH	TOWIEST	TREAGUE
TOCCATA	TOMFOOL	TORMENT	TOWKAYS	TREBLED
TOCCATE	TOMMIED	TORMINA	TOWLINE	TRECKED
TOCKIER	TOMMIES	TORNADE	TOWMOND	TREDDLE
TOCKING	TOMMING	TORPEFY	TOWMONS	TREEWAX
TOCKLEY	TOMPION	TORPORS	TOWMONT	TREHALA
TODDIES	TOMPONS	TORQUED	TOWNEES	TREILLE
TODDING	TOMTITS	TORQUER	TOWNISH	TREKKED
TODDLED	TONALLY	TORREFY	TOWNLET	TREKKER
TODDLER	TONDINI	TORRENT	TOWPATH	TREMBLE
TODDLES	TONDINO	TORRIFY	TOWROPE	TREMBLY
TOEBIES	TONEARM	TORSIVE	TOWSACK	TREMOLO
TOECLIP	TONETTE	TORTONI	TOWZIER	TRENDED
TOEHOLD	TONGERS	TORTRIX	TOWZING	TRENTAL
TOEIEST	TONGING	TORULIN	TOXEMIA	TREPANG
TOELIKE	TONGMAN	TORULUS	TOXEMIC	TRESSES
TOESHOE	TONGMEN	TOSHACH	TOXICAL	TREYBIT
TOETOES	TONGUED	TOSSERS	TOXINES	TRIAGED
TOFFEES	TONGUES	TOSSPOT	TOXOIDS	TRIARCH
TOFFIES	TONKING	TOSSUPS	TOYINGS	TRIATIC
TOFFISH	TONLETS	TOSTADA	TOYLIKE	TRIAXON
TOFUTTI	TONNAGS	TOSTADO	TOYLSOM	TRIAZIN
TOGATED	TONNEAU	TOTABLE	TOYSHOP	TRIBADY
TOGGERY	TONNELL	TOTALED	TOYTOWN	TRIBALS
TOGGING	TONNISH	TOTALLY	TRACERY	TRIBBLE

TRIBUTE	TRIVETS	TRUSTOR	TUMOURS	TUSSLED
TRICARS	TRIVIUM	TRYMATA	TUMPING	TUSSLES
TRICEPS	TRIZONE	TRYOUTS	TUMULTS	TUSSOCK
TRICING	TROAKED	TRYPSIN	TUMULUS	TUSSORS
TRICKED	TROCHAL	TRYPTIC	TUNABLY	TUSSUCK
TRICKER	TROCHAR	TRYSAIL	TUNDISH	TUSSURS
TRICKIE	TROCHEE	TRYSTED	TUNDUNS	TUTANIA
TRICKLY	TROCHIL	TRYSTER	TUNEFUL	TUTELAR
TRICKSY	TROCHUS	TRYSTES	TUNEUPS	TUTENAG
TRICLAD	TROCKED	TSADDIK	TUNICAE	TUTORED
TRICORN	TROCKEN	TSADDIQ	TUNICIN	TUTOYED
TRICOTS	TRODDEN	TSAMBAS	TUNIEST	TUTOYER
TRIDARN	TROELIE	TSANTSA	TUNINGS	TUTRESS
TRIDENT	TROFFER	TSARISM	TUNNAGE	TUTSANS
TRIDUUM	TROGGED	TSATSKE	TUNNELS	TUTSING
TRIFFER	TROGONS	TSKTSKS	TUNNIES	TUTTIES
TRIFFIC	TROIKAS	TSOORIS	TUNNING	TUTTING
TRIFFID	TROILUS	TSOTSIS	TUPELOS	TUTWORK
TRIFOLD	TROKING	TUATARA	TUPPING	TUXEDOS
TRIFOLY	TROLAND	TUATERA	TUPUNAS	TUYERES
TRIFORM	TROLLED	TUBAIST	TURACOU	TWADDLE
TRIGAMY	TROLLER	TUBBERS	TURBAND	TWADDLY
TRIGGED	TROLLEY	TUBBIER	TURBANS	TWAFALD
TRIGGER	TROMMEL	TUBBING	TURBANT	TWANGED
TRIGLOT	TROMPED	TUBBISH	TURBARY	TWANGER
TRIGRAM	TROOLIE	TUBEFUL	TURBETH	TWANGLE
TRILITH	TROPHIC	TUBFAST	TURBITH	TWANKAY
TRILLED	TROPICS	TUBFISH	TURBOND	TWASOME
TRILLER	TROPINS	TUBFULS	TURBOTS	TWATTLE
TRILOBE	TROTHED	TUBIFEX	TURDION	TWEAKED
TRILOGY	TROTTED	TUBISTS	TURDOID	TWEAKER
TRIMMER	TROTTER	TUBLIKE	TURFING	TWEENER
TRIMTAB	TROTYLS	TUBULAR	TURFMAN	TWEENIE
TRINARY	TROUGHS	TUBULES	TURFMEN	TWEERED
TRINING	TROULED	TUCHUNS	TURFSKI	TWEETED
TRINITY	TROUPED	TUCKERS	TURGORS	TWEETER
TRINKUM	TROUPER	TUCKETS	TURISTA	TWEEZED
TRIONYM	TROVERS	TUCKING	TURKEYS	TWEEZER
TRIOXID	TROWTHS	TUFFETS	TURKOIS	TWEEZES
TRIPART	TRUANCY	TUFTERS	TURMOIL	TWELFTH
TRIPERY	TRUANTS	TUFTILY	TURNDUN	TWELVES
TRIPIER	TRUCAGE	TUFTING	TURNERY	TWIBILL
TRIPLED	TRUCING	TUGBOAT	TURNING	TWIBILS
TRIPLET	TRUCKED	TUGGERS	TURNKEY	TWICERS
TRIPLEX	TRUCKER	TUGGING	TURNOFF	TWIDDLE
TRIPODY	TRUCKIE	TUGHRAS	TURNONS	TWIDDLY
TRIPOLI	TRUCKLE	TUGHRIK	TURPETH	TWIFOLD
TRIPPED	TRUDGED	TUGRIKS	TURTLED	TWIGGED
TRIPPER	TRUDGER	TUILLES	TURTLER	TWIGGEN
TRIPPET	TRUDGES	TUILYIE	TURTLES	TWIGGER
TRIPTAN	TRUEING	TUITION	TUSCHES	TWIGHTS
TRISECT	TRUEMAN	TUKTOOS	TUSHERY	TWIGLOO
TRISMIC	TRUEMEN	TULWARS	TUSHKER	TWILLED
TRISOMY	TRUMEAU	TUMBLED	TUSKARS	TWILTED
TRISULS	TRUMPED	TUMBRIL	TUSKERS	TWINGED
TRITIDE	TRUMPET	TUMESCE	TUSKING	TWINIER
TRITIUM	TRUNCAL	TUMIDLY	TUSSAHS	TWINING
TRITOMA	TRUNKED	TUMMIES	TUSSARS	TWINJET
TRITONE	TRUNNEL	TUMMLER	TUSSEHS	TWINKED
TRIUMPH	TRUSTEE	TUMORAL	TUSSIVE	TWINKIE

TWINKLE	UBEROUS	UNBLOCK	UNCURLS	UNHANDY
TWINKLY	UDDERED	UNBLOWN	UNCURSE	UNHAPPY
TWINNED	UFOLOGY	UNBOLTS	UNDEIFY	UNHARDY
TWIRLED	UILLEAN	UNBONES	UNDERNS	UNHASPS
TWIRLER	UJAMAAS	UNBORNE	UNDOCKS	UNHASTY
TWISCAR	UKELELE	UNBOSOM	UNDOING	UNHEADS
TWISTOR	UKULELE	UNBOUND	UNDRAWN	UNHEARD
TWITCHY	ULEXITE	UNBOWED	UNDRIED	UNHEEDY
TWITTED	ULIKONS	UNBOXED	UNDRUNK	UNHELED
TWITTEN	ULLAGED	UNBOXES	UNDULAR	UNHELES
TWITTER	ULLINGS	UNBRACE	UNDYING	UNHELMS
TWIZZLE	ULNARIA	UNBRAID	UNEARED	UNHINGE
TWOCCER	ULPANIM	UNBRAKE	UNEASES	UNHIRED
TWOCKER	ULTIMAS	UNBROKE	UNEATEN	UNHITCH
TWOFERS	ULULANT	UNBUILD	UNEDGED	UNHIVED
TWOFOLD	ULULATE	UNBULKY	UNENDED	UNHIVES
TWONESS	UMBELED	UNBURNT	UNEQUAL	UNHOARD
TWOONIE	UMBONAL	UNCAGED	UNFACTS	UNHOODS
TWOSOME	UMBONES	UNCAKED	UNFADED	UNHOOKS
TWYERES	UMBONIC	UNCAKES	UNFAIRS	UNHOOPS
TWYFOLD	UMBRAGE	UNCANNY	UNFAITH	UNHOPED
TYCOONS	UMBRERE	UNCARTS	UNFAKED	UNHORSE
TYLOPOD	UMBRILS	UNCASED	UNFAMED	UNHOUSE
TYLOTES	UMBROSE	UNCEDED	UNFANCY	UNHUMAN
TYMBALS	UMFAZIS	UNCHAIN	UNFAZED	UNHUSKS
TYMPANA	UMIACKS	UNCHAIR	UNFENCE	UNIBODY
TYMPANI	UMLUNGU	UNCHARM	UNFEUED	UNIBROW
TYMPANO	UMPTEEN	UNCHECK	UNFIRED	UNICITY
TYMPANS	UMWELTS	UNCHILD	UNFITLY	UNICORN
TYMPANY	UMWHILE	UNCHOKE	UNFIXED	UNIFACE
TYPABLE	UNACTED	UNCIALS	UNFIXES	UNIFIED
TYPEBAR	UNADDED	UNCINAL	UNFLESH	UNIFIER
TYPESET	UNADEPT	UNCINUS	UNFLUSH	UNIFIES
TYPHOON	UNADULT	UNCITED	UNFOLDS	UNIFORM
TYPHOSE	UNAGING	UNCIVIL	UNFOOLS	UNIQUER
TYPHOUS	UNAIDED	UNCLAMP	UNFORMS	UNIQUES
TYPICAL	UNAIMED	UNCLASP	UNFOUND	UNISIZE
TYPIEST	UNAKING	UNCLEAN	UNFREED	UNISONS
TYPINGS	UNAKITE	UNCLEFT	UNFREES	UNITAGE
TYPISTS	UNALIKE	UNCLEWS	UNFROCK	UNITARY
TYPTOED	UNALIST	UNCLING	UNFROZE	UNITING
TYRANNY	UNAPTLY	UNCLIPT	UNFUMED	UNITION
TYRANTS	UNASKED	UNCLOAK	UNFUNNY	UNITIVE
TYRONES	UNAWAKE	UNCLOGS	UNFUSED	UNITIZE
TYRONIC	UNAWARE	UNCLOUD	UNFUSSY	UNJADED
TYSTIES	UNBAKED	UNCOCKS	UNGILDS	UNJOINT
TYTHING	UNBALED	UNCODED	UNGIRDS	UNKEMPT
TZADDIK	UNBARED	UNCOMIC	UNGLOVE	UNKINGS
TZADDIQ	UNBARKS	UNCORDS	UNGLUES	UNKINKS
TZARDOM	UNBATED	UNCORKS	UNGODLY	UNKNITS
TZARINA	UNBEGET	UNCOUTH	UNGOWNS	UNKNOTS
TZARISM	UNBEGOT	UNCOVER	UNGROWN	UNKNOWN
TZARIST	UNBEGUN	UNCOWLS	UNGUARD	UNLADED
TZETSES	UNBEING	UNCRAZY	UNGUENT	UNLADEN
TZETZES	UNBENDS	UNCROSS	UNGULAE	UNLAWED
TZIGANY	UNBINDS	UNCROWN	UNGULAR	UNLEARN
TZIMMES	UNBITTS	UNCTION	UNGYVED	UNLEVEL
TZITZIS	UNBLENT	UNCUFFS	UNGYVES	UNLIKED
TZITZIT	UNBLESS	UNCURBS	UNHABLE	UNLINED
UAKARIS	UNBLIND	UNCURED	UNHAIRS	UNLINES

UNLINKS	UNRESTS	UNSTOCK	UNWOMAN	UPHOARD
UNLIVED	UNRIMED	UNSTOWS	UNWOOED	UPHOIST
UNLOBED	UNRIPER	UNSTUFT	UNWORKS	UPHOORD
UNLOCKS	UNRIVEN	UNSTUNG	UNWORTH	UPHROES
UNLOOSE	UNROLLS	UNSUNNY	UNWOUND	UPKEEPS
UNLORDS	UNROPES	UNSURED	UNWOVEN	UPLANDS
UNLOVED	UNROUGH	UNSURER	UNWRAPS	UPLEADS
UNLOVES	UNROUND	UNSWEET	UNWRITE	UPLEANS
UNLUCKY	UNROVEN	UNSWEPT	UNWROTE	UPLEANT
UNMACHO	UNROYAL	UNSWORE	UNWRUNG	UPLEAPT
UNMAKER	UNRUFFE	UNSWORN	UNYOKED	UPLIFTS
UNMAKES	UNRULED	UNTAKEN	UNYOKES	UPLIGHT
UNMANLY	UNRULES	UNTAXED	UNYOUNG	UPLOADS
UNMARRY	UNSAINT	UNTAXES	UNZONED	UPLYING
UNMASKS	UNSAVED	UNTEACH	UPBEARS	UPMAKER
UNMEANT	UNSAWED	UNTENTS	UPBEATS	UPPILED
UNMERRY	UNSCARY	UNTENTY	UPBINDS	UPPROPS
UNMETED	UNSCREW	UNTHAWS	UPBLOWN	UPREACH
UNMEWED	UNSEAMS	UNTHINK	UPBOILS	UPRESTS
UNMIXED	UNSEELS	UNTOMBS	UPBORNE	UPRIGHT
UNMIXES	UNSEWED	UNTRACK	UPBOUND	UPRIVER
UNMOLDS	UNSEXED	UNTRIMS	UPBRAID	UPROARS
UNMORAL	UNSHAPE	UNTRULY	UPBRAYS	UPROLLS
UNMOULD	UNSHARP	UNTRUST	UPBROKE	UPSHIFT
UNMOUNT	UNSHELL	UNTRUTH	UPBUILT	UPSHOOT
UNMOVED	UNSHENT	UNTUNED	UPBURST	UPSHOTS
UNNEATH	UNSHEWN	UNTUNES	UPCHEER	UPSIDES
UNNERVE	UNSHIFT	UNTURFS	UPCHUCK	UPSIZED
UNNESTS	UNSHIPS	UNTURNS	UPCOAST	UPSIZES
UNNOBLE	UNSHOED	UNTWINE	UPCOMES	UPSKILL
UNNOISY	UNSHOES	UNTWIST	UPCOURT	UPSPOKE
UNOFTEN	UNSHOOT	UNTYING	UPCURLS	UPSTAGE
UNOILED	UNSHORN	UNURGED	UPCURVE	UPSTAIR
UNPACKS	UNSHOUT	UNUSUAL	UPDARTS	UPSTATE
UNPAGED	UNSHOWN	UNVAILS	UPDATED	UPSTAYS
UNPAINT	UNSHOWY	UNVEXED	UPDATES	UPSTEPS
UNPANEL	UNSHUTS	UNVISOR	UPDIVED	UPSTOOD
UNPAPER	UNSINEW	UNVITAL	UPDIVES	UPSURGE
UNPAVED	UNSIZED	UNVOCAL	UPDRAFT	UPSWAYS
UNPICKS	UNSLICK	UNVOICE	UPDRAGS	UPSWEEP
UNPILED	UNSLING	UNWAGED	UPDRAWN	UPSWEPT
UNPINKT	UNSLUNG	UNWAKED	UPDRIED	UPSWING
UNPLUGS	UNSMOTE	UNWARIE	UPENDED	UPSWUNG
UNPLUMB	UNSNAGS	UNWATER	UPFIELD	UPTAKEN
UNPLUME	UNSNARL	UNWAXED	UPFILLS	UPTALKS
UNPOPED	UNSNECK	UNWAYED	UPFLING	UPTEMPO
UNPOPES	UNSOLID	UNWEALS	UPFLOWS	UPTHREW
UNPOSED	UNSONCY	UNWEARY	UPFLUNG	UPTHROW
UNPRAYS	UNSONSY	UNWEAVE	UPFRONT	UPTIGHT
UNPROPS	UNSOOTE	UNWELDY	UPFURLS	UPTILTS
UNPURSE	UNSOULS	UNWHIPT	UPGANGS	UPTOWNS
UNQUEEN	UNSOUND	UNWHITE	UPGAZED	UPTYING
UNQUIET	UNSPARS	UNWILLS	UPGAZES	UPVALUE
UNQUOTE	UNSPEAK	UNWINDS	UPGIRDS	UPWAFTS
UNRAKED	UNSPELL	UNWIPED	UPGOING	UPWHIRL
UNRAKES	UNSPOKE	UNWIRED	UPGRADE	UPWOUND
UNRAZED	UNSPOOL	UNWITCH	UPGROWS	UPWRAPS
UNREADY	UNSTAID	UNWITTY	UPHAUDS	URACHUS
UNREAVE	UNSTEPS	UNWIVED	UPHEAVE	URACILS
UNREELS	UNSTICK	UNWIVES	UPHILLS	URAEMIA

URAEMIC	VACCINE	VAPORED	VELIGER	VERMINY
URALITE	VACKING	VAPORER	VELLETS	VERMUTH
URANIAN	VACUATE	VAPOURS	VELLONS	VERNANT
URANINS	VACUIST	VAPOURY	VELLUMS	VERONAL
URANIUM	VACUITY	VAQUERO	VELURED	VERRELS
URANYLS	VACUOLE	VARECHS	VELURES	VERRUCA
URBANER	VACUOUS	VAREUSE	VELVETS	VERSIFY
URCEOLI	VACUUMS	VARIANT	VELVETY	VERSINS
URCHINS	VAGALLY	VARIATE	VENALLY	VERTIGO
UREDIAL	VAGGING	VARIETY	VENATIC	VERTING
UREDINE	VAGINAE	VARIOLE	VENATOR	VERVAIN
UREDIUM	VAGINAS	VARMENT	VENDEES	VERVELS
UREMIAS	VAGITUS	VARMINT	VENDERS	VERVENS
URETERS	VAGRANT	VARNISH	VENDING	VERVETS
URETHRA	VAGROMS	VARROAS	VENDISS	VESICAE
URGENCE	VAGUELY	VARSITY	VENDORS	VESICLE
URGENCY	VAGUEST	VARUSES	VENDUES	VESPERS
URIDINE	VAGUING	VARVELS	VENEFIC	VESPIDS
URINANT	VAHANAS	VARYING	VENENES	VESPOID
URINARY	VAIVODE	VASCULA	VENERER	VESSELS
URINOSE	VAKEELS	VASSALS	VENEWES	VESTALS
URNLIKE	VALANCE	VASTEST	VENGERS	VESTIGE
URODELE	VALENCY	VASTITY	VENGING	VESTING
UROLITH	VALETAS	VATABLE	VENINES	VETIVER
UROLOGY	VALGOID	VATFULS	VENISON	VETKOEK
UROMERE	VALGOUS	VATICAL	VENNELS	VETOING
UROSOME	VALIANT	VATTERS	VENTAGE	VETTING
UROPODS	VALIDLY	VATTING	VENTAIL	VETTURA
URTEXTS	VALKYRS	VAUCHED	VENTANA	VEXEDLY
URTICAS	VALLARY	VAUCHES	VENTIGE	VEXILLA
USAUNCE	VALLATE	VAUDOOS	VENTILS	VEXINGS
USEABLY	VALLEYS	VAUDOUX	VENTING	VIADUCT
USEFULS	VALLUMS	VAULTED	VENTRAL	VIALLED
USELESS	VALONEA	VAULTER	VENTRED	VIBICES
USHERED	VALUATE	VAUNCED	VENTURE	VIBIEST
USUALLY	VALUERS	VAUNCES	VENULES	VIBISTS
USUCAPT	VALUING	VAUNTED	VENUSES	VIBRANT
USURERS	VALUTAS	VAUNTER	VERANDA	VIBRATE
USURESS	VALVATE	VAUNTIE	VERBALS	VIBRATO
USURIES	VALVING	VAURIEN	VERBENA	VIBRION
USURING	VALVULA	VAUTING	VERBIDS	VIBRIOS
USUROUS	VALVULE	VAVASOR	VERBIFY	VICARLY
USWARDS	VAMOSED	VAWARDS	VERBILE	VICEROY
UTILISE	VAMOSES	VAWNTIE	VERBING	VICINAL
UTILITY	VAMPING	VAWTING	VERDANT	VICIOUS
UTMOSTS	VAMPISH	VEDETTE	VERDICT	VICOMTE
UTOPIAS	VANADIC	VEEPEES	VERDINS	VICTIMS
UTOPISM	VANDALS	VEERIES	VERDURE	VICTORS
UTOPIST	VANDYKE	VEGANIC	VERGERS	VICTORY
UTTERED	VANESSA	VEGETAL	VERGING	VICTRIX
UTTERLY	VANILLA	VEGGIES	VERIDIC	VICTUAL
UVEITIC	VANITAS	VEGGING	VERISMO	VICUGNA
UVEITIS	VANLOAD	VEHICLE	VERISMS	VICUNAS
UVULARS	VANNERS	VEILIER	VERLANS	VIDAMES
UXORIAL	VANNING	VEILING	VERMEIL	VIDEOED
VACANCE	VANPOOL	VEINIER	VERMELL	VIDETTE
VACANCY	VANTAGE	VEINING	VERMIAN	VIDICON
VACATED	VANWARD	VEINLET	VERMILS	VIDIMUS
VACATUR	VAPIDER	VEINULE	VERMILY	VIDUAGE
VACCINA	VAPIDLY	VELAMEN	VERMINS	VIDUITY

VIDUOUS	VISITES	VOLUBLE	WADMALS	WALLAHS
VIELLES	VISNOMY	VOLUBLY	WADMELS	WALLERS
VIEWIER	VISUALS	VOLUMED	WADMOLL	WALLEYE
VIEWING	VITALLY	VOLUMES	WADMOLS	WALLIER
VIGOROS	VITAMER	VOLUSPA	WADSETS	WALLIES
VIGOURS	VITAMIN	VOLUTED	WAENESS	WALLING
VIHARAS	VITELLI	VOLUTES	WAESUCK	WALLOPS
VIHUELA	VITESSE	VOLUTIN	WAFERED	WALNUTS
VILAYET	VITEXES	VOLVATE	WAFFIES	WALTIER
VILIACO	VITIATE	VOLVING	WAFFING	WALTZED
VILIAGO	VITRAIN	VOLVULI	WAFFLED	WALTZER
VILLAGE	VITRAUX	VOMICAE	WAFFLER	WALTZES
VILLAIN	VITREUM	VOMICAS	WAFFLES	WAMBLED
VILLANS	VITRICS	VOMITER	WAFTAGE	WAMBLES
VILLANY	VITRIFY	VOMITOS	WAFTING	WAMEFOU
VILLEIN	VITRIOL	VOMITUS	WAFTURE	WAMEFUL
VILLOSE	VITTATE	VOODOOS	WAGERER	WAMMULS
VILLOUS	VITTLED	VORLAGE	WAGGERY	WAMPEES
VIMANAS	VITTLES	VORRING	WAGGING	WAMPISH
VIMINAL	VIVACES	VOTABLE	WAGGISH	WAMPUMS
VINCULA	VIVAING	VOTIVES	WAGGLED	WAMUSES
VINEWED	VIVARIA	VOUCHED	WAGGLER	WANDOOS
VINTAGE	VIVENCY	VOUCHEE	WAGGLES	WANGANS
VINTING	VIVERRA	VOUCHER	WAGGONS	WANGLED
VINTNER	VIVIDER	VOUCHES	WAGONER	WANGLES
VINYLIC	VIVIDLY	VOUDOUN	WAGSOME	WANGUNS
VIOLATE	VIVIFIC	VOUDOUS	WAGTAIL	WANHOPE
VIOLENT	VIXENLY	VOULGES	WAHINES	WANIGAN
VIOLINS	VIZARDS	VOUVRAY	WAIATAS	WANIONS
VIOLIST	VIZIERS	VOWELLY	WAIFING	WANKIER
VIOLONE	VIZORED	VOWLESS	WAIFISH	WANKING
VIRAGOS	VIZSLAS	VOYAGED	WAILFUL	WANKSTA
VIRALLY	VIZYING	VOYAGER	WAILING	WANNABE
VIRANDA	VIZZIED	VOYAGES	WAINAGE	WANNESS
VIRANDO	VIZZIES	VOYEURS	WAINING	WANNEST
VIRELAI	VOCABLE	VROOMED	WAIRING	WANNING
VIRELAY	VOCABLY	VUGGIER	WAIRUAS	WANNISH
VIREMIA	VOCALIC	VUGHIER	WAITING	WANTAGE
VIREMIC	VOCALLY	VULCANS	WAITRON	WANTING
VIRGERS	VOCULAR	VULGARS	WAIVERS	WANTONS
VIRGINS	VOCULES	VULGATE	WAIVING	WANZING
VIRGULE	VOETSAK	VULNING	WAIVODE	WAPITIS
VIROSES	VOETSEK	VULPINE	WAIWODE	WAPPEND
VIROSIS	VOGIEST	VULTURE	WAKAMES	WAPPING
VIRUSES	VOGUERS	VULTURN	WAKANDA	WARAGIS
VISAGED	VOGUIER	VULVATE	WAKEFUL	WARATAH
VISAGES	VOGUING	VUMMING	WAKEMAN	WARBIER
VISARDS	VOGUISH	VUTTIER	WAKEMEN	WARDIAN
VISCINS	VOICING	VYINGLY	WAKENED	WARDOGS
VISCOID	VOIDEES	WABAINS	WAKIKIS	WARDROP
VISCOSE	VOIDING	WABBLED	WAKINGS	WAREHOU
VISCOUS	VOITURE	WABBLER	WALDOES	WARFARE
VISCUMS	VOIVODE	WABOOMS	WALIEST	WARISON
VISIBLE	VOLANTE	WACKEST	WALISES	WARKING
VISIBLY	VOLCANO	WACKIER	WALKERS	WARLIKE
VISIERS	VOLLEYS	WACKILY	WALKING	WARLING
VISILES	VOLOSTS	WADABLE	WALKUPS	WARLOCK
VISIONS	VOLPINO	WADDIED	WALKWAY	WARLORD
VISITED	VOLTAGE	WADINGS	WALLABA	WARMEST
VISITEE	VOLUBIL	WADMAAL	WALLABY	WARMING

WARMISH	WAULKER	WEBFOOT	WENCHER	WHEMMLE
WARMTHS	WAURING	WEBINAR	WENDING	WHENUAS
WARNING	WAVELET	WEBLESS	WENNIER	WHENWES
WARPAGE	WAVEOFF	WEBLIKE	WENNISH	WHEREAS
WARPATH	WAVERED	WEBLISH	WERGELD	WHEREBY
WARPING	WAVERER	WEBMAIL	WERGELT	WHEREIN
WARRAND	WAVESON	WEBPAGE	WERGILD	WHEREOF
WARRANS	WAVICLE	WEBSITE	WERSHER	WHERESO
WARRANT	WAVIEST	WEBWORK	WERWOLF	WHERETO
WARRAYS	WAVINGS	WEBWORM	WESTERN	WHERRET
WARREYS	WAWAING	WEDDERS	WESTIES	WHERVES
WARRING	WAWLING	WEDDING	WETBACK	WHETHER
WARRIOR	WAXABLE	WEDELED	WETLAND	WHETTED
WARSAWS	WAXBILL	WEDELNS	WETNESS	WHETTER
WARSHIP	WAXEYES	WEDGIER	WETSUIT	WHEUGHS
WARSLED	WAXINGS	WEDGIES	WETTERS	WHEWING
WARSLER	WAXLIKE	WEDGING	WETTEST	WHEYIER
WARTHOG	WAXWEED	WEDLOCK	WETTIES	WHEYISH
WARTIER	WAXWING	WEEDERY	WETTING	WHICKER
WARTIME	WAXWORK	WEEDIER	WETWARE	WHIDAHS
WARWOLF	WAXWORM	WEEDILY	WEYWARD	WHIDDED
WARWORK	WAYBILL	WEEDING	WEZANDS	WHIDDER
WARWORN	WAYFARE	WEEKDAY	WHACKED	WHIFFED
WARZONE	WAYGONE	WEEKEND	WHACKER	WHIFFER
WASABIS	WAYLAID	WEENIER	WHACKOS	WHIFFET
WASHDAY	WAYLAYS	WEENIES	WHAIZLE	WHIFFLE
WASHERY	WAYLESS	WEEPIER	WHALERS	WHIGGED
WASHILY	WAYMARK	WEEPIES	WHALERY	WHILERE
WASHINS	WAYMENT	WEEPILY	WHALING	WHILING
WASHPOT	WAYPOST	WEEPING	WHAMMED	WHIMMED
WASHRAG	WAYWARD	WEETEST	WHAMMOS	WHIMPER
WASHTUB	WAYWODE	WEETING	WHAMPLE	WHIMPLE
WASHUPS	WAYWORN	WEEVILS	WHANAUS	WHIMSEY
WASPIER	WAZZOCK	WEEVILY	WHANGAM	WHINERS
WASPIES	WEAKENS	WEEWEED	WHANGED	WHINGED
WASPISH	WEAKEST	WEEWEES	WHANGEE	WHINGER
WASSAIL	WEAKONS	WEFTAGE	WHAPPED	WHINIER
WASTAGE	WEALTHS	WEFTING	WHAPPER	WHINING
WASTELS	WEALTHY	WEIGELA	WHARFED	WHIPCAT
WASTERS	WEANELS	WEIGHED	WHARFIE	WHIPPED
WASTERY	WEANERS	WEIGHTS	WHARVES	WHIPPER
WATAPES	WEANING	WEIGHTY	WHATNOT	WHIPPET
WATCHED	WEAPONS	WEIRDED	WHATSIS	WHIPRAY
WATCHER	WEARIED	WEIRDIE	WHATSIT	WHIPSAW
WATCHES	WEARIER	WEIRDLY	WHATTEN	WHIRLED
WATCHET	WEARIES	WEISING	WHEATEN	WHIRLER
WATERER	WEARILY	WEIZING	WHEECHS	WHIRRED
WATTAGE	WEARING	WELAWAY	WHEELER	WHIRTLE
WATTAPE	WEASAND	WELCHED	WHEELIE	WHISHED
WATTEST	WEASONS	WELCHER	WHEENGE	WHISHES
WATTLED	WEAVERS	WELCOME	WHEEPED	WHISHTS
WATTLES	WEAVING	WELDING	WHEEPLE	WHISKED
WAUCHTS	WEAZAND	WELDORS	WHEESHT	WHISKER
WAUFFED	WEAZENS	WELFARE	WHEEZED	WHISKET
WAUGHED	WEBBIER	WELKING	WHEEZER	WHISKEY
WAUGHTS	WEBBIES	WELLIES	WHEEZES	WHISPER
WAUKERS	WEBBING	WELLING	WHEEZLE	WHISTED
WAUKING	WEBCAMS	WELSHED	WHELKED	WHISTLE
WAULING	WEBCAST	WELSHER	WHELMED	WHITELY
WAULKED	WEBFEET	WENCHED	WHELPED	WHITENS

WHITEYS	WIGGERY	WINGTIP	WOGGISH	WOOZIER
WHITHER	WIGGIER	WINIEST	WOGGLES	WOOZILY
WHITISH	WIGGING	WINKING	WOIWODE	WOPPING
WHITLOW	WIGGLED	WINKLED	WOLFISH	WORDING
WHITTAW	WIGGLES	WINLESS	WOLFKIN	WORDISH
WHITTLE	WIGHTED	WINNERS	WOLFRAM	WORKBAG
WHIZZED	WIGHTLY	WINNING	WOLLIES	WORKBOX
WHIZZER	WIGLESS	WINNLES	WOLVERS	WORKFUL
WHIZZES	WIGLETS	WINNOCK	WOLVING	WORKING
WHOLISM	WIGLIKE	WINNOWS	WOLVISH	WORKMAN
WHOLIST	WIGWAGS	WINSEYS	WOMANLY	WORKMEN
WHOMBLE	WIGWAMS	WINSOME	WOMBATS	WORKSHY
WHOMMLE	WIKIUPS	WINTERY	WOMBING	WORKUPS
WHOMPED	WILDCAT	WIPEOUT	WOMMERA	WORLDED
WHOOBUB	WILDEST	WIPPENS	WOMMITS	WORLDLY
WHOOFED	WILDING	WIREMAN	WONKIER	WORMERS
WHOOPED	WILDISH	WIREMEN	WONNING	WORMERY
WHOOPEE	WILEFUL	WIRETAP	WONTING	WORMFLY
WHOOPER	WILIEST	WIREWAY	WONTONS	WORMIER
WHOOPIE	WILLEYS	WIRIEST	WOOBUTS	WORMILS
WHOOPLA	WILLFUL	WIRILDA	WOODBIN	WORMING
WHOOSIS	WILLIAM	WIRINGS	WOODCUT	WORMISH
WHOOTED	WILLIED	WIRRAHS	WOODIER	WORRALS
WHOPPED	WILLIES	WISARDS	WOODIES	WORRELS
WHOPPER	WILLING	WISDOMS	WOODING	WORRIER
WHORING	WILLOWS	WISEASS	WOODLOT	WORRIES
WHORISH	WILLOWY	WISEGUY	WOODMAN	WORRITS
WHORLED	WILTJAS	WISHFUL	WOODMEN	WORSENS
WHORTLE	WIMBLED	WISHING	WOODSIA	WORSHIP
WHUMMLE	WIMBLES	WISPILY	WOODWAX	WORTHED
WHUMPED	WIMBREL	WISPISH	WOOFERS	WOSBIRD
WHUPPED	WIMPIER	WISSING	WOOFIER	WOTCHER
WHYDAHS	WIMPING	WISTFUL	WOOFING	WOTTEST
WHYEVER	WIMPISH	WISTING	WOOFTER	WOTTETH
WIBBLED	WIMPLED	WISTITI	WOOINGS	WOUBITS
WIBBLES	WIMPLES	WITCHED	WOOLDED	WOULDST
WICCANS	WINCERS	WITCHEN	WOOLDER	WOUNDED
WICKAPE	WINCEYS	WITCHES	WOOLENS	WOURALI
WICKEDS	WINCHED	WITGATS	WOOLERS	WOWFEST
WICKENS	WINCHER	WITHINS	WOOLFAT	WOWSERS
WICKERS	WINCHES	WITLESS	WOOLHAT	WRACKED
WICKETS	WINCING	WITLOOF	WOOLIER	WRANGED
WICKIES	WINDACS	WITNEYS	WOOLIES	WRAPPED
WICKING	WINDAGE	WITTIER	WOOLLED	WRASSES
WICKIUP	WINDBAG	WITTILY	WOOLLEN	WRAWLED
WICKYUP	WINDGUN	WITTING	WOOLMAN	WRAXLED
WIDDERS	WINDIER	WITTOLS	WOOLMEN	WRAXLES
WIDDIES	WINDIGO	WITWALL	WOOLSEY	WREAKER
WIDDLED	WINDILY	WIVERNS	WOOMERA	WREATHY
WIDDLES	WINDOCK	WIZARDS	WOONING	WRECKED
WIDEOUT	WINDOWS	WIZENED	WOOPIES	WRECKER
WIDGETS	WINDOWY	WIZIERS	WOOPSES	WRETHED
WIDGIES	WINDROW	WIZZENS	WOORALI	WRICKED
WIDOWED	WINDSES	WOADWAX	WOORARA	WRIGGLY
WIDOWER	WINDWAY	WOBBLED	WOORARI	WRIGHTS
WIELDED	WINESAP	WOBBLER	WOOSELL	WRINGER
WIELDER	WINGBOW	WOBBLES	WOOSELS	WRINKLY
WIFEDOM	WINGING	WOENESS	WOOSHED	WRITERS
WIFTIER	WINGMAN	WOESOME	WOOSHES	WRITHED
WIGEONS	WINGMEN	WOFULLY	WOOTZES	WRITHEN

WRIZLED	YAMMERS	YEUKING	YUGARIE	ZEBRULA
WROATHS	YAMULKA	YIBBLES	YUKATAS	ZEBRULE
WRONGED	YANKERS	YIDAKIS	YUKIEST	ZECCHIN
WRONGLY	YANKING	YIKKERS	YUKKIER	ZECHINS
WROOTED	YANQUIS	YIPPERS	YUKKING	ZEDOARY
WROUGHT	YANTRAS	YIPPIES	YUMMIER	ZELANTS
WRYBILL	YAOURTS	YIPPING	YUMMIES	ZELATOR
WRYNECK	YAPOCKS	YIRDING	YUMPIES	ZELKOVA
WRYNESS	YAPPIER	YIRKING	YUMPING	ZEMSTVA
WRYTHEN	YAPPIES	YIRRING	YUPPIES	ZEMSTVO
WUDDING	YAPPING	YMOLTEN	YUPPIFY	ZENAIDA
WUDJULA	YAPSTER	YNAMBUS	ZABETAS	ZENANAS
WULLING	YAQONAS	YOBBERY	ZABTIEH	ZENDIKS
WUNNERS	YARDANG	YOBBISH	ZACATON	ZENITHS
WURLEYS	YARDARM	YOBBISM	ZADDICK	ZEOLITE
WURLIES	YARDERS	YOBBOES	ZADDIKS	ZEPHYRS
WURZELS	YARKING	YOCKING	ZAFFARS	ZEPPOLE
WUSSIER	YARNERS	YODELED	ZAFFIRS	ZEPPOLI
WUSSIES	YARNING	YODELER	ZAGGING	ZEREBAS
WUTHERS	YARPHAS	YODLERS	ZAIKAIS	ZEROING
WUZZLED	YARRANS	YODLING	ZAITECH	ZESTERS
WUZZLES	YASHMAC	YOGHURT	ZAKUSKA	ZESTFUL
WYSIWYG	YASHMAK	YOGINIS	ZAKUSKI	ZESTIER
WYVERNS	YASMAKS	YOGISMS	ZAMANGS	ZESTING
XANTHAM	YATAGAN	YOGURTS	ZAMARRA	ZETETIC
XANTHAN	YATTERS	YOHIMBE	ZAMARRO	ZEUGMAS
XANTHIC	YAUPERS	YOICKED	ZAMBUCK	ZEUXITE
XANTHIN	YAUPING	YOJANAS	ZAMBUKS	ZIBETHS
XENOPUS	YAUPONS	YOKINGS	ZAMOUSE	ZIFFIUS
XERAFIN	YAUTIAS	YOKKING	ZAMPONE	ZIGANKA
XERARCH	YAWLING	YOLKIER	ZAMPONI	ZIGGING
XERASIA	YAWNERS	YOMPING	ZANANAS	ZIGZAGS
XEROMAS	YAWNIER	YONDERS	ZANDERS	ZIKURAT
XEROSIS	YAWNING	YONKERS	ZANELLA	ZILCHES
XEROTES	YAWPING	YONNIES	ZANJERO	ZILLAHS
XEROXED	YCLEEPE	YORKERS	ZANYING	ZILLION
XEROXES	YCLEPED	YORKIES	ZANYISH	ZIMMERS
XERUSES	YEADING	YORKING	ZANYISM	ZIMOCCA
XIPHOID	YEALDON	YORPING	ZAPATEO	ZINCATE
XYLENES	YEALMED	YOUKING	ZAPPERS	ZINCIER
XYLENOL	YEANING	YOUNGER	ZAPPING	ZINCIFY
XYLIDIN	YEARNER	YOUNGLY	ZAPTIAH	ZINCING
XYLITOL	YEASTED	YOUNGTH	ZAPTIEH	ZINCKED
XYLOMAS	YEEDING	YOUNKER	ZARAPES	ZINCODE
XYLONIC	YEELINS	YOUPONS	ZAREBAS	ZINCOID
XYLOSES	YEGGMAN	YOUTHEN	ZAREEBA	ZINGANI
XYSTERS	YEGGMEN	YOUTHLY	ZARIBAS	ZINGANO
YABBERS	YELLERS	YOWLERS	ZARNECS	ZINGARA
YABBIED	YELLING	YOWLEYS	ZARNICH	ZINGARE
YABBIES	YELLOCH	YOWLING	ZEALANT	ZINGARI
YACHTED	YELLOWS	YPERITE	ZEALFUL	ZINGARO
YACHTER	YELLOWY	YPLIGHT	ZEALOTS	ZINGELS
YACHTIE	YELMING	YPSILON	ZEALOUS	ZINGERS
YACKING	YELPING	YSHENDS	ZEBECKS	ZINGIER
YAFFLES	YEMMERS	YSLAKED	ZEBRAIC	ZINGING
YAGGERS	YENNING	YTTRIAS	ZEBRANO	ZINKIER
YAKHDAN	YERDING	YTTRIUM	ZEBRASS	ZINKIFY
YAKKERS	YESHIVA	YUCKERS	ZEBRINA	ZINKING
YAKKING	YESSING	YUCKIER	ZEBRINE	ZINNIAS
YAMALKA	YETTIES	YUCKING	ZEBROID	ZIPLESS

ZIPLOCK	ZOCCOLO	ZONURES	ZOOTIER	ZYGOMAS
ZIPPERS	ZODIACS	ZOOECIA	ZOOTOMY	ZYGOSES
ZIPPIER	ZOECIUM	ZOOGAMY	ZOOTYPE	ZYGOSIS
ZIPPING	ZOEFORM	ZOOGENY	ZOOZOOS	ZYGOTES
ZIRCONS	ZOISITE	ZOOGLEA	ZORBING	ZYGOTIC
ZITHERN	ZOMBIES	ZOOGONY	ZORGITE	ZYMASES
ZITHERS	ZOMBIFY	ZOOIDAL	ZORILLA	ZYMITES
ZIZANIA	ZONALLY	ZOOLITE	ZORILLE	ZYMOGEN
ZIZZING	ZONATED	ZOOLITH	ZORILLO	ZYMOMES
ZIZZLED	ZONINGS	ZOOLOGY	ZORINOS	ZYMOSAN
ZIZZLES	ZONKING	ZOOMING	ZOSTERS	ZYMOSES
ZLOTIES	ZONULAE	ZOONING	ZOUAVES	ZYMOSIS
ZLOTYCH	ZONULAR	ZOONITE	ZOYSIAS	ZYMOTIC
ZOARIAL	ZONULAS	ZOONOMY	ZUFFOLI	ZYMURGY
ZOARIUM	ZONULES	ZOOPERY	ZUFFOLO	ZYTHUMS
ZOCALOS	ZONULET	ZOOTAXY	ZYDECOS	ZYZZYVA

Couplets

ABACTOR	ACROBAT	ACONITE	ANOETIC	AGEISTS	SAGIEST
ABATERS	ABREAST	ACORNED	DRACONE	AGELESS	ALGESES
ABATORS	RABATOS	ACQUIST	ACQUITS	AGENDUM	GUDEMAN
ABDUCES	SCUBAED	ACRIDER	CARRIED	AGENTED	NEGATED
ABETTER	BERETTA	ACROGEN	CORNAGE	AGGADAH	HAGGADA
ABIDDEN	BANDIED	ACTINGS	CASTING	AGGRADE	GARAGED
ABIOSES	ISOBASE	ACUTEST	SCUTATE	AGISTOR	ORGIAST
ABLATED	DATABLE	ADAPTER	READAPT	AGNAMED	MANAGED
ABLATES	ASTABLE	ADDICTS	DIDACTS	AGNISES	SEASING
ABLINGS	SABLING	ADDREST	RADDEST	AGNIZES	SEAZING
ABLUENT	TUNABLE	ADDUCES	SCAUDED	AGNOMEN	NONGAME
ABOUNDS	BAUSOND	ADERMIN	INARMED	AGNOSIC	ANGICOS
ABRASAX	ABRAXAS	ADHARMA	HARAMDA	AGONIES	AGONISE
ABRIDGE	BRIGADE	ADHERED	REDHEAD	AGONIST	GITANOS
ABSENTS	BASNETS	ADHERER	REHEARD	AGRISES	GASSIER
ABYEING	EBAYING	ADIPSIA	ASPIDIA	AGUISED	GAUDIES
ABYSMAL	BALSAMY	ADMIRAL	AMILDAR	AIBLINS	BILIANS
ACANTHI	TACHINA	ADMIRED	MARDIED	AIDLESS	DEASILS
ACARINE	CARINAE	ADONIZE	ANODIZE	AILANTO	ALATION
ACATERS	CARATES	ADOPTER	READOPT	AILMENT	ALIMENT
ACATOUR	AUTOCAR	ADORERS	DROSERA	AIRBASE	ARABISE
ACCITES	ASCETIC	ADORNER	READORN	AIRIEST	IRISATE
ACCOILS	CALICOS	ADUSTED	SUDATED	AIRPORT	PARITOR
ACCOMPT	COMPACT	ADVENED	DAVENED	AIRTING	RAITING
ACCOYLD	CACODYL	ADVERSE	EVADERS	ALANYLS	NASALLY
ACCRUAL	CARACUL	ADVERTS	STARVED	ALBUGOS	SUBGOAL
ACCRUED	CARDECU	ADVISER	VARDIES	ALCADES	SCALADE
ACCUSED	SUCCADE	ADVISES	DISSAVE	ALCAICS	CICALAS
ACERBIC	BRECCIA	ADWARES	SEAWARD	ALCOVES	COEVALS
ACEROUS	CAROUSE	ADWOMEN	WOMANED	ALDOSES	LASSOED
ACETALS	LACTASE	AEDILES	DEISEAL	ALEGARS	LAAGERS
ACETOSE	COATEES	AEGISES	ASSIEGE	ALEMBIC	CEMBALI
ACETYLS	SCYTALE	AERIEST	SERIATE	ALEPINE	ELAPINE
ACHENES	ENCHASE	AEROSOL	ROSEOLA	ALETHIC	ETHICAL
ACHIEST	AITCHES	AFFAIRS	RAFFIAS	ALEVINS	VALINES
ACHIRAL	RACHIAL	AFFIXER	REAFFIX	ALEYING	YEALING
ACIDEST	DACITES	AFFYING	YAFFING	ALFAKIS	KAFILAS
ACIFORM	FORMICA	AFREETS	FEASTER	ALIENED	DELAINE
ACNODAL	CALANDO	AGAMETE	AGEMATE	ALINING	NAILING
ACNODES	DEACONS	AGAROSE	OARAGES	ALISMAS	SALAMIS
ACOLYTE	COTYLAE	AGEINGS	SIGNAGE	ALISONS	SIALONS

ALIUNDE	UNIDEAL	ANGINAS	INANGAS	ARGYLES	GRAYLES
ALKANET	KANTELA	ANGLIFY	FLAYING	ARIETTE	ITERATE
ALLAYER	AREALLY	ANGUINE	GUANINE	ARISTAS	TARSIAS
ALLEDGE	ALLEGED	ANGUISH	HAUSING	ARKITES	KARITES
ALLICES	CAILLES	ANICUTS	NAUTICS	ARMINGS	MARGINS
ALLISES	SALLIES	ANKLING	LANKING	ARMLOCK	LOCKRAM
ALLODIA	ALODIAL	ANNELID	LINDANE	ARMREST	SMARTER
ALLONGE	GALLEON	ANNOYED	ANODYNE	ARNOTTO	RATTOON
ALLOVER	OVERALL	ANSWERS	RAWNESS	AROINTS	RATIONS
ALLUDED	DUALLED	ANTHEMS	HETMANS	ARRIDES	RAIDERS
ALLUDES	ALUDELS	ANTIBUG	TABUING	ARRIERO	ROARIER
ALLURED	UDALLER	ANTICLY	CANTILY	ARRIVES	VARIERS
ALLURES	LAURELS	ANTIFLU	FLUTINA	ARROBAS	RASBORA
ALMANAC	MANCALA	ANTINGS	STANING	ARSHINE	HERNIAS
ALMONDS	DOLMANS	ANTIQUE	QUINATE	ARSHINS	SHAIRNS
ALMONER	NEMORAL	ANTISEX	SEXTAIN	ARSINES	SARNIES
ALMUCES	MACULES	ANTRUMS	UNSMART	ARTSMAN	MANTRAS
ALMUDES	MEDUSAL	ANUROUS	URANOUS	ARUGULA	AUGURAL
ALNICOS	OILCANS	ANYMORE	ROMNEYA	ASCITES	ECTASIS
ALOGIAS	LAOGAIS	APEDOMS	POMADES	ASCITIC	SCIATIC
ALPEENS	SPELEAN	APELIKE	PEALIKE	ASEPSIS	ASPISES
ALSIKES	ASSLIKE	APERCUS	SCAUPER	ASININE	INSANIE
ALYSSUM	ASYLUMS	APERIES	EPEIRAS	ASKINGS	GASKINS
AMABILE	AMIABLE	APHESES	SPAHEES	ASPERGE	PRESAGE
AMANDLA	MANDALA	APHETIC	HEPATIC	ASPORTS	PASTORS
AMARANT	MARANTA	APHIDES	DIPHASE	ASPREAD	PARADES
AMATION	ANIMATO	APICALS	SPACIAL	ASQUINT	QUINTAS
AMBARIS	MARABIS	APLENTY	PENALTY	ASSARTS	SASTRAS
AMBOINA	BONAMIA	APNOEAS	PAESANO	ASSENTS	SNASTES
AMBONES	BEMOANS	APNOEIC	PAEONIC	ASSERTS	TRASSES
AMEARST	RETAMAS	APOLLOS	PALOLOS	ASSIGNS	SASSING
AMELIAS	MALAISE	APOMICT	POTAMIC	ASSUAGE	SAUSAGE
AMENDED	DEADMEN	APOSTIL	TOPSAIL	ASSUMED	MEDUSAS
AMENING	MEANING	APOSTLE	PELOTAS	ASSURED	RUDASES
AMENITY	ANYTIME	APPENDS	SNAPPED	ASSURER	RASURES
AMENTIA	ANIMATE	APPLIES	LAPPIES	ASSURES	SARUSES
AMERCER	CREAMER	APPOSED	PEAPODS	ASTARTS	STRATAS
AMIDASE	SEAMAID	APPOSER	POPERAS	ASTHENY	SHANTEY
AMIDINE	DIAMINE	APPRESS	SAPPERS	ASTHMAS	MATSAHS
AMIDINS	DIAMINS	APPRISE	SAPPIER	ASTRALS	TARSALS
AMIDONE	DOMAINE	APPRIZE	ZAPPIER	ASTRAND	TARANDS
AMISSES	MESSIAS	APTOTES	TEAPOTS	ASTUTER	STATURE
AMITIES	ATIMIES	ARAYSED	DARESAY	ASTYLAR	SATYRAL
AMMETER	METAMER	ARAYSES	ASSAYER	ATELIER	REALTIE
AMMINES	MISNAME	ARBITER	RAREBIT	ATHAMES	HAMATES
AMNESIA	ANEMIAS	ARBORES	BRASERO	ATHEIST	STAITHE
AMNESIC	CINEMAS	ARCADES	ASCARED	ATLATLS	TALLATS
AMOOVES	VAMOOSE	ARCHERS	CRASHER	ATOCIAS	COAITAS
AMPERES	EMPARES	ARCHILS	CARLISH	ATOPIES	OPIATES
AMRITAS	TAMARIS	ARCHLET	TRACHLE	ATRIUMS	MATSURI
AMULETS	MULETAS	ARCMINS	NARCISM	ATTONES	NOTATES
ANADEMS	MAENADS	ARCTANS	CANTARS	ATTRIST	ATTRITS
ANAPEST	PEASANT	ARCTOID	CAROTID	AUCTION	CAUTION
ANCILIA	LACINIA	AREFIED	FEDARIE	AUGMENT	MUTAGEN
ANCONES	SONANCE	ARETTED	TREATED	AULDEST	SALUTED
ANCRESS	CASERNS	ARGALIS	GARIALS	AULNAGE	LEGUAAN
ANDVILE	ANVILED	ARGHANS	HANGARS	AUNTIES	SINUATE
ANERGIC	GRECIAN	ARGLING	GLARING	AUTOCUE	COUTEAU
ANESTRA	SANTERA	ARGONON	ORGANON	AUTOING	OUTGAIN
ANETHOL	ETHANOL	ARGUERS	SUGARER	AUTOPSY	PAYOUTS

AVAILED	VEDALIA	BARRETS	BARTERS	BENDIER	INBREED
AVALING	VAGINAL	BARRIES	BRASIER	BENISON	BONNIES
AVARICE	CAVIARE	BARYTES	BETRAYS	BENTHIC	BITCHEN
AVENGED	VENDAGE	BASALLY	SALABLY	BERDASH	BRASHED
AVENGER	ENGRAVE	BASHERS	BRASHES	BERGAMA	MEGABAR
AVENGES	GENEVAS	BASHLIK	KIBLAHS	BERRIED	BRIERED
AVENIRS	RAVINES	BASIONS	BONSAIS	BERTHES	SHERBET
AVERTED	TAVERED	BASSEST	BASSETS	BESCOUR	OBSCURE
AVGASES	SAVAGES	BASTARD	TABARDS	BESINGS	BIGNESS
AVIATIC	VIATICA	BASTLES	STABLES	BESLIME	BESMILE
AVIETTE	EVITATE	BATBOYS	BOBSTAY	BESPAKE	BESPEAK
AVISING	VISAING	BATCHER	BRACHET	BESTEAD	DEBATES
AVOCETS	OCTAVES	BATISTE	BISTATE	BESTILL	BILLETS
AVODIRE	AVOIDER	BATTERS	TABRETS	BESTORM	MOBSTER
AWAKENS	WAKANES	BATTLED	BLATTED	BESTREW	WEBSTER
AWELESS	WEASELS	BAUBLES	BUBALES	BESTRID	BISTRED
AWESOME	WAESOME	BAUERAS	SUBAREA	BESTUCK	BUCKETS
AWMRIES	SEMIRAW	BAWBLES	WABBLES	BETIDED	DEBITED
BABBLED	BLABBED	BAWLERS	WARBLES	BHAKTAS	SABKHAT
BABIEST	TABBIES	BAWLEYS	BYELAWS	BHINDIS	BINDHIS
BABOOSH	HABOOBS	BAWLING	BLAWING	BICOLOR	BROCOLI
BACCIES	SEBACIC	BEADIER	BEARDIE	BICORNS	BICRONS
BACKERS	REBACKS	BEAKERS	BERAKES	BIFTERS	FIBSTER
BACKOUT	OUTBACK	BEARERS	BREARES	BILBOES	LOBBIES
BACKPAY	PAYBACK	BEATIER	EBRIATE	BILLERS	REBILLS
BAETYLS	BEASTLY	BECALMS	SCAMBLE	BILOBED	LOBBIED
BAGARRE	BARRAGE	BECRUST	BECURST	BILTONG	BOLTING
BAGASSE	SEABAGS	BEDERAL	BLEARED	BIMBOES	MOBBIES
BAGFULS	BAGSFUL	BEDIGHT	BIGHTED	BINGOES	BIOGENS
BAGGERS	BEGGARS	BEDLAMS	BELDAMS	BIOGENY	OBEYING
BAGNIOS	GABIONS	BEDLESS	BLESSED	BIOPICS	BIOPSIC
BAGUETS	TUBAGES	BEDRALS	BLADERS	BIPEDAL	PIEBALD
BAKINGS	BASKING	BEDRAPE	PREBADE	BIPOLAR	PARBOIL
BALDING	BLADING	BEDROCK	BROCKED	BIRDIES	BRIDIES
BALEENS	ENABLES	BEDSORE	SOBERED	BIRDING	BRIDING
BALLAST	BALLATS	BEDTIME	BETIMED	BIRSIER	RIBIERS
BALLUTE	BULLATE	BEDUINS	BUNDIES	BIRSLED	BRIDLES
BALSAMS	SAMBALS	BEDUSTS	BESTUDS	BIRSLES	RIBLESS
BAMPOTS	SPAMBOT	BEECHES	BESEECH	BISTORT	BITTORS
BANDARS	SANDBAR	BEEFIER	FREEBIE	BITTURS	TURBITS
BANDIER	BRAINED	BEEGAHS	BHAGEES	BIZARRE	BRAZIER
BANDIES	BASINED	BEENTOS	BONESET	BLATHER	HALBERT
BANDORE	BROADEN	BEETING	BEIGNET	BLEARER	ERRABLE
BANGERS	GRABENS	BEEYARD	BERAYED	BLEATER	RETABLE
BANKERS	BARKENS	BEEZERS	BREEZES	BLENDER	REBLEND
BANTAMS	BATSMAN	BEFANAS	FANBASE	BLETHER	HERBLET
BANTERS	BARNETS	BEFLUMS	FUMBLES	BLINDER	BRINDLE
BAPTISM	BITMAPS	BEGIRDS	BRIDGES	BLOATED	LOBATED
BARAZAS	BAZAARS	BEGUINS	BUNGIES	BLOBBED	BOBBLED
BARBIES	RABBIES	BELACED	DEBACLE	BLOGGER	BOGGLER
BARDING	BRIGAND	BELATED	BLEATED	BLONDES	BOLDENS
BARGING	GARBING	BELAYED	DYEABLE	BLOODED	BOODLED
BARISTA	BARTSIA	BELGARD	GARBLED	BLOOMER	REBLOOM
BARKEEP	PREBAKE	BELTERS	TREBLES	BLOTTED	BOTTLED
BARKIER	BRAKIER	BELTMAN	LAMBENT	BLOTTER	BOTTLER
BARKING	BRAKING	BELUGAS	BLAGUES	BLOUSED	DOUBLES
BARLESS	BRALESS	BEMETES	BETEEMS	BLOUSES	BOLUSES
BAROLOS	ROBALOS	BEMIRED	BERIMED	BLOWERS	BOWLERS
BARONET	REBOANT	BEMUSED	EMBUSED	BLOWFLY	FLYBLOW
BARONGS	BROGANS	BEMUSES	EMBUSES	BLOWING	BOWLING

BLOWSES	BOWLESS	BRAIRDS	BRIARDS	BUYOUTS	OUTBUYS
BLOWUPS	UPBLOWS	BRAIZES	ZERIBAS	BYREMAN	MYRBANE
BLUBBED	BUBBLED	BRANDER	REBRAND	CACHETS	CATCHES
BLUBBER	BUBBLER	BRANLES	BRANSLE	CACHING	CHACING
BLUDGER	BURGLED	BRASHER	HERBARS	CACKLED	CLACKED
BLUEING	BULGINE	BRASSED	SERDABS	CACTOID	OCTADIC
BLUEISH	HELIBUS	BRAWEST	WABSTER	CADRANS	CANARDS
BLUIEST	SUBTILE	BRAWLED	WARBLED	CAESTUS	CUESTAS
BLUNDER	BUNDLER	BRAWLER	WARBLER	CAIMANS	MANIACS
BLUNGED	BUNGLED	BRAWLIE	WIRABLE	CAITIVE	VICIATE
BLUNGER	BUNGLER	BREAKUP	UPBREAK	CAKIEST	TACKIES
BLUNGES	BUNGLES	BREDIES	DERBIES	CALALUS	CLAUSAL
BLUSHER	BURHELS	BRETONS	SORBENT	CALAMUS	MACULAS
BLUSHES	BUSHELS	BRIBERS	RIBBERS	CALDERA	CRAALED
BOATELS	OBLATES	BRIBING	RIBBING	CALENDS	CANDLES
BOCAGES	BOSCAGE	BRICOLE	CORBEIL	CALIBER	CALIBRE
BODICES	CEBOIDS	BRIGUES	RUGBIES	CALICES	CELIACS
BOMBERS	MOBBERS	BRINING	INBRING	CALICHE	CHALICE
BOMBING	MOBBING	BRISTLY	TRILBYS	CALIMAS	CAMAILS
BONDAGE	DOGBANE	BRISTOL	STROBIL	CALIPER	REPLICA
BONIEST	EBONIST	BRITTLE	TRIBLET	CALKING	LACKING
BOODIES	DOOBIES	BROMINS	MISBORN	CALLOPS	SCALLOP
BOOGERS	GOOBERS	BROOSES	SORBOSE	CALLOSE	LOCALES
BOOGIES	GOOBIES	BROUZES	SUBZERO	CALLUNA	LACUNAL
BOOHING	HOBOING	BRUCKLE	BUCKLER	CALMANT	CLAMANT
BOOKERS	REBOOKS	BRUISED	BURDIES	CALMEST	CAMLETS
BOOKIER	BROOKIE	BRUMOUS	UMBROUS	CALQUES	CLAQUES
BOOKIES	BOOKSIE	BRUSHES	BUSHERS	CALTROP	PROCTAL
BOONGAS	GABOONS	BRUSKER	BURKERS	CALVARY	CAVALRY
BOOSTER	REBOOTS	BRUTELY	BUTLERY	CALYCES	CYCLASE
BOOZERS	REBOZOS	BRUTERS	BURSTER	CALYCLE	CECALLY
BORACIC	BRACCIO	BUCKSAW	SAWBUCK	CAMARON	NARCOMA
BORDURE	BOURDER	BUDDERS	REDBUDS	CAMBREL	CLAMBER
BOREENS	ENROBES	BUFFERS	REBUFFS	CAMOTES	COMATES
BORIDES	DISROBE	BUFFEST	BUFFETS	CAMPERS	SCAMPER
BORKING	BROKING	BUGLING	BULGING	CAMPLED	CLAMPED
BORSCHT	BORTSCH	BUILDUP	UPBUILD	CANDIES	INCASED
BORTIER	ORBITER	BUISTED	SUBEDIT	CANDOUR	CAUDRON
BOSHTER	BOTHERS	BULGHUR	BURGHUL	CANFULS	CANSFUL
BOSSEST	BOSSETS	BULKERS	BURLESK	CANGLES	GLANCES
BOSSIER	RIBOSES	BULLOUS	LOBULUS	CANGUES	UNCAGES
BOUCHES	SUBECHO	BUMMLED	MUMBLED	CANKERS	SNACKER
BOUGETS	OUTBEGS	BUNDIST	DUSTBIN	CANNERS	SCANNER
BOULDER	DOUBLER	BUNTALS	TULBANS	CANNIER	NARCEIN
BOULTED	DOUBLET	BURDASH	RHABDUS	CANTRED	TRANCED
BOULTER	TROUBLE	BURIALS	RAILBUS	CANULAE	LACUNAE
BOUNCED	BUNCOED	BURLERS	BURRELS	CANULAR	LACUNAR
BOUNDEN	UNBONED	BURNOUT	OUTBURN	CANULAS	LACUNAS
BOUSIER	OUREBIS	BURPING	UPBRING	CANYONS	SONANCY
BOUTONS	UNBOOTS	BURSERA	SABREUR	CAPABLE	PACABLE
BOWELED	ELBOWED	BURYING	RUBYING	CAPERER	PRERACE
BOWINGS	BOWSING	BUSBIES	SUBBIES	CAPITAL	PLACITA
BOWLDER	LOWBRED	BUSIEST	SUBSITE	CAPITAN	CAPTAIN
BOWLEGS	WEBLOGS	BUSINGS	BUSSING	CAPIZES	CAPSIZE
BOWSERS	BROWSES	BUSTICS	CUBISTS	CAPLETS	PLACETS
BOXWOOD	WOODBOX	BUSTIER	RUBIEST	CAPLINS	INCLASP
BOYARDS	BYROADS	BUSTING	TUBINGS	CAPORAL	CRAPOLA
BRADOON	ONBOARD	BUSTLES	SUBLETS	CAPOUCH	PACHUCO
BRAHMAS	SAMBHAR	BUTANES	SUNBEAT	CAPTION	PACTION
BRAILLE	LIBERAL	BUTENES	SUBTEEN	CARACKS	CRACKAS

CARBEEN	CARBENE	CESSPIT	SEPTICS	CHOKEYS	HOCKEYS
CARBONS	CORBANS	CETANES	TENACES	CHOKING	HOCKING
CARDERS	SCARRED	CHACHKA	KACHCHA	CHOLENT	NOTCHEL
CAREERS	CREASER	CHACOES	COACHES	CHOLERS	ORCHELS
CARGOED	CORDAGE	CHAINED	ECHIDNA	CHOLINE	HELICON
CARHOPS	COPRAHS	CHAINES	INCHASE	CHOOSER	SOROCHE
CARIOUS	CURIOSA	CHAKRAS	CHARKAS	CHOPINE	PHOCINE
CARNEYS	SCENARY	CHALKED	HACKLED	CHOPINS	PHONICS
CAROCHE	COACHER	CHALLIE	HELICAL	CHORDAE	ROACHED
CAROLED	ORACLED	CHAMISA	CHIASMA	CHORDAL	DORLACH
CAROMED	COMRADE	CHAMISO	CHAMOIS	CHORING	OCHRING
CAROTIN	CORTINA	CHANCER	CHANCRE	CHORISM	CHRISOM
CARPING	CRAPING	CHANGED	GANCHED	CHORIST	OSTRICH
CARRIES	SCARIER	CHANGES	GANCHES	CHOROID	OCHROID
CARROTS	TROCARS	CHANSON	NONCASH	CHORTEN	NOTCHER
CARSEYS	SCRAYES	CHANTER	TRANCHE	CHOUSES	HOCUSES
CARTOON	CORANTO	CHAPKAS	PACHAKS	CHOWDER	COWHERD
CARVERS	CRAVERS	CHARGES	CREAGHS	CHOWSED	COWSHED
CARVING	CRAVING	CHARIOT	HARICOT	CHROMAS	MORCHAS
CASABAS	CASSABA	CHARMED	MARCHED	CHUNDER	CHURNED
CASAVAS	CASSAVA	CHARMER	MARCHER	CHYLOUS	SLOUCHY
CASCADE	SACCADE	CHARNEL	LARCHEN	CHYMIST	TYCHISM
CASQUES	SACQUES	CHARPAI	HAIRCAP	CHYPRES	CYPHERS
CASSOCK	COSSACK	CHARTED	RATCHED	CIDARIS	SCIARID
CASTLED	SCLATED	CHARTER	RECHART	CILICES	ICICLES
CASTLES	SCLATES	CHASTEN	NATCHES	CINGULA	GLUCINA
CASTOFF	OFFCAST	CHATTEL	LATCHET	CINQUES	QUINCES
CASTORS	COSTARS	CHATTER	RATCHET	CIPOLIN	PICOLIN
CASUALS	CAUSALS	CHAWING	CHINWAG	CIRCARS	RICRACS
CATALOS	COASTAL	CHEAPED	PEACHED	CIRCLES	CLERICS
CATCHER	RECATCH	CHEAPER	PEACHER	CIRRATE	ERRATIC
CATCHUP	UPCATCH	CHECKER	RECHECK	CISTERN	CRETINS
CATHOLE	CHOLATE	CHEEPED	DEPECHE	CITATOR	RICOTTA
CATLING	TALCING	CHEERED	REECHED	CITHERN	CITHREN
CATLINS	TINCALS	CHEERLY	LECHERY	CITIZEN	ZINCITE
CATSUPS	UPCASTS	CHELOID	HELCOID	CITOLAS	STOICAL
CATTILY	TACITLY	CHELONE	ECHELON	CLADDER	CRADLED
CAUDLES	CEDULAS	CHEMISE	SCHEMIE	CLANGER	GLANCER
CAULOME	LEUCOMA	CHEMIST	MITCHES	CLAQUER	LACQUER
CAUSEYS	CAYUSES	CHENARS	RANCHES	CLARINO	CLARION
CAUSING	SAUCING	CHENETS	TENCHES	CLASHES	SEALCHS
CAUSTIC	CICUTAS	CHERISH	SHRIECH	CLASPED	SCALPED
CAUTELS	SULCATE	CHESILS	CHISELS	CLASSED	DECLASS
CAVEATS	VACATES	CHETAHS	HATCHES	CLASSES	SACLESS
CAVERNS	CRAVENS	CHEVETS	VETCHES	CLAVIES	VESICAL
CAWKERS	WACKERS	CHEVIES	SEVICHE	CLEANER	RECLEAN
CEASING	INCAGES	CHEWERS	RECHEWS	CLEANUP	UNPLACE
CEILING	CIELING	CHIASMS	SCHISMA	CLEFTED	DEFLECT
CELESTA	SELECTA	CHICEST	HECTICS	CLEUCHS	CULCHES
CELOSIA	COALISE	CHICLES	CLICHES	CLEUGHS	GULCHES
CENSING	SCENING	CHICONS	COCHINS	CLIMATE	METICAL
CENTILE	LICENTE	CHIDERS	HERDICS	CLIMBER	RECLIMB
CENTRED	CREDENT	CHIELDS	CHILDES	CLINGER	CRINGLE
CERAMIC	RACEMIC	CHIGRES	SCREIGH	CLINKED	NICKLED
CERIUMS	MURICES	CHIKORS	CHOKRIS	CLINKER	CRINKLE
CEROTIC	ORECTIC	CHIMERS	MICHERS	CLIPPER	CRIPPLE
CERTIFY	RECTIFY	CHIMING	MICHING	CLOBBER	COBBLER
CERVIDS	SCRIVED	CHIPSET	PITCHES	CLOCKED	COCKLED
CESIUMS	MISCUES	CHIVIES	VICHIES	CLOCKER	COCKLER
CESSERS	CRESSES	CHOICER	CHOREIC	CLODDED	CODDLED

CLOGGED	COGGLED	CONSENT	NOCENTS	CREMATE	MEERCAT
CLOISON	SCOLION	CONSIST	TOCSINS	CREMONA	ROMANCE
CLOKING	LOCKING	CONSORT	CROTONS	CREMSIN	MINCERS
CLONERS	CORNELS	CONSULT	UNCOLTS	CREOLES	RECLOSE
CLOSEST	CLOSETS	CONSUME	MUSCONE	CREPING	PERCING
CLOSURE	COLURES	CONURES	ROUNCES	CRETISM	METRICS
CLOTTER	CROTTLE	CONVEYS	COVYNES	CRIMINA	MINICAR
CLOVERS	VELCROS	COOKERS	RECOOKS	CRIMSON	MICRONS
CLUEING	LUCIGEN	COOKOUT	OUTCOOK	CRISPED	DISCERP
CLUMBER	CRUMBLE	COOLANT	OCTANOL	CRISPER	PRICERS
CLUMPER	CRUMPLE	COOLERS	CREOSOL	CROQUET	ROCQUET
CLUNKER	CRUNKLE	COOLEST	OCELOTS	CROSSED	SCORSED
CNEMIAL	MELANIC	COOLING	LOCOING	CROSSES	SCORSES
COAGENT	COGNATE	COOPERS	SCOOPER	CROUPED	PRODUCE
COALTAR	CROTALA	COOSERS	ROSCOES	CROUPER	PROCURE
COARSER	CORREAS	COOTERS	SCOOTER	CROWERS	SCOWRER
COATING	COTINGA	COPITAS	PSOATIC	CROWNED	DECROWN
COCAINE	OCEANIC	COPOUTS	OCTOPUS	CROWNER	RECROWN
COCKERS	RECOCKS	COPTERS	PROSECT	CRUDEST	CRUSTED
COCKILY	COLICKY	COPULAR	CUPOLAR	CRUELTY	CUTLERY
CODDLES	SCOLDED	CORCASS	CORSACS	CRUISED	DISCURE
CODEINA	OCEANID	CORDATE	REDCOAT	CRUIVES	CURSIVE
CODLING	LINGCOD	CORDERS	RECORDS	CRUSADE	SCAURED
CODRIVE	DIVORCE	CORELLA	OCELLAR	CRUSTAL	CURTALS
CODROVE	VOCODER	CORKIER	ROCKIER	CRYINGS	SCRYING
COENURI	NOURICE	CORKING	ROCKING	CUDDLES	SCUDDLE
COFFERS	SCOFFER	CORNERS	SCORNER	CUFFLES	SCUFFLE
COGENER	CONGREE	CORNILY	LYRICON	CUISHES	CUSHIES
COGNISE	COIGNES	CORNUAL	COURLAN	CULMENS	MESCLUN
COHEIRS	HEROICS	CORONAS	RACOONS	CULTIER	UTRICLE
COIFFES	OFFICES	CORONER	CROONER	CUMBERS	SCUMBER
COILERS	RECOILS	CORPSES	PROCESS	CUMMERS	SCUMMER
COLEADS	SOLACED	CORSIVE	VOICERS	CUNNERS	SCUNNER
COLITIS	SOLICIT	COSIERS	CRIOSES	CUPELED	DECUPLE
COLLOPS	SCOLLOP	COSMIST	SITCOMS	CUPFULS	CUPSFUL
COLLUDE	LOCULED	COSTEAN	OCTANES	CUPPERS	SCUPPER
COLOBUS	SUBCOOL	COSTING	GNOSTIC	CUPRITE	PICTURE
COLONES	CONSOLE	COTTISE	SCOTTIE	CURACAO	CURACOA
COLORER	RECOLOR	COUNSEL	UNCLOSE	CURAGHS	SCRAUGH
COMARBS	CRAMBOS	COUPLET	OCTUPLE	CURATED	TRADUCE
COMBATS	TOMBACS	COUPONS	SOUPCON	CURDIER	CURRIED
COMBERS	RECOMBS	COURIES	SCOURIE	CURDLES	SCUDLER
COMBIER	MICROBE	COURTED	EDUCTOR	CURNIER	REINCUR
COMICES	MOCCIES	COUTILS	OCULIST	CURPELS	SCRUPLE
COMPARE	COMPEAR	COUZINS	ZINCOUS	CURTAIL	TRUCIAL
COMPEER	COMPERE	COVERER	RECOVER	CURTAIN	TURACIN
COMPILE	POLEMIC	COWRIES	SCOWRIE	CURTESY	CURTSEY
COMPOST	COMPOTS	COYOTES	OOCYTES	CUSPATE	TEACUPS
COMUSES	MUSCOSE	CRADLES	SCALDER	CUSSING	SCUSING
CONARIA	OCARINA	CRAFTED	FRACTED	CUTOFFS	OFFCUTS
CONCENT	CONNECT	CRAFTER	REFRACT	CYCLISE	CYLICES
CONDOES	SECONDO	CRAMPIT	PTARMIC	CYSTEIN	CYSTINE
CONDORS	CORDONS	CRANING	RANCING	CYTASES	ECSTASY
CONDUIT	NOCTUID	CRANIUM	CUMARIN	DABBLES	SLABBED
CONGAED	DECAGON	CRAPPIE	EPICARP	DABSTER	TABERDS
CONGIUS	SOUCING	CRASHED	ECHARDS	DADDLES	SADDLED
CONICAL	LACONIC	CREASES	SEARCES	DAFTIES	FADIEST
CONIINE	INCONIE	CRECHES	SCREECH	DAGGLES	SLAGGED
CONKERS	RECKONS	CREDITS	DIRECTS	DAIDLES	LADDIES
CONKING	NOCKING	CREEPED	PRECEDE	DAIKERS	DARKIES

DALLIED	DIALLED	DEFROST	FROSTED	DETENUS	DETUNES
DALTONS	SANDLOT	DEFUSER	REFUSED	DETERGE	GREETED
DAMAGER	MEGARAD	DEHORTS	SHORTED	DETICKS	STICKED
DAMMERS	SMARMED	DEIDEST	TEDDIES	DETORTS	DOTTERS
DAMPEST	STAMPED	DEIFIED	EDIFIED	DETRACT	TRACTED
DAMPISH	PHASMID	DEIFIES	EDIFIES	DEUCING	EDUCING
DANDIER	DRAINED	DEINDEX	INDEXED	DEUTONS	SNOUTED
DANDIES	SDAINED	DEISTIC	DICIEST	DEVEINS	ENDIVES
DANGLED	GLADDEN	DEKARES	SKEARED	DEVOLVE	EVOLVED
DANGLER	GNARLED	DELATES	STEALED	DEWITTS	TWISTED
DANKEST	STANKED	DELATOR	LEOTARD	DEWLAPS	SPAWLED
DANTONS	DONNATS	DELENDA	LADENED	DHANSAK	KHANDAS
DARINGS	GRADINS	DELIGHT	LIGHTED	DHURRIE	HURRIED
DARLING	LARDING	DELIMIT	LIMITED	DIALYSE	EYLIADS
DARSHAN	DHARNAS	DELIRIA	IRIDEAL	DIASTEM	MISDATE
DARTING	TRADING	DELVING	DEVLING	DIATOMS	MASTOID
DARTLES	SLARTED	DEMANDS	MADDENS	DIAXONS	DIOXANS
DASHERS	SHADERS	DEMERGE	EMERGED	DIAZINS	DIZAINS
DASHING	SHADING	DEMESNE	SEEDMEN	DIBBLER	DRIBBLE
DATARIA	RADIATA	DEMISED	MISDEED	DICHTED	DITCHED
DAUNTED	UNDATED	DEMOING	MENDIGO	DICINGS	DISCING
DAWDING	WADDING	DEMOUNT	MOUNTED	DICKENS	SNICKED
DAWDLED	WADDLED	DEMURES	RESUMED	DICKERS	SCRIKED
DAWTIES	WAISTED	DENDRON	DONNERD	DICTIER	ICTERID
DAYWORK	WORKDAY	DENGUES	UNEDGES	DIDDLER	RIDDLED
DEAIRED	READIED	DENIALS	SNAILED	DIEDRAL	DRAILED
DEANERS	ENDEARS	DENNETS	STENNED	DIEHARD	DIHEDRA
DEARIES	READIES	DENSITY	DESTINY	DIEOFFS	OFFSIDE
DEASOIL	ISOLEAD	DENTALS	SLANTED	DIGESTS	DISGEST
DEAVING	EVADING	DENTELS	NESTLED	DIGNITY	TIDYING
DEBASES	SEABEDS	DENTING	TENDING	DIGONAL	LOADING
DEBTORS	STROBED	DENUDER	ENDURED	DILUENT	UNTILED
DECAMPS	SCAMPED	DEPERMS	PREMEDS	DILUTES	DUELIST
DECANES	ENCASED	DEPICTS	DISCEPT	DIMNESS	MISSEND
DECERNS	SCERNED	DEPLANE	PANELED	DINDLES	SLIDDEN
DECIDER	DECRIED	DEPLOYS	PODLEYS	DINGERS	ENGIRDS
DECILES	DELICES	DEPONES	SPONDEE	DINGEYS	DYEINGS
DECKELS	DECKLES	DEPOSAL	PEDALOS	DINKEST	KINDEST
DECKOED	DECOKED	DEPOSED	SEEDPOD	DINKEYS	KIDNEYS
DECODER	RECODED	DEPOSER	REPOSED	DINKIES	KINDIES
DECREED	RECEDED	DEPOSES	SPEEDOS	DINKING	KINDING
DECREET	ERECTED	DERAYED	YEARDED	DINNERS	ENDRINS
DECREWS	SCREWED	DERNIER	NERDIER	DINNLES	LINDENS
DECRIES	DEICERS	DERVISH	SHRIVED	DINTING	TINDING
DECTETS	DETECTS	DESANDS	SADDENS	DIOXIDS	IXODIDS
DEDIMUS	MUDDIES	DESCEND	SCENDED	DIPHONE	PHONIED
DEDUCES	SEDUCED	DESCENT	SCENTED	DIPNETS	STIPEND
DEEDEST	STEEDED	DESERVE	SEVERED	DIPNOAN	NONPAID
DEEDILY	YIELDED	DESIGNS	SDEIGNS	DIRHAMS	MIDRASH
DEEDING	DEIGNED	DESIRES	RESIDES	DIRTIED	TIDDIER
DEEPEST	STEEPED	DESKILL	SKILLED	DISCOER	SCODIER
DEFACER	REFACED	DESMANS	MADNESS	DISEASE	SEASIDE
DEFAULT	FAULTED	DESMINE	SIDEMEN	DISEURS	SUDSIER
DEFIANT	FAINTED	DESNOOD	SNOODED	DISGOWN	DOWSING
DEFIERS	SERIFED	DESPISE	PEDESIS	DISHORN	DRONISH
DEFILED	FIELDED	DESUGAR	SUGARED	DISMAYD	MIDDAYS
DEFOCUS	FOCUSED	DESYNES	ENDYSES	DISMAYL	LADYISM
DEFORMS	SERFDOM	DETAILS	DILATES	DISPELS	DISPLES
DEFOULS	FLOUSED	DETENTE	NEDETTE	DISPLED	PIDDLES
DEFROCK	FROCKED	DETENTS	STENTED	DISPONE	SPINODE

DISROOT	TOROIDS	DRAPPIE	PREPAID	EARNERS	REEARNS
DISSEAT	SAIDEST	DRAWEES	RESAWED	EARTHED	HEARTED
DISSERT	STRIDES	DRAWING	WARDING	EARTHEN	HEARTEN
DISSING	SIDINGS	DRAYAGE	YARDAGE	EARWIGS	GAWSIER
DISTUNE	DUNITES	DRAYING	YARDING	EBAYERS	EYEBARS
DITCHES	SICHTED	DRAYMAN	YARDMAN	EBONIES	EBONISE
DITHERS	SHIRTED	DRAYMEN	YARDMEN	ECHOIST	TOISECH
DITHIOL	LITHOID	DREADED	READDED	ECONOMY	MONOECY
DITONES	STONIED	DREADLY	LADDERY	EDENTAL	LATENED
DIURONS	DURIONS	DRESSER	REDRESS	EDGINGS	SNIGGED
DIVERGE	GRIEVED	DRILLER	REDRILL	EDITION	TENIOID
DIVISOR	VIROIDS	DROGUET	GROUTED	EELIEST	STEELIE
DOCKERS	REDOCKS	DROICHS	ORCHIDS	EEVNING	EVENING
DODGERS	GORSEDD	DROOMES	SMOORED	EFTSOON	FESTOON
DODGING	GODDING	DROPLET	PRETOLD	EGGLERS	LEGGERS
DODMANS	ODDSMAN	DROPOUT	OUTDROP	EGOISMS	MISGOES
DOGATES	DOTAGES	DROWSED	SWORDED	EGOISTS	STOGIES
DOGEATE	GOATEED	DRUGGED	GRUDGED	EGOTISE	GOETIES
DOGLEGS	SLOGGED	DRUGGER	GRUDGER	EILDING	ELIDING
DOGLIKE	GODLIKE	DRUMBLE	RUMBLED	EISWEIN	WIENIES
DOGSHIP	GODSHIP	DRUPELS	SLURPED	ELATION	TOENAIL
DOILIES	IDOLISE	DRUSIER	DURRIES	ELCHEES	LEECHES
DOLINAS	LADINOS	DUALINS	SUNDIAL	ELECTOR	ELECTRO
DONATED	NODATED	DUALIST	TULADIS	ELEGIES	ELEGISE
DONGLES	GOLDENS	DUCTILE	DULCITE	ELEGIST	ELEGITS
DONGOLA	GONDOLA	DUDDIER	RUDDIED	ELEMENT	TELEMEN
DONINGS	ONDINGS	DUELERS	ELUDERS	ELOGIST	LOGIEST
DONNERT	TENDRON	DUETTOS	TESTUDO	ELOPERS	LEPROSE
DONNIES	ONDINES	DUFFEST	STUFFED	ELUATES	SETUALE
DOODLER	DROOLED	DUGITES	GIUSTED	ELUENTS	UNSTEEL
DOOFERS	FORDOES	DUGONGS	GUNDOGS	ELUTION	OUTLINE
DOOKETS	STOOKED	DUIKERS	DUSKIER	EMAILED	LIMEADE
DOOLANS	ONLOADS	DUKKAHS	DUKKHAS	EMBLICS	LIMBECS
DOOMILY	MOODILY	DULCIAN	INCUDAL	EMBRUED	UMBERED
DOORMAN	MADRONO	DULOSIS	SOLIDUS	EMENDER	REEDMEN
DOORMEN	MORENDO	DUMAIST	STADIUM	EMERGES	MERGEES
DOPINGS	PONGIDS	DUMMIER	IMMURED	EMICANT	NEMATIC
DORISED	SODDIER	DUMMIES	MEDIUMS	EMITTER	TERMITE
DORISES	DOSSIER	DUMPIER	UMPIRED	EMONGES	GENOMES
DORMANT	MORDANT	DUMPLES	SLUMPED	EMOTING	MITOGEN
DORMINS	NIMRODS	DUNGING	NUDGING	EMPALER	PREMEAL
DORTERS	RODSTER	DUNNEST	STUNNED	EMPANEL	EMPLANE
DOSAGES	SEADOGS	DUNNIER	INURNED	EMPARED	PREMADE
DOSSERS	DROSSES	DUNNIES	UNDINES	EMPORIA	MEROPIA
DOTCOMS	TOMCODS	DUNSHES	SNUSHED	EMPTIES	SEPTIME
DOTIEST	STOITED	DUNTING	TUNDING	EMPTINS	PIMENTS
DOTTLER	DOTTREL	DUOTONE	OUTDONE	EMPTION	PIMENTO
DOURINE	NEUROID	DUPIONS	UNIPODS	EMULGES	LEGUMES
DOUSING	GUIDONS	DURANCE	UNRACED	EMUNGED	GUDEMEN
DOWAGER	WORDAGE	DURIANS	SUNDARI	ENAMELS	MELENAS
DOWNERS	WONDERS	DURMAST	MUSTARD	ENAMOUR	NEUROMA
DOWNIER	WINDORE	DUSTERS	TRUSSED	ENCAVED	VENDACE
DOWSERS	DROWSES	DWARVES	SWARVED	ENCHARM	MARCHEN
DRAFTER	REDRAFT	DWINDLE	WINDLED	ENCLASP	SPANCEL
DRAGEES	GREASED	DWINING	WINDING	ENCLAVE	VALENCE
DRAGNET	GRANTED	DYELINE	NEEDILY	ENCODER	ENCORED
DRAGOON	GADROON	EARFLAP	PARAFLE	ENCODES	SECONDE
DRAINER	RANDIER	EARLIER	LEARIER	ENCORES	NECROSE
DRAPERS	SPARRED	EARLIES	REALISE	ENCRATY	NECTARY
DRAPING	PARDING	EARLIKE	LEAKIER	ENDARCH	RANCHED

ENDINGS	SENDING	ERATHEM	THERMAE	FALCONS	FLACONS
ENDITED	TEINDED	ERECTER	REERECT	FALLERS	REFALLS
ENDNOTE	TENONED	EREPSIN	REPINES	FALLOUT	OUTFALL
ENDOWER	REENDOW	ERGATES	RESTAGE	FALSERS	FLASERS
ENDURES	ENSURED	ERINITE	NITERIE	FALSIES	FILASSE
ENDWISE	SINEWED	ERISTIC	RICIEST	FAMINES	INFAMES
ENEWING	WEENING	EROTICS	TERCIOS	FANGLED	FLANGED
ENFOLDS	FONDLES	ERRANTS	RANTERS	FANGLES	FLANGES
ENFRAME	FREEMAN	ERRATUM	MATURER	FANKLED	FLANKED
ENGINED	NEEDING	ERUPTED	REPUTED	FANNELL	FLANNEL
ENGINER	INGENER	ERYNGOS	GROYNES	FANTAIL	TAILFAN
ENGLISH	SHINGLE	ESCROCS	SOCCERS	FARCERS	SCARFER
ENGLUTS	GLUTENS	ESPADAS	PASSADE	FARCIES	FIACRES
ENGORES	NEGROES	ESPANOL	NOPALES	FARDENS	SNARFED
ENGUARD	RAUNGED	ESPIERS	PRESSIE	FARFELS	RAFFLES
ENJOYER	REENJOY	ESPOUSE	POSEUSE	FARMERS	FRAMERS
ENLIGHT	LIGHTEN	ESQUIRE	QUERIES	FARMING	FRAMING
ENLOCKS	SLOCKEN	ESSOYNE	NOYESES	FARMOST	FORMATS
ENMOVED	VENOMED	ESTEEMS	MESTEES	FARSIDE	FRAISED
ENOLOGY	NEOLOGY	ESTHETE	TEETHES	FASTENS	FATNESS
ENQUIRE	INQUERE	ESTOILE	ETOILES	FASTERS	STRAFES
ENRACED	RECANED	ESTREPE	STEEPER	FASTEST	SAFTEST
ENRINGS	GINNERS	ESTRUAL	SALUTER	FATSOES	FOSSATE
ENROUGH	ROUGHEN	ETALAGE	GALEATE	FAUTORS	FOUTRAS
ENSIGNS	SENSING	ETALONS	TOLANES	FAVORER	OVERFAR
ENSKIED	SKEINED	ETAMINE	MATINEE	FEATHER	TEREFAH
ENSKIES	KINESES	ETATIST	TATTIES	FECHTER	FETCHER
ENSLAVE	LEAVENS	ETCHERS	RETCHES	FEEDERS	REFEEDS
ENSNARE	RENNASE	ETHIONS	HISTONE	FEEDING	FEIGNED
ENSNARL	LANNERS	ETHIOPS	OPHITES	FEELERS	REFEELS
ENSOULS	NOUSLES	ETHNICS	STHENIC	FEELING	FLEEING
ENSTAMP	TAPSMEN	ETTLING	LETTING	FELLATE	LEAFLET
ENSTEEP	STEEPEN	EUMONGS	MUNGOES	FELTIER	FERTILE
ENSTYLE	TENSELY	EVANISH	VAHINES	FEMINAL	INFLAME
ENTAMES	MEANEST	EVENTER	EVERNET	FEODARY	FORAYED
ENTASIA	TAENIAS	EVOKERS	REVOKES	FERNIER	REFINER
ENTERIC	ENTICER	EVOLUTE	VELOUTE	FERROUS	FURORES
ENTERON	TENONER	EVOLVER	REVOLVE	FETIALS	SEALIFT
ENTOPIC	NEPOTIC	EXACTER	EXCRETA	FETICHE	FITCHEE
ENTOTIC	TONETIC	EXAMPLE	EXEMPLA	FETTLES	LEFTEST
ENTOZOA	OZONATE	EXCEPTS	EXPECTS	FEUTRED	REFUTED
ENTRAIN	TRANNIE	EXCIDES	EXCISED	FEUTRES	REFUTES
ENTRUST	NUTTERS	EXCITOR	XEROTIC	FICKLED	FLICKED
ENTWIST	TWINSET	EXCURSE	EXCUSER	FICKLER	FLICKER
ENWOUND	UNOWNED	EXPANDS	SPANDEX	FIERIER	REIFIER
EPACRID	PERACID	EXPERTS	SEXPERT	FILAREE	LEAFIER
EPARCHS	PARCHES	EXPIRES	PREXIES	FILLERS	REFILLS
EPARCHY	PREACHY	EXPOSED	PODEXES	FILMERS	REFILMS
EPEIRIC	EPICIER	EXPOSIT	POXIEST	FILMSET	LEFTISM
EPHEBOS	PHOEBES	EXTINES	SIXTEEN	FINALIS	FINIALS
EPIGRAM	PRIMAGE	EYELIDS	SEEDILY	FINGERS	FRINGES
EPILATE	PILEATE	EYESPOT	PEYOTES	FINITES	NIFTIES
EPIMERE	PREEMIE	FACIEND	FANCIED	FINKING	KNIFING
EPINAOS	SENOPIA	FACTORS	FORCATS	FIRELIT	FITLIER
EPISODE	POESIED	FACTURE	FURCATE	FIREPOT	PIEFORT
EPISTLE	PELITES	FAIENCE	FIANCEE	FIRLOTS	FLORIST
EPOXIDE	EPOXIED	FAINEST	NAIFEST	FIRMEST	FREMITS
EPSILON	PINOLES	FAINNES	FANNIES	FISTING	SIFTING
EQUATOR	QUORATE	FAINTER	FENITAR	FITNESS	INFESTS
EQUINAL	QUINELA	FAIRISH	HAIRIFS	FITTERS	TITFERS

FITTING	TIFTING	GABBLER	GRABBLE	GIRDERS	RIDGERS
FIZZERS	FRIZZES	GABELLE	GELABLE	GIRLOND	LORDING
FLARIER	FRAILER	GABNASH	NASHGAB	GIRNING	RINGING
FLATCAR	FRACTAL	GADGETS	STAGGED	GIRONNY	ROYNING
FLECKER	FRECKLE	GAHNITE	HEATING	GIRSHES	SIGHERS
FLEMISH	HIMSELF	GALERES	REGALES	GIRTHED	RIGHTED
FLENSER	FRESNEL	GALLEIN	NIGELLA	GIRTING	RINGGIT
FLESHED	SHELFED	GALLICA	GLACIAL	GITTERN	RETTING
FLESHER	HERSELF	GALLIES	GALLISE	GLACIER	GRACILE
FLETTON	FONTLET	GALLING	GINGALL	GLADIER	GLAIRED
FLIRTED	TRIFLED	GALLNUT	NUTGALL	GLAIKET	TAGLIKE
FLIRTER	TRIFLER	GALLONS	GOLLANS	GLAIRES	GRAILES
FLITING	LIFTING	GALORES	GAOLERS	GLEAVES	SELVAGE
FLOORER	FORLORE	GAMBIST	GAMBITS	GLEEING	NEGLIGE
FLOOSIE	FOLIOSE	GAMBLER	GAMBREL	GLEEMAN	MELANGE
FLORETS	LOFTERS	GAMETES	METAGES	GLIBBER	GRIBBLE
FLOURED	FOULDER	GAMIEST	SIGMATE	GLIMPSE	MEGILPS
FLUATES	SULFATE	GAMMERS	GRAMMES	GLINTED	TINGLED
FLUERIC	LUCIFER	GAMONES	MANGOES	GLISTER	GRISTLE
FLUIEST	SULFITE	GANGING	NAGGING	GLOATER	LEGATOR
FLUSHED	SHEDFUL	GANSEYS	GAYNESS	GLOIRES	GLORIES
FLUTIER	FUTILER	GANTING	TANGING	GLOMERA	GOMERAL
FLUVIAL	VIALFUL	GAOLING	GOALING	GLONOIN	LOONING
FLYOVER	OVERFLY	GARNERS	RANGERS	GLOSSED	GODLESS
FOALING	LOAFING	GASLESS	GLASSES	GLOSSER	REGLOSS
FOCUSER	REFOCUS	GASPERS	SPARGES	GLOVERS	GROVELS
FOCUSES	FUCOSES	GASSERS	GRASSES	GLOWERS	REGLOWS
FOISTER	FORTIES	GASTERS	STAGERS	GLOWING	GOWLING
FOLDERS	REFOLDS	GASTRIC	TRAGICS	GLUEING	LUGEING
FOLDUPS	UPFOLDS	GATEWAY	GETAWAY	GLUGGED	GUGGLED
FONDLER	FORLEND	GAUDGIE	GUIDAGE	GLUIEST	UGLIEST
FONDUED	FOUNDED	GAUFERS	GAUFRES	GLUTTED	GUTTLED
FORAMEN	FOREMAN	GAUNTED	UNGATED	GNARRED	GRANDER
FORBARE	FORBEAR	GEARING	NAGGIER	GNASHED	HAGDENS
FORESTS	FOSTERS	GELATOS	LEGATOS	GOALIES	SOILAGE
FORETOP	POOFTER	GELDING	NIGGLED	GODDENS	GODSEND
FORFEIT	TOFFIER	GEMMATE	TAGMEME	GODLING	LODGING
FORMERS	REFORMS	GENOISE	SOIGNEE	GOLOSHE	SHOOGLE
FORRAYS	ORFRAYS	GENTLED	GLENTED	GONGING	NOGGING
FORWARD	FROWARD	GENTLES	LENGEST	GONIFFS	OFFINGS
FOUNDER	REFOUND	GENUINE	INGENUE	GOODIES	SOOGIED
FOUTERS	FOUTRES	GENUSES	NEGUSES	GOOLIES	OLOGIES
FRANGER	GRANFER	GERENTS	REGENTS	GOORIES	GOOSIER
FRENUMS	SURFMEN	GERMING	MERGING	GOOSIES	SOOGIES
FRESHER	REFRESH	GESTATE	TAGETES	GORGETS	TOGGERS
FRESHET	HEFTERS	GIBBONS	SOBBING	GORINGS	GRINGOS
FRESHIE	HEIFERS	GILDING	GLIDING	GOSLING	OGLINGS
FRETFUL	TRUFFLE	GILLERS	GRILLES	GOWANED	WAGONED
FRETSAW	WAFTERS	GILLNET	TELLING	GRADDAN	GRANDAD
FRONTER	REFRONT	GIMMERS	MEGRIMS	GRADERS	REGARDS
FUGLIER	GULFIER	GINGALS	LAGGINS	GRADING	NIGGARD
FUGLING	GULFING	GINGELY	GLEYING	GRADINI	RAIDING
FULNESS	UNSELFS	GINGKOS	GINKGOS	GRAFTER	REGRAFT
FUNDERS	REFUNDS	GINNELS	LENSING	GRAHAMS	GRAMASH
FUNDIES	INFUSED	GINNERY	RENYING	GRANDAM	GRANDMA
FUNFAIR	RUFFIAN	GINNIER	REINING	GRANTER	REGRANT
FURANES	UNSAFER	GINSHOP	POSHING	GRAPING	PARGING
FUROLES	OURSELF	GIPPERS	GRIPPES	GRAPLIN	PARLING
FUSIBLE	SUBFILE	GIRAFFE	RIFFAGE	GRASPER	SPARGER
FUSTIER	SURFEIT	GIRASOL	GLORIAS	GRATING	TARGING

GRAVELS	VERGLAS	HALAKAH	HALAKHA	HIDLING	HILDING
GRAVURE	VERRUGA	HALITES	HELIAST	HIELAND	INHALED
GREASER	REGEARS	HALITUS	THULIAS	HIGHTED	THIGHED
GREATER	REGRATE	HALLANS	NALLAHS	HILLERS	RELLISH
GREENED	RENEGED	HALLOED	HOLLAED	HILLOES	HOLLIES
GREETER	REGREET	HALLOOS	HOLLOAS	HILTING	LITHING
GREMIAL	LAMIGER	HALLOWS	SHALLOW	HINDGUT	UNDIGHT
GRIEVES	REGIVES	HALTERE	LEATHER	HINGING	NIGHING
GRIFFIN	RIFFING	HALTING	LATHING	HINTERS	NITHERS
GRINDED	REDDING	HAMBLES	SHAMBLE	HINTING	NITHING
GRINDER	REGRIND	HAMMERS	SHAMMER	HIPBONE	HOPBINE
GRINNED	RENDING	HANDERS	HARDENS	HIPPENS	SHIPPEN
GRIPMAN	RAMPING	HANDLES	HANDSEL	HIPPIES	SHIPPIE
GROANER	ORANGER	HANDOFF	OFFHAND	HIRINGS	SHIRING
GROOMER	REGROOM	HANGOUT	TOHUNGA	HIRSELS	HIRSLES
GROOVED	OVERDOG	HANGUPS	UPHANGS	HISSELF	SELFISH
GROSERS	GROSSER	HANJARS	RHANJAS	HITTERS	TITHERS
GROSSED	SODGERS	HANKERS	HARKENS	HITTING	TITHING
GROUPER	REGROUP	HANTING	TANGHIN	HOARSEN	SENHORA
GROUPIE	PIROGUE	HAPLESS	PLASHES	HODDENS	SHODDEN
GROWERS	REGROWS	HAPLONT	NAPHTOL	HOEDOWN	WOODHEN
GROWNUP	UPGROWN	HARDASS	SRADHAS	HOLDUPS	UPHOLDS
GRUEING	GUNGIER	HARDIER	HARRIED	HOLINGS	LONGISH
GRUELED	REGLUED	HARDMEN	HERDMAN	HOLSTER	HOSTLER
GRUMOSE	MORGUES	HAREEMS	MAHSEER	HOMAGES	OHMAGES
GRUNGES	SNUGGER	HARELDS	HERALDS	HONGIES	SHOEING
GRUNTED	TRUDGEN	HARISSA	SHARIAS	HOODMAN	MANHOOD
GRUSHIE	GUSHIER	HARPIES	SHARPIE	HOOPING	POOHING
GRUTTEN	TURGENT	HARVEST	THRAVES	HOPPERS	SHOPPER
GUBBINS	SUBBING	HASSLED	SLASHED	HORMONE	MOORHEN
GUDDLES	SLUDGED	HASSOCK	SHACKOS	HORRENT	NORTHER
GULLIES	LIGULES	HASTIER	SHERIAT	HORSING	SHORING
GULPERS	SPLURGE	HASTING	TASHING	HORSTES	TOSHERS
GUNDIES	SUEDING	HATFULS	HATSFUL	HOSTING	TOSHING
GUNLESS	GUNSELS	HATTING	TATHING	HOTCHES	SHOCHET
GUNSHIP	PUSHING	HAULING	NILGHAU	HOTLINE	NEOLITH
GURGING	RUGGING	HAVINGS	SHAVING	HOTTING	TONIGHT
GURRIES	SURGIER	HAWKIES	WEAKISH	HOUTING	THOUING
GURSHES	GUSHERS	HAYRIDE	HYDRIAE	HOWEVER	WHOEVER
GUSHING	SUGHING	HAZMATS	MATZAHS	HOWLETS	THOWELS
GUSTIER	GUTSIER	HEADPIN	PINHEAD	HUDDLER	HURDLED
GUSTILY	GUTSILY	HEAVERS	RESHAVE	HUMECTS	MUTCHES
GUSTING	GUTSING	HEEDING	NEIGHED	HUMIDOR	RHODIUM
GUTLESS	TUGLESS	HEELERS	REHEELS	HUMITES	TUMSHIE
GUTROTS	ROTGUTS	HEIRESS	HERISSE	HUNGANS	UNHANGS
GUTTIER	TURGITE	HELIMEN	HEMLINE	HURLIES	LUSHIER
GUYLING	UGLYING	HELLERI	HELLIER	HURRIES	RUSHIER
GYMNAST	SYNTAGM	HELLERS	SHELLER	HURTFUL	RUTHFUL
GYMPIES	PYGMIES	HEMPIES	IMPHEES	HURTLES	HUSTLER
GYRATED	TRAGEDY	HEPCATS	PATCHES	HUSHERS	SHUSHER
HACKLES	SHACKLE	HEPTADS	SPATHED	HYACINE	HYAENIC
HACKSAW	KWACHAS	HERMITS	MITHERS	HYALINS	LINHAYS
HADARIM	HARAMDI	HERNIAL	INHALER	HYDRATE	THREADY
HAEMINS	HEMINAS	HEROINS	INSHORE	HYDROUS	SHROUDY
HAGBORN	HORNBAG	HEROISM	MOREISH	HYLISTS	STYLISH
HAGDONS	SANDHOG	HERRIED	REHIRED	ICECAPS	IPECACS
HAGRIDE	HEADRIG	HERRIES	REHIRES	ICELESS	SIECLES
HAILERS	SHALIER	HESPING	PHESING	ICHNITE	NITCHIE
HAILING	NILGHAI	HEURISM	MUSHIER	ICINESS	INCISES
HAIQUES	QUASHIE	HICATEE	TEACHIE	IDEATUM	TAEDIUM

IDENTIC	INCITED	INSULIN	INULINS	JOUNCES	JUNCOES
IGNITOR	RIOTING	INSULSE	SILENUS	JOURNOS	SOJOURN
IGNOBLE	INGLOBE	INSURER	RUINERS	JOYPOPS	POPJOYS
ILLICIT	ILLITIC	INSURES	SUNRISE	JUGFULS	JUGSFUL
ILLIPES	PILLIES	INTAGLI	TAILING	JUJITSU	JUJUIST
ILLUDES	SULLIED	INTENSE	TENNIES	JUMARED	MUDEJAR
IMBOSOM	MIOMBOS	INTENTS	TENNIST	KAISERS	KARSIES
IMBOWER	WOMBIER	INTERNS	TINNERS	KALMIAS	KAMILAS
IMBRUTE	TERBIUM	INTIMAE	MINIATE	KANGHAS	KHANGAS
IMPAINT	TIMPANI	INTINES	TINNIES	KANTING	TANKING
IMPALED	IMPLEAD	INTONED	NOINTED	KARAMUS	KUMARAS
IMPALES	PALMIES	INTONES	TENSION	KARYONS	RYOKANS
IMPANEL	MANIPLE	INTORTS	TRITONS	KASBAHS	SABKHAS
IMPASSE	PESSIMA	INTRADA	RADIANT	KASHERS	SHAKERS
IMPASTE	PASTIME	INTWIST	NITWITS	KAYOING	OKAYING
IMPASTO	MATIPOS	INVADED	VIDENDA	KEELERS	SLEEKER
IMPEDES	SEMIPED	INVADER	RAVINED	KEENEST	KETENES
IMPLATE	PALMIET	INVERTS	STRIVEN	KEENING	KNEEING
IMPONES	PEONISM	INVITER	VITRINE	KEEPING	PEEKING
IMPORTS	TROPISM	INVITES	VINIEST	KEESTER	SKEETER
IMPOSES	MOPSIES	INWRAPS	RIPSAWN	KEGGERS	SKEGGER
IMPOSTS	MISSTOP	IODATED	TOADIED	KEISTER	KIESTER
IMPRESA	SAMPIRE	IODATES	TOADIES	KEITLOA	OATLIKE
IMPREST	PERMITS	IODIDES	IODISED	KELLIES	SKELLIE
IMPUGNS	SPUMING	IODINES	IONISED	KELSONS	SLOKENS
IMPURER	PRIMEUR	IOLITES	OILIEST	KELTIES	SLEEKIT
IMPUTER	TUMPIER	IONIUMS	NIMIOUS	KENOTIC	KETONIC
INAPTLY	PTYALIN	IONIZER	IRONIZE	KEPHIRS	PERKISH
INCANTS	STANNIC	IONOMER	MOONIER	KERRIAS	SARKIER
INCESTS	INSECTS	IRELESS	RESILES	KETMIAS	MISTAKE
INCISED	INDICES	IRISING	NIGIRIS	KEYINGS	YESKING
INCLUDE	NUCLIDE	IRKSOME	SMOKIER	KEYRING	YERKING
INDEWED	WIDENED	IRONERS	ROSINER	KIDDERS	SKIDDER
INDEXER	REINDEX	IRONING	ROINING	KIDNAPS	SKIDPAN
INDITER	NITRIDE	IRRUPTS	STIRRUP	KILLERS	RESKILL
INDITES	TINEIDS	ISOSPIN	SINOPIS	KILTING	KITLING
INDOORS	SORDINO	ISOTONE	TOONIES	KIMMERS	SKIMMER
INDRAWN	WINNARD	ISSUANT	SUSTAIN	KIMONOS	MONOSKI
INDUSIA	SUIDIAN	ISSUERS	RISUSES	KINDLES	SLINKED
INDWELT	WINTLED	ITCHIER	TICHIER	KINGCUP	PUCKING
INFARES	SERAFIN	IVORIST	VISITOR	KINGPIN	PINKING
INFEFTS	STIFFEN	IVRESSE	REVISES	KINSHIP	PINKISH
INFIDEL	INFIELD	JACKIES	JACKSIE	KIPPERS	SKIPPER
INGESTS	SIGNETS	JACKMAN	MANJACK	KIRNING	RINKING
INHUMER	RHENIUM	JALOUSE	JEALOUS	KIRPANS	PARKINS
INISLED	LINDIES	JAMBOKS	SJAMBOK	KISSING	SKIINGS
INKPOTS	INKSPOT	JAMBONE	JOBNAME	KISTFUL	LUTFISK
INLAYER	NAILERY	JAMBULS	JUMBALS	KITSCHY	SHTICKY
INLIERS	RESILIN	JAMMIES	JEMIMAS	KNEADER	NAKEDER
INNAGES	SEANING	JANTIER	NARTJIE	KNEIDEL	LIKENED
INNINGS	SINNING	JANTIES	TAJINES	KNITTER	TRINKET
INQUEST	QUINTES	JARFULS	JARSFUL	KNURLED	RUNKLED
INSANER	INSNARE	JAWINGS	JIGSAWN	KOORIES	ROOKIES
INSCAPE	PINCASE	JAYVEES	VEEJAYS	KRAKENS	SKANKER
INSEAMS	SAMISEN	JERBILS	JIRBLES	KREESED	SKEERED
INSIDER	SNIDIER	JERKINS	JINKERS	KUMARIS	RUMAKIS
INSTATE	SATINET	JITTERS	TRIJETS	KUMITES	MISTEUK
INSTEPS	SPINETS	JOINERS	REJOINS	KURSAAL	RUSALKA
INSULAE	INULASE	JOLLITY	JOLTILY	KYANISE	YANKIES
INSULAR	URINALS	JOLTERS	JOSTLER	KYLIKES	SKYLIKE

LABELER	RELABEL	LIAISES	SILESIA	LOTHEST	SHOTTLE
LABOURS	SUBORAL	LICHENS	LINCHES	LOTIONS	SOLITON
LABRUMS	LUMBARS	LIERNES	RELINES	LOUNDED	NODULED
LACINGS	SCALING	LIGATED	TAIGLED	LOUVARS	VALOURS
LADINGS	LIGANDS	LIGHTER	RELIGHT	LOVABLE	VOLABLE
LADRONS	LARDONS	LIGNANS	LINSANG	LOVINGS	SOLVING
LADYISH	SHADILY	LIGNINS	LININGS	LOWERED	ROWELED
LAGERED	REGALED	LIGROIN	ROILING	LOWPING	PLOWING
LAIKERS	SERKALI	LIGULAS	LUGSAIL	LOWSEST	SLOWEST
LAIRAGE	REGALIA	LIKINGS	SILKING	LOXYGEN	XYLOGEN
LAISSES	LASSIES	LILTING	TILLING	LUCITES	LUETICS
LAKIEST	TALKIES	LIMACEL	MICELLA	LUCUMOS	OSCULUM
LAKINGS	SLAKING	LIMACES	MALICES	LUDSHIP	SULPHID
LAMINAL	MANILLA	LIMACON	MALONIC	LUMINED	UNLIMED
LAMINAR	RAILMAN	LIMITER	MILTIER	LUMPENS	PLENUMS
LAMMIES	MELISMA	LIMMERS	SLIMMER	LUMPERS	RUMPLES
LAMPING	PALMING	LIMNERS	MERLINS	LUMPIER	PLUMIER
LANCERS	RANCELS	LIMPEST	LIMPETS	LUMPING	PLUMING
LANGARS	RAGLANS	LINCHET	TINCHEL	LUNATED	UNDEALT
LANGUID	LAUDING	LINEMAN	MELANIN	LUNGIES	SLUEING
LANIARD	NADIRAL	LINGAMS	MALIGNS	LUNKERS	RUNKLES
LAPPING	PALPING	LINGUAE	UNAGILE	LURRIES	SURLIER
LARIATS	LATRIAS	LINGUAL	LINGULA	LUSHING	SHULING
LARMIER	MARLIER	LINIEST	LINTIES	LUSKING	SULKING
LASINGS	SIGNALS	LINSEYS	LYSINES	LUTITES	TITULES
LASKETS	SKLATES	LINTIER	NITRILE	LYCHEES	SLEECHY
LASQUES	SQUEALS	LIONELS	NIELLOS	LYDDITE	TIDDLEY
LATINOS	TALIONS	LIPPENS	NIPPLES	MACABER	MACABRE
LATTICE	TACTILE	LIQUATE	TEQUILA	MADRONE	ROADMEN
LAUNCED	UNLACED	LISTERS	RELISTS	MAGIANS	SIAMANG
LAVAGES	SALVAGE	LITOTES	TOILETS	MAGNONS	SONGMAN
LAWINGS	SWALING	LITTERY	TRITELY	MAGPIES	MISPAGE
LAYINGS	SLAYING	LITTLIE	TILLITE	MAIMERS	RAMMIES
LAYOUTS	OUTLAYS	LIVINGS	SLIVING	MAISTRY	SYMITAR
LAYOVER	OVERLAY	LIVVERS	SILVERY	MAKEUPS	UPMAKES
LAYTIME	MEATILY	LOACHES	OSCHEAL	MAKINGS	MASKING
LEACHER	RELACHE	LOAFERS	SAFROLE	MALANGA	NAGMAAL
LEAGUER	REGULAE	LOATHER	RATHOLE	MALICHO	MOCHILA
LEAKING	LINKAGE	LOATHLY	TALLYHO	MANATIS	STAMINA
LEARNER	RELEARN	LOBBERS	SLOBBER	MANDOLA	MONADAL
LEASHED	SHEALED	LOCKERS	RELOCKS	MANDRIL	RIMLAND
LEAVIER	VEALIER	LOCKETS	LOCKSET	MANEGES	MENAGES
LEAVING	VEALING	LOCKUPS	UPLOCKS	MANGELS	MANGLES
LECHWES	WELCHES	LOCOMEN	MONOCLE	MANIHOC	MOHICAN
LEEPING	PEELING	LOCULES	OCELLUS	MANITOS	STAMNOI
LEERING	REELING	LOCUSTA	TALCOUS	MANITOU	TINAMOU
LEESING	SEELING	LOFTIER	TREFOIL	MANKIER	RAMEKIN
LEEWAYS	WEASELY	LOGGERS	SLOGGER	MANPACK	PACKMAN
LEGGISM	MIGGLES	LOMEINS	MOLINES	MANRENT	REMNANT
LEIGERS	LIEGERS	LOMENTS	MELTONS	MANROPE	REPOMAN
LEIRING	LINGIER	LOMPISH	PHLOMIS	MANTEEL	TELEMAN
LEISLER	RELLIES	LOOKERS	RELOOKS	MANTRAP	RAMPANT
LEMURES	RELUMES	LOOKOUT	OUTLOOK	MANTUAS	TAMANUS
LENGTHY	THEGNLY	LOOKUPS	UPLOOKS	MAORMOR	MORMAOR
LENTISK	TINKLES	LOOMING	MOOLING	MAPLESS	SAMPLES
LESSONS	SONLESS	LOOPING	POOLING	MARBLED	RAMBLED
LETTERN	NETTLER	LOOSEST	LOTOSES	MARBLER	RAMBLER
LEVERED	REVELED	LOOTING	TOOLING	MARCONI	MINORCA
LEWDEST	SWELTED	LOPPERS	PROPELS	MARENGO	MEGARON
LEXISES	SILEXES	LORDOMA	MALODOR	MARITAL	MARTIAL

MARKERS	REMARKS	MIKRONS	MORKINS	MOUSTED	SMOUTED
MARMITE	TRAMMIE	MILDEST	MISTLED	MOUTERS	OESTRUM
MAROONS	ROMANOS	MILLETS	MISTELL	MOWINGS	SOWMING
MARQUES	MASQUER	MILREIS	SLIMIER	MUCHELS	MULCHES
MARRANO	ORRAMAN	MIMESES	MISSEEM	MUCOIDS	MUSCOID
MARRIES	SIMARRE	MINCEUR	NUMERIC	MUDGERS	SMUDGER
MARRUMS	MURRAMS	MINDERS	REMINDS	MUGGERS	SMUGGER
MARTIAN	TAMARIN	MINDSET	MISTEND	MUISTED	TEDIUMS
MARTING	MIGRANT	MINIMUS	MINIUMS	MUNDANE	UNNAMED
MASALAS	SALAAMS	MINUEND	UNMINED	MURDERS	SMURRED
MASCOTS	SCAMTOS	MIREXES	REMIXES	MURLAIN	RUMINAL
MASHIER	MISHEAR	MISDOER	MOIDERS	MURREES	RESUMER
MASHIES	MESSIAH	MISEASE	SIAMESE	MUSIMON	OMNIUMS
MASHING	SHAMING	MISERLY	MISRELY	MUSINGS	MUSSING
MASHUPS	SMASHUP	MISHAPS	PASHIMS	MUSKLES	SKELUMS
MASONRY	MORNAYS	MISPLAN	PLASMIN	MUSMONS	SUMMONS
MASQUES	SQUAMES	MISSEES	SEMISES	MUSSELS	SUMLESS
MASSIER	SARMIES	MISSOUT	SUMOIST	MUTANDA	TAMANDU
MASSIVE	MAVISES	MISTERS	SMITERS	MUTUALS	UMLAUTS
MASTERS	STREAMS	MISTERY	SMYTRIE	MUTUELS	MUTULES
MASTICH	TACHISM	MISTLES	SMILETS	MUTULAR	TUMULAR
MATCHER	REMATCH	MISTRAL	RAMTILS	MYOSOTE	TOYSOME
MATLESS	SAMLETS	MITERER	TRIREME	MYTHIER	THYMIER
MATRONS	TRANSOM	MITISES	STIMIES	NANDINE	NANNIED
MATROSS	STROAMS	MITOSES	SOMITES	NAPPIES	PINESAP
MATTERS	SMATTER	MITTENS	SMITTEN	NARKING	RANKING
MATURES	STRUMAE	MODELER	REMODEL	NASTILY	SAINTLY
MAUGRES	MURAGES	MODERNS	RODSMEN	NASUTES	UNSEATS
MAULERS	SERUMAL	MODULES	MOUSLED	NATRONS	NONARTS
MAUMETS	SUMMATE	MOITHER	MOTHIER	NATTERS	RATTENS
MAUVEIN	MAUVINE	MOLLAHS	OLLAMHS	NATURAE	TAUREAN
MAXIMIN	MINIMAX	MOMENTO	MOOTMEN	NAVARIN	NIRVANA
MAZIEST	MESTIZA	MOMENTS	MONTEMS	NEAPING	PEANING
MEANERS	RENAMES	MOMUSES	MOUSMES	NEBULAS	UNBALES
MEANIES	NEMESIA	MONARCH	NOMARCH	NEGATON	TONNAGE
MEDAKAS	SMAAKED	MONAULS	SOLANUM	NEITHER	THEREIN
MEDALET	METALED	MONGERS	MORGENS	NERVIER	VERNIER
MEDICOS	MISCODE	MONISMS	NOMISMS	NESTLES	NETLESS
MEDUSAN	SUDAMEN	MONITOR	TROMINO	NETTIER	TENTIER
MEERING	REGIMEN	MONOMER	MOORMEN	NETTING	TENTING
MEETING	TEEMING	MONOSIS	SIMOONS	NETTLES	TELNETS
MEGASSE	MESSAGE	MONTANE	NONMEAT	NEURONS	NONUSER
MEGILLA	MILLAGE	MOONLET	TOOLMEN	NEXUSES	UNSEXES
MEINEYS	MENYIES	MOORIER	ROOMIER	NHANDUS	UNHANDS
MELICKS	MICKLES	MOORING	ROOMING	NICKERS	SNICKER
MELLAYS	MESALLY	MOORVAS	VAROOMS	NICTATE	TETANIC
MENDERS	REMENDS	MOOTING	TOOMING	NIDINGS	SINDING
MERCERY	REMERCY	MOPPIER	POMPIER	NIFFERS	SNIFFER
MERELLS	SMELLER	MORAINE	ROMAINE	NIPPERS	SNIPPER
MERINOS	MERSION	MORONIC	OMICRON	NIPTERS	PTERINS
MERISIS	MISSIER	MOROSER	ROOMERS	NITROUS	TURIONS
MERISMS	SIMMERS	MORTALS	STROMAL	NOIRISH	ROINISH
MERLOTS	MOLTERS	MOSHPIT	PHOTISM	NONETTI	TONTINE
MESEEMS	SEMEMES	MOTIVED	VOMITED	NONPAST	PANTONS
MESETAS	SEAMSET	MOTTIER	OMITTER	NONSTOP	PONTONS
MESTERS	RESTEMS	MOULDER	REMOULD	NOODLES	SNOOLED
METRING	TERMING	MOUSERS	SMOUSER	NOOKIER	ROOINEK
METTLES	STEMLET	MOUSING	SOUMING	NORITIC	TIRONIC
MIDTERM	TRIMMED	MOUSSED	SMOUSED	NOSHERS	SENHORS
MIGRATE	RAGTIME	MOUSSES	SMOUSES	NOSTOCS	ONCOSTS

NOTCHES	TECHNOS	OTTERED	TETRODE	PARIAHS	RAPHIAS
NOTEPAD	TONEPAD	OUGHTED	TOUGHED	PARIANS	PIRANAS
NOTICES	SECTION	OUTACTS	OUTCAST	PARKIES	SPARKIE
NOUGATS	OUTSANG	OUTDOER	OUTRODE	PARODIC	PICADOR
NOUNIER	REUNION	OUTDRAW	OUTWARD	PAROLES	REPOSAL
NOVALIA	VALONIA	OUTGUNS	OUTSUNG	PARPING	RAPPING
NOWHERE	WHEREON	OUTHIRE	ROUTHIE	PARROTS	RAPTORS
NOWTIER	TOWNIER	OUTJEST	OUTJETS	PARROTY	PORTRAY
NUCLEUS	NUCULES	OUTLIED	TOLUIDE	PARSONS	SANPROS
NURDLED	RUNDLED	OUTNESS	TONUSES	PARTERS	PRATERS
NURSING	URNINGS	OUTPASS	PASSOUT	PARTIAL	PATRIAL
NURSLES	RUNLESS	OUTPOST	OUTTOPS	PARTURE	RAPTURE
NURTURE	UNTRUER	OUTPULL	PULLOUT	PARTYER	PETRARY
NUZZLES	SNUZZLE	OUTPUTS	PUTOUTS	PARURES	UPREARS
OARIEST	OTARIES	OUTRIGS	RIGOUTS	PARVISE	PAVISER
OARSMAN	RAMONAS	OUTROLL	ROLLOUT	PASEARS	SARAPES
OBDURES	ROSEBUD	OUTRUNS	RUNOUTS	PASSADO	POSADAS
ODDNESS	SODDENS	OUTSELL	SELLOUT	PASSELS	SAPLESS
ODORISE	OROIDES	OUTSETS	SETOUTS	PASSING	SPAINGS
OESTRAL	OLESTRA	OUTSIDE	TEDIOUS	PASSMAN	SAMPANS
OEUVRES	OVERUSE	OUTSINS	USTIONS	PASTELS	STAPLES
OFFENDS	SENDOFF	OUTSPED	SPOUTED	PASTEUP	PUPATES
OFFERER	REOFFER	OUTSTEP	TOUPETS	PASTILS	SPITALS
OFFPUTS	PUTOFFS	OUTTAKE	TAKEOUT	PATENTS	PATTENS
OFFSETS	SETOFFS	OUTTURN	TURNOUT	PATRICK	TRIPACK
OFFTAKE	TAKEOFF	OUTWALK	WALKOUT	PATROLS	PORTALS
OGRISMS	SIMORGS	OUTWASH	WASHOUT	PATROON	PRONOTA
OILCUPS	UPCOILS	OUTWITH	WITHOUT	PATTERN	REPTANT
OILLETS	TOLLIES	OUTWORK	WORKOUT	PATTIES	TAPETIS
OILNUTS	ULTIONS	OVARIAL	VARIOLA	PATTLES	PELTAST
OLIVERS	VIOLERS	OVERATE	OVEREAT	PAULINS	SPINULA
OLIVETS	VIOLETS	OVERLIE	RELIEVO	PAUNCES	UNCAPES
OMELETS	TELOMES	OVERMEN	VENOMER	PAUPERS	UPSPEAR
OMNEITY	OMNIETY	OVERNEW	REWOVEN	PAYINGS	SPAYING
ONAGERS	ORANGES	OVERPLY	PLOVERY	PAYSLIP	SAPPILY
ONEYERS	ONEYRES	OVERRED	REDROVE	PEACODS	PEASCOD
ONSTAGE	TANGOES	OVERRUN	RUNOVER	PEANUTS	PESAUNT
OOMPAHS	SHAMPOO	OVERSAD	SAVORED	PEARTER	TAPERER
OORALIS	OORIALS	OVERTIP	PIVOTER	PECKIER	PICKEER
OOZIEST	ZOOIEST	OWRIEST	TOWSIER	PEDALED	PLEADED
OPCODES	SCOOPED	OYSTERS	STOREYS	PEDANTS	PENTADS
OPERONS	SNOOPER	PACKERS	REPACKS	PEDDERS	SPREDDE
OPINING	PIONING	PADANGS	PADNAGS	PEDDLES	SPELDED
OPPRESS	PORPESS	PADRONI	PONIARD	PEDICEL	PEDICLE
OPPUGNS	POPGUNS	PAIDLED	PLAIDED	PEDLERS	SPELDER
OPSONIC	POCOSIN	PAINIMS	PIANISM	PEERIES	SEEPIER
OPUNTIA	UTOPIAN	PALASES	PLAASES	PEERING	PREEING
ORATING	ROATING	PALATES	PATELAS	PEEVERS	PREEVES
ORBIEST	SORBITE	PALETTE	PELTATE	PEISING	PIGSNIE
ORDERER	REORDER	PALLIER	PERILLA	PELORIC	POLICER
OREIDES	OSIERED	PALLONE	PLEONAL	PENCILS	SPLENIC
ORGONES	OROGENS	PALMARY	PALMYRA	PENNATE	PENTANE
ORPHISM	ROMPISH	PALSHIP	SHIPLAP	PENNIES	PINENES
ORRISES	ROSIERS	PALSIER	PARLIES	PENSELS	SPLEENS
OSETRAS	OSSETRA	PANDITS	SANDPIT	PENSIVE	VESPINE
OSPREYS	PYROSES	PANGENS	PENANGS	PEPPIER	PREPPIE
OSSETER	STEREOS	PANIERS	RAPINES	PEPTIDE	PIPETED
OSSUARY	SUASORY	PANNERS	SPANNER	PEPTISE	TIPPEES
OSTENTS	TESTONS	PANTINE	PINNATE	PERCALE	REPLACE
OSTIATE	TOASTIE	PARETIC	PICRATE	PERCENT	PRECENT

PERCEPT	PRECEPT	PLASHER	SPHERAL	POWNIES	WINESOP
PERCUSS	SPRUCES	PLASMIC	PSALMIC	POWTERS	PROWEST
PERDURE	REPURED	PLECTRE	PRELECT	PRAETOR	PRORATE
PEREION	PIONEER	PLERION	PROLINE	PRAWNED	PREDAWN
PERFECT	PREFECT	PLEROMA	RAMPOLE	PRAWNER	PREWARN
PERFORM	PREFORM	PLOATED	TADPOLE	PREARMS	RAMPERS
PERILED	REPLIED	PLODDED	PODDLED	PREDOOM	PROMOED
PERITUS	PUIREST	PLODGES	SPLODGE	PREEDIT	TEPIDER
PERJINK	PREJINK	PLOPPED	POPPLED	PREFILE	PRELIFE
PERLITE	REPTILE	PLOTFUL	TOPFULL	PREIFES	PRIEFES
PERORAL	PREORAL	PLOUTER	POULTER	PREMIER	REPRIME
PERSUES	PERUSES	PLOWERS	REPLOWS	PRENTED	PRETEND
PERTUSE	REPUTES	PLUGGED	PUGGLED	PREPAYS	YAPPERS
PERUSER	REPURES	PLUMBER	REPLUMB	PREPONE	PROPENE
PERVING	PREVING	PLUMBIC	UPCLIMB	PRESHIP	SHIPPER
PESTERS	PRESETS	PLUMOSE	PUMELOS	PRESONG	SPONGER
PESTIER	RESPITE	PLUNGED	PUNGLED	PRESSES	SPERSES
PETALED	PLEATED	PLUNGES	PUNGLES	PRESSOR	PROSERS
PETASOS	SAPOTES	PLUSSES	PUSSELS	PRESUME	SUPREME
PETITES	PETTIES	PLUTEUS	PUSTULE	PRETEEN	TERPENE
PETROLS	REPLOTS	PLUTONS	PULTONS	PREVISE	PRIEVES
PHAETON	PHONATE	POCOSEN	POONCES	PREWRAP	WRAPPER
PHENOMS	SHOPMEN	PODIUMS	SPODIUM	PRINTER	REPRINT
PHILTER	PHILTRE	POGONIP	POOPING	PRISONS	SPINORS
PHRASED	SHARPED	POINDER	PROINED	PRISSED	SPIDERS
PHYTOID	TYPHOID	POISERS	PROSSIE	PROETTE	TREETOP
PICAROS	PROSAIC	POISONS	POISSON	PROGENY	PYROGEN
PICENES	PIECENS	POITREL	POLITER	PROLLED	REDPOLL
PICKETS	SKEPTIC	POLDERS	PRESOLD	PRONAOS	SOPRANO
PICKLER	PRICKLE	POLINGS	SLOPING	PROOFER	REPROOF
PIGNORA	PORANGI	POLLERS	REPOLLS	PROPERS	PROSPER
PIGNUTS	STUPING	POLOIST	TOPSOIL	PROTIST	TROPIST
PIGSNYS	SPYINGS	POODLES	SPOOLED	PROTORE	TROOPER
PILEUPS	UPPILES	PORGIES	SERPIGO	PROYNES	PYRONES
PILLAUS	PILULAS	PORKERS	PROKERS	PRUNERS	SPURNER
PINANGS	SPANING	PORKING	PROKING	PRUSIKS	SPRUIKS
PINCHES	SPHENIC	PORTAGE	POTAGER	PRYINGS	SPRINGY
PINDARI	PRIDIAN	PORTEND	PROTEND	PSALMED	SAMPLED
PINGLES	SPIGNEL	PORTICO	PROOTIC	PSEUDOS	SPOUSED
PINIONS	SPINONI	PORTING	TROPING	PUDDERS	SPUDDER
PINNERS	SPINNER	PORTOUS	UPROOTS	PUDDLES	SPUDDLE
PINOCLE	PLEONIC	POSINGS	POSSING	PUISNES	SUPINES
PIOLETS	PISTOLE	POSNETS	STEPSON	PULSANT	PULTANS
PIONIES	SINOPIE	POSSERS	PROSSES	PULSION	UPSILON
PIPINGS	SIPPING	POSTBOY	POTBOYS	PUMPERS	REPUMPS
PIPLESS	SIPPLES	POSTERN	PRONEST	PUNCHER	UNPERCH
PISMIRE	PRIMSIE	POSTING	STOPING	PUNIEST	PUNTIES
PISSANT	PTISANS	POSTMEN	TOPSMEN	PUNKIES	SPUNKIE
PISSERS	PRISSES	POTASSA	SAPOTAS	PUNNETS	UNSPENT
PISTOLS	POSTILS	POTLUCK	PUTLOCK	PUNSTER	PUNTERS
PITIERS	TIPSIER	POUDERS	POUDRES	PURITAN	UPTRAIN
PITSAWS	SAWPITS	POULPES	UPSLOPE	PURLERS	SLURPER
PLACITS	PLASTIC	POUNCED	UNCOPED	PURSIER	UPRISER
PLACOID	PODALIC	POUNCES	UNCOPES	PURSUED	USURPED
PLAGUES	PLUSAGE	POUNDER	UNROPED	PURSUER	USURPER
PLAICES	SPECIAL	POURERS	REPOURS	PUTTERS	SPUTTER
PLAITED	TALIPED	POURIES	SOUPIER	PUTTIED	TITUPED
PLAITER	PLATIER	POURSUE	UPROUSE	PUZZELS	PUZZLES
PLANERS	REPLANS	POUSSES	SPOUSES	PYEMIAS	YAMPIES
PLANETS	PLATENS	POUSSIN	SPINOUS	PYRALID	RAPIDLY

PYRITES	STRIPEY	RELIVER	REVILER	RIMLESS	SMILERS
PYROPES	YOPPERS	REMEIDS	REMISED	RIPTIDE	TIDERIP
QUEERER	REQUERE	REMORAS	ROAMERS	RISTRAS	STIRRAS
QUELEAS	SEQUELA	REMORSE	ROEMERS	RITTERS	TERRITS
QUERIER	REQUIRE	RENAGUE	UNEAGER	RITUALS	TRISULA
QUERIST	REQUITS	RENNETS	TENNERS	RIVALED	VALIDER
QUESTER	REQUEST	RENOWNS	WONNERS	RIVERET	RIVETER
QUIETER	REQUITE	REPEATS	RETAPES	RIVETED	VERDITE
QUINNAT	QUINTAN	REPINED	RIPENED	RIVIERA	VAIRIER
RABATTE	TABARET	REPINER	RIPENER	ROADIES	SOREDIA
RACISTS	SACRIST	REPLIES	SPIELER	RODENTS	SNORTED
RACKERS	RERACKS	RERISEN	RESINER	ROGUING	ROUGING
RAGGIES	SAGGIER	REROLLS	ROLLERS	ROLLTOP	TROLLOP
RAGTAGS	TAGRAGS	REROOFS	ROOFERS	ROOTLET	TOOTLER
RAGWEED	WAGERED	RESEEDS	SEEDERS	RORTERS	TERRORS
RAILERS	RERAILS	RESELLS	SELLERS	RORTIER	TERROIR
RAKINGS	SARKING	RESHOWS	SHOWERS	ROSALIA	SOLARIA
RALLIES	SALLIER	RESIDUE	UREIDES	ROSYING	SIGNORY
RAMSONS	RANSOMS	RESIGHT	SIGHTER	ROTATED	TROATED
RAMSTAM	TAMMARS	RESISTS	SISTERS	ROTATES	TOASTER
RANDOMS	RODSMAN	RESIZES	SEIZERS	ROTCHIE	THEORIC
RASHERS	SHARERS	RESKEWS	SKEWERS	ROTULAE	TORULAE
RASSLED	SARDELS	RESTIFF	STIFFER	ROTULAS	TORULAS
RATLIKE	TALKIER	RESTING	STINGER	ROUSANT	SANTOUR
RATOONS	SANTOOR	RESTYLE	TERSELY	ROUSING	SOURING
RATTILY	TARTILY	RESURGE	REURGES	ROWDILY	WORDILY
RATTING	TARTING	RETAKES	SAKERET	ROWINGS	WORSING
RAUNCHY	UNCHARY	RETELLS	TELLERS	ROWTING	TROWING
RAUNGES	UNGEARS	RETHINK	THINKER	ROYSTER	STROYER
RAVAGES	SAVAGER	RETICLE	TIERCEL	RUBACES	SUBRACE
RAWHEAD	WARHEAD	RETIRER	TERRIER	RUBELLA	RULABLE
RAYLESS	SLAYERS	RETRACK	TRACKER	RUINOUS	URINOUS
REALTOR	RELATOR	RETREAD	TREADER	RUNDLET	TRUNDLE
REAMERS	SMEARER	RETREES	STEERER	RUNNETS	STUNNER
REAMIER	REREMAI	RETRIMS	TRIMERS	RUSTRES	TRUSSER
REAPERS	SPEARER	RETUNDS	UNDREST	SABELLA	SALABLE
REARISE	RERAISE	RETURNS	TURNERS	SACBUTS	SUBACTS
REASONS	SENORAS	REUTTER	UTTERER	SACHETS	SCATHES
REAVAIL	VELARIA	REVAMPS	VAMPERS	SACKBUT	SUBTACK
REAVING	VINEGAR	REVENUE	UNREEVE	SACKERS	SCREAKS
REBORES	SOBERER	REVIEWS	VIEWERS	SACRIFY	SCARIFY
REBUSES	SUBSERE	REWAKED	WREAKED	SADDISH	SIDDHAS
RECITED	TIERCED	REWAKEN	WAKENER	SAGENES	SENEGAS
RECLUSE	RECULES	REWEIGH	WEIGHER	SAIMINS	SIMIANS
RECULED	ULCERED	REWELDS	WELDERS	SALADES	SALSAED
RECURED	REDUCER	REWIDEN	WIDENER	SALINES	SILANES
REDACTS	SCARTED	REWINDS	WINDERS	SALOONS	SOLANOS
REDBAIT	TRIBADE	REWIRED	WEIRDER	SALTANT	TALANTS
REDDEST	TEDDERS	REWIRES	SWEIRER	SALTISH	TAHSILS
REDDLES	SLEDDER	REWORDS	SWORDER	SALTOED	SOLATED
REDLINE	RELINED	REWORKS	WORKERS	SALUTES	TALUSES
REDWING	WRINGED	REWOUND	WOUNDER	SAMOYED	SOMEDAY
REEDILY	YIELDER	REWRAPS	WARPERS	SANDERS	SARSDEN
REESTED	STEERED	RHUMBAS	SAMBHUR	SANGERS	SERANGS
REFUTAL	TEARFUL	RIBAUDS	SUBARID	SANIOUS	SUASION
REGRESS	SERGERS	RIBBONS	ROBBINS	SANNIES	SIENNAS
REGROWN	WRONGER	RICKEYS	YICKERS	SANNUPS	UNSNAPS
REISSUE	SEISURE	RIDGIER	RIGIDER	SANSEIS	SASINES
REIVING	RIEVING	RIKISHA	SHIKARI	SANTOLS	STANOLS
RELEVES	SLEEVER	RILIEST	SILTIER	SANTONS	SONANTS

SANTURS	SUNSTAR	SHICKER	SKRIECH	SPIRTED	STRIPED
SAPOURS	UPSOARS	SHINERS	SHRINES	SPURIAE	UPRAISE
SARCOUS	SOUCARS	SHIRKED	SHRIKED	SPUTNIK	UPKNITS
SAROSES	SEROSAS	SHIRRAS	SIRRAHS	SPYWARE	YAWPERS
SARSNET	TRANSES	SHIVERS	SHRIVES	STABBED	TEBBADS
SAUCIER	URICASE	SHLOCKY	SHYLOCK	STACKET	TACKETS
SAUNTED	UNSATED	SHOUTED	SOUTHED	STALKER	TALKERS
SAVINES	VINASSE	SHOUTER	SOUTHER	STANDEE	STEANED
SAVIOUR	VARIOUS	SHOVERS	SHROVES	STARDOM	TSARDOM
SAVORER	SEROVAR	SHYSTER	THYRSES	STARTED	TETRADS
SAWDERS	SWEARDS	SICKLED	SLICKED	STARTUP	UPSTART
SAWYERS	SWAYERS	SIDEWAY	WAYSIDE	STATELY	STYLATE
SAXTUBA	SUBTAXA	SIDLERS	SLIDERS	STATING	TASTING
SCAMPIS	SPASMIC	SIDLING	SLIDING	STATINS	TANISTS
SCAPING	SPACING	SIERRAN	SNARIER	STATUTE	TAUTEST
SCEDULE	SECLUDE	SIESTAS	TASSIES	STAYING	STYGIAN
SCHOUTS	SCOUTHS	SIEVING	VISEING	STEEVES	VESTEES
SCHTICK	TCHICKS	SIGNARY	SYRINGA	STELLAR	TELLARS
SCHTIKS	SHTICKS	SIGNING	SINGING	STEMING	TEMSING
SCOURGE	SCROUGE	SILOING	SOILING	STERVED	VERDETS
SCOWING	SOWCING	SILVERS	SLIVERS	STEWERS	WESTERS
SCOWLER	SCROWLE	SIPHONS	SONSHIP	STICKUP	UPTICKS
SCREAKY	YACKERS	SIPPLED	SLIPPED	STIDDIE	TIDDIES
SCREICH	SCRIECH	SITTINE	TINIEST	STINGOS	TOSSING
SCRIEVE	SERVICE	SITUSES	TISSUES	STIPELS	TIPLESS
SCULKED	SUCKLED	SIZEIST	SIZIEST	STIPPLE	TIPPLES
SDEIGNE	SEEDING	SKIVING	VIKINGS	STIRING	TIRINGS
SEAMIER	SERIEMA	SKLATED	STALKED	STIRRED	STRIDER
SEAWORM	WOMERAS	SKREIGH	SKRIEGH	STOKERS	STROKES
SECKELS	SECKLES	SKRYING	SKYRING	STOMPER	TROMPES
SEEKING	SKEEING	SLAMMED	SMALMED	STONERN	TONNERS
SEETHED	SHEETED	SLEEPRY	YELPERS	STONILY	TYLOSIN
SEETHER	SHEETER	SLEWING	SWINGLE	STONING	TONINGS
SEEWING	SWEEING	SLIPWAY	WASPILY	STONNED	TENDONS
SEITENS	SESTINE	SLITTED	STILTED	STOOKER	STROOKE
SELFIST	STIFLES	SLOPIER	SPOILER	STOOLED	TOLEDOS
SELSYNS	SLYNESS	SMOKILY	SOYMILK	STOPPLE	TOPPLES
SEMMITS	TSIMMES	SMOODGE	SMOOGED	STOTTIE	TOTTIES
SENNITS	SINNETS	SNAFUED	UNDEAFS	STOUTEN	TENUTOS
SENSUAL	UNSEALS	SNEAPED	SPEANED	STOVERS	VOTRESS
SEPHENS	SPHENES	SNICKET	TICKENS	STOVING	VOTINGS
SEPTATE	SPATTEE	SNOOPED	SPOONED	STOWAGE	TOWAGES
SERENER	SNEERER	SNOOTED	STOODEN	STRAINT	TRANSIT
SERRANS	SNARERS	SNORERS	SORNERS	STRAWEN	WANTERS
SERVERS	VERSERS	SNORING	SORNING	STREELS	TRESSEL
SERVEWE	WEEVERS	SNOWING	WONINGS	STREETY	SYRETTE
SERVING	VERSING	SOLANDS	SOLDANS	STRETTE	TETTERS
SERVLET	SVELTER	SOLDIER	SOLIDER	STREWED	WRESTED
SESELIS	SESSILE	SOLLERS	SORELLS	STREWER	WRESTER
SESTETS	TSETSES	SOMBERS	SOMBRES	STROWED	WORSTED
SETTEES	TESTEES	SOREXES	XEROSES	STUDDIE	STUDIED
SETTING	TESTING	SOULDAN	UNLOADS	STUDENT	STUNTED
SEWINGS	SWINGES	SOVIETS	STOVIES	STUDIES	TISSUED
SHAITAN	TAHINAS	SOWARRY	YARROWS	STUMBLE	TUMBLES
SHAPEUP	UPHEAPS	SOWINGS	SOWSING	STURNUS	UNTRUSS
SHAWLIE	WHAISLE	SPALTED	STAPLED	STURTED	TRUSTED
SHEIKHS	SHIKSEH	SPEEDER	SPEERED	STUSHIE	TUSHIES
SHEITAN	STHENIA	SPINARS	SPRAINS	STYLITE	TESTILY
SHEWELS	WELSHES	SPIRANT	SPRAINT	STYLIZE	ZESTILY
SHIATSU	THIASUS	SPIRITS	TRIPSIS	STYRENE	YESTERN

SUBDEAN	UNBASED	TARTLET	TATTLER	UNITIES	UNITISE
SUEABLE	USEABLE	TATUING	TAUTING	UNLADES	UNLEADS
SUITORS	TSOURIS	TAWIEST	TWAITES	UNLIVES	UNVEILS
SULLENS	UNSELLS	TAWNIER	TINWARE	UNMATED	UNTAMED
SULPHUR	UPHURLS	TAXWISE	WAXIEST	UNNAILS	UNSLAIN
SUMATRA	TRAUMAS	TEABOWL	TOWABLE	UNNOTED	UNTONED
SUNDECK	UNDECKS	TEAZELS	TEAZLES	UNRAVEL	VENULAR
SUNDERS	UNDRESS	TEAZING	TZIGANE	UNRIVET	VENTURI
SUNLIKE	UNLIKES	TEETERS	TERETES	UNROOST	UNROOTS
SUNROOF	UNROOFS	TEMENOS	TONEMES	UNSEENS	UNSENSE
SUNROOM	UNMOORS	TEMPLAR	TRAMPLE	UNSPILT	UNSPLIT
SUNSPOT	UNSTOPS	TENDRIL	TRINDLE	UNSTACK	UNTACKS
SUNSUIT	UNSUITS	TENOURS	TONSURE	UNSTUCK	UNTUCKS
SUNTRAP	UNSTRAP	TENSIVE	VENITES	UNSWEAR	UNWARES
SUNWARD	UNDRAWS	THIRSTS	THRISTS	UNTAMES	UNTEAMS
SUPPING	UPPINGS	THIRSTY	THRISTY	UNWIRES	UNWISER
SURAMIN	URANISM	THRAWED	WRATHED	UPDATER	UPRATED
SURGING	URGINGS	TICKLER	TRICKLE	UPDRAWS	UPWARDS
SWADDIE	WADDIES	TILTING	TITLING	UPSPAKE	UPSPEAK
SWAGGER	WAGGERS	TITANIS	TITIANS	UPSWARM	WARMUPS
SWALIER	WAILERS	TOOLSET	TOOTLES	UPSWELL	UPWELLS
SWALLOW	WALLOWS	TOPWORK	WORKTOP	UPWINDS	WINDUPS
SWANKER	WANKERS	TORPEDO	TROOPED	VAILING	VIALING
SWAPPER	WAPPERS	TORTILE	TRIOLET	VALETED	VELATED
SWARDED	WADDERS	TORTIVE	VIRETOT	VALISES	VESSAIL
SWATTED	WADSETT	TORTURE	TROUTER	VAMPIER	VAMPIRE
SWATTER	TEWARTS	TOSSILY	TYLOSIS	VENTERS	VENTRES
SWEEPER	WEEPERS	TOWNIES	TWONIES	VENTOSE	VOTEENS
SWIGGER	WIGGERS	TOWTING	WOTTING	VIRGATE	VITRAGE
SWILLER	WILLERS	TRAVOIS	VIATORS	VIRINOS	VIRIONS
SWINDGE	SWINGED	TREVETS	VETTERS	VIRTUAL	VITULAR
SWINDLE	WINDLES	TRIDUAN	UNITARD	VODOUNS	VOUDONS
SWINGER	WINGERS	TRISHAW	WRAITHS	VOLATIC	VOLTAIC
SWINKER	WINKERS	TRIVIAL	VITRAIL	WANGLER	WRANGLE
SWIPIER	WISPIER	TROWELS	WORTLES	WARNERS	WARRENS
SWIRLED	WILDERS	TUBULIN	UNBUILT	WASHIER	WEARISH
SWISHED	WHISSED	TUFTIER	TURFITE	WEIRING	WINGIER
SWISHER	WISHERS	TUILZIE	UTILIZE	WELKINS	WINKLES
SWISHES	WHISSES	TULCHAN	UNLATCH	WELTING	WINGLET
SWOONED	WOODENS	TUMBLER	TUMBREL	WENCHES	WHENCES
SWOOPED	WOOPSED	TURKIES	TUSKIER	WESANDS	WESSAND
SWOUNED	UNSOWED	TURNIPS	UNSTRIP	WESKITS	WISKETS
TABLEAU	TABULAE	TURNUPS	UPTURNS	WESTLIN	WINTLES
TACKLED	TALCKED	TWEEDLE	TWEELED	WETHERS	WRETHES
TACTICS	TICTACS	TWINERS	WINTERS	WHEEDLE	WHEELED
TAKEUPS	UPTAKES	TWINTER	WRITTEN	WHITIER	WITHIER
TALLEST	TALLETS	TWIRING	WRITING	WHITIES	WITHIES
TALLOWY	TOLLWAY	ULICONS	UNCOILS	WHITING	WITHING
TAMARAS	TARAMAS	UNAIRED	URANIDE	WHITRET	WHITTER
TAMPANS	TAPSMAN	UNALIVE	UNVAILE	WIGGLER	WRIGGLE
TANGLER	TRANGLE	UNBARES	UNBEARS	WILLEST	WILLETS
TANGRAM	TRANGAM	UNCAPED	UNPACED	WILTING	WITLING
TANNAHS	THANNAS	UNCASES	USANCES	WINKLER	WRINKLE
TANNERY	TYRANNE	UNDRAPE	UNPARED	WISENTS	WITNESS
TANNEST	TENANTS	UNFILDE	UNFILED	ZAFFERS	ZAFFRES
TANTARA	TARTANA	UNFURLS	URNFULS	ZANIEST	ZEATINS
TARDIER	TARRIED	UNGLUED	UNGULED		

Triplets

ABASING	BAAINGS	BISNAGA	ANIMIST	INTIMAS	SANTIMI
ABETTOR	BATTERO	TABORET	ANKLETS	ASKLENT	LANKEST
ABLEISM	EMBAILS	LAMBIES	ANOINTS	NATIONS	ONANIST
ABORDED	BOARDED	ROADBED	ANOPIAS	ANOPSIA	PAISANO
ABORTED	BORATED	TABORED	ANTEING	ANTIGEN	GENTIAN
ABORTER	ARBORET	TABORER	ANTHERS	HARTENS	THENARS
ABREACT	BEARCAT	CABARET	ANTIARS	ARTISAN	TSARINA
ABREGES	BAREGES	BARGEES	ANTICKS	CATKINS	CATSKIN
ABRUPTS	SUBPART	UPBRAST	ANTIRED	DETRAIN	TRAINED
ABSCISE	SCABIES	SEBASIC	ANURIAS	SAURIAN	URANIAS
ABSEILS	ISABELS	LABISES	AORISTS	ARISTOS	SATORIS
ACARIDS	ASCARID	CARDIAS	APPERIL	APPLIER	ARIPPLE
ACCRUES	ACCURSE	ACCUSER	APPLETS	LAPPETS	STAPPLE
ACERBER	CEREBRA	REBRACE	APPULSE	PAPULES	UPLEAPS
ACETINS	CANIEST	CINEAST	APTNESS	PATNESS	PESANTS
ACHINGS	CASHING	CHASING	ARBUTES	BURSATE	SURBATE
ACROTER	CREATOR	REACTOR	ARCHING	CHAGRIN	CHARING
ACTINAL	ALICANT	ANTICAL	ARCTIID	TRIACID	TRIADIC
ACTINON	CANTION	CONTAIN	AREFIES	FAERIES	FREESIA
ACTIONS	ATONICS	CATIONS	ARENITE	RETINAE	TRAINEE
ACTRESS	CASTERS	RECASTS	ARGENTS	GARNETS	STRANGE
ADMIRER	MARDIER	MARRIED	ARGUSES	SAUGERS	USAGERS
ADONISE	ANODISE	SODAINE	ARISHES	RASHIES	SHERIAS
ADORING	GRADINO	ROADING	ARISTAE	ASTERIA	ATRESIA
ADPRESS	SPADERS	SPREADS	ARKOSES	RESOAKS	SOAKERS
AETHERS	HEATERS	REHEATS	ARMADAS	MADRASA	RAMADAS
AFFRETS	RESTAFF	STAFFER	ARMFULS	ARMSFUL	FULMARS
AGELAST	ALGATES	LASTAGE	ARMPITS	IMPARTS	MISPART
AGGRESS	SAGGERS	SEGGARS	ARRESTS	RASTERS	STARERS
AGNAMES	MANAGES	SAGAMEN	ARRISES	RAISERS	SIERRAS
AGRASTE	GASTREA	TEARGAS	ARTICLE	RECITAL	TALCIER
AGREGES	RAGGEES	REGGAES	ASCENTS	SECANTS	STANCES
AILERON	ALERION	ALIENOR	ASCIANS	CASSINA	SANCAIS
AIRDATE	RADIATE	TIARAED	ASEPTIC	PACIEST	SPICATE
AIRNING	INGRAIN	RAINING	ASPHALT	SPATHAL	TAPLASH
AIRPOST	AIRSTOP	PAROTIS	ASPINES	PANSIES	SAPIENS
AIRSHOT	SHORTIA	THORIAS	ASRAMAS	SAMARAS	SAMSARA
AISLING	NILGAIS	SAILING	ASTHORE	EARSHOT	HAROSET
ALBATAS	ATABALS	BALATAS	ASTONED	DONATES	ONSTEAD
ALERTLY	ELYTRAL	RETALLY	ASUNDER	DANSEUR	DAUNERS
ALIBIES	BAILIES	BIALIES	ATHIRST	RATTISH	TARTISH
ALIGNED	DEALING	LEADING	ATRETIC	CATTIER	CITRATE
ALINERS	NAILERS	RENAILS	ATTORNS	RATTONS	ROTTANS
ALTESSE	STEALES	TEASELS	ATTRITE	TATTIER	TITRATE
AMBEERS	BEAMERS	BESMEAR	ATTUNED	NUTATED	TAUNTED
AMBERED	BREAMED	EMBREAD	AUDILES	DEASIUL	DUALISE
AMENDES	DEMEANS	SEEDMAN	AUNTERS	NATURES	SAUNTER
AMERCED	CREAMED	RACEMED	AUTOMEN	NOTAEUM	OUTNAME
AMERCES	CAREMES	RACEMES	AVENTRE	NERVATE	VETERAN
AMNIONS	MANSION	ONANISM	AVIDEST	DATIVES	VISTAED
AMORETS	MAESTRO	OMERTAS	AVOWERS	OVERSAW	REAVOWS
AMOUNTS	MOUTANS	OUTMANS	AWNINGS	SNAWING	WANINGS
AMTRACS	RAMCATS	TARMACS	BABBLER	BLABBER	BRABBLE
AMUSERS	ASSUMER	MASSEUR	BACKETS	BACKSET	SETBACK
ANCHORS	ARCHONS	RANCHOS	BAILOUT	OBITUAL	TABOULI
ANGELED	GELANDE	GLEANED	BALDEST	BLASTED	STABLED
ANGELIC	ANGLICE	GALENIC	BALDIES	DIABLES	DISABLE
ANGELUS	LAGUNES	LANGUES	BANSHEE	BEENAHS	SHEBEAN

BARBELS	RABBLES	SLABBER	CARINAL	CLARAIN	CRANIAL
BARBETS	RABBETS	STABBER	CARIOSE	ORACIES	SCORIAE
BASEMEN	BEMEANS	BENAMES	CARLOTS	CROTALS	SCROTAL
BASSIER	BRAISES	BRASSIE	CARPERS	SCARPER	SCRAPER
BASTION	BONITAS	OBTAINS	CARTERS	CRATERS	TRACERS
BATHERS	BERTHAS	BREATHS	CARTING	CRATING	TRACING
BATTIER	BIRETTA	RATBITE	CASEINS	CASSINE	INCASES
BATTLER	BLATTER	BRATTLE	CASEMEN	EMACSEN	MENACES
BEADERS	DEBASER	SABERED	CATTIES	STATICE	TIETACS
BEADMEN	BEDEMAN	BENAMED	CATTISH	CHATTIS	TACHIST
BEARDED	BREADED	DEBEARD	CENTARE	CRENATE	REENACT
BEATERS	BERATES	REBATES	CENTAUR	UNCRATE	UNTRACE
BEDROOM	BOREDOM	BROOMED	CENTERS	CENTRES	TENRECS
BEDRUGS	BUDGERS	REDBUGS	CENTIMO	ENTOMIC	TONEMIC
BELDAME	BEMEDAL	EMBALED	CERESIN	SCRIENE	SINCERE
BELLIED	DELIBLE	LIBELED	CERIPHS	CIPHERS	SPHERIC
BEMIRES	BERIMES	BIREMES	CERITES	RECITES	TIERCES
BESORTS	SORBETS	STROBES	CESSION	COSINES	OSCINES
BETRIMS	TIMBERS	TIMBRES	CESTODE	ESCOTED	TEDESCO
BIGENER	BREINGE	REBEGIN	CESTOID	COEDITS	COTISED
BIMETAL	LIMBATE	TIMBALE	CESURAL	RECUSAL	SECULAR
BINDERS	INBREDS	REBINDS	CHALETS	LATCHES	SATCHEL
BLISTER	BRISTLE	RIBLETS	CHAPTER	PATCHER	REPATCH
BLUDIER	BUILDER	REBUILD	CHARISM	CHIMARS	CHRISMA
BLURBED	BURBLED	RUBBLED	CHASERS	CRASHES	ESCHARS
BOILERS	LIBEROS	REBOILS	CHETNIK	KITCHEN	THICKEN
BOLSTER	BOLTERS	LOBSTER	CHILDER	CHIRLED	ELDRICH
BORINGS	ROBINGS	SORBING	CHINING	INCHING	NICHING
BOSSING	GIBSONS	OBSIGNS	CHIRTED	DITCHER	RICHTED
BOULLES	LOBULES	SOLUBLE	CHOKERS	HOCKERS	SHOCKER
BOUNDER	REBOUND	UNROBED	CHOLERA	CHORALE	CHOREAL
BOURNES	UNROBES	UNSOBER	CHORALS	LORCHAS	SCHOLAR
BREEDER	BREERED	REBREED	CHORDEE	COHERED	OCHERED
BRIDALS	LABRIDS	RIBALDS	CHOREAS	ORACHES	ROACHES
BRIEFED	DEBRIEF	FIBERED	CHOREUS	CHOUSER	ROUCHES
BRISURE	BRUISER	BURIERS	CHOUSED	DOUCHES	HOCUSED
BUGLERS	BULGERS	BURGLES	CIERGES	GRECISE	GRIECES
BUMMELS	BUMMLES	MUMBLES	CINDERS	DISCERN	RESCIND
BUNTIER	TRIBUNE	TURBINE	CINEOLS	CONSEIL	INCLOSE
BURNIES	RUBINES	SUBERIN	CITHERS	ESTRICH	RICHEST
CACKLER	CLACKER	CRACKLE	CLARIES	ECLAIRS	SCALIER
CAFILAS	FACIALS	FASCIAL	CLASHER	LARCHES	RASCHEL
CAGANER	CARNAGE	CRANAGE	CLEANED	ELANCED	ENLACED
CAHIERS	CASHIER	ERIACHS	CLIENTS	LECTINS	STENCIL
CAIRNED	CARNIED	DANCIER	CLOSERS	CRESOLS	ESCROLS
CAISSON	CASINOS	CASSINO	CLOTURE	CLOUTER	COULTER
CAKINGS	CASKING	SACKING	CODEINS	CONDIES	SECONDI
CALKERS	LACKERS	SLACKER	CODILLE	COLLIDE	COLLIED
CALVERS	CARVELS	CLAVERS	COEXIST	COXIEST	EXOTICS
CAMBERS	CEMBRAS	CRAMBES	COINFER	CONIFER	INFORCE
CANALED	CANDELA	DECANAL	COINTER	NOTICER	RECTION
CANDORS	CARDONS	DACRONS	CONATUS	NOCTUAS	TOUCANS
CANGLED	CLANGED	GLANCED	CONDERS	CORSNED	SCORNED
CANINES	ENCINAS	NANCIES	CONTOUR	CORNUTO	CROUTON
CANTHUS	CHAUNTS	STAUNCH	CONTUSE	ECONUTS	UNCOEST
CAPELIN	PANICLE	PELICAN	COPERED	PRECODE	PROCEED
CAPERED	PEARCED	PREACED	COPIERS	COPSIER	PERSICO
CAPOTES	SCOPATE	TOECAPS	COPULAS	CUPOLAS	SCOPULA
CAPSTAN	CAPTANS	CATNAPS	COPYISM	MISCOPY	MYOPICS
CARGOES	CORSAGE	SOCAGER			

CORKERS	RECORKS	ROCKERS	DEPRIVE	PREDIVE	PRIEVED
CORNICE	CROCEIN	CROCINE	DERATED	REDATED	TREADED
CORVETS	COVERTS	VECTORS	DERIVER	REDRIVE	RIVERED
COSIEST	COTISES	OECISTS	DESERTS	DESSERT	TRESSED
COSMINE	INCOMES	MESONIC	DESINED	NEDDIES	SDEINED
COUPERS	CROUPES	RECOUPS	DESTINE	ENDITES	STEINED
COURSED	SCOURED	SOURCED	DESTOCK	DOCKETS	STOCKED
COURSER	CRUORES	SCOURER	DESTROY	ROYSTED	STROYED
COUTERS	CROUTES	SCOUTER	DEWATER	TARWEED	WATERED
COUTHER	RETOUCH	TOUCHER	DIALING	GLIADIN	LAIDING
COUVERT	CUTOVER	OVERCUT	DIESELS	IDLESSE	SEIDELS
CRASSER	SCARERS	SCARRES	DIETING	EDITING	IGNITED
CREASED	DECARES	SEARCED	DIETIST	DITTIES	TIDIEST
CREEING	ENERGIC	GENERIC	DILATER	REDTAIL	TRAILED
CREMINI	CRIMINE	MINCIER	DIMPLES	MISPLED	SIMPLED
CREPIER	PIERCER	REPRICE	DIPTERA	PARTIED	PIRATED
CRISPEN	PINCERS	PRINCES	DIRTIES	DITSIER	TIDIERS
CRUDDLE	CUDDLER	CURDLED	DISHING	HIDINGS	SHINDIG
CRUELLS	CULLERS	SCULLER	DISNEST	DISSENT	SNIDEST
CRUISER	CURRIES	SUCRIER	DISPORT	TORPIDS	TRIPODS
CRUISES	CRUSIES	CUISSER	DIVERTS	STRIVED	VERDITS
CTENOID	DEONTIC	NOTICED	DOLINES	INDOLES	SONDELI
CUATROS	SURCOAT	TURACOS	DOMINES	EMODINS	MISDONE
CURTEST	CUTTERS	SCUTTER	DONDERS	NODDERS	SNODDER
CUTLETS	CUTTLES	SCUTTLE	DOOMIER	MOIDORE	MOODIER
CUTLINE	LINECUT	TUNICLE	DORSELS	RODLESS	SOLDERS
DABBLER	DRABBLE	RABBLED	DOTTELS	DOTTLES	SLOTTED
DAILIES	LIAISED	SEDILIA	DOWRIES	ROWDIES	WEIRDOS
DAIMONS	DOMAINS	MADISON	DRAGGLE	GARGLED	RAGGLED
DALLIER	DIALLER	RALLIED	DRAPIER	PARRIED	RAPIDER
DANGERS	GANDERS	GARDENS	DRAUNTS	DURANTS	TUNDRAS
DAPPLES	SAPPLED	SLAPPED	DREAMER	REARMED	REDREAM
DARKEST	STARKED	STRAKED	DREIDLS	RIDDLES	SLIDDER
DARNERS	ERRANDS	SNARRED	DROGUES	GOURDES	GROUSED
DARNING	NARDING	RANDING	DROLEST	OLDSTER	STRODLE
DAUBERS	EARBUDS	SUBEDAR	DROWNED	ROWNDED	WONDRED
DAWDLER	DRAWLED	WADDLER	DUELING	ELUDING	INDULGE
DAWDLES	SWADDLE	WADDLES	DUFFELS	DUFFLES	SLUFFED
DAWNERS	WANDERS	WARDENS	DUNGERS	GERUNDS	NUDGERS
DEADEST	SEDATED	STEADED	DUSTIER	REDUITS	STUDIER
DEALERS	LEADERS	REDEALS	DUSTPAN	STANDUP	UPSTAND
DEBITOR	DEORBIT	ORBITED	EAGLING	GEALING	LIGNAGE
DEBONER	ENROBED	REDBONE	EARFULS	FERULAS	REFUSAL
DECANTS	DESCANT	SCANTED	EARPLUG	GRAUPEL	PLAGUER
DECRIAL	RADICEL	RADICLE	EATCHES	ESCHEAT	TEACHES
DEIFIER	EDIFIER	REIFIED	EIGHTHS	HEIGHTS	HIGHEST
DELAYER	LAYERED	RELAYED	EKISTIC	ICKIEST	TICKIES
DELETES	SLEETED	STEELED	ELANETS	LATEENS	LEANEST
DEMIREP	EPIDERM	IMPEDER	ELAPSES	PLEASES	SAPELES
DENIERS	NEREIDS	RESINED	ELICHES	HELICES	LICHEES
DENTARY	TRAYNED	TYRANED	ELISION	ISOLINE	LIONISE
DENTINS	INDENTS	INTENDS	ELITISM	LIMIEST	LIMITES
DENTIST	DISTENT	STINTED	ELUANTS	LUNATES	UNLASTE
DENTURE	RETUNED	TENURED	ELUTORS	OUTLERS	TROULES
DENUDES	DUDEENS	DUENDES	EMANATE	ENEMATA	MANATEE
DEPAINT	PAINTED	PATINED	EMERITA	EMIRATE	MEATIER
DEPARTS	DRAPETS	PETARDS	EMIGRES	REGIMES	REMIGES
DEPORTS	REDTOPS	SPORTED	EMOTERS	METEORS	REMOTES
DEPRAVE	PERVADE	REPAVED	EMPTING	PIGMENT	TEMPING
DEPRESS	PRESSED	SPERSED	EMULING	GUMLINE	LEGUMIN

EMULSIN	LUMINES	UNLIMES	GALLATE	GALLETA	TALLAGE
ENAMORS	MOANERS	OARSMEN	GANGERS	GRANGES	NAGGERS
ENDARTS	STANDER	STARNED	GAPINGS	GASPING	PAGINGS
ENDGAME	MANEGED	MENAGED	GARGLES	LAGGERS	RAGGLES
ENERVES	EVENERS	VENEERS	GARMENT	MARGENT	RAGMENT
ENGRAMS	GERMANS	MANGERS	GARNISH	RASHING	SHARING
ENISLED	ENSILED	LINSEED	GARRETS	GARTERS	GRATERS
ENLARGE	GENERAL	GLEANER	GARVIES	GRAVIES	RIVAGES
ENRIVEN	INNERVE	NERVINE	GASPIER	PRISAGE	SPAIRGE
ENSUING	GUNNIES	INGENUS	GASTING	GATINGS	STAGING
ENTOILS	LIONETS	ONLIEST	GAULTER	TEGULAR	TRAGULE
ENTREAT	RATTEEN	TERNATE	GELANTS	LANGEST	TANGLES
ENTREES	RETENES	TEENERS	GELATED	LEGATED	TEAGLED
ENVIOUS	NIVEOUS	VEINOUS	GELIDER	LEDGIER	LEIDGER
ENVIROS	RENVOIS	VERSION	GEMINAL	LEAMING	MEALING
ENWRAPS	PAWNERS	SPAWNER	GEMMIER	GREMMIE	IMMERGE
EOLITHS	HOLIEST	HOSTILE	GENESIS	SEEINGS	SIGNEES
EOSINIC	ICONISE	NICOISE	GERMINS	MERINGS	MINGERS
EPACRIS	SCRAPIE	SPACIER	GESTAPO	POSTAGE	POTAGES
EPIGONS	PIGEONS	PINGOES	GINGERY	GREYING	NIGGERY
ERBIUMS	IMBRUES	IMBURSE	GIRDING	GRIDING	RIDGING
ESPARTO	PROTEAS	SEAPORT	GIRDLED	GLIDDER	GRIDDLE
ESPYING	PEYSING	PIGSNEY	GIRNELS	LINGERS	SLINGER
ESSOINS	OSSEINS	SESSION	GLAIRIN	LAIRING	RAILING
ESTRAYS	STAYERS	STAYRES	GLOBINS	GOBLINS	LOBINGS
ESTREAT	RESTATE	RETASTE	GLORIED	GODLIER	GOLDIER
ESTRINS	INSERTS	SINTERS	GNOMISH	HOMINGS	MOSHING
ESTRIOL	LOITERS	TOILERS	GOGLETS	LOGGETS	TOGGLES
ESTRUMS	MUSTERS	STUMERS	GOITERS	GOITRES	GORIEST
ETATISM	MATIEST	MATTIES	GOONIES	ISOGONE	NOOGIES
ETHYLIC	LECYTHI	TECHILY	GORPING	GROPING	PORGING
ETOURDI	IODURET	OUTRIDE	GOSTERS	GROSETS	STORGES
FALSEST	FATLESS	FESTALS	GRASPED	SPADGER	SPARGED
FANCIES	FASCINE	FIANCES	GRAYEST	GYRATES	STAGERY
FARTING	INGRAFT	RAFTING	GREENER	REGREEN	RENEGER
FASTIES	FIESTAS	FISSATE	GREISLY	GRIESLY	GRISELY
FATHERS	HAFTERS	SHAFTER	GREMLIN	MERLING	MINGLER
FEALING	FINAGLE	LEAFING	GRINGAS	RAGINGS	SIRGANG
FELSITE	LEFTIES	LIEFEST	GRIPMEN	IMPREGN	PERMING
FELTERS	REFLETS	TELFERS	GUERDON	UNDERGO	UNGORED
FERRIED	REFIRED	REFRIED	GUILERS	LIGURES	LURGIES
FERRIES	REFIRES	REFRIES	GUNTERS	GURNETS	SURGENT
FERULES	FUELERS	REFUELS	GUSTFUL	GUTFULS	GUTSFUL
FIFTIES	IFFIEST	STIFFIE	HAIRNET	INEARTH	THERIAN
FIGHTER	FREIGHT	REFIGHT	HALSING	LASHING	SHALING
FISHERS	SERFISH	SHERIFS	HAMMALS	MAHMALS	MASHLAM
FISSURE	FUSSIER	SURFIES	HAPTENE	HEPTANE	PHENATE
FLANEUR	FRENULA	FUNERAL	HAPTICS	PATHICS	SPATHIC
FLOATER	FLOREAT	REFLOAT	HARPERS	PHRASER	SHARPER
FLOODER	FLOORED	REFLOOD	HASLETS	HATLESS	SHELTAS
FLOWING	FOWLING	WOLFING	HASTENS	SNATHES	SNEATHS
FLUENTS	NESTFUL	NETFULS	HAWSERS	SWASHER	WASHERS
FLUSTER	FLUTERS	RESTFUL	HAWSING	SHAWING	WASHING
FOETORS	FOOTERS	REFOOTS	HEARERS	REHEARS	SHEARER
FOOTIES	FOOTSIE	OOFIEST	HEEDERS	HEREDES	SHEERED
FORPITS	PROFITS	SPORTIF	HEGARIS	HEGIRAS	HIRAGES
FRANTIC	INFARCT	INFRACT	HELIUMS	HUMLIES	MUHLIES
FRATERS	RAFTERS	STRAFER	HENRIES	INHERES	RESHINE
FRITURE	FRUITER	TURFIER	HEROONS	ONSHORE	SOREHON
GALIOTS	LATIGOS	SALIGOT	HEWINGS	SHEWING	WHINGES

HIDDERS	REDDISH	SHIDDER	LICKERS	RICKLES	SLICKER
HINDERS	NERDISH	SHRINED	LIMINGS	SLIMING	SMILING
HOLIDAY	HYALOID	HYOIDAL	LIMOSES	LISSOME	SMOILES
HOMERIC	MOCHIER	MORICHE	LINGOTS	TIGLONS	TOLINGS
HOTPOTS	HOTSPOT	POTSHOT	LINGUAS	NILGAUS	SALUING
HUNTERS	SHUNTER	UNHERST	LINKERS	RELINKS	SLINKER
HURTING	UNGIRTH	UNRIGHT	LINKUPS	SKULPIN	UPLINKS
HUSTLES	LUSHEST	SLEUTHS	LINTERS	SLINTER	SNIRTLE
ICKLEST	STICKLE	TICKLES	LIPPERS	RIPPLES	SLIPPER
IGNITER	TIERING	TIGRINE	LIPREAD	PEDRAIL	PREDIAL
IMMURES	MUMSIER	RUMMIES	LISTEES	TELESIS	TIELESS
IMPETUS	IMPUTES	UPTIMES	LISTETH	LITHEST	THISTLE
IMPOSER	PROMISE	SEMIPRO	LITERAL	TALLIER	TRIELLA
INANEST	STANINE	TANNIES	LOADERS	ORDEALS	RELOADS
INCHERS	NICHERS	RICHENS	LOANERS	ORLEANS	RELOANS
INCISAL	SALICIN	SINICAL	LOMENTA	OMENTAL	TELAMON
INGINES	INSIGNE	SEINING	LORISES	LOSSIER	RISSOLE
INGROUP	POURING	ROUPING	LOTUSES	SOLUTES	TOUSLES
INKLESS	KINLESS	SILKENS	LOUDENS	NODULES	NOUSLED
INKLING	KILNING	LINKING	LOUDEST	OULDEST	TOUSLED
INLACES	SANICLE	SCALENI	LOUNDER	ROUNDEL	ROUNDLE
INROADS	ORDAINS	SADIRON	LOURIES	LOUSIER	SOILURE
INSCULP	SCULPIN	UNCLIPS	LOUVERS	LOUVRES	VELOURS
INSPIRE	SNIPIER	SPINIER	LUCARNE	NUCLEAR	UNCLEAR
INSTARS	SANTIRS	STRAINS	LUSTIER	RULIEST	RUTILES
INTAKES	KENTIAS	TANKIES	LUSTING	LUTINGS	SINGULT
INTERIM	MINTIER	TERMINI	LUSTRED	RUSTLED	STRUDEL
INTONER	NOINTER	TERNION	MAILERS	REALISM	REMAILS
INURING	RUINING	URINING	MALATES	MALTASE	TAMALES
IRATELY	REALITY	TEARILY	MALISON	MONIALS	SOMNIAL
IRENICS	SERICIN	SIRENIC	MANITUS	SANTIMU	TSUNAMI
ISMATIC	ITACISM	SIMATIC	MANURES	MURENAS	SURNAME
ISOMERS	MOISERS	MOSSIER	MAPPERS	PAMPERS	PREAMPS
ISONOME	MOONIES	NOISOME	MARACAS	MARASCA	MASCARA
ISOTRON	NITROSO	TORSION	MASCLES	MESCALS	SCAMELS
KAROROS	KARROOS	KORORAS	MASTERY	MAYSTER	STREAMY
KARTERS	KRATERS	STARKER	MASTICS	MISACTS	MISCAST
KASHRUT	KHURTAS	TUSHKAR	MASTING	MATINGS	TAMINGS
KELTERS	KESTREL	SKELTER	MEDLING	MELDING	MINGLED
KILTERS	KIRTLES	KLISTER	MEETERS	REMEETS	TEEMERS
KINDERS	KINREDS	REDSKIN	MELOIDS	MIDSOLE	SMOILED
KISTING	KITINGS	SKITING	MENTORS	MONSTER	MONTRES
KITTELS	KITTLES	SKITTLE	MERANTI	MINARET	RAIMENT
KREESES	RESEEKS	SEEKERS	MERCHES	SCHEMER	SCHMEER
LADDERS	RADDLES	SADDLER	MESSILY	MILSEYS	SMILEYS
LAMENTS	MANTELS	MANTLES	MILADIS	MISDIAL	MISLAID
LAMITER	MALTIER	MARLITE	MINTAGE	TEAMING	TEGMINA
LAPPERS	RAPPELS	SLAPPER	MIOTICS	MISTICO	SOMITIC
LAPSING	PALINGS	SAPLING	MIRIEST	MISTIER	RIMIEST
LATENTS	LATTENS	TALENTS	MISDIET	MISEDIT	STIMIED
LAUNDER	LURDANE	RUNDALE	MISLIES	MISSILE	SIMILES
LEAPING	PEALING	PLEAING	MISMATE	SEMIMAT	TAMMIES
LEASING	LINAGES	SEALING	MISUSER	MUSSIER	SURMISE
LEISTER	RETILES	STERILE	MONTURE	MOUNTER	REMOUNT
LENDERS	RELENDS	SLENDER	MOOTEST	MOTTOES	TOOMEST
LENTILS	LINTELS	TELLINS	MOPIEST	OPTIMES	STOMPIE
LEOPARD	PAROLED	PRELOAD	MOTHERS	SMOTHER	THERMOS
LEPTINS	PINTLES	PLENIST	MOTIEST	MOTTIES	TITMOSE
LIBRATE	TABLIER	TRIABLE	MUNSTER	MUNTERS	STERNUM
LICENSE	SELENIC	SILENCE	MUREINS	MURINES	NEURISM

MUTISMS	SUMMIST	SUMMITS	PINIEST	PINITES	TIEPINS
NAGARIS	SANGRIA	SARANGI	PINNETS	SPINNET	TENPINS
NAIVEST	NATIVES	VAINEST	PINTOES	POINTES	PONTIES
NEEDERS	SERENED	SNEERED	PISHERS	RESHIPS	SERIPHS
NEPETAS	PENATES	PESANTE	PISTONS	POSTINS	SPINTOS
NEPHRIC	PHRENIC	PINCHER	PITTERS	SPITTER	TIPSTER
NESTING	SENTING	TENSING	PLANATE	PLANTAE	PLATANE
NESTLER	RELENTS	SLENTER	PLANTAS	PLATANS	SALTPAN
NESTORS	STONERS	TENSORS	PLESSOR	SLOPERS	SPLORES
NETTERS	TENTERS	TESTERN	POOREST	POOTERS	STOOPER
NEWSIER	WEINERS	WIENERS	POPSTER	STOPPER	TOPPERS
NICKELS	NICKLES	SLICKEN	POSEURS	SEROPUS	SOUPERS
NIDGETS	STEDING	STINGED	POSTMAN	TAMPONS	TOPSMAN
NITRITE	NITTIER	TINTIER	POTHERS	STROPHE	THORPES
NOOSERS	SEROONS	SOONERS	POTTERS	PROTEST	SPOTTER
NOSIEST	SONTIES	STONIES	POTTIES	SPOTTIE	TIPTOES
NUPTIAL	PATULIN	UNPLAIT	POULDER	POULDRE	PROULED
NUTSIER	TRIUNES	UNITERS	PRAYERS	RESPRAY	SPRAYER
OBSERVE	OBVERSE	VERBOSE	PREASED	RESPADE	SPEARED
OERSTED	ROSETED	TEREDOS	PRESELL	RESPELL	SPELLER
OOLITES	OSTIOLE	STOOLIE	PRESIDE	SPEIRED	SPIERED
OPERANT	PRONATE	PROTEAN	PRESSER	REPRESS	SPERRES
OPPOSER	POOPERS	PROPOSE	PRISING	RISPING	SPIRING
OPTIONS	POSITON	POTIONS	PRUDENT	PRUNTED	UPTREND
ORIGINS	SIGNIOR	SIGNORI	PRUINES	PURINES	UPRISEN
ORPINES	PIONERS	PROINES	PUDSIER	SIRUPED	UPDRIES
OSSELET	TELOSES	TOELESS	PULIEST	PUTELIS	STIPULE
OSTLERS	STEROLS	TORSELS	PULSATE	PUTEALS	SPATULE
OUTDARE	OUTREAD	READOUT	PUSLEYS	PUSSLEY	SPULYES
OUTSERT	STOUTER	TOUTERS	PUSSIER	SUSPIRE	UPRISES
PAINTER	PERTAIN	REPAINT	QUAREST	QUARTES	QUATRES
PANDIES	PANSIED	SPAINED	RANDIES	SANDIER	SARDINE
PANTLER	PLANTER	REPLANT	RANKEST	STARKEN	TANKERS
PAPERER	PREPARE	REPAPER	RASHEST	SHASTER	TRASHES
PARISON	PORINAS	SOPRANI	RATTANS	TANTRAS	TARTANS
PARKEES	RESPEAK	SPEAKER	RATTERS	RESTART	STARTER
PARKERS	REPARKS	SPARKER	RATTIER	RETRAIT	TARTIER
PARTING	PRATING	TRAPING	REBATER	TABRERE	TEREBRA
PARTLET	PLATTER	PRATTLE	RECURES	RESCUER	SECURER
PARTONS	PATRONS	TARPONS	REDCAPS	SCARPED	SCRAPED
PARULIS	SPIRULA	UPRISAL	REDNESS	RESENDS	SENDERS
PASCUAL	PAUCALS	SCAPULA	REDOUND	ROUNDED	UNDERDO
PASTERS	REPASTS	SPAREST	REEVING	REGIVEN	VEERING
PATTERS	SPATTER	TAPSTER	REMADES	REMEADS	SMEARED
PEARLIN	PLAINER	PRALINE	RENTERS	RERENTS	STERNER
PEASING	SPAEING	SPINAGE	RENTING	RINGENT	TERNING
PEELERS	SLEEPER	SPEELER	RERISES	SERRIES	SIRREES
PENSILS	SPINELS	SPLINES	RESEAUS	SEASURE	UREASES
PENSION	PINONES	SPINONE	RESIFTS	SIFTERS	STRIFES
PERICON	PONCIER	PORCINE	RESPLIT	SPIRTLE	TRIPLES
PERIGON	PIROGEN	PONGIER	RESTOCK	ROCKETS	STOCKER
PERIQUE	REEQUIP	REPIQUE	RESTUFF	STUFFER	TRUFFES
PERNODS	PONDERS	RESPOND	RESTUMP	STUMPER	SUMPTER
PERSING	PINGERS	SPRINGE	RETEARS	SERRATE	TEARERS
PERTEST	PETTERS	PRETEST	RETIRAL	RETRIAL	TRAILER
PERUSAL	PLEURAS	SERPULA	RETIRED	RETRIED	TIREDER
PHYTONS	PYTHONS	TYPHONS	RETRAIN	TERRAIN	TRAINER
PICKERS	RIPECKS	SPICKER	RETRATE	RETREAT	TREATER
PIERROT	PORTIER	PRERIOT	RETWIST	TWISTER	WITTERS
PIGSKIN	PIKINGS	SPIKING	REUSING	RUEINGS	SIGNEUR

REVISIT	STIVIER	VISITER		SNOTTIE	TONIEST	TONITES
REVUIST	STUIVER	VIRTUES		SONNETS	STONNES	TENSONS
REWARMS	SWARMER	WARMERS		SPARTHE	TEPHRAS	THREAPS
REWEARS	SWEARER	WEARERS		SPELDIN	SPINDLE	SPLINED
RHETORS	ROTHERS	SHORTER		SPROUTS	STROUPS	STUPORS
RICKETS	STICKER	TICKERS		STERNED	TENDERS	TENDRES
RINGLET	TINGLER	TRINGLE		STEWARD	STRAWED	WRASTED
RIOTERS	ROISTER	RORIEST		STEWING	TWINGES	WESTING
RIPPLET	TIPPLER	TRIPPLE		STORMER	TERMORS	TREMORS
RISQUES	SQUIERS	SQUIRES		STOTTER	STRETTO	TOTTERS
RONDURE	ROUNDER	UNORDER		STOWING	TOWINGS	TOWSING
ROOSTER	ROOTERS	TOREROS		STRETTA	TARTEST	TATTERS
ROTTENS	SNOTTER	STENTOR		STRETTI	TITTERS	TRITEST
ROWDIER	WORDIER	WORRIED		STRINGY	STYRING	TRYINGS
RUCKLES	SCULKER	SUCKLER		SUNBELT	UNBELTS	UNBLEST
RUMPIES	SPUMIER	UMPIRES		SUNNIER	UNREINS	UNRISEN
RUSSETS	TRUSSES	TUSSERS		SWATHER	THAWERS	WREATHS
RUTTERS	TRUSTER	TURRETS		SWELTER	WELTERS	WRESTLE
SACHEMS	SAMECHS	SCHEMAS		SWIPING	WIPINGS	WISPING
SALIVAS	SALVIAS	VASSAIL		SWITHER	WITHERS	WRITHES
SALLETS	STELLAS	TASSELL		TAIVERS	VASTIER	VERITAS
SALVETE	VALETES	VELETAS		TEWHITS	WETTISH	WHITEST
SALVING	SLAVING	VALSING		THAIRMS	THIRAMS	THRIMSA
SEAGULL	SULLAGE	ULLAGES		THEATER	THEATRE	THEREAT
SEEDLIP	SPEILED	SPIELED		TRAVELS	VARLETS	VESTRAL
SEINERS	SEREINS	SERINES		UNHEALS	UNLEASH	UNSHALE
SENDUPS	SUSPEND	UPSENDS		UNIPEDS	UNSPIDE	UNSPIED
SERVANT	TAVERNS	VERSANT		VERSUTE	VERTUES	VESTURE
SETWALL	SWALLET	WALLETS		WARLESS	WARSLES	WRASSLE
SHREIKS	SHRIEKS	SHRIKES		WARSTLE	WASTREL	WRASTLE
SHUTING	TUSHING	UNSIGHT		WEATHER	WHEREAT	WREATHE
SISTRUM	TRISMUS	TRUISMS		WENDIGO	WIDGEON	WONGIED
SITELLA	TAILLES	TALLIES		WHERRIT	WHIRRET	WRITHER
SKIRRET	SKIRTER	STRIKER				

Chapter 8: Variants

One of the confusing things about the English language is the number of variant spellings that exist. But to a Scrabble player, variant spellings can be a great opportunity. If you know that a word can end in -EY as well as -Y, for example, then you have an extra possibility for playing it – and for using up more of your letters.

American spellings are one great source of variants – think of all the -RE words that are spelt -ER in the US, for example. But there are also many other variations, which you will find in the list below. This list contains most of the common variant spellings in English; the words are listed in alphabetical order.

Not included in this list are the most obvious set of variants – verbs that end in -IZE or -ISE. Obviously, there are simply far too many of these to include; instead, you will find a list of all the verbs ending in -ISE that don't have a variant ending in -IZE, as well as a list for the reverse case.

Variants

ABATER – ABATOR	AESTIVAL – ESTIVAL	ALOE – ALE
ABETTER – ABETTOR	AESTIVATE – ESTIVATE	ALOES – ALES
ABSCISSAE – ABSCISSE	AETHER – ETHER	ALTHAEA – ALTHEA
ACALEPHAE – ACALEPHE	AETHEREAL – ETHEREAL	ALTHAEAS – ALTHEAS
ACCEPTER – ACCEPTOR	AETHERIC – ETHERIC	AMMOCOETE – AMMOCETE
ACCOUTRE – ACCOUTER	AETHERS – ETHERS	AMOEBA – AMEBA
ACHAENIA – ACHENIA	AETIOLOGY – ETIOLOGY	AMOEBAE – AMEBAE
ACHAENIUM – ACHENIUM	AGAPAE – AGAPE	AMOEBAEAN – AMOEBEAN
ACRE – ACER	AGISTER – AGISTOR	AMOEBAN – AMEBAN
ADAPTER – ADAPTOR	AGLY – AGLEY	AMOEBAS – AMEBAS
ADDABLE – ADDIBLE	ALAE – ALE	AMOEBEAN – AMEBEAN
ADDRESSER – ADDRESSOR	ALIENER – ALIENOR	AMOEBIC – AMEBIC
ADJURER – ADJUROR	ALKIE – ALKY	AMOEBOID – AMEBOID
ADJUSTER – ADJUSTOR	ALL – AL	AMYGDALAE – AMYGDALE
ADVISER – ADVISOR	ALLAY – ALAY	ANAEMIA – ANEMIA
AEDILE – EDILE	ALLAYED – ALAYED	ANAEMIAS – ANEMIAS
AEDILES – EDILES	ALLAYING – ALAYING	ANAEMIC – ANEMIC
AEGIS – EGIS	ALLAYS – ALAYS	ANAPAEST – ANAPEST
AEGISES – EGISES	ALLEE – ALEE	ANAPAESTS – ANAPESTS
AEMULE – EMULE	ALLEGGE – ALEGGE	ANIMATER – ANIMATOR
AEMULED – EMULED	ALLEGGED – ALEGGED	ANOESTRA – ANESTRA
AEMULES – EMULES	ALLEGGES – ALEGGES	ANOESTRI – ANESTRI
AEMULING – EMULING	ALLEGGING – ALEGGING	ANOESTRUM – ANESTRUM
AEOLIAN – EOLIAN	ALLERION – ALERION	ANOESTRUS – ANESTRUS
AEOLIPILE – EOLIPILE	ALLERIONS – ALERIONS	ANOETIC – ANETIC
AEON – EON	ALLEYED – ALEYED	ANOMIE – ANOMY
AEONIAN – EONIAN	ALLIGARTA – ALIGARTA	ANOXAEMIA – ANOXEMIA
AEONS – EONS	ALLOD – ALOD	ANOXAEMIC – ANOXEMIC
AERIE – AERY	ALLODIA – ALODIA	ANTAE – ANTE
AEROS – EROS	ALLODIAL – ALODIAL	ANVILLED – ANVILED
AERUGO – ERUGO	ALLODIUM – ALODIUM	ANVILLING – ANVILING
AERUGOS – ERUGOS	ALLODIUMS – ALODIUMS	APNOEA – APNEA
AESTHESES – ESTHESES	ALLODS – ALODS	APNOEAL – APNEAL
AESTHESIA – ESTHESIA	ALLOW – ALOW	APNOEAS – APNEAS
AESTHESIS – ESTHESIS	ALLS – ALS	APNOEIC – APNEIC
AESTHETE – ESTHETE	ALLURE – ALURE	APOGAEIC – APOGEIC
AESTHETES – ESTHETES	ALLURES – ALURES	APPALL – APPAL
AESTHETIC – ESTHETIC	ALLY – ALLEY	APPALLS – APPALS

APPERILL – APPERIL
APPERILLS – APPERILS
APPLY – APPLEY
APPOINTER – APPOINTOR
ARBOUR – ARBOR
ARCHAEI – ARCHEI
ARCHAEUS – ARCHEUS
ARDOUR – ARDOR
AREOLAE – AREOLE
ARMER – ARMOR
ARMOUR – ARMOR
ARRESTER – ARRESTOR
ARSY – ARSEY
ASPERSER – ASPERSOR
ASPIRATAE – ASPIRATE
ASSENTER – ASSENTOR
ASSERTER – ASSERTOR
ASSIGNER – ASSIGNOR
ASSISTER – ASSISTOR
ASSURER – ASSUROR
ATHENAEUM – ATHENEUM
ATTESTER – ATTESTOR
ATTRACTER – ATTRACTOR
AUGMENTER – AUGMENTOR
AUNTIE – AUNTY
AUREOLAE – AUREOLE
AUTOECISM – AUTECISM
AVERTABLE – AVERTIBLE
AWMRIE – AWMRY
AZOTAEMIA – AZOTEMIA
AZOTAEMIC – AZOTEMIC
BADDIE – BADDY
BAEL – BEL
BAELS – BELS
BAGGIE – BAGGY
BAILER – BAILOR
BAILEY – BAILIE
BAILLIE – BAILIE
BAILLIES – BAILIES
BALL – BAL
BALLADIN – BALADIN
BALLADINE – BALADINE
BALLADINS – BALADINS
BALLED – BALED
BALLER – BALER
BALLERS – BALERS
BALLING – BALING
BALLISTA – BALISTA
BALLISTAE – BALISTAE
BALLISTAS – BALISTAS
BALLS – BALS
BARBELL – BARBEL
BARBELLS – BARBELS
BARBIE – BARBY
BARDIE – BARDY
BARMIE – BARMY
BARNY – BARNEY
BARRATER – BARRATOR
BARRE – BARER
BARRELLED – BARRELED

BARRIE – BARRY
BASTILLE – BASTILE
BASTILLES – BASTILES
BATSMAN – BATMAN
BATTELLED – BATTELED
BATTERIE – BATTERY
BAWTIE – BAWTY
BAYADERE – BAYADEER
BEADSMAN – BEADMAN
BEANIE – BEANY
BEARDIE – BEARDY
BEDELL – BEDEL
BEDELLS – BEDELS
BEDESMAN – BEDEMAN
BEGLAMOUR – BEGLAMOR
BEHAVIOUR – BEHAVIOR
BEIN – BIEN
BELABOUR – BELABOR
BELL – BEL
BELLIED – BELIED
BELLIES – BELIES
BELLOW – BELOW
BELLOWS – BELOWS
BELLS – BELS
BELLYING – BELYING
BERE – BEER
BETTER – BETTOR
BEVELLED – BEVELED
BEVELLER – BEVELER
BEVELLERS – BEVELERS
BEVELLING – BEVELING
BEVER – BEVOR
BHEESTIE – BHEESTY
BICOLOUR – BICOLOR
BIGGIE – BIGGY
BILLED – BILED
BILLIE – BILLY
BILLING – BILING
BINGOES – BINGES
BISTRE – BISTER
BITTER – BITTOR
BITTIE – BITTY
BITTOUR – BITTOR
BLAEST – BLEST
BLARE – BLAER
BLASTIE – BLASTY
BLIMY – BLIMEY
BLOCKIE – BLOCKY
BLOOEY – BLOOIE
BLOWIE – BLOWY
BLUDIE – BLUDY
BOATSMAN – BOATMAN
BOET – BET
BOETS – BETS
BOGEY – BOGIE – BOGY
BOLLIX – BOLIX
BOLLIXED – BOLIXED
BOLLIXES – BOLIXES
BOLLIXING – BOLIXING
BOLSHIE – BOLSHY

BONDSMAN – BONDMAN
BONEY – BONIE – BONY
BONNIE – BONNY
BONSELLA – BONSELA
BONSELLAS – BONSELAS
BOOBIE – BOOBY
BOODIE – BOODY
BOOGEY – BOOGIE – BOOGY
BOOKIE – BOOKY
BOOKSIE – BOOKSY
BOOTIE – BOOTY
BOOZY – BOOZEY
BORRELL – BORREL
BORSTALL – BORSTAL
BORSTALLS – BORSTALS
BOTHIE – BOTHY
BOULLE – BOULE
BOULLES – BOULES
BOWELLED – BOWELED
BOWELLING – BOWELING
BOWLLIKE – BOWLIKE
BOWSEY – BOWSIE
BRAILLED – BRAILED
BRAILLING – BRAILING
BRAKESMAN – BRAKEMAN
BRASSIE – BRASSY
BRAVOED – BRAVED
BRAVOES – BRAVES
BRAWLIE – BRAWLY
BREI – BRIE
BREIS – BRIES
BRERE – BREER
BREY – BRIE
BRICKIE – BRICKY
BRIDESMAN – BRIDEMAN
BRIMFULL – BRIMFUL
BROWNIE – BROWNY
BULLBAR – BULBAR
BULLGINE – BULGINE
BULLGINES – BULGINES
BULLRUSH – BULRUSH
BULLWADDY – BULWADDY
BUNCOED – BUNCED
BUNGEY – BUNGIE – BUNGY
BUNJIE – BUNJY
BUNKOED – BUNKED
BUPPIE – BUPPY
BURLY – BURLEY
BURRELL – BURREL
BURRELLS – BURRELS
BURSAE – BURSE
BUSHELLED – BUSHELED
BUSHELLER – BUSHELER
BUSHIE – BUSHY
BY – BEY
CABBAGY – CABBAGEY
CABBIE – CABBY
CABRE – CABER
CADASTRE – CADASTER
CADDIE – CADDY

CAECA – CECA
CAECAL – CECAL
CAECALLY – CECALLY
CAECITIS – CECITIS
CAECUM – CECUM
CAERULE – CERULE
CAERULEAN – CERULEAN
CAESAREAN – CESAREAN
CAESARIAN – CESARIAN
CAESIOUS – CESIOUS
CAESIUM – CESIUM
CAESIUMS – CESIUMS
CAESTUS – CESTUS
CAESTUSES – CESTUSES
CAESURA – CESURA
CAESURAE – CESURAE
CAESURAL – CESURAL
CAESURAS – CESURAS
CAGY – CAGEY
CAKY – CAKEY
CALIBRE – CALIBER
CALICOES – CALICES
CALLALOO – CALALOO
CALLALOOS – CALALOOS
CALLID – CALID
CALLIDITY – CALIDITY
CALLIPASH – CALIPASH
CALLIPEE – CALIPEE
CALLIPEES – CALIPEES
CALLIPER – CALIPER
CALLIPERS – CALIPERS
CALORIE – CALORY
CAMELLIA – CAMELIA
CAMELLIAS – CAMELIAS
CANALLED – CANALED
CANALLING – CANALING
CANCELLED – CANCELED
CANCELLER – CANCELER
CANDIE – CANDY
CANDOUR – CANDOR
CANNIE – CANNY
CANOE – CANE
CANOED – CANED
CANOER – CANER
CANOERS – CANERS
CANOES – CANES
CANTER – CANTOR
CAPELLET – CAPELET
CAPELLETS – CAPELETS
CAPELLINE – CAPELINE
CARDIAE – CARDIAE
CARDIE – CARDY
CARNEY – CARNIE – CARNY
CAROLLED – CAROLED
CAROLLER – CAROLER
CAROLLERS – CAROLERS
CAROLLING – CAROLING
CARRELL – CARREL
CARRELLS – CARRELS
CASTER – CASTOR

CASTRATER – CASTRATOR
CATTIE – CATTY
CAUSAE – CAUSE
CAVIE – CAVY
CAVILLED – CAVILED
CAVILLER – CAVILER
CAVILLERS – CAVILERS
CAVILLING – CAVILING
CEIL – CIEL
CEILED – CIELED
CEILING – CIELING
CEILINGS – CIELINGS
CEILS – CIELS
CELL – CEL
CELLS – CELS
CENSER – CENSOR
CENTINELL – CENTINEL
CENTONELL – CENTONEL
CENTRE – CENTER
CESURAE – CESURE
CHACOES – CHACES
CHALLAH – CHALAH
CHALLAHS – CHALAHS
CHALLAN – CHALAN
CHALLANED – CHALANED
CHALLANS – CHALANS
CHALLIE – CHALLY
CHALLOT – CHALOT
CHALLOTH – CHALOTH
CHAMBRE – CHAMBER
CHANCRE – CHANCER
CHANCY – CHANCEY
CHANTER – CHANTOR
CHANTEY – CHANTIE – CHANTY
CHAPPIE – CHAPPY
CHARLEY – CHARLIE
CHEAPIE – CHEAPY
CHERE – CHEER
CHEWIE – CHEWY
CHILLI – CHILI
CHILLIES – CHILIES
CHILLIS – CHILIS
CHIMAERA – CHIMERA
CHIMAERAS – CHIMERAS
CHIMAERIC – CHIMERIC
CHIMBLY – CHIMBLEY
CHINKIE – CHINKY
CHIPPIE – CHIPPY
CHISELLED – CHISELED
CHISELLER – CHISELER
CHOCKFULL – CHOCKFUL
CHOENIX – CHENIX
CHOENIXES – CHENIXES
CHOKY – CHOKEY
CHOLAEMIA – CHOLEMIA
CHOLLA – CHOLA
CHOLLAS – CHOLAS
CHOLLERS – CHOLERS
CHOOSY – CHOOSEY
CHRISTIE – CHRISTY

CHRONAXIE – CHRONAXY
CHUCKIE – CHUCKY
CIGGIE – CIGGY
CLAMOUR – CLAMOR
CLANGER – CLANGOR
CLANGOUR – CLANGOR
CLASSABLE – CLASSIBLE
CLIQUY – CLIQUEY
COAEVAL – COEVAL
COAEVALS – COEVALS
COELIAC – CELIAC
COELIACS – CELIACS
COELOM – CELOM
COELOMATA – CELOMATA
COELOMIC – CELOMIC
COELOMS – CELOMS
COENACLE – CENACLE
COENACLES – CENACLES
COENOBITE – CENOBITE
COHABITER – COHABITOR
COLL – COL
COLLED – COLED
COLLIE – COLLY
COLLIES – COLIES
COLLINEAR – COLINEAR
COLLINS – COLINS
COLLOCATE – COLOCATE
COLLS – COLS
COLLY – COLY
COLOUR – COLOR
COLY – COLEY
COMAE – COME
COMMENTER – COMMENTOR
COMMIE – COMMY
COMPACTER – COMPACTOR
COMPANDER – COMPANDOR
COMPERE – COMPEER
COMPTABLE – COMPTIBLE
CONCENTRE – CONCENTER
CONCHAE – CONCHE
CONCHIE – CONCHY
CONCOCTER – CONCOCTOR
CONDEMNER – CONDEMNOR
CONDER – CONDOR
CONFIRMER – CONFIRMOR
CONGAED – CONGED
CONGOES – CONGES
CONJURER – CONJUROR
CONNECTER – CONNECTOR
CONQUERER – CONQUEROR
CONSIGNER – CONSIGNOR
CONSULTER – CONSULTOR
CONTEMNER – CONTEMNOR
CONVENER – CONVENOR
CONVERTER – CONVERTOR
CONVEYER – CONVEYOR
CONY – CONEY
COOED – COED
COOKEY – COOKIE – COOKY
COOLIE – COOLY

COOLLY – COOLY
COONTIE – COONTY
CORBELLED – CORBELED
CORBIE – CORBY
CORRECTER – CORRECTOR
CORRUPTER – CORRUPTOR
CORY – COREY
COSEY – COSIE – COSY
COSTAE – COSTE
COTYLAE – COTYLE
COUR – COR
COUTHIE – COUTHY
COWRIE – COWRY
COZEY – COZIE – COZY
CRAMBOES – CRAMBES
CRAMOISIE – CRAMOISY
CRAPPIE – CRAPPY
CREEPIE – CREEPY
CRENELLED – CRENELED
CREPY – CREPEY
CRICKY – CRICKEY
CROPFULL – CROPFUL
CROPPIE – CROPPY
CROWDIE – CROWDY
CRUELLER – CRUELER
CRUELLEST – CRUELEST
CRUELLS – CRUELS
CRUMMIE – CRUMMY
CRUNCHIE – CRUNCHY
CRUSADOES – CRUSADES
CRUSIE – CRUSY
CUDDIE – CUDDY
CUDGELLED – CUDGELED
CUDGELLER – CUDGELER
CULLET – CULET
CULLETS – CULETS
CUPELLED – CUPELED
CUPELLER – CUPELER
CUPELLERS – CUPELERS
CUPELLING – CUPELING
CUPULAE – CUPULE
CURIAE – CURIE
CURNY – CURNEY
CURRIE – CURRY
CURSER – CURSOR
CURTSY – CURTSEY
CURVY – CURVEY
CUSHIE – CUSHY
CUTESIE – CUTESY
CUTEY – CUTIE
CYMAE – CYME
DAE – DE
DAEDAL – DEDAL
DAEDALIAN – DEDALIAN
DAEMON – DEMON
DAEMONIC – DEMONIC
DAEMONS – DEMONS
DALLE – DALE
DALLES – DALES
DARKEY – DARKIE – DARKY

DARRE – DARER
DARTRE – DARTER
DEARIE – DEARY
DEAWIE – DEAWY
DECALITRE – DECALITER
DECALLED – DECALED
DECALLING – DECALING
DECAMETRE – DECAMETER
DECENTRE – DECENTER
DECILITRE – DECILITER
DECIMETRE – DECIMETER
DECKOED – DECKED
DECOLOUR – DECOLOR
DEFAECATE – DEFECATE
DEFLATER – DEFLATOR
DEFUELLED – DEFUELED
DEI – DIE
DEID – DIED
DEIL – DIEL
DEKALITRE – DEKALITER
DEKAMETRE – DEKAMETER
DELL – DEL
DELLS – DELS
DEMEANOUR – DEMEANOR
DEPICTER – DEPICTOR
DERE – DEER
DESMAN – DEMAN
DESOLATER – DESOLATOR
DETECTER – DETECTOR
DEVELLED – DEVELED
DEVELLING – DEVELING
DEVILLED – DEVILED
DEVILLING – DEVILING
DEVISER – DEVISOR
DEXIE – DEXY
DEY – DIE
DHOLL – DHOL
DHOLLS – DHOLS
DIABLERIE – DIABLERY
DIAERESES – DIERESES
DIAERESIS – DIERESIS
DIAERETIC – DIERETIC
DIALLED – DIALED
DIALLER – DIALER
DIALLERS – DIALERS
DIALLING – DIALING
DIALLINGS – DIALINGS
DIALLIST – DIALIST
DIALLISTS – DIALISTS
DIARRHOEA – DIARRHEA
DICKEY – DICKIE – DICKY
DIDDLY – DIDDLEY
DIDIE – DIDY
DIFFUSER – DIFFUSOR
DIGESTER – DIGESTOR
DILATER – DILATOR
DILUTER – DILUTOR
DINGOED – DINGED
DINGOES – DINGES
DINGY – DINGEY

DINKEY – DINKIE – DINKY
DIOECIOUS – DIECIOUS
DIOESTRUS – DIESTRUS
DIOPTRE – DIOPTER
DIRECTER – DIRECTOR
DISCANDIE – DISCANDY
DISCOED – DISCED
DISCOLOUR – DISCOLOR
DISFAVOUR – DISFAVOR
DISHONOUR – DISHONOR
DISMALLER – DISMALER
DISRUPTER – DISRUPTOR
DISTILL – DISTIL
DISTILLS – DISTILS
DITTOED – DITTED
DIXIE – DIXY
DOBBIE – DOBBY
DOBIE – DOBY
DOE – DE
DOEN – DEN
DOER – DOOR
DOGEY – DOGIE – DOGY
DOGGIE – DOGGY
DOLL – DOL
DOLLED – DOLED
DOLLING – DOLING
DOLLS – DOLS
DOLOUR – DOLOR
DOMINOES – DOMINES
DONER – DONOR
DONSIE – DONSY
DOOLIE – DOOLY
DOORSMAN – DOORMAN
DOOZIE – DOOZY
DOPY – DOPEY
DORE – DOER
DORMIE – DORMY
DOUR – DOR
DOVEKEY – DOVEKIE
DOWELLED – DOWELED
DOWELLING – DOWELING
DOXIE – DOXY
DOYLY – DOYLEY
DRACAENA – DRACENA
DRACAENAS – DRACENAS
DRAPPIE – DRAPPY
DREIGH – DRIEGH
DRIVELLED – DRIVELED
DRIVELLER – DRIVELER
DROLLER – DROLER
DROLLEST – DROLEST
DRUGGIE – DRUGGY
DRY – DREY
DUCKIE – DUCKY
DUDDIE – DUDDY
DUELLED – DUELED
DUELLER – DUELER
DUELLERS – DUELERS
DUELLING – DUELING
DUELLIST – DUELIST

DUELLISTS - DUELISTS
DULLNESS - DULNESS
DULLY - DULY
DURRIE - DURRY
DYSPNOEA - DYSPNEA
DYSPNOEAL - DYSPNEAL
DYSPNOEAS - DYSPNEAS
DYSPNOEIC - DYSPNEIC
EAGRE - EAGER
EATERIE - EATERY
ECHOED - ECHED
ECHOES - ECHES
EDUCABLE - EDUCIBLE
EERIE - EERY
EFFECTER - EFFECTOR
EISELL - EISEL
EISELLS - EISELS
ELL - EL
ELLOPS - ELOPS
ELLOPSES - ELOPSES
ELLS - ELS
EMBALLED - EMBALED
EMBALLING - EMBALING
EN - IN
ENACTION - INACTION
ENACTIONS - INACTIONS
ENACTIVE - INACTIVE
ENAMELLED - ENAMELED
ENAMELLER - ENAMELER
ENAMOUR - ENAMOR
ENARCH - INARCH
ENARCHED - INARCHED
ENARCHES - INARCHES
ENARCHING - INARCHING
ENARM - INARM
ENARMED - INARMED
ENARMING - INARMING
ENARMS - INARMS
ENCAGE - INCAGE
ENCAGED - INCAGED
ENCAGES - INCAGES
ENCAGING - INCAGING
ENCASE - INCASE
ENCASED - INCASED
ENCASES - INCASES
ENCASING - INCASING
ENCAVE - INCAVE
ENCAVED - INCAVED
ENCAVES - INCAVES
ENCAVING - INCAVING
ENCHASE - INCHASE
ENCHASED - INCHASED
ENCHASES - INCHASES
ENCHASING - INCHASING
ENCLASP - INCLASP
ENCLASPED - INCLASPED
ENCLASPS - INCLASPS
ENCLOSE - INCLOSE
ENCLOSED - INCLOSED
ENCLOSER - INCLOSER

ENCLOSERS - INCLOSERS
ENCLOSES - INCLOSES
ENCLOSING - INCLOSING
ENCLOSURE - INCLOSURE
ENCREASE - INCREASE
ENCREASED - INCREASED
ENCREASES - INCREASES
ENCRUST - INCRUST
ENCRUSTED - INCRUSTED
ENCRUSTS - INCRUSTS
ENCUMBER - INCUMBER
ENCUMBERS - INCUMBERS
ENDAMOEBA - ENDAMEBA
ENDART - INDART
ENDARTED - INDARTED
ENDARTING - INDARTING
ENDARTS - INDARTS
ENDEAVOUR - ENDEAVOR
ENDEW - INDEW
ENDEWED - INDEWED
ENDEWING - INDEWING
ENDEWS - INDEWS
ENDITE - INDITE
ENDITED - INDITED
ENDITES - INDITES
ENDITING - INDITING
ENDORSE - INDORSE
ENDORSED - INDORSED
ENDORSEE - INDORSEE
ENDORSEES - INDORSEES
ENDORSER - ENDORSOR - INDORSER
ENDORSERS - INDORSERS
ENDORSES - INDORSES
ENDORSING - INDORSING
ENDORSOR - INDORSOR
ENDORSORS - INDORSORS
ENDOW - INDOW
ENDOWED - INDOWED
ENDOWING - INDOWING
ENDOWS - INDOWS
ENDUE - INDUE
ENDUED - INDUED
ENDUES - INDUES
ENDUING - INDUING
ENFANT - INFANT
ENFANTS - INFANTS
ENFEOFF - INFEOFF
ENFEOFFED - INFEOFFED
ENFEOFFS - INFEOFFS
ENFESTED - INFESTED
ENFIX - INFIX
ENFIXED - INFIXED
ENFIXES - INFIXES
ENFIXING - INFIXING
ENFLAME - INFLAME
ENFLAMED - INFLAMED
ENFLAMES - INFLAMES
ENFLAMING - INFLAMING
ENFOLD - INFOLD
ENFOLDED - INFOLDED

ENFOLDER - INFOLDER
ENFOLDERS - INFOLDERS
ENFOLDING - INFOLDING
ENFOLDS - INFOLDS
ENFORCE - INFORCE
ENFORCED - INFORCED
ENFORCES - INFORCES
ENFORCING - INFORCING
ENFORM - INFORM
ENFORMED - INFORMED
ENFORMING - INFORMING
ENFORMS - INFORMS
ENGINE - INGINE
ENGINES - INGINES
ENGLOBE - INGLOBE
ENGLOBED - INGLOBED
ENGLOBES - INGLOBES
ENGLOBING - INGLOBING
ENGRAFT - INGRAFT
ENGRAFTED - INGRAFTED
ENGRAFTS - INGRAFTS
ENGRAIN - INGRAIN
ENGRAINED - INGRAINED
ENGRAINS - INGRAINS
ENGRAM - INGRAM
ENGROOVE - INGROOVE
ENGROOVED - INGROOVED
ENGROOVES - INGROOVES
ENGROSS - INGROSS
ENGROSSED - INGROSSED
ENGROSSES - INGROSSES
ENGULF - INGULF
ENGULFED - INGULFED
ENGULFING - INGULFING
ENGULFS - INGULFS
ENGULPH - INGULPH
ENGULPHED - INGULPHED
ENGULPHS - INGULPHS
ENHEARSE - INHEARSE
ENHEARSED - INHEARSED
ENHEARSES - INHEARSES
ENISLE - INISLE
ENISLED - INISLED
ENISLES - INISLES
ENISLING - INISLING
ENLACE - INLACE
ENLACED - INLACED
ENLACES - INLACES
ENLACING - INLACING
ENLOCK - INLOCK
ENLOCKED - INLOCKED
ENLOCKING - INLOCKING
ENLOCKS - INLOCKS
ENMESH - INMESH
ENMESHED - INMESHED
ENMESHES - INMESHES
ENMESHING - INMESHING
ENNAGE - INNAGE
ENNAGES - INNAGES
ENQUIRE - INQUIRE

ENQUIRED – INQUIRED
ENQUIRER – INQUIRER
ENQUIRERS – INQUIRERS
ENQUIRES – INQUIRES
ENQUIRIES – INQUIRIES
ENQUIRING – INQUIRING
ENQUIRY – INQUIRY
ENROLL – ENROL
ENROLLS – ENROLS
ENS – INS
ENSCONCE – INSCONCE
ENSCONCED – INSCONCED
ENSCONCES – INSCONCES
ENSCROLL – INSCROLL
ENSCROLLS – INSCROLLS
ENSEAM – INSEAM
ENSEAMED – INSEAMED
ENSEAMING – INSEAMING
ENSEAMS – INSEAMS
ENSHEATH – INSHEATH
ENSHEATHE – INSHEATHE
ENSHEATHS – INSHEATHS
ENSHELL – INSHELL
ENSHELLED – INSHELLED
ENSHELLS – INSHELLS
ENSHELTER – INSHELTER
ENSHRINE – INSHRINE
ENSHRINED – INSHRINED
ENSHRINES – INSHRINES
ENSNARE – INSNARE
ENSNARED – INSNARED
ENSNARER – INSNARER
ENSNARERS – INSNARERS
ENSNARES – INSNARES
ENSNARING – INSNARING
ENSORCELL – ENSORCEL
ENSOUL – INSOUL
ENSOULED – INSOULED
ENSOULING – INSOULING
ENSOULS – INSOULS
ENSPHERE – INSPHERE
ENSPHERED – INSPHERED
ENSPHERES – INSPHERES
ENSURE – INSURE
ENSURED – INSURED
ENSURER – INSURER
ENSURERS – INSURERS
ENSURES – INSURES
ENSURING – INSURING
ENSWATHE – INSWATHE
ENSWATHED – INSWATHED
ENSWATHES – INSWATHES
ENSWEPT – INSWEPT
ENTAMOEBA – ENTAMEBA
ENTENDER – INTENDER
ENTENDERS – INTENDERS
ENTER – INTER
ENTERS – INTERS
ENTHRAL – INTHRAL
ENTHRALL – ENTHRAL – INTHRALL

ENTHRALLS – ENTHRALS –
  INTHRALLS
ENTHRALS – INTHRALS
ENTHRONE – INTHRONE
ENTHRONED – INTHRONED
ENTHRONES – INTHRONES
ENTIRE – INTIRE
ENTITLE – INTITLE
ENTITLED – INTITLED
ENTITLES – INTITLES
ENTITLING – INTITLING
ENTOMB – INTOMB
ENTOMBED – INTOMBED
ENTOMBING – INTOMBING
ENTOMBS – INTOMBS
ENTRANT – INTRANT
ENTRANTS – INTRANTS
ENTREAT – INTREAT
ENTREATED – INTREATED
ENTREATS – INTREATS
ENTRENCH – INTRENCH
ENTROLD – INTROLD
ENTRUST – INTRUST
ENTRUSTED – INTRUSTED
ENTRUSTS – INTRUSTS
ENTWINE – INTWINE
ENTWINED – INTWINED
ENTWINES – INTWINES
ENTWINING – INTWINING
ENTWIST – INTWIST
ENTWISTED – INTWISTED
ENTWISTS – INTWISTS
ENURE – INURE
ENURED – INURED
ENUREMENT – INUREMENT
ENURES – INURES
ENURING – INURING
ENVEIGLE – INVEIGLE
ENVEIGLED – INVEIGLED
ENVEIGLES – INVEIGLES
ENVIABLE – INVIABLE
ENVIABLY – INVIABLY
ENVIOUS – INVIOUS
ENWALL – INWALL
ENWALLED – INWALLED
ENWALLING – INWALLING
ENWALLS – INWALLS
ENWIND – INWIND
ENWINDING – INWINDING
ENWINDS – INWINDS
ENWOUND – INWOUND
ENWRAP – INWRAP
ENWRAPPED – INWRAPPED
ENWRAPS – INWRAPS
ENWREATHE – INWREATHE
EPICENTRE – EPICENTER
EPIGAEAL – EPIGEAL
EPIGAEAN – EPIGEAN
EPIGAEOUS – EPIGEOUS
EQUALLED – EQUALED

EQUALLING – EQUALING
ER – OR
ERECTER – ERECTOR
ERODABLE – ERODIBLE
ESCALLOP – ESCALOP
ESCALLOPS – ESCALOPS
ESCROLL – ESCROL
ESCROLLS – ESCROLS
EUDAEMON – EUDEMON
EUDAEMONS – EUDEMONS
EUPNOEA – EUPNEA
EUPNOEAS – EUPNEAS
EUPNOEIC – EUPNEIC
EVADABLE – EVADIBLE
EVILLER – EVILER
EVILLEST – EVILEST
EVOE – EVE
EXACTER – EXACTOR
EXCERPTER – EXCERPTOR
EXCITER – EXCITOR
EXECUTER – EXECUTOR
EXHIBITER – EXHIBITOR
EXPANDER – EXPANDOR
EXPEDITER – EXPEDITOR
EXTOLL – EXTOL
EXTOLLS – EXTOLS
EYRE – EYER
EYRIE – EYRY
FAE – FE
FAECAL – FECAL
FAECES – FECES
FAERIE – FAERY
FAITOUR – FAITOR
FANNELL – FANNEL
FANNELLS – FANNELS
FANTASIE – FANTASY
FARCIE – FARCY
FAUNULAE – FAUNULE
FAVELL – FAVEL
FAVELLA – FAVELA
FAVELLAS – FAVELAS
FAVER – FAVOR
FAVOUR – FAVOR
FAYRE – FAYER
FEDERARIE – FEDERARY
FEINT – FIENT
FEINTS – FIENTS
FEIST – FIEST
FEOFFER – FEOFFOR
FER – FOR
FERE – FEER
FERLIE – FERLY
FERMENTER – FERMENTOR
FERRELLED – FERRELED
FERULAE – FERULE
FERVOUR – FERVOR
FEY – FIE – FY
FIBRE – FIBER
FIBRILLAR – FIBRILAR
FICOES – FICES

FIDDLY – FIDDLEY
FILL – FIL
FILLAGREE – FILAGREE
FILLE – FILE
FILLED – FILED
FILLER – FILER
FILLERS – FILERS
FILLES – FILES
FILLET – FILET
FILLETED – FILETED
FILLETING – FILETING
FILLETS – FILETS
FILLIBEG – FILIBEG
FILLIBEGS – FILIBEGS
FILLING – FILING
FILLINGS – FILINGS
FILLISTER – FILISTER
FILLO – FILO
FILLOS – FILOS
FILLS – FILS
FIRE – FIER
FLAKY – FLAKEY
FLATTIE – FLATTY
FLAVOUR – FLAVOR
FLEECIE – FLEECY
FLOOEY – FLOOIE
FLOOSIE – FLOOSY
FLOOZIE – FLOOZY
FLORULAE – FLORULE
FLOSSIE – FLOSSY
FLOUR – FLOR
FLUKY – FLUKEY
FLUNKEY – FLUNKIE – FLUNKY
FLUTY – FLUTEY
FLY – FLEY
FOE – FE
FOEDARIE – FEDARIE
FOEDARIES – FEDARIES
FOEN – FEN
FOES – FES
FOETAL – FETAL
FOETATION – FETATION
FOETICIDE – FETICIDE
FOETID – FETID
FOETIDER – FETIDER
FOETIDEST – FETIDEST
FOETIDLY – FETIDLY
FOETOR – FETOR
FOETORS – FETORS
FOETUS – FETUS
FOETUSES – FETUSES
FOGEY – FOGIE – FOGY
FOLEY – FOLIE
FOLKIE – FOLKY
FOLLIES – FOLIES
FOODIE – FOODY
FOOTIE – FOOTY
FOOTSIE – FOOTSY
FORESTALL – FORESTAL
FORGOER – FORGER

FORGOERS – FORGERS
FORGOES – FORGES
FOSSAE – FOSSE
FOUR – FOR
FOUTRE – FOUTER
FOVEOLAE – FOVEOLE
FOXIE – FOXY
FRAENA – FRENA
FRAENUM – FRENUM
FRAENUMS – FRENUMS
FRERE – FREER
FRIVOLLED – FRIVOLED
FRIVOLLER – FRIVOLER
FROWIE – FROWY
FUELLED – FUELED
FUELLER – FUELER
FUELLERS – FUELERS
FUELLING – FUELING
FULFILL – FULFIL
FULFILLS – FULFILS
FULGOUR – FULGOR
FULLNESS – FULNESS
FUNDIE – FUNDY
FUNNELLED – FUNNELED
GAED – GED
GAEN – GEN
GALL – GAL
GALLABEA – GALABEA
GALLABEAH – GALABEAH
GALLABEAS – GALABEAS
GALLABIA – GALABIA
GALLABIAH – GALABIAH
GALLABIAS – GALABIAS
GALLABIEH – GALABIEH
GALLABIYA – GALABIYA
GALLANT – GALANT
GALLIOT – GALIOT
GALLIOTS – GALIOTS
GALLIPOT – GALIPOT
GALLIPOTS – GALIPOTS
GALLIVANT – GALIVANT
GALLOOT – GALOOT
GALLOOTS – GALOOTS
GALLOP – GALOP
GALLOPADE – GALOPADE
GALLOPED – GALOPED
GALLOPING – GALOPING
GALLOPS – GALOPS
GALLOWSES – GALOWSES
GALLS – GALS
GALLUMPH – GALUMPH
GALLUMPHS – GALUMPHS
GALLY – GALLEY
GAMBADOES – GAMBADES
GAMBOLLED – GAMBOLED
GAMY – GAMEY
GARBAGY – GARBAGEY
GARVEY – GARVIE
GASTRAEA – GASTREA
GASTRAEAS – GASTREAS

GATER – GATOR
GAUCIE – GAUCY
GAUFRE – GAUFER
GAVELLED – GAVELED
GAVELLING – GAVELING
GAWSIE – GAWSY
GELLANT – GELANT
GELLANTS – GELANTS
GESSOED – GESSED
GESSOES – GESSES
GEY – GIE
GILLET – GILET
GILLETS – GILETS
GILLIE – GILLY
GILPY – GILPEY
GIMBALLED – GIMBALED
GIMMER – GIMMOR
GINGALL – GINGAL
GINGALLS – GINGALS
GINGELLI – GINGELI
GINGELLIS – GINGELIS
GINGELLY – GINGELY
GINGELY – GINGELEY
GINGILLI – GINGILI
GINGILLIS – GINGILIS
GIRLIE – GIRLY
GLAMOUR – GLAMOR
GLASSIE – GLASSY
GLEBAE – GLEBE
GLUTAEAL – GLUTEAL
GLUTAEI – GLUTEI
GLUTAEUS – GLUTEUS
GLYCAEMIA – GLYCEMIA
GLYCAEMIC – GLYCEMIC
GLYCOLLIC – GLYCOLIC
GNOMAE – GNOME
GOEL – GEL
GOELS – GELS
GOER – GOOR
GOEY – GEY
GOITRE – GOITER
GOLOSHOES – GOLOSHES
GOODIE – GOODY
GOOEY – GOEY
GOOLEY – GOOLIE – GOOLY
GOONEY – GOONIE – GOONY
GOORIE – GOORY
GOOSY – GOOSEY
GORBLIMY – GORBLIMEY
GORE – GOER
GOSPELLER – GOSPELER
GOWNSMAN – GOWNMAN
GOY – GOEY
GRAECISE – GRECISE
GRAECISED – GRECISED
GRAECISES – GRECISES
GRAECIZE – GRECIZE
GRAECIZED – GRECIZED
GRAECIZES – GRECIZES
GRANNIE – GRANNY

GRANTER – GRANTOR
GRAPY – GRAPEY
GRAVELLED – GRAVELED
GRAVELLY – GRAVELY
GREENIE – GREENY
GREISLY – GRIESLY
GREMMIE – GREMMY
GRIESIE – GRIESY
GRIPY – GRIPEY
GROUPIE – GROUPY
GROVELLED – GROVELED
GROVELLER – GROVELER
GRUELLED – GRUELED
GRUELLER – GRUELER
GRUELLERS – GRUELERS
GRUELLING – GRUELING
GRUMPHIE – GRUMPHY
GULL – GUL
GULLABLE – GULLIBLE
GULLS – GULS
GULLY – GULLEY – GULY
GUSSIE – GUSSY
GUSTIE – GUSTY
GYNAECIA – GYNECIA
GYNAECIUM – GYNECIUM
GYNAECOID – GYNECOID
GYNIE – GYNY
GYNNY – GYNNEY
GYNOECIA – GYNECIA
GYNOECIUM – GYNECIUM
GYPPIE – GYPPY
HAE – HE
HAEM – HEM
HAEMAL – HEMAL
HAEMATAL – HEMATAL
HAEMATEIN – HEMATEIN
HAEMATIC – HEMATIC
HAEMATICS – HEMATICS
HAEMATIN – HEMATIN
HAEMATINS – HEMATINS
HAEMATITE – HEMATITE
HAEMATOID – HEMATOID
HAEMATOMA – HEMATOMA
HAEMIC – HEMIC
HAEMIN – HEMIN
HAEMINS – HEMINS
HAEMOCOEL – HEMOCOEL
HAEMOCYTE – HEMOCYTE
HAEMOID – HEMOID
HAEMOSTAT – HEMOSTAT
HAEMS – HEMS
HAEN – HEN
HAEREDES – HEREDES
HAERES – HERES
HAES – HES
HAET – HET
HAETS – HETS
HALLAL – HALAL
HALLALLED – HALALLED
HALLALS – HALALS

HALLING – HALING
HALLO – HALO
HALLOAED – HALLOED
HALLOED – HALOED
HALLOES – HALOES
HALLOING – HALOING
HALLOOED – HALLOED
HALLOS – HALOS
HALLOUMI – HALOUMI
HALLOUMIS – HALOUMIS
HALOED – HALED
HALOES – HALES
HANKIE – HANKY
HANSELLED – HANSELED
HARBOUR – HARBOR
HAVIOUR – HAVIOR
HAWKEY – HAWKIE
HEADACHY – HEADACHEY
HEADSMAN – HEADMAN
HEID – HIED
HELLED – HELED
HELLING – HELING
HELLO – HELO
HELLOED – HELLED
HELLOS – HELOS
HEMPIE – HEMPY
HENNAED – HENNED
HERDSMAN – HERDMAN
HEROE – HERE
HEROES – HERES
HESITATER – HESITATOR
HEY – HIE
HICKEY – HICKIE
HILLOAED – HILLOED
HILLOED – HILLED
HIPPIE – HIPPY
HIRSELLED – HIRSELED
HOAED – HOED
HOAGIE – HOAGY
HOE – HE
HOER – HER
HOERS – HERS
HOES – HES
HOLLIES – HOLIES
HOLLOAED – HOLLOED
HOLLOOED – HOLLOED
HOLLY – HOLY
HOLY – HOLEY
HOMEY – HOMIE – HOMY
HOMOEOBOX – HOMEOBOX
HOMOEOSES – HOMEOSES
HOMOEOSIS – HOMEOSIS
HOMOEOTIC – HOMEOTIC
HONER – HONOR
HONKEY – HONKIE – HONKY
HONOUR – HONOR
HOODIE – HOODY
HOOKY – HOOKEY
HOOLEY – HOOLIE – HOOLY
HORE – HOER

HORSY – HORSEY
HOSTELLED – HOSTELED
HOSTELLER – HOSTELER
HOTTIE – HOTTY
HOUSELLED – HOUSELED
HOVELLED – HOVELED
HOVELLING – HOVELING
HOWDIE – HOWDY
HULLOAED – HULLOED
HULLOED – HULLED
HULLOOED – HULLOED
HUMIDER – HUMIDOR
HUMOUR – HUMOR
HUNDREDER – HUNDREDOR
HUNKEY – HUNKIE – HUNKY
HURLY – HURLEY
HYAENA – HYENA
HYAENAS – HYENAS
HYAENIC – HYENIC
HYDRAEMIA – HYDREMIA
HYMENAEAL – HYMENEAL
HYMENAEAN – HYMENEAN
HYPOED – HYPED
HYPOGAEA – HYPOGEA
HYPOGAEAL – HYPOGEAL
HYPOGAEAN – HYPOGEAN
HYPOGAEUM – HYPOGEUM
HYPOPNOEA – HYPOPNEA
IDEALLESS – IDEALESS
IDOLATER – IDOLATOR
IDYLL – IDYL
IDYLLIST – IDYLIST
IDYLLISTS – IDYLISTS
IDYLLS – IDYLS
IGNITABLE – IGNITIBLE
IGNITER – IGNITOR
ILLIAD – ILIAD
ILLIADS – ILIADS
IMAGOES – IMAGES
IMPACTER – IMPACTOR
IMPASTOED – IMPASTED
IMPEDER – IMPEDOR
IMPELLER – IMPELLOR
IMPOSTER – IMPOSTOR
INCENSER – INCENSOR
INCENTRE – INCENTER
INCONIE – INCONY
INDENTER – INDENTOR
INDICTER – INDICTOR
INDORSER – INDORSOR
INFECTER – INFECTOR
INFERABLE – INFERIBLE
INFLATER – INFLATOR
INFLICTER – INFLICTOR
INHABITER – INHABITOR
INHIBITER – INHIBITOR
INSTALL – INSTAL
INSTALLS – INSTALS
INSTILL – INSTIL
INSTILLS – INSTILS

INTENABLE – INTENIBLE
INTHRALL – INTHRAL
INTHRALLS – INTHRALS
INTIMAE – INTIME
INVENTER – INVENTOR
INVERTER – INVERTOR
ISCHAEMIA – ISCHEMIA
ISCHAEMIC – ISCHEMIC
ISLESMAN – ISLESMAN
JACKSIE – JACKSY
JAILER – JAILOR
JARVEY – JARVIE
JASY – JASEY
JAUNTIE – JAUNTY
JAXIE – JAXY
JEELIE – JEELY
JEWELLED – JEWELED
JEWELLER – JEWELER
JEWELLERS – JEWELERS
JEWELLING – JEWELING
JIMMIE – JIMMY
JINGALL – JINGAL
JINGALLS – JINGALS
JIVY – JIVEY
JOHNNIE – JOHNNY
JOKY – JOKEY
JOLL – JOL
JOLLED – JOLED
JOLLING – JOLING
JOLLS – JOLS
JOLLY – JOLLEY
JOUR – JOR
JOY – JOEY
JUMBIE – JUMBY
JUNKIE – JUNKY
KAED – KED
KAIE – KAY
KANAE – KANE
KARSY – KARSEY
KEIR – KIER
KEIRS – KIERS
KEISTER – KIESTER
KEISTERS – KIESTERS
KELPIE – KELPY
KELTIE – KELTY
KEMBOED – KEMBED
KENNELLED – KENNELED
KERNELLED – KERNELED
KIDDIE – KIDDY
KILOLITRE – KILOLITER
KILOMETRE – KILOMETER
KILTIE – KILTY
KINDIE – KINDY
KLUDGY – KLUDGEY
KOOKIE – KOOKY
KRONER – KRONOR
KY – KEY
KYLOE – KYLE
KYLOES – KYLES
LABELLED – LABELED

LABELLER – LABELER
LABELLERS – LABELERS
LABELLING – LABELING
LABOUR – LABOR
LACUNAE – LACUNE
LACY – LACEY
LAERED – LERED
LAERING – LERING
LAEVIGATE – LEVIGATE
LAEVO – LEVO
LAEVULIN – LEVULIN
LAEVULINS – LEVULINS
LAEVULOSE – LEVULOSE
LALDIE – LALDY
LAMBIE – LAMBY
LAMMIE – LAMMY
LANDSMAN – LANDMAN
LAPELLED – LAPELED
LAPSABLE – LAPSIBLE
LARE – LAER
LASSOES – LASSES
LAURELLED – LAURELED
LAVOLTAED – LAVOLTED
LAZOED – LAZED
LAZOES – LAZES
LEADSMAN – LEADMAN
LEFTIE – LEFTY
LEI – LIE
LEIGER – LIEGER
LEIGERS – LIEGERS
LEIR – LIER
LEIRS – LIERS
LEIS – LIES
LERE – LEER
LERNAEAN – LERNEAN
LESSER – LESSOR
LETTRE – LETTER
LEUCAEMIA – LEUCEMIA
LEUCAEMIC – LEUCEMIC
LEUKAEMIA – LEUKEMIA
LEVELLED – LEVELED
LEVELLER – LEVELER
LEVELLERS – LEVELERS
LEVELLING – LEVELING
LEY – LIE
LEZZIE – LEZZY
LIBELLANT – LIBELANT
LIBELLED – LIBELED
LIBELLEE – LIBELEE
LIBELLEES – LIBELEES
LIBELLER – LIBELER
LIBELLERS – LIBELERS
LIBELLING – LIBELING
LIBELLOUS – LIBELOUS
LICENSER – LICENSOR
LIGULAE – LIGULE
LIMPSY – LIMPSEY
LIMY – LIMEY
LINESMAN – LINEMAN
LINKSMAN – LINKMAN

LINNY – LINNEY
LINTIE – LINTY
LINY – LINEY
LIPAEMIA – LIPEMIA
LIPPIE – LIPPY
LIRE – LIER
LITHOED – LITHED
LITRE – LITER
LIVER – LIVOR
LIVRE – LIVER
LLAMA – LAMA
LLAMAS – LAMAS
LOCATER – LOCATOR
LOCKSMAN – LOCKMAN
LODICULAE – LODICULE
LOESS – LESS
LOESSES – LESSES
LOGGIE – LOGGY
LOGIE – LOGY
LONGAEVAL – LONGEVAL
LOOEY – LOOIE
LOONEY – LOONIE – LOONY
LOUR – LOR
LOURIE – LOURY
LOUVRE – LOUVER
LOWRIE – LOWRY
LOYALLER – LOYALER
LOYALLEST – LOYALEST
LUCKIE – LUCKY
LUNULAE – LUNULE
LUSTRE – LUSTER
LUVVIE – LUVVY
MACABRE – MACABER
MACERATER – MACERATOR
MACULAE – MACULE
MAE – ME
MAENAD – MENAD
MAENADS – MENADS
MAES – MES
MAILL – MAIL
MAILLS – MAILS
MAINER – MAINOR
MAINOUR – MAINOR
MALARKY – MALARKEY
MALL – MAL
MALLAM – MALAM
MALLAMS – MALAMS
MALLANDER – MALANDER
MALLEATE – MALEATE
MALLEATES – MALEATES
MALLS – MALS
MALODOUR – MALODOR
MAMEY – MAMIE
MAMMEY – MAMMIE – MAMMY
MANDRILL – MANDRIL
MANDRILLS – MANDRILS
MANGABY – MANGABEY
MANGOES – MANGES
MANGY – MANGEY
MANILLA – MANILA

MANILLAS – MANILAS
MANTOES – MANTES
MARAE – MARE
MARAES – MARES
MARKSMAN – MARKMAN
MARSHALL – MARSHAL
MARSHALLS – MARSHALS
MARVELLED – MARVELED
MASHIE – MASHY
MATY – MATEY
MAUGRE – MAUGER
MAZY – MAZEY
MEAGRE – MEAGER
MEALIE – MEALY
MEANIE – MEANY
MEDALLED – MEDALED
MEDALLING – MEDALING
MEDALLIST – MEDALIST
MEDIAEVAL – MEDIEVAL
MEIN – MIEN
MEINEY – MEINIE – MEINY
MEINS – MIENS
MELL – MEL
MELLS – MELS
MENSAE – MENSE
MERE – MEER
MERELL – MEREL
MERELLS – MERELS
MESOGLOEA – MESOGLEA
MESOPHYLL – MESOPHYL
METALLED – METALED
METALLING – METALING
METALLISE – METALISE
METALLIST – METALIST
METALLIZE – METALIZE
METOPAE – METOPE
METRE – METER
MICELLAE – MICELLE
MICKY – MICKEY
MIDDIE – MIDDY
MIDGIE – MIDGY
MILER – MILOR
MILL – MIL
MILLAGE – MILAGE
MILLAGES – MILAGES
MILLE – MILE
MILLER – MILER
MILLERS – MILERS
MILLES – MILES
MILLIARY – MILIARY
MILLS – MILS
MIMSY – MIMSEY
MINAE – MINE
MINER – MINOR
MINNIE – MINNY
MISCOLOUR – MISCOLOR
MISENROLL – MISENROL
MITRE – MITER
MIXABLE – MIXIBLE
MOBBIE – MOBBY

MOBIE – MOBY
MOCHIE – MOCHY
MODELLED – MODELED
MODELLER – MODELER
MODELLERS – MODELERS
MODELLING – MODELING
MOE – ME
MOER – MOOR
MOERED – MERED
MOERING – MERING
MOES – MES
MOGGIE – MOGGY
MOLL – MOL
MOLLA – MOLA
MOLLAS – MOLAS
MOLLIE – MOLLY
MOLLIES – MOLIES
MOLLS – MOLS
MOLLY – MOLY
MONEY – MONIE – MONY
MOOLY – MOOLEY
MOPY – MOPEY
MORAE – MORE
MORALL – MORAL
MORALLS – MORALS
MORE – MOER
MORSELLED – MORSELED
MORTGAGER – MORTGAGOR
MOSSIE – MOSSY
MOTTOES – MOTTES
MOUSEY – MOUSIE – MOUSY
MUCHELL – MUCHEL
MUCHELLS – MUCHELS
MUCOSAE – MUCOSE
MULLED – MULED
MULLEY – MULEY
MULLEYS – MULEYS
MULLING – MULING
MULMULL – MULMUL
MULMULLS – MULMULS
MURAENA – MURENA
MURAENAS – MURENAS
MURALLED – MURALED
MURRY – MURREY
MUSKIE – MUSKY
MYALL – MYAL
MYXAMOEBA – MYXAMEBA
MYXOEDEMA – MYXEDEMA
NAE – NE
NAEVE – NEVE
NAEVES – NEVES
NAEVI – NEVI
NAEVOID – NEVOID
NAEVUS – NEVUS
NALLA – NALA
NALLAS – NALAS
NANNIE – NANNY
NANOMETRE – NANOMETER
NAPPIE – NAPPY
NARGHILLY – NARGHILY

NARRATER – NARRATOR
NATURAE – NATURE
NEBULAE – NEBULE
NEGATER – NEGATOR
NEGLECTER – NEGLECTOR
NEIF – NIEF
NEIFS – NIEFS
NEIGHBOUR – NEIGHBOR
NEIVE – NIEVE
NEIVES – NIEVES
NELLIE – NELLY
NELLIES – NELIES
NESTER – NESTOR
NETTIE – NETTY
NEWELL – NEWEL
NEWELLS – NEWELS
NEWSIE – NEWSY
NICKELLED – NICKELED
NIE – NY
NIGHTIE – NIGHTY
NILL – NIL
NILLS – NILS
NIRLIE – NIRLY
NITERIE – NITERY
NITRE – NITER
NIXIE – NIXY
NOOKIE – NOOKY
NOSHERIE – NOSHERY
NOSY – NOSEY
NOVELLAE – NOVELLE
OBLIGER – OBLIGOR
OBOE – OBE
OBOES – OBES
OBSEQUIE – OBSEQUY
OCHRE – OCHER
OCHRY – OCHREY
ODOUR – ODOR
OECOLOGY – ECOLOGY
OECUMENIC – ECUMENIC
OEDEMA – EDEMA
OEDEMAS – EDEMAS
OEDEMATA – EDEMATA
OENOLOGY – ENOLOGY
OENOPHILE – ENOPHILE
OES – ES
OESOPHAGI – ESOPHAGI
OESTRAL – ESTRAL
OESTRIN – ESTRIN
OESTRINS – ESTRINS
OESTRIOL – ESTRIOL
OESTRIOLS – ESTRIOLS
OESTROGEN – ESTROGEN
OESTRONE – ESTRONE
OESTRONES – ESTRONES
OESTROUS – ESTROUS
OESTRUM – ESTRUM
OESTRUMS – ESTRUMS
OESTRUS – ESTRUS
OESTRUSES – ESTRUSES
OFFERER – OFFEROR

OLDIE – OLDY
OLIGAEMIA – OLIGEMIA
OLIGAEMIC – OLIGEMIC
OLPAE – OLPE
OMBRE – OMBER
OMNEITIES – OMNIETIES
OMNEITY – OMNIETY
ONEYRE – ONEYER
ONIE – ONY
ORANGERIE – ORANGERY
ORANGY – ORANGEY
ORGANDIE – ORGANDY
OUR – OR
OUTDOER – OUTDOOR
OUTRE – OUTER
OUTWILLED – OUTWILED
OVERLIE – OVERLY
OVERSMAN – OVERMAN
OWRE – OWER
PACY – PACEY
PAEAN – PEAN
PAEANS – PEANS
PAEDERAST – PEDERAST
PAEDOLOGY – PEDOLOGY
PAEON – PEON
PAEONIES – PEONIES
PAEONS – PEONS
PAEONY – PEONY
PALAESTRA – PALESTRA
PALL – PAL
PALLED – PALED
PALLET – PALET
PALLETS – PALETS
PALLETTE – PALETTE
PALLETTES – PALETTES
PALLIER – PALIER
PALLIEST – PALIEST
PALLING – PALING
PALLS – PALS
PALLY – PALY
PALMIE – PALMY
PANATELLA – PANATELA
PANELLED – PANELED
PANELLING – PANELING
PANELLIST – PANELIST
PANETELLA – PANETELA
PANNIKELL – PANNIKEL
PANTIE – PANTY
PAPULAE – PAPULE
PARADER – PARADOR
PARAE – PARE
PARCELLED – PARCELED
PARDIE – PARDY
PARKIE – PARKY
PARLOUR – PARLOR
PARLY – PARLEY
PASSABLE – PASSIBLE
PASSADOES – PASSADES
PASTER – PASTOR
PASTIE – PASTY

PATELLA – PATELA
PATELLAS – PATELAS
PATINAE – PATINE
PATINAED – PATINED
PATTIE – PATTY
PAVIOUR – PAVIOR
PAWNER – PAWNOR
PAYER – PAYOR
PEAVY – PEAVEY
PEDALLED – PEDALED
PEDALLER – PEDALER
PEDALLERS – PEDALERS
PEDALLING – PEDALING
PEERIE – PEERY
PEKOE – PEKE
PEKOES – PEKES
PENCILLED – PENCILED
PENCILLER – PENCILER
PENNAE – PENNE
PERAEA – PEREA
PERAEON – PEREON
PERAEONS – PEREONS
PERAEOPOD – PEREOPOD
PERDIE – PERDY
PERE – PEER
PERENTIE – PERENTY
PERFECTER – PERFECTOR
PERICOPAE – PERICOPE
PERILLED – PERILED
PERILLING – PERILING
PERINAEUM – PERINEUM
PETALLED – PETALED
PETRE – PETER
PHAENOGAM – PHENOGAM
PHILLABEG – PHILABEG
PHILLIBEG – PHILIBEG
PHILTRE – PHILTER
PHOENIX – PHENIX
PHOENIXES – PHENIXES
PHONY – PHONEY
PHYLAE – PHYLE
PIASTRE – PIASTER
PICKADILL – PICKADIL
PICOMETRE – PICOMETER
PIGGIE – PIGGY
PIGMAEAN – PIGMEAN
PIGSNEY – PIGSNIE – PIGSNY
PILAE – PILE
PILLAR – PILAR
PILLAU – PILAU
PILLAUS – PILAUS
PILLED – PILED
PILLING – PILING
PILLINGS – PILINGS
PILLOW – PILOW
PILLOWS – PILOWS
PILULAE – PILULE
PINKEY – PINKIE – PINKY
PINNIE – PINNY
PINNOED – PINNED

PINNULAE – PINNULE
PINY – PINEY
PIONY – PIONEY
PISCINAE – PISCINE
PISTOLLED – PISTOLED
PIXIE – PIXY
PLAGUY – PLAGUEY
PLEDGER – PLEDGOR
PLIE – PLY
PLIMSOLL – PLIMSOL
PLIMSOLLS – PLIMSOLS
PLISKIE – PLISKY
PLOOKIE – PLOOKY
PLOTTIE – PLOTTY
PLOUKIE – PLOUKY
PLUMULAE – PLUMULE
PODDIE – PODDY
POENOLOGY – PENOLOGY
POEP – PEP
POEPS – PEPS
POET – PET
POETS – PETS
POGY – POGEY
POINTSMAN – POINTMAN
POKEY – POKIE – POKY
POLEIS – POLIES
POLKAED – POLKED
POLL – POL
POLLED – POLED
POLLER – POLER
POLLERS – POLERS
POLLICES – POLICES
POLLICIE – POLLICY
POLLICIES – POLICIES
POLLICY – POLICY
POLLIES – POLIES
POLLING – POLING
POLLINGS – POLINGS
POLLS – POLS
POLLY – POLY
POLONIE – POLONY
POLY – POLEY
POMMELLED – POMMELED
POMMIE – POMMY
PONCY – PONCEY
PONY – PONEY
POPSIE – POPSY
PORAE – PORE
PORAES – PORES
PORGIE – PORGY
PORTALLED – PORTALED
POSTILLED – POSTILED
POSY – POSEY
POTAE – POTE
POTAES – POTES
POTSIE – POTSY
POUDRE – POUDER
POULDRE – POULDER
POWNEY – POWNIE – POWNY
POWRE – POWER

PRAEAMBLE – PREAMBLE
PRAECIPE – PRECIPE
PRAECIPES – PRECIPES
PRAEDIAL – PREDIAL
PRAEFECT – PREFECT
PRAEFECTS – PREFECTS
PRAELECT – PRELECT
PRAELECTS – PRELECTS
PRAENOMEN – PRENOMEN
PRAESES – PRESES
PRAESIDIA – PRESIDIA
PRAETOR – PRETOR
PRAETORS – PRETORS
PRATIE – PRATY
PRE – PER
PREDICTER – PREDICTOR
PREFILLED – PREFILED
PREIF – PRIEF
PREIFE – PRIEFE
PREIFES – PRIEFES
PREIFS – PRIEFS
PREMIE – PREMY
PREPPIE – PREPPY
PRESSER – PRESSOR
PRICY – PRICEY
PRIER – PRIOR
PRIMAEVAL – PRIMEVAL
PROCESSER – PROCESSOR
PROEM – PREM
PROEMS – PREMS
PROLLED – PROLED
PROLLER – PROLER
PROLLERS – PROLERS
PROLLING – PROLING
PROMISER – PROMISOR
PROMOTER – PROMOTOR
PROPELLER – PROPELLOR
PROTECTER – PROTECTOR
PROTESTER – PROTESTOR
PROVIDER – PROVIDOR
PRY – PREY
PUDSY – PUDSEY
PUGGIE – PUGGY
PULL – PUL
PULLED – PULED
PULLER – PULER
PULLERS – PULERS
PULLI – PULI
PULLING – PULING
PULLS – PULS
PULLUS – PULUS
PULVILLIO – PULVILIO
PUMIE – PUMY
PUMMELLED – PUMMELED
PUNKEY – PUNKIE – PUNKY
PUPILLAGE – PUPILAGE
PUPILLAR – PUPILAR
PUPILLARY – PUPILARY
PURE – PUER
PURPIE – PURPY

PUSSLY – PUSSLEY
PUTTIE – PUTTY
PYAEMIA – PYEMIA
PYAEMIAS – PYEMIAS
PYAEMIC – PYEMIC
PYGMAEAN – PYGMEAN
PYORRHOEA – PYORRHEA
QUAESTOR – QUESTOR
QUAESTORS – QUESTORS
QUEENIE – QUEENY
QUESTER – QUESTOR
QUINELLA – QUINELA
QUINELLAS – QUINELAS
QUITTER – QUITTOR
RAFTSMAN – RAFTMAN
RAMILLIE – RAMILIE
RAMILLIES – RAMILIES
RANCOUR – RANCOR
RANDIE – RANDY
RAPHAE – RAPHE
RAPPELLED – RAPPELED
RAVELLED – RAVELED
RAVELLER – RAVELER
RAVELLERS – RAVELERS
RAVELLING – RAVELING
RAZER – RAZOR
RE – ER
READEDIFY – REEDIFY
REALLIE – REALLY
REALTER – REALTOR
REALTIE – REALTY
REBATOES – REBATES
RECALL – RECAL
RECALLS – RECALS
RECENTRE – RECENTER
RECOVERER – RECOVEROR
REDIALLED – REDIALED
REDISTILL – REDISTIL
REDOES – REDES
REDRESSER – REDRESSOR
REECHIE – REECHY
REECHOED – REECHED
REECHOES – REECHES
REEKIE – REEKY
REFELL – REFEL
REFILLED – REFILED
REFILLING – REFILING
REFLECTER – REFLECTOR
REFUELLED – REFUELED
REGRATER – REGRATOR
REINSTALL – REINSTAL
REIVE – RIEVE
REIVER – RIEVER
REIVERS – RIEVERS
REIVES – RIEVES
REIVING – RIEVING
REJECTER – REJECTOR
RELATER – RELATOR
RELEASER – RELEASOR
RELIE – RELY

RELLIES – RELIES
RELLISH – RELISH
RELLISHED – RELISHED
RELLISHES – RELISHES
REMITTER – REMITTOR
RENY – RENEY
REPOSALL – REPOSAL
REPOSALLS – REPOSALS
REPRESSER – REPRESSOR
REQUESTER – REQUESTOR
RESHOES – RESHES
RESISTER – RESISTOR
RESPONSER – RESPONSOR
RETAILER – RETAILOR
RETINAE – RETINE
REVELLED – REVELED
REVELLER – REVELER
REVELLERS – REVELERS
REVELLING – REVELING
REVERIE – REVERY
REVISER – REVISOR
REVIVER – REVIVOR
RHAPHAE – RHAPHE
RHODIE – RHODY
RICY – RICEY
RIGOLL – RIGOL
RIGOLLS – RIGOLS
RIGOUR – RIGOR
RILLE – RILE
RILLED – RILED
RILLES – RILES
RILLING – RILING
RIMAE – RIME
RINSABLE – RINSIBLE
RITORNELL – RITORNEL
RIVALLED – RIVALED
RIVALLESS – RIVALESS
RIVALLING – RIVALING
RIZZER – RIZZOR
ROADSMAN – ROADMAN
ROARIE – ROARY
RODSMAN – RODMAN
ROE – RE
ROED – RED
ROES – RES
ROOFIE – ROOFY
ROOKIE – ROOKY
ROOMIE – ROOMY
ROPY – ROPEY
RORIE – RORY
ROUGHIE – ROUGHY
ROWELLED – ROWELED
ROWELLING – ROWELING
RUMOUR – RUMOR
SABRE – SABER
SAECULUM – SECULUM
SAECULUMS – SECULUMS
SAILER – SAILOR
SALL – SAL
SALLAD – SALAD

SALLADS – SALADS
SALLAL – SALAL
SALLALS – SALALS
SALLE – SALE
SALLES – SALES
SALLET – SALET
SALLETS – SALETS
SALTIE – SALTY
SALTIRE – SALTIER
SALTOED – SALTED
SALTPETRE – SALTPETER
SALVER – SALVOR
SALVOED – SALVED
SALVOES – SALVES
SANDALLED – SANDALED
SAPOUR – SAPOR
SAPRAEMIA – SAPREMIA
SAPRAEMIC – SAPREMIC
SARNEY – SARNIE
SATURATER – SATURATOR
SAVER – SAVOR
SAVIOUR – SAVIOR
SAVOUR – SAVOR
SAVVY – SAVVEY
SCALAE – SCALE
SCALLAWAG – SCALAWAG
SCALLED – SCALED
SCALLY – SCALY
SCAPAED – SCAPED
SCARPAED – SCARPED
SCARRE – SCARER
SCARY – SCAREY
SCEPTRE – SCEPTER
SCLERAE – SCLERE
SCOPAE – SCOPE
SCRATCHIE – SCRATCHY
SCREICH – SCRIECH
SCREICHED – SCRIECHED
SCREICHS – SCRIECHS
SCROGGIE – SCROGGY
SCRUMMIE – SCRUMMY
SCRUNCHIE – SCRUNCHY
SCULL – SCUL
SCULLS – SCULS
SECRETER – SECRETOR
SEEDSMAN – SEEDMAN
SEELIE – SEELY
SEIS – SIES
SEISER – SEISOR
SEIZER – SEIZOR
SELL – SEL
SELLAE – SELLE
SELLE – SELE
SELLES – SELES
SELLS – SELS
SEMPRE – SEMPER
SEPALLED – SEPALED
SEPULCHRE – SEPULCHER
SERE – SEER
SERRAE – SERRE

SERRE – SERER
SETTLER – SETTLOR
SHAKOES – SHAKES
SHALLOT – SHALOT
SHALLOTS – SHALOTS
SHALY – SHALEY
SHANTY – SHANTEY
SHARESMAN – SHAREMAN
SHARPIE – SHARPY
SHAWLEY – SHAWLIE
SHEENEY – SHEENIE – SHEENY
SHEILING – SHIELING
SHEILINGS – SHIELINGS
SHELLDUCK – SHELDUCK
SHELTIE – SHELTY
SHERE – SHEER
SHIMMY – SHIMMEY
SHINNY – SHINNEY
SHIRE – SHIER
SHOE – SHE
SHOED – SHED
SHOES – SHES
SHOOED – SHOED
SHORE – SHOER
SHORESMAN – SHOREMAN
SHORTIE – SHORTY
SHOVELLED – SHOVELED
SHOVELLER – SHOVELER
SHREIK – SHRIEK
SHREIKED – SHRIEKED
SHREIKING – SHRIEKING
SHREIKS – SHRIEKS
SIBYLLIC – SIBYLIC
SIDESMAN – SIDEMAN
SIGNALLED – SIGNALED
SIGNALLER – SIGNALER
SIGNER – SIGNOR
SILICULAE – SILICULE
SILIQUAE – SILIQUE
SILKIE – SILKY
SILLER – SILER
SILLERS – SILERS
SILOED – SILED
SIZEIST – SIZIEST
SKELLIE – SKELLY
SKELLUM – SKELUM
SKELLUMS – SKELUMS
SKILLFUL – SKILFUL
SKIVIE – SKIVY
SKOLLIE – SKOLLY
SKREIGH – SKRIEGH
SKREIGHED – SKRIEGHED
SKREIGHS – SKRIEGHS
SKYRE – SKYER
SLATY – SLATEY
SLY – SLEY
SMARTIE – SMARTY
SMOKY – SMOKEY
SMOOTHIE – SMOOTHY
SNAKY – SNAKEY

SNIVELLED – SNIVELED
SNIVELLER – SNIVELER
SNOTTIE – SNOTTY
SNOWSHOED – SNOWSHED
SNUGGERIE – SNUGGERY
SOAPIE – SOAPY
SOEVER – SEVER
SOFTIE – SOFTY
SOLLAR – SOLAR
SOLLARS – SOLARS
SOLLER – SOLER
SOLLERET – SOLERET
SOLLERETS – SOLERETS
SOLLERS – SOLERS
SOLOED – SOLED
SOMBRE – SOMBER
SONSIE – SONSY
SORELL – SOREL
SORELLS – SORELS
SPACY – SPACEY
SPADESMAN – SPADEMAN
SPADOES – SPADES
SPAED – SPED
SPALLE – SPALE
SPALLES – SPALES
SPAMMIE – SPAMMY
SPARE – SPAER
SPARKIE – SPARKY
SPARRE – SPARER
SPECTRE – SPECTER
SPEIL – SPIEL
SPEILED – SPIELED
SPEILING – SPIELING
SPEILS – SPIELS
SPEIR – SPIER
SPEIRED – SPIERED
SPEIRING – SPIERING
SPEIRS – SPIERS
SPELAEAN – SPELEAN
SPHAERE – SPHERE
SPHAERES – SPHERES
SPICAE – SPICE
SPICULAE – SPICULE
SPICY – SPICEY
SPIE – SPY
SPIKY – SPIKEY
SPILLED – SPILED
SPILLIKIN – SPILIKIN
SPILLING – SPILING
SPILLINGS – SPILINGS
SPINAE – SPINE
SPINNY – SPINNEY
SPINULAE – SPINULE
SPIRAEA – SPIREA
SPIRAEAS – SPIREAS
SPIRALLED – SPIRALED
SPIRE – SPIER
SPLENDOUR – SPLENDOR
SPOONY – SPOONEY
SPOTTIE – SPOTTY

SPUNKIE – SPUNKY
SPURRY – SPURREY
SQUADDIE – SQUADDY
SQUAMAE – SQUAME
SQUIRE – SQUIER
STAGGIE – STAGGY
STAGY – STAGEY
STALLED – STALED
STALLING – STALING
STANZOES – STANZES
STATER – STATOR
STAYRE – STAYER
STEAMIE – STEAMY
STEELIE – STEELY
STELAE – STELE
STELLA – STELA
STELLAR – STELAR
STENTOUR – STENTOR
STERE – STEER
STEY – STIE – STY
STIFFIE – STIFFY
STILLED – STILED
STILLING – STILING
STIMIE – STIMY
STOEP – STEP
STOEPS – STEPS
STOGEY – STOGIE – STOGY
STOLLEN – STOLEN
STOMODAEA – STOMODEA
STONY – STONEY
STORY – STOREY
STOURIE – STOURY
STOWRE – STOWER
STRIDER – STRIDOR
STRIPY – STRIPEY
STROBILAE – STROBILE
STUBBIE – STUBBY
STYMIE – STYMY
SUBBIE – SUBBY
SUBPOENA – SUBPENA
SUBPOENAS – SUBPENAS
SUCCOUR – SUCCOR
SUITER – SUITOR
SURE – SUER
SURFIE – SURFY
SURVIVER – SURVIVOR
SUSPENSER – SUSPENSOR
SWABBIE – SWABBY
SWADDIE – SWADDY
SWAGSMAN – SWAGMAN
SWANKEY – SWANKIE – SWANKY
SWANNIE – SWANNY
SWEENY – SWEENEY
SWEETIE – SWEETY
SWIFTIE – SWIFTY
SWILLER – SWILER
SWILLERS – SWILERS
SWIVELLED – SWIVELED
SWORDSMAN – SWORDMAN
SWY – SWEY

SYMBOLLED – SYMBOLED
TABER – TABOR
TABOUR – TABOR
TACKY – TACKEY
TAE – TE
TAED – TED
TAEDIUM – TEDIUM
TAEDIUMS – TEDIUMS
TAEL – TEL
TAELS – TELS
TAENIA – TENIA
TAENIAE – TENIAE
TAENIAS – TENIAS
TAENIASES – TENIASES
TAENIASIS – TENIASIS
TAENIOID – TENIOID
TAES – TES
TAILER – TAILOR
TALKIE – TALKY
TALLENT – TALENT
TALLENTS – TALENTS
TALLER – TALER
TAMMIE – TAMMY
TANGIE – TANGY
TANGOED – TANGED
TASSELL – TASSEL
TASSELLED – TASSELED
TASSELLS – TASSELS
TATTIE – TATTY
TAWNY – TAWNEY
TAXER – TAXOR
TEAED – TEED
TEASELLED – TEASELED
TEASELLER – TEASELER
TEAZELLED – TEAZELED
TECHIE – TECHY
TEDDIE – TEDDY
TELAE – TELE
TELEVISER – TELEVISOR
TELL – TEL
TELLS – TELS
TENDRE – TENDER
TENOUR – TENOR
TENSER – TENSOR
TENTIE – TENTY
TEQUILLA – TEQUILA
TEQUILLAS – TEQUILAS
TERMER – TERMOR
TESTAE – TESTE
TESTRILL – TESTRIL
TESTRILLS – TESTRILS
THAE – THE
THALLI – THALI
THEATRE – THEATER
THERMAE – THERME
THICKIE – THICKY
THRALLDOM – THRALDOM
THRUSTER – THRUSTOR
THY – THEY
THYMY – THYMEY

TICKY – TICKEY
TIDDLY – TIDDLEY
TILL – TIL
TILLED – TILED
TILLER – TILER
TILLERS – TILERS
TILLING – TILING
TILLINGS – TILINGS
TILLS – TILS
TIMBRE – TIMBER
TINNIE – TINNY
TINSELLED – TINSELED
TIRE – TIER
TIROES – TIRES
TITRE – TITER
TITTIE – TITTY
TOASTIE – TOASTY
TOE – TE
TOEA – TEA
TOEAS – TEAS
TOED – TED
TOENAIL – TENAIL
TOENAILS – TENAILS
TOES – TES
TOGAE – TOGE
TOGAED – TOGED
TOLLBOOTH – TOLBOOTH
TOLLED – TOLED
TOLLIE – TOLLY
TOLLING – TOLING
TOLLINGS – TOLINGS
TONSILLAR – TONSILAR
TONY – TONEY
TOOTSIE – TOOTSY
TOPFULL – TOPFUL
TOPSMAN – TOPMAN
TORMENTER – TORMENTOR
TORNADOES – TORNADES
TOTALLED – TOTALED
TOTALLING – TOTALING
TOTTIE – TOTTY
TOUGHIE – TOUGHY
TOUR – TOR
TOWELLED – TOWELED
TOWELLING – TOWELING
TOWIE – TOWY
TOWNIE – TOWNY
TOXAEMIA – TOXEMIA
TOXAEMIAS – TOXEMIAS
TOXAEMIC – TOXEMIC
TOY – TOEY
TRAMELL – TRAMEL
TRAMELLED – TRAMELED
TRAMELLS – TRAMELS
TRANNIE – TRANNY
TRAVELLED – TRAVELED
TRAVELLER – TRAVELER
TREY – TRIE – TRY
TRIALLIST – TRIALIST
TRICKIE – TRICKY

TRICOLOUR – TRICOLOR
TRIER – TRIOR
TRIPY – TRIPEY
TROELIE – TROELY
TROLLY – TROLLEY
TROWELLED – TROWELED
TROWELLER – TROWELER
TRUSTER – TRUSTOR
TUBAE – TUBE
TULLE – TULE
TULLES – TULES
TUMOUR – TUMOR
TUNNELLED – TUNNELED
TUNNELLER – TUNNELER
TUSHIE – TUSHY
TUSSER – TUSSOR
TWEENIE – TWEENY
TWIBILL – TWIBIL
TWIBILLS – TWIBILS
TWIRE – TWIER
TWISTER – TWISTOR
TYPY – TYPEY
TYRE – TYER
TYROES – TYRES
UMBELLED – UMBELED
UMBRAE – UMBRE
UMBRE – UMBER
UMPIE – UMPY
UNDOER – UNDER
UNFILLED – UNFILED
UNICOLOUR – UNICOLOR
UNMITRE – UNMITER
UNSHOED – UNSHED
UNSONSIE – UNSONSY
UNTILLED – UNTILED
UNWARIE – UNWARY
UPSY – UPSEY
URAEMIA – UREMIA
URAEMIAS – UREMIAS
URAEMIC – UREMIC
VAGINULAE – VAGINULE
VALLONIA – VALONIA
VALLONIAS – VALONIAS
VALOUR – VALOR
VALVULAE – VALVULE
VAMPIRE – VAMPIER
VAPOUR – VAPOR
VAUNTIE – VAUNTY
VAVASOUR – VAVASOR
VELLUM – VELUM
VENDABLE – VENDIBLE
VENDER – VENDOR
VENTRE – VENTER
VERDERER – VERDEROR
VERRY – VERREY
VIAE – VIE
VIALLED – VIALED
VIALLING – VIALING
VIGOUR – VIGOR

VILLIAGO – VILIAGO
VILLIAGOS – VILIAGOS
VIOLATER – VIOLATOR
VIRAEMIA – VIREMIA
VIRAEMIAS – VIREMIAS
VIRAEMIC – VIREMIC
VIRE – VIER
VISAED – VISED
VISITER – VISITOR
VISNOMIE – VISNOMY
VITAE – VITE
VLEIS – VLIES
VOLAE – VOLE
VOLVAE – VOLVE
WADDIE – WADDY
WADMOLL – WADMOL
WADMOLLS – WADMOLS
WAE – WE
WALLED – WALED
WALLER – WALER
WALLERS – WALERS
WALLIE – WALLY
WALLIER – WALIER
WALLIES – WALIES
WALLIEST – WALIEST
WALLING – WALING
WALLY – WALY
WANY – WANEY
WARRANTER – WARRANTOR
WASPIE – WASPY
WASTERIE – WASTERY
WASTRIE – WASTRY
WAVY – WAVEY
WEASELLED – WEASELED
WEASELLER – WEASELER
WEASELLY – WEASELY
WEBBIE – WEBBY
WEDGIE – WEDGY
WEENIE – WEENY
WEEPIE – WEEPY
WEEVILLED – WEEVILED
WEEVILLY – WEEVILY
WEIL – WIEL
WEILS – WIELS
WEINER – WIENER
WEINERS – WIENERS
WEIRDIE – WEIRDY
WELDER – WELDOR
WELLAWAY – WELAWAY
WELLIE – WELLY
WERE – WEER
WHEELIE – WHEELY
WHEELSMAN – WHEELMAN
WHIMSY – WHIMSEY
WHINY – WHINEY
WHISKY – WHISKEY
WHITY – WHITEY
WHOSOEVER – WHOSEVER
WHY – WHEY

WIDDIE – WIDDY
WIFEY – WIFIE
WILLED – WILED
WILLEY – WILLIE – WILLY
WILLFUL – WILFUL
WILLFULLY – WILFULLY
WILLING – WILING
WINOES – WINES
WINY – WINEY
WOE – WE
WOODIE – WOODY
WOODSMAN – WOODMAN
WOOLIE – WOOLY
WOOLLED – WOOLED
WOOLLEN – WOOLEN
WOOLLENS – WOOLENS
WOOLLIER – WOOLIER
WOOLLIES – WOOLIES
WOOLLIEST – WOOLIEST
WOOLLY – WOOLY
WOOSELL – WOOSEL
WOOSELLS – WOOSELS
WURLEY – WURLIE
YABBIE – YABBY
YACHTSMAN – YACHTMAN
YAE – YE
YAPPIE – YAPPY
YAWY – YAWEY
YIPPIE – YIPPY
YODELLED – YODELED
YODELLER – YODELER
YODELLERS – YODELERS
YODELLING – YODELING
YUPPIE – YUPPY
ZAFFRE – ZAFFER
ZIBELLINE – ZIBELINE
ZILLA – ZILA
ZILLAS – ZILAS
ZIRCALLOY – ZIRCALOY
ZOAEA – ZOEA
ZOAEAE – ZOEAE
ZOAEAS – ZOEAS
ZOEA – ZEA
ZOEAL – ZEAL
ZOEAS – ZEAS
ZONAE – ZONE
ZONULAE – ZONULE
ZOOEA – ZOEA
ZOOEAE – ZOEAE
ZOOEAL – ZOEAL
ZOOEAS – ZOEAS
ZOOECIA – ZOECIA
ZOOECIUM – ZOECIUM
ZOOGLOEA – ZOOGLEA
ZOOGLOEAE – ZOOGLEAE
ZOOGLOEAL – ZOOGLEAL
ZOOGLOEAS – ZOOGLEAS

ISE not IZE

ABSCISE	CROSSWISE	IMPRECISE	PIECEWISE	SUBINCISE
ADVISE	CRUISE	IMPROVISE	POISE	SUCCISE
AIRWISE	DACQUOISE	INCISE	POLONAISE	SUCHWISE
ALTARWISE	DEBRUISE	LEASTWISE	PORPOISE	SUNRISE
ANGLEWISE	DEMISE	LIAISE	PORTOISE	SUNWISE
ANISE	DESPISE	LIKEWISE	PRACTISE	SUPERVISE
ANTINOISE	DEVISE	LONGWISE	PRAISE	SURMISE
ANYWISE	DISGUISE	LYONNAISE	PRECISE	TABLEWISE
APPRAISE	DISPRAISE	MAINPRISE	PREMISE	TAMISE
ARAISE	DROPWISE	MALAISE	PREVISE	TAPERWISE
ARCHWISE	EARTHRISE	MANWISE	PROMISE	TAXWISE
ARISE	ECOSSAISE	MAPWISE	RAISE	TEAMWISE
BEARNAISE	EDGEWISE	MARQUISE	READVISE	TELEVISE
BENDWISE	EGLOMISE	MAUVAISE	REARISE	TENTWISE
BEPRAISE	ELSEWISE	MISADVISE	REMISE	THUSWISE
BETISE	ENDWISE	MISE	RERAISE	TOISE
BOXERCISE	EPRISE	MISPOISE	REREVISE	TORTOISE
BRANDISE	EPUISE	MISPRAISE	RERISE	TRAVOISE
BROADWISE	EQUIPOISE	MISRAISE	REVISE	TREATISE
BRUISE	EXCISE	MOONRISE	RINGWISE	TRENISE
CAMISE	EXERCISE	MORTISE	RISE	TURQUOISE
CERISE	FADAISE	NICOISE	SCARFWISE	UNMORTISE
CHAISE	FANWISE	NOISE	SEXERCISE	UNPRAISE
CHAMISE	FESSWISE	NOWISE	SHOALWISE	UNPRECISE
CHASTISE	FLATWISE	OTHERWISE	SIDEWISE	UNWISE
CHEMISE	FRAISE	OUTRAISE	SLANTWISE	UPRAISE
CHORDWISE	FRAMBOISE	OVERPOISE	SLOPEWISE	UPRISE
CLOCKWISE	FRANCHISE	OVERWISE	SNAKEWISE	VALISE
COASTWISE	FROISE	PAIRWISE	SOMEWISE	VISE
COMBWISE	FRONTWISE	PAISE	SOUBISE	WALISE
CONCISE	FUNDRAISE	PALEWISE	SPEISE	WARPWISE
COTISE	GENOISE	PARADISE	SPIREWISE	WEDGEWISE
COTTISE	GUESTWISE	PARVISE	SPOKEWISE	WEFTWISE
COVETISE	GUISE	PAVISE	SPOONWISE	WIDTHWISE
CRABWISE	HIGHRISE	PENNYWISE	STAIRWISE	WISE
CRISE	HOISE	PENTISE	STEPWISE	

IZE not ISE

ASSIZE	DOWNSIZE	MULTISIZE	PINTSIZE	SUPERSIZE
BAIZE	GOLDSIZE	OUTPRIZE	RESEIZE	UNDERSIZE
BITESIZE	HAZARDIZE	OUTSIZE	RESIZE	UNISIZE
CAPSIZE	MIDSIZE	OVERPRIZE	RIGHTSIZE	UPSIZE
DISPRIZE	MIRANDIZE	OVERSIZE	SIZE	

Chapter 9: Hooks

Hooks are words that can be transformed into other valid words by the addition of a single letter at the beginning or the end. Such words are called hooks because they allow other words to be 'hung' on them: if you wish to play a word which has a letter that will go with a hook already on the board, you can 'hang' the new word on the hook by playing the new word perpendicular to it, forming the hook word in the process.

Hooks that form valid words with a letter added to their beginning are known as front hooks; those that take a letter at the end are, naturally enough, end hooks. Many words are both front hooks and end hooks. As an example, the word HOOK itself is both a front hook and an end hook, as it can form SHOOK (or CHOOK) and HOOKS (or HOOKA or HOOKY).

Hooks by hook word

The two lists in this section are short words – of two and three letters – that act as hooks. These are listed alphabetically, with the word itself in **bold** and the word formed by hooking shown after each root. The first list contains all the two–letter words, the second all the threes.

Hooks (ordered by root word)

Two-letter root words

AA	CAD	VAE	BAH	**AL**
BAA	DAD	WAE	DAH	AAL
CAA	FAD	YAE	FAH	BAL
FAA	GAD	**AG**	HAH	DAL
MAA	HAD	BAG	LAH	GAL
AAH	LAD	CAG	NAH	JAL
AAL	MAD	DAG	PAH	MAL
AAS	PAD	FAG	RAH	PAL
AB	RAD	GAG	YAH	SAL
CAB	SAD	HAG	AHA	ALA
DAB	TAD	JAG	AHI	ALB
FAB	WAD	LAG	AHS	ALE
GAB	YAD	MAG	**AI**	ALF
JAB	ADD	NAG	JAI	ALL
KAB	ADO	RAG	KAI	ALP
LAB	ADS	SAG	RAI	ALS
NAB	ADZ	TAG	SAI	ALT
SAB	**AE**	VAG	TAI	**AM**
TAB	DAE	WAG	WAI	BAM
WAB	FAE	YAG	AIA	CAM
ABA	GAE	ZAG	AID	DAM
ABB	HAE	AGA	AIL	GAM
ABO	KAE	AGE	AIM	HAM
ABS	MAE	AGO	AIN	JAM
ABY	NAE	AGS	AIR	KAM
AD	SAE	**AH**	AIS	LAM
BAD	TAE	AAH	AIT	MAM

NAM	AAS	AWE	BEY	ODE
PAM	BAS	AWL	BEZ	DEB
RAM	DAS	AWN	**BI**	DEE
SAM	EAS	**AX**	OBI	DEF
TAM	FAS	FAX	BIB	DEG
YAM	GAS	LAX	BID	DEI
AMA	HAS	MAX	BIG	DEL
AMI	KAS	PAX	BIN	DEN
AMP	LAS	RAX	BIO	DEV
AMU	MAS	SAX	BIS	DEW
AN	NAS	TAX	BIT	DEX
BAN	PAS	WAX	BIZ	DEY
CAN	RAS	ZAX	**BO**	**DI**
DAN	TAS	AXE	ABO	DIB
EAN	VAS	**AY**	OBO	DID
FAN	WAS	BAY	BOA	DIE
GAN	ZAS	CAY	BOB	DIF
HAN	ASH	DAY	BOD	DIG
MAN	ASK	FAY	BOG	DIM
NAN	ASP	GAY	BOH	DIN
PAN	ASS	HAY	BOI	DIP
RAN	**AT**	JAY	BOK	DIS
SAN	BAT	KAY	BON	DIT
TAN	CAT	LAY	BOO	DIV
VAN	EAT	MAY	BOP	**DO**
WAN	FAT	NAY	BOR	ADO
ANA	GAT	PAY	BOS	UDO
AND	HAT	RAY	BOT	DOB
ANE	KAT	SAY	BOW	DOC
ANI	LAT	TAY	BOX	DOD
ANN	MAT	WAY	BOY	DOE
ANT	NAT	YAY	**BY**	DOF
ANY	OAT	AYE	ABY	DOG
AR	PAT	AYS	BYE	DOH
BAR	QAT	AYU	BYS	DOL
CAR	RAT	**BA**	**CH**	DOM
EAR	SAT	ABA	ACH	DON
FAR	TAT	OBA	ECH	DOO
GAR	VAT	BAA	ICH	DOP
JAR	WAT	BAC	OCH	DOR
LAR	ATE	BAD	CHA	DOS
MAR	ATT	BAG	CHE	DOT
OAR	**AW**	BAH	CHI	DOW
PAR	CAW	BAL	**DA**	DOY
SAR	DAW	BAM	ODA	**EA**
TAR	FAW	BAN	DAB	KEA
VAR	HAW	BAP	DAD	LEA
WAR	JAW	BAR	DAE	PEA
YAR	KAW	BAS	DAG	SEA
ARB	LAW	BAT	DAH	TEA
ARC	MAW	BAY	DAK	YEA
ARD	NAW	**BE**	DAL	ZEA
ARE	PAW	OBE	DAM	EAN
ARF	RAW	BED	DAN	EAR
ARK	SAW	BEE	DAP	EAS
ARM	TAW	BEG	DAS	EAT
ARS	VAW	BEL	DAW	EAU
ART	WAW	BEN	DAY	**ED**
ARY	YAW	BES	**DE**	BED
AS	AWA	BET	IDE	FED

GED	ELF	ESS	FEW	**HE**
KED	ELK	EST	FEY	CHE
LED	ELL	**ET**	FEZ	SHE
MED	ELM	BET	**GI**	THE
NED	ELS	FET	GIB	HEH
PED	ELT	GET	GID	HEM
RED	**EM**	HET	GIE	HEN
SED	FEM	JET	GIF	HEP
TED	GEM	KET	GIG	HER
WED	HEM	LET	GIN	HES
ZED	MEM	MET	GIO	HET
EDH	REM	NET	GIP	HEW
EDS	WEM	PET	GIS	HEX
EE	EME	RET	GIT	HEY
BEE	EMO	SET	**GO**	**HI**
CEE	EMS	TET	AGO	AHI
DEE	EMU	VET	EGO	CHI
FEE	**EN**	WET	YGO	GHI
GEE	BEN	YET	GOA	KHI
JEE	DEN	ETA	GOB	PHI
LEE	EEN	ETH	GOD	HIC
MEE	FEN	**EX**	GOE	HID
NEE	GEN	DEX	GON	HIE
PEE	HEN	HEX	GOO	HIM
REE	KEN	KEX	GOR	HIN
SEE	MEN	LEX	GOS	HIP
TEE	PEN	REX	GOT	HIS
VEE	REN	SEX	GOV	HIT
WEE	SEN	TEX	GOX	**HM**
ZEE	TEN	VEX	GOY	OHM
EEK	WEN	WEX	**GU**	HMM
EEL	YEN	YEX	GUB	**HO**
EEN	END	ZEX	GUE	MHO
EF	ENE	EXO	GUL	OHO
DEF	ENG	**FA**	GUM	PHO
KEF	ENS	FAA	GUN	RHO
NEF	**ER**	FAB	GUP	THO
REF	FER	FAD	GUR	WHO
TEF	HER	FAE	GUS	ZHO
EFF	PER	FAG	GUT	HOA
EFS	SER	FAH	GUV	HOB
EFT	ERA	FAN	GUY	HOC
EH	ERE	FAP	**HA**	HOD
FEH	ERF	FAR	AHA	HOE
HEH	ERG	FAS	CHA	HOG
PEH	ERK	FAT	SHA	HOH
REH	ERN	FAW	WHA	HOI
YEH	ERR	FAX	HAD	HOM
EHS	ERS	FAY	HAE	HON
EL	**ES**	**FE**	HAG	HOO
BEL	BES	FED	HAH	HOP
CEL	FES	FEE	HAJ	HOS
DEL	HES	FEG	HAM	HOT
EEL	LES	FEH	HAN	HOW
GEL	MES	FEM	HAO	HOX
MEL	OES	FEN	HAP	HOY
SEL	PES	FER	HAS	**ID**
TEL	RES	FES	HAT	AID
ZEL	TES	FET	HAW	BID
ELD	YES	FEU	HAY	CID

DID	QIS	KAW	LOX	MOO
FID	SIS	KAY	LOY	MOP
GID	TIS	**KI**	**MA**	MOR
HID	VIS	SKI	AMA	MOS
KID	WIS	KID	SMA	MOT
LID	XIS	KIF	MAA	MOU
MID	ISH	KIN	MAC	MOW
NID	ISM	KIP	MAD	MOY
RID	ISO	KIR	MAE	MOZ
TID	**IT**	KIS	MAG	**MU**
VID	AIT	KIT	MAK	AMU
YID	BIT	**KO**	MAL	EMU
IDE	CIT	KOA	MAM	UMU
IDS	DIT	KOB	MAN	MUD
IF	FIT	KOI	MAP	MUG
DIF	GIT	KON	MAR	MUM
GIF	HIT	KOP	MAS	MUN
KIF	KIT	KOR	MAT	MUS
RIF	LIT	KOS	MAW	MUT
SIF	NIT	KOW	MAX	MUX
IFF	PIT	**KY**	MAY	**MY**
IFS	RIT	SKY	**ME**	MYC
IN	SIT	KYE	EME	**NA**
AIN	TIT	KYU	MED	ANA
BIN	WIT	**LA**	MEE	MNA
DIN	ZIT	ALA	MEG	NAB
FIN	ITA	LAB	MEL	NAE
GIN	ITS	LAC	MEM	NAG
HIN	**JA**	LAD	MEN	NAH
JIN	JAB	LAG	MES	NAM
KIN	JAG	LAH	MET	NAN
LIN	JAI	LAM	MEU	NAP
PIN	JAK	LAP	MEW	NAS
RIN	JAL	LAR	**MI**	NAT
SIN	JAM	LAS	AMI	NAW
TIN	JAP	LAT	MIB	NAY
VIN	JAR	LAV	MIC	**NE**
WIN	JAW	LAW	MID	ANE
YIN	JAY	LAX	MIG	ENE
ZIN	**JO**	LAY	MIL	ONE
INK	JOB	**LI**	MIM	NEB
INN	JOE	LIB	MIR	NED
INS	JOG	LID	MIS	NEE
IO	JOL	LIE	MIX	NEF
BIO	JOR	LIG	MIZ	NEG
GIO	JOT	LIN	**MM**	NEK
ION	JOW	LIP	HMM	NEP
IOS	JOY	LIS	UMM	NET
IS	**KA**	LIT	**MO**	NEW
AIS	AKA	**LO**	EMO	**NO**
BIS	OKA	LOB	MOA	ONO
CIS	SKA	LOD	MOB	NOB
DIS	KAB	LOG	MOC	NOD
GIS	KAE	LOO	MOD	NOG
HIS	KAF	LOP	MOE	NOH
KIS	KAI	LOR	MOG	NOM
LIS	KAK	LOS	MOI	NON
MIS	KAM	LOT	MOL	NOO
NIS	KAS	LOU	MOM	NOR
PIS	KAT	LOW	MON	NOS

NOT	JOE	WON	ORB	FOX
NOW	MOE	YON	ORC	GOX
NOX	ROE	ONE	ORD	HOX
NOY	TOE	ONO	ORE	LOX
NU	VOE	ONS	ORF	NOX
GNU	WOE	ONY	ORS	POX
NUB	OES	**OO**	ORT	SOX
NUN	**OF**	BOO	**OS**	VOX
NUR	DOF	COO	BOS	WOX
NUS	OOF	DOO	COS	OXO
NUT	WOF	GOO	DOS	OXY
NY	OFF	HOO	GOS	**OY**
ANY	OFT	LOO	HOS	BOY
ONY	**OH**	MOO	IOS	COY
SNY	BOH	NOO	KOS	DOY
NYE	DOH	POO	LOS	FOY
NYS	FOH	ROO	MOS	GOY
OB	HOH	TOO	NOS	HOY
BOB	NOH	WOO	OOS	JOY
COB	OOH	ZOO	POS	LOY
DOB	POH	OOF	SOS	MOY
FOB	SOH	OOH	WOS	NOY
GOB	OHM	OOM	YOS	SOY
HOB	OHO	OON	ZOS	TOY
JOB	OHS	OOP	OSE	OYE
KOB	**OI**	OOR	**OU**	OYS
LOB	BOI	OOS	FOU	**PA**
MOB	HOI	OOT	LOU	SPA
NOB	KOI	**OP**	MOU	PAC
ROB	MOI	BOP	SOU	PAD
SOB	POI	COP	YOU	PAH
YOB	OIK	DOP	OUD	PAL
OBA	OIL	FOP	OUK	PAM
OBE	**OM**	HOP	OUP	PAN
OBI	DOM	KOP	OUR	PAP
OBO	HOM	LOP	OUT	PAR
OBS	MOM	MOP	**OW**	PAS
OD	NOM	OOP	BOW	PAT
BOD	OOM	POP	COW	PAV
COD	POM	SOP	DOW	PAW
DOD	ROM	TOP	HOW	PAX
GOD	SOM	WOP	JOW	PAY
HOD	TOM	OPE	KOW	**PE**
LOD	YOM	OPS	LOW	APE
MOD	OMS	OPT	MOW	OPE
NOD	**ON**	**OR**	NOW	PEA
POD	BON	BOR	POW	PEC
ROD	CON	COR	ROW	PED
SOD	DON	DOR	SOW	PEE
TOD	EON	FOR	TOW	PEG
YOD	FON	GOR	VOW	PEH
ODA	GON	JOR	WOW	PEN
ODD	HON	KOR	YOW	PEP
ODE	ION	LOR	OWE	PER
ODS	KON	MOR	OWL	PES
OE	MON	NOR	OWN	PET
DOE	NON	OOR	OWT	PEW
FOE	OON	TOR	**OX**	**PI**
GOE	SON	VOR	BOX	PIA
HOE	TON	ORA	COX	PIC

PIE	PSI	UTE	GUM	PUS
PIG	SIB	TEA	HUM	SUS
PIN	SIC	TEC	LUM	WUS
PIP	SIF	TED	MUM	YUS
PIR	SIK	TEE	RUM	USE
PIS	SIM	TEF	SUM	**UT**
PIT	SIN	TEG	TUM	BUT
PIU	SIP	TEL	VUM	CUT
PIX	SIR	TEN	YUM	GUT
PO	SIS	TES	UMM	HUT
APO	SIT	TET	UMP	JUT
UPO	SIX	TEW	UMU	MUT
POA	**SO**	TEX	**UN**	NUT
POD	DSO	**TI**	BUN	OUT
POH	ISO	TIC	DUN	PUT
POI	SOB	TID	FUN	RUT
POL	SOC	TIE	GUN	TUT
POM	SOD	TIG	HUN	UTA
POO	SOG	TIL	JUN	UTE
POP	SOH	TIN	MUN	UTS
POS	SOL	TIP	NUN	UTU
POT	SOM	TIS	PUN	**WE**
POW	SON	TIT	RUN	AWE
POX	SOP	TIX	SUN	EWE
POZ	SOS	**TO**	TUN	OWE
QI	SOT	TOC	UNI	WEB
QIS	SOU	TOD	UNS	WED
RE	SOV	TOE	**UP**	WEE
ARE	SOW	TOG	CUP	WEM
ERE	SOX	TOM	DUP	WEN
IRE	SOY	TON	GUP	WET
ORE	**ST**	TOO	HUP	WEX
PRE	EST	TOP	OUP	WEY
URE	PST	TOR	PUP	**WO**
REB	STY	TOT	SUP	TWO
REC	**TA**	TOW	TUP	WOE
RED	ETA	TOY	YUP	WOF
REE	ITA	**UG**	UPO	WOG
REF	UTA	BUG	UPS	WOK
REG	TAB	DUG	**UR**	WON
REH	TAD	FUG	BUR	WOO
REI	TAE	HUG	CUR	WOP
REM	TAG	JUG	FUR	WOS
REN	TAI	LUG	GUR	WOT
REO	TAJ	MUG	LUR	WOW
REP	TAK	PUG	NUR	WOX
RES	TAM	RUG	OUR	**XI**
RET	TAN	TUG	PUR	XIS
REV	TAO	VUG	SUR	**YA**
REW	TAP	YUG	URB	PYA
REX	TAR	UGH	URD	RYA
REZ	TAS	UGS	URE	YAD
SH	TAT	**UH**	URN	YAE
ASH	TAU	DUH	URP	YAG
ISH	TAV	HUH	**US**	YAH
SHA	TAW	PUH	BUS	YAK
SHE	TAX	**UM**	GUS	YAM
SHH	TAY	BUM	JUS	YAP
SHY	**TE**	CUM	MUS	YAR
SI	ATE	FUM	NUS	YAW

YAY	PYE	YEW	**YU**	ZAS
YE	RYE	YEX	AYU	ZAX
AYE	SYE	**YO**	KYU	**ZO**
BYE	TYE	YOB	YUG	AZO
DYE	WYE	YOD	YUK	DZO
EYE	YEA	YOK	YUM	ZOA
HYE	YEH	YOM	YUP	ZOL
KYE	YEN	YON	YUS	ZOO
LYE	YEP	YOS	**ZA**	ZOS
NYE	YES	YOU	ZAG	
OYE	YET	YOW	ZAP	

Three-letter root words

AAH	LACE	YADS	SAGO	RAID
AAHS	MACE	**ADZ**	AGOG	SAID
AAL	PACE	ADZE	AGON	WAID
BAAL	RACE	**AFF**	**AGS**	AIDE
KAAL	TACE	BAFF	BAGS	AIDS
PAAL	ACED	CAFF	CAGS	**AIL**
TAAL	ACER	DAFF	DAGS	BAIL
AALS	ACES	FAFF	FAGS	FAIL
AAS	**ACH**	GAFF	GAGS	HAIL
BAAS	BACH	HAFF	HAGS	JAIL
CAAS	EACH	NAFF	JAGS	KAIL
FAAS	MACH	RAFF	LAGS	MAIL
KAAS	NACH	WAFF	MAGS	NAIL
MAAS	RACH	YAFF	NAGS	PAIL
ABA	TACH	AFFY	RAGS	RAIL
BABA	ACHE	**AFT**	SAGS	SAIL
CABA	ACHY	BAFT	TAGS	TAIL
YABA	**ACT**	DAFT	VAGS	VAIL
ABAC	FACT	HAFT	WAGS	WAIL
ABAS	PACT	RAFT	YAGS	AILS
ABB	TACT	SAFT	ZAGS	**AIM**
ABBA	ACTA	WAFT	**AHA**	KAIM
ABBE	ACTS	**AGA**	HAHA	MAIM
ABBS	**ADD**	GAGA	TAHA	SAIM
ABO	WADD	JAGA	**AHI**	AIMS
ABOS	ADDS	NAGA	AHIS	**AIN**
ABS	ADDY	RAGA	**AHS**	CAIN
CABS	**ADO**	SAGA	AAHS	FAIN
DABS	DADO	AGAR	DAHS	GAIN
FABS	FADO	AGAS	FAHS	HAIN
GABS	SADO	**AGE**	HAHS	KAIN
JABS	ADOS	CAGE	LAHS	LAIN
KABS	**ADS**	GAGE	PAHS	MAIN
LABS	BADS	MAGE	RAHS	NAIN
NABS	CADS	PAGE	YAHS	PAIN
SABS	DADS	RAGE	**AIA**	RAIN
TABS	FADS	SAGE	RAIA	SAIN
WABS	GADS	WAGE	AIAS	TAIN
ABY	HADS	AGED	**AID**	VAIN
BABY	LADS	AGEE	CAID	WAIN
GABY	MADS	AGEN	GAID	AINE
ABYE	NADS	AGER	KAID	AINS
ABYS	PADS	AGES	LAID	**AIR**
ACE	RADS	**AGO**	MAID	FAIR
DACE	TADS	DAGO	PAID	GAIR
FACE	WADS	KAGO	QAID	HAIR

LAIR	ALBE	ALTO	KANE	APOD
MAIR	ALBS	ALTS	LANE	APOS
PAIR	**ALE**	**AMA**	MANE	**APP**
SAIR	BALE	CAMA	NANE	YAPP
VAIR	DALE	GAMA	PANE	APPS
WAIR	EALE	KAMA	SANE	**APT**
AIRN	GALE	LAMA	TANE	RAPT
AIRS	HALE	MAMA	VANE	APTS
AIRT	KALE	SAMA	WANE	**ARB**
AIRY	MALE	AMAH	ANES	BARB
AIS	PALE	AMAS	ANEW	CARB
DAIS	RALE	**AMI**	**ANI**	DARB
JAIS	SALE	KAMI	BANI	GARB
KAIS	TALE	RAMI	MANI	WARB
PAIS	VALE	AMIA	RANI	ARBA
RAIS	WALE	AMID	ANIL	ARBS
SAIS	YALE	AMIE	ANIS	**ARC**
TAIS	ALEC	AMIN	**ANN**	MARC
WAIS	ALEE	AMIR	CANN	NARC
AIT	ALEF	AMIS	JANN	ARCH
BAIT	ALES	**AMP**	ANNA	ARCO
GAIT	ALEW	CAMP	ANNO	ARCS
RAIT	**ALF**	DAMP	ANNS	**ARD**
TAIT	CALF	GAMP	**ANT**	BARD
WAIT	HALF	LAMP	BANT	CARD
AITS	ALFA	RAMP	CANT	EARD
AITU	ALFS	SAMP	DANT	FARD
AKA	**ALL**	TAMP	GANT	HARD
HAKA	BALL	VAMP	HANT	LARD
KAKA	CALL	AMPS	KANT	MARD
TAKA	FALL	**AMU**	LANT	NARD
WAKA	GALL	NAMU	PANT	PARD
AKE	HALL	AMUS	RANT	SARD
BAKE	LALL	**ANA**	SANT	WARD
CAKE	MALL	KANA	VANT	YARD
FAKE	PALL	LANA	WANT	ARDS
HAKE	SALL	MANA	ANTA	**ARE**
JAKE	TALL	NANA	ANTE	BARE
LAKE	WALL	RANA	ANTI	CARE
MAKE	ALLS	TANA	ANTS	DARE
RAKE	ALLY	ANAL	**ANY**	FARE
SAKE	**ALP**	ANAN	CANY	GARE
TAKE	CALP	ANAS	MANY	HARE
WAKE	PALP	**AND**	WANY	LARE
AKED	SALP	BAND	ZANY	MARE
AKEE	ALPS	FAND	**APE**	NARE
AKES	**ALS**	HAND	CAPE	PARE
ALA	AALS	LAND	GAPE	RARE
GALA	BALS	MAND	JAPE	TARE
MALA	DALS	PAND	NAPE	VARE
NALA	GALS	RAND	PAPE	WARE
TALA	MALS	SAND	RAPE	YARE
ALAE	PALS	WAND	TAPE	AREA
ALAN	SALS	ANDS	APED	ARED
ALAP	ALSO	**ANE**	APER	AREG
ALAR	**ALT**	BANE	APES	ARES
ALAS	DALT	CANE	APEX	ARET
ALAY	HALT	FANE	**APO**	AREW
ALB	MALT	GANE	CAPO	**ARF**
ALBA	SALT	JANE	GAPO	BARF

ZARF	OARY	TATT	BAWN	BALE
ARFS	VARY	WATT	DAWN	BALK
ARK	WARY	**AUA**	FAWN	BALL
BARK	ARYL	PAUA	LAWN	BALM
CARK	**ASH**	**AUF**	MAWN	BALS
DARK	BASH	CAUF	PAWN	BALU
HARK	CASH	HAUF	RAWN	**BAM**
JARK	DASH	LAUF	SAWN	BAMS
KARK	FASH	AUFS	YAWN	**BAN**
LARK	GASH	**AUK**	AWNS	BANC
MARK	HASH	BAUK	AWNY	BAND
NARK	LASH	CAUK	**AXE**	BANE
PARK	MASH	JAUK	SAXE	BANG
RARK	PASH	WAUK	AXED	BANI
SARK	RASH	AUKS	AXEL	BANK
WARK	SASH	**AVA**	AXES	BANS
YARK	TASH	CAVA	**AYE**	BANT
ARKS	WASH	FAVA	BAYE	**BAP**
ARM	ASHY	JAVA	AYES	BAPS
BARM	**ASK**	KAVA	**AYS**	BAPU
FARM	BASK	LAVA	BAYS	**BAR**
HARM	CASK	TAVA	CAYS	KBAR
MARM	HASK	AVAL	DAYS	BARB
WARM	MASK	AVAS	FAYS	BARD
ARMS	TASK	**AVE**	GAYS	BARE
ARMY	ASKS	CAVE	HAYS	BARF
ARS	**ASP**	EAVE	JAYS	BARK
BARS	GASP	FAVE	KAYS	BARM
CARS	HASP	GAVE	LAYS	BARN
EARS	JASP	HAVE	MAYS	BARP
FARS	RASP	LAVE	NAYS	BARS
GARS	WASP	NAVE	PAYS	**BAS**
JARS	ASPS	PAVE	RAYS	ABAS
LARS	**ASS**	RAVE	SAYS	OBAS
MARS	BASS	SAVE	TAYS	BASE
OARS	JASS	WAVE	WAYS	BASH
PARS	LASS	AVEL	YAYS	BASK
SARS	MASS	AVER	**AYU**	BASS
TARS	PASS	AVES	AYUS	BAST
VARS	SASS	**AVO**	**AZO**	**BAT**
WARS	TASS	AVOS	LAZO	BATE
ARSE	**ATE**	AVOW	AZON	BATH
ARSY	BATE	**AWA**	**BAA**	BATS
ART	CATE	KAWA	BAAL	BATT
CART	DATE	PAWA	BAAS	**BAY**
DART	FATE	TAWA	**BAC**	BAYE
FART	GATE	WAWA	ABAC	BAYS
GART	HATE	AWAY	BACH	BAYT
HART	LATE	**AWE**	BACK	**BED**
KART	MATE	WAWE	BACS	ABED
MART	PATE	AWED	**BAD**	BEDE
PART	RATE	AWEE	BADE	BEDS
TART	SATE	AWES	BADS	BEDU
WART	TATE	**AWL**	**BAG**	**BEE**
ARTI	WATE	BAWL	BAGH	BEEF
ARTS	YATE	PAWL	BAGS	BEEN
ARTY	ATES	WAWL	**BAH**	BEEP
ARY	**ATT**	YAWL	BAHT	BEER
MARY	BATT	AWLS	**BAL**	BEES
NARY	MATT	**AWN**	BALD	BEET

BEG	BITS	ABOS	BUNA	CAMS
BEGO	BITT	OBOS	BUND	**CAN**
BEGS	**BIZ**	BOSH	BUNG	SCAN
BEL	BIZE	BOSK	BUNK	CANE
BELL	**BOA**	BOSS	BUNN	CANG
BELS	BOAB	**BOT**	BUNS	CANN
BELT	BOAK	BOTA	BUNT	CANS
BEN	BOAR	BOTH	**BUR**	CANT
BEND	BOAS	BOTS	BURA	CANY
BENE	BOAT	BOTT	BURB	**CAP**
BENI	**BOB**	**BOW**	BURD	CAPA
BENJ	BOBA	BOWL	BURG	CAPE
BENS	BOBS	BOWR	BURK	CAPH
BENT	**BOD**	BOWS	BURL	CAPI
BES	BODE	**BOX**	BURN	CAPO
OBES	BODS	BOXY	BURP	CAPS
BEST	BODY	**BOY**	BURR	**CAR**
BET	**BOG**	BOYF	BURS	SCAR
ABET	BOGS	BOYG	BURY	CARB
YBET	BOGY	BOYO	**BUS**	CARD
BETA	**BOH**	BOYS	BUSH	CARE
BETE	BOHO	**BRA**	BUSK	CARK
BETH	BOHS	BRAD	BUSS	CARL
BETS	**BOI**	BRAE	BUST	CARN
BEY	BOIL	BRAG	BUSY	CARP
OBEY	BOIS	BRAK	**BUT**	CARR
BEYS	**BOK**	BRAN	ABUT	CARS
BIB	BOKE	BRAS	BUTE	CART
BIBB	BOKO	BRAT	BUTS	**CAT**
BIBS	BOKS	BRAW	BUTT	SCAT
BID	**BON**	BRAY	**BUY**	CATE
ABID	EBON	**BRO**	BUYS	CATS
BIDE	BONA	BROD	**BYE**	**CAW**
BIDI	BOND	BROG	ABYE	SCAW
BIDS	BONE	BROO	BYES	CAWK
BIG	BONG	BROS	**BYS**	CAWS
BIGA	BONK	BROW	ABYS	**CAY**
BIGG	BONY	**BRR**	**CAA**	CAYS
BIGS	**BOO**	BRRR	CAAS	**CEE**
BIN	BOOB	**BRU**	**CAB**	CEES
BIND	BOOH	BRUS	SCAB	**CEL**
BINE	BOOK	BRUT	CABA	CELL
BING	BOOL	BRUX	CABS	CELS
BINK	BOOM	**BUB**	**CAD**	CELT
BINS	BOON	BUBA	ECAD	**CEP**
BINT	BOOR	BUBO	SCAD	CEPE
BIO	BOOS	BUBS	CADE	CEPS
BIOG	BOOT	BUBU	CADI	**CHA**
BIOS	**BOP**	**BUD**	CADS	CHAD
BIS	BOPS	BUDA	**CAG**	CHAI
IBIS	**BOR**	BUDI	SCAG	CHAL
OBIS	BORA	BUDO	CAGE	CHAM
BISE	BORD	BUDS	CAGS	CHAO
BISH	BORE	**BUG**	CAGY	CHAP
BISK	BORK	BUGS	**CAM**	CHAR
BIST	BORM	**BUM**	SCAM	CHAS
BIT	BORN	BUMF	CAMA	CHAT
OBIT	BORS	BUMP	CAME	CHAV
BITE	BORT	BUMS	CAMO	CHAW
BITO	**BOS**	**BUN**	CAMP	CHAY

CHE	CONS	SCRY	DAMS	DEVA
ACHE	CONY	**CUB**	**DAN**	DEVS
ECHE	**COO**	CUBE	DANG	**DEW**
OCHE	COOF	CUBS	DANK	DEWS
CHEF	COOK	**CUD**	DANS	DEWY
CHER	COOL	SCUD	DANT	**DEX**
CHEW	COOM	CUDS	**DAP**	DEXY
CHEZ	COON	**CUE**	DAPS	**DEY**
CHI	COOP	CUED	**DAS**	DEYS
CHIA	COOS	CUES	ODAS	**DIB**
CHIB	COOT	**CUM**	DASH	DIBS
CHIC	**COP**	SCUM	**DAW**	**DID**
CHID	SCOP	**CUP**	ADAW	DIDO
CHIK	COPE	SCUP	DAWD	DIDY
CHIN	COPS	CUPS	DAWK	**DIE**
CHIP	COPY	**CUR**	DAWN	DIEB
CHIS	**COR**	SCUR	DAWS	DIED
CHIT	CORD	CURB	DAWT	DIEL
CHIV	CORE	CURD	**DAY**	DIES
CHIZ	CORF	CURE	DAYS	DIET
CID	CORK	CURF	**DEB**	**DIF**
ACID	CORM	CURL	DEBE	DIFF
CIDE	CORN	CURN	DEBS	DIFS
CIDS	CORS	CURR	DEBT	**DIG**
CIG	CORY	CURS	**DEE**	DIGS
CIGS	**COS**	CURT	IDEE	**DIM**
CIS	ECOS	**CUT**	DEED	DIME
CIST	COSE	SCUT	DEEK	DIMP
CIT	COSH	CUTE	DEEM	DIMS
CITE	COSS	CUTS	DEEN	**DIN**
CITO	COST	**CWM**	DEEP	DINE
CITS	COSY	CWMS	DEER	DING
CITY	**COT**	**DAB**	DEES	DINK
COB	SCOT	DABS	DEET	DINO
COBB	COTE	**DAD**	DEEV	DINS
COBS	COTH	DADA	**DEF**	DINT
COD	COTS	DADO	DEFI	**DIP**
ECOD	COTT	DADS	DEFT	DIPS
CODA	**COW**	**DAE**	DEFY	DIPT
CODE	SCOW	DAES	**DEG**	**DIS**
CODS	COWK	**DAG**	DEGS	DISA
COG	COWL	DAGO	**DEI**	DISC
SCOG	COWP	DAGS	DEID	DISH
COGS	COWS	**DAH**	DEIF	DISK
COL	COWY	ODAH	DEIL	DISS
COLA	**COX**	DAHL	**DEL**	**DIT**
COLD	COXA	DAHS	DELE	ADIT
COLE	COXY	**DAK**	DELF	EDIT
COLL	**COY**	DAKS	DELI	DITA
COLS	COYS	**DAL**	DELL	DITE
COLT	**COZ**	ODAL	DELO	DITS
COLY	COZE	UDAL	DELS	DITT
CON	COZY	DALE	DELT	DITZ
ICON	**CRU**	DALI	**DEN**	**DIV**
COND	ECRU	DALS	DENE	DIVA
CONE	CRUD	DALT	DENI	DIVE
CONF	CRUE	**DAM**	DENS	DIVI
CONI	CRUS	DAME	DENT	DIVS
CONK	CRUX	DAMN	DENY	**DOB**
CONN	**CRY**	DAMP	**DEV**	DOBS

DOBY	DORY	**EAN**	EAUX	DEEN
DOC	**DOS**	BEAN	**EBB**	FEEN
DOCK	ADOS	DEAN	EBBS	KEEN
DOCO	UDOS	GEAN	**ECH**	PEEN
DOCS	DOSE	JEAN	EECH	REEN
DOD	DOSH	LEAN	HECH	SEEN
DODO	DOSS	MEAN	LECH	TEEN
DODS	DOST	PEAN	PECH	WEEN
DOE	**DOT**	REAN	SECH	**EFF**
DOEK	DOTE	SEAN	TECH	JEFF
DOEN	DOTH	WEAN	YECH	MEFF
DOER	DOTS	YEAN	ECHE	TEFF
DOES	DOTY	EANS	ECHO	EFFS
DOF	**DOW**	**EAR**	ECHT	**EFS**
DOFF	DOWD	BEAR	**ECO**	KEFS
DOG	DOWF	DEAR	DECO	NEFS
DOGE	DOWL	FEAR	SECO	REFS
DOGS	DOWN	GEAR	ECOD	TEFS
DOGY	DOWP	HEAR	ECOS	**EFT**
DOH	DOWS	LEAR	**ECU**	DEFT
DOHS	DOWT	NEAR	ECUS	HEFT
DOL	**DOY**	PEAR	**EDH**	LEFT
IDOL	DOYS	REAR	EDHS	REFT
DOLE	**DRY**	SEAR	**EDS**	WEFT
DOLL	ADRY	TEAR	BEDS	EFTS
DOLS	DRYS	WEAR	FEDS	**EGG**
DOLT	**DSO**	YEAR	GEDS	TEGG
DOM	ODSO	EARD	KEDS	YEGG
DOME	DSOS	EARL	MEDS	EGGS
DOMS	**DUB**	EARN	NEDS	EGGY
DOMY	DUBS	EARS	PEDS	**EGO**
DON	**DUD**	**EAS**	REDS	BEGO
UDON	DUDE	CEAS	TEDS	REGO
DONA	DUDS	KEAS	WEDS	SEGO
DONE	**DUE**	LEAS	ZEDS	VEGO
DONG	DUED	PEAS	**EEK**	EGOS
DONS	DUEL	SEAS	DEEK	**EHS**
DOO	DUES	TEAS	GEEK	FEHS
DOOB	DUET	YEAS	KEEK	HEHS
DOOK	**DUG**	ZEAS	LEEK	PEHS
DOOL	DUGS	EASE	MEEK	REHS
DOOM	**DUI**	EAST	PEEK	**EIK**
DOON	DUIT	EASY	REEK	REIK
DOOR	**DUN**	**EAT**	SEEK	SEIK
DOOS	DUNE	BEAT	TEEK	EIKS
DOP	DUNG	FEAT	WEEK	**EKE**
DOPA	DUNK	GEAT	**EEL**	DEKE
DOPE	DUNS	HEAT	FEEL	LEKE
DOPS	DUNT	JEAT	HEEL	PEKE
DOPY	**DUO**	LEAT	JEEL	REKE
DOR	DUOS	MEAT	KEEL	EKED
ODOR	**DUP**	NEAT	PEEL	EKES
DORB	DUPE	PEAT	REEL	**ELD**
DORE	DUPS	SEAT	SEEL	GELD
DORK	**DYE**	TEAT	TEEL	HELD
DORM	DYED	EATH	WEEL	MELD
DORP	DYER	EATS	EELS	SELD
DORR	DYES	**EAU**	EELY	TELD
DORS	**DZO**	BEAU	**EEN**	VELD
DORT	DZOS	EAUS	BEEN	WELD

YELD	LEME	TENS	SERS	**EVO**
ELDS	MEME	WENS	VERS	LEVO
ELF	SEME	YENS	ERST	EVOE
DELF	TEME	**EON**	**ESS**	EVOS
PELF	EMES	AEON	CESS	**EWE**
SELF	EMEU	JEON	FESS	EWER
ELFS	**EMO**	NEON	JESS	EWES
ELK	DEMO	PEON	LESS	**EWK**
WELK	MEMO	EONS	MESS	EWKS
YELK	EMOS	**ERA**	NESS	**EWT**
ELKS	**EMS**	SERA	SESS	NEWT
ELL	FEMS	VERA	ESSE	EWTS
BELL	GEMS	ERAS	**EST**	**EXO**
CELL	HEMS	**ERE**	BEST	EXON
DELL	MEMS	BERE	FEST	**EYE**
FELL	REMS	CERE	GEST	EYED
HELL	TEMS	DERE	HEST	EYEN
JELL	WEMS	FERE	JEST	EYER
KELL	**EMU**	GERE	KEST	EYES
MELL	EMUS	HERE	LEST	**FAA**
PELL	**END**	LERE	NEST	FAAN
SELL	BEND	MERE	PEST	FAAS
TELL	FEND	PERE	REST	**FAB**
VELL	HEND	SERE	TEST	FABS
WELL	LEND	WERE	VEST	**FAD**
YELL	MEND	ERED	WEST	FADE
ELLS	PEND	ERES	YEST	FADO
ELM	REND	EREV	ZEST	FADS
HELM	SEND	**ERF**	ESTS	FADY
YELM	TEND	KERF	**ETA**	**FAG**
ELMS	VEND	SERF	BETA	FAGS
ELMY	WEND	TERF	FETA	**FAH**
ELS	ENDS	**ERG**	GETA	FAHS
BELS	**ENE**	BERG	KETA	**FAN**
CELS	BENE	ERGO	META	FAND
DELS	DENE	ERGS	SETA	FANE
EELS	GENE	**ERK**	WETA	FANG
GELS	MENE	BERK	ZETA	FANK
MELS	NENE	JERK	ETAS	FANO
SELS	PENE	MERK	ETAT	FANS
TELS	SENE	NERK	**ETH**	**FAR**
ZELS	TENE	PERK	BETH	AFAR
ELSE	ENES	SERK	HETH	FARD
ELT	ENEW	YERK	METH	FARE
BELT	**ENG**	ZERK	TETH	FARL
CELT	LENG	ERKS	ETHE	FARM
DELT	MENG	**ERN**	ETHS	FARO
FELT	ENGS	DERN	**EUK**	FARS
GELT	**ENS**	FERN	NEUK	FART
KELT	BENS	HERN	YEUK	**FAS**
MELT	CENS	KERN	EUKS	FASH
PELT	DENS	PERN	**EVE**	FAST
TELT	FENS	TERN	LEVE	**FAT**
WELT	GENS	ERNE	MEVE	FATE
YELT	HENS	ERNS	NEVE	FATS
ELTS	KENS	**ERR**	YEVE	**FAW**
EME	LENS	SERR	EVEN	FAWN
DEME	PENS	ERRS	EVER	FAWS
FEME	RENS	**ERS**	EVES	**FAY**
HEME	SENS	HERS	EVET	OFAY

FAYS	FIND	FRAB	OGAM	AGEN
FED	FINE	FRAE	GAMA	GENA
FEDS	FINI	FRAG	GAMB	GENE
FEE	FINK	FRAP	GAME	GENS
FEEB	FINO	FRAS	GAMP	GENT
FEED	FINS	FRAT	GAMS	GENU
FEEL	**FIR**	FRAU	GAMY	**GEO**
FEEN	FIRE	FRAY	**GAN**	GEOS
FEER	FIRK	**FRO**	GANE	**GET**
FEES	FIRM	AFRO	GANG	GETA
FEET	FIRN	FROE	GANS	GETS
FEG	FIRS	FROG	GANT	**GHI**
FEGS	**FIT**	FROM	**GAP**	GHIS
FEH	FITS	FROS	GAPE	**GIB**
FEHM	FITT	FROW	GAPO	GIBE
FEHS	**FIX**	**FUB**	GAPS	GIBS
FEM	FIXT	FUBS	GAPY	**GID**
FEME	**FIZ**	**FUD**	**GAR**	GIDS
FEMS	FIZZ	FUDS	AGAR	**GIE**
FEN	**FLU**	**FUG**	GARB	GIED
FEND	FLUB	FUGS	GARE	GIEN
FENI	FLUE	FUGU	GARI	GIES
FENS	FLUS	**FUM**	GARS	**GIF**
FENT	FLUX	FUME	GART	GIFT
FER	**FOB**	FUMS	**GAS**	**GIG**
FERE	FOBS	FUMY	AGAS	GIGA
FERM	**FOE**	**FUN**	GASH	GIGS
FERN	FOEN	FUND	GASP	**GIN**
FES	FOES	FUNG	GAST	AGIN
FESS	**FOG**	FUNK	**GAT**	GING
FEST	FOGS	FUNS	GATE	GINK
FET	FOGY	**FUR**	GATH	GINN
FETA	**FOH**	FURL	GATS	GINS
FETE	FOHN	FURR	**GAU**	**GIO**
FETS	FOHS	FURS	GAUD	AGIO
FETT	**FON**	FURY	GAUM	GIOS
FEU	FOND	**GAB**	GAUN	**GIP**
FEUD	FONE	GABS	GAUP	GIPS
FEUS	FONS	GABY	GAUR	**GIS**
FEY	FONT	**GAD**	GAUS	EGIS
FEYS	**FOP**	EGAD	**GAY**	GISM
FIB	FOPS	IGAD	GAYS	GIST
FIBS	**FOR**	GADE	**GED**	**GIT**
FID	FORA	GADI	AGED	GITE
FIDO	FORB	GADS	GEDS	GITS
FIDS	FORD	**GAE**	**GEE**	**GJU**
FIE	FORE	GAED	AGEE	GJUS
FIEF	FORK	GAEN	OGEE	**GNU**
FIER	FORM	GAES	GEED	GNUS
FIG	FORT	**GAG**	GEEK	**GOA**
FIGO	**FOU**	GAGA	GEEP	GOAD
FIGS	FOUD	GAGE	GEES	GOAF
FIL	FOUL	GAGS	GEEZ	GOAL
FILA	FOUR	**GAL**	**GEL**	GOAS
FILE	FOUS	EGAL	GELD	GOAT
FILL	**FOX**	GALA	GELS	**GOB**
FILM	FOXY	GALE	GELT	GOBO
FILO	**FOY**	GALL	**GEM**	GOBS
FILS	FOYS	GALS	GEMS	GOBY
FIN	**FRA**	**GAM**	**GEN**	**GOD**

GODS	**GUP**	**HAO**	HERN	KHIS
GOE	GUPS	CHAO	HERO	PHIS
YGOE	**GUR**	**HAP**	HERS	THIS
GOEL	GURL	CHAP	HERY	HISH
GOER	GURN	WHAP	**HES**	HISN
GOES	GURS	HAPS	SHES	HISS
GOEY	GURU	HAPU	HESP	HIST
GON	**GUS**	**HAS**	HEST	**HIT**
AGON	GUSH	CHAS	**HET**	CHIT
GONE	GUST	HASH	KHET	SHIT
GONG	**GUT**	HASK	SHET	WHIT
GONK	GUTS	HASP	WHET	HITS
GONS	**GUV**	HAST	HETE	**HOA**
GOO	GUVS	**HAT**	HETH	WHOA
GOOD	**GUY**	BHAT	HETS	HOAR
GOOF	GUYS	CHAT	**HEW**	HOAS
GOOG	**GYM**	GHAT	CHEW	HOAX
GOOK	GYMP	KHAT	PHEW	**HOB**
GOOL	GYMS	PHAT	SHEW	HOBO
GOON	**GYP**	SHAT	THEW	HOBS
GOOP	GYPS	THAT	WHEW	**HOC**
GOOR	**HAD**	WHAT	HEWN	CHOC
GOOS	CHAD	HATE	HEWS	HOCK
GOR	SHAD	HATH	**HEY**	**HOD**
GORA	HADE	HATS	THEY	SHOD
GORE	HADJ	**HAW**	WHEY	HODS
GORI	HADS	CHAW	HEYS	**HOE**
GORM	**HAE**	SHAW	**HIC**	SHOE
GORP	THAE	THAW	CHIC	HOED
GORY	WHAE	HAWK	HICK	HOER
GOS	HAED	HAWM	**HID**	HOES
EGOS	HAEM	HAWS	CHID	**HOG**
GOSH	HAEN	**HAY**	WHID	CHOG
GOSS	HAES	CHAY	HIDE	SHOG
GOT	HAET	SHAY	**HIE**	HOGG
GOTH	**HAG**	HAYS	HIED	HOGH
GOV	SHAG	**HEH**	HIES	HOGS
GOVS	HAGG	HEHS	**HIM**	**HOH**
GOY	HAGS	**HEM**	SHIM	PHOH
GOYS	**HAH**	AHEM	WHIM	HOHA
GUB	SHAH	THEM	HIMS	HOHS
GUBS	HAHA	HEME	**HIN**	**HOI**
GUE	HAHS	HEMP	CHIN	HOIK
AGUE	**HAJ**	HEMS	SHIN	**HOM**
GUES	HAJI	**HEN**	THIN	WHOM
GUL	HAJJ	THEN	WHIN	HOMA
GULA	**HAM**	WHEN	HIND	HOME
GULE	CHAM	HEND	HING	HOMO
GULF	SHAM	HENS	HINS	HOMS
GULL	WHAM	HENT	HINT	HOMY
GULP	HAME	**HEP**	**HIP**	**HON**
GULS	HAMS	HEPS	CHIP	CHON
GULY	**HAN**	HEPT	SHIP	PHON
GUM	KHAN	**HER**	WHIP	THON
GUMP	SHAN	CHER	HIPS	HOND
GUMS	THAN	HERB	HIPT	HONE
GUN	HAND	HERD	**HIS**	HONG
GUNG	HANG	HERE	AHIS	HONK
GUNK	HANK	HERL	CHIS	HONS
GUNS	HANT	HERM	GHIS	**HOO**

SHOO	HUIS	LICK	IGGS	WINN
HOOD	**HUM**	MICK	**ILK**	INNS
HOOF	CHUM	NICK	BILK	**INS**
HOOK	HUMA	PICK	MILK	AINS
HOON	HUMF	RICK	SILK	BINS
HOOP	HUMP	SICK	ILKA	DINS
HOOT	HUMS	TICK	ILKS	FINS
HOP	**HUN**	WICK	**ILL**	GINS
CHOP	SHUN	ICKY	BILL	HINS
SHOP	HUNG	**ICY**	CILL	JINS
WHOP	HUNH	RICY	DILL	KINS
HOPE	HUNK	**IDE**	FILL	LINS
HOPS	HUNS	AIDE	GILL	PINS
HOS	HUNT	BIDE	HILL	RINS
MHOS	**HUP**	CIDE	JILL	SINS
OHOS	WHUP	EIDE	KILL	TINS
PHOS	HUPS	HIDE	LILL	VINS
RHOS	**HUT**	NIDE	MILL	WINS
ZHOS	BHUT	RIDE	NILL	YINS
HOSE	CHUT	SIDE	PILL	ZINS
HOSS	PHUT	TIDE	RILL	**ION**
HOST	SHUT	VIDE	SILL	CION
HOT	HUTS	WIDE	TILL	LION
PHOT	**HYE**	IDEA	VILL	PION
SHOT	HYED	IDEE	WILL	IONS
WHOT	HYEN	IDEM	YILL	**IOS**
HOTE	HYES	IDES	ZILL	BIOS
HOTS	**HYP**	**IDS**	ILLS	GIOS
HOW	HYPE	AIDS	ILLY	**IRE**
CHOW	HYPO	BIDS	**IMP**	CIRE
DHOW	HYPS	CIDS	DIMP	DIRE
SHOW	**ICE**	FIDS	GIMP	FIRE
WHOW	BICE	GIDS	JIMP	HIRE
HOWE	DICE	KIDS	LIMP	LIRE
HOWF	FICE	LIDS	PIMP	MIRE
HOWK	LICE	MIDS	SIMP	SIRE
HOWL	MICE	NIDS	WIMP	TIRE
HOWS	NICE	RIDS	IMPI	VIRE
HOY	PICE	TIDS	IMPS	WIRE
AHOY	RICE	VIDS	**INK**	IRED
HOYA	SICE	YIDS	BINK	IRES
HOYS	TICE	**IFF**	DINK	**IRK**
HUB	VICE	BIFF	FINK	BIRK
CHUB	WICE	DIFF	GINK	DIRK
HUBS	ICED	JIFF	JINK	FIRK
HUE	ICER	KIFF	KINK	KIRK
HUED	ICES	MIFF	LINK	LIRK
HUER	**ICH**	NIFF	MINK	MIRK
HUES	DICH	RIFF	OINK	YIRK
HUG	LICH	TIFF	PINK	IRKS
CHUG	MICH	ZIFF	RINK	**ISH**
THUG	RICH	IFFY	SINK	BISH
HUGE	SICH	**IFS**	TINK	DISH
HUGS	TICH	DIFS	WINK	EISH
HUGY	WICH	KIFS	INKS	FISH
HUH	ICHS	RIFS	INKY	HISH
HUHU	**ICK**	**IGG**	**INN**	KISH
HUI	DICK	BIGG	GINN	NISH
HUIA	HICK	MIGG	JINN	PISH
HUIC	KICK	RIGG	LINN	WISH

ISM	**JAW**	JUDY	KEDS	KITS
GISM	JAWS	**JUG**	**KEF**	**KOA**
JISM	**JAY**	JUGA	KEFS	KOAN
ISMS	JAYS	JUGS	**KEG**	KOAP
ISO	**JEE**	**JUN**	SKEG	KOAS
MISO	AJEE	JUNK	KEGS	**KOB**
PISO	JEED	**JUS**	**KEN**	KOBO
ISOS	JEEL	GJUS	SKEN	KOBS
ITA	JEEP	JUST	KENO	**KOI**
DITA	JEER	**JUT**	KENS	KOIS
PITA	JEES	JUTE	KENT	**KON**
VITA	JEEZ	JUTS	**KEP**	IKON
ITAS	**JET**	**KAB**	SKEP	KOND
ITS	JETE	KABS	KEPI	KONK
AITS	JETS	**KAE**	KEPS	KONS
BITS	**JEU**	KAED	KEPT	**KOP**
CITS	JEUX	KAES	**KET**	KOPH
DITS	**JEW**	**KAF**	SKET	KOPS
FITS	JEWS	KAFS	KETA	**KOR**
GITS	**JIB**	**KAI**	KETE	KORA
HITS	JIBB	KAID	KETO	KORE
KITS	JIBE	KAIE	KETS	KORO
LITS	JIBS	KAIF	**KEY**	KORS
NITS	**JIG**	KAIK	KEYS	KORU
PITS	JIGS	KAIL	**KHI**	**KOS**
RITS	**JIN**	KAIM	KHIS	KOSS
SITS	DJIN	KAIN	**KID**	**KOW**
TITS	JINK	KAIS	SKID	KOWS
WITS	JINN	**KAK**	KIDS	**KUE**
ZITS	JINS	KAKA	**KIF**	KUEH
IVY	JINX	KAKI	KIFF	KUES
JIVY	**JIZ**	KAKS	KIFS	**KYE**
TIVY	JIZZ	**KAM**	**KIN**	KYES
IWI	**JOB**	KAMA	AKIN	**KYU**
KIWI	JOBE	KAME	SKIN	KYUS
IWIS	JOBS	KAMI	KINA	**LAB**
JAB	**JOE**	**KAS**	KIND	BLAB
JABS	SJOE	OKAS	KINE	FLAB
JAG	JOES	SKAS	KING	SLAB
JAGA	JOEY	**KAT**	KINK	LABS
JAGG	**JOG**	IKAT	KINO	**LAC**
JAGS	JOGS	SKAT	KINS	LACE
JAI	**JOL**	KATA	**KIP**	LACK
JAIL	JOLE	KATI	SKIP	LACS
JAIS	JOLL	KATS	KIPE	LACY
JAK	JOLS	**KAW**	KIPP	**LAD**
JAKE	JOLT	SKAW	KIPS	BLAD
JAKS	**JOR**	KAWA	**KIR**	CLAD
JAM	JORS	KAWS	KIRK	GLAD
JAMB	**JOT**	**KAY**	KIRN	LADE
JAMS	JOTA	OKAY	KIRS	LADS
JAP	JOTS	KAYO	**KIS**	LADY
JAPE	**JOW**	KAYS	SKIS	**LAG**
JAPS	JOWL	**KEA**	KISH	BLAG
JAR	JOWS	KEAS	KISS	CLAG
AJAR	**JOY**	**KEB**	KIST	FLAG
JARK	JOYS	KEBS	**KIT**	SLAG
JARL	**JUD**	**KED**	SKIT	LAGS
JARP	JUDO	AKED	KITE	**LAH**
JARS	JUDS	EKED	KITH	BLAH

LAHS	ALAY	ULES	LINO	FLOP
LAM	BLAY	LESS	LINS	GLOP
BLAM	CLAY	LEST	LINT	PLOP
CLAM	FLAY	**LET**	LINY	SLOP
FLAM	PLAY	BLET	**LIP**	LOPE
GLAM	SLAY	LETS	BLIP	LOPS
SLAM	LAYS	**LEU**	CLIP	**LOR**
LAMA	**LEA**	LEUD	FLIP	FLOR
LAMB	FLEA	**LEV**	SLIP	LORD
LAME	ILEA	LEVA	LIPA	LORE
LAMP	OLEA	LEVE	LIPE	LORN
LAMS	PLEA	LEVO	LIPO	LORY
LAP	LEAD	LEVY	LIPS	**LOS**
ALAP	LEAF	**LEW**	**LIS**	LOSE
CLAP	LEAK	ALEW	LISK	LOSH
FLAP	LEAL	BLEW	LISP	LOSS
KLAP	LEAM	CLEW	LIST	LOST
PLAP	LEAN	FLEW	**LIT**	**LOT**
SLAP	LEAP	PLEW	ALIT	BLOT
LAPS	LEAR	SLEW	FLIT	CLOT
LAR	LEAS	LEWD	GLIT	PLOT
ALAR	LEAT	**LEX**	SLIT	SLOT
LARD	**LED**	FLEX	LITE	LOTA
LARE	BLED	ILEX	LITH	LOTE
LARI	FLED	PLEX	LITS	LOTH
LARK	GLED	ULEX	LITU	LOTI
LARN	PLED	**LEY**	**LOB**	LOTO
LARS	SLED	BLEY	BLOB	LOTS
LAS	**LEE**	FLEY	GLOB	**LOU**
ALAS	ALEE	GLEY	SLOB	CLOU
LASE	BLEE	SLEY	LOBE	LOUD
LASH	FLEE	LEYS	LOBI	LOUN
LASS	GLEE	**LEZ**	LOBO	LOUP
LAST	SLEE	LEZZ	LOBS	LOUR
LAT	LEED	**LIB**	**LOD**	LOUS
BLAT	LEEK	GLIB	ALOD	LOUT
CLAT	LEEP	LIBS	CLOD	**LOW**
FLAT	LEER	**LID**	PLOD	ALOW
PLAT	LEES	GLID	LODE	BLOW
SLAT	LEET	OLID	LODS	CLOW
LATE	**LEG**	SLID	**LOG**	FLOW
LATH	CLEG	LIDO	BLOG	GLOW
LATI	FLEG	LIDS	CLOG	PLOW
LATS	GLEG	**LIE**	FLOG	SLOW
LATU	LEGS	PLIE	SLOG	LOWE
LAV	**LEI**	LIED	LOGE	LOWN
LAVA	GLEI	LIEF	LOGO	LOWP
LAVE	VLEI	LIEN	LOGS	LOWS
LAVS	LEIR	LIER	LOGY	LOWT
LAW	LEIS	LIES	**LOO**	**LOY**
BLAW	**LEK**	LIEU	LOOF	CLOY
CLAW	LEKE	**LIG**	LOOK	PLOY
FLAW	LEKS	LIGS	LOOM	LOYS
SLAW	LEKU	**LIN**	LOON	**LUD**
LAWK	**LEP**	BLIN	LOOP	LUDE
LAWN	LEPS	LIND	LOOR	LUDO
LAWS	LEPT	LINE	LOOS	LUDS
LAX	**LES**	LING	LOOT	**LUG**
FLAX	ALES	LINK	**LOP**	GLUG
LAY	OLES	LINN	CLOP	PLUG

SLUG	MAMA	**MEG**	**MIL**	**MOL**
LUGE	MAMS	MEGA	MILD	MOLA
LUGS	**MAN**	MEGS	MILE	MOLD
LUM	MANA	**MEL**	MILK	MOLE
ALUM	MAND	MELA	MILL	MOLL
GLUM	MANE	MELD	MILO	MOLS
PLUM	MANG	MELL	MILS	MOLT
SLUM	MANI	MELS	MILT	MOLY
LUMA	MANO	MELT	**MIM**	**MOM**
LUMP	MANS	**MEM**	MIME	MOME
LUMS	MANY	MEME	**MIR**	MOMI
LUR	**MAP**	MEMO	AMIR	MOMS
BLUR	MAPS	MEMS	EMIR	**MON**
SLUR	**MAR**	**MEN**	SMIR	MONA
LURE	MARA	AMEN	MIRE	MONG
LURK	MARC	OMEN	MIRI	MONK
LURS	MARD	MEND	MIRK	MONO
LUV	MARE	MENE	MIRO	MONS
LUVS	MARG	MENG	MIRS	MONY
LUX	MARK	MENO	MIRV	**MOO**
FLUX	MARL	MENT	MIRY	MOOD
LUXE	MARM	MENU	**MIS**	MOOI
LYE	MARS	**MES**	AMIS	MOOK
LYES	MART	EMES	MISE	MOOL
LYM	MARY	MESA	MISO	MOON
LYME	**MAS**	MESE	MISS	MOOP
LYMS	AMAS	MESH	MIST	MOOR
MAA	MASA	MESS	**MIX**	MOOS
MAAR	MASE	**MET**	MIXT	MOOT
MAAS	MASH	META	MIXY	**MOP**
MAC	MASK	METE	**MIZ**	MOPE
MACE	MASS	METH	MIZZ	MOPS
MACH	MAST	METS	**MNA**	MOPY
MACK	MASU	**MEU**	MNAS	**MOR**
MACS	**MAT**	EMEU	**MOA**	MORA
MAD	MATE	MEUS	MOAI	MORE
MADE	MATH	**MEW**	MOAN	MORN
MADS	MATS	SMEW	MOAS	MORS
MAE	MATT	MEWL	MOAT	MORT
MAES	MATY	MEWS	**MOB**	**MOS**
MAG	**MAW**	**MHO**	MOBE	EMOS
MAGE	MAWK	MHOS	MOBS	MOSE
MAGG	MAWN	**MIB**	MOBY	MOSH
MAGI	MAWR	MIBS	**MOC**	MOSK
MAGS	MAWS	**MIC**	MOCH	MOSS
MAK	**MAX**	EMIC	MOCK	MOST
MAKE	MAXI	MICA	MOCS	**MOT**
MAKI	**MAY**	MICE	**MOD**	MOTE
MAKO	MAYA	MICH	MODE	MOTH
MAKS	MAYO	MICK	MODI	MOTI
MAL	MAYS	MICO	MODS	MOTS
MALA	**MED**	MICS	**MOE**	MOTT
MALE	MEDS	**MID**	MOER	MOTU
MALI	**MEE**	AMID	MOES	**MOU**
MALL	SMEE	IMID	**MOG**	MOUE
MALM	MEED	MIDI	SMOG	MOUP
MALS	MEEK	MIDS	MOGS	MOUS
MALT	MEER	**MIG**	**MOI**	**MOW**
MAM	MEES	MIGG	MOIL	MOWA
IMAM	MEET	MIGS	MOIT	MOWN

MOWS	NANS	**NIL**	NOSY	**OAT**
MOY	**NAP**	ANIL	**NOT**	BOAT
MOYA	KNAP	NILL	KNOT	COAT
MOYL	SNAP	NILS	SNOT	DOAT
MOYS	NAPA	**NIM**	NOTA	GOAT
MOZ	NAPE	NIMB	NOTE	MOAT
MOZE	NAPS	NIMS	NOTT	OATH
MOZO	**NAS**	**NIP**	**NOW**	OATS
MOZZ	ANAS	SNIP	ANOW	**OBA**
MUD	MNAS	NIPA	ENOW	BOBA
MUDS	**NAT**	NIPS	GNOW	SOBA
MUG	GNAT	**NIS**	KNOW	OBAS
SMUG	NATS	ANIS	SNOW	**OBE**
MUGG	**NAW**	UNIS	NOWL	JOBE
MUGS	GNAW	NISH	NOWN	LOBE
MUM	SNAW	NISI	NOWS	MOBE
MUMM	**NAY**	**NIT**	NOWT	ROBE
MUMP	NAYS	KNIT	NOWY	OBES
MUMS	**NEB**	SNIT	**NOY**	OBEY
MUMU	SNEB	UNIT	NOYS	**OBI**
MUN	NEBS	NITE	**NUB**	LOBI
MUNG	**NED**	NITS	KNUB	OBIA
MUNI	SNED	**NIX**	SNUB	OBIS
MUNS	NEDS	NIXE	NUBS	OBIT
MUNT	**NEE**	NIXY	**NUN**	**OBO**
MUS	KNEE	**NOB**	NUNS	GOBO
AMUS	SNEE	KNOB	**NUR**	HOBO
EMUS	NEED	SNOB	KNUR	KOBO
MUSE	NEEM	NOBS	NURD	LOBO
MUSH	NEEP	**NOD**	NURL	ZOBO
MUSK	**NEF**	SNOD	NURR	OBOE
MUSO	NEFS	NODE	NURS	OBOL
MUSS	**NEG**	NODI	**NUS**	OBOS
MUST	NEGS	NODS	ANUS	**OBS**
MUT	**NEK**	**NOG**	GNUS	BOBS
SMUT	NEKS	SNOG	ONUS	COBS
MUTE	**NEP**	NOGG	**NUT**	DOBS
MUTI	NEPS	NOGS	KNUT	FOBS
MUTS	**NET**	**NOM**	NUTS	GOBS
MUTT	NETE	NOMA	**NYE**	HOBS
MYC	NETS	NOME	SNYE	JOBS
MYCS	NETT	NOMS	NYED	KOBS
NAB	**NEW**	**NON**	NYES	LOBS
SNAB	ANEW	ANON	**OAF**	MOBS
NABE	ENEW	NONA	GOAF	NOBS
NABK	KNEW	NONE	LOAF	ROBS
NABS	NEWS	NONG	OAFS	SOBS
NAG	NEWT	NONI	**OAK**	YOBS
KNAG	**NIB**	**NOO**	BOAK	**OCA**
SNAG	SNIB	NOOK	SOAK	COCA
NAGA	NIBS	NOON	OAKS	LOCA
NAGS	**NID**	NOOP	OAKY	SOCA
NAM	NIDE	**NOR**	**OAR**	OCAS
NAME	NIDI	NORI	BOAR	**OCH**
NAMS	**NIE**	NORK	HOAR	COCH
NAMU	ONIE	NORM	ROAR	LOCH
NAN	NIED	**NOS**	SOAR	MOCH
ANAN	NIEF	ONOS	VOAR	ROCH
NANA	NIES	NOSE	OARS	OCHE
NANE		NOSH	OARY	**ODA**

CODA	BOHO	COLE	SONS	POOP
SODA	COHO	DOLE	TONS	ROOP
ODAH	SOHO	GOLE	WONS	SOOP
ODAL	TOHO	HOLE	ONST	YOOP
ODAS	OHOS	JOLE	**ONY**	OOPS
ODD	**OHS**	MOLE	BONY	**OOR**
ODDS	BOHS	NOLE	CONY	BOOR
ODE	DOHS	POLE	MONY	DOOR
BODE	FOHS	ROLE	PONY	GOOR
CODE	HOHS	SOLE	TONY	LOOR
LODE	OOHS	TOLE	**ONYX**	MOOR
MODE	SOHS	VOLE	**OOF**	POOR
NODE	**OIK**	OLEA	COOF	**OOS**
RODE	HOIK	OLEO	GOOF	BOOS
YODE	OIKS	OLES	HOOF	COOS
ODEA	**OIL**	**OLM**	LOOF	DOOS
ODES	BOIL	HOLM	POOF	GOOS
ODS	COIL	OLMS	ROOF	LOOS
BODS	FOIL	**OMS**	WOOF	MOOS
CODS	MOIL	COMS	YOOF	POOS
DODS	NOIL	DOMS	OOFS	ROOS
GODS	ROIL	HOMS	OOFY	WOOS
HODS	SOIL	MOMS	**OOH**	ZOOS
LODS	TOIL	NOMS	BOOH	OOSE
MODS	OILS	OOMS	POOH	OOSY
NODS	OILY	POMS	OOHS	**OOT**
PODS	**OKA**	ROMS	**OOM**	BOOT
RODS	HOKA	SOMS	BOOM	COOT
SODS	OKAS	TOMS	COOM	FOOT
TODS	OKAY	**ONE**	DOOM	HOOT
YODS	**OKE**	BONE	LOOM	LOOT
ODSO	BOKE	CONE	ROOM	MOOT
OES	COKE	DONE	SOOM	POOT
DOES	HOKE	FONE	TOOM	ROOT
FOES	JOKE	GONE	ZOOM	SOOT
GOES	LOKE	HONE	OOMS	TOOT
HOES	MOKE	LONE	**OON**	WOOT
JOES	POKE	NONE	BOON	ZOOT
MOES	ROKE	PONE	COON	OOTS
NOES	SOKE	RONE	DOON	**OPE**
ROES	TOKE	SONE	GOON	COPE
TOES	WOKE	TONE	HOON	DOPE
VOES	YOKE	ZONE	LOON	HOPE
WOES	OKEH	ONER	MOON	LOPE
OFF	OKES	ONES	NOON	MOPE
BOFF	**OLD**	**ONO**	NOON	NOPE
COFF	BOLD	MONO	POON	POPE
DOFF	COLD	ONOS	ROON	ROPE
GOFF	FOLD	**ONS**	SOON	TOPE
KOFF	GOLD	CONS	TOON	OPED
TOFF	HOLD	DONS	WOON	OPEN
OFFS	MOLD	EONS	ZOON	OPES
OFT	SOLD	FONS	OONS	**OPS**
COFT	TOLD	GONS	OONT	BOPS
LOFT	WOLD	HONS	**OOP**	COPS
SOFT	YOLD	IONS	COOP	DOPS
TOFT	OLDS	KONS	GOOP	FOPS
OHM	OLDY	MONS	HOOP	HOPS
OHMS	**OLE**	OONS	LOOP	KOPS
OHO	BOLE	PONS	MOOP	LOPS

MOPS	BORS	DOUR	ROWT	PAPE
OOPS	CORS	FOUR	TOWT	PAPS
POPS	DORS	HOUR	OWTS	**PAR**
SOPS	HORS	JOUR	**OXY**	SPAR
TOPS	JORS	LOUR	BOXY	PARA
WOPS	KORS	POUR	COXY	PARD
OPT	MORS	SOUR	DOXY	PARE
OPTS	TORS	TOUR	FOXY	PARK
ORA	VORS	YOUR	POXY	PARP
BORA	**ORT**	OURN	**OYE**	PARR
FORA	BORT	OURS	OYER	PARS
GORA	DORT	**OUT**	OYES	PART
HORA	FORT	BOUT	OYEZ	**PAS**
KORA	MORT	DOUT	**OYS**	SPAS
MORA	PORT	GOUT	BOYS	UPAS
SORA	RORT	HOUT	COYS	PASE
TORA	SORT	LOUT	DOYS	PASH
ORAD	TORT	NOUT	FOYS	PASS
ORAL	WORT	POUT	GOYS	PAST
ORB	ORTS	ROUT	HOYS	**PAT**
DORB	**OSE**	SOUT	JOYS	SPAT
FORB	COSE	TOUT	LOYS	PATE
SORB	DOSE	OUTS	MOYS	PATH
ORBS	HOSE	**OVA**	NOYS	PATS
ORBY	LOSE	NOVA	SOYS	PATU
ORC	MOSE	OVAL	TOYS	PATY
TORC	NOSE	**OWE**	**PAC**	**PAV**
ORCA	OOSE	HOWE	PACA	PAVE
ORCS	POSE	LOWE	PACE	PAVS
ORD	ROSE	YOWE	PACK	**PAW**
BORD	TOSE	OWED	PACO	SPAW
CORD	OSES	OWER	PACS	PAWA
FORD	**OUD**	OWES	PACT	PAWK
LORD	FOUD	**OWL**	PACY	PAWL
SORD	LOUD	BOWL	**PAD**	PAWN
WORD	OUDS	COWL	PADI	PAWS
ORDO	**OUK**	DOWL	PADS	**PAY**
ORDS	BOUK	FOWL	**PAH**	APAY
ORE	DOUK	GOWL	OPAH	SPAY
BORE	GOUK	HOWL	PAHS	PAYS
CORE	JOUK	JOWL	**PAL**	**PEA**
DORE	POUK	NOWL	OPAL	PEAG
FORE	SOUK	SOWL	PALE	PEAK
GORE	TOUK	YOWL	PALL	PEAL
HORE	YOUK	OWLS	PALM	PEAN
KORE	ZOUK	OWLY	PALP	PEAR
LORE	OUKS	**OWN**	PALS	PEAS
MORE	**OUP**	DOWN	PALY	PEAT
PORE	COUP	GOWN	**PAM**	**PEC**
RORE	DOUP	LOWN	SPAM	SPEC
SORE	LOUP	MOWN	PAMS	PECH
TORE	MOUP	NOWN	**PAN**	PECK
WORE	NOUP	POWN	SPAN	PECS
YORE	ROUP	SOWN	PAND	**PED**
ORES	SOUP	TOWN	PANE	APED
ORF	OUPA	OWNS	PANG	OPED
CORF	OUPH	**OWT**	PANS	SPED
ORFE	OUPS	DOWT	PANT	PEDS
ORFS	**OUR**	LOWT	**PAP**	**PEE**
ORS	COUR	NOWT	PAPA	EPEE

PEED	PICE	POLK	PROP	**PYA**
PEEK	PICK	POLL	PROS	PYAS
PEEL	PICS	POLO	PROW	PYAT
PEEN	**PIE**	POLS	**PRY**	**PYE**
PEEP	SPIE	POLT	SPRY	PYES
PEER	PIED	POLY	PRYS	PYET
PEES	PIER	**POM**	**PSI**	**QAT**
PEG	PIES	POME	PSIS	QATS
PEGH	PIET	POMO	**PUB**	**QUA**
PEGS	**PIG**	POMP	PUBE	AQUA
PEH	PIGS	POMS	PUBS	QUAD
PEHS	**PIN**	**POO**	**PUD**	QUAG
PEN	SPIN	POOD	SPUD	QUAI
OPEN	PINA	POOF	PUDS	QUAT
PEND	PINE	POOH	PUDU	QUAY
PENE	PING	POOK	**PUG**	**RAD**
PENI	PINK	POOL	SPUG	BRAD
PENK	PINS	POON	PUGH	DRAD
PENS	PINT	POOP	PUGS	GRAD
PENT	PINY	POOR	**PUH**	ORAD
PEP	**PIP**	POOS	PUHA	PRAD
PEPO	PIPA	POOT	**PUL**	TRAD
PEPS	PIPE	**POP**	PULA	RADE
PER	PIPI	POPE	PULE	RADS
APER	PIPS	POPS	PULI	**RAG**
PERE	PIPY	**POS**	PULK	BRAG
PERI	**PIR**	APOS	PULL	CRAG
PERK	PIRL	EPOS	PULP	DRAG
PERM	PIRN	POSE	PULS	FRAG
PERN	PIRS	POSH	PULU	RAGA
PERP	**PIS**	POSS	PULY	RAGE
PERT	PISE	POST	**PUN**	RAGG
PERV	PISH	POSY	SPUN	RAGI
PES	PISO	**POT**	PUNA	RAGS
APES	PISS	SPOT	PUNG	**RAH**
OPES	**PIT**	POTE	PUNK	RAHS
PESO	SPIT	POTS	PUNS	**RAI**
PEST	PITA	POTT	PUNT	RAIA
PET	PITH	**POW**	PUNY	RAID
SPET	PITS	POWN	**PUP**	RAIK
PETS	PITY	POWS	PUPA	RAIL
PEW	**PIU**	**POX**	PUPS	RAIN
SPEW	PIUM	POXY	PUPU	RAIS
PEWS	**PIX**	**POZ**	**PUR**	RAIT
PHI	PIXY	POZZ	SPUR	**RAJ**
PHIS	PIXY	**PRE**	PURE	RAJA
PHIZ	**PLU**	PREE	PURI	**RAM**
PHO	PLUE	PREM	PURL	CRAM
PHOH	PLUG	PREP	PURR	DRAM
PHON	PLUM	PREX	PURS	GRAM
PHOS	PLUS	PREY	**PUS**	PRAM
PHOT	**POA**	PREZ	OPUS	TRAM
PIA	POAS	**PRO**	PUSH	RAMI
PIAL	**POD**	PROA	PUSS	RAMP
PIAN	APOD	PROB	**PUT**	RAMS
PIAS	SPOD	PROD	PUTS	**RAN**
PIC	PODS	PROF	PUTT	BRAN
EPIC	**POI**	PROG	PUTZ	CRAN
SPIC	POIS	PROM	**PUY**	GRAN
PICA	**POL**	PROO	PUYS	RANA
	POLE			

RAND	ERED	IRES	**RIM**	**ROK**
RANG	IRED	ORES	BRIM	GROK
RANI	REDD	TRES	CRIM	ROKE
RANK	REDE	URES	GRIM	ROKS
RANT	REDO	RESH	PRIM	ROKY
RAP	REDS	REST	TRIM	**ROM**
CRAP	**REE**	**RET**	RIMA	FROM
DRAP	BREE	ARET	RIME	PROM
FRAP	CREE	FRET	RIMS	ROMA
TRAP	DREE	TRET	RIMU	ROMP
WRAP	FREE	RETE	RIMY	ROMS
RAPE	GREE	RETS	**RIN**	**ROO**
RAPS	PREE	**REV**	BRIN	BROO
RAPT	TREE	EREV	GRIN	PROO
RAS	REED	REVS	TRIN	ROOD
BRAS	REEF	**REW**	RIND	ROOF
ERAS	REEK	AREW	RINE	ROOK
FRAS	REEL	BREW	RING	ROOM
RASE	REEN	CREW	RINK	ROON
RASH	REES	DREW	RINS	ROOP
RASP	**REF**	GREW	**RIP**	ROOS
RAST	TREF	TREW	DRIP	ROOT
RAT	REFS	REWS	GRIP	**ROT**
BRAT	REFT	**REX**	TRIP	GROT
DRAT	**REG**	GREX	RIPE	TROT
FRAT	AREG	PREX	RIPP	VROT
GRAT	DREG	**REZ**	RIPS	ROTA
PRAT	REGO	PREZ	RIPT	ROTE
TRAT	REGS	TREZ	**RIT**	ROTI
RATA	**REH**	**RHO**	BRIT	ROTL
RATE	REHS	RHOS	CRIT	ROTO
RATH	**REI**	**RIA**	FRIT	ROTS
RATO	BREI	ARIA	GRIT	**ROW**
RATS	REIF	RIAL	WRIT	AROW
RATU	REIK	RIAS	RITE	BROW
RAW	REIN	**RIB**	RITS	CROW
BRAW	REIS	CRIB	RITT	DROW
CRAW	**REM**	DRIB	RITZ	FROW
DRAW	CREM	FRIB	**RIZ**	GROW
RAWN	PREM	RIBA	FRIZ	PROW
RAWS	REMS	RIBS	RIZA	TROW
RAY	**REN**	**RID**	**ROB**	VROW
BRAY	BREN	ARID	PROB	ROWS
CRAY	GREN	GRID	ROBE	ROWT
DRAY	WREN	IRID	ROBS	**RUB**
FRAY	REND	RIDE	**ROC**	DRUB
GRAY	RENK	RIDS	CROC	GRUB
PRAY	RENS	**RIF**	ROCH	RUBE
TRAY	RENT	RIFE	ROCK	RUBS
RAYA	RENY	RIFF	ROCS	RUBY
RAYS	**REO**	RIFS	**ROD**	**RUC**
REB	REOS	RIFT	BROD	RUCK
REBS	**REP**	**RIG**	PROD	RUCS
REC	PREP	BRIG	TROD	**RUD**
RECK	REPO	FRIG	RODE	CRUD
RECS	REPP	GRIG	RODS	RUDD
RED	REPS	PRIG	**ROE**	RUDE
ARED	**RES**	TRIG	FROE	RUDS
BRED	ARES	RIGG	ROED	**RUE**
CRED	ERES	RIGS	ROES	CRUE

GRUE	SALL	SEEK	SHES	**SKY**
TRUE	SALP	SEEL	SHET	ESKY
RUED	SALS	SEEM	SHEW	SKYF
RUER	SALT	SEEN	**SHY**	SKYR
RUES	**SAM**	SEEP	ASHY	**SNY**
RUG	SAMA	SEER	**SIB**	SNYE
DRUG	SAME	SEES	SIBB	**SOB**
FRUG	SAMP	**SEG**	SIBS	SOBA
TRUG	SAMS	SEGO	**SIC**	SOBS
RUGA	**SAN**	SEGS	SICE	**SOC**
RUGS	SAND	**SEI**	SICH	SOCA
RUM	SANE	SEIF	SICK	SOCK
ARUM	SANG	SEIK	SICS	SOCS
DRUM	SANK	SEIL	**SIF**	**SOD**
GRUM	SANS	SEIR	SIFT	SODA
RUME	SANT	SEIS	**SIK**	SODS
RUMP	**SAP**	**SEL**	SIKA	**SOG**
RUMS	SAPS	SELD	SIKE	SOGS
RUN	**SAR**	SELE	**SIM**	**SOH**
RUND	ASAR	SELF	SIMA	SOHO
RUNE	KSAR	SELL	SIMI	SOHS
RUNG	OSAR	SELS	SIMP	**SOL**
RUNS	TSAR	**SEN**	SIMS	SOLA
RUNT	SARD	SENA	**SIN**	SOLD
RUT	SARI	SEND	SIND	SOLE
BRUT	SARK	SENE	SINE	SOLI
RUTH	SARS	SENS	SING	SOLO
RUTS	**SAT**	SENT	SINH	SOLS
RYA	SATE	**SER**	SINK	**SOM**
RYAL	SATI	USER	SINS	SOMA
RYAS	**SAU**	SERA	**SIP**	SOME
RYE	SAUL	SERE	SIPE	SOMS
TRYE	SAUT	SERF	SIPS	SOMY
RYES	**SAV**	SERK	**SIR**	**SON**
SAB	SAVE	SERR	SIRE	SONE
SABE	SAVS	SERS	SIRI	SONG
SABS	**SAW**	**SET**	SIRS	SONS
SAC	SAWN	SETA	**SIS**	**SOP**
SACK	SAWS	SETS	PSIS	SOPH
SACS	**SAX**	SETT	SISS	SOPS
SAD	SAXE	**SEW**	SIST	**SOS**
SADE	**SAY**	SEWN	**SIT**	DSOS
SADI	SAYS	SEWS	ISIT	ISOS
SADO	**SEA**	**SEX**	SITE	SOSS
SAG	ASEA	SEXT	SITH	**SOT**
SAGA	SEAL	SEXY	SITS	SOTH
SAGE	SEAM	**SEY**	SITZ	SOTS
SAGO	SEAN	SEYS	**SKA**	**SOU**
SAGS	SEAR	**SHA**	SKAG	SOUK
SAGY	SEAS	SHAD	SKAS	SOUL
SAI	SEAT	SHAG	SKAT	SOUM
SAIC	**SEC**	SHAH	SKAW	SOUP
SAID	SECH	SHAM	**SKI**	SOUR
SAIL	SECO	SHAN	SKID	SOUS
SAIM	SECS	SHAT	SKIM	SOUT
SAIN	SECT	SHAW	SKIN	**SOV**
SAIR	**SED**	SHAY	SKIO	SOVS
SAIS	USED	**SHE**	SKIP	**SOW**
SAL	**SEE**	SHEA	SKIS	SOWF
SALE	SEED	SHED	SKIT	SOWL

SOWM	**SUS**	TARE	TEES	TIER
SOWN	SUSS	TARN	**TEF**	TIES
SOWP	SUSU	TARO	TEFF	**TIG**
SOWS	**SYE**	TARP	TEFS	TIGE
SOY	SYED	TARS	**TEG**	TIGS
SOYA	SYEN	TART	TEGG	**TIL**
SOYS	SYES	**TAS**	TEGS	TILE
SPA	**SYN**	ETAS	TEGU	TILL
SPAE	SYNC	ITAS	**TEL**	TILS
SPAG	SYND	UTAS	TELA	TILT
SPAM	SYNE	TASH	TELD	**TIN**
SPAN	**TAB**	TASK	TELE	TIND
SPAR	STAB	TASS	TELL	TINE
SPAS	TABI	**TAT**	TELS	TING
SPAT	TABS	ETAT	TELT	TINK
SPAW	TABU	STAT	**TEN**	TINS
SPAY	**TAD**	TATE	ETEN	TINT
SPAZ	TADS	TATH	STEN	TINY
SPY	**TAE**	TATS	TEND	**TIP**
ESPY	TAED	TATT	TENE	TIPI
SRI	TAEL	TATU	TENS	TIPS
SRIS	TAES	**TAU**	TENT	TIPT
STY	**TAG**	TAUS	**TES**	**TIS**
STYE	STAG	TAUT	ATES	UTIS
SUB	TAGS	**TAV**	UTES	**TIT**
SUBA	**TAI**	TAVA	TEST	TITE
SUBS	TAIG	TAVS	**TET**	TITI
SUD	TAIL	**TAW**	STET	TITS
SUDD	TAIN	STAW	TETE	**TOC**
SUDS	TAIS	TAWA	TETH	ATOC
SUE	TAIT	TAWS	TETS	TOCK
SUED	**TAK**	TAWT	**TEW**	TOCO
SUER	TAKA	**TAX**	STEW	TOCS
SUES	TAKE	TAXA	TEWS	**TOD**
SUET	TAKI	TAXI	**TEX**	TODS
SUI	TAKS	**TAY**	TEXT	TODY
SUID	TAKY	STAY	**THE**	**TOE**
SUIT	**TAM**	TAYS	ETHE	TOEA
SUK	TAME	**TEA**	THEE	TOED
SUKH	TAMP	TEAD	THEM	TOES
SUKS	TAMS	TEAK	THEN	TOEY
SUM	**TAN**	TEAL	THEW	**TOG**
SUMO	TANA	TEAM	THEY	TOGA
SUMP	TANE	TEAR	**THO**	TOGE
SUMS	TANG	TEAS	THON	TOGS
SUN	TANH	TEAT	THOU	**TOM**
SUNG	TANK	**TEC**	**TIC**	ATOM
SUNK	TANS	TECH	ETIC	TOMB
SUNN	**TAO**	TECS	OTIC	TOME
SUNS	TAOS	**TED**	TICE	TOMO
SUP	**TAP**	STED	TICH	TOMS
SUPE	ATAP	TEDS	TICK	**TON**
SUPS	STAP	TEDY	TICS	TONE
SUQ	TAPA	**TEE**	**TID**	TONG
SUQS	TAPE	TEED	TIDE	TONK
SUR	TAPS	TEEK	TIDS	TONS
SURA	TAPU	TEEL	TIDY	TONY
SURD	**TAR**	TEEM	**TIE**	**TOO**
SURE	STAR	TEEN	STIE	TOOK
SURF	TARA	TEER	TIED	TOOL

TOOM	TUNG	HUGS	**UNS**	URPS
TOON	TUNS	JUGS	BUNS	**USE**
TOOT	TUNY	LUGS	DUNS	FUSE
TOP	**TUP**	MUGS	FUNS	MUSE
ATOP	TUPS	PUGS	GUNS	RUSE
STOP	**TUT**	RUGS	HUNS	USED
TOPE	TUTS	TUGS	MUNS	USER
TOPH	TUTU	VUGS	NUNS	USES
TOPI	**TWA**	YUGS	PUNS	**UTA**
TOPO	TWAE	**UKE**	RUNS	KUTA
TOPS	TWAL	BUKE	SUNS	UTAS
TOR	TWAS	CUKE	TUNS	**UTE**
TORA	TWAT	DUKE	**UPO**	BUTE
TORC	TWAY	JUKE	UPON	CUTE
TORE	**TWO**	LUKE	**UPS**	JUTE
TORI	TWOS	NUKE	CUPS	LUTE
TORN	**TYE**	PUKE	DUPS	MUTE
TORO	STYE	YUKE	GUPS	UTES
TORR	TYED	UKES	HUPS	**UTS**
TORS	TYEE	**ULE**	OUPS	BUTS
TORT	TYER	DULE	PUPS	CUTS
TORY	TYES	GULE	SUPS	GUTS
TOT	**TYG**	HULE	TUPS	HUTS
STOT	TYGS	MULE	YUPS	JUTS
TOTE	**UDO**	PULE	UPSY	MUTS
TOTS	BUDO	RULE	**URB**	NUTS
TOW	JUDO	TULE	BURB	OUTS
STOW	KUDO	YULE	CURB	PUTS
TOWN	LUDO	ULES	URBS	RUTS
TOWS	UDON	ULEX	**URD**	TUTS
TOWT	UDOS	**ULU**	BURD	**UTU**
TOWY	**UDS**	LULU	CURD	KUTU
TOY	BUDS	PULU	NURD	TUTU
TOYO	CUDS	SULU	SURD	UTUS
TOYS	DUDS	ZULU	TURD	**UVA**
TRY	FUDS	ULUS	URDE	UVAE
TRYE	JUDS	**UMM**	URDS	UVAS
TRYP	LUDS	MUMM	URDY	**VAC**
TSK	MUDS	**UMP**	**URE**	VACS
TSKS	OUDS	BUMP	CURE	**VAE**
TUB	PUDS	DUMP	DURE	UVAE
STUB	RUDS	GUMP	IURE	VAES
TUBA	SUDS	HUMP	JURE	**VAG**
TUBE	WUDS	JUMP	LURE	VAGI
TUBS	**UEY**	LUMP	MURE	VAGS
TUG	QUEY	MUMP	PURE	**VAN**
TUGS	**UEYS**	PUMP	SURE	VANE
TUI	**UFO**	RUMP	UREA	VANG
ETUI	BUFO	SUMP	URES	VANS
PTUI	UFOS	TUMP	**URN**	VANT
TUIS	**UGH**	YUMP	BURN	**VAR**
TUM	EUGH	UMPH	CURN	VARA
STUM	PUGH	UMPS	DURN	VARE
TUMP	SUGH	UMPY	GURN	VARS
TUMS	VUGH	**UMU**	OURN	VARY
TUN	UGHS	MUMU	TURN	**VAS**
STUN	**UGS**	**UNI**	URNS	AVAS
TUNA	BUGS	MUNI	**URP**	KVAS
TUND	DUGS	UNIS	BURP	UVAS
TUNE	FUGS	UNIT	RURP	VASA

VASE	VOLS	WARP	WEXE	WOOD
VAST	VOLT	WARS	**WEY**	WOOF
VAT	**VOR**	WART	SWEY	WOOL
VATS	VORS	WARY	WEYS	WOON
VATU	**VOW**	**WAS**	**WHA**	WOOS
VAU	AVOW	TWAS	WHAE	WOOT
VAUS	VOWS	WASE	WHAM	**WOP**
VAUT	**VUG**	WASH	WHAP	SWOP
VAV	VUGG	WASM	WHAT	WOPS
VAVS	VUGH	WASP	**WHO**	**WOS**
VAW	VUGS	WAST	WHOA	TWOS
VAWS	**VUM**	**WAT**	WHOM	WOST
VEE	OVUM	SWAT	WHOP	**WOT**
VEEP	VUMS	TWAT	WHOT	SWOT
VEER	**WAB**	WATE	WHOW	WOTS
VEES	SWAB	WATS	**WHY**	**WOW**
VEG	WABS	WATT	WHYS	WOWF
VEGA	**WAD**	**WAW**	**WIG**	WOWS
VEGO	SWAD	WAWA	SWIG	**WRY**
VET	WADD	WAWE	TWIG	AWRY
EVET	WADE	WAWL	WIGS	**WUD**
VETO	WADI	WAWS	**WIN**	WUDS
VETS	WADS	**WAX**	TWIN	WUDU
VEX	WADT	WAXY	WIND	**WUS**
VEXT	WADY	**WAY**	WINE	WUSS
VIA	**WAE**	AWAY	WING	**WYE**
VIAE	TWAE	SWAY	WINK	WYES
VIAL	WAES	TWAY	WINN	**WYN**
VIAS	**WAG**	WAYS	WINO	WYND
VID	SWAG	**WEB**	WINS	WYNN
AVID	WAGE	WEBS	WINY	WYNS
VIDE	WAGS	**WED**	**WIS**	**XIS**
VIDS	**WAI**	AWED	IWIS	AXIS
VIE	WAID	OWED	YWIS	**YAD**
VIED	WAIF	WEDS	WISE	DYAD
VIER	WAIL	**WEE**	WISH	YADS
VIES	WAIN	AWEE	WISP	**YAG**
VIEW	WAIR	SWEE	WISS	YAGI
VIG	WAIS	TWEE	WIST	YAGS
VIGA	WAIT	WEED	**WIT**	**YAH**
VIGS	**WAN**	WEEK	TWIT	AYAH
VIM	HWAN	WEEL	WITE	YAHS
VIMS	SWAN	WEEM	WITH	**YAK**
VIN	WAND	WEEN	WITS	KYAK
VINA	WANE	WEEP	**WIZ**	YAKS
VINE	WANG	WEER	SWIZ	**YAM**
VINO	WANK	WEES	**WOE**	LYAM
VINS	WANS	WEET	WOES	YAMS
VINT	WANT	**WEM**	**WOF**	**YAP**
VINY	WANY	WEMB	WOFS	YAPP
VIS	**WAP**	WEMS	**WOG**	YAPS
VISA	SWAP	**WEN**	WOGS	**YAR**
VISE	WAPS	WENA	**WOK**	KYAR
VOE	**WAR**	WEND	WOKE	YARD
EVOE	WARB	WENS	WOKS	YARE
VOES	WARD	WENT	**WON**	YARK
VOL	WARE	**WET**	WONK	YARN
VOLA	WARK	WETA	WONS	YARR
VOLE	WARM	WETS	WONT	**YAW**
VOLK	WARN	**WEX**	**WOO**	YAWL

YAWN	OYES	**YOD**	YUKY	ZHOS
YAWP	PYES	YODE	**YUM**	**ZIG**
YAWS	RYES	YODH	YUMP	ZIGS
YAWY	SYES	YODS	**YUP**	**ZIN**
YAY	TYES	**YOK**	YUPS	ZINC
YAYS	WYES	YOKE	**YUS**	ZINE
YEA	YESK	YOKS	AYUS	ZING
YEAD	YEST	**YOM**	KYUS	ZINS
YEAH	**YET**	YOMP	**ZAG**	**ZIP**
YEAN	PYET	**YON**	ZAGS	ZIPS
YEAR	YETI	YOND	**ZAP**	**ZIT**
YEAS	YETT	YONI	ZAPS	ZITE
YEN	**YEW**	YONT	**ZEA**	ZITI
EYEN	YEWS	**YOU**	ZEAL	ZITS
HYEN	**YGO**	YOUK	ZEAS	**ZIZ**
SYEN	YGOE	YOUR	**ZED**	ZIZZ
YENS	**YID**	YOUS	ZEDS	**ZOL**
YEP	YIDS	**YOW**	**ZEE**	ZOLS
YEPS	**YIN**	YOWE	MZEE	**ZOO**
YES	AYIN	YOWL	ZEES	ZOOM
AYES	PYIN	YOWS	**ZEK**	ZOON
BYES	TYIN	**YUG**	ZEKS	ZOOS
DYES	YINS	YUGA	**ZEL**	ZOOT
EYES	**YIP**	YUGS	ZELS	**ZOS**
HYES	YIPE	**YUK**	**ZEP**	DZOS
KYES	YIPS	YUKE	ZEPS	**ZZZ**
LYES	**YOB**	YUKO	**ZHO**	ZZZS
NYES	YOBS	YUKS	DZHO	

Hooks by hook letter

This set of lists contains hooks of two to eight letters, arranged alphabetically by hook letter rather than by root word. Front hooks and back hooks are shown for each letter in turn. Inflections of eight-letter words that end in -S have been omitted to save space, as these words are both obvious and numerous.

Hooks (ordered by hook-letter)

A – Front-hooks

Two letters to three

A-AH	A-DO	A-IT	A-NE	A-WE
A-AL	A-GO	A-KA	A-NY	A-YE
A-AS	A-HA	A-LA	A-PE	A-YU
A-BA	A-HI	A-MA	A-PO	A-ZO
A-BO	A-ID	A-MI	A-RE	
A-BY	A-IN	A-MU	A-SH	
A-CH	A-IS	A-NA	A-TE	

Three letters to four

A-AHS	A-BET	A-BYS	A-DOS	A-GAR
A-ALS	A-BID	A-CHE	A-DRY	A-GAS
A-BAC	A-BOS	A-CID	A-EON	A-GED
A-BAS	A-BUT	A-DAW	A-FAR	A-GEE
A-BED	A-BYE	A-DIT	A-FRO	A-GEN

A-GIN	A-LAR	A-NAN	A-REG	A-VAS
A-GIO	A-LAS	A-NAS	A-RES	A-VID
A-GON	A-LAY	A-NEW	A-RET	A-VOW
A-GUE	A-LEE	A-NIL	A-REW	A-WAY
A-HEM	A-LES	A-NIS	A-RIA	A-WED
A-HIS	A-LEW	A-NON	A-RID	A-WEE
A-HOY	A-LIT	A-NOW	A-ROW	A-WRY
A-IDE	A-LOD	A-NUS	A-RUM	A-XIS
A-IDS	A-LOW	A-PAY	A-SAR	A-YAH
A-INS	A-LUM	A-PED	A-SEA	A-YES
A-ITS	A-MAS	A-PER	A-SHY	A-YIN
A-JAR	A-MEN	A-PES	A-TAP	A-YUS
A-JEE	A-MID	A-POD	A-TES	
A-KED	A-MIR	A-POS	A-TOC	
A-KIN	A-MIS	A-QUA	A-TOM	
A-LAP	A-MUS	A-RED	A-TOP	

Four letters to five

A-AHED	A-DEEM	A-GRIN	A-LURE	A-PODS
A-ARTI	A-DITS	A-GUES	A-MAIN	A-POOP
A-BACK	A-DORE	A-HEAD	A-MASS	A-PORT
A-BACS	A-DOWN	A-HEAP	A-MATE	A-PSIS
A-BAFT	A-DOZE	A-HENT	A-MAUT	A-READ
A-BAND	A-DRAD	A-HIGH	A-MAZE	A-REAL
A-BASE	A-DUST	A-HIND	A-MEER	A-REAR
A-BASH	A-EGIS	A-HING	A-MEND	A-REDD
A-BASK	A-EONS	A-HINT	A-MENE	A-REDE
A-BATE	A-EROS	A-HOLD	A-MENT	A-RETE
A-BEAM	A-FARS	A-HULL	A-MICE	A-RETS
A-BEAR	A-FEAR	A-IDES	A-MIDS	A-RIAS
A-BETS	A-FIRE	A-IRED	A-MINE	A-RIEL
A-BIDE	A-FOOT	A-ISLE	A-MINO	A-RIOT
A-BLED	A-FORE	A-ITCH	A-MIRS	A-RISE
A-BLET	A-FOUL	A-JUGA	A-MISS	A-ROMA
A-BLOW	A-FRIT	A-KING	A-MITY	A-ROSE
A-BODE	A-FROS	A-LACK	A-MOLE	A-RUMS
A-BOIL	A-GAIN	A-LAND	A-MONG	A-SCOT
A-BOMA	A-GAMA	A-LANE	A-MORT	A-SHED
A-BOON	A-GAPE	A-LANG	A-MOVE	A-SHES
A-BORD	A-GARS	A-LANT	A-MUCK	A-SHET
A-BORE	A-GAST	A-LAPS	A-MUSE	A-SIDE
A-BORT	A-GATE	A-LATE	A-NANA	A-SKER
A-BOUT	A-GAVE	A-LAYS	A-NEAR	A-SKEW
A-BRAY	A-GAZE	A-LEFT	A-NIGH	A-SPIC
A-BRIM	A-GENE	A-LIAS	A-NILS	A-STIR
A-BRIN	A-GENT	A-LIEN	A-NODE	A-STUN
A-BRIS	A-GILA	A-LIKE	A-NOLE	A-SWAY
A-BUNA	A-GING	A-LINE	A-NOLE	A-SWIM
A-BUTS	A-GIOS	A-LIST	A-PACE	A-TAPS
A-BUZZ	A-GISM	A-LIVE	A-PAGE	A-TILT
A-BYES	A-GIST	A-LODS	A-PAID	A-TOCS
A-CIDS	A-GLEE	A-LOFT	A-PART	A-TOKE
A-COCK	A-GLEY	A-LOIN	A-PAYS	A-TOLL
A-COLD	A-GLOW	A-LONE	A-PEAK	A-TOMS
A-CORN	A-GONE	A-LONG	A-PEEK	A-TONE
A-CRED	A-GONS	A-LOOF	A-PERT	A-TONY
A-CUTE	A-GOOD	A-LOUD	A-PHIS	A-TRIP
A-DAWS	A-GORA	A-LOWE	A-PIAN	A-URES
A-DAYS	A-GREE	A-LUMS	A-PISH	A-URIC

A-VAIL	A-VINE	A-WARD	A-WEEL	A-YINS
A-VALE	A-VISE	A-WARE	A-WING	A-YONT
A-VANT	A-VOID	A-WARN	A-WOKE	A-ZINE
A-VAST	A-VOWS	A-WASH	A-WORK	A-ZOIC
A-VERS	A-WAIT	A-WAVE	A-YAHS	A-ZYME
A-VERT	A-WAKE	A-WAYS	A-YELP	

Five letters to six

A-AHING	A-DREAD	A-LAYED	A-RETES	A-TOKES
A-ARTIS	A-DRIFT	A-LEGGE	A-RIDER	A-TOLLS
A-BANDS	A-DROIT	A-LEVIN	A-RIELS	A-TONAL
A-BASED	A-DUSTS	A-LIENS	A-RIGHT	A-TONED
A-BASER	A-EDILE	A-LIGHT	A-RILED	A-TONER
A-BASES	A-EMULE	A-LINED	A-RISEN	A-TONES
A-BATED	A-ERUGO	A-LINER	A-RISES	A-TONIC
A-BATES	A-ETHER	A-LINES	A-ROMAS	A-TOPIC
A-BATTU	A-FEARS	A-LOGIA	A-ROUND	A-TRIAL
A-BEARS	A-FIELD	A-LOINS	A-ROUSE	A-TWAIN
A-BIDED	A-FLAME	A-LURES	A-SCEND	A-TWEEL
A-BIDER	A-FLOAT	A-MATED	A-SCENT	A-TWEEN
A-BIDES	A-FREET	A-MATES	A-SCOTS	A-TWIXT
A-BLATE	A-FRESH	A-MAUTS	A-SEITY	A-TYPIC
A-BLAZE	A-FRITS	A-MAZED	A-SHAKE	A-UNTIE
A-BLEST	A-FRONT	A-MAZES	A-SHAME	A-URATE
A-BLETS	A-GAMAS	A-MEERS	A-SHETS	A-VAILS
A-BLING	A-GAMIC	A-MENDS	A-SHIER	A-VALES
A-BLINS	A-GAPES	A-MENED	A-SHINE	A-VAUNT
A-BLOOM	A-GATES	A-MENTA	A-SHORE	A-VENGE
A-BLUSH	A-GAZED	A-MIDST	A-SIDES	A-VENUE
A-BOARD	A-GEIST	A-MINES	A-SKERS	A-VERSE
A-BODED	A-GENES	A-MISES	A-SLAKE	A-VERTS
A-BODES	A-GENTS	A-MOLES	A-SLANT	A-VISED
A-BOMAS	A-GHAST	A-MOOVE	A-SLEEP	A-VISES
A-BORAL	A-GILAS	A-MORAL	A-SLOPE	A-VITAL
A-BORDS	A-GINGS	A-MOUNT	A-SLOSH	A-VOIDS
A-BORNE	A-GISMS	A-MOVED	A-SMEAR	A-VOUCH
A-BORTS	A-GISTS	A-MOVES	A-SPICK	A-VOWED
A-BOUND	A-GLARE	A-MUCKS	A-SPICS	A-VOWER
A-BOUTS	A-GLEAM	A-MUSED	A-SPINE	A-WAITS
A-BRAID	A-GOING	A-MUSER	A-SPIRE	A-WAKED
A-BRAYS	A-GORAS	A-MUSES	A-SPORT	A-WAKEN
A-BRINS	A-GOUTY	A-NANAS	A-SPOUT	A-WAKES
A-BROAD	A-GREED	A-NEARS	A-SQUAT	A-WARDS
A-BUNAS	A-GREES	A-NEATH	A-STARE	A-WARNS
A-BURST	A-GREGE	A-NIGHT	A-START	A-WATCH
A-BUSED	A-GRISE	A-NODAL	A-STERN	A-WEARY
A-BUSES	A-GRIZE	A-NODES	A-STONE	A-WEIGH
A-CATER	A-GUISE	A-NOINT	A-STONY	A-WHEEL
A-CATES	A-HOLDS	A-NOLES	A-STOOP	A-WHILE
A-CETYL	A-HORSE	A-NOMIC	A-STRAY	A-WHIRL
A-CIDER	A-IDANT	A-PHONY	A-STRUT	A-WOKEN
A-CORNS	A-IRING	A-PICAL	A-STUNS	A-WRACK
A-CRAWL	A-ISLED	A-PIECE	A-SWARM	A-WRONG
A-CROSS	A-ISLES	A-RABIC	A-SWING	A-XENIC
A-CUTER	A-KIMBO	A-RABIS	A-SWIRL	A-ZINES
A-CUTES	A-LANDS	A-RAISE	A-SWOON	A-ZONAL
A-DAWED	A-LANTS	A-REACH	A-TAATA	A-ZYMES
A-DEEMS	A-LARUM	A-READS	A-TELIC	
A-DOORS	A-LATED	A-REDES	A-THROB	

Six letters to seven

A-BANDED	A-DUSTED	A-MAZING	A-ROUSED	A-SUNDER
A-BASHED	A-EDILES	A-MENAGE	A-ROUSER	A-TAATAS
A-BASHES	A-EGISES	A-MENDED	A-ROUSES	A-TACTIC
A-BASING	A-EMULED	A-MENDER	A-RUGOLA	A-TAXIES
A-BATING	A-EMULES	A-MENING	A-SCARED	A-THEISM
A-BETTED	A-EOLIAN	A-MENTAL	A-SCENDS	A-THEIST
A-BETTER	A-EONIAN	A-MENTUM	A-SCENTS	A-THIRST
A-BETTOR	A-ERUGOS	A-MERCER	A-SCONCE	A-THRILL
A-BIDDEN	A-ETHERS	A-MERCES	A-SCRIBE	A-THWART
A-BIDERS	A-FEARED	A-MISSES	A-SEPSES	A-TINGLE
A-BIDING	A-FREETS	A-MONGST	A-SEPSIS	A-TONERS
A-BIOTIC	A-GAINST	A-MOOVED	A-SEPTIC	A-TONICS
A-BLINGS	A-GAMETE	A-MOOVES	A-SEXUAL	A-TONIES
A-BODING	A-GEISTS	A-MOTION	A-SHAMED	A-TONING
A-BOUGHT	A-GENTRY	A-MOUNTS	A-SHAMES	A-TROPHY
A-BOUNDS	A-GINNER	A-MOVING	A-SHIEST	A-TROPIN
A-BRAIDS	A-GRASTE	A-MUSERS	A-SHIVER	A-UNTIES
A-BRAYED	A-GRISED	A-MUSING	A-SKLENT	A-URATES
A-BREAST	A-GRISES	A-MUSIVE	A-SLAKED	A-VAILED
A-BRIDGE	A-GRIZES	A-NEARED	A-SLAKES	A-VAUNTS
A-BROACH	A-GROUND	A-NOESES	A-SOCIAL	A-VENGED
A-BROADS	A-GUISED	A-NOESIS	A-SPERSE	A-VENGER
A-BUBBLE	A-GUISES	A-NOETIC	A-SPICKS	A-VENGES
A-BUSING	A-HEIGHT	A-NOINTS	A-SPINES	A-VENTRE
A-BUTTED	A-HUNGRY	A-NOTHER	A-SPIRED	A-VENUES
A-BUTTER	A-ISLING	A-PAYING	A-SPIRES	A-VERTED
A-BYSSAL	A-ITCHES	A-PHASIC	A-SPORTS	A-VIATIC
A-CANTHI	A-LARUMS	A-PHESES	A-SPRAWL	A-VIATOR
A-CATERS	A-LAYING	A-PHONIC	A-SPREAD	A-VISING
A-CAUDAL	A-LEGGED	A-PHOTIC	A-SPROUT	A-VOIDED
A-CERATE	A-LEGGES	A-PLENTY	A-SQUINT	A-VOIDER
A-CEROUS	A-LENGTH	A-POSTIL	A-STABLE	A-VOWERS
A-CETYLS	A-LEVINS	A-PTERIA	A-STARTS	A-VOWING
A-CHIRAL	A-LIASES	A-PTOTIC	A-STATIC	A-WAITED
A-CLINIC	A-LIGHTS	A-QUIVER	A-STELIC	A-WAITER
A-CORNED	A-LINERS	A-RACHIS	A-STONED	A-WAKENS
A-CUTELY	A-LINING	A-RAISED	A-STONES	A-WAKING
A-CUTEST	A-LONELY	A-RAISES	A-STOUND	A-WARDED
A-CYCLIC	A-LUMINA	A-REALLY	A-STRAND	A-WARDER
A-DAWING	A-LUMINE	A-REDING	A-STRICT	A-WARNED
A-DEEMED	A-MASSED	A-RETTED	A-STRIDE	A-WHEELS
A-DHARMA	A-MASSES	A-RIPPLE	A-STYLAR	A-ZYMITE
A-DREADS	A-MATING	A-RISING	A-SUDDEN	

Seven letters to eight

A-BANDING	A-BRAIDED	A-CAULINE	A-EMULING	A-GINNERS
A-BASHING	A-BRAYING	A-CENTRIC	A-ESTHETE	A-GLIMMER
A-BATABLE	A-BRIDGED	A-CERATED	A-ESTIVAL	A-GLITTER
A-BEARING	A-BRIDGES	A-CHROMIC	A-ETHERIC	A-GLOSSAL
A-BEGGING	A-BROOKED	A-COSMISM	A-FEARING	A-GNOSTIC
A-BETTERS	A-BUTMENT	A-COSMIST	A-FEBRILE	A-GRAPHIC
A-BETTING	A-BUTTALS	A-DEEMING	A-FLUTTER	A-GREEING
A-BETTORS	A-BUTTERS	A-DHARMAS	A-GAMETES	A-GRISING
A-BIDINGS	A-BUTTING	A-DREADED	A-GENESES	A-GUISING
A-BOUNDED	A-CANTHUS	A-DUSTING	A-GENESIS	A-KINESES
A-BRACHIA	A-CAUDATE	A-DYNAMIC	A-GENETIC	A-KINESIS

A-KINETIC	A-MOUNTED	A-SCRIBED	A-STONING	A-VENTRES
A-LEGGING	A-MUSETTE	A-SCRIBES	A-STONISH	A-VENTURE
A-LIGHTED	A-NEARING	A-SEISMIC	A-STOUNDS	A-VERSION
A-LOGICAL	A-NEURISM	A-SEITIES	A-STUNNED	A-VERTING
A-LUMINES	A-NODALLY	A-SEPTATE	A-SYNERGY	A-VIATORS
A-MASSING	A-NOINTED	A-SEPTICS	A-SYSTOLE	A-VOIDERS
A-MAZEDLY	A-NOINTER	A-SHAMING	A-TECHNIC	A-VOIDING
A-MEIOSES	A-PHONICS	A-SHINESS	A-THEISMS	A-VOUCHED
A-MEIOSIS	A-PHONIES	A-SLAKING	A-THEISTS	A-VOUCHER
A-MENAGED	A-PIARIST	A-SOCIALS	A-TONALLY	A-VOUCHES
A-MENAGES	A-PLASTIC	A-SPARKLE	A-TREMBLE	A-WAITERS
A-MENDERS	A-POSTILS	A-SPERSED	A-TROPHIC	A-WAITING
A-MENDING	A-PRACTIC	A-SPERSES	A-TROPINE	A-WAKENED
A-MERCERS	A-PYRETIC	A-SPHERIC	A-TROPINS	A-WAKENER
A-MIDMOST	A-PYREXIA	A-SPIRANT	A-TROPISM	A-WAKINGS
A-MIDSHIP	A-RAISING	A-SPIRING	A-TWITTER	A-WANTING
A-MISSING	A-REACHED	A-SPORTED	A-TYPICAL	A-WARDERS
A-MITOSES	A-REACHES	A-STARTED	A-VAILING	A-WARDING
A-MITOSIS	A-READING	A-STERNAL	A-VARICES	A-WARNING
A-MITOTIC	A-RETTING	A-STEROID	A-VAUNTED	A-WEARIED
A-MOOVING	A-ROUSERS	A-STHENIA	A-VENGERS	A-WEATHER
A-MORALLY	A-ROUSING	A-STHENIC	A-VENGING	A-ZYGOSES
A-MORTISE	A-RUGOLAS	A-STONIED	A-VENTAIL	A-ZYMITES
A-MOTIONS	A-SCENDED	A-STONIES	A-VENTRED	

Eight letters to nine

A-BASEMENT	A-ETIOLOGY	A-MOROSITY	A-SEXUALLY	A-TEMPORAL
A-BASHLESS	A-FOREHAND	A-MORTISED	A-SKEWNESS	A-THEISTIC
A-BATEMENT	A-FORESAID	A-MORTISES	A-SMOULDER	A-THEMATIC
A-BIOGENIC	A-FORETIME	A-MOUNTING	A-SPERSING	A-THEOLOGY
A-BODEMENT	A-GELASTIC	A-MUSETTES	A-SPIRANTS	A-TONALITY
A-BOUNDING	A-GENTRIES	A-MUSINGLY	A-SPIRATED	A-TONICITY
A-BRAIDING	A-GNOSTICS	A-MYOTONIA	A-SPLENIUM	A-TROPHIED
A-BRIDGING	A-HISTORIC	A-NEURISMS	A-SPORTING	A-TROPHIES
A-BROOKING	A-HUNGERED	A-NOINTERS	A-STARTING	A-TROPINES
A-BUILDING	A-ISLELESS	A-NOINTING	A-STEROIDS	A-TROPISMS
A-BUTMENTS	A-LACKADAY	A-NUCLEATE	A-STHENIAS	A-VASCULAR
A-CELLULAR	A-LIENABLE	A-PATHETIC	A-STOMATAL	A-VAUNTING
A-CEPHALIC	A-LIGHTING	A-PERIODIC	A-STONYING	A-VENGEFUL
A-CHROMOUS	A-LIKENESS	A-PERTNESS	A-STOUNDED	A-VENTAILE
A-COSMISMS	A-LITERACY	A-PETALOUS	A-STRADDLE	A-VENTAILS
A-COSMISTS	A-LITERATE	A-PHERESES	A-STRINGED	A-VENTRING
A-CRITICAL	A-LIVENESS	A-PHERESIS	A-STRINGER	A-VENTURES
A-CUTENESS	A-LONENESS	A-PIARISTS	A-STUNNING	A-VERSIONS
A-DREADING	A-LUMINOUS	A-PLANETIC	A-SYLLABIC	A-VIRULENT
A-EOLIPILE	A-MAZEMENT	A-PRIORITY	A-SYMMETRY	A-VOCATION
A-ESTHESES	A-MENAGING	A-PYREXIAS	A-SYNAPSES	A-VOIDABLE
A-ESTHESIA	A-MENDABLE	A-RACHISES	A-SYNAPSIS	A-VOIDANCE
A-ESTHESIS	A-MIDSHIPS	A-REACHING	A-SYNDETIC	A-VOUCHERS
A-ESTHETES	A-MORALISM	A-RHYTHMIC	A-SYNDETON	A-VOUCHING
A-ESTHETIC	A-MORALIST	A-SCENDING	A-SYNERGIA	A-WAKENERS
A-ESTIVATE	A-MORALITY	A-SCRIBING	A-SYSTOLES	A-WAKENING
A-ETHEREAL	A-MORNINGS	A-SEPALOUS	A-SYSTOLIC	

A – End-hooks

Two letters to three

AB-A	AW-A	GO-A	OD-A	UT-A
AG-A	BA-A	HO-A	OR-A	YE-A
AH-A	BO-A	IT-A	PE-A	ZO-A
AI-A	CH-A	KO-A	PI-A	
AL-A	ER-A	MA-A	PO-A	
AM-A	ET-A	MO-A	SH-A	
AN-A	FA-A	OB-A	TE-A	

Three letters to four

ABB-A	FET-A	LOT-A	PAW-A	SOL-A
ACT-A	FIL-A	LUM-A	PIC-A	SOM-A
ALB-A	FOR-A	MAL-A	PIN-A	SOY-A
ALF-A	GAG-A	MAM-A	PIP-A	SUB-A
AMI-A	GAL-A	MAN-A	PIT-A	SUR-A
ANN-A	GAM-A	MAR-A	PRO-A	TAK-A
ANT-A	GEN-A	MAS-A	PUH-A	TAN-A
ARB-A	GET-A	MAY-A	PUL-A	TAP-A
ARE-A	GIG-A	MEG-A	PUN-A	TAR-A
BET-A	GOR-A	MEL-A	PUP-A	TAV-A
BIG-A	GUL-A	MES-A	RAG-A	TAW-A
BOB-A	HAH-A	MET-A	RAI-A	TAX-A
BON-A	HOH-A	MIC-A	RAJ-A	TEL-A
BOR-A	HOM-A	MOL-A	RAN-A	TOE-A
BOT-A	HOY-A	MON-A	RAT-A	TOG-A
BUB-A	HUI-A	MOR-A	RAY-A	TOR-A
BUD-A	HUM-A	MOW-A	RIB-A	TUB-A
BUN-A	IDE-A	MOY-A	RIM-A	TUN-A
BUR-A	ILK-A	NAG-A	RIZ-A	URE-A
CAB-A	JAG-A	NAN-A	ROM-A	VAR-A
CAM-A	JOT-A	NAP-A	ROT-A	VAS-A
CAP-A	JUG-A	NIP-A	RUG-A	VEG-A
CHI-A	KAK-A	NOM-A	SAG-A	VIG-A
COD-A	KAM-A	NON-A	SAM-A	VIN-A
COL-A	KAT-A	NOT-A	SEN-A	VIS-A
COX-A	KAW-A	OBI-A	SER-A	VOL-A
DAD-A	KET-A	ODE-A	SET-A	WAW-A
DEV-A	KIN-A	OLE-A	SHE-A	WEN-A
DIS-A	KOR-A	ORC-A	SIK-A	WET-A
DIT-A	LAM-A	OUP-A	SIM-A	WHO-A
DIV-A	LAV-A	PAC-A	SOB-A	YUG-A
DON-A	LEV-A	PAP-A	SOC-A	
DOP-A	LIP-A	PAR-A	SOD-A	

Four letters to five

ABAC-A	BAST-A	CALP-A	COAL-A	DERM-A
AFAR-A	BATT-A	CANN-A	COCO-A	DICT-A
ALAP-A	BORN-A	CART-A	COMM-A	DONG-A
ANAN-A	BUFF-A	CELL-A	CONI-A	DOON-A
BACH-A	BULL-A	CHAR-A	COST-A	DORB-A
BALS-A	BURK-A	CHAY-A	COTT-A	DORS-A
BAND-A	BURS-A	CHIC-A	DARG-A	DOUM-A
BANI-A	CALL-A	CHIN-A	DELT-A	DOUR-A

DOWN-A	HYEN-A	MUSH-A	PUNK-A	SPIN-A
DRAM-A	IDOL-A	NERK-A	QUIN-A	SUNN-A
DURR-A	KAIK-A	NORI-A	RAGG-A	TAIG-A
ERIC-A	KANG-A	NORM-A	RAIT-A	TALE-A
FANG-A	KIND-A	NULL-A	RAST-A	TANG-A
FAUN-A	KIPP-A	PACT-A	RATH-A	TANK-A
FELL-A	LAIK-A	PAIS-A	ROOS-A	TEGU-A
FEST-A	LEPT-A	PALE-A	SAKI-A	TEST-A
FETT-A	LEZZ-A	PALL-A	SALP-A	THAN-A
FLOR-A	LIMB-A	PAND-A	SALS-A	THEM-A
FOND-A	LIMP-A	PANG-A	SANG-A	TIAR-A
FOSS-A	LING-A	PARK-A	SANS-A	TINE-A
GALE-A	LONG-A	PARR-A	SCOP-A	TONG-A
GAMB-A	LOOF-A	PASH-A	SCUT-A	TONK-A
GENU-A	LUFF-A	PAST-A	SELL-A	TORT-A
GRAM-A	LUTE-A	PELT-A	SENS-A	TREF-A
GRAN-A	MANG-A	PERE-A	SEPT-A	TRON-A
GUAN-A	MANI-A	PIET-A	SERR-A	UNCI-A
HAIK-A	MARK-A	PILE-A	SESS-A	VEST-A
HAKE-A	MASS-A	PINT-A	SHAM-A	VILL-A
HALF-A	MENT-A	PLAY-A	SHAY-A	VIOL-A
HALM-A	MISS-A	POLK-A	SHIV-A	VOLT-A
HAST-A	MOCH-A	PONG-A	SIDH-A	WALL-A
HATH-A	MOLL-A	POOK-A	SIGN-A	WHAT-A
HERM-A	MOOL-A	PORT-A	SOFT-A	WINN-A
HOND-A	MUGG-A	PRIM-A	SORD-A	WISH-A
HOOK-A	MULL-A	PUCK-A	SORT-A	YACK-A
HOST-A	MUNG-A	PULK-A	SPAZ-A	YURT-A
HOVE-A	MURR-A	PUNG-A	SPIC-A	ZILL-A

Five letters to six

AMENT-A	CORNU-A	HALAL-A	OCHRE-A	SCARP-A
AMRIT-A	CRACK-A	HALLO-A	ORBIT-A	SENOR-A
ANTAR-A	CREST-A	HEDER-A	ORGAN-A	SHIRR-A
ARGAL-A	CRUST-A	HEMIN-A	PAGOD-A	SHISH-A
BERTH-A	CUBIC-A	HILLO-A	PARER-A	SOLER-A
BILBO-A	CUTCH-A	HOLLO-A	PATER-A	SPIRE-A
BOCCI-A	EGEST-A	HULLO-A	PATIN-A	STELL-A
BOONG-A	EJECT-A	KAING-A	PENNI-A	STERN-A
CABAL-A	ENTER-A	KORUN-A	PETAR-A	STRIG-A
CAMIS-A	EPOCH-A	KUTCH-A	PLANT-A	STRUM-A
CARDI-A	EXACT-A	LATER-A	PLASM-A	TALUK-A
CHANG-A	FASCI-A	LORIC-A	QUANT-A	TAPET-A
CHARK-A	FAVEL-A	MAXIM-A	QUINO-A	TARSI-A
CHART-A	FIEST-A	MIASM-A	QUINT-A	TORAN-A
CHICH-A	FRISK-A	MINIM-A	QUOTH-A	TREIF-A
CHORD-A	FRUST-A	MONER-A	RHUMB-A	TUNIC-A
CHORE-A	GLOSS-A	NYMPH-A	SAHIB-A	VALET-A
CONCH-A	GRAMP-A	OBELI-A	SATYR-A	YOJAN-A

Six letters to seven

ABOMAS-A	ARABIC-A	CHIASM-A	COTING-A	DRACHM-A
ACANTH-A	ASHRAM-A	CHIMER-A	CROTAL-A	EMBLEM-A
ADDEND-A	BUZUKI-A	CHOLER-A	CURIOS-A	EROTIC-A
ALUMIN-A	CANDID-A	CHRISM-A	CYATHI-A	EXOTIC-A
ANALOG-A	CANTAL-A	CODEIN-A	DEJECT-A	FAVELL-A
ANONYM-A	CEMENT-A	CORTIN-A	DEODAR-A	FORMIC-A

GALLET-A	LOCUST-A	OSMUND-A	ROTUND-A	SQUILL-A
GALLIC-A	LOMENT-A	PAISAN-A	SCHISM-A	SULTAN-A
GERMIN-A	MADRAS-A	PERSON-A	SECRET-A	TAMBUR-A
GRAVID-A	MANDIR-A	PLACIT-A	SELECT-A	TARTAN-A
GUNNER-A	MANIOC-A	POTASS-A	SENHOR-A	TAVERN-A
INFANT-A	MARKKA-A	PROPYL-A	SEQUEL-A	TEMPER-A
INGEST-A	MICELL-A	QUININ-A	SERING-A	TRISUL-A
KHALIF-A	MOMENT-A	ROBUST-A	SHEIKH-A	TYMPAN-A
LAVOLT-A	NANDIN-A	ROSACE-A	SIGNOR-A	VIATIC-A

Seven letters to eight

ABSCISS-A	BROUGHT-A	FASCIST-A	MRIDANG-A	STROBIL-A
AMYGDAL-A	CHAMPAC-A	HEPATIC-A	NYMPHAE-A	SYNTAGM-A
ANAPHOR-A	CHARISM-A	JAVELIN-A	PERFECT-A	TAMANDU-A
ANGELIC-A	CISTERN-A	MANDIOC-A	PIGNOLI-A	TAMBOUR-A
ANTEFIX-A	CONSULT-A	MARCHES-A	QUILLAI-A	THERIAC-A
ARBORET-A	DEMENTI-A	MARINER-A	RAKSHAS-A	TORMENT-A
AUTOMAT-A	DIASTEM-A	MATADOR-A	SALICET-A	TOURIST-A
BASILIC-A	DULCIAN-A	MELODIC-A	SARMENT-A	UNGUENT-A
BOTANIC-A	EPITHEM-A	MOLLUSC-A	SCIATIC-A	
BRONCHI-A	EXCERPT-A	MONSTER-A	SIGNORI-A	

Eight letters to nine

AQUATINT-A	DIDRACHM-A	HIERATIC-A	NICOTIAN-A	SLIVOVIC-A
ARGUMENT-A	DIPLOMAT-A	HYPODERM-A	PARAMENT-A	SOUVLAKI-A
BOUSOUKI-A	ESOTERIC-A	HYPOTHEC-A	PHANTASM-A	
BOUZOUKI-A	EXANTHEM-A	JAMBOLAN-A	PHILOMEL-A	
CALYPTER-A	FANFARON-A	MAIASAUR-A	POZZOLAN-A	
CANEPHOR-A	HARMONIC-A	MATACHIN-A	PRINCIPI-A	

B – Front-hooks

Two letters to three

B-AA	B-AT	B-IN	B-OO	B-UN
B-AD	B-AY	B-IO	B-OP	B-UR
B-AG	B-ED	B-IS	B-OR	B-US
B-AH	B-EE	B-IT	B-OS	B-UT
B-AL	B-EL	B-OB	B-OW	B-YE
B-AM	B-EN	B-OD	B-OX	
B-AN	B-ES	B-OH	B-OY	
B-AR	B-ET	B-OI	B-UG	
B-AS	B-ID	B-ON	B-UM	

Three letters to four

B-AAL	B-AIL	B-ANT	B-ASK	B-EAN
B-AAS	B-AIT	B-ARB	B-ASS	B-EAR
B-ABA	B-AKE	B-ARD	B-ATE	B-EAT
B-ABY	B-ALE	B-ARE	B-ATT	B-EAU
B-ACH	B-ALL	B-ARF	B-AUK	B-EDS
B-ADS	B-ALS	B-ARK	B-AWL	B-EEN
B-AFF	B-AND	B-ARM	B-AWN	B-EGO
B-AFT	B-ANE	B-ARS	B-AYE	B-ELL
B-AGS	B-ANI	B-ASH	B-AYS	B-ELS

B-ELT	B-ISH	B-OAR	B-ORD	B-RIN
B-END	B-ITS	B-OAT	B-ORE	B-RIT
B-ENE	B-LAB	B-OBA	B-ORS	B-ROD
B-ENS	B-LAD	B-OBS	B-ORT	B-ROO
B-ERE	B-LAG	B-ODE	B-OUK	B-ROW
B-ERG	B-LAH	B-ODS	B-OUT	B-RUT
B-ERK	B-LAM	B-OFF	B-OWL	B-UDO
B-EST	B-LAT	B-OHO	B-OXY	B-UDS
B-ETA	B-LAW	B-OHS	B-OYS	B-UFO
B-ETH	B-LAY	B-OIL	B-RAD	B-UGS
B-HAT	B-LED	B-OKE	B-RAG	B-UKE
B-HUT	B-LEE	B-OLD	B-RAN	B-UMP
B-ICE	B-LET	B-OLE	B-RAS	B-UNS
B-IDE	B-LEW	B-ONE	B-RAT	B-URB
B-IDS	B-LEY	B-ONY	B-RAW	B-URD
B-IFF	B-LIN	B-OOH	B-RAY	B-URN
B-IGG	B-LIP	B-OOM	B-RED	B-URP
B-ILK	B-LOB	B-OON	B-REE	B-UTE
B-ILL	B-LOG	B-OOR	B-REI	B-UTS
B-INK	B-LOT	B-OOS	B-REN	B-YES
B-INS	B-LOW	B-OOT	B-REW	
B-IOS	B-LUR	B-OPS	B-RIG	
B-IRK	B-OAK	B-ORA	B-RIM	

Four letters to five

B-AALS	B-AYES	B-ILLS	B-LEED	B-LUNT
B-ABAS	B-EACH	B-ILLY	B-LEEP	B-LURS
B-ACCA	B-EANS	B-INGO	B-LEES	B-LUSH
B-ADDY	B-EARD	B-INKS	B-LEND	B-OAKS
B-AFFY	B-EARS	B-IOTA	B-LENT	B-OARS
B-AILS	B-EAST	B-IRKS	B-LESS	B-OAST
B-AIRN	B-EATH	B-ITCH	B-LEST	B-OATS
B-AITS	B-EATS	B-LABS	B-LETS	B-OBAS
B-AKED	B-EAUS	B-LACK	B-LEYS	B-OBOL
B-AKES	B-EAUX	B-LADE	B-LIMP	B-OCHE
B-ALAS	B-EECH	B-LADS	B-LIMY	B-ODES
B-ALES	B-EERY	B-LADY	B-LIND	B-OFFS
B-ALKY	B-EGAD	B-LAER	B-LING	B-OGLE
B-ALLS	B-ELLS	B-LAGS	B-LINK	B-OHOS
B-ALLY	B-ELTS	B-LAHS	B-LINS	B-OILS
B-ALMS	B-ENDS	B-LAIN	B-LINY	B-OINK
B-ANAL	B-ENES	B-LAME	B-LIPS	B-OKES
B-ANDS	B-ERES	B-LAMS	B-LIST	B-OLDS
B-ANES	B-ERGS	B-LAND	B-LITE	B-OLES
B-ANNS	B-ERKS	B-LANK	B-LIVE	B-ONCE
B-ANTS	B-ESES	B-LARE	B-LOBS	B-ONER
B-ARBS	B-ESTS	B-LASE	B-LOCK	B-ONES
B-ARDS	B-ETAS	B-LASH	B-LOGS	B-ONIE
B-ARED	B-ETHS	B-LAST	B-LOKE	B-ONUS
B-ARES	B-EVER	B-LATE	B-LOOM	B-OOFY
B-ARFS	B-HAJI	B-LATS	B-LOOP	B-OOHS
B-ARKS	B-HANG	B-LAUD	B-LORE	B-OOMS
B-ARMS	B-HOOT	B-LAWN	B-LOTS	B-OONS
B-ARMY	B-HUTS	B-LAWS	B-LOWN	B-OOSE
B-ASKS	B-ICES	B-LAYS	B-LOWS	B-OOTS
B-ATES	B-IDES	B-LAZE	B-LUDE	B-OOZE
B-AUKS	B-IFFY	B-LEAK	B-LUES	B-OOZY
B-AWLS	B-IGGS	B-LEAR	B-LUFF	B-ORAL
B-AWNS	B-ILKS	B-LEAT	B-LUNK	B-ORDS

B-ORES   B-RAIN   B-RENS   B-ROIL   B-UKES
B-ORTS   B-RAKE   B-RENT   B-ROKE   B-UMBO
B-OUKS   B-RAND   B-REWS   B-ROOD   B-UMPH
B-OURN   B-RANK   B-RICK   B-ROOK   B-UMPS
B-OUTS   B-RANT   B-RIDE   B-ROOM   B-UMPY
B-OWED   B-RASH   B-RIGS   B-ROOS   B-UNCE
B-OWER   B-RAST   B-RILL   B-ROSE   B-UNCO
B-OWES   B-RATS   B-RIMS   B-ROSY   B-UNDE
B-OWLS   B-RAVE   B-RINE   B-ROWS   B-UNDY
B-OWSE   B-RAWN   B-RING   B-RUIN   B-URBS
B-OXEN   B-RAWS   B-RINK   B-RULE   B-URDS
B-OXER   B-RAYS   B-RINS   B-RUME   B-URNS
B-OXES   B-RAZE   B-RISE   B-RUNG   B-URPS
B-RACE   B-READ   B-RISK   B-RUNT   B-URSA
B-RACH   B-REAK   B-RITS   B-RUSH   B-USED
B-RACK   B-REAM   B-RITT   B-RUSK   B-USES
B-RADS   B-REDE   B-ROAD   B-RUST   B-UTES
B-RAGS   B-REED   B-ROCH   B-RUTS
B-RAID   B-REES   B-ROCK   B-UDOS
B-RAIL   B-REIS   B-RODS   B-UFOS

Five letters to six

B-ABIES   B-EARDS   B-LATER   B-LUNGE   B-RACER
B-ABOON   B-EARED   B-LAUDS   B-LUNKS   B-RACES
B-ACCAS   B-EASTS   B-LAWED   B-LUNTS   B-RACKS
B-ACHED   B-EATEN   B-LAZED   B-LURRY   B-RAGGY
B-ACHES   B-EATER   B-LAZES   B-OAKED   B-RAIDS
B-ACKER   B-EGGAR   B-LEACH   B-OASTS   B-RAILS
B-ADDER   B-EGGED   B-LEAKS   B-OATER   B-RAINS
B-ADMAN   B-EIGNE   B-LEAKY   B-OBOLS   B-RAINY
B-ADMEN   B-ELATE   B-LEARS   B-OCHES   B-RAIRD
B-AGGER   B-ENDED   B-LEARY   B-OFFED   B-RAISE
B-AGGIE   B-ENDER   B-LEATS   B-OGLES   B-RAKED
B-AILED   B-HAJIS   B-LEEPS   B-OILED   B-RAKES
B-AIRNS   B-HANGS   B-LENDS   B-OILER   B-RANCH
B-AKING   B-HOOTS   B-LIGHT   B-OINKS   B-RANDS
B-ALDER   B-ICKER   B-LIMEY   B-OLDEN   B-RANDY
B-ALLOT   B-IDENT   B-LIMPS   B-OLDER   B-RANKS
B-ALLOW   B-IGGED   B-LINDS   B-OMBER   B-RANTS
B-ANANA   B-ILLER   B-LINGS   B-ONCES   B-RASES
B-ANGER   B-INGLE   B-LINKS   B-ONERS   B-RATTY
B-ANGLE   B-INNED   B-LITES   B-OOHED   B-RAVED
B-ANKER   B-IONIC   B-LITHE   B-OOSES   B-RAVER
B-ANTED   B-IOTAS   B-LOBBY   B-OOZED   B-RAVES
B-ARISH   B-ISHES   B-LOCKS   B-OOZES   B-RAWER
B-ARKED   B-ITCHY   B-LOKES   B-ORALS   B-RAWLY
B-ARRAS   B-LACKS   B-LOOEY   B-ORATE   B-RAWNS
B-ARRET   B-LADED   B-LOOIE   B-ORDER   B-RAYED
B-ARROW   B-LADER   B-LOOMS   B-OTHER   B-RAZED
B-ASHED   B-LADES   B-LOOPS   B-OUGHT   B-RAZER
B-ASHES   B-LAMED   B-LORES   B-OUNCE   B-RAZES
B-ASKED   B-LAMER   B-LOTTO   B-OVATE   B-REACH
B-ASSED   B-LAMES   B-LOUSE   B-OVINE   B-READS
B-ASSES   B-LANCH   B-LOUSY   B-OWING   B-READY
B-ASSET   B-LANDS   B-LOWED   B-OWLED   B-REAKS
B-ASTER   B-LANKS   B-LOWER   B-OWLER   B-REAMS
B-ATMAN   B-LANKY   B-LOWSE   B-OWNED   B-REAST
B-EAGLE   B-LARES   B-LUDES   B-OXERS   B-REDED
B-EANED   B-LASTS   B-LUFFS   B-RACED   B-REDES

B-REECH	B-RIDGE	B-ROILS	B-RULES	B-UNION
B-REEDS	B-RIGHT	B-ROKED	B-RUMAL	B-UNKED
B-REEKS	B-RILLS	B-ROKER	B-RUMES	B-URGER
B-REEST	B-RINES	B-ROKES	B-RUNCH	B-URIAL
B-REGMA	B-RINGS	B-ROMAL	B-RUNTS	B-URNED
B-REIST	B-RINKS	B-ROODS	B-RUSHY	B-URPED
B-RENNE	B-RISES	B-ROOKS	B-RUSTS	B-URSAE
B-RENTS	B-RISKS	B-ROOMS	B-UDDER	B-USHER
B-REVET	B-RISKY	B-ROOMY	B-UGGED	B-USING
B-REWED	B-RITTS	B-ROOSE	B-UMBLE	B-UTTER
B-RIBES	B-ROACH	B-ROSES	B-UMBOS	
B-RICHT	B-ROADS	B-ROUGH	B-UMPED	
B-RICKS	B-ROCKS	B-ROWED	B-UNCES	
B-RIDES	B-ROGUE	B-RUINS	B-UNCOS	

Six letters to seven

B-ABYING	B-EGGING	B-LETTED	B-OINKED	B-RAKING
B-ACHING	B-ELATED	B-LIGHTS	B-OLDENS	B-RAMBLE
B-ACKERS	B-ELATES	B-LINGER	B-OLDEST	B-RANDED
B-ADDIES	B-ENDERS	B-LINKED	B-OMBERS	B-RANKED
B-ADLAND	B-ENDING	B-LINKER	B-ONDING	B-RASHED
B-AFFIES	B-HISTIE	B-LINNED	B-ONEYER	B-RASHER
B-AGGERS	B-ICKERS	B-LIPPED	B-ONUSES	B-RASHES
B-AGGIES	B-IDENTS	B-LISSES	B-OODLES	B-RASHLY
B-AILING	B-IGGING	B-LISTER	B-OOFIER	B-RASSES
B-ALLIES	B-INGLES	B-LITHER	B-OOHING	B-RATTLE
B-ALLIUM	B-INGOES	B-LOBBED	B-OOZIER	B-RAUNCH
B-ALLONS	B-INNING	B-LOCKED	B-OOZILY	B-RAVERS
B-ALLOTS	B-IONICS	B-LOCKER	B-OOZING	B-RAVING
B-ALLOWS	B-ITCHED	B-LOGGER	B-ORATED	B-RAWEST
B-ANALLY	B-ITCHES	B-LOOMED	B-ORATES	B-RAYING
B-ANANAS	B-LACKED	B-LOOPED	B-ORDERS	B-RAZERS
B-ANGERS	B-LACKER	B-LOOPER	B-ORDURE	B-RAZING
B-ANGLED	B-LADDER	B-LOTTED	B-OTHERS	B-REAMED
B-ANGLES	B-LADERS	B-LOTTER	B-OUCHES	B-REASTS
B-ANKERS	B-LADING	B-LOUSED	B-OUGHTS	B-REDING
B-ANTING	B-LAGGED	B-LOUSES	B-OULDER	B-REEDER
B-ARISTA	B-LAGGER	B-LOWERS	B-OUNCES	B-REESTS
B-ARKING	B-LAMING	B-LOWING	B-OVATES	B-REISTS
B-ARRACK	B-LANDER	B-LOWSED	B-OVINES	B-RENNES
B-ARRETS	B-LANKED	B-LOWSES	B-OWLERS	B-RENTER
B-ARROWS	B-LANKER	B-LUBBER	B-OWLING	B-REVETS
B-ASHING	B-LANKLY	B-LUFFED	B-OWNING	B-RICKED
B-ASKING	B-LARNEY	B-LUNGED	B-OXLIKE	B-RICKLE
B-ASSETS	B-LASHES	B-LUNGER	B-RABBLE	B-RIDGED
B-ASSIST	B-LASTED	B-LUNGES	B-RACERS	B-RIDGES
B-ASTERS	B-LASTER	B-LUNKER	B-RACHES	B-RIDING
B-ATONED	B-LATEST	B-LUNTED	B-RACHET	B-RIGHTS
B-EAGLED	B-LATHER	B-LUSHED	B-RACING	B-RIMING
B-EAGLES	B-LATTER	B-LUSHER	B-RACKET	B-RIMMED
B-EANING	B-LAUDED	B-LUSHES	B-RADDED	B-RIMMER
B-EARDED	B-LAWING	B-LUSTER	B-RAGGED	B-RINDED
B-EARING	B-LAZING	B-OATERS	B-RAIDED	B-RINGER
B-EATERS	B-LEAKER	B-OBECHE	B-RAIDER	B-RISKED
B-EATING	B-LEARED	B-OCCIES	B-RAILED	B-RISKER
B-EECHES	B-LEEPED	B-OFFING	B-RAINED	B-ROCHES
B-EERIER	B-LENDER	B-OILERS	B-RAIRDS	B-ROCKED
B-EERILY	B-LESSER	B-OILERY	B-RAISED	B-ROCKET
B-EGGARS	B-LESSES	B-OILING	B-RAISES	B-RODDED

B-ROGUES	B-ROOKIE	B-RUMMER	B-UGGING	B-URGERS
B-ROILED	B-ROOMED	B-RUNTED	B-ULLING	B-URIALS
B-ROKERS	B-ROOSES	B-RUSHED	B-UMBLES	B-URNING
B-ROKING	B-ROTHER	B-RUSHER	B-UMPING	B-URPING
B-ROMALS	B-ROUGHS	B-RUSHES	B-UNDIES	B-USHERS
B-RONZER	B-ROUGHT	B-UCKERS	B-UNIONS	B-UTTERS
B-ROOKED	B-RUCKLE	B-UDDERS	B-UNKING	

Seven letters to eight

B-ADLANDS	B-LARNEYS	B-LOUSING	B-RAIDING	B-RICHTER
B-AILMENT	B-LASTERS	B-LOWBALL	B-RAILING	B-RICKING
B-ALLIUMS	B-LASTING	B-LOWDOWN	B-RAINIER	B-RICKLES
B-ANALITY	B-LATHERS	B-LUBBERS	B-RAINILY	B-RIDGING
B-ANTINGS	B-LAUDING	B-LUFFING	B-RAINING	B-RIGHTEN
B-ARISTAS	B-LEACHED	B-LUNGERS	B-RAISING	B-RIGHTER
B-ARRACKS	B-LEACHER	B-LUNGING	B-RAMBLED	B-RIGHTLY
B-ARTISAN	B-LEACHES	B-LUNKERS	B-RAMBLES	B-RIMLESS
B-ASHLESS	B-LEARIER	B-LUNTING	B-RANCHED	B-RIMMERS
B-ASSISTS	B-LEARING	B-LUSHERS	B-RANCHER	B-RIMMING
B-ATONING	B-LEEPING	B-LUSHING	B-RANCHES	B-RINGERS
B-EAGLING	B-LENDERS	B-LUSTERS	B-RANDIES	B-RINGING
B-EARDING	B-LENDING	B-OARFISH	B-RANDING	B-RISKING
B-EARINGS	B-LETTING	B-OATLIKE	B-RANKING	B-ROACHED
B-EARLIKE	B-LIGHTED	B-OBECHES	B-RASHEST	B-ROACHES
B-EATABLE	B-LIGHTER	B-OINKING	B-RASHING	B-ROADWAY
B-EATINGS	B-LIMBING	B-OLDENED	B-RATCHET	B-ROCKETS
B-EERIEST	B-LINKERS	B-OLDNESS	B-RATLING	B-RODDING
B-ELATING	B-LINKING	B-ONDINGS	B-RATPACK	B-ROGUERY
B-ENDINGS	B-LINNING	B-OOFIEST	B-RATTIER	B-ROGUISH
B-ENDWAYS	B-LIPPING	B-OOZIEST	B-RATTISH	B-ROILING
B-ENDWISE	B-LISTERS	B-ORATING	B-RATTLED	B-RONZERS
B-ESPOUSE	B-LITHELY	B-ORDERED	B-RATTLES	B-ROOKIES
B-ETACISM	B-LITHEST	B-ORDERER	B-REACHED	B-ROOKING
B-ITCHIER	B-LOBBING	B-ORDURES	B-REACHER	B-ROOMIER
B-ITCHILY	B-LOCKAGE	B-OWLLIKE	B-REACHES	B-ROOMING
B-ITCHING	B-LOCKERS	B-RABBLED	B-READING	B-ROTHERS
B-LACKING	B-LOCKING	B-RABBLER	B-REAKING	B-RUMMERS
B-LADDERS	B-LOGGERS	B-RABBLES	B-REAMING	B-RUNCHES
B-LADDERY	B-LOGGING	B-RACHETS	B-REASTED	B-RUSHERS
B-LADINGS	B-LOOMING	B-RACHIAL	B-REECHED	B-RUSHIER
B-LAGGERS	B-LOOPERS	B-RACINGS	B-REECHES	B-RUSHING
B-LAGGING	B-LOOPING	B-RACKETS	B-REEDERS	B-RUSTING
B-LANCHED	B-LOTTERS	B-RADDING	B-REEDING	B-ULLINGS
B-LANCHES	B-LOTTING	B-RAGGIER	B-REGMATA	B-URNINGS
B-LANKEST	B-LOUSIER	B-RAGGING	B-RENNING	B-UTTERED
B-LANKING	B-LOUSILY	B-RAIDERS	B-REVISES	

Eight letters to nine

B-AILMENTS	B-LACKLAND	B-LEACHING	B-LOGGINGS	B-ORDERERS
B-ARTISANS	B-LADDERED	B-LEARIEST	B-LOUSIEST	B-ORDERING
B-EASTINGS	B-LAGGINGS	B-LENDINGS	B-LOWBALLS	B-RABBLERS
B-EERINESS	B-LANCHING	B-LIGHTERS	B-LOWDOWNS	B-RABBLING
B-ELATEDLY	B-LANKNESS	B-LIGHTING	B-LUSTERED	B-RACKETED
B-ESPOUSED	B-LASTINGS	B-LINDWORM	B-LUSTROUS	B-RAGGIEST
B-ESPOUSES	B-LATHERED	B-LOCKABLE	B-OILERIES	B-RAGGINGS
B-ETACISMS	B-LATHERER	B-LOCKAGES	B-OLDENING	B-RAIDINGS
B-ITCHIEST	B-LEACHERS	B-LOCKINGS	B-OOZINESS	B-RAINIEST

B-RAINLESS	B-RATLINGS	B-REACHING	B-RIDGINGS	B-ROADWAYS
B-RAINWASH	B-RATPACKS	B-REASTING	B-RIGHTENS	B-ROOMIEST
B-RAMBLING	B-RATTIEST	B-REECHING	B-RIGHTEST	B-RUSHIEST
B-RANCHERS	B-RATTLING	B-REEDINGS	B-RIGHTISH	B-RUSHINGS
B-RANCHING	B-RAUNCHED	B-REVETTED	B-RINGINGS	B-RUSHLIKE
B-RASHNESS	B-RAUNCHES	B-RICHTEST	B-ROACHING	B-URSIFORM
B-RATCHETS	B-REACHERS	B-RICKYARD	B-ROADSIDE	B-UTTERING

B – End-hooks

Two letters to three

AB-B	DI-B	JA-B	MI-B	RE-B
AL-B	DO-B	JO-B	MO-B	SI-B
AR-B	FA-B	KA-B	NA-B	SO-B
BI-B	GI-B	KO-B	NE-B	TA-B
BO-B	GO-B	LA-B	NO-B	UR-B
DA-B	GU-B	LI-B	NU-B	WE-B
DE-B	HO-B	LO-B	OR-B	YO-B

Three letters to four

BAR-B	CHI-B	FEE-B	HER-B	SIB-B
BIB-B	COB-B	FLU-B	JAM-B	TOM-B
BOA-B	CUR-B	FOR-B	JIB-B	WAR-B
BOO-B	DIE-B	FRA-B	LAM-B	WEM-B
BUR-B	DOO-B	GAM-B	NIM-B	
CAR-B	DOR-B	GAR-B	PRO-B	

Four letters to five

ACER-B	COUR-B	NEEM-B	SLUR-B	ZINE-B
BLUR-B	CUBE-B	PLUM-B	THRO-B	
COOM-B	DEMO-B	SLUB-B	ZEBU-B	

Five letters to six

SCRAM-B	SUPER-B

Six letters to seven

POTHER-B	PROVER-B	REPLUM-B

C – Front-hooks

Two letters to three

C-AA	C-AT	C-HI	C-OO	C-UM
C-AB	C-AW	C-ID	C-OP	C-UP
C-AD	C-AY	C-IS	C-OR	C-UR
C-AG	C-EE	C-IT	C-OS	C-UT
C-AM	C-EL	C-OB	C-OW	
C-AN	C-HA	C-OD	C-OX	
C-AR	C-HE	C-ON	C-OY	

Three letters to four

C-AAS	C-AUK	C-HOW	C-OCH	C-OXY
C-ABA	C-AVA	C-HUB	C-ODA	C-OYS
C-ABS	C-AVE	C-HUG	C-ODE	C-RAG
C-ADS	C-AYS	C-HUM	C-ODS	C-RAM
C-AFF	C-EAS	C-HUT	C-OFF	C-RAN
C-AGE	C-ELL	C-IDE	C-OFT	C-RAP
C-AGS	C-ELS	C-IDS	C-OHO	C-RAW
C-AID	C-ELT	C-ILL	C-OIL	C-RAY
C-AIN	C-ENS	C-ION	C-OKE	C-RED
C-AKE	C-ERE	C-IRE	C-OLD	C-REE
C-ALF	C-ESS	C-ITS	C-OLE	C-REM
C-ALL	C-HAD	C-LAD	C-OMS	C-REW
C-ALP	C-HAM	C-LAG	C-ONE	C-RIB
C-AMA	C-HAO	C-LAM	C-ONS	C-RIM
C-AMP	C-HAP	C-LAP	C-ONY	C-RIT
C-ANE	C-HAS	C-LAT	C-OOF	C-ROC
C-ANN	C-HAT	C-LAW	C-OOM	C-ROW
C-ANT	C-HAW	C-LAY	C-OON	C-RUD
C-ANY	C-HAY	C-LEG	C-OOP	C-RUE
C-APE	C-HER	C-LEW	C-OOS	C-UDS
C-APO	C-HEW	C-LIP	C-OOT	C-UKE
C-ARB	C-HIC	C-LOD	C-OPE	C-UPS
C-ARD	C-HID	C-LOG	C-OPS	C-URB
C-ARE	C-HIN	C-LOP	C-ORD	C-URD
C-ARK	C-HIP	C-LOT	C-ORE	C-URE
C-ARS	C-HIS	C-LOU	C-ORF	C-URN
C-ART	C-HIT	C-LOW	C-ORS	C-UTE
C-ASH	C-HOC	C-LOY	C-OSE	C-UTS
C-ASK	C-HOG	C-OAT	C-OUP	
C-ATE	C-HON	C-OBS	C-OUR	
C-AUF	C-HOP	C-OCA	C-OWL	

Four letters to five

C-ABAS	C-ANNA	C-AVER	C-HANT	C-HILI
C-ABLE	C-ANNS	C-AVES	C-HAPS	C-HILL
C-ACHE	C-ANON	C-AWED	C-HARD	C-HINS
C-ADDY	C-ANTS	C-AXON	C-HARE	C-HIPS
C-AGED	C-APED	C-EASE	C-HARK	C-HITS
C-AGER	C-APER	C-ELLS	C-HARM	C-HIVE
C-AGES	C-APES	C-ELTS	C-HART	C-HIZZ
C-AIDS	C-APOS	C-EORL	C-HATS	C-HOCK
C-AINS	C-ARBS	C-ERED	C-HAVE	C-HOGS
C-AIRN	C-ARDS	C-ERES	C-HAWK	C-HOKE
C-AKED	C-ARED	C-ERIC	C-HAWS	C-HOMA
C-AKES	C-ARES	C-ERNE	C-HAYS	C-HONS
C-ALFS	C-ARET	C-EROS	C-HEAP	C-HOOF
C-ALIF	C-ARKS	C-ESSE	C-HEAT	C-HOOK
C-ALLS	C-ARLE	C-HACK	C-HECK	C-HOPS
C-ALMS	C-ARSE	C-HADS	C-HELP	C-HORE
C-ALPS	C-ARTS	C-HAFF	C-HERE	C-HOSE
C-AMAS	C-ASKS	C-HAFT	C-HEST	C-HOUT
C-AMIS	C-ATES	C-HAIN	C-HETH	C-HOWK
C-AMPS	C-AUKS	C-HAIR	C-HEWS	C-HOWS
C-AMUS	C-AULD	C-HAMS	C-HICK	C-HUBS
C-ANAL	C-AVAS	C-HANG	C-HIDE	C-HUCK
C-ANES	C-AVEL	C-HANK	C-HILD	C-HUFF

C-HUGS	C-LEVE	C-LUNG	C-OVEN	C-RIMS
C-HUMP	C-LICK	C-LUNK	C-OVER	C-RINE
C-HUMS	C-LIED	C-OAST	C-OWED	C-RIPE
C-HUNK	C-LIES	C-OATS	C-OWER	C-RISE
C-HURL	C-LIFT	C-OBIA	C-OWLS	C-RISP
C-HYLE	C-LIMB	C-OCAS	C-OXES	C-RITS
C-IDES	C-LIME	C-ODAS	C-OYER	C-ROCK
C-ILIA	C-LINE	C-ODES	C-RACK	C-ROCS
C-ILLS	C-LING	C-OFFS	C-RAFT	C-RONE
C-INCH	C-LINK	C-OHOS	C-RAGS	C-ROOK
C-IONS	C-LINT	C-OILS	C-RAKE	C-ROON
C-IRES	C-LIPE	C-OKES	C-RAMP	C-RORE
C-LACK	C-LIPS	C-OLDS	C-RAMS	C-ROST
C-LADE	C-LOAM	C-OLES	C-RANK	C-ROUP
C-LADS	C-LOCK	C-OMER	C-RAPE	C-ROUT
C-LAGS	C-LODS	C-ONES	C-RAPS	C-ROWS
C-LAME	C-LOGS	C-ONTO	C-RARE	C-RUCK
C-LAMP	C-LOKE	C-ONUS	C-RASH	C-RUDE
C-LAMS	C-LONE	C-OOFS	C-RATE	C-RUDS
C-LANG	C-LOOP	C-OOMS	C-RAVE	C-RUES
C-LANK	C-LOOT	C-OONS	C-RAWS	C-RUMP
C-LAPS	C-LOPS	C-OOPS	C-RAYS	C-RUSE
C-LASH	C-LOSE	C-OOTS	C-RAZE	C-RUSH
C-LASS	C-LOTE	C-OOZE	C-REAK	C-RUST
C-LAST	C-LOTH	C-OPAL	C-REAM	C-TENE
C-LATS	C-LOTS	C-OPED	C-REDO	C-UKES
C-LAVE	C-LOUD	C-OPEN	C-REDS	C-ULEX
C-LAWS	C-LOUR	C-OPES	C-REED	C-UNDY
C-LAYS	C-LOUS	C-ORAL	C-REEK	C-URBS
C-LEAN	C-LOUT	C-ORBY	C-REEL	C-URDS
C-LEAR	C-LOVE	C-ORDS	C-REES	C-URDY
C-LEAT	C-LOWN	C-ORES	C-REMS	C-URES
C-LEEK	C-LOWS	C-OSES	C-REST	C-URNS
C-LEEP	C-LOYS	C-OUCH	C-REWS	C-UTES
C-LEFT	C-LUCK	C-OULD	C-RIBS	C-UTIS
C-LEGS	C-LUES	C-OUPS	C-RICK	
C-LEPT	C-LUMP	C-OURS	C-RIME	

Five letters to six

C-ABBED	C-ANKER	C-AVELS	C-HANGS	C-HEDER
C-ABLED	C-ANNAS	C-AVERS	C-HANKS	C-HELPS
C-ABLER	C-ANTAR	C-AWING	C-HANTS	C-HEMIC
C-ABLES	C-ANTED	C-AXONS	C-HAPPY	C-HERRY
C-ABLET	C-ANTIC	C-EASED	C-HARDS	C-HESTS
C-ACHED	C-ANYON	C-EASES	C-HARED	C-HETHS
C-ACHES	C-APERS	C-ENTER	C-HARES	C-HEWED
C-AGERS	C-APING	C-ENTRY	C-HARKS	C-HEWER
C-AGING	C-ARETS	C-EORLS	C-HARMS	C-HICKS
C-AIRNS	C-ARKED	C-ERING	C-HARRY	C-HIDED
C-AKING	C-ARLES	C-ERNED	C-HARTS	C-HIDER
C-ALIFS	C-ARSES	C-ERNES	C-HASTE	C-HIDES
C-ALLEE	C-ARSEY	C-ESSES	C-HAUNT	C-HILLS
C-ALLOW	C-ARTEL	C-HACKS	C-HAWED	C-HILLY
C-AMASS	C-ASHED	C-HAFFS	C-HAWKS	C-HINKY
C-AMBER	C-ASHES	C-HAFTS	C-HAZAN	C-HINTS
C-AMPED	C-ASKED	C-HAINS	C-HEAPS	C-HIPPY
C-AMPLE	C-ASTER	C-HAIRS	C-HEAPY	C-HIVED
C-AMPLY	C-AUDAD	C-HAMMY	C-HEATS	C-HIVES
C-ANGLE	C-AUGHT	C-HANCE	C-HECKS	C-HOCKS

C-HOKED	C-LEATS	C-LYING	C-RAFTS	C-RISPS
C-HOKES	C-LEAVE	C-OASTS	C-RAGGY	C-ROCKS
C-HOKEY	C-LEEKS	C-OATER	C-RAKED	C-RONES
C-HOLLA	C-LEEPS	C-OBIAS	C-RAKES	C-ROOKS
C-HOMAS	C-LEFTS	C-OCHES	C-RAMPS	C-ROONS
C-HOOFS	C-LEUCH	C-OCKER	C-RANCH	C-RORES
C-HOOKS	C-LEUGH	C-ODDER	C-RANKS	C-ROTAL
C-HOPPY	C-LEVER	C-ODIST	C-RANTS	C-ROTCH
C-HORAL	C-LEVIS	C-OFFED	C-RAPED	C-ROTON
C-HOSEN	C-LICKS	C-OFFER	C-RAPES	C-ROUPS
C-HOSES	C-LIFTS	C-OILED	C-RARES	C-ROUPY
C-HOUGH	C-LIMAX	C-OILER	C-RASES	C-ROUSE
C-HOUSE	C-LIMBS	C-OLDER	C-RATCH	C-ROUTE
C-HOUTS	C-LIMES	C-OLDIE	C-RATED	C-ROUTS
C-HOWKS	C-LINCH	C-OLLIE	C-RATER	C-ROWDY
C-HUBBY	C-LINES	C-OMBER	C-RATES	C-ROWED
C-HUCKS	C-LINGS	C-OMERS	C-RAVED	C-ROWER
C-HUFFS	C-LINGY	C-ONIUM	C-RAVEN	C-RUCKS
C-HUFFY	C-LINKS	C-ONNED	C-RAVER	C-RUDDY
C-HUMPS	C-LINTS	C-OOPED	C-RAVES	C-RUDER
C-HUNKS	C-LOAMS	C-OORIE	C-RAWLY	C-RUDES
C-HUNKY	C-LOCKS	C-OOZES	C-RAYON	C-RUMEN
C-HURLS	C-LOGGY	C-OPALS	C-RAZED	C-RUMMY
C-HYLES	C-LOKES	C-OPENS	C-RAZES	C-RUMPS
C-ILIUM	C-LONER	C-OPING	C-REACH	C-RUMPY
C-ITHER	C-LOOPS	C-OPTER	C-REAKS	C-RUNCH
C-IVIES	C-LOOTS	C-ORALS	C-REAMS	C-RURAL
C-LACKS	C-LOSED	C-ORDER	C-REAMY	C-RUSES
C-LADES	C-LOSER	C-OSIER	C-REATE	C-RUSTS
C-LAMES	C-LOSES	C-OSMIC	C-REDOS	C-RUSTY
C-LAMMY	C-LOTES	C-OTTAR	C-REEDS	C-TENES
C-LAMPS	C-LOUGH	C-OTTER	C-REEKS	C-UMBER
C-LANKS	C-LOURS	C-OUPED	C-REEKY	C-UPPED
C-LANKY	C-LOUTS	C-OURIE	C-REELS	C-UPPER
C-LASTS	C-LOVER	C-OUTER	C-RESTS	C-URARE
C-LATCH	C-LOVES	C-OVARY	C-REWED	C-URARI
C-LAVER	C-LOWNS	C-OVENS	C-RIANT	C-URATE
C-LAVES	C-LUCKS	C-OVERS	C-RICKS	C-URIAL
C-LAWED	C-LUCKY	C-OVERT	C-RIMED	C-URITE
C-LAWER	C-LUMPS	C-OWING	C-RIMES	C-UTTER
C-LAYED	C-LUMPY	C-OWLED	C-RINES	C-YCLED
C-LEANS	C-LUNCH	C-OWRIE	C-RIPES	C-YESES
C-LEARS	C-LUNKS	C-RACKS	C-RISES	

Six letters to seven

C-ABLETS	C-ANGLES	C-ASHIER	C-HALLAH	C-HARMER
C-ABLING	C-ANKERS	C-ASHING	C-HALLAN	C-HASTEN
C-ACHING	C-ANTARS	C-ASKING	C-HALLOT	C-HATTED
C-ACUMEN	C-ANTING	C-ASTERS	C-HALUTZ	C-HATTER
C-ADDIES	C-ANYONS	C-ASTRAL	C-HAMLET	C-HAUNTS
C-AIRNED	C-ARABIN	C-AULDER	C-HAMPER	C-HAWING
C-ALLEES	C-ARIOSE	C-EASING	C-HANCES	C-HAZANS
C-ALLOWS	C-ARKING	C-ENSURE	C-HANGED	C-HAZZAN
C-AMBERS	C-ARLING	C-ENTERS	C-HANGER	C-HEAPED
C-AMELIA	C-AROUSE	C-ERNING	C-HANTED	C-HEAPER
C-AMISES	C-ARRACK	C-EROTIC	C-HAPPED	C-HEATED
C-AMPING	C-ARRECT	C-HACKED	C-HARING	C-HEATER
C-AMUSES	C-ARTELS	C-HAINED	C-HARKED	C-HEDERS
C-ANGLED	C-ARTFUL	C-HAIRED	C-HARMED	C-HELPED

C-HEWERS	C-LAMBER	C-LOPPED	C-OWLING	C-RINGED
C-HEWING	C-LAMMED	C-LOSERS	C-RACKED	C-RINGER
C-HIDDEN	C-LAMMER	C-LOSING	C-RACKER	C-RIPPLE
C-HIDERS	C-LAMPED	C-LOTTED	C-RACKET	C-RISPED
C-HIDING	C-LAMPER	C-LOTTER	C-RACKLE	C-RITTER
C-HILLED	C-LANGER	C-LOUGHS	C-RAFTED	C-ROCHES
C-HILLER	C-LANKED	C-LOURED	C-RAFTER	C-ROCHET
C-HIPPED	C-LAPPED	C-LOUTED	C-RAGGED	C-ROCKED
C-HIPPER	C-LAPPER	C-LOVERS	C-RAKING	C-ROCKET
C-HIPPIE	C-LASHED	C-LOWNED	C-RAMMED	C-ROOKED
C-HITTER	C-LASHER	C-LUBBER	C-RAMMER	C-ROQUET
C-HIVING	C-LASHES	C-LUCKED	C-RAMPED	C-ROSIER
C-HIZZED	C-LASSES	C-LUMBER	C-RAMPER	C-ROSSER
C-HIZZES	C-LASSIS	C-LUMPED	C-RANKED	C-ROTONS
C-HOCKED	C-LATTER	C-LUMPER	C-RANKER	C-ROUPED
C-HOCKER	C-LAVERS	C-LUNKER	C-RANKLE	C-ROUTES
C-HOKIER	C-LAWING	C-LUSTER	C-RANKLY	C-ROWERS
C-HOKING	C-LAYING	C-OATERS	C-RAPIER	C-ROWING
C-HOLLAS	C-LEANED	C-OCKERS	C-RAPING	C-RUDDED
C-HOOFED	C-LEANER	C-ODISTS	C-RAPPED	C-RUDDLE
C-HOOKED	C-LEANLY	C-OFFERS	C-RAPPER	C-RUDELY
C-HOPPED	C-LEARED	C-OFFING	C-RASHED	C-RUDEST
C-HOPPER	C-LEAVED	C-OILERS	C-RASHER	C-RUMBLE
C-HORDED	C-LEAVER	C-OILING	C-RASHES	C-RUMBLY
C-HOUGHS	C-LEAVES	C-OLDEST	C-RATERS	C-RUMENS
C-HOUSED	C-LEEPED	C-OLDIES	C-RATING	C-RUMPED
C-HOUSER	C-LICHES	C-OLDISH	C-RAUNCH	C-RUMPLE
C-HOUSES	C-LICKED	C-OLLIES	C-RAVENS	C-RUMPLY
C-HUCKLE	C-LICKER	C-OMBERS	C-RAVERS	C-RUNKLE
C-HUFFED	C-LIFTED	C-ONIUMS	C-RAVING	C-RUSHED
C-HUFFER	C-LIMBED	C-ONNING	C-RAYONS	C-RUSHER
C-HUGGED	C-LIMBER	C-OOPING	C-RAZING	C-RUSHES
C-HUGGER	C-LINGER	C-OPTERS	C-REAKED	C-RUSTED
C-HUMMED	C-LINKED	C-ORACLE	C-REAMED	C-ULEXES
C-HUMPED	C-LINKER	C-ORDERS	C-REAMER	C-ULLING
C-HUNTER	C-LIPPED	C-OSIERS	C-REATES	C-UMBERS
C-HUPPAH	C-LIPPER	C-OTTARS	C-REELED	C-UNDIES
C-HUTZPA	C-LIPPIE	C-OTTERS	C-REMATE	C-UPPERS
C-ILICES	C-LITTER	C-OUCHED	C-RESTED	C-UPPING
C-INCHED	C-LIVERS	C-OUCHES	C-RIBBED	C-URARES
C-INCHES	C-LOBBER	C-OUPING	C-RIBBER	C-URARIS
C-LACKED	C-LOCKED	C-OURIER	C-RICKED	C-URATES
C-LACKER	C-LOCKER	C-OUTERS	C-RICKEY	C-URITES
C-LADDER	C-LOGGED	C-OUTHER	C-RIMING	C-UTISES
C-LADDIE	C-LOGGER	C-OUVERT	C-RIMMER	C-UTTERS
C-LAGGED	C-LONERS	C-OVERED	C-RIMPLE	

Seven letters to eight

C-ABLINGS	C-AROUSER	C-ENTERED	C-HAMLETS	C-HARMERS
C-AMASSES	C-AROUSES	C-ENTRIES	C-HAMPERS	C-HARMFUL
C-AMBERED	C-ARRACKS	C-ENTRISM	C-HANDLER	C-HARMING
C-AMELIAS	C-ARRIAGE	C-ENTRIST	C-HANGERS	C-HAROSET
C-ANGLING	C-ASHLESS	C-HACKING	C-HANGING	C-HARPIES
C-ANNULAR	C-ASTABLE	C-HADARIM	C-HANTING	C-HARRIER
C-ANTINGS	C-ASTEISM	C-HAINING	C-HAPLESS	C-HASTENS
C-APSIDAL	C-AULDEST	C-HAIRING	C-HAPPIER	C-HATTERS
C-ARABINS	C-ENSURED	C-HALLAHS	C-HAPPIES	C-HATTING
C-AROUSAL	C-ENSURER	C-HALLANS	C-HAPPING	C-HAUNTED
C-AROUSED	C-ENSURES	C-HALLOTH	C-HARKING	C-HAUNTER

C-HAZANIM	C-HUPPAHS	C-LIPPING	C-RACKETS	C-RIPPLED
C-HAZZANS	C-HUTZPAH	C-LITORAL	C-RACKING	C-RIPPLER
C-HEAPING	C-HUTZPAS	C-LITTERS	C-RAFTERS	C-RIPPLES
C-HEATERS	C-INCHING	C-LOBBERS	C-RAFTING	C-RISPING
C-HEATING	C-LACKERS	C-LOCKERS	C-RAGGIER	C-RITTERS
C-HELPING	C-LACKING	C-LOCKING	C-RAMMERS	C-ROCHETS
C-HERRIED	C-LADDERS	C-LOGGERS	C-RAMMING	C-ROCKERY
C-HERRIES	C-LADDIES	C-LOGGIER	C-RAMPERS	C-ROCKETS
C-HEWABLE	C-LAGGING	C-LOGGING	C-RAMPING	C-ROCKING
C-HICKORY	C-LAMBERS	C-LOPPING	C-RANCHED	C-ROOKERY
C-HIDINGS	C-LAMMERS	C-LOSABLE	C-RANCHES	C-ROOKING
C-HILDING	C-LAMMING	C-LOSINGS	C-RANKEST	C-ROQUETS
C-HILLERS	C-LAMPERS	C-LOTTERS	C-RANKING	C-ROSIERS
C-HILLIER	C-LAMPING	C-LOTTING	C-RANKISH	C-ROSSERS
C-HILLING	C-LANGERS	C-LOURING	C-RANKLED	C-ROTCHES
C-HINKIER	C-LANKIER	C-LOUTING	C-RANKLES	C-ROUCHES
C-HIPPIER	C-LANKING	C-LOVERED	C-RAPPERS	C-ROUPIER
C-HIPPIES	C-LAPPERS	C-LOWNING	C-RAPPING	C-ROUPILY
C-HIPPING	C-LAPPING	C-LUBBERS	C-RASHERS	C-ROUPING
C-HIRLING	C-LASHERS	C-LUCKIER	C-RASHING	C-ROWDIES
C-HITTERS	C-LASHING	C-LUCKING	C-RATCHES	C-RUDDIER
C-HITTING	C-LATCHED	C-LUMBERS	C-RAUNCHY	C-RUDDING
C-HIZZING	C-LATCHES	C-LUMPERS	C-RAVENED	C-RUDDLED
C-HOCKING	C-LAWLESS	C-LUMPIER	C-RAVINGS	C-RUDDLES
C-HOKIEST	C-LAWLIKE	C-LUMPING	C-REAKING	C-RUMBLED
C-HOLLERS	C-LEANERS	C-LUMPISH	C-REAMERS	C-RUMBLES
C-HOOFING	C-LEANEST	C-LUNCHES	C-REAMIER	C-RUMMIER
C-HOOKIES	C-LEANING	C-LUNKERS	C-REAMING	C-RUMMIES
C-HOOKING	C-LEARING	C-LUSTERS	C-REEKIER	C-RUMPING
C-HOPPERS	C-LEAVERS	C-OCREATE	C-REELING	C-RUMPLED
C-HOPPIER	C-LEAVING	C-OFFERED	C-REMAINS	C-RUMPLES
C-HOPPING	C-LEEPING	C-OLDNESS	C-REMATED	C-RUNCHES
C-HORDING	C-LEMMING	C-ORACLES	C-REMATES	C-RUNKLED
C-HOUSERS	C-LICKERS	C-OSMOSES	C-RESTING	C-RUNKLES
C-HOUSING	C-LICKING	C-OTTERED	C-RIBBERS	C-RUSHERS
C-HUCKLES	C-LIMBERS	C-OUCHING	C-RIBBING	C-RUSHING
C-HUFFIER	C-LIMBING	C-OULDEST	C-RIBWORK	C-RUSTIER
C-HUFFING	C-LINCHES	C-OVARIES	C-RICKETS	C-RUSTILY
C-HUGGERS	C-LINGERS	C-OVERAGE	C-RICKING	C-RUSTING
C-HUGGING	C-LINGIER	C-OVERALL	C-RIMMERS	C-ULLINGS
C-HUMMING	C-LINKERS	C-OVERING	C-RIMPLED	C-UMBERED
C-HUMPING	C-LINKING	C-OVERLET	C-RIMPLES	C-UMBROUS
C-HUNKIER	C-LIPPERS	C-OVERTLY	C-RINGERS	C-UNIFORM
C-HUNTERS	C-LIPPIES	C-RACKERS	C-RINGING	C-UPPINGS

Eight letters to nine

C-AMPHORIC	C-ENTRISTS	C-HAZZANIM	C-HUFFIEST	C-LICKINGS
C-ANNULATE	C-HALUTZIM	C-HEATABLE	C-HUNKIEST	C-LINGIEST
C-AROUSALS	C-HANDLERS	C-HEATINGS	C-HUTZPAHS	C-LIPPINGS
C-AROUSERS	C-HANUKIAH	C-HEMOSTAT	C-LANKIEST	C-LITTERED
C-AROUSING	C-HAPPIEST	C-HERRYING	C-LAPBOARD	C-LOCKINGS
C-ARRIAGES	C-HARMLESS	C-HIDLINGS	C-LAPPERED	C-LOGGIEST
C-ASTEISMS	C-HAROSETH	C-HILLIEST	C-LAPPINGS	C-LUCKIEST
C-AVIARIES	C-HAROSETS	C-HINKIEST	C-LASHINGS	C-LUMPIEST
C-EASELESS	C-HASTENED	C-HIPPIEST	C-LATCHING	C-LUSTERED
C-ENSURERS	C-HASTENER	C-HIPPINGS	C-LAVATION	C-OFFERING
C-ENSURING	C-HATTERED	C-HOPPIEST	C-LEANINGS	C-OTTERING
C-ENTERING	C-HAUNTERS	C-HOPPINGS	C-LEANNESS	C-OVERABLE
C-ENTRISMS	C-HAUNTING	C-HOROLOGY	C-LEAVINGS	C-OVERAGES

C-OVERALLS	C-RANKNESS	C-RESTLESS	C-ROQUETED	C-RUMPLING
C-OVERLETS	C-RAUNCHED	C-RETINOID	C-ROQUETTE	C-RUNKLING
C-OVERSLIP	C-RAUNCHES	C-RIBBINGS	C-ROUPIEST	C-RUSTIEST
C-OVERTURE	C-RAVENING	C-RIBWORKS	C-RUDDIEST	C-RUSTLESS
C-RACKINGS	C-REAMIEST	C-RIMELESS	C-RUDDLING	C-UMBERING
C-RAFTSMAN	C-REEKIEST	C-RIMPLING	C-RUDENESS	C-UNIFORMS
C-RAFTSMEN	C-REMASTER	C-RINGINGS	C-RUMBLIER	C-UPBEARER
C-RAGGIEST	C-REMATING	C-RIPPLERS	C-RUMBLING	
C-RANCHING	C-RENATURE	C-RIPPLING	C-RUMMIEST	
C-RANKLING	C-RESTINGS	C-ROCKETED	C-RUMPLIER	

C – End-hooks

Two letters to three

AR-C	HO-C	MO-C	PE-C	SO-C
BA-C	LA-C	MY-C	PI-C	TE-C
DO-C	MA-C	OR-C	RE-C	TI-C
HI-C	MI-C	PA-C	SI-C	TO-C

Three letters to four

ABA-C	CHI-C	MAR-C	TOR-C
ALE-C	DIS-C	SAI-C	ZIN-C
BAN-C	HUI-C	SYN-C	

Four letters to five

ANTI-C	COSE-C	LOTI-C	SERA-C	VARE-C
ARTI-C	DARI-C	MAGI-C	TARO-C	YOGI-C
BOBA-C	DURO-C	MALI-C	TOPI-C	YONI-C
CODE-C	ILEA-C	MANI-C	TORI-C	
CONI-C	ILIA-C	RABI-C	TRON-C	

Five letters to six

ACINI-C	CHOLI-C	FUNDI-C	LENTI-C	ORGIA-C
AGAMI-C	COCCI-C	FUNGI-C	LIMBI-C	PARSE-C
BUSTI-C	CULTI-C	IAMBI-C	MANIA-C	THYMI-C
CALPA-C	FILMI-C	KALPA-C	MYTHI-C	TRAGI-C

Six letters to seven

ALKALI-C	EMBOLI-C	NUCLEI-C	PYLORI-C	THALLI-C
CARDIA-C	EPHEBI-C	PHALLI-C	RHOMBI-C	TROPHI-C
COLONI-C	ISTHMI-C	PRIAPI-C	SCORIA-C	

Seven letters to eight

AMMONIA-C	CHIASMI-C	ELENCHI-C	RHYTHMI-C	TYMPANI-C
AMNESIA-C	CHORAGI-C	EPIGONI-C	SYLLABI-C	
APHASIA-C	CHOREGI-C	NURAGHI-C	THALAMI-C	
BULIMIA-C	DACTYLI-C	OMPHALI-C	TSUNAMI-C	

Eight letters to nine

EGOMANIA-C	MACARONI-C	PRODROMI-C	VIRTUOSI-C
FASCISTI-C	PARANOIA-C	SYMPOSIA-C	ZOOPHORI-C
INSOMNIA-C	PAROEMIA-C	TROCHILI-C	

D – Front-hooks

Two letters to three

D-AB	D-AW	D-IN	D-ON	D-UH
D-AD	D-AY	D-IS	D-OO	D-UN
D-AE	D-EE	D-IT	D-OP	D-UP
D-AG	D-EF	D-OB	D-OR	D-YE
D-AH	D-EL	D-OD	D-OS	D-ZO
D-AL	D-EN	D-OE	D-OW	
D-AM	D-EX	D-OF	D-OY	
D-AN	D-ID	D-OH	D-SO	
D-AS	D-IF	D-OM	D-UG	

Three letters to four

D-ABS	D-EAR	D-INK	D-ORB	D-RIB
D-ACE	D-ECO	D-INS	D-ORE	D-RIP
D-ADO	D-EEK	D-IRE	D-ORS	D-ROW
D-ADS	D-EEN	D-IRK	D-ORT	D-RUB
D-AFF	D-EFT	D-ISH	D-OSE	D-RUG
D-AFT	D-EKE	D-ITA	D-OUK	D-RUM
D-AGO	D-ELF	D-ITS	D-OUP	D-SOS
D-AGS	D-ELL	D-JIN	D-OUR	D-UDS
D-AHS	D-ELS	D-OAT	D-OUT	D-UGS
D-AIS	D-ELT	D-OBS	D-OWL	D-UKE
D-ALE	D-EME	D-ODS	D-OWN	D-ULE
D-ALS	D-EMO	D-OES	D-OWT	D-UMP
D-ALT	D-ENE	D-OFF	D-OXY	D-UNS
D-AMP	D-ENS	D-OHS	D-OYS	D-UPS
D-ANT	D-ERE	D-OLE	D-RAD	D-URE
D-ARB	D-ERN	D-OMS	D-RAG	D-URN
D-ARE	D-HOW	D-ONE	D-RAM	D-YAD
D-ARK	D-ICE	D-ONS	D-RAP	D-YES
D-ART	D-ICH	D-OOM	D-RAT	D-ZHO
D-ASH	D-ICK	D-OON	D-RAW	D-ZOS
D-ATE	D-IFF	D-OOR	D-RAY	
D-AWN	D-IFS	D-OOS	D-REE	
D-AYS	D-ILL	D-OPE	D-REG	
D-EAN	D-IMP	D-OPS	D-REW	

Four letters to five

D-ABBA	D-ALLY	D-ARIS	D-EANS	D-EKED
D-ACES	D-ALTS	D-ARKS	D-EARN	D-EKES
D-ADDY	D-AMPS	D-ARTS	D-EARS	D-ELFS
D-ADOS	D-ANCE	D-ASHY	D-EATH	D-ELLS
D-AFFY	D-ANTS	D-ATES	D-EAVE	D-ELTS
D-AINE	D-ARBS	D-AUNT	D-ECAD	D-EMES
D-AIRY	D-ARED	D-AWED	D-ECOS	D-EMIC
D-ALES	D-ARES	D-AWNS	D-EELY	D-EMIT

D-EMOS	D-IRKS	D-OWED	D-READ	D-ROWS
D-EMPT	D-ITAS	D-OWER	D-REAM	D-RUBS
D-ENES	D-ITCH	D-OWLS	D-REAR	D-RUGS
D-ERED	D-JINN	D-OWLY	D-RECK	D-RUMS
D-ERES	D-JINS	D-OWNS	D-REED	D-RUSE
D-ERNS	D-OATS	D-OWSE	D-REES	D-UKES
D-EROS	D-OFFS	D-OWTS	D-REGS	D-ULES
D-ESSE	D-OILY	D-RACK	D-RENT	D-UMBO
D-EVIL	D-OLES	D-RAFF	D-REST	D-UMPY
D-EXES	D-ONER	D-RAFT	D-RIBS	D-UNCE
D-HOLE	D-OOMS	D-RAGS	D-RICE	D-URES
D-HOLS	D-OOZY	D-RAIL	D-RIFT	D-URNS
D-HOWS	D-OPED	D-RAIN	D-RILL	D-WALE
D-ICED	D-OPES	D-RAKE	D-RINK	D-WANG
D-ICER	D-ORAD	D-RAMS	D-RIPS	D-WELL
D-ICES	D-ORBS	D-RANK	D-RIPT	D-WELT
D-ICKY	D-ORTS	D-RANT	D-RIVE	D-WILE
D-ILLS	D-OSES	D-RAPE	D-ROIL	D-WINE
D-ILLY	D-OUKS	D-RAPS	D-ROLE	D-YADS
D-IMPS	D-OUMA	D-RATS	D-ROLL	D-ZHOS
D-INGO	D-OUPS	D-RAVE	D-RONE	
D-INKS	D-OUTS	D-RAWN	D-ROOK	
D-INKY	D-OVEN	D-RAWS	D-ROOP	
D-IOTA	D-OVER	D-RAYS	D-ROVE	

Five letters to six

D-ABBAS	D-EDUCE	D-INNER	D-RAGEE	D-RONES
D-ABBED	D-EDUCT	D-IOTAS	D-RAGGY	D-ROOKS
D-ACKER	D-EGGED	D-IRKED	D-RAILS	D-ROOPS
D-ADDED	D-EIDER	D-ISHES	D-RAINS	D-ROOPY
D-ADDLE	D-EJECT	D-ITHER	D-RAKES	D-ROUTH
D-AFTER	D-EKING	D-JEBEL	D-RANTS	D-ROVED
D-AGGER	D-ELATE	D-JEMBE	D-RAPED	D-ROVER
D-AMPED	D-ELOPE	D-JINNI	D-RAPER	D-ROVES
D-AMPLY	D-ELUDE	D-JINNS	D-RAPES	D-ROWND
D-ANGER	D-ELVER	D-OATER	D-RAWER	D-RUGGY
D-ANGLE	D-ELVES	D-OCKER	D-RAWLY	D-RUMLY
D-ANKER	D-EMITS	D-ODDER	D-RAYED	D-RUMMY
D-ANTED	D-EMOTE	D-OFFED	D-READS	D-RUSES
D-APPLE	D-EMURE	D-OFFER	D-REAMS	D-UDDER
D-ARGLE	D-ERING	D-OILED	D-REAMY	D-UMBER
D-ARKED	D-ESSES	D-OLENT	D-REARS	D-UMBOS
D-ASHED	D-EVILS	D-ONNED	D-RECKS	D-UMPED
D-ASHES	D-EXIES	D-OPING	D-RICES	D-UNCES
D-AUNTS	D-HOLES	D-ORMER	D-RIFTS	D-UNDER
D-AVENS	D-HOOLY	D-OTTER	D-RIFTY	D-UNITE
D-AWING	D-HURRA	D-OUGHT	D-RILLS	D-UNKED
D-AWNED	D-ICERS	D-OUMAS	D-RINKS	D-UPPED
D-AWNER	D-ICIER	D-OUTED	D-RIVEL	D-URNED
D-EANED	D-ICING	D-OUTER	D-RIVEN	D-WALES
D-EARED	D-ICKER	D-OVENS	D-RIVER	D-WANGS
D-EARLY	D-IGGED	D-OVERS	D-RIVES	D-WELLS
D-EARNS	D-IMPLY	D-OWING	D-ROGER	D-WILES
D-EARTH	D-INGLE	D-OWNED	D-ROGUE	D-WINED
D-EAVED	D-INKED	D-OWNER	D-ROILS	D-WINES
D-EAVES	D-INKER	D-RAFFS	D-ROLES	
D-ECADS	D-INNED	D-RAFTS	D-ROLLS	

Six letters to seven

D-ACKERS	D-EFTEST	D-INNING	D-RAGGLE	D-ROOPED
D-ADDIES	D-EGGING	D-IREFUL	D-RAILED	D-ROUGHT
D-ADDING	D-EJECTA	D-IRKING	D-RAINED	D-ROUTHS
D-ADDLED	D-EJECTS	D-ITCHED	D-RAMMED	D-ROVERS
D-ADDLES	D-ELAPSE	D-ITCHES	D-RANTED	D-ROVING
D-AFFIES	D-ELATED	D-IZZARD	D-RAPERS	D-ROWNDS
D-AGGERS	D-ELATES	D-JEBELS	D-RAPIER	D-RUBBED
D-ALLIED	D-ELOPED	D-JEMBES	D-RAPING	D-RUBBER
D-ALLIES	D-ELOPES	D-JIBBAH	D-RAPPED	D-RUGGED
D-AMPING	D-ELUDED	D-OATERS	D-RATTED	D-RUGGER
D-ANGERS	D-ELUDER	D-OCKERS	D-RAUGHT	D-RUMBLE
D-ANGLED	D-ELUDES	D-OFFERS	D-RAWING	D-RUMMER
D-ANGLER	D-ELVERS	D-OFFING	D-RAYING	D-UBIETY
D-ANGLES	D-EMERGE	D-OLLIES	D-READER	D-UCKERS
D-ANTING	D-EMOTED	D-ONNING	D-REAMED	D-UDDERS
D-APPLES	D-EMOTES	D-OODLES	D-REAMER	D-ULLING
D-ARGLES	D-EMURED	D-ORMERS	D-REARER	D-ULOSES
D-ARKING	D-EMURES	D-OTTERS	D-RIBBED	D-ULOSIS
D-ARLING	D-EPOSES	D-OUCHED	D-RIBBER	D-UMPIES
D-ASHIER	D-EVOLVE	D-OUCHES	D-RIBLET	D-UMPING
D-ASHING	D-HURRAS	D-OUTERS	D-RIFTED	D-UNITES
D-AUDING	D-ICIEST	D-OUTING	D-RILLED	D-UNKING
D-AUNTER	D-ICINGS	D-OVENED	D-RIPPED	D-UNNEST
D-AWNERS	D-ICKERS	D-OVERED	D-RIPPER	D-UNSHED
D-AWNING	D-ICKIER	D-OWLIER	D-RIVELS	D-UPPING
D-EANING	D-IGGING	D-OWNERS	D-RIVERS	D-URNING
D-EARING	D-IGNIFY	D-OWNING	D-RIVING	D-WELLED
D-EARTHS	D-IMPLED	D-RABBET	D-ROGERS	D-WINDLE
D-EATHLY	D-INGLES	D-RABBLE	D-ROGUES	D-WINING
D-EAVING	D-INGOES	D-RAFTED	D-ROILED	D-YESTER
D-EDUCED	D-INKIER	D-RAFTER	D-ROLLED	
D-EDUCES	D-INKING	D-RAGEES	D-ROLLER	
D-EDUCTS	D-INNERS	D-RAGGED	D-ROOKED	

Seven letters to eight

D-ADDLING	D-ELUSORY	D-JELLABA	D-RAMMING	D-RIPPING
D-ALLYING	D-EMERGED	D-JIBBAHS	D-RANTING	D-ROILING
D-ANGERED	D-EMERGES	D-OLOROSO	D-RAPIERS	D-ROLLING
D-ANGLERS	D-EMERSED	D-ONENESS	D-RAPPING	D-ROOKING
D-ANGLING	D-EMITTED	D-OUCHING	D-RATTING	D-ROOPIER
D-ARRAIGN	D-EMOTING	D-OVENING	D-RAWINGS	D-ROOPING
D-ASHIEST	D-EMOTION	D-OVERING	D-READERS	D-ROVINGS
D-AUNTERS	D-EMURING	D-OWLIEST	D-READING	D-ROWNDED
D-AWNINGS	D-ENOUNCE	D-RABBETS	D-REAMERS	D-RUBBERS
D-ECURIES	D-EPILATE	D-RABBLED	D-REAMIER	D-RUBBING
D-EDUCING	D-EPURATE	D-RABBLER	D-REAMING	D-RUGGERS
D-EJECTED	D-ESCRIBE	D-RABBLES	D-REARING	D-RUGGIER
D-ELAPSED	D-EVOLVED	D-RAFFISH	D-RIBBERS	D-RUGGING
D-ELAPSES	D-EVOLVES	D-RAFTERS	D-RIBBING	D-RUMBLED
D-ELATING	D-HOOLIES	D-RAFTING	D-RIBLETS	D-RUMBLES
D-ELATION	D-HURRIES	D-RAGGIER	D-RIFTIER	D-RUMMERS
D-ELOPING	D-ICKIEST	D-RAGGING	D-RIFTING	D-RUMMIES
D-ELUDERS	D-INGOING	D-RAGGLED	D-RILLING	D-UPLYING
D-ELUDING	D-INKIEST	D-RAGGLES	D-RINKING	D-WELLING
D-ELUSION	D-ITCHING	D-RAILING	D-RIPPERS	D-WINDLED
D-ELUSIVE	D-IZZARDS	D-RAINING	D-RIPPIER	D-WINDLES

Eight letters to nine

D-ALLIANCE	D-ELATIONS	D-EPILATED	D-IREFULLY	D-RIFTLESS
D-ANGERING	D-ELUSIONS	D-EPILATES	D-JELLABAH	D-RIVELLED
D-ANGLINGS	D-EMERGING	D-EPILATOR	D-JELLABAS	D-ROLLINGS
D-ARRAIGNS	D-EMERSION	D-EPURATED	D-RABBLERS	D-ROOPIEST
D-EBAUCHES	D-EMISSION	D-EPURATES	D-RABBLING	D-ROUTHIER
D-ECAUDATE	D-EMISSIVE	D-ESCRIBED	D-RAFTINGS	D-ROWNDING
D-EDUCIBLE	D-EMITTING	D-ESCRIBES	D-RAFTSMAN	D-RUBBINGS
D-EDUCTION	D-EMOTIONS	D-EVALUATE	D-RAFTSMEN	D-RUGGIEST
D-EDUCTIVE	D-EMULSIFY	D-EVOLVING	D-RAGGIEST	D-RUMBLING
D-EJECTING	D-ENERVATE	D-EXTRORSE	D-RAGGLING	D-UBIETIES
D-EJECTION	D-ENOUNCED	D-IGNIFIED	D-REAMIEST	D-WELLINGS
D-ELAPSING	D-ENOUNCES	D-IGNIFIES	D-RIFTIEST	D-WINDLING

D – End-hooks

Two letters to three

AD-D	DO-D	KI-D	NO-D	TE-D
AI-D	EL-D	LA-D	OD-D	TI-D
AN-D	EN-D	LI-D	OR-D	TO-D
AR-D	FA-D	LO-D	OU-D	UR-D
BA-D	FE-D	MA-D	PA-D	WE-D
BE-D	GI-D	ME-D	PE-D	YA-D
BI-D	GO-D	MI-D	PO-D	YO-D
BO-D	HA-D	MO-D	RE-D	
DA-D	HI-D	MU-D	SO-D	
DI-D	HO-D	NE-D	TA-D	

Three letters to four

ACE-D	CRU-D	GAU-D	LEE-D	PIE-D
AGE-D	CUE-D	GEE-D	LEU-D	POO-D
AKE-D	CUR-D	GEL-D	LEW-D	PRO-D
AMI-D	DAW-D	GIE-D	LIE-D	QUA-D
APE-D	DEE-D	GOA-D	LIN-D	RAI-D
APO-D	DEI-D	GOO-D	LOR-D	RAN-D
ARE-D	DIE-D	HAE-D	LOU-D	RED-D
AWE-D	DOW-D	HAN-D	MAN-D	REE-D
AXE-D	DUE-D	HEN-D	MAR-D	REN-D
BAL-D	DYE-D	HER-D	MEE-D	RIN-D
BAN-D	EAR-D	HIE-D	MEL-D	ROE-D
BAR-D	ECO-D	HIN-D	MEN-D	ROO-D
BEN-D	EKE-D	HOE-D	MIL-D	RUD-D
BIN-D	ERE-D	HON-D	MOL-D	RUE-D
BON-D	EYE-D	HOO-D	MOO-D	RUN-D
BOR-D	FAN-D	HUE-D	NEE-D	SAI-D
BRA-D	FAR-D	HYE-D	NIE-D	SAN-D
BRO-D	FEE-D	ICE-D	NUR-D	SAR-D
BUN-D	FEN-D	IRE-D	NYE-D	SEE-D
BUR-D	FEU-D	JEE-D	OPE-D	SEL-D
CAR-D	FIN-D	KAE-D	ORA-D	SEN-D
CHA-D	FON-D	KAI-D	OWE-D	SHA-D
CHI-D	FOR-D	KIN-D	PAN-D	SHE-D
COL-D	FOU-D	KON-D	PAR-D	SIN-D
CON-D	FUN-D	LAR-D	PEE-D	SKI-D
COR-D	GAE-D	LEA-D	PEN-D	SOL-D

SUD-D	TAE-D	TIN-D	WAD-D	WIN-D
SUE-D	TEA-D	TOE-D	WAI-D	WOO-D
SUI-D	TEE-D	TUN-D	WAN-D	WYN-D
SUR-D	TEL-D	TYE-D	WAR-D	YAR-D
SYE-D	TEN-D	USE-D	WEE-D	YEA-D
SYN-D	TIE-D	VIE-D	WEN-D	YON-D

Four letters to five

ABBE-D	CAPE-D	DYKE-D	HARE-D	LOBE-D
ABLE-D	CARE-D	EASE-D	HATE-D	LOME-D
ACHE-D	CASE-D	EAVE-D	HAUL-D	LOOR-D
ACNE-D	CAUL-D	ECHE-D	HAZE-D	LOPE-D
ACRE-D	CAVE-D	EDGE-D	HEAL-D	LOSE-D
ADZE-D	CEDE-D	ELAN-D	HEAR-D	LOUN-D
AGUE-D	CERE-D	ERNE-D	HELE-D	LOVE-D
AIDE-D	CHAR-D	FACE-D	HIDE-D	LOWE-D
ALAN-D	CIDE-D	FADE-D	HIKE-D	LOWN-D
ALKY-D	CITE-D	FAKE-D	HIRE-D	LUBE-D
ALOE-D	CLOU-D	FAME-D	HIVE-D	LUGE-D
AMEN-D	CLUE-D	FARE-D	HOAR-D	LURE-D
ANTE-D	CODE-D	FATE-D	HOKE-D	LUTE-D
APAY-D	COKE-D	FAUR-D	HOLE-D	LYSE-D
AREA-D	COLE-D	FAZE-D	HOME-D	LYTE-D
ARED-D	CONE-D	FETE-D	HONE-D	MACE-D
ARLE-D	COPE-D	FIFE-D	HOPE-D	MANE-D
ARSE-D	CORE-D	FIKE-D	HOSE-D	MASE-D
AXLE-D	COSE-D	FILE-D	HOVE-D	MATE-D
BAKE-D	COTE-D	FINE-D	HYPE-D	MAUN-D
BALE-D	COUR-D	FIRE-D	IDLE-D	MAZE-D
BANE-D	COVE-D	FLUE-D	ILIA-D	MENE-D
BARE-D	COZE-D	FRAU-D	ISLE-D	MERE-D
BASE-D	CREE-D	FREE-D	IZAR-D	METE-D
BATE-D	CROW-D	FUME-D	JADE-D	MEVE-D
BAYE-D	CUBE-D	FUSE-D	JAPE-D	MIKE-D
BEAR-D	CURE-D	FUZE-D	JIBE-D	MIME-D
BEMA-D	DALE-D	FYKE-D	JIVE-D	MINE-D
BETE-D	DARE-D	GADI-D	JOBE-D	MIRE-D
BIDE-D	DATE-D	GAGE-D	JOKE-D	MONA-D
BIKE-D	DAZE-D	GAME-D	JOLE-D	MOPE-D
BILE-D	DEKE-D	GAPE-D	JUKE-D	MOSE-D
BLEE-D	DELE-D	GATE-D	KITE-D	MOTE-D
BLIN-D	DERE-D	GAZE-D	KNEE-D	MOVE-D
BLUE-D	DICE-D	GIBE-D	LACE-D	MOZE-D
BOAR-D	DIKE-D	GIVE-D	LADE-D	MULE-D
BODE-D	DINE-D	GLEE-D	LAIR-D	MURE-D
BOKE-D	DITE-D	GLUE-D	LAKE-D	MUSE-D
BONE-D	DIVE-D	GOOL-D	LAME-D	MUTE-D
BOOR-D	DOLE-D	GORE-D	LASE-D	NAME-D
BORE-D	DOME-D	GRAN-D	LATE-D	NAPE-D
BOUN-D	DOPE-D	GREE-D	LAVE-D	NIDE-D
BRAN-D	DOSE-D	GRIN-D	LAZE-D	NIXE-D
BREE-D	DOTE-D	GRUE-D	LEME-D	NOMA-D
BREI-D	DOVE-D	GUAR-D	LERE-D	NOSE-D
BROO-D	DOZE-D	GYBE-D	LIAR-D	NOTE-D
BYDE-D	DREE-D	GYRE-D	LIKE-D	NOUL-D
BYKE-D	DUDE-D	GYVE-D	LIME-D	NUKE-D
CAGE-D	DUKE-D	HADE-D	LINE-D	OCTA-D
CAKE-D	DUPE-D	HALE-D	LITE-D	OGLE-D
CANE-D	DURE-D	HAME-D	LIVE-D	OOZE-D

PACE-D	RARE-D	SIDE-D	THIR-D	VISE-D
PAGE-D	RASE-D	SILE-D	TICE-D	VOLE-D
PALE-D	RATE-D	SINE-D	TIDE-D	VOTE-D
PANE-D	RAVE-D	SIPE-D	TILE-D	WADE-D
PARE-D	RAZE-D	SIRE-D	TIME-D	WAGE-D
PATE-D	READ-D	SITE-D	TINE-D	WAKE-D
PAVE-D	REDE-D	SIZE-D	TIRE-D	WALE-D
PAYS-D	REKE-D	SKEE-D	TOGE-D	WAME-D
PENE-D	RICE-D	SLUE-D	TOKE-D	WANE-D
PIKE-D	RILE-D	SNEE-D	TOLE-D	WARE-D
PILE-D	RIME-D	SOLE-D	TONE-D	WAVE-D
PINE-D	RIPE-D	SOLI-D	TOPE-D	WEAL-D
PIPE-D	RIVE-D	SORE-D	TOSE-D	WEIR-D
PIZE-D	ROBE-D	SOWN-D	TOTE-D	WEXE-D
PLEA-D	RODE-D	SPAE-D	TOZE-D	WIEL-D
PLIE-D	ROKE-D	SPAR-D	TREE-D	WIFE-D
POKE-D	ROPE-D	SPAY-D	TRIE-D	WILE-D
POLE-D	ROSE-D	SPIE-D	TRUE-D	WINE-D
PORE-D	ROTE-D	SPUE-D	TUBE-D	WIPE-D
POSE-D	ROVE-D	STED-D	TUNE-D	WIRE-D
POTE-D	RULE-D	STEN-D	TWEE-D	WISE-D
POWN-D	RUNE-D	STIE-D	TYNE-D	WITE-D
PREE-D	RYKE-D	STYE-D	TYPE-D	WIVE-D
PUKE-D	SABE-D	SURE-D	TYRE-D	WOOL-D
PULE-D	SAFE-D	SWEE-D	ULNA-D	WYLE-D
PURE-D	SANE-D	SYNE-D	UNBE-D	WYTE-D
PYNE-D	SATE-D	SYPE-D	URGE-D	YEAR-D
QUAY-D	SAVE-D	TABI-D	VADE-D	YIKE-D
RABI-D	SCAN-D	TAME-D	VALI-D	YOKE-D
RACE-D	SEEL-D	TAPE-D	VANE-D	YOWE-D
RAGE-D	SERE-D	TARE-D	VICE-D	YUKE-D
RAKE-D	SHAN-D	TEEN-D	VINE-D	ZONE-D
RANI-D	SHOE-D	TEME-D	VIOL-D	
RAPE-D	SHOW-D	THEE-D	VIRE-D	

Five letters to six

ABASE-D	ANELE-D	BEARE-D	BOUSE-D	BUTTE-D
ABATE-D	ANGLE-D	BECKE-D	BOWNE-D	CABLE-D
ABIDE-D	ANKLE-D	BEDYE-D	BOWSE-D	CACHE-D
ABODE-D	APPAY-D	BELEE-D	BOYAR-D	CADGE-D
ABUSE-D	ARGAN-D	BELIE-D	BRACE-D	CALVE-D
ACARI-D	ARGLE-D	BELLE-D	BRAKE-D	CANOE-D
ADDLE-D	ARGUE-D	BERME-D	BRAVE-D	CARTE-D
ADORE-D	ATONE-D	BILGE-D	BRAZE-D	CARVE-D
AERIE-D	AVALE-D	BINGE-D	BREDE-D	CASTE-D
AFEAR-D	AVISE-D	BIRLE-D	BRIAR-D	CAUDA-D
AGAMI-D	AVIZE-D	BITTE-D	BRIBE-D	CAUSE-D
AGAZE-D	AVYZE-D	BLADE-D	BRIDE-D	CEASE-D
AGREE-D	AWAKE-D	BLAME-D	BRINE-D	CEAZE-D
AISLE-D	AZOTE-D	BLARE-D	BROKE-D	CENSE-D
ALATE-D	BADGE-D	BLAZE-D	BRUTE-D	CERNE-D
ALEYE-D	BAIZE-D	BLUME-D	BUDGE-D	CESSE-D
ALINE-D	BARBE-D	BODGE-D	BUFFE-D	CHACE-D
AMATE-D	BARDE-D	BOGIE-D	BUGLE-D	CHAFE-D
AMAZE-D	BARGE-D	BOMBE-D	BULGE-D	CHARE-D
AMBLE-D	BARRE-D	BOOSE-D	BUNCE-D	CHASE-D
AMENE-D	BASSE-D	BOOZE-D	BUNDE-D	CHIDE-D
AMOVE-D	BASTE-D	BOTTE-D	BURKE-D	CHIEL-D
AMUSE-D	BATHE-D	BOUGE-D	BUTLE-D	CHIME-D

CHINE-D	DROWN-D	FOYLE-D	HOISE-D	MEASE-D
CHIVE-D	DWINE-D	FOYNE-D	HOOVE-D	MEDIA-D
CHOKE-D	EAGLE-D	FRAME-D	HORDE-D	MEDLE-D
CHORE-D	EDUCE-D	FRIZE-D	HORSE-D	MENGE-D
CHUTE-D	ELATE-D	FUDGE-D	HOUSE-D	MENSE-D
CLEPE-D	ELIDE-D	FUGLE-D	IMAGE-D	MERGE-D
CLIPE-D	ELOPE-D	FUGUE-D	IMBUE-D	METHO-D
CLOKE-D	ELUDE-D	GABLE-D	INDUE-D	METRE-D
CLONE-D	ELUTE-D	GAFFE-D	INKLE-D	MEUSE-D
CLOSE-D	EMCEE-D	GAMME-D	INURE-D	MICHE-D
CLOYE-D	EMOTE-D	GARBE-D	IRONE-D	MIEVE-D
CLYPE-D	EMOVE-D	GARRE-D	ISSUE-D	MILLE-D
COATE-D	EMULE-D	GAUGE-D	JAMBE-D	MILOR-D
COCCI-D	EMURE-D	GEARE-D	JESSE-D	MINCE-D
COMBE-D	ENDUE-D	GERNE-D	JOULE-D	MINGE-D
CONGE-D	ENSUE-D	GESSE-D	JUDGE-D	MITRE-D
CONNE-D	ENURE-D	GLARE-D	JUICE-D	MOBLE-D
COOEE-D	ERASE-D	GLAZE-D	KEDGE-D	MODGE-D
COPSE-D	ERODE-D	GLIDE-D	KENTE-D	MONIE-D
COSIE-D	ETTLE-D	GLIME-D	KERNE-D	MOOVE-D
COSTE-D	EVADE-D	GLOBE-D	KERVE-D	MORNE-D
COUPE-D	EVITE-D	GLOVE-D	KITHE-D	MOUSE-D
COURE-D	EVOKE-D	GLOZE-D	KLUGE-D	MOYLE-D
COZIE-D	EXEME-D	GOOSE-D	KNIFE-D	MUDGE-D
CRAKE-D	EXILE-D	GORGE-D	KNIVE-D	MUSSE-D
CRANE-D	EXTOL-D	GOSSE-D	KYNDE-D	NACRE-D
CRAPE-D	EXUDE-D	GOUGE-D	KYTHE-D	NAPPE-D
CRATE-D	FABLE-D	GRACE-D	LADLE-D	NEESE-D
CRAVE-D	FADGE-D	GRADE-D	LANCE-D	NEEZE-D
CRAZE-D	FAINE-D	GRAPE-D	LANDE-D	NERVE-D
CREPE-D	FALSE-D	GRATE-D	LAPSE-D	NICHE-D
CREWE-D	FARCE-D	GRAVE-D	LATHE-D	NOISE-D
CRIME-D	FARSE-D	GRAZE-D	LEARE-D	NOOSE-D
CRINE-D	FAYNE-D	GRIDE-D	LEASE-D	NUDGE-D
CROME-D	FEARE-D	GRIME-D	LEAVE-D	NURSE-D
CURSE-D	FEASE-D	GRIPE-D	LEDGE-D	OCHRE-D
CURVE-D	FEAZE-D	GRISE-D	LEGGE-D	OPINE-D
CYCLE-D	FEESE-D	GRONE-D	LENSE-D	ORATE-D
DAINE-D	FEEZE-D	GROPE-D	LEVEE-D	OUTRE-D
DAMME-D	FENCE-D	GROVE-D	LIGAN-D	OVATE-D
DANCE-D	FESSE-D	GRYDE-D	LIGGE-D	PAIRE-D
DARRE-D	FIBRE-D	GUIDE-D	LITHE-D	PANNE-D
DAUBE-D	FIDGE-D	GUILE-D	LOAVE-D	PARGE-D
DEARE-D	FILLE-D	GUISE-D	LODGE-D	PARLE-D
DEAVE-D	FITTE-D	GUNGE-D	LONGE-D	PARSE-D
DEEVE-D	FLAKE-D	GURGE-D	LOOSE-D	PASSE-D
DEICE-D	FLAME-D	GUYLE-D	LOTTE-D	PASTE-D
DELVE-D	FLARE-D	HALSE-D	LOUPE-D	PATTE-D
DEMAN-D	FLITE-D	HALVE-D	LOURE-D	PAUSE-D
DEUCE-D	FLUKE-D	HASTE-D	LOUSE-D	PEACE-D
DINGE-D	FLUME-D	HAUSE-D	LOWNE-D	PEASE-D
DIRKE-D	FLUTE-D	HAWSE-D	LOWSE-D	PEAZE-D
DODGE-D	FLYPE-D	HEAVE-D	LUNGE-D	PECKE-D
DONNE-D	FLYTE-D	HEDGE-D	MACLE-D	PEECE-D
DORSA-D	FORCE-D	HEEZE-D	MAILE-D	PEEPE-D
DOUSE-D	FORGE-D	HEFTE-D	MANGE-D	PEEVE-D
DOWSE-D	FORME-D	HELVE-D	MARLE-D	PEISE-D
DRAPE-D	FORTE-D	HERSE-D	MASSE-D	PEIZE-D
DRONE-D	FOSSE-D	HERYE-D	MATTE-D	PENNE-D
DROVE-D	FOULE-D	HINGE-D	MEANE-D	PERCE-D

PERVE-D	REEDE-D	SERGE-D	SPARE-D	TEMSE-D
PETAR-D	REEVE-D	SERRE-D	SPAUL-D	TENSE-D
PEYSE-D	REGAR-D	SERVE-D	SPICE-D	TERNE-D
PHASE-D	REIVE-D	SHADE-D	SPIKE-D	TESTE-D
PHESE-D	RELIE-D	SHAKE-D	SPILE-D	TETRA-D
PHONE-D	REMAN-D	SHALE-D	SPINE-D	THEME-D
PIECE-D	REMEN-D	SHAME-D	SPIRE-D	THOLE-D
PIQUE-D	RENNE-D	SHAPE-D	SPITE-D	THROE-D
PLACE-D	RENTE-D	SHARE-D	SPOKE-D	TINGE-D
PLANE-D	RESEE-D	SHAVE-D	SPORE-D	TITHE-D
PLATE-D	RETIE-D	SHIEL-D	SPRED-D	TITLE-D
PLONG-D	RETRO-D	SHINE-D	SPREE-D	TOAZE-D
PLUME-D	REUSE-D	SHIRE-D	SPUME-D	TODDE-D
POISE-D	REVIE-D	SHITE-D	STAGE-D	TOGAE-D
PONCE-D	REWIN-D	SHORE-D	STAKE-D	TOILE-D
PORGE-D	RHYME-D	SHOVE-D	STALE-D	TOUSE-D
POSSE-D	RIDGE-D	SHREW-D	STANE-D	TOUZE-D
POUKE-D	RIFLE-D	SHROW-D	STARE-D	TOWSE-D
POUPE-D	RIFTE-D	SHULE-D	STATE-D	TOWZE-D
POWRE-D	RILLE-D	SHUTE-D	STAVE-D	TRACE-D
POYSE-D	RINSE-D	SIDLE-D	STEAR-D	TRADE-D
PRATE-D	ROATE-D	SIEGE-D	STEDE-D	TRAPE-D
PREVE-D	ROGUE-D	SIEVE-D	STEEL-D	TRICE-D
PRICE-D	ROOSE-D	SINGE-D	STEME-D	TRINE-D
PRIDE-D	ROTTE-D	SITHE-D	STILE-D	TROKE-D
PRIME-D	ROUGE-D	SKATE-D	STIME-D	TROPE-D
PRISE-D	ROUSE-D	SKITE-D	STIPE-D	TRUCE-D
PRIZE-D	ROUTE-D	SKIVE-D	STIRE-D	TWINE-D
PROBE-D	ROYNE-D	SKYRE-D	STIVE-D	TWIRE-D
PROKE-D	RUCHE-D	SKYTE-D	STOKE-D	TYTHE-D
PROLE-D	RUFFE-D	SLAKE-D	STOLE-D	UNCLE-D
PROSE-D	RYMME-D	SLATE-D	STONE-D	UNITE-D
PROVE-D	SABLE-D	SLAVE-D	STOPE-D	UNTIE-D
PRUNE-D	SABRE-D	SLICE-D	STORE-D	UPTIE-D
PULSE-D	SAINE-D	SLIDE-D	STOUN-D	URINE-D
PUNCE-D	SALUE-D	SLIME-D	STOVE-D	USURE-D
PUREE-D	SALVE-D	SLIPE-D	STOWN-D	VAGUE-D
PURGE-D	SASSE-D	SLIVE-D	STUPE-D	VALSE-D
PURSE-D	SAUCE-D	SLOPE-D	STYLE-D	VALUE-D
PUSLE-D	SAUTE-D	SMILE-D	STYME-D	VALVE-D
QUAKE-D	SCALE-D	SMOKE-D	STYRE-D	VARVE-D
QUEME-D	SCAPE-D	SMORE-D	STYTE-D	VAUTE-D
QUEUE-D	SCARE-D	SNAKE-D	SUEDE-D	VAWTE-D
QUIRE-D	SCENE-D	SNARE-D	SUITE-D	VEALE-D
QUITE-D	SCOPE-D	SNIPE-D	SURGE-D	VENGE-D
QUOTE-D	SCORE-D	SNOKE-D	SWAGE-D	VERGE-D
QUYTE-D	SCREE-D	SNORE-D	SWALE-D	VERSE-D
RAILE-D	SCUSE-D	SOARE-D	SWEAR-D	VISIE-D
RAINE-D	SEAME-D	SOLAN-D	SWIPE-D	VOGUE-D
RAISE-D	SEARE-D	SOLVE-D	SWIVE-D	VOICE-D
RANCE-D	SEASE-D	SOOLE-D	SWOUN-D	VOLVE-D
RANGE-D	SEAZE-D	SOOTE-D	TABER-D	WAITE-D
RANKE-D	SEDGE-D	SOUCE-D	TABLE-D	WAIVE-D
RAPPE-D	SEGUE-D	SOUSE-D	TARGE-D	WANZE-D
RAYLE-D	SEINE-D	SOWCE-D	TARRE-D	WARRE-D
RAZEE-D	SEISE-D	SOWLE-D	TASTE-D	WASTE-D
REAME-D	SEIZE-D	SOWSE-D	TAWSE-D	WEAVE-D
REAVE-D	SEMEE-D	SPACE-D	TEASE-D	WEDGE-D
RECCE-D	SENSE-D	SPADE-D	TEAZE-D	WEETE-D
REDYE-D	SENTE-D	SPANE-D	TEENE-D	WEFTE-D

WEISE-D	WHALE-D	WHITE-D	WINGE-D	WORSE-D
WEIZE-D	WHILE-D	WHORE-D	WITHE-D	YODLE-D
WELKE-D	WHINE-D	WINCE-D	WOLVE-D	ZINKE-D

Six letters to seven

ABDUCE-D	AVENGE-D	BRIGUE-D	COFFLE-D	DEFACE-D
ABJURE-D	AVIATE-D	BROCHE-D	COGGLE-D	DEFAME-D
ABLATE-D	AVULSE-D	BRONZE-D	COHERE-D	DEFILE-D
ABRADE-D	AWHAPE-D	BROWSE-D	COIFFE-D	DEFINE-D
ACCEDE-D	BABBLE-D	BRUISE-D	COIGNE-D	DEFUSE-D
ACCITE-D	BAFFLE-D	BUBBLE-D	COLLAR-D	DEFUZE-D
ACCRUE-D	BANGLE-D	BUCKLE-D	COLLIE-D	DEGREE-D
ACCUSE-D	BASQUE-D	BUDDLE-D	COLOBI-D	DELATE-D
ADDUCE-D	BATTLE-D	BUMBLE-D	CONCHE-D	DELETE-D
ADHERE-D	BEAGLE-D	BUMMLE-D	CONGEE-D	DELIME-D
ADJURE-D	BEDAZE-D	BUNDLE-D	CONJEE-D	DELOPE-D
ADMIRE-D	BEETLE-D	BUNGLE-D	COORIE-D	DELUDE-D
ADVENE-D	BEGAZE-D	BURBLE-D	CORPSE-D	DELUGE-D
ADVISE-D	BEHAVE-D	BURGLE-D	COSTAR-D	DEMISE-D
AEMULE-D	BEHOVE-D	BUSTLE-D	COTISE-D	DEMODE-D
AERATE-D	BEJADE-D	BUTTLE-D	COUCHE-D	DEMOTE-D
AFFEAR-D	BELACE-D	BYLINE-D	COUPLE-D	DEMURE-D
AFFINE-D	BELATE-D	CACKLE-D	COURIE-D	DENOTE-D
AGNAME-D	BELOVE-D	CADDIE-D	COURSE-D	DENUDE-D
AGNISE-D	BEMETE-D	CAJOLE-D	CRADLE-D	DEPONE-D
AGNIZE-D	BEMIRE-D	CALQUE-D	CREASE-D	DEPOSE-D
AGRISE-D	BEMUSE-D	CAMPLE-D	CREATE-D	DEPUTE-D
AGRIZE-D	BENAME-D	CANDIE-D	CREESE-D	DERATE-D
AGRYZE-D	BERAKE-D	CANDLE-D	CRINGE-D	DERIDE-D
AGUISE-D	BERATE-D	CANGLE-D	CROSSE-D	DERIVE-D
AGUIZE-D	BERIME-D	CANTLE-D	CROUPE-D	DESINE-D
ALCOVE-D	BERTHE-D	CARNIE-D	CRUISE-D	DESIRE-D
ALEGGE-D	BETIDE-D	CASQUE-D	CUDDLE-D	DESYNE-D
ALLEGE-D	BETIME-D	CASTLE-D	CUFFLE-D	DETUNE-D
ALLUDE-D	BEWARE-D	CAUDLE-D	CURATE-D	DEVISE-D
ALLURE-D	BEZZLE-D	CENTRE-D	CURDLE-D	DEVOTE-D
AMENDE-D	BINGLE-D	CERATE-D	CURRIE-D	DIBBLE-D
AMERCE-D	BIRDIE-D	CESTOI-D	CUTTLE-D	DIDDLE-D
AMOOVE-D	BIRSLE-D	CHAINE-D	DABBLE-D	DILATE-D
ANNEXE-D	BISTRE-D	CHANCE-D	DADDLE-D	DILUTE-D
ANSATE-D	BLENDE-D	CHANGE-D	DAGGLE-D	DIMPLE-D
APPOSE-D	BLOUSE-D	CHARGE-D	DAIDLE-D	DINDLE-D
ARAISE-D	BLOWSE-D	CHASSE-D	DAMAGE-D	DINNLE-D
ARAYSE-D	BLOWZE-D	CHAUFE-D	DANDLE-D	DISMAY-D
ARCADE-D	BLUDGE-D	CHEESE-D	DANGLE-D	DISPLE-D
AROUSE-D	BLUNGE-D	CHILDE-D	DAPPLE-D	DISUSE-D
ARRIDE-D	BOBBLE-D	CHIRRE-D	DARKLE-D	DIVIDE-D
ARRIVE-D	BOGGLE-D	CHOUSE-D	DARTLE-D	DIVINE-D
ASHAME-D	BOODIE-D	CHOWSE-D	DAWDLE-D	DONATE-D
ASLAKE-D	BOODLE-D	CHROME-D	DAZZLE-D	DOODLE-D
ASPIRE-D	BOOGIE-D	CIRCLE-D	DEBASE-D	DORISE-D
ASSIZE-D	BORATE-D	CLEAVE-D	DEBATE-D	DORIZE-D
ASSUME-D	BOTTLE-D	CLICHE-D	DEBONE-D	DOTTLE-D
ASSURE-D	BOUNCE-D	CLIQUE-D	DECIDE-D	DOUBLE-D
ASTONE-D	BRAIDE-D	CLOTHE-D	DECKLE-D	DOUCHE-D
ATTIRE-D	BRAISE-D	COBBLE-D	DECODE-D	DREDGE-D
ATTUNE-D	BREEZE-D	COCKLE-D	DECOKE-D	DROMON-D
AURATE-D	BRIDGE-D	CODDLE-D	DECREE-D	DROWSE-D
AVAILE-D	BRIDLE-D	COERCE-D	DEDUCE-D	DRUDGE-D

DUMPLE-D	FACETE-D	GRAINE-D	INCASE-D	LIAISE-D
ECLOSE-D	FADDLE-D	GREASE-D	INCAVE-D	LIBATE-D
EFFACE-D	FANGLE-D	GREAVE-D	INCEDE-D	LIGATE-D
EFFERE-D	FANKLE-D	GREETE-D	INCISE-D	LOATHE-D
EFFUSE-D	FARCIE-D	GRIECE-D	INCITE-D	LOBATE-D
ELANCE-D	FEAGUE-D	GRIEVE-D	INCUSE-D	LOCATE-D
ELAPSE-D	FEEBLE-D	GRILLE-D	INDITE-D	LOCULE-D
EMBACE-D	FERLIE-D	GRIPPE-D	INDUCE-D	LOUNGE-D
EMBALE-D	FERULE-D	GROOVE-D	INFAME-D	LOUVRE-D
EMBASE-D	FETTLE-D	GROUSE-D	INFUSE-D	LUMINE-D
EMBRUE-D	FEUTRE-D	GRUDGE-D	INHALE-D	LUNATE-D
EMERGE-D	FICKLE-D	GUDDLE-D	INHERE-D	LUSTRE-D
EMMOVE-D	FIDDLE-D	GUGGLE-D	INHUME-D	LUXATE-D
EMPALE-D	FIGURE-D	GUIMPE-D	INISLE-D	LYRATE-D
EMPARE-D	FISSLE-D	GURGLE-D	INJURE-D	MACKLE-D
EMULGE-D	FIXATE-D	GUSSIE-D	INLACE-D	MACULE-D
EMUNGE-D	FIZZLE-D	GUTTLE-D	INSURE-D	MADAME-D
ENABLE-D	FLANGE-D	GUZZLE-D	INTONE-D	MALGRE-D
ENCAGE-D	FLEDGE-D	GYRATE-D	INVADE-D	MALICE-D
ENCASE-D	FLEECE-D	HACKLE-D	INVITE-D	MANAGE-D
ENCAVE-D	FLENSE-D	HAGGLE-D	INVOKE-D	MANEGE-D
ENCODE-D	FLOUSE-D	HAMBLE-D	IODATE-D	MANGLE-D
ENCORE-D	FONDLE-D	HANDLE-D	IODISE-D	MANTLE-D
ENDITE-D	FONDUE-D	HASSLE-D	IODIZE-D	MANURE-D
ENDURE-D	FOOTLE-D	HEARSE-D	IONISE-D	MARBLE-D
ENERVE-D	FOOZLE-D	HECKLE-D	IONIZE-D	MASCLE-D
ENFACE-D	FORAGE-D	HEDDLE-D	JABBLE-D	MATURE-D
ENFIRE-D	FOUTRE-D	HIGGLE-D	JANGLE-D	MAUGRE-D
ENFREE-D	FRAISE-D	HIRPLE-D	JAUNCE-D	MEASLE-D
ENGAGE-D	FRAPPE-D	HIRSLE-D	JAUNSE-D	MEDDLE-D
ENGINE-D	FRIDGE-D	HOBBLE-D	JEELIE-D	MEGARA-D
ENGORE-D	FRIEZE-D	HOCKLE-D	JERQUE-D	MENACE-D
ENISLE-D	FRINGE-D	HODDLE-D	JIGGLE-D	MENAGE-D
ENLACE-D	FUDDLE-D	HOGTIE-D	JIMMIE-D	METTLE-D
ENMOVE-D	FUMBLE-D	HOMAGE-D	JINGLE-D	MICATE-D
ENNUYE-D	FUZZLE-D	HONDLE-D	JIRBLE-D	MIDDLE-D
ENRACE-D	GABBLE-D	HOPPLE-D	JOGGLE-D	MINGLE-D
ENRAGE-D	GAGGLE-D	HOWDIE-D	JOSTLE-D	MINUTE-D
ENROBE-D	GAMBLE-D	HUDDLE-D	JOUNCE-D	MISCUE-D
ENSILE-D	GARAGE-D	HUMBLE-D	JUGGLE-D	MISTLE-D
ENSURE-D	GARBLE-D	HURDLE-D	JUMBLE-D	MISUSE-D
ENTAME-D	GARGLE-D	HURTLE-D	JUNGLE-D	MIZZLE-D
ENTICE-D	GAROTE-D	HUSTLE-D	JUSTLE-D	MOBBLE-D
ENZONE-D	GELATE-D	ICICLE-D	KECKLE-D	MOTIVE-D
EQUATE-D	GENTLE-D	IDEATE-D	KIBBLE-D	MOTTLE-D
ERMINE-D	GHESSE-D	IGNITE-D	KIDDIE-D	MOUSLE-D
ESCAPE-D	GIGGLE-D	IGNORE-D	KINDLE-D	MOUSSE-D
ESTATE-D	GILLIE-D	ILLUDE-D	KIRTLE-D	MUDDLE-D
EUCHRE-D	GIRDLE-D	ILLUME-D	KITTLE-D	MUFFLE-D
EVINCE-D	GLAIRE-D	IMBASE-D	KLUDGE-D	MUMBLE-D
EVOLVE-D	GLAIVE-D	IMBIBE-D	KREESE-D	MUNITE-D
EVULSE-D	GLANCE-D	IMBRUE-D	LAIPSE-D	MUSCLE-D
EXCIDE-D	GLEDGE-D	IMMURE-D	LALLAN-D	MUTATE-D
EXCISE-D	GOATEE-D	IMPALE-D	LANATE-D	MUTINE-D
EXCITE-D	GOBBLE-D	IMPAVE-D	LANGUE-D	MUZZLE-D
EXCUSE-D	GOGGLE-D	IMPEDE-D	LATERA-D	NANNIE-D
EXHALE-D	GOITRE-D	IMPONE-D	LAUNCE-D	NATURE-D
EXHUME-D	GOLLAN-D	IMPOSE-D	LEAGUE-D	NEEDLE-D
EXPIRE-D	GOOGLE-D	IMPUTE-D	LEGATE-D	NEGATE-D
EXPOSE-D	GOWLAN-D	INCAGE-D	LENITE-D	NESTLE-D

NETTLE-D	PIFFLE-D	REBORE-D	REVIVE-D	SHOTTE-D
NIBBLE-D	PIMPLE-D	REBUKE-D	REVOKE-D	SHRIKE-D
NICKLE-D	PINGLE-D	RECANE-D	REVOTE-D	SHRINE-D
NIDATE-D	PIRATE-D	RECEDE-D	REWAKE-D	SHRIVE-D
NIGGLE-D	PLAGUE-D	RECITE-D	REWIRE-D	SHROVE-D
NIPPLE-D	PLEASE-D	RECODE-D	REZONE-D	SICKLE-D
NOBBLE-D	PLEDGE-D	RECULE-D	RIDDLE-D	SIFFLE-D
NODDLE-D	PLODGE-D	RECURE-D	RIFFLE-D	SILAGE-D
NODULE-D	PLONGE-D	RECUSE-D	RIMPLE-D	SIMPLE-D
NONAGE-D	PLUNGE-D	REDATE-D	RIPPLE-D	SINGLE-D
NOODGE-D	PODDLE-D	REDDLE-D	ROOTLE-D	SIPPLE-D
NOODLE-D	POINTE-D	REDUCE-D	ROTATE-D	SIZZLE-D
NOTATE-D	POLICE-D	REFACE-D	RUBBLE-D	SKLATE-D
NOTICE-D	POLYPE-D	REFILE-D	RUCKLE-D	SKRIKE-D
NOUSLE-D	POMADE-D	REFINE-D	RUDDLE-D	SLEAVE-D
NUANCE-D	POONCE-D	REFIRE-D	RUFFLE-D	SLEDGE-D
NUBBLE-D	POOTLE-D	REFUGE-D	RUMBLE-D	SLEEVE-D
NURDLE-D	POPPLE-D	REFUSE-D	RUMPLE-D	SLUDGE-D
NURSLE-D	POTCHE-D	REFUTE-D	RUNDLE-D	SLUICE-D
NUTATE-D	POUFFE-D	REGALE-D	RUNKLE-D	SMOILE-D
NUZZLE-D	POUNCE-D	REGLUE-D	RUSTLE-D	SMOOGE-D
OBDURE-D	PRAISE-D	REHEAR-D	RUSTRE-D	SMOUSE-D
OBJURE-D	PRANCE-D	REHIRE-D	SADDLE-D	SMOYLE-D
OBLIGE-D	PREACE-D	RELACE-D	SAGGAR-D	SMUDGE-D
OPAQUE-D	PREASE-D	RELATE-D	SALUTE-D	SNEBBE-D
OPIATE-D	PREDYE-D	RELINE-D	SAMPLE-D	SNEEZE-D
OPPOSE-D	PREEVE-D	RELIVE-D	SAPPLE-D	SNOOZE-D
ORACLE-D	PREVUE-D	RELUME-D	SAVAGE-D	SNUBBE-D
OSMOSE-D	PRIEFE-D	REMATE-D	SCARRE-D	SNUDGE-D
OUGLIE-D	PRIEVE-D	REMBLE-D	SCATHE-D	SOLACE-D
OUTLIE-D	PRINCE-D	REMEDE-D	SCERNE-D	SOLATE-D
OUTVIE-D	PROINE-D	REMISE-D	SCHEME-D	SOMBRE-D
OUTWAR-D	PROTEI-D	REMOVE-D	SCLATE-D	SOOGEE-D
OUTWIN-D	PROVEN-D	RENAME-D	SCONCE-D	SOOGIE-D
PADDLE-D	PSYCHE-D	RENEGE-D	SCORSE-D	SOOTHE-D
PAIDLE-D	PUDDLE-D	REPAVE-D	SCRAPE-D	SOPITE-D
PALACE-D	PUGGLE-D	REPINE-D	SCRIBE-D	SORTIE-D
PALATE-D	PUMICE-D	REPONE-D	SCRIKE-D	SOUPLE-D
PARADE-D	PUNGLE-D	REPOSE-D	SCRIVE-D	SOURCE-D
PAROLE-D	PUPATE-D	REPURE-D	SCROME-D	SOWSSE-D
PARPEN-D	PURFLE-D	REPUTE-D	SCRUZE-D	SOZZLE-D
PATINE-D	PURPLE-D	RESCUE-D	SCULLE-D	SPALLE-D
PEARCE-D	PURSUE-D	RESHOE-D	SCUNGE-D	SPARGE-D
PEBBLE-D	PUTTIE-D	RESIDE-D	SCYTHE-D	SPARKE-D
PEDDLE-D	PUZZLE-D	RESILE-D	SDAINE-D	SPARRE-D
PEENGE-D	QUAERE-D	RESITE-D	SEARCE-D	SPATHE-D
PEOPLE-D	QUICHE-D	RESIZE-D	SECEDE-D	SPERRE-D
PERSUE-D	RABBLE-D	RESKUE-D	SECURE-D	SPERSE-D
PERUKE-D	RACEME-D	RESOLE-D	SEDATE-D	SPHERE-D
PERUSE-D	RADDLE-D	RESUME-D	SEDUCE-D	SPLICE-D
PESTLE-D	RAFFLE-D	RETAPE-D	SEETHE-D	SPLINE-D
PETTLE-D	RAGGLE-D	RETILE-D	SEMBLE-D	SPONGE-D
PHEESE-D	RAMBLE-D	RETIME-D	SERENE-D	SPOUSE-D
PHEEZE-D	RANKLE-D	RETIRE-D	SETTLE-D	SPRUCE-D
PHRASE-D	RASSLE-D	RETUNE-D	SEVERE-D	SPULYE-D
PIAFFE-D	RATTLE-D	RETYPE-D	SHEAVE-D	SPURNE-D
PICKLE-D	RAUNGE-D	REURGE-D	SHELVE-D	SQUARE-D
PICOTE-D	RAVAGE-D	REVERE-D	SHINNE-D	SQUIRE-D
PIDDLE-D	RAVINE-D	REVILE-D	SHOOLE-D	STABLE-D
PIERCE-D	REBATE-D	REVISE-D	SHOPPE-D	STAPLE-D

STARVE-D	TACKLE-D	TREBLE-D	UNLINE-D	VOYAGE-D
STATUE-D	TAIGLE-D	TRIAGE-D	UNLIVE-D	WABBLE-D
STAYNE-D	TAMMIE-D	TRIFLE-D	UNLOVE-D	WADDIE-D
STEALE-D	TANGLE-D	TRIPLE-D	UNPILE-D	WADDLE-D
STEANE-D	TATTLE-D	TROMPE-D	UNPOPE-D	WAFFLE-D
STEARE-D	TEAGLE-D	TROULE-D	UNRAKE-D	WAGGLE-D
STEDDE-D	TEAZLE-D	TROUPE-D	UNROBE-D	WAMBLE-D
STEEVE-D	TEETHE-D	TRUDGE-D	UNROPE-D	WANGLE-D
STEMME-D	TEMPLE-D	TRYSTE-D	UNRULE-D	WARBLE-D
STEPPE-D	TENURE-D	TUMBLE-D	UNSHOE-D	WARRAN-D
STERVE-D	THIEVE-D	TURBAN-D	UNSURE-D	WARSLE-D
STIFLE-D	THRIVE-D	TURTLE-D	UNTAME-D	WATTLE-D
STIMIE-D	THRONE-D	TUSSLE-D	UNTILE-D	WEEWEE-D
STIRRE-D	TICKLE-D	TWEEZE-D	UNTUNE-D	WHEEZE-D
STODGE-D	TIDDLE-D	TWINGE-D	UNWIRE-D	WHINGE-D
STONNE-D	TIERCE-D	ULLAGE-D	UNWIVE-D	WIBBLE-D
STOOGE-D	TINGLE-D	UMPIRE-D	UNYOKE-D	WIDDLE-D
STOOPE-D	TINKLE-D	UNBALE-D	UPDATE-D	WIGGLE-D
STRAFE-D	TIPPLE-D	UNBARE-D	UPDIVE-D	WILLIE-D
STRAKE-D	TIPTOE-D	UNBONE-D	UPGAZE-D	WIMBLE-D
STRIPE-D	TISSUE-D	UNCAGE-D	UPPILE-D	WIMPLE-D
STRIVE-D	TITTLE-D	UNCAKE-D	UPRATE-D	WINDLE-D
STROBE-D	TITULE-D	UNCAPE-D	UPSIZE-D	WINKLE-D
STROKE-D	TODDLE-D	UNCASE-D	VACATE-D	WINTLE-D
STYMIE-D	TOGATE-D	UNCOPE-D	VALETE-D	WOBBLE-D
SUBDUE-D	TOGGLE-D	UNDATE-D	VAMOSE-D	WRAXLE-D
SUCKLE-D	TONGUE-D	UNEDGE-D	VAUNCE-D	WRETHE-D
SUDATE-D	TOOTLE-D	UNFREE-D	VELATE-D	WRITHE-D
SUPPLE-D	TOPPLE-D	UNGLUE-D	VELURE-D	WUZZLE-D
SUTTLE-D	TORQUE-D	UNGYVE-D	VENTRE-D	YABBIE-D
SUTURE-D	TOUCHE-D	UNHELE-D	VISAGE-D	ZIZZLE-D
SWARVE-D	TOUSLE-D	UNHIVE-D	VISITE-D	ZONATE-D
SWATHE-D	TOUZLE-D	UNLACE-D	VITTLE-D	
SWERVE-D	TOWMON-D	UNLADE-D	VIZZIE-D	
SWINGE-D	TRANCE-D	UNLIKE-D	VOLUME-D	
SWOUNE-D	TRAYNE-D	UNLIME-D	VOLUTE-D	

Seven letters to eight

ABRIDGE-D	AGATIZE-D	APPRISE-D	ATTRITE-D	BECURSE-D
ABROOKE-D	AGENISE-D	APPRIZE-D	ATTUITE-D	BEDRAPE-D
ABSCISE-D	AGENIZE-D	APPROVE-D	AUDIBLE-D	BEDUNCE-D
ABSOLVE-D	AGGRACE-D	ARABISE-D	AUREOLE-D	BEELINE-D
ACCINGE-D	AGGRADE-D	ARABIZE-D	AURICLE-D	BEGRIME-D
ACCRETE-D	AGGRATE-D	ARCHIVE-D	AVENTRE-D	BEGUILE-D
ACCURSE-D	AGITATE-D	ARCUATE-D	AVERAGE-D	BEHOOVE-D
ACERATE-D	AGONISE-D	ARRANGE-D	AZOTISE-D	BEKNAVE-D
ACETATE-D	AGONIZE-D	ARTICLE-D	AZOTIZE-D	BELIEVE-D
ACHIEVE-D	ALLEDGE-D	ASCRIBE-D	BACCATE-D	BEPROSE-D
ACQUIRE-D	ALLEGGE-D	ASKANCE-D	BACKHOE-D	BEREAVE-D
ACTUATE-D	AMENAGE-D	ASPERGE-D	BAGPIPE-D	BERHYME-D
ACYLATE-D	ANALYSE-D	ASPERSE-D	BALANCE-D	BESHAME-D
ADJUDGE-D	ANALYZE-D	ASSIEGE-D	BALLADE-D	BESIEGE-D
ADONISE-D	ANIMATE-D	ASSUAGE-D	BALLADE-D	BESLAVE-D
ADONIZE-D	ANODISE-D	ASSWAGE-D	BANDAGE-D	BESLIME-D
ADULATE-D	ANODIZE-D	ATHEISE-D	BAPTISE-D	BESMILE-D
ADVANCE-D	ANTICKE-D	ATHEIZE-D	BAPTIZE-D	BESMOKE-D
AFFEARE-D	ANTIQUE-D	ATOMISE-D	BARBATE-D	BESPICE-D
AFFORCE-D	APANAGE-D	ATOMIZE-D	BARRAGE-D	BETEEME-D
AGATISE-D	APPEASE-D	ATTACHE-D	BAUCHLE-D	BETITLE-D
			BECRIME-D	

BEWHORE-D	COGNIZE-D	CRUMBLE-D	DIFFUSE-D	EMPERCE-D
BICYCLE-D	COLLAGE-D	CRUMPLE-D	DISABLE-D	EMPLACE-D
BIVALVE-D	COLLATE-D	CRUNKLE-D	DISCAGE-D	EMPLANE-D
BLOOSME-D	COLLIDE-D	CRUSADE-D	DISCASE-D	EMPLOYE-D
BRABBLE-D	COLLUDE-D	CUITTLE-D	DISCIDE-D	EMPLUME-D
BRAILLE-D	COLOGNE-D	CULTURE-D	DISCURE-D	EMULATE-D
BRAMBLE-D	COMBINE-D	CUNEATE-D	DISEASE-D	ENCHAFE-D
BRANGLE-D	COMMOVE-D	CURETTE-D	DISEDGE-D	ENCHASE-D
BRATTLE-D	COMMUNE-D	CURVATE-D	DISHOME-D	ENCLAVE-D
BREATHE-D	COMMUTE-D	CUSPATE-D	DISLIKE-D	ENCLOSE-D
BREENGE-D	COMPARE-D	CYANIDE-D	DISPACE-D	ENDORSE-D
BREINGE-D	COMPERE-D	CYANISE-D	DISPONE-D	ENFLAME-D
BREVETE-D	COMPETE-D	CYANIZE-D	DISPOSE-D	ENFORCE-D
BRIGADE-D	COMPILE-D	CYCLISE-D	DISPUTE-D	ENFRAME-D
BRINDLE-D	COMPOSE-D	CYCLIZE-D	DISRATE-D	ENGLOBE-D
BRISTLE-D	COMPUTE-D	DEALATE-D	DISROBE-D	ENGORGE-D
BRITTLE-D	CONACRE-D	DEBRIDE-D	DISSAVE-D	ENGRACE-D
BROCADE-D	CONCAVE-D	DECEASE-D	DISTUNE-D	ENGRAVE-D
BRODDLE-D	CONCEDE-D	DECEIVE-D	DISYOKE-D	ENHANCE-D
BROMATE-D	CONCISE-D	DECLARE-D	DIVERGE-D	ENLARGE-D
BROMISE-D	CONDOLE-D	DECLINE-D	DIVERSE-D	ENNOBLE-D
BROMIZE-D	CONDONE-D	DECUPLE-D	DIVORCE-D	ENOUNCE-D
BUMBAZE-D	CONDUCE-D	DECURVE-D	DIVULGE-D	ENPLANE-D
CABBAGE-D	CONFIDE-D	DEFENCE-D	DIVULSE-D	ENQUIRE-D
CADENCE-D	CONFINE-D	DEFENSE-D	DOCKISE-D	ENRANGE-D
CALCINE-D	CONFUSE-D	DEFLATE-D	DOCKIZE-D	ENSLAVE-D
CALIBRE-D	CONFUTE-D	DEFORCE-D	DOGGONE-D	ENSNARE-D
CALYCLE-D	CONGREE-D	DEGLAZE-D	DRABBLE-D	ENSTYLE-D
CAPSIZE-D	CONGRUE-D	DEGRADE-D	DRAGGLE-D	ENTAYLE-D
CAPSULE-D	CONJURE-D	DEHISCE-D	DRIBBLE-D	ENTHUSE-D
CAPTIVE-D	CONNIVE-D	DELAPSE-D	DRIZZLE-D	ENTITLE-D
CAPTURE-D	CONNOTE-D	DELEAVE-D	DRUMBLE-D	ENTWINE-D
CAPUCHE-D	CONSOLE-D	DELOUSE-D	DUALISE-D	EPILATE-D
CARCASE-D	CONSUME-D	DEMEANE-D	DUALIZE-D	EPISTLE-D
CAROUSE-D	CONTUSE-D	DEMERGE-D	DWINDLE-D	EPURATE-D
CASCADE-D	CONVENE-D	DEMERSE-D	EBONISE-D	EROTISE-D
CASEATE-D	CONVIVE-D	DENTATE-D	EBONIZE-D	EROTIZE-D
CAUDATE-D	CONVOKE-D	DEPLANE-D	EBRIATE-D	ESCRIBE-D
CAYENNE-D	COPPICE-D	DEPLETE-D	ECHOISE-D	ESLOYNE-D
CENSURE-D	CORNICE-D	DEPLORE-D	ECHOIZE-D	ESPOUSE-D
CHALICE-D	CORNUTE-D	DEPLUME-D	ECLIPSE-D	ESQUIRE-D
CHARQUI-D	CORRADE-D	DEPRAVE-D	EDUCATE-D	ESTREPE-D
CHAUNCE-D	CORRODE-D	DEPRIVE-D	EFFORCE-D	EVIRATE-D
CHAUNGE-D	COSTATE-D	DERANGE-D	EFFULGE-D	EVITATE-D
CHELATE-D	COSTUME-D	DESCALE-D	EGOTISE-D	EVOCATE-D
CHICANE-D	COTTAGE-D	DESERVE-D	EGOTIZE-D	EVOLUTE-D
CHORTLE-D	COTTISE-D	DESPISE-D	ELEGISE-D	EXAMINE-D
CHUCKLE-D	COWHIDE-D	DESPITE-D	ELEGIZE-D	EXAMPLE-D
CILIATE-D	CRACKLE-D	DESTINE-D	ELEVATE-D	EXCLUDE-D
CITRATE-D	CRANKLE-D	DETERGE-D	ELOCUTE-D	EXCRETE-D
CLAVATE-D	CREMATE-D	DETRUDE-D	EMANATE-D	EXCURSE-D
CLEANSE-D	CRENATE-D	DEVALUE-D	EMBATHE-D	EXECUTE-D
CLIMATE-D	CREVICE-D	DEVIATE-D	EMBLAZE-D	EXPENSE-D
CLOSURE-D	CRIBBLE-D	DEVOICE-D	EMBOGUE-D	EXPIATE-D
CLOTURE-D	CRIMPLE-D	DEVOLVE-D	EMBRACE-D	EXPLODE-D
COALISE-D	CRINATE-D	DIALYSE-D	EMBRAVE-D	EXPLORE-D
COALIZE-D	CRINKLE-D	DIALYZE-D	EMBRUTE-D	EXPULSE-D
COCKADE-D	CRIPPLE-D	DIARISE-D	EMICATE-D	EXPUNGE-D
COCKEYE-D	CROODLE-D	DIARIZE-D	EMPAIRE-D	EXPURGE-D
COGNISE-D	CRUDDLE-D	DICTATE-D	EMPAYRE-D	EXTRUDE-D

FALCATE-D	GRUMBLE-D	INWEAVE-D	MISMATE-D	OUTSIZE-D
FANFARE-D	GRUNTLE-D	IRIDISE-D	MISMOVE-D	OUTVOTE-D
FATIGUE-D	GUMSHOE-D	IRIDIZE-D	MISNAME-D	OUTWILE-D
FEATURE-D	GUTTATE-D	IRISATE-D	MISPAGE-D	OVERAGE-D
FELLATE-D	HACHURE-D	IRONISE-D	MISRATE-D	OVERAWE-D
FENAGLE-D	HALTERE-D	IRONIZE-D	MISRULE-D	OVERDYE-D
FERRULE-D	HAMBONE-D	ISOLATE-D	MISTIME-D	OVEREYE-D
FIBROSE-D	HASTATE-D	ITEMISE-D	MISTUNE-D	OVERSEE-D
FILIATE-D	HERBAGE-D	ITEMIZE-D	MISTYPE-D	OVERUSE-D
FINAGLE-D	HEROISE-D	ITERATE-D	MISYOKE-D	OVULATE-D
FINANCE-D	HEROIZE-D	JALOUSE-D	MONOCLE-D	OXALATE-D
FINESSE-D	HOGNOSE-D	JAWBONE-D	MONTAGE-D	OXIDATE-D
FISSURE-D	HYDRATE-D	KEYNOTE-D	MORTICE-D	OXIDISE-D
FLAMBEE-D	ICONISE-D	KNAPPLE-D	MORTISE-D	OXIDIZE-D
FLOUNCE-D	ICONIZE-D	KNOBBLE-D	MULTURE-D	OZONATE-D
FOLIAGE-D	IDOLISE-D	KNUBBLE-D	MURIATE-D	OZONISE-D
FOLIATE-D	IDOLIZE-D	KNUCKLE-D	MYTHISE-D	OZONIZE-D
FORBODE-D	ILLAPSE-D	KYANISE-D	MYTHIZE-D	PACKAGE-D
FORMATE-D	IMAGINE-D	KYANIZE-D	NARRATE-D	PALMATE-D
FORPINE-D	IMBATHE-D	LABIATE-D	NECROSE-D	PALPATE-D
FORSLOE-D	IMBLAZE-D	LACTATE-D	NICTATE-D	PANCAKE-D
FORTUNE-D	IMBRUTE-D	LAICISE-D	NITRATE-D	PANICLE-D
FOVEATE-D	IMBURSE-D	LAICIZE-D	NITRIDE-D	PANTILE-D
FRAZZLE-D	IMITATE-D	LAIRISE-D	NOURSLE-D	PARABLE-D
FRECKLE-D	IMMERGE-D	LAIRIZE-D	NURTURE-D	PARBAKE-D
FRIBBLE-D	IMMERSE-D	LARVATE-D	OBELISE-D	PASSAGE-D
FRIZZLE-D	IMPASTE-D	LATTICE-D	OBELIZE-D	PASTURE-D
FROGEYE-D	IMPINGE-D	LEASOWE-D	OBLIQUE-D	PATINAE-D
FROUNCE-D	IMPLATE-D	LECTURE-D	OBSCURE-D	PECTISE-D
FRUMPLE-D	IMPLETE-D	LEISURE-D	OBSERVE-D	PECTIZE-D
FULMINE-D	IMPLODE-D	LIBRATE-D	OBTRUDE-D	PEDICLE-D
FURCATE-D	IMPLORE-D	LICENCE-D	OBVIATE-D	PENANCE-D
FURNACE-D	IMPROVE-D	LICENSE-D	OCCLUDE-D	PENNATE-D
GABELLE-D	IMPULSE-D	LINEATE-D	OCTUPLE-D	PENTICE-D
GALEATE-D	INCENSE-D	LIONISE-D	OCULATE-D	PENTISE-D
GALLISE-D	INCHASE-D	LIONIZE-D	ODORISE-D	PEPTISE-D
GALLIZE-D	INCLINE-D	LIQUATE-D	ODORIZE-D	PEPTIZE-D
GALOCHE-D	INCLOSE-D	LOZENGE-D	OPERATE-D	PERDURE-D
GALOSHE-D	INCLUDE-D	MACHINE-D	OUTBAKE-D	PERFUME-D
GAROTTE-D	INCURVE-D	MANACLE-D	OUTCROW-D	PERFUSE-D
GARROTE-D	INDORSE-D	MANDATE-D	OUTDARE-D	PERJURE-D
GAVOTTE-D	INDULGE-D	MASSAGE-D	OUTDATE-D	PERMUTE-D
GAZETTE-D	INFLAME-D	MAULGRE-D	OUTDURE-D	PERTUSE-D
GEMMATE-D	INFLATE-D	MEASURE-D	OUTFACE-D	PERVADE-D
GESTATE-D	INFORCE-D	MEDIATE-D	OUTFIRE-D	PETIOLE-D
GESTURE-D	INGLOBE-D	MESSAGE-D	OUTGAZE-D	PHILTRE-D
GHILLIE-D	INHERCE-D	MIDSIZE-D	OUTHEAR-D	PHONATE-D
GLIMPSE-D	INNERVE-D	MIDWIFE-D	OUTHIRE-D	PICKAXE-D
GLOBATE-D	INQUERE-D	MIDWIVE-D	OUTHYRE-D	PICRATE-D
GOLOSHE-D	INQUIRE-D	MIGRATE-D	OUTLINE-D	PICTURE-D
GRABBLE-D	INSNARE-D	MINIATE-D	OUTLIVE-D	PILEATE-D
GRADATE-D	INSPIRE-D	MISCITE-D	OUTLOVE-D	PILLAGE-D
GRANNIE-D	INSTATE-D	MISCODE-D	OUTMODE-D	PINNATE-D
GRAPPLE-D	INTERNE-D	MISDATE-D	OUTMOVE-D	PIPETTE-D
GRECISE-D	INTITLE-D	MISFARE-D	OUTNAME-D	PISTOLE-D
GRECIZE-D	INTRUDE-D	MISFILE-D	OUTPACE-D	PLACATE-D
GRIDDLE-D	INTWINE-D	MISFIRE-D	OUTRACE-D	PLANCHE-D
GRIMACE-D	INVERSE-D	MISHEAR-D	OUTRAGE-D	PLICATE-D
GRIZZLE-D	INVOICE-D	MISLIKE-D	OUTRATE-D	PLUMAGE-D
GRUBBLE-D	INVOLVE-D	MISLIVE-D	OUTRAVE-D	POETISE-D

POETIZE-D	QUACKLE-D	REPRICE-D	SCANTLE-D	SNIRTLE-D
POLEAXE-D	QUIBBLE-D	REPRIME-D	SCAPPLE-D	SNOOZLE-D
POLLUTE-D	QUIDDLE-D	REPRISE-D	SCEDULE-D	SNUFFLE-D
POMMELE-D	QUIESCE-D	REPRIVE-D	SCEPTRE-D	SNUGGLE-D
PORTAGE-D	QUINCHE-D	REPRIZE-D	SCHAPPE-D	SNUZZLE-D
POSTURE-D	RABATTE-D	REPROBE-D	SCHOOLE-D	SOLVATE-D
POTHOLE-D	RADIATE-D	REPROVE-D	SCIENCE-D	SOUFFLE-D
POURSUE-D	RAILCAR-D	REPRYVE-D	SCOURGE-D	SPACKLE-D
PRANCKE-D	RAMPAGE-D	REPULSE-D	SCOURSE-D	SPAIRGE-D
PRANKLE-D	RAMPIRE-D	REQUERE-D	SCREEVE-D	SPANGLE-D
PRATTLE-D	RAPTURE-D	REQUIRE-D	SCRIEVE-D	SPARKLE-D
PRAUNCE-D	RAWBONE-D	REQUITE-D	SCROOGE-D	SPECKLE-D
PREASSE-D	RAWHIDE-D	REQUOTE-D	SCROUGE-D	SPICATE-D
PREBAKE-D	REALISE-D	RERAISE-D	SCROWLE-D	SPINDLE-D
PRECEDE-D	REALIZE-D	REROUTE-D	SCRUPLE-D	SPLODGE-D
PRECISE-D	REALLIE-D	RESCALE-D	SCUDDLE-D	SPLURGE-D
PRECODE-D	REARGUE-D	RESCORE-D	SCUFFLE-D	SPREAZE-D
PRECURE-D	REAWAKE-D	RESEIZE-D	SCUMBLE-D	SPREEZE-D
PREDATE-D	REBADGE-D	RESERVE-D	SCUTTLE-D	SPRINGE-D
PREFACE-D	REBRACE-D	RESHAPE-D	SDEIGNE-D	SPULYIE-D
PREFADE-D	RECEIVE-D	RESHAVE-D	SECLUDE-D	SPULZIE-D
PREFILE-D	RECENSE-D	RESHINE-D	SECONDE-D	SQUEEZE-D
PREFIRE-D	RECLINE-D	RESLATE-D	SECRETE-D	SQUIDGE-D
PRELUDE-D	RECLOSE-D	RESOLVE-D	SELVAGE-D	STARTLE-D
PREMISE-D	RECOUPE-D	RESPACE-D	SENSATE-D	STATURE-D
PREMOVE-D	RECOURE-D	RESPADE-D	SERIATE-D	STEEPLE-D
PREPARE-D	RECOYLE-D	RESPIRE-D	SERRATE-D	STICKLE-D
PREPAVE-D	RECRATE-D	RESPITE-D	SERUEWE-D	STIDDIE-D
PREPONE-D	RECUILE-D	RESTAGE-D	SERVEWE-D	STIPPLE-D
PREPOSE-D	RECURVE-D	RESTATE-D	SERVICE-D	STIPULE-D
PRESAGE-D	RECYCLE-D	RESTOKE-D	SHACKLE-D	STOPPLE-D
PRESIDE-D	REDLINE-D	RESTORE-D	SHAMBLE-D	STRAYVE-D
PRESUME-D	REEVOKE-D	RESTYLE-D	SHEATHE-D	STRIATE-D
PRETAPE-D	REFENCE-D	RESURGE-D	SHINGLE-D	STRODLE-D
PRETYPE-D	REFEREE-D	RETASTE-D	SHMOOSE-D	STUBBLE-D
PREVENE-D	REFLATE-D	RETINUE-D	SHMOOZE-D	STUMBLE-D
PREVISE-D	REFORGE-D	RETITLE-D	SHOGGLE-D	STYLISE-D
PREWIRE-D	REFRAME-D	RETRACE-D	SHOOGIE-D	STYLIZE-D
PRICKLE-D	REGAUGE-D	RETRATE-D	SHOOGLE-D	SUBDUCE-D
PROBATE-D	REGLAZE-D	REUNITE-D	SHRIEVE-D	SUBLATE-D
PROCURE-D	REGORGE-D	REVALUE-D	SHUFFLE-D	SUBLIME-D
PRODUCE-D	REGRADE-D	REVENGE-D	SHUTTLE-D	SUBSIDE-D
PROFANE-D	REGRATE-D	REVENUE-D	SIAMESE-D	SUBSUME-D
PROFILE-D	REGREDE-D	REVERSE-D	SIAMEZE-D	SUBVENE-D
PROLATE-D	REHINGE-D	REVOICE-D	SIGMATE-D	SUFFICE-D
PROMISE-D	REHOUSE-D	REVOLVE-D	SILENCE-D	SUFFUSE-D
PROMOTE-D	REIMAGE-D	REWEAVE-D	SINUATE-D	SUICIDE-D
PRONATE-D	REISSUE-D	RHOMBOI-D	SIRNAME-D	SULCATE-D
PROPAGE-D	REJOICE-D	RIPOSTE-D	SITUATE-D	SULFATE-D
PROPALE-D	REJUDGE-D	ROMANCE-D	SKELLIE-D	SUMMATE-D
PROPONE-D	RELAPSE-D	ROSETTE-D	SKIFFLE-D	SUNBAKE-D
PROPOSE-D	RELEASE-D	RUINATE-D	SKITTLE-D	SUPPOSE-D
PRORATE-D	RELIEVE-D	RUMMAGE-D	SKUTTLE-D	SURBASE-D
PROVIDE-D	REMERGE-D	RUPTURE-D	SKYDIVE-D	SURBATE-D
PROVINE-D	RENAGUE-D	SALTATE-D	SMOODGE-D	SURFACE-D
PROVOKE-D	RENEGUE-D	SALVAGE-D	SMUGGLE-D	SURMISE-D
PULSATE-D	REPIQUE-D	SARDINE-D	SNABBLE-D	SURNAME-D
PURPOSE-D	REPLACE-D	SATIATE-D	SNAFFLE-D	SURVIVE-D
PURTRAY-D	REPLATE-D	SCABBLE-D	SNIFFLE-D	SUSPIRE-D
PUSTULE-D	REPLETE-D	SCAMBLE-D	SNIGGLE-D	SWADDLE-D

SWINDGE-D	TRILOBE-D	UNCURSE-D	UPCLOSE-D	VITIATE-D
SWINDLE-D	TRINDLE-D	UNDERGO-D	UPCURVE-D	WALLEYE-D
SWINGLE-D	TRIPPLE-D	UNDRAPE-D	UPGRADE-D	WARFARE-D
SWIZZLE-D	TROUBLE-D	UNFENCE-D	UPHEAVE-D	WARSTLE-D
SYMBOLE-D	TROUNCE-D	UNGLOVE-D	UPRAISE-D	WAYFARE-D
SYNAPSE-D	TRUCKLE-D	UNHINGE-D	UPROUSE-D	WELCOME-D
SYRINGE-D	TRUFFLE-D	UNHORSE-D	UPSCALE-D	WHAISLE-D
TALLAGE-D	TRUNDLE-D	UNHOUSE-D	UPSTAGE-D	WHAIZLE-D
TAMARIN-D	TRUSTEE-D	UNITISE-D	UPSTARE-D	WHEEDLE-D
TAPPICE-D	TUILYIE-D	UNITIZE-D	UPSURGE-D	WHEENGE-D
TARTANE-D	TUILZIE-D	UNLOOSE-D	UPVALUE-D	WHEEPLE-D
TEENAGE-D	TUMESCE-D	UNMITRE-D	URINATE-D	WHEEZLE-D
TERRACE-D	TURBINE-D	UNNERVE-D	UTILISE-D	WHEMMLE-D
TEXTURE-D	TWADDLE-D	UNNOBLE-D	UTILIZE-D	WHIFFLE-D
THIMBLE-D	TWANGLE-D	UNPLACE-D	VACUATE-D	WHIMPLE-D
TITRATE-D	TWATTLE-D	UNPLUME-D	VALANCE-D	WHISTLE-D
TONSURE-D	TWEEDLE-D	UNPURSE-D	VALUATE-D	WHITTLE-D
TOPLINE-D	TWIDDLE-D	UNQUOTE-D	VAMOOSE-D	WHOMBLE-D
TORTURE-D	TWINKLE-D	UNREAVE-D	VAMPIRE-D	WHOMMLE-D
TRACHLE-D	TWIZZLE-D	UNREEVE-D	VANDYKE-D	WHUMMLE-D
TRADUCE-D	TYRANNE-D	UNSCALE-D	VANTAGE-D	WOODBIN-D
TRAIPSE-D	ULULATE-D	UNSENSE-D	VARIATE-D	WRANGLE-D
TRAMPLE-D	UMBRAGE-D	UNSHALE-D	VENTURE-D	WRASSLE-D
TRAPEZE-D	UNAWAKE-D	UNSHAPE-D	VERDURE-D	WRASTLE-D
TREACLE-D	UNBRACE-D	UNSTATE-D	VESTURE-D	WREATHE-D
TREADLE-D	UNBRAKE-D	UNTRACE-D	VIBRATE-D	WRESTLE-D
TREDDLE-D	UNCHOKE-D	UNTWINE-D	VICIATE-D	WRIGGLE-D
TREMBLE-D	UNCLOSE-D	UNVAILE-D	VINTAGE-D	WRINKLE-D
TRICKLE-D	UNCRATE-D	UNVOICE-D	VIOLATE-D	YCLEEPE-D

Eight letters to nine

ABDICATE-D	AMBULATE-D	ARBORIZE-D	BADINAGE-D	BESOOTHE-D
ABERRATE-D	AMORTISE-D	ARCHAISE-D	BALDPATE-D	BESPOUSE-D
ABNEGATE-D	AMORTIZE-D	ARCHAIZE-D	BANALISE-D	BILOBATE-D
ABROGATE-D	AMPUTATE-D	AREOLATE-D	BANALIZE-D	BIRDLIME-D
ABSTERGE-D	ANGULATE-D	ARILLATE-D	BARBECUE-D	BLOCKADE-D
ACCOLADE-D	ANKYLOSE-D	ARMATURE-D	BARBEQUE-D	BLONDINE-D
ACCORAGE-D	ANNALISE-D	ARROGATE-D	BAREBONE-D	BLOVIATE-D
ACCOUTRE-D	ANNALIZE-D	ASPERATE-D	BARNACLE-D	BLUENOSE-D
ACERBATE-D	ANNOTATE-D	ASPIRATE-D	BECHANCE-D	BOLDFACE-D
ACIERATE-D	ANNOUNCE-D	ASSEMBLE-D	BECLOTHE-D	BOMBARDE-D
ACTIVATE-D	ANNULATE-D	ASSONATE-D	BEDABBLE-D	BOTANISE-D
ACTIVISE-D	ANTECEDE-D	ASTRINGE-D	BEDAGGLE-D	BOTANIZE-D
ACTIVIZE-D	ANTEDATE-D	ATCHIEVE-D	BEDAZZLE-D	BRATTICE-D
ACULEATE-D	ANTICISE-D	ATHETISE-D	BEDIMPLE-D	BRETTICE-D
ADUNCATE-D	ANTICIZE-D	ATHETIZE-D	BEFRINGE-D	BROMELIA-D
ADVOCATE-D	ANTIDOTE-D	ATMOLYSE-D	BEFUDDLE-D	BULLDOZE-D
AFFIANCE-D	APERTURE-D	ATMOLYZE-D	BEGIRDLE-D	BURNOOSE-D
AFFRONTE-D	APHETISE-D	ATTICISE-D	BEGRUDGE-D	BURNOUSE-D
AFTEREYE-D	APHETIZE-D	ATTICIZE-D	BEJUMBLE-D	BUTYLATE-D
AGGRIEVE-D	APHORISE-D	AUTOLYSE-D	BELITTLE-D	CALAMINE-D
ALBITISE-D	APHORIZE-D	AUTOLYZE-D	BEMINGLE-D	CALCEATE-D
ALBITIZE-D	APPANAGE-D	AUTOMATE-D	BEMUDDLE-D	CALORISE-D
ALIENATE-D	APPETISE-D	AUTOTYPE-D	BEMUFFLE-D	CALORIZE-D
ALKALISE-D	APPETIZE-D	AVIANISE-D	BEMUZZLE-D	CANALISE-D
ALKALIZE-D	APPLIQUE-D	AVIANIZE-D	BENEFICE-D	CANALIZE-D
ALKYLATE-D	APPRAISE-D	BACKBONE-D	BEPIMPLE-D	CANONISE-D
ALLIGATE-D	APRICATE-D	BACKDATE-D	BEPRAISE-D	CANONIZE-D
ALLOCATE-D	ARBORISE-D	BACKFIRE-D	BESMUDGE-D	CANOODLE-D

CANTHARI-D	CONCLUDE-D	DELEGATE-D	DISTANCE-D	ENSPHERE-D
CANULATE-D	CONCRETE-D	DELIBATE-D	DISTASTE-D	ENSWATHE-D
CAPITATE-D	CONDENSE-D	DEMONISE-D	DISUNITE-D	ENTANGLE-D
CAPONISE-D	CONFLATE-D	DEMONIZE-D	DISVALUE-D	ENTHRONE-D
CAPONIZE-D	CONGLOBE-D	DENATURE-D	DIVAGATE-D	ENTRANCE-D
CAPRIOLE-D	CONSERVE-D	DENOTATE-D	DIVINISE-D	ENVEIGLE-D
CARACOLE-D	CONSPIRE-D	DENOUNCE-D	DIVINIZE-D	ENVELOPE-D
CARAPACE-D	CONSTATE-D	DENUDATE-D	DOMICILE-D	ENVISAGE-D
CARINATE-D	CONSTRUE-D	DEPEOPLE-D	DOMINATE-D	EPILOGUE-D
CASEMATE-D	CONTINUE-D	DEPILATE-D	DOWNSIZE-D	EQUALISE-D
CASTRATE-D	CONTRIVE-D	DEPURATE-D	DOWNZONE-D	EQUALIZE-D
CATALYSE-D	CONVERGE-D	DEPUTISE-D	DUBITATE-D	EQUIPAGE-D
CATALYZE-D	CONVERSE-D	DEPUTIZE-D	DUCHESSE-D	ERADIATE-D
CATENATE-D	CONVINCE-D	DEROGATE-D	DUNGAREE-D	ERGOTISE-D
CAVITATE-D	CONVOLVE-D	DESCRIBE-D	DYNAMISE-D	ERGOTIZE-D
CENTUPLE-D	CONVULSE-D	DESCRIVE-D	DYNAMITE-D	ERUCTATE-D
CHASTISE-D	COPULATE-D	DESOLATE-D	DYNAMIZE-D	ESCALADE-D
CHIVAREE-D	COQUETTE-D	DETHRONE-D	EBIONISE-D	ESCALATE-D
CHROMISE-D	CORDELLE-D	DETONATE-D	EBIONIZE-D	ESCALOPE-D
CHROMIZE-D	CORELATE-D	DEVELOPE-D	ECHINATE-D	ESTIMATE-D
CICERONE-D	CORONATE-D	DIAGNOSE-D	EFFIERCE-D	ESTIVATE-D
CINCTURE-D	COROTATE-D	DIALOGUE-D	ELONGATE-D	ESTRANGE-D
CIVILISE-D	CORVETTE-D	DIAPAUSE-D	ELUVIATE-D	ETERNISE-D
CIVILIZE-D	CREASOTE-D	DIGITATE-D	EMACIATE-D	ETERNIZE-D
CLODPATE-D	CRENELLE-D	DIGITISE-D	EMBATTLE-D	ETHERISE-D
COADMIRE-D	CREOLISE-D	DIGITIZE-D	EMBEZZLE-D	ETHERIZE-D
COALESCE-D	CREOLIZE-D	DIMERISE-D	EMBOLISE-D	ETHICISE-D
COASSUME-D	CREOSOTE-D	DIMERIZE-D	EMBOLIZE-D	ETHICIZE-D
COCREATE-D	CREVASSE-D	DISABUSE-D	EMENDATE-D	ETHYLATE-D
CODERIVE-D	CRISPATE-D	DISAGREE-D	EMIGRATE-D	ETIOLATE-D
COENDURE-D	CRISTATE-D	DISBURSE-D	EMMARBLE-D	EULOGISE-D
COEQUATE-D	CRITIQUE-D	DISCIPLE-D	EMPEOPLE-D	EULOGIZE-D
COEVOLVE-D	CROSSTIE-D	DISCLOSE-D	EMPERISE-D	EUPHUISE-D
COGITATE-D	CRUSTATE-D	DISCOURE-D	EMPERIZE-D	EUPHUIZE-D
COGNOSCE-D	CULTRATE-D	DISGORGE-D	EMPIERCE-D	EVACUATE-D
COHOBATE-D	CUMULATE-D	DISGRACE-D	EMPLONGE-D	EVALUATE-D
COIFFURE-D	CURARISE-D	DISGRADE-D	EMPURPLE-D	EVANESCE-D
COINCIDE-D	CURARIZE-D	DISGUISE-D	ENCHARGE-D	EVENTISE-D
COINHERE-D	CURLICUE-D	DISHABLE-D	ENCIRCLE-D	EVENTIZE-D
COINSURE-D	CUTINISE-D	DISHORSE-D	ENCLOTHE-D	EVIDENCE-D
COLLAPSE-D	CUTINIZE-D	DISHOUSE-D	ENCRADLE-D	EVULGATE-D
COLLOGUE-D	DARRAINE-D	DISINURE-D	ENCREASE-D	EXCAVATE-D
COLLOQUE-D	DATABASE-D	DISLEAVE-D	ENDAMAGE-D	EXCHANGE-D
COLOCATE-D	DATELINE-D	DISLODGE-D	ENERGISE-D	EXECRATE-D
COLONISE-D	DEADLINE-D	DISPENCE-D	ENERGIZE-D	EXERCISE-D
COLONIZE-D	DEAERATE-D	DISPENSE-D	ENERVATE-D	EXHUMATE-D
COLORISE-D	DEBOUCHE-D	DISPERSE-D	ENFEEBLE-D	EXORCISE-D
COLORIZE-D	DEBRUISE-D	DISPLACE-D	ENFIERCE-D	EXORCIZE-D
COMANAGE-D	DECENTRE-D	DISPLODE-D	ENFILADE-D	EXPEDITE-D
COMEDDLE-D	DECIMATE-D	DISPLUME-D	ENGIRDLE-D	EXTUBATE-D
COMINGLE-D	DECLASSE-D	DISPONGE-D	ENGRIEVE-D	EXUVIATE-D
COMMENCE-D	DECORATE-D	DISPRIZE-D	ENGROOVE-D	FABULATE-D
COMMERCE-D	DECOUPLE-D	DISPROVE-D	ENHEARSE-D	FABULISE-D
COMMERGE-D	DECREASE-D	DISPUNGE-D	ENKINDLE-D	FABULIZE-D
COMPESCE-D	DEDICATE-D	DISPURSE-D	ENLUMINE-D	FANTASIE-D
COMPLETE-D	DEFECATE-D	DISSEISE-D	ENRAUNGE-D	FARADISE-D
COMPRISE-D	DEFILADE-D	DISSEIZE-D	ENSAMPLE-D	FARADIZE-D
COMPRIZE-D	DEGREASE-D	DISSERVE-D	ENSCONCE-D	FASCIATE-D
COMPULSE-D	DEIONISE-D	DISSOLVE-D	ENSHRINE-D	FASCICLE-D
CONCEIVE-D	DEIONIZE-D	DISSUADE-D	ENSILAGE-D	FATIGATE-D

FEDERATE-D	HUMANIZE-D	JUGULATE-D	MAXIMISE-D	MUSTACHE-D
FEMINISE-D	IDEALISE-D	JULIENNE-D	MAXIMIZE-D	MUTILATE-D
FEMINIZE-D	IDEALIZE-D	JUMBOISE-D	MEDICATE-D	NASALISE-D
FIBERISE-D	ILLUMINE-D	JUMBOIZE-D	MEDICINE-D	NASALIZE-D
FIBERIZE-D	IMMANTLE-D	KEELHALE-D	MEDITATE-D	NAUSEATE-D
FILAGREE-D	IMMINGLE-D	KEFUFFLE-D	MELANISE-D	NAVIGATE-D
FILIGREE-D	IMMOLATE-D	KEYSTONE-D	MELANIZE-D	NEBULISE-D
FILTRATE-D	IMMUNISE-D	KLONDIKE-D	MELODISE-D	NEBULIZE-D
FINALISE-D	IMMUNIZE-D	KLONDYKE-D	MELODIZE-D	NECKLACE-D
FINALIZE-D	IMPLEDGE-D	KREASOTE-D	MEMBRANE-D	NEGATIVE-D
FLATLINE-D	IMPLUNGE-D	KREOSOTE-D	MEMORISE-D	NICKNAME-D
FLUIDISE-D	IMPRESSE-D	LACERATE-D	MEMORIZE-D	NICOTINE-D
FLUIDIZE-D	IMPURPLE-D	LAMBASTE-D	METALISE-D	NODALISE-D
FOCALISE-D	INCHOATE-D	LAMINATE-D	METALIZE-D	NODALIZE-D
FOCALIZE-D	INCORPSE-D	LANGUAGE-D	MICROCAR-D	NOMADISE-D
FOOTNOTE-D	INCREASE-D	LAPIDATE-D	MILITATE-D	NOMADIZE-D
FOREBODE-D	INCUBATE-D	LATERISE-D	MINIMISE-D	NOMINATE-D
FOREDATE-D	INDAGATE-D	LATERIZE-D	MINIMIZE-D	NOSEDIVE-D
FORENAME-D	INDICATE-D	LATINISE-D	MISATONE-D	NOTARISE-D
FORHAILE-D	INDURATE-D	LATINIZE-D	MISFRAME-D	NOTARIZE-D
FORHOOIE-D	INFAMISE-D	LAUREATE-D	MISGAUGE-D	NOVELISE-D
FORJUDGE-D	INFAMIZE-D	LEGALISE-D	MISGRADE-D	NOVELIZE-D
FORWASTE-D	INFRINGE-D	LEGALIZE-D	MISGUIDE-D	NUCLEATE-D
FRACTURE-D	INGROOVE-D	LEVERAGE-D	MISJUDGE-D	NUMERATE-D
FRANCISE-D	INHEARSE-D	LEVIGATE-D	MISLEEKE-D	OBDURATE-D
FRANCIZE-D	INHUMATE-D	LEVITATE-D	MISLODGE-D	OBLIGATE-D
FREEBASE-D	INITIATE-D	LIBERATE-D	MISMETRE-D	OBSOLETE-D
FUMIGATE-D	INNOVATE-D	LIGATURE-D	MISPARSE-D	OBTURATE-D
GANGRENE-D	INSCONCE-D	LIGULATE-D	MISPLACE-D	OBVOLUTE-D
GARGOYLE-D	INSCRIBE-D	LINOTYPE-D	MISPOISE-D	OCCUPATE-D
GARROTTE-D	INSHRINE-D	LIQUESCE-D	MISPRICE-D	OCELLATE-D
GEFUFFLE-D	INSOLATE-D	LITIGATE-D	MISPRISE-D	OPALESCE-D
GEMINATE-D	INSPHERE-D	LOBULATE-D	MISPRIZE-D	OPPILATE-D
GENERATE-D	INSTANCE-D	LOCALISE-D	MISQUOTE-D	OPSONISE-D
GESNERIA-D	INSULATE-D	LOCALIZE-D	MISRAISE-D	OPSONIZE-D
GLACIATE-D	INSWATHE-D	LOCOMOTE-D	MISROUTE-D	OPTIMISE-D
GLISSADE-D	INTHRONE-D	LOCULATE-D	MISSHAPE-D	OPTIMIZE-D
GRADUATE-D	INTIMATE-D	LOGICISE-D	MISSPACE-D	ORDINATE-D
GRAECISE-D	INTITULE-D	LOGICIZE-D	MISSTATE-D	ORGANISE-D
GRAECIZE-D	INTONATE-D	LOOPHOLE-D	MISSTYLE-D	ORGANIZE-D
GRATINEE-D	INTRIGUE-D	LORICATE-D	MISTITLE-D	OSCITATE-D
GUNKHOLE-D	INTUBATE-D	LUNULATE-D	MISTRACE-D	OSCULATE-D
HARANGUE-D	INUNDATE-D	LUSTRATE-D	MISVALUE-D	OUTARGUE-D
HARDNOSE-D	INVEAGLE-D	LYOPHILE-D	MITIGATE-D	OUTBLAZE-D
HARDWIRE-D	INVEIGLE-D	LYRICISE-D	MOBILISE-D	OUTBRAVE-D
HEADLINE-D	INVOCATE-D	LYRICIZE-D	MOBILIZE-D	OUTBRIBE-D
HEBETATE-D	INVOLUTE-D	MACARISE-D	MODERATE-D	OUTBULGE-D
HEBRAISE-D	IODINATE-D	MACARIZE-D	MODULATE-D	OUTCASTE-D
HEBRAIZE-D	IRRIGATE-D	MACERATE-D	MONETISE-D	OUTCHIDE-D
HEMOLYSE-D	IRRITATE-D	MACULATE-D	MONETIZE-D	OUTCURSE-D
HEMOLYZE-D	JACULATE-D	MADERISE-D	MONOTONE-D	OUTDANCE-D
HEPATISE-D	JALOUSIE-D	MADERIZE-D	MOONFACE-D	OUTDODGE-D
HEPATIZE-D	JAPANISE-D	MAINLINE-D	MORALISE-D	OUTFABLE-D
HERNIATE-D	JAPANIZE-D	MALAXATE-D	MORALIZE-D	OUTFENCE-D
HESITATE-D	JAROVISE-D	MALLEATE-D	MORTGAGE-D	OUTGLARE-D
HOMINISE-D	JAROVIZE-D	MANICURE-D	MOTIVATE-D	OUTGUIDE-D
HOMINIZE-D	JAUNDICE-D	MARINADE-D	MOTORISE-D	OUTPLACE-D
HOOKNOSE-D	JEALOUSE-D	MARINATE-D	MOTORIZE-D	OUTPRICE-D
HOTHOUSE-D	JOINTURE-D	MASSACRE-D	MUCKRAKE-D	OUTPRIZE-D
HUMANISE-D	JUBILATE-D	MATURATE-D	MURICATE-D	OUTQUOTE-D

OUTRAISE-D	PENALISE-D	PROGRADE-D	REHANDLE-D	ROMANISE-D
OUTRANGE-D	PENALIZE-D	PROLAPSE-D	REHEARSE-D	ROMANIZE-D
OUTSCORE-D	PENSIONE-D	PROLOGUE-D	REIGNITE-D	ROSTRATE-D
OUTSERVE-D	PERCEIVE-D	PROLONGE-D	REILLUME-D	ROTAVATE-D
OUTSHAME-D	PERMEATE-D	PROMULGE-D	REIMPOSE-D	ROTOVATE-D
OUTSHINE-D	PERORATE-D	PROROGUE-D	REINCITE-D	ROULETTE-D
OUTSKATE-D	PEROXIDE-D	PROTRUDE-D	REINDUCE-D	ROYALISE-D
OUTSMILE-D	PERSPIRE-D	PTYALISE-D	REINFUSE-D	ROYALIZE-D
OUTSMOKE-D	PERSUADE-D	PTYALIZE-D	REINJURE-D	RUMINATE-D
OUTSNORE-D	PERSWADE-D	PULVILLE-D	REINSURE-D	RURALISE-D
OUTSTARE-D	PERVIATE-D	PUMICATE-D	REINVADE-D	RURALIZE-D
OUTSTATE-D	PHYSIQUE-D	PUNCTATE-D	REINVITE-D	SABOTAGE-D
OUTTRADE-D	PICOWAVE-D	PUNCTURE-D	REINVOKE-D	SAGINATE-D
OUTVALUE-D	PINAFORE-D	PURCHASE-D	REJUGGLE-D	SALINISE-D
OUTVOICE-D	PINNACLE-D	PURLICUE-D	REKINDLE-D	SALINIZE-D
OUTWASTE-D	PINTSIZE-D	PYRITISE-D	RELEGATE-D	SALIVATE-D
OVERBAKE-D	PIPELINE-D	PYRITIZE-D	RELOCATE-D	SANGUINE-D
OVERCROW-D	PIRLICUE-D	PYROLISE-D	RELUMINE-D	SANITATE-D
OVERCURE-D	PLEASURE-D	PYROLIZE-D	REMARQUE-D	SANITISE-D
OVERDARE-D	POLARISE-D	PYROLYSE-D	REMIGATE-D	SANITIZE-D
OVERDOSE-D	POLARIZE-D	PYROLYZE-D	RENATURE-D	SAPPHIRE-D
OVERHALE-D	POLEMISE-D	QUADRATE-D	RENEGADE-D	SATIRISE-D
OVERHATE-D	POLEMIZE-D	QUAGMIRE-D	RENFORCE-D	SATIRIZE-D
OVERHEAR-D	POLONISE-D	QUANTISE-D	RENOUNCE-D	SATURATE-D
OVERHOPE-D	POLONIZE-D	QUANTIZE-D	RENOVATE-D	SCAVENGE-D
OVERHYPE-D	POPULATE-D	RACEMISE-D	RENVERSE-D	SCHEDULE-D
OVERLADE-D	PORPOISE-D	RACEMIZE-D	REOPPOSE-D	SCHMOOSE-D
OVERLIVE-D	PORTIERE-D	RADICATE-D	REPARTEE-D	SCHMOOZE-D
OVERLOVE-D	POSTCODE-D	RAMPAUGE-D	REPEOPLE-D	SCLEROSE-D
OVERMINE-D	POSTDATE-D	REACCEDE-D	REPERUSE-D	SCRABBLE-D
OVERNAME-D	POSTPONE-D	REACCUSE-D	REPHRASE-D	SCRAMBLE-D
OVERRAKE-D	POSTPOSE-D	READVISE-D	REPLEDGE-D	SCRATTLE-D
OVERRATE-D	POULTICE-D	REAROUSE-D	REPLUNGE-D	SCRIBBLE-D
OVERRULE-D	POURTRAY-D	REASSUME-D	REPREEVE-D	SCRIGGLE-D
OVERSAVE-D	PRACTICE-D	REASSURE-D	REPRIEVE-D	SCROUNGE-D
OVERSIZE-D	PRACTISE-D	REBOTTLE-D	REPURSUE-D	SCROWDGE-D
OVERTIME-D	PREAMBLE-D	RECENTRE-D	REQUOYLE-D	SCRUMPLE-D
OVERTIRE-D	PRECLUDE-D	RECHANGE-D	REREVISE-D	SELVEDGE-D
OVERTURE-D	PREGUIDE-D	RECHARGE-D	RESADDLE-D	SEMIDOME-D
OVERTYPE-D	PREJUDGE-D	RECIRCLE-D	RESALUTE-D	SEMINATE-D
OVERURGE-D	PREMIERE-D	RECLOTHE-D	RESAMPLE-D	SEMINOMA-D
OVERVOTE-D	PRENTICE-D	RECOUPLE-D	RESECURE-D	SENTENCE-D
PAGANISE-D	PREPASTE-D	RECOURSE-D	RESEMBLE-D	SEPARATE-D
PAGANIZE-D	PREPENSE-D	RECREATE-D	RESETTLE-D	SEPTUPLE-D
PAGINATE-D	PREPLACE-D	REDAMAGE-D	RESINATE-D	SEQUENCE-D
PALISADE-D	PREPRICE-D	REDARGUE-D	RESINISE-D	SERENADE-D
PALLIATE-D	PRERINSE-D	REDECIDE-D	RESINIZE-D	SEROTYPE-D
PAPALISE-D	PRESCORE-D	REDEFINE-D	RESONATE-D	SEXTUPLE-D
PAPALIZE-D	PRESERVE-D	REDIVIDE-D	RESOURCE-D	SHAUCHLE-D
PARALYSE-D	PRESHAPE-D	REDOUBLE-D	RESPLICE-D	SHIVAREE-D
PARALYZE-D	PRESLICE-D	REEMERGE-D	RESTABLE-D	SHOWCASE-D
PATINATE-D	PRESOLVE-D	REENGAGE-D	RETACKLE-D	SHUNPIKE-D
PATINISE-D	PRESSURE-D	REEXPOSE-D	RETRIEVE-D	SIBILATE-D
PATINIZE-D	PRESTORE-D	REFIGURE-D	RIDICULE-D	SIDELINE-D
PATRIATE-D	PRETASTE-D	REFRINGE-D	RIGIDISE-D	SIDERATE-D
PECULATE-D	PREUNITE-D	REGELATE-D	RIGIDIZE-D	SILICATE-D
PEDICURE-D	PREVALUE-D	REGROOVE-D	RIVALISE-D	SIMILISE-D
PEDIGREE-D	PRIMROSE-D	REGULATE-D	RIVALIZE-D	SIMILIZE-D
PEDUNCLE-D	PRODNOSE-D	REGULISE-D	ROBOTISE-D	SIMONISE-D
PEJORATE-D	PROGNOSE-D	REGULIZE-D	ROBOTIZE-D	SIMONIZE-D

SIMULATE-D	STAMPEDE-D	TARTRATE-D	ULCERATE-D	URBANIZE-D
SINICISE-D	STARGAZE-D	TELETYPE-D	ULTIMATE-D	URTICATE-D
SINICIZE-D	STELLATE-D	TELEVISE-D	UNBOTTLE-D	VAGINATE-D
SIRENISE-D	STOCKADE-D	TENTACLE-D	UNBRIDLE-D	VALIDATE-D
SIRENIZE-D	STRADDLE-D	TETANISE-D	UNBUCKLE-D	VALORISE-D
SIRONISE-D	STRAGGLE-D	TETANIZE-D	UNBUNDLE-D	VALORIZE-D
SIRONIZE-D	STRANGLE-D	THEORISE-D	UNCHARGE-D	VAMBRACE-D
SLIPCASE-D	STRAVAGE-D	THEORIZE-D	UNCINATE-D	VAPORISE-D
SNOWSHOE-D	STREIGNE-D	THRAPPLE-D	UNCLOTHE-D	VAPORIZE-D
SOBERISE-D	STRICKLE-D	THROPPLE-D	UNCOUPLE-D	VAPULATE-D
SOBERIZE-D	STRIDDLE-D	THROTTLE-D	UNCREATE-D	VARICOSE-D
SODOMISE-D	STRINKLE-D	TIDIVATE-D	UNDAZZLE-D	VARITYPE-D
SODOMIZE-D	STRODDLE-D	TINCTURE-D	UNDERAGE-D	VEGETATE-D
SOLARISE-D	STRUGGLE-D	TINPLATE-D	UNDERUSE-D	VELARISE-D
SOLARIZE-D	STUPRATE-D	TIPPYTOE-D	UNDOUBLE-D	VELARIZE-D
SOLECISE-D	SUBERISE-D	TITIVATE-D	UNDULATE-D	VENENATE-D
SOLECIZE-D	SUBERIZE-D	TITUBATE-D	UNHEARSE-D	VENERATE-D
SOLIDATE-D	SUBITISE-D	TOLERATE-D	UNICYCLE-D	VERJUICE-D
SOMNIATE-D	SUBITIZE-D	TORQUATE-D	UNIONISE-D	VESICATE-D
SONICATE-D	SUBLEASE-D	TOTALISE-D	UNIONIZE-D	VIGNETTE-D
SORORISE-D	SUBMERGE-D	TOTALIZE-D	UNIVALVE-D	VIRILISE-D
SORORIZE-D	SUBMERSE-D	TRABEATE-D	UNMANTLE-D	VIRILIZE-D
SPECIATE-D	SUBSERVE-D	TRAMLINE-D	UNMINGLE-D	VITALISE-D
SPECTATE-D	SUBTITLE-D	TRANSUDE-D	UNMUFFLE-D	VITALIZE-D
SPOLIATE-D	SUBTRUDE-D	TRANSUME-D	UNMUZZLE-D	VOCALISE-D
SPRACKLE-D	SUBVERSE-D	TRAUCHLE-D	UNPEOPLE-D	VOCALIZE-D
SPRADDLE-D	SUFFLATE-D	TRAVERSE-D	UNPRAISE-D	VOLITATE-D
SPRANGLE-D	SULPHATE-D	TREASURE-D	UNPUZZLE-D	VOLPLANE-D
SPRATTLE-D	SUNBATHE-D	TREPHINE-D	UNRETIRE-D	VOLUMISE-D
SPREATHE-D	SUPERATE-D	TRESSURE-D	UNRIDDLE-D	VOLUMIZE-D
SPREETHE-D	SUPINATE-D	TRIANGLE-D	UNRUFFLE-D	VOUTSAFE-D
SPRINGAL-D	SURCEASE-D	TRICYCLE-D	UNSADDLE-D	VOWELISE-D
SPRINKLE-D	SURPLICE-D	TRITIATE-D	UNSETTLE-D	VOWELIZE-D
SPUILZIE-D	SURPRISE-D	TRIVALVE-D	UNSLUICE-D	WARDROBE-D
SQUABBLE-D	SURPRIZE-D	TRUNCATE-D	UNSPHERE-D	WHEYFACE-D
SQUATTLE-D	SYLLABLE-D	TUBERCLE-D	UNSWATHE-D	WOMANISE-D
SQUEEGEE-D	TABULATE-D	TUBULATE-D	UNTACKLE-D	WOMANIZE-D
SQUIGGLE-D	TAILGATE-D	TUNICATE-D	UNTANGLE-D	WORMHOLE-D
SQUILGEE-D	TAILPIPE-D	TUTORISE-D	UNTHRONE-D	
STAGNATE-D	TALLIATE-D	TUTORIZE-D	URBANISE-D	

E – Front-hooks

Two letters to three

E-AN	E-CH	E-ME	E-ON	E-WE
E-AR	E-EL	E-MO	E-RE	E-YE
E-AS	E-EN	E-MU	E-ST	
E-AT	E-GO	E-NE	E-TA	

Three letters to four

E-ACH	E-CAD	E-ECH	E-IDE	E-MIR
E-ALE	E-CHE	E-ELS	E-ISH	E-MOS
E-ARD	E-COD	E-GAD	E-KED	E-MUS
E-ARS	E-COS	E-GAL	E-MES	E-NEW
E-AVE	E-CRU	E-GIS	E-MEU	E-NOW
E-BON	E-DIT	E-GOS	E-MIC	E-ONS

E-PEE	E-RED	E-SPY	E-THE	E-VET
E-PIC	E-RES	E-TAS	E-TIC	E-VOE
E-POS	E-REV	E-TAT	E-TUI	E-YEN
E-RAS	E-SKY	E-TEN	E-UGH	E-YES

Four letters to five

E-AGER	E-GEST	E-MACS	E-PEES	E-STOP
E-ALES	E-HING	E-MAIL	E-PICS	E-TAPE
E-ARDS	E-IKON	E-MEER	E-POXY	E-TATS
E-ARED	E-KING	E-MEND	E-PROM	E-TENS
E-AVES	E-LAIN	E-MEUS	E-QUID	E-TUIS
E-BONY	E-LAND	E-MIRS	E-QUIP	E-TWEE
E-BOOK	E-LATE	E-MONG	E-RASE	E-UGHS
E-CADS	E-LINT	E-MOTE	E-REVS	E-VADE
E-CLAT	E-LITE	E-MOVE	E-RICK	E-VENT
E-CRUS	E-LOGE	E-MULE	E-RING	E-VERT
E-DICT	E-LOGY	E-MURE	E-RODE	E-VERY
E-DITS	E-LOIN	E-NEMA	E-ROSE	E-VETS
E-DUCE	E-LOPE	E-NEWS	E-SCAR	E-VITE
E-DUCT	E-LOPS	E-NORM	E-SCOT	E-WEST
E-EVEN	E-LUDE	E-NOWS	E-SILE	E-WHOW
E-GADS	E-LUTE	E-PACT	E-SKER	

Five letters to six

E-AGERS	E-LANDS	E-MOTES	E-QUIDS	E-SPRIT
E-AGLET	E-LAPSE	E-MOVED	E-QUINE	E-STATE
E-ASTER	E-LATED	E-MOVES	E-QUIPS	E-STEEM
E-BOOKS	E-LATER	E-MULED	E-RASED	E-STOPS
E-CARTE	E-LEGIT	E-MULES	E-RASER	E-STRAY
E-CHARD	E-LICIT	E-MURED	E-RASES	E-STRUM
E-CLATS	E-LINTS	E-MURES	E-RICKS	E-TALON
E-CLOSE	E-LITES	E-NATES	E-RODED	E-TAMIN
E-CURIE	E-LOGES	E-NEMAS	E-RODES	E-TAPES
E-DICTS	E-LOINS	E-NERVE	E-ROSES	E-TERNE
E-DITED	E-LOPED	E-NEWED	E-SCAPE	E-THANE
E-DUCES	E-LOPER	E-NODAL	E-SCARP	E-TOILE
E-DUCTS	E-LOPES	E-NOSES	E-SCARS	E-TRIER
E-ECHED	E-LUDES	E-PACTS	E-SCOTS	E-TYPIC
E-ECHES	E-LUTED	E-PARCH	E-SCROW	E-VADED
E-EVENS	E-LUTES	E-PERDU	E-SCUDO	E-VADES
E-GALLY	E-MAILS	E-PICAL	E-SILES	E-VENTS
E-GESTS	E-MEERS	E-POSES	E-SKERS	E-VERTS
E-IDENT	E-MENDS	E-PRISE	E-SKIES	E-VILER
E-IDOLA	E-MERGE	E-PROMS	E-SPIAL	E-VOLVE
E-IKONS	E-MESES	E-PULIS	E-SPIED	
E-ITHER	E-METIC	E-QUANT	E-SPIER	
E-LANCE	E-MOTED	E-QUATE	E-SPIES	

Six letters to seven

E-AGLETS	E-CHARDS	E-DITING	E-LAPSES	E-LOPERS
E-ASTERN	E-CLOSED	E-ECHING	E-LECTOR	E-LOPING
E-ASTERS	E-CLOSES	E-IRENIC	E-LEGIST	E-LUTING
E-BAYING	E-COTYPE	E-LANCED	E-LEGITS	E-MAILED
E-BONIST	E-CURIES	E-LANCES	E-LICHES	E-MENDED
E-CARTES	E-DENTAL	E-LAPSED	E-LOGIES	E-MENDER

E-MERGED	E-NERVES	E-SCAPED	E-STATED	E-TRIERS
E-MERGES	E-NEWING	E-SCAPES	E-STATES	E-UPHROE
E-METICS	E-PERDUE	E-SCARPS	E-STEEMS	E-VADING
E-MICATE	E-PICENE	E-SCRIBE	E-STOVER	E-VANISH
E-MONGST	E-QUANTS	E-SCROLL	E-STRAYS	E-VENTED
E-MOTION	E-QUINES	E-SCROWS	E-STRICH	E-VENTER
E-MOTIVE	E-QUITES	E-SERINE	E-STRUMS	E-VERTED
E-MOVING	E-RASERS	E-SPIALS	E-TALONS	E-VICTOR
E-MULING	E-RASING	E-SPIERS	E-TAMINE	E-VILEST
E-MUNGED	E-RASURE	E-SPOUSE	E-TAMINS	E-VOLUTE
E-MURING	E-RECTOR	E-SPRITS	E-TERNAL	E-VOLVED
E-NATION	E-RODENT	E-SPYING	E-THANES	E-VOLVES
E-NERVED	E-RODING	E-SQUIRE	E-TOILES	

Seven letters to eight

E-BONISTS	E-MERSION	E-PICENES	E-SCRIBES	E-TYPICAL
E-CAUDATE	E-METICAL	E-QUALITY	E-SCROLLS	E-UPHROES
E-CLOSING	E-MICATED	E-QUIPPED	E-SERINES	E-VACUATE
E-COSTATE	E-MICATES	E-QUIPPER	E-SPECIAL	E-VALUATE
E-COTYPES	E-MICTION	E-RADIATE	E-SPOUSAL	E-VENTERS
E-DENTATE	E-MIGRANT	E-RASURES	E-SPOUSED	E-VENTING
E-LANCING	E-MIGRATE	E-RECTION	E-SPOUSES	E-VERSION
E-LAPSING	E-MISSILE	E-RECTORS	E-SQUIRED	E-VERTING
E-LECTION	E-MISSION	E-RODENTS	E-SQUIRES	E-VICTORS
E-LECTORS	E-MISSIVE	E-SCALADE	E-STATING	E-VOCABLE
E-LEGISTS	E-MOTIONS	E-SCALADO	E-STEEMED	E-VOLUTED
E-LEVATOR	E-MUNGING	E-SCALIER	E-STOPPED	E-VOLUTES
E-MAILING	E-NATIONS	E-SCALLOP	E-STOVERS	E-VOLVING
E-MENDERS	E-NERVATE	E-SCAPING	E-STRANGE	E-VULGATE
E-MENDING	E-NERVING	E-SCARPED	E-STRAYED	
E-MERGING	E-PHORATE	E-SCRIBED	E-TAMINES	

Eight letters to nine

E-CARINATE	E-MICATING	E-RADIATED	E-STEEMING	E-VANISHED
E-COMMERCE	E-MICTIONS	E-RADIATES	E-STOPPAGE	E-VANISHES
E-GRESSING	E-MIGRANTS	E-RADICANT	E-STOPPING	E-VENTINGS
E-IRENICAL	E-MIGRATED	E-RADICATE	E-STRANGER	E-VENTLESS
E-IRENICON	E-MIGRATES	E-RECTIONS	E-STRANGES	E-VERSIONS
E-JACULATE	E-MISSIONS	E-ROSTRATE	E-STRAYING	E-VINCIBLE
E-LATERITE	E-MOTIONAL	E-SCALADES	E-STRICHES	E-VINCIBLY
E-LECTIONS	E-MOTIVITY	E-SCALLOPS	E-THIONINE	E-VOCATION
E-LECTRESS	E-NUCLEATE	E-SCARPING	E-VACUATED	E-VOCATIVE
E-LEVATORS	E-NUMERATE	E-SCRIBING	E-VACUATES	E-VOLUTION
E-LOCUTION	E-PHORATES	E-SPOUSALS	E-VAGINATE	E-VULGATES
E-LOCUTORY	E-PICRITIC	E-SPOUSING	E-VALUABLE	
E-MENDABLE	E-PISTOLET	E-SQUIRESS	E-VALUATED	
E-MERGENCE	E-QUIPPERS	E-SQUIRING	E-VALUATES	
E-MERSIONS	E-QUIPPING	E-STABLISH	E-VALUATOR	

E – End-hooks

Two letters to three

AG-E	AN-E	AT-E	AX-E	BE-E
AL-E	AR-E	AW-E	AY-E	BY-E

CH-E	GI-E	LI-E	OP-E	TE-E
DA-E	GO-E	MA-E	OR-E	TI-E
DE-E	GU-E	ME-E	OS-E	TO-E
DI-E	HA-E	MO-E	OW-E	UR-E
DO-E	HI-E	NA-E	OY-E	US-E
EM-E	HO-E	NE-E	PE-E	UT-E
EN-E	ID-E	NY-E	PI-E	WE-E
ER-E	JO-E	OB-E	RE-E	WO-E
FA-E	KA-E	OD-E	SH-E	YA-E
FE-E	KY-E	ON-E	TA-E	

Three letters to four

ABB-E	COL-E	FIR-E	KIN-E	MOB-E	
ABY-E	CON-E	FLU-E	KIP-E	MOD-E	
ACH-E	COP-E	FON-E	KIT-E	MOL-E	
ADZ-E	COR-E	FOR-E	KOR-E	MOM-E	
AGE-E	COS-E	FRA-E	LAC-E	MOP-E	
AID-E	COT-E	FRO-E	LAD-E	MOR-E	
AIN-E	COZ-E	FUM-E	LAM-E	MOS-E	
AKE-E	CRU-E	GAD-E	LAR-E	MOT-E	
ALA-E	CUB-E	GAG-E	LAS-E	MOU-E	
ALB-E	CUR-E	GAL-E	LAT-E	MOZ-E	
ALE-E	CUT-E	GAM-E	LAV-E	MUS-E	
AMI-E	DAL-E	GAN-E	LEK-E	MUT-E	
ANT-E	DAM-E	GAP-E	LEV-E	NAB-E	
ARS-E	DEB-E	GAR-E	LIN-E	NAM-E	
AWE-E	DEL-E	GAT-E	LIP-E	NAN-E	
BAD-E	DEN-E	GEN-E	LIT-E	NAP-E	
BAL-E	DIM-E	GIB-E	LOB-E	NET-E	
BAN-E	DIN-E	GIT-E	LOD-E	NID-E	
BAR-E	DIT-E	GON-E	LOG-E	NIT-E	
BAS-E	DIV-E	GOR-E	LOP-E	NIX-E	
BAT-E	DOG-E	GUL-E	LOR-E	NOD-E	
BAY-E	DOL-E	HAD-E	LOS-E	NOM-E	
BED-E	DOM-E	HAM-E	LOT-E	NON-E	
BEN-E	DON-E	HAT-E	LOW-E	NOS-E	
BET-E	DOP-E	HEM-E	LUD-E	NOT-E	
BID-E	DOR-E	HER-E	LUG-E	OBO-E	
BIN-E	DOS-E	HET-E	LUR-E	OCH-E	
BIS-E	DOT-E	HID-E	LUX-E	OOS-E	
BIT-E	DUD-E	HOM-E	LYM-E	ORF-E	
BIZ-E	DUN-E	HON-E	MAC-E	PAC-E	
BOD-E	DUP-E	HOP-E	MAD-E	PAL-E	
BOK-E	EAS-E	HOS-E	MAG-E	PAN-E	
BON-E	ECH-E	HOT-E	MAK-E	PAP-E	
BOR-E	ELS-E	HOW-E	MAL-E	PAR-E	
BRA-E	ERN-E	HUG-E	MAN-E	PAS-E	
BUT-E	ESS-E	HYP-E	MAR-E	PAT-E	
CAD-E	ETH-E	IDE-E	MAS-E	PAV-E	
CAG-E	EVO-E	JAK-E	MAT-E	PEN-E	
CAM-E	FAD-E	JAP-E	MEM-E	PER-E	
CAN-E	FAN-E	JET-E	MEN-E	PIC-E	
CAP-E	FAR-E	JIB-E	MES-E	PIN-E	
CAR-E	FAT-E	JOB-E	MET-E	PIP-E	
CAT-E	FEM-E	JOL-E	MIC-E	PIS-E	
CEP-E	FER-E	JUT-E	MIL-E	PLU-E	
CID-E	FET-E	KAI-E	MIM-E	POL-E	
CIT-E	FIL-E	KAM-E	MIR-E	POM-E	
COD-E	FIN-E	KET-E	MIS-E	POP-E	

POS-E	RUB-E	SOL-E	TIT-E	WAG-E
POT-E	RUD-E	SOM-E	TOG-E	WAN-E
PRE-E	RUM-E	SON-E	TOM-E	WAR-E
PUB-E	RUN-E	SPA-E	TON-E	WAS-E
PUL-E	SAB-E	STY-E	TOP-E	WAT-E
PUR-E	SAD-E	SUP-E	TOR-E	WAW-E
RAD-E	SAG-E	SUR-E	TOT-E	WEX-E
RAG-E	SAL-E	SYN-E	TRY-E	WHA-E
RAP-E	SAM-E	TAK-E	TUB-E	WIN-E
RAS-E	SAN-E	TAM-E	TUN-E	WIS-E
RAT-E	SAT-E	TAN-E	TWA-E	WIT-E
RED-E	SAV-E	TAP-E	TYE-E	WOK-E
RET-E	SAX-E	TAR-E	URD-E	YAR-E
RID-E	SEL-E	TAT-E	UVA-E	YGO-E
RIF-E	SEN-E	TEL-E	VAN-E	YIP-E
RIM-E	SER-E	TEN-E	VAR-E	YOD-E
RIN-E	SIC-E	TET-E	VAS-E	YOK-E
RIP-E	SIK-E	THE-E	VIA-E	YOW-E
RIT-E	SIN-E	TIC-E	VID-E	YUK-E
ROB-E	SIP-E	TID-E	VIN-E	ZIN-E
ROD-E	SIR-E	TIG-E	VIS-E	ZIT-E
ROK-E	SIT-E	TIL-E	VOL-E	
ROT-E	SNY-E	TIN-E	WAD-E	

Four letters to five

ABAS-E	BATH-E	CARS-E	CRAP-E	FEES-E
ABID-E	BEAR-E	CART-E	CREM-E	FEHM-E
AGEN-E	BECK-E	CAST-E	CREW-E	FESS-E
AGOG-E	BELL-E	CEAS-E	CRIM-E	FIER-E
AGON-E	BERM-E	CENS-E	CRIS-E	FILL-E
AINE-E	BIGA-E	CESS-E	CRUD-E	FITT-E
ALAN-E	BING-E	CHAP-E	CRUS-E	FLAK-E
ALBE-E	BIRL-E	CHAR-E	CURS-E	FLAM-E
ALGA-E	BITT-E	CHAS-E	CYMA-E	FLIT-E
ALOW-E	BLAD-E	CHAV-E	DAUB-E	FORM-E
AMEN-E	BLAM-E	CHER-E	DEAR-E	FORT-E
AMID-E	BLAT-E	CHID-E	DEER-E	FOSS-E
AMIN-E	BOMB-E	CHIN-E	DEEV-E	FOUL-E
AMUS-E	BOOS-E	CHIV-E	DENS-E	FRAP-E
ANIL-E	BORD-E	CHUT-E	DHOL-E	FRAT-E
ANIS-E	BORE-E	CLAD-E	DING-E	FRIS-E
ANSA-E	BORN-E	CLAM-E	DIRK-E	FRIZ-E
ANTA-E	BOTT-E	CLIP-E	DIXI-E	FUGU-E
APOD-E	BOWS-E	CLON-E	DONE-E	FUSE-E
AQUA-E	BRAK-E	CLOT-E	DOOL-E	FUZE-E
AREA-E	BRED-E	CLOY-E	DORE-E	GAFF-E
ARED-E	BRER-E	COAT-E	DORS-E	GAMB-E
ARET-E	BRIN-E	COHO-E	DOUC-E	GARB-E
ARIS-E	BRIS-E	COMA-E	DOWL-E	GEAR-E
ATOK-E	BROS-E	COMB-E	DOWS-E	GEES-E
AURA-E	BRUT-E	CONN-E	DRAP-E	GEST-E
AVAL-E	BUFF-E	COPS-E	EATH-E	GING-E
AXIL-E	BUND-E	CORS-E	EMYD-E	GLAD-E
AXON-E	BURK-E	COST-E	ERAS-E	GLED-E
AZYM-E	BURS-E	COUP-E	EROS-E	GLID-E
BARB-E	BUTT-E	COUR-E	FAIN-E	GLIM-E
BARD-E	CADE-E	COXA-E	FARL-E	GLOB-E
BASS-E	CADI-E	CRAM-E	FARS-E	GLUM-E
BAST-E	CARL-E	CRAN-E	FEAR-E	GLUT-E

GOLP-E	MACH-E	PLAT-E	SENT-E	SYCE-E
GOOS-E	MAIL-E	PLEB-E	SERR-E	TACH-E
GOSS-E	MAIR-E	PLUM-E	SETA-E	TASS-E
GRAD-E	MANG-E	POIS-E	SHAD-E	TAWS-E
GRAM-E	MANS-E	POSS-E	SHAM-E	TEAD-E
GRAT-E	MARA-E	POUK-E	SHIN-E	TEAS-E
GRAV-E	MARG-E	PRAT-E	SHIR-E	TEEN-E
GRID-E	MARL-E	PRIM-E	SHIT-E	TELA-E
GRIM-E	MARS-E	PROB-E	SHIV-E	TEMS-E
GRIP-E	MASS-E	PROS-E	SHOP-E	TENS-E
GRIS-E	MATT-E	PRYS-E	SHOT-E	TERF-E
GRUM-E	MEAN-E	PULS-E	SHUL-E	TERN-E
GUID-E	MENG-E	PUPA-E	SHUT-E	TEST-E
GUNG-E	MERL-E	PURE-E	SIDH-E	THAN-E
GUYS-E	MEUS-E	PURS-E	SING-E	THEM-E
HAST-E	MEZZ-E	QUAT-E	SIRE-E	THIN-E
HAUT-E	MICH-E	QUIN-E	SITH-E	THRO-E
HAWS-E	MILL-E	QUIT-E	SKAT-E	TING-E
HEAR-E	MINA-E	RACH-E	SKEN-E	TOGA-E
HEFT-E	MING-E	RAGE-E	SKIT-E	TOIL-E
HERO-E	MINK-E	RAIL-E	SKYR-E	TOPE-E
HERS-E	MIXT-E	RAIN-E	SLAT-E	TOPH-E
HERY-E	MOOS-E	RAIS-E	SLID-E	TORS-E
HING-E	MORA-E	RAKE-E	SLIM-E	TORT-E
HIRE-E	MORN-E	RAMI-E	SLIP-E	TOWS-E
HORS-E	MORS-E	RANG-E	SLOP-E	TRAD-E
IMID-E	MOST-E	RANK-E	SMIT-E	TRAP-E
INBY-E	MOTT-E	RARE-E	SNAR-E	TRIN-E
IRON-E	MOUS-E	RATH-E	SNIP-E	TRIP-E
ISNA-E	MOYL-E	RAZE-E	SOAR-E	TROD-E
JAMB-E	MURR-E	REAM-E	SOLD-E	TRON-E
JASP-E	MUSS-E	REED-E	SONS-E	TROP-E
JESS-E	NACH-E	RENT-E	SOOL-E	TUBA-E
JINN-E	NEUM-E	RIFT-E	SOOT-E	TUFF-E
KANA-E	NOUL-E	RILL-E	SORE-E	TURM-E
KENT-E	NOVA-E	RIMA-E	SOUS-E	TWIN-E
KERN-E	NURS-E	RINS-E	SOWL-E	TWIT-E
KITH-E	OBES-E	RONT-E	SOWN-E	TYND-E
KNOW-E	OBOL-E	ROOS-E	SOWS-E	ULNA-E
KYND-E	ODYL-E	ROUL-E	SPAN-E	UNDE-E
LAND-E	OUPH-E	ROUT-E	SPAR-E	UNIT-E
LAPS-E	OXID-E	RUFF-E	SPAT-E	UPBY-E
LARE-E	OXIM-E	RUGA-E	SPIC-E	URDE-E
LATH-E	PAIR-E	SAIC-E	SPIK-E	URSA-E
LEAR-E	PAIS-E	SAIN-E	SPIN-E	VAIR-E
LEAS-E	PARA-E	SALL-E	SPIT-E	VAUT-E
LEES-E	PARS-E	SALS-E	SPOD-E	VEAL-E
LEFT-E	PASS-E	SASS-E	STAG-E	VEHM-E
LENS-E	PAST-E	SAUT-E	STAR-E	VENA-E
LEVE-E	PEAG-E	SCAR-E	STAT-E	VERS-E
LITH-E	PEAR-E	SCOP-E	STED-E	VILD-E
LONG-E	PEAS-E	SCUT-E	STEM-E	VITA-E
LOOS-E	PECK-E	SEAM-E	STIM-E	VOLA-E
LOUP-E	PEEP-E	SEAR-E	STIR-E	VOLT-E
LOUR-E	PENI-E	SEAS-E	STOA-E	WACK-E
LOUS-E	PERV-E	SEIS-E	STOP-E	WAID-E
LOWN-E	PHON-E	SELL-E	SUED-E	WAIT-E
LOWS-E	PILA-E	SEME-E	SUIT-E	WAST-E
LUNG-E	PIOY-E	SEMI-E	SWAG-E	WEEK-E
MAAR-E	PLAN-E	SENS-E	SYBO-E	WEET-E

WEFT-E	WHIT-E	WOOS-E	ZOEA-E
WELK-E	WING-E	WRIT-E	ZONA-E
WHIN-E	WITH-E	YOUS-E	

Five letters to six

AGORA-E	COATE-E	FRORN-E	LIPID-E	PINNA-E
ALLEL-E	COIGN-E	FUNDI-E	LOATH-E	PLAST-E
ALMUD-E	COLON-E	FURAN-E	LOBOS-E	PLEAS-E
ALULA-E	COMIC-E	FURCA-E	LOCAL-E	PLICA-E
AMEBA-E	CONCH-E	FUROL-E	LUNGE-E	PLONG-E
AMEND-E	CONGE-E	FUROR-E	LUNGI-E	POINT-E
AMPUL-E	CONIN-E	FUSIL-E	LUPIN-E	POLYP-E
ANCON-E	COOMB-E	GALEA-E	LYSIN-E	POTCH-E
ANNEX-E	CORPS-E	GAMIN-E	LYTTA-E	POULP-E
ANYON-E	COSTA-E	GEMMA-E	MADAM-E	PREDY-E
AORTA-E	COTTA-E	GEMOT-E	MALIC-E	PREIF-E
AVAIL-E	COUCH-E	GENOM-E	MAMMA-E	PRIEF-E
AVERS-E	COUPE-E	GLAIR-E	MEATH-E	PROIN-E
BACCA-E	COURS-E	GLEBA-E	MEDIA-E	PROYN-E
BARGE-E	CREES-E	GOURD-E	MENSA-E	PSYCH-E
BATTU-E	CROSS-E	GRAIL-E	MERGE-E	PURIN-E
BERTH-E	CROUP-E	GRAIN-E	MISER-E	PUTTI-E
BETID-E	CROUT-E	GRAND-E	MISSA-E	QUART-E
BLEND-E	CULPA-E	GREES-E	MONGO-E	QUICH-E
BLOND-E	CURAT-E	GREET-E	MORAL-E	QUINT-E
BLOWS-E	CURIA-E	GRIFF-E	MURRE-E	RALLY-E
BOCCI-E	CUTTO-E	GRILL-E	MUSCA-E	RAPPE-E
BOORD-E	DECAD-E	GROSZ-E	NOMAD-E	RAVIN-E
BOURN-E	DEMUR-E	GUIMP-E	NOULD-E	REBIT-E
BRAID-E	DERAT-E	GUTTA-E	NUCHA-E	RECIT-E
BREES-E	DEVOT-E	GYROS-E	OCREA-E	RECUR-E
BRIBE-E	DILDO-E	HALID-E	OCTAN-E	REDIA-E
BROCH-E	DONNE-E	HEARS-E	OLEIN-E	REDON-E
BROOS-E	DOOLE-E	HEAST-E	OPPOS-E	REGAL-E
BROWS-E	DORIS-E	HERMA-E	ORACH-E	REPIN-E
BUBAL-E	DREAR-E	HEXAD-E	ORANG-E	REPOS-E
BULLA-E	DROWS-E	HOARS-E	ORCIN-E	RESID-E
BUNJE-E	ENZYM-E	HORST-E	ORPIN-E	RESIT-E
BURSA-E	EOSIN-E	HUMAN-E	OSMOL-E	ROTCH-E
CAMES-E	EPRIS-E	HYDRA-E	OUTBY-E	RUBIN-E
CAMIS-E	EQUIP-E	HYPHA-E	PALEA-E	SABIN-E
CANNA-E	EXPOS-E	IMPED-E	PALLA-E	SAITH-E
CAPOT-E	FACET-E	INCUS-E	PARDI-E	SALAD-E
CARAT-E	FACIA-E	INDOL-E	PAREV-E	SALLE-E
CARDI-E	FARCI-E	INFER-E	PARKI-E	SALPA-E
CAUDA-E	FASTI-E	IODID-E	PAROL-E	SAROD-E
CAUSA-E	FAUNA-E	IODIN-E	PASSE-E	SASIN-E
CELLA-E	FEMAL-E	JAMBE-E	PATIN-E	SAVIN-E
CHAIN-E	FERIA-E	JINNE-E	PATTE-E	SCALA-E
CHAIS-E	FILOS-E	KARAT-E	PAVAN-E	SCATH-E
CHANG-E	FINAL-E	KINAS-E	PAVIS-E	SCHMO-E
CHELA-E	FITCH-E	LAMIA-E	PELTA-E	SCOPA-E
CHILD-E	FLORA-E	LARVA-E	PENNA-E	SCRAP-E
CHIRR-E	FONDU-E	LASSI-E	PERDU-E	SCRAY-E
CHORE-E	FORBY-E	LATHE-E	PETIT-E	SCULL-E
CHOWS-E	FORME-E	LAURA-E	PHEER-E	SELLA-E
CLAVI-E	FOSSA-E	LAWIN-E	PHOCA-E	SERIN-E
CLOTH-E	FOVEA-E	LETHE-E	PHYLA-E	SERRA-E
CNIDA-E	FRISE-E	LIBRA-E	PICOT-E	SEVER-E

SHOOL-E	STEAN-E	TAMIN-E	TRIOS-E	VALET-E
SHOTT-E	STEAR-E	TAMIS-E	TRIST-E	VALIS-E
SILEN-E	STEDD-E	TANGI-E	TROAD-E	VENIN-E
SILVA-E	STELA-E	TEETH-E	TROMP-E	VERST-E
SITHE-E	STONN-E	TENIA-E	TRYST-E	VERTU-E
SKEAN-E	STOOP-E	TERRA-E	TUYER-E	VILLA-E
SKRIK-E	STOUR-E	TESTA-E	TWYER-E	VIRTU-E
SNATH-E	STRIA-E	TESTE-E	ULNAR-E	VISIT-E
SOOTH-E	STRIP-E	THECA-E	UMBRA-E	VITTA-E
SOURS-E	STYLI-E	THEIN-E	UNBAR-E	VOLVA-E
SOZIN-E	SUMMA-E	THERM-E	UNCAP-E	VULVA-E
SPALL-E	SWATH-E	THORP-E	UNCIA-E	WALIS-E
SPARK-E	SWING-E	THROW-E	UNCUT-E	WATAP-E
SPARS-E	SWITH-E	TIBIA-E	UNRIP-E	WHEAR-E
SPICA-E	SWOUN-E	TOLAN-E	UNTIL-E	ZOAEA-E
SPINA-E	SYLVA-E	TOROS-E	UPTAK-E	ZOMBI-E
SPRIT-E	TALEA-E	TOUCH-E	URBAN-E	ZOOEA-E
SPURN-E	TALPA-E	TOXIN-E	UREAS-E	
STEAL-E	TAMAL-E	TRANS-E	UVULA-E	

Six letters to seven

ABOLLA-E	BENZIN-E	CICADA-E	DIOXID-E	FRIJOL-E
ACQUIT-E	BENZOL-E	CINEOL-E	DIVERS-E	GALOSH-E
ADONIS-E	BERLIN-E	CITRIN-E	DOLENT-E	GANOIN-E
ADVISE-E	BESPAT-E	CLEANS-E	DOMAIN-E	GARROT-E
AFFAIR-E	BETEEM-E	CLOACA-E	DOMINE-E	GENTIL-E
AFFEAR-E	BHISTI-E	COCAIN-E	DURESS-E	GERMAN-E
ALANIN-E	BICORN-E	CODEIN-E	EMETIN-E	GLOSSA-E
ALEXIN-E	BLINTZ-E	COELOM-E	EMPLOY-E	GLYCIN-E
ALIDAD-E	BOTONE-E	COMMER-E	ENGAGE-E	GOLOSH-E
ALSOON-E	BOUCHE-E	COMMOT-E	ENNUYE-E	GOODBY-E
ALTERN-E	BOUCLE-E	COMPER-E	ENTETE-E	GOUGER-E
ALUMIN-E	BREATH-E	COMPOS-E	EPERDU-E	GRADIN-E
ALUMNA-E	BREVET-E	COMPOT-E	EPIGON-E	GRANDE-E
AMIDIN-E	BROMID-E	CONCHA-E	EPIMER-E	GRATIN-E
AMOEBA-E	BROMIN-E	CONSOL-E	EPUISE-E	GUANAS-E
ANATAS-E	BRUCIN-E	COPULA-E	ESCAPE-E	GUANIN-E
ANILIN-E	BUGGAN-E	CORNEA-E	ETAMIN-E	HALTER-E
ANTICK-E	CAGOUL-E	CORONA-E	EUCAIN-E	HAPTEN-E
ANTLIA-E	CAMERA-E	COSMIN-E	EXEDRA-E	HARMIN-E
APHTHA-E	CANULA-E	COUCHE-E	EXTERN-E	HERNIA-E
ARABIS-E	CAPRIC-E	CRISTA-E	EXUVIA-E	HEROIN-E
ARCSIN-E	CARDIA-E	CRUSTA-E	FACULA-E	HYALIN-E
AREOLA-E	CARINA-E	CUPULA-E	FASCIA-E	HYDRAS-E
ARISTA-E	CARLIN-E	CYANID-E	FECULA-E	HYDRIA-E
ARSHIN-E	CAROCH-E	CYANIN-E	FERULA-E	HYDRID-E
ARTIST-E	CARPAL-E	DEFAST-E	FETICH-E	IMPING-E
ASPERS-E	CASERN-E	DEMAIN-E	FIANCE-E	IMPROV-E
ATTACH-E	CATENA-E	DEMEAN-E	FIBROS-E	INFANT-E
ATTRIT-E	CAVIAR-E	DENTIN-E	FIBULA-E	INFULA-E
AUGUST-E	CELLOS-E	DETENT-E	FITCHE-E	INGENU-E
AURORA-E	CESURA-E	DETENU-E	FLAMBE-E	INSULA-E
AXILLA-E	CHAETA-E	DEVISE-E	FLAVIN-E	INTERN-E
BAGASS-E	CHIMER-E	DEVOTE-E	FOLIOS-E	INTIMA-E
BAILLI-E	CHINES-E	DHOOTI-E	FORBAD-E	INULAS-E
BALLAD-E	CHOANA-E	DIAMIN-E	FOREBY-E	INVITE-E
BEGRIM-E	CHOPIN-E	DIAZIN-E	FORMAT-E	ISATIN-E
BEGUIN-E	CHORAL-E	DILUTE-E	FRAPPE-E	ISOBAR-E
BELDAM-E	CHORDA-E	DIOXAN-E	FRIAND-E	ISOGON-E

ISOMER-E	MOUSME-E	PICOTE-E	SAVANT-E	SUMMAT-E
JAGHIR-E	MUCOSA-E	PILULA-E	SCALAR-E	SYLVIN-E
JASMIN-E	MURRIN-E	PINKEY-E	SCHOOL-E	SYMBOL-E
JUBILE-E	MYELIN-E	PISTOL-E	SCLERA-E	SYNURA-E
KAGOUL-E	NANDIN-E	PLANCH-E	SCORIA-E	TABULA-E
KAINIT-E	NARCOS-E	PLANTA-E	SCOURS-E	TAENIA-E
KAOLIN-E	NATURA-E	PLATAN-E	SCROWL-E	TARTAN-E
LACUNA-E	NEBULA-E	PLEDGE-E	SDEIGN-E	TARTAR-E
LADRON-E	NEURON-E	PLEURA-E	SECOND-E	TEGULA-E
LAMINA-E	NITRID-E	POLEAX-E	SECRET-E	TIMBAL-E
LEASOW-E	NITRIL-E	POMMEL-E	SEROSA-E	TOLUID-E
LEGATE-E	NOVENA-E	PONTIL-E	SHEATH-E	TOLUOL-E
LEUCIN-E	NYMPHA-E	PRANCK-E	SIGNOR-E	TONNAG-E
LIGULA-E	OBLIGE-E	PRECIS-E	SITULA-E	TORULA-E
LINGUA-E	OCHREA-E	PRISER-E	SIXAIN-E	TRITON-E
LISSOM-E	OCTETT-E	PROTYL-E	SKATOL-E	TROCHE-E
LORICA-E	OLEFIN-E	PURLIN-E	SODAIN-E	TROPIN-E
LUCERN-E	ORIGAN-E	PYRROL-E	SOIGNE-E	TUNICA-E
LUNULA-E	OUVERT-E	QUININ-E	SPARTH-E	TUSSOR-E
LURDAN-E	PAIOCK-E	RADIAL-E	SPHAER-E	UNBORN-E
MACULA-E	PAJOCK-E	RADULA-E	SPHEAR-E	UNGULA-E
MARLIN-E	PALAMA-E	RATLIN-E	SPIREM-E	UNLAST-E
MARQUE-E	PANGEN-E	RECOUP-E	SPREDD-E	UNVAIL-E
MATRIC-E	PAPULA-E	REFUGE-E	SPRING-E	VAGINA-E
MAUVIN-E	PARDAL-E	REGINA-E	SQUAMA-E	VERDIT-E
MEDUSA-E	PAROLE-E	REGULA-E	STAITH-E	VERSIN-E
MEGASS-E	PARVIS-E	REQUIT-E	STATIC-E	VESICA-E
MESTOM-E	PATERA-E	RETINA-E	STRANG-E	VISITE-E
MICELL-E	PATINA-E	RETIRE-E	STRIGA-E	VOLANT-E
MODERN-E	PENSIL-E	REVERS-E	STROOK-E	VOMICA-E
MODIST-E	PEPSIN-E	RIPOST-E	STRUMA-E	WREATH-E
MONTAN-E	PEPTID-E	ROSIER-E	SUBTIL-E	ZONULA-E
MOOLVI-E	PESANT-E	ROTULA-E	SUCCOS-E	
MORULA-E	PICKAX-E	SAFROL-E	SULFID-E	

Seven letters to eight

ABSCISS-E	ATABRIN-E	CARACOL-E	DECIDUA-E	EULOGIA-E
ABSINTH-E	ATROPIN-E	CARDECU-E	DECLASS-E	EXAMINE-E
ACALEPH-E	AUREOLA-E	CERESIN-E	DEVELOP-E	EXCLUDE-E
ACANTHA-E	AUTOMAT-E	CHALAZA-E	DEXTRIN-E	EXHEDRA-E
ACICULA-E	AVELLAN-E	CHLORID-E	DISPONE-E	FALCULA-E
ACKNOWN-E	BACKBIT-E	CHLORIN-E	DIVORCE-E	FAUNULA-E
ACQUIRE-E	BALADIN-E	CINEAST-E	DOMICIL-E	FILARIA-E
ACRIDIN-E	BALISTA-E	COCHLEA-E	DOVECOT-E	FIMBRIA-E
ACTINIA-E	BARCHAN-E	COLICIN-E	DRACHMA-E	FINALIS-E
AFFRONT-E	BARGEES-E	COMPLIN-E	DUCHESS-E	FISTULA-E
AGACANT-E	BARYTON-E	CONTRAT-E	DUVETYN-E	FLORULA-E
AGLYCON-E	BENEFIC-E	CONTROL-E	DYSODIL-E	FLUORID-E
ALEURON-E	BESTRID-E	CORYPHE-E	ECDYSON-E	FLUORIN-E
ALKALIN-E	BIOPHOR-E	COURANT-E	ECHIDNA-E	FOLKMOT-E
ALKALIS-E	BOMBARD-E	CRANNOG-E	EMERITA-E	FORMULA-E
AMPHORA-E	BROADAX-E	CREATIN-E	EMPLOYE-E	FOSSULA-E
AMPULLA-E	BURNOUS-E	CROCEIN-E	EMPRESS-E	FOVEOLA-E
AMYGDAL-E	CABEZON-E	CURARIS-E	ENDORSE-E	FRACTUR-E
ANCILLA-E	CAESURA-E	CYPSELA-E	ENVELOP-E	FUCHSIN-E
ANETHOL-E	CAFFEIN-E	CYSTEIN-E	ESCALOP-E	FURCULA-E
ANTENNA-E	CANNULA-E	DARRAIN-E	ETATISM-E	FUSAROL-E
ANTIGEN-E	CAPELIN-E	DAUPHIN-E	ETATIST-E	GELATIN-E
ARMILLA-E	CARABIN-E	DEBOUCH-E	ETOURDI-E	GENERAL-E

GERMAIN-E	LIVEYER-E	OUTRANG-E	RATTLIN-E	SULPHID-E
GINGIVA-E	LOCUSTA-E	OUTWRIT-E	REHEARS-E	SUNBATH-E
GIRASOL-E	LUPULIN-E	OUVRIER-E	RELEASE-E	SUSPENS-E
GLIADIN-E	LYOPHIL-E	OXYPHIL-E	RETRAIT-E	SYLPHID-E
GRAMARY-E	MALEFIC-E	PAENULA-E	RHABDOM-E	SYMBIOT-E
GRANDAM-E	MAMILLA-E	PAPILLA-E	RIBSTON-E	SYMITAR-E
GRAPLIN-E	MARCHES-E	PARVENU-E	ROCKABY-E	SYNONYM-E
GRATINE-E	MARQUIS-E	PATELLA-E	RUSSULA-E	TABORIN-E
GRAVIDA-E	MASTICH-E	PENSION-E	SALICIN-E	TACHISM-E
HALIDOM-E	MATADOR-E	PERIDOT-E	SALVAGE-E	TACHIST-E
HALIMOT-E	MATELOT-E	PERIGON-E	SAPHENA-E	TEREBRA-E
HEGUMEN-E	MAUVAIS-E	PEROXID-E	SAPONIN-E	TESSERA-E
HEMATIN-E	MAUVEIN-E	PERSONA-E	SARCINA-E	THERMIT-E
HEMIPOD-E	MAXILLA-E	PFENNIG-E	SAUTOIR-E	THIAMIN-E
HETAERA-E	MEDULLA-E	PIANIST-E	SCAPULA-E	THIAZIN-E
HOLESOM-E	MEGAPOD-E	PICOLIN-E	SCHMELZ-E	THIAZOL-E
HOLYDAM-E	MESQUIN-E	PINNULA-E	SCHMOOS-E	THIONIN-E
IMPRESS-E	MESQUIT-E	PISCINA-E	SCHMOOZ-E	TOLIDIN-E
INCONNU-E	METAMER-E	PLACCAT-E	SCISSIL-E	TORCHER-E
INDAMIN-E	MEZQUIT-E	PLANULA-E	SCOPULA-E	TRACHEA-E
INDIGEN-E	MICELLA-E	PLAUDIT-E	SCURRIL-E	TRAVOIS-E
INDORSE-E	MINUTIA-E	PLIMSOL-E	SECONDE-E	TRIAZIN-E
INDULIN-E	MISWRIT-E	PLUMULA-E	SELVAGE-E	TRICORN-E
INERTIA-E	MONDAIN-E	PORPESS-E	SEQUELA-E	TRIOXID-E
INFAUNA-E	MONOPOD-E	PORTESS-E	SERPULA-E	TRIPTAN-E
INHUMAN-E	MORPHIN-E	PORTIER-E	SESTETT-E	URETHAN-E
INTERNE-E	MUSICAL-E	POTLACH-E	SEXTETT-E	URETHRA-E
ISOCHOR-E	NARCEIN-E	POULARD-E	SILICON-E	VACCINE-E
JACINTH-E	NARWHAL-E	PRACTIC-E	SILIQUA-E	VALVULA-E
JEALOUS-E	NEBBISH-E	PRECAVA-E	SKYBORN-E	VENTAIL-E
KERMESS-E	NEGLIGE-E	PREMIER-E	SMARAGD-E	VERRUCA-E
LACINIA-E	NEURULA-E	PREPUPA-E	SOLANIN-E	VITAMIN-E
LAMBAST-E	NICOTIN-E	PROLONG-E	SPICULA-E	WANNABE-E
LAMELLA-E	NOCTURN-E	PROMISE-E	SPINULA-E	WOODBIN-E
LANOLIN-E	NOTITIA-E	PROTEAS-E	SPIRULA-E	XANTHIN-E
LARGESS-E	NOVELLA-E	PROTEGE-E	SQUILLA-E	XYLIDIN-E
LICENCE-E	ONCOGEN-E	PROTEID-E	STAMPED-E	ZECCHIN-E
LICENSE-E	OOTHECA-E	PTERYLA-E	STEARIN-E	ZOOGLEA-E
LIGROIN-E	OUTCAST-E	PTOMAIN-E	STROBIL-E	ZYMOGEN-E
LINGULA-E	OUTCHID-E	QUADRAT-E	SUCCUBA-E	

Eight letters to nine

ABORIGIN-E	BACCHANT-E	CAPONIER-E	CURCUMIN-E	DISSEISE-E
ABSCISSA-E	BACKSLID-E	CAPSOMER-E	CURTALAX-E	DISSEIZE-E
ACANTHIN-E	BALLADIN-E	CARTOUCH-E	CUSPIDOR-E	DISTRAIT-E
ACETAMID-E	BALLISTA-E	CATHEDRA-E	CUTICULA-E	DISULFID-E
AFFRONTE-E	BANDEROL-E	CERCARIA-E	CYANAMID-E	ECCLESIA-E
ALIZARIN-E	BASILICA-E	CHAPERON-E	DANCETTE-E	ECSTASIS-E
ALTERNAT-E	BASOPHIL-E	CHLORDAN-E	DARRAIGN-E	EMPHASIS-E
AMYGDALA-E	BAUDRICK-E	CIRRIPED-E	DEBONAIR-E	ENDAMEBA-E
ANGUIPED-E	BENZIDIN-E	CISTERNA-E	DEBUTANT-E	ENDOSMOS-E
ANTEFIXA-E	BERBERIN-E	CLAUSULA-E	DECLASSE-E	ENSHEATH-E
ANTISTAT-E	BLASTULA-E	COCHLEAR-E	DEDICATE-E	ENSHRINE-E
APOLOGIA-E	BOUTONNE-E	COMATULA-E	DELEGATE-E	ENTAMEBA-E
APPRAISE-E	BRANCHIA-E	CONCOURS-E	DEMIVOLT-E	ENWREATH-E
ASPIRATA-E	BRASSIER-E	CONFERVA-E	DESPOTAT-E	EPHEDRIN-E
AURICULA-E	BRUCELLA-E	CONFRONT-E	DETRAQUE-E	EPHEMERA-E
AVENTAIL-E	CACOMIXL-E	CORPORAL-E	DIPLOMAT-E	EPIFAUNA-E
AVIFAUNA-E	CANEPHOR-E	CROSSBIT-E	DIRIGISM-E	EPITHECA-E

ETRANGER-E	LANDSLID-E	PASTORAL-E	RACHILLA-E	SYPHILIS-E
EUCARYOT-E	LAVALIER-E	PATHOGEN-E	RATIONAL-E	TESSELLA-E
EUKARYOT-E	LODICULA-E	PENTOSAN-E	REAEDIFY-E	TETROXID-E
EXIGEANT-E	MAGDALEN-E	PENUMBRA-E	REFORMAT-E	THEREFOR-E
FENESTRA-E	MAMMILLA-E	PEREGRIN-E	RELOCATE-E	THIOPHEN-E
FIBRILLA-E	MANDARIN-E	PERIODID-E	REMEDIAT-E	THYROXIN-E
FIGURANT-E	MANDOLIN-E	PETECHIA-E	REPLICAS-E	TOLUIDIN-E
FISSIPED-E	MARGARIN-E	PHENAZIN-E	RESTRING-E	TORCHIER-E
FROSTBIT-E	MESCALIN-E	PHENETOL-E	RETINULA-E	TRACHEID-E
FURFUROL-E	METHADON-E	PHOSPHID-E	RHODAMIN-E	TRICHINA-E
GAILLARD-E	MILLEPED-E	PHOSPHIN-E	RICERCAR-E	TRITICAL-E
GARAGIST-E	MILLIPED-E	PHOSPHOR-E	SAFRANIN-E	TROCHLEA-E
GASTNESS-E	MISCEGEN-E	PHOTOGEN-E	SARABAND-E	TURQUOIS-E
GASTRULA-E	MORTGAGE-E	PINNIPED-E	SCELERAT-E	TYRANNIS-E
GLABELLA-E	MULTIPED-E	PLACENTA-E	SCLEREID-E	UNDERBIT-E
GLYCERIN-E	MULTITON-E	PLEONAST-E	SEMIMATT-E	VAGINULA-E
GRANDSIR-E	MUSCADIN-E	POLYPHON-E	SEMUNCIA-E	VERATRIN-E
GUANIDIN-E	MYXAMEBA-E	PONTIFIC-E	SENSILLA-E	VERTEBRA-E
HANDWRIT-E	NIGROSIN-E	POSTCAVA-E	SERAPHIN-E	VESICULA-E
HARMALIN-E	NUBECULA-E	PRETERIT-E	SHEEPCOT-E	VIBRISSA-E
HEPATICA-E	OENOPHIL-E	PRIMITIA-E	SHIGELLA-E	VIGILANT-E
HISTAMIN-E	OSTRACOD-E	PROLAMIN-E	SILICULA-E	VISAGIST-E
HISTIDIN-E	OVERBORN-E	PROTAMIN-E	SIMPLIST-E	VITELLIN-E
HOSPITAL-E	PALESTRA-E	PROTOXID-E	SLUGHORN-E	VULSELLA-E
INSHEATH-E	PALMIPED-E	PROVEDOR-E	SNAKEBIT-E	WHEREFOR-E
INTERESS-E	PALPEBRA-E	PUERPERA-E	SQUADRON-E	XYLOIDIN-E
INTERVAL-E	PANTALON-E	QUADRIGA-E	STROBILA-E	YERSINIA-E
INTIMIST-E	PARAFFIN-E	QUARTETT-E	STRONGYL-E	ZOOGLOEA-E
ISOCHRON-E	PAROCHIN-E	QUINOLIN-E	SUBCOSTA-E	
KHALIFAT-E	PARVOLIN-E	QUINTETT-E	SYNOPSIS-E	

F – Front-hooks

Two letters to three

F-AA	F-AS	F-EM	F-OB	F-OY
F-AB	F-AT	F-EN	F-OE	F-UG
F-AD	F-AW	F-ER	F-OH	F-UM
F-AE	F-AX	F-ES	F-ON	F-UN
F-AG	F-AY	F-ET	F-OP	F-UR
F-AH	F-ED	F-ID	F-OR	
F-AN	F-EE	F-IN	F-OU	
F-AR	F-EH	F-IT	F-OX	

Three letters to four

F-AAS	F-AKE	F-AVE	F-EMS	F-INS
F-ABS	F-ALL	F-AWN	F-END	F-IRE
F-ACE	F-AND	F-AYS	F-ENS	F-IRK
F-ACT	F-ANE	F-EAR	F-ERE	F-ISH
F-ADO	F-ARD	F-EAT	F-ERN	F-ITS
F-ADS	F-ARE	F-EDS	F-ESS	F-LAB
F-AFF	F-ARM	F-EEL	F-EST	F-LAG
F-AGS	F-ARS	F-EEN	F-ETA	F-LAM
F-AHS	F-ART	F-EHS	F-ICE	F-LAP
F-AIL	F-ASH	F-ELL	F-IDS	F-LAT
F-AIN	F-ATE	F-ELT	F-ILL	F-LAW
F-AIR	F-AVA	F-EME	F-INK	F-LAX

F-LAY	F-LOP	F-OOT	F-OYS	F-RIZ
F-LEA	F-LOR	F-OPS	F-RAG	F-ROE
F-LED	F-LOW	F-ORA	F-RAP	F-ROM
F-LEE	F-LUX	F-ORB	F-RAS	F-ROW
F-LEG	F-OBS	F-ORD	F-RAT	F-RUG
F-LEW	F-OES	F-ORE	F-RAY	F-UDS
F-LEX	F-OHS	F-ORT	F-REE	F-UGS
F-LEY	F-OIL	F-OUD	F-RET	F-UNS
F-LIP	F-OLD	F-OUR	F-RIB	F-USE
F-LIT	F-ONE	F-OWL	F-RIG	
F-LOG	F-ONS	F-OXY	F-RIT	

Four letters to five

F-ABLE	F-AWNY	F-LAIR	F-LORY	F-RAGS
F-ACED	F-AXED	F-LAKE	F-LOSH	F-RAIL
F-ACER	F-AXES	F-LAKY	F-LOSS	F-RANK
F-ACES	F-AYRE	F-LAME	F-LOTA	F-RAPE
F-ACTS	F-EARS	F-LAMS	F-LOTE	F-RAPS
F-ADDY	F-EASE	F-LANK	F-LOUR	F-RATE
F-ADOS	F-EAST	F-LAPS	F-LOUT	F-RATS
F-AERY	F-EATS	F-LARE	F-LOWN	F-RAYS
F-AGIN	F-ECHT	F-LASH	F-LOWS	F-REAK
F-AILS	F-EELS	F-LATS	F-LUES	F-REED
F-AINE	F-ELLS	F-LAWN	F-LUFF	F-REES
F-AINS	F-ELTS	F-LAWS	F-LUKE	F-RESH
F-AIRS	F-EMES	F-LAYS	F-LUMP	F-RETS
F-AIRY	F-EMMY	F-LEAM	F-LUNG	F-RIBS
F-AKED	F-ENDS	F-LEAS	F-LUNK	F-RIGS
F-AKES	F-ERES	F-LEER	F-LUSH	F-RILL
F-ALLS	F-ERNS	F-LEES	F-LUTE	F-RISE
F-ANAL	F-ESSE	F-LEET	F-LYTE	F-RISK
F-ANDS	F-ESTS	F-LEGS	F-OGLE	F-RITS
F-ANES	F-ETAS	F-LEME	F-OILS	F-RITT
F-ANGA	F-ETCH	F-LEYS	F-OLDS	F-RITZ
F-ANON	F-EVER	F-LICK	F-OLIO	F-ROCK
F-ARDS	F-EWER	F-LIED	F-ONLY	F-ROES
F-ARED	F-EYED	F-LIER	F-OOTS	F-RONT
F-ARES	F-EYER	F-LIES	F-ORBS	F-RORE
F-ARLE	F-ICES	F-LIMP	F-ORBY	F-RORY
F-ARMS	F-ILLS	F-LING	F-ORDO	F-ROST
F-ARSE	F-ILLY	F-LINT	F-ORDS	F-ROWS
F-ARTS	F-INCH	F-LIPS	F-ORES	F-RUGS
F-ASCI	F-INKS	F-LISK	F-ORTS	F-RUMP
F-ATES	F-IRED	F-LITE	F-OSSA	F-RUSH
F-AULD	F-IRES	F-LITS	F-OUDS	F-RUST
F-AVAS	F-IRKS	F-LOCK	F-OURS	F-UGLY
F-AVEL	F-ITCH	F-LOGS	F-OWLS	F-UNDY
F-AVER	F-LABS	F-LONG	F-OXES	F-USED
F-AVES	F-LACK	F-LOOR	F-OYER	F-USES
F-AWNS	F-LAGS	F-LOPS	F-RACK	

Five letters to six

F-ABLED	F-ACTOR	F-AIRER	F-ANGAS	F-ARLES
F-ABLER	F-ADDLE	F-AKING	F-ANGLE	F-ARMED
F-ABLES	F-AERIE	F-ALLOW	F-ANION	F-ARMER
F-ACERS	F-AILED	F-ALTER	F-ANKLE	F-ARROW
F-ACING	F-AIRED	F-AMINE	F-ARCED	F-ARSED

F-ARSES	F-IRING	F-LENSE	F-LUFFS	F-RATCH
F-ASHED	F-IRKED	F-LETCH	F-LUMPS	F-RATER
F-ASHES	F-ISHES	F-LEXES	F-LUNKS	F-RAYED
F-ASTER	F-ITCHY	F-LICKS	F-LURRY	F-REAKS
F-AWNED	F-LACKS	F-LIERS	F-LUSHY	F-REEST
F-AWNER	F-LAIRS	F-LIGHT	F-LUTED	F-REMIT
F-AXING	F-LAKED	F-LIMPS	F-LUTER	F-RENNE
F-AYRES	F-LAKER	F-LINCH	F-LUTES	F-RICHT
F-EARED	F-LAKES	F-LINGS	F-LUXES	F-RIDGE
F-EASED	F-LAMED	F-LINTS	F-LYING	F-RIGHT
F-EASES	F-LAMER	F-LINTY	F-LYTED	F-RIGID
F-EASTS	F-LAMES	F-LIPPY	F-LYTES	F-RILLS
F-EATER	F-LANCH	F-LISKS	F-ODDER	F-RISES
F-EERIE	F-LANES	F-LITED	F-OGLES	F-RISKS
F-ENDED	F-LANKS	F-LITES	F-OILED	F-RISKY
F-ENDER	F-LARES	F-LOCKS	F-OLDER	F-RITES
F-ESSES	F-LASER	F-LONGS	F-OLIOS	F-RITTS
F-ESTER	F-LATUS	F-LOOEY	F-ONNED	F-ROCKS
F-ETTLE	F-LAWED	F-LOOIE	F-ORMER	F-RONTS
F-EWEST	F-LAWNS	F-LOPPY	F-OTHER	F-ROSTS
F-EYING	F-LAXES	F-LORAL	F-OUGHT	F-RUGAL
F-ICHES	F-LAYED	F-LOSSY	F-OUTER	F-RUMPS
F-ICKLE	F-LAYER	F-LOTAS	F-OUTRE	F-RUMPY
F-IGGED	F-LEAMS	F-LOTES	F-OWLED	F-RUSTS
F-ILIAL	F-LEDGE	F-LOURS	F-OWLER	F-UGGED
F-ILLER	F-LEDGY	F-LOURY	F-OYERS	F-UMBLE
F-INGAN	F-LEECH	F-LOUSE	F-RAILS	F-UNDER
F-INKED	F-LEERS	F-LOUTS	F-RAISE	F-UNKED
F-INNED	F-LEETS	F-LOWED	F-RANKS	F-USING
F-INNER	F-LEMES	F-LOWER	F-RAPPE	F-UTILE

Six letters to seven

F-ABLING	F-ARROWS	F-INCHES	F-LATTER	F-LOOSIE
F-ACTION	F-ARSING	F-INGANS	F-LAUNCH	F-LOPPED
F-ACTIVE	F-ASHERY	F-INKING	F-LAWING	F-LOPPER
F-ACTORS	F-ASHING	F-INNERS	F-LAYERS	F-LOSSES
F-ACTUAL	F-ASTERS	F-INNING	F-LAYING	F-LOURED
F-ACTURE	F-ATTEST	F-IRKING	F-LECHES	F-LOUSED
F-ADDLED	F-AWNERS	F-ITCHES	F-LEDGED	F-LOUSES
F-ADDLES	F-AWNIER	F-LACKED	F-LEDGES	F-LOUTED
F-AERIES	F-AWNING	F-LACKER	F-LEEING	F-LOWERS
F-AILING	F-EARFUL	F-LAGGED	F-LEERED	F-LOWERY
F-AIREST	F-EARING	F-LAGGER	F-LEGGED	F-LOWING
F-AIRILY	F-EASING	F-LAKERS	F-LEMING	F-LUBBER
F-AIRING	F-EASTED	F-LAKIER	F-LENSED	F-LUFFED
F-AIRWAY	F-EASTER	F-LAKING	F-LENSES	F-LUMMOX
F-ALCADE	F-EATING	F-LAMING	F-LICKED	F-LUMPED
F-ALLOWS	F-ENDERS	F-LAMMED	F-LICKER	F-LUNKER
F-ALTERS	F-ENDING	F-LANGER	F-LIGHTS	F-LUSHED
F-AMINES	F-ERNING	F-LANKED	F-LIMPED	F-LUSHER
F-ANGLED	F-ESTERS	F-LANKER	F-LINGER	F-LUSHES
F-ANGLES	F-ETCHED	F-LAPPED	F-LINTED	F-LUSTER
F-ANIONS	F-ETCHER	F-LAPPER	F-LIPPED	F-LUTERS
F-ANKLED	F-ETCHES	F-LASERS	F-LIPPER	F-LUTING
F-ANKLES	F-ETTLED	F-LASHED	F-LITING	F-LUTIST
F-ARCING	F-ETTLES	F-LASHER	F-LITTER	F-LYINGS
F-ARMERS	F-ICKLER	F-LASHES	F-LOCKED	F-LYTING
F-ARMING	F-IGGING	F-LASKET	F-LOGGED	F-OILING
F-ARRANT	F-INCHED	F-LATTEN	F-LOGGER	F-OLLIES

F-ONDING
F-ONNING
F-ORGONE
F-ORMERS
F-ORPINE
F-OTHERS
F-OULDER
F-OUTERS
F-OUTRED
F-OWLERS
F-OWLING
F-OXLIKE
F-OXTAIL
F-RABBIT
F-RAGGED

F-RAILER
F-RAILLY
F-RAISED
F-RAISES
F-RANGER
F-RANKED
F-RANKER
F-RANKLY
F-RAPPED
F-RAPPEE
F-RAPPES
F-RASSES
F-RATERS
F-RAUGHT
F-RAYING

F-RAZZLE
F-REAKED
F-REMITS
F-RESHES
F-RETTED
F-RICHTS
F-RIDGED
F-RIDGES
F-RIGGED
F-RIGGER
F-RIGHTS
F-RILLED
F-RINGED
F-RIPPER
F-RISKED

F-RISKER
F-RITTED
F-RITTER
F-RITZES
F-RIZZER
F-ROCKED
F-ROMAGE
F-RONTES
F-ROSTED
F-ROTHER
F-ROUGHY
F-ROUNCE
F-RUGGED
F-RUMPED
F-RUMPLE

F-RUSHED
F-RUSHES
F-UCKERS
F-UGGING
F-UGLIER
F-ULLAGE
F-ULLING
F-UMBLES
F-UNDIES
F-UNFAIR
F-UNKING
F-UNNEST

Seven letters to eight

F-ABLINGS
F-ACTIONS
F-ACTURES
F-ADDLING
F-AIRINGS
F-AIRWAYS
F-ALCADES
F-ALLOWED
F-ALTERED
F-ALTERER
F-ANGLING
F-ANKLING
F-ARCINGS
F-ARMINGS
F-ARROWED
F-AWNIEST
F-AWNINGS
F-EARLESS
F-EASTERS
F-EASTING
F-ESTIVAL
F-ETCHERS
F-ETCHING
F-ETTLING
F-ICKLEST
F-IRELESS
F-LABELLA
F-LACKERS
F-LACKING
F-LAGGERS

F-LAGGING
F-LAKIEST
F-LAMMING
F-LANCHED
F-LANCHES
F-LANGERS
F-LANKING
F-LAPPERS
F-LAPPING
F-LASHERS
F-LASHING
F-LASKETS
F-LATTENS
F-LAWLESS
F-LECTION
F-LEDGIER
F-LEECHED
F-LEECHES
F-LEERING
F-LEGGING
F-LENSING
F-LETCHED
F-LETCHES
F-LICHTER
F-LICKERS
F-LICKING
F-LIGHTED
F-LIMPING
F-LINCHES
F-LINGERS

F-LINTIER
F-LINTING
F-LIPPERS
F-LIPPING
F-LITTERS
F-LOCKING
F-LOGGERS
F-LOGGING
F-LOOSIES
F-LOPPERS
F-LOPPIER
F-LOPPIES
F-LOPPING
F-LOSSIER
F-LOUNDER
F-LOURIER
F-LOURING
F-LOUSING
F-LOUTING
F-LOWERED
F-LUBBERS
F-LUFFING
F-LUMPING
F-LUNKERS
F-LURRIES
F-LUSHERS
F-LUSHEST
F-LUSHIER
F-LUSHING
F-LUSTERS

F-LUTINGS
F-LUTISTS
F-ORPINES
F-OUTRING
F-OXTAILS
F-RACKING
F-RAGGING
F-RAGMENT
F-RAISING
F-RANGERS
F-RANKERS
F-RANKEST
F-RANKING
F-RAPPING
F-RATCHES
F-RAZZLES
F-REAKING
F-REEDMAN
F-REEDMEN
F-RETTING
F-RICHTED
F-RICKING
F-RIDGING
F-RIGGERS
F-RIGGING
F-RIGHTED
F-RIGHTEN
F-RIGIDER
F-RIGIDLY
F-RILLING

F-RINGING
F-RIPPERS
F-RISKERS
F-RISKFUL
F-RISKIER
F-RISKILY
F-RISKING
F-RITTERS
F-RITTING
F-RIZZERS
F-ROCKING
F-ROMAGES
F-ROSTING
F-ROTHERS
F-ROUNCES
F-RUGGING
F-RUMPING
F-RUMPLED
F-RUMPLES
F-RUSHING
F-UGLIEST
F-ULLAGES
F-UNCTION
F-UNFAIRS
F-UNHOUSE
F-USELESS
F-UTILITY

Eight letters to nine

F-ACTUALLY
F-ALLOWING
F-ALTERERS
F-ALTERING
F-ARROWING
F-ASHERIES
F-EASTINGS
F-IBERISES

F-LABELLUM
F-LACKERED
F-LAGGINGS
F-LANCHING
F-LAPPINGS
F-LASHINGS
F-LAUGHTER
F-LAUNCHED

F-LAUNCHES
F-LECTIONS
F-LEDGIEST
F-LEECHING
F-LEERINGS
F-LETCHING
F-LIGHTING
F-LINTIEST

F-LITTERED
F-LOCKINGS
F-LOGGINGS
F-LOPPIEST
F-LOSSIEST
F-LOUNDERS
F-LOURIEST
F-LOWERIER

F-LOWERING
F-LUMMOXES
F-LUSHIEST
F-LUSHNESS
F-LUSTERED
F-LUSTRATE
F-LUXMETER
F-RACKINGS

F-RAGGINGS	F-RECKLING	F-RIGHTFUL	F-RISKIEST	F-UNCTIONS
F-RAGMENTS	F-RICHTING	F-RIGHTING	F-ROCKINGS	F-UNHOUSES
F-RANKNESS	F-RIGGINGS	F-RIGIDEST	F-ROCKLESS	
F-RATCHING	F-RIGHTENS	F-RIGIDITY	F-RUMPLING	

F – End-hooks

Two letters to three

AL-F	DO-F	GI-F	NE-F	RE-F
AR-F	EF-F	IF-F	OF-F	SI-F
DE-F	EL-F	KA-F	OO-F	TE-F
DI-F	ER-F	KI-F	OR-F	WO-F

Three letters to four

ALE-F	CUR-F	GUL-F	NIE-F	SER-F
BAR-F	DEI-F	HOO-F	POO-F	SKY-F
BEE-F	DEL-F	HOW-F	PRO-F	SOW-F
BOY-F	DIF-F	HUM-F	REE-F	SUR-F
BUM-F	DOF-F	KAI-F	REI-F	TEF-F
CHE-F	DOW-F	KIF-F	RIF-F	WAI-F
CON-F	FIE-F	LEA-F	ROO-F	WOO-F
COO-F	GOA-F	LIE-F	SEI-F	WOW-F
COR-F	GOO-F	LOO-F	SEL-F	

Four letters to five

BRIE-F	HOWF-F	PROO-F	SKEE-F
GANE-F	KALI-F	SCAR-F	SNAR-F
GONE-F	MOTI-F	SCUR-F	SOWF-F
HOUF-F	PILA-F	SHEA-F	SPIF-F

Five letters to six

BELIE-F	DECAF-F	GONIF-F	PILAF-F	RELIE-F

Six letters to seven

SHERIF-F

G – Front-hooks

Two letters to three

G-AB	G-AS	G-ET	G-NU	G-OX
G-AD	G-AT	G-HI	G-OB	G-OY
G-AE	G-AY	G-ID	G-OD	G-UM
G-AG	G-ED	G-IF	G-OE	G-UN
G-AL	G-EE	G-IN	G-ON	G-UP
G-AM	G-EL	G-IO	G-OO	G-UR
G-AN	G-EM	G-IS	G-OR	G-US
G-AR	G-EN	G-IT	G-OS	G-UT

Three letters to four

G-ABS	G-ASH	G-INN	G-OAF	G-RAN
G-ABY	G-ASP	G-INS	G-OAT	G-RAT
G-ADS	G-ATE	G-IOS	G-OBO	G-RAY
G-AFF	G-AVE	G-ISM	G-OBS	G-REE
G-AGA	G-AYS	G-ITS	G-ODS	G-REN
G-AGE	G-EAN	G-JUS	G-OES	G-REW
G-AGS	G-EAR	G-LAD	G-OFF	G-REX
G-AID	G-EAT	G-LAM	G-OLD	G-RID
G-AIN	G-EDS	G-LED	G-OLE	G-RIG
G-AIR	G-EEK	G-LEE	G-ONE	G-RIM
G-AIT	G-ELD	G-LEG	G-ONS	G-RIN
G-ALA	G-ELS	G-LEI	G-OOF	G-RIP
G-ALE	G-ELT	G-LEY	G-OON	G-RIT
G-ALL	G-EMS	G-LIB	G-OOP	G-ROK
G-ALS	G-ENE	G-LID	G-OOR	G-ROT
G-AMA	G-ENS	G-LIT	G-OOS	G-ROW
G-AMP	G-ERE	G-LOB	G-ORA	G-RUB
G-ANE	G-EST	G-LOP	G-ORE	G-RUE
G-ANT	G-ETA	G-LOW	G-OUK	G-RUM
G-APE	G-HAT	G-LUG	G-OUT	G-ULE
G-APO	G-HIS	G-LUM	G-OWL	G-UMP
G-ARB	G-IDS	G-NAT	G-OWN	G-UNS
G-ARE	G-ILL	G-NAW	G-OYS	G-UPS
G-ARS	G-IMP	G-NOW	G-RAD	G-URN
G-ART	G-INK	G-NUS	G-RAM	G-UTS

Four letters to five

G-ABLE	G-EANS	G-LAIK	G-LOBS	G-ONER
G-AGED	G-EARS	G-LAIR	G-LODE	G-OOFS
G-AGER	G-EATS	G-LAMS	G-LOOM	G-OOFY
G-AGES	G-ELDS	G-LAND	G-LOOP	G-OONS
G-AIDS	G-ELTS	G-LARE	G-LOPS	G-OOPS
G-AINS	G-EMMA	G-LASS	G-LORY	G-OOSE
G-AIRS	G-EMMY	G-LAZE	G-LOSS	G-OOSY
G-AITS	G-ENES	G-LAZY	G-LOST	G-ORAL
G-ALAS	G-ERES	G-LEAM	G-LOUT	G-ORES
G-ALES	G-ERNE	G-LEAN	G-LOVE	G-OUKS
G-ALLS	G-ESSE	G-LEED	G-LOWS	G-OUTS
G-ALLY	G-ESTS	G-LEEK	G-LUES	G-OWLS
G-AMAS	G-ETAS	G-LEES	G-LUGS	G-OWNS
G-AMBO	G-EYER	G-LEET	G-LUMS	G-OXES
G-AMIN	G-HAST	G-LEIS	G-LUTE	G-RACE
G-AMPS	G-HATS	G-LENS	G-NATS	G-RADE
G-ANTS	G-HAUT	G-LENT	G-NOME	G-RADS
G-APED	G-HEST	G-LEYS	G-NOWS	G-RAFF
G-APER	G-HOST	G-LIAS	G-OAFS	G-RAFT
G-APES	G-ILLS	G-LIBS	G-OARY	G-RAIL
G-APOS	G-ILLY	G-LIFT	G-OATS	G-RAIN
G-ARBS	G-IMPS	G-LIKE	G-OBOS	G-RAMP
G-ARIS	G-INKS	G-LIME	G-ODSO	G-RAMS
G-ARUM	G-IRON	G-LINT	G-OFFS	G-RANA
G-ASPS	G-ISMS	G-LISK	G-OLDS	G-RAND
G-ATES	G-LACE	G-LITS	G-OLDY	G-RANT
G-AUNT	G-LADE	G-LOAM	G-OLES	G-RAPE
G-AVEL	G-LADS	G-LOBE	G-OLPE	G-RASP
G-AZON	G-LADY	G-LOBI	G-OMER	G-RATE

G-RAVE	G-RIDE	G-RIPS	G-ROTS	G-RYKE
G-RAYS	G-RIDS	G-RIPT	G-ROUP	G-RYPE
G-RAZE	G-RIFF	G-RISE	G-ROUT	G-ULES
G-REED	G-RIFT	G-RITS	G-ROVE	G-UMBO
G-REEK	G-RIGS	G-ROAN	G-ROWS	G-UMPS
G-REEN	G-RILL	G-ROIN	G-RUBS	G-UNDY
G-REES	G-RIME	G-ROKS	G-RUED	G-URGE
G-REGO	G-RIMY	G-ROMA	G-RUES	G-URNS
G-REIN	G-RIND	G-RONE	G-RUFF	G-URUS
G-RENS	G-RINS	G-ROOF	G-RUME	G-WINE
G-REWS	G-RIOT	G-ROOM	G-RUMP	G-YELD
G-RICE	G-RIPE	G-ROPE	G-RUNT	

Five letters to six

G-ABBED	G-ERNED	G-LOPPY	G-RAINY	G-RIPES
G-ABIES	G-ERNES	G-LOSSY	G-RAMPS	G-RISES
G-ABLED	G-ESSES	G-LOUTS	G-RANDS	G-RIVET
G-ABLES	G-HARRY	G-LOVED	G-RANGE	G-ROANS
G-ABLET	G-HAZEL	G-LOVER	G-RANTS	G-ROINS
G-ABOON	G-HOSTS	G-LOVES	G-RAPED	G-ROMAS
G-ADDED	G-IGGED	G-LOWED	G-RAPES	G-RONES
G-ADDER	G-ILLER	G-LOWER	G-RASPS	G-ROOFS
G-AGERS	G-IMPED	G-LUMPS	G-RATED	G-ROOMS
G-AGGER	G-INGLE	G-LUMPY	G-RATER	G-ROPED
G-AGING	G-INNED	G-LUNCH	G-RATES	G-ROPER
G-ALANT	G-INNER	G-LUTES	G-RAVED	G-ROPES
G-ALLEY	G-IRONS	G-NAMMA	G-RAVEL	G-ROSET
G-ALLOW	G-LACES	G-NATTY	G-RAVEN	G-ROUGH
G-AMBIT	G-LADES	G-NOMES	G-RAVER	G-ROUND
G-AMBLE	G-LAIKS	G-NOMIC	G-RAVES	G-ROUPS
G-AMBOS	G-LAIRS	G-NOSES	G-RAYED	G-ROUPY
G-AMINE	G-LAIRY	G-OBANG	G-RAYLE	G-ROUSE
G-AMINS	G-LANCE	G-OBOES	G-RAZED	G-ROUTS
G-AMMON	G-LANDS	G-ODSOS	G-RAZER	G-ROVED
G-ANGER	G-LARES	G-OFFED	G-RAZES	G-ROVES
G-ANTED	G-LAZED	G-OFFER	G-REAVE	G-ROWER
G-APERS	G-LAZES	G-OLDEN	G-REEDS	G-ROWTH
G-APING	G-LEAMS	G-OLDER	G-REEDY	G-ROYNE
G-ARGLE	G-LEANS	G-OLLER	G-REENS	G-RUBBY
G-ARISH	G-LEAVE	G-OLPES	G-REGOS	G-RUFFS
G-ARRET	G-LEDGE	G-OMERS	G-REINS	G-RUING
G-ARUMS	G-LEEKS	G-ONERS	G-RESES	G-RUMES
G-ASHED	G-LEETS	G-ONION	G-REWED	G-RUMLY
G-ASHES	G-LIFTS	G-ONIUM	G-REXES	G-RUMPS
G-ASPER	G-LIKES	G-OORIE	G-RICER	G-RUMPY
G-ASSED	G-LIMED	G-OOSES	G-RICES	G-RUNTS
G-ASSES	G-LIMES	G-ORALS	G-RIDES	G-RYKES
G-ASTER	G-LINTS	G-ORGIA	G-RIEVE	G-UMBOS
G-AUGER	G-LINTY	G-OWLED	G-RIFFS	G-UMPED
G-AUNTS	G-LISKS	G-OWNED	G-RIFTS	G-UNITE
G-AVELS	G-LOAMS	G-RACED	G-RILLE	G-UNMAN
G-AZONS	G-LOBBY	G-RACES	G-RILLS	G-URGED
G-EARED	G-LOBED	G-RAFFS	G-RIMED	G-URGES
G-ELATE	G-LOBES	G-RAFTS	G-RIMES	G-URNED
G-ELDER	G-LOBUS	G-RAILE	G-RINDS	G-USHER
G-EMOTE	G-LOOMS	G-RAILS	G-RIOTS	G-UTTER
G-ENDER	G-LOOPS	G-RAINE	G-RIPED	
G-ENTRY	G-LOOPY	G-RAINS	G-RIPER	

Six letters to seven

G-ABLETS	G-HOSTED	G-LOOPED	G-RATINE	G-ROPERS
G-ABLING	G-HOSTLY	G-LOPPED	G-RATING	G-ROPING
G-ADDERS	G-IGGING	G-LORIES	G-RAUNCH	G-ROSETS
G-ADDING	G-IMMIES	G-LOSSES	G-RAVELS	G-ROSSER
G-AGGERS	G-IMPING	G-LOUTED	G-RAVERS	G-ROUGHS
G-ALLEYS	G-INGLES	G-LOVERS	G-RAVING	G-ROUNDS
G-ALLIED	G-INNERS	G-LOVING	G-RAYING	G-ROUPED
G-ALLIES	G-INNING	G-LOWERS	G-RAYLES	G-ROUSED
G-ALLIUM	G-IRONIC	G-LOWING	G-RAZERS	G-ROUSER
G-ALLONS	G-IZZARD	G-LUGGED	G-RAZING	G-ROUSES
G-ALLOWS	G-LACIER	G-LUTEAL	G-REAVED	G-ROUTED
G-AMBITS	G-LADDER	G-OBANGS	G-REAVES	G-ROUTER
G-AMBLED	G-LADDIE	G-OFFERS	G-REEKED	G-ROWERS
G-AMBLER	G-LAIRED	G-OFFING	G-REGALE	G-ROWING
G-AMBLES	G-LANCED	G-OLDENS	G-REINED	G-ROWTHS
G-AMINES	G-LANCER	G-OLDEST	G-RENNED	G-ROYNES
G-AMMONS	G-LANCES	G-OLDISH	G-RICERS	G-RUBBED
G-ANGERS	G-LANDES	G-OLLERS	G-RICING	G-RUBBER
G-ANTING	G-LASSES	G-OLLIES	G-RIDDED	G-RUBBLE
G-ARGLED	G-LASSIE	G-OOFIER	G-RIDDER	G-RUEING
G-ARGLES	G-LAZIER	G-OOSIER	G-RIDDLE	G-RUFFED
G-ARRETS	G-LAZILY	G-ORGIAS	G-RIDING	G-RUFFLY
G-ASEITY	G-LAZING	G-OUTFLY	G-RIEVER	G-RUMBLE
G-ASHING	G-LEAMED	G-OWLING	G-RIEVES	G-RUMBLY
G-ASKING	G-LEANED	G-OWNING	G-RIFTED	G-RUMMER
G-ASPERS	G-LEANER	G-RABBLE	G-RIGGED	G-RUMPED
G-ASTERS	G-LEAVES	G-RACING	G-RILLED	G-RUNTED
G-ASTRAL	G-LEDGED	G-RACKLE	G-RILLES	G-ULLING
G-AUDING	G-LEDGES	G-RAFTED	G-RIMIER	G-UMPING
G-AUGERS	G-LEEING	G-RAFTER	G-RIMING	G-UNDIES
G-AUNTER	G-LEGGER	G-RAILES	G-RIMMER	G-UNITES
G-AUNTLY	G-LIBBED	G-RAINED	G-RINDED	G-UNLESS
G-EARING	G-LIBBER	G-RAINES	G-RIPERS	G-UNLOCK
G-ELATED	G-LIMING	G-RANGER	G-RIPING	G-UNSHIP
G-ELATES	G-LIMMER	G-RANGES	G-RIPPED	G-UNSHOT
G-ELDERS	G-LINTED	G-RANTED	G-RIPPER	G-URGING
G-ELDING	G-LISTEN	G-RANTER	G-RIPPLE	G-URNING
G-EMOTES	G-LISTER	G-RAPIER	G-RISING	G-USHERS
G-ENDERS	G-LITTER	G-RAPING	G-RITTED	G-UTTERS
G-ENLOCK	G-LOBATE	G-RASPED	G-RITTER	G-YMPING
G-ERNING	G-LOBING	G-RASPER	G-RIVETS	
G-ESTATE	G-LOBOSE	G-RASSES	G-ROINED	
G-HASTED	G-LOBULE	G-RATERS	G-ROOMED	
G-HAZELS	G-LOOMED	G-RATIFY	G-ROOMER	

Seven letters to eight

G-ALLISES	G-EARINGS	G-HARRIES	G-LANCING	G-LINTING
G-ALLIUMS	G-EARLESS	G-HASTING	G-LANDERS	G-LISTENS
G-ALLOWED	G-ELASTIC	G-HOSTING	G-LASSIES	G-LISTERS
G-ALLYING	G-ELATING	G-INNINGS	G-LAZIEST	G-LITTERS
G-AMBLERS	G-ELATION	G-IZZARDS	G-LEAMING	G-LITTERY
G-AMBLING	G-ELDINGS	G-LABELLA	G-LEANERS	G-LOAMING
G-ANGLING	G-ENLOCKS	G-LADDIES	G-LEANING	G-LOBATED
G-ARGLING	G-ENTRIES	G-LAIRIER	G-LIBBING	G-LOBULAR
G-ARISHES	G-ESTATED	G-LAIRING	G-LIMMERS	G-LOBULES
G-ASKINGS	G-ESTATES	G-LANCERS	G-LINTIER	G-LOOMING

G-LOOPIER	G-OOSIEST	G-REAVING	G-RIPPING	G-RUBBLED
G-LOOPING	G-OUTWEED	G-REEDIER	G-RIPPLES	G-RUBBLES
G-LOPPIER	G-RABBLED	G-REEDILY	G-RITTERS	G-RUFFING
G-LOPPING	G-RABBLER	G-REEKING	G-RITTING	G-RUMBLED
G-LOSSIER	G-RABBLES	G-REGALES	G-ROINING	G-RUMBLER
G-LOUTING	G-RAFTERS	G-REINING	G-ROOMERS	G-RUMBLES
G-LOVINGS	G-RAFTING	G-RENNING	G-ROOMING	G-RUMMEST
G-LOWERED	G-RAINIER	G-RIDDERS	G-ROSSERS	G-RUMNESS
G-LUGGING	G-RAINING	G-RIDDLED	G-ROUCHES	G-RUMPING
G-LUMPIER	G-RANGERS	G-RIDDLES	G-ROUNDED	G-UNHOUSE
G-LUMPILY	G-RANTERS	G-RIEVERS	G-ROUNDER	G-UNLOCKS
G-LUMPISH	G-RANTING	G-RIEVING	G-ROUPING	G-UNMAKER
G-LUNCHED	G-RANULAR	G-RIFTING	G-ROUSERS	G-UNPAPER
G-LUNCHES	G-RASPERS	G-RIGGING	G-ROUSING	G-UNSHIPS
G-NATTIER	G-RASPING	G-RILLING	G-ROUTERS	G-UNSTICK
G-OATLIKE	G-RATINGS	G-RIMIEST	G-ROUTING	G-UNSTOCK
G-OFFERED	G-RAVELED	G-RINDING	G-ROWABLE	G-UTTERED
G-OLDENED	G-RAVELLY	G-RINNING	G-ROWINGS	
G-ONENESS	G-RAVINGS	G-RIPPERS	G-RUBBERS	
G-OOFIEST	G-RAYLING	G-RIPPIER	G-RUBBING	

Eight letters to nine

G-ALLOWING	G-LISTENED	G-NATTIEST	G-RATIFIER	G-ROUTINGS
G-AMBLINGS	G-LITTERED	G-OFFERING	G-RATIFIES	G-RUBBLING
G-ANTELOPE	G-LOOPIEST	G-OLDENING	G-RAUNCHED	G-RUMBLERS
G-ASEITIES	G-LOPPIEST	G-OUTFLIES	G-RAUNCHES	G-RUMBLIER
G-ELATIONS	G-LOSSIEST	G-OUTWEEDS	G-RAVELING	G-RUMBLING
G-ESTATING	G-LOSSLESS	G-RABBLERS	G-RAVELLED	G-UNFOUGHT
G-HOSTINGS	G-LOVELESS	G-RABBLING	G-REEDIEST	G-UNHOUSES
G-LAIRIEST	G-LOWERING	G-RAFTINGS	G-REENGAGE	G-UNMAKERS
G-LANDLESS	G-LUGGABLE	G-RAINIEST	G-RIDDLING	G-UNPAPERS
G-LAZINESS	G-LUMPIEST	G-RAINLESS	G-RIMINESS	G-UNSTICKS
G-LEANINGS	G-LUNCHING	G-RAPESEED	G-ROUNDERS	G-UNSTOCKS
G-LINTIEST	G-MELINITE	G-RATIFIED	G-ROUNDING	G-UTTERING

G – End-hooks

Two letters to three

BA-G	EN-G	JO-G	MU-G	TA-G
BE-G	ER-G	LA-G	NA-G	TE-G
BI-G	FA-G	LI-G	NE-G	TI-G
BO-G	FE-G	LO-G	NO-G	TO-G
DA-G	GI-G	MA-G	PE-G	WO-G
DE-G	HA-G	ME-G	PI-G	YA-G
DI-G	HO-G	MI-G	RE-G	YU-G
DO-G	JA-G	MO-G	SO-G	ZA-G

Three letters to four

AGO-G	BON-G	CAN-G	FRA-G	GOO-G
ARE-G	BOY-G	DAN-G	FRO-G	GUN-G
BAN-G	BRA-G	DIN-G	FUN-G	HAG-G
BIG-G	BRO-G	DON-G	GAN-G	HAN-G
BIN-G	BUN-G	DUN-G	GIN-G	HIN-G
BIO-G	BUR-G	FAN-G	GON-G	HOG-G

HON-G	MIG-G	PLU-G	SAN-G	TEG-G
HUN-G	MON-G	PRO-G	SHA-G	TIN-G
JAG-G	MUG-G	PUN-G	SIN-G	TON-G
KIN-G	MUN-G	QUA-G	SKA-G	TUN-G
LIN-G	NOG-G	RAG-G	SON-G	VAN-G
MAG-G	NON-G	RAN-G	SPA-G	VUG-G
MAN-G	PAN-G	RIG-G	SUN-G	WAN-G
MAR-G	PEA-G	RIN-G	TAI-G	WIN-G
MEN-G	PIN-G	RUN-G	TAN-G	ZIN-G

Four letters to five

AGIN-G	BLIN-G	COHO-G	RUIN-G	SWAN-G
AKIN-G	BOON-G	GULA-G	SKEG-G	THIN-G
ALAN-G	BRIN-G	HYLE-G	SPAN-G	THON-G
BEIN-G	CLAN-G	KAIN-G	STUN-G	TYIN-G

Five letters to six

ACTIN-G	GAMIN-G	LYSIN-G	RAVIN-G	SERIN-G
BARON-G	GOBAN-G	MATIN-G	RAWIN-G	SEWIN-G
BASIN-G	KOBAN-G	MIRIN-G	RICIN-G	SPAIN-G
BELON-G	LAKIN-G	PAVIN-G	ROBIN-G	TAKIN-G
CONIN-G	LAWIN-G	PHOTO-G	ROSIN-G	TAMIN-G
COVIN-G	LAYIN-G	POTIN-G	SARIN-G	ZAMAN-G
ELDIN-G	LIKIN-G	PROLE-G	SATIN-G	
ELFIN-G	LININ-G	PURIN-G	SAVIN-G	

Six letters to seven

BIFFIN-G	DOBBIN-G	HODDIN-G	OUTRUN-G	ROBBIN-G
BIGGIN-G	DUBBIN-G	HOGGIN-G	OUTSIN-G	RUFFIN-G
BOBBIN-G	FARCIN-G	HOISIN-G	OUTWIN-G	SEISIN-G
BOFFIN-G	FECKIN-G	JERKIN-G	OVERDO-G	SEIZIN-G
BUGGIN-G	FEERIN-G	LAGGIN-G	PARKIN-G	STATIN-G
BUSKIN-G	FIRKIN-G	LEGGIN-G	PERFIN-G	TANNIN-G
CALKIN-G	FLEEIN-G	MARLIN-G	PERKIN-G	TELLIN-G
CARLIN-G	GASKIN-G	MARTIN-G	PICKIN-G	TIFFIN-G
CATALO-G	GERMIN-G	MATTIN-G	PIGGIN-G	TREPAN-G
CATLIN-G	GITTIN-G	MERLIN-G	PIPPIN-G	TROPIN-G
CODLIN-G	GLOBIN-G	MINGIN-G	POSTIN-G	UNAKIN-G
COFFIN-G	GRADIN-G	MUFFIN-G	PUFFIN-G	VERSIN-G
COPPIN-G	GRATIN-G	MUNTIN-G	PURLIN-G	WASHIN-G
CUFFIN-G	HARMIN-G	MURLIN-G	RAISIN-G	WELKIN-G
CYCLIN-G	HARPIN-G	NOGGIN-G	RATLIN-G	WITHIN-G
CYMLIN-G	HENNIN-G	NUBBIN-G	RENNIN-G	
DENTIN-G	HIPPIN-G	OUTRAN-G	RIGLIN-G	

Seven letters to eight

ASPIRIN-G	GALOPIN-G	MAHJONG-G	RELAXIN-G	TABORIN-G
CHITLIN-G	GELATIN-G	MORPHIN-G	RESILIN-G	UNDERDO-G
CREATIN-G	GLAIRIN-G	PEARLIN-G	SCULPIN-G	
CRISPIN-G	HALFLIN-G	PUMPKIN-G	SPELDIN-G	
EASTLIN-G	LITTLIN-G	RATTLIN-G	SPONGIN-G	
FINIKIN-G	MAFFLIN-G	RAVELIN-G	STEARIN-G	

Eight letters to nine

ABSCISIN-G	DAMASKIN-G	INVERTIN-G	SNEESHIN-G	WARFARIN-G
BALLADIN-G	FINICKIN-G	LICHENIN-G	SPELDRIN-G	
BULLETIN-G	GOLLIWOG-G	SECRETIN-G	TABOURIN-G	

H – Front-hooks

Two letters to three

H-AD	H-AY	H-IN	H-OM	H-UH
H-AE	H-EH	H-IS	H-ON	H-UM
H-AG	H-EM	H-IT	H-OO	H-UN
H-AH	H-EN	H-MM	H-OP	H-UP
H-AM	H-ER	H-OB	H-OS	H-UT
H-AN	H-ES	H-OD	H-OW	H-YE
H-AS	H-ET	H-OE	H-OX	
H-AT	H-EX	H-OH	H-OY	
H-AW	H-ID	H-OI	H-UG	

Three letters to four

H-ADS	H-ARK	H-EME	H-ODS	H-ORE
H-AFF	H-ARM	H-EMS	H-OES	H-ORS
H-AFT	H-ART	H-END	H-OHS	H-OSE
H-AGS	H-ASH	H-ENS	H-OIK	H-OUR
H-AHA	H-ASK	H-ERE	H-OKA	H-OUT
H-AHS	H-ASP	H-ERN	H-OKE	H-OWE
H-AIL	H-ATE	H-ERS	H-OLD	H-OWL
H-AIN	H-AUF	H-EST	H-OLE	H-OYS
H-AIR	H-AVE	H-ETH	H-OLM	H-UGS
H-AKA	H-AYS	H-ICK	H-OMS	H-ULE
H-AKE	H-EAR	H-IDE	H-ONE	H-UMP
H-ALE	H-EAT	H-ILL	H-ONS	H-UNS
H-ALF	H-ECH	H-INS	H-OOF	H-UPS
H-ALL	H-EEL	H-IRE	H-OON	H-UTS
H-ALT	H-EFT	H-ISH	H-OOP	H-WAN
H-AND	H-EHS	H-ITS	H-OOT	H-YEN
H-ANT	H-ELD	H-OAR	H-OPE	H-YES
H-ARD	H-ELL	H-OBO	H-OPS	
H-ARE	H-ELM	H-OBS	H-ORA	

Four letters to five

H-ABLE	H-ANCE	H-ATES	H-EAVE	H-EROS
H-AILS	H-ANDS	H-AUFS	H-ECHT	H-ESTS
H-AINS	H-ANSA	H-AULD	H-EDGE	H-ETHS
H-AIRS	H-ANTS	H-AUNT	H-EDGY	H-EUGH
H-AIRY	H-ARDS	H-AVER	H-EELS	H-EWER
H-AKES	H-ARED	H-AVES	H-EFTS	H-EXED
H-ALES	H-ARES	H-AWED	H-ELLS	H-EXES
H-ALFA	H-ARKS	H-AZAN	H-ELMS	H-EYED
H-ALFS	H-ARMS	H-EARD	H-EMES	H-IDES
H-ALLS	H-ARTS	H-EARS	H-EMIC	H-ILLS
H-ALMA	H-ASHY	H-EAST	H-ENDS	H-ILLY
H-ALMS	H-ASKS	H-EATH	H-ERES	H-INKY
H-ALTS	H-ASPS	H-EATS	H-ERNS	H-IRED

H-IRES	H-OKES	H-OOFS	H-OURS	H-OXES
H-ITCH	H-OLDS	H-OONS	H-OUTS	H-ULES
H-OARS	H-OLES	H-OOPS	H-OVEL	H-UMPH
H-OARY	H-OLLA	H-OOTS	H-OVEN	H-UMPS
H-OAST	H-OLMS	H-OPED	H-OVER	H-UMPY
H-OBOS	H-OMER	H-OPES	H-OWES	H-URDS
H-OHED	H-ONER	H-ORAL	H-OWLS	H-YENS
H-OIKS	H-ONES	H-OSES	H-OWRE	

Five letters to six

H-ACKEE	H-ARBOR	H-EATER	H-IRING	H-OSIER
H-ACKER	H-ARISH	H-EAVED	H-ISHES	H-OTTER
H-AFTER	H-ARKED	H-EAVES	H-ITCHY	H-OUSEL
H-AGLET	H-ARLED	H-EDGED	H-ITHER	H-OUTED
H-AILED	H-ARMED	H-EDGER	H-OARED	H-OVELS
H-AIRED	H-ARMER	H-EDGES	H-OASTS	H-OVERS
H-ALFAS	H-ARROW	H-EIGHT	H-OBOES	H-OWLED
H-ALLEL	H-ARTAL	H-ELVES	H-OCKER	H-OWLER
H-ALLOT	H-ASHED	H-EMMER	H-OGGIN	H-OWLET
H-ALLOW	H-ASHES	H-ENDED	H-OHING	H-OWRES
H-ALMAS	H-AUGHT	H-ERSES	H-OLDEN	H-UGGED
H-ALOED	H-AUNTS	H-ETHER	H-OLDER	H-UMBLE
H-ALOES	H-AVENS	H-EUGHS	H-OLLAS	H-UMPED
H-ALTER	H-AVERS	H-EWERS	H-OLLER	H-UMPTY
H-AMATE	H-AWING	H-EXACT	H-OMBRE	H-UPPED
H-AMBLE	H-AZANS	H-EXING	H-OMERS	H-USHER
H-ANGER	H-EARDS	H-EYING	H-ONERS	
H-ANKER	H-EARTH	H-ILLER	H-OOPED	
H-ANTED	H-EASTS	H-INTER	H-OPING	

Six letters to seven

H-ABDABS	H-AMBLES	H-AUTEUR	H-IDLING	H-OUSELS
H-ACKEES	H-ANGERS	H-EARING	H-INKIER	H-OUTING
H-ACKERS	H-ANKERS	H-EARTHS	H-INTERS	H-OVERED
H-ADDIES	H-ANTING	H-EATERS	H-ITCHED	H-OWLERS
H-ADDING	H-APLITE	H-EATING	H-ITCHES	H-OWLETS
H-AFTERS	H-ARBORS	H-EAVING	H-OARIER	H-OWLING
H-AGGADA	H-ARBOUR	H-EDGERS	H-OARING	H-UGGING
H-AGLETS	H-ARKING	H-EDGIER	H-OCKERS	H-ULLING
H-AILING	H-ARLING	H-EDGING	H-OGGINS	H-UMBLES
H-AIRIER	H-ARMERS	H-EIGHTH	H-OLLERS	H-UMPIES
H-AIRING	H-ARMFUL	H-EIGHTS	H-OLLIES	H-UMPING
H-ALBERT	H-ARMING	H-EMMERS	H-OMBRES	H-UPPING
H-ALLELS	H-ARROWS	H-ENDING	H-OOPING	H-USHERS
H-ALLOWS	H-ASHIER	H-ERRING	H-OSIERS	
H-ALTERS	H-ASHING	H-EUREKA	H-OSIERY	
H-AMATES	H-AUDING	H-EXACTS	H-OSTLER	
H-AMBLED	H-AUNTER	H-EXARCH	H-OTTERS	

Seven letters to eight

H-AGGADAH	H-AIRLESS	H-ALBERTS	H-APLITES	H-ARROWED
H-AGGADAS	H-AIRLIKE	H-ALLOWED	H-APLITIC	H-ARUSPEX
H-AGGADIC	H-AIRLINE	H-ALTERED	H-ARBORED	H-ASHIEST
H-AGGADOT	H-AIRLOCK	H-AMBLING	H-ARBOURS	H-AUNTERS
H-AIRIEST	H-ALATION	H-AMBONES	H-ARMLESS	H-AUTEURS

H-EARINGS	H-EIGHTHS	H-INKIEST	H-OROLOGY	H-OVERING
H-EATABLE	H-ERRINGS	H-ITCHIER	H-OSTLERS	H-USHERED
H-EATINGS	H-EUREKAS	H-ITCHILY	H-OTTERED	
H-EDGIEST	H-EXAMINE	H-ITCHING	H-OUTINGS	
H-EDGINGS	H-EXARCHY	H-OARIEST	H-OVERFLY	

Eight letters to nine

H-AGGADAHS	H-AIRLOCKS	H-ARBOURED	H-EXAMINES	H-OOLACHAN
H-AGGADOTH	H-ALATIONS	H-ARMONICA	H-ITCHIEST	H-OSIERIES
H-AIRBRUSH	H-ALLOWING	H-ARQUEBUS	H-ODOGRAPH	H-OTTERING
H-AIRINESS	H-ALTERING	H-ARROWING	H-ODOMETER	H-USHERING
H-AIRLINES	H-ARBOROUS	H-ESSONITE	H-ODOMETRY	

H – End-hooks

Two letters to three

AA-H	ED-H	HO-H	PA-H	UG-H
AS-H	ET-H	IS-H	PE-H	YA-H
BA-H	FA-H	LA-H	PO-H	YE-H
BO-H	FE-H	NA-H	RE-H	
DA-H	HA-H	NO-H	SH-H	
DO-H	HE-H	OO-H	SO-H	

Three letters to four

AMA-H	EAT-H	LIT-H	PAS-H	SIN-H
ARC-H	FAS-H	LOS-H	PAT-H	SIT-H
BAC-H	GAS-H	LOT-H	PEC-H	SOP-H
BAG-H	GAT-H	MAC-H	PEG-H	SOT-H
BAS-H	GOS-H	MAS-H	PHO-H	SUK-H
BAT-H	GOT-H	MAT-H	PIS-H	TAN-H
BET-H	GUS-H	MES-H	PIT-H	TAS-H
BIS-H	HAS-H	MET-H	POO-H	TAT-H
BOO-H	HAT-H	MIC-H	POS-H	TEC-H
BOS-H	HET-H	MOC-H	PUG-H	TET-H
BOT-H	HIS-H	MOS-H	PUS-H	TIC-H
BUS-H	HOG-H	MOT-H	RAS-H	TOP-H
CAP-H	HUN-H	MUS-H	RAT-H	UMP-H
COS-H	KIS-H	NIS-H	RES-H	VUG-H
COT-H	KIT-H	NOS-H	ROC-H	WAS-H
DAS-H	KOP-H	OAT-H	RUT-H	WIS-H
DIS-H	KUE-H	ODA-H	SEC-H	WIT-H
DOS-H	LAS-H	OKE-H	SHA-H	YEA-H
DOT-H	LAT-H	OUP-H	SIC-H	YOD-H

Four letters to five

ABAS-H	BIMA-H	BURG-H	DOSE-H	GART-H
AIRT-H	BOOT-H	CANE-H	DUNS-H	GIRT-H
ALMA-H	BRAS-H	CHIC-H	EPHA-H	GRIT-H
ALME-H	BRIT-H	CLOT-H	FLUS-H	GULP-H
ARIS-H	BROG-H	CRIT-H	FORT-H	GURS-H
BAIT-H	BRUS-H	CRUS-H	FRIT-H	HEAT-H
BAND-H	BUMP-H	DADA-H	FROS-H	HORA-H
BEAT-H	BUND-H	DONA-H	GALA-H	HUMP-H

KANE-H	MEAT-H	ROWT-H	SUBA-H	TOOT-H
KHET-H	MERC-H	SANG-H	SUMP-H	TORA-H
LAIC-H	MUST-H	SCAT-H	SURA-H	TORC-H
LEAS-H	MYNA-H	SIRI-H	SWAT-H	TROT-H
LEIS-H	NEAT-H	SLOT-H	SYNC-H	WOOS-H
LOTA-H	PLUS-H	SMIT-H	TAIS-H	WORT-H
MANE-H	PUJA-H	SOLA-H	TAVA-H	
MARA-H	RAJA-H	SOOT-H	TENT-H	
MARC-H	RAYA-H	SOUT-H	THIG-H	
MARS-H	ROUT-H	STAP-H	TILT-H	

Five letters to six

ALIYA-H	FINIS-H	KIBLA-H	POOJA-H	STOUT-H
ANKUS-H	GALUT-H	KYBOS-H	PRUTA-H	SUMAC-H
ARRIS-H	GAMAS-H	LAMED-H	PUNKA-H	SUNNA-H
ASPIS-H	GANJA-H	LAVAS-H	PURDA-H	SWART-H
CAMAS-H	GARIS-H	LIROT-H	RAKIS-H	TANNA-H
COHOS-H	GRUMP-H	LOOFA-H	RUPIA-H	THANA-H
COMET-H	HALVA-H	MATZA-H	SAMEK-H	TOROT-H
COPRA-H	HAMZA-H	MATZO-H	SCARP-H	TREFA-H
COSEC-H	HEART-H	MINIS-H	SCART-H	VAREC-H
CREES-H	HIGHT-H	MOLLA-H	SCOUT-H	WAIRS-H
DALED-H	HIJRA-H	MOOLA-H	SHEIK-H	WALLA-H
DARGA-H	HOOKA-H	MULLA-H	SHIVA-H	WIRRA-H
DELIS-H	HURRA-H	NALLA-H	SIRRA-H	ZIBET-H
DOURA-H	HUZZA-H	NULLA-H	SKART-H	ZILLA-H
DUKKA-H	IMPIS-H	PALLA-H	SMOOT-H	ZIZIT-H
EIGHT-H	INWIT-H	PARIS-H	SNEES-H	
FATWA-H	KHEDA-H	PERIS-H	SPART-H	
FELLA-H	KIBBE-H	POLIS-H	SPILT-H	

Six letters to seven

AARRGH-H	CHUPPA-H	MATZOT-H	QABALA-H	SUCCOT-H
AGGADA-H	FILMIS-H	MEGILP-H	SABBAT-H	SUKKOT-H
AGOROT-H	GRAMAS-H	MEZUZA-H	SABKHA-H	TALLIS-H
ALIYOT-H	HAGGIS-H	MIKVOT-H	SAHIBA-H	TALLIT-H
BABOOS-H	HALALA-H	MISSIS-H	SHANTI-H	TEREFA-H
BILLYO-H	HALLOT-H	OUTWIT-H	SHARIA-H	THANNA-H
BUSHWA-H	HEIGHT-H	PARKIS-H	SHIKSE-H	TURBIT-H
CADDIS-H	HUTZPA-H	PITARA-H	SIMURG-H	UNGIRT-H
CHALLA-H	LUCHOT-H	POORIS-H	STEALT-H	
CHALOT-H	MASTIC-H	PRUTOT-H	STIRRA-H	

Seven letters to eight

AGGADOT-H	HAFTARA-H	KABBALA-H	MEZUZOT-H	SHEHITA-H
AMARANT-H	HAGGADA-H	KASHRUT-H	NARGILE-H	TZITZIT-H
BEGORRA-H	HALAKHA-H	KETUBOT-H	OCTOPUS-H	VERANDA-H
CABBALA-H	HAROSET-H	KHALIFA-H	PEISHWA-H	YESHIVA-H
CHALLOT-H	HOSANNA-H	MADRASA-H	RABBITO-H	
CHUTZPA-H	HYDRANT-H	MASTABA-H	SAVANNA-H	
GALABEA-H	JAMBIYA-H	MEGILLA-H	SCAMPIS-H	
GALABIA-H	JELLABA-H	MESHUGA-H	SHAMMAS-H	

Eight letters to nine

ALLELUIA-H	GALLABIA-H	HAPHTARA-H	PARASHOT-H	TELESTIC-H
CHAROSET-H	HAFTAROT-H	INTIFADA-H	SANDARAC-H	YESHIVOT-H
DAHABIYA-H	HAFTOROT-H	KHANSAMA-H	SHAMIANA-H	
DJELLABA-H	HAGGADOT-H	MADRASSA-H	SHECHITA-H	
GALABIYA-H	HALACHOT-H	MAHARAJA-H	SHILLALA-H	
GALLABEA-H	HALAKHOT-H	MESHUGGA-H	TALLITOT-H	

I – Front-hooks

Two letters to three

I-CH	I-ON	I-RE	I-SO
I-DE	I-OS	I-SH	I-TA

Three letters to four

I-BIS	I-GAD	I-LEX	I-RED	I-SOS
I-CON	I-KAT	I-MAM	I-RES	I-TAS
I-DEE	I-KON	I-MID	I-RID	I-URE
I-DOL	I-LEA	I-ONS	I-SIT	I-WIS

Four letters to five

I-CONS	I-GAPO	I-MAMS	I-RADE	I-SLED
I-DANT	I-KANS	I-MIDS	I-RATE	I-TEMS
I-DEAL	I-KATS	I-MINE	I-RIDS	I-VIED
I-DEES	I-KONS	I-MINO	I-RING	I-VIES
I-DENT	I-LEAL	I-NANE	I-RONE	
I-DOLS	I-MAGE	I-ODIC	I-SHES	

Five letters to six

I-BICES	I-DANTS	I-LEXES	I-ODISM	I-RONES
	I-DEALS	I-MAGES	I-ONIUM	I-SATIN
I-BISES	I-DENTS	I-MINES	I-RATER	I-SLING
I-CONES	I-GAPOS	I-NERTS	I-RIDES	I-TEMED
I-CONIC	I-GUANA	I-NYALA	I-RISES	

Six letters to seven

I-GUANAS	I-NYALAS	I-ONIUMS	I-SATINS
I-MAGISM	I-ODISMS	I-RISING	I-SOLATE

Seven letters to eight

I-CONICAL	I-SABELLA	I-SOLATED	I-SOLATES
I-MAGISMS	I-SLANDER		

Eight letters to nine

I-CONICITY	I-SABELLAS	I-SOLATING	I-SOLATION
I-ODOMETRY	I-SLANDERS		

I – End-hooks

Two letters to three

AH-I	CH-I	KA-I	PO-I
AM-I	DE-I	KO-I	RE-I
AN-I	HO-I	MO-I	TA-I
BO-I	JA-I	OB-I	UN-I

Three letters to four

ANT-I	FIN-I	MAL-I	NOR-I	SIR-I
ART-I	GAD-I	MAN-I	PAD-I	SOL-I
BAN-I	GAR-I	MAX-I	PEN-I	TAB-I
BEN-I	GOR-I	MID-I	PER-I	TAK-I
BID-I	HAJ-I	MIR-I	PIP-I	TAX-I
BUD-I	IMP-I	MOA-I	PUL-I	TIP-I
CAD-I	KAK-I	MOD-I	PUR-I	TIT-I
CAP-I	KAM-I	MOM-I	QUA-I	TOP-I
CHA-I	KAT-I	MOO-I	RAG-I	TOR-I
CON-I	KEP-I	MOT-I	RAM-I	VAG-I
DAL-I	LAR-I	MUN-I	RAN-I	WAD-I
DEF-I	LAT-I	MUT-I	ROT-I	YAG-I
DEL-I	LOB-I	NID-I	SAD-I	YET-I
DEN-I	LOT-I	NIS-I	SAR-I	YON-I
DIV-I	MAG-I	NOD-I	SAT-I	ZIT-I
FEN-I	MAK-I	NON-I	SIM-I	

Four letters to five

ABAC-I	CURL-I	JINN-I	OBOL-I	SOLD-I
BASS-I	CURS-I	KIBE-I	PALP-I	SOLE-I
BAST-I	DASH-I	KORA-I	PARD-I	STOA-I
BEST-I	DILL-I	LANA-I	PARK-I	SWAM-I
BIND-I	DISC-I	LASS-I	PART-I	TANG-I
BLIN-I	FAST-I	LATH-I	PILE-I	TARS-I
BUFF-I	FERM-I	LENT-I	POOR-I	TAWA-I
BUST-I	FILM-I	LICH-I	PRIM-I	TEMP-I
CAMP-I	FRAT-I	LIMB-I	PULL-I	TOPH-I
CARD-I	FUND-I	LOGO-I	PUTT-I	TOPO-I
CARP-I	FUNG-I	LUNG-I	RANG-I	TORI-I
CEIL-I	GLOB-I	MACH-I	REIK-I	TORS-I
CELL-I	HADJ-I	MAND-I	ROST-I	VILL-I
COAT-I	HAJJ-I	MODI-I	SAMP-I	VOLT-I
COMB-I	HANG-I	MOOL-I	SCUD-I	XYST-I
CORN-I	HONG-I	MURR-I	SENT-I	ZIMB-I
CROC-I	HOUR-I	MYTH-I	SERA-I	
CULT-I	IAMB-I	NIMB-I	SHOG-I	

Five letters to six

ANNUL-I	COLON-I	EQUAL-I	JIHAD-I	NEROL-I
ARGAL-I	CUBIT-I	FRACT-I	JOWAR-I	PILOT-I
AVANT-I	DENAR-I	GARDA-I	KAIKA-I	PIROG-I
CAROL-I	DEWAN-I	GLUTE-I	KROON-I	POLYP-I
CHICH-I	DJINN-I	HAIKA-I	KULAK-I	RHOMB-I
CHILL-I	DUETT-I	HERMA-I	MANAT-I	SCAMP-I
CLYPE-I	EPHOR-I	JEHAD-I	MOIRA-I	SENSE-I

SHALL-I	SMALT-I	STELA-I	YOGIN-I
SILEN-I	SOLID-I	TAPET-I	

Six letters to seven

ABOMAS-I	DACTYL-I	EPIGON-I	MARTIN-I	RHYTHM-I
ACANTH-I	DAKOIT-I	GRADIN-I	OBLAST-I	SECOND-I
AFGHAN-I	DEMENT-I	HALLAL-I	PAESAN-I	SHIKAR-I
BANDAR-I	DENARI-I	HELLER-I	QAWWAL-I	SIGNOR-I
CHIASM-I	ELENCH-I	JAMPAN-I	REVERS-I	TYMPAN-I

Seven letters to eight

BRAHMAN-I	CONDUCT-I	FASCISM-I	PARCHES-I	TROCHIL-I
CALAMAR-I	CORNETT-I	FASCIST-I	PERFECT-I	ZECCHIN-I
CAPITAN-I	COTHURN-I	HETAIRA-I	SIGNIOR-I	
CONCEPT-I	DRACHMA-I	KOFTGAR-I	STROBIL-I	
CONCERT-I	DUUMVIR-I	MARCHES-I	TANDOOR-I	

Eight letters to nine

ASTRAGAL-I	EUCALYPT-I	PASTORAL-I	QUARTETT-I	TRIUMVIR-I
CANNELON-I	LEYLANDI-I	PEDIPALP-I	QUINTETT-I	ZAMINDAR-I
CHORIAMB-I	MATACHIN-I	PHOSPHOR-I	RICERCAR-I	ZEMINDAR-I
DECEMVIR-I	MOSASAUR-I	PORTOLAN-I	STRELITZ-I	

J – Front-hooks

Two letters to three

J-AB	J-AM	J-EE	J-OE	J-UG
J-AG	J-AR	J-ET	J-OR	J-UN
J-AI	J-AW	J-IN	J-OW	J-US
J-AL	J-AY	J-OB	J-OY	J-UT

Three letters to four

J-ABS	J-ASP	J-ERK	J-OBE	J-UDS
J-AGA	J-ASS	J-ESS	J-OBS	J-UGS
J-AGS	J-AUK	J-EST	J-OES	J-UKE
J-AIL	J-AVA	J-IFF	J-OKE	J-UMP
J-AIS	J-AYS	J-ILL	J-OLE	J-URE
J-AKE	J-EAN	J-IMP	J-ORS	J-UTE
J-ANE	J-EAT	J-INK	J-OUK	J-UTS
J-ANN	J-EEL	J-INN	J-OUR	
J-APE	J-EFF	J-INS	J-OWL	
J-ARK	J-ELL	J-ISM	J-OYS	
J-ARS	J-EON	J-IVY	J-UDO	

Four letters to five

J-AGAS	J-ALAP	J-APED	J-ASPS	J-AVEL
J-AGER	J-AMBO	J-APER	J-AUKS	J-AWED
J-AILS	J-ANES	J-APES	J-AUNT	J-EANS
J-AKES	J-ANNS	J-ARKS	J-AVAS	J-EATS

J-EELS	J-IFFY	J-OBES	J-OWED	J-UNCO
J-EELY	J-ILLS	J-OINT	J-OWLS	J-UNTO
J-EFFS	J-IMMY	J-OKES	J-OWLY	J-UPON
J-ELLS	J-INGO	J-OLES	J-UDOS	J-UTES
J-EMMY	J-INKS	J-ONES	J-UKES	
J-ERKS	J-INNS	J-OUKS	J-UMBO	
J-ESSE	J-ISMS	J-OURS	J-UMPS	
J-ESTS	J-NANA	J-OUST	J-UMPY	

Five letters to six

J-ABBED	J-APERS	J-AVELS	J-INKER	J-UGGED
J-ACKER	J-APERY	J-AWING	J-NANAS	J-UMBLE
J-AGERS	J-APING	J-EANED	J-OINTS	J-UMBOS
J-AGGER	J-ARGON	J-EFFED	J-OTTER	J-UMPED
J-AILED	J-ARRAH	J-ESSES	J-OUNCE	J-UNCOS
J-ALAPS	J-ASPER	J-ESTER	J-OUSTS	J-UNCUS
J-AMBER	J-ASPIS	J-IGGED	J-OWING	J-UNKED
J-AMBOS	J-ASSES	J-IMPLY	J-OWLED	J-UNKET
J-ANGLE	J-AUNTS	J-INGLE	J-OWLER	
J-ANKER	J-AUNTY	J-INKED	J-UDDER	

Six letters to seven

J-ACKERS	J-ANKERS	J-IMMIES	J-OSTLER	J-UDDERS
J-AGGERS	J-ARGONS	J-INGLES	J-OTTERS	J-UGGING
J-AGGIES	J-ASPERS	J-INGOES	J-OUNCES	J-UMBLES
J-AILING	J-AUNTIE	J-INKERS	J-OUSTED	J-UMPING
J-AMBERS	J-AWLESS	J-INKING	J-OUSTER	J-UNCATE
J-ANGLED	J-EFFING	J-OCULAR	J-OWLERS	J-UNKING
J-ANGLER	J-ESTERS	J-OINTED	J-OWLIER	
J-ANGLES	J-IGGING	J-OLLIES	J-OWLING	

Seven letters to eight

J-AMBONES	J-APERIES	J-OINTING	J-OUSTING	J-UNCTION
J-ANGLERS	J-ASPISES	J-OSTLERS	J-OWLIEST	
J-ANGLING	J-AUNTIES	J-OUSTERS	J-UDDERED	

Eight letters to nine

J-ANGLINGS	J-ASPEROUS	J-OCULARLY	J-UNCTIONS

J – End-hooks

Two letters to three

HA-J	TA-J

Three letters to four

BEN-J	HAD-J	HAJ-J

K – Front-hooks

Two letters to three

K-AB	K-AW	K-ET	K-IS	K-OR
K-AE	K-AY	K-EX	K-IT	K-OS
K-AI	K-EA	K-HI	K-OB	K-OW
K-AM	K-ED	K-ID	K-OI	K-YE
K-AS	K-EF	K-IF	K-ON	K-YU
K-AT	K-EN	K-IN	K-OP	

Three letters to four

K-AAL	K-ARK	K-ERN	K-ITS	K-OFF
K-AAS	K-ART	K-EST	K-IWI	K-ONS
K-ABS	K-AVA	K-ETA	K-LAP	K-OPS
K-AGO	K-AWA	K-HAN	K-NAG	K-ORA
K-AID	K-AYS	K-HAT	K-NAP	K-ORE
K-AIL	K-BAR	K-HET	K-NEE	K-ORS
K-AIM	K-EAS	K-HIS	K-NEW	K-SAR
K-AIN	K-EDS	K-ICK	K-NIT	K-UDO
K-AIS	K-EEK	K-IDS	K-NOB	K-UTA
K-AKA	K-EEL	K-IFF	K-NOT	K-UTU
K-ALE	K-EEN	K-IFS	K-NOW	K-VAS
K-AMA	K-EFS	K-ILL	K-NUB	K-YAK
K-AMI	K-ELL	K-INK	K-NUR	K-YAR
K-ANA	K-ELT	K-INS	K-NUT	K-YES
K-ANE	K-ENS	K-IRK	K-OBO	K-YUS
K-ANT	K-ERF	K-ISH	K-OBS	

Four letters to five

K-AIDS	K-EDGY	K-ICKY	K-NITS	K-RAIT
K-AILS	K-EECH	K-ILLS	K-NOBS	K-RANG
K-AIMS	K-EELS	K-INKS	K-NOCK	K-RILL
K-AINS	K-ELLS	K-INKY	K-NOLL	K-RONE
K-ALES	K-ELTS	K-IRKS	K-NOUT	K-ROON
K-ALIF	K-EMPT	K-IWIS	K-NOWN	K-SARS
K-AMAS	K-ERNE	K-LANG	K-NOWS	K-UDOS
K-AMIS	K-ERNS	K-LAPS	K-NUBS	K-ULAN
K-ANAS	K-EROS	K-LICK	K-NURL	K-URUS
K-ANES	K-ESTS	K-LONG	K-NURR	K-UTAS
K-ANGA	K-ETAS	K-LOOF	K-NURS	K-UTIS
K-ANTS	K-ETCH	K-LUGE	K-NUTS	K-UTUS
K-ARKS	K-EVIL	K-LUTZ	K-OBOS	K-VELL
K-ARSY	K-EXES	K-NAGS	K-OFFS	K-YACK
K-ARTS	K-EYED	K-NAPS	K-OKRA	K-YAKS
K-AVAS	K-HATS	K-NAVE	K-OMBU	K-YANG
K-AWED	K-HETH	K-NEED	K-ORES	
K-BARS	K-HETS	K-NIFE	K-OSES	
K-EDGE	K-HORS	K-NISH	K-RAFT	

Five letters to six

K-ABAKA	K-ALIFS	K-ANTED	K-AURIS	K-EDGER
K-ABAYA	K-ALONG	K-ARKED	K-AWING	K-EDGES
K-ABELE	K-ANGAS	K-ARRIS	K-EBBED	K-EGGED
K-AINGA	K-ANTAR	K-ARSEY	K-EDGED	K-EGGER

K-EIGHT	K-ICKER	K-LONGS	K-NOCKS	K-RATER
K-EMBED	K-ILLER	K-LOOFS	K-NOLLS	K-RILLS
K-ENTIA	K-INDIE	K-LUGED	K-NUBBY	K-RISES
K-ERNED	K-INGLE	K-LUGES	K-NURLS	K-ROONS
K-ERNES	K-INKED	K-NAGGY	K-NURRS	K-ULANS
K-ETTLE	K-INKLE	K-NAVES	K-OBANG	K-VASES
K-EVILS	K-IRKED	K-NICKS	K-OKRAS	K-VELLS
K-EYING	K-ISHES	K-NIFES	K-OMBUS	K-VETCH
K-HETHS	K-LATCH	K-NIGHT	K-RAFTS	K-YACKS
K-HODJA	K-LICKS	K-NOBBY	K-RAITS	K-YANGS

Six letters to seven

K-ABAKAS	K-EDGING	K-ICKERS	K-LINKER	K-NUBBLE
K-ABAYAS	K-EECHES	K-ICKIER	K-LISTER	K-NUBBLY
K-ABELES	K-EGGERS	K-IDLING	K-LUGING	K-NURLED
K-AINGAS	K-EGGING	K-INDIES	K-LUTZES	K-OBANGS
K-AMISES	K-ENOSES	K-INGLES	K-NAPPED	K-ONNING
K-ANTARS	K-ENOSIS	K-INKIER	K-NAPPER	K-RATERS
K-ANTING	K-ERNING	K-INKING	K-NICKER	K-RIMMER
K-ARKING	K-ETCHES	K-INKLES	K-NIGHTS	K-RISING
K-EBBING	K-ETTLES	K-INSHIP	K-NISHES	K-VETCHY
K-EDGERS	K-HANJAR	K-IRKING	K-NOBBLE	
K-EDGIER	K-HODJAS	K-LAPPED	K-NOCKED	

Seven letters to eight

K-ALEWIFE	K-INKIEST	K-NAGGIER	K-NOBBIER	K-NUBBLES
K-EDGIEST	K-INSHIPS	K-NAPPERS	K-NOBBLED	K-NURLING
K-ETAMINE	K-LAPPING	K-NAPPING	K-NOBBLES	K-OSMOSES
K-ETCHING	K-LATCHES	K-NICKERS	K-NOCKING	K-RIMMERS
K-HANJARS	K-LINKERS	K-NIGHTED	K-NUBBIER	K-VETCHES
K-ICKIEST	K-LISTERS	K-NIGHTLY	K-NUBBLED	

Eight letters to nine

K-ALEWIVES	K-INKINESS	K-NICKERED	K-NUBBIEST	K-VETCHIER
K-ENOSISES	K-NAGGIEST	K-NOBBIEST	K-NUBBLIER	
K-ETAMINES	K-NEVELLED	K-NOBBLING	K-NUBBLING	

K – End-hooks

Two letters to three

AR-K	EE-K	JA-K	OI-K	WO-K
AS-K	EL-K	KA-K	OU-K	YA-K
BO-K	ER-K	MA-K	SI-K	YO-K
DA-K	IN-K	NE-K	TA-K	YU-K

Three letters to four

BAC-K	BIN-K	BOR-K	BUS-K	COO-K
BAL-K	BIS-K	BOS-K	CAR-K	COR-K
BAN-K	BOA-K	BRA-K	CAW-K	COW-K
BAR-K	BON-K	BUN-K	CHI-K	DAN-K
BAS-K	BOO-K	BUR-K	CON-K	DAW-K

DEE-K	HOI-K	MAS-K	PIN-K	SOC-K
DIN-K	HON-K	MAW-K	POL-K	SOU-K
DIS-K	HOO-K	MEE-K	POO-K	SUN-K
DOC-K	HOW-K	MIC-K	PUL-K	TAN-K
DOE-K	HUN-K	MIL-K	PUN-K	TAS-K
DOO-K	JAR-K	MIR-K	RAI-K	TEA-K
DOR-K	JIN-K	MOC-K	RAN-K	TEE-K
DUN-K	JUN-K	MON-K	REC-K	TIC-K
FAN-K	KAI-K	MOO-K	REE-K	TIN-K
FIN-K	KIN-K	MOS-K	REI-K	TOC-K
FIR-K	KIR-K	MUS-K	REN-K	TON-K
FOR-K	KON-K	NAB-K	RIN-K	TOO-K
FUN-K	LAC-K	NOO-K	ROC-K	VOL-K
GEE-K	LAR-K	NOR-K	ROO-K	WAN-K
GIN-K	LAW-K	PAC-K	RUC-K	WAR-K
GON-K	LEA-K	PAR-K	SAC-K	WEE-K
GOO-K	LEE-K	PAW-K	SAN-K	WIN-K
GUN-K	LIN-K	PEA-K	SAR-K	WON-K
HAN-K	LIS-K	PEC-K	SEE-K	YAR-K
HAS-K	LOO-K	PEE-K	SEI-K	YES-K
HAW-K	LUR-K	PEN-K	SER-K	YOU-K
HIC-K	MAC-K	PER-K	SIC-K	
HOC-K	MAR-K	PIC-K	SIN-K	

Four letters to five

ABAC-K	CHAW-K	FRIS-K	SKIN-K	SWAN-K
ABAS-K	CHIC-K	GLEE-K	SLEE-K	TALA-K
ALEC-K	CHIN-K	GREE-K	SMEE-K	TARO-K
BLIN-K	CHOC-K	KAMI-K	SMIR-K	THAN-K
BLOC-K	CHOW-K	KULA-K	SNAR-K	THEE-K
BOBA-K	CLAN-K	MALI-K	SNOW-K	THIN-K
BORA-K	CLON-K	PLAN-K	SPAN-K	TOPE-K
BRAN-K	CRAN-K	PULI-K	SPAR-K	TORS-K
BRIN-K	CREE-K	REIN-K	SPEC-K	TRON-K
BRIS-K	CROC-K	SAIC-K	SPIC-K	TWIN-K
BROO-K	DRAC-K	SAME-K	SPIN-K	UPTA-K
BRUS-K	ERIC-K	SCUL-K	SPUN-K	WAUL-K
CAUL-K	FLAN-K	SHAN-K	STAR-K	
CHAL-K	FLIC-K	SHIR-K	STIR-K	
CHAR-K	FLOC-K	SHOO-K	STUN-K	

Five letters to six

ANTIC-K	EMBAR-K	MEDIC-K	PANIC-K	UMIAC-K
ASPIC-K	IMBAR-K	MELIC-K	REBEC-K	UNBAR-K
BEGUN-K	JAMBO-K	MUSIC-K	RESEE-K	ZEBEC-K
DEBAR-K	KALPA-K	PACHA-K	SQUAW-K	

Six letters to seven

AMTRAC-K	DISBAR-K	LIMBEC-K	OUTRAN-K
BOOBOO-K	FINNAC-K	OOMIAC-K	TIETAC-K
CALPAC-K	GWEDUC-K	OUTBAR-K	TOMBAC-K

Seven letters to eight

ALMANAC-K	BAUDRIC-K	OVERRAN-K	PRACTIC-K	SHOEPAC-K
BALDRIC-K	FORERAN-K	POLITIC-K	SHELLAC-K	TAMARIS-K

Eight letters to nine

BERGAMAS-K	OVERTHIN-K

L – Front-hooks

Two letters to three

L-AB	L-AT	L-ES	L-OB	L-OW
L-AD	L-AW	L-ET	L-OD	L-OX
L-AG	L-AX	L-EX	L-OO	L-OY
L-AH	L-AY	L-ID	L-OP	L-UG
L-AM	L-EA	L-IN	L-OR	L-UM
L-AR	L-ED	L-IS	L-OS	L-UR
L-AS	L-EE	L-IT	L-OU	L-YE

Three letters to four

L-ABS	L-ASS	L-ESS	L-OBS	L-OUP
L-ACE	L-ATE	L-EST	L-OCA	L-OUR
L-ADS	L-AUF	L-EVE	L-OCH	L-OUT
L-AGS	L-AVA	L-EVO	L-ODE	L-OWE
L-AHS	L-AVE	L-ICE	L-ODS	L-OWN
L-AID	L-AWN	L-ICH	L-OFT	L-OWT
L-AIN	L-AYS	L-ICK	L-OKE	L-OYS
L-AIR	L-AZO	L-IDS	L-ONE	L-UDO
L-AKE	L-EAN	L-ILL	L-OOF	L-UDS
L-ALL	L-EAR	L-IMP	L-OOM	L-UGS
L-AMA	L-EAS	L-INK	L-OON	L-UKE
L-AMP	L-EAT	L-INN	L-OOP	L-ULU
L-ANA	L-ECH	L-INS	L-OOR	L-UMP
L-AND	L-EEK	L-ION	L-OOS	L-URE
L-ANE	L-EFT	L-IRE	L-OOT	L-UTE
L-ANT	L-EKE	L-IRK	L-OPE	L-YAM
L-ARD	L-EME	L-ITS	L-OPS	L-YES
L-ARE	L-END	L-OAF	L-ORD	
L-ARK	L-ENG	L-OBE	L-ORE	
L-ARS	L-ENS	L-OBI	L-OSE	
L-ASH	L-ERE	L-OBO	L-OUD	

Four letters to five

L-ACED	L-AKIN	L-ANTS	L-AURA	L-EACH
L-ACER	L-ALLS	L-APSE	L-AVAS	L-EANS
L-ACES	L-AMAS	L-ARCH	L-AVER	L-EARN
L-AGER	L-AMIA	L-ARDS	L-AVES	L-EARS
L-AIDS	L-AMPS	L-ARES	L-AWED	L-EASE
L-AIRS	L-ANAS	L-ARIS	L-AWNS	L-EAST
L-AIRY	L-ANCE	L-ARKS	L-AWNY	L-EATS
L-AKED	L-ANDS	L-ARUM	L-AXES	L-EAVE
L-AKES	L-ANES	L-AUFS	L-AYIN	L-EDGE

L-EDGY	L-ESTS	L-ITAS	L-OPED	L-OWLY
L-EECH	L-ETCH	L-LAMA	L-OPES	L-OWNS
L-EERY	L-ETHE	L-OAFS	L-ORAL	L-OWSE
L-EFTS	L-EUGH	L-OAST	L-ORDS	L-OWTS
L-EGAL	L-EVER	L-OATH	L-ORES	L-OXES
L-EGER	L-EXES	L-OBES	L-OSES	L-UDOS
L-EGGY	L-ILLS	L-OBOS	L-OTIC	L-ULUS
L-EISH	L-IMPS	L-ODES	L-OTTO	L-UMPS
L-EMES	L-INCH	L-OKES	L-OUMA	L-UMPY
L-EMMA	L-INGO	L-ONER	L-OUPS	L-URES
L-ENDS	L-INKS	L-OOFS	L-OURS	L-USER
L-ENES	L-INKY	L-OOMS	L-OUTS	L-UTES
L-ENGS	L-INNS	L-OONS	L-OVER	L-YAMS
L-ERED	L-IONS	L-OOPS	L-OWED	L-YARD
L-ERES	L-IRKS	L-OOSE	L-OWER	
L-ESES	L-ISLE	L-OOTS	L-OWES	

Five letters to six

L-ACERS	L-ARVAL	L-ECHED	L-INGLE	L-ORATE
L-ACHES	L-ASHED	L-ECHES	L-INGOT	L-OTHER
L-ACING	L-ASHES	L-EDGED	L-INKED	L-OTTER
L-ACKER	L-ASSES	L-EDGER	L-INKER	L-OTTOS
L-ADDER	L-ASTER	L-EDGES	L-INNED	L-OUMAS
L-AGERS	L-ATRIA	L-EGERS	L-INTEL	L-OUPED
L-AGGER	L-AURAE	L-EGGED	L-INTER	L-OURIE
L-AIDED	L-AURAS	L-EGGER	L-IRKED	L-OUTED
L-AIRED	L-AURIC	L-EMMAS	L-ISLES	L-OVERS
L-AKING	L-AVERS	L-ENDER	L-ITHER	L-OWING
L-ALANG	L-AWFUL	L-ENVOY	L-IZARD	L-OWNED
L-AMBER	L-AWING	L-ERING	L-LAMAS	L-OWRIE
L-AMENT	L-AYINS	L-ESSES	L-OAVES	L-UGGED
L-AMIAS	L-EANED	L-ETHAL	L-OCKER	L-UMBER
L-AMPED	L-EARED	L-EVITE	L-OCULI	L-UMPED
L-ANGER	L-EARNS	L-EXEME	L-OFTER	L-UNARY
L-ANKER	L-EASED	L-ICHES	L-OLLER	L-USERS
L-APPEL	L-EASER	L-ICKER	L-ONELY	L-USHER
L-APSES	L-EASES	L-IGGED	L-ONERS	
L-ARKED	L-EASTS	L-IMBED	L-OOPED	
L-AROID	L-EAVED	L-IMPED	L-OOSES	
L-ARUMS	L-EAVES	L-IMPLY	L-OPING	

Six letters to seven

L-ACKERS	L-ASHING	L-EECHED	L-ETHALS	L-INKING
L-ADDERS	L-ASTERS	L-EECHES	L-EUGHEN	L-INNING
L-ADDIES	L-AUDING	L-EERIER	L-EVITES	L-INTELS
L-AGGERS	L-AWLESS	L-EERILY	L-EXEMES	L-INTERS
L-AIDING	L-AWNIER	L-EFTEST	L-ICKERS	L-IONISE
L-AIRIER	L-EANING	L-EGALLY	L-IGGING	L-IONIZE
L-AIRING	L-EARING	L-EGGERS	L-IGNIFY	L-IRKING
L-ALANGS	L-EARNED	L-EGGIER	L-IGNITE	L-IZARDS
L-AMBERS	L-EARNER	L-EGGING	L-IMPING	L-OBELIA
L-AMENTS	L-EASERS	L-EMURES	L-INCHES	L-OCKERS
L-AMPING	L-EASING	L-ENDERS	L-INDIES	L-OCULAR
L-ANGERS	L-EAVING	L-ENDING	L-INGLES	L-OCULUS
L-APPELS	L-ECHING	L-ENVOYS	L-INGOES	L-OLLERS
L-ARCHES	L-EDGERS	L-ETCHED	L-INGOTS	L-OLLIES
L-ARKING	L-EDGIER	L-ETCHES	L-INKERS	L-OMENTA

L-OOPING	L-OURIER	L-OVERLY	L-OXYGEN	L-UMBERS
L-OTTERS	L-OUTING	L-OWLIER	L-UGGING	L-UMPING
L-OUPING	L-OVERED	L-OWNING	L-ULLING	L-USHERS

Seven letters to eight

L-ABILITY	L-AZURITE	L-EPIDOTE	L-IONISER	L-ONENESS
L-ACERATE	L-EARNERS	L-ETCHING	L-IONISES	L-OURIEST
L-AIRIEST	L-EARNING	L-EVIRATE	L-IONIZED	L-OWLIEST
L-AMBLING	L-EDGIEST	L-EVITATE	L-IONIZER	L-OXYGENS
L-ANGERED	L-EECHING	L-IGNEOUS	L-IONIZES	L-UMBERED
L-ANGUISH	L-EERIEST	L-IGNITES	L-ITERATE	
L-AUREATE	L-EGALITY	L-IMPINGS	L-OBELIAS	
L-AWFULLY	L-EGGIEST	L-INCHPIN	L-OCULATE	
L-AWNIEST	L-ENDINGS	L-IONISED	L-OMENTUM	

Eight letters to nine

L-ACERATED	L-EPIDOTES	L-IGNIFIED	L-IONISING	L-OCULATED
L-AMBLINGS	L-ETCHINGS	L-IGNIFIES	L-IONIZERS	L-OMENTUMS
L-AZURITES	L-EVIRATES	L-IMITABLE	L-IONIZING	L-UMBERING
L-EARNINGS	L-EVITATED	L-INCHPINS	L-ITERATES	
L-EERINESS	L-EVITATES	L-IONISERS	L-OCELLATE	

L – End-hooks

Two letters to three

AA-L	DA-L	JA-L	OI-L	TI-L
AI-L	DE-L	JO-L	OW-L	ZO-L
AL-L	DO-L	MA-L	PA-L	
AW-L	EE-L	ME-L	PO-L	
BA-L	EL-L	MI-L	SO-L	
BE-L	GU-L	MO-L	TE-L	

Three letters to four

ANA-L	DEI-L	JAI-L	ORA-L	SEE-L
ANI-L	DEL-L	JAR-L	OVA-L	SEI-L
ARY-L	DIE-L	JEE-L	PAL-L	SEL-L
AVA-L	DOL-L	JOL-L	PAW-L	SOU-L
AVE-L	DOO-L	JOW-L	PEA-L	SOW-L
AXE-L	DOW-L	KAI-L	PEE-L	TAE-L
BAA-L	DUE-L	LEA-L	PIA-L	TAI-L
BAL-L	EAR-L	MAL-L	PIR-L	TEA-L
BEL-L	FAR-L	MAR-L	POL-L	TEE-L
BOI-L	FEE-L	MEL-L	POO-L	TEL-L
BOO-L	FIL-L	MEW-L	PUL-L	TIL-L
BOW-L	FOU-L	MIL-L	PUR-L	TOO-L
BUR-L	FUR-L	MOI-L	RAI-L	TWA-L
CAR-L	GAL-L	MOL-L	REE-L	VIA-L
CEL-L	GOA-L	MOO-L	RIA-L	WAI-L
CHA-L	GOE-L	MOY-L	ROT-L	WAW-L
COL-L	GOO-L	NIL-L	RYA-L	WEE-L
COO-L	GUL-L	NOW-L	SAI-L	WOO-L
COW-L	GUR-L	NUR-L	SAL-L	YAW-L
CUR-L	HER-L	OBO-L	SAU-L	YOW-L
DAH-L	HOW-L	ODA-L	SEA-L	ZEA-L

Four letters to five

ALGA-L	DRAW-L	KETO-L	PEAR-L	SPAW-L
ALKY-L	DURA-L	KNAR-L	PERI-L	SPIE-L
ALLY-L	DYNE-L	KNEE-L	PICA-L	SURA-L
ANNA-L	EASE-L	KNUR-L	PIPA-L	SWAY-L
AREA-L	FAVE-L	LEME-L	PROW-L	SWEE-L
AURA-L	FETA-L	LEVE-L	PUPA-L	TEPA-L
AWEE-L	FORE-L	LOCA-L	QUAI-L	THIO-L
BABE-L	FUSE-L	LORE-L	RATA-L	THIR-L
BABU-L	GAVE-L	LOSE-L	RATE-L	TRIO-L
BEDE-L	GENA-L	MAIL-L	RAVE-L	TUBA-L
BETE-L	GIBE-L	MERE-L	RIVA-L	TWEE-L
BORA-L	GLIA-L	MERI-L	RIVE-L	UREA-L
BORE-L	GNAR-L	MESA-L	ROMA-L	UVEA-L
BRAW-L	GORA-L	MESE-L	ROTA-L	VASA-L
BROO-L	GROW-L	META-L	RUBE-L	VENA-L
BUBA-L	GRUE-L	MODE-L	RUGA-L	VINA-L
CABA-L	HAZE-L	MOLA-L	SAME-L	VINY-L
CAME-L	HORA-L	MONA-L	SCOW-L	VITA-L
CAVE-L	HOSE-L	MORA-L	SCUL-L	WHEE-L
CECA-L	HOTE-L	MORE-L	SEGO-L	WHIR-L
COMA-L	HOVE-L	MOTE-L	SERA-L	YODE-L
COXA-L	IDEA-L	MURA-L	SETA-L	YOKE-L
CRAW-L	IDYL-L	MYAL-L	SHAW-L	ZOEA-L
CREE-L	ILEA-L	NAVE-L	SHEA-L	ZONA-L
CRUE-L	ILIA-L	NEVE-L	SHOO-L	ZORI-L
DATA-L	INTI-L	NOTA-L	SIZE-L	ZYGA-L
DEBE-L	JUGA-L	OCTA-L	SNAR-L	
DHOL-L	JURA-L	PANE-L	SORA-L	
DITA-L	JURE-L	PAPA-L	SORE-L	

Five letters to six

ACETA-L	COSTA-L	HOUSE-L	NUCHA-L	RIGOL-L
AECIA-L	CREWE-L	HYPHA-L	OMASA-L	RONDE-L
AMIDO-L	CRURA-L	JAMBU-L	OSTIA-L	RONNE-L
ANIMA-L	CURIA-L	KERNE-L	PALEA-L	RUSSE-L
ANTRA-L	DERMA-L	KHAYA-L	PARRA-L	SACRA-L
AORTA-L	DORSA-L	KNAWE-L	PASSE-L	SAMBA-L
APNEA-L	DORSE-L	LABIA-L	PASTE-L	SANTO-L
APPAL-L	DRIVE-L	LARVA-L	PENCE-L	SCRAW-L
ASSAI-L	DRUPE-L	LENTI-L	PENNA-L	SCROW-L
ATRIA-L	EISEL-L	LUTEA-L	PETRE-L	SCUTA-L
BABOO-L	ENROL-L	MAMMA-L	PINNA-L	SEPTA-L
BARBE-L	EXTOL-L	MANGA-L	PLICA-L	SERAI-L
BARRE-L	FACIA-L	MANGE-L	PODIA-L	SHOVE-L
BEDEL-L	FAUNA-L	MEDIA-L	PORTA-L	SIGNA-L
BEIGE-L	FAVEL-L	MENSA-L	PRIMA-L	SOREL-L
BORDE-L	FERIA-L	MENTA-L	QUINO-L	SORTA-L
BUFFE-L	FESTA-L	MEREL-L	RANCE-L	SPINA-L
BURSA-L	FLORA-L	MISSA-L	RAPPE-L	SPINE-L
CAECA-L	FLOTE-L	MONGO-L	RECAL-L	STIPE-L
CARTE-L	FOVEA-L	MORAL-L	RECTA-L	STOMA-L
CARVE-L	FURCA-L	MORSE-L	REDIA-L	SWIVE-L
CAUDA-L	GAMBO-L	MUSSE-L	REFEL-L	TASSE-L
CAUSA-L	GRAVE-L	NEWEL-L	REGNA-L	TEASE-L
CHAPE-L	GROVÉ-L	NITRY-L	RETIA-L	TEAZE-L
CORBE-L	HANSE-L	NORMA-L	RIDGE-L	TECTA-L

TELIA-L	TINEA-L	UMBRE-L	VESTA-L	XENIA-L
TERCE-L	TOMIA-L	UNCIA-L	VISTA-L	ZOOEA-L
TERGA-L	TORSE-L	VANDA-L	VULVA-L	
THECA-L	TRAVE-L	VARVE-L	WASTE-L	
TIBIA-L	UMBRA-L	VERVE-L	WOOSE-L	

Six letters to seven

ADNEXA-L	CONCHA-L	GINGAL-L	MULMUL-L	STIGMA-L
ALODIA-L	CORNEA-L	GLOSSA-L	NATURA-L	STRATA-L
AMENTA-L	CORNUA-L	HEDERA-L	NOMINA-L	STROMA-L
ANGINA-L	CORONA-L	HERNIA-L	NYMPHA-L	TAPETA-L
APNOEA-L	CORYZA-L	INSTAL-L	OMENTA-L	TASSEL-L
AURORA-L	CRANIA-L	INSTIL-L	OPTIMA-L	TERTIA-L
BARBEL-L	CRESTA-L	INTIMA-L	ORBITA-L	THERME-L
BORREL-L	CRISSA-L	ISCHIA-L	PALLIA-L	TIERCE-L
BURREL-L	CRUSTA-L	JEJUNA-L	PLEURA-L	TIMBRE-L
CAMBIA-L	CUBICA-L	JINGAL-L	POINTE-L	TOPFUL-L
CAMERA-L	DISMAY-L	LACUNA-L	QUANTA-L	TRAMEL-L
CAPITA-L	DISTIL-L	LAMINA-L	QUINTA-L	TRIVIA-L
CARINA-L	ELUVIA-L	LATERA-L	REGINA-L	TROCHI-L
CARREL-L	ELYTRA-L	LEXICA-L	RETINA-L	TWIBIL-L
CENTRA-L	ENCINA-L	LIMINA-L	ROSTRA-L	UREDIA-L
CESURA-L	ENTERA-L	LINGUA-L	RUMINA-L	VAGINA-L
CHAETA-L	EPOCHA-L	LOCHIA-L	SALIVA-L	VESICA-L
CHANCE-L	ESCROL-L	LUMINA-L	SATYRA-L	VIMINA-L
CHORDA-L	ETHOXY-L	LUSTRA-L	SCLERA-L	WADMOL-L
CHOREA-L	EXUVIA-L	MAXIMA-L	SCROTA-L	WOOSEL-L
CHORIA-L	FANNEL-L	MEDUSA-L	SEMINA-L	ZOARIA-L
CHROME-L	FASCIA-L	MIASMA-L	SEROSA-L	
CHROMY-L	FEMORA-L	MINIMA-L	SHRIVE-L	
CLOACA-L	FULFIL-L	MUCHEL-L	STADIA-L	
COLONE-L	GENERA-L	MUCOSA-L	STERNA-L	

Seven letters to eight

ABOMASA-L	CHIASMA-L	GALANGA-L	MINUTIA-L	RESIDUA-L
ACHENIA-L	CHRISMA-L	GANGLIA-L	MONILIA-L	SABURRA-L
ACROMIA-L	CINEREA-L	GERMINA-L	MYCELIA-L	SAGITTA-L
AECIDIA-L	COMITIA-L	GINGIVA-L	NOUMENA-L	SOREDIA-L
ALLODIA-L	CONARIA-L	GONIDIA-L	OOGONIA-L	SPECTRA-L
ALLUVIA-L	CONIDIA-L	HYDROXY-L	OOTHECA-L	SPLENIA-L
AMPHORA-L	CORPORA-L	HYMENIA-L	PATAGIA-L	STAMINA-L
ANTENNA-L	CRIMINA-L	HYPOGEA-L	PERIDIA-L	STOMATA-L
APPERIL-L	CROPFUL-L	ILLUVIA-L	PERINEA-L	SULFURY-L
AQUARIA-L	DECIDUA-L	IMPERIA-L	PERSONA-L	SYNOVIA-L
ARCHAEA-L	DIHEDRA-L	INDICIA-L	PESSIMA-L	TEGMINA-L
BASIDIA-L	DILUVIA-L	INDUSIA-L	PISCINA-L	TESSERA-L
BIENNIA-L	DIPTERA-L	INERTIA-L	PLIMSOL-L	TESTRIL-L
BORSTAL-L	DUODENA-L	INFAUNA-L	PODAGRA-L	TORMINA-L
BRACHIA-L	DYSPNEA-L	INTHRAL-L	PRECAVA-L	TRACHEA-L
BRECCIA-L	ENTHRAL-L	KHEDIVA-L	PREPUPA-L	TYMPANA-L
BRIMFUL-L	ENTOZOA-L	LIXIVIA-L	PRONOTA-L	URETHRA-L
CAESURA-L	EROTICA-L	LOCUSTA-L	PROSOMA-L	VACCINA-L
CANDIDA-L	EXCRETA-L	MALARIA-L	PUDENDA-L	VIATICA-L
CAROUSE-L	EXORDIA-L	MANDRIL-L	PUPARIA-L	VISCERA-L
CEREBRA-L	EXTREMA-L	MARSHAL-L	PYGIDIA-L	ZOOGLEA-L
CHALAZA-L	FILARIA-L	METAZOA-L	PYREXIA-L	
CHAMISA-L	FIMBRIA-L	METHOXY-L	REPOSAL-L	

Eight letters to nine

ABDOMINA-L	CISTERNA-L	FORESTAL-L	POSTCAVA-L	SYMPODIA-L
AGNOMINA-L	CLAUSTRA-L	GYMNASIA-L	PRESIDIA-L	SYMPOSIA-L
AMBROSIA-L	COLLEGIA-L	HEPATICA-L	PRIMITIA-L	SYNCYTIA-L
ANAPHORA-L	COLLUVIA-L	HERBARIA-L	PROTOZOA-L	SYNEDRIA-L
ANECDOTA-L	CONFERVA-L	HYPOGAEA-L	PTERYGIA-L	TEGMENTA-L
ANGELICA-L	CONTINUA-L	LISTERIA-L	PUERPERA-L	TENTORIA-L
ANTEFIXA-L	CRITERIA-L	MAGNESIA-L	PYCNIDIA-L	THERIACA-L
ANTIMONY-L	DECENNIA-L	MANUBRIA-L	PYORRHEA-L	TRAPEZIA-L
ASPHYXIA-L	DEMENTIA-L	MARSUPIA-L	REDISTIL-L	TRICHINA-L
AVIFAUNA-L	DIARRHEA-L	MENSTRUA-L	REINSTAL-L	TRIENNIA-L
BACTERIA-L	DICHASIA-L	MESOGLEA-L	RHIZOBIA-L	TRIFORIA-L
BASILICA-L	DYSPNOEA-L	MESOPHYL-L	RITORNEL-L	TRIHEDRA-L
BLASTEMA-L	DYSTOCIA-L	MILIARIA-L	SACRARIA-L	UNDERSEA-L
BOTANICA-L	ECCLESIA-L	MISENROL-L	SCIATICA-L	UREDINIA-L
BRANCHIA-L	EFFLUVIA-L	MOSCHATE-L	SEMUNCIA-L	UROPYGIA-L
BRONCHIA-L	ENDOSTEA-L	OCCIPITA-L	SENSORIA-L	VACCINIA-L
CACUMINA-L	ENSORCEL-L	PALESTRA-L	SIGNORIA-L	VERTEBRA-L
CALCANEA-L	EPENDYMA-L	PALPEBRA-L	SPORIDIA-L	VESTIGIA-L
CALVARIA-L	EPHEMERA-L	PANNIKEL-L	SPOROZOA-L	VIBRISSA-L
CATHEDRA-L	EPICEDIA-L	PAROEMIA-L	STOMODEA-L	ZOOGLOEA-L
CENTINEL-L	EPIFAUNA-L	PENUMBRA-L	SUBCOSTA-L	
CENTONEL-L	ERYTHEMA-L	PETECHIA-L	SUBMENTA-L	
CERCARIA-L	FENESTRA-L	PICKADIL-L	SUDAMINA-L	
CHOCKFUL-L	FORAMINA-L	PLACENTA-L	SULPHURY-L	

M – Front-hooks

Two letters to three

M-AA	M-AT	M-ES	M-OI	M-OY
M-AD	M-AW	M-ET	M-OM	M-UG
M-AE	M-AX	M-HO	M-ON	M-UM
M-AG	M-AY	M-ID	M-OO	M-UN
M-AL	M-ED	M-IS	M-OP	M-US
M-AM	M-EE	M-NA	M-OR	M-UT
M-AN	M-EL	M-OB	M-OS	
M-AR	M-EM	M-OD	M-OU	
M-AS	M-EN	M-OE	M-OW	

Three letters to four

M-AAS	M-ALS	M-ARY	M-ELS	M-ICE
M-ACE	M-ALT	M-ASH	M-ELT	M-ICH
M-ACH	M-AMA	M-ASK	M-EME	M-ICK
M-ADS	M-ANA	M-ASS	M-EMO	M-IDS
M-AGE	M-AND	M-ATE	M-EMS	M-IFF
M-AGS	M-ANE	M-ATT	M-END	M-IGG
M-AID	M-ANI	M-AWN	M-ENE	M-ILK
M-AIL	M-ANY	M-AYS	M-ENG	M-ILL
M-AIM	M-ARC	M-EAN	M-ERE	M-INK
M-AIN	M-ARD	M-EAT	M-ERK	M-IRE
M-AIR	M-ARE	M-EDS	M-ESS	M-IRK
M-AKE	M-ARK	M-EEK	M-ETA	M-ISO
M-ALA	M-ARM	M-EFF	M-ETH	M-NAS
M-ALE	M-ARS	M-ELD	M-EVE	M-OAT
M-ALL	M-ART	M-ELL	M-HOS	M-OBE

M-OBS	M-OMS	M-OPE	M-OYS	M-URE
M-OCH	M-ONO	M-OPS	M-UDS	M-USE
M-ODE	M-ONS	M-ORA	M-UGS	M-UTE
M-ODS	M-ONY	M-ORE	M-ULE	M-UTS
M-OES	M-OON	M-ORS	M-UMM	M-ZEE
M-OIL	M-OOP	M-ORT	M-UMP	
M-OKE	M-OOR	M-OSE	M-UMU	
M-OLD	M-OOS	M-OUP	M-UNI	
M-OLE	M-OOT	M-OWN	M-UNS	

Four letters to five

M-ACED	M-ANNA	M-EKKA	M-IRES	M-ORES
M-ACER	M-ANTA	M-ELDS	M-IRKS	M-ORRA
M-ACES	M-ANUS	M-ELLS	M-ISOS	M-ORTS
M-ACHE	M-ARCH	M-ELTS	M-ITCH	M-OSES
M-AGES	M-ARCS	M-EMES	M-OATS	M-OTTO
M-AGMA	M-ARES	M-EMOS	M-OBES	M-OUCH
M-AIDS	M-ARIA	M-ENDS	M-ODAL	M-OULD
M-AILS	M-ARID	M-ENES	M-ODES	M-OUPS
M-AIMS	M-ARKS	M-ENGS	M-OILS	M-OURN
M-AINS	M-ARLE	M-ERED	M-OKES	M-OUST
M-AIRS	M-ARMS	M-ERES	M-OLDS	M-OVER
M-AKES	M-ARSE	M-ERKS	M-OLDY	M-OWED
M-ALAR	M-ARTS	M-ESES	M-OLES	M-OWER
M-ALAS	M-ASHY	M-ESNE	M-OLLA	M-ULES
M-ALES	M-ASKS	M-ETHS	M-ONER	M-UMPS
M-ALLS	M-ATES	M-ETIC	M-ONIE	M-UNIS
M-ALMS	M-AWED	M-EVES	M-ONOS	M-URES
M-ALTS	M-AXED	M-ICKY	M-OONS	M-URVA
M-AMAS	M-AXES	M-IFFY	M-OOPS	M-USED
M-AMBO	M-AXIS	M-IGGS	M-OOSE	M-USER
M-AMIE	M-EANS	M-ILIA	M-OOTS	M-USES
M-ANAS	M-EASE	M-ILKS	M-OPED	M-UTES
M-ANES	M-EATH	M-ILLS	M-OPES	M-UTIS
M-ANGA	M-EATS	M-INKS	M-OPUS	M-ZEES
M-ANIS	M-EFFS	M-IRED	M-ORAL	

Five letters to six

M-ACERS	M-ALLEE	M-ARLED	M-AXING	M-ETHOS
M-ACHES	M-ALLOW	M-ARLES	M-EAGER	M-ETHYL
M-ACING	M-AMBOS	M-ARRIS	M-EAGRE	M-ETTLE
M-ADDED	M-AMIES	M-ARROW	M-EANED	M-ICHED
M-ADDER	M-AMMON	M-ARSES	M-EASED	M-ICHES
M-ADMAN	M-ANANA	M-ARTEL	M-EASES	M-ICKLE
M-ADMEN	M-ANENT	M-ASCOT	M-EASLE	M-ILIUM
M-AGGIE	M-ANGAS	M-ASHED	M-EATHE	M-ILLER
M-AGISM	M-ANGEL	M-ASHES	M-EKKAS	M-IMBAR
M-AGMAS	M-ANGER	M-ASKED	M-ELDER	M-INGLE
M-AIDED	M-ANGLE	M-ASKER	M-EMBER	M-INION
M-AILED	M-ANNAS	M-ASSED	M-ENDED	M-INTER
M-AIMED	M-ANTAS	M-ASSES	M-ENDER	M-IRING
M-AIMER	M-ANTES	M-ASTER	M-ERING	M-ISLED
M-AKING	M-ANTIC	M-ATOKE	M-ERSES	M-ISTLE
M-ALATE	M-ANTIS	M-AUGER	M-ESNES	M-ITHER
M-ALIGN	M-ANTRA	M-AURIS	M-ESSES	M-OCKER
M-ALINE	M-ARISH	M-AVENS	M-ESTER	M-ODALS
M-ALIST	M-ARKED	M-AWING	M-ETAGE	M-ODIST

M-OILED	M-ORALS	M-OUPED	M-UGGED	M-URINE
M-OILER	M-ORGAN	M-OUSTS	M-UMBLE	M-URVAS
M-OLDER	M-ORGUE	M-OUTER	M-UMPED	M-USERS
M-OLLAS	M-ORRIS	M-OVERS	M-UNIFY	M-USHER
M-OLLIE	M-OTHER	M-OWING	M-UNITE	M-USING
M-OOPED	M-OTTOS	M-OZZIE	M-UNTIN	M-UTTER
M-OPING	M-OUGHT	M-UDDER	M-URENA	

Six letters to seven

M-ADDERS	M-ARCHED	M-EASING	M-ITCHED	M-OUSTED
M-ADDING	M-ARCHER	M-EASLES	M-ITCHES	M-OUTERS
M-AGGIES	M-ARCHES	M-ELDERS	M-OCCIES	M-OUTHER
M-AGISMS	M-ARGENT	M-ELDING	M-OCKERS	M-OZZIES
M-AGNATE	M-ARKING	M-EMBERS	M-ODISTS	M-UCKERS
M-AIDING	M-ARLING	M-ENDERS	M-OILERS	M-UDDERS
M-AILING	M-ARROWS	M-ENDING	M-OILING	M-UGGING
M-AIMERS	M-ARROWY	M-ESTERS	M-OLLIES	M-ULLING
M-AIMING	M-ARTELS	M-ETAGES	M-OMENTA	M-UMBLES
M-ALATES	M-ASCOTS	M-ETHANE	M-ONEYER	M-UMPING
M-ALIGNS	M-ASHIER	M-ETHOXY	M-OOPING	M-UNITED
M-ALINES	M-ASHING	M-ETHYLS	M-OORIER	M-UNITES
M-ALISON	M-ASHMAN	M-ETTLED	M-OPUSES	M-UNTINS
M-ALLEES	M-ASHMEN	M-ETTLES	M-ORALLY	M-URENAS
M-ALLOWS	M-ASKERS	M-ICHING	M-ORGANS	M-URINES
M-AMMONS	M-ASKING	M-ICKLER	M-ORGUES	M-USEFUL
M-ANANAS	M-ASTERS	M-IFFIER	M-ORPHIC	M-USHERS
M-ANGELS	M-ATOKES	M-IMBARS	M-ORRICE	M-UTASES
M-ANGERS	M-AVISES	M-INGLES	M-OTHERS	M-UTTERS
M-ANGLED	M-AXILLA	M-INIONS	M-OUCHED	
M-ANGLER	M-EAGRES	M-INTERS	M-OUCHES	
M-ANGLES	M-EANING	M-IRITIS	M-OULDER	
M-ARABIS	M-EARING	M-ISTLES	M-OUPING	

Seven letters to eight

M-ACERATE	M-ARCHERS	M-EAGERLY	M-IFFIEST	M-ORRICES
M-ADWOMAN	M-ARCHING	M-EMETICS	M-ISOGAMY	M-ORRISES
M-ADWOMEN	M-ARGENTS	M-ENDINGS	M-ITCHING	M-OUCHING
M-AGISTER	M-ARISHES	M-ENOLOGY	M-OATLIKE	M-OUSTING
M-AGNATES	M-ARRIAGE	M-ERISTIC	M-OMENTUM	M-UNIFIED
M-AIDLESS	M-ARROWED	M-ETHANAL	M-ONEYERS	M-UNIFIES
M-ALIGNED	M-ASHIEST	M-ETHANES	M-OORIEST	M-UNITING
M-ALIGNER	M-ASKINGS	M-ETHANOL	M-ORALISM	M-UNITION
M-ALISONS	M-AXILLAE	M-ETHOXYL	M-ORALIST	M-UTTERED
M-ANGLERS	M-AXILLAR	M-ETHYLIC	M-ORALITY	M-UTTERER
M-ANGLING	M-AXILLAS	M-ICKLEST	M-ORATORY	

Eight letters to nine

M-ACERATED	M-ANGULATE	M-ETHANOIC	M-ISOGAMIC	M-USEFULLY
M-ACRODONT	M-ARRIAGES	M-ETHANOLS	M-OMENTUMS	M-UTTERERS
M-AGISTERS	M-ARROWING	M-ETHOXIDE	M-ORALISMS	M-UTTERING
M-ALIGNERS	M-AXILLARY	M-ETHYLATE	M-ORALISTS	
M-ALIGNING	M-ENARCHES	M-ETHYLENE	M-UNIFYING	
M-AMMONITE	M-ETHANALS	M-IFFINESS	M-UNITIONS	

M – End-hooks

Two letters to three

AI-M	GU-M	KA-M	NO-M	TA-M
AR-M	HA-M	LA-M	OH-M	TO-M
BA-M	HE-M	MA-M	OO-M	UM-M
DA-M	HI-M	ME-M	PA-M	WE-M
DI-M	HM-M	MI-M	PO-M	YA-M
DO-M	HO-M	MO-M	RE-M	YO-M
EL-M	IS-M	MU-M	SI-M	YU-M
FE-M	JA-M	NA-M	SO-M	

Three letters to four

BAL-M	FER-M	KAI-M	PRE-M	TEE-M
BAR-M	FIL-M	LEA-M	PRO-M	THE-M
BOO-M	FIR-M	LOO-M	ROO-M	TOO-M
BOR-M	FOR-M	MAL-M	SAI-M	WAR-M
CHA-M	FRO-M	MAR-M	SEA-M	WAS-M
COO-M	GAU-M	MUM-M	SEE-M	WEE-M
COR-M	GIS-M	NEE-M	SHA-M	WHA-M
DEE-M	GOR-M	NOR-M	SKI-M	WHO-M
DOO-M	HAE-M	PAL-M	SOU-M	ZOO-M
DOR-M	HAW-M	PER-M	SOW-M	
FAR-M	HER-M	PIU-M	SPA-M	
FEH-M	IDE-M	PLU-M	TEA-M	

Four letters to five

ABRI-M	DENI-M	HAUL-M	REAL-M	STUM-M
ABYS-M	FLAM-M	MALA-M	REAR-M	THAR-M
ALAR-M	FLEA-M	MAXI-M	RETE-M	THRU-M
BREE-M	FORA-M	MINI-M	SATE-M	TOTE-M
BROO-M	GOLE-M	MODE-M	SEIS-M	TUIS-M
CHAR-M	HAKA-M	PASH-M	SHAW-M	
CHAS-M	HARE-M	PURI-M	SPAS-M	

Five letters to six

BALSA-M	COPAL-M	MESTO-M	PURIS-M	TELES-M
BESEE-M	DODGE-M	MONTE-M	SADIS-M	YOGIS-M
CENTU-M	LINGA-M	MURRA-M	SCRAW-M	
CHIAS-M	MALIS-M	MUTIS-M	SHTUM-M	
CONDO-M	MERIS-M	PARTI-M	SPIRE-M	

Six letters to seven

ANIMIS-M	FASCIS-M	MANTRA-M	MISTER-M
BUCKRA-M	GOPURA-M	MISSEE-M	PREWAR-M

Seven letters to eight

CLASSIS-M	FINALIS-M	JIHADIS-M	TITANIS-M
CYMBALO-M	JEHADIS-M		

Eight letters to nine

LITERATI-M   MEPHITIS-M   MRIDANGA-M

N – Front-hooks

Two letters to three

N-AB	N-AT	N-ID	N-ON	N-UN
N-AE	N-AW	N-IS	N-OO	N-UR
N-AG	N-AY	N-IT	N-OR	N-US
N-AH	N-ED	N-OB	N-OS	N-UT
N-AM	N-EE	N-OD	N-OW	N-YE
N-AN	N-EF	N-OH	N-OX	
N-AS	N-ET	N-OM	N-OY	

Three letters to four

N-ABS	N-ARC	N-ERK	N-ITS	N-OUP
N-ACH	N-ARD	N-ESS	N-OBS	N-OUT
N-ADS	N-ARE	N-EST	N-ODE	N-OVA
N-AFF	N-ARK	N-EUK	N-ODS	N-OWL
N-AGA	N-ARY	N-EVE	N-OES	N-OWN
N-AGS	N-AVE	N-EWT	N-OIL	N-OWT
N-AIL	N-AYS	N-ICE	N-OLE	N-OYS
N-AIN	N-EAR	N-ICK	N-OMS	N-UKE
N-ALA	N-EAT	N-IDE	N-ONE	N-UNS
N-AMU	N-EDS	N-IDS	N-OON	N-URD
N-ANA	N-EFS	N-IFF	N-OOP	N-UTS
N-ANE	N-ENE	N-ILL	N-OPE	N-YES
N-APE	N-EON	N-ISH	N-OSE	

Four letters to five

N-ACHE	N-ARES	N-EONS	N-ODES	N-OUPS
N-ACRE	N-ARIS	N-ERKS	N-OILS	N-OVEL
N-AGAS	N-ARKS	N-ESTS	N-OILY	N-OVUM
N-AILS	N-ATES	N-EUKS	N-OINT	N-OWED
N-AKED	N-AUNT	N-EVER	N-OLES	N-OWLS
N-ALAS	N-AVAL	N-EVES	N-OMEN	N-OWTS
N-ANAS	N-AVEL	N-EWER	N-ONCE	N-OXES
N-ANCE	N-AVES	N-EWTS	N-ONES	N-OYES
N-ANNA	N-EARS	N-ICER	N-OONS	N-UKES
N-APED	N-EATH	N-IDES	N-OOPS	N-URDS
N-APES	N-EATS	N-IFFY	N-OOSE	N-URDY
N-ARCO	N-EDDY	N-ILLS	N-OPAL	N-YAFF
N-ARCS	N-EMPT	N-IMPS	N-OSES	
N-ARDS	N-ENES	N-ODAL	N-OULD	

Five letters to six

N-ABBED	N-AILED	N-APRON	N-AUNTS	N-EATER
N-ACHES	N-AIVER	N-ARKED	N-AVELS	N-EBBED
N-ACRED	N-ANNAS	N-ARRAS	N-EARED	N-ESSES
N-ACRES	N-APERY	N-ARROW	N-EARLY	N-ESTER
N-AGGER	N-APING	N-AUGHT	N-EATEN	N-ETHER

N-ETTLE	N-ICKLE	N-OGGIN	N-OSIER	N-UMBER
N-EWEST	N-IMBED	N-OINTS	N-OTARY	N-UMPTY
N-ICHED	N-ISHES	N-ONCES	N-OTHER	N-UNCLE
N-ICHES	N-ITHER	N-OOSES	N-OUGHT	N-UTTER
N-ICKER	N-ODDER	N-OPALS	N-OVELS	N-YAFFS

Six letters to seven

N-AGGERS	N-AYWORD	N-EOLITH	N-ONUSES	N-UNCLES
N-AILING	N-EARING	N-ESTERS	N-OODLES	N-UNDINE
N-APHTHA	N-EBBING	N-ETTLED	N-OOLOGY	N-UNHOOD
N-APRONS	N-EDDIES	N-ETTLES	N-OUGHTS	N-UNLIKE
N-ARKING	N-EDDISH	N-ICHING	N-OVATED	N-UNSHIP
N-ARROWS	N-EGRESS	N-ICKERS	N-OYESES	N-UTTERS
N-ASCENT	N-EITHER	N-IFFIER	N-ULLING	N-YAFFED
N-ATRIUM	N-EMESES	N-OGGINS	N-UMBERS	
N-AUGHTS	N-EMESIS	N-OINTED	N-UMBLES	

Seven letters to eight

N-AINSELL	N-ATRIUMS	N-ETTLING	N-OVATION	N-UNHOODS
N-APERIES	N-AYWORDS	N-IFFIEST	N-ULLINGS	N-UNSHIPS
N-ARRASES	N-EARLIER	N-OINTING	N-UMBERED	N-YAFFING
N-ARROWED	N-EOLITHS	N-OTARIES	N-UNDINES	

Eight letters to nine

N-AINSELLS	N-AVICULAR	N-EGRESSES	N-OOLOGIES	N-UMBERING
N-APHTHOUS	N-AVIGATOR	N-EOLITHIC	N-OOSPHERE	
N-ARROWING	N-EARLIEST	N-EVERMORE	N-OVATIONS	

N – End-hooks

Two letters to three

AI-N	EA-N	HO-N	NO-N	TE-N
AN-N	EE-N	IN-N	NU-N	TI-N
AW-N	ER-N	IO-N	OO-N	TO-N
BA-N	FA-N	KI-N	OW-N	UR-N
BE-N	FE-N	KO-N	PA-N	WE-N
BI-N	GI-N	LI-N	PE-N	WO-N
BO-N	GO-N	MA-N	PI-N	YE-N
DA-N	GU-N	ME-N	RE-N	YO-N
DE-N	HA-N	MO-N	SI-N	
DI-N	HE-N	MU-N	SO-N	
DO-N	HI-N	NA-N	TA-N	

Three letters to four

AGE-N	BAR-N	CAN-N	DAM-N	EVE-N
AGO-N	BEE-N	CAR-N	DAW-N	EXO-N
AIR-N	BOO-N	CHI-N	DEE-N	EYE-N
ALA-N	BOR-N	CON-N	DOE-N	FAA-N
AMI-N	BRA-N	COO-N	DOO-N	FAW-N
ANA-N	BUN-N	COR-N	DOW-N	FEE-N
AZO-N	BUR-N	CUR-N	EAR-N	FER-N

FIR-N	KIR-N	NOW-N	SAI-N	TOR-N
FOE-N	KOA-N	OPE-N	SAW-N	TOW-N
FOH-N	LAR-N	OUR-N	SEA-N	UDO-N
GAE-N	LAW-N	PAW-N	SEE-N	UPO-N
GAU-N	LEA-N	PEA-N	SEW-N	WAI-N
GIE-N	LIE-N	PEE-N	SHA-N	WAR-N
GIN-N	LIN-N	PER-N	SKI-N	WEE-N
GOO-N	LOO-N	PHO-N	SOW-N	WIN-N
GUR-N	LOR-N	PIA-N	SPA-N	WOO-N
HAE-N	LOU-N	PIR-N	SUN-N	WYN-N
HER-N	LOW-N	POO-N	SYE-N	YAR-N
HEW-N	MAW-N	POW-N	TAI-N	YAW-N
HIS-N	MOA-N	RAI-N	TAR-N	YEA-N
HOO-N	MOO-N	RAW-N	TEE-N	ZOO-N
HYE-N	MOR-N	REE-N	THE-N	
JIN-N	MOW-N	REI-N	THO-N	
KAI-N	NOO-N	ROO-N	TOO-N	

Four letters to five

ABRI-N	DOZE-N	LADE-N	RIPE-N	SPAW-N
AMMO-N	DRAW-N	LATE-N	RISE-N	SPUR-N
ATMA-N	DROW-N	LEAR-N	RIVE-N	STAR-N
BAKE-N	ERGO-N	LIKE-N	ROMA-N	STOW-N
BALU-N	FANO-N	LIMA-N	ROTA-N	TABU-N
BLAW-N	FLAW-N	LIME-N	ROTO-N	TAKE-N
BLOW-N	FLOW-N	LINE-N	ROUE-N	TAKI-N
BRAW-N	FROW-N	LIVE-N	ROVE-N	TAPE-N
BROW-N	GIRO-N	LODE-N	RUME-N	TOKE-N
BURA-N	GIVE-N	LOGO-N	SAMA-N	TOLA-N
CAMA-N	GNAW-N	LOSE-N	SAME-N	TORA-N
CAPO-N	GREE-N	MAYA-N	SARI-N	TOYO-N
CHAI-N	GROW-N	MIRI-N	SATI-N	TREE-N
CLOW-N	GYRO-N	MOTE-N	SEME-N	TWEE-N
CODE-N	HALO-N	NOME-N	SHAW-N	VARA-N
CONI-N	HAVE-N	OCTA-N	SHEW-N	VEGA-N
COPE-N	HEBE-N	OWSE-N	SHOO-N	WAKE-N
COVE-N	HERO-N	PATE-N	SHOW-N	WHEE-N
COZE-N	HOSE-N	PAVE-N	SHUL-N	WIDE-N
CROW-N	HOTE-N	PREE-N	SILE-N	WOKE-N
DEAR-N	HOVE-N	PURI-N	SIRE-N	WOVE-N
DEMO-N	HUMA-N	QUEY-N	SKEE-N	YEAR-N
DIVA-N	JOMO-N	RAMI-N	SOKE-N	YEVE-N
DJIN-N	KNOW-N	RATA-N	SOLA-N	YOGI-N
DOOR-N	KORU-N	RAVE-N	SOLO-N	YOUR-N
DOVE-N	KULA-N	REDO-N	SOMA-N	ZUPA-N

Five letters to six

ALDER-N	BARRE-N	CAUSE-N	DOLMA-N	GLUTE-N
ALTER-N	BESEE-N	CAVER-N	DRIVE-N	GODSO-N
AMEBA-N	BITTE-N	CEDAR-N	FARCI-N	GRAVE-N
AMNIO-N	BOREE-N	CHICO-N	FLAME-N	HASTE-N
ARISE-N	BRAZE-N	CHOSE-N	FRORE-N	HAUSE-N
ASTER-N	BROKE-N	CLOVE-N	FROZE-N	HEAVE-N
AWAKE-N	CALLA-N	COMMO-N	GAZOO-N	HOOVE-N
AWOKE-N	CANTO-N	CRAVE-N	GEMMA-N	INTER-N
BABOO-N	CARBO-N	CRIME-N	GLAZE-N	INTRO-N
BANIA-N	CARVE-N	DOGMA-N	GLOBI-N	JOTUN-N

KRONE-N	NORMA-N	REEDE-N	SILVA-N	TRIGO-N
LARGE-N	PAISA-N	REPLA-N	SITHE-N	UNDER-N
LATHE-N	PANTO-N	RESAW-N	SLIVE-N	UNSEW-N
LATTE-N	PARKI-N	RESEE-N	SLOVE-N	VERVE-N
LEAVE-N	PATTE-N	RESEW-N	SOLEI-N	VILLA-N
LIGGE-N	PEASE-N	RESOW-N	SPOKE-N	VODOU-N
LOIPE-N	PERCE-N	ROTTE-N	STOLE-N	WARRE-N
LONGA-N	PHONO-N	SANTO-N	STONE-N	WEDEL-N
LOOSE-N	PHOTO-N	SCHUL-N	STRAW-N	WEETE-N
LOUPE-N	PIECE-N	SCREE-N	STREW-N	WHITE-N
MACRO-N	PLATE-N	SEAME-N	STROW-N	WICCA-N
MANNA-N	POLEY-N	SERRA-N	SYLVA-N	WIVER-N
MEDIA-N	PROVE-N	SEXTO-N	TAVER-N	WORSE-N
MICRO-N	RABBI-N	SHAKE-N	THORO-N	WROKE-N
MODER-N	RAPPE-N	SHAMA-N	THRAW-N	
MURRE-N	RATIO-N	SHAPE-N	THROW-N	
MURRI-N	RATOO-N	SHAVE-N	TORTE-N	

Six letters to seven

ABELIA-N	ENVIRO-N	PATTER-N	RIPSAW-N	UNDRAW-N
ACKNOW-N	EPIZOA-N	PHALLI-N	SALTER-N	UNLADE-N
ALKALI-N	GELATI-N	POSTER-N	SHIPPO-N	UNROVE-N
AMOEBA-N	GODDAM-N	PREWAR-N	SHOTTE-N	UNWOVE-N
ANLAGE-N	HOARSE-N	PROTEA-N	SHRIVE-N	UPBLOW-N
BETAKE-N	HOMELY-N	PROTEI-N	SIERRA-N	UPDRAW-N
BITTER-N	INWOVE-N	QUINTA-N	SILVER-N	UPGROW-N
BRAHMA-N	JIGSAW-N	REDRAW-N	SMIDGE-N	UPRISE-N
BRONZE-N	LAMPER-N	REFLOW-N	SOLITO-N	UPTAKE-N
CAPITA-N	LETTER-N	REGIME-N	STONER-N	URANIA-N
CHALLA-N	MEDUSA-N	REGIVE-N	STRIVE-N	UTOPIA-N
CHASTE-N	MISSEE-N	REGROW-N	STROKE-N	VIBRIO-N
CHIRRE-N	MONERA-N	RERISE-N	TAMARI-N	VOUDOU-N
CITHER-N	NUCLEI-N	RESHOW-N	TERTIA-N	WESTER-N
COARSE-N	ORARIA-N	RETAKE-N	TESTER-N	WRITHE-N
CRYPTO-N	OUTSEE-N	REWAKE-N	THRIVE-N	YESTER-N
EASTER-N	PAPAYA-N	REWOKE-N	TORULI-N	ZITHER-N
EMBRYO-N	PASTER-N	REWOVE-N	TRUDGE-N	

Seven letters to eight

ACANTHI-N	CONIDIA-N	FORSAKE-N	OUTFLOW-N	QUARTER-N
ACTINIA-N	DEFROZE-N	GALLICA-N	OUTGIVE-N	REARISE-N
ALFAQUI-N	DILUVIA-N	HACKSAW-N	OUTGNAW-N	REAWAKE-N
ALIZARI-N	DIPTERA-N	HISTRIO-N	OUTGROW-N	REAWOKE-N
APHELIA-N	DISLIKE-N	HYPOGEA-N	OUTTAKE-N	RECHOSE-N
AQUARIA-N	ECTOZOA-N	LEATHER-N	OVERSEE-N	REDRIVE-N
ARCADIA-N	ELECTRO-N	MAGNETO-N	OVERSEW-N	REFROZE-N
ARCHAEA-N	ENFROZE-N	MALARIA-N	OVERSOW-N	REGALIA-N
ASCIDIA-N	ENGRAVE-N	METAZOA-N	PANACEA-N	RESHAVE-N
AURELIA-N	ENLARGE-N	MISDRAW-N	PARAZOA-N	RESPOKE-N
BEREAVE-N	ENTOZOA-N	MISGIVE-N	PARTAKE-N	ROSARIA-N
BESPOKE-N	FEDAYEE-N	MISGROW-N	PELORIA-N	RUBELLA-N
BESTREW-N	FILARIA-N	MISKNOW-N	PERTAKE-N	SLATTER-N
BESTROW-N	FLITTER-N	MISTAKE-N	PETITIO-N	SOUTHER-N
BOHEMIA-N	FLYBLOW-N	MYCELIA-N	PIMENTO-N	SPREDDE-N
CHONDRI-N	FORESEE-N	NORTHER-N	POLYZOA-N	STROOKE-N
CODRIVE-N	FORFAIR-N	OPHIURA-N	PRESHOW-N	THROMBI-N
COLLAGE-N	FORGIVE-N	OUTDRAW-N	PUNALUA-N	UNBROKE-N

UNFROZE-N	UNSHAPE-N	UPBROKE-N	UPTHROW-N	WHIPSAW-N
UNLOOSE-N	UNSPOKE-N	UPSPOKE-N	VITELLI-N	WREATHE-N

Eight letters to nine

AMBROSIA-N	EPICEDIA-N	MISCHOSE-N	OVERGIVE-N	SANNYASI-N
AMPHIBIA-N	FELLATIO-N	MISDRIVE-N	OVERGROW-N	SCHLIERE-N
BACTERIA-N	FOREKNOW-N	MISSHAPE-N	OVERLADE-N	SCHNECKE-N
BASILICA-N	FORESHEW-N	MISSPOKE-N	OVERRIPE-N	SEPTARIA-N
CALCANEA-N	FORESHOW-N	MISTHROW-N	OVERTAKE-N	SIGHTSEE-N
CALVARIA-N	FORSPOKE-N	MOLLUSCA-N	PANDEMIA-N	SPATLESE-N
CARETAKE-N	HERBARIA-N	OUTBROKE-N	PLANARIA-N	SPOROZOA-N
CASTELLA-N	HYDROZOA-N	OUTDRIVE-N	PRECHOSE-N	STRONTIA-N
CERCARIA-N	HYPOGAEA-N	OUTSPOKE-N	PREFROZE-N	SUBTOPIA-N
COLLEGIA-N	MAGNESIA-N	OUTTHROW-N	PROTOZOA-N	WINDBLOW-N
DEMERARA-N	MALVASIA-N	OVERBLOW-N	REPTILIA-N	WIREDRAW-N
DISPROVE-N	MARSUPIA-N	OVERDRAW-N	RESTRIVE-N	WITHDRAW-N
DYSTOPIA-N	MAUSOLEA-N	OVERFLOW-N	ROUGHHEW-N	

O – Front-hooks

Two letters to three

O-AR	O-CH	O-KA	O-OM	O-RE
O-AT	O-DA	O-NE	O-ON	O-UP
O-BA	O-DE	O-NO	O-OP	O-UR
O-BE	O-ES	O-NY	O-OR	O-UT
O-BI	O-HM	O-OF	O-OS	O-WE
O-BO	O-HO	O-OH	O-PE	O-YE

Three letters to four

O-ARS	O-DAL	O-KAY	O-ONS	O-RES
O-ARY	O-DAS	O-LEA	O-OPS	O-SAR
O-BAS	O-DOR	O-LES	O-OSE	O-TIC
O-BES	O-DSO	O-LID	O-PAH	O-UDS
O-BEY	O-FAY	O-MEN	O-PAL	O-UPS
O-BIS	O-GAM	O-NIE	O-PED	O-URN
O-BIT	O-GEE	O-NOS	O-PEN	O-UTS
O-BOS	O-HOS	O-NUS	O-PES	O-VUM
O-CHE	O-INK	O-OHS	O-PUS	O-WED
O-DAH	O-KAS	O-OMS	O-RAD	O-YES

Four letters to five

O-AKED	O-DOUR	O-LENT	O-PINE	O-UNDY
O-ARED	O-DSOS	O-LIVE	O-PING	O-UPAS
O-AVES	O-FAYS	O-LOGY	O-PIUM	O-VARY
O-BANG	O-FLAG	O-MASA	O-RACH	O-VERS
O-BEYS	O-GAMS	O-MEGA	O-RACY	O-VERT
O-BIAS	O-GEES	O-OBIT	O-RANG	O-VINE
O-BITS	O-GIVE	O-OHED	O-RANT	O-VOID
O-BOLE	O-GLED	O-OPED	O-RATE	O-WING
O-CHER	O-HING	O-OSES	O-READ	O-ZONE
O-DAHS	O-HONE	O-PAHS	O-RIEL	
O-DALS	O-INKS	O-PALS	O-SCAR	
O-DORS	O-KAYS	O-PENS	O-UNCE	

Five letters to six

O-BANGS	O-GIVES	O-OSIER	O-RANGY	O-URALI
O-BENTO	O-INKED	O-PALED	O-RANTS	O-URARI
O-BITER	O-LINGO	O-PENED	O-RATED	O-VINES
O-BLAST	O-LIVER	O-PINED	O-RATES	O-VOIDS
O-BLATE	O-LIVES	O-PINES	O-READS	O-WRIER
O-BOLES	O-MENED	O-PIUMS	O-RIELS	O-YESES
O-BOLUS	O-MENTA	O-PULUS	O-SCARS	O-ZONES
O-CELLI	O-OBITS	O-PUSES	O-STEAL	
O-EDEMA	O-OHING	O-RACHE	O-STENT	
O-FLAGS	O-OLOGY	O-RALLY	O-TITIS	
O-GAMIC	O-OPING	O-RANGE	O-UNCES	

Six letters to seven

O-BENTOS	O-ESTRAL	O-MENTUM	O-RANGER	O-URALIS
O-BLASTS	O-ESTRIN	O-MICRON	O-RANGES	O-URARIS
O-BOVATE	O-ESTRUM	O-MIKRON	O-RATING	O-UTMOST
O-CARINA	O-ESTRUS	O-NANISM	O-RATION	O-VARIES
O-CELLAR	O-INKING	O-PACIFY	O-ROTUND	O-VERBID
O-CREATE	O-KIMONO	O-PENING	O-STENTS	O-VERSET
O-DONATE	O-LIVERS	O-PINING	O-STRICH	O-WRIEST
O-DORISE	O-LOGIES	O-PINION	O-UAKARI	O-YESSES
O-DORIZE	O-MENING	O-POSSUM	O-UGLIED	O-ZONATE
O-EDEMAS	O-MENTAL	O-RACHES	O-UGLIES	

Seven letters to eight

O-CARINAS	O-EDEMATA	O-KIMONOS	O-OLOGIST	O-UROLOGY
O-DONATES	O-ENOLOGY	O-MICRONS	O-PINIONS	O-VARIOLE
O-DORISED	O-ESTRINS	O-MIKRONS	O-POSSUMS	O-VARIOUS
O-DORISES	O-ESTRIOL	O-MISSION	O-RANGIER	O-VERBIDS
O-DORIZED	O-ESTRONE	O-MISSIVE	O-RATIONS	O-VERSETS
O-DORIZES	O-ESTROUS	O-NANISMS	O-STOMATE	O-ZONATED
O-ECOLOGY	O-ESTRUMS	O-OLOGIES	O-UAKARIS	

Eight letters to nine

O-DORISING	O-ESTRIOLS	O-OLOGISTS	O-RANGIEST	O-VERMINED
O-DORIZING	O-ESTROGEN	O-PACIFIED	O-STOMATES	O-ZONATION
O-ECUMENIC	O-ESTRONES	O-PACIFIER	O-STRICHES	
O-ENOPHILE	O-ESTRUSES	O-PACIFIES	O-UROSCOPY	
O-ESOPHAGI	O-MISSIONS	O-PINIONED	O-VARIOLES	

O – End-hooks

Two letters to three

AB-O	EM-O	IS-O	ON-O	UP-O
AD-O	EX-O	LO-O	OX-O	WO-O
AG-O	GI-O	MO-O	PO-O	ZO-O
BI-O	GO-O	NO-O	RE-O	
BO-O	HA-O	OB-O	TA-O	
DO-O	HO-O	OH-O	TO-O	

Three letters to four

ALS-O	DIN-O	KEN-O	MIR-O	SAD-O
ALT-O	DOC-O	KET-O	MIS-O	SAG-O
ANN-O	DOD-O	KIN-O	MON-O	SEC-O
ARC-O	ECH-O	KOB-O	MOZ-O	SEG-O
BEG-O	ERG-O	KOR-O	MUS-O	SKI-O
BIT-O	FAD-O	LEV-O	ODS-O	SOH-O
BOH-O	FAN-O	LID-O	OLE-O	SOL-O
BOK-O	FAR-O	LIN-O	ORD-O	SUM-O
BOY-O	FID-O	LIP-O	PAC-O	TAR-O
BRO-O	FIG-O	LOB-O	PEP-O	TOC-O
BUB-O	FIL-O	LOG-O	PES-O	TOM-O
BUD-O	FIN-O	LOT-O	PIS-O	TOP-O
CAM-O	GAP-O	LUD-O	POL-O	TOR-O
CAP-O	GOB-O	MAK-O	POM-O	TOY-O
CHA-O	HER-O	MAN-O	PRO-O	VEG-O
CIT-O	HOB-O	MAY-O	RAT-O	VET-O
DAD-O	HOM-O	MEM-O	RED-O	VIN-O
DAG-O	HYP-O	MEN-O	REG-O	WIN-O
DEL-O	JUD-O	MIC-O	REP-O	YUK-O
DID-O	KAY-O	MIL-O	ROT-O	

Four letters to five

AMID-O	CHIN-O	GUAN-O	MOTT-O	REST-O
AMIN-O	CHOC-O	GUST-O	MUCH-O	RODE-O
BANC-O	COMB-O	HALL-O	MUNG-O	RONE-O
BARD-O	COMM-O	HELL-O	NACH-O	RUMP-O
BASH-O	COMP-O	HILL-O	NARC-O	SALT-O
BASS-O	COND-O	HOWS-O	NUTS-O	SANG-O
BAST-O	CORN-O	HULL-O	PANT-O	SANK-O
BEAN-O	CORS-O	IMID-O	PARE-O	SANT-O
BENT-O	CRED-O	JAMB-O	PASE-O	SCUD-O
BERK-O	CUFF-O	JELL-O	PEST-O	SEXT-O
BIFF-O	CUSS-O	JOCK-O	PHON-O	SICK-O
BING-O	CYAN-O	KARO-O	PHOT-O	SKIM-O
BOFF-O	DECK-O	KEEN-O	PIAN-O	SOCK-O
BOMB-O	DING-O	KEMB-O	PILA-O	SOLD-O
BONG-O	DIPS-O	KOND-O	PING-O	SORB-O
BUCK-O	DISC-O	LASS-O	PINK-O	SORD-O
BUFF-O	DITT-O	LENT-O	PINT-O	STEN-O
BUNK-O	DRAC-O	LIMB-O	PONG-O	TACH-O
BURR-O	DUMB-O	LING-O	PORN-O	TANG-O
BUTE-O	FANG-O	LITH-O	POSH-O	TEMP-O
CACA-O	FATS-O	MACH-O	POTT-O	TORS-O
CAME-O	FILL-O	MAIK-O	PRIM-O	TRIG-O
CAMP-O	FLEX-O	MANG-O	PROM-O	TRUG-O
CANS-O	FORD-O	MENT-O	PROS-O	VERS-O
CANT-O	FUNG-O	METH-O	PULA-O	VIDE-O
CARB-O	GADS-O	MEZZ-O	PUNT-O	VIRE-O
CELL-O	GAMB-O	MILK-O	PUTT-O	WACK-O
CENT-O	GARB-O	MIME-O	QUIN-O	WALD-O
CHAD-O	GECK-O	MOLT-O	QUIP-O	WHAM-O
CHIA-O	GISM-O	MONG-O	RATO-O	YUCK-O
CHIC-O	GODS-O	MOSS-O	REAL-O	ZINC-O

Five letters to six

AMMON-O	CRYPT-O	LIVED-O	REECH-O	THICK-O
BILLY-O	DINER-O	MEDIC-O	RIGHT-O	TOLED-O
BRILL-O	DORAD-O	MORPH-O	ROMAN-O	TRILL-O
BROCH-O	DUETT-O	NYMPH-O	SHACK-O	VIGOR-O
BRONC-O	ERING-O	PEDAL-O	SHEEP-O	VOMIT-O
CARDI-O	FASCI-O	PLONK-O	SMALT-O	WEIRD-O
CHARR-O	FRANC-O	PREST-O	SOLAN-O	WHACK-O
CHEAP-O	GIUST-O	PSEUD-O	SPEED-O	WHATS-O
CHEER-O	HALLO-O	PSYCH-O	STALK-O	
CHOCK-O	HOLLO-O	QUART-O	STERE-O	
CHURR-O	HULLO-O	RABAT-O	STING-O	
CONCH-O	LIBER-O	RANCH-O	STINK-O	

Six letters to seven

BANDIT-O	CYMBAL-O	PAESAN-O	PUMMEL-O	TAMARA-O
BATTER-O	GRADIN-O	PAISAN-O	RABBIT-O	TYMPAN-O
BRACER-O	MAGNET-O	PAMPER-O	REVERS-O	VERISM-O
BUDGER-O	MOMENT-O	PIMENT-O	SECOND-O	WHERES-O
CANTIC-O	NITROS-O	PRIMER-O	SERRAN-O	

Seven letters to eight

ARMIGER-O	CORNETT-O	INTAGLI-O	PRELUDI-O	VIGOROS-O
CAPITAN-O	COURANT-O	LEGGIER-O	RANCHER-O	ZECCHIN-O
CLASSIC-O	EXPRESS-O	MONTANT-O	SESTETT-O	
COMMAND-O	FASCISM-O	PERFECT-O	SOMBRER-O	
CONCERT-O	FLAMING-O	POLITIC-O	STAMPED-O	

Eight letters to nine

CABALLER-O	MAGNIFIC-O	PORTOLAN-O	QUINTETT-O
CAPRICCI-O	MANIFEST-O	PULVILLI-O	SOLFEGGI-O
DESTRUCT-O	PASTICCI-O	QUARTETT-O	

P – Front-hooks

Two letters to three

P-AD	P-AX	P-ET	P-OM	P-UG
P-AH	P-AY	P-HI	P-OO	P-UH
P-AL	P-EA	P-HO	P-OP	P-UN
P-AM	P-ED	P-IN	P-OS	P-UP
P-AN	P-EE	P-IS	P-OW	P-UR
P-AR	P-EH	P-IT	P-OX	P-US
P-AS	P-EN	P-OD	P-RE	P-UT
P-AT	P-ER	P-OH	P-SI	P-YA
P-AW	P-ES	P-OI	P-ST	P-YE

Three letters to four

P-AAL	P-ADS	P-AID	P-AIR	P-ALL
P-ACE	P-AGE	P-AIL	P-AIS	P-ALP
P-ACT	P-AHS	P-AIN	P-ALE	P-ALS

P-AND	P-EEN	P-INK	P-ONE	P-REP
P-ANE	P-EHS	P-INS	P-ONS	P-REX
P-ANT	P-EKE	P-ION	P-ONY	P-REZ
P-APE	P-ELF	P-ISH	P-OOF	P-RIG
P-ARD	P-ELL	P-ISO	P-OOH	P-RIM
P-ARE	P-ELT	P-ITA	P-OON	P-ROB
P-ARK	P-END	P-ITS	P-OOP	P-ROD
P-ARS	P-ENE	P-LAP	P-OOR	P-ROM
P-ART	P-ENS	P-LAT	P-OOS	P-ROO
P-ASH	P-EON	P-LAY	P-OOT	P-ROW
P-ASS	P-ERE	P-LEA	P-OPE	P-SIS
P-ATE	P-ERK	P-LED	P-OPS	P-TUI
P-AUA	P-ERN	P-LEW	P-ORE	P-UDS
P-AVE	P-EST	P-LEX	P-ORT	P-UGH
P-AWA	P-HAT	P-LIE	P-OSE	P-UGS
P-AWL	P-HEW	P-LOD	P-OUK	P-UKE
P-AWN	P-HIS	P-LOP	P-OUR	P-ULE
P-AYS	P-HOH	P-LOT	P-OUT	P-ULU
P-EAN	P-HON	P-LOW	P-OWN	P-UMP
P-EAR	P-HOS	P-LOY	P-OXY	P-UNS
P-EAS	P-HOT	P-LUG	P-RAD	P-UPS
P-EAT	P-HUT	P-LUM	P-RAM	P-URE
P-ECH	P-ICE	P-ODS	P-RAT	P-UTS
P-EDS	P-ICK	P-OKE	P-RAY	P-YES
P-EEK	P-ILL	P-OLE	P-REE	P-YET
P-EEL	P-IMP	P-OMS	P-REM	P-YIN

Four letters to five

P-AALS	P-ARES	P-ENES	P-LACE	P-LUGS
P-ACED	P-ARIS	P-EONS	P-LACK	P-LUMP
P-ACER	P-ARKS	P-EPOS	P-LAID	P-LUMS
P-ACES	P-ARLE	P-ERES	P-LAIN	P-LUNK
P-ACTA	P-ARSE	P-ERKS	P-LANE	P-LUSH
P-ACTS	P-ARTI	P-ERNS	P-LANK	P-OINT
P-ADDY	P-ARTS	P-ERST	P-LANT	P-OKES
P-AEON	P-ARTY	P-ESKY	P-LAPS	P-OLES
P-AGED	P-ARVO	P-ESTS	P-LASH	P-OLIO
P-AGER	P-ATES	P-HANG	P-LAST	P-ONCE
P-AGES	P-AVER	P-HARE	P-LATE	P-ONES
P-AILS	P-AVES	P-HOHS	P-LATS	P-OOFS
P-AINS	P-AVID	P-HONE	P-LAYS	P-OOFY
P-AIRS	P-AWED	P-HONS	P-LEAD	P-OOHS
P-ALAS	P-AWLS	P-HOTS	P-LEAS	P-OONS
P-ALAY	P-AWNS	P-HUTS	P-LEAT	P-OOPS
P-ALES	P-AXES	P-HYLA	P-LIED	P-OOTS
P-ALLS	P-EACH	P-HYLE	P-LIER	P-OPES
P-ALLY	P-EANS	P-ICKY	P-LIES	P-ORAL
P-ALMS	P-EARL	P-ILEA	P-LING	P-ORES
P-ALPS	P-EARS	P-ILLS	P-LINK	P-ORGY
P-ANCE	P-EASE	P-IMPS	P-LODS	P-ORTS
P-ANDS	P-EATS	P-INCH	P-LONG	P-OSES
P-ANES	P-EELS	P-INGO	P-LOOK	P-OTTO
P-ANGA	P-EERY	P-INKS	P-LOPS	P-OUCH
P-ANTS	P-EGGY	P-INKY	P-LOTS	P-OUKS
P-APER	P-EKES	P-INTO	P-LOWS	P-OURS
P-APES	P-ELFS	P-IONS	P-LOYS	P-OUTS
P-ARCH	P-ELLS	P-ISOS	P-LUCK	P-OWER
P-ARDS	P-ELTS	P-ITAS	P-LUES	P-OWNS
P-ARED	P-ENDS	P-ITCH	P-LUFF	P-OWRE

P-OXES	P-REIF	P-RIMS	P-ROOF	P-UKES
P-RADS	P-REMS	P-RIMY	P-RORE	P-ULES
P-RAMS	P-RENT	P-RINK	P-ROSE	P-ULUS
P-RANA	P-REPS	P-RISE	P-ROST	P-UMPS
P-RANG	P-REST	P-ROBE	P-ROSY	P-UNCE
P-RANK	P-RIAL	P-ROBS	P-ROUL	P-UNTO
P-RASE	P-RICE	P-RODS	P-ROVE	P-UPAS
P-RATE	P-RICK	P-ROIN	P-ROWS	P-URES
P-RATS	P-RICY	P-ROKE	P-RUDE	P-URGE
P-RAWN	P-RIDE	P-ROLE	P-RUNE	P-USES
P-RAYS	P-RIGS	P-ROLL	P-RUNT	P-YINS
P-REED	P-RILL	P-ROMS	P-SHAW	
P-REEN	P-RIMA	P-RONE	P-SORA	
P-REES	P-RIME	P-RONG	P-UGHS	

Five letters to six

P-ACERS	P-EANED	P-ITCHY	P-LUNKS	P-REENS
P-ACING	P-EARLS	P-LACED	P-LURRY	P-REEVE
P-ACKER	P-EARLY	P-LACER	P-LUSHY	P-REFER
P-ADDED	P-EARST	P-LACES	P-LYING	P-REFIX
P-ADDER	P-EASED	P-LACET	P-ODIUM	P-REIFS
P-ADDLE	P-EASES	P-LACKS	P-OINTS	P-REMAN
P-AEONS	P-ECHED	P-LAIDS	P-OLDER	P-REMEN
P-AGERS	P-EERIE	P-LANCH	P-OLIOS	P-REMIX
P-AGING	P-EGGED	P-LANES	P-OLLER	P-RENTS
P-AIRED	P-ELITE	P-LANKS	P-ONCES	P-REPAY
P-AIRER	P-ELVES	P-LANTS	P-ONTIC	P-RESES
P-ALAPA	P-ENDED	P-LATED	P-OOHED	P-RESET
P-ALATE	P-ERNED	P-LATEN	P-OOPED	P-RESTO
P-ALAYS	P-ERSES	P-LATER	P-OPERA	P-RESTS
P-ALTER	P-ESTER	P-LAYED	P-OSIER	P-RETAX
P-ANGAS	P-ETHER	P-LAYER	P-OTHER	P-REVUE
P-ANTED	P-ETTLE	P-LEACH	P-OTTER	P-REXES
P-APERS	P-HANGS	P-LEADS	P-OTTOS	P-RIALS
P-APERY	P-HARES	P-LEASE	P-OUNCE	P-RICED
P-APISH	P-HAROS	P-LEATS	P-OUPED	P-RICER
P-APISM	P-HEEZE	P-LEDGE	P-OURIE	P-RICES
P-ARISH	P-HONED	P-LEUCH	P-OUTED	P-RICEY
P-ARKED	P-HONER	P-LEUGH	P-OUTER	P-RICKS
P-ARLED	P-HONES	P-LEXES	P-OWRES	P-RIDES
P-ARLES	P-HONEY	P-LIERS	P-RAISE	P-RIEVE
P-ARPEN	P-HOOEY	P-LIGHT	P-RANAS	P-RILLS
P-ARRAS	P-HYLIC	P-LINGS	P-RANCE	P-RIMED
P-ARSED	P-ICKER	P-LINKS	P-RANKS	P-RIMER
P-ARSES	P-ICKLE	P-LODGE	P-RASES	P-RIMES
P-ARSON	P-IGGED	P-LONGE	P-RATED	P-RIMUS
P-ARTIS	P-ILEUM	P-LONGS	P-RATER	P-RINKS
P-ARVOS	P-ILEUS	P-LOOKS	P-RATES	P-RISER
P-ASHED	P-IMPED	P-LOUGH	P-RAWNS	P-RISES
P-ASHES	P-IMPLY	P-LOVER	P-RAXES	P-RIVET
P-ASSED	P-INGLE	P-LOWED	P-RAYED	P-ROBED
P-ASSES	P-INION	P-LOWER	P-REACH	P-ROBES
P-ASTER	P-INKED	P-LUCKS	P-REACT	P-ROINS
P-AVENS	P-INKER	P-LUCKY	P-REARM	P-ROKED
P-AVERS	P-INNED	P-LUFFS	P-REBID	P-ROKER
P-AVISE	P-INNER	P-LUMMY	P-REBUY	P-ROKES
P-AWING	P-IONIC	P-LUMPS	P-RECUT	P-ROLES
P-AWNED	P-IRATE	P-LUMPY	P-REDRY	P-ROLLS
P-AWNER	P-ISHES	P-LUNGE	P-REDYE	P-RONES

P-ROOFS	P-ROULS	P-RUDES	P-UDDER	P-URGES
P-ROPER	P-ROVED	P-RUNED	P-UGGED	P-URINE
P-RORES	P-ROVEN	P-RUNES	P-UMPED	P-USHER
P-ROSED	P-ROVER	P-RUNTS	P-UNCES	P-UTTER
P-ROSES	P-ROVES	P-SHAWS	P-UPPED	
P-ROSIT	P-ROWER	P-SORAS	P-URGED	
P-ROTON	P-ROYNE	P-TOSES	P-URGER	

Six letters to seven

P-ACKERS	P-ENFOLD	P-LASHED	P-LUSHLY	P-RECEDE
P-ACTION	P-ENSILE	P-LASHER	P-LUTEAL	P-RECENT
P-ADDERS	P-ENTICE	P-LASHES	P-ODIUMS	P-RECEPT
P-ADDIES	P-EONISM	P-LASTER	P-OINTED	P-RECESS
P-ADDING	P-ERNING	P-LATENS	P-OLLERS	P-RECIPE
P-ADDLED	P-ESTERS	P-LATINA	P-OLLIES	P-RECODE
P-ADDLES	P-ETHERS	P-LATTER	P-ONDING	P-RECOOK
P-AEONIC	P-ETTLED	P-LAYERS	P-OODLES	P-RECOUP
P-AGINGS	P-ETTLES	P-LAYING	P-OOFIER	P-RECURE
P-AIREST	P-HANGED	P-LAYOFF	P-OOHING	P-RECUTS
P-AIRING	P-HATTER	P-LEADED	P-OOPING	P-REDATE
P-ALAPAS	P-HEEZED	P-LEADER	P-OPERAS	P-REDIAL
P-ALATED	P-HEEZES	P-LEASED	P-ORCINE	P-REDYED
P-ALATES	P-HIZZES	P-LEASER	P-ORGIES	P-REDYES
P-ALLIUM	P-HONERS	P-LEASES	P-ORTHOS	P-REEDIT
P-ALTERS	P-HONEYS	P-LEDGED	P-OTHERS	P-REEVED
P-ANELED	P-HONIED	P-LEDGER	P-OTTERS	P-REEVES
P-ANTHER	P-HONING	P-LEDGES	P-OUCHED	P-REFACE
P-ANTING	P-HUTTED	P-LESSOR	P-OUCHES	P-REFECT
P-ANTLER	P-ICKERS	P-LIABLE	P-OULDER	P-REFERS
P-APISMS	P-ICKIER	P-LIGHTS	P-OUNCES	P-REFILE
P-APPOSE	P-ICKILY	P-LINKED	P-OUPING	P-REFILL
P-ARABLE	P-ICKLER	P-LINKER	P-OUTERS	P-REFIRE
P-ARCHED	P-IGGING	P-LISSES	P-OUTHER	P-REFORM
P-ARCHES	P-IMPING	P-LODGED	P-OUTING	P-REFUND
P-ARISES	P-IMPLED	P-LODGES	P-OZZIES	P-REHEAT
P-ARKING	P-INCASE	P-LONGED	P-RABBLE	P-RELATE
P-ARLING	P-INCHED	P-LONGES	P-RAISED	P-RELOAD
P-ARPENS	P-INCHER	P-LOPPED	P-RAISER	P-REMADE
P-ARPENT	P-INCHES	P-LOTTED	P-RAISES	P-REMEET
P-ARSING	P-INFALL	P-LOTTER	P-RANCED	P-REMISE
P-ARSONS	P-INFOLD	P-LOUGHS	P-RANCES	P-REMISS
P-ARTIER	P-INGLES	P-LOVERS	P-RANGED	P-REMOLD
P-ARTIES	P-INGOES	P-LOWBOY	P-RANKED	P-REMOVE
P-ASHING	P-INIONS	P-LOWERS	P-RANKLE	P-RENAME
P-ASTERN	P-INKING	P-LOWING	P-RATERS	P-RENTED
P-ASTERS	P-INNATE	P-LUCKED	P-RATING	P-REPACK
P-ATRIAL	P-INNERS	P-LUFFED	P-RATTLE	P-REPAID
P-AVISES	P-INNING	P-LUGGED	P-RAYING	P-REPAVE
P-AWNERS	P-INWORK	P-LUGGER	P-REACTS	P-REPAYS
P-AWNING	P-ITCHED	P-LUMBER	P-REARMS	P-REPLAN
P-EANING	P-ITCHES	P-LUMPED	P-REAVER	P-REPONE
P-EASING	P-LACERS	P-LUMPEN	P-REBIDS	P-REPOSE
P-EATERY	P-LACETS	P-LUMPER	P-REBILL	P-REPPED
P-ECHING	P-LACING	P-LUNGED	P-REBIND	P-RESALE
P-EERIER	P-LAIDED	P-LUNGER	P-REBOIL	P-RESELL
P-EGGING	P-LANATE	P-LUNGES	P-REBOOK	P-RESENT
P-ELITES	P-LANKED	P-LUNKER	P-REBORN	P-RESETS
P-ENATES	P-LANNER	P-LUSHER	P-REBUYS	P-RESHIP
P-ENDING	P-LAPPED	P-LUSHES	P-RECAST	P-RESHOW

P-RESIDE	P-REVISE	P-RIEVES	P-ROKING	P-UBERTY
P-RESIFT	P-REVUES	P-RIGGED	P-ROLLED	P-UCKERS
P-RESOAK	P-REWARM	P-RIGGER	P-ROLLER	P-UDDERS
P-RESOLD	P-REWASH	P-RILLED	P-ROOFED	P-UGGING
P-RESORT	P-REWIRE	P-RIMERS	P-ROOFER	P-ULLING
P-RESTED	P-REWORK	P-RIMING	P-ROPERS	P-UMPING
P-RESTER	P-REWORN	P-RIMMED	P-ROSIER	P-UNTIES
P-RESTOS	P-REWRAP	P-RIMMER	P-ROSILY	P-UPPING
P-RESUME	P-REZZES	P-RINKED	P-ROSING	P-URANIC
P-RETAPE	P-RICERS	P-RISERS	P-ROTONS	P-URGERS
P-RETELL	P-RICIER	P-RISING	P-ROVERS	P-URGING
P-RETEST	P-RICING	P-RIVETS	P-ROVING	P-URINES
P-RETOLD	P-RICKED	P-ROBAND	P-ROYNES	P-USHERS
P-RETRIM	P-RICKER	P-ROBING	P-RUDERY	P-UTTERS
P-RETYPE	P-RICKLE	P-RODDED	P-RUDISH	
P-REVERB	P-RICKLY	P-ROINED	P-RUNTED	
P-REVIEW	P-RIDING	P-ROKERS	P-SALTER	

Seven letters to eight

P-ACTIONS	P-INCASES	P-LOPPING	P-RANKLED	P-REDATED
P-ADDLING	P-INCHERS	P-LOTTERS	P-RANKLES	P-REDATES
P-AIRINGS	P-INCHING	P-LOTTING	P-RATINGS	P-REDRAFT
P-AIRWISE	P-INFALLS	P-LOWBOYS	P-RATTLED	P-REDRIED
P-ALIFORM	P-INFOLDS	P-LOWLAND	P-RATTLER	P-REDRIES
P-ALIMONY	P-INNINGS	P-LUCKIER	P-RATTLES	P-REDRILL
P-ALLIUMS	P-INWORKS	P-LUCKILY	P-REACHED	P-REEDITS
P-ALTERED	P-ITCHIER	P-LUCKING	P-REACHER	P-REELECT
P-ALTERER	P-ITCHILY	P-LUFFING	P-REACHES	P-REENACT
P-ANELING	P-ITCHING	P-LUGGERS	P-REACTED	P-REERECT
P-ANTHERS	P-LACINGS	P-LUGGING	P-READAPT	P-REEVING
P-ANTINGS	P-LAIDING	P-LUGHOLE	P-READMIT	P-REFACED
P-ANTLERS	P-LANCHED	P-LUMBAGO	P-REALLOT	P-REFACES
P-ARABLES	P-LANCHES	P-LUMBERS	P-REALTER	P-REFECTS
P-ARCHING	P-LANKING	P-LUMMIER	P-REAPPLY	P-REFIGHT
P-ARISHES	P-LANNERS	P-LUMPENS	P-REARMED	P-REFILED
P-ARPENTS	P-LAPPING	P-LUMPERS	P-REAVERS	P-REFILES
P-ARTICLE	P-LASHERS	P-LUMPIER	P-REBILLS	P-REFILLS
P-ARTISAN	P-LASHING	P-LUMPING	P-REBINDS	P-REFIRED
P-ARTWORK	P-LASTERS	P-LUMPISH	P-REBIRTH	P-REFIRES
P-EARLIER	P-LATINAS	P-LUNGERS	P-REBOARD	P-REFIXED
P-EARLIES	P-LAYBACK	P-LUNGING	P-REBOILS	P-REFIXES
P-ECTASES	P-LAYOFFS	P-LUNKERS	P-REBOOKS	P-REFOCUS
P-EERIEST	P-LAYTIME	P-LUSHEST	P-REBOUND	P-REFORMS
P-ENCHANT	P-LEACHED	P-LUSHIER	P-REBUILD	P-REFROZE
P-ENFOLDS	P-LEACHES	P-LYINGLY	P-REBUILT	P-REFUNDS
P-ENLIGHT	P-LEADERS	P-OINTING	P-RECASTS	P-REGNANT
P-ENOLOGY	P-LEADING	P-OOFIEST	P-RECEDED	P-REHEATS
P-ENTICED	P-LEASERS	P-ORTOLAN	P-RECEDES	P-REJUDGE
P-ENTICES	P-LEASING	P-OSTMARK	P-RECEPTS	P-RELATES
P-ENTOMIC	P-LEASURE	P-OTTERED	P-RECHECK	P-RELOADS
P-EONISMS	P-LEATHER	P-OUCHING	P-RECHOSE	P-REMEETS
P-ETTLING	P-LEDGERS	P-OUTINGS	P-RECIPES	P-REMISED
P-HANGING	P-LESSORS	P-RABBLES	P-RECITED	P-REMISES
P-HARMING	P-LIGHTED	P-RAISERS	P-RECLEAN	P-REMIXED
P-HEEZING	P-LIGHTER	P-RAISING	P-RECODED	P-REMIXES
P-HISHING	P-LINKERS	P-RANCING	P-RECODES	P-REMOLDS
P-HONEYED	P-LINKING	P-RANGING	P-RECOOKS	P-REMORSE
P-HUTTING	P-LODGING	P-RANKING	P-RECURED	P-REMOVED
P-ICKIEST	P-LONGING	P-RANKISH	P-RECURES	P-REMOVES

P-RENAMES	P-RESELLS	P-RESUMER	P-REVISIT	P-RINKING
P-RENTING	P-RESENTS	P-RESUMES	P-REVISOR	P-ROBANDS
P-REORDER	P-RESERVE	P-RETAPED	P-REWARMS	P-RODDING
P-REPACKS	P-RESHAPE	P-RETAPES	P-REWEIGH	P-ROINING
P-REPAVED	P-RESHIPS	P-RETASTE	P-REWIRED	P-ROLLERS
P-REPAVES	P-RESHOWN	P-RETELLS	P-REWIRES	P-ROLLING
P-REPLACE	P-RESHOWS	P-RETESTS	P-REWORKS	P-ROOFERS
P-REPLANS	P-RESIDED	P-RETRAIN	P-REWRAPS	P-ROOFING
P-REPLANT	P-RESIDER	P-RETREAT	P-RICIEST	P-ROSIEST
P-REPONED	P-RESIDES	P-RETRIAL	P-RICKERS	P-ROVINGS
P-REPONES	P-RESIFTS	P-RETRIMS	P-RICKETS	P-SALTERS
P-REPOSED	P-RESOAKS	P-RETYPED	P-RICKING	P-UDDERED
P-REPOSES	P-RESOLVE	P-RETYPES	P-RICKLES	P-UNITION
P-REPPING	P-RESORTS	P-REUNION	P-RIEVING	P-UNITIVE
P-REPRESS	P-RESPLIT	P-REUNITE	P-RIGGERS	P-URGINGS
P-REPRICE	P-RESTAMP	P-REVALUE	P-RIGGING	P-UTTERED
P-REPRINT	P-RESTERS	P-REVERBS	P-RIGGISH	P-UTTERER
P-RESALES	P-RESTING	P-REVIEWS	P-RILLING	
P-RESCIND	P-RESTORE	P-REVISED	P-RIMMERS	
P-RESCORE	P-RESUMED	P-REVISES	P-RIMMING	

Eight letters to nine

P-ACTIONED	P-LIGHTING	P-REBOILED	P-REFILLED	P-REPACKED
P-ALTERERS	P-LOWLANDS	P-REBOOKED	P-REFIRING	P-REPASTED
P-ALTERING	P-LUCKIEST	P-REBOUGHT	P-REFIXING	P-REPAVING
P-ARTICLES	P-LUGHOLES	P-REBUILDS	P-REFORMAT	P-REPAYING
P-ARTISANS	P-LUMBAGOS	P-REBUTTAL	P-REFORMED	P-REPLACED
P-ARTWORKS	P-LUMMIEST	P-REBUYING	P-REFREEZE	P-REPLACES
P-EARLIEST	P-LUMPIEST	P-RECEDING	P-REFROZEN	P-REPLANTS
P-EATERIES	P-LUSHIEST	P-RECENSOR	P-REFUNDED	P-REPONING
P-ENCHANTS	P-LUSHNESS	P-RECEPTOR	P-REGNANCY	P-REPOSING
P-ENLIGHTS	P-NEUMATIC	P-RECESSED	P-REGROWTH	P-REPRICED
P-ENTANGLE	P-OENOLOGY	P-RECESSES	P-REHANDLE	P-REPRICES
P-ENTICING	P-ORTHOSES	P-RECHARGE	P-REHARDEN	P-REPRINTS
P-ETIOLATE	P-ORTOLANS	P-RECHECKS	P-REHEATED	P-RERECORD
P-HONEYING	P-OSTMARKS	P-RECHOOSE	P-REHEATER	P-REREVIEW
P-ICKINESS	P-OTTERING	P-RECHOSEN	P-REIMPOSE	P-RESCHOOL
P-INFOLDED	P-RAISINGS	P-RECISION	P-REINFORM	P-RESCINDS
P-INKINESS	P-RANKINGS	P-RECLEANS	P-REINSERT	P-RESCORED
P-INNATELY	P-RANKLING	P-RECODING	P-REINVITE	P-RESCORES
P-INSETTER	P-RATTLERS	P-RECOOKED	P-REJUDGED	P-RESCREEN
P-ITCHIEST	P-RATTLING	P-RECURING	P-REJUDGES	P-RESCRIPT
P-ITCHINGS	P-REABSORB	P-REDATING	P-RELATION	P-RESEASON
P-LACELESS	P-REACCUSE	P-REDEFINE	P-RELAUNCH	P-RESELECT
P-LANCHING	P-REACHERS	P-REDESIGN	P-RELOADED	P-RESENTED
P-LASHINGS	P-REACHING	P-REDIGEST	P-RELOCATE	P-RESENTER
P-LATINISE	P-REACTING	P-REDRILLS	P-REMARKET	P-RESERVED
P-LATINIZE	P-READAPTS	P-REDRYING	P-REMISING	P-RESERVER
P-LATITUDE	P-READJUST	P-REDYEING	P-REMIXING	P-RESERVES
P-LAYBACKS	P-READMITS	P-REEDITED	P-REMODIFY	P-RESETTLE
P-LAYTIMES	P-REALLOTS	P-REELECTS	P-REMOLDED	P-RESHAPED
P-LEACHING	P-REALTERS	P-REENACTS	P-REMOTION	P-RESHAPES
P-LEADINGS	P-REARMING	P-REERECTS	P-REMOVING	P-RESHOWED
P-LEASABLE	P-REASSIGN	P-REEXPOSE	P-RENOTIFY	P-RESIDENT
P-LEASINGS	P-REASSURE	P-REFACING	P-RENUMBER	P-RESIDERS
P-LEASURES	P-REBIDDEN	P-REFERRED	P-REOBTAIN	P-RESIDING
P-LEATHERS	P-REBILLED	P-REFERRER	P-REOCCUPY	P-RESIFTED
P-LIGHTERS	P-REBIRTHS	P-REFIGURE	P-REORDAIN	P-RESOAKED
P-LIGHTFUL	P-REBOARDS	P-REFILING	P-REORDERS	P-RESOLVED

P-RESOLVES	P-RETAPING	P-REUNITES	P-REWASHED	P-ROSTRATE
P-RESORTED	P-RETASTED	P-REVALUED	P-REWASHES	P-RUDERIES
P-RESTAMPS	P-RETASTES	P-REVALUES	P-REWEIGHS	P-UBERTIES
P-RESTORED	P-RETESTED	P-REVIEWED	P-REWIRING	P-UNGENTLY
P-RESTORES	P-RETRAINS	P-REVIEWER	P-REWORKED	P-UNITIONS
P-RESTRESS	P-RETREATS	P-REVISING	P-RIGGINGS	P-USTULATE
P-RESTRIKE	P-RETRIALS	P-REVISION	P-ROOFINGS	P-UTTERERS
P-RESUMERS	P-RETYPING	P-REVISITS	P-ROOFLESS	P-UTTERING
P-RESUMING	P-REUNIONS	P-REVISORS	P-ROSELIKE	
P-RESURVEY	P-REUNITED	P-REWARMED	P-ROSINESS	

P – End-hooks

Two letters to three

AL-P	GI-P	LA-P	PA-P	TO-P
AM-P	GU-P	LI-P	PE-P	UM-P
AS-P	HA-P	LO-P	PI-P	UR-P
BA-P	HE-P	MA-P	PO-P	WO-P
BO-P	HI-P	MO-P	RE-P	YA-P
DA-P	HO-P	NA-P	SI-P	YE-P
DI-P	JA-P	NE-P	SO-P	YU-P
DO-P	KI-P	OO-P	TA-P	ZA-P
FA-P	KO-P	OU-P	TI-P	

Three letters to four

ALA-P	GAS-P	LEA-P	PRE-P	TAM-P
BAR-P	GAU-P	LEE-P	PRO-P	TAR-P
BEE-P	GEE-P	LIS-P	PUL-P	TRY-P
BUM-P	GOO-P	LOO-P	RAM-P	TUM-P
BUR-P	GOR-P	LOU-P	RAS-P	VEE-P
CAM-P	GUL-P	LOW-P	REP-P	WAR-P
CAR-P	GUM-P	LUM-P	RIP-P	WAS-P
CHA-P	GYM-P	MOO-P	ROM-P	WEE-P
CHI-P	HAS-P	MOU-P	ROO-P	WHA-P
COO-P	HEM-P	MUM-P	RUM-P	WHO-P
COW-P	HES-P	NEE-P	SAL-P	WIS-P
DAM-P	HOO-P	NOO-P	SAM-P	YAP-P
DEE-P	HUM-P	PAL-P	SEE-P	YAW-P
DIM-P	JAR-P	PAR-P	SIM-P	YOM-P
DOR-P	JEE-P	PEE-P	SKI-P	YUM-P
DOW-P	KIP-P	PER-P	SOU-P	
FRA-P	KOA-P	POM-P	SOW-P	
GAM-P	LAM-P	POO-P	SUM-P	

Four letters to five

BICE-P	CRIM-P	PRIM-P	SLEE-P	SWEE-P
BLEE-P	CRIS-P	SALE-P	SLUM-P	TRAM-P
CHAM-P	FLIM-P	SCAM-P	SLUR-P	WHEE-P
CHUM-P	GRAM-P	SCAR-P	STIR-P	WHOM-P
CLAM-P	GRUM-P	SCOW-P	STOW-P	
CRAM-P	PLUM-P	SCUL-P	STUM-P	
CREE-P	POLY-P	SKIM-P	SWAM-P	

Five letters to six

ESCAR-P	SCRIM-P	SHLEP-P	TRICE-P
SCRAW-P	SCRUM-P	THREE-P	

Six letters to seven

BEDLAM-P	MANTRA-P	SCHLEP-P

Seven letters to eight

AUTOCAR-P	MINICAM-P

Q – Front-hooks

Two letters to three

Q-AT	Q-IS

Three letters to four

Q-AID	Q-UEY

Four letters to five

Q-AIDS	Q-UEYS

Q – End-hooks

Four letters to five

TALA-Q

R – Front-hooks

Two letters to three

R-AD	R-AW	R-EN	R-IT	R-UM
R-AG	R-AX	R-ES	R-OB	R-UN
R-AH	R-AY	R-ET	R-OD	R-UT
R-AI	R-ED	R-EX	R-OE	R-YA
R-AM	R-EE	R-HO	R-OM	R-YE
R-AN	R-EF	R-ID	R-OO	
R-AS	R-EH	R-IF	R-OW	
R-AT	R-EM	R-IN	R-UG	

Three letters to four

R-ACE	R-AFT	R-AHS	R-AIN	R-ALE
R-ACH	R-AGA	R-AIA	R-AIS	R-AMI
R-ADS	R-AGE	R-AID	R-AIT	R-AMP
R-AFF	R-AGS	R-AIL	R-AKE	R-ANA

R-AND	R-EEK	R-ICK	R-ODS	R-OSE
R-ANI	R-EEL	R-ICY	R-OES	R-OUP
R-ANT	R-EEN	R-IDE	R-OIL	R-OUT
R-APE	R-EFS	R-IDS	R-OKE	R-OWT
R-APT	R-EFT	R-IFF	R-OLE	R-UDS
R-ARE	R-EGO	R-IFS	R-OMS	R-UGS
R-ARK	R-EHS	R-IGG	R-ONE	R-ULE
R-ASH	R-EIK	R-ILL	R-OOF	R-UMP
R-ASP	R-EKE	R-INK	R-OOM	R-UNS
R-ATE	R-EMS	R-INS	R-OON	R-URP
R-AVE	R-END	R-ITS	R-OOP	R-USE
R-AWN	R-ENS	R-OAR	R-OOS	R-UTS
R-AYS	R-EST	R-OBE	R-OOT	R-YES
R-EAN	R-HOS	R-OBS	R-OPE	
R-EAR	R-ICE	R-OCH	R-ORE	
R-EDS	R-ICH	R-ODE	R-ORT	

Four letters to five

R-ABID	R-AMIS	R-EARS	R-HONE	R-OPED
R-ACED	R-AMPS	R-EAST	R-ICED	R-OPES
R-ACER	R-AMUS	R-EAVE	R-ICER	R-ORAL
R-ACES	R-ANAS	R-ECCE	R-ICES	R-ORES
R-ACHE	R-ANCE	R-ECCO	R-IDES	R-ORTS
R-AGAS	R-ANDS	R-EDDY	R-IGGS	R-OSES
R-AGED	R-ANIS	R-EECH	R-ILLS	R-OUPS
R-AGEE	R-ANTS	R-EELS	R-INKS	R-OUST
R-AGER	R-APED	R-EGAL	R-OARS	R-OUTS
R-AGES	R-APER	R-EGMA	R-OARY	R-OVEN
R-AHED	R-APES	R-EGOS	R-OAST	R-OVER
R-AIAS	R-ARED	R-EIKS	R-OBES	R-OWED
R-AIDS	R-ARES	R-EKED	R-ODES	R-OWER
R-AILS	R-ARKS	R-EKES	R-OILS	R-OWTS
R-AINE	R-ASPS	R-EMIT	R-OILY	R-ULES
R-AINS	R-ATES	R-ENDS	R-OKES	R-UMBO
R-AITS	R-AVEL	R-ENEW	R-OLES	R-UMPS
R-AKED	R-AVER	R-EPOS	R-ONES	R-UMPY
R-AKEE	R-AVES	R-ESES	R-OOFS	R-URPS
R-AKES	R-AWNS	R-ESTS	R-OOFY	R-URUS
R-ALES	R-AXED	R-ETCH	R-OOMS	R-USES
R-ALLY	R-AXES	R-EVET	R-OONS	
R-AMEN	R-AYAH	R-EXES	R-OOPS	
R-AMIE	R-EACH	R-HEME	R-OOSE	
R-AMIN	R-EANS	R-HIES	R-OOTS	

Five letters to six

R-ABIES	R-AHING	R-ANCHO	R-ASHED	R-AYAHS
R-ACERS	R-AIDED	R-ANGER	R-ASHES	R-AZURE
R-ACHES	R-AIDER	R-ANKER	R-ASPER	R-EALES
R-ACING	R-AILED	R-ANKLE	R-ASSES	R-EARED
R-ACKER	R-AKEES	R-ANTED	R-ASTER	R-EARLY
R-ADDED	R-AKING	R-APERS	R-AUGHT	R-EASTS
R-ADDER	R-AMATE	R-APHIS	R-AVELS	R-EAVED
R-ADDLE	R-AMBLE	R-APING	R-AVENS	R-EAVES
R-ADIOS	R-AMENS	R-APPEL	R-AVERS	R-EBOOK
R-AFTER	R-AMIES	R-APTLY	R-AVINE	R-EDUCE
R-AGERS	R-AMINS	R-AREFY	R-AWING	R-EFFED
R-AGING	R-AMPED	R-ARKED	R-AXING	R-EGEST

R-EGRET	R-ENVOI	R-ICHED	R-OCKER	R-OUTED
R-EJECT	R-ENVOY	R-ICHES	R-OILED	R-OUTER
R-EKING	R-EROSE	R-ICIER	R-OLLER	R-OVERS
R-ELAND	R-ESILE	R-ICING	R-ONION	R-OWING
R-ELATE	R-ESTER	R-ICKER	R-OOPED	R-UDDER
R-ELIDE	R-ETAPE	R-ICKLE	R-OOSES	R-UGGED
R-EMAIL	R-EVERT	R-ICTAL	R-OPING	R-UMBLE
R-EMEND	R-EVERY	R-ICTUS	R-OSIER	R-UMBOS
R-EMITS	R-EVETS	R-IDENT	R-OTARY	R-UMPED
R-EMOTE	R-EVOKE	R-IGGED	R-OTHER	R-UNLET
R-EMOVE	R-EXINE	R-INKED	R-OTTER	R-UNRIG
R-ENDED	R-HEMES	R-IZARD	R-OUGHT	R-URBAN
R-ENDER	R-HEXES	R-OARED	R-OUNCE	R-USHER
R-ENEWS	R-HONES	R-OASTS	R-OUPED	R-UTILE
R-ENTER	R-ICERS	R-OCHES	R-OUSTS	R-UTTER

Six letters to seven

R-ABIDER	R-APPORT	R-EJECTS	R-ETCHED	R-ONNING
R-ACKERS	R-ARKING	R-ELANDS	R-ETCHES	R-OOFIER
R-ADDING	R-ASHING	R-ELAPSE	R-EVERTS	R-OOPING
R-ADDLED	R-ASPERS	R-ELATED	R-EVILER	R-OSIERS
R-ADDLES	R-ASPISH	R-ELATER	R-EVOKED	R-OTHERS
R-AFTERS	R-ASTERS	R-ELATES	R-EVOKER	R-OTTERS
R-AGGIES	R-ATTRAP	R-EMAILS	R-EVOKES	R-OUCHES
R-AGINGS	R-AZURES	R-EMENDS	R-EVOLVE	R-OUGHLY
R-AIDERS	R-EARING	R-EMERGE	R-EXINES	R-OUNCES
R-AIDING	R-EASTED	R-EMOTER	R-HACHIS	R-OUPING
R-AILING	R-EAVING	R-EMOTES	R-ICHING	R-OUSTED
R-ALLIED	R-EBOOKS	R-EMOVED	R-ICIEST	R-OUSTER
R-ALLIES	R-ECLOSE	R-EMOVES	R-ICKERS	R-OUTERS
R-AMBLED	R-EDDISH	R-ENDERS	R-IGGING	R-OUTING
R-AMBLER	R-EDUCED	R-ENDING	R-IMPLED	R-OYSTER
R-AMBLES	R-EDUCES	R-ENEWED	R-INKING	R-UDDERS
R-AMENTA	R-EECHED	R-ENTERS	R-INNING	R-UGGING
R-AMPING	R-EECHES	R-ENVOIS	R-IZARDS	R-UMBLES
R-ANCHOS	R-EFFING	R-ENVOYS	R-OARIER	R-UMPIES
R-ANGERS	R-EGALLY	R-EPOSES	R-OARING	R-UMPING
R-ANKERS	R-EGENCE	R-EPRISE	R-OCKERS	R-UNLESS
R-ANKLED	R-EGENCY	R-ESILES	R-OILIER	R-UNRIGS
R-ANKLES	R-EGESTS	R-ESTATE	R-OILING	R-USHERS
R-ANTING	R-EGRESS	R-ESTERS	R-OLLERS	R-UTTERS
R-APPELS	R-EGRETS	R-ETAPES	R-ONIONS	

Seven letters to eight

R-ABIETIC	R-ATTRAPS	R-ELATING	R-EQUITES	R-OARIEST
R-ADDLING	R-EASTING	R-ELATION	R-ESTATED	R-OILIEST
R-ADULATE	R-ECLOSED	R-ELATIVE	R-ESTATES	R-OOFIEST
R-ALLYING	R-ECLOSES	R-EMAILED	R-ETCHING	R-OTARIES
R-AMBLERS	R-EDUCING	R-EMENDED	R-EVERTED	R-OUSTERS
R-AMBLING	R-EDUCTOR	R-EMERGED	R-EVOKERS	R-OUSTING
R-AMENTUM	R-EECHING	R-EMERGES	R-EVOKING	R-OUTINGS
R-ANKLING	R-EGALITY	R-EMITTED	R-EVOLUTE	R-OYSTERS
R-ANTINGS	R-EGENCES	R-EMITTER	R-EVOLVED	R-UNROUND
R-APHIDES	R-EJECTED	R-EMOTION	R-EVOLVER	R-URALITE
R-APPORTS	R-EJECTOR	R-EMOVING	R-EVOLVES	
R-APTNESS	R-ELAPSED	R-ENEWING	R-EVULSED	
R-AREFIED	R-ELAPSES	R-ENFORCE	R-HEMATIC	
R-AREFIES	R-ELATERS	R-ENOUNCE	R-ICTUSES	

Eight letters to nine

R-AMBLINGS	R-EGRESSES	R-EMENDING	R-ENOUNCED	R-EVULSION
R-ANTIPOLE	R-EJECTING	R-EMERGING	R-ENOUNCES	R-OYSTERED
R-AREFYING	R-EJECTION	R-EMIGRATE	R-ERADIATE	R-OYSTERER
R-ECLOSING	R-EJECTIVE	R-EMISSION	R-ESTATING	R-UNCINATE
R-EDUCIBLE	R-EJECTORS	R-EMISSIVE	R-EVALUATE	R-UNROUNDS
R-EDUCTION	R-ELAPSING	R-EMITTERS	R-EVERSION	R-URALITES
R-EDUCTIVE	R-ELATEDLY	R-EMITTING	R-EVERTING	
R-EDUCTORS	R-ELATIONS	R-EMOTIONS	R-EVOCABLE	
R-EGENCIES	R-ELATIVES	R-ENFORCED	R-EVOLVERS	
R-EGRESSED	R-EMAILING	R-ENFORCES	R-EVOLVING	

R – End-hooks

Two letters to three

AI-R	FE-R	KO-R	NU-R	TA-R
BA-R	GO-R	LA-R	OO-R	TO-R
BO-R	GU-R	LO-R	OU-R	YA-R
DO-R	HE-R	MA-R	PA-R	
EA-R	JA-R	MI-R	PE-R	
ER-R	JO-R	MO-R	PI-R	
FA-R	KI-R	NO-R	SI-R	

Three letters to four

ACE-R	DEE-R	HUE-R	OYE-R	TEA-R
AGA-R	DOE-R	ICE-R	PAR-R	TEE-R
AGE-R	DOO-R	JEE-R	PEA-R	TIE-R
ALA-R	DOR-R	LEA-R	PEE-R	TOR-R
AMI-R	DYE-R	LEE-R	PIE-R	TYE-R
APE-R	EVE-R	LEI-R	POO-R	USE-R
AVE-R	EWE-R	LIE-R	PUR-R	VEE-R
BEE-R	EYE-R	LOO-R	RUE-R	VIE-R
BOA-R	FEE-R	LOU-R	SAI-R	WAI-R
BOO-R	FIE-R	MAA-R	SEA-R	WEE-R
BOW-R	FOU-R	MAW-R	SEE-R	YAR-R
BRR-R	FUR-R	MEE-R	SEI-R	YEA-R
BUR-R	GAU-R	MOE-R	SER-R	YOU-R
CAR-R	GOE-R	MOO-R	SKY-R	
CHA-R	GOO-R	NUR-R	SOU-R	
CHE-R	HOA-R	ONE-R	SPA-R	
CUR-R	HOE-R	OWE-R	SUE-R	

Four letters to five

ABLE-R	BIKE-R	CAGE-R	CITE-R	CYMA-R
AIDE-R	BINE-R	CANE-R	CLOU-R	DARE-R
ANTA-R	BITE-R	CAPE-R	CODE-R	DATE-R
AREA-R	BLAE-R	CARE-R	COME-R	DAZE-R
AURA-R	BLUE-R	CATE-R	COPE-R	DECO-R
BAKE-R	BOLA-R	CAVE-R	CORE-R	DICE-R
BALE-R	BONE-R	CEDE-R	COVE-R	DIKE-R
BARE-R	BORE-R	CHAI-R	CUBE-R	DIME-R
BASE-R	BREE-R	CHAR-R	CURE-R	DINE-R
BIDE-R	BRIE-R	CIDE-R	CUTE-R	DIRE-R

DIVE-R	HOPE-R	MINO-R	RAVE-R	TALE-R
DONE-R	HOSE-R	MISE-R	RAZE-R	TAME-R
DOPE-R	HOVE-R	MITE-R	RICE-R	TAPE-R
DOSE-R	HUGE-R	MODE-R	RIDE-R	TATE-R
DOTE-R	HYPE-R	MOLA-R	RIFE-R	TIGE-R
DOVE-R	IDLE-R	MOPE-R	RIME-R	TILE-R
DOZE-R	JAPE-R	MOVE-R	RIPE-R	TIME-R
DUPE-R	JIBE-R	MUSE-R	RISE-R	TITE-R
EASE-R	JIVE-R	MUTE-R	RIVE-R	TOKE-R
EDGE-R	JOKE-R	NAME-R	ROKE-R	TOLA-R
EIDE-R	KITE-R	NAZI-R	ROPE-R	TONE-R
ETHE-R	KNUR-R	NEVE-R	ROTO-R	TOPE-R
FACE-R	LACE-R	NICE-R	ROVE-R	TOTE-R
FADE-R	LADE-R	NITE-R	RUDE-R	TRIE-R
FAKE-R	LAKE-R	NIXE-R	RULE-R	TRIO-R
FARE-R	LAME-R	NOSE-R	RYPE-R	TRUE-R
FAVE-R	LASE-R	NOTE-R	SABE-R	TRYE-R
FERE-R	LATE-R	NUDE-R	SAFE-R	TUBA-R
FIFE-R	LAVE-R	OCHE-R	SAGE-R	TUBE-R
FILA-R	LEVE-R	OGLE-R	SAKE-R	TUNE-R
FILE-R	LIFE-R	ONCE-R	SANE-R	TWEE-R
FINE-R	LIKE-R	PACE-R	SAVE-R	ULNA-R
FIRE-R	LINE-R	PAGE-R	SERE-R	UNDE-R
FIVE-R	LITE-R	PALE-R	SHEA-R	URGE-R
FLEE-R	LIVE-R	PAPE-R	SHIR-R	VELA-R
FREE-R	LONE-R	PARE-R	SHOE-R	VILE-R
FUME-R	LOPE-R	PATE-R	SIDE-R	VINE-R
GAGE-R	LOSE-R	PAVE-R	SIKE-R	VIVE-R
GAME-R	LOVE-R	PIKE-R	SILE-R	VOLA-R
GAPE-R	LOWE-R	PILA-R	SIMA-R	VOTE-R
GATE-R	LUGE-R	PILE-R	SIZE-R	WADE-R
GAZE-R	LUNA-R	PIPE-R	SKEE-R	WAGE-R
GIBE-R	LURE-R	PLIE-R	SLEE-R	WAKE-R
GIVE-R	LUTE-R	POKE-R	SMIR-R	WALE-R
GLUE-R	MACE-R	POLE-R	SNEE-R	WATE-R
GNAR-R	MAKE-R	PORE-R	SOFA-R	WAVE-R
GONE-R	MALA-R	POSE-R	SOLA-R	WHIR-R
GULA-R	MANO-R	PUCE-R	SOLE-R	WIDE-R
HALE-R	MASE-R	PUKE-R	SORE-R	WIPE-R
HATE-R	MATE-R	PULE-R	SPAE-R	WIRE-R
HAVE-R	MAYO-R	PURE-R	SPIE-R	WISE-R
HAZE-R	MAZE-R	QUAI-R	SPUE-R	WIVE-R
HIDE-R	MERE-R	RACE-R	STAR-R	YARE-R
HIKE-R	METE-R	RAGE-R	SUPE-R	YOKE-R
HILA-R	MILE-R	RAKE-R	SURE-R	ZONE-R
HIRE-R	MILO-R	RAPE-R	SWEE-R	
HIVE-R	MIME-R	RARE-R	SYKE-R	
HOME-R	MINA-R	RASE-R	TAKE-R	
HONE-R	MINE-R	RATE-R	TALA-R	

Five letters to six

ABASE-R	ALINE-R	ATONE-R	BEARE-R	BLATE-R
ABATE-R	ALULA-R	AWARE-R	BELIE-R	BLAZE-R
ABIDE-R	AMBLE-R	BADGE-R	BESTI-R	BODGE-R
ABUSE-R	AMPLE-R	BANDA-R	BINGE-R	BOMBE-R
ACUTE-R	AMUSE-R	BARBE-R	BIRLE-R	BONIE-R
ADORE-R	ANCHO-R	BASSE-R	BITTE-R	BONZE-R
AERIE-R	ANGLE-R	BASTE-R	BLADE-R	BOOZE-R
AGILE-R	ARGUE-R	BATHE-R	BLAME-R	BORDE-R

BOWSE-R	DANCE-R	GRATE-R	LOWSE-R	PRONE-R
BRACE-R	DAUBE-R	GRAVE-R	LUNGE-R	PROSE-R
BRAVE-R	DEARE-R	GRAZE-R	MACHE-R	PROVE-R
BRAZE-R	DEICE-R	GRICE-R	MAILE-R	PRUNE-R
BRIBE-R	DELVE-R	GRIPE-R	MANDI-R	PULSE-R
BRINE-R	DENSE-R	GROPE-R	MANGE-R	PURGE-R
BROKE-R	DINGE-R	GUIDE-R	MATTE-R	PURSE-R
BRUTE-R	DODGE-R	GUILE-R	MAUVE-R	QUAKE-R
BUDGE-R	DORSE-R	GUISE-R	MEANE-R	QUARE-R
BUFFE-R	DOUCE-R	GUSLA-R	MENTO-R	QUEUE-R
BUGLE-R	DOUSE-R	GUYLE-R	MERGE-R	QUOTE-R
BULGE-R	DOVIE-R	HALSE-R	MICHE-R	RADGE-R
BURKE-R	DOWIE-R	HALVE-R	MILLE-R	RAILE-R
BURSA-R	DOWSE-R	HAWSE-R	MINCE-R	RAISE-R
BUTLE-R	DRAPE-R	HEARE-R	MINGE-R	RANGE-R
BUTTE-R	DRIVE-R	HEAVE-R	MOUSE-R	RANKE-R
CABLE-R	DROLE-R	HEDGE-R	MUDGE-R	RAPPE-R
CADGE-R	DRONE-R	HEFTE-R	MUGGA-R	RATHE-R
CALVE-R	DROVE-R	HINGE-R	NAIVE-R	REAME-R
CANOE-R	EERIE-R	HITHE-R	NAPPE-R	REAVE-R
CANTO-R	ELATE-R	HOMIE-R	NERVE-R	RECTO-R
CARTE-R	ELOPE-R	HOOVE-R	NICHE-R	REEDE-R
CARVE-R	ELUDE-R	HOUSE-R	NOBLE-R	REIVE-R
CASTE-R	EMOTE-R	ICKLE-R	NOOSE-R	RELIE-R
CAUSE-R	ERASE-R	IMAGE-R	NUDGE-R	RENTE-R
CAVIE-R	EVADE-R	INANE-R	NURSE-R	RHYME-R
CELLA-R	EVOKE-R	IRATE-R	OBESE-R	RIDGE-R
CENSE-R	EXILE-R	IRONE-R	OLIVE-R	RIEVE-R
CESSE-R	FABLE-R	ISSUE-R	OORIE-R	RIFLE-R
CHADO-R	FAINE-R	JAMBE-R	OURIE-R	RINSE-R
CHAFE-R	FALSE-R	JASPE-R	OWRIE-R	ROOSE-R
CHASE-R	FARCE-R	JUDGE-R	PAIRE-R	RORIE-R
CHIDE-R	FEARE-R	JUICE-R	PANDA-R	ROTTE-R
CHIME-R	FENCE-R	KEDGE-R	PANNE-R	ROUSE-R
CHINA-R	FILLE-R	KNIFE-R	PARSE-R	ROUTE-R
CHOKE-R	FITTE-R	KNOWE-R	PASSE-R	SALVE-R
CIRCA-R	FLAKE-R	KRONE-R	PASTE-R	SALVO-R
CLAVE-R	FLAME-R	LADLE-R	PATTE-R	SAMBA-R
CLEVE-R	FLEXO-R	LANCE-R	PAUSE-R	SANGA-R
CLONE-R	FLUTE-R	LANDE-R	PECKE-R	SANSA-R
CLOSE-R	FOLIA-R	LAPSE-R	PEEPE-R	SAUCE-R
CLOVE-R	FORCE-R	LARGE-R	PEEVE-R	SCALA-R
COATE-R	FORGE-R	LATHE-R	PENNE-R	SCALE-R
COMBE-R	FORME-R	LATTE-R	PHONE-R	SCARE-R
CONDO-R	FOULE-R	LEASE-R	PHYLA-R	SCORE-R
CONGE-R	FOXIE-R	LEAVE-R	PIECE-R	SEAME-R
CONNE-R	FRAME-R	LEDGE-R	PLACE-R	SEARE-R
COSIE-R	FRATE-R	LEFTE-R	PLANE-R	SEINE-R
COSTA-R	FRIZE-R	LEGGE-R	PLATE-R	SEISE-R
COSTE-R	GAFFE-R	LENTO-R	POISE-R	SEIZE-R
COTTA-R	GAMME-R	LIEGE-R	POKIE-R	SELLE-R
COUPE-R	GAUGE-R	LIEVE-R	POSSE-R	SERGE-R
COZIE-R	GIMME-R	LIGGE-R	PRATE-R	SERVE-R
CRATE-R	GINGE-R	LITHE-R	PRICE-R	SHADE-R
CRAVE-R	GLAZE-R	LODGE-R	PRIME-R	SHAKE-R
CROZE-R	GLIDE-R	LOGIE-R	PRISE-R	SHAME-R
CRUDE-R	GLOVE-R	LONGE-R	PRIZE-R	SHAPE-R
CURSE-R	GORGE-R	LOOSE-R	PROBE-R	SHARE-R
CYCLE-R	GOUGE-R	LOTTE-R	PROKE-R	SHAVE-R
DAMME-R	GRADE-R	LOUSE-R	PROLE-R	SHINE-R

SHIVE-R	SOARE-R	STOVE-R	TOWSE-R	VOICE-R
SHORE-R	SOLDE-R	STYLE-R	TRACE-R	VULVA-R
SHOVE-R	SOLVE-R	SUAVE-R	TRADE-R	WACKE-R
SIDLE-R	SONDE-R	SUITE-R	TRITE-R	WAITE-R
SIEGE-R	SORDO-R	SUMMA-R	TROVE-R	WAIVE-R
SINGE-R	SPACE-R	SURGE-R	TWICE-R	WASTE-R
SKATE-R	SPADE-R	SWAGE-R	TWINE-R	WEAVE-R
SKIVE-R	SPARE-R	SWIPE-R	UNITE-R	WEETE-R
SLAKE-R	SPICE-R	TASTE-R	USAGE-R	WHALE-R
SLATE-R	SPIDE-R	TAWIE-R	USURE-R	WHINE-R
SLAVE-R	SPIKE-R	TEASE-R	UVULA-R	WHITE-R
SLICE-R	SPINA-R	TEENE-R	VAGUE-R	WINCE-R
SLIDE-R	STAGE-R	TENNE-R	VALUE-R	WINGE-R
SLIVE-R	STALE-R	TENSE-R	VEALE-R	WITHE-R
SLOPE-R	STARE-R	TERSE-R	VENGE-R	WOLVE-R
SMILE-R	STATE-R	TESTE-R	VERGE-R	WORSE-R
SMITE-R	STELA-R	TITHE-R	VERSE-R	WRITE-R
SMOKE-R	STIVE-R	TITLE-R	VILLA-R	YODLE-R
SNARE-R	STOKE-R	TOILE-R	VIRGE-R	
SNIDE-R	STONE-R	TONNE-R	VISIE-R	
SNIPE-R	STOPE-R	TOUSE-R	VOGIE-R	
SNORE-R	STORE-R	TOWIE-R	VOGUE-R	

Six letters to seven

ABJURE-R	BIRKIE-R	CANULA-R	CRINGE-R	DEVISE-R
ABRADE-R	BITTIE-R	CARNIE-R	CROSSE-R	DIBBLE-R
ACCEDE-R	BLAGUE-R	CATTIE-R	CROUPE-R	DICKIE-R
ACCUSE-R	BLENDE-R	CHANCE-R	CRUISE-R	DIDDLE-R
ADDUCE-R	BLITHE-R	CHANGE-R	CUDDLE-R	DILATE-R
ADHERE-R	BLONDE-R	CHARGE-R	CUISSE-R	DILUTE-R
ADJURE-R	BLOWIE-R	CHASTE-R	CUPOLA-R	DINKIE-R
ADMIRE-R	BLUDGE-R	CHAUFE-R	CUPULA-R	DIVIDE-R
ADVISE-R	BLUDIE-R	CHEQUE-R	CURDLE-R	DIVINE-R
ALLEGE-R	BLUNGE-R	CHEWIE-R	CURRIE-R	DOCILE-R
ALLURE-R	BODGIE-R	CHILDE-R	CUSHIE-R	DOGGIE-R
ALNAGE-R	BOGGLE-R	CHOICE-R	DABBLE-R	DONSIE-R
AMENDE-R	BONNIE-R	CHOOSE-R	DAMAGE-R	DOODLE-R
AMERCE-R	BOODLE-R	CHOUSE-R	DANDLE-R	DOTTLE-R
APPOSE-R	BOOKIE-R	CHUKKA-R	DANGLE-R	DOUBLE-R
AREOLA-R	BOTTLE-R	CIRCLE-R	DAWDLE-R	DREARE-R
AROUSE-R	BOUNCE-R	CLAMBE-R	DAZZLE-R	DREDGE-R
ARRIVE-R	BRAIDE-R	CLAQUE-R	DEBASE-R	DRUDGE-R
ASPIRE-R	BRIDLE-R	CLAVIE-R	DEBATE-R	DUCKIE-R
ASSIZE-R	BRONZE-R	CLEAVE-R	DEBONE-R	DUDDIE-R
ASSUME-R	BROWSE-R	COARSE-R	DECIDE-R	EFFACE-R
ASSURE-R	BRUISE-R	COBBLE-R	DECODE-R	EMPALE-R
ASTUTE-R	BUBBLE-R	COCKLE-R	DECREE-R	ENABLE-R
AVENGE-R	BUCKLE-R	CODDLE-R	DEFACE-R	ENCODE-R
AXILLA-R	BUMBLE-R	COERCE-R	DEFAME-R	ENDURE-R
BABBLE-R	BUNDLE-R	COHERE-R	DEFILE-R	ENGAGE-R
BAFFLE-R	BUNGLE-R	COLLIE-R	DEFINE-R	ENGINE-R
BAGGIE-R	BURBLE-R	COMAKE-R	DEFUSE-R	ENROBE-R
BARDIE-R	BUSHIE-R	COPULA-R	DELUDE-R	ENSURE-R
BARMIE-R	BUSTLE-R	COUCHE-R	DEMURE-R	ENTICE-R
BARRIE-R	BYLINE-R	COUPLE-R	DENUDE-R	ESCAPE-R
BATTLE-R	CACKLE-R	COURIE-R	DEPOSE-R	EVOLVE-R
BEAGLE-R	CAJOLE-R	COURSE-R	DERIDE-R	EXCITE-R
BEETLE-R	CANDLE-R	CRADLE-R	DERIVE-R	EXCUSE-R
BEHAVE-R	CANNIE-R	CREASE-R	DESIRE-R	EXHUME-R

EXPIRE-R	HANDLE-R	LAMBIE-R	NOOKIE-R	RADULA-R
EXPOSE-R	HECKLE-R	LAMINA-R	NOTICE-R	RAFFLE-R
FACULA-R	HEMPIE-R	LEAGUE-R	NUZZLE-R	RAMBLE-R
FEEBLE-R	HIGGLE-R	LEGATO-R	OBLIGE-R	RANDIE-R
FERLIE-R	HIPPIE-R	LIGULA-R	OBTUSE-R	RANULA-R
FETTLE-R	HOARSE-R	LINTIE-R	OFFICE-R	RATTLE-R
FIBULA-R	HOBBLE-R	LIPPIE-R	ONLINE-R	RAUCLE-R
FICKLE-R	HOMAGE-R	LITTLE-R	OPAQUE-R	RAVAGE-R
FIDDLE-R	HOODIE-R	LOATHE-R	OPPOSE-R	REBATE-R
FIERCE-R	HOOLIE-R	LOCATE-R	ORANGE-R	REBUKE-R
FIGURE-R	HOPPLE-R	LOGGIE-R	ORNATE-R	RECITE-R
FLANGE-R	HUDDLE-R	LOONIE-R	OSCULA-R	REDUCE-R
FLEECE-R	HUMANE-R	LOUNGE-R	OUTLIE-R	REEKIE-R
FLENSE-R	HUMBLE-R	LOURIE-R	PADDLE-R	REFINE-R
FOLKIE-R	HUNKIE-R	LUCKIE-R	PALMIE-R	REFUSE-R
FONDLE-R	HURDLE-R	LUNULA-R	PAPULA-R	REFUTE-R
FOOTIE-R	HUSTLE-R	MACULA-R	PARADE-R	REGALE-R
FOOTLE-R	IGNITE-R	MANAGE-R	PARKIE-R	REGULA-R
FOOZLE-R	IGNORE-R	MANGLE-R	PASTIE-R	RELATE-R
FORAGE-R	IMBIBE-R	MANURE-R	PAVISE-R	RELIVE-R
FREEZE-R	IMPALE-R	MARBLE-R	PEDDLE-R	REMAKE-R
FROWIE-R	IMPEDE-R	MARINE-R	PEERIE-R	REMOTE-R
FUDDLE-R	IMPOSE-R	MASHIE-R	PEOPLE-R	REMOVE-R
FUMBLE-R	IMPURE-R	MASQUE-R	PERUSE-R	RENEGE-R
FUTILE-R	IMPUTE-R	MATURE-R	PHRASE-R	REPINE-R
GABBLE-R	INCITE-R	MEAGRE-R	PIAFFE-R	REPOSE-R
GAMBLE-R	INCOME-R	MEALIE-R	PICKLE-R	RESCUE-R
GARBLE-R	INDITE-R	MEDDLE-R	PIDDLE-R	RESIDE-R
GARGLE-R	INDUCE-R	MENACE-R	PIERCE-R	RESUME-R
GAUCHE-R	INFUSE-R	MICKLE-R	PIFFLE-R	RETAKE-R
GAUCIE-R	INHALE-R	MIDDLE-R	PIGGIE-R	RETIRE-R
GAWSIE-R	INHUME-R	MILLIE-R	PILULA-R	REVERE-R
GENTLE-R	INJURE-R	MINGLE-R	PINGLE-R	REVILE-R
GIGGLE-R	INSANE-R	MINUTE-R	PLAGUE-R	REVISE-R
GIRDLE-R	INSIDE-R	MISUSE-R	PLANTA-R	REVIVE-R
GIRLIE-R	INSULA-R	MOCHIE-R	PLASTE-R	REVOKE-R
GIRNIE-R	INSURE-R	MOROSE-R	PLEASE-R	RIDDLE-R
GLANCE-R	INTONE-R	MORULA-R	PLEDGE-R	RIFFLE-R
GOBBLE-R	INVADE-R	MOSSIE-R	PLUNGE-R	RIPPLE-R
GOGGLE-R	INVITE-R	MOTTLE-R	POINTE-R	ROARIE-R
GOODIE-R	INVOKE-R	MOUSIE-R	POLICE-R	ROOFIE-R
GOONIE-R	IODISE-R	MUDDLE-R	POLITE-R	ROOKIE-R
GRAINE-R	IODIZE-R	MUFFLE-R	POTAGE-R	ROOMIE-R
GRAMMA-R	IONISE-R	MUMBLE-R	POTCHE-R	RUFFLE-R
GRANDE-R	IONIZE-R	MUSKIE-R	POUNCE-R	RUMBLE-R
GRANGE-R	JANGLE-R	MUZZLE-R	PRAISE-R	RUSTLE-R
GREASE-R	JERQUE-R	NAPPIE-R	PRANCE-R	SADDLE-R
GREETE-R	JINGLE-R	NEBULA-R	PREMIE-R	SALTIE-R
GRIEVE-R	JOGGLE-R	NEEDLE-R	PUDDLE-R	SALUTE-R
GRILLE-R	JOSTLE-R	NEGATE-R	PUGGIE-R	SAMPLE-R
GRIPPE-R	JUGGLE-R	NESTLE-R	PUMICE-R	SAVAGE-R
GROOVE-R	JUGULA-R	NETTIE-R	PUNKIE-R	SCARCE-R
GROUSE-R	JUMBLE-R	NETTLE-R	PURFLE-R	SCHEME-R
GRUDGE-R	JUNKIE-R	NEWSIE-R	PURPLE-R	SCORSE-R
GRUNGE-R	KIDDIE-R	NIBBLE-R	PURSUE-R	SCOUSE-R
GUSTIE-R	KIDGIE-R	NIGGLE-R	PUTTIE-R	SCRAPE-R
GUTTLE-R	KINDLE-R	NIMBLE-R	PUZZLE-R	SCRIBE-R
GUZZLE-R	KITTLE-R	NIRLIE-R	QUARTE-R	SCULLE-R
HACKLE-R	KOOKIE-R	NOBBLE-R	QUINTA-R	SCYTHE-R
HAGGLE-R	LACUNA-R	NONUSE-R	RABBLE-R	SECEDE-R

SECURE-R	SOOTHE-R	STRIVE-R	TINGLE-R	UPMAKE-R
SEDATE-R	SPALLE-R	STROKE-R	TINKLE-R	UPRISE-R
SEDUCE-R	SPARGE-R	STYLIE-R	TINNIE-R	URBANE-R
SEELIE-R	SPARKE-R	SUBDUE-R	TIPPLE-R	VISITE-R
SEETHE-R	SPARRE-R	SUBTLE-R	TODDLE-R	VOYAGE-R
SEMINA-R	SPARSE-R	SUCKLE-R	TOGGLE-R	WABBLE-R
SEMPLE-R	SPENCE-R	SUPPLE-R	TOOTLE-R	WADDLE-R
SERENE-R	SPLICE-R	SURFIE-R	TORQUE-R	WAFFLE-R
SETTLE-R	SPONGE-R	SVELTE-R	TOTTIE-R	WAGGLE-R
SEVERE-R	SPRUCE-R	SWATHE-R	TOUCHE-R	WALLIE-R
SHELVE-R	SPURNE-R	SWERVE-R	TOUTIE-R	WANGLE-R
SHOPPE-R	SQUARE-R	SWINGE-R	TOWNIE-R	WARBLE-R
SHRIVE-R	STABLE-R	SWITHE-R	TRIFLE-R	WARSLE-R
SILKIE-R	STAPLE-R	TABULA-R	TROUPE-R	WASPIE-R
SIMPLE-R	STARVE-R	TACKLE-R	TROUSE-R	WEBBIE-R
SIZZLE-R	STEALE-R	TALKIE-R	TRUDGE-R	WEDGIE-R
SKIVIE-R	STEEVE-R	TANGIE-R	TRYSTE-R	WEENIE-R
SLEDGE-R	STELLA-R	TANGLE-R	TUMBLE-R	WEEPIE-R
SLEEVE-R	STEMME-R	TATTIE-R	TURTLE-R	WHEEZE-R
SMOUSE-R	STEPPE-R	TATTLE-R	TWEEZE-R	WHINGE-R
SMUDGE-R	STIEVE-R	TAWTIE-R	UNGULA-R	WIGGLE-R
SNEEZE-R	STIFLE-R	TECHIE-R	UNIQUE-R	WINKLE-R
SNOOZE-R	STIRRE-R	TEETHE-R	UNMAKE-R	WOBBLE-R
SNUBBE-R	STODGE-R	TEGULA-R	UNRIPE-R	WOODIE-R
SOAPIE-R	STOOPE-R	TENTIE-R	UNSAFE-R	WOOLIE-R
SOCAGE-R	STRAFE-R	THRIVE-R	UNSURE-R	WRITHE-R
SOLACE-R	STRIDE-R	THROWE-R	UNTRUE-R	YAPPIE-R
SOMBRE-R	STRIKE-R	TICKLE-R	UNWISE-R	ZONULA-R
SONSIE-R	STRIPE-R	TIDDLE-R	UPDATE-R	

Seven letters to eight

ABRIDGE-R	AUSTERE-R	CANNULA-R	CONCEDE-R	DECLINE-R
ABSOLVE-R	BAGPIPE-R	CAPABLE-R	CONCISE-R	DEFLATE-R
ACHIEVE-R	BALANCE-R	CAPTURE-R	CONDOLE-R	DEFORCE-R
ACICULA-R	BANDAGE-R	CAROUSE-R	CONDONE-R	DEGRADE-R
ACQUIRE-R	BAPTISE-R	CENSURE-R	CONDUCE-R	DEJEUNE-R
ADVANCE-R	BAPTIZE-R	CHAPPIE-R	CONFIDE-R	DELOUSE-R
ADVERSE-R	BEARDIE-R	CHARLIE-R	CONFINE-R	DEMERGE-R
AGITATO-R	BEGINNE-R	CHICANE-R	CONFUTE-R	DEPLETE-R
AIRLINE-R	BEGUILE-R	CHINKIE-R	CONJURE-R	DEPLORE-R
AMPULLA-R	BELIEVE-R	CHIPPIE-R	CONNIVE-R	DEPRAVE-R
ANALYSE-R	BEREAVE-R	CHORTLE-R	CONSOLE-R	DEPRIVE-R
ANALYZE-R	BESIEGE-R	CHUCKLE-R	CONSUME-R	DERANGE-R
ANIMATE-R	BESLAVE-R	CINGULA-R	CONVENE-R	DESERVE-R
ANIMATO-R	BICYCLE-R	CLEANSE-R	CONVOKE-R	DESPISE-R
ANTIQUE-R	BLASTIE-R	COCHLEA-R	CORRODE-R	DETERGE-R
APPEASE-R	BLOCKIE-R	CODRIVE-R	COSTUME-R	DIALYSE-R
APPRISE-R	BOLSHIE-R	COGNISE-R	COTTAGE-R	DIALYZE-R
APPRIZE-R	BONDAGE-R	COGNIZE-R	COUTHIE-R	DIFFUSE-R
APPROVE-R	BOOKSIE-R	COLLEGE-R	COWRITE-R	DISABLE-R
ARRANGE-R	BRABBLE-R	COLLIDE-R	CRAPPIE-R	DISLIKE-R
ASPERGE-R	BRAILLE-R	COLLUDE-R	CREEPIE-R	DISPONE-R
ASPERSE-R	BRASSIE-R	COMBINE-R	CRIPPLE-R	DISPOSE-R
ASSUAGE-R	BRAWLIE-R	COMMUNE-R	CRUMMIE-R	DISPUTE-R
ATOMISE-R	BREATHE-R	COMMUTE-R	CRUSADE-R	DISROBE-R
ATOMIZE-R	BRICKIE-R	COMPARE-R	CUTESIE-R	DIVORCE-R
ATTACHE-R	BRITTLE-R	COMPILE-R	DAYTALE-R	DIVULGE-R
AUGUSTE-R	BROWNIE-R	COMPOSE-R	DECEIVE-R	DOGGONE-R
AULNAGE-R	BRUSQUE-R	COMPUTE-R	DECLARE-R	DOMINEE-R

DRABBLE-R	GRUMBLE-R	NURTURE-R	PROFILE-R	SECRETE-R
DRIBBLE-R	HAGRIDE-R	OBLIQUE-R	PROFUSE-R	SERVICE-R
DRUGGIE-R	HEXAPLA-R	OBSCENE-R	PROMISE-R	SHACKLE-R
ECLIPSE-R	IDOLISE-R	OBSCURE-R	PROMOTE-R	SHEATHE-R
EMBLAZE-R	IDOLIZE-R	OBSERVE-R	PROPOSE-R	SHEENIE-R
EMBRACE-R	IGNOBLE-R	OBTRUDE-R	PROVIDE-R	SHINGLE-R
EMPLOYE-R	IMAGINE-R	OCCLUDE-R	PROVISO-R	SHUFFLE-R
ENCHASE-R	IMMENSE-R	OFFSIDE-R	PROVOKE-R	SHUTTLE-R
ENCLOSE-R	IMMERSE-R	OUTLINE-R	QUEENIE-R	SILENCE-R
ENDORSE-R	IMPINGE-R	OUTLIVE-R	QUIBBLE-R	SINCERE-R
ENFORCE-R	IMPLORE-R	OUTRIDE-R	QUIDDLE-R	SKELLIE-R
ENGRAVE-R	IMPROVE-R	OUTROPE-R	RAGTIME-R	SKYDIVE-R
ENHANCE-R	INCENSE-R	OUTSIDE-R	RAMPAGE-R	SMUGGLE-R
ENLARGE-R	INCLINE-R	OUTVOTE-R	REALISE-R	SNIFFLE-R
ENNOBLE-R	INCLOSE-R	OVERDYE-R	REALIZE-R	SNIGGLE-R
ENQUIRE-R	INDORSE-R	OVERLIE-R	RECEIVE-R	SNOTTIE-R
ENSLAVE-R	INDULGE-R	OVERSEE-R	RECLINE-R	SNUFFLE-R
ENSNARE-R	INFLAME-R	OXIDISE-R	RECYCLE-R	SPAMMIE-R
EPISTLE-R	INFLATE-R	OXIDIZE-R	REDLINE-R	SPANGLE-R
ESPOUSE-R	INQUIRE-R	OZONISE-R	REECHIE-R	SPARKIE-R
EXAMINE-R	INSNARE-R	OZONIZE-R	REGRATE-R	SPARKLE-R
EXCLUDE-R	INSPIRE-R	PACKAGE-R	REISSUE-R	SPATULA-R
EXCRETE-R	INTENSE-R	PAPILLA-R	REJOICE-R	SPECULA-R
EXECUTE-R	INTRUDE-R	PARTAKE-R	RELAPSE-R	SPICULA-R
EXEMPLA-R	INVOLVE-R	PASSAGE-R	RELEASE-R	SPINDLE-R
EXPLODE-R	ITEMISE-R	PASTURE-R	RELIEVE-R	SPLURGE-R
EXPLORE-R	ITEMIZE-R	PATELLA-R	RENEGUE-R	SPOTTIE-R
EXPUNGE-R	JAUNTIE-R	PECULIA-R	REPLACE-R	SPRINGE-R
EXTREME-R	JAWBONE-R	PEPTISE-R	REPROVE-R	SPUNKIE-R
EXTRUDE-R	JOYRIDE-R	PEPTIZE-R	REPULSE-R	SQUEEZE-R
FERTILE-R	JUSTICE-R	PERFUME-R	REQUIRE-R	STAGGIE-R
FINAGLE-R	KEYNOTE-R	PERJURE-R	REQUITE-R	STARTLE-R
FINESSE-R	KILLDEE-R	PERVADE-R	RESERVE-R	STEAMIE-R
FISTULA-R	KNUCKLE-R	PILLAGE-R	RESHAPE-R	STEELIE-R
FLEECIE-R	LAMELLA-R	PINNULA-R	RESOLVE-R	STIBBLE-R
FLOSSIE-R	LECTURE-R	PLACATE-R	RESTORE-R	STICKLE-R
FORESEE-R	LICENCE-R	PLANULA-R	RETRACE-R	STIPPLE-R
FORGIVE-R	LICENSE-R	PLOOKIE-R	REUNITE-R	STOURIE-R
FORMULA-R	LINGULA-R	PLOTTIE-R	REVENGE-R	STRANGE-R
FORSAKE-R	LIONISE-R	PLOUKIE-R	REVENUE-R	STUBBIE-R
FOVEOLA-R	LIONIZE-R	PLUMULA-R	REVERSE-R	STUMBLE-R
FRAGILE-R	LOWLIFE-R	POETISE-R	REVOLVE-R	STYLISE-R
FRENULA-R	MAMILLA-R	POETIZE-R	REWRITE-R	STYLIZE-R
FRIBBLE-R	MASSAGE-R	POLLUTE-R	ROMANCE-R	SUBLIME-R
FRIZZLE-R	MAXILLA-R	POSTURE-R	ROSEOLA-R	SUBSIDE-R
FULSOME-R	MEASURE-R	POTHOLE-R	ROUTHIE-R	SUBTILE-R
FURCULA-R	MEDULLA-R	PRATTLE-R	RUBEOLA-R	SUFFICE-R
GABELLE-R	MICELLA-R	PRECISE-R	RUMMAGE-R	SUPPOSE-R
GANGLIA-R	MIDLIFE-R	PREFACE-R	SALVAGE-R	SUPREME-R
GAROTTE-R	MILLINE-R	PRELUDE-R	SANDBUR-R	SURFACE-R
GARROTE-R	MISLIKE-R	PREPARE-R	SCAMBLE-R	SURMISE-R
GESTURE-R	MISTAKE-R	PREPPIE-R	SCAPULA-R	SURNAME-R
GLASSIE-R	MODERNE-R	PRESAGE-R	SCAVAGE-R	SURVIVE-R
GLIMPSE-R	MORTICE-R	PRESIDE-R	SCOURGE-R	SWADDLE-R
GOSPODA-R	MORTISE-R	PRESUME-R	SCREEVE-R	SWANKIE-R
GRABBLE-R	MULTURE-R	PRIMSIE-R	SCROUGE-R	SWANNIE-R
GRAPPLE-R	MUNDANE-R	PRIVATE-R	SCRUPLE-R	SWINDLE-R
GREENIE-R	NARRATE-R	PROCURE-R	SCUFFLE-R	SWIZZLE-R
GRIMACE-R	NEURULA-R	PRODUCE-R	SCUTTLE-R	TEENAGE-R
GRIZZLE-R	NEWCOME-R	PROFANE-R	SECONDE-R	TOASTIE-R

TONTINE-R	TROUBLE-R	UNWARIE-R	VENTURE-R	WELCOME-R
TOPLINE-R	TROUNCE-R	UPGRADE-R	VERBOSE-R	WHEEDLE-R
TOPSIDE-R	TRUCKLE-R	UPHEAVE-R	VERDITE-R	WHEELIE-R
TORTURE-R	TRUNDLE-R	UPRAISE-R	VESTURE-R	WHIFFLE-R
TOUSTIE-R	TWADDLE-R	UPSTAGE-R	VEXILLA-R	WHISTLE-R
TRADUCE-R	TWANGLE-R	UPSTATE-R	VIBRATO-R	WHITTLE-R
TRAMPLE-R	TWATTLE-R	UTILISE-R	VILLAGE-R	WINSOME-R
TREADLE-R	TWEEDLE-R	UTILIZE-R	VINTAGE-R	WRANGLE-R
TREMBLE-R	TWIDDLE-R	VALVULA-R	VIOLATE-R	WREATHE-R
TRIBUTE-R	TWINKLE-R	VARIOLA-R	WARFARE-R	WRESTLE-R
TRICKIE-R	UNITISE-R	VASCULA-R	WARSTLE-R	WRIGGLE-R
TRIPPLE-R	UNITIZE-R	VAUNTIE-R	WAYFARE-R	

Eight letters to nine

ABSOLUTE-R	CLAUSULA-R	DISPROVE-R	GLADSOME-R	MINIMIZE-R
ABSTRUSE-R	CLITELLA-R	DISSOLVE-R	GLISSADE-R	MISGUIDE-R
ALKALISE-R	COALMINE-R	DISSUADE-R	GREWSOME-R	MISJUDGE-R
ALKALIZE-R	COINSURE-R	DISUNITE-R	GRUESOME-R	MISPRISE-R
ANNOUNCE-R	COLONISE-R	DOWNCOME-R	HANDSOME-R	MISPRIZE-R
ANTILIFE-R	COLONIZE-R	DRICKSIE-R	HARANGUE-R	MISQUOTE-R
ANTINUKE-R	COLORISE-R	DYNAMITE-R	HARDLINE-R	MISSHAPE-R
APHORISE-R	COLORIZE-R	EMBEZZLE-R	HEADLINE-R	MOBILISE-R
APHORIZE-R	COMANAGE-R	ENERGISE-R	HESITATE-R	MOBILIZE-R
APPETISE-R	COMMENCE-R	ENERGIZE-R	HOROLOGE-R	MODERATO-R
APPETIZE-R	COMPLETE-R	ENFEEBLE-R	HUMANISE-R	MORALISE-R
APPRAISE-R	CONCEIVE-R	ENKINDLE-R	HUMANIZE-R	MORALIZE-R
ARCHAISE-R	CONCLUDE-R	ENTANGLE-R	IDEALISE-R	MORTGAGE-R
ARCHAIZE-R	CONDENSE-R	ENVELOPE-R	IDEALIZE-R	MUCKRAKE-R
ARTIFICE-R	CONSERVE-R	EQUALISE-R	ILLUMINE-R	MULTIUSE-R
ASSEMBLE-R	CONSPIRE-R	EQUALIZE-R	IMMUNISE-R	NAVICULA-R
ASTRINGE-R	CONSTRUE-R	ESCALADE-R	IMMUNIZE-R	NEBBISHE-R
AURICULA-R	CONTINUE-R	ESTRANGE-R	IMPOLITE-R	NEBULISE-R
BACKBITE-R	CONTRIVE-R	ETHERISE-R	IMPRESSE-R	NEBULIZE-R
BARBECUE-R	CONVERSE-R	ETHERIZE-R	INCREASE-R	NICKNAME-R
BARRETTE-R	CONVINCE-R	EULOGISE-R	INFRINGE-R	NONDANCE-R
BASELINE-R	CRIBELLA-R	EULOGIZE-R	INSCRIBE-R	NOVELISE-R
BEGRUDGE-R	CRUNCHIE-R	EXCHANGE-R	INTIMATE-R	NOVELIZE-R
BELITTLE-R	CUTICULA-R	EXERCISE-R	INTRIGUE-R	NUISANCE-R
BLASTULA-R	DECOUPLE-R	EXORCISE-R	INVEIGLE-R	OBLIGATO-R
BLOCKADE-R	DEGREASE-R	EXORCIZE-R	KLONDIKE-R	OPERCULA-R
BLUELINE-R	DEIONISE-R	EXPEDITE-R	KLONDYKE-R	OPTIMISE-R
BOMBARDE-R	DEIONIZE-R	FARADISE-R	LEGALISE-R	OPTIMIZE-R
BOTANISE-R	DENOUNCE-R	FARADIZE-R	LEGALIZE-R	OPUSCULA-R
BOTANIZE-R	DESCRIBE-R	FIBRILLA-R	LINOTYPE-R	ORGANISE-R
BULLDOZE-R	DESOLATE-R	FINALISE-R	LITERATO-R	ORGANIZE-R
CANONISE-R	DETHRONE-R	FINALIZE-R	LOCALISE-R	OUTPLACE-R
CANONIZE-R	DEVELOPE-R	FLAGELLA-R	LOCALIZE-R	OVERCOME-R
CANOODLE-R	DIALOGUE-R	FLATLINE-R	MACERATE-R	OVERRIDE-R
CAPITULA-R	DIGITISE-R	FLEXTIME-R	MAINLINE-R	OVERRULE-R
CARABINE-R	DIGITIZE-R	FLUIDISE-R	MASSACRE-R	OVERTIME-R
CARACOLE-R	DISBURSE-R	FLUIDIZE-R	MAXIMISE-R	PAGANISE-R
CARETAKE-R	DISCLOSE-R	FOREBODE-R	MAXIMIZE-R	PAGANIZE-R
CASTRATE-R	DISCRETE-R	FRACTURE-R	MEDICINE-R	PARALYSE-R
CASTRATO-R	DISGORGE-R	FREEBASE-R	MELODISE-R	PARALYZE-R
CATALYSE-R	DISGRACE-R	FRONTAGE-R	MELODIZE-R	PENDICLE-R
CATALYZE-R	DISGUISE-R	GARROTTE-R	MEMORISE-R	PENSIONE-R
CHASTISE-R	DISPENSE-R	GASTRULA-R	MEMORIZE-R	PERCEIVE-R
CIVILISE-R	DISPERSE-R	GLABELLA-R	MINIBIKE-R	PERFECTO-R
CIVILIZE-R	DISPLACE-R	GLADIOLA-R	MINIMISE-R	PERSUADE-R

PERVERSE-R	REDOUBLE-R	SCRABBLE-R	STRADDLE-R	UNBUNDLE-R
PHALANGE-R	REHEARSE-R	SCRAMBLE-R	STRAGGLE-R	UNCHASTE-R
PLEASURE-R	REINSURE-R	SCRIBBLE-R	STRANGLE-R	UNCOUPLE-R
POLARISE-R	RENOUNCE-R	SCROGGIE-R	STROBILA-R	UNDERLIE-R
POLARIZE-R	REPRIEVE-R	SCROUNGE-R	STRUGGLE-R	UNIONISE-R
POSITIVE-R	RESEMBLE-R	SCRUMMIE-R	SUBPHYLA-R	UNIONIZE-R
POSSIBLE-R	RESOLUTE-R	SCUTELLA-R	SUNBATHE-R	UNRIDDLE-R
POSTPONE-R	RESPONSE-R	SENSIBLE-R	SURPRISE-R	UNSTABLE-R
PRACTICE-R	RETICULA-R	SENTENCE-R	SUSPENSE-R	VAPORISE-R
PRACTISE-R	RETINULA-R	SEQUENCE-R	TAILGATE-R	VAPORIZE-R
PREJUDGE-R	RETRIEVE-R	SERENADE-R	TELEVISE-R	VESICULA-R
PRESBYTE-R	RIDICULE-R	SHUNPIKE-R	TESSELLA-R	VIGNETTE-R
PRESERVE-R	RINGSIDE-R	SIDELINE-R	THEORISE-R	VITALISE-R
PROLONGE-R	ROSTELLA-R	SIGHTSEE-R	THEORIZE-R	VITALIZE-R
PUNCTURE-R	SANITISE-R	SKYWRITE-R	THROTTLE-R	VOCALISE-R
PURCHASE-R	SANITIZE-R	SNOWSHOE-R	TOTALISE-R	VOCALIZE-R
PYROLYSE-R	SATIRISE-R	SPIRILLA-R	TOTALIZE-R	WARDROBE-R
PYROLYZE-R	SATIRIZE-R	SPRINKLE-R	TRAVERSE-R	WOMANISE-R
QUANTISE-R	SATURATE-R	SQUABBLE-R	TREASURE-R	WOMANIZE-R
QUANTIZE-R	SCAVENGE-R	SQUIGGLE-R	TREPHINE-R	
REASSURE-R	SCHEDULE-R	STAMPEDE-R	TRICYCLE-R	
RECHARGE-R	SCHMOOZE-R	STARGAZE-R	TROCHLEA-R	

S – Front-hooks

Two letters to three

S-AB	S-AW	S-EX	S-MA	S-OW
S-AD	S-AX	S-HA	S-NY	S-OX
S-AE	S-AY	S-HE	S-OB	S-OY
S-AG	S-EA	S-IF	S-OD	S-PA
S-AI	S-ED	S-IN	S-OH	S-UM
S-AL	S-EE	S-IS	S-OM	S-UN
S-AM	S-EL	S-IT	S-ON	S-UP
S-AN	S-EN	S-KA	S-OP	S-UR
S-AR	S-ER	S-KI	S-OS	S-US
S-AT	S-ET	S-KY	S-OU	S-YE

Three letters to four

S-ABS	S-ALT	S-CAG	S-EAS	S-ERE
S-ADO	S-AMA	S-CAM	S-EAT	S-ERF
S-AFT	S-AMP	S-CAN	S-ECH	S-ERK
S-AGA	S-AND	S-CAR	S-ECO	S-ERR
S-AGE	S-ANE	S-CAT	S-EEK	S-ERS
S-AGO	S-ANT	S-CAW	S-EEL	S-ESS
S-AGS	S-ARD	S-COG	S-EEN	S-ETA
S-AID	S-ARK	S-COP	S-EGO	S-HAD
S-AIL	S-ARS	S-COT	S-EIK	S-HAG
S-AIM	S-ASH	S-COW	S-ELD	S-HAH
S-AIN	S-ASS	S-CRY	S-ELF	S-HAM
S-AIR	S-ATE	S-CUD	S-ELL	S-HAN
S-AIS	S-AVE	S-CUM	S-ELS	S-HAT
S-AKE	S-AWN	S-CUP	S-EME	S-HAW
S-ALE	S-AXE	S-CUR	S-END	S-HAY
S-ALL	S-AYS	S-CUT	S-ENE	S-HES
S-ALP	S-CAB	S-EAN	S-ENS	S-HET
S-ALS	S-CAD	S-EAR	S-ERA	S-HEW

S-HIM	S-KIT	S-NIB	S-ORT	S-TAY
S-HIN	S-LAB	S-NIP	S-OUK	S-TED
S-HIP	S-LAG	S-NIT	S-OUP	S-TEN
S-HIT	S-LAM	S-NOB	S-OUR	S-TET
S-HOD	S-LAP	S-NOD	S-OUT	S-TEW
S-HOE	S-LAT	S-NOG	S-OWL	S-TIE
S-HOG	S-LAW	S-NOT	S-OWN	S-TOP
S-HOO	S-LAY	S-NOW	S-OYS	S-TOT
S-HOP	S-LED	S-NUB	S-PAM	S-TOW
S-HOT	S-LEE	S-NYE	S-PAN	S-TUB
S-HOW	S-LEW	S-OAK	S-PAR	S-TUM
S-HUN	S-LEY	S-OAR	S-PAS	S-TUN
S-HUT	S-LID	S-OBA	S-PAT	S-TYE
S-ICE	S-LIP	S-OBS	S-PAW	S-UDS
S-ICH	S-LIT	S-OCA	S-PAY	S-UGH
S-ICK	S-LOB	S-ODA	S-PEC	S-ULU
S-IDE	S-LOG	S-ODS	S-PED	S-UMP
S-ILK	S-LOP	S-OFT	S-PET	S-UNS
S-ILL	S-LOT	S-OHO	S-PEW	S-UPS
S-IMP	S-LOW	S-OHS	S-PIC	S-URD
S-INK	S-LUG	S-OIL	S-PIE	S-URE
S-INS	S-LUM	S-OKE	S-PIN	S-WAB
S-IRE	S-LUR	S-OLD	S-PIT	S-WAD
S-ITS	S-MEE	S-OLE	S-POD	S-WAG
S-JOE	S-MEW	S-OMS	S-POT	S-WAN
S-KAS	S-MIR	S-ONE	S-PRY	S-WAP
S-KAT	S-MOG	S-ONS	S-PUD	S-WAT
S-KAW	S-MUG	S-OOM	S-PUG	S-WAY
S-KEG	S-MUT	S-OON	S-PUN	S-WEE
S-KEN	S-NAB	S-OOP	S-PUR	S-WEY
S-KEP	S-NAG	S-OOT	S-TAB	S-WIG
S-KET	S-NAP	S-OPS	S-TAG	S-WIZ
S-KID	S-NAW	S-ORA	S-TAP	S-WOP
S-KIN	S-NEB	S-ORB	S-TAR	S-WOT
S-KIP	S-NED	S-ORD	S-TAT	S-YEN
S-KIS	S-NEE	S-ORE	S-TAW	S-YES

Four letters to five

S-ABED	S-AMEN	S-CALL	S-COLD	S-CREE
S-ABLE	S-AMPS	S-CALP	S-CONE	S-CREW
S-ADOS	S-ANDS	S-CAMP	S-COOP	S-CRIM
S-AGAS	S-ANES	S-CAMS	S-COOT	S-CROG
S-AGER	S-ANGA	S-CANS	S-COPE	S-CROW
S-AGES	S-ANSA	S-CANT	S-COPS	S-CUDS
S-AIDS	S-ANTS	S-CAPA	S-CORE	S-CUFF
S-AIGA	S-ARDS	S-CAPE	S-CORN	S-CULL
S-AILS	S-ARED	S-CAPI	S-COTS	S-CUPS
S-AIMS	S-ARIS	S-CARE	S-COUP	S-CURF
S-AINE	S-ARKS	S-CARP	S-COUR	S-CURS
S-AINS	S-ATES	S-CARS	S-COWL	S-CUTE
S-AIRS	S-AUNT	S-CART	S-COWP	S-CUTS
S-AKES	S-AVER	S-CATS	S-COWS	S-EANS
S-ALES	S-AVES	S-CAUP	S-CRAB	S-EARS
S-ALLY	S-AWED	S-CAWS	S-CRAG	S-EASE
S-ALPS	S-AXES	S-CENT	S-CRAM	S-EATS
S-ALTO	S-CABS	S-CHAV	S-CRAN	S-ECCO
S-ALTS	S-CADS	S-CION	S-CRAP	S-EDGE
S-AMAS	S-CAFF	S-COFF	S-CRAW	S-EDGY
S-AMBO	S-CAGS	S-COGS	S-CRAY	S-EELS

S-EELY	S-HILL	S-KIDS	S-LOVE	S-NIPS
S-EGOS	S-HIMS	S-KIER	S-LOWS	S-NITS
S-EINE	S-HINS	S-KIFF	S-LUES	S-NOBS
S-ELFS	S-HIPS	S-KILL	S-LUFF	S-NODS
S-ELLS	S-HIRE	S-KINK	S-LUGS	S-NOGS
S-EMES	S-HISH	S-KINS	S-LUIT	S-NOOK
S-ENDS	S-HIST	S-KIPS	S-LUMP	S-NOOP
S-ENVY	S-HITS	S-KITE	S-LUMS	S-NOUT
S-EPIC	S-HIVE	S-KITS	S-LUNG	S-NOWS
S-ERED	S-HOCK	S-KOFF	S-LUNK	S-NOWY
S-ERES	S-HOED	S-KYTE	S-LURS	S-NUBS
S-ERIC	S-HOER	S-LABS	S-LUSH	S-NUFF
S-ERKS	S-HOES	S-LACK	S-MACK	S-NYES
S-ERRS	S-HOGS	S-LADE	S-MAIK	S-OAKS
S-EVEN	S-HONE	S-LAGS	S-MALL	S-OARS
S-EVER	S-HOOK	S-LAID	S-MALM	S-OBAS
S-EWER	S-HOON	S-LAIN	S-MALT	S-OCAS
S-EXED	S-HOOT	S-LAKE	S-MARM	S-ODAS
S-EXES	S-HOPE	S-LAMS	S-MART	S-ODIC
S-EYEN	S-HOPS	S-LANE	S-MASH	S-OILS
S-HACK	S-HORE	S-LANG	S-MAZE	S-OILY
S-HADE	S-HORN	S-LANK	S-MEEK	S-OKES
S-HADS	S-HOTE	S-LANT	S-MEES	S-OLDS
S-HAFT	S-HOTS	S-LAPS	S-MELL	S-OLES
S-HAGS	S-HOUT	S-LASH	S-MELT	S-OLID
S-HAHS	S-HOVE	S-LATE	S-MERK	S-ONCE
S-HAKE	S-HOWS	S-LATS	S-MEWS	S-ONES
S-HALE	S-HUCK	S-LAVE	S-MILE	S-ONLY
S-HALL	S-HULE	S-LAWS	S-MIRK	S-OOMS
S-HALM	S-HUNS	S-LAYS	S-MIRS	S-OOPS
S-HALT	S-HUNT	S-LEEK	S-MITE	S-OOTS
S-HAME	S-HUSH	S-LEEP	S-MOCK	S-ORAL
S-HAMS	S-HUTS	S-LEER	S-MOGS	S-ORBS
S-HAND	S-ICES	S-LEET	S-MOKE	S-ORDO
S-HANK	S-IDES	S-LEPT	S-MOKO	S-ORDS
S-HAPS	S-IDLE	S-LEYS	S-MOLT	S-ORES
S-HARD	S-ILEX	S-LICE	S-MOOR	S-ORRA
S-HARE	S-ILKS	S-LICK	S-MOOT	S-ORTS
S-HARK	S-ILLS	S-LIER	S-MORE	S-OUKS
S-HARN	S-ILLY	S-LILY	S-MOTE	S-OUPS
S-HARP	S-IMPS	S-LIME	S-MUGS	S-OURS
S-HASH	S-INKS	S-LIMY	S-MUSH	S-OUTS
S-HAUL	S-INKY	S-LING	S-MUTS	S-OWED
S-HAVE	S-IRED	S-LINK	S-NABS	S-OWER
S-HAWM	S-IRES	S-LIPE	S-NAGS	S-OWLS
S-HAWS	S-IRIS	S-LIPS	S-NAIL	S-OWSE
S-HAYS	S-IZAR	S-LITS	S-NAPS	S-PACE
S-HEAL	S-KAIL	S-LIVE	S-NARE	S-PACY
S-HEAR	S-KART	S-LOAN	S-NARK	S-PAIL
S-HEEL	S-KATS	S-LOBS	S-NARY	S-PAIN
S-HELL	S-KAWS	S-LOGS	S-NEAP	S-PALE
S-HEND	S-KEEF	S-LOID	S-NEBS	S-PALL
S-HENT	S-KEEN	S-LOOM	S-NECK	S-PAMS
S-HERD	S-KEET	S-LOOP	S-NEDS	S-PANE
S-HERE	S-KEGS	S-LOOT	S-NEED	S-PANG
S-HETS	S-KELL	S-LOPE	S-NIBS	S-PANS
S-HEWN	S-KELP	S-LOPS	S-NICK	S-PARD
S-HEWS	S-KENS	S-LOSH	S-NIDE	S-PARE
S-HIED	S-KEPS	S-LOTH	S-NIES	S-PARK
S-HIES	S-KETS	S-LOTS	S-NIFF	S-PARS

S-PART	S-POOL	S-TATE	S-TONK	S-WAIL
S-PATE	S-POON	S-TATS	S-TONY	S-WAIN
S-PATS	S-POOR	S-TAWS	S-TOOK	S-WALE
S-PAUL	S-POOT	S-TAYS	S-TOOL	S-WALY
S-PAWL	S-PORE	S-TEAD	S-TOPE	S-WANG
S-PAWN	S-PORT	S-TEAK	S-TOPS	S-WANK
S-PAWS	S-POSH	S-TEAL	S-TORE	S-WANS
S-PAYS	S-POTS	S-TEAM	S-TORY	S-WAPS
S-PEAK	S-POUT	S-TEAR	S-TOSS	S-WARD
S-PEAL	S-PRAD	S-TEDS	S-TOTS	S-WARE
S-PEAN	S-PRAT	S-TEED	S-TOUN	S-WARM
S-PEAR	S-PRAY	S-TEEK	S-TOUR	S-WART
S-PEAT	S-PREE	S-TEEL	S-TOUT	S-WASH
S-PECK	S-PRIG	S-TEEM	S-TOWN	S-WATS
S-PECS	S-PROD	S-TEEN	S-TOWS	S-WAYS
S-PEED	S-PROG	S-TEER	S-TRAD	S-WEAL
S-PEEL	S-PUDS	S-TEIL	S-TRAP	S-WEAR
S-PEER	S-PUER	S-TELA	S-TRAY	S-WEED
S-PELL	S-PUGS	S-TELE	S-TREW	S-WEEL
S-PELT	S-PULE	S-TELL	S-TRIG	S-WEEP
S-PEND	S-PUMY	S-TEME	S-TRIP	S-WEER
S-PENT	S-PUNK	S-TEMS	S-TROP	S-WEES
S-PERM	S-PURS	S-TEND	S-TROW	S-WEET
S-PETS	S-PYRE	S-TENS	S-TROY	S-WEIR
S-PEWS	S-QUAD	S-TENT	S-TUBS	S-WELL
S-PIAL	S-QUAT	S-TERN	S-TUCK	S-WELT
S-PICA	S-QUID	S-TETS	S-TUFF	S-WEPT
S-PICE	S-QUIT	S-TEWS	S-TUMP	S-WEYS
S-PICK	S-QUIZ	S-TICH	S-TUMS	S-WIGS
S-PICS	S-TABS	S-TICK	S-TUNG	S-WILL
S-PIED	S-TACK	S-TIED	S-TUNS	S-WINE
S-PIER	S-TAGS	S-TIES	S-TYED	S-WING
S-PIES	S-TAIG	S-TIFF	S-TYES	S-WINK
S-PIKE	S-TAIN	S-TILE	S-TYRE	S-WIPE
S-PILE	S-TAKE	S-TILL	S-TYTE	S-WIRE
S-PILL	S-TALE	S-TILT	S-UGHS	S-WISH
S-PINA	S-TALK	S-TIME	S-ULUS	S-WISS
S-PINE	S-TALL	S-TING	S-UMPH	S-WITH
S-PINK	S-TAMP	S-TINK	S-UMPS	S-WITS
S-PINS	S-TANE	S-TINT	S-URDS	S-WIVE
S-PINY	S-TANG	S-TIRE	S-URES	S-WOON
S-PITS	S-TANK	S-TIVY	S-URGE	S-WOPS
S-PLAT	S-TAPS	S-TOCK	S-USES	S-WORD
S-PLAY	S-TARE	S-TOIT	S-WABS	S-WORE
S-PODS	S-TARN	S-TOKE	S-WACK	S-WORN
S-POKE	S-TARS	S-TOLE	S-WADS	S-WOTS
S-POOF	S-TART	S-TONE	S-WAGE	S-YENS
S-POOK	S-TASH	S-TONG	S-WAGS	

Five letters to six

S-ABBED	S-AGGER	S-ALTER	S-ASHED	S-AWING
S-ABLED	S-AIGAS	S-ALTOS	S-ASHES	S-CABBY
S-ABLES	S-AILED	S-AMBOS	S-ASSED	S-CAFFS
S-ACKER	S-AIRED	S-AMPLE	S-ASSES	S-CALLS
S-ACRED	S-AIRER	S-ANCHO	S-AUGER	S-CALPS
S-ADDER	S-ALARY	S-ANGAS	S-AUNTS	S-CAMEL
S-ADDLE	S-ALINE	S-ANGER	S-AVANT	S-CAMPI
S-AFTER	S-ALLEE	S-APPLE	S-AVERS	S-CAMPS
S-AGENE	S-ALLOW	S-ARGUS	S-AVINE	S-CANTS

S-CANTY	S-CROME	S-HARPY	S-IRING	S-LOOPS
S-CAPAS	S-CROWS	S-HAUGH	S-IZARS	S-LOOTS
S-CAPED	S-CRUMP	S-HAULS	S-KAILS	S-LOPED
S-CAPES	S-CUFFS	S-HAVEN	S-KARTS	S-LOPER
S-CARED	S-CULCH	S-HAVER	S-KEENS	S-LOPES
S-CARER	S-CULLS	S-HAVES	S-KEETS	S-LOPPY
S-CARES	S-CURFS	S-HAWED	S-KELLS	S-LOUGH
S-CARPS	S-CURRY	S-HAWMS	S-KELLY	S-LOWED
S-CARRY	S-CURVY	S-HEALS	S-KELPS	S-LOWER
S-CARTS	S-CUTCH	S-HEARS	S-KERRY	S-LOWLY
S-CATCH	S-CUTES	S-HEATH	S-KETCH	S-LUFFS
S-CATTY	S-DAINE	S-HEAVE	S-KIDDY	S-LUMMY
S-CAUPS	S-DEIGN	S-HEELS	S-KIERS	S-LUMPS
S-CENTS	S-EANED	S-HELLS	S-KILLS	S-LUMPY
S-CERNE	S-EARED	S-HELVE	S-KINKS	S-LURRY
S-CHAVS	S-EASED	S-HENDS	S-KITED	S-LUSHY
S-CHOUT	S-EASES	S-HERDS	S-KITES	S-MACKS
S-CIONS	S-EATER	S-HERRY	S-KOFFS	S-MAIKS
S-CLAVE	S-EDGED	S-HEUCH	S-KRANS	S-MALLS
S-CLIFF	S-EDGES	S-HEUGH	S-KYTES	S-MALMS
S-COFFS	S-EDILE	S-HEWED	S-LACKS	S-MALMY
S-COLDS	S-EDUCE	S-HEWER	S-LADES	S-MALTS
S-CONES	S-EGGAR	S-HILLS	S-LAKED	S-MARMS
S-COOCH	S-ELECT	S-HINNY	S-LAKER	S-MARTS
S-COOPS	S-ELFED	S-HIPPO	S-LAKES	S-MATCH
S-COOTS	S-ELVES	S-HIRED	S-LANES	S-MAZES
S-COPED	S-ENATE	S-HIRES	S-LANTS	S-MEATH
S-COPES	S-ENDED	S-HISTS	S-LATCH	S-MELLS
S-CORED	S-ENDER	S-HIVER	S-LATED	S-MELTS
S-CORER	S-ENTRY	S-HIVES	S-LATER	S-MERKS
S-CORES	S-ERING	S-HOCKS	S-LAVED	S-MEUSE
S-CORIA	S-ERRED	S-HOERS	S-LAVER	S-MIDDY
S-CORNS	S-ESSES	S-HONKY	S-LAVES	S-MIDGE
S-CORSE	S-ETTLE	S-HOOKS	S-LAYED	S-MIGHT
S-COUPS	S-EVENS	S-HOOTS	S-LAYER	S-MILER
S-COURS	S-EVERY	S-HOPPY	S-LEAVE	S-MILES
S-COUTH	S-EWERS	S-HOUGH	S-LEAZE	S-MIRKS
S-COWED	S-EXING	S-HOUSE	S-LEDGE	S-MIRKY
S-COWLS	S-EXIST	S-HOUTS	S-LEECH	S-MITER
S-COWPS	S-HACKS	S-HOVED	S-LEEKS	S-MITES
S-CRABS	S-HADED	S-HOVEL	S-LEEPS	S-MOCKS
S-CRAGS	S-HADES	S-HOVER	S-LEETS	S-MOGGY
S-CRAMS	S-HAFTS	S-HOVES	S-LICKS	S-MOKES
S-CRANS	S-HAKES	S-HUCKS	S-LIEVE	S-MOKOS
S-CRAPE	S-HALED	S-HUGGY	S-LIGHT	S-MOLTS
S-CRAPS	S-HALES	S-HULES	S-LIMED	S-MOOCH
S-CRAWL	S-HALMS	S-HUNTS	S-LIMES	S-MOORS
S-CRAWS	S-HAMBA	S-HYING	S-LINGS	S-MOOTS
S-CRAYS	S-HAMED	S-ICKER	S-LINKS	S-MORES
S-CREAK	S-HAMES	S-ICKLE	S-LINKY	S-MOUCH
S-CREAM	S-HAMMY	S-IDLED	S-LIPPY	S-MOUSE
S-CREED	S-HANDS	S-IDLER	S-LIVED	S-MOYLE
S-CREES	S-HANDY	S-IDLES	S-LIVEN	S-MUDGE
S-CREWS	S-HANKS	S-ILLER	S-LIVER	S-MURRY
S-CRIED	S-HARDS	S-IMPLY	S-LIVES	S-MUTCH
S-CRIES	S-HARED	S-INGLE	S-LOANS	S-NAGGY
S-CRIMP	S-HARES	S-INKER	S-LOBBY	S-NAILS
S-CRIMS	S-HARKS	S-INNED	S-LOGAN	S-NAKED
S-CRINE	S-HARNS	S-INNER	S-LOIDS	S-NAPPY
S-CROGS	S-HARPS	S-INTER	S-LOOMS	S-NARES

S-NARKS	S-PARKS	S-PORED	S-TARTS	S-TOOLS
S-NARKY	S-PARKY	S-PORES	S-TATER	S-TOPED
S-NATCH	S-PARRY	S-PORTS	S-TATES	S-TOPER
S-NEAPS	S-PARSE	S-PORTY	S-TATUS	S-TOPES
S-NEATH	S-PARTS	S-POTTY	S-TAWED	S-TORES
S-NECKS	S-PATES	S-POUTS	S-TEADS	S-TOUNS
S-NEEZE	S-PAULS	S-POUTY	S-TEAKS	S-TOURS
S-NELLY	S-PAVIN	S-PRANG	S-TEALS	S-TOUTS
S-NICKS	S-PAWLS	S-PRATS	S-TEAMS	S-TOWED
S-NIDES	S-PAWNS	S-PRAYS	S-TEARS	S-TOWER
S-NIFFS	S-PAYED	S-PREED	S-TEDDY	S-TRADS
S-NIFFY	S-PEAKS	S-PREES	S-TEELS	S-TRAIK
S-NIFTY	S-PEALS	S-PRENT	S-TEEMS	S-TRAIN
S-NIPPY	S-PEANS	S-PRIER	S-TEENS	S-TRAIT
S-NOBBY	S-PEARS	S-PRIGS	S-TEERS	S-TRAMP
S-NOOKS	S-PEATS	S-PRINT	S-TEILS	S-TRAPS
S-NOOPS	S-PECKS	S-PRODS	S-TELAE	S-TRASS
S-NOWED	S-PECKY	S-PROGS	S-TELES	S-TRAYS
S-NUBBY	S-PEELS	S-PRONG	S-TELIC	S-TRESS
S-NUDGE	S-PEERS	S-PRYER	S-TELLS	S-TREWS
S-NUFFS	S-PEISE	S-PUDDY	S-TEMED	S-TRICK
S-OAKED	S-PELLS	S-PUERS	S-TEMES	S-TRIDE
S-OAKEN	S-PELTS	S-PUGGY	S-TENCH	S-TRIGS
S-OAKER	S-PENCE	S-PULES	S-TENDS	S-TRIKE
S-OARED	S-PENDS	S-PUNKS	S-TENTS	S-TRIPE
S-OAVES	S-PERMS	S-PUNKY	S-TERES	S-TRIPS
S-OBOLE	S-PERSE	S-PURGE	S-TERNS	S-TRIPY
S-ODIUM	S-PERST	S-PYRES	S-TEWED	S-TRODE
S-OFTEN	S-PHENE	S-QUADS	S-TICKS	S-TROKE
S-OFTER	S-PICAS	S-QUAIL	S-TICKY	S-TROLL
S-OILED	S-PICKS	S-QUARE	S-TIFFS	S-TROUT
S-OLDER	S-PIERS	S-QUARK	S-TILED	S-TROVE
S-OLEIN	S-PIGHT	S-QUASH	S-TILES	S-TROWS
S-OLIVE	S-PIKED	S-QUATS	S-TILLS	S-TROYS
S-OLLER	S-PIKER	S-QUIDS	S-TILLY	S-TRUCK
S-OMBER	S-PIKES	S-QUIFF	S-TILTS	S-TUBBY
S-OMBRE	S-PIKEY	S-QUILL	S-TIMED	S-TUCKS
S-ONCES	S-PILED	S-QUINT	S-TIMES	S-TUFFS
S-OOPED	S-PILES	S-QUIRE	S-TINGS	S-TUMPS
S-ORBED	S-PILLS	S-QUIRT	S-TINKS	S-TUMPY
S-OUGHT	S-PINAS	S-QUITS	S-TINTS	S-TYING
S-OUPED	S-PINED	S-TABLE	S-TINTY	S-TYLER
S-OUTER	S-PINES	S-TACKS	S-TIRED	S-TYRED
S-OWING	S-PINKS	S-TAGGY	S-TIRES	S-TYRES
S-OWLED	S-PINNY	S-TAIGS	S-TITCH	S-UDDER
S-PACED	S-PINTO	S-TAINS	S-TOCKS	S-UNBED
S-PACER	S-PLASH	S-TAKES	S-TOCKY	S-UNDER
S-PACES	S-PLATS	S-TALER	S-TOITS	S-UNHAT
S-PACEY	S-PLAYS	S-TALES	S-TOKED	S-UNKET
S-PAILS	S-PODDY	S-TALKS	S-TOKER	S-UNLIT
S-PAINS	S-POKED	S-TALKY	S-TOKES	S-UNSET
S-PALES	S-POKES	S-TALLS	S-TOLED	S-UPPED
S-PALLS	S-PONGY	S-TAMPS	S-TOLES	S-UPPER
S-PANED	S-POOFS	S-TANGS	S-TOMIA	S-URGED
S-PANES	S-POOFY	S-TANKS	S-TONED	S-URGER
S-PANGS	S-POOKS	S-TAPES	S-TONER	S-URGES
S-PARED	S-POOLS	S-TARED	S-TONES	S-UTILE
S-PARER	S-POONS	S-TARES	S-TONEY	S-WADDY
S-PARES	S-POOTS	S-TARNS	S-TONKS	S-WAGED
S-PARGE	S-PORAL	S-TARRY	S-TONNE	S-WAGER

S-WAGES	S-WARTY	S-WEEPY	S-WINGS	S-WIVED
S-WAILS	S-WASHY	S-WEETS	S-WINGY	S-WIVES
S-WAINS	S-WATCH	S-WEIRS	S-WINKS	S-WOONS
S-WALED	S-WAYED	S-WELLS	S-WIPED	S-WOOPS
S-WALES	S-WEALS	S-WELTS	S-WIPER	S-WOOSH
S-WANKS	S-WEARS	S-WIFTY	S-WIPES	S-WORDS
S-WANKY	S-WEELS	S-WILLS	S-WIRES	S-WOUND
S-WARDS	S-WEENY	S-WINES	S-WITCH	
S-WARMS	S-WEEPS	S-WINGE	S-WITHE	

Six letters to seven

S-ABLING	S-CLAVES	S-CROTAL	S-HACKED	S-HIRING
S-ACKERS	S-CLIFFS	S-CRUMMY	S-HACKLE	S-HIVERS
S-ADDLED	S-COFFED	S-CRUMPS	S-HADING	S-HOCKED
S-ADDLES	S-COFFER	S-CRUMPY	S-HAFTED	S-HOCKER
S-AGENES	S-COGGED	S-CRUNCH	S-HAFTER	S-HODDEN
S-AGGERS	S-COLDER	S-CRYING	S-HAGGED	S-HOEING
S-AILING	S-COLLOP	S-CUDDLE	S-HALING	S-HOGGED
S-AIREST	S-COOPED	S-CUFFED	S-HALLOT	S-HOOTER
S-AIRING	S-COOPER	S-CUFFLE	S-HALLOW	S-HOPPED
S-ALINES	S-COOTCH	S-CULLED	S-HAMBLE	S-HOPPER
S-ALLEES	S-COOTER	S-CULLER	S-HAMING	S-HOTTED
S-ALLIED	S-COPING	S-CULTCH	S-HAMMED	S-HOUGHS
S-ALLIES	S-COPULA	S-CUMBER	S-HAMMER	S-HOUSES
S-ALLOWS	S-CORERS	S-CUMMER	S-HANKED	S-HOUTED
S-ALTERN	S-CORING	S-CUNNER	S-HARING	S-HOVELS
S-ALTERS	S-CORNED	S-CUPPER	S-HARKED	S-HOVERS
S-AMPLER	S-CORNER	S-CURRED	S-HARPED	S-HOVING
S-ANCHOS	S-CORSES	S-CUTTER	S-HARPER	S-HUNTED
S-ANGERS	S-COUPED	S-CUTTLE	S-HASHED	S-HUNTER
S-APPLES	S-COURED	S-CUZZES	S-HASHES	S-HUSHED
S-ARKING	S-COURIE	S-DAINED	S-HATTER	S-HUSHER
S-ARMIES	S-COURSE	S-DAINES	S-HAUGHS	S-HUSHES
S-ASHING	S-COUTER	S-DEIGNS	S-HAULED	S-IDLERS
S-AUGERS	S-COUTHS	S-EANING	S-HAVERS	S-IDLING
S-AUNTER	S-COWING	S-EARING	S-HAVING	S-IGNIFY
S-CABBED	S-COWLED	S-EASING	S-HAWING	S-IGNORE
S-CALLED	S-COWPED	S-EATERS	S-HEALED	S-ILEXES
S-CALLOP	S-COWRIE	S-EATING	S-HEARER	S-IMPLED
S-CAMELS	S-CRAGGY	S-EDGIER	S-HEATHS	S-IMPLEX
S-CAMMED	S-CRANCH	S-EDUCED	S-HEATHY	S-INGLES
S-CAMPED	S-CRANNY	S-EDUCES	S-HEAVED	S-INKERS
S-CAMPER	S-CRAPED	S-EELIER	S-HEAVES	S-INKIER
S-CANNED	S-CRAPES	S-EGGARS	S-HEELED	S-INKING
S-CANNER	S-CRAPPY	S-ELECTS	S-HELLED	S-INNERS
S-CANTED	S-CRATCH	S-ELFING	S-HELLER	S-INNING
S-CANTER	S-CRAWLS	S-ELFISH	S-HELVED	S-INTERS
S-CANTLE	S-CRAWLY	S-ENATES	S-HELVES	S-IRENIC
S-CAPING	S-CREAKS	S-ENDERS	S-HEUCHS	S-JAMBOK
S-CARERS	S-CREAKY	S-ENDING	S-HEUGHS	S-KEGGER
S-CARING	S-CREAMS	S-ENSATE	S-HEWERS	S-KELPED
S-CARPED	S-CREEDS	S-ENSILE	S-HEWING	S-KELTER
S-CARPER	S-CREWED	S-ENVIES	S-HIDDER	S-KENNED
S-CARTED	S-CRIMPS	S-ERRING	S-HILLED	S-KEPPED
S-CARVES	S-CRIMPY	S-ETTLED	S-HIPPED	S-KIDDED
S-CATTED	S-CRINES	S-ETTLES	S-HIPPEN	S-KIDDER
S-CERNED	S-CROGGY	S-EXISTS	S-HIPPER	S-KILLED
S-CERNES	S-CROMED	S-EXPERT	S-HIPPIE	S-KIMMER
S-CHOUTS	S-CROMES	S-EXTANT	S-HIPPOS	S-KINKED

S-KIPPED	S-LOWEST	S-NIFFED	S-PECKED	S-QUIRTS
S-KIPPER	S-LOWING	S-NIFFER	S-PEELED	S-QUITCH
S-KITING	S-LOWISH	S-NIGGER	S-PEELER	S-TABBED
S-KITTLE	S-LUBBER	S-NIGGLE	S-PEERED	S-TABLED
S-LACKED	S-LUFFED	S-NIPPED	S-PEISES	S-TABLES
S-LACKER	S-LUGGED	S-NIPPER	S-PELLED	S-TACKED
S-LAGGED	S-LUGGER	S-NODDED	S-PELTER	S-TACKER
S-LAKERS	S-LUMBER	S-NODDER	S-PENCES	S-TACKET
S-LAKING	S-LUMPED	S-NOGGED	S-PERSES	S-TAGGED
S-LAMMED	S-LUSHED	S-NUBBED	S-PHENES	S-TAGGER
S-LAMMER	S-LUSHES	S-NUDGED	S-PHENIC	S-TAKING
S-LANDER	S-MALLED	S-NUDGES	S-PICKER	S-TALKED
S-LANGER	S-MARTED	S-NUZZLE	S-PIGHTS	S-TALKER
S-LAPPED	S-MARTEN	S-OAKERS	S-PIKERS	S-TAMPED
S-LAPPER	S-MASHED	S-OARING	S-PIKING	S-TAMPER
S-LASHED	S-MASHER	S-OBOLES	S-PILING	S-TANGED
S-LASHER	S-MASHES	S-ODIUMS	S-PILLED	S-TANKED
S-LASHES	S-MASHUP	S-OFTEST	S-PINIER	S-TANNIC
S-LATHER	S-MATTER	S-OILIER	S-PINNER	S-TAPPED
S-LATTER	S-MEATHS	S-OILING	S-PINNET	S-TARING
S-LAVERS	S-MELLED	S-OLIVES	S-PINTOS	S-TARRED
S-LAVING	S-MELTED	S-OLLERS	S-PITTED	S-TARTED
S-LAVISH	S-MELTER	S-OMBERS	S-PITTEN	S-TARTER
S-LAYERS	S-MEUSES	S-OMBRES	S-PITTER	S-TARTLY
S-LAYING	S-MIDGES	S-OOPING	S-PLASHY	S-TASHED
S-LEAVED	S-MIGHTS	S-ORBING	S-PLAYED	S-TASHES
S-LEAVES	S-MILERS	S-OUPING	S-PLODGE	S-TATERS
S-LEAZES	S-MIRKER	S-OUTERS	S-PODIUM	S-TATUED
S-LEDGED	S-MITERS	S-OUTHER	S-POKING	S-TAWING
S-LEDGER	S-MITTEN	S-OWLING	S-PONGED	S-TEAMED
S-LEDGES	S-MOCKED	S-PACERS	S-POOLED	S-TEAMER
S-LENDER	S-MOILED	S-PACIER	S-POOLER	S-TEARED
S-LICKED	S-MOLDER	S-PACING	S-POORER	S-TEDDED
S-LICKER	S-MOORED	S-PAINED	S-PORING	S-TEEMED
S-LIGHTS	S-MOOTED	S-PALLED	S-PORTED	S-TEENED
S-LIMIER	S-MOTHER	S-PANGED	S-PORTER	S-TEERED
S-LIMING	S-MOUSED	S-PANING	S-POSHES	S-TELLAR
S-LIMMER	S-MOUSER	S-PANNED	S-POTTED	S-TEMPLE
S-LIMPSY	S-MOUSES	S-PANNER	S-POTTER	S-TENDED
S-LINGER	S-MOYLED	S-PARERS	S-POUTED	S-TENTED
S-LINKED	S-MOYLES	S-PARGED	S-POUTER	S-TERNAL
S-LINKER	S-MUDGED	S-PARGES	S-PRANGS	S-TERNED
S-LINTER	S-MUDGER	S-PARING	S-PRAYED	S-TEWING
S-LIPPED	S-MUDGES	S-PARKED	S-PRAYER	S-TIBIAL
S-LIPPER	S-MUGGED	S-PARKER	S-PRIEST	S-TICKED
S-LITHER	S-MUGGER	S-PARKIE	S-PRINTS	S-TICKER
S-LITTER	S-MUSHED	S-PARKLY	S-PUDDER	S-TICKLE
S-LIVERS	S-MUSHES	S-PARRED	S-PUDDLE	S-TIFFED
S-LIVING	S-NAGGED	S-PARSER	S-PUNKIE	S-TILING
S-LOBBER	S-NAILED	S-PARTAN	S-PURGES	S-TILLED
S-LOGANS	S-NAPPED	S-PATHED	S-PURRED	S-TILLER
S-LOGGED	S-NAPPER	S-PATHIC	S-PUTTER	S-TILTED
S-LOGGER	S-NEAPED	S-PATTED	S-QUAILS	S-TILTER
S-LOOMED	S-NEBBED	S-PATTEE	S-QUARER	S-TIMING
S-LOPERS	S-NECKED	S-PATTER	S-QUARKS	S-TINGED
S-LOPING	S-NEEZED	S-PAVINS	S-QUELCH	S-TINKER
S-LOPPED	S-NEEZES	S-PAWNED	S-QUILLS	S-TINTED
S-LOTTED	S-NIBBED	S-PAWNER	S-QUINTS	S-TINTER
S-LOTTER	S-NICKED	S-PAYING	S-QUIRED	S-TIPPLE
S-LOUGHS	S-NICKER	S-PEANED	S-QUIRES	S-TIRING

S-TIRRED	S-TOUTER	S-UDDERS	S-WALLET	S-WIGGER
S-TOCKED	S-TOWAGE	S-UGGING	S-WALLOW	S-WILLED
S-TOITED	S-TOWERS	S-ULLAGE	S-WANKED	S-WILLER
S-TOKERS	S-TOWING	S-UNBEDS	S-WANKER	S-WINDLE
S-TOKING	S-TRAIKS	S-UNBELT	S-WANNED	S-WINERY
S-TOMIUM	S-TRAINS	S-UNDECK	S-WAPPED	S-WINGED
S-TONERS	S-TRAITS	S-UNHATS	S-WAPPER	S-WINGER
S-TONIER	S-TRAMPS	S-UNLESS	S-WARDED	S-WINGES
S-TONIES	S-TRAPPY	S-UNLIKE	S-WARMED	S-WINISH
S-TONING	S-TRICKS	S-UNROOF	S-WARMER	S-WINKED
S-TONISH	S-TRIKES	S-UNSETS	S-WASHED	S-WINKER
S-TONKED	S-TRIPES	S-UNSUIT	S-WASHER	S-WIPERS
S-TONKER	S-TRIPEY	S-UNWISE	S-WASHES	S-WIPING
S-TONNES	S-TROKED	S-UPPERS	S-WATTER	S-WISHED
S-TOOLED	S-TROKES	S-UPPING	S-WAYING	S-WISHER
S-TOPERS	S-TROLLS	S-URGENT	S-WEARER	S-WISHES
S-TOPING	S-TROUTS	S-URGERS	S-WEEING	S-WISSES
S-TOPPED	S-TROWED	S-URGING	S-WEEPER	S-WITCHY
S-TOPPER	S-TUBBED	S-WADDIE	S-WEETED	S-WITHER
S-TOPPLE	S-TUMBLE	S-WADDLE	S-WEETEN	S-WIVING
S-TORIES	S-TUMPED	S-WAGERS	S-WEETER	S-WIZZES
S-TOSSES	S-TUNNED	S-WAGGED	S-WEIRED	S-WOONED
S-TOTTED	S-TUSHIE	S-WAGGER	S-WELLED	S-WOPPED
S-TOTTER	S-TYLERS	S-WAGING	S-WELTED	S-WORDED
S-TOTTIE	S-TYRING	S-WALIER	S-WELTER	S-WOTTED
S-TOURIE	S-UCKERS	S-WALING	S-WIGGED	S-WOUNDS

Seven letters to eight

S-ADDLING	S-CATTILY	S-CRAPING	S-CURRIED	S-HACKLER
S-ALLOWED	S-CATTING	S-CRAPPED	S-CURRIER	S-HACKLES
S-ALLYING	S-CERNING	S-CRAPPER	S-CURRIES	S-HADDOCK
S-ANGUINE	S-CHAPPED	S-CRAWLED	S-CURRING	S-HAFTERS
S-ARGUSES	S-CHILLER	S-CRAWLER	S-CURVIER	S-HAFTING
S-ASHLESS	S-COFFERS	S-CREAKED	S-CUTCHES	S-HAGGING
S-AUNTERS	S-COFFING	S-CREAMED	S-CUTTERS	S-HALLOWS
S-CABBING	S-COGGING	S-CREAMER	S-CUTTLED	S-HAMBLED
S-CALLOPS	S-COLLOPS	S-CREWING	S-CUTTLES	S-HAMBLES
S-CAMMING	S-COOCHES	S-CRIBBLE	S-CUTWORK	S-HAMMERS
S-CAMPERS	S-COOPERS	S-CRIMPED	S-DAINING	S-HAMMING
S-CAMPING	S-COOPING	S-CRIMPER	S-DEIGNED	S-HANKING
S-CANDENT	S-COOTERS	S-CROMING	S-EARINGS	S-HARKING
S-CANNERS	S-COPULAE	S-CRUMMIE	S-EATINGS	S-HARPERS
S-CANNING	S-COPULAS	S-CRUMPED	S-EDGIEST	S-HARPIES
S-CANTEST	S-CORIOUS	S-CRUMPLE	S-EDITION	S-HARPING
S-CANTIER	S-CORNERS	S-CRUNCHY	S-EDUCING	S-HASHING
S-CANTILY	S-CORNING	S-CRYINGS	S-EDUCTOR	S-HATTERS
S-CANTING	S-COUPING	S-CUDDLED	S-EELIEST	S-HAULING
S-CANTLED	S-COURIES	S-CUDDLES	S-ELECTED	S-HAVINGS
S-CANTLES	S-COURING	S-CUFFING	S-ELECTEE	S-HEADING
S-CARIOSE	S-COURSED	S-CUFFLED	S-ELECTOR	S-HEALING
S-CARIOUS	S-COURSES	S-CUFFLES	S-ELFHOOD	S-HEARERS
S-CARLESS	S-COUTERS	S-CULCHES	S-ENDINGS	S-HEARING
S-CARPERS	S-COUTHER	S-CULLERS	S-ENTRIES	S-HEATHER
S-CARPING	S-COWLING	S-CULLING	S-ETTLING	S-HEAVING
S-CARRIER	S-COWPING	S-CULLION	S-EXPERTS	S-HEELING
S-CARTING	S-COWRIES	S-CUMBERS	S-FORZATI	S-HEILING
S-CATCHES	S-CRABBED	S-CUMMERS	S-FORZATO	S-HELLERS
S-CATTERY	S-CRAGGED	S-CUNNERS	S-HACKING	S-HELLIER
S-CATTIER	S-CRAMMED	S-CUPPERS	S-HACKLED	S-HELLING

S-HELVING	S-LANGERS	S-MELLING	S-NODDING	S-PLASHED
S-HENDING	S-LAPPERS	S-MELTERS	S-NOGGING	S-PLASHER
S-HERRIES	S-LAPPING	S-MELTING	S-NUBBIER	S-PLASHES
S-HIDDERS	S-LASHERS	S-MIDDIES	S-NUBBING	S-PLATTED
S-HILLING	S-LASHING	S-MIRKIER	S-NUDGING	S-PLATTER
S-HINNIED	S-LATCHES	S-MIRKILY	S-NUZZLED	S-PLAYING
S-HINNIES	S-LATHERS	S-MITHERS	S-NUZZLES	S-PLODGED
S-HIPLESS	S-LEAVING	S-MOCKING	S-OFTENER	S-PLODGES
S-HIPPENS	S-LEDGERS	S-MOILING	S-OILIEST	S-PODIUMS
S-HIPPIES	S-LEECHES	S-MOLDERS	S-OMNIFIC	S-PONGIER
S-HIPPING	S-LEEPING	S-MOOCHED	S-ORDINES	S-PONGING
S-HITLESS	S-LICKERS	S-MOOCHER	S-PACIEST	S-PONTOON
S-HITTING	S-LICKING	S-MOOCHES	S-PAINING	S-POOKING
S-HOCKERS	S-LIGHTED	S-MOORING	S-PALLING	S-POOLERS
S-HOCKING	S-LIGHTER	S-MOOTING	S-PANGING	S-POOLING
S-HOGGING	S-LIGHTLY	S-MOTHERS	S-PANNERS	S-PORTERS
S-HOOTERS	S-LIMIEST	S-MOTHERY	S-PANNING	S-PORTIER
S-HOOTING	S-LIMMERS	S-MOUCHED	S-PARABLE	S-PORTING
S-HOPPERS	S-LINGERS	S-MOUCHES	S-PARGING	S-POTTERS
S-HOPPIER	S-LINKERS	S-MOULDER	S-PARKERS	S-POTTIER
S-HOPPING	S-LINKING	S-MOUSERS	S-PARKIER	S-POTTIES
S-HOTTING	S-LINTERS	S-MOUSING	S-PARKIES	S-POTTING
S-HOUTING	S-LIPLESS	S-MOYLING	S-PARKING	S-POUTERS
S-HOVELED	S-LIPPERS	S-MUDGERS	S-PARKISH	S-POUTIER
S-HUNTERS	S-LIPPIER	S-MUDGING	S-PARLING	S-POUTING
S-HUNTING	S-LIPPING	S-MUGGING	S-PARRIER	S-PRATTLE
S-HUSHERS	S-LITTERS	S-MUSHING	S-PARRING	S-PRAYERS
S-HUSHING	S-LIVERED	S-MUTCHED	S-PARTANS	S-PRAYING
S-HUTTING	S-LOBBERS	S-MUTCHES	S-PATTERS	S-PREEING
S-IGNORES	S-LOGGERS	S-NAGGIER	S-PATTING	S-PRIGGED
S-INKIEST	S-LOGGING	S-NAGGING	S-PAWNERS	S-PRIGGER
S-IRONISE	S-LOOMING	S-NAILERY	S-PAWNING	S-PRINTED
S-IRONIZE	S-LOPPIER	S-NAILING	S-PEAKING	S-PRINTER
S-JAMBOKS	S-LOPPING	S-NAPLESS	S-PEANING	S-PUDDERS
S-KEGGERS	S-LOTTERS	S-NAPPERS	S-PECKIER	S-PUDDING
S-KELLIES	S-LOTTING	S-NAPPIER	S-PECKING	S-PUDDLES
S-KELPING	S-LOWDOWN	S-NAPPING	S-PECTATE	S-PUGGIES
S-KELTERS	S-LOWINGS	S-NARKIER	S-PEELERS	S-PUNKIER
S-KENNING	S-LOWNESS	S-NATCHES	S-PEELING	S-PUNKIES
S-KEPPING	S-LUBBERS	S-NEAPING	S-PEERING	S-PURLING
S-KERRIES	S-LUFFING	S-NEBBING	S-PELLING	S-PURRING
S-KETCHES	S-LUGGERS	S-NECKING	S-PELTERS	S-PUTTERS
S-KIDDERS	S-LUGGING	S-NEEZING	S-PENDING	S-QUADDED
S-KIDDIER	S-LUMBERS	S-NIBBING	S-PERSING	S-QUAILED
S-KIDDING	S-LUMMIER	S-NICKERS	S-PETTING	S-QUAREST
S-KILLIES	S-LUMPIER	S-NICKING	S-PIGHTED	S-QUASHED
S-KILLING	S-LUMPING	S-NIFFERS	S-PIKELET	S-QUASHER
S-KIMMERS	S-LURRIES	S-NIFFIER	S-PILINGS	S-QUASHES
S-KINKING	S-LUSHIER	S-NIFFING	S-PILLAGE	S-QUINIES
S-KINLESS	S-LUSHING	S-NIFTIER	S-PILLING	S-QUIRING
S-KIPPERS	S-MALLING	S-NIGGERS	S-PINIEST	S-QUIRTED
S-KIPPING	S-MARTENS	S-NIGGLED	S-PINNERS	S-QUIZZES
S-KITTLED	S-MARTING	S-NIGGLER	S-PINNETS	S-TABBING
S-KITTLES	S-MASHERS	S-NIGGLES	S-PINNIES	S-TABLING
S-LACKERS	S-MASHING	S-NIPPERS	S-PINNING	S-TACKERS
S-LACKING	S-MASHUPS	S-NIPPIER	S-PIRATED	S-TACKETS
S-LAGGING	S-MATCHED	S-NIPPILY	S-PIRLING	S-TACKING
S-LAMMERS	S-MATCHES	S-NIPPING	S-PITCHER	S-TAGGERS
S-LAMMING	S-MATTERS	S-NOBBIER	S-PITTERS	S-TAGGIER
S-LANDERS	S-MEARING	S-NOBBILY	S-PITTING	S-TAGGING

S-TAKEOUT	S-TIDDIES	S-TOWABLE	S-ULLAGES	S-WEARING
S-TALKERS	S-TIFFING	S-TOWAGES	S-UNBAKED	S-WEENIES
S-TALKIER	S-TILLAGE	S-TOWAWAY	S-UNBELTS	S-WEEPERS
S-TALKING	S-TILLERS	S-TOWINGS	S-UNBLIND	S-WEEPIER
S-TALLAGE	S-TILLIER	S-TRAIKED	S-UNBLOCK	S-WEEPING
S-TAMPERS	S-TILLING	S-TRAINED	S-UNBURNT	S-WEETEST
S-TAMPING	S-TILTERS	S-TRAINER	S-UNCHOKE	S-WEETING
S-TANGING	S-TILTING	S-TRAMMEL	S-UNDECKS	S-WEIRING
S-TANKING	S-TINGING	S-TRAMPED	S-UNDRESS	S-WELLING
S-TANNATE	S-TINKERS	S-TRANGLE	S-UNROOFS	S-WELTERS
S-TAPPING	S-TINKING	S-TRAPPED	S-UNSUITS	S-WELTING
S-TARINGS	S-TINTERS	S-TRAPPER	S-URGINGS	S-WIGGERS
S-TARRIER	S-TINTIER	S-TRASSES	S-WADDIES	S-WIGGING
S-TARRING	S-TINTING	S-TRESSED	S-WADDLED	S-WILLERS
S-TARTING	S-TIPPLED	S-TRESSES	S-WADDLER	S-WILLING
S-TARTISH	S-TIPPLER	S-TRICKLE	S-WADDLES	S-WINDLED
S-TASHING	S-TIPPLES	S-TRIDENT	S-WAGGERS	S-WINDLES
S-TEAMERS	S-TIRRING	S-TRIGGED	S-WAGGING	S-WINGERS
S-TEAMING	S-TITCHES	S-TRIPIER	S-WAINING	S-WINGIER
S-TEARING	S-TOCCATA	S-TRIPPED	S-WALIEST	S-WINGING
S-TEDDIES	S-TOCKIER	S-TRIPPER	S-WALLETS	S-WINGMAN
S-TEDDING	S-TOCKING	S-TROKING	S-WALLOWS	S-WINGMEN
S-TEEMING	S-TOITING	S-TROLLED	S-WAMPISH	S-WINKERS
S-TEENING	S-TONIEST	S-TROLLER	S-WANKERS	S-WINKING
S-TEERING	S-TONINGS	S-TROPHIC	S-WANKIER	S-WISHERS
S-TELLING	S-TONKERS	S-TROWING	S-WANKING	S-WISHING
S-TEMPLES	S-TONKING	S-TRUMPET	S-WANNING	S-WISSING
S-TENCHES	S-TOOLING	S-TUBBIER	S-WAPPERS	S-WITCHED
S-TENDING	S-TOOSHIE	S-TUBBING	S-WAPPING	S-WITCHES
S-TENTING	S-TOPLESS	S-TUMBLED	S-WARDING	S-WITHERS
S-TERNING	S-TOPPERS	S-TUMBLER	S-WARMERS	S-WOONING
S-TICKERS	S-TOPPING	S-TUMBLES	S-WARMING	S-WOOSHED
S-TICKIES	S-TOPPLED	S-TUMPIER	S-WASHERS	S-WOOSHES
S-TICKING	S-TOPPLES	S-TUMPING	S-WASHIER	S-WOPPING
S-TICKLED	S-TOTTERS	S-TUNNING	S-WASHING	S-WORDING
S-TICKLER	S-TOTTIES	S-TUSHIES	S-WATCHES	S-WOTTING
S-TICKLES	S-TOTTING	S-UBEROUS	S-WEARERS	S-WOUNDED

Eight letters to nine

S-ALLOWING	S-CRANCHES	S-CRUMPLED	S-EDUCTIVE	S-HAMBLING
S-ARCOLOGY	S-CRAPPERS	S-CRUMPLES	S-EDUCTORS	S-HARPINGS
S-CAMPINGS	S-CRAPPIER	S-CRUNCHED	S-ELECTEES	S-HATTERED
S-CANNINGS	S-CRAPPING	S-CRUNCHES	S-ELECTING	S-HEADINGS
S-CANTIEST	S-CRATCHES	S-CRUNCHIE	S-ELECTION	S-HEALINGS
S-CANTLING	S-CRAWLERS	S-CUDDLING	S-ELECTIVE	S-HEARINGS
S-CARPINGS	S-CRAWLIER	S-CUFFLING	S-ELECTORS	S-HEATHERS
S-CATTIEST	S-CRAWLING	S-CULLINGS	S-ELFHOODS	S-HEATHIER
S-CHILLERS	S-CREAKIER	S-CULLIONS	S-ELFISHLY	S-HELLFIRE
S-CHILLING	S-CREAKING	S-CULTCHES	S-EXERCISE	S-HINNYING
S-COOTCHED	S-CREAMERS	S-CUMBERED	S-FORZANDI	S-HIPPINGS
S-COOTCHES	S-CREAMING	S-CURRIERS	S-FORZANDO	S-HOPPIEST
S-COPULATE	S-CRIBBLED	S-CURRYING	S-FORZATOS	S-HOPPINGS
S-CORELESS	S-CRIBBLES	S-CURVIEST	S-GRAFFITI	S-HOUTINGS
S-COURSING	S-CRIMPERS	S-CUTTLING	S-GRAFFITO	S-HOVELING
S-CRABBING	S-CRIMPIER	S-CUTWORKS	S-HACKLERS	S-HOVELLED
S-CRAGGIER	S-CRIMPING	S-DEIGNING	S-HACKLING	S-HOVELLER
S-CRAGGILY	S-CRUMMIER	S-EDITIONS	S-HADDOCKS	S-HUNTINGS
S-CRAMMING	S-CRUMMIES	S-EDUCIBLE	S-HALLOWED	S-IGNIFIED
S-CRANCHED	S-CRUMPING	S-EDUCTION	S-HALLOWER	S-IGNIFIES

S-IMPLEXES	S-MOTHERED	S-PORTIEST	S-TICKLERS	S-TUBBIEST
S-IRONISED	S-MOUCHING	S-PORTLESS	S-TICKLING	S-TUMBLERS
S-IRONISES	S-MOULDERS	S-POTTIEST	S-TICKSEED	S-TUMBLING
S-IRONIZED	S-MUTCHING	S-POUTIEST	S-TILLAGES	S-TUMPIEST
S-IRONIZES	S-NAGGIEST	S-POUTINGS	S-TILLIEST	S-TUNNINGS
S-KETCHING	S-NAPPIEST	S-PRATTLED	S-TILLINGS	S-UNBATHED
S-KILLINGS	S-NARKIEST	S-PRATTLES	S-TILTINGS	S-UNBEATEN
S-KIPPERED	S-NICKERED	S-PRAYINGS	S-TINTIEST	S-UNBLINDS
S-KITTLING	S-NIFFIEST	S-PRIGGERS	S-TINTINGS	S-UNBLOCKS
S-LAGGINGS	S-NIFTIEST	S-PRIGGING	S-TINTLESS	S-UNBONNET
S-LAMMINGS	S-NIGGERED	S-PRINTERS	S-TIPPLERS	S-UNBRIGHT
S-LANGUAGE	S-NIGGLERS	S-PRINTING	S-TIPPLING	S-UNBURNED
S-LASHINGS	S-NIGGLING	S-PUDDINGS	S-TOCCATAS	S-UNCHOKES
S-LATHERED	S-NIPPIEST	S-PUNKIEST	S-TOCKIEST	S-UNSTRUCK
S-LAUGHTER	S-NOBBIEST	S-PURLINGS	S-TONELESS	S-UNTANNED
S-LAVISHLY	S-NUBBIEST	S-PURRINGS	S-TOPPINGS	S-WADDLERS
S-LICKINGS	S-NUZZLING	S-PUTTERED	S-TOPPLING	S-WADDLING
S-LIGHTERS	S-OILINESS	S-PUTTERER	S-TOTTERED	S-WALLOWED
S-LIGHTEST	S-PARABLES	S-QUADDING	S-TOWAWAYS	S-WALLOWER
S-LIGHTING	S-PARKIEST	S-QUAILING	S-TRAIKING	S-WANKIEST
S-LIGHTISH	S-PATTERED	S-QUASHERS	S-TRAINERS	S-WARMINGS
S-LIMINESS	S-PECKIEST	S-QUASHING	S-TRAINING	S-WASHIEST
S-LIMPSIER	S-PECTATES	S-QUELCHED	S-TRAMMELS	S-WASHINGS
S-LIPPERED	S-PECULATE	S-QUELCHES	S-TRAMPING	S-WEARINGS
S-LIPPIEST	S-PIGHTING	S-QUINCHED	S-TRANGLES	S-WEEPIEST
S-LIVERING	S-PIKELETS	S-QUINCHES	S-TRAPLINE	S-WEEPINGS
S-LOPPIEST	S-PILLAGES	S-QUIRTING	S-TRAPPERS	S-WELLHEAD
S-LOWDOWNS	S-PILLINGS	S-QUITCHES	S-TRAPPIER	S-WELLINGS
S-LUMBERED	S-PINDLING	S-TABLINGS	S-TRAPPING	S-WELTERED
S-LUMBERER	S-PINELIKE	S-TACKINGS	S-TRESSING	S-WINDLING
S-LUMMIEST	S-PINNINGS	S-TACKLESS	S-TRICKLED	S-WINERIES
S-LUMPIEST	S-PITTINGS	S-TAGGIEST	S-TRICKLES	S-WINGBEAT
S-LUSHIEST	S-PLASHERS	S-TAKEOUTS	S-TRIGGING	S-WINGEING
S-MASHINGS	S-PLASHIER	S-TALKIEST	S-TRIPIEST	S-WINGIEST
S-MATCHING	S-PLASHING	S-TALKINGS	S-TRIPLING	S-WISHINGS
S-MATTERED	S-PLATTERS	S-TALLAGES	S-TRIPPERS	S-WITCHIER
S-MELTINGS	S-PLATTING	S-TAMPINGS	S-TRIPPING	S-WITCHING
S-MIRKIEST	S-PLODGING	S-TANNATES	S-TROLLERS	S-WITHERED
S-MOCKINGS	S-PONGIEST	S-TARRIEST	S-TROLLING	S-WOOSHING
S-MOLDERED	S-PONTOONS	S-TARRINGS	S-TROSSERS	S-WORDLESS
S-MOOCHERS	S-PORTABLE	S-TEAMINGS	S-TROUTING	S-WORDPLAY
S-MOOCHING	S-PORTANCE	S-TICKINGS	S-TRUMPETS	S-WOUNDING

S – End-hooks

Two letters to three

AA-S	BI-S	EN-S	ID-S	ME-S
AB-S	BO-S	ER-S	IF-S	MI-S
AD-S	BY-S	ES-S	IN-S	MO-S
AG-S	DA-S	FA-S	IO-S	MU-S
AH-S	DI-S	FE-S	IT-S	NA-S
AI-S	DO-S	GI-S	KA-S	NO-S
AL-S	EA-S	GO-S	KI-S	NU-S
AR-S	ED-S	GU-S	KO-S	NY-S
AS-S	EF-S	HA-S	LA-S	OB-S
AY-S	EH-S	HE-S	LI-S	OD-S
BA-S	EL-S	HI-S	LO-S	OE-S
BE-S	EM-S	HO-S	MA-S	OH-S

OM-S	PA-S	SI-S	UN-S	YO-S
ON-S	PE-S	SO-S	UP-S	YU-S
OO-S	PI-S	TA-S	UT-S	ZA-S
OP-S	PO-S	TE-S	WO-S	ZO-S
OR-S	QI-S	TI-S	XI-S	
OY-S	RE-S	UG-S	YE-S	

Three letters to four

AAH-S	ASP-S	BOY-S	CUT-S	DUD-S
AAL-S	ATE-S	BRA-S	CWM-S	DUE-S
ABA-S	AUF-S	BRO-S	DAB-S	DUG-S
ABB-S	AUK-S	BRU-S	DAD-S	DUN-S
ABO-S	AVA-S	BUB-S	DAE-S	DUO-S
ABY-S	AVE-S	BUD-S	DAG-S	DUP-S
ACE-S	AVO-S	BUG-S	DAH-S	DYE-S
ACT-S	AWE-S	BUM-S	DAK-S	DZO-S
ADD-S	AWL-S	BUN-S	DAL-S	EAN-S
ADO-S	AWN-S	BUR-S	DAM-S	EAR-S
AGA-S	AXE-S	BUS-S	DAN-S	EAT-S
AGE-S	AYE-S	BUT-S	DAP-S	EAU-S
AHI-S	AYU-S	BUY-S	DAW-S	EBB-S
AIA-S	BAA-S	BYE-S	DAY-S	ECO-S
AID-S	BAC-S	CAA-S	DEB-S	ECU-S
AIL-S	BAD-S	CAB-S	DEE-S	EDH-S
AIM-S	BAG-S	CAD-S	DEG-S	EEL-S
AIN-S	BAL-S	CAG-S	DEL-S	EFF-S
AIR-S	BAM-S	CAM-S	DEN-S	EFT-S
AIT-S	BAN-S	CAN-S	DEV-S	EGG-S
AKE-S	BAP-S	CAP-S	DEW-S	EGO-S
ALA-S	BAR-S	CAR-S	DEY-S	EIK-S
ALB-S	BAS-S	CAT-S	DIB-S	EKE-S
ALE-S	BAT-S	CAW-S	DIE-S	ELD-S
ALF-S	BAY-S	CAY-S	DIF-S	ELF-S
ALL-S	BED-S	CEE-S	DIG-S	ELK-S
ALP-S	BEE-S	CEL-S	DIM-S	ELL-S
ALT-S	BEG-S	CEP-S	DIN-S	ELM-S
AMA-S	BEL-S	CHA-S	DIP-S	ELT-S
AMI-S	BEN-S	CHI-S	DIS-S	EME-S
AMP-S	BET-S	CID-S	DIT-S	EMO-S
AMU-S	BEY-S	CIG-S	DIV-S	EMU-S
ANA-S	BIB-S	CIT-S	DOB-S	END-S
AND-S	BID-S	COB-S	DOC-S	ENE-S
ANE-S	BIG-S	COD-S	DOD-S	ENG-S
ANI-S	BIN-S	COG-S	DOE-S	EON-S
ANN-S	BIO-S	COL-S	DOG-S	ERA-S
ANT-S	BIT-S	CON-S	DOH-S	ERE-S
APE-S	BOA-S	COO-S	DOL-S	ERG-S
APO-S	BOB-S	COP-S	DOM-S	ERK-S
APP-S	BOD-S	COR-S	DON-S	ERN-S
APT-S	BOG-S	COS-S	DOO-S	ERR-S
ARB-S	BOH-S	COT-S	DOP-S	EST-S
ARC-S	BOI-S	COW-S	DOR-S	ETA-S
ARD-S	BOK-S	COY-S	DOS-S	ETH-S
ARE-S	BOO-S	CRU-S	DOT-S	EUK-S
ARF-S	BOP-S	CUB-S	DOW-S	EVE-S
ARK-S	BOR-S	CUD-S	DOY-S	EVO-S
ARM-S	BOS-S	CUE-S	DRY-S	EWE-S
ART-S	BOT-S	CUP-S	DSO-S	EWK-S
ASK-S	BOW-S	CUR-S	DUB-S	EWT-S

EYE-S	GEM-S	HOB-S	JOY-S	LET-S
FAA-S	GEN-S	HOD-S	JUD-S	LEY-S
FAB-S	GEO-S	HOE-S	JUG-S	LIB-S
FAD-S	GET-S	HOG-S	JUT-S	LID-S
FAG-S	GHI-S	HOH-S	KAB-S	LIE-S
FAH-S	GIB-S	HOM-S	KAE-S	LIG-S
FAN-S	GID-S	HON-S	KAF-S	LIN-S
FAR-S	GIE-S	HOP-S	KAI-S	LIP-S
FAT-S	GIG-S	HOS-S	KAK-S	LIT-S
FAW-S	GIN-S	HOT-S	KAT-S	LOB-S
FAY-S	GIO-S	HOW-S	KAW-S	LOD-S
FED-S	GIP-S	HOY-S	KAY-S	LOG-S
FEE-S	GIT-S	HUB-S	KEA-S	LOO-S
FEG-S	GJU-S	HUE-S	KEB-S	LOP-S
FEH-S	GNU-S	HUG-S	KED-S	LOS-S
FEM-S	GOA-S	HUI-S	KEF-S	LOT-S
FEN-S	GOB-S	HUM-S	KEG-S	LOU-S
FES-S	GOD-S	HUN-S	KEN-S	LOW-S
FET-S	GOE-S	HUP-S	KEP-S	LOY-S
FEU-S	GON-S	HUT-S	KET-S	LUD-S
FEY-S	GOO-S	HYE-S	KEY-S	LUG-S
FIB-S	GOS-S	HYP-S	KHI-S	LUM-S
FID-S	GOV-S	ICE-S	KID-S	LUR-S
FIG-S	GOY-S	ICH-S	KIF-S	LUV-S
FIL-S	GUB-S	IDE-S	KIN-S	LYE-S
FIN-S	GUE-S	IGG-S	KIP-S	LYM-S
FIR-S	GUL-S	ILK-S	KIR-S	MAA-S
FIT-S	GUM-S	ILL-S	KIS-S	MAC-S
FLU-S	GUN-S	IMP-S	KIT-S	MAD-S
FOB-S	GUP-S	INK-S	KOA-S	MAE-S
FOE-S	GUR-S	INN-S	KOB-S	MAG-S
FOG-S	GUT-S	ION-S	KOI-S	MAK-S
FOH-S	GUV-S	IRE-S	KON-S	MAL-S
FON-S	GUY-S	IRK-S	KOP-S	MAM-S
FOP-S	GYM-S	ISM-S	KOR-S	MAN-S
FOU-S	GYP-S	ISO-S	KOS-S	MAP-S
FOY-S	HAD-S	ITA-S	KOW-S	MAR-S
FRA-S	HAE-S	IWI-S	KUE-S	MAS-S
FRO-S	HAG-S	JAB-S	KYE-S	MAT-S
FUB-S	HAH-S	JAG-S	KYU-S	MAW-S
FUD-S	HAM-S	JAI-S	LAB-S	MAY-S
FUG-S	HAP-S	JAK-S	LAC-S	MED-S
FUM-S	HAT-S	JAM-S	LAD-S	MEE-S
FUN-S	HAW-S	JAP-S	LAG-S	MEG-S
FUR-S	HAY-S	JAR-S	LAH-S	MEL-S
GAB-S	HEH-S	JAW-S	LAM-S	MEM-S
GAD-S	HEM-S	JAY-S	LAP-S	MES-S
GAE-S	HEN-S	JEE-S	LAR-S	MET-S
GAG-S	HEP-S	JET-S	LAS-S	MEU-S
GAL-S	HER-S	JEW-S	LAT-S	MEW-S
GAM-S	HET-S	JIB-S	LAV-S	MHO-S
GAN-S	HEW-S	JIG-S	LAW-S	MIB-S
GAP-S	HEY-S	JIN-S	LAY-S	MIC-S
GAR-S	HIE-S	JOB-S	LEA-S	MID-S
GAT-S	HIM-S	JOE-S	LEE-S	MIG-S
GAU-S	HIN-S	JOG-S	LEG-S	MIL-S
GAY-S	HIP-S	JOL-S	LEI-S	MIR-S
GED-S	HIS-S	JOR-S	LEK-S	MIS-S
GEE-S	HIT-S	JOT-S	LEP-S	MNA-S
GEL-S	HOA-S	JOW-S	LES-S	MOA-S

MOB-S	OBA-S	PED-S	REG-S	SEW-S
MOC-S	OBE-S	PEE-S	REH-S	SEY-S
MOD-S	OBI-S	PEG-S	REI-S	SHE-S
MOE-S	OBO-S	PEH-S	REM-S	SIB-S
MOG-S	OCA-S	PEN-S	REN-S	SIC-S
MOL-S	ODA-S	PEP-S	REO-S	SIM-S
MOM-S	ODD-S	PET-S	REP-S	SIN-S
MON-S	ODE-S	PEW-S	RET-S	SIP-S
MOO-S	OFF-S	PHI-S	REV-S	SIR-S
MOP-S	OHM-S	PHO-S	REW-S	SIS-S
MOR-S	OHO-S	PIA-S	RHO-S	SIT-S
MOS-S	OIK-S	PIC-S	RIA-S	SKA-S
MOT-S	OIL-S	PIE-S	RIB-S	SKI-S
MOU-S	OKA-S	PIG-S	RID-S	SOB-S
MOW-S	OKE-S	PIN-S	RIF-S	SOC-S
MOY-S	OLD-S	PIP-S	RIG-S	SOD-S
MUD-S	OLE-S	PIR-S	RIM-S	SOG-S
MUG-S	OLM-S	PIS-S	RIN-S	SOH-S
MUM-S	ONE-S	PIT-S	RIP-S	SOL-S
MUN-S	ONO-S	PLU-S	RIT-S	SOM-S
MUS-S	OOF-S	POA-S	ROB-S	SON-S
MUT-S	OOH-S	POD-S	ROC-S	SOP-S
MYC-S	OOM-S	POI-S	ROD-S	SOS-S
NAB-S	OON-S	POL-S	ROE-S	SOT-S
NAG-S	OOP-S	POM-S	ROK-S	SOU-S
NAM-S	OOT-S	POO-S	ROM-S	SOV-S
NAN-S	OPE-S	POP-S	ROO-S	SOW-S
NAP-S	OPT-S	POS-S	ROT-S	SOY-S
NAT-S	ORB-S	POT-S	ROW-S	SPA-S
NAY-S	ORC-S	POW-S	RUB-S	SRI-S
NEB-S	ORD-S	PRO-S	RUC-S	SUB-S
NED-S	ORE-S	PRY-S	RUD-S	SUD-S
NEF-S	ORF-S	PSI-S	RUE-S	SUE-S
NEG-S	ORT-S	PUB-S	RUG-S	SUK-S
NEK-S	OSE-S	PUD-S	RUM-S	SUM-S
NEP-S	OUD-S	PUG-S	RUN-S	SUN-S
NET-S	OUK-S	PUL-S	RUT-S	SUP-S
NEW-S	OUP-S	PUN-S	RYA-S	SUQ-S
NIB-S	OUR-S	PUP-S	RYE-S	SUS-S
NID-S	OUT-S	PUR-S	SAB-S	SYE-S
NIE-S	OWE-S	PUS-S	SAC-S	TAB-S
NIL-S	OWL-S	PUT-S	SAG-S	TAD-S
NIM-S	OWN-S	PUY-S	SAI-S	TAE-S
NIP-S	OWT-S	PYA-S	SAL-S	TAG-S
NIT-S	OYE-S	PYE-S	SAM-S	TAI-S
NOB-S	PAC-S	QAT-S	SAN-S	TAK-S
NOD-S	PAD-S	RAD-S	SAP-S	TAM-S
NOG-S	PAH-S	RAG-S	SAR-S	TAN-S
NOM-S	PAL-S	RAH-S	SAV-S	TAO-S
NOW-S	PAM-S	RAI-S	SAW-S	TAP-S
NOY-S	PAN-S	RAM-S	SAY-S	TAR-S
NUB-S	PAP-S	RAP-S	SEA-S	TAS-S
NUN-S	PAR-S	RAT-S	SEC-S	TAT-S
NUR-S	PAS-S	RAW-S	SEE-S	TAU-S
NUT-S	PAT-S	RAY-S	SEG-S	TAV-S
NYE-S	PAV-S	REB-S	SEI-S	TAW-S
OAF-S	PAW-S	REC-S	SEL-S	TAY-S
OAK-S	PAY-S	RED-S	SEN-S	TEA-S
OAR-S	PEA-S	REE-S	SER-S	TEC-S
OAT-S	PEC-S	REF-S	SET-S	TED-S

TEE-S	TUN-S	VAT-S	WEE-S	YEA-S
TEF-S	TUP-S	VAU-S	WEM-S	YEN-S
TEG-S	TUT-S	VAV-S	WEN-S	YEP-S
TEL-S	TWA-S	VAW-S	WET-S	YEW-S
TEN-S	TWO-S	VEE-S	WEY-S	YID-S
TET-S	TYE-S	VET-S	WHY-S	YIN-S
TEW-S	TYG-S	VIA-S	WIG-S	YIP-S
TIC-S	UDO-S	VID-S	WIN-S	YOB-S
TID-S	UEY-S	VIE-S	WIS-S	YOD-S
TIE-S	UFO-S	VIG-S	WIT-S	YOK-S
TIG-S	UGH-S	VIM-S	WOE-S	YOU-S
TIL-S	UKE-S	VIN-S	WOF-S	YOW-S
TIN-S	ULE-S	VOE-S	WOG-S	YUG-S
TIP-S	ULU-S	VOL-S	WOK-S	YUK-S
TIT-S	UMP-S	VOR-S	WON-S	YUP-S
TOC-S	UNI-S	VOW-S	WOO-S	ZAG-S
TOD-S	URB-S	VUG-S	WOP-S	ZAP-S
TOE-S	URD-S	VUM-S	WOT-S	ZEA-S
TOG-S	URE-S	WAB-S	WOW-S	ZED-S
TOM-S	URN-S	WAD-S	WUD-S	ZEE-S
TON-S	URP-S	WAE-S	WUS-S	ZEK-S
TOP-S	USE-S	WAG-S	WYE-S	ZEL-S
TOR-S	UTA-S	WAI-S	WYN-S	ZEP-S
TOT-S	UTE-S	WAN-S	YAD-S	ZHO-S
TOW-S	UTU-S	WAP-S	YAG-S	ZIG-S
TOY-S	UVA-S	WAR-S	YAH-S	ZIN-S
TSK-S	VAC-S	WAT-S	YAK-S	ZIP-S
TUB-S	VAE-S	WAW-S	YAM-S	ZIT-S
TUG-S	VAG-S	WAY-S	YAP-S	ZOL-S
TUI-S	VAN-S	WEB-S	YAW-S	ZOO-S
TUM-S	VAR-S	WED-S	YAY-S	ZZZ-S

Four letters to five

ABAC-S	AGER-S	ALME-S	ANTI-S	ATUA-S
ABBA-S	AGHA-S	ALOD-S	APAY-S	AULA-S
ABBE-S	AGIO-S	ALOE-S	APER-S	AUNE-S
ABET-S	AGLU-S	ALTO-S	APOD-S	AUNT-S
ABLE-S	AGMA-S	ALUM-S	APSE-S	AURA-S
ABRI-S	AGON-S	AMAH-S	APSO-S	AUTO-S
ABUT-S	AGUE-S	AMAS-S	AQUA-S	AVEL-S
ABYE-S	AIDE-S	AMBO-S	ARAK-S	AVER-S
ABYS-S	AIGA-S	AMEN-S	ARAR-S	AVOW-S
ACAI-S	AIRN-S	AMIA-S	ARBA-S	AWAY-S
ACCA-S	AIRT-S	AMID-S	AREA-S	AWDL-S
ACER-S	AITU-S	AMIE-S	ARET-S	AWOL-S
ACHE-S	AKEE-S	AMIN-S	ARIA-S	AXEL-S
ACID-S	ALAN-S	AMIR-S	ARIL-S	AXIL-S
ACME-S	ALAP-S	AMIS-S	ARLE-S	AXLE-S
ACNE-S	ALAY-S	AMLA-S	ARNA-S	AXON-S
ACRE-S	ALBA-S	AMMO-S	ARSE-S	AYAH-S
ACYL-S	ALCO-S	AMOK-S	ARTI-S	AYIN-S
ADAW-S	ALEC-S	AMYL-S	ARUM-S	AYRE-S
ADIT-S	ALEF-S	ANGA-S	ARVO-S	AZAN-S
ADZE-S	ALEW-S	ANIL-S	ARYL-S	AZON-S
AEON-S	ALFA-S	ANKH-S	ATAP-S	AZYM-S
AERO-S	ALGA-S	ANNA-S	ATMA-S	BAAL-S
AFAR-S	ALIF-S	ANOA-S	ATOC-S	BABA-S
AFRO-S	ALKO-S	ANTA-S	ATOK-S	BABE-S
AGAR-S	ALMA-S	ANTE-S	ATOM-S	BABU-S

BACH-S	BELL-S	BLIP-S	BOZO-S	BURN-S
BACK-S	BELT-S	BLOB-S	BRAD-S	BURP-S
BAEL-S	BEMA-S	BLOC-S	BRAE-S	BURR-S
BAFF-S	BEND-S	BLOG-S	BRAG-S	BUSK-S
BAFT-S	BENE-S	BLOT-S	BRAK-S	BUST-S
BAGH-S	BENI-S	BLOW-S	BRAN-S	BUTE-S
BAHT-S	BENT-S	BLUB-S	BRAS-S	BUTT-S
BAIL-S	BERE-S	BLUE-S	BRAT-S	BYDE-S
BAIT-S	BERG-S	BLUR-S	BRAW-S	BYKE-S
BAJU-S	BERK-S	BOAB-S	BRAY-S	BYRE-S
BAKE-S	BERM-S	BOAK-S	BREE-S	BYRL-S
BALD-S	BEST-S	BOAR-S	BREI-S	BYTE-S
BALE-S	BETA-S	BOAT-S	BREN-S	CABA-S
BALK-S	BETE-S	BOBA-S	BRER-S	CACA-S
BALL-S	BETH-S	BOCK-S	BREW-S	CADE-S
BALM-S	BHEL-S	BODE-S	BREY-S	CADI-S
BALU-S	BHUT-S	BOEP-S	BRIE-S	CAFE-S
BANC-S	BIBB-S	BOET-S	BRIG-S	CAFF-S
BAND-S	BICE-S	BOFF-S	BRIK-S	CAGE-S
BANE-S	BIDE-S	BOHO-S	BRIM-S	CAID-S
BANG-S	BIDI-S	BOIL-S	BRIN-S	CAIN-S
BANK-S	BIER-S	BOKE-S	BRIO-S	CAKE-S
BANT-S	BIFF-S	BOKO-S	BRIS-S	CALF-S
BAPU-S	BIGG-S	BOLA-S	BRIT-S	CALK-S
BARB-S	BIKE-S	BOLD-S	BROD-S	CALL-S
BARD-S	BILE-S	BOLE-S	BROG-S	CALM-S
BARE-S	BILK-S	BOLL-S	BROO-S	CALO-S
BARF-S	BILL-S	BOLO-S	BROW-S	CALP-S
BARK-S	BIMA-S	BOLT-S	BRUT-S	CAMA-S
BARM-S	BIND-S	BOMA-S	BUAT-S	CAME-S
BARN-S	BINE-S	BOMB-S	BUBA-S	CAMO-S
BARP-S	BING-S	BOND-S	BUBU-S	CAMP-S
BASE-S	BINK-S	BONE-S	BUCK-S	CANE-S
BASK-S	BINT-S	BONG-S	BUDA-S	CANG-S
BAST-S	BIOG-S	BONK-S	BUDI-S	CANN-S
BATE-S	BIRD-S	BOOB-S	BUDO-S	CANT-S
BATH-S	BIRK-S	BOOH-S	BUFF-S	CAPA-S
BATT-S	BIRL-S	BOOK-S	BUFO-S	CAPE-S
BAUD-S	BIRO-S	BOOL-S	BUHL-S	CAPH-S
BAUK-S	BIRR-S	BOOM-S	BUHR-S	CAPO-S
BAUR-S	BISE-S	BOON-S	BUIK-S	CARB-S
BAWD-S	BISK-S	BOOR-S	BUKE-S	CARD-S
BAWL-S	BITE-S	BOOT-S	BULB-S	CARE-S
BAWN-S	BITO-S	BORA-S	BULK-S	CARK-S
BAWR-S	BITT-S	BORD-S	BULL-S	CARL-S
BAYE-S	BIZE-S	BORE-S	BUMF-S	CARN-S
BAYT-S	BLAB-S	BORK-S	BUMP-S	CARP-S
BEAD-S	BLAD-S	BORM-S	BUNA-S	CARR-S
BEAK-S	BLAE-S	BORT-S	BUND-S	CART-S
BEAM-S	BLAG-S	BOSK-S	BUNG-S	CASA-S
BEAN-S	BLAH-S	BOTA-S	BUNK-S	CASE-S
BEAR-S	BLAM-S	BOTT-S	BUNN-S	CASK-S
BEAT-S	BLAT-S	BOUK-S	BUNT-S	CAST-S
BEAU-S	BLAW-S	BOUN-S	BUOY-S	CATE-S
BECK-S	BLAY-S	BOUT-S	BURA-S	CAUK-S
BEDE-S	BLEB-S	BOWL-S	BURB-S	CAUL-S
BEEF-S	BLEE-S	BOWR-S	BURD-S	CAUM-S
BEEP-S	BLET-S	BOYF-S	BURG-S	CAUP-S
BEER-S	BLEY-S	BOYG-S	BURK-S	CAVA-S
BEET-S	BLIN-S	BOYO-S	BURL-S	CAVE-S

CAWK-S	CLEF-S	COST-S	DAFF-S	DENT-S
CEDE-S	CLEG-S	COTE-S	DAGO-S	DERE-S
CEDI-S	CLEM-S	COTH-S	DAHL-S	DERM-S
CEIL-S	CLEW-S	COTT-S	DALE-S	DERN-S
CELL-S	CLIP-S	COUP-S	DALI-S	DERO-S
CELT-S	CLOD-S	COUR-S	DALT-S	DERV-S
CENT-S	CLOG-S	COVE-S	DAME-S	DESK-S
CEPE-S	CLON-S	COWK-S	DAMN-S	DEVA-S
CERE-S	CLOP-S	COWL-S	DAMP-S	DHAK-S
CERO-S	CLOT-S	COWP-S	DANG-S	DHAL-S
CERT-S	CLOU-S	COZE-S	DANK-S	DHOL-S
CETE-S	CLOW-S	CRAB-S	DANT-S	DHOW-S
CHAD-S	CLOY-S	CRAG-S	DARB-S	DIAL-S
CHAI-S	CLUB-S	CRAM-S	DARE-S	DICE-S
CHAL-S	CLUE-S	CRAN-S	DARG-S	DICK-S
CHAM-S	COAL-S	CRAP-S	DARI-S	DICT-S
CHAO-S	COAT-S	CRAW-S	DARK-S	DIDO-S
CHAP-S	COBB-S	CRAY-S	DARN-S	DIEB-S
CHAR-S	COCA-S	CRED-S	DART-S	DIET-S
CHAT-S	COCK-S	CREE-S	DATE-S	DIFF-S
CHAV-S	COCO-S	CREM-S	DATO-S	DIKA-S
CHAW-S	CODA-S	CREW-S	DAUB-S	DIKE-S
CHAY-S	CODE-S	CRIB-S	DAUD-S	DILL-S
CHEF-S	COED-S	CRIM-S	DAUR-S	DIME-S
CHEW-S	COFF-S	CRIT-S	DAUT-S	DIMP-S
CHIA-S	COHO-S	CROC-S	DAWD-S	DINE-S
CHIB-S	COIF-S	CROG-S	DAWK-S	DING-S
CHIC-S	COIL-S	CROP-S	DAWN-S	DINK-S
CHIK-S	COIN-S	CROW-S	DAWT-S	DINO-S
CHIN-S	COIR-S	CRUD-S	DAZE-S	DINT-S
CHIP-S	COIT-S	CRUE-S	DEAD-S	DIOL-S
CHIT-S	COKE-S	CUBE-S	DEAL-S	DIRK-S
CHIV-S	COLA-S	CUFF-S	DEAN-S	DIRL-S
CHOC-S	COLD-S	CUIF-S	DEAR-S	DIRT-S
CHOG-S	COLE-S	CUIT-S	DEAW-S	DISA-S
CHON-S	COLL-S	CUKE-S	DEBE-S	DISC-S
CHOP-S	COLT-S	CULL-S	DEBT-S	DISK-S
CHOW-S	COMA-S	CULM-S	DECK-S	DITA-S
CHUB-S	COMB-S	CULT-S	DECO-S	DITE-S
CHUG-S	COME-S	CUNT-S	DEED-S	DITT-S
CHUM-S	COMM-S	CURB-S	DEEM-S	DIVA-S
CIAO-S	COMP-S	CURD-S	DEEN-S	DIVE-S
CIDE-S	CONE-S	CURE-S	DEEP-S	DIVI-S
CIEL-S	CONF-S	CURF-S	DEER-S	DJIN-S
CILL-S	CONK-S	CURL-S	DEET-S	DOAB-S
CINE-S	CONN-S	CURN-S	DEEV-S	DOAT-S
CION-S	COOF-S	CURR-S	DEFI-S	DOCK-S
CIRE-S	COOK-S	CUSK-S	DEID-S	DOCO-S
CIRL-S	COOL-S	CUSP-S	DEIL-S	DODO-S
CIST-S	COOM-S	CUTE-S	DEKE-S	DOEK-S
CITE-S	COON-S	CYAN-S	DELE-S	DOER-S
CIVE-S	COOP-S	CYMA-S	DELF-S	DOFF-S
CLAD-S	COOT-S	CYME-S	DELI-S	DOGE-S
CLAG-S	COPE-S	CYST-S	DELL-S	DOIT-S
CLAM-S	CORD-S	CYTE-S	DELO-S	DOJO-S
CLAN-S	CORE-S	CZAR-S	DELT-S	DOLE-S
CLAP-S	CORK-S	DACE-S	DEME-S	DOLL-S
CLAT-S	CORM-S	DACK-S	DEMO-S	DOLT-S
CLAW-S	CORN-S	DADA-S	DENE-S	DOME-S
CLAY-S	COSE-S	DADO-S	DENI-S	DONA-S

DONG-S	DULE-S	ERIC-S	FECK-S	FLEG-S
DOOB-S	DULL-S	ERNE-S	FEEB-S	FLEW-S
DOOK-S	DUMA-S	ERUV-S	FEED-S	FLEY-S
DOOL-S	DUMB-S	ESNE-S	FEEL-S	FLIC-S
DOOM-S	DUMP-S	ESSE-S	FEEN-S	FLIM-S
DOOR-S	DUNE-S	ETAT-S	FEER-S	FLIP-S
DOPA-S	DUNG-S	ETEN-S	FELL-S	FLIR-S
DOPE-S	DUNK-S	ETNA-S	FELT-S	FLIT-S
DORB-S	DUNT-S	ETUI-S	FEME-S	FLOC-S
DORK-S	DUPE-S	EUGH-S	FEND-S	FLOE-S
DORM-S	DURA-S	EURO-S	FENI-S	FLOG-S
DORP-S	DURE-S	EVEN-S	FENT-S	FLOP-S
DORR-S	DURN-S	EVET-S	FEOD-S	FLOR-S
DORT-S	DURO-S	EVIL-S	FERE-S	FLOW-S
DOSE-S	DURR-S	EWER-S	FERM-S	FLUB-S
DOTE-S	DUSK-S	EXAM-S	FERN-S	FLUE-S
DOUC-S	DUST-S	EXEC-S	FEST-S	FOAL-S
DOUK-S	DWAM-S	EXIT-S	FETA-S	FOAM-S
DOUM-S	DYAD-S	EXON-S	FETE-S	FOHN-S
DOUP-S	DYER-S	EXPO-S	FETT-S	FOID-S
DOUT-S	DYKE-S	EXUL-S	FEUD-S	FOIL-S
DOVE-S	DYNE-S	EYAS-S	FIAR-S	FOIN-S
DOWD-S	DZHO-S	EYER-S	FIAT-S	FOLD-S
DOWL-S	EALE-S	EYOT-S	FICE-S	FOLK-S
DOWN-S	EARD-S	EYRA-S	FICO-S	FOND-S
DOWP-S	EARL-S	EYRE-S	FIDO-S	FONT-S
DOWT-S	EARN-S	FACE-S	FIEF-S	FOOD-S
DOZE-S	EASE-S	FACT-S	FIER-S	FOOL-S
DRAB-S	EAST-S	FADE-S	FIFE-S	FOOT-S
DRAG-S	EAVE-S	FADO-S	FIGO-S	FORB-S
DRAM-S	EBON-S	FAFF-S	FIKE-S	FORD-S
DRAP-S	ECAD-S	FAIK-S	FILE-S	FORE-S
DRAT-S	ECHE-S	FAIL-S	FILL-S	FORK-S
DRAW-S	ECHO-S	FAIN-S	FILM-S	FORM-S
DRAY-S	ECRU-S	FAIR-S	FILO-S	FORT-S
DREE-S	EDGE-S	FAKE-S	FIND-S	FOUD-S
DREG-S	EDIT-S	FALL-S	FINE-S	FOUL-S
DREK-S	EEVN-S	FAME-S	FINI-S	FOUR-S
DREY-S	EGAD-S	FAND-S	FINK-S	FOWL-S
DRIB-S	EGER-S	FANE-S	FINO-S	FRAB-S
DRIP-S	EGMA-S	FANG-S	FIRE-S	FRAG-S
DROP-S	EILD-S	FANK-S	FIRK-S	FRAP-S
DROW-S	EKKA-S	FANO-S	FIRM-S	FRAS-S
DRUB-S	ELAN-S	FARD-S	FIRN-S	FRAT-S
DRUG-S	EMEU-S	FARE-S	FISC-S	FRAU-S
DRUM-S	EMIR-S	FARL-S	FISK-S	FRAY-S
DUAD-S	EMIT-S	FARM-S	FIST-S	FREE-S
DUAL-S	EMMA-S	FARO-S	FITT-S	FRET-S
DUAN-S	EMMY-S	FART-S	FIVE-S	FRIB-S
DUAR-S	EMPT-S	FAST-S	FLAB-S	FRIG-S
DUCE-S	EMYD-S	FATE-S	FLAG-S	FRIT-S
DUCK-S	ENEW-S	FAUN-S	FLAK-S	FROE-S
DUCT-S	ENOL-S	FAUT-S	FLAM-S	FROG-S
DUDE-S	ENOW-S	FAVA-S	FLAN-S	FROW-S
DUEL-S	EORL-S	FAVE-S	FLAP-S	FRUG-S
DUET-S	EPEE-S	FAWN-S	FLAT-S	FUCK-S
DUFF-S	EPHA-S	FAZE-S	FLAW-S	FUEL-S
DUIT-S	EPIC-S	FEAL-S	FLAY-S	FUFF-S
DUKA-S	EREV-S	FEAR-S	FLEA-S	FUGU-S
DUKE-S	ERGO-S	FEAT-S	FLEE-S	FUJI-S

FULL-S	GENA-S	GOER-S	GULE-S	HAUD-S
FUME-S	GENE-S	GOFF-S	GULF-S	HAUF-S
FUND-S	GENT-S	GOGO-S	GULL-S	HAUL-S
FUNG-S	GENU-S	GOLD-S	GULP-S	HAVE-S
FUNK-S	GERE-S	GOLE-S	GUMP-S	HAWK-S
FURL-S	GERM-S	GOLF-S	GUNK-S	HAWM-S
FURR-S	GEST-S	GOLP-S	GURL-S	HAZE-S
FUSE-S	GETA-S	GONG-S	GURN-S	HEAD-S
FUST-S	GEUM-S	GONK-S	GURU-S	HEAL-S
FUZE-S	GHAT-S	GOOD-S	GUST-S	HEAP-S
FYCE-S	GHEE-S	GOOF-S	GYAL-S	HEAR-S
FYKE-S	GIBE-S	GOOG-S	GYBE-S	HEAT-S
FYLE-S	GIFT-S	GOOK-S	GYMP-S	HEBE-S
FYRD-S	GIGA-S	GOOL-S	GYRE-S	HECK-S
GADE-S	GILA-S	GOON-S	GYRO-S	HEED-S
GADI-S	GILD-S	GOOP-S	GYTE-S	HEEL-S
GAFF-S	GILL-S	GOOR-S	GYVE-S	HEFT-S
GAGE-S	GILT-S	GORA-S	HAAF-S	HEID-S
GAID-S	GIMP-S	GORE-S	HAAR-S	HEIL-S
GAIN-S	GING-S	GORI-S	HABU-S	HEIR-S
GAIR-S	GINK-S	GORM-S	HACK-S	HELE-S
GAIT-S	GIRD-S	GORP-S	HADE-S	HELL-S
GAJO-S	GIRL-S	GOTH-S	HAEM-S	HELM-S
GALA-S	GIRN-S	GOUK-S	HAET-S	HELO-S
GALE-S	GIRO-S	GOUT-S	HAFF-S	HELP-S
GALL-S	GIRR-S	GOWD-S	HAFT-S	HEME-S
GAMA-S	GIRT-S	GOWF-S	HAGG-S	HEMP-S
GAMB-S	GISM-S	GOWK-S	HAHA-S	HEND-S
GAME-S	GIST-S	GOWL-S	HAIK-S	HENT-S
GAMP-S	GITE-S	GOWN-S	HAIL-S	HERB-S
GANG-S	GIVE-S	GRAB-S	HAIN-S	HERD-S
GANT-S	GLAD-S	GRAD-S	HAIR-S	HERE-S
GAOL-S	GLAM-S	GRAM-S	HAJI-S	HERL-S
GAPE-S	GLED-S	GRAN-S	HAKA-S	HERM-S
GAPO-S	GLEE-S	GRAV-S	HAKE-S	HERN-S
GARB-S	GLEI-S	GRAY-S	HAKU-S	HERO-S
GARI-S	GLEN-S	GREE-S	HALE-S	HESP-S
GASP-S	GLEY-S	GREN-S	HALF-S	HEST-S
GAST-S	GLIA-S	GREW-S	HALL-S	HETE-S
GATE-S	GLIB-S	GREY-S	HALM-S	HETH-S
GATH-S	GLIM-S	GRID-S	HALO-S	HICK-S
GAUD-S	GLIT-S	GRIG-S	HALT-S	HIDE-S
GAUM-S	GLOB-S	GRIN-S	HAME-S	HIGH-S
GAUP-S	GLOM-S	GRIP-S	HAND-S	HIKE-S
GAUR-S	GLOP-S	GRIT-S	HANG-S	HILL-S
GAUS-S	GLOW-S	GROG-S	HANK-S	HILT-S
GAWD-S	GLUE-S	GROK-S	HANT-S	HIND-S
GAWK-S	GLUG-S	GROT-S	HAPU-S	HING-S
GAWP-S	GLUM-S	GROW-S	HARD-S	HINT-S
GAZE-S	GLUT-S	GRUB-S	HARE-S	HIOI-S
GEAL-S	GNAR-S	GRUE-S	HARK-S	HIRE-S
GEAN-S	GNAT-S	GUAN-S	HARL-S	HIST-S
GEAR-S	GNAW-S	GUAR-S	HARM-S	HIVE-S
GEAT-S	GNOW-S	GUCK-S	HARN-S	HOAR-S
GECK-S	GOAD-S	GUDE-S	HARO-S	HOBO-S
GEEK-S	GOAF-S	GUES-S	HARP-S	HOCK-S
GEEP-S	GOAL-S	GUFF-S	HART-S	HOER-S
GEIT-S	GOAT-S	GUGA-S	HASK-S	HOGG-S
GELD-S	GOBO-S	GUID-S	HASP-S	HOGH-S
GELT-S	GOEL-S	GULA-S	HATE-S	HOIK-S

HOKE-S	HYPO-S	JIBB-S	KAON-S	KIRK-S
HOKI-S	IAMB-S	JIBE-S	KAPA-S	KIRN-S
HOLD-S	ICER-S	JIFF-S	KAPH-S	KIST-S
HOLE-S	ICON-S	JILL-S	KARA-S	KITE-S
HOLK-S	IDEA-S	JILT-S	KARK-S	KITH-S
HOLM-S	IDEE-S	JINK-S	KARN-S	KIVA-S
HOLT-S	IDLE-S	JINN-S	KART-S	KIWI-S
HOMA-S	IDOL-S	JIRD-S	KATA-S	KLAP-S
HOME-S	IDYL-S	JISM-S	KATI-S	KLIK-S
HOMO-S	IGLU-S	JIVE-S	KAVA-S	KNAG-S
HOND-S	IKAN-S	JOBE-S	KAWA-S	KNAP-S
HONE-S	IKAT-S	JOCK-S	KAYO-S	KNAR-S
HONG-S	IKON-S	JOEY-S	KAZI-S	KNEE-S
HONK-S	IMAM-S	JOHN-S	KBAR-S	KNIT-S
HOOD-S	IMID-S	JOIN-S	KECK-S	KNOB-S
HOOF-S	IMPI-S	JOKE-S	KEEF-S	KNOP-S
HOOK-S	INFO-S	JOLE-S	KEEK-S	KNOT-S
HOON-S	INTI-S	JOLL-S	KEEL-S	KNOW-S
HOOP-S	IOTA-S	JOLT-S	KEEN-S	KNUB-S
HOOT-S	IRID-S	JOMO-S	KEEP-S	KNUR-S
HOPE-S	IRON-S	JOOK-S	KEET-S	KNUT-S
HORA-S	ISBA-S	JOTA-S	KEIR-S	KOAN-S
HORI-S	ISLE-S	JOUK-S	KELL-S	KOAP-S
HORN-S	ITEM-S	JOUR-S	KELP-S	KOBO-S
HOSE-S	IXIA-S	JOWL-S	KELT-S	KOEL-S
HOST-S	IZAR-S	JUBA-S	KEMB-S	KOFF-S
HOUF-S	JAAP-S	JUBE-S	KEMP-S	KOHA-S
HOUR-S	JACK-S	JUCO-S	KENO-S	KOHL-S
HOUT-S	JADE-S	JUDO-S	KENT-S	KOJI-S
HOVE-S	JAFA-S	JUJU-S	KEPI-S	KOLA-S
HOWE-S	JAGA-S	JUKE-S	KERB-S	KOLO-S
HOWF-S	JAGG-S	JUKU-S	KERF-S	KONK-S
HOWK-S	JAIL-S	JUMP-S	KERN-S	KOOK-S
HOWL-S	JAKE-S	JUNK-S	KERO-S	KOPH-S
HOYA-S	JAMB-S	JUPE-S	KEST-S	KORA-S
HUCK-S	JANE-S	JUST-S	KETA-S	KORE-S
HUER-S	JANN-S	JUTE-S	KHAF-S	KORU-S
HUFF-S	JAPE-S	JUVE-S	KHAN-S	KOTO-S
HUHU-S	JARK-S	KADE-S	KHAT-S	KRAB-S
HUIA-S	JARL-S	KADI-S	KHET-S	KSAR-S
HULA-S	JARP-S	KAGO-S	KHOR-S	KUDO-S
HULE-S	JASP-S	KAGU-S	KHUD-S	KUDU-S
HULK-S	JATO-S	KAID-S	KIBE-S	KUFI-S
HULL-S	JAUK-S	KAIE-S	KICK-S	KUIA-S
HUMA-S	JAUP-S	KAIF-S	KIEF-S	KUKU-S
HUMF-S	JAVA-S	KAIK-S	KIER-S	KULA-S
HUMP-S	JEAN-S	KAIL-S	KIKE-S	KURI-S
HUNK-S	JEAT-S	KAIM-S	KILL-S	KURU-S
HUNT-S	JEDI-S	KAIN-S	KILN-S	KUTA-S
HURL-S	JEEL-S	KAKA-S	KILO-S	KUTI-S
HURT-S	JEEP-S	KAKI-S	KILP-S	KUTU-S
HUSK-S	JEER-S	KALE-S	KILT-S	KUZU-S
HUSO-S	JEFE-S	KALI-S	KINA-S	KVAS-S
HWYL-S	JEFF-S	KAMA-S	KIND-S	KYAK-S
HYEN-S	JEHU-S	KAME-S	KINE-S	KYAR-S
HYKE-S	JELL-S	KAMI-S	KING-S	KYAT-S
HYLA-S	JERK-S	KANA-S	KINK-S	KYBO-S
HYLE-S	JEST-S	KANE-S	KINO-S	KYLE-S
HYMN-S	JETE-S	KANG-S	KIPE-S	KYND-S
HYPE-S	JIAO-S	KANT-S	KIPP-S	KYPE-S

KYTE-S	LEUD-S	LOOM-S	MAIM-S	MENE-S
LACE-S	LIAR-S	LOON-S	MAIN-S	MENG-S
LACK-S	LICK-S	LOOP-S	MAIR-S	MENU-S
LADE-S	LIDO-S	LOOT-S	MAKE-S	MEOU-S
LAER-S	LIEF-S	LOPE-S	MAKI-S	MEOW-S
LAIC-S	LIEN-S	LORD-S	MAKO-S	MERC-S
LAID-S	LIER-S	LORE-S	MALA-S	MERE-S
LAIK-S	LIEU-S	LOSE-S	MALE-S	MERI-S
LAIR-S	LIFE-S	LOTA-S	MALI-S	MERK-S
LAKE-S	LIFT-S	LOTE-S	MALL-S	MERL-S
LAKH-S	LIKE-S	LOTO-S	MALM-S	MESA-S
LALL-S	LILL-S	LOUN-S	MALT-S	MESE-S
LAMA-S	LILO-S	LOUP-S	MAMA-S	METE-S
LAMB-S	LILT-S	LOUR-S	MANA-S	METH-S
LAME-S	LIMA-S	LOUT-S	MANE-S	MEVE-S
LAMP-S	LIMB-S	LOVE-S	MANG-S	MEWL-S
LANA-S	LIME-S	LOWE-S	MANI-S	MEZE-S
LAND-S	LIMN-S	LOWN-S	MANO-S	MICA-S
LANE-S	LIMO-S	LOWP-S	MARA-S	MICK-S
LANK-S	LIMP-S	LOWT-S	MARC-S	MICO-S
LANT-S	LIND-S	LUAU-S	MARE-S	MIDI-S
LARD-S	LINE-S	LUBE-S	MARG-S	MIEN-S
LARE-S	LING-S	LUCE-S	MARK-S	MIFF-S
LARI-S	LINK-S	LUCK-S	MARL-S	MIGG-S
LARK-S	LINN-S	LUDE-S	MARM-S	MIHI-S
LARN-S	LINO-S	LUDO-S	MART-S	MIKE-S
LASE-S	LINT-S	LUFF-S	MASA-S	MILD-S
LAST-S	LION-S	LUGE-S	MASE-S	MILE-S
LATH-S	LIPO-S	LULL-S	MASK-S	MILK-S
LATU-S	LIRA-S	LULU-S	MAST-S	MILL-S
LAUD-S	LIRK-S	LUMA-S	MASU-S	MILO-S
LAUF-S	LISK-S	LUMP-S	MATE-S	MILT-S
LAVA-S	LISP-S	LUNA-S	MATH-S	MIME-S
LAVE-S	LIST-S	LUNE-S	MATT-S	MINA-S
LAWK-S	LITE-S	LUNG-S	MAUD-S	MIND-S
LAWN-S	LITH-S	LUNK-S	MAUL-S	MINE-S
LAZE-S	LIVE-S	LUNT-S	MAUT-S	MING-S
LAZO-S	LOAD-S	LURE-S	MAWK-S	MINI-S
LEAD-S	LOAF-S	LURK-S	MAWR-S	MINK-S
LEAF-S	LOAM-S	LUSK-S	MAXI-S	MINO-S
LEAK-S	LOAN-S	LUST-S	MAYA-S	MINT-S
LEAM-S	LOBE-S	LUTE-S	MAYO-S	MIRE-S
LEAN-S	LOBO-S	LUXE-S	MAZE-S	MIRK-S
LEAP-S	LOCH-S	LWEI-S	MEAD-S	MIRV-S
LEAR-S	LOCK-S	LYAM-S	MEAL-S	MISE-S
LEAT-S	LOCO-S	LYME-S	MEAN-S	MISO-S
LEEK-S	LODE-S	LYNE-S	MEAT-S	MIST-S
LEEP-S	LOFT-S	LYRE-S	MECK-S	MITE-S
LEER-S	LOGE-S	LYSE-S	MEED-S	MITT-S
LEET-S	LOGO-S	LYTE-S	MEER-S	MOAN-S
LEFT-S	LOID-S	MAAR-S	MEET-S	MOAT-S
LEHR-S	LOIN-S	MABE-S	MEFF-S	MOBE-S
LEIR-S	LOIR-S	MACE-S	MEIN-S	MOCH-S
LEME-S	LOKE-S	MACH-S	MELA-S	MOCK-S
LEND-S	LOLL-S	MACK-S	MELD-S	MODE-S
LENG-S	LOMA-S	MAGE-S	MELL-S	MOER-S
LENO-S	LOME-S	MAGG-S	MELT-S	MOFO-S
LERE-S	LONG-S	MAID-S	MEME-S	MOHR-S
LERP-S	LOOF-S	MAIK-S	MEMO-S	MOIL-S
LEST-S	LOOK-S	MAIL-S	MEND-S	MOIT-S

MOJO-S	MURK-S	NIDE-S	ODAL-S	PACO-S
MOKE-S	MURL-S	NIEF-S	ODOR-S	PACT-S
MOKI-S	MURR-S	NIFE-S	ODSO-S	PADI-S
MOKO-S	MUSE-S	NIFF-S	ODYL-S	PAGE-S
MOLA-S	MUSK-S	NIGH-S	OFAY-S	PAIK-S
MOLD-S	MUSO-S	NILL-S	OGAM-S	PAIL-S
MOLE-S	MUST-S	NIMB-S	OGEE-S	PAIN-S
MOLL-S	MUTE-S	NINE-S	OGLE-S	PAIR-S
MOLT-S	MUTI-S	NIPA-S	OGRE-S	PALE-S
MOME-S	MUTT-S	NIRL-S	OHIA-S	PALL-S
MONA-S	MYNA-S	NITE-S	OINK-S	PALM-S
MONG-S	MYTH-S	NIXE-S	OINT-S	PALP-S
MONK-S	MYXO-S	NOAH-S	OKAY-S	PAND-S
MONO-S	MZEE-S	NOCK-S	OKEH-S	PANE-S
MOOD-S	NAAM-S	NODE-S	OKRA-S	PANG-S
MOOK-S	NAAN-S	NOEL-S	OKTA-S	PANT-S
MOOL-S	NABE-S	NOGG-S	OLEO-S	PAPA-S
MOON-S	NABK-S	NOIL-S	OLIO-S	PAPE-S
MOOP-S	NADA-S	NOIR-S	OLLA-S	PARA-S
MOOR-S	NAFF-S	NOLE-S	OLPE-S	PARD-S
MOOT-S	NAGA-S	NOLL-S	OMBU-S	PARE-S
MOPE-S	NAIF-S	NOLO-S	OMEN-S	PARK-S
MORA-S	NAIK-S	NOMA-S	OMER-S	PARP-S
MORE-S	NAIL-S	NOME-S	OMIT-S	PARR-S
MORN-S	NALA-S	NONA-S	OMOV-S	PART-S
MORT-S	NAME-S	NONE-S	ONCE-S	PASE-S
MOSE-S	NANA-S	NONG-S	ONER-S	PAST-S
MOSK-S	NAPA-S	NONI-S	OONT-S	PATE-S
MOST-S	NAPE-S	NOOK-S	OOSE-S	PATH-S
MOTE-S	NARC-S	NOON-S	OOZE-S	PATU-S
MOTH-S	NARD-S	NOOP-S	OPAH-S	PAUA-S
MOTI-S	NARE-S	NORI-S	OPAL-S	PAUL-S
MOTT-S	NARK-S	NORK-S	OPEN-S	PAVE-S
MOTU-S	NAVE-S	NORM-S	OPPO-S	PAWA-S
MOUE-S	NAZE-S	NOSE-S	ORAL-S	PAWK-S
MOUP-S	NAZI-S	NOTE-S	ORCA-S	PAWL-S
MOVE-S	NEAL-S	NOUL-S	ORDO-S	PAWN-S
MOWA-S	NEAP-S	NOUN-S	ORFE-S	PEAG-S
MOXA-S	NEAR-S	NOUP-S	ORLE-S	PEAK-S
MOYA-S	NEAT-S	NOVA-S	ORZO-S	PEAL-S
MOYL-S	NECK-S	NOWL-S	OTTO-S	PEAN-S
MOZE-S	NEED-S	NOWT-S	OULK-S	PEAR-S
MOZO-S	NEEM-S	NUDE-S	OUMA-S	PEAT-S
MUCK-S	NEEP-S	NUFF-S	OUPA-S	PEBA-S
MUFF-S	NEIF-S	NUKE-S	OUPH-S	PECH-S
MUGG-S	NEMA-S	NULL-S	OUST-S	PECK-S
MUID-S	NEMN-S	NUMB-S	OUZO-S	PEEK-S
MUIL-S	NENE-S	NURD-S	OVAL-S	PEEL-S
MUIR-S	NEON-S	NURL-S	OVEL-S	PEEN-S
MULE-S	NERD-S	NURR-S	OVEN-S	PEEP-S
MULL-S	NERK-S	OAST-S	OVER-S	PEER-S
MUMM-S	NEST-S	OATH-S	OWRE-S	PEGH-S
MUMP-S	NETE-S	OBEY-S	OXER-S	PEIN-S
MUMU-S	NETT-S	OBIA-S	OXID-S	PEKE-S
MUNG-S	NEUK-S	OBIT-S	OXIM-S	PELA-S
MUNI-S	NEUM-S	OBOE-S	OYER-S	PELE-S
MUNT-S	NEVE-S	OBOL-S	PAAL-S	PELF-S
MUON-S	NEWT-S	OCHE-S	PACA-S	PELL-S
MURA-S	NEXT-S	OCTA-S	PACE-S	PELT-S
MURE-S	NICK-S	ODAH-S	PACK-S	PEND-S

PENE-S	PLOD-S	PRIG-S	QUIN-S	REEK-S
PENI-S	PLOP-S	PRIM-S	QUIP-S	REEL-S
PENK-S	PLOT-S	PROA-S	QUIT-S	REEN-S
PENT-S	PLOW-S	PROB-S	QUOD-S	REGO-S
PEON-S	PLOY-S	PROD-S	QUOP-S	REIF-S
PEPO-S	PLUE-S	PROF-S	RABI-S	REIK-S
PERE-S	PLUG-S	PROG-S	RACE-S	REIN-S
PERI-S	PLUM-S	PROM-S	RACK-S	REKE-S
PERK-S	POCK-S	PROP-S	RAFF-S	REND-S
PERM-S	POEM-S	PROS-S	RAFT-S	RENT-S
PERN-S	POEP-S	PROW-S	RAGA-S	REPO-S
PERP-S	POET-S	PUBE-S	RAGE-S	REPP-S
PERT-S	POGO-S	PUCE-S	RAGG-S	REST-S
PERV-S	POKE-S	PUCK-S	RAGI-S	RETE-S
PESO-S	POLE-S	PUDU-S	RAIA-S	RHEA-S
PEST-S	POLK-S	PUER-S	RAID-S	RIAL-S
PHOH-S	POLL-S	PUFF-S	RAIK-S	RIBA-S
PHON-S	POLO-S	PUGH-S	RAIL-S	RICE-S
PHOT-S	POLT-S	PUHA-S	RAIN-S	RICK-S
PHUT-S	POLY-S	PUJA-S	RAIT-S	RIDE-S
PIAN-S	POME-S	PUKE-S	RAJA-S	RIEL-S
PICA-S	POMO-S	PUKU-S	RAKE-S	RIEM-S
PICK-S	POMP-S	PULA-S	RAKI-S	RIFF-S
PIER-S	POND-S	PULE-S	RAKU-S	RIFT-S
PIET-S	PONE-S	PULI-S	RALE-S	RIGG-S
PIKA-S	PONG-S	PULK-S	RAMI-S	RILE-S
PIKE-S	PONK-S	PULL-S	RAMP-S	RILL-S
PIKI-S	PONT-S	PULP-S	RANA-S	RIME-S
PILE-S	POOD-S	PULU-S	RAND-S	RIMU-S
PILI-S	POOF-S	PUMA-S	RANI-S	RIND-S
PILL-S	POOH-S	PUMP-S	RANK-S	RINE-S
PIMA-S	POOK-S	PUNA-S	RANT-S	RING-S
PIMP-S	POOL-S	PUNG-S	RAPE-S	RINK-S
PINA-S	POON-S	PUNK-S	RARE-S	RIOT-S
PINE-S	POOP-S	PUNT-S	RARK-S	RIPE-S
PING-S	POOT-S	PUPA-S	RASE-S	RIPP-S
PINK-S	POPE-S	PUPU-S	RASP-S	RISE-S
PINT-S	PORE-S	PURE-S	RATA-S	RISK-S
PION-S	PORK-S	PURI-S	RATE-S	RISP-S
PIOY-S	PORN-S	PURL-S	RATH-S	RITE-S
PIPA-S	PORT-S	PURR-S	RATO-S	RITT-S
PIPE-S	POSE-S	PUTT-S	RATU-S	RIVA-S
PIPI-S	POST-S	PYAT-S	RAUN-S	RIVE-S
PIRL-S	POTE-S	PYET-S	RAVE-S	RIVO-S
PIRN-S	POTT-S	PYIN-S	RAWN-S	RIZA-S
PISE-S	POUF-S	PYNE-S	RAYA-S	ROAD-S
PISO-S	POUK-S	PYOT-S	RAZE-S	ROAM-S
PITA-S	POUR-S	PYRE-S	READ-S	ROAN-S
PITH-S	POUT-S	PYRO-S	REAK-S	ROAR-S
PIUM-S	POWN-S	QADI-S	REAL-S	ROBE-S
PIZE-S	PRAD-S	QAID-S	REAM-S	ROCK-S
PLAN-S	PRAM-S	QOPH-S	REAN-S	RODE-S
PLAP-S	PRAO-S	QUAD-S	REAP-S	ROIL-S
PLAT-S	PRAT-S	QUAG-S	REAR-S	ROIN-S
PLAY-S	PRAU-S	QUAI-S	RECK-S	ROJI-S
PLEA-S	PRAY-S	QUAT-S	REDD-S	ROKE-S
PLEB-S	PREE-S	QUAY-S	REDE-S	ROLE-S
PLEW-S	PREM-S	QUEY-S	REDO-S	ROLF-S
PLIE-S	PREP-S	QUID-S	REED-S	ROLL-S
PLIM-S	PREY-S	QUIM-S	REEF-S	ROMA-S

ROMP-S	SAGE-S	SEEP-S	SIJO-S	SLOE-S
RONE-S	SAGO-S	SEER-S	SIKA-S	SLOG-S
RONT-S	SAIC-S	SEGO-S	SIKE-S	SLOP-S
ROOD-S	SAID-S	SEIF-S	SILD-S	SLOT-S
ROOF-S	SAIL-S	SEIL-S	SILE-S	SLOW-S
ROOK-S	SAIM-S	SEIR-S	SILK-S	SLUB-S
ROOM-S	SAIN-S	SEKT-S	SILL-S	SLUE-S
ROON-S	SAIR-S	SELE-S	SILO-S	SLUG-S
ROOP-S	SAKE-S	SELF-S	SILT-S	SLUM-S
ROOT-S	SAKI-S	SELL-S	SIMA-S	SLUR-S
ROPE-S	SALE-S	SEME-S	SIMI-S	SLUT-S
RORE-S	SALP-S	SEMI-S	SIMP-S	SMEE-S
RORT-S	SALT-S	SENA-S	SIND-S	SMEW-S
ROSE-S	SAMA-S	SEND-S	SINE-S	SMIR-S
ROST-S	SAME-S	SENT-S	SING-S	SMIT-S
ROTA-S	SAMP-S	SEPT-S	SINH-S	SMOG-S
ROTE-S	SAND-S	SERE-S	SINK-S	SMUG-S
ROTI-S	SANE-S	SERF-S	SIPE-S	SMUR-S
ROTL-S	SANG-S	SERK-S	SIRE-S	SMUT-S
ROTO-S	SANT-S	SERR-S	SIRI-S	SNAB-S
ROUE-S	SARD-S	SETT-S	SIST-S	SNAG-S
ROUL-S	SARI-S	SEXT-S	SITE-S	SNAP-S
ROUM-S	SARK-S	SHAD-S	SIZE-S	SNAR-S
ROUP-S	SATE-S	SHAG-S	SKAG-S	SNAW-S
ROUT-S	SATI-S	SHAH-S	SKAT-S	SNEB-S
ROVE-S	SAUL-S	SHAM-S	SKAW-S	SNED-S
ROWT-S	SAUT-S	SHAN-S	SKEE-S	SNEE-S
RUBE-S	SAVE-S	SHAW-S	SKEG-S	SNIB-S
RUCK-S	SAXE-S	SHAY-S	SKEN-S	SNIG-S
RUDD-S	SCAB-S	SHEA-S	SKEO-S	SNIP-S
RUDE-S	SCAD-S	SHED-S	SKEP-S	SNIT-S
RUER-S	SCAG-S	SHET-S	SKER-S	SNOB-S
RUFF-S	SCAM-S	SHEW-S	SKET-S	SNOD-S
RUIN-S	SCAN-S	SHIM-S	SKEW-S	SNOG-S
RUKH-S	SCAR-S	SHIN-S	SKID-S	SNOT-S
RULE-S	SCAT-S	SHIP-S	SKIM-S	SNOW-S
RUME-S	SCAW-S	SHIR-S	SKIN-S	SNUB-S
RUMP-S	SCOG-S	SHIT-S	SKIO-S	SNUG-S
RUND-S	SCOP-S	SHIV-S	SKIP-S	SNYE-S
RUNE-S	SCOT-S	SHOE-S	SKIT-S	SOAK-S
RUNG-S	SCOW-S	SHOG-S	SKOL-S	SOAP-S
RUNT-S	SCUD-S	SHOO-S	SKUA-S	SOAR-S
RURP-S	SCUG-S	SHOP-S	SKUG-S	SOBA-S
RURU-S	SCUL-S	SHOT-S	SKYF-S	SOCA-S
RUSA-S	SCUM-S	SHOW-S	SKYR-S	SOCK-S
RUSE-S	SCUP-S	SHRI-S	SLAB-S	SODA-S
RUSK-S	SCUR-S	SHUL-S	SLAE-S	SOFA-S
RUST-S	SCUT-S	SHUN-S	SLAG-S	SOFT-S
RUTH-S	SCYE-S	SHUT-S	SLAM-S	SOIL-S
RYAL-S	SEAL-S	SHWA-S	SLAP-S	SOJA-S
RYKE-S	SEAM-S	SIAL-S	SLAT-S	SOKE-S
RYND-S	SEAN-S	SIBB-S	SLAW-S	SOLA-S
RYOT-S	SEAR-S	SICE-S	SLAY-S	SOLD-S
SABE-S	SEAT-S	SICK-S	SLED-S	SOLE-S
SACK-S	SECH-S	SIDA-S	SLEW-S	SOLO-S
SADE-S	SECT-S	SIDE-S	SLEY-S	SOMA-S
SADI-S	SEED-S	SIEN-S	SLIM-S	SONE-S
SADO-S	SEEK-S	SIFT-S	SLIP-S	SONG-S
SAFE-S	SEEL-S	SIGH-S	SLIT-S	SOOK-S
SAGA-S	SEEM-S	SIGN-S	SLOB-S	SOOL-S

SOOM-S	STEW-S	TABU-S	TEHR-S	TOFU-S
SOOP-S	STIE-S	TACE-S	TEIL-S	TOGA-S
SOOT-S	STIM-S	TACH-S	TELE-S	TOGE-S
SOPH-S	STIR-S	TACK-S	TELL-S	TOHO-S
SORA-S	STOA-S	TACO-S	TEME-S	TOIL-S
SORB-S	STOB-S	TACT-S	TEMP-S	TOIT-S
SORD-S	STOP-S	TAEL-S	TEND-S	TOKE-S
SORE-S	STOT-S	TAHA-S	TENE-S	TOKO-S
SORN-S	STOW-S	TAHR-S	TENT-S	TOLA-S
SORT-S	STUB-S	TAIG-S	TEPA-S	TOLE-S
SOTH-S	STUD-S	TAIL-S	TERF-S	TOLL-S
SOUK-S	STUM-S	TAIN-S	TERM-S	TOLT-S
SOUL-S	STUN-S	TAIT-S	TERN-S	TOLU-S
SOUM-S	STYE-S	TAKA-S	TEST-S	TOMB-S
SOUP-S	SUBA-S	TAKE-S	TETE-S	TOME-S
SOUR-S	SUCK-S	TAKI-S	TETH-S	TOMO-S
SOUT-S	SUDD-S	TALA-S	TEXT-S	TONE-S
SOWF-S	SUER-S	TALC-S	THAN-S	TONG-S
SOWL-S	SUET-S	TALE-S	THAR-S	TONK-S
SOWM-S	SUGH-S	TALK-S	THAW-S	TOOL-S
SOWP-S	SUID-S	TALL-S	THEE-S	TOOM-S
SOYA-S	SUIT-S	TAME-S	THEN-S	TOON-S
SPAE-S	SUKH-S	TAMP-S	THEW-S	TOOT-S
SPAG-S	SULK-S	TANA-S	THIG-S	TOPE-S
SPAM-S	SULU-S	TANG-S	THIN-S	TOPH-S
SPAN-S	SUMO-S	TANH-S	THOU-S	TOPI-S
SPAR-S	SUMP-S	TANK-S	THUD-S	TOPO-S
SPAT-S	SUNK-S	TAPA-S	THUG-S	TORA-S
SPAW-S	SUNN-S	TAPE-S	TIAR-S	TORC-S
SPAY-S	SUPE-S	TAPU-S	TICE-S	TORE-S
SPEC-S	SURA-S	TARA-S	TICK-S	TORO-S
SPEK-S	SURD-S	TARE-S	TIDE-S	TORR-S
SPET-S	SURE-S	TARN-S	TIER-S	TORT-S
SPEW-S	SURF-S	TARO-S	TIFF-S	TOSA-S
SPIC-S	SUSU-S	TARP-S	TIFT-S	TOSE-S
SPIE-S	SWAB-S	TART-S	TIGE-S	TOTE-S
SPIF-S	SWAD-S	TASK-S	TIKA-S	TOUK-S
SPIK-S	SWAG-S	TATE-S	TIKE-S	TOUN-S
SPIM-S	SWAN-S	TATH-S	TIKI-S	TOUR-S
SPIN-S	SWAP-S	TATT-S	TILE-S	TOUT-S
SPIT-S	SWAT-S	TATU-S	TILL-S	TOWN-S
SPIV-S	SWAY-S	TAUT-S	TILT-S	TOWT-S
SPOD-S	SWEE-S	TAVA-S	TIME-S	TOYO-S
SPOT-S	SWEY-S	TAWA-S	TIND-S	TOZE-S
SPUD-S	SWIG-S	TAWT-S	TINE-S	TRAD-S
SPUE-S	SWIM-S	TAXI-S	TING-S	TRAM-S
SPUG-S	SWOB-S	TEAD-S	TINK-S	TRAP-S
SPUR-S	SWOP-S	TEAK-S	TINT-S	TRAT-S
STAB-S	SWOT-S	TEAL-S	TIPI-S	TRAY-S
STAG-S	SYCE-S	TEAM-S	TIRE-S	TREE-S
STAP-S	SYEN-S	TEAR-S	TIRL-S	TREK-S
STAR-S	SYKE-S	TEAT-S	TIRO-S	TRES-S
STAT-S	SYLI-S	TECH-S	TIRR-S	TRET-S
STAW-S	SYNC-S	TEEL-S	TITI-S	TREW-S
STAY-S	SYND-S	TEEM-S	TOAD-S	TREY-S
STED-S	SYNE-S	TEEN-S	TOCK-S	TRIE-S
STEM-S	SYPE-S	TEER-S	TOCO-S	TRIG-S
STEN-S	SYPH-S	TEFF-S	TOEA-S	TRIM-S
STEP-S	TAAL-S	TEGG-S	TOFF-S	TRIN-S
STET-S	TABI-S	TEGU-S	TOFT-S	TRIO-S

TRIP-S	UPDO-S	VOLK-S	WEAR-S	WIST-S
TROD-S	URAO-S	VOLT-S	WEED-S	WITE-S
TROG-S	UREA-S	VOTE-S	WEEK-S	WITH-S
TRON-S	URGE-S	VRIL-S	WEEL-S	WIVE-S
TROT-S	URVA-S	VROU-S	WEEM-S	WOAD-S
TROW-S	USER-S	VROW-S	WEEN-S	WOCK-S
TROY-S	UVEA-S	VUGG-S	WEEP-S	WOLD-S
TRUE-S	VADE-S	VUGH-S	WEET-S	WOLF-S
TRUG-S	VAIL-S	VULN-S	WEFT-S	WOMB-S
TRYP-S	VAIR-S	WAAC-S	WEID-S	WONK-S
TSAR-S	VALE-S	WACK-S	WEIL-S	WONT-S
TUAN-S	VALI-S	WADD-S	WEIR-S	WOOD-S
TUBA-S	VAMP-S	WADE-S	WEKA-S	WOOF-S
TUBE-S	VANE-S	WADI-S	WELD-S	WOOL-S
TUCK-S	VANG-S	WADT-S	WELK-S	WOON-S
TUFA-S	VANT-S	WAFF-S	WELL-S	WORD-S
TUFF-S	VARA-S	WAFT-S	WELT-S	WORK-S
TUFT-S	VARE-S	WAGE-S	WEMB-S	WORM-S
TULE-S	VASE-S	WAIF-S	WEND-S	WORT-S
TUMP-S	VAST-S	WAIL-S	WENT-S	WRAP-S
TUNA-S	VATU-S	WAIN-S	WERO-S	WREN-S
TUND-S	VAUT-S	WAIR-S	WEST-S	WRIT-S
TUNE-S	VEAL-S	WAIT-S	WETA-S	WUDU-S
TUNG-S	VEEP-S	WAKA-S	WEXE-S	WULL-S
TURD-S	VEER-S	WAKE-S	WHAM-S	WYLE-S
TURF-S	VEGA-S	WAKF-S	WHAP-S	WYND-S
TURK-S	VEGO-S	WALD-S	WHAT-S	WYNN-S
TURM-S	VEIL-S	WALE-S	WHEN-S	WYTE-S
TURN-S	VEIN-S	WALI-S	WHET-S	XYST-S
TUSK-S	VELD-S	WALK-S	WHEW-S	YAAR-S
TUTU-S	VELE-S	WALL-S	WHEY-S	YACK-S
TWAE-S	VELL-S	WAME-S	WHID-S	YAFF-S
TWAL-S	VEND-S	WAND-S	WHIG-S	YAGI-S
TWAT-S	VENT-S	WANE-S	WHIM-S	YALE-S
TWAY-S	VERB-S	WANG-S	WHIN-S	YANG-S
TWIG-S	VERT-S	WANK-S	WHIP-S	YANK-S
TWIN-S	VEST-S	WANT-S	WHIR-S	YAPP-S
TWIT-S	VIAL-S	WAQF-S	WHIT-S	YARD-S
TYEE-S	VIBE-S	WARB-S	WHOP-S	YARK-S
TYER-S	VICE-S	WARD-S	WHUP-S	YARN-S
TYKE-S	VIER-S	WARE-S	WICK-S	YARR-S
TYMP-S	VIEW-S	WARK-S	WIDE-S	YATE-S
TYNE-S	VIGA-S	WARM-S	WIEL-S	YAUD-S
TYPE-S	VILL-S	WARN-S	WIFE-S	YAUP-S
TYPO-S	VINA-S	WARP-S	WILD-S	YAWL-S
TYPP-S	VINE-S	WART-S	WILE-S	YAWN-S
TYRE-S	VINO-S	WASE-S	WILI-S	YAWP-S
TYRO-S	VINT-S	WASM-S	WILL-S	YEAD-S
TZAR-S	VIOL-S	WASP-S	WILT-S	YEAH-S
UDAL-S	VIRE-S	WAST-S	WIMP-S	YEAN-S
UDON-S	VIRL-S	WATT-S	WIND-S	YEAR-S
ULAN-S	VISA-S	WAUK-S	WINE-S	YECH-S
ULNA-S	VISE-S	WAUL-S	WING-S	YEDE-S
ULVA-S	VITA-S	WAUR-S	WINK-S	YEED-S
UMBO-S	VIVA-S	WAVE-S	WINN-S	YEGG-S
UNAI-S	VIVE-S	WAWA-S	WINO-S	YELK-S
UNAU-S	VLEI-S	WAWE-S	WIPE-S	YELL-S
UNCE-S	VOAR-S	WAWL-S	WIRE-S	YELM-S
UNCO-S	VOID-S	WEAL-S	WISE-S	YELP-S
UNIT-S	VOLE-S	WEAN-S	WISP-S	YELT-S

YERD-S	YLKE-S	YOUK-S	ZARF-S	ZING-S
YERK-S	YMPE-S	YOUR-S	ZATI-S	ZITI-S
YESK-S	YOCK-S	YOWE-S	ZEAL-S	ZOBO-S
YEST-S	YODH-S	YOWL-S	ZEBU-S	ZOBU-S
YETI-S	YOGA-S	YUAN-S	ZEIN-S	ZOEA-S
YETT-S	YOGH-S	YUCA-S	ZERK-S	ZONE-S
YEUK-S	YOGI-S	YUCK-S	ZERO-S	ZONK-S
YEVE-S	YOKE-S	YUFT-S	ZEST-S	ZOOM-S
YIKE-S	YOLK-S	YUGA-S	ZETA-S	ZOON-S
YILL-S	YOMP-S	YUKE-S	ZEZE-S	ZORI-S
YIPE-S	YONI-S	YUKO-S	ZIFF-S	ZOUK-S
YIRD-S	YOOF-S	YULE-S	ZILA-S	ZULU-S
YIRK-S	YOOP-S	YUMP-S	ZILL-S	ZUPA-S
YIRR-S	YORE-S	YURT-S	ZIMB-S	ZURF-S
YITE-S	YORK-S	YUZU-S	ZINC-S	ZYME-S
YLEM-S	YORP-S	ZACK-S	ZINE-S	

Five letters to six

AALII-S	ADAGE-S	AGLOO-S	ALGOR-S	AMICE-S
AARTI-S	ADAPT-S	AGOGE-S	ALGUM-S	AMIDE-S
ABACA-S	ADDER-S	AGONE-S	ALIBI-S	AMIGA-S
ABAKA-S	ADDIO-S	AGORA-S	ALIEN-S	AMIGO-S
ABAMP-S	ADDLE-S	AGREE-S	ALIGN-S	AMINE-S
ABAND-S	ADEEM-S	AGRIA-S	ALINE-S	AMMAN-S
ABASE-S	ADEPT-S	AGUTI-S	ALIYA-S	AMMON-S
ABATE-S	ADHAN-S	AHOLD-S	ALKIE-S	AMNIO-S
ABAYA-S	ADIEU-S	AIDER-S	ALKYD-S	AMOLE-S
ABBES-S	ADMIN-S	AIMER-S	ALKYL-S	AMOUR-S
ABBEY-S	ADMIT-S	AINGA-S	ALLAY-S	AMOVE-S
ABBOT-S	ADOBE-S	AIOLI-S	ALLEE-S	AMOWT-S
ABCEE-S	ADOBO-S	AIRER-S	ALLEL-S	AMPUL-S
ABEAR-S	ADOPT-S	AIRTH-S	ALLEY-S	AMRIT-S
ABELE-S	ADORE-S	AISLE-S	ALLOD-S	AMUCK-S
ABHOR-S	ADORN-S	AIVER-S	ALLOT-S	AMUSE-S
ABIDE-S	ADUKI-S	AIZLE-S	ALLOW-S	ANANA-S
ABLET-S	ADULT-S	AJIVA-S	ALLOY-S	ANATA-S
ABMHO-S	ADUST-S	AJUGA-S	ALLYL-S	ANCHO-S
ABODE-S	ADVEW-S	AJWAN-S	ALMAH-S	ANCLE-S
ABOHM-S	AERIE-S	AKELA-S	ALMEH-S	ANDRO-S
ABOMA-S	AFARA-S	AKENE-S	ALMUD-S	ANEAR-S
ABORD-S	AFEAR-S	AKITA-S	ALMUG-S	ANELE-S
ABORT-S	AFRIT-S	ALAAP-S	ALOHA-S	ANGEL-S
ABOUT-S	AFTER-S	ALAMO-S	ALOIN-S	ANGER-S
ABOVE-S	AGAMA-S	ALAND-S	ALPHA-S	ANGLE-S
ABRAY-S	AGAMI-S	ALANG-S	ALTAR-S	ANGLO-S
ABRIN-S	AGAPE-S	ALANT-S	ALTER-S	ANGST-S
ABSEY-S	AGATE-S	ALAPA-S	ALURE-S	ANIMA-S
ABSIT-S	AGAVE-S	ALARM-S	ALWAY-S	ANIME-S
ABUNA-S	AGENE-S	ALATE-S	AMATE-S	ANIMI-S
ABUSE-S	AGENT-S	ALBUM-S	AMAUT-S	ANION-S
ABYSM-S	AGGER-S	ALCID-S	AMAZE-S	ANISE-S
ACCOY-S	AGGIE-S	ALDEA-S	AMBAN-S	ANKER-S
ACKEE-S	AGGRO-S	ALDER-S	AMBER-S	ANKLE-S
ACKER-S	AGILA-S	ALDOL-S	AMBIT-S	ANNAL-S
ACORN-S	AGING-S	ALECK-S	AMBLE-S	ANNAT-S
ACTIN-S	AGISM-S	ALEPH-S	AMEBA-S	ANNOY-S
ACTON-S	AGIST-S	ALERT-S	AMEER-S	ANNUL-S
ACTOR-S	AGITA-S	ALEYE-S	AMEND-S	ANODE-S
ACUTE-S	AGLET-S	ALGIN-S	AMENT-S	ANOLE-S

ANTAR-S	ASANA-S	AZOLE-S	BATON-S	BETEL-S
ANTIC-S	ASCOT-S	AZOTE-S	BATTA-S	BETON-S
ANTRE-S	ASDIC-S	AZOTH-S	BAULK-S	BETTA-S
ANVIL-S	ASHET-S	AZUKI-S	BAVIN-S	BEVEL-S
ANYON-S	ASIDE-S	AZURE-S	BAYLE-S	BEVER-S
AORTA-S	ASKER-S	AZYME-S	BAYOU-S	BEVOR-S
APHID-S	ASPEN-S	BABEL-S	BAZAR-S	BEVUE-S
APIOL-S	ASPER-S	BABKA-S	BAZOO-S	BEWET-S
APISM-S	ASPIC-S	BABOO-S	BEANO-S	BEWIG-S
APNEA-S	ASPRO-S	BABUL-S	BEARD-S	BEZEL-S
APODE-S	ASSAI-S	BACCA-S	BEARE-S	BEZIL-S
APPAL-S	ASSAM-S	BACCO-S	BEAST-S	BHAJI-S
APPAY-S	ASSAY-S	BACHA-S	BEATH-S	BHANG-S
APPEL-S	ASSES-S	BACON-S	BEAUT-S	BHOOT-S
APPLE-S	ASSET-S	BADGE-S	BEBOP-S	BHUNA-S
APPRO-S	ASSOT-S	BAGEL-S	BECAP-S	BIALI-S
APPUI-S	ASTER-S	BAGIE-S	BECKE-S	BIALY-S
APPUY-S	ASTUN-S	BAHUT-S	BEDEL-S	BIBLE-S
APRON-S	ATIGI-S	BAIRN-S	BEDEW-S	BICEP-S
ARABA-S	ATMAN-S	BAIZA-S	BEDIM-S	BIDER-S
ARAME-S	ATOKE-S	BAIZE-S	BEDYE-S	BIDET-S
ARBOR-S	ATOLL-S	BAJAN-S	BEFIT-S	BIDON-S
ARDEB-S	ATONE-S	BAJRA-S	BEFOG-S	BIELD-S
ARDOR-S	ATTAP-S	BAJRI-S	BEGAR-S	BIFFO-S
ARDRI-S	ATTAR-S	BAKER-S	BEGEM-S	BIGHA-S
AREAD-S	ATTIC-S	BAKRA-S	BEGET-S	BIGHT-S
ARECA-S	AUDAD-S	BALER-S	BEGIN-S	BIGOT-S
AREDE-S	AUDIO-S	BALOO-S	BEGUM-S	BIJOU-S
ARENA-S	AUDIT-S	BALSA-S	BEIGE-S	BIKER-S
ARENE-S	AUGER-S	BALTI-S	BEING-S	BIKIE-S
AREPA-S	AUGHT-S	BALUN-S	BEKAH-S	BILBO-S
ARETE-S	AUGUR-S	BAMBI-S	BELAH-S	BILGE-S
ARETT-S	AUMIL-S	BANAK-S	BELAR-S	BIMAH-S
ARGAL-S	AURUM-S	BANCO-S	BELAY-S	BIMBO-S
ARGAN-S	AUXIN-S	BANDA-S	BELEE-S	BINDI-S
ARGIL-S	AVAIL-S	BANDH-S	BELGA-S	BINER-S
ARGLE-S	AVALE-S	BANIA-S	BELIE-S	BINGE-S
ARGOL-S	AVERT-S	BANJO-S	BELLE-S	BINGO-S
ARGON-S	AVIAN-S	BANTU-S	BELON-S	BINIT-S
ARGOT-S	AVION-S	BARBE-S	BELOW-S	BIOME-S
ARGUE-S	AVISE-S	BARCA-S	BEMAD-S	BIONT-S
ARHAT-S	AVISO-S	BARDE-S	BEMUD-S	BIOTA-S
ARIEL-S	AVIZE-S	BARDO-S	BENDY-S	BIPED-S
ARISE-S	AVOID-S	BARGE-S	BENET-S	BIPOD-S
ARMER-S	AVYZE-S	BARON-S	BENNE-S	BIRLE-S
ARMET-S	AWAIT-S	BARRA-S	BENNI-S	BIRSE-S
ARMIL-S	AWAKE-S	BARRE-S	BENTO-S	BIRTH-S
ARMOR-S	AWARD-S	BARYE-S	BEPAT-S	BISON-S
ARNUT-S	AWARN-S	BASAN-S	BERAY-S	BITER-S
AROBA-S	AWETO-S	BASIC-S	BERET-S	BIZZO-S
AROHA-S	AWNER-S	BASIL-S	BERME-S	BLACK-S
AROID-S	AXIOM-S	BASIN-S	BEROB-S	BLADE-S
AROMA-S	AXION-S	BASON-S	BERTH-S	BLAFF-S
ARPEN-S	AXITE-S	BASSE-S	BERYL-S	BLAIN-S
ARRAY-S	AXOID-S	BASSO-S	BESEE-S	BLAME-S
ARRET-S	AXONE-S	BASTE-S	BESET-S	BLAND-S
ARROW-S	AYRIE-S	BASTI-S	BESIT-S	BLANK-S
ARSON-S	AZIDE-S	BASTO-S	BESOM-S	BLARE-S
ARTEL-S	AZINE-S	BATHE-S	BESOT-S	BLART-S
ARTIC-S	AZLON-S	BATIK-S	BESTI-S	BLAST-S

BLATT-S	BONGO-S	BRAZE-S	BUILD-S	CALVE-S
BLAUD-S	BONNE-S	BREAD-S	BUIST-S	CAMAN-S
BLAZE-S	BONZE-S	BREAK-S	BULGE-S	CAMAS-S
BLEAK-S	BOONG-S	BREAM-S	BULSE-S	CAMEL-S
BLEAR-S	BOORD-S	BREDE-S	BUMBO-S	CAMEO-S
BLEAT-S	BOOSE-S	BREED-S	BUMPH-S	CAMPO-S
BLEED-S	BOOST-S	BREER-S	BUNCE-S	CANAL-S
BLEEP-S	BOOTH-S	BREID-S	BUNCO-S	CANEH-S
BLEND-S	BOOZE-S	BRENT-S	BUNDH-S	CANER-S
BLERT-S	BORAK-S	BRERE-S	BUNDT-S	CANID-S
BLIMP-S	BORAL-S	BREVE-S	BUNDU-S	CANNA-S
BLIND-S	BORDE-S	BRIAR-S	BUNIA-S	CANOE-S
BLING-S	BOREE-S	BRIBE-S	BUNJE-S	CANON-S
BLINI-S	BORER-S	BRICK-S	BUNKO-S	CANSO-S
BLINK-S	BORGO-S	BRIDE-S	BUNYA-S	CANTO-S
BLITE-S	BORON-S	BRIEF-S	BURAN-S	CAPER-S
BLOAT-S	BOSOM-S	BRIER-S	BURET-S	CAPLE-S
BLOCK-S	BOSON-S	BRILL-S	BURGH-S	CAPON-S
BLOKE-S	BOSUN-S	BRINE-S	BURIN-S	CAPOT-S
BLOND-S	BOTEL-S	BRING-S	BURKA-S	CAPUL-S
BLOOD-S	BOTTE-S	BRINK-S	BURKE-S	CARAP-S
BLOOM-S	BOUGE-S	BRISE-S	BUROO-S	CARAT-S
BLOOP-S	BOUGH-S	BRISK-S	BURQA-S	CARBO-S
BLORE-S	BOULE-S	BRITH-S	BURRO-S	CARDI-S
BLUDE-S	BOULT-S	BRITT-S	BURSA-S	CARER-S
BLUET-S	BOUND-S	BRIZE-S	BURSE-S	CARES-S
BLUEY-S	BOURD-S	BROAD-S	BURST-S	CARET-S
BLUFF-S	BOURG-S	BROCH-S	BUSSU-S	CARGO-S
BLUID-S	BOURN-S	BROCK-S	BUSTI-S	CARLE-S
BLUME-S	BOUSE-S	BROGH-S	BUTEO-S	CAROB-S
BLUNK-S	BOVID-S	BROIL-S	BUTLE-S	CAROL-S
BLUNT-S	BOWAT-S	BROKE-S	BUTTE-S	CAROM-S
BLURB-S	BOWEL-S	BROME-S	BUTUT-S	CARSE-S
BLURT-S	BOWER-S	BROMO-S	BUTYL-S	CARTA-S
BLYPE-S	BOWET-S	BRONC-S	BUYER-S	CARTE-S
BOARD-S	BOWNE-S	BROND-S	BWANA-S	CARVE-S
BOART-S	BOWSE-S	BROOD-S	BWAZI-S	CASCO-S
BOAST-S	BOXER-S	BROOK-S	BYLAW-S	CASTE-S
BOBAC-S	BOYAR-S	BROOL-S	BYWAY-S	CATER-S
BOBAK-S	BOYLA-S	BROOM-S	CABAL-S	CAULD-S
BOBOL-S	BRAAI-S	BROSE-S	CABER-S	CAULK-S
BOCCA-S	BRACE-S	BROTH-S	CABIN-S	CAUSE-S
BOCCE-S	BRACH-S	BROWN-S	CABLE-S	CAVAS-S
BOCCI-S	BRACK-S	BRUGH-S	CABOB-S	CAVEL-S
BOCHE-S	BRACT-S	BRUIN-S	CABOC-S	CAVER-S
BODGE-S	BRAID-S	BRUIT-S	CACAO-S	CAVIE-S
BODLE-S	BRAIL-S	BRULE-S	CACHE-S	CAVIL-S
BOFFO-S	BRAIN-S	BRUME-S	CADEE-S	CAXON-S
BOGAN-S	BRAKE-S	BRUNT-S	CADET-S	CEASE-S
BOGEY-S	BRAME-S	BRUST-S	CADGE-S	CEAZE-S
BOGIE-S	BRAND-S	BRUTE-S	CADIE-S	CEBID-S
BOGLE-S	BRANK-S	BUAZE-S	CADRE-S	CEDAR-S
BOHEA-S	BRANT-S	BUBAL-S	CAGER-S	CEDER-S
BOING-S	BRAST-S	BUBBA-S	CAGOT-S	CEIBA-S
BOINK-S	BRAVA-S	BUCHU-S	CAHOW-S	CEILI-S
BOITE-S	BRAVE-S	BUCKO-S	CAIRD-S	CELEB-S
BOMBE-S	BRAVO-S	BUCKU-S	CAIRN-S	CELLO-S
BOMBO-S	BRAWL-S	BUDGE-S	CALIF-S	CELOM-S
BONCE-S	BRAWN-S	BUFFO-S	CALLA-S	CENSE-S
BONER-S	BRAZA-S	BUGLE-S	CALPA-S	CENTO-S

CEORL-S	CHINA-S	CLAMP-S	COATE-S	COPER-S
CERCI-S	CHINE-S	CLANG-S	COATI-S	COPRA-S
CERGE-S	CHINK-S	CLANK-S	COBIA-S	COPSE-S
CERIA-S	CHINO-S	CLARO-S	COBLE-S	CORAL-S
CERNE-S	CHIRK-S	CLART-S	COBRA-S	CORBE-S
CESSE-S	CHIRL-S	CLASP-S	COBZA-S	CORER-S
CESTA-S	CHIRM-S	CLAST-S	COCCO-S	COREY-S
CETYL-S	CHIRO-S	CLAUT-S	COCOA-S	CORGI-S
CHACE-S	CHIRP-S	CLAVE-S	CODEC-S	CORNU-S
CHACK-S	CHIRR-S	CLAVI-S	CODEN-S	CORSE-S
CHACO-S	CHIRT-S	CLEAN-S	CODER-S	CORSO-S
CHADO-S	CHIRU-S	CLEAR-S	CODON-S	COSEC-S
CHAFE-S	CHIVE-S	CLEAT-S	COGIE-S	COSET-S
CHAFF-S	CHOCK-S	CLECK-S	COGON-S	COSEY-S
CHAFT-S	CHOCO-S	CLEEK-S	COGUE-S	COSIE-S
CHAIN-S	CHOIR-S	CLEEP-S	COHAB-S	COSTE-S
CHAIR-S	CHOKE-S	CLEFT-S	COHOE-S	COTAN-S
CHALK-S	CHOKO-S	CLEIK-S	COHOG-S	COTTA-S
CHAMP-S	CHOLA-S	CLEPE-S	COIGN-S	COUGH-S
CHANG-S	CHOLI-S	CLERK-S	COLBY-S	COUNT-S
CHANK-S	CHOLO-S	CLEVE-S	COLEY-S	COUPE-S
CHANT-S	CHOMA-S	CLICK-S	COLIC-S	COURB-S
CHAPE-S	CHOMP-S	CLIFF-S	COLIN-S	COURE-S
CHARA-S	CHOOF-S	CLIFT-S	COLOG-S	COURT-S
CHARD-S	CHOOK-S	CLIMB-S	COLON-S	COUTH-S
CHARE-S	CHOOM-S	CLIME-S	COLOR-S	COVEN-S
CHARK-S	CHORD-S	CLINE-S	COLZA-S	COVER-S
CHARM-S	CHORE-S	CLING-S	COMBE-S	COVET-S
CHARR-S	CHOSE-S	CLINK-S	COMBI-S	COVEY-S
CHART-S	CHOTT-S	CLINT-S	COMBO-S	COVIN-S
CHASE-S	CHOUT-S	CLIPE-S	COMER-S	COWAL-S
CHASM-S	CHOWK-S	CLOAK-S	COMET-S	COWAN-S
CHAWK-S	CHUCK-S	CLOAM-S	COMIC-S	COWER-S
CHAYA-S	CHUFA-S	CLOCK-S	COMMA-S	COYPU-S
CHEAP-S	CHUFF-S	CLOFF-S	COMMO-S	COZEN-S
CHEAT-S	CHUMP-S	CLOKE-S	COMPO-S	COZEY-S
CHECK-S	CHUNK-S	CLOMP-S	COMPT-S	COZIE-S
CHEEK-S	CHURL-S	CLONE-S	COMTE-S	CRAAL-S
CHEEP-S	CHURN-S	CLONK-S	CONCH-S	CRACK-S
CHEER-S	CHURR-S	CLOOP-S	CONDO-S	CRAFT-S
CHEKA-S	CHUSE-S	CLOOT-S	CONEY-S	CRAIC-S
CHELA-S	CHUTE-S	CLOSE-S	CONGA-S	CRAIG-S
CHELP-S	CHYLE-S	CLOTE-S	CONGE-S	CRAKE-S
CHEMO-S	CHYME-S	CLOTH-S	CONGO-S	CRAME-S
CHERT-S	CIBOL-S	CLOUD-S	CONIA-S	CRAMP-S
CHEST-S	CIDER-S	CLOUR-S	CONIC-S	CRANE-S
CHETH-S	CIGAR-S	CLOUT-S	CONIN-S	CRANK-S
CHICA-S	CIMAR-S	CLOVE-S	CONNE-S	CRAPE-S
CHICK-S	CISCO-S	CLOYE-S	CONTE-S	CRARE-S
CHICO-S	CITAL-S	CLOZE-S	CONTO-S	CRATE-S
CHIDE-S	CITER-S	CLUCK-S	CONVO-S	CRAVE-S
CHIEF-S	CITES-S	CLUMP-S	COOEE-S	CRAWL-S
CHIEL-S	CIVET-S	CLUNK-S	COOER-S	CRAZE-S
CHILD-S	CIVIC-S	CLYPE-S	COOEY-S	CREAK-S
CHILE-S	CIVIE-S	COACT-S	COOMB-S	CREAM-S
CHILI-S	CLACH-S	COALA-S	COOPT-S	CREDO-S
CHILL-S	CLACK-S	COAPT-S	COOZE-S	CREED-S
CHIMB-S	CLADE-S	COARB-S	COPAL-S	CREEK-S
CHIME-S	CLAIM-S	COAST-S	COPAY-S	CREEL-S
CHIMP-S	CLAME-S		COPEN-S	CREEP-S

CREME-S	CUSEC-S	DECAD-S	DIGHT-S	DOUAR-S
CRENA-S	CUSSO-S	DECAF-S	DIGIT-S	DOUBT-S
CREPE-S	CUTEY-S	DECAL-S	DIKER-S	DOUGH-S
CREST-S	CUTIE-S	DECAY-S	DILDO-S	DOULA-S
CREWE-S	CUTIN-S	DECKO-S	DILLI-S	DOUMA-S
CRICK-S	CUTUP-S	DECOR-S	DIMER-S	DOURA-S
CRIER-S	CUVEE-S	DECOY-S	DINAR-S	DOUSE-S
CRIME-S	CYCAD-S	DEEVE-S	DINER-S	DOVEN-S
CRIMP-S	CYCLE-S	DEFAT-S	DINGE-S	DOVER-S
CRINE-S	CYCLO-S	DEFER-S	DINIC-S	DOWAR-S
CRIPE-S	CYDER-S	DEFOG-S	DIODE-S	DOWEL-S
CRISE-S	CYMAR-S	DEGUM-S	DIOTA-S	DOWER-S
CRISP-S	CYMOL-S	DEICE-S	DIPSO-S	DOWLE-S
CRITH-S	CYNIC-S	DEIGN-S	DIRAM-S	DOWSE-S
CROAK-S	CYTON-S	DEISM-S	DIRGE-S	DOXIE-S
CROCK-S	DABBA-S	DEIST-S	DIRKE-S	DOYEN-S
CROFT-S	DACHA-S	DEKKO-S	DISCO-S	DOZEN-S
CROMB-S	DADAH-S	DELAY-S	DISME-S	DOZER-S
CROME-S	DAGGA-S	DELFT-S	DITAL-S	DRAFF-S
CRONE-S	DAINE-S	DELPH-S	DITTO-S	DRAFT-S
CROOK-S	DAKER-S	DELTA-S	DIVAN-S	DRAIL-S
CROOL-S	DALED-S	DELVE-S	DIVER-S	DRAIN-S
CROON-S	DALLE-S	DEMAN-S	DIVOT-S	DRAKE-S
CRORE-S	DAMAN-S	DEMIT-S	DIWAN-S	DRAMA-S
CROUP-S	DAMAR-S	DEMOB-S	DIXIE-S	DRANT-S
CROUT-S	DANCE-S	DEMON-S	DIXIT-S	DRAPE-S
CROWD-S	DANIO-S	DEMUR-S	DIZEN-S	DRAWL-S
CROWN-S	DARAF-S	DENAR-S	DJINN-S	DREAD-S
CROZE-S	DARCY-S	DENAY-S	DOBIE-S	DREAM-S
CRUCK-S	DARER-S	DENET-S	DOBLA-S	DREAR-S
CRUDE-S	DARGA-S	DENIM-S	DOBRA-S	DRECK-S
CRUEL-S	DARIC-S	DEPOT-S	DOBRO-S	DRERE-S
CRUET-S	DARRE-S	DEPTH-S	DODGE-S	DRICE-S
CRUMB-S	DARZI-S	DERAT-S	DOGEY-S	DRIER-S
CRUMP-S	DASHI-S	DERAY-S	DOGIE-S	DRIFT-S
CRUOR-S	DATAL-S	DERIG-S	DOGMA-S	DRILL-S
CRUSE-S	DATER-S	DERMA-S	DOHYO-S	DRINK-S
CRUST-S	DATTO-S	DERRO-S	DOING-S	DRIVE-S
CRUVE-S	DATUM-S	DERTH-S	DOLCE-S	DROID-S
CRWTH-S	DAUBE-S	DESSE-S	DOLMA-S	DROIL-S
CRYPT-S	DAULT-S	DETER-S	DOLOR-S	DROIT-S
CTENE-S	DAUNT-S	DEUCE-S	DONAH-S	DROLE-S
CUBEB-S	DAVEN-S	DEVEL-S	DONEE-S	DROLL-S
CUBER-S	DAVIT-S	DEVIL-S	DONGA-S	DROME-S
CUBIC-S	DAWAH-S	DEVON-S	DONKO-S	DRONE-S
CUBIT-S	DAYAN-S	DEVOT-S	DONNA-S	DROOB-S
CULET-S	DAZER-S	DEWAN-S	DONNE-S	DROOG-S
CUMEC-S	DEAIR-S	DEWAR-S	DONOR-S	DROOK-S
CUMIN-S	DEARE-S	DEXIE-S	DONUT-S	DROOL-S
CUPEL-S	DEARN-S	DHOBI-S	DOOLE-S	DROOP-S
CUPID-S	DEATH-S	DHOLE-S	DOONA-S	DROUK-S
CUPPA-S	DEAVE-S	DHOLL-S	DOORN-S	DROVE-S
CURAT-S	DEBAG-S	DHOTI-S	DOPER-S	DROWN-S
CURER-S	DEBAR-S	DHUTI-S	DORAD-S	DRUID-S
CURET-S	DEBEL-S	DIAZO-S	DORBA-S	DRUNK-S
CURIA-S	DEBIT-S	DICER-S	DOREE-S	DRUPE-S
CURIE-S	DEBUD-S	DICHT-S	DORSE-S	DRUSE-S
CURIO-S	DEBUG-S	DICOT-S	DOSEH-S	DRYAD-S
CURSE-S	DEBUT-S	DIDIE-S	DOSER-S	DRYER-S
CURVE-S	DEBYE-S	DIENE-S	DOTER-S	DSOBO-S

DSOMO-S	ELAIN-S	ENVOI-S	EXEAT-S	FEINT-S
DUBBO-S	ELAND-S	ENVOY-S	EXEEM-S	FEIST-S
DUCAT-S	ELATE-S	ENZYM-S	EXEME-S	FELID-S
DUETT-S	ELBOW-S	EOSIN-S	EXERT-S	FELLA-S
DUKKA-S	ELCHI-S	EPACT-S	EXILE-S	FELON-S
DULIA-S	ELDER-S	EPHAH-S	EXINE-S	FEMAL-S
DULSE-S	ELDIN-S	EPHOD-S	EXIST-S	FEMME-S
DUMBO-S	ELECT-S	EPHOR-S	EXODE-S	FEMUR-S
DUNAM-S	ELEMI-S	EPOCH-S	EXPAT-S	FENCE-S
DUNCE-S	ELFIN-S	EPODE-S	EXPEL-S	FEOFF-S
DUOMO-S	ELIAD-S	EPOPT-S	EXTOL-S	FERAL-S
DUPER-S	ELIDE-S	EPROM-S	EXTRA-S	FERIA-S
DURAL-S	ELINT-S	EQUAL-S	EXUDE-S	FERMI-S
DURES-S	ELITE-S	EQUID-S	EXULT-S	FESSE-S
DUROC-S	ELOGE-S	EQUIP-S	EXURB-S	FESTA-S
DUROY-S	ELOIN-S	ERASE-S	EYRIE-S	FETOR-S
DURRA-S	ELOPE-S	ERBIA-S	FABLE-S	FETTA-S
DURUM-S	ELPEE-S	ERECT-S	FACER-S	FETWA-S
DURZI-S	ELSIN-S	ERGON-S	FACET-S	FEUAR-S
DUVET-S	ELUDE-S	ERGOT-S	FACIA-S	FEVER-S
DWAAL-S	ELUTE-S	ERICA-S	FADER-S	FIBER-S
DWALE-S	ELVAN-S	ERICK-S	FADGE-S	FIBRE-S
DWALM-S	ELVER-S	ERODE-S	FAENA-S	FIBRO-S
DWANG-S	EMAIL-S	EROSE-S	FAGIN-S	FICHE-S
DWARF-S	EMBAR-S	ERROR-S	FAGOT-S	FICHU-S
DWAUM-S	EMBAY-S	ERUCT-S	FAINE-S	FICIN-S
DWEEB-S	EMBED-S	ERUGO-S	FAINT-S	FIDGE-S
DWELL-S	EMBER-S	ERUPT-S	FAITH-S	FIELD-S
DWILE-S	EMBOG-S	ERVIL-S	FAKER-S	FIEND-S
DWINE-S	EMBOW-S	ESCAR-S	FAKIR-S	FIENT-S
DYING-S	EMCEE-S	ESCOT-S	FALSE-S	FIERE-S
DYNEL-S	EMEER-S	ESILE-S	FANAL-S	FIFER-S
EAGER-S	EMEND-S	ESKAR-S	FANGA-S	FIFTH-S
EAGLE-S	EMMER-S	ESKER-S	FANGO-S	FIGHT-S
EAGRE-S	EMMET-S	ESSAY-S	FANON-S	FILER-S
EARTH-S	EMMEW-S	ESTER-S	FANUM-S	FILET-S
EASEL-S	EMOTE-S	ESTOC-S	FAQIR-S	FILLE-S
EASER-S	EMOVE-S	ESTOP-S	FARAD-S	FILLO-S
EASLE-S	EMULE-S	ESTRO-S	FARCE-S	FILMI-S
EATER-S	EMURE-S	ETAGE-S	FARER-S	FILTH-S
EBBET-S	EMYDE-S	ETAPE-S	FARLE-S	FINAL-S
EBOOK-S	ENACT-S	ETHAL-S	FARSE-S	FINCA-S
ECLAT-S	ENARM-S	ETHER-S	FASCI-S	FINER-S
EDEMA-S	ENATE-S	ETHIC-S	FATSO-S	FIORD-S
EDGER-S	ENDER-S	ETHYL-S	FATWA-S	FIQUE-S
EDICT-S	ENDEW-S	ETTIN-S	FAULD-S	FIRER-S
EDILE-S	ENDOW-S	ETTLE-S	FAULT-S	FIRIE-S
EDUCE-S	ENDUE-S	ETUDE-S	FAUNA-S	FIRST-S
EDUCT-S	ENEMA-S	ETWEE-S	FAUVE-S	FIRTH-S
EEJIT-S	ENIAC-S	EUPAD-S	FAVOR-S	FITNA-S
EEVEN-S	ENJOY-S	EUSOL-S	FAYNE-S	FITTE-S
EGEST-S	ENMEW-S	EVADE-S	FAYRE-S	FIVER-S
EGGAR-S	ENNOG-S	EVENT-S	FEARE-S	FIXER-S
EGGER-S	ENNUI-S	EVERT-S	FEASE-S	FJELD-S
EGRET-S	ENOKI-S	EVICT-S	FEAST-S	FJORD-S
EIDER-S	ENROL-S	EVITE-S	FEAZE-S	FLACK-S
EIGHT-S	ENSEW-S	EVOKE-S	FECHT-S	FLAFF-S
EIKON-S	ENSUE-S	EXACT-S	FEESE-S	FLAIL-S
EISEL-S	ENTER-S	EXALT-S	FEEZE-S	FLAIR-S
EJECT-S	ENURE-S	EXCEL-S	FEIGN-S	FLAKE-S

FLAME-S	FORTE-S	FURAN-S	GEBUR-S	GLEDE-S
FLAMM-S	FORUM-S	FUROL-S	GECKO-S	GLEED-S
FLANK-S	FORZA-S	FUROR-S	GEEST-S	GLEEK-S
FLARE-S	FOSSA-S	FURZE-S	GEIST-S	GLEET-S
FLASK-S	FOSSE-S	FUSEE-S	GELEE-S	GLENT-S
FLAWN-S	FOUAT-S	FUSEL-S	GEMEL-S	GLIDE-S
FLEAM-S	FOUET-S	FUSIL-S	GEMOT-S	GLIFF-S
FLECK-S	FOULE-S	FUTON-S	GENET-S	GLIFT-S
FLEER-S	FOUND-S	FUZEE-S	GENIE-S	GLIKE-S
FLEET-S	FOUNT-S	FUZIL-S	GENIP-S	GLIME-S
FLEME-S	FOUTH-S	FYTTE-S	GENOA-S	GLINT-S
FLEXO-S	FOVEA-S	GABLE-S	GENOM-S	GLISK-S
FLICK-S	FOWTH-S	GADDI-S	GENRE-S	GLOAM-S
FLIER-S	FOXIE-S	GADGE-S	GENRO-S	GLOAT-S
FLIMP-S	FOYER-S	GADID-S	GEODE-S	GLOBE-S
FLING-S	FOYLE-S	GADJE-S	GEOID-S	GLOGG-S
FLINT-S	FOYNE-S	GADSO-S	GERAH-S	GLOOM-S
FLIRT-S	FRACT-S	GAFFE-S	GERBE-S	GLOOP-S
FLISK-S	FRAIL-S	GAGER-S	GERLE-S	GLOST-S
FLITE-S	FRAIM-S	GAITT-S	GERNE-S	GLOUT-S
FLOAT-S	FRAME-S	GALAH-S	GESSE-S	GLOVE-S
FLOCK-S	FRANC-S	GALEA-S	GESTE-S	GLOZE-S
FLONG-S	FRANK-S	GALOP-S	GETUP-S	GLUER-S
FLOOD-S	FRAUD-S	GALUT-S	GHAST-S	GLUME-S
FLOOR-S	FREAK-S	GALVO-S	GHAUT-S	GLUON-S
FLORA-S	FREER-S	GAMAY-S	GHAZI-S	GLUTE-S
FLOTA-S	FREET-S	GAMBA-S	GHOST-S	GLYPH-S
FLOTE-S	FREIT-S	GAMBE-S	GHOUL-S	GNARL-S
FLOUR-S	FREMD-S	GAMBO-S	GHYLL-S	GNARR-S
FLOUT-S	FREON-S	GAMER-S	GIANT-S	GNOME-S
FLUFF-S	FRERE-S	GAMIN-S	GIBEL-S	GOBAN-S
FLUID-S	FRIAR-S	GAMMA-S	GIBER-S	GODET-S
FLUKE-S	FRIER-S	GAMME-S	GIBLI-S	GODSO-S
FLUME-S	FRILL-S	GAMUT-S	GIGOT-S	GOFER-S
FLUMP-S	FRISE-S	GANEF-S	GIGUE-S	GOGGA-S
FLUNK-S	FRISK-S	GANEV-S	GILET-S	GOING-S
FLUOR-S	FRIST-S	GANJA-S	GIMEL-S	GOLEM-S
FLURR-S	FRITH-S	GANOF-S	GIMME-S	GOLPE-S
FLUTE-S	FRITT-S	GAPER-S	GINGE-S	GOMBO-S
FLUYT-S	FRIZE-S	GARBE-S	GIPON-S	GOMER-S
FLYBY-S	FROCK-S	GARBO-S	GIPPO-S	GOMPA-S
FLYER-S	FROND-S	GARRE-S	GIRON-S	GONAD-S
FLYPE-S	FRONT-S	GARTH-S	GIRTH-S	GONEF-S
FLYTE-S	FROST-S	GARUM-S	GISMO-S	GONER-S
FOEHN-S	FROTH-S	GATER-S	GIUST-S	GONIF-S
FOGEY-S	FROWN-S	GATOR-S	GIVEN-S	GONOF-S
FOGIE-S	FRUIT-S	GAUGE-S	GIVER-S	GOOLD-S
FOGLE-S	FRUMP-S	GAUJE-S	GIZMO-S	GOOSE-S
FOIST-S	FRUST-S	GAULT-S	GLACE-S	GOPAK-S
FOLEY-S	FRYER-S	GAUNT-S	GLADE-S	GORAL-S ⟩
FOLIE-S	FUDGE-S	GAUZE-S	GLAIK-S	GORGE-S
FOLIO-S	FUERO-S	GAVEL-S	GLAIR-S	GORSE-S
FONDA-S	FUGIE-S	GAVOT-S	GLAND-S	GOSHT-S
FONDU-S	FUGIO-S	GAYAL-S	GLARE-S	GOSSE-S
FORAM-S	FUGLE-S	GAZAL-S	GLAUM-S	GOUGE-S
FORAY-S	FUGUE-S	GAZAR-S	GLAUR-S	GOURA-S
FORCE-S	FUMER-S	GAZER-S	GLAZE-S	GOURD-S
FOREL-S	FUMET-S	GAZON-S	GLEAM-S	GOWAN-S
FORGE-S	FUNDI-S	GAZOO-S	GLEAN-S	GRAAL-S
FORME-S	FURAL-S	GEARE-S	GLEBE-S	GRACE-S

GRADE-S	GRUNT-S	HANAP-S	HEXYL-S	HOVEL-S
GRAFF-S	GRYCE-S	HANCE-S	HIDER-S	HOVER-S
GRAFT-S	GRYDE-S	HANGI-S	HIGHT-S	HOWFF-S
GRAIL-S	GRYKE-S	HANSA-S	HIJAB-S	HOWRE-S
GRAIN-S	GRYPE-S	HANSE-S	HIJRA-S	HOYLE-S
GRAIP-S	GUACO-S	HAOLE-S	HIKER-S	HUDNA-S
GRAMA-S	GUANA-S	HAOMA-S	HIKOI-S	HUDUD-S
GRAME-S	GUANO-S	HARAM-S	HILLO-S	HULLO-S
GRAMP-S	GUARD-S	HAREM-S	HIMBO-S	HUMAN-S
GRAND-S	GUAVA-S	HARIM-S	HINGE-S	HUMOR-S
GRANT-S	GUEST-S	HASTE-S	HIPPO-S	HUMPH-S
GRAPE-S	GUIDE-S	HATER-S	HIREE-S	HURRA-S
GRAPH-S	GUILD-S	HAUGH-S	HIRER-S	HURST-S
GRASP-S	GUILE-S	HAULD-S	HITHE-S	HUTIA-S
GRATE-S	GUILT-S	HAULM-S	HIVER-S	HUZZA-S
GRAVE-S	GUIMP-S	HAUNT-S	HIZEN-S	HYDRA-S
GRAZE-S	GUIRO-S	HAUSE-S	HOARD-S	HYDRO-S
GREAT-S	GUISE-S	HAVEN-S	HOAST-S	HYENA-S
GREBE-S	GULAG-S	HAVER-S	HODAD-S	HYLEG-S
GRECE-S	GULPH-S	HAVOC-S	HODJA-S	HYMEN-S
GREED-S	GUMBO-S	HAWSE-S	HOGAN-S	HYNDE-S
GREEN-S	GUMMA-S	HAYER-S	HOGEN-S	HYOID-S
GREET-S	GUNGE-S	HAYLE-S	HOICK-S	HYPER-S
GREGO-S	GURGE-S	HAZAN-S	HOISE-S	HYSON-S
GREIN-S	GUSLA-S	HAZEL-S	HOIST-S	HYTHE-S
GRESE-S	GUSLE-S	HAZER-S	HOKUM-S	ICHOR-S
GREVE-S	GUSLI-S	HEALD-S	HOLLA-S	ICING-S
GRICE-S	GUSTO-S	HEARD-S	HOLLO-S	ICKER-S
GRIDE-S	GUTTA-S	HEARE-S	HOLON-S	IDANT-S
GRIEF-S	GUYLE-S	HEART-S	HOMER-S	IDEAL-S
GRIFF-S	GUYOT-S	HEAST-S	HOMEY-S	IDENT-S
GRIFT-S	GUYSE-S	HEATH-S	HOMIE-S	IDIOM-S
GRIKE-S	GYELD-S	HEAVE-S	HOMME-S	IDIOT-S
GRIME-S	GYNAE-S	HEBEN-S	HONAN-S	IDLER-S
GRIND-S	GYNIE-S	HECHT-S	HONDA-S	IDYLL-S
GRIOT-S	GYOZA-S	HEDER-S	HONER-S	IFTAR-S
GRIPE-S	GYPPO-S	HEDGE-S	HONEY-S	IGAPO-S
GRISE-S	GYRON-S	HEEZE-S	HONGI-S	IGLOO-S
GRIST-S	HABIT-S	HEIST-S	HONOR-S	IHRAM-S
GRITH-S	HACEK-S	HEJAB-S	HOOEY-S	ILIAD-S
GRIZE-S	HADJI-S	HEJRA-S	HOOKA-S	ILLTH-S
GROAN-S	HAICK-S	HELIO-S	HOORD-S	IMAGE-S
GROAT-S	HAIKU-S	HELLO-S	HOOVE-S	IMAGO-S
GROIN-S	HAINT-S	HELOT-S	HOPER-S	IMARI-S
GROMA-S	HAJJI-S	HELVE-S	HORAH-S	IMAUM-S
GRONE-S	HAKAM-S	HEMIN-S	HORDE-S	IMBAR-S
GROOF-S	HAKEA-S	HENGE-S	HORME-S	IMBED-S
GROOM-S	HAKIM-S	HENNA-S	HORSE-S	IMBUE-S
GROPE-S	HALAL-S	HENRY-S	HORST-S	IMIDE-S
GROUF-S	HALER-S	HEPAR-S	HOSEL-S	IMINE-S
GROUP-S	HALFA-S	HEROE-S	HOSER-S	IMMEW-S
GROUT-S	HALID-S	HERON-S	HOSEY-S	IMMIT-S
GROVE-S	HALLO-S	HERSE-S	HOSTA-S	IMPEL-S
GROWL-S	HALMA-S	HERYE-S	HOTEL-S	IMPOT-S
GRUEL-S	HALON-S	HEUCH-S	HOUFF-S	INANE-S
GRUFE-S	HALSE-S	HEUGH-S	HOUGH-S	INARM-S
GRUFF-S	HALVA-S	HEVEA-S	HOUND-S	INCLE-S
GRUME-S	HALVE-S	HEWER-S	HOURI-S	INCOG-S
GRUMP-S	HAMAL-S	HEXAD-S	HOUSE-S	INCUR-S
	HAMZA-S	HEXER-S	HOVEA-S	INDEW-S

INDIE-S	JAUNT-S	KAMIK-S	KIGHT-S	KRILL-S
INDOL-S	JAVEL-S	KANEH-S	KIKOI-S	KROON-S
INDOW-S	JAWAN-S	KANGA-S	KILEY-S	KRUBI-S
INDRI-S	JAXIE-S	KANJI-S	KILIM-S	KUDZU-S
INDUE-S	JEBEL-S	KANZU-S	KIMBO-S	KUGEL-S
INERT-S	JEHAD-S	KAPOK-S	KININ-S	KUKRI-S
INFER-S	JELAB-S	KAPPA-S	KIOSK-S	KULAK-S
INGAN-S	JELLO-S	KARAT-S	KIPPA-S	KULAN-S
INGLE-S	JEMBE-S	KARMA-S	KIRRI-S	KULFI-S
INGOT-S	JERID-S	KAROO-S	KISAN-S	KURRE-S
INION-S	JESSE-S	KARRI-S	KITER-S	KURTA-S
INKER-S	JETON-S	KARST-S	KITHE-S	KUSSO-S
INKLE-S	JEWEL-S	KASHA-S	KLANG-S	KVELL-S
INLAY-S	JEWIE-S	KATTI-S	KLICK-S	KWELA-S
INLET-S	JHALA-S	KAUGH-S	KLONG-S	KYACK-S
INNER-S	JIBER-S	KAURI-S	KLOOF-S	KYANG-S
INORB-S	JIGOT-S	KAVAS-S	KLUGE-S	KYLIE-S
INPUT-S	JIHAD-S	KAYAK-S	KNACK-S	KYLIN-S
INRUN-S	JINNI-S	KAYLE-S	KNARL-S	KYLOE-S
INSET-S	JIRGA-S	KAZOO-S	KNAUR-S	KYNDE-S
INTEL-S	JIVER-S	KEBAB-S	KNAVE-S	KYRIE-S
INTER-S	JNANA-S	KEBAR-S	KNAWE-S	KYTHE-S
INTRO-S	JOCKO-S	KEBOB-S	KNEAD-S	LAARI-S
INULA-S	JODEL-S	KEDGE-S	KNEEL-S	LABDA-S
INURE-S	JOINT-S	KEENO-S	KNELL-S	LABEL-S
INURN-S	JOIST-S	KEEVE-S	KNIFE-S	LABOR-S
INVAR-S	JOKER-S	KEFIR-S	KNIVE-S	LACER-S
INWIT-S	JORAM-S	KEHUA-S	KNOCK-S	LACET-S
IODID-S	JORUM-S	KELEP-S	KNOLL-S	LADEN-S
IODIN-S	JOTUN-S	KELIM-S	KNOSP-S	LADER-S
IONIC-S	JOUAL-S	KEMBO-S	KNOUT-S	LADLE-S
IPPON-S	JOULE-S	KENAF-S	KNOWE-S	LAGAN-S
IRADE-S	JOUST-S	KENDO-S	KNOWN-S	LAGER-S
IROKO-S	JOWAR-S	KENTE-S	KNURL-S	LAHAR-S
IRONE-S	JUDGE-S	KEREL-S	KNURR-S	LAICH-S
ISLET-S	JUGAL-S	KERMA-S	KOALA-S	LAIGH-S
ISSEI-S	JUGUM-S	KERNE-S	KOBAN-S	LAIKA-S
ISSUE-S	JUICE-S	KERVE-S	KOFTA-S	LAIRD-S
ISTLE-S	JULEP-S	KESAR-S	KOINE-S	LAKER-S
IXORA-S	JUMAR-S	KETOL-S	KOKER-S	LAKIN-S
IXTLE-S	JUMBO-S	KEVEL-S	KOKRA-S	LAKSA-S
IZARD-S	JUNCO-S	KEVIL-S	KOKUM-S	LAMED-S
IZZAT-S	JUNTA-S	KHADI-S	KOMBU-S	LAMIA-S
JABOT-S	JUNTO-S	KHAKI-S	KONBU-S	LANAI-S
JACAL-S	JUPON-S	KHAPH-S	KONDO-S	LANCE-S
JAGER-S	JURAT-S	KHAYA-S	KOORI-S	LANDE-S
JAGIR-S	JUREL-S	KHAZI-S	KOPEK-S	LAPEL-S
JAGRA-S	JUROR-S	KHEDA-S	KOPJE-S	LAPIN-S
JAKEY-S	KAAMA-S	KHETH-S	KOPPA-S	LAPJE-S
JALAP-S	KABAB-S	KHOJA-S	KORAT-S	LAPSE-S
JALOP-S	KABAR-S	KHOUM-S	KORMA-S	LAREE-S
JAMBE-S	KABOB-S	KIAAT-S	KOTOW-S	LARGE-S
JAMBO-S	KACHA-S	KIANG-S	KRAAL-S	LARGO-S
JAMBU-S	KAFIR-S	KIBBE-S	KRAFT-S	LARUM-S
JAPAN-S	KAHAL-S	KIBBI-S	KRAIT-S	LARVA-S
JAPER-S	KAIAK-S	KIBEI-S	KRANG-S	LASER-S
JARTA-S	KAIKA-S	KIBLA-S	KRAUT-S	LASSI-S
JARUL-S	KALAM-S	KIDDO-S	KREEP-S	LASSO-S
JASEY-S	KALIF-S	KIDEL-S	KRENG-S	LASSU-S
JASPE-S	KALPA-S	KIEVE-S	KREWE-S	LATAH-S

LATEN-S	LIDAR-S	LORAN-S	MAFIA-S	MATER-S
LATHE-S	LIEGE-S	LOREL-S	MAFIC-S	MATEY-S
LATHI-S	LIFER-S	LORIC-S	MAGIC-S	MATIN-S
LATKE-S	LIGAN-S	LOSEL-S	MAGMA-S	MATLO-S
LATTE-S	LIGER-S	LOSER-S	MAGOT-S	MATTE-S
LAUAN-S	LIGGE-S	LOTAH-S	MAHOE-S	MATZA-S
LAUCH-S	LIGHT-S	LOTTE-S	MAHUA-S	MATZO-S
LAUGH-S	LIGNE-S	LOTTO-S	MAHWA-S	MAUND-S
LAUND-S	LIKEN-S	LOUGH-S	MAIKO-S	MAURI-S
LAURA-S	LIKER-S	LOUIE-S	MAILE-S	MAUVE-S
LAVER-S	LIKIN-S	LOUMA-S	MAILL-S	MAVEN-S
LAVRA-S	LILAC-S	LOUND-S	MAIRE-S	MAVIE-S
LAWIN-S	LIMAN-S	LOUPE-S	MAISE-S	MAVIN-S
LAYER-S	LIMBA-S	LOURE-S	MAIST-S	MAXIM-S
LAYIN-S	LIMBO-S	LOUSE-S	MAIZE-S	MAYBE-S
LAYUP-S	LIMEN-S	LOVAT-S	MAJOR-S	MAYOR-S
LAZAR-S	LIMEY-S	LOVER-S	MAKAR-S	MAZER-S
LEARE-S	LIMIT-S	LOVEY-S	MAKER-S	MAZUT-S
LEARN-S	LIMMA-S	LOWAN-S	MALAM-S	MBIRA-S
LEASE-S	LIMPA-S	LOWER-S	MALAR-S	MEANE-S
LEAST-S	LINAC-S	LOWND-S	MALIK-S	MEARE-S
LEAVE-S	LINEN-S	LOWNE-S	MALVA-S	MEASE-S
LEAZE-S	LINER-S	LOWSE-S	MALWA-S	MEATH-S
LEBEN-S	LINGA-S	LOZEN-S	MAMBA-S	MECCA-S
LEDGE-S	LININ-S	LUBRA-S	MAMBO-S	MEDAL-S
LEDUM-S	LINUM-S	LUCRE-S	MAMEE-S	MEDIA-S
LEEAR-S	LIPID-S	LUFFA-S	MAMEY-S	MEDIC-S
LEESE-S	LIPIN-S	LUGER-S	MAMIE-S	MEDLE-S
LEGAL-S	LISLE-S	LUMEN-S	MAMMA-S	MEITH-S
LEGER-S	LITER-S	LUNAR-S	MANAT-S	MEKKA-S
LEGGE-S	LITHE-S	LUNET-S	MANDI-S	MELEE-S
LEGIT-S	LITHO-S	LUNGE-S	MANEH-S	MELIC-S
LEHUA-S	LITRE-S	LUNGI-S	MANGA-S	MELIK-S
LEMAN-S	LIVEN-S	LUPIN-S	MANGE-S	MELON-S
LEMEL-S	LIVER-S	LURER-S	MANGO-S	MENAD-S
LEMMA-S	LIVOR-S	LURGI-S	MANIA-S	MENGE-S
LEMON-S	LIVRE-S	LURVE-S	MANIC-S	MENSA-S
LEMUR-S	LLAMA-S	LUSER-S	MANNA-S	MENSE-S
LENSE-S	LLANO-S	LUTER-S	MANOR-S	MENTO-S
LENTO-S	LOAVE-S	LYASE-S	MANSE-S	MERDE-S
LEONE-S	LOCAL-S	LYCEE-S	MANTA-S	MEREL-S
LEPER-S	LOCUM-S	LYCRA-S	MANTO-S	MERGE-S
LEPRA-S	LODEN-S	LYING-S	MANUL-S	MERIL-S
LESBO-S	LODGE-S	LYMPH-S	MAPLE-S	MERIT-S
LETHE-S	LOGAN-S	LYRIC-S	MAQUI-S	MERLE-S
LETUP-S	LOGIC-S	LYSIN-S	MARAE-S	MERSE-S
LEVEE-S	LOGIE-S	LYSOL-S	MARAH-S	MESEL-S
LEVEL-S	LOGIN-S	LYSSA-S	MARGE-S	MESNE-S
LEVER-S	LOGON-S	LYTHE-S	MARID-S	MESON-S
LEVIN-S	LOHAN-S	LYTTA-S	MARKA-S	METAL-S
LEZZA-S	LOLOG-S	MACAW-S	MARLE-S	METER-S
LIANA-S	LONER-S	MACER-S	MARON-S	METHO-S
LIANE-S	LONGA-S	MACHE-S	MAROR-S	METIC-S
LIANG-S	LONGE-S	MACHO-S	MARRI-S	METIF-S
LIARD-S	LOOEY-S	MACLE-S	MARSE-S	METOL-S
LIBEL-S	LOOFA-S	MACON-S	MASER-S	METRE-S
LIBER-S	LOOIE-S	MACRO-S	MASON-S	METRO-S
LIBRA-S	LOORD-S	MADAM-S	MASSA-S	MEUSE-S
LICHI-S	LOOSE-S	MADGE-S	MASSE-S	MEZZE-S
LICHT-S	LOPER-S	MADRE-S	MATAI-S	MEZZO-S

MHORR-S	MONIE-S	MUNTU-S	NEBEL-S	NOSER-S
MIAOU-S	MONTE-S	MURAL-S	NEELD-S	NOSEY-S
MIAOW-S	MONTH-S	MURID-S	NEELE-S	NOTER-S
MIASM-S	MOOLA-S	MURRA-S	NEEMB-S	NOULE-S
MIAUL-S	MOOLI-S	MURRE-S	NEESE-S	NOVEL-S
MICHE-S	MOOVE-S	MURRI-S	NEEZE-S	NOVUM-S
MICHT-S	MOPED-S	MURTI-S	NEIGH-S	NOWAY-S
MICRO-S	MOPER-S	MURVA-S	NEIVE-S	NOYAU-S
MIDGE-S	MORAL-S	MUSAR-S	NEPER-S	NUBIA-S
MIDST-S	MORAS-S	MUSER-S	NEPIT-S	NUDGE-S
MIEVE-S	MORAT-S	MUSET-S	NERAL-S	NUDIE-S
MIGHT-S	MORAY-S	MUSIC-S	NERKA-S	NULLA-S
MILER-S	MOREL-S	MUSIT-S	NEROL-S	NURSE-S
MILKO-S	MORIA-S	MUSSE-S	NERVE-S	NYAFF-S
MILLE-S	MORNE-S	MUSTH-S	NETOP-S	NYALA-S
MILOR-S	MORON-S	MUTHA-S	NEUME-S	NYLON-S
MILPA-S	MORPH-S	MUTON-S	NEVEL-S	NYMPH-S
MIMEO-S	MORRA-S	MVULE-S	NEWEL-S	NYSSA-S
MIMER-S	MORRO-S	MYALL-S	NEWIE-S	OAKER-S
MIMIC-S	MORSE-S	MYLAR-S	NGAIO-S	OAKUM-S
MINAR-S	MOSEY-S	MYNAH-S	NGANA-S	OATER-S
MINCE-S	MOTEL-S	MYOMA-S	NGATI-S	OBANG-S
MINER-S	MOTET-S	MYOPE-S	NGOMA-S	OBEAH-S
MINGE-S	MOTIF-S	MYRRH-S	NICAD-S	OBJET-S
MINIM-S	MOTOR-S	MYSID-S	NICHE-S	OBOLE-S
MINKE-S	MOTTE-S	NABLA-S	NICHT-S	OCCAM-S
MINOR-S	MOTTO-S	NABOB-S	NICOL-S	OCCUR-S
MIRIN-S	MOTZA-S	NACHE-S	NIDOR-S	OCEAN-S
MIRTH-S	MOULD-S	NACHO-S	NIECE-S	OCHER-S
MIRZA-S	MOULT-S	NACRE-S	NIEVE-S	OCHRE-S
MISER-S	MOUND-S	NADIR-S	NIGER-S	OCKER-S
MITER-S	MOUNT-S	NAEVE-S	NIGHT-S	OCTAD-S
MITRE-S	MOURN-S	NAGOR-S	NIHIL-S	OCTAL-S
MIXEN-S	MOUSE-S	NAHAL-S	NIKAU-S	OCTAN-S
MIXER-S	MOUST-S	NAIAD-S	NINJA-S	OCTET-S
MIXUP-S	MOUTH-S	NAIRA-S	NINON-S	OCTYL-S
MIZEN-S	MOVER-S	NAIRU-S	NINTH-S	ODEON-S
MNEME-S	MOVIE-S	NAIVE-S	NIQAB-S	ODEUM-S
MOBIE-S	MOWER-S	NAKER-S	NISEI-S	ODISM-S
MOBLE-S	MOWRA-S	NAKFA-S	NISSE-S	ODIST-S
MOCHA-S	MOXIE-S	NALED-S	NITER-S	ODIUM-S
MODAL-S	MOYLE-S	NALLA-S	NITON-S	ODOUR-S
MODEL-S	MPRET-S	NAMER-S	NITRE-S	ODYLE-S
MODEM-S	MUCIN-S	NANCE-S	NITRO-S	OFFAL-S
MODER-S	MUCOR-S	NANDU-S	NIXER-S	OFFER-S
MODGE-S	MUCRO-S	NANNA-S	NIXIE-S	OFLAG-S
MOGUL-S	MUDGE-S	NAPOO-S	NIZAM-S	OGGIN-S
MOHEL-S	MUDIR-S	NAPPA-S	NKOSI-S	OGHAM-S
MOHUR-S	MUDRA-S	NAPPE-S	NOBLE-S	OGIVE-S
MOIRE-S	MUFTI-S	NARCO-S	NOINT-S	OGLER-S
MOIST-S	MUGGA-S	NASAL-S	NOISE-S	OGRES-S
MOLAR-S	MUIST-S	NASHI-S	NOMAD-S	OILER-S
MOLLA-S	MUJIK-S	NAUNT-S	NONCE-S	OJIME-S
MOMMA-S	MULCT-S	NAVAR-S	NONET-S	OKAPI-S
MONAD-S	MULEY-S	NAVEL-S	NONYL-S	OLDEN-S
MONAL-S	MULGA-S	NAVEW-S	NOOSE-S	OLDIE-S
MONDE-S	MULLA-S	NAWAB-S	NOPAL-S	OLEIN-S
MONDO-S	MULSE-S	NAZIR-S	NORIA-S	OLEUM-S
MONEY-S	MUNGA-S	NEAFE-S	NORMA-S	OLIVE-S
MONGO-S	MUNGO-S	NEBEK-S	NORTH-S	OLLAV-S

OLLER-S	OVINE-S	PASEO-S	PEYSE-S	PLACE-S
OLLIE-S	OVIST-S	PASHA-S	PHAGE-S	PLACK-S
OMBER-S	OVOID-S	PASHM-S	PHANG-S	PLAGE-S
OMBRE-S	OVOLO-S	PASSE-S	PHARE-S	PLAID-S
OMEGA-S	OVULE-S	PASTA-S	PHASE-S	PLAIN-S
OMLAH-S	OWCHE-S	PASTE-S	PHEER-S	PLAIT-S
OMRAH-S	OWLER-S	PATEN-S	PHENE-S	PLANE-S
ONCER-S	OWLET-S	PATER-S	PHEON-S	PLANK-S
ONION-S	OWNER-S	PATIN-S	PHESE-S	PLANT-S
ONIUM-S	OXBOW-S	PATIO-S	PHIAL-S	PLASM-S
ONLAY-S	OXEYE-S	PATTE-S	PHOCA-S	PLATE-S
ONSET-S	OXIDE-S	PAUSE-S	PHONE-S	PLATY-S
OOBIT-S	OXIME-S	PAVAN-S	PHONO-S	PLAYA-S
OOMPH-S	OXLIP-S	PAVEN-S	PHOTO-S	PLAZA-S
OOTID-S	OXTER-S	PAVER-S	PIANO-S	PLEAD-S
OPEPE-S	OZEKI-S	PAVIN-S	PIBAL-S	PLEAT-S
OPERA-S	OZONE-S	PAWAW-S	PICOT-S	PLEBE-S
OPINE-S	OZZIE-S	PAWER-S	PICRA-S	PLEON-S
OPIUM-S	PACER-S	PAYEE-S	PICUL-S	PLIER-S
OPSIN-S	PACHA-S	PAYER-S	PIECE-S	PLING-S
OPTER-S	PADLE-S	PAYOR-S	PIEND-S	PLINK-S
OPTIC-S	PADMA-S	PEACE-S	PIERT-S	PLOAT-S
ORANG-S	PADRE-S	PEAGE-S	PIETA-S	PLONG-S
ORANT-S	PAEAN-S	PEARE-S	PIGHT-S	PLONK-S
ORATE-S	PAEON-S	PEARL-S	PIKAU-S	PLOOK-S
ORBIT-S	PAGAN-S	PEASE-S	PIKER-S	PLOUK-S
ORCIN-S	PAGER-S	PEAZE-S	PIKEY-S	PLUCK-S
ORDER-S	PAGLE-S	PECAN-S	PIKUL-S	PLUFF-S
OREAD-S	PAGOD-S	PECKE-S	PILAF-S	PLUMB-S
ORGAN-S	PAGRI-S	PEDAL-S	PILAO-S	PLUME-S
ORGIA-S	PAINT-S	PEDRO-S	PILAU-S	PLUMP-S
ORGUE-S	PAIRE-S	PEECE-S	PILAW-S	PLUNK-S
ORIBI-S	PAISA-S	PEEOY-S	PILEA-S	PLYER-S
ORIEL-S	PALAY-S	PEEPE-S	PILER-S	POAKA-S
ORIXA-S	PALET-S	PEEVE-S	PILOT-S	POAKE-S
ORLON-S	PALKI-S	PEISE-S	PILOW-S	POBOY-S
ORLOP-S	PAMPA-S	PEIZE-S	PINGO-S	PODGE-S
ORMER-S	PANCE-S	PEKAN-S	PINKO-S	POGEY-S
ORPIN-S	PANDA-S	PEKIN-S	PINNA-S	POGGE-S
ORTHO-S	PANEL-S	PEKOE-S	PINON-S	POILU-S
ORVAL-S	PANGA-S	PELMA-S	PINOT-S	POIND-S
OSCAR-S	PANIC-S	PELTA-S	PINTA-S	POINT-S
OSHAC-S	PANIM-S	PENCE-S	PINTO-S	POISE-S
OSIER-S	PANNE-S	PENGO-S	PINUP-S	POKAL-S
OSMIC-S	PANTO-S	PENIE-S	PIOYE-S	POKER-S
OSMOL-S	PAPAW-S	PENNE-S	PIPAL-S	POKEY-S
OTHER-S	PAPER-S	PENNI-S	PIPER-S	POKIE-S
OTTAR-S	PAREO-S	PERAI-S	PIPET-S	POLAR-S
OTTER-S	PARER-S	PERCE-S	PIPIT-S	POLER-S
OUBIT-S	PAREU-S	PERDU-S	PIPUL-S	POLEY-S
OUCHT-S	PARGE-S	PERIL-S	PIQUE-S	POLIO-S
OUGHT-S	PARGO-S	PERSE-S	PIRAI-S	POLJE-S
OUIJA-S	PARKA-S	PERVE-S	PISCO-S	POLKA-S
OUNCE-S	PARKI-S	PESTO-S	PISTE-S	POLYP-S
OUPHE-S	PARLE-S	PETAL-S	PITON-S	POMBE-S
OUSEL-S	PAROL-S	PETAR-S	PITTA-S	PONCE-S
OUTER-S	PARRA-S	PETER-S	PIVOT-S	PONEY-S
OUTRO-S	PARSE-S	PETRE-S	PIXEL-S	PONGA-S
OUZEL-S	PARTI-S	PEWEE-S	PIXIE-S	PONGO-S
OVATE-S	PARVO-S	PEWIT-S	PIZZA-S	PONZU-S

POOJA-S	PRINT-S	PYLON-S	RAGER-S	REBBE-S
POOKA-S	PRION-S	PYRAN-S	RAGGA-S	REBEC-S
POORI-S	PRIOR-S	PYXIE-S	RAHUI-S	REBEL-S
POORT-S	PRISE-S	QANAT-S	RAILE-S	REBID-S
POOVE-S	PRISM-S	QIBLA-S	RAINE-S	REBOP-S
POPPA-S	PRIZE-S	QORMA-S	RAIRD-S	REBUT-S
PORAE-S	PROBE-S	QUACK-S	RAISE-S	REBUY-S
PORER-S	PROEM-S	QUAFF-S	RAITA-S	RECAL-S
PORGE-S	PROIN-S	QUAIL-S	RAJAH-S	RECAP-S
PORNO-S	PROKE-S	QUAIR-S	RAKEE-S	RECCE-S
PORTA-S	PROLE-S	QUAKE-S	RAKER-S	RECCO-S
POSER-S	PROLL-S	QUALM-S	RALPH-S	RECIT-S
POSHO-S	PROMO-S	QUANT-S	RAMEE-S	RECON-S
POSIT-S	PRONE-S	QUARK-S	RAMEN-S	RECTO-S
POSSE-S	PRONG-S	QUART-S	RAMET-S	RECUR-S
POTAE-S	PRONK-S	QUBIT-S	RAMIE-S	RECUT-S
POTIN-S	PROOF-S	QUEAN-S	RAMIN-S	REDAN-S
POTOO-S	PRORE-S	QUEEN-S	RANCE-S	REDIA-S
POTTO-S	PROSE-S	QUEER-S	RANEE-S	REDIP-S
POUKE-S	PROSO-S	QUELL-S	RANGE-S	REDON-S
POULE-S	PROUL-S	QUEME-S	RANGI-S	REDUB-S
POULP-S	PROVE-S	QUENA-S	RANID-S	REDYE-S
POULT-S	PROWL-S	QUERN-S	RANKE-S	REEDE-S
POUND-S	PROYN-S	QUEST-S	RAPER-S	REEST-S
POUPE-S	PRUDE-S	QUEUE-S	RAPHE-S	REEVE-S
POWAN-S	PRUNE-S	QUEYN-S	RAPID-S	REFEL-S
POWER-S	PRUNT-S	QUICK-S	RAPPE-S	REFER-S
POWIN-S	PRYER-S	QUIET-S	RASER-S	REFFO-S
POWND-S	PSALM-S	QUIFF-S	RASSE-S	REFIT-S
POWRE-S	PSEUD-S	QUILL-S	RATAL-S	REGAL-S
POYNT-S	PSHAW-S	QUILT-S	RATAN-S	REGAR-S
POYOU-S	PSION-S	QUINA-S	RATEL-S	REGGO-S
POYSE-S	PSORA-S	QUINE-S	RATER-S	REGIE-S
PRAAM-S	PSYCH-S	QUINO-S	RATHA-S	REGUR-S
PRAHU-S	PSYOP-S	QUINT-S	RATIO-S	REHAB-S
PRANA-S	PUCAN-S	QUIPO-S	RATOO-S	REHEM-S
PRANG-S	PUDGE-S	QUIPU-S	RAVEL-S	REIGN-S
PRANK-S	PUDOR-S	QUIRE-S	RAVEN-S	REIKI-S
PRASE-S	PUGIL-S	QUIRK-S	RAVER-S	REINK-S
PRATE-S	PUJAH-S	QUIRT-S	RAVIN-S	REIRD-S
PRAWN-S	PUKER-S	QUIST-S	RAWIN-S	REIST-S
PREEN-S	PULAO-S	QUITE-S	RAYAH-S	REIVE-S
PREIF-S	PULER-S	QUOIF-S	RAYLE-S	REJIG-S
PRENT-S	PULKA-S	QUOIN-S	RAYNE-S	REKEY-S
PREOP-S	PULSE-S	QUOIT-S	RAYON-S	RELAY-S
PRESE-S	PUMIE-S	QUOLL-S	RAZEE-S	RELET-S
PREST-S	PUNCE-S	QUONK-S	RAZER-S	RELIC-S
PREVE-S	PUNGA-S	QUOTA-S	RAZOO-S	RELIE-S
PRIAL-S	PUNJI-S	QUOTE-S	RAZOR-S	REMAN-S
PRICE-S	PUNKA-S	QUYTE-S	REACT-S	REMAP-S
PRICK-S	PUNTO-S	RABAT-S	READD-S	REMEN-S
PRIDE-S	PUPIL-S	RABBI-S	REALM-S	REMIT-S
PRIEF-S	PURDA-S	RACER-S	REALO-S	RENAY-S
PRIER-S	PUREE-S	RACHE-S	REAME-S	RENEW-S
PRILL-S	PURGE-S	RACON-S	REARM-S	RENEY-S
PRIMA-S	PURIM-S	RADAR-S	REAST-S	RENGA-S
PRIME-S	PURIN-S	RADGE-S	REATA-S	RENIG-S
PRIMO-S	PURSE-S	RADIO-S	REATE-S	RENIN-S
PRIMP-S	PUSLE-S	RADON-S	REAVE-S	RENNE-S
PRINK-S	PUTON-S	RAGEE-S	REBAR-S	RENTE-S

REOIL-S	RIPER-S	ROYNE-S	SALSE-S	SCAPE-S
REPAY-S	RISER-S	ROYST-S	SALTO-S	SCARE-S
REPEG-S	RISHI-S	ROZET-S	SALUE-S	SCARF-S
REPEL-S	RIVAL-S	ROZIT-S	SALVE-S	SCARP-S
REPIN-S	RIVEL-S	RUANA-S	SALVO-S	SCART-S
REPOT-S	RIVER-S	RUBEL-S	SAMAN-S	SCATH-S
REPRO-S	RIVET-S	RUBIN-S	SAMBA-S	SCATT-S
RERIG-S	RIYAL-S	RUBLE-S	SAMBO-S	SCAUD-S
RERUN-S	ROAST-S	RUCHE-S	SAMEK-S	SCAUP-S
RESAW-S	ROATE-S	RUDIE-S	SAMFU-S	SCAUR-S
RESAY-S	ROBIN-S	RUFFE-S	SAMPI-S	SCENA-S
RESEE-S	ROBLE-S	RUING-S	SANGA-S	SCEND-S
RESET-S	ROBOT-S	RULER-S	SANGH-S	SCENE-S
RESEW-S	RODEO-S	RUMAL-S	SANGO-S	SCENT-S
RESID-S	ROGER-S	RUMBA-S	SANKO-S	SCHAV-S
RESIN-S	ROGUE-S	RUMBO-S	SANSA-S	SCHMO-S
RESIT-S	ROIST-S	RUMEN-S	SANTO-S	SCHUL-S
RESOD-S	ROJAK-S	RUMOR-S	SAPAN-S	SCHWA-S
RESOW-S	ROKER-S	RUMPO-S	SAPOR-S	SCION-S
RESTO-S	ROLAG-S	RUPEE-S	SARAN-S	SCLIM-S
RETAG-S	ROMAL-S	RUPIA-S	SAREE-S	SCOFF-S
RETEM-S	ROMAN-S	RURAL-S	SARGE-S	SCOLD-S
RETIE-S	ROMEO-S	RUSMA-S	SARGO-S	SCONE-S
RETRO-S	RONDE-S	RUTIN-S	SARIN-S	SCOOG-S
REUSE-S	RONDO-S	RYBAT-S	SAROD-S	SCOOP-S
REVEL-S	RONEO-S	RYMME-S	SASER-S	SCOOT-S
REVET-S	RONIN-S	SABAL-S	SASIN-S	SCOPA-S
REVIE-S	RONTE-S	SABER-S	SASSE-S	SCOPE-S
REVUE-S	ROOSA-S	SABIN-S	SATAI-S	SCORE-S
REWED-S	ROOSE-S	SABIR-S	SATAY-S	SCORN-S
REWET-S	ROOST-S	SABLE-S	SATIN-S	SCOUG-S
REWIN-S	ROPER-S	SABOT-S	SATYR-S	SCOUP-S
REWTH-S	ROQUE-S	SABRA-S	SAUBA-S	SCOUR-S
RHEME-S	ROSET-S	SABRE-S	SAUCE-S	SCOUT-S
RHEUM-S	ROSHI-S	SADDO-S	SAUCH-S	SCOWL-S
RHIME-S	ROSIN-S	SADHE-S	SAUGH-S	SCOWP-S
RHINE-S	ROSIT-S	SADHU-S	SAULT-S	SCRAB-S
RHINO-S	ROSTI-S	SADZA-S	SAUNA-S	SCRAE-S
RHOMB-S	ROTAN-S	SAHEB-S	SAUNT-S	SCRAG-S
RHONE-S	ROTON-S	SAHIB-S	SAUTE-S	SCRAM-S
RHUMB-S	ROTOR-S	SAICE-S	SAVER-S	SCRAN-S
RHYME-S	ROTTE-S	SAICK-S	SAVEY-S	SCRAP-S
RHYNE-S	ROUEN-S	SAIGA-S	SAVIN-S	SCRAT-S
RIATA-S	ROUGE-S	SAINT-S	SAVOR-S	SCRAW-S
RICER-S	ROUGH-S	SAITH-S	SAVOY-S	SCRAY-S
RICHT-S	ROULE-S	SAJOU-S	SAWAH-S	SCREE-S
RICIN-S	ROUND-S	SAKAI-S	SAWER-S	SCREW-S
RIDER-S	ROUSE-S	SAKER-S	SAYED-S	SCRIM-S
RIDGE-S	ROUST-S	SAKIA-S	SAYER-S	SCRIP-S
RIEVE-S	ROUTE-S	SALAD-S	SAYID-S	SCROD-S
RIFLE-S	ROUTH-S	SALAL-S	SAYON-S	SCROG-S
RIGHT-S	ROVER-S	SALEP-S	SCAFF-S	SCROW-S
RIGID-S	ROWAN-S	SALET-S	SCAIL-S	SCRUB-S
RIGOL-S	ROWEL-S	SALLE-S	SCALD-S	SCRUM-S
RIGOR-S	ROWEN-S	SALMI-S	SCALE-S	SCUBA-S
RILLE-S	ROWER-S	SALOL-S	SCALL-S	SCUFF-S
RIMER-S	ROWME-S	SALON-S	SCALP-S	SCUFT-S
RINSE-S	ROWND-S	SALOP-S	SCAMP-S	SCULK-S
RIOJA-S	ROWTH-S	SALPA-S	SCANT-S	SCULL-S
RIPEN-S	ROYAL-S	SALSA-S	SCAPA-S	SCULP-S

SCURF-S	SHACK-S	SHOJI-S	SIVER-S	SLEEP-S
SCUSE-S	SHADE-S	SHOLA-S	SIXER-S	SLEET-S
SCUTE-S	SHAFT-S	SHOOK-S	SIXMO-S	SLICE-S
SDAYN-S	SHAKE-S	SHOOL-S	SIXTE-S	SLICK-S
SDEIN-S	SHAKO-S	SHOOT-S	SIXTH-S	SLIDE-S
SEAME-S	SHALE-S	SHORE-S	SIZAR-S	SLIME-S
SEASE-S	SHALM-S	SHORL-S	SIZEL-S	SLING-S
SEAZE-S	SHAMA-S	SHORT-S	SIZER-S	SLINK-S
SEBUM-S	SHAME-S	SHOTE-S	SKAIL-S	SLIPE-S
SECCO-S	SHAND-S	SHOTT-S	SKALD-S	SLIVE-S
SEDAN-S	SHANK-S	SHOUT-S	SKANK-S	SLOAN-S
SEDER-S	SHAPE-S	SHOVE-S	SKART-S	SLOID-S
SEDGE-S	SHARD-S	SHOWD-S	SKATE-S	SLOJD-S
SEDUM-S	SHARE-S	SHOYU-S	SKATT-S	SLOOM-S
SEGAR-S	SHARK-S	SHRED-S	SKEAN-S	SLOOP-S
SEGNO-S	SHARN-S	SHREW-S	SKEAR-S	SLOOT-S
SEGOL-S	SHARP-S	SHROW-S	SKEEN-S	SLOPE-S
SEGUE-S	SHAUL-S	SHRUB-S	SKEER-S	SLORM-S
SEINE-S	SHAVE-S	SHRUG-S	SKEET-S	SLOTH-S
SEISE-S	SHAWL-S	SHTIK-S	SKEGG-S	SLOYD-S
SEISM-S	SHAWM-S	SHTUP-S	SKEIN-S	SLUBB-S
SEIZE-S	SHAYA-S	SHUCK-S	SKELF-S	SLUFF-S
SELAH-S	SHCHI-S	SHULE-S	SKELL-S	SLUIT-S
SELLA-S	SHEAF-S	SHUNT-S	SKELM-S	SLUMP-S
SELLE-S	SHEAL-S	SHURA-S	SKELP-S	SLURB-S
SELVA-S	SHEAR-S	SHUTE-S	SKENE-S	SLURP-S
SEMEN-S	SHEEL-S	SHYER-S	SKIER-S	SLUSE-S
SEMIE-S	SHEEN-S	SIBYL-S	SKIFF-S	SLYPE-S
SENNA-S	SHEER-S	SICHT-S	SKILL-S	SMAAK-S
SENOR-S	SHEET-S	SICKO-S	SKIMO-S	SMACK-S
SENSE-S	SHEIK-S	SIDER-S	SKIMP-S	SMAIK-S
SEPAD-S	SHELF-S	SIDHA-S	SKINK-S	SMALL-S
SEPAL-S	SHELL-S	SIDLE-S	SKIRL-S	SMALM-S
SEPIA-S	SHEND-S	SIEGE-S	SKIRR-S	SMALT-S
SEPOY-S	SHEOL-S	SIENT-S	SKIRT-S	SMARM-S
SERAC-S	SHERD-S	SIETH-S	SKITE-S	SMART-S
SERAI-S	SHEVA-S	SIEUR-S	SKIVE-S	SMAZE-S
SERGE-S	SHIAI-S	SIEVE-S	SKLIM-S	SMEAR-S
SERIF-S	SHIEL-S	SIGHT-S	SKOAL-S	SMEEK-S
SERIN-S	SHIER-S	SIGIL-S	SKOFF-S	SMELL-S
SERON-S	SHIFT-S	SIGLA-S	SKOOL-S	SMELT-S
SEROW-S	SHILL-S	SIGMA-S	SKORT-S	SMERK-S
SERRA-S	SHINE-S	SILEN-S	SKRAN-S	SMILE-S
SERRE-S	SHIRE-S	SILER-S	SKRIK-S	SMIRK-S
SERUM-S	SHIRK-S	SILVA-S	SKULK-S	SMIRR-S
SERVE-S	SHIRR-S	SIMAR-S	SKULL-S	SMITE-S
SERVO-S	SHIRT-S	SIMBA-S	SKUNK-S	SMITH-S
SETON-S	SHISO-S	SIMUL-S	SKYER-S	SMOCK-S
SETUP-S	SHIST-S	SINEW-S	SKYRE-S	SMOKE-S
SEVEN-S	SHITE-S	SINGE-S	SKYTE-S	SMOKO-S
SEVER-S	SHIVA-S	SIREE-S	SLACK-S	SMOLT-S
SEWAN-S	SHIVE-S	SIREN-S	SLADE-S	SMOOR-S
SEWAR-S	SHLEP-S	SIRIH-S	SLAKE-S	SMOOT-S
SEWEL-S	SHLUB-S	SIROC-S	SLANE-S	SMORE-S
SEWEN-S	SHMEK-S	SIRRA-S	SLANG-S	SMOUT-S
SEWER-S	SHOAL-S	SIRUP-S	SLANT-S	SMOWT-S
SEWIN-S	SHOAT-S	SISAL-S	SLART-S	SNACK-S
SEXER-S	SHOCK-S	SITAR-S	SLATE-S	SNAFU-S
SEXTO-S	SHOER-S	SITHE-S	SLAVE-S	SNAIL-S
SEYEN-S	SHOGI-S	SITUP-S	SLEEK-S	SNAKE-S

SNARE-S	SOREE-S	SPEND-S	SQUEG-S	STILT-S
SNARF-S	SOREL-S	SPERM-S	SQUIB-S	STIME-S
SNARK-S	SORGO-S	SPEUG-S	SQUID-S	STING-S
SNARL-S	SORRA-S	SPIAL-S	SQUIT-S	STINK-S
SNATH-S	SOTOL-S	SPICA-S	STACK-S	STINT-S
SNEAD-S	SOUCE-S	SPICE-S	STADE-S	STIPA-S
SNEAK-S	SOUGH-S	SPICK-S	STAFF-S	STIPE-S
SNEAP-S	SOUND-S	SPIDE-S	STAGE-S	STIRE-S
SNECK-S	SOUSE-S	SPIEL-S	STAIG-S	STIRK-S
SNEER-S	SOUTH-S	SPIER-S	STAIN-S	STIRP-S
SNELL-S	SOWAR-S	SPIFF-S	STAIR-S	STIVE-S
SNICK-S	SOWCE-S	SPIKE-S	STAKE-S	STOAT-S
SNIDE-S	SOWER-S	SPILE-S	STALE-S	STOCK-S
SNIFF-S	SOWFF-S	SPILL-S	STALK-S	STOEP-S
SNIFT-S	SOWLE-S	SPINA-S	STALL-S	STOIC-S
SNIPE-S	SOWND-S	SPINE-S	STAMP-S	STOIT-S
SNIRT-S	SOWNE-S	SPINK-S	STAND-S	STOKE-S
SNOEK-S	SOWSE-S	SPIRE-S	STANE-S	STOLE-S
SNOKE-S	SOWTH-S	SPIRT-S	STANG-S	STOMA-S
SNOOD-S	SOYLE-S	SPITE-S	STANK-S	STOMP-S
SNOOK-S	SOZIN-S	SPLAT-S	STAPH-S	STOND-S
SNOOL-S	SPACE-S	SPLAY-S	STARE-S	STONE-S
SNOOP-S	SPADE-S	SPLIT-S	STARK-S	STONK-S
SNOOT-S	SPADO-S	SPODE-S	STARN-S	STONN-S
SNORE-S	SPAER-S	SPOIL-S	STARR-S	STOOK-S
SNORT-S	SPAHI-S	SPOKE-S	START-S	STOOL-S
SNOUT-S	SPAIL-S	SPOOF-S	STATE-S	STOOP-S
SNOWK-S	SPAIN-S	SPOOK-S	STAUN-S	STOOR-S
SNUFF-S	SPAIT-S	SPOOL-S	STAVE-S	STOPE-S
SOARE-S	SPALD-S	SPOOM-S	STEAD-S	STORE-S
SOAVE-S	SPALE-S	SPOON-S	STEAK-S	STORK-S
SOBER-S	SPALL-S	SPOOR-S	STEAL-S	STORM-S
SOCLE-S	SPALT-S	SPOOT-S	STEAM-S	STOTT-S
SODOM-S	SPANE-S	SPORE-S	STEAN-S	STOUN-S
SOFAR-S	SPANG-S	SPORT-S	STEAR-S	STOUP-S
SOFTA-S	SPANK-S	SPOUT-S	STEDD-S	STOUR-S
SOGER-S	SPARE-S	SPRAG-S	STEDE-S	STOUT-S
SOKAH-S	SPARK-S	SPRAT-S	STEED-S	STOVE-S
SOKEN-S	SPART-S	SPRAY-S	STEEK-S	STOWP-S
SOKOL-S	SPASM-S	SPRED-S	STEEL-S	STRAD-S
SOLAH-S	SPATE-S	SPREE-S	STEEM-S	STRAE-S
SOLAN-S	SPAUL-S	SPREW-S	STEEN-S	STRAG-S
SOLAR-S	SPAWL-S	SPRIG-S	STEEP-S	STRAP-S
SOLDE-S	SPAWN-S	SPRIT-S	STEER-S	STRAW-S
SOLER-S	SPAYD-S	SPROD-S	STEIL-S	STRAY-S
SOLID-S	SPEAK-S	SPROG-S	STEIN-S	STREP-S
SOLON-S	SPEAL-S	SPRUE-S	STELE-S	STREW-S
SOLUM-S	SPEAN-S	SPRUG-S	STELL-S	STRIG-S
SOLVE-S	SPEAR-S	SPUER-S	STEME-S	STRIP-S
SOMAN-S	SPEAT-S	SPULE-S	STEND-S	STROP-S
SONAR-S	SPECK-S	SPUME-S	STENO-S	STROW-S
SONCE-S	SPEED-S	SPUNK-S	STENT-S	STROY-S
SONDE-S	SPEEL-S	SPURN-S	STERE-S	STRUM-S
SONIC-S	SPEER-S	SPURT-S	STERN-S	STRUT-S
SONNE-S	SPEIL-S	SPYAL-S	STICH-S	STUCK-S
SONSE-S	SPEIR-S	SPYRE-S	STICK-S	STUFF-S
SOOLE-S	SPELD-S	SQUAB-S	STIFF-S	STULL-S
SOOTE-S	SPELK-S	SQUAD-S	STILB-S	STULM-S
SOOTH-S	SPELL-S	SQUAT-S	STILE-S	STUMP-S
SOPOR-S	SPELT-S	SQUAW-S	STILL-S	STUNT-S

STUPA-S	SWILL-S	TANGA-S	TENUE-S	THUJA-S
STUPE-S	SWINE-S	TANGI-S	TEPAL-S	THUMB-S
STURT-S	SWING-S	TANGO-S	TEPEE-S	THUMP-S
STYLE-S	SWINK-S	TANKA-S	TEPOY-S	THUNK-S
STYLO-S	SWIPE-S	TANNA-S	TERAI-S	THURL-S
STYME-S	SWIRE-S	TAPER-S	TERCE-S	THUYA-S
STYRE-S	SWIRL-S	TAPET-S	TEREK-S	THYME-S
STYTE-S	SWIVE-S	TAPIR-S	TERFE-S	TIARA-S
SUBAH-S	SWONE-S	TAPPA-S	TERNE-S	TIBIA-S
SUBER-S	SWOON-S	TARGE-S	TERRA-S	TICAL-S
SUBHA-S	SWOOP-S	TAROC-S	TESLA-S	TIGER-S
SUCRE-S	SWORD-S	TAROK-S	TESTE-S	TIGHT-S
SUDOR-S	SWOUN-S	TAROT-S	TETRA-S	TIGON-S
SUEDE-S	SYBBE-S	TARRE-S	TETRI-S	TIKKA-S
SUGAN-S	SYBIL-S	TASAR-S	TEWEL-S	TILAK-S
SUGAR-S	SYBOE-S	TASER-S	TEWIT-S	TILDE-S
SUING-S	SYBOW-S	TASSE-S	THACK-S	TILER-S
SUINT-S	SYCEE-S	TASTE-S	THAGI-S	TILTH-S
SUITE-S	SYLPH-S	TATAR-S	THALI-S	TIMBO-S
SUJEE-S	SYLVA-S	TATER-S	THANA-S	TIMER-S
SULFA-S	SYMAR-S	TATIE-S	THANE-S	TIMON-S
SUMAC-S	SYNCH-S	TATOU-S	THANK-S	TINCT-S
SUMMA-S	SYNOD-S	TAUBE-S	THARM-S	TINEA-S
SUMPH-S	SYNTH-S	TAUNT-S	THEBE-S	TINGE-S
SUNNA-S	SYRAH-S	TAUON-S	THEEK-S	TITAN-S
SUNUP-S	SYREN-S	TAUPE-S	THEFT-S	TITER-S
SUPER-S	SYRUP-S	TAVAH-S	THEGN-S	TITHE-S
SURAH-S	SYSOP-S	TAVER-S	THEIC-S	TITLE-S
SURAT-S	SYTHE-S	TAWAI-S	THEIN-S	TITRE-S
SURGE-S	SYVER-S	TAWER-S	THEIR-S	TITUP-S
SURRA-S	TAATA-S	TAWSE-S	THEME-S	TOAST-S
SUSHI-S	TABER-S	TAXER-S	THEOW-S	TOAZE-S
SUTOR-S	TABLA-S	TAXOL-S	THERE-S	TODAY-S
SUTRA-S	TABLE-S	TAXON-S	THERM-S	TODDE-S
SUTTA-S	TABOO-S	TAXOR-S	THESE-S	TOGUE-S
SWAGE-S	TABOR-S	TAYRA-S	THESP-S	TOILE-S
SWAIL-S	TABUN-S	TAZZA-S	THETA-S	TOING-S
SWAIN-S	TACAN-S	TEADE-S	THETE-S	TOISE-S
SWALE-S	TACET-S	TEASE-S	THICK-S	TOKAY-S
SWAMI-S	TACHE-S	TEAZE-S	THIGH-S	TOKEN-S
SWAMP-S	TACHO-S	TEEND-S	THILL-S	TOKER-S
SWANK-S	TAFIA-S	TEENE-S	THING-S	TOLAN-S
SWARD-S	TAHOU-S	TEGUA-S	THINK-S	TOLAR-S
SWARF-S	TAIGA-S	TEIID-S	THIOL-S	TOLYL-S
SWARM-S	TAINT-S	TEIND-S	THIRD-S	TOMAN-S
SWATH-S	TAIRA-S	TELCO-S	THIRL-S	TONDO-S
SWAYL-S	TAKER-S	TELLY-S	THOFT-S	TONER-S
SWEAL-S	TAKHI-S	TEMPO-S	THOLE-S	TONGA-S
SWEAR-S	TAKIN-S	TEMPT-S	THONG-S	TONIC-S
SWEAT-S	TALAK-S	TEMSE-S	THORN-S	TONNE-S
SWEDE-S	TALAQ-S	TENDU-S	THORP-S	TOOTH-S
SWEEL-S	TALAR-S	TENET-S	THOWL-S	TOPEE-S
SWEEP-S	TALER-S	TENGE-S	THRAW-S	TOPEK-S
SWEER-S	TALMA-S	TENIA-S	THREE-S	TOPER-S
SWEET-S	TALON-S	TENNE-S	THRID-S	TOPHE-S
SWEIR-S	TALPA-S	TENNO-S	THRIP-S	TOPIC-S
SWELL-S	TALUK-S	TENON-S	THROB-S	TOQUE-S
SWELT-S	TAMAL-S	TENOR-S	THROE-S	TORAH-S
SWERF-S	TAMER-S	TENSE-S	THROW-S	TORAN-S
SWIFT-S	TAMIN-S	TENTH-S	THRUM-S	TORIC-S

TORSE-S	TROAK-S	TWEEN-S	UNLAY-S	VANDA-S
TORSK-S	TROAT-S	TWEER-S	UNLID-S	VAPOR-S
TORSO-S	TROCK-S	TWEET-S	UNMAN-S	VARAN-S
TORTA-S	TRODE-S	TWERP-S	UNMEW-S	VAREC-S
TORTE-S	TROKE-S	TWIER-S	UNPAY-S	VARIA-S
TOTAL-S	TROLL-S	TWILL-S	UNPEG-S	VARNA-S
TOTEM-S	TROMP-S	TWILT-S	UNPEN-S	VARVE-S
TOTER-S	TRONA-S	TWINE-S	UNPIN-S	VAULT-S
TOUGH-S	TRONC-S	TWINK-S	UNRIG-S	VAUNT-S
TOUSE-S	TRONE-S	TWIRE-S	UNRIP-S	VAUTE-S
TOUZE-S	TRONK-S	TWIRL-S	UNSAY-S	VAWTE-S
TOWEL-S	TROOP-S	TWIRP-S	UNSET-S	VEALE-S
TOWER-S	TROPE-S	TWIST-S	UNSEW-S	VEENA-S
TOWIE-S	TROTH-S	TWITE-S	UNTIE-S	VEGAN-S
TOWSE-S	TROUT-S	TWOER-S	UNTIN-S	VEGIE-S
TOWZE-S	TROVE-S	TWYER-S	UNWIT-S	VELAR-S
TOXIC-S	TRUCE-S	TYLER-S	UNZIP-S	VELDT-S
TOXIN-S	TRUCK-S	TYPTO-S	UPBOW-S	VENEY-S
TOYER-S	TRUGO-S	TYRAN-S	UPEND-S	VENGE-S
TOYON-S	TRULL-S	TYTHE-S	UPJET-S	VENIN-S
TOZIE-S	TRUMP-S	UDDER-S	UPLAY-S	VENOM-S
TRACE-S	TRUNK-S	UGALI-S	UPPER-S	VENUE-S
TRACK-S	TRUST-S	UHLAN-S	UPRUN-S	VERGE-S
TRACT-S	TRUTH-S	UHURU-S	UPSEE-S	VERSE-S
TRADE-S	TRYER-S	UKASE-S	UPSET-S	VERSO-S
TRAIK-S	TRYKE-S	ULAMA-S	UPSEY-S	VERST-S
TRAIL-S	TRYST-S	ULCER-S	UPTAK-S	VERTU-S
TRAIN-S	TSADE-S	ULEMA-S	UPTIE-S	VERVE-S
TRAIT-S	TSADI-S	ULMIN-S	URALI-S	VESPA-S
TRAMP-S	TSUBA-S	ULTRA-S	URARE-S	VESTA-S
TRANK-S	TUART-S	ULYIE-S	URARI-S	VEXER-S
TRANQ-S	TUATH-S	ULZIE-S	URASE-S	VEXIL-S
TRANT-S	TUBER-S	UMAMI-S	URATE-S	VEZIR-S
TRAPE-S	TUFFE-S	UMBEL-S	URBIA-S	VIAND-S
TRATT-S	TUGRA-S	UMBER-S	UREDO-S	VICAR-S
TRAVE-S	TUINA-S	UMBLE-S	URENA-S	VIDEO-S
TRAWL-S	TUISM-S	UMBRA-S	URGER-S	VIFDA-S
TREAD-S	TUKTU-S	UMBRE-S	URIAL-S	VIGIA-S
TREAT-S	TULIP-S	UMIAC-S	URINE-S	VIGIL-S
TRECK-S	TULLE-S	UMIAK-S	URITE-S	VIGOR-S
TREEN-S	TULPA-S	UMIAQ-S	URMAN-S	VILLA-S
TREMA-S	TUMOR-S	UMPIE-S	URSID-S	VINAL-S
TREND-S	TUNER-S	UNARM-S	URSON-S	VINCA-S
TREST-S	TUNIC-S	UNBAG-S	URUBU-S	VINER-S
TRIAC-S	TUPEK-S	UNBAN-S	USAGE-S	VINEW-S
TRIAD-S	TUPIK-S	UNBAR-S	USHER-S	VINYL-S
TRIAL-S	TUPLE-S	UNBED-S	USNEA-S	VIOLA-S
TRIBE-S	TUQUE-S	UNCAP-S	USQUE-S	VIPER-S
TRICE-S	TURBO-S	UNCLE-S	USUAL-S	VIREO-S
TRICK-S	TURME-S	UNDAM-S	USURE-S	VIRGA-S
TRIER-S	TUTEE-S	UNFIT-S	USURP-S	VIRGE-S
TRIGO-S	TUTOR-S	UNGAG-S	UTTER-S	VIRTU-S
TRIKE-S	TUTTI-S	UNGET-S	UVULA-S	VISIE-S
TRILL-S	TUYER-S	UNGOD-S	VAGUE-S	VISIT-S
TRINE-S	TWAIN-S	UNGUM-S	VAKIL-S	VISNE-S
TRIOL-S	TWANG-S	UNHAT-S	VALET-S	VISON-S
TRIOR-S	TWANK-S	UNION-S	VALOR-S	VISOR-S
TRIPE-S	TWEAK-S	UNITE-S	VALSE-S	VISTA-S
TRITE-S	TWEED-S	UNJAM-S	VALUE-S	VISTO-S
TROAD-S	TWEEL-S	UNLAW-S	VALVE-S	VITAL-S

VIVAT-S	WAUFF-S	WHOOF-S	WRICK-S	YOKER-S
VIVDA-S	WAUGH-S	WHOOP-S	WRING-S	YOUNG-S
VIVER-S	WAULK-S	WHOOT-S	WRIST-S	YOURT-S
VIXEN-S	WAVER-S	WHORE-S	WRITE-S	YOUTH-S
VIZIR-S	WAVEY-S	WHORL-S	WRONG-S	YOWIE-S
VIZOR-S	WAXER-S	WHORT-S	WROOT-S	YRNEH-S
VOCAB-S	WAZIR-S	WHUMP-S	WURST-S	YUCCA-S
VOCAL-S	WAZOO-S	WICCA-S	WUSHU-S	YULAN-S
VODKA-S	WEALD-S	WIDEN-S	WUXIA-S	YUPON-S
VODOU-S	WEAMB-S	WIDOW-S	XEBEC-S	YURTA-S
VODUN-S	WEAVE-S	WIDTH-S	XENIA-S	ZABRA-S
VOEMA-S	WEBER-S	WIELD-S	XENON-S	ZAIRE-S
VOGUE-S	WECHT-S	WIFEY-S	XYLAN-S	ZAKAT-S
VOICE-S	WEDEL-S	WIFIE-S	XYLEM-S	ZAMAN-S
VOILE-S	WEDGE-S	WIGAN-S	XYLOL-S	ZAMBO-S
VOLET-S	WEEKE-S	WIGGA-S	XYLYL-S	ZAMIA-S
VOLTE-S	WEFTE-S	WIGHT-S	YABBA-S	ZANJA-S
VOLVA-S	WEIGH-S	WILGA-S	YACCA-S	ZANTE-S
VOLVE-S	WEIRD-S	WILJA-S	YACHT-S	ZANZA-S
VOMER-S	WEISE-S	WINCE-S	YACKA-S	ZANZE-S
VOMIT-S	WEIZE-S	WINGE-S	YAGER-S	ZAYIN-S
VOTER-S	WELKE-S	WINZE-S	YAHOO-S	ZAZEN-S
VOUGE-S	WENGE-S	WIPER-S	YAIRD-S	ZEBEC-S
VOWEL-S	WHACK-S	WIRER-S	YAKKA-S	ZEBRA-S
VOWER-S	WHALE-S	WITAN-S	YAKOW-S	ZEBUB-S
VOXEL-S	WHANG-S	WITHE-S	YAMEN-S	ZERDA-S
VOZHD-S	WHARE-S	WIVER-S	YAMUN-S	ZHOMO-S
VRAIC-S	WHARF-S	WIZEN-S	YAPOK-S	ZIBET-S
VROOM-S	WHATA-S	WOALD-S	YAPON-S	ZIGAN-S
VROUW-S	WHAUP-S	WODGE-S	YARCO-S	ZILLA-S
VULVA-S	WHAUR-S	WOLVE-S	YARFA-S	ZIMBI-S
WACKE-S	WHEAL-S	WOMAN-S	YARTA-S	ZINCO-S
WACKO-S	WHEAT-S	WONGA-S	YARTO-S	ZINEB-S
WADER-S	WHEEL-S	WONGI-S	YEALM-S	ZINKE-S
WAFER-S	WHEEN-S	WOOER-S	YEARD-S	ZIPPO-S
WAGER-S	WHEEP-S	WOOLD-S	YEARN-S	ZIRAM-S
WAGGA-S	WHEFT-S	WOOSE-S	YEAST-S	ZIZEL-S
WAGON-S	WHELK-S	WORLD-S	YECCH-S	ZLOTY-S
WAHOO-S	WHELM-S	WORSE-S	YENTA-S	ZOAEA-S
WAIFT-S	WHELP-S	WORST-S	YENTE-S	ZOCCO-S
WAIST-S	WHERE-S	WORTH-S	YERBA-S	ZOISM-S
WAITE-S	WHIFF-S	WOULD-S	YIELD-S	ZOIST-S
WAIVE-S	WHIFT-S	WOUND-S	YIRTH-S	ZOMBI-S
WAKEN-S	WHILE-S	WOVEN-S	YITIE-S	ZONDA-S
WAKER-S	WHINE-S	WRACK-S	YOBBO-S	ZONER-S
WALDO-S	WHIRL-S	WRANG-S	YODEL-S	ZOOEA-S
WALER-S	WHIRR-S	WRAST-S	YODLE-S	ZOOID-S
WALLA-S	WHISK-S	WRATH-S	YOGEE-S	ZORIL-S
WANZE-S	WHIST-S	WRAWL-S	YOGIN-S	ZORRO-S
WASTE-S	WHITE-S	WREAK-S	YOICK-S	ZUPAN-S
WATAP-S	WHOLE-S	WRECK-S	YOJAN-S	
WATER-S	WHOMP-S	WREST-S	YOKEL-S	

Six letters to seven

ABASER-S	ABDUCT-S	ABLATE-S	ABRADE-S	ABRUPT-S
ABASIA-S	ABELIA-S	ABLAUT-S	ABRAID-S	ABSEIL-S
ABATER-S	ABIDER-S	ABLING-S	ABRAZO-S	ABSENT-S
ABATOR-S	ABJECT-S	ABOLLA-S	ABREGE-S	ABSORB-S
ABDUCE-S	ABJURE-S	ABOUND-S	ABROAD-S	ABSURD-S

ABULIA-S	ADVECT-S	AJOWAN-S	ALTEZA-S	ANOMIE-S
ABUSER-S	ADVENE-S	AKEAKE-S	ALTHEA-S	ANONYM-S
ABVOLT-S	ADVENT-S	AKEDAH-S	ALUDEL-S	ANOPIA-S
ABWATT-S	ADVERB-S	AKHARA-S	ALUMIN-S	ANORAK-S
ACACIA-S	ADVERT-S	ALALIA-S	AMADOU-S	ANOXIA-S
ACAJOU-S	ADVICE-S	ALANIN-S	AMATOL-S	ANSWER-S
ACANTH-S	ADVISE-S	ALANYL-S	AMAZON-S	ANTARA-S
ACARID-S	ADWARD-S	ALARUM-S	AMBAGE-S	ANTHEM-S
ACATER-S	ADWARE-S	ALASKA-S	AMBARI-S	ANTHER-S
ACCEDE-S	ADZUKI-S	ALBATA-S	AMBEER-S	ANTIAR-S
ACCEND-S	AEDILE-S	ALBEDO-S	AMBLER-S	ANTICK-S
ACCENT-S	AEMULE-S	ALBERT-S	AMELIA-S	ANTING-S
ACCEPT-S	AERATE-S	ALBINO-S	AMENDE-S	ANTLER-S
ACCITE-S	AERIAL-S	ALBITE-S	AMERCE-S	ANTRUM-S
ACCLOY-S	AEROBE-S	ALBUGO-S	AMIDIN-S	ANURAN-S
ACCOIL-S	AERUGO-S	ALCADE-S	AMIDOL-S	ANURIA-S
ACCORD-S	AETHER-S	ALCAIC-S	AMMINE-S	ANYONE-S
ACCOST-S	AFFAIR-S	ALCOOL-S	AMNION-S	ANYWAY-S
ACCREW-S	AFFEAR-S	ALCOVE-S	AMOEBA-S	AORIST-S
ACCRUE-S	AFFECT-S	ALDOSE-S	AMOMUM-S	AOUDAD-S
ACCUSE-S	AFFEER-S	ALDRIN-S	AMOOVE-S	APACHE-S
ACEDIA-S	AFFINE-S	ALEGAR-S	AMORCE-S	APEDOM-S
ACETAL-S	AFFIRM-S	ALEGGE-S	AMORET-S	APERCU-S
ACETIN-S	AFFORD-S	ALERCE-S	AMOUNT-S	APICAL-S
ACETYL-S	AFFRAP-S	ALEVIN-S	AMPERE-S	APLITE-S
ACHAGE-S	AFFRAY-S	ALEXIA-S	AMPULE-S	APLOMB-S
ACHENE-S	AFFRET-S	ALEXIN-S	AMRITA-S	APNOEA-S
ACHING-S	AFGHAN-S	ALFAKI-S	AMTMAN-S	APOGEE-S
ACHKAN-S	AFREET-S	ALGATE-S	AMTRAC-S	APOLLO-S
ACKNOW-S	AFTOSA-S	ALIDAD-S	AMULET-S	APOLOG-S
ACMITE-S	AGAMID-S	ALIGHT-S	AMUSER-S	APORIA-S
ACNODE-S	AGARIC-S	ALINER-S	AMUSIA-S	APOZEM-S
ACQUIT-S	AGEING-S	ALIPED-S	AMYLUM-S	APPAIR-S
ACTANT-S	AGEISM-S	ALISMA-S	AMYTAL-S	APPALL-S
ACTING-S	AGEIST-S	ALISON-S	ANADEM-S	APPEAL-S
ACTION-S	AGENDA-S	ALIYAH-S	ANALOG-S	APPEAR-S
ACTIVE-S	AGGADA-S	ALKALI-S	ANANKE-S	APPEND-S
ACTUAL-S	AGNAIL-S	ALKANE-S	ANARCH-S	APPLET-S
ACTURE-S	AGNAME-S	ALKENE-S	ANATTA-S	APPORT-S
ACUMEN-S	AGNATE-S	ALKINE-S	ANATTO-S	APPOSE-S
ADAGIO-S	AGNISE-S	ALKYNE-S	ANCHOR-S	APTOTE-S
ADDEEM-S	AGNIZE-S	ALLEGE-S	ANCOME-S	ARAARA-S
ADDEND-S	AGOGIC-S	ALLELE-S	ANCONE-S	ARABIN-S
ADDICT-S	AGOUTA-S	ALLICE-S	ANEMIA-S	ARABLE-S
ADDOOM-S	AGOUTI-S	ALLIUM-S	ANGICO-S	ARAISE-S
ADDUCE-S	AGRAFE-S	ALLUDE-S	ANGINA-S	ARALIA-S
ADDUCT-S	AGREGE-S	ALLURE-S	ANGLER-S	ARAMID-S
ADENYL-S	AGRISE-S	ALMAIN-S	ANGORA-S	ARAYSE-S
ADHERE-S	AGRIZE-S	ALMNER-S	ANICCA-S	ARBOUR-S
ADJIGO-S	AGRYZE-S	ALMOND-S	ANICUT-S	ARBUTE-S
ADJOIN-S	AGUISE-S	ALMUCE-S	ANILIN-S	ARCADE-S
ADJURE-S	AGUIZE-S	ALMUDE-S	ANIMAL-S	ARCANA-S
ADJUST-S	AHIMSA-S	ALNAGE-S	ANKLET-S	ARCHER-S
ADLAND-S	AIGLET-S	ALNICO-S	ANLACE-S	ARCHIL-S
ADMIRE-S	AIGRET-S	ALOGIA-S	ANLAGE-S	ARCHON-S
ADNOUN-S	AIKIDO-S	ALPACA-S	ANNEAL-S	ARCING-S
ADORER-S	AIRBAG-S	ALPEEN-S	ANNEXE-S	ARCMIN-S
ADREAD-S	AIRGAP-S	ALPHYL-S	ANNONA-S	ARCSEC-S
ADSORB-S	AIRING-S	ALPINE-S	ANNUAL-S	ARCSIN-S
ADSUKI-S	AIRWAY-S	ALSIKE-S	ANOINT-S	ARCTAN-S

ARCTIC-S	ASRAMA-S	AUSUBO-S	BAILIE-S	BARLOW-S
ARDOUR-S	ASSAIL-S	AUTEUR-S	BAILLI-S	BARNET-S
AREOLA-S	ASSART-S	AUTHOR-S	BAILOR-S	BARNEY-S
AREOLE-S	ASSENT-S	AUTISM-S	BAININ-S	BAROCK-S
ARGALA-S	ASSERT-S	AUTIST-S	BAITER-S	BAROLO-S
ARGALI-S	ASSIGN-S	AUTUMN-S	BAJADA-S	BARONG-S
ARGAND-S	ASSIST-S	AVAILE-S	BAJREE-S	BARQUE-S
ARGENT-S	ASSIZE-S	AVATAR-S	BAKING-S	BARRAT-S
ARGHAN-S	ASSOIL-S	AVAUNT-S	BAKKIE-S	BARREL-S
ARGUER-S	ASSORT-S	AVENGE-S	BALATA-S	BARREN-S
ARGYLE-S	ASSUME-S	AVENIR-S	BALBOA-S	BARRET-S
ARGYLL-S	ASSURE-S	AVENUE-S	BALEEN-S	BARRIE-S
ARIOSO-S	ASTART-S	AVIATE-S	BALKER-S	BARRIO-S
ARISTA-S	ASTERT-S	AVIDIN-S	BALLAD-S	BARROW-S
ARISTO-S	ASTHMA-S	AVOCET-S	BALLAN-S	BARTER-S
ARKITE-S	ASTONE-S	AVOSET-S	BALLAT-S	BARTON-S
ARKOSE-S	ASTRAL-S	AVOURE-S	BALLER-S	BARYON-S
ARMADA-S	ASYLUM-S	AVOWAL-S	BALLET-S	BARYTA-S
ARMFUL-S	ATAATA-S	AVOWER-S	BALLON-S	BARYTE-S
ARMING-S	ATABAL-S	AVOYER-S	BALLOT-S	BASALT-S
ARMLET-S	ATABEG-S	AVRUGA-S	BALLOW-S	BASHAW-S
ARMOUR-S	ATABEK-S	AVULSE-S	BALLUP-S	BASHER-S
ARMPIT-S	ATAMAN-S	AWAKEN-S	BALSAM-S	BASION-S
ARMURE-S	ATAXIA-S	AWHAPE-S	BAMBOO-S	BASKET-S
ARNICA-S	ATAXIC-S	AWHEEL-S	BAMMER-S	BASNET-S
AROINT-S	ATHAME-S	AWMRIE-S	BAMPOT-S	BASQUE-S
AROLLA-S	ATLATL-S	AWNING-S	BANANA-S	BASSET-S
AROUSE-S	ATOCIA-S	AXILLA-S	BANDAR-S	BASTER-S
AROYNT-S	ATOMIC-S	AXSEED-S	BANDER-S	BASTLE-S
ARPENT-S	ATONER-S	AYWORD-S	BANDIT-S	BASUCO-S
ARRACK-S	ATONIA-S	AZALEA-S	BANDOG-S	BATATA-S
ARREAR-S	ATONIC-S	AZIONE-S	BANGER-S	BATBOY-S
ARREST-S	ATRIUM-S	AZOLLA-S	BANGLE-S	BATHER-S
ARRIDE-S	ATTACK-S	BAAING-S	BANIAN-S	BATLER-S
ARRIVE-S	ATTAIN-S	BABACO-S	BANKER-S	BATLET-S
ARROBA-S	ATTASK-S	BABBLE-S	BANKET-S	BATOON-S
ARROYO-S	ATTEND-S	BABLAH-S	BANKIT-S	BATTEL-S
ARSHIN-S	ATTENT-S	BABOOL-S	BANNER-S	BATTEN-S
ARSINE-S	ATTEST-S	BABOON-S	BANNET-S	BATTER-S
ARTIST-S	ATTIRE-S	BACKER-S	BANTAM-S	BATTIK-S
ASARUM-S	ATTONE-S	BACKET-S	BANTER-S	BATTLE-S
ASCEND-S	ATTORN-S	BACKIE-S	BANYAN-S	BATTUE-S
ASCENT-S	ATTRAP-S	BACKRA-S	BANZAI-S	BAUBEE-S
ASCIAN-S	ATTRIT-S	BACKUP-S	BAOBAB-S	BAUBLE-S
ASHAME-S	ATTUNE-S	BADDIE-S	BARAZA-S	BAUERA-S
ASHCAN-S	AUBADE-S	BADGER-S	BARBEL-S	BAWBEE-S
ASHKEY-S	AUBURN-S	BAETYL-S	BARBER-S	BAWBLE-S
ASHLAR-S	AUCUBA-S	BAFFLE-S	BARBET-S	BAWLER-S
ASHLER-S	AUDILE-S	BAGFUL-S	BARBIE-S	BAWLEY-S
ASHRAM-S	AUDING-S	BAGGER-S	BARBUT-S	BAWTIE-S
ASIAGO-S	AUGEND-S	BAGGIE-S	BARDIE-S	BAXTER-S
ASKANT-S	AUGITE-S	BAGGIT-S	BAREGE-S	BAYAMO-S
ASKARI-S	AUGUST-S	BAGNIO-S	BARGEE-S	BAYARD-S
ASKING-S	AUKLET-S	BAGUET-S	BARHOP-S	BAYYAN-S
ASLAKE-S	AUMAIL-S	BAGUIO-S	BARITE-S	BAZAAR-S
ASPECT-S	AUNTER-S	BAGWIG-S	BARIUM-S	BEACON-S
ASPICK-S	AUNTIE-S	BAHADA-S	BARKAN-S	BEADER-S
ASPINE-S	AURATE-S	BAILEE-S	BARKEN-S	BEADLE-S
ASPIRE-S	AURIST-S	BAILER-S	BARKER-S	BEAGLE-S
ASPORT-S	AURORA-S	BAILEY-S	BARLEY-S	BEAKER-S

BEAMER-S	BEHEAD-S	BESMUT-S	BIGEYE-S	BLONDE-S
BEANIE-S	BEHEST-S	BESNOW-S	BIGGIE-S	BLOUSE-S
BEARER-S	BEHIND-S	BESOIN-S	BIGGIN-S	BLOWBY-S
BEATER-S	BEHOLD-S	BESORT-S	BIGGON-S	BLOWER-S
BEAVER-S	BEHOOF-S	BESPIT-S	BIGWIG-S	BLOWIE-S
BEBUNG-S	BEHOTE-S	BESPOT-S	BIKING-S	BLOWSE-S
BECALL-S	BEHOVE-S	BESTAR-S	BIKINI-S	BLOWUP-S
BECALM-S	BEHOWL-S	BESTIR-S	BIKKIE-S	BLOWZE-S
BECKET-S	BEIGEL-S	BESTOW-S	BILBOA-S	BLUDGE-S
BECKON-S	BEIGNE-S	BESTUD-S	BILIAN-S	BLUING-S
BECLOG-S	BEJADE-S	BETAKE-S	BILKER-S	BLUNGE-S
BECOME-S	BEJANT-S	BETEEM-S	BILLER-S	BOATEL-S
BECURL-S	BEKNOT-S	BETHEL-S	BILLET-S	BOATER-S
BEDAMN-S	BELACE-S	BETIDE-S	BILLIE-S	BOATIE-S
BEDAUB-S	BELATE-S	BETIME-S	BILLON-S	BOBBER-S
BEDAZE-S	BELAUD-S	BETISE-S	BILLOW-S	BOBBIN-S
BEDBUG-S	BELDAM-S	BETOIL-S	BILLYO-S	BOBBLE-S
BEDDER-S	BELEAP-S	BETRAY-S	BINDER-S	BOBCAT-S
BEDECK-S	BELIEF-S	BETRIM-S	BINDHI-S	BOBLET-S
BEDELL-S	BELIER-S	BETTER-S	BINDLE-S	BOBWIG-S
BEDLAM-S	BELLOW-S	BETTOR-S	BINGER-S	BOCAGE-S
BEDPAN-S	BELONG-S	BEURRE-S	BINGHI-S	BOCCIA-S
BEDRAL-S	BELOVE-S	BEWAIL-S	BINGLE-S	BOCCIE-S
BEDROP-S	BELTER-S	BEWARE-S	BINIOU-S	BODACH-S
BEDRUG-S	BELUGA-S	BEWEEP-S	BIODOT-S	BODDLE-S
BEDSIT-S	BEMAUL-S	BEWORM-S	BIOGEN-S	BODEGA-S
BEDUCK-S	BEMEAN-S	BEWRAP-S	BIONIC-S	BODGER-S
BEDUIN-S	BEMETE-S	BEWRAY-S	BIOPIC-S	BODGIE-S
BEDUMB-S	BEMIRE-S	BEYLIC-S	BIOTIC-S	BODICE-S
BEDUNG-S	BEMIST-S	BEYLIK-S	BIOTIN-S	BODING-S
BEDUST-S	BEMOAN-S	BEYOND-S	BIPACK-S	BODKIN-S
BEEBEE-S	BEMOCK-S	BEZANT-S	BIRDER-S	BODRAG-S
BEEGAH-S	BEMOIL-S	BEZOAR-S	BIRDIE-S	BOFFIN-S
BEENAH-S	BEMUSE-S	BEZZLE-S	BIREME-S	BOGART-S
BEENTO-S	BENAME-S	BHAGEE-S	BIRKIE-S	BOGGER-S
BEEPER-S	BENDAY-S	BHAJAN-S	BIRLER-S	BOGGLE-S
BEETLE-S	BENDEE-S	BHAJEE-S	BIRSLE-S	BOGOAK-S
BEEZER-S	BENDER-S	BHAKTA-S	BISECT-S	BOGONG-S
BEFALL-S	BENNET-S	BHAKTI-S	BISHOP-S	BOHUNK-S
BEFANA-S	BENUMB-S	BHARAL-S	BISMAR-S	BOILER-S
BEFLAG-S	BENZAL-S	BHAVAN-S	BISQUE-S	BOLDEN-S
BEFLEA-S	BENZIL-S	BHAWAN-S	BISTER-S	BOLERO-S
BEFLUM-S	BENZIN-S	BHIKHU-S	BISTRE-S	BOLETE-S
BEFOAM-S	BENZOL-S	BHINDI-S	BISTRO-S	BOLIDE-S
BEFOOL-S	BENZYL-S	BHISTI-S	BITING-S	BOLINE-S
BEFOUL-S	BEPELT-S	BIBBER-S	BITMAP-S	BOLSON-S
BEFRET-S	BEPUFF-S	BIBBLE-S	BITSER-S	BOLTER-S
BEGALL-S	BERAKE-S	BIBLES-S	BITTER-S	BOMBER-S
BEGAZE-S	BERATE-S	BICARB-S	BITTIE-S	BOMMIE-S
BEGGAR-S	BERGEN-S	BICKER-S	BITTOR-S	BONACI-S
BEGIFT-S	BERIME-S	BICKIE-S	BITTUR-S	BONBON-S
BEGILD-S	BERLEY-S	BICORN-S	BIZONE-S	BONDER-S
BEGIRD-S	BERLIN-S	BICRON-S	BLADER-S	BONDUC-S
BEGLAD-S	BERRET-S	BIDDER-S	BLAGUE-S	BONHAM-S
BEGNAW-S	BERTHA-S	BIDENT-S	BLAMER-S	BONING-S
BEGRIM-S	BERTHE-S	BIDING-S	BLANCO-S	BONISM-S
BEGUIN-S	BESEEM-S	BIFACE-S	BLAZER-S	BONIST-S
BEGULF-S	BESIDE-S	BIFFER-S	BLAZON-S	BONITA-S
BEGUNK-S	BESIGH-S	BIFFIN-S	BLENDE-S	BONITO-S
BEHAVE-S	BESING-S	BIFTER-S	BLIGHT-S	BONNET-S

BONNIE-S	BOUGHT-S	BRIGHT-S	BUMBAG-S	BUSKER-S
BONOBO-S	BOUGIE-S	BRIGUE-S	BUMBLE-S	BUSKET-S
BONSAI-S	BOULLE-S	BRILLO-S	BUMKIN-S	BUSKIN-S
BONXIE-S	BOUNCE-S	BRINER-S	BUMMEL-S	BUSTEE-S
BOOBIE-S	BOURNE-S	BROCHE-S	BUMMER-S	BUSTER-S
BOOBOO-S	BOURSE-S	BROCHO-S	BUMMLE-S	BUSTIC-S
BOOCOO-S	BOUTON-S	BROGAN-S	BUMPER-S	BUSTLE-S
BOODIE-S	BOVATE-S	BROGUE-S	BUNDLE-S	BUTANE-S
BOODLE-S	BOVINE-S	BROKER-S	BUNGEE-S	BUTENE-S
BOOGER-S	BOVVER-S	BROLGA-S	BUNGER-S	BUTLER-S
BOOGEY-S	BOWFIN-S	BROMAL-S	BUNGEY-S	BUTTER-S
BOOGIE-S	BOWGET-S	BROMID-S	BUNGIE-S	BUTTLE-S
BOOHAI-S	BOWING-S	BROMIN-S	BUNGLE-S	BUTTON-S
BOOHOO-S	BOWLEG-S	BRONCO-S	BUNION-S	BUYOFF-S
BOOJUM-S	BOWLER-S	BRONZE-S	BUNJEE-S	BUYOUT-S
BOOKER-S	BOWPOT-S	BROOSE-S	BUNJIE-S	BUZUKI-S
BOOKIE-S	BOWSAW-S	BROUGH-S	BUNKER-S	BUZZER-S
BOOKOO-S	BOWSER-S	BROUZE-S	BUNKUM-S	BYELAW-S
BOOMER-S	BOWSEY-S	BROWSE-S	BUNNET-S	BYGONE-S
BOONER-S	BOWSIE-S	BROWST-S	BUNNIA-S	BYLANE-S
BOONGA-S	BOWWOW-S	BRUCIN-S	BUNSEN-S	BYLINE-S
BOORDE-S	BOWYER-S	BRUISE-S	BUNTAL-S	BYNAME-S
BOORKA-S	BOXCAR-S	BRULOT-S	BUNTER-S	BYPATH-S
BOOTEE-S	BOXFUL-S	BRUNET-S	BUNYIP-S	BYPLAY-S
BOOTIE-S	BOXING-S	BRUTER-S	BUPPIE-S	BYRLAW-S
BOOZER-S	BOYARD-S	BUBALE-S	BUQSHA-S	BYRNIE-S
BOPEEP-S	BRAATA-S	BUBBLE-S	BURBLE-S	BYROAD-S
BOPPER-S	BRACER-S	BUCKER-S	BURBOT-S	BYROOM-S
BORAGE-S	BRAHMA-S	BUCKET-S	BURDEN-S	BYTALK-S
BORANE-S	BRAIRD-S	BUCKIE-S	BURDIE-S	BYWORD-S
BORATE-S	BRAISE-S	BUCKLE-S	BUREAU-S	BYWORK-S
BORDAR-S	BRAIZE-S	BUCKRA-S	BURGEE-S	BYZANT-S
BORDEL-S	BRANLE-S	BUDDER-S	BURGER-S	CABALA-S
BORDER-S	BRASCO-S	BUDDHA-S	BURGLE-S	CABANA-S
BOREEN-S	BRASIL-S	BUDDLE-S	BURGOO-S	CABBIE-S
BORIDE-S	BRAVER-S	BUDGER-S	BURHEL-S	CABLER-S
BORING-S	BRAYER-S	BUDGET-S	BURIAL-S	CABLET-S
BORNYL-S	BRAZEN-S	BUDGIE-S	BURIER-S	CABRIE-S
BORROW-S	BRAZER-S	BUFFER-S	BURITI-S	CABRIO-S
BORSHT-S	BRAZIL-S	BUFFET-S	BURKER-S	CABRIT-S
BORSIC-S	BREARE-S	BUGEYE-S	BURLAP-S	CACHET-S
BORZOI-S	BREAST-S	BUGGAN-S	BURLER-S	CACHOU-S
BOSBOK-S	BREATH-S	BUGGER-S	BURLEY-S	CACKLE-S
BOSCHE-S	BREDIE-S	BUGGIN-S	BURNER-S	CACOON-S
BOSKET-S	BREESE-S	BUGLER-S	BURNET-S	CADAGA-S
BOSQUE-S	BREEST-S	BUGLET-S	BURNIE-S	CADAGI-S
BOSSET-S	BREEZE-S	BUGONG-S	BURPEE-S	CADDIE-S
BOSTON-S	BREHON-S	BUGOUT-S	BURREL-S	CADGER-S
BOTHAN-S	BREIST-S	BUGSHA-S	BURRER-S	CADUAC-S
BOTHER-S	BRENNE-S	BUHUND-S	BURROW-S	CAEOMA-S
BOTHIE-S	BRETON-S	BUIBUI-S	BURSAR-S	CAESAR-S
BOTNET-S	BREVET-S	BUKSHI-S	BURTON-S	CAFARD-S
BOTTLE-S	BREWER-S	BULBEL-S	BUSBAR-S	CAFILA-S
BOTTOM-S	BRIARD-S	BULBIL-S	BUSBOY-S	CAFTAN-S
BOUBOU-S	BRIBEE-S	BULBUL-S	BUSERA-S	CAGMAG-S
BOUCHE-S	BRIBER-S	BULGER-S	BUSHEL-S	CAGOUL-S
BOUCLE-S	BRIDAL-S	BULGUR-S	BUSHER-S	CAHIER-S
BOUDIN-S	BRIDGE-S	BULKER-S	BUSHIE-S	CAHOOT-S
BOUFFE-S	BRIDIE-S	BULLER-S	BUSHWA-S	CAILLE-S
BOUGET-S	BRIDLE-S	BULLET-S	BUSING-S	CAIMAC-S

CAIMAN-S	CANTON-S	CASHEW-S	CERMET-S	CHEVIN-S
CAIQUE-S	CANTOR-S	CASHOO-S	CEROON-S	CHEVRE-S
CAJOLE-S	CANULA-S	CASING-S	CERUSE-S	CHEWER-S
CAKING-S	CANVAS-S	CASINO-S	CERVID-S	CHEWET-S
CALALU-S	CANYON-S	CASITA-S	CESIUM-S	CHEWIE-S
CALCAR-S	CAPFUL-S	CASKET-S	CESSER-S	CHIACK-S
CALESA-S	CAPLES-S	CASQUE-S	CESTUI-S	CHIASM-S
CALICO-S	CAPLET-S	CASSIA-S	CESURA-S	CHIBOL-S
CALIGO-S	CAPLIN-S	CASTER-S	CESURE-S	CHICHA-S
CALIMA-S	CAPOTE-S	CASTLE-S	CETANE-S	CHICHI-S
CALIPH-S	CAPPER-S	CASTOR-S	CHABUK-S	CHICLE-S
CALKER-S	CAPRID-S	CASUAL-S	CHACMA-S	CHICON-S
CALKIN-S	CAPSID-S	CATALO-S	CHADAR-S	CHIDER-S
CALLAN-S	CAPTAN-S	CATENA-S	CHADOR-S	CHIELD-S
CALLEE-S	CAPTOR-S	CATGUT-S	CHAFER-S	CHIGGA-S
CALLER-S	CARACK-S	CATKIN-S	CHAGAN-S	CHIGOE-S
CALLET-S	CARACT-S	CATLIN-S	CHAINE-S	CHIGRE-S
CALLOP-S	CARAFE-S	CATNAP-S	CHAISE-S	CHIKOR-S
CALLOW-S	CARATE-S	CATNEP-S	CHAKRA-S	CHILDE-S
CALPAC-S	CARBON-S	CATNIP-S	CHALAH-S	CHILLI-S
CALQUE-S	CARBOY-S	CATSUP-S	CHALAN-S	CHIMAR-S
CALTHA-S	CARCEL-S	CATTIE-S	CHALEH-S	CHIMER-S
CALVER-S	CARDER-S	CAUDLE-S	CHALET-S	CHIMLA-S
CAMAIL-S	CARDIA-S	CAUKER-S	CHALLA-S	CHINAR-S
CAMBER-S	CARDIE-S	CAUSAL-S	CHANCE-S	CHIRRE-S
CAMERA-S	CARDON-S	CAUSER-S	CHANGE-S	CHISEL-S
CAMESE-S	CAREEN-S	CAUSEY-S	CHAPEL-S	CHITAL-S
CAMION-S	CAREER-S	CAUTEL-S	CHAPES-S	CHITIN-S
CAMISA-S	CAREME-S	CAUTER-S	CHAPKA-S	CHITON-S
CAMISE-S	CARFUL-S	CAVEAT-S	CHARET-S	CHOCHO-S
CAMLET-S	CARHOP-S	CAVERN-S	CHARGE-S	CHOCKO-S
CAMMIE-S	CARIBE-S	CAVIAR-S	CHARKA-S	CHOICE-S
CAMOTE-S	CARINA-S	CAVIER-S	CHARRO-S	CHOKER-S
CAMPER-S	CARLES-S	CAVING-S	CHARTA-S	CHOKEY-S
CAMPLE-S	CARLIN-S	CAVORT-S	CHASER-S	CHOKRA-S
CANADA-S	CARLOT-S	CAWING-S	CHASSE-S	CHOKRI-S
CANARD-S	CARNAL-S	CAWKER-S	CHATON-S	CHOLER-S
CANCAN-S	CARNET-S	CAYMAN-S	CHATTA-S	CHOLLA-S
CANCEL-S	CARNEY-S	CAYUSE-S	CHATTI-S	CHOOSE-S
CANCER-S	CARNIE-S	CEBOID-S	CHAUFE-S	CHOPIN-S
CANCHA-S	CARPAL-S	CEDULA-S	CHAUFF-S	CHORAL-S
CANDID-S	CARPEL-S	CEILER-S	CHAUNT-S	CHOREA-S
CANDIE-S	CARPER-S	CELIAC-S	CHAWER-S	CHOREE-S
CANDLE-S	CARPET-S	CELLAR-S	CHAZAN-S	CHOUGH-S
CANDOR-S	CARRAT-S	CEMBRA-S	CHEAPO-S	CHOUSE-S
CANFUL-S	CARREL-S	CEMENT-S	CHEBEC-S	CHOWRI-S
CANGLE-S	CARROM-S	CENOTE-S	CHEDER-S	CHOWSE-S
CANGUE-S	CARROT-S	CENSER-S	CHEERO-S	CHRISM-S
CANINE-S	CARSEY-S	CENSOR-S	CHEESE-S	CHROMA-S
CANING-S	CARTEL-S	CENTAL-S	CHEGOE-S	CHROME-S
CANKER-S	CARTER-S	CENTER-S	CHEMIC-S	CHROMO-S
CANNEL-S	CARTON-S	CENTRE-S	CHENAR-S	CHUKAR-S
CANNER-S	CARVEL-S	CENTUM-S	CHENET-S	CHUKKA-S
CANNON-S	CARVER-S	CERATE-S	CHEQUE-S	CHUKOR-S
CANOER-S	CASABA-S	CEREAL-S	CHERUB-S	CHUPPA-S
CANOLA-S	CASAVA-S	CERIPH-S	CHERUP-S	CHURRO-S
CANTAL-S	CASBAH-S	CERISE-S	CHESIL-S	CHYACK-S
CANTAR-S	CASEIN-S	CERITE-S	CHETAH-S	CHYMIC-S
CANTER-S	CASERN-S	CERIUM-S	CHEVEN-S	CHYPRE-S
CANTLE-S	CASHAW-S		CHEVET-S	CICADA-S

CICALA-S	COBBER-S	COLURE-S	COOSIN-S	COTTAR-S
CICERO-S	COBBLE-S	COMAKE-S	COOTER-S	COTTER-S
CICUTA-S	COBNUT-S	COMARB-S	COOTIE-S	COTTID-S
CIERGE-S	COBURG-S	COMART-S	COPALM-S	COTTON-S
CIGGIE-S	COBWEB-S	COMATE-S	COPECK-S	COTWAL-S
CILICE-S	COCAIN-S	COMBAT-S	COPIER-S	COTYLE-S
CIMIER-S	COCCID-S	COMBER-S	COPING-S	COTYPE-S
CINDER-S	COCHIN-S	COMBLE-S	COPITA-S	COUCAL-S
CINEMA-S	COCKER-S	COMEDO-S	COPLOT-S	COUCHE-S
CINEOL-S	COCKET-S	COMFIT-S	COPOUT-S	COUGAN-S
CINQUE-S	COCKLE-S	COMICE-S	COPPER-S	COUGAR-S
CIPHER-S	COCKUP-S	COMING-S	COPPIN-S	COULEE-S
CIRCAR-S	COCOON-S	COMMER-S	COPPLE-S	COUPEE-S
CIRCLE-S	CODDER-S	COMMIE-S	COPPRA-S	COUPER-S
CIRQUE-S	CODDLE-S	COMMIT-S	COPRAH-S	COUPLE-S
CITHER-S	CODEIA-S	COMMON-S	COPTER-S	COUPON-S
CITOLA-S	CODEIN-S	COMMOT-S	COPULA-S	COURIE-S
CITOLE-S	CODGER-S	COMPAS-S	COQUET-S	COURSE-S
CITRAL-S	CODING-S	COMPEL-S	CORBAN-S	COUSIN-S
CITRIN-S	CODIST-S	COMPER-S	CORBEL-S	COUTER-S
CITRON-S	CODLIN-S	COMPOT-S	CORBIE-S	COUTIL-S
CIVISM-S	COEDIT-S	CONCHA-S	CORDER-S	COUZIN-S
CLAMOR-S	COELOM-S	CONCHE-S	CORDON-S	COVENT-S
CLAQUE-S	COEMPT-S	CONCHO-S	CORIUM-S	COVERT-S
CLARET-S	COERCE-S	CONCUR-S	CORKER-S	COVING-S
CLAUSE-S	COEVAL-S	CONDER-S	CORKIR-S	COVYNE-S
CLAVER-S	COFFEE-S	CONDIE-S	CORMEL-S	COWAGE-S
CLAVIE-S	COFFER-S	CONDOM-S	CORNEA-S	COWARD-S
CLAWER-S	COFFIN-S	CONDOR-S	CORNEL-S	COWBOY-S
CLAXON-S	COFFLE-S	CONFAB-S	CORNER-S	COWPAT-S
CLEAVE-S	COGGER-S	CONFER-S	CORNET-S	COWPEA-S
CLEEVE-S	COGGIE-S	CONFIT-S	CORONA-S	COWPIE-S
CLEOME-S	COGGLE-S	CONGEE-S	COROZO-S	COWRIE-S
CLERIC-S	COGITO-S	CONGER-S	CORPSE-S	COYDOG-S
CLERID-S	COGNAC-S	CONGOU-S	CORRAL-S	COYOTE-S
CLEUCH-S	COGWAY-S	CONIMA-S	CORREA-S	COYPOU-S
CLEUGH-S	COHEAD-S	CONINE-S	CORRIE-S	COZIER-S
CLICHE-S	COHEIR-S	CONIUM-S	CORSAC-S	CRACKA-S
CLIENT-S	COHERE-S	CONJEE-S	CORSET-S	CRADLE-S
CLINIC-S	COHORN-S	CONKER-S	CORSEY-S	CRAMBE-S
CLIQUE-S	COHORT-S	CONNER-S	CORTIN-S	CRAMBO-S
CLITIC-S	COHOST-S	CONOID-S	CORVEE-S	CRAPLE-S
CLIVIA-S	COHUNE-S	CONSOL-S	CORVET-S	CRATER-S
CLOACA-S	COIFFE-S	CONSUL-S	CORVID-S	CRATON-S
CLOCHE-S	COIGNE-S	CONTRA-S	CORYMB-S	CRATUR-S
CLONER-S	COILER-S	CONURE-S	CORYZA-S	CRAVAT-S
CLOQUE-S	COINER-S	CONVEY-S	COSECH-S	CRAVEN-S
CLOSER-S	COJOIN-S	CONVOY-S	COSHER-S	CRAVER-S
CLOSET-S	COLDIE-S	COOING-S	COSIER-S	CRAYER-S
CLOTHE-S	COLEAD-S	COOKER-S	COSIGN-S	CRAYON-S
CLOUGH-S	COLLAR-S	COOKEY-S	COSINE-S	CREACH-S
CLOVER-S	COLLET-S	COOKIE-S	COSMEA-S	CREAGH-S
CLUSIA-S	COLLIE-S	COOLER-S	COSMID-S	CREASE-S
COAITA-S	COLLOP-S	COOLIE-S	COSMIN-S	CREATE-S
COALER-S	COLONE-S	COOLTH-S	COSSET-S	CRECHE-S
COATEE-S	COLOUR-S	COOMBE-S	COSSIE-S	CREDIT-S
COATER-S	COLTAN-S	COOPER-S	COSTAL-S	CREESE-S
COAXER-S	COLTER-S	COORIE-S	COSTAR-S	CREMOR-S
COBAEA-S	COLUGO-S	COOSEN-S	COSTER-S	CRENEL-S
COBALT-S	COLUMN-S	COOSER-S	COTISE-S	CREOLE-S

CREPON-S	CUPFUL-S	DACOIT-S	DATIVE-S	DEFANG-S
CRESOL-S	CUPOLA-S	DACRON-S	DATURA-S	DEFEAT-S
CRESYL-S	CUPPER-S	DACTYL-S	DAUBER-S	DEFECT-S
CRETIC-S	CUPRUM-S	DADDLE-S	DAUNER-S	DEFEND-S
CRETIN-S	CUPULE-S	DAEMON-S	DAUTIE-S	DEFIER-S
CREWEL-S	CURAGH-S	DAFTAR-S	DAWDLE-S	DEFILE-S
CRINGE-S	CURARA-S	DAFTIE-S	DAWNER-S	DEFINE-S
CRINUM-S	CURARE-S	DAGABA-S	DAWTIE-S	DEFLEA-S
CRITIC-S	CURARI-S	DAGGER-S	DAYBED-S	DEFOAM-S
CROCHE-S	CURATE-S	DAGGLE-S	DAYBOY-S	DEFORM-S
CROJIK-S	CURBER-S	DAGOBA-S	DAZZLE-S	DEFOUL-S
CRONET-S	CURDLE-S	DAHLIA-S	DEACON-S	DEFRAG-S
CROOVE-S	CURFEW-S	DAHOON-S	DEADEN-S	DEFRAY-S
CROSSE-S	CURIET-S	DAIDLE-S	DEADER-S	DEFUEL-S
CROTAL-S	CURITE-S	DAIKER-S	DEAFEN-S	DEFUND-S
CROTON-S	CURIUM-S	DAIKON-S	DEALER-S	DEFUSE-S
CROUPE-S	CURLER-S	DAIMIO-S	DEANER-S	DEFUZE-S
CROUTE-S	CURLEW-S	DAIMON-S	DEARIE-S	DEGAME-S
CROWEA-S	CURPEL-S	DAIMYO-S	DEARTH-S	DEGAMI-S
CROWER-S	CURRAN-S	DAKOIT-S	DEASIL-S	DEGERM-S
CROZER-S	CURRIE-S	DALASI-S	DEBARK-S	DEGOUT-S
CRUISE-S	CURSER-S	DALEDH-S	DEBASE-S	DEGREE-S
CRUIVE-S	CURSOR-S	DALETH-S	DEBATE-S	DEGUST-S
CRUMEN-S	CURTAL-S	DALLOP-S	DEBEAK-S	DEHORN-S
CRUSET-S	CURVET-S	DALTON-S	DEBONE-S	DEHORT-S
CRUSIE-S	CUSHAT-S	DAMAGE-S	DEBTEE-S	DEICER-S
CRUZIE-S	CUSHAW-S	DAMASK-S	DEBTOR-S	DEJECT-S
CRYING-S	CUSHIE-S	DAMMAR-S	DEBUNK-S	DEKARE-S
CRYPTO-S	CUSPID-S	DAMMER-S	DEBURR-S	DELATE-S
CUATRO-S	CUSSER-S	DAMNER-S	DECADE-S	DELEAD-S
CUBAGE-S	CUSTOM-S	DAMPEN-S	DECAFF-S	DELETE-S
CUBANE-S	CUTLAS-S	DAMPER-S	DECAMP-S	DELICE-S
CUBICA-S	CUTLER-S	DAMSEL-S	DECANE-S	DELICT-S
CUBISM-S	CUTLET-S	DAMSON-S	DECANT-S	DELIME-S
CUBIST-S	CUTOFF-S	DANCER-S	DECARB-S	DELIST-S
CUBOID-S	CUTOUT-S	DANDER-S	DECARE-S	DELOPE-S
CUCKOO-S	CUTTER-S	DANDLE-S	DECCIE-S	DELUDE-S
CUDDEN-S	CUTTLE-S	DANGER-S	DECEIT-S	DELUGE-S
CUDDIE-S	CUTTOE-S	DANGLE-S	DECERN-S	DELVER-S
CUDDIN-S	CYANID-S	DANTON-S	DECIDE-S	DEMAIN-S
CUDDLE-S	CYANIN-S	DAPHNE-S	DECILE-S	DEMAND-S
CUDGEL-S	CYBORG-S	DAPPER-S	DECIME-S	DEMARK-S
CUEIST-S	CYBRID-S	DAPPLE-S	DECKEL-S	DEMAST-S
CUESTA-S	CYCLER-S	DARBAR-S	DECKER-S	DEMEAN-S
CUFFIN-S	CYCLIN-S	DARGAH-S	DECKLE-S	DEMENT-S
CUFFLE-S	CYGNET-S	DARGLE-S	DECLAW-S	DEMISE-S
CUISSE-S	CYMBAL-S	DARING-S	DECOCT-S	DEMIST-S
CUITER-S	CYMENE-S	DARKEN-S	DECODE-S	DEMOTE-S
CULLAY-S	CYMLIN-S	DARKEY-S	DECOKE-S	DEMURE-S
CULLER-S	CYPHER-S	DARKIE-S	DECREE-S	DENGUE-S
CULLET-S	CYPRES-S	DARKLE-S	DECREW-S	DENIAL-S
CULMEN-S	CYPRID-S	DARNEL-S	DECTET-S	DENIER-S
CULTER-S	CYSTID-S	DARNER-S	DEDUCE-S	DENNET-S
CULVER-S	CYTASE-S	DARTER-S	DEDUCT-S	DENOTE-S
CUMBER-S	CYTODE-S	DARTLE-S	DEEJAY-S	DENTAL-S
CUMBIA-S	CZAPKA-S	DARTRE-S	DEEPEN-S	DENTEL-S
CUMMER-S	DABBER-S	DASHER-S	DEEPIE-S	DENTIL-S
CUMMIN-S	DABBLE-S	DASSIE-S	DEEWAN-S	DENTIN-S
CUNDUM-S	DACITE-S	DATCHA-S	DEFACE-S	DENUDE-S
CUNNER-S	DACKER-S	DATING-S	DEFAME-S	DEODAR-S

DEPART-S	DHURRA-S	DIPNET-S	DOGNAP-S	DOTARD-S
DEPEND-S	DIABLE-S	DIPOLE-S	DOLINA-S	DOTCOM-S
DEPERM-S	DIACID-S	DIPPER-S	DOLINE-S	DOTING-S
DEPICT-S	DIADEM-S	DIQUAT-S	DOLLAR-S	DOTTEL-S
DEPLOY-S	DIALER-S	DIRDAM-S	DOLLOP-S	DOTTER-S
DEPONE-S	DIALOG-S	DIRDUM-S	DOLMAN-S	DOTTLE-S
DEPORT-S	DIAMIN-S	DIRECT-S	DOLMEN-S	DOUANE-S
DEPOSE-S	DIAPER-S	DIRHAM-S	DOLOUR-S	DOUBLE-S
DEPUTE-S	DIAPIR-S	DIRHEM-S	DOMAIN-S	DOUCET-S
DERAIL-S	DIATOM-S	DIRIGE-S	DOMETT-S	DOUCHE-S
DERATE-S	DIAXON-S	DIRNDL-S	DOMINE-S	DOURAH-S
DERHAM-S	DIAZIN-S	DISARM-S	DOMINO-S	DOUSER-S
DERIDE-S	DIBBER-S	DISBAR-S	DONATE-S	DOUTER-S
DERIVE-S	DIBBLE-S	DISBUD-S	DONDER-S	DOWLNE-S
DESALT-S	DIBBUK-S	DISCUS-S	DONGLE-S	DOWNER-S
DESAND-S	DICAST-S	DISEUR-S	DONING-S	DOWSER-S
DESERT-S	DICING-S	DISMAL-S	DONJON-S	DOWSET-S
DESIGN-S	DICKER-S	DISMAN-S	DONKEY-S	DOYLEY-S
DESINE-S	DICKEY-S	DISMAY-S	DONNAT-S	DOZING-S
DESIRE-S	DICKIE-S	DISOWN-S	DONNEE-S	DRACHM-S
DESIST-S	DICTUM-S	DISPEL-S	DONNOT-S	DRAGEE-S
DESMAN-S	DIDACT-S	DISPLE-S	DONZEL-S	DRAGON-S
DESMID-S	DIDDER-S	DISTIL-S	DOOBIE-S	DRAPER-S
DESORB-S	DIDDLE-S	DISUSE-S	DOOCOT-S	DRAPET-S
DESPOT-S	DIEDRE-S	DITHER-S	DOODAD-S	DRAUNT-S
DESYNE-S	DIEOFF-S	DITONE-S	DOODAH-S	DRAWEE-S
DETAIL-S	DIESEL-S	DITTAY-S	DOODLE-S	DRAWER-S
DETAIN-S	DIETER-S	DIURON-S	DOODOO-S	DRAZEL-S
DETECT-S	DIFFER-S	DIVERT-S	DOOFER-S	DREARE-S
DETENT-S	DIGEST-S	DIVEST-S	DOOKET-S	DREDGE-S
DETENU-S	DIGGER-S	DIVIDE-S	DOOLAN-S	DREIDL-S
DETEST-S	DIGLOT-S	DIVINE-S	DOOLEE-S	DRIVEL-S
DETICK-S	DIKAST-S	DIVING-S	DOOLIE-S	DRIVER-S
DETORT-S	DIKDIK-S	DIZAIN-S	DOOSRA-S	DROGER-S
DETOUR-S	DIKKOP-S	DJEBEL-S	DOOWOP-S	DROGUE-S
DETUNE-S	DIKTAT-S	DJEMBE-S	DOOZER-S	DROICH-S
DEUTON-S	DILATE-S	DOATER-S	DOOZIE-S	DROMON-S
DEVALL-S	DILDOE-S	DOBBER-S	DOPANT-S	DRONER-S
DEVEIN-S	DILUTE-S	DOBBIE-S	DOPING-S	DRONGO-S
DEVEST-S	DIMBLE-S	DOBBIN-S	DOPPER-S	DROOME-S
DEVICE-S	DIMMER-S	DOBLON-S	DOPPIE-S	DROUTH-S
DEVISE-S	DIMOUT-S	DOBSON-S	DOPPIO-S	DROVER-S
DEVOIR-S	DIMPLE-S	DOCENT-S	DORADO-S	DROWND-S
DEVORE-S	DIMWIT-S	DOCKEN-S	DORBUG-S	DROWSE-S
DEVOTE-S	DINDLE-S	DOCKER-S	DORISE-S	DRUDGE-S
DEVOUR-S	DINERO-S	DOCKET-S	DORIZE-S	DRUPEL-S
DEVVEL-S	DINGER-S	DOCTOR-S	DORMER-S	DRYING-S
DEWANI-S	DINGEY-S	DODDER-S	DORMIN-S	DRYLOT-S
DEWITT-S	DINGLE-S	DODDLE-S	DORPER-S	DUALIN-S
DEWLAP-S	DINKEY-S	DODGEM-S	DORSAL-S	DUBBER-S
DEWOOL-S	DINKIE-S	DODGER-S	DORSEL-S	DUBBIN-S
DEWORM-S	DINKUM-S	DODKIN-S	DORSER-S	DUCKER-S
DEXTER-S	DINNER-S	DODMAN-S	DORTER-S	DUCKIE-S
DEZINC-S	DINNLE-S	DOFFER-S	DOSAGE-S	DUDDER-S
DHAMMA-S	DIOBOL-S	DOGATE-S	DOSSAL-S	DUDEEN-S
DHARMA-S	DIOXAN-S	DOGDOM-S	DOSSEL-S	DUDISM-S
DHARNA-S	DIOXID-S	DOGEAR-S	DOSSER-S	DUELER-S
DHOORA-S	DIOXIN-S	DOGGER-S	DOSSIL-S	DUELLO-S
DHOOTI-S	DIPLOE-S	DOGGIE-S	DOTAGE-S	DUENDE-S
DHURNA-S	DIPLON-S	DOGLEG-S	DOTANT-S	DUENNA-S

DUETTO-S	ECHARD-S	EMBASE-S	ENGORE-S	EPONYM-S
DUFFEL-S	ECHIUM-S	EMBLEM-S	ENGRAM-S	EPOPEE-S
DUFFER-S	ECHOER-S	EMBLIC-S	ENGULF-S	EQUANT-S
DUFFLE-S	ECLAIR-S	EMBOIL-S	ENHALO-S	EQUATE-S
DUGITE-S	ECLOSE-S	EMBOSK-S	ENIGMA-S	EQUINE-S
DUGONG-S	ECONUT-S	EMBRUE-S	ENISLE-S	EQUIPE-S
DUGOUT-S	ECTYPE-S	EMBRYO-S	ENJAMB-S	ERASER-S
DUHKHA-S	ECURIE-S	EMERGE-S	ENJOIN-S	ERBIUM-S
DUIKER-S	ECZEMA-S	EMEROD-S	ENLACE-S	ERGATE-S
DUKKAH-S	EDGING-S	EMETIC-S	ENLARD-S	ERIACH-S
DUKKHA-S	EDIBLE-S	EMETIN-S	ENLINK-S	ERINGO-S
DULCET-S	EDITOR-S	EMEUTE-S	ENLIST-S	ERLANG-S
DUMDUM-S	EFFACE-S	EMIGRE-S	ENLOCK-S	ERMINE-S
DUMPER-S	EFFECT-S	EMMOVE-S	ENMOVE-S	EROTIC-S
DUMPLE-S	EFFEIR-S	EMODIN-S	ENNAGE-S	ERRAND-S
DUNDER-S	EFFERE-S	EMOTER-S	ENNEAD-S	ERRANT-S
DUNGER-S	EFFING-S	EMPALE-S	ENOUGH-S	ERRATA-S
DUNITE-S	EFFORT-S	EMPARE-S	ENRACE-S	ERRING-S
DUNKER-S	EFFRAY-S	EMPARL-S	ENRAGE-S	ERYNGO-S
DUNLIN-S	EFFUSE-S	EMPART-S	ENRANK-S	ESCAPE-S
DUOLOG-S	EGENCE-S	EMPIRE-S	ENRING-S	ESCARP-S
DUPION-S	EGGCUP-S	EMPLOY-S	ENROBE-S	ESCHAR-S
DUPLET-S	EGGLER-S	EMPUSA-S	ENROLL-S	ESCHEW-S
DURANT-S	EGGNOG-S	EMPUSE-S	ENROOT-S	ESCORT-S
DURBAR-S	EGOISM-S	EMULGE-S	ENSEAL-S	ESCROC-S
DURDUM-S	EGOIST-S	EMUNGE-S	ENSEAM-S	ESCROL-S
DURGAH-S	EIGHTH-S	ENABLE-S	ENSEAR-S	ESCROW-S
DURGAN-S	EIRACK-S	ENAMEL-S	ENSERF-S	ESCUDO-S
DURIAN-S	EISELL-S	ENAMOR-S	ENSIGN-S	ESLOIN-S
DURION-S	ELANCE-S	ENCAGE-S	ENSILE-S	ESPADA-S
DURRIE-S	ELANET-S	ENCALM-S	ENSOUL-S	ESPIAL-S
DUSKEN-S	ELAPID-S	ENCAMP-S	ENSURE-S	ESPIER-S
DUSTER-S	ELAPSE-S	ENCASE-S	ENTAIL-S	ESPRIT-S
DUSTUP-S	ELATER-S	ENCAVE-S	ENTAME-S	ESSIVE-S
DUYKER-S	ELCHEE-S	ENCINA-S	ENTICE-S	ESSOIN-S
DYADIC-S	ELDING-S	ENCODE-S	ENTIRE-S	ESTATE-S
DYBBUK-S	ELEGIT-S	ENCORE-S	ENTOIL-S	ESTEEM-S
DYEING-S	ELENCH-S	ENCYST-S	ENTOMB-S	ESTRAY-S
DYNAMO-S	ELEVEN-S	ENDART-S	ENTRAP-S	ESTRIN-S
DYNAST-S	ELEVON-S	ENDEAR-S	ENTREE-S	ESTRUM-S
DYNEIN-S	ELICHE-S	ENDING-S	ENVIER-S	ETALON-S
DYNODE-S	ELICIT-S	ENDITE-S	ENVIRO-S	ETAMIN-S
DYVOUR-S	ELIXIR-S	ENDIVE-S	ENWALL-S	ETCHER-S
DZEREN-S	ELODEA-S	ENDRIN-S	ENWIND-S	ETHANE-S
EAGLET-S	ELOIGN-S	ENDURE-S	ENWOMB-S	ETHENE-S
EARBOB-S	ELOPER-S	ENDURO-S	ENWRAP-S	ETHION-S
EARBUD-S	ELSHIN-S	ENERVE-S	ENZIAN-S	ETHNIC-S
EARCON-S	ELTCHI-S	ENFACE-S	ENZONE-S	ETHYNE-S
EARFUL-S	ELUANT-S	ENFANT-S	ENZYME-S	ETOILE-S
EARING-S	ELUATE-S	ENFIRE-S	EOLITH-S	ETRIER-S
EARLAP-S	ELUDER-S	ENFOLD-S	EONISM-S	ETYMON-S
EARNER-S	ELUENT-S	ENFORM-S	EOSINE-S	EUCAIN-S
EARWIG-S	ELUTOR-S	ENFREE-S	EPARCH-S	EUCHRE-S
EASTER-S	EMBACE-S	ENGAGE-S	EPAULE-S	EUMONG-S
EATAGE-S	EMBAIL-S	ENGAOL-S	EPEIRA-S	EUMUNG-S
EATCHE-S	EMBALE-S	ENGILD-S	EPHEBE-S	EUNUCH-S
EATING-S	EMBALL-S	ENGINE-S	EPIGON-S	EUOUAE-S
EBAYER-S	EMBALM-S	ENGIRD-S	EPILOG-S	EUPHON-S
ECARTE-S	EMBANK-S	ENGLUT-S	EPIMER-S	EUPNEA-S
ECBOLE-S	EMBARK-S	ENGOBE-S	EPOCHA-S	EUREKA-S

EVADER-S	FACTUM-S	FAWNER-S	FILMER-S	FLOWER-S
EVEJAR-S	FADDLE-S	FEAGUE-S	FILTER-S	FLUATE-S
EVENER-S	FADEIN-S	FEARER-S	FIMBLE-S	FLUENT-S
EVINCE-S	FADEUR-S	FECIAL-S	FINALE-S	FLUGEL-S
EVOKER-S	FADING-S	FECULA-S	FINDER-S	FLUTER-S
EVOLUE-S	FAERIE-S	FEDORA-S	FINEER-S	FLYBOY-S
EVOLVE-S	FAGGOT-S	FEEBLE-S	FINGAN-S	FLYING-S
EVOVAE-S	FAIBLE-S	FEEDER-S	FINGER-S	FLYOFF-S
EVULSE-S	FAILLE-S	FEELER-S	FINIAL-S	FLYWAY-S
EVZONE-S	FAINNE-S	FEERIE-S	FINING-S	FOAMER-S
EXACTA-S	FAITOR-S	FEERIN-S	FINITE-S	FODDER-S
EXACUM-S	FAJITA-S	FEIJOA-S	FINJAN-S	FOETOR-S
EXAMEN-S	FAKEER-S	FELINE-S	FINNAC-S	FOGBOW-S
EXARCH-S	FALCON-S	FELLAH-S	FINNAN-S	FOGDOG-S
EXCAMB-S	FALLAL-S	FELLER-S	FINNER-S	FOGGER-S
EXCEED-S	FALLER-S	FELLOE-S	FIORIN-S	FOGLES-S
EXCEPT-S	FALLOW-S	FELLOW-S	FIPPLE-S	FOGRAM-S
EXCIDE-S	FALSER-S	FELTER-S	FIRING-S	FOIBLE-S
EXCISE-S	FALSIE-S	FEMALE-S	FIRKIN-S	FOISON-S
EXCITE-S	FALTER-S	FENCER-S	FIRLOT-S	FOLATE-S
EXCUSE-S	FAMINE-S	FENDER-S	FIRMAN-S	FOLDER-S
EXEMPT-S	FANDOM-S	FENNEC-S	FIRMER-S	FOLDUP-S
EXHALE-S	FANEGA-S	FENNEL-S	FISCAL-S	FOLIUM-S
EXHORT-S	FANFIC-S	FERBAM-S	FISGIG-S	FOLKIE-S
EXHUME-S	FANGLE-S	FERLIE-S	FISHER-S	FOLLOW-S
EXILER-S	FANION-S	FERREL-S	FISSLE-S	FOMENT-S
EXOGEN-S	FANJET-S	FERRET-S	FITCHE-S	FOMITE-S
EXONYM-S	FANKLE-S	FERRUM-S	FITTER-S	FONDLE-S
EXOPOD-S	FANNEL-S	FERULA-S	FIXATE-S	FONDUE-S
EXOTIC-S	FANNER-S	FERULE-S	FIXING-S	FOODIE-S
EXPAND-S	FANTAD-S	FERVOR-S	FIXURE-S	FOOTER-S
EXPECT-S	FANTOD-S	FESCUE-S	FIZGIG-S	FOOTIE-S
EXPEND-S	FANTOM-S	FESTAL-S	FIZZEN-S	FOOTLE-S
EXPERT-S	FAQUIR-S	FESTER-S	FIZZER-S	FOOTRA-S
EXPIRE-S	FARCER-S	FETIAL-S	FIZZLE-S	FOOZLE-S
EXPORT-S	FARCIE-S	FETTER-S	FLACON-S	FORAGE-S
EXPOSE-S	FARCIN-S	FETTLE-S	FLAGON-S	FORBID-S
EXPUGN-S	FARDEL-S	FEUTRE-S	FLAKER-S	FORCAT-S
EXSECT-S	FARDEN-S	FEWMET-S	FLAMBE-S	FORCER-S
EXSERT-S	FARFAL-S	FEWTER-S	FLAMEN-S	FOREST-S
EXTEND-S	FARFEL-S	FIACRE-S	FLAMER-S	FORGER-S
EXTENT-S	FARINA-S	FIANCE-S	FLANGE-S	FORGET-S
EXTERN-S	FARMER-S	FIASCO-S	FLASER-S	FORHOO-S
EXTINE-S	FARREN-S	FIAUNT-S	FLAUNE-S	FORHOW-S
EXTIRP-S	FARROW-S	FIBBER-S	FLAUNT-S	FORINT-S
EXTOLL-S	FASCIA-S	FIBRIL-S	FLAUTA-S	FORKER-S
EXTORT-S	FASTEN-S	FIBRIN-S	FLAVIN-S	FORMAL-S
EYALET-S	FASTER-S	FIBULA-S	FLAVOR-S	FORMAT-S
EYEBAR-S	FASTIE-S	FICKLE-S	FLAYER-S	FORMER-S
EYECUP-S	FATHER-S	FICTOR-S	FLECHE-S	FORMOL-S
EYEFUL-S	FATHOM-S	FIDDLE-S	FLEDGE-S	FORMYL-S
EYELET-S	FATSIA-S	FIDGET-S	FLEECE-S	FORPET-S
EYELID-S	FATTEN-S	FIESTA-S	FLENSE-S	FORPIT-S
EYLIAD-S	FATWAH-S	FIGJAM-S	FLEXOR-S	FORRAY-S
FABLER-S	FAUCAL-S	FIGURE-S	FLIGHT-S	FORSAY-S
FABRIC-S	FAUCET-S	FILFOT-S	FLORAL-S	FOSSIL-S
FACADE-S	FAUTOR-S	FILING-S	FLORET-S	FOSSOR-S
FACIAL-S	FAVELA-S	FILLER-S	FLORIN-S	FOSTER-S
FACING-S	FAVISM-S	FILLET-S	FLOTEL-S	FOTHER-S
FACTOR-S	FAVOUR-S	FILLIP-S	FLOUSE-S	FOULIE-S

FOURTH-S	FUNNEL-S	GAMMER-S	GEDACT-S	GIMBAL-S
FOUSSA-S	FURANE-S	GAMMON-S	GEEBAG-S	GIMLET-S
FOUTER-S	FUREUR-S	GAMONE-S	GEEGAW-S	GIMMAL-S
FOUTRA-S	FURFUR-S	GANDER-S	GEEZAH-S	GIMMER-S
FOUTRE-S	FURKID-S	GANGER-S	GEEZER-S	GIMMIE-S
FOWLER-S	FURLER-S	GANGUE-S	GEGGIE-S	GIMMOR-S
FOXING-S	FUROLE-S	GANJAH-S	GEISHA-S	GINGAL-S
FRAGOR-S	FURORE-S	GANNET-S	GELADA-S	GINGER-S
FRAISE-S	FURROW-S	GANOID-S	GELANT-S	GINGKO-S
FRAMER-S	FUSAIN-S	GANOIN-S	GELATE-S	GINGLE-S
FRAPPE-S	FUSION-S	GANSEY-S	GELATI-S	GINKGO-S
FRATER-S	FUSSER-S	GAOLER-S	GELATO-S	GINNEL-S
FRAZIL-S	FUSTET-S	GAPING-S	GELCAP-S	GINNER-S
FREEZE-S	FUSTIC-S	GAPPER-S	GELDER-S	GIPPER-S
FREMIT-S	FUSTOC-S	GARAGE-S	GEMOTE-S	GIPSEN-S
FRENUM-S	FUTSAL-S	GARBLE-S	GENDER-S	GIRDER-S
FRESCO-S	FUTURE-S	GARCON-S	GENEVA-S	GIRDLE-S
FRIAND-S	FUZZLE-S	GARDEN-S	GENNEL-S	GIRKIN-S
FRICHT-S	FYLFOT-S	GARGET-S	GENNET-S	GIRLIE-S
FRIDGE-S	GABBER-S	GARGLE-S	GENOME-S	GIRNEL-S
FRIEND-S	GABBLE-S	GARIAL-S	GENTLE-S	GIRNER-S
FRIEZE-S	GABBRO-S	GARJAN-S	GENTOO-S	GITANA-S
FRIGHT-S	GABION-S	GARLIC-S	GERBIL-S	GITANO-S
FRIGOT-S	GABLET-S	GARNER-S	GERENT-S	GIVING-S
FRINGE-S	GABOON-S	GARNET-S	GERMAN-S	GIZZEN-S
FRIPON-S	GADDER-S	GAROTE-S	GERMEN-S	GLAIRE-S
FRISEE-S	GADGET-S	GARRAN-S	GERMIN-S	GLAIVE-S
FRISKA-S	GADGIE-S	GARRET-S	GERUND-S	GLAMOR-S
FRIVOL-S	GADOID-S	GARRON-S	GETTER-S	GLANCE-S
FRIZER-S	GAFFER-S	GARROT-S	GEWGAW-S	GLAZER-S
FROING-S	GAGAKU-S	GARRYA-S	GEYSER-S	GLEAVE-S
FROISE-S	GAGGER-S	GARTER-S	GHARRI-S	GLEDGE-S
FROLIC-S	GAGGLE-S	GARUDA-S	GHAZAL-S	GLIDER-S
FROWST-S	GAINER-S	GARVEY-S	GHAZEL-S	GLIOMA-S
FRUICT-S	GAITER-S	GARVIE-S	GHERAO-S	GLOBIN-S
FRYING-S	GALAGE-S	GASBAG-S	GHESSE-S	GLOIRE-S
FRYPAN-S	GALAGO-S	GASCON-S	GHETTO-S	GLORIA-S
FUCKER-S	GALENA-S	GASKET-S	GHIBLI-S	GLOSSA-S
FUCKUP-S	GALERE-S	GASKIN-S	GIAOUR-S	GLOVER-S
FUCOID-S	GALIOT-S	GASPER-S	GIBBER-S	GLOWER-S
FUCOSE-S	GALLET-S	GASSER-S	GIBBET-S	GLUCAN-S
FUDDLE-S	GALLEY-S	GASTER-S	GIBBON-S	GLURGE-S
FUELER-S	GALLON-S	GATEAU-S	GIBLET-S	GLUTEN-S
FUGATO-S	GALLOP-S	GATHER-S	GIBSON-S	GLYCAN-S
FUHRER-S	GALLOW-S	GATING-S	GIDGEE-S	GLYCIN-S
FULFIL-S	GALOOT-S	GAUCHO-S	GIDJEE-S	GLYCOL-S
FULGOR-S	GALORE-S	GAUFER-S	GIFTEE-S	GLYCYL-S
FULHAM-S	GALUTH-S	GAUFRE-S	GIGGIT-S	GNAWER-S
FULLAM-S	GALYAC-S	GAUGER-S	GIGGLE-S	GNOMON-S
FULLAN-S	GALYAK-S	GAUPER-S	GIGLET-S	GOALIE-S
FULLER-S	GAMBET-S	GAVAGE-S	GIGLOT-S	GOANNA-S
FULMAR-S	GAMBIA-S	GAVIAL-S	GIGOLO-S	GOATEE-S
FUMADO-S	GAMBIR-S	GAWKER-S	GILCUP-S	GOBANG-S
FUMAGE-S	GAMBIT-S	GAWPER-S	GILDER-S	GOBBET-S
FUMBLE-S	GAMBLE-S	GAYDAR-S	GILGAI-S	GOBBLE-S
FUNDER-S	GAMBOL-S	GAZABO-S	GILGIE-S	GOBIID-S
FUNDIE-S	GAMETE-S	GAZEBO-S	GILLER-S	GOBLET-S
FUNGAL-S	GAMINE-S	GAZING-S	GILLET-S	GOBLIN-S
FUNKER-S	GAMING-S	GAZOON-S	GILLIE-S	GODDAM-S
FUNKIA-S	GAMMAT-S	GAZUMP-S	GILPEY-S	GODDEN-S

GODOWN-S	GOZZAN-S	GUAIAC-S	GYPSUM-S	HANGUP-S
GODSON-S	GRABEN-S	GUANAY-S	GYRASE-S	HANJAR-S
GODWIT-S	GRADER-S	GUANGO-S	GYRATE-S	HANKER-S
GOFFER-S	GRADIN-S	GUANIN-S	GYRENE-S	HANKIE-S
GOGGLE-S	GRAHAM-S	GUANXI-S	GYTTJA-S	HANSEL-S
GOGLET-S	GRAILE-S	GUBBAH-S	HABOOB-S	HANSOM-S
GOITER-S	GRAINE-S	GUDDLE-S	HACKEE-S	HANTLE-S
GOITRE-S	GRAITH-S	GUENON-S	HACKER-S	HAPPEN-S
GOLDEN-S	GRAKLE-S	GUFFAW-S	HACKIE-S	HAPTEN-S
GOLFER-S	GRAMMA-S	GUFFIE-S	HACKLE-S	HAPTIC-S
GOLLAN-S	GRAMME-S	GUGGLE-S	HADDIE-S	HAPUKA-S
GOLLAR-S	GRAMPA-S	GUGLET-S	HADITH-S	HAPUKU-S
GOLLER-S	GRANGE-S	GUIDER-S	HADJEE-S	HARBOR-S
GOLLOP-S	GRAPLE-S	GUIDON-S	HADRON-S	HARDEN-S
GOMBRO-S	GRAPPA-S	GUILER-S	HAEMIN-S	HAREEM-S
GOMOKU-S	GRATER-S	GUIMPE-S	HAFFET-S	HARELD-S
GOMUTI-S	GRATIN-S	GUINEA-S	HAFFIT-S	HARIRA-S
GOMUTO-S	GRAVEL-S	GUISER-S	HAFTER-S	HARKEN-S
GONGYO-S	GRAVER-S	GUITAR-S	HAGBUT-S	HARLOT-S
GONIFF-S	GRAYLE-S	GUIZER-S	HAGDEN-S	HARMAN-S
GONOPH-S	GRAZER-S	GULDEN-S	HAGDON-S	HARMEL-S
GOOBER-S	GREASE-S	GULLER-S	HAGGLE-S	HARMER-S
GOODBY-S	GREAVE-S	GULLET-S	HAGLET-S	HARMIN-S
GOODIE-S	GREECE-S	GULLEY-S	HAIDUK-S	HARPER-S
GOOGLE-S	GREESE-S	GULPER-S	HAILER-S	HARPIN-S
GOOGOL-S	GREETE-S	GUMMER-S	HAIQUE-S	HARROW-S
GOOLEY-S	GREIGE-S	GUMNUT-S	HAIRDO-S	HARTAL-S
GOOLIE-S	GRICER-S	GUNDOG-S	HAIRIF-S	HARTEN-S
GOONDA-S	GRIECE-S	GUNITE-S	HAIRST-S	HASLET-S
GOONEY-S	GRIEVE-S	GUNNEL-S	HAJJAH-S	HASSAR-S
GOONIE-S	GRIFFE-S	GUNNER-S	HAKEEM-S	HASSEL-S
GOORAL-S	GRIGRI-S	GUNSEL-S	HALALA-S	HASSLE-S
GOORIE-S	GRILLE-S	GUNTER-S	HALIDE-S	HASTEN-S
GOOROO-S	GRILSE-S	GUNYAH-S	HALITE-S	HATFUL-S
GOOSEY-S	GRINGA-S	GURAMI-S	HALLAH-S	HATPEG-S
GOPHER-S	GRINGO-S	GURGLE-S	HALLAL-S	HATPIN-S
GOPURA-S	GRIPER-S	GURJUN-S	HALLAN-S	HATRED-S
GORGER-S	GRIPPE-S	GURLET-S	HALLEL-S	HATTER-S
GORGET-S	GRISON-S	GURNET-S	HALLOA-S	HAULER-S
GORGIA-S	GRIVET-S	GURNEY-S	HALLOO-S	HAUSEN-S
GORGIO-S	GROCER-S	GURRAH-S	HALLOW-S	HAUYNE-S
GORGON-S	GROMET-S	GUSHER-S	HALOID-S	HAVING-S
GORHEN-S	GROOVE-S	GUSLAR-S	HALSER-S	HAVIOR-S
GORING-S	GROPER-S	GUSSET-S	HALTER-S	HAWALA-S
GOSLET-S	GROSER-S	GUSSIE-S	HALVAH-S	HAWKER-S
GOSPEL-S	GROSET-S	GUTFUL-S	HALVER-S	HAWKEY-S
GOSSAN-S	GROTTO-S	GUTROT-S	HAMADA-S	HAWKIE-S
GOSSIB-S	GROUGH-S	GUTSER-S	HAMATE-S	HAWSER-S
GOSSIP-S	GROUND-S	GUTTER-S	HAMAUL-S	HAYING-S
GOSTER-S	GROUSE-S	GUTTLE-S	HAMBLE-S	HAYMOW-S
GOTCHA-S	GROVEL-S	GUTZER-S	HAMLET-S	HAYSEL-S
GOTHIC-S	GROVET-S	GUYLER-S	HAMMAL-S	HAZARD-S
GOUGER-S	GROWER-S	GUZZLE-S	HAMMAM-S	HAZING-S
GOUJON-S	GROWTH-S	GWEDUC-S	HAMMER-S	HAZMAT-S
GOURDE-S	GROYNE-S	GYMBAL-S	HAMPER-S	HAZZAN-S
GOUTTE-S	GRUDGE-S	GYMMAL-S	HAMZAH-S	HEADER-S
GOVERN-S	GRUGRU-S	GYMPIE-S	HANDER-S	HEALEE-S
GOWFER-S	GRUMPH-S	GYNNEY-S	HANDLE-S	HEALER-S
GOWLAN-S	GRUNGE-S	GYPPER-S	HANGAR-S	HEALTH-S
GOWPEN-S	GRYFON-S	GYPPIE-S	HANGER-S	HEAPER-S

HEARER-S	HEXONE-S	HOLLOO-S	HUBCAP-S	IAMBIC-S
HEARSE-S	HEXOSE-S	HOLLOW-S	HUCKLE-S	ICECAP-S
HEARTH-S	HEYDAY-S	HOLMIA-S	HUDDLE-S	ICICLE-S
HEASTE-S	HEYDEY-S	HOMAGE-S	HUFFER-S	IDEATE-S
HEATER-S	HICCUP-S	HOMBRE-S	HUGGER-S	IGNARO-S
HEAUME-S	HICKEY-S	HOMING-S	HUIPIL-S	IGNITE-S
HEAVEN-S	HICKIE-S	HONCHO-S	HULLER-S	IGNORE-S
HEAVER-S	HIDAGE-S	HONDLE-S	HULLOA-S	IGUANA-S
HEBONA-S	HIDDER-S	HONKER-S	HULLOO-S	ILLIAD-S
HECKLE-S	HIDING-S	HONKEY-S	HUMATE-S	ILLIPE-S
HECTIC-S	HIGGLE-S	HONKIE-S	HUMBLE-S	ILLITE-S
HECTOR-S	HIGHER-S	HONOUR-S	HUMBUG-S	ILLUDE-S
HEDDLE-S	HIGHTH-S	HOODIA-S	HUMECT-S	ILLUME-S
HEDERA-S	HIJACK-S	HOODIE-S	HUMHUM-S	ILLUPI-S
HEDGER-S	HIJRAH-S	HOODOO-S	HUMINT-S	IMAGER-S
HEEDER-S	HILLER-S	HOOFER-S	HUMITE-S	IMARET-S
HEEHAW-S	HILLOA-S	HOOKAH-S	HUMLIE-S	IMBALM-S
HEELER-S	HINDER-S	HOOKER-S	HUMMEL-S	IMBARK-S
HEEZIE-S	HINGER-S	HOOKEY-S	HUMMER-S	IMBASE-S
HEFTER-S	HINTER-S	HOOKUP-S	HUMMUM-S	IMBIBE-S
HEGARI-S	HIPPEN-S	HOOLEY-S	HUMOUR-S	IMBIZO-S
HEGIRA-S	HIPPIE-S	HOOLIE-S	HUMPEN-S	IMBOSK-S
HEIFER-S	HIPPIN-S	HOOPER-S	HUMPER-S	IMBRUE-S
HEIGHT-S	HIRAGE-S	HOOPLA-S	HUMVEE-S	IMMASK-S
HEINIE-S	HIRING-S	HOOPOE-S	HUNGAN-S	IMMUNE-S
HEJIRA-S	HIRPLE-S	HOOPOO-S	HUNGER-S	IMMURE-S
HELIUM-S	HIRSEL-S	HOORAH-S	HUNKER-S	IMPACT-S
HELLER-S	HIRSLE-S	HOORAY-S	HUNKEY-S	IMPAIR-S
HELMER-S	HISSER-S	HOOTER-S	HUNKIE-S	IMPALA-S
HELMET-S	HITHER-S	HOOVER-S	HUNTER-S	IMPALE-S
HELPER-S	HITTER-S	HOPDOG-S	HUPPAH-S	IMPARK-S
HEMINA-S	HOAGIE-S	HOPPER-S	HURDEN-S	IMPARL-S
HEMMER-S	HOAXER-S	HOPPLE-S	HURDLE-S	IMPART-S
HEMPIE-S	HOBBER-S	HORKEY-S	HURLER-S	IMPAVE-S
HENBIT-S	HOBBIT-S	HORNER-S	HURLEY-S	IMPAWN-S
HENLEY-S	HOBBLE-S	HORNET-S	HURRAH-S	IMPEDE-S
HENNER-S	HOBDAY-S	HORROR-S	HURRAY-S	IMPEND-S
HENNIN-S	HOBJOB-S	HORSON-S	HURTER-S	IMPHEE-S
HEPCAT-S	HOBNOB-S	HORSTE-S	HURTLE-S	IMPING-S
HEPTAD-S	HOCKER-S	HOSIER-S	HUSHER-S	IMPONE-S
HERALD-S	HOCKEY-S	HOSTEL-S	HUSKER-S	IMPORT-S
HERBAL-S	HOCKLE-S	HOSTIE-S	HUSSAR-S	IMPOSE-S
HERBAR-S	HODDEN-S	HOTBED-S	HUSSIF-S	IMPOST-S
HERDEN-S	HODDIN-S	HOTDOG-S	HUSTLE-S	IMPROV-S
HERDER-S	HODDLE-S	HOTPOT-S	HUTZPA-S	IMPUGN-S
HERDIC-S	HOGGER-S	HOTROD-S	HUZOOR-S	IMPUTE-S
HERIOT-S	HOGGET-S	HOTTER-S	HUZZAH-S	INANGA-S
HERMIT-S	HOGGIN-S	HOTTIE-S	HYAENA-S	INBRED-S
HERNIA-S	HOGNUT-S	HOUDAH-S	HYALIN-S	INCAGE-S
HEROIC-S	HOGTIE-S	HOUDAN-S	HYBRID-S	INCANT-S
HEROIN-S	HOIDEN-S	HOUSEL-S	HYDRID-S	INCASE-S
HEROON-S	HOISIN-S	HOUSER-S	HYDYNE-S	INCAVE-S
HETERO-S	HOLARD-S	HOWDAH-S	HYLISM-S	INCEDE-S
HETMAN-S	HOLDER-S	HOWDIE-S	HYLIST-S	INCENT-S
HEWING-S	HOLDUP-S	HOWKER-S	HYMNAL-S	INCEPT-S
HEXACT-S	HOLING-S	HOWLER-S	HYPATE-S	INCEST-S
HEXADE-S	HOLISM-S	HOWLET-S	HYPHEN-S	INCHER-S
HEXANE-S	HOLIST-S	HOYDEN-S	HYPNIC-S	INCISE-S
HEXENE-S	HOLLER-S	HRYVNA-S	HYPNUM-S	INCITE-S
HEXING-S	HOLLOA-S	HUBBUB-S	HYSSOP-S	INCLIP-S

INCOME-S	INSIST-S	ISOMER-S	JEREED-S	JOWARI-S
INCUSE-S	INSOLE-S	ISOPOD-S	JERKER-S	JOWLER-S
INDABA-S	INSOUL-S	ISSUER-S	JERKIN-S	JOYPOP-S
INDART-S	INSPAN-S	ISTANA-S	JERQUE-S	JUBBAH-S
INDENE-S	INSTAL-S	ITALIC-S	JERRID-S	JUBHAH-S
INDENT-S	INSTAR-S	IXODID-S	JERSEY-S	JUBILE-S
INDICT-S	INSTEP-S	IZZARD-S	JESSIE-S	JUDDER-S
INDIGO-S	INSTIL-S	JABBER-S	JESTEE-S	JUDGER-S
INDITE-S	INSULA-S	JABBLE-S	JESTER-S	JUDOGI-S
INDIUM-S	INSULT-S	JABIRU-S	JESUIT-S	JUDOKA-S
INDOLE-S	INSURE-S	JACANA-S	JETLAG-S	JUGFUL-S
INDOOR-S	INTAKE-S	JACARE-S	JETSAM-S	JUGGLE-S
INDUCE-S	INTEND-S	JACKAL-S	JETSOM-S	JUGLET-S
INDUCT-S	INTENT-S	JACKER-S	JETSON-S	JUICER-S
INDULT-S	INTERN-S	JACKET-S	JETTON-S	JUJUBE-S
INDUNA-S	INTIMA-S	JAEGER-S	JETWAY-S	JUMART-S
INFALL-S	INTINE-S	JAGGER-S	JEZAIL-S	JUMBAL-S
INFAME-S	INTOMB-S	JAGHIR-S	JHATKA-S	JUMBIE-S
INFANT-S	INTONE-S	JAGUAR-S	JIBBAH-S	JUMBLE-S
INFARE-S	INTORT-S	JAILER-S	JIBBER-S	JUMPER-S
INFECT-S	INTRON-S	JAILOR-S	JICAMA-S	JUNGLE-S
INFEFT-S	INTUIT-S	JAMBEE-S	JIGGER-S	JUNGLI-S
INFEST-S	INTURN-S	JAMBER-S	JIGGLE-S	JUNIOR-S
INFILL-S	INTUSE-S	JAMBOK-S	JIGJIG-S	JUNKER-S
INFIRM-S	INULIN-S	JAMBUL-S	JIGSAW-S	JUNKET-S
INFLOW-S	INVADE-S	JAMJAR-S	JIHADI-S	JUNKIE-S
INFOLD-S	INVENT-S	JAMMER-S	JILBAB-S	JUPATI-S
INFORM-S	INVERT-S	JAMPAN-S	JILGIE-S	JURANT-S
INFUSE-S	INVEST-S	JAMPOT-S	JILLET-S	JURIST-S
INGATE-S	INVITE-S	JANDAL-S	JILTER-S	JUSTER-S
INGENU-S	INVOKE-S	JANGLE-S	JIMJAM-S	JUSTLE-S
INGEST-S	INWALL-S	JANKER-S	JIMMIE-S	JYMOLD-S
INGINE-S	INWARD-S	JANSKY-S	JINGAL-S	KABAKA-S
INGULF-S	INWICK-S	JAPING-S	JINGLE-S	KABALA-S
INHALE-S	INWIND-S	JARFUL-S	JINKER-S	KABAYA-S
INHAUL-S	INWORK-S	JARGON-S	JIRBLE-S	KABELE-S
INHERE-S	INWRAP-S	JARINA-S	JISSOM-S	KABIKI-S
INHOOP-S	INYALA-S	JAROOL-S	JITNEY-S	KABUKI-S
INHUME-S	IODATE-S	JARRAH-S	JITTER-S	KACCHA-S
INISLE-S	IODIDE-S	JARVEY-S	JOANNA-S	KAFFIR-S
INJECT-S	IODINE-S	JARVIE-S	JOBBER-S	KAFILA-S
INJERA-S	IODISE-S	JASMIN-S	JOBBIE-S	KAFTAN-S
INJURE-S	IODISM-S	JASPER-S	JOCKEY-S	KAGOOL-S
INKLES-S	IODIZE-S	JASSID-S	JOGGER-S	KAGOUL-S
INKPOT-S	IOLITE-S	JATAKA-S	JOGGLE-S	KAHUNA-S
INLACE-S	IONISE-S	JAUNCE-S	JOINER-S	KAIKAI-S
INLAND-S	IONIUM-S	JAUNSE-S	JOJOBA-S	KAINGA-S
INLIER-S	IONIZE-S	JAWARI-S	JOLLEY-S	KAINIT-S
INLOCK-S	IONONE-S	JAWING-S	JOLLOP-S	KAISER-S
INMATE-S	IPECAC-S	JAYGEE-S	JOLTER-S	KAIZEN-S
INNAGE-S	IRENIC-S	JAYVEE-S	JORDAN-S	KAKAPO-S
INNING-S	IRONER-S	JAZZBO-S	JOSEPH-S	KALIAN-S
INPOUR-S	IRRUPT-S	JAZZER-S	JOSHER-S	KALIPH-S
INROAD-S	ISABEL-S	JEELIE-S	JOSKIN-S	KALIUM-S
INSEAM-S	ISATIN-S	JEERER-S	JOSSER-S	KALMIA-S
INSECT-S	ISLAND-S	JEHADI-S	JOSTLE-S	KALONG-S
INSEEM-S	ISOBAR-S	JEMIMA-S	JOTTER-S	KALPAC-S
INSERT-S	ISOGON-S	JENNET-S	JOTUNN-S	KALPAK-S
INSHIP-S	ISOHEL-S	JERBIL-S	JOUNCE-S	KAMALA-S
INSIDE-S	ISOLOG-S	JERBOA-S	JOURNO-S	KAMELA-S

KAMILA-S	KERSEY-S	KINKLE-S	KUMITE-S	LANGUE-S
KAMSIN-S	KETENE-S	KINONE-S	KUMMEL-S	LANGUR-S
KANAKA-S	KETMIA-S	KINRED-S	KUNKAR-S	LANNER-S
KANBAN-S	KETONE-S	KIPPER-S	KUNKUR-S	LANUGO-S
KANGHA-S	KETOSE-S	KIRBEH-S	KURGAN-S	LAOGAI-S
KANTAR-S	KETTLE-S	KIRPAN-S	KURVEY-S	LAPDOG-S
KANTEN-S	KEWPIE-S	KIRTAN-S	KWACHA-S	LAPFUL-S
KANTHA-S	KEYING-S	KIRTLE-S	KWAITO-S	LAPPEL-S
KAOLIN-S	KEYPAD-S	KISHKA-S	KWANZA-S	LAPPER-S
KARAIT-S	KEYPAL-S	KISHKE-S	KYOGEN-S	LAPPET-S
KARAKA-S	KEYSET-S	KISMAT-S	LAAGER-S	LAPPIE-S
KARAMU-S	KEYWAY-S	KISMET-S	LABIAL-S	LAPSER-S
KARATE-S	KGOTLA-S	KISSEL-S	LABLAB-S	LAPTOP-S
KARITE-S	KHALAT-S	KISSER-S	LABOUR-S	LARDER-S
KARORO-S	KHALIF-S	KITBAG-S	LABRET-S	LARDON-S
KARROO-S	KHANDA-S	KITING-S	LABRID-S	LARGEN-S
KARSEY-S	KHANGA-S	KITSET-S	LABRUM-S	LARGES-S
KARTER-S	KHANUM-S	KITTEL-S	LACING-S	LARIAT-S
KARYON-S	KHARIF-S	KITTEN-S	LACKER-S	LARKER-S
KASBAH-S	KHAYAL-S	KITTLE-S	LACKEY-S	LARNEY-S
KASHER-S	KHAZEN-S	KITTUL-S	LACTAM-S	LARRUP-S
KATANA-S	KHEDAH-S	KLAXON-S	LACUNA-S	LASCAR-S
KATHAK-S	KHILAT-S	KLEPHT-S	LACUNE-S	LASHER-S
KATION-S	KHILIM-S	KLEPTO-S	LADDER-S	LASING-S
KATIPO-S	KHODJA-S	KLUDGE-S	LADDIE-S	LASKET-S
KEASAR-S	KHURTA-S	KNAWEL-S	LADING-S	LASQUE-S
KEAVIE-S	KIAUGH-S	KNIFER-S	LADINO-S	LASSIE-S
KEBBIE-S	KIBBEH-S	KNIGHT-S	LADLER-S	LASTER-S
KEBELE-S	KIBBLE-S	KNOWER-S	LADRON-S	LATEEN-S
KEBLAH-S	KIBLAH-S	KOBANG-S	LAGENA-S	LATENT-S
KECKLE-S	KICKER-S	KOBOLD-S	LAGEND-S	LATEST-S
KEDDAH-S	KICKUP-S	KOCHIA-S	LAGGEN-S	LATHEE-S
KEDGER-S	KIDDER-S	KOKAKO-S	LAGGER-S	LATHER-S
KEEKER-S	KIDDIE-S	KONFYT-S	LAGGIN-S	LATIGO-S
KEELER-S	KIDDLE-S	KOODOO-S	LAGOON-S	LATINA-S
KEELIE-S	KIDLET-S	KOOLAH-S	LAGUNA-S	LATINO-S
KEENER-S	KIDNAP-S	KOPECK-S	LAGUNE-S	LATRIA-S
KEEPER-S	KIDNEY-S	KOPPIE-S	LAIKER-S	LATRON-S
KEFFEL-S	KIDULT-S	KORERO-S	LAIPSE-S	LATTEN-S
KEGGER-S	KIDVID-S	KORKIR-S	LAISSE-S	LATTIN-S
KEGLER-S	KIEKIE-S	KORORA-S	LAKING-S	LAUDER-S
KEKSYE-S	KIERIE-S	KORUNA-S	LALANG-S	LAUNCE-S
KELOID-S	KIKUYU-S	KOSHER-S	LALDIE-S	LAUREL-S
KELPER-S	KILERG-S	KOTWAL-S	LALLAN-S	LAURYL-S
KELPIE-S	KILLER-S	KOULAN-S	LAMBDA-S	LAVABO-S
KELSON-S	KILLIE-S	KOUMIS-S	LAMBER-S	LAVAGE-S
KELTER-S	KILLUT-S	KOUMYS-S	LAMBIE-S	LAVEER-S
KELTIE-S	KILTER-S	KOUSSO-S	LAMEDH-S	LAVOLT-S
KELVIN-S	KILTIE-S	KOWHAI-S	LAMENT-S	LAWINE-S
KEMBLA-S	KIMCHI-S	KOWTOW-S	LAMINA-S	LAWING-S
KEMPER-S	KIMMER-S	KRAKEN-S	LAMMER-S	LAWYER-S
KEMPLE-S	KIMONO-S	KRATER-S	LAMMIE-S	LAXISM-S
KENNEL-S	KINARA-S	KREESE-S	LAMPAD-S	LAXIST-S
KENNER-S	KINASE-S	KRUBUT-S	LAMPER-S	LAYING-S
KENNET-S	KINCOB-S	KUCHEN-S	LANCER-S	LAYOFF-S
KENTIA-S	KINDER-S	KUDLIK-S	LANCET-S	LAYOUT-S
KEPHIR-S	KINDIE-S	KULTUR-S	LANDAU-S	LAZULI-S
KERMES-S	KINDLE-S	KUMARA-S	LANDER-S	LEADEN-S
KERNEL-S	KINEMA-S	KUMARI-S	LANGAR-S	LEADER-S
KERRIA-S	KINGLE-S	KUMERA-S	LANGER-S	LEAGUE-S

LEAKER-S	LIBERO-S	LIQUID-S	LOONIE-S	LUTEIN-S
LEANER-S	LIBIDO-S	LIQUOR-S	LOOPER-S	LUTING-S
LEAPER-S	LIBKEN-S	LISPER-S	LOOSEN-S	LUTIST-S
LEASER-S	LIBLAB-S	LISTEE-S	LOOSIE-S	LUTITE-S
LEASOW-S	LICHEE-S	LISTEL-S	LOOTER-S	LUVVIE-S
LEAVEN-S	LICHEN-S	LISTEN-S	LOPPER-S	LUXATE-S
LEAVER-S	LICKER-S	LISTER-S	LOQUAT-S	LUZERN-S
LEBBEK-S	LICTOR-S	LITCHI-S	LORCHA-S	LYCEUM-S
LECHER-S	LIDGER-S	LITHIA-S	LORING-S	LYCHEE-S
LECHWE-S	LIEGER-S	LITTER-S	LORIOT-S	LYNAGE-S
LECTIN-S	LIERNE-S	LITTLE-S	LOSING-S	LYRISM-S
LECTOR-S	LIFTER-S	LIVEDO-S	LOSLYF-S	LYRIST-S
LEDDEN-S	LIGAND-S	LIVIER-S	LOTION-S	LYSATE-S
LEDGER-S	LIGASE-S	LIVING-S	LOTTER-S	LYSINE-S
LEEWAY-S	LIGATE-S	LIVYER-S	LOUDEN-S	MABELA-S
LEFTIE-S	LIGGER-S	LIZARD-S	LOUNGE-S	MACACO-S
LEGATE-S	LIGNAN-S	LIZZIE-S	LOURIE-S	MACHAN-S
LEGATO-S	LIGNIN-S	LOADEN-S	LOUSER-S	MACHER-S
LEGEND-S	LIGNUM-S	LOADER-S	LOUVAR-S	MACKLE-S
LEGGER-S	LIGULA-S	LOAFER-S	LOUVER-S	MACOYA-S
LEGGIN-S	LIGULE-S	LOANER-S	LOUVRE-S	MACRON-S
LEGION-S	LIGURE-S	LOATHE-S	LOVAGE-S	MACULA-S
LEGIST-S	LIKING-S	LOBBER-S	LOVING-S	MACULE-S
LEGLAN-S	LIMAIL-S	LOBING-S	LOWBOY-S	MADAFU-S
LEGLEN-S	LIMBEC-S	LOBOLA-S	LOWING-S	MADAME-S
LEGLET-S	LIMBER-S	LOBOLO-S	LOWNES-S	MADCAP-S
LEGLIN-S	LIMING-S	LOBULE-S	LOWRIE-S	MADDEN-S
LEGONG-S	LIMMER-S	LOCALE-S	LOZELL-S	MADDER-S
LEGUME-S	LIMNER-S	LOCATE-S	LUBBER-S	MADTOM-S
LEHAIM-S	LIMPER-S	LOCHAN-S	LUCERN-S	MADURO-S
LEIGER-S	LIMPET-S	LOCKER-S	LUCITE-S	MAELID-S
LEIPOA-S	LINAGE-S	LOCKET-S	LUCKIE-S	MAENAD-S
LEKVAR-S	LINDEN-S	LOCKUP-S	LUCUMA-S	MAFFIA-S
LENDER-S	LINEUP-S	LOCULE-S	LUCUMO-S	MAFTIR-S
LENGTH-S	LINGAM-S	LOCUST-S	LUETIC-S	MAGGIE-S
LENITE-S	LINGEL-S	LODGER-S	LUGGER-S	MAGGOT-S
LENTIL-S	LINGER-S	LOERIE-S	LUGGIE-S	MAGIAN-S
LENTOR-S	LINGLE-S	LOFTER-S	LUGING-S	MAGILP-S
LENVOY-S	LINGOT-S	LOGGAT-S	LULLER-S	MAGISM-S
LEPTIN-S	LINGUA-S	LOGGER-S	LUMBAR-S	MAGLEV-S
LEPTON-S	LINHAY-S	LOGGIA-S	LUMBER-S	MAGNET-S
LESION-S	LINING-S	LOGION-S	LUMINE-S	MAGNON-S
LESSEE-S	LINKER-S	LOGJAM-S	LUMPEN-S	MAGNUM-S
LESSEN-S	LINKUP-S	LOGLOG-S	LUMPER-S	MAGPIE-S
LESSON-S	LINNET-S	LOGOFF-S	LUNATE-S	MAGUEY-S
LESSOR-S	LINNEY-S	LOGOUT-S	LUNGAN-S	MAHEWU-S
LETHAL-S	LINSEY-S	LOGWAY-S	LUNGEE-S	MAHMAL-S
LETHEE-S	LINTEL-S	LOITER-S	LUNGER-S	MAHOUT-S
LETTER-S	LINTER-S	LOLIGO-S	LUNGIE-S	MAHSIR-S
LETTRE-S	LINTIE-S	LOLIUM-S	LUNGYI-S	MAHZOR-S
LEUCIN-S	LINTOL-S	LOLLER-S	LUNKER-S	MAIDAN-S
LEUKON-S	LIONEL-S	LOLLOP-S	LUNULE-S	MAIDEN-S
LEVANT-S	LIONET-S	LOMEIN-S	LUNYIE-S	MAIGRE-S
LEVIER-S	LIPASE-S	LOMENT-S	LUPINE-S	MAIHEM-S
LEVITE-S	LIPIDE-S	LONGAN-S	LURDAN-S	MAILER-S
LEXEME-S	LIPOID-S	LONGER-S	LURDEN-S	MAIMER-S
LEZZIE-S	LIPOMA-S	LOOFAH-S	LURKER-S	MAINOR-S
LIAISE-S	LIPPEN-S	LOOKER-S	LUSHER-S	MAKEUP-S
LIBATE-S	LIPPER-S	LOOKUP-S	LUSTER-S	MAKING-S
LIBBER-S	LIPPIE-S	LOONEY-S	LUSTRE-S	MAKUTU-S

MALATE-S	MARCEL-S	MAWKIN-S	MENTOR-S	MIGNON-S
MALGRE-S	MARGAY-S	MAWMET-S	MENUDO-S	MIHRAB-S
MALICE-S	MARGIN-S	MAXIXE-S	MENYIE-S	MIKADO-S
MALIGN-S	MARINA-S	MAYDAY-S	MERCAT-S	MIKRON-S
MALINE-S	MARINE-S	MAYHEM-S	MERCER-S	MIKVAH-S
MALISM-S	MARKER-S	MAYING-S	MERELL-S	MIKVEH-S
MALKIN-S	MARKET-S	MAYPOP-S	MERGEE-S	MILADI-S
MALLAM-S	MARKKA-S	MAYVIN-S	MERGER-S	MILAGE-S
MALLEE-S	MARKUP-S	MAZARD-S	MERING-S	MILDEN-S
MALLET-S	MARLIN-S	MAZHBI-S	MERINO-S	MILDEW-S
MALLOW-S	MARMOT-S	MAZOUT-S	MERISM-S	MILIEU-S
MALMAG-S	MAROON-S	MAZUMA-S	MERKIN-S	MILKER-S
MALTED-S	MARQUE-S	MEADOW-S	MERLIN-S	MILLER-S
MALTHA-S	MARRAM-S	MEAGRE-S	MERLON-S	MILLET-S
MALTOL-S	MARRER-S	MEALER-S	MERLOT-S	MILLIE-S
MAMLUK-S	MARRON-S	MEALIE-S	MEROME-S	MILNEB-S
MAMMAL-S	MARROW-S	MEANER-S	MESAIL-S	MILORD-S
MAMMEE-S	MARRUM-S	MEANIE-S	MESCAL-S	MILSEY-S
MAMMER-S	MARTEL-S	MEASLE-S	MESETA-S	MILTER-S
MAMMET-S	MARTEN-S	MEATHE-S	MESSAN-S	MIMBAR-S
MAMMEY-S	MARTIN-S	MEAZEL-S	MESTEE-S	MIMOSA-S
MAMMIE-S	MARTYR-S	MEDAKA-S	MESTER-S	MINBAR-S
MAMMON-S	MARVEL-S	MEDDLE-S	MESTOM-S	MINCER-S
MAMZER-S	MARVER-S	MEDIAL-S	METAGE-S	MINDER-S
MANAGE-S	MASALA-S	MEDIAN-S	METATE-S	MINGER-S
MANANA-S	MASCLE-S	MEDICK-S	METEOR-S	MINGLE-S
MANATI-S	MASCON-S	MEDICO-S	METEPA-S	MINING-S
MANAWA-S	MASCOT-S	MEDINA-S	METHOD-S	MINION-S
MANCHE-S	MASHER-S	MEDIUM-S	METHYL-S	MINIUM-S
MANDIR-S	MASHIE-S	MEDLAR-S	METIER-S	MINNIE-S
MANDOM-S	MASHUA-S	MEDLEY-S	METOPE-S	MINNOW-S
MANEGE-S	MASHUP-S	MEDUSA-S	METRIC-S	MINTER-S
MANGAL-S	MASJID-S	MEEKEN-S	METTLE-S	MINUET-S
MANGEL-S	MASKEG-S	MEEMIE-S	METUMP-S	MINUTE-S
MANGER-S	MASKER-S	MEETER-S	MEVROU-S	MINYAN-S
MANGLE-S	MASLIN-S	MEGILP-S	MEWLER-S	MIOMBO-S
MANIAC-S	MASQUE-S	MEGOHM-S	MEZAIL-S	MIOTIC-S
MANILA-S	MASSIF-S	MEGRIM-S	MEZCAL-S	MIRAGE-S
MANIOC-S	MASTER-S	MEHNDI-S	MEZUZA-S	MIRITI-S
MANITO-S	MASTIC-S	MEINEY-S	MGANGA-S	MIRROR-S
MANITU-S	MASULA-S	MEINIE-S	MIASMA-S	MISACT-S
MANNAN-S	MATICO-S	MEISHI-S	MICATE-S	MISADD-S
MANNER-S	MATING-S	MELANO-S	MICELL-S	MISAIM-S
MANOAO-S	MATIPO-S	MELDER-S	MICHER-S	MISCUE-S
MANRED-S	MATLOW-S	MELENA-S	MICKEY-S	MISCUT-S
MANTEL-S	MATOKE-S	MELICK-S	MICKLE-S	MISEAT-S
MANTID-S	MATRIC-S	MELLAY-S	MICRON-S	MISERE-S
MANTLE-S	MATRON-S	MELLOW-S	MIDAIR-S	MISFIT-S
MANTRA-S	MATSAH-S	MELOID-S	MIDDAY-S	MISHAP-S
MANTUA-S	MATTER-S	MELTER-S	MIDDEN-S	MISHIT-S
MANUAL-S	MATTIE-S	MELTON-S	MIDDIE-S	MISHMI-S
MANUKA-S	MATTIN-S	MEMBER-S	MIDDLE-S	MISKAL-S
MANURE-S	MATURE-S	MEMOIR-S	MIDGET-S	MISKEN-S
MAPLES-S	MATZAH-S	MENACE-S	MIDGIE-S	MISKEY-S
MAPPER-S	MATZOH-S	MENAGE-S	MIDGUT-S	MISLAY-S
MARABI-S	MAUGRE-S	MENDER-S	MIDLEG-S	MISLIE-S
MARACA-S	MAULER-S	MENEER-S	MIDRIB-S	MISPEN-S
MARARI-S	MAULVI-S	MENHIR-S	MIDWAY-S	MISSAL-S
MARAUD-S	MAUMET-S	MENIAL-S	MIELIE-S	MISSAY-S
MARBLE-S	MAUVIN-S	MENTEE-S	MIGGLE-S	MISSEE-S

MISSEL-S	MONTEM-S	MUCATE-S	MUSANG-S	NANDIN-S
MISSET-S	MONTRE-S	MUCHEL-S	MUSCAT-S	NANDOO-S
MISTAL-S	MOOLAH-S	MUCKER-S	MUSCID-S	NANISM-S
MISTER-S	MOOLEY-S	MUCKLE-S	MUSCLE-S	NANKIN-S
MISTLE-S	MOOLOO-S	MUCLUC-S	MUSEUM-S	NANNIE-S
MISUSE-S	MOOLVI-S	MUCOID-S	MUSHER-S	NANOBE-S
MITHER-S	MOONER-S	MUCOSA-S	MUSICK-S	NANOOK-S
MITTEN-S	MOORVA-S	MUDBUG-S	MUSING-S	NAPALM-S
MIZUNA-S	MOOTER-S	MUDCAP-S	MUSJID-S	NAPKIN-S
MIZZEN-S	MOPANE-S	MUDCAT-S	MUSKEG-S	NAPPER-S
MIZZLE-S	MOPANI-S	MUDDER-S	MUSKET-S	NAPPIE-S
MNEMON-S	MOPOKE-S	MUDDLE-S	MUSKIE-S	NAPRON-S
MOANER-S	MOPPER-S	MUDEYE-S	MUSKIT-S	NARDOO-S
MOBBER-S	MOPPET-S	MUDGER-S	MUSKLE-S	NARROW-S
MOBBIE-S	MORALE-S	MUDHEN-S	MUSLIN-S	NARWAL-S
MOBBLE-S	MORALL-S	MUESLI-S	MUSMON-S	NASARD-S
MOBCAP-S	MORCHA-S	MUFFIN-S	MUSROL-S	NASION-S
MOBILE-S	MOREEN-S	MUFFLE-S	MUSSEL-S	NASUTE-S
MOBLOG-S	MORGAN-S	MUFLON-S	MUSTEE-S	NATION-S
MOCKER-S	MORGAY-S	MUGFUL-S	MUSTER-S	NATIVE-S
MOCKUP-S	MORGEN-S	MUGGAR-S	MUTANT-S	NATRON-S
MOCOCK-S	MORGUE-S	MUGGEE-S	MUTASE-S	NATTER-S
MOCUCK-S	MORION-S	MUGGER-S	MUTATE-S	NATURE-S
MODENA-S	MORKIN-S	MUGGUR-S	MUTINE-S	NAUGHT-S
MODERN-S	MORNAY-S	MUGHAL-S	MUTISM-S	NAUSEA-S
MODIST-S	MORPHO-S	MUKLUK-S	MUTTER-S	NAUTIC-S
MODULE-S	MORROW-S	MUKTUK-S	MUTTON-S	NAVAID-S
MOFFIE-S	MORSEL-S	MULETA-S	MUTUAL-S	NAYSAY-S
MOGGAN-S	MORTAL-S	MULLAH-S	MUTUCA-S	NEAFFE-S
MOGGIE-S	MORTAR-S	MULLEN-S	MUTUEL-S	NEATEN-S
MOGHUL-S	MORULA-S	MULLER-S	MUTULE-S	NEBBUK-S
MOHAIR-S	MOSAIC-S	MULLET-S	MUTUUM-S	NEBECK-S
MOHAWK-S	MOSHER-S	MULLEY-S	MUUMUU-S	NEBULA-S
MOIDER-S	MOSQUE-S	MULMUL-S	MUZHIK-S	NEBULE-S
MOILER-S	MOSSER-S	MULTUM-S	MUZJIK-S	NECKER-S
MOISER-S	MOSSIE-S	MUMBLE-S	MUZZLE-S	NECTAR-S
MOKORO-S	MOTETT-S	MUMMER-S	MYCELE-S	NEEDER-S
MOKSHA-S	MOTHER-S	MUMMIA-S	MYELIN-S	NEEDLE-S
MOLDER-S	MOTILE-S	MUMPER-S	MYELON-S	NEGATE-S
MOLEST-S	MOTION-S	MUNDIC-S	MYGALE-S	NEINEI-S
MOLINE-S	MOTIVE-S	MUNITE-S	MYOGEN-S	NEKTON-S
MOLLAH-S	MOTLEY-S	MUNSHI-S	MYOPIA-S	NELLIE-S
MOLLIE-S	MOTMOT-S	MUNTER-S	MYOPIC-S	NELSON-S
MOLOCH-S	MOTSER-S	MUNTIN-S	MYOSIN-S	NEOCON-S
MOLTER-S	MOTTLE-S	MUPPET-S	MYOTIC-S	NEPETA-S
MOMENT-S	MOTUCA-S	MURAGE-S	MYRIAD-S	NEPHEW-S
MOMISM-S	MOUJIK-S	MURDER-S	MYRICA-S	NEREID-S
MOMMET-S	MOULIN-S	MUREIN-S	MYRTLE-S	NERINE-S
MOMSER-S	MOUSER-S	MURENA-S	MYSOST-S	NERITE-S
MOMZER-S	MOUSIE-S	MURINE-S	MYSTIC-S	NEROLI-S
MONAUL-S	MOUSLE-S	MURLAN-S	MYXOMA-S	NERVER-S
MONEME-S	MOUSME-S	MURLIN-S	MZUNGU-S	NESTER-S
MONETH-S	MOUSSE-S	MURMUR-S	NABBER-S	NESTLE-S
MONGER-S	MOUTAN-S	MURRAM-S	NACKET-S	NESTOR-S
MONGOE-S	MOUTER-S	MURRAY-S	NAGANA-S	NETFUL-S
MONGOL-S	MOUTON-S	MURREE-S	NAGARI-S	NETTER-S
MONIAL-S	MOWDIE-S	MURREN-S	NAGGER-S	NETTIE-S
MONISM-S	MOWING-S	MURREY-S	NAILER-S	NETTLE-S
MONIST-S	MOZZIE-S	MURRHA-S	NALLAH-S	NEURON-S
MONKEY-S	MOZZLE-S	MURRIN-S	NAMING-S	NEUTER-S

NEWBIE-S	NOOKIE-S	OBEISM-S	ONBEAT-S	ORMOLU-S
NEWELL-S	NOONER-S	OBELIA-S	ONCOME-S	OROGEN-S
NEWSIE-S	NOOSER-S	OBENTO-S	ONCOST-S	OROIDE-S
NEWTON-S	NORITE-S	OBEYER-S	ONDINE-S	ORPHAN-S
NHANDU-S	NORMAL-S	OBIISM-S	ONDING-S	ORPINE-S
NIACIN-S	NORMAN-S	OBJECT-S	ONEYER-S	ORRICE-S
NIBBLE-S	NORSEL-S	OBJURE-S	ONEYRE-S	OSCINE-S
NICHER-S	NOSEAN-S	OBLAST-S	ONFALL-S	OSCULE-S
NICKAR-S	NOSHER-S	OBLATE-S	ONFLOW-S	OSETRA-S
NICKEL-S	NOSING-S	OBLIGE-S	ONLOAD-S	OSMATE-S
NICKER-S	NOSODE-S	OBLONG-S	ONSIDE-S	OSMIUM-S
NICKLE-S	NOSTOC-S	OBOIST-S	ONWARD-S	OSMOLE-S
NICKUM-S	NOTATE-S	OBSIGN-S	ONYCHA-S	OSMOSE-S
NIDATE-S	NOTICE-S	OBTAIN-S	OOCYST-S	OSMUND-S
NIDGET-S	NOTION-S	OBTEND-S	OOCYTE-S	OSPREY-S
NIDING-S	NOUGAT-S	OBTEST-S	OOLITE-S	OSSEIN-S
NIELLO-S	NOUGHT-S	OBTUND-S	OOLITH-S	OSTENT-S
NIFFER-S	NOUSLE-S	OBVERT-S	OOLONG-S	OSTLER-S
NIGGER-S	NOVENA-S	OCCULT-S	OOMIAC-S	OTTAVA-S
NIGGLE-S	NOVICE-S	OCELOT-S	OOMIAK-S	OUGLIE-S
NIGIRI-S	NOYADE-S	OCICAT-S	OOMPAH-S	OULONG-S
NILGAI-S	NOZZER-S	OCTANE-S	OORALI-S	OURALI-S
NILGAU-S	NOZZLE-S	OCTANT-S	OORIAL-S	OURANG-S
NIMMER-S	NUANCE-S	OCTAVE-S	OPAQUE-S	OURARI-S
NIMROD-S	NUBBIN-S	OCTAVO-S	OPCODE-S	OUREBI-S
NINCOM-S	NUBBLE-S	OCTETT-S	OPENER-S	OUSTER-S
NINCUM-S	NUBUCK-S	OCTROI-S	OPERON-S	OUTACT-S
NIPPER-S	NUCHAL-S	OCTUOR-S	OPHITE-S	OUTADD-S
NIPPLE-S	NUCULE-S	OCULAR-S	OPIATE-S	OUTAGE-S
NIPTER-S	NUDGER-S	OECIST-S	OPIOID-S	OUTASK-S
NISGUL-S	NUDISM-S	OEDEMA-S	OPPOSE-S	OUTBAR-S
NITHER-S	NUDIST-S	OEUVRE-S	OPPUGN-S	OUTBEG-S
NITRID-S	NUDNIK-S	OFFCUT-S	OPTANT-S	OUTBID-S
NITRIL-S	NUFFIN-S	OFFEND-S	OPTIME-S	OUTBUY-S
NITRYL-S	NUGGAR-S	OFFICE-S	OPTION-S	OUTEAT-S
NITWIT-S	NUGGET-S	OFFING-S	ORACHE-S	OUTFIT-S
NOBBLE-S	NULLAH-S	OFFPUT-S	ORACLE-S	OUTGUN-S
NOCAKE-S	NUMBAT-S	OFFSET-S	ORANGE-S	OUTHIT-S
NOCENT-S	NUMBER-S	OGDOAD-S	ORATOR-S	OUTING-S
NOCHEL-S	NUMDAH-S	OGLING-S	ORBITA-S	OUTJET-S
NOCKET-S	NUMNAH-S	OGRISM-S	ORCEIN-S	OUTJUT-S
NOCTUA-S	NUNCIO-S	OHMAGE-S	ORCHAT-S	OUTLAW-S
NODDER-S	NUNCLE-S	OIKIST-S	ORCHEL-S	OUTLAY-S
NODDLE-S	NURDLE-S	OILCAN-S	ORCHID-S	OUTLER-S
NODULE-S	NURHAG-S	OILCUP-S	ORCHIL-S	OUTLET-S
NOGGIN-S	NURSER-S	OILLET-S	ORCINE-S	OUTLIE-S
NOMADE-S	NURSLE-S	OILNUT-S	ORDAIN-S	OUTMAN-S
NOMISM-S	NUTATE-S	OILWAY-S	ORDEAL-S	OUTPUT-S
NONAGE-S	NUTLET-S	OLEATE-S	ORDURE-S	OUTRED-S
NONANE-S	NUTMEG-S	OLEFIN-S	OREIDE-S	OUTRIG-S
NONART-S	NUTRIA-S	OLEINE-S	ORFRAY-S	OUTROW-S
NONCOM-S	NUTTER-S	OLFACT-S	ORGASM-S	OUTRUN-S
NONEGO-S	NUZZER-S	OLINGO-S	ORGEAT-S	OUTSAY-S
NONFAN-S	NUZZLE-S	OLIVER-S	ORGONE-S	OUTSEE-S
NONGAY-S	NYANZA-S	OLIVET-S	ORIENT-S	OUTSET-S
NONUSE-S	NYBBLE-S	OLLAMH-S	ORIGAN-S	OUTSIN-S
NONWAR-S	NYMPHO-S	OMELET-S	ORIGIN-S	OUTSIT-S
NOODGE-S	OARAGE-S	OMERTA-S	ORIOLE-S	OUTSUM-S
NOODLE-S	OBDURE-S	OMNIUM-S	ORISHA-S	OUTTOP-S
NOOGIE-S	OBECHE-S	ONAGER-S	ORISON-S	OUTVIE-S

OUTWAR-S	PAMPER-S	PASEAR-S	PEDLAR-S	PESEWA-S
OUTWIN-S	PANADA-S	PASHIM-S	PEDLER-S	PESHWA-S
OUTWIT-S	PANAMA-S	PASHKA-S	PEELER-S	PESTER-S
OVATOR-S	PANDAR-S	PASSEL-S	PEENGE-S	PESTLE-S
OVISAC-S	PANDER-S	PASSER-S	PEEPER-S	PETARA-S
OVONIC-S	PANDIT-S	PASTEL-S	PEEPUL-S	PETARD-S
OXCART-S	PANEER-S	PASTER-S	PEERIE-S	PETHER-S
OXFORD-S	PANFUL-S	PASTIE-S	PEEVER-S	PETITE-S
OXGANG-S	PANGEN-S	PASTIL-S	PEEWEE-S	PETNAP-S
OXGATE-S	PANICK-S	PASTOR-S	PEEWIT-S	PETREL-S
OXHEAD-S	PANIER-S	PATACA-S	PEINCT-S	PETROL-S
OXHIDE-S	PANISC-S	PATELA-S	PELAGE-S	PETSAI-S
OXLAND-S	PANISK-S	PATENT-S	PELHAM-S	PETTER-S
OXSLIP-S	PANNER-S	PATHIC-S	PELITE-S	PETTLE-S
OXTAIL-S	PANTER-S	PATINA-S	PELLET-S	PEWTER-S
OXYGEN-S	PANTIE-S	PATINE-S	PELLUM-S	PEYOTE-S
OXYMEL-S	PANTON-S	PATROL-S	PELMET-S	PEYOTL-S
OYSTER-S	PANTUN-S	PATRON-S	PELOID-S	PEZANT-S
OZAENA-S	PANZER-S	PATTEN-S	PELOTA-S	PHARMA-S
OZALID-S	PAPAIN-S	PATTER-S	PELTER-S	PHASOR-S
PABLUM-S	PAPAYA-S	PATTIE-S	PELVIC-S	PHEERE-S
PACHAK-S	PAPISM-S	PATTLE-S	PENANG-S	PHEESE-S
PACKER-S	PAPIST-S	PATZER-S	PENCEL-S	PHEEZE-S
PACKET-S	PAPULE-S	PAUCAL-S	PENCIL-S	PHENOL-S
PADANG-S	PARADE-S	PAULIN-S	PENFUL-S	PHENOM-S
PADAUK-S	PARAGE-S	PAUNCE-S	PENNAL-S	PHENYL-S
PADDER-S	PARAMO-S	PAUPER-S	PENNER-S	PHIZOG-S
PADDLE-S	PARANG-S	PAUSER-S	PENNON-S	PHLEGM-S
PADNAG-S	PARAPH-S	PAVAGE-S	PENSEE-S	PHLOEM-S
PADOUK-S	PARCEL-S	PAVANE-S	PENSEL-S	PHOBIA-S
PADSAW-S	PARDAH-S	PAVING-S	PENSIL-S	PHOBIC-S
PAELLA-S	PARDAL-S	PAVIOR-S	PENSUM-S	PHOEBE-S
PAESAN-S	PARDON-S	PAVISE-S	PENTAD-S	PHONER-S
PAGING-S	PARENT-S	PAVONE-S	PENTEL-S	PHONEY-S
PAGODA-S	PARGET-S	PAWNCE-S	PENTYL-S	PHONIC-S
PAIDLE-S	PARIAH-S	PAWNEE-S	PENULT-S	PHONON-S
PAIGLE-S	PARIAL-S	PAWNER-S	PEOPLE-S	PHOTIC-S
PAINIM-S	PARIAN-S	PAWNOR-S	PEPINO-S	PHOTOG-S
PAIOCK-S	PARING-S	PAWPAW-S	PEPLUM-S	PHOTON-S
PAISAN-S	PARKEE-S	PAYDAY-S	PEPPER-S	PHRASE-S
PAJAMA-S	PARKER-S	PAYING-S	PEPSIN-S	PHREAK-S
PAJOCK-S	PARKIE-S	PAYNIM-S	PEPTIC-S	PHYLLO-S
PAKAHI-S	PARKIN-S	PAYOFF-S	PEPTID-S	PHYLON-S
PAKEHA-S	PARLAY-S	PAYOLA-S	PERDUE-S	PHYSED-S
PAKIHI-S	PARLEY-S	PAYOUT-S	PEREON-S	PHYSIC-S
PAKOKO-S	PARLOR-S	PEACOD-S	PERFIN-S	PHYSIO-S
PAKORA-S	PAROLE-S	PEAHEN-S	PERIOD-S	PHYTIN-S
PALACE-S	PARPEN-S	PEANUT-S	PERKIN-S	PHYTOL-S
PALAGI-S	PARRAL-S	PEAPOD-S	PERMIE-S	PHYTON-S
PALAPA-S	PARREL-S	PEARCE-S	PERMIT-S	PIAFFE-S
PALATE-S	PARROT-S	PEAVEY-S	PERNOD-S	PIAZZA-S
PALING-S	PARSEC-S	PEBBLE-S	PERONE-S	PICARA-S
PALKEE-S	PARSER-S	PECHAN-S	PERRON-S	PICARO-S
PALLAH-S	PARSON-S	PECKER-S	PERSON-S	PICENE-S
PALLET-S	PARTAN-S	PECTEN-S	PERSUE-S	PICKER-S
PALLOR-S	PARTER-S	PECTIN-S	PERUKE-S	PICKET-S
PALMER-S	PARTON-S	PEDALO-S	PERUSE-S	PICKIN-S
PALMIE-S	PARURA-S	PEDANT-S	PESADE-S	PICKLE-S
PALOLO-S	PARURE-S	PEDDER-S	PESANT-S	PICKUP-S
PALTER-S	PASCAL-S	PEDDLE-S	PESETA-S	PICNIC-S

PICONG-S	PIRATE-S	PODSOL-S	PORISM-S	PREACT-S
PIDDLE-S	PIRAYA-S	PODZOL-S	PORKER-S	PREAMP-S
PIDGIN-S	PISHER-S	POEPOL-S	POROSE-S	PREARM-S
PIECEN-S	PISSER-S	POETIC-S	PORTAL-S	PREASE-S
PIECER-S	PISTIL-S	POFFLE-S	PORTER-S	PREBID-S
PIERCE-S	PISTOL-S	POGOER-S	POSADA-S	PREBUY-S
PIERID-S	PISTON-S	POGROM-S	POSEUR-S	PRECUT-S
PIFFLE-S	PISTOU-S	POHIRI-S	POSING-S	PREDYE-S
PIGEON-S	PITARA-S	POINTE-S	POSNET-S	PREEVE-S
PIGGIE-S	PITAYA-S	POISER-S	POSOLE-S	PREFAB-S
PIGGIN-S	PITIER-S	POISON-S	POSSER-S	PREFER-S
PIGLET-S	PITMAN-S	POITIN-S	POSSES-S	PREIFE-S
PIGNUT-S	PITSAW-S	POLDER-S	POSSET-S	PRELIM-S
PIGOUT-S	PITTER-S	POLEYN-S	POSSIE-S	PREMED-S
PIGPEN-S	PITURI-S	POLICE-S	POSSUM-S	PREMIE-S
PIGSNY-S	PIUPIU-S	POLING-S	POSTER-S	PRENUP-S
PIKAKE-S	PIZZLE-S	POLLAN-S	POSTIE-S	PREPAY-S
PIKING-S	PLACER-S	POLLEE-S	POSTIL-S	PRESET-S
PILAFF-S	PLACET-S	POLLEN-S	POSTIN-S	PRESTO-S
PILEUP-S	PLACIT-S	POLLER-S	POSTOP-S	PRETOR-S
PILFER-S	PLAGUE-S	POLYOL-S	POTAGE-S	PREVUE-S
PILING-S	PLAICE-S	POLYPE-S	POTBOY-S	PREWYN-S
PILLAR-S	PLAINT-S	POMACE-S	POTCHE-S	PREYER-S
PILLAU-S	PLANER-S	POMADE-S	POTEEN-S	PRICER-S
PILLIE-S	PLANET-S	POMELO-S	POTENT-S	PRIEFE-S
PILLOW-S	PLANTA-S	POMMEL-S	POTFUL-S	PRIEST-S
PILOTI-S	PLAQUE-S	POMMIE-S	POTGUN-S	PRIEVE-S
PILULA-S	PLASMA-S	POMPEY-S	POTHER-S	PRIMER-S
PILULE-S	PLATAN-S	POMPOM-S	POTION-S	PRINCE-S
PIMENT-S	PLATEN-S	POMPON-S	POTPIE-S	PRISER-S
PIMPLE-S	PLATER-S	POMROY-S	POTSIE-S	PRISON-S
PINANG-S	PLAYER-S	PONCHO-S	POTTER-S	PRIVET-S
PINATA-S	PLEASE-S	PONDER-S	POTTLE-S	PRIZER-S
PINCER-S	PLEDGE-S	PONDOK-S	POTZER-S	PROBER-S
PINDAN-S	PLEIAD-S	PONGEE-S	POUDER-S	PROBIT-S
PINDER-S	PLENUM-S	PONGID-S	POUDRE-S	PROFIT-S
PINEAL-S	PLEUCH-S	PONTIL-S	POUFFE-S	PROIGN-S
PINENE-S	PLEUGH-S	PONTON-S	POULPE-S	PROINE-S
PINGER-S	PLEURA-S	POODLE-S	POUNCE-S	PROJET-S
PINGLE-S	PLEXOR-S	POOGYE-S	POURER-S	PROKER-S
PINION-S	PLIGHT-S	POOJAH-S	POURIE-S	PROLAN-S
PINITE-S	PLINTH-S	POOLER-S	POUSSE-S	PROLEG-S
PINKEN-S	PLISSE-S	POONAC-S	POUTER-S	PROLER-S
PINKEY-S	PLODGE-S	POONCE-S	POWDER-S	PROLOG-S
PINKIE-S	PLONGE-S	POOPER-S	POWNEY-S	PROMPT-S
PINNER-S	PLONKO-S	POOTER-S	POWNIE-S	PROPEL-S
PINNET-S	PLOUGH-S	POOTLE-S	POWTER-S	PROPER-S
PINNIE-S	PLOVER-S	POPERA-S	POWWAW-S	PROPYL-S
PINOLE-S	PLOWER-S	POPGUN-S	POWWOW-S	PROSER-S
PINTLE-S	PLUNGE-S	POPJOY-S	POYSON-S	PROTEA-S
PINYON-S	PLURAL-S	POPLAR-S	POZOLE-S	PROTON-S
PIOLET-S	PLUTON-S	POPLIN-S	PRAISE-S	PROTYL-S
PIONER-S	PNEUMA-S	POPPER-S	PRAJNA-S	PROVER-S
PIONEY-S	POCHAY-S	POPPET-S	PRANCE-S	PROYNE-S
PIPAGE-S	POCKET-S	POPPIT-S	PRANCK-S	PRUINA-S
PIPING-S	PODDIE-S	POPPLE-S	PRATER-S	PRUINE-S
PIPKIN-S	PODDLE-S	POPRIN-S	PRATIE-S	PRUNER-S
PIPPIN-S	PODITE-S	POPSIE-S	PRAWLE-S	PRUSIK-S
PIQUET-S	PODIUM-S	PORGIE-S	PRAYER-S	PRYING-S
PIRANA-S	PODLEY-S	PORINA-S	PREACE-S	PSEUDO-S

PSOCID-S	PURINE-S	QUAVER-S	RAIDER-S	RATTEN-S
PSYCHE-S	PURIRI-S	QUBYTE-S	RAILER-S	RATTER-S
PSYCHO-S	PURISM-S	QUEEST-S	RAISER-S	RATTLE-S
PSYLLA-S	PURIST-S	QUELEA-S	RAISIN-S	RATTON-S
PSYWAR-S	PURLER-S	QUETHE-S	RAIYAT-S	RAUNGE-S
PTERIN-S	PURLIN-S	QUEUER-S	RAKING-S	RAVAGE-S
PTISAN-S	PURPIE-S	QUEZAL-S	RALLYE-S	RAVINE-S
PUBLIC-S	PURPLE-S	QUICHE-S	RAMADA-S	RAVING-S
PUCKER-S	PURSER-S	QUIDAM-S	RAMBLA-S	RAWING-S
PUCKLE-S	PURSEW-S	QUIGHT-S	RAMBLE-S	RAYLES-S
PUDDEN-S	PURSUE-S	QUINCE-S	RAMCAT-S	RAYLET-S
PUDDER-S	PURVEY-S	QUINIE-S	RAMJET-S	RAZURE-S
PUDDLE-S	PUSHER-S	QUININ-S	RAMMEL-S	RAZZIA-S
PUEBLO-S	PUSHUP-S	QUINOA-S	RAMMER-S	RAZZLE-S
PUFFER-S	PUSLEY-S	QUINOL-S	RAMMLE-S	READER-S
PUFFIN-S	PUSSEL-S	QUINTA-S	RAMONA-S	REAGIN-S
PUGGIE-S	PUSSER-S	QUINTE-S	RAMPER-S	REAMER-S
PUGGLE-S	PUTEAL-S	QUINZE-S	RAMROD-S	REAPER-S
PUGREE-S	PUTELI-S	QUIPPU-S	RAMSON-S	REARER-S
PUISNE-S	PUTLOG-S	QUIVER-S	RAMTIL-S	REASON-S
PUKEKO-S	PUTOFF-S	QUOHOG-S	RANCEL-S	REAVER-S
PULING-S	PUTOUT-S	QUOIST-S	RANCHO-S	REAVOW-S
PULKHA-S	PUTTEE-S	QUOKKA-S	RANCOR-S	REBACK-S
PULLER-S	PUTTER-S	QUORUM-S	RANDAN-S	REBAIT-S
PULLET-S	PUTTIE-S	QUOTER-S	RANDEM-S	REBATE-S
PULLEY-S	PUTURE-S	QUOTUM-S	RANDIE-S	REBATO-S
PULLUP-S	PUZZEL-S	QWERTY-S	RANDOM-S	REBECK-S
PULPER-S	PUZZLE-S	RABATO-S	RANDON-S	REBILL-S
PULPIT-S	PYCNIC-S	RABBET-S	RANGER-S	REBIND-S
PULQUE-S	PYCNON-S	RABBIN-S	RANKER-S	REBITE-S
PULSAR-S	PYEMIA-S	RABBIT-S	RANKLE-S	REBOIL-S
PULSER-S	PYGARG-S	RABBLE-S	RANSEL-S	REBOOK-S
PULTAN-S	PYJAMA-S	RACEME-S	RANSOM-S	REBOOT-S
PULTON-S	PYKNIC-S	RACHET-S	RANTER-S	REBORE-S
PULTUN-S	PYRENE-S	RACING-S	RANULA-S	REBOZO-S
PULVER-S	PYRITE-S	RACISM-S	RANZEL-S	REBUFF-S
PULVIL-S	PYROLA-S	RACIST-S	RAPHIA-S	REBUKE-S
PULWAR-S	PYRONE-S	RACKER-S	RAPIER-S	RECALL-S
PUMELO-S	PYROPE-S	RACKET-S	RAPINE-S	RECANE-S
PUMICE-S	PYRROL-S	RACOON-S	RAPIST-S	RECANT-S
PUMMEL-S	PYTHON-S	RADDLE-S	RAPPEE-S	RECAST-S
PUMPER-S	PYURIA-S	RADIAL-S	RAPPEL-S	RECEDE-S
PUNCTO-S	QABALA-S	RADIAN-S	RAPPER-S	RECEPT-S
PUNDIT-S	QASIDA-S	RADIUM-S	RAPTOR-S	RECHEW-S
PUNGLE-S	QAWWAL-S	RADOME-S	RASCAL-S	RECIPE-S
PUNKAH-S	QIGONG-S	RADULA-S	RASHER-S	RECITE-S
PUNKER-S	QINDAR-S	RAFALE-S	RASHIE-S	RECKON-S
PUNKEY-S	QINTAR-S	RAFFIA-S	RASPER-S	RECOAL-S
PUNKIE-S	QIVIUT-S	RAFFLE-S	RASSLE-S	RECOAT-S
PUNKIN-S	QUAERE-S	RAFTER-S	RASTER-S	RECOCK-S
PUNNER-S	QUAGGA-S	RAGBAG-S	RASURE-S	RECODE-S
PUNNET-S	QUAHOG-S	RAGGEE-S	RATBAG-S	RECOIL-S
PUNTEE-S	QUAICH-S	RAGGLE-S	RATEEN-S	RECOIN-S
PUNTER-S	QUAIGH-S	RAGING-S	RATINE-S	RECOMB-S
PUPATE-S	QUAKER-S	RAGINI-S	RATING-S	RECOOK-S
PUPPET-S	QUANGO-S	RAGLAN-S	RATION-S	RECORD-S
PURANA-S	QUARTE-S	RAGMAN-S	RATITE-S	RECORK-S
PURDAH-S	QUARTO-S	RAGOUT-S	RATLIN-S	RECOUP-S
PURFLE-S	QUASAR-S	RAGTAG-S	RATOON-S	RECTOR-S
PURGER-S	QUATRE-S	RAGTOP-S	RATTAN-S	RECTUM-S

RECULE-S	REGENT-S	REMISE-S	RESEDA-S	REVERT-S
RECURE-S	REGEST-S	REMOLD-S	RESEED-S	REVEST-S
RECUSE-S	REGGAE-S	REMORA-S	RESEEK-S	REVEUR-S
REDACT-S	REGILD-S	REMOTE-S	RESELL-S	REVIEW-S
REDATE-S	REGIME-S	REMOVE-S	RESEND-S	REVILE-S
REDBAY-S	REGINA-S	REMUDA-S	RESENT-S	REVISE-S
REDBUD-S	REGION-S	RENAIL-S	RESHIP-S	REVIVE-S
REDBUG-S	REGIVE-S	RENAME-S	RESHOE-S	REVOKE-S
REDCAP-S	REGLET-S	RENDER-S	RESHOW-S	REVOLT-S
REDDEN-S	REGLOW-S	RENEGE-S	RESIDE-S	REVOTE-S
REDDER-S	REGLUE-S	RENEST-S	RESIFT-S	REWAKE-S
REDDLE-S	REGRET-S	RENNET-S	RESIGN-S	REWARD-S
REDEAL-S	REGROW-S	RENNIN-S	RESILE-S	REWARM-S
REDEAR-S	REGULO-S	RENOWN-S	RESIST-S	REWEAR-S
REDEEM-S	REHANG-S	RENTAL-S	RESITE-S	REWELD-S
REDEYE-S	REHEAR-S	RENTER-S	RESIZE-S	REWIND-S
REDFIN-S	REHEAT-S	RENVOI-S	RESKEW-S	REWIRE-S
REDIAL-S	REHEEL-S	RENVOY-S	RESKUE-S	REWORD-S
REDLEG-S	REHIRE-S	REOPEN-S	RESOAK-S	REWORK-S
REDOCK-S	REITER-S	REPACK-S	RESOLE-S	REWRAP-S
REDOUT-S	REIVER-S	REPAIR-S	RESORB-S	REXINE-S
REDOWA-S	REJECT-S	REPARK-S	RESORT-S	REZERO-S
REDRAW-S	REJOIN-S	REPAST-S	RESPOT-S	REZONE-S
REDTOP-S	REKNIT-S	REPAVE-S	RESTEM-S	RHANJA-S
REDUCE-S	REKNOT-S	REPEAL-S	RESTER-S	RHAPHE-S
REDUIT-S	RELACE-S	REPEAT-S	RESULT-S	RHEBOK-S
REEARN-S	RELAND-S	REPENT-S	RESUME-S	RHETOR-S
REEBOK-S	RELATE-S	REPERK-S	RETACK-S	RHODIE-S
REEDER-S	RELEND-S	REPINE-S	RETAIL-S	RHUMBA-S
REEDIT-S	RELENT-S	REPLAN-S	RETAIN-S	RHYMER-S
REEFER-S	RELEVE-S	REPLAY-S	RETAKE-S	RHYTHM-S
REEKER-S	RELICT-S	REPLOT-S	RETAMA-S	RHYTON-S
REELER-S	RELIEF-S	REPLOW-S	RETAPE-S	RIALTO-S
REEMIT-S	RELIER-S	REPOLL-S	RETARD-S	RIBALD-S
REFACE-S	RELINE-S	REPONE-S	RETEAM-S	RIBAND-S
REFALL-S	RELINK-S	REPORT-S	RETEAR-S	RIBAUD-S
REFECT-S	RELIST-S	REPOSE-S	RETELL-S	RIBBER-S
REFEED-S	RELIVE-S	REPOST-S	RETENE-S	RIBBON-S
REFEEL-S	RELOAD-S	REPOUR-S	RETEST-S	RIBIBE-S
REFILE-S	RELOAN-S	REPUGN-S	RETILE-S	RIBIER-S
REFILL-S	RELOCK-S	REPULP-S	RETIME-S	RIBLET-S
REFILM-S	RELOOK-S	REPUMP-S	RETINA-S	RIBOSE-S
REFIND-S	RELUCT-S	REPURE-S	RETINE-S	RICHEN-S
REFINE-S	RELUME-S	REPUTE-S	RETINT-S	RICKER-S
REFIRE-S	REMADE-S	REQUIN-S	RETIRE-S	RICKEY-S
REFLAG-S	REMAIL-S	REQUIT-S	RETOOL-S	RICKLE-S
REFLET-S	REMAIN-S	RERACK-S	RETORT-S	RICRAC-S
REFLOW-S	REMAKE-S	RERAIL-S	RETOUR-S	RIDDER-S
REFOLD-S	REMAND-S	REREAD-S	RETREE-S	RIDDLE-S
REFOOT-S	REMARK-S	RERENT-S	RETRIM-S	RIDGEL-S
REFORM-S	REMATE-S	RERISE-S	RETUND-S	RIDGER-S
REFUEL-S	REMBLE-S	REROLL-S	RETUNE-S	RIDGIL-S
REFUGE-S	REMEAD-S	REROOF-S	RETURF-S	RIDING-S
REFUND-S	REMEDE-S	RESAIL-S	RETURN-S	RIDLEY-S
REFUSE-S	REMEET-S	RESALE-S	RETYPE-S	RIEVER-S
REFUTE-S	REMEID-S	RESCUE-S	REURGE-S	RIFFLE-S
REGAIN-S	REMELT-S	RESEAL-S	REVAMP-S	RIFLER-S
REGALE-S	REMEND-S	RESEAT-S	REVEAL-S	RIFLIP-S
REGARD-S	REMIND-S	RESEAU-S	REVERB-S	RIGGER-S
REGEAR-S	REMINT-S	RESECT-S	REVERE-S	RIGHTO-S

RIGLIN-S	RONZER-S	RUMAKI-S	SAIYID-S	SANTON-S
RIGOLL-S	ROOFER-S	RUMBLE-S	SAKIEH-S	SANTUR-S
RIGOUR-S	ROOFIE-S	RUMKIN-S	SALAAM-S	SAPELE-S
RIGOUT-S	ROOKIE-S	RUMMER-S	SALADE-S	SAPOTA-S
RILLET-S	ROOMER-S	RUMOUR-S	SALAMI-S	SAPOTE-S
RIMAYE-S	ROOMIE-S	RUMPLE-S	SALINA-S	SAPOUR-S
RIMMER-S	ROOSER-S	RUNDLE-S	SALINE-S	SAPPAN-S
RIMPLE-S	ROOTER-S	RUNKLE-S	SALIVA-S	SAPPER-S
RINGER-S	ROOTLE-S	RUNLET-S	SALLAD-S	SAPPLE-S
RINSER-S	ROPING-S	RUNNEL-S	SALLAL-S	SARAPE-S
RIOTER-S	ROQUET-S	RUNNER-S	SALLEE-S	SARDAR-S
RIPECK-S	RORTER-S	RUNNET-S	SALLET-S	SARDEL-S
RIPOFF-S	ROSACE-S	RUNOFF-S	SALLOW-S	SARMIE-S
RIPOST-S	ROSBIF-S	RUNOUT-S	SALMON-S	SARNEY-S
RIPPER-S	ROSCOE-S	RUNRIG-S	SALOON-S	SARNIE-S
RIPPLE-S	ROSIER-S	RUNWAY-S	SALOOP-S	SARODE-S
RIPRAP-S	ROSSER-S	RUPIAH-S	SALPID-S	SARONG-S
RIPSAW-S	ROSTER-S	RUSHEE-S	SALTER-S	SARSAR-S
RISING-S	ROSULA-S	RUSHER-S	SALTIE-S	SARSEN-S
RISKER-S	ROTATE-S	RUSSEL-S	SALUKI-S	SARTOR-S
RISQUE-S	ROTCHE-S	RUSSET-S	SALUTE-S	SASHAY-S
RISTRA-S	ROTGUT-S	RUSSIA-S	SALVER-S	SASINE-S
RITARD-S	ROTHER-S	RUSTIC-S	SALVIA-S	SASTRA-S
RITTER-S	ROTOLO-S	RUSTLE-S	SALVOR-S	SATANG-S
RITUAL-S	ROTTAN-S	RUSTRE-S	SAMAAN-S	SATARA-S
RIVAGE-S	ROTTEN-S	RUTILE-S	SAMARA-S	SATEEN-S
RIVLIN-S	ROTTER-S	RUTTER-S	SAMBAL-S	SATIRE-S
RIZARD-S	ROTULA-S	RYOKAN-S	SAMBAR-S	SATORI-S
RIZZAR-S	ROTUND-S	RYPECK-S	SAMBUR-S	SATRAP-S
RIZZER-S	ROUBLE-S	SABBAT-S	SAMECH-S	SATYRA-S
RIZZOR-S	ROUCHE-S	SABINE-S	SAMEKH-S	SAUCER-S
ROADEO-S	ROUCOU-S	SABKHA-S	SAMFOO-S	SAUGER-S
ROADIE-S	ROUNCE-S	SACBUT-S	SAMIEL-S	SAULGE-S
ROAMER-S	ROUSER-S	SACHEM-S	SAMITE-S	SAULIE-S
ROARER-S	ROUTER-S	SACHET-S	SAMITI-S	SAUREL-S
ROBALO-S	ROVING-S	SACKER-S	SAMLET-S	SAVAGE-S
ROBAND-S	ROWING-S	SACQUE-S	SAMLOR-S	SAVANT-S
ROBBER-S	ROZZER-S	SACRAL-S	SAMOSA-S	SAVATE-S
ROBBIN-S	RUBACE-S	SACRUM-S	SAMPAN-S	SAVINE-S
ROBING-S	RUBATO-S	SADDEN-S	SAMPLE-S	SAVING-S
ROCHET-S	RUBBER-S	SADDHU-S	SAMSHU-S	SAVIOR-S
ROCKER-S	RUBBLE-S	SADDLE-S	SANCAI-S	SAVOUR-S
ROCKET-S	RUBIGO-S	SADISM-S	SANCHO-S	SAVVEY-S
ROCOCO-S	RUBINE-S	SADIST-S	SANDAL-S	SAWDER-S
RODENT-S	RUBOFF-S	SAETER-S	SANDEK-S	SAWING-S
RODING-S	RUBOUT-S	SAFARI-S	SANDER-S	SAWLOG-S
ROEMER-S	RUBRIC-S	SAFROL-S	SANDHI-S	SAWNEY-S
ROGNON-S	RUCKLE-S	SAGBUT-S	SANGAR-S	SAWPIT-S
ROLFER-S	RUCOLA-S	SAGENE-S	SANGER-S	SAWYER-S
ROLLER-S	RUDDER-S	SAGGAR-S	SANJAK-S	SAXAUL-S
ROMAGE-S	RUDDLE-S	SAGGER-S	SANNIE-S	SAYING-S
ROMAJI-S	RUEING-S	SAGOIN-S	SANNOP-S	SAYYID-S
ROMANO-S	RUELLE-S	SAGUIN-S	SANNUP-S	SAZHEN-S
ROMCOM-S	RUFFIN-S	SAHIBA-S	SANPAN-S	SCAITH-S
ROMPER-S	RUFFLE-S	SAIKEI-S	SANPRO-S	SCALAR-S
RONDEL-S	RUGGER-S	SAILER-S	SANSAR-S	SCALER-S
RONION-S	RUGOLA-S	SAILOR-S	SANSEI-S	SCAMEL-S
RONNEL-S	RUGOSA-S	SAIMIN-S	SANTAL-S	SCAMPI-S
RONNIE-S	RUINER-S	SAIQUE-S	SANTIR-S	SCAMTO-S
RONYON-S	RULING-S	SAITHE-S	SANTOL-S	SCARAB-S

SCARER-S	SCROBE-S	SEISIN-S	SETTER-S	SHINNE-S
SCARPA-S	SCROLL-S	SEISOR-S	SETTLE-S	SHIPPO-S
SCARPH-S	SCROME-S	SEITAN-S	SETULE-S	SHIRRA-S
SCARRE-S	SCROOP-S	SEITEN-S	SEWAGE-S	SHISHA-S
SCARTH-S	SCRORP-S	SEIZER-S	SEWING-S	SHIVAH-S
SCATHE-S	SCROTE-S	SEIZIN-S	SEXISM-S	SHIVER-S
SCAZON-S	SCROWL-S	SEIZOR-S	SEXIST-S	SHIVOO-S
SCENIC-S	SCRUFF-S	SELECT-S	SEXPOT-S	SHLEPP-S
SCERNE-S	SCRUMP-S	SELKIE-S	SEXTAN-S	SHLOCK-S
SCHELM-S	SCRUNT-S	SELLER-S	SEXTET-S	SHLUMP-S
SCHEMA-S	SCRUTO-S	SELSYN-S	SEXTON-S	SHMEAR-S
SCHEME-S	SCRUZE-S	SEMBLE-S	SHACKO-S	SHMOCK-S
SCHISM-S	SCRYER-S	SEMEME-S	SHADER-S	SHMUCK-S
SCHIST-S	SCRYNE-S	SEMMIT-S	SHADOW-S	SHNOOK-S
SCHIZO-S	SCULLE-S	SEMSEM-S	SHADUF-S	SHODER-S
SCHLEP-S	SCULPT-S	SENATE-S	SHAIKH-S	SHOFAR-S
SCHLUB-S	SCUNGE-S	SENDAL-S	SHAIRD-S	SHOGUN-S
SCHMOE-S	SCYTHE-S	SENDER-S	SHAIRN-S	SHOLOM-S
SCHOOL-S	SDAINE-S	SENDUP-S	SHAKER-S	SHOOLE-S
SCHORL-S	SDEIGN-S	SENECA-S	SHALLI-S	SHOORA-S
SCHOUT-S	SEABAG-S	SENEGA-S	SHALOM-S	SHOPPE-S
SCHRIK-S	SEABED-S	SENHOR-S	SHALOT-S	SHORAN-S
SCHROD-S	SEADOG-S	SENILE-S	SHAMAN-S	SHORER-S
SCHTIK-S	SEAHOG-S	SENIOR-S	SHAMBA-S	SHOTTE-S
SCHUIT-S	SEALCH-S	SENNET-S	SHAMER-S	SHOUGH-S
SCHUYT-S	SEALER-S	SENNIT-S	SHAMOY-S	SHOUSE-S
SCILLA-S	SEALGH-S	SENORA-S	SHANTI-S	SHOVEL-S
SCIROC-S	SEAMER-S	SENSEI-S	SHAPER-S	SHOVER-S
SCLAFF-S	SEANCE-S	SENSOR-S	SHARER-S	SHOWER-S
SCLATE-S	SEARAT-S	SEPHEN-S	SHARIA-S	SHREEK-S
SCLAVE-S	SEARCE-S	SEPIUM-S	SHARIF-S	SHREIK-S
SCLERA-S	SEASON-S	SEPTET-S	SHAUGH-S	SHRIEK-S
SCLERE-S	SEATER-S	SEPTIC-S	SHAVER-S	SHRIFT-S
SCLIFF-S	SEAWAN-S	SEPTUM-S	SHAVIE-S	SHRIKE-S
SCONCE-S	SEAWAY-S	SEQUEL-S	SHEATH-S	SHRILL-S
SCORER-S	SEBATE-S	SEQUIN-S	SHEAVE-S	SHRIMP-S
SCORSE-S	SECANT-S	SERAIL-S	SHEEPO-S	SHRINE-S
SCOTER-S	SECEDE-S	SERANG-S	SHEEVE-S	SHRINK-S
SCOTIA-S	SECERN-S	SERAPE-S	SHEIKH-S	SHRIVE-S
SCOUSE-S	SECKEL-S	SERAPH-S	SHEILA-S	SHROFF-S
SCOUTH-S	SECKLE-S	SERDAB-S	SHEKEL-S	SHROOM-S
SCOWTH-S	SECOND-S	SEREIN-S	SHELTA-S	SHROUD-S
SCOZZA-S	SECPAR-S	SERENE-S	SHELVE-S	SHROVE-S
SCRAMB-S	SECRET-S	SERGER-S	SHEQEL-S	SHTCHI-S
SCRAPE-S	SECTOR-S	SERIAL-S	SHERIA-S	SHTETL-S
SCRAWL-S	SECURE-S	SERINE-S	SHERIF-S	SHTICK-S
SCRAWM-S	SEDATE-S	SERIPH-S	SHERPA-S	SHTOOK-S
SCRAWP-S	SEDUCE-S	SERMON-S	SHEUCH-S	SHTUCK-S
SCRAYE-S	SEEDER-S	SEROON-S	SHEUGH-S	SHUFTI-S
SCREAK-S	SEEING-S	SEROSA-S	SHEWEL-S	SHYPOO-S
SCREAM-S	SEEKER-S	SERRAN-S	SHEWER-S	SIALID-S
SCREED-S	SEEMER-S	SERVAL-S	SHIBAH-S	SIALON-S
SCREEN-S	SEESAW-S	SERVER-S	SHIELD-S	SICKEE-S
SCREET-S	SEETHE-S	SESAME-S	SHIKAR-S	SICKEN-S
SCRIBE-S	SEGGAR-S	SESELI-S	SHIKSA-S	SICKIE-S
SCRIKE-S	SEGHOL-S	SESTET-S	SHIKSE-S	SICKLE-S
SCRIMP-S	SEICHE-S	SESTON-S	SHINDY-S	SIDDHA-S
SCRINE-S	SEIDEL-S	SETOFF-S	SHINER-S	SIDDHI-S
SCRIPT-S	SEINER-S	SETOUT-S	SHINES-S	SIDDUR-S
SCRIVE-S	SEISER-S	SETTEE-S	SHINJU-S	SIDING-S

SIDLER-S	SITTAR-S	SMIDGE-S	SONATA-S	SPENCE-S
SIECLE-S	SITTER-S	SMIGHT-S	SONDER-S	SPENSE-S
SIEGER-S	SIXAIN-S	SMILER-S	SONERI-S	SPERRE-S
SIENNA-S	SIZING-S	SMILET-S	SONNET-S	SPERSE-S
SIERRA-S	SIZISM-S	SMILEY-S	SONTAG-S	SPEWER-S
SIESTA-S	SIZIST-S	SMITER-S	SOOGEE-S	SPHAER-S
SIFAKA-S	SIZZLE-S	SMOILE-S	SOOGIE-S	SPHEAR-S
SIFFLE-S	SKAITH-S	SMOKER-S	SOOJEY-S	SPHENE-S
SIFTER-S	SKARTH-S	SMOOGE-S	SOONER-S	SPHERE-S
SIGHER-S	SKATER-S	SMOOTH-S	SOOTHE-S	SPICER-S
SIGNAL-S	SKATOL-S	SMOUSE-S	SOPITE-S	SPIDER-S
SIGNEE-S	SKEANE-S	SMOYLE-S	SORAGE-S	SPIGHT-S
SIGNER-S	SKELUM-S	SMRITI-S	SORBET-S	SPIGOT-S
SIGNET-S	SKEWER-S	SMUDGE-S	SORDOR-S	SPIKER-S
SIGNOR-S	SKIBOB-S	SNARER-S	SORELL-S	SPILTH-S
SILAGE-S	SKIDOO-S	SNASTE-S	SORGHO-S	SPINAL-S
SILANE-S	SKIING-S	SNATHE-S	SORING-S	SPINAR-S
SILENE-S	SKIVER-S	SNEATH-S	SORNER-S	SPINEL-S
SILENT-S	SKLATE-S	SNEBBE-S	SORREL-S	SPINET-S
SILICA-S	SKLENT-S	SNEEZE-S	SORROW-S	SPINOR-S
SILKEN-S	SKLIFF-S	SNIPER-S	SORTAL-S	SPINTO-S
SILKIE-S	SKREEN-S	SNIVEL-S	SORTER-S	SPIRAL-S
SILLER-S	SKRIKE-S	SNOOZE-S	SORTIE-S	SPIREA-S
SILVAN-S	SKRIMP-S	SNORER-S	SOUARI-S	SPIREM-S
SILVER-S	SKRUMP-S	SNUBBE-S	SOUCAR-S	SPIRIC-S
SIMIAN-S	SKRYER-S	SNUDGE-S	SOUDAN-S	SPIRIT-S
SIMILE-S	SKYCAP-S	SOAKER-S	SOUPER-S	SPITAL-S
SIMKIN-S	SKYLAB-S	SOAPER-S	SOUPLE-S	SPLAKE-S
SIMLIN-S	SKYWAY-S	SOAPIE-S	SOURCE-S	SPLEEN-S
SIMMER-S	SLAIRG-S	SOARER-S	SOURSE-S	SPLENT-S
SIMNEL-S	SLAKER-S	SOBBER-S	SOUTAR-S	SPLICE-S
SIMOOM-S	SLALOM-S	SOBOLE-S	SOUTER-S	SPLIFF-S
SIMOON-S	SLATER-S	SOCAGE-S	SOUTIE-S	SPLINE-S
SIMORG-S	SLAVER-S	SOCCER-S	SOVIET-S	SPLINT-S
SIMPAI-S	SLAVEY-S	SOCIAL-S	SOVRAN-S	SPLORE-S
SIMPER-S	SLAYER-S	SOCKET-S	SOWCAR-S	SPONGE-S
SIMPLE-S	SLEAVE-S	SODDEN-S	SOWING-S	SPOUSE-S
SIMURG-S	SLEAZE-S	SODGER-S	SOWSSE-S	SPRAIN-S
SINDON-S	SLEDGE-S	SODIUM-S	SOWTER-S	SPRANG-S
SINGER-S	SLEEVE-S	SOFFIT-S	SOZINE-S	SPRAWL-S
SINGLE-S	SLEIGH-S	SOFTEN-S	SOZZLE-S	SPREAD-S
SINKER-S	SLEUTH-S	SOFTIE-S	SPACER-S	SPREDD-S
SINNER-S	SLICER-S	SOIREE-S	SPADER-S	SPRING-S
SINNET-S	SLIDER-S	SOLACE-S	SPAHEE-S	SPRINT-S
SINTER-S	SLIEVE-S	SOLAND-S	SPAING-S	SPRITE-S
SIPHON-S	SLIGHT-S	SOLANO-S	SPALLE-S	SPROUT-S
SIPPER-S	SLIPUP-S	SOLATE-S	SPARER-S	SPRUCE-S
SIPPET-S	SLIVER-S	SOLDAN-S	SPARGE-S	SPRUIK-S
SIPPLE-S	SLOGAN-S	SOLDER-S	SPARID-S	SPRUIT-S
SIRCAR-S	SLOKEN-S	SOLERA-S	SPARKE-S	SPULYE-S
SIRDAR-S	SLOPER-S	SOLION-S	SPARRE-S	SPUNGE-S
SIRKAR-S	SLOUGH-S	SOLIVE-S	SPARTH-S	SPURGE-S
SIRRAH-S	SLOVEN-S	SOLLAR-S	SPATHE-S	SPURNE-S
SIRREE-S	SLUDGE-S	SOLLER-S	SPAULD-S	SPYING-S
SISKIN-S	SLUICE-S	SOLUTE-S	SPAVIE-S	SQUAIL-S
SISSOO-S	SMALTO-S	SOLVER-S	SPAVIN-S	SQUALL-S
SISTER-S	SMEATH-S	SOMBER-S	SPAYAD-S	SQUAME-S
SITCOM-S	SMEETH-S	SOMBRE-S	SPECIE-S	SQUARE-S
SITHEN-S	SMEGMA-S	SOMITE-S	SPEEDO-S	SQUARK-S
SITREP-S	SMEUSE-S	SONANT-S	SPEISE-S	SQUAWK-S

SQUEAK-S	STOGEY-S	STYLER-S	SUNRAY-S	TAENIA-S
SQUEAL-S	STOGIE-S	STYLET-S	SUNSET-S	TAFFIA-S
SQUIER-S	STOKER-S	STYMIE-S	SUNTAN-S	TAGGEE-S
SQUILL-S	STOLON-S	SUBACT-S	SUPAWN-S	TAGGER-S
SQUINT-S	STONER-S	SUBBIE-S	SUPINE-S	TAGINE-S
SQUIRE-S	STONNE-S	SUBDEB-S	SUPPER-S	TAGRAG-S
SQUIRM-S	STOOGE-S	SUBDEW-S	SUPPLE-S	TAGUAN-S
SQUIRR-S	STOOPE-S	SUBDUE-S	SURBED-S	TAHINA-S
SQUIRT-S	STOPER-S	SUBFEU-S	SURFER-S	TAHINI-S
SRADHA-S	STORER-S	SUBGUM-S	SURFIE-S	TAHSIL-S
STABLE-S	STOREY-S	SUBLET-S	SURGER-S	TAIAHA-S
STACTE-S	STORGE-S	SUBLOT-S	SURIMI-S	TAIGLE-S
STADDA-S	STOTIN-S	SUBMIT-S	SURREY-S	TAILER-S
STADIA-S	STOUND-S	SUBNET-S	SURVEY-S	TAILLE-S
STAGER-S	STOURE-S	SUBORN-S	SUSLIK-S	TAILOR-S
STAITH-S	STOUTH-S	SUBSET-S	SUTLER-S	TAILYE-S
STALAG-S	STOVER-S	SUBURB-S	SUTTEE-S	TAIPAN-S
STAMEN-S	STOWER-S	SUBWAY-S	SUTTLE-S	TAIVER-S
STANCE-S	STOWND-S	SUCCAH-S	SUTURE-S	TAJINE-S
STANOL-S	STOWRE-S	SUCCES-S	SWAGER-S	TAKAHE-S
STANZA-S	STRAFE-S	SUCCOR-S	SWARTH-S	TAKEUP-S
STANZE-S	STRAFF-S	SUCCUS-S	SWARVE-S	TAKING-S
STANZO-S	STRAIK-S	SUCKEN-S	SWATHE-S	TALANT-S
STAPLE-S	STRAIN-S	SUCKER-S	SWAYER-S	TALBOT-S
STARER-S	STRAIT-S	SUCKET-S	SWEARD-S	TALCUM-S
STARVE-S	STRAKE-S	SUCKLE-S	SWERVE-S	TALENT-S
STATER-S	STRAMP-S	SUDATE-S	SWEVEN-S	TALION-S
STATIC-S	STRAND-S	SUDDEN-S	SWILER-S	TALKER-S
STATIN-S	STRATA-S	SUDDER-S	SWINGE-S	TALKIE-S
STATOR-S	STRATH-S	SUDSER-S	SWIPER-S	TALLAT-S
STATUA-S	STREAK-S	SUFFER-S	SWIPLE-S	TALLET-S
STATUE-S	STREAM-S	SUITER-S	SWIVEL-S	TALLIT-S
STAYER-S	STREEK-S	SUITOR-S	SWIVET-S	TALLOL-S
STAYNE-S	STREEL-S	SUKKAH-S	SWOUND-S	TALLOT-S
STAYRE-S	STREET-S	SULDAN-S	SWOUNE-S	TALLOW-S
STEALE-S	STRENE-S	SULFID-S	SWOWND-S	TALMUD-S
STEANE-S	STRICK-S	SULFUR-S	SWOWNE-S	TALUKA-S
STEARE-S	STRIDE-S	SULKER-S	SYLVAN-S	TALWEG-S
STEDDE-S	STRIFE-S	SULLEN-S	SYLVIA-S	TAMALE-S
STEEVE-S	STRIFT-S	SULPHA-S	SYLVIN-S	TAMANU-S
STELLA-S	STRIKE-S	SULTAN-S	SYMBOL-S	TAMARA-S
STEMMA-S	STRING-S	SUMACH-S	SYNCOM-S	TAMARI-S
STEMME-S	STRIPE-S	SUMMAT-S	SYNDET-S	TAMBAC-S
STEPPE-S	STRIVE-S	SUMMER-S	SYNDIC-S	TAMBAK-S
STEREO-S	STROAM-S	SUMMIT-S	SYNROC-S	TAMBER-S
STEROL-S	STROBE-S	SUMMON-S	SYNTAN-S	TAMBUR-S
STERVE-S	STROKE-S	SUMPIT-S	SYPHER-S	TAMEIN-S
STEVEN-S	STROLL-S	SUNBED-S	SYPHON-S	TAMINE-S
STEWER-S	STROMB-S	SUNBOW-S	SYSTEM-S	TAMING-S
STIFLE-S	STROND-S	SUNDAE-S	TABARD-S	TAMISE-S
STIGMA-S	STROUD-S	SUNDER-S	TABERD-S	TAMMAR-S
STIGME-S	STROUP-S	SUNDEW-S	TABLET-S	TAMMIE-S
STILET-S	STROUT-S	SUNDOG-S	TABOUR-S	TAMPAN-S
STIMIE-S	STRUMA-S	SUNDRA-S	TABRET-S	TAMPER-S
STINGO-S	STRUNT-S	SUNDRI-S	TABULI-S	TAMPON-S
STIPEL-S	STUCCO-S	SUNGAR-S	TACKER-S	TANDEM-S
STIRRA-S	STUDIO-S	SUNHAT-S	TACKET-S	TANGIE-S
STIRRE-S	STUMER-S	SUNKET-S	TACKLE-S	TANGLE-S
STIVER-S	STUPID-S	SUNKIE-S	TACTIC-S	TANGUN-S
STODGE-S	STUPOR-S	SUNNAH-S	TADDIE-S	TANIST-S

TANKER-S	TEACUP-S	TERCIO-S	THWACK-S	TISICK-S
TANKIA-S	TEAGLE-S	TEREDO-S	THWART-S	TISSUE-S
TANNAH-S	TEAMER-S	TERETE-S	THYMOL-S	TITBIT-S
TANNER-S	TEAPOT-S	TERMER-S	THYRSE-S	TITFER-S
TANNIE-S	TEAPOY-S	TERMOR-S	TICKEN-S	TITHER-S
TANNIN-S	TEARER-S	TERRET-S	TICKER-S	TITIAN-S
TANNOY-S	TEASEL-S	TERRIT-S	TICKET-S	TITLER-S
TANREC-S	TEASER-S	TERROR-S	TICKEY-S	TITOKI-S
TANTRA-S	TEAZEL-S	TERTIA-S	TICKLE-S	TITTER-S
TANUKI-S	TEAZLE-S	TESTEE-S	TICTAC-S	TITTIE-S
TAONGA-S	TEBBAD-S	TESTER-S	TICTOC-S	TITTLE-S
TAPALO-S	TECHIE-S	TESTON-S	TIDBIT-S	TITTUP-S
TAPETI-S	TECHNO-S	TETHER-S	TIDDLE-S	TITULE-S
TAPIST-S	TECKEL-S	TETRAD-S	TIDIER-S	TOCHER-S
TAPPER-S	TECTUM-S	TETRYL-S	TIDING-S	TOCSIN-S
TAPPET-S	TEDDER-S	TETTER-S	TIEPIN-S	TODDLE-S
TARAMA-S	TEDDIE-S	TEWART-S	TIERCE-S	TOEBIE-S
TARAND-S	TEDIUM-S	TEWHIT-S	TIEROD-S	TOECAP-S
TARBOY-S	TEEMER-S	TEXTER-S	TIETAC-S	TOERAG-S
TARCEL-S	TEENER-S	THAIRM-S	TIFFIN-S	TOETOE-S
TARGET-S	TEEPEE-S	THALER-S	TIGLON-S	TOFFEE-S
TARIFF-S	TEETER-S	THANAH-S	TILING-S	TOGGER-S
TARING-S	TEETHE-S	THANNA-S	TILLER-S	TOGGLE-S
TARMAC-S	TEFLON-S	THAWER-S	TILTER-S	TOILER-S
TARPAN-S	TEKKIE-S	THEAVE-S	TIMBAL-S	TOILET-S
TARPON-S	TELEDU-S	THEINE-S	TIMBER-S	TOISON-S
TARROW-S	TELEGA-S	THEISM-S	TIMBRE-S	TOITOI-S
TARSAL-S	TELESM-S	THEIST-S	TIMING-S	TOLANE-S
TARSEL-S	TELFER-S	THENAR-S	TIMIST-S	TOLEDO-S
TARSIA-S	TELLAR-S	THERME-S	TINAJA-S	TOLING-S
TARTAN-S	TELLEN-S	THIBET-S	TINCAL-S	TOLLER-S
TARTAR-S	TELLER-S	THIBLE-S	TINDAL-S	TOLLIE-S
TARZAN-S	TELLIN-S	THICKO-S	TINDER-S	TOLSEL-S
TASKER-S	TELNET-S	THIEVE-S	TINEID-S	TOLSEY-S
TASLET-S	TELOME-S	THIRAM-S	TINFUL-S	TOLTER-S
TASSEL-S	TELSON-S	THIRST-S	TINGLE-S	TOLUID-S
TASSET-S	TEMPEH-S	THIVEL-S	TINKER-S	TOLUOL-S
TASSIE-S	TEMPER-S	THORIA-S	TINKLE-S	TOLUYL-S
TASTER-S	TEMPLE-S	THORON-S	TINNER-S	TOLZEY-S
TATAMI-S	TENACE-S	THORPE-S	TINNIE-S	TOMBAC-S
TATLER-S	TENAIL-S	THOWEL-S	TINPOT-S	TOMBAK-S
TATSOI-S	TENANT-S	THRALL-S	TINSEL-S	TOMBOC-S
TATTER-S	TENDER-S	THRANG-S	TINSEY-S	TOMBOY-S
TATTIE-S	TENDON-S	THRAVE-S	TINTER-S	TOMCAT-S
TATTLE-S	TENDRE-S	THREAD-S	TIPCAT-S	TOMCOD-S
TATTOO-S	TENNER-S	THREAP-S	TIPOFF-S	TOMPON-S
TATTOW-S	TENOUR-S	THREAT-S	TIPPEE-S	TOMTIT-S
TAUIWI-S	TENPIN-S	THREEP-S	TIPPER-S	TONEME-S
TAUPIE-S	TENREC-S	THRENE-S	TIPPET-S	TONGER-S
TAUTEN-S	TENSON-S	THRIFT-S	TIPPLE-S	TONGUE-S
TAUTOG-S	TENSOR-S	THRILL-S	TIPTOE-S	TONING-S
TAVERN-S	TENTER-S	THRIST-S	TIPTOP-S	TONITE-S
TAWHAI-S	TENURE-S	THRIVE-S	TIPULA-S	TONKER-S
TAWING-S	TENUTO-S	THROAT-S	TIPUNA-S	TONLET-S
TAWNEY-S	TENZON-S	THRONE-S	TIRADE-S	TONNAG-S
TAWPIE-S	TEOPAN-S	THRONG-S	TIRAGE-S	TONNER-S
TAXEME-S	TEPHRA-S	THROWE-S	TIRING-S	TONSIL-S
TAXING-S	TERBIA-S	THRUST-S	TIRITI-S	TONSOR-S
TAXITE-S	TERCEL-S	THUGGO-S	TIRRIT-S	TOOART-S
TCHICK-S	TERCET-S	THULIA-S	TISANE-S	TOOLER-S

TOONIE-S	TREVIS-S	TUGRIK-S	TYPING-S	UNEDGE-S
TOORIE-S	TRIAGE-S	TUILLE-S	TYPIST-S	UNFACT-S
TOOTER-S	TRIBAL-S	TUKTOO-S	TYRANT-S	UNFAIR-S
TOOTLE-S	TRICAR-S	TULADI-S	TYSTIE-S	UNFOLD-S
TOPPER-S	TRICEP-S	TULBAN-S	TZETSE-S	UNFOOL-S
TOPPLE-S	TRICOT-S	TULWAR-S	TZETZE-S	UNFORM-S
TOQUET-S	TRIENE-S	TUMBLE-S	UAKARI-S	UNFREE-S
TORANA-S	TRIFLE-S	TUMOUR-S	UJAMAA-S	UNFURL-S
TORERO-S	TRIGON-S	TUMULT-S	ULICON-S	UNGEAR-S
TOROID-S	TRIJET-S	TUNDRA-S	ULIKON-S	UNGILD-S
TORPID-S	TRILBY-S	TUNDUN-S	ULLAGE-S	UNGIRD-S
TORPOR-S	TRIMER-S	TUNEUP-S	ULLING-S	UNGLUE-S
TORQUE-S	TRIODE-S	TUNING-S	ULSTER-S	UNGOWN-S
TORRET-S	TRIOSE-S	TUNNEL-S	ULTIMA-S	UNGYVE-S
TORSEL-S	TRIPLE-S	TUPELO-S	ULTION-S	UNHAIR-S
TORULA-S	TRIPOD-S	TUPUNA-S	UMBREL-S	UNHAND-S
TOSHER-S	TRISUL-S	TURACO-S	UMBRIL-S	UNHANG-S
TOSSER-S	TRITON-S	TURBAN-S	UMFAZI-S	UNHASP-S
TOSSUP-S	TRIUNE-S	TURBIT-S	UMIACK-S	UNHEAD-S
TOTARA-S	TRIVET-S	TURBOT-S	UMLAUT-S	UNHEAL-S
TOTTER-S	TROADE-S	TUREEN-S	UMPIRE-S	UNHELE-S
TOTTIE-S	TROCAR-S	TURGOR-S	UMWELT-S	UNHELM-S
TOUCAN-S	TROCHE-S	TURION-S	UNBALE-S	UNHIVE-S
TOUCHE-S	TROGON-S	TURKEY-S	UNBARE-S	UNHOOD-S
TOUPEE-S	TROIKA-S	TURNER-S	UNBARK-S	UNHOOK-S
TOUPET-S	TROMPE-S	TURNIP-S	UNBEAR-S	UNHOOP-S
TOURER-S	TROPIC-S	TURNON-S	UNBELT-S	UNHUSK-S
TOURIE-S	TROPIN-S	TURNUP-S	UNBEND-S	UNIPED-S
TOUSER-S	TROTYL-S	TURRET-S	UNBIND-S	UNIPOD-S
TOUSLE-S	TROUGH-S	TURTLE-S	UNBITT-S	UNIQUE-S
TOUTER-S	TROULE-S	TUSCHE-S	UNBOLT-S	UNISON-S
TOUZLE-S	TROUPE-S	TUSHIE-S	UNBONE-S	UNITER-S
TOWAGE-S	TROUSE-S	TUSKAR-S	UNBOOT-S	UNKING-S
TOWARD-S	TROVER-S	TUSKER-S	UNCAGE-S	UNKINK-S
TOWBAR-S	TROWEL-S	TUSSAH-S	UNCAKE-S	UNKNIT-S
TOWHEE-S	TROWTH-S	TUSSAR-S	UNCAPE-S	UNKNOT-S
TOWING-S	TRUANT-S	TUSSEH-S	UNCART-S	UNLACE-S
TOWKAY-S	TRUDGE-S	TUSSER-S	UNCASE-S	UNLADE-S
TOWMON-S	TRUFFE-S	TUSSLE-S	UNCIAL-S	UNLEAD-S
TOWNEE-S	TRUISM-S	TUSSOR-S	UNCLEW-S	UNLIKE-S
TOWNIE-S	TRYING-S	TUSSUR-S	UNCLIP-S	UNLIME-S
TOWSER-S	TRYOUT-S	TUTSAN-S	UNCLOG-S	UNLINE-S
TOXINE-S	TRYSTE-S	TUXEDO-S	UNCOCK-S	UNLINK-S
TOXOID-S	TSAMBA-S	TUYERE-S	UNCOIL-S	UNLIVE-S
TOYING-S	TSETSE-S	TWAITE-S	UNCOLT-S	UNLOAD-S
TRACER-S	TSKTSK-S	TWEEZE-S	UNCOPE-S	UNLOCK-S
TRADER-S	TSOTSI-S	TWELVE-S	UNCORD-S	UNLORD-S
TRAGIC-S	TUBAGE-S	TWIBIL-S	UNCORK-S	UNLOVE-S
TRAMEL-S	TUBBER-S	TWICER-S	UNCOWL-S	UNMAKE-S
TRANCE-S	TUBFUL-S	TWIGHT-S	UNCUFF-S	UNMASK-S
TRANSE-S	TUBING-S	TWINER-S	UNCURB-S	UNMOLD-S
TRAPAN-S	TUBIST-S	TWINGE-S	UNCURL-S	UNMOOR-S
TRAUMA-S	TUBULE-S	TWOFER-S	UNDEAF-S	UNNAIL-S
TRAVEL-S	TUCHUN-S	TWONIE-S	UNDECK-S	UNNEST-S
TRAYNE-S	TUCKER-S	TWYERE-S	UNDERN-S	UNPACK-S
TREBLE-S	TUCKET-S	TYCOON-S	UNDINE-S	UNPICK-S
TREMIE-S	TUFFET-S	TYLOTE-S	UNDOCK-S	UNPILE-S
TREMOR-S	TUFTER-S	TYMBAL-S	UNDOER-S	UNPLUG-S
TREPAN-S	TUGGER-S	TYMPAN-S	UNDRAW-S	UNPOPE-S
TREVET-S	TUGHRA-S	TYPHON-S	UNEASE-S	UNPRAY-S

UNPROP-S	UPCOME-S	UPTOWN-S	VARVEL-S	VERVET-S
UNRAKE-S	UPCURL-S	UPTURN-S	VASSAL-S	VESPER-S
UNREEL-S	UPDART-S	UPWAFT-S	VATFUL-S	VESPID-S
UNREIN-S	UPDATE-S	UPWARD-S	VATTER-S	VESSEL-S
UNREST-S	UPDIVE-S	UPWELL-S	VAUDOO-S	VESTAL-S
UNROBE-S	UPDRAG-S	UPWIND-S	VAUNCE-S	VESTEE-S
UNROLL-S	UPDRAW-S	UPWRAP-S	VAWARD-S	VETOER-S
UNROOF-S	UPFILL-S	URACIL-S	VEALER-S	VETTER-S
UNROOT-S	UPFLOW-S	URANIA-S	VECTOR-S	VEXING-S
UNROPE-S	UPFOLD-S	URANIN-S	VEEJAY-S	VIATOR-S
UNRULE-S	UPFURL-S	URANYL-S	VEEPEE-S	VIBIST-S
UNSEAL-S	UPGANG-S	URCHIN-S	VEGGIE-S	VIBRIO-S
UNSEAM-S	UPGAZE-S	UREASE-S	VEILER-S	VICTIM-S
UNSEAT-S	UPGIRD-S	UREIDE-S	VEINER-S	VICTOR-S
UNSEEL-S	UPGROW-S	UREMIA-S	VELCRO-S	VICUNA-S
UNSEEN-S	UPHANG-S	URETER-S	VELETA-S	VIDAME-S
UNSELF-S	UPHAUD-S	URGING-S	VELLET-S	VIELLE-S
UNSELL-S	UPHEAP-S	URINAL-S	VELLON-S	VIEWER-S
UNSHIP-S	UPHILL-S	URNFUL-S	VELLUM-S	VIGORO-S
UNSHOE-S	UPHOLD-S	URNING-S	VELOUR-S	VIGOUR-S
UNSHUT-S	UPHROE-S	UROPOD-S	VELURE-S	VIHARA-S
UNSNAG-S	UPHURL-S	URTEXT-S	VELVET-S	VIKING-S
UNSNAP-S	UPKEEP-S	URTICA-S	VENDEE-S	VILLAN-S
UNSOUL-S	UPKNIT-S	USAGER-S	VENDER-S	VIMANA-S
UNSPAR-S	UPLAND-S	USANCE-S	VENDIS-S	VIOLER-S
UNSTEP-S	UPLEAD-S	USEFUL-S	VENDOR-S	VIOLET-S
UNSTOP-S	UPLEAN-S	USTION-S	VENDUE-S	VIOLIN-S
UNSTOW-S	UPLEAP-S	USURER-S	VENEER-S	VIRAGO-S
UNSUIT-S	UPLIFT-S	USURES-S	VENENE-S	VIRGER-S
UNTACK-S	UPLINK-S	USWARD-S	VENEWE-S	VIRGIN-S
UNTAME-S	UPLOAD-S	UTMOST-S	VENGER-S	VIRINO-S
UNTEAM-S	UPLOCK-S	UTOPIA-S	VENINE-S	VIRION-S
UNTENT-S	UPLOOK-S	UVULAR-S	VENIRE-S	VIROID-S
UNTHAW-S	UPMAKE-S	VACATE-S	VENITE-S	VIROSE-S
UNTILE-S	UPPILE-S	VACUUM-S	VENNEL-S	VIRTUE-S
UNTOMB-S	UPPING-S	VAGINA-S	VENTER-S	VISAGE-S
UNTRIM-S	UPPROP-S	VAGROM-S	VENTIL-S	VISARD-S
UNTUCK-S	UPRATE-S	VAHANA-S	VENTRE-S	VISCIN-S
UNTUNE-S	UPREAR-S	VAHINE-S	VENULE-S	VISCUM-S
UNTURF-S	UPREST-S	VAKEEL-S	VERBAL-S	VISIER-S
UNTURN-S	UPRISE-S	VALETA-S	VERBID-S	VISILE-S
UNVAIL-S	UPRIST-S	VALETE-S	VERDET-S	VISION-S
UNVEIL-S	UPROAR-S	VALINE-S	VERDIN-S	VISITE-S
UNWARE-S	UPROLL-S	VALISE-S	VERDIT-S	VISUAL-S
UNWEAL-S	UPROOT-S	VALKYR-S	VERGER-S	VITRIC-S
UNWILL-S	UPSEND-S	VALLEY-S	VERISM-S	VITTLE-S
UNWIND-S	UPSHOT-S	VALLUM-S	VERIST-S	VIVACE-S
UNWIRE-S	UPSIDE-S	VALOUR-S	VERITE-S	VIZARD-S
UNWIVE-S	UPSIZE-S	VALUER-S	VERLAN-S	VIZIER-S
UNWORK-S	UPSOAR-S	VALUTA-S	VERMIL-S	VIZSLA-S
UNWRAP-S	UPSTAY-S	VAMOSE-S	VERMIN-S	VIZZIE-S
UNYOKE-S	UPSTEP-S	VAMPER-S	VERREL-S	VOCULE-S
UPBEAR-S	UPSTIR-S	VANDAL-S	VERSAL-S	VODOUN-S
UPBEAT-S	UPSWAY-S	VANNER-S	VERSER-S	VOGUER-S
UPBIND-S	UPTAKE-S	VAPOUR-S	VERSET-S	VOICER-S
UPBLOW-S	UPTALK-S	VARECH-S	VERSIN-S	VOIDEE-S
UPBOIL-S	UPTEAR-S	VARIER-S	VERSTE-S	VOIDER-S
UPBRAY-S	UPTICK-S	VARLET-S	VERTUE-S	VOLLEY-S
UPCAST-S	UPTILT-S	VAROOM-S	VERVEL-S	VOLOST-S
UPCOIL-S	UPTIME-S	VARROA-S	VERVEN-S	VOLUME-S

VOLUTE-S	WANGUN-S	WEEPIE-S	WILLER-S	WOOLER-S
VOMICA-S	WANING-S	WEEVER-S	WILLET-S	WOOLIE-S
VOMITO-S	WANION-S	WEEVIL-S	WILLEY-S	WOOPIE-S
VOODOO-S	WANKER-S	WEEWEE-S	WILLIE-S	WOOSEL-S
VOTEEN-S	WANTER-S	WEIGHT-S	WILLOW-S	WORKER-S
VOTING-S	WANTON-S	WEINER-S	WILTJA-S	WORKUP-S
VOTIVE-S	WAPITI-S	WEIRDO-S	WIMBLE-S	WORMER-S
VOUDON-S	WAPPER-S	WELDER-S	WIMPLE-S	WORMIL-S
VOUDOU-S	WARAGI-S	WELDOR-S	WINCER-S	WORRAL-S
VOULGE-S	WARBLE-S	WELKIN-S	WINCEY-S	WORREL-S
VOYAGE-S	WARDEN-S	WELLIE-S	WINDAC-S	WORRIT-S
VOYEUR-S	WARDER-S	WELTER-S	WINDER-S	WORSEN-S
VULCAN-S	WARDOG-S	WESAND-S	WINDLE-S	WORSET-S
VULGAR-S	WARMER-S	WESKIT-S	WINDOW-S	WORTLE-S
WABAIN-S	WARMTH-S	WESTER-S	WINDUP-S	WOUBIT-S
WABBLE-S	WARMUP-S	WESTIE-S	WINGER-S	WOWSER-S
WABOOM-S	WARNER-S	WETHER-S	WINKER-S	WRAITH-S
WACKER-S	WARPER-S	WETTER-S	WINKLE-S	WRASSE-S
WADDER-S	WARRAN-S	WETTIE-S	WINNER-S	WRAXLE-S
WADDIE-S	WARRAY-S	WEZAND-S	WINNLE-S	WREATH-S
WADDLE-S	WARREN-S	WHACKO-S	WINNOW-S	WRETHE-S
WADING-S	WARREY-S	WHALER-S	WINSEY-S	WRIGHT-S
WADMAL-S	WARSAW-S	WHAMMO-S	WINTER-S	WRITER-S
WADMEL-S	WARSLE-S	WHANAU-S	WINTLE-S	WRITHE-S
WADMOL-S	WASABI-S	WHARVE-S	WIPING-S	WROATH-S
WADSET-S	WASHER-S	WHEECH-S	WIPPEN-S	WUNNER-S
WAFFIE-S	WASHIN-S	WHEEZE-S	WIRING-S	WURLEY-S
WAFFLE-S	WASHUP-S	WHENCE-S	WIRRAH-S	WURLIE-S
WAFTER-S	WASPIE-S	WHENUA-S	WISARD-S	WURZEL-S
WAGGER-S	WASTEL-S	WHENWE-S	WISDOM-S	WUTHER-S
WAGGLE-S	WASTER-S	WHERVE-S	WISENT-S	WUZZLE-S
WAGGON-S	WATAPE-S	WHEUGH-S	WISHER-S	WYVERN-S
WAHINE-S	WATTLE-S	WHIDAH-S	WISKET-S	XEROMA-S
WAIATA-S	WAUCHT-S	WHINER-S	WITGAT-S	XYLENE-S
WAILER-S	WAUGHT-S	WHINGE-S	WITHER-S	XYLOMA-S
WAIRUA-S	WAUKER-S	WHISHT-S	WITHIN-S	XYLOSE-S
WAITER-S	WAVING-S	WHITEN-S	WITNEY-S	XYSTER-S
WAIVER-S	WAXEYE-S	WHITEY-S	WITTER-S	YABBER-S
WAKAME-S	WAXING-S	WHYDAH-S	WITTOL-S	YABBIE-S
WAKANE-S	WAYLAY-S	WIBBLE-S	WIVERN-S	YACKER-S
WAKIKI-S	WEAKEN-S	WICCAN-S	WIZARD-S	YAFFLE-S
WAKING-S	WEAKON-S	WICKED-S	WIZIER-S	YAGGER-S
WALISE-S	WEALTH-S	WICKEN-S	WIZZEN-S	YAKKER-S
WALKER-S	WEANEL-S	WICKER-S	WOBBLE-S	YAMMER-S
WALKUP-S	WEANER-S	WICKET-S	WOGGLE-S	YANKER-S
WALLAH-S	WEAPON-S	WIDDER-S	WOLFER-S	YANKIE-S
WALLER-S	WEARER-S	WIDDIE-S	WOLVER-S	YANQUI-S
WALLET-S	WEASEL-S	WIDDLE-S	WOMBAT-S	YANTRA-S
WALLIE-S	WEASON-S	WIDGET-S	WOMERA-S	YAOURT-S
WALLOP-S	WEAVER-S	WIDGIE-S	WOMMIT-S	YAPOCK-S
WALLOW-S	WEAZEN-S	WIENER-S	WONDER-S	YAPPER-S
WALNUT-S	WEBBIE-S	WIENIE-S	WONING-S	YAPPIE-S
WAMBLE-S	WEBCAM-S	WIGEON-S	WONNER-S	YAQONA-S
WAMMUL-S	WEBLOG-S	WIGGER-S	WONTON-S	YARDER-S
WAMPEE-S	WEDDER-S	WIGGLE-S	WOOBUT-S	YARNER-S
WAMPUM-S	WEDELN-S	WIGLET-S	WOODEN-S	YARPHA-S
WANDER-S	WEDGIE-S	WIGWAG-S	WOODIE-S	YARRAN-S
WANDOO-S	WEEDER-S	WIGWAM-S	WOOFER-S	YARROW-S
WANGAN-S	WEENIE-S	WIKIUP-S	WOOING-S	YASMAK-S
WANGLE-S	WEEPER-S	WILDER-S	WOOLEN-S	YATTER-S

YAUPER-S	YOGURT-S	ZAFFAR-S	ZENANA-S	ZODIAC-S
YAUPON-S	YOJANA-S	ZAFFER-S	ZENDIK-S	ZOMBIE-S
YAUTIA-S	YOKING-S	ZAFFIR-S	ZENITH-S	ZONING-S
YAWNER-S	YONDER-S	ZAFFRE-S	ZEPHYR-S	ZONULA-S
YAWPER-S	YONKER-S	ZAIKAI-S	ZEREBA-S	ZONULE-S
YEELIN-S	YONNIE-S	ZAMANG-S	ZERIBA-S	ZONURE-S
YELLER-S	YOPPER-S	ZAMBUK-S	ZESTER-S	ZOOZOO-S
YELLOW-S	YORKER-S	ZANANA-S	ZEUGMA-S	ZORINO-S
YELPER-S	YORKIE-S	ZANDER-S	ZIBETH-S	ZOSTER-S
YEMMER-S	YOUPON-S	ZAPPER-S	ZIGZAG-S	ZOUAVE-S
YETTIE-S	YOWLER-S	ZARAPE-S	ZILLAH-S	ZOYSIA-S
YICKER-S	YOWLEY-S	ZAREBA-S	ZIMMER-S	ZYDECO-S
YIDAKI-S	YSHEND-S	ZARIBA-S	ZINGEL-S	ZYGOMA-S
YIKKER-S	YTTRIA-S	ZARNEC-S	ZINGER-S	ZYGOSE-S
YIPPER-S	YUCKER-S	ZEALOT-S	ZINNIA-S	ZYGOTE-S
YIPPIE-S	YUKATA-S	ZEATIN-S	ZIPPER-S	ZYMASE-S
YNAMBU-S	YUMPIE-S	ZEBECK-S	ZIRCON-S	ZYMITE-S
YODLER-S	YUPPIE-S	ZEBRAS-S	ZITHER-S	ZYMOME-S
YOGINI-S	ZABETA-S	ZECHIN-S	ZIZZLE-S	ZYTHUM-S
YOGISM-S	ZADDIK-S	ZELANT-S	ZOCALO-S	

Seven letters to eight

ABACTOR-S	ABUTTER-S	ACQUITE-S	ADMIRER-S	AGENISE-S
ABALONE-S	ACADEME-S	ACRASIA-S	ADONISE-S	AGENIZE-S
ABANDON-S	ACALEPH-S	ACRASIN-S	ADONIZE-S	AGEUSIA-S
ABATURE-S	ACANTHA-S	ACREAGE-S	ADOPTEE-S	AGGADAH-S
ABDOMEN-S	ACAPNIA-S	ACRIDIN-S	ADOPTER-S	AGGRACE-S
ABETTAL-S	ACARINE-S	ACROBAT-S	ADORNER-S	AGGRADE-S
ABETTER-S	ACATOUR-S	ACROGEN-S	ADRENAL-S	AGGRATE-S
ABETTOR-S	ACCEDER-S	ACRONYM-S	ADULATE-S	AGINNER-S
ABFARAD-S	ACCIDIA-S	ACROTER-S	ADVANCE-S	AGISTER-S
ABHENRY-S	ACCIDIE-S	ACRYLIC-S	ADVISEE-S	AGISTOR-S
ABIDING-S	ACCINGE-S	ACRYLYL-S	ADVISER-S	AGITATE-S
ABIGAIL-S	ACCLAIM-S	ACTINIA-S	ADVISOR-S	AGITPOP-S
ABJOINT-S	ACCOAST-S	ACTINON-S	AERATOR-S	AGLYCON-S
ABJURER-S	ACCOMPT-S	ACTUATE-S	AEROBAT-S	AGNOMEN-S
ABLATOR-S	ACCOUNT-S	ACUSHLA-S	AEROBIC-S	AGNOSIA-S
ABLEISM-S	ACCOURT-S	ACYLATE-S	AEROGEL-S	AGONISE-S
ABLEIST-S	ACCRETE-S	ACYLOIN-S	AEROSAT-S	AGONIST-S
ABLUENT-S	ACCRUAL-S	ADAMANT-S	AEROSOL-S	AGONIZE-S
ABORTEE-S	ACCURSE-S	ADAPTER-S	AFFAIRE-S	AGRAFFE-S
ABORTER-S	ACCUSAL-S	ADAPTOR-S	AFFEARE-S	AIDANCE-S
ABOULIA-S	ACCUSER-S	ADDUCER-S	AFFIANT-S	AILANTO-S
ABRADER-S	ACEQUIA-S	ADENINE-S	AFFICHE-S	AILERON-S
ABREACT-S	ACEROLA-S	ADENOID-S	AFFIXER-S	AILETTE-S
ABRIDGE-S	ACETATE-S	ADENOMA-S	AFFLICT-S	AILMENT-S
ABROOKE-S	ACETONE-S	ADERMIN-S	AFFOORD-S	AINSELL-S
ABROSIA-S	ACHARYA-S	ADHARMA-S	AFFORCE-S	AIRBASE-S
ABSCIND-S	ACHIEVE-S	ADHERER-S	AFFRONT-S	AIRBOAT-S
ABSCISE-S	ACHIOTE-S	ADHIBIT-S	AFGHANI-S	AIRCREW-S
ABSCOND-S	ACHOLIA-S	ADIPOSE-S	AGAMETE-S	AIRDATE-S
ABSENCE-S	ACICULA-S	ADIPSIA-S	AGAMOID-S	AIRDROP-S
ABSINTH-S	ACOLYTE-S	ADJOINT-S	AGAMONT-S	AIRFARE-S
ABSOLVE-S	ACOLYTH-S	ADJOURN-S	AGAROSE-S	AIRFLOW-S
ABSTAIN-S	ACONITE-S	ADJUDGE-S	AGATISE-S	AIRFOIL-S
ABTHANE-S	ACOUCHI-S	ADJUNCT-S	AGATIZE-S	AIRGLOW-S
ABUSAGE-S	ACQUEST-S	ADJURER-S	AGELAST-S	AIRHEAD-S
ABUSION-S	ACQUIRE-S	ADJUROR-S	AGEMATE-S	AIRHOLE-S
ABUTTAL-S	ACQUIST-S	ADMIRAL-S	AGENDUM-S	AIRLIFT-S

AIRLINE-S	ALLEDGE-S	AMMIRAL-S	ANKLONG-S	APPROOF-S
AIRLOCK-S	ALLEGER-S	AMMONAL-S	ANKLUNG-S	APPROVE-S
AIRMAIL-S	ALLEGGE-S	AMMONIA-S	ANNATTA-S	APPULSE-S
AIRPARK-S	ALLEGRO-S	AMNESIA-S	ANNATTO-S	APRAXIA-S
AIRPLAY-S	ALLHEAL-S	AMNESIC-S	ANNELID-S	APRICOT-S
AIRPORT-S	ALLICIN-S	AMNIOTE-S	ANNICUT-S	APYRASE-S
AIRPOST-S	ALLOBAR-S	AMORISM-S	ANNOYER-S	AQUAFER-S
AIRSHED-S	ALLONGE-S	AMORIST-S	ANNULAR-S	AQUATIC-S
AIRSHIP-S	ALLONYM-S	AMOROSA-S	ANNULET-S	AQUAVIT-S
AIRSHOT-S	ALLOVER-S	AMOROSO-S	ANOBIID-S	AQUIFER-S
AIRSHOW-S	ALLOXAN-S	AMOSITE-S	ANODISE-S	AQUILON-S
AIRSIDE-S	ALLSEED-S	AMOTION-S	ANODIZE-S	ARABESK-S
AIRSTOP-S	ALLURER-S	AMPHORA-S	ANODYNE-S	ARABICA-S
AIRTIME-S	ALMANAC-S	AMPOULE-S	ANOLYTE-S	ARABISE-S
AIRWARD-S	ALMEMAR-S	AMPUTEE-S	ANONYMA-S	ARABIZE-S
AIRWAVE-S	ALMIRAH-S	AMREETA-S	ANOPSIA-S	ARANEID-S
AISLING-S	ALMONER-S	AMTRACK-S	ANOSMIA-S	ARAROBA-S
AJUTAGE-S	ALNAGER-S	AMYGDAL-S	ANTACID-S	ARBITER-S
AKRASIA-S	ALODIUM-S	AMYLASE-S	ANTBEAR-S	ARBLAST-S
AKVAVIT-S	ALOETIC-S	AMYLENE-S	ANTBIRD-S	ARBORET-S
ALAMEDA-S	ALPACCA-S	AMYLOID-S	ANTENNA-S	ARCADIA-S
ALAMODE-S	ALPHORN-S	AMYLOSE-S	ANTHILL-S	ARCANUM-S
ALANINE-S	ALTERER-S	ANAEMIA-S	ANTIENT-S	ARCHFOE-S
ALANNAH-S	ALTERNE-S	ANAGOGE-S	ANTIGEN-S	ARCHINE-S
ALASTOR-S	ALTESSE-S	ANAGRAM-S	ANTILOG-S	ARCHING-S
ALATION-S	ALTEZZA-S	ANALGIA-S	ANTIQUE-S	ARCHIVE-S
ALBIZIA-S	ALTHAEA-S	ANALYSE-S	ANTLION-S	ARCHLET-S
ALBUMEN-S	ALTHORN-S	ANALYST-S	ANTONYM-S	ARCHWAY-S
ALBUMIN-S	ALTOIST-S	ANALYTE-S	APADANA-S	ARCKING-S
ALCAIDE-S	ALUMINA-S	ANALYZE-S	APAGOGE-S	ARCSINE-S
ALCALDE-S	ALUMINE-S	ANAPEST-S	APANAGE-S	ARCTIID-S
ALCAYDE-S	ALUMIUM-S	ANAPHOR-S	APAREJO-S	ARDRIGH-S
ALCAZAR-S	ALUNITE-S	ANATASE-S	APATITE-S	AREAWAY-S
ALCHERA-S	ALVEOLE-S	ANATMAN-S	APEHOOD-S	ARENITE-S
ALCOHOL-S	ALYSSUM-S	ANCHUSA-S	APEPSIA-S	ARGONON-S
ALCOPOP-S	AMALGAM-S	ANCIENT-S	APHAGIA-S	ARGYRIA-S
ALCORZA-S	AMANDLA-S	ANCILLA-S	APHAKIA-S	ARIETTA-S
ALECOST-S	AMANITA-S	ANDANTE-S	APHASIA-S	ARIETTE-S
ALEMBIC-S	AMARANT-S	ANDIRON-S	APHASIC-S	ARMBAND-S
ALENCON-S	AMARONE-S	ANDROID-S	APHONIA-S	ARMHOLE-S
ALEPINE-S	AMASSER-S	ANDVILE-S	APHONIC-S	ARMIGER-S
ALERION-S	AMATEUR-S	ANELACE-S	APLANAT-S	ARMILLA-S
ALEURON-S	AMATION-S	ANEMONE-S	APLASIA-S	ARMLOAD-S
ALEXINE-S	AMBIENT-S	ANERGIA-S	APOCARP-S	ARMLOCK-S
ALFALFA-S	AMBLING-S	ANEROID-S	APOCOPE-S	ARMOIRE-S
ALFAQUI-S	AMBOINA-S	ANETHOL-S	APOLUNE-S	ARMORER-S
ALFORJA-S	AMBOYNA-S	ANEURIN-S	APOMICT-S	ARMREST-S
ALGEBRA-S	AMBROID-S	ANGAKOK-S	APOSTIL-S	ARNATTO-S
ALGESIA-S	AMBSACE-S	ANGARIA-S	APOSTLE-S	ARNOTTO-S
ALICANT-S	AMENAGE-S	ANGEKOK-S	APOTHEM-S	AROUSAL-S
ALIDADE-S	AMENDER-S	ANGIOMA-S	APPARAT-S	AROUSER-S
ALIENEE-S	AMENTIA-S	ANGLING-S	APPAREL-S	ARRAIGN-S
ALIENER-S	AMERCER-S	ANGLIST-S	APPEASE-S	ARRANGE-S
ALIENOR-S	AMESACE-S	ANHINGA-S	APPERIL-S	ARRAYAL-S
ALIGNER-S	AMIDASE-S	ANILINE-S	APPLAUD-S	ARRAYER-S
ALIMENT-S	AMIDINE-S	ANIMATE-S	APPLIER-S	ARREEDE-S
ALIQUOT-S	AMIDONE-S	ANIMISM-S	APPOINT-S	ARRIAGE-S
ALIZARI-S	AMILDAR-S	ANIMIST-S	APPOSER-S	ARRIERO-S
ALKANET-S	AMIRATE-S	ANISEED-S	APPRISE-S	ARRIVAL-S
ALLAYER-S	AMMETER-S	ANISOLE-S	APPRIZE-S	ARRIVER-S

ARSENAL-S	ATHEISM-S	AWAKING-S	BAKLAWA-S	BARONNE-S
ARSENIC-S	ATHEIST-S	AWARDEE-S	BALADIN-S	BAROQUE-S
ARSHEEN-S	ATHEIZE-S	AWARDER-S	BALANCE-S	BARRACE-S
ARSHINE-S	ATHLETA-S	AWAYDAY-S	BALDRIC-S	BARRACK-S
ARTICLE-S	ATHLETE-S	AWLBIRD-S	BALISTA-S	BARRAGE-S
ARTISAN-S	ATHODYD-S	AWLWORT-S	BALKING-S	BARRICO-S
ARTISTE-S	ATISHOO-S	AXEBIRD-S	BALLADE-S	BARRIER-S
ARTWORK-S	ATOMISE-S	AXILLAR-S	BALLANT-S	BARRING-S
ARUGOLA-S	ATOMISM-S	AXINITE-S	BALLAST-S	BARROOM-S
ARUGULA-S	ATOMIST-S	AXOLOTL-S	BALLING-S	BARTEND-S
ASCARID-S	ATOMIZE-S	AXONEME-S	BALLIUM-S	BARTSIA-S
ASCETIC-S	ATRESIA-S	AZIMUTH-S	BALLOON-S	BARWARE-S
ASCRIBE-S	ATROPIA-S	AZOTISE-S	BALLUTE-S	BARWOOD-S
ASEPTIC-S	ATROPIN-S	AZOTIZE-S	BALONEY-S	BARYTON-S
ASHCAKE-S	ATTACHE-S	AZULEJO-S	BAMBINO-S	BASCULE-S
ASHFALL-S	ATTAINT-S	AZURINE-S	BANDAGE-S	BASENJI-S
ASHRAMA-S	ATTEMPT-S	AZURITE-S	BANDANA-S	BASHING-S
ASHTRAY-S	ATTRACT-S	AZYMITE-S	BANDARI-S	BASHLIK-S
ASINICO-S	ATTRIST-S	BAALISM-S	BANDEAU-S	BASHLYK-S
ASKANCE-S	ATTRITE-S	BAASKAP-S	BANDING-S	BASINET-S
ASOCIAL-S	ATTUITE-S	BABASSU-S	BANDITO-S	BASMATI-S
ASPERGE-S	AUBERGE-S	BABBITT-S	BANDOOK-S	BASOCHE-S
ASPERSE-S	AUCTION-S	BABBLER-S	BANDORA-S	BASSETT-S
ASPHALT-S	AUDIBLE-S	BABESIA-S	BANDORE-S	BASSIST-S
ASPIRER-S	AUDIENT-S	BABICHE-S	BANDROL-S	BASSOON-S
ASPIRIN-S	AUDITEE-S	BABUCHE-S	BANDSAW-S	BASTARD-S
ASSAGAI-S	AUDITOR-S	BABUDOM-S	BANDURA-S	BASTIDE-S
ASSAULT-S	AUFGABE-S	BABUISM-S	BANGING-S	BASTILE-S
ASSAYER-S	AUGMENT-S	BABYSIT-S	BANGKOK-S	BASTING-S
ASSEGAI-S	AUGURER-S	BACALAO-S	BANKING-S	BASTION-S
ASSEVER-S	AUGUSTE-S	BACCARA-S	BANKSIA-S	BATAVIA-S
ASSHOLE-S	AULNAGE-S	BACHCHA-S	BANNOCK-S	BATCHER-S
ASSIEGE-S	AURELIA-S	BACKFIT-S	BANOFFI-S	BATFOWL-S
ASSIZER-S	AUREOLA-S	BACKHOE-S	BANQUET-S	BATGIRL-S
ASSUAGE-S	AUREOLE-S	BACKING-S	BANSELA-S	BATHMAT-S
ASSUMER-S	AURICLE-S	BACKLOG-S	BANSHEE-S	BATHTUB-S
ASSURED-S	AUSFORM-S	BACKLOT-S	BANSHIE-S	BATISTE-S
ASSURER-S	AUSPICE-S	BACKOUT-S	BANTENG-S	BATTERO-S
ASSUROR-S	AUSTRAL-S	BACKPAY-S	BANTING-S	BATTILL-S
ASSWAGE-S	AUTARCH-S	BACKSAW-S	BAPTISE-S	BATTING-S
ASTASIA-S	AUTOCAR-S	BACKSET-S	BAPTISM-S	BATTLER-S
ASTATKI-S	AUTOCUE-S	BACKSEY-S	BAPTIST-S	BATTUTA-S
ASTEISM-S	AUTOMAT-S	BACLAVA-S	BAPTIZE-S	BAUCHLE-S
ASTERIA-S	AUTONYM-S	BACONER-S	BARACAN-S	BAUDRIC-S
ASTERID-S	AUTOPEN-S	BACULUM-S	BARBELL-S	BAULKER-S
ASTHORE-S	AUTOPUT-S	BADLAND-S	BARBOLA-S	BAUXITE-S
ASTILBE-S	AUTOVAC-S	BAFFLER-S	BARBULE-S	BAWCOCK-S
ASTOUND-S	AUXETIC-S	BAGARRE-S	BARCHAN-S	BAWDKIN-S
ASTRICT-S	AVARICE-S	BAGASSE-S	BARDISM-S	BAWDRIC-S
ASTROID-S	AVENGER-S	BAGGAGE-S	BARGAIN-S	BAWLING-S
ATABRIN-S	AVENTRE-S	BAGGING-S	BARGEST-S	BAWNEEN-S
ATAGHAN-S	AVERAGE-S	BAGPIPE-S	BARGOON-S	BAYONET-S
ATALAYA-S	AVERTER-S	BAGWORM-S	BARILLA-S	BAYWOOD-S
ATAVISM-S	AVIATOR-S	BAHADUR-S	BARISTA-S	BAZOOKA-S
ATAVIST-S	AVIETTE-S	BAILIFF-S	BARKEEP-S	BAZOUKI-S
ATEBRIN-S	AVIONIC-S	BAILLIE-S	BARKHAN-S	BEADING-S
ATELIER-S	AVOCADO-S	BAILOUT-S	BARMAID-S	BEAGLER-S
ATEMOYA-S	AVODIRE-S	BAINITE-S	BARMKIN-S	BEAMING-S
ATHANOR-S	AVOIDER-S	BAITING-S	BAROCCO-S	BEAMLET-S
ATHEISE-S	AWAITER-S	BAKLAVA-S	BARONET-S	BEANBAG-S

BEARCAT-S	BEGROAN-S	BESIEGE-S	BILEVEL-S	BLAUBOK-S
BEARDIE-S	BEGUILE-S	BESLAVE-S	BILIMBI-S	BLAWORT-S
BEARHUG-S	BEGUINE-S	BESLIME-S	BILLBUG-S	BLEATER-S
BEARING-S	BEHAVER-S	BESMEAR-S	BILLING-S	BLEEDER-S
BEASTIE-S	BEHIGHT-S	BESMILE-S	BILLION-S	BLEEPER-S
BEATING-S	BEHOOVE-S	BESMOKE-S	BILLYOH-S	BLELLUM-S
BEATNIK-S	BEIGNET-S	BESPEAK-S	BILSTED-S	BLENDER-S
BEAUFET-S	BEJEWEL-S	BESPEED-S	BILTONG-S	BLESBOK-S
BEAUFIN-S	BEKNAVE-S	BESPICE-S	BIMETAL-S	BLESSER-S
BEBEERU-S	BELABOR-S	BESPORT-S	BIMORPH-S	BLETHER-S
BEBLOOD-S	BELAYER-S	BESPOUT-S	BINDING-S	BLEWART-S
BECASSE-S	BELCHER-S	BESTAIN-S	BINOCLE-S	BLINDER-S
BECHALK-S	BELDAME-S	BESTEAD-S	BIOCHIP-S	BLINKER-S
BECHARM-S	BELGARD-S	BESTIAL-S	BIOCIDE-S	BLINTZE-S
BECLASP-S	BELIEVE-S	BESTICK-S	BIOFACT-S	BLISTER-S
BECLOAK-S	BELLBOY-S	BESTILL-S	BIOFILM-S	BLITHER-S
BECLOUD-S	BELLEEK-S	BESTORM-S	BIOFUEL-S	BLITZER-S
BECLOWN-S	BELLHOP-S	BESTREW-S	BIOHERM-S	BLOATER-S
BECRAWL-S	BELLING-S	BESTROW-S	BIOPHOR-S	BLOCKER-S
BECRIME-S	BELLOCK-S	BESWARM-S	BIOTECH-S	BLOCKIE-S
BECROWD-S	BELOVED-S	BETAINE-S	BIOTITE-S	BLOGGER-S
BECRUST-S	BELTING-S	BETEEME-S	BIOTOPE-S	BLOOMER-S
BECURSE-S	BELTWAY-S	BETHANK-S	BIOTRON-S	BLOOPER-S
BEDAWIN-S	BEMADAM-S	BETHINK-S	BIOTYPE-S	BLOOSME-S
BEDDING-S	BEMEDAL-S	BETHORN-S	BIPLANE-S	BLOSSOM-S
BEDERAL-S	BEMOUTH-S	BETHUMB-S	BIPRISM-S	BLOTTER-S
BEDEVIL-S	BENCHER-S	BETHUMP-S	BIRDDOG-S	BLOUBOK-S
BEDGOWN-S	BENDING-S	BETITLE-S	BIRDING-S	BLOUSON-S
BEDIGHT-S	BENDLET-S	BETOKEN-S	BIRETTA-S	BLOWGUN-S
BEDIZEN-S	BENEFIT-S	BETREAD-S	BIRIANI-S	BLOWJOB-S
BEDLAMP-S	BENIGHT-S	BETROTH-S	BIRLING-S	BLOWOFF-S
BEDMATE-S	BENISON-S	BETTING-S	BIRLINN-S	BLOWOUT-S
BEDOUIN-S	BENOMYL-S	BETTONG-S	BIRYANI-S	BLUBBER-S
BEDPOST-S	BENTHON-S	BETWEEN-S	BISCUIT-S	BLUCHER-S
BEDRAIL-S	BENZENE-S	BEVELER-S	BISMUTH-S	BLUDGER-S
BEDRAPE-S	BENZINE-S	BEVOMIT-S	BISNAGA-S	BLUECAP-S
BEDROCK-S	BENZOIN-S	BEWHORE-S	BISTORT-S	BLUEFIN-S
BEDROLL-S	BENZOLE-S	BEZIQUE-S	BITTERN-S	BLUEGUM-S
BEDROOM-S	BENZOYL-S	BEZZANT-S	BITTING-S	BLUEING-S
BEDSIDE-S	BEPAINT-S	BHANGRA-S	BITTOCK-S	BLUEJAY-S
BEDSORE-S	BEPEARL-S	BHISHTI-S	BITTOUR-S	BLUETIT-S
BEDTICK-S	BEPROSE-S	BHISTEE-S	BITUMEN-S	BLUETTE-S
BEDTIME-S	BEQUEST-S	BHISTIE-S	BIVALVE-S	BLUFFER-S
BEDUNCE-S	BERBERE-S	BIASING-S	BIVINYL-S	BLUNDER-S
BEDWARD-S	BEREAVE-S	BIBCOCK-S	BIVOUAC-S	BLUNGER-S
BEDWARF-S	BERETTA-S	BIBELOT-S	BIZARRE-S	BLUNKER-S
BEEFALO-S	BERGAMA-S	BIBLIST-S	BIZARRO-S	BLURTER-S
BEEHIVE-S	BERGERE-S	BICOLOR-S	BIZNAGA-S	BLUSHER-S
BEELINE-S	BERGYLT-S	BICORNE-S	BLABBER-S	BLUSHET-S
BEERAGE-S	BERHYME-S	BICYCLE-S	BLACKEN-S	BLUSTER-S
BEETLER-S	BERLINE-S	BIDARKA-S	BLADDER-S	BOARDER-S
BEEYARD-S	BERSEEM-S	BIDDING-S	BLADING-S	BOASTER-S
BEFFANA-S	BERSERK-S	BIFOCAL-S	BLAGGER-S	BOATFUL-S
BEFLECK-S	BESAINT-S	BIGENER-S	BLAGUER-S	BOATING-S
BEGGING-S	BESCOUR-S	BIGFOOT-S	BLANKET-S	BOBBITT-S
BEGHARD-S	BESEEKE-S	BIGGING-S	BLARNEY-S	BOBECHE-S
BEGINNE-S	BESHAME-S	BIGHEAD-S	BLASTER-S	BOBOTIE-S
BEGLOOM-S	BESHINE-S	BIGHORN-S	BLASTIE-S	BOBSLED-S
BEGONIA-S	BESHOUT-S	BIKEWAY-S	BLATHER-S	BOBSTAY-S
BEGRIME-S	BESHREW-S	BILAYER-S	BLATTER-S	BOBTAIL-S

BODHRAN-S	BOSCAGE-S	BRAIDER-S	BROCKET-S	BUGWORT-S
BODIKIN-S	BOSHBOK-S	BRAILLE-S	BROCOLI-S	BUILDER-S
BOERBUL-S	BOSKAGE-S	BRAMBLE-S	BRODDLE-S	BUILDUP-S
BOFFOLA-S	BOSQUET-S	BRANDER-S	BRODKIN-S	BUKKAKE-S
BOGBEAN-S	BOSSBOY-S	BRANNER-S	BROIDER-S	BUKSHEE-S
BOGGARD-S	BOSSDOM-S	BRANSLE-S	BROILER-S	BULBLET-S
BOGGART-S	BOSSISM-S	BRANTLE-S	BROKAGE-S	BULGHUR-S
BOGGLER-S	BOTANIC-S	BRASERO-S	BROKING-S	BULGINE-S
BOGLAND-S	BOTARGO-S	BRASIER-S	BROMATE-S	BULIMIA-S
BOGWOOD-S	BOTCHER-S	BRASSET-S	BROMIDE-S	BULIMIC-S
BOGYISM-S	BOTHOLE-S	BRASSIE-S	BROMINE-S	BULKAGE-S
BOHEMIA-S	BOTTEGA-S	BRATTLE-S	BROMISE-S	BULLACE-S
BOHRIUM-S	BOTTINE-S	BRAVADO-S	BROMISM-S	BULLBAR-S
BOILING-S	BOTTLER-S	BRAVERA-S	BROMIZE-S	BULLBAT-S
BOILOFF-S	BOTULIN-S	BRAVURA-S	BROMMER-S	BULLDOG-S
BOLIVAR-S	BOUCHEE-S	BRAWLER-S	BRONCHO-S	BULLING-S
BOLIVIA-S	BOUCLEE-S	BRAZIER-S	BRONZER-S	BULLION-S
BOLLARD-S	BOUDOIR-S	BREADTH-S	BROODER-S	BULLOCK-S
BOLLOCK-S	BOUILLI-S	BREAKER-S	BROOKIE-S	BULLPEN-S
BOLOGNA-S	BOULDER-S	BREAKUP-S	BROTHEL-S	BULWARK-S
BOLONEY-S	BOULTER-S	BREATHE-S	BROTHER-S	BUMBAZE-S
BOLSHIE-S	BOUNCER-S	BRECCIA-S	BROWNIE-S	BUMBLER-S
BOLSTER-S	BOUNDER-S	BRECHAM-S	BROWSER-S	BUMBOAT-S
BOLTING-S	BOUQUET-S	BRECHAN-S	BRUCHID-S	BUMELIA-S
BOMBARD-S	BOURBON-S	BREEDER-S	BRUCINE-S	BUMMALO-S
BOMBAST-S	BOURDER-S	BREENGE-S	BRUCITE-S	BUMMOCK-S
BOMBING-S	BOURDON-S	BREINGE-S	BRUHAHA-S	BUMPING-S
BOMBLET-S	BOURKHA-S	BREVIER-S	BRUISER-S	BUMPKIN-S
BOMBORA-S	BOURLAW-S	BREWAGE-S	BRUITER-S	BUNDIST-S
BONAMIA-S	BOURREE-S	BREWING-S	BRULYIE-S	BUNDLER-S
BONANZA-S	BOURSIN-S	BREWPUB-S	BRULZIE-S	BUNDOOK-S
BONDAGE-S	BOUTADE-S	BREWSKI-S	BRUMMER-S	BUNGLER-S
BONDING-S	BOUVIER-S	BRICKIE-S	BRUSHER-S	BUNRAKU-S
BONESET-S	BOWHEAD-S	BRICKLE-S	BRUSHUP-S	BUNTING-S
BONFIRE-S	BOWKNOT-S	BRICOLE-S	BRUTING-S	BUOYAGE-S
BONIATO-S	BOWLDER-S	BRIDLER-S	BRUTISM-S	BURBLER-S
BONKING-S	BOWLFUL-S	BRIDOON-S	BRUXISM-S	BURDOCK-S
BONNOCK-S	BOWLINE-S	BRIEFER-S	BUBBLER-S	BURETTE-S
BONSELA-S	BOWLING-S	BRIGADE-S	BUBINGA-S	BURGAGE-S
BOOBIRD-S	BOWSHOT-S	BRIGAND-S	BUBUKLE-S	BURGEON-S
BOOBOOK-S	BOWYANG-S	BRIMING-S	BUCCINA-S	BURGHER-S
BOODLER-S	BOXBALL-S	BRIMMER-S	BUCKEEN-S	BURGHUL-S
BOOKEND-S	BOXHAUL-S	BRINDLE-S	BUCKEYE-S	BURGLAR-S
BOOKFUL-S	BOXROOM-S	BRINGER-S	BUCKING-S	BURGOUT-S
BOOKING-S	BOXWOOD-S	BRINJAL-S	BUCKLER-S	BURKITE-S
BOOKLET-S	BOYCHIK-S	BRIOCHE-S	BUCKRAM-S	BURLESK-S
BOOMING-S	BOYCOTT-S	BRIQUET-S	BUCKSAW-S	BURNING-S
BOOMKIN-S	BOYHOOD-S	BRISKEN-S	BUCOLIC-S	BURNOUT-S
BOOMLET-S	BRABBLE-S	BRISKET-S	BUDDING-S	BURRELL-S
BOOSTER-S	BRACERO-S	BRISTLE-S	BUDGERO-S	BURRHEL-S
BOOTLEG-S	BRACHAH-S	BRISTOL-S	BUDWORM-S	BURRITO-S
BORAZON-S	BRACHET-S	BRISURE-S	BUFFALO-S	BURSEED-S
BORDURE-S	BRACING-S	BRITSKA-S	BUFFING-S	BURSTER-S
BOREDOM-S	BRACKEN-S	BRITTLE-S	BUFFOON-S	BURTHEN-S
BORNEOL-S	BRACKET-S	BRITZKA-S	BUGABOO-S	BURWEED-S
BORNITE-S	BRADAWL-S	BROADEN-S	BUGBANE-S	BUSGIRL-S
BORONIA-S	BRADOON-S	BROCADE-S	BUGBEAR-S	BUSHIDO-S
BOROUGH-S	BRAGGER-S	BROCAGE-S	BUGGANE-S	BUSHING-S
BORSCHT-S	BRAHMAN-S	BROCARD-S	BUGGING-S	BUSHPIG-S
BORSTAL-S	BRAHMIN-S	BROCHAN-S	BUGSEED-S	BUSHTIT-S

BUSHWAH-S	CAJUPUT-S	CANAKIN-S	CARAVAN-S	CASSATA-S
BUSKING-S	CALALOO-S	CANASTA-S	CARAVEL-S	CASSAVA-S
BUSLOAD-S	CALAMAR-S	CANBANK-S	CARAWAY-S	CASSENA-S
BUSSING-S	CALCINE-S	CANDELA-S	CARBARN-S	CASSENE-S
BUSTARD-S	CALCITE-S	CANDIDA-S	CARBEEN-S	CASSINA-S
BUSTIER-S	CALCIUM-S	CANDLER-S	CARBENE-S	CASSINE-S
BUSTING-S	CALDERA-S	CANDOCK-S	CARBIDE-S	CASSINO-S
BUSTLER-S	CALDRON-S	CANDOUR-S	CARBINE-S	CASSOCK-S
BUSUUTI-S	CALECHE-S	CANELLA-S	CARBORA-S	CASSONE-S
BUTANOL-S	CALIBER-S	CANIKIN-S	CARCAKE-S	CASSPIR-S
BUTCHER-S	CALIBRE-S	CANNACH-S	CARCASE-S	CASTING-S
BUTMENT-S	CALICHE-S	CANNING-S	CARDECU-S	CASTOCK-S
BUTTOCK-S	CALICLE-S	CANNOLI-S	CARDIAC-S	CASTOFF-S
BUTYRAL-S	CALIPEE-S	CANNULA-S	CARDING-S	CASUIST-S
BUTYRIN-S	CALIPER-S	CANTALA-S	CARDOON-S	CATALOG-S
BUTYRYL-S	CALIVER-S	CANTATA-S	CARFARE-S	CATALPA-S
BUVETTE-S	CALKING-S	CANTATE-S	CARIAMA-S	CATAPAN-S
BUYABLE-S	CALLANT-S	CANTDOG-S	CARIBOU-S	CATARRH-S
BUYBACK-S	CALLBOY-S	CANTEEN-S	CARIERE-S	CATASTA-S
BUZZARD-S	CALLING-S	CANTICO-S	CARIOCA-S	CATAWBA-S
BUZZCUT-S	CALLOSE-S	CANTINA-S	CARIOLE-S	CATBIRD-S
BUZZING-S	CALLUNA-S	CANTING-S	CARJACK-S	CATBOAT-S
BUZZWIG-S	CALMANT-S	CANTION-S	CARLINE-S	CATCALL-S
BYCOKET-S	CALMING-S	CANTLET-S	CARLING-S	CATCHER-S
BYLINER-S	CALOMEL-S	CANTRAP-S	CARLOAD-S	CATCHUP-S
BYPLACE-S	CALORIC-S	CANTRED-S	CARLOCK-S	CATCLAW-S
BYWONER-S	CALORIE-S	CANTREF-S	CARMINE-S	CATECHU-S
CABARET-S	CALOTTE-S	CANTRIP-S	CARNAGE-S	CATELOG-S
CABBAGE-S	CALOYER-S	CANZONA-S	CAROCHE-S	CATERAN-S
CABBALA-S	CALPACK-S	CANZONE-S	CAROLER-S	CATERER-S
CABEZON-S	CALPAIN-S	CAPELAN-S	CAROMEL-S	CATFACE-S
CABILDO-S	CALTRAP-S	CAPELET-S	CAROTID-S	CATFALL-S
CABINET-S	CALTROP-S	CAPELIN-S	CAROTIN-S	CATHEAD-S
CABLING-S	CALUMBA-S	CAPERER-S	CAROUSE-S	CATHECT-S
CABOMBA-S	CALUMET-S	CAPITAL-S	CARPALE-S	CATHODE-S
CABOOSE-S	CALYCLE-S	CAPITAN-S	CARPARK-S	CATHOLE-S
CACIQUE-S	CALYPSO-S	CAPITOL-S	CARPING-S	CATHOOD-S
CACKLER-S	CALZONE-S	CAPORAL-S	CARPOOL-S	CATJANG-S
CACODYL-S	CAMARON-S	CAPPING-S	CARPORT-S	CATLING-S
CACOLET-S	CAMBISM-S	CAPRATE-S	CARRACK-S	CATMINT-S
CACONYM-S	CAMBIST-S	CAPRICE-S	CARRACT-S	CATSKIN-S
CADAVER-S	CAMBIUM-S	CAPROCK-S	CARRECT-S	CATSPAW-S
CADDICE-S	CAMBOGE-S	CAPSIZE-S	CARRELL-S	CATSUIT-S
CADELLE-S	CAMBREL-S	CAPSTAN-S	CARRIER-S	CATTABU-S
CADENCE-S	CAMBRIC-S	CAPSULE-S	CARRION-S	CATTAIL-S
CADENZA-S	CAMELIA-S	CAPTAIN-S	CARRYON-S	CATTALO-S
CADMIUM-S	CAMELID-S	CAPTION-S	CARTAGE-S	CATWALK-S
CAESIUM-S	CAMELOT-S	CAPTIVE-S	CARTFUL-S	CATWORM-S
CAESURA-S	CAMISIA-S	CAPTURE-S	CARTOON-S	CAUDATE-S
CAFFEIN-S	CAMOGIE-S	CAPUCHE-S	CARTWAY-S	CAUDRON-S
CAFFILA-S	CAMOODI-S	CAPUERA-S	CARVING-S	CAULKER-S
CAGANER-S	CAMORRA-S	CARABAO-S	CASCADE-S	CAULOME-S
CAGEFUL-S	CAMPANA-S	CARABID-S	CASCARA-S	CAUSTIC-S
CAGOULE-S	CAMPHOL-S	CARABIN-S	CASEASE-S	CAUTION-S
CAISSON-S	CAMPHOR-S	CARACAL-S	CASEATE-S	CAVALLA-S
CAITIFF-S	CAMPING-S	CARACOL-S	CASEOSE-S	CAVETTO-S
CAITIVE-S	CAMPION-S	CARACUL-S	CASERNE-S	CAVIARE-S
CAJAPUT-S	CAMPONG-S	CARAMEL-S	CASETTE-S	CAVILER-S
CAJEPUT-S	CAMPOUT-S	CARANNA-S	CASHIER-S	CAYENNE-S
CAJOLER-S	CAMWOOD-S	CARAUNA-S	CASSABA-S	CAZIQUE-S

CEASING-S	CHAMLET-S	CHEDITE-S	CHLORID-S	CIGARET-S
CEDILLA-S	CHAMPAC-S	CHEEPER-S	CHLORIN-S	CILIATE-S
CEDRATE-S	CHAMPAK-S	CHEERER-S	CHOBDAR-S	CINEAST-S
CEILIDH-S	CHAMPER-S	CHEERIO-S	CHOCTAW-S	CINEOLE-S
CEILING-S	CHANCEL-S	CHEETAH-S	CHOLATE-S	CINEREA-S
CELADON-S	CHANCER-S	CHEFDOM-S	CHOLENT-S	CINERIN-S
CELESTA-S	CHANCRE-S	CHEKIST-S	CHOLERA-S	CIPOLIN-S
CELESTE-S	CHANGER-S	CHELATE-S	CHOLINE-S	CIRCLER-S
CELLIST-S	CHANNEL-S	CHELLUP-S	CHOMMIE-S	CIRCLET-S
CELLOSE-S	CHANNER-S	CHELOID-S	CHOMPER-S	CIRCLIP-S
CELLULE-S	CHANOYO-S	CHELONE-S	CHONDRE-S	CIRCUIT-S
CELOSIA-S	CHANOYU-S	CHEMISE-S	CHOOKIE-S	CISSING-S
CEMBALO-S	CHANSON-S	CHEMISM-S	CHOOSER-S	CISSOID-S
CENACLE-S	CHANTER-S	CHEMIST-S	CHOPINE-S	CISTERN-S
CENSURE-S	CHANTEY-S	CHEQUER-S	CHOPPER-S	CISTRON-S
CENTAGE-S	CHANTIE-S	CHEROOT-S	CHORALE-S	CITADEL-S
CENTARE-S	CHANTOR-S	CHERVIL-S	CHORDEE-S	CITATOR-S
CENTAUR-S	CHAPATI-S	CHESNUT-S	CHORINE-S	CITHARA-S
CENTAVO-S	CHAPEAU-S	CHESSEL-S	CHORION-S	CITHERN-S
CENTILE-S	CHAPLET-S	CHETNIK-S	CHORISM-S	CITHREN-S
CENTIME-S	CHAPPAL-S	CHETRUM-S	CHORIST-S	CITIZEN-S
CENTIMO-S	CHAPPIE-S	CHEVIOT-S	CHORIZO-S	CITRATE-S
CENTNER-S	CHAPTER-S	CHEVRET-S	CHOROID-S	CITRINE-S
CENTRAL-S	CHARACT-S	CHEVRON-S	CHORRIE-S	CITTERN-S
CENTRUM-S	CHARADE-S	CHEWINK-S	CHORTEN-S	CLABBER-S
CEPHEID-S	CHARGER-S	CHIANTI-S	CHORTLE-S	CLACHAN-S
CERAMAL-S	CHARIOT-S	CHIASMA-S	CHOUSER-S	CLACKER-S
CERAMIC-S	CHARISM-S	CHIBOUK-S	CHOWDER-S	CLADDER-S
CERASIN-S	CHARKHA-S	CHICANA-S	CHRISOM-S	CLADDIE-S
CERATIN-S	CHARLEY-S	CHICANE-S	CHROMEL-S	CLADISM-S
CERESIN-S	CHARLIE-S	CHICANO-S	CHROMYL-S	CLADIST-S
CERUMEN-S	CHARMER-S	CHICKEE-S	CHRONIC-S	CLADODE-S
CERVEZA-S	CHARNEL-S	CHICKEN-S	CHRONON-S	CLAIMER-S
CESSION-S	CHARPAI-S	CHIDING-S	CHUCKER-S	CLAMBER-S
CESSPIT-S	CHARPIE-S	CHIFFON-S	CHUCKIE-S	CLAMMER-S
CESTODE-S	CHARPOY-S	CHIGGER-S	CHUCKLE-S	CLAMOUR-S
CESTOID-S	CHARQUI-S	CHIGNON-S	CHUDDAH-S	CLAMPER-S
CEVICHE-S	CHARTER-S	CHIKARA-S	CHUDDAR-S	CLANGER-S
CHABOUK-S	CHARVER-S	CHIKHOR-S	CHUDDER-S	CLANGOR-S
CHACHKA-S	CHASING-S	CHILIAD-S	CHUGGER-S	CLAPNET-S
CHADDAR-S	CHASTEN-S	CHILIOI-S	CHUKKAR-S	CLAPPER-S
CHADDOR-S	CHATBOT-S	CHILLER-S	CHUKKER-S	CLAQUER-S
CHAEBOL-S	CHATEAU-S	CHILLUM-S	CHUMLEY-S	CLARAIN-S
CHAFFER-S	CHATTEL-S	CHIMERA-S	CHUNDER-S	CLARINO-S
CHAGRIN-S	CHATTER-S	CHIMERE-S	CHUNNEL-S	CLARION-S
CHALAZA-S	CHAUFER-S	CHIMLEY-S	CHUNNER-S	CLARKIA-S
CHALCID-S	CHAUMER-S	CHIMNEY-S	CHUNTER-S	CLASHER-S
CHALDER-S	CHAUNCE-S	CHINDIT-S	CHUPATI-S	CLASPER-S
CHALICE-S	CHAUNGE-S	CHINKIE-S	CHUPPAH-S	CLASSER-S
CHALLAH-S	CHAUVIN-S	CHINONE-S	CHURNER-S	CLASSIC-S
CHALLAN-S	CHAYOTE-S	CHINOOK-S	CHUTIST-S	CLASSON-S
CHALLIE-S	CHAZZAN-S	CHINWAG-S	CHUTNEE-S	CLASTIC-S
CHALONE-S	CHAZZEN-S	CHIPPER-S	CHUTNEY-S	CLATTER-S
CHALUPA-S	CHEAPEN-S	CHIPPIE-S	CHUTZPA-S	CLAUCHT-S
CHAMADE-S	CHEAPIE-S	CHIPSET-S	CHYMIST-S	CLAUGHT-S
CHAMBER-S	CHEATER-S	CHIRPER-S	CHYTRID-S	CLAVIER-S
CHAMFER-S	CHECHIA-S	CHIRRUP-S	CIBOULE-S	CLAYPAN-S
CHAMISA-S	CHECKER-S	CHITLIN-S	CICHLID-S	CLEANER-S
CHAMISE-S	CHECKUP-S	CHITTER-S	CICOREE-S	CLEANSE-S
CHAMISO-S	CHEDDAR-S	CHLORAL-S	CIELING-S	CLEANUP-S

CLEARER-S	COCKPIT-S	COLORED-S	CONDONE-S	COOLANT-S
CLEAVER-S	COCOMAT-S	COLORER-S	CONDUCE-S	COONCAN-S
CLERUCH-S	COCONUT-S	COLUMEL-S	CONDUCT-S	COONDOG-S
CLICKER-S	COCOPAN-S	COMAKER-S	CONDUIT-S	COONTIE-S
CLICKET-S	COCOTTE-S	COMATIK-S	CONDYLE-S	COPAIBA-S
CLIMATE-S	COCOYAM-S	COMBINE-S	CONFECT-S	COPAIVA-S
CLIMBER-S	COCTION-S	COMBING-S	CONFIDE-S	COPEPOD-S
CLINGER-S	CODDLER-S	COMBLES-S	CONFINE-S	COPIHUE-S
CLINKER-S	CODEINA-S	COMBUST-S	CONFIRM-S	COPILOT-S
CLIPART-S	CODEINE-S	COMFORT-S	CONFORM-S	COPPICE-S
CLIPPER-S	CODETTA-S	COMFREY-S	CONFUSE-S	COPSHOP-S
CLIPPIE-S	CODICIL-S	COMIQUE-S	CONFUTE-S	COPYBOY-S
CLITTER-S	CODILLA-S	COMITIA-S	CONGEAL-S	COPYCAT-S
CLOBBER-S	CODILLE-S	COMMAND-S	CONGEST-S	COPYISM-S
CLOCKER-S	CODLING-S	COMMEND-S	CONGREE-S	COPYIST-S
CLOGGER-S	CODRIVE-S	COMMENT-S	CONGRUE-S	COQUINA-S
CLOISON-S	COEHORN-S	COMMERE-S	CONIFER-S	COQUITO-S
CLONING-S	COELIAC-S	COMMODE-S	CONIINE-S	CORACLE-S
CLONISM-S	COELOME-S	COMMOTE-S	CONJECT-S	CORANTO-S
CLOSEUP-S	COENACT-S	COMMOVE-S	CONJOIN-S	CORBEAU-S
CLOSING-S	COENURE-S	COMMUNE-S	CONJURE-S	CORBEIL-S
CLOSURE-S	COEQUAL-S	COMMUTE-S	CONNECT-S	CORBINA-S
CLOTBUR-S	COERCER-S	COMPACT-S	CONNING-S	CORDAGE-S
CLOTTER-S	COERECT-S	COMPAGE-S	CONNIVE-S	CORDIAL-S
CLOTURE-S	COESITE-S	COMPAND-S	CONNOTE-S	CORDING-S
CLOUTER-S	COEXERT-S	COMPARE-S	CONQUER-S	CORDITE-S
CLOWDER-S	COEXIST-S	COMPART-S	CONSEIL-S	CORDOBA-S
CLUBBER-S	COFFRET-S	COMPEAR-S	CONSENT-S	COREIGN-S
CLUDGIE-S	COFOUND-S	COMPEER-S	CONSIGN-S	CORELLA-S
CLUMBER-S	COGENCE-S	COMPEND-S	CONSIST-S	CORIVAL-S
CLUMPER-S	COGENER-S	COMPERE-S	CONSOLE-S	CORIXID-S
CLUNKER-S	COGGING-S	COMPETE-S	CONSORT-S	CORKAGE-S
CLUPEID-S	COGNATE-S	COMPILE-S	CONSTER-S	CORNAGE-S
CLUSTER-S	COGNISE-S	COMPING-S	CONSULT-S	CORNCOB-S
CLUTTER-S	COGNIZE-S	COMPLIN-S	CONSUME-S	CORNETT-S
CLYSTER-S	COHABIT-S	COMPLOT-S	CONTACT-S	CORNICE-S
COACHEE-S	COHERER-S	COMPORT-S	CONTAIN-S	CORNIST-S
COACHER-S	COHIBIT-S	COMPOSE-S	CONTECK-S	CORNROW-S
COACTOR-S	COINAGE-S	COMPOST-S	CONTEMN-S	CORNUTE-S
COADMIT-S	COINFER-S	COMPOTE-S	CONTEND-S	CORNUTO-S
COAEVAL-S	COINING-S	COMPTER-S	CONTENT-S	COROLLA-S
COAGENT-S	COINTER-S	COMPUTE-S	CONTEST-S	CORONAL-S
COALBIN-S	COITION-S	COMRADE-S	CONTEXT-S	CORONEL-S
COALISE-S	COLETIT-S	COMSYMP-S	CONTORT-S	CORONER-S
COALIZE-S	COLIBRI-S	CONACRE-S	CONTOUR-S	CORONET-S
COALPIT-S	COLICIN-S	CONCAVE-S	CONTRAT-S	CORPORA-S
COALTAR-S	COLLAGE-S	CONCEAL-S	CONTROL-S	CORRADE-S
COAMING-S	COLLARD-S	CONCEDE-S	CONTUND-S	CORRECT-S
COARSEN-S	COLLATE-S	CONCEIT-S	CONTUSE-S	CORRIDA-S
COASTER-S	COLLECT-S	CONCENT-S	CONVECT-S	CORRODE-S
COATING-S	COLLEEN-S	CONCEPT-S	CONVENE-S	CORRUPT-S
COBBLER-S	COLLEGE-S	CONCERN-S	CONVENT-S	CORSAGE-S
COCAINE-S	COLLIDE-S	CONCERT-S	CONVERT-S	CORSAIR-S
COCCOID-S	COLLIER-S	CONCHIE-S	CONVICT-S	CORSIVE-S
COCHAIR-S	COLLING-S	CONCISE-S	CONVIVE-S	CORSLET-S
COCHLEA-S	COLLOID-S	CONCOCT-S	CONVOKE-S	CORSNED-S
COCKADE-S	COLLUDE-S	CONCORD-S	COOKING-S	CORTEGE-S
COCKEYE-S	COLOGNE-S	CONCREW-S	COOKOFF-S	CORTINA-S
COCKLER-S	COLONEL-S	CONDEMN-S	COOKOUT-S	CORULER-S
COCKNEY-S	COLONIC-S	CONDOLE-S	COOKTOP-S	CORVINA-S

CORYPHE-S	COWPOKE-S	CRINITE-S	CUBBING-S	CUTBACK-S
COSINES-S	COWRITE-S	CRINKLE-S	CUBHOOD-S	CUTBANK-S
COSMINE-S	COWSHED-S	CRINOID-S	CUBICLE-S	CUTDOWN-S
COSMISM-S	COWSKIN-S	CRIOLLO-S	CUCKOLD-S	CUTICLE-S
COSMIST-S	COWSLIP-S	CRIPPLE-S	CUDBEAR-S	CUTIKIN-S
COSSACK-S	COWTREE-S	CRISPEN-S	CUDDLER-S	CUTLINE-S
COSTARD-S	COXCOMB-S	CRISPER-S	CUDWEED-S	CUTOVER-S
COSTEAN-S	COZENER-S	CRISPIN-S	CUFFLES-S	CUTTAGE-S
COSTREL-S	CRABBER-S	CRITTER-S	CUISINE-S	CUTTING-S
COSTUME-S	CRACKER-S	CRITTUR-S	CUISSER-S	CUTWORK-S
COTERIE-S	CRACKET-S	CROAKER-S	CUITTLE-S	CUTWORM-S
COTHURN-S	CRACKLE-S	CROCEIN-S	CULCHIE-S	CUVETTE-S
COTINGA-S	CRACKUP-S	CROCHET-S	CULICID-S	CYANATE-S
COTLAND-S	CRACOWE-S	CROCKET-S	CULLING-S	CYANIDE-S
COTTAGE-S	CRADLER-S	CROFTER-S	CULLION-S	CYANINE-S
COTTIER-S	CRAFTER-S	CROMACK-S	CULOTTE-S	CYANISE-S
COTTISE-S	CRAMMER-S	CROMBEC-S	CULPRIT-S	CYANITE-S
COTTOWN-S	CRAMPER-S	CROODLE-S	CULTISM-S	CYANIZE-S
COUCHEE-S	CRAMPET-S	CROONER-S	CULTIST-S	CYCASIN-S
COUCHER-S	CRAMPIT-S	CROPFUL-S	CULTURE-S	CYCLASE-S
COUGHER-S	CRAMPON-S	CROPPER-S	CULVERT-S	CYCLING-S
COUGUAR-S	CRANAGE-S	CROPPIE-S	CUMARIN-S	CYCLISE-S
COULOIR-S	CRANIUM-S	CROQUET-S	CUMQUAT-S	CYCLIST-S
COULOMB-S	CRANKLE-S	CROSIER-S	CUMSHAW-S	CYCLIZE-S
COULTER-S	CRANNOG-S	CROSSER-S	CUMULET-S	CYCLOID-S
COUNCIL-S	CRAPAUD-S	CROTTLE-S	CUNETTE-S	CYCLONE-S
COUNSEL-S	CRAPOLA-S	CROUPER-S	CUNNING-S	CYMBALO-S
COUNTER-S	CRAPPER-S	CROUPON-S	CUPCAKE-S	CYMLING-S
COUPLER-S	CRAPPIE-S	CROUTON-S	CUPELER-S	CYPRIAN-S
COUPLET-S	CRASHER-S	CROWBAR-S	CUPGALL-S	CYSTEIN-S
COUPURE-S	CRAVING-S	CROWDER-S	CUPHEAD-S	CYSTINE-S
COURAGE-S	CRAWDAD-S	CROWDIE-S	CUPPING-S	CYSTOID-S
COURANT-S	CRAWLER-S	CROWNER-S	CUPRITE-S	CYTOSOL-S
COURIER-S	CREAMER-S	CROWNET-S	CURACAO-S	CZARDOM-S
COURLAN-S	CREANCE-S	CROZIER-S	CURACOA-S	CZARINA-S
COURSER-S	CREASER-S	CRUBEEN-S	CURATOR-S	CZARISM-S
COURTER-S	CREATIN-S	CRUCIAN-S	CURBING-S	CZARIST-S
COUTURE-S	CREATOR-S	CRUDDLE-S	CURCHEF-S	DABBLER-S
COUVADE-S	CREEPER-S	CRUISER-S	CURCUMA-S	DABSTER-S
COUVERT-S	CREEPIE-S	CRUISIE-S	CURDLER-S	DADAISM-S
COVELET-S	CREMATE-S	CRUIZIE-S	CURETTE-S	DADAIST-S
COVERER-S	CREMINI-S	CRULLER-S	CURLING-S	DADDOCK-S
COVERUP-S	CREMONA-S	CRUMBER-S	CURRACH-S	DAFFING-S
COVETER-S	CREOSOL-S	CRUMBLE-S	CURRAGH-S	DAGGING-S
COWBANE-S	CRESSET-S	CRUMBUM-S	CURRANT-S	DAGLOCK-S
COWBELL-S	CRESTON-S	CRUMMIE-S	CURRENT-S	DAGWOOD-S
COWBIND-S	CRETISM-S	CRUMPET-S	CURRIER-S	DAIMOKU-S
COWBIRD-S	CREVICE-S	CRUMPLE-S	CURSING-S	DAKOITI-S
COWFLAP-S	CREWCUT-S	CRUNKLE-S	CURSIVE-S	DALAPON-S
COWFLOP-S	CRIBBER-S	CRUNODE-S	CURTAIL-S	DALGYTE-S
COWGIRL-S	CRIBBLE-S	CRUPPER-S	CURTAIN-S	DALLIER-S
COWHAGE-S	CRICKET-S	CRUSADE-S	CURTANA-S	DAMAGER-S
COWHAND-S	CRICOID-S	CRUSADO-S	CURTAXE-S	DAMBROD-S
COWHEEL-S	CRIMINI-S	CRUSHER-S	CURTSEY-S	DAMIANA-S
COWHERB-S	CRIMMER-S	CRUSIAN-S	CUSHION-S	DAMOSEL-S
COWHERD-S	CRIMPER-S	CRUZADO-S	CUSTARD-S	DAMOZEL-S
COWHIDE-S	CRIMPLE-S	CRYOGEN-S	CUSTOCK-S	DAMPING-S
COWLICK-S	CRIMSON-S	CRYONIC-S	CUSTODE-S	DANAZOL-S
COWLING-S	CRINGER-S	CRYPTON-S	CUSTREL-S	DANCING-S
COWPLOP-S	CRINGLE-S	CRYSTAL-S	CUTAWAY-S	DANDLER-S

DANELAW-S	DECAGON-S	DELIMIT-S	DESPISE-S	DIARIZE-S
DANGLER-S	DECALOG-S	DELIVER-S	DESPITE-S	DIASTEM-S
DANSEUR-S	DECAPOD-S	DELOUSE-S	DESPOIL-S	DIASTER-S
DAPHNIA-S	DECAYER-S	DELTOID-S	DESPOND-S	DIATRON-S
DAPHNID-S	DECEASE-S	DELUDER-S	DESSERT-S	DIAZINE-S
DAPSONE-S	DECEIVE-S	DEMAGOG-S	DESTAIN-S	DIAZOLE-S
DAQUIRI-S	DECIARE-S	DEMAINE-S	DESTINE-S	DIBBLER-S
DARIOLE-S	DECIBEL-S	DEMAYNE-S	DESTOCK-S	DICAMBA-S
DARLING-S	DECIDER-S	DEMEANE-S	DESTROY-S	DICHORD-S
DARNING-S	DECIDUA-S	DEMENTI-S	DESUGAR-S	DICOTYL-S
DAROGHA-S	DECIMAL-S	DEMERGE-S	DETENTE-S	DICTATE-S
DARRAIN-S	DECKING-S	DEMERIT-S	DETENUE-S	DICTION-S
DARRAYN-S	DECLAIM-S	DEMERSE-S	DETERGE-S	DIDAKAI-S
DARSHAN-S	DECLARE-S	DEMESNE-S	DETINUE-S	DIDAKEI-S
DASHEEN-S	DECLINE-S	DEMETON-S	DETRACT-S	DIDDLER-S
DASHEKI-S	DECODER-S	DEMIGOD-S	DETRAIN-S	DIDDLEY-S
DASHIKI-S	DECOLOR-S	DEMIREP-S	DETRUDE-S	DIDICOI-S
DASHPOT-S	DECORUM-S	DEMOTIC-S	DEUTZIA-S	DIDICOY-S
DASTARD-S	DECOYER-S	DEMOUNT-S	DEVALUE-S	DIEBACK-S
DASYPOD-S	DECREER-S	DENDRON-S	DEVELOP-S	DIEDRAL-S
DASYURE-S	DECREET-S	DENIZEN-S	DEVIANT-S	DIEHARD-S
DATARIA-S	DECRIAL-S	DENTINE-S	DEVIATE-S	DIESTER-S
DAUBING-S	DECRIER-S	DENTIST-S	DEVILET-S	DIETHER-S
DAUNDER-S	DECROWN-S	DENTURE-S	DEVISAL-S	DIETHYL-S
DAUNTER-S	DECRYPT-S	DENUDER-S	DEVISEE-S	DIETINE-S
DAUNTON-S	DECUMAN-S	DEODAND-S	DEVISER-S	DIETING-S
DAUPHIN-S	DECUPLE-S	DEODARA-S	DEVISOR-S	DIETIST-S
DAVIDIA-S	DECURIA-S	DEODATE-S	DEVLING-S	DIFFUSE-S
DAWBAKE-S	DECURVE-S	DEONTIC-S	DEVOICE-S	DIGAMMA-S
DAWCOCK-S	DEERLET-S	DEORBIT-S	DEVOLVE-S	DIGGING-S
DAWDLER-S	DEFACER-S	DEPAINT-S	DEVOTEE-S	DIGICAM-S
DAWNING-S	DEFAMER-S	DEPECHE-S	DEWATER-S	DIGITAL-S
DAYBOOK-S	DEFAULT-S	DEPLANE-S	DEWCLAW-S	DIGLYPH-S
DAYCARE-S	DEFENCE-S	DEPLETE-S	DEWDROP-S	DIGOXIN-S
DAYGLOW-S	DEFENSE-S	DEPLORE-S	DEWFALL-S	DIGRAPH-S
DAYMARE-S	DEFICIT-S	DEPLUME-S	DEXTRAN-S	DILATER-S
DAYMARK-S	DEFILER-S	DEPOSAL-S	DEXTRIN-S	DILATOR-S
DAYROOM-S	DEFINER-S	DEPOSER-S	DHANSAK-S	DILEMMA-S
DAYSACK-S	DEFLATE-S	DEPOSIT-S	DHOOTIE-S	DILLING-S
DAYSIDE-S	DEFLECT-S	DEPRAVE-S	DHOURRA-S	DILUENT-S
DAYSTAR-S	DEFORCE-S	DEPRIVE-S	DHURRIE-S	DILUTEE-S
DAYTALE-S	DEFRAUD-S	DEPSIDE-S	DIABASE-S	DILUTER-S
DAYTIME-S	DEFROCK-S	DERAIGN-S	DIABOLO-S	DILUTOR-S
DAYWORK-S	DEFROST-S	DERANGE-S	DIADROM-S	DIMETER-S
DAZZLER-S	DEFUNCT-S	DERIDER-S	DIAGRAM-S	DIMORPH-S
DEADBOY-S	DEFUSER-S	DERIVER-S	DIAGRID-S	DINETTE-S
DEADEYE-S	DEGLAZE-S	DERMOID-S	DIALECT-S	DINGBAT-S
DEADPAN-S	DEGRADE-S	DERRICK-S	DIALING-S	DINMONT-S
DEALATE-S	DEHISCE-S	DESCALE-S	DIALIST-S	DIOCESE-S
DEALING-S	DEICIDE-S	DESCANT-S	DIALLER-S	DIOPTER-S
DEASIUL-S	DEICTIC-S	DESCEND-S	DIALYSE-S	DIOPTRE-S
DEASOIL-S	DEIFIER-S	DESCENT-S	DIALYZE-S	DIORAMA-S
DEBACLE-S	DEISEAL-S	DESERVE-S	DIAMIDE-S	DIORISM-S
DEBASER-S	DEJEUNE-S	DESIRER-S	DIAMINE-S	DIORITE-S
DEBATER-S	DELAINE-S	DESKILL-S	DIAMOND-S	DIOXANE-S
DEBEARD-S	DELAPSE-S	DESKTOP-S	DIANOIA-S	DIOXIDE-S
DEBITOR-S	DELATOR-S	DESMINE-S	DIAPASE-S	DIPHONE-S
DEBONER-S	DELAYER-S	DESMOID-S	DIAPSID-S	DIPLOID-S
DEBRIDE-S	DELEAVE-S	DESNOOD-S	DIARISE-S	DIPLOMA-S
DEBRIEF-S	DELIGHT-S	DESPAIR-S	DIARIST-S	DIPLONT-S

DIPNOAN-S	DISPONE-S	DOGSLED-S	DRAINER-S	DUELLER-S
DIPPING-S	DISPORT-S	DOGTOWN-S	DRAPIER-S	DUFFING-S
DIPSHIT-S	DISPOSE-S	DOGTROT-S	DRAPPIE-S	DUKEDOM-S
DIPTERA-S	DISPOST-S	DOGVANE-S	DRASTIC-S	DULCIAN-S
DIPTYCA-S	DISPRED-S	DOGWOOD-S	DRAUGHT-S	DULCITE-S
DIPTYCH-S	DISPUTE-S	DOITKIN-S	DRAWBAR-S	DULCOSE-S
DIQUARK-S	DISRANK-S	DOLLDOM-S	DRAWING-S	DULLARD-S
DIREMPT-S	DISRATE-S	DOLLIER-S	DRAWLER-S	DUMAIST-S
DIRTBAG-S	DISROBE-S	DOLPHIN-S	DRAYAGE-S	DUMPBIN-S
DISABLE-S	DISROOT-S	DOMAINE-S	DREADER-S	DUMPING-S
DISAVOW-S	DISRUPT-S	DOMICIL-S	DREAMER-S	DUNGEON-S
DISBAND-S	DISSAVE-S	DOMINEE-S	DREDGER-S	DUNNAGE-S
DISBARK-S	DISSEAT-S	DOMINIE-S	DREIDEL-S	DUNNART-S
DISCAGE-S	DISSECT-S	DONATOR-S	DRESSER-S	DUNNING-S
DISCANT-S	DISSENT-S	DONGOLA-S	DREVILL-S	DUNNITE-S
DISCARD-S	DISSERT-S	DONNISM-S	DRIBBER-S	DUNNOCK-S
DISCASE-S	DISTAFF-S	DONSHIP-S	DRIBBLE-S	DUOTONE-S
DISCEPT-S	DISTAIN-S	DOODLER-S	DRIBLET-S	DUPATTA-S
DISCERN-S	DISTEND-S	DOORMAT-S	DRIFTER-S	DURABLE-S
DISCERP-S	DISTICH-S	DOORWAY-S	DRILLER-S	DURAMEN-S
DISCIDE-S	DISTILL-S	DOPATTA-S	DRINKER-S	DURANCE-S
DISCOER-S	DISTOME-S	DOPIAZA-S	DRIPPER-S	DURESSE-S
DISCOID-S	DISTORT-S	DOPPING-S	DRIVING-S	DURMAST-S
DISCORD-S	DISTUNE-S	DORHAWK-S	DRIZZLE-S	DUSTBIN-S
DISCURE-S	DISTURB-S	DORLACH-S	DROGHER-S	DUSTING-S
DISDAIN-S	DISTYLE-S	DORMANT-S	DROGUET-S	DUSTOFF-S
DISEASE-S	DISYOKE-S	DORNECK-S	DROMOND-S	DUSTPAN-S
DISEDGE-S	DITCHER-S	DORNICK-S	DROPLET-S	DUSTRAG-S
DISEUSE-S	DIURNAL-S	DORNOCK-S	DROPOUT-S	DUUMVIR-S
DISFAME-S	DIVERGE-S	DORTOUR-S	DROPPER-S	DUVETYN-S
DISFORM-S	DIVERSE-S	DOSSIER-S	DROPPLE-S	DVANDVA-S
DISGEST-S	DIVIDER-S	DOTTREL-S	DROSERA-S	DVORNIK-S
DISGOWN-S	DIVINER-S	DOUBLER-S	DROSTDY-S	DWELLER-S
DISGUST-S	DIVISOR-S	DOUBLET-S	DROUGHT-S	DWINDLE-S
DISHELM-S	DIVORCE-S	DOUBTER-S	DROVING-S	DYELINE-S
DISHFUL-S	DIVULGE-S	DOUCEUR-S	DROWNER-S	DYESTER-S
DISHING-S	DIVULSE-S	DOUCINE-S	DRUBBER-S	DYEWEED-S
DISHOME-S	DIZZARD-S	DOULEIA-S	DRUDGER-S	DYEWOOD-S
DISHORN-S	DJIBBAH-S	DOURINE-S	DRUGGER-S	DYNAMIC-S
DISHPAN-S	DOATING-S	DOVECOT-S	DRUGGET-S	DYSODIL-S
DISHRAG-S	DOCKAGE-S	DOVEKEY-S	DRUGGIE-S	DYSPNEA-S
DISJECT-S	DOCKING-S	DOVEKIE-S	DRUMBLE-S	DYSURIA-S
DISJOIN-S	DOCKISE-S	DOVELET-S	DRUMLIN-S	EANLING-S
DISJUNE-S	DOCKIZE-S	DOWAGER-S	DRUMMER-S	EARACHE-S
DISLEAF-S	DOCQUET-S	DOWNBOW-S	DRYBEAT-S	EARBALL-S
DISLIKE-S	DODGING-S	DOYENNE-S	DRYWALL-S	EARDROP-S
DISLIMB-S	DODOISM-S	DOZENTH-S	DRYWELL-S	EARDRUM-S
DISLIMN-S	DOESKIN-S	DRABBER-S	DUALISE-S	EARFLAP-S
DISLINK-S	DOGBANE-S	DRABBET-S	DUALISM-S	EARLDOM-S
DISLOAD-S	DOGBOLT-S	DRABBLE-S	DUALIST-S	EARLOBE-S
DISMASK-S	DOGCART-S	DRABLER-S	DUALIZE-S	EARLOCK-S
DISMAST-S	DOGEATE-S	DRACENA-S	DUBBING-S	EARMARK-S
DISMAYL-S	DOGEDOM-S	DRACHMA-S	DUBNIUM-S	EARMUFF-S
DISNEST-S	DOGFACE-S	DRACONE-S	DUCKING-S	EARNEST-S
DISOBEY-S	DOGGING-S	DRAFTEE-S	DUCKPIN-S	EARNING-S
DISPACE-S	DOGGONE-S	DRAFTER-S	DUCTING-S	EARPICK-S
DISPARK-S	DOGGREL-S	DRAGGER-S	DUCTULE-S	EARPLUG-S
DISPART-S	DOGHOLE-S	DRAGGLE-S	DUDGEON-S	EARRING-S
DISPEND-S	DOGSHIP-S	DRAGNET-S	DUDHEEN-S	EARSHOT-S
DISPLAY-S	DOGSKIN-S	DRAGOON-S	DUELIST-S	EARWORM-S

EASTING-S	EJECTOR-S	EMPANEL-S	ENGLOOM-S	ENWHEEL-S
EASTLIN-S	EKISTIC-S	EMPAYRE-S	ENGORGE-S	EOBIONT-S
EATABLE-S	EKPWELE-S	EMPERCE-S	ENGRACE-S	EPACRID-S
EATERIE-S	ELASTIC-S	EMPEROR-S	ENGRAFF-S	EPAGOGE-S
EBAUCHE-S	ELASTIN-S	EMPIRIC-S	ENGRAFT-S	EPAULET-S
EBAYING-S	ELATION-S	EMPLACE-S	ENGRAIL-S	EPAZOTE-S
EBBTIDE-S	ELATIVE-S	EMPLANE-S	ENGRAIN-S	EPEEIST-S
EBONISE-S	ELECTEE-S	EMPLOYE-S	ENGRASP-S	EPEIRID-S
EBONIST-S	ELECTOR-S	EMPLUME-S	ENGRAVE-S	EPERGNE-S
EBONITE-S	ELECTRO-S	EMPOWER-S	ENGUARD-S	EPHEDRA-S
EBONIZE-S	ELEGIAC-S	EMPRISE-S	ENGULPH-S	EPIBLEM-S
ECBOLIC-S	ELEGISE-S	EMPRIZE-S	ENHANCE-S	EPICARP-S
ECDYSON-S	ELEGIST-S	EMPTIER-S	ENJOYER-S	EPICEDE-S
ECHAPPE-S	ELEGIZE-S	EMPTING-S	ENLARGE-S	EPICENE-S
ECHELLE-S	ELEMENT-S	EMPTION-S	ENLIGHT-S	EPICIER-S
ECHELON-S	ELEVATE-S	EMPYEMA-S	ENLIVEN-S	EPICISM-S
ECHIDNA-S	ELFHOOD-S	EMULATE-S	ENNOBLE-S	EPICIST-S
ECHOISE-S	ELFLAND-S	EMULSIN-S	ENOLASE-S	EPICURE-S
ECHOISM-S	ELFLOCK-S	EMULSOR-S	ENOUNCE-S	EPIDERM-S
ECHOIST-S	ELISION-S	ENABLER-S	ENPLANE-S	EPIDOTE-S
ECHOIZE-S	ELITISM-S	ENACTOR-S	ENPRINT-S	EPIGONE-S
ECLIPSE-S	ELITIST-S	ENAMINE-S	ENQUIRE-S	EPIGRAM-S
ECLOGUE-S	ELLIPSE-S	ENAMOUR-S	ENRANGE-S	EPILATE-S
ECOCIDE-S	ELLWAND-S	ENATION-S	ENRHEUM-S	EPIMERE-S
ECORCHE-S	ELMWOOD-S	ENCHAFE-S	ENROBER-S	EPISCIA-S
ECOTAGE-S	ELOCUTE-S	ENCHAIN-S	ENROUGH-S	EPISODE-S
ECOTONE-S	ELOGIST-S	ENCHANT-S	ENROUND-S	EPISOME-S
ECOTOUR-S	ELOGIUM-S	ENCHARM-S	ENSHELL-S	EPISTLE-S
ECOTYPE-S	ELOINER-S	ENCHASE-S	ENSLAVE-S	EPITAPH-S
ECTASIA-S	ELUSION-S	ENCHEER-S	ENSNARE-S	EPITHEM-S
ECTHYMA-S	ELUTION-S	ENCLASP-S	ENSNARL-S	EPITHET-S
ECTOPIA-S	ELUVIUM-S	ENCLAVE-S	ENSTAMP-S	EPITOME-S
ECUELLE-S	EMANATE-S	ENCLOSE-S	ENSTEEP-S	EPITOPE-S
EDIFICE-S	EMBATHE-S	ENCLOUD-S	ENSTYLE-S	EPIZOAN-S
EDIFIER-S	EMBLAZE-S	ENCODER-S	ENSURER-S	EPOXIDE-S
EDITING-S	EMBLOOM-S	ENCRUST-S	ENSWEEP-S	EPSILON-S
EDITION-S	EMBOGUE-S	ENCRYPT-S	ENTASIA-S	EPURATE-S
EDUCATE-S	EMBOSOM-S	ENDEMIC-S	ENTAYLE-S	EQUATOR-S
EDUCTOR-S	EMBOUND-S	ENDERON-S	ENTENTE-S	EQUINIA-S
EELFARE-S	EMBOWEL-S	ENDGAME-S	ENTERER-S	ERASION-S
EELPOUT-S	EMBOWER-S	ENDIRON-S	ENTERIC-S	ERASURE-S
EELWORM-S	EMBRACE-S	ENDLEAF-S	ENTERON-S	ERATHEM-S
EEVNING-S	EMBRAID-S	ENDNOTE-S	ENTHRAL-S	ERECTER-S
EFFACER-S	EMBRAVE-S	ENDOGEN-S	ENTHUSE-S	ERECTOR-S
EFFENDI-S	EMBREAD-S	ENDOPOD-S	ENTICER-S	EREMITE-S
EFFORCE-S	EMBROIL-S	ENDORSE-S	ENTITLE-S	EREPSIN-S
EFFULGE-S	EMBROWN-S	ENDOWER-S	ENTRAIL-S	ERINITE-S
EFTSOON-S	EMBRUTE-S	ENDPLAY-S	ENTRAIN-S	ERISTIC-S
EGALITE-S	EMBRYON-S	ENDSHIP-S	ENTRANT-S	ERLKING-S
EGGHEAD-S	EMENDER-S	ENDURER-S	ENTREAT-S	ERMELIN-S
EGOTISE-S	EMERALD-S	ENERGID-S	ENTRISM-S	ERODENT-S
EGOTISM-S	EMERITA-S	ENFELON-S	ENTRIST-S	ERODIUM-S
EGOTIST-S	EMEROID-S	ENFEOFF-S	ENTRUST-S	EROSION-S
EGOTIZE-S	EMETINE-S	ENFEVER-S	ENTWINE-S	EROTEMA-S
EIDETIC-S	EMICATE-S	ENFLAME-S	ENTWIST-S	EROTEME-S
EIDOLON-S	EMIRATE-S	ENFORCE-S	ENVAULT-S	EROTISE-S
EIGHTVO-S	EMITTER-S	ENFRAME-S	ENVELOP-S	EROTISM-S
EILDING-S	EMOTION-S	ENGAGER-S	ENVENOM-S	EROTIZE-S
EINKORN-S	EMPAIRE-S	ENGINER-S	ENVIRON-S	ERRATIC-S
EISWEIN-S	EMPALER-S	ENGLOBE-S	ENVYING-S	ERRHINE-S

ERUDITE-S	EUTEXIA-S	EXPOSIT-S	FALLING-S	FECHTER-S
ESCALOP-S	EVACUEE-S	EXPOUND-S	FALLOFF-S	FEDARIE-S
ESCAPEE-S	EVANGEL-S	EXPULSE-S	FALLOUT-S	FEDERAL-S
ESCAPER-S	EVASION-S	EXPUNCT-S	FALSISM-S	FEEDBAG-S
ESCHEAT-S	EVENING-S	EXPUNGE-S	FAMILLE-S	FEEDING-S
ESCOLAR-S	EVENTER-S	EXPURGE-S	FANATIC-S	FEEDLOT-S
ESCRIBE-S	EVERNET-S	EXSCIND-S	FANBASE-S	FEELBAD-S
ESCROLL-S	EVERTOR-S	EXTERNE-S	FANCIER-S	FEELING-S
ESCUAGE-S	EVICTEE-S	EXTINCT-S	FANFARE-S	FEERING-S
ESERINE-S	EVICTOR-S	EXTRACT-S	FANFOLD-S	FEIGNER-S
ESLOYNE-S	EVIDENT-S	EXTRAIT-S	FANGLES-S	FELAFEL-S
ESPARTO-S	EVIRATE-S	EXTREAT-S	FANNELL-S	FELICIA-S
ESPOUSE-S	EVITATE-S	EXTREME-S	FANNING-S	FELLATE-S
ESQUIRE-S	EVOCATE-S	EXTRUDE-S	FANTAIL-S	FELSITE-S
ESSAYER-S	EVOLUTE-S	EXUDATE-S	FANTASM-S	FELSPAR-S
ESSENCE-S	EVOLVER-S	EXURBIA-S	FANTAST-S	FELTING-S
ESSOYNE-S	EXABYTE-S	EYEBALL-S	FANTEEG-S	FELUCCA-S
ESTHETE-S	EXACTER-S	EYEBANK-S	FANWORT-S	FELWORT-S
ESTOILE-S	EXACTOR-S	EYEBATH-S	FANZINE-S	FEMITER-S
ESTOVER-S	EXALTER-S	EYEBEAM-S	FARADAY-S	FENAGLE-S
ESTRADE-S	EXAMINE-S	EYEBOLT-S	FARAWAY-S	FENCING-S
ESTREAT-S	EXAMPLE-S	EYEBROW-S	FARCEUR-S	FENITAR-S
ESTREPE-S	EXCERPT-S	EYEFOLD-S	FARCING-S	FENLAND-S
ESTRIOL-S	EXCHEAT-S	EYEHOLE-S	FARDAGE-S	FENURON-S
ESTRONE-S	EXCIMER-S	EYEHOOK-S	FARDING-S	FEOFFEE-S
ETACISM-S	EXCIPLE-S	EYELIAD-S	FARINHA-S	FEOFFER-S
ETAERIO-S	EXCITER-S	EYELIFT-S	FARMING-S	FEOFFOR-S
ETAGERE-S	EXCITON-S	EYESHOT-S	FARRAGO-S	FERMATA-S
ETALAGE-S	EXCITOR-S	EYESORE-S	FARRIER-S	FERMENT-S
ETAMINE-S	EXCLAIM-S	EYESPOT-S	FARRUCA-S	FERMION-S
ETATISM-S	EXCLAVE-S	EYEWINK-S	FARSIDE-S	FERMIUM-S
ETCHANT-S	EXCLUDE-S	FABLING-S	FARTHEL-S	FERNING-S
ETCHING-S	EXCRETE-S	FACEBAR-S	FARTLEK-S	FERRATE-S
ETERNAL-S	EXCURSE-S	FACIEND-S	FASCINE-S	FERRITE-S
ETESIAN-S	EXCUSAL-S	FACTICE-S	FASCISM-S	FERRUGO-S
ETHANAL-S	EXCUSER-S	FACTION-S	FASCIST-S	FERRULE-S
ETHANOL-S	EXECUTE-S	FACTOID-S	FASHION-S	FERVOUR-S
ETHICAL-S	EXEGETE-S	FACTURE-S	FASTING-S	FESTOON-S
ETHINYL-S	EXEMPLE-S	FADAISE-S	FATBACK-S	FETCHER-S
ETHMOID-S	EXERGUE-S	FADDISM-S	FATBIRD-S	FETICHE-S
ETHOXYL-S	EXHAUST-S	FADDIST-S	FATHEAD-S	FETLOCK-S
ETHYNYL-S	EXHIBIT-S	FADEOUT-S	FATIGUE-S	FETTLER-S
ETIOLIN-S	EXHUMER-S	FAGGING-S	FATLING-S	FEUDING-S
ETRENNE-S	EXIGENT-S	FAGOTER-S	FATTISM-S	FEUDIST-S
EUCAINE-S	EXOCARP-S	FAHLORE-S	FATTIST-S	FIANCEE-S
EUCLASE-S	EXODERM-S	FAIENCE-S	FATWOOD-S	FIBROID-S
EUCRITE-S	EXODIST-S	FAILING-S	FAUCHON-S	FIBROIN-S
EUDEMON-S	EXOMION-S	FAILURE-S	FAUNIST-S	FIBROMA-S
EUGARIE-S	EXOTISM-S	FAINNES-S	FAUNULE-S	FIBROSE-S
EUGENIA-S	EXPANSE-S	FAINTER-S	FAUVISM-S	FIBSTER-S
EUGENIC-S	EXPENSE-S	FAIRING-S	FAUVIST-S	FICTION-S
EUGENOL-S	EXPIATE-S	FAIRWAY-S	FAVELLA-S	FIDDLER-S
EUGLENA-S	EXPIRER-S	FAITHER-S	FAVORER-S	FIDDLEY-S
EULOGIA-S	EXPLAIN-S	FAITOUR-S	FAVRILE-S	FIDEISM-S
EUPHROE-S	EXPLANT-S	FALAFEL-S	FAWNING-S	FIDEIST-S
EUPLOID-S	EXPLODE-S	FALBALA-S	FAYENCE-S	FIEFDOM-S
EUPNOEA-S	EXPLOIT-S	FALCADE-S	FAZENDA-S	FIELDER-S
EUSTELE-S	EXPLORE-S	FALCULA-S	FEASTER-S	FIFTEEN-S
EUSTYLE-S	EXPOSAL-S	FALDAGE-S	FEATHER-S	FIGHTER-S
EUTAXIA-S	EXPOSER-S		FEATURE-S	FIGMENT-S

FIGURER-S	FLANNEL-S	FLUERIC-S	FOOTWAY-S	FOXFIRE-S
FIGWORT-S	FLANNEN-S	FLUFFER-S	FOOZLER-S	FOXHOLE-S
FILABEG-S	FLAPPER-S	FLUIDIC-S	FOPLING-S	FOXHUNT-S
FILACER-S	FLAREUP-S	FLUNKER-S	FORAGER-S	FOXSHIP-S
FILAREE-S	FLASHER-S	FLUNKEY-S	FORAMEN-S	FOXSKIN-S
FILARIA-S	FLASKET-S	FLUNKIE-S	FORAYER-S	FOXTAIL-S
FILASSE-S	FLATBED-S	FLUORID-S	FORBEAR-S	FOXTROT-S
FILAZER-S	FLATCAP-S	FLUORIN-S	FORBODE-S	FOYBOAT-S
FILBERD-S	FLATCAR-S	FLUSHER-S	FOREARM-S	FRACTAL-S
FILBERT-S	FLATLET-S	FLUSTER-S	FOREBAY-S	FRACTUR-S
FILCHER-S	FLATTEN-S	FLUTINA-S	FORECAR-S	FRAENUM-S
FILEMOT-S	FLATTER-S	FLUTING-S	FOREGUT-S	FRAKTUR-S
FILIATE-S	FLATTIE-S	FLUTIST-S	FORELAY-S	FRAMING-S
FILIBEG-S	FLATTOP-S	FLUTTER-S	FORELEG-S	FRANGER-S
FILLING-S	FLAUGHT-S	FLUXION-S	FORELIE-S	FRANION-S
FILMDOM-S	FLAVINE-S	FLYAWAY-S	FOREPAW-S	FRANKER-S
FILMSET-S	FLAVONE-S	FLYBACK-S	FORERUN-S	FRAUGHT-S
FINAGLE-S	FLAVOUR-S	FLYBANE-S	FORESAY-S	FRAWZEY-S
FINANCE-S	FLEABAG-S	FLYBELT-S	FORESEE-S	FRAYING-S
FINBACK-S	FLEAPIT-S	FLYBLOW-S	FORETOP-S	FRAZZLE-S
FINDING-S	FLECKER-S	FLYBOAT-S	FOREVER-S	FRECKLE-S
FINDRAM-S	FLEECER-S	FLYBOOK-S	FORFAIR-S	FREEBEE-S
FINESSE-S	FLEECIE-S	FLYHAND-S	FORFEIT-S	FREEBIE-S
FINFOOT-S	FLEERER-S	FLYOVER-S	FORFEND-S	FREEDOM-S
FINMARK-S	FLEHMEN-S	FLYPAST-S	FORGING-S	FREEGAN-S
FINNACK-S	FLENSER-S	FLYTIER-S	FORGIVE-S	FREESIA-S
FINNOCK-S	FLESHER-S	FLYTING-S	FORGOER-S	FREEWAY-S
FIREARM-S	FLETTON-S	FLYTRAP-S	FORHENT-S	FREEZER-S
FIREBUG-S	FLEURET-S	FOAMING-S	FORKFUL-S	FREIGHT-S
FIREDOG-S	FLEURON-S	FOCUSER-S	FORLANA-S	FRESHEN-S
FIREPAN-S	FLEXION-S	FOGGAGE-S	FORLEND-S	FRESHER-S
FIREPOT-S	FLEXURE-S	FOGHORN-S	FORLESE-S	FRESHET-S
FIRRING-S	FLICKER-S	FOGYDOM-S	FORLORN-S	FRESHIE-S
FISHEYE-S	FLINDER-S	FOGYISM-S	FORMANT-S	FRESNEL-S
FISHGIG-S	FLINGER-S	FOILING-S	FORMATE-S	FRETSAW-S
FISHING-S	FLIPPER-S	FOISTER-S	FORMICA-S	FRETTER-S
FISHNET-S	FLIRTER-S	FOLACIN-S	FORMING-S	FRIANDE-S
FISHWAY-S	FLITTER-S	FOLDING-S	FORMULA-S	FRIBBLE-S
FISSION-S	FLIVVER-S	FOLDOUT-S	FORPINE-S	FRIGATE-S
FISSURE-S	FLOATEL-S	FOLIAGE-S	FORSAKE-S	FRIGGER-S
FISTFUL-S	FLOATER-S	FOLIATE-S	FORSLOE-S	FRIJOLE-S
FISTULA-S	FLOGGER-S	FOLIOLE-S	FORSLOW-S	FRILLER-S
FITCHET-S	FLOKATI-S	FOLKMOT-S	FORTLET-S	FRIPPER-S
FITCHEW-S	FLOODER-S	FOLKWAY-S	FORTUNE-S	FRIPPET-S
FITMENT-S	FLOORER-S	FONDANT-S	FORWARD-S	FRISBEE-S
FITTING-S	FLOOSIE-S	FONDLER-S	FORWARN-S	FRISEUR-S
FIVEPIN-S	FLOOZIE-S	FONTINA-S	FORZATO-S	FRISKER-S
FIXATIF-S	FLOPPER-S	FONTLET-S	FOSSICK-S	FRISKET-S
FIXTURE-S	FLORIST-S	FOODISM-S	FOUDRIE-S	FRISSON-S
FIZZGIG-S	FLORULE-S	FOOLING-S	FOUETTE-S	FRISURE-S
FIZZING-S	FLOSSER-S	FOOTAGE-S	FOUGADE-S	FRITTER-S
FLACKER-S	FLOSSIE-S	FOOTBAG-S	FOULARD-S	FRITURE-S
FLACKET-S	FLOTAGE-S	FOOTBAR-S	FOULDER-S	FRIZZER-S
FLAFFER-S	FLOTSAM-S	FOOTBOY-S	FOULING-S	FRIZZLE-S
FLAGGER-S	FLOUNCE-S	FOOTING-S	FOUMART-S	FROGBIT-S
FLAMBEE-S	FLOUTER-S	FOOTLER-S	FOUNDER-S	FROGEYE-S
FLAMFEW-S	FLOWAGE-S	FOOTLES-S	FOURGON-S	FROGLET-S
FLANEUR-S	FLUBBER-S	FOOTPAD-S	FOVEOLA-S	FROMAGE-S
FLANGER-S	FLUBDUB-S	FOOTROT-S	FOVEOLE-S	FRONTAL-S
FLANKER-S	FLUENCE-S	FOOTSIE-S	FOWLING-S	FRONTON-S

FROSTED-S	GADWALL-S	GARROTE-S	GETTING-S	GLOBULE-S
FROTHER-S	GAFFING-S	GARVOCK-S	GHARIAL-S	GLOCHID-S
FROUNCE-S	GAGSTER-S	GASAHOL-S	GHERKIN-S	GLONOIN-S
FROWARD-S	GAHNITE-S	GASKING-S	GHILGAI-S	GLOSSER-S
FROWNER-S	GAINING-S	GASOHOL-S	GHILLIE-S	GLOVING-S
FRUCTAN-S	GAINSAY-S	GASPING-S	GHOULIE-S	GLOZING-S
FRUITER-S	GALABEA-S	GASSING-S	GIARDIA-S	GLUCINA-S
FRUMPLE-S	GALABIA-S	GASTREA-S	GIGABIT-S	GLUCOSE-S
FRUSTUM-S	GALANGA-S	GASTRIN-S	GIGATON-S	GLUEPOT-S
FUCHSIA-S	GALATEA-S	GATEWAY-S	GIGGLER-S	GLUTTON-S
FUCHSIN-S	GALETTE-S	GAUDGIE-S	GILBERT-S	GLYCINE-S
FUCKING-S	GALILEE-S	GAUFFER-S	GILDING-S	GLYCOSE-S
FUCKOFF-S	GALIPOT-S	GAUGING-S	GILLION-S	GLYPTAL-S
FUCKWIT-S	GALLANT-S	GAULTER-S	GILLNET-S	GLYPTIC-S
FUDDLER-S	GALLATE-S	GAVOTTE-S	GILTCUP-S	GNASHER-S
FUEHRER-S	GALLEIN-S	GAZANIA-S	GIMMICK-S	GNAWING-S
FUELLER-S	GALLEON-S	GAZELLE-S	GINGALL-S	GNOCCHI-S
FUGUIST-S	GALLETA-S	GAZETTE-S	GINGELI-S	GNOMIST-S
FULCRUM-S	GALLICA-S	GAZOOKA-S	GINGHAM-S	GNOSTIC-S
FULFILL-S	GALLIOT-S	GEARING-S	GINGILI-S	GOBBLER-S
FULGOUR-S	GALLISE-S	GEDECKT-S	GINNING-S	GOBIOID-S
FULLAGE-S	GALLIUM-S	GEEBUNG-S	GINSENG-S	GOBURRA-S
FULMINE-S	GALLIZE-S	GEECHEE-S	GINSHOP-S	GODDAMN-S
FUMBLER-S	GALLNUT-S	GEEKDOM-S	GIRAFFE-S	GODETIA-S
FUMETTE-S	GALLOON-S	GEELBEK-S	GIRASOL-S	GODHEAD-S
FUNCTOR-S	GALLOOT-S	GELATIN-S	GIRDING-S	GODHOOD-S
FUNDING-S	GALOCHE-S	GELDING-S	GIRDLER-S	GODLING-S
FUNERAL-S	GALOPIN-S	GELLANT-S	GIRLOND-S	GODROON-S
FUNFAIR-S	GALOSHE-S	GEMCLIP-S	GIROLLE-S	GODSEND-S
FUNFEST-S	GALUMPH-S	GEMMATE-S	GIROSOL-S	GODSHIP-S
FUNGOID-S	GAMBADE-S	GEMMULE-S	GISARME-S	GODSLOT-S
FUNICLE-S	GAMBADO-S	GEMSBOK-S	GITTERN-S	GODWARD-S
FUNSTER-S	GAMBIER-S	GENAPPE-S	GIZZARD-S	GOGGLER-S
FURCATE-S	GAMBIST-S	GENERAL-S	GJETOST-S	GOLDARN-S
FURFAIR-S	GAMBLER-S	GENERIC-S	GLACIAL-S	GOLDBUG-S
FURIOSO-S	GAMBOGE-S	GENETIC-S	GLACIER-S	GOLDEYE-S
FURLANA-S	GAMBREL-S	GENETTE-S	GLADDEN-S	GOLDURN-S
FURLONG-S	GAMELAN-S	GENIPAP-S	GLADDIE-S	GOLFING-S
FURNACE-S	GAMINES-S	GENISTA-S	GLADDON-S	GOLIARD-S
FURRIER-S	GAMMOCK-S	GENITAL-S	GLAIRIN-S	GOLIATH-S
FURRING-S	GANACHE-S	GENITOR-S	GLAMOUR-S	GOLLAND-S
FURTHER-S	GANGING-S	GENIZAH-S	GLANCER-S	GOLOSHE-S
FUSAROL-S	GANGREL-S	GENLOCK-S	GLASSIE-S	GOMBEEN-S
FUSHION-S	GANGSTA-S	GENOISE-S	GLAZIER-S	GOMERAL-S
FUSILLI-S	GANGWAY-S	GENOMIC-S	GLAZING-S	GOMEREL-S
FUSSPOT-S	GANOINE-S	GENSENG-S	GLEAMER-S	GOMERIL-S
FUSTIAN-S	GANTLET-S	GENTIAN-S	GLEANER-S	GONDOLA-S
FUTCHEL-S	GARBAGE-S	GENTILE-S	GLEENIE-S	GONOPOD-S
FUTHARC-S	GARBLER-S	GEODUCK-S	GLENOID-S	GOODBYE-S
FUTHARK-S	GARBLES-S	GEOFACT-S	GLEYING-S	GOOMBAH-S
FUTHORC-S	GARBOIL-S	GEOMANT-S	GLIADIN-S	GOOMBAY-S
FUTHORK-S	GARBURE-S	GEORGIC-S	GLIDING-S	GOPURAM-S
FUTTOCK-S	GARDANT-S	GERBERA-S	GLIMMER-S	GORCOCK-S
GABBARD-S	GARGLER-S	GERENUK-S	GLIMPSE-S	GORCROW-S
GABBART-S	GARIGUE-S	GERMAIN-S	GLISTEN-S	GORDITA-S
GABBLER-S	GARLAND-S	GERMANS-S	GLISTER-S	GORILLA-S
GABELLE-S	GARMENT-S	GESTALT-S	GLITTER-S	GORMAND-S
GABFEST-S	GAROTTE-S	GESTAPO-S	GLOATER-S	GORSEDD-S
GADLING-S	GAROUPA-S	GESTATE-S	GLOBOID-S	GORSOON-S
GADROON-S	GARPIKE-S	GESTURE-S	GLOBOSE-S	GOSHAWK-S

GOSLING-S	GREENER-S	GRYSBOK-S	GYMNAST-S	HAMMADA-S
GOSPORT-S	GREENIE-S	GUANACO-S	GYMSLIP-S	HAMMOCK-S
GOSSOON-S	GREENTH-S	GUANASE-S	GYPLURE-S	HAMSTER-S
GOTHITE-S	GREETER-S	GUANINE-S	GYPSTER-S	HANAPER-S
GOUACHE-S	GREGALE-S	GUARANA-S	GYRATOR-S	HANDBAG-S
GOUGERE-S	GREISEN-S	GUARANI-S	GYROCAR-S	HANDCAR-S
GOURAMI-S	GREMIAL-S	GUARDEE-S	HABITAN-S	HANDFUL-S
GOURMET-S	GREMLIN-S	GUARDER-S	HABITAT-S	HANDGUN-S
GOWLAND-S	GREMMIE-S	GUAYULE-S	HABITUE-S	HANDISM-S
GOWNBOY-S	GRENADE-S	GUDGEON-S	HACHURE-S	HANDJAR-S
GRABBER-S	GREYHEN-S	GUERDON-S	HACKBUT-S	HANDLER-S
GRABBLE-S	GREYING-S	GUEREZA-S	HACKING-S	HANDLES-S
GRACILE-S	GREYLAG-S	GUERITE-S	HACKLER-S	HANDOFF-S
GRACKLE-S	GRIBBLE-S	GUESSER-S	HACKLET-S	HANDOUT-S
GRADATE-S	GRICING-S	GUESTEN-S	HACKNEY-S	HANDSAW-S
GRADDAN-S	GRIDDER-S	GUICHET-S	HACKSAW-S	HANDSEL-S
GRADINE-S	GRIDDLE-S	GUIDAGE-S	HADEDAH-S	HANDSET-S
GRADUAL-S	GRIEFER-S	GUIDING-S	HADROME-S	HANGDOG-S
GRAFTER-S	GRIEVER-S	GUILDER-S	HAFFLIN-S	HANGING-S
GRAINER-S	GRIFFIN-S	GUIPURE-S	HAFNIUM-S	HANGOUT-S
GRAMMAR-S	GRIFFON-S	GUISARD-S	HAFTARA-S	HANGTAG-S
GRANDAD-S	GRIFTER-S	GUISING-S	HAGBOLT-S	HANUMAN-S
GRANDAM-S	GRILLER-S	GUMBALL-S	HAGDOWN-S	HAPKIDO-S
GRANDEE-S	GRIMACE-S	GUMBOIL-S	HAGGADA-S	HAPLITE-S
GRANDMA-S	GRINDER-S	GUMBOOT-S	HAGGARD-S	HAPLOID-S
GRANDPA-S	GRINNER-S	GUMDROP-S	HAGGLER-S	HAPLONT-S
GRANFER-S	GRIPPER-S	GUMLINE-S	HAGRIDE-S	HAPTENE-S
GRANGER-S	GRIPPLE-S	GUMMING-S	HAHNIUM-S	HARAMDA-S
GRANITA-S	GRISKIN-S	GUMMITE-S	HAINING-S	HARAMDI-S
GRANITE-S	GRISTER-S	GUMMOSE-S	HAIRCAP-S	HARBOUR-S
GRANNAM-S	GRISTLE-S	GUMSHOE-S	HAIRCUT-S	HARDBAG-S
GRANNIE-S	GRITTER-S	GUMTREE-S	HAIRNET-S	HARDHAT-S
GRANNOM-S	GRIZZLE-S	GUMWEED-S	HAIRPIN-S	HARDOKE-S
GRANOLA-S	GROANER-S	GUMWOOD-S	HALACHA-S	HARDPAN-S
GRANTEE-S	GROCKLE-S	GUNBOAT-S	HALAKAH-S	HARDTOP-S
GRANTER-S	GROGRAM-S	GUNFIRE-S	HALAKHA-S	HARELIP-S
GRANTOR-S	GROMMET-S	GUNLOCK-S	HALALAH-S	HARIANA-S
GRANULE-S	GROOMER-S	GUNNAGE-S	HALAVAH-S	HARICOT-S
GRAPHIC-S	GROOVER-S	GUNNERA-S	HALBERD-S	HARIJAN-S
GRAPLIN-S	GROSERT-S	GUNNING-S	HALBERT-S	HARISSA-S
GRAPNEL-S	GROSSER-S	GUNPLAY-S	HALCYON-S	HARLING-S
GRAPPLE-S	GROUPER-S	GUNPORT-S	HALFLIN-S	HARMALA-S
GRASPER-S	GROUPIE-S	GUNROOM-S	HALFWIT-S	HARMINE-S
GRASSER-S	GROUSER-S	GUNSHIP-S	HALIBUT-S	HARMOST-S
GRASSUM-S	GROUTER-S	GUNSHOT-S	HALIDOM-S	HAROSET-S
GRATING-S	GROWING-S	GUNWALE-S	HALIMOT-S	HARPING-S
GRAUPEL-S	GROWLER-S	GURGLET-S	HALLALI-S	HARPIST-S
GRAVIDA-S	GROWNUP-S	GURNARD-S	HALLIAN-S	HARPOON-S
GRAVING-S	GRUBBER-S	GURRIER-S	HALLING-S	HARRIER-S
GRAVURE-S	GRUBBLE-S	GURUDOM-S	HALLION-S	HARSHEN-S
GRAYLAG-S	GRUDGER-S	GURUISM-S	HALLWAY-S	HARSLET-S
GRAYOUT-S	GRUELER-S	GUTCHER-S	HALLYON-S	HARUMPH-S
GRAZIER-S	GRUMBLE-S	GUTSFUL-S	HALOGEN-S	HARVEST-S
GRAZING-S	GRUMMET-S	GUTTATE-S	HALOUMI-S	HASBIAN-S
GREASER-S	GRUNGER-S	GUTTLER-S	HALTERE-S	HASSIUM-S
GREATEN-S	GRUNION-S	GUYLINE-S	HALTING-S	HASSOCK-S
GRECIAN-S	GRUNTER-S	GUZZLER-S	HALYARD-S	HASTING-S
GRECISE-S	GRUNTLE-S	GWEDUCK-S	HAMBONE-S	HATBAND-S
GRECIZE-S	GRUYERE-S	GWINIAD-S	HAMBURG-S	HATCHEL-S
GRECQUE-S	GRYPHON-S	GWYNIAD-S	HAMBURG-S	HATCHER-S

HATCHET-S	HELICON-S	HILLOCK-S	HOOSGOW-S	HURDLER-S
HATRACK-S	HELIPAD-S	HILLTOP-S	HOPBIND-S	HURLBAT-S
HATTING-S	HELLCAT-S	HINDGUT-S	HOPBINE-S	HURLING-S
HATTOCK-S	HELLERI-S	HINDLEG-S	HOPEFUL-S	HURRIER-S
HAUBERK-S	HELLIER-S	HINTING-S	HOPHEAD-S	HURTLES-S
HAULAGE-S	HELLION-S	HIPBONE-S	HOPLITE-S	HUSBAND-S
HAULIER-S	HELPING-S	HIPLINE-S	HOPPING-S	HUSKING-S
HAUNTER-S	HEMAGOG-S	HIPPING-S	HOPPLER-S	HUSTLER-S
HAUTBOY-S	HEMATIC-S	HIPSTER-S	HOPSACK-S	HUSWIFE-S
HAUTEUR-S	HEMATIN-S	HIREAGE-S	HOPTOAD-S	HUTCHIE-S
HAVARTI-S	HEMIOLA-S	HIRLING-S	HORDEIN-S	HUTMENT-S
HAVEOUR-S	HEMIONE-S	HIRUDIN-S	HORDOCK-S	HUTTING-S
HAVEREL-S	HEMIPOD-S	HISSING-S	HORIZON-S	HUTZPAH-S
HAVIOUR-S	HEMLINE-S	HISTONE-S	HORMONE-S	HYACINE-S
HAWBUCK-S	HEMLOCK-S	HISTRIO-S	HORNBAG-S	HYALINE-S
HAWKBIT-S	HENBANE-S	HITCHER-S	HORNBUG-S	HYALITE-S
HAWKING-S	HENCOOP-S	HOARDER-S	HORNFUL-S	HYALOID-S
HAYBAND-S	HENPECK-S	HOARSEN-S	HORNING-S	HYDATID-S
HAYCOCK-S	HEPARIN-S	HOATZIN-S	HORNIST-S	HYDRANT-S
HAYFORK-S	HEPATIC-S	HOBBLER-S	HORNITO-S	HYDRASE-S
HAYLAGE-S	HEPSTER-S	HOBNAIL-S	HORNLET-S	HYDRATE-S
HAYLOFT-S	HEPTANE-S	HOBODOM-S	HORSING-S	HYDRIDE-S
HAYRACK-S	HEPTOSE-S	HOBOISM-S	HOSANNA-S	HYDROID-S
HAYRICK-S	HERBAGE-S	HOECAKE-S	HOSPICE-S	HYDROMA-S
HAYRIDE-S	HERBIST-S	HOEDOWN-S	HOSTAGE-S	HYGEIST-S
HAYSEED-S	HERBLET-S	HOGBACK-S	HOSTILE-S	HYGIENE-S
HAYWARD-S	HERDBOY-S	HOGGING-S	HOSTING-S	HYGROMA-S
HAYWIRE-S	HERETIC-S	HOGHOOD-S	HOSTLER-S	HYLDING-S
HEADAGE-S	HERITOR-S	HOGMANE-S	HOTCAKE-S	HYLOIST-S
HEADEND-S	HERLING-S	HOGNOSE-S	HOTFOOT-S	HYMNIST-S
HEADFUL-S	HEROINE-S	HOGWARD-S	HOTHEAD-S	HYPERON-S
HEADING-S	HEROISE-S	HOGWEED-S	HOTLINE-S	HYPNONE-S
HEADPIN-S	HEROISM-S	HOISTER-S	HOTLINK-S	HYPONEA-S
HEADRIG-S	HEROIZE-S	HOKONUI-S	HOTSHOT-S	HYPONYM-S
HEADSET-S	HERRING-S	HOLDALL-S	HOTSPOT-S	HYPOXIA-S
HEADWAY-S	HERSALL-S	HOLDING-S	HOTSPUR-S	IAMBIST-S
HEALING-S	HERSHIP-S	HOLDOUT-S	HOTTING-S	ICEBALL-S
HEARING-S	HESSIAN-S	HOLIBUT-S	HOUNDER-S	ICEBERG-S
HEARKEN-S	HESSITE-S	HOLIDAY-S	HOUNGAN-S	ICEBOAT-S
HEARSAY-S	HETAERA-S	HOLLAND-S	HOUSING-S	ICEFALL-S
HEARTEN-S	HETAIRA-S	HOLMIUM-S	HOUTING-S	ICEPACK-S
HEATHEN-S	HEUREKA-S	HOLSTER-S	HOVERER-S	ICEWINE-S
HEATHER-S	HEURISM-S	HOLYDAM-S	HOWLING-S	ICHNITE-S
HEATING-S	HEXAGON-S	HOLYDAY-S	HRYVNIA-S	ICONISE-S
HEAVING-S	HEXAPLA-S	HOMAGER-S	HRYVNYA-S	ICONIZE-S
HEBENON-S	HEXAPOD-S	HOMBURG-S	HUANACO-S	ICTERIC-S
HECKLER-S	HEXEREI-S	HOMEBOY-S	HUDDLER-S	ICTERID-S
HECTARE-S	HEXOSAN-S	HOMELYN-S	HUFFING-S	IDLESSE-S
HEDGING-S	HEYDUCK-S	HOMINES-S	HUFFKIN-S	IDOLISE-S
HEDONIC-S	HIBACHI-S	HOMINID-S	HUITAIN-S	IDOLISM-S
HEELING-S	HICATEE-S	HOMMOCK-S	HUMBLER-S	IDOLIST-S
HEELTAP-S	HIDALGA-S	HOMOLOG-S	HUMDRUM-S	IDOLIZE-S
HEGEMON-S	HIDALGO-S	HOMONYM-S	HUMERAL-S	IDYLIST-S
HEGUMEN-S	HIDEOUT-S	HONOREE-S	HUMIDOR-S	IGARAPE-S
HEIGHTH-S	HIDLING-S	HONORER-S	HUMMAUM-S	IGNATIA-S
HEIRDOM-S	HIGGLER-S	HOOCHIE-S	HUMMING-S	IGNITER-S
HEISTER-S	HIGHBOY-S	HOODLUM-S	HUMMOCK-S	IGNITOR-S
HEITIKI-S	HIGHTOP-S	HOOFROT-S	HUMOGEN-S	IGNORER-S
HEKTARE-S	HIGHWAY-S	HOOKLET-S	HUNDRED-S	IGUANID-S
HELIAST-S	HILDING-S	HOOLOCK-S	HUNTING-S	IJTIHAD-S

IKEBANA-S	INCIPIT-S	INITIAL-S	INVOICE-S	JACKLEG-S
ILKADAY-S	INCISOR-S	INJOINT-S	INVOKER-S	JACKPOT-S
ILLAPSE-S	INCITER-S	INJUNCT-S	INVOLVE-S	JACKSIE-S
ILLEGAL-S	INCLASP-S	INJURER-S	INWEAVE-S	JACOBIN-S
ILLOGIC-S	INCLINE-S	INKBLOT-S	IODISER-S	JACONET-S
IMAGINE-S	INCLOSE-S	INKHORN-S	IODIZER-S	JACUZZI-S
IMAGING-S	INCLUDE-S	INKLING-S	IODURET-S	JADEITE-S
IMAGISM-S	INCOMER-S	INKSPOT-S	IONISER-S	JAGHIRE-S
IMAGIST-S	INCONNU-S	INKWELL-S	IONIZER-S	JALAPIN-S
IMAMATE-S	INCRUST-S	INKWOOD-S	IONOGEN-S	JALOUSE-S
IMBATHE-S	INCURVE-S	INLAYER-S	IONOMER-S	JAMADAR-S
IMBIBER-S	INDAMIN-S	INNERVE-S	IPOMOEA-S	JAMBART-S
IMBLAZE-S	INDEXER-S	INNYARD-S	IRIDISE-S	JAMBIER-S
IMBOSOM-S	INDICAN-S	INOSINE-S	IRIDIUM-S	JAMBIYA-S
IMBOWER-S	INDICIA-S	INOSITE-S	IRIDIZE-S	JAMBONE-S
IMBROWN-S	INDIGEN-S	INQILAB-S	IRISATE-S	JAMBOOL-S
IMBRUTE-S	INDITER-S	INQUERE-S	IRONING-S	JAMDANI-S
IMBURSE-S	INDORSE-S	INQUEST-S	IRONISE-S	JAMPANI-S
IMITANT-S	INDOXYL-S	INQUIET-S	IRONIST-S	JANGLER-S
IMITATE-S	INDRAFT-S	INQUIRE-S	IRONIZE-S	JANITOR-S
IMMERGE-S	INDUCER-S	INSANIE-S	ISAGOGE-S	JANIZAR-S
IMMERSE-S	INDULGE-S	INSCAPE-S	ISATINE-S	JANNOCK-S
IMPAINT-S	INDULIN-S	INSCULP-S	ISOAMYL-S	JARGOON-S
IMPALER-S	INDWELL-S	INSHELL-S	ISOBARE-S	JARHEAD-S
IMPANEL-S	INEARTH-S	INSIDER-S	ISOBASE-S	JARLDOM-S
IMPASSE-S	INERTIA-S	INSIGHT-S	ISOBATH-S	JARRING-S
IMPASTE-S	INFANTA-S	INSINEW-S	ISOCHOR-S	JASMINE-S
IMPASTO-S	INFANTE-S	INSNARE-S	ISODONT-S	JAUNTIE-S
IMPEARL-S	INFARCT-S	INSPECT-S	ISODOSE-S	JAVELIN-S
IMPEDER-S	INFAUNA-S	INSPIRE-S	ISOFORM-S	JAWBONE-S
IMPEDOR-S	INFEOFF-S	INSTALL-S	ISOGONE-S	JAWFALL-S
IMPERIL-S	INFERNO-S	INSTANT-S	ISOGRAM-S	JAWHOLE-S
IMPINGE-S	INFIDEL-S	INSTATE-S	ISOGRIV-S	JAWLINE-S
IMPLANT-S	INFIELD-S	INSTILL-S	ISOHYET-S	JAYBIRD-S
IMPLATE-S	INFIGHT-S	INSULAR-S	ISOKONT-S	JAYWALK-S
IMPLEAD-S	INFIMUM-S	INSULIN-S	ISOLATE-S	JEEPNEY-S
IMPLETE-S	INFLAME-S	INSURED-S	ISOLEAD-S	JEERING-S
IMPLODE-S	INFLATE-S	INSURER-S	ISOLINE-S	JELLABA-S
IMPLORE-S	INFLECT-S	INSWING-S	ISOMERE-S	JEMADAR-S
IMPOSER-S	INFLICT-S	INTEGER-S	ISONOME-S	JEMIDAR-S
IMPOUND-S	INFORCE-S	INTERIM-S	ISOPACH-S	JEOFAIL-S
IMPOWER-S	INFRACT-S	INTERNE-S	ISOSPIN-S	JEOPARD-S
IMPREGN-S	INFUSER-S	INTHRAL-S	ISOTACH-S	JERKING-S
IMPRESA-S	INGENER-S	INTITLE-S	ISOTONE-S	JERQUER-S
IMPRESE-S	INGENUE-S	INTONER-S	ISOTOPE-S	JERREED-S
IMPREST-S	INGLOBE-S	INTRADA-S	ISOTRON-S	JESTING-S
IMPRINT-S	INGOING-S	INTRANT-S	ISOTYPE-S	JETBEAD-S
IMPROVE-S	INGRAFT-S	INTREAT-S	ISOZYME-S	JETFOIL-S
IMPULSE-S	INGRAIN-S	INTROIT-S	ITACISM-S	JETPORT-S
IMPUTER-S	INGRATE-S	INTRUDE-S	ITCHING-S	JEWELER-S
INBEING-S	INGROUP-S	INTRUST-S	ITEMISE-S	JEZEBEL-S
INBOARD-S	INGULPH-S	INTWINE-S	ITEMIZE-S	JIBBING-S
INBOUND-S	INHABIT-S	INTWIST-S	ITERATE-S	JIBBOOM-S
INBREAK-S	INHALER-S	INULASE-S	IVORIST-S	JIGABOO-S
INBREED-S	INHAUST-S	INVADER-S	IVRESSE-S	JIGAJIG-S
INBRING-S	INHERCE-S	INVALID-S	JACAMAR-S	JIGAJOG-S
INBURST-S	INHERIT-S	INVEIGH-S	JACINTH-S	JIGGING-S
INCENSE-S	INHIBIN-S	INVERSE-S	JACKDAW-S	JILLION-S
INCHASE-S	INHIBIT-S	INVITEE-S	JACKEEN-S	JINGALL-S
INCHPIN-S	INHUMER-S	INVITER-S	JACKING-S	JINGLER-S

JINGLET-S	KAMICHI-S	KHAMSIN-S	KNAPPLE-S	LADYBUG-S
JINJILI-S	KAMPONG-S	KHANATE-S	KNEADER-S	LADYCOW-S
JIPYAPA-S	KAMSEEN-S	KHANJAR-S	KNEECAP-S	LADYISM-S
JOBBING-S	KANTELA-S	KHEDIVA-S	KNEELER-S	LADYKIN-S
JOBNAME-S	KANTELE-S	KHEDIVE-S	KNEEPAD-S	LAETARE-S
JOCKNEY-S	KAOLINE-S	KHIRKAH-S	KNEEPAN-S	LAGGARD-S
JODHPUR-S	KARAISM-S	KHOTBAH-S	KNESSET-S	LAGGING-S
JOGGING-S	KARAKIA-S	KHOTBEH-S	KNEVELL-S	LAICISE-S
JOGGLER-S	KARAKUL-S	KHUTBAH-S	KNICKER-S	LAICISM-S
JOGTROT-S	KARANGA-S	KIBITKA-S	KNIFING-S	LAICIZE-S
JOHNNIE-S	KARAOKE-S	KICKOFF-S	KNITTER-S	LAIRAGE-S
JOHNSON-S	KARENGO-S	KIDDIER-S	KNITTLE-S	LAIRISE-S
JOINDER-S	KAROSHI-S	KIDLING-S	KNOBBER-S	LAIRIZE-S
JOINING-S	KARTING-S	KIDSKIN-S	KNOBBLE-S	LAKEBED-S
JOINTER-S	KASHMIR-S	KIESTER-S	KNOCKER-S	LAKELET-S
JOLLIER-S	KASHRUT-S	KIKUMON-S	KNOLLER-S	LALIQUE-S
JOLLYER-S	KATCINA-S	KILLCOW-S	KNOTTER-S	LALLAND-S
JONQUIL-S	KATHODE-S	KILLDEE-S	KNOWHOW-S	LALLING-S
JOSTLER-S	KATORGA-S	KILLICK-S	KNOWING-S	LAMBADA-S
JOTTING-S	KATSURA-S	KILLING-S	KNUBBLE-S	LAMBAST-S
JOURNAL-S	KATYDID-S	KILLJOY-S	KNUCKLE-S	LAMBERT-S
JOURNEY-S	KAUPAPA-S	KILLOCK-S	KOFTGAR-S	LAMBING-S
JOUSTER-S	KAYAKER-S	KILOBAR-S	KOKANEE-S	LAMBKIN-S
JOYANCE-S	KAYOING-S	KILOBIT-S	KOKOWAI-S	LAMELLA-S
JOYRIDE-S	KEBBOCK-S	KILORAD-S	KOLBASI-S	LAMETER-S
JUBILEE-S	KEBBUCK-S	KILOTON-S	KOMATIK-S	LAMIGER-S
JUDOIST-S	KEELAGE-S	KILTING-S	KOPIYKA-S	LAMINAL-S
JUGGING-S	KEELING-S	KIMCHEE-S	KOTOWER-S	LAMININ-S
JUGGLER-S	KEELSON-S	KINCHIN-S	KOUPREY-S	LAMITER-S
JUGHEAD-S	KEENING-S	KINDLER-S	KREMLIN-S	LAMMING-S
JUGULAR-S	KEEPING-S	KINDLES-S	KREUZER-S	LAMPERN-S
JUJITSU-S	KEEPNET-S	KINDRED-S	KRIMMER-S	LAMPING-S
JUJUISM-S	KEESTER-S	KINESIC-S	KRULLER-S	LAMPION-S
JUJUIST-S	KEGELER-S	KINETIC-S	KRYPTON-S	LAMPOON-S
JUJUTSU-S	KEGLING-S	KINETIN-S	KRYTRON-S	LAMPREY-S
JUKSKEI-S	KEISTER-S	KINFOLK-S	KUFIYAH-S	LAMPUKA-S
JUMBLER-S	KEITLOA-S	KINGCUP-S	KUMQUAT-S	LAMPUKI-S
JUMBUCK-S	KELLAUT-S	KINGDOM-S	KUNZITE-S	LAMSTER-S
JUMELLE-S	KEMPING-S	KINGLES-S	KURSAAL-S	LANDING-S
JUMPING-S	KENNETT-S	KINGLET-S	KYANISE-S	LANDLER-S
JUMPOFF-S	KENNING-S	KINGPIN-S	KYANITE-S	LANEWAY-S
JUNCATE-S	KERAMIC-S	KINSHIP-S	KYANIZE-S	LANGAHA-S
JUNIPER-S	KERATIN-S	KIPPAGE-S	LABARUM-S	LANGLEY-S
JUSSIVE-S	KERBAYA-S	KIPSKIN-S	LABELER-S	LANGREL-S
JUSTICE-S	KERBING-S	KIRIMON-S	LABIATE-S	LANGUET-S
JUVENAL-S	KERNING-S	KIRKING-S	LABORER-S	LANGUOR-S
KABADDI-S	KERNITE-S	KIRKTON-S	LABROID-S	LANIARD-S
KABBALA-S	KEROGEN-S	KISTFUL-S	LACQUER-S	LANITAL-S
KACHCHA-S	KERYGMA-S	KITCHEN-S	LACQUEY-S	LANOLIN-S
KACHERA-S	KESTREL-S	KITENGE-S	LACTASE-S	LANTANA-S
KACHERI-S	KETCHUP-S	KITHARA-S	LACTATE-S	LANTERN-S
KACHINA-S	KETUBAH-S	KITLING-S	LACTEAL-S	LANYARD-S
KAGOULE-S	KEYCARD-S	KLAVERN-S	LACTONE-S	LAPPING-S
KAHAWAI-S	KEYHOLE-S	KLAVIER-S	LACTOSE-S	LAPSANG-S
KAINITE-S	KEYLINE-S	KLEAGLE-S	LACUNAR-S	LAPTRAY-S
KAJAWAH-S	KEYNOTE-S	KLEZMER-S	LADANUM-S	LAPWING-S
KAJEPUT-S	KEYSTER-S	KLINKER-S	LADETTE-S	LAPWORK-S
KAKODYL-S	KEYWORD-S	KLISTER-S	LADHOOD-S	LARDOON-S
KALIMBA-S	KHADDAR-S	KNACKER-S	LADRONE-S	LARMIER-S
KAMERAD-S	KHALIFA-S	KNAPPER-S	LADYBOY-S	LASAGNA-S

LASAGNE-S	LEGATOR-S	LIGNOSE-S	LOCATOR-S	LULIBUB-S
LASHING-S	LEGGING-S	LIGROIN-S	LOCKAGE-S	LUMBAGO-S
LASHKAR-S	LEGGISM-S	LIMACEL-S	LOCKFUL-S	LUMBANG-S
LASSOCK-S	LEGHORN-S	LIMACON-S	LOCKING-S	LUMPKIN-S
LASSOER-S	LEGITIM-S	LIMBECK-S	LOCKJAW-S	LUNATIC-S
LASTAGE-S	LEGROOM-S	LIMEADE-S	LOCKNUT-S	LUNCHER-S
LASTING-S	LEGUAAN-S	LIMEPIT-S	LOCKOUT-S	LUNETTE-S
LATAKIA-S	LEGUMIN-S	LIMITED-S	LOCKRAM-S	LUNGFUL-S
LATCHET-S	LEGWEAR-S	LIMITER-S	LOCKSET-S	LUPANAR-S
LATENCE-S	LEGWORK-S	LIMPING-S	LOCOISM-S	LUPULIN-S
LATERAL-S	LEHAYIM-S	LIMPKIN-S	LODGING-S	LURCHER-S
LATHING-S	LEIDGER-S	LINALOL-S	LOGANIA-S	LURDANE-S
LATILLA-S	LEISLER-S	LINCHET-S	LOGBOOK-S	LURKING-S
LATITAT-S	LEISTER-S	LINDANE-S	LOGGING-S	LUSTRUM-S
LATOSOL-S	LEISURE-S	LINEAGE-S	LOGLINE-S	LUTFISK-S
LATRINE-S	LEKKING-S	LINECUT-S	LOGROLL-S	LUTHERN-S
LATTICE-S	LEMMING-S	LINGCOD-S	LOGWOOD-S	LUTHIER-S
LAUGHER-S	LEMPIRA-S	LINGUAL-S	LONGBOW-S	LYCOPOD-S
LAUNDER-S	LENDING-S	LINGULA-S	LONGING-S	LYDDITE-S
LAUWINE-S	LENIENT-S	LINKAGE-S	LOOFFUL-S	LYMITER-S
LAVOLTA-S	LENTISK-S	LINKBOY-S	LOOKISM-S	LYMPHAD-S
LAVROCK-S	LENTOID-S	LINOCUT-S	LOOKIST-S	LYNCHER-S
LAWBOOK-S	LEOPARD-S	LINSANG-S	LOOKOUT-S	LYNCHET-S
LAWLAND-S	LEOTARD-S	LINSEED-S	LOONING-S	LYRICON-S
LAWSUIT-S	LEPORID-S	LINURON-S	LOOPING-S	LYSOGEN-S
LAXATOR-S	LEPTOME-S	LIONCEL-S	LOOSING-S	MACADAM-S
LAYAWAY-S	LEQUEAR-S	LIONISE-S	LOOTING-S	MACAQUE-S
LAYBACK-S	LESBIAN-S	LIONISM-S	LOPPING-S	MACERAL-S
LAYETTE-S	LETDOWN-S	LIONIZE-S	LORDING-S	MACHAIR-S
LAYLOCK-S	LETTERN-S	LIPEMIA-S	LORDKIN-S	MACHETE-S
LAYOVER-S	LETTING-S	LIPPING-S	LORDOMA-S	MACHINE-S
LAYTIME-S	LETTUCE-S	LIPREAD-S	LORETTE-S	MACHREE-S
LAZARET-S	LEUCINE-S	LIPURIA-S	LORGNON-S	MACHZOR-S
LEACHER-S	LEUCITE-S	LIQUATE-S	LORIMER-S	MACRAME-S
LEADING-S	LEUCOMA-S	LIQUEUR-S	LORINER-S	MACRAMI-S
LEADOFF-S	LEUKOMA-S	LIRIOPE-S	LORRELL-S	MACUMBA-S
LEAFAGE-S	LEVATOR-S	LISPING-S	LOUNDER-S	MADDOCK-S
LEAFBUD-S	LEVELER-S	LISPUND-S	LOUNGER-S	MADEIRA-S
LEAFLET-S	LEVERET-S	LISTING-S	LOURING-S	MADISON-S
LEAGUER-S	LEVULIN-S	LITERAL-S	LOVEBUG-S	MADLING-S
LEAKAGE-S	LEWISIA-S	LITHATE-S	LOWBALL-S	MADONNA-S
LEANING-S	LEXICON-S	LITHITE-S	LOWBROW-S	MADOQUA-S
LEARNER-S	LIAISON-S	LITHIUM-S	LOWDOWN-S	MADRASA-S
LEASING-S	LIBBARD-S	LITTLIE-S	LOWLAND-S	MADRONA-S
LEASOWE-S	LIBELEE-S	LITTLIN-S	LOWLIFE-S	MADRONE-S
LEASURE-S	LIBELER-S	LIVELOD-S	LOWVELD-S	MADRONO-S
LEATHER-S	LIBERAL-S	LIVENER-S	LOXYGEN-S	MADWORT-S
LEAVING-S	LIBRATE-S	LIVEYER-S	LOZENGE-S	MADZOON-S
LECHAIM-S	LICENCE-S	LLANERO-S	LUBBARD-S	MAESTRO-S
LECTERN-S	LICENSE-S	LOADING-S	LUCARNE-S	MAFFICK-S
LECTION-S	LICHWAY-S	LOAFING-S	LUCENCE-S	MAFFLIN-S
LECTURE-S	LICKING-S	LOANING-S	LUCERNE-S	MAFIOSO-S
LECTURN-S	LIFEWAY-S	LOATHER-S	LUCIFER-S	MAGALOG-S
LECYTHI-S	LIFTBOY-S	LOBBYER-S	LUCIGEN-S	MAGENTA-S
LEECHEE-S	LIFTOFF-S	LOBEFIN-S	LUDSHIP-S	MAGNATE-S
LEERING-S	LIGGING-S	LOBELET-S	LUGEING-S	MAGNETO-S
LEEWARD-S	LIGHTEN-S	LOBELIA-S	LUGGAGE-S	MAHATMA-S
LEFTISM-S	LIGHTER-S	LOBSTER-S	LUGHOLE-S	MAHJONG-S
LEFTIST-S	LIGNAGE-S	LOBWORM-S	LUGSAIL-S	MAHONIA-S
LEGATEE-S	LIGNITE-S	LOCATER-S	LUGWORM-S	MAHSEER-S

MAHUANG-S	MANIPLE-S	MASHLIM-S	MEDRESE-S	METAMER-S
MAIDISM-S	MANITOU-S	MASHLIN-S	MEDULLA-S	METATAG-S
MAILBAG-S	MANJACK-S	MASHLUM-S	MEDUSAN-S	METAYER-S
MAILCAR-S	MANKIND-S	MASKING-S	MEERCAT-S	METCAST-S
MAILING-S	MANNITE-S	MASQUER-S	MEERKAT-S	METHANE-S
MAILLOT-S	MANNOSE-S	MASSAGE-S	MEETING-S	METHINK-S
MAILVAN-S	MANPACK-S	MASSEUR-S	MEGABAR-S	METICAL-S
MAIMING-S	MANRENT-S	MASTABA-S	MEGABIT-S	METISSE-S
MAINOUR-S	MANROPE-S	MASTICH-S	MEGAFOG-S	METONYM-S
MAINTOP-S	MANSARD-S	MASTIFF-S	MEGAHIT-S	METOPON-S
MAISTER-S	MANSION-S	MASTOID-S	MEGAPOD-S	METRIST-S
MAJAGUA-S	MANTEAU-S	MATADOR-S	MEGARAD-S	MEZQUIT-S
MAJORAT-S	MANTEEL-S	MATCHER-S	MEGARON-S	MEZUZAH-S
MALACCA-S	MANTLET-S	MATCHET-S	MEGASSE-S	MICELLA-S
MALACIA-S	MANTRAM-S	MATCHUP-S	MEGATON-S	MICELLE-S
MALAISE-S	MANTRAP-S	MATELOT-S	MEGILLA-S	MICHING-S
MALANGA-S	MANUMEA-S	MATILDA-S	MEGILPH-S	MICROBE-S
MALARIA-S	MANUMIT-S	MATINEE-S	MEISTER-S	MICROHM-S
MALEATE-S	MANURER-S	MATOOKE-S	MELANGE-S	MICTION-S
MALICHO-S	MANWARD-S	MATRICE-S	MELANIC-S	MIDCULT-S
MALISON-S	MANYATA-S	MATSURI-S	MELANIN-S	MIDDLER-S
MALLARD-S	MAORMOR-S	MATTING-S	MELILOT-S	MIDIRON-S
MALLING-S	MAPPING-S	MATTOCK-S	MELISMA-S	MIDLAND-S
MALMSEY-S	MAPPIST-S	MATTOID-S	MELLITE-S	MIDLINE-S
MALODOR-S	MAQUILA-S	MATURER-S	MELODIA-S	MIDLIST-S
MALTASE-S	MARABOU-S	MATWEED-S	MELODIC-S	MIDMOST-S
MALTING-S	MARANTA-S	MATZOON-S	MELTAGE-S	MIDNOON-S
MALTOSE-S	MARASCA-S	MAULGRE-S	MELTEMI-S	MIDRIFF-S
MALWARE-S	MARBLER-S	MAUNDER-S	MELTING-S	MIDSHIP-S
MAMAGUY-S	MARCATO-S	MAUTHER-S	MELTITH-S	MIDSOLE-S
MAMELON-S	MARCHER-S	MAUVEIN-S	MEMENTO-S	MIDTERM-S
MAMMOCK-S	MARCONI-S	MAUVINE-S	MENACER-S	MIDTOWN-S
MAMMOTH-S	MAREMMA-S	MAWSEED-S	MENAZON-S	MIDWEEK-S
MAMPARA-S	MARGENT-S	MAWTHER-S	MENDIGO-S	MIDWIFE-S
MAMPOER-S	MARGOSA-S	MAXILLA-S	MENDING-S	MIDWIVE-S
MANACLE-S	MARIMBA-S	MAXIMAL-S	MENFOLK-S	MIDYEAR-S
MANAGER-S	MARINER-S	MAXIMIN-S	MENORAH-S	MIGRANT-S
MANAKIN-S	MARKHOR-S	MAXIMUM-S	MENTHOL-S	MIGRATE-S
MANATEE-S	MARKING-S	MAXWELL-S	MENTION-S	MILEAGE-S
MANCALA-S	MARLINE-S	MAYBIRD-S	MERANTI-S	MILFOIL-S
MANCHET-S	MARLING-S	MAYPOLE-S	MERCHET-S	MILITIA-S
MANDALA-S	MARLITE-S	MAYSTER-S	MERFOLK-S	MILKING-S
MANDATE-S	MARMITE-S	MAYWEED-S	MERGING-S	MILKSOP-S
MANDIOC-S	MARMOSE-S	MAZURKA-S	MERLING-S	MILLAGE-S
MANDIRA-S	MARPLOT-S	MAZZARD-S	MERMAID-S	MILLDAM-S
MANDOLA-S	MARQUEE-S	MEACOCK-S	MERONYM-S	MILLIER-S
MANDORA-S	MARQUES-S	MEANDER-S	MEROPIA-S	MILLIME-S
MANDREL-S	MARRANO-S	MEANING-S	MERSION-S	MILLINE-S
MANDRIL-S	MARRIED-S	MEASURE-S	MESCLUM-S	MILLING-S
MANGLER-S	MARRIER-S	MEATAXE-S	MESCLUN-S	MILLION-S
MANGOLD-S	MARSALA-S	MECONIN-S	MESHING-S	MILLRUN-S
MANHOLE-S	MARSHAL-S	MEDACCA-S	MESHUGA-S	MIMMICK-S
MANHOOD-S	MARTEXT-S	MEDALET-S	MESQUIT-S	MINARET-S
MANHUNT-S	MARTIAN-S	MEDDLER-S	MESSAGE-S	MINCING-S
MANIHOC-S	MARTINI-S	MEDEVAC-S	MESSIAH-S	MINDING-S
MANIHOT-S	MARTLET-S	MEDIANT-S	MESTESO-S	MINDSET-S
MANIKIN-S	MARYBUD-S	MEDIATE-S	MESTINO-S	MINEOLA-S
MANILLA-S	MASCARA-S	MEDICAL-S	MESTIZA-S	MINERAL-S
MANILLE-S	MASHING-S	MEDIGAP-S	MESTIZO-S	MINETTE-S
MANIOCA-S	MASHLAM-S	MEDIVAC-S	MESTOME-S	MINEVER-S

MINGLER-S	MISLUCK-S	MODERNE-S	MOPHEAD-S	MUDWORT-S
MINIATE-S	MISMAKE-S	MODICUM-S	MORAINE-S	MUEDDIN-S
MINIBAR-S	MISMARK-S	MODISTE-S	MORDANT-S	MUEZZIN-S
MINICAB-S	MISMATE-S	MODULAR-S	MORDENT-S	MUFFLER-S
MINICAM-S	MISMEET-S	MOELLON-S	MORELLE-S	MUGGING-S
MINICAR-S	MISMOVE-S	MOFETTE-S	MORELLO-S	MUGSHOT-S
MINICOM-S	MISNAME-S	MOHICAN-S	MORICHE-S	MUGWORT-S
MINIKIN-S	MISPAGE-S	MOIDORE-S	MORISCO-S	MUGWUMP-S
MINILAB-S	MISPART-S	MOINEAU-S	MORLING-S	MUKHTAR-S
MINIMAL-S	MISPLAN-S	MOISTEN-S	MORMAOR-S	MULATTA-S
MINIMUM-S	MISPLAY-S	MOITHER-S	MORNING-S	MULATTO-S
MINISKI-S	MISRATE-S	MOJARRA-S	MOROCCO-S	MULLEIN-S
MINIVAN-S	MISREAD-S	MOLASSE-S	MORPHEW-S	MULLION-S
MINIVER-S	MISRULE-S	MOLDING-S	MORPHIA-S	MULLITE-S
MINIVET-S	MISSEAT-S	MOLERAT-S	MORPHIN-S	MULLOCK-S
MINNICK-S	MISSEEM-S	MOLIMEN-S	MORRELL-S	MULMULL-S
MINNOCK-S	MISSEND-S	MOLINET-S	MORRHUA-S	MULTURE-S
MINORCA-S	MISSILE-S	MOLLUSC-S	MORRICE-S	MUMBLER-S
MINSTER-S	MISSION-S	MOLLUSK-S	MORRION-S	MUMMING-S
MINTAGE-S	MISSIVE-S	MOMENTO-S	MORSURE-S	MUMMOCK-S
MINUEND-S	MISSORT-S	MONACID-S	MORTICE-S	MUNCHER-S
MIRACLE-S	MISSOUT-S	MONARCH-S	MORTISE-S	MUNNION-S
MIRADOR-S	MISSTEP-S	MONARDA-S	MORWONG-S	MUNSTER-S
MIRBANE-S	MISSTOP-S	MONAXON-S	MOSELLE-S	MUNTING-S
MISAVER-S	MISSUIT-S	MONDAIN-S	MOSHING-S	MUNTJAC-S
MISBILL-S	MISTAKE-S	MONERAN-S	MOSHPIT-S	MUNTJAK-S
MISBIND-S	MISTBOW-S	MONEYER-S	MOSTEST-S	MUNTRIE-S
MISCALL-S	MISTELL-S	MONGREL-S	MOTTLER-S	MUONIUM-S
MISCAST-S	MISTEND-S	MONIKER-S	MOUCHER-S	MURAENA-S
MISCITE-S	MISTERM-S	MONILIA-S	MOUFLON-S	MURGEON-S
MISCODE-S	MISTICO-S	MONITOR-S	MOULAGE-S	MURIATE-S
MISCOIN-S	MISTIME-S	MONOCLE-S	MOULDER-S	MURLAIN-S
MISCOOK-S	MISTING-S	MONOCOT-S	MOULTER-S	MURRAGH-S
MISDATE-S	MISTRAL-S	MONOFIL-S	MOUNTER-S	MURRAIN-S
MISDEAL-S	MISTUNE-S	MONOLOG-S	MOURNER-S	MURRION-S
MISDEED-S	MISTYPE-S	MONOMER-S	MOUSAKA-S	MURTHER-S
MISDEEM-S	MISUSER-S	MONONYM-S	MOUSING-S	MUSCONE-S
MISDIAL-S	MISWEEN-S	MONOPOD-S	MOUSMEE-S	MUSETTE-S
MISDIET-S	MISWEND-S	MONOSKI-S	MOUTHER-S	MUSICAL-S
MISDOER-S	MISWORD-S	MONSOON-S	MOVABLE-S	MUSIMON-S
MISDRAW-S	MISYOKE-S	MONSTER-S	MOVIOLA-S	MUSKONE-S
MISEASE-S	MITERER-S	MONTAGE-S	MOWBURN-S	MUSKRAT-S
MISEDIT-S	MITOGEN-S	MONTANE-S	MOZETTA-S	MUSPIKE-S
MISFALL-S	MITSVAH-S	MONTANT-S	MRIDANG-S	MUSTANG-S
MISFARE-S	MITUMBA-S	MONTERO-S	MUCHELL-S	MUSTARD-S
MISFEED-S	MITZVAH-S	MONTURE-S	MUCIGEN-S	MUTAGEN-S
MISFILE-S	MIXDOWN-S	MONURON-S	MUDBATH-S	MUZZLER-S
MISFIRE-S	MIXTION-S	MOOCHER-S	MUDDLER-S	MWALIMU-S
MISFORM-S	MIXTURE-S	MOOKTAR-S	MUDFLAP-S	MYALGIA-S
MISGIVE-S	MIZMAZE-S	MOOLVIE-S	MUDFLAT-S	MYALISM-S
MISGROW-S	MOBBING-S	MOONBOW-S	MUDFLOW-S	MYALIST-S
MISHEAR-S	MOBBISM-S	MOONEYE-S	MUDHOLE-S	MYCELLA-S
MISHMEE-S	MOBSTER-S	MOONLET-S	MUDHOOK-S	MYELINE-S
MISJOIN-S	MOCHELL-S	MOONSET-S	MUDIRIA-S	MYELOMA-S
MISKEEP-S	MOCHILA-S	MOORAGE-S	MUDLARK-S	MYLODON-S
MISKICK-S	MOCKAGE-S	MOORHEN-S	MUDPACK-S	MYNHEER-S
MISKNOW-S	MOCKING-S	MOORILL-S	MUDROCK-S	MYOGRAM-S
MISLEAD-S	MOCKNEY-S	MOORING-S	MUDROOM-S	MYOSOTE-S
MISLIKE-S	MODELER-S	MOORLOG-S	MUDSCOW-S	MYOTOME-S
MISLIVE-S	MODELLO-S	MOOTING-S	MUDSILL-S	MYOTUBE-S

MYRBANE-S	NELUMBO-S	NOCTURN-S	NUNHOOD-S	OFFCAST-S
MYRINGA-S	NEMESIA-S	NODDING-S	NUNSHIP-S	OFFENCE-S
MYRRHOL-S	NEOLITH-S	NOGGING-S	NUPTIAL-S	OFFENSE-S
MYTHISE-S	NEONATE-S	NOINTER-S	NURSING-S	OFFEREE-S
MYTHISM-S	NEOTYPE-S	NOMARCH-S	NURTURE-S	OFFERER-S
MYTHIST-S	NEPHRON-S	NOMBRIL-S	NUTCASE-S	OFFEROR-S
MYTHIZE-S	NERVINE-S	NOMINAL-S	NUTGALL-S	OFFICER-S
NAARTJE-S	NERVING-S	NOMINEE-S	NUTMEAL-S	OFFLOAD-S
NACARAT-S	NERVULE-S	NONACID-S	NUTMEAT-S	OFFRAMP-S
NACELLE-S	NERVURE-S	NONAGON-S	NUTPICK-S	OFFSCUM-S
NACRITE-S	NESTFUL-S	NONBANK-S	NUTTING-S	OFFSIDE-S
NAGAPIE-S	NESTING-S	NONBOOK-S	NUTWOOD-S	OFFTAKE-S
NAGMAAL-S	NESTLER-S	NONCOLA-S	NUZZLER-S	OGREISM-S
NAILING-S	NETBALL-S	NONETTE-S	NYLGHAI-S	OILBIRD-S
NAILSET-S	NETHEAD-S	NONETTO-S	NYLGHAU-S	OILCAMP-S
NAIVETE-S	NETIZEN-S	NONFACT-S	NYMPHET-S	OILHOLE-S
NAMASTE-S	NETSUKE-S	NONPAST-S	OAKLING-S	OILSEED-S
NAMETAG-S	NETTING-S	NONPLAY-S	OARLOCK-S	OILSKIN-S
NANDINA-S	NETTLER-S	NONSKED-S	OARWEED-S	OINOMEL-S
NANDINE-S	NETWORK-S	NONSTOP-S	OATCAKE-S	OKIMONO-S
NANKEEN-S	NEURINE-S	NONSUIT-S	OATMEAL-S	OLDSTER-S
NANODOT-S	NEURISM-S	NONUPLE-S	OBELISE-S	OLEARIA-S
NAPHTHA-S	NEURITE-S	NONUSER-S	OBELISK-S	OLEFINE-S
NAPHTOL-S	NEUROMA-S	NONWORD-S	OBELISM-S	OLESTRA-S
NARCEEN-S	NEURONE-S	NOONDAY-S	OBELIZE-S	OLICOOK-S
NARCEIN-S	NEURULA-S	NOONING-S	OBLIGEE-S	OLIGIST-S
NARCISM-S	NEUSTON-S	NORIMON-S	OBLIGER-S	OLIVINE-S
NARCIST-S	NEUTRAL-S	NORLAND-S	OBLIGOR-S	OLOGIST-S
NARCOMA-S	NEUTRON-S	NORTENA-S	OBLIQUE-S	OLOGOAN-S
NARCOSE-S	NEWBORN-S	NORTENO-S	OBSCURE-S	OLOROSO-S
NARGILE-S	NEWSBOY-S	NORTHER-S	OBSERVE-S	OLYCOOK-S
NARRATE-S	NIBBLER-S	NORWARD-S	OBTRUDE-S	OLYKOEK-S
NARTJIE-S	NIBLICK-S	NOSEBAG-S	OBVERSE-S	OMENTUM-S
NARWHAL-S	NICOTIN-S	NOSEGAY-S	OBVIATE-S	OMICRON-S
NASHGAB-S	NICTATE-S	NOSTRIL-S	OCARINA-S	OMIKRON-S
NATRIUM-S	NIDDICK-S	NOSTRUM-S	OCCIPUT-S	OMITTER-S
NATURAL-S	NIGELLA-S	NOTABLE-S	OCCLUDE-S	ONANISM-S
NAVARCH-S	NIGGARD-S	NOTAEUM-S	OCEANID-S	ONANIST-S
NAVARHO-S	NIGGLER-S	NOTCHEL-S	OCTAGON-S	ONCOGEN-S
NAVARIN-S	NIGHTIE-S	NOTCHER-S	OCTANOL-S	ONDATRA-S
NAVETTE-S	NIHONGA-S	NOTELET-S	OCTAPLA-S	ONGOING-S
NAYWARD-S	NILGHAI-S	NOTEPAD-S	OCTETTE-S	ONLINER-S
NAYWORD-S	NILGHAU-S	NOTHING-S	OCTOPOD-S	ONSTEAD-S
NEATNIK-S	NINEPIN-S	NOTICER-S	OCTUPLE-S	ONYCHIA-S
NEBBICH-S	NIOBATE-S	NOTITIA-S	OCULIST-S	OOLAKAN-S
NECKING-S	NIOBITE-S	NOURICE-S	ODALISK-S	OOMIACK-S
NECKLET-S	NIOBIUM-S	NOURSLE-S	ODALLER-S	OOPHYTE-S
NECKTIE-S	NIRVANA-S	NOUSELL-S	ODDBALL-S	OOSPERM-S
NECROSE-S	NITCHIE-S	NOVELLA-S	ODDMENT-S	OOSPORE-S
NEDETTE-S	NITERIE-S	NOWHERE-S	ODONATE-S	OPALINE-S
NEEDFUL-S	NITHING-S	NOYANCE-S	ODORANT-S	OPENING-S
NEEDLER-S	NITINOL-S	NUCLEIN-S	ODORISE-S	OPERAND-S
NEEDLES-S	NITPICK-S	NUCLEON-S	ODORIZE-S	OPERANT-S
NEGATER-S	NITRATE-S	NUCLIDE-S	ODYLISM-S	OPERATE-S
NEGATON-S	NITRIDE-S	NUDNICK-S	ODYSSEY-S	OPHIURA-S
NEGATOR-S	NITRILE-S	NULLING-S	OENOMEL-S	OPINION-S
NEGLECT-S	NITRITE-S	NUMERAL-S	OERSTED-S	OPORICE-S
NEGLIGE-S	NOBBLER-S	NUMERIC-S	OESTRIN-S	OPOSSUM-S
NEGROID-S	NOCTUID-S	NUNATAK-S	OESTRUM-S	OPPIDAN-S
NEGRONI-S	NOCTULE-S	NUNDINE-S	OFFBEAT-S	OPPOSER-S

OPSONIN-S	OUTCALL-S	OUTPART-S	OUTWORK-S	OXYPHIL-S
OPTIMUM-S	OUTCAST-S	OUTPEEP-S	OUTYELL-S	OXYSALT-S
OPUNTIA-S	OUTCOME-S	OUTPEER-S	OUTYELP-S	OXYSOME-S
OPUSCLE-S	OUTCOOK-S	OUTPLAN-S	OUVRAGE-S	OXYTONE-S
OQUASSA-S	OUTCROP-S	OUTPLAY-S	OUVRIER-S	OZONATE-S
ORALISM-S	OUTCROW-S	OUTPLOD-S	OVATION-S	OZONIDE-S
ORALIST-S	OUTDARE-S	OUTPLOT-S	OVERACT-S	OZONISE-S
ORARIAN-S	OUTDATE-S	OUTPOLL-S	OVERAGE-S	OZONIZE-S
ORARION-S	OUTDOER-S	OUTPORT-S	OVERALL-S	PABULUM-S
ORARIUM-S	OUTDOOR-S	OUTPOST-S	OVERARM-S	PACEWAY-S
ORATION-S	OUTDRAG-S	OUTPOUR-S	OVERAWE-S	PACHISI-S
ORBITAL-S	OUTDRAW-S	OUTPRAY-S	OVERBET-S	PACHUCO-S
ORBITER-S	OUTDROP-S	OUTPULL-S	OVERBID-S	PACKAGE-S
ORCHARD-S	OUTDUEL-S	OUTRACE-S	OVERBUY-S	PACKING-S
ORCINOL-S	OUTDURE-S	OUTRAGE-S	OVERCUT-S	PACKWAY-S
ORDERER-S	OUTEARN-S	OUTRANK-S	OVERDOG-S	PACTION-S
ORDINAL-S	OUTEDGE-S	OUTRATE-S	OVERDUB-S	PADDING-S
ORDINAR-S	OUTFACE-S	OUTRAVE-S	OVERDYE-S	PADDLER-S
ORDINEE-S	OUTFALL-S	OUTREAD-S	OVEREAT-S	PADDOCK-S
OREGANO-S	OUTFAST-S	OUTRIDE-S	OVEREGG-S	PADELLA-S
OREWEED-S	OUTFAWN-S	OUTRING-S	OVEREYE-S	PADLOCK-S
ORGANIC-S	OUTFEEL-S	OUTROAR-S	OVERGET-S	PADRONE-S
ORGANON-S	OUTFIND-S	OUTROCK-S	OVERHIT-S	PADSHAH-S
ORGANUM-S	OUTFIRE-S	OUTROLL-S	OVERJOY-S	PAENULA-S
ORGANZA-S	OUTFLOW-S	OUTROOP-S	OVERLAP-S	PAEONIC-S
ORGIAST-S	OUTFOOL-S	OUTROOT-S	OVERLAY-S	PAESANO-S
ORIFICE-S	OUTFOOT-S	OUTROPE-S	OVERLET-S	PAGEANT-S
ORIGAMI-S	OUTGAIN-S	OUTSAIL-S	OVERLIE-S	PAGEBOY-S
ORIGANE-S	OUTGATE-S	OUTSELL-S	OVERMAN-S	PAGEFUL-S
OROPESA-S	OUTGAZE-S	OUTSERT-S	OVERNET-S	PAGURID-S
ORPHISM-S	OUTGIVE-S	OUTSHOT-S	OVERPAY-S	PAHLAVI-S
ORPHREY-S	OUTGLOW-S	OUTSIDE-S	OVERRED-S	PAILFUL-S
ORTOLAN-S	OUTGNAW-S	OUTSING-S	OVERREN-S	PAILLON-S
OSMIATE-S	OUTGOER-S	OUTSIZE-S	OVERRUN-S	PAINTER-S
OSMUNDA-S	OUTGRIN-S	OUTSOAR-S	OVERSEA-S	PAIOCKE-S
OSSELET-S	OUTGROW-S	OUTSOLE-S	OVERSEE-S	PAIRIAL-S
OSSETER-S	OUTHAUL-S	OUTSPAN-S	OVERSET-S	PAIRING-S
OSSETRA-S	OUTHEAR-S	OUTSTAY-S	OVERSEW-S	PAISANA-S
OSSICLE-S	OUTHIRE-S	OUTSTEP-S	OVERSOW-S	PAISANO-S
OSTEOID-S	OUTHOWL-S	OUTSULK-S	OVERSUP-S	PAISLEY-S
OSTEOMA-S	OUTHUNT-S	OUTSWIM-S	OVERTIP-S	PAJOCKE-S
OSTIOLE-S	OUTHYRE-S	OUTTAKE-S	OVERTOP-S	PAKAPOO-S
OSTMARK-S	OUTJEST-S	OUTTALK-S	OVERUSE-S	PAKFONG-S
OTALGIA-S	OUTJUMP-S	OUTTASK-S	OVERWET-S	PAKTONG-S
OTOCYST-S	OUTKEEP-S	OUTTELL-S	OVICIDE-S	PALABRA-S
OTOLITH-S	OUTKICK-S	OUTTROT-S	OVIDUCT-S	PALADIN-S
OTTOMAN-S	OUTKILL-S	OUTTURN-S	OVOIDAL-S	PALATAL-S
OUABAIN-S	OUTLAND-S	OUTVOTE-S	OVULATE-S	PALAVER-S
OUAKARI-S	OUTLAST-S	OUTWAIT-S	OWRELAY-S	PALAZZO-S
OUGUIYA-S	OUTLEAD-S	OUTWALK-S	OXALATE-S	PALETOT-S
OULAKAN-S	OUTLEAP-S	OUTWARD-S	OXAZINE-S	PALETTE-S
OUSTITI-S	OUTLIER-S	OUTWEAR-S	OXBLOOD-S	PALFREY-S
OUTBACK-S	OUTLINE-S	OUTWEED-S	OXHEART-S	PALIKAR-S
OUTBAKE-S	OUTLIVE-S	OUTWEEP-S	OXIDANT-S	PALINKA-S
OUTBARK-S	OUTLOOK-S	OUTWELL-S	OXIDASE-S	PALLIUM-S
OUTBAWL-S	OUTLOVE-S	OUTWICK-S	OXIDATE-S	PALLONE-S
OUTBEAM-S	OUTMODE-S	OUTWILE-S	OXIDISE-S	PALMFUL-S
OUTBRAG-S	OUTMOVE-S	OUTWILL-S	OXIDIZE-S	PALMIET-S
OUTBULK-S	OUTNAME-S	OUTWIND-S	OXONIUM-S	PALMIST-S
OUTBURN-S	OUTPACE-S	OUTWING-S	OXYACID-S	PALMTOP-S

PALMYRA-S	PARFAIT-S	PATROON-S	PEMICAN-S	PEROXID-S
PALOOKA-S	PARGANA-S	PATTERN-S	PENANCE-S	PERPEND-S
PALPATE-S	PARGING-S	PATULIN-S	PENDANT-S	PERPENT-S
PALSHIP-S	PARISON-S	PAUSING-S	PENDENT-S	PERRIER-S
PAMPEAN-S	PARITOR-S	PAVIOUR-S	PENDULE-S	PERSALT-S
PAMPERO-S	PARKADE-S	PAVISER-S	PENFOLD-S	PERSICO-S
PAMPOEN-S	PARKING-S	PAVISSE-S	PENGUIN-S	PERSIST-S
PANACEA-S	PARKOUR-S	PAVLOVA-S	PENICIL-S	PERSONA-S
PANACHE-S	PARKWAY-S	PAWNAGE-S	PENLITE-S	PERTAIN-S
PANCAKE-S	PARLOUR-S	PAXIUBA-S	PENNAME-S	PERTAKE-S
PANDECT-S	PAROLEE-S	PAYABLE-S	PENNANT-S	PERTURB-S
PANDOOR-S	PARONYM-S	PAYBACK-S	PENNINE-S	PERUSAL-S
PANDORA-S	PAROTID-S	PAYFONE-S	PENOCHE-S	PERUSER-S
PANDORE-S	PARPANE-S	PAYLOAD-S	PENSION-S	PERVADE-S
PANDOUR-S	PARPEND-S	PAYMENT-S	PENSTER-S	PERVERT-S
PANDURA-S	PARPENT-S	PAYROLL-S	PENTACT-S	PESAUNT-S
PANGENE-S	PARQUET-S	PAYSAGE-S	PENTANE-S	PETCOCK-S
PANGRAM-S	PARRIER-S	PAYSLIP-S	PENTENE-S	PETIOLE-S
PANICLE-S	PARROCK-S	PEACHER-S	PENTHIA-S	PETRALE-S
PANICUM-S	PARSING-S	PEACOAT-S	PENTICE-S	PETTING-S
PANNAGE-S	PARSLEY-S	PEACOCK-S	PENTISE-S	PETUNIA-S
PANNICK-S	PARSNEP-S	PEAFOWL-S	PENTODE-S	PEYTRAL-S
PANNIER-S	PARSNIP-S	PEARLER-S	PENTOSE-S	PEYTREL-S
PANNING-S	PARTAKE-S	PEARLIN-S	PENUCHE-S	PFENNIG-S
PANOCHA-S	PARTIAL-S	PEASANT-S	PENUCHI-S	PHAEISM-S
PANOCHE-S	PARTIER-S	PEASCOD-S	PEONAGE-S	PHAETON-S
PANPIPE-S	PARTING-S	PEBRINE-S	PEONISM-S	PHALLIN-S
PANTHER-S	PARTITA-S	PECCAVI-S	PEOPLER-S	PHANTOM-S
PANTILE-S	PARTLET-S	PECKING-S	PEPSINE-S	PHARAOH-S
PANTINE-S	PARTNER-S	PECTASE-S	PEPTALK-S	PHASING-S
PANTING-S	PARTURE-S	PECTATE-S	PEPTIDE-S	PHASMID-S
PANTLER-S	PARTYER-S	PECTISE-S	PEPTISE-S	PHEAZAR-S
PANTOUM-S	PARVENU-S	PECTIZE-S	PEPTIZE-S	PHELLEM-S
PAPADAM-S	PARVISE-S	PECTOSE-S	PEPTONE-S	PHENATE-S
PAPADOM-S	PASCHAL-S	PEDAGOG-S	PERACID-S	PHILTER-S
PAPADUM-S	PASQUIL-S	PEDALER-S	PERAEON-S	PHILTRE-S
PAPERER-S	PASSADE-S	PEDDLER-S	PERCALE-S	PHOBISM-S
PAPHIAN-S	PASSADO-S	PEDICAB-S	PERCENT-S	PHOBIST-S
PAPILIO-S	PASSAGE-S	PEDICEL-S	PERCEPT-S	PHONATE-S
PAPOOSE-S	PASSATA-S	PEDICLE-S	PERCHER-S	PHONEME-S
PAPRICA-S	PASSING-S	PEDOCAL-S	PERCOID-S	PHORATE-S
PAPRIKA-S	PASSION-S	PEDRAIL-S	PERDURE-S	PHOTISM-S
PARABLE-S	PASSIVE-S	PEDRERO-S	PEREION-S	PHRASER-S
PARACME-S	PASSKEY-S	PEEBEEN-S	PEREIRA-S	PHYLLID-S
PARADER-S	PASSOUT-S	PEELING-S	PERFECT-S	PHYTANE-S
PARADOR-S	PASTERN-S	PEERAGE-S	PERFORM-S	PIAFFER-S
PARAFLE-S	PASTEUP-S	PEGGING-S	PERFUME-S	PIANINO-S
PARAGON-S	PASTIME-S	PEISHWA-S	PERFUSE-S	PIANISM-S
PARANYM-S	PASTINA-S	PEKEPOO-S	PERGOLA-S	PIANIST-S
PARAPET-S	PASTING-S	PELAGIC-S	PERIAPT-S	PIARIST-S
PARASOL-S	PASTURE-S	PELICAN-S	PERIDOT-S	PIASABA-S
PARATHA-S	PATAMAR-S	PELISSE-S	PERIGEE-S	PIASAVA-S
PARBAKE-S	PATBALL-S	PELLACH-S	PERIGON-S	PIASTER-S
PARBOIL-S	PATCHER-S	PELLACK-S	PERILLA-S	PIASTRE-S
PARDALE-S	PATELLA-S	PELLOCK-S	PERIOST-S	PIBROCH-S
PARDNER-S	PATHWAY-S	PELORIA-S	PERIQUE-S	PICACHO-S
PAREIRA-S	PATIENT-S	PELOTON-S	PERIWIG-S	PICADOR-S
PARELLA-S	PATRIAL-S	PELTAST-S	PERJURE-S	PICAMAR-S
PARELLE-S	PATRICK-S	PELTING-S	PERLITE-S	PICCOLO-S
PARETIC-S	PATRIOT-S	PEMBINA-S	PERMUTE-S	PICKAXE-S

PICKEER-S	PINGUIN-S	PLASHET-S	PLUMPER-S	POMFRET-S
PICKING-S	PINHEAD-S	PLASMID-S	PLUMULE-S	POMPANO-S
PICKLER-S	PINHOLE-S	PLASMIN-S	PLUNDER-S	POMPELO-S
PICKMAW-S	PINITOL-S	PLASMON-S	PLUNGER-S	POMPION-S
PICKOFF-S	PINKEYE-S	PLASTER-S	PLUNKER-S	POMPOON-S
PICOLIN-S	PINKING-S	PLASTIC-S	PLUSAGE-S	PONCEAU-S
PICOTEE-S	PINNACE-S	PLASTID-S	PLUVIAL-S	PONDAGE-S
PICQUET-S	PINNING-S	PLATANE-S	PLYWOOD-S	PONIARD-S
PICRATE-S	PINNOCK-S	PLATEAU-S	POACHER-S	PONTAGE-S
PICRITE-S	PINNULA-S	PLATINA-S	POBLANO-S	PONTIFF-S
PICTURE-S	PINNULE-S	PLATING-S	POCHARD-S	PONTOON-S
PIDDLER-S	PINOCLE-S	PLATOON-S	POCHOIR-S	POOFTAH-S
PIDDOCK-S	PINTADO-S	PLATTER-S	POCKARD-S	POOFTER-S
PIDGEON-S	PINTAIL-S	PLAUDIT-S	POCKPIT-S	POPADUM-S
PIEBALD-S	PINTANO-S	PLAYACT-S	POCOSEN-S	POPCORN-S
PIECING-S	PINWALE-S	PLAYBOY-S	POCOSIN-S	POPEDOM-S
PIEFORT-S	PINWEED-S	PLAYDAY-S	POCOSON-S	POPERIN-S
PIEHOLE-S	PINWORK-S	PLAYLET-S	PODAGRA-S	POPETTE-S
PIERAGE-S	PINWORM-S	PLAYOFF-S	PODCAST-S	POPOVER-S
PIERCER-S	PIONEER-S	PLAYPEN-S	PODESTA-S	POPSTER-S
PIERROT-S	PIONING-S	PLEADER-S	PODITIC-S	POPULAR-S
PIETISM-S	PIPEAGE-S	PLEASER-S	POETISE-S	PORCINI-S
PIETIST-S	PIPEFUL-S	PLEATER-S	POETIZE-S	PORIFER-S
PIFFERO-S	PIPETTE-S	PLECTRE-S	POGONIA-S	PORKPIE-S
PIFFLER-S	PIRAGUA-S	PLEDGEE-S	POGONIP-S	PORRECT-S
PIGBOAT-S	PIRANHA-S	PLEDGER-S	POINDER-S	PORRIGO-S
PIGFACE-S	PIROGUE-S	PLEDGET-S	POINTEL-S	PORTAGE-S
PIGFEED-S	PIROQUE-S	PLEDGOR-S	POINTER-S	PORTEND-S
PIGGING-S	PISCINA-S	PLENIPO-S	POISSON-S	PORTENT-S
PIGHTLE-S	PISHOGE-S	PLENISM-S	POITREL-S	PORTICO-S
PIGLING-S	PISMIRE-S	PLENIST-S	POKEFUL-S	PORTION-S
PIGMEAT-S	PISSANT-S	PLEOPOD-S	POLACCA-S	PORTRAY-S
PIGMENT-S	PISSOIR-S	PLERION-S	POLACRE-S	POSAUNE-S
PIGNOLI-S	PISTOLE-S	PLEROMA-S	POLARON-S	POSEUSE-S
PIGSKIN-S	PITAPAT-S	PLEROME-S	POLEAXE-S	POSITIF-S
PIGSNEY-S	PITARAH-S	PLESSOR-S	POLECAT-S	POSITON-S
PIGSNIE-S	PITCHER-S	PLEXURE-S	POLEMIC-S	POSTAGE-S
PIGTAIL-S	PITFALL-S	PLICATE-S	POLENTA-S	POSTBAG-S
PIGWEED-S	PITHEAD-S	PLIMSOL-S	POLICER-S	POSTBOY-S
PIKELET-S	PITPROP-S	PLINKER-S	POLITIC-S	POSTDOC-S
PILCHER-S	PITTING-S	PLISKIE-S	POLLACK-S	POSTEEN-S
PILCORN-S	PITTITE-S	PLODDER-S	POLLARD-S	POSTERN-S
PILCROW-S	PITUITA-S	PLONKER-S	POLLING-S	POSTING-S
PILGRIM-S	PITUITE-S	PLOSION-S	POLLIST-S	POSTURE-S
PILLAGE-S	PIVOTER-S	PLOSIVE-S	POLLOCK-S	POTABLE-S
PILLING-S	PLACARD-S	PLOTTER-S	POLLUTE-S	POTAGER-S
PILLION-S	PLACATE-S	PLOTTIE-S	POLOIST-S	POTASSA-S
PILLOCK-S	PLACCAT-S	PLOUTER-S	POLONIE-S	POTBOIL-S
PILSNER-S	PLACEBO-S	PLOWBOY-S	POLYCOT-S	POTCHER-S
PIMENTO-S	PLACING-S	PLOWTER-S	POLYENE-S	POTENCE-S
PINBALL-S	PLACKET-S	PLUCKER-S	POLYGAM-S	POTHEAD-S
PINBONE-S	PLACOID-S	PLUGGER-S	POLYGON-S	POTHEEN-S
PINCASE-S	PLAFOND-S	PLUGOLA-S	POLYMER-S	POTHERB-S
PINCHER-S	PLAGIUM-S	PLUMAGE-S	POLYNIA-S	POTHOLE-S
PINDARI-S	PLAGUER-S	PLUMBER-S	POLYNYA-S	POTHOOK-S
PINDOWN-S	PLAITER-S	PLUMBUM-S	POLYOMA-S	POTICHE-S
PINESAP-S	PLANCHE-S	PLUMCOT-S	POLYPED-S	POTLINE-S
PINFALL-S	PLANNER-S	PLUMIST-S	POLYPOD-S	POTLUCK-S
PINFOLD-S	PLANTER-S	PLUMMET-S	POMATUM-S	POTOROO-S
PINGLER-S	PLASHER-S	PLUMPEN-S	POMEROY-S	POTSHOP-S

POTSHOT-S	PREEDIT-S	PRETYPE-S	PROMMER-S	PUDDING-S
POTTAGE-S	PREEMIE-S	PRETZEL-S	PROMOTE-S	PUDDLER-S
POTTEEN-S	PREEMPT-S	PREVAIL-S	PRONATE-S	PUDDOCK-S
POUFTAH-S	PREENER-S	PREVENE-S	PRONEUR-S	PUFFING-S
POUFTER-S	PREFACE-S	PREVENT-S	PRONOUN-S	PUGAREE-S
POULARD-S	PREFADE-S	PREVERB-S	PROOFER-S	PUGGING-S
POULDER-S	PREFECT-S	PREVIEW-S	PROOTIC-S	PUGGREE-S
POULDRE-S	PREFILE-S	PREVISE-S	PROPAGE-S	PUGMARK-S
POULTER-S	PREFILL-S	PREWARM-S	PROPALE-S	PUKATEA-S
POUNCER-S	PREFIRE-S	PREWARN-S	PROPANE-S	PULDRON-S
POUNCET-S	PREFORM-S	PREWIRE-S	PROPEND-S	PULLMAN-S
POUNDAL-S	PREFUND-S	PREWORK-S	PROPENE-S	PULLOUT-S
POUNDER-S	PREGAME-S	PREWRAP-S	PROPHET-S	PULSATE-S
POURING-S	PREHEAT-S	PREZZIE-S	PROPJET-S	PULSION-S
POURSEW-S	PREHEND-S	PRIBBLE-S	PROPONE-S	PULTOON-S
POURSUE-S	PRELATE-S	PRICING-S	PROPOSE-S	PULTURE-S
POUSSIE-S	PRELECT-S	PRICKER-S	PRORATE-S	PUMICER-S
POUSSIN-S	PRELOAD-S	PRICKET-S	PROSECT-S	PUMMELO-S
POUTHER-S	PRELUDE-S	PRICKLE-S	PROSING-S	PUMPION-S
POUTINE-S	PREMEET-S	PRIGGER-S	PROSOMA-S	PUMPKIN-S
POUTING-S	PREMIER-S	PRIMAGE-S	PROSPER-S	PUNALUA-S
POWHIRI-S	PREMISE-S	PRIMATE-S	PROSSIE-S	PUNCHER-S
PRABBLE-S	PREMIUM-S	PRIMERO-S	PROSTIE-S	PUNNING-S
PRAETOR-S	PREMOLD-S	PRIMEUR-S	PROTEAN-S	PUNSTER-S
PRAIRIE-S	PREMOLT-S	PRIMINE-S	PROTECT-S	PUPUNHA-S
PRAISER-S	PREMOVE-S	PRIMING-S	PROTEGE-S	PURFLER-S
PRALINE-S	PRENAME-S	PRIMMER-S	PROTEID-S	PURGING-S
PRANCER-S	PREPACK-S	PRIMULA-S	PROTEIN-S	PURITAN-S
PRANCKE-S	PREPARE-S	PRINCES-S	PROTEND-S	PURLIEU-S
PRANKLE-S	PREPAVE-S	PRINKER-S	PROTEST-S	PURLINE-S
PRATING-S	PREPLAN-S	PRINTER-S	PROTHYL-S	PURLING-S
PRATTLE-S	PREPONE-S	PRISAGE-S	PROTIST-S	PURLOIN-S
PRAUNCE-S	PREPOSE-S	PRISERE-S	PROTIUM-S	PURPORT-S
PRAWLIN-S	PREPPIE-S	PRIVADO-S	PROTORE-S	PURPOSE-S
PRAWNER-S	PREPREG-S	PRIVATE-S	PROTYLE-S	PURPURA-S
PRAYING-S	PREPUCE-S	PROBAND-S	PROULER-S	PURPURE-S
PREASSE-S	PREPUPA-S	PROBANG-S	PROVAND-S	PURRING-S
PREAVER-S	PREQUEL-S	PROBATE-S	PROVANT-S	PURSUAL-S
PREBAKE-S	PRESAGE-S	PROBLEM-S	PROVEND-S	PURSUER-S
PREBEND-S	PRESALE-S	PROCARP-S	PROVERB-S	PURSUIT-S
PREBILL-S	PRESELL-S	PROCEED-S	PROVIDE-S	PURTRAY-S
PREBIND-S	PRESENT-S	PROCTOR-S	PROVINE-S	PURVIEW-S
PREBOIL-S	PRESHIP-S	PROCURE-S	PROVING-S	PUSHPIN-S
PREBOOK-S	PRESHOW-S	PRODDER-S	PROVISO-S	PUSHROD-S
PRECAST-S	PRESIDE-S	PRODRUG-S	PROVOKE-S	PUSSLEY-S
PRECEDE-S	PRESIFT-S	PRODUCE-S	PROVOST-S	PUSTULE-S
PRECENT-S	PRESOAK-S	PRODUCT-S	PROWLER-S	PUTCHER-S
PRECEPT-S	PRESORT-S	PROETTE-S	PRUNING-S	PUTCHUK-S
PRECIPE-S	PRESSER-S	PROFANE-S	PRURIGO-S	PUTDOWN-S
PRECISE-S	PRESSIE-S	PROFFER-S	PSALTER-S	PUTLOCK-S
PRECODE-S	PRESTER-S	PROFILE-S	PSAMMON-S	PUTTIER-S
PRECOOK-S	PRESUME-S	PROGGER-S	PSCHENT-S	PUTTING-S
PRECOOL-S	PRETAPE-S	PROGRAM-S	PSIONIC-S	PUTTOCK-S
PRECURE-S	PRETEEN-S	PROJECT-S	PSYCHIC-S	PUZZLER-S
PREDATE-S	PRETELL-S	PROLATE-S	PSYLLID-S	PYAEMIA-S
PREDAWN-S	PRETEND-S	PROLINE-S	PTARMIC-S	PYCNITE-S
PREDICT-S	PRETERM-S	PROLLER-S	PTOMAIN-S	PYEBALD-S
PREDIVE-S	PRETEST-S	PROLONG-S	PTYALIN-S	PYRALID-S
PREDOOM-S	PRETEXT-S	PROMINE-S	PUCCOON-S	PYRAMID-S
PREDUSK-S	PRETRIM-S	PROMISE-S	PUCELLE-S	PYREXIA-S

PYROGEN-S	QUINTIC-S	RAMPION-S	REALIGN-S	REDBIRD-S
PYRRHIC-S	QUINTIN-S	RAMPIRE-S	REALISE-S	REDBONE-S
PYRROLE-S	QUIPPER-S	RAMPOLE-S	REALISM-S	REDCOAT-S
PYTHIUM-S	QUITTAL-S	RANCHER-S	REALIST-S	REDDING-S
QABALAH-S	QUITTER-S	RANCOUR-S	REALIZE-S	REDFOOT-S
QAWWALI-S	QUITTOR-S	RANGING-S	REALLIE-S	REDHEAD-S
QUACKER-S	QUIXOTE-S	RANGOLI-S	REALLOT-S	REDLINE-S
QUACKLE-S	QUIZZER-S	RANKING-S	REALTER-S	REDNECK-S
QUADRAT-S	QUODLIN-S	RANKISM-S	REALTIE-S	REDOUBT-S
QUADRIC-S	QUOITER-S	RANKLES-S	REALTOR-S	REDOUND-S
QUAFFER-S	QUOMODO-S	RANPIKE-S	REAMEND-S	REDPOLL-S
QUAHAUG-S	RABANNA-S	RANSACK-S	REARGUE-S	REDRAFT-S
QUAKING-S	RABATTE-S	RANTING-S	REARISE-S	REDREAM-S
QUANNET-S	RABBITO-S	RAOULIA-S	REAVAIL-S	REDRILL-S
QUANTIC-S	RABBLER-S	RAPHIDE-S	REAWAKE-S	REDRIVE-S
QUARREL-S	RABBONI-S	RAPLOCH-S	REBADGE-S	REDROOT-S
QUARTAN-S	RACCOON-S	RAPPING-S	REBATER-S	REDSKIN-S
QUARTER-S	RACEWAY-S	RAPPORT-S	REBEGIN-S	REDTAIL-S
QUARTET-S	RACKETT-S	RAPTURE-S	REBIRTH-S	REDUCER-S
QUARTIC-S	RACKFUL-S	RAREBIT-S	REBLEND-S	REDWARE-S
QUASHEE-S	RACKING-S	RASBORA-S	REBLOOM-S	REDWING-S
QUASHER-S	RACLOIR-S	RASCHEL-S	REBOARD-S	REDWOOD-S
QUASHIE-S	RACQUET-S	RASPING-S	REBOUND-S	REEDBED-S
QUASSIA-S	RADIANT-S	RASTRUM-S	REBRACE-S	REEDING-S
QUASSIN-S	RADIATA-S	RATABLE-S	REBREED-S	REEFING-S
QUAYAGE-S	RADIATE-S	RATAFEE-S	REBUILD-S	REEJECT-S
QUEENIE-S	RADICAL-S	RATAFIA-S	REBUKER-S	REELECT-S
QUELLER-S	RADICEL-S	RATATAT-S	RECEIPT-S	REELING-S
QUERIDA-S	RADICLE-S	RATCHET-S	RECEIVE-S	REENACT-S
QUERIER-S	RAFFLER-S	RATFINK-S	RECENSE-S	REENDOW-S
QUERIST-S	RAFTING-S	RATHOLE-S	RECHART-S	REENJOY-S
QUESTER-S	RAGBOLT-S	RATLINE-S	RECHATE-S	REENTER-S
QUESTOR-S	RAGGING-S	RATLING-S	RECHEAT-S	REEQUIP-S
QUETZAL-S	RAGHEAD-S	RATPACK-S	RECHECK-S	REERECT-S
QUEUING-S	RAGMENT-S	RATTAIL-S	RECITAL-S	REEVOKE-S
QUEYNIE-S	RAGTIME-S	RATTEEN-S	RECITER-S	REEXPEL-S
QUIBBLE-S	RAGWEED-S	RATTING-S	RECLAIM-S	REFENCE-S
QUIBLIN-S	RAGWORK-S	RATTLER-S	RECLAME-S	REFEREE-S
QUICKEN-S	RAGWORM-S	RATTLIN-S	RECLASP-S	REFIGHT-S
QUICKIE-S	RAGWORT-S	RATTOON-S	RECLEAN-S	REFINER-S
QUIDDIT-S	RAIDING-S	RATTRAP-S	RECLIMB-S	REFLATE-S
QUIDDLE-S	RAILBED-S	RAUPATU-S	RECLINE-S	REFLECT-S
QUIESCE-S	RAILCAR-S	RAURIKI-S	RECLOSE-S	REFLOAT-S
QUIETEN-S	RAILING-S	RAVAGER-S	RECLUSE-S	REFLOOD-S
QUIETER-S	RAILWAY-S	RAVELER-S	RECOLOR-S	REFORGE-S
QUILLAI-S	RAIMENT-S	RAVELIN-S	RECOUNT-S	REFOUND-S
QUILLET-S	RAINBOW-S	RAVENER-S	RECOURE-S	REFRACT-S
QUILLON-S	RAINOUT-S	RAVIOLI-S	RECOVER-S	REFRAIN-S
QUILTER-S	RAISING-S	RAWHEAD-S	RECOWER-S	REFRAME-S
QUINCHE-S	RAKEOFF-S	RAWHIDE-S	RECOYLE-S	REFRONT-S
QUINELA-S	RALLIER-S	REACHER-S	RECRATE-S	REFUGEE-S
QUININA-S	RAMAKIN-S	REACTOR-S	RECROWN-S	REFUSAL-S
QUININE-S	RAMBLER-S	READAPT-S	RECRUIT-S	REFUSER-S
QUINNAT-S	RAMEKIN-S	READING-S	RECTION-S	REFUTAL-S
QUINOID-S	RAMILIE-S	READMIT-S	RECUILE-S	REFUTER-S
QUINONE-S	RAMPAGE-S	READOPT-S	RECURVE-S	REGALER-S
QUINTAL-S	RAMPART-S	READORN-S	RECUSAL-S	REGALIA-S
QUINTAN-S	RAMPICK-S	READOUT-S	RECYCLE-S	REGATTA-S
QUINTAR-S	RAMPIKE-S	REAGENT-S	REDBACK-S	REGAUGE-S
QUINTET-S	RAMPING-S	REALGAR-S	REDBAIT-S	REGENCE-S

REGIMEN-S	RENEWER-S	RESIDUE-S	REUNION-S	RIGHTEN-S
REGLAZE-S	RENNASE-S	RESIGHT-S	REUNITE-S	RIGHTER-S
REGORGE-S	RENNING-S	RESILIN-S	REUTTER-S	RIGLING-S
REGOSOL-S	RENTIER-S	RESINER-S	REVALUE-S	RIKISHA-S
REGRADE-S	RENTING-S	RESKILL-S	REVELER-S	RIKSHAW-S
REGRAFT-S	REOCCUR-S	RESLATE-S	REVENGE-S	RIMFIRE-S
REGRANT-S	REOFFER-S	RESMELT-S	REVENUE-S	RIMLAND-S
REGRATE-S	REORDER-S	RESOJET-S	REVERER-S	RIMMING-S
REGREDE-S	REPAINT-S	RESOLVE-S	REVERIE-S	RIMROCK-S
REGREEN-S	REPANEL-S	RESOUND-S	REVERSE-S	RIMSHOT-S
REGREET-S	REPAPER-S	RESPACE-S	REVERSI-S	RINGBIT-S
REGRIND-S	REPINER-S	RESPADE-S	REVERSO-S	RINGGIT-S
REGROOM-S	REPIQUE-S	RESPEAK-S	REVEUSE-S	RINGING-S
REGROUP-S	REPLACE-S	RESPECT-S	REVILER-S	RINGLET-S
REGULAR-S	REPLANT-S	RESPELL-S	REVISAL-S	RINGTAW-S
REHINGE-S	REPLATE-S	RESPIRE-S	REVISER-S	RINGWAY-S
REHOUSE-S	REPLEAD-S	RESPITE-S	REVISIT-S	RINSING-S
REIFIER-S	REPLETE-S	RESPLIT-S	REVISOR-S	RIOTING-S
REIMAGE-S	REPLICA-S	RESPOND-S	REVIVAL-S	RIOTISE-S
REINCUR-S	REPLIER-S	RESPOOL-S	REVIVER-S	RIOTIZE-S
REINTER-S	REPLUMB-S	RESPRAY-S	REVIVOR-S	RIPCORD-S
REISSUE-S	REPOINT-S	RESTACK-S	REVOICE-S	RIPENER-S
REITBOK-S	REPOSAL-S	RESTAFF-S	REVOKER-S	RIPIENO-S
REJOICE-S	REPOSER-S	RESTAGE-S	REVOLVE-S	RIPOSTE-S
REJONEO-S	REPOSIT-S	RESTAMP-S	REVUIST-S	RIPPIER-S
REJOURN-S	REPOWER-S	RESTART-S	REWAKEN-S	RIPPLER-S
REJUDGE-S	REPPING-S	RESTATE-S	REWEAVE-S	RIPPLET-S
RELABEL-S	REPRICE-S	RESTING-S	REWEIGH-S	RIPSTOP-S
RELACHE-S	REPRIME-S	RESTOCK-S	REWIDEN-S	RIPTIDE-S
RELAPSE-S	REPRINT-S	RESTOKE-S	REWRITE-S	RISIBLE-S
RELATER-S	REPRISE-S	RESTORE-S	REYNARD-S	RISOTTO-S
RELATOR-S	REPRIVE-S	RESTUFF-S	RHABDOM-S	RISPING-S
RELAXER-S	REPRIZE-S	RESTUMP-S	RHENIUM-S	RISSOLE-S
RELAXIN-S	REPROBE-S	RESTYLE-S	RHIZINE-S	RIVERET-S
RELEARN-S	REPROOF-S	RESUMER-S	RHIZOID-S	RIVETER-S
RELEASE-S	REPROVE-S	RESURGE-S	RHIZOME-S	RIVIERA-S
RELIEVE-S	REPRYVE-S	RETABLE-S	RHODIUM-S	RIVIERE-S
RELIEVO-S	REPTILE-S	RETAKER-S	RHODORA-S	RIVULET-S
RELIGHT-S	REPULSE-S	RETASTE-S	RHUBARB-S	RIZZART-S
RELIQUE-S	REPUNIT-S	RETHINK-S	RHYMIST-S	ROADBED-S
RELIVER-S	REQUERE-S	RETICLE-S	RHYTINA-S	ROADING-S
RELLENO-S	REQUEST-S	RETINAL-S	RIBBAND-S	ROADWAY-S
REMAKER-S	REQUIEM-S	RETINOL-S	RIBBING-S	ROAMING-S
REMANET-S	REQUIRE-S	RETINUE-S	RIBCAGE-S	ROARING-S
REMANIE-S	REQUITE-S	RETIRAL-S	RIBIBLE-S	ROASTER-S
REMBLAI-S	REQUOTE-S	RETIREE-S	RIBSTON-S	ROBINIA-S
REMERGE-S	RERAISE-S	RETIRER-S	RIBWORK-S	ROBOTIC-S
REMNANT-S	REROUTE-S	RETITLE-S	RIBWORT-S	ROBUSTA-S
REMODEL-S	RESCALE-S	RETOTAL-S	RICKSHA-S	ROCKIER-S
REMORSE-S	RESCIND-S	RETRACE-S	RICOTTA-S	ROCKING-S
REMOULD-S	RESCORE-S	RETRACK-S	RIDDLER-S	ROCKLAY-S
REMOUNT-S	RESCUER-S	RETRACT-S	RIDGING-S	ROCKOON-S
REMOVAL-S	RESEIZE-S	RETRAIN-S	RIDOTTO-S	ROCQUET-S
REMOVER-S	RESERVE-S	RETRAIT-S	RIEMPIE-S	RODDING-S
REMUAGE-S	RESHAPE-S	RETRATE-S	RIFFAGE-S	RODEWAY-S
REMUEUR-S	RESHAVE-S	RETREAD-S	RIFFLER-S	RODSTER-S
RENAGUE-S	RESHINE-S	RETREAT-S	RIFFOLA-S	ROEBUCK-S
RENEGER-S	RESHOOT-S	RETRIAL-S	RIFLING-S	ROGALLO-S
RENEGUE-S	RESIANT-S	RETSINA-S	RIGGALD-S	ROISTER-S
RENEWAL-S	RESIDER-S	RETWIST-S	RIGGING-S	ROKELAY-S

ROLFING-S	ROUSTER-S	SACKAGE-S	SAMSARA-S	SAVARIN-S
ROLLBAR-S	ROUTINE-S	SACKBUT-S	SAMSHOO-S	SAVELOY-S
ROLLICK-S	ROUTING-S	SACKFUL-S	SAMURAI-S	SAVIOUR-S
ROLLING-S	ROWBOAT-S	SACKING-S	SANCTUM-S	SAVORER-S
ROLLMOP-S	ROWLOCK-S	SACRING-S	SANDBAG-S	SAWBILL-S
ROLLOCK-S	ROWOVER-S	SACRIST-S	SANDBAR-S	SAWBUCK-S
ROLLOUT-S	ROYALET-S	SADDLER-S	SANDBOY-S	SAWDUST-S
ROLLWAY-S	ROYSTER-S	SADHANA-S	SANDBUR-S	SAWMILL-S
ROMAIKA-S	ROZELLE-S	SADIRON-S	SANDDAB-S	SAXHORN-S
ROMAINE-S	RUBABOO-S	SAFFIAN-S	SANDHOG-S	SAXTUBA-S
ROMANCE-S	RUBASSE-S	SAFFRON-S	SANDING-S	SAZERAC-S
ROMANZA-S	RUBBING-S	SAFROLE-S	SANDLOT-S	SCABBLE-S
ROMAUNT-S	RUBDOWN-S	SAGENES-S	SANDPIT-S	SCAFFIE-S
ROMNEYA-S	RUBELLA-S	SAGGARD-S	SANGHAT-S	SCAGLIA-S
RONDINO-S	RUBEOLA-S	SAGGING-S	SANGOMA-S	SCALADE-S
RONDURE-S	RUBICON-S	SAGITTA-S	SANGRIA-S	SCALADO-S
RONTGEN-S	RUCHING-S	SAGOUIN-S	SANICLE-S	SCALAGE-S
ROOFING-S	RUCTION-S	SAGUARO-S	SANTERA-S	SCALARE-S
ROOFTOP-S	RUDDOCK-S	SAHIBAH-S	SANTERO-S	SCALDER-S
ROOIKAT-S	RUDERAL-S	SAHIWAL-S	SANTOOR-S	SCALEUP-S
ROOINEK-S	RUELLIA-S	SAHUARO-S	SANTOUR-S	SCALING-S
ROOMFUL-S	RUFFIAN-S	SAILING-S	SANYASI-S	SCALLOP-S
ROOSTER-S	RUFFLER-S	SAIMIRI-S	SAOUARI-S	SCALPEL-S
ROOTAGE-S	RUFIYAA-S	SAKERET-S	SAPAJOU-S	SCALPER-S
ROOTCAP-S	RUGGING-S	SAKIYEH-S	SAPHEAD-S	SCAMBLE-S
ROOTING-S	RUINATE-S	SAKSAUL-S	SAPHENA-S	SCAMMER-S
ROOTLES-S	RUINING-S	SALAMON-S	SAPIENT-S	SCAMPER-S
ROOTLET-S	RULLION-S	SALBAND-S	SAPLING-S	SCANDAL-S
ROPEWAY-S	RULLOCK-S	SALCHOW-S	SAPONIN-S	SCANDIA-S
RORQUAL-S	RUMBLER-S	SALFERN-S	SAPPHIC-S	SCANNER-S
ROSACEA-S	RUMMAGE-S	SALICET-S	SAPROBE-S	SCANTLE-S
ROSAKER-S	RUMPLES-S	SALICIN-S	SAPSAGO-S	SCAPPLE-S
ROSALIA-S	RUNAWAY-S	SALIENT-S	SAPWOOD-S	SCAPULA-S
ROSEBAY-S	RUNBACK-S	SALIGOT-S	SARAFAN-S	SCARFER-S
ROSEBUD-S	RUNDALE-S	SALLIER-S	SARANGI-S	SCARLET-S
ROSEHIP-S	RUNDLET-S	SALPIAN-S	SARCASM-S	SCARPER-S
ROSELLA-S	RUNDOWN-S	SALTANT-S	SARCINA-S	SCATOLE-S
ROSELLE-S	RUNNING-S	SALTATE-S	SARCODE-S	SCATTER-S
ROSEOLA-S	RUNNION-S	SALTCAT-S	SARCOID-S	SCAUPER-S
ROSETTE-S	RUNOVER-S	SALTERN-S	SARCOMA-S	SCAVAGE-S
ROSIERE-S	RUPTURE-S	SALTIER-S	SARDANA-S	SCEDULE-S
ROSINER-S	RUSALKA-S	SALTINE-S	SARDINE-S	SCEPTER-S
ROSINOL-S	RUSHING-S	SALTING-S	SARKING-S	SCEPTIC-S
ROSOLIO-S	RUSSULA-S	SALTIRE-S	SARMENT-S	SCEPTRE-S
ROSTRUM-S	RUSTING-S	SALTPAN-S	SARSDEN-S	SCHANSE-S
ROTATOR-S	RUSTLER-S	SALUTER-S	SARSNET-S	SCHANZE-S
ROTCHIE-S	RUSTLES-S	SALVAGE-S	SASHIMI-S	SCHAPPE-S
ROTIFER-S	RUTTING-S	SALVETE-S	SATCHEL-S	SCHEMER-S
ROTUNDA-S	RYEPECK-S	SALVING-S	SATIATE-S	SCHEMIE-S
ROUGHEN-S	SABATON-S	SAMADHI-S	SATINET-S	SCHERZO-S
ROUGHER-S	SABAYON-S	SAMBHAR-S	SATSUMA-S	SCHISMA-S
ROUGHIE-S	SABBATH-S	SAMBHUR-S	SATYRAL-S	SCHLEPP-S
ROUILLE-S	SABELLA-S	SAMBUCA-S	SATYRID-S	SCHLICH-S
ROULADE-S	SABKHAH-S	SAMBUKE-S	SAUCIER-S	SCHLOCK-S
ROULEAU-S	SABKHAT-S	SAMISEN-S	SAUNTER-S	SCHLONG-S
ROUMING-S	SABREUR-S	SAMITHI-S	SAURIAN-S	SCHLUMP-S
ROUNDEL-S	SABURRA-S	SAMOVAR-S	SAUSAGE-S	SCHMEAR-S
ROUNDER-S	SACATON-S	SAMOYED-S	SAUTOIR-S	SCHMECK-S
ROUNDLE-S	SACCADE-S	SAMPIRE-S	SAVANNA-S	SCHMEER-S
ROUNDUP-S	SACCULE-S	SAMPLER-S	SAVANTE-S	SCHMOCK-S

SCHMUCK-S	SCUDDER-S	SEEDLIP-S	SERVEWE-S	SHASLIK-S
SCHNOOK-S	SCUDDLE-S	SEEDPOD-S	SERVICE-S	SHASTER-S
SCHNORR-S	SCUDLER-S	SEELING-S	SERVILE-S	SHASTRA-S
SCHOLAR-S	SCUFFER-S	SEEMING-S	SERVING-S	SHATTER-S
SCHOOLE-S	SCUFFLE-S	SEEPAGE-S	SERVLET-S	SHAVING-S
SCHTICK-S	SCULKER-S	SEETHER-S	SESSION-S	SHAWLEY-S
SCHTOOK-S	SCULLER-S	SEGMENT-S	SESTETT-S	SHAWLIE-S
SCHTUCK-S	SCULPIN-S	SEINING-S	SESTINA-S	SHEARER-S
SCIARID-S	SCUMBAG-S	SEISING-S	SESTINE-S	SHEATHE-S
SCIATIC-S	SCUMBER-S	SEISURE-S	SETBACK-S	SHEBANG-S
SCIENCE-S	SCUMBLE-S	SEIZING-S	SETLINE-S	SHEBEAN-S
SCISSEL-S	SCUMMER-S	SEIZURE-S	SETTING-S	SHEBEEN-S
SCISSIL-S	SCUNNER-S	SELECTA-S	SETTLER-S	SHEDDER-S
SCISSOR-S	SCUPPER-S	SELFDOM-S	SETTLOR-S	SHEDFUL-S
SCIURID-S	SCUTAGE-S	SELFING-S	SETUALE-S	SHEENEY-S
SCOFFER-S	SCUTTER-S	SELFISM-S	SETWALL-S	SHEENIE-S
SCOLDER-S	SCUTTLE-S	SELFIST-S	SEVENTH-S	SHEETER-S
SCOLLOP-S	SCYTALE-S	SELLOFF-S	SEVERAL-S	SHEHITA-S
SCOOPER-S	SCYTHER-S	SELLOUT-S	SEVICHE-S	SHEIKHA-S
SCOOTER-S	SDEIGNE-S	SELTZER-S	SEVRUGA-S	SHEITAN-S
SCOPULA-S	SEABANK-S	SELVAGE-S	SEXFOIL-S	SHELLAC-S
SCORING-S	SEABIRD-S	SEMINAR-S	SEXPERT-S	SHELLER-S
SCORNER-S	SEABOOT-S	SEMIPED-S	SEXTAIN-S	SHELTER-S
SCORPER-S	SEACOCK-S	SEMIPRO-S	SEXTANT-S	SHELTIE-S
SCORSER-S	SEAFOLK-S	SEMITAR-S	SEXTETT-S	SHELVER-S
SCOTOMA-S	SEAFOOD-S	SENATOR-S	SEXTILE-S	SHERANG-S
SCOTTIE-S	SEAFOWL-S	SENDING-S	SEXTUOR-S	SHERBET-S
SCOURER-S	SEAGULL-S	SENDOFF-S	SEYSURE-S	SHEREEF-S
SCOURGE-S	SEAHAWK-S	SENECIO-S	SFUMATO-S	SHERIAT-S
SCOURIE-S	SEAKALE-S	SENHORA-S	SHABBLE-S	SHERIFF-S
SCOURSE-S	SEALANT-S	SENOPIA-S	SHACKLE-S	SHEROOT-S
SCOUSER-S	SEALIFT-S	SENSATE-S	SHADING-S	SHIATSU-S
SCOUTER-S	SEALINE-S	SENSING-S	SHADOOF-S	SHIATZU-S
SCOWDER-S	SEALING-S	SENSISM-S	SHAFTER-S	SHICKER-S
SCOWLER-S	SEAMAID-S	SENSIST-S	SHAHADA-S	SHICKSA-S
SCOWRER-S	SEAMARK-S	SENTIMO-S	SHAHDOM-S	SHIDDER-S
SCOWRIE-S	SEAMSET-S	SEPIOST-S	SHAITAN-S	SHIFTER-S
SCRAICH-S	SEAPORT-S	SEPPUKU-S	SHAKEUP-S	SHIKARI-S
SCRAIGH-S	SEARING-S	SEPTAGE-S	SHAKING-S	SHIKKER-S
SCRAPER-S	SEASIDE-S	SEPTIME-S	SHAKUDO-S	SHIKSEH-S
SCRAPIE-S	SEASURE-S	SEPTUOR-S	SHALLON-S	SHIMAAL-S
SCRAUCH-S	SEATING-S	SEQUENT-S	SHALLOP-S	SHIMMER-S
SCRAUGH-S	SEAWALL-S	SEQUOIA-S	SHALLOT-S	SHIMMEY-S
SCREEVE-S	SEAWANT-S	SERAFIN-S	SHALLOW-S	SHINDIG-S
SCREICH-S	SEAWARD-S	SERFAGE-S	SHALWAR-S	SHINGLE-S
SCREIGH-S	SEAWARE-S	SERFDOM-S	SHAMBLE-S	SHINKIN-S
SCREWER-S	SEAWEED-S	SERGING-S	SHAMINA-S	SHINNEY-S
SCREWUP-S	SEAWORM-S	SERIATE-S	SHAMMER-S	SHIPFUL-S
SCRIBER-S	SECEDER-S	SERICIN-S	SHAMPOO-S	SHIPLAP-S
SCRIECH-S	SECLUDE-S	SERICON-S	SHANTEY-S	SHIPPEN-S
SCRIENE-S	SECONAL-S	SERIEMA-S	SHANTIH-S	SHIPPER-S
SCRIEVE-S	SECONDE-S	SERINGA-S	SHAPEUP-S	SHIPPIE-S
SCROOGE-S	SECRETE-S	SERKALI-S	SHAPING-S	SHIPPON-S
SCROTUM-S	SECTION-S	SEROVAR-S	SHARIAH-S	SHIPWAY-S
SCROUGE-S	SECULAR-S	SERPENT-S	SHARIAT-S	SHIRKER-S
SCROWLE-S	SECULUM-S	SERPIGO-S	SHARING-S	SHITAKE-S
SCROYLE-S	SECURER-S	SERRANO-S	SHARKER-S	SHITTAH-S
SCRUPLE-S	SEDUCER-S	SERRATE-S	SHARPEN-S	SHITTIM-S
SCRYING-S	SEEDBED-S	SERUEWE-S	SHARPER-S	SHIVITI-S
SCUCHIN-S	SEEDING-S	SERVANT-S	SHARPIE-S	SHMATTE-S

SHMOOSE-S	SIGANID-S	SKIDDOO-S	SLICKEN-S	SNEERER-S
SHMOOZE-S	SIGHTER-S	SKIDLID-S	SLICKER-S	SNEEZER-S
SHOCHET-S	SIGMATE-S	SKIDPAN-S	SLIDDER-S	SNICKER-S
SHOCKER-S	SIGMOID-S	SKIDWAY-S	SLIDING-S	SNICKET-S
SHOEING-S	SIGNAGE-S	SKIFFLE-S	SLIMMER-S	SNIFFER-S
SHOEPAC-S	SIGNING-S	SKILLET-S	SLINGER-S	SNIFFLE-S
SHOGGLE-S	SIGNIOR-S	SKIMMER-S	SLINKER-S	SNIFTER-S
SHONEEN-S	SIGNORA-S	SKIMMIA-S	SLINTER-S	SNIGGER-S
SHOOGIE-S	SIGNORE-S	SKINFUL-S	SLIOTAR-S	SNIGGLE-S
SHOOGLE-S	SILENCE-S	SKINKER-S	SLIPOUT-S	SNIGLET-S
SHOOTER-S	SILESIA-S	SKINNER-S	SLIPPER-S	SNIPING-S
SHOPBOY-S	SILICLE-S	SKIPPER-S	SLIPWAY-S	SNIPPER-S
SHOPFUL-S	SILICON-S	SKIPPET-S	SLITHER-S	SNIPPET-S
SHOPHAR-S	SILIQUA-S	SKIRRET-S	SLITTER-S	SNIRTLE-S
SHOPPER-S	SILIQUE-S	SKIRTER-S	SLOBBER-S	SNOOKER-S
SHORING-S	SILLOCK-S	SKITTER-S	SLOCKEN-S	SNOOPER-S
SHORTEN-S	SILURID-S	SKITTLE-S	SLOGGER-S	SNOOZER-S
SHORTIA-S	SIMARRE-S	SKIVING-S	SLOTTER-S	SNOOZLE-S
SHORTIE-S	SIMILOR-S	SKOLLIE-S	SLOWING-S	SNORING-S
SHOTGUN-S	SIMITAR-S	SKREEGH-S	SLUBBER-S	SNORKEL-S
SHOTPUT-S	SIMPKIN-S	SKREIGH-S	SLUGGER-S	SNORTER-S
SHOTTLE-S	SIMPLER-S	SKRIECH-S	SLUMBER-S	SNOTTER-S
SHOUTER-S	SIMULAR-S	SKRIEGH-S	SLUMGUM-S	SNOTTIE-S
SHOVING-S	SIMURGH-S	SKUDLER-S	SLUMISM-S	SNOWCAP-S
SHOWGHE-S	SINDING-S	SKULKER-S	SLUMMER-S	SNOWCAT-S
SHOWING-S	SINGING-S	SKULPIN-S	SLURPER-S	SNUBBER-S
SHOWOFF-S	SINGLET-S	SKUMMER-S	SMACKER-S	SNUFFER-S
SHRIEVE-S	SINGULT-S	SKUTTLE-S	SMARAGD-S	SNUFFLE-S
SHRIGHT-S	SINKAGE-S	SKYDIVE-S	SMARTEN-S	SNUGGLE-S
SHRIVEL-S	SINKING-S	SKYHOME-S	SMARTIE-S	SNUZZLE-S
SHRIVER-S	SINOPIA-S	SKYHOOK-S	SMASHER-S	SOAKAGE-S
SHTETEL-S	SINUATE-S	SKYJACK-S	SMASHUP-S	SOAKING-S
SHUCKER-S	SIRGANG-S	SKYLARK-S	SMATTER-S	SOARING-S
SHUDDER-S	SIRLOIN-S	SKYLINE-S	SMEARER-S	SOBBING-S
SHUFFLE-S	SIRNAME-S	SKYSAIL-S	SMEDDUM-S	SOCAGER-S
SHUNNER-S	SIROCCO-S	SKYSURF-S	SMELLER-S	SOCCAGE-S
SHUNTER-S	SISTRUM-S	SKYWALK-S	SMELTER-S	SOCIATE-S
SHUSHER-S	SITELLA-S	SKYWARD-S	SMICKER-S	SOCKEYE-S
SHUTEYE-S	SITFAST-S	SLABBER-S	SMICKET-S	SOFABED-S
SHUTOFF-S	SITTING-S	SLACKEN-S	SMIDGEN-S	SOGGING-S
SHUTOUT-S	SITUATE-S	SLACKER-S	SMIDGIN-S	SOILAGE-S
SHUTTER-S	SIXAINE-S	SLADANG-S	SMILING-S	SOILING-S
SHUTTLE-S	SIXTEEN-S	SLAMMER-S	SMIRKER-S	SOILURE-S
SHYLOCK-S	SIZEISM-S	SLANDER-S	SMOKEHO-S	SOJOURN-S
SHYSTER-S	SIZEIST-S	SLANGER-S	SMOKING-S	SOLACER-S
SIAMANG-S	SIZZLER-S	SLANTER-S	SMOLDER-S	SOLANIN-S
SIAMESE-S	SJAMBOK-S	SLAPPER-S	SMOODGE-S	SOLANUM-S
SIAMEZE-S	SKANGER-S	SLASHER-S	SMOTHER-S	SOLDADO-S
SIBLING-S	SKANKER-S	SLATHER-S	SMOUSER-S	SOLDIER-S
SIBSHIP-S	SKATING-S	SLATING-S	SMUDGER-S	SOLERET-S
SICKBAY-S	SKATOLE-S	SLATTER-S	SMUGGLE-S	SOLFEGE-S
SICKBED-S	SKEETER-S	SLEDDER-S	SMYTRIE-S	SOLICIT-S
SICKOUT-S	SKEGGER-S	SLEDGER-S	SNABBLE-S	SOLIDUM-S
SIDEARM-S	SKELDER-S	SLEEKEN-S	SNACKER-S	SOLIPED-S
SIDEBAR-S	SKELLIE-S	SLEEKER-S	SNAFFLE-S	SOLITON-S
SIDECAR-S	SKELLUM-S	SLEEPER-S	SNAPPER-S	SOLOIST-S
SIDEWAY-S	SKELTER-S	SLEEVER-S	SNAPTIN-S	SOLUBLE-S
SIENITE-S	SKEPFUL-S	SLEIGHT-S	SNARING-S	SOLVATE-S
SIEVERT-S	SKEPTIC-S	SLENTER-S	SNARLER-S	SOLVENT-S
SIFTING-S	SKIDDER-S	SLICING-S	SNEAKER-S	SOMEONE-S

SOMEWAY-S	SPARKER-S	SPLURGE-S	STADIAL-S	STENTOR-S
SONANCE-S	SPARKIE-S	SPODIUM-S	STADIUM-S	STEPNEY-S
SONDAGE-S	SPARKLE-S	SPOILER-S	STAFFER-S	STEPPER-S
SONDELI-S	SPAROID-S	SPONDEE-S	STAGGER-S	STEPSON-S
SONGKOK-S	SPARRER-S	SPONDYL-S	STAGGIE-S	STERLET-S
SONHOOD-S	SPARROW-S	SPONGER-S	STAGING-S	STERNUM-S
SONSHIP-S	SPARTAN-S	SPONGIN-S	STAINER-S	STEROID-S
SOOPING-S	SPARTHE-S	SPONSON-S	STAITHE-S	STERTOR-S
SOOTHER-S	SPASTIC-S	SPONSOR-S	STALKER-S	STEWARD-S
SOPHISM-S	SPATTEE-S	SPOOFER-S	STAMINA-S	STEWBUM-S
SOPHIST-S	SPATTER-S	SPOOLER-S	STAMMEL-S	STEWING-S
SOPPING-S	SPATULA-S	SPOONEY-S	STAMMER-S	STEWPAN-S
SOPRANO-S	SPATULE-S	SPOORER-S	STAMPER-S	STEWPOT-S
SORBATE-S	SPATZLE-S	SPORRAN-S	STANDBY-S	STHENIA-S
SORBENT-S	SPAWNER-S	SPORTER-S	STANDEE-S	STIBBLE-S
SORBITE-S	SPEAKER-S	SPORULE-S	STANDER-S	STIBINE-S
SORBOSE-S	SPEARER-S	SPOTTER-S	STANDUP-S	STIBIUM-S
SORDINE-S	SPECIAL-S	SPOTTIE-S	STANIEL-S	STICKER-S
SOREHON-S	SPECKLE-S	SPOUSAL-S	STANINE-S	STICKLE-S
SORGHUM-S	SPECTER-S	SPOUTER-S	STANNEL-S	STICKUM-S
SORNING-S	SPECTRE-S	SPRAINT-S	STANNUM-S	STICKUP-S
SOROBAN-S	SPEEDER-S	SPRAYER-S	STANYEL-S	STIDDIE-S
SOROCHE-S	SPEEDUP-S	SPREAGH-S	STAPLER-S	STIFFEN-S
SORTING-S	SPEELER-S	SPREAZE-S	STAPPLE-S	STIFFIE-S
SOSATIE-S	SPELDER-S	SPREDDE-S	STARDOM-S	STIFLER-S
SOSSING-S	SPELDIN-S	SPREEZE-S	STARING-S	STILLER-S
SOTTING-S	SPELLER-S	SPRIGHT-S	STARKEN-S	STILTER-S
SOUBISE-S	SPELTER-S	SPRINGE-S	STARKER-S	STINGER-S
SOUFFLE-S	SPELUNK-S	SPUDDER-S	STARLET-S	STINKER-S
SOULDAN-S	SPENCER-S	SPUDDLE-S	STARNIE-S	STINTER-S
SOUMING-S	SPENDER-S	SPULYIE-S	STARTER-S	STIPEND-S
SOUNDER-S	SPERTHE-S	SPULZIE-S	STARTLE-S	STIPPLE-S
SOUPCON-S	SPHAERE-S	SPUMONE-S	STARTUP-S	STIPULE-S
SOUPFIN-S	SPHEARE-S	SPUMONI-S	STARVER-S	STIRRAH-S
SOUPLES-S	SPHERIC-S	SPUNKIE-S	STASHIE-S	STIRRER-S
SOURING-S	SPICULE-S	SPURNER-S	STATICE-S	STIRRUP-S
SOUROCK-S	SPIEGEL-S	SPURRER-S	STATION-S	STISHIE-S
SOURSOP-S	SPIELER-S	SPURREY-S	STATISM-S	STOCKER-S
SOUSING-S	SPIGNEL-S	SPURTER-S	STATIST-S	STODGER-S
SOUSLIK-S	SPILING-S	SPURTLE-S	STATIVE-S	STOITER-S
SOUTANE-S	SPILITE-S	SPURWAY-S	STATURE-S	STOKVEL-S
SOUTHER-S	SPILLER-S	SPUTNIK-S	STATUTE-S	STOLLEN-S
SOWBACK-S	SPINACE-S	SPUTTER-S	STEALER-S	STOMACH-S
SOYBEAN-S	SPINDLE-S	SPYHOLE-S	STEALTH-S	STOMACK-S
SOYMILK-S	SPINNER-S	SPYWARE-S	STEAMER-S	STOMATE-S
SPACING-S	SPINNET-S	SQUACCO-S	STEAMIE-S	STOMIUM-S
SPACKLE-S	SPINNEY-S	SQUALOR-S	STEARIN-S	STOMPER-S
SPADGER-S	SPINODE-S	SQUARER-S	STEELIE-S	STOMPIE-S
SPAEING-S	SPINOFF-S	SQUEEZE-S	STEEPEN-S	STONING-S
SPAIRGE-S	SPINOUT-S	SQUIDGE-S	STEEPER-S	STONKER-S
SPALLER-S	SPINULE-S	SQUILLA-S	STEEPLE-S	STOOKER-S
SPAMBOT-S	SPIRAEA-S	SQUIRES-S	STEERER-S	STOOKIE-S
SPAMMER-S	SPIRANT-S	SRADDHA-S	STEMBOK-S	STOOLIE-S
SPAMMIE-S	SPIREME-S	STABBER-S	STEMLET-S	STOOPER-S
SPANCEL-S	SPIRTLE-S	STABILE-S	STEMMER-S	STOPGAP-S
SPANGLE-S	SPIRULA-S	STABLER-S	STEMPEL-S	STOPING-S
SPANIEL-S	SPITTER-S	STACKER-S	STEMPLE-S	STOPOFF-S
SPANKER-S	SPITTLE-S	STACKET-S	STEMSON-S	STOPPER-S
SPANNER-S	SPLICER-S	STACKUP-S	STENCIL-S	STOPPLE-S
SPARGER-S	SPLODGE-S	STADDLE-S	STENGAH-S	STORAGE-S

STORMER-S	SUBCELL-S	SUCKLER-S	SURBASE-S	SWINGER-S
STOTTER-S	SUBCLAN-S	SUCKLES-S	SURBATE-S	SWINGLE-S
STOTTIE-S	SUBCODE-S	SUCRASE-S	SURCOAT-S	SWINKER-S
STOUTEN-S	SUBCOOL-S	SUCRIER-S	SURFACE-S	SWINNEY-S
STOVING-S	SUBCULT-S	SUCROSE-S	SURFEIT-S	SWIPPLE-S
STOWAGE-S	SUBDEAN-S	SUCTION-S	SURFING-S	SWISHER-S
STOWING-S	SUBDUAL-S	SUFFARI-S	SURGEON-S	SWITHER-S
STRAFER-S	SUBDUCE-S	SUFFETE-S	SURGING-S	SWIZZLE-S
STRAINT-S	SUBDUCT-S	SUFFICE-S	SURLOIN-S	SWOBBER-S
STRANGE-S	SUBDUER-S	SUFFUSE-S	SURMISE-S	SWOFFER-S
STRATUM-S	SUBEDAR-S	SUGARER-S	SURNAME-S	SWOONER-S
STRAYER-S	SUBEDIT-S	SUGGEST-S	SURTOUT-S	SWOOPER-S
STRAYVE-S	SUBERIN-S	SUGGING-S	SURVEIL-S	SWOPPER-S
STRETTA-S	SUBFILE-S	SUICIDE-S	SURVIEW-S	SWORDER-S
STRETTO-S	SUBFUSC-S	SUIDIAN-S	SURVIVE-S	SWOTTER-S
STREWER-S	SUBFUSK-S	SUIPLAP-S	SUSPECT-S	SWOZZLE-S
STRIATE-S	SUBGOAL-S	SUITING-S	SUSPEND-S	SYENITE-S
STRIDER-S	SUBHEAD-S	SULFATE-S	SUSPIRE-S	SYLPHID-S
STRIDOR-S	SUBIDEA-S	SULFIDE-S	SUSTAIN-S	SYLVINE-S
STRIGIL-S	SUBITEM-S	SULFITE-S	SWABBER-S	SYLVITE-S
STRIKER-S	SUBJECT-S	SULFONE-S	SWABBIE-S	SYMBION-S
STRIPER-S	SUBJOIN-S	SULLAGE-S	SWADDIE-S	SYMBIOT-S
STRIVER-S	SUBLATE-S	SULPHID-S	SWADDLE-S	SYMBOLE-S
STROBIL-S	SUBLIME-S	SULPHUR-S	SWAGGER-S	SYMITAR-S
STRODLE-S	SUBLINE-S	SULTANA-S	SWAGGIE-S	SYMPTOM-S
STROKER-S	SUBMENU-S	SUMATRA-S	SWALING-S	SYNAGOG-S
STROOKE-S	SUBPART-S	SUMMAND-S	SWALLET-S	SYNANON-S
STROPHE-S	SUBPENA-S	SUMMATE-S	SWALLOW-S	SYNAPSE-S
STROWER-S	SUBPLOT-S	SUMMING-S	SWAMPER-S	SYNAPTE-S
STROYER-S	SUBRACE-S	SUMMIST-S	SWANKER-S	SYNCARP-S
STRUDEL-S	SUBRENT-S	SUMOIST-S	SWANKEY-S	SYNCHRO-S
STUBBIE-S	SUBRING-S	SUMPTER-S	SWANKIE-S	SYNCOPE-S
STUBBLE-S	SUBRULE-S	SUNBAKE-S	SWANNIE-S	SYNDING-S
STUDDIE-S	SUBSALE-S	SUNBATH-S	SWANPAN-S	SYNFUEL-S
STUDDLE-S	SUBSECT-S	SUNBEAM-S	SWAPPER-S	SYNODAL-S
STUDENT-S	SUBSERE-S	SUNBELT-S	SWARMER-S	SYNONYM-S
STUDIER-S	SUBSIDE-S	SUNBIRD-S	SWASHER-S	SYNOVIA-S
STUFFER-S	SUBSIST-S	SUNBURN-S	SWATHER-S	SYNTAGM-S
STUIVER-S	SUBSITE-S	SUNDARI-S	SWATTER-S	SYNTHON-S
STUMBLE-S	SUBSOIL-S	SUNDECK-S	SWAYING-S	SYRETTE-S
STUMMEL-S	SUBSONG-S	SUNDIAL-S	SWAZZLE-S	SYRINGA-S
STUMPER-S	SUBSUME-S	SUNDOWN-S	SWEARER-S	SYRINGE-S
STUNNER-S	SUBTACK-S	SUNGLOW-S	SWEATER-S	SYRPHID-S
STURMER-S	SUBTASK-S	SUNLAMP-S	SWEDGER-S	SYSTOLE-S
STUSHIE-S	SUBTEEN-S	SUNLAND-S	SWEENEY-S	SYSTYLE-S
STUTTER-S	SUBTEND-S	SUNRISE-S	SWEEPER-S	TABANID-S
STYLING-S	SUBTEST-S	SUNROOF-S	SWEETEN-S	TABARET-S
STYLISE-S	SUBTEXT-S	SUNROOM-S	SWEETIE-S	TABETIC-S
STYLIST-S	SUBTONE-S	SUNSPOT-S	SWELLER-S	TABINET-S
STYLITE-S	SUBTYPE-S	SUNSTAR-S	SWELTER-S	TABLEAU-S
STYLIZE-S	SUBUNIT-S	SUNSUIT-S	SWERVER-S	TABLIER-S
STYLOID-S	SUBVENE-S	SUNTRAP-S	SWIDDEN-S	TABLING-S
STYPTIC-S	SUBVERT-S	SUNWARD-S	SWIFTER-S	TABLOID-S
STYRENE-S	SUBZONE-S	SUPPAWN-S	SWIFTIE-S	TABORER-S
SUASION-S	SUCCADE-S	SUPPORT-S	SWIGGER-S	TABORET-S
SUBADAR-S	SUCCEED-S	SUPPOSE-S	SWILLER-S	TABORIN-S
SUBAREA-S	SUCCOUR-S	SUPREME-S	SWIMMER-S	TABOULI-S
SUBATOM-S	SUCCUBA-S	SUPREMO-S	SWINDGE-S	TABRERE-S
SUBBASE-S	SUCCUMB-S	SURAMIN-S	SWINDLE-S	TACHISM-S
SUBBING-S	SUCKING-S	SURANCE-S	SWINGBY-S	TACHIST-S

TACHYON-S	TANKARD-S	TEETHER-S	THANGKA-S	TIETACK-S
TACKING-S	TANKFUL-S	TEKTITE-S	THANKER-S	TIFFING-S
TACKLER-S	TANKING-S	TELAMON-S	THANNAH-S	TIGHTEN-S
TACKLES-S	TANKINI-S	TELECOM-S	THAWING-S	TIKANGA-S
TACNODE-S	TANLING-S	TELEOST-S	THEATER-S	TILAPIA-S
TACRINE-S	TANNAGE-S	TELERAN-S	THEATRE-S	TILLAGE-S
TACTION-S	TANNATE-S	TELFORD-S	THEELIN-S	TILLING-S
TACTISM-S	TANNING-S	TELLING-S	THEELOL-S	TILLITE-S
TADPOLE-S	TANTARA-S	TELPHER-S	THENAGE-S	TILTING-S
TAEDIUM-S	TANTRUM-S	TEMBLOR-S	THEOLOG-S	TIMARAU-S
TAFFETA-S	TANYARD-S	TEMPERA-S	THEORBO-S	TIMBALE-S
TAGGANT-S	TAPERER-S	TEMPEST-S	THEOREM-S	TIMBREL-S
TAGGING-S	TAPHOLE-S	TEMPLAR-S	THEORIC-S	TIMEOUT-S
TAGLINE-S	TAPIOCA-S	TEMPLET-S	THERIAC-S	TIMOLOL-S
TAGMEME-S	TAPPICE-S	TEMPTER-S	THERIAN-S	TINAMOU-S
TAILARD-S	TAPPING-S	TEMPURA-S	THERMAL-S	TINCHEL-S
TAILFAN-S	TAPROOM-S	TENDRIL-S	THERMEL-S	TINFOIL-S
TAILFIN-S	TAPROOT-S	TENDRON-S	THERMIT-S	TINGLER-S
TAILING-S	TAPSTER-S	TENFOLD-S	THIAMIN-S	TINHORN-S
TAILLES-S	TARAMEA-S	TENNIST-S	THIAZIN-S	TINKLER-S
TAILLIE-S	TARDYON-S	TENONER-S	THIAZOL-S	TINNING-S
TAILZIE-S	TARRIER-S	TENSION-S	THICKEN-S	TINTACK-S
TAKEOFF-S	TARRING-S	TENTAGE-S	THICKET-S	TINTING-S
TAKEOUT-S	TARROCK-S	TENTFUL-S	THICKIE-S	TINTYPE-S
TALAUNT-S	TARSEAL-S	TENTIGO-S	THIGGER-S	TINWARE-S
TALAYOT-S	TARSIER-S	TENTING-S	THILLER-S	TINWORK-S
TALIPAT-S	TARTANA-S	TEQUILA-S	THIMBLE-S	TIPCART-S
TALIPED-S	TARTANE-S	TERAOHM-S	THINKER-S	TIPPING-S
TALIPOT-S	TARTARE-S	TERBIUM-S	THINNER-S	TIPPLER-S
TALKING-S	TARTINE-S	TEREBRA-S	THIONIN-S	TIPSTER-S
TALLAGE-S	TARTLET-S	TERGITE-S	THIONYL-S	TIRASSE-S
TALLBOY-S	TARTUFE-S	TERMITE-S	THISTLE-S	TITANIA-S
TALLENT-S	TARWEED-S	TERNION-S	THORITE-S	TITHING-S
TALLIER-S	TASKBAR-S	TERPENE-S	THORIUM-S	TITLARK-S
TALLITH-S	TASKING-S	TERRACE-S	THOUGHT-S	TITLING-S
TALLYHO-S	TASSELL-S	TERRAIN-S	THREAVE-S	TITLIST-S
TALOOKA-S	TASTING-S	TERRANE-S	THRIMSA-S	TITRANT-S
TAMANDU-S	TATOUAY-S	TERREEN-S	THRIVER-S	TITRATE-S
TAMARAO-S	TATTING-S	TERRENE-S	THROWER-S	TITULAR-S
TAMARAU-S	TATTLER-S	TERRIER-S	THRUPUT-S	TOASTER-S
TAMARIN-S	TAUHINU-S	TERRINE-S	THRUWAY-S	TOASTIE-S
TAMASHA-S	TAUNTER-S	TERROIR-S	THRYMSA-S	TOBACCO-S
TAMBALA-S	TAURINE-S	TERSION-S	THUGGEE-S	TOCCATA-S
TAMBOUR-S	TAUTAUG-S	TERTIAL-S	THULITE-S	TOCKLEY-S
TAMBURA-S	TAVERNA-S	TERTIAN-S	THULIUM-S	TODDLER-S
TAMPALA-S	TAXABLE-S	TESTATE-S	THUMPER-S	TOECLIP-S
TAMPING-S	TAXICAB-S	TESTERN-S	THUNDER-S	TOEHOLD-S
TAMPION-S	TAXIWAY-S	TESTING-S	THWAITE-S	TOENAIL-S
TANADAR-S	TEABOWL-S	TESTOON-S	THYLOSE-S	TOESHOE-S
TANAGER-S	TEACAKE-S	TESTRIL-S	THYMINE-S	TOFUTTI-S
TANAGRA-S	TEACART-S	TESTUDO-S	THYROID-S	TOGGLER-S
TANBARK-S	TEACHER-S	TETANIC-S	TICKING-S	TOHEROA-S
TANDOOR-S	TEAMING-S	TETOTUM-S	TICKLER-S	TOHUNGA-S
TANGELO-S	TEAROOM-S	TETRACT-S	TIDDLER-S	TOILING-S
TANGENT-S	TEASHOP-S	TETRODE-S	TIDDLEY-S	TOISECH-S
TANGHIN-S	TEASING-S	TEUCHAT-S	TIDERIP-S	TOKAMAK-S
TANGLER-S	TEATIME-S	TEXTILE-S	TIDEWAY-S	TOKOMAK-S
TANGRAM-S	TEAWARE-S	TEXTURE-S	TIEBACK-S	TOLIDIN-S
TANIWHA-S	TECHNIC-S	THALWEG-S	TIERCEL-S	TOLLAGE-S
TANKAGE-S	TECTITE-S	THANAGE-S	TIERCET-S	TOLLBAR-S

TOLLING-S	TOSTADA-S	TRAPPER-S	TRINKUM-S	TRYPSIN-S
TOLLWAY-S	TOSTADO-S	TRASHER-S	TRIOLET-S	TRYSAIL-S
TOLUATE-S	TOTIENT-S	TRAVAIL-S	TRIONYM-S	TRYSTER-S
TOLUENE-S	TOTTING-S	TRAWLER-S	TRIOXID-S	TSADDIK-S
TOLUIDE-S	TOUCHER-S	TRAWLEY-S	TRIPACK-S	TSADDIQ-S
TOLUOLE-S	TOUCHUP-S	TRAYBIT-S	TRIPLET-S	TSANTSA-S
TOMBACK-S	TOUGHEN-S	TRAYFUL-S	TRIPOLI-S	TSARDOM-S
TOMBOLA-S	TOUGHIE-S	TREACLE-S	TRIPPER-S	TSARINA-S
TOMBOLO-S	TOURACO-S	TREADER-S	TRIPPET-S	TSARISM-S
TOMFOOL-S	TOURING-S	TREADLE-S	TRIPPLE-S	TSARIST-S
TOMPION-S	TOURISM-S	TREAGUE-S	TRIPTAN-S	TSATSKE-S
TONDINO-S	TOURIST-S	TREASON-S	TRIREME-S	TSIGANE-S
TONEARM-S	TOURNEY-S	TREATER-S	TRISECT-S	TSUNAMI-S
TONEPAD-S	TOUSING-S	TREDDLE-S	TRISEME-S	TUATARA-S
TONETIC-S	TOWAWAY-S	TREETOP-S	TRISHAW-S	TUATERA-S
TONETTE-S	TOWBOAT-S	TREFOIL-S	TRISOME-S	TUBAIST-S
TONIGHT-S	TOWHEAD-S	TREHALA-S	TRISULA-S	TUBBING-S
TONNAGE-S	TOWLINE-S	TREILLE-S	TRITIDE-S	TUBEFUL-S
TONNEAU-S	TOWMOND-S	TREKKER-S	TRITIUM-S	TUBFAST-S
TONNELL-S	TOWMONT-S	TREMBLE-S	TRITOMA-S	TUBULIN-S
TONSURE-S	TOWNLET-S	TREMOLO-S	TRITONE-S	TUFTING-S
TONTINE-S	TOWPATH-S	TRENAIL-S	TRIUMPH-S	TUGBOAT-S
TOOLBAG-S	TOWROPE-S	TRENISE-S	TRIVIUM-S	TUGGING-S
TOOLBAR-S	TOWSACK-S	TRENTAL-S	TRIZONE-S	TUGHRIK-S
TOOLING-S	TOXEMIA-S	TREPANG-S	TROCHAR-S	TUILYIE-S
TOOLKIT-S	TOYSHOP-S	TRESSEL-S	TROCHEE-S	TUILZIE-S
TOOLSET-S	TRACEUR-S	TRESTLE-S	TROCHIL-S	TUITION-S
TOOTLER-S	TRACHEA-S	TREYBIT-S	TROELIE-S	TULCHAN-S
TOOTSIE-S	TRACHLE-S	TRIACID-S	TROFFER-S	TUMBLER-S
TOPARCH-S	TRACING-S	TRIADIC-S	TROLAND-S	TUMBREL-S
TOPCOAT-S	TRACKER-S	TRIARCH-S	TROLLER-S	TUMBRIL-S
TOPKICK-S	TRACTOR-S	TRIATIC-S	TROLLEY-S	TUMESCE-S
TOPKNOT-S	TRADING-S	TRIAXON-S	TROLLOP-S	TUMMLER-S
TOPLINE-S	TRADUCE-S	TRIAZIN-S	TROMINO-S	TUMSHIE-S
TOPMAST-S	TRAFFIC-S	TRIBADE-S	TROMMEL-S	TUNICIN-S
TOPONYM-S	TRAGULE-S	TRIBBLE-S	TROOLIE-S	TUNICLE-S
TOPPING-S	TRAILER-S	TRIBLET-S	TROOPER-S	TUNNAGE-S
TOPSAIL-S	TRAINEE-S	TRIBUNE-S	TROPINE-S	TUNNING-S
TOPSIDE-S	TRAINER-S	TRIBUTE-S	TROPISM-S	TURACIN-S
TOPSOIL-S	TRAIPSE-S	TRICKER-S	TROPIST-S	TURACOU-S
TOPSPIN-S	TRAITOR-S	TRICKLE-S	TROTTER-S	TURBAND-S
TOPWORK-S	TRAJECT-S	TRICLAD-S	TROUBLE-S	TURBANT-S
TORCHER-S	TRAMCAR-S	TRICORN-S	TROUNCE-S	TURBETH-S
TORCHON-S	TRAMELL-S	TRIDARN-S	TROUPER-S	TURBINE-S
TORDION-S	TRAMMEL-S	TRIDENT-S	TROUSER-S	TURBITH-S
TORGOCH-S	TRAMMIE-S	TRIDUUM-S	TROUTER-S	TURBOND-S
TORMENT-S	TRAMPER-S	TRIELLA-S	TRUCAGE-S	TURDION-S
TORNADE-S	TRAMPET-S	TRIFFID-S	TRUCKER-S	TURFING-S
TORNADO-S	TRAMPLE-S	TRIFLER-S	TRUCKIE-S	TURFITE-S
TORPEDO-S	TRAMWAY-S	TRIGGER-S	TRUCKLE-S	TURFSKI-S
TORQUER-S	TRANCHE-S	TRIGLOT-S	TRUDGEN-S	TURGITE-S
TORRENT-S	TRANECT-S	TRIGRAM-S	TRUDGER-S	TURISTA-S
TORSADE-S	TRANGAM-S	TRILITH-S	TRUFFLE-S	TURMOIL-S
TORSION-S	TRANGLE-S	TRILLER-S	TRUMPET-S	TURNDUN-S
TORTONI-S	TRANKUM-S	TRILOBE-S	TRUNDLE-S	TURNING-S
TORTURE-S	TRANNIE-S	TRIMMER-S	TRUNNEL-S	TURNKEY-S
TORULIN-S	TRANSIT-S	TRIMTAB-S	TRUSSER-S	TURNOFF-S
TOSHACH-S	TRANSOM-S	TRINDLE-S	TRUSTEE-S	TURNOUT-S
TOSSING-S	TRANTER-S	TRINGLE-S	TRUSTER-S	TURPETH-S
TOSSPOT-S	TRAPEZE-S	TRINKET-S	TRUSTOR-S	TURTLER-S

TUSHKAR-S	TZARIST-S	UNITAGE-S	UNSTRAP-S	UPSURGE-S
TUSHKER-S	TZIGANE-S	UNITARD-S	UNSTRIP-S	UPSWARM-S
TUSKING-S	UDALLER-S	UNITING-S	UNSWEAR-S	UPSWEEP-S
TUSSOCK-S	UKELELE-S	UNITION-S	UNTHINK-S	UPSWELL-S
TUSSORE-S	UKULELE-S	UNITISE-S	UNTRACE-S	UPSWING-S
TUSSUCK-S	ULEXITE-S	UNITIZE-S	UNTRACK-S	UPTEMPO-S
TUTANIA-S	ULULATE-S	UNJOINT-S	UNTREAD-S	UPTHROW-S
TUTELAR-S	UMBRAGE-S	UNKNOWN-S	UNTRUST-S	UPTRAIN-S
TUTENAG-S	UMBRERE-S	UNLEARN-S	UNTRUTH-S	UPTREND-S
TUTOYER-S	UMLUNGU-S	UNLEVEL-S	UNTWINE-S	UPVALUE-S
TUTTING-S	UNAKITE-S	UNLOOSE-S	UNTWIST-S	UPWHIRL-S
TUTWORK-S	UNALIST-S	UNMAKER-S	UNTYING-S	URAEMIA-S
TWADDLE-S	UNAWARE-S	UNMITER-S	UNVAILE-S	URALITE-S
TWANGER-S	UNBEGET-S	UNMITRE-S	UNVISOR-S	URANIDE-S
TWANGLE-S	UNBEING-S	UNMOULD-S	UNVOICE-S	URANISM-S
TWANKAY-S	UNBLIND-S	UNMOUNT-S	UNWATER-S	URANITE-S
TWASOME-S	UNBLOCK-S	UNNERVE-S	UNWEAVE-S	URANIUM-S
TWATTLE-S	UNBOSOM-S	UNNOBLE-S	UNWOMAN-S	UREDINE-S
TWEAKER-S	UNBRACE-S	UNORDER-S	UNWORTH-S	URETHAN-S
TWEEDLE-S	UNBRAID-S	UNPAINT-S	UNWRITE-S	URETHRA-S
TWEENER-S	UNBRAKE-S	UNPANEL-S	UPBRAID-S	URGENCE-S
TWEENIE-S	UNBUILD-S	UNPAPER-S	UPBREAK-S	URICASE-S
TWEETER-S	UNCHAIN-S	UNPLACE-S	UPBRING-S	URIDINE-S
TWEEZER-S	UNCHAIR-S	UNPLAIT-S	UPBUILD-S	URINATE-S
TWELFTH-S	UNCHARM-S	UNPLUMB-S	UPBURST-S	URODELE-S
TWIBILL-S	UNCHECK-S	UNPLUME-S	UPCHEER-S	UROLITH-S
TWIDDLE-S	UNCHILD-S	UNPURSE-S	UPCHUCK-S	UROMERE-S
TWIGGER-S	UNCHOKE-S	UNQUEEN-S	UPCLIMB-S	UROSOME-S
TWIGLOO-S	UNCLAMP-S	UNQUIET-S	UPCLOSE-S	USAUNCE-S
TWINING-S	UNCLASP-S	UNQUOTE-S	UPCURVE-S	USUCAPT-S
TWINJET-S	UNCLOAK-S	UNRAVEL-S	UPDATER-S	USURPER-S
TWINKIE-S	UNCLOSE-S	UNREAVE-S	UPDRAFT-S	UTENSIL-S
TWINKLE-S	UNCLOUD-S	UNREEVE-S	UPFLING-S	UTILISE-S
TWINSET-S	UNCOVER-S	UNRIGHT-S	UPGOING-S	UTILIZE-S
TWINTER-S	UNCRATE-S	UNRIVET-S	UPGRADE-S	UTOPIAN-S
TWIRLER-S	UNCROWN-S	UNROOST-S	UPHEAVE-S	UTOPISM-S
TWISCAR-S	UNCTION-S	UNROUND-S	UPHOARD-S	UTOPIST-S
TWISTER-S	UNCURSE-S	UNSAINT-S	UPHOIST-S	UTRICLE-S
TWISTOR-S	UNDIGHT-S	UNSCALE-S	UPHOORD-S	UTTERER-S
TWITTEN-S	UNDOING-S	UNSCREW-S	UPLIGHT-S	VACANCE-S
TWITTER-S	UNDRAPE-S	UNSENSE-S	UPMAKER-S	VACATUR-S
TWIZZLE-S	UNEARTH-S	UNSHALE-S	UPRAISE-S	VACCINA-S
TWOCCER-S	UNEQUAL-S	UNSHAPE-S	UPRIGHT-S	VACCINE-S
TWOCKER-S	UNFAITH-S	UNSHELL-S	UPRISAL-S	VACUATE-S
TWOFOLD-S	UNFENCE-S	UNSHIFT-S	UPRISER-S	VACUIST-S
TWOONIE-S	UNFROCK-S	UNSHOOT-S	UPRIVER-S	VACUOLE-S
TWOSOME-S	UNGIRTH-S	UNSHOUT-S	UPROUSE-S	VAGRANT-S
TYCHISM-S	UNGLOVE-S	UNSIGHT-S	UPSCALE-S	VAIVODE-S
TYLOPOD-S	UNGUARD-S	UNSINEW-S	UPSHIFT-S	VALANCE-S
TYLOSIN-S	UNGUENT-S	UNSLING-S	UPSHOOT-S	VALENCE-S
TYPEBAR-S	UNHEART-S	UNSNARL-S	UPSILON-S	VALIANT-S
TYPESET-S	UNHINGE-S	UNSNECK-S	UPSKILL-S	VALONEA-S
TYPHOID-S	UNHOARD-S	UNSPEAK-S	UPSPEAK-S	VALONIA-S
TYPHOON-S	UNHORSE-S	UNSPELL-S	UPSPEAR-S	VALUATE-S
TYRANNE-S	UNHOUSE-S	UNSPOOL-S	UPSTAGE-S	VALVULE-S
TZADDIK-S	UNIBROW-S	UNSTACK-S	UPSTAIR-S	VAMOOSE-S
TZADDIQ-S	UNICORN-S	UNSTATE-S	UPSTAND-S	VAMPING-S
TZARDOM-S	UNIFACE-S	UNSTEEL-S	UPSTARE-S	VAMPIRE-S
TZARINA-S	UNIFIER-S	UNSTICK-S	UPSTART-S	VANDYKE-S
TZARISM-S	UNIFORM-S	UNSTOCK-S	UPSTATE-S	VANESSA-S

VANILLA-S	VERRUGA-S	VITAMIN-S	WALKWAY-S	WAVERER-S
VANLOAD-S	VERSANT-S	VITESSE-S	WALLABA-S	WAVESON-S
VANNING-S	VERSINE-S	VITIATE-S	WALLEYE-S	WAVICLE-S
VANPOOL-S	VERSING-S	VITRAGE-S	WALLING-S	WAWLING-S
VANTAGE-S	VERSION-S	VITRAIN-S	WALTZER-S	WAXBILL-S
VAPORER-S	VERTIGO-S	VITREUM-S	WAMEFOU-S	WAXWEED-S
VAQUERO-S	VERVAIN-S	VITRINE-S	WAMEFUL-S	WAXWING-S
VAREUSE-S	VESICLE-S	VITRIOL-S	WANGLER-S	WAXWORK-S
VARIANT-S	VESSAIL-S	VIVERRA-S	WANHOPE-S	WAXWORM-S
VARIATE-S	VESTIGE-S	VOCABLE-S	WANIGAN-S	WAYBILL-S
VARIOLA-S	VESTING-S	VOCALIC-S	WANKSTA-S	WAYFARE-S
VARIOLE-S	VESTURE-S	VOCODER-S	WANNABE-S	WAYMARK-S
VARMENT-S	VETERAN-S	VOGUING-S	WANTAGE-S	WAYMENT-S
VARMINT-S	VETIVER-S	VOICING-S	WANTING-S	WAYPOST-S
VARYING-S	VETKOEK-S	VOIDING-S	WARATAH-S	WAYSIDE-S
VASSAIL-S	VETTURA-S	VOITURE-S	WARBLER-S	WAYWODE-S
VAULTER-S	VIADUCT-S	VOIVODE-S	WARDING-S	WAZZOCK-S
VAUNTER-S	VIALFUL-S	VOLANTE-S	WARDROP-S	WEARING-S
VAURIEN-S	VIBRANT-S	VOLCANO-S	WARFARE-S	WEASAND-S
VAVASOR-S	VIBRATE-S	VOLPINO-S	WARHEAD-S	WEATHER-S
VEDALIA-S	VIBRATO-S	VOLTAGE-S	WARISON-S	WEAVING-S
VEDETTE-S	VIBRION-S	VOLUSPA-S	WARLING-S	WEAZAND-S
VEERING-S	VICEROY-S	VOLUTIN-S	WARLOCK-S	WEBBING-S
VEGETAL-S	VICIATE-S	VOMITER-S	WARLORD-S	WEBCAST-S
VEHICLE-S	VICOMTE-S	VORLAGE-S	WARMING-S	WEBINAR-S
VEILING-S	VICTUAL-S	VOUCHEE-S	WARNING-S	WEBMAIL-S
VEINING-S	VICUGNA-S	VOUCHER-S	WARPAGE-S	WEBPAGE-S
VEINLET-S	VIDETTE-S	VOUDOUN-S	WARPATH-S	WEBSITE-S
VEINULE-S	VIDICON-S	VOUVRAY-S	WARPING-S	WEBSTER-S
VELIGER-S	VIDUAGE-S	VOYAGER-S	WARRAND-S	WEBWORK-S
VELOUTE-S	VIEWING-S	VULGATE-S	WARRANT-S	WEBWORM-S
VENATOR-S	VIHUELA-S	VULTURE-S	WARRIOR-S	WEDDING-S
VENDACE-S	VILAYET-S	VULTURN-S	WARSHIP-S	WEDGING-S
VENDAGE-S	VILIACO-S	WABBLER-S	WARSLER-S	WEDLOCK-S
VENDING-S	VILIAGO-S	WABSTER-S	WARSTLE-S	WEEDING-S
VENERER-S	VILLAGE-S	WADDING-S	WARTHOG-S	WEEKDAY-S
VENISON-S	VILLAIN-S	WADDLER-S	WARTIME-S	WEEKEND-S
VENOMER-S	VILLEIN-S	WADMAAL-S	WARWORK-S	WEEPING-S
VENTAGE-S	VINASSE-S	WADMOLL-S	WARZONE-S	WEFTAGE-S
VENTAIL-S	VINEGAR-S	WADSETT-S	WASHDAY-S	WEIGELA-S
VENTANA-S	VINTAGE-S	WAESUCK-S	WASHING-S	WEIGHER-S
VENTIGE-S	VINTNER-S	WAFFLER-S	WASHOUT-S	WEIRDIE-S
VENTING-S	VIOLATE-S	WAFTAGE-S	WASHPOT-S	WELCHER-S
VENTRAL-S	VIOLENT-S	WAFTING-S	WASHRAG-S	WELCOME-S
VENTURE-S	VIOLIST-S	WAFTURE-S	WASHTUB-S	WELDING-S
VENTURI-S	VIOLONE-S	WAGERER-S	WASSAIL-S	WELFARE-S
VERANDA-S	VIRANDA-S	WAGGLER-S	WASTAGE-S	WELLING-S
VERBENA-S	VIRANDO-S	WAGONER-S	WASTING-S	WELSHER-S
VERBILE-S	VIRELAI-S	WAGTAIL-S	WASTREL-S	WELTING-S
VERBING-S	VIRELAY-S	WAILING-S	WASTRIE-S	WENCHER-S
VERDICT-S	VIREMIA-S	WAINAGE-S	WATCHER-S	WENDIGO-S
VERDITE-S	VIRETOT-S	WAISTER-S	WATCHET-S	WERGELD-S
VERDURE-S	VIRGATE-S	WAITING-S	WATERER-S	WERGELT-S
VERISMO-S	VIRGULE-S	WAITRON-S	WATTAGE-S	WERGILD-S
VERMEIL-S	VISCOSE-S	WAIVODE-S	WATTAPE-S	WESSAND-S
VERMELL-S	VISIBLE-S	WAIWODE-S	WATTLES-S	WESTERN-S
VERMUTH-S	VISITEE-S	WAKANDA-S	WAULING-S	WESTING-S
VERNIER-S	VISITER-S	WAKENER-S	WAULKER-S	WESTLIN-S
VERONAL-S	VISITOR-S	WALKING-S	WAVELET-S	WETBACK-S
VERRUCA-S	VITAMER-S	WALKOUT-S	WAVEOFF-S	WETLAND-S

WETSUIT-S	WHITTLE-S	WISEGUY-S	WRINGER-S	ZABTIEH-S
WETTING-S	WHIZZER-S	WISHING-S	WRINKLE-S	ZACATON-S
WETWARE-S	WHOLISM-S	WISTITI-S	WRITHER-S	ZAITECH-S
WHACKER-S	WHOLIST-S	WITCHEN-S	WRITING-S	ZAMARRA-S
WHAISLE-S	WHOMBLE-S	WITHOUT-S	WRONGER-S	ZAMARRO-S
WHAIZLE-S	WHOMMLE-S	WITLING-S	WRYBILL-S	ZAMBUCK-S
WHALING-S	WHOOBUB-S	WITLOOF-S	WRYNECK-S	ZAMOUSE-S
WHAMPLE-S	WHOOPEE-S	WITTING-S	WUDJULA-S	ZANELLA-S
WHANGAM-S	WHOOPER-S	WITWALL-S	XANTHAM-S	ZANJERO-S
WHANGEE-S	WHOOPIE-S	WOBBLER-S	XANTHAN-S	ZANYISM-S
WHAPPER-S	WHOOPLA-S	WOIWODE-S	XANTHIN-S	ZAPATEO-S
WHARFIE-S	WHOPPER-S	WOLFING-S	XERAFIN-S	ZAPTIAH-S
WHATNOT-S	WHORTLE-S	WOLFKIN-S	XERASIA-S	ZAPTIEH-S
WHATSIT-S	WHUMMLE-S	WOLFRAM-S	XIPHOID-S	ZAREEBA-S
WHEATEN-S	WICKAPE-S	WOLVING-S	XYLENOL-S	ZARNICH-S
WHEEDLE-S	WICKING-S	WOMMERA-S	XYLIDIN-S	ZEALANT-S
WHEELER-S	WICKIUP-S	WONNING-S	XYLITOL-S	ZEBRANO-S
WHEELIE-S	WICKYUP-S	WOODBIN-S	XYLOGEN-S	ZEBRINA-S
WHEENGE-S	WIDENER-S	WOODCUT-S	YACHTER-S	ZEBRINE-S
WHEEPLE-S	WIDEOUT-S	WOODHEN-S	YACHTIE-S	ZEBRULA-S
WHEESHT-S	WIDGEON-S	WOODLOT-S	YAKHDAN-S	ZEBRULE-S
WHEEZER-S	WIDOWER-S	WOODSIA-S	YAMALKA-S	ZECCHIN-S
WHEEZLE-S	WIELDER-S	WOOFTER-S	YAMULKA-S	ZELATOR-S
WHEMMLE-S	WIFEDOM-S	WOOLDER-S	YAPSTER-S	ZELKOVA-S
WHERRET-S	WIGGING-S	WOOLFAT-S	YARDAGE-S	ZEMSTVO-S
WHERRIT-S	WIGGLER-S	WOOLHAT-S	YARDANG-S	ZENAIDA-S
WHETTER-S	WILDCAT-S	WOOLLEN-S	YARDARM-S	ZEOLITE-S
WHICKER-S	WILDING-S	WOOLSEY-S	YARDING-S	ZEPPOLE-S
WHIDDER-S	WILLIAM-S	WOOMERA-S	YASHMAC-S	ZETETIC-S
WHIFFER-S	WIMBREL-S	WOORALI-S	YASHMAK-S	ZEUXITE-S
WHIFFET-S	WINCHER-S	WOORARA-S	YATAGAN-S	ZIGANKA-S
WHIFFLE-S	WINCING-S	WOORARI-S	YAWNING-S	ZIKURAT-S
WHIMPER-S	WINDAGE-S	WOOSELL-S	YAWPING-S	ZILLION-S
WHIMPLE-S	WINDBAG-S	WORDAGE-S	YCLEEPE-S	ZIMOCCA-S
WHIMSEY-S	WINDGUN-S	WORDING-S	YEALDON-S	ZINCATE-S
WHINGER-S	WINDIGO-S	WORKBAG-S	YEALING-S	ZINCITE-S
WHINING-S	WINDING-S	WORKDAY-S	YEAREND-S	ZINCODE-S
WHIPCAT-S	WINDLES-S	WORKING-S	YEARNER-S	ZITHERN-S
WHIPPER-S	WINDOCK-S	WORKOUT-S	YELLING-S	ZIZANIA-S
WHIPPET-S	WINDORE-S	WORKTOP-S	YELLOCH-S	ZOCCOLO-S
WHIPRAY-S	WINDROW-S	WORRIER-S	YELPING-S	ZOISITE-S
WHIPSAW-S	WINDWAY-S	WORSHIP-S	YESHIVA-S	ZONULET-S
WHIRLER-S	WINESAP-S	WORSTED-S	YIELDER-S	ZOOGLEA-S
WHIRRET-S	WINESOP-S	WOSBIRD-S	YOBBISM-S	ZOOLITE-S
WHIRTLE-S	WINGBOW-S	WOUNDER-S	YODELER-S	ZOOLITH-S
WHISKER-S	WINGLET-S	WOURALI-S	YOGHURT-S	ZOONITE-S
WHISKET-S	WINGTIP-S	WRANGLE-S	YOHIMBE-S	ZOOTYPE-S
WHISKEY-S	WINKING-S	WRAPPER-S	YOUNGER-S	ZORBING-S
WHISPER-S	WINKLER-S	WRASSLE-S	YOUNGTH-S	ZORGITE-S
WHISTLE-S	WINNARD-S	WRASTLE-S	YOUNKER-S	ZORILLA-S
WHITHER-S	WINNING-S	WREAKER-S	YOUTHEN-S	ZORILLE-S
WHITING-S	WINNOCK-S	WREATHE-S	YOWLING-S	ZORILLO-S
WHITLOW-S	WIPEOUT-S	WRECKER-S	YPERITE-S	ZYMOGEN-S
WHITRET-S	WIRETAP-S	WRESTER-S	YPSILON-S	ZYMOSAN-S
WHITTAW-S	WIREWAY-S	WRESTLE-S	YTTRIUM-S	ZYMOTIC-S
WHITTER-S	WIRILDA-S	WRIGGLE-S	YUGARIE-S	ZYZZYVA-S

Eight letters to nine

BULGINES-S	PRELATES-S	SKIFFLES-S	TARANTAS-S	TRICKLES-S
ESQUIRES-S	PROCURES-S	SPARKLES-S	TARTINES-S	TYRANNES-S
NERVINES-S	SALTINES-S	SPECKLES-S	TREADLES-S	

T – Front-hooks

Two letters to three

T-AB	T-AT	T-EN	T-IT	T-OY
T-AD	T-AW	T-ES	T-OD	T-UG
T-AE	T-AX	T-ET	T-OE	T-UM
T-AG	T-AY	T-EX	T-OM	T-UN
T-AI	T-EA	T-HE	T-ON	T-UP
T-AM	T-ED	T-HO	T-OO	T-UT
T-AN	T-EE	T-ID	T-OP	T-WO
T-AR	T-EF	T-IN	T-OR	T-YE
T-AS	T-EL	T-IS	T-OW	

Three letters to four

T-AAL	T-AYS	T-HEW	T-OOM	T-RIP
T-ABS	T-EAR	T-HEY	T-OON	T-ROD
T-ACE	T-EAS	T-HIN	T-OOT	T-ROT
T-ACH	T-EAT	T-HIS	T-OPE	T-ROW
T-ACT	T-ECH	T-HON	T-OPS	T-RUE
T-ADS	T-EDS	T-HUG	T-ORA	T-RUG
T-AGS	T-EEK	T-ICE	T-ORC	T-RYE
T-AHA	T-EEL	T-ICH	T-ORE	T-SAR
T-AIL	T-EEN	T-ICK	T-ORS	T-UGS
T-AIN	T-EFF	T-IDE	T-ORT	T-ULE
T-AIS	T-EFS	T-IDS	T-OSE	T-UMP
T-AIT	T-EGG	T-IFF	T-OUK	T-UNS
T-AKA	T-ELD	T-ILL	T-OUR	T-UPS
T-AKE	T-ELL	T-INK	T-OUT	T-URD
T-ALA	T-ELS	T-INS	T-OWN	T-URN
T-ALE	T-ELT	T-IRE	T-OWT	T-UTS
T-ALL	T-EME	T-ITS	T-OYS	T-UTU
T-AMP	T-EMS	T-IVY	T-RAD	T-WAE
T-ANA	T-END	T-ODS	T-RAM	T-WAS
T-ANE	T-ENE	T-OES	T-RAP	T-WAT
T-APE	T-ENS	T-OFF	T-RAT	T-WAY
T-ARE	T-ERF	T-OFT	T-RAY	T-WEE
T-ARS	T-ERN	T-OHO	T-REE	T-WIG
T-ART	T-EST	T-OIL	T-REF	T-WIN
T-ASH	T-ETH	T-OKE	T-RES	T-WIT
T-ASK	T-HAE	T-OLD	T-RET	T-WOS
T-ASS	T-HAN	T-OLE	T-REW	T-YES
T-ATE	T-HAT	T-OMS	T-REZ	T-YIN
T-ATT	T-HAW	T-ONE	T-RIG	
T-AVA	T-HEM	T-ONS	T-RIM	
T-AWA	T-HEN	T-ONY	T-RIN	

Four letters to five

T-AALS	T-EARS	T-HURL	T-RAIN	T-ROWS
T-ABID	T-EASE	T-ICED	T-RAIT	T-RUCK
T-ABLE	T-EATS	T-ICES	T-RAMP	T-RUED
T-ACES	T-EDDY	T-ICKY	T-RAMS	T-RUER
T-ACHE	T-EELS	T-IDES	T-RANK	T-RUES
T-ACTS	T-EFFS	T-ILLS	T-RANT	T-RUGS
T-AFFY	T-EGGS	T-ILLY	T-RAPE	T-RULY
T-AGMA	T-ELLS	T-IMID	T-RAPS	T-RUMP
T-AIGA	T-EMES	T-IMPS	T-RAPT	T-RUST
T-AILS	T-EMPT	T-INKS	T-RASH	T-RUTH
T-AINS	T-ENDS	T-IRED	T-RATS	T-RYKE
T-AITS	T-ENES	T-IRES	T-RAVE	T-SADE
T-AKES	T-EPEE	T-ITCH	T-RAYS	T-SADI
T-AKIN	T-ERAS	T-OAST	T-READ	T-SARS
T-ALAR	T-ERES	T-OFFS	T-RECK	T-SUBA
T-ALAS	T-ERNE	T-OHOS	T-REED	T-ULES
T-ALES	T-ERNS	T-OILS	T-REEN	T-UMPS
T-ALKY	T-ESTS	T-OKAY	T-REES	T-UMPY
T-ALLS	T-ETHS	T-OKES	T-REIF	T-URDS
T-ALLY	T-EUGH	T-OLES	T-REND	T-URNS
T-ALMA	T-EXES	T-ONER	T-REST	T-URPS
T-AMIN	T-HACK	T-ONES	T-RETS	T-UTUS
T-AMIS	T-HANK	T-ONUS	T-REWS	T-WAES
T-AMPS	T-HARM	T-OOMS	T-RIAL	T-WAIN
T-ANAS	T-HAWS	T-OONS	T-RICE	T-WANG
T-ANGA	T-HEBE	T-OOTS	T-RICK	T-WANK
T-ANNA	T-HEED	T-OPED	T-RIDE	T-WATS
T-ANTI	T-HEFT	T-OPES	T-RIFF	T-WAYS
T-APED	T-HEIR	T-ORCS	T-RIGS	T-WEAK
T-APER	T-HEME	T-ORES	T-RILL	T-WEED
T-APES	T-HENS	T-ORTS	T-RIMS	T-WEEL
T-ARED	T-HERE	T-OSES	T-RINE	T-WEEN
T-ARES	T-HERM	T-OUCH	T-RINS	T-WEER
T-ARTS	T-HESP	T-OUKS	T-RIPE	T-WEET
T-ARTY	T-HETE	T-OURS	T-RIPS	T-WICE
T-ASAR	T-HEWS	T-OUTS	T-RITE	T-WIGS
T-ASKS	T-HICK	T-OWED	T-ROAD	T-WILL
T-ATES	T-HIGH	T-OWER	T-ROCK	T-WILT
T-AULD	T-HILL	T-OWNS	T-RODE	T-WINE
T-AUNT	T-HING	T-OWSE	T-RODS	T-WINK
T-AVAS	T-HINS	T-OWTS	T-ROKE	T-WINS
T-AVER	T-HOLE	T-OYER	T-ROLL	T-WINY
T-AWED	T-HONG	T-RACE	T-ROMP	T-WIRE
T-AWNY	T-HORN	T-RACK	T-RONE	T-WIST
T-AXED	T-HOSE	T-RADE	T-ROOP	T-WITE
T-AXES	T-HOWL	T-RADS	T-ROPE	T-WITS
T-AXIS	T-HUGS	T-RAGI	T-ROTS	
T-AXON	T-HUMP	T-RAIK	T-ROUT	
T-EACH	T-HUNK	T-RAIL	T-ROVE	

Five letters to six

T-ABBED	T-ACKER	T-AKING	T-ALLOW	T-AMINS
T-ABLED	T-AGGER	T-ALANT	T-ALMAS	T-AMPED
T-ABLES	T-AIGAS	T-ALKIE	T-ALMUD	T-ANGAS
T-ABLET	T-AILED	T-ALLIS	T-AMBER	T-ANGLE
T-ACHES	T-AIVER	T-ALLOT	T-AMINE	T-ANKER

T-ANNAS	T-ESTER	T-INKLE	T-RAYNE	T-RUSTS
T-ANNOY	T-ETHER	T-INNED	T-READS	T-RUSTY
T-ANTRA	T-HACKS	T-INNER	T-RECKS	T-RUTHS
T-APERS	T-HALER	T-INTER	T-REENS	T-RYKES
T-APING	T-HANKS	T-IRADE	T-RENDS	T-SADES
T-ARRAS	T-HARMS	T-IRING	T-RESTS	T-SADIS
T-ARROW	T-HATCH	T-ISSUE	T-REVET	T-SAMBA
T-ASHED	T-HAWED	T-ITCHY	T-RIALS	T-SORES
T-ASHES	T-HEAVE	T-ITHER	T-RIBES	T-SUBAS
T-ASKED	T-HEBES	T-MESES	T-RICED	T-UGGED
T-ASKER	T-HEFTS	T-OASTS	T-RICES	T-UMBLE
T-ASSES	T-HEIRS	T-OCHER	T-RICKS	T-UMPED
T-ASSET	T-HEIST	T-OILED	T-RIFLE	T-UPPED
T-ASTER	T-HEMES	T-OILER	T-RILLS	T-URBAN
T-AUGHT	T-HENCE	T-OKAYS	T-RIMER	T-URNED
T-AUNTS	T-HERES	T-OLLER	T-RINES	T-WAINS
T-AURIC	T-HERMS	T-OLLIE	T-RIPES	T-WAITE
T-AVERS	T-HESPS	T-ONERS	T-RITES	T-WANGS
T-AVERT	T-HETES	T-OORIE	T-RIVET	T-WANKS
T-AWING	T-HEWED	T-OPING	T-ROADS	T-WANKY
T-AXING	T-HICKS	T-OTHER	T-ROCKS	T-WEEDS
T-AXITE	T-HIGHS	T-OTTER	T-RODES	T-WEEDY
T-AXMAN	T-HILLS	T-OURIE	T-ROKED	T-WEELS
T-AXMEN	T-HINGS	T-OUTED	T-ROKES	T-WEENS
T-AXONS	T-HOLED	T-OUTER	T-ROLLS	T-WEENY
T-CHICK	T-HOLES	T-OWING	T-ROMPS	T-WEEST
T-EAGLE	T-HONGS	T-OYERS	T-RONES	T-WEETS
T-EARED	T-HORNS	T-RACED	T-ROOPS	T-WIGGY
T-EASED	T-HORNY	T-RACER	T-ROPED	T-WIGHT
T-EASEL	T-HOUGH	T-RACES	T-ROPES	T-WILLS
T-EASER	T-HOWLS	T-RACKS	T-ROUGH	T-WILLY
T-EASES	T-HUMPS	T-RAIKS	T-ROULE	T-WILTS
T-ECHED	T-HUNKS	T-RAILS	T-ROUSE	T-WINED
T-EMPTS	T-HURLS	T-RAINS	T-ROUTS	T-WINES
T-ENDED	T-ICHES	T-RAITS	T-ROVER	T-WINGE
T-ENDER	T-ICING	T-RAMPS	T-ROVES	T-WINKS
T-ENTER	T-ICKER	T-RANCE	T-ROWED	T-WIRED
T-ENURE	T-ICKLE	T-RANKS	T-ROWEL	T-WIRES
T-EPEES	T-IGGED	T-RANTS	T-ROWTH	T-WISTS
T-ERBIA	T-ILLER	T-RAPED	T-RUCKS	T-WITCH
T-ERNED	T-INGLE	T-RAPES	T-RUFFE	T-WITES
T-ERNES	T-INKED	T-RAVEL	T-RUING	
T-ERROR	T-INKER	T-RAVES	T-RUMPS	

Six letters to seven

T-ABLETS	T-ALLIED	T-ANTARA	T-CHICKS	T-ENSILE
T-ABLING	T-ALLIES	T-ANTRUM	T-EAGLED	T-ENTERS
T-ACKERS	T-ALLOTS	T-ARROWS	T-EAGLES	T-ENURED
T-ACNODE	T-ALLOWS	T-ARSIER	T-EARFUL	T-ENURES
T-ACTION	T-ALMUDS	T-ARTIER	T-EARING	T-ERBIAS
T-ACTUAL	T-AMBERS	T-ARTILY	T-EASELS	T-ERBIUM
T-ADDIES	T-AMINES	T-ASHING	T-EASERS	T-ERNING
T-AFFIES	T-AMISES	T-ASKERS	T-EASING	T-ERRORS
T-AGGERS	T-AMPING	T-ASKING	T-EDDIES	T-ESTATE
T-AILING	T-ANGLED	T-ASSETS	T-EMPTED	T-ESTERS
T-AIVERS	T-ANGLER	T-ASTERS	T-ENABLE	T-ETCHED
T-ALANTS	T-ANGLES	T-AUNTER	T-ENDERS	T-ETHERS
T-ALIPED	T-ANKERS	T-AWNIER	T-ENDING	T-HACKED
T-ALKIES	T-ANNOYS	T-AXITES	T-ENFOLD	T-HALERS

T-HANKED	T-IRADES	T-RAPING	T-RIVETS	T-UMBREL
T-HANKER	T-IRITIS	T-RAPPED	T-ROATED	T-UMBRIL
T-HAWING	T-IRONIC	T-RAPPER	T-ROCHES	T-UMPING
T-HEATER	T-ISSUED	T-RASHED	T-ROCKED	T-UNABLE
T-HEAVES	T-ISSUES	T-RASHER	T-ROKING	T-UPPING
T-HEISTS	T-ITCHES	T-RASHES	T-ROLLED	T-URGENT
T-HELVES	T-OCHERS	T-RASSES	T-ROLLER	T-URNING
T-HEREAT	T-OFFISH	T-RAVELS	T-ROMPED	T-WADDLE
T-HEREBY	T-OILERS	T-RAYNES	T-ROOPED	T-WADDLY
T-HEREIN	T-OILING	T-READER	T-ROPING	T-WAITES
T-HEREOF	T-OLLERS	T-REASON	T-ROTTED	T-WANGLE
T-HEREON	T-OLLIES	T-RECKED	T-ROTTER	T-WATTLE
T-HERETO	T-OMENTA	T-REDDLE	T-ROUBLE	T-WEAKER
T-HERMAE	T-ONUSES	T-REMBLE	T-ROUGHS	T-WEENIE
T-HERMIT	T-OTTERS	T-RENAIL	T-ROULES	T-WEETED
T-HETHER	T-OUCHED	T-RENDED	T-ROUNCE	T-WEETER
T-HICKIE	T-OUCHES	T-RENTAL	T-ROUPED	T-WIDDLE
T-HIGHED	T-OUGHLY	T-REVETS	T-ROUSER	T-WIGGED
T-HILLER	T-OUTERS	T-RIBLET	T-ROUSES	T-WIGGER
T-HITHER	T-OUTING	T-RICING	T-ROUTER	T-WIGHTS
T-HOLING	T-RACERS	T-RICKED	T-ROVERS	T-WILLED
T-HORNED	T-RACING	T-RICKER	T-ROWELS	T-WILTED
T-HUMPED	T-RACKED	T-RICKLE	T-ROWING	T-WINGED
T-HUMPER	T-RACKER	T-RICKLY	T-ROWTHS	T-WINGES
T-ICKERS	T-RAIKED	T-RIDENT	T-RUCKED	T-WINIER
T-ICKLER	T-RAILED	T-RIFLED	T-RUCKLE	T-WINING
T-IGGING	T-RAILER	T-RIFLER	T-RUEING	T-WINKED
T-ILLITE	T-RAINED	T-RIFLES	T-RUFFES	T-WINKLE
T-INGLES	T-RAMMED	T-RIGGED	T-RUFFLE	T-WINNED
T-INKERS	T-RAMMEL	T-RIGGER	T-RUMPED	T-WINTER
T-INKING	T-RAMPED	T-RILLED	T-RUNDLE	T-WIRING
T-INKLED	T-RAMPER	T-RIMERS	T-RUNNEL	T-WISTED
T-INKLES	T-RANCED	T-RIMMED	T-RUSTED	T-WITCHY
T-INNERS	T-RANCES	T-RIMMER	T-SAMBAS	T-WITTED
T-INNING	T-RANSOM	T-RIPPED	T-UCKERS	T-WITTER
T-INTERS	T-RANTED	T-RIPPER	T-UGGING	T-ZADDIK
T-INWORK	T-RANTER	T-RIPPLE	T-UMBLES	

Seven letters to eight

T-ABLINGS	T-ARTIEST	T-HATCHED	T-ISSUING	T-RANSOMS
T-ACNODES	T-ASKINGS	T-HATCHER	T-ITCHIER	T-RANTERS
T-ACONITE	T-ASSWAGE	T-HATCHES	T-OCHERED	T-RANTING
T-ACTIONS	T-ASTABLE	T-HEATERS	T-OMENTUM	T-RAPPERS
T-ADVANCE	T-AUNTERS	T-HEMATIC	T-OTTERED	T-RAPPING
T-AILERON	T-AUTONYM	T-HERMITS	T-OUCHING	T-RASHERS
T-ALIPEDS	T-AWNIEST	T-HICKIES	T-RACINGS	T-RASHING
T-ALLISES	T-EAGLING	T-HICKISH	T-RACKERS	T-RAVELED
T-ALLNESS	T-EARDROP	T-HILLERS	T-RACKING	T-RAVELER
T-ALLOWED	T-EARLESS	T-HIRLING	T-RAIKING	T-REACHER
T-ALLYING	T-EASELED	T-HORNIER	T-RAILERS	T-READERS
T-ANGLERS	T-EMPTING	T-HORNILY	T-RAILING	T-READING
T-ANGLING	T-ENFOLDS	T-HORNING	T-RAINING	T-REASONS
T-ANNATES	T-ENTERED	T-HUMPERS	T-RAMMELS	T-RECKING
T-ANNOYED	T-ENURING	T-HUMPING	T-RAMMIES	T-REDDLED
T-ANTARAS	T-ERBIUMS	T-ILLITES	T-RAMMING	T-REDDLES
T-ANTRUMS	T-ESTATES	T-INKLING	T-RAMPERS	T-REMBLED
T-APELIKE	T-HACKING	T-INNINGS	T-RAMPING	T-REMBLES
T-ARRASES	T-HANKERS	T-INWORKS	T-RANCHES	T-RENAILS
T-ARROWED	T-HANKING	T-IRELESS	T-RANCING	T-RENDING

T-RENTALS	T-ROATING	T-RUCKLES	T-WADDLED	T-WILLIES
T-REVISES	T-ROCKING	T-RUCKMAN	T-WADDLER	T-WILLING
T-RIBLETS	T-ROLLERS	T-RUCKMEN	T-WADDLES	T-WILTING
T-RICKERS	T-ROLLING	T-RUFFLED	T-WANGLED	T-WINGING
T-RICKING	T-ROMPING	T-RUFFLES	T-WANGLER	T-WINIEST
T-RICKLES	T-ROOPING	T-RUMPING	T-WANGLES	T-WINKING
T-RIFLERS	T-ROSSERS	T-RUNDLED	T-WATTLED	T-WINKLED
T-RIFLING	T-ROTTERS	T-RUNDLES	T-WATTLES	T-WINKLER
T-RIGGERS	T-ROTTING	T-RUNNELS	T-WEEDIER	T-WINKLES
T-RIGGING	T-ROUBLES	T-RUNNION	T-WEENIES	T-WINNING
T-RILLING	T-ROUCHES	T-RUSTIER	T-WEETING	T-WINTERS
T-RIMMERS	T-ROUNCES	T-RUSTILY	T-WIDDLED	T-WISTING
T-RIMMING	T-ROUPING	T-RUSTING	T-WIDDLES	T-WITCHED
T-RIPPERS	T-ROUSERS	T-RUTHFUL	T-WIGGERS	T-WITCHES
T-RIPPIER	T-ROUTERS	T-UBEROUS	T-WIGGIER	T-WITTERS
T-RIPPING	T-ROUTING	T-UMBRELS	T-WIGGING	T-WITTING
T-RIPPLED	T-ROWELED	T-UMBRILS	T-WIGHTED	T-ZADDIKS
T-RIPPLER	T-RUCKING	T-URGENCY	T-WIGLESS	
T-RIPPLES	T-RUCKLED	T-URNINGS	T-WIGLIKE	

Eight letters to nine

T-ACONITES	T-HEMATICS	T-RACHITIS	T-RIMESTER	T-WADDLERS
T-ACTUALLY	T-HEREAWAY	T-RACKINGS	T-RIMMINGS	T-WADDLING
T-AILERONS	T-HEREFROM	T-RAILHEAD	T-RIPPLERS	T-WANGLERS
T-ALLIABLE	T-HEREINTO	T-RAILLESS	T-RIPPLING	T-WANGLING
T-ALLOWING	T-HERENESS	T-RAINBAND	T-ROLLINGS	T-WATTLING
T-ANGLINGS	T-HEREUNTO	T-RAINLESS	T-ROUSSEAU	T-WEEDIEST
T-ANNOYING	T-HEREUPON	T-RAMPINGS	T-ROUTINGS	T-WIDDLING
T-ARROWING	T-HEREWITH	T-RANSOMED	T-ROWELING	T-WIGGIEST
T-ARTINESS	T-HITHERTO	T-RAPPINGS	T-ROWELLED	T-WIGHTING
T-AURIFORM	T-HORNBILL	T-RAVELERS	T-RUCKLING	T-WINGEING
T-AUTOLOGY	T-HORNIEST	T-RAVELING	T-RUFFLING	T-WINKLERS
T-AUTONYMS	T-HORNLESS	T-RAVELLED	T-RUMPLESS	T-WINKLING
T-EARDROPS	T-HORNLIKE	T-RAVELLER	T-RUNNIONS	T-WINNINGS
T-EMPTINGS	T-HUMBLING	T-REACHERS	T-RUSTABLE	T-WITCHIER
T-ENTERING	T-INKLINGS	T-READINGS	T-RUSTIEST	T-WITCHING
T-ERRORIST	T-ITCHIEST	T-REDDLING	T-RUSTLESS	T-WITTERED
T-HATCHERS	T-OCHERING	T-REMBLING	T-RUTHLESS	T-WITTINGS
T-HATCHING	T-OTTERING	T-RIFLINGS	T-URGENTLY	T-ZADDIKIM

T – End-hooks

Two letters to three

AI-T	EF-T	JO-T	NO-T	RE-T
AL-T	EL-T	KA-T	NU-T	SI-T
AN-T	ES-T	KI-T	OF-T	SO-T
AR-T	FA-T	LA-T	OO-T	TA-T
AT-T	FE-T	LI-T	OP-T	TE-T
BA-T	GI-T	LO-T	OR-T	TI-T
BE-T	GO-T	MA-T	OU-T	TO-T
BI-T	GU-T	ME-T	OW-T	WE-T
BO-T	HA-T	MO-T	PA-T	WO-T
DI-T	HE-T	MU-T	PE-T	YE-T
DO-T	HI-T	NA-T	PI-T	
EA-T	HO-T	NE-T	PO-T	

Three letters to four

AIR-T	DOL-T	KEN-T	PEN-T	TAI-T
ARE-T	DOR-T	KEP-T	PER-T	TAR-T
BAH-T	DOS-T	KIS-T	PES-T	TAT-T
BAN-T	DOW-T	LAS-T	PHO-T	TAU-T
BAS-T	DUE-T	LEA-T	PIE-T	TAW-T
BAT-T	DUI-T	LEE-T	PIN-T	TEA-T
BAY-T	DUN-T	LEP-T	POL-T	TEL-T
BEE-T	EAS-T	LES-T	POO-T	TEN-T
BEL-T	ECH-T	LIN-T	POS-T	TES-T
BEN-T	ERS-T	LIS-T	POT-T	TEX-T
BES-T	ETA-T	LOO-T	PUN-T	TIL-T
BIN-T	EVE-T	LOS-T	PUT-T	TIN-T
BIS-T	FAR-T	LOU-T	PYA-T	TIP-T
BIT-T	FAS-T	LOW-T	PYE-T	TOO-T
BOA-T	FEE-T	MAL-T	QUA-T	TOR-T
BOO-T	FEN-T	MAR-T	RAI-T	TOW-T
BOR-T	FES-T	MAS-T	RAN-T	TWA-T
BOT-T	FET-T	MAT-T	RAP-T	UNI-T
BRA-T	FIT-T	MEE-T	RAS-T	VAN-T
BRU-T	FIX-T	MEL-T	REF-T	VAS-T
BUN-T	FON-T	MEN-T	REN-T	VAU-T
BUS-T	FOR-T	MIL-T	RES-T	VEX-T
BUT-T	FRA-T	MIS-T	RIF-T	VIN-T
CAN-T	GAN-T	MIX-T	RIP-T	VOL-T
CAR-T	GAR-T	MOA-T	RIT-T	WAD-T
CEL-T	GAS-T	MOI-T	ROO-T	WAI-T
CHA-T	GEL-T	MOL-T	ROW-T	WAN-T
CHI-T	GEN-T	MOO-T	RUN-T	WAR-T
CIS-T	GIF-T	MOR-T	SAL-T	WAS-T
COL-T	GIS-T	MOS-T	SAN-T	WAT-T
COO-T	GOA-T	MOT-T	SAU-T	WEE-T
COS-T	GUS-T	MUN-T	SEA-T	WEN-T
COT-T	HAE-T	MUS-T	SEC-T	WHA-T
CUR-T	HAN-T	MUT-T	SEN-T	WHO-T
DAL-T	HAS-T	NET-T	SET-T	WIS-T
DAN-T	HEN-T	NEW-T	SEX-T	WON-T
DAW-T	HEP-T	NOT-T	SHA-T	WOO-T
DEB-T	HES-T	NOW-T	SHE-T	WOS-T
DEE-T	HIN-T	OBI-T	SIF-T	YES-T
DEF-T	HIP-T	ONS-T	SIS-T	YET-T
DEL-T	HIS-T	OON-T	SKA-T	YON-T
DEN-T	HOO-T	PAC-T	SKI-T	ZOO-T
DIE-T	HOS-T	PAN-T	SOU-T	
DIN-T	HUN-T	PAR-T	SPA-T	
DIP-T	JOL-T	PAS-T	SUE-T	
DIT-T	JUS-T	PEA-T	SUI-T	

Four letters to five

ABLE-T	ARET-T	BLAT-T	BREN-T	CAPO-T
AGAS-T	AVAS-T	BLUE-T	BRIT-T	CARE-T
AGEN-T	AVER-T	BLUR-T	BRUS-T	CHAP-T
ALAN-T	BEAU-T	BOAR-T	BUND-T	CHAR-T
ALEF-T	BEGO-T	BOAS-T	BURN-T	CHER-T
AMEN-T	BENE-T	BOOS-T	BURS-T	CHOU-T
ANNA-T	BERE-T	BRAN-T	CADE-T	CIVE-T
APER-T	BIDE-T	BRAS-T	CANS-T	CLAP-T

CLEF-T	FLIR-T	LACE-T	QUIN-T	STOT-T
CLIP-T	FLIT-T	LEAN-T	REES-T	STUN-T
CLOU-T	FREE-T	LEAP-T	REIS-T	SURA-T
COME-T	FRIS-T	LEAS-T	REPO-T	SWAP-T
COMP-T	FRIT-T	LIAR-T	RICH-T	SWEE-T
COOP-T	FROS-T	LICH-T	RIVE-T	SWOP-T
COOS-T	FUME-T	LUNE-T	ROOS-T	TACE-T
COSE-T	GAIT-T	MANA-T	ROSE-T	TAIN-T
COUR-T	GAUN-T	MANE-T	SAIN-T	TAPE-T
COVE-T	GEES-T	MAYS-T	SAIS-T	TARO-T
CRUE-T	GENE-T	MEAN-T	SALE-T	TEMP-T
CRUS-T	GLEE-T	MEIN-T	SAUL-T	TENE-T
CURE-T	GLEN-T	MERI-T	SAYS-T	TORO-T
CURS-T	GOSH-T	MICH-T	SCAN-T	TRAP-T
DEAL-T	GRAN-T	MIDS-T	SCAR-T	TRAT-T
DELF-T	GREE-T	MORA-T	SCAT-T	TRES-T
DENE-T	GRIP-T	MOTE-T	SHIR-T	TWEE-T
DICH-T	GRIS-T	MOUS-T	SHOO-T	VALE-T
DIXI-T	GUES-T	MUSE-T	SHOT-T	VELD-T
DOES-T	HADS-T	NIGH-T	SHUN-T	VERS-T
DRIP-T	HAIN-T	NONE-T	SICH-T	VIVA-T
DROP-T	HAUL-T	ONCE-T	SIEN-T	VOLE-T
DUET-T	HEAR-T	OUCH-T	SIGH-T	WAIF-T
EARS-T	HECH-T	OVER-T	SKAT-T	WAIS-T
ERGO-T	HELO-T	PAIN-T	SKEE-T	WARS-T
EVEN-T	HIGH-T	PALE-T	SKIN-T	WEES-T
EVER-T	HOAS-T	PEAR-T	SLEE-T	WELK-T
EWES-T	HORS-T	PIER-T	SLIP-T	WHIP-T
EXUL-T	INGO-T	PIPE-T	SPAR-T	WISH-T
FACE-T	ISLE-T	PIPI-T	SPUR-T	WRAP-T
FAIN-T	JOIN-T	PLAN-T	STAR-T	YEAS-T
FEIS-T	JURA-T	PLEA-T	STEN-T	YOUR-T
FILE-T	KARA-T	POOR-T	STEP-T	
FIRS-T	KEMP-T	PRAT-T	STOA-T	
FLEE-T	KORA-T	PROS-T	STOP-T	

Five letters to six

ABLES-T	BLAES-T	CORSE-T	FERES-T	HAUGH-T
ADMIX-T	BLUES-T	COVEN-T	FIDGE-T	HAULS-T
AGHAS-T	BONNE-T	COVER-T	FILLE-T	HEIGH-T
AMIDS-T	BOUGE-T	CRONE-T	FINES-T	HONES-T
ANIGH-T	BOUGH-T	CRUSE-T	FLIES-T	IDLES-T
ANKLE-T	BREES-T	CURIE-T	FORES-T	JUMAR-T
APPLE-T	BREIS-T	CURVE-T	FORGE-T	KAPUT-T
ARPEN-T	BREVE-T	CUTES-T	FORGO-T	LAMES-T
ARTIS-T	BROWS-T	DELIS-T	FREES-T	LANCE-T
ASSOT-T	BUDGE-T	DIKAS-T	FROWS-T	LATEN-T
ASTER-T	BUFFE-T	DIVER-T	GABLE-T	LAXES-T
AURIS-T	BUGLE-T	DIVES-T	GADGE-T	LEARN-T
BARBE-T	CABLE-T	DONNA-T	GAINS-T	LIKES-T
BARES-T	CACHE-T	DOUCE-T	GAMBE-T	LINGO-T
BARRA-T	CAPLE-T	DOUGH-T	GAMES-T	LIVES-T
BARRE-T	CATCH-T	DOWSE-T	GAMMA-T	LOCUS-T
BASAL-T	CHARE-T	DRAPE-T	GARRE-T	LOWES-T
BASES-T	CLASP-T	DREAM-T	GORGE-T	MALIS-T
BASSE-T	CLOSE-T	DRIES-T	GROVE-T	MATZO-T
BECKE-T	COHOS-T	DUPLE-T	HAIRS-T	MERES-T
BEMIX-T	COMMO-T	EAGLE-T	HALES-T	MIDGE-T
BENNE-T	COMPO-T	FAVES-T	HALLO-T	MILLE-T

MODES-T	PRESE-T	ROUGH-T	SPINE-T	TRIAC-T
MOLES-T	PRIES-T	RUDES-T	SPOIL-T	TRUES-T
MONGS-T	PUCES-T	RUSSE-T	STEAL-T	TUFFE-T
MOTET-T	PURES-T	SADIS-T	STILE-T	TURBO-T
MUSCA-T	PURIS-T	SAFES-T	STRIP-T	TYRAN-T
MUTES-T	RABBI-T	SAGES-T	STYLE-T	UNFIX-T
NUDES-T	RACHE-T	SAIDS-T	SUMMA-T	UNMIX-T
OCTAN-T	RARES-T	SALLE-T	SURES-T	UNPEN-T
OCTET-T	RAYLE-T	SANES-T	SWEER-T	UNWON-T
OLIVE-T	REDIP-T	SCEAT-T	SWEIR-T	VERSE-T
PALES-T	REFEL-T	SCREE-T	SWIVE-T	VERVE-T
PARGE-T	REGES-T	SCRIP-T	TABLE-T	WAUGH-T
PATEN-T	RELIC-T	SCULP-T	TAMES-T	WAURS-T
PEARS-T	REMIX-T	SERES-T	TAPIS-T	WEIGH-T
PIERS-T	RENNE-T	SHIES-T	TARGE-T	WHISH-T
PIQUE-T	REPOS-T	SILEN-T	TASSE-T	WIDES-T
PLACE-T	RETES-T	SMILE-T	TAVER-T	WISES-T
PLAIN-T	RILLE-T	SONNE-T	TERCE-T	WORSE-T
PLANE-T	RIPES-T	SORES-T	TOILE-T	WRIES-T
POSSE-T	ROQUE-T	SOUGH-T	TOQUE-T	

Six letters to seven

ACUTES-T	CONTRA-T	LAMBER-T	POLLEN-T	SPRAIN-T
ADJOIN-T	CORNET-T	LANGUE-T	POSHES-T	STALES-T
AERIES-T	COSIES-T	LARGES-T	POSIES-T	STRAIN-T
ALKANE-T	COUPLE-T	LAZIES-T	POUNCE-T	SUBPAR-T
ANIMIS-T	COZIES-T	LITHES-T	PRONES-T	TAIVER-T
ARCHES-T	CROCHE-T	LOGIES-T	QUARTE-T	TEMPLE-T
ARTIES-T	CRUDES-T	LONGES-T	QUINTE-T	TENNIS-T
ATTAIN-T	CULVER-T	LOOSES-T	RACKET-T	TENSES-T
ATTASK-T	CURRAN-T	LOWSES-T	RADGES-T	THATCH-T
BABIES-T	DEARES-T	LUNIES-T	RADIAN-T	THOUGH-T
BALLAN-T	DECREE-T	LUSHES-T	RAGMEN-T	TIDIES-T
BARGES-T	DEWLAP-T	MANCHE-T	RANKES-T	TIERCE-T
BASSES-T	DIPLON-T	MANTLE-T	RASHES-T	TINIES-T
BASSET-T	DOUBLE-T	MATIES-T	REALES-T	TONIES-T
BEDROP-T	DROGUE-T	MAUVES-T	REDEAL-T	TOWIES-T
BEIGNE-T	DROLES-T	MEANES-T	REPLAN-T	TOWMON-T
BELEAP-T	EASIES-T	MEDIAN-T	REWRAP-T	TRIPLE-T
BEMEAN-T	EPAULE-T	MIGHTS-T	RICHES-T	TRITES-T
BEWRAP-T	FAINES-T	MISHAP-T	RIPPLE-T	TURBAN-T
BORSCH-T	FALSES-T	MISKEN-T	RIZZAR-T	UGLIES-T
BOSQUE-T	FASCIS-T	MOLINE-T	ROOTLE-T	UNCLIP-T
BOSSES-T	FITCHE-T	MONTAN-T	ROSIES-T	UPLEAN-T
BRAVES-T	FITTES-T	NAIVES-T	RUBIES-T	UPLEAP-T
BROUGH-T	FOULES-T	NOBLES-T	RUNDLE-T	VAGUES-T
BUSIES-T	FOXIES-T	NOSIES-T	SABKHA-T	WACKES-T
CALLAN-T	GASHES-T	OAKIES-T	SEAWAN-T	WADSET-T
CANTLE-T	GRAVES-T	ORGIAS-T	SESTET-T	WALIES-T
CHEVRE-T	GROSER-T	OVERGO-T	SEXTAN-T	WARRAN-T
CIRCLE-T	GURGLE-T	PAIRES-T	SEXTET-T	WAVIES-T
CLOSES-T	HACKLE-T	PALMIE-T	SHARIA-T	WHEESH-T
COMMIX-T	HOLIES-T	PARPEN-T	SHERIA-T	WHITES-T
COMPAS-T	HOMIES-T	PELTAS-T	SINGLE-T	WOULDS-T
COMPOS-T	INANES-T	PERCEN-T	SLEIGH-T	ZANIES-T
CONGES-T	JINGLE-T	PINIES-T	SNIDES-T	ZONULE-T
CONSUL-T	KENNET-T	PLEDGE-T	SPARES-T	
CONTES-T	KINGLE-T	POKIES-T	SPAVIE-T	

Seven letters to eight

ANGRIES-T	DOTTLES-T	INTERNE-T	OUTLEAP-T	SISSIES-T
ARTSIES-T	DOWDIES-T	IRONIES-T	PALMIES-T	SMOKIES-T
BACCARA-T	DREARES-T	JAGGIES-T	PALSIES-T	SOAPIES-T
BAGGIES-T	DRIBBLE-T	JAMMIES-T	PAPPIES-T	SODDIES-T
BALDIES-T	DUCKIES-T	JANTIES-T	PARKIES-T	SOMBRES-T
BANDIES-T	DUMMIES-T	JEHADIS-T	PASSMEN-T	SOOTHES-T
BARDIES-T	DUMPIES-T	JEMMIES-T	PASTIES-T	SPANGLE-T
BARRIES-T	DUNNIES-T	JERKIES-T	PEERIES-T	SPARKLE-T
BASEMEN-T	EARLIES-T	JETTIES-T	PERSICO-T	SPRUCES-T
BAWDIES-T	EMONGES-T	JIHADIS-T	PETTIES-T	SQUARES-T
BIRKIES-T	EMPTIES-T	JOLLIES-T	PHONIES-T	STABLES-T
BITTIES-T	FANCIES-T	JUNGLIS-T	PIGGIES-T	STEEVES-T
BLONDES-T	FATTIES-T	JUNKIES-T	PISTOLE-T	STONIES-T
BLOWIES-T	FEEBLES-T	KHALIFA-T	PLANCHE-T	SULKIES-T
BODGIES-T	FENNIES-T	KITTLES-T	PLATIES-T	SUNBURN-T
BONNIES-T	FERLIES-T	LAMBIES-T	PLUSHES-T	SUNNIES-T
BOOKIES-T	FICKLES-T	LINTIES-T	POCKIES-T	SUPPLES-T
BOSSIES-T	FINALIS-T	LIPPIES-T	POPPIES-T	SURFIES-T
BRASHES-T	FLAKIES-T	LITTLES-T	PORKIES-T	SWISHES-T
BRINIES-T	FLASHES-T	LOATHES-T	POTTIES-T	SYMBION-T
BUDDIES-T	FLUSHES-T	LOOBIES-T	PREPLAN-T	TACKIES-T
BUGGIES-T	FOLKIES-T	LOONIES-T	PRIVIES-T	TALKIES-T
BULLIES-T	FOOTIES-T	LOPPIES-T	PUGGIES-T	TANGIES-T
BUSHIES-T	FOVEOLE-T	LOURIES-T	PUNKIES-T	TARDIES-T
BUTCHES-T	FRESHES-T	LUCKIES-T	PURPLES-T	TARRIES-T
CANZONE-T	FUNNIES-T	MARABOU-T	PUSSIES-T	TATTIES-T
CARNIES-T	FURRIES-T	MARDIES-T	QUARTET-T	TAWNIES-T
CASEMEN-T	GAUDIES-T	MARMOSE-T	QUINTET-T	TECHIES-T
CATTIES-T	GAWKIES-T	MASHIES-T	RAGGIES-T	TEGUMEN-T
CHEWIES-T	GENTLES-T	MATURES-T	RAMMIES-T	TELETEX-T
CHOICES-T	GIDDIES-T	MEAGRES-T	RANDIES-T	TIDDIES-T
CHOKIES-T	GIRLIES-T	MEALIES-T	READIES-T	TINNIES-T
CISSIES-T	GLOBULE-T	MERRIES-T	REDREAM-T	TOFFIES-T
CLASSIS-T	GOODIES-T	MICKLES-T	REGIMEN-T	TOTTIES-T
COCKIES-T	GOONIES-T	MINUTES-T	RELEARN-T	TOWNIES-T
COMBIES-T	GOOSIES-T	MISDEAL-T	REMOTES-T	TRANCHE-T
CONGREE-T	GROSSES-T	MISPLAN-T	RETRAIT-T	TRICKLE-T
CONJOIN-T	GROUSES-T	MISSIES-T	ROOFIES-T	UNIQUES-T
CONTRAS-T	GUMMIES-T	MOODIES-T	ROOKIES-T	UNLEARN-T
CRAZIES-T	GUTTIES-T	MOONIES-T	ROOMIES-T	UTOPIAS-T
CROSSES-T	HABITAN-T	MOSSIES-T	ROOTIES-T	VEINULE-T
CUSHIES-T	HANDCAR-T	MOTTIES-T	ROUNDLE-T	VETIVER-T
CUTTIES-T	HAPPIES-T	MOUSIES-T	ROWDIES-T	WALLIES-T
DAFFIES-T	HARDIES-T	MOWBURN-T	RUDDIES-T	WASPIES-T
DANDIES-T	HEAVIES-T	MUDDIES-T	RUMMIES-T	WEARIES-T
DEBBIES-T	HEMPIES-T	MUSKIES-T	SAFARIS-T	WEBBIES-T
DEMURES-T	HENNIES-T	MYLODON-T	SALTIES-T	WEDGIES-T
DICKIES-T	HIPPIES-T	NAPPIES-T	SASSIES-T	WEENIES-T
DIDDIES-T	HISSIES-T	NASTIES-T	SAVAGES-T	WEEPIES-T
DILLIES-T	HOODIES-T	NEDDIES-T	SAVVIES-T	WHITIES-T
DINGIES-T	HOOKIES-T	NETTIES-T	SECURES-T	WITHIES-T
DINKIES-T	HOOLIES-T	NEWSIES-T	SEDATES-T	WOODIES-T
DIPLOMA-T	HUMBLES-T	NIFTIES-T	SEMIMAT-T	WOOLIES-T
DIRTIES-T	HUMPIES-T	NONUPLE-T	SERENES-T	WUSSIES-T
DISJOIN-T	HUNKIES-T	NOOKIES-T	SHINIES-T	YAPPIES-T
DIVINES-T	HUSKIES-T	OCTUPLE-T	SHIPMEN-T	YUMMIES-T
DIZZIES-T	INDICAN-T	OPAQUES-T	SILKIES-T	
DODDIES-T	INDIGEN-T	ORANGES-T	SILLIES-T	
DOGGIES-T	INSCULP-T	OUTBURN-T	SIMPLES-T	

Eight letters to nine

AUGUSTES-T	CRUSTIES-T	MASTODON-T	SECRETES-T	STICKIES-T
BACKDROP-T	DAINTIES-T	MISLEARN-T	SEPTUPLE-T	STINGIES-T
BEARDIES-T	DAYDREAM-T	MODERNES-T	SEXTUPLE-T	STRANGES-T
BLASTIES-T	DISCOVER-T	MULTIPLE-T	SHEENIES-T	STUBBIES-T
BLOCKIES-T	DISTRAIN-T	NEUROMAS-T	SHODDIES-T	STUMPIES-T
BLOODIES-T	DOGGONES-T	OBLIQUES-T	SICKLIES-T	STURDIES-T
BOLSHIES-T	DREARIES-T	OBSCURES-T	SKELLIES-T	SUBLIMES-T
BRASSIES-T	DRUGGIES-T	OUTDREAM-T	SKILLIES-T	SUPREMES-T
BRICKIES-T	EXTREMES-T	OUTLEARN-T	SLUSHIES-T	SWANKIES-T
BRITTLES-T	FLEECIES-T	OVERBURN-T	SMELLIES-T	SWANNIES-T
BROWNIES-T	FLIMSIES-T	OVERLEAP-T	SMOOTHES-T	TAWDRIES-T
BUBBLIES-T	FLOPPIES-T	OVERPLAN-T	SNOTTIES-T	THINGIES-T
CABRIOLE-T	FLOSSIES-T	OVERSLIP-T	SPAMMIES-T	TIDDLIES-T
CHAPPIES-T	FOREMEAN-T	PEARLIES-T	SPARKIES-T	TOASTIES-T
CHATTIES-T	FRILLIES-T	PLACEMEN-T	SPIFFIES-T	TRANSFIX-T
CHERRIES-T	FRIZZIES-T	PLOTTIES-T	SPOONIES-T	TRENDIES-T
CHILLIES-T	GLASSIES-T	POLYGLOT-T	SPORTIES-T	TRUSTIES-T
CHINKIES-T	GLOSSIES-T	PRECISES-T	SPOTTIES-T	UNTIDIES-T
CHIPPIES-T	GREASIES-T	PREPPIES-T	SPRINGLE-T	VIDEOTEX-T
CHITTIES-T	GREENIES-T	PRETTIES-T	SPUNKIES-T	WHEELIES-T
CHOCCIES-T	GRISLIES-T	PRISSIES-T	SPURRIES-T	WHIMSIES-T
CHUMMIES-T	HARTBEES-T	PRIVATES-T	STAGGIES-T	WHINNIES-T
COMPLAIN-T	HEARTIES-T	QUEENIES-T	STANCHES-T	WHIRLIES-T
CONCISES-T	JAUNTIES-T	RESTRAIN-T	STEADIES-T	WINDBURN-T
CRAPPIES-T	LANDDROS-T	SAVORIES-T	STEAMIES-T	WOBBLIES-T
CREEPIES-T	LAVISHES-T	SCANTIES-T	STEELIES-T	WOOLLIES-T
CRUMMIES-T	LOVELIES-T	SCURVIES-T	STEGODON-T	WORTHIES-T

U – Front-hooks

Two letters to three

U-DO	U-MU	U-RE	U-TE
U-MM	U-PO	U-TA	

Three letters to four

U-DAL	U-LEX	U-RES	U-TES
U-DON	U-NIS	U-SED	U-TIS
U-DOS	U-NIT	U-SER	U-VAE
U-LES	U-PAS	U-TAS	U-VAS

Four letters to five

U-DALS	U-NITS	U-RASE	U-RIAL	U-SING
U-DONS	U-PEND	U-RATE	U-RINE	U-SURE
U-LAMA	U-PLAY	U-REAL	U-RITE	U-TILE
U-NARY	U-PLED	U-REDO	U-SAGE	U-VEAL
U-NITE	U-RARE	U-RENT	U-SERS	

Five letters to six

U-LAMAS	U-LOSES	U-NITER	U-NOWED	U-PENDS
U-LEXES	U-NEATH	U-NITES	U-PASES	U-PHANG

U-PLAID	U-PREST	U-RATES	U-RITES	U-SAGES
U-PLAYS	U-PRISE	U-REDIA	U-ROSES	U-SURED
U-PLEAD	U-PROLL	U-REDOS	U-RUBUS	U-SURER
U-PLINK	U-PROSE	U-RESES	U-RUSES	U-SURES
U-PLOOK	U-RARES	U-RIALS	U-SABLE	U-SWARD
U-PRATE	U-RASES	U-RINES	U-SAGER	

Six letters to seven

U-NEARED	U-PLEADS	U-PRAISE	U-PRISER	U-SWARDS
U-NEATEN	U-PLIGHT	U-PRATED	U-PRISES	
U-NITERS	U-PLINKS	U-PRATES	U-PROLLS	
U-PENDED	U-PLOOKS	U-PREACH	U-REDIAL	
U-PHANGS	U-PLYING	U-PRESTS	U-SURING	

Seven letters to eight

U-PENDING	U-PLINKED	U-PRAISES	U-PRISING
U-PLAYING	U-PRAISED	U-PRATING	U-PROLLED
U-PLIGHTS	U-PRAISER	U-PRISERS	

Eight letters to nine

U-PHANGING	U-PLIGHTED	U-PLINKING	U-PRAISING	U-PREACHES
U-PLEADING	U-PLIGHTER	U-PRAISERS	U-PREACHED	U-PROLLING

U – End-hooks

Two letters to three

AM-U	EM-U	LO-U	PI-U	UM-U
AY-U	FE-U	ME-U	SO-U	UT-U
EA-U	KY-U	MO-U	TA-U	YO-U

Three letters to four

AIT-U	GEN-U	LIT-U	PUL-U	TEG-U
BAL-U	GUR-U	MAS-U	PUP-U	THO-U
BAP-U	HAP-U	MEN-U	RAT-U	TUT-U
BED-U	HUH-U	MOT-U	RIM-U	VAT-U
BUB-U	KOR-U	MUM-U	SUS-U	WUD-U
EME-U	LAT-U	NAM-U	TAB-U	
FRA-U	LEK-U	PAT-U	TAP-U	
FUG-U	LIE-U	PUD-U	TAT-U	

Four letters to five

BANT-U	BUSS-U	JAMB-U	PEND-U	VERT-U
BATT-U	CENT-U	KAWA-U	PIKA-U	
BITO-U	CORN-U	LASS-U	PILA-U	
BUCK-U	FOND-U	MUNT-U	QUIP-U	
BUND-U	HAIK-U	PARE-U	TEND-U	

Five letters to six

CONGO-U   HALER-U   MANAT-U

Six letters to seven

MANITO-U   SUBMEN-U   TAMARA-U   TURACO-U

V – Front-hooks

Two letters to three

V-AE	V-AS	V-ET	V-IS	V-OX
V-AG	V-AT	V-EX	V-OE	V-UG
V-AN	V-AW	V-ID	V-OR	V-UM
V-AR	V-EE	V-IN	V-OW	

Three letters to four

V-AGS	V-ANT	V-END	V-ILL	V-OLE
V-AIL	V-ARE	V-ERA	V-INS	V-ORS
V-AIN	V-ARS	V-ERS	V-IRE	V-ROT
V-AIR	V-ARY	V-EST	V-ITA	V-ROW
V-ALE	V-EGO	V-ICE	V-LEI	V-UGH
V-AMP	V-ELD	V-IDE	V-OAR	V-UGS
V-ANE	V-ELL	V-IDS	V-OES	

Four letters to five

V-AGUE	V-ARIA	V-ERST	V-IRED	V-OMER
V-AILS	V-ARNA	V-ESTS	V-IRES	V-OMIT
V-AIRS	V-AUNT	V-ETCH	V-IRID	V-OUCH
V-AIRY	V-EALE	V-EXED	V-ISIT	V-OWED
V-ALES	V-EERY	V-EXES	V-ITAS	V-OWER
V-AMPS	V-EGOS	V-IBEX	V-LEIS	V-ROOM
V-ANES	V-ELDS	V-ICED	V-LIES	V-ROWS
V-ANTS	V-ELLS	V-ICES	V-OARS	V-UGHS
V-ARES	V-ENDS	V-ILLS	V-OLES	V-ULVA

Five letters to six

V-AGILE	V-ARIAS	V-EALES	V-ERSES	V-OMITS
V-AGUED	V-ARNAS	V-EGGED	V-ERVEN	V-ORANT
V-AGUES	V-ASTER	V-ELATE	V-EXING	V-OTARY
V-AILED	V-ATMAN	V-ENDED	V-ICING	V-OWING
V-ALINE	V-AUNTS	V-ENDER	V-IRING	V-ROOMS
V-ALLEY	V-AUNTY	V-ENDUE	V-IZARD	V-ULVAS
V-AMPED	V-AWARD	V-ENTER	V-OMERS	

Six letters to seven

V-ACATES	V-AIRIER	V-AMPING	V-AWARDS	V-ENATIC
V-ACUATE	V-ALGOID	V-ASSAIL	V-EGGING	V-ENDERS
V-ACUITY	V-ALINES	V-AUNTER	V-ELATED	V-ENDING
V-AILING	V-ALLEYS	V-AUNTIE	V-ELITES	V-ENDUES

V-ENTAIL	V-ESTRAL	V-IBICES	V-OCULAR	V-OUCHES
V-ENTERS	V-ETCHES	V-IZARDS	V-OUCHED	V-ROOMED

Seven letters to eight

V-AGILITY	V-AUNTERS	V-ENTAILS	V-ICELESS	V-OUCHING
V-AIRIEST	V-ENATION	V-ENTAYLE	V-ICELIKE	V-ROOMING
V-ALLEYED	V-ENDINGS	V-ERISTIC	V-IRIDIAN	
V-ASSAILS	V-ENOLOGY	V-ERMINED	V-OTARIES	

Eight letters to nine

V-ACUITIES	V-ENATIONS	V-ENTAYLES	V-IDEOGRAM	V-INDICATE

V – End-hooks

Two letters to three

DE-V	GO-V	LA-V	RE-V	TA-V
DI-V	GU-V	PA-V	SO-V	

Three letters to four

CHA-V	DEE-V	MIR-V
CHI-V	ERE-V	PER-V

Four letters to five

GANE-V	OLLA-V	PARE-V

W – Front-hooks

Two letters to three

W-AB	W-AS	W-EM	W-IS	W-OS
W-AD	W-AT	W-EN	W-IT	W-OW
W-AE	W-AW	W-ET	W-OE	W-OX
W-AG	W-AX	W-EX	W-OF	W-US
W-AI	W-AY	W-HA	W-ON	W-YE
W-AN	W-ED	W-HO	W-OO	
W-AR	W-EE	W-IN	W-OP	

Three letters to four

W-ABS	W-AIS	W-ARD	W-AUK	W-EEN
W-ADD	W-AIT	W-ARE	W-AVE	W-EFT
W-ADS	W-AKA	W-ARK	W-AWA	W-ELD
W-AFF	W-AKE	W-ARM	W-AWE	W-ELK
W-AFT	W-ALE	W-ARS	W-AWL	W-ELL
W-AGE	W-ALL	W-ART	W-AYS	W-ELT
W-AGS	W-AND	W-ARY	W-EAN	W-EMS
W-AID	W-ANE	W-ASH	W-EAR	W-END
W-AIL	W-ANT	W-ASP	W-EDS	W-ENS
W-AIN	W-ANY	W-ATE	W-EEK	W-ERE
W-AIR	W-ARB	W-ATT	W-EEL	W-EST

W-ETA	W-HIM	W-ICE	W-ISH	W-OPS
W-HAE	W-HIN	W-ICH	W-ITS	W-ORD
W-HAM	W-HIP	W-ICK	W-OES	W-ORE
W-HAP	W-HIT	W-IDE	W-OKE	W-ORT
W-HAT	W-HOA	W-ILL	W-OLD	W-RAP
W-HEN	W-HOM	W-IMP	W-ONS	W-REN
W-HET	W-HOP	W-INK	W-OOF	W-RIT
W-HEW	W-HOT	W-INN	W-OON	W-UDS
W-HEY	W-HOW	W-INS	W-OOS	W-YES
W-HID	W-HUP	W-IRE	W-OOT	

Four letters to five

W-ADDS	W-ARTY	W-EXES	W-HIZZ	W-OOZY
W-ADDY	W-ASHY	W-HACK	W-HOLE	W-ORDS
W-AGED	W-ASPS	W-HALE	W-HOOF	W-ORTS
W-AGER	W-ATAP	W-HAMS	W-HOOP	W-OULD
W-AGES	W-AUKS	W-HANG	W-HOOT	W-OVEN
W-AGON	W-AVER	W-HAPS	W-HOPS	W-OWED
W-AIDE	W-AVES	W-HARE	W-HORE	W-OXEN
W-AILS	W-AWES	W-HATS	W-HOSE	W-RACK
W-AINS	W-AWLS	W-HEAL	W-HUMP	W-RANG
W-AIRS	W-AXED	W-HEAR	W-HUPS	W-RAPS
W-AITS	W-AXES	W-HEAT	W-ICKY	W-RAPT
W-AKED	W-EANS	W-HEEL	W-IDES	W-RAST
W-AKES	W-EARS	W-HEFT	W-ILLS	W-RATE
W-ALES	W-EAVE	W-HELM	W-ILLY	W-RATH
W-ALLS	W-ECHT	W-HELP	W-IMPS	W-REAK
W-ALLY	W-EDGE	W-HENS	W-INCH	W-RECK
W-AMUS	W-EDGY	W-HERE	W-INKS	W-RENS
W-ANDS	W-EELS	W-HETS	W-INNS	W-REST
W-ANES	W-EFTS	W-HEWS	W-IRED	W-RICK
W-ANNA	W-ELDS	W-HEYS	W-IRES	W-RING
W-ANTS	W-ELKS	W-HIMS	W-ITCH	W-RITE
W-ARBS	W-ELLS	W-HINS	W-OLDS	W-RITS
W-ARDS	W-ELTS	W-HIPS	W-OMEN	W-ROKE
W-ARED	W-ENDS	W-HIPT	W-OOFS	W-RONG
W-ARES	W-EROS	W-HISH	W-OOFY	W-ROOT
W-ARKS	W-ESTS	W-HISS	W-OONS	W-ROTE
W-ARMS	W-ETAS	W-HIST	W-OOPS	W-RUNG
W-ARTS	W-EXED	W-HITS	W-OOSE	W-USES

Five letters to six

W-ACKER	W-ANGLE	W-AVERS	W-EXING	W-HELPS
W-ADDED	W-ANION	W-AXING	W-HACKS	W-HENCE
W-ADDER	W-ANKER	W-EANED	W-HALED	W-HERES
W-ADDLE	W-ANKLE	W-EARED	W-HALER	W-HERRY
W-AFTER	W-ANTED	W-EASEL	W-HALES	W-HEUGH
W-AGERS	W-ARKED	W-EAVED	W-HAMMY	W-HEWED
W-AGGER	W-ARMED	W-EAVES	W-HANGS	W-HILLY
W-AGING	W-ARMER	W-EBBED	W-HARES	W-HINGE
W-AGONS	W-ARRAY	W-EDGED	W-HEALS	W-HINNY
W-AILED	W-ASHED	W-EDGES	W-HEARE	W-HIPPY
W-AIRED	W-ASHEN	W-EIGHT	W-HEATS	W-HISTS
W-AIVER	W-ASHES	W-ELDER	W-HEELS	W-HOLES
W-AKING	W-ASTER	W-ENDED	W-HEEZE	W-HOLLY
W-ALLOW	W-ATAPS	W-ESTER	W-HEFTS	W-HOOFS
W-AMBLE	W-AUGHT	W-ETHER	W-HELMS	W-HOOPS

W-HOOSH	W-INDOW	W-ISHES	W-OUNDY	W-RESTS
W-HOOTS	W-INKED	W-ITCHY	W-OVENS	W-RETCH
W-HUMPS	W-INKER	W-ITHER	W-OWING	W-RICKS
W-ICHES	W-INKLE	W-IZARD	W-RACKS	W-RIGHT
W-ICKER	W-INNED	W-ONNED	W-RASSE	W-RINGS
W-IGGED	W-INNER	W-OOSES	W-RATHS	W-RITES
W-ILLER	W-INTER	W-ORMER	W-REAKS	W-ROOTS
W-IMPED	W-IRING	W-OUBIT	W-RECKS	

Six letters to seven

W-ACKERS	W-ARTIER	W-HAPPED	W-HIZZES	W-ITCHED
W-ADDERS	W-ASHERY	W-HEELED	W-HOLISM	W-ITCHES
W-ADDIES	W-ASHIER	W-HEELER	W-HOLIST	W-IZARDS
W-ADDING	W-ASHING	W-HEEZED	W-HOOFED	W-OLLIES
W-ADDLED	W-ASPISH	W-HEEZES	W-HOOPED	W-ONNING
W-ADDLES	W-ASSAIL	W-HELMED	W-HOOPER	W-OOFIER
W-AFFIES	W-ASTERS	W-HELPED	W-HOOPLA	W-OORALI
W-AFTERS	W-ATTEST	W-HEREAT	W-HOOTED	W-OOZIER
W-AGGERS	W-AUGHTS	W-HEREBY	W-HOPPED	W-OOZILY
W-AILING	W-AXLIKE	W-HEREIN	W-HOPPER	W-ORMERS
W-AIRING	W-EANING	W-HEREOF	W-HUMPED	W-OUBITS
W-AIVERS	W-EARING	W-HEREON	W-HUPPED	W-OURALI
W-ALLIES	W-EASELS	W-HERETO	W-ICKERS	W-RACKED
W-ALLOWS	W-EAVING	W-HETHER	W-IGGING	W-RANGED
W-AMBLED	W-EBBING	W-HEUGHS	W-ILLEST	W-RAPPED
W-AMBLES	W-EDGIER	W-HEWING	W-IMPING	W-RAPPER
W-AMUSES	W-EDGING	W-HIDDER	W-IMPISH	W-RASSES
W-ANGLED	W-EIGHTS	W-HINGED	W-IMPLED	W-RASSLE
W-ANGLER	W-EIGHTY	W-HINGER	W-INCHED	W-REAKED
W-ANGLES	W-ELDERS	W-HINGES	W-INCHER	W-RECKED
W-ANIONS	W-ELDING	W-HIPPED	W-INCHES	W-RESTED
W-ANKERS	W-ENDING	W-HIPPER	W-INDIGO	W-RESTER
W-ANTING	W-ESTERS	W-HISHED	W-INDOWS	W-RICKED
W-APPEND	W-ETHERS	W-HISHES	W-INKERS	W-RIGHTS
W-ARKING	W-HACKED	W-HISSED	W-INKING	W-RINGED
W-ARLING	W-HACKER	W-HISSES	W-INKLED	W-RINGER
W-ARMERS	W-HALERS	W-HISTED	W-INKLES	W-ROOTED
W-ARMING	W-HALING	W-HITHER	W-INNERS	W-ROUGHT
W-ARRANT	W-HAMMED	W-HITTER	W-INNING	W-ULLING
W-ARRAYS	W-HANGED	W-HIZZED	W-INTERS	

Seven letters to eight

W-ADDLING	W-ASTABLE	W-HELMING	W-HISSING	W-HOPPING
W-AGELESS	W-EANLING	W-HELPING	W-HISTING	W-HUMPING
W-ALLEYED	W-EARINGS	W-HERRIED	W-HITHERS	W-HUPPING
W-ALLOWED	W-EASELED	W-HERRIES	W-HITTERS	W-INCHERS
W-AMBLING	W-EDGIEST	W-HIDDERS	W-HIZZING	W-INCHING
W-ANGLERS	W-EDGINGS	W-HINGERS	W-HOLISMS	W-INDIGOS
W-ANGLING	W-ELDINGS	W-HINGING	W-HOLISTS	W-INDOWED
W-ANTHILL	W-HACKERS	W-HINNIED	W-HOOFING	W-INKLING
W-ANTINGS	W-HACKING	W-HINNIES	W-HOOPERS	W-INNARDS
W-ARMINGS	W-HAMMING	W-HIPLIKE	W-HOOPING	W-INNINGS
W-ARRAYED	W-HANGING	W-HIPPIER	W-HOOPLAS	W-IRELESS
W-ARTIEST	W-HAPPING	W-HIPPING	W-HOOSHED	W-ITCHIER
W-ARTLESS	W-HEELERS	W-HIPSTER	W-HOOSHES	W-ITCHING
W-ASHIEST	W-HEELING	W-HIRLING	W-HOOTING	W-OOFIEST
W-ASSAILS	W-HEEZING	W-HISHING	W-HOPPERS	W-OORALIS

W-OOZIEST	W-RACKING	W-RASSLED	W-RESTERS	W-RICKING
W-OULDEST	W-RANGING	W-RASSLES	W-RESTING	W-RINGERS
W-OURALIS	W-RAPPERS	W-REAKING	W-RETCHED	W-RINGING
W-RACKFUL	W-RAPPING	W-RECKING	W-RETCHES	W-ROOTING

Eight letters to nine

W-ALLOWING	W-EANLINGS	W-HERENESS	W-HIRLINGS	W-ITCHINGS
W-AMBLINGS	W-EDGEWISE	W-HEREUNTO	W-HITHERED	W-ITCHWEED
W-ANGLINGS	W-HACKINGS	W-HEREUPON	W-HOLESOME	W-OOZINESS
W-ANTHILLS	W-HEATLESS	W-HEREWITH	W-HOLISTIC	W-RAPPINGS
W-ARRAYING	W-HEELINGS	W-HERRYING	W-HOOSHING	W-RASSLING
W-ASHERIES	W-HEELLESS	W-HINNYING	W-HOPPINGS	W-RINGINGS
W-ASHINESS	W-HELPLESS	W-HIPPIEST	W-IMPISHLY	
W-ASSAILED	W-HEREFROM	W-HIPPINGS	W-INDOWING	
W-ASSAILER	W-HEREINTO	W-HIPSTERS	W-ITCHIEST	

W – End-hooks

Two letters to three

BO-W	HE-W	LO-W	PA-W	TO-W
DA-W	HO-W	MA-W	PE-W	WO-W
DE-W	JA-W	ME-W	PO-W	YA-W
DO-W	JO-W	MO-W	RE-W	YE-W
FA-W	KA-W	NA-W	SO-W	YO-W
FE-W	KO-W	NE-W	TA-W	
HA-W	LA-W	NO-W	TE-W	

Three letters to four

ALE-W	BRA-W	ENE-W	SHE-W	VIE-W
ANE-W	BRO-W	FRO-W	SKA-W	WHO-W
ARE-W	CHA-W	PRO-W	SPA-W	
AVO-W	CHE-W	SHA-W	THE-W	

Four letters to five

BEDE-W	PAPA-W	SINE-W	VINE-W
KOTO-W	PAWA-W	SYBO-W	VROU-W
NAVE-W	PILA-W	THRO-W	

Five letters to six

BARRO-W	HOLLO-W	MORRO-W	REVIE-W
BURRO-W	MATLO-W	OUTRO-W	UNCLE-W
HALLO-W	MISSA-W	PURSE-W	

Six letters to seven

DAYGLO-W	FITCHE-W

Seven letters to eight

BUDGERO-W   RICKSHA-W

Eight letters to nine

KABELJOU-W

X – Front-hooks

Two letters to three

X-IS

Four letters to five

X-ERIC   X-YLEM

Five letters to six

X-YLEMS

Six letters to seven

X-EROSES   X-EROTIC

Eight letters to nine

X-ENOPHILE

X – End-hooks

Two letters to three

BO-X	HO-X	MU-X	RE-X	TI-X
DE-X	LA-X	NO-X	SI-X	WE-X
FA-X	LO-X	PA-X	SO-X	WO-X
GO-X	MA-X	PI-X	TA-X	YE-X
HE-X	MI-X	PO-X	TE-X	ZA-X

Three letters to four

APE-X	EAU-X	JEU-X	PRE-X
BRU-X	FLU-X	JIN-X	ULE-X
CRU-X	HOA-X	ONY-X	

Four letters to five

BEAU-X	CODE-X	LIMA-X	MURE-X	SORE-X
BORA-X	FORE-X	LURE-X	PYRE-X	TELE-X
CARE-X	GALA-X	MALA-X	REDO-X	VIBE-X
CHOU-X	LATE-X	MIRE-X	SILE-X	VITE-X

Five letters to six

ADIEU-X	BIJOU-X	BOYAU-X	DUPLE-X

Six letters to seven

BATEAU-X	CADEAU-X	GATEAU-X	MINIMA-X	SIMPLE-X
BUREAU-X	COTEAU-X	MILIEU-X	RESEAU-X	TRIPLE-X

Seven letters to eight

BANDEAU-X	CHAPEAU-X	JAMBEAU-X	OCTUPLE-X	TABLEAU-X
BATTEAU-X	CHATEAU-X	MANTEAU-X	PLATEAU-X	TONNEAU-X
BERCEAU-X	COUTEAU-X	MORCEAU-X	RONDEAU-X	TRUMEAU-X
CAMAIEU-X	FABLIAU-X	NOUVEAU-X	ROULEAU-X	

Eight letters to nine

ABOIDEAU-X	ABOITEAU-X	FLAMBEAU-X	MULTIPLE-X	PRIEDIEU-X

Y – Front-hooks

Two letters to three

Y-AD	Y-AW	Y-ET	Y-OD	Y-UG
Y-AE	Y-AY	Y-EX	Y-OM	Y-UM
Y-AG	Y-EA	Y-GO	Y-ON	Y-UP
Y-AH	Y-EH	Y-ID	Y-OS	Y-US
Y-AM	Y-EN	Y-IN	Y-OU	
Y-AR	Y-ES	Y-OB	Y-OW	

Three letters to four

Y-ABA	Y-AWL	Y-ELL	Y-INS	Y-OUR
Y-ADS	Y-AWN	Y-ELM	Y-IRK	Y-OWE
Y-AFF	Y-AYS	Y-ELT	Y-OBS	Y-OWL
Y-AGS	Y-BET	Y-ENS	Y-ODE	Y-UGS
Y-AHS	Y-EAN	Y-ERK	Y-ODS	Y-UKE
Y-ALE	Y-EAR	Y-EST	Y-OKE	Y-ULE
Y-APP	Y-EAS	Y-EUK	Y-OLD	Y-UMP
Y-ARD	Y-ECH	Y-EVE	Y-OOF	Y-UPS
Y-ARE	Y-EGG	Y-GOE	Y-OOP	Y-WIS
Y-ARK	Y-ELD	Y-IDS	Y-ORE	
Y-ATE	Y-ELK	Y-ILL	Y-OUK	

Four letters to five

Y-ABBA	Y-ARKS	Y-CLAD	Y-EGGS	Y-EUKS
Y-ACCA	Y-ATES	Y-COND	Y-ELKS	Y-EVEN
Y-AGER	Y-AULD	Y-DRAD	Y-ELLS	Y-EVES
Y-ALES	Y-AWED	Y-EANS	Y-ELMS	Y-EXED
Y-AMEN	Y-AWLS	Y-EARD	Y-ELTS	Y-EXES
Y-APPS	Y-AWNS	Y-EARN	Y-ERKS	Y-FERE
Y-ARCO	Y-AWNY	Y-EARS	Y-ESES	Y-ILLS
Y-ARDS	Y-BORE	Y-EAST	Y-ESTS	Y-IRKS

Y-LIKE	Y-OOPS	Y-OWED	Y-SAME	Y-UMPS
Y-MOLT	Y-ORES	Y-OWES	Y-TOST	Y-UPON
Y-OGEE	Y-OUKS	Y-OWLS	Y-UKES	
Y-OKES	Y-OURN	Y-RAPT	Y-ULAN	
Y-OOFS	Y-OURS	Y-RENT	Y-ULES	

Five letters to six

Y-ABBAS	Y-ARKED	Y-EANED	Y-EXING	Y-SHEND
Y-ACCAS	Y-ARROW	Y-EARDS	Y-ICKER	Y-SHENT
Y-ACKER	Y-AWING	Y-EARLY	Y-IRKED	Y-ULANS
Y-AGERS	Y-AWNED	Y-EARNS	Y-OGEES	Y-UMPED
Y-AGGER	Y-AWNER	Y-EASTS	Y-OWING	Y-UMPIE
Y-AKKAS	Y-BLENT	Y-EMMER	Y-OWLED	Y-WROKE
Y-AMENS	Y-BOUND	Y-ESSES	Y-OWLER	
Y-ANKER	Y-BRENT	Y-ESTER	Y-PIGHT	
Y-ANTRA	Y-CLEPT	Y-EUKED	Y-PLAST	

Six letters to seven

Y-ACKERS	Y-AWNIER	Y-EARNER	Y-MOLTEN	Y-UCKERS
Y-AGGERS	Y-AWNING	Y-EASTED	Y-OWLERS	Y-UMPIES
Y-ANKERS	Y-CLEPED	Y-EMMERS	Y-OWLING	Y-UMPING
Y-ARKING	Y-EANING	Y-EUKING	Y-PLIGHT	
Y-ARROWS	Y-EARDED	Y-ICKERS	Y-SHENDS	
Y-AWNERS	Y-EARNED	Y-IRKING	Y-SLAKED	

Seven letters to eight

Y-ATAGHAN	Y-BOUNDEN	Y-EARDING	Y-EARNING
Y-AWNIEST	Y-CLEEPED	Y-EARLIES	Y-EASTING
Y-AWNINGS	Y-EANLING	Y-EARNERS	Y-OURSELF

Eight letters to nine

Y-ATAGHANS	Y-EANLINGS	Y-RAVISHED
Y-CLEEPING	Y-EARNINGS	Y-SHENDING

Y – End-hooks

Two letters to three

AB-Y	DE-Y	HE-Y	MA-Y	SH-Y
AN-Y	DO-Y	HO-Y	MO-Y	SO-Y
AR-Y	FA-Y	JA-Y	NA-Y	ST-Y
BA-Y	FE-Y	JO-Y	NO-Y	TA-Y
BE-Y	GO-Y	KA-Y	ON-Y	TO-Y
BO-Y	GU-Y	LA-Y	OX-Y	WE-Y
DA-Y	HA-Y	LO-Y	PA-Y	YA-Y

Three letters to four

ACH-Y	AIR-Y	ARM-Y	ASH-Y	BOD-Y
ADD-Y	ALA-Y	ARS-Y	AWA-Y	BOG-Y
AFF-Y	ALL-Y	ART-Y	AWN-Y	BON-Y

BOX-Y	DOT-Y	JUD-Y	OOS-Y	TAK-Y
BRA-Y	EAS-Y	LAC-Y	ORB-Y	TED-Y
BUR-Y	EEL-Y	LAD-Y	OWL-Y	THE-Y
BUS-Y	EGG-Y	LEV-Y	PAC-Y	TID-Y
CAG-Y	ELM-Y	LIN-Y	PAL-Y	TIN-Y
CAN-Y	FAD-Y	LOG-Y	PAT-Y	TOD-Y
CHA-Y	FOG-Y	LOR-Y	PIN-Y	TOE-Y
CIT-Y	FOX-Y	MAN-Y	PIP-Y	TON-Y
COL-Y	FRA-Y	MAR-Y	PIT-Y	TOR-Y
CON-Y	FUM-Y	MAT-Y	PIX-Y	TOW-Y
COP-Y	FUR-Y	MIR-Y	POL-Y	TUN-Y
COR-Y	GAB-Y	MIX-Y	POS-Y	TWA-Y
COS-Y	GAM-Y	MOB-Y	POX-Y	UMP-Y
COW-Y	GAP-Y	MOL-Y	PRE-Y	UPS-Y
COX-Y	GOB-Y	MON-Y	PUL-Y	URD-Y
COZ-Y	GOE-Y	MOP-Y	PUN-Y	VAR-Y
DEF-Y	GOR-Y	NIX-Y	QUA-Y	VIN-Y
DEN-Y	GUL-Y	NOS-Y	REN-Y	WAD-Y
DEW-Y	HER-Y	NOW-Y	RIM-Y	WAN-Y
DEX-Y	HOM-Y	OAK-Y	ROK-Y	WAR-Y
DID-Y	HUG-Y	OAR-Y	RUB-Y	WAX-Y
DOB-Y	ICK-Y	OBE-Y	SAG-Y	WIN-Y
DOG-Y	IFF-Y	OIL-Y	SEX-Y	YAW-Y
DOM-Y	ILL-Y	OKA-Y	SHA-Y	YUK-Y
DOP-Y	INK-Y	OLD-Y	SOM-Y	
DOR-Y	JOE-Y	OOF-Y	SPA-Y	

Four letters to five

ABBE-YACID-Y	BEEF-Y	BULL-Y	COLL-Y	DAUB-Y
AGON-Y	BEER-Y	BUMP-Y	COMB-Y	DEAR-Y
ALAR-Y	BELL-Y	BUND-Y	COMM-Y	DEAW-Y
ANNO-Y	BEND-Y	BUNG-Y	CONE-Y	DECO-Y
ANTS-Y	BENT-Y	BUNN-Y	CONK-Y	DEED-Y
APER-Y	BIFF-Y	BUNT-Y	COOK-Y	DEIF-Y
ARSE-Y	BIGG-Y	BURL-Y	COOL-Y	DELL-Y
ARTS-Y	BILL-Y	BURR-Y	COOM-Y	DICE-Y
ATOM-Y	BING-Y	BUSH-Y	COPS-Y	DICK-Y
ATOP-Y	BITS-Y	BUSK-Y	CORE-Y	DICT-Y
AUNT-Y	BITT-Y	BUST-Y	CORK-Y	DIKE-Y
BAFF-Y	BLAD-Y	BUTT-Y	CORN-Y	DILL-Y
BALD-Y	BLIN-Y	BUZZ-Y	COSE-Y	DING-Y
BALK-Y	BLOW-Y	CAGE-Y	COVE-Y	DINK-Y
BALL-Y	BLUE-Y	CAKE-Y	COZE-Y	DIRT-Y
BALM-Y	BONE-Y	CALM-Y	CRAP-Y	DISH-Y
BAND-Y	BOOB-Y	CAMP-Y	CRUD-Y	DITS-Y
BANT-Y	BOOK-Y	CANN-Y	CRUS-Y	DITT-Y
BARB-Y	BOOM-Y	CANT-Y	CULL-Y	DITZ-Y
BARD-Y	BOOT-Y	CARB-Y	CULT-Y	DOGE-Y
BARK-Y	BORT-Y	CARD-Y	CURD-Y	DOLL-Y
BARM-Y	BOSK-Y	CARN-Y	CURL-Y	DONS-Y
BARN-Y	BOSS-Y	CARR-Y	CURN-Y	DOOL-Y
BASS-Y	BOTH-Y	CASK-Y	CURR-Y	DOOM-Y
BATT-Y	BOTT-Y	CHAR-Y	CUSH-Y	DOPE-Y
BAWD-Y	BOYS-Y	CHEW-Y	CUTE-Y	DORK-Y
BEAD-Y	BRAK-Y	CHIV-Y	DAFF-Y	DORM-Y
BEAK-Y	BRIN-Y	COAL-Y	DAIS-Y	DORT-Y
BEAM-Y	BROS-Y	COBB-Y	DAMP-Y	DOWD-Y
BEAN-Y	BUFF-Y	COCK-Y	DARK-Y	DOWL-Y
BEAT-Y	BULK-Y	COLE-Y	DASH-Y	DOWN-Y

DUCK-Y	GERM-Y	HOOT-Y	LIND-Y	MOSS-Y
DULL-Y	GILL-Y	HORN-Y	LINE-Y	MOTE-Y
DUMP-Y	GIMP-Y	HORS-Y	LING-Y	MOTH-Y
DUNG-Y	GINN-Y	HOSE-Y	LINK-Y	MOTT-Y
DURO-Y	GIPS-Y	HUFF-Y	LINN-Y	MOUS-Y
DURR-Y	GIRL-Y	HULK-Y	LINT-Y	MUCK-Y
DUSK-Y	GLAD-Y	HULL-Y	LOAM-Y	MUGG-Y
DUST-Y	GLOB-Y	HUMP-Y	LOFT-Y	MULE-Y
DYKE-Y	GLUE-Y	HUNK-Y	LOLL-Y	MUMM-Y
EARL-Y	GOAT-Y	HURL-Y	LOON-Y	MUMS-Y
EBON-Y	GOLD-Y	HUSH-Y	LOOP-Y	MURK-Y
EMPT-Y	GOOD-Y	HUSK-Y	LORD-Y	MURL-Y
EVER-Y	GOOF-Y	HUSS-Y	LOSS-Y	MURR-Y
FAIR-Y	GOOK-Y	IRON-Y	LOUR-Y	MUSH-Y
FAKE-Y	GOOL-Y	ITCH-Y	LOUS-Y	MUSK-Y
FAWN-Y	GOON-Y	JACK-Y	LOVE-Y	MUSS-Y
FELL-Y	GOOP-Y	JAGG-Y	LUCK-Y	MUST-Y
FELT-Y	GOOR-Y	JAKE-Y	LUMP-Y	MUZZ-Y
FEND-Y	GOOS-Y	JANN-Y	LUSH-Y	MYTH-Y
FERN-Y	GORM-Y	JAZZ-Y	LUST-Y	NARK-Y
FEST-Y	GOUT-Y	JEEL-Y	MALM-Y	NEED-Y
FIER-Y	GRAV-Y	JELL-Y	MALT-Y	NERD-Y
FILL-Y	GRIM-Y	JERK-Y	MANG-Y	NETT-Y
FILM-Y	GRIP-Y	JIFF-Y	MARD-Y	NEWS-Y
FISH-Y	GRIS-Y	JIMP-Y	MARL-Y	NIFF-Y
FIST-Y	GUCK-Y	JIVE-Y	MASH-Y	NIRL-Y
FIZZ-Y	GULF-Y	JOKE-Y	MASS-Y	NOIL-Y
FLAK-Y	GULL-Y	JOLL-Y	MAST-Y	NOOK-Y
FLAM-Y	GULP-Y	JOLT-Y	MATE-Y	NOSE-Y
FLAW-Y	GUNG-Y	JOWL-Y	MAWK-Y	NOUN-Y
FLAX-Y	GUNK-Y	JUMP-Y	MAZE-Y	NOWT-Y
FLOR-Y	GURL-Y	JUNK-Y	MEAL-Y	NURD-Y
FLUE-Y	GUSH-Y	KELL-Y	MEAN-Y	NUTS-Y
FOAM-Y	GUST-Y	KELP-Y	MEAT-Y	ONER-Y
FOLK-Y	GUTS-Y	KELT-Y	MEIN-Y	PACE-Y
FOOD-Y	GYPS-Y	KEMP-Y	MELT-Y	PALL-Y
FOOT-Y	HAIL-Y	KICK-Y	MERC-Y	PALM-Y
FORA-Y	HAIR-Y	KILT-Y	MESH-Y	PALS-Y
FORB-Y	HAND-Y	KIND-Y	MESS-Y	PAND-Y
FORK-Y	HANK-Y	KINK-Y	MICK-Y	PANS-Y
FORT-Y	HARD-Y	KISS-Y	MIFF-Y	PANT-Y
FROW-Y	HARP-Y	KOOK-Y	MILK-Y	PARD-Y
FUBS-Y	HASH-Y	LACE-Y	MILT-Y	PARK-Y
FUFF-Y	HAST-Y	LAIR-Y	MING-Y	PARR-Y
FULL-Y	HEAD-Y	LAMB-Y	MINT-Y	PART-Y
FUND-Y	HEAP-Y	LANK-Y	MIRK-Y	PAST-Y
FUNK-Y	HEED-Y	LARD-Y	MISS-Y	PATS-Y
FURR-Y	HEFT-Y	LARK-Y	MIST-Y	PAWK-Y
FUSS-Y	HEMP-Y	LATH-Y	MIZZ-Y	PEAK-Y
FUST-Y	HERB-Y	LAWN-Y	MOCH-Y	PEAT-Y
FUZZ-Y	HILL-Y	LEAD-Y	MOLD-Y	PECK-Y
GALL-Y	HISS-Y	LEAF-Y	MOLL-Y	PEER-Y
GAMA-Y	HOAR-Y	LEAK-Y	MOOD-Y	PEON-Y
GAME-Y	HOKE-Y	LEAN-Y	MOOL-Y	PERK-Y
GASP-Y	HOLE-Y	LEAR-Y	MOON-Y	PEST-Y
GAUD-Y	HOME-Y	LEER-Y	MOOR-Y	PHON-Y
GAUM-Y	HONE-Y	LEFT-Y	MOPE-Y	PICK-Y
GAWK-Y	HONK-Y	LEZZ-Y	MOPS-Y	PIET-Y
GEEK-Y	HOOD-Y	LIMB-Y	MORA-Y	PIKE-Y
GENT-Y	HOOK-Y	LIME-Y	MOSE-Y	PINE-Y

PINK-Y	REED-Y	SILK-Y	TELL-Y	WANK-Y
PION-Y	REEF-Y	SILL-Y	TENT-Y	WANT-Y
PITH-Y	REEK-Y	SILT-Y	TEST-Y	WARB-Y
PLAT-Y	REIF-Y	SINK-Y	THAW-Y	WART-Y
PLUM-Y	REKE-Y	SISS-Y	THEW-Y	WASH-Y
POCK-Y	REST-Y	SLAT-Y	TICH-Y	WASP-Y
POKE-Y	RICE-Y	SLIM-Y	TICK-Y	WAVE-Y
POLE-Y	RIFT-Y	SLOP-Y	TILL-Y	WEAR-Y
POLL-Y	RILE-Y	SNAR-Y	TINT-Y	WEED-Y
PONE-Y	RIND-Y	SNIP-Y	TIPS-Y	WEEN-Y
PONG-Y	RISK-Y	SNOW-Y	TIZZ-Y	WEEP-Y
POOF-Y	RITZ-Y	SOAP-Y	TOAD-Y	WELL-Y
POPS-Y	ROAR-Y	SOFT-Y	TOCK-Y	WHIN-Y
PORK-Y	ROCK-Y	SOIL-Y	TOFF-Y	WHIT-Y
PORN-Y	ROIL-Y	SONS-Y	TOLL-Y	WICK-Y
PORT-Y	ROOF-Y	SOOT-Y	TONE-Y	WIFE-Y
POSE-Y	ROOK-Y	SOPH-Y	TOSH-Y	WILL-Y
POTS-Y	ROOM-Y	SOUP-Y	TOSS-Y	WIMP-Y
POTT-Y	ROOP-Y	SPEW-Y	TOWN-Y	WIND-Y
POUT-Y	ROOT-Y	SPIC-Y	TOWS-Y	WINE-Y
POWN-Y	ROPE-Y	SPIK-Y	TRIP-Y	WING-Y
POZZ-Y	RORT-Y	SPIN-Y	TUFT-Y	WISP-Y
PRAT-Y	ROUP-Y	STAG-Y	TUMP-Y	WITH-Y
PREM-Y	RUDD-Y	STEW-Y	TURF-Y	WOMB-Y
PREX-Y	RUMP-Y	STIM-Y	TUSH-Y	WONK-Y
PRIM-Y	RUNT-Y	STUD-Y	TUSK-Y	WOOD-Y
PROS-Y	RUSH-Y	SUCK-Y	TWIN-Y	WOOF-Y
PUDS-Y	RUST-Y	SUDS-Y	TYPE-Y	WOOL-Y
PUFF-Y	SALL-Y	SUET-Y	UNCO-Y	WORD-Y
PULP-Y	SALT-Y	SULK-Y	UNIT-Y	WORM-Y
PUNK-Y	SAME-Y	SUNN-Y	VAIR-Y	WUSS-Y
PUNT-Y	SAND-Y	SURF-Y	VAMP-Y	YAPP-Y
PURS-Y	SARK-Y	SWAM-Y	VAST-Y	YAWN-Y
PUSH-Y	SASS-Y	TACK-Y	VEAL-Y	YECH-Y
PUSS-Y	SAVE-Y	TALC-Y	VEER-Y	YEST-Y
PUTT-Y	SCAR-Y	TALK-Y	VEIL-Y	YEUK-Y
RAGG-Y	SEAM-Y	TALL-Y	VEIN-Y	YOLK-Y
RAIN-Y	SEED-Y	TANG-Y	VIBE-Y	YUCK-Y
RAND-Y	SEEL-Y	TANK-Y	VIEW-Y	ZEST-Y
RANG-Y	SEEP-Y	TANS-Y	VUGG-Y	ZINC-Y
RASP-Y	SERR-Y	TART-Y	VUGH-Y	ZING-Y
READ-Y	SESE-Y	TATT-Y	WACK-Y	ZOOT-Y
REAM-Y	SHAD-Y	TEAR-Y	WADD-Y	
REDD-Y	SHIN-Y	TECH-Y	WALL-Y	
	SHOW-Y	TEEN-Y	WANE-Y	

Five letters to six

AMBER-Y	BEAUT-Y	BLOKE-Y	BRAIN-Y	BROOD-Y
ANGST-Y	BEECH-Y	BLOOD-Y	BRAND-Y	BROOM-Y
APPLE-Y	BENCH-Y	BLOOM-Y	BRANK-Y	BROTH-Y
ARMOR-Y	BETON-Y	BLOWS-Y	BRASH-Y	BROWN-Y
ARROW-Y	BIELD-Y	BLUES-Y	BRASS-Y	BROWS-Y
AUGUR-Y	BITCH-Y	BLUID-Y	BRAWL-Y	BRUSH-Y
BAKER-Y	BLANK-Y	BOOKS-Y	BRAWN-Y	BUNCH-Y
BALLS-Y	BLASH-Y	BOOZE-Y	BREAD-Y	CAIRN-Y
BARON-Y	BLAST-Y	BOSOM-Y	BRIAR-Y	CARBO-Y
BAULK-Y	BLEAK-Y	BOTCH-Y	BRICK-Y	CARSE-Y
BEACH-Y	BLEAR-Y	BOWER-Y	BRIER-Y	CATCH-Y
BEARD-Y	BLOCK-Y	BOWSE-Y	BRISK-Y	CAUSE-Y

CEDAR-Y	CRUST-Y	FLUTE-Y	JAUNT-Y	PLUCK-Y
CHAFF-Y	CURVE-Y	FOLKS-Y	KECKS-Y	PLUFF-Y
CHALK-Y	CUTES-Y	FOOTS-Y	KLUTZ-Y	PLUMP-Y
CHAMP-Y	DAINT-Y	FORTH-Y	KNACK-Y	PLUNK-Y
CHANT-Y	DANCE-Y	FREAK-Y	KNARL-Y	PLUSH-Y
CHARR-Y	DEATH-Y	FREET-Y	KNOLL-Y	POACH-Y
CHASM-Y	DENAR-Y	FREIT-Y	KNURL-Y	POINT-Y
CHEAP-Y	DIMPS-Y	FRIAR-Y	KORUN-Y	PONCE-Y
CHECK-Y	DINGE-Y	FRILL-Y	LAUGH-Y	POUCH-Y
CHEEK-Y	DJINN-Y	FRISK-Y	LEACH-Y	PRANK-Y
CHEER-Y	DOUGH-Y	FRIZZ-Y	LEMON-Y	PRICE-Y
CHERT-Y	DOWER-Y	FROST-Y	LIMPS-Y	PRICK-Y
CHEST-Y	DRAFF-Y	FROTH-Y	LINEN-Y	PRIOR-Y
CHILL-Y	DRAFT-Y	FROWS-Y	LIVER-Y	PRISM-Y
CHINK-Y	DRAPE-Y	FRUIT-Y	LOATH-Y	PRISS-Y
CHIRP-Y	DRAWL-Y	FRUMP-Y	LOWER-Y	PUNCH-Y
CHOKE-Y	DREAM-Y	GALAX-Y	LUNAR-Y	PUSLE-Y
CHUCK-Y	DREAR-Y	GAMES-Y	MANGE-Y	QUACK-Y
CHUFF-Y	DRECK-Y	GHOST-Y	MARSH-Y	QUALM-Y
CHUNK-Y	DRESS-Y	GLAIR-Y	MAUND-Y	QUEEN-Y
CIDER-Y	DRIFT-Y	GLASS-Y	MEDLE-Y	QUINS-Y
CLANK-Y	DROLL-Y	GLAUR-Y	MEREL-Y	QUIRK-Y
CLART-Y	DROOL-Y	GLEAM-Y	MIGHT-Y	RAKER-Y
CLASS-Y	DROOP-Y	GLEET-Y	MISER-Y	RATAN-Y
CLECK-Y	DROPS-Y	GLINT-Y	MISSA-Y	REAST-Y
CLIFF-Y	DROSS-Y	GLITZ-Y	MONOS-Y	REECH-Y
CLIFT-Y	DROWS-Y	GLOOM-Y	MOPER-Y	REEST-Y
CLING-Y	DUPER-Y	GLOOP-Y	MOTOR-Y	REPLA-Y
CLOUD-Y	DWEEB-Y	GLOSS-Y	MOULD-Y	RESIN-Y
CLUCK-Y	EARTH-Y	GNARL-Y	MOUSE-Y	RHEUM-Y
CLUMP-Y	EATER-Y	GOOSE-Y	MOUTH-Y	RIGHT-Y
CLUNK-Y	EGGER-Y	GOURD-Y	MURRA-Y	RIVER-Y
COACH-Y	EIGHT-Y	GOWAN-Y	MURRE-Y	ROOTS-Y
COCKS-Y	EMBUS-Y	GRAIN-Y	NIGHT-Y	ROPER-Y
COLON-Y	FAINT-Y	GRAPE-Y	NITER-Y	ROSET-Y
COLOR-Y	FAKER-Y	GRASS-Y	NOMAD-Y	ROSIN-Y
CONCH-Y	FAULT-Y	GREED-Y	NOTCH-Y	ROUGH-Y
CONVO-Y	FEIST-Y	GREEN-Y	OCCAM-Y	RUDER-Y
CORSE-Y	FELON-Y	GRIPE-Y	OCHER-Y	SAMEL-Y
COUNT-Y	FILTH-Y	GROSZ-Y	OCHRE-Y	SATIN-Y
COUTH-Y	FINER-Y	GROUP-Y	OILER-Y	SAUGH-Y
CRACK-Y	FITCH-Y	GROUT-Y	ONION-Y	SAVOR-Y
CRAFT-Y	FIXIT-Y	GROWL-Y	ORANG-Y	SCALL-Y
CRAMP-Y	FLAKE-Y	GRUFF-Y	ORBIT-Y	SCANT-Y
CRANK-Y	FLASH-Y	GRUMP-Y	OSIER-Y	SCARE-Y
CRAWL-Y	FLECK-Y	GUANA-Y	OWLER-Y	SCATT-Y
CREAK-Y	FLESH-Y	GUILT-Y	PAEON-Y	SCAUR-Y
CREAM-Y	FLIMS-Y	HAULM-Y	PAINT-Y	SCREW-Y
CREEK-Y	FLINT-Y	HEARS-Y	PAPER-Y	SCURF-Y
CREEP-Y	FLIRT-Y	HEART-Y	PARLE-Y	SCUZZ-Y
CREPE-Y	FLISK-Y	HEATH-Y	PATCH-Y	SEVER-Y
CRESS-Y	FLOAT-Y	HERES-Y	PEACH-Y	SHALE-Y
CRICK-Y	FLOCK-Y	HITCH-Y	PEARL-Y	SHAND-Y
CRIMP-Y	FLOSS-Y	HORSE-Y	PETAR-Y	SHARN-Y
CRISP-Y	FLOUR-Y	HOUSE-Y	PHONE-Y	SHARP-Y
CROAK-Y	FLUFF-Y	HUMUS-Y	PITCH-Y	SHEAF-Y
CROUP-Y	FLUKE-Y	HURRA-Y	PLASH-Y	SHEEN-Y
CROWD-Y	FLUNK-Y	JACKS-Y	PLONK-Y	SHEEP-Y
CRUMB-Y	FLURR-Y	JALOP-Y	PLOOK-Y	SHEET-Y
CRUMP-Y	FLUSH-Y	JAPER-Y	PLOUK-Y	SHELF-Y

SHELL-Y	SNAKE-Y	STEEL-Y	THICK-Y	UNSEX-Y
SHIFT-Y	SNARK-Y	STEEP-Y	THING-Y	VAPOR-Y
SHIRT-Y	SNARL-Y	STEER-Y	THORN-Y	VAULT-Y
SHOAL-Y	SNEAK-Y	STICK-Y	THUMB-Y	VAUNT-Y
SHORT-Y	SNEER-Y	STIFF-Y	THYME-Y	VETCH-Y
SHOUT-Y	SNELL-Y	STILL-Y	TIGER-Y	VICAR-Y
SINEW-Y	SNIDE-Y	STILT-Y	TILER-Y	VINER-Y
SIRUP-Y	SNIFF-Y	STING-Y	TITCH-Y	VOGUE-Y
SKANK-Y	SNIFT-Y	STINK-Y	TITUP-Y	VOLAR-Y
SKEAR-Y	SNOOP-Y	STINT-Y	TOAST-Y	WAFER-Y
SKEER-Y	SNOOT-Y	STOCK-Y	TOOTH-Y	WARRE-Y
SKELL-Y	SNORT-Y	STONE-Y	TOOTS-Y	WATER-Y
SKILL-Y	SNOUT-Y	STORE-Y	TORCH-Y	WAVER-Y
SKIMP-Y	SNUFF-Y	STORM-Y	TOUCH-Y	WEENS-Y
SKUNK-Y	SODOM-Y	STOUR-Y	TOUGH-Y	WEIRD-Y
SLANG-Y	SOREL-Y	STRAW-Y	TOWER-Y	WHACK-Y
SLANT-Y	SPACE-Y	STRIP-Y	TRAMP-Y	WHEAT-Y
SLATE-Y	SPARK-Y	STUFF-Y	TRASH-Y	WHEEL-Y
SLAVE-Y	SPAWN-Y	STUMP-Y	TREAT-Y	WHELK-Y
SLEEK-Y	SPEAR-Y	SUGAR-Y	TREND-Y	WHIFF-Y
SLEEP-Y	SPECK-Y	SWAMP-Y	TRESS-Y	WHIMS-Y
SLEET-Y	SPEED-Y	SWANK-Y	TRICK-Y	WHINE-Y
SLIMS-Y	SPEND-Y	SWARD-Y	TRIPE-Y	WHIRL-Y
SLINK-Y	SPICE-Y	SWART-Y	TROLL-Y	WHIRR-Y
SLOOM-Y	SPIFF-Y	SWASH-Y	TROUT-Y	WHISK-Y
SLOSH-Y	SPIKE-Y	SWATH-Y	TRUST-Y	WHITE-Y
SLUBB-Y	SPOOF-Y	SWEAT-Y	TRUTH-Y	WHIZZ-Y
SLUMP-Y	SPOOK-Y	SWEEP-Y	TWANG-Y	WIELD-Y
SLUSH-Y	SPOON-Y	SWEET-Y	TWANK-Y	WINCE-Y
SMALM-Y	SPORT-Y	SWIFT-Y	TWEAK-Y	WITCH-Y
SMARM-Y	SPOSH-Y	SWING-Y	TWEED-Y	WOODS-Y
SMART-Y	SPOUT-Y	SWIPE-Y	TWEEL-Y	WORTH-Y
SMEAR-Y	SPUNK-Y	SWIRL-Y	TWEEN-Y	WOUND-Y
SMELL-Y	STAGE-Y	SWISH-Y	TWERP-Y	WRATH-Y
SMILE-Y	STALK-Y	SWOON-Y	TWILL-Y	WRIST-Y
SMIRK-Y	STARR-Y	SWOOP-Y	TWIRL-Y	YEAST-Y
SMIRR-Y	STEAD-Y	SYLPH-Y	TWIRP-Y	YOUTH-Y
SMITH-Y	STEAM-Y	SYRUP-Y	TWIST-Y	
SMOKE-Y	STEDD-Y	TAWER-Y	UMBER-Y	
SNAIL-Y	STEED-Y	TEENS-Y	UNRED-Y	

Six letters to seven

ALMOND-Y	BOBBER-Y	CARVER-Y	COPPER-Y	DODGER-Y
ANALOG-Y	BOCKED-Y	CASTOR-Y	COSHER-Y	DOGGER-Y
ANARCH-Y	BOILER-Y	CAUTER-Y	COTTON-Y	DOUGHT-Y
APOLOG-Y	BRANCH-Y	CHANCE-Y	CRAMES-Y	DOWLNE-Y
ARCHER-Y	BRAVER-Y	CHINCH-Y	CREESH-Y	DRAPER-Y
ARMOUR-Y	BREATH-Y	CHINTZ-Y	CRUNCH-Y	DROICH-Y
AUTUMN-Y	BREWER-Y	CHOOSE-Y	CURSOR-Y	DROUTH-Y
BALSAM-Y	BRIBER-Y	CHURCH-Y	CUTLER-Y	DUDDER-Y
BATTER-Y	BROKER-Y	CINDER-Y	CYCLER-Y	DYNAST-Y
BEAVER-Y	BUGGER-Y	CIRCUS-Y	DACOIT-Y	DYVOUR-Y
BEGGAR-Y	BURSAR-Y	CITRUS-Y	DAKOIT-Y	EPARCH-Y
BIBBER-Y	BUTLER-Y	CLIQUE-Y	DAUBER-Y	EPONYM-Y
BILLOW-Y	BUTTER-Y	CLOVER-Y	DEANER-Y	EUPHON-Y
BINDER-Y	BUTTON-Y	CLUTCH-Y	DIARCH-Y	EXARCH-Y
BIOGEN-Y	CANKER-Y	COLOUR-Y	DIDDLE-Y	FACTOR-Y
BLIGHT-Y	CANNER-Y	COOKER-Y	DITHER-Y	FAGGOT-Y
BLOTCH-Y	CARROT-Y	COOPER-Y	DODDER-Y	FARMER-Y

FERRET-Y	KLUDGE-Y	PEPPER-Y	SHRILL-Y	TALLOW-Y
FIBBER-Y	KOLHOZ-Y	PHLEGM-Y	SHRIMP-Y	TANNER-Y
FIDDLE-Y	KOLKOZ-Y	PICKER-Y	SHROUD-Y	TATTER-Y
FIDGET-Y	KVETCH-Y	PILFER-Y	SHTICK-Y	THATCH-Y
FISHER-Y	LADDER-Y	PILLOW-Y	SIGNOR-Y	THIRST-Y
FLAUNT-Y	LATHER-Y	PIZAZZ-Y	SILVER-Y	THREAD-Y
FLAVOR-Y	LECHER-Y	PLAGUE-Y	SINTER-Y	THRIFT-Y
FLIGHT-Y	LENGTH-Y	PLOVER-Y	SKETCH-Y	THRILL-Y
FLOWER-Y	LITTER-Y	POTHER-Y	SLAVER-Y	THRIST-Y
FORGER-Y	LOLLOP-Y	POTTER-Y	SLEECH-Y	THROAT-Y
FOUGHT-Y	LOTTER-Y	POWDER-Y	SLOUCH-Y	TIDDLE-Y
FRATCH-Y	MAGGOT-Y	PREACH-Y	SLOUGH-Y	TIMBER-Y
FRATER-Y	MAPPER-Y	PROBIT-Y	SLUTCH-Y	TINDER-Y
FROWST-Y	MARROW-Y	PUCKER-Y	SMOOCH-Y	TISSUE-Y
FULLER-Y	MARTYR-Y	PUFFER-Y	SMOOTH-Y	TITTUP-Y
FURROW-Y	MASTER-Y	QUARTZ-Y	SMUTCH-Y	TOGGER-Y
GADGET-Y	MATTER-Y	QUAVER-Y	SNATCH-Y	TOTTER-Y
GAGGER-Y	MEADOW-Y	QUEACH-Y	SNITCH-Y	TRACER-Y
GALANT-Y	MELLOW-Y	QUIVER-Y	SPICER-Y	TRICKS-Y
GARGET-Y	MENSCH-Y	RABBIT-Y	SPIDER-Y	TRIPOD-Y
GEODES-Y	MERCER-Y	RACKET-Y	SPIKER-Y	TURNER-Y
GINGER-Y	MILDEW-Y	RAGGED-Y	SPIRIT-Y	TWITCH-Y
GINNER-Y	MISTER-Y	RAISIN-Y	SPLASH-Y	TYMPAN-Y
GLITCH-Y	MOCKER-Y	RATTER-Y	SPLEEN-Y	UNHAND-Y
GOSSIP-Y	MODEST-Y	RAUNCH-Y	SPRAWL-Y	UNREAD-Y
GRAVEL-Y	MONGER-Y	RECTOR-Y	SPRING-Y	UNTENT-Y
GROCER-Y	MORALL-Y	RIBBON-Y	SQUALL-Y	VALLAR-Y
GROUCH-Y	MORASS-Y	RIFLER-Y	SQUASH-Y	VAPOUR-Y
GROWTH-Y	MORTAR-Y	ROBBER-Y	SQUAWK-Y	VELVET-Y
GRUMPH-Y	MOTHER-Y	ROCKER-Y	SQUEAK-Y	VERMIL-Y
GULLER-Y	MOUSER-Y	RUBBER-Y	SQUIFF-Y	VERMIN-Y
GUNNER-Y	MUMMER-Y	RUBBIT-Y	SQUINT-Y	VICTOR-Y
GUTTER-Y	MUTTON-Y	RUSSET-Y	SQUIRM-Y	VILLAN-Y
HACKER-Y	NAILER-Y	SALLOW-Y	SQUISH-Y	WAGGER-Y
HAUGHT-Y	NATTER-Y	SATRAP-Y	STAGER-Y	WASHER-Y
HEALTH-Y	NAUGHT-Y	SAVOUR-Y	STARCH-Y	WASTER-Y
HELLER-Y	NECTAR-Y	SCRAWL-Y	STARTS-Y	WEALTH-Y
HENNER-Y	NIGGER-Y	SCREAK-Y	STATUS-Y	WEASEL-Y
HERBAR-Y	NOSHER-Y	SCRIMP-Y	STENCH-Y	WEEDER-Y
HICCUP-Y	NUGGET-Y	SCRUFF-Y	STREAK-Y	WEEVIL-Y
HOGGER-Y	NURSER-Y	SCRUMP-Y	STREAM-Y	WEIGHT-Y
HONEST-Y	NUTTER-Y	SCRUNT-Y	STREET-Y	WHALER-Y
HOSIER-Y	ORANGE-Y	SEALER-Y	STRING-Y	WIGGER-Y
IMAGER-Y	ORATOR-Y	SENSOR-Y	STRIPE-Y	WILLOW-Y
ISOGON-Y	OROGEN-Y	SERVER-Y	SUCCOR-Y	WINDOW-Y
JAGGER-Y	OVULAR-Y	SHADOW-Y	SULFUR-Y	WINTER-Y
JARGON-Y	PALMAR-Y	SHEATH-Y	SUMMAR-Y	WORMER-Y
JASPER-Y	PANICK-Y	SHINNE-Y	SUMMER-Y	WREATH-Y
JITTER-Y	PARROT-Y	SHIVER-Y	SURGER-Y	YELLOW-Y
JOBBER-Y	PASTIL-Y	SHLOCK-Y	SUTLER-Y	
JOINER-Y	PAUNCH-Y	SHLUMP-Y	SWARTH-Y	
KITSCH-Y	PEDLAR-Y	SHOWER-Y	SWITCH-Y	
KITTEN-Y	PEDLER-Y	SHRIEK-Y	TACKET-Y	

Seven letters to eight

ACTRESS-Y	ANTONYM-Y	AUTARCH-Y	BISCUIT-Y	BLOOMER-Y
ADVISOR-Y	APOCARP-Y	AXILLAR-Y	BLADDER-Y	BLOSSOM-Y
ANTILOG-Y	APOPLEX-Y	BASILAR-Y	BLANKET-Y	BLUBBER-Y
ANTIQUE-Y	AUDITOR-Y	BASTARD-Y	BLISTER-Y	BLUSTER-Y

BOTCHER-Y	DROLLER-Y	HYDROPS-Y	PUDDING-Y	SOLDIER-Y
BOULDER-Y	DROUGHT-Y	HYPONYM-Y	PUPILAR-Y	SOLICIT-Y
BRAZIER-Y	DRUDGER-Y	INCISOR-Y	QUACKER-Y	SOVKHOZ-Y
BROIDER-Y	ENACTOR-Y	INTRADA-Y	QUIDDIT-Y	SPINACH-Y
BULLOCK-Y	ENDARCH-Y	JANIZAR-Y	QUIZZER-Y	SPINNER-Y
BULRUSH-Y	ENDOGEN-Y	JEALOUS-Y	RAINBOW-Y	SPLOTCH-Y
BURGLAR-Y	ENGINER-Y	JEOPARD-Y	RECOVER-Y	SPOOFER-Y
BUTCHER-Y	ENTREAT-Y	JUGGLER-Y	REFINER-Y	SPUTTER-Y
CABBAGE-Y	EUPLOID-Y	KNACKER-Y	REVISOR-Y	SQUELCH-Y
CACONYM-Y	EVANGEL-Y	KOLKHOS-Y	RHUBARB-Y	SQUOOSH-Y
CAJOLER-Y	FARRIER-Y	KOLKHOZ-Y	ROLLICK-Y	STAGGER-Y
CALAMAR-Y	FASHION-Y	LACUNAR-Y	ROTATOR-Y	STEALTH-Y
CANTICO-Y	FEATHER-Y	LAMINAR-Y	RUBBISH-Y	STEMMER-Y
CARTOON-Y	FLACKER-Y	LEATHER-Y	SACRIST-Y	STOMACH-Y
CENTAUR-Y	FLATTER-Y	LYSOGEN-Y	SADDLER-Y	STRETCH-Y
CHAFFER-Y	FLAVOUR-Y	MERONYM-Y	SAFFRON-Y	STUDENT-Y
CHANCER-Y	FEATHER-Y	METONYM-Y	SAMPLER-Y	SULPHUR-Y
CHATTER-Y	FLICKER-Y	MILITAR-Y	SAVAGER-Y	SUNBEAM-Y
CHEATER-Y	FLUSTER-Y	MONARCH-Y	SAWDUST-Y	SYNCARP-Y
CHEDDAR-Y	FLUTTER-Y	MONITOR-Y	SCATTER-Y	SYNONYM-Y
CHEVRON-Y	FRIPPER-Y	MONOLOG-Y	SCHLEPP-Y	TABLOID-Y
CHIEFER-Y	FROTHER-Y	MONOPOD-Y	SCHLOCK-Y	TASSELL-Y
CHIFFON-Y	FRUITER-Y	MULLOCK-Y	SCHLUMP-Y	THEOLOG-Y
CHIRRUP-Y	FURRIER-Y	MUSTARD-Y	SCHMALZ-Y	THICKET-Y
CIRCUIT-Y	GARBAGE-Y	NAVARCH-Y	SCHMOOZ-Y	THUNDER-Y
CITATOR-Y	GEALOUS-Y	NEBBISH-Y	SCRATCH-Y	TITULAR-Y
CLATTER-Y	GIMMICK-Y	NEGATOR-Y	SCREECH-Y	TOPARCH-Y
CLERUCH-Y	GLAZIER-Y	NITPICK-Y	SCRUNCH-Y	TOPONYM-Y
CLUSTER-Y	GLIBBER-Y	NOMARCH-Y	SCULLER-Y	TOURIST-Y
CLUTTER-Y	GLIDDER-Y	ORANGER-Y	SEMINAR-Y	TRASHER-Y
COBBLER-Y	GLIMMER-Y	ORDINAR-Y	SHATTER-Y	TRIARCH-Y
COLLIER-Y	GLITTER-Y	OUTWEAR-Y	SHELTER-Y	TRICKER-Y
CONCEIT-Y	GLUTTON-Y	OVERMAN-Y	SHIMMER-Y	TRIFFID-Y
COSTUME-Y	GOLIARD-Y	PARADOX-Y	SHMALTZ-Y	TRIPPER-Y
COTTAGE-Y	GREENER-Y	PARONYM-Y	SHUDDER-Y	TROLLOP-Y
CRAUNCH-Y	GRILLER-Y	PATCHER-Y	SIGNIOR-Y	TUMULAR-Y
CREAMER-Y	GRINDER-Y	PEACOCK-Y	SKITTER-Y	TUSSOCK-Y
CROOKER-Y	GROWLER-Y	PEASANT-Y	SLABBER-Y	TUTELAR-Y
CRYOGEN-Y	GYRATOR-Y	PEDAGOG-Y	SLATTER-Y	TWITTER-Y
CURATOR-Y	HAPLOID-Y	PEDDLER-Y	SLEEPER-Y	UNCLOUD-Y
CURRANT-Y	HARMOST-Y	PERCHER-Y	SLIDDER-Y	UNTRUST-Y
CURRIER-Y	HASSOCK-Y	PHANTOM-Y	SLIPPER-Y	UNWATER-Y
CUSHION-Y	HATCHER-Y	PIZZAZZ-Y	SLITHER-Y	UNWORTH-Y
CUSTARD-Y	HATCHET-Y	PLASTER-Y	SLOBBER-Y	VARNISH-Y
DASTARD-Y	HEATHER-Y	PLUMBER-Y	SLUMBER-Y	VAUNTER-Y
DELIVER-Y	HEGEMON-Y	POLYGAM-Y	SMELTER-Y	VAVASOR-Y
DEMAGOG-Y	HEGUMEN-Y	POLYGON-Y	SMOTHER-Y	VILLAIN-Y
DILATOR-Y	HEXAPOD-Y	POLYMER-Y	SMUGGER-Y	VINEGAR-Y
DIPLOID-Y	HEXARCH-Y	POLYPOD-Y	SNICKER-Y	WARRANT-Y
DONATOR-Y	HILLOCK-Y	PRIGGER-Y	SNIPPET-Y	WHISKER-Y
DRAUGHT-Y	HOMOLOG-Y	PRINTER-Y	SNOTTER-Y	WHISPER-Y
DREAMER-Y	HOMONYM-Y	PSALTER-Y	SNUGGER-Y	
	HUMMOCK-Y			

Eight letters to nine

ADULATOR-Y	ANTIPHON-Y	BIOGRAPH-Y	BRIMFULL-Y	CHARCOAL-Y
ALLOPATH-Y	ASPERSOR-Y	BLEACHER-Y	BUSINESS-Y	CHICANER-Y
ALLOTTER-Y	ASSERTOR-Y	BLIZZARD-Y	CALCULAR-Y	CINNAMON-Y
AMPULLAR-Y	AUXILIAR-Y	BOUTIQUE-Y	CAPSULAR-Y	COLOPHON-Y
ANAGLYPH-Y	BACILLAR-Y	BRANCHER-Y	CHANDLER-Y	CONNIVER-Y

CONTRAST-Y	FORMULAR-Y	MILLINER-Y	POLYARCH-Y	SQUIRREL-Y
COSTUMER-Y	FREEBOOT-Y	MOUNTAIN-Y	POLYMATH-Y	STIPULAR-Y
CREMATOR-Y	GOSSAMER-Y	MYOGRAPH-Y	POLYONYM-Y	STITCHER-Y
CROTCHET-Y	GRANULAR-Y	MYSTAGOG-Y	POLYPHON-Y	SUBAHDAR-Y
CURSITOR-Y	HAWTHORN-Y	NARRATOR-Y	PREDATOR-Y	SUBLIMIT-Y
DANDRUFF-Y	HEADACHE-Y	NONSTICK-Y	PRODITOR-Y	SUBLUNAR-Y
DAYDREAM-Y	HEPTARCH-Y	NUMMULAR-Y	PROVISOR-Y	TAUTONYM-Y
DEMOCRAT-Y	HIERARCH-Y	OENOPHIL-Y	PULSATOR-Y	TELEPATH-Y
DEVIATOR-Y	HISTOGEN-Y	OKEYDOKE-Y	PUPILLAR-Y	TETRAPOD-Y
DICTATOR-Y	HUCKSTER-Y	OLIGARCH-Y	RADIATOR-Y	TETRARCH-Y
DIRECTOR-Y	HYPERNYM-Y	OPSIMATH-Y	RAKEHELL-Y	THEOSOPH-Y
DISCOVER-Y	IMMODEST-Y	ORTHODOX-Y	SCAPULAR-Y	TREACHER-Y
EDUCATOR-Y	IMPLICIT-Y	OSTEOGEN-Y	SCHMALTZ-Y	TRIPLOID-Y
ELEVATOR-Y	INCENSOR-Y	OUTDOORS-Y	SCOUTHER-Y	TRIUMVIR-Y
EMANATOR-Y	INVENTOR-Y	OVERWEAR-Y	SECRETOR-Y	UNHEALTH-Y
EMBRACER-Y	JEWELLER-Y	PALPATOR-Y	SEIGNEUR-Y	UNTHRIFT-Y
ENGRAVER-Y	LAUDATOR-Y	PAPILLAR-Y	SEIGNIOR-Y	VEXILLAR-Y
EPIGRAPH-Y	LOGOMACH-Y	PARAFFIN-Y	SERGEANT-Y	VILLAGER-Y
ETHNARCH-Y	MAGISTER-Y	PATHOGEN-Y	SERJEANT-Y	VISCOUNT-Y
EUDAEMON-Y	MALINGER-Y	PEDERAST-Y	SINGSONG-Y	WHIFFLER-Y
EVOCATOR-Y	MAMILLAR-Y	PENTARCH-Y	SINGULAR-Y	WHIPCORD-Y
EXECUTOR-Y	MANDATOR-Y	PERFUMER-Y	SLAISTER-Y	ZAMINDAR-Y
EXEMPLAR-Y	MAXILLAR-Y	PERIPTER-Y	SOAPSUDS-Y	ZEMINDAR-Y
EXPIATOR-Y	MEDIATOR-Y	PHOTOGEN-Y	SPLINTER-Y	ZOOMORPH-Y
FLOURISH-Y	MEDULLAR-Y	PHYLARCH-Y	SPLUTTER-Y	
FOOTWEAR-Y	MIGRATOR-Y	PISCATOR-Y	SQUEAKER-Y	

Z – Front-hooks

Two letters to three

Z-AG	Z-EA	Z-EL	Z-IN	Z-OS
Z-AS	Z-ED	Z-EX	Z-IT	
Z-AX	Z-EE	Z-HO	Z-OO	

Three letters to four

Z-AGS	Z-ELS	Z-IFF	Z-ONE	Z-OUK
Z-ANY	Z-ERK	Z-ILL	Z-OOM	Z-ULU
Z-ARF	Z-EST	Z-INS	Z-OON	
Z-EAS	Z-ETA	Z-ITS	Z-OOS	
Z-EDS	Z-HOS	Z-OBO	Z-OOT	

Four letters to five

Z-AMBO	Z-AYIN	Z-EXES	Z-OBOS	Z-OPPO
Z-AMIA	Z-ERKS	Z-HOMO	Z-ONER	Z-OUKS
Z-ANTE	Z-EROS	Z-ILLS	Z-ONES	Z-ULUS
Z-ARFS	Z-ESTS	Z-INKY	Z-OOMS	Z-UPAS
Z-AXES	Z-ETAS	Z-LOTE	Z-OONS	

Five letters to six

Z-AMBOS	Z-ANTES	Z-HOMOS	Z-ITHER
Z-AMIAS	Z-AYINS	Z-IGGED	Z-ONERS
Z-ANANA	Z-ESTER	Z-INKED	

Six letters to seven

Z-ANANAS	Z-INCITE	Z-OOGAMY	Z-OOLITE	Z-ORBING
Z-ESTERS	Z-INKIER	Z-OOGENY	Z-OOLITH	
Z-IGGING	Z-INKING	Z-OOIDAL	Z-OOLOGY	

Seven letters to eight

Z-INCITES	Z-ONETIME	Z-OOLITHS	Z-OOLOGIC	Z-OOSPERM
Z-INKIEST	Z-OOLITES	Z-OOLITIC	Z-OOPHYTE	Z-OOSPORE

Eight letters to nine

Z-OOGAMETE	Z-OOGENIES	Z-OOPHYTES	Z-OOSPORES
Z-OOGAMIES	Z-OOLOGIES	Z-OOPHYTIC	Z-OOSPORIC
Z-OOGAMOUS	Z-OOLOGIST	Z-OOSPERMS	

Z – End-hooks

Two letters to three

AD-Z	BI-Z	MI-Z	PO-Z
BE-Z	FE-Z	MO-Z	RE-Z

Three letters to four

CHE-Z	GEE-Z	MIZ-Z	POZ-Z	SIT-Z
CHI-Z	JEE-Z	MOZ-Z	PRE-Z	SPA-Z
DIT-Z	JIZ-Z	OYE-Z	PUT-Z	ZIZ-Z
FIZ-Z	LEZ-Z	PHI-Z	RIT-Z	

Four letters to five

BORT-Z	FRIT-Z	GREN-Z	SPAZ-Z	WARE-Z
CAPI-Z	FRIZ-Z	MILT-Z	SPIT-Z	WHIZ-Z
CHIZ-Z	GLIT-Z	PLOT-Z	SWIZ-Z	WOOT-Z

Five letters to six

PIZZA-Z	QUART-Z	SPELT-Z	SPRIT-Z

Six letters to seven

PIZZAZ-Z	SCHNOZ-Z

Blockers

Blockers are the opposite of hooks – words which **cannot** have a letter added at the beginning or end. These are extremely useful to know, as they allow you to close whole sections of the board to your opponents.

The following lists show blockers of two to six letters in length. Not included in the five and six-letter lists are words with endings that obviously preclude a single letter being added at the back: -ED, -J, -S, -X, -Y and -Z.

Two-letter words

FY	XU

Three-letter words

AUE	GEY	NTH	SEZ	WOX
BEZ	GOX	NYS	SHH	YAE
CAZ	HEX	OXO	SIX	YEH
CLY	HMM	PAX	SLY	YEX
CUZ	HOX	PHT	SMA	YOS
DUH	JAL	PLY	SOX	ZAS
DUX	KEX	POH	SWY	ZAX
FAE	LOX	PST	TAJ	ZEX
FAP	LUZ	PYX	THY	ZOA
FAX	MUX	QIS	TIX	ZUZ
FEW	NAE	RAX	TUX	
FEZ	NAH	RHY	TWP	
FLY	NOH	SAE	VLY	
FRY	NOX	SAZ	VOX	

Four-letter words

AAHS	AROW	BEVY	BOXY	CEPS
ABBS	ASEA	BHAT	BRRR	CHEZ
ABLY	AVOS	BIBS	BRUX	CHIS
ABOS	AWRY	BIDS	BUBO	CIGS
ACHY	AXAL	BIEN	BUBS	CITO
ADRY	AYUS	BIGS	BUDS	CITS
AESC	BAAS	BINS	BUGS	CITY
AGLY	BABY	BIOS	BUMS	COAX
AHEM	BADE	BISH	BUNS	COBS
AHIS	BADS	BIST	BURY	COCH
AHOY	BAGS	BLEW	BUSY	CODS
AJAR	BAMS	BOBS	BUYS	COFT
AJEE	BANS	BODS	CAAS	COKY
ALAE	BAPS	BODY	CAGY	COLS
ALBS	BATS	BOGS	CAKY	COLY
ALEE	BAYS	BOGY	CALX	COMS
ALIT	BEDS	BOHS	CANY	CONY
ALSO	BEDU	BOIS	CAPS	COPY
ANEW	BEEN	BOKS	CASH	CORF
ANOW	BEES	BONA	CAUF	CORY
APEX	BEGS	BOPS	CAVY	COSH
APTS	BELS	BORS	CAYS	COSS
AREG	BENJ	BOSH	CEES	COSY
AREW	BENS	BOTS	CELS	COWY

COXY	DOPY	FAHS	GAGS	HEPT
COYS	DORY	FAIX	GALS	HISN
COZY	DOSH	FALX	GAMY	HIYA
CRUX	DOSS	FANS	GANS	HOAX
CUBS	DOST	FASH	GAPS	HOBS
CUED	DOTH	FAUX	GAPY	HODS
CUES	DOTS	FAWS	GARE	HOHA
CURT	DOTY	FEDS	GASH	HOKA
CWMS	DOUN	FEET	GATS	HOLP
DABS	DOUX	FEGS	GAYS	HOLY
DADS	DOWF	FEHS	GAZY	HOMS
DAES	DOXY	FEMS	GEDS	HOMY
DAFT	DOYS	FENS	GEED	HOSS
DAGS	DOZY	FETS	GEEZ	HOYS
DAKS	DREW	FEUS	GELS	HUED
DAMS	DRYS	FEYS	GEMS	HUES
DANS	DUBS	FIBS	GENS	HUGY
DAPS	DUCI	FIDS	GEOS	HUIC
DAVY	DUDS	FIFI	GERT	HUIS
DEAF	DUED	FIGS	GETS	HUNG
DEBS	DUES	FIKY	GHIS	HUNH
DEEK	DUGS	FILS	GIBS	HWAN
DEFT	DULY	FINS	GIDS	HYED
DEFY	DUOS	FITS	GIED	HYES
DEGS	DUPS	FIXT	GIEN	HYPS
DELS	DUSH	FLED	GIES	HYTE
DEMY	DUTY	FLIX	GIGS	IBIS
DENY	DYED	FLUX	GINS	ICHS
DESI	DYES	FOBS	GITS	IDEM
DEUS	DZOS	FOCI	GIZZ	IDLY
DEVS	EASY	FOEN	GJUS	IGAD
DEWS	EBBS	FOES	GLEG	ILKA
DEWY	ECOD	FOGS	GNUS	INIA
DEXY	ECUS	FOGY	GOAS	INLY
DEYS	EDDO	FOHS	GOBS	INRO
DIBS	EDHS	FONE	GOBY	IURE
DIDY	EHED	FONS	GOES	JABS
DIED	EINA	FOPS	GOEY	JAGS
DIEL	ELHI	FOUS	GORY	JAIS
DIES	ELMY	FOXY	GOVS	JAKS
DIFS	ELSE	FOYS	GOYS	JAMS
DIGS	EMUS	FOZY	GREX	JAPS
DIMS	EMYS	FRAE	GUBS	JARS
DINS	ENUF	FROM	GULS	JASS
DIPT	EOAN	FUCI	GULY	JASY
DISS	ESPY	FUDS	GUMS	JAWS
DIVS	EUGE	FUGS	GUNS	JAXY
DIXY	EUOI	FUMS	GUPS	JAYS
DOBS	EVOE	FUMY	GUVS	JAZY
DOBY	EVOS	FUNS	GYMS	JEED
DOCS	EWKS	FURS	GYNY	JEES
DODS	EYES	FURY	GYRI	JEEZ
DOEN	EYNE	FUSC	HAED	JEON
DOGS	EYRY	FUTZ	HAEN	JETS
DOGY	FAAN	GABS	HAES	JEUX
DOHS	FAAS	GABY	HAZY	JEWS
DOMS	FABS	GAED	HEHS	JIBS
DOMY	FADS	GAEN	HELD	JIGS
DOOS	FADY	GAES	HEMS	JINX
DOPS	FAGS	GAGA	HEPS	JIVY

JIZZ	LACS	MIPS	NOYS	PTUI
JOBS	LACY	MIRO	NUNS	PUBS
JOCO	LANX	MIRY	NYAS	PUIR
JOES	LARS	MIXY	NYED	PUKA
JOGS	LATI	MNAS	OAKY	PULY
JOKY	LAVS	MOAI	OBIS	PUNS
JOLS	LECH	MOAS	OCCY	PUNY
JONG	LEKE	MOBS	ODDS	PUPS
JORS	LEKS	MOBY	ODEA	PUTS
JOSH	LEKU	MOCS	OHMS	PUTZ
JOSS	LEPS	MODS	OKAS	PUYS
JOTS	LEVA	MOES	OLEA	PYAS
JOWS	LEVO	MOLS	ONST	PYES
JOYS	LEVY	MOLY	ONYX	PYIC
JUDS	LEWD	MOMI	OPTS	QATS
JUDY	LIDS	MOMS	ORFS	QUEP
JUGS	LIGS	MONS	ORYX	RACA
JURY	LIPA	MONY	OSAR	RAHS
JUTS	LIRE	MOOI	OYEZ	RAZZ
JYNX	LIRI	MOPY	PACS	REBS
KAAL	LITU	MOSH	PADS	RECS
KAAS	LOCI	MOTS	PALY	REFS
KABS	LORN	MOWN	PAPS	REFT
KAED	LUDS	MOWS	PATY	REHS
KAES	LUNY	MOYS	PAVS	RELY
KAFS	LUVS	MOZZ	PEDS	RENK
KAIS	LYCH	MUDS	PEGS	RENY
KAKS	LYES	MUNS	PEHS	REOS
KEAS	LYMS	MYCS	PEPS	RHOS
KEBS	LYNX	NADS	PFFT	RHUS
KEDS	LYRA	NAIN	PFUI	RIFS
KEFS	MAAS	NAMS	PHAT	ROED
KEKS	MADE	NAMU	PHEW	ROKY
KEPT	MADS	NANS	PHIZ	ROPY
KESH	MAES	NAOI	PHOS	ROUX
KETE	MAGS	NAOS	PIAS	RUBY
KEWL	MAKS	NAVY	PIGS	RUCS
KEYS	MALS	NAYS	PILY	RUNS
KHIS	MANY	NEFS	PIPS	RYAS
KIFS	MAPS	NEGS	PIPY	RYES
KILD	MARY	NEKS	PIRS	RYFE
KIRS	MATS	NEPS	PISS	SABS
KISH	MATY	NESH	PITY	SACS
KNEW	MAWN	NESS	PIXY	SAFT
KOAS	MAWS	NETS	PLEX	SAGS
KOBS	MAZY	NEVI	POAS	SAGY
KOIS	MEDS	NIDI	POCO	SAMS
KOPS	MEGS	NIDS	POGY	SAPS
KORO	MELS	NIED	POKY	SASH
KORS	MEMS	NIMS	POLS	SAVS
KOSS	MENO	NISI	POMS	SAWN
KOWS	METS	NIXY	PONS	SAWS
KRIS	MHOS	NODI	PONY	SCRY
KUEH	MIBS	NOES	POOS	SECO
KUES	MICS	NOMS	PORY	SECS
KUNA	MIGS	NOPE	POSY	SEEN
KUNE	MIHA	NOSH	POWS	SEES
KYES	MILS	NOSY	PREZ	SEGS
KYNE	MINX	NOTT	PRUH	SEIK
KYUS	MINY	NOUS	PSST	SELD

SELS	SUBS	TODS	VIDS	YAGS
SENE	SUCH	TODY	VIGS	YALD
SEPS	SUES	TOED	VIMS	YAPS
SESH	SUKS	TOES	VINS	YAWS
SETS	SUMS	TOEY	VIVO	YAWY
SEWN	SUNG	TOGS	VIZY	YAYS
SEWS	SUNS	TOLD	VOES	YBET
SEXY	SUPS	TONS	VOLS	YEBO
SEYS	SUQS	TORN	VORS	YEPS
SHAT	SUSS	TOWY	VROT	YEWS
SHMO	SWUM	TOYS	VUGS	YGOE
SHOD	SYED	TREZ	VUMS	YIDS
SIBS	SYES	TSKS	WADY	YIPS
SICS	TADS	TUGS	WANY	YMPT
SIES	TAED	TUNY	WARY	YOBS
SIMS	TAES	TUPS	WAVY	YODS
SINS	TAKS	TUTS	WAWS	YOKS
SIPS	TAKY	TUZZ	WAXY	YOLD
SIRS	TALI	TWAS	WEBS	YOND
SITS	TAMS	TWOS	WEDS	YOWS
SITZ	TAOS	TYDE	WEMS	YUCH
SIZY	TAUS	TYGS	WENA	YUGS
SJOE	TAVS	TYPY	WENS	YUKS
SKAS	TAXA	UNDO	WERE	YUKY
SKIS	TECS	UPGO	WERT	YUNX
SKRY	TEDY	UPSY	WETS	YUPS
SOBS	TEES	UVAE	WHAE	YUTZ
SOCS	TEFS	UVAS	WHIO	YWIS
SODS	TEGS	VACS	WHOA	ZAGS
SOGS	TELD	VAES	WHOT	ZANY
SOHO	TELS	VAGI	WHYS	ZAPS
SOHS	TELT	VAGS	WICH	ZEAS
SOLS	THAE	VAIN	WILY	ZEDS
SOME	THAT	VANS	WIRY	ZEKS
SOMS	THEY	VARS	WOES	ZELS
SOMY	THIS	VATS	WOFS	ZEPS
SOON	THUS	VAUS	WOGS	ZIGS
SOPS	TICS	VAVS	WOKS	ZINS
SORI	TIDS	VAWS	WONS	ZIPS
SOSS	TIDY	VEES	WOST	ZITE
SOTS	TIGS	VERA	WOWF	ZITS
SOVS	TILS	VERD	WOWS	ZIZZ
SOYS	TINS	VETO	WUDS	ZOLS
SPED	TINY	VEXT	WYCH	ZOOS
SPRY	TIPT	VIAE	WYES	ZZZS
SRIS	TITS	VIAS	WYNS	
STEY	TOBY	VIBS	YABA	

Five-letter words (except words ending in '-ED', '-J', '-S', '-X', '-Y' or '-Z')

AARGH	ABOIL	ACOCK	ADYTA	AGAST
ABACI	ABORE	ACOLD	AESIR	AGGRI
ABACK	ABRAM	ACRID	AFALD	AGLEE
ABAFT	ABRIM	ADOWN	AFIRE	AGLOW
ABASH	ABUNE	ADOZE	AFOOT	AGOOD
ABASK	ACERB	ADRAD	AFORE	AGRIN
ABEAM	ACHOO	ADSUM	AFOUL	AHEAD
ABLOW	ACMIC	ADUNC	AGAIN	AHEAP

AHENT	ASTIR	BORIC	CRASH	DUING
AHIGH	ASWIM	BORNA	CREPT	DUMKA
AHIND	ASYLA	BOWIE	CROCI	DUNCH
AHINT	ATILT	BOXEN	CRONK	DUNNO
AHULL	ATRIP	BRAVI	CROST	DUNSH
AHURU	AULIC	BREEM	CRUSH	DUOMI
AIDOI	AULOI	BREME	CUFFO	DURST
AINEE	AURAL	BRUNG	CUING	DUTCH
AITCH	AURAR	BRUSK	CUISH	DWELT
ALACK	AUREI	BUFFA	CUNEI	EHING
ALANE	AVAST	BUFFI	CURCH	ELMEN
ALBEE	AWASH	BUILT	CURLI	EMONG
ALEFT	AWATO	BURNT	CURSI	ENLIT
ALGAE	AWAVE	BUTCH	CURST	ENORM
ALGAL	AWEEL	BUXOM	CWTCH	ETYMA
ALGID	AWORK	BYSSI	CYANO	EVHOE
ALIKE	AXIAL	CABRE	CYBER	EVOHE
ALIVE	AXILE	CACTI	CYMAE	EWHOW
ALOFT	AYELP	CAESE	DAWEN	EYRIR
ALONE	AYGRE	CAJON	DAYCH	FATAL
ALOOF	AYONT	CAJUN	DAYNT	FAUGH
ALOUD	AZIDO	CALID	DEALT	FAURD
ALOWE	AZOIC	CANST	DEASH	FAVER
ALTHO	AZURN	CAPUT	DEDAL	FAYER
AMAIN	BAITH	CARPI	DEERE	FECAL
AMICI	BAKEN	CECAL	DEFFO	FECIT
AMINO	BANAL	CECUM	DEMIC	FEHME
AMNIA	BARER	CERIC	DEMPT	FERER
AMNIC	BARIC	CESTI	DESHI	FETAL
AMONG	BASHO	CHAPT	DIACT	FETCH
AMORT	BASSI	CHAVE	DICTA	FETID
ANILE	BASTA	CHERE	DIDST	FEWER
ANSAE	BATCH	CHIAO	DINGO	FEYER
ANTAE	BEDAD	CHIMO	DINNA	FILAR
APACE	BEEDI	CHODE	DIRER	FILCH
APAGE	BEGAD	CHOTA	DISCI	FILUM
APAID	BEGAN	CHYND	DITCH	FINCH
APART	BEGAT	CILIA	DOCHT	FLITT
APAYD	BEGOT	CINCH	DOEST	FLOSH
APEAK	BELCH	CINCT	DOETH	FLOWN
APEEK	BERKO	CIPPI	DOGGO	FLUNG
APERT	BESAT	CIRRI	DOILT	FOCAL
APGAR	BESAW	CIVIL	DOLCI	FOLIC
APIAN	BIFID	CLAPT	DOLIA	FORDO
APOOP	BIGAE	CLASH	DOMAL	FOUER
APORT	BINAL	CLIPT	DOMIC	FRACK
APTER	BIRCH	CLOMB	DONER	FRAPE
AQUAE	BITOU	CLUNG	DORIC	FRATI
AREAE	BIVIA	COMAE	DOTAL	FRENA
AREAL	BLAER	COMAL	DOWNA	FROSH
AREAR	BLASE	COOST	DRACK	FRUSH
AREDD	BLAWN	CORAM	DRACO	FUBAR
AREIC	BLIST	CORNI	DRANK	FUGAL
ARERE	BLIVE	CORNO	DRAVE	FUNGO
ARIKI	BLOWN	COUDE	DRAWN	FURTH
ARIOT	BLUER	COULD	DRENT	GADJO
AROSE	BOEUF	COURD	DREST	GANCH
ARUHE	BOLAR	COXAE	DRIPT	GARNI
ASKEW	BONZA	COXAL	DROPT	GAYER
ASKOI	BOREL	COYER	DUCAL	GEESE

GELID	HOWSO	LEPID	MOSTE	PACTA
GENAL	HUGER	LEPTA	MOTEN	PADRI
GENIC	HUMIC	LEUCO	MUCHO	PAISE
GENII	HUMID	LIART	MUCIC	PAKKA
GENUA	HUNCH	LIBRI	MUCID	PALER
GESSO	HUTCH	LITAI	MULCH	PALPI
GEYAN	ICTIC	LIVID	MULSH	PAOLI
GEYER	ILEAC	LOACH	MUNCH	PAOLO
GHEST	ILEAL	LOAST	MUSHA	PAPAL
GIGHE	ILIAC	LOBAR	MUTER	PAPPI
GINZO	IMIDO	LOGOI	MYOID	PARAE
GIRSH	IMINO	LOSEN	NAEVI	PARVE
GLIAL	IMSHI	LOTIC	NANUA	PAVID
GLODE	INAPT	LOYAL	NARIC	PAYSD
GNASH	INBYE	LUACH	NARRE	PEART
GNAWN	INCUT	LUCID	NATAL	PELON
GOBBI	INEPT	LUDIC	NAUCH	PENAL
GOBBO	INERM	LUMME	NAVAL	PENDU
GOIER	INFRA	LURCH	NEGRO	PEPLA
GONIA	INTIL	LURID	NEIST	PERCH
GONNA	INTRA	LYARD	NEMPT	PEREA
GONZO	INUST	LYART	NEVER	PETTI
GOPIK	IODIC	LYCEA	NEWER	PETTO
GOTTA	ISNAE	LYNCH	NGWEE	PHPHT
GOYIM	JEUNE	LYTIC	NICER	PHYLE
GRANA	JINGO	MAARE	NIDAL	PIEZO
GREEK	JIRRE	MACHI	NIMBI	PIING
GRIPT	JOKOL	MADID	NITID	PILAE
GROWN	JOMON	MANET	NIVAL	PILAR
GRYPT	JURAL	MAPAU	NOHOW	PILCH
GULAR	KAMME	MARCH	NOMEN	PILEI
GULCH	KANAE	MARIA	NOMOI	PILUM
GURSH	KASME	MAYAN	NOOIT	PINCH
GWINE	KAURU	MAYST	NOTAL	PLENA
GYRAL	KAWAU	MEANT	NOTUM	PLESH
HABLE	KEECH	MEDII	NOVAE	POOCH
HADAL	KEMPT	MEINT	NOXAL	PORCH
HADST	KENCH	MENSH	NUDER	POUPT
HAITH	KIDGE	MERCH	NUDZH	PRATT
HANCH	KINDA	MERER	NUGAE	PRESA
HARSH	KIORE	MESAL	NUMEN	PRIMI
HASTA	KLIEG	MESIC	NUTSO	PROST
HATHA	KNELT	MEYNT	NYING	PROUD
HAULT	KNISH	MICRA	OATEN	PRYSE
HAUTE	KORAI	MIKRA	OBIIT	PSOAE
HEAME	KOTCH	MILCH	OBOLI	PSOAI
HEMAL	KOURA	MILIA	OGMIC	PUBIC
HEWGH	KRONA	MINAE	OHMIC	PUCER
HIANT	KYDST	MISCH	OHONE	PUCKA
HILAR	LABRA	MISDO	OIDIA	PUDIC
HILCH	LAEVO	MISGO	OLEIC	PUKKA
HILUM	LAITH	MITCH	OLPAE	PULIK
HINAU	LARCH	MIXTE	ONCET	PULLI
HOING	LAXER	MODII	ORGIC	PULMO
HOKKU	LAZZI	MOHUA	OSSIA	PUPAE
HOOCH	LAZZO	MOLAL	OTAKU	PUPAL
HOTCH	LEANT	MOLTO	OUTDO	PURER
HOTEN	LEAPT	MOOSE	OUTGO	PUTID
HOVEN	LEASH	MORAE	OVOLI	PUTTO
HOWBE	LEISH	MOSSO	OWSEN	PYGAL

PYOID	SESSA	STAID	TONDI	VILDE
PYRAL	SETAE	STASH	TONKA	VILLI
PYRIC	SETAL	STEPT	TOPHI	VIMEN
QUALE	SHAKT	STOAE	TOPOI	VINIC
QUASI	SHALT	STOAI	TORII	VIOLD
QUAYD	SHASH	STOLN	TORSI	VIRAL
QUOAD	SHAWN	STONG	TRAPT	VIRID
QURSH	SHERE	STOOD	TRIFF	VITAE
RABID	SHEWN	STOPT	TRILD	VIVID
RADII	SHIUR	STUMM	TRUER	VOILA
RAGDE	SHONE	STUNG	TRYMA	VOLAE
RAMAL	SHOON	STUNK	TUBAE	VOLTA
RAREE	SHOPE	STURE	TUBAL	VOLTI
RARER	SHORN	SUCCI	TUBAR	VOULU
RASTA	SHOWN	SUENT	TUMID	VULGO
RAUPO	SHULN	SULCI	TYIYN	VYING
RECTI	SHUSH	SULFO	TYNDE	WAIDE
REDID	SIDHE	SUPRA	TYPAL	WANLE
REJON	SIELD	SURAL	ULNAD	WANNA
RELIT	SIKER	SWACK	ULNAE	WARST
REMET	SINCE	SWANG	ULPAN	WAXEN
RENAL	SITKA	SWAPT	UNAPT	WELCH
RERAN	SKEEF	SWARE	UNBID	WELKT
RESAT	SKINT	SWEPT	UNDEE	WELSH
REWAN	SKOSH	SWOLN	UNDID	WENCH
REWON	SLAID	SWOPT	UNDUE	WERSH
RHYTA	SLAIN	SWORE	UNDUG	WHAMO
RIFER	SLANK	SWORN	UNETH	WHICH
RIMAE	SLASH	SWUNG	UNGOT	WHILK
RORAL	SLEER	SYKER	UNHIP	WHIPT
RORIC	SLEPT	TABID	UNKID	WHOSE
RORID	SLIER	TACIT	UNMET	WHOSO
RUBAI	SLIPT	TAGMA	UNRID	WIDER
RUGAE	SLISH	TAISH	UNSOD	WILCO
RUNIC	SLUNG	TAKEN	UNWET	WINCH
RYPER	SLUNK	TANTI	UPBYE	WINNA
SAFER	SLYER	TANTO	UPLIT	WISER
SAGUM	SMASH	TAPEN	UPRAN	WISHA
SAIST	SMOTE	TARDO	UPTER	WISHT
SALIC	SMUSH	TAULD	URAEI	WOFUL
SAMEN	SNASH	TAZZE	URDEE	WOKKA
SANER	SNOEP	TEACH	UREAL	WOMEN
SAPID	SNUCK	TELOI	UREIC	WOMYN
SATEM	SNUSH	TEMPI	URENT	WOWEE
SAYNE	SOCKO	TEPID	URNAL	WOXEN
SAYST	SODIC	TEUCH	UTERI	WRAPT
SCAND	SOLDI	TEUGH	UVEAL	WRATE
SCAPI	SOLDO	THAIM	VACUA	WROTE
SCUDI	SOPRA	THELF	VAGAL	WROTH
SEELD	SORAL	THEMA	VAIRE	WRUNG
SEFER	SORBO	THIEF	VALID	WRYER
SEGNI	SORDA	THILK	VAPID	XERIC
SENGI	SORER	THINE	VASAL	XOANA
SENSA	SOUCT	THOLI	VATIC	XYLIC
SENTI	SPAKE	THOSE	VAUCH	XYSTI
SENZA	SPARD	THRAE	VEHME	YARER
SEPIC	SPAZA	THREW	VELUM	YAULD
SERAL	SPENT	TICCA	VENAE	YBORE
SERER	SPRAD	TIDAL	VENAL	YCLAD
SERIC	SPUTA	TIMID	VERRA	YCOND

YDRAD	YOGIC	YRENT	ZILCH	ZOWIE
YEVEN	YOKUL	YRIVD	ZLOTE	ZUZIM
YEWEN	YOMIM	YSAME	ZOEAE	ZYGAL
YFERE	YONIC	YTOST	ZOEAL	ZYGON
YINCE	YOURN	YUCCH	ZONAE	ZYMIC
YLIKE	YOUSE	YUCKO	ZOPPA	
YMOLT	YRAPT	YUMMO	ZOPPO	

Six-letter words (except words ending in '-ED', '-J', '-S', '-X', '-Y' or '-Z')

AAHING	AGILER	ANETIC	ASLEEP	AZONAL
ABATTU	AGLARE	ANGOLA	ASLOPE	AZONIC
ABEIGH	AGLEAM	ANIGHT	ASLOSH	AZOTIC
ABLAZE	AGOING	ANISIC	ASMEAR	BAALIM
ABLEST	AGONAL	ANKUSH	ASPOUT	BABIER
ABLOOM	AGONIC	ANNULI	ASQUAT	BACCAE
ABLUSH	AGORAE	ANODAL	ASSOTT	BACULA
ABOARD	AGUISH	ANODIC	ASTARE	BADDER
ABORAL	AHCHOO	ANOMIC	ASTOOP	BADMAN
ABORNE	AHORSE	ANOUGH	ASTRUT	BADMEN
ABULIC	AIDANT	ANOXIC	ASWARM	BAGMAN
ABURST	AIDFUL	ANTRAL	ASWING	BAGMEN
ACETIC	AIDMAN	ANURAL	ASWIRL	BALDER
ACETUM	AIDMEN	ANURIC	ASWOON	BALING
ACHIER	AIKONA	ANYHOW	ATAVIC	BANING
ACIDER	AIMFUL	AORTAE	ATELIC	BANISH
ACIDIC	AIRMAN	AORTAL	ATHROB	BARBAL
ACINAR	AIRMEN	AORTIC	ATOKAL	BARDIC
ACINIC	AKATEA	APEMAN	ATONAL	BAREST
ACKNEW	AKIMBO	APEMEN	ATOPIC	BARFUL
ACRAWL	ALBEIT	APIECE	ATWAIN	BARING
ACULEI	ALDERN	APNEAL	ATWEEL	BARISH
ACUTER	ALEXIC	APNEIC	ATWEEN	BARMAN
ADIPIC	ALIBLE	APODAL	ATWIXT	BARMEN
ADMIXT	ALLYOU	APPAID	ATYPIC	BASEST
ADNATE	ALMOST	APPAYD	AUDIAL	BASSER
ADRIFT	ALULAE	APTEST	AVANTI	BATMAN
ADROIT	ALULAR	APTING	AVERSE	BATMEN
ADYTUM	ALUMNI	ARCANE	AVIDER	BAYMAN
ADZING	ALVINE	ARCHEI	AVITAL	BAYMEN
AECIAL	AMARNA	ARDENT	AVOUCH	BEATEN
AECIUM	AMBACH	AREACH	AWARER	BECAME
AEDINE	AMBUSH	ARGULI	AWATCH	BEDASH
AEFALD	AMEBAE	ARGUTE	AWEIGH	BEDIDE
AERIER	AMEBAN	ARIDER	AWEING	BEDRID
AFAWLD	AMEBIC	ARIGHT	AWHATO	BEDYDE
AFEARD	AMIDIC	ARILLI	AWHETO	BEFELD
AFFYDE	AMIDST	ARIOSI	AWHILE	BEFELL
AFIELD	AMINIC	ARISEN	AWHIRL	BEFORE
AFLAME	AMMINO	AROUND	AWOKEN	BEGILT
AFLOAT	AMMONO	ARRIBA	AWRACK	BEGIRT
AFRAID	AMORAL	ARRISH	AWRONG	BEGONE
AFRESH	AMYLIC	ARSENO	AWSOME	BEHALF
AFRONT	ANCILE	ARSINO	AXEMAN	BEHELD
AGAMIC	ANCORA	ASHAKE	AXEMEN	BELIKE
AGAPAE	ANEATH	ASHINE	AXENIC	BELIVE
AGAPAI	ANEMIC	ASHORE	AXONAL	BEMATA
AGHAST	ANENST	ASLANT	AXONIC	BEMIXT

BENIGN	BROMIC	CELLAE	COWMEN	DEBOSH
BEREFT	BROOCH	CENDRE	COXIER	DECANI
BESANG	BRUMAL	CENTAI	COXING	DECENT
BESEEN	BRUNCH	CERCAL	COYEST	DEEDER
BESTAD	BRUTAL	CERING	COYING	DEEING
BESUNG	BUCCAL	CERULE	COYISH	DEEPER
BETING	BUFFEL	CHADRI	COZING	DEFFER
BETOOK	BULBAR	CHANGA	CREANT	DEFTER
BETROD	BULLAE	CHELAE	CREDAL	DEGAGE
BEWENT	BUMALO	CHEVAL	CRIANT	DEIDER
BEWEPT	BURSAE	CHICER	CRIBLE	DEIFER
BIAXAL	BURSAL	CHOLIC	CRIMEN	DEIFIC
BIFOLD	BUSIER	CHORIC	CRINAL	DEKING
BIFORM	BUSMAN	CHOSEN	CRISIC	DELISH
BIGGER	BUSMEN	CHOUSH	CROTCH	DELTIC
BILING	BUYING	CHYLDE	CROUCH	DELUXE
BIMBLE	BYDING	CICALE	CROUSE	DENSER
BINATE	BYKING	CIDING	CRUDER	DERING
BINMAN	BYLIVE	CILIUM	CRURAL	DERMAL
BINMEN	BYPAST	CISTIC	CRUTCH	DERMIC
BIRKEN	CAAING	CITING	CUBING	DETACH
BISSON	CABMAN	CITRIC	CUBITI	DEVOID
BITTEN	CABMEN	CLASPT	CUEING	DEVOUT
BIVIUM	CADENT	CLATCH	CULPAE	DEWIER
BLAEST	CADMIC	CLECHE	CULTIC	DEWING
BLAISE	CAECAL	CLENCH	CUMULI	DEXTRO
BLAIZE	CAECUM	CLEVER	CUNEAL	DIAMYL
BLANCH	CAGIER	CLINAL	CUPMAN	DICIER
BLATER	CAGING	CLINCH	CUPMEN	DIEING
BLEACH	CAKIER	CLONAL	CUPRIC	DIKIER
BLENCH	CALAMI	CLONIC	CURIAE	DIKING
BLOOIE	CALASH	CLOVEN	CURIAL	DINFUL
BLOTTO	CALCIC	CLUING	CURING	DINING
BLUEST	CALLID	CLUNCH	CURSAL	DINKER
BLUIER	CALMER	CLYING	CURTER	DIREST
BLUISH	CAMASH	CLYPEI	CURULE	DISCAL
BOGMAN	CAMSHO	CNIDAE	CUSPAL	DISTAL
BOGMEN	CANAPE	COAXAL	CUTCHA	DITTIT
BOKING	CANIER	COBRIC	CYANIC	DJINNI
BOLDER	CANNAE	COCCAL	CYMOID	DOABLE
BOLETI	CANNOT	COCCIC	CYMOSE	DOGMAN
BOLLEN	CARDAN	COGENT	CYSTIC	DOGMEN
BONIER	CARDIO	COHOSH	CYTISI	DOITIT
BONZER	CARMAN	COITAL	CYTOID	DOLING
BOOING	CARMEN	COKIER	DADGUM	DOLIUM
BOREAL	CAROLI	COKING	DAEDAL	DOMIER
BOSHTA	CARRON	COMADE	DAEING	DOMING
BOSKER	CARTOP	COMETH	DAFTER	DOPIER
BOSSER	CARVEN	COMODO	DAIMEN	DORMIE
BOWMAN	CASEIC	COMOSE	DAMMIT	DORSAD
BOWMEN	CASINI	CONGII	DANISH	DORSUM
BOXIER	CATCHT	CONING	DANKER	DOSING
BOYING	CATTLE	COOCOO	DARKER	DOTIER
BOYISH	CAUDAD	COSING	DAWISH	DOTISH
BRAWER	CAUDAE	COSMIC	DAYLIT	DOUCER
BREACH	CAUGHT	COSTAE	DAZING	DOURER
BREECH	CAUSAE	COTTAE	DEAFER	DOVIER
BREGMA	CAUSEN	COWIER	DEARER	DOVING
BRICHT	CEDARN	COWISH	DEAWIE	DOVISH
BROKEN	CEDING	COWMAN	DEBILE	DOWIER

DOWING	ENOLIC	FELSIC	FONDER	GARDAI
DOZIER	ENRAPT	FENMAN	FONTAL	GARISH
DREAMT	ENRICH	FENMEN	FOOBAR	GASHER
DREICH	EOCENE	FEODAL	FORANE	GASLIT
DREIGH	EOTHEN	FEREST	FORBYE	GASMAN
DRENCH	EPHORI	FERIAE	FORDID	GASMEN
DRIEGH	EPICAL	FERIAL	FOREDO	GATVOL
DRIEST	EPODIC	FERINE	FOREGO	GAUNCH
DRIVEN	EQUALI	FERRIC	FORGAT	GAYEST
DROLER	EREMIC	FERVID	FORGOT	GAZIER
DROMIC	ERENOW	FETING	FORMEE	GEASON
DROMOI	ERUCIC	FETISH	FORRAD	GEDDIT
DRYEST	ERUVIM	FEUDAL	FORREN	GEEING
DRYISH	ERUVIN	FEUING	FORRIT	GEMINI
DUCTAL	ETERNE	FEWEST	FOSSAE	GEMMAE
DUDING	ETYMIC	FEYEST	FOUEST	GEMMAN
DUDISH	ETYPIC	FEYING	FOULER	GEMMEN
DUEFUL	EURIPI	FIFING	FOVEAE	GENIAL
DUELLI	EWGHEN	FIKIER	FOVEAL	GEODIC
DUETTI	EWKING	FIKING	FOXIER	GESTIC
DUKING	EXEUNT	FIKISH	FOZIER	GEYEST
DULLER	EXILIC	FILIAL	FRACTI	GIBING
DUMBER	EXODIC	FILMIC	FRAENA	GIDDAP
DUMELA	EXODOI	FILOSE	FRANCO	GIDDUP
DUMOSE	EXONIC	FINEST	FREEST	GIEING
DUNNER	EXTOLD	FINISH	FRENCH	GIGMAN
DUPING	EYEING	FINITO	FRENNE	GIGMEN
DURING	FABBER	FINSKO	FRIGID	GILDEN
DUSKER	FACEUP	FISTIC	FROREN	GIUSTO
DYABLE	FACIAE	FITFUL	FRORNE	GLAZEN
DYKIER	FACILE	FIXIVE	FROZEN	GLEBAE
DYKING	FADIER	FLANCH	FRUGAL	GLOBAL
EADISH	FAECAL	FLAXEN	FRUSTA	GLUIER
EASIER	FAINER	FLEECH	FULCRA	GLUING
EASSEL	FAIRER	FLEMIT	FULGID	GLUISH
EASSIL	FAKING	FLENCH	FULVID	GLUNCH
ECESIC	FALLEN	FLETCH	FUMIER	GLUTEI
ECHINI	FAMING	FLIEST	FUMING	GNAMMA
ECHOIC	FAMISH	FLINCH	FUMULI	GNOMAE
EDENIC	FAMULI	FLITCH	FUNDIC	GNOMIC
EFFETE	FARAND	FLOCCI	FUNEST	GOETIC
EGESTA	FARFET	FLOOIE	FUNGIC	GOIEST
EIDENT	FARING	FLORAE	FUNNER	GOLDER
EIDOLA	FASCIO	FLORID	FURCAE	GONION
EIKING	FATING	FLOUSH	FURCAL	GONIUM
EKUELE	FATTER	FLUIER	FURDER	GOOIER
ELDEST	FAUNAE	FLUISH	FUSILE	GORIER
ELMIER	FAUNAL	FLYEST	FUSING	GOTTEN
ELVISH	FAURER	FLYMAN	FUSUMA	GOWDER
EMBOST	FAVEST	FLYMEN	FUZING	GOYISH
EMDASH	FAVOSE	FLYSCH	FYKING	GRANUM
EMMESH	FAXING	FODGEL	GAEING	GRAVEN
ENARCH	FAYEST	FOEMAN	GAGING	GRAYER
ENCASH	FAYING	FOEMEN	GAGMAN	GREEBO
ENDASH	FAZING	FOETAL	GAGMEN	GREYER
ENGILT	FEATER	FOETID	GAIJIN	GRINCH
ENGIRT	FECUND	FOGASH	GALEAE	GRIPLE
ENLEVE	FEEING	FOGMAN	GAMASH	GROSZE
ENMESH	FEHMIC	FOGMEN	GAMEST	GRUING
ENODAL	FEIRIE	FOLIAR	GAMIER	GRUTCH

GRYSIE	HOLMIC	INTIME	KOKOPU	LIEFER
GUNMAN	HOLPEN	INTIRE	KONAKI	LIENAL
GUNMEN	HOMIER	INTOWN	KONEKE	LIEVER
GUNNEN	HOOROO	INWITH	KONINI	LIFULL
GUTTAE	HOOTCH	INWORN	KORARI	LIGGEN
GUYING	HOOVEN	IRATER	KOTARE	LIKEST
GYBING	HOPING	IRIDAL	KOTUKU	LIKUTA
GYLDEN	HORMIC	IRIDIC	KOUROI	LIMBIC
GYMNIC	HORRID	IRITIC	KRONEN	LIMNIC
GYRANT	HOSING	IRREAL	KRONER	LIMPID
GYRING	HOWZAT	ITERUM	KRONOR	LIMULI
GYROSE	HOWZIT	ITSELF	KRONUR	LINEAL
GYVING	HOXING	JACENT	KROONI	LINEAR
HABILE	HOYING	JADING	KULAKI	LINIER
HADDEN	HUDDEN	JADISH	KUTCHA	LINISH
HAEING	HUDDUP	JANTEE	KYBOSH	LIPOIC
HAEMAL	HUGEST	JEEING	LABARA	LIROTH
HAEMIC	HUMERI	JEJUNE	LABILE	LITHIC
HAIKAI	HUPIRO	JEWING	LABIUM	LITTEN
HAINCH	HYDRAE	JIBING	LACTIC	LIVEST
HAKARI	HYDRIC	JIMPER	LAESIE	LOBULI
HALERU	HYEING	JIMSON	LAICAL	LOCULI
HALEST	HYENIC	JINGKO	LAKISH	LOGIER
HALFEN	HYETAL	JINNEE	LAMEST	LOIPEN
HAMOSE	HYMNIC	JIVIER	LAMIAE	LOMATA
HAMULI	HYPHAE	JIVING	LAMISH	LOMING
HANGUL	HYPHAL	JOBING	LANOSE	LOOING
HANIWA	HYPING	JOCOSE	LARGER	LOOSER
HARDER	HYPOID	JOCUND	LARINE	LOOTEN
HARISH	IATRIC	JOKIER	LAROID	LORATE
HATING	IBIDEM	JOKING	LARVAE	LOREAL
HAUDEN	ICEMAN	JOLING	LARVAL	LOTHER
HAULST	ICEMEN	JOVIAL	LATHEN	LOUCHE
HAUNCH	ICONIC	JOWING	LATISH	LOUDER
HAWKIT	IDEATA	JOYFUL	LAURAE	LOUING
HAZIER	IDLEST	JOYING	LAURIC	LOUPEN
HEARIE	IDOLUM	JUBATE	LAVASH	LOUPIT
HEISHI	IMIDIC	JUGATE	LAWEST	LOWSER
HELIAC	IMMANE	JUKING	LAWFUL	LOWSIT
HELING	IMMESH	KAEING	LAWMAN	LOXING
HEMOID	INANER	KAMAHI	LAWMEN	LUBING
HEMPEN	INARCH	KANUKA	LAXEST	LUBRIC
HEPPER	INBENT	KAONIC	LAYMAN	LUCENT
HERMAI	INBORN	KAPUKA	LAYMEN	LUCKEN
HETING	INCAVI	KAPUTT	LEALER	LUITEN
HEYING	INCAVO	KARMIC	LEARNT	LUNIER
HIATAL	INCUBI	KAWING	LEETLE	LUPPEN
HIEING	INCULT	KEIGHT	LEFTER	LURING
HIEMAL	INDIGN	KEKENO	LEGMAN	LUTEUM
HIKING	INFELT	KEPPEN	LEGMEN	LUTTEN
HIPPIC	INFERE	KEPPIT	LEKKER	LYFULL
HISPID	INFIMA	KERERU	LENGER	LYSING
HITMAN	INGRAM	KEWLER	LENTEN	LYTTAE
HITMEN	INGRUM	KIBOSH	LENTIC	MAAING
HOAING	INKJET	KIPPEN	LERING	MACING
HODMAN	INLAID	KIRSCH	LESBIC	MADMAN
HODMEN	INMESH	KLATCH	LEWDER	MADMEN
HOHING	INMOST	KLOOCH	LIBANT	MAGYAR
HOLDEN	INRUSH	KNITCH	LIBRAE	MAINER
HOLIER	INTACT	KOKIRI	LIEDER	MAKUTA

MALEIC	MISMET	NESHER	OMIGOD	PENIAL
MALIBU	MISSAE	NETHER	ONAGRI	PENILE
MALIST	MISSAW	NEUMIC	ONIRIC	PENILL
MALLEI	MISUST	NEURAL	ONRUSH	PENMAN
MALOTI	MITIER	NEVOID	OPTING	PENMEN
MAMAKO	MITRAL	NEWEST	ORBIER	PENNAE
MAMAKU	MIXIER	NEWISH	ORGANA	PENNIA
MAMMAE	MIXING	NICEST	ORGIAC	PEPFUL
MANAIA	MNEMIC	NICISH	ORIHOU	PERAEA
MANATU	MODICA	NIELLI	OSTEAL	PERDIE
MANENT	MODISH	NIGHER	OSTIAL	PEREIA
MANFUL	MODULI	NIOBIC	OSTIUM	PERFET
MANQUE	MODULO	NIRLIT	OTIOSE	PERISH
MANTIC	MOIRAI	NITRIC	OTITIC	PERITI
MAOMAO	MOKIHI	NIXING	OUTATE	PERNIO
MARISH	MONACT	NOBBUT	OUTBYE	PERTER
MASING	MONISH	NOBLER	OUTDID	PHAEIC
MATATA	MONOAO	NODOSE	OUTSAT	PHATIC
MATIER	MOOING	NOGAKU	OUTSAW	PHOCAE
MAUGER	MOPIER	NONFAT	OUTWON	PHONAL
MAUNNA	MOPING	NONMAN	OWLISH	PHYLAE
MAUVER	MOPISH	NONMEN	OWRIER	PHYLAR
MAWGER	MORBID	NONPAR	OXALIC	PHYLIC
MAWING	MORISH	NORDIC	OXIDIC	PHYLUM
MAXING	MORSAL	NOSIER	OZONIC	PIANIC
MAYEST	MORYAH	NOSTOI	PACTUM	PIAZZE
MAYHAP	MOSHAV	NOSTRO	PAINCH	PICINE
MAZIER	MOSING	NOTING	PAIRER	PICRIC
MEAGER	MOTIER	NOTOUR	PALEAE	PIEING
MEATAL	MOUGHT	NOULDE	PALEAL	PIEMAN
MEDIAD	MOZING	NOUNAL	PALEST	PIEMEN
MEDIAE	MUCOSE	NOWISE	PALIER	PIERST
MEEKER	MULISH	NOYING	PALISH	PILEUM
MEIKLE	MUONIC	NUBILE	PALLAE	PILOSE
MENSAE	MURKER	NUCHAE	PALLID	PINETA
MENSAL	MUSCAE	NUDEST	PALPAL	PINKER
MEREST	MUTEST	NUKING	PANINI	PINNAE
MERMAN	MUTING	NUMINA	PANINO	PINNAL
MERMEN	MUXING	NUTANT	PAPISH	PINXIT
MESIAD	MYSELF	OAFISH	PAPYRI	PINYIN
MESIAL	MYTHIC	OAKIER	PARDEE	PIONIC
MESIAN	MYTHOI	OBESER	PARDIE	PIOPIO
METING	MYXOID	OBIING	PARERA	PIPIER
MEVING	NAFFER	OBITAL	PAREVE	PIRNIE
MEWING	NAIANT	OBITER	PARISH	PIRNIT
MIDCAP	NAIFER	OBTECT	PARORE	PIROGI
MIKING	NAIVER	OCELLI	PARTIM	PITHOI
MILDER	NAPING	OCHONE	PASSEE	PITMEN
MILIUM	NARIAL	OCREAE	PASSIM	PIZING
MILKEN	NARINE	OCTOPI	PATAKA	PLACID
MIMING	NASIAL	ODDEST	PATIKI	PLAGAL
MIMMER	NASTIC	ODDISH	PAUSAL	PLANAR
MINIER	NATANT	OGAMIC	PAWING	PLEACH
MINISH	NAUTCH	OGIVAL	PEARST	PLENCH
MIRCHI	NEANIC	OGRISH	PEASEN	PLEXAL
MIRIER	NEARER	OIDIUM	PEASON	PLIANT
MIRING	NEATER	OILMAN	PECTIC	PLICAE
MISATE	NEBISH	OILMEN	PEDATE	PLICAL
MISDID	NEFAST	OMASAL	PEEING	PLONGD
MISLIT	NERVAL	OMASUM	PELTAE	PLUTEI

PODIAL	QUENCH	RENKER	SAIRER	SHAKEN
POISHA	QUETCH	REPAND	SAKKOI	SHAPEN
POKIER	QUINIC	REROSE	SALEWD	SHARON
POLISH	QUOOKE	RESAID	SALPAE	SHAVEN
POLYPI	QUOTHA	RESAWN	SALWAR	SHAZAM
POMATO	QURUSH	RESEEN	SAMIER	SHEESH
POMMEE	RACIAL	RESEWN	SANCTA	SHOULD
PONENT	RACIER	RESHOD	SANEST	SHRANK
PONTAL	RADDER	RESHOT	SANING	SHREWD
PONTIC	RADGER	RESOWN	SAPEGO	SHROWD
POOING	RADISH	RETIAL	SAPFUL	SHRUNK
POOKIT	RAHING	RETOOK	SARING	SHTOOM
POPISH	RAKISH	RETORE	SATING	SHTUMM
PORIER	RAMATE	RETORN	SATIVE	SHYEST
POSHER	RAMEAL	RETRAL	SAYEST	SHYING
POSIER	RAMOSE	RETROD	SBIRRI	SHYISH
POSTAL	RAMULI	RETUSE	SBIRRO	SIALIC
POTASH	RANCID	REWORE	SCALAE	SICCAN
POTATO	RANINE	RHINAL	SCATCH	SICCAR
POTING	RAPHAE	RHIZIC	SCEATT	SICKER
POTMAN	RAPINI	RHODIC	SCHULN	SIFREI
POTMEN	RAPPEN	RHOTIC	SCIENT	SIGLOI
POUKIT	RAREST	RICHER	SCOLIA	SIGLUM
POXIER	RARING	RICTAL	SCOOCH	SILENI
POXING	RATHER	RIDDEN	SCOOSH	SILING
PRELAW	RAUCID	RIFEST	SCOPAE	SILVAE
PREMAN	RAVISH	RILIER	SCORCH	SIMIAL
PREMEN	RAWARU	RILING	SCOTCH	SINFUL
PREMIA	RAWISH	RIMOSE	SCRYDE	SINING
PRIMAL	RAXING	RIPEST	SCULCH	SIPING
PROGUN	REALER	RODMAN	SCUTAL	SIRING
PRONER	REALIA	RODMEN	SCUTCH	SISTRA
PRONTO	RECHIE	ROKIER	SCUTUM	SITHEE
PROSIT	RECKAN	ROOPIT	SCYPHI	SITING
PROWAR	RECLAD	ROPIER	SEAMAN	SITTEN
PROWER	RECTAL	RORIER	SEAMEN	SIWASH
PRUTAH	REDIAE	ROSCID	SEARCH	SIZIER
PSORIC	REDIPT	ROSEAL	SEARER	SKEIGH
PUCEST	REDONE	ROTING	SECESH	SKITCH
PUDENT	REDREW	ROUPET	SECUND	SKOLIA
PUIRER	REECHO	ROUPIT	SEDENT	SKOOSH
PUKING	REEDEN	RUBATI	SEDILE	SKYIER
PULIER	REFELL	RUBBET	SEIKER	SKYING
PULPAL	REFELT	RUBIER	SEJANT	SKYISH
PUNCTA	REFLEW	RUEFUL	SELDOM	SKYLIT
PUNIER	REGAVE	RUGATE	SELLAE	SKYMAN
PUNISH	REGILT	RUGOSE	SEMEIA	SKYMEN
PUREST	REGNAL	RULIER	SEMPER	SLATCH
PURING	REGNUM	RURBAN	SEMPRE	SLEAZO
PUTRID	REGREW	RUSHEN	SENITI	SLEEST
PUTSCH	REGULI	RUSINE	SENRYU	SLIEST
PUTTEN	REHASH	RYKING	SENSUM	SLIVEN
PYEMIC	REHUNG	SACCOI	SEPMAG	SLOOSH
PYNING	REKING	SADDER	SEPTAL	SLOWER
PYONER	RELAID	SAFEST	SEREST	SLUING
PYXING	RELATA	SAFING	SERRAE	SLYEST
QUAINT	RELIDE	SAFTER	SETOSE	SLYISH
QUALIA	RELISH	SAGEST	SEXFID	SMALTI
QUATCH	REMIXT	SAGIER	SEXIER	SMATCH
QUEINT	REMOUD	SAIDST	SEXING	SMEECH

SMIRCH	STOLEN	TECTAL	TOPMAN	UNCIAE
SMOOSH	STOLID	TEDIER	TOPMEN	UNCINI
SMOUCH	STOMAL	TEEING	TOROSE	UNCLAD
SNEESH	STOMIA	TEGMEN	TOROTH	UNCOER
SNIDER	STONEN	TELIAL	TORRID	UNCOOL
SOAKEN	STOUSH	TELIUM	TORTEN	UNCUTE
SOBEIT	STRATI	TEMENE	TOSING	UNDEAD
SOBFUL	STRAWN	TENIAE	TOSSEN	UNDEAR
SOCMAN	STREWN	TENSER	TOTHER	UNDONE
SOCMEN	STRIAE	TENUTI	TOTING	UNDREW
SODAIC	STRIPT	TERAPH	TOWIER	UNEATH
SOEVER	STRODE	TERATA	TOYISH	UNEVEN
SOFTER	STRONG	TERBIC	TOYMAN	UNFELT
SOLEIN	STROVE	TERGAL	TOYMEN	UNFINE
SOLEMN	STROWN	TERGUM	TOZING	UNFIRM
SOLGEL	STRUCK	TERRAE	TRAGAL	UNFIXT
SOLIDI	STRUNG	TERSER	TREFAH	UNFOND
SOLING	STYING	TESTAE	TREIFA	UNGAIN
SOMATA	SUABLE	THECAE	TRENCH	UNGILT
SOMONI	SUAVER	THECAL	TREPID	UNGLAD
SORBIC	SUBITO	THENAL	TRIACT	UNGORD
SORDID	SUBMAN	THENCE	TRIFID	UNGUAL
SOREST	SUBSEA	THETCH	TRILLO	UNHEWN
SOUGHT	SULCAL	THETIC	TRINAL	UNHUNG
SOURER	SUMMAE	THOLOI	TRISTE	UNHURT
SPEECH	SUNKEN	THORIC	TRITER	UNIFIC
SPERST	SUNLIT	THRASH	TROPPO	UNITAL
SPETCH	SUPERB	THRAWN	TROUCH	UNJUST
SPICAE	SURBET	THRESH	TRUEST	UNKEND
SPINAE	SUREST	THRICE	TRUING	UNKENT
SPLOSH	SUTILE	THROVE	TRYPAN	UNKEPT
SPOILT	SWATCH	THROWN	TSKING	UNKIND
SPOKEN	SWEERT	THRUSH	TUATUA	UNLAID
SPORAL	SWEIRT	THYINE	TUBATE	UNLASH
SPRACK	SWOOSH	THYMIC	TUFOLI	UNLEAL
SPRAID	SYEING	THYRSI	TUMULI	UNLICH
SPRENT	SYLVAE	TIBIAE	TUNIER	UNLOST
SPRIER	SYNING	TICING	TURBID	UNMADE
SPRONG	SYPING	TIEING	TURFEN	UNMARD
SPRUNG	TAEING	TIFOSI	TURGID	UNMEEK
SPRUSH	TAIHOA	TIFOSO	TUSSAL	UNMEET
SPRYER	TAISCH	TIGLIC	TUTMAN	UNMESH
SPUING	TAKIER	TINEAL	TUTMEN	UNMIXT
SPUTUM	TALEAE	TINIER	TWEEST	UNMOWN
SQUUSH	TALLER	TINING	TWILIT	UNOPEN
STALER	TALPAE	TINMAN	TYEING	UNPAID
STALKO	TAMEST	TINMEN	TYKISH	UNPENT
STANCH	TAPING	TITMAN	TYNING	UNPURE
STANCK	TAPPIT	TITMEN	TYPIER	UNREAL
STATAL	TARNAL	TITULI	UBIQUE	UNRENT
STATIM	TAUGHT	TOEIER	UGSOME	UNRUDE
STEARD	TAUHOU	TOEING	ULNARE	UNSAID
STEELD	TAURIC	TOFORE	ULTIMO	UNSAWN
STELAE	TAUTER	TOLUIC	UMBRAE	UNSENT
STELAI	TAUTIT	TOMATO	UMBRAL	UNSEWN
STELAR	TAVERT	TOMBAL	UNBEEN	UNSHOD
STERIC	TAWIER	TOMBIC	UNBENT	UNSOFT
STEYER	TAXMAN	TOMIAL	UNBORE	UNSOLD
STINKO	TAXMEN	TONANT	UNCAST	UNSOWN
STITCH	TEAING	TOOMER	UNCHIC	UNSPUN

UNSUNG	URSINE	VISCID	WHITER	YEOMEN
UNSUNK	USABLE	VISIVE	WHOMSO	YEVING
UNTOLD	UVULAE	VISTAL	WHOOSH	YEXING
UNTORN	VACANT	VITTAE	WIDEST	YIKING
UNTROD	VADOSE	VOGIER	WIDISH	YIPPEE
UNVEXT	VAGILE	VOLAGE	WIFING	YITTEN
UNWELL	VAGUER	VOLING	WILFUL	YOWING
UNWEPT	VAINER	VOLVAE	WILIER	YPIGHT
UNWISH	VALVAL	VORAGO	WILING	YPLAST
UNWIST	VALVAR	VORANT	WIMMIN	YSHENT
UNWONT	VANMAN	VORPAL	WIRIER	YTTRIC
UNWORN	VANMEN	VOSTRO	WISEST	YUKIER
UPBLEW	VARSAL	VULVAE	WISING	YUKING
UPBORE	VASTER	VULVAL	WITHAL	YWROKE
UPDOVE	VATMAN	VULVAR	WITING	ZAFTIG
UPDREW	VATMEN	WABBIT	WOEFUL	ZANIER
UPGIRT	VEDUTA	WAEFUL	WORSER	ZAPATA
UPGONE	VEDUTE	WAIRSH	WOWFER	ZELOSO
UPGREW	VEGETE	WANDLE	WOWING	ZEROTH
UPGUSH	VEHMIC	WANIER	WRENCH	ZINCIC
UPHAND	VEINAL	WANKLE	WRETCH	ZIPTOP
UPHELD	VELOCE	WANNEL	WROKEN	ZIZITH
UPHILD	VENIAL	WANNER	WRYEST	ZOAEAE
UPHOVE	VENOSE	WARIER	WRYING	ZOECIA
UPHUNG	VERIER	WARING	WYLING	ZOETIC
UPLAID	VERLIG	WARMAN	WYTING	ZOFTIG
UPMOST	VERMAL	WARMEN	XENIAL	ZONOID
UPPISH	VERNAL	WASHEN	XENIUM	ZOOEAE
UPROSE	VIABLE	WASSUP	XOANON	ZOOEAL
UPRUSH	VIBIER	WAURST	XYLOID	ZOOIER
UPRYST	VICING	WAVIER	XYSTOI	ZOONAL
UPSENT	VIDUAL	WAXIER	YAKUZA	ZOONIC
UPTOOK	VILLAE	WEXING	YAREST	ZUFOLI
UPTORE	VILLAR	WEYARD	YAWING	ZUFOLO
UPTORN	VINEAL	WHATEN	YBLENT	ZYGOID
UPWENT	VINIER	WHATNA	YBOUND	ZYMOID
URACHI	VINING	WHATSO	YBRENT	
URATIC	VIRENT	WHEARE	YCLEPT	
UREMIC	VIRILE	WHILOM	YEDING	
URETIC	VIRING	WHILST	YEOMAN	

Chapter 10: Anagrams

A vital skill for the keen Scrabble player is the ability to find anagrams for sets of letters. This is the real essence of Scrabble, which, after all, is about rearranging letters on your rack to find the highest scoring combination to place on the board.

The most useful anagrams, of course, are those of seven and eight letters, as these are essential for scoring 50-point bonuses. Having the component letters of a bonus word is great – but you still have to be able to get it onto the board to obtain the bonus. Even if there are useful hooks in place on the board, you need these to be in the right place – other words and the limits of board space may well keep your bonus word out of the game. This is where anagrams come in so useful. If you have the letters for one bonus word, it's invaluable to know if the same letters will work in a different combination. A good knowledge of bonus-length anagrams allows you to adapt a good rack to the situation on the board. This enables you to play bonus words more easily – or at the very least, to avoid wasting time hunting for combinations that aren't there.

This section is particularly useful when you are trying to learn from your mistakes after a game or tournament. If you had a rack which you were sure could yield a bonus word, but couldn't find it, you can check the anagram lists to find whether you were on the right lines.

The letter sets are listed alphabetically, according to the alphabetical order of their component letters (eg all sets containing A come before those with B and no A).

Seven-letter anagrams

AAAADNP	APADANA	AAABFLL	FALBALA	AAABRSX	ABRASAX
AAAALTY	ATALAYA	AAABGIL	GALABIA		ABRAXAS
AAAARRS	ARAARAS	AAABHLQ	QABALAH	AAABRSZ	BARAZAS
AAAASTT	ATAATAS	AAABILX	ABAXIAL		BAZAARS
AAABBCL	CABBALA	AAABIPS	PIASABA	AAABSTT	BATATAS
AAABBKL	KABBALA	AAABISS	ABASIAS	AAACCIS	ACACIAS
AAABBLS	BABALAS	AAABITV	BATAVIA	AAACCLM	MALACCA
AAABCCR	BACCARA	AAABKKS	KABAKAS	AAACCLP	ALPACCA
AAABCIR	ARABICA	AAABKLS	KABALAS	AAACCLR	CARACAL
AAABCLO	BACALAO	AAABKLV	BAKLAVA	AAACCRS	CASCARA
AAABCLS	CABALAS	AAABKLW	BAKLAWA	AAACDGS	CADAGAS
AAABCLV	BACLAVA	AAABKPS	BAASKAP	AAACDIR	ARCADIA
AAABCMR	CARAMBA	AAABKSY	KABAYAS	AAACDLU	ACAUDAL
AAABCNR	BARACAN	AAABLLW	WALLABA	AAACDMM	MACADAM
AAABCNS	CABANAS	AAABLMT	TAMBALA	AAACDNS	CANADAS
AAABCOR	CARABAO	AAABLPR	PALABRA	AAACEHR	ARCHAEA
AAABCSS	CASABAS	AAABLQS	QABALAS	AAACENP	PANACEA
	CASSABA	AAABLST	ALBATAS	AAACGNT	AGACANT
AAABCTW	CATAWBA		ATABALS	AAACHHL	HALACHA
AAABDFR	ABFARAD		BALATAS	AAACHLZ	CHALAZA
AAABDGS	DAGABAS	AAABMOS	ABOMASA	AAACHNT	ACANTHA
AAABDHS	BAHADAS	AAABMST	MASTABA	AAACHRY	ACHARYA
AAABDJS	BAJADAS	AAABNNR	RABANNA	AAACILM	MALACIA
AAABDLM	LAMBADA	AAABNNS	BANANAS	AAACIMR	CARIAMA
AAABDNN	BANDANA	AAABORR	ARAROBA	AAACINP	ACAPNIA
AAABEGL	GALABEA	AAABRST	BRAATAS	AAACINR	ACARIAN

AAACIRS	ACRASIA	**AAAEGNP**	APANAGE	**AAAIKRS**	AKRASIA
AAACJMR	JACAMAR	**AAAEHLT**	ALTHAEA	**AAAILLS**	ALALIAS
AAACJNS	JACANAS	**AAAEIMN**	ANAEMIA	**AAAILMR**	MALARIA
AAACLLV	CAVALLA	**AAAELMP**	PALAMAE	**AAAILNX**	ANAXIAL
AAACLMN	ALMANAC	**AAAELSZ**	AZALEAS	**AAAILPS**	APLASIA
	MANCALA	**AAAEMRT**	TARAMEA	**AAAILRS**	ARALIAS
AAACLMR	CALAMAR	**AAAENST**	ANATASE	**AAAILRT**	TALARIA
AAACLNT	CANTALA	**AAAERWY**	AREAWAY	**AAAIMNT**	AMANITA
AAACLPS	ALPACAS	**AAAFFLL**	ALFALFA	**AAAINPS**	PAISANA
AAACLPT	CATALPA	**AAAFHRT**	HAFTARA	**AAAIPRX**	APRAXIA
AAACLRZ	ALCAZAR	**AAAFIRT**	RATAFIA	**AAAIPSV**	PIASAVA
AAACMNP	CAMPANA	**AAAFNRS**	SARAFAN	**AAAIQRU**	AQUARIA
AAACMRS	MARACAS	**AAAFRWY**	FARAWAY	**AAAISST**	ASTASIA
	MARASCA	**AAAGGLN**	GALANGA	**AAAISTW**	WAIATAS
	MASCARA	**AAAGHIP**	APHAGIA	**AAAISTX**	ATAXIAS
AAACNNR	CARANNA	**AAAGHLN**	LANGAHA	**AAAJKST**	JATAKAS
AAACNPT	CATAPAN	**AAAGHNT**	ATAGHAN	**AAAJMPS**	PAJAMAS
AAACNRS	ARCANAS	**AAAGHPR**	AGRAPHA	**AAAJMSU**	UJAMAAS
AAACNRT	NACARAT	**AAAGILN**	ANALGIA	**AAAKKMR**	MARKKAA
AAACNRU	CARAUNA	**AAAGINR**	ANGARIA	**AAAKKNS**	KANAKAS
AAACNRV	CARAVAN	**AAAGINZ**	GAZANIA	**AAAKKRS**	KARAKAS
AAACNST	CANASTA	**AAAGIPT**	PATAGIA	**AAAKLMS**	KAMALAS
AAACNTT	CANTATA	**AAAGISS**	ASSAGAI	**AAAKLMY**	YAMALKA
AAACPRX	CARAPAX	**AAAGJMU**	MAJAGUA	**AAAKLSS**	ALASKAS
AAACPST	PATACAS	**AAAGKNR**	KARANGA	**AAAKMMU**	MAMAKAU
AAACRWY	CARAWAY	**AAAGLMM**	AMALGAM	**AAAKNST**	KATANAS
AAACSST	CASSATA	**AAAGLMN**	MALANGA	**AAAKPPU**	KAUPAPA
AAACSSV	CASAVAS		NAGMAAL	**AAALLPT**	PALATAL
	CASSAVA	**AAAGLNO**	ANALOGA	**AAALMPT**	TAMPALA
AAACSTT	CATASTA	**AAAGLNS**	LASAGNA	**AAALMRS**	MARSALA
AAADDMO	AMADODA	**AAAGLRS**	ARGALAS	**AAALMSS**	MASALAS
AAADELM	ALAMEDA	**AAAGMMT**	MAGMATA		SALAAMS
AAADFRY	FARADAY	**AAAGMNR**	ANAGRAM	**AAALNNT**	LANTANA
AAADGGH	AGGADAH	**AAAGMNS**	SAGAMAN	**AAALNPT**	APLANAT
	HAGGADA	**AAAGMTT**	TAGMATA	**AAALPPS**	PALAPAS
AAADGGS	AGGADAS	**AAAGNNS**	NAGANAS	**AAALRRY**	ARRAYAL
AAADGIL	ADAGIAL	**AAAGNPR**	PARGANA	**AAALWYY**	LAYAWAY
AAADGRS	SAGRADA	**AAAGNRR**	NGARARA	**AAAMMPR**	MAMPARA
AAADHHS	SHAHADA	**AAAGNRT**	TANAGRA	**AAAMNNS**	MANANAS
AAADHMM	HAMMADA	**AAAGNRU**	GUARANA	**AAAMNNT**	ANATMAN
AAADHMR	ADHARMA	**AAAGNTY**	YATAGAN	**AAAMNPS**	PANAMAS
	HARAMDA	**AAAHHKL**	HALAKAH	**AAAMNRT**	AMARANT
AAADHMS	HAMADAS		HALAKHA		MARANTA
AAADHNS	SADHANA	**AAAHHLL**	HALALAH	**AAAMNSS**	SAMAANS
AAADHWY	HADAWAY	**AAAHHLV**	HALAVAH	**AAAMNST**	ATAMANS
AAADILX	ADAXIAL	**AAAHIKP**	APHAKIA	**AAAMNSW**	MANAWAS
AAADIMN	DAMIANA	**AAAHIKW**	KAHAWAI	**AAAMNTY**	MANYATA
AAADIRT	DATARIA	**AAAHINR**	HARIANA	**AAAMORT**	TAMARAO
	RADIATA	**AAAHIPS**	APHASIA	**AAAMPPU**	PAPAUMA
AAADJMR	JAMADAR	**AAAHIST**	TAIAHAS	**AAAMPRT**	PATAMAR
AAADKNW	WAKANDA	**AAAHJKW**	KAJAWAH	**AAAMRRZ**	ZAMARRA
AAADLMN	AMANDLA	**AAAHKRS**	AKHARAS	**AAAMRSS**	ASRAMAS
	MANDALA	**AAAHLLS**	HALALAS		SAMARAS
AAADLMW	WADMAAL	**AAAHLMR**	HARMALA		SAMSARA
AAADMNT	ADAMANT	**AAAHLNN**	ALANNAH	**AAAMRST**	TAMARAS
AAADMPP	PAPADAM	**AAAHLSW**	HAWALAS		TARAMAS
AAADMRS	ARMADAS	**AAAHMMT**	MAHATMA	**AAAMRTU**	TAMARAU
	MADRASA	**AAAHMRS**	ASHRAMA	**AAANNSV**	SAVANNA
	RAMADAS	**AAAHMST**	TAMASHA	**AAANNSZ**	ZANANAS
AAADNPS	PANADAS	**AAAHNSV**	VAHANAS	**AAANNTT**	ANNATTA
AAADNRS	SARDANA	**AAAHPRT**	PARATHA	**AAANPPY**	PAPAYAN
AAADNRT	TANADAR	**AAAHRTW**	WARATAH	**AAANRST**	ANTARAS
AAADWYY	AWAYDAY	**AAAIKKR**	KARAKIA	**AAANRTT**	TANTARA
AAAEGLT	GALATEA	**AAAIKLT**	LATAKIA		TARTANA

AAAANSTT	ANATTAS	AABCKLY	LAYBACK	AABDIOT	BIODATA
AAAOOPRZ	PARAZOA	AABCKNN	CANBANK	AABDIRS	ABRAIDS
AAAPPRT	APPARAT	AABCKPY	BACKPAY	AABDLLS	BALLADS
AAAPPSY	PAPAYAS		PAYBACK	AABDLMS	LAMBDAS
AAAPRSS	APSARAS	AABCKRR	BARRACK	AABDLNS	SALBAND
AAAPSST	PASSATA	AABCKRS	BACKRAS	AABDLRW	BRADAWL
AAAPTTU	TAUPATA	AABCKSW	BACKSAW	AABDMNR	ARMBAND
AAARSST	SATARAS	AABCLMU	CALUMBA	AABDNNO	ABANDON
AAARSTV	AVATARS	AABCLPY	CAPABLY	AABDNOR	BANDORA
AAARTTT	RATATAT	AABCLSY	SCYBALA	AABDNRS	BANDARS
AAARTTU	TUATARA	AABCMMU	MACUMBA		SANDBAR
AAARTXY	ATARAXY	AABCMST	TAMBACS	AABDNRU	BANDURA
AABBBOS	BAOBABS	AABCMSU	SAMBUCA	AABDNSW	BANDSAW
AABBCEG	CABBAGE	AABCNRR	CARBARN	AABDORS	ABROADS
AABBCGY	CABBAGY	AABCORR	CARBORA	AABDORV	BRAVADO
AABBCMO	CABOMBA	AABCORT	ABACTOR	AABDORX	BROADAX
AABBCOS	BABACOS		ACROBAT	AABDRRS	DARBARS
AABBDGR	GABBARD	AABCOTT	CATBOAT	AABDRRW	DRAWBAR
AABBDHS	HABDABS	AABCRSS	SCARABS	AABDRST	BASTARD
AABBEGN	BEANBAG	AABCSUU	AUCUBAS		TABARDS
AABBEIS	BABESIA	AABCTTU	CATTABU	AABDRSU	SUBADAR
AABBELT	BATABLE	AABDDEL	ADDABLE	AABDRSY	BAYARDS
AABBERT	BARBATE	AABDDEN	ABANDED	AABDSTU	DATABUS
AABBGRT	GABBART	AABDDER	ABRADED	AABEELT	EATABLE
AABBHLS	BABLAHS	AABDDIK	KABADDI	AABEEMN	AMEBEAN
AABBHST	SABBATH	AABDDIN	BANDAID	AABEEMO	AMOEBAE
AABBLLS	LABLABS	AABDDLN	BADLAND	AABEERZ	ZAREEBA
AABBLOR	BARBOLA	AABDDNS	SANDDAB	AABEFFL	AFFABLE
AABBLOS	BALBOAS	AABDEFL	FADABLE	AABEFFN	BEFFANA
AABBSST	SABBATS	AABDEGM	GAMBADE	AABEFGL	FLEABAG
AABBSSU	BABASSU	AABDEGN	BANDAGE	AABEFGU	AUFGABE
AABBSTY	BABYSAT	AABDEHS	ABASHED	AABEFNS	BEFANAS
AABCCEL	ACCABLE	AABDEIR	BRAAIED		FANBASE
AABCCER	BACCARE	AABDEIS	DIABASE	AABEGGG	BAGGAGE
AABCCET	BACCATE	AABDEKW	DAWBAKE	AABEGGR	GARBAGE
AABCCHH	BACHCHA	AABDELL	BALLADE	AABEGLR	ALGEBRA
AABCCIR	BRACCIA	AABDELT	ABLATED	AABEGMR	BERGAMA
AABCDIM	DICAMBA		DATABLE		MEGABAR
AABCDIR	CARABID	AABDELW	WADABLE	AABEGMS	AMBAGES
AABCEFR	FACEBAR	AABDEMM	BEMADAM	AABEGRR	BAGARRE
AABCEKR	BACKARE	AABDEMN	BEADMAN		BARRAGE
AABCELN	BALANCE	AABDEMS	SAMBAED	AABEGSS	BAGASSE
AABCELP	CAPABLE	AABDENU	BANDEAU		SEABAGS
	PACABLE	AABDERR	ABRADER	AABEGST	ATABEGS
AABCELT	ACTABLE	AABDERS	ABRADES	AABEGSU	ABUSAGE
AABCEMR	MACABER	AABDERY	ABRAYED	AABEHLT	HATABLE
	MACABRE	AABDESU	AUBADES	AABEHNT	ABTHANE
AABCEMS	AMBSACE	AABDGHN	HANDBAG	AABEHRS	EARBASH
AABCEOS	COBAEAS	AABDGHR	HARDBAG	AABEHSS	ABASHES
AABCERR	BARRACE	AABDGMO	GAMBADO	AABEIKN	IKEBANA
AABCERT	ABREACT	AABDGNS	SANDBAG	AABEILM	AMABILE
	BEARCAT	AABDGOS	DAGOBAS		AMIABLE
	CABARET	AABDHMS	BADMASH	AABEILN	ABELIAN
AABCFKT	FATBACK	AABDHNT	HATBAND	AABEILS	ABELIAS
AABCHHR	BRACHAH	AABDHNY	HAYBAND	AABEILT	LABIATE
AABCHIR	BRACHIA	AABDHRS	BARDASH	AABEILX	ABAXILE
AABCHMT	AMBATCH	AABDHRU	BAHADUR	AABEIOR	AEROBIA
AABCHNR	BARCHAN	AABDIIS	BASIDIA	AABEIRS	AIRBASE
AABCHOR	ABROACH	AABDIKR	BIDARKA		ARABISE
AABCHSS	CASBAHS	AABDILN	BALADIN	AABEIRZ	ARABIZE
AABCILM	CAMBIAL	AABDIMR	BARMAID	AABEJLL	JELLABA
AABCINR	CARABIN	AABDINR	BANDARI	AABEJMU	JAMBEAU
AABCIOP	COPAIBA	AABDINS	INDABAS	AABEKLM	MAKABLE
AABCITX	TAXICAB	AABDINT	TABANID	AABEKLT	TAKABLE

AABEKNS	SEABANK	AABGILM	MAILBAG	AABINSW	WABAINS
AABEKPR	PARBAKE	AABGIMS	GAMBIAS	AABINSZ	BANZAIS
AABEKRS	ARABESK	AABGINR	BARGAIN	AABIORS	ABROSIA
AABEKRY	KERBAYA	AABGINS	ABASING	AABIORT	AIRBOAT
AABEKST	ATABEKS		BAAINGS	AABIPUX	PAXIUBA
AABELLL	LABELLA		BISNAGA	AABIRST	BARISTA
AABELLN	BALNEAL	AABGINT	ABATING		BARTSIA
AABELLO	ABOLLAE	AABGINZ	BIZNAGA	AABIRSZ	ZARIBAS
AABELLR	EARBALL	AABGIRS	AIRBAGS	AABISSW	WASABIS
AABELLS	SABELLA	AABGMNY	MANGABY	AABISTT	ABATTIS
	SALABLE	AABGOSZ	GAZABOS	AABJMRT	JAMBART
AABELMN	NAMABLE	AABGRST	RATBAGS	AABKMST	TAMBAKS
AABELMS	MABELAS	AABHHIS	SAHIBAH	AABKNNS	KANBANS
AABELMT	TAMABLE	AABHHKS	SABKHAH	AABKNRS	BARKANS
AABELNO	ABALONE	AABHHRU	BRUHAHA	AABKNRT	TANBARK
AABELNR	BANALER	AABHHSS	SHABASH	AABKOOZ	BAZOOKA
AABELNS	BANSELA	AABHINS	HASBIAN	AABKRST	TASKBAR
AABELPP	PAPABLE	AABHINT	HABITAN	AABLLNS	BALLANS
AABELPR	PARABLE	AABHISS	SAHIBAS	AABLLNT	BALLANT
AABELPY	PAYABLE	AABHITT	HABITAT	AABLLNY	BANALLY
AABELRS	ARABLES	AABHJNS	BHAJANS	AABLLOR	ALLOBAR
AABELRT	RATABLE	AABHKNR	BARKHAN	AABLLOS	ABOLLAS
AABELSS	BALASES	AABHKSS	KASBAHS	AABLLPT	PATBALL
AABELST	ABLATES		SABKHAS	AABLLST	BALLAST
	ASTABLE	AABHKST	BHAKTAS		BALLATS
AABELSV	SAVABLE		SABKHAT	AABLLSY	BASALLY
AABELSY	SAYABLE	AABHLRS	BHARALS		SALABLY
AABELTT	ABETTAL	AABHLTY	BATHYAL	AABLLWY	WALLABY
AABELTU	TABLEAU	AABHMNR	BRAHMAN	AABLMRS	RAMBLAS
	TABULAE	AABHMRS	BRAHMAS	AABLMRU	LABARUM
AABELTV	VATABLE		SAMBHAR	AABLMSS	BALSAMS
AABELTX	TAXABLE	AABHMSS	SHAMBAS		SAMBALS
AABELWX	WAXABLE	AABHMTT	BATHMAT	AABLMST	LAMBAST
AABEMNO	AMOEBAN	AABHNSV	BHAVANS	AABLMSY	ABYSMAL
AABEMNS	BASEMAN	AABHNSW	BHAWANS		BALSAMY
AABEMOS	AMOEBAS	AABHSSW	BASHAWS	AABLNTT	BLATANT
AABENNW	WANNABE	AABIILX	BIAXIAL	AABLORT	ABLATOR
AABENRT	ANTBEAR	AABIILZ	ALBIZIA	AABLOSV	LAVABOS
AABENTY	ABEYANT	AABIJMY	JAMBIYA	AABLPRU	PABULAR
AABEORT	AEROBAT	AABIKLM	KALIMBA	AABLPYY	PAYABLY
AABERRW	BARWARE	AABIKNS	BANKSIA	AABLRST	ARBLAST
AABERSS	ABASERS	AABILLN	ALBINAL	AABLRSU	SUBALAR
AABERST	ABATERS	AABILLR	BARILLA	AABLRTU	TABULAR
	ABREAST	AABILLS	LABIALS	AABLRTY	RATABLY
AABERSU	BAUERAS	AABILMN	BIMANAL	AABLSST	BASALTS
	SUBAREA	AABILMS	BAALISM	AABLSSY	ABYSSAL
AABERSZ	ZAREBAS	AABILMY	AMIABLY	AABLSTU	ABLAUTS
AABERTT	RABATTE	AABILNS	BASINAL	AABLTTU	ABUTTAL
	TABARET	AABILOU	ABOULIA	AABLTXY	TAXABLY
AABERTU	ABATURE	AABILRS	BASILAR	AABMNOT	BOATMAN
AABESTZ	ZABETAS	AABILST	BALISTA	AABMNOY	AMBOYNA
AABETTU	BATTEAU	AABILSU	ABULIAS	AABMNST	BANTAMS
AABETUX	BATEAUX	AABIMMR	MARIMBA		BATSMAN
AABFFLY	AFFABLY	AABIMNO	AMBOINA	AABMORU	MARABOU
AABFILU	FABLIAU		BONAMIA	AABMOSY	BAYAMOS
AABFLRU	FABULAR	AABIMOS	ABOMASI	AABMRSS	SAMBARS
AABGGRS	RAGBAGS	AABIMRS	AMBARIS	AABMRTU	TAMBURA
AABGGRY	GARBAGY		MARABIS	AABMSST	TSAMBAS
AABGGSS	GASBAGS	AABIMST	BASMATI	AABMSSY	AMBASSY
AABGHNR	BHANGRA	AABINNS	BANIANS	AABNNOZ	BONANZA
AABGHNS	GABNASH	AABINOU	OUABAIN	AABNNSY	BANYANS
	NASHGAB	AABINRS	ARABINS	AABNOST	SABATON
AABGHSW	BAGWASH	AABINRT	ATABRIN	AABNOSY	SABAYON
AABGIIL	ABIGAIL	AABINST	ABSTAIN	AABNSYY	BAYYANS

AABORRS	ARROBAS	**AACCLOS**	CLOACAS	**AACDHST**	DATCHAS
	RASBORA	**AACCLPS**	CALPACS	**AACDIIS**	ASCIDIA
AABORST	ABATORS	**AACCLPT**	PLACCAT	**AACDILR**	RADICAL
	RABATOS	**AACCLRS**	CALCARS	**AACDINS**	SCANDIA
AABORSZ	ABRAZOS	**AACCLRU**	ACCRUAL	**AACDINT**	ANTACID
AABOTTY	ATTABOY		CARACUL	**AACDINV**	VANADIC
AABQSUU	SUBAQUA	**AACCLSU**	ACCUSAL	**AACDIOR**	ACAROID
AABRRST	BARRATS	**AACCLTW**	CATCLAW	**AACDIRS**	ACARIDS
AABRRSU	SABURRA	**AACCMOS**	MACACOS		ASCARID
AABRRUV	BRAVURA	**AACCNNS**	CANCANS		CARDIAS
AABRSTY	BARYTAS	**AACCNVY**	VACANCY	**AACDJKW**	JACKDAW
AABSSSY	SASSABY	**AACCORU**	CURACAO	**AACDKSY**	DAYSACK
AABSTTW	ABWATTS		CURACOA	**AACDLNO**	ACNODAL
AABSTUX	SAXTUBA	**AACCOST**	ACCOAST		CALANDO
	SUBTAXA	**AACCOTT**	TOCCATA	**AACDLNS**	SCANDAL
AABTTTU	BATTUTA	**AACCRRT**	CARRACT	**AACDLOR**	CARLOAD
AACCDEI	CICADAE	**AACCRSS**	CARCASS	**AACDLOS**	SCALADO
AACCDEM	MEDACCA	**AACCRST**	CARACTS	**AACDLPR**	PLACARD
AACCDES	CASCADE	**AACDDEL**	DECADAL	**AACDMPS**	MADCAPS
	SACCADE	**AACDDER**	ARCADED	**AACDNRS**	CADRANS
AACCDII	ACCIDIA	**AACDDHR**	CHADDAR		CANARDS
AACCDIR	CARDIAC	**AACDDIN**	CANDIDA	**AACDOOV**	AVOCADO
AACCDIS	CICADAS	**AACDDRW**	CRAWDAD	**AACDPRU**	CRAPAUD
AACCDSU	CADUACS	**AACDEEM**	ACADEME	**AACDRSS**	CSARDAS
AACCEFT	CATFACE	**AACDEFL**	FALCADE	**AACDRSZ**	CZARDAS
AACCEKR	CARCAKE	**AACDEFS**	FACADES	**AACEEGR**	ACREAGE
AACCELO	CLOACAE	**AACDEHM**	CHAMADE	**AACEEHR**	EARACHE
AACCENV	VACANCE	**AACDEHR**	CHARADE	**AACEEHT**	CHAETAE
AACCERS	CARCASE	**AACDEHT**	CATHEAD	**AACEEKT**	TEACAKE
AACCEST	SACCATE	**AACDEII**	AECIDIA	**AACEELN**	ANELACE
AACCHHK	CHACHKA	**AACDEIL**	ALCAIDE	**AACEEMR**	CAMERAE
	KACHCHA	**AACDEIN**	AIDANCE	**AACEEMS**	AMESACE
AACCHIM	MACCHIA	**AACDEIR**	CARDIAE	**AACEENT**	CATENAE
AACCHIN	CHICANA	**AACDEIS**	ACEDIAS	**AACEERT**	ACERATE
AACCHIR	ARCHAIC	**AACDELL**	ALCALDE	**AACEESS**	CASEASE
AACCHKS	KACCHAS	**AACDELN**	CANALED	**AACEEST**	CASEATE
AACCHLN	CLACHAN		CANDELA	**AACEETT**	ACETATE
AACCHMP	CHAMPAC		DECANAL	**AACEFIS**	FASCIAE
AACCHMS	CHACMAS	**AACDELP**	PALACED	**AACEFLT**	FALCATE
AACCHNN	CANNACH	**AACDELR**	CALDERA	**AACEFLU**	FACULAE
AACCHNS	CANCHAS		CRAALED	**AACEFMN**	FACEMAN
AACCHOR	CAROACH	**AACDELS**	ALCADES	**AACEFRR**	CARFARE
AACCHRT	CHARACT		SCALADE	**AACEFRS**	CARAFES
AACCILM	ACCLAIM	**AACDELY**	ALCAYDE	**AACEGGR**	AGGRACE
AACCILS	ALCAICS	**AACDEMY**	ACADEMY	**AACEGHN**	GANACHE
	CICALAS	**AACDENR**	DRACENA	**AACEGHS**	ACHAGES
AACCILU	ACICULA	**AACDENV**	ADVANCE	**AACEGIP**	AGAPEIC
AACCIMS	CAIMACS	**AACDENZ**	CADENZA	**AACEGKP**	PACKAGE
AACCIMT	ACMATIC	**AACDEPS**	SCAPAED	**AACEGKS**	SACKAGE
AACCINS	ANICCAS	**AACDERS**	ARCADES	**AACEGLS**	SCALAGE
AACCINV	VACCINA		ASCARED	**AACEGNR**	CAGANER
AACCIOR	CARIOCA	**AACDERV**	CADAVER		CARNAGE
AACCIPT	PICCATA	**AACDERY**	DAYCARE		CRANAGE
AACCIRT	ACRATIC	**AACDETU**	CAUDATE	**AACEGRT**	CARTAGE
AACCITT	ATACTIC	**AACDETV**	VACATED	**AACEGSV**	SCAVAGE
AACCJKR	CARJACK	**AACDEUX**	CADEAUX	**AACEHIN**	ACHENIA
AACCKLP	CALPACK	**AACDFIR**	FARADIC	**AACEHIR**	ARCHAEI
AACCKRR	CARRACK	**AACDFRS**	CAFARDS	**AACEHKR**	KACHERA
AACCKRS	CARACKS	**AACDGGI**	AGGADIC	**AACEHKS**	ASHCAKE
	CRACKAS	**AACDGHI**	HAGADIC	**AACEHLP**	ACALEPH
AACCLLO	CLOACAL	**AACDGIS**	CADAGIS	**AACEHLR**	ALCHERA
AACCLLT	CATCALL	**AACDHMR**	DRACHMA	**AACEHLT**	CHAETAL
AACCLOP	POLACCA	**AACDHNR**	HANDCAR	**AACEHNO**	CHOANAE
AACCLOR	CARACOL	**AACDHRS**	CHADARS	**AACEHNP**	PANACHE

AACEHNR	ACHARNE	AACEORS	ROSACEA	AACHINT	ACANTHI
AACEHPP	APPEACH	AACEPRT	CAPRATE		TACHINA
AACEHPS	APACHES	AACEPRU	CAPUERA	AACHIPR	CHARPAI
AACEHPU	CHAPEAU	AACEPRV	PRECAVA		HAIRCAP
AACEHRT	TRACHEA	AACEPWY	PACEWAY	AACHIPS	APHASIC
AACEHST	ACHATES	AACERSS	CAESARS	AACHIPT	CHAPATI
AACEHTT	ATTACHE	AACERST	ACATERS	AACHIRS	ARACHIS
AACEHTU	CHATEAU		CARATES	AACHIRT	CITHARA
AACEILM	CAMELIA	AACERSU	CAESURA	AACHITY	CYATHIA
AACEIMN	ANAEMIC	AACERSZ	SAZERAC	AACHKMN	HACKMAN
AACEIMU	CAMAIEU	AACERTT	TEACART	AACHKMP	CHAMPAK
AACEINR	ACARINE	AACERTU	ARCUATE	AACHKNS	ACHKANS
	CARINAE	AACERWY	RACEWAY	AACHKPS	CHAPKAS
AACEIQU	ACEQUIA	AACESTV	CAVEATS		PACHAKS
AACEIRV	AVARICE		VACATES	AACHKRS	CHAKRAS
	CAVIARE	AACESTX	EXACTAS		CHARKAS
AACEIST	ECTASIA	AACETTU	ACTUATE	AACHKRT	HATRACK
AACEJLS	JACALES	AACETUV	VACUATE	AACHKRY	HAYRACK
AACEJRS	JACARES	AACFFIL	CAFFILA	AACHKSW	HACKSAW
AACEKNP	PANCAKE	AACFILS	CAFILAS		KWACHAS
AACEKNS	ASKANCE		FACIALS	AACHLLN	CHALLAN
AACEKOT	OATCAKE		FASCIAL	AACHLLS	CHALLAS
AACELLN	CANELLA	AACFILU	FAUCIAL	AACHLMS	CHASMAL
AACELLS	SACELLA	AACFINT	FANATIC	AACHLNS	CHALANS
AACELLT	LACTEAL	AACFISS	FASCIAS	AACHLNT	CANTHAL
AACELMN	MANACLE	AACFLLT	CATFALL	AACHLPP	CHAPPAL
AACELMR	CAMERAL	AACFLLU	FALCULA	AACHLPS	PASCHAL
	CARAMEL	AACFLLY	FALLACY	AACHLPU	CHALUPA
	CERAMAL	AACFLPT	FLATCAP	AACHLST	CALTHAS
	MACERAL	AACFLRT	FLATCAR	AACHLSU	ACUSHLA
AACELMU	MACULAE		FRACTAL	AACHMNP	CHAPMAN
AACELNP	CAPELAN	AACFLRU	FACULAR	AACHMNS	MACHANS
AACELNS	ANLACES	AACFLSU	FAUCALS	AACHMSY	YASHMAC
AACELNT	LACTEAN	AACFLTU	FACTUAL	AACHNOP	PANOCHA
AACELNU	CANULAE	AACFNST	CAFTANS	AACHNOU	HUANACO
	LACUNAE	AACFRRU	FARRUCA	AACHNPX	PANCHAX
AACELNV	VALANCE	AACGGMS	CAGMAGS	AACHNRS	ANARCHS
AACELOR	ACEROLA	AACGHNS	CHAGANS	AACHNRV	NAVARCH
AACELOV	COAEVAL	AACGILL	GALLICA	AACHNRY	ANARCHY
AACELPR	CARPALE		GLACIAL	AACHNSS	ASHCANS
AACELPS	PALACES	AACGILM	MAGICAL	AACHNST	ACANTHS
AACELPT	PLACATE	AACGILS	SCAGLIA	AACHNSU	ANCHUSA
AACELRS	SCALARE	AACGINT	AGNATIC	AACHNSZ	CHAZANS
AACELRV	CARAVEL	AACGIRS	AGARICS	AACHNZZ	CHAZZAN
AACELSS	CALESAS	AACGIRV	AGRAVIC	AACHRRT	CATARRH
AACELST	ACETALS	AACGISU	GUAIACS	AACHRST	CHARTAS
	LACTASE	AACGJNT	CATJANG	AACHRSW	CARWASH
AACELTT	LACTATE	AACGLOT	CATALOG	AACHRTU	AUTARCH
AACELTV	CLAVATE	AACGLOU	COAGULA	AACHRWY	ARCHWAY
AACELTY	ACYLATE	AACGLSY	GALYACS	AACHSSW	CASHAWS
AACEMMR	MACRAME	AACGNOU	GUANACO	AACHSTT	CHATTAS
AACEMNS	CASEMAN	AACHHKR	CHARKHA	AACIILN	ANCILIA
AACEMNV	CAVEMAN	AACHHLL	CHALLAH		LACINIA
AACEMOS	CAEOMAS	AACHHLS	CHALAHS	AACIIMS	CAMISIA
AACEMPR	PARACME	AACHIKL	HALAKIC	AACIINP	APICIAN
AACEMQU	MACAQUE	AACHIKN	KACHINA	AACIINT	ACTINIA
AACEMRS	CAMERAS	AACHIKR	CHIKARA	AACIITV	AVIATIC
AACEMSS	CAMASES	AACHILO	ACHOLIA		VIATICA
AACENRT	CATERAN	AACHILR	ACHIRAL	AACIJLP	JALAPIC
AACENSS	CASSENA		RACHIAL	AACIJMS	JICAMAS
AACENST	CATENAS	AACHILT	CALATHI	AACIKLL	ALKALIC
AACENTT	CANTATE	AACHIMR	MACHAIR	AACIKLR	CLARKIA
AACENTY	CYANATE	AACHIMS	CHAMISA	AACIKNN	CANAKIN
AACEOPT	PEACOAT		CHIASMA	AACIKNT	KATCINA

AACIKRT	AKRATIC
AACILLN	ANCILLA
AACILLS	CALLAIS
AACILMR	MAILCAR
AACILMS	CALIMAS
	CAMAILS
AACILNP	CALPAIN
AACILNR	CARINAL
	CLARAIN
	CRANIAL
AACILNT	ACTINAL
	ALICANT
	ANTICAL
AACILOS	ASOCIAL
AACILOX	COAXIAL
AACILPS	APICALS
	SPACIAL
AACILPT	CAPITAL
	PLACITA
AACILRR	RAILCAR
AACILTT	CATTAIL
AACILTV	VATICAL
AACIMMR	MACRAMI
AACIMNO	MANIOCA
AACIMNS	CAIMANS
	MANIACS
AACIMNY	ANIMACY
AACIMOR	ACROMIA
AACIMPR	PICAMAR
AACIMSS	CAMISAS
AACIMTY	CYMATIA
AACINNT	CANTINA
AACINOR	CONARIA
	OCARINA
AACINPT	CAPITAN
	CAPTAIN
AACINRS	ACRASIN
	ARNICAS
	CARINAS
	SARCINA
AACINRT	ANTICAR
AACINRZ	CZARINA
AACINSS	ASCIANS
	CASSINA
	SANCAIS
AACINST	SATANIC
AACIOPT	TAPIOCA
AACIOPV	COPAIVA
AACIOST	ATOCIAS
	COAITAS
AACIPPR	PAPRICA
AACIPRS	PICARAS
AACIPRX	APRAXIC
AACIQTU	AQUATIC
AACIRSS	ASCARIS
AACIRST	CARITAS
AACIRSV	CAVIARS
AACISSS	CASSIAS
AACISST	CASITAS
AACISTT	ASTATIC
AACISTX	ATAXICS
AACJKLS	JACKALS
AACJKMN	JACKMAN
	MANJACK
AACJKSS	JACKASS
AACJOSU	ACAJOUS
AACJPTU	CAJAPUT
AACKLPS	KALPACS
AACKLTW	CATWALK
AACKMNP	MANPACK
	PACKMAN
AACKMRT	AMTRACK
AACKNRS	RANSACK
AACKPRR	CARPARK
AACKPRT	RATPACK
AACKPSZ	CZAPKAS
AACKPWX	PACKWAX
AACKPWY	PACKWAY
AACKRRS	ARRACKS
AACKSTT	ATTACKS
AACLLNS	CALLANS
AACLLNT	CALLANT
AACLLNU	CALLUNA
	LACUNAL
AACLLOO	CALALOO
AACLLOR	CORALLA
AACLLSU	CALALUS
	CLAUSAL
AACLLVY	CAVALLY
AACLMNO	COALMAN
AACLMNT	CALMANT
	CLAMANT
AACLMRU	MACULAR
AACLMST	LACTAMS
AACLMSU	CALAMUS
	MACULAS
AACLNNO	ANCONAL
AACLNNU	CANNULA
AACLNOS	CANOLAS
AACLNPY	CLAYPAN
AACLNRS	CARNALS
AACLNRU	CANULAR
	LACUNAR
AACLNST	CANTALS
AACLNSU	CANULAS
	LACUNAS
AACLOPR	CAPORAL
	CRAPOLA
AACLOPT	OCTAPLA
AACLORT	COALTAR
	CROTALA
AACLORZ	ALCORZA
AACLOST	CATALOS
	COASTAL
AACLOTT	CATTALO
AACLOTV	OCTAVAL
AACLPRS	CARPALS
AACLPRT	CALTRAP
AACLPSS	PASCALS
AACLPSU	PASCUAL
	PAUCALS
	SCAPULA
AACLPTY	PLAYACT
AACLRSS	LASCARS
	RASCALS
	SACRALS
	SCALARS
AACLRST	CASTRAL
AACLRTY	LACTARY
AACLRVY	CALVARY
	CAVALRY
AACLSSU	CASUALS
	CAUSALS
AACLSTT	SALTCAT
AACLSTU	ACTUALS
AACLSUV	VASCULA
AACLTTU	TACTUAL
AACMMOT	COMMATA
AACMNOR	CAMARON
	NARCOMA
AACMNRU	ARCANUM
AACMNSY	CAYMANS
AACMORR	CAMORRA
AACMORS	SARCOMA
AACMORT	MARCATO
AACMOSY	MACOYAS
AACMRRT	TRAMCAR
AACMRSS	SARCASM
AACMRST	AMTRACS
	RAMCATS
	TARMACS
AACNNOZ	CANZONA
AACNOST	SACATON
AACNOTZ	ZACATON
AACNPRT	CANTRAP
AACNPST	CAPSTAN
	CAPTANS
	CATNAPS
AACNRST	ARCTANS
	CANTARS
AACNRTU	CURTANA
AACNSSV	CANVASS
AACNSTT	ACTANTS
AACNSTU	ASCAUNT
AACOPPR	APOCARP
AACORST	OSTRACA
AACORTU	ACATOUR
	AUTOCAR
AACOTUV	AUTOVAC
AACPRSS	SCARPAS
AACPSTW	CATSPAW
AACRRST	CARRATS
AACRRSU	CURARAS
AACRSTV	CRAVATS
AACRTTT	ATTRACT
AACRTUV	VACATUR
AACRTUY	ACTUARY
AACRTWY	CARTWAY
AACTUWY	CUTAWAY
AADDDEN	ADDENDA
AADDEGM	DAMAGED
AADDEHH	HADEDAH
AADDEIL	ALIDADE
AADDEMM	MADAMED
AADDEMN	DEADMAN
AADDENP	DEADPAN
AADDEOR	DEODARA
AADDEPR	PARADED
AADDEPT	ADAPTED
AADDERS	ADREADS
AADDERW	AWARDED
AADDESX	ADDAXES

AADDGNR	GRADDAN	AADEINS	NAIADES	AADERSY	ARAYSED
	GRANDAD	AADEINZ	ZENAIDA		DARESAY
AADDHKR	KHADDAR	AADEIPS	DIAPASE	AADERTU	AURATED
AADDHRS	SRADDHA	AADEIRS	ARAISED	AADESSY	ASSAYED
AADDIIK	DIDAKAI	AADEIRT	AIRDATE	AADFLTW	TWAFALD
AADDIIV	DAVIDIA		RADIATE	AADFMSU	MADAFUS
AADDILS	ALIDADS		TIARAED	AADFNRR	FARRAND
AADDIMS	DADAISM	AADEITV	AVIATED	AADFNST	FANTADS
AADDIST	DADAIST	AADEITW	AWAITED	AADFRST	DAFTARS
AADDLNS	ADLANDS	AADEJMR	JEMADAR	AADGGHR	HAGGARD
AADDMRY	DRAMADY	AADEKKY	KAYAKED	AADGGLR	LAGGARD
AADDNVV	DVANDVA	AADEKLR	KRAALED	AADGGOT	AGGADOT
AADDOSU	AOUDADS	AADEKLS	ASLAKED	AADGGRS	SAGGARD
AADDRST	DASTARD	AADEKMR	KAMERAD	AADGHIL	HIDALGA
AADDRSW	ADWARDS	AADEKMS	MEDAKAS	AADGHOR	DAROGHA
AADDSST	STADDAS		SMAAKED	AADGHRS	DARGAHS
AADEEFR	AFEARED	AADEKPR	PARKADE	AADGIIR	GIARDIA
AADEEGH	HEADAGE	AADELLP	PADELLA	AADGIMM	DIGAMMA
AADEELT	DEALATE	AADELLY	ALLAYED	AADGIMO	AGAMOID
AADEEMT	EDEMATA	AADELMN	LEADMAN	AADGIMR	DIAGRAM
AADEENR	ANEARED	AADELMO	ALAMODE	AADGIMS	AGAMIDS
AADEERT	AERATED	AADELMR	ALARMED	AADGINW	ADAWING
AADEERW	AWARDEE	AADELMX	MALAXED	AADGIOS	ADAGIOS
AADEFFR	AFFEARD	AADELNR	ADRENAL	AADGIOT	AGATOID
AADEFGL	FALDAGE	AADELNT	LANATED	AADGIRV	GRAVIDA
AADEFGR	FARDAGE	AADELNW	DANELAW	AADGLLW	GADWALL
AADEFHT	FATHEAD	AADELNX	ADNEXAL	AADGLMY	AMYGDAL
AADEFIS	FADAISE	AADELPR	PARDALE	AADGLNO	GONADAL
AADEFLU	AEFAULD	AADELPT	PALATED	AADGLNR	GARLAND
AADEFNZ	FAZENDA	AADELRT	LATERAD	AADGLNS	SLADANG
AADEFTW	FATWAED	AADELRU	RADULAE	AADGLRU	GRADUAL
AADEGGR	AGGRADE	AADELRY	ALREADY	AADGMNR	GRANDAM
	GARAGED	AADELSS	SALADES		GRANDMA
AADEGHR	RAGHEAD		SALSAED	AADGMNS	GADSMAN
AADEGLS	GELADAS	AADELTU	ADULATE	AADGMOT	DOGMATA
AADEGMN	AGNAMED	AADELTY	DAYTALE	AADGMRS	SMARAGD
	MANAGED	AADEMMN	MANMADE	AADGNPR	GRANDPA
AADEGMR	DAMAGER	AADEMMS	MADAMES	AADGNPS	PADANGS
	MEGARAD	AADEMNO	ADENOMA		PADNAGS
AADEGMS	DAMAGES	AADEMNS	ANADEMS	AADGNRS	ARGANDS
AADEGNS	AGENDAS		MAENADS	AADGNRT	GARDANT
AADEGRT	GRADATE	AADEMNT	MANDATE	AADGNRY	YARDANG
AADEGRV	RAVAGED	AADEMRY	DAYMARE	AADGOPR	PODAGRA
AADEGRY	DRAYAGE	AADEMSS	AMASSED	AADGOPS	PAGODAS
	YARDAGE	AADENNT	ANDANTE	AADGRSU	GARUDAS
AADEGSV	SAVAGED	AADENRV	VERANDA	AADGRSY	GAYDARS
AADEHIR	AIRHEAD	AADENRW	AWARNED	AADHHPS	PADSHAH
AADEHJR	JARHEAD	AADENST	ANSATED	AADHHRT	HARDHAT
AADEHKS	AKEDAHS	AADENSU	SAUNAED	AADHILS	DAHLIAS
AADEHMN	HEADMAN	AADENSW	WEASAND	AADHIMR	HADARIM
AADEHMS	ASHAMED	AADENWZ	WEAZAND		HARAMID
AADEHPS	SAPHEAD	AADEPRR	PARADER	AADHIMS	SAMADHI
AADEHPW	AWHAPED	AADEPRS	ASPREAD	AADHINP	DAPHNIA
AADEHRW	RAWHEAD		PARADES	AADHJNR	HANDJAR
	WARHEAD	AADEPRT	ADAPTER	AADHKNS	DHANSAK
AADEHWY	HEADWAY		READAPT		KHANDAS
AADEIKK	KAIAKED	AADEPSS	ESPADAS	AADHKNY	YAKHDAN
AADEILR	RADIALE		PASSADE	AADHLRY	HALYARD
AADEILV	AVAILED	AADEPWW	PAWAWED	AADHMMS	DHAMMAS
	VEDALIA	AADERRS	ARRASED	AADHMNR	HARDMAN
AADEIMR	MADEIRA	AADERRW	AWARDER	AADHMRS	DHARMAS
AADEIMS	AMIDASE	AADERRY	ARRAYED	AADHNPR	HARDPAN
	SEAMAID	AADERSW	ADWARES	AADHNRS	DARSHAN
AADEINR	ARANEID		SEAWARD		DHARNAS

AADHNSW	HANDSAW	AADLMNO	MANDOLA			POSADAS
AADHPRS	PARDAHS		MONADAL	AADOPTT	DOPATTA
AADHRSS	HARDASS	AADLMNU	LADANUM	AADORWY	ROADWAY
	SRADHAS	AADLMOR	ARMLOAD	AADOSTT	TOSTADA
AADHRSZ	HAZARDS	AADLMPS	LAMPADS	AADOWWX	WOADWAX
AADHRWY	HAYWARD	AADLMSW	WADMALS	AADPSSW	PADSAWS
AADHSWY	WASHDAY	AADLNOP	DALAPON	AADPSSY	SPAYADS
AADIILR	DIARIAL	AADLNOV	VANLOAD	AADPSYY	PAYDAYS
AADIINO	DIANOIA	AADLNOZ	DANAZOL	AADPTTU	DUPATTA
AADIINR	DIARIAN	AADLNRY	LANYARD	AADQRTU	QUADRAT
AADIIPS	ADIPSIA	AADLNSS	SANDALS	AADRRSS	SARDARS
	ASPIDIA	AADLNSU	LANDAUS	AADRSTU	DATURAS
AADIJMN	JAMDANI	AADLNSV	VANDALS	AADRSTY	DAYSTAR
AADIKLY	ILKADAY	AADLOPY	PAYLOAD	AADRSVW	VAWARDS
AADILLO	ALLODIA	AADLPPU	APPLAUD	AADRWWY	WAYWARD
	ALODIAL	AADLPRS	PARDALS	AAEEFFR	AFFEARE
AADILMR	ADMIRAL	AADLPYY	PLAYDAY	AAEEFGL	LEAFAGE
	AMILDAR	AADLRRU	RADULAR	AAEEFRT	RATAFEE
AADILMT	MATILDA	AADLRSU	RADULAS	AAEEGKL	LEAKAGE
AADILNP	PALADIN	AADMMRS	DAMMARS	AAEEGLT	ETALAGE
AADILNR	LANIARD	AADMNNO	MADONNA		GALEATE
	NADIRAL	AADMNNS	SANDMAN	AAEEGMN	AMENAGE
AADILPS	APSIDAL	AADMNOR	MADRONA	AAEEGMT	AGAMETE
AADILRS	RADIALS		MANDORA		AGEMATE
AADILRT	TAILARD		MONARDA	AAEEGRV	AVERAGE
AADILSS	DALASIS		ROADMAN	AAEEGST	EATAGES
AADILST	STADIAL	AADMNOW	ADWOMAN	AAEEHRT	HETAERA
AADILTV	DATIVAL	AADMNRS	MANSARD	AAEEINT	TAENIAE
AADILWY	WAYLAID	AADMNRW	MANWARD	AAEEKKS	AKEAKES
AADIMNR	MANDIRA	AADMNRY	DRAYMAN	AAEEKLS	SEAKALE
AADIMNS	MAIDANS		YARDMAN	AAEEKRW	REAWAKE
AADIMNY	DAYANIM	AADMNSY	DAYSMAN	AAEELMT	MALEATE
AADIMOR	DIORAMA	AADMNTU	MUTANDA	AAEELOR	AREOLAE
AADIMOT	DOMATIA		TAMANDU	AAEELPT	PALEATE
AADIMRS	ARAMIDS	AADMOPP	PAPADOM	AAEELRT	LAETARE
AADINNN	NANDINA	AADMOQU	MADOQUA	AAEEMNT	EMANATE
AADINNP	PANDANI	AADMORT	MATADOR		ENEMATA
AADINPT	PINTADA	AADMOSU	AMADOUS		MANATEE
AADINRR	DARRAIN	AADMPPU	PAPADUM	AAEEMRT	AMREETA
AADINRS	RADIANS	AADMRRY	YARDARM	AAEEMTX	MEATAXE
AADINRT	INTRADA	AADMRSU	MARAUDS	AAEEPPS	APPEASE
	RADIANT	AADMRSZ	MAZARDS	AAEEPRT	PATERAE
AADINRV	VIRANDA	AADMRZZ	MAZZARD	AAEERST	AERATES
AADINRW	WARDIAN	AADMSYY	MAYDAYS	AAEERSW	SEAWARE
AADINSV	NAVAIDS	AADNNOT	NOTANDA	AAEERTU	AUREATE
AADINSY	NAYSAID	AADNNRS	RANDANS	AAEERTW	TEAWARE
AADIOPZ	DOPIAZA	AADNOPR	PANDORA	AAEERTX	EXARATE
AADIPTX	TAXPAID	AADNORT	ONDATRA	AAEFFGR	AGRAFFE
AADIQSS	QASIDAS	AADNORY	ANYROAD	AAEFFIR	AFFAIRE
AADIRRW	AIRWARD	AADNPRS	PANDARS	AAEFFLL	FALAFEL
AADIRSU	SUDARIA	AADNPRU	PANDURA	AAEFFNR	FANFARE
AADISST	STADIAS	AADNRRW	WARRAND	AAEFFRS	AFFEARS
AADJLNS	JANDALS	AADNRRY	DARRAYN	AAEFFTT	TAFFETA
AADKMRY	DAYMARK	AADNRSS	NASARDS	AAEFGNS	FANEGAS
AADKMSS	DAMASKS	AADNRST	ASTRAND	AAEFGRS	AGRAFES
AADKNRT	TANKARD		TARANDS	AAEFGTW	WAFTAGE
AADKPSU	PADAUKS	AADNRTY	TANYARD	AAEFIRR	AIRFARE
AADKRWW	AWKWARD	AADNRVW	VANWARD	AAEFKLO	OAKLEAF
AADLLLN	LALLAND	AADNRWY	NAYWARD	AAEFLLV	FAVELLA
AADLLMR	MALLARD	AADOPRR	PARADOR	AAEFLPR	EARFLAP
AADLLNW	LAWLAND	AADOPRS	PARADOS		PARAFLE
AADLLPU	PALUDAL	AADOPRT	ADAPTOR	AAEFLRS	RAFALES
AADLLSS	SALLADS	AADOPRX	PARADOX	AAEFLSV	FAVELAS
AADLMNN	LANDMAN	AADOPSS	PASSADO	AAEFMRT	FERMATA

AAEFQRU	AQUAFER	AAEGMRT	REGMATA	AAEHPRZ	PHEAZAR
AAEFRRW	WARFARE	AAEGMSS	MASSAGE	AAEHPSW	AWHAPES
AAEFRWY	WAYFARE	AAEGMTT	METATAG	AAEHPSX	HAPAXES
AAEGGLS	GALAGES	AAEGNNP	PANNAGE	AAEHRSY	HEARSAY
AAEGGNO	ANAGOGE	AAEGNNT	TANNAGE	AAEHSTT	HASTATE
AAEGGOP	APAGOGE	AAEGNOP	APOGEAN	AAEIKLN	AKENIAL
AAEGGRS	GARAGES	AAEGNPW	PAWNAGE	AAEILLX	AXILLAE
AAEGGRT	AGGRATE	AAEGNRR	ARRANGE	AAEILMN	LAMINAE
AAEGGSV	GAVAGES	AAEGNRT	TANAGER	AAEILMS	AMELIAS
AAEGHLU	HAULAGE	AAEGNST	AGNATES		MALAISE
AAEGHLY	HAYLAGE	AAEGNSU	GUANASE	AAEILNN	ALANINE
AAEGHNT	THANAGE	AAEGNTV	VANTAGE	AAEILNO	AEOLIAN
AAEGILR	LAIRAGE	AAEGNTW	WANTAGE	AAEILNT	ANTLIAE
	REGALIA	AAEGORS	AGAROSE	AAEILOR	OLEARIA
AAEGILS	ALGESIA		OARAGES	AAEILPX	EPAXIAL
AAEGINP	NAGAPIE	AAEGPRR	PARERGA	AAEILRS	AERIALS
AAEGINR	ANERGIA	AAEGPRS	PARAGES	AAEILRU	AURELIA
AAEGINV	VAGINAE	AAEGPRW	WARPAGE	AAEILRV	REAVAIL
AAEGINW	WAINAGE	AAEGPSS	PASSAGE		VELARIA
AAEGIPR	IGARAPE	AAEGPSV	PAVAGES	AAEILSS	ALIASES
AAEGIRR	ARRIAGE	AAEGPSY	PAYSAGE	AAEILSV	AVAILES
AAEGISS	ASSEGAI	AAEGQUY	QUAYAGE	AAEILSX	ALEXIAS
AAEGIST	AGATISE	AAEGRRV	RAVAGER	AAEIMMT	IMAMATE
AAEGISU	AGEUSIA	AAEGRST	AGRASTE	AAEIMNS	AMNESIA
AAEGITT	AGITATE		GASTREA		ANEMIAS
AAEGITZ	AGATIZE		TEARGAS	AAEIMNT	AMENTIA
AAEGJTU	AJUTAGE	AAEGRSV	RAVAGES		ANIMATE
AAEGKNT	TANKAGE		SAVAGER	AAEIMPY	PYAEMIA
AAEGKOS	SOAKAGE	AAEGRTT	REGATTA	AAEIMRT	AMIRATE
AAEGLLR	GLAREAL	AAEGSSU	ASSUAGE	AAEIMRU	URAEMIA
AAEGLLT	GALLATE		SAUSAGE	AAEIMTV	AMATIVE
	GALLETA	AAEGSSV	AVGASES	AAEINNO	AEONIAN
	TALLAGE		SAVAGES	AAEINPS	PAESANI
AAEGLMN	GAMELAN	AAEGSSW	ASSWAGE	AAEINPT	PATINAE
AAEGLMT	GAMETAL	AAEGSTU	GATEAUS	AAEINST	ENTASIA
AAEGLNN	ANLAGEN	AAEGSTW	WASTAGE		TAENIAS
AAEGLNR	ALNAGER	AAEGTTW	WATTAGE	AAEIPPS	APEPSIA
AAEGLNS	ALNAGES	AAEGTUX	GATEAUX	AAEIPRR	PAREIRA
	ANLAGES	AAEGTWY	GATEWAY	AAEIPRS	SPIRAEA
	GALENAS		GETAWAY	AAEIPRT	APTERIA
	LAGENAS	AAEHHPR	RHAPHAE	AAEIPTT	APATITE
	LASAGNE	AAEHHPT	APHTHAE	AAEIRRT	TARAIRE
AAEGLNU	AULNAGE	AAEHILP	APHELIA	AAEIRSS	ARAISES
	LEGUAAN	AAEHIRT	HETAIRA	AAEIRST	ARISTAE
AAEGLOP	APOGEAL	AAEHKNT	KHANATE		ASTERIA
AAEGLRR	REALGAR	AAEHKPS	PAKEHAS		ATRESIA
AAEGLRS	ALEGARS	AAEHKST	TAKAHES	AAEIRSX	XERASIA
	LAAGERS	AAEHKSW	SEAHAWK	AAEIRTT	ARIETTA
AAEGLST	AGELAST	AAEHLLL	ALLHEAL	AAEIRTV	VARIATE
	ALGATES	AAEHLMT	HEMATAL	AAEIRTW	AWAITER
	LASTAGE	AAEHLNT	ETHANAL	AAEIRVW	AIRWAVE
AAEGLSV	LAVAGES	AAEHLPS	PHASEAL	AAEISTT	SATIATE
	SALVAGE	AAEHLPX	HEXAPLA	AAEISTV	AVIATES
AAEGLSX	GALAXES	AAEHLRT	TREHALA	AAEISTX	ATAXIES
AAEGMNO	MANGEAO	AAEHLST	ALTHEAS	AAEITUX	EUTAXIA
AAEGMNR	MANAGER	AAEHLTT	ATHLETA	AAEJMST	MAATJES
AAEGMNS	AGNAMES	AAEHMSS	ASHAMES	AAEJNRT	NAARTJE
	MANAGES	AAEHMST	ATHAMES	AAEJOPR	APAREJO
	SAGAMEN		HAMATES	AAEKKOR	KARAOKE
AAEGMNT	GATEMAN	AAEHMTT	THEMATA	AAEKKRY	KAYAKER
	MAGENTA	AAEHNPR	HANAPER	AAEKLMS	KAMELAS
	MAGNATE	AAEHNPS	SAPHENA	AAEKLNS	ALKANES
	NAMETAG	AAEHNSY	HYAENAS	AAEKLNT	ALKANET
AAEGMPR	RAMPAGE				KANTELA

AAEKLSS	ASLAKES
AAEKMNW	WAKEMAN
AAEKMRR	EARMARK
AAEKMRS	SEAMARK
AAEKMSW	WAKAMES
AAEKNNS	ANANKES
AAEKNSW	AWAKENS
	WAKANES
AAEKNUW	UNAWAKE
AAEKPRT	PARTAKE
AAEKPTU	PUKATEA
AAEKRSS	KEASARS
AAEKRST	KARATES
AAELLLM	LAMELLA
AAELLNV	AVELLAN
AAELLNZ	ZANELLA
AAELLPR	PARELLA
AAELLPS	PAELLAS
AAELLPT	PATELLA
AAELLRT	LATERAL
AAELLRY	ALLAYER
	AREALLY
AAELLSW	SEAWALL
AAELLTV	VALLATE
AAELMMR	ALMEMAR
AAELMMT	LEMMATA
AAELMNT	AMENTAL
AAELMNU	ALUMNAE
AAELMOT	OATMEAL
AAELMPT	PALMATE
AAELMRW	MALWARE
AAELMST	MALATES
	MALTASE
	TAMALES
AAELMSX	MALAXES
AAELMSY	AMYLASE
AAELNNS	ANNEALS
AAELNOP	APNOEAL
AAELNOV	VALONEA
AAELNPR	PREANAL
AAELNPT	PLANATE
	PLANTAE
	PLATANE
AAELNPU	PAENULA
AAELNRS	ARSENAL
AAELNSS	ANLASES
AAELNST	SEALANT
AAELNSY	ANALYSE
AAELNTT	TETANAL
AAELNTY	ANALYTE
AAELNTZ	ZEALANT
AAELNWY	LANEWAY
AAELNYZ	ANALYZE
AAELORR	AREOLAR
AAELORS	AREOLAS
AAELORU	AUREOLA
AAELOTX	OXALATE
AAELPPR	APPAREL
AAELPPS	APPEALS
AAELPPT	PALPATE
AAELPPU	PAPULAE
AAELPRS	EARLAPS
AAELPRT	APTERAL
AAELPRV	PALAVER
AAELPSS	PALASES
	PLAASES
AAELPST	PALATES
	PATELAS
AAELPTT	TAPETAL
AAELPTU	PLATEAU
AAELPTY	APETALY
AAELRST	TARSEAL
AAELRTV	LARVATE
AAELRTZ	LAZARET
AAELRVY	ALVEARY
AAELSST	ATLASES
AAELSTT	SALTATE
AAELSTV	VALETAS
AAELSTZ	ALTEZAS
AAELSUX	ASEXUAL
AAELSWX	SEALWAX
AAELTUV	VALUATE
AAELTVV	VALVATE
AAELTZZ	ALTEZZA
AAELWWY	WELAWAY
AAEMMMR	MAREMMA
AAEMMMT	MAMMATE
AAEMMNT	MEATMAN
AAEMMNU	MANUMEA
AAEMMOT	OMMATEA
AAEMNNT	EMANANT
AAEMNOR	AMARONE
AAEMNPP	PAMPEAN
AAEMNPS	SPAEMAN
AAEMNPT	PEATMAN
AAEMNRT	RAMENTA
AAEMNRU	MURAENA
AAEMNST	NAMASTE
AAEMNTU	MANTEAU
AAEMOTY	ATEMOYA
AAEMOTZ	METAZOA
AAEMQSU	SQUAMAE
AAEMRSS	AMASSER
AAEMRST	AMEARST
	RETAMAS
AAEMRTU	AMATEUR
AAEMSSS	AMASSES
AAENNNT	ANTENNA
AAENNST	ANNATES
AAENNSZ	ZENANAS
AAENNTT	TANNATE
AAENNTV	VENTANA
AAENOPS	APNOEAS
	PAESANO
AAENOSZ	OZAENAS
AAENPPR	PARPANE
AAENPSS	PAESANS
AAENPST	ANAPEST
	PEASANT
AAENPSV	PAVANES
AAENPSX	PANAXES
AAENPTT	EPATANT
AAENRRT	NARRATE
AAENRSS	NARASES
AAENRST	ANESTRA
	SANTERA
AAENRTT	TARTANE
AAENRTU	NATURAE
	TAUREAN
AAENRTV	TAVERNA
AAENRUW	UNAWARE
AAENRUZ	AZUREAN
AAENSSU	NAUSEAS
AAENSSV	VANESSA
AAENSSW	SEAWANS
AAENSTV	SAVANTE
AAENSTW	SEAWANT
AAEOPTZ	ZAPATEO
AAEORRT	AERATOR
AAEORRU	AURORAE
AAEORST	AEROSAT
AAEPPRS	APPEARS
AAEPPRT	PARAPET
AAEPRSS	PASEARS
	SARAPES
AAEPRST	PETARAS
AAEPRSY	APYRASE
AAEPRSZ	ZARAPES
AAEPRTY	PEATARY
AAEPSTW	WATAPES
AAEPTTW	WATTAPE
AAERRRS	ARREARS
AAERRRY	ARRAYER
AAERRSS	ARRASES
AAERRST	ERRATAS
AAERRTT	TARTARE
AAERSST	SEARATS
AAERSSY	ARAYSES
	ASSAYER
AAERSTU	AURATES
AAERSTW	AWAREST
AAERTTU	TUATERA
AAESSTV	SAVATES
AAESSWY	SEAWAYS
AAFFILN	AFFINAL
AAFFILX	AFFIXAL
AAFFIMS	MAFFIAS
AAFFINS	SAFFIAN
AAFFINT	AFFIANT
AAFFIRS	AFFAIRS
	RAFFIAS
AAFFIST	TAFFIAS
AAFFLRS	FARFALS
AAFFPRS	AFFRAPS
AAFFRSY	AFFRAYS
AAFFRSZ	ZAFFARS
AAFGHIN	AFGHANI
AAFGHNS	AFGHANS
AAFGLMN	FLAGMAN
AAFGORR	FARRAGO
AAFHIKL	KHALIFA
AAFHINR	FARINHA
AAFHLLS	ASHFALL
AAFHLWY	HALFWAY
AAFHSTW	FATWAHS
AAFIILR	FILARIA
AAFIJST	FAJITAS
AAFIKLS	ALFAKIS
	KAFILAS
AAFIKSS	SIFAKAS
AAFILNT	FANTAIL
	TAILFAN

AAFILQU	ALFAQUI	**AAGHRSW**	WASHRAG	**AAGLLVY**	VAGALLY
AAFINNT	INFANTA	**AAGHSTY**	SAGATHY	**AAGLMMS**	MALMAGS
AAFINNU	INFAUNA	**AAGIINT**	IGNATIA	**AAGLMNS**	MANGALS
AAFINRS	FARINAS	**AAGIKNS**	KAINGAS	**AAGLNOR**	GRANOLA
AAFINTT	ANTIFAT	**AAGIKNT**	TIKANGA	**AAGLNOS**	ANALOGS
AAFIPRT	PARFAIT	**AAGIKNW**	AWAKING	**AAGLNOY**	ANALOGY
AAFIRSS	SAFARIS	**AAGIKNZ**	ZIGANKA	**AAGLNPS**	LAPSANG
AAFIRSU	FUSARIA	**AAGILMY**	MYALGIA	**AAGLNRS**	LANGARS
AAFIRUY	RUFIYAA	**AAGILNN**	ANGINAL		RAGLANS
AAFIRWY	FAIRWAY	**AAGILNO**	LOGANIA	**AAGLNRU**	ANGULAR
AAFISST	FATSIAS	**AAGILNP**	PAGINAL	**AAGLNSU**	LAGUNAS
AAFJLLW	JAWFALL	**AAGILNS**	AGNAILS	**AAGLNTY**	GALANTY
AAFJLOR	ALFORJA	**AAGILNV**	AVALING	**AAGLORU**	ARUGOLA
AAFKNST	KAFTANS		VAGINAL	**AAGLRST**	GASTRAL
AAFLLLS	FALLALS	**AAGILNY**	ALAYING	**AAGLRUU**	ARUGULA
AAFLLTY	FATALLY	**AAGILOS**	ALOGIAS		AUGURAL
AAFLMPR	FRAMPAL		LAOGAIS	**AAGLRVX**	GRAVLAX
AAFLNOR	FORLANA	**AAGILOT**	OTALGIA	**AAGLSST**	STALAGS
AAFLNRU	FURLANA	**AAGILPS**	PALAGIS	**AAGMMNS**	MAGSMAN
AAFLNUU	FAUNULA	**AAGILRS**	ARGALIS	**AAGMMRR**	GRAMMAR
AAFLSTU	FLAUTAS		GARIALS	**AAGMMRS**	GRAMMAS
AAFLWYY	FLYAWAY	**AAGILSV**	GAVIALS	**AAGMMST**	GAMMATS
AAFMNRT	RAFTMAN	**AAGILTW**	WAGTAIL	**AAGMMTU**	GUMMATA
AAFMNST	FANTASM	**AAGIMNO**	ANGIOMA	**AAGMMUY**	MAMAGUY
AAFNRRT	FARRANT	**AAGIMNS**	MAGIANS	**AAGMNNR**	GRANNAM
AAFNSTT	FANTAST		SIAMANG	**AAGMNOS**	SANGOMA
AAFNSTY	FANTASY	**AAGIMNT**	AMATING	**AAGMNOT**	AGAMONT
AAFOSST	AFTOSAS	**AAGIMNZ**	AMAZING	**AAGMNPR**	PANGRAM
AAGGHNT	HANGTAG	**AAGINNS**	ANGINAS	**AAGMNPY**	PANGAMY
AAGGIJN	JAGAING		INANGAS	**AAGMNRS**	RAGMANS
AAGGILN	GANGLIA	**AAGINNW**	WANIGAN	**AAGMNRT**	TANGRAM
AAGGJRY	JAGGARY	**AAGINOS**	AGNOSIA		TRANGAM
AAGGKSU	GAGAKUS	**AAGINPY**	APAYING	**AAGMNSW**	SWAGMAN
AAGGLMO	MAGALOG	**AAGINRR**	ARRAIGN	**AAGMNSZ**	ZAMANGS
AAGGLOS	GALAGOS	**AAGINRS**	NAGARIS	**AAGMOPY**	APOGAMY
AAGGLRY	GRAYLAG		SANGRIA	**AAGMORS**	MARGOSA
AAGGMNS	MGANGAS		SARANGI	**AAGMOSU**	AGAMOUS
AAGGNOY	ANAGOGY	**AAGINRT**	GRANITA	**AAGMPRS**	GRAMPAS
AAGGNST	GANGSTA	**AAGINRU**	GUARANI	**AAGMRRY**	GRAMARY
AAGGNTT	TAGGANT	**AAGINRZ**	ZINGARA	**AAGMRSY**	MARGAYS
AAGGNWY	GANGWAY	**AAGINST**	AGAINST	**AAGNNOS**	GOANNAS
AAGGQSU	QUAGGAS		AGITANS	**AAGNNRU**	RUNANGA
AAGGRSS	SAGGARS		ANTISAG	**AAGNNSW**	WANGANS
AAGGRST	RAGTAGS		GITANAS	**AAGNOPR**	PARAGON
	TAGRAGS	**AAGINSU**	IGUANAS	**AAGNORS**	ANGORAS
AAGHHRR	AARRGHH	**AAGINSV**	VAGINAS	**AAGNORZ**	ORGANZA
AAGHILR	GHARIAL	**AAGINSY**	GAINSAY	**AAGNOST**	TAONGAS
AAGHINN	ANHINGA	**AAGINTY**	ANTIGAY	**AAGNPRS**	PARANGS
AAGHJNS	GANJAHS	**AAGINWW**	WAWAING	**AAGNRRS**	GARRANS
AAGHKNS	KANGHAS	**AAGIOSS**	ASIAGOS	**AAGNRRY**	GRANARY
	KHANGAS	**AAGIOTT**	AGITATO	**AAGNRSS**	SANGARS
AAGHKNT	THANGKA	**AAGIPRS**	AIRGAPS	**AAGNRTV**	VAGRANT
AAGHLNT	GNATHAL	**AAGIPRU**	PIRAGUA	**AAGNSST**	SATANGS
AAGHLOS	GASAHOL	**AAGIRRY**	ARGYRIA	**AAGNSTU**	TAGUANS
AAGHLSZ	GHAZALS	**AAGIRSW**	WARAGIS	**AAGNSUY**	GUANAYS
AAGHMNN	HANGMAN	**AAGISTT**	SAGITTA	**AAGOPRU**	GAROUPA
AAGHMNU	MAHUANG	**AAGJNRS**	GARJANS	**AAGOPSS**	SAPSAGO
AAGHMNW	WHANGAM	**AAGJRSU**	JAGUARS	**AAGORSU**	SAGUARO
AAGHMRS	GRAHAMS	**AAGKKNO**	ANGAKOK	**AAGOSTU**	AGOUTAS
	GRAMASH	**AAGKLSY**	GALYAKS	**AAGPPRS**	GRAPPAS
AAGHNRS	ARGHANS	**AAGKOOZ**	GAZOOKA	**AAGRRSY**	GARRYAS
	HANGARS	**AAGKORT**	KATORGA	**AAGRSUV**	AVRUGAS
AAGHNST	SANGHAT	**AAGLLNS**	LALANGS	**AAGTTUU**	TAUTAUG
AAGHQUU	QUAHAUG	**AAGLLNT**	GALLANT	**AAHHIRS**	SHARIAH

AAHHJJS	HAJJAHS	AAHLLWY	HALLWAY	AAIIRVV	VIVARIA
AAHHLLS	HALLAHS	AAHLMMS	HAMMALS	AAIJLNP	JALAPIN
AAHHLSV	HALVAHS		MAHMALS	AAIJMNP	JAMPANI
AAHHMSZ	HAMZAHS		MASHLAM	AAIJMNT	ANTIJAM
AAHHNNT	THANNAH	AAHLMRS	MARSHAL	AAIJNRS	JARINAS
AAHHNPT	NAPHTHA	AAHLMRU	HAMULAR	AAIJNRZ	JANIZAR
AAHHNST	THANAHS	AAHLMST	MALTHAS	AAIJNST	TINAJAS
AAHHOPR	PHARAOH	AAHLMSU	HAMAULS	AAIJPPY	JIPYAPA
AAHIIMT	HIMATIA	AAHLNPX	PHALANX	AAIJRSW	JAWARIS
AAHIJNR	HARIJAN	AAHLNRW	NARWHAL	AAIKLLN	ALKALIN
AAHIKOR	AKIRAHO	AAHLPRS	PHRASAL	AAIKLLS	ALKALIS
AAHIKPS	PAKAHIS	AAHLPST	ASPHALT	AAIKLMS	KALMIAS
AAHIKRT	KITHARA		SPATHAL		KAMILAS
AAHILLL	HALLALI		TAPLASH	AAIKLNP	PALINKA
AAHILLN	HALLIAN	AAHLRSS	ASHLARS	AAIKLNS	KALIANS
AAHILMR	ALMIRAH	AAHLRST	HARTALS	AAIKLPR	PALIKAR
AAHILMS	SHIMAAL	AAHLRSW	SHALWAR	AAIKMNN	MANAKIN
AAHILMT	THALAMI	AAHMMMS	HAMMAMS	AAIKMNR	RAMAKIN
AAHILNT	THALIAN	AAHMMNS	MASHMAN	AAIKMOR	ROMAIKA
AAHILPV	PAHLAVI	AAHMMSS	SHAMMAS	AAIKMRS	KARAISM
AAHILSW	SAHIWAL	AAHMNNU	HANUMAN	AAIKNRS	KINARAS
AAHILSY	ALIYAHS	AAHMNRS	HARMANS	AAIKNST	TANKIAS
AAHIMNO	MAHONIA	AAHMNSS	SHAMANS	AAIKORU	OUAKARI
AAHIMNS	SHAMINA	AAHMNTX	XANTHAM	AAIKOSY	SOKAIYA
AAHIMNZ	HAZANIM	AAHMOPR	AMPHORA	AAIKPPR	PAPRIKA
AAHIMSS	AHIMSAS	AAHMPRS	PHARMAS	AAIKPRR	AIRPARK
AAHINOP	APHONIA	AAHMQSU	QUAMASH	AAIKRSS	ASKARIS
AAHINPP	PAPHIAN	AAHMRSS	ASHRAMS	AAIKRST	KARAITS
AAHINPR	PIRANHA	AAHMSST	ASTHMAS	AAIKRSU	UAKARIS
AAHINST	SHAITAN		MATSAHS	AAIKSTT	ASTATKI
	TAHINAS	AAHMSSU	MASHUAS	AAIKTVV	AKVAVIT
AAHINTW	TANIWHA	AAHMSTZ	HAZMATS	AAILLLP	PALLIAL
AAHIPRS	PARIAHS		MATZAHS	AAILLLT	LATILLA
	RAPHIAS	AAHNNOS	HOSANNA	AAILLMM	MAMILLA
AAHIPRT	PITARAH	AAHNNST	TANNAHS	AAILLMN	LAMINAL
AAHIPTZ	ZAPTIAH		THANNAS		MANILLA
AAHIRRS	HARIRAS	AAHNNTX	XANTHAN	AAILLMR	ARMILLA
AAHIRSS	HARISSA	AAHNOPR	ANAPHOR	AAILLMX	MAXILLA
	SHARIAS	AAHNORT	ATHANOR	AAILLNT	LANITAL
AAHIRST	SHARIAT	AAHNORV	NAVARHO	AAILLNV	VANILLA
AAHIRSV	VIHARAS	AAHNRTX	ANTHRAX	AAILLPP	PAPILLA
AAHIRTV	HAVARTI	AAHNRTY	RHATANY	AAILLRX	AXILLAR
AAHISTW	TAWHAIS	AAHNSUW	WHANAUS	AAILLSV	SALIVAL
AAHJKNR	KHANJAR	AAHNSZZ	HAZZANS	AAILLSX	AXILLAS
AAHJKST	JHATKAS	AAHORSU	SAHUARO	AAILLUV	ALLUVIA
AAHJNRS	HANJARS	AAHPPRS	PARAPHS	AAILLXY	AXIALLY
	RHANJAS	AAHPRSY	YARPHAS	AAILMMN	MAILMAN
AAHJRRS	JARRAHS	AAHPRTW	WARPATH	AAILMMR	AMMIRAL
AAHKKST	KATHAKS	AAHPTWY	PATHWAY	AAILMMS	MIASMAL
AAHKLRS	LASHKAR	AAHRSSS	HASSARS	AAILMMX	MAXIMAL
AAHKLST	KHALATS	AAHRSST	SHASTRA	AAILMNR	LAMINAR
AAHKLSY	KHAYALS	AAHRSTY	ASHTRAY		RAILMAN
AAHKMSY	YASHMAK	AAHRTTW	ATHWART	AAILMNS	ALMAINS
AAHKNST	KANTHAS	AAHSSSY	SASHAYS		ANIMALS
AAHKNSU	KAHUNAS	AAIIKKS	KAIKAIS		LAMINAS
AAHKPSS	PASHKAS	AAIIKSZ	ZAIKAIS		MANILAS
AAHKPSU	HAPUKAS	AAIILMR	AIRMAIL	AAILMNT	MATINAL
AAHKRSS	RAKSHAS	AAIILPR	PAIRIAL	AAILMNU	ALUMINA
AAHLLLS	HALLALS	AAIILPT	TILAPIA	AAILMNV	MAILVAN
AAHLLNS	HALLANS	AAIILRZ	ALIZARI	AAILMPS	IMPALAS
	NALLAHS	AAIINNZ	ANZIANI	AAILMQU	MAQUILA
AAHLLOS	HALLOAS	AAIINRT	ANTIAIR	AAILMRT	MARITAL
AAHLLPS	PALLAHS	AAIINTT	TITANIA		MARTIAL
AAHLLSW	WALLAHS	AAIINZZ	ZIZANIA	AAILMSS	ALISMAS

	SALAMIS	AAIMRTU	TIMARAU	AAISTTV	ATAVIST
AAILMSU	AUMAILS	AAIMSST	STASIMA	AAISTUY	YAUTIAS
AAILNNS	ALANINS	AAIMSSU	AMUSIAS	AAITWXY	TAXIWAY
AAILNOT	AILANTO	AAIMSTT	TATAMIS	AAJJMRS	JAMJARS
	ALATION	AAIMSTV	ATAVISM	AAJKLWY	JAYWALK
AAILNOV	NOVALIA	AAIMSUV	MAUVAIS	AAJKMNR	JARKMAN
	VALONIA	AAINNRU	URANIAN	AAJKNSS	SANJAKS
AAILNPS	SALPIAN	AAINNRV	NAVARIN	AAJMNPS	JAMPANS
AAILNPT	PLATINA		NIRVANA	AAJMNZZ	JAZZMAN
AAILNRU	ULNARIA	AAINOPS	ANOPIAS	AAJMORR	MOJARRA
AAILNRY	LANIARY		ANOPSIA	AAJMORT	MAJORAT
AAILNSS	SALINAS		PAISANO	AAJMPSY	PYJAMAS
AAILNST	LATINAS	AAINORR	ORARIAN	AAJNNOS	JOANNAS
AAILNSY	INYALAS	AAINORV	OVARIAN	AAJNOSW	AJOWANS
AAILNTV	VALIANT	AAINOST	ATONIAS	AAJNOSY	YOJANAS
AAILNTY	ANALITY	AAINOSX	ANOXIAS	AAJNPRS	PRAJNAS
AAILORS	ROSALIA	AAINPPS	PAPAINS	AAJOPSU	SAPAJOU
	SOLARIA	AAINPRS	PARIANS	AAKKLPS	KALPAKS
AAILORU	RAOULIA		PIRANAS	AAKKLRU	KARAKUL
AAILORV	OVARIAL	AAINPSS	PAISANS	AAKKMOT	TOKAMAK
	VARIOLA	AAINPST	PASTINA	AAKKMRS	MARKKAS
AAILORZ	ZOARIAL		PATINAS	AAKKOPS	KAKAPOS
AAILOST	SOLATIA		PINATAS	AAKKSUZ	ZAKUSKA
AAILPPT	APPALTI		TAIPANS	AAKLMPU	LAMPUKA
AAILPRS	PARIALS	AAINRST	ANTIARS	AAKLMRY	MALARKY
AAILPRT	PARTIAL		ARTISAN	AAKLMUY	YAMULKA
	PATRIAL		TSARINA	AAKLNOO	OOLAKAN
AAILPRY	AIRPLAY	AAINRSU	ANURIAS	AAKLNOU	OULAKAN
AAILPST	SPATIAL		SAURIAN	AAKLOOP	PALOOKA
AAILPTT	TALIPAT		URANIAS	AAKLOOT	TALOOKA
AAILPZZ	PALAZZI	AAINRSV	SAVARIN	AAKLRSU	KURSAAL
AAILQWW	QAWWALI	AAINRTV	VARIANT		RUSALKA
AAILRRV	ARRIVAL	AAINRTW	ANTIWAR	AAKLSSU	SAKSAUL
AAILRST	LARIATS	AAINRTZ	TZARINA	AAKLSTU	TALUKAS
	LATRIAS	AAINSST	ISTANAS	AAKLWWY	WALKWAY
AAILRTT	RATTAIL	AAINSSY	SANYASI	AAKMMNR	MARKMAN
AAILRTV	TRAVAIL	AAINSTT	ATTAINS	AAKMNSU	MANUKAS
AAILRWY	RAILWAY	AAINSTV	VANITAS	AAKMORU	AMOKURA
AAILSSS	ASSAILS	AAINTTT	ATTAINT	AAKMOSU	MOUSAKA
AAILSSV	SALIVAS	AAINTTU	TUTANIA	AAKMRSU	KARAMUS
	SALVIAS	AAINTTX	ANTITAX		KUMARAS
	VASSAIL	AAIOPRS	APORIAS	AAKMRUZ	MAZURKA
AAILSSW	WASSAIL	AAIOPRT	ATROPIA	AAKMRWY	WAYMARK
AAILTTT	LATITAT	AAIOPRV	OVIPARA	AAKMSSY	YASMAKS
AAIMMMT	MAMMATI	AAIORRS	ROSARIA	AAKNNTU	NUNATAK
AAIMMNO	AMMONIA	AAIORSU	SAOUARI	AAKNORS	ANORAKS
AAIMMSS	MIASMAS	AAIORTV	AVIATOR	AAKNRST	KANTARS
AAIMNNO	OMNIANA	AAIPPRS	APPAIRS	AAKNSST	ASKANTS
AAIMNNT	ANTIMAN	AAIPPRU	PUPARIA	AAKNSTW	WANKSTA
AAIMNOS	ANOSMIA	AAIPPTT	PITAPAT	AAKNSWZ	KWANZAS
AAIMNOT	AMATION	AAIPRST	PITARAS	AAKNTWY	TWANKAY
	ANIMATO	AAIPRSY	PIRAYAS	AAKOOPP	PAKAPOO
AAIMNPT	TIMPANA	AAIPRTT	PARTITA	AAKOPRS	PAKORAS
AAIMNRS	MARINAS	AAIPSTY	PITAYAS	AAKORST	OSTRAKA
AAIMNRT	MARTIAN	AAIPSZZ	PIAZZAS	AAKPRWY	PARKWAY
	TAMARIN	AAIQSSU	QUASSIA	AAKRSTU	KATSURA
AAIMNST	MANATIS	AAIQTUV	AQUAVIT	AAKRTUY	AUTARKY
	STAMINA	AAIRSST	ARISTAS	AAKSSTT	ATTASKS
AAIMNSV	VIMANAS		TARSIAS	AAKSTTT	ATTASKT
AAIMNTX	TAXIMAN	AAIRSTT	STRIATA	AAKSTUY	YUKATAS
AAIMRRS	MARARIS	AAIRSTY	RAIYATS	AALLLNS	LALLANS
AAIMRST	AMRITAS	AAIRSUW	WAIRUAS	AALLLSS	SALLALS
	TAMARIS	AAIRSWY	AIRWAYS	AALLMMS	MALLAMS
AAIMRSU	SAMURAI	AAIRSZZ	RAZZIAS	AALLMPU	AMPULLA

AALLNOX	ALLOXAN	AALOSTT	SALTATO	AAMPSSY	AMPASSY
AALLNPU	PLANULA	AALOSVW	AVOWALS	AAMRSST	MATRASS
AALLNSY	ALANYLS	AALOTTY	TALAYOT	AAMRSSU	ASARUMS
	NASALLY	AALPPRU	PAPULAR	AAMRSTU	SUMATRA
AALLNVY	NAVALLY	AALPPRY	PAPYRAL		TRAUMAS
AALLORS	AROLLAS	AALPRRS	PARRALS	AAMRTTY	TRYMATA
AALLOSZ	AZOLLAS	AALPRSW	ASPRAWL	AAMRTWY	TRAMWAY
AALLOTV	LAVOLTA	AALPRSY	PARLAYS	AAMSSTU	SATSUMA
AALLPPS	APPALLS	AALPRTY	LAPTRAY	AANNNOS	ANNONAS
AALLPPY	PAPALLY	AALPSTU	SPATULA	AANNOTT	ANNATTO
AALLRUY	AURALLY	AALQSWW	QAWWALS	AANNPSS	SANPANS
AALLRVY	VALLARY	AALRSST	ASTRALS	AANNPSW	SWANPAN
AALLSTT	ATLATLS		TARSALS	AANNRSU	ANURANS
	TALLATS	AALRSTT	STRATAL	AANNSYZ	NYANZAS
AALLUVV	VALVULA	AALRSTU	AUSTRAL	AANOQSY	YAQONAS
AALMMMS	MAMMALS	AALRSTY	ASTYLAR	AANORST	TORANAS
AALMMNO	AMMONAL		SATYRAL	AANORTT	ARNATTO
AALMMNS	ALMSMAN	AALSSSV	VASSALS	AANOSST	SONATAS
AALMMNT	MALTMAN	AALSSTU	ASSAULT	AANOSTT	ANATTOS
AALMNOS	SALAMON	AALSSUX	SAXAULS	AANPPSS	SAPPANS
AALMNOY	ANOMALY	AALSTUV	VALUTAS	AANPRST	PARTANS
AALMNPS	NAPALMS	AALSWYY	WAYLAYS		SPARTAN
AALMNSU	MANUALS	AAMMMRY	MAMMARY		TARPANS
AALMORT	ALAMORT	AAMMNRT	MANTRAM		TRAPANS
AALMORY	MAYORAL	AAMMNST	AMTMANS	AANPRSU	PURANAS
AALMOST	AMATOLS	AAMMOTY	MYOMATA	AANPSST	PASSANT
AALMPRY	PALMARY	AAMMRRS	MARRAMS	AANQRTU	QUARTAN
	PALMYRA	AAMMRST	RAMSTAM	AANRRSW	WARRANS
AALMPSS	PLASMAS		TAMMARS	AANRRSY	YARRANS
AALMRRU	RAMULAR	AAMMSUZ	MAZUMAS	AANRRTW	WARRANT
AALMRSU	ALARUMS	AAMNNNS	MANNANS	AANRSSS	SANSARS
AALMSSU	MASULAS	AAMNNOY	ANONYMA	AANRSTT	RATTANS
AALMSTY	AMYTALS	AAMNOOS	MANOAOS		TANTRAS
AALMTTU	MULATTA	AAMNORR	MARRANO		TARTANS
AALNNRU	ANNULAR		ORRAMAN	AANRSTY	YANTRAS
AALNNSU	ANNUALS	AAMNORS	OARSMAN	AANRSTZ	TARZANS
AALNPRT	PLANTAR		RAMONAS	AANRUWY	RUNAWAY
AALNPRU	LUPANAR	AAMNORT	AMORANT	AANSSTT	TSANTSA
AALNPST	PLANTAS	AAMNORZ	ROMANZA	AANSSTV	SAVANTS
	PLATANS	AAMNOSZ	AMAZONS	AANSSTZ	STANZAS
	SALTPAN	AAMNOTU	AUTOMAN	AANSSVY	NAYSAYS
AALNPUU	PUNALUA	AAMNOTY	ANATOMY	AANSTTT	STATANT
AALNQTU	QUANTAL	AAMNPRT	MANTRAP	AANSTUV	AVAUNTS
AALNRRU	RANULAR		RAMPANT	AANSWYY	ANYWAYS
AALNRSU	RANULAS	AAMNPRY	PARANYM	AAOORRW	WOORARA
AALNRSW	NARWALS	AAMNPSS	PASSMAN	AAOPSST	POTASSA
AALNRTT	LATRANT		SAMPANS		SAPOTAS
AALNRTU	NATURAL	AAMNPST	TAMPANS	AAOQSSU	OQUASSA
AALNSST	SANTALS		TAPSMAN	AAORRSU	AURORAS
AALNSTT	SALTANT	AAMNPTY	TYMPANA	AAORRSV	VARROAS
	TALANTS	AAMNRST	ARTSMAN	AAORSTT	TOTARAS
AALNSTU	SULTANA		MANTRAS	AAORSVV	VAVASOR
AALNSTY	ANALYST	AAMNRUY	MANUARY	AAOSTTV	OTTAVAS
AALNTTU	TALAUNT	AAMNSTU	MANTUAS	AAOTTUY	TATOUAY
AALOPPT	APPALTO		TAMANUS	AAOTWWY	TOWAWAY
AALOPRS	PARASOL	AAMOORS	AMOROSA	AAPPSWW	PAWPAWS
AALOPST	TAPALOS	AAMOPRS	PARAMOS	AAPRRSU	PARURAS
AALOPSY	PAYOLAS	AAMORRZ	ZAMARRO	AAPRRTT	RATTRAP
AALOPVV	PAVLOVA	AAMORSV	SAMOVAR	AAPRSST	SATRAPS
AALOPZZ	PALAZZO	AAMORTY	AMATORY	AAPRSTT	ATTRAPS
AALORRU	AURORAL	AAMOSSS	SAMOSAS	AAPRSTY	SATRAPY
AALORST	ALASTOR	AAMOSTT	STOMATA	AAPRTUU	RAUPATU
AALORSU	AROUSAL	AAMOTTU	AUTOMAT	AAPRTWY	PARTWAY
AALORTX	LAXATOR	AAMPRRT	RAMPART	AAPZZZZ	PAZZAZZ

AAQRSSU	QUASARS	**ABBDNOX**	BANDBOX	**ABBHISY**	BABYISH
AARRSSS	SARSARS	**ABBEESU**	BAUBEES	**ABBHJSU**	JUBBAHS
AARRSTT	TARTARS	**ABBEESW**	BAWBEES	**ABBHOOS**	BABOOSH
AARRSWY	WARRAYS	**ABBEFST**	FABBEST		HABOOBS
AARSSST	ASSARTS	**ABBEGIR**	GABBIER	**ABBHRRU**	RHUBARB
	SASTRAS	**ABBEGLR**	GABBLER	**ABBHTTU**	BATHTUB
AARSSTT	ASTARTS		GRABBLE	**ABBIIMN**	BAMBINI
	STRATAS	**ABBEGLS**	GABBLES	**ABBIJLS**	JILBABS
AARSSTY	SATYRAS	**ABBEGNO**	BOGBEAN	**ABBILLS**	LIBLABS
AARSSWW	WARSAWS	**ABBEGNU**	BUGBANE	**ABBILOR**	BILOBAR
AASSTTU	STATUAS	**ABBEGRR**	GRABBER	**ABBILOS**	BILBOAS
ABBBDEL	BABBLED	**ABBEGRS**	GABBERS	**ABBILOT**	BOBTAIL
	BLABBED	**ABBEGRU**	BUGBEAR	**ABBILSU**	BUBALIS
ABBBELR	BABBLER	**ABBEHLS**	SHABBLE	**ABBIMNO**	BAMBINO
	BLABBER	**ABBEILT**	BITABLE	**ABBIMSU**	BABUISM
	BRABBLE	**ABBEIRS**	BARBIES	**ABBINOR**	RABBONI
ABBBELS	BABBLES		RABBIES	**ABBINRS**	RABBINS
ABBBELU	ABUBBLE	**ABBEIST**	BABIEST	**ABBIORT**	RABBITO
ABBBITT	BABBITT		TABBIES	**ABBIRST**	RABBITS
ABBCDER	CRABBED	**ABBEISW**	SWABBIE	**ABBIRTY**	RABBITY
ABBCDES	SCABBED	**ABBEISY**	YABBIES	**ABBISTY**	BABYSIT
ABBCEHI	BABICHE	**ABBEJLS**	JABBLES	**ABBKLOU**	BLAUBOK
ABBCEHU	BABUCHE	**ABBEJRS**	JABBERS	**ABBLLOX**	BOXBALL
ABBCEIS	CABBIES	**ABBELLR**	BARBELL	**ABBLLRU**	BULLBAR
ABBCELR	CLABBER	**ABBELMR**	BRAMBLE	**ABBLLTU**	BULLBAT
ABBCELS	SCABBLE	**ABBELNS**	SNABBLE	**ABBLMRY**	BRAMBLY
ABBCERR	CRABBER	**ABBELOR**	BELABOR	**ABBLOOS**	BABOOLS
ABBCGIN	CABBING	**ABBELPR**	PRABBLE	**ABBMOOR**	BOMBORA
ABBCIIS	BIBASIC	**ABBELRR**	RABBLER	**ABBMOOS**	BAMBOOS
ABBCIKT	BACKBIT	**ABBELRS**	BARBELS	**ABBMOST**	BOMBAST
ABBCIRS	BICARBS		RABBLES	**ABBMOTU**	BUMBOAT
ABBCKUY	BUYBACK		SLABBER	**ABBNOOS**	BABOONS
ABBCOST	BOBCATS	**ABBELRU**	BARBULE	**ABBOORU**	RUBABOO
ABBCOTY	ABBOTCY	**ABBELRW**	WABBLER	**ABBORSS**	ABSORBS
ABBCRYY	CRYBABY	**ABBELSU**	BAUBLES	**ABBOSTY**	BATBOYS
ABBDDEL	DABBLED		BUBALES		BOBSTAY
ABBDDER	DRABBED	**ABBELSW**	BAWBLES	**ABBQSUY**	SQUABBY
ABBDEFR	FRABBED		WABBLES	**ABBRSSU**	BUSBARS
ABBDEGL	GABBLED	**ABBELUY**	BUYABLE	**ABBRSTU**	BARBUTS
ABBDEGR	GRABBED	**ABBEMUZ**	BUMBAZE	**ABBSSSU**	SUBBASS
ABBDEIT	TABBIED	**ABBENRS**	NABBERS	**ABCCCHI**	BACCHIC
ABBDEIY	YABBIED	**ABBEORS**	EARBOBS	**ABCCEIR**	ACERBIC
ABBDEJL	JABBLED	**ABBEOTX**	BEATBOX		BRECCIA
ABBDELR	DABBLER	**ABBERRS**	BARBERS	**ABCCEIS**	BACCIES
	DRABBLE	**ABBERST**	BARBETS		SEBACIC
	RABBLED		RABBETS	**ABCCEOS**	BACCOES
ABBDELS	DABBLES		STABBER	**ABCCHII**	BACCHII
	SLABBED	**ABBERSW**	SWABBER	**ABCCHTY**	BYCATCH
ABBDELW	WABBLED	**ABBERSY**	YABBERS	**ABCCILU**	CUBICAL
ABBDERR	DRABBER	**ABBESSU**	SUBBASE	**ABCCIMR**	CAMBRIC
ABBDERS	DABBERS	**ABBFIRT**	FRABBIT	**ABCCINU**	BUCCINA
ABBDERT	DRABBET	**ABBGGIN**	GABBING	**ABCCIOR**	BORACIC
ABBDEST	STABBED	**ABBGHSU**	GUBBAHS		BRACCIO
	TEBBADS	**ABBGIJN**	JABBING	**ABCCIOS**	BOCCIAS
ABBDESU	BEDAUBS	**ABBGINN**	NABBING	**ABCCISU**	CUBICAS
ABBDESW	SWABBED	**ABBGINR**	BARBING	**ABCCKOW**	BAWCOCK
ABBDGIN	DABBING	**ABBGINS**	SABBING	**ABCCKTU**	CUTBACK
ABBDHIJ	DJIBBAH	**ABBGINT**	TABBING	**ABCCOOR**	BAROCCO
ABBDILR	LIBBARD	**ABBGINU**	BUBINGA	**ABCCOOT**	TOBACCO
ABBDINR	RIBBAND	**ABBGINY**	BABYING	**ABCCSUU**	SUCCUBA
ABBDITY	DABBITY	**ABBGMSU**	BUMBAGS	**ABCDDEU**	ABDUCED
ABBDLRU	LUBBARD	**ABBGOOU**	BUGABOO	**ABCDEEH**	BEACHED
ABBDMOR	BOMBARD	**ABBGORS**	GABBROS	**ABCDEEL**	BELACED
ABBDMOU	BABUDOM	**ABBHIJS**	JIBBAHS		DEBACLE

ABCDEEM	EMBACED	ABCEHRT	BATCHER	ABCENOZ	CABEZON
ABCDEHT	BATCHED		BRACHET	ABCENRU	UNBRACE
ABCDEHU	DEBAUCH	ABCEHST	BATCHES	ABCENSU	CUBANES
ABCDEIK	DIEBACK	ABCEIIT	ABIETIC	ABCEOOS	CABOOSE
ABCDEIN	CABINED	ABCEIKS	BACKIES	ABCEORR	BRACERO
ABCDEIP	PEDICAB	ABCEIKT	TIEBACK	ABCEORS	BORACES
ABCDEIR	CARBIDE	ABCEILL	ICEBALL	ABCEORU	CORBEAU
ABCDEKL	BLACKED	ABCEILM	ALEMBIC	ABCEORV	CABOVER
ABCDEKR	REDBACK		CEMBALI	ABCERRS	BRACERS
ABCDELO	CODABLE	ABCEILR	CALIBER	ABCERSU	RUBACES
ABCDEOR	BROCADE		CALIBRE		SUBRACE
ABCDERS	DECARBS	ABCEILT	CITABLE	ABCESSS	ABSCESS
ABCDERT	BRACTED	ABCEIMO	AMOEBIC	ABCESTW	WEBCAST
ABCDERU	CUDBEAR	ABCEINR	CARBINE	ABCFIKN	FINBACK
ABCDESU	ABDUCES	ABCEINT	CABINET	ABCFIKT	BACKFIT
	SCUBAED	ABCEIOR	AEROBIC	ABCFILO	BIFOCAL
ABCDHIO	ICHABOD	ABCEIOT	ICEBOAT	ABCFIOT	BIOFACT
ABCDHOR	CHOBDAR	ABCEIRS	ASCRIBE	ABCFIRS	FABRICS
ABCDHOS	BODACHS		CABRIES	ABCFKLY	FLYBACK
ABCDIIS	DIBASIC		CARBIES	ABCFLOO	COBLOAF
ABCDILO	CABILDO		CARIBES	ABCFNOS	CONFABS
ABCDILR	BALDRIC	ABCEIRZ	ZEBRAIC	ABCGHIN	BACHING
ABCDINS	ABSCIND	ABCEISS	ABSCISE	ABCGHKO	HOGBACK
ABCDIRS	SCABRID		SCABIES	ABCGIKN	BACKING
ABCDIRT	CATBIRD		SEBASIC	ABCGILN	CABLING
ABCDIRU	BAUDRIC	ABCEITT	TABETIC	ABCGINR	BRACING
ABCDIRW	BAWDRIC	ABCEJST	ABJECTS	ABCGKLO	BACKLOG
ABCDISU	SUBACID	ABCEKLN	BLACKEN	ABCGMSU	SCUMBAG
ABCDNOS	ABSCOND	ABCEKLO	BECLOAK	ABCHHII	HIBACHI
ABCDOOR	CORDOBA	ABCEKLR	BLACKER	ABCHILS	CHABLIS
ABCDORR	BROCARD	ABCEKNR	BRACKEN	ABCHIMT	BATHMIC
ABCDSTU	ABDUCTS	ABCEKRS	BACKERS	ABCHIOT	COHABIT
ABCEEHS	BEACHES		REBACKS	ABCHKOU	CHABOUK
ABCEEHU	EBAUCHE	ABCEKRT	BRACKET	ABCHKSU	CHABUKS
ABCEELS	BELACES	ABCEKST	BACKETS	ABCHKTU	HACKBUT
ABCEEMR	EMBRACE		BACKSET	ABCHKUW	HAWBUCK
ABCEEMS	EMBACES		SETBACK	ABCHNOR	BROCHAN
ABCEENR	CARBEEN	ABCEKSY	BACKSEY	ABCHNRU	BRAUNCH
	CARBENE	ABCEKTW	WETBACK	ABCHNRY	BRANCHY
ABCEENS	ABSENCE	ABCELLS	BECALLS	ABCHOSX	CASHBOX
ABCEERR	ACERBER	ABCELLU	BULLACE	ABCHOTT	CHATBOT
	CEREBRA	ABCELMO	CEMBALO	ABCHPSU	HUBCAPS
	REBRACE	ABCELMR	CAMBREL	ABCIILL	BACILLI
ABCEERU	BERCEAU		CLAMBER	ABCIILN	ALBINIC
ABCEESS	BECASSE	ABCELMS	BECALMS	ABCIILS	BASILIC
ABCEESU	BECAUSE		SCAMBLE	ABCIILT	ALBITIC
ABCEFIS	BIFACES	ABCELOP	PLACEBO	ABCIIMN	MINICAB
ABCEGIR	RIBCAGE	ABCELOV	VOCABLE	ABCIIMS	IAMBICS
ABCEGMO	CAMBOGE	ABCELPS	BECLASP	ABCIIOR	CIBORIA
ABCEGOR	BROCAGE	ABCELPU	BLUECAP	ABCIIOT	ABIOTIC
ABCEGOS	BOCAGES	ABCELPY	BYPLACE	ABCIJNO	JACOBIN
	BOSCAGE	ABCELRS	CABLERS	ABCIKLT	BACKLIT
ABCEGSU	CUBAGES	ABCELRU	CURABLE	ABCIKPS	BIPACKS
ABCEHKL	BECHALK	ABCELRW	BECRAWL	ABCIKSY	SICKBAY
ABCEHKO	BACKHOE	ABCELST	CABLETS	ABCILNO	COALBIN
ABCEHLO	CHAEBOL	ABCELSU	BASCULE	ABCILOU	ABOULIC
ABCEHLU	BAUCHLE	ABCEMRS	CAMBERS	ABCILRS	SCRIBAL
ABCEHMR	BECHARM		CEMBRAS	ABCILTU	CUBITAL
	BRECHAM		CRAMBES	ABCIMMS	CAMBISM
	CHAMBER		WEBCAMS	ABCIMMU	CAMBIUM
	CHAMBRE	ABCEMSW	EXCAMBS	ABCIMST	CAMBIST
ABCEHNR	BRECHAN	ABCEMSX	EXCAMBS	ABCIMSU	CUMBIAS
ABCEHOS	BASOCHE	ABCENOR	BACONER	ABCINOR	CORBINA
ABCEHRS	BRACHES	ABCENOS	BEACONS	ABCINOS	BONACIS
		ABCENOW	COWBANE		

ABCINOT	BOTANIC	ABDDEEZ	BEDAZED		SABERED
ABCIORR	BARRICO	ABDDEIL	ADDIBLE	ABDEERT	BERATED
ABCIORS	CABRIOS	ABDDEIN	ABIDDEN		BETREAD
ABCIORU	CARIBOU		BANDIED		DEBATER
ABCIOUV	BIVOUAC	ABDDEIR	BRAIDED		REBATED
ABCIRST	CABRITS	ABDDEIS	BADDIES		TABERED
ABCIRTY	BARYTIC	ABDDELR	BLADDER	ABDEERW	BEWARED
ABCISSS	ABSCISS	ABDDELU	BLAUDED	ABDEERY	BEEYARD
ABCJOSU	JACOBUS	ABDDENR	BRANDED		BERAYED
ABCKLLY	BLACKLY	ABDDEOR	ABORDED	ABDEESS	DEBASES
ABCKLOT	BACKLOT		BOARDED		SEABEDS
ABCKMOT	TOMBACK		ROADBED	ABDEEST	BESTEAD
ABCKMRU	BUCKRAM	ABDDEOY	DEADBOY		DEBATES
ABCKMUZ	ZAMBUCK	ABDDERW	BEDWARD	ABDEESZ	BEDAZES
ABCKNNO	BANNOCK	ABDDEST	BADDEST	ABDEETT	ABETTED
ABCKNRU	RUNBACK	ABDDESY	DAYBEDS	ABDEETX	BETAXED
ABCKNSU	SUNBACK	ABDDHIS	BADDISH	ABDEFFL	BAFFLED
ABCKNTU	CUTBANK	ABDDHSU	BUDDHAS	ABDEFLT	FLATBED
ABCKORS	BAROCKS	ABDDINS	DISBAND	ABDEFLU	LEAFBUD
ABCKORY	ROCKABY	ABDDLLO	ODDBALL	ABDEFOR	FORBADE
ABCKOSW	SOWBACK	ABDDMOR	DAMBROD	ABDEFOS	SOFABED
ABCKOTU	BACKOUT	ABDEEFG	FEEDBAG	ABDEFRW	BEDWARF
	OUTBACK	ABDEEFL	FEELBAD	ABDEFST	BEDFAST
ABCKPSU	BACKUPS	ABDEEGL	BEAGLED	ABDEGGL	BLAGGED
ABCKRSU	BUCKRAS	ABDEEGR	REBADGE	ABDEGGR	BRAGGED
ABCKSTU	SACKBUT	ABDEEGZ	BEGAZED	ABDEGHI	BIGHEAD
	SUBTACK	ABDEEHO	OBEAHED	ABDEGHR	BEGHARD
ABCKSUW	BUCKSAW	ABDEEHS	BEHEADS	ABDEGIN	BEADING
	SAWBUCK	ABDEEHT	BEATHED	ABDEGIR	ABRIDGE
ABCLLOY	CALLBOY	ABDEEHV	BEHAVED		BRIGADE
ABCLMNU	CLUBMAN	ABDEEIR	BEADIER	ABDEGLM	GAMBLED
ABCLMOY	CYMBALO		BEARDIE	ABDEGLN	BANGLED
ABCLMSY	CYMBALS	ABDEEJS	BEJADES	ABDEGLR	BELGARD
ABCLMUU	BACULUM	ABDEEJT	JETBEAD		GARBLED
ABCLNOS	BLANCOS	ABDEEKL	LAKEBED	ABDEGLS	BEGLADS
ABCLNOY	BALCONY	ABDEEKR	BERAKED	ABDEGNO	BONDAGE
ABCLNSU	SUBCLAN	ABDEEKS	DEBEAKS		DOGBANE
ABCLOOX	COALBOX	ABDEELL	LABELED	ABDEGOS	BODEGAS
ABCLOST	COBALTS	ABDEELM	BELDAME	ABDEGRS	BADGERS
ABCLOVY	VOCABLY		BEMEDAL	ABDEHIL	HIDABLE
ABCLRUY	CURABLY		EMBALED	ABDEHIT	HABITED
ABCMOPS	MOBCAPS	ABDEELN	ENABLED	ABDEHLM	HAMBLED
ABCMORS	COMARBS	ABDEELR	BEDERAL	ABDEHLR	HALBERD
	CRAMBOS		BLEARED	ABDEHOW	BOWHEAD
ABCMOST	COMBATS	ABDEELS	BEADLES	ABDEHRS	BERDASH
	TOMBACS	ABDEELT	BELATED		BRASHED
ABCMRSS	SCRAMBS		BLEATED	ABDEHRT	BREADTH
ABCNORS	CARBONS	ABDEELY	BELAYED	ABDEHSU	SUBHEAD
	CORBANS		DYEABLE	ABDEIIL	ALIBIED
ABCORRW	CROWBAR	ABDEEMN	BEADMEN	ABDEIKT	BATIKED
ABCORSS	BRASCOS		BEDEMAN	ABDEILP	BIPEDAL
ABCORSX	BOXCARS		BENAMED		PIEBALD
ABCORSY	CARBOYS	ABDEEMR	AMBERED	ABDEILR	BALDIER
ABCOSSU	BASUCOS		BREAMED		BEDRAIL
ABCSSTU	SACBUTS		EMBREAD		BRAILED
	SUBACTS	ABDEEMS	EMBASED		RAILBED
ABDDDEL	BLADDED	ABDEEMT	BEDMATE		RIDABLE
ABDDDER	BRADDED	ABDEEMY	EMBAYED	ABDEILS	BALDIES
ABDDEEJ	BEJADED	ABDEEMZ	BEMAZED		DIABLES
ABDDEER	BEARDED	ABDEEPR	BEDRAPE		DISABLE
	BREADED		PREBADE	ABDEILT	LIBATED
	DEBEARD	ABDEERR	BARREED	ABDEILU	AUDIBLE
ABDDEES	DEBASED	ABDEERS	BEADERS	ABDEILY	BEADILY
ABDDEET	DEBATED		DEBASER	ABDEIMO	AMEBOID

ABDEIMR	EMBRAID
ABDEIMS	IMBASED
ABDEINR	BANDIER
	BRAINED
ABDEINS	BANDIES
	BASINED
ABDEINW	BEDAWIN
ABDEIRR	BARDIER
	BRAIDER
	BRIARED
	RABIDER
ABDEIRS	ABIDERS
	BARDIES
	BRAISED
	DARBIES
	SEABIRD
	SIDEBAR
ABDEIRT	REDBAIT
	TRIBADE
ABDEIRU	DAUBIER
ABDEIRW	BAWDIER
ABDEIRX	AXEBIRD
ABDEISS	BIASSED
ABDEIST	BASTIDE
ABDEISU	SUBIDEA
ABDEISW	BAWDIES
ABDEJRU	ABJURED
ABDEKLN	BLANKED
ABDEKLU	BAULKED
ABDEKNR	BRANKED
ABDEKNU	UNBAKED
ABDEKRS	DEBARKS
ABDELMP	BEDLAMP
ABDELMR	MARBLED
	RAMBLED
ABDELMS	BEDLAMS
	BELDAMS
ABDELMW	WAMBLED
ABDELMY	EMBAYLD
ABDELNR	BLANDER
ABDELNU	UNBALED
ABDELOR	LABORED
ABDELOS	ALBEDOS
ABDELOT	BLOATED
	LOBATED
ABDELOW	DOWABLE
ABDELPU	DUPABLE
ABDELPY	PYEBALD
ABDELRR	DRABLER
ABDELRS	BEDRALS
	BLADERS
ABDELRT	BLARTED
ABDELRU	DURABLE
ABDELRW	BRAWLED
	WARBLED
ABDELRY	DRYABLE
ABDELST	BALDEST
	BLASTED
	STABLED
ABDELSU	BELAUDS
ABDELTT	BATTLED
	BLATTED
ABDELTU	ABLUTED
ABDEMMO	MAMBOED
ABDEMNO	ABDOMEN
ABDEMNS	BEDAMNS
ABDEMRU	RUMBAED
ABDENNR	BRANNED
ABDENOR	BANDORE
	BROADEN
ABDENOT	BATONED
ABDENOY	NAEBODY
ABDENPS	BEDPANS
ABDENRR	BRANDER
	REBRAND
ABDENRS	BANDERS
ABDENRT	BARTEND
ABDENRU	UNBARED
ABDENRW	BRAWNED
ABDENSS	BADNESS
ABDENSU	SUBDEAN
	UNBASED
ABDENSY	BENDAYS
ABDENTU	UNBATED
ABDEOOT	TABOOED
ABDEORR	ARBORED
	BOARDER
	BROADER
	REBOARD
ABDEORT	ABORTED
	BORATED
	TABORED
ABDEORV	BRAVOED
ABDEOST	BOASTED
ABDEOTU	BOUTADE
ABDEQSU	BASQUED
ABDERSS	BRASSED
	SERDABS
ABDERST	DABSTER
	TABERDS
ABDERSU	DAUBERS
	EARBUDS
	SUBEDAR
ABDERSV	ADVERBS
ABDERSY	REDBAYS
ABDERTY	DRYBEAT
ABDERUY	DAUBERY
ABDETTU	ABUTTED
ABDFIRT	FATBIRD
ABDGGIN	BADGING
ABDGGOR	BOGGARD
ABDGIIN	ABIDING
ABDGILN	BALDING
	BLADING
ABDGINN	BANDING
ABDGINO	ABODING
ABDGINR	BARDING
	BRIGAND
ABDGINT	DINGBAT
ABDGINU	DAUBING
ABDGINW	WINDBAG
ABDGIRT	DIRTBAG
ABDGLNO	BOGLAND
ABDGLUY	LADYBUG
ABDGNOS	BANDOGS
ABDGORS	BODRAGS
ABDHHOS	DOBHASH
ABDHIIT	ADHIBIT
ABDHILS	BALDISH
ABDHMOR	RHABDOM
ABDHMSU	BUDMASH
ABDHMTU	MUDBATH
ABDHNOR	BODHRAN
ABDHNSU	HUSBAND
ABDHOSY	HOBDAYS
ABDHRSU	BURDASH
	RHABDUS
ABDIINO	ANOBIID
ABDIJRY	JAYBIRD
ABDIKNW	BAWDKIN
ABDIKRS	DISBARK
ABDILMO	BIMODAL
ABDILOO	DIABOLO
ABDILOR	LABROID
ABDILOT	TABLOID
ABDILRS	BRIDALS
	LABRIDS
	RIBALDS
ABDILRW	AWLBIRD
ABDILRY	RABIDLY
ABDILUY	AUDIBLY
ABDILWY	BAWDILY
ABDIMNR	BIRDMAN
ABDIMOR	AMBROID
ABDIMRS	BARDISM
ABDIMRY	MAYBIRD
ABDINOR	INBOARD
ABDINOT	BANDITO
ABDINRS	RIBANDS
ABDINRT	ANTBIRD
ABDINRU	UNBRAID
ABDINST	BANDITS
ABDIOSU	BADIOUS
ABDIPRU	UPBRAID
ABDIRRS	BRAIRDS
	BRIARDS
ABDIRSS	DISBARS
ABDIRSU	RIBAUDS
	SUBARID
ABDIRTY	TRIBADY
ABDKNOO	BANDOOK
ABDKOOY	DAYBOOK
ABDLLNY	BLANDLY
ABDLLOR	BOLLARD
ABDLNOR	BANDROL
ABDLORY	BROADLY
ABDLOSU	BUSLOAD
ABDLOYY	LADYBOY
ABDLRUY	DURABLY
ABDLRYY	BYRLADY
ABDLSUU	SUBDUAL
ABDMNNO	BONDMAN
ABDMRUY	MARYBUD
ABDNOOR	BRADOON
	ONBOARD
ABDNOPR	PROBAND
ABDNORS	ROBANDS
ABDNOSU	ABOUNDS
	BAUSOND
ABDNOSX	SANDBOX
ABDNOSY	SANDBOY
ABDNOVY	ANYBODY

ABDNRSU	SANDBUR	ABEEJRS	BAJREES	ABEERST	BEATERS
ABDNRTU	TURBAND	ABEEKLR	BLEAKER		BERATES
ABDNSTY	STANDBY	ABEEKLS	KABELES		REBATES
ABDOORW	BARWOOD	ABEEKNT	BETAKEN	ABEERSV	BEAVERS
ABDOOWY	BAYWOOD	ABEEKNV	BEKNAVE	ABEERSW	BEWARES
ABDORRS	BORDARS	ABEEKNY	EYEBANK	ABEERSY	EBAYERS
ABDORSS	ADSORBS	ABEEKPR	BARKEEP		EYEBARS
ABDORSY	BOYARDS		PREBAKE	ABEERSZ	ZEREBAS
	BYROADS	ABEEKPS	BESPAKE	ABEERTT	ABETTER
ABDOSYY	DAYBOYS		BESPEAK		BERETTA
ABDRRSU	DURBARS	ABEEKRR	BREAKER	ABEERVY	BEAVERY
ABDRSSU	ABSURDS	ABEEKRS	BEAKERS	ABEERWY	BEWEARY
ABDRSTU	BUSTARD		BERAKES	ABEESST	SEBATES
ABDRUZZ	BUZZARD	ABEEKST	BETAKES	ABEESWX	BEESWAX
ABEEEGR	BEERAGE	ABEELLR	LABELER	ABEETXY	EXABYTE
ABEEELS	SEEABLE		RELABEL	ABEFFIS	BAFFIES
ABEEELV	EYEABLE	ABEELLY	EYEBALL	ABEFFLR	BAFFLER
ABEEEMY	EYEBEAM	ABEELMM	EMBLEMA	ABEFFLS	BAFFLES
ABEEERV	BEREAVE	ABEELMS	EMBALES	ABEFFOT	OFFBEAT
ABEEFFL	EFFABLE	ABEELMT	BEAMLET	ABEFGIL	FILABEG
ABEEFLM	FLAMBEE	ABEELMZ	EMBLAZE	ABEFGLS	BEFLAGS
ABEEFLO	BEEFALO	ABEELNP	PLEBEAN	ABEFGST	GABFEST
ABEEFLS	BEFLEAS	ABEELNR	ENABLER	ABEFILN	FINABLE
ABEEFTU	BEAUFET	ABEELNS	BALEENS	ABEFILR	FRIABLE
ABEEGGS	GEEBAGS		ENABLES	ABEFILS	FAIBLES
ABEEGHR	HERBAGE	ABEELNT	TENABLE	ABEFILU	FIBULAE
ABEEGHS	BEEGAHS	ABEELNU	NEBULAE	ABEFILX	FIXABLE
	BHAGEES	ABEELOR	EARLOBE	ABEFINU	BEAUFIN
ABEEGLL	GABELLE	ABEELPR	BEPEARL	ABEFIRT	BAREFIT
	GELABLE	ABEELPS	BELEAPS	ABEFITY	BEATIFY
ABEEGLR	BEAGLER	ABEELPT	BELEAPT	ABEFLLS	BEFALLS
ABEEGLS	BEAGLES	ABEELQU	EQUABLE	ABEFLLU	BALEFUL
ABEEGLT	GETABLE	ABEELRR	BLEARER	ABEFLLY	FLYABLE
ABEEGNR	REBEGAN		ERRABLE	ABEFLMS	FLAMBES
ABEEGPW	WEBPAGE	ABEELRT	BLEATER	ABEFLNU	BANEFUL
ABEEGRR	GERBERA		RETABLE	ABEFLNY	FLYBANE
ABEEGRS	ABREGES	ABEELRY	BELAYER	ABEFLRS	FABLERS
	BAREGES	ABEELST	BELATES	ABEFLRY	FRYABLE
	BARGEES	ABEELSU	SUEABLE	ABEFMOS	BEFOAMS
ABEEGRU	AUBERGE		USEABLE	ABEFMRS	FERBAMS
ABEEGRW	BREWAGE	ABEELSV	BESLAVE	ABEFORR	FORBARE
ABEEGSZ	BEGAZES	ABEELSW	SEWABLE		FORBEAR
ABEEHJS	BHAJEES	ABEEMNS	BASEMEN	ABEFORX	FAREBOX
ABEEHLW	HEWABLE		BEMEANS	ABEFORY	FOREBAY
ABEEHMS	BESHAME		BENAMES	ABEFPRS	PREFABS
ABEEHMT	EMBATHE	ABEEMNT	BEMEANT	ABEGGIR	BAGGIER
ABEEHNN	HENBANE	ABEEMRS	AMBEERS	ABEGGIS	BAGGIES
ABEEHNS	BANSHEE		BEAMERS	ABEGGLR	BLAGGER
	BEENAHS		BESMEAR	ABEGGMO	GAMBOGE
	SHEBEAN	ABEEMRV	EMBRAVE	ABEGGNU	BUGGANE
ABEEHNT	BENEATH	ABEEMSS	EMBASES	ABEGGRR	BRAGGER
ABEEHRT	BREATHE	ABEEMST	EMBASTE	ABEGGRS	BAGGERS
ABEEHRV	BEHAVER	ABEENNW	BAWNEEN		BEGGARS
ABEEHSV	BEHAVES	ABEENRV	VERBENA	ABEGGRU	BURGAGE
ABEEHTY	EYEBATH	ABEENRY	BEANERY	ABEGGRY	BEGGARY
ABEEIKR	BEAKIER	ABEEORS	AEROBES	ABEGHNS	SHEBANG
ABEEILS	BAILEES	ABEEORT	ABORTEE	ABEGHOR	BEGORAH
ABEEIMR	BEAMIER	ABEEPRS	PREBASE	ABEGHRU	BEARHUG
ABEEINS	BEANIES	ABEEPST	BESPATE	ABEGIKL	BAGLIKE
ABEEINT	BETAINE	ABEERRS	BEARERS	ABEGILV	GIVABLE
ABEEIRT	BEATIER		BREARES	ABEGIMN	BEAMING
	EBRIATE	ABEERRT	REBATER	ABEGIMR	GAMBIER
ABEEIST	BEASTIE		TABRERE	ABEGIMT	MEGABIT
ABEEJMS	JAMBEES		TEREBRA	ABEGINN	BEANING

ABEGINO	BEGONIA		HALBERT		WIRABLE
ABEGINR	BEARING	ABEHLSS	BLASHES	ABEILRV	BILAYER
ABEGINS	SABEING	ABEHMNO	HAMBONE	ABEILSS	ABSEILS
ABEGINT	BEATING	ABEHNOS	HEBONAS		ISABELS
ABEGINV	ABYEING	ABEHNRY	ABHENRY		LABISES
	EBAYING	ABEHRRS	BRASHER	ABEILST	ABLEIST
ABEGIPP	BAGPIPE		HERBARS		ALBITES
ABEGKLU	BULKAGE	ABEHRRY	HERBARY		ASTILBE
ABEGKOR	BROKAGE	ABEHRSS	BASHERS		BASTILE
ABEGKOS	BOSKAGE		BRASHES		BESTIAL
ABEGLLS	BEGALLS	ABEHRST	BATHERS		BLASTIE
ABEGLMR	GAMBLER		BERTHAS		LIBATES
	GAMBREL		BREATHS		STABILE
ABEGLMS	GAMBLES	ABEHRTY	BREATHY	ABEILSW	BEWAILS
ABEGLNR	BRANGLE	ABEIILL	BAILLIE	ABEILSY	BAILEYS
ABEGLNS	BANGLES	ABEIILS	ALIBIES	ABEILSZ	SIZABLE
ABEGLOR	ALBERGO		BAILIES	ABEILVV	BIVALVE
ABEGLOT	GLOBATE		BIALIES	ABEIMNP	PEMBINA
ABEGLRR	GARBLER	ABEIINN	BIENNIA	ABEIMNR	MIRBANE
ABEGLRS	GARBLES	ABEIINT	BAINITE	ABEIMNT	AMBIENT
ABEGLRU	BLAGUER	ABEIJMR	JAMBIER	ABEIMRR	BARMIER
ABEGLSS	BAGLESS	ABEIJNS	BASENJI	ABEIMRS	AMBRIES
ABEGLST	GABLETS	ABEIKKS	BAKKIES	ABEIMSS	IMBASES
ABEGLSU	BELUGAS	ABEIKLL	LIKABLE	ABEIMSU	MAUBIES
	BLAGUES	ABEIKLR	BALKIER	ABEINOT	NIOBATE
ABEGMOR	EMBARGO	ABEIKLS	SKIABLE	ABEINPT	BEPAINT
ABEGMRU	UMBRAGE	ABEIKLT	BATLIKE	ABEINRR	BARNIER
ABEGMST	GAMBETS	ABEIKNR	INBREAK	ABEINRT	ATEBRIN
ABEGNNT	BANTENG	ABEIKNT	BEATNIK	ABEINRW	WEBINAR
ABEGNOR	BEGROAN	ABEIKRR	BARKIER	ABEINRZ	ZEBRINA
ABEGNOS	NOSEBAG		BRAKIER	ABEINSS	SABINES
ABEGNRS	BANGERS	ABEIKWY	BIKEWAY	ABEINST	BANTIES
	GRABENS	ABEILLN	LINABLE		BASINET
ABEGNSW	BEGNAWS	ABEILLO	LOBELIA		BESAINT
ABEGOPY	PAGEBOY	ABEILLP	PLIABLE		BESTAIN
ABEGORR	BEGORRA	ABEILLR	BRAILLE	ABEINTT	TABINET
ABEGORS	BORAGES		LIBERAL	ABEIORS	ISOBARE
ABEGORX	GEARBOX	ABEILLS	BALLIES	ABEIOSS	ABIOSES
ABEGOSZ	GAZEBOS	ABEILLV	LIVABLE		ISOBASE
ABEGOTT	BOTTEGA	ABEILMN	MINABLE	ABEIOST	BOATIES
ABEGOUY	BUOYAGE	ABEILMR	BALMIER	ABEIOTV	OBVIATE
ABEGRRU	GARBURE		LAMBIER	ABEIPST	BAPTISE
ABEGRST	BARGEST		MIRABLE	ABEIPTZ	BAPTIZE
ABEGSTU	BAGUETS		REMBLAI	ABEIRRR	BARRIER
	TUBAGES	ABEILMS	ABLEISM	ABEIRRS	BARRIES
ABEHILR	HIRABLE		EMBAILS		BRASIER
ABEHIMO	BOHEMIA		LAMBIES	ABEIRRT	ARBITER
ABEHIMS	BEAMISH	RAEILMT	BIMETAL		RAREBIT
ABEHIMT	IMBATHE		LIMBATE	ABEIRRW	WARBIER
ABEHINS	BANSHIE		TIMBALE	ABEIRRZ	BIZARRE
ABEHIRS	BEARISH	ABEILMU	BUMELIA		BRAZIER
ABEHISU	BEAUISH	ABEILMW	WEBMAIL	ABEIRSS	BASSIER
ABEHITU	HABITUE	ABEILMX	MIXABLE		BRAISES
ABEHITZ	ZABTIEH	ABEILMY	BEAMILY		BRASSIE
ABEHKLS	KEBLAHS	ABEILMZ	IMBLAZE	ABEIRST	BAITERS
ABEHKNT	BETHANK	ABEILNP	BIPLANE		BARITES
ABEHKRU	HAUBERK	ABEILNS	LESBIAN		REBAITS
ABEHKTU	KETUBAH	ABEILOS	OBELIAS		TERBIAS
ABEHLMS	HAMBLES	ABEILPT	PATIBLE	ABEIRSX	BRAXIES
	SHAMBLE	ABEILRS	BAILERS	ABEIRSZ	BRAIZES
ABEHLNT	BENTHAL	ABEILRT	LIBRATE		ZERIBAS
ABEHLNU	UNHABLE		TABLIER	ABEIRTT	BATTIER
ABEHLRS	HERBALS		TRIABLE		BIRETTA
ABEHLRT	BLATHER	ABEILRW	BRAWLIE		RATBITE

Code	Word(s)
ABEIRTV	VIBRATE
ABEIRUX	EXURBIA
ABEISSS	BIASSES
ABEISTT	BATISTE
	BISTATE
ABEISTW	BAWTIES
ABEISUV	ABUSIVE
ABEITUX	BAUXITE
ABEJLUY	BLUEJAY
ABEJMNO	JAMBONE
	JOBNAME
ABEJMNS	ENJAMBS
ABEJMRS	JAMBERS
ABEJMUX	JAMBEUX
ABEJNOS	BANJOES
ABEJNOW	JAWBONE
ABEJNST	BEJANTS
ABEJORS	JERBOAS
ABEJRRU	ABJURER
ABEJRSU	ABJURES
ABEKKKU	BUKKAKE
ABEKLLY	BLEAKLY
ABEKLMS	KEMBLAS
ABEKLNR	BLANKER
ABEKLNT	BLANKET
ABEKLOP	POKABLE
ABEKLRS	BALKERS
ABEKLRU	BAULKER
ABEKMNS	EMBANKS
ABEKMRS	EMBARKS
ABEKMSU	SAMBUKE
ABEKNRS	BANKERS
	BARKENS
ABEKNRU	UNBRAKE
ABEKNST	BANKETS
ABEKNSU	SUNBAKE
ABEKOOR	ABROOKE
ABEKOTU	OUTBAKE
ABEKPRU	BREAKUP
	UPBREAK
ABEKRRS	BARKERS
ABEKSST	BASKETS
ABELLMN	BELLMAN
ABELLMS	EMBALLS
ABELLNT	NETBALL
ABELLOS	LOSABLE
ABELLOV	LOVABLE
	VOLABLE
ABELLRS	BALLERS
ABELLRU	RUBELLA
	RULABLE
ABELLST	BALLETS
ABELLTU	BALLUTE
	BULLATE
ABELMMR	MEMBRAL
ABELMMS	EMBALMS
ABELMNT	BELTMAN
	LAMBENT
ABELMNU	ALBUMEN
ABELMOV	MOVABLE
ABELMRR	MARBLER
	RAMBLER
ABELMRS	AMBLERS
	BLAMERS
	LAMBERS
	MARBLES
	RAMBLES
ABELMRT	LAMBERT
ABELMSU	BEMAULS
ABELMSW	WAMBLES
ABELMTU	MUTABLE
ABELNOS	BONSELA
ABELNOT	NOTABLE
ABELNOW	OWNABLE
ABELNOY	BALONEY
ABELNRS	BRANLES
	BRANSLE
ABELNRT	BRANTLE
ABELNRU	NEBULAR
ABELNRY	BLARNEY
ABELNSU	NEBULAS
	UNBALES
ABELNSY	BYLANES
ABELNSZ	BENZALS
ABELNTU	ABLUENT
	TUNABLE
ABELNTY	TENABLY
ABELOPR	ROPABLE
ABELOPS	POSABLE
ABELOPT	POTABLE
ABELORR	LABORER
ABELORS	LABROSE
ABELORT	BLOATER
ABELORU	RUBEOLA
ABELORW	ROWABLE
ABELOSS	BOLASES
ABELOST	BOATELS
	OBLATES
ABELOSV	ABSOLVE
ABELOSW	SOWABLE
ABELOTT	TOTABLE
ABELOTV	VOTABLE
ABELOTW	TEABOWL
	TOWABLE
ABELPRU	PUBERAL
ABELPTY	TYPABLE
ABELQUY	EQUABLY
ABELRRS	BARRELS
ABELRRW	BRAWLER
	WARBLER
ABELRSS	BARLESS
	BRALESS
ABELRST	ALBERTS
	BATLERS
	BLASTER
	LABRETS
	STABLER
ABELRSV	VERBALS
ABELRSW	BAWLERS
	WARBLES
ABELRSY	BARLEYS
ABELRSZ	BLAZERS
ABELRTT	BATTLER
	BLATTER
	BRATTLE
ABELRTW	BLEWART
ABELRUZ	ZEBRULA
ABELRVY	BRAVELY
ABELSST	BASTLES
	STABLES
ABELSSU	SUBSALE
ABELSTT	BATLETS
	BATTELS
	BATTLES
	BLATEST
	TABLETS
ABELSTU	SUBLATE
ABELSTY	BAETYLS
	BEASTLY
ABELSUY	USEABLY
ABELSWY	BAWLEYS
	BYELAWS
ABELTWY	BELTWAY
ABEMMOS	MAMBOES
ABEMMRS	BAMMERS
ABEMNOS	AMBONES
	BEMOANS
ABEMNOT	BOATMEN
ABEMNRY	BYREMAN
	MYRBANE
ABEMNST	BATSMEN
ABEMNSU	SUNBEAM
ABEMNSY	BYNAMES
ABEMORT	BROMATE
ABEMOTU	OUTBEAM
ABEMRST	TAMBERS
ABEMRSW	BESWARM
ABEMSSY	EMBASSY
ABENNOR	BARONNE
ABENNOS	NANOBES
ABENNRR	BRANNER
ABENNRS	BANNERS
ABENNST	BANNETS
ABENORS	BORANES
ABENORT	BARONET
	REBOANT
ABENORW	RAWBONE
ABENORZ	ZEBRANO
ABENOST	ONBEATS
ABENOSY	SOYBEAN
ABENOTY	BAYONET
ABENPSU	SUBPENA
ABENQTU	BANQUET
ABENRRS	BARRENS
ABENRRU	URBANER
ABENRST	BANTERS
	BARNETS
ABENRSU	UNBARES
	UNBEARS
ABENRSY	BARNEYS
ABENRSZ	BRAZENS
ABENRUX	EXURBAN
ABENSST	ABSENTS
	BASNETS
ABENSTT	BATTENS
ABENSTU	BUTANES
	SUNBEAT
ABENSTZ	BEZANTS
ABENTZZ	BEZZANT
ABEOOST	SEABOOT
ABEOOTV	OBOVATE
ABEOPRS	SAPROBE

ABEOPRT	PROBATE		BASSETS		BASKING
ABEOQRU	BAROQUE	ABESSSY	ABYSSES	ABGIKNU	BAUKING
ABEORRS	ARBORES	ABESSTT	BASSETT	ABGIKST	KITBAGS
	BRASERO	ABESTTU	BATTUES	ABGILLN	BALLING
ABEORRT	ABORTER	ABFFGIN	BAFFING	ABGILMN	AMBLING
	ARBORET	ABFFIIL	BAILIFF		BALMING
	TABORER	ABFFINO	BANOFFI		BLAMING
ABEORST	BOASTER	ABFFLOO	BOFFOLA		LAMBING
	BOATERS	ABFFLOU	BUFFALO	ABGILMS	GIMBALS
	BORATES	ABFGILN	FABLING	ABGILNR	BLARING
	REBATOS	ABFGINR	BARFING	ABGILNS	ABLINGS
	SORBATE	ABFGLSU	BAGFULS		SABLING
ABEORSU	AEROBUS		BAGSFUL	ABGILNT	TABLING
ABEORSV	BRAVOES	ABFGOOT	FOOTBAG	ABGILNW	BAWLING
ABEORSX	BORAXES	ABFHIST	BATFISH		BLAWING
ABEORSY	ROSEBAY	ABFHLSU	BASHFUL	ABGILNZ	BLAZING
ABEORSZ	BEZOARS	ABFIILR	BIFILAR	ABGILOR	GARBOIL
ABEORTT	ABETTOR	ABFIIMR	FIMBRIA	ABGILRT	BATGIRL
	BATTERO	ABFILRU	FIBULAR	ABGIMMN	BAMMING
	TABORET	ABFILSU	FIBULAS	ABGIMRS	GAMBIRS
ABEOSTV	BOVATES	ABFIMOR	FIBROMA	ABGIMST	GAMBIST
ABEPRSU	UPBEARS	ABFLOTU	BOATFUL		GAMBITS
ABEPRSW	BEWRAPS	ABFLOTW	BATFOWL	ABGINNN	BANNING
ABEPRTW	BEWRAPT	ABFLOTY	FLYBOAT	ABGINNR	BARNING
ABEPRTY	TYPEBAR	ABFOORT	FOOTBAR	ABGINNT	BANTING
ABEPSTU	UPBEATS	ABFOOTY	FOYBOAT	ABGINOS	BAGNIOS
ABEQRSU	BARQUES	ABFSTTU	TUBFAST		GABIONS
ABEQSSU	BASQUES	ABGGGIN	BAGGING	ABGINOT	BOATING
ABERRST	BARRETS	ABGGIIT	GIGABIT	ABGINRR	BARRING
	BARTERS	ABGGILN	GABLING	ABGINRS	SABRING
ABERRSU	BURSERA	ABGGILY	BAGGILY	ABGINRV	BRAVING
	SABREUR	ABGGINN	BANGING	ABGINRY	BRAYING
ABERRSV	BRAVERS	ABGGINR	BARGING	ABGINRZ	BRAZING
ABERRSY	BRAYERS		GARBING	ABGINSS	BASSING
ABERRSZ	BRAZERS	ABGGIST	BAGGITS	ABGINST	BASTING
ABERRUV	BRAVURE	ABGGISW	BAGWIGS	ABGINSU	ABUSING
ABERRVY	BRAVERY	ABGGNOS	GOBANGS	ABGINTT	BATTING
ABERSSS	BRASSES	ABGGNSU	BUGGANS	ABGINTU	ANTIBUG
ABERSST	BASTERS	ABGGORT	BOGGART		TABUING
	BESTARS	ABGHHSU	HAGBUSH	ABGINTW	BATWING
	BRASSET	ABGHILN	BLAHING	ABGINTY	BAYTING
	BREASTS	ABGHINS	BASHING	ABGIOPT	PIGBOAT
ABERSSU	ABUSERS	ABGHINT	BATHING	ABGIOSU	BAGUIOS
	BUSERAS	ABGHLOT	HAGBOLT	ABGKKNO	BANGKOK
	RUBASSE	ABGHLRU	BURGHAL	ABGKNOS	KOBANGS
	SURBASE	ABGHMOO	GOOMBAH	ABGKOOS	BOGOAKS
ABERSSZ	ZEBRASS	ABGHMRU	HAMBURG	ABGKORW	WORKBAG
ABERSTT	BATTERS	ABGHNOR	HAGBORN	ABGLLMU	GUMBALL
	TABRETS		HORNBAG	ABGLMNU	LUMBANG
ABERSTU	ARBUTES	ABGHOTU	ABOUGHT	ABGLMOS	GAMBOLS
	BURSATE	ABGHSSU	BUGSHAS	ABGLMOU	LUMBAGO
	SURBATE	ABGHSTU	HAGBUTS	ABGLMSY	GYMBALS
ABERSTV	BRAVEST	ABGIILN	BAILING	ABGLNOO	BOLOGNA
ABERSTW	BRAWEST	ABGIINS	BIASING	ABGLOOT	TOOLBAG
	WABSTER	ABGIINT	BAITING	ABGLORS	BROLGAS
ABERSTX	BAXTERS	ABGIINZ	BAIZING	ABGLORT	RAGBOLT
ABERSTY	BARYTES	ABGIJMN	JAMBING	ABGLOSU	ALBUGOS
	BETRAYS	ABGIJOO	JIGABOO		SUBGOAL
ABERSUU	BUREAUS	ABGIKLN	BALKING	ABGLRRU	BURGLAR
ABERSWY	BEWRAYS	ABGIKNN	BANKING	ABGMNOY	BOGYMAN
ABERTTU	ABUTTER	ABGIKNO	BOAKING	ABGMOOY	GOOMBAY
ABERTTY	BATTERY	ABGIKNR	BARKING	ABGMORW	BAGWORM
ABERUUX	BUREAUX		BRAKING	ABGNOOR	BARGOON
ABESSST	BASSEST	ABGIKNS	BAKINGS	ABGNOOS	BOONGAS

	GABOONS	ABIILLS	BAILLIS	ABILRSU	BURIALS
ABGNOPR	PROBANG	ABIILMN	MINILAB		RAILBUS
ABGNORS	BARONGS	ABIILMU	BULIMIA	ABILRSZ	BRAZILS
	BROGANS	ABIILNQ	INQILAB	ABILSTU	TABULIS
ABGNOTU	GUNBOAT	ABIILNS	AIBLINS	ABILSYZ	SIZABLY
ABGNOWY	BOWYANG		BILIANS	ABIMMRS	MIMBARS
ABGOORT	BOTARGO	ABIILOV	BOLIVIA	ABIMMTU	MITUMBA
ABGOPST	POSTBAG	ABIILRY	BILIARY	ABIMNRS	MINBARS
ABGORRU	GOBURRA	ABIILST	STIBIAL	ABIMOSS	BIOMASS
ABGORST	BOGARTS	ABIILTY	ABILITY	ABIMPST	BAPTISM
ABGORTU	OUTBRAG	ABIIMNR	MINIBAR		BITMAPS
ABGOTTU	TUGBOAT	ABIIMSS	MISBIAS	ABIMRSS	BISMARS
ABGSSTU	SAGBUTS	ABIIMST	IAMBIST	ABIMRST	IMBRAST
ABHHISS	SHIBAHS	ABIINNS	BAININS	ABIMRSU	BARIUMS
ABHHJSU	JUBHAHS	ABIINOR	ROBINIA	ABIMRTT	TRIMTAB
ABHHKOT	KHOTBAH	ABIINRY	BIRYANI	ABIMTTY	AMBITTY
ABHHKTU	KHUTBAH	ABIIOSS	ABIOSIS	ABINNSU	BUNNIAS
ABHHSUW	BUSHWAH	ABIJLNR	BRINJAL	ABINOOR	BORONIA
ABHHSUY	HUSHABY	ABIJNOT	ABJOINT	ABINOOT	BONIATO
ABHIINT	INHABIT	ABIJRSU	JABIRUS	ABINORT	TABORIN
ABHIKLS	BASHLIK	ABIKKSU	KABUKIS	ABINORW	RAINBOW
	KIBLAHS	ABIKLLY	BALKILY	ABINOSS	BASIONS
ABHIKST	BHAKTIS	ABIKLMN	LAMBKIN		BONSAIS
ABHIKTW	HAWKBIT	ABIKLOR	KILOBAR	ABINOST	BASTION
ABHILNO	HOBNAIL	ABIKLOS	KOLBASI		BONITAS
ABHILOS	ABOLISH	ABIKMNR	BARMKIN		OBTAINS
ABHILTU	HALIBUT	ABIKMRS	IMBARKS	ABINOSU	ABUSION
ABHIMNR	BRAHMIN	ABIKNST	BANKITS	ABINRST	BRISANT
ABHIMRS	MIHRABS	ABIKOUZ	BAZOUKI	ABINRTV	VIBRANT
ABHIMSZ	MAZHBIS	ABIKRST	BRITSKA	ABIOORR	ARBORIO
ABHINST	ABSINTH	ABIKRTZ	BRITZKA	ABIORRS	BARRIOS
ABHIOOS	BOOHAIS	ABIKSTT	BATTIKS	ABIORRZ	BIZARRO
ABHIOPS	PHOBIAS	ABIKUUZ	BUZUKIA	ABIORSS	ISOBARS
ABHIORS	BOARISH	ABILLMN	BILLMAN	ABIORST	ORBITAS
ABHIORT	BOTHRIA	ABILLMU	BALLIUM	ABIORTV	VIBRATO
ABHIOST	ISOBATH	ABILLMY	BALMILY	ABIPRTY	BIPARTY
ABHIOSU	HAUBOIS	ABILLNP	PINBALL	ABIPSTT	BAPTIST
ABHISTU	HABITUS	ABILLPY	PLIABLY	ABIRTTY	TRAYBIT
ABHKLSY	BASHLYK	ABILLSW	SAWBILL	ABISSST	BASSIST
ABHKORU	BOURKHA	ABILLSY	SYLLABI	ABISTTU	TUBAIST
ABHKRSU	KURBASH	ABILLTT	BATTILL	ABJJOOS	JOJOBAS
ABHLMSY	SHAMBLY	ABILLWX	WAXBILL	ABJKMOS	JAMBOKS
ABHLOUX	BOXHAUL	ABILLWY	WAYBILL		SJAMBOK
ABHLRSY	BRASHLY	ABILMMS	IMBALMS	ABJLMOO	JAMBOOL
ABHLRTU	HURLBAT	ABILMNU	ALBUMIN	ABJLMSU	JAMBULS
ABHMNOS	BONHAMS	ABILMOX	MAILBOX		JUMBALS
ABHMNSU	BUSHMAN	ABILMRT	TIMBRAL	ABJOSZZ	JAZZBOS
ABHMRSU	RHUMBAS	ABILMST	TIMBALS	ABKLLNY	BLANKLY
	SAMBHUR	ABILNOS	ALBINOS	ABKLOOW	LAWBOOK
ABHMSUY	MAYBUSH	ABILNOT	BITONAL	ABKLOTX	TALKBOX
ABHNOST	BOTHANS	ABILNOZ	BIZONAL	ABKLRUW	BULWARK
ABHNSTU	SUNBATH	ABILNRY	BAIRNLY	ABKLSSY	SKYLABS
ABHOPRS	BARHOPS	ABILOPR	BIPOLAR	ABKLSTY	BYTALKS
ABHORRS	HARBORS		PARBOIL	ABKMNOO	BOOKMAN
ABHORRU	HARBOUR	ABILORS	BAILORS	ABKMOST	TOMBAKS
ABHOTUY	HAUTBOY	ABILORT	ORBITAL	ABKMSUZ	ZAMBUKS
ABHPSTY	BYPATHS	ABILORV	BOLIVAR	ABKNNNO	NONBANK
ABHQSSU	BUQSHAS	ABILOST	OBLASTI	ABKNRSU	UNBARKS
ABHRSTU	TARBUSH	ABILOTU	BAILOUT	ABKNRUU	BUNRAKU
ABHSSUW	BUSHWAS		OBITUAL	ABKOORS	BOORKAS
ABHSTUW	WASHTUB		TABOULI	ABKORTU	OUTBARK
ABIIINR	BIRIANI	ABILRRY	LIBRARY	ABKSSTU	SUBTASK
ABIIKKS	KABIKIS	ABILRSS	BRASILS	ABLLLOW	LOWBALL
ABIIKKT	KIBITKA	ABILRST	TRIBALS	ABLLLUY	LULLABY

ABLLNOO	BALLOON
ABLLNOS	BALLONS
ABLLOOS	LOBOLAS
ABLLOPR	PROBALL
ABLLORR	ROLLBAR
ABLLORT	TOLLBAR
ABLLORU	LOBULAR
ABLLOST	BALLOTS
ABLLOSU	BULLOSA
ABLLOSW	BALLOWS
ABLLOTY	TALLBOY
ABLLOVY	LOVABLY
ABLLPSU	BALLUPS
ABLLRUY	BULLARY
ABLMMOU	BUMMALO
ABLMNOU	UMBONAL
ABLMOOT	TOMBOLA
ABLMOPS	APLOMBS
ABLMORS	BROMALS
ABLMOSY	LAMBOYS
ABLMOVY	MOVABLY
ABLMPSU	PABLUMS
ABLMPUU	PABULUM
ABLMRSU	LABRUMS
	LUMBARS
ABLMSTY	TYMBALS
ABLMTUY	MUTABLY
ABLNOOP	POBLANO
ABLNOSZ	BLAZONS
ABLNOTU	BUTANOL
ABLNOTY	NOTABLY
ABLNRSU	SLURBAN
ABLNSTU	BUNTALS
	TULBANS
ABLNTUY	TUNABLY
ABLOORS	BAROLOS
	ROBALOS
ABLOORT	TOOLBAR
ABLOORY	OBOLARY
ABLOPYY	PLAYBOY
ABLORST	BORSTAL
ABLORSU	LABOURS
	SUBORAL
ABLORSW	BARLOWS
ABLORTW	BLAWORT
ABLORUW	BOURLAW
ABLOSST	OBLASTS
ABLOSTT	TALBOTS
ABLOSTV	ABVOLTS
ABLOSTX	SALTBOX
ABLOSUV	SUBOVAL
ABLOTUW	OUTBAWL
ABLPRSU	BURLAPS
ABLPSUY	PLAYBUS
ABLPSYY	BYPLAYS
ABLRSWY	BYRLAWS
ABLRTUU	TUBULAR
ABLRTUY	BUTYRAL
ABLSTTU	BUTTALS
ABMMNOS	MOBSMAN
ABMNSTU	NUMBATS
ABMNSUY	YNAMBUS
ABMOORR	BARROOM
ABMOOSW	WABOOMS

ABMOOSZ	BAZOOMS
ABMOPST	BAMPOTS
	SPAMBOT
ABMORTU	TAMBOUR
ABMOSTU	SUBATOM
ABMOSTW	WOMBATS
ABMRSSU	SAMBURS
ABMRSTU	TAMBURS
ABNOORS	SOROBAN
ABNOORZ	BORAZON
ABNOOSS	BASSOON
ABNOOST	BATOONS
ABNORST	BARTONS
ABNORSY	BARYONS
ABNORTY	BARYTON
ABNOSSU	BONASUS
ABNOTUY	BUOYANT
ABNRSTU	TURBANS
ABNRSUU	AUBURNS
ABNRTTU	TURBANT
ABNSTUW	BAWSUNT
ABNSTYZ	BYZANTS
ABOOPSX	SOAPBOX
ABOORTW	ROWBOAT
ABOOTTW	TOWBOAT
ABORRSU	ARBOURS
ABORRSW	BARROWS
ABORSTU	ABORTUS
	OUTBARS
	ROBUSTA
	RUBATOS
	TABOURS
ABORSTW	TOWBARS
ABORSTY	TARBOYS
ABOSSUU	AUSUBOS
ABOSSWW	BOWSAWS
ABOSTUU	AUTOBUS
ABPRSTU	ABRUPTS
	SUBPART
	UPBRAST
ABPRSUY	UPBRAYS
ABRRSSU	BURSARS
ABRRSUY	BURSARY
ABRRTUY	TURBARY
ABRSTUU	ARBUTUS
ABSSUWY	SUBWAYS
ACCCILY	ACYCLIC
ACCDDEE	ACCEDED
ACCDDEI	CADDICE
ACCDEEN	CADENCE
ACCDEER	ACCEDER
ACCDEES	ACCEDES
ACCDEHK	CHACKED
ACCDEHN	CHANCED
ACCDEHO	COACHED
ACCDEHT	CATCHED
ACCDEII	ACCIDIE
ACCDEIO	ACCOIED
ACCDEIT	ACCITED
ACCDEIU	CADUCEI
ACCDEKL	CACKLED
	CLACKED
ACCDEKO	COCKADE
ACCDEKR	CRACKED

ACCDENS	ACCENDS
ACCDENY	CADENCY
ACCDEOT	COACTED
ACCDEOY	ACCOYED
ACCDERU	ACCRUED
	CARDECU
ACCDESU	ACCUSED
	SUCCADE
ACCDFIL	FLACCID
ACCDHIL	CHALCID
ACCDILS	SCALDIC
ACCDINS	SCANDIC
ACCDIOT	CACTOID
	OCTADIC
ACCDKNO	CANDOCK
ACCDKOW	DAWCOCK
ACCDLOY	ACCOYLD
	CACODYL
ACCDORS	ACCORDS
ACCEEHL	CALECHE
ACCEEHO	COACHEE
ACCEELN	CENACLE
ACCEENR	CREANCE
ACCEERT	ACCRETE
ACCEFIT	FACTICE
ACCEFLU	FELUCCA
ACCEGIN	ACCINGE
ACCEGOS	SOCCAGE
ACCEHHI	CHECHIA
ACCEHIL	CALICHE
	CHALICE
ACCEHIM	MACCHIE
ACCEHIN	CHICANE
ACCEHLN	CHANCEL
ACCEHLO	COCHLEA
ACCEHNO	CONCHAE
ACCEHNR	CHANCER
	CHANCRE
ACCEHNS	CHANCES
ACCEHNT	CATCHEN
ACCEHNU	CHAUNCE
ACCEHNY	CHANCEY
ACCEHOR	CAROCHE
	COACHER
ACCEHOS	CHACOES
	COACHES
ACCEHPU	CAPUCHE
ACCEHRS	CREACHS
ACCEHRT	CATCHER
	RECATCH
ACCEHST	CACHETS
	CATCHES
ACCEHTT	CATHECT
ACCEHTU	CATECHU
ACCEHXY	CACHEXY
ACCEIKP	ICEPACK
ACCEIKR	CACKIER
ACCEILL	CALICLE
ACCEILN	CALCINE
ACCEILO	COELIAC
ACCEILS	CALICES
	CELIACS
ACCEILT	CALCITE
ACCEIMR	CERAMIC

	RACEMIC	ACCHIMS	CHASMIC	ACCIRRS	CIRCARS
ACCEINO	COCAINE	ACCHINO	CHICANO		RICRACS
	OCEANIC	ACCHIOP	PICACHO	ACCIRST	ARCTICS
ACCEINV	VACCINE	ACCHIOR	COCHAIR	ACCISTT	TACTICS
ACCEIPR	CAPRICE	ACCHIOT	CHAOTIC		TICTACS
ACCEIPS	ICECAPS	ACCHIOU	ACOUCHI	ACCISTU	CAUSTIC
	IPECACS	ACCHIRS	SCRAICH		CICUTAS
ACCEIPV	PECCAVI	ACCHJSU	JACCHUS	ACCKLOR	CARLOCK
ACCEIQU	CACIQUE	ACCHKOY	HAYCOCK	ACCKLRY	CRACKLY
ACCEIRS	CARICES	ACCHKSY	CHYACKS	ACCKMOR	CROMACK
ACCEIRT	CREATIC	ACCHLNO	CONCHAL	ACCKOPR	CAPROCK
ACCEIST	ACCITES	ACCHLTU	CLAUCHT	ACCKOSS	CASSOCK
	ASCETIC	ACCHNOS	CONCHAS		COSSACK
ACCEITT	ECTATIC	ACCHNRS	SCRANCH	ACCKOST	CASTOCK
ACCEKLR	CACKLER	ACCHNRU	CRAUNCH	ACCKPRU	CRACKUP
	CLACKER	ACCHOPU	CAPOUCH	ACCLOSU	COUCALS
	CRACKLE		PACHUCO	ACCLOSY	ACCLOYS
ACCEKLS	CACKLES	ACCHORR	CARROCH	ACCMNOY	CACONYM
ACCEKMO	MEACOCK	ACCHOSU	CACHOUS	ACCMOOT	COCOMAT
ACCEKOP	PEACOCK	ACCHOTW	CHOCTAW	ACCMOOY	COCOYAM
ACCEKOS	SEACOCK	ACCHOUY	ACOUCHY	ACCMOPT	ACCOMPT
ACCEKPU	CUPCAKE	ACCHPTU	CATCHUP		COMPACT
ACCEKRR	CRACKER		UPCATCH	ACCMRUU	CURCUMA
ACCEKRT	CRACKET	ACCHRRU	CURRACH	ACCNNOO	COONCAN
ACCELLY	CALYCLE	ACCHRST	SCRATCH	ACCNOOP	COCOPAN
	CECALLY	ACCHRSU	SCRAUCH	ACCNOOR	RACCOON
ACCELNO	CONCEAL	ACCHSSU	SUCCAHS	ACCNOOS	CACOONS
ACCELNS	CANCELS	ACCIILN	ACLINIC	ACCNOTT	CONTACT
ACCELOR	CORACLE	ACCIINT	ACTINIC	ACCNOTU	ACCOUNT
ACCELOT	CACOLET	ACCIIST	ASCITIC	ACCOORT	COACTOR
ACCELRS	CARCELS		SCIATIC	ACCOPTY	COPYCAT
ACCELSU	SACCULE	ACCIKRR	CARRICK	ACCOQSU	SQUACCO
ACCELSY	CALYCES	ACCIKRS	CARSICK	ACCORSS	CORCASS
	CYCLASE	ACCILLU	CALCULI		CORSACS
ACCEMNU	CACUMEN	ACCILMO	COMICAL	ACCORTU	ACCOURT
ACCENOR	CONACRE	ACCILMU	CALCIUM	ACCOSST	ACCOSTS
ACCENOS	ASCONCE	ACCILNO	CONICAL	ACCRSTU	ACCURST
ACCENOT	COENACT		LACONIC	ACDDDEI	CADDIED
ACCENOV	CONCAVE	ACCILNY	CYNICAL	ACDDDEL	CLADDED
ACCENPT	PECCANT	ACCILOR	CALORIC	ACDDDEU	ADDUCED
ACCENRS	CANCERS	ACCILOS	ACCOILS	ACDDDKO	DADDOCK
ACCENST	ACCENTS		CALICOS	ACDDEEF	DEFACED
ACCEOPY	CACOEPY	ACCILOV	VOCALIC	ACDDEEL	DECALED
ACCEORW	CRACOWE	ACCILRU	CRUCIAL	ACDDEER	CEDARED
ACCEOTT	TOCCATE	ACCILRY	ACRYLIC	ACDDEES	DECADES
ACCEPRY	PECCARY	ACCILSS	CLASSIC	ACDDEEY	DECAYED
ACCEPST	ACCEPTS	ACCILST	CLASTIC	ACDDEHR	CHEDDAR
ACCERRS	SCARCER	ACCILSU	SACCULI	ACDDEHY	DAYCHED
ACCERRT	CARRECT	ACCIMOT	COMATIC	ACDDEIL	CLADDIE
ACCERSS	ARCSECS	ACCIMOZ	ZIMOCCA	ACDDEIN	CANDIED
ACCERSU	ACCRUES	ACCIMRU	CUMARIC	ACDDEIS	CADDIES
	ACCURSE	ACCINNO	CANONIC	ACDDEIU	DECIDUA
	ACCUSER	ACCINOP	CANOPIC	ACDDELN	CANDLED
ACCERSW	ACCREWS	ACCINOR	ACRONIC	ACDDELO	CLADODE
ACCESSU	ACCUSES	ACCINOS	COCAINS	ACDDELR	CLADDER
ACCESSY	CYCASES	ACCINOT	CANTICO		CRADLED
ACCFIIP	PACIFIC	ACCINRU	CRUCIAN	ACDDELS	SCALDED
ACCFILY	CALCIFY	ACCINSW	WICCANS	ACDDELU	CAUDLED
ACCGHIN	CACHING	ACCINSY	CYCASIN	ACDDEMU	DUCDAME
	CHACING	ACCIOPR	CAPROIC	ACDDEOP	DECAPOD
ACCGNOS	COGNACS	ACCIORS	SCORIAC	ACDDERU	ADDUCER
ACCHHIS	CHICHAS	ACCIORT	ACROTIC	ACDDESU	ADDUCES
ACCHHKU	KUCHCHA	ACCIOST	OCICATS		SCAUDED
ACCHIKS	CHIACKS	ACCIPRT	PRACTIC	ACDDHHU	CHUDDAH

ACDDHIS	CADDISH	ACDEERT	CATERED	ACDEHNR	ENDARCH
ACDDHKO	HADDOCK		CEDRATE		RANCHED
ACDDHOR	CHADDOR		CERATED	ACDEHNT	CHANTED
ACDDHRU	CHUDDAR		CREATED	ACDEHOP	POACHED
ACDDIIS	DIACIDS		REACTED	ACDEHOR	CHORDAE
ACDDIKZ	ZADDICK	ACDEERY	DECAYER		ROACHED
ACDDINS	CANDIDS	ACDEEST	TEDESCA	ACDEHOS	COHEADS
ACDDIRS	DISCARD	ACDEETT	TACETED	ACDEHOT	CATHODE
ACDDIRY	DRYADIC	ACDEETU	EDUCATE	ACDEHPP	CHAPPED
ACDDIST	ADDICTS	ACDEETX	EXACTED	ACDEHPR	PARCHED
	DIDACTS	ACDEFFH	CHAFFED	ACDEHPT	PATCHED
ACDDISY	DYADICS	ACDEFFS	DECAFFS	ACDEHPU	CUPHEAD
ACDDKMO	MADDOCK	ACDEFGO	DOGFACE	ACDEHRR	CHARRED
ACDDKOP	PADDOCK	ACDEFHU	CHAUFED	ACDEHRS	CRASHED
ACDDSSY	CADDYSS	ACDEFIN	FACIEND		ECHARDS
ACDDSTU	ADDUCTS		FANCIED	ACDEHRT	CHARTED
ACDEEES	DECEASE		FARCIED		RATCHED
ACDEEFF	EFFACED	ACDEFIR	FARCIED	ACDEHSS	CHASSED
ACDEEFN	ENFACED	ACDEFKL	FLACKED	ACDEHST	SCATHED
ACDEEFR	DEFACER	ACDEFRS	SCARFED	ACDEHSY	DAYCHES
	REFACED	ACDEFRT	CRAFTED	ACDEHTT	CHATTED
ACDEEFS	DEFACES		FRACTED	ACDEHTW	WATCHED
ACDEEFT	FACETED	ACDEGGL	CLAGGED	ACDEHTY	YACHTED
ACDEEGL	GLACEED	ACDEGGR	CRAGGED	ACDEHUV	VAUCHED
ACDEEGN	ENCAGED	ACDEGGS	SCAGGED	ACDEIIR	ACIDIER
ACDEEHL	LEACHED	ACDEGHN	CHANGED	ACDEILL	CEDILLA
ACDEEHP	CHEAPED		GANCHED	ACDEILM	CAMELID
	PEACHED	ACDEGHR	CHARGED		CLAIMED
ACDEEHR	REACHED	ACDEGIN	INCAGED		DECIMAL
ACDEEHT	CHEATED	ACDEGIR	CADGIER		DECLAIM
ACDEEIR	DECIARE	ACDEGIS	DISCAGE		MALICED
ACDEEJT	DEJECTA	ACDEGKO	DOCKAGE		MEDICAL
ACDEEKR	CREAKED	ACDEGLN	CANGLED	ACDEILN	INLACED
ACDEELL	CADELLE		CLANGED	ACDEILR	DECRIAL
ACDEELN	CLEANED		GLANCED		RADICEL
	ELANCED	ACDEGLO	DECALOG		RADICLE
	ENLACED	ACDEGNO	CONGAED	ACDEILS	SCAILED
ACDEELR	CLEARED		DECAGON	ACDEILT	CITADEL
	CREEDAL	ACDEGNU	UNCAGED		DELTAIC
	DECLARE	ACDEGOR	CARGOED		DIALECT
	RELACED		CORDAGE		EDICTAL
ACDEELS	DESCALE	ACDEGRS	CADGERS	ACDEILV	CAVILED
ACDEELT	CLEATED	ACDEGST	GEDACTS	ACDEIMT	MICATED
ACDEELV	CLEAVED	ACDEHHN	HANCHED	ACDEIMV	MEDIVAC
ACDEEMN	MENACED	ACDEHHT	HATCHED	ACDEIMY	MEDIACY
ACDEEMO	CAMEOED	ACDEHIN	CHAINED	ACDEINO	CODEINA
ACDEEMR	AMERCED		ECHIDNA		OCEANID
	CREAMED	ACDEHIP	EDAPHIC	ACDEINR	CAIRNED
	RACEMED	ACDEHIR	CHAIRED		CARNIED
ACDEEMV	MEDEVAC	ACDEHIX	HEXADIC		DANCIER
ACDEENR	ENRACED	ACDEHKL	CHALKED	ACDEINS	CANDIES
	RECANED		HACKLED		INCASED
ACDEENS	DECANES	ACDEHKR	CHARKED	ACDEINV	INCAVED
	ENCASED	ACDEHKS	SHACKED	ACDEINY	CYANIDE
ACDEENT	ENACTED	ACDEHKT	THACKED	ACDEIOS	CODEIAS
ACDEENV	ENCAVED	ACDEHKW	WHACKED	ACDEIPR	EPACRID
	VENDACE	ACDEHLN	LANCHED		PERACID
ACDEEPR	CAPERED	ACDEHLR	CHALDER	ACDEIPS	DISPACE
	PEARCED	ACDEHLS	CLASHED	ACDEIRR	ACRIDER
	PREACED	ACDEHLT	LATCHED		CARRIED
ACDEEPS	ESCAPED	ACDEHMP	CHAMPED	ACDEIRS	CARDIES
ACDEERS	CREASED	ACDEHMR	CHARMED		DARCIES
	DECARES		MARCHED		RADICES
	SEARCED	ACDEHMS	CHASMED		SIDECAR
		ACDEHMT	MATCHED		

ACDEIRU	DECURIA		CEDULAS	**ACDESTT**	SCATTED
ACDEISS	DISCASE	**ACDELSW**	DECLAWS	**ACDESTV**	ADVECTS
ACDEIST	ACIDEST	**ACDELTT**	CLATTED	**ACDFIIT**	FATIDIC
	DACITES	**ACDELTU**	CLAUTED	**ACDFIIY**	ACIDIFY
ACDEISV	ADVICES	**ACDELWW**	DEWCLAW	**ACDFIOT**	FACTOID
ACDEITT	DICTATE	**ACDEMMR**	CRAMMED	**ACDGGIN**	CADGING
ACDEITY	EDACITY	**ACDEMMS**	SCAMMED	**ACDGIIM**	DIGICAM
ACDEJLO	CAJOLED	**ACDEMNU**	DECUMAN	**ACDGIKN**	DACKING
ACDEJNU	JAUNCED	**ACDEMOR**	CAROMED	**ACDGINN**	DANCING
ACDEKKN	KNACKED		COMRADE	**ACDGINO**	GONADIC
ACDEKLM	MACKLED	**ACDEMPR**	CRAMPED	**ACDGINR**	CARDING
ACDEKLN	CLANKED	**ACDEMPS**	DECAMPS	**ACDGKLO**	DAGLOCK
ACDEKLO	CLOAKED		SCAMPED	**ACDGNOT**	CANTDOG
ACDEKLS	SLACKED	**ACDENNS**	SCANNED	**ACDGORT**	DOGCART
ACDEKLT	TACKLED	**ACDENNT**	CANDENT	**ACDHIIL**	CHILIAD
	TALCKED	**ACDENNU**	NUANCED	**ACDHIMR**	DHARMIC
ACDEKLU	CAULKED	**ACDENOR**	ACORNED	**ACDHIOP**	PHACOID
ACDEKMS	SMACKED		DRACONE	**ACDHIRY**	DIARCHY
ACDEKNR	CRANKED	**ACDENOS**	ACNODES	**ACDHLOR**	CHORDAL
ACDEKNS	SNACKED		DEACONS		DORLACH
ACDEKNU	UNCAKED	**ACDENOT**	TACNODE	**ACDHMRS**	DRACHMS
ACDEKOR	CROAKED	**ACDENPR**	PRANCED	**ACDHNOW**	COWHAND
ACDEKQU	QUACKED	**ACDENPT**	PANDECT	**ACDHOOT**	CATHOOD
ACDEKRS	DACKERS	**ACDENPU**	UNCAPED	**ACDHOPR**	POCHARD
ACDEKRT	TRACKED		UNPACED	**ACDHORR**	ORCHARD
ACDEKRW	WRACKED	**ACDENRS**	DANCERS	**ACDHORS**	CHADORS
ACDEKRY	KEYCARD	**ACDENRT**	CANTRED	**ACDHRUY**	DUARCHY
ACDEKST	STACKED		TRANCED	**ACDHRYY**	DYARCHY
ACDEKSW	SWACKED	**ACDENRU**	DURANCE	**ACDIIIN**	INDICIA
ACDELLS	SCALLED		UNRACED	**ACDIIJT**	JADITIC
ACDELMM	CLAMMED	**ACDENRY**	ARDENCY	**ACDIINN**	INDICAN
ACDELMP	CAMPLED	**ACDENSS**	ASCENDS	**ACDIINO**	CONIDIA
	CLAMPED	**ACDENST**	DECANTS	**ACDIINR**	ACRIDIN
ACDELMS	MASCLED		DESCANT	**ACDIIOS**	ISODICA
ACDELMU	MACULED		SCANTED	**ACDIIRS**	CIDARIS
ACDELNO	CELADON	**ACDENSU**	UNCASED		SCIARID
ACDELNR	CANDLER	**ACDENTU**	UNACTED	**ACDIIRT**	ARCTIID
ACDELNS	CALENDS	**ACDENUV**	VAUNCED		TRIACID
	CANDLES	**ACDEOPS**	PEACODS		TRIADIC
ACDELNT	CANTLED		PEASCOD	**ACDIITY**	ACIDITY
ACDELNU	LAUNCED	**ACDEOPT**	COAPTED	**ACDIKLS**	SKALDIC
	UNLACED	**ACDEORR**	CORRADE	**ACDILLO**	CODILLA
ACDELOP	PEDOCAL	**ACDEORS**	SARCODE	**ACDILMO**	DOMICAL
ACDELOR	CAROLED	**ACDEORT**	CORDATE	**ACDILMS**	CLADISM
	ORACLED		REDCOAT	**ACDILNO**	NODICAL
ACDELOS	COLEADS	**ACDEOST**	COASTED	**ACDILNU**	DULCIAN
	SOLACED	**ACDEOTT**	CODETTA		INCUDAL
ACDELOT	LOCATED	**ACDEOUV**	COUVADE	**ACDILOP**	PLACOID
ACDELOV	ALCOVED	**ACDEPPR**	CRAPPED		PODALIC
ACDELPP	CLAPPED	**ACDEPRS**	REDCAPS	**ACDILOR**	CORDIAL
ACDELPS	CLASPED		SCARPED	**ACDILOT**	COTIDAL
	SCALPED		SCRAPED	**ACDILPU**	PALUDIC
ACDELQU	CALQUED	**ACDEPSU**	SCAUPED	**ACDILRT**	TRICLAD
ACDELRR	CRADLER	**ACDEQSU**	CASQUED	**ACDILRY**	ACRIDLY
ACDELRS	CRADLES	**ACDERRS**	CARDERS	**ACDILST**	CLADIST
	SCALDER		SCARRED	**ACDILTW**	WILDCAT
ACDELRT	CLARTED	**ACDERST**	REDACTS	**ACDILTY**	DACTYLI
ACDELRU	CAULDER		SCARTED	**ACDIMMU**	CADMIUM
ACDELRW	CRAWLED	**ACDERSU**	CRUSADE	**ACDIMNO**	MANDIOC
ACDELSS	CLASSED		SCAURED		MONACID
	DECLASS	**ACDERTT**	DETRACT		MONADIC
ACDELST	CASTLED		TRACTED		NOMADIC
	SCLATED	**ACDERTU**	CURATED	**ACDIMNY**	DYNAMIC
ACDELSU	CAUDLES		TRADUCE	**ACDIMOO**	CAMOODI

ACDIMOT	COADMIT
ACDINNO	NONACID
ACDINRU	IRACUND
ACDINST	DISCANT
ACDINSW	WINDACS
ACDINSY	CYANIDS
ACDIOPR	PARODIC
	PICADOR
ACDIORR	CORRIDA
ACDIORS	SARCOID
ACDIORT	ARCTOID
	CAROTID
ACDIOST	DACOITS
ACDIOSZ	ZODIACS
ACDIOTY	DACOITY
ACDIOXY	OXYACID
ACDIPRS	CAPRIDS
ACDIPSS	CAPSIDS
ACDIPTY	DIPTYCA
ACDIQRU	QUADRIC
ACDIRST	DRASTIC
ACDIRTU	DATURIC
ACDISST	DICASTS
ACDITUV	VIADUCT
ACDJNTU	ADJUNCT
ACDKLOP	PADLOCK
ACDKLSY	SKYCLAD
ACDKMOO	MOCKADO
ACDKMPU	MUDPACK
ACDKOPR	POCKARD
ACDLLOR	COLLARD
ACDLLUY	DUCALLY
ACDLNOR	CALDRON
ACDLNOT	COTLAND
ACDLOWY	LADYCOW
ACDLSTY	DACTYLS
ACDMMNO	COMMAND
ACDMNOP	COMPAND
ACDMOOW	CAMWOOD
ACDMORZ	CZARDOM
ACDMPSU	MUDCAPS
ACDMSTU	MUDCATS
ACDNOOR	CARDOON
ACDNORS	CANDORS
	CARDONS
	DACRONS
ACDNORU	CANDOUR
	CAUDRON
ACDOPST	PODCAST
ACDORST	COSTARD
ACDORSU	CRUSADO
ACDORSW	COWARDS
ACDORUZ	CRUZADO
ACDRSTU	CUSTARD
ACDRSUU	CARDUUS
ACEEEPS	ESCAPEE
ACEEEUV	EVACUEE
ACEEFFR	EFFACER
ACEEFFS	EFFACES
ACEEFHN	ENCHAFE
ACEEFIN	FAIENCE
	FIANCEE
ACEEFLU	FECULAE
ACEEFMN	FACEMEN
ACEEFNS	ENFACES
ACEEFNY	FAYENCE
ACEEFPR	PREFACE
ACEEFRS	REFACES
ACEEGIL	ELEGIAC
ACEEGNR	ENGRACE
ACEEGNS	ENCAGES
ACEEGNT	CENTAGE
ACEEGOT	ECOTAGE
ACEEGSU	ESCUAGE
ACEEHHT	CHEETAH
ACEEHIP	CHEAPIE
ACEEHIT	HICATEE
	TEACHIE
ACEEHIV	ACHIEVE
ACEEHKO	HOECAKE
ACEEHKS	HACKEES
ACEEHLR	LEACHER
	RELACHE
ACEEHLS	LEACHES
ACEEHLT	CHELATE
ACEEHMP	EMPEACH
ACEEHMR	MACHREE
ACEEHMT	MACHETE
ACEEHNN	ENHANCE
ACEEHNP	CHEAPEN
ACEEHNS	ACHENES
	ENCHASE
ACEEHOR	OCHREAE
ACEEHPP	ECHAPPE
ACEEHPR	CHEAPER
	PEACHER
ACEEHPS	PEACHES
ACEEHRR	REACHER
ACEEHRS	REACHES
ACEEHRT	CHEATER
	HECTARE
	RECHATE
	RECHEAT
	RETEACH
	TEACHER
ACEEHST	EATCHES
	ESCHEAT
	TEACHES
ACEEHTT	THECATE
ACEEHTX	EXCHEAT
ACEEILP	CALIPEE
ACEEIMT	EMICATE
ACEEINR	CINEREA
ACEEINU	EUCAINE
ACEEIRR	CARIERE
ACEEISV	VESICAE
ACEEJKN	JACKEEN
ACEEKNP	KNEECAP
ACEELLN	NACELLE
ACEELLS	CALLEES
ACEELMP	EMPLACE
ACEELMR	RECLAME
ACEELNR	CLEANER
	RECLEAN
ACEELNS	CLEANSE
	ELANCES
	ENLACES
	SCALENE
ACEELNT	LATENCE
ACEELNV	ENCLAVE
	VALENCE
ACEELPR	PERCALE
	REPLACE
ACEELPT	CAPELET
ACEELRR	CLEARER
ACEELRS	ALERCES
	CEREALS
	RELACES
	RESCALE
	SCLERAE
ACEELRT	TREACLE
ACEELRU	CAERULE
ACEELRV	CLEAVER
ACEELST	CELESTA
	SELECTA
ACEELSU	EUCLASE
ACEELSV	CLEAVES
ACEELVX	EXCLAVE
ACEEMNR	MENACER
ACEEMNS	CASEMEN
	EMACSEN
	MENACES
ACEEMNT	CEMENTA
ACEEMNV	CAVEMEN
ACEEMRR	AMERCER
	CREAMER
ACEEMRS	AMERCES
	CAREMES
	RACEMES
ACEEMRT	CREMATE
	MEERCAT
ACEEMSS	CAMESES
ACEEMSZ	ECZEMAS
ACEENNP	PENANCE
ACEENNR	NARCEEN
ACEENNT	CANTEEN
ACEENNY	CAYENNE
ACEENOR	CORNEAE
ACEENOT	ACETONE
ACEENRS	CAREENS
	CASERNE
	ENRACES
	RECANES
ACEENRT	CENTARE
	CRENATE
	REENACT
ACEENSS	CASSENE
	ENCASES
	SEANCES
	SENECAS
ACEENST	CETANES
	TENACES
ACEENSV	ENCAVES
ACEENTU	CUNEATE
ACEEORS	ACEROSE
ACEEORT	OCREATE
ACEEOSS	CASEOSE
ACEEOST	ACETOSE
	COATEES
ACEEOTV	EVOCATE
ACEEPRR	CAPERER
	PRERACE

ACEEPRS	ESCAPER	ACEFORR	FORECAR	ACEGNOR	ACROGEN
	PEARCES	ACEFOTU	OUTFACE		CORNAGE
	PERCASE	ACEFRRS	FARCERS	ACEGNOT	COAGENT
	PREACES		SCARFER		COGNATE
	RESPACE	ACEFRRT	CRAFTER	ACEGNSU	CANGUES
ACEEPSS	ESCAPES		REFRACT		UNCAGES
ACEEPST	PECTASE	ACEFRRU	FARCEUR	ACEGORS	CARGOES
ACEEPTT	PECTATE	ACEFRSU	SURFACE		CORSAGE
ACEERRS	CAREERS	ACEFRTU	FACTURE		SOCAGER
	CREASER		FURCATE	ACEGORU	COURAGE
ACEERRT	CATERER	ACEFSTU	FAUCETS	ACEGOSS	SOCAGES
	RECRATE	ACEGHLO	GALOCHE	ACEGOSW	COWAGES
	RETRACE	ACEGHNR	CHANGER	ACEGOTT	COTTAGE
	TERRACE	ACEGHNS	CHANGES	ACEGRTU	TRUCAGE
ACEERSS	CREASES		GANCHES	ACEGSTU	SCUTAGE
	SEARCES	ACEGHNU	CHAUNGE	ACEGTTU	CUTTAGE
ACEERST	CERATES	ACEGHOU	GOUACHE	ACEHHLS	CHALEHS
	CREATES	ACEGHOW	COWHAGE	ACEHHLT	HATCHEL
	ECARTES	ACEGHRR	CHARGER	ACEHHNS	HANCHES
	SECRETA	ACEGHRS	CHARGES	ACEHHRT	HATCHER
ACEERSU	CESURAE		CREAGHS	ACEHHRU	HACHURE
ACEERTX	EXACTER	ACEGHRT	GERTCHA	ACEHHRX	HEXARCH
	EXCRETA	ACEGHRU	GAUCHER	ACEHHST	CHETAHS
ACEERVZ	CERVEZA	ACEGILL	ELLAGIC		HATCHES
ACEESSS	ASCESES	ACEGILN	ANGELIC	ACEHHTT	HATCHET
ACEESST	ECTASES		ANGLICE	ACEHIKR	KACHERI
ACEESTT	CASETTE		GALENIC	ACEHIKS	HACKIES
ACEFFHI	AFFICHE	ACEGILP	PELAGIC	ACEHILL	CHALLIE
ACEFFHR	CHAFFER	ACEGILR	GLACIER		HELICAL
ACEFFIN	CAFFEIN		GRACILE	ACEHILM	LECHAIM
ACEFFIS	SCAFFIE	ACEGILS	ALGESIC	ACEHILR	CHARLIE
ACEFFOR	AFFORCE	ACEGILT	ALGETIC	ACEHILT	ALETHIC
ACEFFST	AFFECTS	ACEGIMO	CAMOGIE		ETHICAL
ACEFGIP	PIGFACE	ACEGIMR	GRIMACE	ACEHIMN	MACHINE
ACEFGLU	CAGEFUL	ACEGIMT	GAMETIC	ACEHIMP	IMPEACH
ACEFGOT	GEOFACT	ACEGINO	COINAGE	ACEHIMR	CHIMERA
ACEFHMR	CHAMFER	ACEGINP	PEACING	ACEHIMS	CHAMISE
ACEFHOR	ARCHFOE	ACEGINR	ANERGIC	ACEHIMT	HEMATIC
ACEFHRS	CHAFERS		GRECIAN	ACEHINN	ENCHAIN
ACEFHRU	CHAUFER	ACEGINS	CEASING	ACEHINR	ARCHINE
ACEFHSU	CHAUFES		INCAGES	ACEHINS	CHAINES
ACEFIIL	FELICIA	ACEGINV	VEGANIC		INCHASE
ACEFILL	ICEFALL	ACEGINY	GYNECIA	ACEHINT	CHANTIE
ACEFILM	MALEFIC	ACEGINZ	CEAZING	ACEHINY	HYACINE
ACEFILR	FILACER	ACEGIOP	APOGEIC		HYAENIC
ACEFILS	FECIALS	ACEGIRT	CIGARET	ACEHIOT	ACHIOTE
ACEFINN	FINANCE	ACEGIRU	GAUCIER	ACEHIPP	CHAPPIE
ACEFINR	FANCIER	ACEGIRW	GAWCIER	ACEHIPR	CHARPIE
ACEFINS	FANCIES	ACEGIST	CAGIEST	ACEHIPT	APHETIC
	FASCINE	ACEGJKL	JACKLEG		HEPATIC
	FIANCES	ACEGKLO	LOCKAGE	ACEHIRR	CHARIER
ACEFINU	UNIFACE	ACEGKLR	GRACKLE	ACEHIRS	CAHIERS
ACEFIRS	FARCIES	ACEGKMO	MOCKAGE		CASHIER
	FIACRES	ACEGKOR	CORKAGE		ERIACHS
ACEFITV	FACTIVE	ACEGLLO	COLLAGE	ACEHIRT	THERIAC
ACEFITY	ACETIFY	ACEGLNO	CONGEAL	ACEHIRV	ARCHIVE
ACEFKLR	FLACKER	ACEGLNR	CLANGER	ACEHISS	CHAISES
ACEFKLT	FLACKET		GLANCER	ACEHIST	ACHIEST
ACEFLRU	CAREFUL	ACEGLNS	CANGLES		AITCHES
ACEFLSU	FECULAS		GLANCES	ACEHITY	YACHTIE
ACEFNNO	FACONNE	ACEGLOT	CATELOG	ACEHITZ	ZAITECH
ACEFNRT	CANTREF	ACEGLOU	CAGOULE	ACEHKLR	HACKLER
ACEFNRU	FURNACE	ACEGLPS	GELCAPS	ACEHKLS	HACKLES
ACEFOPR	PROFACE	ACEGMOP	COMPAGE		SHACKLE

ACEHKLT	HACKLET	**ACEHNNR**	CHANNER	**ACEHRTW**	WATCHER
ACEHKMN	HACKMEN	**ACEHNNT**	ENCHANT	**ACEHRTY**	YACHTER
ACEHKNY	HACKNEY	**ACEHNOP**	PANOCHE	**ACEHRXY**	EXARCHY
ACEHKOT	HOTCAKE	**ACEHNPS**	PECHANS	**ACEHSSS**	CHASSES
ACEHKRS	HACKERS	**ACEHNRR**	RANCHER	**ACEHSST**	SACHETS
ACEHKRW	WHACKER		RANCHES		SCATHES
ACEHKRY	HACKERY	**ACEHNRS**	CHENARS	**ACEHSSW**	CASHEWS
ACEHLLP	PELLACH		RANCHES	**ACEHSTW**	WATCHES
ACEHLLS	SHELLAC	**ACEHNRT**	CHANTER	**ACEHSTX**	HEXACTS
ACEHLLT	HELLCAT		TRANCHE	**ACEHSUV**	VAUCHES
ACEHLMT	CHAMLET	**ACEHNSS**	SCHANSE	**ACEHTTU**	TEUCHAT
ACEHLMY	ALCHEMY	**ACEHNST**	CHASTEN	**ACEHTTW**	WATCHET
ACEHLNN	CHANNEL		NATCHES	**ACEIILM**	CIMELIA
ACEHLNO	CHALONE	**ACEHNSU**	NAUCHES	**ACEIILS**	LAICISE
ACEHLNP	PLANCHE	**ACEHNSZ**	SCHANZE	**ACEIILT**	CILIATE
ACEHLNR	CHARNEL	**ACEHNTT**	ETCHANT	**ACEIILZ**	LAICIZE
	LARCHEN	**ACEHNTU**	UNTEACH	**ACEIIPS**	EPISCIA
ACEHLNS	LANCHES	**ACEHNTY**	CHANTEY	**ACEIITV**	CAITIVE
ACEHLOP	EPOCHAL	**ACEHNZZ**	CHAZZEN		VICIATE
ACEHLOR	CHOLERA	**ACEHOOT**	OOTHECA	**ACEIJKS**	JACKIES
	CHORALE	**ACEHOPR**	POACHER		JACKSIE
	CHOREAL	**ACEHOPS**	CHEAPOS	**ACEIKLS**	SACLIKE
ACEHLOS	LOACHES		EPOCHAS	**ACEIKLT**	CATLIKE
	OSCHEAL		POACHES	**ACEIKMR**	KERAMIC
ACEHLOT	CATHOLE		SHOEPAC	**ACEIKNT**	ANTICKE
	CHOLATE	**ACEHORS**	CHOREAS	**ACEIKOP**	PAIOCKE
ACEHLPS	CHAPELS		ORACHES	**ACEIKPR**	EARPICK
ACEHLPT	CHAPLET		ROACHES	**ACEIKPW**	WICKAPE
ACEHLPY	CHEAPLY	**ACEHOSS**	CHAOSES	**ACEIKPX**	PICKAXE
ACEHLRS	CLASHER	**ACEHOTY**	CHAYOTE	**ACEIKRS**	EIRACKS
	LARCHES	**ACEHPPS**	SCHAPPE	**ACEIKRT**	TACKIER
	RASCHEL	**ACEHPRS**	EPARCHS	**ACEIKRW**	WACKIER
ACEHLRT	ARCHLET		PARCHES	**ACEIKSS**	SEASICK
	TRACHLE	**ACEHPRT**	CHAPTER	**ACEIKST**	CAKIEST
ACEHLRY	CHARLEY		PATCHER		TACKIES
ACEHLSS	CLASHES		REPATCH	**ACEIKTT**	TIETACK
	SEALCHS	**ACEHPRU**	UPREACH	**ACEILLL**	ALLELIC
ACEHLST	CHALETS	**ACEHPRY**	EPARCHY	**ACEILLM**	LIMACEL
	LATCHES		PREACHY		MICELLA
	SATCHEL	**ACEHPSS**	CHAPESS	**ACEILLS**	ALLICES
ACEHLTT	CHATTEL	**ACEHPST**	HEPCATS		CAILLES
	LATCHET		PATCHES	**ACEILLX**	LEXICAL
ACEHMNP	CHAPMEN	**ACEHQUY**	QUEACHY	**ACEILMN**	CNEMIAL
ACEHMNR	ENCHARM	**ACEHRRS**	ARCHERS		MELANIC
	MARCHEN		CRASHER	**ACEILMR**	CALMIER
ACEHMNS	MANCHES	**ACEHRRT**	CHARTER		CLAIMER
ACEHMNT	MANCHET		RECHART		MIRACLE
ACEHMPR	CHAMPER	**ACEHRRV**	CHARVER		RECLAIM
ACEHMRR	CHARMER	**ACEHRRX**	XERARCH	**ACEILMS**	LIMACES
	MARCHER	**ACEHRRY**	ARCHERY		MALICES
ACEHMRS	MACHERS	**ACEHRSS**	CHASERS	**ACEILMT**	CLIMATE
	MARCHES		CRASHES		METICAL
	MESARCH		ESCHARS	**ACEILMX**	EXCLAIM
	SCHMEAR	**ACEHRST**	ARCHEST	**ACEILMY**	MYCELIA
ACEHMRT	MATCHER		CHARETS	**ACEILNN**	ENCINAL
	REMATCH		CHASTER	**ACEILNP**	CAPELIN
ACEHMRU	CHAUMER		RACHETS		PANICLE
ACEHMSS	SACHEMS		RATCHES		PELICAN
	SAMECHS	**ACEHRSU**	ARCHEUS	**ACEILNR**	CARLINE
	SCHEMAS	**ACEHRSV**	VARECHS	**ACEILNS**	INLACES
ACEHMST	MATCHES	**ACEHRSW**	CHAWERS		SANICLE
ACEHMTT	MATCHET	**ACEHRSX**	EXARCHS		SCALENI
ACEHMTY	ECTHYMA	**ACEHRSY**	HYRACES	**ACEILNU**	CAULINE
ACEHMTZ	CHAMETZ	**ACEHRTT**	CHATTER	**ACEILOR**	CALORIE
			RATCHET		

	CARIOLE		NANCIES	**ACEIPTV**	CAPTIVE
	COALIER	**ACEINNT**	ANCIENT	**ACEIQRU**	ACQUIRE
	LORICAE	**ACEINNY**	CYANINE	**ACEIQSU**	CAIQUES
ACEILOS	CELOSIA	**ACEINOP**	APNOEIC	**ACEIQTU**	ACQUITE
	COALISE		PAEONIC	**ACEIQUZ**	CAZIQUE
ACEILOT	ALOETIC	**ACEINOS**	ACINOSE	**ACEIRRR**	CARRIER
ACEILOZ	COALIZE	**ACEINOT**	ACONITE	**ACEIRRS**	CARRIES
ACEILPR	CALIPER		ANOETIC		SCARIER
	REPLICA	**ACEINPR**	CAPRINE	**ACEIRRT**	CIRRATE
ACEILPS	PLAICES	**ACEINPS**	INSCAPE		ERRATIC
	SPECIAL		PINCASE	**ACEIRRW**	AIRCREW
ACEILPT	PLICATE	**ACEINPT**	PICANTE	**ACEIRRZ**	CRAZIER
ACEILPU	PECULIA	**ACEINRR**	CARNIER	**ACEIRST**	ATRESIC
ACEILRR	CERRIAL	**ACEINRS**	ARCSINE		CRISTAE
ACEILRS	CLARIES		ARSENIC		RACIEST
	ECLAIRS		CARNIES		STEARIC
	SCALIER		CERASIN	**ACEIRSU**	SAUCIER
ACEILRT	ARTICLE	**ACEINRT**	CANTIER		URICASE
	RECITAL		CERATIN	**ACEIRSV**	CARVIES
	TALCIER		CERTAIN		CAVIERS
ACEILRU	AURICLE		CREATIN		VARICES
ACEILRV	CALIVER		CRINATE		VISCERA
	CAVILER		NACRITE	**ACEIRSZ**	CRAZIES
	CLAVIER		TACRINE	**ACEIRTT**	ATRETIC
	VALERIC	**ACEINSS**	CASEINS		CATTIER
	VELARIC		CASSINE		CITRATE
ACEILRY	CLAYIER		INCASES	**ACEISSS**	ASCESIS
ACEILSS	SALICES	**ACEINST**	ACETINS	**ACEISST**	ASCITES
ACEILST	ASTELIC		CANIEST		ECTASIS
	ELASTIC		CINEAST	**ACEISTT**	CATTIES
	LACIEST	**ACEINSU**	EUCAINS		STATICE
	LATICES	**ACEINSV**	INCAVES		TIETACS
	SALICET	**ACEINSY**	CYANISE	**ACEISTV**	ACTIVES
ACEILSV	CLAVIES	**ACEINTT**	NICTATE	**ACEISVV**	VIVACES
	VESICAL		TETANIC	**ACEITTV**	CAVETTI
ACEILTT	LATTICE	**ACEINTU**	TUNICAE	**ACEITTX**	EXTATIC
	TACTILE	**ACEINTV**	VENATIC	**ACEITUX**	AUXETIC
ACEILVW	WAVICLE	**ACEINTX**	INEXACT	**ACEJKMN**	JACKMEN
ACEIMMS	CAMMIES	**ACEINTY**	CYANITE	**ACEJKOP**	PAJOCKE
ACEIMNO	ENCOMIA	**ACEINTZ**	ZINCATE	**ACEJKRS**	JACKERS
ACEIMNP	PEMICAN	**ACEINYZ**	CYANIZE	**ACEJKST**	JACKETS
ACEIMNR	CARMINE	**ACEIOOZ**	ZOOECIA	**ACEJLOR**	CAJOLER
ACEIMNS	AMNESIC	**ACEIOPT**	ECTOPIA	**ACEJLOS**	CAJOLES
	CINEMAS	**ACEIORS**	CARIOSE	**ACEJNOS**	CAJONES
ACEIMNT	EMICANT		ORACIES	**ACEJNOT**	JACONET
	NEMATIC		SCORIAE	**ACEJNOY**	JOYANCE
ACEIMOR	COREMIA	**ACEIORT**	EROTICA	**ACEJNSU**	JAUNCES
ACEIMOV	VOMICAE	**ACEIOST**	SOCIATE	**ACEJNTU**	JUNCATE
ACEIMPR	CAMPIER	**ACEIOTX**	EXOTICA	**ACEJPTU**	CAJEPUT
ACEIMPY	PYAEMIC	**ACEIPPR**	CRAPPIE	**ACEJRTT**	TRAJECT
ACEIMRT	MATRICE		EPICARP	**ACEKKNR**	KNACKER
ACEIMRU	URAEMIC	**ACEIPPT**	TAPPICE	**ACEKLLP**	PELLACK
ACEIMSS	CAMISES	**ACEIPRR**	CRAPIER	**ACEKLMS**	MACKLES
ACEIMST	ACMITES	**ACEIPRS**	EPACRIS	**ACEKLNR**	CRANKLE
	ETACISM		SCRAPIE	**ACEKLNS**	SLACKEN
	MICATES		SPACIER	**ACEKLOR**	EARLOCK
	SEMATIC	**ACEIPRT**	PARETIC	**ACEKLPS**	SPACKLE
ACEIMSU	CAESIUM		PICRATE	**ACEKLPT**	PLACKET
ACEIMTX	TAXEMIC	**ACEIPST**	ASEPTIC	**ACEKLQU**	QUACKLE
ACEINNP	PINNACE		PACIEST	**ACEKLRS**	CALKERS
ACEINNR	CANNIER		SPICATE		LACKERS
	NARCEIN	**ACEIPSU**	AUSPICE		SLACKER
ACEINNS	CANINES	**ACEIPSZ**	CAPIZES	**ACEKLRT**	TACKLER
	ENCINAS		CAPSIZE	**ACEKLRU**	CAULKER

ACEKLST	TACKLES	**ACELMNS**	ENCALMS	**ACELORY**	CALOYER
ACEKLSY	LACKEYS	**ACELMOR**	CAROMEL	**ACELOSS**	SOLACES
ACEKMNP	PACKMEN	**ACELMOT**	CAMELOT	**ACELOST**	ALECOST
ACEKMOR	COMAKER	**ACELMOU**	CAULOME		LACTOSE
ACEKMOS	COMAKES		LEUCOMA		LOCATES
ACEKMRS	SMACKER	**ACELMPR**	CLAMPER		SCATOLE
ACEKNOS	NOCAKES	**ACELMPS**	CAMPLES		TALCOSE
ACEKNPR	PRANCKE	**ACELMRS**	MARCELS	**ACELOSV**	ALCOVES
ACEKNRR	CRANKER	**ACELMRY**	CAMELRY		COEVALS
ACEKNRS	CANKERS	**ACELMSS**	MASCLES	**ACELOTT**	CALOTTE
	SNACKER		MESCALS	**ACELOTU**	OCULATE
ACEKNRY	CANKERY		SCAMELS	**ACELOTY**	ACOLYTE
ACEKNST	NACKETS	**ACELMST**	CALMEST		COTYLAE
ACEKNSU	UNCAKES		CAMLETS	**ACELOUV**	VACUOLE
ACEKORR	CROAKER	**ACELMSU**	ALMUCES	**ACELPPR**	CLAPPER
ACEKPPR	PREPACK		MACULES	**ACELPPS**	SCAPPLE
ACEKPRS	PACKERS	**ACELMSZ**	MEZCALS	**ACELPRS**	CARPELS
	REPACKS	**ACELMTU**	CALUMET		CLASPER
ACEKPST	PACKETS	**ACELNNO**	ALENCON		CRAPLES
ACEKQRU	QUACKER	**ACELNNS**	CANNELS		PARCELS
ACEKRRS	RACKERS	**ACELNNU**	UNCLEAN		PLACERS
	RERACKS	**ACELNNY**	LYNCEAN		RECLASP
ACEKRRT	RETRACK	**ACELNOP**	NOPLACE		SCALPER
	TRACKER	**ACELNOR**	CORNEAL	**ACELPRT**	PLECTRA
ACEKRSS	SACKERS	**ACELNOS**	SECONAL	**ACELPRY**	PRELACY
	SCREAKS	**ACELNOT**	LACTONE	**ACELPSS**	CAPLESS
ACEKRST	RACKETS	**ACELNOZ**	CALZONE	**ACELPST**	CAPLETS
	RESTACK	**ACELNPS**	ENCLASP		PLACETS
	RETACKS		SPANCEL	**ACELPSU**	CAPSULE
	STACKER	**ACELNPT**	CLAPNET		SCALEUP
	TACKERS	**ACELNPU**	CLEANUP		SPECULA
ACEKRSU	CAUKERS		UNPLACE		UPSCALE
ACEKRSW	CAWKERS	**ACELNRS**	LANCERS	**ACELPSY**	CYPSELA
	WACKERS		RANCELS	**ACELPTY**	ECTYPAL
ACEKRSY	SCREAKY	**ACELNRT**	CENTRAL	**ACELPUU**	CUPULAE
	YACKERS	**ACELNRU**	LUCARNE	**ACELQRU**	CLAQUER
ACEKRTT	RACKETT		NUCLEAR		LACQUER
ACEKRTY	RACKETY		UNCLEAR	**ACELQSU**	CALQUES
ACEKSST	CASKETS	**ACELNRY**	LARCENY		CLAQUES
ACEKSTT	STACKET	**ACELNST**	CANTLES	**ACELQUY**	LACQUEY
	TACKETS		CENTALS	**ACELRRS**	CARRELS
ACEKSTW	WACKEST		LANCETS	**ACELRRU**	RAUCLER
ACEKSUW	WAESUCK		SCANTLE	**ACELRRW**	CRAWLER
ACEKTTY	TACKETY	**ACELNSU**	CENSUAL	**ACELRSS**	CARLESS
ACELLMO	CALOMEL		LACUNES		CLASSER
ACELLMY	MYCELLA		LAUNCES		SCALERS
ACELLNU	NUCLEAL		UNLACES		SCLERAS
ACELLNY	CLEANLY		UNSCALE	**ACELRST**	CARTELS
ACELLOR	CORELLA	**ACELNTT**	CANTLET		CLARETS
	OCELLAR	**ACELNTY**	LATENCY		CRESTAL
ACELLOS	CALLOSE	**ACELNVY**	VALENCY		SCARLET
	LOCALES	**ACELOPR**	POLACRE		TARCELS
ACELLOT	COLLATE	**ACELOPS**	ESCALOP	**ACELRSU**	CESURAL
ACELLPS	SCALPEL	**ACELOPT**	POLECAT		RECUSAL
ACELLPY	CLYPEAL	**ACELOPU**	COPULAE		SECULAR
ACELLRR	CARRELL	**ACELOQU**	COEQUAL	**ACELRSV**	CALVERS
ACELLRS	CALLERS	**ACELORR**	CAROLER		CARVELS
	CELLARS	**ACELORS**	CLAROES		CLAVERS
	RECALLS		COALERS	**ACELRSW**	CLAWERS
	SCLERAL		ESCOLAR	**ACELRTT**	CLATTER
ACELLRY	CLEARLY		ORACLES	**ACELRTY**	TREACLY
ACELLST	CALLETS		RECOALS	**ACELSSS**	CLASSES
ACELMMR	CLAMMER		SOLACER		SACLESS
ACELMNO	COALMEN	**ACELORT**	LOCATER	**ACELSST**	CASTLES

	SCLATES	ACENOSS	CASSONE		CAROUSE
ACELSSU	CLAUSES	ACENOST	COSTEAN	ACEORSW	CROWEAS
ACELSSV	SCLAVES		OCTANES	ACEORSX	COAXERS
ACELSTU	CAUTELS	ACENOTT	ATTONCE	ACEORTU	OUTRACE
	SULCATE	ACENOTV	CENTAVO	ACEORTV	OVERACT
ACELSTY	ACETYLS	ACENPRR	PRANCER	ACEORTX	EXACTOR
	SCYTALE	ACENPRS	PRANCES	ACEOSSU	CASEOUS
ACELSUU	ACULEUS	ACENPRU	PRAUNCE	ACEOSTT	COSTATE
ACELSUX	EXCUSAL	ACENPST	CATNEPS	ACEOSTU	ACETOUS
ACELSXY	CALYXES	ACENPSU	PAUNCES	ACEOSTV	AVOCETS
ACELTUY	ACUTELY		UNCAPES		OCTAVES
ACELTXY	EXACTLY	ACENPSW	PAWNCES	ACEOTTV	CAVETTO
ACEMMRR	CRAMMER	ACENPTT	PENTACT	ACEOTUU	AUTOCUE
ACEMMRS	SCAMMER	ACENPTY	PATENCY		COUTEAU
ACEMNOR	CREMONA	ACENRRY	ERRANCY	ACEOTUX	COTEAUX
	ROMANCE	ACENRSS	ANCRESS	ACEPPRR	CRAPPER
ACEMNOS	ANCOMES		CASERNS	ACEPPRS	CAPPERS
ACEMNPS	ENCAMPS	ACENRST	CANTERS	ACEPRRS	CARPERS
ACEMNRT	CREMANT		CARNETS		SCARPER
ACEMNRW	CREWMAN		NECTARS		SCRAPER
ACEMNSU	ACUMENS		RECANTS	ACEPRSS	ESCARPS
ACEMOPR	COMPARE		SCANTER		PARSECS
	COMPEAR		TANRECS		SCRAPES
ACEMOPS	POMACES		TRANCES		SECPARS
ACEMORS	AMORCES	ACENRSU	SURANCE		SPACERS
ACEMORU	MORCEAU	ACENRSV	CAVERNS	ACEPRST	CARPETS
ACEMOSS	COSMEAS		CRAVENS		PREACTS
ACEMOST	CAMOTES	ACENRSY	CARNEYS		PRECAST
	COMATES		SCENARY		SPECTRA
ACEMOSU	MUCOSAE	ACENRSZ	ZARNECS	ACEPRSU	APERCUS
ACEMPRR	CRAMPER	ACENRTT	TRANECT		SCAUPER
ACEMPRS	CAMPERS	ACENRTU	CENTAUR	ACEPRTU	CAPTURE
	SCAMPER		UNCRATE	ACEPSST	ASPECTS
ACEMPRT	CRAMPET		UNTRACE	ACEPSTU	CUSPATE
ACEMPST	CAMPEST	ACENRTY	ENCRATY		TEACUPS
ACEMRSS	SCREAMS		NECTARY	ACEQRTU	RACQUET
ACEMRST	MERCATS	ACENSST	ASCENTS	ACEQSSU	CASQUES
ACEMRSY	CRAMESY		SECANTS		SACQUES
ACEMSSU	CAMUSES		STANCES	ACEQSTU	ACQUEST
ACEMSTT	METCAST	ACENSSU	UNCASES	ACERRRY	RECARRY
ACEMSTU	MUCATES		USANCES	ACERRSS	CRASSER
ACEMSUX	EXACUMS	ACENSTT	CANTEST		SCARERS
ACENNOS	ANCONES	ACENSTU	NUTCASE		SCARRES
	SONANCE	ACENSUU	USAUNCE	ACERRST	CARTERS
ACENNOT	CONNATE	ACENSUV	VAUNCES		CRATERS
ACENNOX	COANNEX	ACEOOPP	APOCOPE		TRACERS
ACENNOY	NOYANCE	ACEOOTZ	ECTOZOA	ACERRSU	CURARES
ACENNOZ	CANZONE	ACEOPRX	EXOCARP	ACERRSV	CARVERS
ACENNRS	CANNERS	ACEOPSS	SCAPOSE		CRAVERS
	SCANNER	ACEOPST	CAPOTES	ACERRSY	CRAYERS
ACENNRY	CANNERY		SCOPATE	ACERRTT	RETRACT
ACENNST	NASCENT		TOECAPS	ACERRTU	TRACEUR
ACENNSU	NUANCES	ACEOPSW	COWPEAS	ACERRTY	TRACERY
ACENNTY	TENANCY	ACEOPTU	OUTPACE	ACERRUV	VERRUCA
ACENOOR	CORONAE	ACEORRS	COARSER	ACERRVY	CARVERY
ACENOPT	PATONCE		CORREAS	ACERSST	ACTRESS
ACENOPU	PONCEAU	ACEORRT	ACROTER		CASTERS
ACENORS	CANOERS		CREATOR		RECASTS
	CARNOSE		REACTOR	ACERSSU	ARCUSES
	COARSEN	ACEORSS	ROSACES		CAUSERS
	CORNEAS	ACEORST	COASTER		CESURAS
	EARCONS		COATERS		SAUCERS
	NARCOSE		RECOATS		SUCRASE
ACENORT	ENACTOR	ACEORSU	ACEROUS	ACERSSV	SCARVES

ACERSSY	CARSEYS	**ACFINRT**	FRANTIC		LACKING
	SCRAYES		INFARCT	**ACGIKNP**	PACKING
ACERSTT	SCATTER		INFRACT	**ACGIKNR**	ARCKING
ACERSTU	ACTURES	**ACFINRY**	CARNIFY		CARKING
	CAUTERS	**ACFIOPY**	OPACIFY		CRAKING
	CRUSTAE	**ACFIOSS**	FIASCOS		RACKING
	CURATES	**ACFIPRY**	CAPRIFY	**ACGIKNS**	CAKINGS
ACERSTY	SECTARY	**ACFIRSY**	SACRIFY		CASKING
ACERTTT	TETRACT		SCARIFY		SACKING
ACERTTU	CURTATE	**ACFISST**	FASCIST	**ACGIKNT**	TACKING
ACERTTX	EXTRACT	**ACFKLRU**	RACKFUL	**ACGIKNV**	VACKING
ACERTTY	CATTERY	**ACFKLSU**	SACKFUL	**ACGIKNY**	YACKING
ACERTUV	CURVATE	**ACFLLOY**	FOCALLY	**ACGILLN**	CALLING
ACERTUX	CURTAXE	**ACFLNOS**	FALCONS	**ACGILLO**	LOGICAL
ACERTUY	CAUTERY		FLACONS	**ACGILMN**	CALMING
ACESSTT	STACTES	**ACFLNSU**	CANFULS	**ACGILMY**	MYALGIC
ACESSTU	CAESTUS		CANSFUL	**ACGILNN**	LANCING
	CUESTAS	**ACFLOPW**	COWFLAP	**ACGILNO**	COALING
ACESSTY	CYTASES	**ACFLOST**	OLFACTS	**ACGILNP**	PLACING
	ECSTASY	**ACFLPSU**	CAPFULS	**ACGILNR**	CARLING
ACESSUY	CAUSEYS	**ACFLRSU**	CARFULS	**ACGILNS**	LACINGS
	CAYUSES	**ACFLRTU**	CARTFUL		SCALING
ACESTTU	ACUTEST	**ACFLRUU**	FURCULA	**ACGILNT**	CATLING
	SCUTATE	**ACFLTTU**	TACTFUL		TALCING
ACESTTY	TESTACY	**ACFLTUY**	FACULTY	**ACGILNU**	CINGULA
ACESTUY	EUSTACY	**ACFMSTU**	FACTUMS		GLUCINA
ACFFHSU	CHAUFFS	**ACFNNOT**	NONFACT	**ACGILNV**	CALVING
ACFFIIT	CAITIFF	**ACFNNUY**	UNFANCY	**ACGILNW**	CLAWING
ACFFIKM	MAFFICK	**ACFNRTU**	FRUCTAN	**ACGILNY**	CLAYING
ACFFILT	AFFLICT	**ACFNSTU**	UNFACTS	**ACGILOS**	CALIGOS
ACFFINS	FANFICS	**ACFORST**	FACTORS	**ACGILOT**	OTALGIC
ACFFINY	FANCIFY		FORCATS	**ACGILRS**	GARLICS
ACFFIRT	TRAFFIC	**ACFORTY**	FACTORY	**ACGIMMN**	CAMMING
ACFFIRY	FARCIFY	**ACFRRTU**	FRACTUR	**ACGIMNO**	COAMING
ACFFLSS	SCLAFFS	**ACFRSTU**	FRACTUS	**ACGIMNP**	CAMPING
ACFFLTU	FACTFUL	**ACGGHIS**	CHIGGAS	**ACGIMNU**	CAUMING
ACFFOST	CASTOFF	**ACGGINR**	GRACING	**ACGINNN**	CANNING
	OFFCAST	**ACGGIOS**	AGOGICS	**ACGINNR**	CRANING
ACFGHIN	CHAFING	**ACGGRSY**	SCRAGGY		RANCING
ACFGINR	FARCING	**ACGHIKN**	HACKING	**ACGINNS**	CANINGS
ACFGINS	FACINGS	**ACGHIMO**	OGHAMIC	**ACGINNT**	CANTING
ACFHIIS	FIASCHI	**ACGHINR**	ARCHING	**ACGINOR**	ORGANIC
ACFHIST	CATFISH		CHAGRIN	**ACGINOS**	AGNOSIC
ACFHISU	FUCHSIA		CHARING		ANGICOS
ACFHLNU	FLAUNCH	**ACGHINS**	ACHINGS	**ACGINOT**	COATING
ACFHNOU	FAUCHON		CASHING		COTINGA
ACFHRTU	FUTHARC		CHASING	**ACGINOX**	COAXING
ACFHRTY	FRATCHY	**ACGHINT**	GNATHIC	**ACGINPP**	CAPPING
ACFIILN	FINICAL	**ACGHINW**	CHAWING	**ACGINPR**	CARPING
ACFIKNN	FINNACK		CHINWAG		CRAPING
ACFIKTY	TACKIFY	**ACGHIOR**	CHORAGI	**ACGINPS**	SCAPING
ACFILNO	FOLACIN	**ACGHIPR**	GRAPHIC		SPACING
ACFILNY	FANCILY	**ACGHIRS**	SCRAIGH	**ACGINRS**	ARCINGS
ACFILOY	COALIFY	**ACGHLTU**	CLAUGHT		RACINGS
ACFILRY	CLARIFY	**ACGHNRU**	GRAUNCH		SACRING
ACFILSS	FISCALS	**ACGHOST**	GOTCHAS		SCARING
ACFIMOR	ACIFORM	**ACGHOSU**	GAUCHOS	**ACGINRT**	CARTING
	FORMICA	**ACGHRRU**	CURRAGH		CRATING
ACFIMRU	FUMARIC	**ACGHRSU**	CURAGHS		TRACING
ACFIMSS	FASCISM		SCRAUGH	**ACGINRV**	CARVING
ACFINNS	FINNACS	**ACGIILN**	ALGINIC		CRAVING
ACFINNY	INFANCY	**ACGIITU**	AUGITIC	**ACGINRZ**	CRAZING
ACFINOT	FACTION	**ACGIJKN**	JACKING	**ACGINSS**	CASINGS
ACFINRS	FARCINS	**ACGIKLN**	CALKING	**ACGINST**	ACTINGS

	CASTING	ACHILST	CHITALS	ACHLMYY	ALCHYMY
ACGINSU	CAUSING	ACHILSY	CLAYISH	ACHLNOS	LOCHANS
	SAUCING	ACHILWY	LICHWAY	ACHLNOY	HALCYON
ACGINSV	CAVINGS	ACHIMNO	MANIHOC	ACHLNSU	NUCHALS
ACGINSW	CAWINGS		MOHICAN	ACHLNTU	TULCHAN
ACGINTT	CATTING	ACHIMOS	CHAMISO		UNLATCH
ACGINUV	VICUGNA		CHAMOIS	ACHLOPR	RAPLOCH
ACGIORT	ARGOTIC	ACHIMOX	CHAMOIX	ACHLOPT	POTLACH
ACGIRST	GASTRIC	ACHIMRS	CHARISM	ACHLORS	CHORALS
	TRAGICS		CHIMARS		LORCHAS
ACGKLLO	GALLOCK		CHRISMA		SCHOLAR
ACGKMMO	GAMMOCK	ACHIMSS	CHIASMS	ACHLORT	TROCHAL
ACGKORV	GARVOCK		SCHISMA	ACHLOSW	SALCHOW
ACGLLPU	CUPGALL	ACHIMST	MASTICH	ACHLOTY	ACOLYTH
ACGLNOR	CLANGOR		TACHISM	ACHLPST	SPLATCH
ACGLNOY	AGLYCON	ACHINNU	UNCHAIN	ACHLTUZ	CHALUTZ
ACGLNSU	GLUCANS	ACHINOP	APHONIC	ACHMNOR	MONARCH
ACGLNSY	GLYCANS	ACHINOY	ONYCHIA		NOMARCH
ACGLOSU	CAGOULS	ACHINPS	SPINACH	ACHMNOU	UNMACHO
ACGLOXY	COXALGY	ACHINRS	CHINARS	ACHMNRU	UNCHARM
ACGMNOP	CAMPONG	ACHINRU	UNCHAIR	ACHMOPR	CAMPHOR
ACGNNOR	CRANNOG	ACHINRZ	ZARNICH	ACHMORS	CHROMAS
ACGNOOT	OCTAGON	ACHINTX	XANTHIC		MORCHAS
ACGNORS	GARCONS	ACHINUV	CHAUVIN	ACHMORZ	MACHZOR
ACGNOSS	GASCONS	ACHIOPS	ISOPACH	ACHMOST	STOMACH
ACGNOSU	COUGANS	ACHIOPT	APHOTIC	ACHMPTU	MATCHUP
ACGORRY	GYROCAR	ACHIORT	CHARIOT	ACHMSSU	SUMACHS
ACGORSU	COUGARS		HARICOT	ACHMSUW	CUMSHAW
ACGORUU	COUGUAR	ACHIOST	ISOTACH	ACHNNOS	CHANSON
ACGOSWY	COGWAYS	ACHIPPS	SAPPHIC		NONCASH
ACGSTTU	CATGUTS	ACHIPST	HAPTICS	ACHNOOY	CHANOYO
ACHHIRS	RHACHIS		PATHICS	ACHNORS	ANCHORS
ACHHISV	CHAVISH		SPATHIC		ARCHONS
ACHHLOT	CHALOTH	ACHIPTU	CHUPATI		RANCHOS
ACHHMSU	CHUMASH	ACHIPTW	WHIPCAT	ACHNORT	CHANTOR
ACHHOST	TOSHACH	ACHIQRU	CHARQUI	ACHNOSS	SANCHOS
ACHHPPU	CHUPPAH	ACHIQSU	QUAICHS	ACHNOST	CHATONS
ACHHTTT	THATCHT	ACHIRRT	TRIARCH	ACHNOSY	ONYCHAS
ACHHTTY	THATCHY	ACHIRTU	HAIRCUT	ACHNOTY	TACHYON
ACHIIKM	KAMICHI	ACHIRTY	CHARITY	ACHNOUY	CHANOYU
ACHIILS	ISCHIAL	ACHISSS	CHASSIS	ACHNOVY	ANCHOVY
ACHIIMS	CHIASMI	ACHISST	SCAITHS	ACHNPSS	SCHNAPS
ACHIINT	CHIANTI	ACHISTT	CATTISH	ACHNPUY	PAUNCHY
ACHIIPS	PACHISI		CHATTIS	ACHNRTY	CHANTRY
ACHIIRV	CHIVARI		TACHIST	ACHNRUY	RAUNCHY
ACHIJKS	HIJACKS	ACHKKRU	CHUKKAR		UNCHARY
ACHIJNT	JACINTH	ACHKKSU	CHUKKAS	ACHNSTU	CANTHUS
ACHIKOS	KOCHIAS	ACHKLST	KLATSCH		CHAUNTS
ACHIKRS	RICKSHA	ACHKMMO	HAMMOCK		STAUNCH
ACHIKRY	HAYRICK	ACHKOPS	HOPSACK	ACHNSTY	SNATCHY
ACHIKSS	SHICKSA	ACHKORS	CHOKRAS	ACHOOSS	CASHOOS
ACHILLO	LOCHIAL	ACHKOSS	HASSOCK	ACHOOST	CAHOOTS
ACHILLP	PHALLIC		SHACKOS	ACHOPRS	CARHOPS
ACHILLS	CHALLIS	ACHKOSW	WHACKOS		COPRAHS
ACHILLT	THALLIC	ACHKOTT	HATTOCK	ACHOPRT	TOPARCH
ACHILMO	MALICHO	ACHKRSU	CHUKARS	ACHOPRY	CHARPOY
	MOCHILA	ACHKSTW	THWACKS	ACHOPSY	POCHAYS
ACHILMS	CHIMLAS	ACHLLOO	ALCOHOL	ACHORRS	CHARROS
ACHILOR	CHORIAL	ACHLLOR	CHLORAL	ACHORRT	TROCHAR
ACHILOS	SCHOLIA	ACHLLOS	CHOLLAS	ACHORST	ORCHATS
ACHILPS	CALIPHS	ACHLLOT	CHALLOT	ACHORSU	AUROCHS
ACHILRS	ARCHILS	ACHLMOP	CAMPHOL	ACHPPSU	CHUPPAS
	CARLISH	ACHLMSY	CHLAMYS	ACHPRSS	SCARPHS
ACHILRY	CHARILY	ACHLMSZ	SCHMALZ	ACHPTUZ	CHUTZPA

ACHRSST	SCARTHS		CATSKIN	**ACILRTY**	CLARITY
ACHRSTY	STARCHY	**ACIKNTT**	TINTACK	**ACILRVY**	VICARLY
ACHRSUU	URACHUS	**ACIKOPS**	PAIOCKS	**ACILRYZ**	CRAZILY
ACHSSTU	CUSHATS	**ACIKORS**	ARKOSIC	**ACILSSS**	CLASSIS
ACHSSTY	STACHYS	**ACIKPRT**	PATRICK	**ACILSSU**	CLUSIAS
ACHSSUW	CUSHAWS		TRIPACK	**ACILSUY**	SAUCILY
ACHSTUW	WAUCHTS	**ACIKPSS**	ASPICKS	**ACILTTY**	CATTILY
ACHSTUY	CYATHUS	**ACIKRST**	KARSTIC		TACITLY
ACIIKNN	CANIKIN	**ACILLLY**	ALLYLIC	**ACILTUV**	VICTUAL
ACIIKRS	AIRSICK	**ACILLMS**	MISCALL	**ACIMMNO**	AMMONIC
ACIILLN	ALLICIN	**ACILLRY**	LYRICAL	**ACIMNOP**	CAMPION
ACIILMM	MIMICAL	**ACILLSS**	SCILLAS	**ACIMNOR**	MARCONI
ACIILMS	LAICISM	**ACILMNO**	LIMACON		MINORCA
ACIILNR	CLARINI		MALONIC	**ACIMNOS**	ANOSMIC
ACIILNS	INCISAL	**ACILMOP**	OILCAMP		CAMIONS
	SALICIN	**ACILMOT**	COMITAL		CONIMAS
	SINICAL	**ACILMPS**	PLASMIC		MANIOCS
ACIILNV	VICINAL		PSALMIC		MASONIC
ACIILOV	VILIACO	**ACILMPY**	CAMPILY	**ACIMNPU**	PANICUM
ACIILPT	APLITIC	**ACILMSU**	MUSICAL	**ACIMNRS**	ARCMINS
ACIILPU	APICULI	**ACILNNO**	CANNOLI		NARCISM
ACIILRY	CILIARY	**ACILNNU**	UNCINAL	**ACIMNRT**	MANTRIC
ACIILSS	SILICAS	**ACILNNY**	CANNILY	**ACIMNRU**	CRANIUM
ACIILST	ITALICS	**ACILNOR**	CLARINO		CUMARIN
ACIILSU	ILIACUS		CLARION	**ACIMNTT**	CATMINT
ACIILSV	CLIVIAS	**ACILNOS**	ALNICOS	**ACIMOOS**	OOMIACS
ACIILTY	LAICITY		OILCANS	**ACIMOPT**	APOMICT
ACIIMMN	MINICAM	**ACILNOU**	INOCULA		POTAMIC
ACIIMMS	MIASMIC	**ACILNOY**	ACYLOIN	**ACIMOSS**	MOSAICS
ACIIMNR	CRIMINA	**ACILNOZ**	CALZONI	**ACIMOST**	ATOMICS
	MINICAR	**ACILNPS**	CAPLINS		MATICOS
ACIIMOT	COMITIA		INCLASP		OSMATIC
ACIIMST	ISMATIC	**ACILNPY**	PLIANCY		SOMATIC
	ITACISM	**ACILNRS**	CARLINS	**ACIMOSV**	VOMICAS
	SIMATIC	**ACILNST**	CATLINS	**ACIMPRT**	CRAMPIT
ACIINNO	ANIONIC		TINCALS		PTARMIC
ACIINNS	NIACINS	**ACILNSU**	UNCIALS	**ACIMPRY**	PRIMACY
ACIINOS	ASINICO	**ACILNTU**	LUNATIC	**ACIMPSS**	SCAMPIS
ACIINOV	AVIONIC	**ACILNTY**	ANTICLY		SPASMIC
ACIINPS	PISCINA		CANTILY	**ACIMPST**	IMPACTS
ACIINTT	TITANIC	**ACILNUV**	VINCULA	**ACIMRSS**	RACISMS
ACIINUX	AUXINIC	**ACILOPT**	CAPITOL	**ACIMRST**	MATRICS
ACIIPPR	PRIAPIC		COALPIT	**ACIMRSY**	MYRICAS
ACIIPRT	PIRATIC		OPTICAL	**ACIMRSZ**	CZARISM
ACIIRST	SATIRIC		TOPICAL	**ACIMSST**	MASTICS
ACIIRTT	TRIATIC	**ACILORR**	RACLOIR		MISACTS
ACIITTX	TAXITIC	**ACILORV**	CORIVAL		MISCAST
ACIJUZZ	JACUZZI	**ACILOSS**	SOCIALS	**ACIMSTT**	TACTISM
ACIKLLY	ALKYLIC	**ACILOST**	CITOLAS	**ACINNOT**	ACTINON
ACIKLNS	CALKINS		STOICAL		CANTION
ACIKLOR	AIRLOCK	**ACILOTV**	VOLATIC		CONTAIN
ACIKLTY	TACKILY		VOLTAIC	**ACINNOZ**	CANZONI
ACIKLWY	WACKILY	**ACILOTX**	TOXICAL	**ACINNST**	INCANTS
ACIKMOO	OOMIACK	**ACILPRT**	CLIPART		STANNIC
ACIKMOT	COMATIK	**ACILPST**	PLACITS	**ACINNSY**	CYANINS
ACIKMPR	RAMPICK		PLASTIC	**ACINNTU**	ANNICUT
ACIKMPW	PICKMAW	**ACILPSU**	SPICULA	**ACINOPT**	CAPTION
ACIKMSU	UMIACKS	**ACILPTY**	TYPICAL		PACTION
ACIKNNP	PANNICK	**ACILRSS**	CRISSAL	**ACINOQU**	COQUINA
ACIKNPS	PANICKS	**ACILRST**	CITRALS	**ACINORR**	CARRION
ACIKNPY	PANICKY	**ACILRSU**	URACILS	**ACINORS**	SARONIC
ACIKNRS	NICKARS	**ACILRSY**	SCARILY	**ACINORT**	CAROTIN
ACIKNST	ANTICKS	**ACILRTU**	CURTAIL		CORTINA
	CATKINS		TRUCIAL	**ACINORV**	CORVINA

ACINOSS	CAISSON	ACIRTUY	RAUCITY	ACLMORS	CLAMORS
	CASINOS	ACISSTT	STATICS	ACLMORU	CLAMOUR
	CASSINO	ACISSTU	CASUIST	ACLMOSU	MUCOSAL
ACINOST	ACTIONS	ACISTTU	CATSUIT	ACLMSTU	TALCUMS
	ATONICS	ACISTUV	VACUIST	ACLMSUU	LUCUMAS
	CATIONS	ACITUVY	VACUITY	ACLMSUY	MASCULY
ACINOSU	ACINOUS	ACJKKSY	SKYJACK	ACLNNOO	NONCOLA
ACINOSY	SYCONIA	ACJKLOW	LOCKJAW	ACLNOOR	CORONAL
ACINOTT	TACTION	ACJKNNO	JANNOCK	ACLNOOT	COOLANT
ACINOTU	AUCTION	ACJKOPS	PAJOCKS		OCTANOL
	CAUTION	ACJKOPT	JACKPOT	ACLNOOV	VOLCANO
ACINPRT	CANTRIP	ACJLORU	JOCULAR	ACLNORU	CORNUAL
ACINPRU	PURANIC	ACJMNTU	MUNTJAC		COURLAN
ACINPRY	CYPRIAN	ACJPTUU	CAJUPUT	ACLNOSS	CLASSON
ACINPSS	PANISCS	ACKKLOY	KOLACKY	ACLNOST	COLTANS
ACINPST	CATNIPS	ACKLLOP	POLLACK	ACLNOSX	CLAXONS
ACINQTU	QUANTIC	ACKLLOY	LAYLOCK	ACLNOUV	UNVOCAL
ACINRSS	ARCSINS	ACKLLSY	SLACKLY	ACLNPSU	UNCLASP
ACINRST	NARCIST	ACKLMNO	LOCKMAN	ACLNRTU	TRUNCAL
ACINRSU	CRUSIAN	ACKLMOR	ARMLOCK	ACLNSTY	SCANTLY
ACINRTT	TANTRIC		LOCKRAM	ACLNSUV	VULCANS
ACINRTU	CURTAIN	ACKLNOU	UNCLOAK	ACLOOPP	ALCOPOP
	TURACIN	ACKLNRY	CRANKLY	ACLOOPR	CARPOOL
ACINSTU	ANICUTS	ACKLOOR	OARLOCK	ACLOORT	LOCATOR
	NAUTICS	ACKLORV	LAVROCK	ACLOOSZ	ZOCALOS
ACINSUV	VICUNAS	ACKLORW	WARLOCK	ACLOPRT	CALTROP
ACIOPRS	PICAROS	ACKLORY	ROCKLAY		PROCTAL
	PROSAIC	ACKLOSS	LASSOCK	ACLOPRU	COPULAR
ACIOPRT	APRICOT	ACKMMMO	MAMMOCK		CUPOLAR
	APROTIC	ACKMNOS	SOCKMAN	ACLOPSU	COPULAS
	PAROTIC	ACKMNRU	RUCKMAN		CUPOLAS
	PATRICO	ACKMOST	STOMACK		SCOPULA
ACIOPST	COPITAS	ACKMOTT	MATTOCK	ACLOPSY	CALYPSO
	PSOATIC	ACKNNOW	ACKNOWN	ACLOPTY	POLYACT
ACIOPTT	APTOTIC	ACKNOSW	ACKNOWS	ACLORRS	CORRALS
ACIOPTY	OPACITY	ACKNPRS	PRANCKS	ACLORST	CARLOTS
ACIORRS	CORSAIR	ACKNPSU	UNPACKS		CROTALS
ACIORSU	CARIOUS	ACKNRTU	UNTRACK		SCROTAL
	CURIOSA	ACKNSTU	UNSTACK	ACLORSU	CAROLUS
ACIORTT	CITATOR		UNTACKS		OCULARS
	RICOTTA	ACKOPRR	PARROCK		OSCULAR
ACIOSST	SCOTIAS	ACKOPSY	YAPOCKS		RUCOLAS
ACIOSSV	OVISACS	ACKORRT	TARROCK	ACLORTY	ACTORLY
ACIPRSS	CASSPIR	ACKOSTW	TOWSACK	ACLORUV	VOCULAR
ACIPRSY	PISCARY	ACKOWZZ	WAZZOCK	ACLORYZ	CORYZAL
ACIPRTT	TIPCART	ACKPSSY	SKYCAPS	ACLOSST	COSTALS
ACIPRVY	PRIVACY	ACKPSTU	STACKUP	ACLOSTU	LOCUSTA
ACIPSST	SPASTIC	ACLLLOY	LOCALLY		TALCOUS
ACIPSTT	TIPCATS	ACLLOOR	COROLLA	ACLOSTW	COTWALS
ACIPTUY	PAUCITY	ACLLOOS	ALCOOLS	ACLPRTY	CRYPTAL
ACIQRTU	QUARTIC	ACLLOPS	CALLOPS	ACLPRUU	CUPULAR
ACIQSTU	ACQUIST		SCALLOP	ACLRSSW	SCRAWLS
	ACQUITS	ACLLORS	COLLARS	ACLRSSY	CRASSLY
ACIRRSS	SIRCARS	ACLLORU	LOCULAR	ACLRSTU	CRUSTAL
ACIRRST	TRICARS	ACLLOSU	CALLOUS		CURTALS
ACIRRSU	CURARIS	ACLLOSW	CALLOWS	ACLRSTY	CRYSTAL
ACIRSST	RACISTS	ACLLOTU	OUTCALL	ACLRSWY	SCRAWLY
	SACRIST	ACLLOVY	VOCALLY	ACLSSTU	CUTLASS
ACIRSSU	CUIRASS	ACLLRYY	ACRYLYL	ACMNOPR	CRAMPON
ACIRSTT	ASTRICT	ACLLSUY	CULLAYS	ACMNOPY	COMPANY
ACIRSTU	URTICAS	ACLMNOO	LOCOMAN	ACMNORS	MACRONS
ACIRSTW	TWISCAR	ACLMNPU	UNCLAMP	ACMNORY	ACRONYM
ACIRSTY	SATYRIC	ACLMNUY	CALUMNY	ACMNOSS	MASCONS
ACIRSTZ	CZARIST	ACLMOPS	COPALMS	ACMNSTU	SANCTUM

ACMOOST	SCOTOMA	ACOPPRS	COPPRAS	ADDEEHL	HEALDED
ACMOPRT	COMPART	ACOPRRT	CARPORT	ADDEEHN	HEADEND
ACMOPSS	COMPASS	ACOPRST	CAPTORS	ADDEEHR	ADHERED
ACMOPST	COMPAST	ACOPSTU	UPCOAST		REDHEAD
ACMOPTU	CAMPOUT	ACOPSTW	COWPATS	ADDEEHS	DEASHED
ACMORRS	CARROMS	ACORRST	CARROTS	ADDEEIR	DEAIRED
ACMORST	COMARTS		TROCARS		READIED
ACMORTW	CATWORM	ACORRTT	TRACTOR	ADDEEIT	IDEATED
ACMOSST	MASCOTS	ACORRTU	CURATOR	ADDEEKN	KNEADED
	SCAMTOS	ACORRTY	CARROTY	ADDEEKR	DAKERED
ACMOSSU	MUCOSAS	ACORSST	CASTORS	ADDEELM	MEDALED
ACMOSTT	TOMCATS		COSTARS	ADDEELN	DELENDA
ACMOSTU	MOTUCAS	ACORSSU	SARCOUS		LADENED
ACMQTUU	CUMQUAT		SOUCARS	ADDEELP	PEDALED
ACMRSSU	SACRUMS	ACORSSW	SOWCARS		PLEADED
ACMRSSW	SCRAWMS	ACORSTT	COTTARS	ADDEELS	DELEADS
ACMSSTU	MUSCATS	ACORSTU	CUATROS	ADDEELT	DELATED
ACMSTUU	MUTUCAS		SURCOAT	ADDEELY	DELAYED
ACMSUUV	VACUUMS		TURACOS	ADDEEMN	AMENDED
ACNNNOS	CANNONS	ACORSTV	CAVORTS		DEADMEN
ACNNNUY	UNCANNY	ACORSTX	OXCARTS	ADDEEMR	DREAMED
ACNNORY	CANONRY	ACORSTY	CASTORY	ADDEEMS	ADDEEMS
ACNNOST	CANTONS	ACORSUU	RAUCOUS	ADDEENS	DEADENS
ACNNOSY	CANYONS	ACORSYZ	CORYZAS	ADDEENV	ADVENED
	SONANCY	ACORTUU	TURACOU		DAVENED
ACNNRSY	SCRANNY	ACOSSZZ	SCOZZAS	ADDEENY	DENAYED
ACNOOPS	POONACS	ACOSTTU	OUTACTS	ADDEEOT	DEODATE
ACNOORS	CORONAS		OUTCAST	ADDEERR	DREADER
	RACOONS	ACOSUUV	VACUOUS	ADDEERS	DEADERS
ACNOORT	CARTOON	ACPPRSY	SCRAPPY	ADDEERT	DERATED
	CORANTO	ACPRSSW	SCRAWPS		REDATED
ACNOPSW	SNOWCAP	ACPSSTU	CATSUPS		TREADED
ACNORRS	RANCORS		UPCASTS	ADDEERY	DERAYED
ACNORRU	RANCOUR	ACPSTUU	USUCAPT		YEARDED
ACNORRY	CARRYON	ACRRSTU	CRATURS	ADDEEST	DEADEST
ACNORST	CANTORS	ACRSTTU	TRACTUS		SEDATED
	CARTONS	ADDDDEL	DADDLED		STEADED
	CONTRAS	ADDDDOR	DODDARD	ADDEEVW	ADVEWED
	CRATONS	ADDDEER	DREADED	ADDEEWX	DEWAXED
ACNORSU	NACROUS		READDED	ADDEFHN	HANDFED
ACNORSY	CRAYONS	ADDDEFL	FADDLED	ADDEFIR	FADDIER
ACNORTT	CONTRAT	ADDDEGL	GLADDED	ADDEFLS	FADDLES
ACNORTU	COURANT	ADDDEIL	DAIDLED	ADDEFLY	FADEDLY
ACNOSSZ	SCAZONS	ADDDEIS	DADDIES	ADDEFNU	UNFADED
ACNOSTT	OCTANTS	ADDDEIW	WADDIED	ADDEFRT	DRAFTED
ACNOSTU	CONATUS	ADDDELN	DANDLED	ADDEFRU	DEFRAUD
	NOCTUAS	ADDDELP	PADDLED	ADDEFRW	DWARFED
	TOUCANS	ADDDELR	RADDLED	ADDEGGL	DAGGLED
ACNOSTW	SNOWCAT	ADDDELS	DADDLES	ADDEGGR	DRAGGED
ACNPRSY	SYNCARP		SADDLED	ADDEGHO	GODHEAD
ACNRRSU	CURRANS	ADDDELW	DAWDLED	ADDEGIL	GLADDIE
ACNRRTU	CURRANT		WADDLED	ADDEGIN	DEADING
ACNRSTU	UNCARTS	ADDDELY	ADDEDLY	ADDEGJU	ADJUDGE
ACNRSUY	UNSCARY	ADDDENO	DEODAND	ADDEGLN	DANGLED
ACNRSWY	SCRAWNY	ADDDENS	ADDENDS		GLADDEN
ACNRTUY	TRUANCY	ADDDENU	UNADDED	ADDEGLR	GLADDER
ACNRUYZ	UNCRAZY	ADDDEQU	QUADDED	ADDEGRS	GADDERS
ACOOPRR	CORPORA	ADDDGIN	DADDING	ADDEGRU	GUARDED
ACOOPRT	ROOTCAP	ADDDHOY	HODADDY	ADDEHIR	DIEHARD
ACOOPSU	OPACOUS	ADDDOOS	DOODADS		DIHEDRA
ACOOPTT	TOPCOAT	ADDEEEM	ADEEMED	ADDEHIS	HADDIES
ACOORTU	TOURACO	ADDEEEY	DEADEYE	ADDEHKS	KEDDAHS
ACOOSTV	OCTAVOS	ADDEEFM	DEFAMED	ADDEHLN	HANDLED
ACOPPRR	PROCARP	ADDEEGR	DEGRADE	ADDEHLS	DALEDHS

ADDEHOR	HOARDED	ADDELSS	SADDLES	ADDGIPY	GIDDYAP
ADDEHRS	SHARDED	ADDELST	STADDLE	ADDGLNO	GLADDON
ADDEHST	HADDEST	ADDELSW	DAWDLES	ADDGMNO	GODDAMN
ADDEIIK	DIDAKEI		SWADDLE	ADDGMOS	GODDAMS
ADDEIIM	DIAMIDE		WADDLES	ADDGOOS	OGDOADS
ADDEIIS	DAISIED	ADDELTW	TWADDLE	ADDGOOW	DAGWOOD
ADDEILL	DALLIED	ADDELTY	DATEDLY	ADDGORW	GODWARD
	DIALLED	ADDELYZ	DAZEDLY	ADDGOSY	DOGDAYS
ADDEILP	PAIDLED	ADDELZZ	DAZZLED	ADDHIKS	KADDISH
	PLAIDED	ADDEMMR	DRAMMED	ADDHILS	LADDISH
ADDEILR	DIEDRAL	ADDEMMW	DWAMMED	ADDHIMS	MADDISH
	DRAILED	ADDEMNS	DEMANDS	ADDHINP	DAPHNID
ADDEILS	DAIDLES		MADDENS	ADDHISS	SADDISH
	LADDIES	ADDEMNU	MAUNDED		SIDDHAS
ADDEILT	DILATED	ADDEMOP	POMADED	ADDHITY	HYDATID
ADDEIMR	ADMIRED	ADDEMRS	MADDERS	ADDHLOO	LADHOOD
	MARDIED	ADDEMRY	DRAMEDY	ADDHOOS	DOODAHS
ADDEIMS	DIADEMS	ADDEMST	MADDEST	ADDHOTY	ATHODYD
ADDEIMX	ADMIXED	ADDEMUW	DWAUMED	ADDHSSU	SADDHUS
ADDEINO	ADENOID	ADDENOR	ADORNED	ADDIINS	DISDAIN
ADDEINP	PANDIED	ADDENOT	DONATED	ADDIIPS	DIAPSID
ADDEINR	DANDIER		NODATED	ADDIKST	TSADDIK
	DRAINED	ADDENOU	DUODENA	ADDIKSZ	ZADDIKS
ADDEINS	DANDIES	ADDENPU	PUDENDA	ADDIKTY	KATYDID
	SDAINED	ADDENRS	DANDERS	ADDIKTZ	TZADDIK
ADDEINT	NIDATED	ADDENRT	DRANTED	ADDILMN	MIDLAND
ADDEINU	UNAIDED	ADDENRU	DAUNDER	ADDILNY	DANDILY
ADDEINV	INVADED	ADDENSS	DESANDS	ADDILOS	DISLOAD
	VIDENDA		SADDENS	ADDIMNO	DIAMOND
ADDEIOR	RADIOED	ADDENSU	ASUDDEN	ADDIMOR	DIADROM
ADDEIOT	IODATED	ADDENSY	SDAYNED	ADDIMRS	DIRDAMS
	TOADIED	ADDENTU	DAUNTED	ADDIMSS	MISADDS
ADDEIOV	AVOIDED		UNDATED	ADDIMSY	DISMAYD
ADDEIPS	PADDIES	ADDEOPT	ADOPTED		MIDDAYS
ADDEIRR	ARRIDED	ADDEORS	DEODARS	ADDINOR	ANDROID
ADDEIRT	TARDIED	ADDEPPR	DRAPPED	ADDINRY	DIANDRY
ADDEIST	TADDIES	ADDEPRS	PADDERS	ADDIPRS	DISPRAD
ADDEISV	ADVISED	ADDEPTU	UPDATED	ADDIQST	TSADDIQ
ADDEISW	SWADDIE	ADDERSS	ADDRESS	ADDIQTZ	TZADDIQ
	WADDIES	ADDERST	ADDREST	ADDIRZZ	DIZZARD
ADDEISY	DAYSIDE		RADDEST	ADDLLRU	DULLARD
ADDEITU	AUDITED	ADDERSW	SWARDED	ADDLNRY	DRYLAND
ADDEJLY	JADEDLY		WADDERS	ADDLOOS	SOLDADO
ADDEJNU	UNJADED	ADDERSY	DRYADES	ADDLTWY	TWADDLY
ADDEJRU	ADJURED	ADDERTT	DRATTED	ADDMNOS	DODMANS
ADDEKLR	DARKLED	ADDESST	SADDEST		ODDSMAN
ADDELLU	ALLUDED	ADDESTU	ADUSTED	ADDMOOS	ADDOOMS
	DUALLED		SUDATED	ADDNNOR	DONNARD
ADDELMW	DWALMED	ADDFHIS	FADDISH	ADDOORS	DORADOS
ADDELNR	DANDLER	ADDFIMS	FADDISM	ADDOPSY	DASYPOD
ADDELNS	DANDLES	ADDFINY	DANDIFY	ADDORST	DOTARDS
ADDELNU	UNLADED	ADDFIST	FADDIST	ADDOSTU	OUTADDS
ADDELPP	DAPPLED	ADDGGIN	GADDING	ADDQSUY	SQUADDY
ADDELPR	PADDLER	ADDGHIN	HADDING	ADEEEFY	FEDAYEE
ADDELPS	PADDLES	ADDGIIR	DIAGRID	ADEEELS	EASELED
ADDELRS	LADDERS	ADDGILN	ADDLING	ADEEELV	DELEAVE
	RADDLES	ADDGIMN	MADDING	ADEEEMN	DEMEANE
	SADDLER	ADDGINO	DADOING	ADEEERR	ARREEDE
ADDELRT	DARTLED	ADDGINP	PADDING	ADEEERX	EXEDRAE
ADDELRW	DAWDLER	ADDGINR	RADDING	ADEEESW	SEAWEED
	DRAWLED	ADDGINU	DAUDING	ADEEFGU	FEAGUED
	WADDLER	ADDGINW	DAWDING	ADEEFHS	SHEAFED
ADDELRY	DREADLY		WADDING	ADEEFIR	AREFIED
	LADDERY	ADDGIOS	GADOIDS		FEDARIE

ADEEFKR	FREAKED	ADEEHNS	DASHEEN		METALED
ADEEFLN	ENDLEAF	ADEEHNT	NETHEAD	ADEELMU	AEMULED
ADEEFLR	FEDERAL	ADEEHNV	HAVENED	ADEELMY	YEALMED
ADEEFLS	DEFLEAS	ADEEHPR	EPHEDRA	ADEELNP	DEPLANE
ADEEFLT	DEFLATE	ADEEHRR	ADHERER		PANELED
ADEEFMR	DEFAMER		REHEARD	ADEELNR	LEARNED
ADEEFMS	DEFAMES	ADEEHRS	ADHERES	ADEELNS	LEADENS
ADEEFNS	DEAFENS		HEADERS	ADEELNT	EDENTAL
ADEEFPR	PREFADE		HEARSED		LATENED
ADEEFRT	DRAFTEE		HEDERAS	ADEELOS	ELODEAS
ADEEFRW	WAFERED		SHEARED	ADEELPR	PEARLED
ADEEFST	DEAFEST	ADEEHRT	EARTHED		PEDALER
	DEFASTE		HEARTED		PLEADER
	DEFEATS	ADEEHRV	HAVERED		REPLEAD
	FEASTED	ADEEHRX	EXHEDRA	ADEELPS	DELAPSE
ADEEGGH	EGGHEAD	ADEEHSS	DEASHES		ELAPSED
ADEEGGL	ALEGGED	ADEEHST	HEADSET		PLEASED
ADEEGGN	ENGAGED	ADEEHSV	SHEAVED		SEPALED
ADEEGLL	ALLEDGE	ADEEHSX	HEXADES	ADEELPT	PETALED
	ALLEGED	ADEEHSY	HAYSEED		PLEATED
ADEEGLM	GLEAMED	ADEEIJT	JADEITE	ADEELQU	EQUALED
ADEEGLN	ANGELED	ADEEILM	EMAILED	ADEELRS	DEALERS
	GELANDE		LIMEADE		LEADERS
	GLEANED	ADEEILN	ALIENED		REDEALS
ADEEGLR	LAGERED		DELAINE	ADEELRT	ALERTED
	REGALED	ADEEILR	LEADIER		ALTERED
ADEEGLT	GELATED	ADEEILS	AEDILES		REDEALT
	LEGATED		DEISEAL		RELATED
	TEAGLED	ADEEILY	EYELIAD		TREADLE
ADEEGLU	LEAGUED	ADEEIMN	DEMAINE	ADEELRV	RAVELED
ADEEGLV	GAVELED	ADEEIMT	MEDIATE	ADEELRW	LEEWARD
ADEEGLZ	DEGLAZE	ADEEINN	ADENINE	ADEELRX	RELAXED
ADEEGMN	ENDGAME	ADEEINS	ANISEED	ADEELRY	DELAYER
	MANEGED	ADEEIRR	READIER		LAYERED
	MENAGED	ADEEIRS	DEARIES		RELAYED
ADEEGMS	DEGAMES		READIES	ADEELST	DELATES
ADEEGNR	ANGERED	ADEEIRW	WEARIED		STEALED
	DERANGE	ADEEISS	DISEASE	ADEELSV	SLEAVED
	ENRAGED		SEASIDE	ADEELSW	SWEALED
	GRANDEE	ADEEIST	IDEATES	ADEELTT	LADETTE
	GRENADE	ADEEISV	ADVISEE	ADEELTV	VALETED
ADEEGNT	AGENTED	ADEEITU	AUDITEE		VELATED
	NEGATED	ADEEITV	DEVIATE	ADEELTX	EXALTED
ADEEGNV	AVENGED	ADEEJSY	DEEJAYS	ADEELTZ	TEAZLED
	VENDAGE	ADEEKNP	KNEEPAD	ADEELUV	DEVALUE
ADEEGOT	DOGEATE	ADEEKNR	KNEADER	ADEELYZ	LAYDEEZ
	GOATEED		NAKEDER	ADEEMNR	AMENDER
ADEEGPR	PREAGED	ADEEKNS	SNEAKED		ENARMED
ADEEGRR	REGRADE	ADEEKNW	WAKENED		MEANDER
ADEEGRS	DRAGEES	ADEEKRS	DEKARES		REAMEND
	GREASED		SKEARED		REEDMAN
ADEEGRU	GUARDEE	ADEEKRW	REWAKED		RENAMED
ADEEGRV	GREAVED		WREAKED	ADEEMNS	AMENDES
ADEEGRW	RAGWEED	ADEEKTW	TWEAKED		DEMEANS
	WAGERED	ADEEKWY	WEEKDAY		SEEDMAN
ADEEGSS	DEGASES	ADEELLP	LAPELED	ADEEMNT	ENTAMED
ADEEHIR	HEADIER	ADEELLS	ALLSEED	ADEEMNY	DEMAYNE
ADEEHJS	HADJEES	ADEELLY	ALLEYED	ADEEMOS	OEDEMAS
ADEEHLR	HEDERAL	ADEELMM	MELAMED	ADEEMPR	EMPARED
ADEEHLS	LEASHED	ADEELMN	LEADMEN		PREMADE
	SHEALED	ADEELMP	EMPALED	ADEEMRR	DREAMER
ADEEHLX	EXHALED	ADEELMR	EMERALD		REARMED
ADEEHMN	HEADMEN	ADEELMS	MEASLED		REDREAM
ADEEHNN	HENNAED	ADEELMT	MEDALET	ADEEMRS	REMADES

	REMEADS
	SMEARED
ADEEMRT	REMATED
ADEEMST	STEAMED
ADEEMSU	MEDUSAE
ADEEMSW	MAWSEED
ADEEMTW	MATWEED
ADEEMWY	MAYWEED
ADEENNS	ENNEADS
ADEENNX	ANNEXED
ADEENPS	SNEAPED
	SPEANED
ADEENRS	DEANERS
	ENDEARS
ADEENRU	UNEARED
ADEENRV	RAVENED
ADEENRY	DEANERY
	RENAYED
	YEAREND
	YEARNED
ADEENST	STANDEE
	STEANED
ADEENSV	ADVENES
ADEENSW	DEEWANS
ADEENTT	DENTATE
ADEEOPT	ADOPTEE
ADEEORS	OREADES
ADEEORW	OARWEED
ADEEPPR	PAPERED
ADEEPRS	PREASED
	RESPADE
	SPEARED
ADEEPRT	ADEPTER
	PREDATE
	RETAPED
	TAPERED
ADEEPRV	DEPRAVE
	PERVADE
	REPAVED
ADEEPSS	PESADES
ADEEPTX	EXAPTED
ADEEQRU	QUAERED
ADEEQTU	EQUATED
ADEERRR	DREARER
ADEERRS	DREARES
	READERS
	REDEARS
	REDSEAR
	REREADS
ADEERRT	RETREAD
	TREADER
ADEERRV	AVERRED
ADEERRW	REDWARE
ADEERSS	RESEDAS
ADEERST	DEAREST
	DERATES
	ESTRADE
	REASTED
	REDATES
	SEDATER
	STEARED
	TASERED
ADEERSV	ADVERSE
	EVADERS
ADEERSW	DRAWEES
	RESAWED
ADEERTT	ARETTED
	TREATED
ADEERTV	AVERTED
	TAVERED
ADEERTW	DEWATER
	TARWEED
	WATERED
ADEERTX	RETAXED
ADEERVW	WAVERED
ADEERWX	REWAXED
ADEESST	SEDATES
ADEESSX	AXSEEDS
ADEESSY	ESSAYED
ADEESTT	ESTATED
ADEESTU	SAUTEED
ADEESTW	SWEATED
ADEESTY	YEASTED
ADEESVY	SAVEYED
ADEESWX	DEWAXES
ADEETUX	EXUDATE
ADEEWWX	WAXWEED
ADEFFFL	FLAFFED
ADEFFGR	GRAFFED
ADEFFIN	AFFINED
ADEFFIP	PIAFFED
ADEFFIR	DAFFIER
ADEFFIS	DAFFIES
ADEFFIX	AFFIXED
ADEFFLM	MAFFLED
ADEFFLO	LEADOFF
ADEFFLR	RAFFLED
ADEFFLW	WAFFLED
ADEFFNY	NYAFFED
ADEFFQU	QUAFFED
ADEFFST	STAFFED
ADEFFUW	WAUFFED
ADEFGGL	FLAGGED
ADEFGGR	FRAGGED
ADEFGLN	FANGLED
	FLANGED
ADEFGNS	DEFANGS
ADEFGOR	FORAGED
ADEFGOT	FAGOTED
ADEFGOU	FOUGADE
ADEFGRS	DEFRAGS
ADEFGRT	GRAFTED
ADEFHIS	DEAFISH
ADEFHIT	FAITHED
ADEFHLS	FLASHED
ADEFHLU	HEADFUL
ADEFHRW	WHARFED
ADEFHST	SHAFTED
ADEFIKL	FADLIKE
ADEFILL	FLAILED
ADEFILS	DISLEAF
ADEFIMN	INFAMED
ADEFIMS	DISFAME
ADEFINR	FRIANDE
ADEFINS	FADEINS
ADEFINT	DEFIANT
	FAINTED
ADEFIRS	FARSIDE
	FRAISED
ADEFIST	DAFTIES
	FADIEST
ADEFITX	FIXATED
ADEFKLN	FANKLED
	FLANKED
ADEFKNR	FRANKED
ADEFKNU	UNFAKED
ADEFLLN	ELFLAND
ADEFLLW	DEWFALL
ADEFLMM	FLAMMED
ADEFLNN	FENLAND
ADEFLOR	ALFREDO
ADEFLOT	FLOATED
ADEFLPP	FLAPPED
ADEFLRS	FARDELS
ADEFLRU	DAREFUL
ADEFLTT	FLATTED
ADEFLTU	DEFAULT
	FAULTED
ADEFMNU	UNFAMED
ADEFMOS	DEFOAMS
ADEFNRS	FARDENS
	SNARFED
ADEFNSU	SNAFUED
	UNDEAFS
ADEFNUZ	UNFAZED
ADEFOOS	SEAFOOD
ADEFORS	FEDORAS
ADEFORV	FAVORED
ADEFORY	FEODARY
	FORAYED
ADEFOTU	FADEOUT
ADEFPPR	FRAPPED
ADEFRRT	DRAFTER
	REDRAFT
ADEFRRW	DWARFER
ADEFRST	STRAFED
ADEFRSU	FADEURS
ADEFRSW	SWARFED
ADEFRSY	DEFRAYS
ADEFRUY	FEUDARY
ADEFSTT	DAFTEST
ADEGGGL	GAGGLED
ADEGGHL	HAGGLED
ADEGGHS	SHAGGED
ADEGGIR	DAGGIER
ADEGGIS	GADGIES
ADEGGIU	GAUDGIE
	GUIDAGE
ADEGGLR	DRAGGLE
	GARGLED
	RAGGLED
ADEGGLS	DAGGLES
	SLAGGED
ADEGGLW	WAGGLED
ADEGGMO	DEMAGOG
ADEGGNS	SNAGGED
ADEGGOP	PEDAGOG
ADEGGPS	SPAGGED
ADEGGRR	DRAGGER
ADEGGRS	DAGGERS
ADEGGRY	RAGGEDY
ADEGGST	GADGETS

	STAGGED	**ADEGLNS**	DANGLES		REGARDS
ADEGGSW	SWAGGED		GLANDES	**ADEGRRU**	GUARDER
ADEGGTY	GADGETY		LAGENDS	**ADEGRSS**	GRASSED
ADEGHIN	HEADING		SLANGED	**ADEGRST**	RADGEST
ADEGHIR	HAGRIDE	**ADEGLNT**	TANGLED	**ADEGRSU**	DESUGAR
	HEADRIG	**ADEGLNU**	LANGUED		SUGARED
ADEGHIS	HIDAGES	**ADEGLNW**	WANGLED	**ADEGRTY**	GYRATED
ADEGHJU	JUGHEAD	**ADEGLOP**	GALOPED		TRAGEDY
ADEGHLU	LAUGHED	**ADEGLOT**	GLOATED	**ADEGRUU**	AUGURED
ADEGHMO	HOMAGED	**ADEGLPU**	PLAGUED	**ADEGRUY**	GAUDERY
ADEGHNP	PHANGED	**ADEGLRS**	DARGLES	**ADEGRYZ**	AGRYZED
ADEGHNS	GNASHED	**ADEGLRU**	RAGULED	**ADEGSSU**	DEGAUSS
	HAGDENS	**ADEGLRY**	GRADELY	**ADEHHKS**	KHEDAHS
ADEGHNW	WHANGED	**ADEGLSS**	GLASSED	**ADEHHOP**	HOPHEAD
ADEGHOR	HAGRODE	**ADEGLTY**	DALGYTE	**ADEHHOT**	HOTHEAD
ADEGHPR	GRAPHED	**ADEGMNS**	GADSMEN	**ADEHHSS**	SHASHED
ADEGHST	GHASTED	**ADEGMNU**	AGENDUM	**ADEHIJS**	JEHADIS
ADEGHUW	WAUGHED		GUDEMAN	**ADEHIKS**	DASHEKI
ADEGILL	GALLIED	**ADEGMOP**	MEGAPOD	**ADEHIKV**	KHEDIVA
ADEGILN	ALIGNED	**ADEGMRU**	MAUGRED	**ADEHILN**	HIELAND
	DEALING	**ADEGNNO**	NONAGED		INHALED
	LEADING	**ADEGNNU**	DUNNAGE	**ADEHILP**	HELIPAD
ADEGILO	GEOIDAL	**ADEGNOP**	PONDAGE	**ADEHILS**	HALIDES
ADEGILR	GLADIER	**ADEGNOR**	GROANED	**ADEHILY**	HEADILY
	GLAIRED	**ADEGNOS**	SONDAGE	**ADEHIMO**	HAEMOID
ADEGILS	SILAGED	**ADEGNOT**	TANGOED	**ADEHINP**	HEADPIN
ADEGILT	LIGATED	**ADEGNOV**	DOGVANE		PINHEAD
	TAIGLED	**ADEGNOW**	GOWANED	**ADEHINR**	HANDIER
ADEGILV	GLAIVED		WAGONED	**ADEHIPP**	HAPPIED
ADEGIMP	MEDIGAP	**ADEGNPR**	PRANGED	**ADEHIPR**	RAPHIDE
ADEGIMS	DEGAMIS	**ADEGNPS**	SPANGED	**ADEHIPS**	APHIDES
ADEGINN	DEANING	**ADEGNPU**	UNPAGED		DIPHASE
ADEGINR	AREDING	**ADEGNRR**	GNARRED	**ADEHIPT**	PITHEAD
	DEARING		GRANDER	**ADEHIRR**	HARDIER
	DERAIGN	**ADEGNRS**	DANGERS		HARRIED
	EARDING		GANDERS	**ADEHIRS**	AIRSHED
	GRADINE		GARDENS		DASHIER
	GRAINED	**ADEGNRT**	DRAGNET		HARDIES
	READING		GRANTED		SHADIER
ADEGINS	AGNISED	**ADEGNRU**	ENGUARD	**ADEHIRT**	AIRTHED
ADEGINV	DEAVING		RAUNGED	**ADEHIRW**	RAWHIDE
	EVADING	**ADEGNRW**	WRANGED	**ADEHIRY**	HAYRIDE
ADEGINW	WINDAGE	**ADEGNST**	STANGED		HYDRIAE
ADEGINY	YEADING	**ADEGNSU**	AUGENDS	**ADEHKNS**	SHANKED
ADEGINZ	AGNIZED	**ADEGNTU**	GAUNTED	**ADEHKNT**	THANKED
ADEGIOT	GODETIA		UNGATED	**ADEHKOR**	HARDOKE
ADEGIRS	AGRISED	**ADEGNTW**	TWANGED	**ADEHKOT**	KATHODE
ADEGIRT	TRIAGED	**ADEGNUW**	UNWAGED	**ADEHKRS**	SHARKED
ADEGIRU	GAUDIER	**ADEGORS**	DOGEARS	**ADEHLLO**	HALLOED
ADEGIRZ	AGRIZED	**ADEGORT**	GAROTED		HOLLAED
ADEGIST	AGISTED	**ADEGORW**	DOWAGER	**ADEHLLP**	LAPHELD
ADEGISU	AGUISED		WORDAGE	**ADEHLMS**	LAMEDHS
	GAUDIES	**ADEGOSS**	DOSAGES	**ADEHLNR**	HANDLER
ADEGISV	VISAGED		SEADOGS	**ADEHLNS**	HANDLES
ADEGIUV	VIDUAGE	**ADEGOST**	DOGATES		HANDSEL
ADEGIUZ	AGUIZED		DOTAGES	**ADEHLOS**	SHOALED
ADEGJLN	JANGLED	**ADEGOTT**	TOGATED	**ADEHLOT**	LOATHED
ADEGLLU	ULLAGED	**ADEGOVY**	VOYAGED	**ADEHLPR**	RALPHED
ADEGLMN	MANGLED	**ADEGPRS**	GRASPED	**ADEHLPS**	PLASHED
ADEGLMR	MALGRED		SPADGER	**ADEHLRS**	HARELDS
ADEGLMU	GLAUMED		SPARGED		HERALDS
ADEGLNN	ENDLANG	**ADEGPRU**	UPGRADE	**ADEHLSS**	HASSLED
ADEGLNR	DANGLER	**ADEGPUZ**	UPGAZED		SLASHED
	GNARLED	**ADEGRRS**	GRADERS	**ADEHLST**	DALETHS

ADEHLSU	SHAULED			DIARIES		DIALERS
ADEHLSW	SHAWLED			DIARISE		REDIALS
ADEHLTY	DEATHLY	ADEIIRZ	DIARIZE		SIDERAL
ADEHMMS	SHAMMED	ADEIISS	DAISIES	ADEILRT	DILATER
ADEHMMW	WHAMMED	ADEIJMR	JEMIDAR		REDTAIL
ADEHMNR	HARDMEN	ADEIKLN	KNAIDEL		TRAILED
	HERDMAN	ADEIKLS	SKAILED	ADEILRU	UREDIAL
ADEHMOP	MOPHEAD	ADEIKLY	KAYLIED	ADEILRV	RIVALED
ADEHMOR	HADROME	ADEIKNS	KANDIES		VALIDER
ADEHMRS	DERHAMS	ADEIKRS	DAIKERS	ADEILRY	READILY
ADEHMSS	SMASHED		DARKIES	ADEILSS	AIDLESS
ADEHNPS	DAPHNES	ADEIKRT	TRAIKED		DEASILS
ADEHNRS	HANDERS	ADEILLL	DIALLEL	ADEILST	DETAILS
	HARDENS	ADEILLR	DALLIER		DILATES
ADEHNRU	UNHEARD		DIALLER	ADEILSU	AUDILES
ADEHNSS	SNASHED		RALLIED		DEASIUL
ADEHNST	HANDSET	ADEILLS	DALLIES		DUALISE
ADEHNSU	UNHEADS		DISLEAL	ADEILSV	DEVISAL
ADEHNTU	HAUNTED		LALDIES	ADEILSY	DIALYSE
ADEHOOP	APEHOOD		SALLIED		EYLIADS
ADEHOPT	POTHEAD	ADEILLT	TALLIED	ADEILUZ	DUALIZE
ADEHOPX	HEXAPOD	ADEILLV	VIALLED	ADEILYZ	DIALYZE
ADEHORR	HOARDER	ADEILLY	IDEALLY	ADEIMMR	MERMAID
ADEHOST	HOASTED	ADEILMM	DILEMMA	ADEIMMS	MISMADE
ADEHOSX	OXHEADS	ADEILMO	MELODIA	ADEIMMT	TAMMIED
ADEHOTW	TOWHEAD	ADEILMP	IMPALED	ADEIMNO	AMIDONE
ADEHPPW	WHAPPED		IMPLEAD		DOMAINE
ADEHPRS	PHRASED	ADEILMS	MAELIDS	ADEIMNR	ADERMIN
	SHARPED		MEDIALS		INARMED
ADEHPST	HEPTADS		MISDEAL	ADEIMNS	DEMAINS
	SPATHED		MISLEAD		MAIDENS
ADEHQSU	QUASHED	ADEILMU	MIAULED		MEDIANS
ADEHRRU	HURRAED	ADEILNN	ANNELID		MEDINAS
ADEHRSS	DASHERS		LINDANE		SIDEMAN
	SHADERS	ADEILNP	PLAINED	ADEIMNT	MEDIANT
ADEHRST	DEARTHS	ADEILNS	DENIALS	ADEIMNU	UNAIMED
	HARDEST		SNAILED	ADEIMOU	MIAOUED
	HARDSET	ADEILNU	ALIUNDE	ADEIMOW	MIAOWED
	HATREDS		UNIDEAL	ADEIMPR	DAMPIER
	THREADS	ADEILNV	ANDVILE	ADEIMPV	IMPAVED
	TRASHED		ANVILED	ADEIMRR	ADMIRER
ADEHRSY	HYDRASE	ADEILNX	INDEXAL		MARDIER
ADEHRTW	THRAWED	ADEILOP	OEDIPAL		MARRIED
	WRATHED	ADEILOR	DARIOLE	ADEIMRS	ADMIRES
ADEHRTY	HYDRATE	ADEILOS	DEASOIL		MARDIES
	THREADY		ISOLEAD		MISREAD
ADEHSST	STASHED	ADEILOU	DOULEIA		SEDARIM
ADEHSSW	SWASHED	ADEILOZ	DIAZOLE		SIDEARM
ADEHSTW	SWATHED	ADEILPP	APPLIED	ADEIMRT	READMIT
ADEHSYY	HEYDAYS	ADEILPR	LIPREAD	ADEIMRY	MIDYEAR
ADEHUZZ	HUZZAED		PEDRAIL	ADEIMST	DIASTEM
ADEIILR	DELIRIA		PREDIAL		MISDATE
	IRIDEAL	ADEILPS	ALIPEDS	ADEIMSV	VIDAMES
ADEIILS	DAILIES		ELAPIDS	ADEIMSX	ADMIXES
	LIAISED		LAIPSED	ADEIMTU	IDEATUM
	SEDILIA		LAPIDES		TAEDIUM
ADEIIMN	AMIDINE		PAIDLES	ADEIMTY	DAYTIME
	DIAMINE		PALSIED	ADEINNN	NANDINE
ADEIINR	DENARII		PLEIADS		NANNIED
ADEIINT	INEDITA	ADEILPT	PLAITED	ADEINNR	NARDINE
ADEIINZ	DIAZINE		TALIPED	ADEINNS	DANNIES
ADEIIPR	PERIDIA	ADEILQU	QUAILED	ADEINOR	ANEROID
ADEIIRS	AIRSIDE	ADEILRR	LARDIER	ADEINOS	ADONISE
	DAIRIES	ADEILRS	DERAILS		ANODISE

	SODAINE		PARTIED	**ADEKLUW**	WAULKED
ADEINOV	NAEVOID		PIRATED	**ADEKMNS**	DESKMAN
ADEINOX	DIOXANE	**ADEIPRV**	VAPIDER	**ADEKMRS**	DEMARKS
ADEINOZ	ADONIZE	**ADEIPSS**	APSIDES	**ADEKNPP**	KNAPPED
	ANODIZE	**ADEIQRU**	QUERIDA	**ADEKNPR**	PRANKED
ADEINPR	PARDINE	**ADEIRRS**	ARRIDES	**ADEKNPS**	SPANKED
ADEINPS	PANDIES		RAIDERS	**ADEKNRR**	KNARRED
	PANSIED	**ADEIRRT**	TARDIER	**ADEKNRS**	DARKENS
	SPAINED		TARRIED	**ADEKNRU**	UNRAKED
ADEINPT	DEPAINT	**ADEIRRV**	ARRIVED	**ADEKNSS**	SANDEKS
	PAINTED	**ADEIRST**	ARIDEST	**ADEKNST**	DANKEST
	PATINED		ASTERID		STANKED
ADEINRR	DRAINER		ASTRIDE	**ADEKNSU**	UNASKED
	RANDIER		DIASTER	**ADEKNSW**	SWANKED
ADEINRS	RANDIES		DISRATE	**ADEKNUW**	UNWAKED
	SANDIER		STAIDER	**ADEKNVY**	VANDYKE
	SARDINE		STAIRED	**ADEKORT**	TROAKED
ADEINRT	ANTIRED		TARDIES	**ADEKPRS**	SPARKED
	DETRAIN		TIRADES	**ADEKPSY**	KEYPADS
	TRAINED	**ADEIRSU**	RESIDUA	**ADEKRST**	DARKEST
ADEINRU	UNAIRED	**ADEIRSV**	ADVISER		STARKED
	URANIDE		VARDIES		STRAKED
ADEINRV	INVADER	**ADEIRSX**	RADIXES	**ADEKRSY**	DARKEYS
	RAVINED	**ADEIRTT**	ATTIRED	**ADELLMS**	SMALLED
ADEINSS	SDAINES	**ADEIRTV**	TARDIVE	**ADELLMU**	MEDULLA
ADEINST	DESTAIN	**ADEIRTY**	DIETARY	**ADELLNR**	LANDLER
	DETAINS	**ADEISSS**	DASSIES	**ADELLNW**	ELLWAND
	INSTEAD	**ADEISST**	DISSEAT	**ADELLOR**	ODALLER
	NIDATES		SAIDEST	**ADELLOW**	ALLOWED
	SAINTED	**ADEISSV**	ADVISES	**ADELLOY**	ALLOYED
	SATINED		DISSAVE	**ADELLPS**	SPALLED
	STAINED	**ADEISSZ**	ASSIZED	**ADELLRS**	LADLERS
ADEINSV	INVADES	**ADEISTU**	DAUTIES	**ADELLRU**	ALLURED
ADEINSW	DEWANIS	**ADEISTV**	AVIDEST		UDALLER
ADEINTT	TAINTED		DATIVES	**ADELLST**	STALLED
ADEINTU	AUDIENT		VISTAED	**ADELLSU**	ALLUDES
ADEINTV	DEVIANT	**ADEISTW**	DAWTIES		ALUDELS
ADEINVV	NAVVIED		WAISTED	**ADELLSV**	DEVALLS
ADEIOPS	ADIPOSE	**ADEISVV**	SAVVIED	**ADELMMS**	SLAMMED
ADEIOPT	OPIATED	**ADEISWY**	SIDEWAY		SMALMED
ADEIORS	ROADIES		WAYSIDE	**ADELMNN**	LANDMEN
	SOREDIA	**ADEITUZ**	DEUTZIA	**ADELMNR**	MANDREL
ADEIORV	AVODIRE	**ADEITWY**	TIDEWAY	**ADELMNT**	MANTLED
	AVOIDER	**ADEJMOR**	MAJORED	**ADELMOR**	EARLDOM
ADEIORX	EXORDIA	**ADEJMRU**	JUMARED	**ADELMOS**	DAMOSEL
ADEIOST	IODATES		MUDEJAR	**ADELMOZ**	DAMOZEL
	TOADIES	**ADEJNSU**	JAUNSED	**ADELMPS**	PSALMED
ADEIOSX	OXIDASE	**ADEJNTU**	JAUNTED		SAMPLED
ADEIOSZ	DIAZOES	**ADEJOPR**	JEOPARD	**ADELMRS**	MEDLARS
ADEIOTX	OXIDATE	**ADEJRRU**	ADJURER	**ADELMRU**	MURALED
ADEIOVV	VAIVODE	**ADEJRSU**	ADJURES	**ADELMSS**	DAMSELS
ADEIOVW	WAIVODE	**ADEJSSU**	JUDASES	**ADELMST**	MALTEDS
ADEIOWW	WAIWODE	**ADEKKNS**	SKANKED	**ADELMSU**	ALMUDES
ADEIPPR	DRAPPIE	**ADEKLNP**	PLANKED		MEDUSAL
	PREPAID	**ADEKLNR**	RANKLED	**ADELMSW**	WADMELS
ADEIPPU	APPUIED	**ADEKLNS**	KALENDS	**ADELMYZ**	MAZEDLY
ADEIPRR	DRAPIER	**ADEKLNY**	NAKEDLY	**ADELNNP**	PLANNED
	PARRIED	**ADEKLOP**	POLKAED	**ADELNNU**	UNLADEN
	RAPIDER	**ADEKLOS**	SKOALED	**ADELNOR**	LADRONE
ADEIPRS	ASPIRED	**ADEKLPP**	KLAPPED	**ADELNOS**	LOADENS
	DESPAIR	**ADEKLRS**	DARKLES	**ADELNOT**	TALONED
	DIAPERS	**ADEKLST**	SKLATED	**ADELNOY**	YEALDON
	PRAISED		STALKED	**ADELNPT**	PLANTED
ADEIPRT	DIPTERA	**ADEKLSY**	YSLAKED	**ADELNPY**	ENDPLAY

ADELNRS	DARNELS	**ADELRSW**	WARSLED		SOMEDAY
	ENLARDS	**ADELRSZ**	DRAZELS	**ADEMOWY**	MEADOWY
	LANDERS	**ADELRTT**	RATTLED	**ADEMPRS**	DAMPERS
	RELANDS	**ADELRTW**	TRAWLED	**ADEMPRT**	TRAMPED
	SLANDER	**ADELRTX**	DEXTRAL	**ADEMPSS**	SPASMED
	SNARLED	**ADELRTY**	LYRATED	**ADEMPST**	DAMPEST
ADELNRU	LAUNDER	**ADELRWW**	WRAWLED		STAMPED
	LURDANE	**ADELRWX**	WRAXLED	**ADEMPSW**	SWAMPED
	RUNDALE	**ADELRZZ**	DAZZLER	**ADEMRRU**	EARDRUM
ADELNRY	DEARNLY	**ADELSST**	DESALTS	**ADEMRST**	SMARTED
ADELNSS	SENDALS	**ADELSTT**	SLATTED	**ADEMRSU**	REMUDAS
ADELNST	DENTALS	**ADELSTU**	AULDEST	**ADEMRSW**	SWARMED
	SLANTED		SALUTED	**ADEMRTU**	MATURED
ADELNSU	UNLADES	**ADELSUV**	AVULSED	**ADEMSST**	DEMASTS
	UNLEADS	**ADELSWY**	SWAYLED	**ADEMSSU**	ASSUMED
ADELNSY	ADENYLS	**ADELSZZ**	DAZZLES		MEDUSAS
ADELNTU	LUNATED	**ADELTTT**	TATTLED	**ADEMTTU**	MUTATED
	UNDEALT	**ADELTTW**	WATTLED	**ADENNOY**	ANNOYED
ADELNTW	WETLAND	**ADELTUV**	VAULTED		ANODYNE
ADELNUW	UNLAWED	**ADELTUX**	LUXATED	**ADENNPS**	SPANNED
ADELOPR	LEOPARD	**ADELTWZ**	WALTZED	**ADENNPT**	PENDANT
	PAROLED	**ADEMMPS**	SPAMMED	**ADENNST**	STANDEN
	PRELOAD	**ADEMMRS**	DAMMERS	**ADENNSU**	DUENNAS
ADELOPS	DEPOSAL		SMARMED	**ADENNSW**	SWANNED
	PEDALOS	**ADEMMRT**	TRAMMED	**ADENNWY**	DEWANNY
ADELOPT	PLOATED	**ADEMNNS**	SANDMEN	**ADENOOP**	NAPOOED
	TADPOLE	**ADEMNNU**	MUNDANE	**ADENOOT**	ODONATE
ADELORS	LOADERS		UNNAMED	**ADENOOZ**	ENDOZOA
	ORDEALS	**ADEMNOR**	MADRONE	**ADENOPR**	APRONED
	RELOADS		ROADMEN		OPERAND
ADELORT	DELATOR	**ADEMNOS**	DAEMONS		PADRONE
	LEOTARD		MASONED		PANDORE
ADELORU	ROULADE		MODENAS	**ADENOPS**	DAPSONE
ADELOSS	ALDOSES		MONADES	**ADENOPT**	NOTEPAD
	LASSOED		NOMADES		TONEPAD
ADELOST	SALTOED	**ADEMNOW**	ADWOMEN	**ADENORR**	ADORNER
	SOLATED		WOMANED		READORN
ADELOSV	SALVOED	**ADEMNPS**	DAMPENS	**ADENORT**	TORNADE
ADELOSW	WALDOES	**ADEMNRS**	DAMNERS	**ADENORU**	RONDEAU
ADELOTT	TOTALED		MANREDS	**ADENOST**	ASTONED
ADELOTU	OUTLEAD		RANDEMS		DONATES
ADELPPP	PLAPPED		REMANDS		ONSTEAD
ADELPPS	DAPPLES	**ADEMNRU**	DURAMEN	**ADENOSU**	DOUANES
	SAPPLED		MANURED	**ADENOSY**	NOYADES
	SLAPPED		MAUNDER	**ADENOTT**	NOTATED
ADELPRS	PEDLARS		UNARMED	**ADENOTV**	NOVATED
ADELPRY	PEDLARY	**ADEMNRY**	DRAYMEN	**ADENOTZ**	ZONATED
ADELPST	SPALTED		YARDMEN	**ADENPPR**	PARPEND
	STAPLED	**ADEMNSS**	DESMANS	**ADENPPS**	APPENDS
ADELPSU	UPLEADS		MADNESS		SNAPPED
ADELPSW	DEWLAPS	**ADEMNST**	TANDEMS	**ADENPPW**	WAPPEND
	SPAWLED	**ADEMNSU**	MEDUSAN	**ADENPRR**	PARDNER
ADELPSY	SPLAYED		SUDAMEN	**ADENPRS**	PANDERS
ADELPTT	PLATTED	**ADEMNSY**	DAYSMEN	**ADENPRU**	UNDRAPE
ADELPTW	DEWLAPT	**ADEMNTU**	UNMATED		UNPARED
ADELPTY	ADEPTLY		UNTAMED	**ADENPRW**	PRAWNED
ADELRRS	LARDERS	**ADEMOOV**	AMOOVED		PREDAWN
ADELRRU	RUDERAL	**ADEMOPS**	APEDOMS	**ADENPST**	PEDANTS
ADELRRW	DRAWLER		POMADES		PENTADS
ADELRSS	RASSLED	**ADEMORR**	ARMORED	**ADENPSW**	SPAWNED
	SARDELS	**ADEMORS**	RADOMES	**ADENPSX**	EXPANDS
ADELRST	DARTLES	**ADEMOSV**	VAMOSED		SPANDEX
	SLARTED	**ADEMOSW**	MEADOWS	**ADENPSY**	DYSPNEA
ADELRSU	LAUDERS	**ADEMOSY**	SAMOYED	**ADENPTU**	UNADEPT

ADENPUV	UNPAVED	ADEORRW	ARROWED		WRASTED
ADENQTU	QUANTED	ADEORRZ	RAZORED	ADERSTY	STRAYED
ADENRRS	DARNERS	ADEORSS	SARODES	ADERSUY	DASYURE
	ERRANDS	ADEORST	DOATERS	ADERSVW	DWARVES
	SNARRED		ROASTED		SWARVED
ADENRRW	REDRAWN		TORSADE	ADERWWY	WEYWARD
ADENRRY	REYNARD		TROADES	ADESSTU	SUDATES
ADENRSS	SANDERS	ADEORSU	AROUSED	ADESSTW	WADSETS
	SARSDEN	ADEORSV	OVERSAD	ADESTTU	STATUED
ADENRST	ENDARTS		SAVORED	ADESTTW	SWATTED
	STANDER	ADEORSW	REDOWAS		WADSETT
	STARNED	ADEORTT	ROTATED	ADFFGIN	DAFFING
ADENRSU	ASUNDER		TROATED	ADFFHNO	HANDOFF
	DANSEUR	ADEORTU	OUTDARE		OFFHAND
	DAUNERS		OUTREAD	ADFFILY	DAFFILY
ADENRSW	DAWNERS		READOUT	ADFFIST	DISTAFF
	WANDERS	ADEORWY	RODEWAY	ADFFLNO	FANFOLD
	WARDENS	ADEORYZ	ZEDOARY	ADFFLOO	OFFLOAD
ADENRSZ	ZANDERS	ADEOSTT	TOASTED	ADFFOOR	AFFOORD
ADENRTT	TRANTED	ADEOTTU	OUTDATE	ADFFORS	AFFORDS
ADENRTU	DAUNTER	ADEOWWY	WAYWODE	ADFGGIN	FADGING
	NATURED	ADEPPRS	DAPPERS	ADFGINN	FANDING
	UNRATED	ADEPPRT	TRAPPED	ADFGINR	FARDING
	UNTREAD	ADEPPRW	WRAPPED	ADFGINS	FADINGS
ADENRTV	VERDANT	ADEPPST	STAPPED	ADFGLLU	GLADFUL
ADENRTX	DEXTRAN	ADEPPSW	SWAPPED	ADFHLNU	HANDFUL
ADENRTY	DENTARY	ADEPPTU	PUPATED	ADFHLNY	FLYHAND
	TRAYNED	ADEPPUY	APPUYED	ADFHLSY	SHADFLY
	TYRANED	ADEPRRS	DRAPERS	ADFHOOS	SHADOOF
ADENRUY	UNREADY		SPARRED	ADFHSSU	SHADUFS
ADENRUZ	UNRAZED	ADEPRRY	DRAPERY	ADFILLU	FLUIDAL
ADENSSS	SADNESS	ADEPRSS	ADPRESS	ADFIMNR	FINDRAM
ADENSSU	SUNDAES		SPADERS	ADFIMNY	DAMNIFY
ADENSSW	WESANDS		SPREADS	ADFINRS	FRIANDS
	WESSAND	ADEPRST	DEPARTS	ADFINRT	INDRAFT
ADENSTT	ATTENDS		DRAPETS	ADFIORS	FORSAID
ADENSTU	SAUNTED		PETARDS	ADFLLYY	LADYFLY
	UNSATED	ADEPRSY	SPRAYED	ADFLMOO	DAMFOOL
ADENSTV	ADVENTS	ADEPRTU	UPDATER	ADFLMPU	MUDFLAP
ADENSTY	STAYNED		UPRATED	ADFLMTU	MUDFLAT
ADENSUV	UNSAVED	ADEPSTT	SPATTED	ADFLNOP	PLAFOND
ADENSUW	UNSAWED	ADEPSTU	UPDATES	ADFLNSY	SANDFLY
ADENSWY	ENDWAYS	ADEPSZZ	SPAZZED	ADFLORU	FOULARD
ADENSWZ	WEZANDS	ADEQRSU	SQUARED	ADFMNOS	FANDOMS
ADENTTU	ATTUNED	ADERRST	DARTERS	ADFMOSU	FUMADOS
	NUTATED		DARTRES	ADFNNOT	FONDANT
	TAUNTED		RETARDS	ADFNOST	FANTODS
ADENTUV	VAUNTED		STARRED	ADFOOPT	FOOTPAD
ADENTUX	UNTAXED		TRADERS	ADFOOTW	FATWOOD
ADENUWX	UNWAXED	ADERRSW	DRAWERS	ADFORRW	FORWARD
ADENUWY	UNWAYED		REDRAWS		FROWARD
ADEOORS	ROADEOS		REWARDS	ADFPRTU	UPDRAFT
ADEOORT	ODORATE		WARDERS	ADGGGIN	DAGGING
ADEOPPS	APPOSED	ADERRSY	YARDERS	ADGGHNO	HANGDOG
	PEAPODS	ADERSSU	ASSURED	ADGGILN	GADLING
ADEOPQU	OPAQUED		RUDASES	ADGGILR	RIGGALD
ADEOPRR	EARDROP	ADERSSW	SAWDERS	ADGGINN	DANGING
ADEOPRT	ADOPTER		SWEARDS	ADGGINO	GOADING
	READOPT	ADERSTT	STARTED	ADGGINR	GRADING
ADEOPRV	VAPORED		TETRADS		NIGGARD
ADEOPSS	SPADOES	ADERSTV	ADVERTS	ADGGINU	GAUDING
ADEOPST	PODESTA		STARVED	ADGHILO	HIDALGO
ADEORRS	ADORERS	ADERSTW	STEWARD	ADGHINN	HANDING
	DROSERA		STRAWED	ADGHINS	DASHING

	SHADING		GRADINS	**ADHILOS**	HALOIDS
ADGHINU	HAUDING	**ADGINRT**	DARTING	**ADHILOY**	HOLIDAY
ADGHIPR	DIGRAPH		TRADING		HYALOID
ADGHIRR	ARDRIGH	**ADGINRU**	DAURING		HYOIDAL
ADGHIRS	DISHRAG	**ADGINRW**	DRAWING	**ADHILRY**	HARDILY
ADGHNNU	HANDGUN		WARDING	**ADHILSY**	LADYISH
ADGHNOS	HAGDONS	**ADGINRY**	DRAYING		SHADILY
	SANDHOG		YARDING	**ADHIMNS**	HANDISM
ADGHNOW	HAGDOWN	**ADGINST**	DATINGS	**ADHIMPS**	DAMPISH
ADGHORW	HOGWARD	**ADGINSU**	AUDINGS		PHASMID
ADGHRSU	DURGAHS	**ADGINSW**	WADINGS	**ADHIMRS**	DIRHAMS
ADGHRTU	DRAUGHT	**ADGINTU**	DAUTING		MIDRASH
ADGIILN	DIALING	**ADGINTW**	DAWTING	**ADHINOT**	ANTHOID
	GLIADIN	**ADGINWY**	GWYNIAD	**ADHINPS**	DISHPAN
	LAIDING	**ADGIORT**	GORDITA	**ADHINPU**	DAUPHIN
ADGIILT	DIGITAL	**ADGIPRU**	PAGURID	**ADHINSS**	SANDHIS
ADGIIMN	MAIDING	**ADGIRSU**	GUISARD	**ADHIOOS**	HOODIAS
ADGIINN	DAINING	**ADGIRZZ**	GIZZARD	**ADHIORS**	HAIRDOS
ADGIINO	GONIDIA	**ADGLLNO**	GOLLAND	**ADHIOST**	TOADISH
ADGIINR	GRADINI	**ADGLMNO**	MANGOLD	**ADHIRSS**	SHAIRDS
	RAIDING	**ADGLNOO**	DONGOLA	**ADHJKOS**	KHODJAS
ADGIINS	SIGANID		GONDOLA	**ADHKKSU**	DUKKAHS
ADGIINU	IGUANID	**ADGLNOR**	GOLDARN		DUKKHAS
ADGIINW	GWINIAD	**ADGLNOW**	GOWLAND	**ADHKORW**	DORHAWK
ADGIIPY	PYGIDIA	**ADGLNOY**	DAYLONG	**ADHKOSU**	SHAKUDO
ADGIJOS	ADJIGOS	**ADGLNRY**	GRANDLY	**ADHLLLO**	HOLDALL
ADGIKNR	DARKING	**ADGLOPS**	LAPDOGS	**ADHLLNO**	HOLLAND
ADGILLN	LADLING	**ADGLOWY**	DAYGLOW	**ADHLMOY**	HOLYDAM
ADGILMN	MADLING	**ADGMNOO**	GOODMAN	**ADHLMPY**	LYMPHAD
ADGILNN	LANDING	**ADGMNOR**	GORMAND	**ADHLORS**	HOLARDS
ADGILNO	DIGONAL	**ADGNOOR**	DRAGOON	**ADHLOYY**	HOLYDAY
	LOADING		GADROON	**ADHMNOO**	HOODMAN
ADGILNR	DARLING	**ADGNOOS**	GOONDAS		MANHOOD
	LARDING	**ADGNOPS**	DOGNAPS	**ADHMNSU**	NUMDAHS
ADGILNS	LADINGS	**ADGNORS**	DRAGONS	**ADHMORY**	HYDROMA
	LIGANDS	**ADGNORU**	AGROUND	**ADHNNSU**	NHANDUS
ADGILNU	LANGUID	**ADGNORY**	ORGANDY		UNHANDS
	LAUDING	**ADGNRRU**	GURNARD	**ADHNNUY**	UNHANDY
ADGILOR	GOLIARD	**ADGNRSU**	DURGANS	**ADHNOOS**	DAHOONS
ADGILOS	DIALOGS	**ADGNRUU**	UNGUARD	**ADHNORS**	HADRONS
ADGILOV	VALGOID	**ADGOOPS**	GOSPODA	**ADHNORU**	UNHOARD
ADGILSU	GLADIUS	**ADGORSW**	WARDOGS	**ADHNOSU**	HOUDANS
ADGILUY	GAUDILY	**ADGORTU**	OUTDRAG	**ADHNOTU**	HANDOUT
ADGIMMN	DAMMING	**ADGPRSU**	UPDRAGS	**ADHNRSU**	DHURNAS
ADGIMNN	DAMNING	**ADGRSTU**	DUSTRAG	**ADHNRSY**	SHANDRY
ADGIMNP	DAMPING	**ADHHIRS**	HARDISH	**ADHNRTY**	HYDRANT
ADGIMNR	MRIDANG	**ADHHIST**	HADITHS	**ADHNRUY**	UNHARDY
ADGINNR	DARNING	**ADHHISW**	WHIDAHS	**ADHOOPT**	HOPTOAD
	NARDING	**ADHHKSU**	DUHKHAS	**ADHOORR**	RHODORA
	RANDING	**ADHHMOS**	SHAHDOM	**ADHOORS**	DHOORAS
ADGINNS	SANDING	**ADHHOSU**	HOUDAHS	**ADHOPRT**	HARDTOP
ADGINNT	DANTING	**ADHHOSW**	HOWDAHS	**ADHOPRU**	UPHOARD
ADGINNW	DAWNING	**ADHHSWY**	WHYDAHS	**ADHOPST**	DASHPOT
ADGINOR	ADORING	**ADHIIJS**	JIHADIS	**ADHORRU**	DHOURRA
	GRADINO	**ADHIIJT**	IJTIHAD	**ADHORSU**	DOURAHS
	ROADING	**ADHIIKS**	DASHIKI	**ADHOSSW**	SHADOWS
ADGINOS	GANOIDS	**ADHIIMS**	MAIDISH	**ADHOSWY**	SHADOWY
ADGINOT	DOATING	**ADHIKNS**	DANKISH	**ADHPRSU**	PURDAHS
ADGINPP	DAPPING	**ADHIKOP**	HAPKIDO	**ADHPSUU**	UPHAUDS
ADGINPR	DRAPING	**ADHIKRS**	DARKISH	**ADHRRSU**	DHURRAS
	PARDING	**ADHIKSU**	HAIDUKS	**ADIIILR**	IRIDIAL
ADGINPS	SPADING	**ADHILMO**	HALIDOM	**ADIIINR**	IRIDIAN
ADGINRR	DARRING	**ADHILNY**	HANDILY	**ADIIKOS**	AIKIDOS
ADGINRS	DARINGS	**ADHILOP**	HAPLOID	**ADIIKOT**	DAKOITI

ADIIKSY	YIDAKIS	**ADILLTY**	TIDALLY	**ADIMRSW**	MISDRAW
ADIILLS	ILLIADS	**ADILLVY**	VALIDLY	**ADIMRSY**	MYRIADS
ADIILMS	MILADIS	**ADILLYY**	DAYLILY	**ADIMSSS**	SADISMS
	MISDIAL	**ADILMNO**	MONDIAL	**ADIMSST**	DISMAST
	MISLAID	**ADILMNR**	MANDRIL	**ADIMSSY**	DISMAYS
ADIILNO	LIANOID		RIMLAND	**ADIMSTU**	DUMAIST
ADIILNV	INVALID	**ADILMNU**	MAUDLIN		STADIUM
ADIILOS	SIALOID	**ADILMOP**	DIPLOMA	**ADIMSWY**	MIDWAYS
ADIILRW	WIRILDA	**ADILMOS**	AMIDOLS	**ADINNNS**	NANDINS
ADIILSS	SIALIDS	**ADILMOU**	ALODIUM	**ADINNOP**	DIPNOAN
ADIILST	DIALIST	**ADILMOY**	AMYLOID		NONPAID
ADIILUV	DILUVIA	**ADILMPS**	PLASMID	**ADINNOR**	ANDIRON
ADIIMMS	MAIDISM	**ADILMSS**	DISMALS	**ADINNPS**	PINDANS
ADIIMNN	INDAMIN	**ADILMSU**	DUALISM	**ADINNRS**	INNARDS
ADIIMNS	AMIDINS	**ADILMSY**	DISMAYL	**ADINNRW**	INDRAWN
	DIAMINS		LADYISM		WINNARD
ADIIMOS	DAIMIOS	**ADILNNS**	INLANDS	**ADINNRY**	INNYARD
ADIIMPV	IMPAVID	**ADILNOR**	ORDINAL	**ADINNSU**	INDUNAS
ADIIMRS	MIDAIRS	**ADILNOS**	DOLINAS	**ADINOOP**	POINADO
ADIIMRU	MUDIRIA		LADINOS	**ADINOPP**	OPPIDAN
ADIIMSS	MISSAID	**ADILNRS**	ALDRINS	**ADINOPR**	PADRONI
ADIINPR	PINDARI	**ADILNRU**	DIURNAL		PONIARD
	PRIDIAN	**ADILNRY**	RANDILY	**ADINOPT**	PINTADO
ADIINST	DISTAIN	**ADILNSS**	ISLANDS	**ADINORR**	ORDINAR
ADIINSU	INDUSIA	**ADILNST**	TINDALS	**ADINORS**	INROADS
	SUIDIAN	**ADILNSU**	DUALINS		ORDAINS
ADIINSV	AVIDINS		SUNDIAL		SADIRON
ADIINSZ	DIAZINS	**ADILOOV**	OVOIDAL	**ADINORT**	DIATRON
	DIZAINS	**ADILOOZ**	ZOOIDAL	**ADINORV**	VIRANDO
ADIIPRS	DIAPIRS	**ADILOPR**	DIPOLAR	**ADINOSX**	DIAXONS
ADIIPXY	PYXIDIA	**ADILORT**	DILATOR		DIOXANS
ADIIQRU	DAQUIRI	**ADILOSZ**	OZALIDS	**ADINOTX**	OXIDANT
ADIIRST	DIARIST	**ADILOTU**	OUTLAID	**ADINPST**	PANDITS
ADIIRTY	ARIDITY	**ADILPRY**	PYRALID		SANDPIT
ADIISSY	SAIYIDS		RAPIDLY	**ADINQRS**	QINDARS
ADIITVY	AVIDITY	**ADILPSS**	SALPIDS	**ADINRRT**	TRIDARN
ADIJMSS	MASJIDS	**ADILPST**	PLASTID	**ADINRST**	INDARTS
ADIJNOS	ADJOINS	**ADILPSY**	DISPLAY	**ADINRSU**	DURIANS
ADIJNOT	ADJOINT	**ADILPTU**	PLAUDIT		SUNDARI
ADIJSSS	JASSIDS	**ADILPVY**	VAPIDLY	**ADINRSW**	INWARDS
ADIKLNY	LADYKIN	**ADILQSU**	SQUALID	**ADINRTU**	TRIDUAN
ADIKLOR	KILORAD	**ADILRSZ**	LIZARDS		UNITARD
ADIKLOS	ODALISK	**ADILRTY**	TARDILY	**ADINSTT**	DISTANT
ADIKLPS	KLIPDAS	**ADILSTU**	DUALIST	**ADINSTU**	UNSTAID
ADIKMNN	MANKIND		TULADIS	**ADINTTY**	DITTANY
ADIKMOS	MIKADOS	**ADILSTY**	STAIDLY	**ADINWWY**	WINDWAY
ADIKMOU	DAIMOKU	**ADILTUY**	DUALITY	**ADIOOPR**	PARODOI
ADIKMSS	DISMASK	**ADIMNNO**	MONDAIN	**ADIOOSW**	WOODSIA
ADIKNOS	DAIKONS	**ADIMNOS**	DAIMONS	**ADIOPRR**	AIRDROP
ADIKNPS	KIDNAPS		DOMAINS	**ADIOPRS**	SPAROID
	SKIDPAN		MADISON	**ADIOPRT**	PAROTID
ADIKNRS	DISRANK	**ADIMNRS**	MANDIRS	**ADIOPRV**	PRIVADO
ADIKOST	DAKOITS	**ADIMNSS**	DISMANS	**ADIOPSU**	ADIPOUS
ADIKOTY	DAKOITY	**ADIMNST**	MANTIDS	**ADIORST**	ASTROID
ADIKPRS	DISPARK	**ADIMOOS**	ISODOMA	**ADIORSU**	SAUROID
ADIKQRU	DIQUARK	**ADIMORR**	MIRADOR	**ADIORSV**	ADVISOR
ADIKSST	DIKASTS	**ADIMOST**	DIATOMS	**ADIORTU**	AUDITOR
ADIKSSU	ADSUKIS		MASTOID	**ADIOSTU**	OUTSAID
ADIKSTT	DIKTATS	**ADIMOSY**	DAIMYOS	**ADIOSVW**	DISAVOW
ADIKSUZ	ADZUKIS	**ADIMOTT**	MATTOID	**ADIPRSS**	SPARIDS
ADIKSWY	SKIDWAY	**ADIMPRY**	PYRAMID	**ADIPRST**	DISPART
ADILLMM	MILLDAM	**ADIMQSU**	QUIDAMS	**ADIQSTU**	DIQUATS
ADILLRY	LAIRDLY	**ADIMRSS**	DISARMS	**ADIRRSS**	SIRDARS
ADILLSY	DISALLY	**ADIMRSU**	RADIUMS	**ADIRRST**	RITARDS

ADIRRSZ	RIZARDS	ADLNRUY	LAUNDRY	ADNOSSU	SOUDANS
ADIRSSU	SARDIUS	ADLNSSU	SULDANS	ADNOSTT	DOTANTS
ADIRSSV	VISARDS	ADLNTUU	UNADULT	ADNOSTU	ASTOUND
ADIRSSW	WISARDS	ADLOPRU	POULARD	ADNPRUW	UPDRAWN
ADIRSTY	SATYRID	ADLOPSU	UPLOADS	ADNPSTU	DUSTPAN
ADIRSUY	DYSURIA	ADLORRW	WARLORD		STANDUP
ADIRSVZ	VIZARDS	ADLORSS	DORSALS		UPSTAND
ADIRSWZ	WIZARDS	ADLORSU	SUDORAL	ADNRSST	STRANDS
ADIRSZZ	IZZARDS	ADLOSSS	DOSSALS	ADNRSSU	SUNDRAS
ADISSST	SADISTS	ADLPSSU	SPAULDS	ADNRSTU	DRAUNTS
ADISSYY	SAYYIDS	ADMMNOS	MANDOMS		DURANTS
ADISTTY	DITTAYS	ADMMNSU	SUMMAND		DURANTS
ADJKOSU	JUDOKAS	ADMNOOR	DOORMAN	ADNRSUW	SUNWARD
ADJLMOR	JARLDOM		MADRONO		UNDRAWS
ADJLUUW	WUDJULA	ADMNOOW	WOODMAN	ADNSSTY	DYNASTS
ADJNORS	JORDANS	ADMNOOZ	MADZOON	ADNSTYY	DYNASTY
ADJNORU	ADJOURN	ADMNOQU	QUONDAM	ADOOPRS	PARODOS
ADJORRU	ADJUROR	ADMNORS	RANDOMS	ADOOPSU	APODOUS
ADJSSTU	ADJUSTS		RODSMAN	ADOOPSW	SAPWOOD
ADKKLOY	KAKODYL	ADMNORT	DORMANT	ADOORSS	DOOSRAS
ADKLMRU	MUDLARK		MORDANT	ADOORWY	DOORWAY
ADKOPSU	PADOUKS	ADMNOSS	DAMSONS	ADOOSTT	TOSTADO
ADKORWY	DAYWORK	ADMNOSU	OSMUNDA	ADOOSUV	VAUDOOS
	WORKDAY	ADMNOSY	DYNAMOS	ADOOWWX	WOODWAX
ADKRSWY	SKYWARD	ADMNSTU	DUSTMAN	ADOPRRW	WARDROP
ADLLMOW	WADMOLL	ADMOORT	DOORMAT	ADORRSU	ARDOURS
ADLLMOY	MODALLY	ADMOORY	DAYROOM	ADORSTW	TOWARDS
ADLLNOW	LOWLAND	ADMOPPU	POPADUM	ADORSUU	ARDUOUS
ADLLNOY	NODALLY	ADMORRS	RAMRODS	ADORSWY	AYWORDS
ADLLOPR	POLLARD	ADMORST	STARDOM	ADORTUW	OUTDRAW
ADLLOPS	DALLOPS		TSARDOM		OUTWARD
ADLLORS	DOLLARS	ADMORSU	MADUROS	ADOUUVX	VAUDOUX
ADLLRWY	DRYWALL	ADMORTW	MADWORT	ADPRSTU	UPDARTS
ADLLTUY	ADULTLY	ADMORTZ	TZARDOM	ADPRSUW	UPDRAWS
ADLMNOS	ALMONDS	ADMRSTU	DURMAST		UPWARDS
	DOLMANS		MUSTARD	ADRSSUW	USWARDS
ADLMNOY	ALMONDY	ADNNOOS	NANDOOS	ADSSTUW	SAWDUST
ADLMOOR	LORDOMA	ADNNOOT	NANODOT	AEEEFLR	EELFARE
	MALODOR	ADNNOOY	NOONDAY	AEEEGGN	ENGAGEE
ADLMORU	MODULAR	ADNNORS	RANDONS	AEEEGKL	KEELAGE
ADLMOSW	WADMOLS	ADNNORT	DONNART	AEEEGLT	LEGATEE
ADLMSTU	TALMUDS	ADNNOST	DANTONS	AEEEGNT	TEENAGE
ADLNNOR	NORLAND		DONNATS	AEEEGPR	PEERAGE
ADLNNSU	SUNLAND	ADNNOSU	ADNOUNS	AEEEGPS	SEEPAGE
ADLNOOR	LARDOON	ADNNOTU	DAUNTON	AEEEGRR	EAGERER
ADLNOOS	DOOLANS	ADNNRTU	DUNNART	AEEEGRT	ETAGERE
	ONLOADS	ADNNRUW	UNDRAWN	AEEEHLS	HEALEES
ADLNOPU	POUNDAL	ADNOOPR	PANDOOR	AEEEILN	ALIENEE
ADLNORS	LADRONS	ADNOORS	NARDOOS	AEEEIRT	EATERIE
	LARDONS	ADNOORT	DONATOR	AEEELRS	RELEASE
ADLNORT	TROLAND		ODORANT	AEEELTV	ELEVATE
ADLNORU	NODULAR		TANDOOR	AEEERVW	REWEAVE
ADLNOSS	SOLANDS		TORNADO	AEEERWY	EYEWEAR
	SOLDANS	ADNOOSW	WANDOOS	AEEFFLL	FELAFEL
ADLNOST	DALTONS	ADNOPRS	PARDONS	AEEFFNS	NEAFFES
	SANDLOT	ADNOPRU	PANDOUR	AEEFFRS	AFFEERS
ADLNOSU	SOULDAN	ADNOPRV	PROVAND	AEEFGLN	FENAGLE
	UNLOADS	ADNOPST	DOPANTS	AEEFGNR	FREEGAN
ADLNOSX	OXLANDS	ADNORRW	NORWARD	AEEFGNT	FANTEEG
ADLNOSY	SYNODAL	ADNORSW	ONWARDS	AEEFGRS	SERFAGE
ADLNOTU	OUTLAND	ADNORTU	ROTUNDA	AEEFGSU	FEAGUES
ADLNPSU	UPLANDS	ADNORTY	TARDYON	AEEFGTW	WEFTAGE
ADLNRSU	LURDANS	ADNORWY	NAYWORD	AEEFHRT	FEATHER
ADLNRUU	UNDULAR				TEREFAH

AEEFILR	FILAREE
	LEAFIER
AEEFILW	ALEWIFE
AEEFIRS	AREFIES
	FAERIES
	FREESIA
AEEFISW	SEAWIFE
AEEFKRS	FAKEERS
AEEFLLT	FELLATE
	LEAFLET
AEEFLMN	ENFLAME
AEEFLMS	FEMALES
AEEFLRT	REFLATE
AEEFLRU	FERULAE
AEEFLRW	WELFARE
AEEFLRY	LEAFERY
AEEFLRZ	ALFEREZ
AEEFLSU	EASEFUL
AEEFLTX	TELEFAX
AEEFMNR	ENFRAME
	FREEMAN
AEEFMRR	REFRAME
AEEFMRT	FERMATE
AEEFOTV	FOVEATE
AEEFPPR	FRAPPEE
AEEFRRS	FEARERS
AEEFRRT	FERRATE
AEEFRST	AFREETS
	FEASTER
AEEFRTU	FEATURE
AEEFRWY	FREEWAY
AEEFSTT	FEATEST
AEEGGLL	ALLEGGE
AEEGGLR	GREGALE
AEEGGLS	ALEGGES
AEEGGLT	GATELEG
AEEGGNR	ENGAGER
AEEGGNS	ENGAGES
AEEGGOP	EPAGOGE
AEEGGRS	AGREGES
	RAGGEES
	REGGAES
AEEGGRU	REGAUGE
AEEGGST	TAGGEES
AEEGGSW	GEEGAWS
AEEGHIR	HIREAGE
AEEGHNT	THENAGE
AEEGHNW	WHANGEE
AEEGHSZ	GEEZAHS
AEEGILL	GALILEE
AEEGILM	MILEAGE
AEEGILN	LINEAGE
AEEGILP	EPIGEAL
AEEGILT	EGALITE
AEEGILW	WEIGELA
AEEGIMR	REIMAGE
AEEGINP	EPIGEAN
AEEGINR	REGINAE
AEEGINS	AGENISE
AEEGINU	EUGENIA
AEEGINZ	AGENIZE
AEEGIPP	PIPEAGE
AEEGIPR	PIERAGE
AEEGIRU	EUGARIE
AEEGISS	AEGISES
	ASSIEGE
AEEGJRS	JAEGERS
AEEGJSY	JAYGEES
AEEGKLL	KLEAGLE
AEEGLLR	ALLEGER
AEEGLLS	ALLEGES
AEEGLLZ	GAZELLE
AEEGLMN	GLEEMAN
	MELANGE
AEEGLMR	GLEAMER
AEEGLMT	MELTAGE
AEEGLNR	ENLARGE
	GENERAL
	GLEANER
AEEGLNT	ELEGANT
AEEGLNU	EUGLENA
AEEGLNV	EVANGEL
AEEGLOR	AEROGEL
AEEGLPR	PEREGAL
AEEGLPS	PELAGES
AEEGLRR	REGALER
AEEGLRS	GALERES
	REGALES
AEEGLRU	LEAGUER
	REGULAE
AEEGLRW	LEGWEAR
AEEGLRY	EAGERLY
AEEGLRZ	REGLAZE
AEEGLSS	AGELESS
	ALGESES
AEEGLST	EAGLETS
	GELATES
	LEGATES
	SEGETAL
	TEAGLES
	TELEGAS
AEEGLSU	LEAGUES
AEEGLSV	GLEAVES
	SELVAGE
AEEGLTT	GALETTE
AEEGLTU	TEGULAE
AEEGLTV	VEGETAL
AEEGMMT	GEMMATE
	TAGMEME
AEEGMNR	GERMANE
AEEGMNS	MANEGES
	MENAGES
AEEGMNT	GATEMEN
AEEGMPR	PREGAME
AEEGMRR	MEAGRER
AEEGMRS	MEAGRES
AEEGMRU	REMUAGE
AEEGMSS	MEGASSE
	MESSAGE
AEEGMST	GAMETES
	METAGES
AEEGNNP	PANGENE
AEEGNNR	ENRANGE
AEEGNNS	ENNAGES
AEEGNOP	PEONAGE
AEEGNPP	GENAPPE
AEEGNRS	ENRAGES
AEEGNRT	GRANTEE
	GREATEN
	NEGATER
	REAGENT
AEEGNRU	RENAGUE
	UNEAGER
AEEGNRV	AVENGER
	ENGRAVE
AEEGNSS	SAGENES
	SENEGAS
AEEGNST	NEGATES
AEEGNSV	AVENGES
	GENEVAS
AEEGNTT	TENTAGE
AEEGNTV	VENTAGE
AEEGOPS	APOGEES
AEEGORV	OVERAGE
AEEGOST	GOATEES
AEEGPRS	ASPERGE
	PRESAGE
AEEGPRU	PUGAREE
AEEGPST	SEPTAGE
AEEGRRS	GREASER
	REGEARS
AEEGRRT	GREATER
	REGRATE
AEEGRRU	REARGUE
AEEGRRW	WAGERER
AEEGRSS	GREASES
AEEGRST	ERGATES
	RESTAGE
AEEGRSV	GREAVES
AEEGRTU	TREAGUE
AEEGRUZ	GUEREZA
AEEGSSW	SEWAGES
AEEGSTT	GESTATE
	TAGETES
AEEGTTZ	GAZETTE
AEEHHNT	HEATHEN
AEEHHRT	HEATHER
AEEHHST	SHEATHE
AEEHHSW	HEEHAWS
AEEHINR	HERNIAE
AEEHIPR	HEAPIER
AEEHIRV	HEAVIER
AEEHIST	ATHEISE
AEEHISV	HEAVIES
AEEHITZ	ATHEIZE
AEEHKMS	HAKEEMS
AEEHKNR	HEARKEN
AEEHKNT	THANKEE
AEEHKRT	HEKTARE
AEEHKRU	HEUREKA
AEEHLNT	LETHEAN
AEEHLPT	HEELTAP
AEEHLRS	HEALERS
AEEHLRT	HALTERE
	LEATHER
AEEHLRV	HAVEREL
AEEHLSS	LEASHES
AEEHLST	LATHEES
AEEHLSW	AWHEELS
AEEHLSX	EXHALES
AEEHLSY	EYELASH
AEEHLTT	ATHLETE

AEEHMNT	METHANE	AEEILNX	ALEXINE	AEEIUVX	EXUVIAE
AEEHMRS	HAREEMS	AEEILPT	EPILATE	AEEJKSS	JAKESES
	MAHSEER		PILEATE	AEEJMSS	JAMESES
AEEHMRT	ERATHEM	AEEILRR	EARLIER	AEEJNST	SEJEANT
	THERMAE		LEARIER	AEEJNTU	JAUNTEE
AEEHMST	MEATHES	AEEILRS	EARLIES	AEEJRSV	EVEJARS
AEEHMSU	HEAUMES		REALISE	AEEJSVY	JAYVEES
AEEHNPS	PEAHENS	AEEILRT	ATELIER		VEEJAYS
AEEHNPT	HAPTENE		REALTIE	AEEKKNO	KOKANEE
	HEPTANE	AEEILRV	LEAVIER	AEEKKOO	KOEKOEA
	PHENATE		VEALIER	AEEKLLT	LAKELET
AEEHNRS	ARSHEEN	AEEILRZ	REALIZE	AEEKLMN	KEELMAN
AEEHNRT	EARTHEN	AEEILTT	AILETTE	AEEKLNS	ALKENES
	HEARTEN	AEEILTV	ELATIVE	AEEKLNT	KANTELE
AEEHNST	ETHANES	AEEIMNN	ENAMINE	AEEKLPS	PALKEES
AEEHNSV	HEAVENS	AEEIMNR	REMANIE	AEEKLRS	LEAKERS
AEEHNSX	HEXANES	AEEIMNS	MEANIES	AEEKLSV	VAKEELS
AEEHNTW	WHEATEN		NEMESIA	AEEKMNS	KAMSEEN
AEEHPRS	HEAPERS	AEEIMNT	ETAMINE	AEEKMNW	WAKEMEN
	RESHAPE		MATINEE	AEEKMRR	REMAKER
	SPHAERE	AEEIMNX	EXAMINE	AEEKMRS	REMAKES
	SPHEARE	AEEIMPR	EMPAIRE	AEEKMRT	MEERKAT
AEEHPRT	PREHEAT	AEEIMRR	REAMIER	AEEKNNN	NANKEEN
AEEHPSS	APHESES		REREMAI	AEEKNNP	KNEEPAN
	SPAHEES	AEEIMRS	SEAMIER	AEEKNRS	SNEAKER
AEEHPUV	UPHEAVE		SERIEMA	AEEKNRT	RETAKEN
AEEHQSU	QUASHEE	AEEIMRT	EMERITA	AEEKNRW	REWAKEN
AEEHRRS	HEARERS		EMIRATE		WAKENER
	REHEARS		MEATIER	AEEKNSS	SKEANES
	SHEARER	AEEIMSS	MISEASE	AEEKNSW	WEAKENS
AEEHRSS	HEARSES		SIAMESE	AEEKORW	REAWOKE
AEEHRST	AETHERS	AEEIMST	STEAMIE	AEEKPRS	PARKEES
	HEATERS	AEEIMSZ	SIAMEZE		RESPEAK
	REHEATS	AEEIMTT	TEATIME		SPEAKER
AEEHRSV	HEAVERS	AEEINPR	PERINEA	AEEKPRT	PERTAKE
	RESHAVE	AEEINRT	ARENITE	AEEKRRT	RETAKER
AEEHRSW	WHEREAS		RETINAE	AEEKRRW	WREAKER
AEEHRTT	THEATER		TRAINEE	AEEKRST	RETAKES
	THEATRE	AEEINST	ETESIAN		SAKERET
	THEREAT	AEEINTV	NAIVETE	AEEKRSU	EUREKAS
AEEHRTV	THREAVE	AEEINVW	INWEAVE	AEEKRSW	REWAKES
AEEHRTW	WEATHER	AEEIORT	ETAERIO	AEEKRTW	TWEAKER
	WHEREAT	AEEIPRR	PEREIRA	AEEKSSS	ASKESES
	WREATHE	AEEIPRS	APERIES	AEEKSTW	WEAKEST
AEEHSST	HEASTES		EPEIRAS	AEELLLS	ALLELES
AEEHSSV	SHEAVES	AEEIPRT	PEATIER	AEELLMS	MALLEES
AEEHSTV	THEAVES	AEEIPSV	PEAVIES	AEELLOV	ALVEOLE
AEEHSWY	EYEWASH	AEEIPTX	EXPIATE	AEELLPR	PARELLE
AEEIIRS	AIERIES	AEEIRRR	ARRIERE	AEELLSS	SALLEES
AEEIKLP	APELIKE	AEEIRRS	REARISE	AEELLST	LEALEST
	PEALIKE		RERAISE	AEELLWY	WALLEYE
AEEIKLR	EARLIKE	AEEIRRT	TEARIER	AEELMNP	EMPANEL
	LEAKIER	AEEIRRW	WEARIER		EMPLANE
AEEIKLT	TEALIKE	AEEIRST	AERIEST	AEELMNR	REELMAN
AEEIKPR	PEAKIER		SERIATE	AEELMNS	ENAMELS
AEEIKSV	KEAVIES	AEEIRSW	WEARIES		MELENAS
AEEILLR	REALLIE	AEEIRTT	ARIETTE	AEELMNT	MANTEEL
AEEILMR	MEALIER		ITERATE		TELEMAN
AEEILMS	MEALIES	AEEIRTV	EVIRATE	AEELMNV	VELAMEN
AEEILNP	ALEPINE	AEEISST	EASIEST	AEELMNY	AMYLENE
	ELAPINE	AEEISVV	EVASIVE	AEELMPR	EMPALER
AEEILNR	ALIENER	AEEITTV	AVIETTE		PREMEAL
AEEILNS	SEALINE		EVITATE	AEELMPS	EMPALES
AEEILNT	LINEATE	AEEITUX	EUTEXIA	AEELMPX	EXAMPLE

	EXEMPLA
AEELMRS	MEALERS
AEELMRT	LAMETER
AEELMSS	MEASLES
AEELMSU	AEMULES
AEELMSZ	MEAZELS
AEELMTU	EMULATE
AEELNNP	ENPLANE
AEELNNR	LERNEAN
AEELNOS	ENOLASE
AEELNPR	REPANEL
AEELNPS	ALPEENS
	SPELEAN
AEELNRR	LEARNER
	RELEARN
AEELNRS	LEANERS
AEELNRT	ALTERNE
	ENTERAL
	ETERNAL
	TELERAN
AEELNRW	RENEWAL
AEELNSS	ENSEALS
AEELNST	ELANETS
	LATEENS
	LEANEST
AEELNSV	ENSLAVE
	LEAVENS
AEELNSW	WEANELS
AEELNTY	ENTAYLE
AEELOPR	PAROLEE
AEELOPX	POLEAXE
AEELORS	AREOLES
AEELORU	AUREOLE
AEELOST	OLEATES
AEELOSW	LEASOWE
AEELPRR	PEARLER
AEELPRS	LEAPERS
	PLEASER
	PRESALE
	RELAPSE
	REPEALS
AEELPRT	PETRALE
	PLEATER
	PRELATE
	REPLATE
AEELPRU	PLEURAE
AEELPSS	ELAPSES
	PLEASES
	SAPELES
AEELPSU	EPAULES
AEELPTT	PALETTE
	PELTATE
AEELPTU	EPAULET
AEELQRU	LEQUEAR
AEELQSU	QUELEAS
	SEQUELA
AEELRRT	ALERTER
	ALTERER
	REALTER
	RELATER
AEELRRV	RAVELER
AEELRRX	RELAXER
AEELRSS	EARLESS
	LEASERS

	RESALES
	RESEALS
	SEALERS
AEELRST	ELATERS
	REALEST
	RELATES
	RESLATE
	STEALER
AEELRSU	LEASURE
AEELRSV	LAVEERS
	LEAVERS
	REVEALS
	SEVERAL
	VEALERS
AEELRSX	RELAXES
AEELRSY	SEALERY
AEELRTX	EXALTER
AEELRUV	REVALUE
AEELSST	ALTESSE
	STEALES
	TEASELS
AEELSSV	SLEAVES
AEELSSW	AWELESS
	WEASELS
AEELSSZ	SLEAZES
AEELSTU	ELUATES
	SETUALE
AEELSTV	SALVETE
	VALETES
	VELETAS
AEELSTX	LATEXES
AEELSTY	EYALETS
AEELSTZ	TEAZELS
	TEAZLES
AEELSWY	LEEWAYS
	WEASELY
AEELTTY	LAYETTE
AEELTVW	WAVELET
AEEMMMR	MAREMME
AEEMMMS	MAMMEES
AEEMMNT	MEATMEN
AEEMMPY	EMPYEMA
AEEMMRT	AMMETER
	METAMER
AEEMMSY	MAMEYES
AEEMNNO	ANEMONE
AEEMNNP	PENNAME
AEEMNOX	AXONEME
AEEMNPR	PRENAME
AEEMNPS	SPAEMEN
AEEMNPT	PEATMEN
AEEMNRS	MEANERS
	RENAMES
AEEMNRT	REMANET
AEEMNSS	ENSEAMS
AEEMNST	ENTAMES
	MEANEST
AEEMNSX	EXAMENS
AEEMOPT	METOPAE
AEEMORT	EROTEMA
AEEMOSW	AWESOME
	WAESOME
AEEMPRS	AMPERES
	EMPARES

AEEMPRT	TEMPERA
AEEMPRY	EMPAYRE
AEEMPST	METEPAS
AEEMPSW	WAMPEES
AEEMPTU	AMPUTEE
AEEMQRU	MARQUEE
AEEMRRS	REAMERS
	SMEARER
AEEMRSS	SEAMERS
AEEMRST	REMATES
	RETEAMS
	STEAMER
	TEAMERS
AEEMRSU	MEASURE
AEEMRTX	EXTREMA
AEEMRTY	METAYER
AEEMSSS	SESAMES
AEEMSST	MESETAS
	SEAMSET
AEEMSTT	METATES
AEEMSTX	TAXEMES
AEENNOT	NEONATE
AEENNOV	NOVENAE
AEENNPT	PENNATE
	PENTANE
AEENNRS	ENSNARE
	RENNASE
AEENNRX	REANNEX
AEENNST	NEATENS
AEENNSX	ANNEXES
AEENNTU	UNEATEN
AEENOPR	PERAEON
AEENOPU	EUPNOEA
AEENORS	ARENOSE
AEENOSS	ANOESES
AEENOSU	AENEOUS
AEENPRS	PANEERS
AEENPST	NEPETAS
	PENATES
	PESANTE
AEENPSU	EUPNEAS
AEENPSW	PAWNEES
AEENPSX	EXPANSE
AEENRRS	EARNERS
	REEARNS
AEENRRT	TERRANE
AEENRRV	RAVENER
AEENRRY	YEARNER
AEENRSS	ENSEARS
AEENRST	EARNEST
	EASTERN
	NEAREST
	RATEENS
AEENRSW	WEANERS
AEENRTT	ENTREAT
	RATTEEN
	TERNATE
AEENRTV	AVENTRE
	NERVATE
	VETERAN
AEENRUV	UNREAVE
AEENSST	ENTASES
	SATEENS
	SENATES

	SENSATE		RETREAT	AEFFLRU	FEARFUL
	STEANES		TREATER	AEFFLRW	WAFFLER
AEENSSU	UNEASES	AEERRTV	AVERTER	AEFFLSW	WAFFLES
AEENSSV	AVENSES	AEERRTW	WATERER	AEFFLSY	YAFFLES
AEENSSW	WAENESS	AEERRVW	WAVERER	AEFFLTU	FATEFUL
AEENSTT	NEATEST	AEERSST	EASTERS	AEFFMRU	EARMUFF
AEENSUV	AVENUES		RESEATS	AEFFNST	NAFFEST
AEENSWZ	WEAZENS		SAETERS	AEFFOVW	WAVEOFF
AEENTTV	NAVETTE		SEAREST	AEFFQRU	QUAFFER
AEENUVW	UNWEAVE		SEATERS	AEFFRST	AFFRETS
AEEOPRT	OPERATE		STEARES		RESTAFF
AEEOPTZ	EPAZOTE		TEASERS		STAFFER
AEEORRS	REAROSE		TESSERA	AEFFRSY	EFFRAYS
AEEORSS	SEROSAE	AEERSSU	RESEAUS	AEFFRSZ	ZAFFERS
AEEORST	ROSEATE		SEASURE		ZAFFRES
AEEORSV	OVERSEA		UREASES	AEFFTTY	TAFFETY
AEEORTV	OVERATE	AEERSSV	ASSEVER	AEFGGGO	FOGGAGE
	OVEREAT	AEERSSY	ESSAYER	AEFGGIR	FAGGIER
AEEORVW	OVERAWE	AEERSTT	ESTREAT	AEFGGLR	FLAGGER
AEEOSUU	EUOUAES		RESTATE	AEFGGMO	MEGAFOG
AEEOSVV	EVOVAES		RETASTE	AEFGGRY	FAGGERY
AEEPPRR	PAPERER	AEERSTU	AUSTERE	AEFGILN	FEALING
	PREPARE	AEERSTW	SWEATER		FINAGLE
	REPAPER	AEERSTX	RETAXES		LEAFING
AEEPPRS	RAPPEES	AEERSUV	VAREUSE	AEFGILO	FOLIAGE
AEEPPRT	PRETAPE	AEERSUX	RESEAUX	AEFGILR	FRAGILE
AEEPPRV	PREPAVE	AEERSVW	WEAVERS	AEFGINR	FEARING
AEEPRRS	REAPERS	AEERSWX	REWAXES	AEFGINS	FEASING
	SPEARER	AEERTTX	EXTREAT	AEFGINT	FEATING
AEEPRRT	PEARTER	AEERTWW	WETWARE	AEFGINZ	FEAZING
	TAPERER	AEERTWX	TREEWAX	AEFGIRT	FRIGATE
AEEPRRV	PREAVER	AEESSSW	SEESAWS	AEFGIRU	REFUGIA
AEEPRSS	ASPERSE	AEESSSY	EYASSES	AEFGITU	FATIGUE
	PARESES	AEESSTT	ESTATES	AEFGLLU	FULLAGE
	PRAESES	AEESSTU	SAUTEES	AEFGLMN	FLAGMEN
	PREASES	AEESSTX	TEXASES	AEFGLNR	FLANGER
	PREASSE	AEESSUX	AUXESES	AEFGLNS	FANGLES
	SERAPES	AEESTTT	TESTATE		FLANGES
AEEPRST	REPEATS	AEESWXY	WAXEYES	AEFGLOT	FLOTAGE
	RETAPES	AEFFFLR	FLAFFER	AEFGLOW	FLOWAGE
AEEPRSV	REPAVES	AEFFGIR	GIRAFFE	AEFGLPU	PAGEFUL
AEEPRSZ	SPREAZE		RIFFAGE	AEFGLRS	REFLAGS
AEEPRTU	EPURATE	AEFFGNR	ENGRAFF	AEFGLRU	RAGEFUL
AEEPRTY	PEATERY	AEFFGRS	GAFFERS	AEFGLUZ	GAZEFUL
AEEPRTZ	TRAPEZE	AEFFGRU	GAUFFER	AEFGMOR	FROMAGE
AEEPSSS	ASEPSES	AEFFHST	HAFFETS	AEFGMSU	FUMAGES
AEEPSST	PESETAS	AEFFINS	AFFINES	AEFGNRR	FRANGER
AEEPSSW	PESEWAS	AEFFIPR	PIAFFER		GRANFER
AEEPSTT	SEPTATE	AEFFIPS	PIAFFES	AEFGNRT	ENGRAFT
	SPATTEE	AEFFIRX	AFFIXER	AEFGOOT	FOOTAGE
AEEPSVY	PEAVEYS		REAFFIX	AEFGORR	FORAGER
AEEQRSU	QUAERES	AEFFIST	TAFFIES	AEFGORS	FORAGES
AEEQSTU	EQUATES	AEFFISW	WAFFIES	AEFGORT	FAGOTER
AEERRRS	REARERS	AEFFISX	AFFIXES	AEFGORV	FORGAVE
AEERRSS	ERASERS	AEFFKOP	OFFPEAK	AEFGRRT	GRAFTER
AEERRST	RETEARS	AEFFKOR	RAKEOFF		REGRAFT
	SERRATE	AEFFKOT	OFFTAKE	AEFGRSU	GAUFERS
	TEARERS		TAKEOFF		GAUFRES
AEERRSU	ERASURE	AEFFLLY	FLYLEAF	AEFHIRT	FAITHER
AEERRSV	REAVERS	AEFFLMW	FLAMFEW	AEFHIRW	WHARFIE
AEERRSW	REWEARS	AEFFLNS	SNAFFLE	AEFHISZ	HAFIZES
	SWEARER	AEFFLRR	RAFFLER	AEFHLLS	FELLAHS
	WEARERS	AEFFLRS	FARFELS	AEFHLOR	FAHLORE
AEERRTT	RETRATE		RAFFLES	AEFHLRS	FLASHER

AEFHLRT	FARTHEL	**AEFIRRR**	FARRIER	**AEFLRSY**	FLAYERS
AEFHLRZ	FAHLERZ	**AEFIRSS**	FRAISES	**AEFLRTT**	FLATTER
AEFHLSS	FLASHES	**AEFIRST**	FAIREST	**AEFLRTU**	REFUTAL
AEFHLTU	HATEFUL	**AEFIRTT**	FATTIER		TEARFUL
AEFHRRT	FARTHER	**AEFISST**	FASTIES	**AEFLRZZ**	FRAZZLE
AEFHRST	FATHERS		FIESTAS	**AEFLSST**	FALSEST
	HAFTERS		FISSATE		FATLESS
	SHAFTER	**AEFISTT**	FATTIES		FESTALS
AEFHRSY	FASHERY	**AEFISTX**	FIXATES	**AEFLSTU**	FLUATES
AEFIILT	FILIATE	**AEFJNST**	FANJETS		SULFATE
AEFIIRS	FAIRIES	**AEFKLNN**	FLANKEN	**AEFMNOR**	FORAMEN
AEFIJLO	JEOFAIL	**AEFKLNR**	FLANKER		FOREMAN
AEFIJOS	FEIJOAS	**AEFKLNS**	FANKLES	**AEFMNRT**	RAFTMEN
AEFIKLN	FANLIKE	**AEFKLOS**	SEAFOLK	**AEFMNRU**	FRAENUM
AEFIKLR	FLAKIER	**AEFKLRS**	FLAKERS	**AEFMORR**	FOREARM
AEFIKLS	FLAKIES	**AEFKLRT**	FARTLEK	**AEFMORS**	FOAMERS
AEFIKLT	FATLIKE	**AEFKLST**	FLASKET	**AEFMORT**	FORMATE
AEFILLM	FAMILLE	**AEFKLUW**	WAKEFUL	**AEFMOUW**	WAMEFOU
AEFILLS	FAILLES	**AEFKNRR**	FRANKER	**AEFMRRS**	FARMERS
AEFILMN	FEMINAL	**AEFKORS**	FORSAKE		FRAMERS
	INFLAME	**AEFLLNN**	FANNELL	**AEFMRRY**	FARMERY
AEFILMR	FLAMIER		FLANNEL	**AEFNNRS**	FANNERS
AEFILNS	FINALES	**AEFLLOT**	FLOATEL	**AEFNNST**	ENFANTS
AEFILNT	INFLATE	**AEFLLRS**	FALLERS	**AEFNOPR**	PROFANE
AEFILNU	INFULAE		REFALLS	**AEFNOPY**	PAYFONE
AEFILNV	FLAVINE	**AEFLLSY**	FALSELY	**AEFNORR**	FORERAN
AEFILOT	FOLIATE	**AEFLLTT**	FLATLET	**AEFNRRS**	FARRENS
AEFILPT	FLEAPIT	**AEFLLTU**	TALEFUL	**AEFNRSS**	FARNESS
AEFILRR	FLARIER	**AEFLLUZ**	ZEALFUL	**AEFNRSU**	FURANES
	FRAILER	**AEFLMNS**	FLAMENS		UNSAFER
AEFILRU	FAILURE	**AEFLMOR**	FEMORAL	**AEFNRSW**	FAWNERS
AEFILRV	FAVRILE	**AEFLMRS**	FLAMERS	**AEFNSST**	FASTENS
AEFILRW	FLAWIER	**AEFLMUW**	WAMEFUL		FATNESS
AEFILRX	FLAXIER	**AEFLMUZ**	MAZEFUL	**AEFNSTT**	FATTENS
AEFILRZ	FILAZER	**AEFLNNN**	FLANNEN	**AEFOPRW**	FOREPAW
AEFILSS	FALSIES	**AEFLNNS**	FANNELS	**AEFORRV**	FAVORER
	FILASSE	**AEFLNOV**	FLAVONE		OVERFAR
AEFILST	FETIALS	**AEFLNRS**	SALFERN	**AEFORRY**	FORAYER
	SEALIFT	**AEFLNRU**	FLANEUR	**AEFORSW**	FORESAW
AEFILTT	FLATTIE		FRENULA	**AEFORSY**	FORESAY
AEFILWY	LIFEWAY		FUNERAL	**AEFORTV**	OVERFAT
AEFIMNR	FIREMAN	**AEFLNSU**	FLAUNES	**AEFOSST**	FATSOES
AEFIMNS	FAMINES	**AEFLNTT**	FLATTEN		FOSSATE
	INFAMES	**AEFLNUU**	FAUNULE	**AEFOSTU**	FEATOUS
AEFIMOR	FOAMIER	**AEFLOOV**	FOVEOLA	**AEFPPRS**	FRAPPES
AEFIMRR	FIREARM	**AEFLOPW**	PEAFOWL	**AEFRRST**	FRATERS
AEFIMRS	MISFARE	**AEFLORS**	LOAFERS		RAFTERS
AEFINNS	FAINNES		SAFROLE		STRAFER
	FANNIES	**AEFLORT**	FLOATER	**AEFRRTY**	FRATERY
AEFINNT	INFANTE		FLOREAT	**AEFRSSS**	FRASSES
AEFINNZ	FANZINE		REFLOAT	**AEFRSST**	FASTERS
AEFINPR	FIREPAN	**AEFLORY**	FORELAY		STRAFES
AEFINRR	REFRAIN	**AEFLOST**	FOLATES	**AEFRSTU**	FAUREST
AEFINRS	INFARES	**AEFLOSW**	SEAFOWL	**AEFRSTW**	FRETSAW
	SERAFIN	**AEFLPPR**	FLAPPER		WAFTERS
AEFINRT	FAINTER	**AEFLPRS**	FELSPAR	**AEFRTTU**	TARTUFE
	FENITAR	**AEFLPRU**	FLAREUP	**AEFRTUW**	WAFTURE
AEFINRW	FAWNIER	**AEFLPRY**	PALFREY	**AEFRWYZ**	FRAWZEY
AEFINRX	XERAFIN	**AEFLRSS**	FALSERS	**AEFSSTT**	FASTEST
AEFINST	FAINEST		FLASERS		SAFTEST
	NAIFEST	**AEFLRST**	FALTERS	**AEFSSUV**	FAVUSES
AEFINSW	FANWISE	**AEFLRSU**	EARFULS	**AEFSTTT**	FATTEST
AEFINTX	ANTEFIX		FERULAS	**AEGGGLS**	GAGGLES
AEFIQRU	AQUIFER		REFUSAL	**AEGGGLU**	LUGGAGE

AEGGGRS	GAGGERS	AEGHIMT	MEGAHIT	AEGILLU	LIGULAE
AEGGGRY	GAGGERY	AEGHINP	HEAPING	AEGILLV	VILLAGE
AEGGHLR	HAGGLER	AEGHINR	HEARING	AEGILLY	AGILELY
AEGGHLS	HAGGLES	AEGHINT	GAHNITE	AEGILLZ	GALLIZE
AEGGHMO	HEMAGOG		HEATING	AEGILMN	GEMINAL
AEGGHSW	EGGWASH	AEGHINV	HEAVING		LEAMING
AEGGIJR	JAGGIER	AEGHINZ	GENIZAH		MEALING
AEGGIJS	JAGGIES	AEGHIOS	HOAGIES	AEGILMR	GREMIAL
AEGGILN	EAGLING	AEGHIRS	HEGARIS		LAMIGER
	GEALING		HEGIRAS	AEGILMS	MILAGES
	LIGNAGE		HIRAGES	AEGILNN	ANELING
AEGGIMS	MAGGIES	AEGHISS	GEISHAS		EANLING
AEGGINR	GEARING	AEGHISZ	GHAZIES		LEANING
	NAGGIER	AEGHLNO	HALOGEN		NEALING
AEGGINS	AGEINGS	AEGHLNT	ALENGTH	AEGILNP	LEAPING
	SIGNAGE	AEGHLOS	GALOSHE		PEALING
AEGGIOS	ISAGOGE	AEGHLRU	LAUGHER		PLEAING
AEGGIRR	RAGGIER	AEGHLSS	SEALGHS	AEGILNR	ALIGNER
AEGGIRS	RAGGIES	AEGHLST	HAGLETS		ENGRAIL
	SAGGIER	AEGHLSZ	GHAZELS		LAERING
AEGGIRT	TAGGIER	AEGHLTW	THALWEG		LEARING
AEGGIRU	GARIGUE	AEGHMNN	HANGMEN		NARGILE
AEGGIST	STAGGIE	AEGHMNO	HOGMANE		REALIGN
AEGGISW	SWAGGIE	AEGHMOR	HOMAGER		REGINAL
AEGGJRS	JAGGERS	AEGHMOS	HOMAGES	AEGILNS	LEASING
AEGGJRY	JAGGERY		OHMAGES		LINAGES
AEGGLNO	AGELONG	AEGHMSU	MESHUGA		SEALING
AEGGLNR	GANGREL	AEGHNOX	HEXAGON	AEGILNT	ATINGLE
AEGGLNS	LAGGENS	AEGHNRS	GNASHER		ELATING
AEGGLRR	GARGLER		HANGERS		GELATIN
AEGGLRS	GARGLES		REHANGS		GENITAL
	LAGGERS		SHERANG		TAGLINE
	RAGGLES	AEGHNRU	NURAGHE	AEGILNU	LINGUAE
AEGGLRW	WAGGLER	AEGHNSS	GNASHES		UNAGILE
AEGGLRY	GREYLAG	AEGHNST	STENGAH	AEGILNV	LEAVING
AEGGLSW	WAGGLES	AEGHOPY	HYPOGEA		VEALING
AEGGMNY	YEGGMAN	AEGHORS	GHERAOS	AEGILNY	ALEYING
AEGGMSS	EGGMASS	AEGHOSS	SEAHOGS		YEALING
AEGGNNU	GUNNAGE	AEGHOST	HOSTAGE	AEGILOS	GOALIES
AEGGNRR	GRANGER	AEGHPRS	SPREAGH		SOILAGE
AEGGNRS	GANGERS	AEGHPST	HATPEGS	AEGILOU	EULOGIA
	GRANGES	AEGHRST	GATHERS	AEGILPS	PAIGLES
	NAGGERS	AEGHSST	GASHEST	AEGILRR	GLARIER
AEGGNSU	GANGUES	AEGIIMN	IMAGINE	AEGILRS	GLAIRES
AEGGRRY	RAGGERY	AEGIKLN	LEAKING		GRAILES
AEGGRSS	AGGRESS		LINKAGE	AEGILRZ	GLAZIER
	SAGGERS	AEGIKLT	GLAIKET	AEGILSS	ALGESIS
	SEGGARS		TAGLIKE		GLASSIE
AEGGRST	GAGSTER	AEGIKNP	PEAKING		LIGASES
	GARGETS	AEGIKNR	REAKING		SILAGES
	STAGGER	AEGIKNS	SINKAGE	AEGILST	AGILEST
	TAGGERS	AEGIKPP	KIPPAGE		AIGLETS
AEGGRSU	GAUGERS	AEGIKPR	GARPIKE		GELATIS
AEGGRSW	SWAGGER	AEGIKRW	GAWKIER		LIGATES
	WAGGERS	AEGIKSW	GAWKIES		TAIGLES
AEGGRSY	YAGGERS	AEGILLL	ILLEGAL	AEGILSV	GLAIVES
AEGGRTY	GARGETY	AEGILLM	MEGILLA	AEGILTU	GLUTAEI
AEGGRWY	WAGGERY		MILLAGE	AEGILTY	EGALITY
AEGGSWW	GEWGAWS	AEGILLN	GALLEIN	AEGIMMR	GAMMIER
AEGHHIT	AHEIGHT		NIGELLA	AEGIMNN	AMENING
AEGHIJR	JAGHIRE	AEGILLP	PILLAGE		MEANING
AEGHIKL	HAGLIKE	AEGILLS	GALLIES	AEGIMNP	PIGMEAN
AEGHILN	HEALING		GALLISE	AEGIMNR	GERMAIN
AEGHILR	LAIGHER	AEGILLT	TILLAGE		GERMINA

	MANGIER		GAINERS	**AEGIRUY**	YUGARIE
	MEARING		GRAINES	**AEGIRUZ**	GAUZIER
	REAMING		REAGINS	**AEGISST**	AGEISTS
AEGIMNS	ENIGMAS		REGAINS		SAGIEST
	GAMINES		REGINAS	**AEGISSU**	AGUISES
	MEASING		SEARING	**AEGISSV**	VISAGES
	SEAMING		SERINGA	**AEGISTU**	AUGITES
AEGIMNT	MINTAGE	**AEGINRT**	GRANITE	**AEGISTY**	GASEITY
	TEAMING		GRATINE	**AEGISTZ**	GAZIEST
	TEGMINA		INGRATE	**AEGISUZ**	AGUIZES
AEGIMOS	IMAGOES		TANGIER	**AEGISYZ**	AZYGIES
AEGIMPR	EPIGRAM		TEARING	**AEGJLNR**	JANGLER
	PRIMAGE	**AEGINRV**	REAVING	**AEGJLNS**	JANGLES
AEGIMPS	MAGPIES		VINEGAR	**AEGJLSS**	JAGLESS
	MISPAGE	**AEGINRW**	WEARING	**AEGJLST**	JETLAGS
AEGIMPT	PIGMEAT	**AEGINRZ**	ZINGARE	**AEGKKNO**	ANGEKOK
AEGIMRR	ARMIGER	**AEGINSS**	AGNISES	**AEGKLOU**	KAGOULE
AEGIMRS	GISARME		SEASING	**AEGKLRS**	GRAKLES
	IMAGERS	**AEGINST**	EASTING	**AEGKMRY**	KERYGMA
	MAIGRES		EATINGS	**AEGKMSS**	MASKEGS
	MIRAGES		GAINEST	**AEGKNOR**	KARENGO
AEGIMRT	MIGRATE		GENISTA	**AEGKNRS**	SKANGER
	RAGTIME		INGATES	**AEGKRSW**	GAWKERS
AEGIMRU	GAUMIER		INGESTA	**AEGKSST**	GASKETS
AEGIMRY	IMAGERY		SEATING	**AEGLLLY**	LEGALLY
AEGIMSS	AGEISMS		TAGINES	**AEGLLNO**	ALLONGE
AEGIMST	GAMIEST		TANGIES		GALLEON
	SIGMATE		TEASING	**AEGLLNR**	LANGREL
AEGIMSV	MISGAVE		TSIGANE	**AEGLLNS**	LEGLANS
AEGINNO	GANOINE	**AEGINSU**	GUINEAS	**AEGLLNT**	GELLANT
AEGINNP	NEAPING	**AEGINSY**	EASYING	**AEGLLNY**	LANGLEY
	PEANING	**AEGINSZ**	AGNIZES	**AEGLLOR**	ALLEGRO
AEGINNR	AGINNER		SEAZING	**AEGLLOT**	TOLLAGE
	EARNING	**AEGINTU**	UNITAGE	**AEGLLRY**	ALLERGY
	ENGRAIN	**AEGINTV**	VINTAGE		GALLERY
	GRANNIE	**AEGINTZ**	TEAZING		LARGELY
	NEARING		TZIGANE		REGALLY
AEGINNS	INNAGES	**AEGINVW**	WEAVING	**AEGLLST**	GALLETS
	SEANING	**AEGIORT**	GOATIER	**AEGLLSU**	SEAGULL
AEGINNT	ANTEING	**AEGIPPR**	GAPPIER		SULLAGE
	ANTIGEN	**AEGIPPS**	PIPAGES		ULLAGES
	GENTIAN	**AEGIPRR**	GRAPIER	**AEGLLSY**	GALLEYS
AEGINNU	ANGUINE	**AEGIPRS**	GASPIER	**AEGLLTU**	GLUTEAL
	GUANINE		PRISAGE	**AEGLMNR**	MANGLER
AEGINNW	WEANING		SPAIRGE	**AEGLMNS**	MANGELS
AEGINNY	YEANING	**AEGIRRZ**	GRAZIER		MANGLES
AEGINOR	ORIGANE	**AEGIRSS**	AGRISES	**AEGLMOR**	GLOMERA
AEGINOS	AGONIES		GASSIER		GOMERAL
	AGONISE	**AEGIRST**	AGISTER	**AEGLMOU**	MOULAGE
AEGINOZ	AGONIZE		AIGRETS	**AEGLMPU**	PLUMAGE
AEGINPP	GENIPAP		GAITERS	**AEGLMRS**	MALGRES
AEGINPR	REAPING		SEAGIRT	**AEGLMRU**	MAULGRE
AEGINPS	PEASING		STAGIER	**AEGLMSV**	MAGLEVS
	SPAEING		STRIGAE	**AEGLMSY**	MYGALES
	SPINAGE		TIRAGES	**AEGLNOS**	ENGAOLS
AEGINPZ	PEAZING		TRIAGES	**AEGLNOT**	TANGELO
AEGINRR	ANGRIER	**AEGIRSV**	GARVIES	**AEGLNPR**	GRAPNEL
	EARRING		GRAVIES	**AEGLNPS**	SPANGLE
	GRAINER		RIVAGES	**AEGLNRS**	ANGLERS
	RANGIER	**AEGIRSW**	EARWIGS		ERLANGS
	REARING		GAWSIER		LANGERS
AEGINRS	ANGRIES	**AEGIRSZ**	AGRIZES		LARGENS
	EARINGS	**AEGIRTV**	VIRGATE		SLANGER
	ERASING		VITRAGE	**AEGLNRT**	TANGLER

	TRANGLE
AEGLNRU	GRANULE
AEGLNRW	WANGLER
	WRANGLE
AEGLNRY	ANGERLY
AEGLNSS	GLASSEN
AEGLNST	GELANTS
	LANGEST
	TANGLES
AEGLNSU	ANGELUS
	LAGUNES
	LANGUES
AEGLNSW	WANGLES
AEGLNSY	LYNAGES
AEGLNTT	GANTLET
AEGLNTU	LANGUET
AEGLNTW	TWANGLE
AEGLNUU	UNGULAE
AEGLNUW	GUNWALE
AEGLOOZ	ZOOGLEA
AEGLOPR	PERGOLA
AEGLORS	GALORES
	GAOLERS
AEGLORT	GLOATER
	LEGATOR
AEGLORV	VORLAGE
AEGLOSS	GLOSSAE
AEGLOST	GELATOS
	LEGATOS
AEGLOSU	GEALOUS
AEGLOSV	LOVAGES
AEGLOTV	VOLTAGE
AEGLPPR	GRAPPLE
AEGLPRS	GRAPLES
AEGLPRU	EARPLUG
	GRAUPEL
	PLAGUER
AEGLPSS	GAPLESS
AEGLPSU	PLAGUES
	PLUSAGE
AEGLPUY	PLAGUEY
AEGLRRU	REGULAR
AEGLRSS	LARGESS
AEGLRST	LARGEST
AEGLRSV	GRAVELS
	VERGLAS
AEGLRSY	ARGYLES
	GRAYLES
AEGLRSZ	GLAZERS
AEGLRTU	GAULTER
	TEGULAR
	TRAGULE
AEGLRTY	GREATLY
AEGLRVY	GRAVELY
AEGLSSS	GASLESS
	GLASSES
AEGLSSU	SAULGES
AEGLSTT	GESTALT
AEGLSTW	TALWEGS
AEGLTUV	VULGATE
AEGLUUY	GUAYULE
AEGLUVY	VAGUELY
AEGMMNS	MAGSMEN
AEGMMRS	GAMMERS

	GRAMMES
AEGMMRU	RUMMAGE
AEGMMSS	SMEGMAS
AEGMNNO	AGNOMEN
	NONGAME
AEGMNOR	MARENGO
	MEGARON
AEGMNOS	GAMONES
	MANGOES
AEGMNOT	GEOMANT
	MAGNETO
	MEGATON
	MONTAGE
AEGMNPY	PYGMEAN
AEGMNRS	ENGRAMS
	GERMANS
	MANGERS
AEGMNRT	GARMENT
	MARGENT
	RAGMENT
AEGMNST	MAGNETS
AEGMNSW	SWAGMEN
AEGMNTU	AUGMENT
	MUTAGEN
AEGMOOR	MOORAGE
AEGMORS	ROMAGES
AEGMOSW	WAGSOME
AEGMOSY	GAYSOME
AEGMOXY	EXOGAMY
AEGMRSU	MAUGRES
	MURAGES
AEGMSUY	MAGUEYS
AEGMSUZ	ZEUGMAS
AEGNNOS	NONAGES
AEGNNOT	NEGATON
	TONNAGE
AEGNNOW	NONWAGE
AEGNNPS	PANGENS
	PENANGS
AEGNNRT	REGNANT
AEGNNRU	GUNNERA
AEGNNST	GANNETS
AEGNNTT	TANGENT
AEGNNTU	TUNNAGE
AEGNOOR	OREGANO
AEGNOPT	PONTAGE
AEGNORR	GROANER
	ORANGER
AEGNORS	ONAGERS
	ORANGES
AEGNORT	NEGATOR
AEGNORW	WAGONER
AEGNORY	ORANGEY
AEGNOST	ONSTAGE
	TANGOES
AEGNOSY	NOSEGAY
AEGNOWY	WAYGONE
AEGNPRS	ENGRASP
AEGNPRT	TREPANG
AEGNRRS	GARNERS
	RANGERS
AEGNRRT	GRANTER
	REGRANT
AEGNRSS	SANGERS

	SERANGS
AEGNRST	ARGENTS
	GARNETS
	STRANGE
AEGNRSU	RAUNGES
	UNGEARS
AEGNRSW	GNAWERS
AEGNRTU	GAUNTER
AEGNRTW	TWANGER
AEGNRTY	AGENTRY
AEGNSSY	GANSEYS
	GAYNESS
AEGNSTT	GESTANT
AEGNTTU	TUTENAG
AEGOORT	ROOTAGE
AEGOPPR	PROPAGE
AEGOPRT	PORTAGE
	POTAGER
AEGOPST	GESTAPO
	POSTAGE
	POTAGES
AEGOPTT	POTTAGE
AEGORRT	GARROTE
AEGORSS	SORAGES
AEGORST	GAROTES
	ORGEATS
	STORAGE
	TOERAGS
AEGORSU	AERUGOS
AEGORTT	GAROTTE
AEGORTU	OUTRAGE
AEGORUV	OUVRAGE
AEGORVY	VOYAGER
AEGOSSU	GASEOUS
AEGOSTU	OUTAGES
AEGOSTW	STOWAGE
	TOWAGES
AEGOSTX	OXGATES
AEGOSVY	VOYAGES
AEGOTTU	OUTGATE
AEGOTTV	GAVOTTE
AEGOTUV	OUTGAVE
AEGOTUZ	OUTGAZE
AEGPPRS	GAPPERS
AEGPRRS	GRASPER
	SPARGER
AEGPRRY	GRAPERY
AEGPRSS	GASPERS
	SPARGES
AEGPRST	PARGETS
AEGPRSU	GAUPERS
AEGPRSW	GAWPERS
AEGPSSU	PEGASUS
AEGPSTU	UPSTAGE
AEGPSUZ	UPGAZES
AEGRRSS	GRASSER
AEGRRST	GARRETS
	GARTERS
	GRATERS
AEGRRSU	ARGUERS
	SUGARER
AEGRRSV	GRAVERS
AEGRRSZ	GRAZERS
AEGRRUU	AUGURER

AEGRRUV	GRAVURE		HELIAST		STAITHE
	VERRUGA	**AEHILSW**	SHAWLIE	**AEHISTZ**	HAZIEST
AEGRSSS	GASSERS		WHAISLE	**AEHISVY**	YESHIVA
	GRASSES	**AEHILTT**	LITHATE	**AEHITTW**	THWAITE
AEGRSST	GASTERS	**AEHILTY**	HYALITE	**AEHJLOW**	JAWHOLE
	STAGERS	**AEHILUV**	VIHUELA	**AEHKMSS**	SAMEKHS
AEGRSSU	ARGUSES	**AEHILVY**	HEAVILY	**AEHKNRS**	HANKERS
	SAUGERS	**AEHILWZ**	WHAIZLE		HARKENS
	USAGERS	**AEHIMMR**	HAMMIER	**AEHKNRT**	THANKER
AEGRSSW	SWAGERS	**AEHIMMS**	MAIHEMS	**AEHKNSZ**	KHAZENS
AEGRSSY	GYRASES	**AEHIMNR**	HARMINE	**AEHKOOR**	HOROEKA
AEGRSTT	TARGETS	**AEHIMNS**	HAEMINS	**AEHKOSS**	SHAKOES
AEGRSTV	GRAVEST		HEMINAS	**AEHKPRS**	PHREAKS
AEGRSTY	GRAYEST	**AEHIMNT**	HEMATIN	**AEHKPSU**	SHAKEUP
	GYRATES	**AEHIMNY**	HYMENIA	**AEHKRRS**	SHARKER
	STAGERY	**AEHIMPS**	PHAEISM	**AEHKRSS**	KASHERS
AEGRSUV	SEVRUGA	**AEHIMRS**	MASHIER		SHAKERS
AEGRSVY	GARVEYS		MISHEAR	**AEHKRSW**	HAWKERS
AEGRSYZ	AGRYZES	**AEHIMSS**	MASHIES	**AEHKSSY**	ASHKEYS
AEGSSSU	GAUSSES		MESSIAH	**AEHKSWY**	HAWKEYS
AEGSTUU	AUGUSTE	**AEHIMST**	ATHEISM	**AEHLLLS**	HALLELS
AEGSTUV	VAGUEST	**AEHINPR**	HEPARIN	**AEHLLOS**	HALLOES
AEGTTTU	GUTTATE	**AEHINPS**	INPHASE	**AEHLLOV**	HELLOVA
AEHHIKS	SHEIKHA	**AEHINPT**	PENTHIA	**AEHLLRS**	HERSALL
AEHHIRS	HASHIER	**AEHINRS**	ARSHINE	**AEHLLST**	LETHALS
AEHHIST	SHEHITA		HERNIAS	**AEHLLUV**	HELLUVA
AEHHLST	HEALTHS	**AEHINRT**	HAIRNET	**AEHLLYZ**	HAZELLY
AEHHLTY	HEALTHY		INEARTH	**AEHLMNO**	MANHOLE
AEHHNRS	HARSHEN		THERIAN	**AEHLMNY**	HYMENAL
AEHHPRS	RHAPHES	**AEHINSS**	HESSIAN	**AEHLMOR**	ARMHOLE
AEHHRRS	HARSHER	**AEHINST**	SHEITAN	**AEHLMPS**	PELHAMS
AEHHRST	HEARTHS		STHENIA	**AEHLMPW**	WHAMPLE
AEHHSSS	SHASHES	**AEHINSV**	EVANISH	**AEHLMRS**	HARMELS
AEHHSST	SHEATHS		VAHINES	**AEHLMRT**	THERMAL
AEHHSTY	SHEATHY	**AEHINSW**	WAHINES	**AEHLMRU**	HUMERAL
AEHIILR	HAILIER	**AEHIORR**	HOARIER	**AEHLMST**	HAMLETS
AEHIIRR	HAIRIER	**AEHIPPR**	HAPPIER	**AEHLNOS**	ENHALOS
AEHIJRS	HEJIRAS	**AEHIPPS**	HAPPIES	**AEHLNOT**	ANETHOL
AEHIKLT	HATLIKE	**AEHIPPT**	EPITAPH		ETHANOL
AEHIKNS	HANKIES	**AEHIPRS**	HARPIES	**AEHLNRT**	ENTHRAL
AEHIKPS	PEAKISH		SHARPIE	**AEHLNSS**	HANSELS
AEHIKRS	SHAKIER	**AEHIPSS**	APHESIS	**AEHLNST**	HANTLES
AEHIKSS	SAKIEHS	**AEHIPSW**	PEISHWA	**AEHLNSU**	UNHEALS
AEHIKST	SHITAKE	**AEHIPTZ**	ZAPTIEH		UNLEASH
AEHIKSW	HAWKIES	**AEHIQSU**	HAIQUES		UNSHALE
	WEAKISH		QUASHIE	**AEHLOPR**	EPHORAL
AEHIKSY	SAKIYEH	**AEHIRRR**	HARRIER	**AEHLOPT**	TAPHOLE
AEHILMN	HELIMAN	**AEHIRRS**	HARRIES	**AEHLORS**	SHOALER
AEHILMO	HEMIOLA	**AEHIRSS**	ARISHES	**AEHLORT**	LOATHER
AEHILMS	LEHAIMS		RASHIES		RATHOLE
AEHILMY	LEHAYIM		SHERIAS	**AEHLOSS**	ASSHOLE
AEHILNR	HERNIAL	**AEHIRST**	HASTIER	**AEHLOST**	LOATHES
	INHALER		SHERIAT	**AEHLPRS**	PLASHER
AEHILNS	INHALES	**AEHIRSV**	ASHIVER		SPHERAL
AEHILNY	HYALINE	**AEHIRSW**	WASHIER	**AEHLPSS**	HAPLESS
AEHILOR	AIRHOLE		WEARISH		PLASHES
AEHILPR	HARELIP	**AEHIRTW**	THAWIER	**AEHLPST**	PLASHET
AEHILPT	HAPLITE	**AEHIRWY**	HAYWIRE	**AEHLPSY**	SHAPELY
AEHILRS	HAILERS	**AEHISST**	ASHIEST	**AEHLRSS**	ASHLERS
	SHALIER		SAITHES		HALSERS
AEHILRT	LATHIER		STASHIE		LASHERS
AEHILRU	HAULIER		TAISHES		SLASHER
AEHILSS	SHEILAS	**AEHISSV**	SHAVIES	**AEHLRST**	HALTERS
AEHILST	HALITES	**AEHISTT**	ATHEIST		HARSLET

	LATHERS	AEHNOSX	HEXOSAN	AEHRRSS	RASHERS
	SLATHER	AEHNPPS	HAPPENS		SHARERS
	THALERS	AEHNPRS	SHARPEN	AEHRRST	TRASHER
AEHLRSU	HAULERS	AEHNPRT	PANTHER	AEHRRTU	URETHRA
AEHLRSV	HALVERS	AEHNPST	HAPTENS	AEHRSST	RASHEST
AEHLRSW	WHALERS	AEHNPSU	UNSHAPE		SHASTER
AEHLRTY	EARTHLY	AEHNPTY	PHYTANE		TRASHES
	HARTELY	AEHNRSS	HARNESS	AEHRSSV	SHAVERS
	HEARTLY	AEHNRST	ANTHERS	AEHRSSW	HAWSERS
	LATHERY		HARTENS		SWASHER
AEHLRWY	WHALERY		THENARS		WASHERS
AEHLSSS	ASHLESS	AEHNRTU	HAUNTER	AEHRSTT	HATTERS
	HASSELS		UNEARTH		RATHEST
	HASSLES		UNHEART		SHATTER
	SLASHES		URETHAN		THREATS
AEHLSST	HASLETS	AEHNRTX	NARTHEX	AEHRSTV	HARVEST
	HATLESS	AEHNSSS	SNASHES		THRAVES
	SHELTAS	AEHNSST	HASTENS	AEHRSTW	SWATHER
AEHLSSY	HAYSELS		SNATHES		THAWERS
AEHLSTT	STEALTH		SNEATHS		WREATHS
AEHLSTW	WEALTHS	AEHNSSU	HAUSENS	AEHRSVW	WHARVES
AEHLSWY	SHAWLEY	AEHNSSZ	SAZHENS	AEHRSWY	WASHERY
AEHLTWY	WEALTHY	AEHNSTY	ASTHENY	AEHRSXY	HYRAXES
AEHMMNS	MASHMEN		SHANTEY	AEHRTUU	HAUTEUR
AEHMMRS	HAMMERS	AEHNSUW	WHENUAS	AEHRTWY	WREATHY
	SHAMMER	AEHNSUY	HAUYNES	AEHSSST	STASHES
AEHMMSS	SHAMMES	AEHNTTW	WHATTEN	AEHSSSW	SWASHES
AEHMMSY	MAYHEMS	AEHOORT	TOHEROA	AEHSSTW	SWATHES
AEHMNOR	MENORAH	AEHOPRT	PHORATE	AEHSTUX	EXHAUST
AEHMNOS	HOSEMAN	AEHOPST	TEASHOP	AEIIKLR	AIRLIKE
AEHMNOT	NATHEMO	AEHORRS	HOARSER	AEIIKNT	KAINITE
AEHMNOY	HAEMONY	AEHORST	ASTHORE	AEIIKSS	SAIKEIS
AEHMNPY	NYMPHAE		EARSHOT	AEIILLT	TAILLIE
AEHMNRU	HUMANER		HAROSET	AEIILMP	LIPEMIA
AEHMNST	ANTHEMS	AEHORSX	HOAXERS	AEIILMR	RAMILIE
	HETMANS	AEHORTU	OUTHEAR	AEIILNN	ANILINE
AEHMOPT	APOTHEM	AEHORTX	OXHEART	AEIILNR	AIRLINE
AEHMORT	TERAOHM	AEHORUV	HAVEOUR	AEIILNX	EXILIAN
AEHMPRS	HAMPERS	AEHORUW	WAREHOU	AEIILRR	LAIRIER
AEHMPTY	EMPATHY	AEHOSTU	ATHEOUS	AEIILRS	LAIRISE
AEHMRRS	HARMERS	AEHPPRS	PERHAPS	AEIILRV	VIRELAI
AEHMRSS	MARSHES	AEHPPRW	WHAPPER	AEIILRZ	LAIRIZE
	MASHERS	AEHPPSU	SHAPEUP	AEIILSS	LIAISES
	SHAMERS		UPHEAPS		SILESIA
	SHMEARS	AEHPRRS	HARPERS	AEIILST	LAITIES
	SMASHER		PHRASER	AEIILSW	LEWISIA
AEHMRST	HAMSTER		SHARPER	AEIILTZ	TAILZIE
AEHMRTU	MAUTHER	AEHPRSS	PHRASES	AEIIMNT	INTIMAE
AEHMRTW	MAWTHER		SERAPHS		MINIATE
AEHMSSS	SMASHES		SHAPERS	AEIIMPR	IMPERIA
AEHMSST	SMEATHS		SHERPAS	AEIIMRT	AIRTIME
AEHMSTT	SHMATTE		SPHAERS	AEIIMRV	VIREMIA
AEHMSTU	HUMATES		SPHEARS	AEIIMST	AMITIES
AEHMSUW	MAHEWUS	AEHPRST	SPARTHE		ATIMIES
AEHMUZZ	MEZUZAH		TEPHRAS	AEIIMTT	IMITATE
AEHNNTU	UNNEATH		THREAPS	AEIINNS	ASININE
AEHNNWY	ANYWHEN	AEHPRSW	PREWASH		INSANIE
AEHNOPT	PHAETON	AEHPRTT	PHATTER	AEIINOP	EPINAOI
	PHONATE	AEHPRTY	THERAPY	AEIINQU	EQUINIA
AEHNOPW	WANHOPE	AEHPSST	SPATHES	AEIINRR	RAINIER
AEHNOPY	HYPONEA	AEHPSSW	PESHWAS	AEIINRS	SENARII
AEHNORS	HOARSEN	AEHPSTY	HYPATES	AEIINRT	INERTIA
	SENHORA	AEHQRSU	QUASHER	AEIINST	ISATINE
AEHNORT	ANOTHER	AEHQSSU	QUASHES	AEIINSX	SIXAINE

AEIINTX	AXINITE	AEIKMRW	MAWKIER	AEILLUV	ELUVIAL
AEIIPRR	PRAIRIE	AEIKMSS	KAMISES	AEILLVX	VEXILLA
AEIIRRV	RIVIERA	AEIKMST	KETMIAS	AEILMMN	MAILMEN
	VAIRIER		MISTAKE	AEILMMR	MALMIER
AEIIRST	AIRIEST	AEIKNNT	NEATNIK	AEILMMS	LAMMIES
	IRISATE	AEIKNPR	RANPIKE		MELISMA
AEIIRSW	AIRWISE	AEIKNRR	NARKIER	AEILMNN	LINEMAN
AEIITTV	VITIATE	AEIKNRS	SNAKIER		MELANIN
AEIJKLM	JAMLIKE	AEIKNRT	KERATIN	AEILMNO	MINEOLA
AEIJKLW	JAWLIKE	AEIKNRW	WANKIER	AEILMNP	IMPANEL
AEIJLNV	JAVELIN	AEIKNSS	KINASES		MANIPLE
AEIJLNW	JAWLINE	AEIKNST	INTAKES	AEILMNR	MANLIER
AEIJLRS	JAILERS		KENTIAS		MARLINE
AEIJLSZ	JEZAILS		TANKIES		MINERAL
AEIJMMR	JAMMIER	AEIKNSW	SWANKIE		RAILMEN
AEIJMMS	JAMMIES	AEIKNSY	KYANISE	AEILMNS	ISLEMAN
	JEMIMAS		YANKIES		MALINES
AEIJMNS	JASMINE	AEIKNSZ	KAIZENS		MENIALS
AEIJNNS	JANNIES	AEIKNTU	UNAKITE		SEMINAL
AEIJNRS	INJERAS	AEIKNTY	KYANITE	AEILMNT	AILMENT
AEIJNRT	JANTIER	AEIKNYZ	KYANIZE		ALIMENT
	NARTJIE	AEIKOST	OAKIEST	AEILMNU	ALUMINE
AEIJNST	JANTIES	AEIKPRR	PARKIER	AEILMOR	LOAMIER
	TAJINES	AEIKPRS	PARKIES	AEILMPR	IMPALER
AEIJNTU	JAUNTIE		SPARKIE		IMPEARL
AEIJRSV	JARVIES	AEIKPRW	PAWKIER		LEMPIRA
AEIJRZZ	JAZZIER	AEIKQRU	QUAKIER		PALMIER
AEIJSSV	JIVEASS	AEIKRRS	KERRIAS	AEILMPS	IMPALES
AEIKKLO	OAKLIKE		SARKIER		PALMIES
AEIKKPS	PIKAKES	AEIKRSS	KAISERS	AEILMPT	IMPLATE
AEIKKST	TAKKIES		KARSIES		PALMIET
AEIKLLW	LAWLIKE	AEIKRST	ARKITES	AEILMRR	LARMIER
AEIKLLY	LEAKILY		KARITES		MARLIER
AEIKLMN	MANLIKE	AEIKRSU	KAURIES	AEILMRS	MAILERS
AEIKLMP	MAPLIKE	AEIKRSW	SKIWEAR		REALISM
AEIKLMR	ARMLIKE	AEIKRSZ	KARZIES		REMAILS
AEIKLNO	KAOLINE	AEIKSSS	ASKESIS	AEILMRT	LAMITER
AEIKLNR	LANKIER	AEIKSTT	TAKIEST		MALTIER
AEIKLNS	ALKINES	AEILLMN	MANILLE		MARLITE
AEIKLNT	ANTLIKE	AEILLNR	RALLINE	AEILMSS	AIMLESS
AEIKLNU	UNALIKE	AEILLNS	AINSELL		MESAILS
AEIKLOR	OARLIKE	AEILLNU	UILLEAN		SAMIELS
AEIKLOT	KEITLOA	AEILLNY	ALIENLY		SEISMAL
	OATLIKE	AEILLOV	ALVEOLI	AEILMSZ	MEZAILS
AEIKLRR	LARKIER	AEILLPR	PALLIER	AEILMTY	LAYTIME
AEIKLRS	LAIKERS		PERILLA		MEATILY
	SERKALI	AEILLPS	ILLAPSE	AEILNNY	INANELY
AEIKLRT	RATLIKE	AEILLPU	PILULAE	AEILNOP	OPALINE
	TALKIER	AEILLPY	EPYLLIA	AEILNOR	AILERON
AEIKLRV	KLAVIER	AEILLQU	LALIQUE		ALERION
AEIKLRW	WARLIKE	AEILLRR	RALLIER		ALIENOR
AEIKLRY	RAYLIKE	AEILLRS	RALLIES	AEILNOS	ANISOLE
AEIKLSS	ALSIKES		SALLIER	AEILNOT	ELATION
	ASSLIKE	AEILLRT	LITERAL		TOENAIL
AEIKLST	LAKIEST		TALLIER	AEILNPR	PEARLIN
	TALKIES		TRIELLA		PLAINER
AEIKLSW	SAWLIKE	AEILLRU	RUELLIA		PRALINE
AEIKLWX	WAXLIKE	AEILLRW	WALLIER	AEILNPS	ALPINES
AEIKMMS	MISMAKE	AEILLSS	ALLISES		PINEALS
AEIKMNP	PIKEMAN		SALLIES		SPANIEL
AEIKMNR	MANKIER	AEILLST	SITELLA		SPLENIA
	RAMEKIN		TAILLES	AEILNPT	PANTILE
AEIKMNS	KINEMAS		TALLIES	AEILNPW	PINWALE
AEIKMPR	RAMPIKE	AEILLSW	WALLIES	AEILNPX	EXPLAIN

Key	Words	Key	Words	Key	Words
AEILNQU	EQUINAL		TALIPES	AEIMNOT	AMNIOTE
	QUINELA	AEILPSY	PAISLEY	AEIMNOU	MOINEAU
AEILNRR	LARNIER	AEILQTU	LIQUATE	AEIMNPR	PERMIAN
AEILNRS	ALINERS		TEQUILA	AEIMNRR	MARINER
	NAILERS	AEILRRS	RAILERS	AEIMNRS	MARINES
	RENAILS		RERAILS		REMAINS
AEILNRT	ENTRAIL	AEILRRT	RETIRAL		SEMINAR
	LATRINE		RETRIAL		SIRNAME
	RATLINE		TRAILER	AEIMNRT	MERANTI
	RELIANT	AEILRSS	AIRLESS		MINARET
	RETINAL		RESAILS		RAIMENT
	TRENAIL		SAILERS	AEIMNRV	VERMIAN
AEILNRV	RAVELIN		SERAILS	AEIMNRW	WIREMAN
AEILNRW	LAWNIER		SERIALS	AEIMNSS	INSEAMS
AEILNRX	RELAXIN	AEILRST	REALIST		SAMISEN
AEILNRY	INLAYER		RETAILS	AEIMNST	ETAMINS
	NAILERY		SALTIER		INMATES
AEILNSS	SALINES		SALTIRE		MAINEST
	SILANES		SLATIER		MANTIES
AEILNST	EASTLIN		TAILERS		TAMEINS
	ELASTIN	AEILRSV	REVISAL		TAMINES
	ENTAILS	AEILRSW	SWALIER	AEIMNSW	MANWISE
	NAILSET		WAILERS	AEIMNTX	TAXIMEN
	SALIENT	AEILRTT	TERTIAL	AEIMNTY	AMENITY
	SALTINE	AEILRTU	URALITE		ANYTIME
	SLAINTE	AEILRTW	WALTIER	AEIMNUV	MAUVEIN
	STANIEL	AEILRTY	IRATELY		MAUVINE
	TENAILS		REALITY	AEIMOOP	IPOMOEA
AEILNSU	INSULAE		TEARILY	AEIMOPR	EMPORIA
	INULASE	AEILRVV	REVIVAL		MEROPIA
AEILNSV	ALEVINS	AEILRVY	VIRELAY	AEIMORR	ARMOIRE
	VALINES	AEILRWY	WEARILY	AEIMOST	AMOSITE
AEILNSW	LAWINES	AEILSSS	LAISSES		ATOMIES
AEILNSX	ALEXINS		LASSIES		ATOMISE
AEILNSY	ELYSIAN	AEILSST	SALTIES		OSMIATE
AEILNTU	ALUNITE	AEILSSU	SAULIES	AEIMOTX	TOXEMIA
AEILNTV	VENTAIL	AEILSSV	VALISES	AEIMOTZ	ATOMIZE
AEILNUV	UNALIVE		VESSAIL	AEIMPRR	RAMPIRE
	UNVAILE	AEILSSW	WALISES	AEIMPRS	IMPRESA
AEILNUW	LAUWINE	AEILSTU	SITULAE		SAMPIRE
AEILNVY	NAIVELY	AEILSTV	ESTIVAL	AEIMPRT	PRIMATE
AEILOPR	PELORIA	AEILSTW	WALIEST	AEIMPRV	VAMPIER
AEILOPS	LEIPOAS	AEILSTY	TAILYES		VAMPIRE
AEILORV	VARIOLE	AEILSTZ	LAZIEST	AEIMPSS	IMPASSE
AEILOST	ISOLATE	AEILTVY	VILAYET		PESSIMA
AEILOTV	VIOLATE	AEILUVX	EXUVIAL	AEIMPST	IMPASTE
AEILPPR	APPERIL	AEIMMMS	MAMMIES		PASTIME
	APPLIER	AEIMMNS	AMMINES	AEIMPSV	IMPAVES
	ARIPPLE		MISNAME	AEIMPSW	MAPWISE
AEILPPS	APPLIES	AEIMMPS	SPAMMIE	AEIMPSY	PYEMIAS
	LAPPIES	AEIMMRR	RAMMIER		YAMPIES
AEILPRS	PALSIER	AEIMMRS	MAIMERS	AEIMRRR	MARRIER
	PARLIES		RAMMIES	AEIMRRS	MARRIES
AEILPRT	PLAITER	AEIMMRT	MARMITE		SIMARRE
	PLATIER		TRAMMIE	AEIMRSS	MASSIER
AEILPRV	PREVAIL	AEIMMSS	SAMMIES		SARMIES
AEILPSS	ESPIALS	AEIMMST	MISMATE	AEIMRST	IMARETS
	LAIPSES		SEMIMAT		MAESTRI
	LAPISES		TAMMIES		MAISTER
	LIPASES	AEIMMZZ	MIZMAZE		MASTIER
	PALSIES	AEIMNNT	MANNITE		MISRATE
AEILPST	APLITES	AEIMNOR	MORAINE		SEMITAR
	PALIEST		ROMAINE		SMARTIE
	PLATIES	AEIMNOS	ANOMIES	AEIMRSU	UREMIAS

AEIMRSV	MISAVER	**AEINPSS**	ASPINES	**AEINSTV**	NAIVEST
AEIMRSW	AWMRIES		PANSIES		NATIVES
	SEMIRAW		SAPIENS		VAINEST
AEIMRSY	RIMAYES	**AEINPST**	PANTIES	**AEINSTW**	AWNIEST
AEIMRTU	MURIATE		PATINES		TAWNIES
AEIMRTV	VITAMER		SAPIENT		WANIEST
AEIMRTW	WARTIME		SPINATE		WANTIES
AEIMSSS	AMISSES	**AEINPSW**	WINESAP	**AEINSTX**	ANTISEX
	MESSIAS	**AEINPTT**	PATIENT		SEXTAIN
AEIMSST	ASTEISM	**AEINPTU**	PETUNIA	**AEINSTZ**	ZANIEST
	MISEATS	**AEINPTY**	PANEITY		ZEATINS
	MISSEAT	**AEINQTU**	ANTIQUE	**AEINSVV**	NAVVIES
	SAMIEST		QUINATE	**AEINSWY**	ANYWISE
	SAMITES	**AEINRRS**	SIERRAN	**AEINTUV**	VAUNTIE
	TAMISES		SNARIER	**AEINTVW**	VAWNTIE
AEIMSSV	MASSIVE	**AEINRRT**	RETRAIN	**AEINTVY**	NAIVETY
	MAVISES		TERRAIN	**AEINTXY**	ANXIETY
AEIMSSW	SWAMIES		TRAINER	**AEIOPRS**	SOAPIER
AEIMSSY	MYIASES	**AEINRSS**	ARSINES	**AEIOPSS**	SOAPIES
AEIMSTT	ETATISM		SARNIES	**AEIOPST**	ATOPIES
	MATIEST	**AEINRST**	ANESTRI		OPIATES
	MATTIES		ANTSIER	**AEIOQSU**	SEQUOIA
AEIMSTZ	MAZIEST		NASTIER	**AEIORRR**	ARRIERO
	MESTIZA		RATINES		ROARIER
AEIMSUV	AMUSIVE		RESIANT	**AEIORST**	OARIEST
AEIMSXX	MAXIXES		RETAINS		OTARIES
AEIMTVZ	AZYMITE		RETINAS	**AEIORSV**	OVARIES
AEINNNS	NANNIES		RETSINA	**AEIOSST**	SOSATIE
AEINNOT	ENATION		STAINER	**AEIOSTT**	OSTIATE
AEINNPR	PANNIER		STARNIE		TOASTIE
AEINNPT	PANTINE		STEARIN	**AEIOSTZ**	AZOTISE
	PINNATE	**AEINRSV**	AVENIRS	**AEIOTZZ**	AZOTIZE
AEINNRS	INSANER		RAVINES	**AEIPPPR**	PAPPIER
	INSNARE	**AEINRTT**	INTREAT	**AEIPPPS**	PAPPIES
AEINNRT	ENTRAIN		ITERANT	**AEIPPRS**	APPRISE
	TRANNIE		NATTIER		SAPPIER
AEINNRU	ANEURIN		NITRATE	**AEIPPRT**	PERIAPT
AEINNSS	SANNIES		TARTINE	**AEIPPRY**	YAPPIER
	SIENNAS		TERTIAN	**AEIPPRZ**	APPRIZE
AEINNST	INANEST	**AEINRTU**	RUINATE		ZAPPIER
	STANINE		TAURINE	**AEIPPSS**	PASPIES
	TANNIES		URANITE	**AEIPPSY**	YAPPIES
AEINNSW	SWANNIE		URINATE	**AEIPRRR**	PARRIER
AEINNSZ	ENZIANS	**AEINRTW**	TAWNIER	**AEIPRRS**	ASPIRER
AEINNTT	ANTIENT		TINWARE		PARRIES
AEINOPS	EPINAOS	**AEINRUV**	VAURIEN		PRAISER
	SENOPIA	**AEINRUW**	UNWARIE		RAPIERS
AEINOPZ	EPIZOAN	**AEINRUZ**	AZURINE		RASPIER
AEINORS	ERASION	**AEINRVV**	VERVAIN		REPAIRS
AEINORT	OTARINE	**AEINRWY**	YAWNIER	**AEIPRRT**	PARTIER
AEINOSS	ANOESIS	**AEINSSS**	SANSEIS	**AEIPRSS**	ASPIRES
AEINOST	ATONIES		SASINES		PARESIS
AEINOSV	EVASION	**AEINSST**	ENTASIS		PARISES
AEINOSZ	AZIONES		NASTIES		PRAISES
AEINOXZ	OXAZINE		SEITANS		SPIREAS
AEINPPP	PANPIPE		SESTINA	**AEIPRST**	PAIREST
AEINPPR	NAPPIER		TANSIES		PARTIES
AEINPPS	NAPPIES		TISANES		PASTIER
	PINESAP	**AEINSSV**	SAVINES		PIASTER
AEINPRS	PANIERS		VINASSE		PIASTRE
	RAPINES	**AEINSTT**	INSTATE		PIRATES
AEINPRT	PAINTER		SATINET		PRATIES
	PERTAIN	**AEINSTU**	AUNTIES		TRAIPSE
	REPAINT		SINUATE	**AEIPRSU**	SPURIAE

	UPRAISE
AEIPRSV	PARVISE
	PAVISER
AEIPRSW	WASPIER
AEIPRTT	PARTITE
AEIPRTV	PRIVATE
AEIPRTW	WIRETAP
AEIPRXY	PYREXIA
AEIPSSS	ASEPSIS
	ASPISES
AEIPSST	PASTIES
	PATSIES
	PETSAIS
	TAPISES
AEIPSSV	PASSIVE
	PAVISES
	PAVISSE
	SPAVIES
AEIPSSW	WASPIES
AEIPSTT	PATTIES
	TAPETIS
AEIPSTU	TAUPIES
AEIPSTV	SPAVIET
AEIPSTW	TAWPIES
AEIPTXY	EPITAXY
AEIQRUV	AQUIVER
AEIQSSU	SAIQUES
AEIRRRT	TARRIER
AEIRRRV	ARRIVER
AEIRRSS	ARRISES
	RAISERS
	SIERRAS
AEIRRST	ARTSIER
	SERRATI
	TARRIES
	TARSIER
AEIRRSV	ARRIVES
	VARIERS
AEIRRTT	RATTIER
	RETRAIT
	TARTIER
AEIRRTW	WARTIER
AEIRRTY	RETIARY
AEIRRVV	VIVERRA
AEIRSSS	SASSIER
AEIRSST	ARSIEST
	ARTSIES
	SAIREST
	SATIRES
	TIRASSE
AEIRSSU	SAURIES
AEIRSSZ	ASSIZER
AEIRSTT	ARTIEST
	ARTISTE
	ATTIRES
	IRATEST
	RATITES
	STRIATE
	TASTIER
	TERTIAS
AEIRSTV	TAIVERS
	VASTIER
	VERITAS
AEIRSTW	WAISTER

	WAITERS
	WARIEST
	WASTRIE
AEIRSVV	SAVVIER
AEIRSVW	WAIVERS
AEIRTTT	ATTRITE
	TATTIER
	TITRATE
AEIRTTV	TAIVERT
AEIRTTW	TAWTIER
AEIRTTX	EXTRAIT
AEIRTUY	AUREITY
AEIRTUZ	AZURITE
AEIRTVY	VARIETY
AEIRWWY	WIREWAY
AEISSSS	SASSIES
AEISSST	SIESTAS
	TASSIES
AEISSSW	WISEASS
AEISSSZ	ASSIZES
AEISSUV	SUASIVE
AEISSUX	AUXESIS
AEISSVV	SAVVIES
AEISTTT	ETATIST
	TATTIES
AEISTTU	SITUATE
AEISTTV	STATIVE
AEISTTW	TAWIEST
	TWAITES
AEISTTX	TAXITES
AEISTTY	SATIETY
AEISTVW	WAVIEST
AEISTWX	TAXWISE
	WAXIEST
AEITTTU	ATTUITE
AEITTTV	VITTATE
AEJJLNU	JEJUNAL
AEJKMNR	JARKMEN
AEJKNRS	JANKERS
AEJKPTU	KAJEPUT
AEJLNUV	JUVENAL
AEJLOSU	JALOUSE
	JEALOUS
AEJLOUZ	AZULEJO
AEJLSSW	JAWLESS
AEJMMRS	JAMMERS
AEJMNZZ	JAZZMEN
AEJMRST	RAMJETS
AEJMSST	JETSAMS
AEJMSSY	JESSAMY
AEJMSTY	MAJESTY
AEJNNOS	JOANNES
AEJNORZ	ZANJERO
AEJNSST	JESSANT
AEJNSSU	JAUNSES
AEJPRSS	JASPERS
AEJPRSY	JASPERY
AEJRSVY	JARVEYS
AEJRSZZ	JAZZERS
AEJSTWY	JETWAYS
AEKKNRS	KRAKENS
	SKANKER
AEKKRSY	YAKKERS
AEKLLTU	KELLAUT

AEKLMOU	LEUKOMA
AEKLNPP	KNAPPLE
AEKLNPR	PRANKLE
AEKLNRS	RANKLES
AEKLNRV	KLAVERN
AEKLNST	ANKLETS
	ASKLENT
	LANKEST
AEKLNSW	KNAWELS
AEKLNSY	ALKYNES
AEKLORY	ROKELAY
AEKLOST	SKATOLE
AEKLOVZ	ZELKOVA
AEKLPPT	PEPTALK
AEKLPRS	SPARKLE
AEKLPSS	SPLAKES
AEKLPSY	KEYPALS
AEKLRRS	LARKERS
AEKLRSS	SLAKERS
AEKLRST	STALKER
	TALKERS
AEKLRSV	LEKVARS
AEKLRSW	WALKERS
AEKLRUW	WAULKER
AEKLSST	LASKETS
	SKLATES
AEKLSTU	AUKLETS
AEKMMNR	MARKMEN
AEKMNOS	SOKEMAN
AEKMNRU	UNMAKER
AEKMNSU	UNMAKES
AEKMOOT	MATOOKE
AEKMOST	MATOKES
AEKMPRU	UPMAKER
AEKMPSU	MAKEUPS
	UPMAKES
AEKMRRS	MARKERS
	REMARKS
AEKMRSS	MASKERS
AEKMRST	MARKETS
AEKMRSU	KUMERAS
AEKNNOP	NONPEAK
AEKNNRS	ENRANKS
AEKNNST	KANTENS
AEKNNTU	UNTAKEN
AEKNOSW	WEAKONS
AEKNPPR	KNAPPER
AEKNPRS	SPANKER
AEKNPSU	UNSPEAK
AEKNPTU	UPTAKEN
AEKNRRS	RANKERS
AEKNRSS	KRANSES
AEKNRST	RANKEST
	STARKEN
	TANKERS
AEKNRSU	UNRAKES
AEKNRSW	SWANKER
	WANKERS
AEKNRSY	YANKERS
AEKNRSZ	KRANZES
AEKNRVY	KNAVERY
AEKNSSU	ANKUSES
AEKNSWY	SWANKEY
AEKOPRS	PRESOAK

AEKORRS	ROSAKER	AELLPTU	PLUTEAL	AELMOST	MALTOSE
AEKORSS	ARKOSES	AELLPTY	PLAYLET	AELMOSY	AMYLOSE
	RESOAKS	AELLQUY	EQUALLY	AELMOTT	MATELOT
	SOAKERS	AELLRRU	ALLURER	AELMPRS	EMPARLS
AEKOSTV	VOETSAK	AELLRST	STELLAR		LAMPERS
AEKOTTU	OUTTAKE		TELLARS		PALMERS
	TAKEOUT	AELLRSU	ALLURES		SAMPLER
AEKPPSU	UPSPAKE		LAURELS	AELMPRT	TEMPLAR
	UPSPEAK	AELLRSW	WALLERS		TRAMPLE
AEKPRRS	PARKERS	AELLRSY	RALLYES	AELMPRY	LAMPREY
	REPARKS	AELLRTY	ALERTLY	AELMPSS	MAPLESS
	SPARKER		ELYTRAL		SAMPLES
AEKPRSS	SPARKES		RETALLY	AELMPST	AMPLEST
AEKPSSY	PASSKEY	AELLRVY	RAVELLY	AELMPSU	AMPULES
AEKPSTU	TAKEUPS	AELLSST	SALLETS	AELMPTU	PLUMATE
	UPTAKES		STELLAS	AELMRRS	MARRELS
AEKQRSU	QUAKERS		TASSELL	AELMRSS	ARMLESS
AEKQSSU	SQUEAKS	AELLSSW	LAWLESS	AELMRST	ARMLETS
AEKQSUY	SQUEAKY	AELLSTT	TALLEST		LAMSTER
AEKRRST	KARTERS		TALLETS		MARTELS
	KRATERS	AELLSTW	SETWALL		TRAMELS
	STARKER		SWALLET	AELMRSU	MAULERS
AEKRSST	SKATERS		WALLETS		SERUMAL
	STRAKES	AELLSTY	STALELY	AELMRSV	MARVELS
	STREAKS	AELLSVY	VALLEYS	AELMRTT	MARTLET
	TASKERS	AELLTUU	ULULATE	AELMRTU	RELATUM
AEKRSSY	KARSEYS	AELLUVV	VALVULE	AELMSST	MATLESS
AEKRSTY	STREAKY	AELMMNO	MAMELON		SAMLETS
AEKRSUW	WAUKERS	AELMMNS	ALMSMEN	AELMSTU	AMULETS
AEKSSSV	KVASSES	AELMMNT	MALTMEN		MULETAS
AEKSSTT	TSATSKE	AELMMOY	MYELOMA	AELNNPR	PLANNER
AEKSWVY	KEYWAYS	AELMMRS	LAMMERS	AELNNPS	PENNALS
AELLMNU	LUMENAL		RAMMELS	AELNNPU	UNPANEL
AELLMRS	SMALLER		RAMMLES	AELNNRS	ENSNARL
AELLMRT	TRAMELL		SLAMMER		LANNERS
AELLMST	MALLETS	AELMMRT	TRAMMEL	AELNNRT	LANTERN
AELLMSU	MALLEUS	AELMMST	STAMMEL	AELNNRU	UNLEARN
AELLMSY	MELLAYS	AELMMSY	MALMSEY	AELNNST	STANNEL
	MESALLY	AELMMNS	LENSMAN	AELNNTU	ANNULET
AELLMTY	METALLY	AELMNOR	ALMONER	AELNOOS	ALSOONE
AELLMWX	MAXWELL		NEMORAL	AELNOPS	ESPANOL
AELLNOP	PALLONE	AELMNOS	MELANOS		NOPALES
	PLEONAL	AELMNOT	LOMENTA	AELNOPT	POLENTA
AELLNOR	LLANERO		OMENTAL	AELNOPU	APOLUNE
AELLNOV	NOVELLA		TELAMON	AELNORS	LOANERS
AELLNOY	ALONELY	AELMNPR	LAMPERN		ORLEANS
AELLNPY	PENALLY	AELMNRS	ALMNERS		RELOANS
AELLNRT	ENTRALL	AELMNRU	NUMERAL	AELNORU	ALEURON
AELLNSS	ALLNESS	AELMNSS	MANLESS	AELNORV	VERONAL
AELLNSW	ENWALLS	AELMNST	LAMENTS	AELNOST	ETALONS
AELLNTT	TALLENT		MANTELS		TOLANES
AELLNUU	LUNULAE		MANTLES	AELNOTV	VOLANTE
AELLNVY	VENALLY	AELMNSU	MENSUAL	AELNOTY	ANOLYTE
AELLORS	ROSELLA	AELMNTT	MANTLET	AELNOUZ	ZONULAE
AELLORT	REALLOT	AELMNTU	NUTMEAL	AELNPPR	PREPLAN
AELLORV	ALLOVER	AELMOPR	PLEROMA	AELNPPY	PLAYPEN
	OVERALL		RAMPOLE	AELNPRS	PLANERS
AELLORY	LOYALER	AELMOPU	AMPOULE		REPLANS
AELLOSS	LOESSAL	AELMOPY	MAYPOLE	AELNPRT	PANTLER
AELLPPS	LAPPELS	AELMORS	MORALES		PLANTER
AELLPRS	SPALLER	AELMORT	MOLERAT		REPLANT
AELLPRU	PLEURAL	AELMORU	MORULAE	AELNPRY	PLENARY
AELLPSS	SPALLES	AELMORV	REMOVAL	AELNPSS	NAPLESS
AELLPST	PALLETS	AELMOSS	MOLASSE	AELNPST	PLANETS

	PLATENS	**AELORTV**	LEVATOR	**AELPSTU**	PULSATE
AELNPSU	UPLEANS	**AELORTY**	ROYALET		PUTEALS
AELNPTU	UPLEANT	**AELORTZ**	ZELATOR		SPATULE
AELNPTX	EXPLANT	**AELORUU**	ROULEAU	**AELPSTZ**	SPATZLE
AELNPTY	APLENTY	**AELORVX**	OVERLAX	**AELPUUV**	UPVALUE
	PENALTY	**AELORVY**	LAYOVER	**AELQRRU**	QUARREL
AELNQUU	UNEQUAL		OVERLAY	**AELQSSU**	LASQUES
AELNRRS	SNARLER	**AELORWY**	OWRELAY		SQUEALS
AELNRSS	RANSELS	**AELOSSS**	LASSOES	**AELQSUZ**	QUEZALS
AELNRST	ANTLERS	**AELOSST**	SOLATES	**AELQTUZ**	QUETZAL
	RENTALS	**AELOSSV**	SALVOES	**AELRRSU**	SURREAL
	SALTERN	**AELOSSW**	LEASOWS	**AELRRSW**	WARSLER
	SLANTER	**AELOSTV**	SOLVATE	**AELRRTT**	RATTLER
	STERNAL	**AELOSTZ**	ZEALOTS	**AELRRTW**	TRAWLER
AELNRSV	VERLANS	**AELOSUZ**	ZEALOUS	**AELRSSS**	RASSLES
AELNRSY	LARNEYS	**AELOSVY**	SAVELOY	**AELRSST**	ARTLESS
AELNRSZ	RANZELS	**AELOTTU**	TOLUATE		LASTERS
AELNRTT	TRENTAL	**AELOTUV**	OVULATE		SALTERS
AELNRTU	NEUTRAL	**AELOTVV**	VOLVATE		SLATERS
AELNRTV	VENTRAL	**AELOTVY**	OVATELY		TARSELS
AELNRUU	NEURULA	**AELPPRS**	LAPPERS	**AELRSSU**	SAURELS
AELNRUV	UNRAVEL		RAPPELS	**AELRSSV**	SALVERS
	VENULAR		SLAPPER		SERVALS
AELNSSU	SENSUAL	**AELPPRY**	REAPPLY		SLAVERS
	UNSEALS	**AELPPSS**	SAPPLES		VERSALS
AELNSSW	AWNLESS	**AELPPST**	APPLETS	**AELRSSW**	WARLESS
AELNSSX	LAXNESS		LAPPETS		WARSLES
AELNSTT	LATENTS		STAPPLE		WRASSLE
	LATTENS	**AELPPSU**	APPULSE	**AELRSSY**	RAYLESS
	TALENTS		PAPULES		SLAYERS
AELNSTU	ELUANTS		UPLEAPS	**AELRSTT**	RATTLES
	LUNATES	**AELPPTU**	UPLEAPT		SLATTER
	UNLASTE	**AELPQSU**	PLAQUES		STARLET
AELNSTV	LEVANTS	**AELPRSV**	PARRELS		STARTLE
AELNSTY	STANYEL	**AELPRSS**	LAPSERS		TATLERS
AELNSTZ	ZELANTS	**AELPRST**	PALTERS	**AELRSTU**	ESTRUAL
AELNSUW	UNWEALS		PERSALT		SALUTER
AELNTUV	ENVAULT		PLASTER	**AELRSTV**	TRAVELS
AELOORS	AEROSOL		PLATERS		VARLETS
	ROSEOLA		PSALTER		VESTRAL
AELOPPR	PROPALE		STAPLER	**AELRSTW**	WARSTLE
AELOPPX	APOPLEX	**AELPRSU**	PERUSAL		WASTREL
AELOPRR	PERORAL		PLEURAS		WRASTLE
	PREORAL		SERPULA	**AELRSTY**	RAYLETS
AELOPRS	PAROLES	**AELPRSW**	PRAWLES	**AELRSUV**	VALUERS
	REPOSAL	**AELPRSY**	PARLEYS	**AELRSVV**	VARVELS
AELOPRT	PROLATE		PARSLEY	**AELRSVY**	SLAVERY
AELOPRV	OVERLAP		PLAYERS	**AELRSWX**	WRAXLES
AELOPST	APOSTLE		REPLAYS	**AELRSWY**	LAWYERS
	PELOTAS		SPARELY	**AELRSZZ**	RAZZLES
AELOPSX	EXPOSAL	**AELPRTT**	PARTLET	**AELRTTT**	TARTLET
AELOPTT	PALETOT		PLATTER		TATTLER
AELOPTU	OUTLEAP		PRATTLE	**AELRTTU**	TUTELAR
AELORRT	REALTOR	**AELPRTY**	PEARTLY	**AELRTUV**	VAULTER
	RELATOR		PEYTRAL	**AELRTWY**	TRAWLEY
AELORSS	LASSOER		PRELATY	**AELRTWZ**	WALTZER
	OARLESS		PTERYLA	**AELSSST**	TASSELS
	SEROSAL	**AELPRUY**	EPULARY	**AELSSTT**	LATESTS
	SOLERAS	**AELPSSS**	PASSELS		SALTEST
AELORST	OESTRAL		SAPLESS		STALEST
	OLESTRA	**AELPSST**	PASTELS		TASLETS
AELORTT	RETOTAL		STAPLES	**AELSSTU**	SALUTES
AELORTU	ROTULAE	**AELPSTT**	PATTLES		TALUSES
	TORULAE		PELTAST	**AELSSTV**	VESTALS

AELSSTW	WASTELS	AEMNOTU	AUTOMEN		TAMPERS
AELSSTX	TAXLESS		NOTAEUM	AEMPRSV	REVAMPS
AELSSTY	LYSATES		OUTNAME		VAMPERS
AELSSUV	AVULSES	AEMNPSS	PASSMEN	AEMPRSW	SWAMPER
AELSSVY	SLAVEYS	AEMNPST	ENSTAMP	AEMPRTT	TRAMPET
AELSSWY	WAYLESS		TAPSMEN	AEMPRTU	TEMPURA
AELSTTT	TATTLES	AEMNPSU	PNEUMAS	AEMPSSU	EMPUSAS
AELSTTW	WATTLES	AEMNPTU	PUTAMEN	AEMPTTT	ATTEMPT
AELSTTY	STATELY	AEMNPTY	PAYMENT	AEMPTTU	TAPETUM
	STYLATE	AEMNRRU	MANURER	AEMQRSU	MARQUES
AELSTUX	LUXATES	AEMNRST	ARTSMEN		MASQUER
AELSTWZ	WALTZES		MARTENS	AEMQSSU	MASQUES
AELSUVY	SUAVELY		SARMENT		SQUAMES
AELSWZZ	SWAZZLE		SMARTEN	AEMRRRS	MARRERS
AELTTTW	TWATTLE	AEMNRSU	MANURES	AEMRRRY	REMARRY
AELTTUX	TEXTUAL		MURENAS	AEMRRST	ARMREST
AELTUVV	VULVATE		SURNAME		SMARTER
AEMMMRS	MAMMERS	AEMNRTU	TRUEMAN	AEMRRSU	ARMURES
AEMMMST	MAMMETS	AEMNRTV	VARMENT	AEMRRSV	MARVERS
AEMMMSV	MAMMEYS	AEMNSSS	MESSANS	AEMRRSW	REWARMS
AEMMNOT	MOMENTA	AEMNSST	STAMENS		SWARMER
AEMMNSS	MESSMAN	AEMNSSU	UNSEAMS		WARMERS
AEMMNTU	AMENTUM	AEMNSTU	UNTAMES	AEMRRTU	ERRATUM
AEMMOPR	MAMPOER		UNTEAMS		MATURER
AEMMORS	MARMOSE	AEMNSTY	AMNESTY	AEMRSST	MASTERS
AEMMORW	WOMMERA	AEMNTTU	NUTMEAT		STREAMS
AEMMPRS	SPAMMER	AEMNTWY	WAYMENT	AEMRSSU	AMUSERS
AEMMRRS	RAMMERS	AEMOORT	TEAROOM		ASSUMER
AEMMRST	STAMMER	AEMOORW	WOOMERA		MASSEUR
AEMMRSY	YAMMERS	AEMOOST	OSTEOMA	AEMRSTT	MATTERS
AEMMRSZ	MAMZERS	AEMOOSV	AMOOVES		SMATTER
AEMMSST	STEMMAS		VAMOOSE	AEMRSTU	MATURES
AEMMSTU	MAUMETS	AEMOPPR	PAMPERO		STRUMAE
	SUMMATE	AEMOPSZ	APOZEMS	AEMRSTW	WARMEST
AEMMSTW	MAWMETS	AEMORRR	ARMORER	AEMRSTY	MASTERY
AEMNNOR	MONERAN	AEMORRS	REMORAS		MAYSTER
AEMNNOS	MANNOSE		ROAMERS		STREAMY
AEMNNOT	MONTANE	AEMORRV	OVERARM	AEMRTTX	MARTEXT
	NONMEAT	AEMORRW	EARWORM	AEMRTTY	MATTERY
AEMNNOU	NOUMENA	AEMORST	AMORETS	AEMRTUU	TRUMEAU
AEMNNOZ	MENAZON		MAESTRO	AEMSSSU	ASSUMES
AEMNNRS	MANNERS		OMERTAS	AEMSSTU	MUTASES
AEMNNRT	MANRENT	AEMORSU	RAMEOUS	AEMSSUW	WAMUSES
	REMNANT	AEMORSW	SEAWORM	AEMSSYZ	ZYMASES
AEMNNSW	NEWSMAN		WOMERAS	AEMSTTU	MUTATES
AEMNNTU	UNMEANT	AEMORSX	XEROMAS	AEMSTUV	MAUVEST
AEMNOPP	PAMPOEN	AEMOSST	OSMATES	AEMSTVZ	ZEMSTVA
AEMNOPR	MANROPE	AEMOSSV	VAMOSES	AEMSUZZ	MEZUZAS
	REPOMAN	AEMOSTT	STOMATE	AENNNOS	NONANES
AEMNOPS	MOPANES	AEMOSTW	TWASOME	AENNNPT	PENNANT
AEMNOPZ	ZAMPONE	AEMOSUZ	ZAMOUSE	AENNOPS	PANNOSE
AEMNORR	ORRAMEN	AEMOSWY	SOMEWAY	AENNORT	NORTENA
AEMNORS	ENAMORS	AEMOTTZ	MOZETTA	AENNORY	ANNOYER
	MOANERS	AEMPPRS	MAPPERS	AENNOSS	NOSEANS
	OARSMEN		PAMPERS	AENNOSV	NOVENAS
AEMNORT	TONEARM		PREAMPS	AENNOSY	ANYONES
AEMNORU	ENAMOUR	AEMPPRY	MAPPERY	AENNOTU	TONNEAU
	NEUROMA	AEMPRRS	PREARMS	AENNPRS	PANNERS
AEMNORV	OVERMAN		RAMPERS		SPANNER
AEMNORY	ANYMORE	AEMPRRT	TRAMPER	AENNQTU	QUANNET
	ROMNEYA	AEMPRRW	PREWARM	AENNRSV	VANNERS
AEMNOSS	MONASES	AEMPRST	EMPARTS	AENNRTT	ENTRANT
AEMNOST	MANTOES		RESTAMP	AENNRTV	VERNANT
AEMNOTT	TOMENTA		STAMPER		

AENNRTY	TANNERY	AENPSST	APTNESS	AENSTWY	TAWNEYS
	TYRANNE		PATNESS	AENTTTU	ATTUENT
AENNSSW	WANNESS		PESANTS	AEOOPPS	PAPOOSE
AENNSTT	TANNEST	AENPSSY	SYNAPSE	AEOOPRS	OROPESA
	TENANTS	AENPSTT	PATENTS	AEOPPPS	PAPPOSE
AENNSTW	WANNEST		PATTENS	AEOPPRS	APPOSER
AENOOTZ	ENTOZOA	AENPSTU	PEANUTS		POPERAS
	OZONATE		PESAUNT	AEOPPRV	APPROVE
AENOPPR	PROPANE	AENPSTW	STEWPAN	AEOPPSS	APPOSES
AENOPRS	PERSONA	AENPSTY	SYNAPTE	AEOPQRU	OPAQUER
AENOPRT	OPERANT	AENPSTZ	PEZANTS	AEOPQSU	OPAQUES
	PRONATE	AENQSTU	EQUANTS	AEOPRRT	PRAETOR
	PROTEAN	AENRRSS	SERRANS		PRORATE
AENOPST	TEOPANS		SNARERS	AEOPRRV	VAPORER
AENOPSU	POSAUNE	AENRRST	ERRANTS	AEOPRSS	SOAPERS
AENOPSV	PAVONES		RANTERS	AEOPRST	ESPARTO
AENOPSW	WEAPONS	AENRRSW	WARNERS		PROTEAS
AENOPTU	AUTOPEN		WARRENS		SEAPORT
AENORRS	SERRANO	AENRRSY	YARNERS	AEOPRTT	PORTATE
AENORRT	ORNATER	AENRRTT	TRANTER	AEOPRTV	OVERAPT
AENORRV	OVERRAN	AENRRTY	TERNARY	AEOPRVY	OVERPAY
AENORSS	REASONS	AENRSSS	SARSENS	AEOPRWY	ROPEWAY
	SENORAS	AENRSST	SARSNET	AEOPSST	PETASOS
AENORST	ATONERS		TRANSES		SAPOTES
	SANTERO	AENRSSW	ANSWERS	AEOPSTT	APTOTES
	SENATOR		RAWNESS		TEAPOTS
	TREASON	AENRSSY	SARNEYS	AEOPSTY	TEAPOYS
AENORSU	ARENOUS	AENRSTT	NATTERS	AEOPSTZ	TOPAZES
AENORTU	OUTEARN		RATTENS	AEOQRTU	EQUATOR
AENORTV	VENATOR	AENRSTU	AUNTERS	AEOQRUV	VAQUERO
AENORWZ	WARZONE		NATURES	AEOQSUU	AQUEOUS
AENORXY	ANOREXY		SAUNTER	AEORRRS	ROARERS
AENOSSS	SEASONS	AENRSTV	SERVANT	AEORRSS	SOARERS
AENOSST	ASTONES		TAVERNS	AEORRST	ROASTER
AENOSSW	WEASONS		VERSANT	AEORRSU	AROUSER
AENOSTT	ATTONES	AENRSTW	STRAWEN	AEORRSV	SAVORER
	NOTATES		WANTERS		SEROVAR
AENOSTU	SOUTANE	AENRSTY	TRAYNES	AEORSSS	SAROSES
AENOSVW	WAVESON	AENRSUW	UNSWEAR		SEROSAS
AENOUUV	NOUVEAU		UNWARES	AEORSST	OSETRAS
AENPPRS	NAPPERS	AENRSUY	SYNURAE		OSSETRA
	PARPENS	AENRSWY	YAWNERS	AEORSSU	AROUSES
	PARSNEP	AENRTTU	TAUNTER	AEORSTT	ROTATES
	SNAPPER	AENRTTY	NATTERY		TOASTER
AENPPRT	PARPENT	AENRTUV	VAUNTER	AEORSUV	AVOURES
AENPPRU	UNPAPER	AENRTUW	UNWATER	AEORSVW	AVOWERS
AENPPST	PETNAPS	AENRUWY	UNWEARY		OVERSAW
AENPRRT	PARTNER	AENSSST	ASSENTS		REAVOWS
AENPRRW	PRAWNER		SNASTES	AEORSVY	AVOYERS
	PREWARN	AENSSTU	NASUTES	AEORTTU	OUTRATE
AENPRST	ARPENTS		UNSEATS	AEORTUV	OUTRAVE
	ENTRAPS	AENSSTX	SEXTANS	AEORTUW	OUTWEAR
	PANTERS	AENSSTY	STAYNES	AEORTVX	OVERTAX
	PARENTS	AENSSTZ	STANZES	AEOSSTV	AVOSETS
	PASTERN	AENSSWY	SAWNEYS	AEOSTTU	OUTEATS
	PERSANT	AENSSXY	SYNAXES	AEOSUVZ	ZOUAVES
	TREPANS	AENSTTT	ATTENTS	AEPPPRU	PREPUPA
AENPRSW	ENWRAPS	AENSTTU	ATTUNES	AEPPRRS	RAPPERS
	PAWNERS		NUTATES	AEPPRRT	TRAPPER
	SPAWNER		TAUTENS	AEPPRRW	PREWRAP
AENPRSZ	PANZERS		TETANUS		WRAPPER
AENPRTT	PATTERN		UNSTATE	AEPPRSS	APPRESS
	REPTANT	AENSTTX	SEXTANT		SAPPERS
AENPRUV	PARVENU	AENSTUX	UNTAXES		

AEPPRST	TAPPERS	AEQRTTU	QUARTET	AFFGINW	WAFFING
AEPPRSU	PAUPERS	AEQRUVY	QUAVERY	AFFGINY	AFFYING
	UPSPEAR	AEQSSSU	QUASSES		YAFFING
AEPPRSW	SWAPPER	AERRSST	ARRESTS	AFFGSUW	GUFFAWS
	WAPPERS		RASTERS	AFFHILN	HAFFLIN
AEPPRSY	PREPAYS		STARERS	AFFHIRS	RAFFISH
	YAPPERS	AERRSSU	ASSURER	AFFHIST	HAFFITS
AEPPRSZ	ZAPPERS		RASURES	AFFIITX	FIXATIF
AEPPSTT	TAPPETS	AERRSTT	RATTERS	AFFIKRS	KAFFIRS
AEPPSTU	PASTEUP		RESTART	AFFILMN	MAFFLIN
	PUPATES		STARTER	AFFILOR	RIFFOLA
AEPQRTU	PARQUET	AERRSTV	STARVER	AFFILPS	PILAFFS
AEPRRRS	SPARRER	AERRSTY	STRAYER	AFFILSY	FALSIFY
AEPRRSS	PARSERS	AERRSUZ	RAZURES	AFFIMRS	AFFIRMS
	RASPERS	AERRSWY	WARREYS	AFFIMST	MASTIFF
	SPARERS	AERRTTY	RATTERY	AFFINRU	FUNFAIR
	SPARRES	AERSSST	ASSERTS		RUFFIAN
	SPARSER		TRASSES	AFFINTY	TIFFANY
AEPRRST	PARTERS	AERSSSU	ASSURES	AFFIORR	FORFAIR
	PRATERS		SARUSES	AFFIRRU	FURFAIR
AEPRRSU	PARURES	AERSSSW	WRASSES	AFFIRST	TARIFFS
	UPREARS	AERSSTT	ASTERTS	AFFIRSU	SUFFARI
AEPRRSW	REWRAPS		STARETS	AFFIRSZ	ZAFFIRS
	WARPERS		STATERS	AFFLOPY	PLAYOFF
AEPRRSY	PRAYERS	AERSSTV	STARVES	AFFLOSY	LAYOFFS
	RESPRAY	AERSSTW	WASTERS	AFFMOPR	OFFRAMP
	SPRAYER	AERSSTY	ESTRAYS	AFFNORS	SAFFRON
AEPRRTU	PARTURE		STAYERS	AFFNORT	AFFRONT
	RAPTURE		STAYRES	AFFOPSY	PAYOFFS
AEPRRTW	REWRAPT	AERSSUV	VARUSES	AFFRSST	STRAFFS
AEPRRTY	PARTYER	AERSSVW	SWARVES	AFGGGIN	FAGGING
	PETRARY	AERSSWY	SAWYERS	AFGGINN	FANGING
AEPRSSS	PASSERS		SWAYERS	AFGGOST	FAGGOTS
AEPRSST	PASTERS	AERSTTT	STRETTA	AFGGOTY	FAGGOTY
	REPASTS		TARTEST	AFGHHIS	HAGFISH
	SPAREST		TATTERS	AFGHINS	FASHING
AEPRSSU	PAUSERS	AERSTTU	ASTUTER	AFGHINT	HAFTING
AEPRSSY	PESSARY		STATURE	AFGHIRS	GARFISH
AEPRSTT	PATTERS	AERSTTV	VATTERS	AFGHLSU	GASHFUL
	SPATTER	AERSTTW	SWATTER	AFGHLTU	FLAUGHT
	TAPSTER		TEWARTS	AFGHRTU	FRAUGHT
AEPRSTU	PASTURE	AERSTTY	YATTERS	AFGIIKN	FAIKING
	UPRATES	AERSTTZ	STARETZ	AFGIILN	FAILING
	UPSTARE	AERSTUU	AUTEURS	AFGIINR	FAIRING
	UPTEARS	AERSTUY	ESTUARY	AFGIINT	FIATING
AEPRSTY	YAPSTER	AERSTVY	STRAYVE	AFGIINW	WAIFING
AEPRSTZ	PATZERS	AERSTWY	WASTERY	AFGIJMS	FIGJAMS
AEPRSUX	ARUSPEX	AERTTTY	TATTERY	AFGIKLN	FLAKING
AEPRSUY	YAUPERS	AERTTUV	VETTURA	AFGILLN	FALLING
AEPRSWY	SPYWARE	AESSSTT	TASSETS	AFGILMN	FLAMING
	YAWPERS	AESSTTT	ATTESTS	AFGILNO	FOALING
AEPRSYY	SPRAYEY		STATUES		LOAFING
AEPRTXY	APTERYX	AESSTTU	VASTEST	AFGILNR	FLARING
AEPSSTU	PETASUS	AESSTUV	SUAVEST	AFGILNS	FALSING
AEPSSZZ	SPAZZES	AESSTUY	EUSTASY	AFGILNT	FATLING
AEPSTTU	UPSTATE	AESSVVY	SAVVEYS	AFGILNU	GAINFUL
AEPSZZZ	PZAZZES	AESTTTU	STATUTE	AFGILNW	FLAWING
AEQRRSU	SQUARER		TAUTEST	AFGILNY	ANGLIFY
AEQRRTU	QUARTER	AESTTTW	WATTEST		FLAYING
AEQRSSU	SQUARES	AFFFGIN	FAFFING	AFGILRU	FIGURAL
AEQRSTU	QUAREST	AFFFLLO	FALLOFF	AFGIMNO	FOAMING
	QUARTES	AFFGGIN	GAFFING	AFGIMNR	FARMING
	QUATRES	AFFGINN	NAFFING		FRAMING
AEQRSUV	QUAVERS				

AFGIMNY	MAGNIFY	AFIILNT	TAILFIN		FUSTIAN
AFGINNN	FANNING	AFIILOR	AIRFOIL		INFAUST
AFGINNS	FINGANS	AFIILRT	AIRLIFT	AFIORST	FAITORS
AFGINNW	FAWNING	AFIILRY	FAIRILY	AFIORTU	FAITOUR
AFGINNY	FAYNING	AFIIMOS	MAFIOSI	AFIORTZ	FORZATI
AFGINOT	ANTIFOG	AFIJNNS	FINJANS	AFIQRSU	FAQUIRS
AFGINRR	FARRING	AFIKLLY	FLAKILY	AFISSTT	SITFAST
AFGINRS	FARSING	AFIKLOT	FLOKATI	AFISSTY	SATISFY
AFGINRT	FARTING	AFIKMNR	FINMARK	AFISTTT	FATTIST
	INGRAFT	AFIKNRT	RATFINK	AFISTUV	FAUVIST
	RAFTING	AFIKNSU	FUNKIAS	AFITTUY	FATUITY
AFGINRY	FRAYING	AFIKRSS	FRISKAS	AFJLRSU	JARFULS
AFGINST	FASTING	AFILLMS	MISFALL		JARSFUL
AFGINTT	FATTING	AFILLNP	PINFALL	AFKLNRY	FRANKLY
AFGINTU	FAUTING	AFILLNS	INFALLS	AFKLNTU	TANKFUL
AFGINTW	WAFTING	AFILLNY	FINALLY	AFKLOWY	FOLKWAY
AFGIOTT	FAGOTTI	AFILLPT	PITFALL	AFKRRTU	FRAKTUR
AFGIRTY	GRATIFY	AFILLPU	PAILFUL	AFLLMPU	PALMFUL
AFGKNOP	PAKFONG	AFILLRY	FRAILLY	AFLLMSU	FULLAMS
AFGKORT	KOFTGAR	AFILLTY	TAILFLY	AFLLNOS	ONFALLS
AFGLLLY	GALLFLY	AFILLUV	FLUVIAL	AFLLNSU	FULLANS
AFGLLUY	FUGALLY		VIALFUL	AFLLOOY	ALOOFLY
AFGLNOS	FLAGONS	AFILLUW	WAILFUL	AFLLORS	FLORALS
AFGLNSU	FUNGALS	AFILMNT	LIFTMAN	AFLLORU	FLORULA
AFGLRYV	GRAYFLY	AFILMOR	ALIFORM	AFLLOSW	FALLOWS
AFGMNOR	FROGMAN	AFILMOY	FOAMILY	AFLLOTU	FALLOUT
AFGMORS	FOGRAMS	AFILMPY	AMPLIFY		OUTFALL
AFGOOTT	FAGOTTO	AFILMSS	FALSISM	AFLLPSU	LAPFULS
AFGORRS	FRAGORS	AFILNPU	PAINFUL	AFLLPUY	PLAYFUL
AFGOSTU	FUGATOS	AFILNSV	FLAVINS	AFLLUWY	AWFULLY
AFHIIRS	FAIRISH	AFILNTU	ANTIFLU	AFLMNOU	MOANFUL
	HAIRIFS		FLUTINA	AFLMORS	FORMALS
AFHIISW	WAIFISH	AFILNTY	FAINTLY	AFLMORU	FORMULA
AFHIKLS	KHALIFS	AFILORW	AIRFLOW	AFLMORW	WOLFRAM
AFHIKRS	KHARIFS	AFILOTX	FOXTAIL	AFLMOST	FLOTSAM
AFHIKUV	KUFIYAH	AFILQUY	QUALIFY	AFLMRSU	ARMFULS
AFHILLN	HALFLIN	AFILRRY	FRIARLY		ARMSFUL
AFHILSS	FALSISH	AFILRSZ	FRAZILS		FULMARS
AFHILTW	HALFWIT	AFILRTY	FRAILTY	AFLMSTU	MASTFUL
AFHIMNU	HAFNIUM	AFILSSY	SALSIFY	AFLMSUU	FAMULUS
AFHINOS	FASHION	AFILSTU	FISTULA	AFLNORT	FRONTAL
AFHINPS	PANFISH	AFILSTY	FALSITY	AFLNOTT	FLOTANT
AFHINTU	UNFAITH	AFILTTY	FATTILY	AFLNPSU	PANFULS
AFHIORS	OARFISH	AFIMNRS	FIRMANS	AFLNRTU	RUNFLAT
AFHIRSS	SHARIFS	AFIMOOS	MAFIOSO	AFLNSTU	FLAUNTS
AFHIRST	RATFISH	AFIMORV	AVIFORM	AFLNTUY	FLAUNTY
AFHISST	FASTISH	AFIMRST	MAFTIRS	AFLOOTW	WOOLFAT
AFHISSW	SAWFISH	AFIMSSS	MASSIFS	AFLOPTT	FLATTOP
AFHISTT	FATTISH	AFIMSSV	FAVISMS	AFLORSS	SAFROLS
AFHISWY	FISHWAY	AFIMSTT	FATTISM	AFLORSU	FUSAROL
AFHKORY	HAYFORK	AFIMSUV	FAUVISM	AFLORSV	FLAVORS
AFHKRTU	FUTHARK	AFIMSUZ	UMFAZIS	AFLORUV	FLAVOUR
AFHLMRU	HARMFUL	AFIMTTY	MATTIFY	AFLORVY	FLAVORY
AFHLMSU	FULHAMS	AFINNNS	FINNANS	AFLORWW	WARWOLF
AFHLOOS	LOOFAHS	AFINNOR	FRANION	AFLOSSU	FOSSULA
AFHLOTY	HAYLOFT	AFINNOS	FANIONS	AFLPRTY	FLYTRAP
AFHLSTU	HATFULS	AFINNOT	FONTINA	AFLPSTY	FLYPAST
	HATSFUL	AFINNST	INFANTS	AFLRTUU	FUTURAL
AFHMOST	FATHOMS	AFINORS	INSOFAR	AFLRTUY	TRAYFUL
AFHOOPT	POOFTAH	AFINRSU	UNFAIRS	AFLSSTU	FUTSALS
AFHOPTU	POUFTAH	AFINRTU	ANTIFUR	AFLSTUV	VATFULS
AFHORSS	SHOFARS	AFINSSU	FUSAINS	AFLSUWY	SWAYFUL
AFIILNS	FINALIS	AFINSTU	FAUNIST	AFLSWYY	FLYWAYS
	FINIALS		FIAUNTS	AFMNNOR	NONFARM

AFMNOOT	FOOTMAN	AGGILNN	ANGLING	AGHHIWY	HIGHWAY
AFMNORT	FORMANT	AGGILNO	GAOLING	AGHHOSW	HOGWASH
AFMNOST	FANTOMS		GOALING	AGHHSSU	SHAUGHS
AFMNRSU	SURFMAN	AGGILNR	ARGLING	AGHHTUY	HAUGHTY
AFMNRTU	TURFMAN		GLARING	AGHIILN	HAILING
AFMOOSS	SAMFOOS	AGGILNS	GINGALS		NILGHAI
AFMORST	FARMOST		LAGGINS	AGHIINN	HAINING
	FORMATS	AGGILNZ	GLAZING	AGHIINR	HAIRING
AFMORSU	AUSFORM	AGGILOS	LOGGIAS	AGHIJRS	JAGHIRS
AFMORTU	FOUMART	AGGIMMN	GAMMING	AGHIKNN	HANKING
AFMOSTT	AFTMOST	AGGIMNN	MANGING	AGHIKNR	HARKING
AFMOSTU	SFUMATO	AGGIMNS	GAMINGS	AGHIKNS	SHAKING
AFNNNOS	NONFANS	AGGIMNU	GAUMING	AGHIKNW	HAWKING
AFNORRW	FORWARN	AGGINNN	GANNING	AGHIKSU	KIAUGHS
AFNORTW	FANWORT	AGGINNP	PANGING	AGHIKSW	GAWKISH
AFNOTUW	OUTFAWN	AGGINNR	RANGING	AGHILLN	HALLING
AFNPRSY	FRYPANS	AGGINNT	GANTING	AGHILNO	HALOING
AFNSSTU	SUNFAST		TANGING	AGHILNR	HARLING
AFOOPPR	APPROOF	AGGINNU	UNAGING	AGHILNS	HALSING
AFOORST	FOOTRAS	AGGINNW	GNAWING		LASHING
AFOORTZ	FORZATO	AGGINOT	GIGATON		SHALING
AFOOTWY	FOOTWAY	AGGINPP	GAPPING	AGHILNT	HALTING
AFORRSW	FARROWS	AGGINPR	GRAPING		LATHING
AFORRSY	FORRAYS		PARGING	AGHILNU	HAULING
	ORFRAYS	AGGINPS	GAPINGS		NILGHAU
AFORSSY	FORSAYS		GASPING	AGHILNV	HALVING
AFORSTU	FAUTORS		PAGINGS	AGHILNW	WHALING
	FOUTRAS	AGGINPU	GAUPING	AGHILNY	NYLGHAI
AFORSUV	FAVOURS	AGGINPW	GAWPING	AGHILOT	GOLIATH
AFOSSSU	FOUSSAS	AGGINRR	GARRING	AGHILRS	LARGISH
AFOSTTU	OUTFAST	AGGINRS	GRINGAS	AGHILRT	ALRIGHT
AFOSTUU	FATUOUS		RACINGS	AGHILST	ALIGHTS
AFPSTUW	UPWAFTS		SIRGANG	AGHIMMN	HAMMING
AGGGGIN	GAGGING	AGGINRT	GRATING	AGHIMNR	HARMING
AGGGHIN	HAGGING		TARGING	AGHIMNS	MASHING
AGGGIJN	JAGGING	AGGINRU	ARGUING		SHAMING
AGGGILN	LAGGING	AGGINRV	GRAVING	AGHIMNW	HAWMING
AGGGIMN	MAGGING	AGGINRY	GRAYING	AGHIMPS	GAMPISH
AGGGINN	GANGING	AGGINRZ	GRAZING	AGHINNO	NIHONGA
	NAGGING	AGGINSS	GASSING	AGHINNT	HANTING
AGGGINR	RAGGING	AGGINST	GASTING		TANGHIN
AGGGINS	SAGGING		GATINGS	AGHINOR	HOARING
AGGGINT	TAGGING		STAGING	AGHINOX	HOAXING
AGGGINU	GAUGING	AGGINSW	SWAGING	AGHINPP	HAPPING
AGGGINV	VAGGING	AGGINSZ	GAZINGS	AGHINPR	HARPING
AGGGINW	WAGGING	AGGINUV	VAGUING	AGHINPS	HASPING
AGGGINZ	ZAGGING	AGGIORS	GORGIAS		PASHING
AGGHHIS	HAGGISH	AGGISWW	WIGWAGS		PHASING
AGGHIIL	GHILGAI	AGGISZZ	ZIGZAGS		SHAPING
AGGHIMN	GINGHAM	AGGLOST	LOGGATS	AGHINPT	PATHING
AGGHINN	HANGING	AGGMNOS	MOGGANS	AGHINRS	GARNISH
AGGHINS	GASHING	AGGMORR	GROGRAM		RASHING
AGGHISW	WAGGISH	AGGMOST	MAGGOTS		SHARING
AGGIIJJ	JIGAJIG	AGGMOTY	MAGGOTY	AGHINRU	NURAGHI
AGGIILS	GILGAIS	AGGMRSU	MUGGARS	AGHINSS	SASHING
AGGIIMN	IMAGING	AGGNOSU	GUANGOS	AGHINST	HASTING
AGGIINN	GAINING	AGGNOSW	WAGGONS		TASHING
AGGIINT	GAITING	AGGNOSX	OXGANGS	AGHINSU	ANGUISH
AGGIINV	GINGIVA	AGGNOSY	SYNAGOG		HAUSING
AGGIJJO	JIGAJOG	AGGNPSU	UPGANGS	AGHINSV	HAVINGS
AGGIKNS	GASKING	AGGNRSU	NUGGARS		SHAVING
AGGIKNW	GAWKING	AGGPRSY	PYGARGS	AGHINSW	HAWSING
AGGILLN	GALLING	AGHHIMN	HIGHMAN		SHAWING
	GINGALL	AGHHINS	HASHING		WASHING

AGHINSY	HAYINGS	AGIILPT	PIGTAIL	AGIKNNW	WANKING
AGHINSZ	HAZINGS	AGIILTY	AGILITY	AGIKNNY	YANKING
AGHINTT	HATTING	AGIIMMN	MAIMING	AGIKNOS	SOAKING
	TATHING	AGIIMMS	IMAGISM	AGIKNOY	KAYOING
AGHINTW	THAWING	AGIIMNN	MAINING		OKAYING
AGHIOST	GOATISH	AGIIMOR	ORIGAMI	AGIKNPR	PARKING
AGHIPSW	PIGWASH	AGIIMST	IMAGIST	AGIKNQU	QUAKING
AGHIQSU	QUAIGHS	AGIINNP	PAINING	AGIKNRR	RARKING
AGHIRRS	GHARRIS	AGIINNR	AIRNING	AGIKNRS	RAKINGS
AGHIRST	GRAITHS		INGRAIN		SARKING
AGHIRSU	GUARISH		RAINING	AGIKNRT	KARTING
AGHIRSY	GRAYISH	AGIINNS	SAINING	AGIKNRW	WARKING
AGHJMNO	MAHJONG	AGIINNW	WAINING	AGIKNRY	YARKING
AGHKOSW	GOSHAWK	AGIINNZ	ZINGANI	AGIKNSS	ASKINGS
AGHLMPU	GALUMPH	AGIINPR	PAIRING		GASKINS
AGHLMSU	MUGHALS	AGIINRS	AIRINGS	AGIKNST	SKATING
AGHLNUY	NYLGHAU		ARISING		STAKING
AGHLOOS	GASOHOL		RAGINIS		TAKINGS
AGHLOSU	GOULASH		RAISING		TASKING
AGHLSTU	GALUTHS		SAIRING	AGIKNSW	WAKINGS
AGHLSTY	GHASTLY	AGIINRT	AIRTING	AGIKNUW	WAUKING
AGHMORY	HYGROMA		RAITING	AGILLLN	LALLING
AGHMRRU	MURRAGH	AGIINRW	WAIRING	AGILLMN	MALLING
AGHNNOU	HOUNGAN	AGIINRZ	ZINGARI	AGILLMU	GALLIUM
AGHNNSU	HUNGANS	AGIINSV	AVISING	AGILLNP	PALLING
	UNHANGS		VISAING	AGILLNU	LINGUAL
AGHNOTU	HANGOUT	AGIINTW	WAITING		LINGULA
	TOHUNGA	AGIINTX	TAXIING	AGILLNW	WALLING
AGHNPSU	HANGUPS	AGIINVV	VIVAING	AGILLNY	ALLYING
	UPHANGS	AGIINVW	WAIVING	AGILLOR	GORILLA
AGHNRST	THRANGS	AGIINVZ	AVIZING	AGILLOT	GALLIOT
AGHNRSU	NURHAGS	AGIJKNU	JAUKING	AGILLRU	LIGULAR
AGHNRUY	AHUNGRY	AGIJLLN	JINGALL	AGILLSU	LIGULAS
AGHNSTU	NAUGHTS	AGIJLNS	JINGALS		LUGSAIL
AGHNSUY	GUNYAHS	AGIJMMN	JAMMING	AGILLYZ	GLAZILY
AGHNTUY	NAUGHTY	AGIJNPP	JAPPING	AGILMMN	LAMMING
AGHOORT	AGOROTH	AGIJNPR	JARPING	AGILMMS	GIMMALS
AGHOQSU	QUAHOGS	AGIJNPS	JAPINGS	AGILMNO	LOAMING
AGHORTW	WARTHOG	AGIJNPU	JAUPING	AGILMNP	LAMPING
AGHPTUY	PAUGHTY	AGIJNRR	JARRING		PALMING
AGHRRSU	GURRAHS	AGIJNSW	JAWINGS	AGILMNR	MARLING
AGHRSTU	TUGHRAS		JIGSAWN	AGILMNS	LINGAMS
AGHRSTY	GYTRASH	AGIJNZZ	JAZZING		MALIGNS
AGHSTUW	WAUGHTS	AGIJSSW	JIGSAWS	AGILMNT	MALTING
AGIIJLN	JAILING	AGIKKNR	KARKING	AGILMNU	MAULING
AGIIKLN	LAIKING	AGIKKNY	YAKKING	AGILMNY	MANGILY
AGIIKLT	GLAIKIT	AGIKLNN	ANKLING	AGILMOS	GLIOMAS
AGIIKNP	PAIKING		LANKING	AGILMPS	MAGILPS
AGIIKNR	RAIKING	AGIKLNO	OAKLING	AGILMPU	PLAGIUM
AGIILMN	MAILING	AGIKLNR	LARKING	AGILMST	STIGMAL
AGIILNN	ALINING	AGIKLNS	LAKINGS	AGILNNO	LOANING
	NAILING		SLAKING	AGILNNP	PLANING
AGIILNR	GLAIRIN	AGIKLNT	TALKING	AGILNNR	LARNING
	LAIRING	AGIKLNW	WALKING	AGILNNS	LIGNANS
	RAILING	AGIKLWY	GAWKILY		LINSANG
AGIILNS	AISLING	AGIKMNR	MARKING	AGILNNT	TANLING
	NILGAIS	AGIKMNS	MAKINGS	AGILNOP	GALOPIN
	SAILING		MASKING	AGILNOR	RANGOLI
AGIILNT	INTAGLI	AGIKNNR	NARKING	AGILNOT	ANTILOG
	TAILING		RANKING	AGILNOV	LOAVING
AGIILNV	VAILING	AGIKNNS	SNAKING	AGILNOZ	LAZOING
	VIALING	AGIKNNT	KANTING	AGILNPP	LAPPING
AGIILNW	WAILING		TANKING		PALPING
AGIILOV	VILIAGO	AGIKNNU	UNAKING	AGILNPR	GRAPLIN

Code	Words	Code	Words	Code	Words
	PARLING	AGIMNRR	MARRING		GITANOS
AGILNPS	LAPSING	AGIMNRS	ARMINGS	AGINOSU	SAGOUIN
	PALINGS		MARGINS	AGINOTU	AUTOING
	SAPLING	AGIMNRT	MARTING		OUTGAIN
AGILNPT	PLATING		MIGRANT	AGINOTV	OVATING
AGILNPW	LAPWING	AGIMNRW	WARMING	AGINOTZ	TOAZING
AGILNPY	PLAYING	AGIMNRY	MYRINGA	AGINOVW	AVOWING
AGILNRT	RATLING	AGIMNSS	MASSING	AGINPPP	PAPPING
AGILNRW	WARLING	AGIMNST	MASTING	AGINPPR	PARPING
AGILNRY	ANGRILY		MATINGS		RAPPING
	NARGILY		TAMINGS	AGINPPS	SAPPING
	RANGILY	AGIMNSU	AMUSING	AGINPPT	TAPPING
	RAYLING	AGIMNSY	MAYINGS	AGINPPW	WAPPING
AGILNSS	LASINGS	AGIMNTT	MATTING	AGINPPY	YAPPING
	SIGNALS	AGIMORS	ISOGRAM	AGINPPZ	ZAPPING
AGILNST	ANGLIST	AGIMORU	GOURAMI	AGINPRR	PARRING
	LASTING	AGIMOSY	ISOGAMY	AGINPRS	PARINGS
	SALTING	AGIMRRT	TRIGRAM		PARSING
	SLATING	AGIMRSU	GURAMIS		RASPING
	STALING	AGIMRTY	TRIGAMY		SPARING
AGILNSU	LINGUAS	AGIMSST	STIGMAS	AGINPRT	PARTING
	NILGAUS	AGIMSWW	WIGWAMS		PRATING
	SALUING	AGINNNP	PANNING		TRAPING
AGILNSV	SALVING	AGINNNT	TANNING	AGINPRW	WARPING
	SLAVING	AGINNNV	VANNING	AGINPRY	PRAYING
	VALSING	AGINNNW	WANNING	AGINPSS	PASSING
AGILNSW	LAWINGS	AGINNOS	GANOINS		SPAINGS
	SWALING	AGINNOT	ATONING	AGINPST	PASTING
AGILNSY	LAYINGS	AGINNOZ	ZINGANO	AGINPSU	PAUSING
	SLAYING	AGINNPP	NAPPING	AGINPSV	PAVINGS
AGILNTY	GIANTLY	AGINNPS	PINANGS	AGINPSY	PAYINGS
AGILNUV	VALUING		SPANING		SPAYING
AGILNUW	WAULING	AGINNPT	PANTING	AGINPTT	PATTING
AGILNVV	VALVING	AGINNPW	PAWNING	AGINPUY	YAUPING
AGILNWW	WAWLING	AGINNRS	SNARING	AGINPWY	YAWPING
AGILNWY	YAWLING	AGINNRT	RANTING	AGINRRT	TARRING
AGILNYZ	LAZYING	AGINNRW	WARNING	AGINRRW	WARRING
AGILOPT	GALIPOT	AGINNRY	YARNING	AGINRST	GASTRIN
AGILORS	GIRASOL	AGINNST	ANTINGS		GRATINS
	GLORIAS		STANING		RATINGS
AGILORW	AIRGLOW	AGINNSU	GUANINS		STARING
AGILOST	GALIOTS	AGINNSW	AWNINGS		TARINGS
	LATIGOS		SNAWING	AGINRSV	RAVINGS
	SALIGOT		WANINGS	AGINRSW	RAWINGS
AGILRSS	SLAIRGS	AGINNTU	ANTIGUN	AGINRSY	SIGNARY
AGILSSY	GASSILY	AGINNTW	WANTING		SYRINGA
AGILSTY	STAGILY	AGINNWY	YAWNING	AGINRTT	RATTING
AGILUYZ	GAUZILY	AGINNWZ	WANZING		TARTING
AGIMMNR	RAMMING	AGINNYZ	ZANYING	AGINRTW	RINGTAW
AGIMMNS	SAMMING	AGINOOO	OOGONIA	AGINRTY	GIANTRY
AGIMMSS	MAGISMS	AGINOOP	POGONIA	AGINRUW	WAURING
AGIMNNN	MANNING	AGINOPR	PIGNORA	AGINRVY	VARYING
AGIMNNO	MOANING		PORANGI	AGINRWY	RINGWAY
AGIMNNR	RINGMAN	AGINOPS	SOAPING	AGINRZZ	RAZZING
AGIMNNS	NAMINGS	AGINORR	ROARING	AGINSSS	ASSIGNS
AGIMNNW	WINGMAN	AGINORS	IGNAROS		SASSING
AGIMNOR	ROAMING		ORIGANS	AGINSSU	SAGUINS
AGIMNOT	MOATING		SIGNORA	AGINSSV	SAVINGS
AGIMNOV	AMOVING		SOARING	AGINSSW	SAWINGS
AGIMNPP	MAPPING	AGINORT	ORATING	AGINSSY	SAYINGS
AGIMNPR	GRIPMAN		ROATING	AGINSTT	STATING
	RAMPING	AGINORZ	ZINGARO		TASTING
AGIMNPT	TAMPING	AGINOSS	SAGOINS	AGINSTU	SAUTING
AGIMNPV	VAMPING	AGINOST	AGONIST	AGINSTV	STAVING

AGINSTW	STAWING
	TAWINGS
	TAWSING
	WASTING
AGINSTX	TAXINGS
AGINSTY	STAYING
	STYGIAN
AGINSUX	GUANXIS
AGINSVW	WAVINGS
AGINSWX	WAXINGS
AGINSWY	SWAYING
AGINTTT	TATTING
AGINTTU	TATUING
	TAUTING
AGINTTV	VATTING
AGINTTW	TAWTING
AGINTUV	VAUTING
AGINTVW	VAWTING
AGINTXY	TAXYING
AGINTYZ	TZIGANY
AGINVYZ	AVYZING
AGINWWX	WAXWING
AGIOPPT	AGITPOP
AGIOPSS	GAPOSIS
AGIORST	AGISTOR
	ORGIAST
AGIORSU	GIAOURS
AGIORSV	VIRAGOS
AGIOSTU	AGOUTIS
AGIOUUV	OUGUIYA
AGIRSTU	GUITARS
AGIRTVY	GRAVITY
AGISTTW	WITGATS
AGISTUV	VAGITUS
AGJLMOS	LOGJAMS
AGJLRUU	JUGULAR
AGJNOOR	JARGOON
AGJNORS	JARGONS
AGJNORY	JARGONY
AGJSTTY	GYTTJAS
AGKLNNO	ANKLONG
AGKLNNU	ANKLUNG
AGKLNOS	KALONGS
AGKLOOS	KAGOOLS
AGKLOST	KGOTLAS
AGKLOSU	KAGOULS
AGKMNOP	KAMPONG
AGKMPRU	PUGMARK
AGKNOPT	PAKTONG
AGKNRSU	KURGANS
AGKORRW	RAGWORK
AGLLNOO	GALLOON
AGLLNOS	GALLONS
	GOLLANS
AGLLNTU	GALLNUT
	NUTGALL
AGLLOOR	ROGALLO
AGLLOOT	GALLOOT
AGLLOPS	GALLOPS
AGLLOPU	PLUGOLA
AGLLORS	GOLLARS
AGLLOSS	GLOSSAL
AGLLOSU	GALLOUS
AGLLOSW	GALLOWS
AGLLOTT	GLOTTAL
AGLLPTY	GLYPTAL
AGLLRSY	ARGYLLS
AGLLRYY	GYRALLY
AGLMMSY	GYMMALS
AGLMOPY	POLYGAM
AGLMORS	GLAMORS
AGLMORU	GLAMOUR
AGLNNOS	LONGANS
AGLNNSU	LUNGANS
AGLNOOO	OLOGOAN
AGLNOOS	LAGOONS
AGLNORU	LANGUOR
AGLNOSS	SLOGANS
AGLNOST	ALONGST
AGLNOSU	LANUGOS
AGLNOSW	GOWLANS
AGLNPSY	SPANGLY
AGLNPUY	GUNPLAY
AGLNRSU	LANGURS
AGLNRUU	UNGULAR
AGLNTUY	GAUNTLY
AGLOOPS	APOLOGS
AGLOOPY	APOLOGY
AGLOORS	GOORALS
AGLOOST	GALOOTS
AGLORSU	RUGOLAS
AGLOSSS	GLOSSAS
AGLOSSW	SAWLOGS
AGLOSUV	VALGOUS
AGLOSWY	LOGWAYS
AGLRSSU	GUSLARS
AGLRSUU	ARGULUS
AGLRSUV	VULGARS
AGLSYYZ	SYZYGAL
AGMMNOS	GAMMONS
AGMMNSU	MAGNUMS
AGMMORY	MYOGRAM
AGMNNOR	GRANNOM
AGMNNOS	MAGNONS
	SONGMAN
AGMNNOT	TONGMAN
AGMNNOW	GOWNMAN
AGMNORS	MORGANS
AGMNORU	ORGANUM
AGMNOST	AMONGST
AGMNSSU	MUSANGS
AGMNSTU	MUSTANG
AGMNSTY	GYMNAST
	SYNTAGM
AGMNSYY	SYNGAMY
AGMOOYZ	ZOOGAMY
AGMOPRR	PROGRAM
AGMOPRU	GOPURAM
AGMORRW	RAGWORM
AGMORSS	ORGASMS
AGMORSV	VAGROMS
AGMORSY	MORGAYS
AGMOSYZ	ZYGOMAS
AGMPRSU	GRAMPUS
AGMPSUZ	GAZUMPS
AGMRSSU	GRASSUM
AGNNNOO	NONAGON
AGNNOOR	ARGONON
	ORGANON
AGNNOST	TONNAGS
AGNNOSY	NONGAYS
AGNNSSU	UNSNAGS
AGNNSTU	TANGUNS
AGNNSUW	WANGUNS
AGNOOSZ	GAZOONS
AGNOQSU	QUANGOS
AGNORRS	GARRONS
AGNORRT	GRANTOR
AGNORSS	SARONGS
AGNORSU	OURANGS
AGNORTU	OUTRANG
AGNOSSS	GOSSANS
AGNOSST	SONTAGS
AGNOSTU	NOUGATS
	OUTSANG
AGNOSZZ	GOZZANS
AGNOTUW	OUTGNAW
AGNPRSS	SPRANGS
AGNRSSU	SUNGARS
AGNRTUY	GAUNTRY
AGOPPST	STOPGAP
AGOPRST	RAGTOPS
AGOPRSU	GOPURAS
AGORRST	GARROTS
AGORRTW	RAGWORT
AGORRTY	GYRATOR
AGORSSU	RUGOSAS
AGORSTU	RAGOUTS
AGORTUY	GRAYOUT
AGOSTTU	TAUTOGS
AGOSUYZ	AZYGOUS
AGSSTUU	AUGUSTS
AHHHISS	HASHISH
AHHIIMS	HAIMISH
AHHIJRS	HIJRAHS
AHHIKKR	KHIRKAH
AHHIKSS	SHAIKHS
AHHIKSW	HAWKISH
AHHIMNU	HAHNIUM
AHHINST	SHANTIH
AHHIPRS	RHAPHIS
AHHISSS	SHISHAS
AHHISSV	SHIVAHS
AHHISTT	SHITTAH
AHHKOOS	HOOKAHS
AHHLLOT	HALLOTH
AHHLRSY	HARSHLY
AHHMPRU	HARUMPH
AHHOORS	HOORAHS
AHHOPRS	SHOPHAR
AHHPPSU	HUPPAHS
AHHPTUZ	HUTZPAH
AHHRRSU	HURRAHS
AHHSUZZ	HUZZAHS
AHIIKPS	PAKIHIS
AHIIKRS	RIKISHA
	SHIKARI
AHIILPS	SILPHIA
AHIILST	LITHIAS
AHIIMNT	THIAMIN
AHIIMSS	SASHIMI
AHIIMST	SAMITHI

AHIINPR	HAIRPIN		THULIAS	AHIPSWY	SHIPWAY
AHIINST	TAHINIS	AHILSTY	HASTILY	AHIRRSS	SHIRRAS
AHIINTU	HUITAIN	AHILSWY	WASHILY		SIRRAHS
AHIINTZ	THIAZIN	AHILSYZ	LAZYISH	AHIRRST	STIRRAH
AHIIPRS	AIRSHIP	AHIMMRS	RAMMISH	AHIRRSW	WIRRAHS
AHIIRTW	TAWHIRI	AHIMNNS	MANNISH	AHIRSST	HAIRSTS
AHIKKSS	KISHKAS	AHIMNNU	INHUMAN	AHIRSTT	ATHIRST
AHIKLPS	KALIPHS	AHIMNOT	MANIHOT		RATTISH
AHIKLRS	LARKISH	AHIMNPS	SHIPMAN		TARTISH
AHIKLSS	SHASLIK	AHIMNRS	HARMINS	AHIRSTW	TRISHAW
AHIKLST	KHILATS	AHIMOPR	MORPHIA		WRAITHS
AHIKLSY	SHAKILY	AHIMORS	MOHAIRS	AHISSTT	STAITHS
AHIKMNS	KHAMSIN	AHIMORZ	RHIZOMA	AHISSTU	SHIATSU
AHIKMRS	KASHMIR	AHIMOSS	SHAMOIS		THIASUS
AHIKMSV	MIKVAHS	AHIMPSS	MISHAPS		
AHIKMSW	MAWKISH		PASHIMS	AHISSTW	WHATSIS
AHIKNRS	RANKISH	AHIMPST	MISHAPT	AHISTTW	WHATSIT
AHIKNSS	SNAKISH	AHIMPSV	VAMPISH	AHISTUZ	SHIATZU
AHIKNSV	KNAVISH	AHIMPSW	WAMPISH	AHITTWW	WHITTAW
AHIKORS	KAROSHI	AHIMRSS	MAHSIRS	AHJOOPS	POOJAHS
AHIKOSW	KOWHAIS	AHIMRST	THAIRMS	AHKKSSU	SUKKAHS
AHIKPRS	PARKISH		THIRAMS	AHKLOOS	KOOLAHS
AHIKRSS	SHIKARS		THRIMSA	AHKLPSU	PULKHAS
AHIKRSW	RIKSHAW	AHIMRSW	WARMISH	AHKMNSU	KHANUMS
AHIKSSS	SHIKSAS	AHIMSSU	HASSIUM	AHKMORR	MARKHOR
AHIKSST	SKAITHS	AHIMSTV	MITSVAH	AHKMOSS	MOKSHAS
AHILLNO	HALLION	AHIMTUZ	AZIMUTH	AHKMOSW	MOHAWKS
AHILLNP	PHALLIN	AHIMTVZ	MITZVAH	AHKMRTU	MUKHTAR
AHILLNT	ANTHILL	AHINNST	TANNISH	AHKNPSU	PUNKAHS
AHILLOS	HILLOAS	AHINNSW	WANNISH	AHKPSUU	HAPUKUS
AHILLRT	ATHRILL	AHINNTX	XANTHIN	AHKRSST	SKARTHS
AHILLSS	SHALLIS	AHINORT	ORTHIAN	AHKRSSU	KASHRUS
AHILLST	TALLISH	AHINOTZ	HOATZIN	AHKRSTU	KASHRUT
AHILLSZ	ZILLAHS	AHINPRS	HARPINS		KHURTAS
AHILLTT	TALLITH	AHINPST	HATPINS		TUSHKAR
AHILLTY	LAITHLY	AHINRSS	ARSHINS	AHLLMOS	MOLLAHS
AHILMMO	MOHALIM		SHAIRNS		OLLAMHS
AHILMMS	MASHLIM	AHINRST	TARNISH	AHLLMSU	MULLAHS
AHILMMY	HAMMILY	AHINRSU	UNHAIRS	AHLLNOS	SHALLON
AHILMNS	MASHLIN	AHINRSV	VARNISH	AHLLNOY	HALLYON
AHILMOP	OMPHALI	AHINRTY	RHYTINA	AHLLNSU	NULLAHS
AHILMOS	HOLMIAS	AHINRVY	HRYVNIA	AHLLOOS	HALLOOS
AHILMOT	HALIMOT	AHINSST	SHANTIS		HOLLOAS
AHILMOU	HALOUMI	AHINSSW	WASHINS	AHLLOPS	SHALLOP
AHILMSU	ALUMISH	AHINSTU	INHAUST	AHLLOST	SHALLOT
AHILNPS	PLANISH	AHINSYZ	ZANYISH	AHLLOSU	HULLOAS
AHILNRS	SHRINAL	AHINTUU	TAUHINU	AHLLOSW	HALLOWS
AHILNRT	INTHRAL	AHIOOST	ATISHOO		SHALLOW
AHILNSS	LASHINS	AHIOPRU	OPHIURA	AHLLOTY	LOATHLY
AHILNSU	INHAULS	AHIOPXY	HYPOXIA		TALLYHO
AHILNSY	HYALINS	AHIORSS	ORISHAS	AHLLPSU	PHALLUS
	LINHAYS	AHIORST	AIRSHOT	AHLLPSY	ALPHYLS
AHILORY	HOARILY		SHORTIA	AHLLPYY	APHYLLY
AHILOTY	ALIYOTH		THORIAS	AHLLRST	THRALLS
AHILOTZ	THIAZOL	AHIORSV	HAVIORS	AHLLSTU	THALLUS
AHILPPS	PALSHIP	AHIORSW	AIRSHOW	AHLMMSU	MASHLUM
	SHIPLAP	AHIORUV	HAVIOUR	AHLMNPY	NYMPHAL
AHILPPY	HAPPILY	AHIPRSS	RASPISH	AHLMNSY	HYMNALS
AHILPRT	PHILTRA	AHIPRST	HARPIST	AHLMNUY	HUMANLY
AHILPSY	APISHLY	AHIPRSU	RUPIAHS	AHLMOOS	MOOLAHS
AHILSST	SALTISH	AHIPRSW	WARSHIP	AHLMORU	HUMORAL
	TAHSILS	AHIPRWY	WHIPRAY	AHLMOSS	SHALOMS
AHILSSV	SLAVISH	AHIPSSW	WASPISH	AHLMSTZ	SHMALTZ
AHILSTU	HALITUS	AHIPSWW	WHIPSAW	AHLMSUU	HAMULUS
				AHLNOPR	ALPHORN

AHLNOPT	HAPLONT	AHOPRSS	PHASORS	AIILRST	LIATRIS
	NAPHTOL	AHOPRTY	ATROPHY	AIILRTV	TRIVIAL
AHLNORT	ALTHORN	AHOPSTW	WASHPOT		VITRAIL
AHLOOPS	HOOPLAS	AHOPTTW	TOWPATH	AIIMMNS	ANIMISM
AHLOOPW	WHOOPLA	AHORRSW	HARROWS	AIIMMNX	MAXIMIN
AHLOOTW	WOOLHAT	AHORSTT	THROATS		MINIMAX
AHLORST	HARLOTS	AHORSTU	AUTHORS	AIIMMSS	MISAIMS
AHLOSST	SHALOTS	AHORSTW	WROATHS	AIIMNNV	MINIVAN
AHLOSTU	OUTLASH	AHORTTY	THROATY	AIIMNOR	AMORINI
AHLOTUU	OUTHAUL	AHOSTUW	OUTWASH	AIIMNPS	PAINIMS
AHLPRSY	SHARPLY		WASHOUT		PIANISM
AHLPRUY	HYPURAL	AHPRRTY	PHRATRY	AIIMNPT	IMPAINT
AHLPSSU	SULPHAS	AHPRSST	SPARTHS		TIMPANI
AHLPSSY	SPLASHY	AHPSSUW	WASHUPS	AIIMNRT	MARTINI
AHMMMOT	MAMMOTH	AHPSTUZ	HUTZPAS	AIIMNSS	SAIMINS
AHMMMUU	HUMMAUM	AHPSXYY	ASPHYXY		SIMIANS
AHMMOSS	SHAMMOS	AHQSSUY	SQUASHY	AIIMNST	ANIMIST
AHMMOSW	WHAMMOS	AHRRSUY	HURRAYS		INTIMAS
AHMNNSU	NUMNAHS	AHRSSSU	HUSSARS		SANTIMI
AHMNNTU	MANHUNT	AHRSSTT	STRATHS	AIIMNTT	IMITANT
AHMNNUU	UNHUMAN	AHRSSTW	SWARTHS	AIIMNTU	MINUTIA
AHMNOPS	SHOPMAN	AHRSTTW	THWARTS	AIIMNTV	VITAMIN
AHMNOPT	PHANTOM	AHRSTWY	SWARTHY	AIIMNTY	AMINITY
AHMNORY	HARMONY	AHRTUWY	THRUWAY	AIIMPRS	IMPAIRS
AHMNOSS	HANSOMS	AHSSSTU	TUSSAHS	AIIMPSS	SIMPAIS
AHMNOSW	SHOWMAN	AIIILMT	MILITIA	AIIMRST	SIMITAR
AHMNRSU	RHAMNUS	AIIILNT	INITIAL	AIIMSST	SAMITIS
AHMNRVY	HYMNARY	AIIILVX	LIXIVIA	AIIMSSY	MYIASIS
AHMOOPS	OOMPAHS	AIIIMRS	SAIMIRI	AIINNOP	PIANINO
	SHAMPOO	AIIKKSW	WAKIKIS	AIINNQU	QUININA
AHMOOSS	SAMSHOO	AIIKMMS	SKIMMIA	AIINNSZ	ZINNIAS
AHMORRU	MORRHUA	AIIKMNN	MANIKIN	AIINNTY	INANITY
AHMORST	HARMOST	AIIKNNT	TANKINI	AIINOPS	SINOPIA
AHMORSZ	MAHZORS	AIIKNST	KAINITS	AIINOTT	NOTITIA
AHMOSSY	SHAMOYS	AIIKRRU	RAURIKI	AIINPPR	RAPPINI
AHMOSTU	MAHOUTS	AIIKRTT	TRAIKIT	AIINPRS	ASPIRIN
AHMOSTZ	MATZOHS	AIILLLP	LAPILLI	AIINPST	PIANIST
AHMOSWY	HAYMOWS	AIILLMN	LIMINAL	AIINRSS	RAISINS
AHMOTTZ	MATZOTH	AIILLMS	LIMAILS	AIINRSY	RAISINY
AHMPSSU	MASHUPS	AIILLMW	WILLIAM	AIINRTV	VITRAIN
	SMASHUP	AIILLNV	VILLAIN	AIINRTZ	TRIAZIN
AHMRRSU	MURRHAS	AIILLQU	QUILLAI	AIINSST	ISATINS
AHMRSTW	WARMTHS	AIILLUV	ILLUVIA	AIINSSX	SIXAINS
AHMRSTY	THRYMSA	AIILMMN	MINIMAL	AIINSTT	TITANIS
AHMSSSU	SAMSHUS	AIILMNN	LAMININ		TITIANS
AHNNSSU	SUNNAHS	AIILMNO	MONILIA	AIINSTV	NAIVIST
AHNOOPR	HARPOON	AIILMNS	MISLAIN	AIIPRST	PIARIST
AHNOPRS	ORPHANS	AIILMNT	INTIMAL	AIIPSTW	WAPITIS
AHNORSS	SHORANS	AIILMNV	VIMINAL	AIIPTTU	PITUITA
AHNORSX	SAXHORN	AIILMRS	SIMILAR	AIISTUW	TAUIWIS
AHNOTTW	WHATNOT	AIILMRT	MILITAR	AIJJMMS	JIMJAMS
AHNPPSS	SHNAPPS	AIILMRY	MILIARY	AIJLORS	JAILORS
AHNPPUU	PUPUNHA	AIILNNS	ANILINS	AIJLORT	TOLARJI
AHNPPUY	UNHAPPY	AIILNOS	LIAISON	AIJLSTW	WILTJAS
AHNPRSU	UNSHARP	AIILNPT	PINTAIL	AIJLYZZ	JAZZILY
AHNPRXY	PHARYNX	AIILNPU	NAUPLII	AIJMNSS	JASMINS
AHNPSSU	UNHASPS	AIILNRY	RAINILY	AIJMORS	ROMAJIS
AHNRSVY	HRYVNAS	AIILNTU	NAUTILI	AIJNORT	JANITOR
AHNRVYY	HRYVNYA	AIILNTV	INVITAL	AIJORSW	JOWARIS
AHNSSTU	SUNHATS	AIILNTY	ANILITY	AIJPSTU	JUPATIS
AHNSTUW	UNTHAWS	AIILOPP	PAPILIO	AIKKMNR	KIRKMAN
AHNSTUY	UNHASTY	AIILORV	RAVIOLI	AIKKMOT	KOMATIK
AHOORSS	SHOORAS	AIILPRU	LIPURIA	AIKKOOW	KOKOWAI
AHOORSY	HOORAYS	AIILQSU	SILIQUA	AIKKOPY	KOPIYKA

AIKKSUZ	ZAKUSKI	AILLQSU	SQUILLA		SPINULA
AIKLLNY	LANKILY	AILLRSU	ARILLUS	AILNPSX	SALPINX
AIKLMMN	MILKMAN	AILLRVY	VIRALLY	AILNPTU	NUPTIAL
AIKLMNN	LINKMAN	AILLSTT	TALLITS		PATULIN
AIKLMNS	MALKINS	AILLSTY	SALTILY		UNPLAIT
AIKLMPU	LAMPUKI	AILLSUZ	LAZULIS	AILNPTY	INAPTLY
AIKLMSS	MISKALS	AILLTVY	VITALLY		PTYALIN
AIKLMSU	KALIUMS	AILLTWW	WITWALL	AILNPUV	PLUVIAN
AIKLNOS	KAOLINS	AILMMOR	IMMORAL	AILNQTU	QUINTAL
AIKLNSY	SNAKILY	AILMMSS	MALISMS	AILNRST	RATLINS
AIKLPWY	PAWKILY	AILMMSY	MYALISM	AILNRSU	INSULAR
AIKLQUY	QUAKILY	AILMMUU	ALUMIUM		URINALS
AIKLRTT	TITLARK	AILMMUW	MWALIMU	AILNRTT	RATTLIN
AIKLSSU	SALUKIS	AILMNNO	NOMINAL	AILNRTY	RIANTLY
AIKLSSY	SKYSAIL	AILMNOP	LAMPION	AILNSST	INSTALS
AIKMMRS	MISMARK	AILMNOS	MALISON	AILNSSU	INSULAS
AIKMMSS	IMMASKS		MONIALS	AILNSSV	SILVANS
AIKMNNS	KINSMAN		SOMNIAL	AILNSTT	LATTINS
AIKMNRS	RANKISM	AILMNOY	ALIMONY	AILNSTU	UNALIST
AIKMNSS	KAMSINS	AILMNPS	MISPLAN	AILNSTY	NASTILY
AIKMNSW	MAWKINS		PLASMIN		SAINTLY
AIKMOOS	OOMIAKS	AILMNPT	IMPLANT	AILNSUV	UNVAILS
AIKMPRS	IMPARKS	AILMNPU	ULPANIM	AILNTTY	NATTILY
AIKMRSU	KUMARIS	AILMNRS	MARLINS	AILNTUV	UNVITAL
	RUMAKIS	AILMNRU	MURLAIN	AILNTWY	TAWNILY
AIKMSST	KISMATS		RUMINAL	AILOORS	OORALIS
AIKNNNS	NANKINS	AILMNSS	MASLINS		OORIALS
AIKNNPS	NAPKINS	AILMNSU	ALUMINS	AILOORW	WOORALI
AIKNOST	KATIONS	AILMOOV	MOVIOLA	AILOPST	APOSTIL
AIKNPRS	KIRPANS	AILMOPS	LIPOMAS		TOPSAIL
	PARKINS	AILMOPT	OPTIMAL	AILOPSY	SOAPILY
AIKNPSS	PANISKS	AILMORS	ORALISM	AILOPTT	TALIPOT
AIKNRST	KIRTANS	AILMOST	SOMITAL	AILOPTV	PIVOTAL
AIKNSTU	TANUKIS	AILMOSY	ISOAMYL	AILOQTU	ALIQUOT
AIKOORT	ROOIKAT	AILMPRS	IMPARLS	AILORSS	SAILORS
AIKOORW	KOROWAI	AILMPRU	PRIMULA	AILORST	ORALIST
AIKOPST	KATIPOS	AILMPST	PALMIST		RIALTOS
AIKORST	TROIKAS	AILMPSY	MISPLAY		SLIOTAR
AIKOSTW	KWAITOS	AILMRST	MISTRAL		TAILORS
AIKRRSS	SIRKARS		RAMTILS	AILORSU	OURALIS
AIKRSST	STRAIKS	AILMRSU	SIMULAR	AILORTY	ORALITY
AIKRTUZ	ZIKURAT	AILMSSS	MISSALS	AILORUW	WOURALI
AILLLNO	LINALOL	AILMSST	MISTALS	AILORUX	UXORIAL
AILLMNU	LUMINAL	AILMSSX	LAXISMS	AILORVY	OLIVARY
AILLMNY	MANLILY	AILMSSY	MISLAYS	AILOSSS	ASSOILS
AILLMOT	MAILLOT	AILMSTU	ULTIMAS	AILOSTT	ALTOIST
AILLMPU	PALLIUM	AILMSTY	MYALIST	AILOSTU	OUTSAIL
AILLMSU	ALLIUMS	AILMSUV	MAULVIS	AILOSTX	OXTAILS
AILLMSW	SAWMILL	AILNNOS	SOLANIN	AILOSWY	OILWAYS
AILLMSY	MISALLY	AILNNOT	ANTLION	AILOTVY	OVALITY
AILLNNO	LANOLIN	AILNNPU	PINNULA	AILPPRU	PUPILAR
AILLNOP	PAILLON	AILNNSU	UNNAILS	AILPPSU	SUIPLAP
AILLNPY	PLAINLY		UNSLAIN	AILPPSY	PAYSLIP
AILLNST	INSTALL	AILNOPY	POLYNIA		SAPPILY
AILLNSV	VILLANS	AILNOQU	AQUILON	AILPPTY	PLATYPI
AILLNSW	INWALLS	AILNOSS	ALISONS	AILPQSU	PASQUIL
AILLNVY	VILLANY		SIALONS	AILPRSS	SPIRALS
AILLORT	LITORAL	AILNOST	LATINOS	AILPRSU	PARULIS
AILLORZ	ZORILLA		TALIONS		SPIRULA
AILLPRS	PILLARS	AILNOTU	OUTLAIN		UPRISAL
AILLPRU	PILULAR	AILNPRW	PRAWLIN	AILPRSY	PYRALIS
AILLPSU	PILLAUS	AILNPSS	SPINALS	AILPSST	PASTILS
	PILULAS	AILNPST	PLAINTS		SPITALS
AILLPUV	PLUVIAL	AILNPSU	PAULINS	AILPSTU	TIPULAS

AILPSTY	PASTILY	AIMNRTV	VARMINT	AINOPSS	PASSION
AILPSWY	SLIPWAY	AIMNRUU	URANIUM	AINOPTT	ANTIPOT
	WASPILY	AIMNSST	SANTIMS	AINOPTU	OPUNTIA
AILQSSU	SQUAILS	AIMNSTT	MATTINS		UTOPIAN
AILQTTU	QUITTAL	AIMNSTU	MANITUS	AINOQSU	QUINOAS
AILQTUY	QUALITY		SANTIMU	AINORST	AROINTS
AILRRVY	RIVALRY		TSUNAMI		RATIONS
AILRSTT	STARLIT	AIMNSUV	MAUVINS	AINORSW	WARISON
AILRSTU	RITUALS	AIMNSUZ	MIZUNAS	AINORTU	RAINOUT
	TRISULA	AIMNSVY	MAYVINS	AINORTW	WAITRON
AILRSTY	TRYSAIL	AIMNSYZ	ZANYISM	AINORTX	TRIAXON
AILRTTU	TITULAR	AIMOPST	IMPASTO	AINOSSU	SANIOUS
AILRTTY	RATTILY		MATIPOS		SUASION
	TARTILY	AIMOPSY	MYOPIAS	AINOSTT	STATION
AILRTUV	VIRTUAL	AIMORRU	ORARIUM	AINOSUX	ANXIOUS
	VITULAR	AIMORST	AMORIST	AINOSVY	SYNOVIA
AILSSSY	SASSILY	AIMORTT	TRITOMA	AINPPRS	PARSNIP
AILSSTU	TISSUAL	AIMORUZ	ZOARIUM	AINPQTU	PIQUANT
AILSSTX	LAXISTS	AIMOSTT	ATOMIST	AINPRSS	SPINARS
AILSSUV	VISUALS	AIMPPSS	PAPISMS		SPRAINS
AILSSVY	SYLVIAS	AIMPPST	MAPPIST	AINPRST	SPIRANT
AILSSVZ	VIZSLAS	AIMPRRY	PRIMARY		SPRAINT
AILSTTY	TASTILY	AIMPRST	ARMPITS	AINPRSU	PRUINAS
AILSTUW	LAWSUIT		IMPARTS	AINPRSW	INWRAPS
AILSVVY	SAVVILY		MISPART		RIPSAWN
AILTTTY	TATTILY	AIMPRSY	PYRAMIS	AINPRTT	TRIPTAN
AIMMMSU	MUMMIAS	AIMQRSU	MARQUIS	AINPRTU	PURITAN
AIMMMUX	MAXIMUM	AIMRSST	TSARISM		UPTRAIN
AIMMNTU	MANUMIT	AIMRSTU	ATRIUMS	AINPSST	PISSANT
AIMMORS	AMORISM		MATSURI		PTISANS
AIMMOSS	MIMOSAS	AIMRSTY	MAISTRY	AINPSSV	SPAVINS
AIMMOST	ATOMISM		SYMITAR	AINPSTU	TIPUNAS
AIMMSUX	MAXIMUS	AIMRSTZ	TZARISM	AINQRST	QINTARS
AIMNNOR	IRONMAN	AIMRSSY	MISSAYS	AINQRTU	QUINTAR
AIMNNOS	AMNIONS	AIMSSTT	STATISM	AINQRUY	QUINARY
	MANSION	AIMSSTU	AUTISMS	AINQSSU	QUASSIN
	ONANISM	AINNNST	TANNINS	AINQSTU	ASQUINT
AIMNNSS	NANISMS	AINNNOPS	SAPONIN		QUINTAS
AIMNNSY	MINYANS	AINNOPT	PINTANO	AINQSUY	YANQUIS
AIMNOOR	AMORINO	AINNOSS	NASIONS	AINRRTY	TRINARY
AIMNOOT	AMOTION	AINNOST	ANOINTS	AINRRUY	URINARY
AIMNOPR	RAMPION		NATIONS	AINRSST	INSTARS
AIMNOPS	MOPANIS		ONANIST		SANTIRS
AIMNOPT	MAINTOP	AINNOSW	WANIONS		STRAINS
	PTOMAIN	AINNPSS	INSPANS	AINRSTT	STRAINT
	TAMPION	AINNPST	SNAPTIN		TRANSIT
	TIMPANO	AINNPTU	UNPAINT	AINRSTU	NUTRIAS
AIMNOPZ	ZAMPONI	AINNQTU	QUINNAT	AINRTTT	TITRANT
AIMNORS	MAINORS		QUINTAN	AINRTUY	UNITARY
AIMNORT	TORMINA	AINNRSU	URANINS	AINSSTT	STATINS
AIMNORU	MAINOUR	AINNRTT	INTRANT		TANISTS
AIMNOST	MANITOS	AINNRTU	URINANT	AINSSTU	ISSUANT
	STAMNOI	AINNSTT	INSTANT		SUSTAIN
AIMNOTU	MANITOU	AINNSTU	UNSAINT	AINSSXY	SYNAXIS
	TINAMOU	AINNTUY	ANNUITY	AINTTVY	TANTIVY
AIMNPST	PITMANS	AINOOPR	PRONAOI	AIOORRW	WOORARI
AIMNPSW	IMPAWNS	AINOORR	ORARION	AIOORSS	ARIOSOS
AIMNPSY	PAYNIMS	AINOORT	ORATION	AIOPPRR	PROPRIA
AIMNPTY	TYMPANI	AINOOTV	OVATION	AIOPRRT	AIRPORT
AIMNRRU	MURRAIN	AINOPPT	APPOINT		PARITOR
AIMNRST	MARTINS	AINOPRS	PARISON	AIOPRST	AIRPOST
AIMNRSU	SURAMIN		PORINAS		AIRSTOP
	URANISM		SOPRANI		PAROTIS
AIMNRTU	NATRIUM	AINOPRT	ATROPIN	AIOPRSV	PAVIORS

AIOPRTT	PATRIOT	**AJLOORS**	JAROOLS	**ALLMNOY**	ALLONYM
AIOPRTY	TOPIARY	**AJLOPPY**	JALOPPY	**ALLMNPU**	PULLMAN
AIOPRUV	PAVIOUR	**AJMNRUY**	JURYMAN	**ALLMOOS**	OSMOLAL
AIOPSTU	UTOPIAS	**AJMOPST**	JAMPOTS	**ALLMORS**	MORALLS
AIORRRW	WARRIOR	**AJMRSTU**	JUMARTS	**ALLMORY**	MORALLY
AIORRSU	OURARIS	**AJNRSTU**	JURANTS	**ALLMOSS**	SLALOMS
AIORRTT	TRAITOR	**AKKKOOS**	KOKAKOS	**ALLMOST**	MALTOLS
AIORRTX	ORATRIX	**AKKKORU**	ROKKAKU	**ALLMOSW**	MALLOWS
AIORSST	AORISTS	**AKKLRSY**	SKYLARK	**ALLMPUU**	PLUMULA
	ARISTOS	**AKKLSWY**	SKYWALK	**ALLMSUV**	VALLUMS
	SATORIS	**AKKMOOT**	TOKOMAK	**ALLNOPS**	POLLANS
AIORSSU	SOUARIS	**AKKNRSU**	KUNKARS	**ALLNOTY**	TONALLY
AIORSSV	SAVIORS	**AKKOOPS**	PAKOKOS	**ALLNOYZ**	ZONALLY
AIORSTU	SAUTOIR	**AKKOQSU**	QUOKKAS	**ALLNRUU**	LUNULAR
AIORSTV	TRAVOIS	**AKLMMSU**	MAMLUKS	**ALLNSTY**	SLANTLY
	VIATORS	**AKLNOSU**	KOULANS	**ALLNTUU**	ULULANT
AIORSTY	OSTIARY	**AKLNOSX**	KLAXONS	**ALLOOPS**	APOLLOS
AIORSUV	SAVIOUR	**AKLOPRW**	LAPWORK		PALOLOS
	VARIOUS	**AKLOSST**	SKATOLS	**ALLOOST**	LATOSOL
AIOSSTT	TATSOIS	**AKLOSTW**	KOTWALS	**ALLOOTX**	AXOLOTL
AIOSSYZ	ZOYSIAS	**AKLOTTU**	OUTTALK	**ALLOPRS**	PALLORS
AIOTTUW	OUTWAIT	**AKLOTUW**	OUTWALK	**ALLOPRY**	PAYROLL
AIPPRRS	RIPRAPS		WALKOUT	**ALLOPSW**	WALLOPS
AIPPRSU	PRIAPUS	**AKLPRSY**	SPARKLY	**ALLORSS**	SOLLARS
AIPPSST	PAPISTS	**AKLPSTU**	UPTALKS	**ALLORWY**	ROLLWAY
AIPRRTT	TRIPART	**AKLPSUW**	WALKUPS	**ALLORYY**	ROYALLY
AIPRSST	RAPISTS	**AKLRSTY**	STARKLY	**ALLOSSW**	SALLOWS
AIPRSSW	RIPSAWS	**AKLRSVY**	VALKYRS	**ALLOSTT**	TALLOTS
AIPRSTU	UPSTAIR	**AKMNORW**	WORKMAN	**ALLOSTV**	LAVOLTS
AIPRSUY	PYURIAS	**AKMNRTU**	TRANKUM	**ALLOSTW**	TALLOWS
AIPRTVY	PRAVITY	**AKMNSSU**	UNMASKS	**ALLOSWW**	SWALLOW
AIPSSTT	TAPISTS	**AKMOORT**	MOOKTAR		WALLOWS
AIPSSTW	PITSAWS	**AKMOOSS**	OAKMOSS	**ALLOSWY**	SALLOWY
	SAWPITS	**AKMORST**	OSTMARK	**ALLOTTY**	TOTALLY
AIPYZZZ	PIZAZZY	**AKMPRSU**	MARKUPS	**ALLOTWY**	TALLOWY
AIPZZZZ	PIZZAZZ	**AKMQTUU**	KUMQUAT		TOLLWAY
AIRRSST	RISTRAS	**AKMRSTU**	MUSKRAT	**ALLOTYY**	LOYALTY
	STIRRAS	**AKMSTUU**	MAKUTUS	**ALLPRSU**	PLURALS
AIRRSZZ	RIZZARS	**AKNNOOS**	NANOOKS	**ALLPSSY**	PSYLLAS
AIRRTZZ	RIZZART	**AKNORSU**	KORUNAS	**ALLQSSU**	SQUALLS
AIRSSSU	RUSSIAS	**AKNORSY**	KARYONS	**ALLQSUY**	SQUALLY
AIRSSTT	ARTISTS		RYOKANS	**ALLRRUY**	RURALLY
	SITTARS	**AKNORTU**	OUTRANK	**ALLRSTU**	LUSTRAL
	STRAITS	**AKOOPRT**	PARTOOK	**ALLRSUY**	LAURYLS
	TSARIST	**AKOORRS**	KAROROS	**ALLSUUY**	USUALLY
AIRSSTU	AURISTS		KARROOS	**ALMMSUW**	WAMMULS
AIRSTTT	ATTRIST		KORORAS	**ALMMSUY**	AMYLUMS
	ATTRITS	**AKOOSTU**	ATOKOUS	**ALMNNUY**	UNMANLY
AIRSTTU	TURISTA	**AKOPRRU**	PARKOUR	**ALMNOOP**	LAMPOON
AIRSTTY	YTTRIAS	**AKORRTW**	ARTWORK	**ALMNOOT**	TOOLMAN
AIRSTTZ	TZARIST	**AKORRWW**	WARWORK	**ALMNOOW**	WOOLMAN
AIRSTVY	VARSITY	**AKORWWX**	WAXWORK	**ALMNOPS**	PLASMON
AIRTUVX	VITRAUX	**AKOSSTU**	OUTASKS	**ALMNOPW**	PLOWMAN
AISSSST	ASSISTS	**AKOSTTU**	OUTTASK	**ALMNORS**	NORMALS
AISSTTT	STATIST	**AKOSTWY**	TOWKAYS	**ALMNORU**	UNMORAL
AISSTTU	AUTISTS	**AKQRSSU**	SQUARKS	**ALMNORY**	ALMONRY
AISTTVY	VASTITY	**AKQSSUW**	SQUAWKS	**ALMNOSS**	SALMONS
AISTUVY	SUAVITY	**AKQSUWY**	SQUAWKY	**ALMNOSU**	MONAULS
AJKMNNU	JUNKMAN	**AKRSSTU**	TUSKARS		SOLANUM
AJKMNTU	MUNTJAK	**AKSSWYY**	SKYWAYS	**ALMNOWY**	WOMANLY
AJKNSSY	JANSKYS	**ALLLOST**	TALLOLS	**ALMNPSU**	SUNLAMP
AJLLRUY	JURALLY	**ALLLOYY**	LOYALLY	**ALMNRSU**	MURLANS
AJLMORY	MAJORLY	**ALLMNOP**	POLLMAN	**ALMNSUU**	ALUMNUS
AJLNORU	JOURNAL	**ALLMNOT**	TOLLMAN	**ALMOOPY**	POLYOMA

ALMOORS	OSMOLAR	ALOPRSU	PARLOUS		ROMANOS
ALMOPPT	PALMTOP	ALOPRSY	PYROLAS	AMNOOTT	OTTOMAN
ALMOPRT	MARPLOT	ALOPSSU	SPOUSAL	AMNOOTZ	MATZOON
ALMORRU	MORULAR	ALOPSUV	VOLUSPA	AMNOPPR	PROPMAN
ALMORSS	SAMLORS	ALOPTUY	OUTPLAY	AMNOPRT	PORTMAN
ALMORST	MORTALS	ALOQRRU	RORQUAL	AMNOPRV	PARONYM
	STROMAL	ALOQRSU	SQUALOR	AMNOPST	POSTMAN
ALMORSU	MORULAS	ALOQSTU	LOQUATS		TAMPONS
ALMORTU	TUMORAL	ALORRST	ROSTRAL		TOPSMAN
ALMOSST	SMALTOS	ALORRSW	WORRALS	AMNOPTU	PANTOUM
ALMOSTW	MATLOWS	ALORSST	SORTALS	AMNOPTY	TYMPANO
ALMOSXY	XYLOMAS	ALORSSU	ROSULAS	AMNORRS	MARRONS
ALMOTTU	MULATTO	ALORSSV	SALVORS	AMNORSS	RAMSONS
ALMRSTY	SMARTLY	ALORSTU	ROTULAS		RANSOMS
ALMRSUU	RAMULUS		TORULAS	AMNORST	MATRONS
ALMRTUU	MUTULAR	ALORSUV	LOUVARS		TRANSOM
	TUMULAR		VALOURS	AMNORSY	MASONRY
ALMSSUY	ALYSSUM	ALORTWW	AWLWORT		MORNAYS
	ASYLUMS	ALORTYY	ROYALTY	AMNORTU	ROMAUNT
ALMSTUU	MUTUALS	ALORUVV	OVULARY	AMNOSST	STAMNOS
	UMLAUTS	ALOSTTU	OUTLAST	AMNOSTU	AMOUNTS
ALNNOOR	NONORAL	ALOSTUW	OUTLAWS		MOUTANS
ALNNOPY	NONPLAY	ALOSTUY	LAYOUTS		OUTMANS
ALNNRSU	UNSNARL		OUTLAYS	AMNOSYZ	ZYMOSAN
ALNNSUU	ANNULUS	ALOSTXY	OXYSALT	AMNOTUY	AUTONYM
ALNOOPR	POLARON	ALPRRSU	LARRUPS	AMNPSTY	TYMPANS
ALNOOPT	PLATOON	ALPRSSU	PULSARS	AMNPTYY	TYMPANY
ALNOOPV	VANPOOL	ALPRSSW	SPRAWLS	AMNQTUU	QUANTUM
ALNOORT	ORTOLAN	ALPRSTY	PSALTRY	AMNRRUY	UNMARRY
ALNOOSS	SALOONS	ALPRSUU	PURSUAL	AMNRSTU	ANTRUMS
	SOLANOS	ALPRSUW	PULWARS		UNSMART
ALNOPPY	PANOPLY	ALPRSWY	SPRAWLY	AMNRTTU	TANTRUM
ALNOPRS	PROLANS	ALQSTUY	SQUATLY	AMNSTTU	MUTANTS
ALNOPSS	SPONSAL	ALRSSUU	RUSSULA	AMNSTUU	AUTUMNS
ALNOPTU	OUTPLAN	ALRSTTY	STARTLY	AMNTUUY	AUTUMNY
ALNOPYY	POLYNYA	ALRSTUU	SUTURAL	AMOOORS	AMOROSO
ALNORST	LATRONS	ALRSTUW	TULWARS	AMOOPRS	PROSOMA
ALNORSU	SOLUNAR	ALRSUUV	UVULARS	AMOOPRT	TAPROOM
ALNORUY	UNROYAL	AMMMNOS	MAMMONS	AMOORSU	AMOROUS
ALNORUZ	ZONULAR	AMMMOSU	AMOMUMS	AMOORSV	MOORVAS
ALNOSST	SANTOLS	AMMNOOR	MOORMAN		VAROOMS
	STANOLS	AMMNOOT	MOOTMAN	AMOORXY	OXYMORA
ALNOSUZ	ZONULAS	AMMNOPS	PSAMMON	AMOPPSY	MAYPOPS
ALNPRUY	PLANURY	AMMNRUY	NUMMARY	AMOPSTT	TOPMAST
ALNPSTU	PULSANT	AMMOORR	MAORMOR	AMORRST	MORTARS
	PULTANS		MORMAOR	AMORRSU	ARMOURS
ALNPTUY	UNAPTLY	AMMOPTU	POMATUM	AMORRSW	MARROWS
ALNPTXY	PLANXTY	AMMORST	MARMOTS	AMORRTY	MORTARY
ALNRSUY	URANYLS	AMMOSXY	MYXOMAS	AMORRUY	ARMOURY
ALNSSTU	SULTANS	AMMPSUW	WAMPUMS	AMORRWY	MARROWY
ALNSSVY	SYLVANS	AMMRRSU	MARRUMS	AMORSST	MATROSS
ALNSTUW	WALNUTS		MURRAMS		STROAMS
ALNSUUU	UNUSUAL	AMMRSUY	SUMMARY	AMORSSY	MORASSY
ALOOPSS	SALOOPS	AMMSSTU	SUMMATS	AMORWWX	WAXWORM
ALOOPYZ	POLYZOA	AMNNOOX	MONAXON	AMOSTUW	OUTSWAM
ALOORRS	SORORAL	AMNNORS	NORMANS	AMOSTUZ	MAZOUTS
ALOPPRS	POPLARS	AMNNOSW	SNOWMAN	AMOSUYZ	AZYMOUS
ALOPPRU	POPULAR	AMNNOSY	ANONYMS	AMPRSST	STRAMPS
ALOPPRY	PROPYLA	AMNNOTT	MONTANT	AMPRSUW	UPSWARM
ALOPPST	LAPTOPS	AMNNOTY	ANTONYM		WARMUPS
ALOPRRS	PARLORS	AMNNOUW	UNWOMAN	AMRRSTU	RASTRUM
ALOPRRU	PARLOUR	AMNNSTU	STANNUM	AMRRSTY	MARTYRS
ALOPRST	PATROLS	AMNOOPP	POMPANO	AMRRSUY	MURRAYS
	PORTALS	AMNOORS	MAROONS	AMRRTYY	MARTYRY

AMRSSTU	STRUMAS
AMRSTTU	STRATUM
ANNNOSY	SYNANON
ANNOPRS	NAPRONS
ANNOPSS	SANNOPS
ANNOPST	NONPAST
	PANTONS
ANNOPTY	POYNANT
ANNORST	NATRONS
	NONARTS
ANNORSW	NONWARS
ANNOSST	SANTONS
	SONANTS
ANNOSTW	WANTONS
ANNOSTY	TANNOYS
ANNOTTY	TANTONY
ANNPSSU	SANNUPS
	UNSNAPS
ANNPSTU	PANTUNS
ANNRTYY	TYRANNY
ANNSSTU	SUNTANS
ANNSSTY	SYNTANS
ANOOPRS	PRONAOS
	SOPRANO
ANOOPRT	PATROON
	PRONOTA
ANOORST	RATOONS
	SANTOOR
ANOORTT	ARNOTTO
	RATTOON
ANOPRRS	SPORRAN
ANOPRSS	PARSONS
	SANPROS
ANOPRST	PARTONS
	PATRONS
	TARPONS
ANOPRSW	PAWNORS
ANOPRTV	PROVANT
ANOPSTT	OPTANTS
ANOPSTU	OUTSPAN
ANOPSUY	YAUPONS
ANORRSW	NARROWS
ANORRWW	WARWORN
ANORSSV	SOVRANS
ANORSTT	ATTORNS
	RATTONS
	ROTTANS
ANORSTU	ROUSANT
	SANTOUR
ANORSTY	AROYNTS
ANORSUU	ANUROUS
	URANOUS
ANORWWY	WAYWORN
ANOSSTZ	STANZOS
ANOSTTU	TOTANUS
ANPPSUW	SUPPAWN
ANPRSSU	UNSPARS
ANPRSTU	SUNTRAP
	UNSTRAP
ANPRSUW	UNWRAPS
ANPRSUY	UNPRAYS
ANPSSUW	SUPAWNS
ANPSTUU	TUPUNAS
ANRSSTU	SANTURS
	SUNSTAR
ANRSSUY	SUNRAYS
ANRSTTU	TRUANTS
ANRSTTY	TYRANTS
ANRSUWY	RUNWAYS
ANSSTTU	TUTSANS
AOOPPRS	APROPOS
AOOPRTT	TAPROOT
AOORRST	ORATORS
AOORRSY	ARROYOS
AOORRTT	ROTATOR
AOORRTU	OUTROAR
AOORRTY	ORATORY
AOORSTT	TOOARTS
AOORSTU	OUTSOAR
AOORSTV	OVATORS
AOOSTTT	TATTOOS
AOOSTUZ	AZOTOUS
AOOTXYZ	ZOOTAXY
AOPPPSU	PAPPOUS
AOPPRRT	RAPPORT
AOPPRST	APPORTS
AOPRRST	PARROTS
	RAPTORS
AOPRRSU	UPROARS
AOPRRSW	SPARROW
AOPRRTY	PARROTY
	PORTRAY
AOPRSST	ASPORTS
	PASTORS
AOPRSSU	SAPOURS
	UPSOARS
AOPRSTU	ASPROUT
AOPRSTW	POSTWAR
AOPRSUV	VAPOURS
AOPRTTU	OUTPART
AOPRTUY	OUTPRAY
AOPRUVY	VAPOURY
AOPSSTU	OUTPASS
	PASSOUT
AOPSTTX	POSTTAX
AOPSTUY	AUTOPSY
	PAYOUTS
AOPSTWY	WAYPOST
AOPSWWW	POWWAWS
AOPTTUU	AUTOPUT
AOQRSTU	QUARTOS
AORRSST	SARTORS
AORRSSU	ASSUROR
AORRSTW	TARROWS
AORRSWY	SOWARRY
	YARROWS
AORSSST	ASSORTS
AORSSTT	STATORS
AORSSTU	SOUTARS
AORSSUV	SAVOURS
AORSSUY	OSSUARY
	SUASORY
AORSTUW	OUTWARS
AORSTUY	YAOURTS
AORSUVY	SAVOURY
AORTUVY	AVOUTRY
AORUVVY	VOUVRAY
AOSSTUY	OUTSAYS
AOSTTTW	TATTOWS
AOSTTUY	OUTSTAY
APPRRUU	PURPURA
APPRSTY	STRAPPY
APPRSUW	UPWRAPS
APPRSUY	PAPYRUS
APRRTUY	PURTRAY
APRSSSU	SURPASS
APRSSWY	PSYWARS
APRSTTU	STARTUP
	UPSTART
APRSTTY	TAPSTRY
APRSUWY	SPURWAY
APSSTUY	UPSTAYS
APSSUWY	UPSWAYS
AQRTUYZ	QUARTZY
AQSTTUY	SQUATTY
ARSSSTU	TUSSARS
ARSSTTU	STRATUS
ARSSTTY	STARTSY
ASSTTUY	STATUSY
AVYYZZZ	ZYZZYVA
BBBDELO	BLOBBED
	BOBBLED
BBBDELU	BLUBBED
	BUBBLED
BBBEILS	BIBBLES
BBBEIOS	BOBBIES
BBBEIRS	BIBBERS
BBBEIRY	BIBBERY
BBBEISU	BUBBIES
BBBELOS	BOBBLES
BBBELRU	BLUBBER
	BUBBLER
BBBELSU	BUBBLES
BBBEORS	BOBBERS
BBBEORY	BOBBERY
BBBGIIN	BIBBING
BBBGINO	BOBBING
BBBHIOS	BOBBISH
BBBHSUU	HUBBUBS
BBBINOS	BOBBINS
BBBIOTT	BOBBITT
BBCCIKO	BIBCOCK
BBCDEHI	CHIBBED
BBCDEIR	CRIBBED
BBCDELO	COBBLED
BBCDELU	CLUBBED
BBCEEHO	BOBECHE
BBCEEIR	BERBICE
BBCEHIN	NEBBICH
BBCEILR	CRIBBLE
BBCEIOR	COBBIER
BBCEIRR	CRIBBER
BBCEISU	CUBBIES
BBCEKKO	KEBBOCK
BBCEKKU	KEBBUCK
BBCELOR	CLOBBER
	COBBLER
BBCELOS	COBBLES
BBCELRU	CLUBBER
BBCEORS	COBBERS
BBCEOSW	COBWEBS
BBCGINO	COBBING

BBCGINU	CUBBING
BBCHISU	CUBBISH
BBCINOU	BUBONIC
BBCRSUY	SCRUBBY
BBDDEIL	DIBBLED
BBDDEIR	DRIBBED
BBDDERU	DRUBBED
BBDEEIR	DEBBIER
BBDEEIS	DEBBIES
BBDEEIT	EBBTIDE
BBDEELP	PEBBLED
BBDEENS	SNEBBED
BBDEEOR	BEROBED
BBDEFLU	FLUBBED
BBDEGIL	GLIBBED
BBDEGLO	GOBBLED
BBDEGRU	GRUBBED
BBDEGSU	BEDBUGS
BBDEHLO	HOBBLED
BBDEIIM	IMBIBED
BBDEIKL	KIBBLED
BBDEILN	NIBBLED
BBDEILO	BILOBED
	LOBBIED
BBDEILR	DIBBLER
	DRIBBLE
BBDEILS	DIBBLES
BBDEILW	WIBBLED
BBDEINS	SNIBBED
BBDEIOS	DOBBIES
BBDEIRR	DRIBBER
BBDEIRS	DIBBERS
BBDEKNO	KNOBBED
BBDELMO	MOBBLED
BBDELMU	BUMBLED
BBDELNO	NOBBLED
BBDELNU	NUBBLED
BBDELOO	BEBLOOD
BBDELOS	BOBSLED
BBDELOW	WOBBLED
BBDELRU	BLURBED
	BURBLED
	RUBBLED
BBDELSU	SLUBBED
BBDEMSU	BEDUMBS
BBDENSU	SNUBBED
BBDEORS	DOBBERS
BBDEOST	STOBBED
BBDEOSW	SWOBBED
BBDERRU	DRUBBER
BBDERSU	DUBBERS
BBDESSU	SUBDEBS
BBDESTU	STUBBED
BBDFLUU	FLUBDUB
BBDGIIN	DIBBING
BBDGINO	DOBBING
BBDGINU	DUBBING
BBDIKSU	DIBBUKS
BBDILRY	DRIBBLY
BBDINOS	DOBBINS
BBDINSU	DUBBINS
BBDIOOR	BOOBIRD
BBDIRUY	RUBBIDY
BBDKSUY	DYBBUKS
BBEEEES	BEEBEES
BBEEERR	BERBERE
BBEEERU	BEBEERU
BBEEIKS	KEBBIES
BBEEIRS	BRIBEES
BBEEIRW	WEBBIER
BBEEISW	WEBBIES
BBEEKLS	LEBBEKS
BBEELPS	PEBBLES
BBEELSS	EBBLESS
BBEENSS	SNEBBES
BBEFILR	FRIBBLE
BBEFIRS	FIBBERS
BBEFIRU	FUBBIER
BBEFIRY	FIBBERY
BBEFLRU	FLUBBER
BBEFRUY	FUBBERY
BBEGIKN	KEBBING
BBEGILR	GLIBBER
	GRIBBLE
BBEGINN	NEBBING
BBEGINW	WEBBING
BBEGIOR	GOBBIER
BBEGIOS	GIBBOSE
BBEGIRS	GIBBERS
BBEGIST	GIBBETS
BBEGLOR	GOBBLER
BBEGLOS	GOBBLES
BBEGLRU	GRUBBLE
BBEGNSU	BEBUNGS
BBEGOST	GOBBETS
BBEGRRU	GRUBBER
BBEHIKS	KIBBEHS
BBEHINS	NEBBISH
BBEHIOS	HOBBIES
BBEHISU	HUBBIES
BBEHLOR	HOBBLER
BBEHLOS	HOBBLES
BBEHMTU	BETHUMB
BBEHORS	HOBBERS
BBEIIKL	BIBLIKE
BBEIILR	RIBIBLE
BBEIILS	BILBIES
BBEIIMR	IMBIBER
BBEIIMS	IMBIBES
BBEIIRR	RIBBIER
BBEIIRS	RIBIBES
BBEIJOS	JOBBIES
BBEIJRS	JIBBERS
BBEIKLS	KIBBLES
BBEILNR	NIBBLER
BBEILNS	NIBBLES
BBEILOS	BILBOES
	LOBBIES
BBEILOT	BIBELOT
BBEILPR	PRIBBLE
BBEILQU	QUIBBLE
BBEILRS	LIBBERS
BBEILRT	TRIBBLE
BBEILSS	BIBLESS
BBEILST	STIBBLE
BBEILSW	WIBBLES
BBEILSY	YIBBLES
BBEIMOS	BIMBOES
	MOBBIES
BBEINOR	NOBBIER
BBEINRU	NUBBIER
BBEIOOS	BOOBIES
BBEIOOT	BOBOTIE
BBEIRRS	BRIBERS
	RIBBERS
BBEIRRY	BRIBERY
BBEIRSU	RUBBIES
BBEIRTU	TUBBIER
BBEISSU	BUSBIES
	SUBBIES
BBEISTU	STUBBIE
BBEJORS	JOBBERS
BBEJORY	JOBBERY
BBEKLNO	KNOBBLE
BBEKLNU	KNUBBLE
BBEKLOS	BLESBOK
BBEKLUU	BUBUKLE
BBEKNOR	KNOBBER
BBEKNSU	NEBBUKS
BBELLOY	BELLBOY
BBELLSU	BULBELS
BBELLTU	BULBLET
BBELMOS	MOBBLES
BBELMOT	BOMBLET
BBELMRU	BUMBLER
BBELMSU	BUMBLES
BBELNOR	NOBBLER
BBELNOS	NOBBLES
BBELNSU	NUBBLES
BBELNSY	NYBBLES
BBELORS	LOBBERS
	SLOBBER
BBELORU	BOERBUL
BBELORW	WOBBLER
BBELORY	LOBBYER
BBELOST	BOBLETS
BBELOSW	WOBBLES
BBELRRU	BURBLER
BBELRSU	BURBLES
	LUBBERS
	RUBBLES
	SLUBBER
BBELSTU	STUBBLE
BBEMNSU	BENUMBS
BBEMORS	BOMBERS
	MOBBERS
BBENOTW	BOWBENT
BBENRSU	SNUBBER
BBENSSU	SNUBBES
BBEOOSY	YOBBOES
BBEORRS	ROBBERS
BBEORRY	ROBBERY
BBEORSS	SOBBERS
BBEORSW	SWOBBER
BBEORYY	YOBBERY
BBEPRUW	BREWPUB
BBERRSU	RUBBERS
BBERRUY	RUBBERY
BBERSTU	TUBBERS
BBFGIIN	FIBBING
BBFGINO	FOBBING
BBFGINU	FUBBING

BBGGIIN	GIBBING	BBLOSWY	BLOWBYS	BCDIIRU	RUBIDIC
BBGGINO	GOBBING	BBLSTUY	STUBBLY	BCDILOO	COLOBID
BBGHINO	HOBBING	BBMOOOX	BOOMBOX	BCDINOW	COWBIND
BBGIIJN	JIBBING	BBNNOOS	BONBONS	BCDIORW	COWBIRD
BBGIILN	LIBBING	BBNOOOS	BONOBOS	BCDIOSU	CUBOIDS
BBGIINN	NIBBING	BBNOORU	BOURBON	BCDIRSY	CYBRIDS
BBGIINR	BRIBING	BBOOOOS	BOOBOOS	BCDKORU	BURDOCK
	RIBBING	BBOOSSY	BOSSBOY	BCDNOSU	BONDUCS
BBGIJNO	JOBBING	BBOOSUU	BOUBOUS	BCDSTUU	SUBDUCT
BBGILLU	BILLBUG	BBORSTU	BURBOTS	BCEEEHN	BEECHEN
BBGILNO	LOBBING	BBOSSUY	BUSBOYS	BCEEEHS	BEECHES
BBGILNU	BULBING	BBRSSUU	SUBURBS		BESEECH
BBGIMNO	BOMBING	BCCEEHS	CHEBECS	BCEEFIN	BENEFIC
	MOBBING	BCCEIIS	BICCIES	BCEEFKL	BEFLECK
BBGINNU	NUBBING	BCCEILO	ECBOLIC	BCEEGIR	ICEBERG
BBGINOO	BOOBING	BCCEILU	CUBICLE	BCEEHIP	EPHEBIC
BBGINOR	ROBBING	BCCEILY	BICYCLE	BCEEHIT	HEBETIC
BBGINOS	GIBBONS	BCCEIOS	BOCCIES	BCEEHLR	BELCHER
	SOBBING	BCCEMOR	CROMBEC	BCEEHLS	BELCHES
BBGINPU	PUBBING	BCCILOU	BUCOLIC	BCEEHNR	BENCHER
BBGINRU	RUBBING	BCCILUY	CUBICLY	BCEEHNS	BENCHES
BBGINSU	GUBBINS	BCCINOO	OBCONIC	BCEEHOS	OBECHES
	SUBBING	BCCISUU	SUCCUBI	BCEEHOU	BOUCHEE
BBGINTU	TUBBING	BCCMOOX	COXCOMB	BCEEIMR	BECRIME
BBGIOSU	GIBBOUS	BCCMSUU	SUCCUMB	BCEEIPS	BESPICE
BBGIOSW	BOBWIGS	BCCNOOR	CORNCOB	BCEEIRS	ESCRIBE
BBHIIOS	HOBBISH	BCDEEHL	BELCHED	BCEEIRT	TEREBIC
BBHIMOS	MOBBISH	BCDEEHN	BENCHED	BCEEKNS	NEBECKS
BBHIOOS	BOOBISH	BCDEEIL	DECIBEL	BCEEKNU	BUCKEEN
BBHIOST	HOBBITS	BCDEEKS	BEDECKS	BCEEKRS	REBECKS
BBHIOSY	YOBBISH	BCDEENU	BEDUNCE	BCEEKST	BECKETS
BBHIRSU	RUBBISH	BCDEHIR	BIRCHED	BCEEKSZ	ZEBECKS
BBHISTU	TUBBISH	BCDEHIT	BITCHED	BCEEKUY	BUCKEYE
BBHJOOS	HOBJOBS	BCDEHNU	BUNCHED	BCEELOS	ECBOLES
BBHKOOS	BOSHBOK	BCDEHOR	BROCHED	BCEELOU	BOUCLEE
BBHNOOS	HOBNOBS	BCDEHOT	BOTCHED	BCEEMOS	BECOMES
BBHOOUW	WHOOBUB	BCDEHOU	DEBOUCH	BCEENOS	OBSCENE
BBHRSUY	SHRUBBY	BCDEIIO	BIOCIDE	BCEENRU	CRUBEEN
BBIIILM	BILIMBI	BCDEIKR	BRICKED	BCEERSU	BECURSE
BBIIKTZ	KIBBITZ	BCDEIKS	SICKBED	BCEFIIS	SEBIFIC
BBIILST	BIBLIST	BCDEIKT	BEDTICK	BCEGIKN	BECKING
BBIISUU	BUIBUIS	BCDEILM	CLIMBED	BCEGLOS	BECLOGS
BBIJMOO	JIBBOOM	BCDEILO	DOCIBLE	BCEHINR	BIRCHEN
BBIJNOS	JIBBONS	BCDEIOS	BODICES	BCEHINT	BENTHIC
BBIKOSS	SKIBOBS		CEBOIDS		BITCHEN
BBIKTUZ	KIBBUTZ	BCDEIRS	SCRIBED	BCEHIOR	BRIOCHE
BBILLSU	BULBILS	BCDEKLO	BLOCKED	BCEHIOT	BIOTECH
BBILLUU	LULIBUB	BCDEKLU	BUCKLED	BCEHIRS	BIRCHES
BBILNOY	NOBBILY	BCDEKOR	BEDROCK	BCEHIST	BITCHES
BBIMMOS	MOBBISM		BROCKED	BCEHITW	BEWITCH
BBIMOSY	YOBBISM	BCDEKOY	BOCKEDY	BCEHLRU	BLUCHER
BBINNSU	NUBBINS	BCDEKSU	BEDUCKS	BCEHNSU	BUNCHES
BBINORS	RIBBONS	BCDELOU	BECLOUD	BCEHORS	BROCHES
	ROBBINS	BCDEMOR	CROMBED	BCEHORT	BOTCHER
BBINORY	RIBBONY	BCDEMRU	CRUMBED	BCEHORW	COWHERB
BBIRTUY	RUBBITY	BCDENOU	BOUNCED	BCEHOSS	BOSCHES
BBJLOOW	BLOWJOB		BUNCOED	BCEHOST	BOTCHES
BBKLNOY	KNOBBLY	BCDEORU	COURBED	BCEHOSU	BOUCHES
BBKLNUY	KNUBBLY	BCDEORW	BECROWD		SUBECHO
BBKLOOU	BLOUBOK	BCDEOSU	SUBCODE	BCEHRSU	CHERUBS
BBKOOOO	BOOBOOK	BCDESUU	SUBDUCE	BCEHRTU	BUTCHER
BBKOOSS	BOSBOKS	BCDHIOR	BICHORD	BCEHSTU	BUTCHES
BBLLSUU	BULBULS	BCDHIRU	BRUCHID	BCEIIKR	BRICKIE
BBLOSUU	BULBOUS	BCDHOOU	CUBHOOD	BCEIIKS	BICKIES

BCEIISV	VIBICES		RECOMBS		BICRONS
BCEIKLM	LIMBECK	BCEMRRU	CRUMBER	BCINORU	RUBICON
BCEIKLO	BLOCKIE	BCEMRSU	CUMBERS	BCINRSU	BRUCINS
BCEIKLR	BRICKLE		SCUMBER	BCINSUU	INCUBUS
BCEIKNR	BRICKEN	BCENORU	BOUNCER	BCIOORT	ROBOTIC
BCEIKRS	BICKERS	BCENOSU	BOUNCES	BCIORSS	BORSICS
BCEIKST	BESTICK	BCEORSS	SCROBES	BCIORST	STROBIC
BCEIKSU	BUCKIES	BCEORSU	BESCOUR	BCIOSTY	SYBOTIC
BCEILMO	EMBOLIC		OBSCURE	BCIRRSU	RUBRICS
BCEILMR	CLIMBER	BCERRSU	CURBERS	BCIRTUY	BUTYRIC
	RECLIMB	BCERSTU	BECRUST	BCISSTU	BUSTICS
BCEILMS	EMBLICS		BECURST		CUBISTS
	LIMBECS	BCESSTU	SUBSECT	BCISTUU	CUBITUS
BCEILNO	BINOCLE	BCFSSUU	SUBFUSC	BCJKMUU	JUMBUCK
BCEILOR	BRICOLE	BCGIKNO	BOCKING	BCKLLOO	BOLLOCK
	CORBEIL	BCGIKNU	BUCKING	BCKLLOU	BULLOCK
BCEILOS	COLBIES	BCGIMNO	COMBING	BCKLNOU	UNBLOCK
BCEILOU	CIBOULE	BCGINNU	BUNCING	BCKLOOX	LOCKBOX
BCEILSY	BEYLICS	BCGINRU	CURBING	BCKMMOU	BUMMOCK
BCEIMNO	COMBINE	BCGORSU	COBURGS	BCKMOSU	BUCKSOM
BCEIMOR	COMBIER	BCGORSY	CYBORGS	BCKNNOO	BONNOCK
	MICROBE	BCHHORS	BORSHCH	BCKNSUU	NUBUCKS
BCEIMOS	COMBIES	BCHIIOP	BIOCHIP	BCKOTTU	BUTTOCK
BCEINOR	BICORNE	BCHIIOT	COHIBIT	BCLMOOU	COULOMB
BCEINOS	EBONICS	BCHIKOU	CHIBOUK	BCLMRUY	CRUMBLY
BCEINOZ	BENZOIC	BCHIKOY	BOYCHIK	BCLOOSU	COLOBUS
BCEINRU	BRUCINE	BCHIKSU	BUCKISH		SUBCOOL
BCEIORS	CORBIES	BCHILMY	CHIMBLY	BCLORTU	CLOTBUR
BCEIRRS	SCRIBER	BCHILOS	CHIBOLS	BCLSTUU	SUBCULT
BCEIRSS	SCRIBES	BCHIMOR	RHOMBIC	BCMMRUU	CRUMBUM
BCEIRSU	SUBERIC	BCHINOR	BRONCHI	BCMOOST	TOMBOCS
BCEIRTU	BRUCITE	BCHIOPR	PIBROCH	BCMORSY	CORYMBS
BCEISST	BISECTS	BCHIOPS	PHOBICS	BCMOSTU	COMBUST
BCEJOST	OBJECTS	BCHLOTY	BLOTCHY	BCNOORS	BRONCOS
BCEJSTU	SUBJECT	BCHLSSU	SCHLUBS	BCNOSTU	COBNUTS
BCEKLLO	BELLOCK	BCHNOOR	BRONCHO	BCNRSUU	UNCURBS
BCEKLOR	BLOCKER	BCHOORS	BROCHOS	BCOOOOS	BOOCOOS
BCEKLRU	BRUCKLE	BCHORST	BORSCHT	BCOOPYY	COPYBOY
	BUCKLER		BORTSCH	BCOOSWY	COWBOYS
BCEKLSU	BUCKLES	BCIIKLN	NIBLICK	BCOOTTY	BOYCOTT
BCEKMOS	BEMOCKS	BCIILMU	BULIMIC	BCTUUZZ	BUZZCUT
BCEKNOS	BECKONS	BCIILOR	COLIBRI	BDDDEIU	BUDDIED
BCEKORT	BROCKET	BCIILSY	SIBYLIC	BDDDELU	BUDDLED
BCEKORU	ROEBUCK	BCIINOS	BIONICS	BDDDEOR	BRODDED
BCEKOSU	BUCKOES	BCIINOT	BIONTIC	BDDEEER	REEDBED
BCEKOTY	BYCOKET	BCIIOPS	BIOPICS	BDDEEES	SEEDBED
BCEKRSU	BUCKERS		BIOPSIC	BDDEEEW	BEDEWED
BCEKSTU	BESTUCK	BCIIOPT	BIOPTIC	BDDEEIL	BIELDED
	BUCKETS	BCIIOST	BIOTICS	BDDEEIR	DEBRIDE
BCELLOW	COWBELL	BCIISTU	BISCUIT	BDDEEIS	BEDSIDE
BCELLSU	SUBCELL	BCIKKOX	KICKBOX	BDDEEIT	BETIDED
BCELMNU	CLUBMEN	BCIKNOS	KINCOBS		DEBITED
BCELMOS	COMBLES	BCIKORT	BROCKIT	BDDEELN	BLENDED
BCELMRU	CLUMBER	BCIKOTT	BITTOCK	BDDEENO	DEBONED
	CRUMBLE	BCILMPU	PLUMBIC	BDDEERS	BEDDERS
BCELMSU	SCUMBLE		UPCLIMB	BDDEESU	DEBUSED
BCELNOW	BECLOWN	BCILOOR	BICOLOR	BDDEETU	DEBUTED
BCELORS	CORBELS		BROCOLI	BDDEGIN	BEDDING
BCELOSU	BOUCLES	BCILPSU	PUBLICS	BDDEGIR	BRIDGED
BCELRSU	BECURLS	BCIMNOU	UMBONIC	BDDEGLU	BLUDGED
BCELSSU	CUBLESS	BCIMSSU	CUBISMS	BDDEIIR	BIRDIED
BCEMNTU	CUMBENT	BCINOOR	BORONIC	BDDEIIS	BIDDIES
BCEMOOS	COOMBES	BCINOOS	BOSONIC	BDDEILN	BLINDED
BCEMORS	COMBERS	BCINORS	BICORNS	BDDEILR	BRIDLED

BDDEILU	BUILDED	BDEEINZ	BEDIZEN	BDEGINO	BOINGED
BDDEINR	BRINDED	BDEEIRR	BERRIED	BDEGINR	BREDING
BDDEIOO	BOODIED		BRIERED	BDEGIOO	BOOGIED
BDDEIRR	REDBIRD	BDEEIRS	BREDIES	BDEGIOR	BODGIER
BDDEIRS	BIDDERS		DERBIES	BDEGIOS	BODGIES
BDDEIRU	BUDDIER	BDEEISS	BESIDES	BDEGIOT	BIGOTED
BDDEISU	BUDDIES	BDEEIST	BETIDES	BDEGIRS	BEGIRDS
BDDELNU	BUNDLED	BDEEIVV	BEVVIED		BRIDGES
BDDELOO	BLOODED	BDEEJLS	DJEBELS	BDEGIRU	BRIGUED
	BOODLED	BDEEJMS	DJEMBES	BDEGISU	BUDGIES
BDDELOR	BRODDLE	BDEEKMO	KEMBOED	BDEGLNU	BLUNGED
BDDELOS	BODDLES	BDEEKRU	REBUKED		BUNGLED
BDDELOU	DOUBLED	BDEELLS	BEDELLS	BDEGLRU	BLUDGER
BDDELSU	BUDDLES	BDEELMR	REMBLED		BURGLED
BDDENOU	BOUNDED	BDEELMS	SEMBLED	BDEGLSU	BLUDGES
BDDEOOR	BROODED	BDEELMU	UMBELED	BDEGNOW	BEDGOWN
BDDEORU	OBDURED	BDEELNR	BLENDER	BDEGNSU	BEDUNGS
BDDEOTU	DOUBTED		REBLEND	BDEGOOY	GOODBYE
BDDERSU	BUDDERS	BDEELNS	BLENDES	BDEGORS	BODGERS
	REDBUDS	BDEELNT	BENDLET	BDEGORU	BUDGERO
BDDESUU	SUBDUED	BDEELOV	BELOVED	BDEGRSU	BEDRUGS
BDDGIIN	BIDDING	BDEELOW	BOWELED		BUDGERS
BDDGINU	BUDDING		ELBOWED		REDBUGS
BDDGIOR	BIRDDOG	BDEELRT	TREBLED	BDEGSTU	BUDGETS
BDDISSU	DISBUDS	BDEELSS	BEDLESS	BDEHINS	BEHINDS
BDEEEFL	FEEBLED		BLESSED	BDEHIRT	BIRTHED
BDEEEIS	BEEDIES	BDEELTT	BLETTED	BDEHLMU	HUMBLED
BDEEELL	DELEBLE	BDEELZZ	BEZZLED	BDEHLOS	BEHOLDS
BDEEELP	BLEEPED	BDEEMOS	BESOMED	BDEHLSU	BLUSHED
BDEEELR	BLEEDER	BDEEMOW	EMBOWED	BDEHMTU	THUMBED
BDEEELT	BEETLED	BDEEMOX	EMBOXED	BDEHORY	HERDBOY
BDEEELV	BEVELED	BDEEMRU	EMBRUED	BDEHOST	HOTBEDS
BDEEEMN	BEDEMEN		UMBERED	BDEHRSU	BRUSHED
BDEEEMT	BEMETED	BDEEMSU	BEMUSED	BDEIIRS	BIRDIES
BDEEENS	BENDEES		EMBUSED		BRIDIES
BDEEEPS	BESPEED	BDEENOR	DEBONER	BDEIIVV	BIVVIED
BDEEERR	BREEDER		ENROBED	BDEIJLR	JIRBLED
	BREERED		REDBONE	BDEIKLN	BLINKED
	REBREED	BDEENOS	DEBONES	BDEIKLU	BUDLIKE
BDEEERZ	BREEZED	BDEENPR	PREBEND	BDEIKMO	KIMBOED
BDEEEST	DEBTEES	BDEENRS	BENDERS	BDEIKNO	BOINKED
BDEEFIR	BRIEFED	BDEEORR	REBORED	BDEIKRS	BRISKED
	DEBRIEF	BDEEORS	BEDSORE	BDEILLU	BULLIED
	FIBERED		SOBERED	BDEILMS	DIMBLES
BDEEFOX	FEEDBOX	BDEEORV	OVERBED	BDEILMW	WIMBLED
BDEEGOR	BEGORED	BDEEORW	BOWERED	BDEILNN	BLINNED
BDEEGOY	BOGEYED	BDEEOSX	SEEDBOX	BDEILNR	BLINDER
BDEEGSU	BUGSEED	BDEERSU	BURSEED		BRINDLE
BDEEHOV	BEHOVED	BDEERUW	BURWEED	BDEILNS	BINDLES
BDEEHRT	BERTHED	BDEESSU	DEBUSES	BDEILNY	BYLINED
BDEEIKL	BEDLIKE	BDEFFLU	BLUFFED	BDEILOP	LOBIPED
BDEEIKN	BEINKED	BDEFILR	FILBERD	BDEILOR	BROILED
BDEEILL	BELLIED	BDEFLMU	FUMBLED	BDEILOS	BOLIDES
	DELIBLE	BDEFLOU	BODEFUL	BDEILOX	BOLIXED
	LIBELED	BDEFOOR	FORBODE	BDEILPP	BLIPPED
BDEEILS	EDIBLES	BDEGGLO	BOGGLED	BDEILRR	BRIDLER
BDEEILV	BEDEVIL	BDEGGOR	BROGGED	BDEILRS	BIRSLED
BDEEIMR	BEMIRED	BDEGHIT	BEDIGHT		BRIDLES
	BERIMED		BIGHTED	BDEILRT	DRIBLET
BDEEIMT	BEDTIME	BDEGHOU	BOUGHED	BDEILRU	BLUDIER
	BETIMED	BDEGILN	BINGLED		BUILDER
BDEEIMX	BEMIXED	BDEGILO	OBLIGED		REBUILD
BDEEINR	BENDIER	BDEGILS	BEGILDS	BDEILSS	BLISSED
	INBREED	BDEGINN	BENDING	BDEILST	BILSTED

BDEILTZ	BLITZED	BDELOOP	BLOOPED	BDEORTU	DOUBTER
BDEIMMR	BRIMMED	BDELOOR	BOODLER		OBTRUDE
BDEIMNR	BIRDMEN	BDELOOS	BOODLES		OUTBRED
BDEIMOR	BROMIDE	BDELORS	BORDELS		REDOUBT
BDEIMRU	IMBRUED	BDELORU	BOULDER	BDEORUV	OVERDUB
BDEIMTU	BITUMED		DOUBLER	BDERRSU	DEBURRS
BDEINOR	INORBED	BDELORW	BOWLDER	BDERSSU	SURBEDS
BDEINOU	BEDOUIN		LOWBRED	BDERSTU	BURSTED
BDEINPR	PREBIND	BDELOST	BOLDEST	BDERSUU	SUBDUER
BDEINRS	BINDERS	BDELOSU	BLOUSED	BDERSUY	RUDESBY
	INBREDS		DOUBLES	BDESSTU	BEDUSTS
	REBINDS	BDELOSW	BLOWSED		BESTUDS
BDEINRY	BINDERY	BDELOTT	BLOTTED	BDESSUU	SUBDUES
BDEINST	BIDENTS		BOTTLED	BDESSUW	SUBDEWS
BDEINSU	BEDUINS	BDELOTU	BOULTED	BDFIILY	BIFIDLY
	BUNDIES		DOUBLET	BDFIIOR	FIBROID
BDEIOOS	BOODIES	BDELOWZ	BLOWZED	BDFIISU	FIDIBUS
	DOOBIES	BDELRRU	BLURRED	BDFIORS	FORBIDS
BDEIORR	BROIDER	BDELRTU	BLURTED	BDGGINO	BODGING
BDEIORS	BORIDES	BDELSSU	BUDLESS	BDGGINU	BUDGING
	DISROBE	BDELSTU	BUSTLED	BDGGLOU	GOLDBUG
BDEIORT	DEBITOR	BDELSWY	LEWDSBY	BDGIINN	BINDING
	DEORBIT	BDELTTU	BUTTLED	BDGIINR	BIRDING
	ORBITED	BDEMNNO	BONDMEN		BRIDING
BDEIORV	OVERBID	BDEMNOU	EMBOUND	BDGIINS	BIDINGS
BDEIORZ	ZEBROID	BDEMOOR	BEDROOM	BDGIIOO	GOBIOID
BDEIOSY	DISOBEY		BOREDOM	BDGIIOS	GOBIIDS
BDEIPRS	PREBIDS		BROOMED	BDGILOO	GLOBOID
BDEIRRS	BIRDERS	BDEMOOS	BOSOMED	BDGIMNU	DUMBING
BDEIRST	BESTRID	BDEMORS	SOMBRED	BDGINNO	BONDING
	BISTRED	BDEMSTU	DUMBEST	BDGINNU	BUNDING
BDEIRSU	BRUISED	BDENNOU	BOUNDEN	BDGINOS	BODINGS
	BURDIES		UNBONED	BDGINOY	BODYING
BDEIRSV	VERBIDS	BDENNSU	UNBENDS	BDGLLOU	BULLDOG
BDEIRTU	BRUITED	BDENORS	BONDERS	BDGLOOT	DOGBOLT
BDEIRTY	BEDIRTY	BDENORU	BOUNDER	BDGMSUU	MUDBUGS
BDEISST	BEDSITS		REBOUND	BDGOOOW	BOGWOOD
BDEISSU	SUBSIDE		UNROBED	BDGOOSY	GOODBYS
BDEISTU	BUISTED	BDENORW	BROWNED	BDGORSU	DORBUGS
	SUBEDIT	BDENORZ	BRONZED	BDHIINS	BHINDIS
BDEITUY	DUBIETY	BDENOST	OBTENDS		BINDHIS
BDEJLMU	JUMBLED	BDENOSY	BEYONDS	BDHINOP	HOPBIND
BDEJORU	OBJURED	BDENOUW	UNBOWED	BDHIOSU	BUSHIDO
BDEKLNU	BLUNKED	BDENOUX	UNBOXED	BDHIRSY	HYBRIDS
BDEKNOO	BOOKEND	BDENRSU	BURDENS	BDHMOOO	HOBODOM
BDEKNOU	BUNKOED	BDENRTU	BRUNTED	BDHNSUU	BUHUNDS
BDEKNSU	DEBUNKS	BDENSSU	SUNBEDS	BDHOOOY	BOYHOOD
BDEKOOR	BROOKED	BDENSTU	SUBTEND	BDIIKNO	BODIKIN
BDELLOR	BEDROLL	BDENSUY	SEBUNDY	BDIILMS	DISLIMB
BDELMMU	BUMMLED	BDEOORR	BROODER	BDIILOR	OILBIRD
	MUMBLED	BDEOORS	BOORDES	BDIILOS	LIBIDOS
BDELMOO	BLOOMED	BDEOOST	BOOSTED	BDIIMNS	MISBIND
BDELMPU	PLUMBED	BDEOPRS	BEDROPS	BDIIMRS	MIDRIBS
BDELMRU	DRUMBLE	BDEOPRT	BEDROPT	BDIISTT	TIDBITS
	RUMBLED	BDEOPST	BEDPOST	BDIKNOR	BRODKIN
BDELMTU	TUMBLED	BDEORRS	BORDERS	BDIKNOS	BODKINS
BDELNOR	BLONDER	BDEORRU	BORDURE	BDILLNY	BLINDLY
BDELNOS	BLONDES		BOURDER	BDILNNU	UNBLIND
	BOLDENS	BDEORSS	DESORBS	BDILNUU	UNBUILD
BDELNOU	UNLOBED	BDEORST	DEBTORS	BDILOOS	DIOBOLS
BDELNRU	BLUNDER		STROBED	BDILPUU	BUILDUP
	BUNDLER	BDEORSU	OBDURES		UPBUILD
BDELNSU	BUNDLES		ROSEBUD	BDILRUY	BUIRDLY
BDELNTU	BLUNTED	BDEORSW	BROWSED	BDILTUY	DIBUTYL

BDIMNPU	DUMPBIN	BEEEKLS	KEBELES	BEEHLST	BETHELS
BDIMNUU	DUBNIUM	BEEELPR	BLEEPER	BEEHMRY	BERHYME
BDIMORS	BROMIDS	BEEELRT	BEETLER	BEEHNNO	HEBENON
BDINNOU	INBOUND	BEEELRV	BEVELER	BEEHNOS	BESHONE
BDINNSU	UNBINDS	BEEELST	BEETLES	BEEHOOV	BEHOOVE
BDINOOR	BRIDOON	BEEEMOS	BEESOME	BEEHOPS	EPHEBOS
BDINOOW	WOODBIN	BEEEMRS	BERSEEM		PHOEBES
BDINOSU	BOUDINS	BEEEMSS	BESEEMS	BEEHORS	HERBOSE
BDINOUY	UNIBODY	BEEEMST	BEMETES	BEEHORW	BEWHORE
BDINPSU	UPBINDS		BETEEMS	BEEHOST	BEHOTES
BDINRSU	SUNBIRD	BEEENNZ	BENZENE	BEEHOSV	BEHOVES
BDINSTU	BUNDIST	BEEENTW	BETWEEN	BEEHPSU	EPHEBUS
	DUSTBIN	BEEEPRS	BEEPERS	BEEHRST	BERTHES
BDIOOOV	OBOVOID	BEEEPSW	BEWEEPS		SHERBET
BDIOORU	BOUDOIR	BEEERSS	BREESES	BEEHRSW	BESHREW
BDIOOST	BIODOTS	BEEERSZ	BEEZERS	BEEHRTY	THEREBY
BDIORSW	WOSBIRD		BREEZES	BEEHRWY	WHEREBY
BDIOSSY	BYSSOID	BEEERTV	BREVETE	BEEHSST	BEHESTS
BDIOSTU	OUTBIDS	BEEFGIN	BEEFING	BEEHSTY	BHEESTY
BDIOSUU	DUBIOUS	BEEFGIT	BIGFEET	BEEIJLU	JUBILEE
BDIRSTU	DISTURB	BEEFILR	FEBRILE	BEEIKLW	WEBLIKE
BDISSUY	SUBSIDY	BEEFILS	BELIEFS	BEEILLR	LIBELER
BDKLOOS	KOBOLDS	BEEFILY	BEEFILY	BEEILLS	BELLIES
BDKNOOU	BUNDOOK	BEEFINT	BENEFIT	BEEILLV	BILEVEL
BDLNOOS	DOBLONS	BEEFIRR	BRIEFER	BEEILMP	EPIBLEM
BDLOOOX	OXBLOOD	BEEFIRS	FRISBEE	BEEILMS	BESLIME
BDMOOSS	BOSSDOM	BEEFLTY	BEETFLY		BESMILE
BDMORUW	BUDWORM	BEEFNRU	FUNEBRE	BEEILNR	BERLINE
BDNNOOY	NONBODY	BEEFORY	FOREBYE	BEEILOS	OBELISE
BDNNOUU	UNBOUND	BEEFRST	BEFRETS	BEEILOZ	OBELIZE
BDNOORU	BOURDON	BEEGGNU	GEEBUNG	BEEILRS	BELIERS
BDNOOSS	DOBSONS	BEEGILL	LEGIBLE	BEEILRV	VERBILE
BDNOOWW	DOWNBOW	BEEGILO	OBLIGEE	BEEILRY	BEERILY
BDNOPUU	UPBOUND	BEEGILS	BEIGELS	BEEILTT	BETITLE
BDNORTU	TURBOND	BEEGILU	BEGUILE	BEEIMRS	BEMIRES
BDNORUW	RUBDOWN	BEEGIMR	BEGRIME		BERIMES
BDNOSTU	OBTUNDS	BEEGINN	BEGINNE		BIREMES
BDOOOWX	BOXWOOD	BEEGINP	BEEPING	BEEIMST	BETIMES
	WOODBOX	BEEGINR	BIGENER	BEEIMSX	BEMIXES
BDORSWY	BYWORDS		BREINGE	BEEINNS	BENNIES
BEEEEFR	FREEBEE		REBEGIN	BEEINNZ	BENZINE
BEEEEKS	BESEEKE	BEEGINS	BEIGNES	BEEINOS	EBONIES
BEEEEMT	BETEEME	BEEGINT	BEETING		EBONISE
BEEEENP	PEEBEEN		BEIGNET	BEEINOT	EBONITE
BEEEFIR	BEEFIER	BEEGINU	BEGUINE	BEEINOZ	EBONIZE
	FREEBIE	BEEGISY	BIGEYES	BEEINPR	PEBRINE
BEEEFLR	FEEBLER	BEEGLNO	ENGLOBE	BEEINRT	BENTIER
BEEEFLS	FEEBLES	BEEGMNO	GOMBEEN	BEEINRZ	ZEBRINE
BEEEFTW	WEBFEET	BEEGMOU	EMBOGUE	BEEINSW	NEWBIES
BEEEGIS	BESIEGE	BEEGNOO	GOBONEE	BEEIORS	EBRIOSE
BEEEGKL	GEELBEK	BEEGNOS	ENGOBES	BEEIOST	TOEBIES
BEEEGNR	BREENGE	BEEGNRS	BERGENS	BEEIQUZ	BEZIQUE
BEEEGRR	BERGERE	BEEGNRU	REBEGUN	BEEIRRS	BERRIES
BEEEHIV	BEEHIVE	BEEGNSU	BUNGEES	BEEIRRV	BREVIER
BEEEHNS	SHEBEEN	BEEGNTU	UNBEGET	BEEIRST	REBITES
BEEEHPS	EPHEBES	BEEGRSU	BURGEES	BEEIRTY	EBRIETY
BEEEIKL	BEELIKE	BEEGSUY	BUGEYES	BEEISST	BETISES
BEEEILL	LIBELEE	BEEHINS	BESHINE	BEEISTT	BETTIES
BEEEILN	BEELINE	BEEHIOP	EPHEBOI	BEEISTW	WEBSITE
BEEEILV	BELIEVE	BEEHIRR	HERBIER	BEEISVV	BEVVIES
BEEEIRR	BEERIER	BEEHIST	BHISTEE	BEEJNSU	BUNJEES
BEEEJLW	BEJEWEL	BEEHKSU	BUKSHEE	BEEJSSU	BEJESUS
BEEEJLZ	JEZEBEL	BEEHLRT	BLETHER	BEEKMOS	BESMOKE
BEEEKLL	BELLEEK		HERBLET	BEEKNOT	BETOKEN

BEEKOPS	BESPOKE		VERBOSE
BEEKORS	REEBOKS	BEEORSY	OBEYERS
BEEKRRS	BERSERK	BEEORTV	OVERBET
BEEKRRU	REBUKER	BEEORWY	EYEBROW
BEEKRSU	REBUKES	BEEOSST	OBESEST
BEELLMN	BELLMEN	BEEPRRV	PREVERB
BEELLOT	LOBELET	BEEPRSU	BURPEES
BEELMMS	EMBLEMS	BEEQSTU	BEQUEST
BEELMNT	BELTMEN	BEERRST	BERRETS
BEELMOW	EMBOWEL	BEERRSU	BEURRES
BEELMRS	REMBLES	BEERRSV	REVERBS
BEELMRT	TREMBLE	BEERRSW	BREWERS
BEELMSS	SEMBLES	BEERRWY	BREWERY
BEELNNO	ENNOBLE	BEERSST	BREESTS
BEELNOZ	BENZOLE	BEERSSU	REBUSES
BEELNRT	REBLENT		SUBSERE
BEELNSU	NEBULES	BEERSTT	BETTERS
BEELOST	BOLETES	BEERSTV	BREVETS
BEELOSV	BELOVES	BEERSTW	BESTREW
BEELOSY	OBESELY		WEBSTER
BEELOTY	EYEBOLT	BEERTTU	BURETTE
BEELPST	BEPELTS	BEESSTU	BUSTEES
BEELRSS	BLESSER	BEETTUV	BUVETTE
BEELRST	BELTERS	BEFFIIS	BIFFIES
	TREBLES	BEFFIRS	BIFFERS
BEELRSY	BERLEYS	BEFFIRU	BUFFIER
BEELRUZ	ZEBRULE	BEFFLRU	BLUFFER
BEELSSS	BLESSES	BEFFOSU	BOUFFES
BEELSSW	WEBLESS	BEFFPSU	BEPUFFS
BEELSZZ	BEZZLES	BEFFRSU	BUFFERS
BEELTTU	BLUETTE		REBUFFS
BEEMMRS	MEMBERS	BEFFSTU	BUFFEST
BEEMNPT	BENEMPT		BUFFETS
BEEMNRY	BYREMEN	BEFGIIL	FILIBEG
BEEMORW	EMBOWER	BEFGIRU	FIREBUG
BEEMOSS	MEBOSES	BEFGIST	BEGIFTS
BEEMOSX	EMBOXES	BEFGLSU	BEGULFS
BEEMRRU	UMBRERE	BEFHOOS	BEHOOFS
BEEMRSU	EMBRUES	BEFILMS	FIMBLES
BEEMRTU	EMBRUTE	BEFILNO	LOBEFIN
BEEMSSU	BEMUSES	BEFILNU	BLUEFIN
	EMBUSES	BEFILOS	FOIBLES
BEENNRS	BRENNES	BEFILOU	BIOFUEL
BEENNST	BENNETS	BEFILPY	PLEBIFY
BEENOOT	BOTONEE	BEFILRT	FILBERT
BEENORR	ENROBER	BEFILRY	BRIEFLY
BEENORS	BOREENS	BEFILSU	FUSIBLE
	ENROBES		SUBFILE
BEENORY	BONEYER	BEFINOR	BONFIRE
BEENOST	BEENTOS	BEFIOOR	BOOFIER
	BONESET	BEFIORS	FIBROSE
BEENRRT	BRENTER	BEFIORX	FIREBOX
BEENSTU	BUTENES	BEFIRST	BIFTERS
	SUBTEEN		FIBSTER
BEENSUV	SUBVENE	BEFIRSU	FUBSIER
BEEOOST	BOOTEES	BEFIRVY	VERBIFY
BEEOPPS	BOPEEPS	BEFITUX	TUBIFEX
BEEOPRR	REPROBE	BEFLLTY	FLYBELT
BEEOPRS	BEPROSE	BEFLLWY	FLYBLEW
BEEORRS	REBORES	BEFLMRU	FUMBLER
	SOBERER	BEFLMSU	BEFLUMS
BEEORRU	BOURREE		FUMBLES
BEEORSV	OBSERVE	BEFLOOS	BEFOOLS
	OBVERSE	BEFLOSU	BEFOULS
BEFLTUU	TUBEFUL
BEFOORR	FORBORE
BEFOOTW	WEBFOOT
BEFSSUU	SUBFEUS
BEGGGIN	BEGGING
BEGGIIS	BIGGIES
BEGGINO	BEGOING
BEGGIOR	BOGGIER
BEGGIRU	BUGGIER
BEGGIST	BIGGEST
BEGGISU	BUGGIES
BEGGITY	BIGGETY
BEGGLOR	BLOGGER
	BOGGLER
BEGGLOS	BOGGLES
BEGGORS	BOGGERS
BEGGRSU	BUGGERS
BEGGRUY	BUGGERY
BEGHHIT	BEHIGHT
BEGHINT	BENIGHT
BEGHISS	BESIGHS
BEGHITT	BETIGHT
BEGHRRU	BURGHER
BEGIILR	BILGIER
BEGIIMT	BIGTIME
BEGIINN	INBEING
BEGIINR	BREIING
BEGIINS	BINGIES
BEGIKMN	KEMBING
BEGIKNR	KERBING
BEGILLN	BELLING
BEGILLY	LEGIBLY
BEGILNO	IGNOBLE
	INGLOBE
BEGILNR	BLINGER
BEGILNS	BINGLES
BEGILNT	BELTING
BEGILNU	BLUEING
	BULGINE
BEGILNY	BELYING
BEGILOR	OBLIGER
BEGILOS	OBLIGES
BEGILRS	GERBILS
BEGILRT	GILBERT
BEGILRU	BULGIER
BEGILST	GIBLETS
BEGIMNR	BERMING
BEGIMRS	BEGRIMS
BEGINNU	UNBEING
BEGINOS	BINGOES
	BIOGENS
BEGINOY	BIOGENY
	OBEYING
BEGINRR	BRINGER
BEGINRS	BINGERS
BEGINRV	VERBING
BEGINRW	BREWING
BEGINRY	BREYING
BEGINSS	BESINGS
	BIGNESS
BEGINST	BESTING
BEGINSU	BEGUINS
	BUNGIES
BEGINTT	BETTING

BEGIOOS	BOOGIES	BEHIMOY	YOHIMBE	BEIINRS	BRINIES
	GOOBIES	BEHINOP	HIPBONE	BEIINST	STIBINE
BEGIORV	OVERBIG		HOPBINE	BEIIOTT	BIOTITE
BEGIOSS	BIGOSES	BEHINST	HENBITS	BEIIRRS	BIRSIER
BEGIOSU	BOUGIES	BEHIOST	BOTHIES		RIBIERS
BEGIRSU	BRIGUES	BEHIOTW	HOWBEIT	BEIIRST	BITSIER
	RUGBIES	BEHIRRT	REBIRTH	BEIIRTT	BITTIER
BEGISSU	GIBUSES	BEHIRST	HERBIST	BEIISTT	BITTIES
BEGKMOS	GEMSBOK	BEHIRSU	BUSHIER	BEIISTV	VIBIEST
BEGKNSU	BEGUNKS	BEHISSU	BUSHIES	BEIISVV	BIVVIES
BEGLLOU	GLOBULE	BEHISTT	THIBETS	BEIISZZ	BIZZIES
BEGLMOO	BEGLOOM	BEHISTZ	ZIBETHS	BEIJLRS	JERBILS
BEGLMRU	GRUMBLE	BEHKKOO	KOKOBEH		JIRBLES
BEGLMUU	BLUEGUM	BEHKORS	RHEBOKS	BEIJLSU	JUBILES
BEGLNOS	BELONGS	BEHLLOP	BELLHOP	BEIJMSU	JUMBIES
BEGLNRU	BLUNGER	BEHLLOX	HELLBOX	BEIJNSU	BUNJIES
	BUNGLER	BEHLMOW	WHOMBLE	BEIKLMS	BLIKSEM
BEGLNSU	BLUNGES	BEHLMRU	HUMBLER	BEIKLNR	BLINKER
	BUNGLES	BEHLMSU	HUMBLES	BEIKLNS	LIBKENS
BEGLOOS	GLOBOSE	BEHLOOT	BOTHOLE	BEIKLOR	BLOKIER
BEGLOOT	BOOTLEG	BEHLORT	BROTHEL	BEIKLOS	OBELISK
BEGLOST	GOBLETS	BEHLOSW	BEHOWLS	BEIKLOW	BOWLIKE
BEGLOSU	GLEBOUS	BEHLRRU	BURRHEL	BEIKLOX	BOXLIKE
BEGLOSW	BOWLEGS	BEHLRSU	BLUSHER	BEIKLRS	BILKERS
	WEBLOGS		BURHELS	BEIKLRU	BULKIER
BEGLOUV	LOVEBUG	BEHLSSU	BLUSHES	BEIKLSY	BEYLIKS
BEGLRSU	BUGLERS		BUSHELS	BEIKLTU	TUBLIKE
	BULGERS	BEHLSTU	BLUSHET	BEIKNRS	BRISKEN
	BURGLES	BEHMNSU	BUSHMEN	BEIKOOR	BOOKIER
BEGLRTY	BERGYLT	BEHMOOY	HOMEBOY		BROOKIE
BEGLSTU	BUGLETS	BEHMORS	HOMBRES	BEIKOOS	BOOKIES
BEGMNOY	BOGYMEN	BEHMOTU	BEMOUTH		BOOKSIE
BEGNNUU	UNBEGUN	BEHMPTU	BETHUMP	BEIKORS	BOSKIER
BEGNOOS	BONGOES	BEHNNOT	BENTHON	BEIKORT	REITBOK
BEGNORU	BURGEON	BEHNORS	BREHONS	BEIKRRS	BRISKER
BEGNOSY	BYGONES	BEHNORT	BETHORN	BEIKRST	BRISKET
BEGNOTT	BETTONG	BEHNOST	BENTHOS	BEIKRSW	BREWSKI
BEGNOTU	UNBEGOT	BEHNRTU	BURTHEN	BEIKRTU	BURKITE
BEGNRSU	BUNGERS	BEHOORT	THEORBO	BEILLMN	BILLMEN
BEGNSUY	BUNGEYS	BEHOOSX	SHOEBOX	BEILLPR	PREBILL
BEGOORS	BOOGERS	BEHOPRT	POTHERB	BEILLRR	BRILLER
	GOOBERS	BEHOPSU	PHOEBUS	BEILLRS	BILLERS
BEGOOSY	BOOGEYS	BEHORRT	BROTHER		REBILLS
BEGORSU	BROGUES	BEHORST	BOSHTER	BEILLRU	BULLIER
BEGOSTU	BOUGETS		BOTHERS	BEILLST	BESTILL
	OUTBEGS	BEHORSU	HERBOUS		BILLETS
BEGOSTW	BOWGETS	BEHORTT	BETROTH	BEILLSU	BULLIES
BEGRRSU	BURGERS	BEHOSTU	BESHOUT	BEILMNR	NIMBLER
BEGRSSU	BURGESS	BEHRRSU	BRUSHER	BEILMNS	MILNEBS
BEHHKOT	KHOTBEH	BEHRSSU	BRUSHES	BEILMOR	EMBROIL
BEHIIST	BHISTIE		BUSHERS	BEILMOS	BEMOILS
BEHIITX	EXHIBIT	BEHRTTU	TURBETH		EMBOILS
BEHIKLO	HOBLIKE	BEIIKKS	BIKKIES		MOBILES
BEHIKNT	BETHINK	BEIIKLN	NIBLIKE		OBELISM
BEHIKRS	KIRBEHS	BEIIKLR	RIBLIKE	BEILMRS	LIMBERS
BEHILMS	BLEMISH	BEIIKRR	BIRKIER	BEILMRT	TIMBREL
BEHILMT	THIMBLE	BEIIKRS	BIRKIES	BEILMRW	WIMBREL
BEHILOS	BOLSHIE	BEIILLS	BILLIES	BEILMSU	SUBLIME
BEHILRT	BLITHER	BEIILMR	LIMBIER	BEILMSW	WIMBLES
BEHILST	THIBLES	BEIILMX	MIXIBLE	BEILNOO	OBELION
BEHILSU	BLUEISH	BEIILRS	RISIBLE	BEILNOS	BOLINES
	HELIBUS	BEIILSV	VISIBLE	BEILNOW	BOWLINE
BEHILSW	WEBLISH	BEIINOT	NIOBITE	BEILNRS	BERLINS
BEHIMOR	BIOHERM	BEIINRR	BRINIER	BEILNRY	BYLINER

BEILNSU	SUBLINE	BEINNOP	PINBONE	BEIRSTT	BITTERS
BEILNSY	BYLINES	BEINNOR	BONNIER	BEIRSTU	BUSTIER
BEILNSZ	BENZILS	BEINNOS	BENISON		RUBIEST
BEILNTZ	BLINTZE		BONNIES	BEIRTTU	TRIBUTE
BEILOOR	LOOBIER	BEINNOZ	BENZOIN	BEIRTTY	TREYBIT
BEILOOS	LOOBIES	BEINNSU	BUNNIES	BEIRTVY	BREVITY
BEILOPR	PREBOIL	BEINNSZ	BENZINS	BEIRUZZ	BUZZIER
BEILOPY	EPIBOLY	BEINOOS	BOONIES	BEISSTU	BUSIEST
BEILOQU	OBLIQUE	BEINOOT	EOBIONT		SUBSITE
BEILORR	BROILER	BEINORT	BORNITE	BEISTTU	BUTTIES
BEILORS	BOILERS	BEINORW	BROWNIE	BEITTWX	BETWIXT
	LIBEROS	BEINOSS	BESOINS	BEJJSUU	JUJUBES
	REBOILS	BEINOST	BONIEST	BEJKOUX	JUKEBOX
BEILORT	TRILOBE		EBONIST	BEJLMRU	JUMBLER
BEILORW	BLOWIER	BEINOSV	BOVINES	BEJLMSU	JUMBLES
BEILORY	BOILERY	BEINOSX	BONXIES	BEJLOSS	JOBLESS
BEILOST	BETOILS	BEINOSZ	BIZONES	BEJORSU	OBJURES
BEILOSW	BLOWIES	BEINOTT	BOTTINE	BEKLNRU	BLUNKER
BEILOSX	BOLIXES	BEINRRS	BRINERS	BEKLOOT	BOOKLET
BEILRRS	BIRLERS	BEINRSU	BURNIES	BEKLRSU	BULKERS
BEILRRU	BURLIER		RUBINES		BURLESK
BEILRSS	BIRSLES		SUBERIN	BEKMNOO	BOOKMEN
	RIBLESS	BEINRSY	BYRNIES	BEKMOSS	EMBOSKS
BEILRST	BLISTER	BEINRTT	BITTERN	BEKMOST	STEMBOK
	BRISTLE	BEINRTU	BUNTIER	BEKNNOW	BEKNOWN
	RIBLETS		TRIBUNE	BEKNORS	BONKERS
BEILRTT	BRITTLE		TURBINE	BEKNORU	UNBROKE
	TRIBLET	BEINSSY	BYSSINE	BEKNOST	BEKNOTS
BEILRTU	REBUILT	BEIOOPT	BIOTOPE	BEKNRSU	BUNKERS
BEILRTY	LIBERTY	BEIOORZ	BOOZIER	BEKOOPR	PREBOOK
BEILRTZ	BLITZER	BEIOOST	BOOTIES	BEKOORS	BOOKERS
BEILRUY	BRULYIE	BEIOPTY	BIOTYPE		REBOOKS
BEILRUZ	BRULZIE	BEIORRT	BORTIER	BEKOPRU	UPBROKE
BEILSSS	BLISSES		ORBITER	BEKORRS	BROKERS
BEILSST	BITLESS	BEIORSS	BOSSIER	BEKORRY	BROKERY
BEILSTU	BLUIEST		RIBOSES	BEKORWW	WEBWORK
	SUBTILE	BEIORST	ORBIEST	BEKOSST	BOSKETS
BEILSTW	BLEWITS		SORBITE	BEKOTTU	KETUBOT
BEILSTZ	BLITZES	BEIORSU	BOUSIER	BEKRRSU	BRUSKER
BEILTTU	BLUETIT		OUREBIS		BURKERS
BEIMMOS	BOMMIES	BEIORSY	BOYSIER	BEKRSSU	BUSKERS
BEIMMRR	BRIMMER	BEIORUV	BOUVIER	BEKSSTU	BUSKETS
BEIMNOR	BROMINE	BEIOSSS	BOSSIES	BELLLMU	BLELLUM
BEIMNTU	BITUMEN	BEIOSSU	SOUBISE	BELLNPU	BULLPEN
BEIMOOR	BOOMIER	BEIOSSW	BOWSIES	BELLORR	BORRELL
BEIMORS	BROMISE	BEIOSTT	BOTTIES	BELLOSU	BOULLES
BEIMORW	IMBOWER	BEIOSTX	BOXIEST		LOBULES
	WOMBIER	BEIOSTY	OBESITY		SOLUBLE
BEIMORZ	BROMIZE	BEIPPSU	BUPPIES	BELLOSW	BELLOWS
BEIMOSS	OBEISMS	BEIPSST	BESPITS	BELLOUV	VOLUBLE
BEIMOSZ	ZOMBIES	BEIQRTU	BRIQUET	BELLRRU	BURRELL
BEIMOTV	BEVOMIT	BEIQSSU	BISQUES	BELLRSU	BULLERS
BEIMPRU	BUMPIER	BEIRRRU	BURRIER	BELLSTU	BULLETS
BEIMRST	BETRIMS	BEIRRSU	BRISURE	BELMMOO	EMBLOOM
	TIMBERS		BRUISER	BELMMRU	MUMBLER
	TIMBRES		BURIERS	BELMMSU	BUMMELS
BEIMRSU	ERBIUMS	BEIRRTU	BRUITER		BUMMLES
	IMBRUES	BEIRSSS	BRISSES		MUMBLES
	IMBURSE	BEIRSST	BESTIRS	BELMNOS	NOMBLES
BEIMRTU	IMBRUTE		BISTERS	BELMNOU	NELUMBO
	TERBIUM		BISTRES	BELMNOY	BENOMYL
BEIMRTY	TIMBERY		BITSERS	BELMNSU	NUMBLES
BEIMSST	BEMISTS		BREISTS	BELMOOR	BLOOMER
BEIMSTU	SUBITEM	BEIRSSU	BRUISES		REBLOOM

BELMOOS	BLOOSME
BELMOOT	BOOMLET
BELMOPR	PROBLEM
BELMORT	TEMBLOR
BELMOSU	EMBOLUS
BELMOSY	SYMBOLE
BELMPRU	PLUMBER
	REPLUMB
BELMRRU	RUMBLER
BELMRSU	LUMBERS
	RUMBLES
	SLUMBER
	UMBRELS
BELMRTU	TUMBLER
	TUMBREL
BELMRTY	TREMBLY
BELMSTU	STUMBLE
	TUMBLES
BELNNOU	UNNOBLE
BELNNTU	UNBLENT
BELNOOR	BORNEOL
BELNOOV	BOLONEY
BELNOST	NOBLEST
BELNOSZ	BENZOLS
BELNOYZ	BENZOYL
BELNRTU	BLUNTER
BELNSSU	UNBLESS
BELNSTU	SUNBELT
	UNBELTS
	UNBLEST
BELNSYZ	BENZYLS
BELOOPR	BLOOPER
BELOORS	BOLEROS
BELOOSS	SOBOLES
BELOPSU	PUEBLOS
BELORSS	ORBLESS
BELORST	BOLSTER
	BOLTERS
	LOBSTER
BELORSU	ROUBLES
BELORSW	BLOWERS
	BOWLERS
BELORSY	SOBERLY
BELORTT	BLOTTER
	BOTTLER
BELORTU	BOULTER
	TROUBLE
BELOSSU	BLOUSES
	BOLUSES
BELOSSW	BLOWSES
	BOWLESS
BELOSTT	BOTTLES
BELOSTU	BOLETUS
BELOSWZ	BLOWZES
BELRRSU	BURLERS
	BURRELS
BELRRTU	BLURTER
BELRSTU	BLUSTER
	BUSTLER
	BUTLERS
	SUBTLER
BELRSUU	SUBRULE
BELRSUY	BURLEYS
BELRTUY	BRUTELY
	BUTLERY
BELSSTU	BUSTLES
	SUBLETS
BELSTTU	BUTTLES
BELSTUU	TUBULES
BEMMNOS	MOBSMEN
BEMMOOS	EMBOSOM
BEMMORR	BROMMER
BEMMRRU	BRUMMER
BEMMRSU	BUMMERS
BEMMSTU	BUMMEST
BEMNORW	EMBROWN
BEMNORY	EMBRYON
BEMNOST	ENTOMBS
BEMNOSU	UMBONES
BEMNOSW	ENWOMBS
BEMNPTY	BYNEMPT
BEMNRSU	NUMBERS
BEMNSTU	NUMBEST
BEMNSUU	SUBMENU
BEMNTTU	BUTMENT
BEMOOPR	PREBOOM
BEMOORS	BOOMERS
BEMORRS	SOMBRER
BEMORSS	SOMBERS
	SOMBRES
BEMORST	BESTORM
	MOBSTER
BEMORSU	UMBROSE
BEMORSW	BEWORMS
BEMORSY	EMBRYOS
BEMORUX	BUXOMER
BEMORWW	WEBWORM
BEMOTUY	MYOTUBE
BEMPRSU	BUMPERS
BEMSSTU	BESMUTS
BEMSSUU	SUBSUME
BEMSTUW	STEWBUM
BENNORU	UNBORNE
BENNORW	NEWBORN
BENNORZ	BRONZEN
BENNOST	BONNETS
BENNOSU	UNBONES
BENNSSU	BUNSENS
BENNSTU	BUNNETS
BENOORS	BOONERS
BENOOST	OBENTOS
BENOPRR	PREBORN
BENOPRU	UPBORNE
BENORRW	BROWNER
BENORRZ	BRONZER
BENORST	BRETONS
	SORBENT
BENORSU	BOURNES
	UNROBES
	UNSOBER
BENORSZ	BRONZES
BENORWY	BYWONER
BENOSSU	BONUSES
BENOSSW	BESNOWS
BENOSTT	BOTNETS
BENOSTU	SUBTONE
BENOSUX	UNBOXES
BENOSUZ	SUBZONE
BENOSWY	NEWSBOY
BENRRSU	BURNERS
BENRSSU	BRUSSEN
BENRSTU	BRUNETS
	BUNTERS
	BURNETS
	BURSTEN
	SUBRENT
BENSSTU	SUBNETS
BEOORSS	BROOSES
	SORBOSE
BEOORST	BOOSTER
	REBOOTS
BEOORSZ	BOOZERS
	REBOZOS
BEOORTY	BOOTERY
BEOPPRS	BOPPERS
BEOPRRS	PROBERS
BEOPRRV	PROVERB
BEOPRST	BESPORT
BEOPSST	BESPOTS
BEOPSTU	BESPOUT
BEOQSSU	BOSQUES
BEOQSTU	BOSQUET
BEOQSUY	OBSEQUY
BEOQTUU	BOUQUET
BEORRSS	RESORBS
BEORRSW	BROWSER
BEORRWY	BEWORRY
BEORSST	BESORTS
	SORBETS
	STROBES
BEORSSU	BOURSES
BEORSSW	BOWSERS
	BROWSES
BEORSTT	BETTORS
BEORSTU	OBTUSER
BEORSTV	OBVERTS
BEORSTW	BESTROW
BEORSTZ	BORTZES
BEORSUU	UBEROUS
BEORSUZ	BROUZES
	SUBZERO
BEORSVV	BOVVERS
BEORSWY	BOWYERS
BEORUVY	OVERBUY
BEOSSST	BOSSEST
	BOSSETS
BEOSSTT	OBTESTS
BEOSSTW	BESTOWS
BEOSSWY	BOWSEYS
BEPRRTU	PERTURB
BEPRSUY	PREBUYS
BEPRTUY	PUBERTY
BEPSTUY	SUBTYPE
BEQRSUU	BRUSQUE
BEQSTUY	QUBYTES
BERRRSU	BURRERS
BERRSTU	BRUTERS
	BURSTER
BERSSTU	BUSTERS
BERSTTU	BUTTERS
BERSTUV	SUBVERT
BERSUZZ	BUZZERS

BERTTUY	BUTTERY	BGGNOSU	BUGONGS	BGILOOY	BIOLOGY
BESSSTU	SUBSETS	BGHHIOY	HIGHBOY	BGILRSU	BUSGIRL
BESSTTU	SUBTEST	BGHIILS	GHIBLIS	BGIMMNU	BUMMING
BESTTUX	SUBTEXT	BGHIINS	BINGHIS	BGIMNNU	NUMBING
BFFGIIN	BIFFING	BGHILST	BLIGHTS	BGIMNOO	BOOMING
BFFGINO	BOFFING	BGHILTY	BLIGHTY	BGIMNOR	BORMING
BFFGINU	BUFFING	BGHINOO	BOOHING	BGIMNOT	TOMBING
BFFIINS	BIFFINS		HOBOING	BGIMNOW	WOMBING
BFFILOO	BOILOFF	BGHINOR	BIGHORN	BGIMNPU	BUMPING
BFFINOS	BOFFINS	BGHINSU	BUSHING	BGIMOSY	BOGYISM
BFFLLUY	BLUFFLY	BGHIPSU	BUSHPIG	BGINNOS	BONINGS
BFFLOOW	BLOWOFF	BGHIRST	BRIGHTS	BGINNOU	BOUNING
BFFNOOU	BUFFOON	BGHLRUU	BULGHUR	BGINNOW	BOWNING
BFFORSU	RUBOFFS		BURGHUL	BGINNRU	BURNING
BFFOSUY	BUYOFFS	BGHMORU	HOMBURG	BGINNTU	BUNTING
BFGIOOT	BIGFOOT	BGHMSUU	HUMBUGS	BGINOOS	BOOSING
BFGIORT	FROGBIT	BGHNORU	HORNBUG	BGINOOT	BOOTING
BFGOOSW	FOGBOWS	BGHOORU	BOROUGH	BGINOOZ	BOOZING
BFHILSU	LUBFISH	BGHORSU	BROUGHS	BGINOPP	BOPPING
BFHIOSX	BOXFISH	BGHORTU	BROUGHT	BGINOPR	PROBING
BFHIRSU	FURBISH	BGHOSTU	BOUGHTS	BGINORS	BORINGS
BFHISTU	TUBFISH	BGIIKLN	BILKING		ROBINGS
BFHLSUY	BUSHFLY	BGIIKNS	BIKINGS		SORBING
BFIILMO	BIOFILM	BGIILLN	BILLING	BGINORZ	ZORBING
BFIILRS	FIBRILS	BGIILMN	LIMBING	BGINOSS	BOSSING
BFIINOR	FIBROIN	BGIILNO	BOILING		GIBSONS
BFIINRS	FIBRINS	BGIILNR	BIRLING		OBSIGNS
BFILMRU	BRIMFUL	BGIILNS	SIBLING	BGINOSU	BOUSING
BFILOTY	LIFTBOY	BGIIMNR	BRIMING	BGINOSW	BOWINGS
BFILSUY	FUSIBLY	BGIIMNU	IMBUING		BOWSING
BFIMOYZ	ZOMBIFY	BGIINNN	BINNING	BGINOSX	BOXINGS
BFINOSW	BOWFINS	BGIINNR	BRINING	BGINOTT	BOTTING
BFIORSS	ROSBIFS		INBRING	BGINOUY	BUOYING
BFIORSU	FIBROUS	BGIINRR	BIRRING	BGINOWW	WINGBOW
BFIRTUY	BRUTIFY	BGIINRT	RINGBIT	BGINPRU	BURPING
BFKLOOU	BOOKFUL	BGIINST	BITINGS		UPBRING
BFKLOOY	FLYBOOK	BGIINTT	BITTING	BGINRRU	BURRING
BFKSSUU	SUBFUSK	BGIKLNU	BULKING	BGINRSU	SUBRING
BFLLOUW	BOWLFUL	BGIKNNO	BONKING	BGINRTU	BRUTING
BFLLOWY	BLOWFLY	BGIKNNU	BUNKING	BGINRUX	BRUXING
	FLYBLOW	BGIKNOO	BOOKING	BGINRUY	BURYING
BFLOSUX	BOXFULS	BGIKNOR	BORKING		RUBYING
BFLOSYY	FLYBOYS		BROKING	BGINSSU	BUSINGS
BFLSTUU	TUBFULS		BURKING		BUSSING
BFOOOTY	FOOTBOY	BGIKNRU	BURKING	BGINSTU	BUSTING
BGGGIIN	BIGGING	BGIKNSU	BUSKING		TUBINGS
BGGGINO	BOGGING	BGILLNO	BOLLING	BGINSUY	BUSYING
BGGGINU	BUGGING	BGILLNU	BULLING	BGINSWY	SWINGBY
BGGHIIS	BIGGISH	BGILMNO	MOBLING	BGINTTU	BUTTING
BGGHIOS	BOGGISH	BGILMNU	BLUMING	BGINUZZ	BUZZING
BGGIILN	BILGING	BGILMOU	GUMBOIL	BGIORSU	RUBIGOS
BGGIINN	BINGING	BGILNOO	BOOLING	BGIORTY	BIGOTRY
BGGIINS	BIGGINS	BGILNOS	GLOBINS	BGIOSSS	GOSSIBS
BGGIISW	BIGWIGS		GOBLINS	BGIUWZZ	BUZZWIG
BGGIITY	BIGGITY		LOBINGS	BGKLOOO	LOGBOOK
BGGILNO	GLOBING	BGILNOT	BILTONG	BGKORSY	GRYSBOK
BGGILNU	BUGLING		BOLTING	BGLMOOS	MOBLOGS
	BULGING	BGILNOW	BLOWING	BGLMRUY	GRUMBLY
			BOWLING	BGLNOOS	OBLONGS
BGGINNO	BONGING	BGILNOY	IGNOBLY	BGLNOOW	LONGBOW
BGGINNU	BUNGING	BGILNRU	BURLING	BGLNOUW	BLOWGUN
BGGINOS	BIGGONS	BGILNRY	BYRLING	BGLOOSU	GLOBOUS
BGGINOU	BOUGING	BGILNSU	BLUINGS	BGLOSSU	BUGLOSS
BGGINSU	BUGGINS	BGILNTU	BUTLING	BGLOSUY	BOGUSLY
BGGNOOS	BOGONGS	BGILOOR	OBLIGOR		

BGLRSUU	BULGURS	**BIILRSY**	RISIBLY	**BIMMORS**	BROMISM
BGMOORS	GOMBROS	**BIILSTW**	TWIBILS	**BIMNOOY**	BIONOMY
BGMOOTU	GUMBOOT	**BIILSVY**	VISIBLY	**BIMNORS**	BROMINS
BGMSSUU	SUBGUMS	**BIIMNOU**	NIOBIUM		MISBORN
BGNOOWY	GOWNBOY	**BIIMNSU**	MINIBUS	**BIMNORW**	IMBROWN
BGNOSSU	SUBSONG	**BIIMOSS**	OBIISMS	**BIMNOSS**	BONISMS
BGOORSU	BURGOOS	**BIIMOSZ**	IMBIZOS	**BIMNOST**	INTOMBS
BGORTUU	BURGOUT	**BIIMPRS**	BIPRISM	**BIMNOSU**	OMNIBUS
BGORTUW	BUGWORT	**BIIMSTU**	STIBIUM	**BIMNOSY**	SYMBION
BGOSTUU	BUGOUTS	**BIINORV**	VIBRION	**BIMOSSS**	BOSSISM
BHHIIST	BHISHTI	**BIINOST**	BIOTINS	**BIMOSTW**	MISTBOW
BHHIKSU	BHIKHUS	**BIINOSU**	BINIOUS	**BIMOSTY**	SYMBIOT
BHIIINN	INHIBIN	**BIIORSV**	VIBRIOS	**BIMRSTU**	BRUTISM
BHIIINT	INHIBIT	**BIIOSUV**	BIVIOUS	**BIMRSUX**	BRUXISM
BHIINRS	BRINISH	**BIIRSTU**	BURITIS	**BIMSSSU**	SUBMISS
BHIIPSS	SIBSHIP	**BIISSTV**	VIBISTS	**BIMSSTU**	SUBMITS
BHIISST	BHISTIS	**BIISTTT**	TITBITS	**BINNOSU**	BUNIONS
BHIKLOS	BLOKISH	**BIJNOSU**	SUBJOIN	**BINOORS**	BONSOIR
BHIKOOS	BOOKISH	**BIKLLUY**	BULKILY	**BINOORT**	BIOTRON
BHIKSSU	BUKSHIS	**BIKLNOT**	INKBLOT	**BINOOST**	BONITOS
BHILLOY	BILLYOH	**BIKLNOY**	LINKBOY	**BINOOSU**	NIOBOUS
BHILLSU	BULLISH	**BIKLRSY**	BRISKLY	**BINORST**	RIBSTON
BHILOTU	HOLIBUT	**BIKMNOO**	BOOMKIN	**BINORSU**	BOURSIN
BHILPSU	PUBLISH	**BIKMNPU**	BUMPKIN	**BINORUW**	UNIBROW
BHILSUY	BUSHILY	**BIKMNSU**	BUMKINS	**BINOSST**	BONISTS
BHIMOOR	RHOMBOI	**BIKMOSS**	IMBOSKS	**BINPSUY**	BUNYIPS
BHIMOOS	HOBOISM	**BIKNSSU**	BUSKINS	**BINRSTU**	INBURST
BHIMOPR	BIMORPH	**BIKORRW**	RIBWORK	**BINRTUY**	BUTYRIN
BHIMOPS	PHOBISM	**BIKSUUZ**	BUZUKIS	**BINSTTU**	UNBITTS
BHIMORT	THROMBI	**BILLNOS**	BILLONS	**BINSTUU**	SUBUNIT
BHIMORU	BOHRIUM	**BILLNOU**	BULLION	**BIOOORS**	ROOIBOS
BHIMSTU	BISMUTH	**BILLOOY**	LOOBILY	**BIOORSZ**	BORZOIS
BHINRSU	BURNISH	**BILLOPX**	PILLBOX	**BIOOSST**	OBOISTS
BHIOOPR	BIOPHOR	**BILLORS**	BRILLOS	**BIOOSUV**	OBVIOUS
BHIOORS	BOORISH	**BILLOSW**	BILLOWS	**BIOPRST**	PROBITS
BHIOOST	BOOSHIT	**BILLOSY**	BILLYOS	**BIOPRTY**	PROBITY
BHIOPSS	BISHOPS	**BILLOUV**	VOLUBIL	**BIORRTU**	BURRITO
BHIOPST	PHOBIST	**BILLOWY**	BILLOWY	**BIORRTW**	RIBWORT
BHIOSWZ	SHOWBIZ	**BILLRUY**	BURLILY	**BIORSST**	BISTROS
BHIRSTU	BRUTISH	**BILLRWY**	WRYBILL	**BIORSTT**	BISTORT
BHIRTTU	TURBITH	**BILMNOR**	NOMBRIL		BITTORS
BHISTTU	BUSHTIT	**BILMOSU**	LIMBOUS	**BIORSUU**	RUBIOUS
BHKNOSU	BOHUNKS	**BILMPUY**	BUMPILY	**BIORTTU**	BITTOUR
BHLRSUU	BULRUSH	**BILMRSU**	UMBRILS	**BIOSTUW**	WOUBITS
BHMOORS	RHOMBOS	**BILMRTU**	TUMBRIL	**BIRSTTU**	BITTURS
BHMORSU	RHOMBUS	**BILMSUU**	BULIMUS		TURBITS
BHMUUZZ	HUMBUZZ	**BILNNOY**	BONNILY	**BISSSTU**	SUBSIST
BHOOOOS	BOOHOOS	**BILNOTU**	BOTULIN	**BISSTTU**	TUBISTS
BHOOPSY	SHOPBOY	**BILNTUU**	TUBULIN	**BISTUUU**	BUSUUTI
BHOOSTW	BOWSHOT		UNBUILT	**BJMOOSU**	BOOJUMS
BHOOSWX	SHOWBOX	**BILOOPT**	POTBOIL	**BJNOORU**	BONJOUR
BHORSST	BORSHTS	**BILOOYZ**	BOOZILY	**BKLNUUY**	UNBULKY
BHPRSUU	BRUSHUP	**BILOPSU**	UPBOILS	**BKLOTUU**	OUTBULK
BIIIKNS	BIKINIS	**BILORST**	BRISTOL	**BKMNSUU**	BUNKUMS
BIIKLOT	KILOBIT		STROBIL	**BKNNOOO**	NONBOOK
BIILLMS	MISBILL	**BILOSSU**	SUBSOIL	**BKNOOTW**	BOWKNOT
BIILLNO	BILLION	**BILOSSY**	BOSSILY	**BKNORSY**	SKYBORN
BIILLOU	BOUILLI	**BILPTUU**	UPBUILT	**BKOOOOS**	BOOKOOS
BIILLTW	TWIBILL	**BILRSTY**	BRISTLY	**BKOORWX**	WORKBOX
BIILNNR	BIRLINN		TRILBYS	**BKORSWY**	BYWORKS
BIILNQU	QUIBLIN	**BILRTTY**	BRITTLY	**BKRSTUU**	KRUBUTS
BIILNTU	INBUILT	**BILRTUY**	TILBURY	**BLLNTUY**	BLUNTLY
BIILNVY	BIVINYL	**BIMMOOS**	IMBOSOM	**BLLOOOS**	LOBOLOS
BIILOSU	BILIOUS		MIOMBOS	**BLLOSUU**	BULLOUS

	LOBULUS	**BOPSSTU**	POSTBUS	**CCEEHOR**	ECORCHE
BLLOSUY	SOLUBLY	**BORRSUW**	BURROWS	**CCEEHOU**	COUCHEE
BLLOUVY	VOLUBLY	**BORSSTW**	BROWSTS	**CCEEHRS**	CRECHES
BLMNPUU	PLUMBUM	**BORSTTU**	TURBOTS		SCREECH
BLMNPUU	UNPLUMB	**BORSTUU**	RUBOUTS	**CCEEILN**	LICENCE
BLMOOOT	TOMBOLO	**BORSTXY**	BOSTRYX	**CCEEILS**	LECCIES
BLMOORW	LOBWORM	**BOSTUUY**	BUYOUTS	**CCEEINR**	ECCRINE
BLMOOSS	BLOSSOM			**CCEEINS**	SCIENCE
BLMOSSY	SYMBOLS	**BPRSTUU**	UPBURST	**CCEEIOR**	CICOREE
BLMOUXY	BUXOMLY	**CCCDIOO**	COCCOID	**CCEEIRS**	RECCIES
BLMRSUY	SLUMBRY	**CCCDIOS**	COCCIDS	**CCEEIRV**	CREVICE
BLMSTUY	STUMBLY	**CCCNOOT**	CONCOCT	**CCEEKOY**	COCKEYE
BLNNOUW	UNBLOWN	**CCCOOSU**	COCCOUS	**CCEELNU**	LUCENCE
BLNOORW	LOWBORN	**CCDEEER**	RECCEED	**CCEELRY**	RECYCLE
BLNOOSS	BOLSONS	**CCDEEHK**	CHECKED	**CCEENRY**	RECENCY
BLNOOSU	BLOUSON	**CCDEEIM**	ECDEMIC	**CCEEORR**	COERCER
BLNOPUW	UPBLOWN	**CCDEEIO**	ECOCIDE	**CCEEORS**	COERCES
BLNORSY	BORNYLS	**CCDEEIR**	RECCIED	**CCEEORT**	COERECT
BLNOSTU	UNBOLTS	**CCDEEIS**	DECCIES	**CCEERSY**	SECRECY
BLOOOTX	TOOLBOX	**CCDEEKL**	CLECKED	**CCEFHRU**	CURCHEF
BLOOPWY	PLOWBOY	**CCDEENO**	CONCEDE	**CCEFNOT**	CONFECT
BLOOQUY	OBLOQUY	**CCDEENY**	DECENCY	**CCEGINY**	GYNECIC
BLOORWW	LOWBROW	**CCDEEOR**	COERCED	**CCEGNOY**	COGENCY
BLOOSWY	LOWBOYS	**CCDEEPS**	SPECCED	**CCEHHIS**	CHICHES
BLOOTUW	BLOWOUT	**CCDEESU**	SUCCEED	**CCEHIKN**	CHICKEN
BLOPSTU	SUBPLOT	**CCDEFLO**	FLOCCED	**CCEHIKU**	CHUCKIE
BLOPSUW	BLOWUPS	**CCDEHIL**	CLICHED	**CCEHILS**	CHICLES
	UPBLOWS	**CCDEHIN**	CINCHED		CLICHES
BLORSTU	BRULOTS	**CCDEHKO**	CHOCKED	**CCEHILU**	CULCHIE
BLOSSTU	SUBLOTS	**CCDEHKU**	CHUCKED	**CCEHIMS**	CHEMICS
BLRTUYY	BUTYRYL	**CCDEHNO**	CONCHED	**CCEHINO**	CONCHIE
BMNOOOW	MOONBOW	**CCDEHOU**	COUCHED	**CCEHINS**	CINCHES
BMNOOSU	UNBOSOM	**CCDEHTW**	CWTCHED	**CCEHINT**	TECHNIC
BMNORUW	MOWBURN	**CCDEIIL**	ICICLED	**CCEHINZ**	ZECCHIN
BMNOSTU	UNTOMBS	**CCDEIIT**	DEICTIC	**CCEHIOR**	CHOICER
BMOOORX	BOXROOM	**CCDEIKL**	CLICKED		CHOREIC
BMOORSY	BYROOMS	**CCDEIKR**	CRICKED	**CCEHIOS**	CHOICES
BMOOSTT	BOTTOMS	**CCDEILR**	CIRCLED	**CCEHIRS**	SCREICH
BMOOSTY	TOMBOYS	**CCDEIMO**	COMEDIC		SCRIECH
BMORSST	STROMBS	**CCDEIOS**	CODICES	**CCEHIST**	CHICEST
BMORSUU	BRUMOUS	**CCDEIOT**	DOCETIC		HECTICS
	UMBROUS	**CCDEKLO**	CLOCKED	**CCEHKLU**	CHUCKLE
BNNRSUU	SUNBURN		COCKLED	**CCEHKMS**	SCHMECK
BNNRTUU	UNBURNT	**CCDEKLU**	CLUCKED	**CCEHKNU**	UNCHECK
BNOOSST	BOSTONS	**CCDEKOR**	CROCKED	**CCEHKOR**	CHOCKER
BNOOSTU	BOUTONS	**CCDELOU**	OCCLUDE	**CCEHKPU**	CHECKUP
	UNBOOTS	**CCDENOO**	CONCEDO	**CCEHKRU**	CHUCKER
BNOOTTY	BOTTONY	**CCDENOS**	SCONCED	**CCEHLOS**	CLOCHES
BNORSSU	SUBORNS	**CCDENOU**	CONDUCE	**CCEHLRU**	CLERUCH
BNORSTU	BURTONS	**CCDEOST**	DECOCTS	**CCEHLSU**	CLEUCHS
BNORSUU	BURNOUS	**CCDHIIL**	CICHLID		CULCHES
BNORTUU	BURNOUT	**CCDIILO**	CODICIL	**CCEHNOS**	CONCHES
	OUTBURN	**CCDIILU**	CULICID	**CCEHOOS**	COOCHES
BNOSSUW	SUNBOWS	**CCDIIOR**	CRICOID	**CCEHORS**	CROCHES
BNOSTTU	BUTTONS	**CCDILOY**	CYCLOID	**CCEHORT**	CROCHET
BNOTTUY	BUTTONY	**CCDILYY**	DICYCLY	**CCEHORU**	COUCHER
BOOPSTW	BOWPOTS	**CCDKLOU**	CUCKOLD	**CCEHOSS**	COSECHS
BOOPSTX	POSTBOX	**CCDNOOR**	CONCORD	**CCEHOSU**	COUCHES
BOOPSTY	POSTBOY	**CCDNOTU**	CONDUCT	**CCEHRSU**	CURCHES
	POTBOYS	**CCEEGNO**	COGENCE	**CCEHSTU**	CUTCHES
BOORRSW	BORROWS	**CCEEHIK**	CHICKEE	**CCEHSTW**	CWTCHES
BOORRTY	ROBOTRY	**CCEEHIV**	CEVICHE	**CCEIILS**	CILICES
BOOSTUW	WOOBUTS	**CCEEHKR**	CHECKER		ICICLES
BOOSWWW	BOWWOWS		RECHECK	**CCEIIMS**	CIMICES

CCEIIPS	PICCIES	**CCENORW**	CONCREW	**CCIILOT**	COLITIC
CCEIIRT	ICTERIC	**CCENOSS**	SCONCES	**CCIILPR**	CIRCLIP
CCEIIST	CECITIS	**CCENOTV**	CONVECT	**CCIILST**	CLITICS
CCEIKLR	CLICKER	**CCEOOTT**	COCOTTE	**CCIINPS**	PICNICS
CCEIKLT	CLICKET	**CCEOPRT**	PERCOCT	**CCIIRST**	CRITICS
CCEIKOR	COCKIER	**CCEORRT**	CORRECT	**CCIIRTU**	CIRCUIT
CCEIKOS	COCKIES	**CCEORRU**	REOCCUR	**CCIISTY**	SICCITY
CCEIKRT	CRICKET	**CCEORSS**	ESCROCS	**CCIKLOW**	COWLICK
CCEIKRY	CRICKEY		SOCCERS	**CCIKLOY**	COCKILY
CCEILMO	CELOMIC	**CCEORTW**	TWOCCER		COLICKY
CCEILNU	NUCLEIC	**CCEOSSU**	SUCCOSE	**CCIKOPT**	COCKPIT
CCEILOT	COCTILE	**CCERTUW**	CREWCUT	**CCILNOO**	COLONIC
CCEILRR	CIRCLER	**CCESSSU**	SUCCESS	**CCILNOU**	COUNCIL
CCEILRS	CIRCLES	**CCFIRUY**	CRUCIFY	**CCILNSY**	CYCLINS
	CLERICS	**CCFLOSU**	FLOCCUS	**CCILOOP**	PICCOLO
CCEILRT	CIRCLET	**CCGHINO**	GNOCCHI	**CCILSTY**	CYCLIST
CCEILSU	CULICES	**CCGIINS**	SICCING	**CCIMNOU**	UNCOMIC
CCEILSY	CYCLISE	**CCGIINT**	TICCING	**CCIMOTY**	MYCOTIC
	CYLICES	**CCGIKNO**	COCKING	**CCINOOT**	COCTION
CCEILTU	CUTICLE	**CCGIKNU**	CUCKING	**CCINORY**	CRYONIC
CCEILYZ	CYCLIZE	**CCGILNY**	CYCLING	**CCINOTV**	CONVICT
CCEIMNO	MECONIC	**CCGKOOR**	GORCOCK	**CCINPSY**	PYCNICS
CCEIMOS	COMICES	**CCHHIIS**	CHICHIS	**CCIOORS**	SIROCCO
	MOCCIES	**CCHHIIT**	ICHTHIC	**CCIOPTU**	OCCIPUT
CCEIMOT	COMETIC	**CCHHILS**	SCHLICH	**CCIORSS**	SCIROCS
CCEIMST	SMECTIC	**CCHHINY**	CHINCHY	**CCIOSTT**	TICTOCS
CCEINOR	CORNICE	**CCHHOOS**	CHOCHOS	**CCIPRTY**	CRYPTIC
	CROCEIN	**CCHHRUY**	CHURCHY	**CCIRSUY**	CIRCUSY
	CROCINE	**CCHIIST**	STICHIC	**CCKMOOS**	MOCOCKS
CCEINOS	CONCISE	**CCHIKMS**	SCHMICK	**CCKMOSU**	MOCUCKS
CCEINOT	CONCEIT	**CCHIKOS**	COCKISH	**CCKNOSU**	UNCOCKS
CCEINRT	CENTRIC	**CCHIKST**	SCHTICK	**CCKOOSU**	CUCKOOS
CCEINSS	SCENICS		TCHICKS	**CCKOPSU**	COCKUPS
CCEIOPP	COPPICE			**CCKOSTU**	CUSTOCK
CCEIOPT	ECTOPIC	**CCHILOR**	CHLORIC	**CCLMSUU**	MUCLUCS
CCEIORS	CICEROS	**CCHIMOR**	CHROMIC	**CCLOOOZ**	ZOCCOLO
CCEIORT	CEROTIC	**CCHIMSY**	CHYMICS	**CCLOPSY**	CYCLOPS
	ORECTIC	**CCHINOR**	CHRONIC	**CCLOSTU**	OCCULTS
CCEIOSS	CISCOES	**CCHINOS**	CHICONS	**CCMOOOR**	MOROCCO
CCEIPST	SCEPTIC		COCHINS	**CCNOOOS**	COCOONS
CCEIRST	CRETICS	**CCHINSU**	SCUCHIN	**CCNOOPU**	PUCCOON
CCEISSU	SUCCISE	**CCHIORY**	CHICORY	**CCNOOTU**	COCONUT
CCEJNOT	CONJECT	**CCHIOTW**	COWITCH	**CCNOPUY**	CONCUPY
CCEKLOR	CLOCKER	**CCHIPSU**	HICCUPS	**CCNORSU**	CONCURS
	COCKLER	**CCHIPSY**	PSYCHIC	**CCNOSSU**	CONCUSS
CCEKLOS	COCKLES	**CCHIPUY**	HICCUPY	**CCOOORS**	ROCOCOS
CCEKNOT	CONTECK	**CCHIRST**	SCRITCH	**CCORSSU**	SUCCORS
CCEKNOY	COCKNEY	**CCHKLOS**	SCHLOCK	**CCORSUU**	SUCCOUR
CCEKOPS	COPECKS	**CCHKMOS**	SCHMOCK	**CCORSUY**	SUCCORY
CCEKOPT	PETCOCK	**CCHKMSU**	SCHMUCK	**CCOSSTU**	STUCCOS
CCEKORS	COCKERS	**CCHKOOS**	CHOCKOS	**CCOSSUU**	SUCCOUS
	RECOCKS	**CCHKOSY**	COCKSHY	**CCSSSUU**	SUCCUSS
CCEKORT	CROCKET	**CCHKPUU**	UPCHUCK	**CDDDEEI**	DECIDED
CCEKOST	COCKETS	**CCHKSTU**	SCHTUCK	**CDDDEEO**	DECODED
CCELLOT	COLLECT	**CCHLSTU**	SCULTCH	**CDDDEEU**	DEDUCED
CCELNOY	CYCLONE	**CCHLTUY**	CLUTCHY	**CDDDELO**	CLODDED
CCELNUY	LUCENCY	**CCHNOOS**	CONCHOS		CODDLED
CCELRSY	CYCLERS	**CCHNRSU**	SCRUNCH	**CDDDELU**	CUDDLED
CCELRYY	CYCLERY	**CCHNRUY**	CRUNCHY	**CDDDERU**	CRUDDED
CCENNOR	CONCERN	**CCHOORS**	SCROOCH	**CDDDESU**	SCUDDED
CCENNOT	CONCENT	**CCHOOST**	SCOOTCH	**CDDEEER**	DECREED
	CONNECT	**CCHOSTU**	SUCCOTH		RECEDED
CCENOPT	CONCEPT	**CCIIILS**	SILICIC	**CDDEEES**	SECEDED
CCENORT	CONCERT	**CCIILNO**	COLICIN	**CDDEEII**	DEICIDE
		CCIILNS	CLINICS		

CDDEEIN	INCEDED	CDEEEHP	CHEEPED	CDEEINT	ENTICED
CDDEEIR	DECIDER		DEPECHE	CDEEINV	EVINCED
	DECRIED	CDEEEHR	CHEERED	CDEEIOS	DIOCESE
CDDEEIS	DECIDES		REECHED	CDEEIOV	DEVOICE
CDDEEIX	EXCIDED	CDEEEHS	CHEESED	CDEEIPR	PIERCED
CDDEEKL	DECKLED	CDEEEIP	EPICEDE	CDEEIPT	PEDETIC
CDDEEKO	DECKOED	CDEEEIV	DECEIVE	CDEEIRR	DECRIER
	DECOKED	CDEEEJT	EJECTED	CDEEIRS	DECRIES
CDDEENO	ENCODED	CDEEEKL	CLEEKED		DEICERS
CDDEENS	DESCEND	CDEEELP	CLEEPED	CDEEIRT	RECITED
	SCENDED	CDEEELR	CREELED		TIERCED
CDDEENU	UNCEDED	CDEEELT	ELECTED	CDEEIST	DECEITS
CDDEEOR	DECODER	CDEEEPR	CREEPED	CDEEISV	DEVICES
	RECODED		PRECEDE	CDEEISX	EXCIDES
CDDEEOS	DECODES	CDEEERR	DECREER		EXCISED
CDDEEOY	DECOYED	CDEEERS	CREESED	CDEEITV	EVICTED
CDDEERU	REDUCED		DECREES	CDEEITX	EXCITED
CDDEESU	DEDUCES		RECEDES	CDEEJNO	CONJEED
	SEDUCED		SECEDER	CDEEJST	DEJECTS
CDDEEUW	CUDWEED	CDEEERT	DECREET	CDEEKKL	KECKLED
CDDEHIL	CHILDED		ERECTED	CDEEKLR	CLERKED
CDDEHIN	CHIDDEN	CDEEESS	SECEDES	CDEEKLS	DECKELS
CDDEHIT	DICHTED	CDEEESX	EXCEEDS		DECKLES
	DITCHED	CDEEFFH	CHEFFED	CDEEKNR	REDNECK
CDDEHNU	DUNCHED	CDEEFHT	FETCHED	CDEEKNS	SNECKED
CDDEHOR	CHORDED	CDEEFII	EDIFICE	CDEEKOS	DECOKES
CDDEHOU	DOUCHED	CDEEFKL	FLECKED	CDEEKPS	SPECKED
CDDEHRU	CHUDDER	CDEEFLT	CLEFTED	CDEEKRS	DECKERS
CDDEIIS	DISCIDE		DEFLECT	CDEEKRT	TRECKED
CDDEINU	INDUCED	CDEEFOR	DEFORCE	CDEEKRW	WRECKED
CDDEIOS	DISCOED	CDEEFST	DEFECTS	CDEELMM	CLEMMED
CDDEISU	CUDDIES	CDEEGIR	GRIECED	CDEELOS	ECLOSED
CDDELOR	CODDLER	CDEEGKT	GEDECKT	CDEELPU	CUPELED
CDDELOS	CODDLES	CDEEGNO	CONGEED		DECUPLE
	SCOLDED	CDEEHIP	CEPHEID	CDEELPY	YCLEPED
CDDELOU	CLOUDED	CDEEHIS	DEHISCE	CDEELRU	RECULED
CDDELRU	CRUDDLE	CDEEHIT	CHEDITE		ULCERED
	CUDDLER	CDEEHIV	CHEVIED	CDEELSU	SCEDULE
	CURDLED	CDEEHKL	HECKLED		SECLUDE
CDDELSU	CUDDLES	CDEEHLP	CHELPED	CDEELUX	EXCLUDE
	SCUDDLE	CDEEHLT	LETCHED	CDEENOR	ENCODER
CDDENOU	UNCODED	CDEEHLW	WELCHED		ENCORED
CDDENSU	CUDDENS	CDEEHMS	SCHEMED	CDEENOS	ENCODES
CDDEORS	CODDERS	CDEEHNW	WENCHED		SECONDE
CDDEORW	CROWDED	CDEEHOR	CHORDEE	CDEENOZ	COZENED
CDDERSU	SCUDDER		COHERED	CDEENRS	DECERNS
CDDESTU	DEDUCTS		OCHERED		SCERNED
CDDGINO	CODDING	CDEEHPR	PERCHED	CDEENRT	CENTRED
CDDHIOR	DICHORD	CDEEHRS	CHEDERS		CREDENT
CDDIIIO	DIDICOI	CDEEHRT	RETCHED	CDEENST	DESCENT
CDDIIKN	NIDDICK	CDEEHRU	EUCHRED		SCENTED
CDDIIOP	DIPODIC	CDEEHST	CHESTED	CDEEOOY	COOEYED
CDDIIOS	DISCOID	CDEEHTT	TETCHED	CDEEOPR	COPERED
CDDIIOY	DIDICOY	CDEEIIT	EIDETIC		PRECODE
CDDIIRU	DRUIDIC	CDEEILN	DECLINE		PROCEED
CDDIKOP	PIDDOCK	CDEEILP	PEDICEL	CDEEORS	RECODES
CDDINSU	CUDDINS		PEDICLE	CDEEORV	COVERED
CDDIORS	DISCORD	CDEEILS	DECILES	CDEEORW	COWERED
CDDKOPU	PUDDOCK		DELICES	CDEEORY	DECOYER
CDDKORU	RUDDOCK	CDEEIMN	ENDEMIC	CDEEOST	CESTODE
CDEEEFL	FLEECED	CDEEIMS	DECIMES		ESCOTED
CDEEEFN	DEFENCE	CDEEINO	CODEINE		TEDESCO
CDEEEHK	CHEEKED	CDEEINR	CEDRINE	CDEEOTV	COVETED
CDEEEHL	LEECHED	CDEEINS	INCEDES	CDEERRU	RECURED

	REDUCER	CDEGORS	CODGERS	CDEHMOP	CHOMPED
CDEERSS	SCREEDS	CDEGOSU	SCOUGED	CDEHMOR	CHROMED
CDEERST	CRESTED	CDEGSUW	GWEDUCS	CDEHMOU	MOUCHED
CDEERSU	RECUSED	CDEHHIL	HILCHED	CDEHMPU	CHUMPED
	REDUCES	CDEHHIT	HITCHED	CDEHMTU	MUTCHED
	RESCUED	CDEHHNU	HUNCHED	CDEHNOR	CHONDRE
	SECURED	CDEHHOT	HOTCHED	CDEHNOT	NOTCHED
	SEDUCER	CDEHHTU	HUTCHED	CDEHNPU	PUNCHED
CDEERSW	DECREWS	CDEHIIL	CEILIDH	CDEHNRU	CHUNDER
	SCREWED	CDEHIIV	CHIVIED		CHURNED
CDEERTU	ERUCTED	CDEHIKN	CHINKED	CDEHNSU	DUNCHES
CDEERUV	DECURVE	CDEHIKO	HOICKED	CDEHNSY	SYNCHED
CDEESSU	SEDUCES	CDEHIKR	CHIRKED	CDEHOOP	POOCHED
CDEESSY	ECDYSES	CDEHIKT	THICKED	CDEHOPP	CHOPPED
CDEESTT	DECTETS	CDEHILL	CHILLED	CDEHOPT	POTCHED
	DETECTS	CDEHILO	CHELOID	CDEHOPU	POUCHED
CDEESUX	EXCUSED		HELCOID	CDEHORT	TORCHED
CDEFFHU	CHUFFED	CDEHILP	DELPHIC	CDEHORW	CHOWDER
CDEFFIL	CLIFFED	CDEHILR	CHILDER		COWHERD
CDEFFIO	COIFFED		CHIRLED	CDEHOSU	CHOUSED
CDEFFLO	COFFLED		ELDRICH		DOUCHES
CDEFFLU	CUFFLED	CDEHILS	CHIELDS		HOCUSED
CDEFFOS	SCOFFED		CHILDES	CDEHOSW	CHOWSED
CDEFFSU	SCUFFED	CDEHILT	LICHTED		COWSHED
CDEFHIL	FILCHED	CDEHIMR	CHIRMED	CDEHOTU	TOUCHED
CDEFHIN	FINCHED	CDEHIMT	MITCHED	CDEHOUV	VOUCHED
CDEFHMO	CHEFDOM	CDEHINN	CHINNED	CDEHPSY	PSYCHED
CDEFHOO	CHOOFED	CDEHINO	HEDONIC	CDEHRRU	CHURRED
CDEFIIT	DEFICIT	CDEHINP	PINCHED	CDEHRSU	CRUSHED
CDEFIKL	FICKLED	CDEHINW	WINCHED	CDEHSSU	DUCHESS
	FLICKED	CDEHIOR	CHOIRED	CDEHSTU	DUTCHES
CDEFILT	CLIFTED	CDEHIOW	COWHIDE	CDEHSTY	SCYTHED
CDEFINO	CONFIDE	CDEHIPP	CHIPPED	CDEIIKR	DICKIER
CDEFKLO	FLOCKED	CDEHIPR	CHIRPED	CDEIIKS	DICKIES
CDEFKOR	DEFROCK	CDEHIPT	PITCHED	CDEIILO	EIDOLIC
	FROCKED	CDEHIQU	QUICHED	CDEIIMR	DIMERIC
CDEFNOR	CORNFED	CDEHIRR	CHIRRED	CDEIINR	DINERIC
CDEFNTU	DEFUNCT	CDEHIRS	CHIDERS	CDEIINS	INCISED
CDEFOSU	DEFOCUS		HERDICS		INDICES
	FOCUSED	CDEHIRT	CHIRTED	CDEIINT	IDENTIC
CDEFRTU	FRUCTED		DITCHER		INCITED
CDEFSUU	FUCUSED		RICHTED	CDEIIOR	ERICOID
CDEGGHU	CHUGGED	CDEHIST	DITCHES	CDEIIOV	OVICIDE
CDEGGLO	CLOGGED		SICHTED	CDEIIRT	DICTIER
	COGGLED	CDEHISU	DUCHIES		ICTERID
CDEGGOR	CROGGED	CDEHITT	CHITTED	CDEIIRV	VERIDIC
CDEGGOS	SCOGGED	CDEHITW	WITCHED	CDEIIST	DEISTIC
CDEGGSU	SCUGGED	CDEHIVV	CHIVVED		DICIEST
CDEGHLU	GULCHED	CDEHIZZ	CHIZZED	CDEIISU	SUICIDE
CDEGHOU	COUGHED	CDEHKLO	HOCKLED	CDEIJST	DISJECT
CDEGIIN	DEICING	CDEHKNU	CHUNKED	CDEIKLN	CLINKED
CDEGIKN	DECKING	CDEHKOO	CHOOKED		NICKLED
CDEGILN	CLINGED	CDEHKOS	SHOCKED	CDEIKLP	PICKLED
CDEGILU	CLUDGIE	CDEHKOT	KOTCHED	CDEIKLS	SICKLED
CDEGINO	COIGNED	CDEHKSU	SHUCKED		SLICKED
CDEGINR	CRINGED	CDEHKUY	HEYDUCK	CDEIKLT	TICKLED
CDEGINU	DEUCING	CDEHLMU	MULCHED	CDEIKMS	MEDICKS
	EDUCING	CDEHLNU	LUNCHED	CDEIKNS	DICKENS
CDEGIOR	ERGODIC	CDEHLNY	LYNCHED		SNICKED
CDEGKOU	GEODUCK	CDEHLOT	CLOTHED	CDEIKNZ	ZINCKED
CDEGKUW	GWEDUCK	CDEHLRU	LURCHED	CDEIKOS	DOCKISE
CDEGLSU	CUDGELS	CDEHMMU	CHUMMED	CDEIKOY	YOICKED
CDEGNSU	SCUNGED	CDEHMNU	MUNCHED	CDEIKOZ	DOCKIZE
CDEGOOS	SCOOGED	CDEHMOO	MOOCHED	CDEIKPR	PRICKED

CDEIKRR	DERRICK	CDEIOPT	PICOTED		CROODLE
CDEIKRS	DICKERS	CDEIORS	DISCOER		CROOLED
	SCRIKED		SCODIER		DECOLOR
CDEIKRT	TRICKED	CDEIORT	CORDITE	CDELOPP	CLOPPED
CDEIKRU	DUCKIER	CDEIORU	COURIED	CDELOPU	COUPLED
CDEIKRW	WRICKED	CDEIORV	CODRIVE	CDELORS	SCOLDER
CDEIKST	DETICKS		DIVORCE	CDELORU	CLOURED
	STICKED	CDEIORW	CROWDIE	CDELORW	CLOWDER
CDEIKSU	DUCKIES	CDEIOST	CESTOID	CDELOST	COLDEST
CDEIKSW	WICKEDS		COEDITS	CDELOSU	DULCOSE
CDEIKSY	DICKEYS		COTISED	CDELOSW	SCOWLED
CDEILLO	CODILLE	CDEIPRS	CRISPED	CDELOTT	CLOTTED
	COLLIDE		DISCERP	CDELOTU	CLOUTED
	COLLIED	CDEIPRT	PREDICT	CDELOUY	DOUCELY
CDEILLU	CULLIED	CDEIPST	DEPICTS	CDELOWY	COWEDLY
CDEILMO	MELODIC		DISCEPT	CDELPSU	SCULPED
CDEILNU	INCLUDE	CDEIRRU	CURDIER	CDELRRU	CURDLER
	NUCLIDE		CURRIED	CDELRSU	CURDLES
CDEILOO	OCELOID	CDEIRST	CREDITS		SCUDLER
CDEILOP	POLICED		DIRECTS	CDELRUY	CRUDELY
CDEILOR	DOCILER	CDEIRSU	CRUISED	CDELSTU	DULCETS
CDEILOS	COLDIES		DISCURE	CDELTTU	CUTTLED
CDEILPP	CLIPPED	CDEIRSV	CERVIDS	CDELTUU	DUCTULE
CDEILPS	SPLICED		SCRIVED	CDEMMNO	COMMEND
CDEILPU	CLUPEID	CDEIRTV	VERDICT	CDEMMOO	COMMODE
CDEILQU	CLIQUED	CDEISST	DISSECT	CDEMMSU	SCUMMED
CDEILRS	CLERIDS	CDEISSY	ECDYSIS	CDEMNNO	CONDEMN
CDEILRU	LUCIDER	CDEITUX	EXCUDIT	CDEMNOP	COMPEND
CDEILST	DELICTS	CDEJNOU	JOUNCED	CDEMOOS	COMEDOS
CDEILSU	SLUICED	CDEKKNO	KNOCKED	CDEMOPT	COMPTED
CDEILTU	DUCTILE	CDEKLNO	CLONKED	CDEMORS	SCROMED
	DULCITE	CDEKLNU	CLUNKED	CDEMORU	DECORUM
CDEIMNO	DEMONIC	CDEKLOW	WEDLOCK	CDEMPRU	CRUMPED
CDEIMOR	DORMICE	CDEKLPU	PLUCKED	CDENNOO	CONDONE
CDEIMOS	MEDICOS	CDEKLRU	RUCKLED	CDENNOT	CONTEND
	MISCODE	CDEKLSU	SCULKED	CDENOOP	POONCED
CDEIMOT	DEMOTIC		SUCKLED	CDENOOR	CROONED
CDEIMPR	CRIMPED	CDEKMOS	SMOCKED	CDENOOS	CONDOES
CDEIMPU	PUMICED	CDEKNOR	DORNECK		SECONDO
CDEIMSU	MISCUED	CDEKNOS	DOCKENS	CDENOPU	POUNCED
CDEINOS	CODEINS	CDEKNRU	DRUCKEN		UNCOPED
	CONDIES	CDEKNSU	SUNDECK	CDENORS	CONDERS
	SECONDI		UNDECKS		CORSNED
CDEINOT	CTENOID	CDEKOOR	CROOKED		SCORNED
	DEONTIC	CDEKORS	DOCKERS	CDENORU	CRUNODE
	NOTICED		REDOCKS	CDENORW	CROWNED
CDEINOU	DOUCINE	CDEKORT	TROCKED		DECROWN
CDEINOZ	ZINCODE	CDEKOST	DESTOCK	CDENOSS	SECONDS
CDEINPR	PRINCED		DOCKETS	CDENOST	DOCENTS
CDEINRS	CINDERS		STOCKED	CDENOSY	ECDYSON
	DISCERN	CDEKRSU	DUCKERS	CDENOTU	COUNTED
	RESCIND	CDEKRTU	TRUCKED	CDENPUY	PUDENCY
CDEINRU	INDUCER	CDELLOU	COLLUDE	CDENRUU	UNCURED
CDEINRY	CINDERY		LOCULED	CDENRUY	DUNCERY
CDEINSU	CUNDIES	CDELLSU	SCULLED	CDEOOPP	COPEPOD
	INCUDES	CDELMOP	CLOMPED	CDEOOPS	OPCODES
	INCUSED	CDELMPU	CLUMPED		SCOOPED
	INDUCES	CDELMSU	MUSCLED	CDEOOPT	COOPTED
CDEINSX	EXSCIND	CDELMTU	MULCTED	CDEOORR	CORRODE
CDEINSZ	DEZINCS	CDELNOO	CONDOLE	CDEOORV	CODROVE
CDEINTT	TINCTED	CDELNOU	ENCLOUD		VOCODER
CDEINTU	UNCITED	CDELNOW	CLOWNED	CDEOOST	SCOOTED
CDEIOOR	COORIED	CDELNOY	CONDYLE	CDEOOTV	DOVECOT
CDEIOPR	PERCOID	CDELOOR	COLORED	CDEOPPR	CROPPED

CDEOPRS	CORPSED	CDHINSU	DUNCISH	CDIOSST	CODISTS
CDEOPRU	CROUPED	CDHIOOR	CHOROID	CDIOSTT	COTTIDS
	PRODUCE		OCHROID	CDIOSTY	CYSTOID
CDEOPSU	SCOUPED	CDHIORS	DROICHS	CDIOTUV	OVIDUCT
CDEOPSW	SCOWPED		ORCHIDS	CDIPRSY	CYPRIDS
CDEOQTU	DOCQUET	CDHIORY	DROICHY	CDIPSSU	CUSPIDS
CDEORRS	CORDERS	CDHIOTU	OUTCHID	CDIRSUY	DYSURIC
	RECORDS	CDHIPTY	DIPTYCH	CDIRTUY	CRUDITY
CDEORRW	CROWDER	CDHIRTY	CHYTRID	CDISSSU	DISCUSS
CDEORSS	CROSSED	CDHKOOR	HORDOCK	CDISSTY	CYSTIDS
	SCORSED	CDHORSS	SCHRODS	CDKMORU	MUDROCK
CDEORSU	COURSED	CDIIILP	LIPIDIC	CDKNNOU	DUNNOCK
	SCOURED	CDIIIOT	IDIOTIC	CDKNOOR	DORNOCK
	SOURCED	CDIIJRU	JURIDIC	CDKNOSU	UNDOCKS
CDEORSW	SCOWDER	CDIILLY	IDYLLIC	CDLNOUU	UNCLOUD
CDEORTU	COURTED	CDIILMO	DOMICIL	CDLOOPY	LYCOPOD
	EDUCTOR	CDIILNY	DICLINY	CDLOSTU	COULDST
CDEORUU	DOUCEUR	CDIILOP	DIPLOIC	CDMMOOO	COMMODO
CDEOSSU	ESCUDOS	CDIIMOS	DISOMIC	CDMNOOS	CONDOMS
CDEOSTU	CUSTODE	CDIINOR	CRINOID	CDMNSUU	CUNDUMS
	DOUCEST	CDIINOT	DICTION	CDMOOST	DOTCOMS
	DOUCETS	CDIINOV	VIDICON		TOMCODS
	SCOUTED	CDIINOZ	ZINCOID	CDMOSUW	MUDSCOW
CDEOSTY	CYTODES	CDIINST	INDICTS	CDNNOTU	CONTUND
CDEOSYZ	ZYDECOS	CDIINTU	DUNITIC	CDNOORS	CONDORS
CDEPRSU	SPRUCED	CDIIOPT	PODITIC		CORDONS
CDEPRTY	DECRYPT	CDIIORS	CIRSOID	CDNORSU	UNCORDS
CDERRSU	SCURRED	CDIIORX	CORIXID	CDNOTUW	CUTDOWN
CDERSTU	CRUDEST	CDIIOSS	CISSOID	CDOOOPT	OCTOPOD
	CRUSTED	CDIIOSV	VISCOID	CDOOOST	DOOCOTS
CDERSUZ	SCRUZED	CDIIOTY	IDIOTCY	CDOOPST	POSTDOC
CDFHIOS	CODFISH	CDIIPRY	PYRIDIC	CDOORRY	CORRODY
CDFIILU	FLUIDIC	CDIIRSU	SCIURID	CDOORST	DOCTORS
CDFIJOR	FJORDIC	CDIKNNU	NUDNICK	CDOOTUW	WOODCUT
CDFILUV	DULCIFY	CDIKNOR	DORNICK	CDOPRTU	PRODUCT
CDFIOOT	OCTOFID	CDIKNOW	WINDOCK	CDOSTUY	CUSTODY
CDFIOSU	FUCOIDS	CDIKNPU	DUCKPIN	CEEEEGH	GEECHEE
CDFNOOU	COFOUND	CDILLOO	COLLOID	CEEEEHL	LEECHEE
CDGHIIN	CHIDING	CDILLUY	LUCIDLY	CEEEELT	ELECTEE
CDGHILO	GLOCHID	CDILMTU	MIDCULT	CEEEFIL	FLEECIE
CDGIIKN	DICKING	CDILNOS	CODLINS	CEEEFLR	FLEECER
CDGIINO	GONIDIC	CDILOTU	DULOTIC	CEEEFLS	FLEECES
CDGIINS	DICINGS	CDILOTY	DICOTYL	CEEEFNR	REFENCE
	DISCING	CDIMMOU	MODICUM	CEEEGNR	REGENCE
CDGIINT	DICTING	CDIMNOO	MONODIC	CEEEGNS	EGENCES
CDGIKNO	DOCKING	CDIMNSU	MUNDICS	CEEEGRS	GREECES
CDGIKNU	DUCKING	CDIMOOR	CORMOID	CEEEHIR	REECHIE
CDGILNO	CODLING	CDIMOOS	COSMOID	CEEEHKS	KEECHES
	LINGCOD	CDIMOSS	COSMIDS	CEEEHLL	ECHELLE
CDGINNO	CONDIGN	CDIMOSU	MUCOIDS	CEEEHLS	ELCHEES
CDGINOR	CORDING		MUSCOID		LEECHES
CDGINOS	CODINGS	CDIMSSU	MUSCIDS	CEEEHNR	ENCHEER
CDGINRU	CURDING	CDIMSTU	DICTUMS	CEEEHPR	CHEEPER
CDGINTU	DUCTING	CDINOOS	CONOIDS	CEEEHRR	CHEERER
CDGNOOO	COONDOG	CDINOOT	ODONTIC	CEEEHRS	REECHES
CDGOOSY	COYDOGS	CDINOSY	SYNODIC	CEEEHSS	CHEESES
CDHIIMO	DOCHMII	CDINOTU	CONDUIT	CEEEINP	EPICENE
CDHIINT	CHINDIT		NOCTUID	CEEEIPR	CREEPIE
CDHIIST	DISTICH	CDINSSY	SYNDICS	CEEEIRV	RECEIVE
CDHILLY	CHILDLY	CDINSTU	INDUCTS	CEEEITV	EVICTEE
CDHILNU	UNCHILD	CDIOOTT	COTTOID	CEEEJRT	REEJECT
CDHILOR	CHLORID	CDIOPRR	RIPCORD	CEEELLU	ECUELLE
CDHILOS	COLDISH	CDIOPSS	PSOCIDS	CEEELPY	YCLEEPE
CDHINOR	CHONDRI	CDIORSV	CORVIDS	CEEELRT	REELECT

CEEELST	CELESTE	CEEHILN	ELENCHI	CEEHOUV	VOUCHEE
CEEELSV	CLEEVES	CEEHILS	ELICHES	CEEHPRR	PERCHER
CEEEMPR	EMPERCE		HELICES	CEEHPRS	PERCHES
CEEENRS	RECENSE		LICHEES	CEEHPRU	UPCHEER
CEEENSS	ESSENCE	CEEHILV	VEHICLE	CEEHQRU	CHEQUER
CEEEPRR	CREEPER	CEEHIMR	CHIMERE	CEEHQSU	CHEQUES
CEEERRT	ERECTER	CEEHIMS	CHEMISE	CEEHQUY	QUEECHY
	REERECT		SCHEMIE	CEEHRST	ETCHERS
CEEERSS	CREESES	CEEHINR	INHERCE		RETCHES
CEEERST	SECRETE	CEEHINS	CHINESE	CEEHRSU	EUCHRES
CEEERSV	SCREEVE	CEEHIOR	CHEERIO	CEEHRSV	CHEVRES
CEEERTX	EXCRETE	CEEHIOS	ECHOISE	CEEHRSW	CHEWERS
CEEETUX	EXECUTE	CEEHIOZ	ECHOIZE		RECHEWS
CEEFFNO	OFFENCE	CEEHIRT	ERETHIC	CEEHRSY	CREESHY
CEEFFOR	EFFORCE		ETHERIC	CEEHRTU	TEUCHER
CEEFFOS	COFFEES		HERETIC	CEEHRTV	CHEVRET
CEEFFST	EFFECTS		TECHIER	CEEHSSS	CHESSES
CEEFHIR	CHIEFER	CEEHIRW	CHEWIER	CEEHSSW	ESCHEWS
CEEFHIT	FETICHE	CEEHISS	SEICHES	CEEHSTV	CHEVETS
	FITCHEE	CEEHIST	TECHIES		VETCHES
CEEFHLS	FLECHES	CEEHISV	CHEVIES	CEEHSTW	CHEWETS
CEEFHRT	FECHTER		SEVICHE	CEEIIKL	ICELIKE
	FETCHER	CEEHISW	CHEWIES	CEEIINR	EIRENIC
CEEFHST	FETCHES	CEEHKLR	HECKLER	CEEIINW	ICEWINE
CEEFINV	VENEFIC	CEEHKLS	HECKLES	CEEIIPR	EPEIRIC
CEEFIRR	FIERCER	CEEHKNP	HENPECK		EPICIER
CEEFKLR	FLECKER	CEEHKNS	KENCHES	CEEIJOR	REJOICE
	FRECKLE	CEEHKST	KETCHES	CEEIKLT	CLEEKIT
CEEFLNU	FLUENCE	CEEHLNO	CHELONE	CEEIKNT	NECKTIE
CEEFLRT	REFLECT		ECHELON	CEEIKPR	PECKIER
CEEFNNS	FENNECS	CEEHLNS	ELENCHS		PICKEER
CEEFNNU	UNFENCE	CEEHLNU	LEUCHEN	CEEIKSS	SICKEES
CEEFNOR	ENFORCE	CEEHLOW	COWHEEL	CEEILLM	MICELLE
CEEFNRS	FENCERS	CEEHLRS	LECHERS	CEEILMX	LEXEMIC
CEEFPRT	PERFECT	CEEHLRW	WELCHER	CEEILNO	CINEOLE
	PREFECT	CEEHLRY	CHEERLY	CEEILNR	RECLINE
CEEFRST	REFECTS		LECHERY	CEEILNS	LICENSE
CEEFSSU	FESCUES	CEEHLSS	CHESSEL		SELENIC
CEEGHIN	EECHING	CEEHLST	LETCHES		SILENCE
CEEGHOS	CHEGOES	CEEHLSW	LECHWES	CEEILNT	CENTILE
CEEGIIP	EPIGEIC		WELCHES		LICENTE
CEEGINP	PEECING	CEEHLSY	LYCHEES	CEEILNU	LEUCINE
CEEGINR	CREEING		SLEECHY	CEEILPS	ECLIPSE
	ENERGIC	CEEHMRS	MERCHES	CEEILPX	EXCIPLE
	GENERIC		SCHEMER	CEEILRS	CEILERS
CEEGINT	GENETIC		SCHMEER	CEEILRT	RETICLE
CEEGINU	EUGENIC	CEEHMRT	MERCHET		TIERCEL
CEEGIRS	CIERGES	CEEHMSS	SCHEMES	CEEILRU	RECUILE
	GRECISE	CEEHNOP	PENOCHE	CEEILSS	ICELESS
	GRIECES	CEEHNPU	PENUCHE		SIECLES
CEEGIRZ	GRECIZE	CEEHNRW	WENCHER	CEEILST	SECTILE
CEEGKOS	GECKOES	CEEHNST	CHENETS	CEEILSV	VESICLE
CEEGLLO	COLLEGE		TENCHES	CEEILTU	LEUCITE
CEEGLNT	NEGLECT	CEEHNSV	CHEVENS	CEEIMMS	SEMEMIC
CEEGLOU	ECLOGUE	CEEHNSW	WENCHES	CEEIMNO	MIOCENE
CEEGNOR	COGENER		WHENCES	CEEIMNT	CENTIME
	CONGREE	CEEHNTU	CHUTNEE	CEEIMRS	MERCIES
CEEGNOS	CONGEES	CEEHORR	COHERER	CEEIMRX	EXCIMER
CEEGNRU	URGENCE	CEEHORS	CHEEROS	CEEIMST	EMETICS
CEEGNRY	REGENCY		CHOREES	CEEINNS	INCENSE
CEEGORT	CORTEGE		COHERES	CEEINOS	SENECIO
CEEGQRU	GRECQUE		ECHOERS	CEEINPR	PERCINE
CEEHHSW	WHEECHS		RECHOSE	CEEINPS	PICENES
CEEHIKM	KIMCHEE	CEEHORT	TROCHEE		PIECENS

CEEINPT	PENTICE	CEELMNT	CLEMENT	CEENPST	PECTENS
CEEINPU	EUPNEIC	CEELMOO	COELOME	CEENRSS	CENSERS
CEEINRS	CERESIN	CEELMOS	CLEOMES		SCERNES
	SCRIENE	CEELMOT	TELECOM		SCREENS
	SINCERE	CEELMOW	WELCOME		SECERNS
CEEINRT	ENTERIC	CEELMSY	MYCELES	CEENRST	CENTERS
	ENTICER	CEELNOS	ENCLOSE		CENTRES
CEEINRV	CERVINE	CEELNPS	PENCELS		TENRECS
CEEINST	ENTICES	CEELNRS	CRENELS	CEENRSU	CENSURE
CEEINSV	EVINCES	CEELNRT	LECTERN	CEENRSY	SCENERY
CEEIOPT	PICOTEE	CEELNRU	LUCERNE	CEENTTU	CUNETTE
CEEIORT	COTERIE	CEELORS	CREOLES	CEEOPRU	RECOUPE
CEEIORV	REVOICE		RECLOSE	CEEOPST	PECTOSE
CEEIOST	COESITE	CEELORT	ELECTOR	CEEOPSU	COUPEES
CEEIPPR	PRECIPE		ELECTRO	CEEOPTY	ECOTYPE
CEEIPRR	CREPIER	CEELORY	RECOYLE	CEEORRS	RESCORE
	PIERCER	CEELOSS	ECLOSES	CEEORRT	ERECTOR
	REPRICE	CEELOSU	COULEES	CEEORRU	RECOURE
CEEIPRS	PIECERS	CEELOTU	ELOCUTE	CEEORRV	COVERER
	PIERCES	CEELOTV	COVELET		RECOVER
	PRECISE	CEELOTX	CELOTEX		RECOWER
	RECIPES	CEELPRT	PLECTRE	CEEORRW	RECOWER
CEEIPRT	RECEIPT		PRELECT	CEEORSU	CEREOUS
CEEIPRU	EPICURE	CEELPRU	CUPELER	CEEORSV	CORVEES
CEEIPSS	SPECIES	CEELRRU	CRUELER	CEEORTV	COVETER
CEEIPST	PECTISE	CEELRSS	SCLERES	CEEORTW	COWTREE
CEEIPTZ	PECTIZE	CEELRST	TERCELS	CEEORTX	COEXERT
CEEIQSU	QUIESCE	CEELRSU	RECLUSE	CEEOTTT	OCTETTE
CEEIRRT	RECITER		RECULES	CEEPPRT	PERCEPT
CEEIRSS	CERISES	CEELRSW	CREWELS		PRECEPT
CEEIRST	CERITES	CEELRTU	LECTURE	CEEPPRU	PREPUCE
	RECITES	CEELRTY	ERECTLY	CEEPPRU	PRECURE
	TIERCES	CEELSST	SELECTS	CEEPRSS	PRECESS
CEEIRSU	ECURIES	CEELSUX	CULEXES	CEEPRST	RECEPTS
CEEIRSV	SCRIEVE	CEELTTU	LETTUCE		RESPECT
	SERVICE	CEEMMOR	COMMERE		SCEPTER
CEEIRTT	TIERCET	CEEMNOW	NEWCOME		SCEPTRE
CEEIRTU	EUCRITE	CEEMNRU	CERUMEN		SPECTER
CEEIRTX	EXCITER	CEEMNRW	CREWMEN		SPECTRE
CEEISSX	EXCISES	CEEMNST	CEMENTS	CEEPRTX	EXCERPT
CEEISTU	CUTESIE	CEEMNSY	CYMENES	CEEPSTX	EXCEPTS
CEEISTX	EXCITES	CEEMOPR	COMPEER		EXPECTS
CEEITTT	TECTITE		COMPERE	CEEPSTY	ECTYPES
CEEITTZ	ZETETIC	CEEMOPT	COMPETE	CEEPSUY	EYECUPS
CEEJNOS	CONJEES	CEEMRRS	MERCERS	CEERRSU	RECURES
CEEJORT	EJECTOR	CEEMRRY	MERCERY		RESCUER
CEEJRST	REJECTS		REMERCY		SECURER
CEEKKLS	KECKLES	CEEMRST	CERMETS	CEERRSW	SCREWER
CEEKKSS	KECKSES	CEEMSTU	TUMESCE	CEERRUV	RECURVE
CEEKLNT	NECKLET	CEEMSTY	MYCETES	CEERSSS	CESSERS
CEEKLPS	SPECKLE	CEENNOU	ENOUNCE		CRESSES
CEEKLSS	SECKELS	CEENNOV	CONVENE	CEERSST	CRESSET
	SECKLES	CEENNRT	CENTNER		RESECTS
CEEKLST	TECKELS	CEENOOT	ECOTONE		SCREETS
CEEKNRS	NECKERS	CEENOPT	POTENCE		SECRETS
CEEKOSS	COKESES	CEENORS	ENCORES	CEERSSU	CERUSES
CEEKOSY	SOCKEYE		NECROSE		CESURES
CEEKPRS	PECKERS	CEENORU	COENURE		RECUSES
CEEKPRY	RYEPECK	CEENORZ	COZENER		RESCUES
CEEKRRW	WRECKER	CEENOST	CENOTES		SECURES
CEELLLU	CELLULE	CEENPRS	SPENCER	CEERSTT	TERCETS
CEELLNO	COLLEEN	CEENPRT	PERCENT	CEERSUX	EXCURSE
CEELLOS	CELLOSE		PRECENT		EXCUSER
CEELLPU	PUCELLE	CEENPSS	SPENCES	CEERTTU	CURETTE
				CEESSTX	EXSECTS

CEESSUX	EXCUSES	CEFORRS	FORCERS	CEGINSS	CESSING
CEETTUV	CUVETTE	CEFORRT	CROFTER	CEGIORT	ERGOTIC
CEFFHRU	CHUFFER	CEFORSS	FRESCOS	CEGIRRS	GRICERS
CEFFIOR	OFFICER	CEFORSU	FOCUSER	CEGKLNO	GENLOCK
CEFFIOS	COIFFES		REFOCUS	CEGKLOR	GROCKLE
	OFFICES	CEFOSSU	FOCUSES	CEGLNOO	COLOGNE
CEFFISU	SUFFICE		FUCOSES	CEGLOOY	ECOLOGY
CEFFLOS	COFFLES	CEFRSUW	CURFEWS	CEGLOSU	GLUCOSE
CEFFLSU	CUFFLES	CEFSSUU	FUCUSES	CEGLOSY	GLYCOSE
	SCUFFLE	CEGGHIR	CHIGGER	CEGNNOO	ONCOGEN
CEFFORS	COFFERS	CEGGHRU	CHUGGER	CEGNOOS	CONGOES
	SCOFFER	CEGGIIS	CIGGIES	CEGNORS	CONGERS
CEFFORT	COFFRET	CEGGIKN	GECKING	CEGNORU	CONGRUE
CEFFRSU	SCUFFER	CEGGIOR	GEORGIC	CEGNORY	CRYOGEN
CEFFSTU	SUFFECT	CEGGIOS	COGGIES	CEGNOST	CONGEST
CEFGHIN	CHEFING	CEGGLOR	CLOGGER	CEGNRUY	URGENCY
CEFGIKN	FECKING	CEGGLOS	COGGLES	CEGNSSU	SCUNGES
CEFGINN	FENCING	CEGGORS	COGGERS	CEGNSTY	CYGNETS
CEFHILR	FILCHER	CEGGPSU	EGGCUPS	CEGOORS	SCROOGE
CEFHILS	FILCHES	CEGHILN	LECHING	CEGORRS	GROCERS
CEFHILY	CHIEFLY	CEGHINO	ECHOING	CEGORRY	GROCERY
CEFHINS	FINCHES	CEGHINP	PECHING	CEGORSU	SCOURGE
CEFHIRY	CHIEFRY	CEGHINT	ETCHING		SCROUGE
CEFHIST	FITCHES	CEGHINW	CHEWING	CEHHILS	HILCHES
CEFHITT	FITCHET	CEGHIOR	CHOREGI	CEHHIOO	HOOCHIE
CEFHITW	FITCHEW	CEGHIOS	CHIGOES	CEHHIRS	CHERISH
CEFHLTU	FUTCHEL	CEGHIRS	CHIGRES		SHRIECH
CEFIILT	FICTILE		SCREIGH	CEHHIRT	HITCHER
CEFIIOR	ORIFICE	CEGHITU	GUICHET	CEHHIST	HITCHES
CEFIITV	FICTIVE	CEGHLSU	CLEUGHS	CEHHITU	HUTCHIE
CEFIKLR	FICKLER		GULCHES	CEHHNSU	HUNCHES
	FLICKER	CEGHORU	COUGHER	CEHHOOS	HOOCHES
CEFIKLS	FICKLES	CEGHRTU	GUTCHER	CEHHOST	HOTCHES
CEFILNT	INFLECT	CEGIILN	CEILING		SHOCHET
CEFILNU	FUNICLE		CIELING	CEHHSSU	SHEUCHS
CEFILRU	FLUERIC	CEGIINP	PIECING	CEHHSTU	HUTCHES
	LUCIFER	CEGIKKN	KECKING	CEHIIKN	CHINKIE
CEFIMOR	COMFIER	CEGIKNN	NECKING	CEHIIKS	HICKIES
CEFIMRY	MERCIFY	CEGIKNP	PECKING	CEHIIKT	THICKIE
CEFINNO	CONFINE	CEGIKNR	RECKING	CEHIILS	CHILIES
CEFINOR	COINFER	CEGIKRU	GUCKIER	CEHIINR	HIRCINE
	CONIFER	CEGILLN	CELLING	CEHIINS	NICEISH
	INFORCE	CEGILMP	GEMCLIP	CEHIINT	ICHNITE
CEFINST	INFECTS	CEGILNP	CLEPING		NITCHIE
CEFIPSY	SPECIFY	CEGILNR	CLINGER	CEHIIPP	CHIPPIE
CEFIRSS	SFERICS		CRINGLE	CEHIIRT	ITCHIER
CEFIRTY	CERTIFY	CEGILNU	CLUEING		TICHIER
	RECTIFY		LUCIGEN	CEHIISV	CHIVIES
CEFISSU	FICUSES	CEGILNW	CLEWING		VICHIES
CEFKLLO	ELFLOCK	CEGILNY	GLYCINE	CEHIKNT	CHETNIK
CEFKLOT	FETLOCK	CEGIMNO	GENOMIC		KITCHEN
CEFKLRY	FRECKLY	CEGIMNU	MUCIGEN		THICKEN
CEFKRSU	FUCKERS	CEGINNR	CERNING	CEHIKNW	CHEWINK
CEFLNOU	FLOUNCE	CEGINNS	CENSING	CEHIKOO	CHOOKIE
CEFLNTU	UNCLEFT		SCENING	CEHIKOR	CHOKIER
CEFLNUY	FLUENCY	CEGINOR	COREIGN	CEHIKOS	CHOKIES
CEFMORY	COMFREY	CEGINOS	COGNISE	CEHIKPS	PECKISH
CEFNORS	CONFERS		COIGNES	CEHIKRR	CHIRKER
CEFNORU	FROUNCE	CEGINOZ	COGNIZE	CEHIKRS	SHICKER
CEFNOSS	CONFESS	CEGINPR	CREPING		SKRIECH
CEFNOST	CONFEST		PERCING	CEHIKRT	THICKER
CEFNOSU	CONFUSE	CEGINRR	CRINGER	CEHIKRW	WHICKER
CEFNOTU	CONFUTE	CEGINRS	CRINGES	CEHIKST	CHEKIST
CEFOPRS	FORCEPS	CEGINRW	CREWING	CEHIKSY	HICKEYS

CEHIKTT	THICKET	CEHIOPU	COPIHUE	CEHLNOT	CHOLENT
CEHILLR	CHILLER	CEHIORR	CHORRIE		NOTCHEL
CEHILMY	CHIMLEY	CEHIORS	COHEIRS	CEHLNRU	LUNCHER
CEHILNO	CHOLINE		HEROICS	CEHLNRY	LYNCHER
	HELICON	CEHIORT	ROTCHIE	CEHLNSU	LUNCHES
CEHILNS	LICHENS		THEORIC	CEHLNSY	LYNCHES
	LINCHES	CEHIOST	ECHOIST	CEHLNTY	LYNCHET
CEHILNT	LINCHET		TOISECH	CEHLOOS	SCHOOLE
	TINCHEL	CEHIOTU	COUTHIE	CEHLORS	CHOLERS
CEHILPR	PILCHER	CEHIOTV	CHEVIOT		ORCHELS
CEHILPS	PILCHES	CEHIPPR	CHIPPER	CEHLORT	CHORTLE
CEHILRT	LICHTER	CEHIPRR	CHIRPER	CEHLOST	CLOTHES
CEHILRV	CHERVIL	CEHIPRS	CERIPHS	CEHLPPS	SCHLEPP
CEHILSS	CHESILS		CIPHERS	CEHLPSS	SCHLEPS
	CHISELS		SPHERIC	CEHLPSU	PLEUCHS
CEHILST	ELTCHIS	CEHIPRT	PITCHER	CEHLQSU	SQUELCH
CEHILSZ	ZILCHES	CEHIPST	CHIPSET	CEHLRRU	LURCHER
CEHILTY	ETHYLIC		PITCHES	CEHLRSU	LURCHES
	LECYTHI	CEHIQSU	QUICHES	CEHMNRU	MUNCHER
	TECHILY	CEHIRRS	CHIRRES	CEHMNSU	MUNCHES
CEHILXY	HEXYLIC	CEHIRRT	RICHTER	CEHMNSY	MENSCHY
CEHIMMO	CHOMMIE	CEHIRST	CITHERS	CEHMOOR	MOOCHER
CEHIMMS	CHEMISM		ESTRICH	CEHMOOS	MOOCHES
CEHIMNY	CHIMNEY		RICHEST	CEHMOPR	CHOMPER
CEHIMOR	HOMERIC	CEHIRSU	CUSHIER	CEHMORS	CHROMES
	MOCHIER	CEHIRSZ	SCHERZI	CEHMORU	MOUCHER
	MORICHE	CEHIRTT	CHITTER	CEHMOSS	SCHMOES
CEHIMOS	ECHOISM	CEHISSU	CUISHES	CEHMOSU	MOUCHES
CEHIMRS	CHIMERS		CUSHIES	CEHMOTZ	CHOMETZ
	MICHERS	CEHISTT	TITCHES	CEHMRTU	CHETRUM
CEHIMRT	THERMIC	CEHISTW	WITCHES	CEHMSTU	HUMECTS
CEHIMRU	RHEUMIC	CEHISZZ	CHIZZES		MUTCHES
CEHIMST	CHEMIST	CEHKKRU	CHUKKER	CEHNNRU	CHUNNER
	MITCHES	CEHKLMO	HEMLOCK	CEHNOOP	HENCOOP
CEHIMSU	ECHIUMS	CEHKLOS	HOCKLES	CEHNOOR	COEHORN
CEHINNO	CHINONE	CEHKLSU	HUCKLES	CEHNORT	CHORTEN
CEHINOP	CHOPINE	CEHKNOU	UNCHOKE		NOTCHER
	PHOCINE	CEHKNSU	KUCHENS	CEHNORV	CHEVRON
CEHINOR	CHORINE	CEHKOOR	KERCHOO	CEHNOST	NOTCHES
CEHINOT	HENOTIC	CEHKORS	CHOKERS		TECHNOS
CEHINOX	CHOENIX		HOCKERS	CEHNOSU	COHUNES
CEHINPR	NEPHRIC		SHOCKER	CEHNPRU	PUNCHER
	PHRENIC	CEHKOST	KOTCHES		UNPERCH
	PINCHER	CEHKOSY	CHOKEYS	CEHNPST	PSCHENT
CEHINPS	PINCHES		HOCKEYS	CEHNPSU	PUNCHES
	SPHENIC	CEHKPTU	KETCHUP	CEHNRRU	CHURNER
CEHINPU	PENUCHI	CEHKRSU	SHUCKER	CEHNRSU	RUNCHES
CEHINQU	QUINCHE	CEHKRUY	HUCKERY	CEHNRTU	CHUNTER
CEHINRR	CHIRREN	CEHKSTU	KUTCHES	CEHNSTU	CHESNUT
CEHINRS	INCHERS	CEHKSTY	SKETCHY	CEHNSTY	STENCHY
	NICHERS	CEHKTVY	KVETCHY	CEHNSUU	EUNUCHS
	RICHENS	CEHLLMO	MOCHELL	CEHNTUY	CHUTNEY
CEHINRT	CITHERN	CEHLLMU	MUCHELL	CEHOOPS	POOCHES
	CITHREN	CEHLLNS	SCHNELL	CEHOORS	CHOOSER
CEHINRW	WINCHER	CEHLLOY	YELLOCH		SOROCHE
CEHINST	ETHNICS	CEHLLPU	CHELLUP	CEHOORT	CHEROOT
	STHENIC	CEHLMOR	CHROMEL	CEHOOSS	CHOOSES
CEHINSU	ECHINUS	CEHLMSS	SCHELMS	CEHOOSY	CHOOSEY
CEHINSV	CHEVINS	CEHLMSU	MUCHELS	CEHOOTU	OUTECHO
CEHINSW	WINCHES		MULCHES	CEHOPPR	CHOPPER
CEHINSZ	ZECHINS	CEHLMSZ	SCHMELZ	CEHOPRS	PORCHES
CEHINTW	WITCHEN	CEHLMUY	CHUMLEY	CEHOPRT	POTCHER
CEHIOPS	HOSPICE	CEHLNNU	CHUNNEL	CEHOPRY	CORYPHE
CEHIOPT	POTICHE	CEHLNOS	NOCHELS	CEHOPST	POTCHES

CEHOPSU	POUCHES	**CEIIMPS**	EPICISM	**CEIKLRT**	TICKLER
CEHORRT	TORCHER	**CEIIMRS**	CIMIERS		TRICKLE
CEHORSS	COSHERS	**CEIIMRV**	VIREMIC	**CEIKLRU**	LUCKIER
CEHORST	HECTORS	**CEIIMSS**	SEISMIC	**CEIKLSS**	SICKLES
	ROCHETS	**CEIIMST**	MISCITE	**CEIKLST**	ICKLEST
	ROTCHES	**CEIIMTT**	TITMICE		STICKLE
	TOCHERS	**CEIINNO**	CONIINE		TICKLES
	TORCHES		INCONIE	**CEIKLSU**	LUCKIES
	TROCHES	**CEIINNR**	CINERIN	**CEIKLSY**	KYLICES
CEHORSU	CHOREUS	**CEIINOR**	ONEIRIC	**CEIKMRS**	SMICKER
	CHOUSER	**CEIINOS**	EOSINIC	**CEIKMRU**	MUCKIER
	ROUCHES		ICONISE	**CEIKMST**	SMICKET
CEHORSY	COSHERY		NICOISE	**CEIKMSY**	MICKEYS
CEHORSZ	SCHERZO	**CEIINOV**	INVOICE	**CEIKNOR**	CONKIER
CEHORTU	COUTHER	**CEIINOZ**	ICONIZE	**CEIKNOT**	KENOTIC
	RETOUCH	**CEIINPS**	PISCINE		KETONIC
	TOUCHER	**CEIINRS**	IRENICS	**CEIKNQU**	QUICKEN
CEHORTW	WOTCHER		SERICIN	**CEIKNRS**	NICKERS
CEHORUV	VOUCHER		SIRENIC		SNICKER
CEHOSSU	CHOUSES	**CEIINRT**	CITRINE	**CEIKNSS**	SICKENS
	HOCUSES		CRINITE	**CEIKNST**	SNICKET
CEHOSSW	CHOWSES		INCITER		TICKENS
CEHOSTU	TOUCHES		NERITIC	**CEIKNSW**	WICKENS
CEHOSUV	VOUCHES	**CEIINRZ**	ZINCIER	**CEIKOOS**	COOKIES
CEHPRSU	CHERUPS	**CEIINSS**	ICINESS	**CEIKOPR**	POCKIER
CEHPRSY	CHYPRES		INCISES	**CEIKOPS**	POCKIES
	CYPHERS	**CEIINST**	INCITES	**CEIKORR**	CORKIER
CEHPRTU	PUTCHER	**CEIINSU**	CUISINE		ROCKIER
CEHPSSY	PSYCHES	**CEIINTZ**	CITIZEN	**CEIKORT**	TOCKIER
CEHQSTU	QUETSCH		ZINCITE	**CEIKOST**	COKIEST
CEHRRSU	CRUSHER	**CEIIOPZ**	EPIZOIC	**CEIKOTT**	KETOTIC
CEHRSSU	CRUSHES	**CEIIPPR**	PIPERIC	**CEIKPRR**	PRICKER
CEHRSTT	STRETCH	**CEIIPRR**	PRICIER	**CEIKPRS**	PICKERS
CEHRSTY	SCYTHER	**CEIIPRS**	SPICIER		RIPECKS
CEHSSTU	TUSCHES	**CEIIPRT**	PICRITE		SPICKER
CEHSSTY	SCYTHES	**CEIIPST**	EPICIST	**CEIKPRT**	PRICKET
CEIIJRU	JUICIER	**CEIIRSS**	CISSIER	**CEIKPRY**	PICKERY
CEIIKKR	KICKIER	**CEIIRST**	ERISTIC	**CEIKPST**	PICKETS
CEIIKLS	SICLIKE		RICIEST		SKEPTIC
CEIIKMS	MICKIES	**CEIIRSU**	CRUISIE	**CEIKQRU**	QUICKER
CEIIKNS	KINESIC	**CEIIRUZ**	CRUIZIE	**CEIKRRS**	RICKERS
CEIIKNT	KINETIC	**CEIISSS**	CISSIES	**CEIKRRT**	TRICKER
CEIIKPR	PICKIER	**CEIISVV**	CIVVIES	**CEIKRSS**	SCRIKES
CEIIKQU	QUICKIE	**CEIITUV**	UVEITIC	**CEIKRST**	RICKETS
CEIIKRT	TRICKIE	**CEIJNST**	INJECTS		STICKER
CEIIKSS	SICKIES	**CEIJRSU**	JUICERS		TICKERS
CEIIKST	EKISTIC	**CEIJSTU**	JUSTICE	**CEIKRSU**	SUCKIER
	ICKIEST	**CEIKKNR**	KNICKER	**CEIKRSW**	WICKERS
	TICKIES	**CEIKKRS**	KICKERS	**CEIKRSY**	RICKEYS
CEIIKSW	WICKIES	**CEIKLMR**	MICKLER		YICKERS
CEIILLS	SILICLE	**CEIKLMS**	MELICKS	**CEIKRTU**	TRUCKIE
CEIILNN	INCLINE		MICKLES	**CEIKRTY**	RICKETY
CEIILNP	PENICIL	**CEIKLNR**	CLINKER	**CEIKRUY**	YUCKIER
CEIILPP	CLIPPIE		CRINKLE	**CEIKSST**	SICKEST
CEIILPT	PELITIC	**CEIKLNS**	NICKELS	**CEIKSTT**	TICKETS
CEIILST	ELICITS		NICKLES	**CEIKSTW**	WICKETS
CEIILTV	LEVITIC		SLICKEN	**CEIKSTY**	TICKEYS
CEIIMMT	MIMETIC	**CEIKLPR**	PICKLER	**CEILLMS**	MICELLS
CEIIMNR	CREMINI		PRICKLE	**CEILLNO**	LIONCEL
	CRIMINE	**CEIKLPS**	PICKLES	**CEILLNU**	NUCELLI
	MINCIER	**CEIKLPU**	CUPLIKE	**CEILLOR**	COLLIER
CEIIMNS	MENISCI	**CEIKLRS**	LICKERS	**CEILLOS**	COLLIES
CEIIMOT	MEIOTIC		RICKLES	**CEILLST**	CELLIST
CEIIMPR	EMPIRIC		SLICKER	**CEILLSU**	CULLIES

CEILMOP	COMPILE		TONEMIC		PRINCES
	POLEMIC	CEIMNRS	CREMSIN	CEINPRY	CYPRINE
CEILMOT	TELOMIC		MINCERS	CEINPST	INCEPTS
CEILMPR	CRIMPLE	CEIMNRU	MINCEUR		INSPECT
CEILNNU	NUCLEIN		NUMERIC		PECTINS
CEILNOP	PINOCLE	CEIMNYZ	ENZYMIC		PEINCTS
	PLEONIC	CEIMOOR	COOMIER	CEINPTY	PYCNITE
CEILNOS	CINEOLS	CEIMOPR	MEROPIC	CEINQSU	CINQUES
	CONSEIL	CEIMOPT	METOPIC		QUINCES
	INCLOSE	CEIMOQU	COMIQUE	CEINRRU	CURNIER
CEILNOT	LECTION	CEIMORR	MORRICE		REINCUR
CEILNOX	LEXICON	CEIMORT	MORTICE	CEINRSS	SCRINES
CEILNPS	PENCILS	CEIMOSX	EXOSMIC	CEINRST	CISTERN
	SPLENIC	CEIMOTT	TOTEMIC		CRETINS
CEILNST	CLIENTS	CEIMOTV	VICOMTE	CEINRSV	CRIVENS
	LECTINS	CEIMOTX	TOXEMIC	CEINRSW	WINCERS
	STENCIL	CEIMOUZ	ZOECIUM	CEINRTT	CITTERN
CEILNSU	LEUCINS	CEIMPRR	CRIMPER	CEINRUV	INCURVE
CEILNTU	CUTLINE	CEIMPRS	SPERMIC	CEINSST	INCESTS
	LINECUT	CEIMPRU	PUMICER		INSECTS
	TUNICLE	CEIMPSU	PUMICES	CEINSSU	INCUSES
CEILOOS	COOLIES	CEIMRST	CRETISM	CEINSTU	NEUSTIC
CEILOPR	PELORIC		METRICS	CEINSTY	CYSTEIN
	POLICER	CEIMRSU	CERIUMS		CYSTINE
CEILOPS	POLICES		MURICES	CEINSWY	WINCEYS
CEILOPT	TOECLIP	CEIMSSU	CESIUMS	CEINTTX	EXTINCT
CEILORS	COILERS		MISCUES	CEINVVY	VIVENCY
	RECOILS	CEINNOS	CONINES	CEIOOPR	OPORICE
CEILORT	CORTILE	CEINNOV	CONNIVE	CEIOORS	COORIES
CEILORU	URCEOLI	CEINNST	INCENTS	CEIOOST	COOTIES
CEILOSS	OSSICLE	CEINOOT	COONTIE	CEIOPPR	CROPPIE
CEILOST	CITOLES	CEINOPR	PERICON	CEIOPPS	COPPIES
CEILOTT	COLETIT		PONCIER	CEIOPRS	COPIERS
CEILPPR	CLIPPER		PORCINE		COPSIER
	CRIPPLE	CEINOPT	ENTOPIC		PERSICO
CEILPRS	SPLICER		NEPOTIC	CEIOPST	POETICS
CEILPSS	SPLICES	CEINORR	CORNIER	CEIOPSU	PICEOUS
CEILPSU	SPICULE	CEINORS	COINERS	CEIOPSW	COWPIES
CEILPSV	PELVICS		CRINOSE	CEIORRS	CIRROSE
CEILQSU	CLIQUES		CRONIES		CORRIES
CEILQUY	CLIQUEY		ORCEINS		CROSIER
CEILRRU	CURLIER		ORCINES		ORRICES
CEILRSS	SLICERS		RECOINS	CEIORRU	COURIER
CEILRST	RELICTS		SERICON	CEIORRZ	CROZIER
CEILRSV	CLIVERS	CEINORT	COINTER	CEIORSS	COSIERS
CEILRSY	CLERISY		NOTICER		CRIOSES
CEILRTT	CLITTER		RECTION	CEIORST	EROTICS
CEILRTU	CULTIER	CEINORU	COENURI		TERCIOS
	UTRICLE		NOURICE	CEIORSU	COURIES
CEILSSS	SCISSEL	CEINORV	CORVINE		SCOURIE
CEILSSU	SLUICES	CEINORY	ORIENCY	CEIORSV	CORSIVE
CEILSTU	LUCITES	CEINOSS	CESSION		VOICERS
	LUETICS		COSINES	CEIORSW	COWRIES
CEILTTU	CUITTLE		OSCINES		SCOWRIE
CEIMMOS	COMMIES	CEINOST	NOTICES	CEIORSZ	COZIERS
CEIMMRR	CRIMMER		SECTION	CEIORTT	COTTIER
CEIMMRU	CRUMMIE	CEINOSV	NOVICES	CEIORTV	EVICTOR
CEIMNNO	MECONIN	CEINOTT	ENTOTIC	CEIORTW	COWRITE
CEIMNOR	INCOMER		TONETIC	CEIORTX	EXCITOR
CEIMNOS	COSMINE	CEINOTX	EXCITON		XEROTIC
	INCOMES	CEINOUV	UNVOICE	CEIORVY	VICEROY
	MESONIC	CEINOVV	CONVIVE	CEIOSSS	COSSIES
CEIMNOT	CENTIMO	CEINPRS	CRISPEN	CEIOSST	COSIEST
	ENTOMIC		PINCERS		COTISES

	OECISTS	**CEKKLNU**	KNUCKLE	**CEKSTTU**	TUCKETS
CEIOSSU	CESIOUS	**CEKKNOR**	KNOCKER	**CELLMOU**	COLUMEL
CEIOSSV	VISCOSE	**CEKKOPS**	KOPECKS	**CELLNOO**	COLONEL
CEIOSTT	COTTISE	**CEKLLOP**	PELLOCK	**CELLORS**	ESCROLL
	SCOTTIE	**CEKLLRY**	CLERKLY	**CELLOST**	COLLETS
CEIOSTV	COSTIVE	**CEKLMNO**	LOCKMEN	**CELLOSU**	LOCULES
CEIOSTW	COWIEST	**CEKLMSU**	MUCKLES		OCELLUS
CEIOSTX	COEXIST	**CEKLNOS**	ENLOCKS		
	COXIEST		SLOCKEN	**CELLOSY**	CLOSELY
	EXOTICS	**CEKLNRU**	CLUNKER	**CELLRRU**	CRULLER
CEIOSTY	SOCIETY		CRUNKLE	**CELLRSU**	CRUELLS
CEIOSTZ	COZIEST	**CEKLORS**	LOCKERS		CULLERS
CEIPPRU	CUPPIER		RELOCKS		SCULLER
CEIPPST	PEPTICS	**CEKLOST**	LOCKETS	**CELLRUY**	CRUELLY
CEIPQTU	PICQUET		LOCKSET	**CELLSSU**	SCULLES
CEIPRRS	CRISPER	**CEKLOTY**	TOCKLEY	**CELLSTU**	CULLETS
	PRICERS	**CEKLPRU**	PLUCKER	**CELMMSU**	MESCLUM
CEIPRSS	SPICERS	**CEKLPSU**	PUCKLES	**CELMNOO**	LOCOMEN
CEIPRST	TRICEPS	**CEKLRSU**	RUCKLES		MONOCLE
CEIPRSY	SPICERY		SCULKER	**CELMNSU**	CULMENS
CEIPRTU	CUPRITE		SUCKLER		MESCLUN
	PICTURE	**CEKLRTU**	TRUCKLE	**CELMOOS**	COELOMS
CEIPRTY	PYRETIC	**CEKLSSU**	SUCKLES	**CELMOPS**	COMPELS
CEIPRXY	PYREXIC	**CEKMNOS**	SOCKMEN	**CELMOPX**	COMPLEX
CEIPSSS	SCEPSIS	**CEKMNOY**	MOCKNEY	**CELMORS**	CORMELS
CEIPSST	CESSPIT	**CEKMNRU**	RUCKMEN	**CELMPRU**	CLUMPER
	SEPTICS	**CEKMORS**	MOCKERS		CRUMPLE
CEIQRSU	CIRQUES	**CEKMORY**	MOCKERY	**CELMSSU**	MUSCLES
CEIRRRU	CURRIER	**CEKMRSU**	MUCKERS	**CELMSUU**	SECULUM
CEIRRSU	CRUISER	**CEKNNSU**	UNSNECK	**CELMSUY**	LYCEUMS
	CURRIES	**CEKNOOV**	CONVOKE	**CELMTUU**	CUMULET
	SUCRIER	**CEKNORR**	CRONKER	**CELNNOU**	NUCLEON
CEIRRTT	CRITTER	**CEKNORS**	CONKERS	**CELNNSU**	NUNCLES
CEIRRTU	RECRUIT		RECKONS	**CELNOOR**	CORONEL
CEIRRTX	RECTRIX	**CEKNORT**	TROCKEN	**CELNOOS**	COLONES
CEIRRUV	CURVIER	**CEKNOST**	NOCKETS		CONSOLE
CEIRSSU	CRUISES	**CEKNRWY**	WRYNECK	**CELNORS**	CLONERS
	CRUSIES	**CEKNSSU**	SUCKENS		CORNELS
	CUISSER	**CEKOOPR**	PRECOOK	**CELNOSU**	COUNSEL
CEIRSSV	SCRIVES	**CEKOOPW**	COWPOKE		UNCLOSE
CEIRSTT	TRISECT	**CEKOORR**	CROOKER	**CELNOTU**	NOCTULE
CEIRSTU	CUITERS	**CEKOORS**	COOKERS	**CELNRSU**	LUCERNS
	CURIETS		RECOOKS	**CELNRTU**	LECTURN
	CURITES	**CEKOORY**	COOKERY	**CELNSUU**	NUCLEUS
	ICTERUS	**CEKOOSY**	COOKEYS		NUCULES
CEIRSTW	TWICERS	**CEKOPRR**	PREROCK	**CELNSUW**	UNCLEWS
CEIRSUV	CRUIVES	**CEKOPST**	POCKETS	**CELOOPR**	PRECOOL
	CURSIVE	**CEKORRS**	CORKERS	**CELOORR**	COLORER
CEIRSUZ	CRUZIES		RECORKS		RECOLOR
CEIRTTU	CUTTIER		ROCKERS	**CELOORS**	COOLERS
CEIRTTX	TECTRIX	**CEKORRY**	ROCKERY		CREOSOL
CEISSSU	CUISSES	**CEKORST**	RESTOCK	**CELOOST**	COOLEST
CEISSTU	CESTUIS		ROCKETS		OCELOTS
	CUEISTS		STOCKER	**CELOPPS**	COPPLES
	CUTISES	**CEKORTW**	TWOCKER	**CELOPRU**	COUPLER
	ICTUSES	**CEKOSST**	SOCKETS	**CELOPSU**	CLOSEUP
CEISTTU	CUTTIES	**CEKPRSU**	PUCKERS		COUPLES
CEJKNOY	JOCKNEY	**CEKPRSY**	RYPECKS		OPUSCLE
CEJKOSY	JOCKEYS	**CEKPRUY**	PUCKERY		UPCLOSE
CEJNOOS	COJONES	**CEKRRTU**	TRUCKER	**CELOPTU**	COUPLET
CEJNORU	CONJURE	**CEKRSSU**	SUCKERS		OCTUPLE
CEJNOSU	JOUNCES	**CEKRSTU**	TUCKERS	**CELOQSU**	CLOQUES
	JUNCOES	**CEKRSUY**	YUCKERS	**CELORRU**	CORULER
CEJOPRT	PROJECT	**CEKSSTU**	SUCKETS	**CELORSS**	CLOSERS
					CRESOLS

Key	Words	Key	Words	Key	Words
	ESCROLS	**CEMNSTU**	CENTUMS	**CENORUV**	UNCOVER
CELORST	COLTERS	**CEMOOPS**	COMPOSE	**CENOSSY**	COYNESS
	CORSLET	**CEMOOPT**	COMPOTE	**CENOSTT**	CONTEST
	COSTREL	**CEMOOTU**	OUTCOME	**CENOSTU**	CONTUSE
	LECTORS	**CEMOPRS**	COMPERS		ECONUTS
CELORSU	CLOSURE	**CEMOPRT**	COMPTER		UNCOEST
	COLURES	**CEMOPST**	COEMPTS	**CENOSTV**	COVENTS
CELORSV	CLOVERS	**CEMOPSU**	UPCOMES	**CENOSVY**	CONVEYS
	VELCROS	**CEMOPTU**	COMPUTE		COVYNES
CELORSW	SCOWLER	**CEMORRS**	CREMORS	**CENOTTX**	CONTEXT
	SCROWLE	**CEMORSS**	SCROMES	**CENPRTY**	ENCRYPT
CELORSY	SCROYLE	**CEMOSSU**	COMUSES	**CENPTUX**	EXPUNCT
CELORTT	CLOTTER		MUSCOSE	**CENRRTU**	CURRENT
	CROTTLE	**CEMOSSY**	MYCOSES	**CENRSSY**	SCRYNES
CELORTU	CLOTURE	**CEMOSTU**	COSTUME	**CENRSTU**	ENCRUST
	CLOUTER	**CEMPRRU**	CRUMPER	**CENRSUU**	UNCURSE
	COULTER	**CEMPRTU**	CRUMPET	**CENRSUW**	UNSCREW
CELORVY	CLOVERY	**CEMRRUY**	MERCURY	**CENRTUY**	CENTURY
CELOSST	CLOSEST	**CEMRSTU**	RECTUMS	**CENSSTY**	ENCYSTS
	CLOSETS	**CEMSSUU**	MUCUSES	**CEOOPRS**	COOPERS
CELOSSU	OSCULES	**CEMSTTU**	TECTUMS		SCOOPER
CELOSSX	COXLESS	**CENNOOR**	NONCORE	**CEOOPRY**	COOPERY
CELOSTY	COTYLES	**CENNOOS**	NEOCONS	**CEOORSS**	COOSERS
CELOSUV	VOCULES	**CENNOOT**	CONNOTE		ROSCOES
CELOTTU	CULOTTE	**CENNORS**	CONNERS	**CEOORST**	COOTERS
CELPRSU	CURPELS	**CENNOST**	CONSENT		SCOOTER
	SCRUPLE		NOCENTS	**CEOORSV**	CROOVES
CELPSUU	CUPULES	**CENNOTT**	CONTENT	**CEOORTU**	ECOTOUR
CELPSUY	CLYPEUS	**CENNOTV**	CONVENT	**CEOORTW**	COWROTE
CELRRSU	CURLERS	**CENNRSU**	CUNNERS	**CEOORVY**	OVERCOY
CELRSSY	CRESYLS		SCUNNER	**CEOOSTY**	COYOTES
CELRSTU	CLUSTER	**CENOOPS**	POCOSEN		OOCYTES
	CULTERS		POONCES	**CEOPPRR**	CROPPER
	CUSTREL	**CENOORR**	CORONER	**CEOPPRS**	COPPERS
	CUTLERS		CROONER	**CEOPPRU**	PRECOUP
	RELUCTS	**CENOORS**	CEROONS	**CEOPPRY**	COPPERY
CELRSTY	CLYSTER	**CENOORT**	CORONET	**CEOPRRS**	SCORPER
CELRSUV	CULVERS	**CENOOSS**	COOSENS	**CEOPRRT**	PORRECT
CELRSUW	CURLEWS	**CENOPRS**	CREPONS	**CEOPRRU**	CROUPER
CELRTTU	CLUTTER	**CENOPRU**	POUNCER		PROCURE
CELRTUU	CULTURE	**CENOPSU**	POUNCES	**CEOPRSS**	CORPSES
CELRTUV	CULVERT		UNCOPES		PROCESS
CELRTUY	CRUELTY	**CENOPSY**	SYNCOPE	**CEOPRST**	COPTERS
	CUTLERY	**CENOPTU**	POUNCET		PROSECT
CELSTTU	CUTLETS	**CENOPTY**	POTENCY	**CEOPRSU**	COUPERS
	CUTTLES	**CENOQRU**	CONQUER		CROUPES
	SCUTTLE	**CENORRS**	CORNERS		RECOUPS
CEMMNOT	COMMENT		SCORNER	**CEOPRTT**	PROTECT
CEMMNOU	COMMUNE	**CENORRW**	CROWNER	**CEOPRUU**	COUPURE
CEMMOOT	COMMOTE		RECROWN	**CEOPRUV**	COVERUP
CEMMOOV	COMMOVE	**CENORSS**	CENSORS	**CEOPSTY**	COTYPES
CEMMORS	COMMERS	**CENORST**	CONSTER	**CEOQRTU**	CROQUET
CEMMOTU	COMMUTE		CORNETS		ROCQUET
CEMMRSU	CUMMERS		CRESTON	**CEOQSTU**	COQUETS
	SCUMMER		CRONETS	**CEORRSS**	CROSSER
CEMNNOT	CONTEMN	**CENORSU**	CONURES		RECROSS
CEMNOOP	COMPONE		ROUNCES		SCORERS
CEMNOOS	ONCOMES	**CENORTT**	CORNETT		SCORSER
CEMNOOY	ECONOMY	**CENORTU**	CORNUTE	**CEORRST**	RECTORS
	MONOECY		COUNTER	**CEORRSU**	COURSER
CEMNOSU	CONSUME		RECOUNT		CRUORES
	MUSCONE		TROUNCE		SCOURER
CEMNRSU	CRUMENS	**CENORTV**	CONVERT	**CEORRSW**	CROWERS
CEMNRTU	CENTRUM	**CENORTW**	CROWNET		SCOWRER

CEORRSY	SORCERY
CEORRSZ	CROZERS
CEORRTU	COURTER
CEORRTY	RECTORY
CEORSSS	CROSSES
	SCORSES
CEORSST	CORSETS
	COSTERS
	ESCORTS
	SCOTERS
	SCROTES
	SECTORS
CEORSSU	COURSES
	SCOURSE
	SCOUSER
	SOURCES
	SUCROSE
CEORSSW	ESCROWS
CEORSSY	CORSEYS
CEORSTT	COTTERS
CEORSTU	COUTERS
	CROUTES
	SCOUTER
CEORSTV	CORVETS
	COVERTS
	VECTORS
CEORTUU	COUTURE
CEORTUV	COUVERT
	CUTOVER
	OVERCUT
CEOSSST	COSSETS
CEOSSSU	SCOUSES
CEOSSSY	SYCOSES
CEOSTTT	OCTETTS
CEOSTTU	CUTTOES
CEPPRRU	CRUPPER
CEPPRSU	CUPPERS
	SCUPPER
CEPRRSU	SPRUCER
CEPRSSU	PERCUSS
	SPRUCES
CEPRSSY	CYPRESS
CEPRSTU	PRECUTS
CEPRSTY	SCEPTRY
CEPRSUW	SCREWUP
CEPRUUV	UPCURVE
CEPSSTU	SUSPECT
CERRSSU	CURSERS
CERRSSY	SCRYERS
CERSSSU	CUSSERS
CERSSTU	CRUSETS
CERSSUZ	SCRUZES
CERSTTU	CURTEST
	CUTTERS
	SCUTTER
CERSTUV	CURVETS
CERSTUY	CURTESY
	CURTSEY
CESSUZZ	SCUZZES
CFFFKOU	FUCKOFF
CFFGINO	COFFING
CFFGINU	CUFFING
CFFHINO	CHIFFON
CFFIIRT	TRIFFIC

CFFIKKO	KICKOFF
CFFIKOP	PICKOFF
CFFILSS	SCLIFFS
CFFINOS	COFFINS
CFFINSU	CUFFINS
CFFKOOO	COOKOFF
CFFMOSU	OFFSCUM
CFFNSUU	UNCUFFS
CFFOSTU	CUTOFFS
	OFFCUTS
CFFRSSU	SCRUFFS
CFFRSUY	SCRUFFY
CFGIINO	COIFING
CFGIKNU	FUCKING
CFGINOR	FORCING
CFHILYY	CHYLIFY
CFHIMYY	CHYMIFY
CFHINSU	FUCHSIN
CFHIOSW	COWFISH
CFHIRST	FRICHTS
CFHORTU	FUTHORC
CFIIIMR	MIRIFIC
CFIIIVV	VIVIFIC
CFIIKNY	FINICKY
CFIILNT	INFLICT
CFIIMNO	OMNIFIC
CFIIMOT	MOTIFIC
CFIIMRY	MICRIFY
CFIINOT	FICTION
CFIINOY	ICONIFY
CFIINYZ	ZINCIFY
CFIIOSS	OSSIFIC
CFIKNNO	FINNOCK
CFIKOSS	FOSSICK
CFIKTUW	FUCKWIT
CFILORS	FROLICS
CFILORU	FLUORIC
CFIMNOR	CONFIRM
CFIMOST	COMFITS
CFINORY	CORNIFY
CFINOST	CONFITS
CFIORST	FICTORS
CFIORSY	SCORIFY
CFIRSTU	FRUICTS
CFISSTU	FUSTICS
CFKLLOU	LOCKFUL
CFKNORU	UNFROCK
CFKOTTU	FUTTOCK
CFKPSUU	FUCKUPS
CFLMRUU	FULCRUM
CFLNORY	CORNFLY
CFLNOUX	CONFLUX
CFLNOUY	FLOUNCY
CFLOOPW	COWFLOP
CFLOPRU	CROPFUL
CFLPSUU	CUPFULS
	CUPSFUL
CFMNOOR	CONFORM
CFMOORT	COMFORT
CFNORTU	FUNCTOR
CFOSSTU	FUSTOCS
CFOSSUU	FUSCOUS
CGGGINO	COGGING
CGGIINR	GRICING

CGGORSY	SCROGGY
CGHHOSU	CHOUGHS
CGHIILM	MILCHIG
CGHIIMN	CHIMING
	MICHING
CGHIINN	CHINING
	INCHING
	NICHING
CGHIINR	RICHING
CGHIINT	ITCHING
CGHIINV	CHIVING
CGHIKNO	CHOKING
	HOCKING
CGHILPY	GLYPHIC
CGHILTY	GLITCHY
CGHINNO	CHIGNON
CGHINOR	CHORING
	OCHRING
CGHINOS	COSHING
CGHINOU	OUCHING
CGHINOW	CHOWING
CGHINRU	RUCHING
CGHINSU	CHUSING
CGHINTU	CHUTING
CGHIOST	GOTHICS
CGHIOSY	GOYISCH
CGHLNOS	SCHLONG
CGHLOSU	CLOUGHS
CGHOORT	TORGOCH
CGHORUY	GROUCHY
CGIIJNU	JUICING
CGIIKKN	KICKING
CGIIKLN	LICKING
CGIIKMM	GIMMICK
CGIIKNN	NICKING
CGIIKNP	PICKING
CGIIKNR	RICKING
CGIIKNS	SICKING
CGIIKNT	TICKING
CGIIKNW	WICKING
CGIILLO	ILLOGIC
CGIILNO	COILING
CGIILNP	CLIPING
CGIILNS	SLICING
CGIIMNN	MINCING
CGIIMNR	CRIMING
CGIINNO	COINING
CGIINNR	CRINING
CGIINNW	WINCING
CGIINNZ	ZINCING
CGIINOR	GIRONIC
CGIINOV	VOICING
CGIINPR	PRICING
CGIINPS	SPICING
CGIINRT	TRICING
CGIINSS	CISSING
CGIKLNO	CLOKING
	LOCKING
CGIKLNU	LUCKING
CGIKMNO	MOCKING
CGIKMNU	MUCKING
CGIKNNO	CONKING
	NOCKING
CGIKNOO	COOKING

CGIKNOP	POCKING	CGINOSV	COVINGS		SHTICKS
CGIKNOR	CORKING	CGINOSW	SCOWING	CHIKSTY	KITSCHY
	ROCKING		SOWCING		SHTICKY
CGIKNOS	SOCKING	CGINOSY	COSYING	CHILLMU	CHILLUM
CGIKNOT	TOCKING	CGINOTT	COTTING	CHILLTY	LICHTLY
CGIKNOW	COWKING	CGINOYZ	COZYING	CHILNOO	HOLONIC
CGIKNOY	YOCKING	CGINPPU	CUPPING	CHILNOR	CHLORIN
CGIKNPU	KINGCUP	CGINRRU	CURRING	CHILNSY	LYCHNIS
	PUCKING	CGINRSU	CURSING	CHILOOS	COOLISH
CGIKNRU	RUCKING	CGINRSY	CRYINGS	CHILORS	ORCHILS
CGIKNSU	SUCKING		SCRYING	CHILORT	TROCHIL
CGIKNTU	TUCKING	CGINRTU	TRUCING	CHILOST	COLTISH
CGIKNUY	YUCKING	CGINRUV	CURVING	CHILPSY	SYLPHIC
CGILLNO	COLLING	CGINSSU	CUSSING	CHILSTU	CULTISH
CGILLNU	CULLING		SCUSING	CHILSUY	CUSHILY
CGILMNU	CULMING	CGINTTU	CUTTING	CHIMMOR	MICROHM
CGILMNY	CYMLING	CGIOOOS	GIOCOSO	CHIMNPY	NYMPHIC
CGILNNO	CLONING	CGIOOST	COGITOS	CHIMOPR	MORPHIC
CGILNNU	UNCLING	CGIOTYZ	ZYGOTIC	CHIMORS	CHORISM
CGILNOO	COOLING	CGKLNOU	GUNLOCK		CHRISOM
	LOCOING	CGLLOSY	GLYCOLS	CHIMRRY	MYRRHIC
CGILNOS	CLOSING	CGLLSYY	GLYCYLS	CHIMRSS	CHRISMS
CGILNOT	COLTING	CGLNOSU	UNCLOGS	CHIMSSS	SCHISMS
CGILNOW	COWLING	CGLOOSU	COLUGOS	CHIMSTY	CHYMIST
CGILNOY	CLOYING	CGNOOSU	CONGOUS		TYCHISM
CGILNPY	CLYPING	CGOORRW	GORCROW	CHINOOR	CHORION
CGILNRU	CURLING	CHHIIKS	HICKISH	CHINOPS	CHOPINS
CGILNSY	GLYCINS	CHHIKOR	CHIKHOR		PHONICS
CGILOOO	OOLOGIC	CHHINOR	RHONCHI	CHINOPY	CIPHONY
CGILORW	COWGIRL	CHHINTU	UNHITCH	CHINORS	CRONISH
CGILOTT	GLOTTIC	CHHIRST	SHRITCH	CHINOST	CHITONS
CGILPSU	GILCUPS	CHHISST	SHTCHIS	CHINOSU	CUSHION
CGILPTU	GILTCUP	CHHISTY	ICHTHYS	CHINPSY	HYPNICS
CGILPTY	GLYPTIC	CHHLOTU	LUCHOTH	CHINQSU	SQUINCH
CGIMNOO	COOMING	CHHNOOS	HONCHOS	CHINRSU	URCHINS
CGIMNOP	COMPING	CHHRTTU	THRUTCH	CHINSTY	SNITCHY
CGIMNOR	CROMING	CHIIILO	CHILIOI	CHINTUW	UNWITCH
CGIMNOS	COMINGS	CHIIKLM	MILCHIK	CHINTYZ	CHINTZY
CGINNNO	CONNING	CHIIKMS	KIMCHIS	CHIOOPR	POCHOIR
CGINNNU	CUNNING	CHIIKNN	KINCHIN	CHIOORS	ISOCHOR
CGINNOP	PONCING	CHIIKSS	SICKISH	CHIOORZ	CHORIZO
CGINNOR	CORNING	CHIILLS	CHILLIS	CHIOPRT	TROPHIC
CGINNOS	CONSIGN	CHIILNT	CHITLIN	CHIOPST	PHOTICS
CGINNPU	PUNCING	CHIILOT	THIOLIC	CHIOPXY	HYPOXIC
CGINNSY	SYNCING	CHIILST	LITCHIS	CHIORST	CHORIST
CGINOOP	COOPING	CHIILTY	ITCHILY		OSTRICH
CGINOOS	COOINGS	CHIIMST	ISTHMIC	CHIORSW	CHOWRIS
CGINOPP	COPPING	CHIIMSU	ISCHIUM	CHIOSST	STICHOS
CGINOPS	COPINGS	CHIINNP	INCHPIN	CHIOSSZ	SCHIZOS
	COPSING	CHIINOT	THIONIC	CHIPRRU	CHIRRUP
	PICONGS	CHIINST	CHITINS	CHIPRRY	PYRRHIC
	SCOPING	CHIIOPT	OPHITIC	CHIPSSY	PHYSICS
CGINOPU	COUPING	CHIIOST	STICHOI	CHIQSTU	SQUITCH
CGINOPW	COWPING	CHIIRRS	SCIRRHI	CHIRRSU	CURRISH
CGINOPY	COPYING	CHIKLLO	HILLOCK	CHIRSTY	CHRISTY
CGINORS	SCORING	CHIKLTY	THICKLY	CHISSST	SCHISTS
CGINORU	COURING	CHIKNOO	CHINOOK	CHISSTU	SCHUITS
CGINORW	CROWING	CHIKORS	CHIKORS	CHISTTU	CHUTIST
CGINORY	GYRONIC		CHOKRIS	CHISTWY	SWITCHY
CGINOSS	COSIGNS	CHIKORY	HICKORY	CHISYZZ	SCHIZZY
CGINOST	COSTING	CHIKOST	THICKOS	CHITTWY	TWITCHY
	GNOSTIC	CHIKPSU	PUCKISH	CHKLOOO	HOOLOCK
CGINOSU	CONGIUS	CHIKRSS	SCHRIKS	CHKLOOT	KLOOTCH
	SOUCING	CHIKSST	SCHTIKS	CHKLOSS	SHLOCKS

CHKLOSY	SHLOCKY	**CIIKLPY**	PICKILY	**CIJNNOO**	CONJOIN
	SHYLOCK	**CIIKMMM**	MIMMICK	**CIJNNTU**	INJUNCT
CHKMMOO	HOMMOCK	**CIIKMNN**	MINNICK	**CIJNOOS**	COJOINS
CHKMMOU	HUMMOCK	**CIIKNPS**	PICKINS	**CIKKLLO**	KILLOCK
CHKMOSS	SHMOCKS	**CIIKNPT**	NITPICK	**CIKKOPT**	TOPKICK
CHKMSSU	SHMUCKS	**CIIKNSW**	INWICKS	**CIKKOTU**	OUTKICK
CHKNOOS	SCHNOOK	**CIIKNTU**	CUTIKIN	**CIKKPSU**	KICKUPS
CHKOOST	SCHTOOK	**CIIKPUW**	WICKIUP	**CIKLLOP**	PILLOCK
CHKORSU	CHUKORS	**CIIKSST**	TISICKS	**CIKLLOR**	ROLLICK
CHKPTUU	PUTCHUK	**CIIKSTT**	STICKIT	**CIKLLOS**	SILLOCK
CHKSSTU	SHTUCKS	**CIILLTY**	LICITLY	**CIKLLOW**	KILLCOW
CHLMOOS	MOLOCHS	**CIILLVY**	CIVILLY	**CIKLLSY**	SLICKLY
CHLMORY	CHROMYL	**CIILNOP**	CIPOLIN	**CIKLLUY**	LUCKILY
CHLMPSU	SCHLUMP		PICOLIN	**CIKLMSU**	MISLUCK
CHLOOSS	SCHOOLS	**CIILNOS**	SILICON	**CIKLMSY**	SMICKLY
CHLOOST	COOLTHS	**CIILNPS**	INCLIPS	**CIKLMUY**	MUCKILY
CHLOPST	SPLOTCH	**CIILNUV**	UNCIVIL	**CIKLNOS**	INLOCKS
CHLORSS	SCHORLS	**CIILNVY**	VINYLIC	**CIKLNRY**	CRINKLY
CHLORTY	CHOLTRY	**CIILOOT**	OOLITIC	**CIKLNSU**	UNSLICK
CHLOSSS	SCHLOSS	**CIILOPT**	POLITIC	**CIKLOOO**	OLICOOK
CHLOSUV	CHYLOUS	**CIILORT**	CORTILI	**CIKLOPY**	POCKILY
	SLOUCHY	**CIILOST**	COLITIS	**CIKLOPZ**	ZIPLOCK
CHLOTYZ	ZLOTYCH		SOLICIT	**CIKLORY**	ROCKILY
CHLSTUY	SLUTCHY	**CIILOTT**	LITOTIC	**CIKLPRY**	PRICKLY
CHMOORS	CHROMOS	**CIILPRY**	PRICILY	**CIKLQUY**	QUICKLY
CHMOOSS	SCHMOOS	**CIILPSY**	SPICILY	**CIKLRTY**	TRICKLY
CHMOOST	SCHTOOM	**CIILSSS**	SCISSIL	**CIKLSTU**	LUSTICK
CHMOOSY	SMOOCHY	**CIILSSV**	SILVICS	**CIKMNNO**	MINNOCK
CHMOOSZ	SCHMOOZ	**CIIMMNO**	MINICOM	**CIKMNSU**	NICKUMS
CHMOSUV	CHYMOUS	**CIIMMRY**	MIMICRY	**CIKMOOS**	MISCOOK
CHMSTUY	SMUTCHY	**CIIMNNO**	NIMONIC	**CIKMORR**	RIMROCK
CHNNOOR	CHRONON	**CIIMNOS**	MISCOIN	**CIKMSSU**	MUSICKS
CHNNOSU	NONSUCH	**CIIMNOT**	MICTION	**CIKMSTU**	STICKUM
CHNOOPS	PONCHOS	**CIIMNRY**	CRIMINY	**CIKNNOP**	PINNOCK
CHNOORS	COHORNS	**CIIMOST**	MIOTICS	**CIKNNOW**	WINNOCK
CHNOORT	TORCHON		MISTICO	**CIKNOSW**	COWSKIN
CHNORRS	SCHNORR		SOMITIC	**CIKNPSU**	UNPICKS
CHNORSY	SYNCHRO	**CIIMOTT**	MITOTIC	**CIKNPSY**	PYKNICS
CHNORTU	COTHURN	**CIIMOTV**	MOTIVIC	**CIKNPTU**	NUTPICK
CHNOSZZ	SCHNOZZ	**CIIMRST**	TRISMIC	**CIKNSTU**	UNSTICK
CHNOTUU	UNCOUTH	**CIIMSSV**	CIVISMS	**CIKOPPT**	POCKPIT
CHNSTUU	TUCHUNS	**CIIMSTV**	VICTIMS	**CIKORRS**	CORKIRS
CHOOPPS	COPSHOP	**CIINNOT**	NICOTIN	**CIKOSTU**	SICKOUT
CHOORST	COHORTS	**CIINNTU**	TUNICIN	**CIKOTUW**	OUTWICK
CHOORSU	OCHROUS	**CIINOOT**	COITION	**CIKPPSU**	PICKUPS
CHOOSST	COHOSTS	**CIINOPR**	PORCINI	**CIKPSTU**	STICKUP
CHOPSSY	PSYCHOS	**CIINOPS**	PSIONIC		UPTICKS
CHOPTUU	TOUCHUP	**CIINORS**	INCISOR		
CHORRSU	CHURROS	**CIINORT**	NORITIC	**CIKPUWY**	WICKYUP
CHORSTU	TROCHUS		TIRONIC	**CIKRSST**	STRICKS
CHOSSTU	SCHOUTS	**CIINPRS**	CRISPIN	**CIKRSTY**	TRICKSY
	SCOUTHS	**CIINQTU**	QUINTIC	**CILLNOS**	COLLINS
CHOSSTW	SCOWTHS	**CIINRST**	CITRINS	**CILLNOU**	CULLION
CHPSSUY	SCYPHUS	**CIINRSU**	RICINUS	**CILLOOR**	CRIOLLO
CHRRSUU	CHURRUS	**CIINSSV**	VISCINS	**CILLOPY**	POLLICY
CHSSTUY	SCHUYTS	**CIINTUY**	UNICITY	**CILLRUY**	CURLILY
CIIILLT	ILLICIT	**CIIORST**	SORITIC	**CILMNOP**	COMPLIN
	ILLITIC	**CIIOSTX**	COXITIS	**CILMNOS**	CLONISM
CIIILNV	INCIVIL	**CIIOSUV**	VICIOUS	**CILMNSY**	CYMLINS
CIIIMNR	CRIMINI	**CIIPRSS**	SPIRICS	**CILMOOS**	LOCOISM
CIIINPT	INCIPIT	**CIIPRTY**	PYRITIC	**CILMSTU**	CULTISM
CIIJLUY	JUICILY	**CIIRSTV**	VITRICS	**CILNOOR**	ORCINOL
CIIKKLL	KILLICK	**CIIRTVX**	VICTRIX	**CILNOOS**	CLOISON
CIIKKMS	MISKICK	**CIJKORS**	CROJIKS		SCOLION
				CILNOPR	PILCORN

CILNORY	CORNILY	CINNOTU	UNCTION	CKLNOTU	LOCKNUT
	LYRICON	CINNSUU	UNCINUS	CKLNUUY	UNLUCKY
CILNOSU	ULICONS	CINOOPR	PORCINO	CKLOOOY	OLYCOOK
	UNCOILS	CINOOPS	OPSONIC	CKLOORW	ROWLOCK
CILNOTU	LINOCUT		POCOSIN	CKLOOTU	LOCKOUT
CILNOXY	XYLONIC	CINOORS	CORONIS	CKLOPSU	LOCKUPS
CILNPSU	INSCULP	CINOOSS	COOSINS		UPLOCKS
	SCULPIN	CINOOSV	OVONICS	CKLOPTU	POTLUCK
	UNCLIPS	CINOPPS	COPPINS		PUTLOCK
CILNPTU	UNCLIPT	CINOPRX	PRINCOX	CKMMMOU	MUMMOCK
CILNSTU	LINCTUS	CINORRT	TRICORN	CKMOPSU	MOCKUPS
CILOOPT	COPILOT	CINORSS	INCROSS	CKNOOOR	ROCKOON
CILOORU	COULOIR	CINORST	CISTRON	CKNORSU	UNCORKS
CILOOSS	COLOSSI		CITRONS	CKNOSTU	UNSTOCK
CILOOST	SCIOLTO		CORNIST	CKNSTUU	UNSTUCK
CILOPRW	PILCROW		CORTINS		UNTUCKS
CILOPRY	PYLORIC	CINORSZ	ZIRCONS	CKOOOPT	COOKTOP
CILOPSU	OILCUPS	CINORTU	RUCTION	CKOOOTU	COOKOUT
	UPCOILS	CINORTY	TYRONIC		OUTCOOK
CILOPSW	COWSLIP	CINOSST	CONSIST	CKOORSU	SOUROCK
CILORST	LICTORS		TOCSINS	CKOORTU	OUTROCK
CILOSTU	COUTILS	CINOSSU	COUSINS	CKOPTTU	PUTTOCK
	OCULIST	CINOSTU	SUCTION	CKORTUW	CUTWORK
CILPRSY	CRISPLY	CINOSUZ	COUZINS	CKOSSTU	TUSSOCK
CILPRTU	CULPRIT		ZINCOUS	CKSSTUU	TUSSUCK
CILRRSU	SCURRIL	CINOTXY	OXYNTIC	CLLMOSU	MOLLUSC
CILRSUU	SURCULI	CINRSTU	INCRUST	CLLOOPS	COLLOPS
CILRSUY	CRUSILY	CIOOPRT	PORTICO		SCOLLOP
CILSTTU	CULTIST		PROOTIC	CLLORSS	SCROLLS
CIMMNSU	CUMMINS	CIOOPSU	COPIOUS	CLLOSUU	LOCULUS
CIMMOSS	COSMISM	CIOOQTU	COQUITO	CLMNOSU	COLUMNS
CIMMOST	COMMITS	CIOORST	OCTROIS	CLMOOPT	COMPLOT
CIMMOTX	COMMIXT	CIOORSU	CORIOUS	CLMOPTU	PLUMCOT
CIMNNOS	NINCOMS	CIOPRST	TROPICS	CLMOSUU	LUCUMOS
CIMNNSU	NINCUMS	CIOPSTY	COPYIST		OSCULUM
CIMNOOR	MORONIC	CIOQRSU	CROQUIS	CLMPRUY	CRUMPLY
	OMICRON	CIORRSU	CIRROUS	CLMSUUU	CUMULUS
CIMNORS	CRIMSON	CIORSSS	SCISSOR	CLNOORT	CONTROL
	MICRONS	CIORSTT	TRICOTS	CLNOOSS	CONSOLS
CIMNOSS	COSMINS	CIORSTU	CITROUS	CLNOOSU	COLONUS
CIMNOSU	CONIUMS	CIORSTV	VICTORS	CLNOSSU	CONSULS
CIMNRSU	CRINUMS	CIORSUU	CURIOUS	CLNOSTU	CONSULT
CIMOORS	MORISCO	CIORTVY	VICTORY		UNCOLTS
CIMOORT	MOTORIC	CIOSSSY	SYCOSIS	CLNOSUW	UNCOWLS
CIMOOST	OSMOTIC	CIOSSUV	VISCOUS	CLNRSUU	UNCURLS
CIMOPSY	COPYISM	CIOTTUY	OUTCITY	CLOOPPW	COWPLOP
	MISCOPY	CIPRSST	SCRIPTS	CLOOPST	COPLOTS
	MYOPICS	CIPRSSU	PRUSSIC	CLOOPTY	POLYCOT
CIMORSU	CORIUMS	CIPRTTY	TRYPTIC	CLOORSU	COLOURS
CIMOSST	COSMIST	CIPRUVY	PYRUVIC	CLOORUY	COLOURY
	SITCOMS	CIPSTTY	STYPTIC	CLOOSTY	CYTOSOL
CIMOSSY	MYCOSIS	CIRRTTU	CRITTUR	CLOPTUY	OCTUPLY
CIMOSTY	MYOTICS	CIRSSTU	RUSTICS	CLORSSW	SCROWLS
CIMOTYZ	ZYMOTIC	CIRSTUY	CITRUSY	CLORSSY	CROSSLY
CIMPRSS	SCRIMPS	CIRTUVY	CURVITY	CLORSUY	CORYLUS
CIMPRSY	SCRIMPY	CISSTUY	CYTISUS	CLORTUY	COURTLY
CIMRSSU	CRISSUM	CJKNNOO	JONNOCK	CLOSSTU	LOCUSTS
CIMRSUU	CURIUMS	CJNORUY	CONJURY	CLPRSUU	UPCURLS
CIMSSTU	MISCUTS	CKKLNUY	KNUCKLY	CLPSSTU	SCULPTS
CIMSSTY	MYSTICS	CKLLMOU	MULLOCK	CMMNOOS	COMMONS
CIMSSUV	VISCUMS	CKLLOOP	POLLOCK	CMMOORS	ROMCOMS
CINNNOU	INCONNU	CKLLOOR	ROLLOCK	CMMOOST	COMMOTS
CINNORU	UNICORN	CKLLORU	RULLOCK	CMMOPSY	COMSYMP
CINNOSU	NUNCIOS	CKLNOSU	UNLOCKS	CMMRSUY	SCRUMMY

CMNNOOS	NONCOMS	CORRSSU	CURSORS	DDDERSU	DUDDERS
CMNOOOT	MONOCOT	CORRSUY	CURSORY	DDDERUY	DUDDERY
CMNOOPY	COMPONY	CORRSSTU	SCRUTOS	DDDESTU	STUDDED
CMNOSSY	SYNCOMS	COSTTUU	CUTOUTS	DDDGINO	DODDING
CMNPTUU	PUNCTUM	DDDDEIL	DIDDLED	DDEEEFX	FEDEXED
CMOOPRT	COMPORT	DDDEEGR	DREDGED	DDEEEGR	DEGREED
CMOOPST	COMPOST	DDDEEHL	HEDDLED	DDEEEIR	DEEDIER
	COMPOTS	DDDEEHS	SHEDDED	DDEEELN	NEEDLED
CMOORSU	CORMOUS	DDDEEIR	DERIDED	DDEEELT	DELETED
CMOOSTY	SCOTOMY	DDDEELM	MEDDLED	DDEEELV	DEVELED
CMORSTU	SCROTUM	DDDEELP	PEDDLED	DDEEELW	WEDELED
CMORTUW	CUTWORM	DDDEELR	REDDLED	DDEEEMN	EMENDED
CMOSSTU	CUSTOMS	DDDEELS	SLEDDED	DDEEEMR	REMEDED
CMPRSSU	SCRUMPS	DDDEELU	DELUDED	DDEEENT	TEENDED
CMPRSUU	CUPRUMS	DDDEEMO	DEMODED	DDEEENW	ENDEWED
CMPRSUY	SCRUMPY	DDDEENS	SNEDDED	DDEEEPS	SPEEDED
CNNOPSY	PYCNONS	DDDEENU	DENUDED	DDEEEST	DEEDEST
CNNORTU	NOCTURN	DDDEERU	UDDERED		STEEDED
CNNORUW	UNCROWN	DDDEEST	STEDDED	DDEEESX	DESEXED
CNNOSUY	UNSONCY	DDDEFIL	FIDDLED	DDEEEWY	DYEWEED
CNOOOPS	POCOSON	DDDEFLU	FUDDLED	DDEEFGL	FLEDGED
CNOOPPR	POPCORN	DDDEGII	GIDDIED	DDEEFII	DEIFIED
CNOOPRU	CROUPON	DDDEGIR	GRIDDED		EDIFIED
CNOOPSU	COUPONS	DDDEGLU	GUDDLED	DDEEFIL	DEFILED
	SOUPCON	DDDEGRU	DRUDGED		FIELDED
CNOORRW	CORNROW	DDDEHIW	WHIDDED	DDEEFIN	DEFINED
CNOORST	CONSORT	DDDEHLO	HODDLED	DDEEFLU	DEEDFUL
	CROTONS	DDDEHLU	HUDDLED	DDEEFNS	DEFENDS
CNOORTT	CONTORT	DDDEHTU	THUDDED	DDEEFSU	DEFUSED
CNOORTU	CONTOUR	DDDEIIK	KIDDIED	DDEEFUZ	DEFUZED
	CORNUTO	DDDEIIR	DIDDIER	DDEEGGL	GLEDGED
	CROUTON	DDDEIIS	DIDDIES	DDEEGIN	DEEDING
CNOOSST	NOSTOCS	DDDEIIV	DIVIDED		DEIGNED
	ONCOSTS	DDDEIKS	SKIDDED	DDEEGIS	DISEDGE
CNOOSTT	COTTONS	DDDEILM	MIDDLED	DDEEGLP	PLEDGED
CNOOSTY	TYCOONS	DDDEILN	DINDLED	DDEEGLS	SLEDGED
CNOOSUU	NOCUOUS	DDDEILP	PIDDLED	DDEEGLU	DELUGED
CNOOSVY	CONVOYS	DDDEILR	DIDDLER	DDEEGNU	UNEDGED
CNOOTTW	COTTOWN		RIDDLED	DDEEGRR	DREDGER
CNOOTTY	COTTONY	DDDEILS	DIDDLES	DDEEGRS	DREDGES
CNOPRTY	CRYPTON	DDDEILT	TIDDLED	DDEEHLS	HEDDLES
CNOPSTU	PUNCTOS	DDDEILW	WIDDLED	DDEEHNU	DUDHEEN
CNORSSU	UNCROSS	DDDEILY	DIDDLEY	DDEEHRS	SHEDDER
CNORSSY	SYNROCS	DDDEIMU	MUDDIED	DDEEILM	DELIMED
CNORTUY	COUNTRY	DDDEIOR	DODDIER	DDEEILR	DREIDEL
CNRSSTU	SCRUNTS	DDDEIOS	DODDIES	DDEEILS	SLEIDED
CNRSTUY	SCRUNTY	DDDEIRS	DIDDERS	DDEEILV	DEVILED
COOORSZ	COROZOS	DDDEIRU	DUDDIER	DDEEILW	WIELDED
COOPRRT	PROCTOR		RUDDIED	DDEEILY	DEEDILY
COOPRSS	SCROOPS	DDDELMU	MUDDLED		YIELDED
COOPRTU	OUTCROP	DDDELNO	NODDLED	DDEEIMN	DENIMED
COOPSTU	COPOUTS	DDDELOO	DOODLED	DDEEIMP	IMPEDED
	OCTOPUS	DDDELOP	PLODDED	DDEEIMS	DEMISED
COOPSUY	COYPOUS		PODDLED		MISDEED
COORSTU	OCTUORS	DDDELOS	DODDLES	DDEEINP	PIENDED
COORSUU	ROUCOUS	DDDELOT	TODDLED	DDEEINR	NEDDIER
COORTUW	OUTCROW	DDDELPU	PUDDLED	DDEEINS	DESINED
COOSSTY	OOCYSTS	DDDELRU	RUDDLED		NEDDIES
COOSTTY	OTOCYST	DDDENOS	SNODDED		SDEINED
COPRRSS	SCRORPS	DDDEOPR	PRODDED	DDEEINT	ENDITED
COPRRTU	CORRUPT	DDDEOQU	QUODDED		TEINDED
COPRSTY	CRYPTOS	DDDEORS	DODDERS	DDEEINW	INDEWED
COPRSUU	CUPROUS	DDDEORY	DODDERY		WIDENED
COPRTUU	UPCOURT	DDDEPSU	SPUDDED	DDEEINX	DEINDEX

	INDEXED	DDEEOTX	DETOXED	DDEGRRU	DRUDGER
DDEEINZ	DIZENED	DDEEPRS	PEDDERS	DDEGRSU	DRUDGES
DDEEIOV	VIDEOED		SPREDDE	DDEGRTU	TRUDGED
DDEEIPS	DEPSIDE	DDEEPRY	PREDYED	DDEHINS	NEDDISH
DDEEIRR	DERIDER	DDEEPTU	DEPUTED	DDEHIOW	HOWDIED
	REDDIER	DDEERRS	REDDERS	DDEHIRS	HIDDERS
	REDRIED	DDEERSS	DRESSED		REDDISH
	RIDERED	DDEERST	REDDEST		SHIDDER
DDEEIRS	DERIDES		TEDDERS	DDEHIRT	THIRDED
	DESIRED	DDEERSW	WEDDERS	DDEHIRW	WHIDDER
	DIEDRES	DDEERTU	DETRUDE	DDEHIRY	HYDRIDE
	RESIDED	DDEESST	STEDDES	DDEHLNO	HONDLED
DDEEIRV	DERIVED	DDEETTU	DUETTED	DDEHLOS	HODDLES
DDEEIRW	WEIRDED	DDEFGIR	FRIDGED	DDEHLRU	HUDDLER
DDEEIST	DEIDEST	DDEFILR	FIDDLER		HURDLED
	TEDDIES	DDEFILS	FIDDLES	DDEHLSU	HUDDLES
DDEEISV	DEVISED	DDEFILY	FIDDLEY	DDEHNOS	HODDENS
DDEEKKO	DEKKOED	DDEFIOR	FOREDID		SHODDEN
DDEELLU	DUELLED	DDEFIRT	DRIFTED	DDEHNOU	HOUNDED
DDEELLW	DWELLED	DDEFISU	FUDDIES	DDEHNRU	HUNDRED
DDEELMO	MODELED	DDEFLNO	FONDLED	DDEHNSU	DUNSHED
DDEELMR	MEDDLER	DDEFLOO	FLOODED	DDEHNUZ	NUDZHED
DDEELMS	MEDDLES	DDEFLRU	FUDDLER	DDEHOSW	SHOWDED
DDEELNO	OLDENED	DDEFLSU	FUDDLES	DDEHRSU	SHUDDER
DDEELNS	LEDDENS	DDEFNOR	FRONDED	DDEHRSY	SHREDDY
DDEELOP	DELOPED	DDEFNOU	FONDUED	DDEIIKR	KIDDIER
DDEELOW	DOWELED		FOUNDED	DDEIIKS	KIDDIES
DDEELOY	YODELED	DDEFNSU	DEFUNDS	DDEIIMS	MIDDIES
DDEELPR	PEDDLER	DDEFORS	FODDERS	DDEIINT	INDITED
DDEELPS	PEDDLES	DDEGGRU	DRUGGED	DDEIINV	DIVINED
	SPELDED		GRUDGED	DDEIIOS	IODIDES
DDEELRS	REDDLES	DDEGHIT	DIGHTED		IODISED
	SLEDDER	DDEGIIR	GIDDIER	DDEIIOX	DIOXIDE
DDEELRT	TREDDLE	DDEGIIS	GIDDIES	DDEIIOZ	IODIZED
DDEELRU	DELUDER	DDEGILR	GIRDLED	DDEIIRT	DIRTIED
DDEELSU	DELUDES		GLIDDER		TIDDIER
DDEEMMO	MODEMED		GRIDDLE	DDEIIRV	DIVIDER
DDEEMOT	DEMOTED	DDEGIMO	DEMIGOD	DDEIIST	STIDDIE
DDEEMRU	DEMURED	DDEGINO	DINGOED		TIDDIES
DDEENNU	UNENDED	DDEGINR	GRINDED	DDEIISV	DIVIDES
DDEENOP	DEPONED		REDDING	DDEIISW	WIDDIES
DDEENOT	DENOTED	DDEGINT	TEDDING	DDEIITT	DITTIED
DDEENOV	DOVENED	DDEGINW	WEDDING	DDEIIVV	DIVVIED
DDEENOW	ENDOWED	DDEGINY	EDDYING	DDEIIZZ	DIZZIED
DDEENOZ	DOZENED	DDEGIOR	DODGIER	DDEIKLN	KINDLED
DDEENPS	DEPENDS	DDEGIRR	GRIDDER	DDEIKLS	KIDDLES
DDEENPU	UPENDED	DDEGKLU	KLUDGED	DDEIKNR	KINDRED
DDEENRS	REDDENS	DDEGLOP	PLODGED	DDEIKOS	KIDDOES
DDEENRT	TRENDED	DDEGLOS	DOGSLED	DDEIKRS	KIDDERS
DDEENRU	DENUDER	DDEGLSU	GUDDLES		SKIDDER
	ENDURED		SLUDGED	DDEILLO	DOLLIED
DDEENST	STENDED	DDEGMOO	DOGEDOM	DDEILLR	DRILLED
DDEENSU	DENUDES	DDEGMOS	DODGEMS	DDEILLU	ILLUDED
	DUDEENS	DDEGMSU	SMUDGED	DDEILMP	DIMPLED
	DUENDES	DDEGNOO	NOODGED	DDEILMR	MIDDLER
DDEENSY	DESYNED	DDEGNOS	GODDENS	DDEILMS	MIDDLES
DDEENTU	DETUNED		GODSEND	DDEILNN	DINNLED
DDEEOOR	RODEOED	DDEGNOU	DUDGEON	DDEILNS	DINDLES
DDEEOPS	DEPOSED	DDEGNSU	SNUDGED		SLIDDEN
	SEEDPOD	DDEGORS	DODGERS	DDEILNW	DWINDLE
DDEEORR	ORDERED		GORSEDD		WINDLED
DDEEORV	DOVERED	DDEGORY	DODGERY	DDEILOR	DROILED
DDEEORW	DOWERED	DDEGOSS	GODDESS	DDEILOS	DILDOES
DDEEOTV	DEVOTED	DDEGOST	STODGED	DDEILOT	DELTOID

DDEILPR	PIDDLER	DDELLOR	DROLLED	DDEOOWY	DYEWOOD
DDEILPS	DISPLED	DDELMOU	MOULDED	DDEOPPR	DROPPED
	PIDDLES	DDELMPU	DUMPLED	DDEOPRR	PRODDER
DDEILPU	DUPLIED	DDELMRU	MUDDLER	DDEOPRW	DEWDROP
DDEILQU	QUIDDLE	DDELMSU	MUDDLES	DDEORSW	DROWSED
DDEILRR	RIDDLER	DDELNOO	NOODLED		SWORDED
DDEILRS	DREIDLS	DDELNOS	NODDLES	DDEPRSS	SPREDDS
	RIDDLES	DDELNOU	LOUNDED	DDEPRSU	PUDDERS
	SLIDDER		NODULED		SPUDDER
DDEILRT	TIDDLER	DDELNOW	LOWNDED	DDERRSU	RUDDERS
DDEILST	TIDDLES	DDELNRU	NURDLED	DDERSSU	SUDDERS
DDEILSW	WIDDLES		RUNDLED	DDGGINO	DODGING
DDEILTU	DILUTED	DDELOOR	DOODLER		GODDING
DDEILTW	TWIDDLE		DROOLED	DDGHINO	HODDING
DDEILTY	LYDDITE	DDELOOS	DOODLES	DDGHOOO	GODHOOD
	TIDDLEY	DDELOOW	WOOLDED	DDGIIKN	KIDDING
DDEIMMU	DUMMIED	DDELOPR	PLODDER	DDGIILN	LIDDING
DDEIMNS	MIDDENS	DDELOPS	PODDLES	DDGIILY	GIDDILY
DDEIMNU	MUEDDIN	DDELORT	TODDLER	DDGIINR	RIDDING
DDEIMOO	MOODIED	DDELORW	WORLDED	DDGIMNU	MUDDING
DDEIMOR	DERMOID	DDELOST	TODDLES	DDGINNO	NODDING
DDEIMOS	DESMOID	DDELOTT	DOTTLED	DDGINOP	PODDING
DDEIMRU	MUDDIER	DDELPRU	PUDDLER	DDGINOR	RODDING
DDEIMSS	DESMIDS	DDELPSU	PUDDLES	DDGINOS	SODDING
DDEIMST	MIDDEST		SPUDDLE	DDGINOT	TODDING
DDEIMSU	DEDIMUS	DDELRSU	RUDDLES	DDGINPU	PUDDING
	MUDDIES	DDELSTU	STUDDLE	DDGINRU	RUDDING
DDEINOP	POINDED	DDEMMRU	DRUMMED	DDGINUW	WUDDING
DDEINOS	NODDIES	DDEMMSU	SMEDDUM	DDGIPUY	GIDDYUP
DDEINOT	DENTOID	DDEMNOS	ODDSMEN	DDGMOOS	DOGDOMS
DDEINOW	INDOWED	DDEMNOT	ODDMENT	DDGOOOW	DOGWOOD
DDEINPS	DISPEND	DDEMNOU	MOUNDED	DDHIIKS	KIDDISH
DDEINRU	UNDRIED	DDEMRSU	MUDDERS	DDHIISS	SIDDHIS
DDEINST	DISTEND	DDENNOR	DENDRON	DDHIKSU	KIDDUSH
DDEINSU	NUDDIES		DONNERD	DDHINOS	HODDINS
DDEINSW	SWIDDEN	DDENOOP	ENDOPOD	DDHIORY	HYDROID
DDEIOOS	DOODIES	DDENOOS	DESNOOD	DDHIRSY	HYDRIDS
DDEIOPS	PODDIES		SNOODED	DDIIIOO	OIDIOID
DDEIORS	DORISED	DDENOPS	DESPOND	DDIIKKS	DIKDIKS
	SODDIER	DDENOPU	POUNDED	DDIIKLS	SKIDLID
DDEIORV	OVERDID	DDENOPW	POWNDED	DDIIKSV	KIDVIDS
DDEIORW	DOWDIER	DDENORS	DONDERS	DDIILOP	DIPLOID
DDEIORZ	DORIZED		NODDERS	DDIIOSX	DIOXIDS
DDEIOSS	SODDIES		SNODDER		IXODIDS
DDEIOST	TODDIES	DDENORT	TRODDEN	DDIIQTU	QUIDDIT
DDEIOSW	DOWDIES	DDENORU	REDOUND	DDIKNOS	DODKINS
DDEIOTT	DITTOED		ROUNDED	DDIKOOS	SKIDDOO
DDEIOWW	WIDOWED		UNDERDO	DDILMUY	MUDDILY
DDEIPPR	DRIPPED	DDENORW	DROWNED	DDILNRS	DIRNDLS
DDEIPRS	DISPRED		ROWNDED	DDILOSY	DYSODIL
DDEIPRU	UPDRIED		WONDRED	DDILOWY	DOWDILY
DDEIPSU	PUDDIES	DDENOSS	ODDNESS	DDILRUY	RUDDILY
DDEIPUV	UPDIVED		SODDENS	DDILTWY	TWIDDLY
DDEIRRS	RIDDERS	DDENOSU	SOUNDED	DDIMOOS	DODOISM
DDEIRRU	RUDDIER	DDENOSW	SOWNDED	DDIMRSU	DIRDUMS
DDEIRSU	RUDDIES	DDENOSY	DYNODES	DDIMSSU	DUDISMS
DDEIRSW	WIDDERS	DDENOUW	WOUNDED	DDINOST	SNODDIT
DDEISSU	DISUSED	DDENPSU	PUDDENS	DDIORTU	TURDOID
DDEISTU	STUDDIE	DDENRSU	DUNDERS	DDIRRUY	DRUIDRY
	STUDIED	DDENSSU	SUDDENS	DDIRRSU	SIDDURS
DDEJRSU	JUDDERS	DDENSTU	STUDDEN	DDLLMOO	DOLLDOM
DDEKMOU	DUKEDOM	DDEOOPR	DROOPED	DDMMSUU	DUMDUMS
DDEKOOR	DROOKED	DDEOORU	ODOURED	DDMNOOR	DROMOND
DDEKORU	DROUKED	DDEOORW	REDWOOD	DDMRSUU	DURDUMS

DDNORSW	DROWNDS	DEEELMS	MESELED	DEEERSV	DESERVE
DDOOOOS	DOODOOS	DEEELNR	NEEDLER		SEVERED
DDORSTY	DROSTDY	DEEELNS	NEEDLES	DEEERSW	RESEWED
DEEEEMX	EXEEMED	DEEELPS	SPEELED		SEWERED
DEEEEWW	WEEWEED	DEEELPT	DEPLETE		SWEERED
DEEEFFR	EFFERED	DEEELRT	DEERLET		WEEDERS
DEEEFLR	FLEERED	DEEELRV	LEVERED	DEEERSY	REDEYES
DEEEFLT	FLEETED		REVELED	DEEERTV	EVERTED
DEEEFNR	ENFREED	DEEELST	DELETES	DEEERTW	TWEERED
DEEEFNS	DEFENSE		SLEETED	DEEERTX	EXERTED
DEEEFRS	FEEDERS		STEELED	DEEERWY	WEEDERY
	REFEEDS	DEEELSV	SLEEVED	DEEESSX	DESEXES
DEEEFRV	FEVERED	DEEELSW	SWEELED	DEEESTV	STEEVED
DEEEFSX	FEDEXES	DEEELTW	TWEEDLE	DEEESTW	SWEETED
DEEEGKL	GLEEKED		TWEELED	DEEETTV	VEDETTE
DEEEGKR	GREEKED	DEEELTX	TELEXED	DEEETTW	TWEETED
DEEEGLP	PLEDGEE	DEEEMMW	EMMEWED	DEEETWZ	TWEEZED
DEEEGLT	GLEETED	DEEEMNR	EMENDER	DEEFFFO	FEOFFED
DEEEGMR	DEMERGE		REEDMEN	DEEFFIN	EFFENDI
	EMERGED	DEEEMNS	DEMESNE	DEEFFOR	OFFERED
DEEEGNP	PEENGED		SEEDMEN	DEEFFST	DEFFEST
DEEEGNR	GREENED	DEEEMNW	ENMEWED	DEEFFSU	EFFUSED
	RENEGED	DEEEMRS	DEMERSE	DEEFGGL	FLEGGED
DEEEGRR	REGREDE		EMERSED	DEEFGIN	FEEDING
DEEEGRS	DEGREES		MEDRESE		FEIGNED
DEEEGRT	DETERGE		REDEEMS	DEEFGIP	PIGFEED
	GREETED		REMEDES	DEEFGLS	FLEDGES
DEEEGST	EGESTED	DEEEMRT	METERED	DEEFGRU	REFUGED
DEEEHKT	THEEKED	DEEEMST	STEEMED	DEEFHLS	FLESHED
DEEEHLS	SHEELED	DEEENPR	PREENED		SHELFED
DEEEHLW	WHEEDLE	DEEENPS	DEEPENS	DEEFHLU	HEEDFUL
	WHEELED	DEEENQU	QUEENED	DEEFHRS	FRESHED
DEEEHNS	SHEENED	DEEENRS	NEEDERS	DEEFIIR	DEIFIER
DEEEHPS	PHEESED		SERENED		EDIFIER
DEEEHPW	WHEEPED		SNEERED		REIFIED
DEEEHPZ	PHEEZED	DEEENRT	ENTERED	DEEFIIS	DEIFIES
DEEEHRS	HEEDERS	DEEENRV	ENERVED		EDIFIES
	HEREDES	DEEENRW	RENEWED	DEEFILN	ENFILED
	SHEERED	DEEENRY	RENEYED	DEEFILR	DEFILER
DEEEHST	SEETHED	DEEENST	STEENED		FERLIED
	SHEETED	DEEENSV	VENDEES		FIELDER
DEEEHTT	TEETHED	DEEENSW	ENSEWED		REFILED
DEEEHWZ	WHEEZED	DEEENSZ	SNEEZED	DEEFILS	DEFILES
DEEEIJL	JEELIED	DEEENTT	DETENTE	DEEFILT	FILETED
DEEEIMR	EMERIED		NEDETTE	DEEFIMS	MISFEED
DEEEINR	NEEDIER	DEEENTU	DETENUE	DEEFINR	DEFINER
DEEEIPS	DEEPIES	DEEENTV	EVENTED		ENFIRED
DEEEIRR	REEDIER	DEEEORW	OREWEED		FENDIER
DEEEIRS	SEEDIER	DEEEOTV	DEVOTEE		REFINED
DEEEIRW	WEEDIER	DEEEPRS	SPEEDER	DEEFINS	DEFINES
DEEEISV	DEVISEE		SPEERED	DEEFINT	FEINTED
DEEEJLW	JEWELED	DEEEPRT	PETERED	DEEFINX	ENFIXED
DEEEJNU	DEJEUNE	DEEEPRU	EPERDUE	DEEFIPR	PRIEFED
DEEEJRR	JERREED	DEEEPRV	PREEVED	DEEFIRR	FERRIED
DEEEJRS	JEREEDS	DEEEPSS	PEDESES		REFIRED
DEEEKLN	KNEELED	DEEEPST	DEEPEST		REFRIED
DEEEKLS	SLEEKED		STEEPED	DEEFIRS	DEFIERS
DEEEKMS	SMEEKED	DEEEQRU	QUEERED		SERIFED
DEEEKNW	WEEKEND	DEEERRS	REEDERS	DEEFIRT	FETIDER
DEEEKRS	KREESED	DEEERRV	REVERED	DEEFIRX	REFIXED
	SKEERED	DEEERSS	RESEEDS	DEEFIRY	REEDIFY
DEEEKRY	REKEYED		SEEDERS	DEEFIRZ	FRIEZED
DEEEKST	STEEKED	DEEERST	REESTED	DEEFIST	DEIFEST
DEEELLV	LEVELED		STEERED	DEEFLLU	FUELLED

DEEFLNS	FLENSED	**DEEGLNS**	LEGENDS	**DEEHOSY**	HOSEYED
DEEFLNU	NEEDFUL	**DEEGLNT**	GENTLED	**DEEHPRS**	SPHERED
DEEFLOT	FEEDLOT		GLENTED	**DEEHRRS**	HERDERS
DEEFLOY	EYEFOLD	**DEEGLOY**	GOLDEYE	**DEEHRSS**	HERDESS
DEEFLRU	FERULED	**DEEGLPR**	PLEDGER	**DEEHRSU**	USHERED
DEEFLRY	DEERFLY	**DEEGLPS**	PLEDGES	**DEEHRSW**	SHREWED
DEEFLSU	DEFUELS	**DEEGLPT**	PLEDGET	**DEEHRTW**	WRETHED
DEEFLTT	FETTLED	**DEEGLRS**	GELDERS	**DEEHSYY**	HEYDEYS
DEEFMOR	FREEDOM		LEDGERS	**DEEHTTW**	WHETTED
DEEFNRS	FENDERS		REDLEGS	**DEEIINT**	DIETINE
DEEFNRU	UNFREED		SLEDGER	**DEEIIPR**	EPEIRID
DEEFNUU	UNFEUED	**DEEGLRU**	GRUELED	**DEEIIRW**	WEIRDIE
DEEFORV	OVERFED		REGLUED	**DEEIIST**	DEITIES
DEEFORZ	DEFROZE	**DEEGLRW**	WERGELD	**DEEIJLL**	JELLIED
DEEFRSU	DEFUSER	**DEEGLSS**	SLEDGES	**DEEIJMM**	JEMMIED
	REFUSED	**DEEGLSU**	DELUGES	**DEEIJTT**	JETTIED
DEEFRSW	SWERFED	**DEEGMNU**	EMUNGED	**DEEIKLL**	KILLDEE
DEEFRTT	FRETTED		GUDEMEN	**DEEIKLN**	KNEIDEL
DEEFRTU	FEUTRED	**DEEGMRS**	DEGERMS		LIKENED
	REFUTED	**DEEGMUW**	GUMWEED	**DEEIKMW**	MIDWEEK
DEEFSSU	DEFUSES	**DEEGNHO**	ENDOGEN	**DEEIKNR**	REINKED
DEEFSTT	DEFTEST	**DEEGNNR**	GRENNED	**DEEIKNS**	ENSKIED
DEEFSUZ	DEFUZES	**DEEGNOR**	ENGORED		SKEINED
DEEGGIS	GIDGEES	**DEEGNRS**	GENDERS	**DEEIKOV**	DOVEKIE
DEEGGLS	GLEDGES	**DEEGNSU**	DENGUES	**DEEILLS**	DELLIES
DEEGHIN	HEEDING		UNEDGES	**DEEILMS**	DELIMES
	NEIGHED	**DEEGOOS**	SOOGEED	**DEEILNO**	ELOINED
DEEGHIR	HEDGIER	**DEEGORR**	ROGERED	**DEEILNR**	REDLINE
DEEGHIW	WEIGHED	**DEEGOSS**	GESSOED		RELINED
DEEGHOW	HOGWEED	**DEEGOSY**	GEODESY	**DEEILNS**	ENISLED
DEEGHRS	HEDGERS	**DEEGOTU**	OUTEDGE		ENSILED
DEEGHSS	GHESSED	**DEEGRRU**	REURGED		LINSEED
DEEGIJS	GIDJEES	**DEEGRSW**	SWEDGER	**DEEILNT**	LENITED
DEEGIKN	DEKEING	**DEEGSSU**	GUESSED	**DEEILNV**	LIVENED
DEEGIKR	KEDGIER	**DEEGSTU**	GUESTED	**DEEILNY**	DYELINE
DEEGILN	DELEING	**DEEHIKV**	KHEDIVE		NEEDILY
DEEGILR	GELIDER	**DEEHILS**	SHIELED	**DEEILOR**	REOILED
	LEDGIER	**DEEHILT**	LETHIED	**DEEILOS**	OILSEED
	LEIDGER	**DEEHINR**	INHERED	**DEEILPR**	PERILED
DEEGIMN	DEEMING	**DEEHIRR**	HERRIED		REPLIED
DEEGIMV	DEMIVEG		REHIRED	**DEEILPS**	SEEDLIP
DEEGINN	ENGINED	**DEEHIRT**	DIETHER		SPEILED
	NEEDING	**DEEHIST**	HEISTED		SPIELED
DEEGINR	DREEING	**DEEHITV**	THIEVED	**DEEILRS**	RESILED
	ENERGID	**DEEHKLW**	WHELKED	**DEEILRT**	RETILED
	GREINED	**DEEHLLO**	HELLOED	**DEEILRV**	DELIVER
	REEDING	**DEEHLLS**	SHELLED		LIVERED
	REIGNED	**DEEHLMW**	WHELMED		RELIVED
DEEGINS	SDEIGNE	**DEEHLNU**	UNHELED		REVILED
	SEEDING	**DEEHLOV**	HOVELED	**DEEILRW**	WIELDER
DEEGINV	DEEVING	**DEEHLPW**	WHELPED	**DEEILRY**	REEDILY
DEEGINW	WEEDING	**DEEHLSV**	SHELVED		YIELDER
DEEGINY	YEEDING	**DEEHLSW**	WELSHED	**DEEILSS**	DIESELS
DEEGIPW	PIGWEED	**DEEHMNR**	HERDMEN		IDLESSE
DEEGIRS	SEDGIER	**DEEHMNS**	MENSHED		SEIDELS
DEEGIRV	DIVERGE	**DEEHMOR**	HOMERED	**DEEILST**	ISLETED
	GRIEVED	**DEEHMRU**	RHEUMED	**DEEILSY**	EYELIDS
DEEGIRW	WEDGIER	**DEEHMUX**	EXHUMED		SEEDILY
DEEGIST	EDGIEST	**DEEHNOY**	HONEYED	**DEEILTU**	DILUTEE
DEEGISW	WEDGIES	**DEEHNPR**	PREHEND	**DEEILTV**	DEVILET
DEEGJRU	REJUDGE	**DEEHNRS**	HERDENS	**DEEILWY**	WEEDILY
DEEGKMO	GEEKDOM	**DEEHNUY**	UNHEEDY	**DEEIMMO**	MIMEOED
DEEGKRS	KEDGERS	**DEEHORS**	RESHOED	**DEEIMMS**	MISDEEM
DEEGLMU	EMULGED	**DEEHORV**	HOVERED	**DEEIMMW**	IMMEWED

DEEIMNO	DOMINEE	DEEIPPT	PEPTIDE	DEEKNNS	SKENNED
DEEIMNR	ERMINED		PIPETED	DEEKNOT	TOKENED
DEEIMNS	DESMINE	DEEIPRS	PRESIDE	DEEKNSY	ENSKYED
	SIDEMEN		SPEIRED	DEEKORV	REVOKED
DEEIMNT	DEMENTI		SPIERED	DEEKOVY	DOVEKEY
DEEIMOR	EMEROID	DEEIPRT	PREEDIT	DEEKPPS	SKEPPED
DEEIMPR	DEMIREP		TEPIDER	DEEKPRU	PERUKED
	EPIDERM	DEEIPRV	DEPRIVE	DEEKRRS	SKERRED
	IMPEDER		PREDIVE	DEEKRSU	RESKUED
DEEIMPS	IMPEDES		PRIEVED	DEEKSTT	SKETTED
	SEMIPED	DEEIPRX	EXPIRED	DEELLMS	SMELLED
DEEIMPT	EMPTIED	DEEIPSS	DESPISE	DEELLNS	SNELLED
DEEIMRS	REMEIDS		PEDESIS	DEELLPS	SPELLED
	REMISED	DEEIPST	DESPITE	DEELLQU	QUELLED
DEEIMRT	DEMERIT	DEEIQRU	QUERIED	DEELLRU	DUELLER
	DIMETER	DEEIQTU	QUIETED	DEELLRW	DWELLER
	MERITED	DEEIRRS	DERRIES	DEELLRY	ELDERLY
	MITERED		DESIRER	DEELLST	STELLED
	RETIMED		REDRIES	DEELLSW	SWELLED
DEEIMRX	REMIXED		RESIDER	DEELMNO	LEMONED
DEEIMSS	DEMISES		SERRIED	DEELMOR	MODELER
DEEIMTT	EMITTED	DEEIRRT	RETIRED		REMODEL
DEEINNP	PENNIED		RETRIED	DEELMPT	TEMPLED
DEEINNS	INDENES		TIREDER	DEELMPU	DEPLUME
DEEINNT	DENTINE	DEEIRRV	DERIVER	DEELMRS	MELDERS
DEEINNU	ENNUIED		REDRIVE	DEELMRU	RELUMED
DEEINNZ	DENIZEN		RIVERED	DEELMST	SMELTED
DEEINOR	ORDINEE	DEEIRRW	REWIRED	DEELMSU	MULESED
DEEINPR	REPINED		WEIRDER	DEELMSY	MEDLEYS
	RIPENED	DEEIRSS	DESIRES	DEELMTT	METTLED
DEEINPW	PINWEED		RESIDES	DEELNOT	DOLENTE
DEEINRR	DERNIER	DEEIRST	DIESTER	DEELNPU	PENDULE
	NERDIER		DIETERS	DEELNRS	LENDERS
DEEINRS	DENIERS		REEDITS		RELENDS
	NEREIDS		REISTED		SLENDER
	RESINED		RESITED	DEELNSS	ENDLESS
DEEINRU	UREDINE	DEEIRSU	RESIDUE	DEELNST	DENTELS
DEEINRW	REWIDEN		UREIDES		NESTLED
	WIDENER	DEEIRSV	DERIVES	DEELNSW	WEDELNS
DEEINRX	INDEXER		DEVISER	DEELNSY	DENSELY
	REINDEX		DIVERSE	DEELNTT	NETTLED
DEEINSS	DESINES		REVISED	DEELOOS	DOOLEES
DEEINST	DESTINE	DEEIRSW	SWEIRED	DEELOPP	PEOPLED
	ENDITES	DEEIRSZ	RESIZED	DEELOPR	DEPLORE
	STEINED	DEEIRTU	ERUDITE	DEELOPS	DELOPES
DEEINSV	DEVEINS	DEEIRTV	RIVETED	DEELOPV	DEVELOP
	ENDIVES		VERDITE	DEELOPX	EXPLODE
DEEINSW	ENDWISE	DEEIRVV	REVIVED	DEELORS	RESOLED
	SINEWED	DEEISSU	DISEUSE	DEELORU	URODELE
DEEINSX	INDEXES	DEEISSV	DEVISES	DEELORV	LOVERED
DEEINTT	DINETTE	DEEISTT	TEDIEST	DEELORW	LOWERED
DEEINTU	DETINUE	DEEISTW	DEWIEST		ROWELED
DEEINTV	EVIDENT	DEEISTX	EXISTED	DEELORY	YODELER
DEEINVW	VINEWED	DEEITTV	VIDETTE	DEELOSU	DELOUSE
DEEINVX	INVEXED	DEEJNOS	JONESED	DEELOTV	DOVELET
DEEINWZ	WIZENED	DEEJNOY	ENJOYED	DEELOTW	TOWELED
DEEIOPS	EPISODE	DEEJQRU	JERQUED	DEELOVV	DEVOLVE
	POESIED	DEEKKRT	TREKKED		EVOLVED
DEEIOPT	EPIDOTE	DEEKLLN	KNELLED	DEELPRS	PEDLERS
DEEIOPX	EPOXIDE	DEEKLLV	KVELLED		SPELDER
	EPOXIED	DEEKLPS	SKELPED	DEELPRU	PRELUDE
DEEIORS	OREIDES	DEEKLRS	SKELDER	DEELPRY	PEDLERY
	OSIERED	DEEKMNS	DESKMEN	DEELPST	PESTLED
DEEIOSV	VOIDEES	DEEKMRS	SMERKED	DEELPTT	PETTLED

DEELRRU	RULERED	DEENOST	DENOTES	DEEORXX	XEROXED
DEELRSS	ELDRESS	DEENPPR	PERPEND	DEEOSTV	DEVOTES
DEELRSU	DUELERS	DEENPRS	SPENDER	DEEOSTX	DETOXES
	ELUDERS	DEENPRT	PRENTED	DEEOTUW	OUTWEED
DEELRSV	DELVERS		PRETEND	DEEPPPR	PREPPED
DEELRSW	REWELDS	DEENPSX	EXPENDS	DEEPPST	STEPPED
	WELDERS	DEENRRS	RENDERS	DEEPPSU	SPEEDUP
DEELRUV	VELURED	DEENRRU	ENDURER	DEEPRRS	SPERRED
DEELSSW	DEWLESS	DEENRSS	REDNESS	DEEPRRU	PERDURE
DEELSTT	SETTLED		RESENDS		REPURED
DEELSTU	TELEDUS		SENDERS	DEEPRSS	DEPRESS
DEELSTW	LEWDEST	DEENRST	STERNED		PRESSED
	SWELTED		TENDERS		SPERSED
DEELSUV	EVULSED		TENDRES	DEEPRST	PRESTED
DEELSVV	DEVVELS	DEENRSU	ENDURES	DEEPRSU	PERDUES
DEELTUX	EXULTED		ENSURED		PERSUED
DEELVXY	VEXEDLY	DEENRSV	VENDERS		PERUSED
DEEMMOV	EMMOVED	DEENRSZ	DZERENS		SUPERED
DEEMMST	STEMMED	DEENRTU	DENTURE	DEEPRSY	PREDYES
DEEMNOR	MODERNE		RETUNED	DEEPRTU	ERUPTED
DEEMNOT	DEMETON		TENURED		REPUTED
DEEMNOU	EUDEMON	DEENRTV	VENTRED	DEEPRTY	RETYPED
DEEMNOV	ENMOVED	DEENSST	DENSEST	DEEPRUV	PREVUED
	VENOMED	DEENSSU	DUENESS	DEEPSTU	DEPUTES
DEEMNOY	MONEYED	DEENSSY	DESYNES	DEEQSTU	QUESTED
DEEMNRS	MENDERS		ENDYSES	DEERRSS	DRESSER
	REMENDS	DEENSTT	DETENTS		REDRESS
DEEMNST	DEMENTS		STENTED	DEERRUV	VERDURE
DEEMNTU	UNMETED	DEENSTU	DETENUS	DEERSSS	DRESSES
DEEMNUW	UNMEWED		DETUNES	DEERSST	DESERTS
DEEMORS	EMERODS	DEENSTX	EXTENDS		DESSERT
DEEMORV	REMOVED	DEENSUV	VENDUES		TRESSED
DEEMORX	EXODERM	DEENSUW	UNSEWED	DEERSSU	DURESSE
DEEMOSS	DEMOSES	DEENSUX	UNSEXED	DEERSTV	STERVED
DEEMOST	DEMOTES	DEENUVX	UNVEXED		VERDETS
DEEMOSY	MOSEYED	DEEOPPY	POPEYED	DEERSTW	STREWED
DEEMPRS	DEPERMS	DEEOPRR	PEDRERO		WRESTED
	PREMEDS	DEEOPRS	DEPOSER	DEERSTX	DEXTERS
DEEMPTT	TEMPTED		REPOSED	DEERSTY	DYESTER
DEEMRRU	DEMURER	DEEOPRW	POWERED	DEERSVW	SWERVED
DEEMRSU	DEMURES	DEEOPSS	DEPOSES	DEERTTU	UTTERED
	RESUMED		SPEEDOS	DEERTUX	EXTRUDE
DEEMSUY	MUDEYES	DEEOPSX	EXPOSED	DEESSTT	DETESTS
DEENNOR	ENDERON		PODEXES	DEESSTV	DEVESTS
DEENNOS	DONNEES	DEEOPXY	EPOXYED	DEESTTT	STETTED
DEENNOT	ENDNOTE	DEEORRR	ORDERER	DEFFFLU	FLUFFED
	TENONED		REORDER	DEFFGRU	GRUFFED
DEENNOV	DOYENNE	DEEORRS	REREDOS	DEFFHIW	WHIFFED
DEENNOZ	ENZONED	DEEORRV	OVERRED	DEFFHOU	HOUFFED
DEENNPT	PENDENT		REDROVE	DEFFHOW	HOWFFED
DEENNST	DENNETS	DEEORST	OERSTED	DEFFIKS	SKIFFED
	STENNED		ROSETED	DEFFILP	PIFFLED
DEENNTZ	TENDENZ		TEREDOS	DEFFILR	RIFFLED
DEENNUY	ENNUYED	DEEORSV	DEVORES	DEFFILS	SIFFLED
DEENOOR	RONEOED	DEEORSW	RESOWED	DEFFIMO	FIEFDOM
DEENOPR	REPONED	DEEORSX	REDOXES	DEFFINS	SNIFFED
DEENOPS	DEPONES	DEEORTT	OTTERED	DEFFIOS	DIEOFFS
	SPONDEE		TETRODE		OFFSIDE
DEENOPT	PENTODE	DEEORTV	REVOTED	DEFFIPS	SPIFFED
DEENORS	ENDORSE	DEEORTW	TOWERED	DEFFIRS	DIFFERS
DEENORT	ERODENT	DEEORTX	OXTERED	DEFFIST	STIFFED
DEENORW	ENDOWER	DEEORTZ	ROZETED	DEFFISU	DIFFUSE
	REENDOW	DEEORUV	OVERDUE	DEFFKOS	SKOFFED
DEENORZ	REZONED	DEEORVY	OVERDYE	DEFFLMU	MUFFLED

DEFFLPU	PLUFFED	**DEFILSU**	SULFIDE		SERFDOM
DEFFLRU	RUFFLED	**DEFILTT**	FLITTED	**DEFMPRU**	FRUMPED
DEFFLSU	DUFFELS	**DEFILTY**	FETIDLY	**DEFNOOR**	FORDONE
	DUFFLES	**DEFILXY**	FIXEDLY	**DEFNORT**	FRONTED
	SLUFFED	**DEFILZZ**	FIZZLED	**DEFNORU**	FOUNDER
DEFFNOR	FORFEND	**DEFIMOR**	DEIFORM		REFOUND
DEFFNOS	OFFENDS	**DEFIMOW**	WIFEDOM	**DEFNORW**	FROWNED
	SENDOFF	**DEFINRS**	FINDERS	**DEFNOST**	FONDEST
DEFFNSU	SNUFFED		FRIENDS	**DEFNOSU**	FONDUES
DEFFOPU	POUFFED		REDFINS	**DEFNPRU**	PREFUND
DEFFORS	DOFFERS		REFINDS	**DEFNRSU**	FUNDERS
DEFFOSW	SOWFFED	**DEFINRU**	UNFIRED		REFUNDS
DEFFRSU	DUFFERS	**DEFINST**	SNIFTED	**DEFNSUU**	UNFUSED
DEFFSTU	DUFFEST	**DEFINSU**	FUNDIES	**DEFOOPR**	PROOFED
	STUFFED		INFUSED	**DEFOOPS**	SPOOFED
DEFGGIR	FRIGGED	**DEFINSY**	DENSIFY	**DEFOORS**	DOOFERS
DEFGGLO	FLOGGED	**DEFINUX**	UNFIXED		FORDOES
DEFGGOR	FROGGED	**DEFINUY**	UNDEIFY	**DEFOORT**	REDFOOT
DEFGGRU	FRUGGED	**DEFIOOS**	FOODIES	**DEFORST**	DEFROST
DEFGINN	FENDING	**DEFIOQU**	QUOIFED		FROSTED
DEFGINR	FRINGED	**DEFIORU**	FOUDRIE	**DEFORTU**	FOUTRED
DEFGINU	FEUDING	**DEFIOST**	FOISTED	**DEFSSUU**	DUFUSES
DEFGINY	DEFYING	**DEFIPRY**	PERFIDY	**DEGGGIL**	GIGGLED
DEFGIOR	FIREDOG	**DEFIRRT**	DRIFTER	**DEGGGIN**	DEGGING
DEFGIRS	FRIDGES	**DEFIRST**	FRISTED	**DEGGGIR**	GRIGGED
DEFGIRT	GRIFTED	**DEFIRTT**	FRITTED	**DEGGGLO**	GOGGLED
DEFGIRU	FIGURED	**DEFIRTU**	FRUITED	**DEGGGLU**	GLUGGED
DEFGIST	FIDGETS	**DEFIRZZ**	FRIZZED		GUGGLED
DEFGITY	FIDGETY	**DEFISTU**	FEUDIST	**DEGGGOR**	GROGGED
DEFGRTU	GRUFTED	**DEFISTW**	SWIFTED	**DEGGHIL**	HIGGLED
DEFHIRS	REDFISH	**DEFKLNU**	FLUNKED	**DEGGHIN**	HEDGING
DEFHIST	SHIFTED	**DEFLLOU**	DOLEFUL	**DEGGHIW**	WHIGGED
DEFHLOO	ELFHOOD	**DEFLLUW**	DEWFULL	**DEGGHOS**	SHOGGED
DEFHLSU	FLUSHED	**DEFLMOS**	SELFDOM	**DEGGIJL**	JIGGLED
	SHEDFUL	**DEFLMPU**	FLUMPED	**DEGGIKN**	KEDGING
DEFHOOW	WHOOFED	**DEFLNOO**	ONEFOLD	**DEGGILN**	GELDING
DEFHORT	FROTHED	**DEFLNOP**	PENFOLD		NIGGLED
DEFHRSU	FRUSHED	**DEFLNOR**	FONDLER	**DEGGILW**	WIGGLED
DEFIILM	MIDLIFE		FORLEND	**DEGGINS**	EDGINGS
DEFIILN	INFIDEL	**DEFLNOS**	ENFOLDS		SNIGGED
	INFIELD		FONDLES	**DEGGINW**	WEDGING
DEFIIMS	FIDEISM	**DEFLNOT**	TENFOLD	**DEGGIOR**	DOGGIER
DEFIIMW	MIDWIFE	**DEFLNRU**	DERNFUL	**DEGGIOS**	DOGGIES
DEFIINU	UNIFIED	**DEFLOOR**	FLOODER	**DEGGIPR**	PRIGGED
DEFIINX	INFIXED		FLOORED	**DEGGIRS**	DIGGERS
DEFIIST	FIDEIST		REFLOOD	**DEGGIRT**	TRIGGED
DEFIKLS	FLISKED	**DEFLOOT**	FOOTLED	**DEGGIRU**	DRUGGIE
DEFIKRS	FRISKED	**DEFLOOZ**	FOOZLED	**DEGGISW**	SWIGGED
DEFILLO	FOLLIED	**DEFLOPP**	FLOPPED	**DEGGITW**	TWIGGED
DEFILLR	FRILLED	**DEFLORS**	FOLDERS	**DEGGJLO**	JOGGLED
DEFILMP	FLIMPED		REFOLDS	**DEGGJLU**	JUGGLED
DEFILNR	FLINDER	**DEFLORT**	TELFORD	**DEGGKSU**	SKUGGED
DEFILNT	FLINTED	**DEFLORU**	FLOURED	**DEGGLOO**	GOOGLED
DEFILNU	UNFILDE		FOULDER	**DEGGLOR**	DOGGREL
	UNFILED	**DEFLOSS**	FLOSSED	**DEGGLOS**	DOGLEGS
DEFILOO	FOLIOED	**DEFLOSU**	DEFOULS		SLOGGED
DEFILOW	OLDWIFE		FLOUSED	**DEGGLOT**	TOGGLED
DEFILPP	FLIPPED	**DEFLOTU**	FLOUTED	**DEGGLPU**	PLUGGED
DEFILPU	UPFIELD	**DEFLPRU**	PURFLED		PUGGLED
DEFILRT	FLIRTED	**DEFLRRU**	FLURRED	**DEGGLRU**	GURGLED
	TRIFLED	**DEFLRUU**	DUREFUL	**DEGGLSU**	SLUGGED
DEFILRU	DIREFUL	**DEFLUZZ**	FUZZLED	**DEGGMSU**	SMUGGED
DEFILSS	FISSLED	**DEFMNUU**	UNFUMED	**DEGGNOO**	DOGGONE
DEFILST	STIFLED	**DEFMORS**	DEFORMS	**DEGGNOS**	SNOGGED

DEGGNOU	GUDGEON	DEGILNO	GLENOID	DEGINRU	DUNGIER
DEGGNSU	SNUGGED	DEGILNP	PINGLED	DEGINRW	REDWING
DEGGOPR	PROGGED	DEGILNS	DINGLES		WRINGED
DEGGORS	DOGGERS		ELDINGS	DEGINRY	YERDING
DEGGORT	TROGGED		ENGILDS	DEGINSS	DESIGNS
DEGGORY	DOGGERY		SINGLED		SDEIGNS
DEGGOSS	DOGGESS	DEGILNT	GLINTED	DEGINST	NIDGETS
DEGGRRU	DRUGGER		TINGLED		STEDING
	GRUDGER	DEGILNU	DUELING		STINGED
DEGGRSU	GRUDGES		ELUDING	DEGINSU	GUNDIES
DEGGRTU	DRUGGET		INDULGE		SUEDING
DEGHHIT	HIGHTED	DEGILNV	DELVING	DEGINSW	SWINDGE
	THIGHED		DEVLING		SWINGED
DEGHHOU	HOUGHED	DEGILNW	WELDING	DEGINSY	DINGEYS
DEGHILN	HINDLEG	DEGILOR	GLORIED		DYEINGS
DEGHILT	DELIGHT		GODLIER	DEGINTU	DUETING
	LIGHTED		GOLDIER	DECINTW	TWINGED
DEGHINN	HENDING	DEGILOU	OUGLIED	DEGINUX	EXUDING
DEGHINO	HONGIED	DEGILRR	GIRDLER	DEGIOOR	GOODIER
DEGHINR	HERDING	DEGILRS	GILDERS	DEGIOOS	GOODIES
DEGHINT	NIGHTED		GIRDLES		SOOGIED
DEGHINW	WHINGED		GLIDERS	DEGIOPR	PODGIER
DEGHIOT	HOGTIED		GRISLED	DEGIORR	GRODIER
DEGHIPT	PIGHTED		LIDGERS	DEGIORT	GOITRED
DEGHIRT	GIRTHED		REGILDS	DEGIPPR	GRIPPED
	RIGHTED		RIDGELS	DEGIPRU	PUDGIER
DEGHIST	SIGHTED	DEGILRU	GUILDER	DEGIPSY	GYPSIED
DEGHITW	WIGHTED	DEGILRW	WERGILD	DEGIQSU	SQUIDGE
DEGHLOO	DOGHOLE	DEGILTZ	GLITZED	DEGIRRS	GIRDERS
DEGHNOT	THONGED	DEGILUV	DIVULGE		RIDGERS
DEGHORR	DROGHER	DEGIMNN	MENDING	DEGIRRU	DURGIER
DEGHORU	ROUGHED	DEGIMNO	DEMOING	DEGIRSS	DIGRESS
DEGHOST	GHOSTED		MENDIGO	DEGIRSU	GUIDERS
DEGHOSU	SOUGHED	DEGIMNS	SMIDGEN	DEGIRTT	GRITTED
DEGHOTU	OUGHTED	DEGIMPU	GUIMPED	DEGISST	DIGESTS
	TOUGHED	DEGIMSS	SMIDGES		DISGEST
DEGIIKR	KIDGIER	DEGIMST	MIDGETS	DEGISSU	GUSSIED
DEGIILL	GILLIED	DEGINNN	DENNING	DEGISTU	DUGITES
DEGIILN	EILDING	DEGINNP	PENDING		GIUSTED
	ELIDING	DEGINNR	GRINNED	DEGISTW	WIDGETS
DEGIIMS	MIDGIES		RENDING	DEGJLNU	JUNGLED
DEGIINN	INDIGEN	DEGINNS	ENDINGS	DEGJRSU	JUDGERS
DEGIINR	DINGIER		SENDING	DEGKKOR	GROKKED
DEGIINS	DINGIES	DEGINNT	DENTING	DEGKLSU	KLUDGES
DEGIINT	DIETING		TENDING	DEGKLUY	KLUDGEY
	EDITING	DEGINNU	ENDUING	DEGLMMO	GLOMMED
	IGNITED	DEGINNV	VENDING	DEGLMOO	GLOOMED
DEGIIPS	GIPSIED	DEGINNW	WENDING	DEGLMOU	MOGULED
DEGIIRR	RIDGIER	DEGINNY	DENYING	DEGLNNO	ENDLONG
	RIGIDER	DEGINOP	PIDGEON	DEGLNOP	PLONGED
DEGIIRS	DIRIGES	DEGINOR	ERODING	DEGLNOS	DONGLES
DEGIISW	WIDGIES		GROINED		GOLDENS
DEGIJLN	JINGLED		IGNORED	DEGLNOU	LOUNGED
DEGIKLO	DOGLIKE		NEGROID	DEGLNPU	PLUNGED
	GODLIKE		REDOING		PUNGLED
DEGILLO	GOLLIED	DEGINOS	DINGOES	DEGLNSU	GULDENS
DEGILLR	GRILLED	DEGINOT	INGOTED	DEGLNUU	UNGLUED
DEGILLU	GULLIED	DEGINOW	WENDIGO		UNGLUED
DEGILLY	GELIDLY		WIDGEON	DEGLOOP	GLOOPED
DEGILMN	MEDLING		WONGIED	DEGLOPP	GLOPPED
	MELDING	DEGINRR	GRINDER	DEGLOPR	PLEDGOR
	MINGLED		REGRIND	DEGLOPS	PLODGES
DEGILMS	MIDLEGS	DEGINRS	DINGERS		SPLODGE
DEGILNN	LENDING		ENGIRDS	DEGLORS	LODGERS

DEGLORW	GROWLED	DEHILLO	HILLOED	DEHISTW	WHISTED
DEGLOSS	GLOSSED	DEHILLS	SHILLED	DEHISVV	SHIVVED
	GODLESS	DEHILMS	DISHELM	DEHIWZZ	WHIZZED
DEGLOST	GOLDEST	DEHILNP	DELPHIN	DEHKNTU	THUNKED
DEGLOTU	GLOUTED	DEHILOT	LITHOED	DEHLLOO	HOLLOED
DEGLSSU	SLUDGES	DEHILPR	HIRPLED	DEHLLOU	HULLOED
DEGLTTU	GLUTTED	DEHILRS	HIRSLED	DEHLMOU	MUDHOLE
	GUTTLED	DEHILRT	THIRLED	DEHLMSU	MULSHED
DEGLUZZ	GUZZLED	DEHILRW	WHIRLED	DEHLNOS	HONDLES
DEGMNOO	GOODMEN	DEHILSS	SHIELDS	DEHLOOS	SHOOLED
DEGMOOR	GROOMED	DEHILTY	DIETHYL	DEHLOOT	TOEHOLD
DEGMOOS	SMOODGE	DEHIMMS	SHIMMED	DEHLOPP	HOPPLED
	SMOOGED	DEHIMMW	WHIMMED	DEHLORS	HOLDERS
DEGMPRU	GRUMPED	DEHIMNS	MEHNDIS	DEHLORW	WHORLED
DEGMRSU	MUDGERS	DEHIMNU	INHUMED	DEHLOSS	SLOSHED
	SMUDGER	DEHIMOP	HEMIPOD	DEHLOST	SLOTHED
DEGMSSU	SMUDGES	DEHIMOR	HEIRDOM	DEHLRRU	HURDLER
DEGNNOU	DUNGEON	DEHIMOS	DISHOME	DEHLRSU	HURDLES
DEGNOOS	NOODGES	DEHIMOT	ETHMOID	DEHLRTU	HURTLED
DEGNOPR	PRONGED	DEHIMRS	DIRHEMS	DEHLSSU	SLUSHED
DEGNOPS	SPONGED	DEHIMRU	HUMIDER	DEHLSTU	HUSTLED
DEGNORU	GUERDON	DEHIMST	SMITHED	DEHMNOO	HOODMEN
	UNDERGO	DEHIMUX	HUMIDEX	DEHMNSU	MUDHENS
	UNGORED	DEHINNS	SHINNED	DEHMOPR	MORPHED
DEGNORW	WRONGED	DEHINNT	THINNED	DEHMOPW	WHOMPED
DEGNOTU	TONGUED	DEHINOP	DIPHONE	DEHMORU	HUMORED
DEGNRSU	DUNGERS		PHONIED	DEHMOST	METHODS
	GERUNDS	DEHINOR	HORDEIN	DEHMOTU	MOUTHED
	NUDGERS	DEHINOS	HOIDENS	DEHMPTU	THUMPED
DEGNRTU	GRUNTED	DEHINOY	HYENOID	DEHMPUW	WHUMPED
	TRUDGEN	DEHINPS	ENDSHIP	DEHMSSU	SMUSHED
DEGNRUU	UNURGED	DEHINRS	HINDERS	DEHNNSU	SHUNNED
DEGNSSU	SNUDGES		NERDISH	DEHNOOR	HONORED
DEGNUVY	UNGYVED		SHRINED	DEHNOOW	HOEDOWN
DEGOORV	GROOVED	DEHINRU	UNHIRED		WOODHEN
	OVERDOG	DEHINUV	UNHIVED	DEHNOPU	UNHOPED
DEGOOST	STOOGED	DEHIOOR	HOODIER	DEHNORS	DEHORNS
DEGOPRU	GROUPED	DEHIOOS	HOODIES	DEHNORT	NORTHED
DEGORRS	DROGERS	DEHIOOT	DHOOTIE		THONDER
DEGORSS	GROSSED	DEHIORS	RHODIES		THORNED
	SODGERS	DEHIORT	THEROID		THRONED
DEGORST	STODGER	DEHIOST	HOISTED	DEHNORU	HOUNDER
DEGORSU	DROGUES	DEHIOSU	HIDEOUS	DEHNOSU	UNSHOED
	GOURDES	DEHIOSV	DOVEISH	DEHNOSY	HOYDENS
	GROUSED	DEHIOSW	HOWDIES	DEHNOTZ	DOZENTH
DEGORTU	DROGUET	DEHIOSX	OXHIDES	DEHNRSU	HURDENS
	GROUTED	DEHIOTU	HIDEOUT	DEHNRTU	THUNDER
DEGOSST	STODGES	DEHIPPS	SHIPPED	DEHNSSU	DUNSHES
DEGOSTU	DEGOUTS	DEHIPPW	WHIPPED		SNUSHED
DEGOSTW	GOWDEST	DEHIRRS	SHIRRED	DEHNSSY	YSHENDS
DEGRRTU	TRUDGER	DEHIRRU	DHURRIE	DEHNSTU	SHUNTED
DEGRSTU	TRUDGES		HURRIED	DEHNSUZ	NUDZHES
DEGSSTU	DEGUSTS	DEHIRRW	WHIRRED	DEHNSYY	HYDYNES
DEHHISW	WHISHED	DEHIRST	DITHERS	DEHOOPT	PHOTOED
DEHHMPU	HUMPHED		SHIRTED	DEHOOPW	WHOOPED
DEHHOOS	HOOSHED	DEHIRSU	HURDIES	DEHOOST	SOOTHED
DEHHSSU	SHUSHED	DEHIRSV	DERVISH	DEHOOSW	WOOSHED
DEHIIKO	HIKOIED		SHRIVED	DEHOOTT	TOOTHED
DEHIINN	HINNIED	DEHIRTV	THRIVED	DEHOOTW	WHOOTED
DEHIIPS	PIEDISH	DEHIRTW	WRITHED	DEHOPPS	SHOPPED
DEHIIRS	DISHIER	DEHIRTY	DITHERY	DEHOPPW	WHOPPED
DEHIKRS	SHIRKED	DEHISSW	SWISHED	DEHORSS	SHODERS
	SHRIKED		WHISSED	DEHORST	DEHORTS
DEHIKSW	WHISKED	DEHISTT	SHITTED		SHORTED

DEHORSV	SHROVED	DEIIOSS	IODISES	DEIKNSW	SWINKED
DEHORSW	SHROWED	DEIIOSX	OXIDISE	DEIKNSY	DINKEYS
DEHORTT	TROTHED	DEIIOSZ	IODIZES		KIDNEYS
DEHORTW	WORTHED	DEIIOXZ	OXIDIZE	DEIKNSZ	ZENDIKS
DEHOSTT	SHOTTED	DEIIPPR	DIPPIER	DEIKNTT	KNITTED
DEHOSTU	SHOUTED	DEIIPRS	PIERIDS	DEIKNTW	TWINKED
	SOUTHED	DEIIPRT	RIPTIDE	DEIKORR	DORKIER
DEHOSTW	SOWTHED		TIDERIP	DEIKOSY	DISYOKE
DEHPPUW	WHUPPED	DEIIRRT	DIRTIER	DEIKPPS	SKIPPED
DEHPSSY	PHYSEDS	DEIIRST	DIRTIES	DEIKQRU	QUIRKED
DEHPTTU	PHUTTED		DITSIER	DEIKRRS	SKIRRED
DEIIIRS	IRIDISE		TIDIERS	DEIKRST	SKIRTED
DEIIIRZ	IRIDIZE	DEIIRTT	TRITIDE	DEIKRSU	DUIKERS
DEIIJMM	JIMMIED	DEIIRTX	EDITRIX		DUSKIER
DEIIKKL	KIDLIKE	DEIIRTZ	DITZIER	DEIKSTY	DYKIEST
DEIIKLS	DISLIKE	DEIIRZZ	DIZZIER	DEIKSVY	SKYDIVE
DEIIKNR	DINKIER	DEIISTT	DIETIST	DEILLMO	MODELLI
DEIIKNS	DINKIES		DITTIES	DEILLMU	ILLUMED
	KINDIES		TIDIEST	DEILLNW	INDWELL
DEIIKST	DIKIEST	DEIISTV	VISITED	DEILLOR	DOLLIER
DEIILLR	DILLIER	DEIISVV	DIVVIES	DEILLOS	DOLLIES
DEIILLS	DILLIES	DEIISZZ	DIZZIES	DEILLOV	LIVELOD
DEIILLW	WILLIED	DEIIVZZ	VIZZIED	DEILLPR	PRILLED
DEIILMN	MIDLINE	DEIJLLO	JOLLIED	DEILLPS	SPILLED
DEIILMP	IMPLIED	DEIJNOR	JOINDER	DEILLQU	QUILLED
DEIILMT	DELIMIT	DEIJNOT	JOINTED	DEILLRR	DRILLER
	LIMITED	DEIJNRU	INJURED		REDRILL
DEIILNS	INISLED	DEIJNSU	DISJUNE	DEILLRT	TRILLED
	LINDIES	DEIJORY	JOYRIDE	DEILLRU	DULLIER
DEIILOS	DOILIES	DEIJOST	JOISTED	DEILLRV	DREVILL
	IDOLISE	DEIJRRS	JERRIDS	DEILLSS	LIDLESS
DEIILOZ	IDOLIZE	DEIJTTU	JUTTIED	DEILLST	STILLED
DEIILPS	LIPIDES	DEIKKNS	SKINKED	DEILLSU	ILLUDES
DEIILRV	LIVIDER	DEIKKRS	SKRIKED		SULLIED
DEIIMMX	IMMIXED	DEIKLLS	DESKILL	DEILLSW	SWILLED
DEIIMNO	DOMINIE		SKILLED	DEILLTW	TWILLED
DEIIMRT	TIMIDER	DEIKLNP	PLINKED	DEILMMP	PLIMMED
DEIIMST	MISDIET	DEIKLNR	KINDLER	DEILMMS	SLIMMED
	MISEDIT	DEIKLNS	KINDLES	DEILMNS	MILDENS
	STIMIED		SLINKED	DEILMNU	LUMINED
DEIIMSZ	MIDSIZE	DEIKLNT	TINKLED		UNLIMED
DEIIMVW	MIDWIVE	DEIKLNU	UNLIKED	DEILMOP	IMPLODE
DEIINOS	IODINES	DEIKLNW	WINKLED	DEILMOR	MOLDIER
	IONISED	DEIKLOP	PODLIKE	DEILMOS	MELOIDS
DEIINOT	EDITION	DEIKLOR	RODLIKE		MIDSOLE
	TENIOID	DEIKLOS	KELOIDS		SMOILED
DEIINOZ	IONIZED	DEIKLRS	SKIRLED	DEILMOY	MYELOID
DEIINRR	RINDIER	DEIKLRT	KIRTLED	DEILMPP	PIMPLED
DEIINRS	INSIDER	DEIKLST	KIDLETS	DEILMPR	RIMPLED
	SNIDIER	DEIKLTT	KITTLED	DEILMPS	DIMPLES
DEIINRT	INDITER	DEIKMMS	SKIMMED		MISPLED
	NITRIDE	DEIKMPS	SKIMPED		SIMPLED
DEIINRU	URIDINE	DEIKMRS	SMIRKED	DEILMPW	WIMPLED
DEIINRV	DIVINER	DEIKNNS	SKINNED	DEILMST	MILDEST
DEIINRW	WINDIER	DEIKNOS	DOESKIN		MISTLED
DEIINSS	INSIDES	DEIKNOV	INVOKED	DEILMSW	MILDEWS
DEIINST	INDITES	DEIKNPR	PRINKED	DEILMWY	MILDEWY
	TINEIDS	DEIKNRR	DRINKER	DEILMXY	MIXEDLY
DEIINSV	DIVINES	DEIKNRS	KINDERS	DEILMZZ	MIZZLED
DEIINTV	INVITED		KINREDS	DEILNNS	DINNLES
DEIIORS	IODISER		REDSKIN		LINDENS
DEIIORT	DIORITE	DEIKNST	DINKEST	DEILNNU	UNLINED
DEIIORV	IVORIED		KINDEST	DEILNOO	EIDOLON
DEIIORZ	IODIZER			DEILNOS	DOLINES

	INDOLES	DEILSST	DELISTS		VOMITED
	SONDELI	DEILSTT	SLITTED	DEIMPPR	PRIMPED
DEILNOT	LENTOID		STILTED	DEIMPRT	DIREMPT
DEILNOU	UNOILED	DEILSTU	DILUTES	DEIMPRU	DUMPIER
DEILNPP	NIPPLED		DUELIST		UMPIRED
DEILNPS	SPELDIN	DEILSTW	WILDEST	DEIMPSU	DUMPIES
	SPINDLE	DEILSTY	DISTYLE	DEIMPTU	IMPUTED
	SPLINED	DEILSUV	DIVULSE	DEIMRRS	SMIRRED
DEILNPU	UNPILED	DEILSZZ	SIZZLED	DEIMRSW	MISDREW
DEILNRT	TENDRIL	DEILTTT	TITTLED	DEIMRSY	SEMIDRY
	TRINDLE	DEILTTU	TITULED	DEIMRUU	UREDIUM
DEILNST	DENTILS	DEILTTV	VITTLED	DEIMSST	DEMISTS
DEILNSW	SWINDLE	DEILTTW	TWILTED	DEIMSSU	MISUSED
	WINDLES	DEILZZZ	ZIZZLED	DEIMSTT	SMITTED
DEILNSY	SNIDELY	DEIMMMU	MUMMIED	DEIMSTU	MUISTED
DEILNTU	DILUENT	DEIMMOT	TOMMIED		TEDIUMS
	UNTILED	DEIMMPR	PRIMMED	DEIMSTY	STYMIED
DEILNTW	INDWELT	DEIMMRS	DIMMERS	DEINNNU	NUNDINE
	WINTLED	DEIMMRT	MIDTERM	DEINNOO	ONIONED
DEILNUV	UNLIVED		TRIMMED	DEINNOP	PINNOED
DEILOOS	DOOLIES	DEIMMRU	DUMMIER	DEINNOR	ENDIRON
DEILOPR	LEPORID		IMMURED	DEINNOS	DONNIES
DEILOPS	DESPOIL	DEIMMST	DIMMEST		ONDINES
	DIPLOES	DEIMMSU	DUMMIES	DEINNOT	INTONED
	DIPOLES		MEDIUMS		NOINTED
	PELOIDS	DEIMNNU	MINUEND	DEINNRS	DINNERS
	SOLIPED		UNMINED		ENDRINS
	SPOILED	DEIMNOP	IMPONED	DEINNRU	DUNNIER
DEILOPT	PILOTED	DEIMNOR	MINORED		INURNED
DEILOPU	EUPLOID	DEIMNOS	DOMINES	DEINNST	DENTINS
DEILORS	SOLDIER		EMODINS		INDENTS
	SOLIDER		MISDONE		INTENDS
DEILORT	DOILTER	DEIMNPS	IMPENDS	DEINNSU	DUNNIES
DEILORW	DOWLIER	DEIMNRS	MINDERS		UNDINES
DEILOSV	LIVEDOS		REMINDS	DEINNSW	ENWINDS
DEILOSY	DOYLIES	DEIMNRU	UNRIMED	DEINNSY	DYNEINS
DEILOTU	OUTLIED	DEIMNSS	DIMNESS	DEINNTU	DUNNITE
	TOLUIDE		MISSEND	DEINNTW	TWINNED
DEILPPR	RIPPLED	DEIMNST	MINDSET	DEINOOZ	OZONIDE
DEILPPS	SIPPLED		MISTEND	DEINOPR	POINDER
	SLIPPED	DEIMNSW	MISWEND		PROINED
DEILPPT	TIPPLED	DEIMNTU	MINUTED	DEINOPS	DISPONE
DEILPPU	UPPILED		MUNITED		SPINODE
DEILPRT	TRIPLED		MUTINED	DEINOPT	POINTED
DEILPRU	PRELUDI		UNTIMED	DEINOQU	QUOINED
DEILPSS	DISPELS	DEIMNUX	UNMIXED	DEINORR	DRONIER
	DISPLES	DEIMOOR	DOOMIER	DEINORS	DINEROS
DEILPSU	DUPLIES		MOIDORE		DONSIER
DEILPTY	TEPIDLY		MOODIER		INDORSE
DEILQTU	QUILTED	DEIMOOS	MOODIES		ORDINES
DEILRRU	LURIDER	DEIMOPR	IMPEDOR		ROSINED
DEILRSS	SIDLERS	DEIMOPS	IMPOSED		SORDINE
	SLIDERS	DEIMORR	REMORID	DEINORU	DOURINE
DEILRSV	DRIVELS	DEIMORS	MISDOER		NEUROID
DEILRSW	SWIRLED		MOIDERS	DEINORW	DOWNIER
	WILDERS	DEIMORU	ERODIUM		WINDORE
DEILRSY	RIDLEYS	DEIMOSS	MISDOES	DEINOSS	ONSIDES
DEILRTU	DILUTER	DEIMOST	DISTOME	DEINOST	DITONES
DEILRTW	TWIRLED		DOMIEST		STONIED
DEILRTY	TIREDLY		MODISTE	DEINPPS	SNIPPED
DEILRVY	DEVILRY		MOISTED	DEINPRS	PINDERS
DEILRWY	WEIRDLY	DEIMOSW	MOWDIES	DEINPRT	PRINTED
DEILRWZ	WRIZLED	DEIMOTT	OMITTED	DEINPST	DIPNETS
DEILRZZ	DRIZZLE	DEIMOTV	MOTIVED		STIPEND

DEINPSU	UNIPEDS	DEIOQTU	QUOITED		TITUPED
	UNSPIDE	DEIORRT	DORTIER	DEIQRSU	SQUIRED
	UNSPIED	DEIORRW	ROWDIER	DEIQRTU	QUIRTED
DEINPUW	UNWIPED		WORDIER	DEIQTTU	QUITTED
DEINRRU	NURDIER		WORRIED	DEIQUZZ	QUIZZED
DEINRST	TINDERS	DEIORSS	DORISES	DEIRRST	STIRRED
DEINRSU	INSURED		DOSSIER		STRIDER
DEINRSV	VERDINS	DEIORST	EDITORS	DEIRRSU	DRUSIER
DEINRSW	REWINDS		ROISTED		DURRIES
	WINDERS		ROSITED	DEIRRSV	DRIVERS
DEINRTT	TRIDENT		SORTIED	DEIRRUX	DRUXIER
DEINRTU	INTRUDE		STEROID	DEIRSST	DISSERT
	TURDINE		STORIED		STRIDES
	UNTIRED		TIERODS	DEIRSSU	DISEURS
	UNTRIDE		TRIODES		SUDSIER
	UNTRIED	DEIORSV	DEVISOR	DEIRSTU	DUSTIER
DEINRTX	DEXTRIN		DEVOIRS		REDUITS
DEINRTY	TINDERY		VISORED		STUDIER
DEINRUW	UNWIRED		VOIDERS	DEIRSTV	DIVERTS
DEINSST	DISNEST	DEIORSW	DOWRIES		STRIVED
	DISSENT		ROWDIES		VERDITS
	SNIDEST		WEIRDOS	DEISSST	DESISTS
DEINSSU	NIDUSES	DEIORSZ	DORIZES	DEISSSU	DISUSES
DEINSSV	VENDISS	DEIORTT	DOTTIER	DEISSTU	STUDIES
DEINSSW	WINDSES	DEIORTU	ETOURDI		TISSUED
DEINSSY	ENDYSIS		IODURET	DEISSTV	DIVESTS
DEINSTT	DENTIST		OUTRIDE	DEISTTW	DEWITTS
	DISTENT	DEIORTZ	ROZITED		TWISTED
	STINTED	DEIORVZ	VIZORED	DEISWZZ	SWIZZED
DEINSTU	DISTUNE	DEIORWW	WIDOWER	DEITTTW	TWITTED
	DUNITES	DEIOSTT	DOTIEST	DEJLOST	JOSTLED
DEINSTY	DENSITY		STOITED	DEJLSTU	JUSTLED
	DESTINY	DEIOSTU	OUTSIDE	DEJOORY	JOYRODE
DEINSUZ	UNSIZED		TEDIOUS	DEJOSTU	JOUSTED
DEINUVW	UNWIVED	DEIOSTV	DOVIEST	DEKKLSU	SKULKED
DEIOORS	ODORISE	DEIOSTW	DOWIEST	DEKKNSU	SKUNKED
	OROIDES	DEIOSTX	EXODIST	DEKLLNO	KNOLLED
DEIOORW	WOODIER	DEIOSTZ	DOZIEST	DEKLLOS	SKOLLED
DEIOORZ	ODORIZE	DEIOSUV	DEVIOUS	DEKLLSU	SKULLED
DEIOOSS	ISODOSE	DEIOTUV	OUTVIED	DEKLNOP	PLONKED
DEIOOST	OSTEOID	DEIOTUW	WIDEOUT	DEKLNPU	PLUNKED
DEIOOSW	WOODIES	DEIPPPU	PUPPIED	DEKLNRU	KNURLED
DEIOOSZ	DOOZIES	DEIPPQU	QUIPPED		RUNKLED
DEIOOVV	VOIVODE	DEIPPRR	DRIPPER	DEKLRSU	SKUDLER
DEIOOWW	WOIWODE	DEIPPRS	DIPPERS	DEKNNOS	NONSKED
DEIOPPP	POPPIED	DEIPPRT	TRIPPED	DEKNNRU	DRUNKEN
DEIOPPS	DOPPIES	DEIPPST	PEPTIDS	DEKNOOS	SNOOKED
DEIOPRS	PERIODS	DEIPPSU	DUPPIES	DEKNOPP	KNOPPED
DEIOPRT	DIOPTER	DEIPRSS	PRISSED	DEKNOPR	PRONKED
	DIOPTRE		SPIDERS	DEKNOQU	QUONKED
	PERIDOT	DEIPRST	SPIRTED	DEKNOST	STONKED
	PROTEID		STRIPED	DEKNOSW	SNOWKED
DEIOPRV	PROVIDE	DEIPRSU	PUDSIER	DEKNOSY	DONKEYS
DEIOPRX	PEROXID		SIRUPED	DEKNOTT	KNOTTED
DEIOPSS	DISPOSE		UPDRIES	DEKNOTU	KNOUTED
DEIOPST	DEPOSIT	DEIPRSY	SPIDERY	DEKNOUY	UNYOKED
	DOPIEST	DEIPSSU	UPSIDES	DEKNPSU	SPUNKED
	PODITES	DEIPSSV	VESPIDS	DEKNRRU	DRUNKER
	POSITED	DEIPSTT	SPITTED	DEKNRSU	DUNKERS
	SOPITED	DEIPSTU	DISPUTE	DEKNRTU	TRUNKED
	TOPSIDE	DEIPSUV	UPDIVES	DEKNSSU	DUSKENS
DEIOPSV	VESPOID	DEIPSUZ	UPSIZED	DEKOOPS	SPOOKED
DEIOPTT	TIPTOED	DEIPSXY	PYXIDES	DEKOOST	DOOKETS
DEIOPTV	PIVOTED	DEIPTTU	PUTTIED		STOOKED

Code	Word(s)	Code	Word(s)	Code	Word(s)
DEKOOTW	KOTOWED	DELNRTU	RUNDLET	DELPRSU	DRUPELS
DEKOPST	DESKTOP		TRUNDLE		SLURPED
DEKORST	STROKED	DELNRUU	UNRULED	DELPSSU	PLUSSED
DEKORWY	KEYWORD	DELNSSU	DULNESS	DELPSTU	DUPLETS
DEKOSSU	KUDOSES	DELNUWY	UNWELDY	DELPSUY	SPULYED
DEKOSVY	SKYDOVE	DELNUZZ	NUZZLED	DELPUZZ	PUZZLED
DEKPRSU	PREDUSK	DELOOPP	PLEOPOD	DELRRSU	SLURRED
DEKRSUY	DUYKERS	DELOOPS	POODLES	DELRSTU	LUSTRED
DEKSSTU	DUSKEST		SPOOLED		RUSTLED
DELLMOO	MODELLO	DELOOPT	POOTLED		STRUDEL
DELLOOW	WOOLLED	DELOORT	ROOTLED	DELRTTU	TURTLED
DELLOPR	PROLLED	DELOORW	WOOLDER	DELSSTU	TUSSLED
	REDPOLL	DELOOSS	DOLOSSE	DELSTTU	SUTTLED
DELLORR	DROLLER	DELOOST	STOOLED	DELUWZZ	WUZZLED
DELLORT	TROLLED		TOLEDOS	DEMMRRU	DRUMMER
DELLOSU	DUELLOS	DELOOSW	DEWOOLS	DEMMSTU	STUMMED
DELLOVW	LOWVELD	DELOOTT	TOOTLED	DEMNOOR	DOORMEN
DELLRWY	DRYWELL	DELOPPP	PLOPPED		MORENDO
DELLSTU	DULLEST		POPPLED	DEMNOOW	WOODMEN
DELMMSU	SLUMMED	DELOPPR	DROPPLE	DEMNORS	MODERNS
DELMNOS	DOLMENS	DELOPPS	SLOPPED		RODSMEN
DELMOOS	SLOOMED	DELOPPT	TOPPLED	DEMNORT	MORDENT
DELMOOW	ELMWOOD	DELOPPY	POLYPED	DEMNORU	MOURNED
DELMOPR	PREMOLD	DELOPRS	POLDERS	DEMNORY	DEMONRY
DELMORS	MOLDERS		PRESOLD	DEMNOST	ENDMOST
	REMOLDS	DELOPRT	DROPLET	DEMNOSU	MENUDOS
	SLORMED		PRETOLD	DEMNOTU	DEMOUNT
	SMOLDER	DELOPRU	POULDER		MOUNTED
DELMORU	MOULDER		POULDRE	DEMNOUV	UNMOVED
	REMOULD		PROULED	DEMNSTU	DUSTMEN
DELMOSU	MODULES	DELOPRW	PROWLED	DEMOOPP	POPEDOM
	MOUSLED	DELOPSU	SOUPLED	DEMOOPR	PREDOOM
DELMOSY	SMOYLED	DELOPSY	DEPLOYS		PROMOED
DELMOTT	MOTTLED		PODLEYS	DEMOOPS	SPOOMED
DELMOTU	MOULTED	DELOPTT	PLOTTED	DEMOORS	DROOMES
DELMOUV	VOLUMED	DELOPTZ	PLOTZED		SMOORED
DELMPPU	PLUMPED	DELORRY	ORDERLY	DEMOORT	MOTORED
DELMPRU	RUMPLED	DELORSS	DORSELS	DEMOORV	VROOMED
DELMPSU	DUMPLES		RODLESS	DEMOOSS	OSMOSED
	SLUMPED		SOLDERS	DEMOOST	SMOOTED
DELMTUY	MUTEDLY	DELORST	DROLEST	DEMOOTT	MOTTOED
DELMUZZ	MUZZLED		OLDSTER	DEMOOTU	OUTMODE
DELNOOS	NOODLES		STRODLE	DEMOPRT	TROMPED
	SNOOLED	DELORSW	WELDORS	DEMOPST	STOMPED
DELNORS	RONDELS	DELORSY	YODLERS	DEMORRS	DORMERS
DELNORT	ENTROLD	DELORTT	DOTTLER	DEMORRU	RUMORED
DELNORU	LOUNDER		DOTTREL	DEMORST	STORMED
	ROUNDEL	DELORTU	TROULED	DEMORSW	DEWORMS
	ROUNDLE	DELORUV	LOUVRED	DEMOSSU	MOUSSED
DELNOSS	OLDNESS	DELOSSS	DOSSELS		SMOUSED
DELNOSU	LOUDENS	DELOSSU	DULOSES	DEMOSTT	DOMETTS
	NODULES	DELOSTT	DOTTELS	DEMOSTU	MOUSTED
	NOUSLED		DOTTLES		SMOUTED
DELNOSW	DOWLNES		SLOTTED	DEMOSTY	MODESTY
DELNOSZ	DONZELS	DELOSTU	LOUDEST	DEMPRSU	DUMPERS
DELNOTW	LETDOWN		OULDEST	DEMPRTU	TRUMPED
DELNOTY	NOTEDLY		TOUSLED	DEMPSTU	STUMPED
DELNOUV	UNLOVED	DELOSYY	DOYLEYS	DEMRRSU	MURDERS
DELNOWY	DOWLNEY	DELOSZZ	SOZZLED		SMURRED
DELNPRU	PLUNDER	DELOTUU	OUTDUEL	DEMSTTU	SMUTTED
DELNRSU	LURDENS	DELOTUV	VOLUTED	DENNORT	DONNERT
	NURDLES	DELOTUZ	TOUZLED		TENDRON
	NURSLED	DELPPRU	PURPLED	DENNORU	ENROUND
	RUNDLES	DELPPSU	SUPPLED	DENNOST	STONNED

	TENDONS
DENNOTU	UNNOTED
	UNTONED
DENNOUW	ENWOUND
	UNOWNED
DENNOUZ	UNZONED
DENNRSU	UNDERNS
DENNSSU	DUNNESS
DENNSTU	DUNNEST
	STUNNED
DENNTUU	UNTUNED
DENOOPS	SNOOPED
	SPOONED
DENOOSS	NOSODES
DENOOST	SNOOTED
	STOODEN
DENOOSW	SWOONED
	WOODENS
DENOOSZ	SNOOZED
DENOOTU	DUOTONE
	OUTDONE
DENOOUW	UNWOOED
DENOPPR	PROPEND
DENOPPU	UNPOPED
DENOPRS	PERNODS
	PONDERS
	RESPOND
DENOPRT	PORTEND
	PROTEND
DENOPRU	POUNDER
	UNROPED
DENOPRV	PROVEND
DENOPSU	UNPOSED
DENOPTY	POYNTED
DENOPUX	EXPOUND
DENORRS	DRONERS
DENORRU	RONDURE
	ROUNDER
	UNORDER
DENORRW	DROWNER
DENORSS	SONDERS
DENORST	RODENTS
	SNORTED
DENORSU	ENDUROS
	RESOUND
	SOUNDER
	UNDOERS
DENORSV	VENDORS
DENORSW	DOWNERS
	WONDERS
DENORSY	YONDERS
DENORUW	REWOUND
	WOUNDER
DENOSTT	SNOTTED
DENOSTU	DEUTONS
	SNOUTED
DENOSUW	SWOUNED
	UNSOWED
DENPRSU	SPURNED
DENPRTU	PRUDENT
	PRUNTED
	UPTREND
DENPSSU	SENDUPS
	SUSPEND
	UPSENDS
DENRSSU	SUNDERS
	UNDRESS
DENRSSY	DRYNESS
DENRSTU	RETUNDS
	UNDREST
DENRSUU	UNSURED
DENSSTY	SYNDETS
DENSSUW	SUNDEWS
DENSTTU	STUDENT
	STUNTED
DENTUVY	DUVETYN
DEOOPPS	OPPOSED
DEOOPRS	SPOORED
DEOOPRT	TORPEDO
	TROOPED
DEOOPST	STOOPED
DEOOPSW	SWOOPED
	WOOPSED
DEOOPSX	EXOPODS
DEOORRT	REDROOT
DEOORST	ROOSTED
DEOORSZ	DOOZERS
DEOORTU	OUTDOER
	OUTRODE
DEOORTW	WROOTED
DEOOSTT	TOOTSED
DEOOSTU	OUTDOES
DEOPPPR	PROPPED
DEOPPQU	QUOPPED
DEOPPRR	DROPPER
DEOPPRS	DOPPERS
DEOPPST	STOPPED
DEOPPSW	SWOPPED
DEOPRRS	DORPERS
DEOPRRU	PROUDER
DEOPRST	DEPORTS
	REDTOPS
	SPORTED
DEOPRSU	POUDERS
	POUDRES
DEOPRSW	POWDERS
DEOPRTU	TROUPED
DEOPRWY	POWDERY
DEOPSST	DESPOTS
DEOPSSU	PSEUDOS
	SPOUSED
DEOPSTT	SPOTTED
DEOPSTU	OUTSPED
	SPOUTED
DEOPTTY	TYPTOED
DEOQRTU	TORQUED
DEORRSS	DORSERS
DEORRST	DORTERS
	RODSTER
DEORRSU	ORDURES
DEORRSV	DROVERS
DEORRSW	REWORDS
	SWORDER
DEORRVY	OVERDRY
DEORSSS	DOSSERS
	DROSSES
DEORSSU	DOUSERS
DEORSSW	DOWSERS
	DROWSES
DEORSTT	DETORTS
	DOTTERS
DEORSTU	DETOURS
	DOUREST
	DOUTERS
	OUTREDS
	REDOUTS
	ROUSTED
DEORSTW	STROWED
	WORSTED
DEORSTY	DESTROY
	ROYSTED
	STROYED
DEORSUV	DEVOURS
DEORTTT	TROTTED
DEORTTU	TUTORED
DEORTUU	OUTDURE
DEORTUW	OUTDREW
DEOSSSW	SOWSSED
DEOSSTW	DOWSETS
DEOSSYY	ODYSSEY
DEOSTTT	STOTTED
DEOSTTU	DUETTOS
	TESTUDO
DEOSTTW	SWOTTED
DEOSTUU	DUTEOUS
DEOSTUX	TUXEDOS
DEOTTUY	TUTOYED
DEPRRSU	SPURRED
DEPRRUY	PRUDERY
DEPRSTU	SPURTED
DEPRSUU	PURSUED
	USURPED
DEPRSUY	SYRUPED
DERRSTU	RUSTRED
DERSSSU	SUDSERS
DERSSTU	DUSTERS
	TRUSSED
DERSTTU	STURTED
	TRUSTED
DERSTTY	TRYSTED
DERSTUU	SUTURED
DERSTUY	RESTUDY
DFFGINO	DOFFING
DFFGINU	DUFFING
DFFIIMR	MIDRIFF
DFFIIRT	TRIFFID
DFFIMOR	DIFFORM
DFFLOOU	FOODFUL
DFFOSTU	DUSTOFF
DFGGIIN	FIDGING
DFGGINU	FUDGING
DFGGOOS	FOGDOGS
DFGHIOS	DOGFISH
DFGIINN	FINDING
DFGIINY	DIGNIFY
DFGILNO	FOLDING
DFGINNO	FONDING
DFGINNU	FUNDING
DFGINOR	FORDING
DFGINOU	FUNGOID
DFGMOOY	FOGYDOM
DFHILSU	DISHFUL

DFHIMSU	MUDFISH	DGHINSU	DUSHING	DGIKNOS	DOGSKIN
DFIKRSU	FURKIDS	DGHINTU	HINDGUT	DGIKNOU	DOUKING
DFILLUY	FLUIDLY		UNDIGHT	DGIKNSU	DUSKING
DFILMMO	FILMDOM	DGHIOOS	GOODISH	DGILLNO	DOLLING
DFILMNU	MINDFUL	DGHIOPS	DOGSHIP	DGILLNU	DULLING
DFILNOP	PINFOLD		GODSHIP	DGILLOV	GODLILY
DFILNOS	INFOLDS	DGHOOPS	HOPDOGS	DGILMNO	MOLDING
DFILORT	TRIFOLD	DGHOOST	HOTDOGS	DGILNOR	GIRLOND
DFILORU	FLUORID	DGHORTU	DROUGHT		LORDING
DFILOSX	SIXFOLD	DGHOTUY	DOUGHTY	DGILNOY	YODLING
DFILOTW	TWIFOLD	DGIIKLN	KIDLING	DGILNSU	UNGILDS
DFILSSU	SULFIDS	DGIIKNN	DINKING	DGILNVY	DYINGLY
DFILTUU	DUTIFUL		KINDING	DGILOPY	PODGILY
DFIMNUY	MUNDIFY	DGIIKNR	DIRKING	DGILOST	DIGLOTS
DFIMOOS	FOODISM	DGIIKNS	DISKING	DGILPUY	PUDGILY
DFIMORS	DISFORM	DGIILLN	DILLING	DGILRUY	GUILDRY
DFINOTU	OUTFIND	DGIILMN	MILDING	DGIMNOO	DOOMING
DFLMOOU	DOOMFUL	DGIILNO	LOIDING	DGIMNPU	DUMPING
DFLMOUW	MUDFLOW	DGIILNR	DIRLING	DGIMOPY	PYGMOID
DFLNOSU	UNFOLDS	DGIILNS	SIDLING	DGIMSTU	MIDGUTS
DFLOORU	ODORFUL		SLIDING	DGINNNO	DONNING
DFLOOTU	FOLDOUT	DGIILNW	WILDING	DGINNNU	DUNNING
DFLOOTW	TWOFOLD	DGIILNY	DINGILY	DGINNOP	PONDING
DFLOPRY	DROPFLY	DGIILRS	RIDGILS	DGINNOR	DRONING
DFLOPSU	FOLDUPS	DGIILRY	RIGIDLY	DGINNOS	DONINGS
	UPFOLDS	DGIIMMN	DIMMING		ONDINGS
DFLOTWY	TWYFOLD	DGIIMNN	MINDING	DGINNOU	UNDOING
DFNNOOO	NONFOOD	DGIIMNS	SMIDGIN	DGINNOW	DOWNING
DFNNOUU	UNFOUND	DGIIMOP	PIGMOID	DGINNRU	DURNING
DFNORUY	FOUNDRY	DGIIMOS	SIGMOID	DGINNSY	SYNDING
DFOORSX	OXFORDS	DGIINNN	DINNING	DGINNTU	DUNTING
DGGGIIN	DIGGING	DGIINNR	RINDING		TUNDING
DGGGINO	DOGGING	DGIINNS	NIDINGS	DGINNUW	WINDGUN
DGGHIOS	DOGGISH		SINDING	DGINNUY	UNDYING
DGGIILN	GILDING	DGIINNT	DINTING	DGINOOW	WOODING
	GLIDING		TINDING	DGINOPP	DOPPING
DGGIINN	DINGING	DGIINNU	INDUING	DGINOPS	DOPINGS
DGGIINR	GIRDING	DGIINNW	DWINING		PONGIDS
	GRIDING		WINDING	DGINORR	DORRING
	RIDGING	DGIINOS	INDIGOS	DGINORS	RODINGS
DGGIINU	GUIDING	DGIINOV	VOIDING	DGINORT	DORTING
DGGIJNU	JUDGING	DGIINOW	WINDIGO	DGINORV	DROVING
DGGILNO	GODLING	DGIINOX	DIGOXIN	DGINORW	WORDING
	LODGING	DGIINPP	DIPPING	DGINOSS	DOSSING
DGGIMNO	MODGING	DGIINPR	PRIDING	DGINOST	DOTINGS
DGGIMNU	MUDGING	DGIINPS	PIDGINS	DGINOSU	DOUSING
DGGINNO	DONGING	DGIINPU	PINGUID		GUIDONS
DGGINNU	DUNGING	DGIINRS	RIDINGS	DGINOSW	DISGOWN
	NUDGING	DGIINRT	DIRTING		DOWSING
DGGINRY	GRYDING	DGIINRV	DRIVING	DGINOSZ	DOZINGS
DGGNOSU	DUGONGS	DGIINRY	YIRDING	DGINOTT	DOTTING
	GUNDOGS	DGIINSS	DISSING	DGINOTU	DOUTING
DGHHOOO	HOGHOOD		SIDINGS	DGINPPU	DUPPING
DGHIILN	HIDLING	DGIINST	TIDINGS	DGINRSU	UNGIRDS
	HILDING	DGIINSV	DIVINGS	DGINRSY	DRYINGS
DGHIINS	DISHING	DGIINTT	DITTING	DGINSSU	SUDSING
	HIDINGS	DGIINTY	DIGNITY	DGINSTU	DUSTING
	SHINDIG		TIDYING	DGIOPRY	PRODIGY
DGHILNO	HOLDING	DGIIORT	TIGROID	DGIOSTW	GODWITS
DGHILNY	HYLDING	DGIJOSU	JUDOGIS	DGIPRSU	UPCIRDS
DGHILOS	GOLDISH	DGIKMNO	KINGDOM	DGIQSUY	SQUIDGY
DGHILPY	DIGLYPH	DGIKNNU	DUNKING	DGISSTU	DISGUST
DGHINOO	HOODING	DGIKNNY	KYNDING	DGLNORU	GOLDURN
DGHINOR	HORDING	DGIKNOO	DOOKING	DGLNOUY	UNGODLY

DGLOOOW	LOGWOOD	DHIPRSY	SYRPHID	DIINORT	DINITRO
DGLOOST	GODSLOT	DHJOPRU	JODHPUR	DIINOSX	DIOXINS
DGLOOSU	DUOLOGS	DHKMOOU	MUDHOOK	DIINRST	NITRIDS
DGLOPSY	SPLODGY	DHKORSY	DROSHKY	DIIOOPS	OPIOIDS
DGLOSYY	DYSLOGY	DHLMOOU	HOODLUM	DIIOPRS	SPIROID
DGMOOUW	GUMWOOD	DHLOOTU	HOLDOUT	DIIORSV	DIVISOR
DGMOPRU	GUMDROP	DHLOPSU	HOLDUPS		VIROIDS
DGMORUU	GURUDOM		UPHOLDS	DIIORTX	TRIOXID
DGNNORU	NONDRUG	DHMMRUU	HUMDRUM	DIIRSTX	DISTRIX
DGNOOOP	GONOPOD	DHMNOVY	HYMNODY	DIITUVV	VIDUITY
DGNOOOR	GODROON	DHNNOOU	NUNHOOD	DIJMSSU	MUSJIDS
DGNOORS	DRONGOS	DHNOOOS	SONHOOD	DIJOSTU	JUDOIST
DGNOOSS	GODSONS	DHNOOSU	UNHOODS	DIKKLSU	KUDLIKS
DGNOOSW	GODOWNS	DHOOOOS	HOODOOS	DIKKOPS	DIKKOPS
DGNOOTW	DOGTOWN	DHOOPRU	UPHOORD	DIKLNOR	LORDKIN
DGNORSU	GROUNDS	DHOORST	HOTRODS	DIKLSTU	KIDULTS
DGNOSSU	SUNDOGS	DHOORSU	RHODOUS	DIKLSUY	DUSKILY
DGOORTT	DOGTROT	DHOPRSU	PUSHROD	DIKMNSU	DINKUMS
DGOPRRU	PRODRUG	DHOPRSY	HYDROPS	DIKNNOS	NONSKID
DGOSTUU	DUGOUTS	DHORSSU	SHROUDS	DIKNNSU	NUDNIKS
DHIILNS	HIDLINS	DHORSTU	DROUTHS	DIKNOOW	INKWOOD
DHIILOT	DITHIOL	DHORSUY	HYDROUS	DIKNORV	DVORNIK
	LITHOID		SHROUDY	DIKOORT	DROOKIT
DHIILSW	WILDISH	DHORTUV	DROUTHY	DIKOOSS	SKIDOOS
DHIIMMS	DIMMISH	DHORXYY	HYDROXY	DIKORTU	DROUKIT
DHIIMNO	HOMINID	DIIIMOS	SIMIOID	DILLMSU	MUDSILL
DHIIMPS	MIDSHIP	DIIIMRU	IRIDIUM	DILLOSY	SOLIDLY
DHIINRU	HIRUDIN	DIIIMSV	DIVISIM	DILLPSY	PSYLLID
DHIIOPX	XIPHOID	DIIINPS	INSIPID	DILLRUY	LURIDLY
DHIIORZ	RHIZOID	DIIJNOS	DISJOIN	DILMNRU	DRUMLIN
DHIIOST	HISTOID	DIIKKNS	KIDSKIN	DILMOOY	DOOMILY
DHIIPST	DIPSHIT	DIIKLNS	DISLINK		MOODILY
DHIKSSU	DUSKISH	DIIKNOT	DOITKIN	DILMORS	MILORDS
DHILLOS	DOLLISH	DIILLST	DISTILL	DILMOST	MISTOLD
DHILLPY	PHYLLID	DIILLVY	LIVIDLY	DILMOSU	SOLIDUM
DHILLSU	DULLISH	DIILMNS	DISLIMN	DILMOSY	ODYLISM
DHILMUY	HUMIDLY	DIILMOO	MODIOLI	DILMPUY	DUMPILY
DHILNOP	DOLPHIN	DIILMOS	IDOLISM	DILMTUY	TUMIDLY
DHILOST	DOLTISH	DIILMST	MIDLIST	DILNNSU	DUNLINS
DHILOSU	LOUDISH	DIILMTY	TIMIDLY	DILNOOS	OODLINS
DHILPSU	LUDSHIP	DIILNNU	INDULIN	DILNOPS	DIPLONS
	SULPHID	DIILNOT	TOLIDIN	DILNOPT	DIPLONT
DHILPSY	SYLPHID	DIILNWY	WINDILY	DILNOQU	QUODLIN
DHILRTY	THIRDLY	DIILNXY	XYLIDIN	DILNORT	INTROLD
DHIMOPR	DIMORPH	DIILOPS	LIPOIDS	DILNOSU	UNSOLID
DHIMORU	HUMIDOR	DIILOST	IDOLIST	DILNOXY	INDOXYL
	RHODIUM	DIILQSU	LIQUIDS	DILNPSU	LISPUND
DHIMOSS	MISSHOD	DIILRSU	SILURID	DILNPSY	SPINDLY
DHIMPSU	DUMPISH	DIILRTY	DIRTILY	DILNSTU	INDULTS
DHINNOS	DONNISH	DIILSST	DISTILS	DILORTU	DILUTOR
DHINNSU	DUNNISH	DIILSTY	IDYLIST	DILORWY	ROWDILY
DHINOPS	DONSHIP	DIILVVY	VIVIDLY		WORDILY
DHINOPY	HYPNOID	DIILYZZ	DIZZILY	DILOSSS	DOSSILS
DHINORS	DISHORN	DIIMNOR	MIDIRON	DILOSSU	DULOSIS
	DRONISH	DIIMNSU	INDIUMS		SOLIDUS
DHINRSU	NURDISH	DIIMORS	DIORISM	DILOSTU	TOLUIDS
DHINSSY	SHINDYS	DIIMOSS	IODISMS	DILOSTY	STYLOID
DHINSTU	TUNDISH	DIIMSSS	DISMISS	DILOTTY	DOTTILY
DHIOOST	DHOOTIS	DIIMSTW	DIMWITS	DILRYZZ	DRIZZLY
DHIOPTY	PHYTOID	DIIMSUV	VIDIMUS	DILSTUY	DUSTILY
	TYPHOID	DIINNOT	TONDINI	DIMMOST	MIDMOST
DHIORSW	WORDISH	DIINNSW	INWINDS	DIMNNOO	MIDNOON
DHIORTY	THYROID	DIINOQU	QUINOID	DIMNNOS	DONNISM
DHIPRSU	PRUDISH	DIINORS	SORDINI	DIMNNOT	DINMONT

DIMNOOS	DOMINOS	DKNOOPS	PONDOKS	DOOPRSY	PROSODY
DIMNOPU	IMPOUND	DKOOOOS	KOODOOS	DOOPRTU	DROPOUT
DIMNORS	DORMINS	DKOOOSZ	ODZOOKS		OUTDROP
	NIMRODS	DLLOOPS	DOLLOPS	DOOPSTU	UPSTOOD
DIMNOTW	MIDTOWN	DLLORWY	WORLDLY	DOORRSS	SORDORS
DIMNOWX	MIXDOWN	DLMNOOY	MYLODON	DOORRTU	DORTOUR
DIMNSSU	NUDISMS	DLMNOSU	UNMOLDS	DOOSUUV	VOUDOUS
DIMOPSU	PODIUMS	DLMNOUU	UNMOULD	DORSSTU	STROUDS
	SPODIUM	DLMOSUU	MODULUS	DORSUVY	DYVOURS
DIMORSW	MISWORD	DLNOOWW	LOWDOWN	DORUVYY	DYVOURY
DIMOSST	MODISTS	DLNOPRU	PULDRON	DPSSTUU	DUSTUPS
DIMOSSU	SODIUMS	DLNOPSY	SPONDYL	EEEEFRR	REFEREE
DIMOSSW	WISDOMS	DLNORSU	UNLORDS	EEEEGTX	EXEGETE
DIMOSTU	DIMOUTS	DLNORUY	ROUNDLY	EEEENTT	ENTETEE
DIMRTUU	TRIDUUM	DLNOSUY	SOUNDLY	EEEEPST	TEEPEES
DIMRUUV	DUUMVIR	DLOOOTW	WOODLOT	EEEEPSV	VEEPEES
DINNOOR	RONDINO	DLOOPPY	POLYPOD	EEEEPSW	PEEWEES
DINNOOT	TONDINO	DLOOPSS	PODSOLS	EEEESWW	WEEWEES
DINNOPR	NONDRIP	DLOOPSZ	PODZOLS	EEEFFFO	FEOFFEE
DINNOPW	PINDOWN	DLOOPTU	OUTPLOD	EEEFFOR	OFFEREE
DINNOSS	SINDONS	DLOOPTY	TYLOPOD	EEEFFRS	EFFERES
DINNOUW	INWOUND	DLOOPUY	DUOPOLY	EEEFGRU	REFUGEE
DINNSUW	UNWINDS	DLOOPWY	PLYWOOD	EEEFHRS	SHEREEF
DINOORS	INDOORS	DLOORSU	DOLOURS	EEEFIRR	REEFIER
	SORDINO	DLOOSTU	OUTSOLD	EEEFIRS	FEERIES
DINOORT	TORDION	DLOOTTU	OUTTOLD	EEEFLRR	FLEERER
DINOOST	ISODONT	DLOPRUY	PROUDLY	EEEFLRS	FEELERS
DINOPSU	DUPIONS	DLORSTY	DRYLOTS		REFEELS
	UNIPODS	DLOSTUW	WOULDST	EEEFLRT	FLEETER
DINORSU	DIURONS	DMMOORU	MUDROOM	EEEFLSS	FEELLESS
	DURIONS	DMNOOOP	MONOPOD	EEEFMNR	FREEMEN
DINORTU	TURDION	DMNOORS	DROMONS	EEEFNRS	ENFREES
DINORWW	WINDROW	DMNOOTW	TOWMOND	EEEFNRV	ENFEVER
DINOSSW	DISOWNS	DMNOSSU	OSMUNDS	EEEFORS	FORESEE
DINOSWW	WINDOWS	DMOOOQU	QUOMODO	EEEFRRS	REEFERS
DINOTUW	OUTWIND	DMORTUW	MUDWORT	EEEFRRZ	FREEZER
DINOWWY	WINDOWY	DNNOORW	NONWORD	EEEFRSZ	FREEZES
DINPSTU	PUNDITS	DNNOOST	DONNOTS	EEEGHNW	WHEENGE
DINPSUW	UPWINDS	DNNORUU	UNROUND	EEEGIKR	GEEKIER
	WINDUPS	DNNORUW	RUNDOWN	EEEGILN	GLEENIE
DINRSSU	SUNDRIS	DNNOSUU	UNSOUND	EEEGILS	ELEGIES
DINSSTU	NUDISTS	DNNOSUW	SUNDOWN		ELEGISE
DIOOPPS	DOPPIOS	DNNOUUW	UNWOUND	EEEGILZ	ELEGIZE
DIOOPRS	SPOROID	DNNRTUU	TURNDUN	EEEGINP	EPIGENE
DIOOPSS	ISOPODS	DNNSTUU	TUNDUNS	EEEGINR	GREENIE
DIOORST	DISROOT	DNOORTU	OROTUND	EEEGIPR	PERIGEE
	TOROIDS	DNOOSUV	VODOUNS	EEEGKLR	KEGELER
DIOORTT	RIDOTTO		VOUDONS	EEEGLMN	GLEEMEN
DIOOSTX	TOXOIDS	DNOOTUW	NUTWOOD	EEEGLNT	GENTEEL
DIOPRST	DISPORT	DNOOUUV	VOUDOUN	EEEGMRR	REMERGE
	TORPIDS	DNOPRUU	ROUNDUP	EEEGMRS	EMERGES
	TRIPODS	DNOPTUW	PUTDOWN		MERGEES
DIOPRTY	TRIPODY	DNOPUUW	UPWOUND	EEEGNNO	NEOGENE
DIPRSST	DISPOST	DNORSST	STRONDS	EEEGNPR	EPERGNE
DIORRST	STRIDOR	DNORSTU	ROTUNDS	EEEGNPS	PEENGES
DIORSTT	DISTORT	DNOSSTU	STOUNDS	EEEGNRR	GREENER
DIOSSTU	STUDIOS	DNOSSTW	STOWNDS		REGREEN
DIOSUUV	VIDUOUS	DNOSSUW	SWOUNDS		RENEGER
DIPRSTU	DISRUPT	DNOSSWW	SWOWNDS	EEEGNRS	RENEGES
DIPSSTU	STUPIDS	DOOOOSV	VOODOOS	EEEGNRU	RENEGUE
DIRSTUY	SURDITY	DOOOPSW	DOOWOPS	EEEGNRV	REVENGE
DJLMOSY	JYMOLDS	DOOORSU	ODOROUS	EEEGNSS	GENESES
DJNNOOS	DONJONS	DOOORTU	OUTDOOR	EEEGNTT	GENETTE
DKNNRUU	UNDRUNK	DOOPRSU	UROPODS	EEEGRRT	GREETER

	REGREET	EEEIRRT	RETIREE	EEEMNSS	NEMESES
EEEGRSS	GREESES	EEEIRRV	REVERIE	EEEMNST	MENTEES
EEEGRST	GREETES	EEEIRST	EERIEST	EEEMORT	EROTEME
EEEGRSZ	GEEZERS	EEEIRSV	VEERIES	EEEMOSY	EYESOME
EEEGRUX	EXERGUE	EEEIRSZ	RESEIZE	EEEMPRT	PREMEET
EEEHILW	WHEELIE	EEEISTW	SWEETIE	EEEMRSS	SEEMERS
EEEHINS	SHEENIE	EEEJLRW	JEWELER	EEEMRST	MEETERS
EEEHIRX	HEXEREI	EEEJNPY	JEEPNEY		REMEETS
EEEHISZ	HEEZIES	EEEJPRS	JEEPERS		TEEMERS
EEEHLNW	ENWHEEL	EEEJRRS	JEERERS	EEEMRTX	EXTREME
EEEHLOY	EYEHOLE	EEEJSST	JESTEES	EEEMSST	ESTEEMS
EEEHLPS	SHEEPLE	EEEKKRS	KEEKERS		MESTEES
EEEHLPW	WHEEPLE	EEEKLLU	UKELELE	EEEMSTT	MEETEST
EEEHLRS	HEELERS	EEEKLMN	KEELMEN	EEEMSTU	EMEUTES
	REHEELS	EEEKLNR	KNEELER	EEENNPT	PENTENE
EEEHLRW	WHEELER	EEEKLNS	SLEEKEN	EEENNRT	ETRENNE
EEEHLST	LETHEES	EEEKLNX	KLEENEX	EEENNSV	VENENES
EEEHLWZ	WHEEZLE	EEEKLPW	EKPWELE	EEENNTT	ENTENTE
EEEHNST	ETHENES	EEEKLRS	KEELERS	EEENNUY	ENNUYEE
EEEHNSX	HEXENES		SLEEKER	EEENPRR	PREENER
EEEHNSY	SHEENEY	EEEKMNS	MEEKENS	EEENPRT	PRETEEN
EEEHPRS	PHEERES	EEEKMST	MEEKEST		TERPENE
EEEHPSS	PHEESES	EEEKNPT	KEEPNET	EEENPRV	PREVENE
EEEHPSZ	PHEEZES	EEEKNRS	KEENERS	EEENPSS	PENSEES
EEEHRRS	SHEERER	EEEKNST	KEENEST	EEENPST	ENSTEEP
EEEHRST	SEETHER		KETENES		STEEPEN
	SHEETER	EEEKORV	REEVOKE	EEENPSW	ENSWEEP
EEEHRTT	TEETHER	EEEKPRS	KEEPERS	EEENPSX	EXPENSE
EEEHRWZ	WHEEZER	EEEKRRS	REEKERS	EEENRRS	SERENER
EEEHSST	SEETHES	EEEKRSS	KREESES		SNEERER
EEEHSSV	SHEEVES		RESEEKS	EEENRRT	ENTERER
EEEHSTT	ESTHETE		SEEKERS		REENTER
	TEETHES	EEEKRST	KEESTER		TERREEN
EEEHSWZ	WHEEZES		SKEETER		TERRENE
EEEIJLS	JEELIES	EEELLRV	LEVELER	EEENRRV	VENERER
EEEIKLL	EELLIKE	EEELMNR	REELMEN	EEENRRW	RENEWER
EEEIKLS	KEELIES	EEELMNT	ELEMENT	EEENRSS	SERENES
EEEIKLY	EYELIKE		TELEMEN	EEENRST	ENTREES
EEEIKRR	REEKIER	EEELMPX	EXEMPLE		RETENES
EEEILRR	LEERIER	EEELMSX	LEXEMES		TEENERS
EEEILRS	SEELIER	EEELNST	STELENE	EEENRSV	ENERVES
EEEILRV	RELIEVE	EEELNSV	ELEVENS		EVENERS
EEEILST	EELIEST	EEELPRS	PEELERS		VENEERS
	STEELIE		SLEEPER	EEENRSZ	SNEEZER
EEEIMMS	MEEMIES		SPEELER	EEENRTV	EVENTER
EEEIMNS	ENEMIES	EEELPRT	REPLETE		EVERNET
EEEIMNT	EMETINE	EEELPRX	REEXPEL	EEENRTW	TWEENER
EEEIMPR	EPIMERE	EEELPST	STEEPLE	EEENRTX	EXTERNE
	PREEMIE	EEELRRS	REELERS	EEENRUV	REVENUE
EEEIMRS	EMERIES	EEELRRV	REVELER		UNREEVE
EEEIMRT	EREMITE	EEELRSV	RELEVES		
EEEINQU	QUEENIE		SLEEVER	EEENSSZ	SNEEZES
EEEINRS	ESERINE	EEELRTV	LEVERET	EEENSTV	EVENEST
EEEINRT	TEENIER	EEELSSS	LESSEES	EEENSTW	SWEETEN
EEEINRW	WEENIER	EEELSSV	SLEEVES	EEENSTX	EXTENSE
EEEINSW	WEENIES	EEELSSY	EYELESS	EEENSVW	VENEWES
EEEINTW	TWEENIE	EEELSTU	EUSTELE	EEENSWY	SWEENEY
EEEIPRR	PEERIER	EEELSTX	TELEXES	EEEOPPS	EPOPEES
EEEIPRS	PEERIES	EEELSTY	EYELETS	EEEORSV	OVERSEE
	SEEPIER	EEELTTX	TELETEX	EEEORSY	EYESORE
EEEIPRW	WEEPIER	EEEMMSS	MESEEMS	EEEORVY	OVEREYE
EEEIPST	EPEEIST		SEMEMES	EEEPPRS	PEEPERS
EEEIPSU	EPUISEE	EEEMNRS	MENEERS	EEEPRSS	PEERESS
EEEIPSW	WEEPIES			EEEPRST	ESTREPE
					STEEPER

EEEPRSV	PEEVERS	EEFHIRT	HEFTIER	EEFISTV	FESTIVE
	PREEVES	EEFHISY	FISHEYE	EEFLLOS	FELLOES
EEEPRSW	SWEEPER	EEFHLMN	FLEHMEN	EEFLLRS	FELLERS
	WEEPERS	EEFHLNS	ENFLESH	EEFLLRU	FUELLER
EEEPRSZ	SPREEZE	EEFHLRS	FLESHER	EEFLLST	FELLEST
EEEQRRU	QUEERER		HERSELF	EEFLLTY	FLEETLY
	REQUERE	EEFHLSS	FLESHES	EEFLMTU	TEEMFUL
EEEQSUZ	SQUEEZE	EEFHNRS	FRESHEN	EEFLNNO	ENFELON
EEERRRV	REVERER	EEFHORT	THEREOF	EEFLNNS	FENNELS
EEERRST	RETREES	EEFHORW	WHEREOF	EEFLNOS	ONESELF
	STEERER	EEFHRRS	FRESHER	EEFLNRS	FLENSER
EEERRSV	RESERVE		REFRESH		FRESNEL
	REVERES	EEFHRRU	FUEHRER	EEFLNSS	FLENSES
	REVERSE	EEFHRSS	FRESHES	EEFLNTU	TEENFUL
	SEVERER	EEFHRST	FRESHET	EEFLOOV	FOVEOLE
EEERRSW	SWEERER		HEFTERS	EEFLORS	FORLESE
EEERSSS	SEERESS	EEFIIMN	FEMINIE	EEFLOTU	OUTFEEL
EEERSTT	TEETERS	EEFIIRR	FIERIER	EEFLRRS	FERRELS
	TERETES		REIFIER	EEFLRRU	FERRULE
EEERSTV	STEEVER	EEFIIRS	REIFIES	EEFLRST	FELTERS
EEERSTW	SWEETER	EEFIKLL	ELFLIKE		REFLETS
EEERSUV	REVEUSE	EEFILLS	FELLIES		TELFERS
EEERSUW	SERUEWE	EEFILLX	FLEXILE	EEFLRSU	FERULES
EEERSVW	SERVEWE	EEFILNO	OLEFINE		FUELERS
	WEEVERS	EEFILNS	FELINES		REFUELS
EEERTTW	TWEETER	EEFILOR	FORELIE	EEFLRTT	FETTLER
EEERTWZ	TWEEZER	EEFILPR	PREFILE	EEFLRTU	FLEURET
EEESSTT	SETTEES		PRELIFE	EEFLRUX	FLEXURE
	TESTEES	EEFILRR	FERLIER	EEFLSTT	FETTLES
EEESSTV	STEEVES	EEFILRS	FERLIES		LEFTEST
	VESTEES		REFILES	EEFLSUY	EYEFULS
EEESTTW	WEETEST		REFLIES	EEFMNOR	FOREMEN
EEESTWZ	TWEEZES		RELIEFS	EEFMNRT	FERMENT
EEFFFNO	ENFEOFF	EEFILRT	FELTIER	EEFMOTT	MOFETTE
EEFFFOR	FEOFFER		FERTILE	EEFMPRU	PERFUME
EEFFGLU	EFFULGE	EEFILST	FELSITE	EEFMSTW	FEWMETS
EEFFINT	FIFTEEN		LEFTIES	EEFMTTU	FUMETTE
EEFFIRS	EFFEIRS		LIEFEST	EEFNORT	OFTENER
EEFFKLS	KEFFELS	EEFILTY	EYELIFT	EEFNORZ	ENFROZE
EEFFNOS	OFFENSE	EEFIMMR	FEMMIER	EEFNRRY	FERNERY
EEFFORR	OFFERER	EEFIMNR	FIREMEN	EEFNRSS	ENSERFS
	REOFFER	EEFIMRT	FEMITER	EEFNRSU	UNFREES
EEFFOST	TOFFEES	EEFINNR	FENNIER	EEFNRTV	FERVENT
EEFFSSU	EFFUSES	EEFINNS	FENNIES	EEFNSSW	FEWNESS
EEFFSTU	SUFFETE	EEFINRR	FERNIER	EEFNSSY	FEYNESS
EEFGILN	FEELING		REFINER	EEFORRV	FOREVER
	FLEEING	EEFINRS	ENFIRES	EEFORRZ	REFROZE
EEFGILT	GEFILTE		FEERINS	EEFORSX	FOREXES
EEFGINR	FEERING		FINEERS	EEFOTTU	FOUETTE
	FEIGNER		REFINES	EEFPRRS	PREFERS
	FREEING	EEFINRT	FEINTER	EEFPRSU	PERFUSE
	REEFING	EEFINSS	FINESSE	EEFRRST	FERRETS
EEFGINS	FEESING	EEFINSX	ENFIXES	EEFRRSU	REFUSER
EEFGINZ	FEEZING	EEFIPRR	PREFIRE	EEFRRTT	FRETTER
EEFGIRR	GRIEFER	EEFIPRS	PREIFES	EEFRRTU	REFUTER
EEFGIST	GIFTEES		PRIEFES	EEFRRTY	FERRETY
EEFGLLU	GLEEFUL	EEFIRRS	FERRIES	EEFRSST	FESTERS
EEFGLOR	FORELEG		REFIRES	EEFRSSU	REFUSES
EEFGLOS	SOLFEGE		REFRIES	EEFRSTT	FETTERS
EEFGORR	REFORGE	EEFIRRT	FERRITE	EEFRSTU	FEUTRES
EEFGORY	FROGEYE	EEFIRSS	FRISEES		REFUTES
EEFGRSU	REFUGES	EEFIRST	FESTIER	EEFRSTW	FEWTERS
EEFHIRS	FRESHIE	EEFIRSX	REFIXES	EEFSSTU	FETUSES
	HEIFERS	EEFIRSZ	FRIEZES	EEGGGIS	GEGGIES

Letters	Anagram	Letters	Anagram	Letters	Anagram
EEGGGLR	GLEGGER	EEGILNT	GENTILE	EEGIRRV	GRIEVER
EEGGHTU	THUGGEE	EEGILOS	ELOGIES	EEGIRSS	SIEGERS
EEGGILN	GLEEING	EEGILPS	SPIEGEL	EEGIRSV	GRIEVES
	NEGLIGE	EEGILRS	LEIGERS		REGIVES
EEGGILR	LEGGIER		LIEGERS	EEGIRTT	TERGITE
EEGGINR	GREEING	EEGILRV	VELIGER	EEGIRTU	GUERITE
EEGGIPS	PEGGIES	EEGILST	ELEGIST	EEGISTV	VESTIGE
EEGGIRS	GREIGES		ELEGITS	EEGKLRS	KEGLERS
EEGGIST	EGGIEST	EEGIMMR	GEMMIER	EEGKNOR	KEROGEN
EEGGISV	VEGGIES		GREMMIE	EEGKNRU	GERENUK
EEGGKRS	KEGGERS		IMMERGE	EEGLLNS	LEGLENS
	SKEGGER	EEGIMNR	MEERING	EEGLLSS	LEGLESS
EEGGLRS	EGGLERS		REGIMEN	EEGLLST	LEGLETS
	LEGGERS	EEGIMNS	SEEMING	EEGLMMU	GEMMULE
EEGGLSS	EGGLESS	EEGIMNT	MEETING	EEGLMOR	GOMEREL
EEGGMNY	YEGGMEN		TEEMING	EEGLMSU	EMULGES
EEGGMSU	MUGGEES	EEGIMNX	EXEMING		LEGUMES
EEGGNNS	GENSENG	EEGIMRR	GERMIER	EEGLNNS	GENNELS
EEGGNOR	ENGORGE	EEGIMRS	EMIGRES	EEGLNOR	ERELONG
EEGGNOY	GEOGENY		REGIMES	EEGLNOU	EUGENOL
EEGGORR	REGORGE		REMIGES	EEGLNOZ	LOZENGE
EEGGORU	GOUGERE	EEGINNP	PEENING	EEGLNRT	GENTLER
EEGGORV	OVEREGG	EEGINNR	ENGINER	EEGLNRY	GREENLY
EEGGPRU	PUGGREE		INGENER	EEGLNST	GENTLES
EEGHILN	HEELING	EEGINNS	ENGINES		LENGEST
EEGHINR	REHINGE		GENNIES	EEGLNSU	LUNGEES
EEGHINT	THEEING		NEESING	EEGLOSS	EGOLESS
EEGHINY	HYGIENE		SNEEING	EEGLPSS	PEGLESS
EEGHINZ	HEEZING	EEGINNT	TEENING	EEGLRRU	GRUELER
EEGHIRW	REWEIGH	EEGINNU	GENUINE	EEGLRST	REGLETS
	WEIGHER		INGENUE	EEGLRSU	REGLUES
EEGHKRS	SKREEGH	EEGINNV	EEVNING	EEGLRTW	WERGELT
EEGHLNU	LEUGHEN		EVENING	EEGLRTY	TELERGY
EEGHMNO	HEGEMON	EEGINNW	ENEWING	EEGMMRY	GEMMERY
EEGHMNU	HEGUMEN		WEENING	EEGMNOS	EMONGES
EEGHNRT	GREENTH	EEGINNZ	NEEZING		GENOMES
EEGHNRY	GREYHEN	EEGINOP	EPIGONE	EEGMNRS	GERMENS
EEGHRTU	TEUGHER	EEGINOS	GENOISE	EEGMNST	SEGMENT
EEGHSSS	GHESSES		SOIGNEE	EEGMNSU	EMUNGES
EEGHSTZ	SHEGETZ	EEGINPP	PEEPING	EEGMNTU	TEGUMEN
EEGIIRS	GRIESIE	EEGINPR	PEERING	EEGMOST	GEMOTES
EEGIJLN	JEELING		PREEING	EEGMRRS	MERGERS
EEGIJNP	JEEPING	EEGINPS	SEEPING	EEGMRTU	GUMTREE
EEGIJNR	JEERING	EEGINPV	PEEVING	EEGNNST	GENNETS
EEGIKKN	KEEKING	EEGINPW	WEEPING	EEGNOPS	PONGEES
EEGIKLL	LEGLIKE	EEGINRS	GREISEN	EEGNORS	ENGORES
EEGIKLM	GEMLIKE	EEGINRT	GENTIER		NEGROES
EEGIKLN	KEELING		INTEGER	EEGNOSX	EXOGENS
EEGIKLP	PEGLIKE		TEERING	EEGNPUX	EXPUNGE
EEGIKNN	KEENING		TREEING	EEGNRSS	NEGRESS
	KNEEING	EEGINRV	REEVING	EEGNRST	GERENTS
EEGIKNP	KEEPING		REGIVEN		REGENTS
	PEEKING		VEERING	EEGNRSV	VENGERS
EEGIKNR	REEKING	EEGINSS	GENESIS	EEGNRSY	GYRENES
EEGIKNS	SEEKING		SEEINGS	EEGNSSU	GENUSES
	SKEEING		SIGNEES		NEGUSES
EEGIKNT	KITENGE	EEGINSW	SEEWING	EEGNSTU	GUESTEN
EEGILLS	GELLIES		SWEEING	EEGOOSS	SOOGEES
EEGILNP	LEEPING	EEGINTV	VENTIGE	EEGOPRT	PROTEGE
	PEELING	EEGINTW	WEETING	EEGORTV	OVERGET
EEGILNR	LEERING	EEGINTX	EXIGENT	EEGOSSS	GESSOES
	REELING	EEGIOST	EGOTISE	EEGPPRR	PREPREG
EEGILNS	LEESING		GOETIES	EEGPRSU	PUGREES
	SEELING	EEGIOTZ	EGOTIZE	EEGPRUX	EXPURGE

EEGRRSS	REGRESS	EEHISST	HESSITE	EEHNSTU	ENTHUSE
	SERGERS	EEHISTV	THIEVES	EEHNSTV	SEVENTH
EEGRRST	REGRETS	EEHKLOY	KEYHOLE	EEHNSTY	ETHYNES
EEGRRSU	RESURGE	EEHKLSS	SHEKELS	EEHNSWW	WHENWES
	REURGES	EEHKOOY	EYEHOOK	EEHOOPW	WHOOPEE
EEGRRSV	VERGERS	EEHKRSS	SHREEKS	EEHOOST	TOESHOE
EEGRRUY	GRUYERE	EEHLLMP	PHELLEM	EEHOPRU	EUPHROE
EEGRSST	REGESTS	EEHLLNS	ENSHELL	EEHOPSS	SHEEPOS
EEGRSSU	GUESSER	EEHLLOS	HELLOES	EEHOPST	HEPTOSE
EEGRSSY	GEYSERS	EEHLLOT	THEELOL	EEHORRV	HOVERER
EEGRSTT	GETTERS	EEHLLRS	HELLERS	EEHORSS	RESHOES
EEGRSTU	GESTURE		SHELLER	EEHORST	HETEROS
EEGRSTY	GREYEST	EEHLLRY	HELLERY	EEHORSU	REHOUSE
EEGSSSU	GUESSES	EEHLMMW	WHEMMLE	EEHORSW	WHERESO
EEHHORU	HOUHERE	EEHLMRS	HELMERS	EEHORTT	THERETO
EEHHRTT	THETHER	EEHLMRT	THERMEL	EEHORTW	WHERETO
EEHHRTW	WHETHER	EEHLMST	HELMETS	EEHORVW	HOWEVER
EEHHSTW	WHEESHT	EEHLNSU	UNHELES		WHOEVER
EEHIINS	HEINIES	EEHLNSY	HENLEYS	EEHOSST	ETHOSES
EEHIKLN	HENLIKE	EEHLORY	HOLEYER	EEHOSSX	HEXOSES
EEHIKLO	HOELIKE	EEHLPRS	HELPERS	EEHOSTW	TOWHEES
EEHILLR	HELLERI	EEHLPRT	TELPHER	EEHOSTY	EYESHOT
	HELLIER	EEHLPSS	PLESHES	EEHPPST	HEPPEST
EEHILMN	HELIMEN	EEHLQSS	SHEQELS	EEHPRSS	SPHERES
	HEMLINE	EEHLRST	SHELTER	EEHPRST	HEPSTER
EEHILNT	THEELIN	EEHLRSV	SHELVER		PETHERS
EEHILOP	PIEHOLE	EEHLRSW	WELSHER		SPERTHE
EEHILPS	EPHELIS	EEHLRSY	SHEERLY		THREEPS
EEHILRS	LEISHER	EEHLSSU	HUELESS	EEHPRTY	PRYTHEE
EEHILRW	WHILERE	EEHLSSV	SHELVES	EEHQSTU	QUETHES
EEHILST	SHELTIE	EEHLSSW	SHEWELS	EEHRRSW	WERSHER
EEHILSX	HELIXES		WELSHES	EEHRRTW	WHERRET
EEHIMMS	MISHMEE	EEHLSTT	SHTETEL	EEHRSSU	RUSHEES
EEHIMNO	HEMIONE	EEHLSTV	THELVES	EEHRSSW	SHEWERS
EEHIMPR	HEMPIER	EEHMMRS	HEMMERS	EEHRSTT	TETHERS
EEHIMPS	HEMPIES	EEHMNNO	NONHEME	EEHRSTW	WETHERS
	IMPHEES	EEHMNNS	MENSHEN		WRETHES
EEHIMPT	EPITHEM	EEHMNOP	PHONEME	EEHRSTZ	HERTZES
EEHIMRS	MESHIER	EEHMNOS	HOSEMEN	EEHRSVW	WHERVES
EEHINNR	HENNIER	EEHMNRU	ENRHEUM	EEHRTTW	WHETTER
EEHINNS	HENNIES	EEHMNRY	MYNHEER	EEHRVWY	WHYEVER
EEHINNY	HYENINE	EEHMNSS	MENSHES	EEHSTUY	SHUTEYE
EEHINOR	HEROINE	EEHMORT	THEOREM	EEIIKKS	KIEKIES
EEHINRR	ERRHINE	EEHMPST	TEMPEHS	EEIIKRS	KIERIES
EEHINRS	HENRIES	EEHMRST	THERMES	EEIILMS	MIELIES
	INHERES	EEHMRUX	EXHUMER	EEIILRV	VEILIER
	RESHINE	EEHMSST	SMEETHS	EEIIMNS	MEINIES
EEHINRT	NEITHER	EEHMSUV	HUMVEES	EEIIMPR	RIEMPIE
	THEREIN	EEHMSUX	EXHUMES	EEIIMRT	EMERITI
EEHINRW	WHEREIN	EEHNNOS	SHONEEN	EEIIMST	ITEMISE
EEHINST	THEINES	EEHNNRS	HENNERS	EEIIMTZ	ITEMIZE
EEHIORS	HEROISE	EEHNNRY	HENNERY	EEIINNS	NEINEIS
EEHIORZ	HEROIZE	EEHNOOR	HONOREE	EEIINRT	ERINITE
EEHIPRT	PRITHEE	EEHNOPT	POTHEEN		NITERIE
EEHIPSV	PEEVISH	EEHNORS	RESHONE	EEIINRV	VEINIER
EEHIPTT	EPITHET	EEHNORT	THEREON	EEIINST	SIENITE
EEHIRRS	HERRIES	EEHNORW	NOWHERE	EEIINSW	EISWEIN
	REHIRES		WHEREON		WIENIES
EEHIRSS	HEIRESS	EEHNOSX	HEXONES	EEIINTV	INVITEE
	HERISSE	EEHNPSS	SEPHENS	EEIIPST	PIETIES
EEHIRST	HEISTER		SPHENES	EEIIRRV	RIVIERE
EEHIRSV	SHRIEVE	EEHNPSW	NEPHEWS	EEIIRVW	VIEWIER
EEHIRTW	THEWIER	EEHNRST	THRENES	EEIISST	SEITIES
EEHIRWY	WHEYIER	EEHNSST	NESHEST	EEIISTV	VISITEE

EEIJKLT	JETLIKE	EEILNNT	LENIENT	EEILSSV	SLIEVES
EEIJKRR	JERKIER	EEILNNV	ENLIVEN	EEILSSW	LEWISES
EEIJKRS	JERKIES	EEILNOR	ELOINER	EEILSSX	LEXISES
EEIJLLS	JELLIES	EEILNOS	OLEINES		SILEXES
EEIJMMR	JEMMIER	EEILNPS	PENSILE	EEILSTV	EVILEST
EEIJMMS	JEMMIES	EEILNPT	PENLITE		LEVITES
EEIJNNS	JENNIES	EEILNRS	LIERNES		LIEVEST
EEIJRRS	JERRIES		RELINES		VELITES
EEIJRTT	JETTIER	EEILNRV	LIVENER	EEILSTX	SEXTILE
EEIJSSS	JESSIES	EEILNSS	ENISLES	EEILSUV	ELUSIVE
EEIJSTT	JETTIES		ENSILES	EEILSVW	WEEVILS
EEIKKRR	KERKIER		SENILES	EEILSZZ	LEZZIES
EEIKKST	TEKKIES		SENSILE	EEILTTX	TEXTILE
EEIKLLS	KELLIES		SILENES	EEILTUX	ULEXITE
	SKELLIE	EEILNST	LENITES	EEILVWY	WEEVILY
EEIKLNT	NETLIKE		LISENTE	EEIMMNS	IMMENSE
EEIKLNY	KEYLINE		SETLINE	EEIMMRS	IMMERSE
EEIKLOT	TOELIKE		TENSILE	EEIMMSS	MIMESES
EEIKLPS	KELPIES	EEILNSY	YEELINS		MISSEEM
EEIKLPT	PIKELET	EEILNTT	ENTITLE	EEIMMST	MISMEET
EEIKLSS	SELKIES	EEILNTV	VEINLET	EEIMNNO	NOMINEE
EEIKLST	KELTIES	EEILNUV	VEINULE	EEIMNNT	EMINENT
	SLEEKIT	EEILOPT	PETIOLE	EEIMNOS	SEMEION
EEIKMNP	PIKEMEN	EEILORS	LOERIES	EEIMNOT	ONETIME
EEIKMPR	KEMPIER	EEILORT	TROELIE	EEIMNRS	ERMINES
EEIKMPS	MISKEEP	EEILORV	OVERLIE	EEIMNRV	MINEVER
EEIKNOS	EIKONES		RELIEVO	EEIMNRW	WIREMEN
EEIKNPY	PINKEYE	EEILOST	ESTOILE	EEIMNSS	INSEEMS
EEIKNRT	KERNITE		ETOILES		MISSEEN
EEIKNSS	ENSKIES	EEILOTZ	ZEOLITE		NEMESIS
	KINESES	EEILPRR	REPLIER		SIEMENS
EEIKNWY	EYEWINK	EEILPRS	REPLIES	EEIMNST	EMETINS
EEIKPRR	PERKIER		SPIELER	EEIMNSW	MISWEEN
EEIKPRS	PESKIER	EEILPRT	PERLITE	EEIMNSY	MEINEYS
EEIKPSW	KEWPIES		REPTILE		MENYIES
EEIKRRS	KERRIES	EEILPRU	PUERILE	EEIMNTT	MINETTE
EEIKRST	KEISTER	EEILPSS	PELISSE	EEIMOPS	EPISOME
	KIESTER	EEILPST	EPISTLE	EEIMOPT	EPITOME
EEIKRSY	SKIEYER		PELITES	EEIMORS	ISOMERE
EEIKSST	SEIKEST	EEILPWY	WEEPILY	EEIMOSS	MEIOSES
EEIKSTT	STEEKIT	EEILQRU	RELIQUE	EEIMOTV	EMOTIVE
EEIKTTT	TEKTITE	EEILRRS	RELIERS	EEIMPRR	PREMIER
EEILLMT	MELLITE	EEILRRV	RELIVER		REPRIME
EEILLNS	NELLIES		REVILER	EEIMPRS	EMPIRES
EEILLPS	ELLIPSE	EEILRSS	IRELESS		EMPRISE
EEILLRS	LEISLER		RESILES		EPIMERS
	RELLIES	EEILRST	LEISTER		IMPRESE
EEILLRT	TREILLE		RETILES		PERMIES
EEILLRV	EVILLER		STERILE		PREMIES
EEILLRY	LEERILY	EEILRSU	LEISURE		PREMISE
EEILLSS	EISELLS	EEILRSV	LEVIERS		SPIREME
EEILLST	TELLIES		RELIVES	EEIMPRT	EMPTIER
EEILLSV	VIELLES		REVILES	EEIMPRZ	EMPRIZE
EEILLSW	WELLIES		SERVILE	EEIMPST	EMPTIES
EEILMMT	MELTEMI		VEILERS		SEPTIME
EEILMNN	LINEMEN	EEILRSX	EXILERS	EEIMQRU	REQUIEM
EEILMNR	ERMELIN	EEILRTT	RETITLE	EEIMRRR	MERRIER
EEILMNS	ISLEMEN	EEILRVY	LIVEYER	EEIMRRS	MERRIES
EEILMNY	MYELINE	EEILSSS	SESELIS	EEIMRRT	MITERER
EEILMPT	IMPLETE		SESSILE		TRIREME
EEILMRT	MELTIER	EEILSST	LISTEES	EEIMRRU	EREMURI
EEILMRV	VERMEIL		TELESIS	EEIMRSS	MERISES
EEILMST	ELMIEST		TIELESS		MESSIER
EEILNNO	LEONINE	EEILSSU	ILEUSES		MISERES

	REMISES		RETINES	EEIPRSV	PREVISE
EEIMRST	MEISTER		TRENISE		PRIEVES
	METIERS		TRIENES	EEIPRSW	SPEWIER
	REEMITS	EEINRSV	ENVIERS	EEIPRSX	EXPIRES
	RETIMES		INVERSE		PREXIES
	TREMIES		VEINERS	EEIPRTT	PETTIER
	TRISEME		VENIRES	EEIPRTY	YPERITE
EEIMRSX	MIREXES		VERSINE	EEIPRVW	PREVIEW
	REMIXES	EEINRSW	NEWSIER	EEIPRZZ	PREZZIE
EEIMRTT	EMITTER		WEINERS	EEIPSSS	SPEISES
	TERMITE		WIENERS	EEIPSTT	PETITES
EEIMSSS	MISSEES	EEINRSX	REXINES		PETTIES
	SEMISES	EEINRTT	NETTIER	EEIPSTW	PEEWITS
EEIMSST	METISSE		TENTIER	EEIQRRU	QUERIER
EEINNNP	PENNINE	EEINRTU	NEURITE		REQUIRE
EEINNPS	PENNIES		RETINUE	EEIQRSU	ESQUIRE
	PINENES		REUNITE		QUERIES
EEINNRS	NERINES		UTERINE	EEIQRTU	QUIETER
EEINNRT	INTERNE	EEINSSS	SENSEIS		REQUITE
EEINNRU	NEURINE	EEINSST	SEITENS	EEIQSTU	EQUITES
EEINNRV	ENRIVEN		SESTINE	EEIRRRT	RETIRER
	INNERVE	EEINSSV	SENVIES		TERRIER
	NERVINE	EEINSSW	NEWSIES	EEIRRSS	RERISES
EEINNRW	WENNIER	EEINSTT	NETTIES		SERRIES
EEINNST	INTENSE	EEINSTV	TENSIVE		SIRREES
	TENNIES		VENITES	EEIRRST	ETRIERS
EEINNSV	VENINES	EEINSTX	EXTINES		REITERS
EEINNTW	ENTWINE		SIXTEEN		RESTIER
EEINNTZ	NETIZEN	EEINSTY	SYENITE		RETIRES
EEINOPR	PEREION	EEIOPPT	EPITOPE		RETRIES
	PIONEER	EEIOPSS	POESIES		TERRIES
EEINOPS	PEONIES	EEIOPST	POETISE	EEIRRSV	REIVERS
EEINORR	ONERIER	EEIOPSX	EPOXIES		REVERSI
EEINOSS	EOSINES	EEIOPTZ	POETIZE		REVISER
EEINPPS	PEPSINE	EEIORRS	ROSIERE		RIEVERS
EEINPRR	REPINER	EEIORSS	SOIREES	EEIRRSW	REWIRES
	RIPENER	EEIORST	EROTISE		SWEIRER
EEINPRS	EREPSIN	EEIORSV	EROSIVE	EEIRRTV	RIVERET
	REPINES	EEIORTZ	EROTIZE		RIVETER
EEINPRT	INEPTER	EEIOSST	ISOETES	EEIRRTW	REWRITE
EEINPRZ	PRENZIE	EEIOSTT	TOEIEST	EEIRRVV	REVIVER
EEINPSS	PENISES	EEIPPPR	PEPPIER	EEIRSSS	SEISERS
EEINPST	PENTISE		PREPPIE	EEIRSST	RESITES
EEINPSV	PENSIVE	EEIPPST	PEPTISE	EEIRSSU	REISSUE
	VESPINE		TIPPEES		SEISURE
EEINQRU	ENQUIRE	EEIPPTT	PIPETTE	EEIRSSV	IVRESSE
	INQUERE	EEIPPTZ	PEPTIZE		REVISES
EEINQSU	EQUINES	EEIPQRU	PERIQUE	EEIRSSZ	RESIZES
EEINQTU	QUIETEN		REEQUIP		SEIZERS
EEINQUY	QUEYNIE		REPIQUE	EEIRSTT	TESTIER
EEINRRS	RERISEN	EEIPQSU	EQUIPES	EEIRSTU	SUETIER
	RESINER	EEIPRRR	PERRIER	EEIRSTV	RESTIVE
EEINRRT	INERTER	EEIPRRS	PERRIES		SIEVERT
	REINTER		PRISERE		STIEVER
	RENTIER		REPRISE		VERIEST
	TERRINE		RESPIRE		VERITES
EEINRRV	NERVIER	EEIPRRV	REPRIVE	EEIRSTW	STEWIER
	VERNIER	EEIPRRW	PREWIRE	EEIRSTZ	ZESTIER
EEINRSS	SEINERS	EEIPRRX	EXPIRER	EEIRSUZ	SEIZURE
	SEREINS	EEIPRRZ	REPRIZE	EEIRSVV	REVIVES
	SERINES	EEIPRSS	ESPIERS	EEIRSVW	REVIEWS
EEINRST	ENTIRES		PRESSIE		VIEWERS
	ENTRIES	EEIPRST	PESTIER	EEIRTVV	VETIVER
	NERITES		RESPITE	EEISSSV	ESSIVES

EEISSTV	VITESSE	EEKPPSU	UPKEEPS	EELMSST	TELESMS
EEISSTW	WESTIES	EEKPRRS	REPERKS	EELMSSU	MULESES
EEISSTX	SEXIEST	EEKPRSU	PERUKES	EELMSTT	METTLES
EEISTTW	WETTIES	EEKRRUZ	KREUZER		STEMLET
EEISTTY	YETTIES	EEKRSST	STREEKS	EELNNSV	VENNELS
EEISTVX	VITEXES	EEKRSSU	RESKUES	EELNOPV	ENVELOP
EEITUXZ	ZEUXITE	EEKRSSW	RESKEWS	EELNOPY	POLYENE
EEJKRRS	JERKERS		SKEWERS	EELNOSV	ELEVONS
EEJLLMU	JUMELLE	EEKRSSY	KERSEYS	EELNOSY	ESLOYNE
EEJLRHY	JEWELRY	EEKRSTY	KEYSTER	EELNOTT	NOTELET
EEJNNST	JENNETS	EEKSSTW	SKEWEST	EELNOTU	TOLUENE
EEJNOOR	REJONEO	EEKSSTY	KEYSETS	EELNPSS	PENSELS
EEJNORS	REJONES	EELLLVY	LEVELLY		SPLEENS
EEJNORY	ENJOYER	EELLMOR	MORELLE	EELNPST	PENTELS
	REENJOY	EELLMOS	MOSELLE	EELNPSY	SPLEENY
EEJNOSS	JONESES	EELLMRS	MERELLS	EELNQUY	QUEENLY
EEJORST	RESOJET		SMELLER	EELNRST	NESTLER
EEJPRRU	PERJURE	EELLMRV	VERMELL		RELENTS
EEJQRRU	JERQUER	EELLNOR	RELLENO		SLENTER
EEJQRSU	JERQUES	EELLNOV	NOVELLE	EELNRSU	UNREELS
EEJRSST	JESTERS	EELLNRS	SNELLER	EELNRTT	LETTERN
EEJRSSY	JERSEYS	EELLNST	TELLENS		NETTLER
EEKKOTV	VETKOEK	EELLNSW	NEWELLS	EELNRUV	NERVULE
EEKKRRT	TREKKER	EELLNUV	UNLEVEL	EELNSSS	LESSENS
EEKKSSY	KEKSYES	EELLOPS	POLLEES	EELNSST	NESTLES
EEKLLNV	KNEVELL	EELLORS	ROSELLE		NETLESS
EEKLLSY	SLEEKLY	EELLORZ	ROZELLE	EELNSSU	UNSEELS
EEKLLUU	UKULELE	EELLPRS	PRESELL	EELNSTT	NETTLES
EEKLMPS	KEMPLES		RESPELL		TELNETS
EEKLMRZ	KLEZMER		SPELLER	EELNSTU	ELUENTS
EEKLNNS	KENNELS	EELLPRT	PRETELL		UNSTEEL
EEKLNOS	KEELSON	EELLPST	PELLETS	EELNSTY	ENSTYLE
EEKLNRS	KERNELS	EELLQRU	QUELLER		TENSELY
EEKLPRS	KELPERS	EELLRSS	RESELLS	EELNSUV	VENULES
EEKLRST	KELTERS		SELLERS	EELNSXY	XYLENES
	KESTREL	EELLRST	RETELLS	EELNTTU	LUNETTE
	SKELTER		TELLERS	EELOPPR	PEOPLER
EEKLSSY	KEYLESS	EELLRSU	RUELLES	EELOPPS	PEOPLES
EEKLSTT	KETTLES	EELLRSW	SWELLER	EELOPPZ	ZEPPOLE
EEKLSTW	KEWLEST	EELLRSY	YELLERS	EELOPRS	ELOPERS
EEKMNOS	SOKEMEN	EELLSTV	VELLETS		LEPROSE
EEKMPRS	KEMPERS	EELMMOP	POMMELE	EELOPRX	EXPLORE
EEKMRSS	KERMESS	EELMMPU	EMPLUME	EELOPSS	ELOPSES
EEKNNRS	KENNERS	EELMNNS	LENSMEN	EELOPTU	EELPOUT
EEKNNST	KENNETS	EELMNOO	OENOMEL	EELORSS	RESOLES
EEKNNTT	KENNETT	EELMNOP	PLEROME	EELORST	SOLERET
EEKNORW	REWOKEN	EELMOPR	PLEROME	EELORSV	RESOLVE
EEKNOSS	KENOSES	EELMOPT	LEPTOME	EELORSY	EROSELY
EEKNOST	KETONES	EELMOPY	EMPLOYE	EELORTT	LORETTE
EEKNOTY	KEYNOTE	EELMORW	EELWORM	EELORTV	OVERLET
EEKNRSS	SKREENS	EELMOST	OMELETS	EELORVV	EVOLVER
EEKNRST	RENKEST		TELOMES		REVOLVE
EEKNSST	KNESSET	EELMPRS	SEMPLER	EELOSSS	LOESSES
EEKNSTU	NETSUKE	EELMPST	PELMETS	EELOSST	OSSELET
EEKOOPP	PEKEPOO		STEMPEL		TELOSES
EEKOPRS	RESPOKE		STEMPLE	EELOSTT	TELEOST
EEKOPTU	OUTKEEP		TEMPLES	EELOSUV	EVOLUES
EEKORRV	REVOKER	EELMPTT	TEMPLET	EELOSVV	EVOLVES
EEKORST	RESTOKE	EELMRST	MELTERS	EELOTUV	EVOLUTE
EEKORSV	EVOKERS		REMELTS		VELOUTE
	REVOKES		RESMELT	EELPPRX	PERPLEX
EEKOSSS	SEKOSES		SMELTER	EELPPSU	PEEPULS
EEKOSST	KETOSES	EELMRSU	LEMURES	EELPQRU	PREQUEL
EEKOSTV	VOETSEK		RELUMES		
		EELMRSW	MEWLERS		

EELPRST	PELTERS	**EEMNOPR**	REPOMEN	**EENNSSU**	UNSEENS
	PETRELS	**EEMNORS**	MOREENS		UNSENSE
	RESPELT	**EEMNORV**	OVERMEN	**EENNSSW**	NEWNESS
	SPELTER		VENOMER	**EENOPPR**	PREPONE
EELPRSU	REPULSE	**EEMNORY**	MONEYER		PROPENE
EELPRSY	SLEEPRY	**EEMNOST**	TEMENOS	**EENOPPT**	PEPTONE
	YELPERS		TONEMES	**EENOPRS**	OPENERS
EELPRTY	PEYTREL	**EEMNOSV**	ENMOVES		PEREONS
EELPRTZ	PRETZEL	**EEMNPRU**	PREMUNE		PERONES
EELPRUX	PLEXURE	**EEMNPTU**	UMPTEEN		REOPENS
EELPRVY	REPLEVY	**EEMNRTU**	TRUEMEN		REPONES
EELPSST	PESTLES	**EEMNSYZ**	ENZYMES	**EENOPST**	OPENEST
EELPSTT	PETTLES	**EEMOOSW**	WOESOME		PENTOSE
EELPSTY	STEEPLY	**EEMOPRR**	EMPEROR		POSTEEN
EELPSUX	EXPULSE	**EEMOPRT**	TEMPORE		POTEENS
EELQRUY	QUEERLY	**EEMOPRV**	PREMOVE	**EENOPTT**	POTTEEN
EELQSSU	SEQUELS	**EEMOPRW**	EMPOWER	**EENOPTY**	NEOTYPE
EELRRSV	VERRELS	**EEMOPST**	METOPES	**EENORRV**	OVERREN
EELRRVY	REVELRY	**EEMORRS**	REMORSE	**EENORSS**	SENORES
EELRSST	STREELS		ROEMERS	**EENORST**	ESTRONE
	TRESSEL	**EEMORRT**	REMOTER	**EENORSY**	ONEYERS
EELRSSU	RULESSE	**EEMORRU**	UROMERE		ONEYRES
EELRSTT	LETTERS	**EEMORRV**	REMOVER	**EENORSZ**	REZONES
	LETTRES	**EEMORST**	EMOTERS	**EENORTV**	OVERNET
	SETTLER		METEORS	**EENORVW**	OVERNEW
	STERLET		REMOTES		REWOVEN
	TRESTLE	**EEMORSV**	REMOVES	**EENOSSW**	WOENESS
EELRSTV	SERVLET	**EEMOSST**	MESTESO	**EENOSSY**	ESSOYNE
	SVELTER	**EEMOTTZ**	MOZETTE		NOYESES
EELRSTW	SWELTER	**EEMPPRT**	PREEMPT	**EENOSTU**	OUTSEEN
	WELTERS	**EEMPRRT**	PRETERM	**EENOSTV**	VENTOSE
	WRESTLE	**EEMPRSS**	EMPRESS		VOTEENS
EELRSTY	RESTYLE	**EEMPRST**	TEMPERS	**EENOSTW**	TOWNEES
	TERSELY	**EEMPRSU**	PRESUME	**EENOSVZ**	EVZONES
EELRSTZ	SELTZER		SUPREME	**EENOTTT**	TONETTE
EELRSUV	VELURES	**EEMPRTT**	TEMPTER	**EENPPRT**	PERPENT
EELRSUX	LUREXES	**EEMPRTU**	PERMUTE	**EENPRST**	PENSTER
EELRSVV	VERVELS	**EEMPSSU**	EMPUSES		PRESENT
EELSSSU	USELESS	**EEMPSTT**	TEMPEST		REPENTS
EELSSSV	VESSELS	**EEMPSTX**	EXEMPTS		SERPENT
EELSSSX	SEXLESS	**EEMRRST**	TERMERS	**EENPRSY**	PYRENES
EELSSTT	SETTLES	**EEMRRSU**	MURREES	**EENPRTV**	PREVENT
EELSSTU	SETULES		RESUMER	**EENPRTY**	PERENTY
EELSSUV	EVULSES	**EEMRRUU**	REMUEUR	**EENPSSS**	SPENSES
EELSTUY	EUSTYLE	**EEMRSST**	MESTERS	**EENPSTU**	PUNTEES
EELSTVV	VELVETS		RESTEMS	**EENPSTW**	ENSWEPT
EELSTVW	TWELVES	**EEMRSSU**	RESUMES	**EENPSTY**	STEPNEY
EELSTWY	SWEETLY	**EEMRSUX**	MUREXES	**EENQSTU**	SEQUENT
EELTVVY	VELVETY	**EEMSSSU**	SMEUSES	**EENRRST**	RENTERS
EEMMNOS	MONEMES	**EEMSSTU**	MUSTEES		RERENTS
EEMMNOT	MEMENTO	**EEMSTTU**	MUSETTE		STERNER
EEMMNSS	MESSMEN	**EENNORT**	ENTERON	**EENRRSU**	ENSURER
EEMMORS	MEROMES		TENONER	**EENRRSV**	NERVERS
EEMMOST	MESTOME	**EENNORU**	NEURONE	**EENRRTY**	REENTRY
EEMMOSU	MOUSMEE	**EENNOSS**	ONENESS	**EENRRUV**	NERVURE
EEMMOSV	EMMOVES	**EENNOSZ**	ENZONES	**EENRSST**	NESTERS
EEMMRST	STEMMER	**EENNOTT**	NONETTE		RENESTS
EEMMRSY	YEMMERS	**EENNOTY**	NEOTENY		RESENTS
EEMMSSS	SEMSEMS	**EENNPRS**	PENNERS		STRENES
EEMMSST	STEMMES	**EENNQUU**	UNQUEEN	**EENRSSU**	ENSURES
EEMNNOV	ENVENOM	**EENNRST**	RENNETS	**EENRSTT**	NETTERS
EEMNNSW	NEWSMEN		TENNERS		TENTERS
EEMNOOS	SOMEONE	**EENNRUV**	UNNERVE		TESTERN
EEMNOOY	MOONEYE	**EENNSST**	SENNETS	**EENRSTU**	NEUTERS

	RETUNES	EEORSUV	OEUVRES		WRESTER
	TENURES		OVERUSE	EERRSUV	REVEURS
	TUREENS	EEORSVW	OVERSEW	EERRSVW	SWERVER
EENRSTV	VENTERS	EEORSXX	XEROXES	EERRSVY	SERVERY
	VENTRES	EEORTUV	OUVERTE	EERRTTU	REUTTER
EENRSTW	WESTERN	EEORTVW	OVERWET		UTTERER
EENRSTX	EXTERNS	EEOSSSY	OYESSES	EERRTTY	RETTERY
EENRSTY	STYRENE	EEOSSTU	OUTSEES	EERSSST	TRESSES
	YESTERN	EEPPPRS	PEPPERS	EERSSTT	RETESTS
EENRSVV	VERVENS	EEPPPRY	PEPPERY		SETTERS
EENRTUV	VENTURE	EEPPRST	STEPPER		STREETS
EENSSST	SETNESS	EEPPRSX	PERSPEX		TERSEST
EENSSSY	SYNESES	EEPPRTY	PRETYPE		TESTERS
EENSSTT	TENSEST	EEPPSST	STEPPES	EERSSTV	REVESTS
EENSSTV	STEVENS	EEPPSTU	STEEPUP		STERVES
EENSSTW	WETNESS	EEPPSUW	UPSWEEP		VERSETS
EENSSUV	VENUSES	EEPPSUY	EUPEPSY		VERSTES
EENSSUX	NEXUSES	EEPRRSS	PRESSER	EERSSTW	STEWERS
	UNSEXES		REPRESS		WESTERS
EENSSVW	SWEVENS		SPERRES	EERSSTX	EXSERTS
EENSTTX	EXTENTS	EEPRRST	PRESTER	EERSSTZ	ZESTERS
EENSTTY	TEENTSY	EEPRRSU	PERUSER	EERSSUX	XERUSES
EENSTUW	UNSWEET		REPURES	EERSSUY	SEYSURE
EENSTVY	SEVENTY	EEPRRSY	PREYERS	EERSSVW	SWERVES
EEOOPRS	OPEROSE	EEPRRTV	PERVERT	EERSTTT	STRETTE
EEOOSTT	TOETOES	EEPRRVY	REPRYVE		TETTERS
EEOPPRS	PREPOSE	EEPRSSS	PRESSES	EERSTTU	TRUSTEE
EEOPPTT	POPETTE		SPERSES	EERSTTV	TREVETS
EEOPPTU	OUTPEEP	EEPRSST	PESTERS		VETTERS
EEOPRRS	REPOSER		PRESETS	EERSTTW	WETTERS
EEOPRRV	REPROVE	EEPRSSU	PERSUES	EERSTTX	TEXTERS
EEOPRRW	REPOWER		PERUSES	EERSTTY	STREETY
EEOPRSS	REPOSES	EEPRSSV	VESPERS		SYRETTE
EEOPRSX	EXPOSER	EEPRSSW	SPEWERS	EERSTUV	VERSUTE
EEOPRTT	PROETTE	EEPRSSX	EXPRESS		VERTUES
	TREETOP	EEPRSTT	PERTEST		VESTURE
EEOPRTU	OUTPEER		PETTERS	EERSTUY	TUYERES
EEOPSSS	SPEOSES		PRETEST	EERSTVV	VERVETS
EEOPSST	POETESS	EEPRSTU	PERTUSE	EERSTWY	TWYERES
EEOPSSU	ESPOUSE		REPUTES	EERTTUX	TEXTURE
	POSEUSE	EEPRSTW	PEWTERS	EESSSTT	SESTETS
EEOPSSX	EXPOSES	EEPRSTX	EXPERTS		TSETSES
EEOPSTU	TOUPEES		SEXPERT	EESSTTT	SESTETT
EEOPSTY	EYESPOT	EEPRSTY	RETYPES	EESSTTU	SUTTEES
	PEYOTES	EEPRSUV	PREVUES	EESSTTX	SEXTETS
EEOPTUW	OUTWEEP	EEPRSXY	PYREXES	EESSTTY	STEYEST
EEOQRTU	REQUOTE	EEPRSZZ	PREZZES	EESSTTZ	TZETSES
EEORRST	RESTORE	EEPRTTX	PRETEXT	EESTTTW	WETTEST
EEORRSV	REVERSO	EEPSSTT	SEPTETS	EESTTTX	SEXTETT
EEORRSZ	REZEROS	EEPSTTU	PUTTEES	EESTTZZ	TZETZES
EEORRTU	REROUTE	EEPSTTY	TYPESET	EFFFINO	INFEOFF
EEORRTV	EVERTOR	EEQRRUY	EQUERRY	EFFFIRU	FUFFIER
EEORRTW	REWROTE	EEQRSTU	QUESTER	EFFFLRU	FLUFFER
EEORSST	OSSETER		REQUEST	EFFFOOR	FEOFFOR
	STEREOS	EEQRSUU	QUEUERS	EFFGIJN	JEFFING
EEORSSX	SOREXES	EEQSSTU	QUEESTS	EFFGINR	REFFING
	XEROSES	EEQSUYZ	SQUEEZY	EFFGINS	EFFINGS
EEORSTT	ROSETTE	EERRSST	RESTERS	EFFGIRS	GRIFFES
EEORSTV	ESTOVER	EERRSSV	SERVERS	EFFGISU	GUFFIES
	OVERSET		VERSERS	EFFGORS	GOFFERS
	REVOTES	EERRSTT	TERRETS	EFFGRRU	GRUFFER
	VETOERS	EERRSTU	URETERS	EFFHILW	WHIFFLE
EEORSTX	XEROTES	EERRSTV	REVERTS	EFFHIRS	SHERIFF
EEORSTY	ESOTERY	EERRSTW	STREWER	EFFHIRU	HUFFIER

EFFHIRW	WHIFFER	EFGGIRR	FRIGGER	EFHINNS	FENNISH
EFFHITW	WHIFFET	EFGGIRU	FUGGIER	EFHINST	FISHNET
EFFHLSU	SHUFFLE	EFGGIRY	FIGGERY	EFHIRSS	FISHERS
EFFHRSU	HUFFERS	EFGGLOR	FLOGGER		SERFISH
EFFIIJS	JIFFIES	EFGGORS	FOGGERS		SHERIFS
EFFIIMR	MIFFIER	EFGHIMS	GEMFISH	EFHIRST	SHIFTER
EFFIINR	NIFFIER	EFGHINT	HEFTING	EFHIRSY	FISHERY
EFFIIST	FIFTIES	EFGHIRT	FIGHTER	EFHISUW	HUSWIFE
	IFFIEST		FREIGHT	EFHLLPU	HELPFUL
	STIFFIE		REFIGHT	EFHLLSY	FLESHLY
EFFIKLS	SKIFFLE	EFGIKNR	KERFING	EFHLNSU	UNFLESH
EFFILLU	LIFEFUL	EFGILLN	FELLING	EFHLOOX	FOXHOLE
EFFILNO	OFFLINE	EFGILMN	FLEMING	EFHLOPU	HOPEFUL
EFFILNS	SNIFFLE	EFGILNR	FLINGER	EFHLOSS	FLOSHES
EFFILPR	PIFFLER	EFGILNS	SELFING	EFHLRSU	FLUSHER
EFFILPS	PIFFLES	EFGILNT	FELTING	EFHLRSY	FRESHLY
EFFILRR	RIFFLER	EFGILNU	FUELING	EFHLSSU	FLUSHES
EFFILRS	RIFFLES	EFGILNX	FLEXING	EFHLSTY	THYSELF
EFFILRY	FIREFLY	EFGILNY	FLEYING	EFHLTTW	TWELFTH
EFFILSS	SIFFLES	EFGILRU	FUGLIER	EFHNORT	FORHENT
EFFIMOS	MOFFIES		GULFIER	EFHOORS	HOOFERS
EFFINRS	NIFFERS	EFGIMNT	FIGMENT	EFHORRT	FROTHER
	SNIFFER	EFGINNP	PFENNIG	EFHORSS	FROSHES
EFFINST	INFEFTS	EFGINNR	FERNING	EFHORST	FOTHERS
	STIFFEN	EFGINOR	FOREIGN	EFHRRSU	FUHRERS
EFFIOPR	PIFFERO	EFGINPR	PERFING	EFHRRTU	FURTHER
EFFIORT	FORFEIT	EFGINRS	FINGERS	EFHRSSU	FRUSHES
	TOFFIER		FRINGES	EFIIKLN	FINLIKE
EFFIORX	FOXFIRE	EFGINRU	GUNFIRE	EFIIKST	FIKIEST
EFFIOST	TOFFIES	EFGINSS	FESSING	EFIILLS	FILLIES
EFFIPRU	PUFFIER	EFGINTT	FETTING	EFIILMR	FILMIER
EFFIRRT	TRIFFER	EFGINTW	WEFTING	EFIILMS	MISFILE
EFFIRST	RESTIFF	EFGIOOR	GOOFIER	EFIILRT	FIRELIT
	STIFFER	EFGIORV	FORGIVE		FITLIER
EFFLLOS	SELLOFF	EFGIRRT	GRIFTER	EFIILRY	FIERILY
EFFLMRU	MUFFLER	EFGIRRU	FIGURER	EFIILSS	FISSILE
EFFLMSU	MUFFLES	EFGIRSU	FIGURES	EFIIMRR	RIMFIRE
EFFLNSU	SNUFFLE	EFGKOOP	OPGEFOK	EFIIMRS	MISFIRE
EFFLOPS	POFFLES	EFGLLSU	FLUGELS	EFIIMST	SEMIFIT
EFFLOSU	SOUFFLE	EFGLNSU	ENGULFS	EFIINNR	FINNIER
EFFLRRU	RUFFLER	EFGLNTU	FULGENT	EFIINPV	FIVEPIN
EFFLRSU	RUFFLES	EFGLORS	GOLFERS	EFIINRT	NIFTIER
EFFLRTU	FRETFUL	EFGLORT	FROGLET	EFIINRU	UNIFIER
	TRUFFLE	EFGLOSS	FOGLESS	EFIINSS	FINISES
EFFNRSU	SNUFFER	EFGMNOR	FROGMEN	EFIINST	FINITES
EFFNRUU	UNRUFFE	EFGNOOR	FORGONE		NIFTIES
EFFNSTU	FUNFEST	EFGNOSU	FUNGOES	EFIINSU	UNIFIES
EFFOORR	OFFEROR	EFGOORR	FORGOER	EFIINSX	INFIXES
EFFOPRR	PROFFER	EFGOORS	FORGOES	EFIIRRR	FIRRIER
EFFOPSU	POUFFES	EFGORRS	FORGERS	EFIIRRT	RIFTIER
EFFORRT	TROFFER	EFGORRU	FERRUGO	EFIIRST	FISTIER
EFFORST	EFFORTS	EFGORRY	FORGERY	EFIIRTW	WIFTIER
EFFORSW	SWOFFER	EFGORST	FORGETS	EFIIRZZ	FIZZIER
EFFOSST	OFFSETS	EFGORSW	GOWFERS	EFIISSV	FISSIVE
	SETOFFS	EFGORTU	FOREGUT	EFIISTW	SWIFTIE
EFFPRSU	PUFFERS	EFHIINS	FINEISH	EFIJLLV	JELLIFY
EFFPRUY	PUFFERY	EFHIIRS	FISHIER	EFIJLOR	FRIJOLE
EFFRSSU	SUFFERS	EFHIJSW	JEWFISH	EFIJLOT	JETFOIL
EFFRSTU	RESTUFF	EFHILMS	FLEMISH	EFIKLNU	FLUNKIE
	STUFFER		HIMSELF	EFIKLOR	FOLKIER
	TRUFFES	EFHILSS	HISSELF	EFIKLOS	FOLKIES
EFFSSUU	SUFFUSE		SELFISH	EFIKLOX	FOXLIKE
EFFSTTU	TUFFETS	EFHILST	LEFTISH	EFIKLRU	FLUKIER
EFGGIOR	FOGGIER	EFHILTY	HEFTILY	EFIKNRS	KNIFERS

EFIKNRU	FUNKIER	EFIMMRU	FERMIUM		STRIFES
EFIKORR	FORKIER	EFIMNOR	FERMION	EFIRSSU	FISSURE
EFIKRRS	FRISKER	EFIMNTT	FITMENT		FUSSIER
EFIKRST	FRISKET	EFIMOST	FOMITES		SURFIES
EFILLMS	MISFELL	EFIMRRS	FIRMERS	EFIRSTT	FITTERS
EFILLOO	FOLIOLE	EFIMRST	FIRMEST		TITFERS
EFILLOS	FOLLIES		FREMITS	EFIRSTU	FUSTIER
EFILLOW	LOWLIFE	EFIMRTY	METRIFY		SURFEIT
EFILLPR	PREFILL	EFIMSTU	FUMIEST	EFIRSTW	SWIFTER
EFILLRR	FRILLER	EFIMTTU	FUMETTI	EFIRSTZ	FRITZES
EFILLRS	FILLERS	EFINNOR	INFERNO	EFIRSUX	FIXURES
	REFILLS	EFINNRS	FINNERS	EFIRSVY	VERSIFY
EFILLST	FILLETS	EFINNRU	FUNNIER	EFIRSZZ	FIZZERS
EFILLUW	WILEFUL	EFINNSU	FUNNIES		FRIZZES
EFILMNT	LIFTMEN	EFINOPR	FORPINE	EFIRTTU	TUFTIER
EFILMNU	FULMINE	EFINPRS	PERFINS		TURFITE
EFILMOT	FILEMOT	EFINRST	SNIFTER	EFIRTUV	FURTIVE
EFILMRS	FILMERS	EFINRSU	INFUSER	EFIRTUX	FIXTURE
	REFILMS	EFINRUY	REUNIFY	EFIRUZZ	FUZZIER
EFILMSS	SELFISM	EFINSST	FITNESS	EFISTTT	FITTEST
EFILMST	FILMSET		INFESTS	EFISTTY	TESTIFY
	LEFTISM	EFINSSU	INFUSES	EFJLSTU	JESTFUL
EFILNNO	NONLIFE	EFINSUX	UNFIXES	EFKLMNO	MENFOLK
EFILNOS	OLEFINS	EFINSZZ	FIZZENS	EFKLMOR	MERFOLK
EFILNOX	FLEXION	EFIOOPR	POOFIER	EFKLNRU	FLUNKER
EFILNSS	FINLESS	EFIOORR	ROOFIER	EFKLNUY	FLUNKEY
EFILOOS	FLOOSIE	EFIOORS	ROOFIES	EFKLOPU	POKEFUL
	FOLIOSE	EFIOORT	FOOTIER	EFKLPSU	SKEPFUL
EFILOOZ	FLOOZIE	EFIOORW	WOOFIER	EFKNRSU	FUNKERS
EFILOPR	PROFILE	EFIOOST	FOOTIES	EFKORRS	FORKERS
EFILORR	FLORIER		FOOTSIE	EFLLORU	FLORULE
EFILORT	LOFTIER		OOFIEST	EFLLOST	FLOTELS
	TREFOIL	EFIOPRR	PORIFER	EFLLOSW	FELLOWS
EFILOSS	FLOSSIE	EFIOPRT	FIREPOT	EFLLRSU	FULLERS
EFILOSU	FOULIES		PIEFORT	EFLLRUY	FULLERY
EFILOSX	SEXFOIL	EFIORRT	ROTIFER	EFLLSSY	FLYLESS
EFILPPR	FLIPPER	EFIORRW	FROWIER	EFLLSTU	FULLEST
EFILPPS	FIPPLES	EFIORSS	FROISES	EFLMOSU	FULSOME
EFILPPU	PIPEFUL	EFIORST	FOISTER	EFLMPRU	FRUMPLE
EFILPRS	PILFERS		FORTIES	EFLMSUU	MUSEFUL
EFILPRY	PILFERY	EFIORTU	OUTFIRE	EFLNNOS	NONSELF
EFILQUY	LIQUEFY	EFIORTV	OVERFIT	EFLNNOU	NONFUEL
EFILRRS	RIFLERS	EFIOSST	SOFTIES	EFLNNSU	FUNNELS
EFILRRT	FLIRTER	EFIOSTX	FOXIEST	EFLNORT	FORLENT
	TRIFLER	EFIOSTZ	FOZIEST	EFLNORU	FLEURON
EFILRRY	RIFLERY	EFIPPRR	FRIPPER	EFLNORW	REFLOWN
EFILRST	FILTERS	EFIPPRT	FRIPPET	EFLNORY	FELONRY
	LIFTERS	EFIPRST	PRESIFT	EFLNOST	TEFLONS
	STIFLER	EFIPRTY	PETRIFY	EFLNOSU	SULFONE
	TRIFLES	EFIRRRU	FURRIER	EFLNOTT	FLETTON
EFILRTT	FLITTER	EFIRRSU	FRISEUR		FONTLET
EFILRTU	FLUTIER		FRISURE	EFLNPSU	PENFULS
	FUTILER		FURRIES	EFLNPUX	FUNPLEX
EFILRTY	FLYTIER		SURFIER	EFLNSSU	FULNESS
EFILRVV	FLIVVER	EFIRRSZ	FRIZERS		UNSELFS
EFILRZZ	FRIZZLE	EFIRRTT	FRITTER	EFLNSTU	FLUENTS
EFILSSS	FISSLES	EFIRRTU	FRITURE		NESTFUL
EFILSST	SELFIST		FRUITER		NETFULS
	STIFLES		TURFIER	EFLNSUY	SYNFUEL
EFILSTT	LEFTIST	EFIRRTY	TERRIFY	EFLNTTU	TENTFUL
EFILSTU	FLUIEST	EFIRRUZ	FURZIER	EFLNTUU	TUNEFUL
	SULFITE	EFIRRZZ	FRIZZER	EFLOORR	FLOORER
EFILSZZ	FIZZLES	EFIRSST	RESIFTS		FORLORE
EFILUVX	FLUXIVE		SIFTERS	EFLOORS	FORSLOE

EFLOORT	FOOTLER	EFNORRT	FRONTER	EGGHIRU	HUGGIER
EFLOORY	FOOLERY		REFRONT	EGGHLOS	SHOGGLE
EFLOORZ	FOOZLER	EFNORRU	FORERUN	EGGHORS	HOGGERS
EFLOOST	FOOTLES	EFNORRW	FROWNER	EGGHORY	HOGGERY
EFLOOSZ	FOOZLES	EFNORST	FRONTES	EGGHOST	HOGGETS
EFLOPPR	FLOPPER	EFNORTU	FORTUNE	EGGHRSU	HUGGERS
EFLORRS	ROLFERS	EFNORTW	FORWENT	EGGIIJR	JIGGIER
EFLORSS	FLOSSER	EFNORUZ	UNFROZE	EGGIILN	GINGELI
EFLORST	FLORETS	EFNOSST	SOFTENS	EGGIILS	GILGIES
	LOFTERS	EFNRSTU	FUNSTER	EGGIINS	SIEGING
EFLORSU	FUROLES	EFOOPRR	PROOFER	EGGIIPR	PIGGIER
	OURSELF		REPROOF	EGGIIPS	PIGGIES
EFLORSW	FLOWERS	EFOOPRS	SPOOFER	EGGIIRW	WIGGIER
	FOWLERS	EFOOPRT	FORETOP	EGGIJLS	JIGGLES
	REFLOWS		POOFTER	EGGIJRS	JIGGERS
	WOLFERS	EFOORRS	REROOFS	EGGIKLN	KEGLING
EFLORSX	FLEXORS		ROOFERS	EGGILLN	GELLING
EFLORTT	FORTLET	EFOORST	FOETORS	EGGILMS	LEGGISM
EFLORTU	FLOUTER		FOOTERS		MIGGLES
EFLORTW	FELWORT		REFOOTS	EGGILNN	LENGING
EFLORVY	FLYOVER	EFOORSW	WOOFERS	EGGILNR	NIGGLER
	OVERFLY	EFOORTW	WOOFTER	EGGILNS	GINGLES
EFLORWW	WERWOLF	EFOPPRY	FOPPERY		LEGGINS
EFLORWY	FLOWERY	EFOPRSS	PROFESS		NIGGLES
EFLOSSS	FLOSSES	EFOPRST	FORPETS		SNIGGLE
EFLOSSU	FLOUSES	EFOPRSU	PROFUSE	EGGILNU	GLUEING
EFLOSTU	FOULEST	EFOPRTU	POUFTER		LUGEING
EFLOTTU	OUTFELT	EFORRSU	FERROUS	EGGILNY	GINGELY
EFLOTUW	OUTFLEW		FURORES		GLEYING
EFLPRRU	PURFLER	EFORRSV	FERVORS	EGGILOR	LOGGIER
EFLPRSU	PURFLES	EFORRTY	TORREFY	EGGILRS	LIGGERS
EFLPRUY	PREYFUL	EFORRUV	FERVOUR	EGGILRW	WIGGLER
EFLPSTU	PESTFUL	EFORSST	FORESTS		WRIGGLE
EFLRRSU	FURLERS		FOSTERS	EGGILST	GIGLETS
EFLRSSU	FURLESS	EFORSSU	FOURSES	EGGILSU	LUGGIES
EFLRSTU	FLUSTER	EFORSTU	FOUTERS	EGGILSW	WIGGLES
	FLUTERS		FOUTRES	EGGIMMN	GEMMING
	RESTFUL	EFORSTW	TWOFERS	EGGIMNN	MENGING
EFLRTTU	FLUTTER	EFOSSTT	SOFTEST	EGGIMNR	GERMING
EFLSSUU	USEFULS	EFOSTWW	WOWFEST		MERGING
EFLSTUZ	ZESTFUL	EFPRTUY	PUTREFY	EGGIMOS	MOGGIES
EFLSUZZ	FUZZLES	EFPSTUY	STUPEFY	EGGIMRU	MUGGIER
EFMNOOT	FOOTMEN	EFRRRSU	SURFERS	EGGINNN	GENNING
EFMNORS	ENFORMS	EFRRSTU	RETURFS	EGGINNR	GERNING
EFMNOST	FOMENTS	EFRRSUU	FUREURS	EGGINNS	GINSENG
EFMNRSU	FRENUMS	EFRRSSU	FUSSERS	EGGINNV	VENGING
	SURFMEN	EFRSTTU	TUFTERS	EGGINRS	GINGERS
EFMNRTU	TURFMEN	EFRSTUU	FUTURES		NIGGERS
EFMOORZ	ZOEFORM	EFSSTTU	FUSTETS		SERGING
EFMOPRR	PERFORM	EGGGIKN	KEGGING		SNIGGER
	PREFORM	EGGGILN	LEGGING	EGGINRU	GRUEING
EFMOPRT	POMFRET	EGGGILR	GIGGLER		GUNGIER
EFMORRS	FORMERS	EGGGILS	GIGGLES	EGGINRV	VERGING
	REFORMS	EGGGINP	PEGGING	EGGINRW	GREWING
EFMOTTU	FUMETTO	EGGGINV	VEGGING	EGGINRY	GINGERY
EFMPRUY	PERFUMY	EGGGLOR	GOGGLER		GREYING
EFMRRSU	FERRUMS	EGGGLOS	GOGGLES		NIGGERY
EFMRTUY	FURMETY	EGGGLSU	GUGGLES	EGGINSS	GESSING
EFNNORT	FORNENT	EGGGNOS	EGGNOGS	EGGINTT	GETTING
EFNNORU	FENURON	EGGHILR	HIGGLER	EGGINTW	TWIGGEN
EFNNOTU	UNOFTEN	EGGHILS	HIGGLES	EGGIORS	SOGGIER
EFNNSTU	FUNNEST	EGGHINP	PEGHING	EGGIPRR	PRIGGER
EFNOOST	EFTSOON	EGGHIRT	THIGGER	EGGIPRU	PUGGIER
	FESTOON			EGGIPRY	PIGGERY

EGGIPSU	PUGGIES	EGHIINT	NIGHTIE	EGHISTY	HYGEIST
EGGIRRS	RIGGERS	EGHIINV	INVEIGH	EGHITWY	WEIGHTY
EGGIRRT	TRIGGER	EGHIKLO	HOGLIKE	EGHLLOU	LUGHOLE
EGGIRRU	RUGGIER	EGHIKNR	GHERKIN	EGHLMPS	PHLEGMS
EGGIRSW	SWIGGER	EGHIKRS	SKREIGH	EGHLMPY	PHLEGMY
	WIGGERS		SKRIEGH	EGHLNOR	LEGHORN
EGGIRTW	TWIGGER	EGHILLN	HELLING	EGHLNPU	ENGULPH
EGGIRUV	VUGGIER	EGHILMN	HELMING	EGHLNST	LENGTHS
EGGIRWY	WIGGERY	EGHILMP	MEGILPH	EGHLNTY	LENGTHY
EGGJLOR	JOGGLER	EGHILNP	HELPING		THEGNLY
EGGJLOS	JOGGLES	EGHILNR	HERLING	EGHLOOS	GOLOSHE
EGGJLRU	JUGGLER	EGHILNS	ENGLISH		SHOOGLE
EGGJLSU	JUGGLES		SHINGLE	EGHLOOT	THEOLOG
EGGJORS	JOGGERS	EGHILNT	ENLIGHT	EGHLOSS	SEGHOLS
EGGLMSU	SMUGGLE		LIGHTEN	EGHLPSU	PLEUGHS
EGGLNOS	LEGONGS	EGHILNV	HELVING	EGHLTUY	TEUGHLY
EGGLNSU	SNUGGLE	EGHILOU	GHOULIE	EGHMMOS	MEGOHMS
EGGLOOS	GOOGLES	EGHILPT	PIGHTLE	EGHMNOU	HUMOGEN
EGGLOOY	GEOLOGY	EGHILRT	LIGHTER	EGHMOSU	GUMSHOE
EGGLORS	LOGGERS		RELIGHT	EGHNOOS	HOGNOSE
	SLOGGER	EGHILSS	SLEIGHS	EGHNORS	GORHENS
EGGLORT	TOGGLER	EGHILST	SLEIGHT	EGHNORU	ENROUGH
EGGLOST	GOGLETS	EGHIMMN	HEMMING		ROUGHEN
	LOGGETS	EGHIMNS	MESHING	EGHNOSU	ENOUGHS
	TOGGLES	EGHIMNT	THEMING	EGHNOTU	TOUGHEN
EGGLOSW	WOGGLES	EGHIMPT	EMPIGHT	EGHNRSU	HUNGERS
EGGLPRU	PLUGGER	EGHINNN	HENNING	EGHOPRS	GOPHERS
EGGLPSU	PUGGLES	EGHINNT	HENTING	EGHORRU	ROUGHER
EGGLRSU	GLURGES	EGHINNU	UNHINGE	EGHORTU	TOUGHER
	GURGLES	EGHINOS	HONGIES	EGHOSTT	GHETTOS
	LUGGERS		SHOEING	EGHOSUU	HUGEOUS
	SLUGGER	EGHINPS	HESPING	EGHRSSU	GURSHES
EGGLRTU	GURGLET		PHESING		GUSHERS
EGGLSTU	GUGLETS	EGHINRR	HERRING	EGHRTUY	THEURGY
EGGMRSU	MUGGERS	EGHINRS	HINGERS	EGIIJKL	JIGLIKE
	SMUGGER	EGHINRT	RIGHTEN	EGIIJLS	JILGIES
EGGNOOY	GEOGONY	EGHINRW	WHINGER	EGIIKLP	PIGLIKE
EGGNRRU	GRUNGER	EGHINRY	HERYING	EGIIKLW	WIGLIKE
EGGNRSU	GRUNGES	EGHINST	NIGHEST	EGIILLS	GILLIES
	SNUGGER	EGHINSW	HEWINGS	EGIILMT	LEGITIM
EGGNSTU	NUGGETS		SHEWING	EGIILNR	LEIRING
EGGNTUY	NUGGETY		WHINGES		LINGIER
EGGOPRR	PROGGER	EGHINSX	HEXINGS	EGIILNS	SEILING
EGGORRS	GORGERS	EGHINTT	TIGHTEN	EGIILNT	LIGNITE
EGGORST	GORGETS	EGHINWW	WHEWING	EGIILNV	VEILING
	TOGGERS	EGHIOOS	SHOOGIE	EGIILNX	EXILING
EGGORSU	GOUGERS	EGHIOPS	PISHOGE	EGIILPS	GILPIES
EGGORTY	TOGGERY	EGHIORS	OGREISH	EGIILRR	GIRLIER
EGGPRUY	PUGGERY	EGHIORU	ROUGHIE	EGIILRS	GIRLIES
EGGRRSU	RUGGERS	EGHIOST	HOGTIES	EGIIMMS	GIMMIES
EGGRSTU	TUGGERS	EGHIOTT	GOTHITE	EGIIMNN	MEINING
EGGSSTU	SUGGEST	EGHIOTU	TOUGHIE	EGIIMNP	IMPINGE
EGHHHIT	HEIGHTH	EGHIOTV	EIGHTVO	EGIIMNR	MINGIER
EGHHIMN	HIGHMEN	EGHIRRT	RIGHTER	EGIIMNT	ITEMING
EGHHIRS	HIGHERS	EGHIRSS	GIRSHES	EGIIMNV	MIEVING
EGHHIST	EIGHTHS		SIGHERS	EGIIMPR	GIMPIER
	HEIGHTS	EGHIRST	RESIGHT	EGIIMPS	PIGMIES
	HIGHEST		SIGHTER	EGIIMRR	GRIMIER
EGHHOSW	SHOWGHE	EGHIRSU	GRUSHIE	EGIIMSV	MISGIVE
EGHHSSU	SHEUGHS		GUSHIER	EGIINNP	PEINING
EGHHSUW	WHEUGHS	EGHIRSY	GREYISH	EGIINNR	GINNIER
EGHIILL	GHILLIE	EGHIRTT	TIGHTER		REINING
EGHIILN	HEILING	EGHIRUV	VUGHIER	EGIINNS	INGINES
EGHIINR	HEIRING	EGHISTW	WEIGHTS		INSIGNE

	SEINING	EGIKNUY	YEUKING		SINGLET
EGIINNV	VEINING	EGILLMN	MELLING		SNIGLET
EGIINOP	EPIGONI	EGILLNO	LOGLINE		TINGLES
EGIINPS	PEISING	EGILLNP	PELLING	EGILNSU	LUNGIES
	PIGSNIE	EGILLNS	LEGLINS		SLUEING
EGIINPZ	PEIZING		LINGELS	EGILNSW	SLEWING
EGIINRR	GIRNIER		LINGLES		SWINGLE
EGIINRT	IGNITER		SELLING	EGILNSZ	ZINGELS
	TIERING	EGILLNT	GILLNET	EGILNTT	ETTLING
	TIGRINE		TELLING		LETTING
EGIINRV	REIVING	EGILLNW	WELLING	EGILNTU	ELUTING
	RIEVING	EGILLNY	YELLING	EGILNTW	WELTING
EGIINRW	WEIRING	EGILLOR	GIROLLE		WINGLET
	WINGIER	EGILLOS	GOLLIES	EGILNUY	GUYLINE
EGIINRZ	ZINGIER	EGILLRR	GRILLER	EGILNVY	LEVYING
EGIINSS	SEISING	EGILLRS	GILLERS	EGILOOS	GOOLIES
EGIINST	IGNITES		GRILLES		OLOGIES
EGIINSV	SIEVING	EGILLST	GILLETS	EGILOPS	EPILOGS
	VISEING	EGILLSU	GULLIES	EGILORS	GLOIRES
EGIINSW	WEISING		LIGULES		GLORIES
EGIINSZ	SEIZING	EGILMMN	LEMMING	EGILOSS	GLIOSES
EGIINTV	EVITING	EGILMMR	GLIMMER	EGILOST	ELOGIST
EGIINTX	EXITING	EGILMMY	GEMMILY		LOGIEST
EGIINVW	VIEWING	EGILMNR	GREMLIN	EGILOSU	OUGLIES
EGIINWZ	WEIZING		MERLING	EGILPPR	GRIPPLE
EGIIOPR	PIEROGI		MINGLER	EGILPRU	GULPIER
EGIIPPS	GIPPIES	EGILMNS	MINGLES	EGILPST	PIGLETS
EGIIPRR	GRIPIER	EGILMNT	MELTING	EGILPSY	GILPEYS
EGIIPRW	PERIWIG	EGILMNU	EMULING	EGILRRU	GURLIER
EGIIPSS	GIPSIES		GUMLINE	EGILRSS	GRILSES
EGIJKNR	JERKING		LEGUMIN	EGILRST	GLISTER
EGIJLLN	JELLING	EGILMNW	MEWLING		GRISTLE
EGIJLNR	JINGLER	EGILMNY	YELMING	EGILRSU	GUILERS
EGIJLNS	JINGLES	EGILMOR	GOMERIL		LIGURES
EGIJLNT	JINGLET	EGILMOS	SEMILOG		LURGIES
EGIJNOS	JINGOES	EGILMOU	ELOGIUM	EGILRSY	GREISLY
EGIJNSS	JESSING	EGILMPS	GLIMPSE		GRIESLY
EGIJNST	JESTING		MEGILPS		GRISELY
EGIJNTT	JETTING	EGILMST	GIMLETS	EGILRTT	GLITTER
EGIKKLN	LEKKING	EGILNNS	GINNELS	EGILRTY	TIGERLY
EGIKLMU	GUMLIKE		LENSING	EGILRUV	VIRGULE
EGIKLNP	KELPING	EGILNOP	ELOPING	EGILRZZ	GRIZZLE
EGIKLNR	ERLKING	EGILNOS	ELOIGNS	EGILSST	LEGISTS
EGIKLNS	KINGLES		LEGIONS	EGILSSW	WIGLESS
EGIKLNT	KINGLET		LIGNOSE	EGILSTU	GLUIEST
EGIKLNW	WELKING		LINGOES		UGLIEST
EGIKLRS	KILERGS		LONGIES	EGILSTW	WIGLETS
EGIKLRU	RUGLIKE	EGILNOT	LENTIGO	EGILSTZ	GLITZES
EGIKLTU	GUTLIKE	EGILNPP	LEPPING	EGIMMRR	GRIMMER
EGIKMNP	KEMPING	EGILNPR	PINGLER	EGIMMRS	GIMMERS
EGIKNNN	KENNING	EGILNPS	PINGLES		MEGRIMS
EGIKNNR	KERNING		SPIGNEL	EGIMMRU	GUMMIER
EGIKNNT	KENTING	EGILNPT	PELTING	EGIMMSU	GUMMIES
EGIKNOV	EVOKING	EGILNPY	YELPING	EGIMMTU	GUMMITE
EGIKNPP	KEPPING	EGILNRS	GIRNELS	EGIMNNN	NEMNING
EGIKNPR	PERKING		LINGERS	EGIMNNO	OMENING
EGIKNRU	GUNKIER		SLINGER	EGIMNNR	RINGMEN
EGIKNRV	KERVING	EGILNRT	RINGLET	EGIMNNS	MENSING
EGIKNRY	KEYRING		TINGLER	EGIMNNW	WINGMEN
	YERKING		TRINGLE	EGIMNOR	MOERING
EGIKNST	KESTING	EGILNRY	RELYING	EGIMNOS	MISGONE
EGIKNSW	SKEWING	EGILNSS	SINGLES	EGIMNOT	EMOTING
EGIKNSY	KEYINGS	EGILNST	GLISTEN		MITOGEN
	YESKING		LESTING	EGIMNOU	MEOUING

EGIMNOV	EMOVING	EGINOOS	GOONIES	EGINRTU	TRUEING
EGIMNOW	MEOWING		ISOGONE	EGINRTV	VERTING
EGIMNPR	GRIPMEN		NOOGIES	EGINRTY	RETYING
	IMPREGN	EGINOPR	PERIGON	EGINRVV	REVVING
	PERMING		PIROGEN	EGINRVY	REVYING
EGIMNPT	EMPTING		PONGIER	EGINSST	INGESTS
	PIGMENT	EGINOPS	EPIGONS		SIGNETS
	TEMPING		PIGEONS	EGINSSW	SEWINGS
EGIMNQU	QUEMING		PINGOES		SWINGES
EGIMNRS	GERMINS	EGINORR	IGNORER	EGINSSY	YESSING
	MERINGS	EGINORS	ERINGOS	EGINSTT	SETTING
	MINGERS		IGNORES		TESTING
EGIMNRT	METRING		REGIONS	EGINSTU	GUNITES
	TERMING		SIGNORE	EGINSTV	VESTING
EGIMNRU	EMURING	EGINORT	GENITOR	EGINSTW	STEWING
EGIMNSS	MESSING	EGINORV	OVERING		TWINGES
EGIMNST	STEMING	EGINORZ	ZEROING		WESTING
	TEMSING	EGINOSU	IGNEOUS	EGINSTZ	ZESTING
EGIMNSU	MEUSING	EGINOSW	WIGEONS	EGINSVX	VEXINGS
EGIMNSW	MEWSING	EGINOSY	ISOGENY	EGINSWY	SWEYING
EGIMORR	GORMIER	EGINOSZ	GINZOES	EGINSZZ	GIZZENS
EGIMORS	OGREISM	EGINOTT	TENTIGO	EGINTTV	VETTING
EGIMOSS	EGOISMS	EGINOTV	VETOING	EGINTTW	WETTING
	MISGOES	EGINPPP	PEPPING	EGIOOPR	GOOPIER
EGIMOST	EGOTISM	EGINPPR	REPPING	EGIOORS	GOORIES
EGIMPSU	GUIMPES	EGINPPS	PIGPENS		GOOSIER
EGIMPSY	GYMPIES	EGINPRS	PERSING	EGIOOSS	GOOSIES
	PYGMIES		PINGERS		SOOGIES
EGIMRSW	MISGREW		SPRINGE	EGIOOST	GOOIEST
EGIMSST	STIGMES	EGINPRU	PUERING	EGIOPPS	GIPPOES
EGINNNP	PENNING	EGINPRV	PERVING	EGIOPRS	PORGIES
EGINNNR	RENNING		PREVING		SERPIGO
EGINNNY	YENNING	EGINPRY	PREYING	EGIOPRU	GROUPIE
EGINNOO	IONOGEN	EGINPSS	GIPSENS		PIROGUE
EGINNOP	OPENING	EGINPSU	SPUEING	EGIORRS	GORSIER
EGINNOR	NEGRONI	EGINPSW	SPEWING	EGIORST	GOITERS
EGINNOV	OVENING	EGINPSY	ESPYING		GOITRES
EGINNPR	PERNING		PEYSING		GORIEST
EGINNPU	PENGUIN		PIGSNEY	EGIORTU	GOUTIER
EGINNRR	GRINNER	EGINPTT	PETTING	EGIORTV	VERTIGO
EGINNRS	ENRINGS	EGINPYY	EPIGYNY	EGIORTZ	ZORGITE
	GINNERS	EGINQUU	QUEUING	EGIORUV	VOGUIER
EGINNRT	RENTING	EGINRRS	ERRINGS	EGIOSST	EGOISTS
	RINGENT		GIRNERS		STOGIES
	TERNING		RINGERS	EGIOSTT	EGOTIST
EGINNRU	ENURING		SERRING	EGIOSTV	VOGIEST
EGINNRV	NERVING	EGINRRW	WRINGER	EGIOTUV	OUTGIVE
EGINNRY	GINNERY	EGINRSS	INGRESS	EGIPPRR	GRIPPER
	RENYING		RESIGNS	EGIPPRS	GIPPERS
EGINNSS	ENSIGNS		SIGNERS		GRIPPES
	SENSING		SINGERS	EGIPPSU	GUPPIES
EGINNST	NESTING	EGINRST	RESTING	EGIPPSY	GYPPIES
	SENTING		STINGER	EGIPRRS	GRIPERS
	TENSING	EGINRSU	REUSING	EGIPRUU	GUIPURE
EGINNSU	ENSUING		RUEINGS	EGIPSSY	GYPSIES
	GUNNIES		SIGNEUR	EGIRRRU	GURRIER
	INGENUS	EGINRSV	SERVING	EGIRRST	GRISTER
EGINNSW	NEWSING		VERSING	EGIRRSU	GURRIES
EGINNSY	GYNNIES	EGINRSW	SWINGER		SURGIER
EGINNTT	NETTING		WINGERS	EGIRRSV	VIRGERS
	TENTING	EGINRSY	SYRINGE	EGIRRTT	GRITTER
EGINNTV	VENTING	EGINRSZ	ZINGERS	EGIRSST	TIGRESS
EGINNVY	ENVYING	EGINRTT	GITTERN	EGIRSSU	GUISERS
EGINOOR	GOONIER		RETTING	EGIRSTU	GUSTIER

	GUTSIER		SPLURGE	EGNORSS	ENGROSS
EGIRSTV	GRIVETS	EGLPRUY	GYPLURE	EGNORST	TONGERS
EGIRSUZ	GUIZERS	EGLRSTU	GURLETS	EGNORSU	SURGEON
EGIRTTU	GUTTIER	EGLRSUU	REGULUS	EGNORSV	GOVERNS
	TURGITE	EGLRSUY	GUYLERS	EGNORSY	ERYNGOS
EGISSSU	GUSSIES	EGLRSYY	GRYSELY		GROYNES
EGISTTU	GUTTIES	EGLRTTU	GUTTLER	EGNORUY	YOUNGER
EGISUWY	WISEGUY	EGLRUZZ	GUZZLER	EGNOSSY	GONYSES
EGJLNSU	JUNGLES	EGLSSTU	GUTLESS	EGNOSTU	TONGUES
EGJLSTU	JUGLETS		TUGLESS	EGNOSXY	OXYGENS
EGJOSTT	GJETOST	EGLSTTU	GUTTLES	EGNPRSU	REPUGNS
EGKLORW	LEGWORK	EGLSTUU	GLUTEUS	EGNPSSU	SPUNGES
EGKMSSU	MUSKEGS	EGLSUZZ	GUZZLES	EGNPSUX	EXPUGNS
EGKNOSY	KYOGENS	EGMMORT	GROMMET	EGNRRTU	GRUNTER
EGLLORS	GOLLERS	EGMMOSU	GUMMOSE	EGNRSTU	GUNTERS
EGLLRSU	GULLERS	EGMMRRU	GRUMMER		GURNETS
EGLLRUY	GULLERY	EGMMRSU	GUMMERS		SURGENT
EGLLSTU	GULLETS	EGMMRTU	GRUMMET	EGNRSUY	GURNEYS
EGLLSUY	GULLEYS	EGMNNOS	SONGMEN	EGNRSYY	SYNERGY
EGLMMRU	GLUMMER	EGMNNOT	TONGMEN	EGNRTTU	GRUTTEN
EGLMNOO	ENGLOOM	EGMNNOW	GOWNMEN		TURGENT
EGLMNOR	MONGREL	EGMNOOS	MONGOES	EGNSUVY	UNGYVES
EGLMOOR	LEGROOM	EGMNORS	MONGERS	EGOOPRS	POGOERS
EGLMSSU	GUMLESS		MORGENS	EGOOPSY	POOGYES
EGLNNSU	GUNNELS	EGMNORU	MURGEON	EGOORRV	GROOVER
EGLNOOY	ENOLOGY	EGMNORY	MONGERY	EGOORSV	GROOVES
	NEOLOGY	EGMNOST	EMONGST	EGOORSY	GOOSERY
EGLNOPS	PLONGES	EGMNOSU	EUMONGS	EGOORTU	OUTGOER
EGLNORS	LONGERS		MUNGOES	EGOORTV	OVERGOT
EGLNORU	LOUNGER	EGMNOSY	MYOGENS	EGOOSST	STOOGES
EGLNOST	LONGEST	EGMNOYZ	ZYMOGEN	EGOOSSY	GOOSEYS
EGLNOSU	LOUNGES	EGMNSTU	NUTMEGS	EGOOSTU	OUTGOES
EGLNOSY	LYSOGEN	EGMNSUU	EUMUNGS	EGOPRRS	GROPERS
EGLNOUV	UNGLOVE	EGMOORR	GROOMER	EGOPRRU	GROUPER
EGLNOXY	LOXYGEN		REGROOM		REGROUP
	XYLOGEN	EGMOOSS	SMOOGES	EGORRSS	GROSERS
EGLNOYZ	LOZENGY	EGMORST	GROMETS		GROSSER
EGLNPRU	PLUNGER	EGMORSU	GRUMOSE	EGORRST	GROSERT
EGLNPSU	PLUNGES		MORGUES	EGORRSU	GROUSER
	PUNGLES	EGMORTU	GOURMET	EGORRSW	GROWERS
EGLNRSU	LUNGERS	EGNNOOS	NONEGOS		REGROWS
EGLNRTU	GRUNTLE	EGNNORT	RONTGEN	EGORRTU	GROUTER
EGLNSSU	GUNLESS	EGNNOSU	GUENONS	EGORRUY	ROGUERY
	GUNSELS	EGNNPTU	PUNGENT	EGORSSS	GROSSES
EGLNSTU	ENGLUTS	EGNNRSU	GUNNERS	EGORSST	GOSTERS
	GLUTENS	EGNNRUY	GUNNERY		GROSETS
EGLNSUU	UNGLUES	EGNNSYY	GYNNEYS		STORGES
EGLOORS	REGOSOL	EGNNTUU	UNGUENT	EGORSSU	GROUSES
EGLOOSY	GOOLEYS	EGNOOPS	PONGOES	EGORSTV	GROVETS
EGLOPRS	PROLEGS	EGNOORS	ORGONES	EGORSUV	VOGUERS
EGLOPSS	GOSPELS		OROGENS	EGORTUW	OUTGREW
EGLOPTU	GLUEPOT	EGNOORY	OROGENY	EGOSSTU	GUSTOES
EGLORRW	GROWLER	EGNOOST	GENTOOS	EGOSSTY	STOGEYS
EGLORSS	GLOSSER	EGNOOSY	GOONEYS	EGOSSYZ	ZYGOSES
	REGLOSS	EGNOOTU	OUTGONE	EGOSTTU	GOUTTES
EGLORSU	REGULOS	EGNOOYZ	ZOOGENY	EGOSTYZ	ZYGOTES
EGLORSV	GLOVERS	EGNOPRS	PRESONG	EGPPRSY	GYPPERS
	GROVELS		SPONGER	EGPRRSU	PURGERS
EGLORSW	GLOWERS	EGNOPRY	PROGENY	EGPRSSU	SPURGES
	REGLOWS		PYROGEN	EGPRSTY	GYPSTER
EGLOSSS	GLOSSES	EGNOPSS	SPONGES	EGPRSUU	UPSURGE
EGLOSST	GOSLETS	EGNOPSW	GOWPENS	EGRRSSU	SURGERS
EGLOSUV	VOULGES	EGNORRW	REGROWN	EGRRSUY	SURGERY
EGLPRSU	GULPERS		WRONGER	EGRSSTU	GUTSERS

EGRSSUV	GYRUSES	EHIKOOS	HOOKIES	EHILSTV	THIVELS
EGRSTTU	GUTTERS	EHIKOST	HOKIEST	EHILSTW	WHISTLE
EGRSTUZ	GUTZERS	EHIKPRS	KEPHIRS	EHILTTU	THULITE
EGRTTUY	GUTTERY		PERKISH	EHILTTW	WHITTLE
EGSSSTU	GUSSETS	EHIKRRS	SHIRKER	EHILTWY	WHITELY
EHHIIMS	HEIMISH	EHIKRSS	SHREIKS	EHIMMRS	SHIMMER
EHHIKSS	SHEIKHS		SHRIEKS	EHIMMSY	SHIMMEY
	SHIKSEH		SHRIKES	EHIMNOS	HOMINES
EHHILLS	HELLISH	EHIKRSU	HUSKIER	EHIMNPS	SHIPMEN
EHHINNS	HENNISH	EHIKRSW	WHISKER	EHIMNRS	MENHIRS
EHHIPRS	HERSHIP	EHIKRSY	SHRIEKY	EHIMNRU	INHUMER
EHHIRST	HITHERS	EHIKSSS	SHIKSES		RHENIUM
EHHIRSU	HUSHIER	EHIKSSU	HUSKIES	EHIMNSU	INHUMES
EHHIRTT	THITHER	EHIKSTW	WHISKET	EHIMNTY	THYMINE
EHHIRTW	WHITHER	EHIKSWY	WHISKEY	EHIMORS	HEROISM
EHHISSW	WHISHES	EHILLMN	HILLMEN		MOREISH
EHHISWY	WHEYISH	EHILLNO	HELLION	EHIMORT	MOITHER
EHHNPSY	HYPHENS	EHILLNS	INSHELL		MOTHIER
EHHOOSS	HOOSHES	EHILLOO	OILHOLE	EHIMORZ	RHIZOME
EHHORTT	THOTHER	EHILLOS	HILLOES	EHIMOST	HOMIEST
EHHRSSU	HUSHERS		HOLLIES	EHIMPPX	PEMPHIX
	SHUSHER	EHILLRS	HILLERS	EHIMPRU	HUMPIER
EHHSSSU	SHUSHES		RELLISH	EHIMPRW	WHIMPER
EHIIIKT	HEITIKI	EHILLRT	THILLER	EHIMPSU	HUMPIES
EHIIKLP	HIPLIKE	EHILLRU	HULLIER	EHIMRST	HERMITS
EHIIKNR	HINKIER	EHILLTY	LITHELY		MITHERS
EHIILLR	HILLIER	EHILMMO	MOHELIM	EHIMRSU	HEURISM
EHIILNP	HIPLINE	EHILMPW	WHIMPLE		MUSHIER
EHIILTT	LITHITE	EHILMSU	HELIUMS	EHIMRTT	THERMIT
EHIIMSS	MEISHIS		HUMLIES	EHIMRTY	MYTHIER
EHIINNS	HINNIES		MUHLIES		THYMIER
EHIINRS	SHINIER	EHILMTT	MELTITH	EHIMSST	THEISMS
EHIINRT	INHERIT	EHILMUW	UMWHILE	EHIMSTU	HUMITES
EHIINRW	WHINIER	EHILNOP	PINHOLE		TUMSHIE
EHIINRZ	RHIZINE	EHILNOT	HOTLINE	EHIMSTY	MYTHISE
EHIINSS	SHINIES		NEOLITH	EHIMSWY	WHIMSEY
EHIIPPR	HIPPIER	EHILNPS	PLENISH	EHIMTYZ	MYTHIZE
EHIIPPS	HIPPIES	EHILNSS	ELSHINS	EHINNNS	HENNINS
	SHIPPIE	EHILNTY	ETHINYL	EHINNRT	THINNER
EHIIPRT	PITHIER	EHILOOR	HOOLIER	EHINNSS	SHINNES
EHIIRSS	HISSIER	EHILOOS	HOOLIES	EHINNSW	WENNISH
EHIIRST	HIRSTIE	EHILOPT	HOPLITE	EHINNSY	SHINNEY
EHIIRTW	WHITIER	EHILOSS	ISOHELS	EHINOPR	PHONIER
	WITHIER	EHILOST	EOLITHS	EHINOPS	PHONIES
EHIISSS	HISSIES		HOLIEST	EHINOPX	PHOENIX
EHIISST	STISHIE		HOSTILE	EHINORR	HORNIER
EHIISTW	WHITIES	EHILPRS	HIRPLES	EHINORS	HEROINS
	WITHIES	EHILPRT	PHILTER		INSHORE
EHIJNNO	JOHNNIE		PHILTRE	EHINOST	ETHIONS
EHIKKRS	SHIKKER	EHILPSS	HIPLESS		HISTONE
EHIKKSS	KISHKES	EHILRRW	WHIRLER	EHINOSU	HEINOUS
EHIKLRU	HULKIER	EHILRSS	HIRSELS	EHINPPS	HIPPENS
EHIKLTU	HUTLIKE		HIRSLES		SHIPPEN
EHIKLTY	LEKYTHI	EHILRST	SLITHER	EHINPSS	HIPNESS
EHIKMNT	METHINK	EHILRSU	HURLIES	EHINRSS	SHINERS
EHIKMSV	MIKVEHS		LUSHIER		SHRINES
EHIKNOS	HONKIES	EHILRSV	SHRIVEL	EHINRST	HINTERS
EHIKNRS	KERNISH	EHILRTU	LUTHIER		NITHERS
EHIKNRT	RETHINK	EHILRTW	WHIRTLE	EHINRSV	SHRIVEN
	THINKER	EHILSSS	SLISHES	EHINRSW	WHINERS
EHIKNRU	HUNKIER	EHILSST	HITLESS	EHINRTV	THRIVEN
EHIKNSS	KNISHES	EHILSTT	LISTETH	EHINRTW	WRITHEN
EHIKNSU	HUNKIES		LITHEST	EHINRTZ	ZITHERN
EHIKOOR	HOOKIER		THISTLE	EHINSSS	SHINESS

EHINSST	SITHENS	EHIRSTZ	ZITHERS	EHLOPSY	SPYHOLE
EHINSTW	WHITENS	EHIRSVY	SHIVERY	EHLORST	HOLSTER
EHINSTZ	ZENITHS	EHIRTTW	WHITRET		HOSTLER
EHINSUV	UNHIVES		WHITTER	EHLORSW	HOWLERS
EHINTUW	UNWHITE	EHIRWZZ	WHIZZER	EHLORTW	WHORTLE
EHIOOPW	WHOOPIE	EHISSSU	HUSSIES	EHLORTY	HELOTRY
EHIOORT	HOOTIER	EHISSSW	SWISHES	EHLOSSS	SLOSHES
EHIOOST	TOOSHIE		WHISSES	EHLOSST	HOSTELS
EHIOPPR	HOPPIER	EHISSTT	THEISTS	EHLOSSU	HOUSELS
EHIOPRS	ROSEHIP	EHISSTU	STUSHIE	EHLOSSV	SHOVELS
EHIOPSS	SOPHIES		TUSHIES	EHLOSTT	LOTHEST
EHIOPST	ETHIOPS	EHISTTW	TEWHITS		SHOTTLE
	OPHITES		WETTISH	EHLOSTW	HOWLETS
EHIORRS	HORSIER		WHITEST		THOWELS
EHIORRT	HERITOR	EHISTWY	WHITEYS	EHLOSTY	THYLOSE
EHIORSS	HOSIERS	EHISUZZ	HUZZIES	EHLOTXY	ETHOXYL
EHIORST	HERIOTS	EHISWZZ	WHIZZES	EHLPPSS	SHLEPPS
	HOISTER	EHJOPSS	JOSEPHS	EHLPRSU	PLUSHER
	SHORTIE	EHJORSS	JOSHERS	EHLPSSU	PLUSHES
	TOSHIER	EHKLNOS	LOKSHEN	EHLRRSU	HURLERS
EHIORSU	HOUSIER	EHKLOOT	HOOKLET	EHLRSSU	LUSHERS
EHIORSW	SHOWIER	EHKLPST	KLEPHTS	EHLRSTU	HURTLES
EHIORSY	HOSIERY	EHKMOOS	SMOKEHO		HUSTLER
EHIORTT	THORITE	EHKMOSY	SKYHOME	EHLRSUY	HURLEYS
EHIORTU	OUTHIRE	EHKNORS	HONKERS	EHLSSSU	SLUSHES
	ROUTHIE	EHKNOSY	HONKEYS	EHLSSTT	SHTETLS
EHIORTV	OVERHIT	EHKNRSU	HUNKERS	EHLSSTU	HUSTLES
EHIOSST	HOSTIES	EHKNSSU	HUNKSES		LUSHEST
EHIOSTT	HOTTIES	EHKNSUY	HUNKEYS		SLEUTHS
EHIOSTY	ISOHYET	EHKOORS	HOOKERS	EHLSTTU	SHUTTLE
EHIPPRS	PRESHIP	EHKOOSY	HOOKEYS	EHMMRSU	HUMMERS
	SHIPPER	EHKORSS	KOSHERS	EHMNNOO	NONHOME
EHIPPRW	WHIPPER	EHKORSW	HOWKERS	EHMNOOR	HORMONE
EHIPPST	HIPPEST	EHKORSY	HORKEYS		MOORHEN
EHIPPTW	WHIPPET	EHKOSSS	SKOSHES	EHMNOPS	PHENOMS
EHIPRSS	PISHERS	EHKRSSU	HUSKERS		SHOPMEN
	RESHIPS	EHKRSTU	TUSHKER	EHMNOST	MONETHS
	SERIPHS	EHLLNSU	UNSHELL	EHMNOSW	SHOWMEN
EHIPRST	HIPSTER	EHLLOOS	HOLLOES	EHMNPSU	HUMPENS
EHIPRSU	PUSHIER	EHLLORS	HOLLERS	EHMNPTY	NYMPHET
EHIPRSW	WHISPER	EHLLOSU	HULLOES	EHMNTTU	HUTMENT
EHIPSTT	PETTISH	EHLLRSU	HULLERS	EHMOOSS	SHMOOSE
EHIPSZZ	PHIZZES	EHLMMOW	WHOMMLE	EHMOOSW	SOMEHOW
EHIRRRU	HURRIER	EHLMMSU	HUMMELS	EHMOOSX	HOMOSEX
EHIRRSS	SHERRIS	EHLMMUW	WHUMMLE	EHMOOSZ	SHMOOZE
EHIRRSU	HURRIES	EHLMNOT	MENTHOL	EHMOPRW	MORPHEW
	RUSHIER	EHLMNOY	HOMELYN	EHMORSS	MOSHERS
EHIRRSV	SHRIVER	EHLMNSU	UNHELMS	EHMORST	MOTHERS
EHIRRTV	THRIVER	EHLMOOS	HOLESOM		SMOTHER
EHIRRTW	WHERRIT	EHLMOPS	PHLOEMS		THERMOS
	WHIRRET	EHLMSSU	MULSHES	EHMORTU	MOUTHER
	WRITHER	EHLMSTY	METHYLS	EHMORTY	MOTHERY
EHIRSSS	HISSERS	EHLNOPS	PHENOLS	EHMOSWY	SOMEWHY
EHIRSSV	SHIVERS	EHLNORT	HORNLET	EHMOTXY	METHOXY
	SHRIVES	EHLNPSY	PHENYLS	EHMPRSU	HUMPERS
EHIRSSW	SWISHER	EHLNRTU	LUTHERN	EHMPRTU	THUMPER
	WISHERS	EHLNTTY	TENTHLY	EHMRRSY	RHYMERS
EHIRSTT	HITTERS	EHLNTYY	ETHYNYL	EHMRRTU	MURTHER
	TITHERS	EHLOOPT	POTHOLE	EHMRSSU	MUSHERS
EHIRSTU	HIRSUTE	EHLOOSS	SHOOLES	EHMRSUU	HUMERUS
EHIRSTV	THRIVES	EHLOOSY	HOOLEYS	EHMRTUV	VERMUTH
EHIRSTW	SWITHER	EHLOPPR	HOPPLER	EHMSSSU	SMUSHES
	WITHERS	EHLOPPS	HOPPLES	EHMSSUU	HUMUSES
	WRITHES	EHLOPSX	PHLOXES	EHNNOOR	NONHERO

EHNNOPR	NEPHRON	EHOPRSW	PRESHOW	EIIKLST	KILTIES
EHNNOPY	HYPNONE	EHOPRSY	PHORESY	EIIKLVY	IVYLIKE
EHNNRSU	SHUNNER	EHOPRTU	POUTHER	EIIKMRR	MIRKIER
EHNNSTU	UNSHENT	EHOPRTY	POTHERY	EIIKNNT	KINETIN
EHNNSUW	UNSHEWN	EHOPRUY	EUPHORY	EIIKNPS	PINKIES
EHNOORR	HONORER	EHOPSSS	SPOSHES	EIIKNRS	SINKIER
EHNOORS	HEROONS	EHOPSST	POSHEST	EIIKNRZ	ZINKIER
	ONSHORE	EHOPSTY	TYPHOSE	EIIKNSS	KINESIS
	SOREHON	EHORRSS	SHORERS	EIIKNST	INKIEST
EHNOPRS	PHONERS	EHORRST	RHETORS	EIIKNTW	TWINKIE
EHNOPRY	HYPERON		ROTHERS	EIIKPRS	SPIKIER
EHNOPSU	EUPHONS		SHORTER	EIIKPSS	PISKIES
EHNOPSY	PHONEYS	EHORRTW	THROWER	EIIKRRS	RISKIER
EHNOPUY	EUPHONY	EHORSST	HORSTES	EIIKRSV	SKIVIER
EHNOPXY	PHENOXY		TOSHERS	EIIKSTT	KITTIES
EHNORRS	HORNERS	EHORSSU	HOUSERS	EIILLMM	MILLIME
EHNORRT	HORRENT	EHORSSV	SHOVERS	EIILLMN	MILLINE
	NORTHER		SHROVES	EIILLMR	MILLIER
EHNORRY	HERONRY	EHORSSW	RESHOWS	EIILLMS	MILLIES
EHNORSS	NOSHERS		SHOWERS	EIILLMT	LIMELIT
	SENHORS	EHORSTT	HOTTERS	EIILLNV	VILLEIN
EHNORST	HORNETS	EHORSTU	SHOUTER	EIILLPS	ILLIPES
	SHORTEN		SOUTHER		PILLIES
	THRENOS	EHORSTW	THROWES	EIILLRS	SILLIER
	THRONES	EHORSTX	EXHORTS	EIILLRT	TILLIER
EHNORSU	UNHORSE	EHORSWY	SHOWERY	EIILLSS	SILLIES
EHNORSW	RESHOWN	EHORTUY	OUTHYRE	EIILLST	ILLITES
EHNORSY	NOSHERY	EHOSSST	HOSTESS	EIILLSW	WILLIES
EHNOSST	HOTNESS	EHOSSSU	SHOUSES	EIILLTT	LITTLIE
EHNOSSU	UNSHOES	EHOSSTT	SHOTTES		TILLITE
EHNOSTT	SHOTTEN	EHOSTTT	HOTTEST	EIILLTV	VITELLI
EHNOSTY	HONESTY	EHOTTTW	WOTTETH	EIILMNV	MILVINE
EHNOSUU	UNHOUSE	EHPRSSU	PUSHERS	EIILMPR	IMPERIL
EHNOTUY	YOUTHEN	EHPRSSY	SYPHERS	EIILMPS	IMPLIES
EHNPRSY	PHRENSY	EHPRSYZ	ZEPHYRS	EIILMPT	LIMEPIT
EHNRSTU	HUNTERS	EHPRTTU	TURPETH	EIILMRR	MIRLIER
	SHUNTER	EHPRTUW	UPTHREW	EIILMRS	MILREIS
	UNHERST	EHQRSSU	QURSHES		SLIMIER
EHNRTWY	WRYTHEN	EHRRSSU	RUSHERS	EIILMRT	LIMITER
EHNSSSU	SNUSHES	EHRRSTU	HURTERS		MILTIER
EHNSSSY	SHYNESS	EHRSSTY	SHYSTER	EIILMSS	MISLIES
EHOOOPS	HOOPOES		THYRSES		MISSILE
EHOOPRS	HOOPERS	EHRSTTU	SHUTTER		SIMILES
EHOOPRW	WHOOPER	EHRSTTW	STREWTH	EIILMST	ELITISM
EHOOPTY	OOPHYTE	EHRSTUW	WUTHERS		LIMIEST
EHOORST	HOOTERS	EHRSTUY	TUSHERY		LIMITES
	RESHOOT	EHRTTTY	THRETTY	EIILMSU	MILIEUS
	SHEROOT	EHSSSTU	TUSSEHS	EIILMSV	MISLIVE
	SHOOTER	EIIILRV	RILIEVI	EIILMUX	MILIEUX
	SOOTHER	EIIILST	ILEITIS	EIILNNS	LINNIES
EHOORSV	HOOVERS	EIIINPR	RIPIENI	EIILNOS	ELISION
EHOORTV	OVERHOT	EIIJMMS	JIMMIES		ISOLINE
EHOOSST	SOOTHES	EIIJMPR	JIMPIER		LIONISE
EHOOSSW	WOOSHES	EIIJSTV	JIVIEST	EIILNOT	ETIOLIN
EHOPPRS	HOPPERS	EIIKKLN	INKLIKE	EIILNOV	OLIVINE
	SHOPPER	EIIKKNR	KINKIER	EIILNOZ	LIONIZE
EHOPPRT	PROPHET	EIIKLLP	LIPLIKE	EIILNPS	SPLENII
EHOPPRW	WHOPPER	EIIKLLS	KILLIES	EIILNRR	NIRLIER
EHOPPSS	SHOPPES	EIIKLMR	MILKIER	EIILNRS	INLIERS
EHOPRRY	ORPHREY	EIIKLMS	MISLIKE		RESILIN
EHOPRST	POTHERS	EIIKLNT	TINLIKE	EIILNRT	LINTIER
	STROPHE	EIIKLPS	PLISKIE		NITRILE
	THORPES	EIIKLRS	SILKIER	EIILNSS	INISLES
EHOPRSU	UPHROES	EIIKLSS	SILKIES	EIILNST	LINIEST

	LINTIES		TINNIES		WISPIER
EIILNTT	INTITLE	EIINNSW	INSINEW	EIIPSTT	PIETIST
EIILNTU	INUTILE	EIINNTV	INVENIT	EIIPTTT	PITTITE
EIILOPR	LIRIOPE	EIINNTW	INTWINE	EIIPTTU	PITUITE
EIILORR	ROILIER	EIINOPR	RIPIENO	EIIRRTZ	RITZIER
EIILORS	SOILIER	EIINOPS	PIONIES	EIIRSSS	SISSIER
EIILORV	RILIEVO		SINOPIE	EIIRSSV	VISIERS
EIILOST	IOLITES	EIINORR	IRONIER	EIIRSTV	REVISIT
	OILIEST	EIINORS	IONISER		STIVIER
EIILPPR	LIPPIER		IRONIES		VISITER
EIILPPS	LIPPIES		IRONISE	EIIRSTW	WIRIEST
EIILPST	SPILITE		NOISIER	EIIRSVZ	VIZIERS
EIILQSU	SILIQUE	EIINORZ	IONIZER	EIIRSWZ	WIZIERS
EIILRST	RILIEST		IRONIZE	EIIRTTW	WITTIER
	SILTIER	EIINOSS	IONISES	EIISSSS	SISSIES
EIILRSV	LIVIERS	EIINOST	INOSITE	EIISSTV	VISITES
EIILRSX	ELIXIRS	EIINOSZ	IONIZES	EIISSTX	SIXTIES
EIILSSV	VISILES	EIINPPR	NIPPIER	EIISSTZ	SIZEIST
EIILSTT	ELITIST	EIINPRS	INSPIRE		SIZIEST
EIILSTU	UTILISE		SNIPIER	EIISTTT	TITTIES
EIILSTW	WILIEST		SPINIER	EIISTUV	UVEITIS
EIILSZZ	LIZZIES	EIINPST	PINIEST	EIISTZZ	TIZZIES
EIILTUY	TUILYIE		PINITES	EIISVZZ	VIZZIES
EIILTUZ	TUILZIE		TIEPINS	EIJKKSU	JUKSKEI
	UTILIZE	EIINPTT	PENTITI	EIJKLRY	JERKILY
EIILTXY	EXILITY	EIINQRU	INQUIRE	EIJKNPR	PERJINK
EIIMMRS	MIMSIER	EIINQSU	QUINIES		PREJINK
EIIMMSS	MIMESIS	EIINQTU	INQUIET	EIJKNRS	JERKINS
EIIMMST	MISTIME	EIINRTT	NITRITE		JINKERS
EIIMMSX	IMMIXES		NITTIER	EIJKNRU	JUNKIER
EIIMNNS	MINNIES		TINTIER	EIJKNSU	JUNKIES
EIIMNPR	PRIMINE	EIINRTV	INVITER	EIJKOST	JOKIEST
EIIMNRT	INTERIM		VITRINE	EIJLLNY	INJELLY
	MINTIER	EIINRTW	TWINIER	EIJLLOR	JOLLIER
	TERMINI	EIINSSS	SEISINS	EIJLLOS	JOLLIES
EIIMNRV	MINIVER	EIINSSZ	SEIZINS	EIJLLST	JILLETS
EIIMNST	MINIEST	EIINSTT	SITTINE	EIJLORT	JOLTIER
EIIMNTV	MINIVET		TINIEST	EIJLORW	JOWLIER
EIIMNTY	NIMIETY	EIINSTU	UNITIES	EIJLRST	JILTERS
EIIMOSS	MEIOSIS		UNITISE	EIJMPRU	JUMPIER
EIIMPRS	PISMIRE	EIINSTV	INVITES	EIJMPST	JIMPEST
	PRIMSIE		VINIEST	EIJNNOS	ENJOINS
EIIMPRW	WIMPIER	EIINSTW	WINIEST	EIJNORS	JOINERS
EIIMPST	PIETISM	EIINSUZ	UNISIZE		REJOINS
EIIMPTY	IMPIETY	EIINTUV	UNITIVE	EIJNORT	JOINTER
EIIMRSS	MERISIS	EIINTUZ	UNITIZE	EIJNORY	JOINERY
	MISSIER	EIIOPTT	PETITIO	EIJNOST	JONTIES
EIIMRST	MIRIEST	EIIORST	RIOTISE	EIJNPRU	JUNIPER
	MISTIER	EIIORSV	IVORIES	EIJNRRU	INJURER
	RIMIEST	EIIORTZ	RIOTIZE	EIJNRSU	INJURES
EIIMSSS	MISSIES	EIIOSTZ	ZOISITE	EIJNSTY	JITNEYS
EIIMSST	MITISES	EIIPPPR	PIPPIER	EIJNTTW	TWINJET
	STIMIES	EIIPPRR	RIPPIER	EIJRSTT	JITTERS
EIIMSSV	MISSIVE	EIIPPRT	TIPPIER		TRIJETS
EIIMSSZ	SIZEISM	EIIPPRZ	ZIPPIER	EIJRTTY	JITTERY
EIIMSTT	MITIEST	EIIPPST	PIPIEST	EIJSSTU	JESUITS
EIIMSTX	MIXIEST	EIIPPSY	YIPPIES	EIJSSUV	JUSSIVE
EIINNNP	NINEPIN	EIIPRRS	SPIRIER	EIJSTTU	JUTTIES
EIINNNS	NINNIES	EIIPRRT	TRIPIER	EIKKLNR	KLINKER
EIINNOS	INOSINE	EIIPRRV	PRIVIER	EIKKLNS	KINKLES
EIINNPS	PINNIES	EIIPRST	PITIERS	EIKKLSY	KYLIKES
EIINNQU	QUININE		TIPSIER		SKYLIKE
EIINNRT	TINNIER	EIIPRSV	PRIVIES	EIKKMNR	KIRKMEN
EIINNST	INTINES	EIIPRSW	SWIPIER	EIKKNRS	SKINKER

EIKKOOR	KOOKIER	
EIKKRSS	SKRIKES	
EIKKRSY	YIKKERS	
EIKKRUY	YUKKIER	
EIKLLNW	INKWELL	
EIKLLOS	SKOLLIE	
EIKLLOW	OWLLIKE	
EIKLLRS	KILLERS	
	RESKILL	
EIKLLST	SKILLET	
EIKLMMN	MILKMEN	
EIKLMNN	LINKMEN	
EIKLMNR	KREMLIN	
EIKLMRS	MILKERS	
EIKLNNS	ENLINKS	
EIKLNNU	NUNLIKE	
EIKLNOS	SONLIKE	
EIKLNPR	PLINKER	
EIKLNRS	LINKERS	
	RELINKS	
	SLINKER	
EIKLNRT	TINKLER	
EIKLNRU	URNLIKE	
EIKLNRW	WINKLER	
	WRINKLE	
EIKLNSS	INKLESS	
	KINLESS	
	SILKENS	
EIKLNST	LENTISK	
	TINKLES	
EIKLNSU	SUNLIKE	
	UNLIKES	
EIKLNSV	KELVINS	
EIKLNSW	WELKINS	
	WINKLES	
EIKLNSY	SKYLINE	
EIKLNTT	KNITTLE	
EIKLNTU	NUTLIKE	
EIKLNTW	TWINKLE	
EIKLOOP	PLOOKIE	
EIKLOPT	POTLIKE	
EIKLOPU	PLOUKIE	
EIKLORY	YOLKIER	
EIKLOTY	TOYLIKE	
EIKLPRY	PERKILY	
EIKLPST	SKELPIT	
EIKLPSU	PUSLIKE	
EIKLPSY	PESKILY	
EIKLRST	KILTERS	
	KIRTLES	
	KLISTER	
EIKLRSU	SULKIER	
EIKLRTT	KITTLER	
EIKLSSS	KISSELS	
EIKLSSU	SULKIES	
EIKLSTT	KITTELS	
	KITTLES	
	SKITTLE	
EIKMMRR	KRIMMER	
EIKMMRS	KIMMERS	
	SKIMMER	
EIKMNNS	KINSMEN	
EIKMNOR	MONIKER	
EIKMNRS	MERKINS	

EIKMNSS	MISKENS	
EIKMNST	MISKENT	
EIKMNSW	MISKNEW	
EIKMORS	IRKSOME	
	SMOKIER	
EIKMOSS	SMOKIES	
EIKMOSY	MISYOKE	
EIKMPST	MISKEPT	
EIKMPSU	MUSPIKE	
EIKMRRS	SMIRKER	
EIKMRRU	MURKIER	
EIKMRSS	KIRMESS	
EIKMRST	MIRKEST	
EIKMRSU	MUSKIER	
EIKMSST	KISMETS	
EIKMSSU	MUSKIES	
EIKMSSY	MISKEYS	
EIKMSTU	KUMITES	
	MISTEUK	
EIKNNOR	EINKORN	
EIKNNOS	KINONES	
EIKNNPS	PINKENS	
EIKNNRS	SKINNER	
EIKNOOR	NOOKIER	
	ROOINEK	
EIKNOOS	NOOKIES	
EIKNOPS	PINKOES	
EIKNORV	INVOKER	
EIKNORW	WONKIER	
EIKNOSS	KENOSIS	
EIKNOSV	INVOKES	
EIKNPRR	PRINKER	
EIKNPRS	PERKINS	
EIKNPRU	PUNKIER	
EIKNPST	PINKEST	
EIKNPSU	PUNKIES	
	SPUNKIE	
EIKNPSY	PINKEYS	
EIKNRSS	SINKERS	
EIKNRST	REKNITS	
	SKINTER	
	STINKER	
	TINKERS	
EIKNRSW	SWINKER	
	WINKERS	
EIKNRTT	KNITTER	
	TRINKET	
EIKNSSU	SUNKIES	
EIKNSTT	KITTENS	
EIKNTTY	KITTENY	
EIKNTUZ	KUNZITE	
EIKOORR	ROOKIER	
EIKOORS	KOORIES	
	ROOKIES	
EIKOOST	STOOKIE	
EIKOPPR	PORKPIE	
EIKOPPS	KOPPIES	
EIKOPRR	PORKIER	
EIKOPRS	PORKIES	
EIKOPST	POKIEST	
EIKORST	ROKIEST	
EIKORSY	YORKIES	
EIKOSST	KETOSIS	
EIKPPRS	KIPPERS	

		SKIPPER
EIKPPST	SKIPPET	
EIKPRSS	SPIKERS	
EIKPRSY	SPIKERY	
EIKPSSS	SKEPSIS	
EIKRRSS	RISKERS	
EIKRRST	SKIRRET	
		SKIRTER
		STRIKER
EIKRSSS	KISSERS	
EIKRSST	STRIKES	
EIKRSSV	SKIVERS	
EIKRSTT	SKITTER	
EIKRSTU	TURKIES	
		TUSKIER
EIKSSTT	KITSETS	
EIKSSTW	WESKITS	
		WISKETS
EIKSSTY	SKYIEST	
EIKSTUY	YUKIEST	
EILLLOS	LOLLIES	
EILLMNU	MULLEIN	
EILLMOS	MOLLIES	
EILLMOT	MELILOT	
EILLMOU	MOUILLE	
EILLMRS	MILLERS	
EILLMST	MILLETS	
		MISTELL
EILLMSU	ILLUMES	
EILLMTU	MULLITE	
EILLNNP	PENNILL	
EILLNOS	LIONELS	
		NIELLOS
EILLNSS	ILLNESS	
EILLNST	LENTILS	
		LINTELS
		TELLINS
EILLNUV	LEVULIN	
EILLOPS	POLLIES	
EILLORU	ROUILLE	
EILLORW	LOWLIER	
EILLORZ	ZORILLE	
EILLOST	OILLETS	
		TOLLIES
EILLOSV	VILLOSE	
EILLOSW	WOLLIES	
EILLPPR	PREPILL	
EILLPRS	SPILLER	
EILLPSS	LIPLESS	
EILLPSU	PILULES	
EILLQTU	QUILLET	
EILLRRT	TRILLER	
EILLRSS	SILLERS	
EILLRST	RILLETS	
		STILLER
		TILLERS
		TRELLIS
EILLRSW	SWILLER	
		WILLERS
EILLRTT	LITTLER	
EILLSST	LISTELS	
EILLSSU	SULLIES	
EILLSTT	LITTLES	
EILLSTU	TUILLES	

EILLSTW	WILLEST
	WILLETS
EILLSWY	WILLEYS
EILMMNO	MOLIMEN
EILMMRS	LIMMERS
	SLIMMER
EILMMRU	LUMMIER
EILMNOO	OINOMEL
EILMNOS	LOMEINS
	MOLINES
EILMNOT	MOLINET
EILMNPS	PLENISM
EILMNRS	LIMNERS
	MERLINS
EILMNSS	SIMNELS
EILMNSU	EMULSIN
	LUMINES
	UNLIMES
EILMNSY	MYELINS
EILMOOS	MOOLIES
EILMOOV	MOOLVIE
EILMOPR	IMPLORE
EILMORR	LORIMER
EILMORS	MOILERS
EILMORT	MOTLIER
EILMOSS	LIMOSES
	LISSOME
	SMOILES
EILMOST	MOTILES
EILMPPS	PIMPLES
EILMPRS	LIMPERS
	PRELIMS
	RIMPLES
	SIMPLER
EILMPRU	LUMPIER
	PLUMIER
EILMPRY	PRIMELY
EILMPSS	SIMPLES
EILMPST	LIMPEST
	LIMPETS
EILMPSU	IMPULSE
EILMPSW	WIMPLES
EILMPSX	SIMPLEX
EILMPSY	LIMPSEY
EILMPTY	EMPTILY
EILMRRU	MURLIER
EILMRRY	MERRILY
EILMRSS	RIMLESS
	SMILERS
EILMRST	MILTERS
EILMRSU	MISRULE
EILMRSV	VERMILS
EILMRSY	MISERLY
	MISRELY
EILMRTY	LYMITER
EILMRVY	VERMILY
EILMSSS	MISSELS
EILMSST	MISTLES
	SMILETS
EILMSSU	MUESLIS
EILMSSY	MESSILY
	MILSEYS
	SMILEYS
EILMSTT	SMITTLE
EILMSTZ	MILTZES
EILMSZZ	MIZZLES
EILMUUV	ELUVIUM
EILNNOR	ONLINER
EILNNPU	PINNULE
EILNNRY	INNERLY
EILNNSS	INNLESS
EILNNST	LINNETS
EILNNSU	UNLINES
EILNNSW	WINNLES
EILNNSY	LINNEYS
EILNOOP	POLONIE
EILNOOR	LOONIER
EILNOOS	LOONIES
EILNOOV	VIOLONE
EILNOPP	PLENIPO
EILNOPR	PLERION
	PROLINE
EILNOPS	EPSILON
	PINOLES
EILNOPT	POINTEL
	PONTILE
	POTLINE
	TOPLINE
EILNORR	LORINER
EILNORS	NEROLIS
EILNORT	RETINOL
EILNOSS	ESLOINS
	INSOLES
	LESIONS
	LIONESS
EILNOST	ENTOILS
	LIONETS
	ONLIEST
EILNOSU	ELUSION
EILNOTU	ELUTION
	OUTLINE
EILNOTV	VIOLENT
EILNOTW	TOWLINE
EILNOVV	INVOLVE
EILNPPS	LIPPENS
	NIPPLES
EILNPRS	PILSNER
EILNPRU	PURLINE
EILNPSS	PENSILS
	SPINELS
	SPLINES
EILNPST	LEPTINS
	PINTLES
	PLENIST
EILNPSU	LINEUPS
	LUPINES
	SPINULE
	UNPILES
EILNPTY	INEPTLY
EILNPUV	VULPINE
EILNRST	LINTERS
	SLINTER
	SNIRTLE
EILNRSV	SILVERN
EILNRTY	INERTLY
EILNRVY	NERVILY
EILNSSS	SINLESS
EILNSST	ENLISTS
	LISTENS
	SILENTS
	TINSELS
EILNSSU	INSULSE
	SILENUS
EILNSSV	SNIVELS
EILNSSW	WINLESS
EILNSSY	LINSEYS
	LYSINES
EILNSTU	LUNIEST
	LUTEINS
	UNTILES
	UTENSIL
EILNSTV	VENTILS
EILNSTW	WESTLIN
	WINTLES
EILNSUV	UNLIVES
	UNVEILS
EILNSUX	LINUXES
EILNSUY	LUNYIES
EILNSVY	SYLVINE
EILNVXY	VIXENLY
EILOOPR	LOOPIER
EILOORS	ORIOLES
EILOORT	TROOLIE
EILOORW	WOOLIER
EILOOSS	LOOSIES
EILOOST	OOLITES
	OSTIOLE
	STOOLIE
EILOOSW	WOOLIES
EILOOTZ	ZOOLITE
EILOPPR	LOPPIER
EILOPPS	LOPPIES
EILOPPZ	ZEPPOLI
EILOPRS	SLOPIER
	SPOILER
EILOPRT	POITREL
	POLITER
EILOPST	PIOLETS
	PISTOLE
EILOPSU	PILEOUS
EILOPSV	PLOSIVE
EILOPTT	PLOTTIE
EILOPTX	EXPLOIT
EILORRS	LORRIES
EILORRU	LOURIER
EILORSS	LORISES
	LOSSIER
	RISSOLE
EILORST	ESTRIOL
	LOITERS
	TOILERS
EILORSU	LOURIES
	LOUSIER
	SOILURE
EILORSV	OLIVERS
	VIOLERS
EILORSW	LOWRIES
EILORTT	TORTILE
	TRIOLET
EILORTU	OUTLIER
EILORTV	OVERLIT
EILOSSV	SOLIVES

EILOSTT	LITOTES		RUTILES	EIMNOOX	EXOMION
	TOILETS	EILRSTY	STYLIER	EIMNOPR	PROMINE
EILOSTU	OUTLIES	EILRSUV	SURVEIL	EIMNOPS	IMPONES
EILOSTV	OLIVETS	EILRSUW	WURLIES		PEONISM
	VIOLETS	EILRSVY	LIVYERS	EIMNOPT	EMPTION
EILOSTW	OWLIEST		SILVERY		PIMENTO
EILOSTZ	ZLOTIES	EILRSZZ	SIZZLER	EIMNORS	MERINOS
EILOTUV	OUTLIVE	EILRTTY	LITTERY		MERSION
EILOTUW	OUTWILE		TRITELY	EIMNOSS	EONISMS
EILPPPY	PEPPILY	EILRTUV	RIVULET	EIMNOST	MESTINO
EILPPRR	RIPPLER	EILSSTT	STILETS		MOISTEN
EILPPRS	LIPPERS	EILSSTW	WITLESS		MONTIES
	RIPPLES	EILSSTY	STYLISE		SENTIMO
	SLIPPER	EILSSVW	SWIVELS	EIMNOSW	WINSOME
EILPPRT	RIPPLET	EILSSZZ	SIZZLES	EIMNOTY	OMNEITY
	TIPPLER	EILSTTT	TITTLES		OMNIETY
	TRIPPLE	EILSTTU	LUTITES	EIMNPSS	MISPENS
EILPPRU	PULPIER		TITULES	EIMNPST	EMPTINS
EILPPSS	PIPLESS	EILSTTV	VITTLES		PIMENTS
	SIPPLES	EILSTTY	STYLITE	EIMNPTU	PINETUM
EILPPST	STIPPLE		TESTILY	EIMNQSU	MESQUIN
	TIPPLES	EILSTVY	SYLVITE	EIMNRRU	MURRINE
EILPPSU	PILEUPS	EILSTYZ	STYLIZE	EIMNRST	ENTRISM
	UPPILES		ZESTILY		MINSTER
EILPPSW	SWIPPLE	EILSUVV	LUVVIES		MINTERS
EILPRSS	LISPERS	EILSWZZ	SWIZZLE		REMINTS
EILPRST	RESPLIT	EILSZZZ	ZIZZLES	EIMNRSU	MUREINS
	SPIRTLE	EILTWZZ	TWIZZLE		MURINES
	TRIPLES	EIMMMOS	MOMMIES		NEURISM
EILPRTT	TRIPLET	EIMMMST	MIMMEST	EIMNRSV	VERMINS
EILPRTX	TRIPLEX	EIMMMSU	MUMMIES	EIMNRTU	MINUTER
EILPRUU	PURLIEU	EIMMNRS	NIMMERS		MUNTRIE
EILPSSS	PLISSES	EIMMNSU	IMMUNES		UNMITER
EILPSST	STIPELS	EIMMOPS	POMMIES		UNMITRE
	TIPLESS	EIMMORS	MEMOIRS	EIMNRVY	VERMINY
EILPSSW	SWIPLES	EIMMOST	TOMMIES	EIMNSSS	SENSISM
EILPSSZ	ZIPLESS	EIMMOSV	MISMOVE	EIMNSST	MISSENT
EILPSTT	SPITTLE	EIMMPRR	PRIMMER	EIMNSSU	MINUSES
EILPSTU	PULIEST	EIMMPRU	PREMIUM	EIMNSTT	MITTENS
	PUTELIS	EIMMRRS	RIMMERS		SMITTEN
	STIPULE	EIMMRRT	TRIMMER	EIMNSTU	MINUETS
EILPSUY	SPULYIE	EIMMRRU	RUMMIER		MINUTES
EILPSUZ	SPULZIE	EIMMRSS	MERISMS		MISTUNE
EILPSZZ	PIZZLES		SIMMERS		MUNITES
EILPTTY	PETTILY	EIMMRST	MISTERM		MUTINES
EILQRTU	QUILTER	EIMMRSU	IMMURES	EIMNSTW	MISWENT
EILQRUU	LIQUEUR		MUMSIER	EIMNSUX	UNMIXES
EILQTUY	QUIETLY		RUMMIES	EIMNSZZ	MIZZENS
EILRRSU	LURRIES	EIMMRSW	SWIMMER	EIMNUZZ	MUEZZIN
	SURLIER	EIMMRSZ	ZIMMERS	EIMOORR	MOORIER
EILRRTW	TWIRLER	EIMMRUY	YUMMIER		ROOMIER
EILRSST	LISTERS	EIMMSST	SEMMITS	EIMOORS	ROOMIES
	RELISTS		TSIMMES	EIMOPPR	MOPPIER
EILRSSV	SILVERS	EIMMSTU	TUMMIES		POMPIER
	SLIVERS	EIMMSTZ	TZIMMES	EIMOPRR	PRIMERO
EILRSSW	SWILERS	EIMMSUY	YUMMIES	EIMOPRS	IMPOSER
EILRSTT	LITTERS	EIMNNOR	IRONMEN		PROMISE
	SLITTER	EIMNNOT	MENTION		SEMIPRO
	STILTER	EIMNOOR	IONOMER	EIMOPRV	IMPROVE
	TESTRIL		MOONIER	EIMOPRW	IMPOWER
	TILTERS	EIMNOOS	ISONOME	EIMOPSS	IMPOSES
	TITLERS		MOONIES		MOPSIES
EILRSTU	LUSTIER		NOISOME	EIMOPST	MOPIEST
	RULIEST	EIMNOOT	EMOTION		OPTIMES

	STOMPIE	EIMRSTU	MUSTIER	EINNTUW	UNTWINE
EIMOPSY	MYOPIES	EIMRSTY	MISTERY	EINOOPZ	EPIZOON
EIMORRW	WORMIER		SMYTRIE	EINOORS	EROSION
EIMORSS	ISOMERS	EIMRTTU	TERTIUM	EINOOST	ISOTONE
	MOISERS	EIMRTUV	VITREUM		TOONIES
	MOSSIER	EIMRTUX	MIXTURE	EINOOSZ	OZONISE
EIMORST	EROTISM	EIMRUZZ	MUZZIER	EINOOTW	TWOONIE
	MOISTER	EIMSSST	MISSETS	EINOOTZ	ZOONITE
	MORTISE	EIMSSSU	MISUSES	EINOOZZ	OZONIZE
	TRISOME	EIMSSSX	SEXISMS	EINOPPR	POPERIN
EIMORSU	MOUSIER	EIMSSTY	STYMIES	EINOPPS	PEPINOS
EIMORSV	VERISMO	EIMSTYZ	ZYMITES	EINOPRR	PORNIER
EIMORTT	MOTTIER	EIMUUVX	EXUVIUM	EINOPRS	ORPINES
	OMITTER	EINNNOS	NONNIES		PIONERS
EIMORTV	VOMITER	EINNNRS	RENNINS		PROINES
EIMORVX	OVERMIX	EINNOOS	IONONES	EINOPRT	POINTER
EIMOSSS	MOSSIES	EINNOPS	PENSION		PROTEIN
EIMOSST	MITOSES		PINONES		PTERION
	SOMITES		SPINONE		REPOINT
EIMOSSU	MOUSIES	EINNOPT	PONTINE		TROPINE
EIMOSTT	MOTIEST	EINNOQU	QUINONE	EINOPRV	PROVINE
	MOTTIES	EINNORS	RONNIES	EINOPSS	SPINOSE
	TITMOSE	EINNORT	INTONER	EINOPST	PINTOES
EIMOSTU	TIMEOUS		NOINTER		POINTES
EIMOSTV	MOTIVES		TERNION		PONTIES
EIMOSTX	EXOTISM	EINNORU	NOUNIER	EINOPSW	POWNIES
EIMOSTZ	MESTIZO		REUNION		WINESOP
EIMOSYZ	ISOZYME	EINNORV	ENVIRON	EINOPSY	PIONEYS
EIMOSZZ	MOZZIES	EINNOSS	SONNIES	EINOPTT	PENTITO
EIMOTTU	TIMEOUT	EINNOST	INTONES	EINOPTU	POUTINE
	TITMOSE		TENSION	EINOQUX	EQUINOX
EIMPRRS	PRIMERS	EINNOSV	VENISON	EINORRS	IRONERS
EIMPRRT	PRETRIM	EINNOSY	YONNIES		ROSINER
EIMPRRU	IMPURER	EINNOTT	NONETTI	EINORSS	ORNISES
	PRIMEUR		TONTINE		SENIORS
EIMPRSS	IMPRESS	EINNOVW	INWOVEN		SONERIS
	PREMISS	EINNPRS	PINNERS		SONSIER
	SIMPERS		SPINNER	EINORST	NORITES
	SPIREMS	EINNPRT	ENPRINT		OESTRIN
EIMPRST	IMPREST	EINNPRU	PUNNIER		ORIENTS
	PERMITS	EINNPST	PINNETS		STONIER
EIMPRSU	RUMPIES		SPINNET		TERSION
	SPUMIER		TENPINS		TRIONES
	UMPIRES	EINNPSY	SPINNEY	EINORSU	URINOSE
EIMPRTU	IMPUTER	EINNRRU	RUNNIER	EINORSV	ENVIROS
	TUMPIER	EINNRSS	SINNERS		RENVOIS
EIMPSST	MISSTEP	EINNRST	INTERNS		VERSION
EIMPSSU	SEPIUMS		TINNERS	EINORSW	SNOWIER
EIMPSTU	IMPETUS	EINNRSU	SUNNIER	EINORTT	TRITONE
	IMPUTES		UNREINS	EINORTU	ROUTINE
	UPTIMES		UNRISEN	EINORTW	NOWTIER
EIMPSTY	MISTYPE	EINNRSW	WINNERS		TOWNIER
EIMPSUY	YUMPIES	EINNRTV	VINTNER	EINORTZ	TRIZONE
EIMQSTU	MESQUIT	EINNRUV	UNRIVEN	EINOSSS	ESSOINS
EIMQTUZ	MEZQUIT	EINNSST	SENNITS		OSSEINS
EIMRRST	RETRIMS		SINNETS		SESSION
	TRIMERS	EINNSSU	SUNNIES	EINOSST	NOSIEST
EIMRRSU	MURRIES	EINNSSY	SINSYNE		SONTIES
EIMRSST	MISTERS	EINNSTT	INTENTS		STONIES
	SMITERS		TENNIST	EINOSSU	SINUOSE
EIMRSSU	MISUSER	EINNSTU	TUNNIES	EINOSSZ	SOZINES
	MUSSIER	EINNSTV	INVENTS	EINOSTT	SNOTTIE
	SURMISE	EINNSUW	UNSINEW		TONIEST
EIMRSSV	VERISMS	EINNSWY	SWINNEY		TONITES
EIMRSTT	METRIST				

EINOSTW	TOWNIES		UNWISER		SOUPIER
	TWONIES	EINRSVW	WIVERNS	EIOPRSX	PROXIES
EINOSTX	TOXINES	EINRSWY	SWINERY	EIOPRTT	POTTIER
EINOSUV	ENVIOUS	EINRTTU	NUTTIER	EIOPRTU	POUTIER
	NIVEOUS	EINRTTW	TWINTER	EIOPRTV	OVERTIP
	VEINOUS		WRITTEN		PIVOTER
EINOTTT	TOTIENT	EINRTUV	UNRIVET	EIOPSSS	POSSIES
EINPPRS	NIPPERS		VENTURI	EIOPSST	POSIEST
	SNIPPER	EINRTUW	UNWRITE		POSTIES
EINPPSS	PEPSINS	EINRTWY	WINTERY		POTSIES
EINPPST	SNIPPET	EINSSST	SENSIST		SEPIOST
EINPPSW	WIPPENS	EINSSSU	SINUSES		SOPITES
EINPRRT	PRINTER	EINSSSY	SYNESIS	EIOPSSU	POUSSIE
	REPRINT	EINSSTU	INTUSES	EIOPSTT	POTTIES
EINPRRU	UNRIPER	EINSSTV	INVESTS		SPOTTIE
EINPRSS	SNIPERS	EINSSTW	WISENTS		TIPTOES
EINPRST	NIPTERS		WITNESS	EIOPSTU	PITEOUS
	PTERINS	EINSSTY	TINSEYS	EIOPSTX	EXPOSIT
EINPRSU	PRUINES	EINSSUW	SUNWISE		POXIEST
	PURINES	EINSSWY	WINSEYS	EIOPSTY	ISOTYPE
	UPRISEN	EINSTTU	TUNIEST	EIOPSZZ	POZZIES
EINPRTU	REPUNIT	EINSTTW	ENTWIST	EIOPTUW	WIPEOUT
EINPSST	INSTEPS		TWINSET	EIOQRTU	QUOITER
	SPINETS	EINSTTY	TENSITY	EIOQTUX	QUIXOTE
EINPSSU	PUISNES	EINSTWY	WITNEYS	EIORRRS	SORRIER
	SUPINES	EINSUVW	UNWIVES	EIORRRT	RORTIER
EINPSTT	SPITTEN	EINSWZZ	WIZZENS		TERROIR
EINPSTU	PUNIEST	EINTTTW	TWITTEN	EIORRRW	WORRIER
	PUNTIES	EINTTUY	TENUITY	EIORRSS	ORRISES
EINPSTW	INSWEPT	EIOOPRR	ROOPIER		ROSIERS
EINPTTY	TINTYPE	EIOOPRV	POOVIER	EIORRST	RIOTERS
EINQRSU	REQUINS	EIOOPST	ISOTOPE		ROISTER
EINQRUU	UNIQUER	EIOOPSW	WOOPIES		RORIEST
EINQRUY	ENQUIRY	EIOORRT	ROOTIER	EIORRSV	REVISOR
EINQSSU	SEQUINS	EIOORST	OORIEST	EIORRSW	WORRIES
EINQSTU	INQUEST		ROOTIES	EIORRUV	OUVRIER
	QUINTES		SOOTIER	EIORRVV	REVIVOR
EINQSUU	UNIQUES		TOORIES	EIORSSS	SEISORS
EINQSUZ	QUINZES	EIOORTZ	ZOOTIER	EIORSST	ROSIEST
EINQTTU	QUINTET	EIOORWZ	WOOZIER		SIROSET
EINQTUU	UNQUIET	EIOOSST	OOSIEST		SORITES
EINRRSS	RINSERS	EIOOSTT	TOOTSIE		SORTIES
EINRRSU	INSURER	EIOOSTZ	OOZIEST		STORIES
	RUINERS		ZOOIEST		TOSSIER
EINRRTU	RUNTIER	EIOPPPR	POPPIER		TRIOSES
EINRSST	ESTRINS	EIOPPPS	POPPIES	EIORSSU	SERIOUS
	INSERTS	EIOPPRS	SOPPIER	EIORSSV	VIROSES
	SINTERS	EIOPPSS	POPSIES	EIORSSX	XEROSIS
EINRSSU	INSURES	EIOPPST	POTPIES	EIORSSZ	SEIZORS
	SUNRISE	EIOPQRU	PIROQUE	EIORSTT	STOITER
EINRSSV	VERSINS	EIOPRRS	PROSIER	EIORSTU	OURIEST
EINRSTT	ENTRIST	EIOPRRT	PIERROT		STOURIE
	RETINTS		PORTIER		TOURIES
	STINTER		PRERIOT		TOUSIER
	TINTERS	EIOPRRU	ROUPIER	EIORSTV	TORSIVE
EINRSTU	NUTSIER	EIOPRSS	POISERS	EIORSTW	OWRIEST
	TRIUNES		PROSSIE		TOWSIER
	UNITERS	EIOPRST	PERIOST	EIORTTT	TOTTIER
EINRSTV	INVERTS		PORIEST	EIORTTU	TOUTIER
	STRIVEN		PROSTIE	EIORTTV	TORTIVE
EINRSTW	TWINERS		REPOSIT		VIRETOT
	WINTERS		RIPOSTE	EIORTUV	VOITURE
EINRSTY	SINTERY		ROPIEST	EIORTUZ	TOUZIER
EINRSUW	UNWIRES	EIOPRSU	POURIES	EIORTWZ	TOWZIER

EIOSSTU	SOUTIES	EIQRSSU	RISQUES	EJKNSTU	JUNKETS
EIOSSTV	SOVIETS		SQUIERS	EJKOORY	JOOKERY
	STOVIES		SQUIRES	EJKORUY	JOUKERY
EIOSTTT	STOTTIE	EIQRSTU	QUERIST	EJLLORY	JOLLYER
	TOTTIES		REQUITS	EJLLOSY	JOLLEYS
EIOSTTU	TOUSTIE	EIQRSUV	QUIVERS	EJLORST	JOLTERS
EIOSTTW	TOWIEST	EIQRTTU	QUITTER		JOSTLER
EIOSTUV	OUTVIES	EIQRUVY	QUIVERY	EJLORSW	JOWLERS
EIOSTUZ	OUTSIZE	EIQRUZZ	QUIZZER	EJLOSST	JOSTLES
EIOSTVV	VOTIVES	EIQSTUU	QUIETUS	EJLOSSY	JOYLESS
EIPPPSU	PUPPIES	EIQSUZZ	QUIZZES	EJLSSTU	JUSTLES
EIPPQRU	QUIPPER	EIRRRST	STIRRER	EJMNRUY	JURYMEN
EIPPRRS	RIPPERS	EIRRSST	STIRRES	EJMOSST	JETSOMS
EIPPRRT	TRIPPER	EIRRSTT	RITTERS	EJMPRSU	JUMPERS
EIPPRSS	SIPPERS		TERRITS	EJNORRU	REJOURN
EIPPRST	TIPPERS	EIRRSTU	RUSTIER	EJNORUY	JOURNEY
EIPPRSU	PURPIES	EIRRSTV	STRIVER	EJNOSST	JETSONS
EIPPRSY	YIPPERS	EIRRSTW	WRITERS	EJNOSTT	JETTONS
EIPPRSZ	ZIPPERS	EIRRSZZ	RIZZERS	EJOORVY	OVERJOY
EIPPRTT	TRIPPET	EIRRTTU	RUTTIER	EJOOSSY	SOOJEYS
EIPPSST	SIPPETS	EIRSSST	RESISTS	EJOPPRT	PROPJET
EIPPSTT	TIPPETS		SISTERS	EJOPRST	PROJETS
EIPPSUY	YUPPIES	EIRSSSU	ISSUERS	EJOPRTT	JETPORT
EIPQSTU	PIQUETS		RISUSES	EJORSSS	JOSSERS
EIPRRSS	PRISERS	EIRSSTT	SITTERS	EJORSTT	JOTTERS
EIPRRST	STRIPER	EIRSSTU	SUITERS	EJORSTU	JOUSTER
EIPRRSU	PURSIER	EIRSSTV	STIVERS	EJOSTTU	OUTJEST
	UPRISER		STRIVES		OUTJETS
EIPRRSZ	PRIZERS		TREVISS	EJPRRUY	PERJURY
EIPRRTU	PURTIER		VERISTS	EJRSSTU	JUSTERS
EIPRRTY	TRIPERY	EIRSSUU	USURIES	EJSSTTU	JUSTEST
EIPRRUV	UPRIVER	EIRSSUV	VIRUSES	EKKLOOY	OLYKOEK
EIPRSSS	PISSERS	EIRSSUW	WUSSIER	EKKLRSU	SKULKER
	PRISSES	EIRSTTT	STRETTI	EKKOPSU	PUKEKOS
EIPRSST	ESPRITS		TITTERS	EKLLMSU	SKELLUM
	PERSIST		TRITEST	EKLLNOR	KNOLLER
	PRIESTS	EIRSTTU	TERTIUS	EKLLRRU	KRULLER
	SITREPS	EIRSTTV	TRIVETS	EKLMMSU	KUMMELS
	SPRIEST	EIRSTTW	RETWIST	EKLMSSU	MUSKLES
	SPRITES		TWISTER		SKELUMS
	STIRPES		WITTERS	EKLNOPR	PLONKER
	STRIPES	EIRSTUV	REVUIST	EKLNORS	SNORKEL
	TRIPSES		STUIVER	EKLNOSS	KELSONS
EIPRSSU	PUSSIER		VIRTUES		SLOKENS
	SUSPIRE	EIRSUVV	SURVIVE	EKLNOSU	LEUKONS
	UPRISES	EIRSUVW	SURVIEW	EKLNPRU	PLUNKER
EIPRSSW	SWIPERS	EIRTTTW	TWITTER	EKLNPSU	SPELUNK
EIPRSTT	PITTERS	EIRTTUV	VUTTIER	EKLNRSU	LUNKERS
	SPITTER	EISSSSW	SWISSES		RUNKLES
	TIPSTER	EISSSTU	SITUSES	EKLNSST	SKLENTS
EIPRSTU	PERITUS		TISSUES	EKLOORS	LOOKERS
	PUIREST	EISSSTW	SWITSES		RELOOKS
EIPRSTV	PRIVETS	EISSSTX	SEXISTS	EKLOPST	KLEPTOS
EIPRSTX	EXTIRPS	EISSSUW	WUSSIES	EKLOSTV	STOKVEL
EIPRSTY	PYRITES	EISSTTY	TYSTIES	EKLRRSU	LURKERS
	STRIPEY	EISSTUV	TUSSIVE	EKLRSSU	SULKERS
EIPRSUU	EURIPUS	EISSTUY	TISSUEY	EKLSTTU	SKUTTLE
EIPRTTU	PUTTIER	EISSTVW	SWIVETS	EKLSTUZ	KLUTZES
EIPRUVW	PURVIEW	EISSWZZ	SWIZZES	EKMMRSU	SKUMMER
EIPSSSU	PUSSIES	EISTTTU	TUTTIES	EKMNORW	WORKMEN
EIPSSTZ	SPITZES	EISTTUW	WETSUIT	EKMNORY	MONKERY
EIPSSUZ	UPSIZES	EJJMNUU	JEJUNUM	EKMNOSU	MUSKONE
EIPSTTU	PUTTIES	EJKMNNU	JUNKMEN	EKMNOSY	MONKEYS
EIPSTTY	TYPIEST	EJKNRSU	JUNKERS	EKMNPTU	UNKEMPT

EKMOOPS	MOPOKES	ELLMRSU	MULLERS	ELMNOST	LOMENTS
EKMORSS	SMOKERS	ELLMSTU	MULLETS		MELTONS
EKMRSTU	MURKEST	ELLMSUV	VELLUMS	ELMNOSY	MYELONS
EKMSSTU	MUSKETS	ELLMSUY	MULLEYS	ELMNOTU	MOULTEN
EKMSSUY	KUMYSES	ELLNNOT	TONNELL	ELMNOTY	YMOLTEN
EKNNOST	NEKTONS	ELLNOOW	WOOLLEN	ELMNPPU	PLUMPEN
EKNOORS	SNOOKER	ELLNOPS	POLLENS	ELMNPSU	LUMPENS
EKNOPSU	UNSPOKE	ELLNOPT	POLLENT		PLENUMS
EKNORST	REKNOTS	ELLNORS	ENROLLS	ELMNPUU	UNPLUME
	STONKER	ELLNOST	STOLLEN	ELMOOPP	POMPELO
	STROKEN	ELLNOSU	NOUSELL	ELMOOPS	POMELOS
	TONKERS	ELLNOSV	VELLONS	ELMOORT	TREMOLO
EKNORSW	KNOWERS	ELLNOSW	SWOLLEN	ELMOOSS	OSMOLES
EKNORSY	YONKERS	ELLNOVY	NOVELLY	ELMOOSY	MOOLEYS
EKNORTT	KNOTTER	ELLNOXY	XYLENOL	ELMOPRT	PREMOLT
EKNORTW	NETWORK	ELLNPSU	UNSPELL	ELMOPRY	POLYMER
EKNORUY	YOUNKER	ELLNSSU	SULLENS	ELMOPSU	PLUMOSE
EKNOSTY	STENOKY		UNSELLS		PUMELOS
EKNOSUY	UNYOKES	ELLNSUU	LUNULES	ELMOPSY	EMPLOYS
EKNPRSU	PUNKERS	ELLOOSW	WOOSELL	ELMORSS	MORSELS
EKNPSTU	PUNKEST	ELLOOSY	LOOSELY	ELMORST	MERLOTS
EKNPSUY	PUNKEYS	ELLOOTU	TOLUOLE		MOLTERS
EKNRTUY	TURNKEY	ELLOPRR	PROLLER	ELMORSU	EMULSOR
EKNSSTU	SUNKETS	ELLOPRS	POLLERS	ELMORTT	MOTTLER
EKOOPRT	PERTOOK		REPOLLS	ELMORTU	MOULTER
EKOOPRV	PROVOKE	ELLOPTU	POLLUTE	ELMOSST	MOLESTS
EKOORRS	KOREROS	ELLORRS	REROLLS	ELMOSSU	MOUSLES
EKOORRY	ROOKERY		ROLLERS	ELMOSSY	SMOYLES
EKOORST	STOOKER	ELLORRT	TROLLER	ELMOSTT	MOTTLES
	STROOKE	ELLORSS	SOLLERS	ELMOSTY	MOTLEYS
EKOORTW	KOTOWER		SORELLS	ELMOSUU	EMULOUS
EKOPPSU	UPSPOKE	ELLORST	TOLLERS	ELMOSUV	VOLUMES
EKOPRRS	PORKERS	ELLORTY	TROLLEY	ELMOSXY	OXYMELS
	PROKERS	ELLORVY	LOVERLY	ELMOSZZ	MOZZLES
EKOPRRW	PREWORK	ELLOSST	TOLSELS	ELMPPRU	PLUMPER
EKOPRUY	KOUPREY	ELLOSTU	OUTSELL	ELMPPSU	PEPLUMS
EKOPTTU	OUTKEPT		SELLOUT	ELMPRSU	LUMPERS
EKORRST	STROKER	ELLOSTX	EXTOLLS		RUMPLES
EKORRSW	REWORKS	ELLOSVY	VOLLEYS	ELMPRUY	PLUMERY
	WORKERS	ELLOSWY	YELLOWS	ELMRSTY	MYRTLES
EKORRSY	YORKERS	ELLOTTU	OUTTELL	ELMRTUU	MULTURE
EKORSST	STOKERS	ELLOTUW	OUTWELL	ELMRTUY	ELYTRUM
	STROKES	ELLOTUY	OUTYELL	ELMRUZZ	MUZZLER
EKORUYY	EURYOKY	ELLOVWY	VOWELLY	ELMSSSU	MUSSELS
EKPPSUU	SEPPUKU	ELLOWYY	YELLOWY		SUMLESS
EKPRSSY	KRYPSES	ELLPRSU	PULLERS	ELMSTUU	MUTUELS
EKRRSSY	SKRYERS	ELLPSTU	PULLETS		MUTULES
EKRSSTU	TUSKERS	ELLPSUW	UPSWELL	ELMSTUW	UMWELTS
EKRSTUY	TURKEYS		UPWELLS	ELMSUZZ	MUZZLES
EKRSUVY	KURVEYS	ELLPSUY	PULLEYS	ELNNOPU	NONUPLE
ELLLORR	LORRELL	ELMMOPS	POMMELS	ELNNORS	RONNELS
ELLLORS	LOLLERS	ELMMOPU	PUMMELO	ELNNOSS	NELSONS
ELLLOSZ	LOZELLS	ELMMORT	TROMMEL	ELNNRSU	RUNNELS
ELLLRSU	LULLERS	ELMMPRU	PLUMMER	ELNNRTU	TRUNNEL
ELLMNOO	MOELLON	ELMMPSU	PUMMELS	ELNNSTU	TUNNELS
ELLMNOP	POLLMEN	ELMMPTU	PLUMMET	ELNOOPT	PELOTON
ELLMNOT	TOLLMEN	ELMMRSU	SLUMMER	ELNOOSS	LOOSENS
ELLMNSU	MULLENS	ELMMRTU	TUMMLER	ELNOOSU	UNLOOSE
ELLMOOR	MORELLO	ELMMSTU	STUMMEL	ELNOOSW	WOOLENS
ELLMORR	MORRELL	ELMNOOT	MOONLET	ELNOOSY	LOONEYS
ELLMOSW	MELLOWS		TOOLMEN	ELNOOSZ	SNOOZLE
ELLMOWY	MELLOWY	ELMNOOW	WOOLMEN	ELNOPRU	PLEURON
ELLMPSU	PELLUMS	ELMNOPW	PLOWMEN	ELNOPRY	PRONELY
ELLMPUU	PLUMULE	ELMNORS	MERLONS	ELNOPST	LEPTONS

ELNOPSY	POLEYNS
ELNOPTU	OPULENT
ELNORSS	NORSELS
ELNORST	LENTORS
ELNORSU	NOURSLE
ELNORTY	ELYTRON
ELNOSSS	LESSONS
	SONLESS
ELNOSST	TELSONS
ELNOSSU	ENSOULS
	NOUSLES
ELNOSSV	SLOVENS
ELNOSSW	LOWNESS
ELNOSTT	TONLETS
ELNOSTU	LENTOUS
ELNOSTV	SOLVENT
ELNOSUV	UNLOVES
ELNOSUZ	ZONULES
ELNOSVY	LENVOYS
ELNOSZZ	NOZZLES
ELNOTTW	TOWNLET
ELNOTUZ	ZONULET
ELNOTVY	NOVELTY
ELNPSST	SPLENTS
ELNPSTU	PENULTS
ELNPSTY	PENTYLS
ELNRSSU	NURSLES
	RUNLESS
ELNRSTU	RUNLETS
ELNRSTY	STERNLY
ELNRSUU	UNRULES
ELNRSUZ	LUZERNS
ELNRUZZ	NUZZLER
ELNSSSU	SUNLESS
ELNSSSY	SELSYNS
	SLYNESS
ELNSTTU	NUTLETS
ELNSUZZ	NUZZLES
	SNUZZLE
ELOOPPS	POEPOLS
ELOOPRS	LOOPERS
	POOLERS
	RESPOOL
	SPOOLER
ELOOPSS	POSOLES
ELOOPST	POOTLES
ELOOPSZ	POZOLES
ELOORST	LOOTERS
	RETOOLS
	ROOTLES
	TOOLERS
ELOORSW	WOOLERS
ELOORTT	ROOTLET
	TOOTLER
ELOOSST	LOOSEST
	LOTOSES
ELOOSSW	WOOSELS
ELOOSTT	TOOLSET
	TOOTLES
ELOOSTU	OUTSOLE
ELOOSWY	WOOLSEY
ELOOTUV	OUTLOVE
ELOPPPS	POPPLES
ELOPPRS	LOPPERS
	PROPELS
ELOPPST	STOPPLE
	TOPPLES
ELOPPSU	POULPES
	UPSLOPE
ELOPPSY	POLYPES
ELOPRRS	PROLERS
ELOPRRU	PROULER
ELOPRRW	PROWLER
ELOPRRY	PYRROLE
ELOPRSS	PLESSOR
	SLOPERS
	SPLORES
ELOPRST	PETROLS
	REPLOTS
ELOPRSU	LEPROUS
	PELORUS
	PERLOUS
	SPORULE
ELOPRSV	PLOVERS
ELOPRSW	PLOWERS
	REPLOWS
ELOPRSX	PLEXORS
ELOPRSY	LEPROSY
ELOPRTT	PLOTTER
ELOPRTU	PLOUTER
	POULTER
ELOPRTW	PLOWTER
ELOPRTY	PROTYLE
ELOPRVY	OVERPLY
	PLOVERY
ELOPSST	TOPLESS
ELOPSSU	SOUPLES
ELOPSTT	POTTLES
ELOPSTU	TUPELOS
ELOPSTY	PEYOTLS
ELOPSTZ	PLOTZES
ELOPTUY	OUTYELP
ELORRSS	SORRELS
ELORRSW	WORRELS
ELORSSS	LESSORS
ELORSST	OSTLERS
	STEROLS
	TORSELS
ELORSSU	LOUSERS
ELORSSV	SOLVERS
ELORSTT	LOTTERS
	SETTLOR
	SLOTTER
	TOLTERS
ELORSTU	ELUTORS
	OUTLERS
	TROULES
ELORSTV	REVOLTS
ELORSTW	TROWELS
	WORTLES
ELORSUV	LOUVERS
	LOUVRES
	VELOURS
ELORSUY	ELUSORY
ELORSVW	WOLVERS
ELORSWY	YOWLERS
ELORTTY	LOTTERY
ELORTVY	OVERTLY
ELOSSTU	LOTUSES
	SOLUTES
	TOUSLES
ELOSSTW	LOWSEST
	SLOWEST
ELOSSTY	SYSTOLE
	TOLSEYS
	TOYLESS
	TYLOSES
ELOSSVW	VOWLESS
ELOSSXY	XYLOSES
ELOSSZZ	SOZZLES
ELOSTTU	OUTLETS
ELOSTTY	TYLOTES
ELOSTUU	LUTEOUS
ELOSTUV	VOLUTES
ELOSTUZ	TOUZLES
ELOSTYZ	TOLZEYS
ELOSWYY	YOWLEYS
ELOSWZZ	SWOZZLE
ELPPRRU	PURPLER
ELPPRSU	PULPERS
	PURPLES
	REPULPS
	SUPPLER
ELPPSSU	SUPPLES
ELPQSUU	PULQUES
ELPRRSU	PURLERS
	SLURPER
ELPRSSU	PULSERS
ELPRSTU	SPURTLE
ELPRSUV	PULVERS
ELPRTUU	PULTURE
ELPRUZZ	PUZZLER
ELPSSSU	PLUSSES
	PUSSELS
ELPSSUU	LUPUSES
ELPSSUY	PUSLEYS
	PUSSLEY
	SPULYES
ELPSTUU	PLUTEUS
	PUSTULE
ELPSUZZ	PUZZELS
	PUZZLES
ELRRSTU	RUSTLER
ELRRTTU	TURTLER
ELRSSSU	RUSSELS
ELRSSTU	LUSTERS
	LUSTRES
	RESULTS
	RUSTLES
	SUTLERS
	ULSTERS
ELRSSTY	STYLERS
ELRSTTU	TURTLES
ELRSTTY	TETRYLS
ELRSTUY	SUTLERY
ELRSTWY	SWELTRY
ELRSUWY	WURLEYS
ELRSUWZ	WURZELS
ELRTTUY	UTTERLY
ELRTUUV	VULTURE
ELSSSTU	TUSSLES
ELSSSUU	LUSUSES

ELSSTTU	SUTTLES	EMNRRUY	UNMERRY	EMRSSTU	ESTRUMS
ELSSTTY	STYLETS	EMNRSSU	RUMNESS		MUSTERS
ELSSTYY	SYSTYLE	EMNRSTU	MUNSTER		STUMERS
ELSUWZZ	WUZZLES		MUNTERS	EMRSTTU	MUTTERS
EMMMOST	MOMMETS		STERNUM	EMRSTYY	MYSTERY
EMMMRSU	MUMMERS	EMOOPRS	OOSPERM	EMSSSTY	SYSTEMS
EMMMRUY	MUMMERY	EMOOPRT	PROMOTE	ENNNOPS	PENNONS
EMMNNOS	MNEMONS	EMOOPRY	POMEROY	ENNNOSW	NONNEWS
EMMNOOR	MONOMER	EMOORRS	MOROSER	ENNNRUY	NUNNERY
	MOORMEN		ROOMERS	ENNOOPR	PRENOON
EMMNOOT	MOMENTO	EMOORST	MOOTERS	ENNOORS	NOONERS
	MOOTMEN	EMOORSU	UROSOME	ENNOORT	NORTENO
EMMNORY	MERONYM	EMOOSSS	OSMOSES	ENNOORZ	NONZERO
EMMNOST	MOMENTS	EMOOSTT	MOOTEST	ENNOOTT	NONETTO
	MONTEMS		MOTTOES	ENNORST	STONERN
EMMNOTU	OMENTUM		TOOMEST		TONNERS
EMMNOTY	METONYM	EMOOSTW	TWOSOME	ENNORSU	NEURONS
EMMOOTY	MYOTOME	EMOOSTY	MYOSOTE		NONUSER
EMMOPRR	PROMMER		TOYSOME	ENNORSW	RENOWNS
EMMORSS	MOMSERS	EMOOSXY	OXYSOME		WONNERS
EMMORSZ	MOMZERS	EMOOTUV	OUTMOVE	ENNORTU	NEUTRON
EMMOSST	MESTOMS	EMOPPRS	MOPPERS	ENNORUV	UNROVEN
EMMOSSU	MOMUSES	EMOPPST	MOPPETS	ENNOSST	SONNETS
	MOUSMES	EMOPPSY	POMPEYS		STONNES
EMMOSYZ	ZYMOMES	EMOPPTU	UPTEMPO		TENSONS
EMMPRSU	MUMPERS	EMOPRRS	ROMPERS	ENNOSSU	NONUSES
EMMPSTU	METUMPS	EMOPRST	STOMPER	ENNOSSW	NOWNESS
EMMRRSU	RUMMERS		TROMPES	ENNOSTU	NEUSTON
EMMRSSU	SUMMERS	EMOPRSU	SUPREMO	ENNOSTW	NEWTONS
EMMRSTU	RUMMEST	EMOPSSU	MOPUSES	ENNOSTZ	TENZONS
EMMRSUY	SUMMERY	EMOPSSY	MYOPSES	ENNOUVW	UNWOVEN
EMMSSUU	MUSEUMS	EMOQSSU	MOSQUES	ENNPRSU	PUNNERS
EMNNOOR	MONERON	EMORRST	STORMER	ENNPSTU	PUNNETS
EMNNOSW	SNOWMEN		TERMORS		UNSPENT
EMNNOWW	NEWMOWN		TREMORS	ENNRRSU	RUNNERS
EMNOOPT	METOPON	EMORRSU	MORSURE	ENNRSTU	RUNNETS
EMNOORS	MOONERS	EMORRSW	WORMERS		STUNNER
EMNOORT	MONTERO	EMORRWY	WORMERY	ENNRSUW	WUNNERS
EMNOOSS	MONOSES	EMORSSS	MOSSERS	ENNSSTU	UNNESTS
EMNOOST	MOONSET	EMORSST	MOTSERS	ENNSTTU	UNTENTS
EMNOOSY	NOYSOME	EMORSSU	MOUSERS	ENNSTUU	UNTUNES
EMNOOTY	ENOMOTY		SMOUSER	ENNSTYY	SYNTENY
EMNOPPR	PROPMEN	EMORSTU	MOUTERS	ENNTTUY	UNTENTY
EMNOPRT	PORTMEN		OESTRUM	ENOOPPR	PROPONE
EMNOPST	POSTMEN	EMORSUV	MEVROUS	ENOOPRS	OPERONS
	TOPSMEN	EMORSUY	MOUSERY		SNOOPER
EMNOPSU	SPUMONE	EMOSSSU	MOUSSES	ENOOPSY	SPOONEY
EMNOPSY	EPONYMS		SMOUSES	ENOORSS	NOOSERS
EMNOPYY	EPONYMY	EMOSSTT	MOSTEST		SEROONS
EMNORRU	MOURNER	EMOSSYZ	ZYMOSES		SOONERS
EMNORSS	SERMONS	EMOSTTT	MOTETTS	ENOORST	ENROOTS
EMNORST	MENTORS	EMOSTVZ	ZEMSTVO	ENOORSU	ONEROUS
	MONSTER	EMOTTTU	TETOTUM	ENOORSW	SWOONER
	MONTRES	EMOTUZZ	MEZUZOT	ENOORSZ	SNOOZER
EMNORTT	TORMENT	EMPPRSU	PUMPERS	ENOOSST	SOONEST
EMNORTU	MONTURE		REPUMPS	ENOOSSZ	SNOOZES
	MOUNTER	EMPPSTU	MUPPETS	ENOOSTT	TESTOON
	REMOUNT	EMPRSTU	RESTUMP	ENOOSTU	UNSOOTE
EMNOSST	STEMSON		STUMPER	ENOOTXY	OXYTONE
EMNOSTU	UNSMOTE		SUMPTER	ENOPPSU	UNPOPES
EMNOSTY	ETYMONS	EMPRTTU	TRUMPET	ENOPRRS	PERRONS
EMNOSXY	EXONYMS	EMPSSTU	SEPTUMS	ENOPRRU	PRONEUR
EMNPSSU	PENSUMS	EMRRSTU	STURMER	ENOPRRW	PREWORN
EMNRRSU	MURRENS	EMRRSUY	MURREYS	ENOPRSS	PERSONS

ENOPRST	POSTERN	ENPSTUW	UNSWEPT	EOPPRSY	PYROPES
	PRONEST	ENRRSSU	NURSERS		YOPPERS
ENOPRSU	UNROPES	ENRRSTU	RETURNS	EOPPSSU	SUPPOSE
ENOPRSY	PROYNES		TURNERS	EOPRRSS	PRESSOR
	PYRONES	ENRRSUU	UNSURER		PROSERS
ENOPRTT	PORTENT	ENRRSUY	NURSERY	EOPRRST	PORTERS
ENOPRTY	ENTROPY	ENRRTUU	NURTURE		PRESORT
ENOPSST	POSNETS		UNTRUER		PRETORS
	STEPSON	ENRRTUY	TURNERY		REPORTS
ENOPSTT	POTENTS	ENRRSTU	UNRESTS		SPORTER
ENOPSUX	XENOPUS	ENRSSWY	WRYNESS	EOPRRSU	POURERS
ENOPSWY	POWNEYS	ENRSTTU	ENTRUST		REPOURS
ENOQTUU	UNQUOTE		NUTTERS	EOPRRSV	PROVERS
ENORRSS	SNORERS	ENRSUZZ	NUZZERS	EOPRRTU	TROUPER
	SORNERS	ENRSVWY	WYVERNS	EOPRSSS	POSSERS
ENORRST	SNORTER	ENRTTUY	NUTTERY		PROSSES
ENORRSZ	RONZERS	ENSSSTU	SUNSETS	EOPRSST	PORTESS
ENORRTT	TORRENT	EOOOPRS	OOSPORE		POSTERS
ENORRUV	OVERRUN	EOOPPRS	OPPOSER		PRESTOS
	RUNOVER		POOPERS		REPOSTS
ENORSSS	SENSORS		PROPOSE		RESPOTS
ENORSST	NESTORS	EOOPPRV	POPOVER		STOPERS
	STONERS	EOOPPSS	OPPOSES	EOPRSSU	POSEURS
	TENSORS	EOOPPRS	SPOORER		SEROPUS
		EOOPRRT	PROTORE		SOUPERS
ENORSSW	WORSENS		TROOPER	EOPRSSW	PROWESS
ENORSSY	SENSORY	EOOPRSS	POROSES	EOPRSSY	OSPREYS
ENORSTT	ROTTENS	EOOPRST	POOREST		PYROSES
	SNOTTER		POOTERS	EUPRSTT	POTTERS
	STENTOR		STOOPER		PROTEST
ENORSTU	TENOURS	EOOPRSW	SWOOPER		SPOTTER
	TONSURE	EOOPRTU	OUTROPE	EOPRSTU	PETROUS
ENORSTY	TYRONES	EOOPRTV	OVERTOP		POSTURE
ENORSUV	NERVOUS	EOOPRTW	TOWROPE		POUTERS
ENORSUW	UNSWORE	EOOPRVY	POOVERY		PROTEUS
ENORSUZ	ZONURES	EOOPRYZ	ZOOPERY		SEPTUOR
ENORSVY	RENVOYS	EOOPSST	STOOPES		SPOUTER
ENORSZZ	NOZZERS	EOOPSSW	WOOPSES		TROUPES
ENORTUW	UNWROTE	EOOPTYZ	ZOOTYPE	EOPRSTW	POWTERS
ENORTUY	TOURNEY	EOORRSS	ROOSERS		PROWEST
ENOSSST	SESTONS	EOORRST	ROOSTER	EOPRSTX	EXPORTS
ENOSSTT	OSTENTS		ROOTERS	EOPRSTZ	POTZERS
	TESTONS		TOREROS	EOPRSUU	POURSUE
ENOSSTU	OUTNESS	EOORRVW	ROWOVER		UPROUSE
	TONUSES	EOORSSS	SOROSES	EOPRSUV	OVERSUP
ENOSSTW	TWONESS	EOORSTT	TOOTERS	EOPRSUW	POURSEW
ENOSSTX	SEXTONS	EOORSVW	OVERSOW	EOPRTTY	POTTERY
ENOSSUW	SWOUNES	EOORTUW	OUTWORE	EOPRTUY	EUTROPY
ENOSSWW	SWOWNES	EOOSSST	OSTOSES	EOPRTVY	POVERTY
ENOSTTU	STOUTEN	EOOSSSU	OSSEOUS	EOPSSSS	POSSESS
	TENUTOS	EOOSSTT	TOOTSES	EOPSSST	POSSETS
ENOSTUU	TENUOUS	EOOSTWZ	WOOTZES	EOPSSSU	POUSSES
ENOTTUW	OUTWENT	EOOTTUV	OUTVOTE		SPOUSES
ENPPRSU	PRENUPS	EOPPPRS	POPPERS	EOPSSTX	SEXPOTS
ENPRRSU	PRUNERS	EOPPPST	POPPETS	EOPSTTU	OUTSTEP
	SPURNER	EOPPRRS	PROPERS		TOUPETS
ENPRSSU	SPURNES		PROSPER	EOPSTTW	STEWPOT
ENPRSTU	PUNSTER	EOPPRSS	OPPRESS	EOPTTUW	OUTWEPT
	PUNTERS		PORPESS	EOQRRTU	TORQUER
ENPRSUU	UNPURSE	EOPPRST	POPSTER	EOQRSTU	QUESTOR
ENPRSWY	PREWYNS		STOPPER		QUOTERS
ENPSSSU	SUSPENS		TOPPERS		ROQUETS
ENPSSTU	UNSTEPS	EOPPRSU	PURPOSE		TORQUES
ENPSTTU	STUPENT	EOPPRSW	SWOPPER	EOQSTTU	TOQUETS
ENPSTUU	TUNEUPS				

EORRRST	RORTERS	**EOSSUYZ**	SOYUZES	**FFHHISU**	HUFFISH
	TERRORS	**EOSTTTW**	WOTTEST	**FFHIINS**	FINFISH
EORRSSS	ROSSERS	**EPPPSTU**	PUPPETS	**FFHIISY**	FISHIFY
EORRSST	RESORTS	**EPPRRTU**	PRERUPT	**FFHIKNU**	HUFFKIN
	ROSTERS	**EPPRRUU**	PURPURE	**FFHILSU**	FISHFUL
	SORTERS	**EPPRSSU**	SUPPERS	**FFHILTY**	FIFTHLY
	STORERS	**EPPSSTU**	UPSTEPS	**FFHILUY**	HUFFILY
EORRSSU	ROUSERS	**EPPSTUW**	UPSWEPT	**FFHIMSU**	MUFFISH
EORRSTT	RETORTS	**EPRRRSU**	SPURRER	**FFHIOST**	TOFFISH
	ROTTERS	**EPRRSSU**	PURSERS	**FFHIOSX**	FOXFISH
	STERTOR	**EPRRSTU**	SPURTER	**FFHOOSW**	SHOWOFF
	TORRETS	**EPRRSUU**	PURSUER	**FFHORSS**	SHROFFS
EORRSTU	RETOURS		USURPER	**FFHOSTU**	SHUTOFF
	ROUSTER	**EPRRSUY**	SPURREY	**FFIILMY**	MIFFILY
	ROUTERS	**EPRRTUU**	RUPTURE	**FFIINST**	TIFFINS
	TOURERS	**EPRSSSU**	PUSSERS	**FFIISUZ**	ZIFFIUS
	TROUSER	**EPRSSTU**	UPRESTS	**FFIKLSS**	SKLIFFS
EORRSTV	TROVERS	**EPRSSTY**	SPRYEST	**FFILLLU**	FULFILL
EORRSTW	STROWER	**EPRSSUU**	PURSUES	**FFILLSU**	FULFILS
EORRSTY	ROYSTER	**EPRSSUW**	PURSEWS	**FFILNSY**	SNIFFLY
	STROYER	**EPRSTTU**	PUTTERS	**FFILOST**	FILFOTS
EORRSZZ	ROZZERS		SPUTTER	**FFILOUZ**	ZUFFOLI
EORRTTT	TROTTER	**EPRSTUU**	PUTURES	**FFILPSS**	SPLIFFS
EORRTTU	TORTURE	**EPRSUVY**	PURVEYS	**FFILPUY**	PUFFILY
	TROUTER	**EQRSTWY**	QWERTYS	**FFILRTY**	FRITFLY
EORSSST	TOSSERS	**ERRSSTU**	RUSTRES	**FFILSTU**	FISTFUL
EORSSSU	SOURSES		TRUSSER	**FFILSTY**	STIFFLY
EORSSTU	ESTROUS	**ERRSSUU**	USURERS	**FFIMNSU**	MUFFINS
	OESTRUS	**ERRSSUY**	SURREYS	**FFINNSU**	NUFFINS
	OUSTERS	**ERRSTTU**	RUTTERS	**FFINOOT**	FINFOOT
	SOUREST		TRUSTER	**FFINOPS**	SPINOFF
	SOUTERS		TURRETS	**FFINOPT**	PONTIFF
	STOURES	**ERRSTTY**	TRYSTER	**FFINPSU**	PUFFINS
	TOUSERS	**ERSSSTU**	RUSSETS	**FFINRSU**	RUFFINS
	TROUSES		TRUSSES	**FFIOPRS**	RIPOFFS
	TUSSORE		TUSSERS	**FFIOPST**	TIPOFFS
EORSSTV	STOVERS	**ERSSSUU**	USURESS	**FFIORTY**	FORTIFY
	VOTRESS	**ERSSTTU**	TUTRESS	**FFIOSST**	SOFFITS
EORSSTW	SOWTERS	**ERSSTTY**	TRYSTES	**FFIQSUY**	SQUIFFY
	STOWERS	**ERSSTUU**	SUTURES	**FFIRTUY**	FRUTIFY
	STOWRES	**ERSSTUY**	RUSSETY	**FFJMOPU**	JUMPOFF
	TOWSERS	**ERSSTXY**	XYSTERS	**FFKLORU**	FORKFUL
	WORSETS	**ERSSUVY**	SURVEYS	**FFLLOOU**	LOOFFUL
EORSSTY	OYSTERS	**ERSTTTU**	STUTTER	**FFLMORU**	FORMFUL
	STOREYS	**ERSTTUX**	URTEXTS	**FFLNSUY**	SNUFFLY
EORSSTZ	ZOSTERS	**FFFGINU**	FUFFING	**FFLOOUZ**	ZUFFOLO
EORSSWW	WOWSERS	**FFFILOT**	LIFTOFF	**FFLOSTY**	FYLFOTS
EORSTTT	STOTTER	**FFFLOSY**	FLYOFFS	**FFNORSU**	RUNOFFS
	STRETTO	**FFGGINO**	GOFFING	**FFNORTU**	TURNOFF
	TOTTERS	**FFGHINU**	HUFFING	**FFOOPST**	STOPOFF
EORSTTU	OUTSERT	**FFGIIMN**	MIFFING	**FFOPSTU**	OFFPUTS
	STOUTER	**FFGIINN**	NIFFING		PUTOFFS
	TOUTERS	**FFGIINR**	GRIFFIN	**FFRRSUU**	FURFURS
			RIFFING	**FGGGIIN**	FIGGING
EORSTTW	SWOTTER	**FFGIINT**	TIFFING	**FGGGINO**	FOGGING
EORSTTX	EXTORTS	**FFGILNU**	LUFFING	**FGGGINU**	FUGGING
EORSTTY	ROSETTY	**FFGIMNU**	MUFFING	**FGGHIIS**	FISHGIG
EORSTUX	SEXTUOR	**FFGINOR**	GRIFFON	**FGGIINT**	GIFTING
EORSUVY	VOYEURS	**FFGINOS**	GONIFFS	**FGGIISS**	FISGIGS
			OFFINGS	**FGGIISZ**	FIZGIGS
EORTTTY	TOTTERY	**FFGINPU**	PUFFING	**FGGIIZZ**	FIZZGIG
EORTTUY	TUTOYER	**FFGINRU**	RUFFING	**FGGILNO**	GOLFING
EOSSSST	STOSSES	**FFGLOOS**	LOGOFFS	**FGGILNU**	FUGLING
EOSSSSW	SOWSSES	**FFGLRUY**	GRUFFLY		GULFING
EOSSTTU	OUTSETS				
	SETOUTS				

FGGILOY	FOGGILY			FHILOOS	FOOLISH
FGGILUY	FUGGILY	FGILNOY	FOYLING	FHILOSW	WOLFISH
FGGINOO	GOOFING	FGILNPU	UPFLING	FHILPSU	SHIPFUL
FGGINOR	FORGING	FGILNPY	FLYPING	FHILPTU	PITHFUL
FGGINOW	GOWFING	FGILNRU	FURLING	FHILSUW	WISHFUL
FGGINUU	FUGUING	FGILNSU	INGULFS	FHINOSU	FUSHION
FGHHIOS	HOGFISH	FGILNSY	FLYINGS	FHINRSU	FURNISH
FGHIINS	FISHING	FGILNTU	FLUTING	FHINSSU	SUNFISH
FGHIINT	INFIGHT	FGILNTY	FLYTING	FHINSTU	UNSHIFT
FGHIIPS	PIGFISH	FGILNUX	FLUXING	FHIOOST	OOFTISH
FGHILST	FLIGHTS	FGILOOY	GOOFILY	FHIOPPS	FOPPISH
FGHILSU	SIGHFUL	FGILORY	GLORIFY	FHIOPSX	FOXSHIP
FGHILTY	FLIGHTY	FGIMNOR	FORMING	FHIORRY	HORRIFY
FGHIMNU	HUMFING	FGIMOSY	FOGYISM	FHIOSST	SOFTISH
FGHINOO	HOOFING	FGINNNO	FONNING	FHIOSTU	OUTFISH
FGHINOU	HOUFING	FGINNNU	FUNNING	FHIPPSU	PUPFISH
FGHINOW	HOWFING	FGINNOY	FOYNING	FHIPSTU	UPSHIFT
FGHIOSY	FOGYISH	FGINOOR	ROOFING	FHIRSST	SHRIFTS
FGHIRST	FRIGHTS	FGINOOT	FOOTING	FHIRSTT	THRIFTS
FGHNOOR	FOGHORN	FGINOOW	WOOFING	FHIRTTY	THRIFTY
FGHORUY	FROUGHY	FGINOPP	FOPPING	FHIRTUY	THURIFY
FGHOTUY	FOUGHTY	FGINOPU	POUFING	FHISSSU	HUSSIFS
FGIIKNN	FINKING	FGINORS	FROINGS	FHISSTU	SHUFTIS
	KNIFING	FGINORT	FORTING	FHKORTU	FUTHORK
FGIIKNR	FIRKING	FGINOST	SOFTING	FHLNORU	HORNFUL
FGIIKNS	FISKING	FGINOSW	SOWFING	FHLNSUU	UNFLUSH
FGIILLN	FILLING	FGINOSX	FOXINGS	FHLOOSY	SHOOFLY
FGIILMN	FILMING	FGINRRU	FURRING	FHLOPSU	SHOPFUL
FGIILNO	FOILING	FGINRSU	SURFING	FHLPSUU	PUSHFUL
FGIILNR	RIFLING	FGINRSY	FRYINGS	FHLRTUU	HURTFUL
FGIILNS	FILINGS	FGINRTU	TURFING		RUTHFUL
FGIILNT	FLITING	FGINSSU	FUSSING	FHNOTUX	FOXHUNT
	LIFTING	FGINSTU	FUSTING	FHOOORS	FORHOOS
FGIILNX	FLIXING	FGINTTU	TUFTING	FHOOORT	HOOFROT
FGIILNY	LIGNIFY	FGINTUZ	FUTZING	FHOOOTT	HOTFOOT
FGIIMNR	FIRMING	FGINUZZ	FUZZING	FHOORSW	FORHOWS
FGIINNN	FINNING	FGIORST	FRIGOTS	FHORSTU	FOURTHS
FGIINNO	FOINING	FGIORTW	FIGWORT	FIIIKNN	FINIKIN
FGIINNS	FININGS	FGISTUU	FUGUIST	FIIKNRS	FIRKINS
FGIINRR	FIRRING	FGJLSUU	JUGFULS	FIIKNYZ	ZINKIFY
FGIINRS	FIRINGS		JUGSFUL	FIILLMO	MILFOIL
FGIINRT	RIFTING	FGLLNUU	LUNGFUL	FIILLMY	FILMILY
FGIINRY	NIGRIFY	FGLLOWY	GLOWFLY	FIILLNS	INFILLS
FGIINRZ	FRIZING	FGLMSUU	MUGFULS	FIILLPS	FILLIPS
FGIINST	FISTING	FGLNORU	FURLONG	FIILLSU	FUSILLI
	SIFTING	FGLNOSU	SONGFUL	FIILNOT	TINFOIL
FGIINSX	FIXINGS	FGLNPUU	UPFLUNG	FIILNTY	NIFTILY
FGIINSY	SIGNIFY	FGLOOUY	UFOLOGY	FIILPRS	RIFLIPS
FGIINTT	FITTING	FGLORSU	FULGORS	FIILPTU	PITIFUL
	TIFTING	FGLORUU	FULGOUR	FIILQUY	LIQUIFY
FGIINZZ	FIZZING	FGLOTUY	GOUTFLY	FIIMMNU	INFIMUM
FGIKLNU	FLUKING	FGLSTUU	GUSTFUL	FIIMNRS	INFIRMS
FGIKNNU	FUNKING		GUTFULS	FIIMSST	MISFITS
FGIKNOR	FORKING		GUTSFUL	FIINORS	FIORINS
FGIKNSY	SKYFING	FGNOORU	FOURGON	FIINOSS	FISSION
FGILLNU	FULLING	FGNORSY	GRYFONS	FIINRTY	NITRIFY
FGILMNU	FLUMING	FGNOSUU	FUNGOUS	FIIOPST	POSITIF
FGILNOO	FOOLING	FHHLSUU	HUSHFUL	FIIPSTY	TIPSIFY
FGILNOP	FOPLING	FHIILMS	FILMISH	FIIRTVY	VITRIFY
FGILNOR	ROLFING	FHIILSY	FISHILY	FIJLLOY	JOLLIFY
FGILNOT	LOFTING	FHIILTY	LITHIFY	FIJSTUY	JUSTIFY
FGILNOU	FOULING	FHIINPS	PINFISH	FIKKLNO	KINFOLK
FGILNOW	FLOWING	FHIKLOS	FOLKISH	FIKLLSU	SKILFUL
	FOWLING	FHILLSU	FULLISH	FIKLLUY	FLUKILY

FIKLNOW	WOLFKIN	FIOORSU	FURIOSO	FOORSSS	FOSSORS
FIKLNSU	SKINFUL	FIOPRST	FORPITS	FOORTTX	FOXTROT
FIKLNUY	FUNKILY		PROFITS	FOPSSTU	FUSSPOT
FIKLRSU	RISKFUL		SPORTIF	FORRSUW	FURROWS
FIKLSTU	KISTFUL	FIOPRSY	PROSIFY	FORRUWY	FURROWY
	LUTFISK	FIOPSTX	POSTFIX	FORSSTW	FROWSTS
FIKNNOS	FINNSKO	FIORRTY	TORRIFY	FORSTWY	FROWSTY
FIKNOSX	FOXSKIN	FIORSUU	FURIOUS	GGGGIIN	GIGGING
FIKRSTU	TURFSKI	FIOSTTU	OUTFITS	GGGHINO	HOGGING
FILLLUW	WILLFUL	FIOTTTU	TOFUTTI	GGGHINU	HUGGING
FILLMOV	MOLLIFY	FIPPUYY	YUPPIFY	GGGIIJN	JIGGING
FILLNUY	NULLIFY	FIRSSTT	STRIFTS	GGGIILN	LIGGING
FILLOTU	TOILFUL	FIRSSUY	RUSSIFY	GGGIINP	PIGGING
FILLOTY	LOFTILY	FKLMOOT	FOLKMOT	GGGIINR	RIGGING
FILLPSU	UPFILLS	FKLORUW	WORKFUL	GGGIINT	TIGGING
FILLSTU	LISTFUL	FKNOSTY	KONFYTS	GGGIINW	WIGGING
FILMNOO	MONOFIL	FKOOORS	FORSOOK	GGGIINZ	ZIGGING
FILMOSU	FOLIUMS	FKRSSUY	SKYSURF	GGGIIST	GIGGITS
FILMSTU	MISTFUL	FLLOOSW	FOLLOWS	GGGIJNO	JOGGING
FILNNUY	FUNNILY	FLLOPTU	PLOTFUL	GGGIJNU	JUGGING
FILNORS	FLORINS		TOPFULL	GGGILNO	LOGGING
FILNORU	FLUORIN	FLLOSSY	LOSLYFS	GGGILNU	LUGGING
FILNOSW	INFLOWS	FLLOSUW	SOULFUL	GGGIMNO	MOGGING
FILNOUX	FLUXION	FLLOUWY	WOFULLY	GGGIMNU	MUGGING
FILNSTU	TINFULS	FLLSTUU	LUSTFUL	GGGINNO	GONGING
FILNTUY	UNFITLY	FLMMOUX	FLUMMOX		NOGGING
FILOOSU	FOLIOUS	FLMNOOU	MOUFLON	GGGINNU	GUNGING
FILOOTW	WITLOOF	FLMNOSU	MUFLONS	GGGINOR	GORGING
FILORST	FIRLOTS	FLMOOOT	TOMFOOL	GGGINOS	SOGGING
	FLORIST	FLMOORS	FORMOLS	GGGINOT	TOGGING
FILORSV	FRIVOLS	FLMOORU	ROOMFUL	GGGINOU	GOUGING
FILORTU	FLORUIT	FLMORSY	FORMYLS	GGGINPU	PUGGING
FILORTY	TRIFOLY	FLMORWY	WORMFLY	GGGINRU	GURGING
FILOSSS	FOSSILS	FLMSUUU	FUMULUS		RUGGING
FILPPUY	PULPIFY	FLNOORR	FORLORN	GGGINSU	SUGGING
FILPSTU	UPLIFTS	FLNOOSU	UNFOOLS	GGGINTU	TUGGING
FILRRUY	FURRILY	FLNOOSW	ONFLOWS	GGHHIIN	HIGHING
FILRSTY	FIRSTLY	FLNRSUU	UNFURLS	GGHHIOS	HOGGISH
FILRYZZ	FRIZZLY		URNFULS	GGHIIJS	JIGGISH
FILSSUY	FUSSILY	FLOOOTU	OUTFOOL	GGHIINN	HINGING
FILSTTU	FLUTIST	FLOOPWX	FOWLPOX		NIGHING
FILSTUW	WISTFUL	FLOORSW	FORSLOW	GGHIINS	SIGHING
FILSTUY	FUSTILY	FLOOTUW	OUTFLOW	GGHIIPS	PIGGISH
FILSTWY	SWIFTLY	FLOPSTU	POTFULS	GGHIIRS	RIGGISH
FILTTUY	TUFTILY	FLOPSUW	UPFLOWS	GGHIITT	THIGGIT
FILUYZZ	FUZZILY	FLOPTUU	POUTFUL	GGHILOS	LOGGISH
FIMMMUY	MUMMIFY	FLOSUUV	FULVOUS	GGHIMSU	MUGGISH
FIMMORS	MISFORM	FLPRSUU	UPFURLS	GGHINNO	HONGING
FIMNORS	INFORMS	FLRSSUU	SULFURS	GGHINOS	HOGGINS
FIMNORU	UNIFORM	FLRSUUY	SULFURY	GGHINSU	GUSHING
FIMOORS	ISOFORM	FMNORSU	UNFORMS		SUGHING
FIMOORV	OVIFORM	FMRSTUU	FRUSTUM	GGHIOSW	WOGGISH
FIMORRT	TRIFORM	FNNNUUY	UNFUNNY	GGHIPSU	PUGGISH
FIMORTY	MORTIFY	FNNOORT	FRONTON	GGHLOSY	SHOGGLY
FIMRTUY	FURMITY	FNOORRW	FORWORN	GGHORSU	GROUGHS
FIMSTYY	MYSTIFY	FNOORSU	SUNROOF	GGHOSTU	THUGGOS
FINOOSS	FOISONS		UNROOFS	GGIIILN	GINGILI
FINOPRS	FRIPONS	FNOPRTU	UPFRONT	GGIIJJS	JIGJIGS
FINOPSU	SOUPFIN	FNRSTUU	UNTURFS	GGIIKNN	KINGING
FINOPTY	PONTIFY	FNSSUUY	UNFUSSY	GGIILLN	GILLING
FINORSS	FRISSON	FNSTTUU	UNSTUFT	GGIILMN	GLIMING
FINORST	FORINTS	FOOOPRT	ROOFTOP	GGIILNP	PIGLING
FINORTY	INTROFY	FOOORTT	FOOTROT	GGIILNR	RIGLING
FINOSSU	FUSIONS	FOOOTTU	OUTFOOT	GGIILNU	GUILING

GGIIMNN	MINGING			PORGING	GHIINZZ	HIZZING
GGIIMNP	GIMPING	GGINOPU	UPGOING		GHIIOPR	PIROGHI
GGIIMNR	GRIMING	GGINOQS	QIGONGS		GHIIRST	TIGRISH
GGIINNN	GINNING	GGINORS	GORINGS		GHIJNOS	JOSHING
GGIINNO	INGOING			GRINGOS	GHIKLNO	HOLKING
GGIINNP	PINGING	GGINORU	ROGUING		GHIKLNU	HULKING
GGIINNR	GIRNING			ROUGING	GHIKNNO	HONKING
	RINGING	GGINORW	GROWING		GHIKNOO	HOOKING
GGIINNS	SIGNING	GGINORZ	GROZING		GHIKNOW	HOWKING
	SINGING	GGINOSS	GOSSING		GHIKNST	KNIGHTS
GGIINNT	TINGING	GGINOUV	VOGUING		GHIKNSU	HUSKING
GGIINNW	WINGING	GGINPPY	GYPPING		GHIKNTY	KYTHING
GGIINNZ	ZINGING	GGINPRU	PURGING		GHIKRTU	TUGHRIK
GGIINPP	GIPPING	GGINRSU	SURGING		GHILLNU	HULLING
GGIINPR	GRIPING			URGINGS	GHILLSU	GULLISH
GGIINPS	PIGGINS	GGINSTU	GUSTING		GHILLTY	LIGHTLY
GGIINRS	GRISING			GUTSINGS	GHILNOS	HOLINGS
GGIINRT	GIRTING	GGINTTU	GUTTING			LONGISH
	RINGGIT	GGIOORS	GORGIOS		GHILNOT	THOLING
GGIINSU	GUISING	GGIPRSY	SPRIGGY		GHILNOW	HOWLING
GGIINSV	GIVINGS	GGLLOOS	LOGLOGS		GHILNPU	INGULPH
GGIINTT	GITTING	GGLOOOS	GOOGOLS		GHILNRU	HURLING
GGIIRRS	GRIGRIS	GGMRSUU	MUGGURS		GHILNSU	LUSHING
GGIJNSU	JUGGINS	GGNOORS	GORGONS			SHULING
GGIKLNU	KLUGING	GGNOOSY	GONGYOS		GHILNSY	SHINGLY
GGIKNOS	GINGKOS	GGRRSUU	GRUGRUS		GHILNTY	NIGHTLY
	GINKGOS	GHHHIIS	HIGHISH		GHILPST	PLIGHTS
GGILLNU	GULLING	GHHHIST	HIGHTHS		GHILPTU	UPLIGHT
GGILMUY	MUGGILY	GHHIINS	HISHING		GHILPTY	YPLIGHT
GGILNNO	LONGING	GHHINSU	HUSHING		GHILRTY	RIGHTLY
GGILNNU	LUNGING	GHHIOPT	HIGHTOP		GHILSST	SLIGHTS
GGILNOS	GOSLING	GHHIRST	SHRIGHT		GHILSTY	SIGHTLY
	OGLINGS	GHHORTU	THROUGH		GHILSUY	GUSHILY
GGILNOV	GLOVING	GHHOSSU	SHOUGHS		GHILTTY	TIGHTLY
GGILNOW	GLOWING	GHHOTTU	THOUGHT		GHILTWY	WIGHTLY
	GOWLING	GHIIIMN	MIHIING		GHIMMNU	HUMMING
GGILNOZ	GLOZING	GHIIKNO	HOIKING		GHIMNNY	HYMNING
GGILNPU	GULPING	GHIIKNT	KITHING		GHIMNOS	GNOMISH
GGILNRU	GURLING	GHIILLN	HILLING			HOMINGS
GGILNSU	LUGINGS	GHIILNR	HIRLING			MOSHING
GGILNUY	GUYLING	GHIILNT	HILTING		GHIMNPU	HUMPING
	UGLYING			LITHING	GHIMNRY	RHYMING
GGILOOS	GIGOLOS	GHIILNW	WHILING		GHIMNSU	MUSHING
GGILOST	GIGLOTS	GHIILRS	GIRLISH		GHIMRSU	SIMURGH
GGILOSY	SOGGILY	GHIINNS	SHINING		GHIMSST	SMIGHTS
GGILRWY	WRIGGLY	GHIINNT	HINTING		GHIMSTT	MIGHTST
GGIMMNU	GUMMING			NITHING	GHINNOP	PHONING
GGIMNNU	MUNGING	GHIINNW	WHINING		GHINNOR	HORNING
GGIMNOR	GORMING	GHIINOS	HOISING		GHINNOS	NOSHING
GGIMNPU	GUMPING	GHIINPP	HIPPING		GHINNOT	NOTHING
GGIMNPY	GYMPING	GHIINPS	PISHING		GHINNTU	HUNTING
GGIMNSU	MUGGINS	GHIINPT	PITHING		GHINOOP	HOOPING
GGINNNU	GUNNING	GHIINRS	HIRINGS			POOHING
GGINNOO	ONGOING			SHIRING	GHINOOS	SHOOING
GGINNOP	PONGING	GHIINSS	HISSING		GHINOOT	HOOTING
GGINNOR	GRONING	GHIINST	HISTING		GHINOOV	HOOVING
GGINNOS	NOGGINS			INSIGHT	GHINOPP	HOPPING
GGINNOT	TONGING			SHITING	GHINOPS	GINSHOP
GGINNOW	GOWNING			SITHING		POSHING
GGINNRU	GURNING	GHIINSW	WISHING		GHINOPY	HYPOING
GGINOOP	POGOING	GHIINTT	HITTING		GHINORS	HORSING
GGINOOS	GOOSING			TITHING		SHORING
GGINOPR	GORPING	GHIINTW	WHITING		GHINORW	WHORING
	GROPING			WITHING		GHINOST	HOSTING

	TOSHING
GHINOSU	HOUSING
GHINOSV	SHOVING
GHINOSW	SHOWING
GHINOTT	HOTTING
	TONIGHT
GHINOTU	HOUTING
	THOUING
GHINPPU	HUPPING
GHINPPY	HYPPING
GHINPSU	GUNSHIP
	PUSHING
GHINRSU	RUSHING
GHINRTU	HURTING
	UNGIRTH
	UNRIGHT
GHINSTU	SHUTING
	TUSHING
	UNSIGHT
GHINTTU	HUTTING
GHINTTY	TYTHING
GHIOPSZ	PHIZOGS
GHIORST	RIGHTOS
GHIORSU	ROGUISH
GHIOSUV	VOGUISH
GHIPRST	SPRIGHT
GHIPRTU	UPRIGHT
GHIPSST	SPIGHTS
GHIPTTU	UPTIGHT
GHIQSTU	QUIGHTS
GHIRSTW	WRIGHTS
GHISTTW	TWIGHTS
GHLMOOO	HOMOLOG
GHLMOSU	MOGHULS
GHLOOSY	SHOOGLY
GHLOPSU	PLOUGHS
GHLORUY	ROUGHLY
GHLOSSU	SLOUGHS
GHLOSTY	GHOSTLY
GHLOSUY	SLOUGHY
GHLOTUY	TOUGHLY
GHMORSU	SORGHUM
GHMOSTU	MUGSHOT
GHMPRSU	GRUMPHS
GHMPRUY	GRUMPHY
GHNOOPS	GONOPHS
GHNOPRY	GRYPHON
GHNORST	THRONGS
GHNORUU	UNROUGH
GHNOSSU	SHOGUNS
GHNOSTU	GUNSHOT
	HOGNUTS
	NOUGHTS
	SHOTGUN
GHNOTUY	YOUNGTH
GHOOOSW	HOOSGOW
GHOOPST	PHOTOGS
GHOOQSU	QUOHOGS
GHOORSS	SORGHOS
GHORSTU	TROUGHS
GHORSTW	GROWTHS
GHORTUW	WROUGHT
GHORTUY	YOGHURT
GHORTWY	GROWTHY

GHOSTUU	OUTGUSH
GIIIKNT	TIKIING
GIIINRS	IRISING
	NIGIRIS
GIIJKNN	JINKING
GIIJLNT	JILTING
GIIJNNO	JOINING
GIIJNNX	JINXING
GIIKKNN	KINKING
GIIKKNR	KIRKING
GIIKLLN	KILLING
GIIKLMN	MILKING
GIIKLNN	INKLING
	KILNING
	LINKING
GIIKLNR	LIRKING
GIIKLNS	LIKINGS
	SILKING
GIIKLNT	KILTING
	KITLING
GIIKNNO	OINKING
GIIKNNP	KINGPIN
	PINKING
GIIKNNR	KIRNING
	RINKING
GIIKNNS	SINKING
GIIKNNT	TINKING
GIIKNNV	KNIVING
GIIKNNW	WINKING
GIIKNNZ	ZINKING
GIIKNPP	KIPPING
GIIKNPS	PIGSKIN
	PIKINGS
	SPIKING
GIIKNRS	GIRKINS
	GRISKIN
	KRISING
	RISKING
GIIKNRY	YIRKING
GIIKNSS	KISSING
	SKIINGS
GIIKNST	KISTING
	KITINGS
	SKITING
GIIKNSV	SKIVING
	VIKINGS
GIIKNTT	KITTING
GIILLLN	LILLING
GIILLMN	MILLING
GIILLNN	NILLING
GIILLNO	GILLION
GIILLNP	PILLING
GIILLNR	RILLING
GIILLNT	LILTING
	TILLING
GIILLNW	WILLING
GIILMNN	LIMNING
GIILMNO	MOILING
GIILMNP	LIMPING
GIILMNS	LIMINGS
	SLIMING
	SMILING
GIILMNT	MILTING
GIILMPR	PILGRIM

GIILMRY	GRIMILY
GIILNNN	LINNING
GIILNNR	NIRLING
GIILNNS	LIGNINS
	LININGS
GIILNNT	LINTING
GIILNNY	INLYING
GIILNOP	PIGNOLI
GIILNOR	LIGROIN
	ROILING
GIILNOS	SILOING
	SOILING
GIILNOT	TOILING
GIILNPP	LIPPING
GIILNPR	PIRLING
GIILNPS	LISPING
	PILINGS
	SLIPING
	SPILING
GIILNRS	RIGLINS
GIILNRT	TIRLING
GIILNST	LISTING
	SILTING
	STILING
	TILINGS
GIILNSV	LIVINGS
	SLIVING
GIILNTT	TILTING
	TITLING
GIILNTW	WILTING
	WITLING
GIILOSS	GLIOSIS
GIILOST	OLIGIST
GIILRST	STRIGIL
GIIMMNN	NIMMING
GIIMMNR	RIMMING
GIIMNNS	MININGS
GIIMNNT	MINTING
GIIMNPP	PIMPING
GIIMNPR	PRIMING
GIIMNPS	IMPINGS
GIIMNPW	WIMPING
GIIMNRT	MITRING
GIIMNRV	MIRVING
GIIMNSS	MISSING
GIIMNST	MISTING
	SMITING
	STIMING
	TIMINGS
GIINNNP	PINNING
GIINNNR	RINNING
GIINNNS	INNINGS
	SINNING
GIINNNT	TINNING
GIINNNW	WINNING
GIINNOP	OPINING
	PIONING
GIINNOR	IRONING
	ROINING
GIINNOS	NOISING
GIINNOT	OINTING
GIINNPP	NIPPING
GIINNPS	SNIPING
GIINNPU	PINGUIN

GIINNRS	RINSING	GIIORSV	ISOGRIV	GILLORS	RIGOLLS
GIINNRT	TRINING	GIJKNNU	JUNKING	GILMMUY	GUMMILY
GIINNRU	INURING	GIJKNOO	JOOKING	GILMNOO	LOOMING
	RUINING	GIJKNOU	JOUKING		MOOLING
	URINING	GIJLLNO	JOLLING	GILMNOR	MORLING
GIINNSW	INSWING	GIJLNOT	JOLTING	GILMNOT	MOLTING
GIINNTT	TINTING	GIJLNOU	JOULING	GILMNOY	MOYLING
GIINNTU	UNITING	GIJLNOW	JOWLING	GILMNPU	LUMPING
GIINNTV	VINTING	GIJLNSU	JUNGLIS		PLUMING
GIINNTW	TWINING	GIJMNPU	JUMPING	GILMNRU	MURLING
GIINOPS	POISING	GIJNOTT	JOTTING	GILMNSU	LIGNUMS
GIINORS	ORIGINS	GIJNRUY	JURYING	GILMPSY	GYMSLIP
	SIGNIOR	GIJNSTU	JUSTING	GILNNOO	GLONOIN
	SIGNORI	GIJNTTU	JUTTING		LOONING
GIINORT	IGNITOR	GIKKNNO	KONKING	GILNNOU	LOUNING
	RIOTING	GIKKNOO	KOOKING	GILNNOW	LOWNING
GIINOSY	YOGINIS	GIKKNOY	YOKKING	GILNNRU	NURLING
GIINOTT	TOITING	GIKKNUY	YUKKING	GILNNSU	UNSLING
GIINPPP	PIPPING	GIKLNOO	LOOKING	GILNNTU	LUNTING
GIINPPR	RIPPING	GIKLNOP	POLKING	GILNNUV	VULNING
GIINPPS	PIPINGS	GIKLNRU	LURKING	GILNOOP	LOOPING
	SIPPING	GIKLNSU	LUSKING		POOLING
GIINPPT	TIPPING		SULKING	GILNOOS	LOGIONS
GIINPPY	YIPPING	GIKMNOS	SMOKING		LOOSING
GIINPPZ	ZIPPING	GIKMNSU	MUSKING		OLINGOS
GIINPQU	PIQUING	GIKNNNO	KONNING		SOLOING
GIINPRS	PRISING	GIKNNOO	KONGONI		SOOLING
	RISPING	GIKNNOS	SNOKING	GILNOOT	LOOTING
	SPIRING	GIKNNOT	TONKING		TOOLING
GIINPRZ	PRIZING	GIKNNOW	KNOWING	GILNOPP	LOPPING
GIINPSS	PISSING	GIKNNOZ	ZONKING	GILNOPR	PROLING
GIINPST	SPITING	GIKNNSU	UNKINGS	GILNOPS	POLINGS
GIINPSW	SWIPING	GIKNOOP	POOKING		SLOPING
	WIPINGS	GIKNOOR	ROOKING	GILNOPT	POLTING
	WISPING	GIKNOOS	SOOKING	GILNOPU	LOUPING
GIINPTT	PITTING	GIKNOPR	PORKING	GILNOPW	LOWPING
GIINPTW	WINGTIP		PROKING		PLOWING
GIINPTY	PITYING	GIKNOPS	SPOKING	GILNOPY	PLOYING
GIINQRU	QUIRING	GIKNOPU	POUKING	GILNORS	LORINGS
GIINQTU	QUITING	GIKNORT	TROKING	GILNORU	LOURING
GIINRRS	SIRRING	GIKNORW	WORKING	GILNOSS	LOSINGS
GIINRRT	TIRRING	GIKNORY	YORKING	GILNOST	LINGOTS
GIINRRY	YIRRING	GIKNOST	STOKING		TIGLONS
GIINRSS	RISINGS	GIKNOSU	SOUKING		TOLINGS
GIINRST	STIRING	GIKNOSY	YOKINGS	GILNOSU	LOUSING
	TIRINGS	GIKNOTU	TOUKING	GILNOSV	LOVINGS
GIINRSV	VIRGINS	GIKNOUY	YOUKING		SOLVING
GIINRSW	WIRINGS	GIKNRSY	SKRYING	GILNOSW	LOWINGS
GIINRTT	RITTING		SKYRING		LOWSING
GIINRTW	TWIRING	GIKNSTU	TUSKING		SLOWING
	WRITING	GIKNSTY	SKYTING		SOWLING
GIINSST	SISTING	GIKRSTU	TUGRIKS	GILNOTT	LOTTING
GIINSSU	ISSUING	GILLLNO	LOLLING	GILNOTU	LOUTING
GIINSSW	WISSING	GILLLNU	LULLING	GILNOTW	LOWTING
GIINSSZ	SIZINGS	GILLMNU	MULLING	GILNOVV	VOLVING
GIINSTT	SITTING	GILLNNU	NULLING	GILNOVW	WOLVING
GIINSTU	SUITING	GILLNOP	POLLING	GILNOWY	YOWLING
GIINSTV	STIVING	GILLNOR	ROLLING	GILNPPU	PULPING
GIINSTW	WISTING	GILLNOT	TOLLING	GILNPRU	PURLING
GIINSVW	SWIVING	GILLNPU	PULLING	GILNPSU	PLUSING
GIINTTT	TITTING	GILLNSU	ULLINGS		PULINGS
GIINTTW	WITTING	GILLNUW	WULLING		PULSING
GIINVYZ	VIZYING	GILLNYY	LYINGLY		PUSLING
GIINZZZ	ZIZZING	GILLOOS	LOLIGOS	GILNPUY	UPLYING

GILNRSU	RULINGS	GIMORSS	OGRISMS		POURING
GILNSSU	NISGULS		SIMORGS		ROUPING
GILNSTU	LUSTING	GIMORSW	MISGROW	GINOPRV	PROVING
	LUTINGS	GIMOSSY	YOGISMS	GINOPRW	POWRING
	SINGULT	GIMOSTU	GOMUTIS	GINOPRY	YORPING
GILNSTY	STYLING	GIMRSSU	SIMURGS	GINOPSS	POSINGS
GILNSUY	LUNGYIS	GIMRSUU	GURUISM		POSSING
GILNVYY	VYINGLY	GINNNOO	NOONING	GINOPST	POSTING
GILOORS	GIROSOL	GINNNOR	RONNING		STOPING
GILOOSS	ISOLOGS	GINNNOW	WONNING	GINOPSU	SOUPING
GILOOST	OLOGIST	GINNNPU	PUNNING	GINOPSY	POYSING
GILOOTW	TWIGLOO	GINNNRU	RUNNING	GINOPTT	POTTING
GILORTT	TRIGLOT	GINNNSU	SUNNING	GINOPTU	POUTING
GILORTY	TRILOGY	GINNNTU	TUNNING	GINOQTU	QUOTING
GILOSTT	GLOTTIS	GINNOOS	NOOSING	GINORRT	RORTING
GILOTUY	GOUTILY	GINNOOW	WOONING	GINORRV	VORRING
GILRSTY	GRISTLY	GINNOOZ	ZOONING	GINORSS	GRISONS
GILRTUY	LITURGY	GINNOPS	SPONGIN		INGROSS
GILRYZZ	GRIZZLY	GINNOPY	PONYING		SIGNORS
GILSTUY	GUSTILY	GINNORS	SNORING		SORINGS
	GUTSILY		SORNING	GINORST	ROSTING
GIMMMNU	MUMMING	GINNORU	GRUNION		SORTING
GIMMNOT	TOMMING	GINNORW	INGROWN		STORING
GIMMNPU	MUMPING	GINNORY	GIRONNY		TRIGONS
GIMMNRY	RYMMING		ROYNING	GINORSU	ROUSING
GIMMNSU	SUMMING	GINNOSS	NOSINGS		SOURING
GIMMNUV	VUMMING	GINNOST	STONING	GINORSV	ROVINGS
GIMMORS	GIMMORS		TONINGS	GINORSW	ROWINGS
GIMNNOO	MOONING	GINNOSW	SNOWING		WORSING
GIMNNOR	MORNING		WONINGS	GINORSY	ROSYING
GIMNNOS	MIGNONS	GINNOSZ	ZONINGS		SIGNORY
GIMNNTU	MUNTING	GINNOTW	WONTING	GINORTT	ROTTING
GIMNOOP	MOOPING	GINNPRU	PRUNING	GINORTU	OUTGRIN
GIMNOOR	MOORING	GINNPTU	PUNTING		OUTRING
	ROOMING	GINNRSU	NURSING		ROUTING
GIMNOOS	SOOMING		URNINGS		TOURING
GIMNOOT	MOOTING	GINNRTU	TURNING	GINORTW	ROWTING
	TOOMING	GINNSTU	TUNINGS		TROWING
GIMNOOV	MOOVING	GINNTTU	NUTTING	GINOSSS	SOSSING
GIMNOOZ	ZOOMING	GINNTUY	UNTYING	GINOSST	STINGOS
GIMNOPP	MOPPING	GINOOPP	POGONIP		TOSSING
GIMNOPR	ROMPING		POOPING	GINOSSU	SOUSING
GIMNOPU	MOUPING	GINOOPR	ROOPING	GINOSSW	SOWINGS
GIMNOPY	YOMPING	GINOOPS	SOOPING		SOWSING
GIMNORS	SMORING	GINOOPT	POOTING	GINOSTT	SOTTING
GIMNORU	ROUMING	GINOORS	ROOSING	GINOSTU	OUSTING
GIMNORW	WORMING	GINOORT	ROOTING		OUTINGS
GIMNOSS	MOSSING	GINOOSS	ISOGONS		OUTSING
GIMNOST	GNOMIST	GINOOST	SOOTING		TOUSING
GIMNOSU	MOUSING	GINOOSW	WOOINGS	GINOSTV	STOVING
	SOUMING	GINOOSY	ISOGONY		VOTINGS
GIMNOSW	MOWINGS	GINOOTT	TOOTING	GINOSTW	STOWING
	SOWMING	GINOPPP	POPPING		TOWINGS
GIMNPPU	PUMPING	GINOPPS	SOPPING		TOWSING
GIMNPRU	RUMPING	GINOPPT	TOPPING	GINOSTY	TOYINGS
GIMNPSU	IMPUGNS	GINOPPU	POUPING	GINOTTT	TOTTING
	SPUMING	GINOPPW	WOPPING	GINOTTU	TOUTING
GIMNPTU	TUMPING	GINOPRS	PROIGNS	GINOTTW	TOWTING
GIMNPUY	YUMPING		PROSING		WOTTING
GIMNSSU	MUSINGS		ROPINGS	GINOTUW	OUTWING
	MUSSING		SPORING	GINOTUZ	TOUZING
GIMNSTU	MUSTING	GINOPRT	PORTING	GINOTWZ	TOWZING
GIMNSTY	STYMING		TROPING	GINPPPU	PUPPING
GIMNUZZ	MUZZING	GINOPRU	INGROUP	GINPPSU	SUPPING

	UPPINGS	GLNORWY	WRONGLY	HHIOSTT	HOTTISH
GINPPTU	TUPPING	GLNOSUW	SUNGLOW	HHISSTW	WHISHTS
GINPRRU	PURRING	GLNOTTU	GLUTTON	HHMMSUU	HUMHUMS
GINPRSS	SPRINGS	GLNOUYY	YOUNGLY	HHMRSTY	RHYTHMS
GINPRSU	PURSING	GLNPSUU	UNPLUGS	HHOOSTT	HOTSHOT
GINPRSY	PRYINGS	GLOOORY	OROLOGY	HIIIKRS	RIKISHI
	SPRINGY	GLOOOTY	OTOLOGY	HIIISTV	SHIVITI
GINPSSY	PIGSNYS	GLOOOYZ	ZOOLOGY	HIIJKNS	HIJINKS
	SPYINGS	GLOOPRS	PROLOGS	HIIKLMS	KHILIMS
GINPSTU	PIGNUTS	GLOORUY	UROLOGY	HIIKNNS	SHINKIN
	STUPING	GLOOSTU	LOGOUTS	HIIKNPS	KINSHIP
GINPSTY	TYPINGS	GLOOTUW	OUTGLOW		PINKISH
GINPSUW	UPSWING	GLOPSTU	PUTLOGS	HIILMTU	LITHIUM
GINPTTU	PUTTING	GLORSSY	GROSSLY	HIILNSY	SHINILY
GINPTUY	UPTYING	GLPRSUY	SPLURGY	HIILPST	SHILPIT
GINPTUZ	PUTZING	GMMOSUU	GUMMOUS	HIILPSU	HUIPILS
GINQTUY	QUYTING	GMMPUUW	MUGWUMP	HIILPTY	PITHILY
GINRRSU	RUNRIGS	GMNNOOS	GNOMONS	HIILRTT	TRILITH
GINRSST	STRINGS	GMNOORU	GUNROOM	HIIMMSS	MISHMIS
GINRSTU	RUSTING	GMNOORW	MORWONG	HIIMNSX	MINXISH
GINRSTY	STRINGY	GMNSTUU	GUMNUTS	HIIMPSW	WIMPISH
	STYRING	GMNSUUZ	MZUNGUS	HIIMRSU	SHIURIM
	TRYINGS	GMOOPRS	POGROMS	HIIMSSS	MISSISH
GINRSUU	USURING	GMOOSTU	GOMUTOS	HIIMSST	MISHITS
GINRTTU	RUTTING	GMORSUU	GRUMOUS	HIIMSTT	SHITTIM
GINSSSU	SUSSING	GMORTUW	MUGWORT	HIINNOT	THIONIN
GINSTTU	TUTSING	GMPSSUY	GYPSUMS	HIINORS	NOIRISH
GINSTTY	STYTING	GMRUYYZ	ZYMURGY		ROINISH
GINTTTU	TUTTING	GNNOORS	ROGNONS	HIINOSS	HOISINS
GIOOPRR	PORRIGO	GNNORUW	UNGROWN	HIINPPS	HIPPINS
GIOORSV	VIGOROS	GNNORYY	GYRONNY	HIINPSS	INSHIPS
GIOPRRU	PRURIGO	GNNOSUW	UNGOWNS	HIINSSW	SWINISH
GIOPSSS	GOSSIPS	GNNOUUY	UNYOUNG	HIINSTW	WITHINS
GIOPSST	SPIGOTS	GNNRUUW	UNWRUNG	HIIOPRS	POHIRIS
GIOPSSY	GOSSIPY	GNNSTUU	UNSTUNG	HIIOPRW	POWHIRI
GIOPSTU	PIGOUTS	GNOOORS	GORSOON	HIIOPRZ	RHIZOPI
GIORRSU	RIGOURS	GNOOOSS	GOSSOON	HIIORST	HISTRIO
GIORSTU	OUTRIGS	GNOOOYZ	ZOOGONY	HIIPSSW	WISPISH
	RIGOUTS	GNOORST	TROGONS	HIIPSXY	PIXYISH
GIORSUV	VIGOURS	GNOPPSU	OPPUGNS	HIISTTT	TITTISH
GIOSSYZ	ZYGOSIS		POPGUNS	HIJNSSU	SHINJUS
GISHWVY	WYSIWYG	GNOPRTU	GUNPORT	HIKLNOT	HOTLINK
GJLMUUU	JUGULUM	GNOPRUW	GROWNUP	HIKLSSU	LUSKISH
GJNOOSU	GOUJONS		UPGROWN	HIKLSUY	HUSKILY
GJNRSUU	GURJUNS	GNOPSTU	POTGUNS	HIKMNOS	MONKISH
GJOORTT	JOGTROT	GNORTUU	OUTRUNG	HIKMOTV	MIKVOTH
GKKNOOS	SONGKOK	GNOSTUU	OUTGUNS	HIKMRSU	MURKISH
GKMOOSU	GOMOKUS		OUTSUNG	HIKMSUZ	MUZHIKS
GLLLOOR	LOGROLL	GNPSUUW	UPSWUNG	HIKNNOR	INKHORN
GLLOOPS	GOLLOPS	GOOOORS	GOOROOS	HIKNNTU	UNTHINK
GLMMSUU	SLUMGUM	GOOPRST	GOSPORT	HIKNOOU	HOKONUI
GLMNOOO	MONOLOG	GOORSTT	GROTTOS	HIKNPSU	PUNKISH
GLMNOOS	MONGOLS	GOORTUW	OUTGROW	HIKNRSS	SHRINKS
GLMNUUU	UMLUNGU	GOPRSUW	UPGROWS	HIKOORS	ROOKISH
GLMOOOR	MOORLOG	GORRSTU	TURGORS	HIKOPSY	SKYPHOI
GLMOOYY	MYOLOGY	GORSTTU	GUTROTS	HILLOPT	HILLTOP
GLMORUW	LUGWORM		ROTGUTS	HILLOPY	LYOPHIL
GLNNOOR	LORGNON	GORSTUY	YOGURTS	HILLPSU	UPHILLS
GLNNSUU	UNSLUNG	HHIIPPS	HIPPISH	HILLRSS	SHRILLS
GLNOOOS	OOLONGS	HHIISTW	WHITISH	HILLRST	THRILLS
GLNOOOY	NOOLOGY	HHIMRTY	RHYTHMI	HILLRSY	SHRILLY
GLNOOPR	PROLONG	HHINORS	HORNISH	HILLRTY	THRILLY
GLNOOPY	POLYGON	HHIOPST	HIPSHOT	HILMMOU	HOLMIUM
GLNOOSU	OULONGS	HHIORSW	WHORISH	HILMOPS	LOMPISH

	PHLOMIS	HINOOPS	INHOOPS	HLMORRY	MYRRHOL
HILMOSS	HOLISMS	HINOORT	HORNITO	HLMOSTY	THYMOLS
HILMOSW	WHOLISM	HINOORZ	HORIZON	HLMPSSU	SHLUMPS
HILMPSU	LUMPISH	HINOOST	INSOOTH	HLMPSUY	SHLUMPY
HILMSSY	HYLISMS	HINOPPS	SHIPPON	HLNOPSY	PHYLONS
HILMSUY	MUSHILY	HINOPSS	SIPHONS	HLOOPSS	SPLOOSH
HILMTUU	THULIUM		SONSHIP	HLOOSTY	SOOTHLY
HILNNTY	NINTHLY	HINORST	HORNIST	HLOOTUW	OUTHOWL
HILNOPY	PHONILY	HINORSU	NOURISH	HLOPRTY	PROTHYL
HILNORY	HORNILY	HINORSY	ROYNISH	HLOPSTY	PHYTOLS
HILNOTY	THIONYL	HINOSST	STONISH	HLORSTY	SHORTLY
HILNPST	PLINTHS	HINOSSW	SNOWISH	HLOTUYY	YOUTHLY
HILOOST	OOLITHS	HINOSTW	TOWNISH	HLPRSUU	SULPHUR
HILOOTT	OTOLITH	HINPPSU	PUSHPIN		UPHURLS
HILOOTZ	ZOOLITH	HINPSSU	UNSHIPS	HMMMSUU	HUMMUMS
HILOPST	LITHOPS	HINPSTY	PHYTINS	HMMNOOY	HOMONYM
HILOPXY	OXYPHIL	HINPTUW	UNWHIPT	HMMOOSU	HOUMMOS
HILORSY	HORSILY	HINRSTU	RUNTISH	HMMRTUY	THRUMMY
HILORTU	UROLITH	HIOOPRS	POORISH	HMNOPSY	NYMPHOS
HILOSST	HOLISTS	HIOOSSV	SHIVOOS	HMNOPYY	HYPONYM
HILOSSW	SLOWISH	HIOOSSW	WHOOSIS	HMNPSUY	HYPNUMS
HILOSTU	LOUTISH	HIOPPPS	POPPISH	HMOOPRS	MORPHOS
HILOSTW	WHOLIST	HIOPPSS	SHIPPOS	HMOORSS	SHROOMS
HILOSTY	HYLOIST	HIOPRSW	WORSHIP	HMOOSST	SMOOTHS
HILOSVW	WOLVISH	HIOPSST	SOPHIST	HMOOSTY	SMOOTHY
HILOSWY	SHOWILY	HIOPSSY	PHYSIOS	HMOOSUU	HOUMOUS
HILOTWW	WHITLOW	HIOPSTU	UPHOIST	HMORSUU	HUMOURS
HILPRUW	UPWHIRL	HIORSSU	SOURISH	HMSTUYZ	ZYTHUMS
HILPSST	SPILTHS	HIORSTY	HISTORY	HNNOOPS	PHONONS
HILPSUY	PUSHILY	HIOSSTT	SOTTISH	HNNORSU	UNSHORN
HILSSTY	HYLISTS	HIOSTTU	OUTHITS	HNNOSTY	SYNTHON
	STYLISH	HIOSTUW	OUTWISH	HNNOSUW	UNSHOWN
HILSTTY	THISTLY	HIOTTUW	OUTWITH	HNOOPST	PHOTONS
HILSTWY	SWITHLY		WITHOUT	HNOOPSU	UNHOOPS
HILSTXY	SIXTHLY	HIQSSUY	SQUISHY	HNOOPTY	TYPHOON
HIMMPSU	MUMPISH	HIRSSTT	THIRSTS	HNOORSS	HORSONS
HIMMRSU	RUMMISH		THRISTS	HNOORST	THORONS
HIMMSTY	MYTHISM	HIRSTTU	RUTTISH	HNOORSU	HONOURS
HIMNOOS	MOONISH	HIRSTTY	THIRSTY	HNOOSTU	UNSHOOT
HIMNOPR	MORPHIN		THRISTY	HNOPSSY	SYPHONS
HIMNSSU	MUNSHIS	HJNNOOS	JOHNSON	HNOPSTY	PHYTONS
HIMNSTU	HUMINTS	HKKLOOS	KOLKHOS		PYTHONS
HIMNSTY	HYMNIST	HKKLOOZ	KOLKHOZ		TYPHONS
HIMOORS	MOORISH	HKKOOSY	SKYHOOK	HNORSTY	RHYTONS
HIMOPRS	ORPHISM	HKKOSTU	SUKKOTH	HNORTUW	UNWORTH
	ROMPISH	HKLOOYZ	KOLHOZY	HNOSTUU	UNSHOUT
HIMOPSS	SOPHISM	HKNOOSS	SHNOOKS	HNOSUWY	UNSHOWY
HIMOPST	MOSHPIT	HKNOOSU	UNHOOKS	HNOTTUU	OUTHUNT
	PHOTISM	HKNOOWW	KNOWHOW	HNRTTUU	UNTRUTH
HIMORST	RIMSHOT	HKNSSUU	UNHUSKS	HNSSTUU	UNSHUTS
HIMORSW	WORMISH	HKOOOPT	POTHOOK	HOOOOPS	HOOPOOS
HIMORTU	THORIUM	HKOOPSU	HOOKUPS	HOOPPST	POTSHOP
HIMOTTY	TIMOTHY	HKOOSST	SHTOOKS	HOOPRST	PORTHOS
HIMPRSS	SHRIMPS	HKOOSVZ	SOVKHOZ	HOOPSSY	SHYPOOS
HIMPRSY	SHRIMPY	HKOPSSY	SKYPHOS	HOOPSTT	HOTPOTS
HIMPRTU	TRIUMPH	HKORSWY	WORKSHY		HOTSPOT
HIMPTUY	PYTHIUM	HLLOOOS	HOLLOOS		POTSHOT
HIMRSTY	RHYMIST	HLLOOSU	HULLOOS	HOOPSTU	UPSHOOT
HIMSSTU	ISTHMUS	HLLOOSW	HOLLOWS	HOOPSTY	TOYSHOP
HIMSTTY	MYTHIST	HLLOPSY	PHYLLOS	HOOQSSU	SQUOOSH
HINNNSU	NUNNISH	HLLPSUY	PLUSHLY	HOORRRS	HORRORS
HINNORT	TINHORN	HLMNOTY	MONTHLY	HOORRST	ORTHROS
HINNOST	TONNISH	HLMNPYY	NYMPHLY	HOORSUZ	HUZOORS
HINNPSU	NUNSHIP	HLMOOSS	SHOLOMS	HOOSTTU	OUTSHOT

HOPRSTU	HOTSPUR	IILNOSV	VIOLINS	IIOPSTY	PIOSITY
HOPRTTU	PRUTOTH	IILNOSY	NOISILY	IIORSSV	VIROSIS
HOPRTUW	UPTHROW	IILNPPY	NIPPILY	IIORSTV	IVORIST
HOPSSSY	HYSSOPS	IILNPUV	PULVINI		VISITOR
HOPSSTU	UPSHOTS	IILNRST	NITRILS	IIOSTTU	OUSTITI
HOPSTTU	SHOTPUT	IILNRSV	RIVLINS	IIPPSUU	PIUPIUS
HOPSTUU	OUTPUSH	IILNSST	INSTILS	IIPRRSU	PURIRIS
HOPSTUY	TYPHOUS	IILOPRT	TRIPOLI	IIPRSST	SPIRITS
HORSTTW	TROWTHS	IILOPST	PILOTIS		TRIPSIS
HORSTUU	OUTRUSH	IILORTV	VITRIOL	IIPRSTU	PITURIS
HOSSTTU	STOUTHS	IILOSTV	VIOLIST	IIPRSTY	SPIRITY
HOSTTUU	SHUTOUT	IILPRVY	PRIVILY	IIPRTVY	PRIVITY
HPPSSUU	PUSHUPS	IILPSST	PISTILS	IIQSTUV	QIVIUTS
HPRTTUU	THRUPUT	IILPSTY	TIPSILY	IIRRSTT	TIRRITS
HRSSTTU	THRUSTS	IILPSWY	WISPILY	IISSSTZ	SIZISTS
HRSSTUY	THYRSUS	IILRTYZ	RITZILY	IISTTZZ	TZITZIS
IIIJJLN	JINJILI	IILSTTT	TITLIST	IITTTZZ	TZITZIT
IIIKMNN	MINIKIN	IILTTUY	UTILITY	IJJMSUU	JUJUISM
IIIKMNS	MINISKI	IILTTWY	WITTILY	IJJSTUU	JUJITSU
IIIMRST	MIRITIS	IIMMMNU	MINIMUM		JUJUIST
IIIRSTT	TIRITIS	IIMMNSU	MINIMUS	IJKLLOY	KILLJOY
IIISTTW	WISTITI		MINIUMS	IJKMOSU	MOUJIKS
IIJKOPR	PIROJKI	IIMNNOS	MINIONS	IJKMSUZ	MUZJIKS
IIJLLNO	JILLION	IIMNOSS	MISSION	IJKNOSS	JOSKINS
IIJMMNY	JIMMINY	IIMNOSU	IONIUMS	IJLLLOV	JOLLILY
IIJMNOS	MISJOIN		NIMIOUS	IJLLOTY	JOLLITY
IIJNNOT	INJOINT	IIMNOTX	MIXTION		JOLTILY
IIKKLNY	KINKILY	IIMNPRT	IMPRINT	IJLMPUY	JUMPILY
IIKKNPS	KIPSKIN	IIMOPSU	IMPIOUS	IJLNOQU	JONQUIL
IIKLLMY	MILKILY	IIMOSST	MITOSIS	IJLNOTY	JOINTLY
IIKLLSY	SILKILY	IIMOSSU	SIMIOUS	IJMOSSS	JISSOMS
IIKLMNP	LIMPKIN	IIMRSST	SMRITIS	IJNNOTU	UNJOINT
IIKLMRY	MIRKILY	IIMRSSU	SURIMIS	IJNORSU	JUNIORS
IIKLNOS	OILSKIN	IIMRSTW	MISWRIT	IJNOTUX	OUTJINX
IIKLPSY	SPIKILY	IIMRTTU	TRITIUM	IJRSSTU	JURISTS
IIKLRSY	RISKILY	IIMRTUV	TRIVIUM	IKKMNOU	KIKUMON
IIKMNOR	KIRIMON	IIMSSSZ	SIZISMS	IKKNNSU	UNKINKS
IIKMNPS	SIMPKIN	IIMSSTT	TIMISTS	IKKNORT	KIRKTON
IIKMNSS	SIMKINS	IIMSSTU	MISSUIT	IKKORRS	KORKIRS
IIKNPPS	PIPKINS	IINNOOP	OPINION	IKKSUUY	KIKUYUS
IIKNSSS	SISKINS	IINNOPS	PINIONS	IKLLOTU	OUTKILL
IIKOSST	OIKISTS		SPINONI	IKLLPSU	UPSKILL
IIKOSTT	TITOKIS	IINNOTU	UNITION	IKLLSTU	KILLUTS
IIKPSUW	WIKIUPS	IINNQSU	QUININS	IKLLSUY	SULKILY
IILLLSY	SILLILY	IINNQTU	QUINTIN	IKLMNPU	LUMPKIN
IILLHNO	MILLION	IINOPSS	ISOSPIN	IKLMOOS	LOOKISM
IILLMSY	SLIMILY		SINOPIS	IKLMOPS	MILKSOP
IILLNOP	PILLION	IINOPST	POITINS	IKLMOSY	SMOKILY
IILLNOZ	ZILLION	IINORST	IRONIST		SOYMILK
IILLNST	INSTILL	IINORSV	VIRINOS	IKLMRUY	MURKILY
IILLNTT	LITTLIN		VIRIONS	IKLMSUY	MUSKILY
IILLPSU	ILLUPIS	IINORTT	INTROIT	IKLNNSU	UNLINKS
IILMNOS	LIONISM	IINOSSV	VISIONS	IKLNOOS	SKOLION
IILMNSS	SIMLINS	IINOSUV	INVIOUS	IKLNOOT	KILOTON
IILMORS	SIMILOR	IINOTTU	TUITION	IKLNOSU	ULIKONS
IILMOSS	LIMOSIS	IINPPPS	PIPPINS	IKLNPSU	LINKUPS
IILMSTU	STIMULI	IINQRUY	INQUIRY		SKULPIN
IILMSTY	MISTILY	IINRTTY	TRINITY		UPLINKS
IILNNOT	NITINOL	IINSSST	INSISTS	IKLNRWY	WRINKLY
IILNNSU	INSULIN	IINSTTU	INTUITS	IKLNTWY	TWINKLY
	INULINS	IINSTTW	INTWIST	IKLOOST	LOOKIST
IILNNTY	TINNILY		NITWITS	IKLOOTT	TOOLKIT
IILNOPT	PINITOL	IIOOSTT	TOITOIS	IKLOSSU	SOUSLIK
IILNORS	SIRLOIN	IIOPRSS	PISSOIR	IKLSSSU	SUSLIKS

IKLSTTU	KITTULS	ILLSTUY	LUSTILY	ILOOSST	SOLOIST
IKMN000	OKIMONO	ILMMRUY	RUMMILY	ILOOSTY	SOOTILY
IKMNOOR	OMIKRON	ILMMSSU	SLUMISM	ILOOWYZ	WOOZILY
IKMNOOS	KIMONOS	ILMMSUU	MIMULUS	ILOPPSY	SOPPILY
	MONOSKI	ILMNOOT	MOONLIT	ILOPRRY	PRIORLY
IKMNORS	MIKRONS	ILMNOOY	MOONILY	ILOPRSY	PROSILY
	MORKINS	ILMNOSU	MOULINS	ILOPRUY	ROUPILY
IKMNOSW	MISKNOW	ILMNRSU	MURLINS	ILOPSST	PISTOLS
IKMNPPU	PUMPKIN	ILMNSSU	MUSLINS		POSTILS
IKMNRSU	RUMKINS	ILMOORY	ROOMILY	ILOPSSX	OXSLIPS
IKMNRTU	TRINKUM	ILMOOSS	MOLOSSI	ILOPSTT	SPOTLIT
IKMOOST	MISTOOK	ILMOOSV	MOOLVIS	ILOPSTU	SLIPOUT
IKMOSSU	KOUMISS	ILMORSW	WORMILS	ILOPSUY	PIOUSLY
IKMPRSS	SKRIMPS	ILMORTU	TURMOIL	ILOQRSU	LIQUORS
IKMSSTU	MUSKITS	ILMOSTY	MOISTLY	ILORRSY	SORRILY
IKNNPSU	PUNKINS	ILMOSUY	MOUSILY	ILORSTU	TROILUS
IKNNPTU	UNPINKT	ILMPSSY	SLIMPSY	ILOSSTY	TOSSILY
IKNNSTU	UNKNITS	ILMPSTU	PLUMIST		TYLOSIS
IKNOOST	ISOKONT	ILMRSSY	LYRISMS	ILOSTTW	WITTOLS
IKNOPRW	PINWORK	ILMSSUY	MUSSILY	ILPPSSU	SLIPUPS
IKNOPST	INKPOTS	ILMSTUY	MUSTILY	ILPPSTU	PULPITS
	INKSPOT	ILMUYZZ	MUZZILY	ILPRSUY	PURSILY
IKNORSW	INWORKS	ILNNOOY	NONOILY	ILPSTTU	UPTILTS
IKNORTW	TINWORK	ILNNOPS	NONSLIP	ILRSSTU	TRISULS
IKNPSTU	SPUTNIK	ILNNORU	LINURON	ILRSSTY	LYRISTS
	UPKNITS	ILNNSUY	SUNNILY	ILRSTUY	RUSTILY
IKORSTU	TURKOIS	ILNOOPS	PLOSION	ILRTTUY	RUTTILY
IKOSSTU	OUTKISS	ILNOOPV	VOLPINO	ILSSTTU	LUTISTS
IKPRSSU	PRUSIKS	ILNOORS	ROSINOL	ILSSTTY	STYLIST
	SPRUIKS	ILNOOSS	SOLIONS	ILSTTUU	TITULUS
IKPRSSY	KRYPSIS	ILNOOST	LOTIONS	IMMMOSS	MOMISMS
ILLLOWY	LOWLILY		SOLITON	IMMNOSS	MONISMS
ILLMNOU	MULLION	ILNOPPS	POPLINS		NOMISMS
ILLMNRU	MILLRUN	ILNOPRU	PURLOIN	IMMNOSU	MUSIMON
ILLMOOR	MOORILL	ILNOPST	PONTILS		OMNIUMS
ILLMOOT	TIMOLOL	ILNOPSU	PULSION	IMMNOUU	MUONIUM
ILLMOPS	PLIMSOL		UPSILON	IMMOOSS	SIMOOMS
ILLMOSU	LOLIUMS	ILNOPSY	YPSILON	IMMOPTU	OPTIMUM
ILLMPUY	LUMPILY	ILNOPYY	POLYNYI	IMMOSSU	OSMIUMS
ILLMSUU	LIMULUS	ILNOQSU	QUINOLS	IMMOSTU	STOMIUM
ILLNOOY	LOONILY	ILNORST	NOSTRIL	IMMOSTW	WOMMITS
ILLNOQU	QUILLON	ILNORSU	SURLOIN	IMMSSTU	MUTISMS
ILLNORU	RULLION	ILNORTU	TORULIN		SUMMIST
ILLNOST	LINTOLS	ILNOSST	TONSILS		SUMMITS
ILLNPUU	LUPULIN	ILNOSSU	INSOULS	IMNNNOU	MUNNION
ILLNSUW	UNWILLS	ILNOSTU	OILNUTS	IMNNOOR	NORIMON
ILLNTUY	NULLITY		ULTIONS	IMNNOSW	MINNOWS
ILLOOPY	LOOPILY	ILNOSTY	STONILY	IMNNSTU	MUNTINS
ILLOORZ	ZORILLO		TYLOSIN	IMNOOPP	POMPION
ILLOPRY	PILLORY	ILNOSWY	SNOWILY	IMNOOPT	TOMPION
ILLOPST	POLLIST	ILNOTUV	VOLUTIN	IMNOORR	MORRION
ILLOPSW	PILLOWS	ILNPRSU	PURLINS	IMNOORS	MORIONS
ILLOPWY	PILLOWY	ILNPSST	SPLINTS	IMNOORT	MONITOR
ILLOSUV	VILLOUS	ILNPSTU	UNSPILT		TROMINO
ILLOSUY	LOUSILY		UNSPLIT	IMNOOSS	MONOSIS
ILLOSWW	WILLOWS	ILNRSTY	NITRYLS		SIMOONS
ILLOTUW	OUTWILL	ILNSSTU	INSULTS	IMNOOST	MOTIONS
ILLOTXY	XYLITOL	ILNSSVY	SYLVINS	IMNOOSU	OMINOUS
ILLOUVV	VOLVULI	ILNTTUY	NUTTILY	IMNOOSY	ISONOMY
ILLOWWY	WILLOWY	ILOOORS	ROSOLIO	IMNOOUX	OXONIUM
ILLPPUY	PULPILY	ILOOPST	POLOIST	IMNOPPU	PUMPION
ILLPSUV	PULVILS		TOPSOIL	IMNOPRW	PINWORM
ILLQSSU	SQUILLS	ILOORST	LORIOTS	IMNOPSU	SPUMONI
ILLRSUY	SURLILY	ILOORTY	OLITORY	IMNORRU	MURRION

IMNORTY	TRIONYM	INOPPST	TOPSPIN	IORTTUW	OUTWRIT
IMNOSST	MONISTS	INOPRSS	PRISONS	IOSSSTT	TSOTSIS
IMNOSSY	MYOSINS		SPINORS	IOSSTTU	OUTSITS
IMNOSVY	VISNOMY	INOPRST	TROPINS	IOSTTUW	OUTWITS
IMNRRSU	MURRINS	INOPRSU	INPOURS	IPPQSUU	QUIPPUS
IMNRSTU	UNTRIMS	INOPSST	PISTONS	IPRRSTU	IRRUPTS
IMOOPRX	PROXIMO		POSTINS		STIRRUP
IMOOSSS	OSMOSIS		SPINTOS	IPRSSTU	PURISTS
IMOOSSU	OSMIOUS	INOPSSU	POUSSIN		SPRUITS
IMOOSTV	VOMITOS		SPINOUS		UPRISTS
IMOPRSS	PORISMS	INOPSTT	TINPOTS		UPSTIRS
IMOPRST	IMPORTS	INOPSTU	SPINOUT	IPRSTUU	PURSUIT
	TROPISM	INORSTT	INTORTS	IPSSSTY	STYPSIS
IMOPRSV	IMPROVS		TRITONS	IPSSTTY	TYPISTS
IMOPRTU	PROTIUM	INORSTU	NITROUS	IPSTTTU	TITTUPS
IMOPSST	IMPOSTS		TURIONS	IPTTTUY	TITTUPY
	MISSTOP	INORSUU	RUINOUS	IQRRSSU	SQUIRRS
IMOPSTU	UTOPISM		URINOUS	IQRSSTU	SQUIRTS
IMORRRS	MIRRORS	INORSUV	UNVISOR	JJSTUUU	JUJUTSU
IMORSST	MISSORT	INOSSTT	STOTINS	JKNOOSU	KUNJOOS
IMORSTU	TOURISM	INOSSTU	OUTSINS	JLLOOPS	JOLLOPS
IMORSTY	TRISOMY		USTIONS	JMOPTUU	OUTJUMP
IMOSSTU	MISSOUT	INOSSUU	SINUOUS	JNNORUY	NONJURY
	SUMOIST	INOSTUW	OUTWINS	JNNOSTU	JOTUNNS
IMOSSVZ	ZYMOSIS	INPRSST	SPRINTS	JNOORSU	JOURNOS
IMOSTTT	TOMTITS	INPRSTU	TURNIPS		SOJOURN
IMOSTUV	VOMITUS		UNSTRIP	JOOPPSY	JOYPOPS
IMOSTUW	OUTSWIM	INPRSTY	TRYPSIN		POPJOYS
IMPRSSU	PURISMS	INQSSTU	SQUINTS	JOSTTUU	OUTJUTS
IMPSSTU	SUMPITS	INQSTUY	SQUINTY	KKLMSUU	MUKLUKS
IMQRSSU	SQUIRMS	INRSTTU	INTRUST	KKLOOYZ	KOLKOZY
IMQRSUY	SQUIRMY	INSSTUU	SUNSUIT	KKMOOSU	SKOOKUM
IMRSSTU	SISTRUM		UNSUITS	KKMSTUU	MUKTUKS
	TRISMUS	INSTTUW	UNTWIST	KKNRSUU	KUNKURS
	TRUISMS	INTTUWY	UNWITTY	KKSSSTT	TSKTSKS
IMRTTUY	YTTRIUM	IOOPRSS	POROSIS	KLLMOSU	MOLLUSK
INNNOOR	NONIRON	IOOPRSV	PROVISO	KLNOOPS	PLONKOS
INNNORU	RUNNION	IOOPSTY	ISOTOPY	KLOOOTU	LOOKOUT
INNOOPS	OPSONIN	IOORSSS	SOROSIS		OUTLOOK
INNOORS	RONIONS	IOORSST	TSOORIS	KLOOPSU	LOOKUPS
INNOOST	NOTIONS	IOORSTT	RISOTTO		UPLOOKS
INNOPSY	PINYONS	IOORSTU	RIOTOUS	KLOSTUU	OUTSULK
INNORST	INTRONS	IOOSSSS	SISSOOS	KLRSTUU	KULTURS
INNOSSU	UNISONS	IOOSSST	OSTOSIS	KMOOORS	MOKOROS
INNOSTU	NONSUIT	IOPPPRT	PITPROP	KMOSSUY	KOUMYSS
INNOSUY	UNNOISY	IOPPPST	POPPITS	KMPRSSU	SKRUMPS
INNOSWW	WINNOWS	IOPPRST	RIPSTOP	KNNNOUW	UNKNOWN
INNQSUY	SQUINNY	IOPPSTT	TIPTOPS	KNNOORW	NONWORK
INNRSTU	INTURNS	IOPRSST	RIPOSTS	KNNOSTU	UNKNOTS
INOOPRT	PORTION	IOPRSSY	PYROSIS	KNOOPTT	TOPKNOT
INOOPSS	POISONS	IOPRSTT	PROTIST	KNOOPRY	KRYPTON
	POISSON		TROPIST	KNORRTY	KRYTRON
INOOPST	OPTIONS	IOPSSTU	PISTOUS	KNORSUW	UNWORKS
	POSITON	IOPSTTU	UTOPIST	KOOOTTU	OUTTOOK
	POTIONS	IOPTTUY	OUTPITY	KOOPRTW	TOPWORK
INOORSS	ORISONS	IOQRTTU	QUITTOR		WORKTOP
INOORST	ISOTRON	IOQSSTU	QUOISTS	KOORTUW	OUTWORK
	NITROSO	IORRSTW	WORRITS		WORKOUT
	TORSION	IORRSZZ	RIZZORS	KOOSSSU	KOUSSOS
INOORSZ	ZORINOS	IORRTTX	TORTRIX	KOOSSUU	SOUKOUS
INOORTT	TORTONI	IORSSTU	SUITORS	KOOSTTU	TUKTOOS
INOOSST	TOISONS		TSOURIS	KOOSTWW	KOWTOWS
INOOSUX	NOXIOUS	IORSTTU	TOURIST	KOPRSUW	WORKUPS
INOPPRS	POPRINS	IORSTTW	TWISTOR	KORTTUW	TUTWORK

LLLMMUU	MULMULL
LLLOOPS	LOLLOPS
LLLOOPY	LOLLOPY
LLMMSUU	MULMULS
LLMOOPR	ROLLMOP
LLMPPUY	PLUMPLY
LLNORSU	UNROLLS
LLOOPRT	ROLLTOP
	TROLLOP
LLOOPSY	POLYOLS
LLOOPTU	OUTPOLL
LLOORTU	OUTROLL
	ROLLOUT
LLOOSTU	TOLUOLS
LLOPRSU	UPROLLS
LLOPTUU	OUTPULL
	PULLOUT
LLORSST	STROLLS
LLOSTUY	TOLUYLS
LLPPSUU	PULLUPS
LMMSTUU	MULTUMS
LMOOOOS	MOOLOOS
LMOORSU	ORMOLUS
LMOOSTY	TOYLSOM
LMOPSUU	PLUMOUS
LMORSSU	MUSROLS
LMRSTUU	LUSTRUM
LMSTTUU	TUMULTS
LMSTUUU	TUMULUS
LNNOOOW	NONWOOL
LNNOPSU	NONPLUS
LNOOPSU	UNSPOOL
LNOOPTU	PULTOON
LNOOSST	STOLONS
LNOPSTU	PLUTONS
	PULTONS
LNOSSUU	UNSOULS
LNPSTUU	PULTUNS
LNRTUUV	VULTURN
LNRTUUY	UNTRULY
LOOOORS	OLOROSO
LOOORST	ROTOLOS
LOOPTTU	OUTPLOT
LOOSSTV	VOLOSTS
LOPPRSY	PROPYLS
LOPPSUU	PULPOUS
LOPPSUY	POLYPUS
LOPRRSY	PYRROLS
LOPRSTY	PROTYLS
LOPRSUY	PYLORUS
LOPRTUY	POULTRY
LOPSSTY	STYLOPS
LORSTTY	TROTYLS
LORSTUU	TORULUS
LOSTTUY	STOUTLY
LPRSSUU	SURPLUS
MMMNOOY	MONONYM
MMNOSSU	MUSMONS
	SUMMONS
MMOOPPS	POMPOMS
MMOOSTT	MOTMOTS
MMOPSTY	SYMPTOM
MMRRSUU	MURMURS
MMSTUUU	MUTUUMS
MMSUUUU	MUUMUUS
MNNOOOS	MONSOON
MNNOORU	MONURON
MNNOSYY	SYNONYM
MNNOTUU	UNMOUNT
MNOOOPP	POMPOON
MNOOOYZ	ZOONOMY
MNOOPPS	POMPONS
MNOOPST	TOMPONS
MNOOPTY	TOPONYM
MNOORSU	SUNROOM
	UNMOORS
MNOOSTU	MOUTONS
MNOOSTW	TOWMONS
MNOOSUY	ONYMOUS
MNOOTTW	TOWMONT
MNORSTU	NOSTRUM
MNOSTTU	MUTTONS
MNOTTUY	MUTTONY
MOOOTYZ	ZOOTOMY
MOOPPSU	POMPOUS
MOOPRSY	POMROYS
MOOPSSU	OPOSSUM
MOOPSTT	TOPMOST
MOORRSW	MORROWS
MOOSTTU	OUTMOST
MOPPRST	PROMPTS
MOPPSSU	POSSUMS
MOPSSUU	SPUMOUS
MOQRSUU	QUORUMS
MOQSTUU	QUOTUMS
MORRSTU	ROSTRUM
MORRSUU	RUMOURS
MORSTUU	TUMOURS
MOSSSTY	MYSOSTS
MOSSTTU	UTMOSTS
MOSSTUU	OUTSUMS
MOSTUUW	OUTSWUM
NNNSUUY	UNSUNNY
NNOOOPR	NONPOOR
NNOOOPT	PONTOON
NNOOPRS	NONPROS
NNOOPRU	PRONOUN
NNOOPSS	SPONSON
NNOOPST	NONSTOP
	PONTONS
NNOORSY	RONYONS
NNOOSTW	WONTONS
NNORSTU	TURNONS
NNORSUW	UNSWORN
NNOSSUY	UNSONSY
NNOSTYY	SYNTONY
NNRSTUU	UNTURNS
NOOOSUZ	OZONOUS
NOOOSVX	SONOVOX
NOOPRSS	SPONSOR
NOOPRST	PROTONS
NOOPSSY	POYSONS
NOOPSUY	YOUPONS
NOORSST	TONSORS
NOORSTU	UNROOST
	UNROOTS
NOORTUW	OUTWORN
NOOTTWY	TOYTOWN
NOPPRSU	UNPROPS
NOPSSTU	SUNSPOT
	UNSTOPS
NOPSTUW	UPTOWNS
NORSTUU	OUTRUNS
	RUNOUTS
NORTTUU	OUTTURN
	TURNOUT
NOSSTUW	UNSTOWS
NPRSTUU	TURNUPS
	UPTURNS
NRSSTTU	STRUNTS
NRSSTUU	STURNUS
	UNTRUSS
NRSTTUU	UNTRUST
OOOOPRT	POTOROO
OOOOSZZ	ZOOZOOS
OOOPRTU	OUTROOP
OOORTTU	OUTROOT
OOPPSST	POSTOPS
OOPRRST	TORPORS
OOPRSSU	SOURSOP
OOPRSTU	PORTOUS
	UPROOTS
OOPRSTV	PROVOST
OOPRTTU	OUTPORT
OOPRTUU	OUTPOUR
OOPSSTT	TOSSPOT
OOPSTTU	OUTPOST
	OUTTOPS
OOPSWWW	POWWOWS
OORRSSW	SORROWS
OORSTUU	ROUTOUS
OORSTUW	OUTROWS
OORTTTU	OUTTROT
OPPPRSU	UPPROPS
OPPRRTU	PURPORT
OPPRSTU	SUPPORT
OPPRSTY	STROPPY
OPPRSUY	PYROPUS
OPRSSTU	SPROUTS
	STROUPS
	STUPORS
OPSSSTU	TOSSUPS
OPSTTUU	OUTPUTS
	PUTOUTS
ORRSTTU	TRUSTOR
ORSSSTU	TUSSORS
ORSSTTU	STROUTS
ORSSUUU	USUROUS
ORSTTUU	SURTOUT
ORSTTUY	TRYOUTS
RSSSTUU	TUSSURS

Eight-letter anagrams

AAAABCLZ	CALABAZA	**AAABDNNN**	BANDANNA	**AAACDKLY**	LACKADAY
AAAABENN	ANABAENA	**AAABDNNS**	BANDANAS	**AAACDMMS**	MACADAMS
AAAABKPS	BAASKAAP	**AAABDNRS**	SARABAND	**AAACDMNY**	ADAMANCY
AAAACCRR	CARACARA	**AAABDNRT**	ABRADANT	**AAACDNNO**	ANACONDA
AAAACGNR	CARAGANA	**AAABEGHL**	GALABEAH	**AAACDNRS**	SANDARAC
AAAACJRR	JARARACA	**AAABEGLL**	GALLABEA	**AAACDOTV**	ADVOCAAT
AAAACLMT	CALAMATA	**AAABEGLS**	GALABEAS	**AAACEGNT**	AGACANTE
AAAACNRS	ANASARCA	**AAABEHNR**	HABANERA	**AAACEGTU**	AGUACATE
AAAADMTV	AMADAVAT	**AAABEHRT**	BARATHEA	**AAACEHIN**	ACHAENIA
AAAADNPS	APADANAS	**AAABEMPR**	PARABEMA	**AAACEHLR**	ARCHAEAL
AAAADTVV	AVADAVAT	**AAABENSS**	ANABASES	**AAACEHLT**	CALATHEA
AAAAHJMR	MAHARAJA	**AAABFLLS**	FALBALAS	**AAACEHLZ**	CHALAZAE
AAAAIKMN	KAMAAINA	**AAABGHIL**	GALABIAH	**AAACEHNR**	ARCHAEAN
AAAAIMPR	ARAPAIMA	**AAABGILL**	GALLABIA	**AAACEHNT**	ACANTHAE
AAAAIRTX	ATARAXIA	**AAABGILS**	GALABIAS	**AAACELNT**	ANALECTA
AAAAJKRR	JARARAKA	**AAABGILY**	GALABIYA	**AAACELST**	CATALASE
AAAAKKMT	TAKAMAKA	**AAABGLNY**	BANGALAY	**AAACENNP**	PANACEAN
AAAAKKNT	KATAKANA	**AAABGLOR**	ALGAROBA	**AAACENPS**	PANACEAS
AAAAKKVV	KAVAKAVA	**AAABGMNQ**	MBAQANGA	**AAACGHNR**	CHARANGA
AAAAKKWW	KAWAKAWA	**AAABGRTU**	RUTABAGA	**AAACGINT**	CAATINGA
AAAAKLMT	KALAMATA	**AAABHLQS**	QABALAHS	**AAACGLSW**	SCALAWAG
AAAALLVV	LAVALAVA	**AAABHMST**	MASTABAH	**AAACGMNP**	CAMPAGNA
AAAALSTY	ATALAYAS	**AAABILTT**	BATTALIA	**AAACGMNR**	ARMAGNAC
AAAAMMTT	MATAMATA	**AAABINSS**	ANABASIS	**AAACHHLS**	HALACHAS
AAAAPPRR	PARAPARA	**AAABIPSS**	PIASABAS	**AAACHILZ**	CHALAZIA
AAAARRSS	SASARARA		PIASSABA	**AAACHIPS**	APHASIAC
AAAABBCHL	CABBALAH	**AAABISTV**	BATAVIAS	**AAACHLLZ**	CHALAZAL
AAABBCLS	CABBALAS	**AAABKLSV**	BAKLAVAS	**AAACHLNR**	ANARCHAL
AAABBELT	ABATABLE	**AAABKLSW**	BAKLAWAS	**AAACHLSZ**	CHALAZAS
AAABBHKL	KABBALAH	**AAABKPSS**	BAASKAPS	**AAACHNST**	ACANTHAS
AAABBILT	ABBATIAL		BAASSKAP	**AAACHRSY**	ACHARYAS
AAABBKLS	KABBALAS	**AAABLLSW**	WALLABAS	**AAACILMN**	MANIACAL
AAABCCMW	MACCABAW	**AAABLMOS**	ABOMASAL	**AAACILMR**	CALAMARI
AAABCCRS	BACCARAS	**AAABLMST**	TAMBALAS	**AAACILMS**	MALACIAS
AAABCCRT	BACCARAT	**AAABLOPR**	PARABOLA	**AAACILOS**	ALOCASIA
AAABCHIR	ABRACHIA	**AAABLPRS**	PALABRAS	**AAACILPR**	CARPALIA
AAABCHLS	CALABASH	**AAABMSST**	MASTABAS	**AAACILRV**	CALVARIA
AAABCHMU	MACAHUBA	**AAABNNRS**	RABANNAS	**AAACILSY**	CALISAYA
AAABCILP	ABAPICAL	**AAABORRS**	ARAROBAS	**AAACIMRS**	CARIAMAS
AAABCINT	ANABATIC	**AAACCELN**	CALCANEA	**AAACINPS**	ACAPNIAS
AAABCIRS	ARABICAS	**AAACCEPR**	CARAPACE	**AAACINTV**	CAVATINA
AAABCITT	CIABATTA	**AAACCILR**	CALCARIA	**AAACIPSU**	SAPUCAIA
AAABCLOS	BACALAOS	**AAACCIMM**	CAIMACAM	**AAACIRRS**	SACRARIA
AAABCLSV	BACLAVAS	**AAACCLMS**	MALACCAS	**AAACIRSS**	ACRASIAS
AAABCNRR	BARRACAN	**AAACCLPS**	ALPACCAS	**AAACIRTX**	ATARAXIC
	BARRANCA	**AAACCLRS**	CARACALS	**AAACJMRS**	JACAMARS
AAABCNRS	BARACANS	**AAACCRSS**	CASCARAS	**AAACKLMN**	ALMANACK
AAABCNRU	CARNAUBA	**AAACCRTT**	CATARACT	**AAACKMRT**	TAMARACK
AAABCORS	CARABAOS	**AAACDDRT**	DATACARD	**AAACLLSV**	CAVALLAS
AAABCPRY	CAPYBARA	**AAACDEIM**	ACADEMIA	**AAACLMNS**	ALMANACS
AAABCSSS	CASSABAS	**AAACDELM**	ACELDAMA		MANCALAS
AAABCSTW	CATAWBAS	**AAACDEMN**	ADAMANCE	**AAACLMRS**	CALAMARS
AAABDEHH	DAHABEAH	**AAACDENR**	DRACAENA	**AAACLMRY**	CALAMARY
AAABDEST	DATABASE	**AAACDEQU**	AQUACADE	**AAACLNST**	CANTALAS
AAABDFRS	ABFARADS	**AAACDETU**	ACAUDATE	**AAACLPST**	CATALPAS
AAABDHHI	DAHABIAH	**AAACDFIR**	FARADAIC	**AAACLRST**	ALCATRAS
AAABDHHL	HABDALAH	**AAACDILR**	CALDARIA	**AAACLRSZ**	ALCAZARS
AAABDHIY	DAHABIYA	**AAACDINR**	ACARIDAN	**AAACMNPS**	CAMPANAS
AAABDIKR	BAIDARKA		ARCADIAN	**AAACMOST**	ATAMASCO
AAABDKNT	DATABANK	**AAACDIRS**	ARCADIAS	**AAACMRSS**	MACASSAR
AAABDLMS	LAMBADAS				MARASCAS

	MASCARAS	**AAADNRST**	TANADARS	**AAAGLMMS**	AMALGAMS
AAACMRSU	AMARACUS	**AAADSWYY**	AWAYDAYS	**AAAGLMNS**	MALANGAS
AAACNNRS	CARANNAS	**AAAEEKRR**	KAREAREA		NAGMAALS
AAACNOPT	CAPONATA	**AAAEGISS**	ASSEGAAI	**AAAGLNSS**	LASAGNAS
AAACNPST	CATAPANS	**AAAEGLMX**	MALAXAGE	**AAAGLNTV**	GALAVANT
AAACNRST	NACARATS	**AAAEGLRT**	ALTARAGE	**AAAGLRRW**	WARRAGAL
AAACNRSU	CARAUNAS	**AAAEGLST**	GALATEAS	**AAAGLRST**	ASTRAGAL
AAACNRSV	CARAVANS	**AAAEGNPP**	APPANAGE	**AAAGMNRS**	ANAGRAMS
AAACNSST	CANASTAS	**AAAEGNPS**	APANAGES	**AAAGMPRR**	PARAGRAM
AAACNSTT	CANTATAS	**AAAEGRST**	GASTRAEA	**AAAGNOPR**	ARAPONGA
AAACRRWY	CARRAWAY	**AAAEHLMT**	HAEMATAL	**AAAGNPRS**	PARASANG
AAACRSWY	CARAWAYS	**AAAEHLST**	ALTHAEAS		PARGANAS
AAACSSST	CASSATAS	**AAAEHMNT**	ANATHEMA	**AAAGNPRU**	ARAPUNGA
AAACSSSV	CASSAVAS	**AAAEHNPS**	ANAPHASE	**AAAGNRST**	TANAGRAS
AAACSSTT	CATASTAS	**AAAEHPTU**	PAHAUTEA	**AAAGNRSU**	GUARANAS
AAACSTWY	CASTAWAY	**AAAEIMNS**	ANAEMIAS	**AAAGNSTY**	YATAGANS
AAADEFGN	FANEGADA	**AAAEKKRT**	KARATEKA	**AAAHHHKL**	HALAKHAH
AAADEFWY	FADEAWAY	**AAAEKTWY**	TAKEAWAY	**AAAHHKLS**	HALAKAHS
AAADEGNP	APANAGED	**AAAELMMN**	ANALEMMA		HALAKHAS
AAADEIMZ	MAZAEDIA	**AAAELMPT**	PALAMATE	**AAAHHLLS**	HALALAHS
AAADEJMP	PAJAMAED	**AAAELMTX**	MALAXATE	**AAAHHLSV**	HALAVAHS
AAADELMS	ALAMEDAS	**AAAELNPT**	PANATELA	**AAAHHPRS**	PARASHAH
	SALAAMED	**AAAELRTV**	LAVATERA	**AAAHHPRT**	HAPHTARA
AAADEMNP	EMPANADA	**AAAEMRST**	TARAMEAS	**AAAHHSTT**	TATAHASH
AAADENTV	VANADATE	**AAAENNSS**	ANANASES	**AAAHIKPS**	APHAKIAS
AAADEPRT	TAPADERA	**AAAENOPR**	PARANOEA	**AAAHIKSW**	KAHAWAIS
AAADFRSY	FARADAYS	**AAAENPRV**	PARAVANE	**AAAHIMNR**	MAHARANI
AAADGGHH	HAGGADAH	**AAAENPST**	ANAPAEST	**AAAHIMNS**	SHAMIANA
AAADGGHS	AGGADAHS	**AAAENSST**	ANATASES	**AAAHIMRT**	HAMARTIA
	HAGGADAS	**AAAEPRST**	SEPARATA	**AAAHINPR**	RAPHANIA
AAADGIMM	GAMMADIA	**AAAERSWY**	AREAWAYS	**AAAHINRS**	HARIANAS
AAADGLMY	AMYGDALA	**AAAERTWY**	TEARAWAY	**AAAHIPSS**	APHASIAS
AAADGLNS	SALADANG	**AAAFFLLS**	ALFALFAS	**AAAHIPTY**	PITAHAYA
AAADHHLV	HAVDALAH	**AAAFHHRT**	HAFTARAH	**AAAHJKSW**	KAJAWAHS
AAADHHSS	SHAHADAS	**AAAFHRST**	HAFTARAS	**AAAHKMNS**	KHANSAMA
AAADHMMS	HAMMADAS	**AAAFINST**	FANTASIA	**AAAHKRSS**	RAKSHASA
AAADHMRS	ADHARMAS	**AAAFINUV**	AVIFAUNA	**AAAHLMRS**	HARMALAS
	HARAMDAS	**AAAFIRST**	RATAFIAS	**AAAHLNNS**	ALANNAHS
	MADRASAH	**AAAFLLWY**	FALLAWAY	**AAAHMMST**	MAHATMAS
AAADHNRT	THANADAR	**AAAFMQRU**	AQUAFARM	**AAAHMNRT**	AMARANTH
AAADHNSS	SADHANAS	**AAAFNRSS**	SARAFANS	**AAAHMRRS**	ASHRAMAS
AAADIILR	RADIALIA	**AAAFRSWY**	FARAWAYS	**AAAHMSST**	TAMASHAS
AAADILLP	PALLADIA	**AAAGGLLN**	GALANGAL	**AAAHNNSV**	SAVANNAH
AAADILRU	ADULARIA	**AAAGGLNS**	GALANGAS	**AAAHNOPR**	ANAPHORA
AAADIMNS	DAMIANAS	**AAAGGLOP**	GALAPAGO	**AAAHNSTY**	ATHANASY
AAADIMNY	ADYNAMIA	**AAAGHINR**	HIRAGANA	**AAAHPRST**	PARATHAS
AAADIRST	DATARIAS	**AAAGHIPR**	AGRAPHIA	**AAAHRSTW**	WARATAHS
	RADIATAS	**AAAGHIPS**	APHAGIAS	**AAAHSWWY**	WASHAWAY
AAADJMRS	JAMADARS	**AAAGHLNS**	LANGAHAS	**AAAHTTWY**	THATAWAY
AAADKLMN	KALAMDAN	**AAAGHNNT**	AGNATHAN	**AAAIIMNP**	APIMANIA
AAADKNSW	WAKANDAS	**AAAGHNSS**	SAGANASH	**AAAIINPR**	APIARIAN
AAADKRRV	AARDVARK	**AAAGHNST**	ATAGHANS	**AAAIKKMM**	KAIMAKAM
AAADLMNQ	QALAMDAN	**AAAGHNTY**	YATAGHAN	**AAAIKKRS**	KARAKIAS
AAADLMNS	AMANDLAS	**AAAGILMM**	MAMALIGA	**AAAIKLST**	LATAKIAS
	MANDALAS	**AAAGILNS**	ANALGIAS	**AAAIKRSS**	AKRASIAS
AAADLMSW	WADMAALS	**AAAGILPT**	PATAGIAL	**AAAILLMR**	MALARIAL
AAADMNST	ADAMANTS	**AAAGILRT**	ALIGARTA	**AAAILLPT**	PALATIAL
AAADMNTU	TAMANDUA	**AAAGIMMT**	GAMMATIA	**AAAILMNR**	MALARIAN
AAADMORT	MATADORA	**AAAGINRR**	AGRARIAN	**AAAILMRS**	MALARIAS
AAADMPPP	PAPPADAM	**AAAGINRS**	ANGARIAS		RASMALAI
AAADMPPS	PAPADAMS	**AAAGINSZ**	GAZANIAS	**AAAILMSV**	MALVASIA
AAADMRSS	MADRASAS	**AAAGISSS**	ASSAGAIS	**AAAILNPR**	PLANARIA
	MADRASSA	**AAAGJMSU**	MAJAGUAS	**AAAILNRU**	AULARIAN
AAADNRSS	SARDANAS	**AAAGKNRS**	KARANGAS	**AAAILPRS**	PARASAIL

AAAILPRV	PARAVAIL		TARTANAS	AABCCHKS	CASHBACK
AAAILPRX	PARAXIAL	AAAORSWY	SOARAWAY	AABCCHKT	BACKCHAT
AAAILPSS	APLASIAS	AAAPPRST	APPARATS	AABCCHNT	BACCHANT
AAAILQRU	AQUARIAL	AAAPQRTU	PARAQUAT	AABCCIMR	CARBAMIC
AAAILRST	SALARIAT	AAAPSSST	PASSATAS	AABCCINN	CANNABIC
AAAIMMQQ	QAIMAQAM	AAARSTTT	RATATATS	AABCCKKP	BACKPACK
AAAIMMST	MIASMATA	AAARSTTU	TUATARAS	AABCCKLL	CALLBACK
AAAIMNRR	MARINARA	AAASTWYY	STAYAWAY	AABCCKLP	BLACKCAP
AAAIMNST	AMANITAS	AABBBDEK	KABABBED	AABCCKLW	CLAWBACK
AAAIMRSU	MAIASAUR	AABBBELS	BABBELAS	AABCCKST	BACKCAST
AAAINNRR	RANARIAN	AABBCDEG	CABBAGED		SCATBACK
AAAINOPR	PARANOIA	AABBCDKN	BACKBAND	AABCCMOT	CATACOMB
AAAINPSS	PAISANAS	AABBCDRS	SCABBARD	AABCCMOY	MACCABOY
AAAINQRU	AQUARIAN	AABBCEGS	CABBAGES	AABCDEIN	ABIDANCE
AAAIPRST	ASPIRATA	AABBCEGY	CABBAGEY	AABCDEIT	ABDICATE
AAAIPRSX	APRAXIAS	AABBCEIS	ABBACIES	AABCDEKT	BACKDATE
AAAIPSSV	PIASAVAS	AABBCEKR	BAREBACK	AABCDELL	CABALLED
	PIASSAVA	AABBCEKT	BACKBEAT	AABCDELN	BALANCED
AAAISSST	ASTASIAS	AABBCINR	BARBICAN	AABCDHKN	BACKHAND
AAAKKTZZ	KAZATZKA	AABBCIRR	BARBARIC	AABCDHKR	HARDBACK
AAAKLMSY	YAMALKAS	AABBCIST	SABBATIC	AABCDIIS	DIABASIC
AAAKLWWY	WALKAWAY	AABBCKST	BACKSTAB	AABCDILL	BALLADIC
AAAKMNRS	NAMASKAR	AABBCMOS	CABOMBAS	AABCDILR	ALDICARB
AAAKMTUU	KAUMATUA	AABBCORS	BARBASCO	AABCDILU	BICAUDAL
AAAKOSWY	SOAKAWAY	AABBDENS	BASEBAND	AABCDIMS	DICAMBAS
AAAKPPSU	KAUPAPAS	AABBDERT	BARBATED	AABCDINT	ABDICANT
AAALLPRX	PARALLAX	AABBDGRS	GABBARDS	AABCDIRS	CARABIDS
AAALLPST	PALATALS	AABBEELR	BEARABLE	AABCDKLN	BACKLAND
AAALMMOR	MALAROMA	AABBEELT	BEATABLE	AABCDKLO	BACKLOAD
AAALMPST	TAMPALAS	AABBEGNS	BEANBAGS	AABCDKNR	BANKCARD
AAALMRSS	MARSALAS	AABBEILL	BAILABLE	AABCDKRW	BACKWARD
AAALNNPT	PLATANNA	AABBEISS	BABESIAS		DRAWBACK
AAALNNST	LANTANAS	AABBEKLN	BANKABLE	AABCDKRY	BACKYARD
AAALNPRT	RATAPLAN	AABBELLM	BLAMABLE	AABCDLNS	SCABLAND
AAALNPST	APLANATS	AABBELLN	BEANBALL	AABCDNRR	BRANCARD
AAALNRTT	TARLATAN	AABBELLS	BASEBALL	AABCDNST	CABSTAND
AAALPRST	SATRAPAL	AABBELNN	BANNABLE	AABCEEFL	FACEABLE
AAALRRSY	ARRAYALS	AABBELOS	BAALEBOS	AABCEEHS	SEABEACH
AAALSWYY	LAYAWAYS	AABBELOT	BOATABLE	AABCEENY	ABEYANCE
AAAMMPRS	MAMPARAS	AABBELRR	BARRABLE	AABCEERS	SCARABEE
AAAMNNST	ANATMANS	AABBELRY	BEARABLY	AABCEERT	ACERBATE
AAAMNOPR	PANORAMA	AABBELSU	ABUSABLE	AABCEFRS	FACEBARS
AAAMNRRY	YARRAMAN	AABBEORT	BAREBOAT	AABCEGOT	CABOTAGE
AAAMNRST	AMARANTS	AABBGRST	GABBARTS	AABCEHKL	HACKABLE
	MARANTAS	AABBHKSU	BABUSHKA	AABCEHLS	CASHABLE
AAAMNSTY	MANYATAS	AABBHSST	SABBATHS	AABCEHMS	AMBACHES
AAAMNTTY	MANYATTA	AABBIILL	BILABIAL	AABCEHNR	BARCHANE
AAAMORST	TAMARAOS	AABBILRT	BARBITAL	AABCEILM	AMICABLE
AAAMOTTU	AUTOMATA	AABBIRSU	BABIRUSA	AABCEIMN	AMBIANCE
AAAMPRST	PATAMARS	AABBLLMY	BLAMABLY	AABCEINR	CARABINE
AAAMPRTT	PATTAMAR	AABBLORS	BARBOLAS	AABCEIRT	BACTERIA
AAAMRRSZ	ZAMARRAS	AABBLSSU	SUBBASAL	AABCEITT	CIABATTE
AAAMRSSS	SAMSARAS	AABBMMOZ	ZAMBOMBA	AABCEKLM	CLAMBAKE
AAAMRSTU	TAMARAUS	AABBSSSU	BABASSUS	AABCEKLP	PACKABLE
AAAMRTTU	TRAUMATA	AABCCCHI	BACCHIAC	AABCEKLR	LACEBARK
AAAMRTZZ	RAZMATAZ	AABCCDET	BACCATED	AABCEKLS	SACKABLE
AAANNSSV	SAVANNAS	AABCCEHK	BACKACHE	AABCEKST	BACKSEAT
AAANNSTT	ANNATTAS	AABCCELS	CASCABEL		SEATBACK
AAANOPRZ	PARAZOAN		CASCABLE	AABCELLL	CALLABLE
AAANORSY	SAYONARA	AABCCERT	BRACCATE	AABCELLP	PLACABLE
AAANPRTV	PARAVANT	AABCCHHS	BACHCHAS	AABCELLR	CABALLER
AAANQTUU	AQUANAUT	AABCCHIN	BACCHIAN	AABCELLS	SCALABLE
AAANRSTT	TANTARAS	AABCCHIS	BISCACHA	AABCELNR	BALANCER
	TARANTAS	AABCCHIZ	BIZCACHA		BARNACLE

AABCELNS	BALANCES	AABCISSS	ABSCISSA	AABDEGHN	HEADBANG
AABCELOR	ALBACORE	AABCISTX	TAXICABS	AABDEGIN	BADINAGE
AABCELPR	CAPABLER	AABCKKLT	TALKBACK	AABDEGIR	BIGARADE
AABCELPS	SPACELAB	AABCKLNO	LOANBACK	AABDEGLR	GRADABLE
AABCELRS	BERASCAL	AABCKLNY	CLAYBANK	AABDEGMS	GAMBADES
AABCELRT	BRACTEAL	AABCKLPS	BACKSLAP	AABDEGNR	BANDAGER
	CARTABLE	AABCKLPY	PLAYBACK	AABDEGNS	BANDAGES
AABCELST	CASTABLE	AABCKLSY	LAYBACKS	AABDEGRR	BARRAGED
AABCELSU	CAUSABLE	AABCKNNS	CANBANKS	AABDEHHI	DAHABIEH
AABCELWY	CABLEWAY	AABCKNPS	SNAPBACK	AABDEHKR	HARDBAKE
AABCEMRT	CRABMEAT	AABCKPRT	BRATPACK	AABDEHMR	HARDBEAM
AABCEMRV	VAMBRACE	AABCKPRW	BACKWRAP	AABDEHNR	BAREHAND
AABCEMSS	AMBSACES	AABCKPSY	BACKPAYS	AABDEILN	BALADINE
AABCENYY	ABEYANCY		PAYBACKS	AABDEILR	RADIABLE
AABCEORS	ACARBOSE	AABCKRRS	BARRACKS	AABDEILT	LABIATED
AABCERRS	BARRACES	AABCKSSW	BACKSAWS	AABDEIOU	ABOIDEAU
AABCERST	ABREACTS	AABCKSTY	BACKSTAY	AABDEIRS	ARABISED
	BEARCATS	AABCKSWY	SWAYBACK	AABDEIRZ	ARABIZED
	CABARETS	AABCLLLO	COALBALL	AABDEISS	DIABASES
	CABRESTA	AABCLLLY	BALLCLAY	AABDEJLL	DJELLABA
AABCERTT	CABRETTA	AABCLLPY	PLACABLY	AABDEJNX	BANJAXED
AABCESSU	ABACUSES	AABCLLSY	SCALABLY	AABDEKPR	PARBAKED
AABCFHKL	HALFBACK	AABCLMRY	CARBAMYL	AABDEKRY	DAYBREAK
AABCFIIL	BIFACIAL	AABCLMSU	CALUMBAS	AABDEKSW	DAWBAKES
AABCFKLL	BACKFALL	AABCLNTY	BLATANCY	AABDELLS	BALLADES
	FALLBACK	AABCLNUU	CUNABULA	AABDELLT	BALLATED
AABCFKLT	FLATBACK	AABCLRRY	CARBARYL	AABDELLU	LAUDABLE
AABCFKST	FASTBACK	AABCLRSU	LABRUSCA	AABDELMN	DAMNABLE
	FATBACKS	AABCMMSU	MACUMBAS	AABDELMS	BALSAMED
AABCGIMO	CAMBOGIA	AABCMSSU	SAMBUCAS	AABDELNS	SANDABLE
AABCGKRY	GRAYBACK	AABCNORR	BARRANCO	AABDELOR	ADORABLE
AABCHHRS	BRACHAHS	AABCNRRS	CARBARNS	AABDELPR	DRAPABLE
AABCHILR	BRACHIAL	AABCORRS	CARBORAS		PARABLED
AABCHINR	BRANCHIA	AABCORST	ABACTORS	AABDELPT	BALDPATE
AABCHKLS	BACKLASH		ACROBATS	AABDELRS	BASELARD
AABCHKLU	BACKHAUL	AABCOSTT	CATBOATS	AABDELRT	TRADABLE
AABCHKRS	SHABRACK	AABCRSTT	ABSTRACT	AABDELRW	DRAWABLE
AABCHKSW	BACKWASH	AABCSTTU	CATTABUS	AABDELRY	READABLY
AABCHLOO	COOLABAH	AABDDEET	DEADBEAT	AABDELSW	SAWBLADE
AABCHMRY	CHAMBRAY	AABDDEGN	BANDAGED	AABDELSY	ABASEDLY
AABCHNRS	BARCHANS	AABDDEHL	BALDHEAD	AABDEMMS	BEMADAMS
AABCIILR	BIRACIAL	AABDDEHN	HEADBAND	AABDEMNS	BEADSMAN
AABCIILS	BASILICA	AABDDEIR	ABRAIDED	AABDEMNT	BANDMATE
AABCIINR	BRAINIAC	AABDDELL	BALLADED	AABDENSU	BANDEAUS
AABCIKLT	TAILBACK	AABDDENR	BRANDADE	AABDENTU	UNABATED
AABCILLR	BACILLAR	AABDDERT	TABARDED	AABDENUX	BANDEAUX
	CABRILLA	AABDDESS	BADASSED	AABDENVW	WAVEBAND
AABCILMS	BALSAMIC	AABDDIKS	KABADDIS	AABDEORS	SEABOARD
	CABALISM	AABDDINZ	ZINDABAD	AABDEORT	TEABOARD
AABCILMY	AMICABLY	AABDDLNS	BADLANDS	AABDEORX	BROADAXE
AABCILNN	CANNIBAL	AABDDMOR	DAMBOARD	AABDERRS	ABRADERS
AABCILNO	ANABOLIC	AABDDMRU	MURDABAD	AABDERRT	TABERDAR
AABCILOR	BRACIOLA	AABDDNSS	SANDDABS	AABDERRW	BEARWARD
AABCILST	BASALTIC	AABDEEHL	BEHEADAL	AABDERTT	RABATTED
	CABALIST	AABDEEHR	BAREHEAD	AABDERTV	VARTABED
AABCINNN	CANNABIN	AABDEELR	READABLE	AABDERWY	WAYBREAD
AABCINNR	CINNABAR	AABDEELT	DATEABLE	AABDESSS	BADASSES
AABCINNS	CANNABIS		DEALBATE	AABDFHLN	FAHLBAND
AABCINOT	BOTANICA	AABDEELV	EVADABLE	AABDGHNS	HANDBAGS
AABCINRS	CARABINS	AABDEELW	WADEABLE	AABDGHRS	HARDBAGS
AABCINSU	BANAUSIC	AABDEEMN	ENDAMEBA	AABDGINN	ABANDING
AABCIOPS	COPAIBAS	AABDEERT	TEABREAD	AABDGINR	ABRADING
AABCIOSS	SCABIOSA	AABDEERY	BAYADEER	AABDGINR	LANDGRAB
AABCIRSS	BRASSICA		BAYADERE	AABDGMOS	GAMBADOS

AABDGNOV	VAGABOND	AABEEGNT	ABNEGATE	AABEGMRS	BERGAMAS
AABDGNSS	SANDBAGS	AABEEHLL	HEALABLE		MEGABARS
AABDGORR	GARBOARD	AABEEHLR	HEARABLE	AABEGMRT	BREGMATA
AABDGORT	TAGBOARD	AABEEHLT	HATEABLE	AABEGMTT	GAMBETTA
AABDGOTU	GADABOUT		HEATABLE	AABEGNOR	BARONAGE
AABDHINR	HAIRBAND	AABEEHMR	HARAMBEE	AABEGORT	ABROGATE
AABDHLLN	HANDBALL	AABEEKLM	MAKEABLE	AABEGOST	SABOTAGE
AABDHLLR	HARDBALL	AABEEKLT	TAKEABLE	AABEGOSZ	GAZABOES
AABDHNST	HATBANDS	AABEEKMT	BAKEMEAT	AABEGRRS	BAGARRES
AABDHNSY	HAYBANDS		MAKEBATE		BARRAGES
AABDHRSU	BAHADURS	AABEEKRW	BAKEWARE	AABEGRSS	BRASSAGE
	SUBAHDAR	AABEELLS	LEASABLE	AABEGSSS	BAGASSES
AABDIILR	BIRADIAL		SALEABLE	AABEGSSU	ABUSAGES
AABDIILS	BASIDIAL		SEALABLE	AABEHIRR	HERBARIA
AABDIKRS	BIDARKAS	AABEELMN	AMENABLE	AABEHJLL	JELLABAH
AABDILLN	BALLADIN		NAMEABLE	AABEHKLS	SHAKABLE
AABDILNS	BALADINS	AABEELMT	TAMEABLE	AABEHLMS	SHAMABLE
AABDIMNO	ABDOMINA	AABEELPR	REAPABLE	AABEHLOT	OATHABLE
AABDIMNR	MADBRAIN	AABEELPT	TAPEABLE	AABEHLPS	SHAPABLE
AABDIMRS	BARMAIDS	AABEELRS	ERASABLE	AABEHLPT	ALPHABET
AABDINNR	RAINBAND	AABEELRT	RATEABLE	AABEHLRS	SHARABLE
AABDINRS	BANDARIS		TEARABLE	AABEHLRW	WARHABLE
AABDINST	TABANIDS	AABEELRW	WEARABLE	AABEHLSV	SHAVABLE
AABDKNNS	SANDBANK	AABEELST	EATABLES	AABEHLSW	WASHABLE
AABDLLRY	BALLADRY		TEASABLE	AABEHNOR	HABANERO
	BALLYARD	AABEELSV	SAVEABLE	AABEHNST	ABTHANES
AABDLLUY	LAUDABLY	AABEEMNO	AMOEBEAN	AABEIJLL	JAILABLE
AABDLMNU	LABDANUM	AABEEMNT	ENTAMEBA	AABEIKLS	KIELBASA
AABDLMNY	DAMNABLY	AABEEMPR	ABAMPERE	AABEIKNS	IKEBANAS
AABDLMRU	ADUMBRAL	AABEENNW	WANNABEE	AABEILLL	ALLIABLE
AABDLNPT	PLATBAND	AABEENOR	ANAEROBE	AABEILLM	MAILABLE
AABDLNSS	SALBANDS	AABEERRT	ABERRATE	AABEILLS	ISABELLA
AABDLOOT	BOATLOAD	AABEERSZ	ZAREEBAS		SAILABLE
AABDLOPR	LAPBOARD	AABEERTT	TRABEATE	AABEILNR	INARABLE
AABDLORR	LABRADOR	AABEFFNS	BEFFANAS	AABEILNS	BANALISE
	LARBOARD	AABEFGLS	FLEABAGS	AABEILNZ	BANALIZE
AABDLORY	ADORABLY	AABEFGSU	AUFGABES	AABEILRS	RAISABLE
AABDLRSW	BRADAWLS	AABEFHKL	HALFBEAK	AABEILRV	VARIABLE
AABDMNNS	BANDSMAN	AABEFLLL	FLABELLA	AABEILST	BALISTAE
AABDMNNY	BANDYMAN	AABEFLMO	FOAMABLE		LABIATES
AABDMNOR	BOARDMAN	AABEFLMR	FARMABLE		SATIABLE
AABDMNRS	ARMBANDS		FRAMABLE	AABEILTV	ABLATIVE
AABDNNOS	ABANDONS	AABEFLMU	FLAMBEAU	AABEIMNR	AMBERINA
AABDNNTU	ABUNDANT	AABEFLTU	FABULATE	AABEIMRS	AMBARIES
AABDNORS	BANDORAS	AABEFNSS	FANBASES	AABEINOZ	ZABAIONE
AABDNPSS	PASSBAND	AABEGGGS	BAGGAGES	AABEINRT	ATABRINE
AABDNRRY	BARNYARD	AABEGGLY	GAGEABLY		RABATINE
AABDNRSS	SANDBARS	AABEGGRS	GARBAGES	AABEINST	BASANITE
AABDNRSU	BANDURAS	AABEGGRY	GARBAGEY	AABEIOTU	ABOITEAU
AABDNSSW	BANDSAWS	AABEGHIL	GALABIEH	AABEIRSS	AIRBASES
AABDORSV	BRAVADOS	AABEGHLN	HANGABLE		ARABISES
AABDORTY	BOATYARD	AABEGHNR	BERGHAAN	AABEIRSV	ABRASIVE
AABDORWY	BROADWAY	AABEGILN	GAINABLE	AABEIRSZ	ARABIZES
	WAYBOARD	AABEGILT	AGITABLE	AABEIRTU	AUBRETIA
AABDRRSS	BRASSARD	AABEGINR	ABEARING		AUBRIETA
AABDRRSW	DRAWBARS	AABEGLLL	GLABELLA	AABEISST	ABATISES
AABDRSST	BASTARDS	AABEGLLM	BALLGAME	AABEJLLS	JELLABAS
AABDRSSU	SUBADARS	AABEGLNW	GNAWABLE	AABEJLMM	JAMMABLE
AABDRSTY	BASTARDY	AABEGLRS	ALGEBRAS	AABEJMUX	JAMBEAUX
AABEEFLN	FLEABANE	AABEGLRT	GLABRATE	AABEJNOZ	ZABAJONE
AABEEGGL	GAGEABLE	AABEGLRU	ARGUABLE	AABEJNSX	BANJAXES
AABEEGKR	BRAKEAGE	AABEGLRZ	GRAZABLE	AABEKLLS	SLAKABLE
	BREAKAGE	AABEGMNR	BARGEMAN	AABEKLLT	TALKABLE
AABEEGLT	ABLEGATE	AABEGMNY	MANGABEY	AABEKLLW	WALKABLE

AABEKLMS	MASKABLE		RATSBANE	AABHMNRS	BRAHMANS
AABEKMNR	BRAKEMAN	AABENRTU	ARBUTEAN	AABHMRSS	SAMBHARS
AABEKNSS	SEABANKS	AABEORRT	ARBORETA	AABHMSTT	BATHMATS
AABEKPRR	PARBREAK	AABEORST	AEROBATS	AABHNOTU	AUTOBAHN
AABEKPRS	PARBAKES		RABATOES	AABHQSSU	SQUABASH
AABEKRRS	BARESARK	AABEOSSU	OUBAASES	AABHRRSU	SURBAHAR
AABEKRSS	ARABESKS	AABEQSUU	USQUABAE	AABIIJLT	JAILBAIT
AABEKRSY	KERBAYAS	AABERRRT	BARRATER	AABIILSZ	ALBIZIAS
AABELLMT	MEATBALL	AABERRSW	BARWARES	AABIILZZ	ALBIZZIA
AABELLNO	LOANABLE	AABERSSU	SUBAREAS	AABIINST	ANTIBIAS
AABELLPP	PALPABLE	AABERSTT	RABATTES	AABIIPST	BAPTISIA
AABELLPS	LAPSABLE		TABARETS	AABIJMSY	JAMBIYAS
AABELLPY	PLAYABLE	AABERSTU	ABATURES	AABIKLMS	KABALISM
AABELLRS	EARBALLS	AABESZZZ	BAZAZZES		KALIMBAS
AABELLSS	SABELLAS	AABETTUX	BATTEAUX	AABIKLST	KABALIST
AABELLSV	SALVABLE	AABFILUX	FABLIAUX	AABIKNSS	BANKSIAS
AABELLSY	SALEABLY	AABFLLST	FASTBALL	AABILLLY	LABIALLY
	SLAYABLE	AABFLOTT	FALTBOAT	AABILLRS	BARILLAS
AABELLUV	VALUABLE		FLATBOAT	AABILLST	BALLISTA
AABELMNY	AMENABLY	AABGGGNN	GANGBANG	AABILMNS	BAILSMAN
AABELMPP	MAPPABLE	AABGGNOT	TABOGGAN	AABILMNU	BIMANUAL
AABELMST	BLASTEMA	AABGGRRT	BRAGGART	AABILMQS	QABALISM
	LAMBASTE	AABGHINS	ABASHING	AABILMSS	BAALISMS
AABELMSU	AMUSABLE	AABGHKRS	SHAGBARK	AABILNNU	BIANNUAL
AABELMTU	AMBULATE	AABGHNRS	BHANGRAS	AABILNOR	BARONIAL
AABELNNT	TANNABLE	AABGHNSS	NASHGABS	AABILNOT	ABLATION
AABELNOS	ABALONES	AABGIILS	ABIGAILS	AABILNRT	BRANTAIL
AABELNOT	ATONABLE	AABGIINR	BRAAIING	AABILNRU	BINAURAL
AABELNPS	ANABLEPS	AABGILMS	MAILBAGS	AABILNTY	BANALITY
AABELNPT	PANTABLE	AABGILNT	ABLATING	AABILOST	SAILBOAT
AABELNPW	PAWNABLE		BANGTAIL	AABILOSU	ABOULIAS
AABELNRY	BALNEARY	AABGIMNS	SAMBAING	AABILOTT	BOATTAIL
AABELNSS	BANSELAS	AABGIMSU	GAMBUSIA	AABILQST	QABALIST
AABELNST	BANALEST	AABGINRS	BARGAINS	AABILRRT	ARBITRAL
AABELOPR	PARABOLE	AABGINRY	ABRAYING	AABILRST	ARBALIST
AABELORR	ARBOREAL	AABGINSS	BISNAGAS	AABILRSU	BALISAUR
AABELOSV	LAVABOES	AABGINSZ	BIZNAGAS	AABILRSY	BASILARY
AABELOVW	AVOWABLE	AABGLLLO	GOALBALL	AABILRVY	VARIABLY
AABELPPR	PALPEBRA	AABGLLRY	BALLYRAG	AABILSST	BALISTAS
AABELPPT	TAPPABLE	AABGLMNU	GALBANUM	AABILSTY	SATIABLY
AABELPRS	PARABLES	AABGLNOW	BANGALOW	AABILSUX	SUBAXIAL
	PARSABLE	AABGLRUY	ARGUABLY	AABIMMRS	MARIMBAS
	PREBASAL	AABGMORR	BAROGRAM	AABIMNNO	BONAMANI
	SPARABLE	AABGNORZ	GARBANZO	AABIMNOS	AMBOINAS
AABELPSS	PASSABLE	AABHHISS	SAHIBAHS		BONAMIAS
AABELPSY	PAYABLES	AABHHKSS	SABKHAHS	AABIMNRU	MANUBRIA
AABELRST	ARBALEST	AABHHORU	BROUHAHA	AABIMORS	AMBROSIA
	RATABLES	AABHHRSU	BRUHAHAS	AABIMRSU	SIMARUBA
AABELRTY	BETRAYAL	AABHIIMP	AMPHIBIA	AABIMSST	BASMATIS
	RATEABLY	AABHIINU	BAUHINIA	AABINNPR	BRAINPAN
AABELSST	BASALTES	AABHIJMY	JAMBIYAH	AABINORS	ABRASION
AABELSTT	ABETTALS	AABHILLR	HAIRBALL	AABINOSU	OUABAINS
	STATABLE	AABHILTU	HABITUAL	AABINRST	ATABRINS
	TASTABLE	AABHIMNR	BRAHMANI		BARTISAN
AABELSTU	TABLEAUS	AABHINSS	HASBIANS	AABINRTZ	BARTIZAN
AABELSTW	WASTABLE	AABHINST	HABITANS	AABINSST	ABSTAINS
AABELSTX	TAXABLES	AABHINTT	HABITANT	AABIORRS	SORBARIA
AABELSWY	SWAYABLE	AABHIRST	TABASHIR	AABIORSS	ABROSIAS
AABELTTU	TABULATE	AABHISTT	HABITATS	AABIORST	AIRBOATS
AABELTUX	TABLEAUX	AABHKLLW	BALLHAWK	AABIORSV	BAVAROIS
AABEMMXY	MYXAMEBA	AABHKNRS	BARKHANS	AABIORTT	ABATTOIR
AABENNSW	WANNABES	AABHKSST	SABKHATS	AABIOSSY	BIOASSAY
AABENRRT	ABERRANT	AABHLLSW	WASHBALL	AABIPSUX	PAXIUBAS
AABENRST	ANTBEARS	AABHLMSY	SHAMABLY	AABIRSST	BARISTAS

	BARTSIAS
AABIRTUY	RUBAIYAT
AABISTUZ	ZAIBATSU
AABJLMNO	JAMBOLAN
AABJMRST	JAMBARTS
AABKLLPR	BALLPARK
AABKMNNS	BANKSMAN
AABKNRST	TANBARKS
AABKOOSZ	BAZOOKAS
AABKOPRS	SOAPBARK
AABKRSST	TASKBARS
AABLLMOR	BALMORAL
AABLLNST	BALLANTS
AABLLORS	ALLOBARS
AABLLORY	ABORALLY
AABLLPPY	PALPABLY
AABLLPRT	TRAPBALL
AABLLPST	PATBALLS
AABLLSST	BALLASTS
AABLLSTU	BLASTULA
AABLLSVY	SALVABLY
AABLLUVY	VALUABLY
AABLMNOR	ABNORMAL
AABLMNTU	AMBULANT
AABLMOST	BLASTOMA
AABLMRSU	LABARUMS
AABLMSST	LAMBASTS
AABLNSSU	SUBNASAL
AABLNTTT	BLATTANT
AABLORST	ABLATORS
AABLOTUY	LAYABOUT
AABLOVWY	AVOWABLY
AABLPSSY	PASSABLY
AABLRRSU	SABURRAL
AABLRSST	ARBLASTS
AABLRSUU	SUBAURAL
AABLSTTU	ABUTTALS
AABMMOSU	ABOMASUM
AABMNNOO	BONAMANO
AABMNOST	BOATSMAN
AABMNOSY	AMBOYNAS
AABMNOTW	BATWOMAN
AABMNRTU	RAMBUTAN
AABMORSU	MARABOUS
AABMORTU	MARABOUT
	TAMBOURA
AABMOSSU	ABOMASUS
AABMRSTU	TAMBURAS
AABNNOST	ABSONANT
AABNNOSZ	BONANZAS
AABNOSST	SABATONS
AABNOSSY	SABAYONS
AABORRRT	BARRATOR
AABORRSS	RASBORAS
AABORRSU	BAROSAUR
AABORSTT	BAROSTAT
AABRRRTY	BARRATRY
AABRRSST	BRASSART
AABRRSSU	SABURRAS
AABRRSUV	BRAVURAS
AABSSTUX	SAXTUBAS
AABSTTTU	BATTUTAS
AACCCDIS	SACCADIC
AACCCFIO	FOCACCIA
AACCCHHU	CACHUCHA
AACCCRUY	ACCURACY
AACCDDES	CASCADED
AACCDEIM	ACADEMIC
AACCDELO	ACCOLADE
AACCDEMS	MEDACCAS
AACCDENU	CADUCEAN
AACCDERR	RACECARD
AACCDERS	CARCASED
	CARDCASE
AACCDESS	CASCADES
	SACCADES
AACCDHIR	CHARACID
AACCDIIS	ACCIDIAS
AACCDIRS	CARDIACS
AACCDOVY	ADVOCACY
AACCEELT	CALCEATE
AACCEENT	CETACEAN
AACCEFLO	COALFACE
AACCEFST	CATFACES
AACCEGOR	ACCORAGE
AACCEGRU	CARUCAGE
AACCEHIX	CACHEXIA
AACCEILN	CALCANEI
AACCEILU	ACICULAE
AACCEIRR	CERCARIA
AACCEKRS	CARCAKES
AACCELLY	CAECALLY
	CALYCEAL
AACCELOR	CARACOLE
AACCELPT	PLACCATE
AACCELRR	CARCERAL
AACCELTY	CALYCATE
AACCEMNU	CUMACEAN
AACCENRT	CARCANET
AACCENSV	VACANCES
AACCENTU	ACUTANCE
AACCERSS	CARCASES
AACCERTU	ACCURATE
	CARUCATE
AACCFGOO	CACAFOGO
AACCFILR	FARCICAL
AACCFLTU	CALCTUFA
AACCGILT	GALACTIC
AACCHHIL	HALACHIC
AACCHHKS	CHACHKAS
	KACHCHAS
AACCHHKT	CHATCHKA
AACCHILL	CAILLACH
AACCHILP	PACHALIC
AACCHINR	ANARCHIC
	CHARACIN
AACCHINS	CHICANAS
AACCHIOR	AIRCOACH
AACCHISV	VISCACHA
AACCHIVZ	VIZCACHA
AACCHLLT	CATCHALL
AACCHLNS	CLACHANS
AACCHLOR	CHARCOAL
AACCHLOT	CACHALOT
AACCHLRS	CLARSACH
AACCHMNO	COACHMAN
AACCHMPS	CHAMPACS
AACCHNNS	CANNACHS
AACCHNOR	CORANACH
AACCHRST	CHARACTS
AACCIINV	VACCINIA
AACCIIST	SCIATICA
AACCILMS	ACCLAIMS
AACCILNV	VACCINAL
AACCILRU	ACICULAR
AACCILSU	ACICULAS
AACCILTT	TACTICAL
AACCIMNU	CACUMINA
AACCINSV	VACCINAS
AACCIORS	CARIOCAS
AACCIORU	CARIACOU
AACCIPRT	APRACTIC
AACCIPTY	CAPACITY
AACCIRTY	CARYATIC
AACCISTT	STACCATI
AACCJKRS	CARJACKS
AACCJKRW	CRACKJAW
AACCJORU	CARCAJOU
	CARJACOU
AACCKKPS	PACKSACK
AACCKLOS	COALSACK
AACCKLPS	CALPACKS
AACCKORT	COATRACK
AACCKRRS	CARRACKS
AACCLLRU	CALCULAR
AACCLLST	CATCALLS
AACCLMNY	CLAMANCY
AACCLOPS	POLACCAS
AACCLORS	CARACOLS
AACCLPRS	CALCSPAR
AACCLPST	PLACCATS
AACCLRSU	ACCRUALS
	CARACULS
	SACCULAR
AACCLSSU	ACCUSALS
AACCLSTW	CATCLAWS
AACCNSTU	ACCUSANT
AACCOPRS	ASCOCARP
AACCORSU	CURACAOS
	CURACOAS
AACCOSST	ACCOASTS
AACCOSTT	STACCATO
	STOCCATA
	TOCCATAS
AACCRRST	CARRACTS
AACDDEHI	ACIDHEAD
AACDDEIL	DAEDALIC
AACDDENV	ADVANCED
AACDDETU	CAUDATED
AACDDGHL	CLADDAGH
AACDDHRS	CHADDARS
AACDDILN	CANDIDAL
AACDDINR	RADICAND
AACDDINS	CANDIDAS
AACDDRSW	CRAWDADS
AACDEEHH	HEADACHE
AACDEEHR	AREACHED
	HEADRACE
AACDEEHS	HEADCASE
AACDEELS	ESCALADE
AACDEEMS	ACADEMES
AACDEEPS	ESCAPADE

Code	Anagram(s)
AACDEERT	ACERATED
AACDEEST	CASEATED
	ESTACADE
AACDEETT	ACETATED
AACDEETU	ECAUDATE
AACDEETV	CAVEATED
AACDEFHR	HARDFACE
AACDEFLS	FALCADES
AACDEFLT	FALCATED
AACDEFNT	CAFTANED
AACDEGGR	AGGRACED
AACDEGKP	PACKAGED
AACDEGMR	DECAGRAM
AACDEHHY	HEADACHY
AACDEHIN	HACIENDA
AACDEHLN	CHALANED
AACDEHLP	CEPHALAD
AACDEHMR	DRACHMAE
AACDEHMS	CHAMADES
AACDEHRS	CHARADES
	HARDCASE
AACDEHRT	CATHEDRA
AACDEHST	CATHEADS
AACDEHTT	ATTACHED
AACDEIIL	AECIDIAL
AACDEIIM	ACIDEMIA
AACDEILM	CAMAILED
AACDEILS	ALCAIDES
	SIDALCEA
AACDEIMN	MAENADIC
AACDEIMS	CAMISADE
AACDEIMT	ACETAMID
AACDEINR	CANARIED
	RADIANCE
AACDEINS	AIDANCES
AACDEIRT	RADICATE
AACDEJNT	ADJACENT
AACDEKNP	PANCAKED
AACDEKNS	ASKANCED
AACDEKTT	ATTACKED
AACDELLN	CALENDAL
	CANALLED
AACDELLS	ALCALDES
AACDELMN	MANACLED
AACDELNR	CALENDAR
	LANDRACE
AACDELNS	CANDELAS
AACDELNV	VALANCED
AACDELOS	CASELOAD
	ESCALADO
AACDELPT	PLACATED
AACDELRS	CALDERAS
AACDELSS	SCALADES
AACDELSY	ALCAYDES
AACDELTT	LACTATED
AACDELTV	CLAVATED
AACDELTY	ACYLATED
AACDENOT	ANECDOTA
AACDENRS	DRACENAS
AACDENRV	ADVANCER
AACDENSV	ADVANCES
	CANVASED
AACDENSZ	CADENZAS
AACDENTU	ADUNCATE
AACDENTV	TADVANCE
AACDEOPS	ESCAPADO
AACDEOTU	AUTOCADE
AACDEOTV	ADVOCATE
AACDEPRS	SCARPAED
AACDEQUY	ADEQUACY
AACDERST	CADASTER
	CADASTRE
AACDERSV	CADAVERS
AACDERSY	DAYCARES
AACDERTU	ARCUATED
AACDESTU	CAUDATES
AACDETTU	ACTUATED
AACDETUV	VACUATED
AACDFLNR	FLANCARD
AACDGGHI	HAGGADIC
AACDGINR	ARCADING
	CARANGID
	CARDIGAN
AACDHHKR	HARDHACK
AACDHHNS	SHADCHAN
AACDHHRS	SHADRACH
AACDHIIS	DICHASIA
AACDHILL	CHILLADA
AACDHILR	DIARCHAL
AACDHIMR	CHADARIM
	DRACHMAI
AACDHINP	HANDICAP
AACDHINR	ARACHNID
AACDHKPR	HARDPACK
AACDHKRT	HARDTACK
AACDHLNP	HANDCLAP
AACDHLOT	CATHODAL
AACDHLRY	CHARLADY
	DYARCHAL
AACDHMMR	DRAMMACH
AACDHMOP	PACHADOM
AACDHMRS	DRACHMAS
AACDHNOW	WAHCONDA
AACDHNRS	HANDCARS
AACDHNRT	HANDCART
AACDHPRS	CRASHPAD
AACDIINS	ASCIDIAN
AACDIIRU	ACIDURIA
AACDILLP	PALLADIC
AACDILMN	MANDALIC
AACDILMT	DALMATIC
AACDILMU	CALADIUM
AACDILNO	DIACONAL
AACDILNR	CARDINAL
AACDILNU	DULCIANA
AACDILNV	VANDALIC
AACDILOZ	ZODIACAL
AACDILPS	CAPSIDAL
AACDILRR	RAILCARD
AACDILRS	RADICALS
AACDIMNO	MANDIOCA
AACDIMNY	ADYNAMIC
	CYANAMID
AACDIMOS	CAMISADO
AACDIMRT	DRAMATIC
AACDINRT	RADICANT
	TRIDACNA
AACDINRY	RADIANCY
AACDINSS	SCANDIAS
AACDINST	ANTACIDS
AACDIOTU	AUTACOID
AACDIRSS	ASCARIDS
AACDIRTY	CARYATID
AACDITUY	AUDACITY
AACDJKSW	JACKDAWS
AACDJQRU	JACQUARD
AACDKLLN	LACKLAND
AACDKPRT	TRACKPAD
AACDKSSY	DAYSACKS
AACDLLUV	CAUDALLY
AACDLNSS	SCANDALS
AACDLORS	CARLOADS
AACDLORT	CARTLOAD
AACDLORY	COALYARD
AACDLOSS	SCALADOS
AACDLOSV	CALVADOS
AACDLPRS	PLACARDS
AACDLRTY	DACTYLAR
AACDMMOR	CARDAMOM
AACDMMRU	CARDAMUM
AACDMNNO	MANCANDO
AACDMNOR	CARDAMON
AACDOOSV	AVOCADOS
AACDORRT	CARTROAD
AACDPRSU	CRAPAUDS
AACEEFIT	FACETIAE
AACEEFLP	PALEFACE
AACEEFNS	FEASANCE
AACEEGIR	ACIERAGE
	AGACERIE
AACEEGLR	CLEARAGE
AACEEGLV	CLEAVAGE
AACEEGNR	CARAGEEN
AACEEGNY	GYNAECEA
AACEEGRS	ACREAGES
	GEARCASE
AACEEHLP	ACALEPHE
AACEEHLT	LEACHATE
AACEEHRS	AREACHES
	EARACHES
AACEEHRT	TRACHEAE
AACEEIMT	EMACIATE
AACEEINN	ENCAENIA
AACEEIRT	ACIERATE
AACEEKRT	CARETAKE
AACEEKST	TEACAKES
AACEELNS	ANELACES
AACEELRT	LACERATE
AACEELST	ESCALATE
AACEELTU	ACULEATE
AACEEMRT	MACERATE
	RACEMATE
AACEEMSS	AMESACES
AACEEMST	CASEMATE
AACEENNT	CATENANE
AACEENRS	CESAREAN
AACEENRW	CANEWARE
AACEENTT	CATENATE
AACEEPRV	PRECAVAE
AACEEPSS	SEASCAPE
AACEERSU	CAESURAE
AACEERTV	ACERVATE

AACEESSS	CASEASES	AACEHMNP	CAMPHANE		CAPITATE
AACEESST	CASEATES	AACEHMRS	MARCHESA	AACEIQSU	ACEQUIAS
AACEESTT	ACETATES	AACEHMSS	CAMASHES	AACEIRSV	AVARICES
AACEETUV	EVACUATE	AACEHMST	SCHEMATA		CAVIARES
AACEETVX	EXCAVATE	AACEHNOR	ARCHAEON	AACEIRTV	VICARATE
AACEFFIN	AFFIANCE	AACEHNPS	PANACHES	AACEISST	ECTASIAS
AACEFHLP	HALFPACE	AACEHPRT	RACEPATH	AACEITTV	ACTIVATE
AACEFILM	FACEMAIL	AACEHPSU	CHAPEAUS		CAVITATE
AACEFILT	CALIFATE	AACEHPUX	CHAPEAUX	AACEJLTU	JACULATE
AACEFIST	FASCIATE	AACEHQTU	CHAQUETA	AACEKKLW	CAKEWALK
AACEFKMS	FACEMASK	AACEHRSS	CHARASES	AACEKLRW	RACEWALK
AACEFLLU	FALCULAE	AACEHRST	TRACHEAS	AACEKMPR	CAPMAKER
AACEFRRS	CARFARES	AACEHRSU	ARCHAEUS	AACEKMRR	CARMAKER
AACEFRRU	FURCRAEA	AACEHRTT	ATTACHER	AACEKNPS	PANCAKES
AACEFRSS	FRACASES		REATTACH	AACEKNSS	ASKANCES
AACEFRST	SEACRAFT	AACEHSTT	ATTACHES	AACEKOST	OATCAKES
AACEFRSX	CARFAXES	AACEHSTU	CHATEAUS	AACEKRTT	ATTACKER
AACEFRTT	ARTEFACT	AACEHTUX	CHATEAUX		REATTACK
AACEGGRS	AGGRACES	AACEIILN	LACINIAE	AACELLMR	MARCELLA
AACEGHNS	GANACHES	AACEIINT	ACTINIAE	AACELLNR	CANALLER
AACEGHNT	CHANTAGE	AACEIIRV	CAVIARIE	AACELLNS	CANELLAS
AACEGILN	ANGELICA	AACEIKMT	KAMACITE	AACELLOT	ALLOCATE
AACEGILT	GLACIATE	AACEILLM	CAMELLIA	AACELLST	CASTELLA
AACEGINR	CANAIGRE	AACEILLN	ALLIANCE		LACTEALS
AACEGINY	GYNAECIA		ANCILLAE	AACELLTY	ALLEYCAT
AACEGIOP	APOGAEIC		CANAILLE	AACELMNP	PLACEMAN
AACEGIRR	CARRIAGE	AACEILMN	ANALCIME	AACELMNS	MANACLES
AACEGIRV	VICARAGE		CALAMINE	AACELMOT	CELOMATA
AACEGKPR	PACKAGER	AACEILMS	CAMELIAS	AACELMRS	CARAMELS
AACEGKPS	PACKAGES	AACEILMT	CALAMITE		CERAMALS
AACEGKRT	TRACKAGE	AACEILNS	CANALISE		MACERALS
AACEGKSS	SACKAGES	AACEILNT	ANALCITE	AACELMTU	MACULATE
AACEGLNY	LANCEGAY		LAITANCE	AACELNNO	ANCONEAL
AACEGLSS	SCALAGES	AACEILNU	ACAULINE	AACELNNU	CANNULAE
AACEGMNO	COMANAGE	AACEILNV	VALENCIA	AACELNOR	LECANORA
AACEGMNP	CAMPAGNE		VALIANCE	AACELNPR	PARLANCE
AACEGNRS	CAGANERS	AACEILNZ	CANALIZE	AACELNPS	CAPELANS
	CARNAGES	AACEILOP	ALOPECIA		SCALEPAN
	CRANAGES	AACEILRT	TAILRACE	AACELNPT	PLACENTA
AACEGRST	CARTAGES	AACEILRV	CAVALIER	AACELNPY	ANYPLACE
AACEGRSV	SCAVAGER	AACEILST	SALICETA	AACELNRT	LACERANT
AACEGSSV	SCAVAGES	AACEIMNS	AMNESIAC	AACELNRY	ARCANELY
AACEHHRU	HUARACHE	AACEIMRS	MACARISE	AACELNST	ANALECTS
AACEHIKN	ICEKHANA		MESARAIC	AACELNSV	VALANCES
AACEHILL	ACHILLEA	AACEIMRZ	MACARIZE	AACELNTU	CANULATE
	HELIACAL	AACEIMTT	CATAMITE		LACUNATE
AACEHILN	ACHENIAL	AACEIMUX	CAMAIEUX		TENACULA
AACEHILP	PHACELIA	AACEINNT	ANTIACNE	AACELORS	ACEROLAS
AACEHIMR	CHIMAERA	AACEINRS	ACARINES	AACELORV	CAVALERO
AACEHIMT	HAEMATIC		CANARIES	AACELOST	CATALOES
AACEHIPT	HEPATICA		CESARIAN	AACELOSU	ACAULOSE
AACEHIRS	ARCHAISE		SARCINAE	AACELOSV	COAEVALS
AACEHIRT	THERIACA	AACEINRT	CARINATE	AACELPRS	CARPALES
AACEHIRZ	ARCHAIZE		CRANIATE	AACELPRT	PLACATER
AACEHKRS	KACHERAS	AACEINRV	VARIANCE	AACELPRV	PRECAVAL
AACEHKSS	ASHCAKES	AACEINST	ESTANCIA	AACELPST	PLACATES
AACEHLNT	CALANTHE	AACEINTV	CAVATINE	AACELPSU	SCAPULAE
AACEHLNU	EULACHAN	AACEIOPR	CAPOEIRA	AACELRSS	SCALARES
AACEHLPS	ACALEPHS	AACEIPPS	PAPACIES	AACELRSU	CAESURAL
AACEHLRS	ALCHERAS	AACEIPRS	AIRSCAPE	AACELRSV	CARAVELS
AACEHLRT	TRACHEAL		AIRSPACE	AACELRTY	ACRYLATE
AACEHLRX	EXARCHAL	AACEIPRT	APRICATE	AACELRWY	CLAYWARE
AACEHLSS	CALASHES	AACEIPSS	CAPIASES		CLEARWAY
AACEHLST	ALCAHEST	AACEIPTT	APATETIC	AACELSST	LACTASES

AACELSTT	LACTATES	AACFJKLP	FLAPJACK	AACHIKNR	CHINKARA
AACELSTY	ACYLATES	AACFKLPT	FLATPACK	AACHIKNS	KACHINAS
	CATALYSE	AACFLLST	CATFALLS	AACHIKNT	KATCHINA
AACELTTY	CATTLEYA	AACFLLSU	FALCULAS	AACHIKRS	CHIKARAS
AACELTYZ	CATALYZE	AACFLOPR	PARFOCAL	AACHILLP	CALIPHAL
AACEMMRS	MACRAMES	AACFLPST	FLATCAPS	AACHILLR	RACHILLA
AACEMNOR	AMORANCE	AACFLRST	FLATCARS	AACHILMS	CHAMISAL
AACEMNPS	SPACEMAN		FRACTALS		CHIASMAL
AACEMNST	CAMSTANE	AACFRRSU	FARRUCAS	AACHILMT	THALAMIC
AACEMPRS	PARACMES	AACFRRTW	WARCRAFT	AACHILNP	CHAPLAIN
AACEMQSU	MACAQUES	AACGGINO	ANAGOGIC	AACHILOS	ACHOLIAS
AACEMRSS	MASSACRE	AACGGIOP	APAGOGIC	AACHILPS	CALIPASH
AACEMSSS	CAMASSES	AACGHILT	TAIGLACH		PASHALIC
AACENOTU	OCEANAUT	AACGHIPR	AGRAPHIC	AACHILPT	HAPTICAL
AACENPRS	PANCREAS	AACGHIRR	CHIRAGRA	AACHILRV	ARCHIVAL
AACENPRT	CATNAPER	AACGHLLO	AGALLOCH	AACHIMNN	CHAINMAN
AACENPST	PASTANCE	AACGHLRU	RUGALACH		CHINAMAN
AACENPSU	SAUCEPAN	AACGHNOR	CHARANGO	AACHIMNP	CHINAMPA
AACENPTT	PANCETTA	AACGHOPZ	GAZPACHO	AACHIMNR	CHAIRMAN
AACENRST	CANASTER	AACGHORU	GUACHARO	AACHIMNS	SHAMANIC
	CATERANS	AACGIIMN	MAGICIAN	AACHIMNT	MATACHIN
AACENRSV	CANVASER	AACGIINR	GARCINIA	AACHIMNZ	CHAZANIM
AACENRTT	REACTANT	AACGILLN	GALLICAN	AACHIMRR	ARMCHAIR
AACENRTY	CATENARY	AACGILLO	ALOGICAL	AACHIMRS	ARCHAISM
AACENRVZ	CZAREVNA	AACGILLS	GALLICAS		CHARISMA
AACENSSS	CASSENAS		GLACIALS		MACHAIRS
AACENSSV	CANVASES	AACGILLU	ALGUACIL	AACHIMSS	CHAMISAS
AACENSTT	CANTATES	AACGILNN	CANALING		CHIASMAS
	CASTANET	AACGILNO	ANALOGIC	AACHIMST	CATHISMA
AACENSTY	CYANATES	AACGILNR	CRAALING	AACHINNT	ACANTHIN
AACENTUV	EVACUANT	AACGILNT	ANTALGIC	AACHINRT	CANTHARI
AACEOPPR	COAPPEAR	AACGILNV	GALVANIC	AACHINSW	CHAINSAW
AACEOPRT	CAPROATE	AACGILOU	GUAIACOL	AACHIPPT	CHAPPATI
AACEOPST	PEACOATS	AACGILOX	COXALGIA	AACHIPRS	CHARPAIS
AACEORSS	ROSACEAS	AACGILRT	TRAGICAL		HAIRCAPS
AACEORSU	ARACEOUS	AACGILSS	SCAGLIAS	AACHIPSS	APHASICS
AACEORTV	CAVEATOR	AACGIMMT	MAGMATIC	AACHIPST	CHAPATIS
AACEOSST	SEACOAST	AACGIMNN	MANGANIC	AACHIPTT	CHAPATTI
AACEPRST	CAPRATES	AACGIMNP	CAMPAIGN	AACHIRST	ARCHAIST
AACEPRSU	CAPUERAS		PANGAMIC		CITHARAS
AACEPSWY	PACEWAYS	AACGIMOP	APOGAMIC	AACHIRTX	TAXIARCH
AACERRTU	ARCATURE	AACGIMRR	MARGARIC	AACHKKOZ	KAZACHOK
AACERSSS	RASCASSE	AACGIMUU	GUAIACUM	AACHKMPS	CHAMPAKS
AACERSSU	CAESURAS	AACGINOT	CONTAGIA	AACHKNSW	HACKSAWN
AACERSSZ	SAZERACS	AACGINPS	SCAPAING	AACHKPSS	SCHAPSKA
AACERSTT	CASTRATE	AACGINTV	VACATING	AACHKRST	HATRACKS
	TEACARTS	AACGISTY	SAGACITY	AACHKRSY	HAYRACKS
AACERSWY	RACEWAYS	AACGJNST	CATJANGS	AACHKSSW	HACKSAWS
AACERTTT	TRACTATE	AACGLMOU	GLAUCOMA	AACHKSTY	HAYSTACK
AACESSSV	CAVASSES	AACGLOST	CATALOGS	AACHLLLU	HALLUCAL
AACESSTT	SCEATTAS	AACGMNRS	CRAGSMAN	AACHLLNS	CHALLANS
AACESTTU	ACTUATES	AACGNOSU	GUANACOS	AACHLLOR	ALACHLOR
AACESTUV	VACUATES	AACGNRVY	VAGRANCY	AACHLMNO	MONACHAL
AACESUWY	CAUSEWAY	AACHHIKL	HALAKHIC	AACHLMOS	CHLOASMA
AACFFILS	CAFFILAS	AACHHIKR	KACHAHRI	AACHLNOO	OOLACHAN
AACFGRST	CRAGFAST	AACHHILR	RHACHIAL	AACHLORT	THORACAL
AACFHMST	CAMSHAFT	AACHHIMS	MASHIACH	AACHLOST	CALATHOS
AACFILLY	FACIALLY	AACHHKRS	CHARKHAS	AACHLPPS	CHAPPALS
AACFILOS	FASCIOLA	AACHHLLS	CHALLAHS	AACHLPSS	PASCHALS
AACFINST	FANATICS	AACHHLOT	HALACHOT	AACHLPSU	CHALUPAS
AACFIRRT	AIRCRAFT	AACHHORU	HUARACHO	AACHLSSU	ACUSHLAS
AACFIRST	FRASCATI	AACHHTWY	HATCHWAY	AACHLSTU	CALATHUS
AACFIRTT	ARTIFACT	AACHIIMR	MARIACHI	AACHMMNR	MARCHMAN
AACFISST	FASCISTA	AACHIKKZ	KAZACHKI	AACHMNNR	RANCHMAN

AACHMNTW	WATCHMAN	AACILNTU	NAUTICAL	AACJKMNS	MANJACKS
AACHMNTY	YACHTMAN	AACILNTY	ANALYTIC	AACJKOOR	JACKAROO
AACHMNUY	NAUMACHY	AACILNUV	NAVICULA	AACJKSTY	JACKSTAY
AACHMORT	ACHROMAT	AACILNVY	VALIANCY	AACJPSTU	CAJAPUTS
	TRACHOMA	AACILOSS	ASOCIALS	AACKKNPS	KNAPSACK
AACHMPRT	CHAMPART	AACILOTT	COATTAIL	AACKLOWY	LOCKAWAY
AACHMPRY	PHARMACY		TAILCOAT	AACKLSTW	CATWALKS
AACHMSSY	YASHMACS	AACILPRU	PIACULAR	AACKMNPS	MANPACKS
AACHNOPS	PANOCHAS	AACILPST	APLASTIC	AACKMNRT	TRACKMAN
AACHNOSU	HUANACOS		CAPITALS	AACKMNST	TACKSMAN
AACHNPRS	SARPANCH	AACILPSZ	CAPSIZAL	AACKMRST	AMTRACKS
AACHNRST	TRASHCAN	AACILPTU	CAPITULA	AACKNRSS	RANSACKS
AACHNRSV	NAVARCHS	AACILPTY	ATYPICAL	AACKORWY	ROCKAWAY
AACHNRVY	NAVARCHY	AACILQRU	ACQUIRAL	AACKPRRS	CARPARKS
AACHNSSU	ANCHUSAS	AACILRRS	RAILCARS	AACKPRST	RATPACKS
AACHNSTU	ACANTHUS	AACILRTY	ALACRITY	AACKPSWY	PACKWAYS
AACHNSZZ	CHAZZANS	AACILRUU	AURICULA	AACKRTWY	TRACKWAY
AACHOPPR	APPROACH	AACILRUV	AVICULAR	AACLLLOO	CALLALOO
AACHOPRR	PARACHOR	AACILSTT	CATTAILS	AACLLMMU	MACALLUM
AACHORTU	RACAHOUT		STATICAL	AACLLMRY	LACRYMAL
AACHOTTU	TACAHOUT	AACILSTY	SALACITY	AACLLNRY	CARNALLY
AACHRRST	CATARRHS	AACIMMNO	AMMONIAC	AACLLNST	CALLANTS
AACHRSTU	AUTARCHS	AACIMMRS	MACARISM	AACLLNSU	CALLUNAS
AACHRSWY	ARCHWAYS		MACRAMIS	AACLLOOS	CALALOOS
AACHRTUY	AUTARCHY		MARASMIC	AACLLRRY	CARRYALL
AACIILMN	ANIMALIC	AACIMNOR	ARMONICA	AACLLRSY	RASCALLY
AACIILMO	MAIOLICA		MACARONI	AACLLSUU	CLAUSULA
AACIILRT	IATRICAL		MAROCAIN	AACLLSUY	CASUALLY
AACIILRV	VICARIAL	AACIMNOS	MANIOCAS		CAUSALLY
AACIILTV	VIATICAL	AACIMNOT	ANATOMIC	AACLLTUY	ACTUALLY
AACIIMNT	ANIMATIC	AACIMORT	AROMATIC	AACLMNNS	CLANSMAN
AACIIMSS	CAMISIAS	AACIMOTX	MAXICOAT	AACLMNSS	CLASSMAN
AACIINNT	ACTINIAN	AACIMPRS	PICAMARS	AACLMNST	CALMANTS
AACIINPR	PICARIAN	AACINNST	CANTINAS	AACLMOTU	COMATULA
AACIINPT	CAPITANI	AACINOPR	PARANOIC	AACLMRRU	MACRURAL
AACIINST	ACTINIAS	AACINOPT	CAPITANO	AACLNNOT	CANTONAL
AACIIRSV	VISCARIA		PACATION	AACLNNRU	CANNULAR
AACIJLMO	MAJOLICA	AACINORS	OCARINAS	AACLNNSU	CANNULAS
AACIJNOP	JAPONICA	AACINORT	RAINCOAT	AACLNOPR	COPLANAR
AACIKLMS	MAILSACK	AACINOTV	VACATION	AACLNOTT	OCTANTAL
AACIKLRS	CLARKIAS	AACINPRT	CANTRAIP	AACLNPSY	CLAYPANS
AACIKMNW	MACKINAW	AACINPST	CAPITANS	AACLNRSU	LACUNARS
AACIKNNS	CANAKINS		CAPTAINS	AACLNRUY	LACUNARY
AACIKNST	KATCINAS	AACINPTY	CAPITAYN	AACLNTVY	VACANTLY
AACIKRTU	AUTARKIC	AACINQTU	ACQUAINT	AACLOOPT	TAPACOLO
AACILLLY	LAICALLY	AACINRSS	ACRASINS	AACLOPRS	CAPORALS
AACILLMR	LACRIMAL		SARCINAS		CRAPOLAS
AACILLMT	CLIMATAL	AACINRST	ARCANIST	AACLOPST	OCTAPLAS
AACILLNS	ANCILLAS	AACINRSZ	CZARINAS	AACLOPTU	TAPACULO
AACILLPY	APICALLY	AACINSSS	CASSINAS	AACLORRU	ORACULAR
AACILLRY	RACIALLY	AACINSTZ	STANZAIC	AACLORST	COALTARS
AACILMNT	CALAMINT	AACIOPST	TAPIOCAS	AACLORSU	CAROUSAL
	CLAIMANT	AACIOPSV	COPAIVAS	AACLORSZ	ALCORZAS
AACILMOR	ACROMIAL	AACIPPRS	PAPRICAS	AACLORUV	VACUOLAR
AACILMOT	ATOMICAL	AACIPRST	ASPARTIC	AACLOSTT	CATTALOS
AACILMRS	MAILCARS	AACIPRTY	RAPACITY	AACLOSUU	ACAULOUS
AACILMTY	CALAMITY	AACIQSTU	AQUATICS	AACLPPRT	CLAPTRAP
AACILNOR	CONARIAL	AACIRRTT	TARTARIC	AACLPRST	CALTRAPS
AACILNPS	CALPAINS	AACIRSTT	CASTRATI	AACLPRSU	CAPSULAR
AACILNRS	CLARAINS	AACIRSTZ	CZARITSA		SCAPULAR
AACILNRV	CARNIVAL	AACIRTVY	CAVITARY	AACLPRTY	CALYPTRA
AACILNST	ALICANTS	AACIRTZZ	CZARITZA	AACLPSSU	SCAPULAS
	SANTALIC	AACISSTW	SWASTICA	AACLPSTY	PLAYACTS
AACILNTT	TANTALIC	AACJKLPS	SLAPJACK	AACLPTTU	CATAPULT

AACLRSTU	CLAUSTRA	AADDEKMS	DAMASKED	AADEEQTU	ADEQUATE
AACLRSUV	VASCULAR	AADDELNS	SANDALED	AADEERSW	AWARDEES
AACLRTUX	CURTALAX	AADDELTU	ADULATED	AADEFFLT	AFFLATED
AACLRWWY	CRAWLWAY	AADDEMNT	MANDATED	AADEFFNR	FANFARED
AACLSSTT	SALTCATS	AADDEMRU	MARAUDED	AADEFFRY	AFFRAYED
AACLSTTY	CATALYST	AADDEMRY	DAYDREAM	AADEFGLS	FALDAGES
AACLSTUY	CASUALTY	AADDENPR	PANDARED	AADEFGRS	FARDAGES
AACMNOOR	MACAROON	AADDENPS	DEADPANS	AADEFHLT	FLATHEAD
AACMNORS	CAMARONS	AADDEORS	DEODARAS	AADEFHST	FATHEADS
	MASCARON	AADDGMNR	GRANDDAM		HEADFAST
	NARCOMAS	AADDGNRS	GRADDANS	AADEFHTW	FATWAHED
AACMNPRY	RAMPANCY		GRANDADS	AADEFILR	FAIRLEAD
AACMNRRU	MACRURAN	AADDGNRU	GRADUAND	AADEFIRS	FARADISE
AACMNRSU	ARCANUMS	AADDHHRS	SHRADDHA		SAFARIED
AACMORRS	CAMORRAS	AADDHIMN	HANDMAID	AADEFIRZ	FARADIZE
AACMORSS	SARCOMAS	AADDHKRS	KHADDARS	AADEFISS	FADAISES
AACMORST	MARCATOS	AADDHRSS	SRADDHAS	AADEFLLR	FALDERAL
AACMRRST	TRAMCARS	AADDIIKS	DIDAKAIS	AADEFLRY	DEFRAYAL
AACMRSSS	SARCASMS	AADDIISV	DAVIDIAS	AADEFLTT	FALDETTA
AACNNOSZ	CANZONAS	AADDILNO	DIANODAL	AADEFNSZ	FAZENDAS
AACNOSST	SACATONS	AADDIMSS	DADAISMS	AADEFRRW	WARFARED
AACNOSTZ	ZACATONS	AADDISST	DADAISTS	AADEFRWY	WAYFARED
AACNOTTY	CATATONY	AADDKMMO	MOKADDAM	AADEGGRS	AGGRADES
AACNPRST	CANTRAPS	AADDLLNY	LANDLADY		SAGGARED
AACNPSST	CAPSTANS	AADDLNRW	LANDWARD	AADEGGRT	AGGRATED
AACNRSTT	TRANSACT	AADDLNRY	YARDLAND	AADEGGRU	GUARDAGE
AACNRSTU	CURTANAS	AADDMMQU	MUQADDAM	AADEGHLN	DANELAGH
AACOORTX	TOXOCARA	AADDNRST	STANDARD	AADEGHNR	HANGARED
AACOPPRS	APOCARPS	AADDNRWY	YARDWAND	AADEGHRS	RAGHEADS
AACOPPRY	APOCARPY	AADDNSVV	DVANDVAS		RHAGADES
AACOPRSU	ACARPOUS	AADDRSST	DASTARDS	AADEGILL	DIALLAGE
AACOPRTU	AUTOCARP	AADDRSTY	DASTARDY	AADEGILT	GLADIATE
AACOPSTV	POSTCAVA	AADEEERT	DEAERATE	AADEGINR	AREADING
AACOPSTY	APOSTACY	AADEEFFR	AFFEARED		DRAINAGE
AACORRTV	VARACTOR	AADEEGHR	GEARHEAD		GARDENIA
AACORSSW	CARASSOW		HEADGEAR	AADEGINT	INDAGATE
AACORSTT	CASTRATO	AADEEGHS	HEADAGES	AADEGIRR	GERARDIA
AACORSTU	ACATOURS	AADEEGHT	HEADGATE	AADEGIRV	GRAVIDAE
	AUTOCARS	AADEEGLM	MEGADEAL	AADEGIST	AGATISED
AACORTTU	ACTUATOR	AADEEGLR	LAAGERED	AADEGITT	AGITATED
	AUTOCRAT	AADEEGLT	GALEATED	AADEGITV	DIVAGATE
AACOSTUV	AUTOVACS	AADEEGMN	AMENAGED	AADEGITZ	AGATIZED
AACPSSTW	CATSPAWS		ENDAMAGE	AADEGJTU	ADJUTAGE
AACRSTTT	ATTRACTS	AADEEGMR	REDAMAGE	AADEGKMR	DEKAGRAM
AACRSTUV	VACATURS	AADEEGNR	GADARENE	AADEGLLT	TALLAGED
AACRSTWY	CARTWAYS	AADEEGRV	AVERAGED	AADEGLMN	MAGDALEN
AACSTUWY	CUTAWAYS	AADEEHMT	MEATHEAD	AADEGLMY	AMYGDALE
AADDDEEH	DEADHEAD	AADEEIRT	ERADIATE	AADEGLNS	SELADANG
AADDDEER	ADREADED	AADEEIRW	AWEARIED	AADEGLOP	GALOPADE
AADDDERW	ADWARDED	AADEEKNW	AWAKENED	AADEGLSV	SALVAGED
AADDDGNR	GRANDDAD	AADEEKRW	REAWAKED	AADEGMNR	GRANDAME
AADDEELT	DEALATED	AADEELNN	ANNEALED	AADEGMPR	RAMPAGED
AADDEFLL	DEADFALL	AADEELPP	APPEALED	AADEGMRS	DAMAGERS
AADDEGGR	AGGRADED	AADEELST	DEALATES		MEGARADS
AADDEGRT	GRADATED	AADEELTV	ALVEATED		SMARAGDE
AADDEHHR	HARDHEAD	AADEEMNS	MAENADES	AADEGMSS	MASSAGED
AADDEHHS	HADEDAHS	AADEEMNT	EMANATED	AADEGNRR	ARRANGED
AADDEHLN	HEADLAND	AADEEMOT	OEDEMATA	AADEGNTV	VANTAGED
AADDEHMN	HANDMADE	AADEEMRR	DEMERARA	AADEGPRY	PAYGRADE
AADDEHRW	HEADWARD	AADEENPT	TAPENADE	AADEGPSS	PASSAGED
AADDEHRZ	HAZARDED	AADEENTT	ANTEDATE	AADEGRST	GRADATES
AADDEILN	DEDALIAN	AADEEPPR	APPEARED	AADEGRSV	SAVEGARD
AADDEILS	ALIDADES	AADEEPPS	APPEASED	AADEGRSY	DRAYAGES
AADDEIRT	RADIATED	AADEEPRS	PASEARED		YARDAGES

AADEGRTU	GRADUATE		RAINDATE	AADEMNST	MANDATES
AADEGSSU	ASSUAGED	AADEINSZ	ZENAIDAS	AADEMNUZ	UNAMAZED
AADEGSSW	ASSWAGED	AADEINTT	ATTAINED	AADEMORT	MATADORE
AADEHHHS	HASHHEAD	AADEIPPR	APPAIRED	AADEMRRU	MARAUDER
AADEHHOR	HOARHEAD	AADEIPRS	PARADISE	AADEMRSS	MADRASES
AADEHILN	NAILHEAD	AADEIPSS	DIAPASES	AADEMRSY	DAYMARES
AADEHILR	HEADRAIL	AADEIPSU	DIAPAUSE	AADEMSSS	ADMASSES
	RAILHEAD	AADEIPTV	ADAPTIVE	AADEMWZZ	ZAMZAWED
AADEHILS	HEADSAIL	AADEIRST	AIRDATES	AADENNST	ANDANTES
AADEHIRR	DIARRHEA		DATARIES	AADENRRT	NARRATED
AADEHIRS	AIRHEADS		RADIATES	AADENRRW	WARRANED
AADEHIWY	HIDEAWAY	AADEIRTV	VARIATED	AADENRSV	VERANDAS
AADEHJRS	JARHEADS	AADEISST	DIASTASE	AADENRTT	TARTANED
AADEHKMR	HEADMARK	AADEISTT	ASTATIDE	AADENSSW	WEASANDS
AADEHLLL	HALALLED		SATIATED	AADENSTY	ASYNDETA
AADEHLLO	HALLOAED	AADEITVW	VIEWDATA	AADENSTZ	STANZAED
AADEHLMP	HEADLAMP	AADEJMPY	PYJAMAED	AADENSWZ	WEAZANDS
AADEHLNR	ANHEDRAL	AADEJMRS	JEMADARS	AADENTUV	AVAUNTED
AADEHLPS	SLAPHEAD	AADEJNNP	JAPANNED	AADEOPRT	TAPADERO
AADEHLRS	ASHLARED	AADEKLLN	LAKELAND	AADEOPST	ADESPOTA
AADEHMNS	HEADSMAN	AADEKLNR	KALENDAR	AADEORRT	AERODART
AADEHMST	MASTHEAD	AADEKLRY	KALEYARD	AADEPPRT	PREADAPT
AADEHNPS	SANDHEAP	AADEKMNR	MANDRAKE	AADEPRRS	PARADERS
AADEHNRV	VERANDAH	AADEKMRS	KAMERADS	AADEPRST	ADAPTERS
AADEHNSX	HANDAXES	AADEKNST	ASKANTED		READAPTS
AADEHPPR	PARAPHED	AADEKNUW	UNAWAKED	AADEPSSS	PASSADES
AADEHPSS	SAPHEADS	AADEKPRS	PARKADES	AADEQRTU	QUADRATE
AADEHRRW	HARDWARE	AADEKSTT	ATTASKED	AADERRRW	REARWARD
AADEHRRZ	HAZARDER	AADELLOS	ALDOLASE	AADERRSW	AWARDERS
AADEHRSS	HARASSED	AADELLPP	APPALLED	AADERRWY	WARRAYED
AADEHRSW	RAWHEADS	AADELLPS	PADELLAS	AADERSST	ASSARTED
	WARHEADS	AADELLRT	DATALLER	AADERSSW	SEAWARDS
AADEHSSY	SASHAYED	AADELLWY	WELLADAY	AADERSTT	ASTARTED
AADEHSTT	HASTATED	AADELMNP	NAPALMED	AADERSTW	EASTWARD
AADEHSTY	HEADSTAY	AADELMNR	ALDERMAN		RADWASTE
AADEHSWY	HEADWAYS		MALANDER	AADERUVY	AYURVEDA
AADEILMS	MALADIES	AADELMNS	DALESMAN	AADFGNNO	FANDANGO
AADEILMU	AUMAILED		LEADSMAN	AADFGRSU	SAUFGARD
AADEILNT	DENTALIA	AADELMOS	ALAMODES	AADFHMNR	FARMHAND
AADEILPR	PRAEDIAL	AADELMPT	PALMATED	AADFHNST	HANDFAST
AADEILPS	PALISADE	AADELMRU	ALARUMED	AADFIINT	INTIFADA
AADEILPT	LAPIDATE	AADELMYZ	AMAZEDLY	AADFIMRS	FARADISM
AADEILRS	SALARIED	AADELNPT	PEATLAND	AADFINRU	UNAFRAID
AADEILRT	LARIATED	AADELNRS	ADRENALS	AADFLLLN	LANDFALL
AADEILSS	ASSAILED	AADELNST	EASTLAND	AADFLLNT	FLATLAND
AADEILSV	VEDALIAS	AADELNSW	DANELAWS	AADFLMNR	FARMLAND
AADEILTT	DILATATE	AADELNSY	ANALYSED	AADFLORW	AARDWOLF
AADEILTV	VALIDATE	AADELNYZ	ANALYZED	AADFLOTW	DATAFLOW
AADEIMNN	AMANDINE	AADELOTX	OXALATED	AADFLOTX	TOADFLAX
AADEIMNP	PANDEMIA	AADELPPT	PALPATED	AADFLOWY	FOLDAWAY
AADEIMNR	MARINADE	AADELPRS	PARDALES	AADFMRRY	FARMYARD
AADEIMNT	ANIMATED	AADELPRY	PARLAYED	AADGGHOT	AGGADOTH
	DIAMANTE	AADELPTY	PLAYDATE		HAGGADOT
AADEIMPZ	DIAZEPAM	AADELQUU	QUAALUDE	AADGGHRS	HAGGARDS
AADEIMRS	MADEIRAS	AADELRSY	SALEYARD	AADGGIMN	DAMAGING
AADEIMRV	MARAVEDI	AADELRTU	RADULATE	AADGGLNN	GANGLAND
AADEIMSS	AMIDASES	AADELRTV	LARVATED	AADGGLRS	LAGGARDS
	SEAMAIDS	AADELRTY	DAYTALER	AADGGRSS	SAGGARDS
AADEIMST	ADAMSITE	AADELSTT	SALTATED	AADGGRST	STAGGARD
	DIASTEMA	AADELSTU	ADULATES	AADGHILS	HIDALGAS
AADEINPT	PATINAED	AADELSTY	DAYTALES	AADGHIPR	DIAGRAPH
AADEINRR	DARRAINE	AADELTUV	VALUATED	AADGHIST	HAGADIST
AADEINRS	ARANEIDS	AADEMNOS	ADENOMAS	AADGHORS	DAROGHAS
AADEINRT	DENTARIA	AADEMNPS	SPADEMAN	AADGHRTU	HATGUARD

AADGIINS	GAINSAID	AADHJNRS	HANDJARS		MAINYARD
AADGIIRS	GIARDIAS	AADHKLOT	KATHODAL	AADIMNRZ	ZAMINDAR
AADGILLO	GLADIOLA	AADHKNSS	DHANSAKS	AADIMNSS	DAMASSIN
AADGILLR	GAILLARD	AADHKNSY	YAKHDANS	AADIMNSU	SUDAMINA
	GALLIARD	AADHLMOY	DALMAHOY	AADIMNUV	VANADIUM
AADGILMR	MADRIGAL	AADHLNPY	HANDPLAY	AADIMORS	DIORAMAS
AADGILNO	DIAGONAL	AADHLNSW	WASHLAND	AADIMPST	MISADAPT
	GONADIAL	AADHLPSS	SLAPDASH	AADIMRSW	MISAWARD
AADGILNS	SALADING	AADHLRSY	HALYARDS	AADIMSTZ	SAMIZDAT
AADGIMMN	MADAMING	AADHLRUY	HAULYARD	AADINNNS	NANDINAS
AADGIMMS	DIGAMMAS	AADHMNNY	HANDYMAN	AADINNOT	ADNATION
AADGIMNR	MRIDANGA	AADHMNOU	OMADHAUN	AADINOPR	PARANOID
AADGIMOS	AGAMOIDS	AADHMOPS	PASHADOM	AADINOPS	DIAPASON
AADGIMPR	PARADIGM	AADHNPRS	HARDPANS	AADINOPT	ADAPTION
AADGIMRS	DIAGRAMS	AADHNRSS	DARSHANS	AADINORT	ANTIDORA
AADGIMRT	GRADATIM	AADHNSSW	HANDSAWS	AADINOTV	AVOIDANT
AADGINPR	PARADING	AADHNSTT	HATSTAND	AADINRRS	DARRAINS
AADGINPT	ADAPTING	AADHRRTW	THRAWARD	AADINRRW	AIRDRAWN
AADGINRR	DARRAIGN	AADHRRYZ	HAZARDRY	AADINRST	INTRADAS
AADGINRU	GUARDIAN	AADHRSWY	HAYWARDS		RADIANTS
AADGINRW	AWARDING	AADHSSWY	WASHDAYS	AADINRSV	VIRANDAS
AADGIQRU	QUADRIGA	AADIILNS	SIALIDAN	AADINRTY	INTRADAY
AADGIRSV	GRAVIDAS	AADIINOS	DIANOIAS	AADIOPRS	DIASPORA
AADGLLSW	GADWALLS	AADIIPSS	ADIPSIAS	AADIOPSZ	DOPIAZAS
AADGLMOR	MALGRADO	AADIJMNS	JAMDANIS	AADIORRT	RADIATOR
AADGLMSY	AMYGDALS	AADIKLLO	ALKALOID	AADIPSUY	UPADAISY
AADGLNOR	LARGANDO	AADIKLLR	KILLADAR	AADIRRSW	AIRWARDS
AADGLNRS	GARLANDS	AADIKLRY	KAILYARD	AADIRRSY	DISARRAY
AADGLNSS	SLADANGS	AADIKLSY	ILKADAYS	AADISTXY	DYSTAXIA
AADGLOOW	AGALWOOD	AADIKMNS	DAMASKIN	AADJNTTU	ADJUTANT
AADGLOPR	PODAGRAL	AADIKNQR	QINDARKA	AADJNTUV	ADJUVANT
AADGLORW	GOALWARD	AADILLLO	ALLODIAL	AADKLMNR	LANDMARK
AADGLPRW	GLADWRAP	AADILLNR	LANDRAIL	AADKLNPR	PARKLAND
AADGLRSU	GRADUALS	AADILLPR	PAILLARD	AADKLRTU	TALUKDAR
AADGMNOP	PAGANDOM		PALLIARD	AADKMNRS	DARKMANS
AADGMNOR	DRAGOMAN	AADILLRS	SILLADAR	AADKMRSY	DAYMARKS
AADGMNOS	GOADSMAN	AADILLRY	RADIALLY	AADKNRST	TANKARDS
AADGMNRS	DRAGSMAN	AADILLSY	DYSLALIA	AADKORWY	WORKADAY
	GRANDAMS	AADILMNN	MAINLAND	AADKPRRW	PARKWARD
	GRANDMAS	AADILMNO	DOMAINAL	AADLLLNS	LALLANDS
AADGMRSS	SMARAGDS			AADLLMPY	LADYPALM
AADGNNQU	QUANDANG	AADILMNP	PLAIDMAN	AADLLMRS	MALLARDS
AADGNPRS	GRANDPAS	AADILMRS	ADMIRALS	AADLLNOY	ANODALLY
AADGNRST	GARDANTS		AMILDARS	AADLLNPY	PLAYLAND
AADGNRSY	YARDANGS	AADILMST	MATILDAS	AADLLNSW	LAWLANDS
AADGNRTU	GUARDANT	AADILNOR	ORDALIAN	AADLMNNS	LANDSMAN
AADGNRUV	VANGUARD	AADILNPR	PRANDIAL	AADLMNOR	MANDORLA
AADGNRWY	DRANGWAY	AADILNPS	PALADINS	AADLMNOS	MANDOLAS
AADGOPRS	PODAGRAS	AADILNRS	LANIARDS	AADLMNSS	LANDMASS
AADGRRUW	GURDWARA	AADILNTT	DILATANT	AADLMNSU	LADANUMS
AADHHIPS	PADISHAH	AADILOPS	PALISADO	AADLMNUU	LAUDANUM
AADHHKNS	SHADKHAN	AADILORR	RAILROAD	AADLMORS	ARMLOADS
AADHHPSS	PADSHAHS	AADILPRS	PARDALIS	AADLNOPR	PARLANDO
AADHHRST	HARDHATS	AADILPRY	LAPIDARY	AADLNOPS	DALAPONS
AADHIINP	APHIDIAN	AADILRRS	RISALDAR		SOAPLAND
AADHILLR	HALLIARD	AADILRST	DIASTRAL	AADLNOST	SALTANDO
AADHILNR	HANDRAIL		TAILARDS	AADLNOSV	VANLOADS
AADHILRV	HAVILDAR			AADLNOSZ	DANAZOLS
AADHIMRS	HARAMDIS	AADILSST	STADIALS	AADLNRSY	LANYARDS
AADHIMSS	SAMADHIS	AADIMNNR	MANDARIN	AADLOPSY	PAYLOADS
AADHINOT	ANTHODIA	AADIMNOR	RADIOMAN	AADLORST	LOADSTAR
AADHINPS	DAPHNIAS	AADIMNOT	MANATOID	AADLORTU	ADULATOR
AADHINRR	HARRIDAN	AADIMNRS	MANDIRAS		LAUDATOR
AADHIPRS	PARISHAD	AADIMNRT	TAMARIND	AADLPPRW	WALDRAPP
		AADIMNRY	DAIRYMAN		

AADLPPSU	APPLAUDS
AADLPSYY	PLAYDAYS
AADMMNOW	MADWOMAN
AADMMNSU	MANDAMUS
AADMNNOS	MADONNAS
AADMNORS	MADRONAS
	MANDORAS
	MONARDAS
	ROADSMAN
AADMNORT	MANDATOR
AADMNRSS	MANSARDS
AADMNRSW	MANWARDS
AADMNSTU	TAMANDUS
AADMOPPP	PAPPADOM
AADMOPPS	PAPADOMS
AADMOQSU	MADOQUAS
AADMORRT	TRAMROAD
AADMORST	MATADORS
AADMPPSU	PAPADUMS
AADMRRSY	YARDARMS
AADMRSZZ	MAZZARDS
AADNNPSU	PANDANUS
AADNOPRS	PANDORAS
AADNOPSS	SANDSOAP
AADNORST	ONDATRAS
AADNORTY	DONATARY
AADNOSUV	VANADOUS
AADNOSWY	NOWADAYS
AADNPRSU	PANDURAS
AADNPSTT	STANDPAT
AADNQRSU	QUADRANS
AADNQRTU	QUADRANT
AADNQRUY	QUANDARY
AADNRRSW	WARRANDS
AADNRRSY	DARRAYNS
AADNRSTY	TANYARDS
AADNRSWY	NAYWARDS
AADOPPRR	PARADROP
AADOPRRS	PARADORS
AADOPRST	ADAPTORS
AADOPRXY	PARADOXY
AADOPSSS	PASSADOS
AADOPSTT	DOPATTAS
AADOPSUY	PADUASOY
AADORSVY	SAVOYARD
AADORSWY	ROADWAYS
AADOSSTT	TOSTADAS
AADPSTTU	DUPATTAS
AADQRSTU	QUADRATS
AADRSSTY	DAYSTARS
AAEEEHRT	HETAERAE
AAEEEMRT	AMEERATE
AAEEFFRS	AFFEARES
AAEEFGLS	LEAFAGES
AAEEFRRS	SEAFARER
AAEEFRST	RATAFEES
AAEEGILN	ALIENAGE
AAEEGILP	EPIGAEAL
AAEEGINP	EPIGAEAN
AAEEGINS	AGENESIA
AAEEGKLS	LEAKAGES
AAEEGLLN	ENALLAGE
AAEEGLRY	LAYERAGE
AAEEGLST	ETALAGES
	STEALAGE
AAEEGLSV	SALVAGEE
AAEEGMNS	AMENAGES
AAEEGMPR	AMPERAGE
AAEEGMST	AGAMETES
	AGEMATES
AAEEGMTY	METAYAGE
AAEEGNRS	SANGAREE
AAEEGNRT	TAGAREEN
AAEEGRST	STEARAGE
AAEEGRSV	AVERAGES
AAEEGRTW	WATERAGE
AAEEHIMR	HAEREMAI
AAEEHKKR	HARAKEKE
AAEEHKRT	HEKETARA
AAEEHLMR	AHEMERAL
AAEEHMNR	HERMAEAN
AAEEHNPS	SAPHENAE
AAEEHPRT	EARTHPEA
	HEARTPEA
AAEEHRST	HETAERAS
AAEEHRTW	AWEATHER
	WHEATEAR
AAEEHRWY	HEREAWAY
AAEEILNT	ALIENATE
AAEEINTT	TAENIATE
AAEEJMNP	JAMPANEE
AAEEKLSS	SEAKALES
AAEEKLTW	LATEWAKE
AAEEKMNS	NAMESAKE
AAEEKMRT	TEAMAKER
AAEEKNRW	AWAKENER
	REAWAKEN
AAEEKPRT	PARAKEET
AAEEKPSS	SEASPEAK
AAEEKQSU	SEAQUAKE
AAEEKRSW	REAWAKES
AAEELLLM	LAMELLAE
AAEELLMR	AMARELLE
AAEELLMT	MALLEATE
AAEELLNV	AVELLANE
AAEELLPT	PATELLAE
AAEELMMT	METAMALE
AAEELMST	MALEATES
AAEELNNR	ANNEALER
	LERNAEAN
AAEELNPS	SEAPLANE
	SPELAEAN
AAEELNPT	PANETELA
AAEELNPU	PAENULAE
AAEELNST	ELASTANE
AAEELORT	AREOLATE
AAEELORU	AUREOLAE
AAEELPPR	APPEALER
AAEELRST	LAETARES
AAEELRTU	LAUREATE
AAEELRTV	VALERATE
AAEELSST	ELASTASE
AAEELTUV	EVALUATE
AAEELVWY	WAYLEAVE
AAEEMMTT	TEAMMATE
AAEEMNPT	NAMETAPE
AAEEMNST	EMANATES
	MANATEES
AAEEMPRS	PARAMESE
AAEEMRST	AMREETAS
AAEEMSTT	SEATMATE
AAEEMSTX	MEATAXES
AAEENNNT	ANTENNAE
AAEENPRT	PARANETE
AAEENRRS	ARRASENE
AAEENRST	ARSENATE
	SERENATA
AAEENRTT	ANTEATER
AAEENSTU	NAUSEATE
AAEEPPRR	APPEARER
	RAPPAREE
	REAPPEAR
AAEEPPRS	APPEASER
AAEEPPSS	APPEASES
AAEEPRST	ASPERATE
	SEPARATE
AAEEPSTT	ASEPTATE
AAEERRWW	REWAREWA
AAEERSSW	SEAWARES
AAEERSTT	STEARATE
AAEERSTW	SEAWATER
	TEAWARES
AAEERSWX	EARWAXES
AAEERSYY	YEASAYER
AAEFFGRS	AGRAFFES
AAEFFGST	STAFFAGE
AAEFFIRS	AFFAIRES
AAEFFLLR	FARFALLE
AAEFFLLS	FALAFELS
AAEFFLPR	PARAFFLE
AAEFFLRT	TAFFAREL
AAEFFNRS	FANFARES
AAEFFRRY	AFFRAYER
AAEFFSTT	TAFFETAS
AAEFGGRT	GRAFTAGE
AAEFGHRW	WHARFAGE
AAEFGINR	AFEARING
AAEFGITT	FATIGATE
AAEFGLLL	FLAGELLA
AAEFGLOT	FLOATAGE
AAEFGRTU	FRAUTAGE
AAEFGSTW	WAFTAGES
AAEFIILR	FILARIAE
AAEFIKLT	KALIFATE
AAEFILTY	FAYALITE
AAEFIMRR	AIRFRAME
AAEFINNT	FAINEANT
AAEFINNU	INFAUNAE
AAEFINPU	EPIFAUNA
AAEFINST	FANTASIE
AAEFINTX	ANTEFIXA
AAEFIRRS	AIRFARES
AAEFKMST	MAKEFAST
AAEFLLSV	FAVELLAS
AAEFLMOT	MEATLOAF
AAEFLMTT	FLATMATE
AAEFLNUU	FAUNULAE
AAEFLPRS	EARFLAPS
	PARAFLES
AAEFLRTW	FLATWARE
AAEFMRST	FERMATAS
AAEFMRSU	FUMARASE

AAEFMRTU	FUMARATE	AAEGIPRU	PERIAGUA	AAEGMRTU	AGERATUM
AAEFQRSU	AQUAFERS	AAEGIRRS	ARRIAGES	AAEGMSSS	MASSAGES
AAEFRRRW	WARFARER	AAEGIRSV	VAGARIES	AAEGMSTT	METATAGS
AAEFRRSW	WARFARES	AAEGISSS	ASSEGAIS	AAEGMTTW	MEGAWATT
AAEFRRWY	WAYFARER	AAEGISST	AGATISES	AAEGNNOP	NEOPAGAN
AAEFRSWY	WAYFARES	AAEGISSU	AGEUSIAS	AAEGNNPS	PANNAGES
AAEFRTTX	AFTERTAX	AAEGISTT	AGITATES	AAEGNNST	TANNAGES
AAEGGINR	GRAINAGE	AAEGISTZ	AGATIZES	AAEGNPST	PAGEANTS
AAEGGIOT	AGIOTAGE	AAEGIVWY	GIVEAWAY	AAEGNPSW	PAWNAGES
AAEGGLNR	LANGRAGE	AAEGJSTU	AJUTAGES	AAEGNRRR	ARRANGER
AAEGGLNU	LANGUAGE	AAEGKNST	TANKAGES	AAEGNRRS	ARRANGES
AAEGGMMR	GRAMMAGE	AAEGKOSS	SOAKAGES	AAEGNRST	STARAGEN
AAEGGNOS	ANAGOGES	AAEGLLMS	SMALLAGE		TANAGERS
AAEGGNOW	WAGONAGE	AAEGLLPR	PELLAGRA	AAEGNRTU	RUNAGATE
AAEGGNRY	GARGANEY	AAEGLLSS	GALLEASS	AAEGNSSU	GUANASES
AAEGGOPR	PARAGOGE	AAEGLLST	GALLATES	AAEGNSTT	STAGNATE
AAEGGOPS	APAGOGES		GALLETAS	AAEGNSTV	VANTAGES
AAEGGRST	AGGRATES		STALLAGE	AAEGNSTW	WANTAGES
AAEGHLNP	PHALANGE		TALLAGES	AAEGNTUV	VAUNTAGE
AAEGHLSU	HAULAGES	AAEGLLTU	GLUTAEAL	AAEGORRT	ARROGATE
AAEGHLSY	HAYLAGES	AAEGLMNS	GAMELANS	AAEGORSS	AGAROSES
AAEGHMRX	HEXAGRAM	AAEGLMNV	GAVELMAN	AAEGORTT	AEGROTAT
AAEGHMSS	GAMASHES	AAEGLMPY	GAMEPLAY	AAEGPPRW	WRAPPAGE
AAEGHNRU	HARANGUE	AAEGLMST	ALMAGEST	AAEGPRSS	PASSAGER
AAEGHNST	THANAGES	AAEGLNOU	ANALOGUE	AAEGPRSW	WARPAGES
AAEGHOPY	HYPOGAEA	AAEGLNPP	LAGNAPPE	AAEGPSSS	PASSAGES
AAEGILLP	PELAGIAL	AAEGLNPT	PLANTAGE	AAEGPSSY	PAYSAGES
AAEGILLR	GALLERIA	AAEGLNRS	ALNAGERS	AAEGQSUY	QUAYAGES
AAEGILLT	ALLIGATE	AAEGLNRT	ARGENTAL	AAEGRRSV	RAVAGERS
AAEGILMS	SEMIGALA	AAEGLNRU	AULNAGER	AAEGRSST	GASTREAS
AAEGILNP	PELAGIAN	AAEGLNSS	LASAGNES	AAEGRSSU	ASSUAGER
AAEGILNR	GERANIAL	AAEGLNSU	AULNAGES	AAEGRSTT	REGATTAS
	REGALIAN		LEGUAANS	AAEGRSTV	STRAVAGE
AAEGILNT	AGENTIAL	AAEGLNTU	ANGULATE	AAEGRSTZ	STARGAZE
	ALGINATE	AAEGLOSV	AASVOGEL	AAEGRSVY	SAVAGERY
AAEGILRS	GASALIER	AAEGLRRS	REALGARS	AAEGSSSU	ASSUAGES
	LAIRAGES		RESALGAR		SAUSAGES
	REGALIAS	AAEGLRRW	WARRAGLE	AAEGSSSV	AVGASSES
AAEGILSS	ALGESIAS	AAEGLRST	AGRESTAL	AAEGSSSW	ASSWAGES
AAEGILSX	GALAXIES	AAEGLRSV	SALVAGER	AAEGSSTV	SAVAGEST
AAEGILTT	TAILGATE	AAEGLRTY	LEGATARY	AAEGSSTW	TASSWAGE
AAEGIMNO	EGOMANIA	AAEGLSST	AGELASTS		WASTAGES
AAEGIMNP	PIGMAEAN		LASTAGES	AAEGSTTW	WATTAGES
AAEGIMNS	MAGNESIA	AAEGLSSV	SALVAGES	AAEGSTWY	GATEWAYS
AAEGIMNT	AGMINATE	AAEGLSVY	SAVAGELY		GETAWAYS
	ENIGMATA	AAEGLTUV	VAULTAGE	AAEHIIRT	HETAIRAI
AAEGIMNZ	MAGAZINE	AAEGMMNR	ENGRAMMA		HETAIRIA
AAEGIMRR	MARRIAGE	AAEGMMNS	GAMESMAN	AAEHILMN	HIELAMAN
AAEGIMRT	GEMATRIA	AAEGMNPY	PYGMAEAN	AAEHILNP	APHELIAN
	MARITAGE	AAEGMNRS	MANAGERS	AAEHILNT	ANTHELIA
AAEGINNR	ANEARING	AAEGMNRT	MAGNETAR	AAEHILPR	PARHELIA
AAEGINPS	NAGAPIES	AAEGMNRV	GRAVAMEN	AAEHIMNT	ANTHEMIA
	PAGANISE	AAEGMNST	MAGENTAS		HAEMATIN
AAEGINPT	PAGINATE		MAGNATES	AAEHIMRU	MAIREHAU
AAEGINPZ	PAGANIZE		NAMETAGS	AAEHINPT	APHANITE
AAEGINRS	ANERGIAS	AAEGMORR	AEROGRAM	AAEHINST	ASTHENIA
	ANGARIES	AAEGMORS	SAGAMORE	AAEHIPST	APATHIES
	ARGINASE	AAEGMPRR	RAMPAGER	AAEHIRST	HETAIRAS
AAEGINRT	AERATING	AAEGMPRS	RAMPAGES	AAEHIRTT	HATTERIA
AAEGINST	SAGINATE	AAEGMPRU	RAMPAUGE	AAEHKLST	ALKAHEST
AAEGINSW	WAINAGES	AAEGMRRV	MARGRAVE	AAEHKMRT	HATMAKER
AAEGINTV	NAVIGATE	AAEGMRRY	GRAMARYE	AAEHKMRY	HAYMAKER
	VAGINATE	AAEGMRSS	MASSAGER	AAEHKNST	KHANATES
AAEGIPRS	IGARAPES	AAEGMRST	MEGASTAR	AAEHKSSW	SEAHAWKS

AAEHLLLS	ALLHEALS	AAEILLPP	PAPILLAE	AAEIMRST	AMIRATES
AAEHLMNT	METHANAL	AAEILLPT	PALLIATE	AAEIMRSU	URAEMIAS
AAEHLMNW	WHALEMAN	AAEILLRT	ARILLATE	AAEIMRTT	AMARETTI
AAEHLMSY	SEALYHAM	AAEILLRV	LAVALIER	AAEIMSUV	MAUVAISE
AAEHLMTU	HAMULATE	AAEILLRY	AERIALLY	AAEINNTT	ANTENATI
AAEHLNOZ	HALAZONE	AAEILLTT	TALLIATE	AAEINORT	AERATION
AAEHLNRT	ANTHERAL	AAEILLTV	ALLATIVE	AAEINORX	ANOREXIA
AAEHLNRW	NARWHALE	AAEILMMX	AXILEMMA	AAEINPPR	PRIAPEAN
AAEHLNST	ETHANALS	AAEILMNN	MELANIAN	AAEINPRS	PANARIES
AAEHLNTX	EXHALANT	AAEILMNT	ALAIMENT	AAEINPRT	ANTIRAPE
AAEHLOPT	APHOLATE		ANTIMALE	AAEINPTT	PATINATE
AAEHLPRS	PEARLASH		LAMINATE	AAEINRRW	RAINWEAR
AAEHLPRX	HEXAPLAR	AAEILMNV	VELAMINA	AAEINRST	ANTISERA
AAEHLPSX	HEXAPLAS	AAEILMRT	MATERIAL		ARTESIAN
AAEHLPUV	UPHEAVAL	AAEILMSS	MALAISES		RATANIES
AAEHLRST	TREHALAS	AAEILNNS	ALANINES		RESINATA
AAEHLRTT	THEATRAL		ANNALISE		SANTERIA
AAEHLSSV	LAVASHES	AAEILNNZ	ANNALIZE		SEATRAIN
AAEHLSTT	ATHLETAS	AAEILNPR	AIRPLANE	AAEINRTT	ATTAINER
AAEHMMOT	HEMATOMA	AAEILNPT	PALATINE		REATTAIN
AAEHMNPT	PATHNAME	AAEILNRU	AURELIAN	AAEINRTU	INAURATE
AAEHMNPY	NYMPHAEA	AAEILNRV	VALERIAN	AAEINRTW	ANTIWEAR
AAEHMNRS	SHAREMAN	AAEILNSS	NASALISE	AAEINRTZ	ATRAZINE
	SHEARMAN	AAEILNSZ	NASALIZE	AAEINSST	ENTASIAS
AAEHMNRT	EARTHMAN	AAEILNTT	ANTLIATE	AAEINSTT	ASTATINE
AAEHMOPR	AMPHORAE	AAEILNTV	AVENTAIL		SANITATE
AAEHMOPT	HEPATOMA	AAEILORS	OLEARIAS		TANAISTE
AAEHMORT	ATHEROMA	AAEILPPS	PAPALISE	AAEINSTV	SANATIVE
AAEHNPRS	HANAPERS	AAEILPPZ	PAPALIZE	AAEINTTT	TITANATE
AAEHNPSS	SAPHENAS	AAEILPRT	PARIETAL	AAEIPPRS	APPRAISE
AAEHNPST	PHEASANT	AAEILPRX	PREAXIAL	AAEIPPSS	APEPSIAS
AAEHNPSY	SYNAPHEA	AAEILPST	STAPELIA	AAEIPRRS	PAREIRAS
AAEHNTTX	XANTHATE	AAEILRRT	ARTERIAL	AAEIPRSS	SPIRAEAS
AAEHPRSZ	PHEAZARS	AAEILRSS	ASSAILER	AAEIPRST	ASPIRATE
AAEHRRSS	HARASSER		REASSAIL		PARASITE
AAEHRSSS	HARASSES		SALARIES		SEPTARIA
AAEHRSSY	HEARSAYS	AAEILRSU	AURELIAS	AAEIPRTT	PATRIATE
AAEHRSTU	ARETHUSA	AAEILRSV	REAVAILS	AAEIPRTZ	TRAPEZIA
AAEHRTWX	EARTHWAX	AAEILRTV	VARIETAL	AAEIPRXY	APYREXIA
AAEIIKNS	AKINESIA	AAEILSTV	AESTIVAL	AAEIPSTT	APATITES
AAEIILMP	LIPAEMIA		SALIVATE	AAEIQRTU	TAQUERIA
AAEIIMRV	VIRAEMIA	AAEILSTX	SAXATILE	AAEIRRRT	TERRARIA
AAEIINSV	AVIANISE	AAEILSWY	AISLEWAY	AAEIRRTV	VERATRIA
AAEIINVZ	AVIANIZE	AAEILTVX	LAXATIVE	AAEIRSST	ASTERIAS
AAEIIPRS	APIARIES	AAEIMMST	IMAMATES		ATRESIAS
AAEIIRSV	AVIARIES	AAEIMNOT	METANOIA	AAEIRSSX	XERASIAS
AAEIJLNV	JAVELINA	AAEIMNOX	ANOXEMIA	AAEIRSTT	ARIETTAS
AAEIJNPS	JAPANISE	AAEIMNPR	PEARMAIN		ARISTATE
AAEIJNPZ	JAPANIZE	AAEIMNPS	PAEANISM	AAEIRSTV	VARIATES
AAEIJNRT	NAARTJIE	AAEIMNPT	IMPANATE	AAEIRSTW	AWAITERS
AAEIKKMZ	KAMIKAZE	AAEIMNRR	MARINERA	AAEIRSVW	AIRWAVES
AAEIKLLN	ALKALINE	AAEIMNRT	ANIMATER	AAEIRTTZ	ZARATITE
AAEIKLLS	ALKALIES		MARINATE	AAEISSTT	SATIATES
	ALKALISE	AAEIMNRZ	MAZARINE	AAEISTUX	EUTAXIAS
AAEIKLLV	LAVALIKE	AAEIMNSS	AMNESIAS	AAEITTVX	TAXATIVE
AAEIKLLZ	ALKALIZE	AAEIMNST	AMENTIAS	AAEJLNOP	JALAPENO
AAEIKLNT	ANTILEAK		ANIMATES	AAEJMNRY	MARYJANE
AAEIKMRR	KRAMERIA	AAEIMNTZ	NIZAMATE	AAEJNNPR	JAPANNER
AAEIKPRT	PARAKITE	AAEIMOPR	PAROEMIA	AAEJNRST	NAARTJES
AAEILLLU	ALLELUIA	AAEIMOTX	TOXAEMIA	AAEJNRTZ	JAZERANT
AAEILLMM	MAMILLAE	AAEIMOTZ	AZOTEMIA	AAEJOPRS	APAREJOS
AAEILLMR	ARMILLAE	AAEIMPRS	ASPERMIA	AAEJRSSV	SVARAJES
AAEILLMX	MAXILLAE		SAPREMIA	AAEJRSSW	SWARAJES
AAEILLNT	ALLANITE	AAEIMPSY	PYAEMIAS	AAEKKORS	KARAOKES

AAEKKRSY	KAYAKERS	AAELMSSY	AMYLASES	AAEMNORS	AMARONES
AAEKLLTY	ALKYLATE	AAELNNNT	ANTENNAL	AAEMNORT	EMANATOR
AAEKLMRW	LAWMAKER	AAELNNOT	NEONATAL	AAEMNOSW	SEAWOMAN
AAEKLMRY	MALARKEY	AAELNNTU	ANNULATE	AAEMNOTZ	METAZOAN
AAEKLNRS	LARNAKES	AAELNOSS	SEASONAL	AAEMNPPS	PAMPEANS
AAEKLNST	ALKANETS	AAELNOSV	VALONEAS	AAEMNPRS	PARMESAN
	KANTELAS	AAELNPRS	PRENASAL		SPEARMAN
AAEKLPRS	ASPARKLE	AAELNPRT	PARENTAL	AAEMNPRT	PARAMENT
AAEKMMPR	MAPMAKER		PARLANTE	AAEMNRRY	YARRAMEN
AAEKMORT	KERATOMA		PATERNAL	AAEMNRST	SARMENTA
AAEKMRRS	EARMARKS		PRENATAL		SEMANTRA
AAEKMRRW	WARMAKER	AAELNPRW	WARPLANE	AAEMNRSU	MURAENAS
AAEKMRSS	SEAMARKS	AAELNPST	PLATANES	AAEMNRTT	ATRAMENT
AAEKNPRT	PARTAKEN		PLEASANT	AAEMNRTW	WATERMAN
AAEKORTY	AKARYOTE	AAELNPSU	PAENULAS	AAEMNSST	NAMASTES
AAEKPRRT	PARTAKER	AAELNPTT	PANTALET	AAEMNSTU	MANTEAUS
AAEKPRST	PARTAKES	AAELNRSS	ARSENALS	AAEMNTUX	MANTEAUX
AAEKPSTU	PUKATEAS	AAELNRST	ASTERNAL	AAEMOPXZ	OXAZEPAM
AAEKSSSV	KAVASSES	AAELNRSY	ANALYSER	AAEMORTT	AMARETTO
	VAKASSES	AAELNRTT	ALTERANT		TERATOMA
AAELLLMR	LAMELLAR		ALTERNAT	AAEMORTX	XEROMATA
AAELLLMS	LAMELLAS		TARLETAN	AAEMOSTT	STEATOMA
AAELLLPR	PARALLEL	AAELNRTX	RELAXANT	AAEMOSTY	ATEMOYAS
AAELLMPU	AMPULLAE	AAELNRYZ	ANALYZER	AAEMOTTU	AUTOMATE
AAELLNPU	PLANULAE	AAELNSST	SEALANTS	AAEMPPSS	PAMPASES
AAELLNSS	NASSELLA	AAELNSSV	ENVASSAL	AAEMPTTU	AMPUTATE
AAELLNSZ	ZANELLAS	AAELNSSY	ANALYSES	AAEMQSTU	SQUAMATE
AAELLORV	ALVEOLAR	AAELNSTT	ATLANTES	AAEMRRTU	ARMATURE
AAELLPRS	PARELLAS	AAELNSTY	ANALYTES	AAEMRSSS	AMASSERS
AAELLPRT	PATELLAR	AAELNSTZ	ZEALANTS	AAEMRSTU	AMATEURS
AAELLPST	PATELLAS	AAELNSWY	LANEWAYS	AAEMRTTU	MATURATE
AAELLRST	LATERALS	AAELNSYZ	ANALYZES	AAENNNST	ANTENNAS
AAELLRSY	ALLAYERS	AAELOPRS	PSORALEA	AAENNOTT	ANNOTATE
AAELLSSW	SEAWALLS	AAELORSU	AUREOLAS	AAENNSTT	STANNATE
AAELLUVV	VALVULAE	AAELORTY	ALEATORY		TANNATES
AAELLWWY	WELLAWAY	AAELOSTX	OXALATES	AAENNSTU	NAUSEANT
AAELLWYY	ALLEYWAY	AAELPPRS	APPARELS	AAENNSTV	VENTANAS
AAELMMNO	MELANOMA	AAELPPST	PALPATES	AAENOPSS	PAESANOS
AAELMMOX	AXOLEMMA	AAELPPSU	APPLAUSE	AAENOQTU	AQUATONE
AAELMMRS	ALMEMARS	AAELPRST	PALESTRA	AAENORRU	AUROREAN
AAELMMTU	MALAMUTE	AAELPRSV	PALAVERS	AAENORST	ANOESTRA
AAELMNOT	MALONATE	AAELPRSY	PARALYSE	AAENORSU	ARANEOUS
AAELMNOX	AXONEMAL	AAELPRTT	TETRAPLA	AAENORTU	AERONAUT
AAELMNPT	PLATEMAN	AAELPRWY	PLAYWEAR	AAENOSST	ASSONATE
AAELMNRT	MATERNAL	AAELPRYZ	PARALYZE	AAENPPRS	PARPANES
AAELMNSS	SALESMAN	AAELPSTU	PLATEAUS	AAENPPRT	APPARENT
AAELMNST	TALESMAN	AAELPSTV	PALSTAVE		TRAPPEAN
AAELMNSW	WEALSMAN	AAELPSWY	PALEWAYS	AAENPRTY	PRYTANEA
AAELMNSY	SEAMANLY	AAELPTUV	VAPULATE	AAENPSST	ANAPESTS
AAELMOST	OATMEALS	AAELPTUX	PLATEAUX		PEASANTS
AAELMOSU	MAUSOLEA	AAELRSST	TARSEALS	AAENPSTT	ANTEPAST
AAELMOTZ	METAZOAL	AAELRSTZ	LAZARETS	AAENPSTY	PEASANTY
AAELMPPY	MAYAPPLE	AAELRTUV	VELATURA	AAENRRRT	NARRATER
AAELMPRT	MALAPERT	AAELRUZZ	ZARZUELA	AAENRRSS	NARRASES
AAELMPRX	EXAMPLAR	AAELRWYY	WAYLAYER	AAENRRST	NARRATES
AAELMPSS	LAMPASES	AAELSSTT	SALTATES	AAENRSST	SANTERAS
	LAMPASSE	AAELSTUV	VALUATES	AAENRSTT	TARTANES
AAELMPST	PLATEASM	AAELSTZZ	ALTEZZAS	AAENRSTV	TAVERNAS
AAELMPTV	VAMPLATE	AAEMMMRS	MAREMMAS		TSAREVNA
AAELMPTY	PLAYMATE	AAEMMNOT	AMMONATE	AAENRSUW	UNAWARES
AAELMRSW	MALWARES	AAEMMNRT	ARMAMENT	AAENRSYY	NAYSAYER
AAELMRSY	LAMASERY	AAEMMNSU	MANUMEAS	AAENRTVZ	TZAREVNA
AAELMRTT	MALTREAT	AAEMMOST	METASOMA	AAENSSSV	VANESSAS
AAELMSST	MALTASES	AAEMMSTT	STEMMATA	AAENSSTV	SAVANTES

AAENSSTW	SEAWANTS	AAFIILNR	FILARIAN	AAGGNNOO	ONGAONGA
AAENSSWY	AWAYNESS	AAFIILRS	FILARIAS	AAGGNSST	GANGSTAS
AAENTTTT	ATTENTAT	AAFIINST	FISTIANA	AAGGNSTT	TAGGANTS
AAEOPPSS	APOAPSES	AAFIKLLY	ALKALIFY	AAGGNSWY	GANGWAYS
AAEOPSTT	APOSTATE	AAFILLNR	RAINFALL	AAGGRSTT	STAGGART
AAEOPSTZ	ZAPATEOS	AAFILLUV	AVAILFUL	AAGHHIMS	MASHGIAH
AAEORRST	AERATORS	AAFILMST	FATALISM	AAGHHINS	SHANGHAI
AAEORSST	AEROSATS	AAFILNNU	INFAUNAL	AAGHHNOS	OANSHAGH
AAEORSTT	AEROSTAT	AAFILNQU	ALFAQUIN	AAGHILNN	HANGNAIL
AAEORTTV	ROTAVATE	AAFILNST	FANTAILS	AAGHILPY	HYPALGIA
AAEPPRRT	TARPAPER		TAILFANS	AAGHILRS	GHARIALS
AAEPPRST	PARAPETS	AAFILOPR	PARAFOIL		HARIGALS
AAEPPSTT	APPESTAT	AAFILQSU	ALFAQUIS	AAGHIMNS	ASHAMING
AAEPQRTU	PARAQUET	AAFILSTT	FATALIST	AAGHIMRT	TAGHAIRM
AAEPRSSY	APYRASES	AAFILTTY	FATALITY	AAGHINNS	ANHINGAS
AAEPRTXY	TAXPAYER	AAFIMNOR	FORAMINA	AAGHINPS	PAGANISH
AAEPSTTW	WATTAPES	AAFIMNOT	ANTIFOAM	AAGHINPW	AWHAPING
AAEPSWXX	PAXWAXES	AAFINNOV	FAVONIAN	AAGHIPRR	AIRGRAPH
AAEPSZZZ	PAZAZZES	AAFINNRS	SAFRANIN	AAGHIRSV	VAGARISH
AAERRRSY	ARRAYERS	AAFINNST	INFANTAS	AAGHKMNY	GYMKHANA
AAERRSST	TARRASES	AAFINNSU	INFAUNAS	AAGHKNST	THANGKAS
AAERRSTT	TARTARES	AAFINRRW	WARFARIN	AAGHLNNS	LANGSHAN
AAERRTTT	TARTRATE	AAFINSTU	FAUSTIAN	AAGHLNPY	ANAGLYPH
AAERSSSY	ASSAYERS	AAFIPRST	PARFAITS	AAGHLOSS	GASAHOLS
AAERSTTU	SATURATE	AAFIRSST	SAFARIST	AAGHMNOY	HOGMANAY
	TUATERAS	AAFIRSUY	RUFIYAAS		MAHOGANY
AAERTTTW	TERAWATT	AAFIRSWY	FAIRWAYS	AAGHMNSU	MAHUANGS
AAERTWWY	WATERWAY	AAFIRTTT	FRITTATA	AAGHMNSW	WHANGAMS
AAESTWWY	WASTEWAY	AAFJLLSW	JAWFALLS	AAGHNOPR	AGRAPHON
AAFFGILS	GAFFSAIL	AAFJLORS	ALFORJAS	AAGHNPRY	PHRYGANA
AAFFHIKY	KAFFIYAH	AAFLLNOV	FLAVANOL	AAGHNSST	SANGHATS
AAFFIILX	AFFIXIAL	AAFLLNUY	FAUNALLY	AAGHOPPR	APOGRAPH
AAFFILRT	TAFFRAIL	AAFLLPRT	PRATFALL	AAGHQSUU	QUAHAUGS
AAFFINPR	PARAFFIN	AAFLLPST	SPATFALL	AAGHRRTU	ARRAUGHT
AAFFINSS	SAFFIANS	AAFLMORV	LAVAFORM	AAGHRSSW	WASHRAGS
AAFFINST	AFFIANTS	AAFLNNOT	NONFATAL	AAGIIKKN	KAIAKING
AAFFLPST	PALSTAFF	AAFLNORS	FORLANAS	AAGIILMN	IMAGINAL
AAFFLSTU	AFFLATUS		SAFRONAL	AAGIILNS	ALIASING
AAFFMNST	STAFFMAN	AAFLNOTT	FLOATANT	AAGIILNV	AVAILING
AAFFNNOR	FANFARON	AAFLNRSU	FURLANAS	AAGIIMNN	MAGAININ
AAFFOORW	FOOFARAW	AAFLSTWY	FLATWAYS	AAGIIMST	ASTIGMIA
AAFGHINS	AFGHANIS	AAFLSWYY	FLYAWAYS	AAGIINNU	IGUANIAN
AAFGHNRU	FRAUGHAN	AAFMNRST	RAFTSMAN	AAGIINRS	ARAISING
AAFGILNO	GOLFIANA	AAFMNSST	FANTASMS	AAGIINST	IGNATIAS
AAFGINTW	FATWAING	AAFMOPRR	PARAFORM	AAGIINTV	AVIATING
AAFGLLNU	LANGLAUF	AAFNPPRT	FRAPPANT	AAGIINTW	AWAITING
AAFGLNRT	FLAGRANT	AAFNSSTT	FANTASTS	AAGIKKNY	KAYAKING
AAFGNNRT	FRAGRANT	AAGGGHNS	GANGSHAG	AAGIKLNO	KAOLIANG
AAFGORRS	FARRAGOS	AAGGGINR	GARAGING	AAGIKLNR	KRAALING
AAFHHIKL	KHALIFAH	AAGGHNST	HANGTAGS	AAGIKLNS	ASLAKING
AAFHHORT	HAFTORAH	AAGGILLN	GANGLIAL	AAGIKMNS	SMAAKING
AAFHIKLS	KHALIFAS	AAGGILNR	GANGLIAR	AAGIKMRS	SKIAGRAM
AAFHIKLT	KHALIFAT	AAGGIMNN	MANAGING	AAGIKNST	TIKANGAS
	KHILAFAT	AAGGIMNR	MARAGING	AAGIKNSW	AWAKINGS
AAFHINRS	FARINHAS	AAGGINNT	ANTIGANG	AAGIKNSZ	ZIGANKAS
AAFHIRST	AIRSHAFT	AAGGINRV	RAVAGING	AAGILLNU	UNIALGAL
AAFHLLSS	ASHFALLS	AAGGINSV	SAVAGING	AAGILLNY	ALLAYING
AAFHLSTW	FLATWASH	AAGGIRST	GARAGIST	AAGILLSS	GALLIASS
AAFHLSTY	LAYSHAFT	AAGGITTW	GIGAWATT	AAGILLTV	GALLIVAT
AAFHORTT	HAFTAROT	AAGGLLLY	LALLYGAG	AAGILLUZ	ALGUAZIL
AAFHRSUU	HAUSFRAU	AAGGLMOS	MAGALOGS	AAGILMMR	MAILGRAM
AAFIILLM	FAMILIAL	AAGGLNOT	TAGALONG	AAGILMNO	MAGNOLIA
AAFIILLR	FILARIAL	AAGGLRSY	GRAYLAGS	AAGILMNR	ALARMING
AAFIILMR	FAMILIAR	AAGGMNNS	GANGSMAN		MARGINAL

AAGILMNX	MALAXING
AAGILMOT	GLIOMATA
AAGILMRY	GRAYMAIL
AAGILMSY	MYALGIAS
AAGILNOS	LOGANIAS
AAGILNOT	GALTONIA
AAGILNPT	PALATING
AAGILNRR	LARRIGAN
AAGILNSS	SALSAING
AAGILNTV	GALIVANT
AAGILNUV	VAGINULA
AAGILOOP	APOLOGIA
AAGILOPT	TOPALGIA
AAGILOSS	AGLOSSIA
AAGILOST	OTALGIAS
AAGILPRY	PLAGIARY
AAGILRRW	WARRIGAL
AAGILRTT	ATTAGIRL
AAGILSTT	SAGITTAL
AAGILSTW	WAGTAILS
AAGIMMRR	MARIGRAM
AAGIMNNN	MANGANIN
AAGIMNNO	AGNOMINA
AAGIMNOS	ANGIOMAS
AAGIMNPS	PAGANISM
AAGIMNRR	MARGARIN
AAGIMNSS	AMASSING
	SIAMANGS
AAGIMNSY	GYMNASIA
AAGIMPTU	PATAGIUM
AAGIMSSV	SAVAGISM
AAGIMSTT	STIGMATA
AAGINNNW	WANNIGAN
AAGINNNY	NANNYGAI
AAGINNOT	AGNATION
AAGINNRW	AWARNING
AAGINNSU	SAUNAING
AAGINNSW	WANIGANS
AAGINNSY	SYNANGIA
AAGINNTV	VAGINANT
AAGINNTW	AWANTING
AAGINORR	RANGIORA
AAGINOSS	AGNOSIAS
AAGINPPY	APPAYING
AAGINPRU	PAGURIAN
AAGINPRW	PARAWING
AAGINPRY	AGRYPNIA
AAGINPST	PAGANIST
AAGINPWW	PAWAWING
AAGINRRS	ARRAIGNS
AAGINRRY	ARRAYING
AAGINRSS	SANGRIAS
	SARANGIS
AAGINRST	GRANITAS
AAGINRSU	GUARANIS
AAGINRSY	ARAYSING
AAGINSST	ASSIGNAT
AAGINSSU	GAUSSIAN
AAGINSSY	ASSAYING
	GAINSAYS
AAGIORTT	AGITATOR
AAGIORTV	AVIGATOR
AAGIPRSU	PIRAGUAS
AAGIRRSY	ARGYRIAS

AAGIRSTV	GRAVITAS
	STRAVAIG
AAGISSTT	SAGITTAS
AAGKKNOS	ANGAKOKS
AAGKLRSV	GRAVLAKS
AAGKNOOR	KANGAROO
AAGKOOSZ	GAZOOKAS
AAGKORST	KATORGAS
AAGLLMOY	ALLOGAMY
AAGLLNOO	LAGOONAL
AAGLLNRY	LARYNGAL
AAGLLNST	GALLANTS
AAGLLOOP	APOLOGAL
AAGLLOPY	POLYGALA
AAGLLOSS	AGLOSSAL
AAGLMNSS	GLASSMAN
AAGLNNOO	ANALOGON
AAGLNORS	GRANOLAS
AAGLNPSS	LAPSANGS
AAGLNQUU	AQUALUNG
AAGLNRRU	GRANULAR
AAGLOPRY	PARALOGY
AAGLORSU	ARUGOLAS
AAGLRRUW	WARRAGUL
AAGLRSTU	GASTRULA
AAGLRSUU	ARUGULAS
AAGMMRRS	GRAMMARS
AAGMMSUY	MAMAGUYS
AAGMNNOR	NANOGRAM
AAGMNNRS	GRANNAMS
AAGMNOPZ	ZAMPOGNA
AAGMNORT	MARTAGON
AAGMNOSS	SANGOMAS
AAGMNOST	AGAMONTS
AAGMNPRS	PANGRAMS
AAGMNRST	TANGRAMS
	TRANGAMS
AAGMNRTU	ARMGAUNT
AAGMNSSW	SWAGSMAN
AAGMNSTY	SYNTAGMA
AAGMORSS	MARGOSAS
AAGMOTUY	AUTOGAMY
AAGMOTYZ	ZYGOMATA
AAGMRSST	MATGRASS
AAGNNNOP	NONPAGAN
AAGNNSTT	STAGNANT
AAGNOPRS	PARAGONS
AAGNOPRT	TRAGOPAN
AAGNORRT	ARROGANT
	TARRAGON
AAGNORSZ	ORGANZAS
AAGNORTU	ARGONAUT
AAGNRSTV	VAGRANTS
AAGNRTUY	GUARANTY
AAGNRTYZ	ZYGANTRA
AAGOPRSU	GAROUPAS
AAGOPSSS	SAPSAGOS
AAGORSSS	SARGASSO
AAGORSSU	SAGUAROS
AAGRRSSY	RAYGRASS
AAGRSSTU	SASTRUGA
AAGRSTUZ	ZASTRUGA
AAGSTTUU	TAUTAUGS
AAHHIIMM	MAHIMAHI

AAHHIINN	HINAHINA
AAHHIKNU	HANUKIAH
AAHHIRSS	SHARIAHS
AAHHKLOT	HALAKHOT
	HALAKOTH
AAHHKMRS	HASHMARK
AAHHKSWW	HAWKSHAW
AAHHMMSS	SHAMMASH
AAHHNNOS	HOSANNAH
AAHHNNST	THANNAHS
AAHHNPST	NAPHTHAS
AAHHOPRS	PHARAOHS
AAHIIKRT	TARAKIHI
AAHIILRT	HAIRTAIL
AAHIJNRS	HARIJANS
AAHIJPRS	RAJASHIP
AAHIKLPS	PASHALIK
AAHIKLST	HALAKIST
AAHIKORW	WHAKAIRO
AAHIKRST	KITHARAS
AAHILLLS	HALLALIS
	SHILLALA
AAHILLNS	HALLIANS
AAHILMNR	HARMALIN
AAHILMRS	ALMIRAHS
AAHILMSS	SHIMAALS
AAHILNNT	INHALANT
AAHILNOT	HALATION
AAHILOPP	HAPLOPIA
AAHILPSV	PAHLAVIS
AAHILPSY	PHYSALIA
AAHILRRZ	ARRHIZAL
AAHILSSW	SAHIWALS
AAHIMNOS	MAHONIAS
AAHIMNPS	PASHMINA
AAHIMNSS	SHAMINAS
AAHIMNZZ	HAZZANIM
AAHIMRSW	RAWMAISH
AAHIMRTY	ARYTHMIA
AAHINOPS	APHONIAS
AAHINPPS	PAPHIANS
AAHINPRS	PIRANHAS
AAHINRSW	RAINWASH
AAHINRTU	HAURIANT
AAHINSST	SHAITANS
AAHINSTW	TANIWHAS
AAHIOPRT	ATROPHIA
AAHIPRST	PITARAHS
AAHIPSTZ	ZAPTIAHS
AAHIPSXY	ASPHYXIA
AAHIRSSS	HARISSAS
AAHIRSST	SHARIATS
AAHIRSTV	HAVARTIS
AAHISTWY	THISAWAY
AAHJKNRS	KHANJARS
AAHKKOOR	HOROKAKA
AAHKLLMR	HALLMARK
AAHKLRSS	LASHKARS
AAHKMOTW	TOMAHAWK
AAHKMSSY	YASHMAKS
AAHKRSSW	SAWSHARK
AAHLLLOO	HALLALOO
AAHLLMRS	MARSHALL
AAHLLOPT	ALLOPATH

AAHLLSWY	HALLWAYS	**AAIINPZZ**	PIAZZIAN	**AAILMNOP**	PALAMINO
AAHLMMSS	MASHLAMS	**AAIINRST**	INTARSIA	**AAILMNOR**	MANORIAL
AAHLMOOS	MASOOLAH	**AAIINSTT**	TITANIAS		MORAINAL
AAHLMOPR	AMPHORAL	**AAIINSZZ**	ZIZANIAS	**AAILMNOX**	MONAXIAL
AAHLMRSS	MARSHALS	**AAIIOPST**	APOSITIA	**AAILMNPS**	PANISLAM
AAHLMSTU	THALAMUS	**AAIIORTZ**	ZOIATRIA	**AAILMNRU**	MANURIAL
AAHLNPST	ASHPLANT	**AAIIPRST**	APIARIST	**AAILMNRY**	LAMINARY
AAHLNRSW	NARWHALS	**AAIIPRVV**	VIVIPARA	**AAILMNSS**	NASALISM
AAHLPRRT	PHRATRAL	**AAIIRSTV**	AVIARIST	**AAILMNST**	STAMINAL
AAHLPSST	ASPHALTS	**AAIIRSTW**	WISTARIA		TALISMAN
AAHLRSSW	SHALWARS	**AAIIRTVX**	AVIATRIX	**AAILMNSU**	ALUMINAS
AAHMNNPU	PANHUMAN	**AAIJLLQU**	QUILLAJA	**AAILMNSV**	MAILVANS
AAHMNNSU	HANUMANS	**AAIJLNPS**	JALAPINS		NAVALISM
AAHMNORT	MARATHON	**AAIJMNPS**	JAMPANIS	**AAILMOPT**	LIPOMATA
AAHMNOST	HOASTMAN	**AAIJNRSY**	JANISARY	**AAILMORR**	ARMORIAL
AAHMNOTX	XANTHOMA	**AAIJNRSZ**	JANIZARS	**AAILMPPS**	PAPALISM
AAHMNPST	PHANTASM	**AAIJNRYZ**	JANIZARY	**AAILMPRT**	PRIMATAL
AAHMNRST	TRASHMAN	**AAIJPPSY**	JIPYAPAS	**AAILMQSU**	MAQUILAS
AAHMNSTX	XANTHAMS	**AAIKKNOS**	SKOKIAAN	**AAILMRST**	ALARMIST
AAHMOPRS	AMPHORAS	**AAIKKSTZ**	KAZATSKI		ALASTRIM
AAHMRSST	STRAMASH	**AAIKLNNN**	ALKANNIN	**AAILMTTU**	ULTIMATA
AAHNNOSS	HOSANNAS	**AAIKLNPS**	PALINKAS	**AAILNNOT**	NATIONAL
AAHNNPSW	SHWANPAN	**AAIKLNST**	NASTALIK	**AAILNNPT**	PLAINANT
AAHNNSTX	XANTHANS	**AAIKLPRS**	PALIKARS		PLANTAIN
AAHNOPRS	ANAPHORS	**AAIKMNNS**	MANAKINS	**AAILNNRU**	LUNARIAN
AAHNORST	ATHANORS	**AAIKMNRS**	RAMAKINS	**AAILNNST**	ANNALIST
AAHNORSV	NAVARHOS	**AAIKMNST**	ANTIMASK		SANTALIN
AAHNOSTT	THANATOS	**AAIKMORS**	ROMAIKAS	**AAILNOPS**	SALOPIAN
AAHNPSTT	PHANTAST	**AAIKMRSS**	KARAISMS	**AAILNOPT**	TALAPOIN
AAHNPSTY	PHANTASY	**AAIKMRST**	TAMARISK	**AAILNORS**	ORINASAL
AAHNTUWY	HUNTAWAY	**AAIKNNTT**	ANTITANK	**AAILNORT**	NOTARIAL
AAHOPRST	PARASHOT	**AAIKORSU**	OUAKARIS		RATIONAL
AAHOPRTU	AUTOHARP	**AAIKPPRS**	PAPRIKAS	**AAILNOST**	AILANTOS
AAHOQSUW	AQUASHOW	**AAIKPRRS**	AIRPARKS		ALATIONS
AAHORSSU	SAHUAROS	**AAIKSSTT**	ASTATKIS	**AAILNOSV**	VALONIAS
AAHPRSTW	WARPATHS	**AAIKSSTV**	SVASTIKA	**AAILNOTV**	LAVATION
AAHPSTWY	PATHWAYS	**AAIKSSTW**	SWASTIKA	**AAILNOTX**	LAXATION
AAHRRTTW	THRAWART	**AAIKSTVV**	AKVAVITS	**AAILNPRU**	PLANURIA
AAHRSSST	SHASTRAS	**AAILLLSS**	SALSILLA	**AAILNPSS**	SALPIANS
AAHRSSTY	ASHTRAYS	**AAILLLST**	LATILLAS	**AAILNPST**	PLATINAS
AAHRSTTW	STRAWHAT	**AAILLLUV**	ALLUVIAL	**AAILNQTU**	ALIQUANT
AAIIILMR	MILIARIA	**AAILLMMM**	MAMMILLA	**AAILNSSY**	ANALYSIS
AAIIIMNR	NIRAMIAI	**AAILLMMR**	MAMILLAR	**AAILNSTV**	VALIANTS
AAIIJJPP	JIPIJAPA	**AAILLMNS**	LAMINALS	**AAILNSTY**	NASALITY
AAIIKKKR	KAKARIKI		MANILLAS	**AAILNTTT**	LATITANT
AAIIKKNN	KINAKINA	**AAILLMNT**	MANTILLA	**AAILNTTY**	NATALITY
AAIILLQU	QUILLAIA	**AAILLMNY**	ANIMALLY	**AAILORRS**	RASORIAL
AAIILMNS	MAINSAIL	**AAILLMPT**	TAILLAMP	**AAILORRV**	VARIOLAR
AAIILMRS	AIRMAILS	**AAILLMRS**	ARMILLAS	**AAILORSS**	ROSALIAS
AAIILNRZ	ALIZARIN	**AAILLMRT**	RAMTILLA	**AAILORSU**	RAOULIAS
AAIILNUX	UNIAXIAL	**AAILLMRX**	MAXILLAR	**AAILORSV**	VARIOLAS
AAIILPRR	RIPARIAL	**AAILLMSX**	MAXILLAS	**AAILPPRU**	PUPARIAL
AAIILPRS	PAIRIALS	**AAILLNOV**	VALLONIA	**AAILPPST**	PAPALIST
AAIILPST	TILAPIAS	**AAILLNPU**	NAUPLIAL	**AAILPRST**	PARTIALS
AAIILRSZ	ALIZARIS	**AAILLNST**	LANITALS		PATRIALS
AAIILRTX	TRIAXIAL	**AAILLNSV**	VANILLAS		TRIAPSAL
AAIILRUX	AUXILIAR	**AAILLPPR**	PAPILLAR	**AAILPRSY**	AIRPLAYS
AAIILTXY	AXIALITY	**AAILLRRY**	ARILLARY	**AAILPSTT**	TALIPATS
AAIIMNNT	AMANITIN	**AAILLRSX**	AXILLARS	**AAILQRSU**	SQUARIAL
	MAINTAIN	**AAILLRXY**	AXILLARY	**AAILQSWW**	QAWWALIS
AAIIMNPX	PANMIXIA	**AAILMMRS**	ALARMISM	**AAILRRSV**	ARRIVALS
AAIINNRT	ANTIARIN		AMMIRALS	**AAILRSTT**	RATTAILS
AAIINOTV	AVIATION	**AAILMMSX**	MAXIMALS	**AAILRSTV**	TRAVAILS
AAIINPRR	RIPARIAN	**AAILMNNT**	LAMANTIN	**AAILRSVY**	SALIVARY

AAILRSWY	RAILWAYS
AAILRTUY	AURALITY
AAILSSSV	VASSAILS
AAILSSSW	WASSAILS
AAILSSTY	STAYSAIL
AAILSTTT	LATITATS
AAIMMNOS	AMMONIAS
AAIMMNST	MAINMAST
AAIMMRSU	SAMARIUM
AAIMNNRT	TRAINMAN
AAIMNOOZ	ZOOMANIA
AAIMNORT	ANIMATOR
	MONTARIA
	TAMANOIR
AAIMNORW	AIRWOMAN
AAIMNOSS	ANOSMIAS
AAIMNOST	AMATIONS
AAIMNOTT	ANTIATOM
AAIMNPRZ	MARZIPAN
AAIMNPST	ANTISPAM
AAIMNPTU	PUTAMINA
AAIMNRRT	TRIMARAN
AAIMNRRU	RANARIUM
AAIMNRST	MARTIANS
	TAMARINS
AAIMNSST	MANTISSA
	SATANISM
	STAMINAS
AAIMNSTU	AMIANTUS
AAIMNSTY	MAINSTAY
AAIMOPRS	MARIPOSA
	PAROSMIA
AAIMPRST	PASTRAMI
AAIMPRSU	MARSUPIA
AAIMQRUU	AQUARIUM
AAIMRRSY	MISARRAY
AAIMRRTY	MARTYRIA
AAIMRSSU	SAMURAIS
AAIMRSTU	TIMARAUS
AAIMSSSY	MISASSAY
AAIMSSTV	ATAVISMS
AAINNOPV	PAVONIAN
AAINNOST	SONATINA
AAINNOTT	NATATION
AAINNOTX	ANATOXIN
AAINNRSV	NAVARINS
	NIRVANAS
AAINNRTU	NUTARIAN
AAINNSST	NAISSANT
AAINNSSY	SANNYASI
AAINOOPS	ANOOPSIA
AAINOPSS	ANOPSIAS
	PAISANOS
AAINORRS	ORARIANS
	ROSARIAN
AAINOTTX	TAXATION
AAINPPRY	PAPYRIAN
AAINPRST	ASPIRANT
	PARTISAN
	SPARTINA
AAINPRTZ	PARTIZAN
AAINPSST	PASTINAS
AAINQRRU	QUARRIAN
AAINQRTU	QUATRAIN
AAINQTTU	AQUATINT
AAINRRSS	SARRASIN
AAINRRSZ	SARRAZIN
AAINRSST	ARTISANS
	TSARINAS
AAINRSSU	SAURIANS
AAINRSSV	SAVARINS
AAINRSTV	VARIANTS
AAINRSTY	SANITARY
AAINRSTZ	TZARINAS
AAINRTWY	TRAINWAY
AAINSSSS	ASSASSIN
AAINSSSY	SANYASIS
AAINSSTT	SATANIST
AAINSTTT	ANTISTAT
	ATTAINTS
AAINSTTU	TUTANIAS
AAINSTTV	AVANTIST
AAINSTTY	SATANITY
AAIOPPSS	APOAPSIS
AAIOPRRT	TROPARIA
AAIOPRST	ATROPIAS
AAIOPRSU	PAROUSIA
AAIOPSTU	AUTOPSIA
AAIORSSU	SAOUARIS
AAIORSTV	AVIATORS
AAIORTUZ	AZOTURIA
AAIPPSTT	PITAPATS
AAIPRSSX	SPARAXIS
AAIPRSTT	PARTITAS
AAIQRSTU	AQUARIST
AAIQSSSU	QUASSIAS
AAIQSTUV	AQUAVITS
AAIRSSTT	TSARITSA
AAIRSTTZ	TSARITZA
AAIRSTWY	STAIRWAY
AAIRTTZZ	TZARITZA
AAISSTTV	ATAVISTS
AAISTWXY	TAXIWAYS
AAJKLSWY	JAYWALKS
AAJMMORR	MARJORAM
AAJMORRS	MOJARRAS
AAJMORST	MAJORATS
AAJOPSSU	SAPAJOUS
AAKKLRSU	KARAKULS
AAKKMMOO	KAMOKAMO
AAKKMOST	TOKAMAKS
AAKKOSUZ	ZAKOUSKA
AAKKSTYZ	KAZATSKY
AAKLMPSU	LAMPUKAS
AAKLMRUY	YARMULKA
AAKLMSUY	YAMULKAS
AAKLNOOS	OOLAKANS
AAKLNOSU	OULAKANS
AAKLOOPS	PALOOKAS
AAKLOOST	TALOOKAS
AAKLPRTY	KALYPTRA
AAKLRSSU	KURSAALS
	RUSALKAS
AAKLSSSU	SAKSAULS
AAKLSWWY	WALKWAYS
AAKMMNRS	MARKSMAN
AAKMORUZ	MAZOURKA
AAKMOSSU	MOUSAKAS
	MOUSSAKA
AAKMRSUZ	MAZURKAS
AAKMRSWY	WAYMARKS
AAKNNSTU	NUNATAKS
AAKNRSYY	SYNKARYA
AAKNSSTW	WANKSTAS
AAKNSTWY	TWANKAYS
AAKOOPPS	PAKAPOOS
AAKOPPRT	PORTAPAK
AAKPRSWY	PARKWAYS
AAKRSSTU	KATSURAS
AALLLSTY	LAYSTALL
AALLMNST	STALLMAN
AALLMNTY	TALLYMAN
AALLMNUY	MANUALLY
AALLMORY	AMORALLY
AALLMPRU	AMPULLAR
AALLMSST	SMALLSAT
AALLNNUY	ANNUALLY
AALLNOST	SANTALOL
AALLNOSX	ALLOXANS
AALLNOTY	ATONALLY
AALLNPRU	PLANULAR
AALLNRTY	TARNALLY
AALLOORW	WALLAROO
AALLORSU	ALLOSAUR
AALLORWY	ROLLAWAY
AALLOSTV	LAVOLTAS
AALLPRST	PLASTRAL
AALLRSTY	ASTRALLY
AALLRUVV	VALVULAR
AALMMNOS	AMMONALS
AALMNORT	MATRONAL
AALMNORU	MONAURAL
AALMNOSS	SALAMONS
AALMNOWY	LAYWOMAN
AALMNPTY	TYMPANAL
AALMNTTU	TANTALUM
AALMNTUU	AUTUMNAL
AALMOOSS	MASSOOLA
AALMOPPR	MALAPROP
AALMOPSX	AXOPLASM
AALMOSTT	STOMATAL
AALMOTXY	XYLOMATA
AALMPPSU	PASPALUM
AALMPRSY	PALMYRAS
AALMPSTY	PLATYSMA
AALMQSUU	SQUAMULA
AALMSTTU	MULATTAS
AALNNNOS	NONNASAL
AALNNNOV	NONNAVAL
AALNNOPP	NONPAPAL
AALNNOPT	PANTALON
AALNNOST	SONANTAL
AALNNPUU	PUNALUAN
AALNNRSU	ANNULARS
AALNNTTY	NATANTLY
AALNNTUU	LUNANAUT
AALNOORS	ORONASAL
AALNOPRT	PATRONAL
AALNOPST	POSTANAL
AALNORUV	ANOVULAR
AALNPRSU	LUPANARS
AALNPSST	SALTPANS

AALNPSUU	PUNALUAS	AANOOPRZ	PARAZOON	ABBCEIRR	CRABBIER
AALNPTWX	WAXPLANT	AANOPRTY	ANATROPY	ABBCEIRS	SCABBIER
AALNRRTY	ARRANTLY	AANORRRT	NARRATOR	ABBCEKLU	BLUEBACK
AALNRSTU	NATURALS	AANORSTT	ARNATTOS	ABBCEKNO	BACKBONE
AALNSSTT	SALTANTS	AANORSTY	SANATORY	ABBCEKNU	BUCKBEAN
AALNSSTU	SULTANAS	AANORTTY	NATATORY	ABBCELLU	CLUBABLE
AALNSSTY	ANALYSTS	AANPPTTY	PATTYPAN	ABBCELRS	CLABBERS
AALNSTTU	TALAUNTS	AANPRSST	SPARTANS		SCRABBLE
	TANTALUS	AANQRSTU	QUARTANS	ABBCELRU	CURBABLE
AALOPPRT	PALPATOR	AANRRSTW	WARRANTS	ABBCELSS	SCABBLES
AALOPPRV	APPROVAL	AANRRTTY	TARTANRY	ABBCERRS	CRABBERS
AALOPPST	APOPLAST	AANRRTWY	WARRANTY	ABBCGINR	CRABBING
AALOPRSS	PARASOLS	AANRSTTU	SATURANT	ABBCGINS	SCABBING
AALOPRST	PASTORAL	AANRSUWY	RUNAWAYS	ABBCGIOR	GABBROIC
AALOPSVV	PAVLOVAS	AANSSSTT	TSANTSAS	ABBCIILL	BIBLICAL
AALOPSZZ	PALAZZOS	AAOORRSW	WOORARAS	ABBCIINR	RABBINIC
AALORSST	ALASTORS	AAOPSSST	POTASSAS	ABBCIKRT	BRICKBAT
AALORSSU	AROUSALS	AAOPSSTY	APOSTASY	ABBCILRY	CRABBILY
AALORSTX	LAXATORS	AAOQSSSU	OQUASSAS	ABBCILSY	SCABBILY
AALORTUV	VALUATOR	AAORSSTT	STAROSTA	ABBCKLOW	BLOWBACK
AALORTVY	LAVATORY	AAORSSVV	VAVASORS	ABBCKLOY	BLACKBOY
AALOSTTY	TALAYOTS		VAVASSOR	ABBCKNRU	BACKBURN
AALPRSTU	PASTURAL	AAORSUVV	VAVASOUR	ABBCKSUY	BUYBACKS
	SPATULAR	AAORSVVY	VAVASORY	ABBCLRSY	SCRABBLY
AALPRSTY	LAPTRAYS	AAOSTTUY	TATOUAYS	ABBDDEEL	BEDDABLE
AALPSSTU	SPATULAS	AAOSTWWY	STOWAWAY	ABBDDEEU	BEDAUBED
AALRRTTY	TARTARLY		TOWAWAYS	ABBDDEIL	BIDDABLE
AALRSSTU	AUSTRALS	AAPRRSTT	RATTRAPS	ABBDDELR	DRABBLED
AALRSSTY	SATYRALS	AAPRSTUU	RAUPATUS	ABBDDEOR	BEDBOARD
AALRSSVY	VASSALRY	AARSTTUY	STATUARY	ABBDDILY	BIDDABLY
AALRSTTW	STALWART	ABBBCDEO	CABOBBED	ABBDEEER	BEEBREAD
AALRSTUY	SALUTARY	ABBBDEEK	KEBABBED	ABBDEEHR	REHABBED
AALSSSTU	ASSAULTS	ABBBDEEL	BEDABBLE	ABBDEEJR	JABBERED
AAMMMSTU	MAMMATUS	ABBBDEKO	KABOBBED	ABBDEELN	BENDABLE
AAMMNPRS	RAMPSMAN	ABBBDELR	BRABBLED	ABBDEERR	BARBERED
AAMMNRST	MANTRAMS	ABBBEILR	BABBLIER	ABBDEERT	RABBETED
AAMMOTXY	MYXOMATA		BRIBABLE	ABBDEERY	YABBERED
AAMMRSSU	MARASMUS	ABBBELMO	BOMBABLE	ABBDEGLR	GRABBLED
AAMNNORS	SONARMAN	ABBBELRR	BRABBLER	ABBDEHOO	BOOBHEAD
AAMNNOSY	ANONYMAS	ABBBELRS	BABBLERS	ABBDEILN	BINDABLE
AAMNORRS	MARRANOS		BLABBERS	ABBDEIRR	DRABBIER
AAMNORSZ	ROMANZAS		BRABBLES	ABBDEIRT	RABBITED
AAMNPRST	MANTRAPS	ABBBELTU	TUBBABLE	ABBDELMO	BABELDOM
AAMNPRSY	PARANYMS	ABBBGILN	BABBLING	ABBDELMR	BRAMBLED
AAMNQSUW	SQUAWMAN		BLABBING	ABBDELNO	BONDABLE
AAMOORSS	AMOROSAS	ABBBHSUY	BUSHBABY	ABBDELNS	SNABBLED
AAMOPRRU	PARAMOUR	ABBBIRTY	BABBITRY	ABBDELRR	DRABBLER
AAMORRSZ	ZAMARROS	ABBBISTT	BABBITTS	ABBDELRS	DABBLERS
AAMORSSU	MOSASAUR	ABBBOORU	RUBBABOO		DRABBLES
AAMORSSV	SAMOVARS	ABBBOSTU	SUBABBOT	ABBDEMOR	BOMBARDE
AAMORSTT	STROMATA	ABBCCKMO	BACKCOMB	ABBDEMUZ	BUMBAZED
AAMOSTTU	AUTOMATS	ABBCDEKN	BACKBEND	ABBDENRU	UNBARBED
AAMPPRST	RAMPARTS	ABBCDELS	SCABBLED	ABBDEORS	ABSORBED
AAMRSSST	SMARTASS	ABBCDERS	SCRABBED	ABBDEORX	BREADBOX
AAMRSSTT	MATTRASS	ABBCDKNO	BACKBOND	ABBDEQSU	SQUABBED
AAMRSSTU	SUMATRAS	ABBCEERU	BARBECUE	ABBDERRS	DRABBERS
AAMRSTWY	TRAMWAYS	ABBCEGIR	CRIBBAGE	ABBDERST	DRABBEST
AAMSSSTU	SATSUMAS	ABBCEHIS	BABICHES		DRABBETS
AANNOSST	ASSONANT	ABBCEHOU	BABOUCHE	ABBDFOOY	BABYFOOD
AANNOSTT	ANNATTOS	ABBCEHOY	BEACHBOY	ABBDGILN	DABBLING
AANNOTTW	NANOWATT	ABBCEHSU	BABUCHES	ABBDGINR	DRABBING
AANNPSSW	SWANPANS	ABBCEHTU	BATHCUBE	ABBDGIOR	GABBROID
AANNRSTY	STANNARY	ABBCEIKT	BACKBITE	ABBDHIJS	DJIBBAHS
AANOOPPX	OPOPANAX	ABBCEILR	BARBICEL	ABBDHIRS	DRABBISH

ABBDHIRT	BIRDBATH	ABBELORU	BELABOUR	ABBKKNOO	BANKBOOK
ABBDHOOY	BABYHOOD	ABBELPRS	PRABBLES	ABBKLOSU	BLAUBOKS
ABBDILNO	BAILBOND	ABBELQSU	SQUABBLE	ABBLLLOW	BLOWBALL
ABBDILRS	LIBBARDS	ABBELRRS	RABBLERS	ABBLLOSX	BOXBALLS
ABBDINRS	RIBBANDS	ABBELRSS	BARBLESS	ABBLLRSU	BULLBARS
ABBDLLOY	BABYDOLL		SLABBERS	ABBLLSTU	BULLBATS
ABBDLMOO	BOMBLOAD	ABBELRSU	BARBULES	ABBLLSUY	SYLLABUB
ABBDLRSU	LUBBARDS	ABBELRSW	WABBLERS	ABBLOPRY	PROBABLY
ABBDMORS	BOMBARDS	ABBELRSY	SLABBERY	ABBMOORS	BOMBORAS
ABBDMOSU	BABUDOMS	ABBELSUY	BUYABLES	ABBMOSST	BOMBASTS
ABBDNORW	BROWBAND	ABBEMOOR	AEROBOMB	ABBMOSTU	BUMBOATS
ABBDOORX	BOXBOARD	ABBEMOSX	BOMBAXES	ABBNRSUU	SUBURBAN
ABBDORRU	RUBBOARD	ABBEMSUZ	BUMBAZES	ABBOORSU	RUBABOOS
ABBEEHRR	REHABBER	ABBENORS	BASEBORN	ABBOSSTY	BOBSTAYS
ABBEEILT	BITEABLE	ABBENORY	NABOBERY	ABCCCIOO	BOCACCIO
ABBEEINR	BEARBINE	ABBENOSS	NABOBESS	ABCCDEHO	CABOCHED
ABBEEJRR	JABBERER	ABBEORRS	ABSORBER	ABCCDHIK	DABCHICK
ABBEEJRS	BEJABERS		REABSORB	ABCCEEHN	BECHANCE
ABBEELOY	OBEYABLE	ABBEORTW	BROWBEAT	ABCCEELP	PECCABLE
ABBEELTU	BLUEBEAT	ABBEQRSU	SQUABBER	ABCCEEOR	CABOCEER
ABBEENOR	BAREBONE	ABBERRRY	BARBERRY	ABCCEFLU	CLUBFACE
ABBEEQRU	BARBEQUE	ABBERRYY	BAYBERRY	ABCCEILR	BRECCIAL
ABBEERTT	BARBETTE	ABBERSST	STABBERS	ABCCEILY	CELIBACY
ABBEESSS	ABBESSES	ABBERSSW	SWABBERS	ABCCEIRS	BRECCIAS
ABBEFFLU	BUFFABLE	ABBESSSU	SUBBASES	ABCCEIRT	BACTERIC
ABBEFILR	FLABBIER	ABBFGINR	FRABBING	ABCCEKMO	COMEBACK
ABBEGIRR	GRABBIER	ABBFILLY	FLABBILY	ABCCESUU	SUCCUBAE
ABBEGIST	GABBIEST	ABBFLOOT	BOBFLOAT	ABCCHISU	BACCHIUS
ABBEGLRR	GRABBLER	ABBGGILN	GABBLING	ABCCHNOO	CABOCHON
ABBEGLRS	GABBLERS	ABBGGINR	GRABBING	ABCCHOSU	CHUBASCO
	GRABBLES	ABBGIJLN	JABBLING	ABCCIKKK	KICKBACK
ABBEGNOS	BOGBEANS	ABBGILNR	RABBLING	ABCCIKKP	PICKBACK
ABBEGNSU	BUGBANES	ABBGILNS	SLABBING	ABCCIKOR	ABRICOCK
ABBEGRRS	GRABBERS	ABBGILNU	BAUBLING	ABCCILOR	CARBOLIC
ABBEGRSU	BUGBEARS	ABBGILNW	WABBLING	ABCCILOT	COBALTIC
ABBEHILS	BABELISH	ABBGINST	STABBING	ABCCILUU	CUBICULA
ABBEHIRS	SHABBIER	ABBGINSU	BUBINGAS	ABCCIMRS	CAMBRICS
ABBEHLSS	SHABBLES	ABBGINSW	SWABBING	ABCCINOR	CARBONIC
ABBEHORT	BATHROBE	ABBGINTY	TABBYING	ABCCINSU	BUCCINAS
ABBEILLL	BILLABLE	ABBGINYY	YABBYING	ABCCIORS	ASCORBIC
ABBEILLO	BOILABLE	ABBGOOSU	BUGABOOS	ABCCKLLO	BALLCOCK
ABBEILMS	BABELISM	ABBHIIMS	BIMBASHI	ABCCKLOX	CLACKBOX
ABBEILNU	BUBALINE	ABBHILSY	SHABBILY	ABCCKOOT	COCKBOAT
ABBEILOT	BILOBATE	ABBHINOS	NABOBISH	ABCCKOSW	BAWCOCKS
ABBEILOV	OBVIABLE	ABBHIORT	RABBITOH	ABCCKSTU	CUTBACKS
ABBEILRS	SLABBIER	ABBHRRSU	RHUBARBS	ABCCLLUY	BUCCALLY
ABBEILRW	WABBLIER	ABBHRRUY	RHUBARBY	ABCCLOOO	COCOBOLA
ABBEILST	BISTABLE	ABBHSTTU	BATHTUBS	ABCCMOOY	MACCOBOY
ABBEIMRU	BERIMBAU	ABBIINOT	BIBATION	ABCCOORS	BAROCCOS
ABBEINTT	TABBINET	ABBILLOT	BOATBILL	ABCCOOST	TOBACCOS
ABBEIRRT	RABBITER	ABBILLSU	SILLABUB	ABCCSSUU	SUCCUBAS
ABBEIRRW	BARBWIRE	ABBILOST	BIOBLAST	ABCDDEER	DECARBED
ABBEISST	TABBISES		BOBTAILS	ABCDDEOR	BROCADED
ABBEISSW	SWABBIES	ABBILOTU	TABBOULI	ABCDDETU	ABDUCTED
ABBEKLOO	BOOKABLE	ABBIMNOS	BAMBINOS	ABCDEEFK	FEEDBACK
ABBELLLU	BLUEBALL		NABOBISM	ABCDEEHL	BLEACHED
ABBELLRS	BARBELLS	ABBIMSSU	BABUISMS	ABCDEEHR	BERDACHE
ABBELMRS	BRAMBLES	ABBINORS	RABBONIS		BREACHED
ABBELNRU	BURNABLE	ABBINORX	BRAINBOX	ABCDEEJT	ABJECTED
ABBELNSS	SNABBLES	ABBINSSU	SUBBASIN	ABCDEEKR	REBACKED
ABBELOOT	BOOTABLE	ABBIORST	RABBITOS	ABCDEELL	BECALLED
ABBELOPR	PROBABLE	ABBIRRTY	RABBITRY	ABCDEELM	BECALMED
ABBELORS	BELABORS	ABBIRSUU	SUBURBIA	ABCDEELS	DEBACLES
	SORBABLE	ABBISSTY	BABYSITS	ABCDEELU	EDUCABLE

ABCDEEMR	CAMBERED	ABCDIRST	CATBIRDS	ABCEGNOR	BONGRACE
	EMBRACED	ABCDIRSU	BAUDRICS	ABCEGORS	BROCAGES
ABCDEEMX	EXCAMBED		SUBACRID	ABCEGOSS	BOSCAGES
ABCDEENO	BEACONED	ABCDIRSW	BAWDRICS	ABCEHITT	BATHETIC
ABCDEEPP	BECAPPED	ABCDKNOW	BACKDOWN	ABCEHKLS	BECHALKS
ABCDEERR	REBRACED	ABCDKOOR	BACKDOOR	ABCEHKOS	BACKHOES
ABCDEETU	ABDUCTEE	ABCDKOOW	BACKWOOD	ABCEHKTW	BETHWACK
ABCDEFLO	BOLDFACE	ABCDKOPR	BACKDROP	ABCEHLNR	BLANCHER
ABCDEGIR	BIRDCAGE	ABCDKORW	BACKWORD	ABCEHLNS	BLANCHES
	CAGEBIRD	ABCDLLNU	CLUBLAND	ABCEHLOR	BACHELOR
ABCDEHIR	BEDCHAIR	ABCDNOSS	ABSCONDS	ABCEHLOS	CHAEBOLS
ABCDEHKO	BACKHOED	ABCDOORS	CORDOBAS	ABCEHLSU	BAUCHLES
ABCDEHLN	BLANCHED	ABCDOORW	CRABWOOD		CHASUBLE
ABCDEHLU	BAUCHLED	ABCDOPRU	CUPBOARD	ABCEHMOT	HECATOMB
	CLUBHEAD	ABCDORRS	BROCARDS	ABCEHMRS	BECHARMS
ABCDEHNR	BRANCHED	ABCDORTU	ABDUCTOR		BRECHAMS
ABCDEHOR	BROACHED	ABCDORUY	OBDURACY		CHAMBERS
ABCDEHOS	CABOSHED	ABCEEEFK	BEEFCAKE	ABCEHNRR	BRANCHER
ABCDEIIT	DIABETIC	ABCEEFNT	BENEFACT		REBRANCH
ABCDEIKS	BACKSIDE	ABCEEHIR	BEACHIER	ABCEHNRS	BRANCHES
	DIEBACKS	ABCEEHLM	BECHAMEL		BRECHANS
ABCDEILR	CALIBRED	ABCEEHLN	ALEBENCH	ABCEHOOT	COHOBATE
ABCDEIPS	PEDICABS	ABCEEHLR	BLEACHER	ABCEHOPU	PABOUCHE
ABCDEIRS	ASCRIBED	ABCEEHLS	BLEACHES	ABCEHORR	BROACHER
	CARBIDES	ABCEEHLW	CHEWABLE	ABCEHORS	BROACHES
ABCDEISS	ABSCISED	ABCEEHRR	BREACHER	ABCEHORU	BAROUCHE
ABCDEKLO	BLOCKADE	ABCEEHRS	BREACHES	ABCEHOSS	BASOCHES
ABCDEKLV	BACKVELD	ABCEEHSU	EBAUCHES	ABCEHRST	BATCHERS
ABCDEKNN	NECKBAND	ABCEEILT	CELIBATE		BRACHETS
ABCDEKNU	UNBACKED		CITEABLE	ABCEHRTT	BRATCHET
ABCDEKRS	REDBACKS	ABCEEIMN	AMBIENCE	ABCEIIRT	RABIETIC
ABCDELMS	SCAMBLED	ABCEEKLY	EYEBLACK	ABCEIKKL	KICKABLE
ABCDELNO	BLANCOED	ABCEELOV	EVOCABLE	ABCEIKLP	PICKABLE
ABCDELOO	CABOODLE	ABCEELRR	CEREBRAL	ABCEIKLR	CRABLIKE
ABCDELRU	BARLEDUC	ABCEELRT	BRACELET	ABCEIKLS	SCABLIKE
ABCDEMNU	DUMBCANE	ABCEEMRR	EMBRACER	ABCEIKST	TIEBACKS
ABCDEMOT	COMBATED	ABCEEMRS	EMBRACES	ABCEIKWZ	ZWIEBACK
ABCDEMRS	SCRAMBED	ABCEENOZ	CABEZONE	ABCEILLR	CRIBELLA
ABCDENRU	UNBRACED	ABCEENRS	CARBEENS	ABCEILLS	ICEBALLS
ABCDENSU	ABDUCENS		CARBENES	ABCEILLT	BALLETIC
ABCDENTU	ABDUCENT	ABCEENRT	CABERNET	ABCEILMS	ALEMBICS
ABCDEORS	BROCADES	ABCEENSS	ABSENCES	ABCEILNN	BINNACLE
ABCDEORW	BECOWARD	ABCEEPRT	BECARPET	ABCEILNO	BIOCLEAN
ABCDEORY	CARBOYED	ABCEERRS	REBRACES		COINABLE
ABCDERSU	CUDBEARS	ABCEERST	ACERBEST	ABCEILNU	BACULINE
ABCDESTU	SUBACTED	ABCEERUX	BERCEAUX	ABCEILOR	ALBICORE
ABCDFKLO	FOLDBACK	ABCEESSS	BECASSES		BRACIOLE
ABCDGINU	ABDUCING	ABCEFIIT	BEATIFIC		CABRIOLE
ABCDHKLO	HOLDBACK	ABCEFIKL	BACKFILE	ABCEILOS	SOCIABLE
ABCDHLNU	CLUBHAND	ABCEFIKR	BACKFIRE	ABCEILRS	CALIBERS
ABCDHORS	CHOBDARS		FIREBACK		CALIBRES
ABCDIILO	BIOCIDAL	ABCEFINO	BONIFACE	ABCEILST	BASILECT
	DIABOLIC	ABCEFLNO	BACLOFEN	ABCEILTT	BITTACLE
ABCDIIMY	CYMBIDIA	ABCEGHIN	BEACHING	ABCEILTU	BACULITE
ABCDIIRT	TRIBADIC	ABCEGIKV	GIVEBACK	ABCEILTY	BIACETYL
ABCDIKLR	BALDRICK	ABCEGILN	BELACING	ABCEIMRW	MICAWBER
ABCDIKLS	BACKSLID	ABCEGIMN	EMBACING	ABCEIMST	BETACISM
ABCDIKRU	BAUDRICK	ABCEGIRS	RIBCAGES	ABCEINOO	COENOBIA
ABCDILLR	BIRDCALL	ABCEGKLL	BLACKLEG	ABCEINRS	BRISANCE
ABCDILOS	CABILDOS	ABCEGKLO	BLOCKAGE		CARBINES
ABCDILOU	CUBOIDAL	ABCEGKMU	MEGABUCK	ABCEINRT	BACTERIN
ABCDILRS	BALDRICS	ABCEGKOR	BROCKAGE	ABCEINRV	VIBRANCE
ABCDINOR	BRACONID	ABCEGKRY	GREYBACK	ABCEINST	BASCINET
ABCDINSS	ABSCINDS	ABCEGMOS	CAMBOGES		CABINETS

ABCEINTU	INCUBATE	ABCELRSU	ARBUSCLE	ABCHIKLS	BLACKISH
ABCEIORS	AEROBICS	ABCELRSW	BECRAWLS	ABCHIKRS	BRACKISH
ABCEIORT	BORACITE		BESCRAWL	ABCHILMO	CHOLIAMB
ABCEIOST	ICEBOATS	ABCELRTT	BRACTLET	ABCHILOO	COOLIBAH
ABCEIRRT	CATBRIER	ABCELSSU	BASCULES	ABCHIMOR	CHORIAMB
	CRIBRATE		SUBSCALE	ABCHIMRU	BRACHIUM
ABCEIRSS	ASCRIBES	ABCELTTU	CUTTABLE	ABCHINOR	BRONCHIA
ABCEIRSW	CRABWISE	ABCEMOOS	CAMBOOSE	ABCHIOOR	BORACHIO
ABCEIRTT	BRATTICE	ABCEMORS	CRAMBOES	ABCHIOST	COHABITS
ABCEIRTY	ACERBITY	ABCEMORT	COMBATER	ABCHIRRT	TRIBRACH
ABCEISSS	ABSCISES	ABCENORS	BACONERS	ABCHKLOT	HACKBOLT
	ABSCISSE	ABCENOSU	SUBOCEAN	ABCHKLOW	HOWLBACK
ABCEISST	ASBESTIC	ABCENOSW	COWBANES	ABCHKMPU	HUMPBACK
ABCEISTT	TABETICS	ABCENOSZ	CABEZONS	ABCHKOOP	CHAPBOOK
ABCEJKLU	BLUEJACK	ABCENOUY	BUOYANCE	ABCHKOOS	CASHBOOK
ABCEJLTY	ABJECTLY	ABCENRSU	UNBRACES	ABCHKOSU	CHABOUKS
ABCEKKRU	BUCKRAKE	ABCENTUX	EXCUBANT	ABCHKRSU	BACKRUSH
ABCEKKSW	SKEWBACK	ABCEOOSS	CABOOSES	ABCHKSTU	HACKBUTS
ABCEKLLO	LOCKABLE	ABCEOPUU	BEAUCOUP	ABCHKSUW	HAWBUCKS
ABCEKLMO	MOCKABLE	ABCEORRS	BRACEROS	ABCHLLUU	CLUBHAUL
ABCEKLNS	BLACKENS	ABCEORST	CABESTRO	ABCHMOTX	MATCHBOX
ABCEKLOO	COOKABLE		CABRESTO	ABCHNORS	BROCHANS
ABCEKLOR	ROCKABLE	ABCEORSU	CORBEAUS	ABCHOORR	ROORBACH
ABCEKLOS	BECLOAKS	ABCEOSUX	SAUCEBOX	ABCHOSTT	CHATBOTS
ABCEKLPU	PALEBUCK	ABCEPSSU	SUBSPACE	ABCHOTWX	WATCHBOX
ABCEKLSS	BACKLESS	ABCERRTU	CARBURET	ABCIIKRR	AIRBRICK
ABCEKLST	BLACKEST	ABCERRWY	CYBERWAR	ABCIILMU	BULIMIAC
ABCEKNOT	BOATNECK	ABCERSSU	SUBRACES	ABCIILOT	BIOTICAL
ABCEKNRS	BRACKENS	ABCERTUU	CUBATURE	ABCIIMNS	MINICABS
ABCEKOOS	BOOKCASE	ABCESSTU	SUBCASTE	ABCIINOT	CIBATION
	CASEBOOK	ABCESSTW	WEBCASTS	ABCIINSS	ABSCISIN
ABCEKORY	ROCKABYE	ABCESSUU	SUBCAUSE	ABCIIORS	ISOBARIC
ABCEKRST	BACKREST	ABCESTUU	SUBACUTE	ABCIIRST	TRIBASIC
	BRACKETS	ABCFIKLL	BACKFILL	ABCIISTY	BASICITY
ABCEKSST	BACKSETS	ABCFIKLN	BLACKFIN	ABCIITUX	BAUXITIC
	SETBACKS	ABCFIKLP	BACKFLIP	ABCIJNOS	JACOBINS
ABCEKSSY	BACKSEYS	ABCFIKLT	BACKLIFT	ABCIKKLL	KICKBALL
ABCEKSTW	WETBACKS		LIFTBACK	ABCIKLST	BACKLIST
ABCELLOS	CLOSABLE	ABCFIKNS	FINBACKS	ABCIKLTU	BUCKTAIL
ABCELLPU	CULPABLE	ABCFIKST	BACKFITS	ABCIKNPS	BACKSPIN
ABCELLRU	BRUCELLA	ABCFILOS	BIFOCALS	ABCIKSSY	SICKBAYS
ABCELLSU	BUCELLAS	ABCFIOST	BIOFACTS	ABCILLNY	BILLYCAN
	BULLACES	ABCFKLLU	FULLBACK	ABCILLRU	LUBRICAL
ABCELMNY	LAMBENCY	ABCFKLLY	BLACKFLY	ABCILLSU	BACILLUS
ABCELMOR	BECLAMOR	ABCFKLOW	BACKFLOW	ABCILLSY	SYLLABIC
ABCELMOS	CEMBALOS	ABCFKLSY	FLYBACKS	ABCILMMO	CIMBALOM
ABCELMRS	CAMBRELS	ABCFKOST	SOFTBACK	ABCILMSU	SUBCLAIM
	CLAMBERS	ABCGGIMO	GAMBOGIC	ABCILNOR	CARBINOL
	SCAMBLER	ABCGHINT	BATCHING	ABCILNOS	COALBINS
	SCRAMBLE	ABCGHKOS	HOGBACKS	ABCILNPU	PUBLICAN
ABCELMRY	CYMBALER	ABCGHNPU	PUNCHBAG	ABCILOOR	COOLIBAR
ABCELMSS	SCAMBLES	ABCGIINN	CABINING	ABCILOSY	SOCIABLY
ABCELNOT	BALCONET	ABCGIKLN	BLACKING	ABCILRRU	RUBRICAL
ABCELNUU	NUBECULA	ABCGIKNS	BACKINGS	ABCIMMSS	CAMBISMS
ABCELOOT	BOOTLACE	ABCGIKNW	WINGBACK	ABCIMMSU	CAMBIUMS
ABCELOPS	PLACEBOS	ABCGILNS	CABLINGS	ABCIMORR	MICROBAR
ABCELOPY	COPYABLE	ABCGINRS	BRACINGS	ABCIMRTU	UMBRATIC
ABCELORT	BROCATEL	ABCGINSU	SCUBAING	ABCIMSST	CAMBISTS
ABCELOST	OBSTACLE	ABCGKLMU	BLACKGUM	ABCINNOS	NONBASIC
ABCELOSV	VOCABLES	ABCGKLOS	BACKLOGS	ABCINORS	CORBINAS
ABCELOTU	BLUECOAT	ABCGLNOX	CLANGBOX	ABCINORU	CONURBIA
ABCELPSS	BECLASPS	ABCGMSSU	SCUMBAGS	ABCINORY	BARYONIC
ABCELPSU	BLUECAPS	ABCHHIIS	HIBACHIS	ABCINOST	BOTANICS
ABCELPSY	BYPLACES	ABCHIIPS	BIPHASIC	ABCINRVY	VIBRANCY

ABCIOPRS	SAPROBIC	ABCORRTU	TURBOCAR	ABDEEERV	BEAVERED
ABCIORRS	BARRICOS	ABCORSSU	SCABROUS		BEREAVED
ABCIORSU	CARIBOUS	ABCOSSTU	SUBCOSTA	ABDEEFGS	FEEDBAGS
ABCIOSSU	SCABIOUS	ABCOSTTU	COTTABUS	ABDEEFIT	TABEFIED
ABCIOSUV	BIVOUACS	ABCRSTTU	SUBTRACT	ABDEEFLM	FLAMBEED
ABCIRSTT	ABSTRICT	ABDDDEEM	BEMADDED	ABDEEFLS	FEELBADS
ABCIRSUV	SUBVICAR	ABDDDEET	ADDEBTED	ABDEEFMO	BEFOAMED
ABCJKOOT	BOOTJACK	ABDDEEEH	BEHEADED	ABDEEFMR	BEDFRAME
	JACKBOOT	ABDDEEEK	DEBEAKED	ABDEEGGL	BEDAGGLE
ABCKKOOR	BOOKRACK	ABDDEEGG	DEBAGGED	ABDEEGGR	BEGGARED
ABCKKORW	BACKWORK	ABDDEEGR	BADGERED	ABDEEGHR	HERBAGED
ABCKLLOR	ROLLBACK		REBADGED	ABDEEGLL	BEGALLED
ABCKLLOS	BALLOCKS	ABDDEEHS	BEDASHED		GABELLED
ABCKLLPU	PULLBACK	ABDDEEHT	DEATHBED	ABDEEGNW	BEGNAWED
ABCKLNNO	NONBLACK	ABDDEEIL	BELADIED	ABDEEGRS	REBADGES
ABCKLOPT	BLACKTOP	ABDDEEKR	DEBARKED	ABDEEGRU	BEDEGUAR
ABCKLOPW	PLOWBACK	ABDDEELU	BELAUDED	ABDEEHIR	BRAEHEID
ABCKLOST	BACKLOTS	ABDDEEMN	BEDAMNED	ABDEEHLS	SHEDABLE
	SLOTBACK		BEMADDEN	ABDEEHLU	BLUEHEAD
ABCKLOSW	SLOWBACK	ABDDEENY	BENDAYED	ABDEEHMS	BESHAMED
ABCKLOTU	BLACKOUT	ABDDEEPR	BEDRAPED	ABDEEHMT	EMBATHED
ABCKMOOR	BACKROOM	ABDDEERR	DEBARRED	ABDEEHNO	BONEHEAD
ABCKMORR	BROCKRAM	ABDDEERS	DEBEARDS	ABDEEHRT	BREATHED
ABCKMOSS	MOSSBACK	ABDDEEST	BEDSTEAD	ABDEEHSS	BEDASHES
ABCKMOST	BACKMOST		BESTADDE	ABDEEHST	BETHESDA
	TOMBACKS	ABDDEGIR	ABRIDGED	ABDEEHTT	BEHATTED
ABCKMRSU	BUCKRAMS		BRIGADED	ABDEEIKL	BEADLIKE
ABCKMSUZ	ZAMBUCKS	ABDDEHMO	HEBDOMAD	ABDEEIKR	BIDARKEE
ABCKNNOS	BANNOCKS	ABDDEHMU	DUMBHEAD	ABDEEILM	EMBAILED
ABCKNORY	CRYOBANK	ABDDEHOY	HOBDAYED	ABDEEILN	DENIABLE
ABCKNRSU	RUNBACKS	ABDDEILS	DISABLED	ABDEEILR	RIDEABLE
ABCKNRTU	TURNBACK	ABDDEILU	AUDIBLED	ABDEEILS	ABSEILED
ABCKNSTU	CUTBANKS		BUDDLEIA		BELADIES
ABCKOORR	ROORBACK	ABDDEINR	BRANDIED	ABDEEILT	DELIBATE
ABCKOORU	BUCKAROO	ABDDEINS	SIDEBAND		EDITABLE
ABCKOPST	BACKSTOP	ABDDEINW	WIDEBAND	ABDEEILV	EVADIBLE
ABCKORUY	BUCKAYRO	ABDDEIRR	BRAIRDED	ABDEEILW	BEWAILED
ABCKOSSW	SOWBACKS	ABDDELOT	DEADBOLT	ABDEEIPR	BEDIAPER
ABCKOSTU	BACKOUTS	ABDDELRS	BLADDERS	ABDEEIRR	BEARDIER
	OUTBACKS	ABDDELRY	BLADDERY	ABDEEIRS	BEARDIES
ABCKSSTU	SACKBUTS	ABDDENNU	UNBANDED	ABDEEIRT	EBRIATED
	SUBTACKS	ABDDENOU	ABOUNDED		REBAITED
ABCKSSUW	BUCKSAWS	ABDDENST	BEDSTAND	ABDEEIST	BEADIEST
	SAWBUCKS	ABDDEORS	ADSORBED		DIABETES
ABCLLNOR	CORNBALL		ROADBEDS	ABDEEITU	BEAUTIED
ABCLLOSY	CALLBOYS	ABDDEOSY	DEADBOYS	ABDEEJMN	ENJAMBED
ABCLLPUY	CULPABLY	ABDDERSW	BEDWARDS	ABDEEJST	JETBEADS
ABCLMMOV	CYMBALOM	ABDDGILN	BLADDING	ABDEEKLS	LAKEBEDS
ABCLMOOO	COLOBOMA	ABDDGINR	BRADDING	ABDEEKMN	EMBANKED
ABCLMOSY	CYMBALOS	ABDDHIOR	RHABDOID	ABDEEKMR	BEDMAKER
ABCLMSUU	BACULUMS	ABDDILMO	LAMBDOID		EMBARKED
ABCLMSUY	SCYBALUM	ABDDILRY	LADYBIRD	ABDEEKNR	BARKENED
ABCLNORY	CARBONYL	ABDDIMNO	BONDMAID		BEDARKEN
ABCLNSSU	SUBCLANS	ABDDINSS	DISBANDS	ABDEEKNV	BEKNAVED
ABCLORXY	CARBOXYL	ABDDIRRY	YARDBIRD	ABDEEKPR	PREBAKED
ABCLOSUV	SUBVOCAL	ABDDLLOS	ODDBALLS	ABDEEKRR	DEBARKER
ABCLSSSU	SUBCLASS	ABDDLUWY	BULWADDY	ABDEELLL	LABELLED
ABCLSUUU	SUBUCULA	ABDDMORS	DAMBRODS	ABDEELLM	EMBALLED
ABCMOORT	MOBOCRAT	ABDEEEFL	BEFLEAED	ABDEELLN	LENDABLE
ABCNNORU	CONURBAN		FEEDABLE	ABDEELLT	BALLETED
ABCNORTY	CORYBANT	ABDEEEFN	BEDEAFEN	ABDEELLW	WELDABLE
ABCNOUVY	BUOYANCY	ABDEEEHR	BEHEADER	ABDEELMM	EMBALMED
ABCORRSS	CROSSBAR	ABDEEELP	BELEAPED	ABDEELMN	MENDABLE
ABCORRSW	CROWBARS	ABDEEEMN	BEMEANED	ABDEELMS	BELDAMES

	BEMEDALS	**ABDEGHIS**	BIGHEADS		IMBALMED
ABDEELMU	BEMAULED	**ABDEGHRS**	BEGHARDS	**ABDEILMN**	MANDIBLE
ABDEELMZ	EMBLAZED	**ABDEGIJN**	BEJADING	**ABDEILMS**	SEMIBALD
ABDEELNS	SENDABLE	**ABDEGILM**	GIMBALED	**ABDEILMZ**	IMBLAZED
ABDEELNT	BANDELET	**ABDEGILN**	BLINDAGE	**ABDEILNR**	BILANDER
ABDEELNV	VENDABLE	**ABDEGILU**	GUIDABLE	**ABDEILNT**	BIDENTAL
ABDEELOR	ERODABLE	**ABDEGIMT**	GAMBITED	**ABDEILNW**	WINDABLE
	LEEBOARD	**ABDEGINO**	GABIONED	**ABDEILNY**	DENIABLY
ABDEELOS	ALBEDOES	**ABDEGINR**	BEARDING	**ABDEILOV**	VOIDABLE
ABDEELPT	BEDPLATE		BREADING	**ABDEILOX**	OXIDABLE
ABDEELRR	BARRELED	**ABDEGINS**	BEADINGS	**ABDEILPP**	DIPPABLE
ABDEELRS	BEDERALS		DEBASING	**ABDEILPS**	PIEBALDS
ABDEELRV	DEVERBAL	**ABDEGINT**	DEBATING	**ABDEILRS**	BEDRAILS
ABDEELRZ	BLAZERED	**ABDEGINZ**	BEDAZING		DISABLER
ABDEELSV	BESLAVED	**ABDEGIPP**	BAGPIPED		RAILBEDS
ABDEELTT	BATTELED	**ABDEGIRR**	ABRIDGER	**ABDEILRT**	LIBRATED
	TABLETED	**ABDEGIRS**	ABRIDGES	**ABDEILRV**	DRIVABLE
ABDEELZZ	BEDAZZLE		BRIGADES	**ABDEILRY**	DIABLERY
ABDEEMNO	BEMOANED	**ABDEGLMO**	GAMBOLED	**ABDEILSS**	DISABLES
ABDEEMNS	BEADSMEN	**ABDEGLNR**	BRANGLED	**ABDEILST**	BALDIEST
	BEDESMAN	**ABDEGLOT**	GLOBATED	**ABDEILSU**	AUDIBLES
ABDEEMRR	EMBARRED	**ABDEGLRS**	BELGARDS	**ABDEILSY**	BIASEDLY
ABDEEMRS	EMBREADS	**ABDEGLRY**	BADGERLY	**ABDEILTU**	DUTIABLE
ABDEEMRV	EMBRAVED	**ABDEGLSU**	SLUGABED	**ABDEILVV**	BIVALVED
ABDEEMST	BEDMATES	**ABDEGMRU**	UMBRAGED	**ABDEIMNR**	BRIDEMAN
ABDEENNR	BANNERED	**ABDEGNOR**	BONDAGER	**ABDEIMOO**	AMOEBOID
ABDEENRT	BANTERED	**ABDEGNOS**	BONDAGES	**ABDEIMOR**	AMBEROID
ABDEENRU	UNBEARED		DOGBANES	**ABDEIMRR**	IMBARRED
ABDEENRY	BARNEYED	**ABDEGNRU**	UNGARBED	**ABDEIMRS**	EMBRAIDS
ABDEENRZ	BRAZENED	**ABDEGOPR**	PEGBOARD	**ABDEINNR**	ENDBRAIN
ABDEENST	ABSENTED	**ABDEGORT**	BOGARTED	**ABDEINOR**	DEBONAIR
ABDEENTT	BATTENED	**ABDEGRSU**	SUBGRADE	**ABDEINOS**	BEDSONIA
ABDEEPRS	BEDRAPES	**ABDEHILL**	BILLHEAD	**ABDEINOT**	OBTAINED
	BESPREAD	**ABDEHILS**	DISHABLE	**ABDEINRS**	BRANDIES
ABDEEPTT	BEPATTED	**ABDEHIMT**	IMBATHED		BRANDISE
ABDEERRT	BARTERED	**ABDEHINS**	BANISHED	**ABDEINST**	BANDIEST
ABDEERRY	RYEBREAD	**ABDEHITU**	HABITUDE	**ABDEINSU**	UNBIASED
ABDEERSS	DEBASERS	**ABDEHKLU**	BULKHEAD	**ABDEINSW**	BEDAWINS
ABDEERST	BETREADS	**ABDEHKNO**	KNOBHEAD	**ABDEINTU**	UNBAITED
	BREASTED	**ABDEHLLN**	HANDBELL	**ABDEIOST**	BEASTOID
	DEBATERS	**ABDEHLLO**	HOLDABLE	**ABDEIOTV**	OBVIATED
ABDEERSY	BEEYARDS	**ABDEHLLU**	BULLHEAD	**ABDEIPRT**	BIPARTED
ABDEERTT	BATTERED	**ABDEHLMS**	SHAMBLED	**ABDEIPST**	BAPTISED
	DRABETTE	**ABDEHLOT**	BOLTHEAD	**ABDEIPTZ**	BAPTIZED
ABDEERTW	WATERBED	**ABDEHLRS**	HALBERDS	**ABDEIRRS**	BRAIDERS
ABDEERTY	BETRAYED	**ABDEHMNO**	HAMBONED	**ABDEIRSS**	SEABIRDS
ABDEERWY	BEWRAYED	**ABDEHMOR**	RHABDOME		SIDEBARS
ABDEESST	BASSETED	**ABDEHMRU**	RHUMBAED	**ABDEIRST**	BARDIEST
	BESTEADS	**ABDEHMSU**	AMBUSHED		BRAIDEST
ABDEFHOO	BOOFHEAD	**ABDEHNTU**	UNBATHED		RABIDEST
ABDEFIIS	BASIFIED	**ABDEHORR**	ABHORRED		REDBAITS
ABDEFILN	FINDABLE		HARBORED		TRIBADES
ABDEFLLO	FOLDABLE	**ABDEHOSW**	BESHADOW	**ABDEIRSU**	DAUBRIES
ABDEFLNU	FUNDABLE		BOWHEADS	**ABDEIRSW**	BAWDRIES
	UNFABLED	**ABDEHRST**	BREADTHS		DAWBRIES
ABDEFLOR	FORDABLE	**ABDEHSSU**	SUBHEADS	**ABDEIRSX**	AXEBIRDS
ABDEFLST	FLATBEDS	**ABDEHTTU**	BUTTHEAD	**ABDEIRTV**	VIBRATED
ABDEFLSU	LEAFBUDS	**ABDEIIRT**	DIATRIBE	**ABDEISST**	BASTIDES
ABDEFNRU	FABURDEN	**ABDEIKMR**	IMBARKED	**ABDEISSU**	DISABUSE
ABDEFOSS	SOFABEDS	**ABDEIKNS**	BANKSIDE		SUBIDEAS
ABDEFRRY	FRYBREAD	**ABDEIKNU**	BAUDEKIN	**ABDEISTU**	DAUBIEST
ABDEFRSW	BEDWARFS	**ABDEILLR**	BRAILLED	**ABDEISTW**	BAWDIEST
ABDEGGIL	DIGGABLE	**ABDEILLS**	SLIDABLE	**ABDEITTU**	DUBITATE
ABDEGGNU	UNBAGGED	**ABDEILMM**	DIMMABLE	**ABDEJNOW**	JAWBONED

ABDEKLSW	SKEWBALD	
ABDEKNNU	UNBANKED	
ABDEKNRU	UNBARKED	
	UNBRAKED	
ABDEKNSU	SUNBAKED	
ABDEKOOR	ABROOKED	
ABDEKOOT	DATEBOOK	
ABDEKORW	BEADWORK	
ABDEKORY	KEYBOARD	
ABDEKOTU	OUTBAKED	
ABDELLMO	MOLDABLE	
ABDELLOR	BEADROLL	
ABDELLOT	BALLOTED	
ABDELMNU	UNBLAMED	
ABDELMPS	BEDLAMPS	
ABDELNOR	BANDEROL	
ABDELNOU	UNDOABLE	
ABDELNOZ	BLAZONED	
ABDELNRY	BENADRYL	
	BYLANDER	
ABDELNSS	BALDNESS	
ABDELNST	BLANDEST	
ABDELORU	LABOURED	
ABDELOSV	ABSOLVED	
ABDELOSW	DOWSABEL	
ABDELPSY	PYEBALDS	
ABDELRRS	DRABLERS	
ABDELRSU	DURABLES	
ABDELRTT	BRATTLED	
ABDELSTU	SUBLATED	
ABDEMNNS	BANDSMEN	
ABDEMNNY	BANDYMEN	
ABDEMNOR	BOARDMEN	
ABDEMNOS	ABDOMENS	
ABDEMORT	BROMATED	
ABDEMRSU	BERMUDAS	
ABDEMRTU	DRUMBEAT	
	UMBRATED	
ABDENNNU	UNBANNED	
ABDENNOS	NOSEBAND	
ABDENOOT	BATOONED	
ABDENORS	BANDORES	
	BROADENS	
ABDENORW	RAWBONED	
ABDENORY	BONEYARD	
ABDENOTW	DOWNBEAT	
ABDENRRS	BRANDERS	
ABDENRRU	UNBARRED	
ABDENRSS	DRABNESS	
ABDENRST	BANDSTER	
	BARTENDS	
ABDENRTU	BREADNUT	
	TURBANED	
ABDENSSU	SUBDEANS	
ABDENSTU	UNBASTED	
ABDENSUU	UNABUSED	
ABDENSWY	BENDWAYS	
ABDENTTU	DEBUTANT	
ABDEOORW	BEARWOOD	
ABDEOPRR	PREBOARD	
ABDEOPRT	PROBATED	
ABDEORRS	ADSORBER	
	BOARDERS	
	REBOARDS	
ABDEORRU	ARBOURED	
ABDEORRW	DRAWBORE	
	WARDROBE	
ABDEORST	BROADEST	
ABDEORSW	SOWBREAD	
ABDEORTU	OBDURATE	
	TABOURED	
ABDEORUX	BORDEAUX	
ABDEOSTU	BOUTADES	
ABDEPRSU	SUPERBAD	
ABDEPRUY	UPBRAYED	
ABDEPSSY	BYPASSED	
ABDERRSU	ABSURDER	
ABDERSST	DABSTERS	
ABDERSSU	SUBEDARS	
	SURBASED	
ABDERSTU	SURBATED	
ABDERSTW	BEDSTRAW	
ABDERSTY	DRYBEATS	
ABDERTUW	DRAWTUBE	
ABDESUWY	SUBWAYED	
ABDFILOR	FORBIDAL	
ABDFIMRR	BIRDFARM	
ABDFIRST	FATBIRDS	
ABDFLOOT	FOLDBOAT	
ABDFNORU	FUNBOARD	
ABDFRSUW	SUBDWARF	
ABDGGORS	BOGGARDS	
ABDGHINR	HANGBIRD	
ABDGIINR	BRAIDING	
ABDGIINS	ABIDINGS	
ABDGILNR	BARDLING	
ABDGILNS	BLADINGS	
ABDGILNU	BLAUDING	
ABDGILOR	GAOLBIRD	
ABDGIMRU	GUIMBARD	
ABDGINNR	BRANDING	
ABDGINNS	BANDINGS	
ABDGINNY	BANDYING	
ABDGINOR	ABORDING	
	BOARDING	
ABDGINRS	BRIGANDS	
ABDGINST	DINGBATS	
ABDGINSU	DAUBINGS	
ABDGINSW	WINDBAGS	
ABDGIRST	DIRTBAGS	
ABDGLNOS	BOGLANDS	
ABDGLOOR	LOGBOARD	
ABDGLSUY	LADYBUGS	
ABDHHSSU	SHADBUSH	
ABDHIIST	ADHIBITS	
	DISHABIT	
ABDHILLN	HANDBILL	
ABDHILNS	BLANDISH	
ABDHINRS	BRANDISH	
ABDHIORS	BROADISH	
ABDHIPRS	BARDSHIP	
ABDHIRTY	BIRTHDAY	
ABDHKNOO	HANDBOOK	
ABDHLNSU	BUSHLAND	
ABDHLORW	BLOWHARD	
ABDHLOSW	SHADBLOW	
ABDHMORS	RHABDOMS	
ABDHMOTU	BADMOUTH	
ABDHMSTU	MUDBATHS	
ABDHNORS	BODHRANS	
ABDHNSSU	HUSBANDS	
ABDHOORT	HARDBOOT	
ABDIIJLR	JAILBIRD	
ABDIILLR	BILLIARD	
ABDIILRR	RAILBIRD	
ABDIIMNR	MIDBRAIN	
ABDIIMSU	BASIDIUM	
ABDIINOS	ANOBIIDS	
	OBSIDIAN	
ABDIINRR	RAINBIRD	
ABDIINTT	BANDITTI	
ABDIIORT	ORIBATID	
ABDIIRTY	RABIDITY	
ABDIJRSY	JAYBIRDS	
ABDIKLNR	BLINKARD	
ABDIKLOU	KILOBAUD	
ABDIKNSW	BAWDKINS	
ABDIKRSS	DISBARKS	
ABDILLRY	BRIDALLY	
	RIBALDLY	
ABDILOOS	DIABOLOS	
ABDILORS	LABROIDS	
ABDILOST	BLASTOID	
	TABLOIDS	
ABDILOTY	TABLOIDY	
ABDILRRY	RIBALDRY	
ABDILRSW	AWLBIRDS	
ABDILRZZ	BLIZZARD	
ABDILSTU	SUBTIDAL	
ABDIMNRS	MISBRAND	
ABDIMORS	AMBROIDS	
ABDIMRSS	BARDISMS	
ABDIMRSY	MAYBIRDS	
ABDINORS	INBOARDS	
ABDINORU	AIRBOUND	
ABDINOST	BANDITOS	
ABDINOTY	ANTIBODY	
ABDINRST	ANTBIRDS	
ABDINRSU	UNBRAIDS	
ABDINRTY	BANDITRY	
ABDIOSUU	SUBAUDIO	
ABDIPRSU	UPBRAIDS	
ABDIRRUY	RIBAUDRY	
ABDJMOOR	DOORJAMB	
ABDKLNOO	BOOKLAND	
ABDKNOOS	BANDOOKS	
ABDKOOSY	DAYBOOKS	
ABDKORSY	SKYBOARD	
ABDLLNOS	SLOBLAND	
ABDLLNUW	BUNDWALL	
ABDLLORS	BOLLARDS	
ABDLNORS	BANDROLS	
ABDLNOSU	SUBNODAL	
ABDLOSSU	BUSLOADS	
ABDLOSYY	LADYBOYS	
ABDLRSUU	SUBDURAL	
ABDLRSUY	ABSURDLY	
ABDLSSUU	SUBDUALS	
ABDLSTUU	SUBADULT	
ABDMNNOS	BONDSMAN	
ABDMNOUW	MAWBOUND	
ABDMOOPR	MOPBOARD	

ABDMRSUY	MARYBUDS	ABEEGNTT	BAGNETTE	ABEEIMRS	AMBERIES
ABDNNNOR	NONBRAND	ABEEGOSZ	GAZEBOES	ABEEIMRT	AMBERITE
ABDNOORS	BRADOONS	ABEEGPSW	WEBPAGES	ABEEIMST	BEAMIEST
ABDNOPRS	PROBANDS	ABEEGRRS	GERBERAS	ABEEINST	BETAINES
ABDNORSU	BAUDRONS	ABEEGRST	ABSTERGE	ABEEINTY	AYENBITE
ABDNORUY	BOUNDARY	ABEEGRSU	AUBERGES	ABEEIPRS	BEPRAISE
ABDNOSSY	SANDBOYS	ABEEGRSW	BREWAGES	ABEEIRTT	BATTERIE
ABDNRRSU	SANDBURR	ABEEGTTU	BAGUETTE	ABEEIRTV	BREVIATE
ABDNRSSU	SANDBURS	ABEEHILR	HIREABLE	ABEEISST	BEASTIES
ABDNRSTU	TURBANDS	ABEEHINT	THEBAINE	ABEEISSV	ABESSIVE
ABDNSSTY	STANDBYS	ABEEHIRS	HEBRAISE	ABEEISTT	BEATIEST
ABDNSTUU	BUTSUDAN	ABEEHIRZ	HEBRAIZE	ABEEISTU	BEAUTIES
ABDOORSW	BARWOODS	ABEEHLLL	HEELBALL	ABEEITUX	BEAUXITE
ABDOORTU	OUTBOARD	ABEEHLLP	HELPABLE	ABEEJMOR	JAMBOREE
ABDOOSSW	BASSWOOD	ABEEHLLR	BEERHALL	ABEEKLOT	KEELBOAT
ABDOOSWY	BAYWOODS		HAREBELL	ABEEKLSS	BEAKLESS
ABDRSSTU	BUSTARDS	ABEEHLSV	BEHALVES	ABEEKLST	BLEAKEST
ABDRSUZZ	BUZZARDS	ABEEHMSS	BESHAMES	ABEEKMNR	BRAKEMEN
ABEEEFLR	REEFABLE	ABEEHMST	EMBATHES		EMBANKER
ABEEEFRS	FREEBASE	ABEEHNNS	HENBANES	ABEEKMRR	REEMBARK
ABEEEGRS	BARGEESE	ABEEHNPP	BEHAPPEN	ABEEKNSV	BEKNAVES
	BEERAGES	ABEEHNSS	BANSHEES	ABEEKNSY	EYEBANKS
ABEEEGRV	BEVERAGE		SHEBEANS	ABEEKOOP	PEEKABOO
ABEEEHTT	HEBETATE	ABEEHNTT	HEBETANT	ABEEKORV	OVERBAKE
ABEEEKLP	KEEPABLE	ABEEHORS	RHEOBASE	ABEEKPRS	BARKEEPS
ABEEELLP	PEELABLE	ABEEHQTU	BEQUEATH		PREBAKES
ABEEELLR	REELABLE	ABEEHRRT	BREATHER	ABEEKPSS	BESPEAKS
ABEEEMSY	EYEBEAMS	ABEEHRST	BREATHES	ABEEKRRS	BREAKERS
ABEEENRT	TENEBRAE		HARTBEES	ABEEKRST	BESTREAK
ABEEENRV	BEREAVEN	ABEEHRSV	BEHAVERS	ABEELLLR	LABELLER
ABEEENST	ABSENTEE	ABEEHSTY	EYEBATHS	ABEELLLS	SELLABLE
ABEEERRT	TEREBRAE	ABEEIKKL	BEAKLIKE	ABEELLLT	TELLABLE
ABEEERRV	BEREAVER	ABEEIKLL	LIKEABLE	ABEELLMT	MELTABLE
ABEEERSV	BEREAVES	ABEEIKLM	BEAMLIKE	ABEELLOT	BALLOTEE
ABEEFFNO	BANOFFEE	ABEEIKLN	BEANLIKE	ABEELLOV	LOVEABLE
ABEEFFTU	BEAUFFET	ABEEIKLR	BEARLIKE	ABEELLRS	LABELERS
ABEEFILL	FILEABLE	ABEEIKLT	BAKELITE		RELABELS
ABEEFILN	FINEABLE	ABEEIKRS	BAKERIES	ABEELLSY	EYEBALLS
ABEEFILR	AFEBRILE	ABEEIKRT	TIEBREAK	ABEELLTT	LETTABLE
	BALEFIRE	ABEEIKST	BEAKIEST	ABEELMMR	EMBALMER
	FIREABLE	ABEEILLN	LIENABLE		EMMARBLE
ABEEFILS	FEASIBLE		LINEABLE	ABEELMNO	BONEMEAL
ABEEFILT	FLEABITE	ABEEILLR	RELIABLE	ABEELMOV	MOVEABLE
ABEEFIRS	FIREBASE	ABEEILLV	LEVIABLE	ABEELMPR	PREAMBLE
ABEEFIST	TABEFIES		LIVEABLE	ABEELMRT	ATREMBLE
ABEEFLLL	FELLABLE	ABEEILLX	EXILABLE	ABEELMRZ	EMBLAZER
ABEEFLLN	BEFALLEN	ABEEILMN	MINEABLE	ABEELMSS	ASSEMBLE
ABEEFLMS	FLAMBEES	ABEEILMS	BELAMIES		BEAMLESS
ABEEFLOS	BEEFALOS	ABEEILNN	BIENNALE	ABEELMST	BEAMLETS
ABEEFORR	FOREBEAR	ABEEILNP	PLEBEIAN	ABEELMSZ	EMBLAZES
ABEEFSTU	BEAUFETS	ABEEILNS	BASELINE	ABEELMTT	EMBATTLE
ABEEGHRS	HERBAGES	ABEEILNU	BANLIEUE	ABEELNOP	BEANPOLE
ABEEGHRT	BERTHAGE	ABEEILNV	ENVIABLE		OPENABLE
ABEEGILV	GIVEABLE	ABEEILPX	EXPIABLE	ABEELNOV	OVENABLE
ABEEGINR	BAREGINE	ABEEILRR	BLEARIER	ABEELNRS	ENABLERS
	BERGENIA	ABEEILRT	LIBERATE	ABEELNRT	RENTABLE
ABEEGIRV	VERBIAGE	ABEEILRW	BEWAILER	ABEELNST	NESTABLE
ABEEGLLR	GABELLER	ABEEILSS	SEISABLE	ABEELNTT	NETTABLE
ABEEGLLS	GABELLES	ABEEILST	SEABLITE	ABEELNTU	TUNEABLE
ABEEGLRS	BEAGLERS	ABEEILSV	EVASIBLE	ABEELOPR	OPERABLE
ABEEGLTT	GETTABLE	ABEEILSZ	SEIZABLE		ROPEABLE
ABEEGMNR	BARGEMEN		SIZEABLE	ABEELOPS	POSEABLE
ABEEGMRT	BREGMATE	ABEEILTV	EVITABLE	ABEELORS	EARLOBES
ABEEGMTY	MEGABYTE	ABEEILVW	VIEWABLE	ABEELORV	OVERABLE

ABEELORX	EXORABLE		BATTERER	ABEGGLRS	BLAGGERS
ABEELOTT	TOTEABLE		BERRETTA	ABEGGLRY	BEGGARLY
ABEELOTV	VOTEABLE	ABEERRTV	VERTEBRA	ABEGGMOS	GAMBOGES
ABEELPRS	BEPEARLS	ABEERRTY	BETRAYER	ABEGGNSU	BUGGANES
ABEELPTT	PETTABLE		TEABERRY	ABEGGRRS	BRAGGERS
ABEELPTY	TYPEABLE	ABEERRWY	BEWRAYER	ABEGGRST	BRAGGEST
ABEELRST	ARBELEST	ABEERSTT	ABETTERS	ABEGGRSU	BURGAGES
	BLEAREST		BERETTAS	ABEGHILP	PHILABEG
	BLEATERS	ABEERSTU	SUBERATE	ABEGHILR	ALBERGHI
	RESTABLE	ABEERTTT	BETATTER	ABEGHINO	OBEAHING
	RETABLES	ABEERTTY	TERABYTE	ABEGHINT	BEATHING
ABEELRSU	REUSABLE	ABEESTXY	EXABYTES	ABEGHINV	BEHAVING
ABEELRSV	BESLAVER	ABEESZZZ	BEZAZZES	ABEGHNSS	SHEBANGS
	SERVABLE	ABEETTUX	EXTUBATE	ABEGHORR	BEGORRAH
ABEELRSY	BELAYERS	ABEFFKOR	BREAKOFF	ABEGHOSU	BAGHOUSE
ABEELRTT	BATTELER	ABEFFLRS	BAFFLERS	ABEGHRRY	HAGBERRY
ABEELRTU	BATELEUR	ABEFFOST	OFFBEATS	ABEGHRST	BARGHEST
	BLEUATRE	ABEFGILS	FILABEGS	ABEGHRSU	BEARHUGS
ABEELSSS	BASELESS	ABEFGILT	GIFTABLE	ABEGIIMS	BIGAMIES
ABEELSST	BATELESS	ABEFGLLR	BERGFALL	ABEGIINO	IBOGAINE
	BEATLESS	ABEFGSST	GABFESTS	ABEGIJTU	BIJUGATE
ABEELSSU	SUBLEASE	ABEFHILS	FISHABLE	ABEGIKNR	BERAKING
ABEELSSV	BESLAVES	ABEFHOOT	HOOFBEAT		BREAKING
ABEELSTT	SEATBELT	ABEFIIMR	FIMBRIAE	ABEGIKNT	BETAKING
	TESTABLE	ABEFIIRS	BASIFIER	ABEGILLN	LABELING
ABEELSTW	STEWABLE	ABEFIISS	BASIFIES	ABEGILMN	EMBALING
ABEELTTW	WETTABLE	ABEFILLL	FALLIBLE	ABEGILNN	ENABLING
ABEEMMNR	MEMBRANE		FILLABLE	ABEGILNR	BLEARING
ABEEMMRU	BUMMAREE	ABEFILLM	FILMABLE	ABEGILNS	SIGNABLE
ABEEMNOR	BEMOANER	ABEFILLO	FOILABLE		SINGABLE
ABEEMNST	BASEMENT	ABEFILLR	FIREBALL	ABEGILNT	BELATING
ABEEMNTT	ABETMENT	ABEFILLT	LIFTABLE		BLEATING
	BATEMENT	ABEFILOT	LIFEBOAT		TANGIBLE
ABEEMRSS	BESMEARS	ABEFILRS	BARFLIES	ABEGILNY	BELAYING
ABEEMRSV	EMBRAVES	ABEFILSU	FABULISE	ABEGILOT	OBLIGATE
ABEENNRT	BANNERET	ABEFILSY	FEASIBLY	ABEGIMNN	BENAMING
ABEENNRU	EBURNEAN	ABEFILTT	FITTABLE	ABEGIMNR	BREAMING
ABEENNSW	BAWNEENS	ABEFILUZ	FABULIZE	ABEGIMNS	BEAMINGS
ABEENNTU	UNBEATEN	ABEFINNR	FIBRANNE		EMBASING
ABEENORS	SEABORNE	ABEFINSU	BEAUFINS		MISBEGAN
ABEENOTZ	BENZOATE	ABEFIORT	BIFORATE	ABEGIMNY	EMBAYING
ABEENRRR	BARRENER		FIREBOAT	ABEGIMRS	GAMBIERS
ABEENRRT	BANTERER	ABEFIRRT	FIREBRAT	ABEGIMST	MEGABITS
ABEENRSS	BARENESS	ABEFITUY	BEAUTIFY	ABEGIMUX	GIAMBEUX
ABEENRST	ABSENTER	ABEFLLMU	BLAMEFUL	ABEGINOR	ABORIGEN
ABEENRSV	VERBENAS	ABEFLLRU	FURLABLE	ABEGINOS	BEGONIAS
ABEENRTT	BATTENER	ABEFLLTU	TABLEFUL	ABEGINRR	BARREING
ABEENSSS	BASENESS	ABEFLMOR	FORMABLE		BERRIGAN
ABEENSTW	NEWSBEAT	ABEFLNRU	FUNEBRAL	ABEGINRS	BEARINGS
ABEEORRV	OVERBEAR	ABEFLNSY	FLYBANES		SABERING
ABEEORSS	BOREASES	ABEFLOTU	OUTFABLE	ABEGINRT	BERATING
ABEEORST	ABORTEES	ABEFLRSU	SURFABLE		REBATING
	REBATOES	ABEFMRSU	SUBFRAME		TABERING
ABEEORTV	OVERBEAT	ABEFOORT	BAREFOOT	ABEGINRW	BEWARING
ABEEOSTX	TEABOXES	ABEFORRS	FORBEARS	ABEGINRY	BERAYING
ABEEPRRU	UPBEARER	ABEFORSY	FOREBAYS	ABEGINST	BEATINGS
ABEEPRRY	PEABERRY	ABEGGGIN	ABEGGING	ABEGINSY	EBAYINGS
ABEEPTTY	PETABYTE	ABEGGHLU	HUGGABLE	ABEGINTT	ABETTING
ABEEQSUU	USQUEBAE	ABEGGILN	BEAGLING	ABEGINTW	WINGBEAT
ABEERRRT	BARTERER	ABEGGINZ	BEGAZING	ABEGIOSS	BIOGASES
ABEERRST	REBATERS	ABEGGIRR	BRAGGIER	ABEGIPPR	BAGPIPER
	TABRERES	ABEGGIST	BAGGIEST	ABEGIPPS	BAGPIPES
	TEREBRAS	ABEGGITY	GIGABYTE	ABEGKLSU	BULKAGES
ABEERRTT	BARRETTE	ABEGGLLU	LUGGABLE	ABEGKORS	BROKAGES

	GROSBEAK	**ABEHLMSS**	SHAMBLES	**ABEIKNRR**	BRANKIER
ABEGKOSS	BOSKAGES	**ABEHLNOT**	BENTHOAL	**ABEIKNRS**	BEARSKIN
ABEGLLLU	GULLABLE	**ABEHLNTU**	HUNTABLE		INBREAKS
ABEGLLOR	BARGELLO	**ABEHLOSW**	SHOWABLE	**ABEIKNST**	BEATNIKS
ABEGLMOR	BEGLAMOR	**ABEHLOTU**	TABOULEH		SNAKEBIT
ABEGLMRS	GAMBLERS	**ABEHLOTY**	HYLOBATE	**ABEIKRST**	BARKIEST
	GAMBRELS	**ABEHLRST**	BLATHERS		BRAKIEST
ABEGLMUY	MEALYBUG		HALBERTS		BREASKIT
ABEGLNRS	BRANGLES	**ABEHLSSS**	BASHLESS	**ABEIKSWY**	BIKEWAYS
ABEGLORW	GROWABLE	**ABEHLSST**	BATHLESS	**ABEILLLM**	MILLABLE
ABEGLRRS	GARBLERS	**ABEHMNOR**	HORNBEAM	**ABEILLLT**	TILLABLE
ABEGLRSS	GARBLESS	**ABEHMNOS**	HAMBONES	**ABEILLLW**	WILLABLE
ABEGLRSU	BLAGUERS	**ABEHMOOR**	REHOBOAM	**ABEILLMM**	LIMBMEAL
ABEGLRUU	BLAGUEUR	**ABEHMRSU**	AMBUSHER	**ABEILLMS**	MISLABEL
ABEGLSTU	GUSTABLE	**ABEHMSSU**	AMBUSHES	**ABEILLNT**	LIBELANT
ABEGMNOS	GAMBESON	**ABEHMSTU**	BUSHMEAT	**ABEILLOS**	ISOLABLE
ABEGMNOY	BOGEYMAN	**ABEHNRSY**	ABHENRYS		LOBELIAS
	MONEYBAG	**ABEHNSTU**	SUNBATHE	**ABEILLOV**	VIOLABLE
ABEGMORT	BERGAMOT	**ABEHORRR**	ABHORRER	**ABEILLPS**	LAPSIBLE
ABEGMRSU	UMBRAGES		HARBORER	**ABEILLQU**	LIQUABLE
ABEGNNST	BANTENGS	**ABEHORST**	BATHORSE	**ABEILLRR**	BRAILLER
ABEGNORS	BEGROANS	**ABEHOSST**	BATHOSES	**ABEILLRS**	BALLSIER
ABEGNOSS	NOSEBAGS	**ABEHOSTX**	HATBOXES		BRAILLES
ABEGNRST	BANGSTER	**ABEHOSXY**	HAYBOXES		LIBERALS
ABEGNRTU	BURGANET	**ABEHPSSU**	SUBPHASE	**ABEILLRY**	BERYLLIA
ABEGNSTU	SUBAGENT	**ABEHRSST**	BRASHEST		BLEARILY
ABEGOORS	BARGOOSE	**ABEHRTUY**	EURYBATH		RELIABLY
ABEGOPSY	PAGEBOYS	**ABEIIKLS**	KIELBASI	**ABEILLST**	BASTILLE
ABEGOSTT	BOTTEGAS	**ABEIILLS**	BAILLIES		LISTABLE
ABEGOSUY	BUOYAGES	**ABEIILMT**	IMITABLE	**ABEILLTT**	TILTABLE
ABEGRRSU	GARBURES	**ABEIILNN**	BIENNIAL	**ABEILMMR**	IMBALMER
ABEGRRUV	BURGRAVE	**ABEIILNR**	BILINEAR	**ABEILMNS**	BAILSMEN
ABEGRSST	BARGESTS	**ABEIILNV**	INVIABLE		BIMENSAL
ABEGRSTU	BARGUEST	**ABEIILPT**	PITIABLE	**ABEILMNT**	BAILMENT
ABEGSSTU	SUBSTAGE	**ABEIILRR**	LIBRAIRE	**ABEILMOR**	BROMELIA
ABEHIKLS	BLEAKISH	**ABEIILRS**	BISERIAL	**ABEILMRR**	MARBLIER
ABEHILLR	HAIRBELL	**ABEIILST**	ALBITISE	**ABEILMRS**	REMBLAIS
ABEHILNR	HIBERNAL		SIBILATE	**ABEILMRW**	WAMBLIER
ABEHILRS	BLASHIER	**ABEIILTV**	VITIABLE	**ABEILMSS**	ABLEISMS
ABEHILTT	HITTABLE	**ABEIILTZ**	ALBITIZE		MISSABLE
	TITHABLE	**ABEIINRR**	BRAINIER	**ABEILMST**	BALMIEST
ABEHIMMS	MEMSAHIB	**ABEIINRS**	BINARIES		BIMETALS
ABEHIMNO	BOHEMIAN	**ABEIINST**	BAINITES		LAMBIEST
ABEHIMOS	BOHEMIAS	**ABEIJLNO**	JOINABLE		TIMBALES
	OBEAHISM	**ABEIJLTU**	JUBILATE	**ABEILMSU**	BUMELIAS
ABEHIMST	IMBATHES	**ABEIJMNN**	BENJAMIN	**ABEILMSW**	WEBMAILS
ABEHINRS	BANISHER	**ABEIJMRS**	JAMBIERS	**ABEILMSZ**	IMBLAZES
ABEHINSS	BANISHES	**ABEIJNSS**	BASENJIS	**ABEILNNW**	WINNABLE
	BANSHIES	**ABEIKLLL**	KILLABLE	**ABEILNOP**	OPINABLE
ABEHINST	ABSINTHE	**ABEIKLLM**	BALMLIKE	**ABEILNOT**	TAILBONE
ABEHIOPU	EUPHOBIA		LAMBLIKE	**ABEILNPS**	BIPLANES
ABEHIORV	BEHAVIOR	**ABEIKLLN**	BALKLINE	**ABEILNPT**	PINTABLE
ABEHIRRS	BRASHIER		LINKABLE	**ABEILNRS**	RINSABLE
ABEHISTU	HABITUES	**ABEIKLLS**	SLABLIKE	**ABEILNRU**	RUINABLE
ABEHISTZ	ZABTIEHS	**ABEIKLNR**	BARNLIKE	**ABEILNSS**	ALBINESS
ABEHJORS	JOBSHARE	**ABEIKLNS**	BLANKIES		LESBIANS
ABEHKLLW	HAWKBELL		SINKABLE	**ABEILNST**	INSTABLE
ABEHKNOR	HORNBEAK	**ABEIKLOS**	KILOBASE	**ABEILNSU**	SABULINE
ABEHKNST	BETHANKS	**ABEIKLOT**	BOATLIKE	**ABEILNTV**	BIVALENT
ABEHKOPS	BAKESHOP	**ABEIKLRU**	BAULKIER	**ABEILNTY**	BINATELY
ABEHKRSU	HAUBERKS	**ABEIKLSS**	KISSABLE	**ABEILNUV**	UNVIABLE
ABEHKSTU	KETUBAHS	**ABEIKLST**	BALKIEST	**ABEILNVY**	ENVIABLY
ABEHLLRT	BETHRALL	**ABEIKLSY**	KIELBASY	**ABEILORR**	BORRELIA
ABEHLMMU	HUMMABLE	**ABEIKNNR**	NINEBARK	**ABEILORS**	BOREALIS

ABEILORT	LABORITE	ABEINRSW	WEBINARS		SMOKABLE
ABEILOTV	BLOVIATE	ABEINRSZ	ZEBRINAS	ABEKLNOW	KNOWABLE
ABEILPPR	RIPPABLE	ABEINRTU	BRAUNITE	ABEKLNRY	BANKERLY
ABEILPPT	TIPPABLE		URBANITE	ABEKLNST	BLANKEST
ABEILPRT	PARTIBLE	ABEINRUZ	URBANIZE		BLANKETS
ABEILPRZ	PRIZABLE	ABEINSSS	BIASNESS	ABEKLNTY	BLANKETY
ABEILPSS	PASSIBLE	ABEINSST	BASINETS	ABEKLORW	WORKABLE
ABEILPST	EPIBLAST		BASSINET	ABEKLRSS	BARKLESS
ABEILRRU	REBURIAL		BESAINTS	ABEKLRSU	BAULKERS
ABEILRRW	BRAWLIER		BESTAINS	ABEKMNNS	BANKSMEN
ABEILRST	BLASTIER	ABEINSSU	UNBIASES	ABEKMNTU	BUNKMATE
	LIBRATES	ABEINSTT	TABINETS	ABEKMSSU	SAMBUKES
	TABLIERS	ABEINTTU	INTUBATE	ABEKNNOT	BANKNOTE
ABEILRSY	BILAYERS	ABEIORRS	ARBORISE	ABEKNRSU	UNBRAKES
ABEILRTT	TITRABLE	ABEIORRZ	ARBORIZE	ABEKNSSU	SUNBAKES
ABEILRTW	WRITABLE	ABEIORSS	ISOBARES	ABEKNSSY	SNEAKSBY
ABEILRYY	BIYEARLY	ABEIORST	SABOTIER	ABEKOORS	ABROOKES
ABEILSST	ABLEISTS	ABEIORTV	ABORTIVE	ABEKOORY	YEARBOOK
	ASTILBES	ABEIOSSS	ISOBASES	ABEKORTU	BREAKOUT
	BASTILES	ABEIOSTV	OBVIATES		OUTBREAK
	BESTIALS	ABEIPRRS	SPARERIB	ABEKOSTU	OUTBAKES
	BLASTIES	ABEIPRST	BAPTISER	ABEKPRSU	BREAKUPS
	STABILES	ABEIPRTZ	BAPTIZER		UPBREAKS
ABEILSSU	ISSUABLE	ABEIPSST	BAPTISES	ABEKRSTY	BASKETRY
	SUASIBLE	ABEIPSTZ	BAPTIZES	ABELLLMU	LABELLUM
ABEILSTU	SUITABLE	ABEIRRRS	BARRIERS	ABELLLOR	ROLLABLE
ABEILSTY	BEASTILY	ABEIRRSS	BRASIERS	ABELLLOT	TOLLABLE
ABEILSUX	BISEXUAL		BRASSIER	ABELLLSY	SYLLABLE
ABEILSVV	BIVALVES	ABEIRRST	ARBITERS	ABELLMOR	OMBRELLA
ABEILSYZ	SIZEABLY		BARRIEST	ABELLMRU	UMBELLAR
ABEIMNPS	PEMBINAS		RAREBITS		UMBRELLA
ABEIMNRS	MIRBANES	ABEIRRSZ	BIZARRES	ABELLNNO	BALLONNE
ABEIMNST	AMBIENTS		BRAZIERS	ABELLNOS	BONSELLA
ABEIMORS	BIRAMOSE	ABEIRRTT	BIRRETTA	ABELLNOT	BALLONET
ABEIMORU	AEROBIUM		BRATTIER	ABELLNRU	RUBELLAN
ABEIMRST	BARMIEST	ABEIRRVY	BREVIARY	ABELLNST	NETBALLS
ABEIMRSU	AUMBRIES	ABEIRRVZ	BRAZIERY	ABELLOPW	PLOWABLE
ABEIMRTV	AMBIVERT	ABEIRSSS	BRASSIES	ABELLORT	BALLOTER
	VERBATIM	ABEIRSSU	AIRBUSES	ABELLOSV	SOLVABLE
ABEIMSSU	IAMBUSES	ABEIRSTT	BIRETTAS	ABELLOTU	LOBULATE
ABEINNOS	BESONIAN	ABEIRSTV	VIBRATES	ABELLOTY	LOBATELY
ABEINNOZ	BEZONIAN	ABEIRSTW	WARBIEST		OBLATELY
ABEINNRR	BRANNIER	ABEIRSTY	BESTIARY	ABELLOVY	LOVEABLY
ABEINNRU	INURBANE		SYBARITE	ABELLRSU	RUBELLAS
ABEINORR	AIRBORNE	ABEIRSUX	EXURBIAS	ABELLRVY	VERBALLY
ABEINORS	BARONIES	ABEIRTTY	YTTERBIA	ABELLSTU	BALLUTES
	SEAROBIN	ABEISSST	BASSIEST	ABELMMSU	SUMMABLE
ABEINORT	BARITONE	ABEISSTT	BATISTES	ABELMNNO	NOBLEMAN
	OBTAINER	ABEISTTT	BATTIEST	ABELMNOZ	EMBLAZON
	REOBTAIN	ABEISTUX	BAUXITES	ABELMNST	SEMBLANT
	TABORINE	ABEISZZZ	BIZAZZES	ABELMNSU	ALBUMENS
ABEINOST	BOTANIES	ABEITTTU	TITUBATE		BLUESMAN
	BOTANISE	ABEJKLOU	KABELJOU	ABELMOOT	MOOTABLE
	NIOBATES	ABEJLMPU	JUMPABLE	ABELMOSU	ALBUMOSE
	OBEISANT	ABEJLSUY	BLUEJAYS	ABELMOSV	MOVABLES
ABEINOTZ	BOTANIZE	ABEJMNOS	JAMBONES	ABELMOTY	METABOLY
ABEINPST	BEPAINTS		JOBNAMES	ABELMOVY	MOVEABLY
ABEINQSU	BASQUINE	ABEJMOOR	JEROBOAM	ABELMPTU	PLUMBATE
ABEINRRW	BRAWNIER	ABEJNORW	JAWBONER	ABELMRRS	MARBLERS
ABEINRST	ATEBRINS	ABEJNOSH	JAWBONES		RAMBLERS
	BANISTER	ABEJOSWX	JAWBOXES	ABELMRST	LAMBERTS
	BARNIEST	ABEJRRSU	ABJURERS	ABELMSSY	ASSEMBLY
ABEINRSU	ANBURIES	ABEKKKSU	BUKKAKES	ABELNNOR	BANNEROL
	URBANISE	ABEKLMOS	ABELMOSK	ABELNNRU	RUNNABLE

ABELNORZ	BLAZONER	ABELSSTU	SUBLATES	ABEOSSST	ASBESTOS
ABELNOSS	BONSELAS	ABELSTUU	SUBULATE	ABEOSTUV	SUBOVATE
ABELNOST	NEOBLAST	ABELSTWY	BELTWAYS	ABEOSTWX	SWEATBOX
	NOTABLES	ABELTTUU	TUBULATE	ABEPRRTU	ABRUPTER
	STONABLE	ABELTTUY	BUTYLATE	ABEPRSSY	PASSERBY
ABELNOSY	BALONEYS	ABEMMNOO	MOONBEAM	ABEPRSTY	TYPEBARS
ABELNPRU	PRUNABLE	ABEMNOST	BOATSMEN	ABEPSSSY	BYPASSES
ABELNPSU	SUBPANEL	ABEMNOTU	UMBONATE	ABEQRSUU	ARQUEBUS
ABELNQTU	BLANQUET	ABEMNOTW	BATWOMEN	ABERRRTY	BARRETRY
ABELNRRY	BARRENLY	ABEMNPRU	PENUMBRA	ABERRSSU	SABREURS
ABELNRSS	BRANSLES	ABEMNRSY	MYRBANES	ABERRTYY	TAYBERRY
ABELNRST	BRANTLES	ABEMNSSU	SUNBEAMS	ABERRWXY	WAXBERRY
ABELNRSY	BLARNEYS	ABEMNSTU	SUBMENTA	ABERSSST	BRASSETS
ABELNRTU	TURNABLE	ABEMNSUY	SUNBEAMY	ABERSSSU	RUBASSES
ABELNRUY	URBANELY	ABEMNTTU	ABUTMENT		SURBASES
ABELNRYZ	BRAZENLY	ABEMORRS	EMBRASOR	ABERSSTU	ABSTRUSE
ABELNSTU	ABLUENTS	ABEMORST	BROMATES		SURBATES
	UNSTABLE	ABEMORSU	AMBEROUS	ABERSSTW	WABSTERS
ABELNSTY	ABSENTLY	ABEMORTZ	BAROMETZ	ABERSTTU	ABUTTERS
ABELNSUU	UNUSABLE	ABEMOSTU	OUTBEAMS	ABERSTUW	WATERBUS
ABELNTUY	TUNEABLY	ABEMRSSW	BESWARMS	ABERTTUY	BUTYRATE
ABELOOTY	TABOOLEY	ABENNORS	BARONNES	ABESSSTT	BASSETTS
ABELOPRT	PORTABLE	ABENNOTU	BUTANONE	ABESSSTU	ASBESTUS
ABELOPRU	POURABLE		NANOTUBE	ABESSTTU	SUBSTATE
ABELOPRV	PROVABLE	ABENNRRS	BRANNERS	ABFFGILN	BAFFLING
ABELOPRY	OPERABLY	ABENOPSU	SUBPOENA	ABFFIILS	BAILIFFS
ABELOPST	POTABLES	ABENORSS	BARONESS	ABFFINOS	BANOFFIS
ABELOPTT	TABLETOP	ABENORST	BARONETS	ABFFLLPU	PUFFBALL
ABELOQTU	QUOTABLE	ABENORSZ	ZEBRANOS	ABFFLOOS	BOFFOLAS
ABELORRS	LABORERS	ABENORTT	BETATRON	ABFFLOST	BLASTOFF
ABELORRU	LABOURER	ABENORTV	BEVATRON	ABFFLOSU	BUFFALOS
	RUBEOLAR	ABENORTY	BARYTONE	ABFFNOTU	BOUFFANT
ABELORST	BLOATERS	ABENOSSW	SAWBONES	ABFGILNS	FABLINGS
	SORTABLE	ABENOSSY	SOYBEANS	ABFGLLOO	GOOFBALL
	STORABLE	ABENOSTY	BAYONETS	ABFGOOST	FOOTBAGS
ABELORSU	RUBEOLAS	ABENPSSU	SUBPENAS	ABFGORUU	FAUBOURG
ABELORSV	ABSOLVER	ABENQSTU	BANQUETS	ABFHIIST	BAITFISH
ABELOSSU	SABULOSE	ABENRRYZ	BRAZENRY	ABFHILLS	FISHBALL
ABELOSSV	ABSOLVES	ABENRSTU	UNBRASTE	ABFHINNO	INFOBAHN
ABELOSTU	ABSOLUTE		URBANEST	ABFHIORS	BOARFISH
ABELOSTW	BESTOWAL	ABENSSSS	BASSNESS	ABFHOOTT	FOOTBATH
	STOWABLE	ABENSTZZ	BEZZANTS	ABFHSSTU	SUBSHAFT
	TEABOWLS	ABEOOSST	SEABOOTS	ABFIILLR	FIBRILLA
ABELOTTU	OUTBLEAT	ABEOPPRY	PAPERBOY	ABFIILMR	FIMBRIAL
ABELOTUZ	OUTBLAZE	ABEOPRSS	SAPROBES	ABFIILRR	FIBRILAR
ABELPRTU	PUBERTAL	ABEOPRST	PROBATES	ABFILLLY	FALLIBLY
ABELQSUU	SUBEQUAL	ABEOPSST	POSTBASE	ABFILNSU	BASINFUL
ABELRRSW	BRAWLERS	ABEOQRSU	BAROQUES	ABFILOTT	BOATLIFT
	WARBLERS	ABEORRRT	BARRETOR	ABFILSTU	FABULIST
ABELRRTU	BARRULET	ABEORRSS	BRASEROS	ABFIMORS	FIBROMAS
ABELRSST	BLASTERS	ABEORRST	ABORTERS	ABFJORSU	FRABJOUS
	STABLERS		ARBORETS	ABFKLLOR	FORKBALL
ABELRSSY	LABRYSES		TABORERS		KORFBALL
ABELRSTT	BATTLERS	ABEORRTU	TABOURER	ABFLLOOS	FOOSBALL
	BLATTERS	ABEORSST	BOASTERS	ABFLLOOT	FOOTBALL
	BRATTLES		SORBATES	ABFLLORU	FOURBALL
ABELRSTU	BALUSTER	ABEORSSY	ROSEBAYS	ABFLLOST	SOFTBALL
	RUSTABLE	ABEORSTT	ABETTORS	ABFLMORY	FORMABLY
ABELRSTW	BLEWARTS		BATTEROS	ABFLNSUU	BUSULFAN
ABELRSUZ	ZEBRULAS		TABORETS	ABFLOSTU	BOASTFUL
ABELRTTU	BURLETTA	ABEORSTU	SABOTEUR		BOATFULS
	REBUTTAL	ABEORTTU	OBTURATE	ABFLOSTW	BATFOWLS
ABELSSSU	SUBSALES		TABOURET	ABFLOSTY	FLYBOATS
ABELSSTT	STABLEST	ABEORTUV	OUTBRAVE	ABFLOSUU	FABULOUS

ABFNORTU	TURBOFAN	ABGILNOT	BLOATING	ABGLOSSU	SUBGOALS
ABFOORST	FOOTBARS		OBLIGANT	ABGLRRSU	BURGLARS
ABFOOSTY	FOYBOATS	ABGILNRT	BLARTING	ABGLRRUY	BURGLARY
ABFORSTU	SURFBOAT		BRATLING	ABGMNOOR	GAMBROON
ABFSSTTU	TUBFASTS	ABGILNRW	BRAWLING	ABGMNOOY	BOOGYMAN
ABGGGILN	BLAGGING		WARBLING	ABGMOOSY	GOOMBAYS
ABGGGINR	BRAGGING	ABGILNST	BLASTING	ABGMORSW	BAGWORMS
ABGGGINS	BAGGINGS		STABLING	ABGNOORS	BARGOONS
ABGGIIST	GIGABITS		TABLINGS	ABGNOORY	BOONGARY
ABGGIJNN	JINGBANG	ABGILNSW	BAWLINGS	ABGNOPRS	PROBANGS
ABGGILMN	GAMBLING	ABGILNTT	BATTLING	ABGNORSU	OSNABURG
ABGGILNR	GARBLING		BLATTING	ABGNOSTU	GUNBOATS
ABGGINNS	BANGINGS	ABGILNTY	TANGIBLY	ABGNOSWY	BOWYANGS
ABGGNNUY	GUNNYBAG	ABGILOOT	OBLIGATO	ABGOORST	BOTARGOS
ABGGNOOT	TOBOGGAN	ABGILORS	GARBOILS	ABGOPSST	POSTBAGS
ABGGORST	BOGGARTS	ABGILORW	BRIGALOW	ABGORRSU	GOBURRAS
ABGHHILL	HIGHBALL	ABGILRST	BATGIRLS	ABGORSTU	OUTBRAGS
ABGHIINT	HABITING	ABGIMMNO	MAMBOING	ABGOSTTU	TUGBOATS
ABGHILMN	HAMBLING	ABGIMNRU	RUMBAING	ABHHIKSS	BAKSHISH
ABGHINRS	BRASHING	ABGIMOSU	BIGAMOUS	ABHHKOST	KHOTBAHS
ABGHINSS	BASHINGS		SUBIMAGO	ABHHKSTU	KHUTBAHS
ABGHINWZ	WHIZBANG	ABGIMSST	GAMBISTS	ABHHRSTU	HATBRUSH
ABGHIOPR	BIOGRAPH	ABGINNNR	BRANNING	ABHHSSUW	BUSHWAHS
ABGHLOST	HAGBOLTS	ABGINNOR	ABORNING	ABHIINRS	BAIRNISH
ABGHMOOS	GOOMBAHS	ABGINNOT	BATONING		BRAINISH
ABGHMORU	BROUGHAM	ABGINNRU	UNBARING	ABHIINST	INHABITS
ABGHMRSU	HAMBURGS	ABGINNRX	BANXRING	ABHIIORZ	RHIZOBIA
ABGHNORS	HORNBAGS	ABGINNST	BANTINGS	ABHIKLLW	HAWKBILL
ABGHORTU	BROUGHTA	ABGINOOR	BIGAROON	ABHIKLOR	KOHLRABI
ABGHOSTU	BUSHGOAT	ABGINOOT	TABOOING	ABHIKLSS	BASHLIKS
ABGHPRSU	SUBGRAPH	ABGINORT	ABORTING	ABHIKSTW	HAWKBITS
ABGIIILN	ALIBIING		BORATING	ABHIKSUZ	BUZKASHI
ABGIIKNT	BATIKING		TABORING	ABHILLPT	PITHBALL
ABGIILNR	BRAILING	ABGINORV	BRAVOING	ABHILNOS	HOBNAILS
ABGIILNS	SAIBLING	ABGINOST	BOASTING	ABHILNOT	BIATHLON
ABGIILNT	LIBATING		BOATINGS	ABHILOPS	BASOPHIL
ABGIILOT	OBLIGATI		BOSTANGI	ABHILRTW	WHIRLBAT
ABGIIMNS	IMBASING	ABGINRRS	BARRINGS	ABHILSST	STABLISH
ABGIIMST	BIGAMIST	ABGINRSS	BRASSING	ABHILSTU	HALIBUTS
ABGIINNO	BIGNONIA	ABGINRST	BRASTING	ABHIMMST	BATHMISM
ABGIINNR	BRAINING	ABGINSST	BASTINGS	ABHIMNRS	BRAHMINS
ABGIINOR	ABORIGIN	ABGINSTT	BATTINGS	ABHINSST	ABSINTHS
ABGIINRS	BRAISING	ABGINSTW	BATSWING	ABHIOSST	ISOBATHS
ABGIINSS	BIASINGS	ABGINTTU	ABUTTING	ABHIOSTU	HAUTBOIS
	BIASSING	ABGIOPST	PIGBOATS	ABHIRRSU	AIRBRUSH
ABGIINST	BAITINGS	ABGIRRSS	RIBGRASS	ABHIRSSS	BRASSISH
ABGIJNRU	ABJURING	ABGKKNOS	BANGKOKS	ABHIRSTT	BRATTISH
ABGIJOOS	JIGABOOS	ABGKORSW	WORKBAGS	ABHJNOOT	JOHNBOAT
ABGIKLNN	BLANKING	ABGLLLOY	GLOBALLY	ABHKLSSY	BASHLYKS
ABGIKLNS	BALKINGS	ABGLLLUY	GULLABLY	ABHKLSUW	BUSHWALK
ABGIKLNU	BAULKING	ABGLLMSU	GUMBALLS	ABHKOOOT	BOATHOOK
ABGIKNNR	BRANKING	ABGLLNUW	BUNGWALL	ABHKORSU	BOURKHAS
ABGIKNNS	BANKINGS	ABGLLORU	GLOBULAR		KOURBASH
ABGIKNRR	RINGBARK	ABGLLRUY	BULLYRAG	ABHKORSV	BOSHVARK
ABGILLMN	LAMBLING	ABGLMNSU	LUMBANGS	ABHLLMOT	MOTHBALL
ABGILLNS	BALLINGS	ABGLMOPU	PLUMBAGO	ABHLLOOY	BALLYHOO
ABGILMNR	MARBLING	ABGLMOSU	LUMBAGOS	ABHLLPSU	PUSHBALL
	RAMBLING	ABGLNOOS	BOLOGNAS	ABHLLSTU	BULLSHAT
ABGILMNS	AMBLINGS	ABGLNOOT	LONGBOAT	ABHLORTW	WHORLBAT
	LAMBINGS	ABGLNOUW	BUNGALOW	ABHLOSUX	BOXHAULS
ABGILMNW	WAMBLING	ABGLOOST	TOOLBAGS	ABHLOSWW	WASHBOWL
ABGILNNT	BANTLING	ABGLOOTY	BATOLOGY	ABHLPSUY	SUBPHYLA
ABGILNNU	UNBALING	ABGLORST	RAGBOLTS	ABHLRSTU	HURLBATS
ABGILNOR	LABORING	ABGLORSU	GLABROUS	ABHLSSTU	SALTBUSH

ABHMNOTY	BOTHYMAN	ABILLPST	SPITBALL	ABIOORTV	OBVIATOR
ABHMNSUU	SUBHUMAN	ABILLRTY	TRIBALLY	ABIOPRSU	BIPAROUS
ABHMOORT	BATHROOM	ABILLSSW	SAWBILLS	ABIOPSTU	SUBTOPIA
ABHMRSSU	SAMBHURS	ABILLSTT	BATTILLS	ABIORRST	ARBORIST
ABHNSSTU	SUNBATHS	ABILLSWX	WAXBILLS	ABIORRSZ	BIZARROS
ABHOORST	TARBOOSH	ABILLSWY	WAYBILLS	ABIORRTV	VIBRATOR
ABHOOSTW	SHOWBOAT	ABILMNOU	OLIBANUM	ABIORSTV	VIBRATOS
ABHORRSU	HARBOURS	ABILMNSU	ALBUMINS	ABIORTUY	OBITUARY
ABHORSTU	TARBOUSH	ABILMOPS	BIOPLASM	ABIPSSTT	BAPTISTS
ABHOSTUY	HAUTBOYS	ABILMORS	LABORISM	ABIRRSTU	AIRBURST
ABHSSTUW	WASHTUBS		MISLABOR	ABIRSSUZ	SUBSIZAR
ABIIINRS	BIRIANIS	ABILMOTU	BUMALOTI	ABIRSTTY	TRAYBITS
ABIIINRY	BIRIYANI	ABILNOOT	BOLTONIA	ABISSSST	BASSISTS
ABIIKKST	KIBITKAS		LOBATION	ABISSTTU	TUBAISTS
ABIIKLSS	BASILISK		OBLATION	ABJKMOSS	SJAMBOKS
ABIILLMR	MILLIBAR	ABILNOPR	PANBROIL	ABJLMOOS	JAMBOOLS
ABIILLTY	LABILITY	ABILNORU	UNILOBAR	ABKKMOOR	BOOKMARK
ABIILMNO	BINOMIAL	ABILNOTU	ABLUTION	ABKLLNOR	BANKROLL
ABIILMNS	ALBINISM		ABUTILON	ABKLOOPY	PLAYBOOK
	MINILABS	ABILNRTU	TRIBUNAL	ABKLOOSW	LAWBOOKS
ABIILMSU	BULIMIAS		TURBINAL	ABKLORTW	BLOWKART
ABIILNOT	LIBATION	ABILNRWY	BRAWNILY	ABKLORWY	WORKABLY
ABIILNQS	INQILABS	ABILOPRS	PARBOILS	ABKLRSUW	BULWARKS
ABIILNRS	BRASILIN	ABILOPST	BIOPLAST	ABKNNNOS	NONBANKS
ABIILNRY	BRAINILY	ABILORST	LABORIST	ABKNNOSW	SNOWBANK
ABIILNRZ	BRAZILIN		ORBITALS	ABKNOPST	STOPBANK
ABIILNST	SIBILANT		STROBILA	ABKNPRTU	BANKRUPT
ABIILNVY	INVIABLY	ABILORSV	BOLIVARS	ABKNRSUU	BUNRAKUS
ABIILOSV	BOLIVIAS	ABILORTY	LIBATORY	ABKOOPSS	PASSBOOK
ABIILPTY	PITIABLY	ABILORUV	BIOVULAR	ABKOORTW	WORKBOAT
ABIIMNOT	AMBITION	ABILOSTU	BAILOUTS	ABKOOSTT	KOTTABOS
ABIIMNRS	BINARISM		TABOULIS	ABKORSTU	OUTBARKS
	MINIBARS	ABILPSSY	PASSIBLY	ABKSSSTU	SUBTASKS
ABIIMSST	IAMBISTS	ABILRSSY	BRASSILY	ABLLLOSW	LOWBALLS
ABIINORS	ROBINIAS	ABILRSUV	SUBVIRAL	ABLLMOOR	BALLROOM
ABIINRSY	BIRYANIS	ABILSSUY	ISSUABLY	ABLLMOPW	BLOWLAMP
ABIIRSSV	VIBRISSA	ABILSTUY	SUITABLY	ABLLMOSY	SMALLBOY
ABIJLNRS	BRINJALS	ABIMMNOO	MAINBOOM	ABLLNOOS	BALLOONS
ABIJLNTU	JUBILANT	ABIMMSTU	MITUMBAS	ABLLNOSW	SNOWBALL
ABIJNOOT	JOBATION	ABIMNOSU	BIMANOUS	ABLLORRS	ROLLBARS
ABIJNOST	ABJOINTS	ABIMNRSU	URBANISM	ABLLORST	BORSTALL
	BANJOIST	ABIMNRTU	TAMBURIN		TOLLBARS
ABIKLLLM	LAMBKILL	ABIMORSU	BIRAMOUS	ABLLORSU	SOURBALL
ABIKLLUY	BAULKILY	ABIMORSY	BOYARISM	ABLLOSTY	TALLBOYS
ABIKLMNS	LAMBKINS	ABIMPSST	BAPTISMS	ABLLRTUY	BRUTALLY
	LAMBSKIN	ABIMRSST	STRABISM	ABLLSSUY	SYLLABUS
ABIKLMOU	KUMBALOI	ABIMRSTT	TRIMTABS	ABLMMOSU	BUMMALOS
ABIKLNRY	BYRLAKIN	ABINNOST	ANTISNOB	ABLMNRUU	ALBURNUM
ABIKLORS	KILOBARS	ABINOORS	BORONIAS		LABURNUM
ABIKLOSS	KOLBASIS	ABINOORT	ABORTION	ABLMOOST	TOMBOLAS
	KOLBASSI	ABINOOST	BONIATOS	ABLMOSTY	MYOBLAST
ABIKLSSY	KISSABLY	ABINOPTX	PAINTBOX	ABLMPSUU	PABULUMS
ABIKMNNR	BRINKMAN	ABINORST	TABORINS	ABLNNOOR	NONLABOR
ABIKMNRS	BARMKINS	ABINORSW	RAINBOWS	ABLNOOPS	POBLANOS
ABIKNORR	IRONBARK	ABINORTU	TABOURIN	ABLNORST	LASTBORN
ABIKOSUZ	BAZOUKIS	ABINORWY	RAINBOWY	ABLNORYZ	BLAZONRY
ABIKRSST	BRITSKAS	ABINOSST	ANTIBOSS	ABLNOSTU	BUTANOLS
ABIKRSTZ	BRITZKAS		BASTIONS	ABLNOSUZ	SUBZONAL
	BRITZSKA	ABINOSSU	ABUSIONS	ABLNRSUU	SUBLUNAR
ABILLLPV	PLAYBILL	ABINOSTT	BOTANIST	ABLNSTUY	UNSTABLY
ABILLMSU	BALLIUMS	ABINRSTU	URBANIST	ABLNSUUY	UNUSABLY
ABILLNPS	PINBALLS	ABINRSTV	VIBRANTS	ABLOOPRR	PROLABOR
ABILLORT	TRILOBAL	ABINRTUY	URBANITY	ABLOORST	BARSTOOL
ABILLOVY	VIOLABLY	ABINTTTU	TITUBANT		TOOLBARS

ABLOORTY	OBLATORY	ACCDEENR	CANCERED	ACCDKOSW	DAWCOCKS
ABLOOSTT	BOOTLAST	ACCDEENS	CADENCES	ACCDLOSY	CACODYLS
ABLOOSTZ	ZOOBLAST	ACCDEENT	ACCENTED	ACCDOOST	STOCCADO
ABLOPRSU	SUBPOLAR	ACCDEEPT	ACCEPTED	ACCDOOXY	CACODOXY
ABLOPRTY	PORTABLY	ACCDEERS	ACCEDERS	ACCDOSUU	CADUCOUS
ABLOPRVY	PROVABLY	ACCDEERT	ACCRETED	ACCEEEPT	ACCEPTEE
ABLOPSUU	PABULOUS	ACCDEERU	CARDECUE	ACCEEHIT	HICCATEE
ABLOPSYY	PLAYBOYS	ACCDEERW	ACCREWED	ACCEEHLO	COCHLEAE
ABLOQTUY	QUOTABLY	ACCDEESS	ACCESSED	ACCEEHLS	CALECHES
ABLORSST	BORSTALS	ACCDEGIN	ACCEDING	ACCEEHOS	COACHEES
ABLORSSU	SUBSOLAR		ACCINGED	ACCEEHRT	CETERACH
ABLORSTW	BLAWORTS	ACCDEHIK	CHIACKED	ACCEEHST	SEECATCH
ABLORSTY	SORTABLY	ACCDEHIL	CHALICED	ACCEEILR	CELERIAC
ABLORSUW	BOURLAWS	ACCDEHIN	CHICANED	ACCEEILS	ECCLESIA
ABLORTUW	OUTBRAWL	ACCDEHKY	CHYACKED	ACCEEINV	VACCINEE
ABLOSSUU	SABULOUS	ACCDEHLT	CLATCHED	ACCEEKLN	NECKLACE
ABLOSTTU	SUBTOTAL	ACCDEHNR	CRANCHED	ACCEELNO	COENACLE
ABLOSTUW	OUTBAWLS	ACCDEHNU	CHAUNCED	ACCEELNR	CANCELER
ABLPRTUY	ABRUPTLY	ACCDEHPU	CAPUCHED		CLARENCE
ABLRSTUY	BUTYRALS	ACCDEIIS	ACCIDIES	ACCEELNS	CENACLES
ABMNTTUY	BUTTYMAN	ACCDEILN	CALCINED	ACCEELOS	COALESCE
ABMOORRS	BARROOMS	ACCDEILO	ECOCIDAL	ACCEELRT	CALCRETE
ABMOPSST	SPAMBOTS	ACCDEILU	CAUDICLE	ACCEENNS	NASCENCE
ABMORSTU	TAMBOURS	ACCDEILY	DELICACY	ACCEENPR	CREPANCE
ABMOSSTU	SUBATOMS	ACCDEINO	DECANOIC	ACCEENRS	CREANCES
ABMRRSUY	BURRAMYS	ACCDEINT	ACCIDENT	ACCEENRT	REACCENT
ABNNNORU	NONURBAN	ACCDEIRT	ACCREDIT	ACCEENST	ACESCENT
ABNOORRT	ROBORANT	ACCDEISU	CAUDICES	ACCEEORT	COCREATE
ABNOORSS	SOROBANS	ACCDEKLR	CRACKLED		CROCEATE
ABNOORSZ	BORAZONS	ACCDEKOS	COCKADES	ACCEEPRT	ACCEPTER
ABNOORYZ	BRYOZOAN	ACCDELLY	CALYCLED		REACCEPT
ABNOOSSS	BASSOONS	ACCDELOY	ACCLOYED	ACCEERST	ACCRETES
ABNORSTY	BARYTONS	ACCDENOR	CONACRED	ACCEERSU	REACCUSE
ABNORTUU	RUNABOUT	ACCDENOV	CONCAVED	ACCEESSS	ACCESSES
ABNOSSSU	BONASSUS	ACCDEORR	ACCORDER	ACCEFFIY	EFFICACY
ABNOSTUX	SUBTAXON	ACCDEOST	ACCOSTED	ACCEFILS	FASCICLE
ABNRSTTU	TURBANTS	ACCDERSU	ACCURSED	ACCEFIST	FACTICES
ABOORRSU	ARBOROUS		CARDECUS	ACCEFLSU	FELUCCAS
ABOORSTW	ROWBOATS	ACCDESSU	SUCCADES	ACCEGINS	ACCINGES
ABOOSTTU	OUTBOAST	ACCDESUU	CADUCEUS	ACCEGKMO	GAMECOCK
ABOOSTTW	TOWBOATS		CAUCUSED	ACCEGNOY	COAGENCY
ABORSSTU	ROBUSTAS	ACCDGHOO	COACHDOG	ACCEGOSS	SOCCAGES
ABPRSSTU	SUBPARTS	ACCDHIIR	DIARCHIC	ACCEHHIS	CHECHIAS
ACCCDIIO	COCCIDIA	ACCDHILS	CHALCIDS	ACCEHHKO	CHECHAKO
ACCCEHIX	CACHEXIC	ACCDHIMO	DOCHMIAC	ACCEHHKT	CHATCHKE
ACCCELRY	CYCLECAR	ACCDHIOR	CHAORDIC		HATCHECK
ACCCENPY	PECCANCY	ACCDHIOT	CATHODIC	ACCEHIKP	CHICKPEA
ACCCFIIL	CALCIFIC	ACCDHIRY	DYARCHIC	ACCEHIKR	AIRCHECK
ACCCHILO	COLCHICA	ACCDHLOR	CLOCHARD	ACCEHILM	ALCHEMIC
ACCCHRTY	CATCHCRY	ACCDIINU	UNACIDIC		CHEMICAL
ACCCIILT	CALCITIC	ACCDIIOT	ACIDOTIC	ACCEHILP	CEPHALIC
ACCCIIPR	CAPRICCI	ACCDIIRT	CARDITIC	ACCEHILS	CALICHES
ACCCILLY	CYCLICAL	ACCDIIST	DICASTIC		CHALICES
ACCCIOPU	CAPUCCIO	ACCDIITY	DICACITY	ACCEHILT	HECTICAL
ACCDDEEN	ACCENDED	ACCDILNU	DUNCICAL	ACCEHIMN	MECHANIC
	CADENCED	ACCDILOY	CALYCOID	ACCEHIMS	SACHEMIC
ACCDDEIS	CADDICES	ACCDILTY	DACTYLIC	ACCEHINO	ANECHOIC
ACCDDEKO	COCKADED	ACCDINOR	CANCROID	ACCEHINR	CHANCIER
ACCDDEOR	ACCORDED		DRACONIC		CHICANER
ACCDDIII	DIACIDIC	ACCDIOOR	CORACOID	ACCEHINS	CHICANES
ACCDDIIT	DIDACTIC	ACCDIORS	SARCODIC	ACCEHINT	ATECHNIC
ACCDEEER	REACCEDE	ACCDIOST	STICCADO		CATECHIN
ACCDEEHT	CACHETED	ACCDITUY	CADUCITY	ACCEHIOS	COACHIES
ACCDEELN	CANCELED	ACCDKNOS	CANDOCKS	ACCEHIRT	CATCHIER

ACCEHKPY	PAYCHECK	ACCEIRTU	CRUCIATE	ACCGIKLN	CACKLING
ACCEHLNS	CHANCELS	ACCEISST	ASCETICS		CLACKING
ACCEHLOR	COCHLEAR	ACCEISTT	ECSTATIC	ACCGIKMR	GIMCRACK
ACCEHLOS	COCHLEAS	ACCEKLNR	CRACKNEL	ACCGIKNR	CRACKING
ACCEHLOT	CATECHOL	ACCEKLRS	CACKLERS	ACCGILOX	COXALGIC
ACCEHLST	CLATCHES		CLACKERS	ACCGINOT	COACTING
ACCEHMNO	COACHMEN		CRACKLES	ACCGINOY	ACCOYING
ACCEHNNO	CHACONNE	ACCEKMOS	MEACOCKS	ACCGINRU	ACCRUING
ACCEHNNY	CYNANCHE	ACCEKNOR	CORNCAKE	ACCGINSU	ACCUSING
ACCEHNOR	CHARNECO	ACCEKOPS	PEACOCKS	ACCGLOOY	CACOLOGY
	ENCROACH	ACCEKOPY	PEACOCKY	ACCHHITT	CHITCHAT
ACCEHNOT	CONCHATE	ACCEKOSS	SEACOCKS	ACCHHMOS	CAMSHOCH
ACCEHNRS	CHANCERS	ACCEKPSU	CUPCAKES	ACCHHMOU	MUCHACHO
	CHANCRES	ACCEKRRS	CRACKERS	ACCHIIMS	CHIASMIC
	CRANCHES	ACCEKRST	CRACKETS	ACCHIIRT	RACHITIC
ACCEHNRY	CHANCERY	ACCELLSY	CALYCLES	ACCHIIST	CHIASTIC
ACCEHNSU	CHAUNCES	ACCELLUV	CALYCULE	ACCHILNO	CHALONIC
ACCEHOPT	CACHEPOT	ACCELMNY	CYCLAMEN	ACCHILNY	CHANCILY
ACCEHORS	CAROCHES	ACCELNOS	CONCEALS	ACCHILOR	ORICHALC
	COACHERS	ACCELNOV	CONCLAVE	ACCHILOT	CATHOLIC
ACCEHPSU	CAPUCHES	ACCELNRU	CARUNCLE	ACCHIMOR	ACHROMIC
ACCEHRST	CATCHERS	ACCELOOT	COLOCATE	ACCHINNO	CINCHONA
	CRATCHES	ACCELORS	CORACLES	ACCHINOS	CHICANOS
ACCEHSST	SCATCHES	ACCELORT	ACROLECT	ACCHINPU	CAPUCHIN
ACCEHSTT	CATHECTS	ACCELOST	CACOLETS	ACCHIOPS	PICACHOS
ACCEHSTU	CATECHUS	ACCELRSY	SCARCELY	ACCHIORS	COCHAIRS
ACCEIIST	CAECITIS	ACCELRTU	CLEARCUT	ACCHIORT	THORACIC
ACCEIKLT	TICKLACE	ACCELSSU	SACCULES		TROCHAIC
ACCEIKPS	ICEPACKS	ACCELSSY	CYCLASES	ACCHIOSU	ACOUCHIS
ACCEIKST	CACKIEST	ACCELWYY	CYCLEWAY	ACCHIRRT	CARRITCH
ACCEILLN	CANCELLI	ACCENNSY	NASCENCY	ACCHIRSS	SCRAICHS
ACCEILLR	CLERICAL	ACCENORR	CORNACRE	ACCHKLOR	CHARLOCK
ACCEILLS	CALICLES	ACCENORS	CONACRES	ACCHKOSY	HAYCOCKS
ACCEILLU	CAULICLE	ACCENORT	ACCENTOR	ACCHLOOT	CACHOLOT
ACCEILLV	CLAVICLE	ACCENOST	COENACTS	ACCHLSTU	CLAUCHTS
ACCEILNS	CALCINES		COSECANT	ACCHMORS	CASCHROM
	SCENICAL	ACCENOSU	CONCAUSE	ACCHNNUY	UNCHANCY
ACCEILNT	CANTICLE	ACCENOSV	CONCAVES	ACCHNOOR	COANCHOR
ACCEILNV	CLAVECIN	ACCEOPRT	ACCEPTOR		CORONACH
ACCEILNY	CALYCINE	ACCEOPTU	OCCUPATE	ACCHNOTU	COUCHANT
ACCEILOP	ALOPECIC	ACCEORSS	ARCCOSES	ACCHNRUY	CRAUNCHY
ACCEILOS	CALICOES	ACCEORST	ECTOSARC	ACCHNTUY	UNCATCHY
	COELIACS	ACCEORSW	CRACOWES	ACCHOOTU	OUTCOACH
ACCEILRV	CERVICAL	ACCEORTU	ACCOUTER	ACCHOPSU	PACHUCOS
ACCEILST	CALCITES		ACCOUTRE	ACCHORTU	CARTOUCH
ACCEILTY	ACETYLIC	ACCEOSSS	SACCOSES	ACCHORTY	OCTARCHY
ACCEIMOS	OCCAMIES	ACCERRST	CARRECTS	ACCHOSTW	CHOCTAWS
ACCEIMRS	CERAMICS	ACCERSST	SCARCEST	ACCHOTTU	OUTCATCH
ACCEINNR	CANCRINE	ACCERSSU	ACCURSES	ACCHPSTU	CATCHUPS
ACCEINOR	COCINERA		ACCUSERS	ACCHRRSU	CURRACHS
ACCEINOS	COCAINES	ACCESSTU	CACTUSES	ACCHRSSU	SCRAUCHS
ACCEINOT	ACETONIC	ACCESSUU	CAUCUSES	ACCHRSTY	SCRATCHY
ACCEINRT	ACENTRIC	ACCFFLTU	CALCTUFF	ACCHRTWY	WATCHCRY
ACCEINSV	VACCINES	ACCFHLTY	CATCHFLY	ACCIIIOT	OITICICA
ACCEINTU	CUNEATIC	ACCFIILT	LACTIFIC	ACCIILLN	CLINICAL
ACCEIOPR	CECROPIA	ACCFIKLL	CALFLICK	ACCIILMT	CLIMATIC
ACCEIOTV	COACTIVE	ACCFLNOO	CONFOCAL	ACCIILNO	ICONICAL
ACCEIPRS	CAPRICES	ACCFOORT	COFACTOR	ACCIILRT	CRITICAL
ACCEIPRT	PRACTICE	ACCGHIKN	CHACKING	ACCIIMNN	CINNAMIC
ACCEIPSV	PECCAVIS	ACCGHINN	CHANCING	ACCIINNO	ANICONIC
ACCEIQSU	CACIQUES	ACCGHINO	COACHING	ACCIINNP	PICCANIN
ACCEIRRR	RICERCAR	ACCGHINT	CATCHING	ACCIINOT	ACONITIC
ACCEIRSU	CAESURIC	ACCGHIOR	CHORAGIC		CATIONIC
	CURACIES	ACCGIINT	ACCITING		ITACONIC

Code	Word	Code	Word	Code	Word
ACCIINPS	CAPSICIN	ACCKMORS	CROMACKS	ACDDEIIM	MEDICAID
ACCIINTY	CYANITIC	ACCKOOOP	COCKAPOO	ACDDEILS	CLADDIES
ACCIIOPT	OCCIPITA	ACCKOOOT	COCKATOO	ACDDEILU	DECIDUAL
ACCIIPST	PASTICCI	ACCKOPRS	CAPROCKS	ACDDEINR	CANDIDER
ACCIIRTX	CICATRIX	ACCKOPRT	CRACKPOT		RIDDANCE
ACCIISST	SCIATICS	ACCKORST	STOCKCAR	ACDDEINT	DEDICANT
ACCIJKMR	JIMCRACK	ACCKOSSS	CASSOCKS	ACDDEINY	CYANIDED
ACCIKKNN	NICKNACK		COSSACKS	ACDDEIPS	DISPACED
ACCIKKRR	RICKRACK	ACCKOSST	CASTOCKS	ACDDEIRT	READDICT
ACCIKKTT	TICKTACK	ACCKPRSU	CRACKUPS	ACDDEISS	CADDISES
ACCIKLOT	COCKTAIL	ACCLLNOY	CYCLONAL		DISCASED
ACCIKNST	CANSTICK	ACCLLOSU	OCCLUSAL	ACDDEISU	DECIDUAS
ACCIKOPR	APRICOCK	ACCLLSUU	CALCULUS	ACDDEITT	DICTATED
ACCIKPRT	PRACTICK	ACCLSSUU	SACCULUS	ACDDEKLO	DEADLOCK
ACCILLUY	CALYCULI	ACCMNOSY	CACONYMS	ACDDEKOR	RADDOCKE
ACCILMOS	COSMICAL	ACCMNOYY	CACONYMY	ACDDELOS	CLADODES
ACCILMOX	CACOMIXL	ACCMOOST	COCOMATS	ACDDELRS	CLADDERS
ACCILMSU	CALCIUMS	ACCMOOSY	COCOYAMS	ACDDENRU	UNCARDED
ACCILMUU	ACICULUM	ACCMOPST	ACCOMPTS	ACDDENTU	ADDUCENT
ACCILNOT	CICLATON		COMPACTS	ACDDEOPS	DECAPODS
	LACTONIC	ACCMOSTU	ACCUSTOM	ACDDEORR	CORRADED
ACCILNOV	VOLCANIC	ACCMRSUU	CURCUMAS	ACDDEORW	COWARDED
ACCILNUV	VULCANIC	ACCNNOOS	COONCANS	ACDDERSU	ADDUCERS
ACCILORS	CALORICS	ACCNOOPS	COCOPANS		CRUSADED
ACCILORT	CORTICAL	ACCNOORS	RACCOONS	ACDDERTU	TRADUCED
ACCILOSS	CLASSICO	ACCNOOTU	COCOANUT	ACDDGILN	CLADDING
ACCILOSV	VOCALICS	ACCNOPTU	OCCUPANT	ACDDGINU	ADDUCING
ACCILPRY	CAPRYLIC	ACCNORTT	CONTRACT	ACDDGINY	CADDYING
ACCILRRU	CIRCULAR	ACCNOSTT	CONTACTS	ACDDHHSU	CHUDDAHS
ACCILRSY	ACRYLICS	ACCNOSTU	ACCOUNTS	ACDDHIIO	DIADOCHI
ACCILSSS	CLASSICS	ACCOORST	COACTORS	ACDDHIMR	DIDRACHM
ACCILSST	CLASTICS	ACCOPSTY	COPYCATS	ACDDHIOY	DIADOCHY
ACCILTUU	CUTICULA	ACCOQSSU	SQUACCOS	ACDDHIRY	HYDRACID
ACCIMNOS	MOCCASIN	ACCORRTY	CARRYCOT	ACDDHKNO	DOCKHAND
ACCIMNTU	CANTICUM	ACCORSTU	ACCOURTS	ACDDHKOS	HADDOCKS
ACCIMOPR	MICROCAP	ACDDDEIS	CADDISED		SHADDOCK
ACCIMORR	MICROCAR	ACDDDEIT	ADDICTED	ACDDHORS	CHADDORS
ACCIMORU	COUMARIC	ACDDDETU	ADDUCTED	ACDDHRSU	CHUDDARS
ACCIMOSZ	ZIMOCCAS	ACDDDKOS	DADDOCKS	ACDDIIOR	CARDIOID
ACCIMPSU	CAPSICUM	ACDDEEES	DECEASED	ACDDILNY	CANDIDLY
ACCIMSTY	CYMATICS	ACDDEEHO	COHEADED	ACDDILRW	WILDCARD
ACCINOOS	OCCASION	ACDDEEHT	DETACHED	ACDDILTY	DIDACTYL
ACCINOOT	COACTION	ACDDEEIT	DEDICATE	ACDDINNU	UNCANDID
ACCINORT	CRATONIC	ACDDEEIU	DECIDUAE	ACDDINSY	DISCANDY
	NARCOTIC	ACDDEEKR	DACKERED	ACDDIRSS	DISCARDS
ACCINORV	CAVICORN	ACDDEELL	DECALLED	ACDDKLNO	DOCKLAND
ACCINOST	CANTICOS	ACDDEELR	DECLARED	ACDDKMOS	MADDOCKS
ACCINOTY	CANTICOY	ACDDEELS	DESCALED	ACDDKOPS	PADDOCKS
	CYANOTIC	ACDDEELW	DECLAWED	ACDDKORY	DOCKYARD
ACCINRSU	CRUCIANS	ACDDEEMP	DECAMPED	ACDDORTU	ADDUCTOR
ACCINSSY	CYCASINS	ACDDEENO	DEACONED	ACDEEEFT	DEFECATE
ACCIOOPP	APOCOPIC	ACDDEENR	CREDENDA	ACDEEEKS	SEEDCAKE
ACCIOPST	SPICCATO	ACDDEENS	ASCENDED	ACDEEEMR	REEDMACE
ACCIORST	ACROSTIC	ACDDEENT	DECADENT	ACDEEENR	CAREENED
ACCIORSY	ISOCRACY		DECANTED	ACDEEENT	ANTECEDE
ACCIOSTT	STICCATO	ACDDEERT	REDACTED	ACDEEERR	CAREERED
ACCIOSTU	ACOUSTIC	ACDDEETU	EDUCATED	ACDEEERS	DECREASE
ACCIRRTT	TRICTRAC	ACDDEETV	ADVECTED	ACDEEESS	DECEASES
ACCIRSTY	SCARCITY	ACDDEGIS	DISCAGED		SEEDCASE
ACCISSTU	CAUSTICS	ACDDEHIK	DICKHEAD	ACDEEFFT	AFFECTED
ACCKKRSU	RUCKSACK	ACDDEHKN	DECKHAND	ACDEEFHN	ENCHAFED
ACCKLLOO	ALCOLOCK	ACDDEHRS	CHEDDARS	ACDEEFIL	CALEFIED
ACCKLORS	CARLOCKS	ACDDEHRY	CHEDDARY	ACDEEFIN	DEFIANCE
ACCKMMRU	CRUMMACK	ACDDEIIL	DEICIDAL	ACDEEFIS	CASEFIED

ACDEEFPR	PREFACED		REPLACED	ACDEFIIP	PACIFIED
ACDEEFRS	DEFACERS	ACDEELRR	DECLARER	ACDEFILN	CANFIELD
	FRESCADE	ACDEELRS	DECLARES	ACDEFILR	FILECARD
ACDEEFRY	FEDERACY		RESCALED		FRICADEL
ACDEEFTT	FACETTED	ACDEELRT	CLARETED	ACDEFINN	FINANCED
ACDEEGLY	DELEGACY		DECRETAL	ACDEFINS	FACIENDS
ACDEEGNR	ENGRACED		TREACLED	ACDEFLOT	OLFACTED
ACDEEHIN	ECHIDNAE	ACDEELRV	CALVERED	ACDEFNOW	FACEDOWN
ACDEEHIR	CHARIDEE		CLAVERED	ACDEFNRU	FURNACED
ACDEEHIV	ACHIEVED	ACDEELSS	DECLASSE	ACDEFORT	FACTORED
ACDEEHKO	COKEHEAD		DESCALES	ACDEFOTU	OUTFACED
ACDEEHLP	PLEACHED	ACDEEMNO	CODENAME	ACDEFRSU	SURFACED
ACDEEHLT	CHELATED	ACDEEMNP	ENCAMPED	ACDEFRTU	FURCATED
ACDEEHMR	DEMARCHE	ACDEEMRS	SCREAMED	ACDEGGRS	SCRAGGED
ACDEEHNN	ENHANCED	ACDEEMRT	CREMATED	ACDEGHLO	GALOCHED
ACDEEHNR	ENARCHED	ACDEEMSV	MEDEVACS	ACDEGHNU	CHAUNGED
ACDEEHNS	ENCASHED	ACDEENNP	PENANCED		GAUNCHED
	ENCHASED	ACDEENNT	TENDANCE	ACDEGIIL	ALGICIDE
ACDEEHPR	PREACHED	ACDEENNY	CAYENNED	ACDEGIKM	MAGICKED
ACDEEHRS	SEARCHED	ACDEENOT	ANECDOTE	ACDEGILN	DECALING
ACDEEHRT	DETACHER	ACDEENRS	ASCENDER	ACDEGIMR	DECIGRAM
	RACHETED		REASCEND		GRIMACED
ACDEEHSS	CHASSEED	ACDEENRT	CANTERED	ACDEGINU	GUIDANCE
ACDEEHST	DETACHES		CRENATED	ACDEGINY	DECAYING
	SACHETED		DECANTER	ACDEGIRS	DISGRACE
ACDEEIIP	EPICEDIA		NECTARED	ACDEGISS	DISCAGES
ACDEEILT	DELICATE		RECANTED	ACDEGIST	CADGIEST
ACDEEILU	AEDICULE	ACDEENRV	CAVERNED	ACDEGKOS	DOCKAGES
ACDEEIMR	CERAMIDE		CRAVENED	ACDEGLLO	COLLAGED
	MEDICARE	ACDEENRY	CARNEYED	ACDEGLOS	DECALOGS
ACDEEIMT	DECIMATE		DECENARY	ACDEGLOU	CLOUDAGE
	EMICATED	ACDEENRZ	CREDENZA	ACDEGNOS	DECAGONS
	MEDICATE	ACDEENSV	VENDACES	ACDEGNRU	UNGRACED
ACDEEINN	DECENNIA	ACDEENTT	DANCETTE	ACDEGORS	CORDAGES
	ENNEADIC	ACDEENTU	CUNEATED	ACDEGOTT	COTTAGED
ACDEEINR	DERACINE	ACDEEOPS	PEASECOD	ACDEHHIN	HAINCHED
ACDEEINU	AUDIENCE	ACDEEORT	DECORATE	ACDEHHNU	HAUNCHED
ACDEEINV	DEVIANCE		RECOATED	ACDEHHRU	HACHURED
ACDEEIPS	DISPEACE	ACDEEOTV	EVOCATED	ACDEHHTT	DETHATCH
ACDEEIRS	DECIARES	ACDEEPPR	RECAPPED		THATCHED
ACDEEJKT	JACKETED	ACDEEPRS	ESCARPED	ACDEHIIP	APHICIDE
ACDEEKLR	LACKERED		RESPACED	ACDEHIJK	HIJACKED
ACDEEKLY	LACKEYED	ACDEEPRT	CARPETED	ACDEHILR	HERALDIC
ACDEEKNR	CANKERED		PREACTED	ACDEHILT	DITHECAL
ACDEEKPR	REPACKED	ACDEEPST	ASPECTED	ACDEHIMM	CHAMMIED
ACDEEKPT	PACKETED	ACDEERRS	SCAREDER	ACDEHIMN	MACHINED
ACDEEKRR	RERACKED	ACDEERRT	CRATERED	ACDEHIMS	SCHIEDAM
ACDEEKRS	SCREAKED		RECRATED	ACDEHINR	INARCHED
ACDEEKRT	RACKETED		RETRACED	ACDEHINS	ECHIDNAS
	RETACKED		TERRACED		INCHASED
ACDEEKST	CASKETED	ACDEERSS	CARESSED	ACDEHIRS	RACHIDES
ACDEELLR	CELLARED	ACDEERST	CEDRATES	ACDEHIRT	THRIDACE
	RECALLED	ACDEERSY	DECAYERS		TRACHEID
ACDEELLS	CADELLES	ACDEESTU	EDUCATES	ACDEHIRV	ARCHIVED
ACDEELMN	ENCALMED	ACDEESUX	CAUDEXES	ACDEHIST	SCAITHED
ACDEELMP	EMPLACED	ACDEESUY	CAUSEYED	ACDEHISU	CHIAUSED
ACDEELNR	CALENDER	ACDEFFHU	CHAUFFED	ACDEHKLO	HEADLOCK
	ENCRADLE	ACDEFFLS	SCLAFFED	ACDEHKLS	SHACKLED
ACDEELNS	CLEANSED	ACDEFFOR	AFFORCED	ACDEHKNU	UNHACKED
ACDEELNT	LANCETED	ACDEFGIN	DEFACING	ACDEHKOV	HAVOCKED
ACDEELNV	ENCLAVED	ACDEFGOS	DOGFACES	ACDEHKRU	ARCHDUKE
ACDEELOR	COLEADER	ACDEFHKU	HEADFUCK	ACDEHKTW	THWACKED
	RECOALED	ACDEFHLN	FLANCHED	ACDEHLNP	PLANCHED
ACDEELPR	PARCELED	ACDEFIIL	DEIFICAL	ACDEHLNR	CHANDLER

ACDEHLNU	LAUNCHED	ACDEILMX	CLIMAXED	ACDEIPRS	EPACRIDS
ACDEHLOS	COALSHED	ACDEILNP	PANICLED		PERACIDS
ACDEHLRS	CHALDERS	ACDEILNU	DULCINEA	ACDEIPRT	PICRATED
ACDEHLRT	TRACHLED	ACDEILNY	ADENYLIC	ACDEIPSS	DISPACES
ACDEHLSS	CHADLESS	ACDEILOS	COALISED		SPADICES
ACDEHMST	SMATCHED	ACDEILOZ	COALIZED	ACDEIPST	SPICATED
ACDEHNOR	ANCHORED	ACDEILPR	PLACIDER	ACDEIPSZ	CAPSIZED
	RONDACHE	ACDEILPS	DISPLACE	ACDEIPTV	CAPTIVED
ACDEHNPU	PAUNCHED	ACDEILPT	PLICATED	ACDEIQRU	ACQUIRED
ACDEHNRU	RAUNCHED	ACDEILRS	DECRIALS	ACDEIRSS	SIDECARS
	UNARCHED		RADICELS	ACDEIRST	ACRIDEST
ACDEHNRY	ENDARCHY		RADICLES	ACDEIRSU	DECURIAS
ACDEHNST	SNATCHED	ACDEILRT	ARTICLED	ACDEIRTT	CITRATED
	STANCHED		LACERTID		TETRACID
ACDEHNSU	UNCASHED	ACDEILRU	AURICLED		TETRADIC
ACDEHNTU	CHAUNTED		RADICULE	ACDEISSS	DISCASES
ACDEHORR	HARDCORE	ACDEILST	CITADELS	ACDEISTT	DICTATES
ACDEHORT	CHORDATE		DIALECTS	ACDEKLNR	CRANKLED
ACDEHORW	COWHEARD	ACDEILSY	ECDYSIAL	ACDEKLPS	SPACKLED
ACDEHOST	CATHODES	ACDEILTT	LATTICED	ACDEKLQU	QUACKLED
ACDEHOUV	AVOUCHED	ACDEILTY	DIACETYL	ACDEKNPR	PRANCKED
ACDEHPPS	SCHAPPED	ACDEIMNO	COMEDIAN	ACDEKNPU	UNPACKED
ACDEHPRS	SCARPHED		DAEMONIC	ACDEKNRU	UNRACKED
ACDEHPST	DESPATCH		DEMONIAC	ACDEKNSU	UNCASKED
ACDEHPSU	CUPHEADS	ACDEIMNP	PANDEMIC	ACDEKNTU	UNTACKED
ACDEHPTU	DEATHCUP	ACDEIMNT	MEDICANT	ACDEKOST	STOCKADE
ACDEHQTU	QUATCHED	ACDEIMOR	COADMIRE	ACDEKRSY	KEYCARDS
ACDEHRRS	CHRESARD		RACEMOID	ACDELLNU	UNCALLED
ACDEHRST	STARCHED	ACDEIMPS	MIDSPACE	ACDELLOR	CAROLLED
ACDEHTUW	WAUCHTED	ACDEIMPT	IMPACTED		COLLARED
ACDEIILN	ALCIDINE	ACDEIMRT	DERMATIC	ACDELLOT	COLLATED
ACDEIILS	LAICISED		TIMECARD	ACDELLSU	CALLUSED
ACDEIILT	CILIATED	ACDEIMST	MISACTED	ACDELMOR	CLAMORED
ACDEIILZ	LAICIZED	ACDEIMSV	MEDIVACS	ACDELMSU	MUSCADEL
ACDEIIMU	AECIDIUM	ACDEINNR	CRANNIED	ACDELNOO	CANOODLE
ACDEIINR	ACRIDINE	ACDEINNT	INCANTED	ACDELNOR	COLANDER
ACDEIINS	SCIAENID	ACDEINOP	CANOPIED		CONELRAD
ACDEIINT	ACTINIDE	ACDEINOS	CODEINAS	ACDELNOS	CELADONS
	CTENIDIA		DIOCESAN	ACDELNPU	UNPLACED
	DIACTINE		OCEANIDS	ACDELNRS	CANDLERS
	INDICATE	ACDEINOT	ACTIONED	ACDELNRY	CALENDRY
ACDEIINU	INDUCIAE		CATENOID	ACDELNST	SCANTLED
ACDEIIRT	RATICIDE	ACDEINOV	VOIDANCE	ACDELNSU	UNSCALED
ACDEIIST	ACIDIEST	ACDEINPT	PEDANTIC	ACDELNUW	UNCLAWED
ACDEIITV	CAVITIED		PENTADIC	ACDELOOW	LACEWOOD
	VATICIDE	ACDEINRR	RANCIDER	ACDELOPS	PEDOCALS
	VICIATED	ACDEINRT	CRINATED	ACDELOPT	CLODPATE
ACDEIJNU	JAUNDICE		DICENTRA	ACDELOPU	CUPOLAED
ACDEIKNP	PANICKED	ACDEINSS	ACIDNESS	ACDELORV	OVERCLAD
ACDEIKNT	ANTICKED	ACDEINST	DANCIEST	ACDELOTU	OCULATED
ACDEIKPX	PICKAXED		DISTANCE	ACDELPPS	SCAPPLED
ACDEILLM	MEDALLIC	ACDEINSY	CYANIDES	ACDELPSU	CAPSULED
ACDEILLN	DECLINAL		CYANISED		UPSCALED
ACDEILLS	CEDILLAS	ACDEINTT	NICTATED	ACDELRRS	CRADLERS
ACDEILLV	CAVILLED	ACDEINTU	INCUDATE	ACDELRSS	SCALDERS
ACDEILMN	MEDCINAL	ACDEINVY	DEVIANCY	ACDELRSW	SCRAWLED
ACDEILMO	CAMELOID	ACDEINYZ	CYANIZED	ACDELRSY	SACREDLY
	MELODICA	ACDEIOPS	DIASCOPE	ACDELSTU	CAULDEST
ACDEILMS	CAMELIDS	ACDEIORS	IDOCRASE		SULCATED
	DECIMALS	ACDEIORT	CERATOID	ACDELSWW	DEWCLAWS
	DECLAIMS	ACDEIORV	COVARIED	ACDEMMRS	SCRAMMED
	MEDICALS	ACDEIOSS	ACIDOSES	ACDEMNOR	ROMANCED
ACDEILMT	CLIMATED	ACDEIOSU	EDACIOUS	ACDEMNSU	DECUMANS
	MALEDICT	ACDEIPPT	TAPPICED	ACDEMOPR	COMPADRE

	COMPARED	ACDEPRTU	CAPTURED	ACDHNORW	CHAWDRON
ACDEMORR	CARROMED	ACDEPSTU	CUSPATED	ACDHNOSW	COWHANDS
ACDEMORS	COMRADES	ACDEQTUU	AQUEDUCT	ACDHOOST	CATHOODS
ACDEMORT	DEMOCRAT	ACDERRSU	CRUSADER	ACDHOOTW	WOODCHAT
ACDEMPSU	CAMPUSED	ACDERRTU	TRADUCER	ACDHOPRS	POCHARDS
ACDEMRSW	SCRAWMED	ACDERSSU	CRUSADES	ACDHOPTU	TOUCHPAD
ACDEMSTU	MUSCADET	ACDERSTT	DETRACTS	ACDHORRS	ORCHARDS
ACDEMUUV	VACUUMED		SCRATTED	ACDHORSY	DYSCHROA
ACDENNNO	CANNONED	ACDERSTU	TRADUCES	ACDIIILN	INDICIAL
	NONDANCE	ACDERTUV	CURVATED	ACDIIINS	INDICIAS
ACDENNNU	UNCANNED	ACDFFHNU	HANDCUFF	ACDIIIPR	DIAPIRIC
ACDENNOR	ORDNANCE	ACDFFIRT	DIFFRACT	ACDIIJLU	JUDICIAL
ACDENNOT	CANTONED	ACDFFLOS	SCAFFOLD	ACDIIKLP	PICKADIL
ACDENNST	SCANDENT	ACDFIILU	FIDUCIAL	ACDIILMS	DISCLAIM
ACDENOPR	ENDOCARP	ACDFILMR	FILMCARD	ACDIILNO	CONIDIAL
ACDENORR	RANCORED	ACDFILOU	FUCOIDAL	ACDIILNS	SCALDINI
ACDENORS	DRACONES	ACDFINOR	FRICANDO	ACDIILOV	OVICIDAL
	ENDOSARC	ACDFIOST	FACTOIDS	ACDIILSU	SUICIDAL
ACDENORT	CARTONED	ACDGHINY	DAYCHING	ACDIILTY	CALIDITY
	NOTECARD	ACDGHOTW	DOGWATCH		DIALYTIC
ACDENORY	CRAYONED		WATCHDOG	ACDIIMNO	DAIMONIC
	DEACONRY	ACDGIILO	DIALOGIC	ACDIIMOR	CORMIDIA
ACDENOST	ENDOCAST	ACDGIIMS	DIGICAMS		DIORAMIC
	TACNODES	ACDGILNN	CANDLING	ACDIIMOT	DIATOMIC
ACDENOSY	CYANOSED	ACDGILNR	CRADLING	ACDIIMSU	ASCIDIUM
ACDENOTT	COATTEND	ACDGILNS	SCALDING	ACDIINNO	CONIDIAN
ACDENOTU	OUTDANCE	ACDGILNU	CAUDLING	ACDIINNS	INDICANS
	UNCOATED	ACDGIMOT	DOGMATIC	ACDIINNT	INDICANT
ACDENPPU	UNCAPPED	ACDGINNS	DANCINGS	ACDIINOP	PINACOID
ACDENPRU	PRAUNCED	ACDGINNY	CANDYING	ACDIINOT	ACTINOID
ACDENPST	PANDECTS	ACDGINRS	CARDINGS		DIATONIC
ACDENRST	CANTREDS	ACDGINSU	SCAUDING	ACDIINPY	PYCNIDIA
ACDENRSU	DURANCES	ACDGIOPR	PODAGRIC	ACDIINRS	ACRIDINS
ACDENRTU	UNCARTED	ACDGKLOS	DAGLOCKS	ACDIIORV	VARICOID
	UNCRATED	ACDGLNOO	GOLCONDA	ACDIIOSS	ACIDOSIS
	UNDERACT	ACDGNOST	CANTDOGS	ACDIIOSX	OXIDASIC
	UNTRACED	ACDGORST	DOGCARTS	ACDIIRSS	SCIARIDS
ACDENRUV	UNCARVED	ACDHIILS	CHILIADS	ACDIIRST	ARCTIIDS
ACDENRVY	VERDANCY	ACDHIINT	TACHINID		CARDITIS
ACDENSST	DESCANTS	ACDHIIPS	DIPHASIC		TRIACIDS
ACDENSUU	UNCAUSED	ACDHIKNP	HANDPICK		TRIADICS
ACDENTTY	DANCETTY	ACDHIKOR	CHOKIDAR	ACDIIRTY	ACRIDITY
ACDEOORS	DOORCASE	ACDHIKOT	KATHODIC	ACDIISST	SADISTIC
ACDEOPRS	SCOREPAD	ACDHILNT	THINCLAD	ACDIKLTU	DUCKTAIL
ACDEOPRU	CROUPADE	ACDHILPR	PILCHARD	ACDIKMOO	COOKMAID
ACDEOPRY	COPYREAD	ACDHILPS	CLAPDISH	ACDIKRRY	RICKYARD
ACDEOPSS	PEASCODS	ACDHIMTW	MIDWATCH	ACDILLOS	CODILLAS
ACDEOPTT	CAPOTTED	ACDHINOR	HADRONIC	ACDILLOU	CAUDILLO
ACDEOPTU	OUTPACED		RHODANIC		LODICULA
ACDEORRS	CORRADES	ACDHINRY	DINARCHY	ACDILLPY	PLACIDLY
ACDEORRT	REDACTOR	ACDHINSW	SANDWICH	ACDILMOR	DROMICAL
ACDEORSS	SARCODES	ACDHIOPS	SCAPHOID	ACDILMOU	MUCOIDAL
ACDEORST	REDCOATS	ACDHIOPY	HYPOACID	ACDILMSS	CLADISMS
ACDEORSU	CAROUSED	ACDHIORY	HYRACOID	ACDILMTU	TALMUDIC
ACDEORTU	AERODUCT	ACDHIPST	DISPATCH	ACDILNOO	CONOIDAL
	EDUCATOR	ACDHIQRU	CHARQUID	ACDILNOR	IRONCLAD
	OUTRACED	ACDHIRRU	CHURIDAR	ACDILNOS	SCALDINO
ACDEORTV	CAVORTED	ACDHKORR	HARDROCK	ACDILNOT	ANTICOLD
ACDEOSTT	CODETTAS	ACDHLNOR	CHALDRON		DALTONIC
	COSTATED		CHLORDAN	ACDILNRY	RANCIDLY
ACDEOSUV	COUVADES		CHONDRAL	ACDILNSU	DULCIANS
ACDEOTTU	OUTACTED	ACDHLORS	DORLACHS	ACDILNSY	SYNDICAL
ACDEPPRS	SCRAPPED	ACDHMNTU	DUTCHMAN	ACDILNUU	NUDICAUL
ACDEPRSW	SCRAWPED	ACDHMORU	MOUCHARD	ACDILOPS	PLACOIDS

ACDILOPY	POLYACID	ACDLORWY	COWARDLY	ACEEFKOR	ECOFREAK
	POLYADIC	ACDLOSWY	LADYCOWS	ACEEFLPU	PEACEFUL
ACDILORS	CORDIALS	ACDLSTUY	DACTYLUS	ACEEFLSS	FACELESS
ACDILORT	DICROTAL	ACDMMNOO	COMMANDO	ACEEFLTV	FACETELY
ACDILOUV	OVIDUCAL	ACDMMNOS	COMMANDS	ACEEFNSY	FAYENCES
ACDILPSU	CUSPIDAL	ACDMNOPS	COMPANDS	ACEEFPRR	PREFACER
ACDILRST	TRICLADS	ACDMNORY	DORMANCY	ACEEFPRS	PREFACES
ACDILSST	CLADISTS		MORDANCY	ACEEFPRT	PERFECTA
ACDILSTW	WILDCATS	ACDMOOPR	MACROPOD		PRAEFECT
ACDIMMSU	CADMIUMS	ACDMOOSW	CAMWOODS	ACEEFPTY	TYPEFACE
ACDIMNOO	CODOMAIN	ACDMORSZ	CZARDOMS	ACEEFRSU	FARCEUSE
	MONOACID	ACDMPRTU	DUMPCART	ACEEGHNR	ENCHARGE
ACDIMNOS	MANDIOCS	ACDNOORR	RONCADOR		RECHANGE
	MONACIDS	ACDNOORS	CARDOONS	ACEEGHNX	EXCHANGE
ACDIMNSU	MUSCADIN	ACDNOORT	ACRODONT	ACEEGHRR	RECHARGE
	SCANDIUM	ACDNOORV	CORDOVAN	ACEEGIKL	CAGELIKE
ACDIMNSY	DYNAMICS	ACDNOOTU	DUCATOON	ACEEGILS	ELEGIACS
ACDIMOOS	CAMOODIS	ACDNORRW	WARDCORN		LEGACIES
ACDIMOST	COADMITS	ACDNORSU	CANDOURS	ACEEGINS	AGENCIES
ACDIMOSY	DOCIMASY		CAUDRONS	ACEEGINT	AGENETIC
ACDINNOO	ANCONOID	ACDNOSTW	DOWNCAST	ACEEGIRS	GRAECISE
ACDINNOS	NONACIDS	ACDNOSUU	ADUNCOUS	ACEEGIRZ	GRAECIZE
ACDINNOY	ANODYNIC	ACDOOPPR	PODOCARP	ACEEGKNR	NECKGEAR
ACDINOPS	SPONDAIC	ACDOOPTY	OCTAPODY	ACEEGKRW	WRECKAGE
ACDINORS	SARDONIC	ACDOORST	OSTRACOD	ACEEGLNY	ELEGANCY
ACDINORT	TORNADIC		SCORDATO	ACEEGLPU	PUCELAGE
ACDINORW	CORDWAIN	ACDOPRST	POSTCARD	ACEEGNNT	TANGENCE
ACDINSST	DISCANTS	ACDOPSST	PODCASTS	ACEEGNOZ	COZENAGE
ACDINSTY	DYNASTIC	ACDORRWY	COWARDRY	ACEEGNRS	ENGRACES
ACDINTUY	ADUNCITY	ACDORSST	COSTARDS	ACEEGNRY	REAGENCY
ACDIOOTU	AUTOCOID	ACDORSSU	CRUSADOS	ACEEGNST	CENTAGES
ACDIOPRS	PICADORS	ACDORSUZ	CRUZADOS	ACEEGNSV	SCAVENGE
	SPORADIC	ACDRSSTU	CUSTARDS	ACEEGORR	RACEGOER
ACDIORRS	CORRIDAS	ACDRSTTU	DUSTCART	ACEEGORV	COVERAGE
ACDIORSS	SARCOIDS	ACDRSTUY	CUSTARDY	ACEEGOST	ECOTAGES
ACDIORST	CAROTIDS	ACEEEFRR	CAREFREE	ACEEGSSU	ESCUAGES
ACDIORTT	DICTATOR	ACEEEGLN	ELEGANCE	ACEEHHRU	HEUCHERA
ACDIOSTX	DOXASTIC	ACEEEGPR	CREEPAGE	ACEEHHST	CHEETAHS
ACDIOSTY	DYSTOCIA	ACEEEGRS	CARGEESE	ACEEHILR	LEACHIER
ACDIOSXY	OXYACIDS	ACEEEIPR	EARPIECE	ACEEHINT	ECHINATE
ACDIPRST	ADSCRIPT	ACEEEIPS	SEAPIECE	ACEEHIPR	PEACHIER
ACDIPSTY	DIPTYCAS	ACEEEKNT	NECKATEE	ACEEHIPS	CHEAPIES
ACDIQRSU	QUADRICS	ACEEELMR	CAMELEER	ACEEHIPT	EPITHECA
ACDIRSST	DRASTICS	ACEEENRR	CAREENER		PETECHIA
ACDIRSTT	DISTRACT	ACEEENRS	ENCREASE	ACEEHIRT	AETHERIC
ACDIRTWY	CITYWARD	ACEEENSV	EVANESCE		HETAERIC
ACDISTUV	VIADUCTS	ACEEEPSS	ESCAPEES	ACEEHIRV	ACHIEVER
ACDJNSTU	ADJUNCTS	ACEEERRR	CAREERER		CHIVAREE
ACDKKLUW	DUCKWALK	ACEEERRT	RECREATE	ACEEHIST	HICATEES
ACDKLOPS	PADLOCKS	ACEEERTT	ETCETERA	ACEEHISV	ACHIEVES
ACDKMMOR	DRAMMOCK	ACEEERTX	EXECRATE	ACEEHITV	ATCHIEVE
ACDKMPSU	MUDPACKS	ACEEESUV	EVACUEES	ACEEHKNS	SKEECHAN
ACDKOPRS	POCKARDS	ACEEFFIN	CAFFEINE	ACEEHKOS	HOECAKES
ACDLLORS	COLLARDS	ACEEFFOR	FOREFACE	ACEEHKTT	HACKETTE
ACDLNNOR	CORNLAND	ACEEFFRS	EFFACERS	ACEEHLMP	EMPLEACH
ACDLNOPR	CROPLAND	ACEEFFRT	AFFECTER	ACEEHLOS	SHOELACE
ACDLNORS	CALDRONS	ACEEFHNS	ENCHAFES	ACEEHLPS	PLEACHES
ACDLNORU	CAULDRON	ACEEFHWY	WHEYFACE	ACEEHLRS	LEACHERS
	CRUNODAL	ACEEFILM	MALEFICE		RELACHES
ACDLNORY	CONDYLAR	ACEEFILR	LIFECARE	ACEEHLSS	LACHESES
ACDLNOST	COTLANDS	ACEEFILS	CALEFIES	ACEEHLST	CHELATES
ACDLNSSU	SUNSCALD	ACEEFINS	FAIENCES	ACEEHLSW	ESCHEWAL
ACDLOOOR	COLORADO		FIANCEES	ACEEHLTV	CHEVALET
ACDLOORT	DOCTORAL	ACEEFISS	CASEFIES	ACEEHMNP	CAMPHENE

ACEEHMNR	MENARCHE		RACEMISE	ACEELNSV	ENCLAVES
ACEEHMRS	CASHMERE	ACEEIMRT	CEMITARE		VALENCES
	MACHREES	ACEEIMRZ	RACEMIZE	ACEELNTT	TENTACLE
	MARCHESE	ACEEIMST	EMICATES	ACEELNTU	NUCLEATE
ACEEHMST	MACHETES	ACEEINNR	NARCEINE	ACEELOPS	ESCALOPE
ACEEHNNR	ENHANCER	ACEEINPS	SAPIENCE		OPALESCE
ACEEHNNS	ENHANCES	ACEEINPT	PATIENCE	ACEELORS	ESCAROLE
ACEEHNPS	CHEAPENS	ACEEINRS	CINEREAS	ACEELORT	CORELATE
ACEEHNRS	ENARCHES		INCREASE		RELOCATE
	ENCHASER		RESIANCE	ACEELOSS	SECALOSE
ACEEHNRV	REVANCHE	ACEEINRT	CENTIARE	ACEELOSV	VOCALESE
ACEEHNSS	ENCASHES		CREATINE	ACEELPPR	PREPLACE
	ENCHASES		INCREATE	ACEELPRR	PRECLEAR
ACEEHOOT	OOTHECAE		ITERANCE		REPLACER
ACEEHOPT	APOTHECE	ACEEINST	CINEASTE	ACEELPRS	PERCALES
ACEEHORT	OCHREATE	ACEEINSU	EUCAINES		REPLACES
ACEEHPPS	ECHAPPES	ACEEINTV	ENACTIVE	ACEELPRT	PRAELECT
ACEEHPRR	PREACHER	ACEEINTX	EXITANCE	ACEELPST	CAPELETS
ACEEHPRS	PEACHERS	ACEEIPPR	PRAECIPE	ACEELPSY	CYPSELAE
	PREACHES	ACEEIPST	SPECIATE	ACEELPTU	PECULATE
ACEEHPRT	ETHERCAP	ACEEIQRU	ACQUIREE	ACEELPTY	CLYPEATE
ACEEHPST	CHEAPEST	ACEEIRRS	CARIERES	ACEELRRS	CLEARERS
ACEEHQSU	QUEACHES		CREASIER	ACEELRSS	CARELESS
ACEEHRRS	REACHERS	ACEEIRSU	CAUSERIE		RESCALES
	RESEARCH	ACEEIRSW	WISEACRE	ACEELRST	CLEAREST
	SEARCHER	ACEEIRTV	CREATIVE		SCELERAT
ACEEHRRT	TREACHER		REACTIVE		TREACLES
ACEEHRSS	SEARCHES	ACEEISTV	VESICATE	ACEELRSV	CERVELAS
ACEEHRST	CHEATERS	ACEEJKNS	JACKEENS		CLEAVERS
	HECTARES	ACEEJKRT	REJACKET	ACEELRTT	RACLETTE
	RECHATES	ACEEKLMR	MACKEREL	ACEELRTU	ULCERATE
	RECHEATS	ACEEKLRT	RETACKLE	ACEELRTV	CERVELAT
	TEACHERS	ACEEKLRW	EELWRACK	ACEELRTX	EXCRETAL
ACEEHRTT	CATHETER	ACEEKMPT	EMPACKET	ACEELSST	CELESTAS
ACEEHRTY	CHEATERY	ACEEKNPS	KNEECAPS		SELECTAS
ACEEHSST	ESCHEATS	ACEEKNRW	NECKWEAR	ACEELSSU	EUCLASES
ACEEHSTX	CATHEXES	ACEEKRRT	RACKETER	ACEELSTT	TELECAST
	EXCHEATS	ACEELLMT	CELLMATE	ACEELSVX	EXCLAVES
ACEEHTTV	CHAVETTE	ACEELLNS	NACELLES	ACEEMMOT	AMMOCETE
ACEEHTWY	WATCHEYE	ACEELLNT	LANCELET	ACEEMNNS	SCENEMAN
ACEEIKLL	LACELIKE	ACEELLOT	OCELLATE	ACEEMNOT	MECONATE
ACEEIKLV	CAVELIKE	ACEELLPT	CAPELLET	ACEEMNPS	SPACEMEN
ACEEIKMR	ICEMAKER	ACEELLRR	CELLARER	ACEEMNRS	MENACERS
ACEEIKNP	PEACENIK		RECALLER	ACEEMNST	CASEMENT
ACEEIKRR	CREAKIER	ACEELLRT	CELLARET	ACEEMOPR	CAMPOREE
ACEEILLM	MICELLAE	ACEELLRV	CREVALLE	ACEEMOPT	COPEMATE
ACEEILLP	CALLIPEE	ACEELLSS	LACELESS	ACEEMORS	RACEMOSE
ACEEILMN	CAMELINE	ACEELMNO	CAMELEON	ACEEMORV	OVERCAME
ACEEILMT	EMETICAL	ACEELMNP	PLACEMEN	ACEEMRRS	AMERCERS
ACEEILMU	LEUCEMIA	ACEELMPS	EMPLACES		CREAMERS
ACEEILNP	CAPELINE	ACEELMRS	RECLAMES		SCREAMER
ACEEILNR	CARELINE		SCLEREMA	ACEEMRRY	CREAMERY
	CINEREAL	ACEELNPR	PRECLEAN	ACEEMRST	CREMATES
	RELIANCE	ACEELNPT	PENTACLE		MEERCATS
ACEEILNS	SALIENCE	ACEELNRR	LARCENER	ACEEMRTW	CREWMATE
ACEEILPS	CALIPEES	ACEELNRS	CLEANERS	ACEENNPS	PENANCES
	ESPECIAL		CLEANSER	ACEENNRS	NARCEENS
ACEEILRS	ESCALIER		RECLEANS	ACEENNRT	ENTRANCE
ACEEILRV	RECEIVAL	ACEELNRU	CERULEAN	ACEENNST	CANTEENS
ACEEIMOT	ACOEMETI	ACEELNRV	VERNACLE	ACEENNSY	CAYENNES
ACEEIMRR	CREAMIER	ACEELNSS	CLEANSES	ACEENOPT	CONEPATE
	REARMICE	ACEELNST	CLEANEST	ACEENORT	CAROTENE
	RECAMIER		LATENCES	ACEENOST	ACETONES
ACEEIMRS	CASIMERE	ACEELNSU	NUCLEASE		NOTECASE

ACEENPRR	PARCENER	**ACEFFISS**	SCAFFIES	**ACEFNPRT**	PENCRAFT
ACEENPRT	PERCEANT	**ACEFFLLU**	FULLFACE	**ACEFNRST**	CANTREFS
	PREENACT	**ACEFFLRS**	SCLAFFER	**ACEFNRSU**	FURNACES
ACEENRRT	RECANTER	**ACEFFORS**	AFFORCES	**ACEFOOPT**	FOOTPACE
	RECREANT	**ACEFGINN**	ENFACING	**ACEFOORT**	FOOTRACE
ACEENRSS	CASERNES	**ACEFGINR**	REFACING	**ACEFOPST**	POSTFACE
ACEENRST	CENTARES	**ACEFGINT**	FACETING	**ACEFORRS**	FORECARS
	ENCASTRE	**ACEFGIPS**	PIGFACES	**ACEFORST**	FORECAST
	REASCENT	**ACEFGLRU**	GRACEFUL	**ACEFORSX**	CARFOXES
	REENACTS	**ACEFGLSU**	CAGEFULS	**ACEFOSTU**	OUTFACES
	SARCENET	**ACEFGOST**	GEOFACTS	**ACEFRRSS**	SCARFERS
ACEENRTU	ENACTURE	**ACEFHIKS**	FISHCAKE	**ACEFRRST**	CRAFTERS
	UNCREATE	**ACEFHISV**	CAVEFISH		REFRACTS
ACEENSSS	CASSENES	**ACEFHLNS**	FLANCHES	**ACEFRRSU**	FARCEURS
ACEENSTX	EXSECANT	**ACEFHMRS**	CHAMFERS		SURFACER
ACEEOQTU	COEQUATE	**ACEFHORS**	ARCHFOES	**ACEFRRTU**	FRACTURE
ACEEORST	CREASOTE	**ACEFHORU**	FAROUCHE	**ACEFRSSU**	SURFACES
ACEEOSSS	CASEOSES	**ACEFHRST**	FRATCHES	**ACEFRSTU**	FACTURES
ACEEOSTT	ECOSTATE	**ACEFHRSU**	CHAUFERS		FURCATES
ACEEOSTV	EVOCATES	**ACEFIILS**	FELICIAS	**ACEGGILN**	CAGELING
ACEEPRRS	CAPERERS	**ACEFIIPR**	PACIFIER		GLACEING
ACEEPRRT	RECARPET	**ACEFIIPS**	PACIFIES	**ACEGGILR**	CLAGGIER
ACEEPRSS	ESCAPERS	**ACEFIIRT**	ARTIFICE	**ACEGGINN**	ENCAGING
	RESPACES	**ACEFIKLL**	CALFLIKE	**ACEGGIOP**	EPAGOGIC
ACEEPRTT	ETTERCAP	**ACEFILLS**	ICEFALLS	**ACEGGIRR**	CRAGGIER
ACEEPRTU	PERACUTE	**ACEFILLY**	FACILELY	**ACEGHIIT**	CHIGETAI
ACEEPRTX	EXCERPTA	**ACEFILOP**	EPIFOCAL	**ACEGHILN**	LEACHING
ACEEPSST	PECTASES	**ACEFILOS**	FASCIOLE	**ACEGHILT**	LICHGATE
ACEEPSSU	AUCEPSES		FOCALISE		TEIGLACH
ACEEPSTT	PECTATES	**ACEFILOZ**	FOCALIZE	**ACEGHINP**	CHEAPING
	SPECTATE	**ACEFILRS**	FILACERS		PEACHING
ACEEPSTY	TYPECASE	**ACEFILRY**	FIRECLAY	**ACEGHINR**	REACHING
ACEERRRT	RETRACER	**ACEFIMNY**	FEMINACY	**ACEGHINT**	CHEATING
ACEERRSS	CARESSER	**ACEFIMPR**	CAMPFIRE		TEACHING
	CREASERS	**ACEFINNS**	FINANCES	**ACEGHLOS**	GALOCHES
ACEERRST	CATERERS	**ACEFINRS**	FANCIERS	**ACEGHLRS**	SCHLAGER
	RECRATES		FRANCISE	**ACEGHLRU**	RUGELACH
	RETRACES	**ACEFINRX**	CARNIFEX	**ACEGHLTY**	LYCHGATE
	TERRACES	**ACEFINRZ**	FRANCIZE	**ACEGHLUY**	GAUCHELY
ACEERRSU	ECRASEUR	**ACEFINSS**	FASCINES	**ACEGHMMU**	CHUMMAGE
ACEERRTU	CREATURE	**ACEFINST**	FANCIEST	**ACEGHMOR**	ECHOGRAM
ACEERRUV	VERRUCAE	**ACEFINSU**	UNIFACES		GRAMOCHE
ACEERSSS	CARESSES	**ACEFIOSS**	FIASCOES	**ACEGHNPU**	CHANGEUP
ACEERSST	CATERESS	**ACEFIPRY**	REPACIFY	**ACEGHNRS**	CHANGERS
	CERASTES	**ACEFIRRT**	CRAFTIER	**ACEGHNRU**	UNCHARGE
ACEERSSU	SURCEASE	**ACEFIRTT**	TRIFECTA	**ACEGHNSU**	CHAUNGES
ACEERSSV	CREVASSE	**ACEFIRTY**	FERACITY		GAUNCHES
ACEERSTU	SECATEUR	**ACEFISST**	FACTISES	**ACEGHOSU**	GOUACHES
ACEERSTX	EXACTERS	**ACEFKLRS**	FLACKERS	**ACEGHOSW**	COWHAGES
ACEERSVZ	CERVEZAS	**ACEFKLRY**	FLACKERY	**ACEGHRRS**	CHARGERS
ACEERTTU	ERUCTATE	**ACEFKLST**	FLACKETS	**ACEGHRTU**	RECAUGHT
ACEESSST	ECSTASES	**ACEFLLSS**	CALFLESS	**ACEGHSTU**	GAUCHEST
ACEESSTT	CASETTES	**ACEFLMNO**	FLAMENCO	**ACEGIIMP**	EPIGAMIC
	CASSETTE	**ACEFLNOR**	FALCONER	**ACEGIINR**	REAGINIC
ACEESTTX	EXACTEST	**ACEFLNOT**	CONFLATE	**ACEGIINV**	VICINAGE
ACEFFGIN	EFFACING		FALCONET	**ACEGIKNR**	CREAKING
ACEFFHIR	CHAFFIER	**ACEFLNRY**	CRANEFLY	**ACEGILLO**	COLLEGIA
ACEFFHIS	AFFICHES	**ACEFLORS**	ALFRESCO	**ACEGILLR**	ALLERGIC
ACEFFHRS	CHAFFERS	**ACEFLRTU**	CRATEFUL	**ACEGILMU**	MUCILAGE
ACEFFHRU	CHAUFFER		FULCRATE	**ACEGILMY**	GLYCEMIA
ACEFFHRY	CHAFFERY	**ACEFLRUU**	FURCULAE	**ACEGILNN**	CLEANING
ACEFFILT	FACELIFT	**ACEFMNOO**	MOONFACE		ELANCING
ACEFFIMS	CAFFEISM	**ACEFNNOS**	FACONNES		ENLACING
ACEFFINS	CAFFEINS	**ACEFNORV**	CONFERVA	**ACEGILNR**	CLEARING

	RELACING				
	RELACING	ACEGKOST	STOCKAGE	ACEHIJNT	JACINTHE
ACEGILNT	CLEATING	ACEGKRTU	TRUCKAGE	ACEHIKLP	KEPHALIC
ACEGILNV	CLEAVING	ACEGLLNO	COLLAGEN	ACEHIKLR	CHALKIER
ACEGILNW	LACEWING	ACEGLLOS	COLLAGES		HACKLIER
ACEGILOS	CALIGOES	ACEGLNOS	CONGEALS	ACEHIKLW	LICHWAKE
ACEGILPS	PELAGICS		LONGCASE	ACEHIKRS	KACHERIS
ACEGILRS	GLACIERS	ACEGLNOT	OCTANGLE	ACEHIKRW	WHACKIER
	GRACILES	ACEGLNOY	AGLYCONE	ACEHILLS	CHALLIES
ACEGILRV	CLAVIGER	ACEGLNRS	CLANGERS	ACEHILLT	HELLICAT
ACEGILRY	GLYCERIA		GLANCERS	ACEHILMN	INCHMEAL
ACEGILSS	GLACISES	ACEGLOST	CATELOGS	ACEHILMO	CHOLEMIA
ACEGILST	GELASTIC	ACEGLOSU	CAGOULES	ACEHILMP	IMPLEACH
	GESTICAL	ACEGMNOY	GEOMANCY	ACEHILMS	CAMELISH
ACEGIMMT	TAGMEMIC	ACEGMNRS	CRAGSMEN		LECHAIMS
ACEGIMNN	MENACING	ACEGMOPS	COMPAGES	ACEHILMY	LECHAYIM
ACEGIMNO	CAMEOING	ACEGMORS	SCARMOGE	ACEHILNP	CEPHALIN
ACEGIMNR	AMERCING	ACEGMRRY	GRAMERCY	ACEHILNT	CHAINLET
	CREAMING	ACEGNNOR	CRANNOGE		CHATLINE
	GERMANIC	ACEGNNOY	CYANOGEN		ETHNICAL
ACEGIMNS	MAGNESIC	ACEGNNRY	REGNANCY	ACEHILOR	HALICORE
ACEGIMNT	MAGNETIC	ACEGNNTY	TANGENCY		HEROICAL
ACEGIMOS	CAMOGIES	ACEGNORS	ACROGENS	ACEHILPR	PARHELIC
ACEGIMOX	EXOGAMIC		CORNAGES	ACEHILPY	PEACHILY
ACEGIMRR	GRIMACER	ACEGNOST	COAGENTS	ACEHILRR	CHARLIER
ACEGIMRS	GRIMACES		COGNATES	ACEHILRS	CHARLIES
ACEGIMTY	MEGACITY	ACEGNSSY	CAGYNESS	ACEHILST	ETHICALS
ACEGINNO	CANOEING	ACEGOORS	CARGOOSE	ACEHILTT	ATHLETIC
ACEGINNR	ENRACING	ACEGOPRY	GEOCARPY		THETICAL
	RECANING	ACEGORSS	CORSAGES	ACEHIMMS	CHAMMIES
ACEGINNS	ENCASING		SOCAGERS	ACEHIMNN	CHAINMEN
ACEGINNT	ENACTING	ACEGORST	ESCARGOT		CHINAMEN
ACEGINNV	ENCAVING	ACEGORSU	COURAGES	ACEHIMNP	CAMPHINE
ACEGINOS	COINAGES	ACEGORTT	COTTAGER	ACEHIMNR	CHAIRMEN
ACEGINOY	GYNOECIA	ACEGORTY	CATEGORY	ACEHIMNS	MACHINES
ACEGINPR	CAPERING	ACEGOSTT	COTTAGES	ACEHIMNT	ANTHEMIC
	PEARCING	ACEGOTTY	COTTAGEY	ACEHIMNU	ACHENIUM
	PREACING	ACEGRSTU	TRUCAGES	ACEHIMPR	CAMPHIRE
ACEGINPS	ESCAPING	ACEGSSTU	SCUTAGES	ACEHIMPT	EMPATHIC
ACEGINRS	CREASING	ACEGSTTU	CUTTAGES		EMPHATIC
	GRECIANS	ACEHHINS	HAINCHES	ACEHIMRS	CHASMIER
	SEARCING	ACEHHIPS	CHEAPISH		CHIMERAS
ACEGINRT	ARGENTIC	ACEHHIRR	HIERARCH		MARCHESI
	CATERING	ACEHHIST	SHECHITA	ACEHIMRT	RHEMATIC
	CITRANGE	ACEHHISU	HUISACHE	ACEHIMSS	CHAMISES
	CREATING	ACEHHLST	HATCHELS	ACEHIMST	HEMATICS
	REACTING	ACEHHLSU	SHAUCHLE		MASTICHE
ACEGINSS	CAGINESS	ACEHHMNN	HENCHMAN		MISTEACH
	CEASINGS	ACEHHNRT	ETHNARCH		TACHISME
ACEGINTT	TACETING	ACEHHNSU	HAUNCHES	ACEHIMTT	THEMATIC
ACEGINTX	EXACTING	ACEHHPRT	HEPTARCH	ACEHIMTZ	MECHITZA
ACEGIOTT	COGITATE	ACEHHRST	HATCHERS	ACEHINNS	ENCHAINS
ACEGIPRS	SPAGERIC	ACEHHRSU	HACHURES	ACEHINOT	ETHANOIC
ACEGIRST	AGRESTIC	ACEHHRTT	THATCHER		INCHOATE
	CIGARETS	ACEHHRTY	HATCHERY	ACEHINOX	HEXANOIC
	ERGASTIC		THEARCHY	ACEHINPS	PAINCHES
ACEGISTU	GAUCIEST	ACEHHRXY	HEXARCHY	ACEHINPT	HAPTENIC
ACEGISTW	GAWCIEST	ACEHHSTT	HATCHETS	ACEHINRS	ARCHINES
ACEGJKLS	JACKLEGS		THATCHES		INARCHES
ACEGKLOS	LOCKAGES	ACEHHTTY	HATCHETY	ACEHINRV	VACHERIN
ACEGKLOV	GAVELOCK	ACEHIIMS	ISCHEMIA	ACEHINSS	ACHINESS
ACEGKLRS	GRACKLES	ACEHIINT	ETHICIAN		INCHASES
ACEGKMOS	MOCKAGES	ACEHIIRT	HETAIRIC	ACEHINST	ASTHENIC
ACEGKORS	CORKAGES		HIERATIC		CHANTIES
ACEGKORW	CAGEWORK	ACEHIJKR	HIJACKER	ACEHINSY	HYACINES

	SYNECHIA	ACEHLMOT	CHAMELOT	ACEHNNOT	NANOTECH
ACEHIOPR	POACHIER	ACEHLMST	CHAMLETS	ACEHNNPT	PENCHANT
ACEHIOST	ACHIOTES	ACEHLNNS	CHANNELS	ACEHNNRS	CHANNERS
	TOISEACH	ACEHLNOS	CHALONES	ACEHNNST	ENCHANTS
ACEHIPPR	CHAPPIER	ACEHLNOU	EULACHON	ACEHNOPR	CANEPHOR
ACEHIPPS	CHAPPIES	ACEHLNPS	PLANCHES		CHAPERON
ACEHIPRS	ASPHERIC	ACEHLNPT	PLANCHET	ACEHNOPS	PANOCHES
	CHARPIES	ACEHLNRS	CHARNELS	ACEHNOPT	CENOTAPH
	PARCHESI	ACEHLNRU	LAUNCHER	ACEHNORR	RANCHERO
	SERAPHIC		RELAUNCH	ACEHNORT	ANCHORET
ACEHIPRT	CHAPITER	ACEHLNST	STANCHEL	ACEHNPRT	PENTARCH
	PATCHIER	ACEHLNSU	LAUNCHES	ACEHNPRU	UNPREACH
	PHREATIC	ACEHLOOT	OOTHECAL	ACEHNPSU	PAUNCHES
ACEHIPST	HEPATICS	ACEHLOPT	POTLACHE	ACEHNRRS	RANCHERS
	PASTICHE	ACEHLORS	CHOLERAS	ACEHNRSS	ARCHNESS
	PISTACHE		CHORALES	ACEHNRST	CHANTERS
ACEHIPTT	PATHETIC	ACEHLORT	CHELATOR		SNATCHER
ACEHIPTW	WHITECAP		CHLORATE		STANCHER
ACEHIQSU	QUAICHES		TROCHLEA		TRANCHES
ACEHIRRR	CHARRIER	ACEHLORU	LEACHOUR	ACEHNRSU	RAUNCHES
ACEHIRSS	CASHIERS	ACEHLOST	CATHOLES	ACEHNRSW	CRENSHAW
	RACHISES		CHOLATES	ACEHNRTT	TRANCHET
ACEHIRST	CHARIEST		ESCHALOT	ACEHNRTU	CHAUNTER
	STICHERA	ACEHLPRT	CHAPTREL	ACEHNSSS	SCHANSES
	THERIACS	ACEHLPRY	CHAPELRY	ACEHNSST	CHASTENS
ACEHIRSU	EUCHARIS	ACEHLPSS	CHAPLESS		SNATCHES
ACEHIRSV	ARCHIVES	ACEHLPST	CHAPLETS		STANCHES
ACEHIRSW	ARCHWISE	ACEHLRSS	CLASHERS	ACEHNSSZ	SCHANZES
ACEHIRTT	CHATTIER		RASCHELS	ACEHNSTT	ETCHANTS
	THEATRIC	ACEHLRST	ARCHLETS	ACEHNSTU	NAUTCHES
ACEHISST	CHASTISE		TRACHLES		UNCHASTE
	TAISCHES	ACEHLRSY	CHARLEYS	ACEHNSTY	CHANTEYS
ACEHISSU	CHIAUSES	ACEHLRTU	ARCHLUTE	ACEHNSTZ	SCHANTZE
ACEHISTT	CHATTIES		TRAUCHLE	ACEHNSZZ	CHAZZENS
	TACHISTE	ACEHLSSS	CASHLESS	ACEHOPPR	COPPERAH
ACEHISTX	CATHEXIS	ACEHLSST	SATCHELS	ACEHOPRR	REPROACH
ACEHISTY	YACHTIES		SLATCHES	ACEHOPRS	POACHERS
ACEHISTZ	ZAITECHS	ACEHLSTT	CHATTELS	ACEHOPSS	SHOEPACS
ACEHKLLS	SHELLACK		LATCHETS	ACEHORRS	HORSECAR
ACEHKLOV	HAVELOCK	ACEHLSTY	CHASTELY	ACEHORRV	OVERARCH
ACEHKLPR	KREPLACH	ACEHMMNR	MARCHMEN	ACEHORST	CHAROSET
ACEHKLRS	HACKLERS	ACEHMNNR	RANCHMEN		THORACES
	SHACKLER	ACEHMNOP	PHONECAM	ACEHORTT	THEOCRAT
ACEHKLSS	SHACKLES	ACEHMNOR	CHOREMAN	ACEHORTU	OUTREACH
ACEHKLST	HACKLETS	ACEHMNRS	ENCHARMS	ACEHORUV	AVOUCHER
	KLATCHES	ACEHMNRT	MERCHANT	ACEHOSSW	SHOWCASE
ACEHKLTY	LATCHKEY	ACEHMNSS	CHESSMAN	ACEHOSTU	CATHOUSE
ACEHKMPU	MUCKHEAP	ACEHMNST	MANCHETS		SOUTACHE
ACEHKNSY	HACKNEYS	ACEHMNTW	WATCHMEN	ACEHOSTY	CHAYOTES
ACEHKOPS	SHOEPACK	ACEHMNTY	YACHTMEN	ACEHOSUV	AVOUCHES
ACEHKORV	HAVOCKER	ACEHMORT	CHROMATE	ACEHOTTU	OUTCHEAT
ACEHKOSS	SHACKOES	ACEHMOST	MOSCHATE	ACEHPPSS	CHAPPESS
ACEHKOST	HOTCAKES	ACEHMPRS	CHAMPERS		SCHAPPES
ACEHKOSW	WHACKOES	ACEHMRRS	CHARMERS	ACEHPRRS	PRECRASH
ACEHKOTU	TUCKAHOE		MARCHERS	ACEHPRST	CHAPTERS
ACEHKRSW	WHACKERS	ACEHMRSS	SCHMEARS		PATCHERS
ACEHKRTW	THWACKER	ACEHMRST	MATCHERS	ACEHPRSU	PURCHASE
ACEHLLMO	MALLECHO	ACEHMRSU	CHAUMERS	ACEHPRTY	PATCHERY
ACEHLLOO	COALHOLE	ACEHMSST	SMATCHES		PETCHARY
ACEHLLOR	ORCHELLA	ACEHMSTT	MATCHETS	ACEHPSTY	SCYPHATE
ACEHLLPS	PELLACHS		SCHMATTE	ACEHQSTU	QUATCHES
ACEHLLSS	SHELLACS	ACEHMSTU	MUSTACHE	ACEHRRSS	CRASHERS
ACEHLLST	HELLCATS	ACEHMSTY	ECTHYMAS	ACEHRRST	CHARTERS
ACEHLLSU	HALLUCES	ACEHNNOP	PANCHEON		RECHARTS

	STARCHER	ACEIKLRY	CREAKILY	ACEILNNR	ENCRINAL
ACEHRRSV	CHARVERS	ACEIKMNN	NICKNAME	ACEILNOR	ACROLEIN
ACEHRRTT	TETRARCH	ACEIKMRS	KERAMICS		COLINEAR
ACEHRSST	STARCHES	ACEIKMRV	MAVERICK		CREOLIAN
ACEHRSSU	CHASSEUR	ACEIKNPS	CAPESKIN		LONICERA
ACEHRSTT	CHATTERS	ACEIKNRR	CRANKIER	ACEILNPS	CAPELINS
	RATCHETS	ACEIKNRS	SKINCARE		PANICLES
ACEHRSTW	WATCHERS	ACEIKNSS	CAKINESS		PELICANS
ACEHRSTY	YACHTERS	ACEIKOPS	PAIOCKES	ACEILNPT	PECTINAL
ACEHRTTY	CHATTERY	ACEIKORR	CROAKIER		PLANETIC
	TRACHYTE	ACEIKPRS	EARPICKS	ACEILNRS	CARLINES
ACEHSSSU	CHAUSSES	ACEIKPSW	WICKAPES		LANCIERS
ACEHSSTT	CHASTEST	ACEIKPSX	PICKAXES	ACEILNRT	CLARINET
ACEHSSTW	SWATCHES	ACEIKQRU	QUACKIER	ACEILNSS	LACINESS
ACEHSTTU	CATHETUS	ACEIKRRV	VRAICKER		SANICLES
	TEUCHATS	ACEIKSTT	TACKIEST	ACEILNST	CANISTEL
ACEHSTTW	WATCHETS		TIETACKS	ACEILNSU	AESCULIN
ACEHTTUZ	ZUCHETTA	ACEIKSTW	WACKIEST		LUNACIES
ACEIIKNT	AKINETIC	ACEILLLT	CLITELLA	ACEILNSY	SALIENCY
ACEIILMN	LIMACINE	ACEILLMR	MICELLAR	ACEILOPR	CAPRIOLE
ACEIILNR	IRENICAL		MILLRACE	ACEILOPT	POETICAL
ACEIILNS	SALICINE	ACEILLMS	LIMACELS	ACEILORR	CARRIOLE
ACEIILNX	ALEXINIC		MICELLAS	ACEILORS	CALORIES
ACEIILSS	LAICISES	ACEILLMT	METALLIC		CALORISE
ACEIILST	CILIATES	ACEILLMY	MYCELIAL		CARIOLES
	SILICATE	ACEILLNT	CLIENTAL	ACEILORT	EROTICAL
ACEIILSZ	LAICIZES	ACEILLOP	CALLIOPE		LORICATE
ACEIIMRS	CASIMIRE	ACEILLOR	ROCAILLE	ACEILORV	ARVICOLE
ACEIIMRV	VIRAEMIC	ACEILLOS	LOCALISE	ACEILORZ	CALORIZE
ACEIIMSS	ASEISMIC	ACEILLOT	LOCALITE	ACEILOSS	CELOSIAS
ACEIIMST	METICAIS		TEOCALLI		COALISES
ACEIIMTU	MAIEUTIC	ACEILLOZ	LOCALIZE	ACEILOST	ALOETICS
ACEIINPS	PISCINAE	ACEILLPR	CALLIPER		COALIEST
ACEIINRS	RIANCIES	ACEILLPS	ALLSPICE		SOCIETAL
ACEIINRT	ARENITIC	ACEILLPY	EPICALLY	ACEILOSU	EUSOCIAL
ACEIINST	ANTICISE	ACEILLRV	CAVILLER	ACEILOSV	VOCALISE
	CANITIES	ACEILLSS	SCALLIES	ACEILOSX	SAXICOLE
ACEIINTV	INACTIVE	ACEILMMO	CAMOMILE	ACEILOSZ	COALIZES
ACEIINTZ	ANTICIZE	ACEILMMR	CLAMMIER	ACEILOTV	LOCATIVE
ACEIIPRS	PIRACIES	ACEILMNN	CLINAMEN	ACEILOVZ	VOCALIZE
ACEIIPSS	EPISCIAS	ACEILMNO	COALMINE	ACEILPPY	PIPECLAY
ACEIIPTX	EPITAXIC	ACEILMNP	MANCIPLE	ACEILPRS	CALIPERS
ACEIIRRT	CRITERIA	ACEILMNS	MELANICS		REPLICAS
ACEIIRSV	VICARIES		MENISCAL		SPIRACLE
ACEIISTT	ATTICISE		MESCALIN	ACEILPRT	PARTICLE
ACEIISTU	ACUITIES	ACEILMNY	MYCELIAN		PRELATIC
ACEIISTV	ACTIVISE	ACEILMOS	CAMISOLE	ACEILPRU	PECULIAR
	CAITIVES	ACEILMPS	MISPLACE	ACEILPSS	SLIPCASE
	CAVITIES	ACEILMPT	PELMATIC		SPECIALS
	VICIATES	ACEILMRS	CLAIMERS	ACEILPST	PLICATES
ACEIITTV	VITICETA		MIRACLES		SEPTICAL
ACEIITTZ	ATTICIZE		RECLAIMS		TIECLASP
ACEIITVZ	ACTIVIZE	ACEILMRT	METRICAL	ACEILPSU	SPICULAE
ACEIJKSS	JACKSIES	ACEILMRY	CREAMILY	ACEILPTY	ETYPICAL
ACEIJMST	MAJESTIC	ACEILMST	CALMIEST	ACEILPXY	EPICALYX
ACEIJNRR	JERRICAN		CLEMATIS	ACEILRRT	CLARTIER
ACEIKKLS	SACKLIKE		CLIMATES	ACEILRRW	CRAWLIER
ACEIKKNR	KNACKIER		METICALS	ACEILRSS	CLASSIER
ACEIKLLM	CLAMLIKE	ACEILMSU	MUSICALE	ACEILRST	ALTRICES
	MILLCAKE	ACEILMSX	CLIMAXES		ARTICLES
ACEIKLLW	CLAWLIKE		EXCLAIMS		RECITALS
ACEIKLLY	CLAYLIKE	ACEILMTU	AMULETIC		SELICTAR
ACEIKLNR	CLANKIER	ACEILNNP	PANNICLE		STERICAL
ACEIKLRT	TALCKIER		PINNACLE	ACEILRSU	AURICLES

ACEILRSV	CALIVERS	ACEINNOT	ENACTION		ENTASTIC
	CAVILERS	ACEINNOZ	CANONIZE		NICTATES
	CLAVIERS	ACEINNPS	PINNACES		TETANICS
	VISCERAL	ACEINNRS	CRANNIES	ACEINSTV	CISTVAEN
ACEILRTT	TRACTILE		NARCEINS		VESICANT
ACEILRTU	RETICULA	ACEINNST	ANCIENTS	ACEINSTY	CYANITES
ACEILRTV	VERTICAL		CANNIEST	ACEINSTZ	ZINCATES
ACEILRTY	LITERACY		INSECTAN	ACEINSYZ	CYANIZES
ACEILRUV	ACERVULI		INSTANCE	ACEINTTU	TUNICATE
ACEILSST	ELASTICS	ACEINNSU	NUISANCE	ACEINTTX	EXCITANT
	SALICETS	ACEINNSY	CYANINES	ACEINTTY	TENACITY
	SCALIEST	ACEINNTU	UNCINATE	ACEINTUV	UNACTIVE
ACEILSTT	LATTICES	ACEINOPR	APOCRINE	ACEIOPRT	APORETIC
	TALCIEST		CAPONIER		OPERATIC
ACEILSTY	CLAYIEST		PROCAINE	ACEIOPST	ECTOPIAS
ACEILSUV	VESICULA	ACEINOPS	CANOPIES	ACEIOPVW	PICOWAVE
ACEILSVW	WAVICLES		CAPONISE	ACEIORSS	SCARIOSE
ACEILTVY	ACTIVELY		PAEONICS	ACEIORSV	COVARIES
ACEIMMNP	PEMMICAN	ACEINOPZ	CAPONIZE		VARICOSE
ACEIMMOS	SEMICOMA	ACEINORS	SCENARIO	ACEIOSST	SOCIATES
ACEIMMRS	RACEMISM	ACEINORT	ACTIONER	ACEIOSSU	CAESIOUS
ACEIMMTT	METAMICT		ANORETIC	ACEIOSTT	OSCITATE
ACEIMNNO	MONECIAN		CREATION	ACEIOTVV	VOCATIVE
ACEIMNOR	CORAMINE		REACTION	ACEIPPRR	CRAPPIER
ACEIMNOT	COINMATE	ACEINORV	VERONICA		PERICARP
ACEIMNOX	ANOXEMIC	ACEINORX	ANOREXIC	ACEIPPRS	CRAPPIES
ACEIMNPS	PEMICANS	ACEINOST	ACONITES		EPICARPS
ACEIMNRS	CARMINES		CANOEIST	ACEIPPST	TAPPICES
	CREMAINS		SONICATE	ACEIPRRS	PERISARC
ACEIMNRU	MANICURE	ACEINOTT	TACONITE	ACEIPRSS	SCRAPIES
ACEIMNSS	AMNESICS	ACEINOTV	CONATIVE	ACEIPRST	CRAPIEST
ACEIMNST	AMNESTIC		INVOCATE		CRISPATE
	SEMANTIC	ACEINOTX	EXACTION		PARETICS
ACEIMNSU	SEMUNCIA	ACEINOPQU	PIQUANCE		PICRATES
ACEIMNSY	SYCAMINE	ACEINPSS	INSCAPES		PRACTISE
ACEIMNTU	NEUMATIC		PINCASES	ACEIPRTV	PRACTIVE
ACEIMOPR	COPREMIA	ACEINPSY	SAPIENCY	ACEIPRTY	APYRETIC
ACEIMOPT	POEMATIC	ACEINPTT	PITTANCE	ACEIPSST	ASEPTICS
ACEIMOTX	TOXAEMIC	ACEINPUY	PICAYUNE		ESCAPIST
ACEIMOTZ	AZOTEMIC	ACEINRRU	CURARINE		SPACIEST
	METAZOIC	ACEINRRY	CINERARY	ACEIPSSU	AUSPICES
ACEIMPRR	CRAMPIER	ACEINRSS	ARCSINES	ACEIPSSZ	CAPSIZES
	MERICARP		ARSENICS	ACEIPSTV	CAPTIVES
ACEIMPRS	PARECISM		CERASINS	ACEIQRRU	ACQUIRER
	SAPREMIC		RACINESS	ACEIQRSU	ACQUIRES
ACEIMPRT	IMPACTER	ACEINRST	CANISTER	ACEIQSTU	ACQUITES
ACEIMPSS	ESCAPISM		CARNIEST	ACEIQSUZ	CAZIQUES
	MISSPACE		CERATINS	ACEIRRRS	CARRIERS
	SCAMPIES		CISTERNA		SCARRIER
ACEIMPST	CAMPIEST		CREATINS	ACEIRRST	ERRATICS
	CAMPSITE		NACRITES	ACEIRRSU	CURARISE
ACEIMPTU	PUMICATE		SCANTIER	ACEIRRSW	AIRCREWS
ACEIMRST	CERAMIST		TACRINES		AIRSCREW
	MATRICES	ACEINRTT	INTERACT	ACEIRRTT	RETRAICT
	MISTRACE	ACEINRTU	ANURETIC	ACEIRRTX	CREATRIX
	SCIMETAR	ACEINRTV	NAVICERT	ACEIRRTY	RETIRACY
ACEIMRTT	TREMATIC	ACEINRTX	XERANTIC	ACEIRRUZ	CURARIZE
ACEIMRTU	MURICATE	ACEINRVY	VICENARY	ACEIRSST	SCARIEST
ACEIMSST	CASTEISM	ACEINSSS	CASSINES	ACEIRSSU	SAUCIERS
	ETACISMS	ACEINSST	CINEASTS		SCAURIES
ACEIMSSU	CAESIUMS		SCANTIES		URICASES
ACEIMSTU	AUTECISM	ACEINSSU	ISSUANCE	ACEIRSSV	VICARESS
ACEIMTTU	MUTICATE	ACEINSSY	CYANISES	ACEIRSTT	CITRATES
ACEINNOS	CANONISE	ACEINSTT	CANTIEST		CRISTATE

	SCATTIER
ACEIRSTU	SURICATE
ACEIRSTZ	CRAZIEST
ACEIRTTU	URTICATE
ACEIRTTV	TRACTIVE
ACEIRTUV	CURATIVE
ACEIRTVY	VERACITY
ACEISSSS	CASSISES
ACEISSST	ECSTASIS
ACEISSSU	SAUCISSE
ACEISSTT	STATICES
ACEISSTU	SAUCIEST
	SUITCASE
ACEISTTT	CATTIEST
ACEISTTU	EUSTATIC
ACEISTTW	SCAWTITE
ACEISTUX	AUXETICS
ACEJKOOR	JACKEROO
ACEJKOPS	PAJOCKES
ACEJLORS	CAJOLERS
ACEJLORY	CAJOLERY
ACEJMRST	SCRAMJET
ACEJNNOO	JONCANOE
ACEJNOST	JACONETS
ACEJNOSY	JOYANCES
ACEJNRRY	JERRYCAN
ACEJNSTU	JUNCATES
ACEJPSTU	CAJEPUTS
ACEJRSTT	TRAJECTS
ACEKKMRU	MUCKRAKE
ACEKKNRS	KNACKERS
ACEKKNRY	KNACKERY
ACEKLLPS	PELLACKS
ACEKLNRS	CRANKLES
ACEKLNSS	SLACKENS
ACEKLNTU	UNTACKLE
ACEKLORS	EARLOCKS
ACEKLORV	LAVEROCK
ACEKLORW	LACEWORK
ACEKLPRS	SPRACKLE
ACEKLPSS	SPACKLES
ACEKLPST	PLACKETS
ACEKLQSU	QUACKLES
ACEKLRSS	SLACKERS
ACEKLRST	TACKLERS
ACEKLRSU	CAULKERS
ACEKLSSS	SACKLESS
ACEKLSST	SLACKEST
	TACKLESS
ACEKMNRT	TRACKMEN
ACEKMNST	TACKSMEN
ACEKMORS	COMAKERS
ACEKMRSS	SMACKERS
ACEKNNOW	ACKNOWNE
ACEKNPRS	PRANCKES
ACEKNPRU	UNPACKER
ACEKNPSS	PACKNESS
ACEKNRSS	SNACKERS
ACEKNRST	CRANKEST
ACEKOORT	CARETOOK
ACEKOORW	COOKWARE
ACEKOPRV	OVERPACK
ACEKOPRW	CAPEWORK
ACEKORRS	CROAKERS
ACEKORRV	OVERRACK
ACEKORSW	CASEWORK
ACEKPPRS	PREPACKS
ACEKPSSY	SKYSCAPE
ACEKQRSU	QUACKERS
ACEKQRUY	QUACKERY
ACEKRRST	RETRACKS
	TRACKERS
ACEKRRTY	RACKETRY
ACEKRSST	RESTACKS
	STACKERS
ACEKRSTT	RACKETTS
ACEKRSTU	RUCKSEAT
ACEKSSTT	STACKETS
ACEKSSUW	WAESUCKS
ACELLLRU	CELLULAR
ACELLMOS	CALOMELS
ACELLMSU	SACELLUM
ACELLMSY	MYCELLAS
ACELLNRU	NUCELLAR
ACELLOPS	COLLAPSE
	ESCALLOP
ACELLORR	CAROLLER
ACELLORS	CORELLAS
ACELLORT	COLLARET
ACELLORV	COVERALL
	OVERCALL
ACELLORW	CALLOWER
ACELLOSS	CALLOSES
	COALLESS
ACELLOST	COLLATES
ACELLOSW	COLESLAW
ACELLOTU	LOCULATE
ACELLOVY	COEVALLY
ACELLPSS	SCALPELS
ACELLRRS	CARRELLS
ACELLRTY	RECTALLY
ACELLSSU	CALLUSES
ACELLSSW	CLAWLESS
ACELLSTU	SCUTELLA
ACELLTWY	CETYWALL
ACELMMOU	MAMELUCO
ACELMMRS	CLAMMERS
ACELMNNS	CLANSMEN
ACELMNOR	AMELCORN
	CORNMEAL
ACELMNOU	COLUMNEA
ACELMNRU	CRUMENAL
ACELMNSS	CALMNESS
	CLASSMEN
ACELMOPT	COMPLEAT
ACELMORR	CLAMORER
ACELMORS	CAROMELS
	SCLEROMA
ACELMORY	CLAYMORE
ACELMOST	CAMELOTS
	MOLECAST
ACELMOSU	CAULOMES
	LEUCOMAS
	MACULOSE
ACELMPRS	CLAMPERS
ACELMPSY	ECLAMPSY
ACELMSSU	LACMUSES
ACELMSTU	CALUMETS
	MUSCATEL
ACELMSUU	SAECULUM
ACELMTUU	CUMULATE
ACELNNNO	CANNELON
ACELNNOS	ALENCONS
ACELNNRS	SCRANNEL
ACELNOOT	ECOTONAL
ACELNOPT	CONEPATL
ACELNORV	NOVERCAL
ACELNOSS	SECONALS
ACELNOST	LACTONES
ACELNOSU	LACUNOSE
ACELNOSZ	CALZONES
ACELNOTV	COVALENT
ACELNOVY	CONVEYAL
ACELNPSS	ENCLASPS
	SPANCELS
ACELNPST	CLAPNETS
ACELNPSU	CLEANUPS
	UNPLACES
ACELNRST	CENTRALS
ACELNRSU	LUCARNES
ACELNRVY	CRAVENLY
ACELNSST	SCANTLES
ACELNSSU	SCALENUS
	UNSCALES
ACELNSTT	CANTLETS
ACELNSTY	SECANTLY
ACELOOSU	ACOELOUS
ACELOPPU	POPULACE
ACELOPRS	PARCLOSE
	POLACRES
ACELOPRT	PECTORAL
ACELOPRU	OPERCULA
ACELOPSS	ESCALOPS
ACELOPST	POLECATS
ACELOPSU	SCOPULAE
ACELOPTU	COPULATE
	OUTPLACE
ACELOPTY	CALOTYPE
ACELOQSU	COEQUALS
ACELORRS	CAROLERS
ACELORRT	RECTORAL
ACELORSS	ESCOLARS
	LACROSSE
	SOLACERS
ACELORST	LOCATERS
	SECTORAL
ACELORSU	CAROUSEL
ACELORSY	CALOYERS
	COARSELY
ACELOSST	ALECOSTS
	COATLESS
	LACTOSES
	SCATOLES
ACELOSTT	CALOTTES
ACELOSTU	LACTEOUS
	LOCUSTAE
	OSCULATE
ACELOSTY	ACOLYTES
ACELOSUV	VACUOLES
ACELOTTY	CATOLYTE
ACELOTXY	ACETOXYL
ACELPPRS	CLAPPERS

	SCRAPPLE	**ACEMPRST**	CRAMPETS	**ACENSSTU**	NUTCASES
ACELPPSS	SCAPPLES	**ACEMPSSU**	CAMPUSES	**ACENSSTW**	NEWSCAST
ACELPRSS	CLASPERS	**ACEMRSST**	SCAMSTER	**ACENSSUU**	USAUNCES
	RECLASPS	**ACEMSSTT**	METCASTS	**ACEOOPPS**	APOCOPES
	SCALPERS	**ACENNNOU**	ANNOUNCE	**ACEOOPSU**	POACEOUS
ACELPRST	SCEPTRAL	**ACENNOSS**	CANONESS	**ACEOORTT**	COROTATE
	SPECTRAL		SONANCES	**ACEOORTV**	EVOCATOR
ACELPRSU	SPECULAR	**ACENNOSY**	NOYANCES		OVERCOAT
ACELPRTY	CALYPTER	**ACENNOSZ**	CANZONES	**ACEOPPRS**	COPPERAS
ACELPSSU	CAPSULES	**ACENNOTT**	COTENANT	**ACEOPRRT**	RECAPTOR
	SCALEUPS	**ACENNOTV**	COVENANT	**ACEOPRST**	POSTRACE
	UPSCALES	**ACENNOTZ**	CANZONET	**ACEOPRSX**	EXOCARPS
ACELPTUU	CUPULATE	**ACENNPRY**	PERNANCY	**ACEOPRTT**	ATTERCOP
ACELPTUY	EUCALYPT	**ACENNRSS**	SCANNERS	**ACEOPRTU**	OUTCAPER
ACELQRSU	CLAQUERS	**ACENNSUY**	SEACUNNY	**ACEOPSTU**	OUTPACES
	LACQUERS	**ACENOORT**	CORONATE		SAUCEPOT
ACELQRUU	CLAQUEUR	**ACENOOTZ**	ECTOZOAN	**ACEORRST**	ACROTERS
ACELQSUY	LACQUEYS	**ACENOPRT**	COPARENT		CREATORS
ACELRRSW	CRAWLERS		PORTANCE		REACTORS
	SCRAWLER	**ACENOPST**	CAPSTONE	**ACEORRSU**	CAROUSER
ACELRSSS	CLASSERS		OPENCAST	**ACEORRTT**	RETROACT
	SCARLESS	**ACENOPSU**	PONCEAUS	**ACEORRTU**	EUROCRAT
ACELRSST	SCARLETS	**ACENOQTU**	COTQUEAN	**ACEORRTV**	CAVORTER
ACELRSSU	RECUSALS	**ACENORRW**	CAREWORN	**ACEORRVW**	OVERCRAW
	SECULARS	**ACENORRY**	CRAYONER	**ACEORSST**	COARSEST
ACELRSTT	CLATTERS	**ACENORSS**	COARSENS		COASTERS
	SCRATTLE		NARCOSES	**ACEORSSU**	CAROUSES
ACELRSTU	RAUCLEST	**ACENORST**	ANCESTOR	**ACEORSTT**	SECTATOR
ACELRTTU	CULTRATE		ENACTORS	**ACEORSTU**	OUTRACES
ACELRTTY	CLATTERY		SARCONET	**ACEORSTV**	OVERACTS
ACELSSTT	TACTLESS		SORTANCE		OVERCAST
ACELSSTU	CUTLASES	**ACENORSU**	CARNEOUS	**ACEORSTX**	EXACTORS
ACELSSTY	SCYTALES		NACREOUS	**ACEORTUY**	EUCARYOT
ACELSSUX	EXCUSALS	**ACENORTT**	CONTRATE	**ACEOSSTU**	SEASCOUT
ACEMMOTY	MYCETOMA	**ACENORTU**	COURANTE	**ACEOSTTT**	COATTEST
ACEMMRRS	CRAMMERS		OUTRANCE	**ACEOSTTU**	OUTCASTE
ACEMMRSS	SCAMMERS	**ACENORTY**	ENACTORY	**ACEOSTTV**	CAVETTOS
ACEMNOOR	COENAMOR	**ACENORUY**	EUCARYON	**ACEOSTUU**	AUTOCUES
ACEMNORR	ROMANCER	**ACENOSSS**	CASSONES	**ACEOTUUX**	COUTEAUX
ACEMNORS	CREMONAS	**ACENOSST**	CONTESSA	**ACEOTUXY**	AUXOCYTE
	ROMANCES		COSTEANS	**ACEPPRRS**	CRAPPERS
ACEMNORU	CUMARONE	**ACENOSSV**	CAVESSON		SCRAPPER
ACEMNOST	CAMSTONE	**ACENOSSY**	CYANOSES	**ACEPRRSS**	SCARPERS
ACEMNPSS	CAMPNESS	**ACENOSTT**	CONSTATE		SCRAPPERS
ACEMNRUY	NUMERACY	**ACENOSTV**	CENTAVOS	**ACEPRRSU**	SUPERCAR
ACEMNSSU	MANCUSES	**ACENOTTU**	TOUCANET	**ACEPRRTU**	CAPTURER
ACEMOORS	ACROSOME	**ACENPRRS**	PRANCERS	**ACEPRSST**	PRECASTS
ACEMOOST	COMATOSE	**ACENPRSU**	ENCARPUS	**ACEPRSSU**	SCAUPERS
ACEMOPRR	COMPARER		PRAUNCES	**ACEPRSTU**	CAPTURES
ACEMOPRS	CAPSOMER	**ACENPSTT**	PENTACTS		PRESCUTA
	COMPARES	**ACENPTTU**	PUNCTATE	**ACEPSTTY**	TYPECAST
	COMPEARS	**ACENRSST**	CRANTSES	**ACEQRSTU**	RACQUETS
	MESOCARP	**ACENRSSU**	SURANCES	**ACEQSSTU**	ACQUESTS
ACEMOPRT	MERCAPTO	**ACENRSTT**	TRANECTS	**ACERRSTT**	RETRACTS
ACEMORRT	CREMATOR		TRANSECT	**ACERRSTU**	TRACEURS
ACEMORRV	OVERCRAM	**ACENRSTU**	CENTAURS	**ACERRSUV**	VERRUCAS
ACEMORSU	RACEMOUS		RECUSANT	**ACERSSST**	CRASSEST
ACEMORSW	CASEWORM		UNCRATES	**ACERSSSU**	SUCRASES
ACEMORSY	SYCAMORE		UNTRACES	**ACERSSTT**	SCATTERS
ACEMORTY	COMETARY	**ACENRSTY**	ANCESTRY	**ACERSSTY**	ACTRESSY
ACEMORUX	MORCEAUX	**ACENRTTU**	TRUNCATE	**ACERSTTT**	TETRACTS
ACEMOSSU	COASSUME	**ACENRTUY**	CENTAURY	**ACERSTTU**	CRUSTATE
ACEMPRRS	CRAMPERS		CYANURET	**ACERSTTX**	EXTRACTS
ACEMPRSS	SCAMPERS	**ACENSSTT**	SCANTEST	**ACERSTTY**	CYTASTER

	SCATTERY	**ACFIMORR**	ARCIFORM	**ACGHIKNT**	THACKING
ACERSTUX	CURTAXES	**ACFIMORS**	FORMICAS	**ACGHIKNW**	WHACKING
ACERTTUW	CUTWATER	**ACFIMOSS**	FASCISMO	**ACGHILNN**	LANCHING
ACFFGHIN	CHAFFING	**ACFIMSSS**	FASCISMS	**ACGHILNS**	CLASHING
ACFFHNOR	CHAFFRON	**ACFINORT**	FRACTION	**ACGHILNT**	LATCHING
ACFFIILO	OFFICIAL	**ACFINOST**	FACTIONS	**ACGHILNU**	LAUCHING
ACFFIIST	CAITIFFS	**ACFINPRS**	SCARFPIN	**ACGHILNY**	ACHINGLY
ACFFIKMS	MAFFICKS	**ACFINRST**	INFARCTS	**ACGHILOR**	OLIGARCH
ACFFILNU	FANCIFUL		INFRACTS	**ACGHIMNP**	CHAMPING
ACFFILST	AFFLICTS	**ACFINSTY**	SANCTIFY	**ACGHIMNR**	CHARMING
ACFFIRST	TRAFFICS	**ACFIOSTU**	FACTIOUS		MARCHING
ACFFKORT	OFFTRACK	**ACFIRTUY**	FURACITY	**ACGHIMNT**	MATCHING
ACFFLOSW	SCOFFLAW	**ACFISSST**	FASCISTS	**ACGHINNR**	RANCHING
ACFFOSST	CASTOFFS	**ACFKLLOR**	ROCKFALL	**ACGHINNT**	CHANTING
	OFFCASTS	**ACFKLORS**	FORSLACK	**ACGHINNU**	UNACHING
	OFFCASTS	**ACFKLOST**	LOCKFAST	**ACGHINOP**	POACHING
ACFGHINU	CHAUFING	**ACFKLRSU**	RACKFULS	**ACGHINOR**	ROACHING
ACFGHITT	CATFIGHT	**ACFKLRUW**	WRACKFUL	**ACGHINPP**	CHAPPING
ACFGIIMN	MAGNIFIC	**ACFKLSSU**	SACKFULS	**ACGHINPR**	PARCHING
ACFGIIPR	CAPRIFIG		SACKSFUL	**ACGHINPT**	NIGHTCAP
ACFGIKLN	FLACKING	**ACFKOSTT**	FATSTOCK		PATCHING
ACFGIKNR	FRACKING	**ACFLMNOO**	MOONCALF	**ACGHINRR**	CHARRING
ACFGINNY	FANCYING	**ACFLNNOO**	NONFOCAL	**ACGHINRS**	ARCHINGS
ACFGINRS	FARCINGS	**ACFLNORY**	FALCONRY		CHAGRINS
	SCARFING	**ACFLOOPS**	FOOLSCAP		CRASHING
ACFGINRT	CRAFTING	**ACFLOPSW**	COWFLAPS	**ACGHINRT**	CHARTING
	FRACTING	**ACFLORSU**	SCROFULA		RATCHING
ACFGITUY	FUGACITY	**ACFLOTTU**	FLOATCUT	**ACGHINRU**	CHURINGA
ACFGKNOP	PACKFONG	**ACFLRRUU**	FURCULAR		NURAGHIC
ACFGLNOR	CORNFLAG	**ACFLRSTU**	CARTFULS	**ACGHINSS**	CHASINGS
ACFHHINW	HAWFINCH	**ACFMOTTU**	FACTOTUM	**ACGHINST**	SCATHING
ACFHIJKS	JACKFISH	**ACFNNOST**	NONFACTS	**ACGHINSW**	CHINWAGS
ACFHILNO	FALCHION	**ACFNRSTU**	FRUCTANS	**ACGHINTT**	CHATTING
ACFHILOS	COALFISH	**ACFRRSTU**	FRACTURS	**ACGHINTW**	WATCHING
ACFHINOU	FAUCHION	**ACGGGILN**	CLAGGING	**ACGHINTY**	YACHTING
ACFHIRSS	SCARFISH	**ACGGGINS**	SCAGGING	**ACGHINUV**	VAUCHING
ACFHIRSW	CRAWFISH	**ACGGHINN**	CHANGING	**ACGHIPRS**	GRAPHICS
ACFHIRSY	CRAYFISH		GANCHING	**ACGHIQTU**	ACQUIGHT
ACFHISSU	FUCHSIAS	**ACGGHINR**	CHARGING	**ACGHIRSS**	SCRAIGHS
ACFHLMRU	CHARMFUL	**ACGGHLUU**	CHUGALUG	**ACGHLLOR**	GRALLOCH
ACFHLTUW	WATCHFUL	**ACGGIINN**	INCAGING	**ACGHLMOO**	LOGOMACH
ACFHMNOR	CHAMFRON	**ACGGIINT**	GIGANTIC	**ACGHLOOY**	CHAOLOGY
ACFHNNOR	CHANFRON	**ACGGIIOS**	ISAGOGIC	**ACGHLSTU**	CLAUGHTS
ACFHNOSU	FAUCHONS	**ACGGILNN**	CANGLING	**ACGHNRYY**	GYNARCHY
ACFHRSTU	FUTHARCS		CLANGING	**ACGHNTUU**	UNCAUGHT
ACFIILST	FISTICAL		GLANCING	**ACGHORSU**	CHORAGUS
ACFIILSV	SALVIFIC	**ACGGILRY**	CRAGGILY	**ACGHPTUU**	UPCAUGHT
ACFIILTY	FACILITY	**ACGGINNO**	CONGAING	**ACGHRRSU**	CURRAGHS
ACFIIMPS	PACIFISM	**ACGGINNU**	UNCAGING	**ACGHRSSU**	SCRAUGHS
ACFIIMSS	FASCISMI	**ACGGINOR**	CARGOING	**ACGIILMN**	CLAIMING
ACFIIPST	PACIFIST	**ACGGIOOR**	CORAGGIO		MALICING
ACFIISST	FASCISTI	**ACGGLNOU**	GLUCAGON	**ACGIILNN**	INLACING
	FASCITIS	**ACGGLRSY**	SCRAGGLY	**ACGIILNO**	LOGICIAN
ACFIKLNS	CALFSKIN	**ACGHHIJK**	HIGHJACK	**ACGIILNS**	SCAILING
ACFIKNNS	FINNACKS	**ACGHHINN**	HANCHING	**ACGIILNU**	LINGUICA
ACFILLSY	FISCALLY	**ACGHHINT**	HATCHING	**ACGIILNV**	CAVILING
ACFILNOR	FORNICAL	**ACGHIIMN**	MICHIGAN	**ACGIILRS**	GRACILIS
ACFILNOS	FOLACINS	**ACGHIINN**	CHAINING	**ACGIIMNT**	MICATING
ACFILNOT	CALIFONT	**ACGHIINR**	CHAIRING	**ACGIIMOS**	ISOGAMIC
ACFILORT	TRIFOCAL	**ACGHIKLN**	CHALKING	**ACGIIMST**	SIGMATIC
ACFILOTU	CLAFOUTI		HACKLING	**ACGIINNS**	INCASING
ACFILRTY	CRAFTILY	**ACGHIKNR**	CHARKING	**ACGIINNV**	INCAVING
ACFILSSY	CLASSIFY	**ACGHIKNS**	HACKINGS	**ACGIINRT**	GRANITIC
ACFILSTU	SULFATIC		SHACKING	**ACGIIPRS**	SPAGIRIC
ACFIMNRU	FRANCIUM				

ACGIJJKO	JICKAJOG	ACGIMMNR	CRAMMING	ACGLOSUU	GLAUCOUS
ACGIJKNS	JACKINGS	ACGIMMNS	SCAMMING	ACGLSSTU	CUTGLASS
ACGIJLNO	CAJOLING	ACGIMNOR	CAROMING	ACGMNOPS	CAMPONGS
ACGIJNNU	JAUNCING	ACGIMNOS	COAMINGS	ACGNNOOT	CONTANGO
ACGIKKNN	KNACKING	ACGIMNPR	CRAMPING	ACGNNORS	CRANNOGS
ACGIKLMN	MACKLING	ACGIMNPS	CAMPINGS	ACGNOOST	OCTAGONS
ACGIKLNN	CLANKING		SCAMPING	ACGNORST	CONGRATS
ACGIKLNO	CLOAKING	ACGIMNSY	GYMNASIC	ACGORRSY	GYROCARS
ACGIKLNS	CALKINGS		SYNGAMIC	ACGORSSW	COWGRASS
	SLACKING	ACGIMOPR	PICOGRAM	ACGORSUU	COUGUARS
ACGIKLNT	TACKLING	ACGIMORS	ORGASMIC	ACGPPSUU	SCUPPAUG
	TALCKING	ACGIMOUU	GUAIOCUM	ACGRSSTU	CUTGRASS
ACGIKLNU	CAULKING	ACGINNNS	CANNINGS	ACHHILPT	PHTHALIC
ACGIKLRY	GARLICKY		SCANNING	ACHHINTW	WHINCHAT
ACGIKMNO	COMAKING	ACGINNNU	NUANCING	ACHHINTY	HYACINTH
ACGIKMNS	SMACKING	ACGINNPR	PRANCING	ACHHIPPR	HIPPARCH
ACGIKNNR	CRANKING	ACGINNPU	UNCAPING	ACHHLLOT	CHALLOTH
ACGIKNNS	SNACKING	ACGINNRT	TRANCING	ACHHLMOS	MASHLOCH
ACGIKNNU	UNCAKING	ACGINNRU	UNCARING	ACHHLNOR	RHONCHAL
ACGIKNOR	CROAKING	ACGINNRY	CARNYING	ACHHLORY	HOLARCHY
ACGIKNPS	PACKINGS	ACGINNST	CANTINGS	ACHHLPRY	PHYLARCH
ACGIKNQU	QUACKING		SCANTING	ACHHLSUY	SHAUCHLY
ACGIKNRS	ARCKINGS	ACGINNSU	UNCASING	ACHHNTTU	NUTHATCH
	RACKINGS	ACGINNUV	VAUNCING		UNTHATCH
ACGIKNRT	TRACKING	ACGINOPT	COAPTING	ACHHOSST	TOSHACHS
ACGIKNRW	WRACKING	ACGINORS	ORGANICS	ACHHPPSU	CHUPPAHS
ACGIKNSS	SACKINGS	ACGINORY	CONGIARY	ACHHPTUZ	CHUTZPAH
ACGIKNST	STACKING	ACGINOST	AGNOSTIC	ACHIIKMS	KAMICHIS
	TACKINGS		COASTING	ACHIILMS	CHILIASM
ACGIKPRS	GRIPSACK		COATINGS	ACHIILPT	HAPLITIC
ACGILLNS	CALLINGS		COTINGAS	ACHIILST	CHILIAST
ACGILMMN	CLAMMING	ACGINPPR	CRAPPING	ACHIINRT	TRICHINA
ACGILMNO	GNOMICAL	ACGINPPS	CAPPINGS	ACHIINST	CHIANTIS
ACGILMNP	CAMPLING	ACGINPRS	CARPINGS	ACHIIPRS	PARCHISI
	CLAMPING		SCARPING	ACHIIPSS	PACHISIS
ACGILMNS	CALMINGS		SCRAPING	ACHIIRST	RACHITIS
ACGILMNU	MACULING	ACGINPSS	SPACINGS	ACHIIRSU	ISCHURIA
ACGILMTU	GLUTAMIC	ACGINPSU	SCAUPING	ACHIJKPW	WHIPJACK
ACGILNNT	CANTLING	ACGINRRS	SCARRING	ACHIJNST	JACINTHS
ACGILNNU	LAUNCING	ACGINRRY	CARRYING	ACHIKKNS	KNACKISH
	UNLACING	ACGINRSS	SACRINGS	ACHIKKSW	KICKSHAW
ACGILNOR	CAROLING	ACGINRST	SCARTING	ACHIKLLW	HICKWALL
	ORACLING		TRACINGS	ACHIKLMY	HICKYMAL
ACGILNOS	SOLACING	ACGINRSU	SCAURING	ACHIKLOR	HAIRLOCK
ACGILNOT	LOCATING	ACGINRSV	CARVINGS	ACHIKLPT	CHALKPIT
ACGILNPP	CLAPPING		CRAVINGS	ACHIKNOP	PACHINKO
ACGILNPS	CLASPING	ACGINRTT	TRACTING	ACHIKNRS	CRANKISH
	PLACINGS	ACGINRTU	CURATING	ACHIKQSU	QUACKISH
	SCALPING	ACGINSST	CASTINGS	ACHIKRSS	RICKSHAS
ACGILNQU	CALQUING	ACGINSTT	SCATTING	ACHIKRSW	RICKSHAW
ACGILNRS	CARLINGS	ACGINSUV	VICUGNAS	ACHIKRSY	HAYRICKS
ACGILNRT	CLARTING	ACGIOORS	GRACIOSO	ACHIKRTW	WHITRACK
ACGILNRU	CINGULAR	ACGIORST	ORGASTIC	ACHIKSSS	SHICKSAS
ACGILNRW	CRAWLING	ACGIORSU	GRACIOUS	ACHILLOR	ORCHILLA
ACGILNSS	CLASSING	ACGIPRSY	SPAGYRIC	ACHILLRT	CLITHRAL
	SCALINGS	ACGJLNOU	CONJUGAL	ACHILMOP	OMPHALIC
ACGILNST	CASTLING	ACGKMMOS	GAMMOCKS	ACHILMOS	MALICHOS
	CATLINGS	ACGKORSV	GARVOCKS		MOCHILAS
	SCLATING	ACGLLPSU	CUPGALLS	ACHILMRS	CHRISMAL
ACGILNSU	GLUCINAS	ACGLMOUU	COAGULUM	ACHILMTY	MYTHICAL
ACGILNTT	CLATTING	ACGLNORS	CLANGORS	ACHILNNS	CLANNISH
ACGILNTU	CLAUTING	ACGLNORU	CLANGOUR	ACHILNOO	HOOLICAN
ACGILNUY	GUANYLIC	ACGLNOSY	AGLYCONS	ACHILNOS	LICHANOS
ACGILRSU	SURGICAL	ACGLOORY	ARCOLOGY	ACHILNPS	CLANSHIP

ACHILOPR	ORPHICAL	
	RHOPALIC	
ACHILOPU	PACHOULI	
ACHILORT	ACROLITH	
ACHILPSY	PHYSICAL	
ACHILPTY	PATCHILY	
ACHILRUY	CHYLURIA	
ACHILRVY	CHIVALRY	
ACHILSWY	LICHWAYS	
ACHILTTY	CHATTILY	
ACHIMMOS	MACHISMO	
	MACHOISM	
ACHIMMST	MISMATCH	
ACHIMNNW	WINCHMAN	
ACHIMNOP	CHAMPION	
ACHIMNOR	CHOIRMAN	
	HARMONIC	
	OMNIARCH	
ACHIMNOS	MANIHOCS	
	MOHICANS	
ACHIMNPT	PITCHMAN	
ACHIMNSU	INASMUCH	
ACHIMOPR	AMPHORIC	
ACHIMOSS	CHAMISOS	
	ISOCHASM	
ACHIMPSS	SCAMPISH	
ACHIMPST	MISPATCH	
ACHIMRSS	CHARISMS	
ACHIMRST	CHARTISM	
ACHIMRTY	ARYTHMIC	
ACHIMSSS	SCHISMAS	
ACHIMSST	MASTICHS	
	TACHISMS	
ACHIMSSU	CHIASMUS	
ACHIMTUY	CYATHIUM	
ACHINNOP	PANCHION	
ACHINNSU	ANCHUSIN	
	UNCHAINS	
ACHINOPR	PAROCHIN	
	PROCHAIN	
ACHINOPS	APHONICS	
ACHINORT	ANORTHIC	
ACHINOST	CHITOSAN	
ACHINOSY	ONYCHIAS	
ACHINOTZ	HOACTZIN	
ACHINPSY	SPINACHY	
ACHINRSU	UNCHAIRS	
ACHINRSZ	ZARNICHS	
ACHINSUV	CHAUVINS	
ACHIOPRT	ATROPHIC	
ACHIOPSS	ISOPACHS	
ACHIORSS	COARSISH	
ACHIORST	ACTORISH	
	CHARIOTS	
	HARICOTS	
ACHIORTV	TOVARICH	
ACHIOSST	ISOTACHS	
ACHIPPSS	SAPPHICS	
ACHIPRRT	PARRITCH	
	PHRATRIC	
ACHIPSTU	CHUPATIS	
ACHIPSTW	WHIPCATS	
ACHIPTTU	CHUPATTI	
ACHIQRSU	CHARQUIS	

ACHIRRST	TRIARCHS	
ACHIRRTY	TRIARCHY	
ACHIRSTT	CHARTIST	
	STRAICHT	
ACHIRSTU	HAIRCUTS	
ACHISSTT	TACHISTS	
ACHISTTY	CHASTITY	
ACHKKORW	HACKWORK	
ACHKKRSU	CHUKKARS	
ACHKMMOS	HAMMOCKS	
ACHKMORS	SHAMROCK	
ACHKNNUU	NUNCHAKU	
ACHKNOOT	CANTHOOK	
ACHKOPSS	HOPSACKS	
ACHKOSSS	HASSOCKS	
ACHKOSSY	HASSOCKY	
ACHKOSTT	HATTOCKS	
ACHLLOOS	ALCOHOLS	
ACHLLORS	CHLORALS	
ACHLLORY	CHORALLY	
ACHLMOPS	CAMPHOLS	
ACHLMSTZ	SCHMALTZ	
ACHLMSYZ	SCHMALZY	
ACHLNOOU	OULACHON	
ACHLNOSY	HALCYONS	
ACHLNSTU	TULCHANS	
ACHLNSTY	STANCHLY	
ACHLOPRS	RAPLOCHS	
ACHLOPRT	CALTHROP	
ACHLOPRY	POLYARCH	
ACHLOPTT	POTLATCH	
ACHLORSS	SCHOLARS	
ACHLOSSW	SALCHOWS	
ACHLOSTY	ACOLYTHS	
ACHLOTWX	WAXCLOTH	
ACHMNORS	MONARCHS	
	NOMARCHS	
ACHMNORY	MONARCHY	
	NOMARCHY	
ACHMNRSU	UNCHARMS	
ACHMNRTU	TRUCHMAN	
ACHMOORT	CHATROOM	
ACHMOPRS	CAMPHORS	
ACHMORSZ	MACHZORS	
ACHMORTU	OUTCHARM	
	OUTMARCH	
ACHMOSST	STOMACHS	
ACHMOSTY	STOMACHY	
ACHMOTTU	OUTMATCH	
ACHMPSTU	MATCHUPS	
ACHMSSUW	CUMSHAWS	
ACHNNORU	UNANCHOR	
ACHNNOSS	CHANSONS	
ACHNOOSY	CHANOYOS	
ACHNORST	CHANTORS	
ACHNORXY	CHRONAXY	
ACHNOSTY	TACHYONS	
ACHNOSUY	CHANOYUS	
ACHNPPSS	SCHNAPPS	
ACHNRSTU	UNSTARCH	
ACHNRSYY	SYNARCHY	
ACHNRTUY	CHAUNTRY	
ACHOORTU	COAUTHOR	
ACHOORTY	CHAYROOT	

ACHOPRST	TOPARCHS	
ACHOPRSY	CHARPOYS	
ACHOPRTY	TOPARCHY	
ACHORRST	TROCHARS	
ACHOTTUW	OUTWATCH	
	WATCHOUT	
ACHPRSTU	PUSHCART	
ACHPSTUZ	CHUTZPAS	
ACHPTTUY	CHUPATTY	
ACHRRTUY	CRAYTHUR	
ACHRSTTU	STRAUCHT	
ACIIILMN	INIMICAL	
ACIIILNV	CIVILIAN	
ACIIINST	ISATINIC	
ACIIKLNO	KAOLINIC	
ACIIKNNN	CANNIKIN	
ACIIKNNS	CANIKINS	
ACIIKNTY	KYANITIC	
ACIIKPRT	PAITRICK	
ACIILLNS	ALLICINS	
ACIILLNV	VANILLIC	
ACIILLSU	SILICULA	
ACIILLSV	SILVICAL	
ACIILLTV	VILLATIC	
ACIILMMS	MISCLAIM	
ACIILMNR	CRIMINAL	
ACIILMNU	ALUMINIC	
ACIILMOT	COMITIAL	
ACIILMPT	PALMITIC	
ACIILMRT	MARLITIC	
ACIILMSS	LAICISMS	
ACIILNOR	IRONICAL	
ACIILNOT	TALIONIC	
ACIILNPS	PISCINAL	
ACIILNPT	PLATINIC	
ACIILNSS	SALICINS	
ACIILOSV	VILIACOS	
ACIILRTT	TRITICAL	
ACIILRTU	URALITIC	
ACIILSST	SILASTIC	
ACIILSTV	SILVATIC	
ACIIMMNP	MINICAMP	
ACIIMMNS	MINICAMS	
ACIIMNNO	AMNIONIC	
ACIIMNNT	MANNITIC	
ACIIMNOR	MORAINIC	
ACIIMNOS	SIMONIAC	
ACIIMNOT	AMNIOTIC	
ACIIMNRS	MINICARS	
ACIIMNST	ACTINISM	
ACIIMNSU	MUSICIAN	
ACIIMNTU	ACTINIUM	
ACIIMNTY	IMITANCY	
	INTIMACY	
	MINACITY	
ACIIMOST	COMITIAS	
	IOTACISM	
ACIIMOTT	AMITOTIC	
ACIIMPRT	PRIMATIC	
ACIIMPRV	VAMPIRIC	
ACIIMRST	SCIMITAR	
ACIIMRTU	MURIATIC	
ACIIMSST	ITACISMS	
ACIIMSTT	ATTICISM	

	MASTITIC	**ACILLNOS**	SCALLION	**ACILPRST**	CLIPARTS
ACIIMSTV	ACTIVISM	**ACILLNUY**	UNCIALLY	**ACILPRSU**	SPICULAR
ACIIMTUV	VIATICUM	**ACILLOQU**	COQUILLA	**ACILPRTU**	PICTURAL
ACIINNOT	INACTION	**ACILLORT**	CLITORAL	**ACILPSST**	PLASTICS
	NICOTIAN	**ACILLORY**	COLLYRIA	**ACILPSUU**	APICULUS
ACIINNQU	CINQUAIN	**ACILLOST**	LOCALIST	**ACILRRTU**	TURRICAL
ACIINNRV	NIRVANIC	**ACILLOSY**	SOCIALLY	**ACILRSTU**	CURTAILS
ACIINNTT	INCITANT	**ACILLOTY**	COITALLY		RUSTICAL
ACIINNTY	CANINITY		LOCALITY	**ACILRTUV**	CULTIVAR
ACIINOPT	OPTICIAN	**ACILLOUV**	COLLUVIA		CURVITAL
ACIINORZ	ZIRCONIA	**ACILLSSY**	CLASSILY	**ACILSSST**	CLASSIST
ACIINOSS	ASINICOS	**ACILMNNY**	CINNAMYL	**ACILSTTY**	SCATTILY
ACIINOSV	AVIONICS	**ACILMNOP**	COMPLAIN	**ACILSTUV**	VICTUALS
ACIINOTT	CITATION	**ACILMNOS**	LACONISM	**ACILSTVY**	SYLVATIC
ACIINPSS	PISCINAS		LIMACONS	**ACIMMOSS**	ACOSMISM
ACIINPTY	ANTIPYIC	**ACILMOOS**	SCOLIOMA	**ACIMMTUY**	CYMATIUM
ACIINRSS	NARCISSI	**ACILMOPR**	PICLORAM	**ACIMNNNO**	CINNAMON
ACIINRSU	URANISCI		PROCLAIM	**ACIMNOOR**	ACROMION
ACIINRTU	URANITIC	**ACILMOPS**	OILCAMPS	**ACIMNOPS**	CAMPIONS
ACIINTTY	ANTICITY	**ACILMOPT**	COMPITAL	**ACIMNORS**	MARCONIS
ACIIOPST	APOSITIC	**ACILMOSV**	VOCALISM		MINORCAS
ACIIORST	AORISTIC	**ACILMPTU**	PLACITUM	**ACIMNORT**	ROMANTIC
ACIIORTV	VICTORIA	**ACILMRTU**	MULTICAR	**ACIMNORU**	CONARIUM
ACIIPPST	PAPISTIC	**ACILMSSS**	CLASSISM		COUMARIN
ACIIRSST	TRIASSIC		MISCLASS	**ACIMNORY**	ACRIMONY
ACIIRSTT	ARTISTIC	**ACILMSSU**	MUSICALS	**ACIMNOSS**	MOCASSIN
	TRIATICS	**ACILMSTY**	MYSTICAL	**ACIMNOST**	MONASTIC
ACIISTTT	ATTICIST	**ACILMTUY**	ULTIMACY	**ACIMNOTU**	ACONITUM
ACIISTTU	AUTISTIC	**ACILNNOS**	CANNOLIS	**ACIMNPSU**	PANICUMS
ACIISTTV	ACTIVIST	**ACILNOOT**	LOCATION	**ACIMNPTY**	TYMPANIC
ACIITTVY	ACTIVITY	**ACILNOOV**	VOCALION	**ACIMNRSS**	NARCISMS
ACIITVVY	VIVACITY	**ACILNOPS**	SALPICON	**ACIMNRSU**	CRANIUMS
ACIJKKPS	SKIPJACK	**ACILNOPT**	PLATONIC		CUMARINS
ACIJKSTW	STICKJAW	**ACILNORS**	CLARINOS	**ACIMNSTT**	CATMINTS
ACIJRSSU	JURASSIC		CLARIONS	**ACIMNSTU**	TSUNAMIC
ACIJSUZZ	JACUZZIS	**ACILNORT**	CILANTRO	**ACIMOOST**	SCOTOMIA
ACIKLMOT	MOCKTAIL		CONTRAIL	**ACIMOPRT**	IMPACTOR
ACIKLMST	MALSTICK	**ACILNOSU**	UNSOCIAL	**ACIMOPST**	APOMICTS
ACIKLNOT	ANTILOCK	**ACILNOSY**	ACYLOINS	**ACIMORST**	ACROTISM
ACIKLNRY	CRANKILY	**ACILNOUV**	UNIVOCAL	**ACIMORSY**	CRAMOISY
ACIKLORS	AIRLOCKS	**ACILNPSS**	INCLASPS	**ACIMOSST**	ACOSMIST
ACIKLORY	CROAKILY		SCALPINS		MASSICOT
ACIKMNST	STICKMAN	**ACILNRSU**	CISLUNAR	**ACIMOSTT**	MASTICOT
ACIKMOOS	OOMIACKS	**ACILNRUY**	CULINARY		STOMATIC
ACIKMOST	COMATIKS		URANYLIC	**ACIMPRST**	CRAMPITS
ACIKMPRS	RAMPICKS	**ACILNSTU**	LUNATICS		PTARMICS
ACIKMPST	MAPSTICK		SULTANIC	**ACIMRRSY**	MISCARRY
ACIKMPSW	PICKMAWS	**ACILNSTY**	SCANTILY	**ACIMRSSZ**	CZARISMS
ACIKMQSU	QUACKISM	**ACILNTTU**	ANTICULT	**ACIMSSST**	MISCASTS
ACIKNNPR	CRANKPIN	**ACILNTTY**	INTACTLY	**ACIMSSTT**	TACTISMS
ACIKNNPS	PANNICKS	**ACILOPRT**	TROPICAL	**ACINNNOO**	NONANOIC
ACIKNORT	ANTIROCK	**ACILOPRV**	VALPROIC	**ACINNOOT**	CONATION
ACIKNSST	CATSKINS	**ACILOPST**	CAPITOLS		INTONACO
ACIKNSTT	TINTACKS		COALPITS	**ACINNOQU**	CONQUIAN
ACIKPRST	PATRICKS		POSTICAL	**ACINNORR**	NARICORN
	TRIPACKS	**ACILORRS**	RACLOIRS	**ACINNOSS**	SCANSION
ACIKSTTY	STATICKY	**ACILORRV**	CORRIVAL	**ACINNOST**	ACTINONS
ACILLLNY	CLINALLY	**ACILORST**	CALORIST		CANONIST
ACILLLOP	POLLICAL	**ACILORSV**	CORIVALS		CANTIONS
ACILLMMY	CLAMMILY	**ACILORTV**	VORTICAL		CONTAINS
ACILLMOS	LOCALISM	**ACILORYZ**	ZIRCALOY		SANCTION
ACILLMSS	MISCALLS	**ACILOSTV**	VOCALIST		SONANTIC
ACILLNOO	COLONIAL	**ACILOTUV**	OUTCAVIL	**ACINNOTU**	CONTINUA
ACILLNOR	CARILLON	**ACILOTVY**	VOCALITY		COUNTIAN

Alphagram	Word	Alphagram	Word	Alphagram	Word
ACINNRTY	TYRANNIC		CITATORY	ACLLMORU	CORALLUM
ACINNSTU	ANNICUTS	ACIORTVY	VORACITY	ACLLMOSU	MOLLUSCA
ACINNSTY	INSTANCY	ACIOSSST	COASSIST	ACLLNNOO	NONLOCAL
ACINOOPR	PICAROON	ACIOSSTY	ISOSTACY	ACLLOORS	COROLLAS
ACINOOTV	VOCATION	ACIOSTUU	CAUTIOUS	ACLLOORT	COLLATOR
ACINOPPT	PANOPTIC	ACIPRRUU	PIRARUCU	ACLLOOSS	COLOSSAL
ACINOPRS	PARSONIC	ACIPRSSS	CASSPIRS	ACLLOPSS	SCALLOPS
ACINOPST	CAPTIONS	ACIPRSTT	TIPCARTS	ACLLORUY	OCULARLY
	PACTIONS	ACIPRTTY	TRIPTYCA	ACLLOSTU	LOCUSTAL
ACINOPTU	ACUPOINT	ACIPSSST	SPASTICS		OUTCALLS
ACINOQSU	COQUINAS	ACIQRSTU	QUARTICS	ACLLOSTY	COSTALLY
ACINORRS	CARRIONS	ACIQSSTU	ACQUISTS	ACLLRSYY	ACRYLYLS
ACINORRT	CARROTIN	ACIRRTTX	TRACTRIX	ACLLRTUU	CULTURAL
	CONTRAIR	ACIRRTUX	CURATRIX	ACLMMNOU	COMMUNAL
ACINORSS	NARCOSIS	ACIRSSST	SACRISTS	ACLMMORW	CLAMWORM
ACINORST	CANTORIS	ACIRSSTT	ASTRICTS	ACLMNOOO	COOLAMON
	CAROTINS	ACIRSSTW	TWISCARS	ACLMNOOR	COLORMAN
	CORTINAS	ACIRSSTY	SACRISTY	ACLMNORU	COLUMNAR
ACINORSV	CORVINAS	ACIRSSTZ	CZARISTS	ACLMNORY	NORMALCY
ACINORTT	TRACTION	ACISSSTU	CASUISTS	ACLMNPSU	UNCLAMPS
ACINORTU	NOCTURIA	ACISSTTU	CATSUITS	ACLMORSU	CLAMOURS
ACINORTY	CARYOTIN	ACISSTUV	VACUISTS	ACLMORTU	CROTALUM
ACINOSSS	CAISSONS	ACISTTUY	ASTUCITY	ACLMPRSU	SCALPRUM
	CASSINOS	ACJKKSSY	SKYJACKS	ACLMRSUU	MUSCULAR
ACINOSSY	CYANOSIS	ACJKLLOR	JACKROLL	ACLMSSTU	MASSCULT
ACINOSTT	OSCITANT	ACJKLOSW	LOCKJAWS	ACLMSTUU	CUSTUMAL
	TACTIONS	ACJKNNOS	JANNOCKS	ACLMSUUV	VASCULUM
ACINOSTU	ANTICOUS	ACJKOPST	JACKPOTS	ACLNNOOS	NONCOLAS
	AUCTIONS	ACJMNSTU	MUNTJACS	ACLNNOOV	NONVOCAL
	CAUTIONS	ACJPSTUU	CAJUPUTS	ACLNNOSS	NONCLASS
ACINOSTW	WAINSCOT	ACKKMOPR	POCKMARK	ACLNOORS	CORONALS
ACINOSWX	COXSWAIN	ACKKORRW	RACKWORK	ACLNOORT	COLORANT
ACINOTTX	TOXICANT	ACKLLOPS	POLLACKS	ACLNOOST	COOLANTS
ACINPQUY	PIQUANCY	ACKLLOSY	LAYLOCKS		OCTANOLS
ACINPRST	CANTRIPS	ACKLLPSU	SKULLCAP	ACLNOOSV	VOLCANOS
ACINPRSY	CYPRIANS	ACKLMNOS	LOCKSMAN	ACLNOPSY	SYNCOPAL
ACINPSTY	SYNAPTIC	ACKLMORS	ARMLOCKS	ACLNORSU	CONSULAR
ACINQSTU	QUANTICS		LOCKRAMS		COURLANS
ACINRSST	NARCISTS	ACKLNOSU	UNCLOAKS	ACLNORTU	CALUTRON
ACINRSSU	CRUSIANS	ACKLOOPW	WOOLPACK	ACLNOSSS	CLASSONS
ACINRSTU	CURTAINS	ACKLOORS	OARLOCKS	ACLNOSTU	CONSULTA
	SATURNIC	ACKLOOSW	WOOLSACK		OSCULANT
	TURACINS	ACKLORSV	LAVROCKS	ACLNPSSU	UNCLASPS
ACINRTTU	TACITURN	ACKLORSW	WARLOCKS	ACLNPTUU	PUNCTUAL
	URTICANT	ACKLORSY	ROCKLAYS	ACLNSSUY	UNCLASSY
ACINSTTY	SANCTITY	ACKLOSSS	LASSOCKS	ACLOOPPS	ALCOPOPS
	SCANTITY	ACKMMMOS	MAMMOCKS	ACLOOPRR	CORPORAL
ACINSTYY	SYNCYTIA	ACKMNOST	STOCKMAN	ACLOOPRS	CARPOOLS
ACIOOPST	SCOTOPIA	ACKMNRTU	TRUCKMAN	ACLOORST	LOCATORS
ACIOOTYZ	ZOOCYTIA	ACKMOSST	STOMACKS	ACLOORWY	COLORWAY
ACIOPRST	APRICOTS	ACKMOSTT	MATTOCKS	ACLOPRRU	PROCURAL
	PISCATOR	ACKNOPSW	SNOWPACK	ACLOPRST	CALTROPS
ACIOPRTT	PROTATIC	ACKNORSU	CRANKOUS	ACLOPRXY	XYLOCARP
ACIOPRTY	POTICARY	ACKNRSTU	UNTRACKS	ACLOPSSU	SCOPULAS
ACIOPSST	POTASSIC	ACKNSSTU	UNSTACKS	ACLOPSSY	CALYPSOS
ACIOPSSU	SPACIOUS	ACKOPRRS	PARROCKS	ACLOPSUU	OPUSCULA
ACIOPSTU	AUTOPSIC	ACKOPRRT	TRAPROCK	ACLORRTU	TORCULAR
	CAPTIOUS	ACKORRST	TARROCKS	ACLORTUW	OUTCRAWL
ACIOPTTU	AUTOPTIC	ACKORSTW	CATWORKS	ACLOSSTU	OUTCLASS
ACIORRSS	CORSAIRS	ACKOSSTW	TOWSACKS	ACLRSSTY	CRYSTALS
ACIORRSU	SCARIOUS	ACKOSWZZ	WAZZOCKS	ACMMNOSY	SCAMMONY
ACIORSTT	CITATORS	ACKPSSTU	STACKUPS	ACMMNOVY	MYOMANCY
	RICOTTAS	ACLLLNOY	CLONALLY	ACMNOOPR	CRAMPOON
ACIORTTY	ATROCITY	ACLLMNOU	COLUMNAL		MONOCARP

ACMNOORR	CROMORNA	ACOSSTTU	OUTCASTS
ACMNOORT	MONOCRAT	ACPSSTUU	USUCAPTS
ACMNOOYZ	ZOOMANCY	ACPSSTUY	PUSSYCAT
ACMNOPRS	CORPSMAN	ADDDEEEL	DELEADED
	CRAMPONS	ADDDEEEM	ADDEEMED
ACMNORSY	ACRONYMS	ADDDEEEN	DEADENED
ACMNSSTU	SANCTUMS	ADDDEEGR	DEGRADED
ACMOOORT	COATROOM	ADDDEEIM	DIADEMED
ACMOOPRS	COPROSMA	ADDDEELR	LADDERED
ACMOORRT	MOTORCAR	ADDDEEMN	DEMANDED
ACMOORUU	COUMAROU		MADDENED
ACMOOSST	SCOTOMAS	ADDDEENR	DANDERED
ACMOPRST	COMPARTS		REDDENDA
ACMOPSTU	CAMPOUTS	ADDDEENS	DESANDED
ACMORRSS	CROSSARM		SADDENED
ACMORSTW	CATWORMS	ADDDEEPS	SEPADDED
	WORMCAST	ADDDEGJU	ADJUDGED
ACMORSTY	COSTMARY	ADDDEIMS	MISADDED
ACMQSTUU	CUMQUATS	ADDDELSW	SWADDLED
ACNNNORY	CANNONRY	ADDDELTW	TWADDLED
ACNNOORT	NONACTOR	ADDDEMNU	ADDENDUM
ACNNOSTT	CONSTANT	ADDDEMOO	ADDOOMED
ACNOOORT	OCTAROON	ADDDENOS	DEODANDS
ACNOOPRT	COPATRON	ADDDENPU	UNPADDED
ACNOORRY	CORONARY	ADDDENRU	DEUDDARN
ACNOORST	CARTOONS	ADDDEOOW	DEADWOOD
	CORANTOS	ADDDEORS	ADDORSED
	OSTRACON	ADDDEOTU	OUTADDED
ACNOORSU	CANOROUS	ADDDEQSU	SQUADDED
ACNOORTU	COURANTO	ADDDGILN	DADDLING
ACNOORTY	CARTOONY	ADDEEEFL	DEFLEAED
	OCTONARY	ADDEEEFN	DEAFENED
ACNOPSSW	SNOWCAPS	ADDEEEFT	DEFEATED
ACNORRSU	RANCOURS	ADDEEEJY	DEEJAYED
ACNORRSY	CARRYONS	ADDEEELN	LEADENED
ACNORRTY	CONTRARY	ADDEEELV	DELEAVED
ACNORSTT	CONTRAST	ADDEEEMN	DEMEANED
	CONTRATS	ADDEEEMR	REMEADED
ACNORSTU	COURANTS	ADDEEENR	DEADENER
ACNORTTU	TURNCOAT		ENDEARED
ACNORTUY	NOCTUARY	ADDEEENW	DANEWEED
ACNOSSTW	SNOWCATS	ADDEEESY	DEADEYES
ACNPRSSY	SYNCARPS	ADDEEFGN	DEFANGED
ACNPRSUY	SPRAUNCY	ADDEEFHN	HANDFEED
ACNPRSYY	SYNCARPY	ADDEEFIL	DEFILADE
ACNRRSTU	CURRANTS	ADDEEFIM	MADEFIED
ACNRRTUY	CURRANTY	ADDEEFLT	DEFLATED
ACOOPRRS	CORPORAS	ADDEEFMO	DEFOAMED
ACOOPRST	COPASTOR	ADDEEFNU	UNDEAFED
	ROOTCAPS	ADDEEFPR	PREFADED
ACOOPSTT	TOPCOATS	ADDEEFRY	DEFRAYED
ACOORSTU	TOURACOS		FEEDYARD
ACOPPRRS	PROCARPS	ADDEEFTT	DEFATTED
ACOPRRST	CARPORTS	ADDEEGGR	DAGGERED
ACOPRRTT	PROTRACT	ADDEEGHR	HARDEDGE
ACORRSTT	TRACTORS	ADDEEGLL	ALLEDGED
ACORRSTU	CURATORS	ADDEEGLN	DANEGELD
ACORRTUY	CARRYOUT	ADDEEGLZ	DEGLAZED
	CURATORY	ADDEEGNR	DANGERED
ACORSSTU	SURCOATS		DERANGED
ACORSSUW	CURASSOW		GANDERED
ACORSSWY	CROSSWAY		GARDENED
ACORSTTY	CRYOSTAT	ADDEEGOR	DOGEARED
ACORSTUU	TURACOUS	ADDEEGRR	DEGRADER

			REGARDED
			REGRADED
	ADDEEGRS	DEGRADES
	ADDEEGSS	DEGASSED
	ADDEEHLR	HERALDED
	ADDEEHLY	ALDEHYDE
	ADDEEHNR	ADHEREND
		HARDENED
	ADDEEHNS	HEADENDS
	ADDEEHNU	UNHEADED
	ADDEEHOP	DOPEHEAD
	ADDEEHRS	REDHEADS
	ADDEEHRT	THREADED
	ADDEEIKR	DAIKERED
	ADDEEILN	DEADLINE
	ADDEEILR	DEADLIER
		DERAILED
		REDIALED
	ADDEEILT	DETAILED
	ADDEEIMT	MEDIATED
	ADDEEINT	DETAINED
	ADDEEINU	UNIDEAED
	ADDEEIPR	DIAPERED
	ADDEEISS	DISEASED
	ADDEEIST	STEADIED
	ADDEEITV	DEVIATED
	ADDEEKMR	DEMARKED
	ADDEEKNR	DARKENED
	ADDEELLM	MEDALLED
	ADDEELLP	PEDALLED
	ADDEELLV	DEVALLED
	ADDEELNO	LOADENED
	ADDEELNP	DEPLANED
	ADDEELNR	ENLARDED
		RELANDED
	ADDEELNU	UNLEADED
	ADDEELOR	RELOADED
	ADDEELPS	DELAPSED
	ADDEELRS	RESADDLE
	ADDEELRT	TREADLED
	ADDEELST	DESALTED
	ADDEELUV	DEVALUED
	ADDEEMNN	DEMANNED
	ADDEEMNP	DAMPENED
	ADDEEMNR	DAMNEDER
		DEMANDER
		REDEMAND
		REMANDED
	ADDEEMST	DEMASTED
	ADDEENPP	APPENDED
	ADDEENPR	PANDERED
	ADDEENPX	EXPANDED
	ADDEENRR	DARNEDER
	ADDEENRT	ENDARTED
	ADDEENRU	DAUNERED
	ADDEENRW	DAWNERED
		WANDERED
		WARDENED
	ADDEENSS	DEADNESS
	ADDEENTT	ATTENDED
		DENTATED
	ADDEENTU	DENUDATE
	ADDEENUV	UNEVADED
	ADDEEOST	DEODATES

ADDEEPRS	RESPADED	ADDEILYZ	DIALYZED	ADDENORU	UNADORED
ADDEEPRT	DEPARTED	ADDEIMOS	SODAMIDE	ADDENPRU	UNDRAPED
	PREDATED	ADDEIMRS	DISARMED	ADDENRST	DARNDEST
ADDEEPRV	DEPRAVED		MISDREAD		STRANDED
	PERVADED	ADDEIMST	MISDATED	ADDENRSU	DAUNDERS
ADDEERRS	DREADERS	ADDEIMSY	DISMAYED	ADDENRTU	DRAUNTED
ADDEERRT	RETARDED	ADDEIMTT	ADMITTED		UNTRADED
ADDEERRW	REWARDED	ADDEINOR	ORDAINED	ADDENRUW	UNWARDED
	WARDERED	ADDEINOS	ADENOIDS	ADDEORTU	OUTDARED
ADDEERRY	DEERYARD		ADONISED	ADDEOTTU	OUTDATED
ADDEERSW	SAWDERED		ANODISED	ADDEPRSU	SUPERADD
ADDEERTT	DERATTED	ADDEINOZ	ADONIZED	ADDEPRTU	UPDARTED
ADDEERTV	ADVERTED		ANODIZED	ADDFFILO	DAFFODIL
ADDEFFOR	AFFORDED	ADDEINPR	DREPANID	ADDFFINR	DANDRIFF
ADDEFIIL	LADIFIED	ADDEINRS	SARDINED	ADDFFNRU	DANDRUFF
ADDEFILT	DEADLIFT	ADDEINRT	INDARTED	ADDFGILN	FADDLING
ADDEFILY	LADYFIED	ADDEINST	DANDIEST	ADDFIMSS	FADDISMS
ADDEFIST	FADDIEST	ADDEIOPR	PARODIED	ADDFISST	FADDISTS
ADDEFLRU	DREADFUL	ADDEIORS	ROADSIDE	ADDGGILN	GLADDING
ADDEFRSU	DEFRAUDS		SIDEROAD	ADDGGORU	GUARDDOG
ADDEGGLR	DRAGGLED	ADDEIOTX	OXIDATED	ADDGIILN	DAIDLING
ADDEGHOS	GODHEADS	ADDEIPPR	DIDAPPER	ADDGIIRS	DIAGRIDS
ADDEGILO	DIALOGED	ADDEIPRS	DISPREAD	ADDGIKNR	GRANDKID
ADDEGILS	GLADDIES	ADDEIPSS	DIPSADES	ADDGILNN	DANDLING
ADDEGINR	DREADING	ADDEIQSU	SQUADDIE	ADDGILNP	PADDLING
	READDING	ADDEIRST	DISRATED	ADDGILNR	RADDLING
ADDEGIRS	DISGRADE	ADDEIRSW	SIDEWARD	ADDGILNS	SADDLING
ADDEGJSU	ADJUDGES	ADDEIRVZ	VIZARDED	ADDGILNW	DAWDLING
ADDEGLNS	GLADDENS	ADDEISSU	DISSUADE		WADDLING
ADDEGLST	GLADDEST	ADDEISSV	DISSAVED	ADDGINPS	PADDINGS
ADDEGNOP	DOGNAPED	ADDEISSW	SWADDIES	ADDGINQU	QUADDING
ADDEGNRU	UNGRADED	ADDEISSY	DAYSIDES	ADDGINSW	WADDINGS
ADDEGPRU	UPGRADED	ADDEJSTU	ADJUSTED	ADDGINWY	WADDYING
ADDEHHIN	HINDHEAD	ADDEKNVY	VANDYKED	ADDGLNOS	GLADDONS
ADDEHHLN	HANDHELD	ADDELLOR	DOLLARED	ADDGMNOS	GODDAMNS
ADDEHILR	DIHEDRAL	ADDELMOS	DOLMADES	ADDGMRUU	MUDGUARD
ADDEHINW	HEADWIND	ADDELNNU	DUNELAND	ADDGOOSW	DAGWOODS
ADDEHIRS	DIEHARDS	ADDELNOO	ONLOADED	ADDGOQSU	GODSQUAD
ADDEHIRW	RAWHIDED	ADDELNOU	DUODENAL	ADDGORSW	GODWARDS
ADDEHLOS	SHEDLOAD		UNLOADED	ADDHHLNO	HANDHOLD
ADDEHMRU	DRUMHEAD	ADDELNPU	PUDENDAL	ADDHIMOO	MAIDHOOD
ADDEHNNU	UNHANDED	ADDELNRS	DANDLERS	ADDHINPS	DAPHNIDS
ADDEHNSU	UNDASHED	ADDELNSU	UNSADDLE	ADDHINRW	HINDWARD
	UNSHADED	ADDELOOR	ELDORADO	ADDHINSY	DANDYISH
ADDEHOPR	DROPHEAD	ADDELOPU	UPLOADED	ADDHIOTY	HYDATOID
ADDEHORW	HEADWORD	ADDELPRS	PADDLERS	ADDHISTY	HYDATIDS
ADDEHOSW	SHADOWED		SPRADDLE	ADDHLOOS	LADHOODS
ADDEHPRU	PURDAHED	ADDELRSS	SADDLERS	ADDHLOOY	LADYHOOD
ADDEHRTY	HYDRATED	ADDELRST	STRADDLE	ADDHOORW	HARDWOOD
ADDEIIKS	DIDAKEIS	ADDELRSW	DAWDLERS	ADDHOSTY	ATHODYDS
ADDEIIMS	DIAMIDES		SWADDLER	ADDIIKMZ	ZADDIKIM
ADDEIINZ	DAIDZEIN		WADDLERS	ADDIILUV	DIVIDUAL
ADDEIIRS	DIARISED	ADDELRSY	SADDLERY	ADDIINOT	ADDITION
ADDEIIRZ	DIARIZED	ADDELRTW	TWADDLER	ADDIINSS	DISDAINS
ADDEIITV	ADDITIVE	ADDELSST	STADDLES	ADDIINTV	DIVIDANT
ADDEIJNO	ADJOINED	ADDELSSW	SWADDLES	ADDIIPSS	DIAPSIDS
ADDEIKNP	KIDNAPED	ADDELSTW	TWADDLES	ADDIKSST	TSADDIKS
ADDEILNS	ISLANDED	ADDEMMNU	UNDAMMED	ADDIKSTY	KATYDIDS
	LANDSIDE	ADDEMMNU	UNDAMNED	ADDIKSTZ	TZADDIKS
ADDEILNT	TIDELAND	ADDEMNPU	UNDAMPED	ADDILLNS	LANDSLID
ADDEILRS	DIEDRALS	ADDEMNST	DAMNDEST	ADDILLNW	WILDLAND
ADDEILSU	DUALISED	ADDEMOSY	DOMESDAY	ADDILMNS	MIDLANDS
ADDEILSY	DIALYSED	ADDENNOT	DANTONED	ADDILNNW	LANDWIND
ADDEILUZ	DUALIZED	ADDENOPR	PARDONED	ADDILOSS	DISLOADS

ADDIMNOS	DIAMONDS		ENSEAMED	ADEEFRTU	FEATURED
ADDIMNSY	DANDYISM	ADEEEMNT	EMENDATE	ADEEGGHS	EGGHEADS
ADDIMNYY	DIDYNAMY	ADEEEMRT	RETEAMED	ADEEGGJR	JAGGEDER
ADDIMORS	DIADROMS	ADEEEMRU	EMERAUDE	ADEEGGLL	ALLEGGED
ADDINNOR	ORDINAND	ADEEENNT	NEATENED	ADEEGGRR	RAGGEDER
ADDINORS	ANDROIDS	ADEEENRR	REEARNED	ADEEGGRS	SAGGERED
	DISADORN	ADEEENRS	ENSEARED	ADEEGGRT	RETAGGED
ADDINQUV	QUIDDANY		SERENADE	ADEEGGRU	REGAUGED
ADDINRWW	WINDWARD	ADEEENTT	ATTENDEE	ADEEGGWW	GEWGAWED
ADDIORTY	ADDITORY		EDENTATE	ADEEGHNR	REHANGED
ADDIQSST	TSADDIQS	ADEEENWZ	WEAZENED	ADEEGHOR	GHERAOED
ADDIQSTZ	TZADDIQS	ADEEEPRS	RAPESEED	ADEEGHRT	GATHERED
ADDIRSZZ	DIZZARDS	ADEEEPRT	DEPARTEE	ADEEGIMN	ADEEMING
ADDKNRRU	DRUNKARD		REPEATED	ADEEGIMR	REIMAGED
ADDLLNOR	LANDLORD	ADEEERRS	ARREEDES	ADEEGINR	REGAINED
ADDLLRSU	DULLARDS	ADEEERST	RESEATED	ADEEGINS	AGENISED
ADDLNNOW	DOWNLAND	ADEEERVW	REWEAVED	ADEEGINZ	AGENIZED
ADDLNOOW	DOWNLOAD	ADEEESSW	SEAWEEDS	ADEEGIRS	DISAGREE
	WOODLAND		SEESAWED	ADEEGISS	ASSIEGED
ADDLNORR	RANDLORD	ADEEFFIR	EFFRAIDE	ADEEGLLS	ALLEDGES
ADDLNORS	LANDDROS	ADEEFGLN	FENAGLED	ADEEGLLT	GALLETED
ADDLOOSS	SOLDADOS	ADEEFHNR	FREEHAND	ADEEGLLV	GAVELLED
ADDLORTY	DOTARDLY	ADEEFHOR	FOREHEAD	ADEEGLNO	ENGAOLED
ADDMOOSY	DOOMSDAY	ADEEFHRT	FATHERED	ADEEGLNR	ENLARGED
ADDNOPWY	PANDOWDY	ADEEFIIR	AERIFIED		LANGERED
ADDNORWW	DOWNWARD	ADEEFILN	ENFILADE		LARGENED
	DRAWDOWN	ADEEFIMS	MADEFIES	ADEEGLNT	DANEGELT
ADDOORRY	DOORYARD		SEMIDEAF	ADEEGLRV	GRAVELED
ADDOORWW	WOODWARD	ADEEFINR	FREDAINE	ADEEGLRZ	REGLAZED
ADDOORWY	WOODYARD	ADEEFIOR	FOEDARIE	ADEEGLSV	SELVAGED
ADDOPSSY	DASYPODS	ADEEFIRR	RAREFIED	ADEEGLSZ	DEGLAZES
ADEEEFFR	AFFEERED	ADEEFIRS	FEDARIES	ADEEGMMO	GAMODEME
ADEEEFNY	FEDAYEEN	ADEEFIRY	REAEDIFY	ADEEGMMT	GEMMATED
ADEEEFRT	DEFEATER	ADEEFIST	SAFETIED	ADEEGMNR	GENDARME
	FEDERATE	ADEEFLLT	FELLATED	ADEEGMNS	ENDGAMES
	REDEFEAT	ADEEFLMN	ENFLAMED	ADEEGMNY	GANYMEDE
ADEEEGLT	DELEGATE	ADEEFLNS	ENDLEAFS		MEGADYNE
ADEEEGNR	RENEGADE	ADEEFLOR	FREELOAD	ADEEGMOP	MEGAPODE
ADEEEGNT	TEENAGED	ADEEFLPR	PEDALFER	ADEEGMOS	MEGADOSE
ADEEEGPS	GAPESEED	ADEEFLRR	DEFERRAL	ADEEGMSS	MESSAGED
ADEEEGRR	REGEARED	ADEEFLRS	FEDERALS	ADEEGNNR	ENDANGER
ADEEEGRS	DEGREASE	ADEEFLRT	DEFLATER		ENRANGED
ADEEEGUW	AGUEWEED		FALTERED	ADEEGNNV	VENDANGE
ADEEEHHW	HEEHAWED		REFLATED	ADEEGNOR	RENEGADO
ADEEEHRS	HAEREDES	ADEEFLSS	FADELESS	ADEEGNRR	DERANGER
ADEEEHRT	REHEATED	ADEEFLST	DEFLATES		GARDENER
ADEEEHRX	EXHEDRAE	ADEEFLSX	FLAXSEED		GARNERED
ADEEEHSY	EYESHADE	ADEEFMNR	ENFRAMED	ADEEGNRS	DERANGES
ADEEEINT	DETAINEE		FREEDMAN		GRANDEES
ADEEEKNW	WEAKENED	ADEEFMOR	DEFOAMER		GRENADES
ADEEELMN	ENAMELED	ADEEFMRR	REFRAMED	ADEEGNRU	DUNGAREE
ADEEELNS	ENSEALED	ADEEFMRS	DEFAMERS		RENAGUED
ADEEELNV	LEAVENED	ADEEFNRU	UNFEARED		UNAGREED
ADEEELPR	REPEALED	ADEEFNSS	DEAFNESS		UNDERAGE
ADEEELRS	RELEASED	ADEEFNST	FASTENED		UNGEARED
	RESEALED	ADEEFNTT	FATTENED	ADEEGNRV	ENGRAVED
ADEEELRV	LAVEERED	ADEEFORR	FOREREAD	ADEEGNSS	AGEDNESS
	REVEALED	ADEEFORT	FOREDATE	ADEEGNSV	VENDAGES
ADEEELST	TEASELED	ADEEFOTV	FOVEATED	ADEEGORT	DEROGATE
ADEEELSV	DELEAVES	ADEEFPRS	PREFADES	ADEEGORV	OVERAGED
ADEEELSW	WEASELED	ADEEFRRT	RAFTERED	ADEEGOST	DOGEATES
ADEEELTV	ELEVATED	ADEEFRRY	DEFRAYER	ADEEGOTW	GOATWEED
ADEEELTZ	TEAZELED		FEDERARY	ADEEGPRS	ASPERGED
ADEEEMNS	DEMEANES	ADEEFRST	DRAFTEES		PRESAGED

ADEEGPRT	PARGETED	ADEEHNST	HASTENED	ADEEILST	LEADIEST
ADEEGRRR	REGARDER		NETHEADS	ADEEILSV	DISLEAVE
ADEEGRRS	REGRADES	ADEEHNTU	UNHEATED	ADEEILSY	EYELIADS
ADEEGRRT	GARRETED	ADEEHOPR	HEADROPE	ADEEIMNR	REMAINED
	GARTERED	ADEEHORS	SOREHEAD	ADEEIMNS	DEMAINES
	REGRATED	ADEEHORV	OVERHEAD		INSEAMED
ADEEGRRU	REARGUED	ADEEHPPU	UPHEAPED	ADEEIMNT	DEMENTIA
	REDARGUE	ADEEHPRS	EPHEDRAS	ADEEIMNX	EXAMINED
ADEEGRSS	DEGASSER		RESHAPED	ADEEIMPR	EMPAIRED
	DRESSAGE	ADEEHPRT	PREDEATH	ADEEIMRR	DREAMIER
ADEEGRST	RESTAGED		THREAPED	ADEEIMRS	MADERISE
ADEEGRSU	GUARDEES	ADEEHPUV	UPHEAVED	ADEEIMRT	DIAMETER
ADEEGRSW	RAGWEEDS	ADEEHRRS	ADHERERS		REMEDIAT
ADEEGRTT	TARGETED		REDSHARE	ADEEIMRZ	MADERIZE
ADEEGSSS	DEGASSES	ADEEHRRT	RETHREAD	ADEEIMSS	SIAMESED
ADEEGSTT	GESTATED		THREADER	ADEEIMST	MEDIATES
ADEEGSWY	EDGEWAYS	ADEEHRST	HEADREST	ADEEIMSZ	SIAMEZED
ADEEGTTZ	GAZETTED	ADEEHRSV	RESHAVED	ADEEIMTT	ADMITTEE
ADEEHHRS	REHASHED	ADEEHRSW	REWASHED		MEDITATE
ADEEHHST	SHEATHED		WASHERED	ADEEINNS	ADENINES
ADEEHIKL	HEADLIKE	ADEEHRTT	HATTERED		ANDESINE
ADEEHILN	HEADLINE		THREATED	ADEEINOP	OEDIPEAN
ADEEHILS	DEISHEAL	ADEEHRTW	WREATHED	ADEEINPR	PINDAREE
ADEEHIRT	DEATHIER	ADEEHSST	HEADSETS	ADEEINPT	DIAPENTE
ADEEHISS	EADISHES	ADEEHSSY	HAYSEEDS	ADEEINRS	ARSENIDE
ADEEHIST	ATHEISED	ADEEIILS	IDEALISE		DENARIES
	HEADIEST	ADEEIILZ	IDEALIZE		DRAISENE
ADEEHISV	ADHESIVE	ADEEIITV	IDEATIVE		NEARSIDE
ADEEHITZ	ATHEIZED	ADEEIJKL	JADELIKE	ADEEINRT	DETAINER
ADEEHKNR	DAKERHEN	ADEEIJMR	JEREMIAD		RETAINED
	HANKERED	ADEEIJRS	JADERIES	ADEEINRV	REINVADE
	HARKENED	ADEEIJST	JADEITES	ADEEINSS	ANISEEDS
ADEEHKPR	PHREAKED	ADEEIKLS	LAKESIDE	ADEEINST	ANDESITE
ADEEHKRS	KASHERED	ADEEIKMR	DIEMAKER	ADEEINTW	ANTIWEED
ADEEHKWW	HAWKWEED	ADEEIKNP	KIDNAPEE	ADEEINVW	INWEAVED
ADEEHKWY	HAWKEYED	ADEEIKSW	WEAKSIDE	ADEEIPRR	RAPIERED
ADEEHLLW	WELLHEAD	ADEEILLO	OEILLADE		REPAIRED
ADEEHLNO	ENHALOED	ADEEILLR	REALLIED	ADEEIPRS	AIRSPEED
ADEEHLNR	REHANDLE	ADEEILMN	ENDEMIAL	ADEEIPTX	EXPIATED
ADEEHLNS	HANSELED	ADEEILMR	REMAILED	ADEEIRRR	DREARIER
ADEEHLNU	UNHEALED		REMEDIAL	ADEEIRRS	DREARIES
ADEEHLRS	ASHLERED	ADEEILMS	LIMEADES		RERAISED
ADEEHLRT	HALTERED	ADEEILMV	MEDIEVAL	ADEEIRST	READIEST
	LATHERED	ADEEILNR	RENAILED		SERIATED
ADEEHLSS	HEADLESS	ADEEILNS	DELAINES		SIDERATE
ADEEHLTY	HEATEDLY	ADEEILNT	DATELINE		STEADIER
ADEEHMMO	HOMEMADE		ENTAILED	ADEEIRSV	READVISE
ADEEHMMR	HAMMERED		LINEATED	ADEEIRTT	ITERATED
ADEEHMNN	MENHADEN	ADEEILPR	PEDALIER	ADEEIRTV	DERIVATE
ADEEHMNS	HEADSMEN	ADEEILPS	PLEIADES		EVIRATED
ADEEHMNT	ANTHEMED	ADEEILPT	DEPILATE		TAIVERED
ADEEHMPR	HAMPERED		EPILATED	ADEEIRTW	WAITERED
ADEEHMSS	EMDASHES		PILEATED	ADEEISSS	DISEASES
ADEEHMST	STEMHEAD	ADEEILRR	DERAILER		SEASIDES
ADEEHNOT	HEADNOTE		RERAILED	ADEEISST	STEADIES
ADEEHNPP	HAPPENED	ADEEILRS	REALISED	ADEEISSV	ADESSIVE
ADEEHNRR	HARDENER		RESAILED		ADVISEES
	REHARDEN		SIDEREAL	ADEEISTU	AUDITEES
ADEEHNRT	ADHERENT	ADEEILRT	DETAILER	ADEEISTV	DEVIATES
	HARTENED		ELATERID		SEDATIVE
	NEATHERD		RETAILED	ADEEITTV	EVITATED
	THREADEN	ADEEILRZ	REALIZED	ADEEITVW	TIDEWAVE
ADEEHNSS	DASHEENS	ADEEILSS	DEISEALS	ADEEKMRR	REMARKED
	ENDASHES		IDEALESS	ADEEKMRT	DEMARKET

	MARKETED	ADEELNTU	UNELATED	ADEEMNSU	UNSEAMED
ADEEKNNR	ENRANKED	ADEELNTV	LEVANTED	ADEEMNSY	DEMAYNES
ADEEKNPS	KNEEPADS	ADEELNTY	ENTAYLED	ADEEMNTU	UNTEAMED
ADEEKNPW	KNAPWEED	ADEELOPS	PEDALOES	ADEEMNTW	METEWAND
ADEEKNRR	DARKENER	ADEELOPX	POLEAXED	ADEEMORS	SEADROME
ADEEKNRS	KNEADERS	ADEELORR	RELOADER	ADEEMORT	MODERATE
ADEEKNST	NAKEDEST	ADEELORU	AUREOLED	ADEEMPPR	PAMPERED
ADEEKORS	RESOAKED	ADEELORV	OVERLADE		REMAPPED
ADEEKPRR	REPARKED	ADEELOST	DESOLATE	ADEEMPRR	PREARMED
ADEEKQSU	SQUEAKED	ADEELOSW	LEASOWED	ADEEMPRT	EMPARTED
ADEEKRST	STREAKED	ADEELPPR	LAPPERED		TAMPERED
ADEEKSWY	WEEKDAYS		RAPPELED	ADEEMPRV	REVAMPED
ADEELLLP	LAPELLED	ADEELPPT	LAPPETED	ADEEMPRY	EMPAYRED
ADEELLMT	METALLED	ADEELPPU	UPLEAPED	ADEEMPST	STAMPEDE
ADEELLMU	MEDULLAE	ADEELPRS	PEDALERS		STEPDAME
ADEELLNP	PANELLED		PLEADERS	ADEEMRRS	DREAMERS
ADEELLNW	ENWALLED		RELAPSED		REDREAMS
ADEELLNY	LEADENLY		REPLEADS	ADEEMRRT	REDREAMT
ADEELLPR	PEDALLER	ADEELPRT	PALTERED	ADEEMRRV	MARVERED
	PREDELLA		REPLATED	ADEEMRRW	REWARMED
ADEELLPS	SEPALLED	ADEELPRY	PARLEYED	ADEEMRRY	DREAMERY
ADEELLPT	PALLETED		REPLAYED	ADEEMRST	MASTERED
	PETALLED	ADEELPSS	DELAPSES		STREAMED
ADEELLQU	EQUALLED	ADEELPST	PEDESTAL	ADEEMRSU	MEASURED
ADEELLRS	SARDELLE	ADEELPTY	PEDATELY	ADEEMRTT	MATTERED
ADEELLRT	TELLARED	ADEELQSU	SQUEALED	ADEEMRTY	METEYARD
ADEELLRU	LAURELED	ADEELRRR	LARDERER	ADEEMSSW	MAWSEEDS
ADEELLRV	RAVELLED	ADEELRRT	TREADLER	ADEEMSTW	MATWEEDS
ADEELLSS	ALLSEEDS	ADEELRRY	READERLY	ADEEMSWY	MAYWEEDS
	LEADLESS	ADEELRST	DESALTER	ADEENNPT	PENNATED
ADEELLTY	ELATEDLY		RESLATED	ADEENNRS	ENSNARED
ADEELLVY	VALLEYED		TREADLES	ADEENNRU	UNEARNED
ADEELLWY	WALLEYED	ADEELRSV	SLAVERED	ADEENNTT	TENANTED
ADEELMNO	LEMONADE	ADEELRSW	LEEWARDS	ADEENNUW	UNWEANED
ADEELMNP	EMPLANED	ADEELRSY	DELAYERS	ADEENNUY	UNYEANED
ADEELMNR	ALDERMEN	ADEELRTV	TRAVELED	ADEENOPW	WEAPONED
ADEELMNS	DALESMEN	ADEELRUV	REVALUED	ADEENORS	REASONED
	EMENDALS	ADEELRWY	LAWYERED	ADEENORV	ENDEAVOR
	LEADSMEN	ADEELSST	DATELESS	ADEENORY	AERODYNE
ADEELMNT	LAMENTED		DETASSEL	ADEENOSS	ADENOSES
ADEELMOR	REMOLADE		TASSELED		SEASONED
ADEELMOS	SOMEDEAL	ADEELSTT	LADETTES	ADEENOST	ENDOSTEA
ADEELMPR	EMPARLED	ADEELSTU	ADULTESE	ADEENOTT	DENOTATE
ADEELMPX	EXAMPLED	ADEELSTY	SEDATELY		DETONATE
ADEELMRS	DEMERSAL	ADEELSUV	DEVALUES	ADEENPPR	ENDPAPER
	EMERALDS	ADEEMMMR	MAMMERED	ADEENPPS	SANDPEEP
ADEELMRT	TRAMELED	ADEEMMRY	YAMMERED	ADEENPRR	PANDERER
ADEELMRV	MARVELED	ADEEMMSS	MESDAMES	ADEENPRT	PARENTED
ADEELMST	MEDALETS	ADEEMMXY	MYXEDEMA	ADEENPRU	UNREAPED
ADEELMTU	EMULATED	ADEEMNNR	MANNERED	ADEENPRX	EXPANDER
ADEELNNP	ENPLANED		REMANNED	ADEENPSW	SNAPWEED
ADEELNNU	UNANELED	ADEEMNOR	DEMEANOR	ADEENPTT	PATENTED
ADEELNOR	OLEANDER		ENAMORED		PATTENED
	RELOANED	ADEEMNOS	DAEMONES	ADEENRRW	WANDERER
ADEELNPS	DEPLANES	ADEEMNOT	NEMATODE	ADEENRSS	DEARNESS
	SPALDEEN	ADEEMNOU	EUDAEMON	ADEENRSU	UNDERSEA
ADEELNPT	ENDPLATE	ADEEMNPR	DAMPENER		UNERASED
ADEELNPU	UPLEANED	ADEEMNPS	SPADEMEN		UNSEARED
ADEELNRT	ANTLERED	ADEEMNPY	EPENDYMA	ADEENRSW	ANSWERED
ADEELNRV	LAVENDER	ADEEMNRS	AMENDERS	ADEENRSY	YEARENDS
ADEELNSU	UNLEASED		MEANDERS	ADEENRTT	ATTENDER
	UNSEALED		REAMENDS		NATTERED
ADEELNSV	ENSLAVED	ADEEMNSS	SEEDSMAN		RATTENED
ADEELNTT	TALENTED	ADEEMNST	STAMENED	ADEENRTU	DENATURE

	UNDERATE		TREADERS	ADEFIINS	SANIFIED
	UNDEREAT	ADEERRSV	ADVERSER	ADEFIINZ	NAZIFIED
ADEENRTV	AVENTRED	ADEERRSW	REDWARES	ADEFIIRR	RARIFIED
ADEENRUV	UNREAVED	ADEERRTT	RETRATED	ADEFIIRT	RATIFIED
ADEENSST	ASSENTED	ADEERRTW	REDWATER	ADEFIIRU	AURIFIED
	SENSATED	ADEERRWY	WARREYED	ADEFILMN	INFLAMED
	STANDEES	ADEERSST	ASSERTED	ADEFILNR	FILANDER
ADEENSSU	DANSEUSE		ESTRADES	ADEFILNT	INFLATED
ADEENSTU	UNSEATED	ADEERSTT	ASTERTED	ADEFILOR	FORELAID
ADEENSTY	ANDESYTE		RESTATED	ADEFILOT	FOLIATED
ADEENTTU	TAUTENED		RETASTED	ADEFILSS	DISLEAFS
ADEENTTV	VENDETTA	ADEERSTW	DEWATERS	ADEFILSY	DAYFLIES
ADEEOPRR	PADERERO		TARWEEDS		LADYFIES
ADEEOPRT	OPERATED		WASTERED	ADEFIMPR	FIREDAMP
ADEEOPST	ADOPTEES	ADEERSTY	ESTRAYED	ADEFIMRS	MISFARED
ADEEORRV	OVERDARE	ADEERTTT	TATTERED	ADEFIMSS	DISFAMES
	OVERDEAR	ADEERTTY	YATTERED	ADEFINPR	PANFRIED
	OVERREAD	ADEERTWW	WARTWEED	ADEFINRR	INFRARED
ADEEORSW	OARWEEDS	ADEERVYY	EVERYDAY	ADEFINRS	FRIANDES
ADEEORVW	OVERAWED	ADEESSSS	ASSESSED	ADEFINRU	UNFAIRED
	REAVOWED	ADEESSTT	SEDATEST	ADEFINYZ	DENAZIFY
ADEEPPRR	DAPPERER	ADEESTTT	ATTESTED	ADEFIORS	FORESAID
	PREPARED	ADEESTUX	EXUDATES	ADEFIRRT	DRAFTIER
ADEEPPRT	PRETAPED	ADEESVVY	SAVVEYED	ADEFIRSS	FARSIDES
ADEEPPRU	PAUPERED	ADEESWWX	WAXWEEDS	ADEFKSST	DESKFAST
ADEEPPRV	PREPAVED	ADEFFGUW	GUFFAWED	ADEFLLLU	LADLEFUL
ADEEPPRW	WAPPERED	ADEFFIMR	AFFIRMED	ADEFLLNS	ELFLANDS
ADEEPRRS	RESPREAD	ADEFFIRR	DRAFFIER	ADEFLLOR	FALDEROL
	SPREADER	ADEFFIRT	TARIFFED	ADEFLLOW	FALLOWED
ADEEPRRT	DEPARTER	ADEFFIST	DAFFIEST	ADEFLLRY	ALDERFLY
ADEEPRRU	UPREARED	ADEFFLNS	SNAFFLED	ADEFLLSW	DEWFALLS
ADEEPRRV	DEPRAVER	ADEFFLOS	LEADOFFS	ADEFLLUY	FEUDALLY
	PERVADER	ADEFFORT	TRADEOFF	ADEFLMRU	DREAMFUL
ADEEPRSS	ASPERSED	ADEFFRST	STRAFFED	ADEFLNNS	FENLANDS
	PREASSED	ADEFGGOT	FAGGOTED	ADEFLNOR	FORELAND
	REPASSED	ADEFGIIS	GASIFIED	ADEFLNRU	DEARNFUL
	RESPADES	ADEFGILN	FINAGLED	ADEFLNTU	FLAUNTED
ADEEPRST	PEDERAST	ADEFGILO	FOLIAGED	ADEFLNUU	UNFEUDAL
	PREDATES	ADEFGILS	GADFLIES	ADEFLNUW	UNFLAWED
	REPASTED		GASFIELD	ADEFLORT	DEFLATOR
	TRAPESED	ADEFGIMN	DEFAMING	ADEFLORV	FLAVORED
ADEEPRSU	PERSUADE	ADEFGIRT	DRIFTAGE	ADEFLORY	FORELADY
ADEEPRSV	DEPRAVES	ADEFGIRU	ARGUFIED	ADEFLPRS	FELDSPAR
	PERVADES	ADEFGITU	FATIGUED	ADEFLPSU	SPADEFUL
ADEEPRSW	PERSWADE	ADEFGLOT	GATEFOLD	ADEFLRSW	SELFWARD
ADEEPRSZ	SPREAZED	ADEFGLRU	FELDGRAU	ADEFLRTU	TRADEFUL
ADEEPRTT	PATTERED	ADEFGNOR	FRONDAGE	ADEFLRTW	LEFTWARD
ADEEPRTU	DEPURATE	ADEFGOSU	FOUGADES	ADEFLRZZ	FRAZZLED
	EPURATED	ADEFHHIS	HEADFISH	ADEFLSTU	DEFAULTS
ADEEPRTZ	TRAPEZED	ADEFHILS	DEALFISH		SULFATED
ADEEPSST	STAPEDES	ADEFHILY	HAYFIELD	ADEFMNRU	UNFRAMED
ADEEPSTT	ADEPTEST	ADEFHIMS	FAMISHED	ADEFMORT	FORMATED
ADEEPSWY	SPEEDWAY	ADEFHKOR	FORKHEAD	ADEFMOSU	FAMOUSED
ADEEQRTU	DETRAQUE	ADEFHLSU	HEADFULS		FUMADOES
ADEEQRUV	QUAVERED	ADEFHLTU	DEATHFUL	ADEFNNNU	UNFANNED
ADEERRMT	RETARDER	ADEFHMOT	FATHOMED	ADEFNOPR	PROFANED
ADEERRRW	REDRAWER	ADEFHNOR	FOREHAND	ADEFNSST	DAFTNESS
	REREWARD	ADEFHOST	SOFTHEAD	ADEFOOSS	SEAFOODS
	REWARDER	ADEFIILN	FINIALED	ADEFORRR	FORRADER
ADEERRST	ARRESTED	ADEFIILR	AIRFIELD	ADEFORRW	FARROWED
	DREAREST	ADEFIILS	LADIFIES		FOREWARD
	RASTERED		SALIFIED	ADEFORRY	FOREYARD
	RETREADS	ADEFIILT	FILIATED		FORRAYED
	SERRATED	ADEFIIMR	RAMIFIED	ADEFORUV	FAVOURED

ADEFOSTU	FADEOUTS	**ADEGILLR**	GLADLIER	**ADEGINWX**	DEWAXING
ADEFPRRT	PREDRAFT		GRILLADE	**ADEGINYZ**	ZYGAENID
ADEFPTUW	UPWAFTED	**ADEGILLS**	GALLISED	**ADEGIORT**	ERGATOID
ADEFRRST	DRAFTERS	**ADEGILLZ**	GALLIZED	**ADEGIOST**	GODETIAS
	REDRAFTS	**ADEGILMN**	MALIGNED	**ADEGIPRR**	PARRIDGE
ADEFRSTW	DWARFEST		MEDALING	**ADEGIPRS**	SPAIRGED
ADEFSSTT	STEDFAST	**ADEGILNN**	LADENING	**ADEGIRWY**	RIDGEWAY
ADEGGGNU	UNGAGGED	**ADEGILNO**	GALENOID	**ADEGISSU**	DISUSAGE
ADEGGIRR	DRAGGIER	**ADEGILNP**	PEDALING	**ADEGISTU**	GAUDIEST
ADEGGIST	DAGGIEST		PLEADING	**ADEGISUV**	VIDUAGES
ADEGGISU	GAUDGIES	**ADEGILNR**	DANGLIER	**ADEGIUWY**	GUIDEWAY
	GUIDAGES		DEARLING	**ADEGJNOR**	JARGONED
ADEGGJLY	JAGGEDLY		DRAGLINE	**ADEGKLOY**	DEKALOGY
ADEGGLNU	ANGLEDUG	**ADEGILNS**	DEALINGS	**ADEGLLNU**	GLANDULE
ADEGGLRS	DRAGGLES		LEADINGS		UNGALLED
ADEGGLRY	RAGGEDLY		SIGNALED	**ADEGLLOP**	GALLOPED
ADEGGMOS	DEMAGOGS	**ADEGILNT**	DELATING	**ADEGLLOR**	GOLLARED
ADEGGMOY	DEMAGOGY	**ADEGILNY**	DELAYING	**ADEGLLOW**	GALLOWED
ADEGGNOW	WAGGONED	**ADEGILOR**	DIALOGER	**ADEGLLSU**	GALLUSED
ADEGGNTU	UNTAGGED	**ADEGILOS**	GOLIASED	**ADEGLMOR**	GLAMORED
ADEGGNUU	UNGAUGED	**ADEGILOU**	DIALOGUE	**ADEGLMOS**	GLADSOME
ADEGGOPS	PEDAGOGS	**ADEGILOY**	IDEALOGY	**ADEGLMPU**	PLUMAGED
ADEGGOPY	PEDAGOGY	**ADEGILRS**	SLAIRGED	**ADEGLMRU**	MAULGRED
ADEGGPRS	SPRAGGED	**ADEGILSS**	GLISSADE	**ADEGLMUY**	AMYGDULE
ADEGGRRS	DRAGGERS	**ADEGILST**	GLADIEST	**ADEGLNOP**	ANGLEPOD
ADEGGRTY	GADGETRY	**ADEGILSV**	DISGAVEL	**ADEGLNOY**	GONDELAY
ADEGHHOS	HOGSHEAD	**ADEGIMNN**	AMENDING	**ADEGLNPS**	SPANGLED
ADEGHILN	HEALDING	**ADEGIMNO**	AMIDOGEN	**ADEGLNRS**	DANGLERS
ADEGHILT	ALIGHTED	**ADEGIMNR**	DREAMING		GLANDERS
	GILTHEAD		MARGINED	**ADEGLNRW**	WRANGLED
ADEGHINR	ADHERING		MIDRANGE	**ADEGLNSS**	GLADNESS
	HEADRING	**ADEGIMOR**	IDEOGRAM	**ADEGLNTW**	TWANGLED
ADEGHINS	DEASHING	**ADEGIMPS**	MEDIGAPS	**ADEGLNUZ**	UNGLAZED
	HEADINGS		MISPAGED	**ADEGLOPP**	GALOPPED
	SHEADING	**ADEGIMRS**	MISGRADE	**ADEGLORV**	OVERGLAD
ADEGHIRR	HAGRIDER	**ADEGIMRT**	MIGRATED	**ADEGLPPR**	GRAPPLED
ADEGHIRS	GARISHED	**ADEGIMST**	SIGMATED	**ADEGLSTY**	DALGYTES
	HAGRIDES	**ADEGINNR**	GRANNIED	**ADEGMMNO**	GAMMONED
	HEADRIGS	**ADEGINNV**	ADVENING	**ADEGMMRU**	RUMMAGED
ADEGHIRT	GRAITHED		DAVENING	**ADEGMNOR**	DRAGOMEN
ADEGHJSU	JUGHEADS	**ADEGINNW**	AWNINGED	**ADEGMNOS**	GOADSMEN
ADEGHLNO	HEADLONG	**ADEGINNY**	DENAYING	**ADEGMNOT**	MONTAGED
	LONGHEAD	**ADEGINOR**	ORGANDIE	**ADEGMNOY**	ENDOGAMY
ADEGHLOS	GALOSHED	**ADEGINOS**	AGONISED	**ADEGMNRS**	DRAGSMEN
ADEGHNNU	UNHANGED		DIAGNOSE	**ADEGMNSU**	AGENDUMS
ADEGHNRT	THRANGED	**ADEGINOZ**	AGONIZED	**ADEGMOPS**	MEGAPODS
ADEGHOOP	PAGEHOOD	**ADEGINPU**	ANGUIPED	**ADEGMORS**	ORGASMED
ADEGHORT	GOATHERD	**ADEGINRR**	DREARING	**ADEGMORW**	WORDGAME
ADEGHRTU	DAUGHTER	**ADEGINRS**	DERAIGNS	**ADEGMPUZ**	GAZUMPED
ADEGHTUW	WAUGHTED		GRADINES	**ADEGNNOR**	ANDROGEN
ADEGIILN	GLIADINE		READINGS		DRAGONNE
ADEGIILP	DIPLEGIA	**ADEGINRT**	DERATING	**ADEGNNPU**	UNPANGED
ADEGIIMN	IMAGINED		GRADIENT	**ADEGNNSU**	DUNNAGES
ADEGIIMS	DIGAMIES		REDATING	**ADEGNOPR**	DOGNAPER
ADEGIINR	DEAIRING		TREADING	**ADEGNOPS**	PONDAGES
ADEGIINT	IDEATING	**ADEGINRY**	DERAYING	**ADEGNOPU**	POUNDAGE
ADEGIIRT	DIGERATI		READYING	**ADEGNORT**	DRAGONET
ADEGIITT	DIGITATE		YEARDING	**ADEGNOSS**	SONDAGES
ADEGIJSW	JIGSAWED	**ADEGINSS**	ASSIGNED	**ADEGNOSV**	DOGVANES
ADEGIKLO	GOADLIKE	**ADEGINST**	SEDATING	**ADEGNPUY**	PYENGADU
ADEGIKNN	KNEADING		STEADING	**ADEGNRRU**	GRANDEUR
ADEGIKNR	DAKERING	**ADEGINSW**	WINDAGES	**ADEGNRST**	DRAGNETS
ADEGILLO	GLADIOLE	**ADEGINTV**	VINTAGED		GRANDEST
ADEGILLP	PILLAGED	**ADEGINVW**	ADVEWING	**ADEGNRSU**	ENGUARDS

ADEGNRUU	UNARGUED		ADEHINOS	ADHESION		ADEHMNOT	METHADON
ADEGNRUZ	GAZUNDER		ADEHINOY	HYOIDEAN			THANEDOM
	UNGRAZED		ADEHINPS	DEANSHIP		ADEHMNRS	HERDSMAN
ADEGOORV	OVERGOAD			HEADPINS		ADEHMNRU	UNHARMED
ADEGOORY	GOODYEAR			PINHEADS		ADEHMNSU	UNSHAMED
ADEGOPPR	PROPAGED		ADEHINPU	DAUPHINE		ADEHMOOP	OOMPAHED
ADEGOPRR	DRAGROPE		ADEHINRT	ANTHERID		ADEHMOOR	HEADROOM
	PROGRADE		ADEHINRU	UNHAIRED		ADEHMOPS	MOPHEADS
ADEGOPRT	PORTAGED		ADEHINSS	DANISHES		ADEHMORS	HADROMES
ADEGORRT	GARROTED			SHANDIES		ADEHMORW	HOMEWARD
ADEGORST	GOADSTER		ADEHINST	HANDIEST		ADEHMOST	HEADMOST
ADEGORSW	DOWAGERS		ADEHINSV	VANISHED		ADEHMOSU	MADHOUSE
	WORDAGES		ADEHIOTT	ATHETOID		ADEHMOSY	SHAMOYED
ADEGORTT	GAROTTED		ADEHIPRS	RAPHIDES		ADEHNNSW	HANDSEWN
ADEGORTU	OUTRAGED		ADEHIPSS	PISSHEAD		ADEHNOPR	ORPHANED
	RAGOUTED		ADEHIPST	PITHEADS		ADEHNOPT	PHONATED
ADEGORTW	WATERDOG			SIDEPATH		ADEHNORS	HARDNOSE
ADEGOTTV	GAVOTTED		ADEHIRRT	TRIHEDRA		ADEHNORV	HANDOVER
ADEGOTUZ	OUTGAZED		ADEHIRRW	HARDWIRE			OVERHAND
ADEGPRRU	UPGRADER		ADEHIRSS	AIRSHEDS		ADEHNOSS	SANDSHOE
ADEGPRSS	SPADGERS			RADISHES		ADEHNOSU	SEAHOUND
ADEGPRSU	UPGRADES		ADEHIRST	HAIRSTED		ADEHNPSU	UNHASPED
ADEGPSTU	UPSTAGED			HARDIEST			UNSHAPED
ADEGRRST	DRAGSTER		ADEHIRSV	RAVISHED		ADEHNPTU	UNPATHED
ADEGRRSU	GUARDERS		ADEHIRSW	DISHWARE		ADEHNRSS	HARDNESS
ADEGRSSU	DESUGARS			RAWHIDES		ADEHNRSU	UNSHARED
	GRADUSES		ADEHIRSY	HAYRIDES		ADEHNRSW	SWANHERD
ADEGTTTU	GUTTATED		ADEHIRVW	HIVEWARD		ADEHNRTU	UNTHREAD
ADEHHIPR	RHAPHIDE		ADEHISST	DASHIEST		ADEHNSST	HANDSETS
ADEHHIPS	HEADSHIP			SHADIEST		ADEHNSSU	SUNSHADE
ADEHHIST	SHITHEAD		ADEHISSW	SIWASHED			UNSASHED
ADEHHNTU	HEADHUNT		ADEHJLOT	JOLTHEAD		ADEHNSUV	UNSHAVED
ADEHHOOR	HOORAHED		ADEHKLNU	LUNKHEAD		ADEHNSUW	UNWASHED
ADEHHOPS	HOPHEADS		ADEHKNRS	REDSHANK		ADEHNTTU	UNHATTED
ADEHHOST	HEADSHOT		ADEHKNSU	UNSHAKED		ADEHNTUW	UNTHAWED
	HOTHEADS		ADEHKORS	HARDOKES		ADEHOOPS	APEHOODS
ADEHHRRU	HURRAHED		ADEHKORW	HEADWORK		ADEHOORW	HAREWOOD
ADEHHRST	THRASHED		ADEHKOST	KATHODES		ADEHOORY	HOORAYED
ADEHHUZZ	HUZZAHED		ADEHLLOO	HALLOOED		ADEHOPRS	RHAPSODE
ADEHIITZ	THIAZIDE			HOLLOAED		ADEHOPST	POTASHED
ADEHIJMS	JEHADISM		ADEHLLOU	HULLOAED			POTHEADS
ADEHIJST	JEHADIST		ADEHLLOW	HALLOWED		ADEHOPSX	HEXAPODS
ADEHIKLN	HANDLIKE		ADEHLLRT	THRALLED		ADEHOPXY	HEXAPODY
ADEHIKLV	KHEDIVAL		ADEHLLRW	HELLWARD		ADEHORRS	HOARDERS
ADEHIKNS	SKINHEAD		ADEHLLSY	DAYSHELL		ADEHORRV	OVERHARD
ADEHIKSS	DASHEKIS		ADEHLMNO	HOMELAND		ADEHORRW	HARROWED
ADEHIKST	SKAITHED		ADEHLMOY	HOLYDAME		ADEHORSW	SHADOWER
ADEHIKSV	KHEDIVAS		ADEHLNRS	HANDLERS		ADEHORTT	THROATED
ADEHILLO	HILLOAED		ADEHLNSS	HANDLESS		ADEHORTU	AUTHORED
ADEHILLP	PHIALLED			HANDSELS			OUTHEARD
	PILLHEAD		ADEHLNST	SHETLAND		ADEHOSTW	TOWHEADS
ADEHILMO	HALIDOME		ADEHLNSU	UNHALSED		ADEHPSTU	DUSTHEAP
ADEHILNR	HARDLINE			UNLASHED		ADEHQSSU	SQUASHED
ADEHILNU	UNHAILED			UNSHALED		ADEHRRUY	HURRAYED
ADEHILPS	HELIPADS		ADEHLNUV	UNHALVED		ADEHRSSY	HYDRASES
ADEHILSV	LAVISHED		ADEHLOOR	HORDEOLA		ADEHRSTY	HYDRATES
ADEHILSW	WHAISLED		ADEHLOOT	TOOLHEAD		ADEHRTTW	THWARTED
ADEHILWZ	WHAIZLED		ADEHLOPS	ASPHODEL		ADEIILMN	LIMNAEID
ADEHIMMS	SHAMMIED			PHOLADES		ADEIILMS	IDEALISM
ADEHIMOT	HEMATOID		ADEHLOPW	PLOWHEAD			MILADIES
ADEHIMRS	MISHEARD		ADEHLPSS	SPLASHED		ADEIILPR	PERIDIAL
	SEMIHARD		ADEHLRRY	HERALDRY		ADEIILRS	LAIRISED
ADEHIMRY	HYDREMIA		ADEHMNNY	HANDYMEN		ADEIILRZ	LAIRIZED
ADEHINOP	DIAPHONE		ADEHMNOS	HANDSOME		ADEIILST	IDEALIST

ADEIILTV	DILATIVE
ADEIILTY	IDEALITY
ADEIIMMS	MISAIMED
ADEIIMNN	INDAMINE
ADEIIMNR	MERIDIAN
ADEIIMNS	AMIDINES
	DIAMINES
ADEIIMNT	MINIATED
ADEIIMPR	IMPAIRED
ADEIIMRS	SEMIARID
ADEIIMTT	IMITATED
ADEIINNS	SANIDINE
ADEIINOT	IDEATION
	IODINATE
	TAENIOID
ADEIINRS	DRAISINE
ADEIINRT	DAINTIER
ADEIINRU	UREDINIA
ADEIINST	ADENITIS
	DAINTIES
ADEIINSZ	DIAZINES
ADEIINTV	VANITIED
ADEIINUV	INDUVIAE
ADEIIPRR	PERRADII
ADEIIPRS	PRESIDIA
ADEIIPST	STAPEDII
ADEIIRSS	AIRSIDES
	DIARISES
ADEIIRST	IRISATED
ADEIIRSZ	DIARIZES
ADEIITTV	TIDIVATE
	VITIATED
ADEIITUV	AUDITIVE
ADEIJMRS	JEMIDARS
ADEIKLLO	KELOIDAL
ADEIKLLR	LARDLIKE
ADEIKLLY	LADYLIKE
ADEIKLNS	SANDLIKE
ADEIKLNW	DAWNLIKE
	WANDLIKE
ADEIKLOT	TOADLIKE
ADEIKLOX	ALKOXIDE
ADEIKLRR	DARKLIER
ADEIKLSW	SIDEWALK
ADEIKMMS	IMMASKED
ADEIKMPR	IMPARKED
ADEIKMRT	TIDEMARK
ADEIKNPR	KIDNAPER
ADEIKNSY	KYANISED
ADEIKNYZ	KYANIZED
ADEIKORT	KERATOID
ADEIKRST	STRAIKED
ADEILLMY	MEDIALLY
ADEILLNN	LANDLINE
ADEILLNU	UNALLIED
ADEILLNV	ANVILLED
ADEILLNW	INWALLED
ADEILLNY	LEYLANDI
ADEILLOR	ARILLODE
ADEILLPR	PALLIDER
	PILLARED
ADEILLPS	ILLAPSED
	SPADILLE
ADEILLRS	DALLIERS
	DIALLERS
ADEILLRT	TRIALLED
ADEILLRV	RIVALLED
ADEILLSW	SIDEWALL
ADEILMMM	MELAMDIM
ADEILMMS	DILEMMAS
ADEILMNO	MELANOID
ADEILMNP	PLAIDMEN
ADEILMNU	UNMAILED
ADEILMNY	MAIDENLY
	MEDIANLY
ADEILMOS	DAMOISEL
	MELODIAS
ADEILMOX	ALDOXIME
ADEILMPP	PALMIPED
ADEILMPR	IMPARLED
ADEILMPS	IMPLEADS
	MISPLEAD
ADEILMPT	IMPLATED
ADEILMRS	DISMALER
ADEILMRY	DREAMILY
ADEILMSS	MAIDLESS
	MISDEALS
	MISLEADS
ADEILMST	MEDALIST
	MISDEALT
ADEILMSY	DYSMELIA
ADEILNNO	NONIDEAL
ADEILNNP	PINELAND
ADEILNNR	INLANDER
ADEILNNS	ANNELIDS
	LINDANES
ADEILNNT	DENTINAL
ADEILNNU	UNNAILED
ADEILNOP	PALINODE
ADEILNOS	NODALISE
ADEILNOT	DELATION
ADEILNOZ	NODALIZE
ADEILNPS	SANDPILE
ADEILNPT	PANTILED
ADEILNPU	PALUDINE
ADEILNRS	ISLANDER
ADEILNSU	UNSAILED
ADEILNSV	ANDVILES
ADEILNTU	UNTAILED
ADEILNTV	DIVALENT
ADEILNUV	UNVAILED
ADEILOPS	EPISODAL
	OPALISED
	SEPALOID
ADEILOPT	PETALOID
ADEILOPZ	OPALIZED
ADEILOQU	ODALIQUE
ADEILORS	DARIOLES
	SOLIDARE
	SOREDIAL
ADEILORT	IDOLATER
	TAILORED
ADEILORV	OVERLAID
ADEILORX	EXORDIAL
ADEILOSS	ASSOILED
	DEASOILS
	ISOLEADS
ADEILOST	DIASTOLE
	ISOLATED
	SODALITE
	SOLIDATE
ADEILOSU	DOULEIAS
ADEILOSZ	DIAZOLES
	SLEAZOID
ADEILOTT	DATOLITE
ADEILOTV	DOVETAIL
	VIOLATED
ADEILPPP	PEDIPALP
ADEILPRS	LIPREADS
	PARSLIED
	PEDRAILS
	SPIRALED
ADEILPRT	DIPTERAL
	TRIPEDAL
ADEILPRU	EPIDURAL
ADEILPRV	DEPRIVAL
ADEILPSS	DESPISAL
ADEILPST	TALIPEDS
ADEILPTU	PLAUDITE
ADEILQSU	SQUAILED
ADEILQTU	LIQUATED
ADEILRRW	DRAWLIER
ADEILRRY	DREARILY
ADEILRST	DILATERS
	LARDIEST
	REDTAILS
ADEILRSU	RESIDUAL
ADEILRSY	DIALYSER
ADEILRTT	DETRITAL
ADEILRTY	DIELYTRA
ADEILRVY	VARIEDLY
ADEILRYZ	DIALYZER
ADEILSSU	DEASIULS
	DUALISES
ADEILSSV	DEVISALS
ADEILSSY	DIALYSES
ADEILSTV	VALIDEST
ADEILSTY	DIASTYLE
	STEADILY
ADEILSUV	DISVALUE
ADEILSUZ	DUALIZES
ADEILSWY	SLIDEWAY
ADEILSXY	DYSLEXIA
ADEILSYZ	DIALYZES
ADEILTTU	ALTITUDE
	LATITUDE
ADEILTVY	DATIVELY
ADEIMMNS	MISNAMED
ADEIMMNU	UNMAIMED
ADEIMMRS	MERMAIDS
ADEIMMST	MISMATED
ADEIMNNO	DEMONIAN
	MONDAINE
ADEIMNOP	DOPAMINE
ADEIMNOR	RADIOMEN
ADEIMNOS	AMIDONES
	DAIMONES
	DOMAINES
	NOMADIES
	NOMADISE
ADEIMNOT	DOMINATE
	NEMATOID

ADEIMNOU	EUDAIMON	**ADEINORU**	DOUANIER	**ADEIOSTX**	OXIDATES
ADEIMNOZ	NOMADIZE	**ADEINOSS**	ADENOSIS	**ADEIOSTZ**	AZOTISED
ADEIMNPW	IMPAWNED		ADONISES	**ADEIOSVV**	VAIVODES
ADEIMNRR	MANRIDER		ANODISES	**ADEIOSVW**	WAIVODES
ADEIMNRS	ADERMINS	**ADEINOST**	ASTONIED	**ADEIOSWW**	WAIWODES
	SIRNAMED		SEDATION	**ADEIOTZZ**	AZOTIZED
ADEIMNRU	MURAENID	**ADEINOSX**	DIOXANES	**ADEIPPRS**	APPRISED
ADEIMNRY	DAIRYMEN	**ADEINOSZ**	ADONIZES		DRAPPIES
ADEIMNRZ	ZEMINDAR		ANODIZES	**ADEIPPRZ**	APPRIZED
ADEIMNSS	SIDESMAN	**ADEINOTT**	ANTIDOTE	**ADEIPRRS**	DRAPIERS
ADEIMNST	MEDIANTS		TETANOID	**ADEIPRSS**	DESPAIRS
	TIDESMAN	**ADEINOTV**	DONATIVE	**ADEIPRST**	DIPTERAS
ADEIMNSU	MAUNDIES	**ADEINPPX**	APPENDIX		RAPIDEST
ADEIMNSY	DYNAMISE	**ADEINPRS**	SPRAINED		SPIRATED
ADEIMNTY	DYNAMITE	**ADEINPRT**	DIPTERAN		TARSIPED
ADEIMNYZ	DYNAMIZE	**ADEINPRU**	UNPAIRED		TRAIPSED
ADEIMORR	AIRDROME		UNREPAID	**ADEIPRSU**	UPRAISED
ADEIMORT	MEDIATOR	**ADEINPST**	DEPAINTS	**ADEIPRSW**	RIPSAWED
ADEIMOSS	SESAMOID	**ADEINPSV**	SPAVINED	**ADEIPRTU**	EUPATRID
ADEIMOST	ATOMISED	**ADEINQTU**	ANTIQUED		PREAUDIT
ADEIMOTZ	ATOMIZED	**ADEINRRS**	DRAINERS	**ADEIPSSX**	SPADIXES
ADEIMPRR	RAMPIRED		SERRANID	**ADEIPSTV**	VAPIDEST
ADEIMPRT	IMPARTED	**ADEINRSS**	ARIDNESS	**ADEIPTTU**	APTITUDE
	PREADMIT		SARDINES	**ADEIQRRU**	QUARRIED
ADEIMPRV	VAMPIRED	**ADEINRST**	DETRAINS	**ADEIQRSU**	QUERIDAS
ADEIMPST	DAMPIEST		RANDIEST	**ADEIQSUY**	QUAYSIDE
	IMPASTED		STRAINED	**ADEIRRSW**	SWARDIER
ADEIMRRS	ADMIRERS	**ADEINRSU**	DENARIUS	**ADEIRRTW**	TAWDRIER
	DISARMER		UNRAISED	**ADEIRRWW**	WIREDRAW
	MARRIEDS		URANIDES	**ADEIRRZZ**	RIZZARED
ADEIMRSS	MISREADS	**ADEINRSV**	INVADERS	**ADEIRSST**	ASTERIDS
	SIDEARMS		SANDIVER		DIASTERS
ADEIMRST	MARDIEST	**ADEINRSY**	SYNEDRIA		DISASTER
	MISRATED	**ADEINRTT**	NITRATED		DISRATES
	READMITS	**ADEINRTU**	DATURINE	**ADEIRSSU**	RADIUSES
ADEIMRSY	MIDYEARS		INDURATE		SUDARIES
ADEIMRTT	ADMITTER		RUINATED	**ADEIRSSV**	ADVISERS
ADEIMRTU	MURIATED		URINATED	**ADEIRSTT**	STRAITED
ADEIMSST	DIASTEMS	**ADEINRUV**	UNVARIED		STRIATED
	MISDATES	**ADEINRVY**	VINEYARD		TARDIEST
ADEIMSTU	TAEDIUMS	**ADEINSST**	DESTAINS	**ADEIRSTW**	TAWDRIES
ADEIMSTY	DAYTIMES		SANDIEST	**ADEIRTTT**	ATTRITED
ADEINNNS	NANDINES	**ADEINSSV**	AVIDNESS		TITRATED
ADEINNOT	ANOINTED		VANESSID	**ADEIRTUV**	DURATIVE
	ANTINODE	**ADEINSSW**	WINDASES	**ADEIRVWY**	DRIVEWAY
ADEINNOV	DEVONIAN	**ADEINSTT**	INSTATED	**ADEISSST**	ASSISTED
ADEINNPT	PINNATED	**ADEINSTU**	AUDIENTS		DISSEATS
ADEINNPU	UNPAINED		SINUATED	**ADEISSSV**	DISSAVES
ADEINNRS	INSNARED	**ADEINSTV**	DEVIANTS	**ADEISSTT**	DISTASTE
ADEINNRZ	RENDZINA	**ADEINSTY**	DESYATIN		STAIDEST
ADEINNSU	UNSANED	**ADEIOPRR**	PRERADIO	**ADEISSTV**	DISTAVES
ADEINNSX	DISANNEX	**ADEIOPRS**	DIASPORE	**ADEISSWY**	SIDEWAYS
ADEINNTU	ANTIDUNE		PARODIES		WAYSIDES
	INUNDATE	**ADEIOPRV**	OVERPAID	**ADEISTTU**	SITUATED
ADEINOPP	PEPONIDA	**ADEIOPSS**	ADIPOSES	**ADEISTUZ**	DEUTZIAS
ADEINOPT	ANTIPODE	**ADEIOPST**	DIOPTASE	**ADEISTWY**	TIDEWAYS
ADEINORR	ORDAINER	**ADEIOPTV**	ADOPTIVE	**ADEITTTU**	ATTITUDE
	REORDAIN	**ADEIORRT**	ADROITER		ATTUITED
ADEINORS	ANEROIDS	**ADEIORST**	ASTEROID	**ADEJLOSU**	JALOUSED
	DONARIES	**ADEIORSV**	AVODIRES	**ADEJMMNU**	UNJAMMED
ADEINORT	AROINTED		AVOIDERS	**ADEJMRRU**	JUMARRED
	DERATION	**ADEIORTT**	TERATOID	**ADEJNRUW**	UNDERJAW
	ORDINATE	**ADEIORTV**	DEVIATOR	**ADEJOPRS**	JEOPARDS
	RATIONED	**ADEIOSSX**	OXIDASES	**ADEJOPRY**	JEOPARDY

ADEJRRSU	ADJURERS	ADELNNNU	UNNANELD	ADELPQUX	QUADPLEX
ADEJRSTU	ADJUSTER	ADELNNOT	LENTANDO	ADELPRRU	LARRUPED
	READJUST	ADELNOPR	PONDERAL	ADELPRSW	SPRAWLED
ADEKLMRY	MARKEDLY	ADELNORS	LADRONES	ADELPRTT	PRATTLED
ADEKLNOX	KLAXONED		SOLANDER	ADELPRTU	PREADULT
ADEKLNPP	KNAPPLED	ADELNORU	UNLOADER	ADELPSTT	SPLATTED
ADEKLNPR	PRANKLED		URODELAN	ADELPSTU	PULSATED
ADEKLNSU	UNSLAKED	ADELNORV	OVERLAND	ADELPUUV	UPVALUED
ADEKLORW	LEADWORK		RONDAVEL	ADELRRSU	RUDERALS
ADEKLPRS	SPARKLED	ADELNOSY	YEALDONS	ADELRRSW	DRAWLERS
ADEKLPTU	UPTALKED	ADELNPRS	SPANDREL	ADELRRTU	ULTRARED
ADEKMNRU	UNMARKED	ADELNPRU	PENDULAR	ADELRSSW	WARDLESS
ADEKMNSU	UNMASKED		UNDERLAP		WRASSLED
ADEKMORS	DARKSOME		UPLANDER	ADELRSTT	STARTLED
ADEKMTUU	MAKUTUED	ADELNPRY	PANDERLY	ADELRSTW	WARSTLED
ADEKNNRU	UNRANKED		REPANDLY		WRASTLED
ADEKNNSS	DANKNESS	ADELNPSY	DYSPNEAL	ADELRSZZ	DAZZLERS
ADEKNOSU	UNSOAKED		ENDPLAYS	ADELRTUY	ADULTERY
ADEKNOTW	TAKEDOWN	ADELNPUY	UNPLAYED	ADELSTTY	STATEDLY
ADEKNRSS	DARKNESS	ADELNRSS	SLANDERS	ADELTTTW	TWATTLED
ADEKNSVY	VANDYKES	ADELNRSU	LAUNDERS	ADEMMNOW	MADWOMEN
ADEKOOTW	TEAKWOOD		LURDANES	ADEMMSTU	SUMMATED
ADEKOSTU	OUTASKED		RUNDALES	ADEMNNNU	UNMANNED
ADEKQSUW	SQUAWKED	ADELNRTU	DENTURAL	ADEMNNOR	NORMANDE
ADELLMOR	MORALLED	ADELNRTY	ARDENTLY	ADEMNNOU	UNMOANED
ADELLMOS	SLALOMED	ADELNRUY	UNDERLAY	ADEMNNRU	MUNDANER
ADELLMRU	MEDULLAR	ADELNSSS	SANDLESS		UNDERMAN
	MURALLED	ADELNSTU	UNSALTED	ADEMNOOR	MAROONED
ADELLMSU	MEDULLAS	ADELNSTW	WETLANDS	ADEMNOPR	POMANDER
ADELLNNU	ANNULLED	ADELNTUU	UNDULATE	ADEMNOPT	TAMPONED
ADELLNPS	SPENDALL	ADELNUUV	UNVALUED	ADEMNORS	MADRONES
ADELLNRS	LANDLERS	ADELNUZZ	UNDAZZLE		RANSOMED
ADELLNSS	LANDLESS	ADELOOPV	LEVODOPA		ROADSMEN
ADELLNSW	ELLWANDS	ADELOORV	OVERLOAD	ADEMNOTU	AMOUNTED
	WALLSEND	ADELOOTW	LATEWOOD		OUTNAMED
ADELLNTY	DENTALLY	ADELOOWW	WOODWALE	ADEMNPPU	UNMAPPED
ADELLNUW	UNWALLED	ADELOPPR	PROPALED	ADEMNPSS	DAMPNESS
ADELLOPW	WALLOPED	ADELOPRS	LEOPARDS	ADEMNRRU	UNDERARM
ADELLORS	ODALLERS		PRELOADS		UNMARRED
ADELLOSW	SALLOWED	ADELOPRT	PORTALED	ADEMNRSU	DURAMENS
ADELLOTT	ALLOTTED		PROLATED		MAUNDERS
	TOTALLED	ADELOPRU	POULARDE		SURNAMED
ADELLOTV	LAVOLTED	ADELOPRW	POLEWARD	ADEMNRTU	UNDREAMT
ADELLOTW	TALLOWED	ADELOPSS	DEPOSALS	ADEMNRUW	UNWARMED
ADELLOVY	LADYLOVE	ADELOPST	TADPOLES	ADEMNSSU	MEDUSANS
ADELLOWW	WALLOWED	ADELOPSU	PALUDOSE	ADEMNSUU	UNAMUSED
ADELLQSU	SQUALLED	ADELOPSY	SEPALODY	ADEMNTTU	UNMATTED
ADELLRSU	UDALLERS	ADELOPTY	PETALODY	ADEMOORT	MODERATO
ADELLTUU	ULULATED	ADELORRV	OVERLARD	ADEMOORV	VAROOMED
ADELMNNS	LANDSMEN	ADELORSS	ROADLESS	ADEMOOST	STOMODEA
ADELMNOS	LODESMAN	ADELORST	DELATORS	ADEMOOSV	VAMOOSED
ADELMNRS	MANDRELS		LEOTARDS	ADEMOPRY	PYODERMA
ADELMOOW	WOODMEAL		LODESTAR	ADEMOPST	STAMPEDO
ADELMOPS	MALPOSED	ADELORSU	ROULADES	ADEMOPSU	MOUSEPAD
ADELMORS	EARLDOMS	ADELORTW	LEADWORT	ADEMORRT	MORTARED
ADELMOSS	DAMOSELS	ADELOSSS	SODALESS	ADEMORRU	ARMOURED
ADELMOSZ	DAMOZELS	ADELOSST	TOADLESS	ADEMORRW	MARROWED
ADELMOTU	MODULATE	ADELOSSW	DOWLASES	ADEMORST	STROAMED
ADELMPRT	TRAMPLED	ADELOSTU	OUTLEADS	ADEMORTU	OUTDREAM
ADELMRRU	DEMURRAL	ADELOSTV	SOLVATED	ADEMORTW	DAMEWORT
ADELMSSY	MASSEDLY	ADELOTUV	OVULATED		WARDMOTE
ADELMSUY	AMUSEDLY	ADELOTUW	OUTLAWED	ADEMOSSY	SAMOYEDS
ADELMTTY	MATTEDLY	ADELOVWY	AVOWEDLY	ADEMPRST	STRAMPED
ADELMTUU	UMLAUTED	ADELPPRY	DAPPERLY	ADEMRRSU	EARDRUMS

ADEMRRTY	MARTYRED	ADENRSSU	DANSEURS	ADEPSUWY	UPSWAYED
ADENNNTU	UNTANNED	ADENRSTU	DAUNTERS	ADEQSTTU	SQUATTED
ADENNORT	NONRATED		TRANSUDE	ADERRSSW	WARDRESS
ADENNOSY	ANODYNES		UNTREADS	ADERRSTT	REDSTART
ADENNOTU	UNATONED	ADENRSTX	DEXTRANS	ADERSSSU	ASSUREDS
ADENNOTW	WANTONED	ADENRSUY	UNDERSAY	ADERSSTW	STEWARDS
ADENNOTY	TANNOYED	ADENRTTU	TRUANTED	ADERSSUY	DASYURES
ADENNPST	PENDANTS	ADENRTTY	TYRANTED	ADERSTTU	STATURED
ADENNRRU	UNDERRAN	ADENRTUX	UNDERTAX	ADERSTUX	SURTAXED
ADENNRTY	TYRANNED	ADENRUWY	UNDERWAY	ADERSTVY	STRAYVED
ADENNRUW	UNWARNED	ADENSSSW	WESSANDS	ADERSTWW	WESTWARD
ADENNSTU	ASTUNNED	ADENSTTU	UNSTATED	ADESSTTW	WADSETTS
ADENNTUW	UNWANTED		UNTASTED	ADFFGIIR	GIRAFFID
ADENOOPS	EPANODOS	ADENSTUW	UNWASTED	ADFFGINS	DAFFINGS
ADENOORT	RATOONED	ADENSTUY	UNSTAYED	ADFFHIRS	DRAFFISH
ADENOORW	WANDEROO		UNSTEADY	ADFFHNOS	HANDOFFS
ADENOOST	ODONATES	ADENSUWY	UNSWAYED	ADFFISST	DISTAFFS
ADENOOTZ	OZONATED	ADEOOPRW	PEARWOOD	ADFFLNOS	FANFOLDS
ADENOPRR	PARDONER	ADEOOPSS	APODOSES	ADFFLOOS	OFFLOADS
ADENOPRS	OPERANDS	ADEOORRT	TOREADOR	ADFFLRUU	FRAUDFUL
	PADRONES	ADEOOTTT	TATTOOED	ADFFNOST	STANDOFF
	PANDORES	ADEOPPRV	APPROVED	ADFFOORS	AFFOORDS
ADENOPRT	PRONATED	ADEOPRRS	EARDROPS	ADFGINNU	UNFADING
ADENOPRX	EXPANDOR	ADEOPRRT	PARROTED	ADFGINRS	FARDINGS
ADENOPSS	DAPSONES		PREDATOR	ADFGINRT	DRAFTING
	SPADONES		PRORATED	ADFGINRW	DWARFING
ADENOPST	NOTEPADS		PROTRADE	ADFHILSY	LADYFISH
	TONEPADS		TEARDROP	ADFHINSS	SANDFISH
ADENOPSU	UNSOAPED	ADEOPRRU	UPROARED	ADFHIOST	TOADFISH
ADENOPSY	DYSPNOEA	ADEOPRST	ADOPTERS	ADFHIRSW	DWARFISH
ADENORRS	ADORNERS		ASPORTED	ADFHLNSU	HANDFULS
	READORNS		PASTORED		HANDSFUL
ADENORRW	NARROWED		READOPTS	ADFHLNSY	FLYHANDS
ADENORST	TORNADES	ADEOPRSU	UPSOARED	ADFHLOST	HOLDFAST
ADENORTT	ATTORNED	ADEOPRTT	TETRAPOD	ADFHOOSS	SHADOOFS
ADENORTW	DANEWORT	ADEOPRUV	VAPOURED	ADFIIILR	FILARIID
	TEARDOWN	ADEOPSST	PODESTAS	ADFIILPY	LAPIDIFY
ADENORTY	AROYNTED	ADEOPSTT	DESPOTAT	ADFILLLN	LANDFILL
ADENORUX	RONDEAUX		POSTDATE	ADFILLMN	FILMLAND
ADENOSST	ONSTEADS	ADEORRSS	DROSERAS	ADFILLNO	NAILFOLD
ADENOTUY	AUTODYNE	ADEORRST	ROADSTER	ADFILLNW	WINDFALL
ADENOUVW	UNAVOWED	ADEORRTW	TARROWED	ADFILMNO	MANIFOLD
ADENPPRS	PARPENDS	ADEORRVW	OVERDRAW	ADFILMRU	FLUIDRAM
ADENPPSU	UNSAPPED	ADEORSST	ASSORTED	ADFILMWW	WINDFLAW
ADENPPTU	UNTAPPED		TORSADES	ADFILRTY	DRAFTILY
ADENPRRS	PARDNERS	ADEORSTU	OUTDARES	ADFIMNRS	FINDRAMS
ADENPRSU	UNDRAPES		OUTREADS	ADFIMORY	FAIRYDOM
	UNSPARED		READOUTS	ADFIMRSW	DWARFISM
ADENPRSW	PREDAWNS	ADEORSTX	EXTRADOS	ADFINORZ	FORZANDI
ADENPRTU	DEPURANT	ADEORSUV	SAVOURED	ADFINRST	INDRAFTS
	UNPARTED	ADEORSWY	RODEWAYS	ADFIORSV	DISFAVOR
ADENPRTY	PEDANTRY	ADEORTTU	OUTRATED	ADFKLLNO	FOLKLAND
ADENPRUW	UNWARPED		OUTTRADE	ADFLLNOW	DOWNFALL
ADENPRUY	UNDERPAY	ADEORTUV	OUTRAVED	ADFLMNOR	LANDFORM
	UNPRAYED	ADEOSSTT	ASSOTTED	ADFLMNOY	MANYFOLD
ADENPSSY	DYSPNEAS	ADEOSTTU	OUTDATES	ADFLMOPR	FRAMPOLD
	SYNAPSED	ADEOSWWY	WAYWODES	ADFLMPSU	MUDFLAPS
ADENQRSU	SQUANDER	ADEOTTTW	TATTOWED	ADFLMSTU	MUDFLATS
ADENRRST	STRANDER	ADEPPRST	STRAPPED	ADFLNOPS	PLAFONDS
ADENRRSY	REYNARDS	ADEPRRTU	RAPTURED	ADFLOOWY	FLOODWAY
ADENRRTU	UNTARRED	ADEPRSTU	PASTURED	ADFLORSU	FOULARDS
ADENRRWY	WARDENRY		UPDATERS	ADFMRSTU	STUDFARM
ADENRSSS	SARSDENS		UPSTARED	ADFNNOST	FONDANTS
ADENRSST	STANDERS	ADEPSTUY	UPSTAYED	ADFNOORZ	FORZANDO

ADFOOPST	FOOTPADS	ADGIINOT	IODATING	ADGINPPR	DRAPPING
ADFOOSTW	FATWOODS	ADGIINOV	AVOIDING	ADGINPTU	UPDATING
ADFOOSWY	FOODWAYS	ADGIINRR	ARRIDING	ADGINRRS	GRANDSIR
ADFORRSW	FORWARDS	ADGIINRS	RAIDINGS	ADGINRST	TRADINGS
	FROWARDS	ADGIINRY	DAIRYING	ADGINRSW	DRAWINGS
ADFPRSTU	UPDRAFTS	ADGIINSS	SIGANIDS		SWARDING
ADGGGILN	DAGGLING	ADGIINSU	IGUANIDS		WARDINGS
ADGGGINR	DRAGGING	ADGIINSV	ADVISING	ADGINRSY	YARDINGS
ADGGGINS	DAGGINGS	ADGIINSW	GWINIADS	ADGINRTT	DRATTING
ADGGHNOS	HANGDOGS	ADGIINTU	AUDITING	ADGINRTU	ANTIDRUG
ADGGHORY	HYDRAGOG	ADGIJNRU	ADJURING	ADGINRTY	TARDYING
ADGGILNN	DANGLING	ADGKILNR	DARKLING	ADGINSTU	ADUSTING
ADGGILNS	GADLINGS	ADGILLNU	ALLUDING		SUDATING
ADGGILRS	RIGGALDS		DUALLING	ADGINSWY	GWYNIADS
ADGGINRS	NIGGARDS	ADGILLNW	WINDGALL	ADGIORST	GORDITAS
ADGGINRU	GUARDING	ADGILLNY	DALLYING	ADGIPRSU	PAGURIDS
ADGGLRSU	SLUGGARD	ADGILLOT	GOLDTAIL	ADGIRSSU	GUISARDS
ADGHHILN	HIGHLAND	ADGILMNS	GILDSMAN	ADGIRSZZ	GIZZARDS
ADGHHIOR	HIGHROAD		MADLINGS	ADGKOOSZ	GADZOOKS
ADGHILLL	GILDHALL	ADGILMNW	DWALMING	ADGLLNOS	GOLLANDS
ADGHILNN	HANDLING	ADGILMOR	MARIGOLD	ADGLMNOS	MANGOLDS
ADGHILOS	HIDALGOS	ADGILNNS	LANDINGS	ADGLMNSU	GUMLANDS
ADGHILPY	DIAGLYPH		SANDLING	ADGLNOOS	DONGOLAS
ADGHILTY	DAYLIGHT	ADGILNNU	UNLADING		GONDOLAS
ADGHINOR	HOARDING	ADGILNOS	LOADINGS	ADGLNORS	GOLDARNS
ADGHINPR	HANDGRIP	ADGILNPP	DAPPLING	ADGLNOSW	GOWLANDS
ADGHINSS	SHADINGS	ADGILNRS	DARLINGS	ADGLOORY	GARDYLOO
ADGHIPRS	DIGRAPHS	ADGILNRT	DARTLING	ADGLOSWY	DAYGLOWS
ADGHIRRS	ARDRIGHS	ADGILNRW	DRAWLING	ADGMNOOR	ONDOGRAM
ADGHIRSS	DISHRAGS	ADGILNRY	DARINGLY	ADGMNORS	GORMANDS
ADGHITTW	TIGHTWAD	ADGILNZZ	DAZZLING	ADGMNORU	GOURMAND
ADGHLNNO	LONGHAND	ADGILOOS	SOLIDAGO	ADGNNOQU	QUANDONG
ADGHNNSU	HANDGUNS	ADGILOPR	PRODIGAL	ADGNNORS	GRANDSON
ADGHNOSS	SANDHOGS	ADGILORS	GOLIARDS	ADGNNRVY	GYNANDRY
ADGHNOSW	HAGDOWNS	ADGILORY	GOLIARDY	ADGNOORS	DRAGOONS
ADGHOOPR	ODOGRAPH		GYROIDAL		GADROONS
ADGHORSW	HOGWARDS	ADGILRVY	GRAVIDLY	ADGNRRSU	GURNARDS
ADGHPSYY	DYSPHAGY	ADGIMMNR	DRAMMING	ADGNRSUU	UNGUARDS
ADGHRSTU	DRAUGHTS	ADGIMMNW	DWAMMING	ADGOOPRS	GOSPODAR
ADGHRTUY	DRAUGHTY	ADGIMNNU	MAUNDING	ADGOPRST	POSTGRAD
ADGIIIRT	TIGRIDIA	ADGIMNOP	POMADING	ADGOPRSU	PODARGUS
ADGIILLN	DIALLING	ADGIMNPS	DAMPINGS	ADGORSTU	OUTDRAGS
ADGIILLO	GLADIOLI	ADGIMNRS	MRIDANGS	ADGORTUU	OUTGUARD
ADGIILNO	GONIDIAL	ADGIMNRY	MARDYING	ADGRSSTU	DUSTRAGS
ADGIILNP	PAIDLING	ADGIMNUW	DWAUMING	ADHHIPRS	HARDSHIP
	PLAIDING	ADGIMOSU	DIGAMOUS	ADHHLOOV	HAVDOLOH
ADGIILNR	DRAILING	ADGINNOR	ADORNING	ADHHMOSS	SHAHDOMS
ADGIILNS	DIALINGS	ADGINNOT	DONATING	ADHHNRTY	HYDRANTH
	GLIADINS	ADGINNPY	PANDYING	ADHIIIKS	DAISHIKI
ADGIILNT	DILATING	ADGINNRS	DARNINGS	ADHIIJMS	JIHADISM
ADGIILPY	PYGIDIAL	ADGINNRT	DRANTING	ADHIIJST	IJTIHADS
ADGIILST	DIGITALS	ADGINNRU	UNDARING		JIHADIST
ADGIILTY	ALGIDITY	ADGINNSS	SANDINGS	ADHIIKSS	DASHIKIS
ADGIIMNR	ADMIRING	ADGINNST	STANDING	ADHIIMPS	AMIDSHIP
ADGIIMNX	ADMIXING	ADGINNSW	DAWNINGS	ADHIINOP	OPHIDIAN
ADGIIMOR	IDIOGRAM	ADGINNSY	SDAYNING	ADHIINRW	WHINIARD
ADGIIMST	DIGAMIST	ADGINNTU	DAUNTING	ADHIJLSY	JADISHLY
ADGIINNR	DRAINING	ADGINOOP	POIGNADO	ADHIKOPS	HAPKIDOS
ADGIINNS	SDAINING	ADGINOOR	RIGADOON	ADHILLMO	HOLLIDAM
ADGIINNT	NIDATING	ADGINOPT	ADOPTING	ADHILLNS	SANDHILL
ADGIINNU	GUANIDIN	ADGINORS	ROADINGS	ADHILLOP	PHALLOID
ADGIINNV	INVADING	ADGINORU	RIGAUDON	ADHILLOT	THALLOID
ADGIINNY	DIGYNIAN	ADGINOST	DOATINGS	ADHILLRY	HYDRILLA
ADGIINOR	RADIOING	ADGINOTY	TOADYING	ADHILMOO	HOMALOID

ADHILMOS	HALIDOMS	ADHOPRSU	UPHOARDS	ADIKKRRW	KIRKWARD
ADHILNOR	RHODINAL	ADHOPRSY	RHAPSODY	ADIKKRRY	KIRKYARD
ADHILNST	HANDLIST	ADHOPSST	DASHPOTS	ADIKLLOR	ROADKILL
ADHILOPS	HAPLOIDS	ADHORRSU	DHOURRAS	ADIKLNPS	LANDSKIP
	SHIPLOAD	ADHORRTY	HYDRATOR	ADIKLNSY	LADYKINS
ADHILOPY	HAPLOIDY	ADHORSTU	TOADRUSH	ADIKLORS	KILORADS
ADHILOST	SHITLOAD	ADHORSWY	SHOWYARD	ADIKLOSS	ODALISKS
ADHILOSY	HOLIDAYS	ADHPSTYY	DYSPATHY	ADIKMNNS	MANKINDS
	HYALOIDS	ADIIINRV	VIRIDIAN	ADIKMOSU	DAIMOKUS
ADHILPSY	LADYSHIP	ADIIIQRU	DAIQUIRI	ADIKMSSS	DISMASKS
ADHIMNOR	RHODAMIN	ADIIKLLN	KALLIDIN	ADIKNNNU	DUNNAKIN
ADHIMNOS	ADMONISH	ADIIKLMM	MILKMAID	ADIKNNST	INKSTAND
ADHIMNOU	HUMANOID	ADIIKLST	TAILSKID	ADIKNOPY	PYINKADO
ADHIMNSS	HANDISMS	ADIIKNOP	PINAKOID	ADIKNPSS	SKIDPANS
ADHIMOPP	AMPHIPOD	ADIIKNST	ANTISKID	ADIKNRSS	DISRANKS
ADHIMPSS	PHASMIDS	ADIIKOST	DAKOITIS	ADIKNRST	STINKARD
ADHIMRTY	MYRIADTH	ADIILLMR	MILLIARD	ADIKPRSS	DISPARKS
ADHINOPY	DIAPHONY	ADIILLNY	IDYLLIAN	ADIKQRSU	DIQUARKS
ADHINPSS	DISHPANS	ADIILLOP	LIPOIDAL	ADIKSSWY	SKIDWAYS
ADHINPSU	DAUPHINS	ADIILLOR	ARILLOID	ADILLLPY	PALLIDLY
ADHINRTW	HANDWRIT	ADIILLST	DIALLIST	ADILLMMS	MILLDAMS
ADHINRWY	WHINYARD	ADIILLUV	DILUVIAL	ADILLMNR	MANDRILL
ADHINSST	STANDISH	ADIILMSS	MISDIALS	ADILLMOU	ALLODIUM
ADHINSTU	DIANTHUS	ADIILNOT	DILATION	ADILLMOV	VILLADOM
ADHIOSTY	TOADYISH	ADIILNSU	INDUSIAL	ADILLMSY	DISMALLY
ADHIPRSW	WARDSHIP	ADIILNSV	INVALIDS	ADILLNPS	LANDSLIP
ADHIPRSY	SHIPYARD	ADIILNSW	WINDSAIL	ADILLOOP	POLOIDAL
ADHIPSTY	DISPATHY	ADIILNTW	TAILWIND	ADILLOPS	SPADILLO
ADHIRTWW	WITHDRAW	ADIILNTY	DAINTILY	ADILLOSW	DISALLOW
ADHITWWY	WIDTHWAY	ADIILNUV	DILUVIAN	ADILLOSY	DISLOYAL
ADHKNORW	HANDWORK		INDUVIAL	ADILLRWY	WILLYARD
ADHKORSW	DORHAWKS	ADIILOPP	DIPLOPIA	ADILLSTY	DISTALLY
ADHKOSSU	SHAKUDOS	ADIILPST	LAPIDIST	ADILMMOS	MODALISM
ADHLLLOS	HOLDALLS	ADIILRST	DISTRAIL	ADILMNNO	MANDOLIN
ADHLLNOR	HANDROLL	ADIILRSW	WIRILDAS	ADILMNOS	SALMONID
ADHLLNOS	HOLLANDS	ADIILSST	DIALISTS	ADILMNRS	MANDRILS
ADHLLNUV	VALLHUND	ADIILSSY	DIALYSIS		RIMLANDS
ADHLMNOO	HANDLOOM	ADIILTVY	VALIDITY	ADILMOOR	MODIOLAR
ADHLMORT	THRALDOM	ADIIMMSS	MAIDISMS	ADILMOPS	DIPLOMAS
ADHLMOSY	HOLYDAMS	ADIIMNNS	INDAMINS		PLASMOID
ADHLMPSY	LYMPHADS	ADIIMPSU	ASPIDIUM	ADILMOPT	DIPLOMAT
ADHLNORW	WALDHORN	ADIIMRST	TRIADISM	ADILMOPY	OLYMPIAD
ADHLNOTU	DUATHLON	ADIIMRSU	MUDIRIAS	ADILMORU	ORDALIUM
ADHLNOUW	DOWNHAUL	ADIINNOT	NIDATION	ADILMOST	MODALIST
ADHLOSYY	HOLYDAYS	ADIINNOZ	DIAZINON	ADILMOSU	ALODIUMS
ADHMNOOS	MANHOODS	ADIINOOT	IODATION	ADILMOSY	AMYLOIDS
ADHMOPRS	DRAMSHOP	ADIINOTU	AUDITION	ADILMOTY	MODALITY
ADHMORSY	HYDROMAS	ADIINPRS	PINDARIS	ADILMPRY	LAMPYRID
ADHNNOOR	HONORAND	ADIINRST	DISTRAIN	ADILMPSS	PLASMIDS
ADHNNORY	NONHARDY	ADIINSST	DISTAINS	ADILMPSU	PALUDISM
ADHNOOTU	AUNTHOOD	ADIINSSU	SUIDIANS	ADILMSSU	DUALISMS
ADHNORSU	UNHOARDS	ADIIOPRS	SPORIDIA	ADILMSSY	DISMAYLS
ADHNOSTU	HANDOUTS	ADIIOPRT	TAPIROID		LADYISMS
	THOUSAND	ADIIOPSS	ADIPOSIS	ADILMTUY	MULTIDAY
ADHNOSUW	UNSHADOW	ADIIORST	TARSIOID	ADILNNNU	NUNDINAL
ADHNOSWW	DOWNWASH	ADIIPRTU	TRIPUDIA	ADILNNOT	NONTIDAL
ADHNRSTY	HYDRANTS	ADIIPRTY	RAPIDITY	ADILNNOV	NONVALID
ADHOOPRS	HOSPODAR	ADIIPSTY	SAPIDITY	ADILNNSU	DISANNUL
ADHOOPST	HOPTOADS	ADIIPTVY	VAPIDITY	ADILNOOR	DOORNAIL
ADHOORRS	RHODORAS	ADIIQRSU	DAQUIRIS	ADILNOOV	VINDALOO
ADHOORSW	ROADSHOW	ADIIRSST	DIARISTS	ADILNOPY	PALINODY
ADHOORYZ	HYDROZOA	ADIIRSTT	DISTRAIT	ADILNORS	ORDINALS
ADHOPRST	HARDTOPS		TRIADIST	ADILNORT	TRINODAL
	POTSHARD	ADIJNOST	ADJOINTS	ADILNOTY	NODALITY

ADILNPRS	SPANDRIL	ADINNORT	ORDINANT	ADKKLOSY	KAKODYLS
ADILNPST	DISPLANT	ADINNORY	NONDAIRY	ADKLMRSU	MUDLARKS
ADILNRSU	DIURNALS	ADINNOTU	NUDATION	ADKLNOPR	DRONKLAP
ADILNRWY	INWARDLY	ADINNRSW	WINNARDS	ADKLOORW	WOODLARK
ADILNSSU	SUNDIALS	ADINNRSY	INNYARDS		WORKLOAD
ADILNSSW	WINDLASS	ADINOOPS	ISOPODAN	ADKMNORW	MARKDOWN
ADILOOPZ	DIPLOZOA	ADINOOPT	ADOPTION	ADKMOORR	DARKROOM
ADILOORT	IDOLATOR	ADINOORT	TANDOORI	ADKNORTU	OUTDRANK
	TOROIDAL	ADINOOTT	DOTATION	ADKNRSTU	STUNKARD
ADILOOSV	OVOIDALS	ADINOPPS	OPPIDANS	ADKOORRW	ROADWORK
ADILOPRT	DIOPTRAL	ADINOPRR	RAINDROP	ADKORRWY	YARDWORK
	TRIPODAL	ADINOPRS	PONIARDS	ADKORSWY	DAYWORKS
ADILOPSS	DISPOSAL	ADINOPRY	PYRANOID		WORKDAYS
ADILOQSU	SQUALOID	ADINOPST	PINTADOS	ADKRSSWY	SKYWARDS
ADILORST	DILATORS		SATINPOD	ADLLLOOY	DOOLALLY
ADILORSY	SOLIDARY	ADINORRS	ORDINARS	ADLLMOSW	WADMOLLS
ADILORTY	ADROITLY	ADINORRY	ORDINARY	ADLLNOPW	PLOWLAND
	DILATORY	ADINORSS	SADIRONS	ADLLNOSW	LOWLANDS
	IDOLATRY	ADINORST	DIATRONS	ADLLOPRS	POLLARDS
ADILOSST	SODALIST		INTRADOS	ADLLORSY	DORSALLY
ADILOSTY	SODALITY	ADINORSU	DINOSAUR	ADLLRSWY	DRYWALLS
ADILPPSY	DISAPPLY	ADINORSV	VIRANDOS	ADLMNNOO	NONMODAL
ADILPRSY	PYRALIDS	ADINORTU	DURATION	ADLMNOOR	MOORLAND
ADILPSST	PLASTIDS	ADINOSTU	SUDATION	ADLMNORY	RANDOMLY
ADILPSSY	DISPLAYS	ADINOSTX	OXIDANTS	ADLMNOSS	MOSSLAND
ADILPSTU	PLAUDITS	ADINOSTY	DYSTONIA	ADLMOORS	LORDOMAS
ADILRTTY	TILTYARD	ADINPSST	SANDPITS		MALODORS
ADILRTWY	TAWDRILY	ADINPSSY	SYNAPSID	ADLMOORU	MALODOUR
ADILRWYZ	WIZARDLY	ADINRRST	TRIDARNS	ADLMOPRW	MOLDWARP
ADILSSTU	DUALISTS	ADINRSSU	SUNDARIS	ADLMOPSY	PSALMODY
ADIMMNOO	AMMONOID	ADINRSTU	UNITARDS	ADLMORSU	MODULARS
ADIMMNOS	MONADISM	ADINRUVZ	UNVIZARD	ADLNNORS	NORLANDS
	NOMADISM	ADINSWWY	WINDWAYS	ADLNNOSW	SNOWLAND
ADIMMNSY	DYNAMISM	ADIOOPRT	PAROTOID	ADLNNOTU	NONADULT
ADIMMOST	AMIDMOST	ADIOOPSS	APODOSIS	ADLNNOTW	TOWNLAND
ADIMMOTU	DOMATIUM	ADIOOSSW	WOODSIAS	ADLNNSSU	SUNLANDS
ADIMMNOS	MONDAINS	ADIOPPST	POSTPAID	ADLNNTUU	UNDULANT
ADIMNNOT	DOMINANT	ADIOPRRS	AIRDROPS	ADLNOORS	LARDOONS
ADIMNOOR	MAINDOOR	ADIOPRSS	SPAROIDS	ADLNOORW	LOANWORD
ADIMNOSS	MADISONS	ADIOPRST	PARODIST	ADLNOPRT	PORTLAND
ADIMNOST	DONATISM		PAROTIDS	ADLNOPRU	PAULDRON
	SAINTDOM	ADIOPRSV	PRIVADOS	ADLNOPSU	POUNDALS
ADIMNOWW	WIDOWMAN	ADIOPRTY	PODIATRY	ADLNOPWY	DOWNPLAY
ADIMNRSW	MISDRAWN	ADIOPSTY	DYSTOPIA		PLAYDOWN
ADIMNRSY	MISANDRY	ADIORRTT	TRADITOR	ADLNORST	TROLANDS
ADIMNSSY	SYSADMIN	ADIORSST	ASTROIDS	ADLNORWY	ONWARDLY
ADIMNSTY	DYNAMIST		SARODIST	ADLNOSST	SANDLOTS
ADIMOPRY	MYRIAPOD	ADIORSSV	ADVISORS	ADLNOSSU	SOULDANS
ADIMOPSY	SYMPODIA	ADIORSTT	STRADIOT	ADLNOSSY	SYNODALS
ADIMORRS	MIRADORS	ADIORSTU	AUDITORS	ADLNOSTU	OUTLANDS
ADIMOSST	MASTOIDS	ADIORSVY	ADVISORY	ADLOOPRU	UROPODAL
ADIMOSTT	MATTOIDS	ADIORTUY	AUDITORY	ADLOORWW	WOOLWARD
ADIMOSTY	TOADYISM	ADIOSSVW	DISAVOWS	ADLOPRSU	POULARDS
ADIMPRSY	PYRAMIDS	ADIPRRTU	PURTRAID	ADLOPRWY	WORDPLAY
ADIMRSSW	MISDRAWS	ADIPRSST	DISPARTS	ADLOPSUU	PALUDOUS
ADIMRSUU	SUDARIUM	ADIRRWYZ	WIZARDRY	ADLOQSUW	OLDSQUAW
ADIMSSST	DISMASTS	ADIRRSTY	SATYRIDS	ADLORRSW	WARLORDS
ADIMSSTU	DUMAISTS	ADIRSSUY	DYSURIAS	ADLORTWY	TOWARDLY
	STADIUMS	ADJKNRUY	JUNKYARD	ADLPRUWY	UPWARDLY
ADINNNTU	INUNDANT	ADJLMORS	JARLDOMS	ADLRRTUY	ULTRADRY
ADINNOOT	DONATION	ADJLSUUW	WUDJULAS	ADMMNOOS	DOOMSMAN
	NODATION	ADJNORSU	ADJOURNS	ADMMNSSU	SUMMANDS
ADINNOPS	DIPNOANS	ADJORRSU	ADJURORS	ADMMNTUU	MUTANDUM
ADINNORS	ANDIRONS	ADJORSTU	ADJUSTOR	ADMNNORY	MONANDRY

ADMNNOSU	SOUNDMAN	ADOOPRSU	SAUROPOD	AEEEELNRT	LATEENER
ADMNNOTU	NOTANDUM	ADOOPSSW	SAPWOODS	AEEEELNRV	VENEREAL
ADMNOOOT	ODONTOMA	ADOORSHY	DOORWAYS	AEEEELNST	SELENATE
ADMNOORS	DOORSMAN	ADOOSSSW	SASSWOOD	AEEEELPRR	REPEALER
	MADRONOS	ADOOSSTT	TOSTADOS	AEEEELQSU	SEQUELAE
ADMNOORW	MOONWARD	ADOPRRSW	WARDROPS	AEEEELRRS	RELEASER
ADMNOOST	MASTODON	ADOPRSSW	PASSWORD	AEEEELRRV	REVEALER
ADMNOOSW	WOODSMAN	ADOPSSSU	SOAPSUDS	AEEEELRSS	RELEASES
ADMNOOSZ	MADZOONS	ADORRSTU	DARTROUS	AEEEELRST	TEASELER
ADMNORST	DORMANTS	ADORSTUW	OUTDRAWS	AEEEELRSW	WEASELER
	MORDANTS		OUTWARDS	AEEEELRTX	AXLETREE
ADMNORSW	SANDWORM	ADORSTUY	SUDATORY	AEEEELSSS	EASELESS
	SWORDMAN	ADORTUVY	ADVOUTRY	AEEEELSTV	ELEVATES
ADMNOSSU	OSMUNDAS	ADPRRTUY	PURTRAYD	AEEEMMRT	METAMERE
ADMNPPSU	SANDPUMP	ADRSSTTU	STARDUST	AEEEMNST	EASEMENT
ADMOOPPP	POPPADOM	ADSSSTUW	SAWDUSTS	AEEEMPRS	PERMEASE
ADMOORRW	WARDROOM	ADSSTUWY	SAWDUSTY	AEEEMPRT	PERMEATE
ADMOORST	DOORMATS	AEEEEELRS	RELEASEE	AEEENNRV	VENEREAN
ADMOORSY	DAYROOMS	AEEEEMRT	EMEERATE	AEEENNTV	VENENATE
ADMOPPPU	POPPADUM	AEEEEFLRS	EELFARES	AEEENPTT	PATENTEE
ADMOPPSU	POPADUMS	AEEEEFRRW	FREEWARE	AEEENRST	SERENATE
ADMORSST	STARDOMS	AEEEEFRTY	AFTEREYE	AEEENRTT	ENTERATE
	TSARDOMS	AEEEEGGNR	REENGAGE	AEEENRTV	ENERVATE
ADMORSTW	MADWORTS	AEEEEGKLS	KEELAGES		VENERATE
ADMORSTZ	TZARDOMS	AEEEEGLLS	LEGALESE	AEEEPRRT	REPARTEE
ADMRSSTU	DURMASTS	AEEEEGLNR	GENERALE		REPEATER
	MUSTARDS	AEEEEGLRT	EGLATERE		REREPEAT
ADMRSTUY	MUSTARDY		REGELATE	AEEEPSTW	SWEETPEA
ADNNOOST	NANODOTS		RELEGATE	AEEERRST	ARRESTEE
ADNNOOSY	NOONDAYS	AEEEEGLRV	LEVERAGE	AEEERRTW	TREEWARE
ADNNORTY	DYNATRON	AEEEEGLST	LEGATEES	AEEERSST	ESTERASE
ADNNOSTU	DAUNTONS	AEEEEGLSV	SELVAGEE		TESSERAE
ADNNRSTU	DUNNARTS	AEEEEGLTV	VEGELATE	AEEERSVW	REWEAVES
ADNOOPRS	PANDOORS	AEEEEGMRT	METERAGE	AEEERTWY	EYEWATER
	SPADROON	AEEEEGNRT	GENERATE	AEEFFLLS	FELAFELS
ADNOOQRU	QUADROON		RENEGATE	AEEFFLRT	TAFFEREL
ADNOORST	DONATORS		TEENAGER	AEEFFLTT	FLATFEET
	ODORANTS	AEEEEGNSS	AGENESES	AEEFFNRT	AFFERENT
	TANDOORS	AEEEEGPRS	PEERAGES	AEEFGILR	FILAGREE
	TORNADOS	AEEEEGPSS	SEEPAGES	AEEFGIRR	FERRIAGE
ADNOORTY	DONATORY	AEEEEGRST	EAGEREST	AEEFGIRS	FEGARIES
ADNOOSVW	ADVOWSON		ETAGERES	AEEFGIRT	FIGEATER
ADNOPRSU	PANDOURS		STEERAGE	AEEFGLNS	FENAGLES
ADNOPRSV	PROVANDS	AEEEEGRSW	SEWERAGE	AEEFGLSU	FUSELAGE
ADNOQRSU	SQUADRON	AEEEEGTTV	VEGETATE	AEEFGNRS	FREEGANS
ADNORRSW	NORWARDS	AEEEEHKLL	KEELHALE	AEEFGNST	FANTEEGS
ADNORSTU	ROTUNDAS	AEEEEHLRT	ETHEREAL	AEEFGRSS	SERFAGES
ADNORSTW	SANDWORT	AEEEEHMPR	EPHEMERA	AEEFGSTW	WEFTAGES
ADNORSTY	TARDYONS	AEEEEHNRS	ENHEARSE	AEEFHIRS	SHEAFIER
ADNORSWY	NAYWORDS	AEEEEHRRS	REHEARSE	AEEFHLLS	SELFHEAL
ADNORSXY	SARDONYX	AEEEEHRRT	REHEATER	AEEFHRST	FEATHERS
ADNORTUW	OUTDRAWN	AEEEEHSTT	AESTHETE	AEEFHRTY	FEATHERY
	UNTOWARD	AEEEEILNS	ALIENEES	AEEFIINR	INFERIAE
ADNORWWY	WANWORDY	AEEEEIMNX	EXAMINEE	AEEFIIRS	AERIFIES
ADNOSSTU	ASTOUNDS	AEEEEIMRT	EMERITAE	AEEFIKLL	LEAFLIKE
ADNOSTTU	OUTSTAND	AEEEEIRST	EATERIES	AEEFIKLW	KALEWIFE
	STANDOUT	AEEEEJNTT	JEANETTE	AEEFIKRR	FREAKIER
ADNPRSSU	SANDSPUR	AEEEEKKPS	KEEPSAKE	AEEFIKRS	FAKERIES
ADNPSSTU	DUSTPANS	AEEEEKMSS	KAMEESES	AEEFIKRW	WAKERIFE
	STANDUPS	AEEEEKMSZ	KAMEEZES	AEEFILMN	FILENAME
	UPSTANDS	AEEEEKNRW	WEAKENER	AEEFILNR	FLANERIE
ADNRSSUW	SUNWARDS	AEEEELLPP	APPELLEE	AEEFILRS	FILAREES
ADOOPPRU	PAUROPOD	AEEEELLST	TELESALE		SERAFILE
ADOOPRRT	TRAPDOOR	AEEEELMNR	ENAMELER	AEEFILRT	FEATLIER

	FRAILTEE	AEEGGPRU	PUGGAREE	AEEGINTV	AGENTIVE
AEEFILST	FEALTIES	AEEGGRSU	REGAUGES		NEGATIVE
	FETIALES	AEEGHIRS	HIREAGES	AEEGINTX	EXIGEANT
	LEAFIEST	AEEGHIRT	HERITAGE	AEEGIPPS	PIPEAGES
AEEFIPSW	SPAEWIFE	AEEGHLOT	HELOTAGE	AEEGIPQU	EQUIPAGE
AEEFIRRR	RAREFIER	AEEGHLRS	SHEARLEG	AEEGIPRS	PIERAGES
AEEFIRRS	RAREFIES	AEEGHLRW	RAGWHEEL	AEEGIPVW	PAGEVIEW
AEEFIRSS	FREESIAS	AEEGHMOP	HOMEPAGE	AEEGIRRS	GREASIER
AEEFIRTT	FETERITA	AEEGHMPR	GRAPHEME	AEEGIRSS	GREASIES
AEEFISST	SAFETIES	AEEGHNRS	SHAGREEN	AEEGIRSU	EUGARIES
AEEFKMNT	FAKEMENT	AEEGHNST	THENAGES	AEEGIRTT	AIGRETTE
AEEFKOPR	FOREPEAK	AEEGHNSW	WHANGEES	AEEGIRTV	ERGATIVE
AEEFKRRY	FREAKERY	AEEGHORS	GHERAOES	AEEGISSS	ASSIEGES
AEEFLLMR	FEMERALL	AEEGHRRT	GATHERER	AEEGISTY	GAYETIES
AEEFLLMT	FLAMELET		REGATHER	AEEGKLLS	KLEAGLES
AEEFLLNR	REFALLEN	AEEGIILW	WEIGELIA	AEEGKMRR	REGMAKER
AEEFLLNV	EVENFALL	AEEGIINR	AEGIRINE	AEEGKNNR	GENNAKER
AEEFLLRW	FAREWELL	AEEGIIRT	AEGIRITE	AEEGLLNR	ALLERGEN
AEEFLLSS	LEAFLESS	AEEGIIST	GAIETIES	AEEGLLPR	PRELEGAL
AEEFLLST	FELLATES	AEEGIKLM	GAMELIKE	AEEGLLRS	ALLEGERS
	LEAFLETS	AEEGIKLT	GATELIKE	AEEGLLSZ	GAZELLES
AEEFLMNS	ENFLAMES	AEEGIKLU	AGUELIKE	AEEGLMNS	MELANGES
AEEFLMOS	FLEASOME	AEEGILLS	GALILEES	AEEGLMNV	GAVELMEN
AEEFLMPR	PREFLAME		LEGALISE	AEEGLMOS	MESOGLEA
AEEFLMSS	FAMELESS	AEEGILLZ	LEGALIZE	AEEGLMPX	MEGAPLEX
	SELFSAME	AEEGILMN	LIEGEMAN	AEEGLMRS	GLEAMERS
AEEFLNRU	FUNEREAL	AEEGILMR	GLEAMIER	AEEGLMRT	TELEGRAM
AEEFLOOV	FOVEOLAE	AEEGILMS	GELSEMIA	AEEGLMRY	MEAGERLY
AEEFLORV	OVERLEAF		MILEAGES		MEAGRELY
AEEFLRRR	REFERRAL	AEEGILNR	ALGERINE	AEEGLMST	MELTAGES
AEEFLRRT	FALTERER	AEEGILNS	ENSILAGE	AEEGLNNR	ENLARGEN
AEEFLRSS	FEARLESS		LINEAGES	AEEGLNNT	ENTANGLE
AEEFLRST	REFLATES	AEEGILNT	GALENITE	AEEGLNOS	GASOLENE
AEEFLRSW	WELFARES		GELATINE	AEEGLNOT	ELONGATE
AEEFLTTT	FLATETTE		LEGATINE	AEEGLNRR	ENLARGER
AEEFMNOR	FOREMEAN	AEEGILNV	INVEAGLE	AEEGLNRS	ENLARGES
	FORENAME	AEEGILOU	EULOGIAE		GENERALS
AEEFMNRS	ENFRAMES	AEEGILPR	PERIGEAL		GLEANERS
AEEFMORS	FEARSOME	AEEGILRS	GASELIER	AEEGLNRT	REGENTAL
AEEFMRRS	REFRAMES	AEEGILST	EGALITES	AEEGLNSU	EUGLENAS
AEEFMRTY	FEMETARY		ELEGIAST	AEEGLNSV	EVANGELS
AEEFNRST	FASTENER	AEEGILSW	WEIGELAS	AEEGLNVY	EVANGELY
	FENESTRA	AEEGILTV	LEVIGATE	AEEGLOOZ	ZOOGLEAE
	REFASTEN	AEEGIMNR	GERMAINE	AEEGLORS	AEROGELS
AEEFNRTT	FATTENER	AEEGIMNT	GEMINATE	AEEGLOST	SEGOLATE
AEEFNSSS	SAFENESS	AEEGIMRS	GAMESIER	AEEGLRRS	REGALERS
AEEFORRV	OVERFEAR		REIMAGES	AEEGLRSS	EELGRASS
AEEFOSTU	FEATEOUS	AEEGIMRT	EMIGRATE		GEARLESS
AEEFRRST	FERRATES		REMIGATE		LARGESSE
AEEFRSST	FEASTERS	AEEGINNT	ANTIGENE	AEEGLRSU	LEAGUERS
AEEFRSTU	FEATURES	AEEGINPR	PERIGEAN	AEEGLRSW	LEGWEARS
AEEFRSWY	FREEWAYS	AEEGINRR	REGAINER	AEEGLRSZ	REGLAZES
AEEFTTUV	FAUVETTE	AEEGINRS	ANERGIES	AEEGLRTU	REGULATE
AEEGGHIW	WEIGHAGE		GESNERIA	AEEGLRUX	EXERGUAL
AEEGGINR	AGREEING	AEEGINRT	GRATINEE	AEEGLSST	GATELESS
AEEGGIRV	AGGRIEVE		INTERAGE	AEEGLSSV	SELVAGES
AEEGGLLS	ALLEGGES	AEEGINRZ	RAZEEING	AEEGLSSW	WAGELESS
AEEGGLOU	AEGLOGUE	AEEGINSS	AGENESIS	AEEGLSSY	EYEGLASS
AEEGGLRS	GREGALES		AGENISES	AEEGLSTT	GALETTES
AEEGGNNR	GANGRENE		ASSIGNEE	AEEGLSTV	VEGETALS
AEEGGNOS	GASOGENE	AEEGINST	SAGENITE	AEEGLTTU	TUTELAGE
AEEGGNOZ	GAZOGENE	AEEGINSU	EUGENIAS	AEEGLTUV	EVULGATE
AEEGGNRS	ENGAGERS	AEEGINSV	ENVISAGE	AEEGMMNR	ENGRAMME
AEEGGOPS	EPAGOGES	AEEGINSZ	AGENIZES	AEEGMMNS	GAMESMEN

AEEGMMOS	GAMESOME	AEEGRRTT	RETARGET	AEEHLMNW	WHALEMEN
AEEGMMST	GEMMATES	AEEGRSST	RESTAGES		WHEELMAN
	TAGMEMES	AEEGRSTT	GREATEST	AEEHLMNY	HYMENEAL
AEEGMNOR	ARGEMONE	AEEGRSTU	TREAGUES	AEEHLMOS	HEALSOME
AEEGMNRS	AGREMENS	AEEGRSTW	STREWAGE	AEEHLMPT	HELPMATE
AEEGMNRT	AGREMENT	AEEGRSUZ	GUEREZAS	AEEHLNOS	ENHALOES
AEEGMNSS	GAMENESS	AEEGSSTT	GESTATES	AEEHLNOT	ANETHOLE
	MAGNESES	AEEGSTTZ	GAZETTES	AEEHLNPT	ELEPHANT
AEEGMNTT	TEGMENTA	AEEHHHSS	HASHEESH	AEEHLNRT	LEATHERN
AEEGMNTZ	GAZEMENT	AEEHHIRT	HEATHIER	AEEHLNSS	HALENESS
AEEGMOOT	OOGAMETE	AEEHHLNZ	HAZELHEN	AEEHLNTX	EXHALENT
AEEGMOST	SOMEGATE	AEEHHNST	ENSHEATH	AEEHLNVY	HEAVENLY
AEEGMPRS	PREGAMES		HEATHENS	AEEHLORS	ARSEHOLE
AEEGMRST	GAMESTER	AEEHHOOP	PAHOEHOE		HALOSERE
	MEAGREST	AEEHHRSS	REHASHES	AEEHLORV	OVERHALE
AEEGMRSU	REMUAGES	AEEHHRST	HEATHERS	AEEHLOSU	ALEHOUSE
AEEGMSSS	MEGASSES		SHEATHER	AEEHLPRT	PLEATHER
	MESSAGES	AEEHHRTY	HEATHERY	AEEHLPST	HEELTAPS
AEEGMSSU	MESSUAGE	AEEHHSST	SHEATHES		PLEASETH
AEEGNNNO	ENNEAGON	AEEHIKLR	HARELIKE	AEEHLPTT	TELEPATH
AEEGNNPS	PANGENES	AEEHIKRS	SHIKAREE	AEEHLRRT	LATHERER
AEEGNNRS	ENRANGES	AEEHILNP	ELAPHINE	AEEHLRST	HALTERES
AEEGNNRT	GENERANT	AEEHILRS	SHIRALEE		LEATHERS
AEEGNNRU	ENRAUNGE	AEEHILRT	ETHERIAL	AEEHLRSV	HAVERELS
AEEGNNRV	ENGRAVEN	AEEHIMNT	HEMATEIN	AEEHLRTT	HEARTLET
AEEGNOPS	PEONAGES		HEMATINE	AEEHLRTY	LEATHERY
AEEGNPPS	GENAPPES	AEEHIMNX	HEXAMINE	AEEHLSST	HATELESS
AEEGNRRT	ETRANGER	AEEHIMPT	EPITHEMA		HEATLESS
AEEGNRRV	ENGRAVER	AEEHIMTT	HEMATITE	AEEHLSTT	ATHLETES
AEEGNRST	ESTRANGE	AEEHINRS	INHEARSE	AEEHLTTY	ETHYLATE
	GRANTEES	AEEHINRT	ATHERINE	AEEHMMRR	HAMMERER
	GREATENS		HERNIATE		REHAMMER
	NEGATERS	AEEHIPRS	PHARISEE	AEEHMNNY	HYMENEAN
	REAGENTS		SPHAIREE	AEEHMNPS	SHEEPMAN
	SEGREANT	AEEHIPST	APHETISE	AEEHMNRS	SHAREMEN
	SERGEANT		HEAPIEST		SHEARMEN
	STERNAGE		HEPATISE	AEEHMNRT	EARTHMEN
AEEGNRSU	RENAGUES	AEEHIPTT	HEPATITE	AEEHMNST	METHANES
AEEGNRSV	AVENGERS	AEEHIPTZ	APHETIZE	AEEHMNTU	ATHENEUM
	ENGRAVES		HEPATIZE	AEEHMNTX	EXANTHEM
AEEGNRTU	GAUNTREE	AEEHIRRS	HEARSIER	AEEHMORW	HOMEWARE
AEEGNRWY	GREENWAY	AEEHIRRT	EARTHIER	AEEHMPRR	HAMPERER
AEEGNSSS	SAGENESS		HEARTIER	AEEHMPSS	EMPHASES
AEEGNSTT	TENTAGES	AEEHIRSS	ASHERIES	AEEHMRSS	MAHSEERS
AEEGNSTV	VENTAGES	AEEHIRST	HEARTIES	AEEHMRST	ERATHEMS
AEEGNTTV	VEGETANT	AEEHIRSV	SHIVAREE	AEEHMRTY	ERYTHEMA
AEEGOPRV	OVERPAGE	AEEHIRTW	WHEATIER	AEEHMSST	MATHESES
AEEGOPSS	SAPEGOES	AEEHISST	ATHEISES	AEEHMTUX	EXHUMATE
AEEGORRV	OVERGEAR		ESTHESIA	AEEHNNSS	SNEESHAN
AEEGORSV	OVERAGES	AEEHISTT	ATHETISE	AEEHNNTX	XANTHENE
AEEGORVV	OVERGAVE		HESITATE	AEEHNOPR	EARPHONE
AEEGOSTX	GEOTAXES	AEEHISTV	HEAVIEST	AEEHNPST	HAPTENES
AEEGPRRS	ASPERGER	AEEHISTZ	ATHEIZES		HEPTANES
	PRESAGER	AEEHITTZ	ATHETIZE		PHENATES
AEEGPRRT	PARGETER	AEEHKLLR	RAKEHELL		STEPHANE
AEEGPRSS	ASPERGES	AEEHKLLU	KEELHAUL	AEEHNRSS	ARSHEENS
	PRESAGES	AEEHKMNS	KHAMSEEN	AEEHNRST	HASTENER
AEEGPRSU	PUGAREES	AEEHKNRR	HANKERER		HEARTENS
AEEGPSST	SEPTAGES		HARKENER	AEEHNRSU	UNHEARSE
AEEGRRRT	REGRATER	AEEHKNRS	HEARKENS	AEEHNRSV	RESHAVEN
AEEGRRSS	GREASERS	AEEHKPRR	PHREAKER	AEEHNRTT	HATERENT
AEEGRRST	REGRATES	AEEHKRST	HEKTARES		THREATEN
AEEGRRSU	REARGUES	AEEHKRSU	HEUREKAS	AEEHNRTU	URETHANE
AEEGRRSW	WAGERERS	AEEHLLSS	SEASHELL	AEEHNRTW	ENWREATH

	WATERHEN
	WREATHEN
AEEHNRWY	ANYWHERE
AEEHNSST	ANTHESES
AEEHNSTU	UNEATHES
AEEHNSTW	ENSWATHE
	WHEATENS
AEEHOPRT	EPHORATE
AEEHOPRV	OVERHEAP
AEEHORRV	OVERHEAR
AEEHORSS	SEAHORSE
	SEASHORE
AEEHORTV	OVERHATE
	OVERHEAT
AEEHOSTU	TEAHOUSE
AEEHPPRS	PRESHAPE
AEEHPRRS	REPHRASE
	RESHAPER
AEEHPRRT	THREAPER
AEEHPRSS	RESHAPES
	SPHAERES
	SPHEARES
AEEHPRST	PREHEATS
	SPREATHE
AEEHPRUV	UPHEAVER
AEEHPSUV	UPHEAVES
AEEHQSSU	QUASHEES
AEEHRRSS	SHEARERS
AEEHRRTU	URETHRAE
AEEHRRTW	WREATHER
AEEHRSSV	RESHAVES
AEEHRSSW	REWASHES
AEEHRSTT	EARTHSET
	THEATERS
	THEATRES
AEEHRSTV	THREAVES
AEEHRSTW	WEATHERS
	WREATHES
AEEHRTVW	WHATEVER
AEEHRTXZ	EXAHERTZ
AEEHSTTW	SAWTEETH
AEEHSTVY	HEAVYSET
AEEIIMRT	METAIRIE
AEEIINRT	INERTIAE
AEEIISST	ASEITIES
AEEIJPRS	JAPERIES
AEEIKKLL	LAKELIKE
AEEIKKLP	PEAKLIKE
AEEIKKLW	LIKEWAKE
AEEIKLLS	SEALLIKE
AEEIKLMS	SEAMLIKE
AEEIKLMU	LEUKEMIA
AEEIKLMZ	MAZELIKE
AEEIKLPT	TAPELIKE
AEEIKLRW	WEAKLIER
AEEIKLST	LEAKIEST
AEEIKLSV	VASELIKE
AEEIKLVW	WAVELIKE
AEEIKMMR	MERIMAKE
AEEIKMNT	KETAMINE
AEEIKNRS	SNEAKIER
AEEIKNRT	ANKERITE
	KREATINE
AEEIKNSS	AKINESES

AEEIKPST	PEAKIEST
AEEIKRRS	RAKERIES
	SKEARIER
AEEIKRTW	TWEAKIER
AEEILLNT	TENAILLE
AEEILLRS	REALLIES
AEEILLRT	LAETRILE
AEEILLST	LEALTIES
AEEILMMN	MELAMINE
AEEILMMT	MEALTIME
AEEILMNS	MELANISE
AEEILMNT	MELANITE
AEEILMNZ	MELANIZE
AEEILMRS	ALMERIES
	MEASLIER
AEEILMRT	EREMITAL
	MATERIEL
	REALTIME
AEEILMST	MEALIEST
	METALISE
AEEILMSV	MALVESIE
AEEILMTZ	METALIZE
AEEILNNS	SELENIAN
AEEILNPR	PERINEAL
AEEILNPS	ALEPINES
	PENALISE
	SEPALINE
AEEILNPT	PETALINE
	TAPELINE
AEEILNPZ	PENALIZE
AEEILNRR	NEARLIER
AEEILNRS	ALIENERS
AEEILNRT	ELATERIN
	ENTAILER
	TREENAIL
AEEILNSS	SEALINES
AEEILNSV	VASELINE
AEEILNSX	ALEXINES
AEEILNTV	ELVANITE
	VENTAILE
AEEILORT	AEROLITE
AEEILOTT	ETIOLATE
AEEILPRR	PEARLIER
AEEILPRS	ESPALIER
	PEARLIES
AEEILPRT	PEARLITE
AEEILPST	EPILATES
AEEILPSW	PALEWISE
AEEILQSU	EQUALISE
AEEILQUX	EXEQUIAL
AEEILQUZ	EQUALIZE
AEEILRRS	REALISER
AEEILRRT	RETAILER
AEEILRRZ	REALIZER
AEEILRSS	REALISES
AEEILRST	ATELIERS
	EARLIEST
	LATERISE
	LEARIEST
	REALTIES
AEEILRSV	VELARISE
AEEILRSY	YEARLIES
AEEILRSZ	REALIZES
	SLEAZIER

AEEILRTT	LATERITE
	LITERATE
AEEILRTV	LEVIRATE
	RELATIVE
AEEILRTZ	LATERIZE
AEEILRVW	LIVEWARE
	REVIEWAL
AEEILRVZ	VELARIZE
AEEILSST	ASTELIES
AEEILSTT	AILETTES
AEEILSTV	ELATIVES
	LEAVIEST
	VEALIEST
AEEILSVW	ALEWIVES
AEEILTTV	LEVITATE
AEEILTUV	ELUVIATE
AEEIMMNT	MEANTIME
AEEIMNNS	ENAMINES
AEEIMNRS	REMANIES
AEEIMNRT	ANTIMERE
AEEIMNRX	EXAMINER
AEEIMNSS	NEMESIAS
AEEIMNST	ETAMINES
	MATINEES
	MISEATEN
	SEMINATE
AEEIMNSX	EXAMINES
AEEIMNUV	MAUVEINE
AEEIMOSS	AMEIOSES
AEEIMPRS	EMPAIRES
AEEIMRRS	SMEARIER
AEEIMRSS	SERIEMAS
AEEIMRST	EMERITAS
	EMIRATES
	REAMIEST
	STEAMIER
AEEIMRTV	VIAMETER
AEEIMSSS	MISEASES
	SIAMESES
AEEIMSST	SEAMIEST
	STEAMIES
AEEIMSSZ	SIAMEZES
AEEIMSTT	ESTIMATE
	ETATISME
	MEATIEST
	TEATIMES
AEEIMSTW	TEAMWISE
AEEINNRS	ANSERINE
AEEINNTV	VENETIAN
AEEINOPS	PAEONIES
AEEINPRS	NAPERIES
AEEINPRT	APERIENT
AEEINPTT	PIANETTE
AEEINRRS	REARISEN
AEEINRRT	RETAINER
AEEINRSS	SENARIES
AEEINRST	ARENITES
	ARSENITE
	RESINATE
	STEARINE
	TRAINEES
AEEINRSU	UNEASIER
AEEINSSS	EASINESS
AEEINSST	ETESIANS

	TENIASES	**AEEJNRST**	SERJEANT	**AEELLPTY**	TELEPLAY
AEEINSSV	VAINESSE	**AEEJOPRT**	PEJORATE	**AEELLRRT**	TERRELLA
AEEINSTT	ANISETTE	**AEEJRTTW**	WATERJET	**AEELLRRV**	RAVELLER
	TETANIES	**AEEKKLWY**	LYKEWAKE	**AEELLSST**	SATELLES
	TETANISE	**AEEKKNOS**	KOKANEES		TESSELLA
AEEINSTV	NAIVETES	**AEEKKPSY**	KEEPSAKY	**AEELLSSZ**	ZEALLESS
AEEINSVW	INWEAVES	**AEEKLLSS**	LEAKLESS	**AEELLSTT**	STELLATE
AEEINTTZ	TETANIZE	**AEEKLLST**	LAKELETS	**AEELLSWY**	WALLEYES
AEEIOOPP	EPOPOEIA		SKELETAL		WEASELLY
AEEIORST	ETAERIOS	**AEEKLMMU**	MAMELUKE	**AEELLTVV**	VALVELET
AEEIPPRR	PAPERIER	**AEEKLMRT**	TELEMARK	**AEELMMTU**	MALEMUTE
AEEIPPSS	APEPSIES	**AEEKLMRY**	YARMELKE	**AEELMNPS**	EMPANELS
AEEIPPST	APPETISE	**AEEKLMSS**	MAKELESS		EMPLANES
AEEIPPSU	EUPEPSIA	**AEEKLNST**	KANTELES		ENSAMPLE
AEEIPPTT	APPETITE	**AEEKLPSS**	PEAKLESS	**AEELMNPT**	PLATEMEN
AEEIPPTZ	APPETIZE	**AEEKLSSW**	WAKELESS	**AEELMNRT**	LAMENTER
AEEIPRRR	RARERIPE	**AEEKLSTY**	EYESTALK	**AEELMNSS**	LAMENESS
	REPAIRER	**AEEKMNSS**	KAMSEENS		MALENESS
AEEIPRRS	PEREIRAS	**AEEKMORV**	MAKEOVER		MANELESS
	SPEARIER	**AEEKMOTY**	YOKEMATE		NAMELESS
AEEIPRST	PARIETES	**AEEKMRRR**	REMARKER		SALESMEN
	PETARIES	**AEEKMRRS**	REMAKERS	**AEELMNST**	MANTEELS
AEEIPRTV	PERVIATE	**AEEKMRRT**	MARKETER		STEELMAN
AEEIPSST	EPITASES		REMARKET		TALESMEN
AEEIPSTT	PEATIEST	**AEEKMRST**	MEERKATS	**AEELMNSW**	WEALSMEN
AEEIPSTX	EPITAXES	**AEEKNNNS**	NANKEENS	**AEELMNSY**	AMYLENES
	EXPIATES	**AEEKNNPS**	KNEEPANS	**AEELMNTT**	MANTELET
AEEIPTVX	EXAPTIVE	**AEEKNORW**	REAWOKEN	**AEELMNTV**	LAVEMENT
AEEIQRSU	QUEASIER	**AEEKNPRT**	PERTAKEN	**AEELMOTT**	MATELOTE
AEEIQRUZ	QUEAZIER	**AEEKNPST**	NETSPEAK	**AEELMPRS**	EMPALERS
AEEIQSTU	EQUISETA	**AEEKNPSU**	SNEAKEUP		RESAMPLE
AEEIRRSS	REARISES	**AEEKNPSW**	NEWSPEAK	**AEELMPRX**	EXEMPLAR
	RERAISES	**AEEKNRSS**	SNEAKERS	**AEELMPRY**	EMPYREAL
AEEIRRST	ARTERIES	**AEEKNRSW**	REWAKENS	**AEELMPSX**	EXAMPLES
	REASTIER		WAKENERS	**AEELMPTT**	PALMETTE
AEEIRRTT	RETRAITE	**AEEKNSSW**	WEAKNESS		TEMPLATE
AEEIRRTW	WATERIER	**AEEKOOPP**	PEEKAPOO	**AEELMRST**	LAMETERS
AEEIRRVW	WAVERIER	**AEEKORRV**	OVERRAKE	**AEELMRTX**	EXTREMAL
AEEIRSST	SERIATES	**AEEKORST**	KERATOSE	**AEELMSSS**	SEAMLESS
AEEIRSTT	ARIETTES		KREASOTE	**AEELMSST**	MATELESS
	ITERATES	**AEEKORTV**	OVERTAKE		MEATLESS
	TEARIEST		TAKEOVER		TAMELESS
	TREATIES	**AEEKORVW**	OVERWEAK	**AEELMSTU**	EMULATES
	TREATISE	**AEEKPRSS**	RESPEAKS	**AEELNNPS**	ENPLANES
AEEIRSTV	EVIRATES		SPEAKERS	**AEELNNRT**	LANNERET
AEEIRSTW	SWEATIER	**AEEKPRST**	PERTAKES	**AEELNNSS**	LEANNESS
	TAWERIES	**AEEKPRTT**	PARKETTE	**AEELNOPR**	PERONEAL
	WASTERIE	**AEEKPRTU**	REUPTAKE	**AEELNOPT**	ANTELOPE
	WEARIEST	**AEEKQRSU**	SQUEAKER	**AEELNORU**	ALEURONE
AEEIRSTY	YEASTIER	**AEEKRRST**	RETAKERS	**AEELNOSS**	ENOLASES
AEEIRSVV	AVERSIVE		STREAKER	**AEELNPPS**	SPALPEEN
AEEISSTX	EXTASIES	**AEEKRRSW**	WREAKERS	**AEELNPRR**	PRERENAL
AEEISSVW	SEAWIVES	**AEEKRSST**	SAKERETS	**AEELNPRS**	REPANELS
AEEISTTT	ETATISTE	**AEEKRSTW**	TWEAKERS	**AEELNPSS**	PALENESS
	STEATITE	**AEELLLPT**	PELLETAL		PANELESS
AEEISTTV	AVIETTES	**AEELLLTT**	TELLTALE	**AEELNQSU**	SQUALENE
	ESTIVATE	**AEELLMMS**	MAMSELLE	**AEELNRRS**	LEARNERS
	EVITATES	**AEELLMSS**	MEALLESS		RELEARNS
AEEISTUX	EUTAXIES	**AEELLNOV**	NOVELLAE	**AEELNRRT**	RELEARNT
	EUTEXIAS	**AEELLOSV**	ALVEOLES	**AEELNRSS**	REALNESS
AEEITTUX	EUTAXITE	**AEELLOTT**	ALLOTTEE	**AEELNRST**	ALTERNES
AEEITUVX	EXUVIATE	**AEELLPRS**	PARELLES		ETERNALS
AEEJLNPT	JETPLANE	**AEELLPTT**	PALLETTE		TELERANS
AEEJLOSU	JEALOUSE		PLATELET	**AEELNRSV**	ENSLAVER

AEELNRSW	RENEWALS	AEELRSST	RESLATES	AEEMPRTT	ATTEMPER
AEELNRTV	LEVANTER		STEALERS	AEEMPSTU	AMPUTEES
	RELEVANT		TEARLESS	AEEMQRRU	REMARQUE
AEELNRTW	TREELAWN		TESSERAL	AEEMQRSU	MARQUEES
AEELNRTX	EXTERNAL	AEELRSSU	LEASURES	AEEMQTTU	MAQUETTE
AEELNRUU	NEURULAE	AEELRSSV	SEVERALS	AEEMRRSS	SMEARERS
AEELNRUV	REVENUAL	AEELRSSW	WARELESS	AEEMRRST	REMASTER
AEELNSST	LATENESS	AEELRSTT	ALERTEST		STREAMER
AEELNSSV	ENSLAVES	AEELRSTU	RESALUTE	AEEMRRSU	MEASURER
	VANELESS	AEELRSTX	EXALTERS	AEEMRRTT	TETRAMER
AEELNSTY	ENTAYLES	AEELRSTY	EASTERLY	AEEMRSST	MASSETER
AEELNTUV	EVENTUAL	AEELRSUV	REVALUES		SEAMSTER
AEELNTVY	VENTAYLE	AEELRSVY	AVERSELY		STEAMERS
AEELOPRS	PAROLEES	AEELSSST	ALTESSES	AEEMRSSU	MEASURES
AEELOPRV	OVERLEAP		SATELESS		REASSUME
AEELOPSX	POLEAXES		SEATLESS	AEEMRSTT	TEAMSTER
AEELOPTT	TOEPLATE	AEELSSTU	SETUALES	AEEMRSTW	STEMWARE
AEELORRS	RELEASOR	AEELSSTV	SALVETES	AEEMRSTY	METAYERS
AEELORST	OLEASTER	AEELSSVW	WAVELESS	AEEMRTWY	YAWMETER
AEELORSU	AUREOLES	AEELSTTT	STATELET	AEEMSSST	SEAMSETS
AEELORSV	OVERSALE	AEELSTTY	LAYETTES	AEEMSSSU	MASSEUSE
AEELORTT	TOLERATE	AEELSTVW	WAVELETS	AEEMSSTU	MEATUSES
AEELORTV	ELEVATOR	AEEMMNRS	MERESMAN	AEEMSTTU	AMUSETTE
	OVERLATE	AEEMMNTZ	MAZEMENT	AEENNOST	NEONATES
AEELORTW	TOLEWARE	AEEMMPSY	EMPYEMAS	AEENNPST	PENTANES
AEELORVZ	OVERZEAL	AEEMMRRV	YAMMERER	AEENNRRS	ENSNARER
AEELOSSW	LEASOWES	AEEMMRST	AMMETERS	AEENNRSS	ENSNARES
AEELOSTV	LOVESEAT		METAMERS		NEARNESS
AEELOTTT	TEETOTAL	AEEMMSST	MESSMATE		RENNASES
AEELPRRS	PEARLERS	AEEMMNOS	ANEMONES	AEENNRTU	ENAUNTER
	RELAPSER	AEEMNNPS	PENNAMES	AEENNRTV	REVENANT
AEELPRRT	PALTERER	AEEMNNRT	REMANENT	AEENNRUX	ANNEXURE
	PREALTER	AEEMNNSS	MEANNESS	AEENNSSS	SANENESS
AEELPRRY	PARLEYER	AEEMNORV	OVERNAME	AEENNSST	NEATNESS
AEELPRSS	PLEASERS	AEEMNORZ	ARMOZEEN	AEENNSTT	SETENANT
	PRESALES	AEEMNOSS	ANEMOSES	AEENOORT	AEROTONE
	RELAPSES	AEEMNOSW	SEAWOMEN	AEENOPRS	PERAEONS
AEELPRST	PETRALES	AEEMNOSX	AXONEMES		PERSONAE
	PLEATERS	AEEMNPRS	PRENAMES	AEENOPSU	EUPNOEAS
	PRELATES		SPEARMEN	AEENORRS	REASONER
	REPLATES	AEEMNPRT	PERMEANT	AEENORRV	OVERNEAR
AEELPRSU	PLEASURE		PETERMAN	AEENORSS	RESEASON
	SERPULAE	AEEMNPRY	EMPYREAN		SEASONER
AEELPRSV	VESPERAL	AEEMNPTV	PAVEMENT	AEENORST	EARSTONE
AEELPRTY	PTERYLAE	AEEMNRST	REMANETS		RESONATE
AEELPRUV	PREVALUE	AEEMNRSU	USERNAME	AEENORTV	OVERNEAT
AEELPSST	SPATLESE	AEEMNRSV	VERSEMAN		RENOVATE
	TAPELESS	AEEMNRSW	MENSWEAR	AEENORVW	OVENWARE
AEELPSTT	PALETTES	AEEMNRTU	NUMERATE	AEENOTTU	OUTEATEN
AEELPSTU	EPAULETS	AEEMNRTV	AVERMENT	AEENPPRT	PETNAPER
AEELPSTV	SEPTLEVA	AEEMNRTW	WATERMEN	AEENPPTT	APPETENT
AEELPSTZ	SPAETZLE	AEEMNRUV	MANEUVER	AEENPQTU	PETANQUE
AEELQRSU	LEQUEARS	AEEMNRVY	EVERYMAN	AEENPRUV	PARVENUE
	SQUEALER	AEEMNSSS	SAMENESS	AEENPSSU	APNEUSES
AEELQSUZ	QUEZALES	AEEMNSST	TAMENESS	AEENPSSX	EXPANSES
AEELRRST	ALTERERS	AEEMNSTU	MANSUETE	AEENPTTY	ANTETYPE
	REALTERS	AEEMNSTW	SWEETMAN	AEENRRRW	WARRENER
	RELATERS	AEEMORST	EROTEMAS	AEENRRSS	RARENESS
AEELRRSV	RAVELERS	AEEMORTV	OVERTAME	AEENRRST	TERRANES
	REVERSAL	AEEMPPRR	PAMPERER	AEENRRSV	RAVENERS
	SLAVERER	AEEMPRRT	TAMPERER	AEENRRSW	ANSWERER
AEELRRSX	RELAXERS	AEEMPRRV	REVAMPER		REANSWER
AEELRRTU	URETERAL	AEEMPRST	TEMPERAS	AEENRRSY	YEARNERS
AEELRRTV	TRAVELER	AEEMPRSY	EMPAYRES	AEENRRTT	NATTERER

	RATTENER	**AEEPRSTU**	EPURATES		TAKEOFFS
AEENRRTU	RENATURE		SUPERATE	**AEFFLMSW**	FLAMFEWS
AEENRRTV	TAVERNER	**AEEPRSTZ**	TRAPEZES	**AEFFLNSS**	SNAFFLES
AEENRSSS	SEARNESS	**AEEPSSTT**	SPATTEES	**AEFFLNTU**	AFFLUENT
AEENRSST	ASSENTER	**AEEQRRUV**	QUAVERER	**AEFFLRRS**	RAFFLERS
	EARNESTS	**AEERRRST**	ARRESTER	**AEFFLRSW**	WAFFLERS
	SARSENET		REARREST	**AEFFLSTU**	FEASTFUL
AEENRSSU	ANURESES	**AEERRSST**	ASSERTER		SUFFLATE
AEENRSSX	XERANSES		REASSERT	**AEFFLSUX**	AFFLUXES
AEENRSTT	ENTREATS		SERRATES	**AEFFMNST**	STAFFMEN
	RATTEENS		TERRASES	**AEFFMRSU**	EARMUFFS
AEENRSTU	SAUTERNE	**AEERRSSU**	ERASURES	**AEFFNNSS**	NAFFNESS
AEENRSTV	AVENTRES		REASSURE	**AEFFNORT**	AFFRONTE
	VETERANS	**AEERRSSW**	SWEARERS	**AEFFORST**	AFFOREST
AEENRSUV	UNREAVES	**AEERRSTT**	RETRATES	**AEFFOSVW**	WAVEOFFS
AEENRTTV	ANTEVERT		RETREATS	**AEFFQRSU**	QUAFFERS
AEENRTTX	EXTERNAT		TREATERS	**AEFFRSST**	RESTAFFS
	EXTRANET	**AEERRSTU**	AUSTERER		STAFFERS
AEENRTTY	ENTREATY		TREASURE	**AEFFRTTU**	TARTUFFE
AEENRTUV	AVENTURE	**AEERRSTV**	AVERTERS	**AEFGGGOS**	FOGGAGES
AEENRVWW	NEWWAVER		TRAVERSE	**AEFGGILR**	FLAGGIER
AEENSSST	SENSATES	**AEERRSTW**	WATERERS	**AEFGGINU**	FEAGUING
AEENSTTV	NAVETTES	**AEERRSVW**	WAVERERS	**AEFGGIST**	FAGGIEST
AEENSUVW	UNWEAVES	**AEERSSSS**	REASSESS	**AEFGGLRS**	FLAGGERS
AEEOPRRT	PATERERO	**AEERSSSU**	SEASURES	**AEFGGMOS**	MEGAFOGS
	PERORATE	**AEERSSSV**	ASSEVERS	**AEFGHINR**	HANGFIRE
AEEOPRST	OPERATES	**AEERSSSY**	ESSAYERS	**AEFGHINS**	SHEAFING
	PROTEASE	**AEERSSTT**	ESTREATS	**AEFGHOSS**	FOGASHES
AEEOPRTT	OPERETTA		RESTATES	**AEFGHTTU**	FUGHETTA
AEEOPSTZ	EPAZOTES		RETASTES	**AEFGIIRS**	GASIFIER
AEEORRSU	REAROUSE	**AEERSSTW**	SWEATERS	**AEFGIISS**	GASIFIES
AEEORRSW	SOWARREE	**AEERSSTZ**	ERSATZES	**AEFGIKLN**	FANGLIKE
AEEORRTV	OVERRATE	**AEERSSUU**	URAEUSES	**AEFGIKNR**	FREAKING
AEEORRVW	OVERWEAR	**AEERSSUV**	VAREUSES	**AEFGILNR**	FINAGLER
AEEORRVY	OVERYEAR	**AEERSTTT**	ATTESTER	**AEFGILNS**	FINAGLES
AEEORSSV	OVERSEAS	**AEERSTTX**	EXTREATS	**AEFGILOS**	FOLIAGES
AEEORSTV	OVEREATS	**AEERSTWW**	WETWARES	**AEFGILRR**	FRAGILER
AEEORSVV	OVERSAVE	**AEERTTTZ**	TERZETTA	**AEFGILTT**	LIFTGATE
AEEORSVW	OVERAWES	**AEERVWYY**	EVERYWAY	**AEFGIMTU**	FUMIGATE
AEEORSVY	OVEREASY	**AEESSSSS**	ASSESSES	**AEFGINRW**	WAFERING
AEEPPPRU	PREPUPAE	**AEESSTTT**	TESTATES	**AEFGINRY**	AREFYING
AEEPPRRR	PREPARER	**AEFFFLRS**	FLAFFERS	**AEFGINST**	FEASTING
AEEPPRRS	PAPERERS	**AEFFGIIL**	EFFIGIAL	**AEFGINTU**	FANTIGUE
	PREPARES	**AEFFGINR**	FIREFANG	**AEFGIORR**	FAIRGOER
	REPAPERS	**AEFFGIRS**	GIRAFFES	**AEFGIRRU**	ARGUFIER
AEEPPRRU	PUERPERA		RIFFAGES	**AEFGIRST**	FRIGATES
AEEPPRST	PREPASTE	**AEFFGNRS**	ENGRAFFS	**AEFGIRSU**	ARGUFIES
	PRETAPES	**AEFFGOST**	OFFSTAGE	**AEFGIRTU**	FIGURATE
AEEPPRSV	PREPAVES	**AEFFGRSU**	GAUFFERS		FRUITAGE
AEEPRRRT	PARTERRE		SUFFRAGE	**AEFGIRTW**	GIFTWARE
AEEPRRSS	ASPERSER	**AEFFHIKY**	KAFFIYEH	**AEFGISTU**	FATIGUES
	SPEARERS		KEFFIYAH	**AEFGLLNO**	LONGLEAF
AEEPRRST	TAPERERS	**AEFFHILL**	HALFLIFE	**AEFGLLOP**	FLAGPOLE
AEEPRRSV	PREAVERS	**AEFFILNY**	AFFINELY	**AEFGLLSS**	FLAGLESS
AEEPRRTT	PATTERER	**AEFFILRW**	WAFFLIER	**AEFGLLSU**	FULLAGES
	PRETREAT	**AEFFILUV**	EFFLUVIA	**AEFGLMNU**	FUGLEMAN
AEEPRRTU	APERTURE	**AEFFIMRR**	AFFIRMER	**AEFGLMOP**	MEGAFLOP
AEEPRSSS	ASPERSES		REAFFIRM	**AEFGLNOX**	FLEXAGON
	PREASSES	**AEFFIMRW**	FARMWIFE	**AEFGLNRS**	FLANGERS
	REPASSES	**AEFFIPRS**	PIAFFERS	**AEFGLNSS**	FANGLESS
AEEPRSST	TRAPESES	**AEFFIRSX**	AFFIXERS	**AEFGLOOR**	FLOORAGE
AEEPRSSZ	SPREAZES	**AEFFKLRU**	FREAKFUL	**AEFGLOPR**	LEAPFROG
AEEPRSTT	PEARTEST	**AEFFKORS**	RAKEOFFS	**AEFGLORW**	GAREFOWL
	PRETASTE	**AEFFKOST**	OFFTAKES	**AEFGLOST**	FLOTAGES

AEFGLOSW	FLOWAGES		INFAMIZE	**AEFILSTT**	FLATTIES
AEFGLPSU	PAGEFULS	**AEFIIMRS**	RAMIFIES	**AEFILSTU**	FISTULAE
AEFGLRTU	GRATEFUL	**AEFIINRT**	FAINTIER	**AEFILSTV**	FESTIVAL
AEFGLSTU	STAGEFUL	**AEFIINRV**	VINIFERA	**AEFILSTW**	FLATWISE
AEFGLTUX	FLUXGATE	**AEFIINSS**	SANIFIES		FLAWIEST
AEFGMNOR	FORGEMAN	**AEFIINST**	FAINITES	**AEFILSTX**	FLAXIEST
AEFGMNRT	FRAGMENT	**AEFIINSZ**	NAZIFIES	**AEFILSWY**	LIFEWAYS
AEFGMORS	FROMAGES	**AEFIIPRT**	APERITIF	**AEFILTUU**	FAUTEUIL
AEFGNNOT	FONTANGE	**AEFIIRRS**	FRIARIES	**AEFIMMMR**	MAMMIFER
AEFGNORT	FRONTAGE		RARIFIES	**AEFIMMRS**	MISFRAME
AEFGNRRS	FRANGERS	**AEFIIRRT**	RATIFIER	**AEFIMNST**	MANIFEST
	GRANFERS	**AEFIIRST**	RATIFIES	**AEFIMORR**	AERIFORM
AEFGNRST	ENGRAFTS	**AEFIIRSU**	AURIFIES	**AEFIMORT**	FORMIATE
AEFGOOPT	FOOTPAGE	**AEFIITVX**	FIXATIVE	**AEFIMOST**	FOAMIEST
AEFGOORT	FOOTGEAR	**AEFIJLOS**	JEOFAILS	**AEFIMRRS**	FIREARMS
AEFGOOST	FOOTAGES	**AEFIKLMO**	FOAMLIKE	**AEFIMRRW**	FIRMWARE
AEFGORRS	FORAGERS	**AEFIKLNU**	FAUNLIKE	**AEFIMRSS**	MISFARES
AEFGORST	FAGOTERS	**AEFIKLNW**	FAWNLIKE	**AEFINNSS**	FAINNESS
AEFGORTT	FROTTAGE	**AEFIKLRV**	FREAKILY		NAIFNESS
AEFGOSSU	FOUGASSE	**AEFIKLST**	FLAKIEST	**AEFINNST**	INFANTES
AEFGRRST	GRAFTERS	**AEFIKMNN**	KNIFEMAN	**AEFINNSZ**	FANZINES
	REGRAFTS	**AEFIKMRR**	FIREMARK	**AEFINOPR**	PINAFORE
AEFHIKRS	FREAKISH	**AEFIKRUW**	WAUKRIFE	**AEFINORS**	FARINOSE
AEFHIKSW	WEAKFISH	**AEFILLMS**	FAMILLES	**AEFINOTT**	FETATION
AEFHILLN	FELLAHIN	**AEFILLNT**	FLATLINE	**AEFINPRS**	FIREPANS
AEFHILLR	FIREHALL	**AEFILLOT**	FELLATIO		PANFRIES
AEFHILLT	TEFILLAH	**AEFILLRW**	FIREWALL	**AEFINRRS**	REFRAINS
AEFHILMS	FISHMEAL	**AEFILMNR**	INFLAMER	**AEFINRRU**	UNFAIRER
AEFHILMT	HALFTIME		RIFLEMAN	**AEFINRRZ**	FRANZIER
AEFHILNS	SHINLEAF	**AEFILMNS**	FLAMINES	**AEFINRSS**	FAIRNESS
AEFHILOR	FORHAILE		INFLAMES		SANSERIF
AEFHILOX	HEXAFOIL		MISFALNE		SERAFINS
AEFHILPP	HALFPIPE	**AEFILMNT**	FILAMENT	**AEFINRST**	FAINTERS
AEFHILRS	FLASHIER	**AEFILMST**	FLAMIEST		FENITARS
AEFHIMSS	FAMISHES	**AEFILMSY**	MAYFLIES	**AEFINRSX**	XERAFINS
AEFHIRST	FAITHERS	**AEFILMTY**	FEMALITY	**AEFINSTT**	FAINTEST
AEFHIRSW	WHARFIES	**AEFILNNR**	INFERNAL	**AEFINSTW**	FAWNIEST
AEFHLMSU	SHAMEFUL	**AEFILNOR**	FORELAIN	**AEFIORTV**	FAVORITE
AEFHLNOT	HALFTONE	**AEFILNOT**	OLEFIANT	**AEFIPRRT**	FIRETRAP
AEFHLNSS	HALFNESS	**AEFILNPS**	LIFESPAN	**AEFIQRSU**	AQUIFERS
AEFHLORS	FAHLORES	**AEFILNRT**	INFLATER	**AEFIRRRS**	FARRIERS
AEFHLPRS	PARFLESH	**AEFILNRU**	FRAULEIN	**AEFIRRRY**	FARRIERY
AEFHLRSS	FLASHERS	**AEFILNST**	INFLATES	**AEFIRRST**	FRATRIES
AEFHLRST	FARTHELS	**AEFILNSV**	FLAVINES	**AEFIRSTW**	WASTRIFE
AEFHLRTY	FATHERLY	**AEFILNTT**	ANTILEFT	**AEFIRTUX**	FIXATURE
AEFHLSST	FLASHEST	**AEFILOOR**	AEROFOIL	**AEFISTTT**	FATTIEST
AEFHLSTU	HASTEFUL	**AEFILORS**	FORESAIL	**AEFKLLOT**	FOLKTALE
AEFHMNRS	FRESHMAN	**AEFILORT**	FLOATIER	**AEFKLMRY**	FLYMAKER
AEFHMORT	FATHOMER	**AEFILOST**	FOLIATES	**AEFKLNRS**	FLANKERS
AEFHNRSW	FERNSHAW	**AEFILPPR**	FLAPPIER	**AEFKLOSS**	SEAFOLKS
AEFHRSST	SHAFTERS	**AEFILPRX**	PREFIXAL	**AEFKLRST**	FARTLEKS
AEFHRSTT	FARTHEST	**AEFILPST**	FLEAPITS	**AEFKLRUW**	WREAKFUL
AEFIIKLW	WAIFLIKE	**AEFILRST**	FLARIEST	**AEFKLSST**	FLASKETS
AEFIILLN	NAILFILE		FLARIEST	**AEFKLSTT**	TALKFEST
AEFIILMS	FAMILIES		FRAILEST	**AEFKNORR**	FORERANK
AEFIILNS	FINALISE	**AEFILRSU**	FAILURES	**AEFKNORS**	FORSAKEN
AEFIILNT	ANTILIFE	**AEFILRSV**	FAVRILES	**AEFKNPRR**	PREFRANK
AEFIILNZ	FINALIZE	**AEFILRSZ**	FILAZERS	**AEFKNRRS**	FRANKERS
AEFIILSS	SALIFIES	**AEFILRTT**	FILTRATE	**AEFKNRST**	FRANKEST
AEFIILST	FETIALIS	**AEFILRTU**	FAULTIER	**AEFKOPRS**	FORSPEAK
	FILIATES		FILATURE	**AEFKORRS**	FORSAKER
AEFIIMNS	INFAMIES	**AEFILRUW**	WEARIFUL	**AEFKORRW**	WORKFARE
	INFAMISE	**AEFILSSS**	FILASSES	**AEFKORSS**	FORSAKES
AEFIIMNZ	FEMINAZI	**AEFILSST**	SEALIFTS	**AEFKORTU**	FREAKOUT
		AEFILSSW	SAWFLIES		

AEFLLMMU	FLAMMULE	AEFLPRSU	FLAREUPS	AEGGGILN	ALEGGING
AEFLLNNS	FANNELLS	AEFLPRSY	PALFREYS	AEGGGINN	ENGAGING
	FLANNELS	AEFLPSUU	PAUSEFUL	AEGGGLSU	LUGGAGES
AEFLLNNU	UNFALLEN	AEFLRSSU	REFUSALS	AEGGHIRS	SHAGGIER
AEFLLORT	FELLATOR	AEFLRSTT	FATTRELS	AEGGHISS	HAGGISES
AEFLLORU	FLORULAE		FLATTERS	AEGGHJRY	JAGGHERY
AEFLLORV	OVERFALL	AEFLRSTU	REFUTALS	AEGGHLRS	HAGGLERS
AEFLLORW	FALLOWER	AEFLRSZZ	FRAZZLES	AEGGHMOS	HEMAGOGS
AEFLLOST	FLOATELS	AEFLRTTU	AFLUTTER	AEGGHMSU	MESHUGGA
AEFLLPSS	FLAPLESS	AEFLRTTY	FLATTERY	AEGGHOPY	GEOPHAGY
AEFLLPTU	PLATEFUL	AEFLSSTU	FLATUSES	AEGGHORU	ROUGHAGE
AEFLLRUW	AWFULLER		SULFATES	AEGGIINV	GINGIVAE
AEFLLRUX	FLEXURAL	AEFLSTTT	FLATTEST	AEGGIJST	JAGGIEST
AEFLLSSW	FLAWLESS	AEFLSTTU	TASTEFUL	AEGGIKNR	KNAGGIER
AEFLLSTT	FLATLETS	AEFLSTUW	WASTEFUL	AEGGILLN	ALLEGING
AEFLLSTY	FESTALLY	AEFMNORS	FORAMENS	AEGGILLR	GRILLAGE
AEFLMNOT	MATFELON	AEFMNRRY	FERRYMAN	AEGGILMN	GLEAMING
AEFLMORU	FORMULAE	AEFMNRST	RAFTSMEN	AEGGILNN	ANGELING
	FUMAROLE	AEFMNRSU	FRAENUMS		GLEANING
AEFLMORW	LEAFWORM	AEFMORRS	FOREARMS	AEGGILNR	GANGLIER
AEFLMOSS	FOAMLESS	AEFMORRT	REFORMAT		LAGERING
AEFLMOSY	FLAYSOME	AEFMORST	FOREMAST		REGALING
AEFLMOTU	FLAMEOUT		FORMATES	AEGGILNS	LIGNAGES
AEFLMPRR	FRAMPLER		MORTSAFE	AEGGILNT	GELATING
AEFLMSUW	WAMEFULS	AEFMORVW	WAVEFORM		LEGATING
AEFLNNNS	FLANNENS	AEFMOSSU	FAMOUSES		TEAGLING
AEFLNNOT	FONTANEL	AEFMOSUW	WAMEFOUS	AEGGILNU	LEAGUING
AEFLNNOY	NONLEAFY	AEFNNSTU	UNFASTEN	AEGGILNV	GAVELING
AEFLNNTY	FENTANYL	AEFNOPRR	PROFANER	AEGGILOT	TALEGGIO
AEFLNOPR	FLAPERON	AEFNOPRS	PROFANES	AEGGILRS	SLAGGIER
	FOREPLAN	AEFNOPSY	PAYFONES	AEGGILRW	WAGGLIER
AEFLNOPT	PANTOFLE	AEFNORRW	FOREWARN	AEGGIMNN	MANEGING
AEFLNORS	FARNESOL	AEFNORST	SEAFRONT		MENAGING
AEFLNORT	FLOREANT	AEFNORSU	FURANOSE	AEGGIMRT	GREGATIM
AEFLNOSV	FLAVONES	AEFNPRSU	SUPERFAN	AEGGIMSU	MISGAUGE
AEFLNRRU	FRENULAR	AEFNRRST	TRANSFER	AEGGINNR	ANGERING
AEFLNRSS	SALFERNS	AEFNRRUY	FUNERARY		ENRAGING
AEFLNRSU	FLANEURS	AEFNRSTU	AFTERSUN	AEGGINNT	AGENTING
	FUNERALS	AEFNSSST	FASTNESS		NEGATING
AEFLNRTU	FLAUNTER	AEFNSSTU	UNSAFEST	AEGGINNU	UNAGEING
AEFLNSST	FLATNESS	AEFNSTUY	UNSAFETY	AEGGINNV	AVENGING
AEFLNSTT	FLATTENS	AEFOORTW	FOOTWEAR	AEGGINOS	SEAGOING
AEFLNSUU	FAUNULES	AEFOPRRT	FOREPART	AEGGINRS	GEARINGS
AEFLNSUY	UNSAFELY	AEFOPRST	FOREPAST		GREASING
AEFLOORS	SEAFLOOR	AEFOPRSW	FOREPAWS		SNAGGIER
AEFLOORV	FOVEOLAR	AEFORRSV	FAVORERS	AEGGINRV	GREAVING
AEFLOOSV	FOVEOLAS	AEFORRSW	FORSWEAR	AEGGINRW	WAGERING
AEFLOPRT	TERAFLOP	AEFORRSY	FORAYERS	AEGGINSS	SIGNAGES
AEFLOPRY	FOREPLAY	AEFORRUV	FAVOURER	AEGGINST	NAGGIEST
AEFLOPSW	PEAFOWLS	AEFORRWY	FOREWARY	AEGGIOPR	ARPEGGIO
AEFLORRV	FLAVORER	AEFORSSY	FORESAYS		GEROPIGA
AEFLORSS	SAFROLES	AEFORSTV	OVERFAST	AEGGIOSS	ISAGOGES
AEFLORST	FLOATERS	AEFORSTW	FORWASTE	AEGGIQRU	QUAGGIER
	FORESTAL		SOFTWARE	AEGGIRRU	GARRIGUE
	REFLOATS	AEFORSTY	FORESTAY	AEGGIRST	RAGGIEST
AEFLORSU	FUSAROLE	AEFOSTTU	OUTFEAST		STAGGIER
AEFLORSY	FORELAYS	AEFOSTUU	FEATUOUS	AEGGIRSU	GARIGUES
AEFLORTW	FLEAWORT	AEFOSTUV	VOUTSAFE	AEGGIRWY	EARWIGGY
AEFLOSSU	FOSSULAE	AEFPRSST	PRESSFAT	AEGGISST	SAGGIEST
AEFLOSSW	SEAFOWLS	AEFRRSST	STRAFERS		STAGGIES
AEFLOSTT	FALSETTO	AEFRSSTW	FRETSAWS	AEGGISSW	SWAGGIES
AEFLPPRS	FLAPPERS	AEFRSTTU	TARTUFES	AEGGISTT	TAGGIEST
AEFLPPRY	FLYPAPER	AEFRSTUW	WAFTURES	AEGGLNPT	EGGPLANT
AEFLPRSS	FELSPARS	AEFRSWYZ	FRAWZEYS	AEGGLNRS	GANGRELS

AEGGLORY	GARGOYLE	AEGHLOSS	GALOSHES	AEGIKNRW	REWAKING
AEGGLOWY	WAYLEGGO	AEGHLOTX	HEXAGLOT		WREAKING
AEGGLRRS	GARGLERS	AEGHLRSU	LAUGHERS	AEGIKNSS	SINKAGES
AEGGLRST	STRAGGLE	AEGHLRTU	LAUGHTER	AEGIKNTW	TWEAKING
AEGGLRSW	WAGGLERS	AEGHLRTY	LETHARGY	AEGIKPPS	KIPPAGES
AEGGLRSY	GREYLAGS	AEGHLSTW	THALWEGS	AEGIKPRS	GARPIKES
AEGGMNNS	GANGSMEN	AEGHMNOP	PHENOGAM	AEGIKSTW	GAWKIEST
AEGGMNOR	GENOGRAM	AEGHMNOS	HOGMANES	AEGILLLS	ILLEGALS
AEGGMORR	ERGOGRAM	AEGHMNOY	HOGMENAY	AEGILLMS	LEGALISM
AEGGMORT	MORTGAGE	AEGHMOPT	APOTHEGM		MEGILLAS
AEGGNNSU	GUNNAGES	AEGHMORS	HOMAGERS		MILLAGES
AEGGNORV	OVERGANG	AEGHMORT	ETHOGRAM	AEGILLNR	ALLERGIN
AEGGNORW	WAGGONER	AEGHMSSU	MESHUGAS	AEGILLNS	GALLEINS
AEGGNRRS	GRANGERS	AEGHNNST	HANGNEST		NIGELLAS
AEGGNRST	GANGSTER	AEGHNOPT	HEPTAGON	AEGILLNU	LINGULAE
AEGGOPRU	GROUPAGE		PATHOGEN	AEGILLNV	GENIALLY
AEGGRSST	GAGSTERS	AEGHNOPY	HYPOGEAN	AEGILLPR	PILLAGER
	STAGGERS	AEGHNORV	HANGOVER	AEGILLPS	PILLAGES
AEGGRSSW	SWAGGERS		OVERHANG		SPILLAGE
AEGGRSTY	STAGGERY	AEGHNOSX	HEXAGONS	AEGILLRU	GUERILLA
AEGHHMSU	MESHUGAH	AEGHNPSW	SPANGHEW	AEGILLRV	VILLAGER
AEGHIJRS	JAGHIRES	AEGHNRSS	GNASHERS	AEGILLSS	GALLISES
AEGHILLM	MEGILLAH		SHERANGS	AEGILLST	LEGALIST
AEGHILLS	SHIGELLA	AEGHNSST	STENGAHS		STILLAGE
AEGHILMT	MEGALITH	AEGHOPPR	PROPHAGE		TILLAGES
AEGHILNR	NARGHILE	AEGHOPPY	APOPHYGE	AEGILLSV	VILLAGES
	NARGILEH	AEGHOPXY	EXOPHAGY	AEGILLSZ	GALLIZES
AEGHILNS	HEALINGS	AEGHORST	SHORTAGE	AEGILLTU	LIGULATE
	LEASHING	AEGHOSST	HOSTAGES	AEGILLTY	LEGALITY
	SHEALING	AEGHOSSU	GASHOUSE	AEGILMMR	AGLIMMER
AEGHILNT	ATHELING	AEGHPRSS	SPREAGHS		LAMMIGER
AEGHILNX	EXHALING	AEGHPRTU	UPGATHER	AEGILMNP	EMPALING
AEGHILPS	SHAGPILE	AEGHRTTU	RETAUGHT	AEGILMNR	GERMINAL
AEGHILRT	LITHARGE	AEGIILLU	AIGUILLE		MALIGNER
	THIRLAGE	AEGIILMN	EMAILING		MALINGER
AEGHILRU	LAUGHIER	AEGIILMO	OLIGEMIA	AEGILMNS	MEASLING
AEGHILST	LAIGHEST	AEGIILMR	REMIGIAL	AEGILMNT	LIGAMENT
AEGHIMNW	WEIGHMAN	AEGIILNN	ALIENING		METALING
AEGHIMPS	MAGESHIP	AEGIILNR	GAINLIER		TEGMINAL
AEGHIMST	MEGAHITS	AEGIILRR	GLAIRIER	AEGILMNU	AEMULING
AEGHINNN	HENNAING	AEGIILTT	LITIGATE	AEGILMNY	YEALMING
AEGHINNT	NAETHING	AEGIILTV	LIGATIVE	AEGILMRS	GREMIALS
AEGHINNV	HAVENING	AEGIIMNR	IMAGINER		LAMIGERS
AEGHINRS	HEARINGS		MIGRAINE		REGALISM
	HEARSING	AEGIIMNS	IMAGINES	AEGILMRX	LEXIGRAM
	SHEARING	AEGIIMTT	MITIGATE	AEGILMTU	MULTIAGE
AEGHINRT	EARTHING	AEGIINNN	NENNIGAI	AEGILNNP	PANELING
	HEARTING	AEGIINNR	ARGININE	AEGILNNR	LEARNING
	INGATHER	AEGIINRR	GRAINIER	AEGILNNS	EANLINGS
AEGHINRV	HAVERING	AEGIIRRT	IRRIGATE		LEANINGS
AEGHINST	GAHNITES	AEGIISTV	VESTIGIA	AEGILNNT	GANTLINE
	HEATINGS	AEGIJLNR	JANGLIER		LATENING
AEGHINSV	HEAVINGS	AEGIKLNS	LINKAGES	AEGILNNU	UNGENIAL
	SHEAVING		SNAGLIKE	AEGILNNW	WEANLING
AEGHINSZ	GENIZAHS	AEGIKLNT	GNATLIKE	AEGILNNY	YEANLING
AEGHINTT	GNATHITE	AEGIKLNW	WEAKLING	AEGILNOR	GERANIOL
AEGHIOPS	ESOPHAGI	AEGIKLOT	GOATLIKE		REGIONAL
AEGHIPPR	EPIGRAPH	AEGIKMNR	REMAKING	AEGILNOS	GASOLINE
AEGHIPRT	GRAPHITE	AEGIKMRW	WIGMAKER	AEGILNOT	GELATION
AEGHIRRS	GHARRIES	AEGIKNNS	SNEAKING		LEGATION
AEGHIRSS	GARISHES	AEGIKNNW	WAKENING	AEGILNPR	GRAPLINE
AEGHLNOS	HALOGENS	AEGIKNPS	SPEAKING		PEARLING
AEGHLNOV	HYALOGEN	AEGIKNRS	SKEARING	AEGILNPS	ELAPSING
AEGHLOPY	HYPOGEAL	AEGIKNRT	RETAKING		PLEASING

AEGILNPT	PLEATING	AEGILRYZ	GLAZIERY	AEGINOPT	PINOTAGE
AEGILNQU	EQUALING	AEGILSSS	GLASSIES	AEGINORR	ORANGIER
AEGILNRR	GNARLIER	AEGILSTZ	GLAZIEST	AEGINORS	IGNAROES
AEGILNRS	ALIGNERS	AEGIMMST	GAMMIEST		ORGANISE
	ENGRAILS	AEGIMNNO	NONIMAGE		ORIGANES
	NARGILES	AEGIMNNR	ENARMING	AEGINORZ	ORGANIZE
	REALIGNS		RENAMING	AEGINOSS	AGONISES
	SALERING	AEGIMNNS	MEANINGS	AEGINOSZ	AGONIZES
	SANGLIER	AEGIMNNT	ENTAMING	AEGINPPR	PAPERING
	SIGNALER	AEGIMNPR	EMPARING	AEGINPPS	GENIPAPS
	SLANGIER	AEGIMNRR	REARMING	AEGINPRS	PREASING
AEGILNRT	ALERTING	AEGIMNRS	GERMAINS		SPEARING
	ALTERING		SMEARING	AEGINPRT	RETAPING
	INTEGRAL	AEGIMNRT	EMIGRANT		TAPERING
	RELATING		REMATING	AEGINPRV	REPAVING
	TANGLIER	AEGIMNRU	GERANIUM	AEGINPRY	REPAYING
	TERAGLIN		MAUNGIER	AEGINPSS	SPAEINGS
	TRIANGLE	AEGIMNSS	GAMINESS		SPINAGES
AEGILNRV	RAVELING	AEGIMNST	MANGIEST	AEGINPSY	GYPSEIAN
AEGILNRX	RELAXING		MINTAGES	AEGINPTY	EGYPTIAN
AEGILNRY	LAYERING		MISAGENT	AEGINQTU	EQUATING
	RELAYING		STEAMING	AEGINRRS	EARRINGS
	YEARLING		TEAMINGS		GRAINERS
AEGILNSS	GAINLESS	AEGIMNSV	VEGANISM	AEGINRRV	AVERRING
	GLASSINE	AEGIMNTU	TEGUMINA	AEGINRSS	ASSIGNER
	LEASINGS		UMANGITE		REASSIGN
	SEALINGS	AEGIMOOS	OOGAMIES		SEARINGS
AEGILNST	EASTLING	AEGIMORR	ARMIGERO		SERINGAS
	GELATINS	AEGIMORS	GORAMIES	AEGINRST	ANGRIEST
	GENITALS	AEGIMORW	WAGMOIRE		ANGSTIER
	STEALING	AEGIMPRS	EPIGRAMS		ASTRINGE
	TAGLINES		PRIMAGES		GANISTER
AEGILNSV	LEAVINGS	AEGIMPRU	UMPIRAGE		GANTRIES
	SLEAVING	AEGIMPSS	MISPAGES		GRANITES
AEGILNSW	SWEALING	AEGIMPST	PIGMEATS		INGRATES
AEGILNSY	YEALINGS	AEGIMQRU	QUAGMIRE		RANGIEST
AEGILNTV	VALETING	AEGIMRRS	ARMIGERS		REASTING
AEGILNTX	EXALTING	AEGIMRRT	RAGTIMER		STEARING
AEGILNTZ	TEAZLING	AEGIMRSS	GISARMES		TASERING
AEGILNUV	VAGINULE	AEGIMRST	MAGISTER	AEGINRSV	VINEGARS
AEGILOPS	SPOILAGE		MIGRATES	AEGINRSW	RESAWING
AEGILOPT	PILOTAGE		RAGTIMES		SWEARING
AEGILORS	GASOLIER		STERIGMA		WEARINGS
	GIRASOLE	AEGIMSST	SIGMATES	AEGINRSY	RESAYING
	SERAGLIO	AEGIMSSU	MISUSAGE		SYNERGIA
AEGILOSS	GOLIASES	AEGIMSTU	GAUMIEST	AEGINRTT	ARETTING
	OILGASES	AEGINNNX	ANNEXING		GNATTIER
	SOILAGES	AEGINNOS	ANGINOSE		TREATING
AEGILOST	LATIGOES		GANOINES	AEGINRTV	AVERTING
	OTALGIES	AEGINNOT	NEGATION		GRIEVANT
AEGILOSU	EULOGIAS	AEGINNPS	SNEAPING		TAVERING
AEGILPPS	SLIPPAGE		SPEANING		VINTAGER
AEGILPPU	PUPILAGE	AEGINNRS	AGINNERS	AEGINRTW	TWANGIER
AEGILPRU	PLAGUIER		EARNINGS		WATERING
AEGILRRU	GLAURIER		ENGRAINS	AEGINRTX	RETAXING
AEGILRSS	GLASSIER		GRANNIES	AEGINRVW	WAVERING
AEGILRST	GLARIEST	AEGINNRV	RAVENING	AEGINRVY	VINEGARY
	REGALIST	AEGINNRY	RENAYING	AEGINRWX	REWAXING
AEGILRSY	GREASILY		YEARNING	AEGINRWY	WEARYING
AEGILRSZ	GLAZIERS	AEGINNST	ANTIGENS	AEGINSST	EASTINGS
AEGILRTT	AGLITTER		GENTIANS		GENISTAS
AEGILRTU	LIGATURE		STEANING		GIANTESS
AEGILRTY	REGALITY	AEGINNSU	GUANINES		SEATINGS
AEGILRVW	LAWGIVER		SANGUINE		TEASINGS

	TSIGANES	**AEGLLORV**	OVERGALL	**AEGLORSU**	GLAREOUS
AEGINSSY	ESSAYING	**AEGLLORY**	ALLEGORY	**AEGLORSV**	VORLAGES
AEGINSTT	ESTATING	**AEGLLOSS**	GAOLLESS	**AEGLORTU**	OUTGLARE
	TANGIEST		GOALLESS	**AEGLORTV**	TRAVELOG
AEGINSTU	SAUTEING	**AEGLLOST**	TOLLAGES	**AEGLORTW**	WATERLOG
	UNITAGES	**AEGLLOTT**	TOLLGATE	**AEGLORTY**	GEOLATRY
AEGINSTV	VINTAGES	**AEGLLRVY**	GRAVELLY	**AEGLOSSW**	GALOWSES
AEGINSTW	SWEATING	**AEGLLSSU**	GALLUSES	**AEGLOSTV**	VOLTAGES
AEGINSTY	YEASTING		SEAGULLS	**AEGLOSUY**	GEALOUSY
AEGINSTZ	TZIGANES		SULLAGES	**AEGLPPRR**	GRAPPLER
AEGINSVW	WEAVINGS	**AEGLMNNO**	MANGONEL	**AEGLPPRS**	GRAPPLES
AEGINSVY	SAVEYING	**AEGLMNOY**	AMYLOGEN	**AEGLPRSU**	EARPLUGS
AEGIOPRR	PROGERIA	**AEGLMNRS**	MANGLERS		GRAUPELS
AEGIORSS	ARGOSIES	**AEGLMNSS**	GLASSMEN		PLAGUERS
AEGIORSV	VIRAGOES	**AEGLMNTU**	GUNMETAL	**AEGLPSSU**	PLUSAGES
AEGIORTV	RAVIGOTE	**AEGLMOPS**	MEGALOPS		PLUSSAGE
AEGIOSTT	GOATIEST	**AEGLMORS**	GOMERALS	**AEGLRRSU**	REGULARS
AEGIOSTU	AGOUTIES	**AEGLMOSU**	MOULAGES	**AEGLRRUV**	VULGARER
AEGIOSTX	GEOTAXIS	**AEGLMOTU**	OUTGLEAM	**AEGLRSTU**	GAULTERS
AEGIPPRT	GRIPTAPE	**AEGLMOTV**	MEGAVOLT		GESTURAL
AEGIPPST	GAPPIEST	**AEGLMPSU**	PLUMAGES		TRAGULES
AEGIPRSS	PRISAGES	**AEGLMRSU**	MAULGRES	**AEGLRTUY**	ARGUTELY
	SPAIRGES	**AEGLMSSU**	GAUMLESS	**AEGLSSTT**	GESTALTS
AEGIPRST	GRAPIEST	**AEGLNNOR**	NONGLARE	**AEGLSSUV**	VALGUSES
AEGIPRTY	PTERYGIA	**AEGLNNPT**	PLANGENT	**AEGLSTUU**	GLUTAEUS
AEGIPSST	GASPIEST	**AEGLNNSY**	LANGSYNE	**AEGLSTUV**	VULGATES
AEGIQRSU	SQUIRAGE	**AEGLNNTU**	UNTANGLE	**AEGLSUUY**	GUAYULES
AEGIRRSS	GRASSIER	**AEGLNOPT**	GANTLOPE	**AEGMMNOR**	GAMMONER
AEGIRRSU	SUGARIER	**AEGLNORY**	YEARLONG	**AEGMMRRU**	RUMMAGER
AEGIRRSZ	GRAZIERS	**AEGLNOST**	TANGELOS	**AEGMMRSU**	RUMMAGES
AEGIRRTY	ARGYRITE	**AEGLNOSU**	ANGULOSE	**AEGMNNOS**	AGNOMENS
AEGIRSST	AGISTERS	**AEGLNPRS**	GRAPNELS	**AEGMNNOT**	MAGNETON
AEGIRSTT	STRIGATE		SPANGLER	**AEGMNORR**	RENOGRAM
AEGIRSTV	VIRGATES		SPRANGLE	**AEGMNORS**	MEGARONS
	VITRAGES	**AEGLNPSS**	PANGLESS	**AEGMNORV**	MANGROVE
AEGIRSUU	AUGURIES		SPANGLES		VENOGRAM
AEGIRSUY	YUGARIES	**AEGLNPST**	SPANGLET	**AEGMNOST**	GEOMANTS
AEGISSST	GASSIEST	**AEGLNRRW**	WRANGLER		MAGNETOS
AEGISSTT	STAGIEST	**AEGLNRSS**	SLANGERS		MEGATONS
AEGISSTW	GAWSIEST	**AEGLNRST**	STRANGLE		MONTAGES
AEGISTUZ	GAUZIEST		TANGLERS	**AEGMNOSX**	MAGNOXES
AEGJLNOR	JARGONEL		TRANGLES	**AEGMNOXY**	XENOGAMY
AEGJLNRS	JANGLERS	**AEGLNRSU**	GRANULES	**AEGMNRST**	GARMENTS
AEGJLTUU	JUGULATE	**AEGLNRSW**	WANGLERS		MARGENTS
AEGKKKNO	ANGEKKOK		WRANGLES		RAGMENTS
AEGKKNOS	ANGEKOKS	**AEGLNRSY**	LARYNGES	**AEGMNRTU**	ARGENTUM
AEGKLLOT	LEKGOTLA	**AEGLNRTW**	TWANGLER		ARGUMENT
AEGKLOSU	KAGOULES	**AEGLNRUY**	GUNLAYER	**AEGMNSSW**	SWAGSMEN
AEGKMNRU	GUNMAKER	**AEGLNSTT**	GANTLETS	**AEGMNSSY**	GAMYNESS
AEGKMRSY	KERYGMAS	**AEGLNSTU**	LANGUETS	**AEGMNSTU**	AUGMENTS
AEGKNORS	KARENGOS	**AEGLNSTW**	TWANGLES		MUTAGENS
AEGKNRSS	SKANGERS	**AEGLNSUW**	GUNWALES	**AEGMOORS**	MOORAGES
AEGLLLMU	GLUMELLA	**AEGLNTTU**	GAUNTLET	**AEGMOPRW**	GAPEWORM
AEGLLNNO	NONLEGAL	**AEGLNTUU**	UNGULATE	**AEGMOPST**	POSTGAME
AEGLLNOS	ALLONGES	**AEGLOOOZ**	ZOOGLOEA	**AEGMORRW**	WORMGEAR
	GALLEONS	**AEGLOOPU**	APOLOGUE	**AEGMORSS**	GOSSAMER
AEGLLNOV	LONGEVAL	**AEGLOORY**	AEROLOGY	**AEGMPRUZ**	GAZUMPER
AEGLLNPS	LANGSPEL		AREOLOGY	**AEGMPSTU**	STUMPAGE
AEGLLNRS	LANGRELS	**AEGLOOSZ**	ZOOGLEAS	**AEGNNOPT**	PENTAGON
AEGLLNST	GELLANTS	**AEGLOPRS**	PERGOLAS	**AEGNNORT**	NEGATRON
AEGLLNSY	LANGLEYS	**AEGLOPRY**	PLAYGOER	**AEGNNOST**	NEGATONS
AEGLLOOZ	ZOOGLEAL	**AEGLOPTT**	PLOTTAGE		TONNAGES
AEGLLOPR	GALLOPER	**AEGLORST**	GLOATERS	**AEGNNPRT**	PREGNANT
AEGLLORS	ALLEGROS		LEGATORS	**AEGNNRSU**	GUNNERAS

AEGNNRTY	GANNETRY	AEGORTTU	TUTORAGE	AEHIKNSS	SNEAKISH
AEGNNSTT	TANGENTS	AEGORTUU	OUTARGUE	AEHIKSST	SHAKIEST
AEGNNSTU	TUNNAGES	AEGORUVY	VOYAGEUR		SHITAKES
AEGNNTUU	UNGUENTA	AEGOSSTU	OUTGASES	AEHIKSSY	SAKIYEHS
AEGNOORS	OREGANOS	AEGOSSTW	STOWAGES	AEHILLNT	THALLINE
AEGNOPRR	PARERGON	AEGOSSYZ	AZYGOSES	AEHILMOS	HEMIOLAS
AEGNOPST	PONTAGES	AEGOSTTU	OUTGATES	AEHILMOT	HALIMOTE
AEGNORRS	GROANERS	AEGOSTTV	GAVOTTES	AEHILMQS	SHEQALIM
AEGNORRY	ORANGERY	AEGOSTUZ	OUTGAZES	AEHILMRU	HAULMIER
AEGNORST	ESTRAGON	AEGPRRSS	GRASPERS	AEHILMSW	LIMEWASH
	NEGATORS		SPARGERS	AEHILMSY	LEHAYIMS
	ORANGEST	AEGPRSTU	UPSTAGER	AEHILNOP	APHELION
	RAGSTONE	AEGPSSTU	UPSTAGES		PHELONIA
	STONERAG	AEGPSSUU	GAUPUSES	AEHILNRS	INHALERS
AEGNORSW	WAGONERS	AEGPSSUW	GAWPUSES	AEHILNRU	INHAULER
AEGNORTT	TETRAGON	AEGQRTUU	TRUQUAGE	AEHILNSY	HYALINES
AEGNORTU	OUTRANGE	AEGRRSSS	GRASSERS	AEHILNTX	ANTHELIX
AEGNORTY	NEGATORY	AEGRRSSU	SUGARERS	AEHILNTZ	ZENITHAL
AEGNORUV	VARGUENO	AEGRRSSY	RYEGRASS	AEHILORS	AIRHOLES
AEGNOSSY	NOSEGAYS	AEGRRSUU	AUGURERS		SHOALIER
AEGNOTUY	AUTOGENY	AEGRRSUV	GRAVURES	AEHILORT	AEROLITH
AEGNPPRU	GUNPAPER		VERRUGAS	AEHILOTZ	THIAZOLE
AEGNPRRS	RESPRANG	AEGRSSSU	SARGUSES	AEHILPRS	EARLSHIP
AEGNPRSS	ENGRASPS	AEGRSSUV	SEVRUGAS		HARELIPS
AEGNPRST	TREPANGS	AEGRSTTY	STRATEGY		PLASHIER
AEGNPRSU	SPEARGUN	AEGRSTUU	AUGUSTER	AEHILPST	HAPLITES
AEGNPRYY	PANEGYRY	AEGSSTUU	AUGUSTES	AEHILRSS	HAIRLESS
AEGNRRST	GRANTERS	AEGSTTTU	GUTTATES	AEHILRSU	HAULIERS
	REGRANTS	AEHHHIST	SHEHITAH	AEHILRSV	LAVISHER
	STRANGER	AEHHIKSS	SHEIKHAS		SHRIEVAL
AEGNRSST	STRANGES	AEHHIMPY	HYPHEMIA	AEHILRTY	EARTHILY
AEGNRSSY	GRAYNESS	AEHHIMTW	HAMEWITH		HEARTILY
AEGNRSTU	STRAUNGE	AEHHINST	INSHEATH	AEHILSST	HELIASTS
AEGNRSTW	TWANGERS	AEHHIPSW	PEISHWAH		SHALIEST
AEGNRSYY	ASYNERGY	AEHHISST	HASHIEST	AEHILSSV	LAVISHES
AEGNSSST	GASTNESS		SHEHITAS	AEHILSSW	SHAWLIES
AEGNSSSY	SYNGASES	AEHHISVY	YESHIVAH		WHAISLES
AEGNSTTU	GAUNTEST	AEHHLNTU	UNHEALTH	AEHILSTT	LATHIEST
	TUTENAGS	AEHHNRSS	HARSHENS		LITHATES
AEGOORST	ROOTAGES	AEHHNRSW	HERNSHAW	AEHILSTY	HYALITES
AEGOORSV	VORAGOES	AEHHORST	HAROSETH	AEHILSUV	VIHUELAS
AEGOOSWY	WAYGOOSE	AEHHRRST	THRASHER	AEHILSWZ	WHAIZLES
AEGOPPRS	PROPAGES	AEHHRSST	HARSHEST	AEHIMMSS	SHAMMIES
AEGOPPST	STOPPAGE		THRASHES	AEHIMMST	HAMMIEST
AEGOPPSU	SUPPEAGO	AEHIIKLR	HAIRLIKE	AEHIMMSW	WHAMMIES
AEGOPRST	PORTAGES	AEHIIKRT	TERAKIHI	AEHIMNNU	INHUMANE
	POTAGERS	AEHIIKST	SHIITAKE	AEHIMNRS	HARMINES
AEGOPRTU	PORTAGUE	AEHIILMO	HEMIOLIA		SHIREMAN
AEGOPSST	GESTAPOS	AEHIILMT	LITHEMIA	AEHIMNSS	SHAMISEN
	POSTAGES	AEHIILNR	HAIRLINE	AEHIMNST	HEMATINS
AEGOPSSU	SPOUSAGE	AEHIILST	HAILIEST	AEHIMNSU	HUMANISE
AEGOPSTT	GATEPOST	AEHIIMNT	THIAMINE	AEHIMNTU	INHUMATE
	POTTAGES	AEHIIMOP	HEMIOPIA	AEHIMNUZ	HUMANIZE
AEGORRRT	GARROTER	AEHIINNT	IANTHINE	AEHIMPRS	SAMPHIRE
	REGRATOR	AEHIINTZ	THIAZINE		SERAPHIM
AEGORRST	GARROTES	AEHIIRRW	WIREHAIR	AEHIMPRT	TERAPHIM
AEGORRTT	GAROTTER	AEHIIRST	HAIRIEST	AEHIMPRX	XERAPHIM
	GARROTTE	AEHIKKLW	HAWKLIKE	AEHIMPSS	EMPHASIS
AEGORSSS	SARGOSES	AEHIKLLO	HALOLIKE		MISSHAPE
AEGORSST	STORAGES	AEHIKLLT	LATHLIKE		PHAEISMS
AEGORSTT	GAROTTES	AEHIKLMS	SHEKALIM	AEHIMPST	MATESHIP
AEGORSTU	OUTRAGES	AEHIKLNP	KEPHALIN		SHIPMATE
AEGORSUV	OUVRAGES	AEHIKLRS	RASHLIKE	AEHIMRRS	MARSHIER
AEGORSVY	VOYAGERS	AEHIKMNZ	KHAZENIM		

AEHIMRSS	MARISHES	**AEHIPSSW**	PEISHWAS	**AEHLNOTY**	ETHANOYL
	MISHEARS	**AEHIPSTZ**	ZAPTIEHS	**AEHLNPRS**	SHRAPNEL
AEHIMSSS	MESSIAHS	**AEHIPSWW**	WASHWIPE	**AEHLNPTY**	ENTHALPY
AEHIMSST	ATHEISMS	**AEHIQSSU**	QUASHIES	**AEHLNRST**	ENTHRALS
	MASHIEST	**AEHIRRRS**	HARRIERS	**AEHLNSST**	NATHLESS
	MATHESIS	**AEHIRRRS**	ARRISHES	**AEHLNSSU**	UNLASHES
AEHIMTUY	EUTHYMIA	**AEHIRRST**	TRASHIER		UNSHALES
AEHINNPZ	PHENAZIN	**AEHIRRSV**	RAVISHER	**AEHLNSTY**	NAYTHLES
AEHINNSS	SHANNIES	**AEHIRRSW**	WAIRSHER	**AEHLNTUZ**	HAZELNUT
AEHINNTX	XANTHEIN	**AEHIRRTW**	WRATHIER	**AEHLOPRT**	PLETHORA
	XANTHINE	**AEHIRSST**	SHERIATS	**AEHLOPSS**	HAPLOSES
AEHINOPS	APHONIES	**AEHIRSSV**	RAVISHES	**AEHLOPST**	TAPHOLES
AEHINOPU	EUPHONIA	**AEHIRSSW**	SWASHIER	**AEHLOPTT**	HOTPLATE
AEHINORT	ANTIHERO	**AEHIRSTU**	THESAURI	**AEHLORST**	LOATHERS
AEHINOTT	THIONATE	**AEHIRSTW**	SWATHIER		RATHOLES
AEHINPPY	EPIPHANY		WATERISH	**AEHLORSY**	HOARSELY
AEHINPRS	HEPARINS	**AEHIRSTY**	HYSTERIA	**AEHLORUV**	OVERHAUL
	PARISHEN	**AEHIRSWY**	HAYWIRES	**AEHLOSSS**	ASSHOLES
	SERAPHIN	**AEHIRTYZ**	YAHRZEIT	**AEHLOSST**	SHOALEST
AEHINPRT	PERIANTH	**AEHISSST**	STASHIES	**AEHLOSTT**	LOATHEST
AEHINPST	PENTHIAS	**AEHISSSW**	SIWASHES	**AEHLPPRT**	THRAPPLE
	THESPIAN	**AEHISSSY**	ESSAYISH	**AEHLPRSS**	PLASHERS
AEHINRRS	SHARNIER	**AEHISSTT**	ATHEISTS		SPLASHER
AEHINRRU	UNHAIRER		HASTIEST	**AEHLPSSS**	SPLASHES
AEHINRSS	ARSHINES		STAITHES	**AEHLPSST**	PATHLESS
AEHINRST	HAIRNETS	**AEHISSTU**	HIATUSES		PLASHETS
	INEARTHS	**AEHISSTW**	WASHIEST	**AEHLPSTU**	SULPHATE
	THERIANS	**AEHISSVY**	YESHIVAS	**AEHLRRTU**	URETHRAL
AEHINRSV	ENRAVISH	**AEHISTTW**	THAWIEST	**AEHLRSS**	SLASHERS
	VANISHER		THWAITES	**AEHLRSST**	HARSLETS
AEHINRSW	SHERWANI	**AEHJLOSW**	JAWHOLES		SLATHERS
AEHINRTU	HAURIENT	**AEHJNNOS**	JOHANNES	**AEHLSSSS**	SASHLESS
AEHINRTW	TARWHINE	**AEHKMOPW**	MOPEHAWK	**AEHLSSTT**	STEALTHS
AEHINRUW	WHARENUI	**AEHKNNSU**	UNSHAKEN	**AEHLSSTW**	THAWLESS
AEHINSSS	ASHINESS	**AEHKNOSW**	HAWKNOSE	**AEHLSSWY**	SHAWLEYS
	HESSIANS	**AEHKNRST**	THANKERS	**AEHLSTTY**	STEALTHY
AEHINSST	ANTHESIS	**AEHKNSSU**	ANKUSHES	**AEHMMRSS**	SHAMMERS
	SHANTIES	**AEHKNSWW**	NEWSHAWK	**AEHMNNPY**	NYMPHEAN
	SHEITANS	**AEHKOOPR**	REAPHOOK	**AEHMNOPR**	MORPHEAN
	STHENIAS	**AEHKOSTU**	SHAKEOUT	**AEHMNORS**	HORSEMAN
AEHINSSV	VANISHES	**AEHKPSSU**	SHAKEUPS		MENORAHS
AEHINSSZ	HAZINESS	**AEHKRRSS**	SHARKERS		RHAMNOSE
AEHINSTT	HESITANT	**AEHLLLTY**	LETHALLY		SHOREMAN
AEHINSTW	INSWATHE	**AEHLLMOP**	LAMPHOLE	**AEHMNOST**	HOASTMEN
AEHINTTT	ANTITHET	**AEHLLMTY**	METHYLAL	**AEHMNOSU**	HOUSEMAN
AEHIOPRS	APHORISE	**AEHLLNRT**	ENTHRALL	**AEHMNPRU**	PREHUMAN
AEHIOPRU	EUPHORIA	**AEHLLNTU**	UNLETHAL	**AEHMNRST**	TRASHMEN
AEHIOPRZ	APHORIZE	**AEHLLORW**	HALLOWER	**AEHMNSTU**	HUMANEST
AEHIOPTT	THIOTEPA	**AEHLLRSS**	HERSALLS	**AEHMOPRT**	METAPHOR
AEHIORRV	OVERHAIR	**AEHLLSST**	HALTLESS	**AEHMOPST**	APOTHEMS
AEHIORST	HOARIEST	**AEHLMMNS**	HELMSMAN	**AEHMORST**	TERAOHMS
AEHIORTU	THIOUREA	**AEHLMNOS**	MANHOLES	**AEHMOSTT**	HEMOSTAT
AEHIPPRS	PAPISHER	**AEHLMNOT**	HOTELMAN	**AEHMOSTU**	OUTSHAME
	SAPPHIRE		METHANOL	**AEHMOSTW**	SOMEWHAT
AEHIPPSS	PAPISHES	**AEHLMNUY**	HUMANELY	**AEHMOSTY**	HOMESTAY
AEHIPPST	EPITAPHS	**AEHLMORS**	ARMHOLES	**AEHMPPRY**	PAMPHREY
	HAPPIEST	**AEHLMOSU**	HAMULOSE	**AEHMPRST**	HAMPSTER
	PEATSHIP	**AEHLMPPT**	PAMPHLET	**AEHMRSSS**	SMASHERS
AEHIPRRS	PHRASIER	**AEHLMPSW**	WHAMPLES	**AEHMRSST**	HAMSTERS
AEHIPRRT	RATHRIPE	**AEHLMRSS**	HARMLESS	**AEHMRSTU**	MAUTHERS
AEHIPRSS	PARISHES	**AEHLMRST**	THERMALS	**AEHMRSTW**	MAWTHERS
	SHARPIES	**AEHLMRSU**	HUMERALS	**AEHMSSSU**	SHAMUSES
AEHIPRST	TRIPHASE	**AEHLNOST**	ANETHOLS	**AEHMSSTT**	SHMATTES
AEHIPRTT	THREAPIT		ETHANOLS	**AEHMSTTY**	AMETHYST

AEHMSUZZ	MEZUZAHS
AEHNNOPT	PANTHEON
AEHNNOTX	XANTHONE
AEHNNPRU	NENUPHAR
AEHNNPSU	UNSHAPEN
AEHNNSUV	UNSHAVEN
AEHNNSUW	UNWASHEN
AEHNOOPT	HANEPOOT
AEHNOPPY	HYPOPNEA
	PAYPHONE
AEHNOPRT	HAPTERON
AEHNOPST	PHAETONS
	PHONATES
	STANHOPE
AEHNOPSW	WANHOPES
AEHNOPSY	HYPONEAS
AEHNOPXY	XENOPHYA
AEHNOQTU	HAQUETON
AEHNORSS	HOARSENS
	SENHORAS
AEHNOSSX	HEXOSANS
AEHNPRSS	SHARPENS
AEHNPRST	PANTHERS
AEHNPSSU	UNSHAPES
AEHNPSTY	PHYTANES
AEHNRSSS	RASHNESS
AEHNRSTU	HAUNTERS
	UNEARTHS
	UNHEARTS
	URETHANS
AEHNRTTU	EARTHNUT
AEHNSSTT	THATNESS
AEHNSSTW	WHATNESS
AEHNSSTY	SHANTEYS
AEHNSTUW	UNSWATHE
AEHOORST	TOHEROAS
AEHOPPRS	PROPHASE
AEHOPRRY	PYORRHEA
AEHOPRSS	PHAROSES
AEHOPRST	PHORATES
	POTSHARE
AEHOPSST	PATHOSES
	POTASHES
	SPATHOSE
	TEASHOPS
AEHOPSTT	HEATSPOT
	POSTHEAT
AEHOPSTU	PHASEOUT
	TAPHOUSE
AEHOQRUU	HUAQUERO
AEHORRRW	HARROWER
AEHORRSV	OVERRASH
AEHORRSW	WARHORSE
AEHORSST	ASTHORES
	EARSHOTS
	HAROSETS
	HOARSEST
AEHORSSW	SAWHORSE
AEHORSTT	RHEOSTAT
AEHORSTU	OUTHEARS
	RATHOUSE
AEHORSTX	OXHEARTS
	THORAXES
AEHORSUV	HAVEOURS
AEHORSVW	OVERWASH
AEHORSWY	HORSEWAY
AEHOSSTU	HOUSESAT
AEHPPRSW	WHAPPERS
AEHPPSSU	SHAPEUPS
AEHPRRSS	PHRASERS
	SHARPERS
AEHPRSST	SHARPEST
	SPARTHES
AEHPRSUX	HARUSPEX
AEHPRSUY	EUPHRASY
AEHPSTTT	PHATTEST
AEHQRSSU	QUASHERS
	SQUASHER
AEHQSSSU	SQUASHES
AEHRRSST	TRASHERS
AEHRRSTU	URETHRAS
AEHRRSTY	TRASHERY
AEHRRTTW	THWARTER
AEHRSSST	SHASTERS
AEHRSSSW	SWASHERS
AEHRSSTT	SHATTERS
AEHRSSTV	HARVESTS
AEHRSSTW	SWATHERS
AEHRSTTY	SHATTERY
AEHRSTUU	HAUTEURS
AEHRSTVZ	SHVARTZE
AEHSSTUX	EXHAUSTS
AEIIINTT	INITIATE
AEIIIRRT	RETIARII
AEIIKLLT	TAILLIKE
AEIIKLNT	KALINITE
AEIIKNRS	KAISERIN
AEIIKNSS	AKINESIS
AEIIKNST	KAINITES
AEIIKRTY	TERIYAKI
AEIILLMR	MILLIARE
	RAMILLIE
AEIILLRS	RAILLIES
AEIILLST	TAILLIES
AEIILLTV	ILLATIVE
AEIILMNN	MAINLINE
AEIILMNS	ALIENISM
	MILESIAN
AEIILMPR	IMPERIAL
AEIILMPS	LIPEMIAS
AEIILMRS	RAMILIES
AEIILMTT	MILITATE
AEIILNNS	ANILINES
AEIILNQU	AQUILINE
	QUINIELA
AEIILNRR	AIRLINER
AEIILNRS	AIRLINES
	SNAILIER
AEIILNRT	INERTIAL
AEIILNSS	SALINISE
AEIILNST	ALIENIST
	LATINISE
	LITANIES
AEIILNSZ	SALINIZE
AEIILNTZ	LATINIZE
AEIILPPT	TAILPIPE
AEIILPRT	LIPARITE
	REPTILIA
AEIILQSU	SILIQUAE
AEIILRSS	LAIRISES
AEIILRST	LAIRIEST
	LISTERIA
AEIILRSV	RIVALISE
	VIRELAIS
AEIILRSZ	LAIRIZES
AEIILRTT	LITERATI
AEIILRVZ	RIVALIZE
AEIILSSS	SILESIAS
AEIILSSW	LEWISIAS
AEIILSTV	VITALISE
AEIILSTX	LAXITIES
AEIILSTZ	TAILZIES
AEIILTVZ	VITALIZE
AEIIMMRT	MARITIME
AEIIMMSX	MAXIMISE
AEIIMMTX	MAXIMITE
AEIIMMXZ	MAXIMIZE
AEIIMNNT	ANTIMINE
AEIIMNRU	URINEMIA
AEIIMNST	MINIATES
AEIIMNSZ	SIMAZINE
AEIIMNTT	INTIMATE
AEIIMNTU	MINUTIAE
AEIIMNTV	VITAMINE
AEIIMOSS	AMEIOSIS
AEIIMPRR	IMPAIRER
AEIIMPSY	EPIMYSIA
AEIIMRSS	MISRAISE
AEIIMRST	AIRTIMES
	SERIATIM
AEIIMRSV	VIREMIAS
AEIIMSTT	IMITATES
AEIINNRS	SIRENIAN
AEIINNRT	TRIENNIA
AEIINNSS	INSANIES
AEIINNTV	INNATIVE
AEIINOTT	NOTITIAE
AEIINPRT	PAINTIER
AEIINPST	PATINISE
	PIANISTE
AEIINPTZ	PATINIZE
AEIINQSU	EQUINIAS
AEIINRRV	RIVERAIN
AEIINRSS	AIRINESS
AEIINRST	INERTIAS
	RAINIEST
AEIINRSY	YERSINIA
AEIINRTZ	TRIAZINE
AEIINSST	ISATINES
	SANITIES
	SANITISE
	TENIASIS
AEIINSSX	SIXAINES
AEIINSTV	VANITIES
AEIINSTX	AXINITES
AEIINSTZ	SANITIZE
AEIINSVV	INVASIVE
AEIINTTT	TITANITE
AEIINTTU	UINTAITE
AEIIPRRS	PRAIRIES
AEIIPRST	PARITIES
AEIIPRSW	PAIRWISE

AEIIPRTZ	TRAPEZII	
AEIIPRZZ	PIZZERIA	
AEIIPSST	EPITASIS	
AEIIPSTX	EPITAXIS	
AEIIRRST	RARITIES	
AEIIRRSV	RIVIERAS	
AEIIRRTT	IRRITATE	
AEIIRSSS	SIRIASES	
AEIIRSST	IRISATES	
	SATIRISE	
AEIIRSTV	VAIRIEST	
AEIIRSTW	WISTERIA	
AEIIRSTX	SEXTARII	
AEIIRSTZ	SATIRIZE	
AEIIRSVV	VIVARIES	
AEIIRTTT	TRITIATE	
AEIIRTVZ	VIZIRATE	
AEIISTTV	VITIATES	
AEIISTVZ	IZVESTIA	
AEIITTTV	TITIVATE	
AEIITTVV	VITATIVE	
AEIJKLZZ	JAZZLIKE	
AEIJLLSS	JAILLESS	
AEIJLMSS	MAJLISES	
AEIJLNSV	JAVELINS	
AEIJLNSW	JAWLINES	
AEIJLOPS	JALOPIES	
AEIJLOSU	JALOUSIE	
AEIJMMST	JAMMIEST	
AEIJMNSS	JASMINES	
AEIJNRST	NARTJIES	
AEIJNRTU	JAUNTIER	
AEIJNSTT	JANTIEST	
AEIJNSTU	JAUNTIES	
AEIJORST	JAROSITE	
AEIJORSV	JAROVISE	
AEIJORVZ	JAROVIZE	
AEIJPSSS	JASPISES	
AEIJSTZZ	JAZZIEST	
AEIKKLLW	LIKEWALK	
AEIKKLMS	MASKLIKE	
AEIKKLNT	TANKLIKE	
AEIKKLPR	PARKLIKE	
AEIKKMNO	KAKIEMON	
AEIKKNRS	SKANKIER	
AEIKLLMP	PALMLIKE	
AEIKLLMS	SELAMLIK	
AEIKLLPY	PLAYLIKE	
AEIKLLSS	KILLASES	
AEIKLLST	SALTLIKE	
AEIKLMOT	MOATLIKE	
AEIKLMST	MASTLIKE	
AEIKLNNP	PANNIKEL	
AEIKLNOS	KAOLINES	
AEIKLNOV	NOVALIKE	
AEIKLNPS	SKIPLANE	
AEIKLNSS	SEALSKIN	
AEIKLNST	LANKIEST	
AEIKLNSW	SWANLIKE	
AEIKLNSY	SNEAKILY	
AEIKLNTU	AUNTLIKE	
AEIKLOPS	SOAPLIKE	
AEIKLOST	KEITLOAS	
AEIKLPRS	SPARLIKE	
AEIKLPRT	TRAPLIKE	AEILLNPY	ALPINELY
AEIKLPSS	KALPISES	AEILLNQU	QUINELLA
AEIKLPSW	WASPLIKE	AEILLNRY	LINEARLY
AEIKLQUY	QUAYLIKE	AEILLNSS	AINSELLS
AEIKLRSS	SERKALIS		NAILLESS
AEIKLRST	LARKIEST		SENSILLA
	STALKIER	AEILLNUV	LAEVULIN
	STARLIKE	AEILLNVY	VENIALLY
AEIKLRSV	KLAVIERS	AEILLOSS	LOESSIAL
AEIKLRTW	WARTLIKE	AEILLOTV	VOLATILE
AEIKLRVY	VALKYRIE	AEILLPPR	APPERILL
AEIKLRWY	WALKYRIE	AEILLPRS	PERILLAS
AEIKLSSS	SAIKLESS	AEILLPSS	ILLAPSES
AEIKLSTT	TALKIEST	AEILLPST	PALLIEST
AEIKMMSS	MISMAKES		PASTILLE
AEIKMNRS	RAMEKINS	AEILLQSU	LALIQUES
AEIKMNST	MANKIEST		SQUILLAE
	MISTAKEN	AEILLQTU	TEQUILLA
AEIKMPRS	RAMPIKES	AEILLRRS	RALLIERS
AEIKMPSS	MISSPEAK	AEILLRRY	RAILLERY
AEIKMRST	MISTAKER	AEILLRSS	RAILLESS
	SITKAMER		SALLIERS
AEIKMSST	MISTAKES	AEILLRST	LITERALS
AEIKMSTW	MAWKIEST		TALLIERS
AEIKNNST	NEATNIKS		TRIELLAS
AEIKNNTU	ANTINUKE	AEILLRSU	RUELLIAS
AEIKNPRR	PRANKIER	AEILLRSY	SERIALLY
AEIKNPRS	RANPIKES	AEILLRTU	TAILLEUR
AEIKNPST	SNAKEPIT	AEILLRVX	VEXILLAR
AEIKNRRS	SNARKIER	AEILLSSS	SAILLESS
AEIKNRST	KERATINS	AEILLSST	SITELLAS
	NARKIEST		TAILLESS
AEIKNRSW	SWANKIER		TALLISES
AEIKNRTW	KNITWEAR	AEILLSTT	SITTELLA
AEIKNSST	SNAKIEST		TALLITES
AEIKNSSW	SWANKIES	AEILLSTW	WALLIEST
AEIKNSSY	KYANISES	AEILLSUV	ALLUSIVE
AEIKNSTU	UNAKITES	AEILLSYZ	SLEAZILY
AEIKNSTV	KISTVAEN	AEILLTUZ	LAZULITE
AEIKNSTW	TWANKIES	AEILMMNS	MELANISM
	WANKIEST	AEILMMNT	IMMANTLE
AEIKNSTY	KYANITES	AEILMMNY	IMMANELY
AEIKNSYZ	KYANIZES	AEILMMOR	MEMORIAL
AEIKOSST	STOKESIA	AEILMMOT	IMMOLATE
AEIKPRRS	SPARKIER	AEILMMRT	TRILEMMA
AEIKPRSS	SPARKIES	AEILMMSS	MELISMAS
AEIKPRST	PARKIEST	AEILMMST	MALMIEST
AEIKPSTW	PAWKIEST	AEILMMTU	MALEMIUT
AEIKQSTU	QUAKIEST	AEILMNNO	MINNEOLA
AEIKRSST	ASTERISK	AEILMNNP	IMPANNEL
	SARKIEST	AEILMNNS	LINESMAN
AEIKRSTW	WATERSKI		MELANINS
AEILLLMO	MALLEOLI	AEILMNOS	LAMINOSE
AEILLLMS	ALLELISM		MINEOLAS
AEILLLNY	LINEALLY		SEMOLINA
AEILLMNS	MANILLES	AEILMNPS	IMPANELS
AEILLMNY	MENIALLY		MANIPLES
AEILLMSS	MAILLESS	AEILMNRS	MARLINES
AEILLMSY	MESIALLY		MINERALS
AEILLNNO	LANOLINE		MISLEARN
AEILLNNS	NAINSELL	AEILMNRT	TERMINAL
AEILLNNU	UNLINEAL		TRAMLINE
AEILLNOR	ALLERION	AEILMNRU	LEMURIAN
AEILLNPS	SPLENIAL	AEILMNSS	ISLESMAN

AEILMNST	AILMENTS
	ALIMENTS
	MANLIEST
	MELANIST
	SMALTINE
AEILMNSU	ALUMINES
AEILMOOV	MOVIEOLA
AEILMOPR	PROEMIAL
AEILMOPS	EPISOMAL
AEILMORS	MORALISE
AEILMORT	AMITROLE
	ROLAMITE
AEILMORZ	MORALIZE
AEILMOST	LOAMIEST
AEILMOSV	SEMIOVAL
AEILMOSW	WAILSOME
AEILMPRS	IMPALERS
	IMPEARLS
	LEMPIRAS
AEILMPRU	PLUMERIA
AEILMPRV	PRIMEVAL
AEILMPSS	PESSIMAL
AEILMPST	IMPLATES
	PALMIEST
	PALMIETS
	PETALISM
	SEPTIMAL
AEILMPTY	PLAYTIME
AEILMQRU	QUALMIER
AEILMRRS	LARMIERS
AEILMRSS	REALISMS
AEILMRST	LAMISTER
	LAMITERS
	MARLIEST
	MARLITES
	MISALTER
AEILMRSY	MISLAYER
	SMEARILY
AEILMRTT	REMITTAL
AEILMRUV	VELARIUM
AEILMSSX	SMILAXES
AEILMSTT	MALTIEST
	METALIST
	SMALTITE
AEILMSTU	SIMULATE
AEILMSTY	LAYTIMES
	STEAMILY
	TALEYSIM
AEILMSUV	MISVALUE
AEILMTTU	MUTILATE
	ULTIMATE
AEILNNOS	SOLANINE
AEILNNPU	PINNULAE
AEILNNRT	INTERNAL
AEILNNSY	INSANELY
AEILNNTY	INNATELY
AEILNOPR	PELORIAN
AEILNOPS	OPALINES
AEILNOPT	ANTIPOLE
AEILNOPU	POULAINE
AEILNORS	AILERONS
	ALERIONS
	ALIENORS
AEILNORT	ORIENTAL
	RELATION
	TAILERON
AEILNORV	OVERLAIN
AEILNOSS	ANISOLES
AEILNOST	ELATIONS
	INSOLATE
	TOENAILS
AEILNOSX	SILOXANE
AEILNOTT	TONALITE
AEILNPPT	PIEPLANT
AEILNPRS	PEARLINS
	PRALINES
AEILNPRT	INTERLAP
	TRAPLINE
	TRIPLANE
AEILNPSS	PAINLESS
	SPANIELS
AEILNPST	PANELIST
	PANTILES
	PLAINEST
AEILNPSU	SPINULAE
AEILNPSW	PINWALES
AEILNPSX	EXPLAINS
AEILNPTT	TINPLATE
AEILNPTY	PENALITY
AEILNQSU	QUINELAS
AEILNQTU	QUANTILE
AEILNRRS	SNARLIER
AEILNRSS	RAINLESS
AEILNRST	ENTRAILS
	LARNIEST
	LATRINES
	RATLINES
	REINSTAL
	RETINALS
	TRENAILS
AEILNRSU	LUNARIES
AEILNRSV	RAVELINS
AEILNRSX	RELAXINS
AEILNRSY	INLAYERS
	SNAILERY
AEILNRTT	RATTLINE
AEILNRTU	AUNTLIER
	RETINULA
	TENURIAL
AEILNRTV	INTERVAL
AEILNRTY	INTERLAY
AEILNSST	EASTLINS
	ELASTINS
	NAILSETS
	SALIENTS
	SALTINES
	STANIELS
AEILNSSU	INULASES
AEILNSSZ	LAZINESS
AEILNSTU	ALUNITES
	INSULATE
AEILNSTV	VENTAILS
AEILNSTW	LAWNIEST
AEILNSUV	UNVAILES
AEILNSUW	LAUWINES
AEILNSUY	UNEASILY
AEILNTVY	NATIVELY
	VENALITY
AEILNUVV	UNIVALVE
AEILOORV	OVARIOLE
AEILOPPR	OILPAPER
AEILOPPT	OPPILATE
AEILOPRS	PELORIAS
	POLARISE
AEILOPRT	EPILATOR
	PETIOLAR
AEILOPRZ	POLARIZE
AEILOPST	SPOLIATE
AEILORRT	RETAILOR
AEILORSS	SOLARISE
AEILORST	SOTERIAL
AEILORSV	OVERSAIL
	VALORISE
	VARIOLES
	VOLARIES
AEILORSY	ROYALISE
AEILORSZ	SOLARIZE
AEILORTT	LITERATO
AEILORTV	VIOLATER
AEILORTZ	TRIAZOLE
AEILORVZ	VALORIZE
AEILORYZ	ROYALIZE
AEILOSST	ISOLATES
AEILOSSX	OXALISES
AEILOSTT	TOTALISE
AEILOSTV	VIOLATES
AEILOTTV	VOLITATE
AEILOTTZ	TOTALIZE
AEILPPQU	APPLIQUE
AEILPPRS	APPERILS
	APPLIERS
AEILPRRS	REPRISAL
AEILPRRT	PALTRIER
	PRETRIAL
AEILPRST	PILASTER
	PLAISTER
	PLAITERS
AEILPRSU	SPIRULAE
AEILPRSV	PREVAILS
AEILPRSW	SLIPWARE
AEILPRTV	LIVETRAP
AEILPRXY	PYREXIAL
AEILPSST	PALSIEST
AEILPSSY	PAISLEYS
AEILPSTT	PLATIEST
AEILPSTY	PTYALISE
AEILPSUV	PLAUSIVE
AEILPTYZ	PTYALIZE
AEILQRSU	SQUAILER
AEILQRTU	QUARTILE
	REQUITAL
AEILQSTU	LIQUATES
	TEQUILAS
AEILQSUY	QUEASILY
AEILQTUY	EQUALITY
AEILRRST	RETIRALS
	RETRIALS
	TRAILERS
AEILRRSU	RURALISE
AEILRRTT	RATTLIER
AEILRRTU	RURALITE
AEILRRTY	LITERARY

AEILRRUZ	RURALIZE	**AEIMNPSX**	PANMIXES		MISRATES
AEILRSST	REALISTS	**AEIMNQRU**	RAMEQUIN		SEMITARS
	SALTIERS	**AEIMNRRS**	MARINERS		SMARTIES
	SALTIRES	**AEIMNRRV**	RIVERMAN	**AEIMRSSV**	MISAVERS
	SLAISTER	**AEIMNRSS**	SEMINARS	**AEIMRSSY**	EMISSARY
AEILRSSV	REVISALS		SIRNAMES	**AEIMRSTT**	MISTREAT
	RIVALESS	**AEIMNRST**	MERANTIS		TERATISM
AEILRSTT	TERTIALS		MINARETS	**AEIMRSTU**	MURIATES
AEILRSTU	URALITES		RAIMENTS		SEMITAUR
AEILRSVV	REVIVALS	**AEIMNRSU**	ANEURISM	**AEIMRSTV**	VITAMERS
AEILRSVY	VIRELAYS	**AEIMNRSY**	SEMINARY	**AEIMRSTW**	WARTIMES
AEILRTTY	ALTERITY	**AEIMNRTT**	INTERMAT	**AEIMRSTX**	MATRIXES
AEILRTUV	VAULTIER		MARTINET	**AEIMRSTY**	SYMITARE
AEILRTUZ	LAZURITE	**AEIMNRTU**	RUMINATE	**AEIMRSWW**	SWIMWEAR
AEILRTVV	TRIVALVE	**AEIMNRTW**	WARIMENT	**AEIMSSST**	ASTEISMS
AEILRTWY	WATERILY	**AEIMNRTY**	TYRAMINE		MASSIEST
AEILRTXZ	ZELATRIX	**AEIMNSSS**	SAMISENS		MASSIEST
AEILSSSV	VESSAILS	**AEIMNSST**	MANTISES		MISSEATS
AEILSSTT	SALTIEST		MATINESS	**AEIMSSTT**	ETATISMS
	SLATIEST	**AEIMNSSU**	ANIMUSES		MASTIEST
AEILSSTW	SWALIEST	**AEIMNSSZ**	MAZINESS		MISSTATE
AEILSTTW	WALTIEST	**AEIMNSUV**	MAUVEINS	**AEIMSSTX**	MASTIXES
AEILSTVY	VILAYETS		MAUVINES	**AEIMSSTZ**	MESTIZAS
AEILSTWY	SWEATILY	**AEIMNTTU**	MATUTINE	**AEIMSTYZ**	AZYMITES
AEILSTYY	YEASTILY	**AEIMNTVZ**	VIZAMENT	**AEIMTTUV**	MUTATIVE
AEIMMMRZ	MAMZERIM	**AEIMOOPS**	IPOMOEAS	**AEINNNOX**	ANNEXION
AEIMMNNT	IMMANENT	**AEIMOPRS**	MEROPIAS	**AEINNOPS**	SAPONINE
AEIMMNOS	SEMINOMA	**AEIMOPSX**	APOMIXES	**AEINNOPV**	PAVONINE
AEIMMNOT	AMMONITE	**AEIMOPTT**	OPTIMATE	**AEINNORS**	RAISONNE
AEIMMNSS	MISNAMES	**AEIMORRS**	ARMOIRES	**AEINNORT**	ANOINTER
AEIMMPRS	SPAMMIER		ARMORIES		INORNATE
AEIMMPSS	SPAMMIES	**AEIMORST**	AMORTISE		REANOINT
AEIMMPST	PSAMMITE		ATOMISER	**AEINNOST**	ENATIONS
AEIMMRRS	SMARMIER	**AEIMORTT**	AMORETTI		SONATINE
AEIMMRST	MARMITES	**AEIMORTZ**	AMORTIZE	**AEINNOTT**	INTONATE
	RAMMIEST		ATOMIZER	**AEINNOTV**	INNOVATE
	TRAMMIES	**AEIMOSST**	AMITOSES		VENATION
AEIMMRTU	IMMATURE		AMOSITES	**AEINNPRS**	PANNIERS
AEIMMSST	MISMATES		ATOMISES	**AEINNPST**	PANTINES
AEIMMSTT	SEMIMATT		OSMIATES	**AEINNRRS**	INSNARER
AEIMMSZZ	MIZMAZES	**AEIMOSTX**	TOXEMIAS	**AEINNRRT**	INERRANT
AEIMNNOT	ANTINOME	**AEIMOSTZ**	ATOMIZES	**AEINNRSS**	INSNARES
	NOMINATE	**AEIMOTTV**	MOTIVATE	**AEINNRST**	ENTRAINS
AEIMNNRS	REINSMAN	**AEIMPRRS**	RAMPIRES		TRANNIES
AEIMNNRT	TRAINMEN	**AEIMPRRT**	IMPARTER	**AEINNRSU**	ANEURINS
AEIMNNST	MANNITES		TRAMPIER		UNARISEN
AEIMNOPT	PTOMAINE	**AEIMPRSS**	IMPRESAS	**AEINNRSW**	SWANNIER
AEIMNORS	MORAINES		MISPARSE	**AEINNRTT**	INTRANET
	ROMAINES		SAMPIRES	**AEINNSST**	INSANEST
	ROMANISE	**AEIMPRST**	APTERISM		STANINES
AEIMNORW	AIRWOMEN		PRIMATES	**AEINNSSV**	VAINNESS
AEIMNORZ	ARMOZINE	**AEIMPRSV**	VAMPIRES	**AEINNSSW**	SWANNIES
	ROMANIZE	**AEIMPRSW**	SWAMPIER	**AEINNSSZ**	ZANINESS
AEIMNOSS	ANEMOSIS	**AEIMPRTU**	APTERIUM	**AEINNSTT**	ANTIENTS
AEIMNOST	AMNIOTES	**AEIMPSSS**	IMPASSES		STANNITE
	MASONITE	**AEIMPSST**	IMPASTES	**AEINNTUV**	UNNATIVE
	MISATONE		PASTIMES	**AEINOPPT**	ANTIPOPE
	SOMNIATE		TIMEPASS	**AEINOPRT**	ATROPINE
AEIMNOSU	MOINEAUS	**AEIMPSTV**	VAMPIEST	**AEINOPSS**	SENOPIAS
AEIMNOSW	WOMANISE	**AEIMQRSU**	MARQUISE	**AEINOPST**	SAPONITE
AEIMNOTZ	MONAZITE	**AEIMRRRS**	MARRIERS	**AEINOPSZ**	EPIZOANS
AEIMNOUX	EXONUMIA	**AEIMRRSS**	SIMARRES	**AEINOPTZ**	TOPAZINE
AEIMNOWZ	WOMANIZE	**AEIMRSST**	ASTERISM	**AEINOQRU**	AEQUORIN
AEIMNPRZ	PRIZEMAN		MAISTERS	**AEINOQTU**	EQUATION
				AEINORRT	ANTERIOR

AEINORRW	IRONWARE
AEINORSS	ERASIONS
	SENSORIA
AEINORST	ANOESTRI
	ARSONITE
	NOTARIES
	NOTARISE
	ROSINATE
	SENORITA
AEINORSV	AVERSION
AEINORTT	TENTORIA
AEINORTZ	NOTARIZE
AEINOSST	ASSIENTO
	ASTONIES
AEINOSSV	EVASIONS
AEINOSSX	SAXONIES
AEINOSTV	STOVAINE
AEINOSTX	SAXONITE
AEINOSXZ	OXAZINES
AEINOTVX	VEXATION
AEINPPPS	PANPIPES
AEINPPRS	SNAPPIER
AEINPPRY	PAPYRINE
AEINPPSS	PINESAPS
AEINPPST	NAPPIEST
AEINPRRT	PRETRAIN
	TERRAPIN
AEINPRRU	UNREPAIR
AEINPRST	PAINTERS
	PANTRIES
	PERTAINS
	PINASTER
	PRISTANE
	REPAINTS
AEINPRSU	UNPRAISE
AEINPRSW	SPAWNIER
AEINPRTT	TRIPTANE
AEINPRTU	PAINTURE
AEINPRTX	EXPIRANT
AEINPSST	SAPIENTS
	STEAPSIN
AEINPSSU	APNEUSIS
AEINPSSW	WINESAPS
AEINPSTT	PATIENTS
AEINPSTU	PETUNIAS
	SUPINATE
AEINPSTY	EPINASTY
AEINPTTY	ANTITYPE
AEINQRTU	ANTIQUER
	QUAINTER
AEINQSTU	ANTIQUES
	QUANTISE
AEINQTTU	EQUITANT
AEINQTUY	ANTIQUEY
AEINQTUZ	QUANTIZE
AEINRRST	RESTRAIN
	RETRAINS
	STRAINER
	TERRAINS
	TRAINERS
	TRANSIRE
AEINRRTT	RETIRANT
AEINRRTV	VERATRIN
AEINRRTW	INTERWAR

AEINRRUW	UNWARIER
AEINRSST	ARTINESS
	RESIANTS
	RETSINAS
	SNARIEST
	STAINERS
	STARNIES
	STEARINS
AEINRSSU	ANURESIS
	SENARIUS
AEINRSSW	WARINESS
AEINRSSX	XERANSIS
AEINRSTT	INTREATS
	NITRATES
	STRAITEN
	TARTINES
	TERTIANS
AEINRSTU	RUINATES
	TAURINES
	URANITES
	URINATES
AEINRSTW	TINWARES
AEINRSUV	VAURIENS
AEINRSUZ	AZURINES
	SUZERAIN
AEINRSVV	VERVAINS
AEINRSZZ	SNAZZIER
AEINRTTU	TAINTURE
AEINRTUV	VAUNTIER
AEINSSST	SAINTESS
	SESTINAS
AEINSSSV	VINASSES
AEINSSTT	ANTSIEST
	INSTATES
	NASTIEST
	SATINETS
	TITANESS
AEINSSTU	SINUATES
AEINSSTX	SEXTAINS
AEINSSVW	WAVINESS
AEINSSWX	WAXINESS
AEINSTTT	NATTIEST
AEINSTTV	TASTEVIN
AEINSTTW	TAWNIEST
AEINSTUV	SUIVANTE
AEINSTWY	YAWNIEST
AEINSUVV	VESUVIAN
AEINTTUU	AUTUNITE
AEIOOPTT	PATOOTIE
AEIOPPST	APPOSITE
AEIOPPRT	PRIORATE
AEIOPRRW	AIRPOWER
AEIOPRSV	VAPORISE
AEIOPRTX	EXPIATOR
AEIOPRVZ	VAPORIZE
AEIOPSST	SOAPIEST
AEIOPTTV	OPTATIVE
AEIOQSSU	SEQUOIAS
AEIORRRS	ARRIEROS
AEIORRSS	ROSARIES
AEIORRST	ROARIEST
	ROTARIES
AEIORRSV	SAVORIER
AEIORSSV	SAVORIES

AEIORSTT	TOASTIER
AEIORSTU	OUTRAISE
	SAUTOIRE
AEIORSTV	TRAVOISE
	VIATORES
	VOTARIES
AEIORSVW	AVOWRIES
AEIORTTV	ROTATIVE
AEIOSSST	SOSATIES
AEIOSSTT	TOASTIES
AEIOSSTZ	AZOTISES
AEIOSTZZ	AZOTIZES
AEIPPPST	PAPPIEST
AEIPPRRS	APPRISER
AEIPPRRT	TRAPPIER
AEIPPRRZ	APPRIZER
AEIPPRSS	APPRISES
AEIPPRST	PERIAPTS
AEIPPRSZ	APPRIZES
AEIPPSST	SAPPIEST
AEIPPSTY	YAPPIEST
AEIPPSTZ	ZAPPIEST
AEIPQRTU	PRATIQUE
AEIPRRRS	PARRIERS
	SPARRIER
AEIPRRSS	ASPIRERS
	PRAISERS
AEIPRRST	PARTIERS
AEIPRRSU	UPRAISER
AEIPRRSY	SPRAYIER
AEIPRRTV	PRIVATER
AEIPRSST	PASTRIES
	PIASTERS
	PIASTRES
	RASPIEST
	TRAIPSES
AEIPRSSU	UPRAISES
AEIPRSSV	PARVISES
	PAVISERS
AEIPRSSX	PRAXISES
AEIPRSTV	PRIVATES
AEIPRSTW	WIRETAPS
AEIPRSTY	ASPERITY
AEIPRSVY	VESPIARY
AEIPRSWW	WARPWISE
AEIPRSXY	PYREXIAS
AEIPRTVY	VARITYPE
AEIPSSST	PASTISES
AEIPSSSV	PASSIVES
	PAVISSES
AEIPSSTT	PASTIEST
AEIPSSTW	WASPIEST
AEIPSSTY	EPISTASY
AEIPSZZZ	PIZAZZES
	PIZZAZES
AEIPTTUV	PUTATIVE
AEIQRRRU	QUARRIER
AEIQRRSU	QUARRIES
AEIQRRTU	QUARTIER
AEIQRUZZ	QUAZZIER
AEIRRRST	STARRIER
	TARRIERS
AEIRRRSV	ARRIVERS
AEIRRSST	TARSIERS

AEIRRSSY	SISERARY	AEKLNPRS	PRANKLES	AEKRRSST	STARKERS
AEIRRSTT	RETRAITS	AEKLNPRT	PLANKTER	AEKRSSTT	STARKEST
	STRAITER	AEKLNRSS	RANKLESS	AEKSSSTT	TSATSKES
	TARRIEST	AEKLNRSV	KLAVERNS	AELLLORY	LOYALLER
AEIRRSTW	STRAWIER	AEKLNSST	TANKLESS	AELLLRTU	TELLURAL
AEIRRSVV	VIVERRAS	AEKLOPRT	LAKEPORT	AELLLSUV	VULSELLA
AEIRRTTT	RETRAITT	AEKLOPRW	ROPEWALK	AELLMNOO	ALLOMONE
AEIRRTTY	TERTIARY	AEKLOPTY	KALOTYPE	AELLMNOZ	MANZELLO
AEIRRVWY	RIVERWAY	AEKLORSY	ROKELAYS	AELLMNST	STALLMEN
AEIRSSST	ASSISTER	AEKLORTV	OVERTALK	AELLMNTY	MENTALLY
	TIRASSES	AEKLORVW	WALKOVER		TALLYMEN
AEIRSSSZ	ASSIZERS	AEKLOSST	SKATOLES	AELLMORR	MORALLER
AEIRSSTT	ARTISTES		STALKOES	AELLMORS	SLALOMER
	ARTSIEST	AEKLOSVZ	ZELKOVAS	AELLMORT	MARTELLO
	STRIATES	AEKLPPST	PEPTALKS	AELLMOSS	LOAMLESS
AEIRSSTV	TRAVISES	AEKLPRRS	SPARKLER	AELLMOTY	TOMALLEY
AEIRSSTW	WAISTERS	AEKLPRSS	SPARKLES	AELLMOYZ	ALLOZYME
	WAITRESS	AEKLPRST	SPARKLET	AELLMPUU	PLUMULAE
	WASTRIES	AEKLRSST	STALKERS	AELLMRST	TRAMELLS
AEIRSTTT	ATTRITES	AEKLRSUW	WAULKERS	AELLMRSY	MERSALYL
	RATTIEST	AEKLSSST	TASKLESS	AELLMSST	SMALLEST
	TARTIEST	AEKMMNRS	MARKSMEN	AELLMSWX	MAXWELLS
	TITRATES	AEKMNRSU	UNMAKERS	AELLNOOT	ATENOLOL
	TRISTATE		UNMAKESR	AELLNOPS	PALLONES
AEIRSTTW	WARTIEST	AEKMOOST	MATOOKES	AELLNOPV	VOLPLANE
AEIRSTTX	EXTRAITS	AEKMOPRT	TOPMAKER	AELLNORS	LLANEROS
AEIRSTTZ	TRISTEZA	AEKMORTW	TEAMWORK	AELLNOSV	NOVELLAS
AEIRSTUZ	AZURITES		WORKMATE	AELLNOWW	ENWALLOW
AEIRSTVY	VESTIARY	AEKMPRRV	VERKRAMP	AELLNPRU	PRUNELLA
AEIRSWWY	WAYWISER	AEKMPRSU	UPMAKERS	AELLNPSS	PLANLESS
	WIREWAYS	AEKMPRTU	UPMARKET	AELLNPTT	PLANTLET
AEIRTTTW	ATWITTER	AEKNNRSS	RANKNESS	AELLNPTU	PLANTULE
AEISSSST	SASSIEST	AEKNORRV	OVERRANK	AELLNRUY	NEURALLY
AEISSSTW	TISWASES	AEKNORUY	EUKARYON		UNREALLY
AEISSSTY	ESSAYIST	AEKNOTTU	OUTTAKEN	AELLNRVY	VERNALLY
AEISSTTT	TASTIEST	AEKNPPRS	KNAPPERS	AELLNSST	TALLNESS
AEISSTTU	SITUATES	AEKNPPSS	SPANSPEK	AELLNSTT	TALLENTS
AEISSTTV	STATIVES	AEKNPRSS	SPANKERS	AELLNTTY	LATENTLY
	VASTIEST	AEKNPSSU	UNSPEAKS	AELLNTUU	LUNULATE
AEISSTVV	SAVVIEST	AEKNRSST	STARKENS	AELLNTUY	LUNATELY
AEISSTWZ	TIZWASES	AEKNRSSW	SWANKERS	AELLOOPS	PALEOSOL
AEISTTTT	TATTIEST	AEKNRSTZ	KRANTZES	AELLOPPR	APPELLOR
AEISTTTU	ATTUITES	AEKNSSTW	SWANKEST	AELLOPRS	REPOSALL
AEISTTTW	TAWTIEST	AEKNSSWY	SWANKEYS	AELLOPRT	PREALLOT
AEJKPSTU	KAJEPUTS	AEKOORSV	OVERSOAK	AELLOPRW	WALLOPER
AEJLNSUV	JUVENALS	AEKOPRRT	PARROKET	AELLOPTY	ALLOTYPE
AEJLORTV	TOLARJEV	AEKOPRSS	PRESOAKS	AELLORRY	ROYALLER
AEJLOSSU	JALOUSES	AEKOPSTU	OUTSPEAK	AELLORSS	ROSELLAS
AEJLOSUY	JEALOUSY		SPEAKOUT	AELLORST	REALLOTS
AEJLOSUZ	AZULEJOS	AEKORRSS	ROSAKERS		ROSTELLA
AEJNORSZ	ZANJEROS	AEKORRWW	WORKWEAR	AELLORSV	ALLOVERS
AEKKKMRU	KRUMKAKE	AEKORSSS	KAROSSES		OVERALLS
AEKKLLWY	LYKEWALK	AEKORSTV	OVERTASK	AELLORSW	SALLOWER
AEKKMNOO	KAKEMONO		VOERTSAK	AELLORTT	ALLOTTER
AEKKNRSS	SKANKERS	AEKORSTW	SEATWORK	AELLORWW	WALLOWER
AEKKOSSS	SAKKOSES	AEKORTUY	EUKARYOT	AELLOSTY	LOYALEST
AEKLLSTU	KELLAUTS	AEKOSTTU	OUTSKATE	AELLOSUV	ALVEOLUS
AEKLMORS	LARKSOME		OUTTAKES	AELLPRSS	SPALLERS
AEKLMOSU	LEUKOMAS		STAKEOUT	AELLPSSY	PLAYLESS
AEKLMRUW	LUKEWARM		TAKEOUTS	AELLPSTY	PLAYLETS
AEKLMRUY	YARMULKE	AEKPPSSU	UPSPEAKS	AELLQRSU	SQUALLER
AEKLNNSS	LANKNESS	AEKPRRSS	SPARKERS	AELLRRSU	ALLURERS
AEKLNOSY	ANKYLOSE	AEKPSSSY	PASSKEYS	AELLRRTY	RETRALLY
AEKLNPPS	KNAPPLES	AEKQRSUW	SQUAWKER	AELLRTTY	LATTERLY

AELLRTVY	TREVALLY	AELMOTVZ	MAZELTOV	AELNPSSS	SNAPLESS
AELLRTYY	LYRATELY	AELMOTYZ	ATMOLYZE		SPANLESS
AELLRWYY	LAWYERLY	AELMPRRT	TRAMPLER	AELNPSSU	SPANSULE
AELLSSST	SALTLESS	AELMPRSS	SAMPLERS	AELNPSTX	EXPLANTS
	TASSELLS	AELMPRST	TEMPLARS	AELNPTTU	PATULENT
AELLSSTW	SETWALLS		TRAMPLES		PETULANT
	SWALLETS	AELMPRSY	LAMPREYS	AELNPTTY	PATENTLY
AELLSSTY	TASSELLY		SAMPLERY	AELNQSUU	UNEQUALS
AELLSTUU	ULULATES	AELMPSUX	AMPLEXUS	AELNRRSS	SNARLERS
AELLSTVY	VESTALLY	AELMQSUU	SQUAMULE	AELNRRTY	ERRANTLY
AELLSUVV	VALVULES	AELMRSST	LAMSTERS	AELNRRUU	NEURULAR
AELLSUXY	SEXUALLY		TRAMLESS	AELNRRUV	NERVULAR
AELMMNOS	MAMELONS	AELMRSTT	MALTSTER	AELNRSST	SALTERNS
AELMMORW	MEALWORM		MARTLETS		SLANTERS
AELMMOSY	MYELOMAS	AELMRSTU	STAUMREL	AELNRSTT	SLATTERN
AELMMRSS	SLAMMERS	AELMRSTY	MASTERLY		TRENTALS
AELMMRST	STRAMMEL	AELMRTUY	MATURELY	AELNRSTU	NEUTRALS
	TRAMMELS	AELMSSSS	MASSLESS	AELNRSTV	VENTRALS
AELMMSST	STAMMELS	AELMSSST	MASTLESS	AELNRSUU	NEURULAS
AELMMSSY	MALMSEYS	AELNNNPU	UNPANNEL	AELNRSUV	UNRAVELS
AELMNNOT	NONMETAL	AELNNOOP	NAPOLEON	AELNRSVY	SYLVANER
AELMNNOU	NOUMENAL	AELNNOOX	NALOXONE	AELNRSXY	LARYNXES
AELMNNRY	MANNERLY	AELNNOPT	PENTANOL	AELNRTTW	TRAWLNET
AELMNNTU	UNMANTLE	AELNNOQU	NONEQUAL	AELNRUWY	UNWARELY
AELMNOPS	NEOPLASM	AELNNORU	NEURONAL	AELNSSST	SALTNESS
	PLEONASM	AELNNOSU	ANNULOSE	AELNSSTY	STANYELS
AELMNORS	ALMONERS	AELNNPRS	PLANNERS	AELNSTUV	ENVAULTS
AELMNOST	SALMONET	AELNNPSU	UNPANELS	AELNSUUX	UNSEXUAL
	TELAMONS	AELNNRSS	ENSNARLS	AELNTTUX	EXULTANT
AELMNOSU	MELANOUS	AELNNRST	LANTERNS	AELOOPRZ	ZOOPERAL
AELMNOWY	LAYWOMEN	AELNNRSU	UNLEARNS	AELOORRS	ROSEOLAR
AELMNOYY	YEOMANLY	AELNNRTU	UNLEARNT	AELOORSS	AEROSOLS
AELMNPRS	LAMPERNS	AELNNSST	STANNELS		ROSEOLAS
AELMNRSU	MENSURAL	AELNNSTU	ANNULETS	AELOORTW	WATERLOO
	NUMERALS	AELNOOTZ	ENTOZOAL	AELOORTZ	ZOOLATER
AELMNSTT	MANTLETS	AELNOPPY	POLYPNEA	AELOPPRS	PROLAPSE
AELMNSTU	NUTMEALS	AELNOPRS	PERSONAL		PROPALES
AELMNSTY	MESNALTY		PSORALEN		SAPROPEL
AELMOOPT	OMOPLATE	AELNOPRV	OVERPLAN	AELOPPSU	PAPULOSE
AELMOORS	SALEROOM	AELNOPST	LAPSTONE	AELOPPTU	POPULATE
AELMOPRR	PREMOLAR		PLEONAST	AELOPPXY	APOPLEXY
	PREMORAL		POLENTAS	AELOPQUY	OPAQUELY
AELMOPRS	PLEROMAS	AELNOPSU	APOLUNES	AELOPRRV	REPROVAL
	RAMPOLES	AELNOPTW	TOWPLANE	AELOPRSS	REPOSALS
AELMOPRT	PROMETAL	AELNORSU	ALEURONS	AELOPRST	PETROSAL
	TEMPORAL		NEUROSAL		POLESTAR
AELMOPSU	AMPOULES	AELNORSV	VERONALS		PROLATES
AELMOPSX	EXOPLASM	AELNORTT	TETRONAL	AELOPRSU	LEAPROUS
AELMOPSY	MAYPOLES		TOLERANT	AELOPRSV	OVERLAPS
	PLAYSOME	AELNORTU	OUTLEARN	AELOPRVY	OVERPLAY
AELMOPTT	METAPLOT	AELNORTY	ORNATELY	AELOPRYZ	PYRAZOLE
	PALMETTO	AELNOSSV	OVALNESS	AELOPSSS	SOAPLESS
AELMORST	MOLERATS	AELNOSTV	VOLANTES	AELOPSST	APOSTLES
AELMORSU	RAMULOSE	AELNOSTY	ANOLYTES	AELOPSSU	ESPOUSAL
AELMORSV	REMOVALS	AELNPPRS	PREPLANS		SEPALOUS
AELMORSY	RAMOSELY	AELNPPRT	PREPLANT	AELOPSSX	EXPOSALS
AELMORTU	EMULATOR	AELNPPSY	PLAYPENS	AELOPSTT	PALETOTS
AELMORTZ	METRAZOL		SPYPLANE	AELOPSTU	OUTLEAPS
AELMOSSS	MOLASSES	AELNPRST	PANTLERS		PETALOUS
AELMOSST	MALTOSES		PLANTERS	AELOPTTU	OUTLEAPT
AELMOSSY	AMYLOSES		REPLANTS	AELORRST	REALTORS
AELMOSTT	MATELOTS	AELNPRSU	PURSLANE		RELATORS
AELMOSTU	SOULMATE		SUPERNAL		RESTORAL
AELMOSTY	ATMOLYSE	AELNPRTY	PLENARTY	AELORSSS	LASSOERS

AELORSST	OLESTRAS		WARSTLER	AEMNOORY	AERONOMY
AELORSTT	RETOTALS	AELRRTVY	VARLETRY	AEMNOOSZ	MESOZOAN
AELORSTU	ROSULATE	AELRSSST	STARLESS	AEMNOOTZ	METAZOON
AELORSTV	LEVATORS	AELRSSSW	WRASSLES	AEMNOPPS	PAMPOENS
	OVERSALT	AELRSSTT	SLATTERS	AEMNOPRS	MANROPES
AELORSTY	ROYALETS		STARLETS		PROSEMAN
AELORSTZ	ZELATORS		STARTLES	AEMNOPRT	EMPATRON
AELORSUU	ROULEAUS	AELRSSTU	SALUTERS	AEMNOPRW	MANPOWER
AELORSVY	LAYOVERS	AELRSSTW	WARSTLES	AEMNORRS	RANSOMER
	OVERLAYS		WARTLESS	AEMNORST	MONSTERA
AELORSWY	OWRELAYS		WASTRELS		ONSTREAM
AELORTTV	VARLETTO		WRASTLES		STOREMAN
AELORTYZ	ZEALOTRY	AELRSSUU	RUSSULAE		TONEARMS
AELORUUX	ROULEAUX	AELRSSUW	WALRUSES	AEMNORSU	ENAMOURS
AELOSSTV	SOLVATES	AELRSTTT	TARTLETS		NEUROMAS
AELOSSTY	ASYSTOLE		TATTLERS	AEMNORSV	OVERMANS
AELOSSVY	SAVELOYS	AELRSTTU	LUSTRATE		OVERSMAN
AELOSTTU	TOLUATES		TUTELARS	AEMNORSY	ROMNEYAS
AELOSTTW	WASTELOT	AELRSTTY	SLATTERY	AEMNORTT	TORMENTA
AELOSTUV	OVULATES	AELRSTUV	VAULTERS	AEMNORTU	ROUTEMAN
AELOSTUY	AUTOLYSE		VESTURAL	AEMNORTY	MONETARY
AELOTUUV	OUTVALUE	AELRSTWY	TRAWLEYS	AEMNORVY	OVERMANY
AELOTUYZ	AUTOLYZE	AELRSTWZ	WALTZERS	AEMNORYY	YEOMANRY
AELPPPRU	PREPUPAL	AELRSUVY	SURVEYAL	AEMNOSTU	NOTAEUMS
AELPPPRY	PREAPPLY	AELRTTTW	TWATTLER		OUTNAMES
AELPPRSS	SLAPPERS	AELRTTUX	TEXTURAL		SEAMOUNT
AELPPSST	STAPPLES	AELRTTUY	TUTELARY	AEMNPRSS	PRESSMAN
AELPPSSU	APPULSES	AELSSSTU	SALTUSES	AEMNPRSU	SUPERMAN
AELPRRRU	LARRUPER	AELSSSTY	STAYLESS	AEMNPSST	ENSTAMPS
AELPRRSW	SPRAWLER	AELSSTTW	WATTLESS		PASSMENT
AELPRRTT	PRATTLER	AELSSWZZ	SWAZZLES	AEMNPSTU	SPUMANTE
AELPRSST	PERSALTS	AELSTTTW	TWATTLES	AEMNPSTY	PAYMENTS
	PLASTERS	AELSTTUU	USTULATE	AEMNQSUW	SQUAWMEN
	PSALTERS	AELSTTUY	ASTUTELY	AEMNRRSU	MANURERS
	STAPLERS	AELUUVVZ	VUVUZELA		SURNAMER
AELPRSSU	PERUSALS	AEMMMOTU	OMMATEUM	AEMNRRUY	NUMERARY
AELPRSSY	PARSLEYS	AEMMMRTY	MAMMETRY	AEMNRSST	SARMENTS
	SPARSELY	AEMMNNOV	MONEYMAN		SMARTENS
AELPRSTT	PARTLETS	AEMMNPRS	RAMPSMEN	AEMNRSSU	SURNAMES
	PLATTERS	AEMMNRRY	MERRYMAN	AEMNRSSW	WARMNESS
	PRATTLES	AEMMNRTU	RAMENTUM	AEMNRSTU	ANESTRUM
	SPLATTER	AEMMOORT	ROOMMATE		MENSTRUA
	SPRATTLE	AEMMOPRS	MAMPOERS		TRANSUME
AELPRSTU	APLUSTRE	AEMMORSS	MARMOSES	AEMNRSTV	VARMENTS
AELPRSTY	PEYTRALS	AEMMORST	MARMOSET	AEMNRSTW	TRANSMEW
	PLASTERY	AEMMORSW	WOMMERAS		TREWSMAN
	PSALTERY	AEMMOSTU	MOUSEMAT	AEMNRSUY	ANEURYSM
AELPRSUY	SUPERLAY	AEMMPRSS	SPAMMERS	AEMNSTTU	NUTMEATS
AELPSSSS	PASSLESS	AEMMRSST	STAMMERS	AEMNSTWY	WAYMENTS
AELPSSST	PASTLESS	AEMMRTUY	MAUMETRY	AEMOOPST	POMATOES
AELPSSTT	PELTASTS	AEMMRTWY	MAWMETRY	AEMOORRW	WAREROOM
AELPSSTU	PULSATES	AEMMSSTU	SUMMATES	AEMOORST	TEAROOMS
	SPATULES	AEMMSSUW	WAMMUSES	AEMOORSW	WOOMERAS
AELPSSTZ	SPATZLES	AEMNNOPW	PENWOMAN	AEMOORTT	AMORETTO
AELPSUUV	UPVALUES	AEMNNORS	MONERANS	AEMOOSST	MAESTOSO
AELQRRSU	QUARRELS		SONARMEN		OSTEOMAS
AELQRSUV	SERVQUAL	AEMNNORT	ORNAMENT	AEMOOSSV	VAMOOSES
AELQRSUY	SQUARELY	AEMNNOSS	MANNOSES	AEMOOSTT	OSTOMATE
AELQSTTU	SQUATTLE	AEMNNOST	MONTANES		TOMATOES
AELQSTUZ	QUETZALS	AEMNNOSZ	MENAZONS	AEMOOSTU	AUTOSOME
AELRRSSW	WARSLERS	AEMNNRST	MANRENTS	AEMOOTTY	TOMATOEY
AELRRSTT	RATTLERS		REMNANTS	AEMOPPRS	PAMPEROS
	STARTLER	AEMNOORR	MAROONER	AEMOPRTW	POMWATER
AELRRSTW	TRAWLERS	AEMNOORT	ANTEROOM		TAPEWORM

AEMOQSSU	SQUAMOSE	AENNORTU	UNORNATE	AENPRSSW	SPAWNERS
AEMORRRS	ARMORERS	AENNORTW	WANTONER	AENPRSTT	PATTERNS
AEMORRRU	ARMOURER	AENNORUX	NEURAXON		TRANSEPT
AEMORRST	REARMOST	AENNORVY	NOVENARY		TRAPNEST
AEMORRSV	OVERARMS	AENNOSSU	UNSEASON	AENPRSTU	PERSAUNT
AEMORRSW	EARWORMS	AENNOSTU	TONNEAUS	AENPRSUV	PARVENUS
AEMORRSY	ROSEMARY	AENNOSTX	NONTAXES	AENPSSST	PASTNESS
AEMORRVW	OVERWARM	AENNOTUX	TONNEAUX	AENPSSSY	SYNAPSES
AEMORSSS	MORASSES	AENNPRSS	SPANNERS	AENPSSTU	PESAUNTS
AEMORSST	MAESTROS	AENNPSSU	PANNUSES	AENPSSTW	STEWPANS
AEMORSSW	SEAWORMS	AENNQSTU	QUANNETS		WASPNEST
AEMORSSY	MAYORESS	AENNRSTT	ENTRANTS	AENPSSTY	SYNAPTES
AEMORSTV	OVERMAST	AENNRSTY	TYRANNES	AENPSSTZ	SPETSNAZ
AEMORSVW	OVERSWAM	AENNRSWY	SWANNERY	AENPSTZZ	SPETZNAZ
AEMORTTU	TAUTOMER	AENNRTTY	TENANTRY	AENQRRTU	QUARTERN
AEMOSSTT	EASTMOST	AENOOPST	TEASPOON	AENQSTTU	QUESTANT
	STOMATES	AENOORRT	RATOONER	AENRRRTY	ERRANTRY
AEMOSSTW	TWASOMES	AENOOSTZ	OZONATES	AENRRSTT	TRANTERS
AEMOSSUZ	ZAMOUSES	AENOPPRS	PROPANES	AENRSSST	SARSNETS
AEMOSSWY	SOMEWAYS	AENOPRSS	PERSONAS	AENRSSTT	TARTNESS
AEMOSTTZ	MOZETTAS		RESPONSA	AENRSSTU	ANESTRUS
AEMOTTZZ	MOZZETTA	AENOPRST	OPERANTS		SAUNTERS
AEMPPRST	PRESTAMP		PRONATES	AENRSSTV	SERVANTS
AEMPRRST	TRAMPERS		PROTEANS		VERSANTS
AEMPRRSW	PREWARMS	AENOPRSY	PYRANOSE	AENRSSUW	UNSWEARS
AEMPRRSY	SPERMARY	AENOPRTT	PATENTOR	AENRSTTU	TAUNTERS
AEMPRSST	RESTAMPS	AENOPRWY	WEAPONRY	AENRSTUV	VAUNTERS
	STAMPERS	AENOPSSU	POSAUNES	AENRSTUW	UNWATERS
AEMPRSSW	SWAMPERS	AENOPSTU	AUTOPENS	AENRSTWY	STERNWAY
AEMPRSTT	TRAMPETS	AENORRRW	NARROWER	AENRTUVY	VAUNTERY
AEMPRSTU	TEMPURAS	AENORRSS	SERRANOS	AENRTUWY	UNWATERY
	UPSTREAM	AENORRST	ANTRORSE	AENRTWYY	ENTRYWAY
AEMPRSUX	SUPERMAX	AENORSST	ASSENTOR	AENSSSTV	VASTNESS
AEMPSSUW	MAWPUSES		SANTEROS	AENSSSTW	WASTNESS
	WAMPUSES		SENATORS	AENSSTTU	TAUTNESS
AEMPSTTT	ATTEMPTS		STARNOSE		UNSTATES
AEMQRSSU	MARQUESS		TREASONS	AENSSTTX	SEXTANTS
	MASQUERS	AENORSSU	ANSEROUS	AENSSTXY	SYNTAXES
AEMRRSST	ARMRESTS		ARSENOUS	AEOOPPPS	PAPPOOSE
AEMRRSSW	SWARMERS	AENORSTT	ORNATEST	AEOOPPSS	PAPOOSES
AEMRRSTU	MATURERS	AENORSTU	OUTEARNS	AEOOPRRT	OPERATOR
AEMRRTUV	VERATRUM	AENORSTV	VENATORS	AEOOPRSS	OROPESAS
AEMRSSSU	ASSUMERS	AENORSTW	STONERAW	AEOOPSTT	POTATOES
	MASSEURS	AENORSUV	RAVENOUS	AEOORRST	SORORATE
AEMRSSTT	MATTRESS	AENORSWZ	WARZONES	AEOORTTT	TATTOOER
	SMARTEST	AENORTTV	TEVATRON	AEOORTTV	ROTOVATE
	SMATTERS	AENORTTX	TETRAXON	AEOPPRRV	APPROVER
AEMRSSTY	MAYSTERS	AENORTTY	ATTORNEY	AEOPPRSS	APPOSERS
AEMRSTTU	MATUREST	AENORTWW	TOWNWEAR	AEOPPRST	TRAPPOSE
	TESTAMUR	AENOSSTU	SOUTANES	AEOPPRSV	APPROVES
AEMRSTTX	MARTEXTS	AENOSSTZ	STANZOES	AEOPQRTU	PAROQUET
AEMRTUUX	TRUMEAUX	AENOSSUU	NAUSEOUS	AEOPQSTU	OPAQUEST
AEMSTTTU	TESTATUM	AENOSSVW	WAVESONS	AEOPRRRT	PARROTER
AENNNPST	PENNANTS	AENOTTUU	AUTOTUNE	AEOPRRRS	ASPERSOR
AENNNTTU	UNTENANT	AENOUUVX	NOUVEAUX	AEOPRRST	PRAETORS
AENNOOTZ	ENTOZOAN	AENPPRSS	PARSNEPS		PRORATES
AENNOPRT	PATRONNE		SNAPPERS	AEOPRRSV	VAPORERS
AENNOPRX	NAPROXEN	AENPPRST	PARPENTS	AEOPRRTV	OVERPART
AENNOPST	PENTOSAN	AENPPRSU	UNPAPERS	AEOPRRUV	VAPOURER
AENNOPUW	UNWEAPON	AENPRRST	PARTNERS	AEOPRRVW	WRAPOVER
AENNORST	NORTENAS	AENPRRSW	PRAWNERS	AEOPRRWW	WARPOWER
	RESONANT		PREWARNS	AEOPRSST	ESPARTOS
AENNORSU	UNREASON	AENPRSST	PASTERNS		PORTASES
AENNORSY	ANNOYERS		RAPTNESS		PROTASES

	SEAPORTS	**AEPPRSSW**	SWAPPERS	**AFFGILNR**	RAFFLING
AEOPRSSU	ASPEROUS	**AEPPSSTU**	PASTEUPS	**AFFGILNW**	WAFFLING
AEOPRSSV	OVERPASS	**AEPQRSTU**	PARQUETS	**AFFGIMRS**	MISGRAFF
	PASSOVER	**AEPRRRSS**	SPARRERS	**AFFGINNY**	NYAFFING
AEOPRSTT	PROSTATE	**AEPRRSSY**	RESPRAYS	**AFFGINQU**	QUAFFING
AEOPRSTU	APTEROUS		SPRAYERS	**AFFGINST**	STAFFING
AEOPRSTV	OVERPAST	**AEPRRSTU**	PARTURES	**AFFGINUW**	WAUFFING
AEOPRSVY	OVERPAYS		PASTURER	**AFFGIORT**	GRAFFITO
AEOPRSWY	ROPEWAYS		RAPTURES	**AFFHILLS**	FALLFISH
AEOPRTWX	WATERPOX	**AEPRRSTY**	PARTYERS	**AFFHILNS**	HAFFLINS
AEOPSSST	POTASSES	**AEPRSSST**	SPARSEST	**AFFHILST**	FLATFISH
AEOPTTUY	AUTOTYPE		TRESPASS	**AFFHILTU**	FAITHFUL
AEOQRSTU	EQUATORS	**AEPRSSTT**	SPATTERS	**AFFIINTY**	AFFINITY
	QUAESTOR		TAPSTERS	**AFFIISTX**	FIXATIFS
AEOQRSUV	VAQUEROS	**AEPRSSTU**	PASTURES	**AFFILLMM**	FLIMFLAM
AEOQRTTU	TORQUATE		UPSTARES	**AFFILMNS**	MAFFLINS
AEOQRTUZ	QUATORZE	**AEPRSSTY**	YAPSTERS	**AFFILORS**	RIFFOLAS
AEORRRST	ARRESTOR	**AEPRSSWY**	SPYWARES	**AFFILSUX**	SUFFIXAL
AEORRSST	ASSERTOR	**AEPRSTTU**	STUPRATE	**AFFIMSST**	MASTIFFS
	ASSORTER		UPSTATER	**AFFINORR**	FORFAIRN
	ORATRESS	**AEPRSTTY**	TAPESTRY	**AFFINOSU**	AFFUSION
	REASSORT	**AEPRSTUX**	SUPERTAX	**AFFINRSU**	FUNFAIRS
	ROASTERS	**AEPRTUVY**	PYRUVATE		RUFFIANS
AEORRSSU	AROUSERS	**AEPSSSSU**	PASSUSES	**AFFIORRS**	FORFAIRS
AEORRSSV	SAVORERS	**AEPSSTTU**	UPSTATES	**AFFIPSTT**	TIPSTAFF
	SEROVARS	**AEQRRSSU**	SQUARERS	**AFFIRRSU**	FURFAIRS
AEORRSTT	ROSTRATE	**AEQRRSTU**	QUARTERS	**AFFIRSSU**	SUFFARIS
AEORRSUV	SAVOURER	**AEQRSSTU**	SQUAREST	**AFFLLOOT**	FOOTFALL
AEORRTTV	OVERTART	**AEQRSTTU**	QUARTETS	**AFFLLTUU**	FAULTFUL
AEORRTUV	AVOUTRER		SQUATTER	**AFFLOOOT**	FOALFOOT
AEORRTZZ	TERRAZZO	**AEQRSTUZ**	QUARTZES	**AFFLOOTT**	FLATFOOT
AEORRVWY	OVERWARY	**AEQRTTTU**	QUARTETT	**AFFLOPSY**	PLAYOFFS
AEORSSSS	ASSESSOR	**AERRSSSU**	ASSURERS	**AFFLORTU**	FORFAULT
AEORSSST	OSSETRAS	**AERRSSTT**	RESTARTS	**AFFLRRUU**	FURFURAL
AEORSSTT	STRATOSE		STARTERS	**AFFMOPRS**	OFFRAMPS
	TOASTERS	**AERRSSTU**	SERRATUS	**AFFNORRS**	SAFFRONS
AEORSSTU	OSSATURE	**AERRSSTV**	STARVERS	**AFFNORST**	AFFRONTS
AEORSSTV	VOTARESS	**AERRSSTY**	STRAYERS	**AFFNORSY**	SAFFRONY
AEORSSTX	STORAXES	**AERRSTUY**	TREASURY	**AFFNRRUU**	FURFURAN
AEORSSUU	ROUSSEAU	**AERSSSST**	STRASSES	**AFGGGILN**	FLAGGING
AEORSTTT	ATTESTOR	**AERSSSTY**	SATYRESS	**AFGGGINR**	FRAGGING
	TESTATOR	**AERSSTTT**	STRETTAS	**AFGGGINS**	FAGGINGS
AEORSTTU	OUTRATES	**AERSSTTU**	STATURES	**AFGGILNN**	FANGLING
	OUTSTARE	**AERSSTTW**	SWATTERS		FLANGING
	SEATROUT	**AERSSTUX**	SURTAXES	**AFGGILOP**	GIGAFLOP
AEORSTUV	OUTRAVES	**AERSSTVY**	STRAYVES	**AFGGINOR**	FORAGING
AEORSTUW	OUTSWARE	**AERSSTXY**	STYRAXES	**AFGGINOT**	FAGOTING
	OUTSWEAR	**AERSTTUV**	VETTURAS	**AFGGINRT**	GRAFTING
	OUTWEARS	**AERSTTVY**	TRAVESTY	**AFGGORTY**	FAGGOTRY
AEORSTVY	OVERSTAY	**AERTTUXY**	TEXTUARY	**AFGHIINT**	FAITHING
AEORSUVW	WAVEROUS	**AESSSTTU**	STATUSES	**AFGHILLN**	HALFLING
AEORSVWY	OVERSWAY	**AESSTTTU**	ASTUTEST	**AFGHILNS**	FLASHING
AEORTUWY	OUTWEARY		STATUTES	**AFGHILNT**	FANLIGHT
	ROUTEWAY	**AFFFFINN**	NIFFNAFF	**AFGHILPS**	FLAGSHIP
AEORTVXY	VEXATORY	**AFFFFIRR**	RIFFRAFF	**AFGHINRT**	FARTHING
AEOSTTTU	OUTSTATE	**AFFFGILN**	FLAFFING	**AFGHINRW**	WHARFING
AEOSTTUW	OUTWASTE	**AFFFLLOS**	FALLOFFS	**AFGHINST**	SHAFTING
AEPPPRSU	PREPUPAS	**AFFGGINR**	GRAFFING	**AFGHIOST**	GOATFISH
AEPPPSSU	PAPPUSES	**AFFGGINS**	GAFFINGS	**AFGHIRSY**	GRAYFISH
AEPPRRST	STRAPPER	**AFFGHIRT**	AFFRIGHT	**AFGHLLUU**	LAUGHFUL
	TRAPPERS	**AFFGIINP**	PIAFFING	**AFGHLNSU**	FLASHGUN
AEPPRRSW	PREWRAPS	**AFFGIINX**	AFFIXING	**AFGHLSTU**	FLAUGHTS
	WRAPPERS	**AFFGIIRT**	GRAFFITI		GHASTFUL
AEPPRSSU	UPSPEARS	**AFFGILMN**	MAFFLING	**AFGHRSTU**	FRAUGHTS

AFGIILLN	FLAILING	AFHIINST	FAINTISH	AFILLPSU	PAILFULS
AFGIILNS	FAILINGS	AFHIKSUY	KUFIYAHS		PAILSFUL
AFGIIMNN	INFAMING	AFHILLNS	HALFLINS	AFILLSUV	VIALFULS
AFGIINNT	FAINTING	AFHILLSW	WALLFISH	AFILLTUY	FAULTILY
AFGIINRS	FAIRINGS	AFHILLSY	FLASHILY	AFILMNOR	FORMALIN
	FRAISING	AFHILOSY	OAFISHLY		INFORMAL
AFGIINTX	FIXATING	AFHILSST	SALTFISH	AFILMNOS	FOILSMAN
AFGIKLNN	FANKLING	AFHILSTT	FLATTISH	AFILMOPR	PALIFORM
	FLANKING	AFHILSTW	HALFWITS	AFILMSSS	FALSISMS
AFGIKNNR	FRANKING	AFHIMNST	MANSHIFT	AFILNNNO	NONFINAL
AFGIKORT	KOFTGARI	AFHIMNSU	HAFNIUMS	AFILNORT	FLATIRON
AFGILLNS	FALLINGS	AFHINOSS	FASHIONS		INFLATOR
AFGILLNT	FLATLING	AFHINOSY	FASHIONY	AFILNOSU	FUSIONAL
AFGILMMN	FLAMMING	AFHINSTU	UNFAITHS	AFILNPPT	FLIPPANT
AFGILMNO	FLAMINGO	AFHIOSSU	FASHIOUS	AFILNRTU	TRAINFUL
AFGILNOS	LOAFINGS	AFHIRSST	STARFISH	AFILNRUY	UNFAIRLY
AFGILNOT	FLOATING	AFHISSWY	FISHWAYS	AFILNSTU	FLUTINAS
AFGILNPP	FLAPPING	AFHKLNTU	THANKFUL		INFLATUS
AFGILNRU	INFRUGAL	AFHKORSX	FOXSHARK	AFILOORT	FAROLITO
AFGILNST	FATLINGS	AFHKORSY	HAYFORKS	AFILORSW	AIRFLOWS
AFGILNTT	FLATTING	AFHKRSTU	FUTHARKS	AFILORTY	FILATORY
AFGILNTU	FAULTING	AFHLLOTU	LOATHFUL	AFILOSTX	FOXTAILS
AFGILORW	GAIRFOWL	AFHLNSUY	UNFLASHY	AFILRSSU	FISSURAL
AFGILSSY	GLASSIFY	AFHLOSTU	OUTFLASH	AFILRSTU	FISTULAR
AFGIMNOS	FOAMINGS	AFHLOSTY	HAYLOFTS	AFILSSTU	FISTULAS
AFGIMNRS	FARMINGS	AFHLRTUW	WRATHFUL	AFILSTTU	FLAUTIST
	FRAMINGS	AFHNOOST	FANTOOSH	AFIMMNOR	MANIFORM
AFGIMNTU	FUMIGANT	AFHOOPST	POOFTAHS	AFIMMNOY	AMMONIFY
AFGIMORS	GASIFORM	AFHOOPTT	FOOTPATH	AFIMMORR	RAMIFORM
AFGIMRST	MISGRAFT	AFHOORST	HAFTOROS	AFIMNOPR	NAPIFORM
AFGINNNS	FANNINGS	AFHOORTT	HAFTOROT	AFIMNORR	RANIFORM
AFGINNRS	SNARFING	AFHOPSTU	POUFTAHS	AFIMNORT	NATIFORM
AFGINNSU	SNAFUING	AFIIKMRS	FAKIRISM	AFIMNOSU	INFAMOUS
AFGINNSW	FAWNINGS	AFIILLLY	FILIALLY	AFIMOOSS	MAFIOSOS
AFGINORV	FAVORING	AFIILLNU	UNFILIAL	AFIMORRU	AURIFORM
AFGINORY	FORAYING	AFIILMMS	FAMILISM	AFIMORRV	VARIFORM
AFGINPPR	FRAPPING	AFIILMNS	FINALISM	AFIMORSV	VASIFORM
AFGINRST	INGRAFTS	AFIILNRU	UNIFILAR	AFIMRSUU	FUSARIUM
	RAFTINGS	AFIILNST	FINALIST	AFIMSSTT	FATTISMS
	STRAFING		TAILFINS	AFIMSSUV	FAUVISMS
AFGINRSW	SWARFING	AFIILNTY	FINALITY	AFINNORS	FRANIONS
AFGINRSY	FRAYINGS	AFIILORS	AIRFOILS	AFINNOST	FONTINAS
AFGINRTU	FIGURANT	AFIILRST	AIRLIFTS	AFINNOTU	FOUNTAIN
AFGINSST	FASTINGS	AFIIMNPR	RIFAMPIN	AFINNRTY	INFANTRY
AFGINSTW	WAFTINGS	AFIIMRSY	FAIRYISM	AFINOPSY	SAPONIFY
AFGINSUY	SANGUIFY	AFIINNOS	SAINFOIN	AFINQTUY	QUANTIFY
AFGIORST	ISOGRAFT		SINFONIA	AFINRSTX	TRANSFIX
AFGIPRTW	GIFTWRAP	AFIINOTX	FIXATION	AFINSSTU	FAUNISTS
AFGKNOPS	PAKFONGS	AFIIORRT	TRIFORIA		FUSTIANS
AFGKORST	KOFTGARS	AFIJKRTU	JAKFRUIT	AFIOOPRR	AIRPROOF
AFGLLNOT	FLATLONG	AFIJMNOR	JANIFORM	AFIORSTU	FAITOROS
AFGLLRUU	FULGURAL	AFIKLNNR	FRANKLIN	AFIORSTZ	SFORZATI
AFGLLRUY	FRUGALLY	AFIKLORT	FORKTAIL	AFIRSTTY	STRATIFY
AFGLLSSU	GLASSFUL	AFIKLOST	FLOKATIS	AFISSSTT	SITFASTS
AFGLLSTU	GASTFULL	AFIKMNNR	FINNMARK	AFISSTTT	FATTISTS
AFGLNNOO	GONFALON	AFIKMNRS	FINMARKS	AFISSTUV	FAUVISTS
AFGLNORU	GROANFUL	AFIKNRST	RATFINKS	AFKLNOTU	OUTFLANK
AFGLNOUW	WAGONFUL	AFIKRSTY	KARSTIFY	AFKLNPRU	PRANKFUL
AFGNNNOO	GONFANON	AFILLLOT	FLOTILLA	AFKLNSTU	TANKFULS
AFGOORTZ	ZOOGRAFT	AFILLMSS	MISFALLS	AFKLORTW	FLATWORK
AFHIILRS	FRAILISH	AFILLMUY	AIMFULLY	AFKLOSWY	FOLKWAYS
AFHIILSS	SAILFISH	AFILLNPS	PINFALLS	AFKMOORT	FOOTMARK
AFHIILST	FISHTAIL	AFILLNPU	PLAINFUL	AFKMORRW	FARMWORK
AFHIIMST	MISFAITH	AFILLPST	PITFALLS	AFKRRSTU	FRAKTURS

AFLLLORY	FLORALLY	**AGGGHINS**	SHAGGING		SLANGING
AFLLLUWY	LAWFULLY	**AGGGILNN**	GANGLING	**AGGILNNT**	GNATLING
AFLLMNUY	MANFULLY	**AGGGILNR**	GARGLING		TANGLING
AFLLMORY	FORMALLY		RAGGLING	**AGGILNNW**	WANGLING
AFLLMPSU	PALMFULS	**AGGGILNS**	LAGGINGS	**AGGILNOP**	GALOPING
AFLLNOOV	FLAVONOL		SLAGGING	**AGGILNOT**	GLOATING
AFLLNOSW	SNOWFALL	**AGGGILNW**	WAGGLING		GOATLING
AFLLNUUW	UNLAWFUL	**AGGGINNS**	GANGINGS	**AGGILNPU**	PLAGUING
AFLLOOTW	FOOTWALL		SNAGGING	**AGGILNPY**	GAPINGLY
AFLLOSTU	FALLOUTS	**AGGGINPS**	SPAGGING	**AGGILNRY**	GRAYLING
	OUTFALLS	**AGGGINRS**	RAGGINGS		RAGINGLY
AFLLRTUY	ARTFULLY	**AGGGINSS**	SAGGINGS	**AGGILNSS**	GLASSING
AFLLSTUW	WASTFULL	**AGGGINST**	STAGGING	**AGGILNSZ**	GLAZINGS
AFLMNNUU	UNMANFUL		TAGGINGS	**AGGIMNRU**	MAUGRING
AFLMNOPR	PLANFORM	**AGGGINSU**	GAUGINGS	**AGGINNOR**	GROANING
AFLMNORU	UNFORMAL	**AGGGINSW**	SWAGGING	**AGGINNOT**	TANGOING
AFLMNOST	LOFTSMAN	**AGGGIYZZ**	ZIGZAGGY	**AGGINNOW**	WAGONING
AFLMOPRT	PLATFORM	**AGGHIILS**	GHILGAIS	**AGGINNPR**	PRANGING
AFLMORRU	FORMULAR	**AGGHILNU**	LAUGHING	**AGGINNPS**	SPANGING
AFLMORSU	FORMULAS	**AGGHILST**	GASLIGHT	**AGGINNRR**	GNARRING
AFLMORSW	WOLFRAMS	**AGGHILSY**	SHAGGILY	**AGGINNRS**	RANGINGS
AFLMORTU	FOULMART	**AGGHIMNO**	HOMAGING	**AGGINNRT**	GRANTING
AFLMORTW	FLATWORM	**AGGHIMNS**	GINGHAMS	**AGGINNRU**	RAUNGING
AFLMOSST	FLOTSAMS	**AGGHINNP**	PHANGING	**AGGINNRW**	WRANGING
AFLMOSUY	FAMOUSLY	**AGGHINNS**	GNASHING	**AGGINNST**	STANGING
AFLNOPRU	APRONFUL		HANGINGS	**AGGINNSW**	GNAWINGS
AFLNORST	FRONTALS	**AGGHINNW**	WHANGING	**AGGINNTU**	GAUNTING
AFLNRTUU	UNARTFUL	**AGGHINPR**	GRAPHING	**AGGINNTW**	TWANGING
AFLNTUUV	VAUNTFUL	**AGGHINST**	GHASTING	**AGGINNUZ**	UNGAZING
AFLNTUUY	UNFAULTY	**AGGHINUW**	WAUGHING	**AGGINORT**	GAROTING
AFLOOSTW	WOOLFATS	**AGGHISTT**	GASTIGHT	**AGGINOST**	GIGATONS
AFLOOTTU	OUTFLOAT	**AGGHJMNO**	MAHJONGG	**AGGINOVY**	VOYAGING
AFLOPSTT	FLATTOPS	**AGGHLOOT**	GOLGOTHA	**AGGINOWY**	WAYGOING
AFLORSSU	FUSAROLS	**AGGIIJJS**	JIGAJIGS	**AGGINPRS**	GRASPING
AFLORSUV	FLAVOURS	**AGGIILNN**	ALIGNING		PARGINGS
AFLORUVY	FLAVOURY	**AGGIILNR**	GLAIRING		SPARGING
AFLOSTUU	FLATUOUS	**AGGIILNS**	SILAGING	**AGGINPSS**	GASPINGS
AFLPRSTY	FLYTRAPS	**AGGIILNT**	LIGATING	**AGGINPUZ**	UPGAZING
AFLPSSTY	FLYPASTS		TAIGLING	**AGGINRSS**	GRASSING
AFLRSTTU	STARTFUL	**AGGIILNV**	GINGIVAL		SIRGANGS
AFLRSTUY	TRAYFULS	**AGGIIMNS**	IMAGINGS	**AGGINRST**	GRATINGS
AFMNNNUY	FUNNYMAN	**AGGIINNR**	GRAINING	**AGGINRSU**	SUGARING
AFMNNORT	FRONTMAN	**AGGIINNS**	AGNISING	**AGGINRSV**	GRAVINGS
AFMNORST	FORMANTS		GAININGS	**AGGINRSZ**	GRAZINGS
AFMNOSUU	UNFAMOUS	**AGGIINNZ**	AGNIZING	**AGGINRTY**	GYRATING
AFMOOPRR	PROFORMA	**AGGIINRS**	AGRISING	**AGGINRUU**	AUGURING
AFMORSSU	AUSFORMS	**AGGIINRT**	TRIAGING	**AGGINRYZ**	AGRYZING
AFMORSTU	FOUMARTS	**AGGIINRZ**	AGRIZING	**AGGINSSS**	GASSINGS
AFMORTUY	FUMATORY	**AGGIINST**	AGISTING	**AGGINSST**	STAGINGS
AFMOSSTU	SFUMATOS	**AGGIINSU**	AGUISING	**AGGINSWY**	GAYWINGS
AFNNOTTY	NONFATTY	**AGGIINUZ**	AGUIZING	**AGGIRTUZ**	ZIGGURAT
AFNORRSW	FORWARNS	**AGGIJJOS**	JIGAJOGS	**AGGKLNNU**	ANGKLUNG
AFNORSTW	FANWORTS	**AGGIJLNN**	JANGLING	**AGGLLLOY**	LOLLYGAG
AFNOSTUW	OUTFAWNS	**AGGIKNSS**	GASKINGS	**AGGLLOOY**	ALGOLOGY
AFOOPPRS	APPROOFS	**AGGILLNS**	GINGALLS	**AGGLMOOR**	LOGOGRAM
AFOOPRRT	RATPROOF	**AGGILLNU**	ULLAGING	**AGGLNOPW**	GANGPLOW
AFOORSTZ	FORZATOS	**AGGILLNY**	GALLYING	**AGGLOORY**	AGROLOGY
	SFORZATO	**AGGILMNN**	MANGLING	**AGGLRSTY**	STRAGGLY
AFOOSTWY	FOOTWAYS	**AGGILMNO**	GLOAMING	**AGGMORRS**	GROGRAMS
AFORSTTW	FORSWATT	**AGGILMNR**	MALGRING	**AGGMOSTY**	MYSTAGOG
AFOSSTTU	OUTFASTS	**AGGILMNU**	GLAUMING	**AGGNOSSY**	SYNAGOGS
AFOSSTUU	FASTUOUS	**AGGILNNO**	GANGLION	**AGGNUWZZ**	ZUGZWANG
AGGGGILN	GAGGLING	**AGGILNNR**	GNARLING	**AGHHIILT**	HIGHTAIL
AGGGHILN	HAGGLING	**AGGILNNS**	ANGLINGS	**AGHHINSS**	SHASHING

AGHHISWY	HIGHWAYS	
AGHHLOTU	ALTHOUGH	
AGHIILNN	INHALING	
AGHIILNS	NILGHAIS	
AGHIINNS	HAININGS	
AGHIINRT	AIRTHING	
AGHIIPRR	HAIRGRIP	
AGHIIRTT	AIRTIGHT	
AGHIJNRT	NIGHTJAR	
AGHIKNNS	SHANKING	
AGHIKNNT	THANKING	
AGHIKNRS	SHARKING	
AGHIKNSS	SHAKINGS	
AGHIKNSW	HAWKINGS	
AGHILLNO	HALLOING	
	HOLLAING	
AGHILLNS	HALLINGS	
AGHILLNT	ALLNIGHT	
AGHILMTY	ALMIGHTY	
AGHILNOO	HOOLIGAN	
AGHILNOR	LONGHAIR	
AGHILNOS	SHOALING	
AGHILNOT	LOATHING	
AGHILNPR	RALPHING	
AGHILNPS	PLASHING	
AGHILNRS	HARLINGS	
	RINGHALS	
AGHILNRY	NARGHILY	
AGHILNSS	HASSLING	
	LASHINGS	
	SLANGISH	
	SLASHING	
AGHILNST	HALTINGS	
	LATHINGS	
AGHILNSU	LANGUISH	
	NILGHAUS	
	SHAULING	
AGHILNSW	SHAWLING	
	WHALINGS	
AGHILNSY	NYLGHAIS	
AGHILOST	GOLIATHS	
AGHILRSY	GARISHLY	
AGHILRTY	GRAITHLY	
AGHILSUY	AGUISHLY	
AGHIMMNS	SHAMMING	
AGHIMMNW	WHAMMING	
AGHIMNPR	PHARMING	
AGHIMNSS	MASHINGS	
	SMASHING	
AGHIMNTY	THINGAMY	
AGHIMOST	OGHAMIST	
AGHIMPRU	GRAPHIUM	
AGHINNOS	NIHONGAS	
AGHINNOT	GNATHION	
AGHINNSS	SNASHING	
AGHINNST	TANGHINS	
AGHINNTU	HAUNTING	
AGHINNTY	ANYTHING	
AGHINORS	ORANGISH	
AGHINOST	HOASTING	
AGHINPPW	WHAPPING	
AGHINPPY	HAPPYING	
AGHINPRS	HARPINGS	
	PHRASING	
	SHARPING	
AGHINPSS	PHASINGS	
	SHAPINGS	
AGHINQSU	QUASHING	
AGHINRRU	HURRAING	
AGHINRRY	HARRYING	
AGHINRSS	SHARINGS	
AGHINRST	TRASHING	
AGHINRTW	THRAWING	
	WRATHING	
AGHINSST	HASTINGS	
	STASHING	
AGHINSSV	SHAVINGS	
AGHINSSW	SWASHING	
	WASHINGS	
AGHINSTT	HATTINGS	
AGHINSTW	SWATHING	
	THAWINGS	
AGHINUZZ	HUZZAING	
AGHIOPRS	ISOGRAPH	
AGHIPRRT	TRIGRAPH	
AGHIRSTT	STRAIGHT	
AGHISSTT	TIGHTASS	
AGHISSTW	SIGHTSAW	
AGHJMNOS	MAHJONGS	
AGHKNOPT	PAKTHONG	
AGHKOSSW	GOSHAWKS	
AGHLLMPU	GALLUMPH	
AGHLMOOR	HOLOGRAM	
AGHLMOOY	HOLOGAMY	
AGHLMPSU	GALUMPHS	
AGHLNOSU	SHOGUNAL	
AGHLNSUY	NYLGHAUS	
AGHLOOSS	GASOHOLS	
AGHLOTUU	OUTLAUGH	
AGHMMOOY	HOMOGAMY	
AGHMNPSU	SPHAGNUM	
AGHMOOPY	OMOPHAGY	
AGHMOPRY	MYOGRAPH	
AGHMORSY	HYGROMAS	
AGHMRRSU	MURRAGHS	
AGHNNOSU	HOUNGANS	
AGHNNSTU	SHANTUNG	
AGHNOORS	SHAGROON	
AGHNORST	STAGHORN	
AGHNOSTU	HANGOUTS	
	TOHUNGAS	
AGHNPRSY	SYNGRAPH	
AGHNTTUU	UNTAUGHT	
AGHOOPYZ	ZOOPHAGY	
AGHOPSSW	SWAGSHOP	
AGHORSTW	WARTHOGS	
AGHRSTTU	STRAUGHT	
AGIIIKMR	KIRIGAMI	
AGIIILNS	LIAISING	
AGIIINNS	INSIGNIA	
AGIIINRV	VIRGINIA	
AGIIKLNS	SKAILING	
AGIIKNNT	ANTIKING	
AGIIKNRT	TRAIKING	
AGIILLLM	MILLIGAL	
AGIILLNV	VIALLING	
AGIILLOV	VILLAGIO	
	VILLIAGO	
AGIILMNP	IMPALING	
AGIILMNS	MAILINGS	
	MISALIGN	
AGIILMNU	MIAULING	
AGIILNNP	PLAINING	
AGIILNNS	NAILINGS	
	SNAILING	
AGIILNNU	INGUINAL	
AGIILNNV	ANVILING	
AGIILNNY	INLAYING	
AGIILNOP	PIGNOLIA	
AGIILNOR	ORIGINAL	
AGIILNOT	INTAGLIO	
	LIGATION	
	TAGLIONI	
AGIILNOX	GLOXINIA	
AGIILNPS	LAIPSING	
AGIILNPT	PLAITING	
AGIILNQU	QUAILING	
AGIILNRS	GLAIRINS	
	RAILINGS	
AGIILNRT	RINGTAIL	
	TRAILING	
AGIILNRV	RIVALING	
	VIRGINAL	
AGIILNSS	AISLINGS	
	SAILINGS	
AGIILNST	TAILINGS	
AGIILNSU	LINGUISA	
AGIILNSW	WAILINGS	
AGIILNTT	LITIGANT	
AGIILNTV	VIGILANT	
AGIILORU	OLIGURIA	
AGIILOSV	VILIAGOS	
AGIILPST	PIGTAILS	
AGIILTVY	VAGILITY	
AGIIMMNS	MAIMINGS	
AGIIMMSS	IMAGISMS	
AGIIMNNR	INARMING	
AGIIMNOR	IGNORAMI	
AGIIMNOU	MIAOUING	
AGIIMNOW	MIAOWING	
AGIIMNPV	IMPAVING	
AGIIMNSS	AMISSING	
AGIIMNST	GIANTISM	
AGIIMNTT	MITIGANT	
AGIIMORS	ORIGAMIS	
AGIIMSST	IMAGISTS	
AGIINNPS	SPAINING	
AGIINNPT	PAINTING	
	PATINING	
AGIINNRS	INGRAINS	
AGIINNRT	TRAINING	
AGIINNRV	RAVINING	
AGIINNST	SAINTING	
	SATINING	
	STAINING	
AGIINNSW	SWAINING	
AGIINNTT	TAINTING	
AGIINOPT	OPIATING	
AGIINORS	SIGNORIA	
AGIINORT	RIGATONI	
AGIINPRS	ASPIRING	
	PAIRINGS	

	PRAISING	AGILLMSU	GALLIUMS		SAPPLING
AGIINPRT	PIRATING	AGILLNOW	ALLOWING		SLAPPING
AGIINRRV	ARRIVING	AGILLNOY	ALLOYING	AGILNPPY	APPLYING
AGIINRSS	RAISINGS	AGILLNPS	SPALLING	AGILNPRS	GRAPLINS
AGIINRTT	ATTIRING	AGILLNRU	ALLURING		SPARLING
AGIINSSZ	ASSIZING		LINGULAR		SPRINGAL
AGIINSTV	VISTAING	AGILLNRY	RALLYING	AGILNPSS	SAPLINGS
AGIINSTW	WAISTING	AGILLNST	STALLING	AGILNPST	PLATINGS
	WAITINGS	AGILLNSU	LINGUALS		SPALTING
AGIISSTV	VISAGIST		LINGULAS		STAPLING
AGIJLLNS	JINGALLS	AGILLNSW	WALLINGS	AGILNPSW	LAPWINGS
AGIJLNPY	JAPINGLY	AGILLNSY	SALLYING		SPAWLING
AGIJMNOR	MAJORING		SIGNALLY	AGILNPSY	PALSYING
AGIJMNRU	JUMARING		SLANGILY		SPLAYING
AGIJNNSU	JAUNSING	AGILLNTY	TALLYING	AGILNPTT	PLATTING
AGIJNNTT	TJANTING	AGILLOOR	GILLAROO	AGILNPUY	UPLAYING
AGIJNNTU	JAUNTING	AGILLOPT	GALLIPOT	AGILNRSS	RASSLING
AGIJNRRS	JARRINGS	AGILLORS	GORILLAS	AGILNRST	RATLINGS
AGIKKNNS	SKANKING	AGILLOST	GALLIOTS		SLARTING
AGIKLMOR	KILOGRAM	AGILLPRY	PLAYGIRL		STARLING
AGIKLNNP	PLANKING	AGILLPUY	PLAGUILY	AGILNRSU	SINGULAR
AGIKLNNR	RANKLING	AGILLSSU	LUGSAILS	AGILNRSW	WARLINGS
AGIKLNOP	POLKAING	AGILLSSY	GLASSILY		WARSLING
AGIKLNOS	OAKLINGS	AGILMMNS	LAMMINGS	AGILNRTT	RATTLING
	SKOALING		SLAMMING	AGILNRTW	TRAWLING
AGIKLNPP	KLAPPING		SMALMING	AGILNRVY	RAVINGLY
AGIKLNST	SKLATING	AGILMNNT	MANTLING	AGILNRWW	WRAWLING
	STALKING	AGILMNPS	LAMPINGS	AGILNRWX	WRAXLING
	TALKINGS		PSALMING	AGILNSST	ANGLISTS
AGIKLNSW	WALKINGS		SAMPLING		LASTINGS
AGIKLNTY	TAKINGLY	AGILMNQU	QUALMING		SALTINGS
AGIKLNUW	WAULKING	AGILMNRS	MARLINGS		SLATINGS
AGIKLORY	KILOGRAY	AGILMNST	MALTINGS	AGILNSSV	SALVINGS
AGIKMNNU	UNMAKING	AGILMOPR	LIPOGRAM	AGILNSSW	SWALINGS
AGIKMNPU	UPMAKING	AGILMORS	ALGORISM	AGILNSTT	SLATTING
AGIKMNRS	MARKINGS	AGILMPSU	PLAGIUMS	AGILNSTU	SALUTING
AGIKMNSS	MASKINGS	AGILNNNP	PLANNING	AGILNSUV	AVULSING
AGIKNNPP	KNAPPING	AGILNNOP	PANGOLIN	AGILNSUW	WAULINGS
AGIKNNPR	PRANKING	AGILNNOS	LOANINGS	AGILNSVY	SAVINGLY
AGIKNNPS	SPANKING	AGILNNPT	PLANTING	AGILNSWW	WAWLINGS
AGIKNNRR	KNARRING	AGILNNRS	SNARLING	AGILNSWY	SWAYLING
AGIKNNRS	RANKINGS	AGILNNSS	LINSANGS	AGILNTTT	TATTLING
AGIKNNRU	UNRAKING	AGILNNST	SLANTING	AGILNTTW	WATTLING
AGIKNNST	STANKING		TANLINGS	AGILNTUV	VAULTING
	TANKINGS	AGILNNUW	UNLAWING	AGILNTUX	LUXATING
AGIKNNSW	SWANKING	AGILNNUY	UNGAINLY	AGILNTWZ	WALTZING
AGIKNORT	TROAKING		UNLAYING	AGILNTXY	TAXINGLY
AGIKNOSS	SOAKINGS	AGILNOOO	OOGONIAL	AGILOOPY	APIOLOGY
AGIKNOST	GOATSKIN	AGILNOOS	ISOGONAL	AGILOORS	GLORIOSA
AGIKNOSY	KAYOINGS	AGILNOPR	PAROLING	AGILOOXY	AXIOLOGY
AGIKNPRS	PARKINGS	AGILNOPS	GALOPINS	AGILOPST	GALIPOTS
	SPARKING	AGILNOPT	PLOATING	AGILORSS	GIRASOLS
AGIKNPTU	UPTAKING	AGILNORS	RANGOLIS	AGILORSW	AIRGLOWS
AGIKNQSU	QUAKINGS	AGILNORT	TRIGONAL	AGILOSST	SALIGOTS
AGIKNRSS	SARKINGS	AGILNOSS	GLOSSINA	AGILRSSY	GRASSILY
AGIKNRST	KARTINGS		LASSOING	AGILSYVZ	SYZYGIAL
	STARKING	AGILNOST	ANTILOGS	AGIMMNPS	SPAMMING
AGIKNSST	SKATINGS		SALTOING	AGIMMNRS	SMARMING
	TASKINGS		SOLATING	AGIMMNRT	TRAMMING
AGILLLNS	LALLINGS	AGILNOSV	SALVOING	AGIMMNTY	TAMMYING
AGILLMNS	MALLINGS	AGILNOTT	TOTALING	AGIMMOSY	MISOGAMY
	SMALLING	AGILNOTY	ANTILOGY	AGIMNNOS	MASONING
AGILLMNU	MULLIGAN	AGILNPPP	PLAPPING	AGIMNNOW	WOMANING
AGILLMNY	MALIGNLY	AGILNPPS	LAPPINGS	AGIMNNRU	MANURING

	UNARMING	**AGINNRTY**	TRAYNING	**AGINPSTT**	SPATTING
AGIMNNSW	SWINGMAN		TYRANING	**AGINPSWY**	YAWPINGS
AGIMNNTU	UNTAMING	**AGINNSTU**	SAUNTING	**AGINPSZZ**	SPAZZING
AGIMNOOV	AMOOVING		STAUNING	**AGINQRSU**	SQUARING
AGIMNORR	ARMORING		UNSATING	**AGINRRST**	STARRING
	ROARMING	**AGINNSTW**	WANTINGS		TARRINGS
AGIMNORS	ORGANISM	**AGINNSTY**	STAYNING	**AGINRRTY**	TARRYING
	ROAMINGS	**AGINNSUY**	UNSAYING	**AGINRSST**	GASTRINS
AGIMNORU	ORIGANUM	**AGINNSWY**	YAWNINGS		STARINGS
AGIMNORY	AGRIMONY	**AGINNTTU**	ATTUNING	**AGINRSSU**	ASSURING
AGIMNOST	ANTISMOG		NUTATING	**AGINRSSY**	SYRINGAS
AGIMNOSV	VAMOSING		TAUNTING	**AGINRSTT**	RATTINGS
AGIMNPPS	MAPPINGS	**AGINNTUV**	VAUNTING		STARTING
AGIMNPRS	RAMPINGS	**AGINNTUX**	UNTAXING	**AGINRSTV**	STARVING
AGIMNPRT	TRAMPING	**AGINNVVY**	NAVVYING	**AGINRSTW**	RINGTAWS
AGIMNPSS	SPASMING	**AGINOOPS**	POGONIAS		STRAWING
AGIMNPST	STAMPING	**AGINOORT**	ROGATION		WRASTING
	TAMPINGS	**AGINOPPS**	APPOSING	**AGINRSTY**	STINGRAY
AGIMNPSV	VAMPINGS	**AGINOPQU**	OPAQUING		STRAYING
AGIMNPSW	SWAMPING	**AGINOPRV**	VAPORING	**AGINRSVW**	SWARVING
AGIMNRRY	MARRYING	**AGINORRS**	GARRISON	**AGINRSVY**	VARYINGS
AGIMNRST	MIGRANTS		ROARINGS	**AGINRSWY**	RINGWAYS
	SMARTING	**AGINORRW**	ARROWING	**AGINRTYY**	GYNIATRY
AGIMNRSW	SWARMING	**AGINORRZ**	RAZORING	**AGINSSTT**	TASTINGS
	WARMINGS	**AGINORSS**	ASSIGNOR	**AGINSSTW**	WASTINGS
AGIMNRSY	MYRINGAS		SIGNORAS	**AGINSSWY**	SWAYINGS
AGIMNRTU	MATURING		SOARINGS	**AGINSTTT**	TATTINGS
AGIMNSSU	ASSUMING	**AGINORST**	ORGANIST	**AGINSTTW**	SWATTING
AGIMNSTT	MATTINGS		ROASTING	**AGINSVVY**	SAVVYING
AGIMNTTU	MUTATING	**AGINORSU**	AROUSING	**AGINSWWX**	WAXWINGS
AGIMORRT	MIGRATOR	**AGINORSV**	SAVORING	**AGIOORSU**	ORAGIOUS
AGIMORSS	ISOGRAMS	**AGINORTT**	ROTATING	**AGIOORSZ**	GRAZIOSO
AGIMORSU	GOURAMIS		TROATING	**AGIOORTU**	AUTOGIRO
AGIMQRUY	QUAGMIRY	**AGINORTV**	GRAVITON	**AGIOPPRT**	AGITPROP
AGIMRRST	TRIGRAMS	**AGINORTY**	GYRATION	**AGIOPPST**	AGITPOPS
AGINNNNY	NANNYING		ORGANITY	**AGIOPRUY**	UROPYGIA
AGINNNOY	ANNOYING	**AGINOSST**	AGONISTS	**AGIORRTT**	GRATTOIR
AGINNNPS	PANNINGS	**AGINOSSU**	SAGOUINS	**AGIORSST**	AGISTORS
	SPANNING	**AGINOSTT**	TANGOIST		ORGIASTS
AGINNNST	TANNINGS		TOASTING	**AGIOSUUY**	OUGUIYAS
AGINNNSV	VANNINGS	**AGINOSTU**	OUTGAINS	**AGIRSSTU**	SASTRUGI
AGINNNSW	SWANNING	**AGINPPRS**	RAPPINGS	**AGIRSTUZ**	ZASTRUGI
AGINNNUW	UNWANING	**AGINPPRT**	TRAPPING	**AGIRTTUY**	GRATUITY
AGINNOOP	NAPOOING	**AGINPPRW**	WRAPPING	**AGJLRSUU**	JUGULARS
AGINNOPR	APRONING	**AGINPPST**	STAPPING	**AGJNOORS**	JARGOONS
AGINNOPT	POIGNANT		TAPPINGS	**AGJNOPST**	JOGPANTS
AGINNORT	IGNORANT	**AGINPPSW**	SWAPPING	**AGKLNNOS**	ANKLONGS
AGINNOST	ASTONING	**AGINPPTU**	PUPATING	**AGKLNNSU**	ANKLUNGS
AGINNOSU	ANGINOUS	**AGINPPUY**	APPUYING	**AGKMMORY**	KYMOGRAM
AGINNOTT	NOTATING	**AGINPRRS**	SPARRING	**AGKMNOPS**	KAMPONGS
AGINNPPS	SNAPPING	**AGINPRRY**	PARRYING	**AGKMPRSU**	PUGMARKS
AGINNPRW	PRAWNING	**AGINPRSS**	PARSINGS	**AGKNOPST**	PAKTONGS
AGINNPST	PANTINGS		PINGRASS	**AGKORRSW**	RAGWORKS
AGINNPSW	SPAWNING		RASPINGS	**AGKORSSW**	GASWORKS
	WINGSPAN	**AGINPRST**	PARTINGS	**AGLLLNOW**	LONGWALL
AGINNPUY	UNPAYING		PRATINGS	**AGLLMOPW**	GLOWLAMP
AGINNQTU	QUANTING	**AGINPRSW**	WARPINGS	**AGLLNOOS**	GALLOONS
AGINNRRS	SNARRING	**AGINPRSY**	PRAYINGS	**AGLLNSTU**	GALLNUTS
AGINNRSS	SNARINGS		SPRAYING		NUTGALLS
AGINNRST	RANTINGS	**AGINPRTU**	UPRATING	**AGLLOORS**	ROGALLOS
	STARNING	**AGINPRTY**	PARTYING	**AGLLOOST**	GALLOOTS
AGINNRSW	WARNINGS	**AGINPSSS**	PASSINGS	**AGLLOPSU**	PLUGOLAS
AGINNRTT	TRANTING	**AGINPSST**	PASTINGS	**AGLLPRSU**	SPURGALL
AGINNRTU	NATURING	**AGINPSSU**	PAUSINGS	**AGLLPSTY**	GLYPTALS

AGLLRUVY	VULGARLY	AGORSTTY	GYROSTAT	AHILLMTU	THALLIUM
AGLMOOTY	ATMOLOGY	AGORSTUY	GRAYOUTS	AHILLNOS	HALLIONS
AGLMOPSY	POLYGAMS	AHHIKKRS	KHIRKAHS	AHILLNPS	PHALLINS
AGLMOPVY	POLYGAMY	AHHIKLSS	SHASHLIK	AHILLNRT	INTHRALL
AGLMORSU	GLAMOURS	AHHILNPT	PHTHALIN	AHILLNST	ANTHILLS
AGLNOOOS	OLOGOANS	AHHILOST	HAILSHOT	AHILLNTW	WANTHILL
AGLNORSU	LANGUORS	AHHILPSW	WHIPLASH	AHILLPST	PHALLIST
AGLNOSST	GLASNOST	AHHIMMSS	MISHMASH	AHILLSTT	TALLITHS
AGLNOSUU	ANGULOUS	AHHIMNSU	HAHNIUMS	AHILLSVY	LAVISHLY
AGLNOSWY	LONGWAYS	AHHINSST	SHANTIHS	AHILMMSS	MASHLIMS
AGLNPSUY	GUNPLAYS	AHHIPRSS	SHARPISH	AHILMNSS	MASHLINS
AGLNRUUV	UNVULGAR	AHHISSTT	SHITTAHS	AHILMOST	HALIMOTS
AGLNSSSU	SUNGLASS	AHHKMOTW	HAWKMOTH		MAILSHOT
AGLNSTUY	YGLAUNST	AHHKRSTU	KASHRUTH	AHILMOSU	HALOUMIS
AGLOOPST	GOALPOST	AHHLMRTY	RHYTHMAL	AHILMQSU	QUALMISH
AGLOOTUY	AUTOLOGY	AHHLNOPT	NAPHTHOL	AHILMTUZ	HALUTZIM
AGLOPRSS	LOPGRASS	AHHLNPTY	NAPHTHYL	AHILNOPS	SIPHONAL
AGLORSSY	GLOSSARY	AHHMPRRU	HARRUMPH	AHILNOPT	OLIPHANT
AGLPSSSY	SPYGLASS	AHHMPRSU	HARUMPHS	AHILNORT	HORNTAIL
AGLRTTUU	GUTTURAL	AHHNORTW	HAWTHORN	AHILNRST	INTHRALS
AGLSTUUY	AUGUSTLY	AHHOPRSS	SHOPHARS	AHILOORT	LOTHARIO
AGMMNOOR	MONOGRAM	AHHOPSTU	APHTHOUS	AHILOPSS	ALPHOSIS
	NOMOGRAM	AHHPSTUZ	HUTZPAHS		HAPLOSIS
AGMMNOOY	MONOGAMY	AHIIILMN	MALIHINI	AHILOPST	HOSPITAL
AGMMOORT	TOMOGRAM	AHIIKRSS	RIKISHAS	AHILOSTU	HALITOUS
AGMMORSY	MYOGRAMS		SHIKARIS	AHILOSTZ	THIAZOLS
AGMMORYZ	ZYMOGRAM	AHIILNPS	PLAINISH	AHILPPSS	PALSHIPS
AGMNNORS	GRANNOMS	AHIILOST	HALIOTIS		SHIPLAPS
AGMNNOSW	GOWNSMAN	AHIILPTW	WHIPTAIL	AHILPRTU	ULTRAHIP
AGMNOOPR	PORNOMAG	AHIILRTY	HILARITY	AHILPSSY	PHYSALIS
AGMNOORS	SONOGRAM	AHIIMNNO	HOMINIAN	AHILPSXY	PHYLAXIS
AGMNOORY	AGRONOMY	AHIIMNOT	HIMATION	AHILRSTY	TRASHILY
AGMNORST	ANGSTROM	AHIIMNRU	MANUHIRI	AHILRTWY	WRATHILY
AGMNORSU	ORGANUMS	AHIIMNST	HISTAMIN	AHIMMNSU	HUMANISM
AGMNSSTU	MUSTANGS		ISTHMIAN	AHIMMORZ	MAHZORIM
AGMNSSTY	GYMNASTS		THIAMINS	AHIMMOSS	SHAMOSIM
	SYNTAGMS	AHIIMOPX	AMPHIOXI	AHIMMOSV	MOSHAVIM
AGMOOOSU	OOGAMOUS	AHIIMRST	ISARITHM	AHIMNOST	HOISTMAN
AGMOOPRY	POROGAMY	AHIIMSSS	SASHIMIS		MANIHOTS
AGMOOTVY	VAGOTOMY	AHIIMSST	SAMITHIS	AHIMNOSW	WOMANISH
AGMOPRRS	PROGRAMS	AHIINOPT	PHOTINIA	AHIMNSTU	HUMANIST
AGMOPRSU	GOPURAMS	AHIINOTT	TITHONIA	AHIMNSTX	XANTHISM
AGMORRSW	RAGWORMS	AHIINPRS	HAIRPINS	AHIMNTUY	HUMANITY
AGMRSSSU	GRASSUMS	AHIINPST	ANTISHIP	AHIMOOSY	YAHOOISM
AGNNNOOS	NONAGONS	AHIINSST	SAINTISH	AHIMOPRS	APHORISM
AGNNOOPT	POONTANG	AHIINSSW	SWAINISH		MORPHIAS
AGNNOORS	ARGONONS	AHIINSTU	HUITAINS	AHIMOPST	OPSIMATH
	ORGANONS	AHIINSTZ	THIAZINS	AHIMORRW	HAIRWORM
AGNNOQTU	QUANTONG	AHIIOPST	HOSPITIA	AHIMPPSS	SAPPHISM
AGNNORSU	NONSUGAR	AHIIPRSS	AIRSHIPS	AHIMPRST	TRAMPISH
AGNNOTUW	OUTGNAWN	AHIKLNRS	RINKHALS	AHIMPSSW	SWAMPISH
AGNORRST	GRANTORS	AHIKLRSY	RAKISHLY	AHIMRSST	SMARTISH
AGNORTUY	NUGATORY	AHIKLSSS	SHASLIKS		THRIMSAS
AGNOSTUW	OUTGNAWS	AHIKMNSS	KHAMSINS	AHIMSSSU	HASSIUMS
AGNPPRSU	UPSPRANG	AHIKMRSS	KASHMIRS	AHIMSSTV	MITSVAHS
AGNRSSTU	NUTGRASS	AHIKNPRS	PRANKISH	AHIMSTUZ	AZIMUTHS
AGOORRTY	ROGATORY	AHIKNPST	TANKSHIP	AHIMSTVZ	MITZVAHS
AGOORTUY	AUTOGYRO	AHIKORRW	HAIRWORK	AHINNNSY	NANNYISH
AGOPPSST	STOPGAPS	AHIKORSS	KAROSHIS	AHINNOPT	ANTIPHON
AGORRSST	GROSSART	AHIKPRSS	SPARKISH	AHINNSTX	XANTHINS
	ROTGRASS	AHIKRSSW	RIKSHAWS	AHINOOPY	HYPONOIA
AGORRSTW	RAGWORTS	AHILLMOU	HALLOUMI	AHINOPRU	OPHIURAN
AGORRSTY	GYRATORS	AHILLMPS	PHALLISM	AHINORST	TRAHISON
AGORRTYY	GYRATORY	AHILLMSS	SMALLISH	AHINOSST	ASTONISH

AHINOSTZ	HOATZINS	AHLMOPTY	POLYMATH	AHRSTUWY	THRUWAYS
AHINPPSS	SNAPPISH	AHLMOSUU	HAMULOUS	AIIILLVX	LIXIVIAL
AHINPRST	TRANSHIP	AHLMSTYZ	SHMALTZY	AIIILMST	MILITIAS
AHINPRSY	SYRPHIAN	AHLNNORT	LANTHORN	AIIILNST	INITIALS
AHINPSWW	WHIPSAWN	AHLNOPRS	ALPHORNS	AIIILRVZ	VIZIRIAL
AHINQSUV	VANQUISH	AHLNOPST	HAPLONTS	AIIIMPRT	PRIMITIA
AHINRSTY	RHYTINAS		NAPHTOLS	AIIIMRSS	SAIMIRIS
AHINRSVY	HRYVNIAS	AHLNORST	ALTHORNS	AIIIRSSS	SIRIASIS
	VARNISHY	AHLNRTWY	THRAWNLY	AIIJKMOT	KOMITAJI
AHINSSTU	INHAUSTS	AHLOOPSW	WHOOPLAS	AIIJNRTX	JANITRIX
AHINSTUU	TAUHINUS	AHLOOSTW	WOOLHATS	AIIKKSUV	SUKIYAKI
AHIOOPPT	PHOTOPIA	AHLOPSST	SLAPSHOT	AIIKLLST	SILKTAIL
AHIOOSST	ATISHOOS	AHLORRTY	HARLOTRY	AIIKLNRR	LARRIKIN
AHIOPRST	APHORIST	AHLORTTU	ULTRAHOT	AIIKMMSS	SKIMMIAS
AHIOPRSU	OPHIURAS	AHLOSTUU	OUTHAULS	AIIKMNNN	MANNIKIN
AHIOPRSV	VAPORISH	AHLRSTUY	LATHYRUS	AIIKMNNS	MANIKINS
AHIOPSXY	HYPOXIAS	AHLRTTWY	THWARTLY	AIIKMNPR	MINIPARK
AHIORSST	AIRSHOTS	AHMMMOST	MAMMOTHS	AIIKNNNP	PANNIKIN
	SHORTIAS	AHMMMSUU	HUMMAUMS	AIIKNNST	TANKINIS
AHIORSSW	AIRSHOWS	AHMNNNOU	NONHUMAN	AIIKORTY	YAKITORI
AHIORSTV	TOVARISH	AHMNNSTU	HUNTSMAN	AIIKRRSU	RAURIKIS
AHIORSUV	HAVIOURS		MANHUNTS	AIIKTTZZ	TZATZIKI
AHIOSTWY	HOISTWAY	AHMNOPST	PHANTOMS	AIILLLMT	MILLTAIL
AHIPPSST	SAPPHIST	AHMNOPTY	PHANTOMY	AIILLLUV	ILLUVIAL
AHIPRSST	HARPISTS	AHMNORRS	RAMSHORN	AIILLMNO	MONILIAL
	STARSHIP	AHMOOPPT	PHOTOMAP	AIILLMRY	MILLIARY
AHIPRSSW	WARSHIPS	AHMOOPSS	SHAMPOOS	AIILLMST	TALLISIM
AHIPRSWY	WHIPRAYS	AHMOORSW	WASHROOM	AIILLMSW	WILLIAMS
AHIPSSWW	WHIPSAWS	AHMOOSSS	SAMSHOOS	AIILLMTT	TALLITIM
AHIPSSWY	SHIPWAYS	AHMOPTYY	MYOPATHY	AIILLNNV	VANILLIN
AHIQRSSU	SQUARISH	AHMORRST	SHORTARM	AIILLNOP	POLLINIA
AHIRRSST	STIRRAHS	AHMORRSU	MORRHUAS	AIILLNOT	ILLATION
AHIRSSTT	STARTISH	AHMORSST	HARMOSTS	AIILLNPT	ANTIPILL
AHIRSSTW	TRISHAWS	AHMORSTY	HARMOSTY	AIILLNSV	VILLAINS
AHISSSTU	SHIATSUS	AHMORTTW	TAMWORTH	AIILLNVY	VILLAINY
AHISSTTW	WHATSITS	AHMORTUW	WARMOUTH	AIILLPRS	SLIPRAIL
AHISSTUZ	SHIATZUS	AHMOSTTW	MOSTWHAT		SPIRILLA
AHISTTWW	WHITTAWS	AHMPSSSU	SMASHUPS	AIILLQSU	QUILLAIS
AHKLOPST	SHOPTALK	AHMPSTYY	SYMPATHY	AIILLUWW	WILLIWAU
AHKLORTW	LATHWORK	AHMQSSUU	MUSQUASH	AIILLWWW	WILLIWAW
AHKMOORR	MARKHOOR	AHMRSSTY	THRYMSAS	AIILMMNS	MINIMALS
AHKMORRS	MARKHORS	AHNNSTYY	SYNANTHY	AIILMNNS	LAMININS
AHKMRSTU	MUKHTARS	AHNOOPPY	APOPHONY	AIILMNOS	MONILIAS
AHKNOTTU	OUTTHANK	AHNOOPRS	HARPOONS	AIILMNOT	LIMATION
AHKNOTUY	THANKYOU	AHNOOPSU	APHONOUS		MILTONIA
AHKRSSTU	KASHRUTS	AHNOORRY	HONORARY	AIILMNPS	ALPINISM
	TUSHKARS	AHNOPPSW	PAWNSHOP	AIILMNPT	PALMITIN
AHLLLOOP	POOLHALL	AHNOPPSY	PANSOPHY	AIILMNTT	MILITANT
AHLLNOOS	SHALLOON	AHNOPSST	SNAPSHOT	AIILMNTU	MINUTIAL
AHLLNOSS	SHALLONS	AHNORSSX	SAXHORNS	AIILMPUV	IMPLUVIA
AHLLNOSY	HALLYONS	AHNORTWW	WANWORTH	AIILMRST	MISTRIAL
AHLLNOTW	TOWNHALL	AHNOSTTW	WHATNOTS		TRIALISM
AHLLNOUW	UNHALLOW	AHNOSTUX	XANTHOUS	AIILMRTY	LIMITARY
AHLLNRTU	TURNHALL	AHNPPSUU	PUPUNHAS		MILITARY
AHLLOPSS	SHALLOPS	AHNRSVYY	HRYVNYAS	AIILMSTV	VITALISM
AHLLOSST	SHALLOTS	AHOOPTYZ	ZOOPATHY	AIILNOPV	PAVILION
AHLLOSSW	SHALLOWS	AHOOSSTY	SOOTHSAY	AIILNOSS	LIAISONS
AHLLOSTU	THALLOUS	AHOOSTTW	SAWTOOTH	AIILNOSV	VISIONAL
AHLLOSTY	TALLYHOS	AHOPSSTW	WASHPOTS	AIILNPST	ALPINIST
AHLLPRVY	PHYLLARY	AHOPSTTW	TOWPATHS		ANTISLIP
AHLMMOPY	LYMPHOMA	AHOPSTUW	SOUTHPAW		PINTAILS
AHLMMSSU	MASHLUMS	AHORTTUW	WATTHOUR		TAILSPIN
AHLMNOOR	HORMONAL	AHOSSTUW	WASHOUTS	AIILNRSU	SILURIAN
AHLMOOPS	OMPHALOS	AHOSSTUY	SOUTHSAY	AIILNSTY	SALINITY

AIILNTTY	LATINITY	AIIORRST	SARTORII		MISALLOT
AIILOPPS	PAPILIOS	AIIORSTT	AORTITIS	AILLMOSY	LOYALISM
AIILORSV	RAVIOLIS	AIIORSTV	OVARITIS	AILLMOTY	MOLALITY
AIILPRSU	LIPURIAS	AIIORTTV	VITIATOR	AILLMPRY	PRIMALLY
AIILQSSU	SILIQUAS	AIIPRRST	AIRSTRIP	AILLMPSU	PALLIUMS
AIILRSTT	TRIALIST	AIIPRSST	PIARISTS	AILLMSSW	SAWMILLS
AIILRTTY	TRIALITY	AIIPRVVY	VIVIPARY	AILLMUUV	ALLUVIUM
AIILRTVY	RIVALITY	AIIPSTTU	PITUITAS	AILLNNOS	LANOLINS
AIILSTTV	VITALIST	AIIRSSTT	SATIRIST	AILLNOPP	PAPILLON
AIILSTTW	WAITLIST		SITARIST	AILLNOPS	PAILLONS
AIILTTVY	VITALITY	AIISSSTY	SYSSITIA	AILLNOPV	PAVILLON
AIIMMMST	MAMMITIS	AIJKKNOU	KINKAJOU	AILLNORT	ANTIROLL
AIIMMNNY	MINYANIM	AIJLLOOR	JILLAROO	AILLNOST	STALLION
AIIMMNSS	ANIMISMS	AIJLLOVY	JOVIALLY	AILLNOSU	ALLUSION
AIIMMNSX	MAXIMINS	AIJLNTUY	JAUNTILY	AILLNOUV	ALLUVION
AIIMMNTY	IMMANITY	AIJLOTVY	JOVIALTY	AILLNPSY	SPINALLY
AIIMMSTX	MAXIMIST	AIJMORTY	MAJORITY	AILLNPTY	PLIANTLY
AIIMNNOS	INSOMNIA	AIJNOPPY	POPINJAY	AILLNSST	INSTALLS
AIIMNNSV	MINIVANS	AIJNORST	JANITORS	AILLOQTU	TOQUILLA
AIIMNPSS	PIANISMS	AIKKMOOR	KORIMAKO	AILLORSY	SAILORLY
	SINAPISM	AIKKMOST	KOMATIKS	AILLORSZ	ZORILLAS
AIIMNPST	IMPAINTS	AIKKNOTY	KANTIKOY	AILLORTT	LITTORAL
	MISPAINT	AIKKOOSW	KOKOWAIS		TORTILLA
AIIMNPSX	PANMIXIS	AIKKOPSY	KOPIYKAS	AILLOSTY	LOYALIST
AIIMNRST	MARTINIS	AIKKOSUZ	ZAKOUSKI	AILLOTTT	TALLITOT
	MISTRAIN	AIKKRTUZ	ZIKKURAT	AILLPPRU	PUPILLAR
AIIMNSST	ANIMISTS	AIKLLLMW	WALKMILL	AILLPPSU	SUPPLIAL
	SAINTISM	AIKLLMRR	RILLMARK	AILLPPTU	PULPITAL
	SAMNITIS	AIKLLMUW	WAUKMILL	AILLPRSY	SPIRALLY
AIIMNSTT	IMITANTS	AIKLLSTY	STALKILY	AILLPRTY	PALTRILY
	TITANISM	AIKLMNNS	LINKSMAN	AILLPSTY	PLAYLIST
AIIMNSTV	NATIVISM	AIKLMPSU	LAMPUKIS	AILLPSUV	PLUVIALS
	VITAMINS	AIKLMPTU	KALUMPIT	AILLPSWY	SPILLWAY
AIIMNTTU	TITANIUM	AIKLNNPS	SNAPLINK	AILLQSSU	SQUILLAS
AIIMOPSX	APOMIXIS	AIKLNPST	LANTSKIP	AILLRSTY	RALLYIST
AIIMORTT	IMITATOR	AIKLNRSY	SNARKILY	AILLRTUY	RITUALLY
	TIMARIOT	AIKLNSWY	SWANKILY	AILLRTWY	WILLYART
AIIMOSST	AMITOSIS	AIKLOSUV	SOUVLAKI	AILLSTWW	WITWALLS
AIIMPPRS	PRIAPISM	AIKLOTTW	KILOWATT	AILLSUVY	VISUALLY
AIIMPRTY	IMPARITY	AIKLPRSY	SPARKILY	AILLWWWY	WILLYWAW
AIIMRSST	SIMITARS	AIKLRSTT	TITLARKS	AILMMNOO	MONOMIAL
AIIMRSTU	TIRAMISU	AIKLSSSY	SKYSAILS	AILMMNUU	ALUMINUM
AIIMRUVV	VIVARIUM	AIKMMNOO	MAKIMONO	AILMMOOR	MAILROOM
AIIMSSTT	MASTITIS	AIKMMRSS	MISMARKS	AILMMORS	MORALISM
AIINNOPS	PIANINOS	AIKMNOOY	YAKIMONO	AILMMORT	IMMORTAL
AIINNOSV	INVASION	AIKMNRSS	RANKISMS	AILMMRSY	SMARMILY
AIINNOTV	NIVATION	AIKMORSS	KOMISSAR	AILMMSSY	MYALISMS
AIINNQSU	QUININAS	AIKMRSTZ	SITZMARK	AILMMSTU	SUMMITAL
AIINNQTU	QUINTAIN	AIKNNOOS	NAINSOOK	AILMMSUU	ALUMIUMS
AIINNSTY	INSANITY	AIKNNSSW	SWANSKIN	AILMMSUW	MWALIMUS
AIINOOSV	AVOISION	AIKNORST	SKIATRON	AILMNNOS	NOMINALS
AIINOPSS	SINOPIAS	AIKNORTY	KARYOTIN	AILMNNOT	MANNITOL
AIINORTT	ANTIRIOT	AIKNOSTT	STOTINKA	AILMNNTU	LUMINANT
	TRITONIA	AIKOORST	ROOIKATS	AILMNOOP	PALOMINO
AIINOSTT	NOTITIAS	AIKPTTUU	PATUTUKI	AILMNOOR	MONORAIL
	OSTINATI	AIKRSSTY	SATYRISK	AILMNOOS	MOONSAIL
AIINPRSS	ASPIRINS	AIKRSTUZ	ZIKURATS	AILMNOOT	MOTIONAL
AIINPSST	PIANISTS	AILLLNOO	LINALOOL	AILMNOPR	PROLAMIN
AIINRRTT	IRRITANT	AILLLNOS	LINALOLS	AILMNOPS	LAMPIONS
AIINRSTV	VITRAINS	AILLLPSU	LAPILLUS	AILMNOPT	PILOTMAN
AIINRSTZ	TRIAZINS	AILLMMSY	SMALMILY	AILMNOPY	PALIMONY
AIINSTTV	NATIVIST	AILLMNQU	QUILLMAN	AILMNORT	TORMINAL
	VISITANT	AILLMNST	STILLMAN	AILMNOSS	MALISONS
AIINTTVY	NATIVITY	AILLMOST	MAILLOTS	AILMNOSU	LAMINOUS

AILMNPSS	MISPLANS	AILNOSUV	AVULSION	AILPSSWY	SLIPWAYS
	PLASMINS	AILNOSVY	SYNOVIAL	AILPSTUY	PLAYSUIT
AILMNPST	IMPLANTS	AILNOTTV	VOLITANT	AILQSTTU	QUITTALS
	MISPLANT	AILNOTTY	TONALITY	AILRRSTU	RURALIST
AILMNPTU	PLATINUM	AILNOTUX	LUXATION	AILRRSTY	STARRILY
AILMNRSU	MURLAINS	AILNPPSY	SNAPPILY	AILRRTUY	RURALITY
AILMNRUY	LUMINARY	AILNPRSU	PURSLAIN	AILRSSTU	TISSULAR
AILMNSTU	SIMULANT	AILNPRSW	PRAWLINS		TRISULAS
AILMOORS	SAILROOM	AILNPRUV	PULVINAR	AILRSSTY	TRYSAILS
AILMOORT	MOTORAIL	AILNPSTU	NUPTIALS	AILRSTTU	ALTRUIST
	MOTORIAL		PATULINS		TITULARS
AILMOOSV	MOVIOLAS		UNPLAITS		ULTRAIST
AILMOPRX	PROXIMAL	AILNPSTY	PTYALINS	AILRSTTY	STRAITLY
AILMORSS	ORALISMS	AILNPSUU	NAUPLIUS	AILRSUVV	SURVIVAL
	SOLARISM	AILNPTTU	TULIPANT	AILRTTUY	TITULARY
AILMORST	MORALIST	AILNQRTU	TRANQUIL	AILSSTUW	LAWSUITS
AILMORSU	SOLARIUM	AILNQSTU	QUINTALS	AIMMMNOU	AMMONIUM
AILMORSY	ROYALISM	AILNQTUY	QUAINTLY	AIMMMSUX	MAXIMUMS
AILMORTY	MOLARITY	AILNRSSU	INSULARS	AIMMNORT	MORTMAIN
	MORALITY	AILNRSTT	RATTLINS	AIMMNOSW	WOMANISM
AILMOSSY	ISOAMYLS	AILNRSTU	LUNARIST	AIMMNPTU	TIMPANUM
AILMOSTT	TOTALISM	AILNRTTU	RUTILANT	AIMMNSTU	MANUMITS
AILMOSTU	SOLATIUM	AILNRUWY	UNWARILY	AIMMORSS	AMORISMS
AILMOSTV	VOLTAISM	AILNSSTU	STUNSAIL	AIMMOSST	ATOMISMS
AILMPPSY	MISAPPLY		UNALISTS		SOMATISM
AILMPRSU	PRIMULAS	AILNSTTU	LUTANIST	AIMMOSSU	MIASMOUS
AILMPSST	PALMISTS	AILNSTUU	NAUTILUS	AIMMPSST	MISSTAMP
	PSALMIST	AILNSYZZ	SNAZZILY	AIMMRRSY	MISMARRY
AILMPSSY	MISPLAYS	AILOOPRT	TROOPIAL	AIMMRSUU	MASURIUM
AILMPSTY	PTYALISM	AILOORRS	SORORIAL	AIMNNOPT	POINTMAN
AILMRRSU	RURALISM	AILOORST	ISOLATOR	AIMNNOSS	MANSIONS
AILMRSST	MISTRALS		OSTIOLAR		ONANISMS
AILMRSSU	SIMULARS	AILOORSW	WOORALIS	AIMNNOTU	ANTIMUON
	SURMISAL	AILOORTV	VIOLATOR		MOUNTAIN
AILMRSTU	ALTRUISM	AILOPRRV	PROVIRAL	AIMNNOTY	ANTIMONY
	MURALIST	AILOPRSU	PLIOSAUR		ANTINOMY
	ULTRAISM	AILOPRTU	TROUPIAL	AIMNNRTU	RUMINANT
AILMSSTY	MYALISTS	AILOPRTY	POLARITY	AIMNOOOZ	ZOONOMIA
AILNNOOT	NOTIONAL	AILOPRUY	POLYURIA	AIMNOORV	OMNIVORA
AILNNORV	NONRIVAL	AILOPSST	APOSTILS	AIMNOOST	AMOTIONS
	NONVIRAL		TOPSAILS	AIMNOOTY	MYOTONIA
AILNNOSS	SOLANINS	AILOPSTT	TALIPOTS	AIMNOPRS	RAMPIONS
AILNNOST	ANTLIONS	AILOQSTU	ALIQUOTS	AIMNOPRT	PROTAMIN
AILNNOSU	UNISONAL	AILORSST	ORALISTS	AIMNOPST	MAINTOPS
AILNNOTU	LUNATION		SLIOTARS		PTOMAINS
AILNNOTV	NONVITAL		SOLARIST		TAMPIONS
AILNNPRU	PINNULAR	AILORSTU	SUTORIAL	AIMNOPTV	PIVOTMAN
AILNNPSU	PINNULAS	AILORSTY	ROYALIST	AIMNOQRU	MAROQUIN
AILNNPTU	UNPLIANT		SOLITARY	AIMNORSU	MAINOURS
AILNNSTU	INSULANT	AILORSUW	WOURALIS	AIMNORTY	MINATORY
AILNOOPT	NOPALITO	AILORSVY	SAVORILY	AIMNOSST	STASIMON
	OPTIONAL	AILORTTU	TUTORIAL	AIMNOSTU	MANITOUS
AILNOOST	SOLATION	AILORTUV	OUTRIVAL		TINAMOUS
AILNOPPT	OPPILANT	AILOSSTT	ALTOISTS	AIMNOSTW	WOMANIST
AILNOPRU	UNIPOLAR	AILOSSTU	OUTSAILS	AIMNOTTU	MUTATION
AILNOPRV	PARVOLIN	AILOSTTT	TOTALIST	AIMNPRYY	PAYNIMRY
AILNOPSY	POLYNIAS	AILOTTTY	TOTALITY	AIMNPSTU	SUMPITAN
AILNOPTV	ANVILTOP	AILPPRUY	PUPILARY	AIMNRRSU	MURRAINS
AILNOPTY	PONYTAIL	AILPPSSU	SUIPLAPS	AIMNRSSU	SURAMINS
AILNOQSU	AQUILONS	AILPPSSY	PAYSLIPS		URANISMS
AILNORST	TONSILAR	AILPQSSU	PASQUILS	AIMNRSTT	TANTRISM
AILNORTZ	TRIZONAL	AILPRSSU	SPIRULAS		TRANSMIT
AILNOSSS	SASSOLIN		UPRISALS	AIMNRSTU	NATRIUMS
AILNOSTY	LANOSITY	AILPRSTU	STIPULAR		NATURISM

AIMNRSTV	VARMINTS	AINOPSSS	PASSIONS	AIORSSST	ASSISTOR
AIMNRSUU	URANIUMS	AINOPSTT	POSTNATI	AIORSSTU	SAUTOIRS
AIMNSSTU	TSUNAMIS	AINOPSTU	OPUNTIAS	AIORSSUV	SAVIOURS
AIMNSSYZ	ZANYISMS		UTOPIANS	AIORSTTU	TOURISTA
AIMNSTTU	ANTISMUT	AINOPSTW	SWAPTION	AIORSTTV	VOTARIST
AIMOPRSS	PROSAISM	AINOPTTU	OUTPAINT	AIORSTUV	VIRTUOSA
AIMOPRST	ATROPISM	AINOPTWY	WAYPOINT	AIOSSSTY	ISOSTASY
	PASTROMI	AINOQRRU	QUARRION	AIOSTTUW	OUTWAITS
AIMOPSST	IMPASTOS	AINOQRSU	NARQUOIS	AIPPRSTY	PAPISTRY
AIMOPSSY	SYMPOSIA	AINORRSW	WARRISON	AIPRSSTU	UPSTAIRS
AIMORRST	ARMORIST	AINORRTT	NITRATOR	AIPRSSTY	SPARSITY
AIMORRSU	ORARIUMS	AINORRTU	URINATOR	AIPYZZZZ	PIZZAZZY
	ROSARIUM	AINORSST	ARSONIST	AIRRSTTY	ARTISTRY
AIMORRUV	VARIORUM	AINORSSW	WARISONS	AIRRSTZZ	RIZZARTS
AIMORSST	AMORISTS	AINORSTT	STRONTIA	AIRSSSTT	TSARISTS
AIMORSSU	OSSARIUM	AINORSTU	RAINOUTS	AIRSSTTT	ATTRISTS
AIMORSTT	TRITOMAS		SUTORIAN	AIRSSTTU	TURISTAS
AIMORSTY	RAMOSITY	AINORSTW	WAITRONS	AIRSSTTZ	TZARISTS
AIMOSSTT	ATOMISTS	AINORSTX	TRIAXONS	AISSSTTT	STATISTS
	SOMATIST	AINORTVY	VANITORY	AJKMNSTU	MUNTJAKS
AIMPPRUU	PUPARIUM	AINOSSSU	SUASIONS	AJKNNOOU	JUNKANOO
AIMPPSST	MAPPISTS	AINOSSTT	STATIONS	AJLNORSU	JOURNALS
AIMPRSST	MISPARTS	AINOSSVY	SYNOVIAS	AJMNNOOR	NONMAJOR
AIMPRSTY	PARTYISM	AINOSTTU	TITANOUS	AJMRSTUY	JURYMAST
AIMRSSST	TSARISMS	AINPPRSS	PARSNIPS	AJORRTUY	JURATORY
AIMRSSTT	MISSTART	AINPPRTT	TRIPPANT	AKKLRSSY	SKYLARKS
AIMRSSTU	MATSURIS	AINPRSST	SPIRANTS	AKKLSSWY	SKYWALKS
AIMRSSTY	SYMITARS		SPRAINTS	AKKMOOST	TOKOMAKS
AIMRSSTZ	TZARISMS	AINPRSTT	TRIPTANS	AKKORSTW	TASKWORK
AIMRSTTU	STRIATUM	AINPRSTU	PURITANS	AKKOSUVZ	KUVASZOK
AIMRTTUY	MATURITY		UPTRAINS	AKLLMRUY	MULLARKY
AIMSSSTT	STATISMS	AINPSSST	PISSANTS	AKLMNOOW	MOONWALK
AINNNOST	SANTONIN	AINPSSSY	SYNAPSIS	AKLMNOPT	PLANKTON
AINNOOTT	NOTATION	AINPSSTU	PUISSANT	AKLOPRSW	LAPWORKS
AINNOOTV	NOVATION	AINPSTTU	PANTSUIT	AKLORSTW	SALTWORK
AINNOOTZ	ZONATION	AINQRSTU	QUINTARS	AKLOSTTU	OUTTALKS
AINNOPRT	ANTIPORN	AINQSSSU	QUASSINS	AKLOSTUW	OUTWALKS
AINNOPSS	SAPONINS	AINQTTUY	QUANTITY		WALKOUTS
AINNOPST	PINTANOS	AINRSSTT	STRAINTS	AKLPRRSU	LARKSPUR
AINNOSST	ONANISTS		TRANSITS	AKMMNOOR	MONOMARK
AINNOTTU	NUTATION	AINRSTTT	TITRANTS	AKMNOOOT	TOKONOMA
AINNPSST	SNAPTINS	AINRSTTU	ANTIRUST	AKMNOOPU	MOKOPUNA
AINNPSTU	UNPAINTS		NATURIST	AKMNRSTU	TRANKUMS
AINNQSTU	QUINNATS	AINRSTTY	TANISTRY	AKMOORST	MOOKTARS
	QUINTANS	AINSSSTU	SUSTAINS	AKMOPRST	POSTMARK
AINNRSTT	INTRANTS	AIOOORRT	ORATORIO	AKMORSST	OSTMARKS
AINNRSTU	INSURANT	AIOORRSW	WOORARIS	AKMQSTUU	KUMQUATS
AINNRSTY	TYRANNIS	AIOORSUV	OVARIOUS	AKMRSSTU	MUSKRATS
AINNSSTT	INSTANTS	AIOPRRST	AIRPORTS	AKNOORST	OSTRAKON
AINNSSTU	UNSAINTS		PARITORS	AKNOOUYZ	YOKOZUNA
AINNSTTY	NYSTATIN	AIOPRRTT	PORTRAIT	AKNOPSTW	SWANKPOT
AINOOPTT	POTATION	AIOPRRST	AIRPOSTS	AKNORSTU	OUTRANKS
AINOORRS	ORARIONS		AIRSTOPS	AKOPRRSU	PARKOURS
AINOORST	ORATIONS		PROSAIST	AKOPRRTW	PARTWORK
AINOORTT	ROTATION		PROTASIS	AKORRSTW	ARTWORKS
AINOOSTT	OSTINATO	AIOPRSTT	PATRIOTS	AKORRSWW	WARWORKS
AINOOSTV	OVATIONS	AIOPRSUV	PAVIOURS	AKORSWWX	WAXWORKS
AINOOTTV	OTTAVINO	AIOPSSTT	PASTITSO	AKOSSTTU	OUTTASKS
AINOPPRT	PARPOINT	AIOPSTTU	UTOPIAST	ALLLOSWY	SALLOWLY
AINOPPST	APPOINTS	AIORRRSW	WARRIORS	ALLLPPUY	PULPALLY
AINOPPTU	PUPATION	AIORRSST	TRAITORS	ALLLPRUY	PLURALLY
AINOPRSS	PARISONS	AIORRSTV	VARISTOR	ALLMNORY	NORMALLY
AINOPRST	ATROPINS	AIORRTTT	TITRATOR	ALLMNOSY	ALLONYMS
AINOPRTV	PROVIANT	AIORRTWY	RYOTWARI	ALLMNPSU	PULLMANS

ALLMOPSX	SMALLPOX	ALNOPRTY	PATRONLY	AMNOOTWY	TOYWOMAN
ALLMORTY	MORTALLY	ALNOPSTU	OUTPLANS	AMNOOTXY	TAXONOMY
ALLMOUWY	MULLOWAY	ALNOPSYY	POLYNYAS	AMNOPRSW	SPANWORM
ALLMPRUU	PLUMULAR	ALNORRWY	NARROWLY	AMNOPRSY	PARONYMS
ALLMTUUY	MUTUALLY	ALNORSVY	SOVRANLY	AMNOPRYY	PARONYMY
ALLNNOOY	NONLOYAL	ALNPPSTU	SUPPLANT	AMNOPSTU	PANTOUMS
ALLNNOUY	NOUNALLY	ALNRRTUU	NURTURAL	AMNORSST	TRANSOMS
ALLNOOPS	PLANOSOL	ALNRTTUY	TRUANTLY	AMNORSTU	ROMAUNTS
ALLNORSS	LASSLORN	ALOOPPRS	PROPOSAL	AMNORSTY	STRAMONY
ALLOOSST	LATOSOLS	ALOOPRST	POSTORAL	AMNOSSYZ	ZYMOSANS
ALLOOSTX	AXOLOTLS	ALOOPRTU	UPROOTAL	AMNOSTUY	AUTONYMS
ALLOPRSY	PAYROLLS	ALOORSUV	VALOROUS	AMNOTTUY	TAUTONYM
ALLOPSTY	POSTALLY	ALOORTYZ	ZOOLATRY	AMNRSTTU	TANTRUMS
ALLOPTYY	ALLOTYPY	ALOPPRSU	POPULARS	AMOOORSS	AMOROSOS
ALLORSST	ALLSORTS	ALOPPRYY	POLYPARY	AMOOPRSS	PROSOMAS
ALLORSWY	ROLLWAYS	ALOPPSSU	SUPPOSAL	AMOOPRST	TAPROOMS
ALLORTUW	ULTRALOW	ALOPPSUU	PAPULOUS	AMOORRTY	MORATORY
ALLORTWW	WALLWORT	ALOPRRSU	PARLOURS	AMOORSTZ	SMORZATO
ALLOSSWW	SWALLOWS		SPORULAR	AMOORTWY	MOTORWAY
ALLOSTWY	TOLLWAYS	ALOPRSTT	PORTLAST	AMOOSSTU	ASTOMOUS
ALLRUUVY	UVULARLY	ALOPRSTU	POSTURAL	AMOOSTVY	VASOTOMY
ALMMNRUU	NUMMULAR		PULSATOR	AMOOTTUY	AUTOTOMY
ALMMORTW	MALTWORM	ALOPRSTY	PASTORLY	AMOPRRST	MARSPORT
ALMNNOOR	NONMORAL	ALOPSSSU	SPOUSALS	AMOPRRSY	PAROXYSM
ALMNOOPS	LAMPOONS	ALOPSSUV	VOLUSPAS	AMOPSSTT	TOPMASTS
ALMNOPSS	PLASMONS	ALOPSTUU	PATULOUS	AMOQSSUU	SQUAMOUS
ALMNORTY	MATRONLY	ALOPSTUY	OUTPLAYS	AMORRTUY	MORTUARY
ALMNOSSU	SOLANUMS	ALOQRRSU	RORQUALS	AMORSTTU	OUTSMART
ALMNPSSU	SUNLAMPS	ALOQRSSU	SQUALORS	AMORSWWX	WAXWORMS
ALMOOPRS	PROSOMAL	ALORRSUY	SURROYAL	AMORTTUY	MUTATORY
ALMOOPRY	PLAYROOM	ALORSTTW	SALTWORT	AMPRSSUW	UPSWARMS
ALMOOPSY	POLYOMAS	ALORSTWW	AWLWORTS	AMPRSTYY	SYMPATRY
ALMOORTU	ALUMROOT	ALORSUVY	SAVOURLY	AMRRSSTU	RASTRUMS
ALMOPPST	LAMPPOST	ALORTUWY	OUTLAWRY	AMRSSTTU	STRATUMS
	PALMTOPS	ALOSSTTU	OUTLASTS	ANNNOSSY	SYNANONS
ALMOPRST	MARPLOTS	ALOSSTXY	OXYSALTS	ANNOOQTU	NONQUOTA
ALMORSUU	RAMULOUS	ALPPSTUY	PLATYPUS	ANNOORST	SONORANT
ALMORSUY	RAMOUSLY	ALPRSSUU	PURSUALS	ANNOPRTY	NONPARTY
ALMOSTTU	MULATTOS	ALPRSTUU	PUSTULAR	ANNOPSST	NONPASTS
ALMPRSTU	PLASTRUM	ALRSSSUU	RUSSULAS	ANNOSSTU	STANNOUS
ALMPSSTY	SYMPLAST	AMMNOORT	MOTORMAN	ANNPRSUY	SPUNYARN
ALMRRTYY	MARTYRLY	AMMNOPSS	PSAMMONS	ANOOPRRT	PRONATOR
ALMRTUUY	TUMULARY	AMMNPTUY	TYMPANUM	ANOOPRSS	SOPRANOS
ALMSSSUY	ALYSSUMS	AMMOORRS	MAORMORS	ANOOPRST	PATROONS
ALNNNOOT	NONTONAL		MORMAORS	ANOORSST	SANTOORS
ALNNOOPR	NONPOLAR	AMMOPSTU	POMATUMS	ANOORSSU	ARSONOUS
ALNNOORS	NONSOLAR	AMMORRWY	ARMYWORM	ANOORSTT	ARNOTTOS
ALNNOORY	NONROYAL	AMNNOOSX	MONAXONS		RATTOONS
ALNNOPSY	NONPLAYS	AMNNOOTT	MONTANTO	ANOORSUU	ANOUROUS
ALNNORRU	NONRURAL	AMNNORSW	MANSWORN	ANOPPPRT	PROPPANT
ALNNOTWY	WANTONLY	AMNNORSY	MANSONRY	ANOPRRSS	SPORRANS
ALNNRSSU	UNSNARLS	AMNNOSTT	MONTANTS	ANOPRSTU	STROUPAN
ALNOOPPR	PROPANOL	AMNNOSTW	TOWNSMAN	ANOPRSTV	PROVANTS
ALNOOPRS	POLARONS	AMNNOSTY	ANTONYMS	ANOPRTTU	TRAPUNTO
ALNOOPRT	PORTOLAN	AMNNOSUW	UNWOMANS	ANOPSSTU	OUTSPANS
	PRONOTAL	AMNNOTTU	MOUNTANT	ANOQRSSU	SQUARSON
ALNOOPST	PLATOONS	AMNNOTVY	ANTONYMY	ANORSSTU	SANTOURS
ALNOOPSV	VANPOOLS	AMNNPSTU	PUNTSMAN	ANORSTVY	SOVRANTY
ALNOOPXY	POLYAXON	AMNNSSTU	STANNUMS	ANORSUVY	UNSAVORY
ALNOOPYZ	POLYZOAN	AMNNSTTU	STUNTMAN	ANOTTUUV	OUTVAUNT
ALNOOPZZ	POZZOLAN	AMNOOPPS	POMPANOS	ANPPSSUW	SUPPAWNS
ALNOORST	ORTOLANS	AMNOOSTT	OTTOMANS	ANPRSSTU	SUNTRAPS
ALNOPRST	PLASTRON	AMNOOSTZ	MATZOONS		UNSTRAPS
ALNOPRTU	PORTULAN	AMNOOTUY	AUTONOMY	ANPRSTUU	PURSUANT

ANRRSTUY	UNSTARRY	BBBGILNU	BLUBBING	BBDEILLR	BELLBIRD
ANRRTTUY	TRUANTRY		BUBBLING	BBDEILQU	QUIBBLED
ANRSSSTU	SUNSTARS	BBBHNOOY	HOBNOBBY	BBDEILRR	DRIBBLER
ANRSSTYY	SYNASTRY	BBBHOOUU	HUBBUBOO	BBDEILRS	DIBBLERS
AOOOPRST	SOAPROOT	BBBIOSTT	BOBBITTS		DRIBBLES
AOOOPRSZ	SPOROZOA	BBBOOSXY	BOBBYSOX	BBDEILRT	DRIBBLET
AOOOPRTZ	PROTOZOA	BBCCIKOS	BIBCOCKS	BBDEILRU	BLUEBIRD
AOOPPRSY	APOSPORY	BBCDEILR	CRIBBLED	BBDEIMOV	DIVEBOMB
AOOPRSSU	SAPOROUS	BBCDERSU	SCRUBBED	BBDEINOR	RIBBONED
AOOPRSTT	TAPROOTS	BBCDIMOY	BOMBYCID	BBDEINRU	UNRIBBED
AOOPRSTU	ATROPOUS	BBCEEHOS	BOBECHES	BBDEIQSU	SQUIBBED
AOOPRSTW	SOAPWORT	BBCEHINS	NEBBICHS	BBDEIRRS	DRIBBERS
AOOPRSUV	VAPOROUS	BBCEHIRU	CHUBBIER	BBDEKLNO	KNOBBLED
AOOPRTTY	POTATORY	BBCEILRS	CRIBBLES	BBDEKLNU	KNUBBLED
AOORRSTT	ROTATORS		SCRIBBLE	BBDELLMU	DUMBBELL
AOORRSTU	OUTROARS	BBCEILRU	CLUBBIER	BBDELLOO	BOBOLLED
AOORRTTY	ROTATORY	BBCEIOST	COBBIEST	BBDELOOS	BEBLOODS
AOORSSTU	OUTSOARS	BBCEIRRS	CRIBBERS	BBDELOSS	BOBSLEDS
AOORSSUV	SAVOROUS	BBCEKKOS	KEBBOCKS	BBDELSTU	STUBBLED
AOORSTUV	OUTSAVOR	BBCEKKSU	KEBBUCKS	BBDENRUU	UNRUBBED
AOPPRRST	RAPPORTS	BBCEKLSU	BLESBUCK	BBDERRSU	DRUBBERS
AOPPRSST	PASSPORT	BBCEKLUU	BLUEBUCK	BBDERSUU	SUBURBED
AOPPRSTU	TRAPPOUS	BBCELORS	CLOBBERS	BBDFLSUU	FLUBDUBS
AOPRRRTY	PARROTRY		COBBLERS	BBDGIILN	DIBBLING
AOPRRSSW	SPARROWS	BBCELORY	COBBLERY	BBDGIINR	DRIBBING
AOPRRSTY	PORTRAYS	BBCELRSU	CLUBBERS	BBDGINRU	DRUBBING
AOPRRTUY	POURTRAY	BBCEMNOU	BUNCOMBE	BBDGINSU	DUBBINGS
AOPRSSTT	STARSPOT	BBCERRSU	SCRUBBER	BBDIIKMU	DIBBUKIM
AOPRSTTU	OUTPARTS	BBCGHIIN	CHIBBING	BBDIKMUY	DYBBUKIM
AOPRSTTY	PYROSTAT	BBCGIINR	CRIBBING	BBDIOORS	BOOBIRDS
AOPRSTUY	OUTPRAYS	BBCGILNO	COBBLING	BBDOSUYY	BUSYBODY
AOPSSSTU	PASSOUTS	BBCGILNU	CLUBBING	BBEEEMSX	BEMBEXES
AOPSSTWY	WAYPOSTS	BBCGINSU	CUBBINGS	BBEEERRS	BERBERES
AOPSTTUU	AUTOPUTS	BBCHILSU	CLUBBISH	BBEEERSU	BEBEERUS
AOPTTUYY	AUTOTYPY	BBCHILUY	CHUBBILY	BBEEHINS	NEBBISHE
AORRSSSU	ASSURORS	BBCHKOOS	BOSCHBOK	BBEEHLOW	BOBWHEEL
AORRSTTW	STARWORT	BBCHKSUU	BUSHBUCK	BBEEIIRR	BERIBERI
AORRTTWW	WARTWORT	BBCILLUY	CLUBBILY	BBEEILPR	PEBBLIER
AORSSTTU	STRATOUS	BBCILMSU	CLUBBISM		PLEBBIER
AORSSTTY	STAROSTY	BBCILRSY	SCRIBBLY	BBEEIMSX	BEMBIXES
AORSTTTU	OUTSTART	BBCILSTU	CLUBBIST	BBEEIMTT	BIMBETTE
AORSUVVY	VOUVRAYS	BBCIPSUU	SUBPUBIC	BBEEINRR	BERBERIN
AOSSTTUY	OUTSTAYS	BBCKLOSU	SUBBLOCK	BBEEIRRS	BERBERIS
APPRRSUU	PURPURAS	BBDDEEIR	DIBBERED	BBEEISTW	WEBBIEST
APRRSTUY	PURTRAYS	BBDDEEMO	DEMOBBED	BBEEJLMU	BEJUMBLE
APRSSTTU	STARTUPS	BBDDEEMU	BEDUMBED	BBEELLLU	BLUEBELL
	UPSTARTS	BBDDEERU	REDUBBED	BBEEOPPR	BEBOPPER
APRSSUWY	SPURWAYS	BBDDEILR	DRIBBLED	BBEFILRR	FRIBBLER
ASVYYZZZ	ZYZZYVAS	BBDDENUU	UNDUBBED	BBEFILRS	FRIBBLES
BBBCEOWY	COBWEBBY	BBDEEGIR	GIBBERED	BBEFILRT	FLIBBERT
BBBDEEKO	KEBOBBED	BBDEEGIT	GIBBETED	BBEFIMOR	FIREBOMB
BBBDEEOR	BEROBBED	BBDEEIJR	JIBBERED	BBEFISTU	FUBBIEST
BBBDENOU	UNBOBBED	BBDEEIST	DEBBIEST	BBEFLRSU	FLUBBERS
BBBEGILN	BLEBBING		EBBTIDES	BBEGIIST	GIBBSITE
BBBEILOR	BLOBBIER	BBDEEMNU	BENUMBED	BBEGILNP	PEBBLING
	BOBBLIER	BBDEENUW	UNWEBBED	BBEGILOR	GLOBBIER
BBBEILRU	BUBBLIER	BBDEEOPP	BEBOPPED	BBEGILRS	GRIBBLES
BBBEILSU	BUBBLIES	BBDEERRU	RUBBERED	BBEGILRY	GLIBBERY
BBBEINOT	BOBBINET	BBDEERSU	SUBBREED	BBEGILST	GLIBBEST
BBBELRSU	BLUBBERS	BBDEFILR	FRIBBLED	BBEGINNS	SNEBBING
	BUBBLERS	BBDEGLRU	GRUBBLED	BBEGINSW	WEBBINGS
BBBELRUY	BLUBBERY	BBDEHORT	THROBBED	BBEGIOST	GOBBIEST
BBBGILNO	BLOBBING	BBDEHRSU	SHRUBBED	BBEGIRRU	GRUBBIER
	BOBBLING	BBDEILLN	BELLBIND	BBEGLORS	GOBBLERS

BBEGLRSU	GRUBBLES	BBELOTUW	BLOWTUBE	BBIKLNOO	BOBOLINK
BBEGRRSU	GRUBBERS	BBELRRSU	BURBLERS	BBILLOVY	BILLYBOY
BBEHINSY	NEBBISHY	BBELRSSU	SLUBBERS	BBILLSUU	LULIBUBS
BBEHIOTW	BOBWHITE	BBELSSTU	STUBBLES	BBILMOSY	LOBBYISM
BBEHLORS	HOBBLERS	BBEMOSXY	BOMBYXES	BBILNOSY	SNOBBILY
BBEHLSUU	BLUEBUSH	BBENORSY	SNOBBERY	BBILOSTY	LOBBYIST
BBEHMSTU	BETHUMBS	BBENRSSU	SNUBBERS	BBILOSUU	BIBULOUS
BBEHORRT	THROBBER	BBEORRXY	BOXBERRY	BBILRSTU	BLURBIST
BBEIILRS	RIBIBLES	BBEORSSW	SWOBBERS	BBILSTUY	STUBBILY
BBEIIMRS	IMBIBERS	BBEPRSUW	BREWPUBS	BBIMMOSS	MOBBISMS
BBEIIRST	RIBBIEST	BBFGILNU	FLUBBING	BBIMNOSS	SNOBBISM
BBEIKNOR	KNOBBIER	BBGGIILN	GLIBBING	BBIMOOSY	BOOBYISM
BBEIKNRU	KNUBBIER	BBGGILNO	GOBBLING	BBIMOSSY	YOBBISMS
BBEILLLU	BLUEBILL	BBGGINRU	GRUBBING	BBINORRY	RIBBONRY
BBEILLNO	BONIBELL	BBGHILNO	HOBBLING	BBJLOOSW	BLOWJOBS
BBEILNRS	NIBBLERS	BBGIIIMN	IMBIBING	BBKLOOSU	BLOUBOKS
BBEILNRU	NUBBLIER	BBGIIJNS	JIBBINGS	BBKOOOOS	BOOBOOKS
BBEILORS	SLOBBIER	BBGIIKLN	KIBBLING	BBLLNNUU	BULNBULN
BBEILORW	WOBBLIER	BBGIILMN	BLIMBING	BBLLOUYY	BULLYBOY
BBEILOST	BIBELOTS	BBGIILNN	NIBBLING	BBNOORSU	BOURBONS
BBEILOSW	WOBBLIES	BBGIILNW	WIBBLING	BBNORSTU	STUBBORN
BBEILPRS	PRIBBLES	BBGIINNS	SNIBBING	BBOOSSSY	BOSSBOYS
BBEILQRU	QUIBBLER	BBGIINRS	RIBBINGS	BCCCIILY	BICYCLIC
BBEILQSU	QUIBBLES	BBGIJNOS	JOBBINGS	BCCDEILY	BICYCLED
BBEILRRU	BURBLIER	BBGIKNNO	KNOBBING	BCCDHIKO	DOBCHICK
	RUBBLIER	BBGILLSU	BILLBUGS	BCCDIKOR	COCKBIRD
BBEILRRY	BILBERRY	BBGILMNO	MOBBLING	BCCEEIRR	CEREBRIC
BBEILRST	STIBBLER	BBGILMNU	BUMBLING	BCCEHIRU	CHERUBIC
	TRIBBLES	BBGILNNO	NOBBLING	BCCEHORS	BESCORCH
BBEILRSU	SLUBBIER	BBGILNNU	NUBBLING	BCCEIIIS	CICISBEI
BBEILSST	STIBBLES	BBGILNOW	WOBBLING	BCCEIILO	LIBECCIO
BBEIMMOT	TIMEBOMB	BBGILNOY	LOBBYING	BCCEIIOS	CICISBEO
BBEIMNOS	BOMBESIN	BBGILNRU	BLURBING	BCCEILOS	ECBOLICS
BBEIMOST	BOMBSITE		BURBLING	BCCEILOY	BIOCYCLE
BBEIMRSU	BRUMBIES		RUBBLING	BCCEILRU	CRUCIBLE
BBEINORS	SNOBBIER	BBGILNSU	SLUBBING	BCCEILRY	BICYCLER
BBEINOST	NOBBIEST	BBGILRUY	GRUBBILY	BCCEILSU	CUBICLES
BBEINRSU	SNUBBIER	BBGIMNOS	BOMBINGS	BCCEILSY	BICYCLES
BBEINSTU	NUBBIEST		MOBBINGS	BCCEMORS	CROMBECS
BBEIOOST	BOBOTIES	BBGINNSU	SNUBBING	BCCEMRUU	CUCUMBER
BBEIORTU	OUTBRIBE	BBGINOSS	SOBBINGS	BCCHIKOY	BOYCHICK
BBEIRSTU	STUBBIER	BBGINOST	STOBBING	BCCIIMOR	MICROBIC
	SUBTRIBE	BBGINOSW	SWOBBING	BCCIISTU	CUBISTIC
BBEISSTU	STUBBIES	BBGINRSU	RUBBINGS	BCCIITUY	CUBICITY
BBEISTTU	TUBBIEST	BBGINSSU	SUBBINGS	BCCIKLLO	COCKBILL
BBEKLNOS	KNOBBLES	BBGINSTU	STUBBING	BCCILMOU	COLUMBIC
BBEKLNSU	KNUBBLES		TUBBINGS	BCCILOOR	BROCCOLI
BBEKLOOU	BLUEBOOK	BBGLOOWY	LOBBYGOW	BCCILOSU	BUCOLICS
BBEKLOSS	BLESBOKS	BBHILOSS	SLOBBISH	BCCINORR	CORNCRIB
BBEKLSUU	BUBUKLES	BBHIMOSY	HOBBYISM	BCCIRTUU	CUCURBIT
BBEKNOOT	BONTEBOK	BBHINOSS	SNOBBISH	BCCLOOOO	COCOBOLO
BBEKNORS	KNOBBERS	BBHINSSU	SNUBBISH	BCCMOOSX	COXCOMBS
BBELLOSY	BELLBOYS	BBHIOOSY	BOOBYISH	BCCMSSUU	SUCCUMBS
BBELLRUY	LUBBERLY	BBHIORTY	HOBBITRY	BCCNOORS	CORNCOBS
BBELLSTU	BULBLETS	BBHIOSTY	HOBBYIST	BCCSSUUU	SUCCUBUS
BBELMOST	BOMBLETS	BBHIRSUY	RUBBISHY	BCDDEEEK	BEDECKED
BBELMRSU	BUMBLERS	BBHKOOSS	BOSHBOKS	BCDDEEKU	BEDUCKED
BBELNORS	NOBBLERS	BBHOOSUW	WHOOBUBS	BCDDEENU	BEDUNCED
BBELOORW	BOBOWLER	BBHRSSUU	SUBSHRUB	BCDDEHIL	CHILDBED
BBELORSS	SLOBBERS	BBIIILMS	BILIMBIS	BCDDESUU	SUBDUCED
BBELORSU	BOERBULS	BBIILLSU	SILLIBUB	BCDEEEHR	BREECHED
BBELORSW	WOBBLERS	BBIILSST	BIBLISTS	BCDEEGLU	BECUDGEL
BBELORSY	LOBBYERS	BBIJMOOS	JIBBOOMS	BCDEEHLN	BLENCHED
	SLOBBERY	BBIKLLOO	BILLBOOK	BCDEEHNR	BEDRENCH

BCDEEHOU	DEBOUCHE	BCDIMOOR	COMORBID	BCEGKMSU	GEMSBUCK
BCDEEIKN	BENEDICK	BCDIMORS	SCOMBRID	BCEGLNOO	CONGLOBE
BCDEEIKR	BICKERED	BCDINOSW	COWBINDS	BCEHIIOT	BIOETHIC
BCDEEILR	CREDIBLE	BCDINRUU	RUBICUND	BCEHIIRT	BITCHIER
BCDEEILS	DECIBELS	BCDIORSW	COWBIRDS	BCEHILMY	CHIMBLEY
BCDEEILU	EDUCIBLE	BCDKNOOO	BOONDOCK	BCEHIMOR	BICHROME
BCDEEIMR	BECRIMED	BCDKORSU	BURDOCKS	BCEHIMRS	BESMIRCH
BCDEEINT	BENEDICT	BCDSSTUU	SUBDUCTS	BCEHIMRU	CHERUBIM
BCDEEIPS	BESPICED	BCEEEFIN	BENEFICE	BCEHINNO	CHINBONE
BCDEEIRS	DESCRIBE	BCEEEFKN	NECKBEEF	BCEHINRU	BUNCHIER
	ESCRIBED	BCEEEHIR	BEECHIER		CHERUBIN
BCDEEIST	BISECTED	BCEEEHRS	BREECHES	BCEHINSU	SUBNICHE
BCDEEJOT	OBJECTED	BCEEENRS	BESCREEN	BCEHIORS	BRIOCHES
BCDEEKMO	BEMOCKED	BCEEERSU	BERCEUSE	BCEHIORT	BOTCHIER
BCDEEKNO	BECKONED	BCEEFILN	FENCIBLE	BCEHIOST	BIOTECHS
BCDEEKRU	REEDBUCK	BCEEFKLS	BEFLECKS	BCEHIRRT	BRICHTER
BCDEEKTU	BUCKETED	BCEEFLTU	CLUBFEET	BCEHIRST	BRITCHES
BCDEELNU	BEUNCLED	BCEEGIRS	ICEBERGS	BCEHIRTY	BITCHERY
BCDEELOR	CORBELED	BCEEHINR	BENCHIER	BCEHLOST	BLOTCHES
BCDEELRU	BECURLED	BCEEHKSU	BUCKSHEE	BCEHLRSU	BLUCHERS
BCDEEMOR	RECOMBED	BCEEHLNR	BLENCHER	BCEHMSTU	BESMUTCH
BCDEENSU	BEDUNCES	BCEEHLNS	BLENCHES	BCEHNOPT	BENCHTOP
BCDEEORV	BEDCOVER	BCEEHLOT	BECLOTHE	BCEHNNRU	BRUNCHER
BCDEEOTT	OBTECTED	BCEEHLRS	BELCHERS	BCEHNRSU	BRUNCHES
BCDEERSU	BECURSED	BCEEHNRS	BENCHERS	BCEHOORS	BROOCHES
BCDEHINS	DISBENCH	BCEEHNRU	UNBREECH	BCEHOPSU	SUBEPOCH
BCDEHLOT	BLOTCHED	BCEEHNTU	BEECHNUT	BCEHORRU	BROCHURE
BCDEHNRU	BRUNCHED	BCEEHOSU	BOUCHEES	BCEHORSS	BORSCHES
BCDEHOOR	BROOCHED	BCEEIILM	IMBECILE	BCEHORST	BOTCHERS
BCDEIIOS	BIOCIDES	BCEEIKRR	BICKERER	BCEHORSW	COWHERBS
BCDEIIRR	RICEBIRD	BCEEILNR	BERNICLE	BCEHORTY	BOTCHERY
BCDEIITU	DECUBITI	BCEEIMRS	BECRIMES	BCEHRSTU	BUTCHERS
BCDEIKRR	REDBRICK	BCEEINOT	CENOBITE	BCEHRTUY	BUTCHERY
BCDEIKSS	SICKBEDS	BCEEIOSX	ICEBOXES	BCEHSTTU	BUTCHEST
BCDEIKST	BEDTICKS	BCEEIPSS	BESPICES	BCEIIKLN	ICEBLINK
BCDEILRY	CREDIBLY		BICEPSES	BCEIIKRR	BRICKIER
BCDEIMNO	COMBINED	BCEEIRSS	ESCRIBES	BCEIIKRS	BRICKIES
BCDEINOU	ICEBOUND	BCEEIRTT	BRETTICE	BCEIILMS	MISCIBLE
BCDEIRSU	CURBSIDE	BCEEJORT	REOBJECT	BCEIILNV	VINCIBLE
BCDEKOOO	CODEBOOK	BCEEKNOR	BECKONER	BCEIILOP	EPIBOLIC
BCDEKORS	BEDROCKS	BCEEKNSU	BUCKEENS	BCEIIMRS	IMBRICES
BCDEKOSS	BEDSOCKS	BCEEKSUY	BUCKEYES	BCEIINRS	INSCRIBE
BCDELMRU	CRUMBLED	BCEELLOT	BELLCOTE	BCEIKLMO	COMBLIKE
BCDELMSU	SCUMBLED	BCEELOOR	BORECOLE	BCEIKLMS	LIMBECKS
BCDELOSU	BECLOUDS	BCEELOSU	BOUCLEES	BCEIKLOO	BOOKLICE
BCDEMNOU	UNCOMBED	BCEELRTU	TUBERCLE	BCEIKLOR	BLOCKIER
BCDEMOOY	COEMBODY	BCEEMMOR	COMEMBER	BCEIKLOS	BLOCKIES
BCDEMORY	CORYMBED	BCEEMNRU	ENCUMBER	BCEIKLRS	BRICKLES
BCDENRUU	UNCURBED	BCEEMRRU	CEREBRUM	BCEIKLTU	BLUETICK
BCDEOORT	CODEBTOR		CUMBERER	BCEIKSST	BESTICKS
BCDEOOWY	COWBOYED	BCEENORS	OBSCENER	BCEILMRS	CLIMBERS
BCDEORSU	OBSCURED	BCEENRSU	CRUBEENS		RECLIMBS
BCDEORSW	BECROWDS	BCEEPRTY	CYBERPET	BCEILNOS	BINOCLES
BCDEOSSU	SUBCODES	BCEERSSU	BECURSES	BCEILNRU	RUNCIBLE
BCDESSUU	SUBDUCES	BCEERSTU	SUBERECT	BCEILNYZ	BENZYLIC
BCDHIRSU	BRUCHIDS	BCEERSXY	CYBERSEX	BCEILORS	BRICOLES
BCDHOOSU	CUBHOODS	BCEERTVY	BREVETCY		CORBEILS
BCDHORSU	SUBCHORD	BCEFFIIR	FEBRIFIC	BCEILOSU	CIBOULES
BCDIIMOR	BROMIDIC	BCEFHISU	SUBCHIEF	BCEILOTU	TUBICOLE
BCDIIPSU	BICUSPID	BCEFILOR	FORCIBLE	BCEILPRU	REPUBLIC
BCDIKLLU	DUCKBILL	BCEGHILN	BELCHING	BCEIMNOR	COMBINER
BCDILMOY	MOLYBDIC	BCEGHINN	BENCHING	BCEIMNOS	COMBINES
BCDILORU	COLUBRID	BCEGIINO	BIOGENIC	BCEIMNRU	INCUMBER
		BCEGIMNO	BECOMING	BCEIMORS	MICROBES

BCEIMOST	COMBIEST
BCEIMOSW	COMBWISE
BCEIMRRU	CRUMBIER
BCEINORS	BICORNES
BCEINORU	BOUNCIER
BCEINOVX	BICONVEX
BCEINRSU	BRUCINES
BCEIOOPS	BIOSCOPE
BCEIOOSS	SCOOBIES
BCEIORRS	CRIBROSE
BCEIORST	BISECTOR
BCEIRRSS	SCRIBERS
BCEIRSTU	BRUCITES
BCEIRTTY	YTTERBIC
BCEJOORT	OBJECTOR
BCEJSSTU	SUBJECTS
BCEKLLNU	BULLNECK
BCEKLLOS	BELLOCKS
BCEKLNOT	BLONCKET
BCEKLNUU	UNBUCKLE
BCEKLORS	BLOCKERS
BCEKLRSU	BUCKLERS
	SUBCLERK
BCEKMSTU	STEMBUCK
BCEKOORU	BUCKEROO
BCEKORST	BROCKETS
BCEKORSU	ROEBUCKS
BCEKOSTY	BYCOKETS
BCELLOSW	COWBELLS
BCELLRUW	WELLCURB
BCELLSSU	SUBCELLS
BCELMOSS	COMBLESS
BCELMRSU	CLUMBERS
	CRUMBLES
BCELMSSU	SCUMBLES
BCELNOSW	BECLOWNS
BCELRSSU	CURBLESS
BCEMRRSU	CRUMBERS
BCEMRSSU	SCUMBERS
BCENOOOX	ECONOBOX
BCENORSU	BOUNCERS
BCEORRSU	OBSCURER
BCEORRWY	COWBERRY
BCEORSSU	BESCOURS
	OBSCURES
BCERSSTU	BECRUSTS
BCESSSTU	SUBSECTS
BCESSTUU	SUBCUTES
BCFIIMOR	MORBIFIC
BCFIIORT	FIBROTIC
BCFILORY	FORCIBLY
BCFIMORU	CUBIFORM
BCFLOOTU	CLUBFOOT
BCFSSSUU	SUBFUSCS
BCGHIINR	BIRCHING
BCGHIINT	BITCHING
BCGHINNU	BUNCHING
BCGHINOR	BROCHING
BCGHINOT	BOTCHING
BCGHINPU	PINCHBUG
BCGHINTU	BUTCHING
BCGIIKNR	BRICKING
BCGIIKST	BIGSTICK
BCGIILMN	CLIMBING
BCGIILOO	BIOLOGIC
BCGIINRS	SCRIBING
BCGIKLNO	BLOCKING
BCGIKLNU	BUCKLING
BCGIKNSU	BUCKINGS
BCGILMNY	CYMBLING
BCGIMNOR	CROMBING
BCGIMNOS	COMBINGS
BCGIMNRU	CRUMBING
BCGIMNUU	CUMBUNGI
BCGINNOU	BOUNCING
	BUNCOING
BCGINORU	COURBING
BCGINRSU	CURBINGS
BCHIILTY	BITCHILY
BCHIIOPS	BIOCHIPS
BCHIIOST	COHIBITS
BCHIISSU	HIBISCUS
BCHIKLOS	BLOCKISH
BCHIKOSU	CHIBOUKS
BCHIKOSY	BOYCHIKS
BCHILNUY	BUNCHILY
BCHILOTY	BOTCHILY
BCHIOORY	CHOIRBOY
BCHIOPRS	PIBROCHS
BCHIORRT	BIRROTCH
BCHIOTTU	OUTBITCH
BCHKNORU	BUCKHORN
BCHKOSTU	BUCKSHOT
BCHLNOUX	LUNCHBOX
BCHLRSUU	CLUBRUSH
BCHNOORS	BRONCHOS
BCHNORSU	BRONCHUS
BCHORSST	BORSCHTS
BCIIILMU	UMBILICI
BCIIIOTT	BIOTITIC
BCIIKLNS	NIBLICKS
BCIILLSY	SIBYLLIC
BCIILMRU	LUMBRICI
BCIILMSU	BULIMICS
BCIILNVY	VINCIBLY
BCIILORS	COLIBRIS
BCIILOTY	BIOLYTIC
BCIIMNOO	BIONOMIC
BCIIMORU	CIBORIUM
BCIIMRSS	SCRIBISM
BCIINORT	BORNITIC
BCIINORV	VIBRONIC
BCIIOPTY	BIOTYPIC
BCIIORST	BISTROIC
	SORBITIC
BCIIOSTT	BISCOTTI
BCIISSTU	BISCUITS
BCIISTUY	BISCUITY
BCIKKNSU	BUCKSKIN
BCIKLOOT	BOOTLICK
BCIKLOST	LOBSTICK
BCIKORRW	CRIBWORK
BCIKOSTT	BITSTOCK
BCILLPUY	PUBLICLY
BCILMOSY	SYMBOLIC
BCILMOTU	OUTCLIMB
BCILMPSU	UPCLIMBS
BCILNOUY	BOUNCILY
BCILOORS	BICOLORS
	BROCOLIS
BCILOORU	BICOLOUR
BCIMORSU	MICROBUS
BCINORSU	BURSICON
	RUBICONS
BCINOSSU	SUBSONIC
BCINOSTU	SUBTONIC
BCINOSUU	INCUBOUS
BCINSTUU	SUBTUNIC
BCIOOPSY	BIOSCOPY
BCIOORST	ROBOTICS
BCIOOSTT	BISCOTTO
BCIOPSTU	SUBOPTIC
	SUBTOPIC
BCIORRSU	CRIBROUS
BCIORSST	CROSSBIT
BCISSTUU	SUBCUTIS
BCJKMSUU	JUMBUCKS
BCKKOOOO	COOKBOOK
BCKLLOOS	BOLLOCKS
BCKLLOSU	BULLOCKS
BCKLLOUY	BULLOCKY
BCKLNOSU	SUNBLOCK
	UNBLOCKS
BCKMMOSU	BUMMOCKS
BCKNNOOS	BONNOCKS
BCKOOOPY	COPYBOOK
BCKOSTTU	BUTTOCKS
BCLMOORU	CLUBROOM
BCLMOOSU	COULOMBS
BCLMOOTU	OUTCLOMB
BCLOORTU	CLUBROOT
BCLOOSSU	SUBCOOLS
BCLORSTU	CLOTBURS
BCLSSTUU	SUBCULTS
BCMMRSUU	CRUMBUMS
BCMORSUU	CUMBROUS
BCMOSSTU	COMBUSTS
BCNNOUUY	UNBOUNCY
BCOOORTW	CROWBOOT
BCOOPSYY	COPYBOYS
BCOORSSW	CROSSBOW
BCOOSTTY	BOYCOTTS
BCORSTTU	OBSTRUCT
BCRSSTUU	SUBCRUST
BCSTUUZZ	BUZZCUTS
BDDDDEEU	DEBUDDED
BDDDEEEM	EMBEDDED
BDDDEEIM	IMBEDDED
BDDDEEIR	DEBRIDED
BDDDEEMU	BEMUDDED
BDDDEENU	UNBEDDED
BDDDELOR	BRODDLED
BDDDENUU	UNBUDDED
BDDEEELL	DEBELLED
BDDEEERS	REEDBEDS
BDDEEESS	SEEDBEDS
BDDEEFIR	BIRDFEED
BDDEEFLU	BEFUDDLE
BDDEEGGU	DEBUGGED
BDDEEGIL	BEGILDED
BDDEEGIR	BEGIRDED

BDDEEGNU	BEDUNGED	BDEEEGNR	BREENGED	BDEEGMSU	BESMUDGE
BDDEEGTU	BUDGETED	BDEEEGRU	BUDGEREE	BDEEGOOY	BOOGEYED
BDDEEHOS	DEBOSHED	BDEEEHST	BEDSHEET	BDEEGORU	BEROUGED
BDDEEIMM	BEDIMMED	BDEEEHTU	HEBETUDE	BDEEGRSV	SVEDBERG
BDDEEIMO	EMBODIED	BDEEEILN	BEELINED	BDEEGRTU	BUDGETER
BDDEEINR	REBIDDEN	BDEEEILV	BELIEVED	BDEEGSSU	BUGSEEDS
BDDEEINT	INDEBTED	BDEEEINS	BENISEED	BDEEHISW	DWEEBISH
BDDEEINW	BINDWEED	BDEEEIRW	DWEEBIER	BDEEHLNO	BEHOLDEN
BDDEEIOR	REBODIED	BDEEEILR	REBELLED	BDEEHLOR	BEHOLDER
BDDEEIRR	REEDBIRD	BDEEEILV	BEVELLED	BDEEHLOW	BEHOWLED
BDDEEIRS	BIRDSEED	BDEEEILMM	EMBLEMED	BDEEHLSU	BUSHELED
	DEBRIDES	BDEEEILPT	BEPELTED	BDEEHMOR	HOMEBRED
BDDEEISS	BEDSIDES	BDEEEILRS	BLEEDERS	BDEEHMRY	BERHYMED
BDDEEKNU	DEBUNKED	BDEEEILRY	BERLEYED	BDEEHOOV	BEHOOVED
BDDEELMU	BEMUDDLE	BDEEEILUW	BLUEWEED	BDEEHORT	BOTHERED
BDDEELNO	BOLDENED	BDEEEMMR	MEMBERED	BDEEHORW	BEWHORED
BDDEENNU	UNBENDED	BDEEEMNS	BEDESMEN	BDEEHOSS	DEBOSHES
BDDEENOT	OBTENDED	BDEEEINTT	BENETTED	BDEEIILL	ELIDIBLE
BDDEENRU	BURDENED	BDEEEPSS	BESPEEDS	BDEEIILN	INEDIBLE
BDDEEORR	BORDERED	BDEEEIRRS	BREEDERS	BDEEIILR	BIELDIER
BDDEEORS	DESORBED		REBREEDS	BDEEIIPT	BEPITIED
BDDEEOSS	DEBOSSED	BDEEEIRRV	REVERBED	BDEEIKRS	KERBSIDE
BDDEEOTT	BEDOTTED	BDEEEIRTT	BETTERED	BDEEIKSS	BEKISSED
BDDEERRU	DEBURRED	BDEEEIRTV	BREVETED	BDEEIILLL	LIBELLED
BDDEESSU	DEBUSSED	BDEEEITTW	BEWETTED	BDEEIILLR	REBILLED
BDDEESTU	BEDUSTED	BDEEFFPU	BEPUFFED	BDEEIILLT	BILLETED
BDDEESUW	SUBDEWED	BDEEFFRU	BUFFERED	BDEEIILLU	ELUDIBLE
BDDEFOOR	FORBODED		REBUFFED	BDEEIILMO	BEMOILED
BDDEGINS	BEDDINGS	BDEEFFTU	BUFFETED		EMBOILED
BDDEIIMO	IMBODIED	BDEEFGGO	BEFOGGED	BDEEIILMP	BEDIMPLE
BDDEILNR	BRINDLED	BDEEFGIT	BEGIFTED	BDEEIILMR	LIMBERED
BDDEILOO	BLOODIED	BDEEFGLU	BEGULFED	BDEEIILMS	BESLIMED
BDDEINNU	UNBIDDEN	BDEEFILR	BELFRIED		BESMILED
BDDEINOU	UNBODIED	BDEEFINN	BEFINNED	BDEEIILNR	LINEBRED
BDDEINRU	UNDERBID	BDEEFINR	BEFRIEND		RENDIBLE
BDDEIORS	DISORBED	BDEEFIRS	DEBRIEFS	BDEEIILNU	UNEDIBLE
	DISROBED	BDEEFIRU	RUBEFIED	BDEEIILNV	VENDIBLE
BDDEIOWY	WIDEBODY	BDEEFITT	BEFITTED	BDEEIILOR	ERODIBLE
BDDEIRRS	REDBIRDS	BDEEFLOO	BEFOOLED		REBOILED
BDDEISSU	SUBSIDED	BDEEFLOU	BEFOULED	BDEEIILOS	OBELISED
BDDEISTU	BUDDIEST	BDEEFOOR	FOREBODE	BDEEIILOT	BETOILED
BDDELMRU	DRUMBLED	BDEEFOOW	BEEFWOOD	BDEEIILOZ	OBELIZED
BDDELOOR	BLOODRED	BDEEFSUU	SUBFEUED	BDEEIILRV	BEDRIVEL
BDDELORS	BRODDLES	BDEEGGIW	BEWIGGED	BDEEIILRW	BEWILDER
BDDENNOU	UNBONDED	BDEEGGMO	EMBOGGED	BDEEIILSV	BEDEVILS
BDDENOTU	OBTUNDED	BDEEGGNU	UNBEGGED	BDEEIILTT	BETITLED
BDDENRUU	UNDERBUD	BDEEGGRU	BEGRUDGE	BDEEIIMNR	BRIDEMEN
BDDEORTU	OBTRUDED		BUGGERED	BDEEIIMOR	EMBODIER
BDDGIINS	BIDDINGS		DEBUGGER	BDEEIIMOS	EMBODIES
BDDGILNU	BUDDLING	BDEEGHIS	BESIGHED	BDEEIIMRT	TIMBERED
BDDGINOR	BRODDING	BDEEGILN	BLEEDING	BDEEIIMST	BEDTIMES
BDDGINSU	BUDDINGS	BDEEGILR	BEGIRDLE		BEMISTED
BDDGINUY	BUDDYING	BDEEGILU	BEGUILED	BDEEIIMSU	EMBUSIED
BDDGIORS	BIRDDOGS	BDEEGIMR	BEGRIMED	BDEEIINOS	EBONISED
BDDGOOSY	DOGSBODY	BDEEGINR	BERINGED	BDEEIINOT	OBEDIENT
BDDHIIRY	DIHYBRID		BREEDING	BDEEIINOZ	EBONIZED
BDDINOOW	WOODBIND		BREINGED	BDEEIINRS	INBREEDS
BDDINOSU	DISBOUND	BDEEGINW	BEDEWING	BDEEIINRT	INTERBED
BDDINPUU	PUDIBUND		BEWINGED	BDEEIINST	BENDIEST
BDDEEEMS	BESEEMED	BDEEGINY	BEDYEING	BDEEIINSW	BENDWISE
BDEEEEMT	BETEEMED	BDEEGKNU	BEGUNKED	BDEEIINSZ	BEDIZENS
BDEEEGIS	BESIEGED	BDEEGLNO	BELONGED	BDEEIORS	REBODIES
BDEEEGMM	BEGEMMED		ENGLOBED	BDEEIORU	BOUDERIE
BDEEEGNO	EDGEBONE	BDEEGMOU	EMBOGUED	BDEEIRRU	REBURIED

BDEEIRRV	RIVERBED
BDEEIRST	BESTRIDE
	BISTERED
BDEEIRSU	DEBRUISE
BDEEIRSY	BIRDSEYE
BDEEIRTT	BITTERED
BDEEISTU	BESUITED
BDEEKMOS	BESMOKED
	EMBOSKED
BDEEKNRU	BUNKERED
	DEBUNKER
BDEEKOOR	REBOOKED
BDEEKORR	BROKERED
BDEELLMU	UMBELLED
BDEELLOW	BELLOWED
	BOWELLED
BDEELLRU	BULLERED
BDEELLRY	REDBELLY
BDEELLTU	BULLETED
BDEELLUW	BULLWEED
BDEELMNO	EMBOLDEN
BDEELMOR	REBELDOM
BDEELMPU	BEPLUMED
BDEELMRT	TREMBLED
BDEELMRU	LUMBERED
BDEELNNO	ENNOBLED
BDEELNRS	BLENDERS
	REBLENDS
BDEELNST	BENDLETS
BDEELNTU	UNBELTED
BDEELORU	REDOUBLE
BDEELOSU	BESOULED
BDEELOSV	BELOVEDS
BDEELRTU	BUTLERED
BDEELRUY	BURLEYED
BDEELSST	DEBTLESS
BDEEMNOT	BODEMENT
	ENTOMBED
BDEEMNOW	ENWOMBED
BDEEMNRU	NUMBERED
BDEEMORR	EMBORDER
BDEEMORS	SOMBERED
BDEEMORW	BEWORMED
BDEEMORY	REEMBODY
BDEEMOSS	EMBOSSED
BDEEMPRU	BUMPERED
BDEEMRTU	EMBRUTED
BDEEMSSU	EMBUSSED
BDEENNOT	BONNETED
BDEENORS	DEBONERS
	REDBONES
BDEENOSW	BESNOWED
BDEENOUY	UNOBEYED
BDEENPRS	PREBENDS
BDEENRRU	BURDENER
BDEENSUV	SUBVENED
BDEEOORT	REBOOTED
BDEEOPRR	REPROBED
BDEEOPRS	BEPROSED
BDEEOPRW	BEPOWDER
BDEEORRR	BORDERER
BDEEORRS	RESORBED
BDEEORRV	OVERBRED
BDEEORSS	BEDSORES
BDEEORST	BESORTED
	BESTRODE
BDEEORSV	OBSERVED
BDEEORTU	OUTBREED
BDEEORTV	OBVERTED
BDEEOSSS	DEBOSSES
	OBSESSED
BDEEOSST	BETOSSED
BDEEOSTT	BESOTTED
	OBTESTED
BDEEOSTW	BESTOWED
BDEEPRRU	PUREBRED
BDEERRTU	TRUEBRED
BDEERRWY	DEWBERRY
BDEERSSU	BURSEEDS
BDEERSUW	BURWEEDS
BDEERTTU	BUTTERED
	REBUTTED
BDEESSSU	DEBUSSES
BDEFIILR	BIRDLIFE
BDEFIIRR	FIREBIRD
BDEFIIRU	RUBIFIED
BDEFIKOR	BIFORKED
BDEFILRS	FILBERDS
BDEFILSU	SUBFIELD
BDEFIMOR	BIFORMED
BDEFINRR	FERNBIRD
BDEFIORS	FIBROSED
BDEFOORS	FORBODES
BDEFOORY	FOREBODY
BDEGHHIR	HIGHBRED
BDEGHILT	BLIGHTED
BDEGHIRT	BEDRIGHT
BDEGHIST	BEDIGHTS
BDEGIILN	BIELDING
BDEGIINT	BETIDING
	DEBITING
BDEGILNN	BLENDING
BDEGILNO	INGLOBED
BDEGINNO	DEBONING
BDEGINNS	BENDINGS
BDEGINOS	OBSIGNED
BDEGINSU	DEBUSING
BDEGINTU	DEBUTING
BDEGIOST	BODGIEST
BDEGLMRU	GRUMBLED
BDEGLNOU	BLUDGEON
BDEGLRSU	BLUDGERS
BDEGNOSW	BEDGOWNS
BDEGOOSY	GOODBYES
BDEGORRY	DOGBERRY
BDEGORSU	BUDGEROS
BDEGORUW	BUDGEROW
BDEHIKOS	KIBOSHED
BDEHILMT	THIMBLED
BDEHIOPS	BISHOPED
BDEHKOSY	KYBOSHED
BDEHLMOW	WHOMBLED
BDEHLSUV	BUSHVELD
BDEHMOOY	HOMEBODY
BDEHOOOO	BOOHOOED
BDEHORSU	BESHROUD
BDEHORSY	HERDBOYS
BDEIIIKN	BIKINIED
BDEIIKLR	BIRDLIKE
BDEIIKTZ	KIBITZED
BDEIILMR	BIRDLIME
BDEIILNY	INEDIBLY
BDEIILRU	BLUIDIER
BDEIILTY	DEBILITY
BDEIIMOS	IMBODIES
BDEIINNZ	BENZIDIN
BDEIIOPS	BIOPSIED
BDEIKMOS	IMBOSKED
BDEIKNOR	BRODEKIN
BDEIKNSU	BUSKINED
BDEILLMU	BDELLIUM
BDEILLNU	UNBILLED
BDEILLNW	WINDBELL
BDEILLOW	BILLOWED
BDEILLOX	BOLLIXED
BDEILMNO	IMBOLDEN
BDEILMOS	SEMIBOLD
BDEILMSU	SUBLIMED
BDEILNNO	BLONDINE
BDEILNOU	UNBOILED
	UNILOBED
BDEILNOY	BODYLINE
BDEILNRS	BLINDERS
	BRINDLES
BDEILNRU	UNBRIDLE
BDEILNST	BLINDEST
BDEILNVY	VENDIBLY
BDEILOOR	BLOODIER
BDEILOOS	BLOODIES
BDEILOPU	UPBOILED
BDEILOQU	OBLIQUED
BDEILORT	TRILOBED
BDEILORV	LOVEBIRD
BDEILOSS	BODILESS
BDEILOSW	DISBOWEL
BDEILPRU	PREBUILD
BDEILQTU	BEDQUILT
BDEILRRS	BRIDLERS
BDEILRRY	LYREBIRD
BDEILRST	BRISTLED
	DRIBLETS
BDEILRSU	BUILDERS
	REBUILDS
BDEILRTT	BRITTLED
BDEILSST	BILSTEDS
BDEILSTU	BLUDIEST
BDEIMNOT	INTOMBED
BDEIMNSU	NIMBUSED
BDEIMNUU	UNIMBUED
BDEIMORR	IMBORDER
	MORBIDER
BDEIMORS	BROMIDES
	BROMISED
BDEIMORY	EMBRYOID
BDEIMORZ	BROMIZED
BDEIMOSS	IMBOSSED
BDEIMRSU	IMBURSED
BDEIMRTU	IMBRUTED
BDEINOOS	NOBODIES
BDEINOOW	WOODBINE
BDEINORV	OVENBIRD
BDEINOSU	BEDOUINS

BDEINOTU	BOUNTIED	BDEMOORS	BEDROOMS	BDGIIOOS	GOBIOIDS
BDEINPRS	PREBINDS		BOREDOMS	BDGILNNO	BLONDING
BDEINRSU	BURNSIDE	BDEMOOSY	SOMEBODY	BDGILNNU	BUNDLING
BDEINRTU	TURBINED	BDEMOOTT	BOTTOMED	BDGILNOO	BLOODING
	UNDERBIT	BDEMSSUU	SUBSUMED		BOODLING
BDEINRUU	UNBURIED	BDENNOTU	DUBONNET	BDGILNOU	DOUBLING
BDEINSUX	SUBINDEX	BDENNOUY	YBOUNDEN	BDGILNOY	BODINGLY
BDEINTTU	UNBITTED	BDENNRUU	UNBURDEN	BDGILNTU	BLINDGUT
BDEIOORR	BROODIER		UNBURNED	BDGILOOS	GLOBOIDS
BDEIORRS	BROIDERS	BDENOORU	EUROBOND	BDGINNOS	BONDINGS
	DISROBER	BDENOOTU	UNBOOTED	BDGINNOU	BOUNDING
BDEIORRU	BOURRIDE	BDENOOTW	BENTWOOD		UNBODING
BDEIORRY	BROIDERY	BDENOPRU	PREBOUND	BDGINOOR	BROODING
BDEIORSS	DISROBES		UNPROBED	BDGINOOY	BOODYING
BDEIORST	DEBITORS	BDENORSU	BOUNDERS	BDGINORS	BIRDSONG
	DEORBITS		REBOUNDS		SONGBIRD
BDEIORSV	OVERBIDS		SUBORNED	BDGINORU	OBDURING
BDEIORTU	TUBEROID	BDENOTTU	BUTTONED	BDGINOTU	DOUBTING
BDEIOSSY	DISOBEYS	BDENRSTU	SUBTREND	BDGINSUU	SUBDUING
BDEIOSUX	SUBOXIDE	BDENRSUU	UNBRUSED	BDGLLOSU	BULLDOGS
BDEIRSSU	DISBURSE	BDENRUUY	UNDERBUY	BDGLOOST	DOGBOLTS
	SUBSIDER	BDENSSTU	SUBTENDS	BDGNRUUY	BURGUNDY
BDEISSSU	SUBSIDES	BDENSTUU	UNBUSTED	BDGOOOSW	BOGWOODS
BDEISSTU	SUBEDITS	BDEOORRS	BROODERS	BDHIIPRW	WHIPBIRD
BDEKLLUY	BULLDYKE	BDEOORRW	BORROWED	BDHILNOS	BLONDISH
BDEKLMOO	BLOKEDOM	BDEOOTUX	OUTBOXED	BDHIMOOR	RHOMBOID
BDEKNOOS	BOOKENDS	BDEOOWWW	BOWWOWED	BDHIMORT	BIRTHDOM
BDEKNOOU	UNBOOKED	BDEOPSST	BEDPOSTS	BDHIMSTU	DUMBSHIT
BDELLOOR	BORDELLO	BDEOPSTU	SUBDEPOT	BDHIMSUU	SUBHUMID
	DOORBELL	BDEORRSU	BORDURES	BDHINOPS	HOPBINDS
BDELLOOX	BOLLOXED		BOURDERS	BDHIORST	BIRDSHOT
BDELLORS	BEDROLLS		SUBORDER	BDHIOSSU	BUSHIDOS
BDELLOUZ	BULLDOZE	BDEORRTU	OBTRUDER	BDHLOOOT	HOTBLOOD
BDELMOOS	BLOOSMED	BDEORRUW	BURROWED	BDHMOOOS	HOBODOMS
BDELMOSY	SYMBOLED	BDEORSSU	ROSEBUDS	BDHNRSUU	UNSHRUBD
BDELMRSU	DRUMBLES	BDEORSTU	DOUBTERS	BDHOOOSY	BOYHOODS
BDELMRUU	DELUBRUM		OBTRUDES	BDIIINRS	BRINDISI
BDELMSTU	STUMBLED		REDOUBTS	BDIIIORV	VIBRIOID
BDELNNOU	UNNOBLED	BDEORSUV	OVERDUBS	BDIIKNOS	BODIKINS
BDELNNUU	UNBUNDLE	BDERSSUU	SUBDUERS	BDIILLNW	WINDBILL
BDELNOOS	DOBLONES	BDERSTUU	SUBTRUDE	BDIILMSS	DISLIMBS
BDELNOSS	BOLDNESS	BDFFIPRU	PUFFBIRD	BDIILMSU	MISBUILD
	BONDLESS	BDFGNOOU	FOGBOUND	BDIILOOS	BIOSOLID
BDELNOST	BLONDEST	BDFIIITY	BIFIDITY	BDIILOQU	OBLIQUID
BDELNOTU	UNBOLTED	BDFIIORS	FIBROIDS	BDIILORS	OILBIRDS
BDELNOUU	UNDOUBLE	BDFILLLO	BILLFOLD	BDIIMNSS	MISBINDS
BDELNOWU	UNBLOWED	BDFILNOO	BLOODFIN	BDIIMRUU	RUBIDIUM
BDELNRSU	BLUNDERS	BDFILSUU	SUBFLUID	BDIIKNORS	BRODKINS
	BUNDLERS	BDFINORU	UNFORBID	BDILLOOY	BLOODILY
BDELOORS	BOODLERS	BDFINRUU	FURIBUND	BDILMORY	MORBIDLY
BDELOORV	OVERBOLD	BDFIRRSU	SURFBIRD	BDILNNSU	SUNBLIND
BDELOOUW	BLUEWOOD	BDFLOTUU	DOUBTFUL		UNBLINDS
BDELORSU	BOULDERS	BDFORSUY	BODYSURF	BDILNOOO	DIOBOLON
	DOUBLERS	BDGGIINR	BRIDGING	BDILNOWW	WINDBLOW
BDELORSW	BOWLDERS	BDGGILNU	BLUDGING	BDILNPRU	PURBLIND
BDELORTU	TROUBLED	BDGGLOSU	GOLDBUGS	BDILNSUU	UNBUILDS
BDELORUU	DOUBLURE	BDGHOOUY	DOUGHBOY	BDILOORY	BROODILY
BDELORUY	BOULDERY	BDGIIKNR	KINGBIRD	BDILOPRY	POLYBRID
BDELOSTU	DOUBLETS	BDGIILNN	BLINDING	BDILOTUU	OUTBUILD
BDELPSUU	SUBDUPLE	BDGIILNR	BRIDLING	BDILPSUU	BUILDUPS
BDEMNNOS	BONDSMEN	BDGIILNU	BUILDING		UPBUILDS
BDEMNOSU	EMBOUNDS	BDGIINNS	BINDINGS	BDILRTUY	TURBIDLY
BDEMNOTU	UNTOMBED	BDGIINRS	BIRDINGS	BDIMNORU	MORIBUND
BDEMNSSU	DUMBNESS	BDGIINRW	BIRDWING	BDIMNOSU	MISBOUND

BDIMNPSU	DUMPBINS
BDIMNSUU	DUBNIUMS
BDIMOOSS	DISBOSOM
BDIMOSTU	MISDOUBT
BDINNOSU	INBOUNDS
BDINNRUW	WINDBURN
BDINOORS	BRIDOONS
BDINOOSW	WOODBINS
BDINORSW	SNOWBIRD
BDINRSSU	SUNBIRDS
BDINRTUU	UNTURBID
BDINSSTU	BUNDISTS
	DUSTBINS
BDIOORSU	BOUDOIRS
BDIOORTY	BOTRYOID
BDIORSSW	WOSBIRDS
BDIORUZZ	BURDIZZO
BDIOSTUY	BODYSUIT
BDIRSSTU	DISTURBS
BDKNOOOR	DOORKNOB
BDKNOOSU	BUNDOOKS
BDKOOORW	WORDBOOK
BDKOORWY	BODYWORK
BDKOOSTU	STUDBOOK
BDLLSTUU	BULLDUST
BDLNOOOU	DOUBLOON
BDLNOOUY	UNBLOODY
BDLNOOWW	BLOWDOWN
BDLOOOSX	OXBLOODS
BDLORSUW	SUBWORLD
BDMOORRS	SMORBROD
BDMOOSSS	BOSSDOMS
BDMORSUW	BUDWORMS
BDNNOOTU	BUNODONT
BDNOOPTU	POTBOUND
BDNOORSU	BOURDONS
BDNOOSUX	SOUNDBOX
BDNOOSWW	DOWNBOWS
BDNOOTUU	OUTBOUND
BDNORSTU	TURBONDS
BDNORSUW	RUBDOWNS
BDOOOSWX	BOXWOODS
BDORUWZZ	BUZZWORD
BEEEEFLN	ENFEEBLE
BEEEEFRS	FREEBEES
BEEEEKSS	BESEEKES
BEEEEMST	BETEEMES
BEEEENPS	PEEBEENS
BEEEENRT	TEREBENE
BEEEENRZ	EBENEZER
BEEEFIRS	FREEBIES
BEEEFIST	BEEFIEST
BEEEFLSS	BEEFLESS
	FEEBLESSE
BEEEFLST	FEEBLEST
BEEEGILN	BELEEING
BEEEGINS	BESEEING
BEEEGIRS	BESIEGER
BEEEGISS	BESIEGES
BEEEGKLS	GEELBEKS
BEEEGNRS	BREENGES
BEEEGORS	GREEBOES
BEEEGRRS	BERGERES
BEEEGRTT	BEGETTER
BEEEHIST	BHEESTIE
BEEEHISV	BEEHIVES
BEEEHLRT	HERBELET
BEEEHLWW	WEBWHEEL
BEEEHNOY	HONEYBEE
BEEEHNSS	SHEBEENS
BEEEILLL	LIBELLEE
BEEEILLS	LIBELEES
BEEEILLT	BILLETEE
BEEEILNS	BEELINES
BEEEILRV	BELIEVER
BEEEILSV	BELIEVES
BEEEINST	EBENISTE
BEEEIRRZ	BREEZIER
BEEEIRST	BEERIEST
BEEEJLSW	BEJEWELS
BEEEJLSZ	JEZEBELS
BEEEJSUZ	BEJEEZUS
BEEEKLLS	BELLEEKS
BEEELLRR	REBELLER
BEEELLRT	BELLETER
BEEELLRV	BEVELLER
BEEELMNS	ENSEMBLE
BEEELMRS	RESEMBLE
BEEELMSY	BESEEMLY
BEEELMZZ	EMBEZZLE
BEEELPRS	BLEEPERS
BEEELRST	BEETLERS
BEEELRSV	BEVELERS
BEEEMMRR	REMEMBER
BEEEMNSU	UNBESEEM
BEEEMRSS	BERSEEMS
BEEENNSZ	BENZENES
BEEENSST	SEBESTEN
BEEENSTW	BETWEENS
BEEEPPPR	BEPEPPER
BEEEPRST	BEPESTER
BEEERSST	BRETESSE
BEEERSTT	BESETTER
BEEESSST	TSESSEBE
BEEFFLMU	BEMUFFLE
BEEFFRTU	BUFFETER
BEEFGILN	FEEBLING
BEEFGINR	BEFINGER
	BEFRINGE
BEEFHILS	FEEBLISH
BEEFIIRS	FIBERISE
BEEFIIRZ	FIBERIZE
BEEFILLT	LIFEBELT
BEEFILLX	FLEXIBLE
BEEFILNU	UNBELIEF
BEEFILRS	BELFRIES
BEEFINST	BENEFITS
BEEFIRRS	BRIEFERS
BEEFIRSS	FRISBEES
BEEFIRST	BRIEFEST
BEEFIRSU	RUBEFIES
BEEFLORU	BEFOULER
BEEFLORW	BEFLOWER
BEEFNORR	FREEBORN
BEEFNRTU	UNBEREFT
BEEFOORT	FREEBOOT
BEEGGNRU	GREENBUG
BEEGGNSU	GEEBUNGS
BEEGHLMR	BERGMEHL
BEEGIILL	ELIGIBLE
BEEGIILX	EXIGIBLE
BEEGILLR	GERBILLE
BEEGILMN	BEMINGLE
BEEGILNP	BLEEPING
BEEGILNT	BEETLING
BEEGILNV	BEVELING
BEEGILOS	OBLIGEES
BEEGILRU	BEGUILER
BEEGILSU	BEGUILES
BEEGIMNT	BEMETING
BEEGIMRS	BEGRIMES
BEEGINNR	BEGINNER
	BENIGNER
BEEGINNS	BEGINNES
BEEGINRR	BREERING
BEEGINRS	BIGENERS
	BREINGES
	REBEGINS
BEEGINRZ	BREEZING
BEEGINST	BEIGNETS
BEEGINSU	BEGUINES
BEEGINSW	BEESWING
BEEGKLUV	KEYBUGLE
BEEGLNOR	BELONGER
BEEGLNOS	ENGLOBES
BEEGMNOS	GOMBEENS
BEEGMNOY	BOGEYMEN
BEEGMOSU	EMBOGUES
BEEGMRSU	SUBMERGE
BEEGNOOW	WOBEGONE
BEEGNOTT	BEGOTTEN
BEEGNRSU	SUBGENRE
	SUNGREBE
BEEGNSTU	UNBEGETS
BEEGOOPR	GEOPROBE
BEEGOPSX	PEGBOXES
BEEHHMOT	BEHEMOTH
BEEHIKLR	HERBLIKE
BEEHIMOT	BOEHMITE
BEEHINSS	BESHINES
	NEBISHES
BEEHIRST	HERBIEST
BEEHIRSV	BESHIVER
BEEHISST	BHISTEES
BEEHKSSU	BUKSHEES
BEEHLLNT	HELLBENT
BEEHLOOR	BOREHOLE
BEEHLOVY	BEHOVELY
BEEHLRSS	HERBLESS
BEEHLRST	BLETHERS
	HERBLETS
BEEHLRSU	BUSHELER
BEEHMORW	HOMEBREW
BEEHMRSY	BERHYMES
BEEHMSTU	SUBTHEME
BEEHNNOS	HEBENONS
BEEHNOOP	NEOPHOBE
BEEHNRRT	BRETHREN
BEEHOOST	BESOOTHE
BEEHOOSV	BEHOOVES
BEEHORSW	BEWHORES
BEEHRRST	SHERBERT

BEEHRSST	SHERBETS	BEEINOSS	EBONISES	BEELRSSS	BLESSERS
BEEHRSSW	BESHREWS	BEEINOST	BETONIES	BEELRSSV	VERBLESS
BEEIILNZ	ZIBELINE		EBONITES	BEELRSUZ	ZEBRULES
BEEIINOS	EBIONISE	BEEINOSZ	EBONIZES	BEELRTUU	TRUEBLUE
BEEIINOZ	EBIONIZE	BEEINPRS	PEBRINES	BEELSSTU	TUBELESS
BEEIINRT	BENITIER	BEEINRSS	NEBRISES	BEELSTTU	BLUETTES
BEEIIORS	BOISERIE	BEEINRSZ	ZEBRINES	BEEMNRRU	NUMBERER
BEEIIPST	BEPITIES	BEEINRTT	REBITTEN		RENUMBER
BEEIIRRR	BRIERIER	BEEINSTT	BENTIEST	BEEMOORS	BORESOME
BEEIIRSS	IBERISES	BEEIOQSU	OBSEQUIE	BEEMOPRT	OBTEMPER
BEEIISTU	UBIETIES	BEEIORSS	SOBERISE	BEEMORRS	SOMBERER
BEEIISTZ	BITESIZE	BEEIORSW	BOWERIES	BEEMORSS	EMBOSSER
BEEIJLSU	JUBILEES	BEEIORSZ	SOBERIZE	BEEMORSW	EMBOWERS
BEEIJORT	BOERTJIE	BEEIORTV	OVERBITE	BEEMOSSS	EMBOSSES
BEEIJSTU	BEJESUIT	BEEIQSUZ	BEZIQUES	BEEMQSUU	EMBUSQUE
BEEIKKRS	BREKKIES	BEEIRRSU	REBURIES	BEEMRRSU	UMBRERES
BEEIKLNY	EYEBLINK	BEEIRRSV	BREVIERS	BEEMRSSU	SUBMERSE
BEEIKLTU	TUBELIKE	BEEIRRTT	BITTERER	BEEMRSTU	EMBRUTES
BEEIKLWY	BIWEEKLY	BEEIRSSU	SUBERISE	BEEMRTTU	UMBRETTE
BEEIKORS	BROEKIES	BEEIRSSV	BREVISES	BEEMRTUZ	ZERUMBET
BEEIKSSS	BEKISSES	BEEIRSSW	BREWISES	BEEMSSSU	EMBUSSES
BEEILLLR	LIBELLER	BEEIRSTU	UBERTIES	BEENNOOS	NONOBESE
BEEILLNO	LOBELINE	BEEIRSUZ	SUBERIZE	BEENNOOT	BOTONNEE
BEEILLNT	BELTLINE	BEEISSTW	WEBSITES	BEENOPTY	TEENYBOP
BEEILLNU	BLUELINE	BEEKMOPR	PEMBROKE	BEENORRS	ENROBERS
BEEILLRS	LIBELERS	BEEKMOSS	BESMOKES	BEENORTU	BOUNTREE
BEEILLRT	BILLETER	BEEKNOPS	BESPOKEN	BEENORTV	VERBOTEN
BEEILLSV	BILEVELS	BEEKNOST	BETOKENS	BEENOSST	BONESETS
BEEILLTT	BELITTLE		STEENBOK	BEENOSTU	TUBENOSE
BEEILLTU	TULLIBEE	BEEKRRSS	BERSERKS	BEENOSTY	BONEYEST
BEEILMOS	EMBOLIES	BEEKRRSU	REBUKERS	BEENPRST	BESPRENT
	EMBOLISE	BEELLMTU	UMBELLET	BEENRSTT	BRENTEST
BEEILMOZ	EMBOLIZE	BEELLORW	BELLOWER	BEENRSTW	BESTREWN
BEEILMPP	BEPIMPLE		REBELLOW	BEENRTTU	BRUNETTE
BEEILMPR	PERIBLEM	BEELLOST	LOBELETS	BEENSSSU	SUBSENSE
BEEILMPS	EPIBLEMS	BEELLSST	BELTLESS	BEENSSTU	SUBTEENS
BEEILMRR	LIMBERER	BEELLSUV	SUBLEVEL		SUBTENSE
BEEILMSS	BESLIMES	BEELMMOP	BEPOMMEL	BEENSSUV	SUBVENES
	BESMILES	BEELMNNO	NOBLEMEN	BEEOORRT	BOORTREE
BEEILNNS	BLENNIES	BEELMNSU	BLUESMEN	BEEOORRV	OVERBORE
BEEILNRS	BERLINES	BEELMOSW	EMBOWELS	BEEOORTT	BEETROOT
BEEILNRY	BERYLINE	BEELMRRT	TREMBLER	BEEOPRRS	REPROBES
BEEILNSS	SENSIBLE	BEELMRRU	LUMBERER	BEEOPRSS	BEPROSES
BEEILNST	STILBENE	BEELMRST	TREMBLES	BEEOPSSU	BESPOUSE
	TENSIBLE	BEELMSTU	BLUESTEM	BEEORRSU	BOURREES
BEEILNSU	NEBULISE	BEELMUZZ	BEMUZZLE	BEEORRSV	OBSERVER
BEEILNUZ	NEBULIZE	BEELNNOR	ENNOBLER		VERBOSER
BEEILORS	EROSIBLE	BEELNNOS	ENNOBLES	BEEORRTU	BOURTREE
BEEILOSS	OBELISES	BEELNOSS	BONELESS	BEEORSST	SOBEREST
BEEILOSZ	OBELIZES		NOBLESSE	BEEORSSU	SUBEROSE
BEEILOTV	LOVEBITE	BEELNOSU	BLUENOSE	BEEORSSV	OBSERVES
BEEILRRT	TERRIBLE		NEBULOSE		OBVERSES
BEEILRSU	BLUESIER	BEELNOSZ	BENZOLES	BEEORSTU	TUBEROSE
BEEILRSV	VERBILES	BEELNSSU	BLUENESS	BEEORSTV	OVERBETS
BEEILRYZ	BREEZILY	BEELNTTU	BETELNUT	BEEORSTW	BESTOWER
BEEILSTT	BETITLES	BEELNTUY	BUTYLENE	BEEORSWY	EYEBROWS
BEEIMORT	BIOMETER	BEELOOST	OBSOLETE	BEEOSSSS	OBSESSES
BEEIMRRU	UMBRIERE	BEELOQRU	BRELOQUE	BEEOSSST	BETOSSES
BEEIMRST	BIMESTER	BEELORTT	REBOTTLE	BEEPPRSU	PREPUBES
BEEIMRTT	EMBITTER	BEELORVW	OVERBLEW	BEEPRRSU	SUPERBER
BEEIMSSU	EMBUSIES	BEELOSTW	STEELBOW	BEEPRRSV	PREVERBS
BEEINNSS	BEINNESS	BEELOSTY	EYEBOLTS	BEEPRSTY	PRESBYTE
BEEINNSZ	BENZINES	BEELPRSS	PREBLESS	BEEQSSTU	BEQUESTS
BEEINORT	TENEBRIO	BEELPRUV	BUPLEVER	BEERRSTW	BREWSTER

BEERRTTU	REBUTTER	BEGHINOT	BEHOTING		MISBEGUN
BEERSSSU	SUBSERES	BEGHINOV	BEHOVING	BEGIMOST	MISBEGOT
BEERSSTW	BESTREWS	BEGHINRT	BERTHING	BEGIMOSY	BOGEYISM
	WEBSTERS		BRIGHTEN	BEGINNNO	NONBEING
BEERSSUV	SUBSERVE	BEGHINST	BENIGHTS	BEGINNNR	BRENNING
	SUBVERSE	BEGHIOST	GOBSHITE	BEGINNNU	UNBENIGN
BEERSTTU	BURETTES	BEGHIRRT	BRIGHTER	BEGINNOR	ENROBING
BEERSTTY	BYSTREET	BEGHLNOU	BUNGHOLE		RINGBONE
BEESTTUV	BUVETTES	BEGHNOTU	BOUGHTEN	BEGINNSU	UNBEINGS
BEFFISTU	BUFFIEST	BEGHORTU	REBOUGHT	BEGINOOS	BESOGNIO
BEFFLRSU	BLUFFERS	BEGHOSTU	BESOUGHT	BEGINORR	REBORING
BEFFLSTU	BLUFFEST	BEGHOSUU	BUGHOUSE	BEGINORS	SOBERING
BEFGIILL	FILLIBEG	BEGHRRSU	BURGHERS	BEGINORW	BOWERING
BEFGIILS	FILIBEGS	BEGIIISS	SIGISBEI	BEGINRRS	BRINGERS
BEFGIINR	BRIEFING	BEGIILLN	LIBELING	BEGINRRY	BERRYING
BEFGILNU	FUNGIBLE	BEGIILLY	ELIGIBLY	BEGINRSV	VERBINGS
BEFGIRSU	FIREBUGS	BEGIILST	BILGIEST	BEGINRSW	BREWINGS
BEFHILSU	BLUEFISH	BEGIIMNR	BEMIRING	BEGINRUY	REBUYING
BEFHINOS	BONEFISH		BERIMING	BEGINSTT	BETTINGS
	FISHBONE	BEGIIMNS	MISBEGIN	BEGINVVY	BEVVYING
BEFHIRSU	BUSHFIRE	BEGIIMNT	BETIMING	BEGKMOSS	GEMSBOKS
	FIREBUSH	BEGIIMNX	BEMIXING	BEGLLORY	GORBELLY
BEFIIRSU	RUBIFIES	BEGIIMNY	BIGEMINY	BEGLLOSU	GLOBULES
BEFILLXY	FLEXIBLY	BEGIINNS	INBEINGS	BEGLLOTU	GLOBULET
BEFILMOR	FORELIMB	BEGIINRT	REBITING	BEGLMOOS	BEGLOOMS
BEFILNOS	LOBEFINS	BEGIINRZ	ZINGIBER	BEGLMRRU	GRUMBLER
BEFILNSU	BLUEFINS	BEGIINTW	BITEWING	BEGLMRSU	GRUMBLES
BEFILOST	BOTFLIES	BEGIIOSS	SIGISBEO	BEGLMSUU	BLUEGUMS
BEFILOSU	BIOFUELS	BEGIKMNO	KEMBOING	BEGLNOUW	BLUEGOWN
BEFILOUY	LIFEBUOY	BEGIKNRS	KERBINGS	BEGLNRSU	BLUNGERS
BEFILRST	FILBERTS	BEGIKNRU	REBUKING		BUNGLERS
BEFILSSU	SUBFILES	BEGILLLU	BLUEGILL	BEGLOOSS	GLOBOSES
BEFINORS	BONFIRES		GULLIBLE	BEGLOOST	BOOTLEGS
BEFIOOST	BOOFIEST	BEGILLNS	BELLINGS	BEGLOSUV	LOVEBUGS
BEFIORSS	FIBROSES	BEGILLNU	BULLGINE	BEGLOTUU	OUTBULGE
BEFIORTT	FOREBITT	BEGILLNY	BELLYING	BEGLRSTY	BERGYLTS
BEFIRSST	FIBSTERS	BEGILMNR	REMBLING	BEGMNOOY	BOOGYMEN
BEFISSTU	FUBSIEST	BEGILMNS	SEMBLING	BEGNOORU	BOURGEON
BEFISSUX	SUBFIXES	BEGILNNY	BENIGNLY	BEGNORSU	BURGEONS
BEFLLLUY	BELLYFUL	BEGILNOR	IGNOBLER	BEGNORTU	BURGONET
BEFLLSTY	FLYBELTS	BEGILNOS	INGLOBES	BEGNOSTT	BETTONGS
BEFLMRSU	FUMBLERS	BEGILNOV	BELOVING	BEGNSSUU	SUBGENUS
BEFLORUW	FURBELOW	BEGILNOW	BOWELING	BEGORRUY	BROGUERY
BEFLSTUU	TUBEFULS	BEGILNRT	TREBLING	BEGPRSUU	SUPERBUG
BEFMOOOR	FOREBOOM	BEGILNSS	BLESSING	BEHHKOST	KHOTBEHS
BEFNOORR	FORBORNE		GLIBNESS	BEHIISST	BHISTIES
BEFNOSSY	FYNBOSES	BEGILNST	BELTINGS	BEHIISTX	EXHIBITS
BEFORRXY	FOXBERRY		BLINGEST	BEHIKLOS	BLOKEISH
BEGGGINS	BEGGINGS	BEGILNSU	BLUEINGS	BEHIKLSU	BUSHLIKE
BEGGIINN	BINGEING		BULGINES	BEHIKNST	BETHINKS
BEGGIINO	BOGIEING	BEGILNTT	BLETTING	BEHIKOSS	KIBOSHES
BEGGILRU	BLUGGIER	BEGILNUW	BLUEWING	BEHILLOS	SHOEBILL
BEGGINOY	BOGEYING	BEGILNZZ	BEZZLING	BEHILLTY	BLITHELY
BEGGIOST	BOGGIEST	BEGILORS	OBLIGERS	BEHILMRW	WHIMBREL
BEGGISTU	BUGGIEST	BEGILRST	GILBERTS	BEHILMST	THIMBLES
BEGGLORS	BLOGGERS	BEGILSTU	BULGIEST	BEHILMTY	BIMETHYL
BEGGOOOS	GOOSEGOB	BEGIMNOS	BESOMING	BEHILNPY	BIPHENYL
BEGHHIST	BEHIGHTS	BEGIMNOW	EMBOWING	BEHILORR	HORRIBLE
BEGHIILP	PHILIBEG	BEGIMNOX	EMBOXING	BEHILORS	BOLSHIER
BEGHIKNT	BEKNIGHT	BEGIMNRU	EMBRUING	BEHILOSS	BOLSHIES
BEGHILRT	BLIGHTER		UMBERING	BEHILRST	BLITHERS
	THERBLIG	BEGIMNSU	BEMUSING	BEHILRTU	THURIBLE
BEGHINOR	NEIGHBOR		EMBUSING	BEHILSTT	BLITHEST
				BEHIMNOO	BONHOMIE

BEHIMOOS	SEMIHOBO	BEIILMOS	MOBILISE	BEILLORV	OVERBILL
BEHIMORS	BIOHERMS	BEIILMOZ	MOBILIZE	BEILLOSU	LIBELOUS
BEHIMOSY	YOHIMBES	BEIILMST	LIMBIEST	BEILLOSX	BOLLIXES
BEHIMRTU	THUMBIER	BEIILMSU	BULIMIES	BEILLPRS	PREBILLS
BEHINNOS	SHINBONE	BEIILNRS	RINSIBLE	BEILLRST	BRILLEST
BEHINOPS	HIPBONES	BEIILRSS	RISIBLES	BEILLSST	BESTILLS
	HOPBINES	BEIILRST	TRILBIES	BEILLSTU	BULLIEST
BEHINOSW	WISHBONE	BEIILRTT	LIBRETTI	BEILMMOS	EMBOLISM
BEHIOOPR	BIOPHORE	BEIILRUZ	BRUILZIE	BEILMNOR	BROMELIN
BEHIPRRT	PREBIRTH	BEIILSSV	VISIBLES	BEILMNOU	NOBELIUM
BEHIRRST	REBIRTHS	BEIILSTT	STILBITE	BEILMNRU	UNLIMBER
BEHIRRSU	BRUSHIER	BEIIMNNR	RENMINBI	BEILMNST	NIMBLEST
BEHIRSST	HERBISTS	BEIIMNNU	BIENNIUM	BEILMNUU	NEBULIUM
BEHIRSSU	HUBRISES	BEIIMNOS	EBIONISM	BEILMOOR	BLOOMIER
BEHIRSSV	HYBRISES	BEIIMRTT	IMBITTER	BEILMORS	EMBROILS
BEHISSTU	BUSHIEST	BEIINNRS	BRINNIES	BEILMOSS	OBELISMS
BEHKOSSY	KYBOSHES	BEIINORS	BRIONIES	BEILMPTU	PLUMBITE
BEHKOTTU	KETUBOTH	BEIINOST	NIOBITES	BEILMRRU	RUMBLIER
BEHLLOOT	BOLTHOLE	BEIINQUU	BIUNIQUE	BEILMRSS	BRIMLESS
BEHLLOOW	BLOWHOLE	BEIINRST	BRINIEST	BEILMRST	TIMBRELS
BEHLLOPS	BELLHOPS	BEIINSST	STIBINES	BEILMRSU	SUBLIMER
BEHLLPSU	BELLPUSH	BEIINSTT	STIBNITE	BEILMRSW	WIMBRELS
BEHLLSSU	SUBSHELL	BEIIOPSS	BIOPSIES	BEILMSSU	LIMBUSES
BEHLMOSW	WHOMBLES	BEIIORST	ORBITIES		SUBLIMES
BEHLMRSU	HUMBLERS	BEIIOSTT	BIOTITES	BEILNNTU	BUNTLINE
BEHLMSTU	HUMBLEST	BEIIRSST	BIRSIEST	BEILNOPS	BONSPIEL
BEHLOOPY	HYPOBOLE	BEIISSTT	BITSIEST	BEILNOSU	NUBILOSE
	LYOPHOBE	BEIISSTU	SUBITISE	BEILNOSW	BOWLINES
BEHLOOST	BOTHOLES	BEIISTTT	BITTIEST	BEILNOVY	BOVINELY
BEHLORST	BROTHELS	BEIISTUZ	SUBITIZE	BEILNRSY	BYLINERS
BEHLOSSU	SLOEBUSH	BEIJLMRU	JUMBLIER	BEILNSSU	SUBLINES
BEHLRRSU	BURRHELS	BEIJMOSU	JUMBOISE	BEILNSSY	SENSIBLY
BEHLRSSU	BLUSHERS	BEIJMOUZ	JUMBOIZE	BEILNSTU	BUSTLINE
BEHLSSSU	BUSHLESS	BEIJNORW	BIJWONER	BEILNSTY	TENSIBLY
BEHLSSTU	BLUSHETS	BEIKKLNO	KNOBLIKE	BEILNSTZ	BLINTZES
BEHMNOTY	BOTHYMEN	BEIKLLOT	BOLTLIKE	BEILOORV	BOILOVER
BEHMOOOX	HOMEOBOX	BEIKLLOW	BOWLLIKE		OVERBOIL
BEHMOOST	BESMOOTH	BEIKLMOT	TOMBLIKE	BEILOOST	LOOBIEST
BEHMOOSY	HOMEBOYS	BEIKLMOW	WOMBLIKE	BEILOPPW	BLOWPIPE
BEHMOSTU	BEMOUTHS	BEIKLNRS	BLINKERS	BEILOPRS	PREBOILS
BEHMPSTU	BETHUMPS	BEIKLOSS	OBELISKS	BEILOPSS	POSSIBLE
BEHNNOST	BENTHONS	BEIKLOST	BLOKIEST	BEILOQRU	BELIQUOR
BEHNNOUY	HONEYBUN	BEIKLOTY	KILOBYTE		OBLIQUER
BEHNORST	BETHORNS	BEIKLRUY	RUBYLIKE	BEILOQSU	OBLIQUES
BEHNRSTU	BURTHENS	BEIKLSTU	BULKIEST	BEILORRS	BROILERS
BEHOOOPZ	ZOOPHOBE	BEIKMNNR	BRINKMEN	BEILORST	STROBILE
BEHOOOST	BOOTHOSE	BEIKNOST	STEINBOK		TRILOBES
BEHOORST	THEORBOS	BEIKNRRY	INKBERRY	BEILORSU	BLOUSIER
BEHOORSX	HORSEBOX	BEIKNRSS	BRISKENS	BEILORSW	BLOWSIER
BEHOOSTX	HOTBOXES	BEIKOORS	BOOKSIER	BEILORTT	BLOTTIER
BEHOOSUY	HOUSEBOY		BROOKIES		LIBRETTO
BEHOPRST	POTHERBS	BEIKOORT	BROOKITE	BEILORWZ	BLOWZIER
BEHORRST	BROTHERS	BEIKOOST	BOOKIEST	BEILOSSY	BIOLYSES
BEHORSSU	ROSEBUSH	BEIKORST	REITBOKS	BEILOSTW	BLOWIEST
BEHORSTT	BETROTHS	BEIKOSST	BOSKIEST	BEILPRTU	PREBUILT
BEHOSSTU	BESHOUTS	BEIKRSST	BRISKEST	BEILPRTV	BLIPVERT
BEHRRSSU	BRUSHERS		BRISKETS	BEILRRRU	BLURRIER
BEHRSTTU	TURBETHS	BEIKRSSW	BREWSKIS	BEILRRTT	BRITTLER
BEIIIKMN	MINIBIKE	BEIKRSTU	BURKITES	BEILRRTY	TERRIBLY
BEIIKRST	BIRKIEST	BEILLMRY	LIMBERLY	BEILRSST	BLISTERS
BEIIKRTZ	KIBITZER	BEILLMSS	LIMBLESS		BRISTLES
BEIIKSTZ	KIBITZES	BEILLMSU	SEMIBULL	BEILRSTT	BRITTLES
BEIILLST	LIBELIST	BEILLNTU	BULLETIN		TRIBLETS
BEIILMMO	IMMOBILE	BEILLORS	BROLLIES	BEILRSTU	BURLIEST

	SUBTILER	**BEIOORTZ**	ROBOTIZE	**BELLNOSU**	BULLNOSE
BEILRSTY	BLISTERY	**BEIOOSSV**	OVIBOSES	**BELLNOSW**	SNOWBELL
BEILRSTZ	BLITZERS	**BEIOOSTZ**	BOOZIEST	**BELLNPSU**	BULLPENS
BEILRSUY	BRULYIES	**BEIOPSTY**	BIOTYPES	**BELLNTUY**	TUNBELLY
BEILRSUZ	BRULZIES	**BEIOQTUU**	BOUTIQUE	**BELLOOSU**	LOBULOSE
BEILRTTY	BITTERLY	**BEIORRST**	ORBITERS	**BELLOOSX**	BOLLOXES
BEILSTTU	BLUETITS	**BEIORRSU**	BOURSIER	**BELLOPTY**	POTBELLY
	SUBTITLE	**BEIORRSW**	BROWSIER	**BELLORTW**	BELLWORT
BEIMMRRS	BRIMMERS	**BEIORRTU**	ROBURITE	**BELLOSST**	BLOTLESS
BEIMNORS	BROMINES	**BEIORSST**	SORBITES		BOLTLESS
BEIMNRUZ	BRUNIZEM	**BEIORSTT**	BORTIEST	**BELLOSSU**	SOLUBLES
BEIMNSSU	NIMBUSES	**BEIORSTY**	SOBRIETY	**BELLOSWY**	SOWBELLY
BEIMNSTU	BITUMENS	**BEIORSUV**	BOUVIERS	**BELLRRSU**	BURRELLS
BEIMOORR	BROOMIER	**BEIOSSST**	BOSSIEST	**BELMMOOS**	EMBLOOMS
BEIMOORS	BOSOMIER	**BEIOSSSU**	SOUBISES	**BELMMRSU**	MUMBLERS
	RIBOSOME	**BEIOSSTU**	BOUSIEST	**BELMNOSU**	NELUMBOS
BEIMOOST	BOOMIEST	**BEIOSSTY**	BOYSIEST	**BELMNOSY**	BENOMYLS
BEIMORRV	OVERBRIM	**BEIOTTZZ**	BOZZETTI	**BELMOORS**	BLOOMERS
BEIMORSS	BROMISES	**BEIPPRSU**	PREPUBIS		REBLOOMS
BEIMORSW	IMBOWERS	**BEIQRSTU**	BRIQUETS	**BELMOORY**	BLOOMERY
BEIMORSZ	BROMIZES	**BEIRRSSU**	BRISURES	**BELMOOSS**	BLOOSMES
BEIMORTY	BIOMETRY		BRUISERS	**BELMOOST**	BOOMLETS
BEIMORYZ	RIBOZYME	**BEIRRSTU**	BRUITERS	**BELMOPRS**	PROBLEMS
BEIMOSSS	IMBOSSES		BURRIEST	**BELMORST**	TEMBLORS
BEIMOSTV	BEVOMITS	**BEIRRTTU**	TRIBUTER	**BELMORSY**	SOMBERLY
BEIMOSTW	WOMBIEST	**BEIRSSTU**	BUSTIERS		SOMBRELY
BEIMOSTY	SYMBIOTE	**BEIRSTTU**	TRIBUTES	**BELMORUW**	RUMBELOW
BEIMPSTU	BUMPIEST	**BEIRSTTY**	TREYBITS	**BELMOSST**	TOMBLESS
BEIMRSSU	IMBURSES	**BEISSSTU**	SUBSITES	**BELMOSSY**	SYMBOLES
BEIMRSTU	IMBRUTES	**BEISSTTU**	BUSTIEST	**BELMPRSU**	PLUMBERS
	RESUBMIT	**BEISTUZZ**	BUZZIEST		REPLUMBS
	TERBIUMS	**BEJKOOST**	JESTBOOK	**BELMPRUY**	PLUMBERY
BEIMSSTU	SUBITEMS	**BEJLMRSU**	JUMBLERS	**BELMRRSU**	RUMBLERS
BEINNOPS	PINBONES	**BEJORTTU**	TURBOJET	**BELMRRUY**	MULBERRY
BEINNOSS	BENISONS	**BEKLNORY**	BROKENLY	**BELMRSSU**	SLUMBERS
	BONINESS	**BEKLNRSU**	BLUNKERS	**BELMRSTU**	STUMBLER
BEINNOST	BONNIEST	**BEKLOOOR**	BOOKLORE		TUMBLERS
BEINNOSZ	BENZOINS	**BEKLOORT**	BROOKLET	**BELMRSUY**	SLUMBERY
BEINNRYZ	ZEBRINNY	**BEKLOOSS**	BOOKLESS	**BELMSSTU**	STUMBLES
BEINNTTU	UNBITTEN	**BEKLOOST**	BOOKLETS	**BELNNNOO**	NONNOBLE
BEINOOST	BONITOES	**BEKLORUV**	OVERBULK	**BELNNOSU**	UNNOBLES
	EOBIONTS	**BEKLRSSU**	BURLESKS	**BELNOORS**	BORNEOLS
BEINORRW	BROWNIER	**BEKMOOPS**	SPEKBOOM	**BELNOOSS**	BOONLESS
BEINORRZ	BRONZIER	**BEKMOSST**	STEMBOKS	**BELNOOSY**	BOLONEYS
BEINORST	BORNITES	**BEKNNORU**	UNBROKEN	**BELNOSTW**	SNOWBELT
	RIBSTONE	**BEKNOOOT**	NOTEBOOK	**BELNOSUU**	NEBULOUS
BEINORSW	BROWNIES	**BEKNOPRU**	UPBROKEN	**BELNOSYZ**	BENZOYLS
BEINORSY	BRYONIES	**BEKNORSY**	SKYBORNE	**BELNOTTU**	UNBOTTLE
BEINORTZ	BRONZITE	**BEKOOORV**	OVERBOOK	**BELNSSTU**	SUNBELTS
BEINOSST	EBONISTS	**BEKOOPRS**	PREBOOKS	**BELNSTTU**	BLUNTEST
BEINOSSX	BOXINESS	**BEKOORST**	BOOKREST	**BELNSTUU**	UNSUBTLE
BEINOSTT	BOTTINES	**BEKOORTU**	OUTBROKE	**BELOOOSX**	LOOSEBOX
BEINOSTU	BOUNTIES	**BEKOOTTX**	TEXTBOOK	**BELOOPRS**	BLOOPERS
BEINRRSY	NISBERRY	**BEKORSWW**	WEBWORKS	**BELOOPRT**	BOLTROPE
BEINRSSU	SUBERINS	**BEKORTUW**	TUBEWORK	**BELOORSW**	ROSEBOWL
BEINRSTT	BITTERNS	**BEKOSSXY**	SKYBOXES	**BELOORVW**	OVERBLOW
BEINRSTU	TRIBUNES	**BEKRSSTU**	BRUSKEST	**BELOOSST**	BOOTLESS
	TURBINES	**BELLLLPU**	BELLPULL	**BELOOTUV**	OBVOLUTE
BEINRSUU	UNBURIES	**BELLLMSU**	BLELLUMS	**BELORRTU**	TROUBLER
BEINRTTU	UNBITTER	**BELLMORT**	MORTBELL	**BELORSST**	BOLSTERS
BEINSSSU	BUSINESS	**BELLMORU**	UMBRELLO		LOBSTERS
BEINSTTU	BUNTIEST	**BELLMRUY**	LUMBERLY	**BELORSSW**	BROWLESS
BEIOOPST	BIOTOPES	**BELLNOPS**	BONSPELL	**BELORSTT**	BLOTTERS
BEIOORST	ROBOTISE	**BELLNORW**	WELLBORN		

	BOTTLERS	BENRSSTU	SUBRENTS	BFILLSSU	BLISSFUL
BELORSTU	BOULTERS	BENRSTUY	SUBENTRY	BFILOSTY	LIFTBOYS
	TROUBLES	BENSSSUY	BUSYNESS	BFIMNORU	NUBIFORM
BELOSSTU	OUTBLESS	BEOOORTV	OVERBOOT	BFIMORTU	TUBIFORM
BELOSTUU	TUBULOSE	BEOORRRW	BORROWER	BFINORYZ	BRONZIFY
BELOSTUY	OBTUSELY		REBORROW	BFIORSTT	FROSTBIT
BELPRSUY	SUPERBLY	BEOORRVW	OVERBROW	BFKLOOSU	BOOKFULS
BELRRSTU	BLURTERS	BEOORSSS	OBSESSOR	BFKLOOSY	FLYBOOKS
BELRSSTU	BLUSTERS		SORBOSES	BFKSSSUU	SUBFUSKS
	BUSTLERS	BEOORSST	BOOSTERS	BFLLNOWY	FLYBLOWN
BELRSSUU	SUBRULES	BEOORSTY	BOTRYOSE	BFLLOSUW	BOWLFULS
BELRSTUY	BLUSTERY	BEOOSTUX	OUTBOXES	BFLLOSWY	FLYBLOWS
BELRTUUU	TUBULURE	BEOOTTZZ	BOZZETTO	BFLOORSU	SUBFLOOR
BELSSTTU	SUBTLEST	BEOPRRSV	PROVERBS	BFNOORTW	BOWFRONT
BELSSTUY	SUBSTYLE	BEOPRSST	BESPORTS	BFOOOSTY	FOOTBOYS
BELSTTUY	SUBTLETY	BEOPSSTU	BESPOUTS	BGGGIINS	BIGGINGS
BEMMOOSS	EMBOSOMS	BEOQSSTU	BOSQUETS	BGGGILNO	BLOGGING
BEMMORRS	BROMMERS	BEOQSTUU	BOUQUETS		BOGGLING
BEMMRRSU	BRUMMERS	BEORRRUW	BURROWER	BGGGINOR	BROGGING
BEMMRRUU	BEMURMUR	BEORRSSW	BROWSERS	BGGGINSU	BUGGINGS
BEMNNSSU	NUMBNESS	BEORRSTU	ROBUSTER	BGGHIINT	BIGHTING
BEMNOORT	TROMBONE	BEORSSSU	SORBUSES	BGGIILNN	BINGLING
BEMNORSW	EMBROWNS	BEORSSTW	BESTROWS		BLINGING
BEMNORSY	EMBRYONS	BEORSSUU	SUBEROUS	BGGIILNO	OBLIGING
BEMNSSUU	SUBMENUS	BEORSTUU	TUBEROUS	BGGIILNY	GIBINGLY
BEMNSTTU	BUTMENTS	BEORSUVY	OVERBUSY	BGGIINNO	BOINGING
BEMNTTUY	BUTTYMEN		OVERBUYS	BGGIINNR	BRINGING
BEMOORRS	SOMBRERO	BEOSSTTU	OBTUSEST	BGGIINRU	BRIGUING
BEMOORTT	BOTTOMER	BEPRRSTU	PERTURBS	BGGILNNU	BLUNGING
BEMORSST	BESTORMS	BEPSSTUY	SUBTYPES		BUNGLING
	MOBSTERS	BEQRRSUU	BRUSQUER	BGGILNRU	BURGLING
	SOMBREST	BERRSSTU	BURSTERS	BGGINOOT	TOBOGGIN
BEMORSSU	MORBUSES	BERRSTUU	SURREBUT	BGGINOOY	BOOGYING
BEMORSWW	WEBWORMS	BERSSTTU	BUTTRESS	BGHHHISU	HIGHBUSH
BEMORTUW	TUBEWORM	BERSSTUV	SUBVERST	BGHHINOR	HIGHBORN
BEMOSTUX	BUXOMEST		SUBVERTS	BGHHIORW	HIGHBROW
BEMOSTUY	MYOTUBES	BESSSSUY	BYSSUSES	BGHHIOSY	HIGHBOYS
BEMRSSTU	BUMSTERS	BESSSTTU	SUBTESTS	BGHIINRT	BIRTHING
BEMSSSUU	SUBSUMES	BESSTTUX	SUBTEXTS	BGHILMNU	HUMBLING
BEMSSTUW	STEWBUMS	BFFFLMUU	BUMFLUFF	BGHILNSU	BLUSHING
BENNNOTU	UNBONNET	BFFGILNU	BLUFFING	BGHILRTY	BRIGHTLY
BENNOOTU	BOUTONNE	BFFGINSU	BUFFINGS	BGHIMNTU	THUMBING
BENNOPYY	PENNYBOY	BFFHORSU	BRUSHOFF	BGHIMOTU	BIGMOUTH
BENNORSW	NEWBORNS	BFFILOOS	BOILOFFS	BGHINORS	BIGHORNS
BENNSSSU	SNUBNESS	BFFLOOSW	BLOWOFFS	BGHINRSU	BRUSHING
BENOORRV	OVERBORN	BFFLOTUU	OUTBLUFF	BGHINRTU	UNBRIGHT
BENOORSU	BURNOOSE	BFFNOOSU	BUFFOONS	BGHINSSU	BUSHINGS
BENORRSU	SUBORNER	BFFNOSUX	SNUFFBOX	BGHIORSU	BROGUISH
BENORRSZ	BRONZERS	BFGHINTU	BUNFIGHT	BGHIPSSU	BUSHPIGS
BENORRTU	TRUEBORN	BFGILMNU	FUMBLING	BGHLRSUU	BULGHURS
BENORRUV	OVERBURN	BFGIOOST	BIGFOOTS		BURGHULS
BENORSST	SORBENTS	BFGIORST	FROGBITS	BGHMORSU	HOMBURGS
BENORSTU	BURSTONE	BFGLLORU	BULLFROG	BGHNORSU	HORNBUGS
	RUBSTONE	BFHIILLS	BILLFISH	BGHNOTUU	UNBOUGHT
BENORSTW	BESTROWN	BFHILOST	FISHBOLT	BGHOOPTU	BOUGHPOT
	BROWNEST	BFHILOSW	BLOWFISH	BGHOORSU	BOROUGHS
BENORSUU	BURNOUSE		FISHBOWL	BGIIJLNR	JIRBLING
BENORSWY	BYWONERS	BFHIMNSU	NUMBFISH	BGIIJLNY	JIBINGLY
BENORTTU	BUTTONER	BFHLLSUU	BLUSHFUL	BGIIKLNN	BLINKING
	REBUTTON	BFIILMOS	BIOFILMS	BGIIKMNO	KIMBOING
BENOSSTU	SUBTONES	BFIINORS	FIBROINS	BGIIKNNO	BOINKING
BENOSSUZ	SUBZONES	BFIIORSS	FIBROSIS	BGIIKNRS	BRISKING
BENOSSWY	NEWSBOYS	BFIKLOOP	FLIPBOOK	BGIILLNS	BILLINGS
BENRRSUY	SUNBERRY	BFILLMRU	BRIMFULL	BGIILMNW	WIMBLING

BGIILNNN	BLINNING	BGILNRRU	BLURRING	BHILLOSY	BILLYOHS
BGIILNNY	BYLINING	BGILNRTU	BLURTING	BHILLPUW	BULLWHIP
BGIILNOR	BROILING	BGILNSTU	BUSTLING	BHILLSTU	BULLSHIT
BGIILNOS	BOILINGS	BGILNTTU	BUTTLING	BHILNSTU	BLUNTISH
BGIILNOX	BOLIXING	BGILOORS	OBLIGORS	BHILORRY	HORRIBLY
BGIILNPP	BLIPPING	BGILRSSU	BUSGIRLS	BHILORUV	BIHOURLY
BGIILNRS	BIRLINGS	BGIMNOOR	BROOMING	BHILOSTU	HOLIBUTS
	BIRSLING	BGIMNOOS	BOOMINGS	BHILOSYY	BOYISHLY
	BRISLING		BOSOMING	BHIMNORT	THROMBIN
BGIILNSS	BLISSING	BGIMNORS	SOMBRING	BHIMOOPR	BIOMORPH
	SIBLINGS	BGIMNORW	RINGWOMB	BHIMOOSS	HOBOISMS
BGIILNTY	BITINGLY	BGIMNPSU	BUMPINGS	BHIMOPRS	BIMORPHS
BGIILNTZ	BLITZING	BGIMOSSY	BOGYISMS	BHIMOPSS	PHOBISMS
BGIIMMNR	BRIMMING	BGINNNOU	UNBONING	BHIMORSU	BOHRIUMS
BGIIMNRS	BRIMINGS	BGINNORU	UNROBING	BHIMORTU	BOTHRIUM
BGIIMNRU	IMBRUING	BGINNORW	BROWNING	BHIMSSTU	BISMUTHS
BGIINNOR	INORBING	BGINNORZ	BRONZING	BHINOPSU	UNBISHOP
BGIINNRS	INBRINGS	BGINNOUW	UNBOWING	BHINORSW	BROWNISH
BGIINORT	ORBITING	BGINNOUX	UNBOXING	BHIOOPRS	BIOPHORS
BGIINRST	RINGBITS	BGINNRSU	BURNINGS	BHIOOPRT	BIOTROPH
BGIINRSU	BRUISING	BGINNRTU	BRUNTING	BHIOPSST	PHOBISTS
BGIINRTU	BRUITING	BGINNSTU	BUNTINGS	BHIRSTTU	TURBITHS
BGIINSTT	BITTINGS	BGINOOST	BONGOIST	BHISSTTU	BUSHTITS
BGIINSTU	BUISTING		BOOSTING	BHKLORUW	BUHLWORK
BGIINVVY	BIVVYING	BGINORST	STROBING	BHKMNOOY	HYMNBOOK
BGIJLMNU	JUMBLING	BGINORSW	BROWSING	BHKNOOOR	HORNBOOK
BGIJNORU	OBJURING	BGINORSZ	ZORBINGS	BHKOOOPS	BOOKSHOP
BGIJOSUU	BIJUGOUS	BGINOSWW	WINGBOWS	BHLLNORU	BULLHORN
BGIKLNNU	BLUNKING	BGINPRSU	UPBRINGS	BHLLOSTU	BULLSHOT
BGIKLNOT	KINGBOLT	BGINRSSU	SUBRINGS	BHLLRSUU	BULLRUSH
BGIKNNOS	BONKINGS	BGINRSTU	BRUSTING	BHLOOOTT	TOLBOOTH
BGIKNNOU	BUNKOING		BRUTINGS	BHLOSTUU	OUTBLUSH
BGIKNOOR	BROOKING		BURSTING	BHLRSUUY	BULRUSHY
BGIKNOOS	BOOKINGS	BGINSSSU	BUSSINGS	BHMNTTUU	THUMBNUT
BGIKNORS	BROKINGS	BGINSSTU	BUSTINGS	BHMOPTTU	THUMBPOT
BGIKNSSU	BUSKINGS	BGINSSWY	SWINGBYS	BHMORSTU	THROMBUS
BGIKNSTU	STINKBUG	BGINSUZZ	BUZZINGS	BHNOOOST	BOSTHOON
BGILLLUY	GULLIBLY	BGISUWZZ	BUZZWIGS	BHNOORTX	BOXTHORN
BGILLNOU	GLOBULIN	BGKLOOOS	LOGBOOKS	BHNOSSUW	SNOWBUSH
BGILLNRU	BULLRING	BGKNOOOS	SONGBOOK	BHOOPSSY	SHOPBOYS
BGILLNSU	BULLINGS	BGKORSSY	GRYSBOKS	BHOORTTU	OUTTHROB
BGILLNUY	BULLYING	BGLLNOOY	OBLONGLY	BHOOSSTW	BOWSHOTS
BGILMMNU	BUMMLING	BGLNOOSW	LONGBOWS	BHPRSSUU	BRUSHUPS
	MUMBLING	BGLNOSUW	BLOWGUNS	BIIKLOST	KILOBITS
BGILMNOO	BLOOMING	BGLOORYV	BRYOLOGY	BIIKNOOT	BOOTIKIN
BGILMNPU	PLUMBING	BGMNOOOR	GOMBROON	BIILLMOR	MORBILLI
BGILMNRU	RUMBLING	BGMOOSTU	GUMBOOTS	BIILLMSS	MISBILLS
BGILMNTU	TUMBLING	BGMORRUW	GRUBWORM	BIILLNOS	BILLIONS
BGILMORY	GORBLIMY	BGNOOSWY	GOWNBOYS	BIILLOSU	BOUILLIS
BGILMOSU	GUMBOILS	BGNOSSSU	SUBSONGS	BIILLSTW	TWIBILLS
BGILMOTU	GUMBOTIL	BGOPRSUU	SUBGROUP	BIILMOTY	MOBILITY
BGILNNOS	SNOBLING	BGORSTUU	BURGOUTS	BIILMSTU	MISBUILT
BGILNNTU	BLUNTING	BGORSTUW	BUGWORTS		SUBLIMIT
BGILNOOP	BLOOPING	BHHIISST	BHISHTIS	BIILNNRS	BIRLINNS
BGILNORT	RINGBOLT	BHIIINNS	INHIBINS	BIILNOOV	OBLIVION
BGILNORY	BORINGLY	BHIIINST	INHIBITS	BIILNORU	UROBILIN
BGILNOST	BILTONGS	BHIIKRSS	BRISKISH	BIILNOTY	NOBILITY
	BOLTINGS	BHIILMPS	BLIMPISH	BIILNQSU	QUIBLINS
BGILNOSU	BLOUSING	BHIIMRST	MISBIRTH	BIILNSTU	SUBTILIN
BGILNOSW	BOWLINGS	BHIIOPRT	PROHIBIT	BIILNSVY	BIVINYLS
BGILNOTT	BLOTTING	BHIIPSSS	SIBSHIPS	BIILNTUY	NUBILITY
	BOTTLING	BHIKLLOO	BILLHOOK	BIILORST	STROBILI
BGILNOTU	BOULTING	BHIKMNTU	THUMBKIN	BIILOSSU	SIBILOUS
BGILNOWY	BOWINGLY	BHILLNOR	HORNBILL	BIILOSSY	BIOLYSIS

BIILSTTW	WITBLITS	**BINORSST**	RIBSTONS	**BNNRSSUU**	SUNBURNS
BIIMMNSY	NIMBYISM	**BINORSSU**	BOURSINS	**BNNRSTUU**	SUNBURNT
BIIMMOSZ	ZOMBIISM	**BINORSUW**	UNIBROWS	**BNOOOSTW**	SNOWBOOT
BIIMHNOSU	NIOBIUMS	**BINRSSTU**	INBURSTS	**BNOOOSUY**	SONOBUOY
BIIMPRSS	BIPRISMS	**BINRSTUY**	BUTYRINS	**BNOORTUW**	BROWNOUT
BIIMSSTU	STIBIUMS	**BINSSTUU**	SUBUNITS	**BNOPRSTU**	POSTBURN
BIINOOTX	BIOTOXIN	**BIOPRRSU**	SUBPRIOR	**BNORRUUW**	UNBURROW
BIINORSV	VIBRIONS	**BIOPRSTW**	BOWSPRIT	**BNORSTUU**	BURNOUTS
BIINOTVY	BOVINITY	**BIORRSTU**	BURRITOS		OUTBURNS
BIINRSTU	BURINIST	**BIORRSTW**	RIBWORTS	**BNORTTUU**	OUTBURNT
BIIQTUUY	UBIQUITY	**BIORSSTT**	BISTORTS	**BNRSSTUU**	SUNBURST
BIIRSSTU	BURSITIS	**BIORSTTU**	BITTOURS	**BOOPSSTY**	POSTBOYS
BIJNOSSU	SUBJOINS	**BIORSTTY**	BOTRYTIS	**BORSTTUU**	OUTBURST
BIKLLSSU	SUBSKILL	**BIORSTUY**	BISTOURY	**BORSTUUY**	BUTYROUS
BIKLNOST	INKBLOTS	**BIOSTTUY**	OBTUSITY	**BPRSSTUU**	UPBURSTS
BIKLNOSY	LINKBOYS	**BIRSSTTU**	SUBTRIST	**CCCDIILY**	DICYCLIC
BIKMNOOS	BOOMKINS	**BIRSSUUV**	SUBVIRUS	**CCCDIOOS**	COCCOIDS
BIKMNPSU	BUMPKINS	**BISSSSTU**	SUBSISTS	**CCCDKLOO**	COLDCOCK
BIKOOSUU	BOUSOUKI	**BISSTUUU**	BUSUUTIS	**CCCEEILT**	ECLECTIC
BIKOOUUZ	BOUZOUKI	**BKKOOORW**	BOOKWORK	**CCCEGOSY**	COCCYGES
BIKORRSW	RIBWORKS		WORKBOOK	**CCCEHIOR**	CHOCCIER
BILLMSUY	BULLYISM	**BKLOSTUU**	OUTBULKS	**CCCEHIOS**	CHOCCIES
BILLNOOU	BOUILLON	**BKMOOORW**	BOOKWORM	**CCCEIIRT**	ECCRITIC
BILLNOSU	BULLIONS	**BKMOORUZ**	ZOMBORUK	**CCCEILNY**	ENCYCLIC
BILLOSUY	BLOUSILY	**BKNNOOOS**	NONBOOKS	**CCCEILUV**	EUCYCLIC
BILLOSWY	BLOWSILY	**BKNOOSTW**	BOWKNOTS	**CCCEOSXY**	COCCYXES
BILLOWYZ	BLOWZILY	**BKORSUWY**	BUSYWORK	**CCCHIORY**	CHICCORY
BILLRRUY	BLURRILY	**BLLLLOOY**	LOBLOLLY	**CCCIINSU**	SUCCINIC
BILLRSWY	WRYBILLS	**BLLMOORW**	BOLLWORM	**CCCILLVY**	CYCLICLY
BILMMPSU	PLUMBISM	**BLLOPTUU**	BULLPOUT	**CCCILNOY**	CYCLONIC
BILMNORS	NOMBRILS	**BLLOTUUY**	OUTBULLY	**CCCILOPY**	CYCLOPIC
BILMOSTU	BOTULISM	**BLMMPSUU**	PLUMBUMS	**CCCINSTU**	SUCCINCT
BILMRSTU	TUMBRILS	**BLMNPSUU**	UNPLUMBS	**CCCIOORS**	SCIROCCO
BILNOSTU	BOTULINS	**BLMOOOST**	TOMBOLOS	**CCCKOORW**	COCKCROW
BILNOSUU	NUBILOUS	**BLMOOOTU**	OUTBLOOM	**CCCNOOST**	CONCOCTS
BILNSTUU	TUBULINS	**BLMOOOTY**	LOBOTOMY	**CCDDEENO**	CONCEDED
BILOOPST	POTBOILS	**BLMOORSW**	LOBWORMS	**CCDDEEOT**	DECOCTED
BILOORST	SORBITOL	**BLMOOSSS**	BLOSSOMS	**CCDDELOU**	OCCLUDED
BILOORTT	BORLOTTI	**BLMOOSSY**	BLOSSOMY	**CCDDENOU**	CONDUCED
BILOPSSY	POSSIBLY	**BLMOPSUU**	PLUMBOUS	**CCDEEENR**	CREDENCE
BILORSST	BRISTOLS	**BLNOOSSU**	BLOUSONS	**CCDEEHIL**	CLICHEED
	STROBILS	**BLNSTUUY**	UNSUBTLY	**CCDEEHLN**	CLENCHED
BILOSSSU	SUBSOILS	**BLOOPSHY**	PLOWBOYS	**CCDEEILN**	LICENCED
BILOSTUY	ISOBUTYL	**BLOORSWW**	LOWBROWS	**CCDEEINS**	SCIENCED
BILOTTUU	OUTBUILT	**BLOOSSTY**	SLYBOOTS	**CCDEEIOP**	CODPIECE
BILSTTUY	SUBTILTY	**BLOOSTUW**	BLOWOUTS	**CCDEEIOS**	ECOCIDES
BIMMOOSS	IMBOSOMS	**BLOPSSTU**	SUBPLOTS	**CCDEEIRV**	CREVICED
BIMMORSS	BROMISMS	**BLORSTUY**	ROBUSTLY	**CCDEEKOR**	COCKERED
BIMNNUUU	UNUNBIUM	**BLOSTUUU**	TUBULOUS		RECOCKED
BIMNORSW	IMBROWNS	**BLRSTUYY**	BUTYRYLS	**CCDEEKOY**	COCKEYED
BIMNOSSY	SYMBIONS	**BMNOOORW**	MONOBROW	**CCDEELRY**	RECYCLED
BIMNOSTY	SYMBIONT	**BMNOOOSW**	MOONBOWS	**CCDEENOR**	CONCEDER
BIMNRRUU	MUIRBURN	**BMNOOOTW**	BOOMTOWN	**CCDEENOS**	CONCEDES
BIMNRUUV	VIBURNUM	**BMNOORRU**	MOORBURN	**CCDEESSU**	SUCCEEDS
BIMOORST	ROBOTISM	**BMNOOSSU**	UNBOSOMS	**CCDEHHRU**	CHURCHED
BIMOSSSS	BOSSISMS	**BMNORSUW**	MOWBURNS	**CCDEHIKT**	TCHICKED
BIMOSSTW	MISTBOWS	**BMNORTUW**	MOWBURNT	**CCDEHILN**	CLINCHED
BIMOSSTY	SYBOTISM	**BMOOORSX**	BOXROOMS	**CCDEHIPU**	HICCUPED
	SYMBIOTS	**BMOORSSU**	SOMBROUS	**CCDEHKLU**	CHUCKLED
BIMRSSTU	BRUTISMS	**BMOORSTU**	MOTORBUS	**CCDEHLTU**	CLUTCHED
BIMRSSUX	BRUXISMS	**BMOORTTY**	BOTTOMRY		DECLUTCH
BINNORTW	TWINBORN	**BMORSSTU**	STROMBUS	**CCDEHNRU**	CRUNCHED
BINOORST	BIOTRONS	**BNNORTUW**	NUTBROWN	**CCDEHOOS**	SCOOCHED
	ISOBRONT	**BNNOTTUU**	UNBUTTON	**CCDEHOOT**	COOTCHED

CCDEHORS	SCORCHED	CCEEHLNS	CLENCHES	CCEHHIIR	CHICHIER
CCDEHORT	CROTCHED	CCEEHORS	ECORCHES	CCEHHINS	CHINCHES
CCDEHORU	CROUCHED	CCEEHOSU	COUCHEES	CCEHHRSU	CHURCHES
CCDEHOST	SCOTCHED	CCEEHRSY	SCREECHY	CCEHIIMR	CHIMERIC
CCDEHRTU	CRUTCHED	CCEEIILS	CICELIES	CCEHIIMS	ISCHEMIC
CCDEHSTU	SCUTCHED	CCEEIIST	CECITIES	CCEHIINZ	ZECCHINI
CCDEIILO	CLEIDOIC	CCEEIKLR	CLECKIER	CCEHIKNP	PINCHECK
CCDEIINO	COINCIDE	CCEEILMU	LEUCEMIC	CCEHIKNS	CHICKENS
CCDEIIRT	CRICETID	CCEEILNR	ENCIRCLE	CCEHIKSU	CHUCKIES
CCDEIIST	DEICTICS		LICENCER	CCEHILNR	CLINCHER
CCDEILOS	SCOLECID	CCEEILNS	LICENCES	CCEHILNS	CLINCHES
CCDEILSY	CYCLISED	CCEEILNT	ELENCTIC	CCEHILOR	CHOLERIC
CCDEILYZ	CYCLIZED	CCEEILPY	EPICYCLE	CCEHILOY	CHOICELY
CCDEINOR	CORNICED	CCEEILRR	RECIRCLE	CCEHILSU	CULCHIES
CCDEINOS	CONCISED	CCEEILRT	ELECTRIC	CCEHILTY	HECTICLY
CCDEINOT	OCCIDENT	CCEEIMNU	ECUMENIC	CCEHINOR	CORNICHE
CCDEIOPP	COPPICED	CCEEINOR	CICERONE		ENCHORIC
CCDEIOPU	OCCUPIED		CROCEINE	CCEHINOS	CONCHIES
CCDEIORT	CODIRECT	CCEEINOV	CONCEIVE	CCEHINOZ	ZECCHINO
CCDEKNOU	UNCOCKED	CCEEINSS	SCIENCES	CCEHINRU	CRUNCHIE
CCDEKOOU	CUCKOOED	CCEEIORS	CICOREES	CCEHINSS	CHICNESS
CCDELNOU	CONCLUDE	CCEEIORV	COERCIVE	CCEHINST	TECHNICS
CCDELORU	OCCLUDER	CCEEIPSS	SPECCIES	CCEHINSZ	ZECCHINS
CCDELOSU	OCCLUDES	CCEEIRSS	CERCISES	CCEHIORT	RICOCHET
CCDELOTU	OCCULTED		ECCRISES	CCEHIOST	CHOICEST
CCDENOOO	COCOONED	CCEEIRSV	CERVICES	CCEHIRSS	SCREICHS
CCDENORU	CONDUCER		CRESCIVE		SCRIECHS
CCDENOSU	CONDUCES		CREVICES	CCEHKLRU	CHUCKLER
CCDEORRU	OCCURRED	CCEEITTU	EUTECTIC	CCEHKLSU	CHUCKLES
CCDEORSU	SUCCORED	CCEEKLOR	COCKEREL	CCEHKMSS	SCHMECKS
CCDEOSTU	STUCCOED	CCEEKNRW	CREWNECK	CCEHKMSU	CHECKSUM
CCDHIIKP	DIPCHICK	CCEEKOSY	COCKEYES	CCEHKNSU	UNCHECKS
CCDHIILO	CICHLOID	CCEELMNY	CLEMENCY	CCEHKORW	CHECKROW
CCDHIILS	CICHLIDS	CCEELNSU	LUCENCES	CCEHKOTU	CHECKOUT
CCDHIIOR	DICHROIC	CCEELOSS	SCOLECES	CCEHKPSU	CHECKUPS
CCDHIIOT	DICHOTIC	CCEELRRY	RECYCLER	CCEHKRSU	CHUCKERS
CCDHINOO	CONCHOID	CCEELRSY	RECYCLES	CCEHLMOR	CROMLECH
CCDIILNU	NUCLIDIC	CCEEMMNO	COMMENCE	CCEHLNNU	UNCLENCH
CCDIILOS	CODICILS	CCEEMMOR	COMMERCE	CCEHLNSU	CLUNCHES
CCDIILSU	CULICIDS	CCEEMOPS	COMPESCE	CCEHLRSU	CLERUCHS
CCDIINOO	CONOIDIC	CCEENNOS	ENSCONCE	CCEHLRUY	CLERUCHY
CCDIINOS	SCINCOID	CCEENORT	CONCRETE	CCEHLSSU	SCULCHES
CCDIINST	DISCINCT	CCEENRST	CRESCENT	CCEHLSTU	CLUTCHES
CCDIIORS	CRICOIDS	CCEEORRS	COERCERS		CULTCHES
CCDIIORT	DICROTIC	CCEEORST	COERECTS	CCEHNRRU	CRUNCHER
CCDILOSY	CYCLOIDS	CCEFFHKO	CHECKOFF	CCEHNRSU	CRUNCHES
CCDINOTU	CONDUCTI	CCEFHRSU	CURCHEFS	CCEHOOSS	SCOOCHES
CCDKLOSU	CUCKOLDS	CCEFIIPS	SPECIFIC	CCEHOOST	COOTCHES
CCDKOOOW	WOODCOCK	CCEFINOT	COINFECT	CCEHORRS	SCORCHER
CCDNOORS	CONCORDS	CCEFIRRU	CRUCIFER	CCEHORSS	SCORCHES
CCDNOSTU	CONDUCTS	CCEFLLOU	FLOCCULE	CCEHORST	CROCHETS
CCEEEILN	LICENCEE	CCEFLOOS	FLOCCOSE		CROTCHES
CCEEFFOT	COEFFECT	CCEFNOST	CONFECTS	CCEHORSU	COUCHERS
CCEEGINR	RECCEING	CCEGHIKN	CHECKING		CROUCHES
CCEEGNOS	COGENCES	CCEGHIOR	CHOREGIC	CCEHORTT	CROTCHET
CCEEHIKS	CHICKEES	CCEGIKLN	CLECKING	CCEHOSST	SCOTCHES
CCEEHILN	ELENCHIC	CCEGILMY	GLYCEMIC	CCEHRSTU	CRUTCHES
CCEEHINZ	ZECCHINE	CCEGILOO	ECOLOGIC		SCUTCHER
CCEEHISV	CEVICHES	CCEGILRY	GLYCERIC	CCEHRTUY	CUTCHERY
CCEEHKNS	SCHNECKE	CCEGINNO	CONGENIC	CCEHSSTU	SCUTCHES
CCEEHKPR	PRECHECK	CCEGINOR	COERCING	CCEIIKLN	NICKELIC
CCEEHKRS	CHECKERS	CCEGINPS	SPECCING	CCEIILNO	COLICINE
	RECHECKS	CCEGINRY	RECCYING	CCEIILNT	ENCLITIC
CCEEHLNR	CLENCHER	CCEGNOOS	COGNOSCE	CCEIILNU	CULICINE

CCEIILOR	LICORICE	CCEIOPRU	OCCUPIER	CCGHINTW	CWTCHING
CCEIILPT	ECLIPTIC	CCEIOPSU	OCCUPIES	CCGIIKLN	CLICKING
CCEIILST	SCILICET	CCEIOPTY	ECOTYPIC	CCGIIKNR	CRICKING
CCEIILTU	LEUCITIC	CCEIORST	CORTICES	CCGIILNR	CIRCLING
CCEIINNO	CONICINE	CCEIOTXY	EXOCYTIC	CCGIILNU	GLUCINIC
CCEIINNR	ENCRINIC	CCEIPSST	SCEPTICS	CCGIKLNO	CLOCKING
CCEIINOR	CICERONI	CCEIRSSU	CIRCUSES		COCKLING
CCEIINTU	CICUTINE	CCEJNOST	CONJECTS	CCGIKLNU	CLUCKING
CCEIIRRT	CIRCITER	CCEKLORS	CLOCKERS	CCGIKNOR	CROCKING
CCEIIRSS	ECCRISIS		COCKLERS	CCGILLOV	GLYCOLIC
CCEIIRST	ICTERICS	CCEKNOST	CONTECKS	CCGILNOY	GLYCONIC
CCEIIRTT	RECTITIC	CCEKNOSY	COCKNEYS	CCGILNSY	CYCLINGS
CCEIIRTU	EUCRITIC	CCEKOPST	PETCOCKS	CCGILOSU	GLUCOSIC
CCEIKKLO	COCKLIKE	CCEKORRY	CROCKERY	CCGINNOS	SCONCING
CCEIKLRS	CLICKERS	CCEKORST	CROCKETS	CCGINOTW	TWOCCING
CCEIKLRU	CLUCKIER	CCEKORSU	COCKSURE	CCGKOORS	GORCOCKS
CCEIKLST	CLICKETS	CCELLOST	COLLECTS	CCHHIITY	ICHTHYIC
CCEIKORS	COCKSIER	CCELMOPT	COMPLECT	CCHHILSS	SCHLICHS
CCEIKOST	COCKIEST	CCELNOSY	CYCLONES	CCHHINOT	CHTHONIC
CCEIKRST	CRICKETS	CCELOPSY	CYCLOPES	CCHHLRUY	CHURCHLY
CCEILMOO	COELOMIC	CCELORTU	OCCULTER	CCHHNRUU	UNCHURCH
CCEILMOP	COMPLICE	CCELOSSY	CYCLOSES	CCHHOOWW	CHOWCHOW
CCEILNOR	CORNICLE	CCELRUUY	CURLYCUE	CCHIINUZ	ZUCCHINI
CCEILNUY	UNICYCLE	CCELSSUY	CYCLUSES	CCHIIORT	ORCHITIC
CCEILOSS	SCOLICES	CCENNORS	CONCERNS	CCHIKMPU	CHIPMUCK
CCEILRRS	CIRCLERS	CCENNOST	CONCENTS	CCHIKORY	CHICKORY
CCEILRRU	CURRICLE		CONNECTS	CCHIKSST	SCHTICKS
CCEILRST	CIRCLETS	CCENOORT	CONCERTO	CCHILNNU	UNCLINCH
CCEILRSY	CRESYLIC	CCENOOTT	CONCETTO	CCHILNUY	UNCHICLY
CCEILRTY	TRICYCLE	CCENOPST	CONCEPTS	CCHINORS	CHRONICS
CCEILRUU	CURLICUE	CCENORST	CONCERTS	CCHINSSU	SCUCHINS
CCEILSSY	CYCLISES	CCENORSW	CONCREWS	CCHIPSSY	PSYCHICS
CCEILSTU	CUTICLES	CCENORTY	CORNETCY	CCHKLOSS	SCHLOCKS
CCEILSYZ	CYCLIZES	CCENOSTV	CONVECTS	CCHKLOSY	SCHLOCKY
CCEIMNOO	ECONOMIC	CCENRRUY	CURRENCY	CCHKMNUU	NUMCHUCK
	ONCOMICE	CCEOOORR	COROCORE	CCHKMOSS	SCHMOCKS
CCEIMOPR	COPREMIC	CCEOORSU	CROCEOUS	CCHKMSSU	SCHMUCKS
CCEIMOST	COSMETIC	CCEOOSTT	COCOTTES	CCHKOOST	COCKSHOT
CCEIMRRU	MERCURIC	CCEOPRUY	REOCCUPY	CCHKOPTU	PUTCHOCK
CCEIMRUV	CERVICUM	CCEORRST	CORRECTS	CCHKOSTU	COCKSHUT
CCEINNOS	INSCONCE	CCEORRSU	REOCCURS	CCHKPSUU	UPCHUCKS
CCEINNOV	CONVINCE		SUCCORER	CCHKSSTU	SCHTUCKS
CCEINOOR	COERCION	CCEORSSU	CROCUSES	CCHLNTUU	UNCLUTCH
CCEINOOZ	CENOZOIC	CCEORSTU	STUCCOER	CCHNRSUY	SCRUNCHY
CCEINOPR	COPRINCE	CCEORSTW	TWOCCERS	CCHOORST	SCROOTCH
CCEINOPT	CONCEPTI	CCEOSSTU	STUCCOES	CCIIIMSV	CIVICISM
CCEINORS	CONCISER	CCERSTUW	CREWCUTS	CCIIIPRT	PICRITIC
	CORNICES	CCESSSUU	CUSCUSES	CCIIKKPW	PICKWICK
	CROCEINS	CCFGILNO	FLOCCING	CCIIKNPY	PICNICKY
CCEINORT	CONCERTI	CCFHKLOU	CHOCKFUL	CCIILNOS	COLICINS
	NECROTIC	CCFIINOR	CORNIFIC	CCIILORT	CLITORIC
CCEINOSS	CONCISES	CCFIIRUX	CRUCIFIX	CCIILPRS	CIRCLIPS
CCEINOST	CONCEITS	CCFIKNOY	COCKNIFY	CCIIMNSY	CYNICISM
CCEINOTT	CONCETTI	CCFILLOU	FLOCCULI	CCIINNSU	CICINNUS
	TECTONIC	CCFILNOT	CONFLICT	CCIINORZ	ZIRCONIC
CCEINOTY	CONCEITY	CCFKLOOT	COCKLOFT	CCIINOTY	CONICITY
CCEINPRT	PRECINCT	CCFLOOOO	LOCOFOCO	CCIIRSTU	CIRCUITS
CCEINRTU	CINCTURE	CCGHHIOU	HICCOUGH	CCIIRTUY	CIRCUITY
CCEINSTY	SYNECTIC	CCGHIINN	CINCHING	CCIKKLOP	LOCKPICK
CCEIOORT	CROCOITE	CCGHIKNO	CHOCKING		PICKLOCK
CCEIOOTX	ECOTOXIC	CCGHIKNU	CHUCKING	CCIKKOTT	TICKTOCK
CCEIOOTZ	ECTOZOIC	CCGHINNO	CONCHING	CCIKLOSW	COWLICKS
CCEIOPPS	COPPICES	CCGHINOS	GNOCCHIS	CCIKNOPR	PRINCOCK
CCEIOPRT	ECTROPIC	CCGHINOU	COUCHING	CCIKOPRS	CROPSICK

CCIKOPST	COCKPITS	CDDEEERW	DECREWED	CDDELNOO	CONDOLED
CCILLOTY	CYCLITOL	CDDEEETT	DETECTED	CDDELOOR	CROODLED
CCILNOOS	COLONICS	CDDEEFOR	DEFORCED	CDDELORS	CODDLERS
CCILNOSU	COUNCILS	CDDEEGLU	CUDGELED	CDDELRSU	CRUDDLES
CCILNSUY	SUCCINYL	CDDEEHIS	DEHISCED		CUDDLERS
CCILOOPS	PICCOLOS	CDDEEHIT	CHEDDITE	CDDELSSU	SCUDDLES
CCILORUU	CURCULIO	CDDEEHNR	DRENCHED	CDDEMNOU	DUNCEDOM
CCILOSSY	CYCLOSIS	CDDEEIIM	MEDICIDE	CDDENNOO	CONDONED
CCILSSTY	CYCLISTS	CDDEEIIS	DEICIDES	CDDENOOR	CORDONED
CCIMNRUU	CURCUMIN	CDDEEIKR	DICKERED	CDDENORU	UNCORDED
CCINOORT	CROTONIC	CDDEEIKT	DETICKED	CDDEOORR	CORRODED
CCINOOST	COCTIONS	CDDEEILN	DECLINED	CDDEOORT	DOCTORED
CCINOPRT	PROCINCT	CDDEEILP	PEDICLED	CDDEOORW	CODEWORD
CCINOPSY	SYNCOPIC	CDDEEINR	CINDERED	CDDEOPRU	PRODUCED
CCINOPTY	PYCNOTIC	CDDEEINZ	DEZINCED	CDDERSSU	SCUDDERS
CCINORSY	CRYONICS	CDDEEIOT	COEDITED	CDDGHILO	GODCHILD
CCINOSTV	CONVICTS	CDDEEIOV	DEVOICED	CDDGILNO	CLODDING
CCIOOPST	SCOTOPIC	CDDEEIPT	DEPICTED		CODDLING
CCIOORSS	SIROCCOS	CDDEEIRS	DECIDERS	CDDGILNU	CUDDLING
CCIOOTXY	OXYTOCIC		DESCRIED	CDDGINRU	CRUDDING
CCIOPRST	COSCRIPT	CDDEEIRT	CREDITED	CDDGINSU	SCUDDING
CCIOPSTU	OCCIPUTS		DIRECTED	CDDHHISU	SHIDDUCH
CCIRSSUY	CIRCUSSY	CDDEEKNU	UNDECKED	CDDHIIRY	DIHYDRIC
CCJNNOTU	CONJUNCT	CDDEEKOR	REDOCKED	CDDHILOS	CLODDISH
CCKKLMUU	MUCKLUCK	CDDEEKOT	DOCKETED	CDDHIORS	DICHORDS
CCKMMORU	CRUMMOCK	CDDEEKUW	DUCKWEED	CDDIIIOS	DIDICOIS
CCKMOOOR	MOORCOCK	CDDEELMO	COMEDDLE	CDDIIKNS	NIDDICKS
CCKNORTU	TURNCOCK	CDDEELPU	DECUPLED	CDDIIOSS	DISCOIDS
CCKOOPRT	CROCKPOT	CDDEELSU	SCEDULED	CDDIIOSY	DIDICOYS
CCKOOPST	STOPCOCK		SECLUDED	CDDIISTY	DYTISCID
CCKOPRSU	COCKSPUR	CDDEELUX	EXCLUDED	CDDIKOPS	PIDDOCKS
CCKOSSTU	CUSTOCKS	CDDEELUY	DEUCEDLY	CDDIORSS	DISCORDS
CCLLOTUY	OCCULTLY	CDDEENOS	SECONDED	CDDKOPSU	PUDDOCKS
CCLMOOPU	COCOPLUM	CDDEENSS	DESCENDS	CDDKORSU	RUDDOCKS
CCLNOOOR	CONCOLOR	CDDEEOPR	PRECODED	CDDMMOUU	MOCUDDUM
CCLOOOSZ	ZOCCOLOS	CDDEEORR	RECORDED	CDDOOORW	CORDWOOD
CCLOORSU	OCCLUSOR	CDDEEORS	DECODERS	CDEEEERX	EXCEEDER
CCMOOORS	MOROCCOS	CDDEERUV	DECURVED	CDEEEFFT	EFFECTED
CCNOOPSU	PUCCOONS	CDDEESUW	CUDWEEDS	CDEEEFHL	FLEECHED
CCNOORSU	CONCOURS	CDDEFIIO	CODIFIED	CDEEEFNR	REFENCED
CCNOOSTU	COCONUTS	CDDEFINO	CONFIDED	CDEEEFNS	DEFENCES
CCOOOORR	COROCORO	CDDEGIIN	DECIDING	CDEEEFRT	REDEFECT
CCOOSSUU	COUSCOUS	CDDEGINO	DECODING		REFECTED
CCOOTTUU	TUCOTUCO	CDDEGINU	DEDUCING	CDEEEHHW	WHEECHED
CCORSSTU	CROSSCUT	CDDEHIOW	COWHIDED	CDEEEHLR	CHEERLED
CCORSSUU	SUCCOURS	CDDEHISU	CHUDDIES		LECHERED
CCOTTUUU	TUCUTUCO	CDDEHRSU	CHUDDERS	CDEEEHMS	SMEECHED
CCRSUUUU	SURUCUCU	CDDEIINT	INDICTED	CDEEEHOR	REECHOED
CCTTUUUU	TUCUTUCU	CDDEIISS	DISCIDES	CDEEEHPS	DEPECHES
CDDDEETU	DEDUCTED	CDDEIISU	SUICIDED		SPEECHED
CDDDEIIS	DISCIDED	CDDEIKOS	DOCKISED	CDEEEHRS	CREESHED
CDDDELRU	CRUDDLED		DOCKSIDE	CDEEEHRW	RECHEWED
CDDDELSU	SCUDDLED	CDDEIKOZ	DOCKIZED	CDEEEHST	TEDESCHE
CDDDIIOY	DIDDICOY	CDDEILLO	COLLIDED	CDEEEHSW	ESCHEWED
CDDEEEEX	EXCEEDED	CDDEILNU	INCLUDED	CDEEEINP	PIECENED
CDDEEEFN	DEFENCED	CDDEILOR	CLODDIER	CDEEEINV	EVIDENCE
CDDEEEFT	DEFECTED	CDDEILRU	CUDDLIER	CDEEEIPS	EPICEDES
CDDEEEIR	REDECIDE	CDDEIMOS	MISCODED	CDEEEIRV	DECEIVER
CDDEEEIV	DECEIVED	CDDEINTU	INDUCTED		RECEIVED
CDDEEEJT	DEJECTED	CDDEIORV	DIVORCED	CDEEEISV	DECEIVES
CDDEEENR	DECERNED	CDDEIRRU	CRUDDIER	CDEEEJRT	REJECTED
CDDEEENT	DECEDENT	CDDEIRSU	DISCURED	CDEEEKNW	NECKWEED
CDDEEEPR	PRECEDED	CDDEKNOU	UNDOCKED	CDEEELLX	EXCELLED
CDDEEERS	SCREEDED	CDDELLOU	COLLUDED	CDEEELNR	CRENELED

CDEEELOS	COLESEED
CDEEELPY	YCLEEPED
CDEEELST	DESELECT
	SELECTED
CDEEELUX	EXCLUDEE
CDEEEMNT	CEMENTED
CDEEEMOR	COREDEEM
CDEEEMPR	EMPERCED
CDEEENNT	TENDENCE
CDEEENOS	SECONDEE
CDEEENRS	RECENSED
	SCREENED
	SECERNED
CDEEENRT	CENTERED
	DECENTER
	DECENTRE
CDEEEPRS	PRECEDES
CDEEEPTX	EXCEPTED
	EXPECTED
CDEEERRS	DECREERS
	SCREEDER
CDEEERSS	RECESSED
	SECEDERS
CDEEERST	DECREETS
	RESECTED
	SCREETED
	SECRETED
CDEEERSV	SCREEVED
CDEEERTT	DETECTER
CDEEERTX	EXCRETED
CDEEESSX	EXCESSED
CDEEESTX	EXSECTED
CDEEETUX	EXECUTED
CDEEFFOR	COFFERED
	EFFORCED
CDEEFHLN	FLENCHED
CDEEFHLT	FLETCHED
CDEEFHNR	FRENCHED
CDEEFIIL	ICEFIELD
CDEEFIIS	EDIFICES
CDEEFIIT	FETICIDE
CDEEFINT	INFECTED
CDEEFKLR	FRECKLED
CDEEFKOR	FOREDECK
CDEEFLST	DEFLECTS
CDEEFNNU	UNFENCED
CDEEFNOR	ENFORCED
CDEEFORR	DEFORCER
CDEEFORS	DEFORCES
	FRESCOED
CDEEFORT	DEFECTOR
CDEEGIIR	REGICIDE
CDEEGINO	GENOCIDE
CDEEGINR	RECEDING
CDEEGINS	SECEDING
CDEEGIOS	GEODESIC
CDEEGIOT	GEODETIC
CDEEGIRS	GRECISED
CDEEGIRU	CUDGERIE
CDEEGIRZ	GRECIZED
CDEEGKST	GEDECKTS
CDEEGLRU	CUDGELER
CDEEGNOR	CONGREED
CDEEHHSU	SHEUCHED
CDEEHHTT	THETCHED
CDEEHIKL	HELIDECK
CDEEHILN	LICHENED
CDEEHILP	CHELIPED
CDEEHILS	CHISELED
CDEEHINR	ENRICHED
	INHERCED
	NICHERED
	RICHENED
CDEEHIOS	ECHOISED
CDEEHIOZ	ECHOIZED
CDEEHIPR	CIPHERED
	DECIPHER
CDEEHIPS	CEPHEIDS
CDEEHIRR	CHERRIED
	DREICHER
CDEEHIRW	RICHWEED
CDEEHISS	DEHISCES
CDEEHIST	CHEDITES
	TEDESCHI
CDEEHITW	ITCHWEED
CDEEHKST	SKETCHED
CDEEHKTV	KVETCHED
CDEEHLMO	LEECHDOM
CDEEHLPU	PLEUCHED
CDEEHLQU	QUELCHED
CDEEHLSU	SCHEDULE
CDEEHMTU	HUMECTED
CDEEHNQU	QUENCHED
CDEEHNRR	DRENCHER
CDEEHNRS	DRENCHES
CDEEHNRT	TRENCHED
CDEEHNRW	WRENCHED
CDEEHNST	STENCHED
CDEEHNUW	UNCHEWED
CDEEHORS	CHORDEES
	COSHERED
CDEEHORT	HECTORED
	TOCHERED
CDEEHPRU	CHERUPED
CDEEHPRY	CYPHERED
CDEEHQTU	QUETCHED
CDEEHRTW	WRETCHED
CDEEHSSU	DUCHESSE
CDEEIILT	ELICITED
CDEEIIMN	MEDICINE
CDEEIIMP	EPIDEMIC
CDEEIINT	INDICTEE
CDEEIIOS	DIOECIES
CDEEIIRT	DIERETIC
CDEEIIST	EIDETICS
CDEEIISV	DECISIVE
CDEEIITT	DIETETIC
CDEEIJNT	INJECTED
CDEEIJOR	REJOICED
CDEEIKLN	NICKELED
CDEEIKMY	MICKEYED
CDEEIKNR	NICKERED
CDEEIKNS	SICKENED
CDEEIKNV	INVECKED
CDEEIKPT	PICKETED
CDEEIKRR	DRECKIER
CDEEIKRT	DETICKER
CDEEIKRW	WICKEDER
	WICKERED
CDEEIKRY	YICKERED
CDEEIKST	TICKSEED
CDEEIKTT	TICKETED
CDEEILNP	PENCILED
	PENDICLE
CDEEILNR	DECLINER
	RECLINED
CDEEILNS	DECLINES
	LICENSED
	SILENCED
CDEEILNT	DENTICLE
CDEEILNU	NUCLEIDE
CDEEILOR	RECOILED
CDEEILPS	ECLIPSED
	PEDICELS
	PEDICLES
CDEEILRS	SCLEREID
CDEEILRT	DERELICT
CDEEILRU	RECUILED
CDEEIMNR	ENDERMIC
CDEEIMNS	CNEMIDES
	ENDEMICS
CDEEIMOR	MEDIOCRE
CDEEIMOS	COMEDIES
CDEEIMPR	PREMEDIC
CDEEIMRS	MISCREED
CDEEIMRV	DECEMVIR
CDEEINNS	INCENSED
CDEEINNT	INCENTED
	INDECENT
CDEEINOR	RECOINED
CDEEINOS	CODEINES
CDEEINPR	PINCERED
CDEEINPS	DISPENCE
CDEEINPT	DEPEINCT
	INCEPTED
	PEINCTED
	PENTICED
CDEEINRU	REINDUCE
CDEEINTU	INDUCTEE
CDEEINTV	INVECTED
CDEEIOPR	RECOPIED
CDEEIORV	CODERIVE
	DIVORCEE
	REVOICED
CDEEIOSS	DIOCESES
CDEEIOSV	DEVOICES
CDEEIPRR	REPRICED
CDEEIPRS	PRECISED
CDEEIPRT	DECREPIT
	DEPICTER
	PRECITED
CDEEIPRU	PEDICURE
CDEEIPST	PECTISED
CDEEIPTZ	PECTIZED
CDEEIQSU	QUIESCED
CDEEIRRS	DECRIERS
	DESCRIER
CDEEIRRT	DIRECTER
	REDIRECT
CDEEIRSS	DESCRIES
CDEEIRST	DESERTIC
	DISCREET

	DISCRETE
CDEEIRSU	DECURIES
CDEEIRSV	DESCRIVE
	SCRIEVED
	SERVICED
CDEEIRTU	CUITERED
	DEUTERIC
CDEEISUV	SEDUCIVE
CDEEITUV	EDUCTIVE
CDEEJKOY	JOCKEYED
CDEEKLNO	ENLOCKED
CDEEKLOR	RELOCKED
CDEEKLPS	SPECKLED
CDEEKMRU	MUCKERED
CDEEKNOR	RECKONED
CDEEKNRS	REDNECKS
CDEEKNRU	UNRECKED
CDEEKOOR	RECOOKED
CDEEKOPT	POCKETED
CDEEKORR	RECORKED
CDEEKORT	ROCKETED
CDEEKORV	OVERDECK
CDEEKORW	ROCKWEED
CDEEKOST	SOCKETED
CDEEKPRU	PUCKERED
CDEEKRSU	SUCKERED
CDEEKRTU	TUCKERED
CDEELLOR	CORDELLE
CDEELLOT	COLLETED
CDEELLPU	CUPELLED
CDEELMOW	WELCOMED
CDEELNOS	ENCLOSED
CDEELNPU	PEDUNCLE
CDEELNTY	DECENTLY
CDEELNUW	UNCLEWED
CDEELOOW	LOCOWEED
CDEELOPU	DECOUPLE
CDEELORS	RECLOSED
CDEELORV	CLOVERED
CDEELORY	RECOYLED
CDEELOSS	CODELESS
CDEELOST	CLOSETED
CDEELOTU	ELOCUTED
CDEELPRU	PRECLUDE
CDEELPSU	DECUPLES
CDEELRTU	LECTURED
	RELUCTED
CDEELRUX	EXCLUDER
CDEELSSU	SCEDULES
	SECLUDES
CDEELSUX	EXCLUDES
CDEEMOPR	COMPERED
CDEEMOPT	COEMPTED
	COMPETED
CDEEMORT	ECTODERM
CDEEMSTU	TUMESCED
CDEENNOR	RECONNED
CDEENNOS	CONDENSE
CDEENNOU	DENOUNCE
	ENOUNCED
CDEENNOV	CONVENED
CDEENNPY	PENDENCY
CDEENNTU	UNDECENT
CDEENNTY	TENDENCY

CDEENOOS	COOSENED
CDEENORR	CORNERED
CDEENORS	CENSORED
	ENCODERS
	NECROSED
	SECONDER
CDEENORT	CENTRODE
CDEENORU	COENDURE
CDEENOSS	SECONDES
CDEENOSY	ECDYSONE
CDEENOTU	DUECENTO
CDEENOTX	COEXTEND
CDEENOVX	CONVEXED
CDEENOVY	CONVEYED
CDEENPRU	PRUDENCE
CDEENRSU	CENSURED
CDEENRUV	VERECUND
CDEENRUW	UNCREWED
CDEENSST	DESCENTS
CDEENSSU	CENSUSED
CDEENSTY	ENCYSTED
CDEEOOPR	COOPERED
CDEEOOTV	DOVECOTE
CDEEOPPR	COPPERED
CDEEOPRS	PRECODES
	PROCEEDS
CDEEOPRU	RECOUPED
CDEEORRR	RECORDER
	RERECORD
CDEEORRS	RESCORED
CDEEORRU	RECOURED
CDEEORST	CORSETED
	ESCORTED
	SECTORED
CDEEORSV	COVERSED
CDEEORSW	ESCROWED
CDEEORSY	DECOYERS
CDEEORTT	COTTERED
	DETECTOR
CDEEORTV	CORVETED
	VECTORED
CDEEOSST	CESTODES
	COSSETED
CDEEOSTT	ESCOTTED
CDEEPPRU	PRECUPED
CDEEPRRU	PRECURED
CDEEPRST	SCEPTRED
CDEERRRU	RECURRED
CDEERRSU	CURSEDER
	REDUCERS
CDEERRUV	RECURVED
CDEERSSU	SEDUCERS
CDEERSUV	DECURVES
CDEERSUX	EXCURSED
CDEERTTU	CURETTED
CDEERTUV	CURVETED

CDEFIIIL	FILICIDE
CDEFIIIT	CITIFIED
CDEFIIOR	CODIFIER
CDEFIIOS	CODIFIES
CDEFIIST	DEFICITS
CDEFIITY	CITYFIED
CDEFINNO	CONFINED
CDEFINNU	INFECUND
CDEFINOR	CONFIDER
	INFORCED
CDEFINOS	CONFIDES
CDEFINOX	CONFIXED
CDEFIORY	RECODIFY
CDEFKORS	DEFROCKS
CDEFLNOU	FLOUNCED
CDEFLORY	FORCEDLY
CDEFNORU	FROUNCED
	UNFORCED
CDEFNOSU	CONFUSED
CDEFNOTU	CONFUTED
CDEFNSTU	DEFUNCTS
CDEFOSSU	FOCUSSED
CDEGHLNU	GLUNCHED
CDEGHORU	GROUCHED
CDEGHRTU	GRUTCHED
CDEGIILP	DIPLEGIC
CDEGIINN	INCEDING
CDEGIINX	EXCIDING
CDEGIKNO	DECKOING
	DECOKING
CDEGIKNS	DECKINGS
CDEGILSU	CLUDGIES
CDEGINNO	ENCODING
CDEGINNS	SCENDING
CDEGINOR	RECODING
CDEGINOS	CODESIGN
	COGNISED
	COSIGNED
CDEGINOY	DECOYING
	GYNECOID
CDEGINOZ	COGNIZED
CDEGINRU	REDUCING
CDEGINRY	DECRYING
CDEGINSU	SEDUCING
CDEGINSY	DYSGENIC
CDEGKOSU	GEODUCKS
CDEGKSUW	GWEDUCKS
CDEGLNOO	COLOGNED
CDEGNORU	CONGRUED
CDEGOORS	SCROOGED
CDEGORSU	SCOURGED
	SCROUGED
CDEGORSW	SCROWDGE
CDEHHNOO	HONCHOED
CDEHIILO	HELICOID
CDEHIILS	CEILIDHS
CDEHIIMO	HOMICIDE
CDEHIIMR	CHIMERID
CDEHIINO	ECHINOID
CDEHIIVV	CHIVVIED
CDEHIKOS	HOICKSED
CDEHIKRW	HERDWICK
CDEHIKST	SKITCHED
CDEHILMR	MERCHILD

CDEHILNR	CHILDREN	CDEIILNO	INDOCILE	CDEILMPR	CRIMPLED
CDEHILOR	CHLORIDE	CDEIILOT	IDIOLECT	CDEILMRU	DULCIMER
CDEHILOS	CHELOIDS	CDEIILPS	DISCIPLE	CDEILMSY	DYSMELIC
CDEHILRT	ELDRITCH	CDEIILPU	PEDICULI	CDEILNOS	INCLOSED
CDEHIMOR	CHROMIDE		PULICIDE	CDEILNOU	NUCLEOID
CDEHIMOT	METHODIC	CDEIILRU	RIDICULE		UNCOILED
CDEHIMRS	SMIRCHED	CDEIIMOS	DIOECISM		UNDOCILE
CDEHINNR	INDRENCH	CDEIIMRT	DIMETRIC	CDEILNRY	CYLINDER
CDEHINOS	HEDONICS	CDEIIMST	MISCITED	CDEILNSU	INCLUDES
CDEHINQU	QUINCHED	CDEIINNT	INCIDENT		NUCLIDES
CDEHINST	SNITCHED	CDEIINOS	DECISION		UNSLICED
CDEHIOOR	CHOREOID		ICONISED	CDEILOOW	WOODLICE
	OCHIDORE	CDEIINOV	INVOICED	CDEILOPS	SCOPELID
CDEHIOSW	COWHIDES	CDEIINOZ	ICONIZED	CDEILOPU	CLUPEOID
CDEHIOTU	OUTCHIDE	CDEIINRT	INDICTER		UPCOILED
CDEHIOTY	THEODICY		INDIRECT	CDEILORS	SCLEROID
CDEHIQTU	QUITCHED		REINDICT	CDEILORU	CLOUDIER
CDEHIRST	DITCHERS	CDEIINTY	CYTIDINE	CDEILORV	COVERLID
CDEHISTT	STITCHED	CDEIIOPR	PERIODIC	CDEILOSS	DISCLOSE
CDEHISTW	SWITCHED	CDEIIOPS	EPISODIC	CDEILOST	DOCILEST
CDEHITTW	TWITCHED	CDEIIOPT	EPIDOTIC	CDEILPPR	CRIPPLED
CDEHKLSU	SHELDUCK	CDEIIOSU	DIECIOUS	CDEILPSU	CLUPEIDS
CDEHKNOU	UNCHOKED	CDEIIOSV	OVICIDES	CDEILRTY	DIRECTLY
CDEHKSUY	HEYDUCKS	CDEIIPPT	PEPTIDIC	CDEILSTU	DULCITES
CDEHLOOR	COHOLDER	CDEIIPRR	CIRRIPED		LUCIDEST
CDEHLOOS	DESCHOOL	CDEIIRST	ICTERIDS	CDEILSXY	DYSLEXIC
	SCHOOLED	CDEIIRTU	DIURETIC	CDEILTTU	CUITTLED
CDEHLORT	CHORTLED	CDEIIRUV	VIRUCIDE	CDEIMMOT	DECOMMIT
CDEHLOSU	SLOUCHED	CDEIISSU	SUICIDES	CDEIMMOX	COMMIXED
CDEHMNTU	DUTCHMEN	CDEIISTT	DICTIEST	CDEIMOOW	WOODMICE
CDEHMOOS	SMOOCHED	CDEIITWY	CITYWIDE	CDEIMORT	MORTICED
CDEHMOSU	SMOUCHED	CDEIJNOO	COJOINED	CDEIMOSS	MISCODES
CDEHMSTU	SMUTCHED	CDEIJSST	DISJECTS	CDEIMOST	DEMOTICS
CDEHNOOP	CHENOPOD	CDEIKLNO	INLOCKED		DOMESTIC
	PONCHOED	CDEIKLNR	CRINKLED	CDEIMPRS	SCRIMPED
CDEHNORS	CHONDRES	CDEIKLNU	UNLICKED	CDEINNOU	UNCOINED
CDEHNRSU	CHUNDERS	CDEIKLOR	CORDLIKE	CDEINNOV	CONNIVED
CDEHOORR	RHEOCORD	CDEIKLOS	SIDELOCK	CDEINOOS	COOSINED
CDEHOOSS	SCOOSHED	CDEIKLPR	PRICKLED	CDEINOOZ	ENDOZOIC
CDEHOOST	COHOSTED	CDEIKLRT	TRICKLED	CDEINORR	CORDINER
CDEHORSU	CHORUSED	CDEIKLRU	LUDERICK	CDEINORS	CONSIDER
CDEHORSW	CHOWDERS	CDEIKLST	STICKLED	CDEINORT	CENTROID
	COWHERDS	CDEIKLWY	WICKEDLY		DOCTRINE
CDEHOSSU	HOCUSSED	CDEIKMSU	MUSICKED	CDEINORU	DECURION
CDEHOSSW	COWSHEDS	CDEIKNPU	UNPICKED	CDEINORV	CODRIVEN
CDEHSSSU	SCHUSSED	CDEIKNTU	TUNICKED	CDEINOST	DEONTICS
CDEIIILS	SILICIDE	CDEIKOSS	DOCKISES	CDEINOSU	DOUCINES
CDEIIIMT	MITICIDE	CDEIKOST	DIESTOCK	CDEINOSZ	ZINCODES
CDEIIIOS	IDIOCIES	CDEIKOSY	YOICKSED	CDEINOTU	EDUCTION
CDEIIIRV	VIRICIDE	CDEIKOSZ	DOCKIZES	CDEINOUV	UNVOICED
CDEIIITV	VITICIDE	CDEIKRRS	DERRICKS	CDEINOVV	CONVIVED
CDEIIKKS	SIDEKICK	CDEIKSTU	DUCKIEST	CDEINPRS	PRESCIND
CDEIIKLS	DISCLIKE	CDEILLOR	COLLIDER	CDEINPRU	UNPRICED
	SICKLIED	CDEILLOS	CODILLES	CDEINPSY	DYSPNEIC
CDEIIKMM	MIMICKED		COLLIDES	CDEINRRU	INCURRED
CDEIIKNR	CIDERKIN	CDEILLOU	LODICULE	CDEINRSS	DISCERNS
CDEIIKNW	INWICKED	CDEILLOY	DOCILELY		RESCINDS
CDEIIKRS	DRICKSIE	CDEILLPU	PELLUCID	CDEINRSU	INDUCERS
CDEIIKRT	DICKTIER	CDEILMMS	SCLIMMED	CDEINRTU	REINDUCT
CDEIIKST	DICKIEST	CDEILMNO	DOLMENIC	CDEINRUV	INCURVED
	STICKIED	CDEILMOP	COMPILED	CDEINSSX	EXSCINDS
CDEIILMM	DILEMMIC		COMPLIED	CDEINSTY	SYNDETIC
CDEIILMO	DOMICILE	CDEILMOS	MELODICS	CDEIOORS	CORODIES
CDEIILNN	INCLINED	CDEILMOV	MYCELOID	CDEIOORT	COEDITOR

CDEIOPRS	PERCOIDS	**CDELNOOR**	CONDOLER	**CDEMPRSU**	SCRUMPED
CDEIOPRT	DEPICTOR	**CDELNOOS**	CONDOLES	**CDENNOOR**	CONDONER
CDEIOPST	DESPOTIC		CONSOLED	**CDENNOOS**	CONDONES
CDEIOPTY	COPYEDIT	**CDELNOOU**	UNCOOLED	**CDENNOOT**	CONNOTED
CDEIORRT	CREDITOR	**CDELNOSS**	COLDNESS	**CDENNOST**	CONTENDS
	DIRECTOR	**CDELNOSU**	ENCLOUDS	**CDENNOUY**	UNCOYNED
CDEIORRV	CODRIVER		UNCLOSED	**CDENOORS**	CONDORES
	DIVORCER	**CDELNOSY**	CONDYLES	**CDENOORT**	CREODONT
CDEIORSS	DISCOERS		SECONDLY	**CDENOOST**	SECODONT
CDEIORST	CORDITES	**CDELNOTU**	UNCOLTED	**CDENOOTT**	COTTONED
CDEIORSU	DISCOURE	**CDELNOUW**	UNCOWLED	**CDENOOVY**	CONVOYED
CDEIORSV	CODRIVES	**CDELNOUY**	UNCLOYED	**CDENORSS**	CORSNEDS
	DISCOVER	**CDELNRUU**	UNCURLED	**CDENORSU**	CRUNODES
	DIVORCES	**CDELNSUY**	SECUNDLY	**CDENORSW**	DECROWNS
CDEIORSW	CROWDIES	**CDELOORS**	COLOREDS	**CDENORTU**	CORNUTED
CDEIORSY	DECISORY		CROODLES		TROUNCED
CDEIORTU	OUTCRIED		DECOLORS	**CDENOSSY**	ECDYSONS
CDEIOSST	CESTOIDS	**CDELOORU**	COLOURED	**CDENOSTU**	CONTUSED
	SCODIEST		DECOLOUR	**CDENRSUU**	UNCURSED
CDEIOSTT	COTTISED	**CDELOORV**	OVERCOLD	**CDENRTUU**	UNDERCUT
CDEIPRSS	DISCERPS	**CDELOOTT**	DOLCETTO	**CDENRUUV**	UNCURVED
CDEIPRST	PREDICTS	**CDELOPSU**	UPCLOSED	**CDEOOPPS**	COPEPODS
	SCRIPTED	**CDELOPTU**	OCTUPLED	**CDEOOPRS**	SCROOPED
CDEIPRSY	CYPRIDES	**CDELORSS**	CORDLESS	**CDEOOPST**	POSTCODE
CDEIPRTU	PICTURED		SCOLDERS	**CDEOORRR**	CORRODER
CDEIPSST	DISCEPTS	**CDELORSU**	CLOSURED	**CDEOORRS**	CORRODES
CDEIPSSU	CUSPIDES	**CDELORSW**	CLOWDERS	**CDEOORSU**	DECOROUS
CDEIRRSU	SCURRIED		SCROWLED	**CDEOORSV**	VOCODERS
CDEIRSSU	DISCURES	**CDELORTU**	CLOTURED	**CDEOOSTV**	DOVECOTS
CDEIRSTU	CRUDITES	**CDELORZZ**	CROZZLED	**CDEOPRRU**	PROCURED
	CURDIEST	**CDELOSSU**	DULCOSES		PRODUCER
	CURTSIED	**CDELOSTU**	COULDEST	**CDEOPRSU**	PRODUCES
CDEIRSTV	VERDICTS		LOCUSTED	**CDEOQSTU**	DOCQUETS
CDEISSST	DISSECTS	**CDELPRSU**	SCRUPLED	**CDEORRSW**	CROWDERS
CDEISSSU	DISCUSES	**CDELPRUU**	UPCURLED	**CDEORRTU**	REDUCTOR
CDEJNORU	CONJURED	**CDELPSTU**	SCULPTED	**CDEORSST**	DOCTRESS
CDEKKLNU	KNUCKLED	**CDELRRSU**	CURDLERS	**CDEORSSU**	SCOURSED
CDEKLMOR	CLERKDOM	**CDELRSSU**	SCUDLERS	**CDEORSSW**	SCOWDERS
CDEKLMOU	DUCKMOLE	**CDELRSUY**	CURSEDLY	**CDEORSTU**	EDUCTORS
CDEKLNOU	UNLOCKED	**CDELRTUU**	CULTURED		SEDUCTOR
CDEKLNRU	CRUNKLED	**CDELRUVY**	CURVEDLY	**CDEORSUU**	DOUCEURS
CDEKLOPU	UPLOCKED	**CDELSSTU**	DUCTLESS	**CDEOSSTU**	CUSTODES
CDEKLORY	YELDROCK	**CDELSSUY**	CUSSEDLY	**CDEPRSTY**	DECRYPTS
CDEKLOSW	WEDLOCKS	**CDELSTTU**	SCUTTLED	**CDEPRUUV**	UPCURVED
CDEKLRTU	TRUCKLED	**CDELSTUU**	DUCTULES	**CDERSTTU**	DESTRUCT
CDEKNOOU	UNCOOKED	**CDEMMNOO**	COMMONED	**CDFIILSU**	FLUIDICS
CDEKNOOV	CONVOKED	**CDEMMNOS**	COMMENDS	**CDFIKMNU**	MINDFUCK
CDEKNORS	DORNECKS	**CDEMMNOU**	COMMUNED	**CDFIKORS**	DISFROCK
CDEKNORU	UNCORKED	**CDEMMOOS**	COMMODES	**CDFKOOTU**	DUCKFOOT
CDEKNSSU	SUNDECKS	**CDEMMOOV**	COMMOVED	**CDFNNOOU**	CONFOUND
CDEKNSUU	UNSUCKED	**CDEMMOTU**	COMMUTED	**CDFNOOSU**	COFOUNDS
CDEKNTUU	UNTUCKED	**CDEMMRSU**	SCRUMMED	**CDGHIILN**	CHILDING
CDEKOPSY	COPYDESK	**CDEMNNOS**	CONDEMNS	**CDGHIILO**	CHILIDOG
CDEKOSST	DESTOCKS	**CDEMNOOW**	COMEDOWN	**CDGHIINS**	CHIDINGS
CDELLNUU	UNCULLED		DOWNCOME	**CDGHIINT**	DICHTING
CDELLOOP	CLODPOLE	**CDEMNOPS**	COMPENDS		DITCHING
CDELLORS	SCROLLED	**CDEMNOSU**	CONSUMED	**CDGHILOS**	GLOCHIDS
CDELLORU	COLLUDER	**CDEMNOTU**	DOCUMENT	**CDGHINNU**	DUNCHING
CDELLOSU	COLLUDES	**CDEMNSUU**	SECUNDUM	**CDGHINOR**	CHORDING
CDELLOTU	CLOUDLET	**CDEMOOPS**	COMPOSED	**CDGHINOU**	DOUCHING
CDELLTUY	DULCETLY	**CDEMOPTU**	COMPUTED	**CDGIINNU**	INDUCING
CDELMNOO	MONOCLED	**CDEMORSU**	DECORUMS	**CDGIINOS**	DISCOING
CDELMNOU	COLUMNED	**CDEMOSTU**	COSTUMED	**CDGIKLNU**	DUCKLING
CDELMPRU	CRUMPLED		CUSTOMED	**CDGIKLOR**	GRIDLOCK

CDGIKNOS	DOCKINGS	CDIINOSV	VIDICONS	CDKOOORW	CORKWOOD
CDGIKNSU	DUCKINGS	CDIINPRY	CYPRINID	CDKORTUW	DUCTWORK
CDGILNOS	CODLINGS	CDIINPTU	PUNDITIC	CDLLLOOP	CLODPOLL
	LINGCODS	CDIINSTT	DISTINCT	CDLNOOOW	COOLDOWN
	SCOLDING	CDIIOORS	SORICOID	CDLNOSUU	UNCLOUDS
CDGILNOU	CLOUDING	CDIIOOSU	DIOICOUS	CDLNOUUY	UNCLOUDY
CDGILNRU	CURDLING	CDIIOPRT	DIOPTRIC	CDLOOOTW	COLTWOOD
CDGINORS	CORDINGS		DIPROTIC	CDLOOPSY	LYCOPODS
CDGINORW	CROWDING		TRIPODIC	CDLOORTY	DOCTORLY
CDGINSTU	DUCTINGS	CDIIOPST	PODITICS	CDLOOSTU	OUTSCOLD
CDGLOOOY	CODOLOGY	CDIIORSU	SCIUROID	CDMNOOPU	COMPOUND
CDGNOOOS	COONDOGS	CDIIORSX	CORIXIDS	CDMNORUU	CORUNDUM
CDGNOOTU	GONODUCT	CDIIOSSS	CISSOIDS	CDMOSSUW	MUDSCOWS
CDHHIILS	CHILDISH	CDIIOSTY	SODICITY	CDNNOOOT	CONODONT
CDHIILTW	TWICHILD	CDIIPTUY	CUPIDITY	CDNNOOTY	CYNODONT
CDHIINST	CHINDITS		PUDICITY	CDNNOSTU	CONTUNDS
CDHIIOOR	CHORIOID	CDIIRSSU	SCIURIDS	CDNOSTUW	CUTDOWNS
CDHIIORT	HIDROTIC	CDIIRSTT	DISTRICT	CDOOOPST	OCTOPODS
	TRICHOID	CDIJNSTU	DISJUNCT	CDOOPSST	POSTDOCS
CDHIIOSZ	SCHIZOID	CDIKKNOW	KICKDOWN	CDOORRUY	CORDUROY
CDHIISST	DISTICHS	CDIKKOPR	DROPKICK	CDOORTUW	OUTCROWD
CDHILNSU	UNCHILDS	CDIKNNSU	NUDNICKS	CDOOSTUW	WOODCUTS
CDHILOOP	CHILOPOD	CDIKNORS	DORNICKS	CDOPRSTU	PRODUCTS
CDHILOOS	DOLICHOS	CDIKNOSW	WINDOCKS	CDORSSUW	CUSSWORD
CDHILORS	CHLORIDS		WINDSOCK	CEEEEGHS	GEECHEES
CDHIMOSU	DOCHMIUS	CDIKNOTW	DOWNTICK	CEEEEHLS	LEECHEES
CDHINNOR	CHONDRIN	CDIKNPSU	DUCKPINS	CEEEEIPY	EYEPIECE
CDHINORY	HYDRONIC	CDILLOOS	COLLOIDS	CEEEEJRT	REJECTEE
CDHIOOPW	WOODCHIP	CDILLOTU	DULCITOL	CEEEELST	ELECTEES
CDHIOORS	CHOROIDS	CDILLOUY	CLOUDILY		SELECTEE
CDHIOORT	TROCHOID	CDILMSTU	MIDCULTS	CEEEEPRS	PRECEESE
CDHIOPRW	WHIPCORD	CDILOOPS	PODSOLIC	CEEEFFIR	EFFIERCE
CDHIOPRY	HYDROPIC	CDILOOPZ	PODZOLIC	CEEEFFRT	EFFECTER
CDHIOPSY	PSYCHOID	CDILOORS	DISCOLOR	CEEEFHLS	FLEECHES
CDHIORRT	TRICHORD	CDILOORT	LORDOTIC	CEEEFILR	FLEECIER
CDHIOSUV	DISVOUCH	CDILOOTY	COTYLOID	CEEEFILS	FLEECIES
CDHIPSTY	DIPTYCHS	CDILOSST	DISCLOST	CEEEFINR	ENFIERCE
CDHIRSTY	CHYTRIDS	CDILOSTY	DICOTYLS	CEEEFLRS	FLEECERS
CDHKOORS	HORDOCKS		SCOLYTID	CEEEFNOR	CONFEREE
CDHLOOPY	COPYHOLD	CDIMMOSU	MODICUMS	CEEEFNRS	REFENCES
CDHNORSU	CHONDRUS	CDIMOORT	MICRODOT	CEEEGIMN	EMCEEING
CDHOOOPW	WOODCHOP	CDINNQUU	QUIDNUNC	CEEEGINS	EGENCIES
CDHOORRU	UROCHORD	CDINOOOR	CORONOID	CEEEGINX	EXIGENCE
CDIIIMNS	MINIDISC	CDINOOTU	NOCTUOID	CEEEGITX	EXEGETIC
CDIIIMNU	INDICIUM	CDINOPSY	DYSPNOIC	CEEEGMNR	MERGENCE
CDIIINSV	INVISCID	CDINORSW	DISCROWN	CEEEGNRS	REGENCES
CDIIIORT	DIORITIC	CDINORTU	INDUCTOR	CEEEGNRV	VERGENCE
CDIIKMNO	DOMINICK	CDINOSTU	CONDUITS	CEEEHIKR	CHEEKIER
CDIIKPST	DIPSTICK		DISCOUNT	CEEEHIRR	CHEERIER
CDIILMOS	DOMICILS		NOCTUIDS		REECHIER
CDIILOPP	DIPLOPIC	CDINOSTY	DYSTONIC	CEEEHIRS	CHEESIER
CDIILOTY	DOCILITY	CDIOOPRS	PROSODIC	CEEEHLLS	ECHELLES
CDIILRUY	URIDYLIC	CDIOORRR	CORRIDOR	CEEEHLRV	CHEVEREL
CDIILSVY	VISCIDLY	CDIOPRRS	RIPCORDS	CEEEHLSS	SLEECHES
CDIILTUV	LUCIDITY	CDIOPRSU	CUSPIDOR	CEEEHMSS	SMEECHES
CDIIMNOU	CONIDIUM	CDIOSSTY	CYSTOIDS	CEEEHNNP	PENNEECH
	MUCINOID	CDIOSTUV	OVIDUCTS	CEEEHNRS	ENCHEERS
	ONCIDIUM	CDJLNOUY	JOCUNDLY	CEEEHORS	REECHOES
CDIIMTUV	MUCIDITY	CDKLNOOW	LOCKDOWN	CEEEHPRS	CHEEPERS
CDIINOOS	ISODICON	CDKLOOOS	OCKODOLS	CEEEHPSS	SPEECHES
	ONISCOID	CDKMMORU	DRUMMOCK	CEEEHRRS	CHEERERS
CDIINORS	CRINOIDS	CDKMORSU	MUDROCKS	CEEEHRSS	CREESHES
CDIINORT	INDICTOR	CDKNNOSU	DUNNOCKS		SECESHER
CDIINOST	DICTIONS	CDKNOORS	DORNOCKS	CEEEHRSW	ESCHEWER

CEEEHRVY	CHEVERYE	CEEENSST	CENTESES	CEEFNRVY	FERVENCY
CEEEHSSS	SECESHES	CEEEPRRS	CREEPERS	CEEFOPRR	PERFORCE
CEEEIJTV	EJECTIVE	CEEEPRRT	PREERECT	CEEFOPRT	PERFECTO
CEEEIKRR	CREEKIER	CEEEPRTX	EXPECTER	CEEFORRS	FRESCOER
CEEEILNN	LENIENCE	CEEERRST	ERECTERS	CEEFORSS	FRESCOES
CEEEILNS	LICENSEE		REERECTS	CEEFORTW	CROWFEET
CEEEILNT	TELECINE		SECRETER	CEEFPRST	PERFECTS
CEEEILRS	CELERIES	CEEERRSU	RESECURE		PREFECTS
CEEEILRT	ERECTILE	CEEERRSV	SCREEVER		
CEEEILTV	CLEVEITE	CEEERRTX	EXCRETER	CEEGHIKN	CHEEKING
	ELECTIVE	CEEERSSS	RECESSES	CEEGHILN	LEECHING
CEEEIMNN	EMINENCE	CEEERSST	SECRETES	CEEGHINP	CHEEPING
CEEEIMPR	EMPIERCE		SESTERCE	CEEGHINR	CHEERING
CEEEIMRR	REREMICE	CEEERSSU	CEREUSES		REECHING
CEEEINNT	ENCEINTE	CEEERSSV	SCREEVES	CEEGHINS	CHEESING
CEEEINPR	PIECENER	CEEERSTX	EXCRETES	CEEGHLOW	COGWHEEL
CEEEINPS	EPICENES	CEEERTTV	CREVETTE	CEEGIINP	EPIGENIC
CEEEINRS	CERESINE	CEEERTUX	EXECUTER	CEEGIJNT	EJECTING
	SCREENIE	CEEESSSX	EXCESSES	CEEGIKLN	CLEEKING
CEEEINSS	ESNECIES	CEEESTUX	EXECUTES	CEEGILNP	CLEEPING
CEEEIOPT	TOEPIECE	CEEFFNOS	OFFENCES	CEEGILNR	CREELING
CEEEIPRR	CREEPIER	CEEFFORS	EFFORCES	CEEGILNT	ELECTING
	CREPERIE	CEEFFORT	EFFECTOR	CEEGILOT	ECLOGITE
CEEEIPRS	CREEPIES	CEEFGILN	FLEECING	CEEGILRS	CLERGIES
CEEEIPRV	PERCEIVE	CEEFHIKR	KERCHIEF	CEEGILRT	TELERGIC
CEEEIRRV	RECEIVER	CEEFHIRY	CHIEFERY	CEEGIMNS	MISCEGEN
CEEEIRSV	RECEIVES	CEEFHISS	CHIEFESS	CEEGINOO	COOEEING
CEEEIRSX	EXERCISE	CEEFHIST	CHIEFEST	CEEGINOR	EROGENIC
CEEEIRTV	ERECTIVE		FETICHES	CEEGINPR	CREEPING
CEEEISSS	ECESISES	CEEFHKLU	CHEEKFUL	CEEGINRS	CREESING
CEEEISTV	EVICTEES	CEEFHLNR	FLENCHER		GENERICS
CEEEJRRT	REJECTER	CEEFHLNS	FLENCHES	CEEGINRT	ERECTING
CEEEJRST	REEJECTS	CEEFHLRT	FLETCHER		GENTRICE
CEEEKNNP	PENNEECK	CEEFHLRU	CHEERFUL	CEEGINST	GENETICS
CEEELLNR	CRENELLE	CEEFHLST	FLETCHES	CEEGINSU	EUGENICS
CEEELLSU	ECUELLES	CEEFHNRS	FRENCHES	CEEGINXY	EXIGENCY
CEEELOPR	OPERCELE	CEEFHORU	FOURCHEE	CEEGIORX	EXOERGIC
CEEELOSS	COLESSEE	CEEFHRST	FECHTERS	CEEGIRSS	GRECISES
CEEELPRT	PREELECT		FETCHERS	CEEGIRSZ	GRECIZES
CEEELPSY	YCLEEPES	CEEFIINT	INFICETE	CEEGLLOR	COLLEGER
CEEELRRV	CLEVERER	CEEFILLY	FLEECILY	CEEGLLOS	COLLEGES
CEEELRST	REELECTS	CEEFILRT	TELFERIC	CEEGLNST	NEGLECTS
	RESELECT	CEEFILRY	FIERCELY	CEEGLOSU	ECLOGUES
CEEELRTT	ELECTRET	CEEFINPP	FIPPENCE	CEEGMMOR	COMMERGE
	TERCELET	CEEFINRT	FRENETIC	CEEGMNOY	CYMOGENE
CEEELSST	CELESTES		INFECTER	CEEGNNOO	ONCOGENE
CEEEMNNS	SCENEMEN		REINFECT	CEEGNNOR	CONGENER
CEEEMNRT	CEMENTER	CEEFIPRT	PERFECTI	CEEGNNPU	PUNGENCE
	CEREMENT	CEEFIRST	FIERCEST	CEEGNORS	COGENERS
	RECEMENT	CEEFKLRS	FLECKERS		CONGREES
CEEEMORT	ECTOMERE		FRECKLES	CEEGNORT	CONGREET
CEEEMPRS	EMPERCES	CEEFKLSS	FECKLESS		COREGENT
CEEEMRTY	CEMETERY	CEEFLNOR	FLORENCE	CEEGNORV	CONVERGE
CEEENNPT	TENPENCE	CEEFLNSU	FLUENCES	CEEGNOTY	ECTOGENY
CEEENNST	SENTENCE	CEEFLNTU	FECULENT	CEEGNRSU	URGENCES
CEEENPRS	PRESENCE	CEEFLRST	REFLECTS	CEEGNRVY	VERGENCY
CEEENPRT	PRETENCE	CEEFNNSU	UNFENCES	CEEGORST	CORTEGES
CEEENQSU	SEQUENCE	CEEFNORR	CONFRERE	CEEGQRSU	GRECQUES
CEEENRRS	RESCREEN		ENFORCER	CEEHHIRS	CHESHIRE
	SCREENER		RECONFER	CEEHHMMN	HENCHMEN
CEEENRRT	RECENTER		RENFORCE	CEEHHSTT	THETCHES
	RECENTRE	CEEFNORS	ENFORCES	CEEHIIST	ETHICISE
CEEENRSS	RECENSES	CEEFNORW	FENCEROW	CEEHIITZ	ETHICIZE
CEEENSSS	ESSENCES	CEEFNOTU	OUTFENCE	CEEHIKLY	CHEEKILY
				CEEHIKMS	KIMCHEES

CEEHIKNW	CHEEWINK	CEEHLORT	RECLOTHE	CEEIINSW	ICEWINES
CEEHILLN	CHENILLE	CEEHLOSS	ECHOLESS	CEEIINVV	EVINCIVE
CEEHILLV	CHEVILLE	CEEHLOSW	COWHEELS	CEEIIPRS	EPICIERS
CEEHILRS	CHISELER	CEEHLQSU	QUELCHES	CEEIIRST	SERICITE
	SCHLIERE	CEEHLRSU	HERCULES	CEEIJNOT	EJECTION
CEEHILRT	TELECHIR	CEEHLRSW	WELCHERS	CEEIJNRT	REINJECT
CEEHILRV	CHEVERIL	CEEHLSSS	CHESSELS	CEEIJORR	REJOICER
CEEHILRW	CLERIHEW	CEEHMNNS	MENSCHEN	CEEIJORS	REJOICES
CEEHILRY	CHEERILY	CEEHMNOR	CHOREMEN	CEEIJRUV	VERJUICE
CEEHILSV	VEHICLES		CHROMENE	CEEIKKLN	NECKLIKE
CEEHILSW	SWELCHIE	CEEHMNSS	CHESSMEN	CEEIKKLO	COKELIKE
CEEHILSY	CHEESILY		MENSCHES	CEEIKKSS	KECKSIES
CEEHIMMS	CHEMMIES	CEEHMORT	COMETHER	CEEIKLMU	LEUKEMIC
CEEHIMRS	CHIMERES	CEEHMOTY	HEMOCYTE	CEEIKLNN	NECKLINE
CEEHIMRT	HERMETIC	CEEHMRSS	SCHEMERS	CEEIKLPR	PICKEREL
CEEHIMSS	CHEMISES		SCHMEERS	CEEIKNRS	SICKENER
	SCHEMIES	CEEHMRST	MERCHETS	CEEIKNST	NECKTIES
CEEHINOR	COINHERE	CEEHNNOW	NOWHENCE	CEEIKPRS	PICKEERS
CEEHINPR	ENCIPHER	CEEHNNRT	ENTRENCH		SPECKIER
CEEHINPT	PHENETIC	CEEHNOPS	PENOCHES	CEEIKPRT	PICKETER
CEEHINPU	EUPHENIC	CEEHNORS	RECHOSEN	CEEIKPST	PECKIEST
CEEHINRR	ENRICHER	CEEHNORT	COHERENT	CEEILLLP	PELLICLE
CEEHINRS	ENRICHES	CEEHNORV	CHEVERON	CEEILLMS	MICELLES
	INHERCES	CEEHNPSU	PENUCHES	CEEILLNT	LENTICEL
CEEHINST	SITHENCE	CEEHNQRU	QUENCHER		LENTICLE
CEEHINSX	CHENIXES	CEEHNQSU	QUENCHES	CEEILMOR	COMELIER
CEEHINTT	ENTHETIC	CEEHNRRT	RETRENCH	CEEILMPS	SEMPLICE
CEEHIORS	CHEERIOS		TRENCHER	CEEILNNT	CENTINEL
CEEHIOSS	ECHOISES	CEEHNRRW	WRENCHER	CEEILNNV	LENIENCY
CEEHIOSU	ICEHOUSE	CEEHNRST	TRENCHES	CEEILNOP	PLIOCENE
CEEHIOSV	COHESIVE	CEEHNRSW	WENCHERS	CEEILNOS	CINEOLES
CEEHIOSZ	ECHOIZES		WRENCHES	CEEILNOT	COTELINE
CEEHIPRR	CIPHERER	CEEHNSST	STENCHES		ELECTION
CEEHIPRT	HERPETIC	CEEHNSTU	CHUTNEES	CEEILNOV	VIOLENCE
CEEHIRRR	CHERRIER	CEEHOOPR	POECHORE	CEEILNPR	PENCILER
CEEHIRRS	CHERRIES	CEEHOORS	RECHOOSE	CEEILNPU	PULICENE
CEEHIRRT	CHERTIER	CEEHOPRS	PRECHOSE	CEEILNPX	CINEPLEX
CEEHIRSS	RICHESSE	CEEHOPRY	CORYPHEE	CEEILNRR	RECLINER
CEEHIRST	CHESTIER	CEEHOPST	SHEEPCOT	CEEILNRS	LICENSER
	HERETICS	CEEHOPTT	POCHETTE		RECLINES
CEEHIRTT	TETCHIER	CEEHORRS	COHERERS		SILENCER
CEEHIRTU	HEURETIC		COSHERER	CEEILNRU	CERULEIN
CEEHIRTV	VETCHIER	CEEHORRT	HECTORER	CEEILNRV	VERNICLE
CEEHISSV	SEVICHES		TORCHERE	CEEILNSS	ENCLISES
CEEHISTT	ESTHETIC	CEEHORSS	ORCHESES		LICENSES
	TECHIEST	CEEHORST	TROCHEES		SILENCES
CEEHISTW	CHEWIEST	CEEHOSUV	VOUCHEES	CEEILNST	CENTILES
CEEHKLPR	KREPLECH	CEEHPRRS	PERCHERS	CEEILNSU	LEUCINES
CEEHKLRS	HECKLERS	CEEHPRRY	PERCHERY	CEEILORR	RECOILER
CEEHKNPS	HENPECKS	CEEHPRSU	UPCHEERS	CEEILORS	CREOLISE
CEEHKRST	RESKETCH	CEEHPSST	SPETCHES	CEEILORZ	CREOLIZE
	SKETCHER	CEEHQRSU	CHEQUERS	CEEILOSS	SOLECISE
CEEHKRTV	KVETCHER	CEEHQSTU	QUETCHES	CEEILOSZ	SOLECIZE
CEEHKSST	SKETCHES	CEEHRSTV	CHEVRETS	CEEILPRS	ECLIPSER
CEEHKSTV	KVETCHES	CEEHRSTW	WRETCHES		PRESLICE
CEEHLMOO	HEMOCOEL	CEEHRTTU	TEUCHTER		RESPLICE
CEEHLMSZ	SCHMELZE	CEEHSTTU	TEUCHEST	CEEILPRV	CREEPILY
CEEHLNOO	HOLOCENE	CEEIIKLP	EPICLIKE	CEEILPSS	ECLIPSES
CEEHLNOS	CHELONES	CEEIIKLV	VICELIKE	CEEILPSX	EXCIPLES
	ECHELONS	CEEIIMPR	EPIMERIC	CEEILQSU	LIQUESCE
CEEHLNOT	ENCLOTHE	CEEIIMRT	EREMITIC	CEEILRST	RETICLES
CEEHLNPS	PLENCHES	CEEIINRT	ICTERINE		SCLERITE
CEEHLNPU	PENUCHLE		REINCITE		TIERCELS
CEEHLNSU	ELENCHUS	CEEIINST	NICETIES		TRISCELE

CEEILRSU	CISELEUR	CEEIOPRS	RECOPIES	CEEKPRRU	PUCKERER
	CISELURE	CEEIOPST	ECTOPIES	CEEKPRSY	RYEPECKS
	RECUILES		PICOTEES	CEEKRRSW	WRECKERS
CEEILRSV	VERSICLE	CEEIORST	COTERIES	CEELLLSU	CELLULES
CEEILRTU	RETICULE		ESOTERIC	CEELLMOU	MOLECULE
CEEILRTY	CELERITY	CEEIORSV	REVOICES	CEELLNOS	COLLEENS
CEEILSSV	CLEVISES	CEEIORSX	EXORCISE	CEELLNOU	NUCLEOLE
	VESICLES	CEEIORTT	EROTETIC	CEELLORT	RECOLLET
	VICELESS	CEEIORTV	ORECTIVE	CEELLOSS	CELLOSES
CEEILSTT	TELESTIC	CEEIORTX	EXOTERIC	CEELLPRU	CUPELLER
	TESTICLE	CEEIORXZ	EXORCIZE	CEELLPSU	PUCELLES
CEEILSTU	LEUCITES	CEEIOSST	COESITES	CEELLRRU	CRUELLER
CEEIMMPY	EMPYEMIC	CEEIOSTV	COVETISE	CEELLRVY	CLEVERLY
CEEIMMRS	MESMERIC	CEEIPPRR	PREPRICE	CEELLSSU	CLUELESS
CEEIMMST	MEMETICS	CEEIPPRS	PRECIPES	CEELLSTY	SELECTLY
CEEIMNNY	EMINENCY	CEEIPPRT	PRECEPIT	CEELMOOS	COELOMES
CEEIMNPS	SPECIMEN	CEEIPPTU	EUPEPTIC	CEELMOPT	COMPLETE
CEEIMNST	CENTIMES	CEEIPRRS	PIERCERS	CEELMORW	WELCOMER
	TENESMIC		PRECISER	CEELMOST	TELECOMS
CEEIMORT	METEORIC		REPRICES	CEELMOSW	WELCOMES
CEEIMOTY	MEIOCYTE	CEEIPRSS	PRECISES	CEELMRTU	ELECTRUM
CEEIMRSX	EXCIMERS	CEEIPRST	CREPIEST	CEELNNOP	PENONCEL
CEEIMSTT	SMECTITE		RECEIPTS	CEELNNOT	CENTONEL
CEEINNOP	PINECONE	CEEIPRSU	EPICURES		NONELECT
CEEINNOT	NEOTENIC	CEEIPSST	PECTISES	CEELNOPU	OPULENCE
CEEINNRS	INCENSER	CEEIPSTZ	PECTIZES	CEELNOPY	LYCOPENE
CEEINNRT	INCENTER	CEEIQSSU	QUIESCES	CEELNORS	ENCLOSER
	INCENTRE	CEEIRRSS	CERRISES		ENSORCEL
CEEINNSS	INCENSES	CEEIRRST	RECITERS	CEELNORT	ELECTRON
	NICENESS	CEEIRRSV	SERVICER	CEELNORU	ENCOLURE
CEEINNST	NESCIENT	CEEIRRSW	SCREWIER	CEELNOSS	ENCLOSES
CEEINOPU	EUPNOEIC	CEEIRRTU	URETERIC	CEELNPTU	CENTUPLE
CEEINORR	ENCIERRO	CEEIRSSV	SCRIEVES	CEELNRST	LECTERNS
CEEINORT	ERECTION		SERVICES	CEELNRSU	LUCERNES
	NEOTERIC	CEEIRSTT	TIERCETS	CEELNRTU	RELUCENT
CEEINORV	OVERNICE	CEEIRSTU	CERUSITE	CEELNRTY	RECENTLY
CEEINORX	EXOCRINE		CUTESIER	CEELNSTU	ESCULENT
CEEINOSS	SENECIOS		EUCRITES	CEELOOVV	COEVOLVE
CEEINOST	ICESTONE	CEEIRSTV	VERTICES	CEELOPRU	OPERCULE
	SEICENTO	CEEIRSTX	EXCITERS		RECOUPLE
CEEINOTV	EVECTION	CEEIRSVX	CERVIXES	CEELORSS	CORELESS
CEEINPRT	PRENTICE	CEEISSST	CITESSES		RECLOSES
	TERPENIC	CEEISTTT	TECTITES		SCLEROSE
CEEINPST	PECTINES	CEEISTTZ	ZETETICS	CEELORST	CORSELET
	PENTICES	CEEISUVX	EXCUSIVE		ELECTORS
CEEINPSX	SIXPENCE	CEEJKOTT	JOCKETTE		ELECTROS
CEEINQRU	QUERCINE	CEEJORRT	REJECTOR		SELECTOR
CEEINRRS	SINCERER	CEEJORST	EJECTORS	CEELORSY	RECOYLES
CEEINRSS	CERESINS	CEEKKNOS	KNEESOCK	CEELORTV	COVERLET
	SCRIENES	CEEKKNPS	KENSPECK	CEELOSSU	COLEUSES
CEEINRST	CENTRIES	CEEKLNPU	PENUCKLE	CEELOSTU	ELOCUTES
	ENTERICS	CEEKLNSS	NECKLESS	CEELOSTV	COVELETS
	ENTICERS	CEEKLNST	NECKLETS	CEELPRST	PLECTRES
	SCIENTER	CEEKLPSS	SPECKLES		PRELECTS
	SECRETIN	CEEKLRSS	CLERKESS	CEELPRSU	CUPELERS
CEEINRSU	INSECURE		RECKLESS	CEELRRTU	LECTURER
	SINECURE	CEEKNORR	RECKONER	CEELRSST	LECTRESS
CEEINRTT	RETICENT	CEEKNRSU	SUCKENER	CEELRSSU	CURELESS
CEEINRTU	CEINTURE	CEEKOPRT	POCKETER		RECLUSES
	ENURETIC	CEEKOPRX	OXPECKER	CEELRSSW	CREWLESS
CEEINSST	CENTESIS	CEEKORRT	CORKTREE	CEELRSTU	CRUELEST
CEEINSTY	CYSTEINE		ROCKETER		LECTURES
CEEIOPPR	PERICOPE	CEEKOSSY	SOCKEYES	CEELRSTY	SECRETLY
CEEIOPPS	EPISCOPE	CEEKOSTT	SOCKETTE	CEELRSUY	SECURELY

CEELSTTU	LETTUCES		RECOURSE	CEFHIIMS	MISCHIEF
CEEMMNTU	CEMENTUM		RESOURCE	CEFHILNR	FLINCHER
CEEMMORS	COMMERES	CEEORRSV	COVERERS	CEFHILNS	FLINCHES
CEEMNORR	CREMORNE		RECOVERS	CEFHILRS	FILCHERS
CEEMNORW	NEWCOMER	CEEORRSW	RECOWERS	CEFHILRT	FLICHTER
CEEMNORY	CEREMONY	CEEORRUV	OVERCURE	CEFHILST	FLITCHES
CEEMNOYZ	COENZYME	CEEORRVY	RECOVERY	CEFHINSU	FUCHSINE
CEEMNRSU	CERUMENS	CEEORSTV	COVETERS	CEFHISTT	FITCHETS
CEEMOORV	COMEOVER	CEEORSTW	COWTREES	CEFHISTU	FUCHSITE
	OVERCOME	CEEORSTX	COEXERTS	CEFHISTW	FITCHEWS
CEEMOORW	OWRECOME		CORTEXES	CEFHKOOR	FOREHOCK
CEEMOOTY	OOMYCETE	CEEORTTV	CORVETTE	CEFHLSSY	FLYSCHES
CEEMOPRS	COMPEERS	CEEORTUX	EXECUTOR	CEFHLSTU	CHESTFUL
	COMPERES	CEEOSSST	CESTOSES		FUTCHELS
CEEMOPST	COMPETES	CEEOSTTT	OCTETTES	CEFIIIST	CITIFIES
CEEMOSSS	COSMESES	CEEPPRST	PERCEPTS	CEFIILLM	MELLIFIC
CEEMSSTU	TUMESCES		PRECEPTS	CEFIILNO	OLEFINIC
CEENNOOS	CONENOSE	CEEPPRSU	PREPUCES	CEFIILRT	CLIFTIER
CEENNORS	ONSCREEN	CEEPRRSU	PRECURES	CEFIILST	FELSITIC
CEENNORT	CRETONNE		PRECURSE	CEFIILTY	FELICITY
CEENNORU	RENOUNCE	CEEPRSST	RESPECTS	CEFIIOPR	OPIFICER
CEENNORV	CONVENER		SCEPTERS	CEFIIORS	ORIFICES
CEENNOST	CENTONES		SCEPTRES	CEFIIPRT	PETRIFIC
CEENNOSU	ENOUNCES		SPECTERS	CEFIIRRT	FERRITIC
CEENNOSV	CONVENES		SPECTRES		TERRIFIC
CEENNRST	CENTNERS	CEEPRSSY	CYPRESES	CEFIISTY	CITYFIES
CEENOOST	ECOTONES	CEEPRSTX	EXCERPTS	CEFIKLOR	FIRELOCK
CEENOPST	POTENCES	CEEPRRSST	RECTRESS		FLOCKIER
CEENOPTW	TWOPENCE	CEERRSSU	RESCUERS	CEFIKLRS	FLICKERS
CEENORRS	RECENSOR		SECURERS	CEFIKLRY	FLICKERY
CEENORSS	NECROSES	CEERRSSW	SCREWERS	CEFIKLST	FICKLEST
CEENORSU	COENURES	CEERRSUV	RECURVES	CEFILLLO	FOLLICLE
CEENORSV	CONSERVE	CEERRTUZ	CREUTZER	CEFILMRU	CRIMEFUL
	CONVERSE	CEERRSST	CRESSETS		MERCIFUL
CEENORSZ	COZENERS	CEERSSTU	SECUREST	CEFILNOT	FLECTION
CEENORTT	TRECENTO	CEERSSTW	SETSCREW	CEFILNST	INFLECTS
CEENORVY	CONVEYER	CEERSSUX	EXCURSES	CEFILNSU	FUNICLES
	RECONVEY		EXCUSERS	CEFILOUV	VOICEFUL
CEENOSVX	CONVEXES	CEERSTTU	CURETTES	CEFILRSU	FLUERICS
CEENPPTU	TUPPENCE	CEERTUXY	EXECUTRY		LUCIFERS
CEENPRSS	SPENCERS	CEESSSTU	CESTUSES	CEFIMOST	COMFIEST
CEENPRST	PERCENTS	CEESTTUV	CUVETTES	CEFINNOR	CONFINER
	PRECENTS	CEFFGHIN	CHEFFING	CEFINNOS	CONFINES
CEENPSSU	SUSPENCE	CEFFHIRU	CHUFFIER	CEFINORS	COINFERS
CEENQSUY	SEQUENCY	CEFFHSTU	CHUFFEST		CONIFERS
CEENRRSU	CENSURER	CEFFIILR	CLIFFIER		FORENSIC
CEENRSSU	CENSURES	CEFFIORS	OFFICERS		FORINSEC
CEENRSTU	UNSECRET	CEFFIORU	COIFFEUR		FORNICES
CEENSSSU	CENSUSES		COIFFURE		INFORCES
CEENSSTU	CUTENESS	CEFFIRSU	SUFFICER	CEFINORT	INFECTOR
CEENSTTU	CUNETTES	CEFFISSU	SUFFICES	CEFINOSX	CONFIXES
CEEOORST	CREOSOTE	CEFFLORU	FORCEFUL	CEFINOTT	CONFETTI
CEEOPRRS	PRESCORE	CEFFLRSU	SCUFFLER	CEFIOPRS	FORCIPES
CEEOPRRT	RECEPTOR	CEFFLSSU	CUFFLESS	CEFIORTY	FEROCITY
CEEOPRTX	EXCEPTOR		SCUFFLES	CEFIRRSU	SCURFIER
CEEOPRTY	CEROTYPE	CEFFORSS	SCOFFERS	CEFIRSTU	FRUTICES
CEEOPSST	PECTOSES	CEFFORST	COFFRETS	CEFIRTUV	FRUCTIVE
CEEOPSTY	ECOTYPES	CEFFRSSU	SCUFFERS	CEFKLLOS	ELFLOCKS
CEEOQTTU	COQUETTE	CEFGHINT	FECHTING	CEFKLOOR	FORELOCK
CEEORRRS	SORCERER		FETCHING	CEFKLOST	FETLOCKS
CEEORRSS	RESCORES	CEFGIKLN	FLECKING	CEFKLPSY	FLYSPECK
CEEORRST	ERECTORS	CEFGILNT	CLEFTING	CEFKLRUW	WRECKFUL
	SECRETOR	CEFGINNS	FENCINGS	CEFLLOSU	FLOSCULE
CEEORRSU	RECOURES	CEFGLNUY	FULGENCY	CEFLNOSU	FLOUNCES

CEFLNRUU	FURUNCLE
CEFLNSTU	SCENTFUL
CEFLOPTY	COPYLEFT
CEFMORSY	COMFREYS
CEFNOOTT	CONFETTO
CEFNORSU	FROUNCES
CEFNORTU	CONFUTER
CEFNOSSU	CONFUSES
CEFNOSTU	CONFUTES
CEFOORST	SOFTCORE
CEFOPRSU	PREFOCUS
CEFORRST	CROFTERS
CEFORSSU	FOCUSERS
CEFORSTU	FRUCTOSE
CEFOSSSU	FOCUSSES
CEGGHIRS	CHIGGERS
CEGGHRSU	CHUGGERS
CEGGILOO	GEOLOGIC
CEGGILOR	CLOGGIER
	COGGLIER
CEGGILRS	SCRIGGLE
CEGGINNO	CONGEING
CEGGINOO	GEOGONIC
CEGGIORS	CROGGIES
	GEORGICS
	SCROGGIE
CEGGLNOY	GLYCOGEN
CEGGLORS	CLOGGERS
CEGHHINT	HECHTING
CEGHIINY	HYGIENIC
CEGHIKLN	HECKLING
CEGHIKNT	KETCHING
CEGHILNP	CHELPING
CEGHILNT	LETCHING
CEGHILNW	WELCHING
CEGHILST	GLITCHES
CEGHIMNS	SCHEMING
CEGHINNW	WENCHING
CEGHINOR	COHERING
	OCHERING
CEGHINPR	PERCHING
CEGHINQU	CHEQUING
CEGHINRS	GRINCHES
CEGHINRT	RETCHING
CEGHINRU	EUCHRING
CEGHINST	CHESTING
	ETCHINGS
CEGHINVY	CHEVYING
CEGHIRSS	SCREIGHS
CEGHIRTU	THEURGIC
CEGHISTU	GUICHETS
CEGHLNSU	GLUNCHES
CEGHMRUY	CHEMURGY
CEGHNORS	GROSCHEN
CEGHORSU	CHOREGUS
	COUGHERS
	GROUCHES
CEGHRSTU	GRUTCHES
	GUTCHERS
CEGIILMO	OLIGEMIC
CEGIILNR	CLINGIER
CEGIILNS	CEILINGS
	CIELINGS
CEGIILNT	GENTILIC

CEGIILOP	EPILOGIC
CEGIILOS	LOGICISE
CEGIILOZ	LOGICIZE
CEGIINNT	ENTICING
CEGIINNV	EVINCING
CEGIINOP	EPIGONIC
CEGIINOS	ISOGENIC
CEGIINPR	PIERCING
CEGIINPS	PIECINGS
CEGIINRT	RECITING
CEGIINSS	GNEISSIC
CEGIINSX	EXCISING
CEGIINTV	EVICTING
CEGIINTX	EXCITING
CEGIIOST	EGOISTIC
CEGIJLOU	LOGJUICE
CEGIKKLN	KECKLING
CEGIKLNR	CLERKING
	RECKLING
CEGIKNNR	RINGNECK
CEGIKNNS	NECKINGS
	SNECKING
CEGIKNPS	PECKINGS
	SPECKING
CEGIKNRT	TRECKING
CEGIKNRW	WRECKING
CEGIKSTU	GUCKIEST
CEGILMMN	CLEMMING
CEGILMNO	COMINGLE
CEGILMPS	GEMCLIPS
CEGILNOO	NEOLOGIC
CEGILNOS	ECLOSING
CEGILNPU	CUPELING
CEGILNRS	CLINGERS
	CRINGLES
CEGILNRU	RECULING
	ULCERING
CEGILNRY	GLYCERIN
CEGILNSU	LUCIGENS
CEGILNSY	GLYCINES
CEGILNTU	CULTIGEN
CEGILRSY	LYSERGIC
CEGIMNOS	GENOMICS
CEGIMNOY	MYOGENIC
CEGIMNSU	MUCIGENS
CEGIMNUY	GYNECIUM
CEGINNOR	ENCORING
CEGINNOZ	COZENING
CEGINNRS	SCERNING
CEGINNRT	CENTRING
CEGINNST	SCENTING
CEGINNSY	ENSIGNCY
	SYNGENIC
CEGINOOP	GEOPONIC
CEGINOOR	OROGENIC
CEGINOOY	COOEYING
CEGINOOZ	ZOOGENIC
CEGINOPR	COPERING
CEGINOPY	PYOGENIC
CEGINORS	COGNISER
	COREIGNS
	COSIGNER
CEGINORT	GERONTIC
CEGINORV	COVERING

CEGINORW	COWERING
CEGINORZ	COGNIZER
CEGINOSS	COGNISES
CEGINOST	ESCOTING
CEGINOSZ	COGNIZES
CEGINOTV	COVETING
CEGINOXY	OXYGENIC
CEGINRRS	CRINGERS
CEGINRRU	RECURING
CEGINRST	CRESTING
CEGINRSU	RECUSING
	RESCUING
	SCUNGIER
	SECURING
CEGINRSW	SCREWING
CEGINRSY	SYNERGIC
CEGINRTU	ERUCTING
CEGINSUX	EXCUSING
CEGIRSTU	SCUTIGER
CEGKLNNO	LONGNECK
CEGKLNOS	GENLOCKS
CEGKLORS	GROCKLES
CEGLLOOU	COLLOGUE
CEGLLORY	GLYCEROL
CEGLLRYY	GLYCERYL
CEGLNOOS	COLOGNES
CEGLNOTY	COGENTLY
CEGLOOOY	OECOLOGY
CEGLOOTY	CETOLOGY
CEGLOSSU	GLUCOSES
CEGLOSSY	GLYCOSES
CEGMNNOO	COGNOMEN
CEGNNOOS	ONCOGENS
CEGNNPUY	PUNGENCY
CEGNOOTY	GONOCYTE
CEGNORSS	CONGRESS
CEGNORSU	CONGRUES
	SCROUNGE
CEGNORSY	CRYOGENS
CEGNORVY	CRYOGENY
CEGNOSST	CONGESTS
CEGNOTYY	CYTOGENY
CEGNRTUY	TURGENCY
CEGOORSS	SCROOGES
CEGORRSU	SCOURGER
	SCROUGER
CEGORSSU	SCOURGES
	SCROUGES
CEHHIIRT	HITCHIER
CEHHINPY	HYPHENIC
CEHHIOOS	HOOCHIES
CEHHIRST	HITCHERS
CEHHISTU	HUTCHIES
CEHHNORU	HURCHEON
CEHHOOSS	COHOSHES
CEHHOOST	HOOTCHES
CEHHOPTY	HYPOTHEC
CEHHOSST	SHOCHETS
CEHHOSSU	CHOUSHES
CEHIIKNR	CHINKIER
CEHIIKNS	CHINKIES
CEHIIKST	THICKIES
CEHIILLR	CHILLIER
CEHIILLS	CHILLIES

CEHIILMO	HEMIOLIC	CEHILNOP	PHENOLIC	CEHINPSU	PENUCHIS
CEHIILMT	LITHEMIC		PINOCHLE	CEHINQSU	QUINCHES
CEHIILNN	LICHENIN	CEHILNOR	CHLORINE	CEHINRSS	RICHNESS
CEHIILNT	LECITHIN	CEHILNOS	CHOLINES	CEHINRST	CHRISTEN
CEHIILOT	EOLITHIC		HELICONS		CITHERNS
CEHIILTY	HELICITY	CEHILNPY	PHENYLIC		CITHRENS
CEHIIMOP	HEMIOPIC	CEHILNSS	CHINLESS		SNITCHER
CEHIIMOS	ISOCHEIM	CEHILNST	LINCHETS	CEHINRSW	WINCHERS
	ISOCHIME		TINCHELS	CEHINRTU	RUTHENIC
CEHIIMPT	MEPHITIC	CEHILOOS	SCHOOLIE	CEHINSST	CHINTSES
CEHIIMRT	HERMITIC	CEHILOPT	CHIPOTLE		SNITCHES
CEHIIMST	ETHICISM		HELICOPT	CEHINSTW	WITCHENS
CEHIINST	ICHNITES	CEHILORS	CEORLISH	CEHINSTZ	CHINTZES
	NITCHIES	CEHILORT	CHLORITE	CEHIOORS	CHOOSIER
CEHIIPPR	CHIPPIER		CLOTHIER		ISOCHORE
CEHIIPPS	CHIPPIES	CEHILORY	HEROICLY	CEHIOPPR	CHOPPIER
CEHIIPPR	CHIRPIER	CEHILPRS	PILCHERS	CEHIOPRS	SOPHERIC
CEHIIPRT	PITCHIER	CEHILPTY	PHYLETIC	CEHIOPRU	EUPHORIC
CEHIIRST	CHRISTIE	CEHILRSV	CHERVILS		POUCHIER
CEHIIRSZ	SCHIZIER	CEHILSTT	LICHTEST	CEHIOPSS	HOSPICES
CEHIIRTT	CHITTIER	CEHILSTW	SWITCHEL	CEHIOPST	POSTICHE
	TITCHIER	CEHILSTY	CHESTILY		POTICHES
	TRICHITE		LECYTHIS	CEHIOPSU	COPIHUES
CEHIIRTW	WITCHIER	CEHILTTY	TETCHILY	CEHIOPTU	EUPHOTIC
CEHIISTT	CHITTIES	CEHIMMOS	CHOMMIES	CEHIORRS	CHORRIES
	ETHICIST	CEHIMMRU	CHUMMIER	CEHIORRT	RHETORIC
	ITCHIEST	CEHIMMSS	CHEMISMS		TORCHIER
	THEISTIC	CEHIMMSU	CHUMMIES	CEHIORRV	OVERRICH
	TICHIEST	CEHIMNNW	WINCHMEN	CEHIORSS	CHORISES
CEHIISVV	CHIVVIES	CEHIMNOP	PHONEMIC		ORCHESIS
CEHIKLPT	KLEPHTIC	CEHIMNOR	CHOIRMEN		ORCHISES
CEHIKLRS	CLERKISH	CEHIMNPT	PITCHMEN	CEHIORST	ROTCHIES
CEHIKLSU	SUCHLIKE	CEHIMNSU	MUNCHIES		THEORICS
CEHIKMOS	HOMESICK	CEHIMNSY	CHIMNEYS	CEHIORSW	CHOWRIES
CEHIKNRU	CHUNKIER	CEHIMOOT	HOMEOTIC	CEHIORTT	TROCHITE
CEHIKNST	CHETNIKS	CEHIMORR	CHROMIER	CEHIORTU	COUTHIER
	KITCHENS	CEHIMORS	CHROMISE		TOUCHIER
	KNITCHES		MORICHES	CEHIOSST	ECHOISTS
	THICKENS	CEHIMORT	CHROMITE		TOISECHS
CEHIKNSW	CHEWINKS		TRICHOME	CEHIOSTV	CHEVIOTS
CEHIKOOS	CHOOKIES	CEHIMORZ	CHROMIZE	CEHIPPRS	CHIPPERS
CEHIKOSS	HOICKSES	CEHIMOSS	ECHOISMS	CEHIPRRS	CHIRPERS
CEHIKOST	CHOKIEST		MISCHOSE	CEHIPRSS	SPHERICS
	THICKOES	CEHIMOST	MOCHIEST	CEHIPRST	PITCHERS
CEHIKRSS	KIRSCHES	CEHIMOTW	CHOWTIME		SPITCHER
	SHICKERS	CEHIMRRS	SMIRCHER	CEHIPSST	CHIPSETS
	SKRIECHS	CEHIMRSS	SMIRCHES	CEHIQSTU	QUITCHES
CEHIKRST	CHIRKEST	CEHIMSST	CHEMISTS	CEHIRSST	STRICHES
CEHIKRSW	WHICKERS	CEHINNOS	CHINONES	CEHIRSTT	CHITTERS
CEHIKSST	CHEKISTS	CEHINNRT	INTRENCH		RESTITCH
	KITSCHES	CEHINOOS	COHESION		RICHTEST
	SKITCHES	CEHINOPR	PROCHEIN		STITCHER
CEHIKSTT	THICKEST	CEHINOPS	CHOPINES	CEHIRSTW	SWITCHER
	THICKETS	CEHINOPT	PHONETIC	CEHIRSTY	HYSTERIC
	THICKSET	CEHINOPU	EUPHONIC	CEHIRTTW	TWITCHER
CEHIKTTY	THICKETY	CEHINORS	CHORINES	CEHIRTWY	WITCHERY
CEHILLPR	PRECHILL	CEHINORT	NOTCHIER	CEHISSTT	STITCHES
CEHILLRS	CHILLERS	CEHINORU	UNHEROIC	CEHISSTU	CUSHIEST
	SCHILLER	CEHINOSY	HYOSCINE	CEHISSTW	SWITCHES
CEHILLST	CHILLEST	CEHINOTY	ONYCHITE	CEHISSUW	SUCHWISE
CEHILMMS	SCHIMMEL	CEHINPRS	PINCHERS	CEHISTTW	TWITCHES
CEHILMOU	HUMICOLE		PINSCHER	CEHKKRSU	CHUKKERS
CEHILMSY	CHIMLEYS	CEHINPRU	PUNCHIER	CEHKLLOS	SKELLOCH
CEHILMTY	METHYLIC		UNCIPHER	CEHKLMOS	HEMLOCKS

CEHKLOOS	KLOOCHES	CEHNOPTU	PUTCHEON		KINESICS
CEHKLORS	SHERLOCK	CEHNORST	CHORTENS	CEIIKNST	KINETICS
CEHKNOSU	SUNCHOKE		NOTCHERS	CEIIKPRR	PRICKIER
	UNCHOKES	CEHNORSV	CHEVRONS	CEIIKPST	PICKIEST
CEHKNPUY	KEYPUNCH	CEHNORTU	CHOUNTER	CEIIKQSU	QUICKIES
CEHKORSS	SHOCKERS	CEHNORVY	CHEVRONY	CEIIKRRT	TRICKIER
CEHKPSTU	KETCHUPS	CEHNOSSZ	SCHNOZES	CEIIKRST	STICKIER
CEHKRSSU	SHUCKERS	CEHNPPRU	PREPUNCH	CEIIKSST	EKISTICS
CEHKRSTU	HUCKSTER	CEHNPRSU	PUNCHERS		STICKIES
CEHLLMOS	MOCHELLS	CEHNPSST	PSCHENTS		
CEHLLMSU	MUCHELLS	CEHNRRSU	CHURNERS	CEIIKTTT	TEKTITIC
	SCHELLUM	CEHNRSTU	CHUNTERS	CEIILLMT	MELLITIC
CEHLLORS	CHOLLERS	CEHNSSSU	SUCHNESS	CEIILLNO	LINOLEIC
CEHLLOSY	YELLOCHS	CEHNSSTU	CHESNUTS	CEIILLOP	POLLICIE
CEHLLOUY	LOUCHELY	CEHNSTTU	CHESTNUT	CEIILLPT	ELLIPTIC
CEHLLPSU	CHELLUPS	CEHNSTUY	CHUTNEYS	CEIILLSS	SILICLES
CEHLMNOU	HOMUNCLE	CEHOOORZ	ZOOCHORE	CEIILLSU	SILICULE
CEHLMORS	CHROMELS	CEHOORSS	CHOOSERS	CEIILMNS	LEMNISCI
CEHLMSUY	CHUMLEYS		SOROCHES	CEIILMNT	LIMNETIC
CEHLNNOU	LUNCHEON	CEHOORST	CHEROOTS	CEIILMNY	MYELINIC
CEHLNNSU	CHUNNELS	CEHOORSU	OCHEROUS	CEIILMOT	CIMOLITE
CEHLNOST	CHOLENTS		OCHREOUS	CEIILNNR	INCLINER
	NOTCHELS	CEHOOSSS	SCOOSHES	CEIILNNS	INCLINES
CEHLNOTU	UNCLOTHE	CEHOOSUW	COWHOUSE	CEIILNOP	PICOLINE
CEHLNPRU	PRELUNCH	CEHOPPRS	CHOPPERS	CEIILNOS	ISOCLINE
CEHLNRSU	LUNCHERS	CEHOPPRY	PROPHECY		SILICONE
CEHLNRSY	LYNCHERS	CEHOPRST	POTCHERS	CEIILNPS	PENICILS
CEHLNSTY	LYNCHETS	CEHOPRSY	CORYPHES	CEIILNQU	CLINIQUE
CEHLOORS	RESCHOOL	CEHORRST	TORCHERS	CEIILNSS	ENCLISIS
CEHLOOSS	SCHOOLES	CEHORSSU	CHORUSES	CEIILOPP	EPIPLOIC
CEHLORRT	CHORTLER		CHOUSERS		EPIPOLIC
CEHLORST	CHORTLES	CEHORSSZ	SCHERZOS	CEIILOPS	POLICIES
CEHLORSU	SLOUCHER	CEHORSTU	SCOUTHER	CEIILORT	ELICITOR
CEHLORTY	HECTORLY		TOUCHERS	CEIILOTZ	ZEOLITIC
CEHLOSSU	SLOUCHES		TROUCHES	CEIILPPS	CLIPPIES
CEHLOSTU	SELCOUTH	CEHORSTW	SCOWTHER	CEIILPRT	PERLITIC
CEHLPPSS	SCHLEPPS	CEHORSUV	VOUCHERS	CEIILPRU	PIRLICUE
CEHLPPSY	SCHLEPPY	CEHOSSSU	HOCUSSES	CEIILPSS	ECLIPSIS
CEHLQSUY	SQUELCHY	CEHOSTTU	COUTHEST	CEIILPTX	EXPLICIT
CEHLRRSU	LURCHERS	CEHOTTUZ	ZUCHETTO	CEIILPTY	PYELITIC
CEHLSSTU	SLUTCHES	CEHPRSTU	PUTCHERS	CEIILQRU	CLIQUIER
CEHLSTUY	LECYTHUS	CEHPSSTU	PUTSCHES	CEIILRSU	SLUICIER
CEHMNRSU	MUNCHERS	CEHRRSSU	CRUSHERS	CEIILRSY	LYRICISE
CEHMNRTU	TRUCHMEN	CEHRSSSU	SCHUSSER	CEIILRTV	VERTICIL
CEHMNSSU	MUCHNESS	CEHRSSTY	SCYTHERS	CEIILRYZ	LYRICIZE
CEHMOORS	MOOCHERS	CEHRSTTY	STRETCHY	CEIILSSS	SCISSILE
	SMOOCHER	CEHSSSSU	SCHUSSES	CEIIMNOT	EMICTION
CEHMOOSS	SCHMOOSE	CEIIILSV	CIVILISE	CEIIMNRS	CREMINIS
	SMOOCHES	CEIIILVZ	CIVILIZE	CEIIMNRU	URINEMIC
CEHMOOSZ	SCHMOOZE	CEIIIMNT	CIMINITE	CEIIMNST	MINCIEST
CEHMOPRS	CHOMPERS	CEIIINSS	SINICISE	CEIIMOPT	EPITOMIC
CEHMORSU	MOUCHERS	CEIIINSV	INCISIVE	CEIIMORS	ISOMERIC
CEHMORUV	OVERMUCH	CEIIINSZ	SINICIZE	CEIIMOST	COMITIES
CEHMOSSU	SMOUCHES	CEIIJSTU	JESUITIC		SEMIOTIC
CEHMRSTU	CHETRUMS		JUICIEST	CEIIMPRR	CRIMPIER
CEHMSSTU	SMUTCHES	CEIIKKST	KICKIEST	CEIIMPRS	EMPIRICS
CEHNNNOU	NUNCHEON	CEIIKLMR	LIMERICK		MISPRICE
CEHNNOPU	PUNCHEON	CEIIKLRS	SICKLIER	CEIIMPSS	EPICISMS
CEHNNOSU	NONESUCH	CEIIKLRT	TICKLIER	CEIIMPTU	PUMICITE
	UNCHOSEN	CEIIKLSS	SICKLIES	CEIIMRRT	TRIMERIC
CEHNNRSU	CHUNNERS	CEIIKMMR	MIMICKER	CEIIMRST	MERISTIC
CEHNOOPS	HENCOOPS	CEIIKMST	KISMETIC		SCIMITER
CEHNOORS	COEHORNS	CEIIKNRZ	ZINCKIER		TRISEMIC
	SCHOONER	CEIIKNSS	ICKINESS	CEIIMRTT	TERMITIC
				CEIIMSST	MISCITES

CEIINNOP	NEPIONIC	CEIKLLTU	CULTLIKE	CEIKSTUY	YUCKIEST
CEIINNOR	IRENICON	CEIKLMOR	CORMLIKE	CEILLMOV	COMELILY
CEIINNOS	CONINES	CEIKLMST	MICKLEST	CEILLNOS	LIONCELS
	OSCININE	CEIKLMSU	SCUMLIKE	CEILLNOU	NUCLEOLI
CEIINNOT	COTININE	CEIKLNPS	SPICKNEL	CEILLOPS	POLLICES
	NICOTINE	CEIKLNRS	CLINKERS	CEILLOQU	COQUILLE
CEIINNRS	CINERINS		CRINKLES	CEILLORS	COLLIERS
CEIINNRT	INTRINCE	CEIKLNRU	CLUNKIER		ORSELLIC
CEIINNST	INSCIENT	CEIKLNSS	SLICKENS	CEILLORY	COLLIERY
CEIINOPR	PECORINI	CEIKLOSV	LOVESICK	CEILLOTU	COUTILLE
CEIINOPS	EPINOSIC	CEIKLOTU	LEUKOTIC	CEILLRTU	TELLURIC
CEIINOPT	EPITONIC	CEIKLPRS	PICKLERS	CEILLSST	CELLISTS
CEIINORS	RECISION		PRICKLES	CEILLSSU	CULLISES
	SORICINE	CEIKLPRU	PLUCKIER	CEILMMUY	MYCELIUM
CEIINOSS	ICONISES	CEIKLRSS	SLICKERS	CEILMNOP	COMPLINE
CEIINOSV	INVOICES	CEIKLRST	STICKLER	CEILMNOT	MONTICLE
CEIINOSX	EXCISION		STRICKLE	CEILMOOP	PICOMOLE
CEIINOSZ	ICONIZES		TICKLERS	CEILMOPR	COMPILER
CEIINOTV	EVICTION		TRICKLES		COMPLIER
CEIINPPR	PRINCIPE	CEIKLRSY	SICKERLY	CEILMOPS	COMPILES
CEIINRSS	SERICINS	CEIKLRTT	TRICKLET		COMPLIES
CEIINRST	CITRINES	CEIKLSST	SLICKEST		POLEMICS
	CRINITES		STICKLES	CEILMOSS	SOLECISM
	INCITERS	CEIKLSSW	WICKLESS	CEILMOSU	COLISEUM
CEIINRSU	INCISURE	CEIKLSTU	LUCKIEST	CEILMPRS	CRIMPLES
	SCIURINE	CEIKMNOR	MONICKER	CEILMPRU	CLUMPIER
CEIINRTU	NEURITIC	CEIKMNST	STICKMEN	CEILMPUU	PECULIUM
CEIINSSU	CUISINES	CEIKMOPT	IMPOCKET	CEILMRSU	CLUMSIER
CEIINSTU	CUTINISE	CEIKMORS	OCKERISM		MUSCLIER
CEIINSTY	CYTISINE	CEIKMRSS	SMICKERS	CEILMTUU	LUTECIUM
	SYENITIC	CEIKMRSU	MUSICKER	CEILNNOT	CONTLINE
CEIINSTZ	CITIZENS	CEIKMSST	SMICKETS	CEILNNSU	NUCLEINS
	ZINCIEST	CEIKMSTU	MUCKIEST	CEILNNSY	SYNCLINE
	ZINCITES	CEIKNNOT	NEKTONIC	CEILNOOS	COLONIES
CEIINTUZ	CUTINIZE	CEIKNNSU	INSUCKEN		COLONISE
CEIIOPRS	IRISCOPE	CEIKNOST	CONKIEST		ECLOSION
CEIIOPRT	PERIOTIC	CEIKNOTY	CYTOKINE	CEILNOOZ	COLONIZE
CEIIOPSW	WICOPIES	CEIKNQSU	QUICKENS	CEILNOPR	PERCOLIN
CEIIOPTT	PICOTITE	CEIKNRSS	SNICKERS		REPLICON
CEIIOSTT	OSTEITIC	CEIKNRST	STRICKEN	CEILNOPS	PINOCLES
CEIIOSTV	SOVIETIC	CEIKNRSU	UNSICKER	CEILNOPT	LEPTONIC
CEIIPRRS	CRISPIER	CEIKNRSY	SNICKERY	CEILNOPY	POLYENIC
CEIIPRST	PICRITES	CEIKNSSS	SICKNESS	CEILNORS	INCLOSER
	PRICIEST	CEIKNSST	SNICKETS		LICENSOR
CEIIPSST	EPICISTS	CEIKOPST	POCKIEST	CEILNOSS	CONSEILS
	SPICIEST	CEIKORRS	ROCKIERS		INCLOSES
CEIIQRTU	CRITIQUE	CEIKORST	CORKIEST	CEILNOST	LECTIONS
CEIIRSST	ERISTICS		ROCKIEST		TELSONIC
CEIIRSSU	CRUISIES		STOCKIER	CEILNOSU	LEUCOSIN
CEIIRSTT	RECTITIS	CEIKORSV	OVERSICK	CEILNOSX	LEXICONS
CEIIRSTV	VERISTIC	CEIKOSSY	YOICKSES	CEILNPRY	PRINCELY
CEIIRSUZ	CRUIZIES	CEIKOSTT	TOCKIEST	CEILNRTU	LINCTURE
CEIISSST	CISSIEST	CEIKPRRS	PRICKERS	CEILNRUV	CULVERIN
CEIISTVV	VIVISECT	CEIKPRST	PRICKETS	CEILNSST	STENCILS
CEIJMORT	MICROJET	CEIKPSST	SKEPTICS	CEILNSTU	CUTLINES
CEIJNORT	INJECTOR		SPICKEST		LINECUTS
CEIJNORU	JOUNCIER	CEIKQSTU	QUICKEST		TUNICLES
CEIJNOUV	CUNJEVOI		QUICKSET	CEILNSUU	UNSLUICE
CEIJRSTU	JUSTICER	CEIKRRST	TRICKERS	CEILOORS	COLORISE
CEIJSSTU	JUSTICES	CEIKRRTY	TRICKERY	CEILOORZ	COLORIZE
CEIKKLOR	CORKLIKE	CEIKRSST	STICKERS	CEILOPPS	POPSICLE
	ROCKLIKE	CEIKRSTU	TRUCKIES	CEILOPRS	POLICERS
CEIKKNRS	KNICKERS	CEIKRTTY	RICKETTY	CEILOPRT	LEPROTIC
CEIKKRRS	SKERRICK	CEIKSSTU	SUCKIEST		PETROLIC

CEILOPRV	PROCLIVE	CEIMOPRX	PROXEMIC	CEINOSSX	COXINESS
CEILOPST	TOECLIPS	CEIMOPRZ	COMPRIZE	CEINOSSZ	COZINESS
CEILOPTU	EPULOTIC	CEIMOQSU	COMIQUES	CEINOSTT	CENTOIST
	POULTICE	CEIMORRS	MORRICES		STENOTIC
CEILOPTY	EPICOTYL	CEIMORRT	MORTICER		TONETICS
	LIPOCYTE	CEIMORST	MORTICES	CEINOSTU	COUNTIES
CEILORST	CLOISTER	CEIMORSX	EXORCISM	CEINOSTX	EXCITONS
	COISTREL	CEIMORSY	ISOCRYME	CEINOSTY	CYTOSINE
	COSTLIER	CEIMORTY	EMICTORY	CEINOSUV	UNVOICES
	CREOLIST	CEIMOSSS	COSMESIS	CEINOSVV	CONVIVES
CEILORTT	CLOTTIER	CEIMOSTV	VICOMTES	CEINOTUX	UNEXOTIC
CEILORTY	CRYOLITE	CEIMPRRS	CRIMPERS	CEINPRSS	CRISPENS
CEILOSSS	OSSICLES		SCRIMPER		PRINCESS
CEILOSST	SOLECIST	CEIMPRRU	CRUMPIER	CEINPRST	SPECTRIN
	SOLSTICE	CEIMPRSU	PUMICERS	CEINPSST	INSPECTS
CEILOSSU	COULISSE	CEIMRRSU	SCRIMURE	CEINPSTY	PYCNITES
CEILOSTT	COLETITS	CEIMRRTU	TURMERIC	CEINRRSU	REINCURS
CEILOTVY	VELOCITY	CEIMRSST	CRETISMS	CEINRSST	CISTERNS
CEILPPRR	CRIPPLER	CEIMSSTY	SYSTEMIC	CEINRSTT	CENTRIST
CEILPPRS	CLIPPERS	CEINNNOT	INNOCENT		CITTERNS
	CRIPPLES	CEINNNOU	INCONNUE	CEINRSTU	CURNIEST
CEILPRSS	SPLICERS	CEINNORS	INCENSOR	CEINRSUV	INCURVES
CEILPRSU	SURPLICE	CEINNORU	NEURONIC	CEINRSVV	CRIVVENS
CEILPRUU	PURLICUE	CEINNORV	CONNIVER	CEINRTTU	INTERCUT
CEILPSSU	SPICULES	CEINNORW	COWINNER		TINCTURE
CEILRRSU	SCURRILE	CEINNOSV	CONNIVES	CEINSSTY	CYSTEINS
CEILRSTT	CLITTERS	CEINNOTU	CONTINUE		CYSTINES
CEILRSTU	CURLIEST	CEINNOTV	COINVENT	CEINSTTX	EXTINCTS
	UTRICLES	CEINNSTY	SYNTENIC	CEIOOPRS	OPORICES
CEILSSSS	SCISSELS	CEINOOPR	PECORINO	CEIOOTUV	OUTVOICE
CEILSTTU	CUITTLES	CEINOOSS	CONIOSES	CEIOOTXX	EXOTOXIC
	CULTIEST	CEINOOST	COONTIES	CEIOPPRS	CROPPIES
CEIMMNNO	MNEMONIC	CEINOOTZ	ENTOZOIC	CEIOPPSY	EPISCOPY
CEIMMNOU	ENCOMIUM		ENZOOTIC	CEIOPRRU	CROUPIER
	MECONIUM	CEINOPPR	CORNPIPE	CEIOPRSS	PERSICOS
CEIMMORT	RECOMMIT	CEINOPPT	PEPTONIC	CEIOPRST	PERSICOT
CEIMMORU	COREMIUM	CEINOPRS	CONSPIRE	CEIOPRSU	PRECIOUS
CEIMMOSX	COMMIXES		INCORPSE	CEIOPRTU	EUTROPIC
CEIMMRRS	CRIMMERS	CEINOPRT	ENTROPIC		OUTPRICE
CEIMMRRU	CRUMMIER		INCEPTOR	CEIOPSST	COPSIEST
CEIMMRSU	CRUMMIES		PRETONIC	CEIOPSSU	SPECIOUS
	SCRUMMIE	CEINOPRV	PROVINCE	CEIORRSS	CROSIERS
	SCUMMIER	CEINOPST	PONCIEST	CEIORRSU	COURIERS
CEIMMRSY	MERYCISM	CEINOPTT	ENTOPTIC	CEIORRSZ	CROZIERS
CEIMNNOO	ENCOMION	CEINOPTU	UNPOETIC	CEIORRTU	COURTIER
CEIMNNOR	NONCRIME	CEINORRS	RESORCIN	CEIORRTW	COWRITER
CEIMNNOS	MECONINS	CEINORRT	TRICORNE	CEIORRUZ	CRUZEIRO
CEIMNNOY	NEOMYCIN	CEINORSS	NECROSIS	CEIORSST	CROSSTIE
CEIMNOOT	EMOTICON		SERICONS	CEIORSSU	SCOURIES
CEIMNOPT	PENTOMIC	CEINORST	COINTERS	CEIORSSV	CORSIVES
CEIMNOPY	EPONYMIC		CORNIEST	CEIORSSW	SCOWRIES
CEIMNORS	CREMOSIN		NOTICERS	CEIORSSX	SIXSCORE
	INCOMERS		RECTIONS	CEIORSTT	COTTIERS
	SERMONIC	CEINORSU	COINSURE	CEIORSTU	CITREOUS
CEIMNORT	INTERCOM		NOURICES		OUTCRIES
CEIMNOSS	COSMINES		ROUNCIES	CEIORSTV	EVICTORS
CEIMNOST	CENTIMOS	CEINORTT	CONTRITE		VORTICES
CEIMNRST	CENTRISM		CORNETTI	CEIORSTW	COWRITES
CEIMNRSU	NUMERICS	CEINORTU	NEUROTIC	CEIORSTX	EXCITORS
CEIMNSSU	MENISCUS		UNEROTIC		EXORCIST
CEIMOOST	COOMIEST	CEINORTV	CONTRIVE	CEIORSVY	VICEROYS
CEIMOOSZ	MESOZOIC	CEINOSSS	CESSIONS	CEIORTTU	TOREUTIC
CEIMOOUZ	ZOOECIUM		COSINESS	CEIOSSSV	VISCOSES
CEIMOPRS	COMPRISE	CEINOSST	SECTIONS	CEIOSSTT	COTTISES

	SCOTTIES	**CEKLOOSS**	COOKLESS	**CELMOSUU**	CUMULOSE
CEIOSSTU	COITUSES	**CEKLOPST**	LOCKSTEP	**CELMOSYY**	CYMOSELY
CEIOSSTX	COEXISTS	**CEKLORSS**	ROCKLESS	**CELMPRSU**	CLUMPERS
CEIPPSTU	CUPPIEST	**CEKLOSSS**	SOCKLESS		CRUMPLES
CEIPQSTU	PICQUETS	**CEKLOSST**	LOCKSETS		SCRUMPLE
CEIPRRSS	CRISPERS	**CEKLOSTY**	TOCKLEYS	**CELMPRTU**	PLECTRUM
CEIPRRST	RESCRIPT	**CEKLPRSU**	PLUCKERS	**CELMPSUU**	SPECULUM
	SCRIPTER	**CEKLRRTU**	TRUCKLER	**CELMSSSU**	SCUMLESS
CEIPRRSU	SPRUCIER	**CEKLRSSU**	SCULLERS	**CELMSSUU**	SECULUMS
CEIPRSST	CRISPEST		SUCKLERS	**CELMSTUU**	CUMULETS
CEIPRSTU	CREPITUS	**CEKLRSTU**	TRUCKLES	**CELNNOSU**	NUCLEONS
	CUPRITES	**CEKLSSSU**	SUCKLESS	**CELNNOTY**	NOCENTLY
	PICTURES	**CEKMNOST**	STOCKMEN	**CELNNOUV**	UNCLOVEN
	PIECRUST	**CEKMNOSY**	MOCKNEYS	**CELNOORS**	CONSOLER
CEIPSSST	CESSPITS	**CEKMNRTU**	TRUCKMEN		CORONELS
CEIRRRSU	CURRIERS	**CEKNNSSU**	UNSNECKS	**CELNOORT**	CONTROLE
	SCURRIER	**CEKNOORV**	CONVOKER	**CELNOORU**	ENCOLOUR
CEIRRRUY	CURRIERY	**CEKNOOSV**	CONVOKES	**CELNOOSS**	CONSOLES
CEIRRSSU	CRUISERS	**CEKNOPST**	PENSTOCK		COOLNESS
	SCURRIES	**CEKNORST**	CRONKEST	**CELNOOVV**	CONVOLVE
	SUCRIERS	**CEKNORTU**	COKERNUT	**CELNOPRT**	PLECTRON
CEIRRSTT	CRITTERS	**CEKNOSTU**	UNSOCKET	**CELNOPUU**	UNCOUPLE
	RESTRICT	**CEKNPRUU**	UNPUCKER	**CELNOPUY**	OPULENCY
	STRICTER	**CEKNRSTU**	STRUCKEN	**CELNORTW**	CROWNLET
CEIRRSTU	CRUSTIER	**CEKNRSWY**	WRYNECKS	**CELNORWY**	CLOWNERY
	RECRUITS	**CEKOOORV**	OVERCOOK	**CELNOSSU**	CLONUSES
CEIRRSUV	SCURVIER	**CEKOOPRS**	PRECOOKS		COUNSELS
CEIRSSSU	CUISSERS	**CEKOOPSW**	COWPOKES		UNCLOSES
	SCISSURE	**CEKOORRS**	ROCKROSE	**CELNOSTU**	NOCTULES
CEIRSSTT	TRISECTS	**CEKOORRW**	COWORKER	**CELNOSUV**	CONVULSE
CEIRSSTU	CITRUSES	**CEKOORRY**	CROOKERY	**CELNOSVY**	SOLVENCY
	CRUSTIES	**CEKOORST**	CROOKEST	**CELNOVXY**	CONVEXLY
	CURTSIES	**CEKOPRST**	SPROCKET	**CELNPTUU**	PUNCTULE
	RICTUSES	**CEKORRTY**	ROCKETRY	**CELNRSTU**	LECTURNS
CEIRSSTV	VICTRESS	**CEKORSST**	RESTOCKS	**CELOOORV**	OVERCOOL
CEIRSSUV	CURSIVES		STOCKERS	**CELOOPRS**	PRECOOLS
	SCURVIES	**CEKORSTW**	TWOCKERS	**CELOOPSS**	CESSPOOL
CEIRSTTU	TUTRICES	**CEKRRSTU**	RESTRUCK	**CELOORRS**	COLORERS
CEIRSTUV	CURVIEST		TRUCKERS		RECOLORS
CEIRSTUY	SECURITY	**CEKRSSUU**	RUCKUSES	**CELOORRU**	COLOURER
CEIRSUZZ	SCUZZIER	**CELLMOSU**	COLUMELS	**CELOORSS**	COLESSOR
CEISSSSU	CISSUSES	**CELLNOOS**	COLONELS		CREOSOLS
CEISSSTU	CISTUSES	**CELLNORS**	ENSCROLL	**CELOORTW**	COLEWORT
CEISTTTU	CUTTIEST	**CELLNSUU**	NUCELLUS	**CELOORVY**	OVERCLOY
CEJKNOSY	JOCKNEYS	**CELLNTUU**	LUCULENT	**CELOOSTU**	CLOSEOUT
CEJLOOSY	JOCOSELY	**CELLNTUY**	LUCENTLY	**CELOPRSS**	CROPLESS
CEJNORRU	CONJURER	**CELLOOQU**	COLLOQUE	**CELOPRSU**	COUPLERS
CEJNORSU	CONJURES	**CELLORSS**	ESCROLLS	**CELOPSSU**	CLOSEUPS
CEJNRTUU	JUNCTURE	**CELLOSSY**	CLOYLESS		OPUSCLES
CEJNSSUU	JUNCUSES	**CELLRRSU**	CRULLERS		UPCLOSES
CEJOPRST	PROJECTS	**CELLRSSU**	SCULLERS	**CELOPSTU**	COUPLETS
CEKKLNRU	KNUCKLER	**CELLRSUY**	SCULLERY		OCTUPLES
CEKKLNSU	KNUCKLES	**CELMMSSU**	MESCLUMS	**CELOPSUU**	OPUSCULE
CEKKNORS	KNOCKERS	**CELMNOOR**	COLORMEN	**CELOPTTU**	OCTUPLET
CEKLLNOR	ROLLNECK	**CELMNOOS**	MONOCLES	**CELOPTUX**	OCTUPLEX
CEKLLOOV	LOVELOCK	**CELMNOTY**	CLOYMENT	**CELORRSU**	CORULERS
CEKLLOPS	PELLOCKS	**CELMNOUY**	UNCOMELY	**CELORSST**	CORSLETS
CEKLLSSU	LUCKLESS	**CELMNSSU**	MESCLUNS		COSTRELS
CEKLMNOS	LOCKSMEN	**CELMNTUU**	MUCULENT		CROSSLET
CEKLNOSS	SLOCKENS	**CELMOOOT**	LOCOMOTE	**CELORSSU**	CLOSURES
CEKLNOST	STENLOCK	**CELMOOPY**	COEMPLOY		SCLEROUS
CEKLNRSU	CLUNKERS	**CELMOOSY**	CLOYSOME	**CELORSSW**	SCOWLERS
	CRUNKLES	**CELMOPSU**	COMPULSE		SCROWLES
CEKLOORV	OVERLOCK	**CELMOPSY**	SYMPLOCE	**CELORSSY**	SCROYLES

CELORSTT	CLOTTERS
	CROTTLES
CELORSTU	CLOTURES
	CLOUTERS
	COULTERS
CELORSTY	COYSTREL
CELORSUU	ULCEROUS
	URCEOLUS
CELORSUY	CROUSELY
CELORTTU	COURTLET
CELORTVY	COVERTLY
CELOSSST	COSTLESS
CELOSTTU	CULOTTES
CELPRRSU	SCRUPLER
CELPRSSU	SCRUPLES
CELPRSTU	RESCULPT
CELPRSUY	SPRUCELY
CELRSSTU	CLUSTERS
	CUSTRELS
CELRSSTY	CLYSTERS
CELRSTTU	CLUTTERS
	SCUTTLER
CELRSTUU	CULTURES
CELRSTUV	CULVERTS
CELRSTUY	CLUSTERY
CELRTTUY	CLUTTERY
CELSSTTU	SCUTTLES
CELSSTUU	CULTUSES
CEMMNOOR	COMMONER
CEMMNOOS	CONSOMME
CEMMNOOY	COMMONEY
CEMMNORU	COMMUNER
CEMMNOST	COMMENTS
CEMMNOSU	COMMUNES
CEMMOOST	COMMOTES
CEMMOOSV	COMMOVES
CEMMORTU	COMMUTER
CEMMOSTU	COMMUTES
CEMMRSSU	SCUMMERS
CEMNNOST	CONTEMNS
CEMNOOPT	CONTEMPO
CEMNOORR	CROMORNE
CEMNOOTY	MONOCYTE
CEMNOPRS	CORPSMEN
CEMNOPTT	CONTEMPT
CEMNORSU	CONSUMER
	MUCRONES
CEMNOSSU	CONSUMES
	MUSCONES
CEMNRSTU	CENTRUMS
CEMOOPRS	COMPOSER
CEMOOPSS	COMPOSES
CEMOOPST	COMPOTES
CEMOOPSY	MYOSCOPE
CEMOORSY	SYCOMORE
CEMOOSSS	COSMOSES
CEMOOSTU	OUTCOMES
CEMOOSTY	CYTOSOME
CEMOPRSS	COMPRESS
CEMOPRST	COMPTERS
CEMOPRTU	COMPUTER
CEMOPSTU	COMPUTES
CEMORSSU	CORMUSES
CEMORSTU	COSTUMER
	CUSTOMER
CEMOSSTU	COSTUMES
CEMOSTUY	COSTUMEY
CEMOTXYY	MYXOCYTE
CEMPRSTU	CRUMPEST
	CRUMPETS
	SPECTRUM
CENNOOPR	CORNPONE
CENNOORV	CONVENOR
CENNOOST	CONNOTES
CENNORRT	CORNRENT
CENNORTU	NOCTURNE
CENNOSST	CONSENTS
CENNOSTT	CONTENTS
CENNOSTV	CONVENTS
CENNRSSU	SCUNNERS
CENOOOTZ	ECTOZOON
CENOOPSS	POCOSENS
CENOORRS	CORONERS
	CROONERS
CENOORST	CORONETS
CENOORSU	CORNEOUS
CENOORSV	CONVERSO
CENOORTT	CORNETTO
CENOORVY	CONVEYOR
CENOPRSU	POUNCERS
CENOPRSY	NECROPSY
CENOPSSY	PYCNOSES
	SYNCOPES
CENOPSTU	POUNCETS
CENOQRSU	CONQUERS
CENOQSTU	CONQUEST
CENORRSS	SCORNERS
CENORRSW	CROWNERS
	RECROWNS
CENORRTU	TROUNCER
CENORSST	CONSTERS
	CRESTONS
CENORSSU	CORNUSES
CENORSTT	CORNETTS
CENORSTU	CONSTRUE
	CORNUTES
	COUNTERS
	RECOUNTS
	TROUNCES
CENORSTV	CONVERTS
CENORSTW	CROWNETS
CENORSUU	CERNUOUS
	COENURUS
CENORSUV	UNCOVERS
CENORSUY	CYNOSURE
CENOSSTT	CONTESTS
CENOSSTU	CONTUSES
	COUNTESS
CENOSTTX	CONTEXTS
CENPRSTY	ENCRYPTS
CENPRTUU	PUNCTURE
CENPSTUX	EXPUNCTS
CENRRSTU	CURRENTS
CENRSSTU	CURTNESS
	ENCRUSTS
CENRSSUU	UNCURSES
CENRSSUW	UNSCREWS
CEOOOPST	OTOSCOPE
CEOOPRRV	OVERCROP
CEOOPRSS	SCOOPERS
CEOOPSWX	COWPOXES
CEOORRVW	OVERCROW
CEOORSST	SCOOTERS
CEOORSTU	ECOTOURS
	OUTSCORE
CEOOSTUV	COVETOUS
CEOPPRRS	CROPPERS
CEOPPRST	PROSPECT
CEOPPRSU	SUPERCOP
CEOPRRRU	PROCURER
CEOPRRSS	SCORPERS
CEOPRRST	PORRECTS
CEOPRRSU	CROUPERS
	PROCURES
CEOPRSST	PROSECTS
CEOPRSSU	CORPUSES
CEOPRSTT	PROTECTS
CEOPRSTW	CROWSTEP
	SCREWTOP
CEOPRSUU	COUPURES
	CUPREOUS
CEOPRSUV	COVERUPS
CEOPRSUW	SUPERCOW
CEOQRSTU	CROQUETS
	ROCQUETS
CEOQRTUY	COQUETRY
CEORRSSS	CROSSERS
	SCORSERS
CEORRSSU	COURSERS
	CURSORES
	SCOURERS
CEORRSSW	SCOWRERS
CEORRSTU	COURTERS
CEORRSTY	CORSETRY
CEORSSST	CROSSEST
CEORSSSU	SCOURSES
	SCOUSERS
	SUCROSES
CEORSSTU	CRUSTOSE
	SCOUTERS
CEORSSUV	CORVUSES
CEORSTUU	COUTURES
	OUTCURSE
CEORSTUV	COUVERTS
	CUTOVERS
	OVERCUTS
CEORSTUY	COURTESY
CEORTUUV	OUTCURVE
CEOSSSTU	COSTUSES
CEOSSTTU	COTTUSES
CEPPRRSU	CRUPPERS
CEPPRSSU	SCUPPERS
CEPPRTUU	UPPERCUT
CEPRSSTU	SPRUCEST
CEPRSSUW	SCREWUPS
CEPRSSUY	CYPRUSES
CEPRSTUU	CUTPURSE
CEPRSUUV	UPCURVES
CEPSSSTU	SUSPECTS
CERSSSUU	RUSCUSES
CERSSTTU	SCUTTERS
CERSSTUY	CURTSEYS

CERSSUUX	EXCURSUS	CFIMNORS	CONFIRMS	CGHIINPP	CHIPPING
CFFFKOSU	FUCKOFFS	CFIMNORU	CUNIFORM	CGHIINPR	CHIRPING
CFFGHINU	CHUFFING		UNCIFORM	CGHIINPT	PITCHING
CFFGIILNO	COIFFING	CFIMOSSU	MISFOCUS	CGHIINQU	QUICHING
CFFGILNO	COFFLING	CFINNOTU	FUNCTION	CGHIINRR	CHIRRING
CFFGILNU	CUFFLING	CFIOPRUY	COPURIFY	CGHIINRT	CHIRTING
CFFGINOS	SCOFFING	CFKLLOSU	LOCKFULS		RICHTING
CFFGINSU	SCUFFING	CFKLRTUU	TRUCKFUL	CGHIINST	ITCHINGS
CFFHINOS	CHIFFONS	CFKNORSU	UNFROCKS		SICHTING
CFFHINOY	CHIFFONY	CFKOSTTU	FUTTOCKS	CGHIINTT	CHITTING
CFFIKKOS	KICKOFFS	CFLLOORU	COLORFUL	CGHIINTW	WITCHING
CFFIKLNU	CUFFLINK	CFLLOPRU	CROPFULL	CGHIINVV	CHIVVING
CFFIKOPS	PICKOFFS	CFLMRSUU	FULCRUMS	CGHIINVY	CHIVVYING
CFFINNOU	UNCOFFIN	CFLMRUUU	FURCULUM	CGHIINZZ	CHIZZING
CFFIRTUY	FRUCTIFY	CFLNOORT	CORNLOFT	CGHIKLNO	HOCKLING
CFFKKNOO	KNOCKOFF	CFLNORSU	SCORNFUL	CGHIKNNU	CHUNKING
CFFKOOOS	COOKOFFS	CFLOOPSU	SCOOPFUL	CGHIKNOO	CHOOKING
CFFMOSSU	OFFSCUMS	CFLOOPSW	COWFLOPS	CGHIKNOS	SHOCKING
CFGHIILN	FILCHING	CFLOPRSU	CROPFULS	CGHIKNOT	KOTCHING
CFGHINOO	CHOOFING	CFMNOORS	CONFORMS	CGHIKNSU	SHUCKING
CFGIIKLN	FICKLING	CFMOORST	COMFORTS	CGHILMNU	MULCHING
	FLICKING	CFNNOORT	CONFRONT	CGHILNNU	LUNCHING
CFGIIKNR	FRICKING	CFNORSTU	FUNCTORS	CGHILNNY	LYNCHING
CFGIKLNO	FLOCKING	CFOOORTW	CROWFOOT	CGHILNOT	CLOTHING
CFGIKNOR	FROCKING	CFRSTUUU	USUFRUCT	CGHILNRU	LURCHING
CFGIKNSU	FUCKINGS	CGGGHINU	CHUGGING	CGHIMMNU	CHUMMING
CFGINORT	CROFTING	CGGGILNO	CLOGGING	CGHIMNNU	MUNCHING
CFGINOSU	FOCUSING		COGGLING	CGHIMNOO	MOOCHING
CFHIINOO	FINOCHIO	CGGGINOR	CROGGING	CGHIMNOP	CHOMPING
CFHIIORR	HORRIFIC	CGGGINOS	COGGINGS	CGHIMNOR	CHROMING
CFHIKORS	ROCKFISH		SCOGGING	CGHIMNOU	MOUCHING
CFHIKSSU	SUCKFISH	CGGGINSU	SCUGGING	CGHIMNPU	CHUMPING
CFHILPTY	FLYPITCH	CGGHILNU	GULCHING	CGHIMNTU	MUTCHING
CFHIMOSS	SCOMFISH	CGGHINOU	COUGHING	CGHIMPSY	SPHYGMIC
CFHIMSSU	SCUMFISH	CGGIILNN	CLINGING	CGHINNOS	CHIGNONS
CFHINSSU	FUCHSINS	CGGIINNO	COIGNING	CGHINNOT	NOTCHING
CFHLOPUU	POUCHFUL	CGGIINNR	CRINGING	CGHINNPU	PUNCHING
CFHORSTU	FUTHORCS	CGGIINRS	GRICINGS	CGHINNRU	CHURNING
CFIIIKNN	FINICKIN	CGGILLOY	CLOGGILY	CGHINNSY	SYNCHING
CFIIILSY	SILICIFY	CGGILRSY	SCRIGGLY	CGHINOOP	POOCHING
CFIIKNNY	FINNICKY	CGGINNSU	SCUNGING	CGHINOOS	CHOOSING
CFIIKNYZ	ZINCKIFY	CGGINOOS	SCOOGING	CGHINOPP	CHOPPING
CFIILMNU	FULMINIC	CGGINORS	SCROGGIN	CGHINOPT	POTCHING
CFIILNST	INFLICTS	CGGINOSU	SCOUGING	CGHINOPU	POUCHING
CFIILNUU	FUNICULI	CGHHIILN	HILCHING	CGHINORT	TORCHING
CFIILOPR	PROLIFIC	CGHHIINT	HITCHING	CGHINOSU	CHOUSING
CFIILPSU	PULSIFIC	CGHHINNU	HUNCHING		HOCUSING
CFIILSTU	SULFITIC	CGHHINOT	HOTCHING	CGHINOSW	CHOWSING
CFIIMNOS	SOMNIFIC	CGHHINTU	HUTCHING	CGHINOTU	TOUCHING
CFIIMOPR	PICIFORM	CGHIIKNN	CHINKING	CGHINOUV	VOUCHING
CFIIMORT	MORTIFIC	CGHIIKNO	HOICKING	CGHINPSY	PSYCHING
CFIINOPT	PONTIFIC	CGHIIKNR	CHIRKING	CGHINPTU	PINCHGUT
CFIINORT	FRICTION	CGHIIKNT	THICKING	CGHINRRU	CHURRING
CFIINOST	FICTIONS	CGHIILLN	CHILLING	CGHINRSU	CRUSHING
CFIKLORY	FROLICKY	CGHIILNR	CHIRLING		RUCHINGS
CFIKLSTU	STICKFUL	CGHIILNT	CHITLING	CGHINSTY	SCYTHING
CFIKNNOS	FINNOCKS		LICHTING	CGHLNOSS	SCHLONGS
CFIKOSSS	FOSSICKS	CGHIIMNR	CHIRMING	CGHNOOOS	SOOCHONG
CFIKPSTU	PUCKFIST	CGHIIMNS	MICHINGS	CGHNOOSU	SOUCHONG
CFIKSTUW	FUCKWITS	CGHIIMNT	MITCHING	CGHOORST	TORGOCHS
CFILMOOR	COLIFORM	CGHIINNN	CHINNING	CGIIILNT	LIGNITIC
CFILNOSU	SULFONIC	CGHIINNP	PINCHING	CGIIINNS	INCISING
CFILRSUU	SULFURIC	CGHIINNW	WINCHING	CGIIINNT	INCITING
CFIMNOOR	CONIFORM	CGHIINOR	CHOIRING	CGIIKLNN	CLINKING

	NICKLING
CGIIKLNP	PICKLING
CGIIKLNS	LICKINGS
	SICKLING
	SLICKING
CGIIKLNT	TICKLING
CGIIKMMS	GIMMICKS
CGIIKMMY	GIMMICKY
CGIIKNNS	SNICKING
CGIIKNNZ	ZINCKING
CGIIKNOY	YOICKING
CGIIKNPR	PRICKING
CGIIKNPS	PICKINGS
CGIIKNRS	SCRIKING
CGIIKNRT	TRICKING
CGIIKNRW	WRICKING
CGIIKNST	STICKING
	TICKINGS
CGIIKNSW	WICKINGS
CGIIKPST	PIGSTICK
CGIILLOS	ILLOGICS
CGIILMOS	LOGICISM
CGIILNOP	POLICING
CGIILNPP	CLIPPING
CGIILNPS	SPLICING
CGIILNQU	CLIQUING
CGIILNSS	SLICINGS
CGIILNSU	SLUICING
CGIILOST	LOGICIST
	LOGISTIC
CGIILRTU	LITURGIC
CGIIMNNO	INCOMING
CGIIMNNS	MINCINGS
CGIIMNPR	CRIMPING
CGIIMNPU	PUMICING
CGIIMNSU	MISCUING
CGIINNOS	COININGS
CGIINNOT	NOTICING
CGIINNPR	PRINCING
CGIINNSU	INCUSING
CGIINNSW	WINCINGS
CGIINNTT	TINCTING
CGIINOOS	ISOGONIC
CGIINOPT	PICOTING
CGIINORT	TRIGONIC
CGIINOST	COTISING
CGIINOSV	VOICINGS
CGIINPRS	CRISPING
	PRICINGS
CGIINRSU	CRUISING
CGIINRSV	SCRIVING
CGIINSSS	CISSINGS
CGIJNNOU	JOUNCING
CGIKKNNO	KNOCKING
CGIKLNNO	CLONKING
CGIKLNNU	CLUNKING
CGIKLNOR	ROCKLING
CGIKLNOS	LOCKINGS
CGIKLNPU	PLUCKING
CGIKLNRU	RUCKLING
CGIKLNSU	SCULKING
	SUCKLING
CGIKMNOS	MOCKINGS
	SMOCKING
CGIKNOOR	CROOKING
CGIKNOOS	COOKINGS
CGIKNORS	ROCKINGS
CGIKNORT	TROCKING
CGIKNORW	CORKWING
CGIKNOST	STOCKING
CGIKNOTW	TWOCKING
CGIKNPSU	KINGCUPS
CGIKNRTU	TRUCKING
CGIKNSSU	SUCKINGS
CGIKNSTU	GUNSTICK
CGIKPSTU	PIGSTUCK
CGILLNOS	COLLINGS
CGILLNOY	COLLYING
CGILLNSU	CULLINGS
	SCULLING
CGILLNUY	CULLYING
CGILMNOP	CLOMPING
CGILMNPU	CLUMPING
CGILMNSU	MUSCLING
CGILMNSY	CYMLINGS
CGILMNTU	MULCTING
CGILMNUU	CINGULUM
	GLUCINUM
CGILMOOY	MYOLOGIC
CGILNNNO	NONCLING
CGILNNOS	CLONINGS
CGILNNOW	CLOWNING
CGILNOOR	COLORING
	CROOLING
CGILNOOY	COOINGLY
CGILNOPP	CLOPPING
CGILNOPU	COUPLING
CGILNORU	CLOURING
CGILNOSS	CLOSINGS
CGILNOSW	COWLINGS
	SCOWLING
CGILNOTT	CLOTTING
CGILNOTU	CLOUTING
CGILNPSU	SCULPING
CGILNRSU	CURLINGS
CGILNRVY	CRYINGLY
CGILNTTU	CUTTLING
CGILOOOZ	ZOOLOGIC
CGILOORU	UROLOGIC
CGILOPRY	COPYGIRL
CGILORSW	COWGIRLS
CGILPSTU	GILTCUPS
CGILPSTY	GLYPTICS
CGIMMNSU	SCUMMING
CGIMNNOO	GNOMONIC
	ONCOMING
CGIMNOPS	COMPINGS
CGIMNOPT	COMPTING
CGIMNOPU	UPCOMING
CGIMNORS	SCROMING
CGIMNPRU	CRUMPING
CGIMRRUY	MICRURGY
CGINNNOS	CONNINGS
CGINNNSU	CUNNINGS
CGINNOOP	POONCING
CGINNOOR	CROONING
CGINNOPU	POUNCING
	UNCOPING
CGINNORS	SCORNING
CGINNORW	CROWNING
CGINNOSS	CONSIGNS
CGINNOTU	COUNTING
CGINOOPS	SCOOPING
CGINOOPT	COOPTING
CGINOOST	SCOOTING
CGINOOTV	COGNOVIT
CGINOPPR	CROPPING
CGINOPRS	CORPSING
CGINOPRU	CROUPING
CGINOPSU	SCOUPING
CGINOPSW	SCOWPING
CGINORSS	CROSSING
	SCORINGS
	SCORSING
CGINORSU	COURSING
	SCOURING
	SOURCING
CGINORTU	COURTING
CGINOSST	GNOSTICS
CGINOSTU	SCOUTING
CGINPPSU	CUPPINGS
CGINPRSU	SPRUCING
CGINRRSU	SCURRING
CGINRRUY	CURRYING
CGINRSSU	CURSINGS
CGINRSSY	SCRYINGS
CGINRSTU	CRUSTING
CGINRSUZ	SCRUZING
CGINSTTU	CUTTINGS
	TUNGSTIC
CGKLNOSU	GUNLOCKS
CGKNOSTU	GUNSTOCK
CGLLOSYY	GLYCOSYL
CGLMOOYY	MYCOLOGY
CGLNOOOY	ONCOLOGY
CGLOOOTY	TOCOLOGY
CGLOOTYY	CYTOLOGY
CGMNNOOR	MONGCORN
CGMNNORU	MUNGCORN
CGNORSUY	SCROUNGY
CGOORRSW	GORCROWS
CHHIIKST	THICKISH
CHHIILTY	HITCHILY
CHHIIPST	PHTHISIC
CHHIKORS	CHIKHORS
CHHILRSU	CHURLISH
CHHIMPSU	CHUMSHIP
CHHIMRTY	RHYTHMIC
CHHKOOPS	HOCKSHOP
CHHNORSU	RHONCHUS
CHHOOPTT	HOTCHPOT
CHIIILOS	CHILIOIS
CHIIINRT	RHINITIC
CHIIKLST	TICKLISH
CHIIKNNS	KINCHINS
CHIIKRST	TRICKISH
CHIIKRTW	WHITRICK
CHIILLLY	CHILLILY
CHIILMSY	HYLICISM
CHIILNNP	LINCHPIN
CHIILNST	CHITLINS
CHIILOPT	HOPLITIC

CHIILORT	TROCHILI	CHIMPSSY	PSYCHISM	CHNORSSY	SYNCHROS
CHIILOST	HOLISTIC	CHIMSSTY	CHYMISTS	CHNORSTU	COTHURNS
CHIILPRY	CHIRPILY		TYCHISMS	CHOOORVZ	ZOOCHORY
CHIILPTY	PITCHILY	CHINOOPT	PHOTONIC	CHOOPPSS	COPSHOPS
CHIILQSU	CLIQUISH	CHINOORS	CHORIONS	CHOOPSTU	OCTOPUSH
CHIILSTY	HYLICIST		ISOCHRON	CHOPSTUU	TOUCHUPS
CHIIMOPT	PHIMOTIC	CHINOORT	ORTHICON	CHORSTTU	SHORTCUT
CHIIMORZ	RHIZOMIC	CHINOPTY	HYPNOTIC	CIIIKNTU	CUITIKIN
CHIIMPRU	PICHURIM		PHYTONIC	CIIILMPT	IMPLICIT
CHIINNPS	INCHPINS		PYTHONIC	CIIILMSU	SILICIUM
CHIINOPS	SIPHONIC		TYPHONIC	CIIILNOV	OLIVINIC
CHIINORT	ORNITHIC	CHINORTU	COTHURNI	CIIILPST	SPILITIC
CHIIORSS	CHORISIS	CHINOSSU	CUSHIONS	CIIILSTV	CIVILIST
CHIIORST	HISTORIC	CHINOSTZ	SCHIZONT	CIIILTVY	CIVILITY
	ORCHITIS	CHINOSUY	CUSHIONY	CIIIMNRS	CRIMINIS
CHIIPPRU	HIPPURIC	CHINSTTU	UNSTITCH	CIIIMNSV	INCIVISM
CHIIRSTT	TRISTICH	CHIOOPPT	PHOTOPIC	CIIINNOS	INCISION
CHIKLLOS	HILLOCKS	CHIOOPRS	POCHOIRS	CIIINNRT	CITRININ
CHIKLLOY	HILLOCKY	CHIOOPTY	OOPHYTIC	CIIINOTY	IONICITY
CHIKLNUY	CHUNKILY	CHIOORSS	ISOCHORS	CIIINPPR	PRINCIPI
CHIKLORS	HORLICKS	CHIOORSU	ICHOROUS	CIIINPST	INCIPITS
CHIKMNNU	MUNCHKIN	CHIOORSZ	CHORIZOS	CIIINTVY	VICINITY
CHIKMNPU	CHIPMUNK	CHIOORTT	ORTHOTIC	CIIJRSTU	JURISTIC
CHIKMNTU	MUTCHKIN	CHIOPRST	STROPHIC	CIIKKLLS	KILLICKS
CHIKNNOP	PHINNOCK	CHIOPSTY	HYPOCIST	CIIKKMSS	MISKICKS
CHIKNOOS	CHINOOKS	CHIOPTTU	OUTPITCH	CIIKLLSY	SICKLILY
CHIKOPTY	KYPHOTIC		PITCHOUT	CIIKLOPT	POLITICK
CHIKORST	TROCHISK	CHIORSSS	CROSSISH	CIIKLPST	LICKSPIT
CHIKOSST	STOCKISH	CHIORSST	CHORISTS		LIPSTICK
CHIKPSYY	PHYSICKY	CHIPRRSU	CHIRRUPS	CIIKLRTY	TRICKILY
CHILLMSU	CHILLUMS	CHIPRRSY	PYRRHICS	CIIKLSTY	STICKILY
CHILLOOT	OILCLOTH	CHIPRRUY	CHIRRUPY	CIIKMMMS	MIMMICKS
CHILMMUY	CHUMMILY	CHIPRTTY	TRIPTYCH	CIIKMNNS	MINNICKS
CHILMOPS	COMPLISH	CHIPSSTY	PSYCHIST	CIIKNOOT	COOTIKIN
CHILMOSU	SCHOLIUM	CHIRRSSU	SCIRRHUS	CIIKNPPR	PINPRICK
CHILMPSU	CLUMPISH	CHISSTTU	CHUTISTS	CIIKNPST	NITPICKS
CHILNNPY	LYNCHPIN	CHKLOOOS	HOOLOCKS		STICKPIN
CHILNOOS	SCHOLION	CHKLOOSY	SHYLOCKS	CIIKNPTY	NITPICKY
CHILNORS	CHLORINS	CHKMMOOS	HOMMOCKS	CIIKNSTU	CUTIKINS
CHILNOSW	CLOWNISH	CHKMMOSU	HUMMOCKS	CIIKPSUW	WICKIUPS
CHILNPUY	PUNCHILY	CHKMMOUY	HUMMOCKY	CIILLMTU	TILLICUM
CHILOOOZ	HOLOZOIC	CHKNOOSS	SCHNOOKS	CIILLNOP	POLLINIC
CHILOOPT	HOLOPTIC	CHKNORSU	CORNHUSK	CIILMOPY	IMPOLICY
CHILOOYZ	HYLOZOIC	CHKOOOPS	COOKSHOP	CIILMOSS	SCIOLISM
CHILOPPY	CHOPPILY	CHKOOSST	SCHTOOKS	CIILMQSU	CLIQUISM
CHILORST	TROCHILS	CHKOPSTU	TUCKSHOP	CIILMRSY	LYRICISM
CHILOSTT	CLOTTISH	CHKPSTUU	PUTCHUKS	CIILNOOT	NOCTILIO
CHILOSYY	COYISHLY	CHLMORSY	CHROMYLS	CIILNOPS	CIPOLINS
CHILOTUV	TOUCHILY	CHLMPSSU	SCHLUMPS		PICOLINS
CHIMMOOR	MICROMHO	CHLMPSUY	SCHLUMPY		PSILOCIN
CHIMMORS	MICROHMS	CHLNOOOP	COLOPHON	CIILNORT	NITROLIC
CHIMMORU	CHROMIUM	CHLOOORU	CHLOROUS	CIILNOSS	SILICONS
CHIMNNOO	NONOHMIC	CHLOPSTY	SPLOTCHY	CIILNOST	COLISTIN
CHIMNOOR	HORMONIC	CHLORTUY	CHOULTRY	CIILOOPT	POLITICO
CHIMNORS	CHRISMON	CHMNOORT	CORNMOTH	CIILOOTZ	ZOOLITIC
CHIMNORW	INCHWORM	CHMNORRU	CRUMHORN	CIILOPPT	POPLITIC
CHIMNOSU	INSOMUCH	CHMOORSU	CHROMOUS	CIILOPST	COLPITIS
CHIMNOSY	CHYMOSIN	CHMOOSYZ	SCHMOOZY		POLITICS
CHIMNOUY	ONYCHIUM	CHNNOORS	CHRONONS		PSILOTIC
CHIMOORU	MOUCHOIR	CHNOOPTT	TOPNOTCH	CIILORST	CLITORIS
CHIMORSS	CHORISMS	CHNOORST	TORCHONS		COISTRIL
	CHRISOMS	CHNOPRSU	SUNPORCH	CIILOSST	SCIOLIST
CHIMORST	CHRISTOM	CHNOPTUU	OUTPUNCH		SOLICITS
CHIMOSTU	MISTOUCH	CHNORRSS	SCHNORRS	CIILOSTY	SOLICITY

CIILOSVV	SLIVOVIC	CIKLLORS	ROLLICKS		STOLONIC
CIILPRSY	CRISPILY	CIKLLORY	ROLLICKY	CILNOOTU	LOCUTION
CIILRSTY	LYRICIST	CIKLLOSS	SILLOCKS	CILNOPRS	PILCORNS
CIILRTUU	UTRICULI	CIKLLOSW	KILLCOWS	CILNOPTU	PLUTONIC
CIILSSSS	SCISSILS	CIKLLPUY	PLUCKILY	CILNORSY	LYRICONS
CIILSTTY	STYLITIC	CIKLMSSU	MISLUCKS	CILNOSTU	LINOCUTS
CIIMMNOS	MINICOMS	CIKLNOST	LINSTOCK	CILNOSUY	COUSINLY
CIIMNOOS	ISONOMIC	CIKLOOOS	OLICOOKS	CILNPSSU	INSCULPS
CIIMNOSS	MISCOINS	CIKLOPST	LOPSTICK		SCULPINS
CIIMNOST	MICTIONS	CIKLOPSU	LIPOSUCK	CILNPSTU	INSCULPT
	MONISTIC	CIKLOSTU	OUTSLICK	CILOOPST	COPILOTS
	NOMISTIC	CIKLOSTY	STOCKILY	CILOOPYZ	POLYZOIC
CIIMNOVY	VIOMYCIN	CIKMNNOS	MINNOCKS	CILOORRT	TRICOLOR
CIIMORST	TRISOMIC	CIKMOORS	SICKROOM	CILOORST	COLORIST
CIIMOSST	MISTICOS	CIKMOOSS	MISCOOKS		CORTISOL
	STOICISM	CIKMOPST	MOPSTICK	CILOORSU	COULOIRS
CIIMOSYZ	ISOZYMIC	CIKMORRS	RIMROCKS	CILOOSSU	SCIOLOUS
CIIMPRST	SCRIMPIT	CIKMSSTU	STICKUMS	CILOPPRY	PROPYLIC
CIIMRSTY	MYRISTIC	CIKNNOOS	COONSKIN	CILOPRRY	PYRROLIC
CIIMRTTU	TRITICUM	CIKNNOPS	PINNOCKS	CILOPRSW	PILCROWS
CIINNNOO	NONIONIC	CIKNNOST	NONSTICK	CILOPRUY	CROUPILY
CIINNORU	UNIRONIC	CIKNNOSW	WINNOCKS		POLYURIC
CIINNOST	NICOTINS	CIKNOPTY	PYKNOTIC	CILOPSSW	COWSLIPS
CIINNSTT	INSTINCT	CIKNOSSW	COWSKINS	CILORSTY	COYSTRIL
CIINNSTU	TUNICINS	CIKNPSTU	NUTPICKS	CILOSSTU	OCULISTS
CIINOOPP	CIOPPINO	CIKNSSTU	UNSTICKS	CILOSSTY	SYSTOLIC
CIINOOSS	CONIOSIS	CIKOPPST	POCKPITS	CILOSSUU	LUSCIOUS
CIINOOST	COITIONS	CIKOPSTT	TIPSTOCK	CILPRSTU	CULPRITS
	ISOTONIC	CIKORTTU	OUTTRICK	CILPSSTU	SCULPSIT
CIINOOTZ	ZOONITIC	CIKOSSTT	STOCKIST	CILRSTTY	STRICTLY
CIINOPRS	PORCINIS	CIKOSSTU	SICKOUTS	CILRSTUY	CRUSTILY
CIINOPSS	PSIONICS	CIKOSTTU	STICKOUT		RUSTICLY
CIINOPSU	OPINICUS	CIKOSTUW	OUTWICKS	CILRSUVY	SCURVILY
CIINORSS	INCISORS	CIKPSSTU	STICKUPS	CILSSTTU	CULTISTS
CIINORST	CROSTINI	CIKPSUWY	WICKYUPS	CIMMOSSS	COSMISMS
CIINORSY	INCISORY	CILLMNOR	CORNMILL	CIMNNOSU	NONMUSIC
CIINOSSS	SCISSION	CILLMSUY	CLUMSILY	CIMNOOOZ	ZOONOMIC
CIINOSTT	STICTION		CULLYISM	CIMNOORS	OMICRONS
CIINOTTY	TONICITY	CILLNOOT	COTILLON	CIMNOORU	CORONIUM
CIINPRSS	CRISPINS	CILLNORS	INSCROLL	CIMNOOTY	MYOTONIC
CIINPSTU	SINCIPUT	CILLNOSU	CULLIONS	CIMNOPRT	COMPRINT
CIINQSTU	QUINTICS		SCULLION	CIMNORSS	CRIMSONS
CIIOOPST	ISOTOPIC	CILLOOOT	OCOTILLO	CIMNORSY	CRONYISM
CIIOPRST	PORISTIC	CILLOORS	CRIOLLOS	CIMNOSTU	MISCOUNT
CIIOPSTT	OPTICIST	CILMMSUY	SCUMMILY	CIMNOSUU	MUCINOUS
CIIOPSTY	ISOTYPIC	CILMNOPS	COMPLINS	CIMNOSUY	SYCONIUM
CIIOQTUX	QUIXOTIC	CILMNOPU	PULMONIC	CIMOOOTZ	ZOOTOMIC
CIIORRWW	WIRRICOW	CILMNOSS	CLONISMS	CIMOORSS	MORISCOS
CIIOTTXY	TOXICITY	CILMNOUU	INOCULUM	CIMOPSSY	COPYISMS
CIIPRRTU	PRURITIC	CILMNUUV	VINCULUM	CIMOSSST	COSMISTS
CIIPRSTU	PURISTIC	CILMOORS	COLORISM	CIMOSTUU	MUTICOUS
CIIRSTTU	TRUISTIC		MISCOLOR	CIMOSTUY	MUCOSITY
CIISSTTY	CYSTITIS	CILMOOSS	LOCOISMS	CIMOSTYZ	ZYMOTICS
CIJKOSTY	JOYSTICK	CILMOPSY	OLYMPICS	CINNNOOT	NONTONIC
CIJNNOOS	CONJOINS	CILMORUX	MICROLUX	CINNNOSU	INCONNUS
CIJNNOOT	CONJOINT	CILMPRSY	SCRIMPLY	CINNOOSS	SCOINSON
CIJNNOTU	JUNCTION	CILMPSUU	SPICULUM	CINNOOST	SCONTION
CIJNNSTU	INJUNCTS	CILMSSTU	CULTISMS	CINNOOTU	CONTINUO
CIJOOSTY	JOCOSITY	CILMSTYY	MYSTICLY	CINNOOTX	NONTOXIC
CIKKLLOS	KILLOCKS	CILNNORY	NONLYRIC	CINNORSU	UNICORNS
CIKKOPST	TOPKICKS	CILNOORS	ORCINOLS	CINNOSTU	UNCTIONS
CIKKOSTU	OUTKICKS	CILNOORU	UNICOLOR	CINNOSTY	SYNTONIC
CIKLLOPR	KILLCROP	CILNOOSS	CLOISONS	CINNQUUX	QUINCUNX
CIKLLOPS	PILLOCKS	CILNOOST	COLONIST	CINOOOPT	COOPTION

CINOOOTZ	ZOONOTIC	CKNOSSTU	UNSTOCKS	CNOOSTTW	COTTOWNS
CINOOPRS	SCORPION	CKNRSTUU	UNSTRUCK	CNOOTTUU	OUTCOUNT
CINOOPRT	PROTONIC	CKOOOPST	COOKTOPS	CNOPRSTY	CRYPTONS
CINOOPSS	POCOSINS	CKOOOSTU	COOKOUTS	CNOPSSTY	POSTSYNC
CINOORST	CROSTINO		OUTCOOKS	CNOSTUUU	UNCTUOUS
CINOOSUV	COVINOUS	CKOOPSTT	STOCKPOT	COOOPSTU	OUTSCOOP
CINOOTXY	OXYTOCIN	CKOORSSU	SOUROCKS	COOOPSTY	OTOSCOPY
CINOPSSY	PYCNOSIS	CKOORSTU	OUTROCKS	COOOPSYZ	ZOOSCOPY
CINOPSTY	SYNOPTIC	CKOPSTTU	PUTTOCKS	COOPPSTU	POSTCOUP
CINORRST	TRICORNS	CKORSTUW	CUTWORKS	COOPRRST	PROCTORS
CINORSST	CISTRONS		SCUTWORK	COOPRSST	TOPCROSS
	CORNISTS	CKOSSSTU	TUSSOCKS	COOPRSTU	OUTCROPS
CINORSTT	CONTRIST	CKOSSTUY	TUSSOCKY	COOPRSUU	CROUPOUS
	STRONTIC	CKSSSTUU	TUSSUCKS	COOPRSUY	UROSCOPY
CINORSTU	RUCTIONS	CLLLOOPT	CLOTPOLL	COORRWWY	WORRYCOW
CINORSUY	COUSINRY	CLLMOSSU	MOLLUSCS	COORSSTU	OUTCROSS
CINORTUX	COTURNIX	CLLOOPSS	SCOLLOPS	COORSTUW	OUTCROWS
CINOSSST	CONSISTS	CLLOOQUY	COLLOQUY	COOSSTTY	OTOCYSTS
CINOSSTU	SUCTIONS	CLMMNOOY	COMMONLY	COPRRSTU	CORRUPTS
CINOSTUV	VISCOUNT	CLMOOOTY	COLOTOMY	DDDDEEIR	DIDDERED
CINRSSTU	INCRUSTS	CLMOOPST	COMPLOTS	DDDDEEOR	DODDERED
CINRSTTU	INSTRUCT	CLMOPSTU	PLUMCOTS	DDDEEEFN	DEFENDED
CINRSTUY	SCRUTINY	CLMOSUUU	CUMULOUS	DDDEEENP	DEPENDED
CIOOOPRS	OOSPORIC	CLNNOOOR	NONCOLOR	DDDEEENR	REDDENED
CIOOOTTX	OTOTOXIC	CLNOORST	CONTROLS	DDDEEENU	UNDEEDED
CIOOOTXZ	ZOOTOXIC	CLNOORTU	CONTROUL	DDDEEERT	TEDDERED
CIOOPRST	PORTICOS		COUNTROL	DDDEEERW	REWEDDED
	PROOTICS	CLNOSSTU	CONSULTS		WEDDERED
CIOOPTYZ	ZOOTYPIC	CLNOSTUY	UNCOSTLY	DDDEEFNU	DEFUNDED
CIOOQSTU	COQUITOS	CLOOOPRT	PROTOCOL	DDDEEFOR	FODDERED
CIOORRWW	WORRICOW	CLOOPPSW	COWPLOPS	DDDEEGIS	DISEDGED
CIOORSSU	SCORIOUS	CLOOPSTY	POLYCOTS	DDDEEHRS	SHREDDED
CIOOSSTU	STOCIOUS	CLOORTUY	LOCUTORY	DDDEEIST	STEDDIED
CIOPSSTY	COPYISTS	CLOOSSSU	COLOSSUS	DDDEEJRU	JUDDERED
CIORRSTU	CURSITOR	CLOOSSTY	CYTOSOLS	DDDEELRT	TREDDLED
CIORSSSS	SCISSORS	CLOPRSTU	SCULPTOR	DDDEENOR	DONDERED
CIORSTUU	RUCTIOUS	CLRSSUUU	SURCULUS		REDDENDO
CIPPRRUU	PURPURIC	CMMNNOOU	UNCOMMON	DDDEENOS	SODDENED
CIPSSTTY	STYPTICS	CMMOPSSY	COMSYMPS	DDDEENUW	UNWEDDED
CIRRSTTU	CRITTURS	CMNOOOST	MONOCOTS	DDDEEORR	DODDERER
CIRSSTUY	CITRUSSY	CMNOOOTY	ONCOTOMY	DDDEEORS	RESODDED
CJNNOOTU	CONJUNTO	CMNOORRW	CORNWORM	DDDEEPRU	PUDDERED
CJNOORRU	CONJUROR	CMNOPSTU	CONSUMPT	DDDEERTU	DETRUDED
CJRSUUUU	SUCURUJU	CMOOPRST	COMPORTS	DDDEGILR	GRIDDLED
CKKNOOTU	KNOCKOUT	CMOOPSST	COMPOSTS	DDDEGNOU	UNGODDED
CKKOORRW	ROCKWORK	CMOPRSUX	SCRUMPOX	DDDEHIRT	THRIDDED
CKLLMOSU	MULLOCKS	CMORSSTU	SCROTUMS	DDDEIILS	DIDDLIES
CKLLMOUY	MULLOCKY	CMORSTUW	CUTWORMS	DDDEIIMS	SMIDDIED
CKLLOOPS	POLLOCKS	CNNOOORT	CONTORNO	DDDEIINV	DIVIDEND
CKLLOORS	ROLLOCKS	CNNORSTU	NOCTURNS	DDDEIIST	DIDDIEST
CKLLORSU	RULLOCKS	CNNORSUW	UNCROWNS		STIDDIED
CKLMMOOS	SLOMMOCK	CNOOOORT	OCTOROON	DDDEILNU	UNLIDDED
CKLMMOSU	SLUMMOCK	CNOOOPSS	POCOSONS	DDDEILNW	DWINDLED
CKLNOSTU	LOCKNUTS	CNOOPPRS	POPCORNS	DDDEILQU	QUIDDLED
CKLOOOSY	OLYCOOKS	CNOOPRSU	CROUPONS	DDDEILRS	DIDDLERS
CKLOORSW	ROWLOCKS	CNOOPSSU	SOUPCONS	DDDEILSY	DIDDLEYS
CKLOOSTU	LOCKOUTS	CNOORRSW	CORNROWS	DDDEILTW	TWIDDLED
CKLOPSTU	POTLUCKS	CNOORRTY	CRYOTRON	DDDEIMOS	DISMODED
	PUTLOCKS	CNOORSST	CONSORTS	DDDEINOR	DENDROID
CKMMMOSU	MUMMOCKS	CNOORSTT	CONTORTS	DDDEINRU	UNDERDID
CKMMORUW	MUCKWORM	CNOORSTU	CONTOURS	DDDEIOST	DODDIEST
CKMNOOOR	MOONROCK		CORNUTOS	DDDEIQSU	SQUIDDED
CKMOOOOR	COOKROOM		CROUTONS	DDDEISTU	DUDDIEST
CKNOOORS	ROCKOONS		OUTSCORN	DDDENORW	DROWNDED

DDDGIILN	DIDDLING	DDEEFMOR	DEFORMED	DDEEIPRS	PRESIDED
DDDIIOOR	DORIDOID	DDEEFNRU	REFUNDED	DDEEIPRV	DEPRIVED
DDEEEEMR	REDEEMED		UNDERFED	DDEEIPSS	DEPSIDES
DDEEEENP	DEEPENED	DDEEFORR	FODDERER		DESPISED
DDEEEERS	RESEEDED	DDEEGGIR	DERIGGED	DDEEIPST	DESPITED
DDEEEERW	DEERWEED	DDEEGGOR	DOGGEDER	DDEEIRRS	DERIDERS
DDEEEFIR	REDEFIED	DDEEGHNU	UNHEDGED	DDEEIRST	REDDIEST
DDEEEFLU	DEFUELED	DDEEGILN	ENGILDED	DDEEIRSV	DIVERSED
DDEEEFLX	DEFLEXED	DDEEGILR	REGILDED	DDEEIRTV	DIVERTED
DDEEEFNR	DEFENDER	DDEEGINR	ENGIRDED	DDEEISST	DESISTED
	FENDERED		ENRIDGED		STEDDIES
DDEEEFNS	DEFENSED	DDEEGINS	DESIGNED	DDEEISTV	DIVESTED
DDEEEFRR	DEFERRED		SDEIGNED	DDEEITTW	DEWITTED
DDEEEGLR	LEDGERED	DDEEGIRV	DIVERGED	DDEEJLLO	JODELLED
DDEEEGMR	DEGERMED	DDEEGISS	DISEDGES	DDEEKNSU	DUSKENED
	DEMERGED	DDEEGIST	DIGESTED	DDEELLMO	MODELLED
DDEEEGNR	DEGENDER	DDEEGJRU	REJUDGED	DDEELLOW	DOWELLED
	GENDERED	DDEEGLNO	GOLDENED	DDEELLOY	YODELLED
DDEEEGRR	REGREDED	DDEEGLNU	UNGELDED	DDEELMOR	MOLDERED
DDEEEGRT	DETERGED	DDEEGMMU	DEGUMMED		REMOLDED
DDEEEHLW	WHEELDED	DDEEGOPS	GODSPEED	DDEELMPU	DEPLUMED
DDEEEHNU	UNHEEDED	DDEEGORS	SODGERED	DDEELMRS	MEDDLERS
DDEEEILS	DIESELED	DDEEGRRS	DREDGERS	DDEELNOU	LOUDENED
DDEEEIMR	REMEDIED	DDEEGSTU	DEGUSTED	DDEELNUW	UNWELDED
	REMEIDED	DDEEHILS	SHIELDED	DDEELOOW	DEWOOLED
DDEEEINR	REDENIED	DDEEHINO	HOIDENED	DDEELOPR	DEPLORED
DDEEEINV	DEVEINED	DDEEHINR	HINDERED		POLDERED
DDEEEIRT	REEDITED	DDEEHIRT	DITHERED	DDEELOPX	EXPLODED
DDEEEIST	DEEDIEST	DDEEHISS	EDDISHES	DDEELOPY	DEPLOYED
	STEEDIED	DDEEHNOR	DEHORNED	DDEELORS	SOLDERED
DDEEELLV	DEVELLED	DDEEHNOY	HOYDENED	DDEELOSU	DELOUSED
DDEEELNW	WEDELNED	DDEEHNSU	DUDHEENS	DDEELOVV	DEVOLVED
DDEEELPT	DEPLETED	DDEEHORT	DEHORTED	DDEELPRS	PEDDLERS
DDEEELRW	REWELDED	DDEEHRRS	SHREDDER	DDEELPRU	PRELUDED
DDEEELSS	DEEDLESS	DDEEHRSS	SHEDDERS	DDEELPRY	PEDDLERY
DDEEELTW	TWEEDLED	DDEEIINT	INEDITED	DDEELPUX	DUPLEXED
DDEEEMNR	REMENDED	DDEEIIRV	REDIVIDE	DDEELRSS	SLEDDERS
DDEEEMNT	DEMENTED	DDEEIILV	DEVILLED	DDEELRST	TREDDLES
DDEEEMPR	DEPERMED	DDEEILMN	MILDENED	DDEELRSU	DELUDERS
DDEEEMRS	DEMERSED	DDEEILMW	MILDEWED	DDEEMNNU	UNMENDED
DDEEENNU	UNNEEDED	DDEEILNR	REDLINED	DDEEMNOR	ENDODERM
DDEEENPX	EXPENDED	DDEEILNT	DENTILED	DDEEMORR	DORMERED
DDEEENRR	RENDERED	DDEEILRS	DREIDELS	DDEEMORW	DEWORMED
DDEEENRT	TENDERED	DDEEILRV	DRIVELED	DDEEMRRU	DEMURRED
DDEEENSU	UNSEEDED	DDEEILRW	WILDERED		MURDERED
DDEEENTT	DENETTED	DDEEILST	DELISTED	DDEENNOR	DONNERED
DDEEENTX	EXTENDED	DDEEIMNP	IMPENDED		REDONNED
DDEEENUW	UNWEEDED	DDEEIMNR	REMINDED	DDEENNOY	ENDODYNE
DDEEERRT	DETERRED	DDEEIMOR	MOIDERED	DDEENNTU	UNDENTED
DDEEERST	DESERTED	DDEEIMSS	MISDEEDS		UNTENDED
DDEEERSV	DESERVED	DDEEIMST	DEMISTED	DDEENOOW	WOODENED
DDEEESTT	DETESTED	DDEEIMTT	DEMITTED	DDEENOPR	PERDENDO
DDEEESTV	DEVESTED	DDEEINNR	DINNERED		PONDERED
DDEEESWY	DYEWEEDS	DDEEINNT	INDENTED	DDEENOPW	PONDWEED
DDEEFFIR	DIFFERED		INTENDED	DDEENORS	ENDORSED
DDEEFFNO	OFFENDED	DDEEINNU	UNDENIED	DDEENORW	WONDERED
DDEEFGGO	DEFOGGED	DDEEINRT	DENDRITE	DDEENOSS	ENDOSSED
DDEEFGIT	FIDGETED	DDEEINRW	REWINDED	DDEENPRS	SPREDDEN
DDEEFINR	FRIENDED	DDEEINST	DESTINED	DDEENRRU	DURNEDER
DDEEFINU	UNDEFIDE		NEDDIEST	DDEENRSU	DENUDERS
	UNDEFIED	DDEEINTU	UNEDITED		SUNDERED
DDEEFLNO	ENFOLDED	DDEEIOPR	PERIODED	DDEENRTU	RETUNDED
DDEEFLOR	REFOLDED	DDEEIPPR	REDIPPED	DDEEOPRT	DEPORTED
DDEEFLOU	DEFOULED	DDEEIPRR	PREDRIED	DDEEOPRW	POWDERED

DDEEOPSS	SEEDPODS		UNDERDOG	DDEILNRT	TRINDLED
DDEEORRW	REWORDED		UNDERGOD	DDEILNRU	UNRIDDLE
DDEEORTT	DETORTED	DDEGNOSS	GODSENDS	DDEILNSW	DWINDLES
DDEEORTU	DETOURED	DDEGNOSU	DUDGEONS		SWINDLED
DDEEORUV	DEVOURED	DDEGOOTU	OUTDODGE	DDEILOPS	DISPLODE
DDEEORVY	OVERDYED	DDEGORSS	GORSEDDS		LOPSIDED
DDEEOTUX	TUXEDOED	DDEGRRSU	DRUDGERS	DDEILOST	DELTOIDS
DDEEPRRU	PERDURED	DDEGRRUY	DRUDGERY	DDEILOSY	DYSODILE
DDEEPRSS	SPREDDES	DDEHILNY	HIDDENLY	DDEILPRS	PIDDLERS
DDEERRUV	VERDURED	DDEHILOO	IDLEHOOD	DDEILPRU	PUDDLIER
DDEERSTU	DETRUDES	DDEHIMOS	DISHOMED	DDEILQRU	QUIDDLER
DDEERTUX	EXTRUDED	DDEHINNU	UNHIDDEN	DDEILQSU	QUIDDLES
DDEFFISU	DIFFUSED	DDEHINOR	DIHEDRON	DDEILRRS	RIDDLERS
DDEFIIIN	NIDIFIED	DDEHIORS	SHODDIER	DDEILRSS	SLIDDERS
DDEFIILM	MIDFIELD	DDEHIOSS	SHODDIES	DDEILRST	STRIDDLE
DDEFIILR	FIDDLIER	DDEHIRSS	SHIDDERS		TIDDLERS
DDEFIIMO	MODIFIED	DDEHIRSW	WHIDDERS	DDEILRSY	SLIDDERY
DDEFIIMW	MIDWIFED	DDEHIRSY	HYDRIDES	DDEILRTW	TWIDDLER
DDEFILNO	INFOLDED	DDEHLRSU	HUDDLERS	DDEILRZZ	DRIZZLED
DDEFILRS	FIDDLERS	DDEHNOOU	UNHOODED	DDEILSTW	TWIDDLES
DDEFILSY	FIDDLEYS	DDEHNPUU	UPHUDDEN	DDEILSTY	LYDDITES
DDEFLNOU	UNFOLDED	DDEHNRSU	HUNDREDS		TIDDLEYS
DDEFLOPU	UPFOLDED	DDEHOOOO	HOODOOED	DDEILSUV	DIVULSED
DDEFLRSU	FUDDLERS	DDEHOOSW	WOODSHED	DDEIMMNU	UNDIMMED
DDEFLRUU	UDDERFUL	DDEHORSU	SHROUDED	DDEIMNNU	UNMINDED
DDEFNNUU	UNFUNDED	DDEHRSSU	SHUDDERS	DDEIMNSU	MUEDDINS
DDEGGINR	DREDGING	DDEHRSUY	SHUDDERY	DDEIMNUV	VIDENDUM
DDEGGLOY	DOGGEDLY	DDEIIIRS	IRIDISED	DDEIMORS	DERMOIDS
DDEGGNOO	DOGGONED	DDEIIIRZ	IRIDIZED	DDEIMOSS	DESMOIDS
DDEGHILN	HEDDLING	DDEIIKLS	DISLIKED	DDEIMOSU	MEDUSOID
DDEGHINS	SHEDDING	DDEIIKRS	KIDDIERS	DDEIMSTU	MUDDIEST
DDEGIINR	DERIDING		SKIDDIER	DDEINNRU	UNRIDDEN
DDEGIIST	GIDDIEST	DDEIILNR	DIELDRIN	DDEINNTU	UNDINTED
DDEGILMN	MEDDLING	DDEIILOS	IDOLISED	DDEINOPS	DISPONED
DDEGILNP	PEDDLING	DDEIILOZ	IDOLIZED	DDEINORS	INDORSED
DDEGILNR	REDDLING	DDEIILRT	TIDDLIER	DDEINORT	TRENDOID
DDEGILNS	SLEDDING	DDEIILST	TIDDLIES	DDEINOSW	DISENDOW
DDEGILNU	DELUDING	DDEIIMSS	SMIDDIES		DISOWNED
	INDULGED	DDEIIMSZ	MIDSIZED		DOWNSIDE
	UNGILDED	DDEIIMVW	MIDWIVED	DDEINOWW	WINDOWED
DDEGILOS	DISLODGE	DDEIINRT	NITRIDED	DDEINPPU	UNDIPPED
DDEGILRS	GRIDDLES	DDEIINTU	UNTIDIED	DDEINPSS	DISPENDS
DDEGILRY	GLIDDERY	DDEIIOPR	PERIODID	DDEINRST	STRIDDEN
DDEGILST	GLIDDEST	DDEIIOPS	DIOPSIDE	DDEINRTU	INTRUDED
DDEGILUV	DIVULGED		DIPODIES	DDEINSST	DISTENDS
DDEGIMOS	DEMIGODS	DDEIIOST	ODDITIES	DDEINSSW	SWIDDENS
DDEGINNS	SNEDDING	DDEIIOSX	DIOXIDES	DDEINSTU	DISTUNED
DDEGINNU	DENUDING		OXIDISED	DDEIOORS	ODORISED
DDEGINRS	REDDINGS	DDEIIOXZ	OXIDIZED	DDEIOORZ	ODORIZED
DDEGINRU	UNGIRDED	DDEIIRSV	DIVIDERS	DDEIOPRS	DROPSIED
DDEGINST	STEDDING	DDEIIRUV	REDUVIID		SPODDIER
DDEGINSW	SWINGDED	DDEIISST	STIDDIES	DDEIOPRV	PROVIDED
	WEDDINGS	DDEIISTT	TIDDIEST	DDEIOPSS	DISPOSED
DDEGINUU	UNGUIDED	DDEIKNRS	KINDREDS	DDEIORRS	DISORDER
DDEGIOST	DODGIEST	DDEIKOOS	SKIDOOED		SORDIDER
DDEGIPRU	UPGIRDED	DDEIKOSY	DISYOKED	DDEIOSST	SODDIEST
DDEGIQSU	SQUIDGED	DDEIKRSS	SKIDDERS	DDEIOSTW	DOWDIEST
DDEGIRRS	GRIDDERS	DDEIKSVY	SKYDIVED	DDEIPRSS	DISPREDS
DDEGJNUU	UNJUDGED	DDEILMOP	IMPLODED	DDEIPRSU	SPUDDIER
DDEGLOPS	SPLODGED	DDEILMOV	DEVILDOM	DDEIPSTU	DISPUTED
DDEGLOSS	DOGSLEDS	DDEILMRS	MIDDLERS	DDEIRSSU	DRUIDESS
DDEGMOOS	DOGEDOMS	DDEILMSU	MUDSLIDE	DDEIRSTU	RUDDIEST
	SMOODGED	DDEILNPS	SPINDLED		STURDIED
DDEGNORU	GROUNDED		SPLENDID	DDEISSTU	STUDDIES

DDEKMOSU	DUKEDOMS	DDGHOOOS	GODHOODS	DDNOORTW	DOWNTROD
DDELLNUU	UNDULLED	DDGIIINO	INDIGOID	DDOORWWY	ROWDYDOW
DDELLOOP	DOLLOPED	DDGIIINV	DIVIDING	DDORSSTY	DROSTDYS
DDELMNOU	UNMOLDED	DDGIIKNS	SKIDDING	DEEEEFRR	REFEREED
DDELMRSU	MUDDLERS	DDGIIKNY	KIDDYING	DEEEEFRZ	DEFREEZE
DDELNORU	UNLORDED	DDGIILMN	MIDDLING	DEEEEGKR	KEDGEREE
DDELNOSY	SODDENLY	DDGIILNN	DINDLING	DEEEEHLR	REHEELED
DDELNRTU	TRUNDLED	DDGIILNP	PIDDLING	DEEEEKMN	MEEKENED
DDELNSUY	SUDDENLY	DDGIILNR	RIDDLING	DEEEELTY	EYELETED
DDELOORS	DOODLERS	DDGIILNT	TIDDLING	DEEEEMMS	MESEEMED
DDELOPRS	PLODDERS	DDGIILNW	WIDDLING	DEEEEMRR	REDEEMER
DDELORST	STRODDLE	DDGILMNU	MUDDLING	DEEEEMST	ESTEEMED
	STRODLED	DDGILNNO	NODDLING	DEEEENPR	DEEPENER
	TODDLERS	DDGILNOO	DOODLING	DEEEENRV	VENEERED
DDELOSYY	DYSODYLE	DDGILNOP	PLODDING	DEEEERTT	TEETERED
DDELPRSU	PUDDLERS		PODDLING	DEEEFFIR	EFFEIRED
DDELPSSU	SPUDDLES	DDGILNOT	TODDLING	DEEEFHLO	FEEDHOLE
DDELSSTU	STUDDLES	DDGILNPU	PUDDLING	DEEEFHST	SHEETFED
DDEMMSSU	SMEDDUMS	DDGILNRU	RUDDLING	DEEEFINR	FINEERED
DDEMNOOU	UNDOOMED	DDGIMNUY	MUDDYING		NEEDFIRE
DDEMNOST	ODDMENTS	DDGIMRSU	DRUDGISM		REDEFINE
DDEMNOUU	DUODENUM	DDGINNOS	NODDINGS	DEEEFIPT	TEPEFIED
DDEMNPUU	PUDENDUM		SNODDING	DEEEFIRS	REDEFIES
DDEMOOTU	OUTMODED	DDGINOPR	PRODDING	DEEEFIRW	FIREWEED
DDENNORS	DENDRONS	DDGINOQU	QUODDING	DEEEFKST	KEFTEDES
DDENNOSU	UNSODDEN	DDGINORS	RODDINGS	DEEEFLLR	REFELLED
DDENOOPS	ENDOPODS	DDGINPSU	PUDDINGS	DEEEFLPT	DEEPFELT
DDENOOSS	DESNOODS		SPUDDING	DEEEFLRR	FERRELED
DDENOOUW	UNWOODED	DDGINPUY	PUDDINGY	DEEEFLRT	FELTERED
DDENOPSS	DESPONDS	DDGINRUY	RUDDYING		TELFERED
DDENORSU	REDOUNDS	DDGINSTU	STUDDING	DEEEFLRU	REFUELED
DDENORTU	ROTUNDED	DDGLORRU	DRUGLORD	DEEEFLRX	REFLEXED
DDENORUW	UNWORDED	DDGOOOSW	DOGWOODS	DEEEFLSX	DEFLEXES
DDENOSST	SNODDEST	DDHILOSY	SHODDILY	DEEEFMNR	FREEDMEN
DDENOSTU	STOUNDED	DDHILSUY	DUDISHLY	DEEEFNRS	ENSERFED
DDENOSTW	STOWNDED	DDHIORSY	HYDROIDS	DEEEFNRT	DEFERENT
DDENOSUW	SWOUNDED	DDHIOSWY	DOWDYISH	DEEEFNSS	DEFENSES
DDENOTTU	DONUTTED	DDHLLOOO	DOLLHOOD	DEEEFNST	ENFESTED
	UNDOTTED	DDHLMOOO	HOODMOLD	DEEEFORV	OVERFEED
DDENRSTU	DURNDEST	DDHLNOOW	HOLDDOWN	DEEEFRRR	DEFERRER
DDENSTUY	SUDDENTY	DDIIIIVV	DIVIDIVI		REFERRED
DDEOOOOV	VOODOOED	DDIIKLSS	SKIDLIDS	DEEEFRRT	FERRETED
DDEOORSW	REDWOODS	DDIILOPS	DIPLOIDS	DEEEFRST	FESTERED
DDEOORWW	ROWDEDOW	DDIILOPY	DIPLOIDY	DEEEFRTT	FETTERED
DDEOOSWY	DYEWOODS	DDIIMMUY	DIDYMIUM	DEEEFRTW	FEWTERED
DDEOOUUV	VOUDOUED	DDIIMRSU	DRUIDISM	DEEEGGPR	REPEGGED
DDEOPRRS	PRODDERS		SIDDURIM	DEEEGHNW	WHEENGED
DDEOPRSW	DEWDROPS	DDIINOPU	DUPONDII	DEEEGILS	ELEGISED
DDEORTUU	OUTDURED	DDIIQSTU	QUIDDITS	DEEEGILZ	ELEGIZED
DDEPRSSU	SPUDDERS	DDIIQTUY	QUIDDITY	DEEEGINS	DESIGNEE
DDFGIILN	FIDDLING	DDIKOOSS	SKIDDOOS	DEEEGIPR	PEDIGREE
DDFGILNU	FUDDLING	DDILOOPP	DIPLOPOD	DEEEGIRR	GREEDIER
DDFIILSU	DISULFID	DDILOOWW	WILDWOOD	DEEEGISS	DIEGESES
DDFIIOSU	FIDDIOUS	DDILORSY	SORDIDLY	DEEEGISW	EDGEWISE
DDFMNOUU	DUMFOUND	DDILOSSY	DYSODILS	DEEEGLPR	REPLEDGE
DDGGIINY	GIDDYING	DDIMOOSS	DODOISMS	DEEEGLPS	PLEDGEES
DDGGILNU	GUDDLING	DDIMOSUY	DIDYMOUS	DEEEGLSS	EDGELESS
DDGGINNO	DINGDONG	DDIMOSWY	DOWDYISM	DEEEGLSV	SELVEDGE
DDGGINOS	DODGINGS	DDINNOWW	DOWNWIND	DEEEGMRR	DEMERGER
DDGGINRU	DRUDGING	DDINOOOT	ODONTOID		REMERGED
DDGHIINW	WHIDDING	DDINOOWW	WOODWIND	DEEEGMRS	DEMERGES
DDGHILNO	HODDLING	DDLLMOOS	DOLLDOMS	DEEEGNNR	ENGENDER
DDGHILNU	HUDDLING	DDLMORSU	DOLDRUMS	DEEEGNRU	RENEGUED
DDGHINTU	THUDDING	DDMNOORS	DROMONDS	DEEEGNRV	REVENGED

DEEEGRRS	REGREDES	DEEEKRSW	RESKEWED		TENDERER
DEEEGRRT	DETERGER		SKEWERED	DEEENRRV	REVEREND
DEEEGRSS	EGRESSED	DEEELLLV	LEVELLED	DEEENRST	RENESTED
DEEEGRST	DETERGES	DEEELLNT	DENTELLE		RESENTED
DEEEGRTT	GETTERED	DEEELLNV	NEVELLED	DEEENRTT	TENTERED
DEEEHHSW	WHEESHED	DEEELLNW	NEWELLED	DEEENRTU	NEUTERED
DEEEHKRS	SHREEKED	DEEELLPR	PREDELLE	DEEENRTX	EXTENDER
DEEEHLMT	HELMETED		REPELLED	DEEENRUV	REVENUED
DEEEHLPW	WHEEPLED	DEEELLPT	PELLETED		UNREEVED
DEEEHLRW	WHEEDLER	DEEELLPX	EXPELLED	DEEENSSS	SEEDNESS
DEEEHLSS	HEEDLESS	DEEELLRT	TELLERED	DEEENSSY	EYEDNESS
DEEEHLSW	WHEEDLES	DEEELLRV	REVELLED	DEEENSTT	DETENTES
DEEEHLWZ	WHEEZLED	DEEELMOS	SOMEDELE		NEDETTES
DEEEHMMR	REHEMMED	DEEELMRT	REMELTED	DEEENSTU	DETENUES
DEEEHMMS	EMMESHED	DEEELNPU	UNPEELED	DEEENSTX	DENTEXES
DEEEHMNS	ENMESHED	DEEELNRS	NEEDLERS	DEEENSUV	VENDEUSE
DEEEHMPS	HEMPSEED	DEEELNRT	RELENTED	DEEEOPRR	PEDERERO
DEEEHMPW	HEMPWEED	DEEELNRU	UNREELED	DEEEOPRT	DEPORTEE
DEEEHPRT	THREEPED	DEEELNSS	LESSENED	DEEEORRZ	REZEROED
DEEEHRTT	TETHERED		NEEDLESS	DEEEORST	STEREOED
DEEEIKLR	DEERLIKE		SELDSEEN	DEEEORSV	OVERSEED
	REEDLIKE	DEEELNSU	UNSEELED	DEEEORSW	OREWEEDS
DEEEIKLS	SEEDLIKE	DEEELNTT	TELNETED	DEEEORVY	OVEREYED
DEEEIKLW	WEEDLIKE	DEEELOPP	DEPEOPLE	DEEEOSTV	DEVOTEES
DEEEILNR	NEEDLIER	DEEELOPV	DEVELOPE	DEEEPPPR	PEPPERED
DEEEILNS	SELENIDE	DEEELPRT	DEPLETER	DEEEPRSS	SPEEDERS
DEEEILRV	RELIEVED		PELTERED	DEEEPRST	ESTREPED
DEEEILTV	DELETIVE		REPLETED		PESTERED
DEEEILVW	WEEVILED	DEEELPST	DEPLETES	DEEEPRSZ	SPREEZED
DEEEIMNS	INSEEMED		STEEPLED	DEEEPRTX	EXPERTED
DEEEIMRS	REMEDIES	DEEELRSS	REDELESS	DEEEQRRU	REQUERED
DEEEIMST	SEEDTIME	DEEELRST	DEERLETS	DEEEQSUZ	SQUEEZED
DEEEINNX	ENDEXINE		STREELED	DEEERRRT	DETERRER
DEEEINRR	REINDEER	DEEELRTT	LETTERED	DEEERRRV	VERDERER
DEEEINRS	NEREIDES	DEEELRTW	TWEEDLER	DEEERRST	DESERTER
	REDENIES		WELTERED	DEEERRSV	DESERVER
DEEEINST	NEEDIEST	DEEELSSS	SEEDLESS		RESERVED
DEEEINSX	ENDEIXES	DEEELSSV	VESSELED		REVERSED
DEEEINTV	EVENTIDE	DEEELSSW	WEEDLESS	DEEERRTV	REVERTED
DEEEIPRS	SPEEDIER	DEEELSTW	TWEEDLES	DEEERSSV	DESERVES
DEEEIPTX	EXPEDITE	DEEELTVV	VELVETED	DEEERSTT	DETESTER
DEEEIRRR	DERRIERE	DEEEMNNT	NEEDMENT		RESETTED
DEEEIRSS	DIERESES	DEEEMNRS	EMENDERS		RETESTED
DEEEIRST	REEDIEST	DEEEMNSS	DEMESNES		SETTERED
DEEEIRSZ	RESEIZED		SEEDSMEN		STREETED
DEEEIRTW	TWEEDIER	DEEEMPRT	TEMPERED	DEEERSTV	REVESTED
DEEEIRVW	REVIEWED	DEEEMPTX	EXEMPTED	DEEERSTW	WESTERED
DEEEISST	SEEDIEST	DEEEMRRU	MURDEREE	DEEERSTX	EXSERTED
	STEEDIES	DEEEMRSS	DEMERSES	DEEERSUW	SERUEWED
DEEEISSV	DEVISEES		MEDRESES	DEEERSVW	SERVEWED
DEEEISTW	WEEDIEST	DEEEMRST	DEEMSTER	DEEERTTT	TETTERED
DEEEJLLW	JEWELLED	DEEENNRT	ENTENDER	DEEERTTV	REVETTED
DEEEJNRU	DEJEUNER	DEEENNUW	UNWEENED	DEEERTTW	REWETTED
DEEEJNSU	DEJEUNES	DEEENOPR	REOPENED	DEEESTTU	SUEDETTE
DEEEJRRS	JERREEDS	DEEENORS	ENDORSEE	DEEESTTV	VEDETTES
DEEEJRSY	JERSEYED	DEEENPRT	REPENTED	DEEFFGLU	EFFULGED
DEEEKLNN	KENNELED		REPETEND	DEEFFGOR	GOFFERED
DEEEKLNR	KERNELED	DEEENPRU	UNPEERED	DEEFFINR	NIFFERED
DEEEKLNU	UNKEELED	DEEENPRV	PREVENED	DEEFFINS	EFFENDIS
DEEEKNSW	WEEKENDS	DEEENPRX	EXPENDER	DEEFFINT	INFEFTED
DEEEKOPW	POKEWEED	DEEENPSS	DEEPNESS	DEEFFIRS	SERIFFED
DEEEKORV	REEVOKED	DEEENPSX	EXPENSED	DEEFFNOR	FOREFEND
DEEEKPRR	REPERKED	DEEENRRR	RENDERER		OFFENDER
DEEEKRST	STREEKED	DEEENRRT	RERENTED		REOFFEND

Key	Anagram	Key	Anagram	Key	Anagram
DEEFFRSU	SUFFERED		FLOWERED	DEEGIINN	INDIGENE
DEEFGGOR	DEFOGGER		REFLOWED	DEEGIISS	DIEGESIS
DEEFGILR	FLEDGIER	DEEFLOST	FEEDLOTS	DEEGIKST	KEDGIEST
DEEFGINR	FINGERED	DEEFLOSY	EYEFOLDS	DEEGILMO	LIEGEDOM
DEEFGINS	FEEDINGS	DEEFLPSU	SPEEDFUL	DEEGILMP	IMPLEDGE
DEEFGINX	FEDEXING	DEEFLRRU	FERRULED	DEEGILMT	GIMLETED
DEEFGIPS	PIGFEEDS	DEEFLRUX	REFLUXED	DEEGILNN	NEEDLING
DEEFGIRT	FIDGETER	DEEFMNOR	ENFORMED	DEEGILNO	ELOIGNED
DEEFGIUW	GUDEWIFE	DEEFMNOT	FOMENTED		LEGIONED
DEEFGLNU	ENGULFED	DEEFMORR	DEFORMER	DEEGILNR	ENGIRDLE
DEEFGLOO	FEELGOOD		REFORMED		LINGERED
DEEFGLUW	GULFWEED	DEEFMORS	FREEDOMS		REEDLING
DEEFGORR	REFORGED	DEEFMPRU	PERFUMED	DEEGILNS	SEEDLING
DEEFGORY	FROGEYED	DEEFNOOR	FOREDONE	DEEGILNT	DELETING
DEEFHIMU	HUMEFIED	DEEFNORZ	DEFROZEN	DEEGILNU	EUGLENID
DEEFHINT	HINDFEET	DEEFNOST	SOFTENED	DEEGILNV	DEVELING
DEEFHLOR	FREEHOLD	DEEFNRRU	REFUNDER	DEEGILNW	WEDELING
DEEFHLRS	FELDSHER	DEEFNSST	DEFTNESS	DEEGILRS	LEIDGERS
DEEFHORT	FOTHERED	DEEFOORR	REROOFED	DEEGILRW	WEREGILD
DEEFIILN	FEDELINI	DEEFOORS	FOREDOES	DEEGILRY	GREEDILY
	LENIFIED	DEEFOORT	FOOTERED	DEEGILST	GELIDEST
DEEFIINT	DEFINITE		REFOOTED		LEDGIEST
DEEFIIRS	DEIFIERS	DEEFOORW	WOODFREE	DEEGIMMR	IMMERGED
	EDIFIERS	DEEFORST	DEFOREST	DEEGIMNN	EMENDING
	FIRESIDE		FORESTED	DEEGIMNR	REMEDING
DEEFIIRV	VERIFIED		FOSTERED	DEEGIMRU	DEMIURGE
DEEFILLR	REFILLED	DEEFORTU	FOUTERED	DEEGINNR	ENRINGED
DEEFILLT	FILLETED	DEEFORUY	FOUREYED	DEEGINNS	ENSIGNED
DEEFILMR	REFILMED	DEEFPRSU	PERFUSED	DEEGINNT	TEENDING
DEEFILMS	MEDFLIES	DEEFRRTU	RETURFED	DEEGINNW	ENDEWING
DEEFILNX	INFLEXED	DEEFRSSU	DEFUSERS	DEEGINOP	PIGEONED
DEEFILPR	PILFERED	DEEGGHHO	HEDGEHOG	DEEGINPS	SPEEDING
	PREFILED	DEEGGHIP	HEDGEPIG	DEEGINRR	DERINGER
DEEFILRS	DEFILERS	DEEGGIJR	JIGGERED	DEEGINRS	DESIGNER
	FIELDERS		REJIGGED		ENERGIDS
DEEFILRT	FILTERED	DEEGGINR	GINGERED		REDESIGN
DEEFIMSS	MISFEEDS		NIGGERED		REEDINGS
DEEFIMTU	TUMEFIED		RENIGGED		RESIGNED
DEEFINRR	INFERRED	DEEGGIRR	DREGGIER	DEEGINRY	REDYEING
DEEFINRS	DEFINERS		RERIGGED	DEEGINSS	DINGESES
DEEFINRZ	FRENZIED	DEEGGLOR	DOGGEREL		EDGINESS
DEEFINSS	FINESSED	DEEGGNOR	ENGORGED		SDEIGNES
DEEFINST	FENDIEST	DEEGGNPU	UNPEGGED		SEEDINGS
	INFESTED	DEEGGNTU	NUGGETED	DEEGINST	INGESTED
DEEFIORS	FORESIDE	DEEGGORR	REGORGED		SIGNETED
DEEFIORT	FOETIDER	DEEGGORT	GORGETED		STEEDING
DEEFIPRR	PREFIRED	DEEGGQSU	SQUEGGED	DEEGINSW	WEEDINGS
DEEFIPRX	PREFIXED	DEEGGRRU	RUGGEDER	DEEGINSX	DESEXING
DEEFIRRV	FERVIDER	DEEGHHIR	HIGHERED	DEEGINZZ	GIZZENED
DEEFIRST	RESIFTED	DEEGHHOP	HEDGEHOP	DEEGIORT	GOITERED
DEEFIRTT	REFITTED	DEEGHHSU	SHEUGHED	DEEGIOST	EGOTISED
DEEFISTT	FETIDEST	DEEGHHUW	WHEUGHED	DEEGIOTZ	EGOTIZED
DEEFLLNU	UNFELLED	DEEGHILS	SLEIGHED	DEEGIPRU	PREGUIDE
DEEFLLOW	FELLOWED	DEEGHINR	REHINGED	DEEGIPSW	PIGWEEDS
DEEFLLRU	FULLERED	DEEGHIST	HEDGIEST	DEEGIRST	DIGESTER
DEEFLNNU	FUNNELED	DEEGHITW	WEIGHTED		ESTRIDGE
DEEFLNOR	ENFOLDER	DEEGHLPU	PLEUGHED		REDIGEST
	FORELEND	DEEGHNRU	HUNGERED	DEEGIRSU	GUDESIRE
DEEFLNSU	NEEDFULS	DEEGHOPR	GOPHERED	DEEGIRSV	DIVERGES
	UNSELFED	DEEGHOPS	SHEEPDOG	DEEGISST	SEDGIEST
DEEFLNTU	DEFLUENT	DEEGHORW	HEDGEROW	DEEGISTW	WEDGIEST
	UNFELTED	DEEGHOSW	HOGWEEDS	DEEGJPRU	PREJUDGE
DEEFLNUX	UNFLEXED	DEEGHOTT	DOGTEETH	DEEGJRSU	REJUDGES
DEEFLORW	DEFLOWER		GHETTOED	DEEGKMOS	GEEKDOMS

DEEGLLOR	GOLLERED	DEEHINTW	WHITENED	DEEIINOZ	DEIONIZE
DEEGLLRU	GRUELLED	DEEHIORS	HEROISED	DEEIINST	DIETINES
DEEGLLUV	GULLEYED	DEEHIORZ	HEROIZED	DEEIINSX	ENDEIXIS
DEEGLNOR	GOLDENER	DEEHIOTX	ETHOXIDE	DEEIIPRS	EPEIRIDS
DEEGLNOU	ENGOULED	DEEHIPRS	HESPERID	DEEIIPRU	PRIEDIEU
DEEGLNOZ	LOZENGED		PERISHED	DEEIIRSS	DIERESIS
DEEGLNRY	LEGENDRY	DEEHIRRS	REDSHIRE	DEEIIRST	SIDERITE
DEEGLOPR	PLEDGEOR	DEEHIRRT	DITHERER	DEEIIRSV	DERISIVE
DEEGLOPS	DOGSLEEP	DEEHIRRW	WHERRIED	DEEIIRSW	WEIRDIES
DEEGLORV	GROVELED	DEEHIRST	DIETHERS	DEEIISSS	DISSEISE
DEEGLORW	GLOWERED	DEEHIRSV	SHIVERED	DEEIISSW	SIDEWISE
	REGLOWED		SHRIEVED	DEEIISSX	DEIXISES
DEEGLOSY	GOLDEYES	DEEHIRSW	SHREWDIE	DEEIISSZ	DISSEIZE
DEEGLPRS	PLEDGERS	DEEHIRTW	WITHERED	DEEIJNNO	ENJOINED
DEEGLPST	PLEDGETS	DEEHIRTY	HEREDITY	DEEIJNOR	REJOINED
DEEGLRSS	SLEDGERS	DEEHKLPS	HELPDESK	DEEIJRTT	JITTERED
DEEGLRSW	WERGELDS	DEEHKNOS	KEESHOND	DEEIKKRV	YIKKERED
DEEGMNOR	MONGERED	DEEHKNRU	HUNKERED	DEEIKLLR	KILLDEER
DEEGMNRU	DUNGMERE	DEEHKORS	KOSHERED	DEEIKLLS	KILLDEES
DEEGMSUW	GUMWEEDS	DEEHLLOR	HOLLERED		SKELLIED
DEEGNNOS	ENDOGENS	DEEHLLOV	HOVELLED	DEEIKLMO	DOMELIKE
DEEGNNOY	ENDOGENY	DEEHLMMW	WHEMMLED	DEEIKLMW	MILKWEED
DEEGNOPU	GEEPOUND	DEEHLMNU	UNHELMED	DEEIKLNN	ENKINDLE
DEEGNORV	GOVERNED	DEEHLMSW	WELDMESH		ENLINKED
DEEGNPRU	REPUGNED	DEEHLNPU	UNHELPED	DEEIKLNR	REKINDLE
DEEGNPUX	EXPUGNED	DEEHLORV	OVERHELD		RELINKED
	EXPUNGED		VERDELHO	DEEIKLNS	SILKENED
DEEGNRUY	UNGREEDY	DEEHLOST	HOSTELED	DEEIKLNU	DUNELIKE
DEEGNSTU	NUTSEDGE	DEEHLOSU	HOUSELED	DEEIKLOV	DOVELIKE
DEEGORST	GOSTERED	DEEHLOSV	SHOVELED	DEEIKLSW	SILKWEED
DEEGOSTU	OUTEDGES	DEEHLPPS	SHLEPPED	DEEIKMSW	MIDWEEKS
DEEGOTUW	GOUTWEED	DEEHLSTU	SLEUTHED	DEEIKMSY	MISKEYED
DEEGPRUX	EXPURGED	DEEHMNRS	HERDSMEN	DEEIKNNP	PINKENED
DEEGRRSU	RESURGED	DEEHMNSU	UNMESHED	DEEIKNRS	DEERSKIN
DEEGRSSW	SWEDGERS	DEEHMORT	MOTHERED	DEEIKNRT	TINKERED
DEEGRSTU	GESTURED	DEEHNOPY	PHONEYED	DEEIKNTT	KITTENED
DEEGRTTU	GUTTERED	DEEHNORR	DEERHORN	DEEIKOSV	DOVEKIES
DEEGSSTU	GUSSETED		DEHORNER	DEEIKPPR	KIPPERED
DEEHHIRT	HITHERED	DEEHNORT	DETHRONE	DEEIKRSU	DUKERIES
DEEHHNPY	HYPHENED		THRENODE	DEEIKRSV	SKIVERED
DEEHHPRS	SHEPHERD	DEEHNOWY	HONEYDEW	DEEIKSTT	DISKETTE
DEEHHRST	THRESHED	DEEHNPRS	PREHENDS	DEEILLMP	IMPELLED
DEEHHRSU	HUSHERED	DEEHNSTU	ENTHUSED		MILLEPED
DEEHIKLR	HERDLIKE	DEEHOORV	HOOVERED	DEEILLNO	NIELLOED
DEEHIKLS	SHEDLIKE	DEEHOPRT	POTHERED	DEEILLOR	ORIELLED
DEEHIKRS	SHREIKED	DEEHORRS	REDHORSE	DEEILLPR	PERILLED
	SHRIEKED	DEEHORRT	DEHORTER	DEEILLRT	TILLERED
DEEHIKSV	KHEDIVES	DEEHORSU	REHOUSED		TREDILLE
DEEHILNS	ENSHIELD	DEEHORSW	RESHOWED	DEEILLRV	RIVELLED
DEEHILRS	HIRSELED		SHOWERED	DEEILLVY	VEILEDLY
	RELISHED	DEEHORTT	HOTTERED	DEEILLWY	WILLEYED
	SHIELDER	DEEHORTX	EXHORTED	DEEILMNU	DEMILUNE
DEEHILSS	HIDELESS	DEEHPRSY	SYPHERED	DEEILMOS	MELODIES
DEEHILSV	DISHEVEL	DEEHRRSW	SHREWDER		MELODISE
DEEHIMMS	IMMESHED	DEEHRTUW	WUTHERED	DEEILMOZ	MELODIZE
DEEHIMNS	INMESHED	DEEIIKLT	TIDELIKE	DEEILMPT	IMPLETED
DEEHIMOP	HEMIPODE	DEEIILNS	SIDELINE	DEEILNOS	ESLOINED
DEEHIMRT	MITHERED	DEEIILRV	LIVERIED		LESIONED
DEEHINPR	EPHEDRIN	DEEIILRW	WIELDIER	DEEILNOT	DELETION
DEEHINRR	HINDERER	DEEIIMRS	DIMERISE		ENTOILED
DEEHINRS	DRISHEEN	DEEIIMRZ	DIMERIZE	DEEILNPP	LIPPENED
	RESHINED	DEEIIMST	ITEMISED	DEEILNRR	REDLINER
DEEHINRT	NITHERED	DEEIIMTZ	ITEMIZED	DEEILNRS	REDLINES
DEEHINST	DISTHENE	DEEIINOS	DEIONISE	DEEILNRU	UNDERLIE

DEEILNSS	IDLENESS	DEEIMNSU	SEMINUDE
	LINSEEDS	DEEIMNTT	MITTENED
DEEILNST	ENLISTED	DEEIMORS	EMEROIDS
	LINTSEED	DEEIMOST	TEDISOME
	LISTENED	DEEIMPRR	PERIDERM
	TINSELED		REPRIMED
DEEILNSV	SNIVELED	DEEIMPRS	DEMIREPS
DEEILNSY	DYELINES		EPIDERMS
DEEILNTT	ENTITLED		IMPEDERS
DEEILNUV	UNLEVIED		PREMISED
	UNVEILED		SIMPERED
DEEILOPT	LEPIDOTE	DEEIMPRX	PREMIXED
	PETIOLED	DEEIMPSS	SEMIPEDS
DEEILORT	DOLERITE	DEEIMRSS	DERMISES
	LOITERED	DEEIMRST	DEMERITS
DEEILORV	EVILDOER		DEMISTER
	OVERIDLE		DIMETERS
DEEILOSS	OILSEEDS		MISTERED
DEEILOTT	TOILETED	DEEIMRTT	REMITTED
DEEILPPR	LIPPERED	DEEIMSSU	MEDIUSES
DEEILPRX	DIPLEXER	DEEINNPR	REPINNED
DEEILPSS	SEEDLIPS	DEEINNRS	SINNERED
DEEILPST	EPISTLED	DEEINNRT	INDENTER
DEEILPSU	EPULIDES		INTENDER
DEEILPSY	SPEEDILY		INTERNED
DEEILRRV	DRIVELER	DEEINNRU	UNREINED
DEEILRST	RELISTED	DEEINNRV	INNERVED
DEEILRSU	LEISURED	DEEINNST	DENTINES
DEEILRSV	DELIVERS		DESINENT
	DESILVER	DEEINNSZ	DENIZENS
	SILVERED	DEEINNTV	INVENTED
	SLIVERED	DEEINNTW	ENTWINED
DEEILRSW	WIELDERS	DEEINNUV	UNENVIED
DEEILRSY	YIELDERS		UNVEINED
DEEILRTT	LITTERED	DEEINOPS	DISPONEE
	RETITLED		OPENSIDE
DEEILRVY	DELIVERY	DEEINORS	INDORSEE
DEEILSSS	IDLESSES		ORDINEES
DEEILSST	TIDELESS	DEEINORT	ORIENTED
DEEILSSV	DEVILESS	DEEINORW	IRONWEED
DEEILSTU	DILUTEES	DEEINOST	SIDENOTE
DEEILSTV	DEVILETS	DEEINOTV	DENOTIVE
DEEILSUV	DELUSIVE	DEEINPPR	NIPPERED
DEEILSVW	SWIVELED	DEEINPRS	SPENDIER
DEEILTUY	YULETIDE	DEEINPSS	DISPENSE
DEEIMMNS	ENDEMISM		PIEDNESS
DEEIMMOS	SEMIDOME	DEEINPST	PENTISED
DEEIMMRS	IMMERSED	DEEINPSU	UNESPIED
	SIMMERED	DEEINPSW	PINWEEDS
DEEIMMSS	MISDEEMS	DEEINQRU	ENQUIRED
DEEIMNOR	DOMINEER		INQUERED
DEEIMNOS	DEMONISE	DEEINQSU	SEQUINED
	DOMINEES	DEEINRRT	INTERRED
DEEIMNOZ	DEMONIZE		TRENDIER
DEEIMNPT	PEDIMENT	DEEINRRV	REDRIVEN
DEEIMNRR	REMINDER	DEEINRRW	REWINDER
	REREMIND	DEEINRSS	DIRENESS
DEEIMNRT	REMINTED	DEEINRST	INSERTED
DEEIMNRV	VERMINED		NERDIEST
DEEIMNSS	DESMINES		RESIDENT
	SIDESMEN		SINTERED
DEEIMNST	DEMENTIS		TRENDIES
	SEDIMENT	DEEINRSU	UREDINES
	TIDESMEN		

DEEINRSV	INVERSED		
DEEINRSW	REWIDENS		
	WIDENERS		
DEEINRSX	INDEXERS		
DEEINRTT	RETINTED		
DEEINRTU	RETINUED		
	REUNITED		
DEEINRTV	INVERTED		
DEEINRTW	WINTERED		
DEEINRTX	DEXTRINE		
DEEINSST	DESTINES		
DEEINSSV	VENDISES		
DEEINSSW	DEWINESS		
	WIDENESS		
DEEINSTT	DINETTES		
	INSETTED		
DEEINSTU	DETINUES		
DEEINSTV	EVIDENTS		
	INVESTED		
DEEINSUZ	UNSEIZED		
DEEINTUV	DUVETINE		
DEEINUVW	UNVIEWED		
DEEIOPRT	PERIDOTE		
	PROTEIDE		
DEEIOPRX	PEROXIDE		
DEEIOPSS	EPISODES		
DEEIOPST	EPIDOTES		
	POETISED		
DEEIOPSX	EPOXIDES		
DEEIOPTZ	POETIZED		
DEEIORRV	OVERRIDE		
DEEIORST	EROTISED		
DEEIORSV	OVERSIDE		
DEEIORSW	DOWERIES		
	WEIRDOES		
DEEIORTU	ETOURDIE		
DEEIORTV	OVEREDIT		
DEEIORTZ	EROTIZED		
DEEIORVW	OVERWIDE		
DEEIOTVX	VIDEOTEX		
DEEIPPQU	EQUIPPED		
DEEIPPRZ	ZIPPERED		
DEEIPPST	PEPTIDES		
	PEPTISED		
DEEIPPTT	PIPETTED		
DEEIPPTZ	PEPTIZED		
DEEIPQRU	REPIQUED		
DEEIPQTU	PIQUETED		
DEEIPRRS	PREDRIES		
	PRESIDER		
	REPRISED		
	RESPIRED		
DEEIPRRV	DEPRIVER		
	REPRIVED		
DEEIPRRW	PREWIRED		
DEEIPRRZ	REPRIZED		
DEEIPRSS	DESPISER		
	DISPERSE		
	PRESIDES		
DEEIPRST	PREEDITS		
	PRIESTED		
	RESPITED		
DEEIPRSU	DUPERIES		
DEEIPRSV	DEPRIVES		

	PREDIVES	DEEKOORR	KOREROED	DEELOPRS	DEPLORES
	PREVISED	DEEKORRW	REWORKED	DEELOPRV	PRELOVED
DEEIPRTT	PITTERED	DEEKORST	RESTOKED	DEELOPRW	REPLOWED
	PRETTIED	DEEKOSVY	DOVEKEYS	DEELOPRX	EXPLODER
DEEIPRTX	EXTIRPED	DEEKRUVY	KURVEYED		EXPLORED
DEEIPSSS	DESPISES	DEELLMOR	MODELLER	DEELOPRY	DEPLOYER
DEEIPSST	DESPITES	DEELLMOW	MELLOWED		REDEPLOY
	SIDESTEP	DEELLMRU	MULLERED	DEELOPSV	DEVELOPS
DEEIPSTT	TEPIDEST	DEELLNOP	POLLENED	DEELOPSX	EXPLODES
DEEIPSTU	DEPUTIES	DEELLNOR	ENROLLED	DEELORRS	RESOLDER
	DEPUTISE		RONDELLE		SOLDERER
DEEIPTUZ	DEPUTIZE	DEELLOPR	REPOLLED	DEELORSV	RESOLVED
DEEIQRRU	REQUIRED	DEELLORR	REROLLED	DEELORSY	YODELERS
DEEIQRSU	ESQUIRED	DEELLORW	ROWELLED	DEELORTT	DOTTEREL
DEEIQRTU	REQUITED		WELLDOER		TOLTERED
DEEIQRUV	QUIVERED	DEELLORY	YODELLER	DEELORTV	REVOLTED
DEEIQTUU	QUIETUDE	DEELLOTW	TOWELLED	DEELORTW	TROWELED
DEEIRRSS	DERRISES	DEELLOTX	EXTOLLED	DEELORTY	DELETORY
	DESIRERS	DEELLOVW	VOWELLED	DEELORUV	LOUVERED
	DRESSIER	DEELLOVY	VOLLEYED	DEELORVV	REVOLVED
	RESIDERS	DEELLOWY	YELLOWED	DEELORVW	OVERLEWD
DEEIRRST	DESTRIER	DEELLPUW	UPWELLED	DEELOSSU	DELOUSES
DEEIRRSU	RUDERIES	DEELLRSU	DUELLERS	DEELOSTV	DOVELETS
DEEIRRSV	DERIVERS	DEELLRSW	DWELLERS	DEELOSVV	DEVOLVES
	REDRIVES	DEELLSSW	WELDLESS	DEELOTUV	EVOLUTED
DEEIRRTV	DIVERTER	DEELLSUX	DUXELLES	DEELPPRU	REPULPED
	VERDITER	DEELMMOP	POMMELED	DEELPRRU	PRELUDER
DEEIRRWW	WIREDREW	DEELMMPU	EMPLUMED	DEELPRSS	SPELDERS
DEEIRRZZ	RIZZERED		PUMMELED	DEELPRSU	PRELUDES
DEEIRSST	DIESTERS	DEELMNOO	MELODEON		REPULSED
	EDITRESS	DEELMNOS	LODESMEN	DEELPRTU	DRUPELET
	RESISTED	DEELMNTU	UNMELTED	DEELPRUV	PULVERED
	SISTERED	DEELMNTW	WELDMENT	DEELPRUX	DUPLEXER
DEEIRSSU	DIURESES	DEELMOOS	DOLESOME	DEELPSUX	DUPLEXES
	REISSUED	DEELMOPR	EMPOLDER		EXPULSED
	RESIDUES	DEELMOPY	EMPLOYED	DEELPTTY	PETTEDLY
DEEIRSSV	DEVISERS	DEELMORS	MODELERS	DEELRSTU	DELUSTER
	DISSERVE		MORSELED		LUSTERED
	DISSEVER		REMODELS		RESULTED
	DIVERSES	DEELMOST	MOLESTED		ULSTERED
DEEIRSTT	TIREDEST	DEELMOSU	DUELSOME	DEELRSTW	LEWDSTER
DEEIRSTU	ERUDITES	DEELMPPU	PEPLUMED		WRESTLED
	SURETIED	DEELMPSU	DEPLUMES	DEELRSTY	RESTYLED
DEEIRSTV	VERDITES	DEELMRUY	DEMURELY	DEELRSUV	REVULSED
DEEIRSTW	WEIRDEST	DEELNNTU	TUNNELED	DEEMMORS	MESODERM
DEEIRTTT	TITTERED	DEELNOOS	LOOSENED	DEEMMRRU	DUMMERER
DEEIRTTV	RIVETTED	DEELNORT	REDOLENT	DEEMMRSU	SUMMERED
DEEIRTTW	WITTERED		RONDELET	DEEMMNRU	UNDERMEN
DEEISSSU	DISEUSES	DEELNORV	OVERLEND	DEEMNNTU	TENENDUM
DEEISTTV	VIDETTES	DEELNOSS	LESSONED	DEEMNOOS	ENDOSOME
DEEJKNTU	JUNKETED	DEELNOSU	ENSOULED		MOONSEED
DEEJPRRU	PERJURED	DEELNOSY	ESLOYNED	DEEMNOQU	QUEENDOM
DEEJPTTU	UPJETTED	DEELNPRS	RESPLEND	DEEMNORR	MODERNER
DEEKKOOY	OKEYDOKE	DEELNPRY	DEPRENYL	DEEMNORS	MODERNES
DEEKLNOS	SLOKENED	DEELNPSU	PENDULES		SERMONED
DEEKLNST	SKLENTED	DEELNRTU	UNDERLET	DEEMNORT	ENTODERM
DEEKLOOR	RELOOKED	DEELNRTY	TENDERLY		MENTORED
DEEKLRSS	SKELDERS	DEELNSSW	LEWDNESS	DEEMNOSS	DEMONESS
DEEKMNOY	MONKEYED	DEELNSTY	ENSTYLED		ENMOSSED
DEEKNNNU	UNKENNED	DEELNTTU	UNLETTED	DEEMNOST	DEMETONS
DEEKNOST	DESKNOTE	DEELNWWY	NEWLYWED	DEEMNOSU	EUDEMONS
DEEKNOTW	KNOTWEED	DEELOORT	RETOOLED	DEEMOOPR	PODOMERE
DEEKNOTY	KEYNOTED	DEELOPPR	LOPPERED		
DEEKNSSW	NEWSDESK	DEELOPRR	DEPLORER		

DEEMOORT	ODOMETER	**DEENPRST**	PRETENDS	**DEEORSST**	DOSSERET
DEEMOPPY	POMPEYED	**DEENRRSU**	ENDURERS		OERSTEDS
DEEMOPRV	PREMOVED		SUNDERER	**DEEORSTT**	ROSETTED
DEEMOPST	DEEPMOST	**DEENRRTU**	RETURNED		TETRODES
DEEMOQRU	QUEERDOM	**DEENRSSU**	RUDENESS	**DEEORSTX**	DEXTROSE
DEEMORRT	TREMORED	**DEENRSTU**	DENTURES	**DEEORSTY**	OYSTERED
DEEMORRW	DEWORMER		SEDERUNT		STOREYED
DEEMORST	MODESTER		UNDERSET	**DEEORSUV**	OVERUSED
DEEMORSW	WORMSEED		UNDESERT	**DEEORSVY**	OVERDYES
DEEMORSX	EXODERMS		UNRESTED	**DEEORTTT**	TOTTERED
DEEMORTU	MOUTERED	**DEENRSUU**	UNDERUSE	**DEEORTTX**	EXTORTED
	UDOMETER	**DEENRSUV**	UNSERVED	**DEEORTUV**	DEVOUTER
DEEMPPRU	REPUMPED		UNVERSED	**DEEOSSUX**	EXODUSES
DEEMPRST	DEMPSTER	**DEENRTUV**	VENTURED	**DEEOSTUW**	OUTWEEDS
DEEMPRSU	PRESUMED	**DEENSSSY**	SYNDESES	**DEEOSTUX**	TUXEDOES
DEEMPRTU	PERMUTED	**DEENSTTU**	UNTESTED	**DEEPPRSU**	SUPPERED
DEEMPSUW	SUMPWEED	**DEENSTUV**	UNVESTED	**DEEPPRTY**	PRETYPED
DEEMRRRU	DEMURRER	**DEENTTUV**	UNVETTED	**DEEPPSSU**	SPEEDUPS
	MURDERER	**DEENTTUW**	UNWETTED	**DEEPRRSU**	PERDURES
DEEMRSTU	DEMUREST	**DEENTUVY**	DUVETYNE	**DEEPRRVY**	REPRYVED
	MUSTERED	**DEEOOPPR**	PEREOPOD	**DEEPRSTU**	PERTUSED
DEEMRTTU	MUTTERED	**DEEOORRV**	OVERDOER	**DEEPRSUW**	PURSEWED
DEEMSSTY	SYSTEMED		OVERRODE	**DEEPRSUY**	PSEUDERY
DEENNNOP	PENNONED	**DEEOORSV**	OVERDOES	**DEEPRTTU**	PUTTERED
DEENNNPU	UNPENNED		OVERDOSE	**DEEPRUVY**	PURVEYED
DEENNOPT	DEPONENT	**DEEOPPRS**	PREPOSED	**DEERRSSS**	DRESSERS
DEENNOPU	UNOPENED	**DEEOPPST**	ESTOPPED	**DEERRSUV**	VERDURES
DEENNORS	ENDERONS	**DEEOPRRR**	PREORDER	**DEERRTTU**	TURRETED
DEENNORW	RENOWNED	**DEEOPRRS**	PEDREROS	**DEERRTUX**	EXTRUDER
DEENNOSS	DONENESS	**DEEOPRRT**	DEPORTER	**DEERSSST**	DESSERTS
DEENNOST	ENDNOTES		PORTERED		STRESSED
	SONNETED		REPORTED	**DEERSSSU**	DURESSES
DEENNOSY	DOYENNES	**DEEOPRRU**	REPOURED	**DEERSSTU**	RUSSETED
DEENNPST	PENDENTS	**DEEOPRRV**	REPROVED	**DEERSSTY**	DYESTERS
DEENNRTU	UNRENTED	**DEEOPRRW**	POWDERER	**DEERSTTU**	TRUSTEED
	UNTENDER	**DEEOPRSS**	DEPOSERS	**DEERSTUV**	VESTURED
DEENNRUV	UNNERVED	**DEEOPRST**	DOPESTER	**DEERSTUX**	EXTRUDES
DEENNSSU	NUDENESS		POSTERED	**DEERSUVY**	SURVEYED
	UNSENSED		REEDSTOP	**DEERTTUX**	TEXTURED
DEENNSTU	UNNESTED		REPOSTED	**DEFFHILW**	WHIFFLED
DEENNTTU	UNNETTED	**DEEOPRSY**	EYEDROPS	**DEFFHLSU**	SHUFFLED
	UNTENTED	**DEEOPRTT**	POTTERED	**DEFFHORS**	SHROFFED
DEENNTUV	UNVENTED		REPOTTED	**DEFFIINT**	TIFFINED
DEENOORT	ENROOTED	**DEEOPRTX**	EXPORTED	**DEFFIIPS**	SPIFFIED
DEENOORV	OVERDONE	**DEEOPRUZ**	DOUZEPER	**DEFFIKLS**	SKIFFLED
DEENOORW	WOODENER	**DEEOPSST**	POSSETED	**DEFFILNS**	SNIFFLED
DEENOOSV	NOSEDOVE	**DEEOPSSU**	ESPOUSED	**DEFFILOV**	FIVEFOLD
DEENOPPR	PREPONED	**DEEOPSTU**	OUTSPEED	**DEFFIMOS**	FIEFDOMS
DEENOPRR	PONDERER	**DEEOQRTU**	REQUOTED	**DEFFIORS**	OFFSIDER
DEENOPRW	PREOWNED		ROQUETED	**DEFFIOSS**	OFFSIDES
DEENOPSS	SPONDEES	**DEEORRRS**	ORDERERS	**DEFFIQSU**	SQUIFFED
DEENOPST	PENTODES		REORDERS	**DEFFIRSU**	DIFFUSER
DEENORRS	ENDORSER	**DEEORRRV**	VERDEROR	**DEFFISSU**	DIFFUSES
DEENORRW	WONDERER	**DEEORRST**	RESORTED	**DEFFISUX**	SUFFIXED
DEENORSS	ENDORSES		RESTORED	**DEFFLNSU**	SNUFFLED
DEENORST	ERODENTS		ROSTERED	**DEFFLOSU**	SOUFFLED
DEENORSW	ENDOWERS	**DEEORRSV**	OVERREDS	**DEFFLRTU**	TRUFFLED
	REENDOWS	**DEEORRTT**	RETORTED	**DEFFNORS**	FORFENDS
	WORSENED	**DEEORRTU**	REROUTED	**DEFFNOSS**	SENDOFFS
DEENORTU	DEUTERON		RETOURED	**DEFFSSUU**	SUFFUSED
DEENOSSS	ENDOSSES	**DEEORRUV**	DEVOURER	**DEFFSTUY**	DYESTUFF
DEENOSST	STENOSED		OVERRUDE	**DEFGGILN**	FLEDGING
DEENPPRS	PERPENDS	**DEEORRVW**	OVERDREW	**DEFGHILT**	FLIGHTED
DEENPRSS	SPENDERS	**DEEORRVY**	OVERDYER	**DEFGHIRT**	FRIGHTED

DEFGIIIN	IGNIFIED	DEFIIMSW	MIDWIFES	DEFLNOOU	UNFOOLED
DEFGIILN	DEFILING	DEFIINOT	NOTIFIED	DEFLNOPS	PENFOLDS
	FIELDING	DEFIINTU	FINITUDE	DEFLNORS	FONDLERS
DEFGIILU	UGLIFIED	DEFIINTY	IDENTIFY		FORLENDS
DEFGIINN	DEFINING	DEFIIOSS	OSSIFIED	DEFLNORU	FLOUNDER
DEFGIINY	DEIFYING	DEFIIOTV	VIDEOFIT		UNFOLDER
	EDIFYING	DEFIIPRU	PURIFIED	DEFLNOST	TENFOLDS
DEFGIIRR	FRIGIDER	DEFIIPSS	FISSIPED	DEFLNRUU	UNFURLED
DEFGIIST	DIGESTIF	DEFIIPTY	TYPIFIED	DEFLNSSU	FUNDLESS
DEFGILNU	INGULFED	DEFIIRRT	DRIFTIER	DEFLNTUU	UNFLUTED
DEFGILRU	DIRGEFUL	DEFIISST	FIDEISTS	DEFLOORS	FLOODERS
DEFGILTY	GIFTEDLY	DEFIITTY	FETIDITY		FORSLOED
DEFGINSU	DEFUSING	DEFILLNU	UNFILLED		REFLOODS
	FEUDINGS	DEFILLPU	UPFILLED	DEFLOORT	FORETOLD
DEFGINTU	UNGIFTED	DEFILMNU	FULMINED	DEFLOORV	OVERFOLD
DEFGINUZ	DEFUZING		UNFILMED	DEFLOOSS	FOODLESS
DEFGIOOW	GOODWIFE	DEFILNNO	NINEFOLD	DEFLOOUW	FUELWOOD
DEFGIORS	FIREDOGS	DEFILNOR	INFOLDER	DEFLOPUW	UPFLOWED
DEFGJORU	FORJUDGE	DEFILNOU	UNFOILED	DEFLORSS	FORDLESS
DEFGMOOY	FOGEYDOM	DEFILNRS	FLINDERS	DEFLORST	TELFORDS
DEFGNORU	UNFORGED	DEFILNRU	UNRIFLED	DEFLORSU	FOULDERS
DEFGOOSX	DOGFOXES		URNFIELD	DEFLPRUU	UPFURLED
DEFHIIMU	HUMIFIED	DEFILNRY	FRIENDLY	DEFLRSUU	DESULFUR
DEFHIINS	FIENDISH	DEFILOPR	PROFILED		SULFURED
	FINISHED	DEFILORR	FLORIDER	DEFMNORU	UNFORMED
DEFHILLO	LIFEHOLD	DEFILORU	FLUORIDE	DEFMOOOR	FOREDOOM
DEFHILSS	DISFLESH	DEFILORV	FRIVOLED	DEFMORSS	SERFDOMS
DEFHINSU	UNFISHED	DEFILOTU	OUTFIELD	DEFNNORT	FRONDENT
DEFHIOOW	WIFEHOOD	DEFILOTY	FOETIDLY	DEFNNOSS	FONDNESS
DEFHIRST	REDSHIFT	DEFILPRU	PRIDEFUL	DEFNNOUW	NEWFOUND
DEFHLOOS	ELFHOODS	DEFILPTU	UPLIFTED	DEFNOOPS	SPOONFED
	SELFHOOD	DEFILRRU	FLURRIED	DEFNOORS	FRONDOSE
DEFHLOSU	FLOUSHED	DEFILRVY	FERVIDLY	DEFNOORU	UNROOFED
DEFHLSSU	SHEDFULS	DEFILRZZ	FRIZZLED	DEFNOORV	OVERFOND
DEFHOOOR	FORHOOED	DEFILSSU	SULFIDES	DEFNOOTU	UNFOOTED
DEFHOORS	SERFHOOD	DEFIMNOR	INFORMED	DEFNOPRS	FORSPEND
DEFHOORW	FORHOWED	DEFIMOPR	PEDIFORM	DEFNORRU	FRONDEUR
DEFIIILV	VILIFIED	DEFIMORY	REMODIFY	DEFNORSU	FOUNDERS
DEFIIIMN	MINIFIED	DEFIMOSW	WIFEDOMS		REFOUNDS
DEFIIINS	NIDIFIES	DEFIMRRU	DRUMFIRE	DEFNORTU	FORTUNED
DEFIIINV	VINIFIED	DEFINNRU	REINFUND	DEFNORUV	OVERFUND
DEFIIIVV	VIVIFIED		UNFRIEND	DEFNOSSW	DOWFNESS
DEFIILLN	INFILLED	DEFINOPR	FORPINED	DEFNPRSU	PREFUNDS
DEFIILLO	OILFIELD	DEFINORW	FOREWIND	DEFNRRUU	UNDERFUR
DEFIILLP	FILLIPED	DEFINRTY	TRENDIFY		UNFURRED
DEFIILLW	WILDLIFE	DEFINSTU	UNSIFTED	DEFNRTUU	UNTURFED
DEFIILMR	MIDLIFER	DEFINTTU	UNFITTED	DEFNTTUU	UNTUFTED
DEFIILMS	MISFIELD	DEFIOORW	FIREWOOD	DEFOORRW	FOREWORD
	MISFILED	DEFIOPRT	PIEDFORT	DEFOORST	REDFOOTS
DEFIILNO	DIOLEFIN		PROFITED	DEFOOSSU	DOOFUSES
DEFIILNS	INFIDELS	DEFIORRU	FROIDEUR	DEFOOTUX	OUTFOXED
	INFIELDS	DEFIORSU	FOUDRIES	DEFORRUW	FURROWED
DEFIILOR	OILFIRED	DEFIORTU	OUTFIRED	DEFORSST	DEFROSTS
DEFIILRW	WILDFIRE	DEFIOTXY	DETOXIFY		FROSTEDS
DEFIILSU	FLUIDISE	DEFIRRST	DRIFTERS	DEFORSTW	FROWSTED
DEFIILTY	FIDELITY	DEFIRSSU	FISSURED	DEGGGIIT	GIGGITED
DEFIILUZ	FLUIDIZE		SURFSIDE	DEGGGILN	GLEDGING
DEFIIMNO	OMNIFIED	DEFISSTU	FEUDISTS	DEGGHINS	HEDGINGS
DEFIIMNR	INFIRMED	DEFKLORY	FORKEDLY	DEGGHIRS	DREGGISH
DEFIIMNU	MUNIFIED	DEFKNORU	UNFORKED	DEGGHLOS	SHOGGLED
DEFIIMOR	MODIFIER	DEFLLOOR	FOLDEROL	DEGGHRSU	SHRUGGED
DEFIIMOS	MODIFIES	DEFLLOOW	FOLLOWED	DEGGIINN	DEIGNING
DEFIIMRS	MISFIRED	DEFLMOSS	SELFDOMS	DEGGILNP	PLEDGING
DEFIIMSS	FIDEISMS	DEFLMPRU	FRUMPLED	DEGGILNS	GELDINGS

	SLEDGING	**DEGIIKNS**	KINGSIDE	**DEGILNOY**	YODELING
	SNIGGLED	**DEGIIKST**	KIDGIEST	**DEGILNPS**	SPELDING
DEGGILNU	DELUGING	**DEGIILMN**	DELIMING	**DEGILNRU**	INDULGER
DEGGILRW	WRIGGLED	**DEGIILNR**	GRIDELIN	**DEGILNRY**	YELDRING
DEGGINNU	UNEDGING	**DEGIILNS**	EILDINGS	**DEGILNSU**	INDULGES
DEGGINRU	UNRIGGED		SIDELING	**DEGILNSV**	DEVLINGS
DEGGINSW	WEDGINGS	**DEGIILNT**	DILIGENT	**DEGILNSW**	SWINGLED
DEGGINUW	UNWIGGED	**DEGIILNV**	DEVILING		WELDINGS
DEGGIORS	DISGORGE	**DEGIILNW**	WIELDING	**DEGILNWY**	WINGEDLY
DEGGIOST	DOGGIEST	**DEGIILNY**	YIELDING	**DEGILOOR**	GOODLIER
DEGGIPRS	SPRIGGED	**DEGIILTU**	DIGITULE	**DEGILOOY**	IDEOLOGY
DEGGIRRU	DRUGGIER	**DEGIILTY**	GELIDITY	**DEGILORV**	OVERGILD
DEGGIRST	STRIGGED	**DEGIIMNP**	IMPEDING	**DEGILOST**	GODLIEST
DEGGIRSU	DRUGGIES		IMPINGED		GOLDIEST
DEGGLMSU	SMUGGLED	**DEGIIMNS**	DEMISING	**DEGILOSZ**	GOLDSIZE
DEGGLNSU	SNUGGLED	**DEGIIMSU**	MISGUIDE	**DEGILPSU**	PULSIDGE
DEGGLORS	DOGGRELS	**DEGIINNP**	PIENDING	**DEGILRRS**	GIRDLERS
DEGGLORY	GORGEDLY	**DEGIINNR**	NIDERING	**DEGILRSU**	GUILDERS
DEGGLRUY	RUGGEDLY	**DEGIINNS**	DESINING		SLUDGIER
DEGGNOOR	DOGGONER		INDIGENS	**DEGILRSW**	WERGILDS
DEGGNOOS	DOGGONES		SDEINING	**DEGILRUV**	DIVULGER
DEGGNORU	UNGORGED	**DEGIINNT**	ENDITING	**DEGILRZZ**	GRIZZLED
DEGGNOSU	GUDGEONS		INDIGENT	**DEGILSUV**	DIVULGES
DEGGRRSU	DRUGGERS		TEINDING	**DEGIMMNO**	MODEMING
	GRUDGERS	**DEGIINNW**	INDEWING	**DEGIMNNS**	MENDINGS
DEGGRSTU	DRUGGETS		WIDENING	**DEGIMNOS**	MENDIGOS
DEGHHILV	HIGHVELD	**DEGIINNX**	INDEXING		SMIDGEON
DEGHIILL	GHILLIED	**DEGIINNZ**	DIZENING	**DEGIMNOT**	DEMOTING
DEGHIINS	DINGHIES	**DEGIINOS**	INDIGOES	**DEGIMNPU**	IMPUGNED
DEGHIKNT	KNIGHTED	**DEGIINOV**	VIDEOING	**DEGIMNRU**	DEMURING
DEGHILNS	HINDLEGS	**DEGIINRS**	DESIRING	**DEGIMNSS**	SMIDGENS
	SHINGLED		RESIDING	**DEGIMOOT**	GOODTIME
DEGHILOU	OUGHLIED		RINGSIDE	**DEGIMOOY**	GEOMYOID
DEGHILPT	PLIGHTED	**DEGIINRT**	DIRIGENT	**DEGIMRSU**	SMUDGIER
DEGHILST	DELIGHTS	**DEGIINRV**	DERIVING	**DEGINNNU**	UNENDING
	SLIGHTED		VIRGINED	**DEGINNOP**	DEPONING
DEGHINNS	SHENDING	**DEGIINRW**	WEIRDING	**DEGINNOT**	DENOTING
DEGHINNU	UNHINGED	**DEGIINST**	DIETINGS	**DEGINNOV**	DOVENING
DEGHIOOS	SHOOGIED		DINGIEST	**DEGINNOW**	ENDOWING
DEGHIOPS	DOGESHIP		EDITINGS	**DEGINNOZ**	DOZENING
DEGHIORU	DOUGHIER		INDIGEST	**DEGINNPS**	SPENDING
DEGHIPST	DESPIGHT	**DEGIINSV**	DEVISING	**DEGINNPU**	UPENDING
	SPIGHTED	**DEGIIRST**	RIDGIEST	**DEGINNRT**	TRENDING
DEGHIQTU	QUIGHTED		RIGIDEST	**DEGINNRU**	ENDURING
DEGHITTW	TWIGHTED	**DEGIISSU**	DISGUISE		UNRINGED
DEGHLNOR	HORNGELD	**DEGIJMSU**	MISJUDGE	**DEGINNSS**	SENDINGS
DEGHLOOS	DOGHOLES	**DEGIKKNO**	DEKKOING	**DEGINNST**	STENDING
	GOLOSHED	**DEGIKLNU**	DUKELING	**DEGINNSU**	UNSIGNED
	SHOOGLED	**DEGIKLOV**	KIDGLOVE	**DEGINNSV**	VENDINGS
DEGHLOPU	PLOUGHED	**DEGIKLRU**	KLUDGIER	**DEGINNSY**	DESYNING
DEGHLORY	HYDROGEL	**DEGIKNNU**	UNKINGED	**DEGINNTU**	DETUNING
DEGHLOSU	SLOUGHED	**DEGILLNU**	DUELLING		UNTINGED
DEGHMOSU	GUMSHOED	**DEGILLNW**	DWELLING	**DEGINNUW**	UNWINGED
DEGHMPRU	GRUMPHED	**DEGILMNO**	MODELING	**DEGINOOR**	RODEOING
DEGHNOOS	HOGNOSED	**DEGILMNS**	GILDSMEN	**DEGINOPR**	PROIGNED
DEGHNORT	THRONGED	**DEGILMOS**	MISLODGE	**DEGINOPS**	DEPOSING
DEGHNORY	HYDROGEN	**DEGILMPS**	GLIMPSED		DISPONGE
DEGHOOSU	DOGHOUSE	**DEGILNNO**	OLDENING		PIDGEONS
DEGHORRS	DROGHERS	**DEGILNNS**	LENDINGS	**DEGINORR**	ORDERING
DEGHPSUU	UPGUSHED	**DEGILNOP**	DELOPING	**DEGINORS**	NEGROIDS
DEGIIIRS	RIGIDISE		DIPLOGEN	**DEGINORU**	GUERIDON
DEGIIIRZ	RIGIDIZE	**DEGILNOS**	GLENOIDS	**DEGINORV**	DOVERING
DEGIIIST	DIGITISE		SIDELONG		RINGDOVE
DEGIIITZ	DIGITIZE	**DEGILNOW**	DOWELING	**DEGINORW**	DOWERING

DEGINOSW	WENDIGOS / WIDGEONS
DEGINOTV	DEVOTING
DEGINOTX	DETOXING
DEGINPRS	SPRINGED
DEGINPSU	DISPUNGE
DEGINPTU	DEPUTING
DEGINRRS	GRINDERS / REGRINDS
DEGINRRY	GRINDERY / REDRYING
DEGINRSS	DRESSING
DEGINRST	STRINGED
DEGINRSU	GRUNDIES
DEGINRSW	REDWINGS
DEGINRSY	SYNERGID / SYRINGED
DEGINSSU	DINGUSES
DEGINSSW	SWINDGES
DEGINSTU	DUNGIEST
DEGINTTU	DUETTING
DEGIOORS	GOODSIRE
DEGIOOST	GOODIEST
DEGIOPRR	PORRIDGE
DEGIOPRT	RIDGETOP
DEGIOPSS	GOSSIPED
DEGIOPST	PODGIEST
DEGIORRU	GOURDIER
DEGIORRV	OVERGIRD
DEGIORST	DIGESTOR / GRODIEST / STODGIER
DEGIOTUU	OUTGUIDE
DEGIPSTU	PUDGIEST
DEGIQSSU	SQUIDGES
DEGIRRTU	TURGIDER
DEGIRSTU	DURGIEST
DEGISSST	DISGESTS
DEGJMNTU	JUDGMENT
DEGLLNOY	GOLDENLY
DEGLLOOP	GOLLOPED
DEGLLOSS	GOLDLESS
DEGLMNOT	LODGMENT
DEGLMOOY	DEMOLOGY
DEGLNOOT	GOLDTONE
DEGLNOUV	UNGLOVED
DEGLNRTU	GRUNTLED
DEGLOOPR	PROLOGED
DEGLOOPY	PEDOLOGY
DEGLOOUU	DUOLOGUE
DEGLOPRS	PLEDGORS
DEGLOPSS	SPLODGES
DEGLPRSU	SPLURGED
DEGMMNUU	UNGUMMED
DEGMOOPR	POGROMED
DEGMOOSS	SMOODGES
DEGMRSSU	SMUDGERS
DEGNNORU	GROUNDEN
DEGNNOSU	DUNGEONS
DEGNNOUW	UNGOWNED
DEGNOORS	DRONGOES
DEGNOOSS	GOODNESS
DEGNOOST	STEGODON
DEGNOPPU	OPPUGNED

DEGNORRU	GROUNDER / REGROUND
DEGNORSU	GUERDONS
DEGNORTU	TRUDGEON
DEGNORUU	UNROUGED
DEGNORYY	GYRODYNE
DEGNPRUU	UNPURGED
DEGNRSTU	TRUDGENS
DEGOORSV	OVERDOGS
DEGOORTT	GROTTOED
DEGORSST	STODGERS
DEGORSTU	DROGUETS
DEGPRSUU	UPSURGED
DEGRRSTU	TRUDGERS
DEHHILTW	WITHHELD
DEHHISTW	WHISHTED
DEHHLSUY	HUSHEDLY
DEHHMRTY	RHYTHMED
DEHHOOSW	WHOOSHED
DEHIIKLS	DISHLIKE
DEHIILLS	HILLSIDE / SIDEHILL
DEHIILLW	WHILLIED
DEHIILNS	LINISHED
DEHIILSV	DEVILISH
DEHIIMMS	SHIMMIED
DEHIIMNS	MINISHED
DEHIIMRU	MUDIRIEH
DEHIIMST	DITHEISM / SMITHIED
DEHIIMSW	WHIMSIED
DEHIINNS	SHINNIED
DEHIINNW	WHINNIED
DEHIINSS	SHINDIES
DEHIINST	SHINTIED
DEHIIPSS	SHIPSIDE
DEHIIRRW	WHIRRIED
DEHIIRST	DISHERIT
DEHIISST	DISHIEST
DEHIISTT	DITHEIST / STITHIED
DEHIJMNO	DEMIJOHN
DEHIKLMS	MILKSHED
DEHIKLOO	HOODLIKE
DEHIKMOS	SHEIKDOM
DEHIKPSU	DUKESHIP
DEHILLOP	PHELLOID
DEHILLRS	SHRILLED
DEHILLRT	THRILLED
DEHILMOS	DEMOLISH
DEHILMPW	WHIMPLED
DEHILMSS	DISHELMS
DEHILMTY	DIMETHYL
DEHILNOR	INHOLDER
DEHILNOY	HONIEDLY
DEHILNPY	DIPHENYL
DEHILOOR	HELIODOR
DEHILOOS	DHOOLIES
DEHILOPS	DEPOLISH / POLISHED
DEHILOTY	HOLYTIDE
DEHILPRT	PHILTRED
DEHILPSU	SULPHIDE
DEHILPSY	SYLPHIDE

DEHILRTW	WRITHLED
DEHILSTW	WHISTLED
DEHILSTY	DIETHYLS
DEHILTTW	WHITTLED
DEHIMNOS	HEDONISM / MONISHED
DEHIMOPS	HEMIPODS
DEHIMORS	HEIRDOMS
DEHIMOSS	DISHOMES
DEHIMOST	ETHMOIDS
DEHIMPRS	SHRIMPED
DEHIMPSY	DEMYSHIP
DEHIMSTU	HUMIDEST
DEHIMSTY	MYTHISED
DEHIMTYZ	MYTHIZED
DEHINOOP	INHOOPED
DEHINOPR	NEPHROID
DEHINOPS	DIPHONES / SIPHONED / SPHENOID
DEHINORS	HORDEINS
DEHINOST	HEDONIST
DEHINPSS	ENDSHIPS
DEHINPSU	PUNISHED
DEHINSUW	UNWISHED
DEHIOOST	DHOOTIES / HOODIEST
DEHIOOVW	WIVEHOOD
DEHIOPRS	SPHEROID
DEHIOPRT	TROPHIED
DEHIORRR	HORRIDER
DEHIORSS	DISHORSE / HIDROSES
DEHIORTU	OUTHIRED
DEHIORTW	WITHEROD / WORTHIED
DEHIORTY	THYREOID
DEHIOSSU	DISHOUSE
DEHIOSSW	SIDESHOW
DEHIOSTU	HIDEOUTS
DEHIPSSU	PSEUDISH
DEHIQSSU	SQUISHED
DEHIRRST	REDSHIRT
DEHIRRSU	DHURRIES
DEHIRSTT	THIRSTED / THRISTED
DEHIRTWW	WITHDREW
DEHKLNOU	ELKHOUND
DEHKNOOU	UNHOOKED
DEHKNSUU	UNHUSKED
DEHKOOSS	SKOOSHED
DEHLLOOO	HOLLOOED
DEHLLOOU	HULLOOED
DEHLLOOW	HOLLOWED
DEHLLOPY	PHYLLODE
DEHLMMOW	WHOMMLED
DEHLMMUW	WHUMMLED
DEHLMOOT	HOTELDOM
DEHLMORY	HYDROMEL
DEHLMOSU	MUDHOLES
DEHLMPSU	SHLUMPED
DEHLNOOW	DOWNHOLE
DEHLNTUY	HUNTEDLY
DEHLOOOW	WOODHOLE

DEHLOOPT	POTHOLED		**DEIIKLMS**	MISLIKED			IRONISED
DEHLOORV	HOLDOVER		**DEIIKLNR**	KINDLIER			IRONSIDE
	OVERHOLD		**DEIIKLNS**	DISLIKEN			RESINOID
DEHLOOSS	HOODLESS		**DEIIKLNV**	DEVILKIN		**DEIINORT**	RETINOID
	SLOOSHED		**DEIIKLRS**	DISLIKER		**DEIINORZ**	IRONIZED
DEHLOOST	TOEHOLDS		**DEIIKLSS**	DISLIKES		**DEIINOST**	EDITIONS
	TOOLSHED		**DEIIKNST**	DINKIEST			SEDITION
DEHLOOSW	WOOLSHED		**DEIIKSVV**	SKIVVIED		**DEIINOSV**	VISIONED
DEHLOPRU	UPHOLDER		**DEIILLMP**	MILLIPED		**DEIINOTY**	IDONEITY
DEHLOPSS	SPLOSHED		**DEIILLMT**	TIDEMILL		**DEIINPPW**	WINDPIPE
DEHLORSU	SHOULDER		**DEIILLST**	DILLIEST		**DEIINPRS**	INSPIRED
DEHLPRUU	UPHURLED		**DEIILMMS**	SEMIMILD		**DEIINPRT**	INTREPID
DEHLRRSU	HURDLERS		**DEIILMNS**	MIDLINES		**DEIINPRY**	PYRIDINE
DEHLRSWY	SHREWDLY		**DEIILMPR**	DIMPLIER		**DEIINPSS**	SIDESPIN
DEHLSTTU	SHUTTLED		**DEIILMRU**	DELIRIUM		**DEIINPTU**	UNPITIED
DEHMMRTU	THRUMMED		**DEIILMST**	DELIMITS		**DEIINQRU**	INQUIRED
DEHMNOOY	HOMODYNE			LIMITEDS		**DEIINQSU**	QUINSIED
DEHMNRUY	UNRHYMED		**DEIILMSU**	SEDILIUM			SQUINIED
DEHMOORS	SHROOMED		**DEIILMSV**	DEVILISM		**DEIINRSS**	INDRISES
DEHMOORW	WHOREDOM			MIDLIVES			INSIDERS
DEHMOOSS	SHMOOSED			MISLIVED		**DEIINRST**	DISINTER
	SMOOSHED		**DEIILMSW**	SEMIWILD			INDITERS
DEHMOOST	SMOOTHED		**DEIILNNU**	INDULINE			NITRIDES
DEHMOOSZ	SHMOOZED		**DEIILNOS**	LIONISED			RINDIEST
DEHMOPRY	HYPODERM		**DEIILNOT**	TOLIDINE		**DEIINRSU**	DISINURE
DEHMORUU	HUMOURED		**DEIILNOZ**	LIONIZED			URIDINES
DEHNNTUU	UNHUNTED		**DEIILNPV**	VILIPEND		**DEIINRSV**	DIVINERS
DEHNOOPU	UNHOOPED		**DEIILNTT**	INTITLED		**DEIINRTU**	UNTIDIER
DEHNOORU	HONOURED		**DEIILNVY**	DIVINELY		**DEIINSST**	INSISTED
DEHNOOSW	HOEDOWNS		**DEIILNXY**	XYLIDINE			SNIDIEST
	WOODHENS		**DEIILOPS**	PLOIDIES			TIDINESS
DEHNOPSY	SYPHONED		**DEIILORS**	IDOLISER		**DEIINSTU**	DISUNITE
DEHNORSU	ENSHROUD		**DEIILORZ**	IDOLIZER			NUDITIES
	HOUNDERS		**DEIILOSS**	IDOLISES			UNITISED
	UNHORSED		**DEIILOSZ**	IDOLIZES			UNTIDIES
DEHNORSY	ENHYDROS		**DEIILPRT**	TRIPLIED		**DEIINSTV**	DIVINEST
DEHNORTY	THRENODY		**DEIILPSS**	SIDESLIP		**DEIINSTW**	WINDIEST
DEHNOSSW	SNOWSHED		**DEIILRST**	REDISTIL		**DEIINTTU**	INTUITED
DEHNOSTZ	DOZENTHS		**DEIILSTU**	UTILISED		**DEIINTTY**	IDENTITY
DEHNOSUU	UNHOUSED		**DEIILSTV**	LIVIDEST		**DEIINTUZ**	UNITIZED
DEHNRSTU	THUNDERS		**DEIILTUV**	DILUTIVE		**DEIIOPRS**	PRESIDIO
DEHNRSUU	UNRUSHED		**DEIILTUY**	TUILYIED		**DEIIOPRT**	DIPTEROI
DEHNRTUY	THUNDERY		**DEIILTUZ**	TUILZIED		**DEIIOPTY**	IDIOTYPE
DEHOOOPP	POPEHOOD			UTILIZED		**DEIIOPZZ**	PEZIZOID
DEHOOPRT	THEROPOD		**DEIIMMRS**	DIMERISM		**DEIIORSS**	IODISERS
DEHOOSSW	SWOOSHED		**DEIIMMST**	MISTIMED		**DEIIORST**	DIORITES
DEHOPRST	POTSHERD		**DEIIMMTT**	IMMITTED		**DEIIORSX**	OXIDISER
DEHORRST	REDSHORT		**DEIIMNOS**	DOMINIES		**DEIIORSZ**	IODIZERS
DEHORTUY	OUTHYRED		**DEIIMNRT**	DIRIMENT		**DEIIORTX**	TRIOXIDE
DEHOSSTU	STOUSHED		**DEIIMNTU**	MUTINIED		**DEIIORTY**	IODYRITE
DEHPPSTU	SHTUPPED		**DEIIMNUV**	VENIDIUM		**DEIIORXZ**	OXIDIZER
DEHPRSSU	SPRUSHED		**DEIIMOSS**	DISOMIES		**DEIIOSSX**	OXIDISES
DEHPRSUU	UPRUSHED		**DEIIMPRU**	PERIDIUM		**DEIIOSTT**	OTITIDES
DEHQSSUU	SQUUSHED		**DEIIMPSS**	DIMPSIES		**DEIIOSXZ**	OXIDIZES
DEHRRSTU	DRUTHERS		**DEIIMRSV**	MISDRIVE		**DEIIPPRR**	DRIPPIER
DEHRSTTU	THRUSTED		**DEIIMSST**	MISDIETS		**DEIIPPST**	DIPPIEST
DEIIIMST	DIMITIES			MISEDITS		**DEIIPRST**	RIPTIDES
DEIIINSV	DIVINISE		**DEIIMSTT**	TIMIDEST			SPIRITED
DEIIINVZ	DIVINIZE		**DEIIMSWW**	MIDWIVES			TIDERIPS
DEIIIRSS	IRIDISES		**DEIINNOP**	PINIONED		**DEIIPRSZ**	DISPRIZE
DEIIIRSZ	IRIDIZES		**DEIINNPP**	PINNIPED		**DEIIPTTY**	TEPIDITY
DEIIIRTV	VIRIDITE		**DEIINNTW**	INTWINED		**DEIIQSTU**	DISQUIET
DEIIISVV	DIVISIVE		**DEIINNUV**	UNDIVINE		**DEIIRRVV**	VIVERRID
DEIIKKLS	DISKLIKE		**DEIINORS**	DERISION		**DEIIRSSU**	DIURESIS

DEIIRSTT	DIRTIEST
	TRITIDES
DEIISSTT	DIETISTS
	DITSIEST
DEIISTTZ	DITZIEST
DEIISTVV	VIVIDEST
DEIISTZZ	DIZZIEST
DEIJNNOU	UNJOINED
DEIJNORS	JOINDERS
DEIJNSSU	DISJUNES
DEIJORRY	JOYRIDER
DEIJORSY	JOYRIDES
DEIKKLNO	KLONDIKE
DEIKKNNU	UNKINKED
DEIKLLOR	LORDLIKE
DEIKLLSS	DESKILLS
DEIKLMMS	SKLIMMED
DEIKLMNU	UNMILKED
DEIKLMRU	DRUMLIKE
DEIKLNNU	UNLINKED
DEIKLNOW	DOWNLIKE
DEIKLNPU	UPLINKED
DEIKLNRS	KINDLERS
DEIKLNRW	WRINKLED
DEIKLNSS	KINDLESS
DEIKLNTW	TWINKLED
DEIKLSSS	DISKLESS
DEIKLSTT	SKITTLED
DEIKLSTU	DUSTLIKE
DEIKMNOO	KIMONOED
DEIKMOSY	MISYOKED
DEIKMPRS	SKRIMPED
DEIKNNOR	DONNIKER
DEIKNNPU	UNPINKED
DEIKNNRU	UNKINDER
DEIKNNSS	KINDNESS
DEIKNORV	OVERKIND
DEIKNORW	INWORKED
DEIKNOSS	DOESKINS
DEIKNRRS	DRINKERS
DEIKNRSS	REDSKINS
DEIKNSSU	UNKISSED
DEIKORSS	DROSKIES
DEIKORST	DORKIEST
DEIKOSSY	DISYOKES
DEIKPRSU	PRUSIKED
	SPRUIKED
DEIKRRSU	SKURRIED
DEIKRSVY	SKYDIVER
DEIKSSTU	DUSKIEST
DEIKSSVY	SKYDIVES
DEILLMNU	UNMILLED
DEILLNSW	INDWELLS
DEILLNTU	UNTILLED
DEILLNUW	UNWILLED
DEILLOOV	LIVELOOD
DEILLOPW	PILLOWED
DEILLORR	LORDLIER
DEILLORS	DOLLIERS
DEILLORT	TROLLIED
DEILLORU	LOUDLIER
DEILLOSV	LIVELODS
DEILLOWW	WILLOWED
DEILLPRR	PREDRILL
DEILLRRS	DRILLERS
	REDRILLS
DEILLRSV	DREVILLS
DEILLSTU	DUELLIST
	DULLIEST
DEILMNOO	MELODION
DEILMNSS	MILDNESS
	MINDLESS
DEILMNSU	MUSLINED
DEILMOOT	DOLOMITE
DEILMOPR	IMPLORED
	IMPOLDER
DEILMOPS	IMPLODES
DEILMORU	LEMUROID
DEILMORV	OVERMILD
DEILMOSS	MIDSOLES
DEILMOST	MELODIST
	MODELIST
	MOLDIEST
DEILMOSU	EMULSOID
DEILMOTV	DEMIVOLT
DEILMPPU	PLUMIPED
DEILMPSU	DISPLUME
	IMPULSED
DEILMPTU	MULTIPED
DEILMRRU	DRUMLIER
DEILMRSU	MISRULED
DEILMSSY	DEMISSLY
DEILMSTU	MUSTELID
DEILNNOT	INDOLENT
DEILNOOS	EIDOLONS
	SOLENOID
DEILNOPT	TOPLINED
DEILNORS	DISENROL
DEILNOSS	SONDELIS
DEILNOST	LENTOIDS
DEILNOSU	DELUSION
	INSOULED
	UNSOILED
DEILNOTU	OUTLINED
DEILNOVV	INVOLVED
DEILNPRS	SPELDRIN
	SPINDLER
DEILNPRU	UNDERLIP
DEILNPSS	SPELDINS
	SPINDLES
DEILNPST	SPLINTED
DEILNRSS	RINDLESS
DEILNRST	SNIRTLED
	TENDRILS
	TRINDLES
DEILNRSW	SWINDLER
DEILNRTU	UNDERLIT
DEILNRTY	TRENDILY
DEILNSST	DINTLESS
DEILNSSV	VILDNESS
DEILNSSW	SWINDLES
	WILDNESS
	WINDLESS
DEILNSTU	DILUENTS
	INSULTED
	UNLISTED
DEILNTTU	UNTILTED
	UNTITLED
DEILNTUY	UNITEDLY
DEILNUWY	UNWIELDY
DEILOOPS	POOLSIDE
DEILOOPW	WOODPILE
DEILOORR	DROOLIER
DEILOPPY	POLYPIDE
DEILOPRS	LEPORIDS
DEILOPRU	PRELUDIO
DEILOPSS	DESPOILS
	DIPLOSES
	SOLIPEDS
DEILOPST	PISTOLED
	POSTILED
DEILOPSU	EUPLOIDS
DEILOPUY	EUPLOIDY
DEILOQRU	LIQUORED
DEILORRW	LOWRIDER
DEILORSS	SOLDIERS
DEILORST	STOLIDER
DEILORSU	SOULDIER
DEILORSY	SOLDIERY
DEILORTY	ELYTROID
DEILOSST	SOLIDEST
DEILOSSV	DISSOLVE
DEILOSTT	DOILTEST
DEILOSTU	SOLITUDE
	TOLUIDES
DEILOSTW	DOWLIEST
DEILOSVW	OLDWIVES
DEILOTUV	OUTLIVED
DEILOTUW	OUTWILED
DEILOTUY	OUTYIELD
DEILPPRT	TRIPPLED
DEILPPST	STIPPLED
DEILPPSU	SUPPLIED
DEILPPTU	PULPITED
DEILPRSS	DRIPLESS
DEILPRSU	SERPULID
DEILPSTT	SPLITTED
DEILPSTU	STIPULED
DEILPSUY	SPULYIED
DEILPSUZ	SPULZIED
DEILPTTU	UPTILTED
DEILRRSU	SLURRIED
DEILRSSY	DRESSILY
DEILRSTU	DILUTERS
	LURIDEST
	STUDLIER
DEILRSVY	DIVERSLY
DEILRSZZ	DRIZZLES
DEILRTVY	DEVILTRY
DEILSSTU	DUELISTS
DEILSSTY	DISTYLES
	STYLISED
DEILSSUV	DIVULSES
DEILSTUY	SEDULITY
DEILSTYZ	STYLIZED
DEILSWZZ	SWIZZLED
DEILTWZZ	TWIZZLED
DEIMMNOO	OMNIMODE
DEIMMNOS	DEMONISM
DEIMMOOV	MOVIEDOM
DEIMMOST	IMMODEST

DEIMMOSV	MISMOVED	DEINNNPU	UNPINNED	DEINPSST	STIPENDS
DEIMMPST	MISDEMPT	DEINNNSU	NUNDINES	DEINPTTU	INPUTTED
DEIMMRST	MIDTERMS	DEINNNTU	UNTINNED		UNPITTED
DEIMMRSU	DRUMMIES	DEINNOOT	NOONTIDE	DEINQSTU	SQUINTED
DEIMMSTU	DUMMIEST	DEINNOPT	ENDPOINT	DEINRRTU	INTRUDER
	SUMMITED	DEINNORS	ENDIRONS	DEINRSSU	INSUREDS
DEIMNNOS	MISDONNE	DEINNORT	INDENTOR		SUNDRIES
DEIMNNOU	UNMONIED	DEINNORU	UNIRONED	DEINRSTT	STRIDENT
DEIMNNSU	MINUENDS	DEINNOWW	WINNOWED		TRIDENTS
DEIMNOOS	DOMINOES	DEINNPRU	UNDERPIN	DEINRSTU	INTRUDES
	MONODIES	DEINNRSU	UNRINSED		NURDIEST
DEIMNOOT	DEMOTION	DEINNRTU	INTURNED	DEINRSTX	DEXTRINS
	MOTIONED	DEINNRUU	UNINURED	DEINRTUW	UNDERWIT
DEIMNOOX	MONOXIDE	DEINNRUV	UNDRIVEN	DEINSSST	DISNESTS
DEIMNOPT	PIEDMONT	DEINNRUW	UNWINDER		DISSENTS
DEIMNORT	DORMIENT	DEINNSTU	DUNNIEST	DEINSSSY	SYNDESIS
DEIMNOST	DEMONIST		DUNNITES	DEINSSTT	DENTISTS
DEIMNOTW	DOWNTIME	DEINNTUU	UNUNITED	DEINSSTU	DISTUNES
DEIMNOWW	WIDOWMEN	DEINNTUW	UNTWINED	DEINSSUU	UNISSUED
DEIMNPRU	UNPRIMED	DEINOOPS	POISONED	DEINSTUU	UNSUITED
DEIMNPSS	MISSPEND	DEINOOPT	OPTIONED	DEINTTUW	UNWITTED
DEIMNPTU	IMPUDENT	DEINOOPW	PINEWOOD	DEIOOPRR	DROOPIER
DEIMNRTU	RUDIMENT	DEINOOSU	IDONEOUS	DEIOORSS	ODORISES
	UNMITRED	DEINOOSZ	OZONIDES	DEIOORSW	WOODSIER
DEIMNSSS	MISSENDS		OZONISED	DEIOORSZ	ODORIZES
DEIMNSST	MINDSETS	DEINOOTV	DEVOTION	DEIOOSSS	ISODOSES
	MISTENDS	DEINOOZZ	OZONIZED	DEIOOSST	OSTEOIDS
DEIMNSSU	UNMISSED	DEINOPPW	DOWNPIPE	DEIOOSTW	WOODIEST
DEIMNSSW	MISWENDS	DEINOPRS	DISPONER	DEIOOSVV	VOIVODES
DEIMNSTU	MISTUNED		POINDERS	DEIOOSWW	WOIWODES
DEIMOORS	MOIDORES		PRISONED	DEIOPRRV	PROVIDER
DEIMOOSS	SODOMIES	DEINOPRT	DIPTERON	DEIOPRSS	DISPOSER
	SODOMISE	DEINOPRU	INPOURED		DROPSIES
DEIMOOST	DOOMIEST	DEINOPRV	PROVINED	DEIOPRST	DIOPTERS
	MOODIEST	DEINOPRY	PYRENOID		DIOPTRES
	SODOMITE	DEINOPSS	DISPONES		DIPTEROS
DEIMOOSZ	SODOMIZE		DOPINESS		PERIDOTS
DEIMOPRS	IMPEDORS	DEINOPSU	UNPOISED		PORTSIDE
	PROMISED	DEINOPTW	DEWPOINT		PROTEIDS
DEIMOPRT	IMPORTED	DEINORRS	INDORSER		RIPOSTED
DEIMOPRV	IMPROVED	DEINORSS	INDORSES		TOPSIDER
DEIMOPST	IMPOSTED		SORDINES	DEIOPRSV	DISPROVE
DEIMORRR	MIRRORED	DEINORST	DRONIEST		PROVIDES
DEIMORRS	MISORDER	DEINORSU	DOURINES	DEIOPRSW	DROPWISE
	MORRISED		SOURDINE	DEIOPRSX	PEROXIDS
DEIMORSS	MISDOERS	DEINORSW	DISOWNER	DEIOPSSS	DISPOSES
DEIMORST	MORTISED		WINDORES	DEIOPSST	DEPOSITS
DEIMORSU	DIMEROUS		WINDROSE		TOPSIDES
	ERODIUMS	DEINORTT	INTORTED	DEIOPSTV	POSTDIVE
	SOREDIUM	DEINORVW	OVERWIND	DEIORRRT	TORRIDER
DEIMORSV	MISDROVE	DEINOSST	DONSIEST	DEIORRSS	DROSSIER
DEIMORUX	EXORDIUM	DEINOSSV	VOIDNESS	DEIORRSW	DROWSIER
DEIMOSST	DISTOMES	DEINOSSZ	DOZINESS	DEIORRSY	DERISORY
	MODISTES	DEINOSTW	DOWNIEST	DEIORRTU	OUTRIDER
DEIMOSTT	DEMOTIST	DEINOSWZ	DOWNSIZE	DEIORRTW	WORRITED
DEIMPRST	DIREMPTS	DEINOTTU	DUETTINO	DEIORRZZ	RIZZORED
DEIMPSTU	DUMPIEST	DEINOTUV	INDEVOUT	DEIORSSS	DOSSIERS
	DUMPSITE	DEINPPRU	UNRIPPED	DEIORSST	STEROIDS
DEIMPSTY	MISTYPED	DEINPPTU	UNTIPPED	DEIORSSU	DESIROUS
DEIMQRSU	SQUIRMED	DEINPPUZ	UNZIPPED	DEIORSSV	DEVISORS
DEIMRSSU	SURMISED	DEINPRST	SPRINTED	DEIORSTT	DORTIEST
DEIMRSTU	DIESTRUM	DEINPRTU	TURNIPED	DEIORSTU	IODURETS
DEIMRSUU	RESIDUUM	DEINPRUZ	UNPRIZED		OUTRIDES
DEINNNOU	INNUENDO				OUTSIDER

	SUITORED	**DELLMOSW**	SWELLDOM		LORDOSES
DEIORSTW	ROWDIEST	**DELLMOSY**	SELDOMLY		ODORLESS
	WORDIEST	**DELLNOPU**	UNPOLLED	**DELOORSV**	OVERSOLD
DEIORSWW	WIDOWERS	**DELLNORU**	UNROLLED	**DELOORSW**	WOOLDERS
DEIORTTX	TETROXID	**DELLNORW**	ROWNDELL	**DELOORTY**	ROOTEDLY
DEIORTUV	OUTDRIVE	**DELLNPUU**	UNPULLED	**DELOORUV**	OVERLOUD
DEIOSSTU	OUTSIDES	**DELLNSSU**	DULLNESS	**DELOOSSW**	WOODLESS
DEIOSSTX	EXODISTS	**DELLOPRS**	REDPOLLS	**DELOOTUV**	OUTLOVED
DEIOSTTT	DOTTIEST	**DELLOPRU**	UPROLLED	**DELOPPRS**	DROPPLES
DEIOSTUW	WIDEOUTS	**DELLOPTU**	POLLUTED	**DELOPPST**	STOPPLED
DEIOSTUZ	OUTSIZED	**DELLORRY**	DROLLERY	**DELOPPSY**	POLYPEDS
DEIPPRRS	DRIPPERS	**DELLORSS**	LORDLESS	**DELOPRST**	DROPLETS
DEIPPRST	STRIPPED	**DELLORST**	DROLLEST	**DELOPRSU**	POULDERS
DEIPPTTU	TITUPPED		STROLLED		POULDRES
DEIPRRTU	IRRUPTED	**DELLOSTY**	OLDSTYLE	**DELOPSTU**	POSTLUDE
	PUTRIDER	**DELLOSVW**	LOWVELDS	**DELORSST**	OLDSTERS
DEIPRSSU	DISPURSE	**DELLOTUW**	OUTDWELL		STRODLES
	SUSPIRED	**DELLRSWY**	DRYWELLS	**DELORSSW**	WORDLESS
DEIPRSTU	DISPUTER	**DELMNOOV**	NOVELDOM	**DELORSTT**	DOTTRELS
	STUPIDER	**DELMNORY**	MODERNLY	**DELORSUY**	DELUSORY
DEIPRSTZ	SPRITZED	**DELMNOSU**	UNSELDOM	**DELOSSUU**	SEDULOUS
DEIPSSTU	DISPUTES	**DELMNOTW**	MELTDOWN	**DELOSTTT**	DOTTLEST
	PUDSIEST	**DELMNPUU**	PENDULUM	**DELOSTTY**	SOTTEDLY
DEIPTTTU	TITTUPED		UNPLUMED	**DELOSTUU**	OUTDUELS
DEIQRRSU	SQUIRRED	**DELMOOSW**	ELMWOODS	**DELOSTUW**	WOULDEST
DEIQRSTU	SQUIRTED	**DELMOPRS**	PREMOLDS	**DELOTTUW**	OUTDWELT
DEIRRSST	STRIDERS	**DELMORSS**	SMOLDERS	**DELOTUVY**	DEVOUTLY
DEIRRSTU	STURDIER	**DELMORSU**	MOULDERS	**DELPSTUU**	PUSTULED
DEIRSSST	DISSERTS		REMOULDS	**DELRSSTU**	STRUDELS
	DISTRESS		SMOULDER	**DELSSSSU**	SUDSLESS
DEIRSSTU	DIESTRUS	**DELMOSTY**	MODESTLY	**DELSSSTU**	DUSTLESS
	DRUSIEST	**DELMRTUU**	MULTURED	**DEMMNOOO**	MONOMODE
	STUDIERS	**DELMTTUU**	TUMULTED	**DEMMNOOS**	DOOMSMEN
	STURDIES	**DELNOOSU**	NODULOSE	**DEMMNOSU**	SUMMONED
DEIRSSUY	DYSURIES		UNLOOSED	**DEMMNSUU**	UNSUMMED
DEIRSTTU	DETRITUS	**DELNOOSZ**	SNOOZLED	**DEMMRRSU**	DRUMMERS
DEIRSTUX	DRUXIEST	**DELNOOWY**	WOODENLY	**DEMMRRUU**	MURMURED
DEIRSUVV	SURVIVED	**DELNOPPU**	UNLOPPED	**DEMMRSTU**	STRUMMED
DEISSSTU	SUDSIEST	**DELNOPRS**	SPLENDOR	**DEMMNOSU**	SOUNDMEN
DEISSTTU	DUSTIEST	**DELNOPUW**	UNPLOWED	**DEMNOOOP**	MONOPODE
DEISTTTU	DUETTIST	**DELNORSU**	LOUNDERS	**DEMNOOPT**	TOMPONED
DEJLOOOR	JORDELOO		NOURSLED	**DEMNOORS**	DOORSMEN
DEJOOPPY	POPJOYED		ROUNDELS	**DEMNOORU**	UNMOORED
DEKKLNOY	KLONDYKE		ROUNDLES	**DEMNOOSS**	ENDOSMOS
DEKKNSTU	STUKKEND		UNSOLDER	**DEMNOOSW**	WOODSMEN
DEKKSSTT	TSKTSKED	**DELNORTU**	ROUNDLET	**DEMNORST**	MORDENTS
DEKLNOOU	UNLOOKED	**DELNORVY**	YONDERLY	**DEMNORSW**	SWORDMEN
DEKLOOPU	UPLOOKED	**DELNOSSU**	LOUDNESS	**DEMNORSY**	SYNDROME
DEKLRSSU	SKUDLERS	**DELNOSSW**	DOWNLESS	**DEMNORUW**	UNWORMED
DEKLSTTU	SKUTTLED	**DELNOSTW**	LETDOWNS	**DEMNOSTU**	DEMOUNTS
DEKMNOSU	UNSMOKED	**DELNOSUU**	UNDULOSE		MUDSTONE
DEKMPRSU	SKRUMPED		UNSOULED	**DEMOOPPS**	POPEDOMS
DEKNNOSS	NONSKEDS	**DELNOSUV**	UNSOLVED	**DEMOOPRR**	PRODROME
DEKNORUW	UNWORKED	**DELNOTWY**	WONTEDLY	**DEMOOPRS**	PREDOOMS
DEKNRSTU	DRUNKEST	**DELNPRSU**	PLUNDERS	**DEMOOPRT**	PROMOTED
DEKNRSUY	UNDERSKY	**DELNRRTU**	TRUNDLER	**DEMOORST**	DOOMSTER
DEKNSSSU	DUSKNESS	**DELNRSTU**	RUNDLETS	**DEMOORSU**	DORMOUSE
DEKOOPRV	PROVOKED		TRUNDLES	**DEMOORTY**	ODOMETRY
DEKOOTWW	KOWTOWED	**DELNSUZZ**	SNUZZLED	**DEMOOSTU**	OUTMODES
DEKOPSST	DESKTOPS	**DELOOORW**	WOODLORE	**DEMOOTUV**	OUTMOVED
DEKORSWY	KEYWORDS	**DELOOPPS**	PLEOPODS	**DEMOPPRT**	PROMPTED
DEKPRSSU	PREDUSKS	**DELOORRV**	OVERLORD	**DEMOPSSU**	POSSUMED
DELLLOOP	LOLLOPED	**DELOORRW**	WORDLORE	**DEMORRUU**	RUMOURED
DELLMOOS	MODELLOS	**DELOORSS**	DOORLESS	**DEMORTUY**	UDOMETRY

DEMPRSTU	DUMPSTER	DENRSSSU	SUNDRESS	DFGIILRY	FRIGIDLY
DENNNSUU	UNSUNNED	DENRSTTU	STRUNTED	DFGIINNS	FINDINGS
DENNOOOZ	ENDOZOON	DENRSTUU	UNRUSTED	DFGIINRT	DRIFTING
DENNOOWZ	DOWNZONE	DENSSTTU	STUDENTS	DFGILNNO	FONDLING
DENNORST	TENDRONS	DENSTTUY	STUDENTY	DFGILNOO	FLOODING
DENNORSU	ENROUNDS	DENSTUVY	DUVETYNS	DFGILNOS	FOLDINGS
DENNOSTU	UNSTONED	DEOOORSW	ROSEWOOD	DFGINNOU	FONDUING
DENNOSTY	SYNDETON	DEOOOSWW	WOODWOSE		FOUNDING
DENNOTUW	UNWONTED	DEOOPPRS	PROPOSED	DFGINNSU	FUNDINGS
DENNPRUU	UNPRUNED	DEOOPPRT	PTEROPOD	DFGINOOR	FORDOING
DENNRRUU	UNDERRUN	DEOOPRRV	PROVEDOR	DFGINOSU	FUNGOIDS
DENNRTUU	UNTURNED	DEOOPRST	DOORSTEP	DFGMOOSY	FOGYDOMS
DENNRTUY	UNTRENDY		TORPEDOS	DFHIIMUY	HUMIDIFY
DENOOORT	OREODONT	DEOOPRTU	UPROOTED	DFHILSSU	DISHFULS
DENOOOTW	WOODNOTE	DEOOPWWW	POWWOWED	DFHIMRSU	DRUMFISH
	WOODTONE	DEOORRST	REDROOTS	DFHINOOT	HINDFOOT
DENOOOVW	OVENWOOD	DEOORRSW	SORROWED	DFHINOPS	FISHPOND
DENOOPPR	PROPONED	DEOORRVW	OVERWORD	DFHISSTU	STUDFISH
DENOOPRS	PRODNOSE	DEOORRWW	OWREWORD	DFHLOOOT	FOOTHOLD
DENOOPSY	POYSONED	DEOORSTU	OUTDOERS	DFHNOOUX	FOXHOUND
DENOORRS	ENDORSOR	DEOORTUV	OUTDROVE	DFIIINVY	DIVINIFY
DENOORTU	UNROOTED	DEOORTUW	OUTROWED	DFIILMTU	MULTIFID
DENOORTX	NEXTDOOR	DEOOTTUV	OUTVOTED	DFIILOSY	SOLIDIFY
DENOOSSW	WOODNESS	DEOPPRRS	DROPPERS	DFIILTUY	FLUIDITY
DENOOSTU	DUOTONES	DEOPPRST	STROPPED	DFIINPRT	DRIFTPIN
DENOPPRS	PROPENDS	DEOPPRSU	PURPOSED	DFIKNOOS	SKINFOOD
DENOPRSS	RESPONDS	DEOPPSSU	SUPPOSED	DFILLOOT	FLOODLIT
DENOPRST	PORTENDS	DEOPRRTU	PROTRUDE	DFILLORY	FLORIDLY
	PROTENDS	DEOPRSTU	POSTURED	DFILLOWW	WILDFOWL
DENOPRSU	POUNDERS		PROUDEST	DFILMMOS	FILMDOMS
DENOPRSV	PROVENDS		SPROUTED	DFILNNOU	NONFLUID
DENOPRUV	UNPROVED	DEOPRSUU	POURSUED	DFILNOPS	PINFOLDS
DENOPSTU	OUTSPEND		UPROUSED	DFILORSU	FLUORIDS
	UNPOSTED	DEOPSSTU	UPTOSSED	DFIMOOOR	IODOFORM
DENOPSTW	STEWPOND	DEORRSST	RODSTERS	DFIMOOSS	FOODISMS
DENOPSUX	EXPOUNDS	DEORRSSW	SWORDERS	DFIMORSS	DISFORMS
DENOPTTU	UNPOTTED	DEORRTTU	TORTURED	DFINOSTU	OUTFINDS
DENOQTUU	UNQUOTED	DEORSSTU	OUTDRESS	DFINRSUW	WINDSURF
DENORRSU	RONDURES	DEORSSTW	WORSTEDS	DFIOOPRS	DISPROOF
	ROUNDERS	DEORSSTY	DESTROYS	DFKMMOPU	DUMMKOPF
	UNORDERS	DEORSSUV	OVERSUDS	DFLMOSUW	MUDFLOWS
DENORRSW	DROWNERS	DEORSTTU	STROUTED	DFLNOOWW	DOWNFLOW
DENORRTU	ROTUNDER	DEORSTUU	OUTDURES	DFLOORUU	ODOURFUL
DENORRUU	ROUNDURE	DEORSTUV	OVERDUST	DFLOOSTU	FOLDOUTS
DENORSSU	DOURNESS	DEORSTUX	DEXTROUS	DFLOOSTW	TWOFOLDS
	RESOUNDS	DEOSSSYY	ODYSSEYS	DFLOPRUU	PROUDFUL
	SOUNDERS	DEOSSTTU	TESTUDOS	DFNOOPRU	PROFOUND
DENORSTU	ROUNDEST	DEPPSSYY	DYSPEPSY	DFNOORSU	FRONDOUS
	TONSURED	DEPRRTUU	RUPTURED	DFNOOTUU	OUTFOUND
	UNSORTED	DEQRSUUY	SURQUEDY	DFOOOORW	WOODROOF
DENORSTY	DRYSTONE	DERSTTTU	STRUTTED	DFOOOSTW	SOFTWOOD
DENORSUU	UNROUSED	DFFGINSU	DUFFINGS	DGGIIINS	DIGGINGS
	UNSOURED	DFFIILUY	FLUIDIFY	DGGIINOS	DOGGINGS
DENORSUW	WOUNDERS	DFFIIMRS	MIDRIFFS	DGGIINRU	DRUGGING
DENORTTU	UNROTTED	DFFIIRST	TRIFFIDS		GRUDGING
DENORTUW	UNDERTOW	DFFIIRTY	TRIFFIDY	DGGHIINT	DIGHTING
DENOSSTU	SOUNDEST	DFFIORSU	DIFFUSOR	DGGIILNR	GIRDLING
DENOSTUW	UNSTOWED	DFFLOORU	FOURFOLD		RIDGLING
DENOTUUV	UNDEVOUT	DFFOORUW	WOODRUFF	DGGIILNS	GILDINGS
DENPRSTU	UPTRENDS	DFFOSSTU	DUSTOFFS		GLIDINGS
DENPRSUU	UNPURSED	DFGGHIOT	DOGFIGHT	DGGIINNO	DINGOING
DENPRTUU	UPTURNED	DFGGIINR	FRIDGING	DGGIINNR	GRINDING
DENPSSSU	SUSPENDS	DFGHILOS	GOLDFISH	DGGIINNW	WINGDING
DENRRTUU	NURTURED	DFGIIIRY	RIGIDIFY	DGGIINRS	GIRDINGS

	RIDGINGS	DGIILNNW	WINDLING	DGILOOTW	GILTWOOD
DGGIINSU	GUIDINGS	DGIILNNY	INDIGNLY	DGILOPSU	SOLPUGID
DGGIKLNU	KLUDGING	DGIILNOR	DROILING	DGILOSTY	STODGILY
DGGILNOP	PLODGING	DGIILNOS	DISLOIGN	DGILRTUY	TURGIDLY
DGGILNOS	GODLINGS	DGIILNPS	DISPLING	DGIMMNRU	DRUMMING
	LODGINGS	DGIILNSS	SLIDINGS	DGIMMNUY	DUMMYING
DGGILNSU	SLUDGING	DGIILNSW	WILDINGS	DGIMNNOU	MOUNDING
DGGIMNSU	SMUDGING	DGIILNTU	DILUTING	DGIMNOOY	MOODYING
DGGINNOO	NOODGING	DGIIMNNS	MINDINGS	DGIMNPSU	DUMPINGS
DGGINNSU	SNUDGING	DGIIMNOS	MISDOING	DGIMOPSY	GIPSYDOM
DGGINOST	STODGING	DGIIMNNO	GONIDIUM	DGINNNSU	DUNNINGS
DGGINRTU	TRUDGING	DGIIMNSS	SMIDGINS	DGINNOOS	SNOODING
DGGIRSTU	DRUGGIST	DGIIMOSS	SIGMOIDS	DGINNOPU	POUNDING
DGHHOOOS	HOGHOODS	DGIIMPUY	PYGIDIUM	DGINNOPW	POWNDING
DGHIILNS	HIDLINGS	DGIINNOP	POINDING	DGINNORU	INGROUND
	HILDINGS	DGIINNOR	NONRIGID		ROUNDING
DGHIIMNT	MIDNIGHT	DGIINNOW	INDOWING	DGINNORW	DROWNING
DGHIIMST	MISDIGHT	DGIINNRW	WINDRING		ROWNDING
DGHIINNW	HINDWING	DGIINNSS	SINDINGS	DGINNOSU	SOUNDING
DGHIINPS	SPHINGID	DGIINNSW	WINDINGS		UNDOINGS
DGHIINRT	THIRDING	DGIINORR	GRIDIRON	DGINNOSW	SOWNDING
DGHIINSS	DISHINGS	DGIINORS	DORISING	DGINNOUW	WOUNDING
	SHINDIGS	DGIINORT	DIGITRON	DGINNSSY	SYNDINGS
DGHIISST	DISSIGHT	DGIINORZ	DORIZING	DGINNSUW	WINDGUNS
DGHIKNOO	KINGHOOD	DGIINOSV	VOIDINGS	DGINOOPR	DROOPING
DGHILLNU	DUNGHILL	DGIINOSW	WINDIGOS	DGINOOPS	GOSPODIN
DGHILNNO	HONDLING	DGIINOSX	DIGOXINS		SPONGOID
DGHILNOS	HOLDINGS	DGIINOTT	DITTOING	DGINOOTU	OUTDOING
DGHILNRU	HURDLING	DGIINOWW	WIDOWING	DGINOPPR	DROPPING
DGHILNSY	HYLDINGS	DGIINPPR	DRIPPING	DGINOPPS	DOPPINGS
DGHILOOR	GIRLHOOD	DGIINPPS	DIPPINGS	DGINORSV	DROVINGS
DGHILPSY	DIGLYPHS	DGIINPUV	UPDIVING	DGINORSW	DROWSING
DGHINNOU	HOUNDING	DGIINRST	STRIDING		SWORDING
DGHINNSU	DUNSHING	DGIINRSV	DRIVINGS		WORDINGS
DGHINNUZ	NUDZHING	DGIINRTY	DIRTYING	DGINOSSW	DISGOWNS
DGHINOSW	SHOWDING	DGIINSSU	DISUSING	DGINOSUY	DIGYNOUS
DGHINOWY	HOWDYING	DGIINTTY	DITTYING	DGINPRUY	UPDRYING
DGHINSTU	HINDGUTS	DGIINVVY	DIVVYING	DGINSSTU	DUSTINGS
	UNDIGHTS	DGIINYZZ	DIZZYING	DGINSTUY	STUDYING
DGHIOORS	DROOGISH	DGIKLOOY	KIDOLOGY	DGIOOPRU	GROUPOID
DGHIOPSS	DOGSHIPS	DGIKMNOS	KINGDOMS	DGIOPRRY	PORRIDGY
	GODSHIPS	DGIKNOOR	DROOKING	DGIOSUYZ	DIZYGOUS
DGHNOTUU	DOUGHNUT	DGIKNOOW	KINGWOOD	DGISSSTU	DISGUSTS
DGHOOOTT	DOGTOOTH	DGIKNORU	DROUKING	DGLNORSU	GOLDURNS
DGHORRUY	ROUGHDRY	DGIKNOSS	DOGSKINS	DGLOOOPY	PODOLOGY
DGHORSTU	DROUGHTS	DGILLNOR	DROLLING	DGLOOOSW	LOGWOODS
DGHORTUY	DROUGHTY		LORDLING	DGLOOOSY	DOSOLOGY
DGIIIMRS	DIRIGISM	DGILLNOY	DOLLYING	DGLOOOXY	DOXOLOGY
DGIIINNT	INDITING	DGILLOOW	GOODWILL	DGLOOSST	GODSLOTS
DGIIINNV	DIVINING	DGILMNOS	MOLDINGS	DGMNNOUU	MUNDUNGO
DGIIINOS	IODISING	DGILMNOU	MOULDING	DGMOOSUW	GUMWOODS
DGIIINOZ	IODIZING	DGILMNPU	DUMPLING	DGMOPRSU	GUMDROPS
DGIIIRTY	RIGIDITY	DGILMSUY	SMUDGILY	DGMOPSYY	GYPSYDOM
DGIIKLNN	KINDLING	DGILNNOO	NOODLING	DGMORSUU	GURUDOMS
DGIIKLNS	KIDLINGS	DGILNNOU	LOUNDING	DGNNORUU	UNGROUND
DGIIKNNR	DRINKING	DGILNNOW	LOWNDING	DGNOOOPS	GONOPODS
DGIILLNR	DRILLING	DGILNNRU	NURDLING	DGNOOORS	GODROONS
DGIILLNS	DILLINGS	DGILNOOR	DROOLING	DGNOOSTW	DOGTOWNS
DGIILLNU	ILLUDING	DGILNOOW	WOOLDING	DGNOOTYZ	ZYGODONT
DGIILLNW	WILDLING	DGILNORS	GIRLONDS	DGOORSTT	DOGTROTS
DGIILLOU	LIGULOID		LORDINGS	DGOPRRSU	PRODRUGS
DGIILMNP	DIMPLING	DGILNORY	YOLDRING	DGOPRSTU	POSTDRUG
DGIILNNN	DINNLING	DGILNOTY	DOTINGLY	DHHILOTW	WITHHOLD
DGIILNNP	PINDLING	DGILNPUY	DUPLYING	DHHIOPPS	PHOSPHID

DHIIIMNS	DIMINISH	**DHLMOOSU**	HOODLUMS	**DIILOPSS**	DIPLOSIS
	MINIDISH	**DHLOOORT**	ROOTHOLD	**DIILOPSY**	YPSILOID
DHIIINST	HISTIDIN	**DHLOORSY**	HYDROSOL	**DIILOQSU**	SOLIQUID
DHIIIOST	HISTIOID	**DHLOOSTU**	HOLDOUTS	**DIILORSU**	SILUROID
	IDIOTISH	**DHLORXYY**	HYDROXYL	**DIILORTU**	UTILIDOR
DHIILOSS	SOLIDISH	**DHLOSSTU**	SHOULDST	**DIILOSST**	IDOLISTS
DHIIMNOO	HOMINOID	**DHMMRSUU**	HUMDRUMS		SOLIDIST
DHIIMNOS	HOMINIDS	**DHMNOOOT**	HOMODONT	**DIILOSTY**	SOLIDITY
DHIIMOST	ISTHMOID	**DHMOOPPU**	PUMPHOOD	**DIILPPRY**	DRIPPILY
DHIIMPSS	MIDSHIPS	**DHMORTUY**	DRYMOUTH	**DIILQSUU**	LIQUIDUS
DHIIMTUY	HUMIDITY	**DHNNOOSU**	NUNHOODS	**DIILRSSU**	SILURIDS
DHIINPSW	WINDSHIP	**DHNOOOSS**	SONHOODS	**DIILSSTY**	IDYLISTS
DHIINRSU	HIRUDINS	**DHNOOSWW**	SHOWDOWN	**DIIMMNOU**	DOMINIUM
DHIINTWW	WITHWIND	**DHNOPSUW**	PUSHDOWN	**DIIMMNOO**	DOMINION
DHIIOPRU	OPHIURID	**DHNORSUU**	UNSHROUD	**DIIMNNSU**	UNDINISM
DHIIOPSX	XIPHOIDS	**DHNORSUW**	DOWNRUSH	**DIIMNOPT**	MIDPOINT
DHIIORSS	HIDROSIS	**DHNOSTUW**	SHUTDOWN	**DIIMNORS**	MIDIRONS
DHIIORSZ	RHIZOIDS	**DHOOOPRT**	ORTHOPOD	**DIIMNSUU**	INDUSIUM
DHIIPSST	DIPSHITS	**DHOOORTX**	ORTHODOX	**DIIMOPRS**	PRISMOID
DHIKNOOW	HOODWINK	**DHOOPRST**	DROPSHOT	**DIIMORSS**	DIORISMS
DHIKORSY	HYDROSKI	**DHOOPRSU**	UPHOORDS	**DIIMPUXY**	PYXIDIUM
DHILLNOW	DOWNHILL	**DHOORSUW**	WOODRUSH	**DIIMRUUV**	DUUMVIRI
DHILLOPY	PHYLLOID	**DHOPRSSU**	PUSHRODS	**DIIMTTUY**	TUMIDITY
DHILLORS	DROLLISH	**DHOPRSYY**	HYDROPSY	**DIINNOSU**	DISUNION
DHILLOST	TOLLDISH	**DIIIKMNS**	MINIDISK	**DIINOOPS**	IODOPSIN
DHILLPSY	PHYLLIDS	**DIIILLQU**	ILLIQUID	**DIINOOPU**	DOUPIONI
DHILMOPY	LYMPHOID	**DIIILTVY**	LIVIDITY	**DIINOQSU**	QUINOIDS
DHILMOSY	MODISHLY	**DIIIMOST**	IDIOTISM	**DIINOSSU**	SINUSOID
DHILNOPS	DOLPHINS	**DIIIMRSU**	IRIDIUMS	**DIINSTUY**	DISUNITY
DHILOPRS	LORDSHIP	**DIIIMTTY**	TIMIDITY	**DIIOPRTY**	PITYROID
DHILOPSS	SLIPSHOD	**DIIINOSV**	DIVISION	**DIIORSST**	SISTROID
DHILORRY	HORRIDLY	**DIIINTVY**	DIVINITY	**DIIORSSV**	DIVISORS
DHILPSSU	LUDSHIPS	**DIIIPRST**	DISPIRIT	**DIIORSTX**	TRIOXIDS
	SULPHIDS	**DIIIRTVY**	VIRIDITY	**DIIORSUV**	VIRUSOID
DHILPSSY	SYLPHIDS	**DIIITVVY**	VIVIDITY	**DIIPSTTY**	TIDYTIPS
DHIMMNOT	MIDMONTH	**DIIJNOSS**	DISJOINS	**DIJOSSTU**	JUDOISTS
DHIMNOST	HINDMOST	**DIIJNOST**	DISJOINT	**DIKLMOOW**	MILKWOOD
DHIMNOSU	UNMODISH	**DIIKKNSS**	KIDSKINS	**DIKLNNOW**	DOWNLINK
DHIMOOOY	OMOHYOID	**DIIKLLNY**	KINDLILY	**DIKLNNUY**	UNKINDLY
DHIMOOSS	MISSHOOD	**DIIKLNSS**	DISLINKS	**DIKLNORS**	LORDKINS
DHIMOPPY	HIPPYDOM	**DIIKNOST**	DOITKINS	**DIKLRUUU**	DURUKULI
DHIMOPRS	DIMORPHS	**DIILLMNR**	MILLRIND	**DIKNOOSW**	INKWOODS
DHIMORSU	HUMIDORS	**DIILLMNW**	WINDMILL		WOODSKIN
	RHODIUMS	**DIILLMOU**	LIMULOID	**DIKNORSV**	DVORNIKS
DHINNOTW	THINDOWN	**DIILLMPY**	LIMPIDLY	**DIKNORTU**	OUTDRINK
DHINOOPR	PHORONID	**DIILLQUY**	LIQUIDLY	**DIKOOSTU**	DITOKOUS
DHINOORS	DISHONOR	**DIILLSST**	DISTILLS	**DILLMNOP**	MILLPOND
DHINOPSS	DONSHIPS	**DIILLSTY**	IDYLLIST	**DILLMSSU**	MUDSILLS
DHINORSS	DISHORNS	**DIILMNSS**	DISLIMNS	**DILLOORS**	DOORSILL
DHINORSU	ROUNDISH	**DIILMOPP**	POMPILID	**DILLOSTY**	STOLIDLY
DHINOTUW	WHODUNIT	**DIILMOSS**	IDOLISMS	**DILLPSSY**	PSYLLIDS
DHINTUWY	WHYDUNIT		SOLIDISM	**DILMNOOS**	SMILODON
DHIOOOPR	IODOPHOR	**DIILMOTY**	MYTILOID	**DILMNORW**	LINDWORM
DHIOOPRZ	RHIZOPOD	**DIILMSST**	MIDLISTS	**DILMNOSW**	SLIMDOWN
DHIOPRSU	PROUDISH	**DIILMUUV**	DILUVIUM	**DILMNRSU**	DRUMLINS
DHIOPSTY	TYPHOIDS	**DIILNNSU**	INDULINS	**DILMOOSU**	MODIOLUS
DHIORSTY	THYROIDS	**DIILNOST**	TOLIDINS	**DILMOSSU**	SOLIDUMS
	THYRSOID	**DIILNOTU**	DILUTION	**DILMOSSY**	ODYLISMS
DHIORSWY	ROWDYISH		TOLUIDIN	**DILNNOOS**	NONSOLID
DHIPRSSY	SYRPHIDS	**DIILNOUV**	DILUVION	**DILNOPST**	DIPLONTS
DHJOPRSU	JODHPURS	**DIILNOXY**	XYLOIDIN	**DILNOPSU**	LISPOUND
DHKMNOOO	MONKHOOD	**DIILNSXY**	XYLIDINS	**DILNOQSU**	QUODLINS
DHKMOOSU	MUDHOOKS	**DIILNTUY**	UNTIDILY	**DILNOSXY**	INDOXYLS
DHLLOPYY	PHYLLODY	**DIILOPRT**	TRIPLOID	**DILNOUWY**	WOUNDILY

DILNPSSU	LISPUNDS
DILNRSUY	SUNDRILY
DILOOPPY	POLYPOID
DILOOPRY	DROOPILY
DILOORSS	LORDOSIS
DILOOSUY	ODIOUSLY
DILOOTUV	VOLUTOID
DILOPRTY	TORPIDLY
DILORRTY	TORRIDLY
DILORSTU	DILUTORS
DILORSWY	DROWSILY
DILOSSTY	STYLOIDS
DILPRTUY	PUTRIDLY
DILPSTUY	STUPIDLY
DILRSTUY	STURDILY
DIMMNORY	MYRMIDON
DIMMOOSU	ISODOMUM
DIMMOSST	MIDMOSTS
DIMNNOOS	MIDNOONS
DIMNNOSS	DONNISMS
DIMNNOST	DINMONTS
DIMNOOOS	ISODOMON
DIMNOOST	MONODIST
DIMNOPSU	IMPOUNDS
DIMNOSSU	MISSOUND
DIMNOSTU	DISMOUNT
DIMNOSTW	MIDTOWNS
DIMNOSUW	UNWISDOM
DIMNOSWX	MIXDOWNS
DIMOOPRR	PRODROMI
DIMOOPRY	MYRIOPOD
DIMOORTW	MODIWORT
DIMOOSST	SODOMIST
DIMOPRSU	MISPROUD
DIMOPSSU	SPODIUMS
DIMORSSW	MISWORDS
DIMORSTY	MIDSTORY
DIMORSWY	ROWDYISM
DIMOSTUY	DUMOSITY
DIMRSTUU	TRIDUUMS
DIMRSUUV	DUUMVIRS
DINNOORS	RONDINOS
DINNOOST	TONDINOS
DINNOPSW	DOWNSPIN
	PINDOWNS
DINOOORW	IRONWOOD
DINOOPSU	DIPNOOUS
DINOORRS	INDORSOR
DINOORST	TORDIONS
DINOORSU	NIDOROUS
DINOOSST	ISODONTS
DINOOSTT	ODONTIST
DINOOSTY	NODOSITY
DINOPRTY	DRYPOINT
DINORSTU	STURNOID
	TURDIONS
DINORSWH	WINDROWS
DINOSTUW	OUTWINDS
DINPRTUY	PUNDITRY
DINRSTUY	INDUSTRY
DIOOPRRT	PRODITOR
DIOOPRRV	PROVIDOR
DIOOPRTX	PROTOXID
DIOORSST	DISROOTS

DIOORSTT	RIDOTTOS
DIOPRSST	DISPORTS
DIOPSSST	DISPOSTS
DIORRSST	STRIDORS
DIORSSTT	DISTORTS
DIOSSTUU	STUDIOUS
DIPRSSTU	DISRUPTS
DIRSSTTU	DISTRUST
DKLNOOOW	LOOKDOWN
DKMNOOOR	KOMONDOR
DKNORTUU	OUTDRUNK
DKOOOPRW	PORKWOOD
DKOOORWW	WOODWORK
DKORSTUW	STUDWORK
DLLMORRU	DRUMROLL
DLLMORSU	SLUMLORD
DLLNORUY	UNLORDLY
DLMNOOSW	SNOWMOLD
DLMNOOSY	MYLODONS
DLMNOOTY	MYLODONT
DLMNOSUU	UNMOULDS
DLMORSUY	SMOULDRY
DLNOOPRU	POULDRON
DLNOOSUU	NODULOUS
DLNOOSWW	LOWDOWNS
	SLOWDOWN
DLNOPRSU	PULDRONS
DLNOPSSY	SPONDYLS
DLNORTUY	ROTUNDLY
DLNOSUUU	UNDULOUS
DLOOOORS	DOLOROSO
DLOOOPSS	SPODOSOL
DLOOORSU	DOLOROUS
DLOOOSTW	WOODLOTS
DLOOPPSY	POLYPODS
DLOOPPUW	PULPWOOD
DLOOPPYY	POLYPODY
DLOOPSTU	OUTPLODS
DLOOPSTY	TYLOPODS
DLOOPSWY	PLYWOODS
DMMOORTO	MOTORDOM
DMMOORSU	MUDROOMS
DMNNOOOT	MONODONT
DMNOOOPS	MONOPODS
DMNOOOPY	MONOPODY
DMNOOSTU	MOONDUST
DMNOOSTW	DOWNMOST
	TOWMONDS
DMOOOQSU	QUOMODOS
DMOOORWW	WOODWORM
	WORMWOOD
DMOPPPUU	PUPPODUM
DMOPPPUY	PUPPYDOM
DMORSTUW	MUDWORTS
DMPPPUUY	MUDPUPPY
DNNOOOWY	NONWOODY
DNNOOPRU	PUNDONOR
DNNOORSW	NONWORDS
DNNOOTWW	DOWNTOWN
DNNORRUU	RUNROUND
DNNORSUU	UNROUNDS
DNNORSUW	RUNDOWNS
DNNORTUW	DOWNTURN
	TURNDOWN

DNNOSSUW	SUNDOWNS
DNNRSTUU	TURNDUNS
DNOOPPRU	PROPOUND
DNOOPRSW	SNOWDROP
DNOOPRUW	DOWNPOUR
DNOOPSUY	DUOPSONY
DNOORSUW	WONDROUS
DNOOSTUW	NUTWOODS
DNOOSTWW	STOWDOWN
DNOOSUUV	VOUDOUNS
DNOOTUUW	OUTWOUND
DNOPRSSU	SUNDROPS
DNOPRSUU	ROUNDUPS
DNOPSTUW	PUTDOWNS
DNORRSUU	SURROUND
DNORSSUY	UNDROSSY
DOOOPPRT	PROTOPOD
DOOOPRST	DOORPOST
	DOORSTOP
DOOORSTU	OUTDOORS
DOOORSUW	SOURWOOD
DOOOSTTU	OUTSTOOD
DOOPRRTW	DROPWORT
DOOPRSTU	DROPOUTS
	OUTDROPS
DOOPRSTW	STOPWORD
DOOPSWWY	POWSOWDY
DOORRSTU	DORTOURS
DOORRSUU	ORDUROUS
DOORSSUU	SUDOROUS
DOSTTUUY	OUTSTUDY
EEEEFNRZ	ENFREEZE
EEEEFRRS	REFEREES
EEEEFRRZ	REFREEZE
EEEEGGRR	GREEGREE
EEEEGMRR	REEMERGE
EEEEGQSU	SQUEEGEE
EEEEGSSX	EXEGESES
EEEEGSTX	EXEGETES
EEEEHTTY	EYETEETH
EEEELLPX	EXPELLEE
EEEELLVY	EYELEVEL
EEEELMST	TELESEME
EEEELNSV	SLEEVEEN
EEEENRRV	VENEERER
EEEEPPRR	REPEREPE
EEEEPPSW	PEESWEEP
EEEEPRRV	REPREEVE
EEEEPTTW	PEETWEET
EEEFFFOS	FEOFFEES
EEEFFLOR	FOREFEEL
EEEFFLTY	EFFETELY
EEEFFNRT	EFFERENT
EEEFFORS	OFFEREES
EEEFFORT	FOREFEET
EEEFFOTU	ETOUFFEE
EEEFFRVW	FEVERFEW
EEEFGMRR	GERMFREE
EEEFGRSU	REFUGEES
EEEFHRSS	SHEREEFS
EEEFIPRR	REPRIEFE
EEEFIPST	TEPEFIES
EEEFIRRT	FREETIER
EEEFIRST	REEFIEST

EEEFLRRS	FLEERERS	EEEGNRST	GREENEST	EEEIKLRS	SKEELIER
EEEFLRSX	REFLEXES	EEEGNRSU	RENEGUES		SLEEKIER
EEEFLSST	FEETLESS	EEEGNRSV	REVENGES	EEEIKLRT	TREELIKE
EEEFLSTT	FLEETEST	EEEGNSTT	GENETTES	EEEIKLSW	WEEKLIES
EEEFNNPY	PENNYFEE	EEEGOPRT	PROTEGEE	EEEIKNSS	KNEESIES
EEEFNORS	FORESEEN	EEEGRRST	GREETERS	EEEIKNTX	EKTEXINE
EEEFNRRT	REFERENT		REGREETS	EEEIKRRS	SKEERIER
EEEFNRSS	FREENESS	EEEGRSSS	EGRESSES	EEEIKRST	REEKIEST
EEEFNRSV	ENFEVERS	EEEGRSUX	EXERGUES	EEEILLRV	REVEILLE
EEEFNRTT	ENFETTER	EEEHHSSW	WHEESHES	EEEILMRS	SEEMLIER
EEEFNRUZ	UNFREEZE	EEEHILRW	EREWHILE	EEEILNNO	EOLIENNE
EEEFORRS	FORESEER		WHEELIER	EEEILNPR	PELERINE
EEEFORRV	OVERFREE	EEEHILSW	WHEELIES	EEEILNRY	EYELINER
EEEFORSS	FORESEES	EEEHINRS	SHEENIER	EEEILNST	ENLISTEE
EEEFRRRR	REFERRER	EEEHINSS	SHEENIES		SELENITE
EEEFRRRT	FERRETER	EEEHINSY	EYESHINE	EEEILNSU	UNSEELIE
EEEFRRSZ	FREEZERS	EEEHIPRS	SHEEPIER	EEEILPRS	SLEEPIER
EEEFRRTT	FETTERER	EEEHIRSS	HERESIES	EEEILRRV	RELIEVER
EEEGGILN	NEGLIGEE	EEEHIRST	ETHERISE	EEEILRST	LEERIEST
EEEGGIRS	EGGERIES		SHEETIER		SLEETIER
EEEGHINT	EIGHTEEN	EEEHIRSX	HEXEREIS		STEELIER
EEEGHLRS	SHEERLEG	EEEHIRTZ	ETHERIZE	EEEILRSV	RELIEVES
EEEGHMNU	HEGUMENE	EEEHIRWZ	WHEEZIER	EEEILRSZ	SLEEZIER
EEEGHNSW	WHEENGES	EEEHKLNO	KNEEHOLE	EEEILRVY	LIVEYERE
EEEGIKST	GEEKIEST	EEEHLLSS	HEELLESS	EEEILSST	SEELIEST
EEEGILMN	LIEGEMEN	EEEHLMNW	WHEELMEN		STEELIES
EEEGILNS	GLEENIES	EEEHLMPT	HELPMEET	EEEILSSW	ELSEWISE
EEEGILNV	ENVEIGLE	EEEHLNSW	ENWHEELS	EEEILSTV	TELEVISE
	LEVEEING	EEEHLNTV	ELEVENTH	EEEILTVW	TELEVIEW
EEEGILPS	ESPIEGLE	EEEHLNTY	ETHYLENE	EEEIMNRU	MEUNIERE
EEEGILRT	GLEETIER	EEEHLNXY	HEXYLENE	EEEIMNST	EMETINES
EEEGILSS	ELEGISES	EEEHLOPP	PEEPHOLE	EEEIMPRR	PREMIERE
EEEGILSZ	ELEGIZES	EEEHLOPW	WEEPHOLE	EEEIMPRS	EMPERIES
EEEGIMNX	EXEEMING	EEEHLOSY	EYEHOLES		EMPERISE
EEEGIMTV	VEGEMITE	EEEHLPSW	WHEEPLES		EPIMERES
EEEGINNR	ENGINEER	EEEHLRSW	WHEELERS		PREEMIES
EEEGINRR	GREENIER	EEEHLSWZ	WHEEZLES	EEEIMPRZ	EMPERIZE
EEEGINRS	ENERGIES	EEEHMMSS	EMMESHES	EEEIMRRS	MISERERE
	ENERGISE	EEEHMNNT	MENTHENE	EEEIMRST	EREMITES
	GREENIES	EEEHMNPS	SHEEPMEN	EEEIMRTT	REMITTEE
	RESEEING	EEEHMNSS	ENMESHES	EEEINNNT	NINETEEN
EEEGINRV	ENGRIEVE	EEEHMNTV	VEHEMENT	EEEINNRT	INTERNEE
EEEGINRZ	ENERGIZE	EEEHNNPT	NEPENTHE		RETINENE
EEEGIPRS	PERIGEES	EEEHNNQU	HENEQUEN	EEEINPRT	PERENTIE
EEEGIRTY	TIGEREYE	EEEHNPRS	ENSPHERE	EEEINQRU	QUEENIER
EEEGISSX	EXEGESIS	EEEHNRSS	HERENESS	EEEINQSU	QUEENIES
EEEGISTV	EGESTIVE	EEEHNRTV	REVEHENT	EEEINQTU	QUEENITE
EEEGITVV	VEGETIVE	EEEHNRVW	WHENEVER	EEEINRRS	SNEERIER
EEEGKLRS	KEGELERS	EEEHNSSS	SNEESHES	EEEINRSS	EERINESS
EEEGLMOS	GLEESOME	EEEHNSSY	SHEENEYS		ESERINES
EEEGLNRT	GREENLET	EEEHORST	SHOETREE	EEEINRST	ETERNISE
EEEGMNOS	MONGEESE	EEEHPRRT	THREEPER		TEENSIER
EEEGMNRT	EMERGENT	EEEHPRSS	HERPESES	EEEINRSV	VENERIES
EEEGMNRU	MERENGUE		PHERESES	EEEINRSW	WEENSIER
EEEGMORT	GEOMETER	EEEHPRST	SPREETHE	EEEINRSZ	SNEEZIER
EEEGMRRS	REMERGES	EEEHRRVW	WHEREVER	EEEINRTT	REINETTE
EEEGNNRS	SENGREEN	EEEHRSST	SEETHERS		TEENTIER
EEEGNPRS	EPERGNES		SHEEREST	EEEINRTZ	ETERNIZE
EEEGNRRS	GREENERS		SHEETERS	EEEINSSW	SWEENIES
	REGREENS	EEEHRSTT	TEETHERS	EEEINSTT	TEENIEST
	RENEGERS	EEEHRSWZ	WHEEZERS	EEEINSTV	EVENTISE
EEEGNRRU	RENEGUER	EEEHSSST	ESTHESES	EEEINSTW	TWEENIES
EEEGNRRV	REVENGER	EEEHSSTT	ESTHETES		WEENIEST
EEEGNRRY	GREENERY	EEEIKLMS	MISLEEKE	EEEINTUX	EUXENITE

EEEEINTVZ	EVENTIZE	EEELMSSS	SEEMLESS	EEEENNSTT	ENTENTES
EEEIPRRV	REPRIEVE	EEELMSST	TEEMLESS	EEENOPRR	REOPENER
EEEIPRST	PEERIEST	EEELNOPV	ENVELOPE	EEENORSV	OVERSEEN
	STEEPIER	EEELNOSV	NOVELESE	EEENORVW	OVERWEEN
EEEIPRSW	SWEEPIER	EEELNQTU	QUEENLET	EEENORVY	EVERYONE
EEEIPSST	EPEEISTS	EEELNRRU	UNREELER	EEENOSTY	EYESTONE
	SEEPIEST	EEELNRSW	NEWSREEL	EEENPPRS	PREPENSE
EEEIPSTW	WEEPIEST	EEELNRSY	SERENELY	EEENPRRS	PREENERS
EEEIQSUX	EXEQUIES	EEELNRTV	NERVELET	EEENPRRT	REPENTER
EEEIRRST	REESTIER	EEELNRTY	TERYLENE	EEENPRST	PRETEENS
	RETIREES	EEELOPPR	REPEOPLE		PRETENSE
EEEIRRSV	REREVISE	EEELORST	SLOETREE		TERPENES
	REVERIES	EEELPPRS	PRESLEEP	EEENPRSV	PREVENES
EEEIRRTV	RETRIEVE	EEELPRSS	PEERLESS	EEENPSST	ENSTEEPS
EEEIRRVW	REREVIEW		SLEEPERS		STEEPENS
	REVIEWER		SPEELERS	EEENPSSW	ENSWEEPS
EEEIRSST	STEERIES	EEELPRST	REPLETES	EEENPSSX	EXPENSES
EEEIRSSV	SEVERIES	EEELPRSX	REEXPELS	EEENRRSS	SNEERERS
EEEIRSSZ	RESEIZES	EEELPRSY	SLEEPERY	EEENRRST	ENTERERS
EEEIRTVX	EXERTIVE	EEELPSST	STEEPLES		REENTERS
EEEISSTW	SWEETIES	EEELPTTY	TELETYPE		RESENTER
EEEJKKNR	KNEEJERK	EEELRRSV	REVELERS		TERREENS
EEEJLLRW	JEWELLER	EEELRRTT	LETTERER		TERRENES
EEEJLRSW	JEWELERS		RELETTER	EEENRRSV	RENVERSE
EEEJNPSY	JEEPNEYS	EEELRSST	TREELESS		VENERERS
EEEKLLSS	KEELLESS	EEELRSSV	SLEEVERS	EEENRRSW	RENEWERS
EEEKLLSU	UKELELES	EEELRSTT	RESETTLE	EEENRRTU	RETURNEE
EEEKLNNR	ENKERNEL	EEELRSTV	LEVERETS	EEENRRTV	REVERENT
EEEKLNRS	KNEELERS		VERSELET	EEENRRUV	REVENUER
EEEKLNSS	SLEEKENS	EEELRSVY	SEVERELY	EEENRSST	SERENEST
EEEKLPSW	EKPWELES	EEELRTVV	VELVERET	EEENRSSU	ENURESES
EEEKLRSS	SLEEKERS	EEELSSTU	EUSTELES	EEENRSSZ	SNEEZERS
EEEKLSST	SLEEKEST	EEELSSTW	WEETLESS	EEENRSTV	EVENTERS
EEEKMNSS	MEEKNESS	EEELSTVY	STEEVELY		EVERNETS
EEEKMORV	OVERMEEK	EEELTTTX	TELETEXT	EEENRSTW	TWEENERS
EEEKMRSS	KERMESSE	EEEMMNRS	MERESMEN	EEENRSTX	EXTERNES
EEEKNNSS	KEENNESS	EEEMMORS	MESOMERE	EEENRSTY	YESTREEN
EEEKNORS	KEROSENE	EEEMMRUZ	MEZEREUM	EEENRSUV	REVENUES
EEEKNORV	OVERKEEN	EEEMNNTT	TENEMENT		UNREEVES
	OVERKNEE	EEEMNORZ	MEZEREON	EEENSSTW	SWEETENS
EEEKNPST	KEEPNETS	EEEMNPRT	PETERMEN		TWEENESS
EEEKOPRV	OVERKEEP	EEEMNRST	ENTREMES	EEENSSWY	SWEENEYS
EEEKORSV	REEVOKES	EEEMNRSV	VERSEMEN	EEEOPPSY	POPESEYE
EEEKRRST	STREEKER	EEEMNRVY	EVERYMEN	EEEOPRRV	OVERPEER
EEEKRSST	KEESTERS	EEEMNSST	MEETNESS	EEEOPRSX	REEXPOSE
	SKEETERS	EEEMNSTW	SWEETMEN	EEEORRSV	OVERSEER
EEELLLRV	LEVELLER	EEEMORRV	EVERMORE	EEEORRSX	XEROSERE
EEELLLSW	SEWELLEL	EEEMORST	EROTEMES	EEEORRSZ	REZEROES
EEELLNOR	ENROLLEE		STEREOME	EEEORSST	EROTESES
EEELLNQU	QUENELLE	EEEMORTV	OVERTEEM	EEEORSSV	OVERSEES
EEELLPRR	REPELLER	EEEMPRRT	RETEMPER	EEEORSSY	EYESORES
EEELLPRX	EXPELLER		TEMPERER	EEEORSVY	OVEREYES
EEELLRRS	RESELLER	EEEMPRSS	EMPRESSE	EEEPPPRR	PEPPERER
EEELLRRT	RETELLER	EEEMPRST	PREMEETS	EEEPPSTU	STEEPEUP
EEELLRRV	REVELLER	EEEMPSSY	EMPYESES	EEEPRRST	PESTERER
EEELLRSV	LEVELERS	EEEMRRTX	EXTREMER	EEEPRRSU	REPERUSE
EEELMNST	ELEMENTS	EEEMRSST	SEMESTER	EEEPRRSV	PERVERSE
	STEELMEN	EEEMRSTX	EXTREMES		PRESERVE
EEELMOPP	EMPEOPLE	EEENNOPR	NEOPRENE	EEEPRRTW	PEWTERER
EEELMOPY	EMPLOYEE	EEENNOSV	VENENOSE	EEEPRSST	ESTREPES
EEELMORT	TELOMERE	EEENNPST	PENTENES		STEEPERS
EEELMOTT	OMELETTE	EEENNRST	ETRENNES	EEEPRSSW	SWEEPERS
EEELMPSX	EXEMPLES	EEENNRUV	UNEVENER	EEEPRSSZ	SPREEZES
EEELMRTU	MULETEER	EEENNSSV	EVENNESS	EEEPSSTT	STEEPEST

EEEPSTTT	SEPTETTE	EEFGLNRY	GREENFLY	EEFILLNY	FELINELY
EEEQRRSU	REQUERES	EEFGLNUV	VENGEFUL	EEFILLRW	FREEWILL
EEEQRRUV	VERQUERE	EEFGLORS	FORELEGS	EEFILLSS	LIFELESS
EEEQRSTU	QUEEREST	EEFGLOSS	SOLFEGES	EEFILMNR	RIFLEMEN
EEEQRSUZ	SQUEEZER	EEFGMNOR	FORGEMEN	EEFILMOS	LIFESOME
EEEQSSUZ	SQUEEZES	EEFGNOOR	FOREGONE	EEFILMST	FISTMELE
EEERRRSV	RESERVER	EEFGOORR	FOREGOER	EEFILMTX	FLEXTIME
	REVERERS	EEFGOORS	FOREGOES	EEFILNOS	FELONIES
	REVERSER	EEFGORRS	REFORGES		OLEFINES
EEERRRTV	REVERTER	EEFGORSY	FROGEYES	EEFILNSS	FINELESS
EEERRSST	STEERERS	EEFHILLR	HELLFIRE	EEFILNUV	NIEVEFUL
EEERRSSV	RESERVES	EEFHILRS	FLESHIER	EEFILORS	FORELIES
	REVERSES		SHELFIER	EEFILPRR	PILFERER
EEERRSTT	RESETTER	EEFHIMSU	HUMEFIES	EEFILPRS	PREFILES
EEERSSTV	SEVEREST	EEFHIRSS	FRESHIES	EEFILRRT	FERTILER
EEERSSTW	SWEEREST	EEFHIRSV	FEVERISH		FILTERER
EEERSSUV	REVEUSES	EEFHIRTY	ETHERIFY		REFILTER
EEERSSUW	SERUEWES	EEFHISST	FETISHES	EEFILRSS	FIRELESS
EEERSSVW	SERVEWES	EEFHISSY	FISHEYES	EEFILRST	FERLIEST
EEERSTTW	TWEETERS	EEFHISTT	HEFTIEST	EEFILRSU	FUSILEER
EEERSTVX	VERTEXES	EEFHLLWY	FLYWHEEL	EEFILSST	FELSITES
EEERSTWZ	TWEEZERS	EEFHLMNS	FLEHMENS	EEFILSSW	WIFELESS
EEESSTTT	SESTETTE	EEFHLMOT	HOMEFELT	EEFILSTT	FELTIEST
EEESSTTV	STEEVEST	EEFHLMST	THEMSELF	EEFILSTY	EYELIFTS
EEESSTTW	SWEETEST	EEFHLNSU	SHEENFUL	EEFIMMST	FEMMIEST
EEESTTTX	SEXTETTE	EEFHLRSS	FLESHERS	EEFIMORT	FORETIME
EEFFFGLU	GEFUFFLE	EEFHLSTY	FLYSHEET	EEFIMRRS	MISREFER
EEFFFKLU	KEFUFFLE	EEFHMNRS	FRESHMEN	EEFIMRST	FEMITERS
EEFFFNOS	ENFEOFFS	EEFHMORR	HEREFROM	EEFIMSTU	TUMEFIES
EEFFFORS	FEOFFERS	EEFHNORT	FOREHENT	EEFINNSS	FINENESS
EEFFGIIS	EFFIGIES	EEFHNRSS	FRESHENS	EEFINNST	FENNIEST
EEFFGINR	EFFERING	EEFHORRT	THEREFOR	EEFINORV	OVERFINE
EEFFGIRR	GREFFIER	EEFHORRW	WHEREFOR	EEFINRRR	INFERRER
EEFFGLSU	EFFULGES	EEFHORSW	FORESHEW	EEFINRRS	REFINERS
EEFFHIKY	KEFFIYEH	EEFHRRSS	FRESHERS	EEFINRRY	REFINERY
EEFFINST	FIFTEENS	EEFHRRSU	FUEHRERS	EEFINRSS	FINESSER
EEFFISUV	EFFUSIVE	EEFHRSST	FRESHEST		RIFENESS
EEFFLNTU	EFFLUENT		FRESHETS	EEFINRST	FERNIEST
EEFFLORT	FOREFELT	EEFIIKLL	LIFELIKE		INFESTER
EEFFLSUX	EFFLUXES	EEFIIKLW	WIFELIKE	EEFINRSU	REINFUSE
EEFFMORR	FREEFORM	EEFIIKRS	FIKERIES	EEFINRSZ	FRENZIES
EEFFMOTT	MOFFETTE	EEFIILLN	LIFELINE	EEFINSSS	FINESSES
EEFFNOSS	OFFENSES	EEFIILMT	LIFETIME	EEFINSTT	FEINTEST
EEFFORRS	OFFERERS	EEFIILNS	LENIFIES	EEFIORRV	OVERRIFE
	REOFFERS	EEFIILRW	WIFELIER	EEFIORSX	ORIFEXES
EEFFORSX	FORFEXES	EEFIIMNN	FEMININE	EEFIPRRS	PREFIRES
EEFFRRSU	SUFFERER	EEFIIMNS	FEMINISE	EEFIPRSX	PREFIXES
EEFFSSTU	SUFFETES	EEFIIMNZ	FEMINIZE	EEFIRRST	FERRITES
EEFGIILR	FILIGREE	EEFIINRS	FINERIES	EEFIRRSU	SUREFIRE
EEFGILNR	FLEERING	EEFIIRRS	REIFIERS	EEFIRRTT	FRETTIER
EEFGILNS	FEELINGS	EEFIIRRT	FREITIER	EEFIRRVY	REVERIFY
EEFGILNT	FLEETING	EEFIIRRV	VERIFIER	EEFIRSTT	FRISETTE
EEFGINNP	PFENNIGE	EEFIIRST	FEISTIER	EEFIRSTY	ESTERIFY
EEFGINRR	FINGERER		FERITIES	EEFIRTTZ	FRIZETTE
	REFRINGE		FIERIEST	EEFISSSW	FESSWISE
EEFGINRS	FEERINGS	EEFIIRSV	VERIFIES	EEFISSTT	FESTIEST
	FEIGNERS	EEFIKLLT	FELTLIKE	EEFISTWW	WEFTWISE
	REEFINGS	EEFIKLMU	FUMELIKE	EEFKNORW	FOREKNEW
EEFGINRV	FEVERING	EEFIKLNR	FERNLIKE	EEFLLLNU	FLUELLEN
EEFGINRZ	FREEZING	EEFIKLRS	SERFLIKE	EEFLLNSS	FELLNESS
EEFGIRRS	GRIEFERS	EEFIKLSU	FUSELIKE	EEFLLORT	FORETELL
EEFGIRRU	REFIGURE	EEFIKMNN	KNIFEMEN	EEFLLORV	OVERFELL
EEFGLLTU	GEFULLTE	EEFIKNNP	PENKNIFE	EEFLLRSU	FUELLERS
EEFGLMNU	FUGLEMEN	EEFILLMT	TELEFILM	EEFLLRXY	REFLEXLY

EEFLLSSS	SELFLESS	EEFORSUV	FEVEROUS	EEGHINWZ	WHEEZING
EEFLMNSU	MENSEFUL	EEFOSSTT	FOSSETTE	EEGHIOTT	GOETHITE
EEFLMORU	FUMEROLE	EEFOSSTU	FOETUSES	EEGHIPRW	PREWEIGH
EEFLMSSU	FUMELESS	EEFOSTTU	FOUETTES	EEGHIRSW	REWEIGHS
EEFLNNOS	ENFELONS	EEFPRSSU	PERFUSES		WEIGHERS
EEFLNORT	FORELENT	EEFRRSSU	REFUSERS	EEGHIRTW	WEIGHTER
EEFLNORU	FLUORENE	EEFRRSTT	FRETTERS	EEGHISST	SIGHTSEE
EEFLNORW	ENFLOWER	EEFRRSTU	REFUTERS	EEGHISTY	EYESIGHT
EEFLNOST	FELSTONE	EEGGGLST	GLEGGEST	EEGHKRSS	SKREEGHS
EEFLNRSS	FERNLESS	EEGGHLLS	EGGSHELL	EEGHLNNT	LENGTHEN
	FLENSERS	EEGGHLOR	HOGGEREL	EEGHMNOS	HEGEMONS
	FRESNELS	EEGGHMSU	MESHUGGE	EEGHMNOY	HEGEMONY
EEFLNRSU	SNEERFUL	EEGGHSTU	THUGGEES	EEGHMNSU	HEGUMENS
EEFLNRTU	REFLUENT	EEGGIJRR	REJIGGER	EEGHMNUY	HEGUMENY
EEFLNSSS	SELFNESS	EEGGIKLN	GLEEKING	EEGHMORT	GEOTHERM
EEFLNSSU	SENSEFUL	EEGGIKNR	GREEKING	EEGHNNRU	ENHUNGER
EEFLNTUV	EVENTFUL	EEGGILNR	LEGERING	EEGHNOOP	GEOPHONE
EEFLOOSV	FOVEOLES	EEGGILNS	NEGLIGES	EEGHNOPS	PHOSGENE
EEFLOOTV	FOVEOLET	EEGGILNT	GLEETING	EEGHNOPY	HYPOGENE
EEFLORRW	FLOWERER	EEGGILNY	GINGELEY	EEGHNRST	GREENTHS
	REFLOWER	EEGGILOR	LEGGIERO	EEGHNRSY	GREYHENS
EEFLORSS	FORLESES	EEGGILST	LEGGIEST	EEGHNSSU	HUGENESS
EEFLORTV	LEFTOVER	EEGGIMNR	EMERGING	EEGHOPTY	GEOPHYTE
EEFLORTW	FLOWERET	EEGGINNP	PEENGING	EEGHORTT	TOGETHER
EEFLORVW	OVERFLEW	EEGGINNR	GREENING	EEGHOSTT	GHETTOES
EEFLORWW	WEREWOLF		RENEGING	EEGHSTTU	TEUGHEST
EEFLOSTU	OUTFEELS	EEGGINRS	GREESING	EEGIILNR	LINGERIE
EEFLOSTV	LOVEFEST	EEGGINRT	GREETING	EEGIILNV	INVEIGLE
EEFLOSUX	FLEXUOSE	EEGGINST	EGESTING	EEGIIMNS	GEMINIES
EEFLRRSU	FERRULES	EEGGINSU	SEGUEING	EEGIINRT	REIGNITE
EEFLRSST	FRETLESS	EEGGIPRR	PREGGIER		RETIEING
EEFLRSTT	FETTLERS	EEGGJLRU	REJUGGLE	EEGIINTV	GENITIVE
EEFLRSTU	FLEURETS	EEGGKRSS	SKEGGERS	EEGIIOST	EGOITIES
EEFLRSUX	FLEXURES	EEGGLNSS	GLEGNESS	EEGIJLNW	JEWELING
	REFLUXES	EEGGLOOR	GEOLOGER	EEGIJLNY	JEELYING
EEFLSSSU	FUSELESS	EEGGNNSS	GENSENGS	EEGIJNRS	JEERINGS
EEFMNORT	FOMENTER	EEGGNORS	ENGORGES	EEGIJOPR	JEREPIGO
EEFMNRRY	FERRYMEN	EEGGORRS	REGORGES	EEGIKLLN	GLENLIKE
EEFMNRST	FERMENTS	EEGGORSU	GOUGERES	EEGIKLLU	GLUELIKE
EEFMORRR	REFORMER	EEGGORSV	OVEREGGS	EEGIKLMR	GERMLIKE
EEFMORST	FRETSOME	EEGGPRRS	PREGGERS	EEGIKLNN	KNEELING
EEFMOSTT	MOFETTES	EEGGPRSU	PUGGREES	EEGIKLNS	KEELINGS
EEFMPRRU	PERFUMER	EEGGQRSU	SQUEGGER		SLEEKING
EEFMPRSU	PERFUMES	EEGHHINT	HEIGHTEN	EEGIKLOT	EKLOGITE
EEFMSTTU	FUMETTES	EEGHIIST	EIGHTIES	EEGIKMNS	SMEEKING
EEFNNORS	ENFROSEN	EEGHIKNT	THEEKING	EEGIKNNS	KEENINGS
EEFNNORZ	ENFROZEN	EEGHIKRS	SKEIGHER	EEGIKNPS	KEEPINGS
EEFNORRZ	REFROZEN	EEGHILNS	HEELINGS	EEGIKNRS	KREESING
EEFNORST	ENFOREST		SHEELING		SKEERING
	RESOFTEN	EEGHILNW	WHEELING	EEGIKNRY	REKEYING
	SOFTENER	EEGHILRS	SLEIGHER	EEGIKNST	KITENGES
EEFNORTU	FOURTEEN	EEGHIMNW	WEIGHMEN		STEEKING
EEFNORTW	FOREWENT	EEGHINNS	SHEENING	EEGILLNV	LEVELING
EEFNOSTT	OFTENEST	EEGHINPS	PHEESING	EEGILMOS	EGLOMISE
EEFNQRTU	FREQUENT	EEGHINPT	PHENGITE	EEGILNOR	ELOIGNER
EEFNRTTU	UNFETTER	EEGHINPW	WHEEPING	EEGILNPS	PEELINGS
EEFOORRT	ROOFTREE	EEGHINPZ	PHEEZING		SLEEPING
EEFOPRRZ	PREFROZE	EEGHINRS	GREENISH		SPEELING
EEFORRST	FORESTER		REHINGES	EEGILNRR	LINGERER
	FOSTERER		SHEERING	EEGILNRS	LEERINGS
	REFOREST	EEGHINST	SEETHING		REELINGS
EEFORRSU	FERREOUS		SHEETING	EEGILNRT	GREENLIT
EEFORRSV	FOREVERS	EEGHINSY	HYGIENES	EEGILNRU	REGULINE
EEFORRTY	FERETORY	EEGHINTT	TEETHING	EEGILNRV	LEVERING

	REVELING				
EEGILNSS	SEELINGS	EEGINOST	EGESTION	EEGLMNTU	EMULGENT
EEGILNST	GENTILES	EEGINPRR	PEREGRIN	EEGLMORS	GOMERELS
	SLEETING	EEGINPRS	SPEERING	EEGLMOSS	GLOSSEME
	STEELING		SPREEING	EEGLNNTU	UNGENTLE
EEGILNSV	SLEEVING	EEGINPRT	PETERING	EEGLNOPY	POLYGENE
EEGILNSW	SWEELING	EEGINPRU	PUREEING	EEGLNOSU	EUGENOLS
EEGILNTW	TWEELING	EEGINPRV	PREEVING	EEGLNOSZ	LOZENGES
EEGILNTX	TELEXING	EEGINPST	STEEPING	EEGLNOTY	TELEGONY
EEGILOPU	EPILOGUE	EEGINPSW	SWEEPING	EEGLNPRU	REPLUNGE
EEGILOSS	GELOSIES		WEEPINGS	EEGLNSTT	GENTLEST
EEGILOSU	EULOGIES	EEGINQRU	QUEERING	EEGLOPRS	GOSPELER
	EULOGISE	EEGINQUU	QUEUEING	EEGLORRV	GROVELER
EEGILOUZ	EULOGIZE	EEGINRRS	RESIGNER	EEGLORVY	LEVOGYRE
EEGILPSS	SPIEGELS	EEGINRRV	REVERING	EEGLRRSU	GRUELERS
EEGILQSU	SQUILGEE	EEGINRSS	GREISENS	EEGLRSTW	WERGELTS
EEGILRSU	REGULISE	EEGINRST	GENTRIES	EEGMMOSU	GEMMEOUS
EEGILRSV	VELIGERS		INTEGERS	EEGMNOST	EMONGEST
EEGILRTV	VERLIGTE		REESTING		GEMSTONE
EEGILRTY	LEGERITY		STEERING	EEGMNOYZ	ZYMOGENE
EEGILRUZ	REGULIZE		STREIGNE	EEGMNSST	SEGMENTS
EEGILSST	ELEGISTS	EEGINRSU	SEIGNEUR	EEGMNTTU	TEGUMENT
EEGIMMNW	EMMEWING	EEGINRSV	SEVERING	EEGMORSU	GRUESOME
EEGIMMRS	GREMMIES		VEERINGS	EEGMORSW	GREWSOME
	IMMERGES	EEGINRSW	RESEWING	EEGMORTY	GEOMETRY
EEGIMMST	GEMMIEST		SEWERING	EEGMRSTU	GUMTREES
EEGIMNNS	MENINGES		SWEERING	EEGNNNOR	NONGREEN
EEGIMNNW	ENMEWING	EEGINRTU	GENITURE	EEGNNORT	ROENTGEN
EEGIMNRS	REGIMENS	EEGINRTV	EVERTING	EEGNNOSS	GONENESS
EEGIMNRT	METERING	EEGINRTW	TWEERING	EEGNNOSV	EVENSONG
	REGIMENT	EEGINRTX	EXERTING	EEGNNOXY	XENOGENY
EEGIMNRU	MERINGUE		GENETRIX	EEGNOORV	ENGROOVE
EEGIMNRY	EMERYING	EEGINSSS	GNEISSES		OVERGONE
EEGIMNSS	SEEMINGS	EEGINSSU	GENIUSES	EEGNOOST	OSTEOGEN
EEGIMNST	MEETINGS	EEGINSTT	GENTIEST	EEGNOPTY	GENOTYPE
	STEEMING	EEGINSTU	EUGENIST	EEGNORST	ESTROGEN
EEGIMNSU	EUGENISM	EEGINSTV	STEEVING	EEGNORSU	GENEROUS
EEGIMRST	GERMIEST		VENTIGES	EEGNORSY	ERYNGOES
EEGINNPR	PREENING	EEGINSTW	SWEETING	EEGNOTYZ	ZYGOTENE
EEGINNQU	QUEENING	EEGINSTX	EXIGENTS	EEGNPRUX	EXPUNGER
EEGINNRS	ENGINERS	EEGINTTV	VIGNETTE	EEGNPSUX	EXPUNGES
	INGENERS	EEGINTTW	TWEETING	EEGNRSSY	GREYNESS
	SERENING	EEGINTUX	TEGUEXIN	EEGNRSUY	GUERNSEY
	SNEERING	EEGINTWZ	TWEEZING	EEGNSSTU	GUESTENS
EEGINNRT	ENTERING	EEGIOPSU	EPIGEOUS	EEGOORRV	REGROOVE
EEGINNRV	ENERVING	EEGIORST	ERGOTISE	EEGOORSV	OVERGOES
EEGINNRW	RENEWING	EEGIORTZ	ERGOTIZE	EEGOPRST	PROTEGES
EEGINNRY	ENGINERY	EEGIORVV	OVERGIVE	EEGOPRSU	SUPEREGO
	RENEYING	EEGIOSST	EGOTISES	EEGORRST	OSTREGER
EEGINNST	STEENING	EEGIOSTZ	EGOTIZES	EEGORRUV	OVERURGE
EEGINNSU	INGENUES	EEGIPRST	PRESTIGE	EEGORRVW	OVERGREW
	UNSEEING	EEGIRRST	REGISTER	EEGORSSS	OGRESSES
EEGINNSV	EEVNINGS	EEGIRRSV	GRIEVERS	EEGORSTU	UROSTEGE
	EVENINGS	EEGIRSTT	GRISETTE	EEGORSTV	OVERGETS
			TERGITES	EEGPPRRS	PREPREGS
EEGINNSW	ENSEWING	EEGIRSTU	GUERITES	EEGPRSUX	EXPURGES
EEGINNSZ	SNEEZING	EEGISSTV	VESTIGES	EEGRRSSU	RESURGES
EEGINNTV	EVENTING	EEGISTTV	VEGETIST	EEGRRSTU	GESTURER
EEGINOOS	OOGENIES	EEGJORSU	GOUJEERS	EEGRRSUY	GRUYERES
EEGINOPR	PERIGONE	EEGKLNOW	WEEKLONG	EEGRSSSU	GUESSERS
EEGINOPS	EPIGONES	EEGKNORS	KEROGENS	EEGRSSTU	GESTURES
EEGINORR	ERIGERON	EEGKNRSU	GERENUKS	EEHHIPSS	SHEEPISH
EEGINORS	ERINGOES	EEGLLRRU	GRUELLER	EEHHIRST	ETHERISH
EEGINORV	VIROGENE	EEGLMMSU	GEMMULES	EEHHIRTW	HEREWITH
EEGINOSS	GENOISES	EEGLMNOP	EMPLONGE	EEHHKKOO	KOHEKOHE

EEHHLLLO	HELLHOLE	EEHINORS	HEROINES	EEHLMMSW	WHEMMLES
EEHHLRST	THRESHEL		NOSHERIE	EEHLMNOT	HOTELMEN
EEHHNOPT	ETHEPHON	EEHINORT	ETHERION	EEHLMOOS	HOLESOME
EEHHNOSU	HENHOUSE		HEREINTO	EEHLMOSS	HOMELESS
EEHHRRST	THRESHER	EEHINPRS	INSPHERE	EEHLMOSY	HEMOLYSE
EEHHRSST	THRESHES	EEHINPRT	NEPHRITE	EEHLMOYZ	HEMOLYZE
EEHHSSTW	WHEESHTS		PREHNITE	EEHLMRST	THERMELS
EEHHSSWW	SHWESHWE		TREPHINE	EEHLNOPT	PHENETOL
EEHIIKLV	HIVELIKE	EEHINPSX	PHENIXES	EEHLNOTT	TELETHON
EEHIJMNR	MIJNHEER	EEHINRRS	ERRHINES	EEHLOPSS	HOPELESS
EEHIKLLT	HELLKITE	EEHINRSS	RESHINES	EEHLOPST	HEELPOST
EEHIKLMO	HOMELIKE	EEHINRTT	THIRTEEN		PESTHOLE
EEHIKLMP	HEMPLIKE	EEHINRTW	WHITENER		TELESHOP
EEHIKLMS	SHEKELIM	EEHIOPPS	HOSEPIPE	EEHLORST	HOSTELER
EEHIKLOS	HOSELIKE	EEHIORSS	HEROISES	EEHLORSV	SHOVELER
EEHIKLRW	WHELKIER	EEHIORST	ISOTHERE	EEHLOSSS	SHOELESS
EEHIKLWY	WHEYLIKE		THEORIES	EEHLOSTY	HOLEYEST
EEHIKRRS	SHRIEKER		THEORISE	EEHLPPRS	SHLEPPER
EEHILLMS	SHLEMIEL	EEHIORSZ	HEROIZES	EEHLPRST	TELPHERS
EEHILLNP	HELPLINE	EEHIORTZ	THEORIZE	EEHLPRSU	SPHERULE
EEHILLRS	HELLERIS	EEHIOSTX	ETHOXIES	EEHLPSSY	PHYLESES
	HELLIERS	EEHIPPST	PSEPHITE	EEHLRSST	SHELTERS
	SHELLIER	EEHIPPTY	EPIPHYTE	EEHLRSSV	SHELVERS
EEHILMNS	HEMLINES	EEHIPRRS	PERISHER	EEHLRSSW	WELSHERS
EEHILMNU	HELENIUM		SPHERIER	EEHLRSTY	SHELTERY
EEHILMOR	HOMELIER	EEHIPRSS	PERISHES	EEHLSSTT	SHTETELS
EEHILNOP	ENOPHILE		PHERESIS	EEHLSSTW	THEWLESS
	NEOPHILE	EEHIPRST	TREESHIP	EEHMMOPR	MORPHEME
EEHILNPW	PINWHEEL	EEHIPRTT	PERTHITE	EEHMMORT	OHMMETER
EEHILNST	THEELINS		TEPHRITE	EEHMNOOS	MOONSHEE
EEHILOPS	PIEHOLES		THREEPIT	EEHMNOPS	PHONEMES
EEHILORT	HOTELIER	EEHIPSST	STEEPISH	EEHMNORS	HORSEMEN
EEHILOSS	HELIOSES	EEHIPSTT	EPITHETS		SHOREMEN
EEHILPRT	HERPTILE		TIPSHEET	EEHMNOSU	HOUSEMEN
EEHILRSS	HEIRLESS	EEHIPSUU	EUPHUISE	EEHMNOSW	SOMEWHEN
	RELISHES	EEHIPUUZ	EUPHUIZE	EEHMNRSU	ENRHEUMS
EEHILRSV	SHELVIER	EEHIQRSU	QUEERISH	EEHMNRSY	MYNHEERS
EEHILSST	LEISHEST	EEHIRRSS	SHERRIES	EEHMNSSU	UNMESHES
	SHELTIES	EEHIRRSV	SHIVERER	EEHMNTTU	UMTEENTH
EEHILSSV	HIVELESS	EEHIRRSW	WHERRIES	EEHMOORT	RHEOTOME
EEHILWYZ	WHEEZILY	EEHIRRTW	WITHERER	EEHMOOSS	HOMEOSES
EEHIMMSS	IMMESHES	EEHIRRTX	HERETRIX	EEHMORST	THEOREMS
	MISHMEES	EEHIRSST	HEISTERS	EEHMORVW	WHOMEVER
EEHIMNOS	HEMIONES	EEHIRSSV	SHRIEVES	EEHMRSUX	EXHUMERS
EEHIMNRS	SHIREMEN	EEHIRSSX	RHEXISES	EEHMSSTY	METHYSES
EEHIMNRT	THEREMIN	EEHIRSTT	ETHERIST	EEHNNOOT	ETHONONE
EEHIMNSS	INMESHES	EEHIRTVY	THIEVERY	EEHNNORT	ENTHRONE
EEHIMOST	HOMESITE	EEHISSST	ESTHESIS	EEHNNOSS	SHONEENS
EEHIMPRS	EMPERISH		HESSITES	EEHNNPPU	UNHEPPEN
EEHIMPRT	HEMIPTER	EEHISSTW	SWEETISH	EEHNNSSS	NESHNESS
EEHIMPST	EPITHEMS	EEHISTTW	THEWIEST	EEHNNSTU	UNNETHES
	HEMPIEST	EEHISTWY	WHEYIEST	EEHNOORS	HONOREES
EEHIMQUV	VEHMIQUE	EEHKLOSY	KEYHOLES	EEHNOPRU	HEREUPON
EEHIMRRU	RHEUMIER	EEHKOOSY	EYEHOOKS	EEHNOPST	POSHTEEN
EEHIMRST	ERETHISM	EEHLLLOW	WELLHOLE		POTHEENS
	ETHERISM	EEHLLMPS	PHELLEMS	EEHNOPTY	HYPNOTEE
EEHIMRTT	THERMITE	EEHLLMSS	HELMLESS		NEOPHYTE
EEHIMSST	MESHIEST	EEHLLNSS	ENSHELLS	EEHNORSS	SENHORES
EEHINNQU	HENEQUIN	EEHLLORV	HOVELLER	EEHNORST	HONESTER
	HENIQUEN	EEHLLOSS	HOLELESS	EEHNORSW	HERONSEW
EEHINNRS	ENSHRINE	EEHLLOST	THEELOLS		NOWHERES
EEHINNRT	INHERENT	EEHLLPSS	HELPLESS	EEHNORTU	HEREUNTO
EEHINNSS	SNEESHIN	EEHLLRSS	SHELLERS	EEHNORTV	OVERHENT
EEHINNST	HENNIEST	EEHLMMNS	HELMSMEN	EEHNOSST	ETHNOSES

EEHNPRSU	UNSPHERE	**EEIILSTV**	LEVITIES	**EEIKLLSS**	SKELLIES
EEHNRTTU	UNTETHER		VEILIEST	**EEIKLMST**	STEMLIKE
EEHNSSTU	ENTHUSES	**EEIILSTW**	LEWISITE	**EEIKLNOS**	NOSELIKE
EEHNSSTV	SEVENTHS	**EEIIMMTT**	MIMETITE	**EEIKLNOV**	OVENLIKE
EEHOOPRS	OOSPHERE	**EEIIMNOT**	MEIONITE	**EEIKLNRU**	RUNELIKE
EEHOOPRV	OVERHOPE	**EEIIMNST**	ENMITIES	**EEIKLNSS**	LIKENESS
EEHOOPSW	WHOOPEES	**EEIIMOST**	MOIETIES	**EEIKLNST**	NESTLIKE
EEHOORSV	OVERSHOE	**EEIIMPRS**	RIEMPIES	**EEIKLNSY**	KEYLINES
EEHOOSST	TOESHOES	**EEIIMRSS**	MISERIES	**EEIKLNTT**	TENTLIKE
EEHOOTTY	EYETOOTH	**EEIIMRST**	ITEMISER	**EEIKLOPP**	POPELIKE
EEHOPPRY	HYPEROPE	**EEIIMRTZ**	ITEMIZER	**EEIKLOPR**	ROPELIKE
EEHOPPSW	PEEPSHOW	**EEIIMSST**	ITEMISES	**EEIKLOPT**	POETLIKE
EEHOPRSU	EUPHROES	**EEIIMSSV**	EMISSIVE	**EEIKLORS**	ROSELIKE
EEHOPRVY	OVERHYPE	**EEIIMSTZ**	ITEMIZES	**EEIKLORT**	LORIKEET
EEHOPSST	HEPTOSES	**EEIINNST**	EINSTEIN	**EEIKLPST**	PIKELETS
EEHORRSV	HOVERERS		NINETIES		SPIKELET
EEHORRSW	RESHOWER	**EEIINORT**	ERIONITE		STEPLIKE
	SHOWERER	**EEIINPPR**	PIPERINE	**EEIKLRST**	TRISKELE
EEHORRTX	EXHORTER	**EEIINPRS**	PINERIES	**EEIKLSTV**	VESTLIKE
EEHORSSU	REHOUSES	**EEIINPRV**	VIPERINE	**EEIKMOOV**	MOVIEOKE
EEHORSVW	WHOSEVER	**EEIINRRV**	RIVERINE	**EEIKMOTX**	KETOXIME
EEHORTTU	THEREOUT	**EEIINRSS**	RESINISE	**EEIKMPSS**	MISKEEPS
EEHORTUW	WHEREOUT		SIRENISE	**EEIKMPST**	KEMPIEST
EEHOSSTY	EYESHOTS	**EEIINRST**	ERINITES	**EEIKMRSS**	KERMISES
EEHPRSST	HEPSTERS		NITERIES	**EEIKNORS**	KEROSINE
	SPERTHES	**EEIINRSV**	VINERIES	**EEIKNORV**	REINVOKE
EEHPRSTU	SUPERHET	**EEIINRSW**	SINEWIER	**EEIKNPSY**	PINKEYES
EEHPRSTY	HYPESTER		WINERIES	**EEIKNRRT**	TINKERER
	PHYSETER	**EEIINRSZ**	RESINIZE	**EEIKNRST**	KERNITES
EEHRRSTW	WHERRETS		SIRENIZE	**EEIKNSWY**	EYEWINKS
EEHRSSSU	RHESUSES	**EEIINRTT**	INTERTIE	**EEIKOQUV**	EQUIVOKE
	USHERESS		RETINITE	**EEIKORSU**	EUROKIES
EEHRSSTW	WERSHEST	**EEIINRTV**	REINVITE	**EEIKPPRR**	KIPPERER
EEHRSTTW	WHETTERS	**EEIINSST**	SIENITES	**EEIKPRST**	PERKIEST
EEHSSTUY	SHUTEYES	**EEIINSSV**	INESSIVE	**EEIKPSST**	PESKIEST
EEIIKKLT	KITELIKE	**EEIINSSW**	EISWEINS	**EEIKRRSS**	SKERRIES
EEIIKLLN	LINELIKE	**EEIINSTT**	ENTITIES	**EEIKRRST**	RESTRIKE
EEIIKLLR	LIKELIER	**EEIINSTV**	INVITEES	**EEIKRSST**	KEISTERS
EEIIKLLT	TILELIKE		VEINIEST		KIESTERS
EEIIKLLV	VEILLIKE	**EEIIOPTZ**	EPIZOITE	**EEIKRSTU**	KEIRETSU
EEIIKLNP	PINELIKE	**EEIIORSS**	OSIERIES	**EEIKSSTY**	SKIEYEST
EEIIKLNV	VEINLIKE	**EEIIPRSS**	PIERISES	**EEIKSTTT**	TEKTITES
	VINELIKE	**EEIIPRSX**	EXPIRIES	**EEILLMPR**	IMPELLER
EEIIKLPP	PIPELIKE	**EEIIPRTT**	EPITRITE	**EEILLMRS**	SMELLIER
EEIIKLRW	WIRELIKE	**EEIIQSTU**	EQUITIES	**EEILLMRU**	REILLUME
EEIIKLSV	VISELIKE	**EEIIQTUV**	QUIETIVE	**EEILLMSS**	LIMELESS
EEIIKLSW	LIKEWISE	**EEIIRRSV**	RIVIERES		SMELLIES
EEIILLMM	MILLIEME	**EEIIRRTV**	TIRRIVEE	**EEILLMST**	MELLITES
EEIILLMT	MELILITE	**EEIIRSTV**	VERITIES	**EEILLNOR**	LONELIER
EEIILLOP	EOLIPILE	**EEIISSTV**	VISITEES	**EEILLNPS**	SPINELLE
EEIILLRV	LIVELIER	**EEIISTVW**	VIEWIEST	**EEILLNSY**	SENILELY
EEIILMNT	ILMENITE	**EEIJKLTU**	JUTELIKE	**EEILLNVV**	VENVILLE
	MELINITE	**EEIJKRST**	JERKIEST	**EEILLOOP**	EOLOPILE
	MENILITE	**EEIJLMSS**	MEJLISES	**EEILLORS**	ORSEILLE
	TIMELINE	**EEIJLNNU**	JULIENNE	**EEILLORV**	LOVELIER
EEIILMRT	TIMELIER	**EEIJLNRT**	JETLINER	**EEILLOSV**	LOVELIES
EEIILMSS	EMISSILE	**EEIJLNUV**	JUVENILE	**EEILLPSS**	ELLIPSES
EEIILNPP	PIPELINE	**EEIJMMST**	JEMMIEST		PILELESS
EEIILNST	LENITIES	**EEIJNNOR**	ENJOINER	**EEILLPSY**	SLEEPILY
EEIILNTV	LENITIVE	**EEIJNRRU**	REINJURE	**EEILLPZZ**	PIZZELLE
EEIILORS	OILERIES	**EEIJSTTT**	JETTIEST	**EEILLRSS**	LEISLERS
EEIILRST	TILERIES	**EEIKKRST**	KERKIEST	**EEILLRST**	TREILLES
EEIILRSV	LIVERIES	**EEIKLLRS**	SKELLIER	**EEILLSSS**	ISLELESS
EEIILRSW	WISELIER	**EEIKLLRY**	KYRIELLE	**EEILLSSV**	VEILLESS

EEILLSTT	STELLITE		VEINLESS	EEILSTUX	ULEXITES
EEILLSTV	EVILLEST		VILENESS	EEILSTVY	STIEVELY
EEILLSTW	WELLSITE		VINELESS	EEIMMNRS	IMMENSER
EEILLTVY	VELLEITY	EEILNSSW	WINELESS	EEIMMORS	MEMORIES
EEILLVWY	WEEVILLY	EEILNSTT	ENTITLES		MEMORISE
EEILMMST	MELTEMIS	EEILNSTV	VEINLETS	EEIMMORZ	MEMORIZE
EEILMNNO	LIMONENE	EEILNSUV	VEINULES	EEIMMOST	SOMETIME
EEILMNNS	LINESMEN	EEILNTUV	VEINULET	EEIMMRRS	IMMERSER
EEILMNNU	ENLUMINE	EEILOPRS	PELORIES	EEIMMRSS	IMMERSES
EEILMNOP	PEMOLINE	EEILOPST	PETIOLES	EEIMMRST	MERISTEM
EEILMNOR	LEMONIER	EEILORRT	LOITERER		MIMESTER
EEILMNRS	ERMELINS	EEILORRV	OVERLIER		MISMETRE
EEILMNRU	LEMURINE	EEILORRW	LOWERIER		STEMMIER
	RELUMINE	EEILORST	LITEROSE	EEIMMRSU	EUMERISM
EEILMNSS	ISLESMEN		TROELIES	EEIMMRTT	TERMTIME
EEILMNSU	SELENIUM	EEILORSV	OVERLIES	EEIMMSSS	MISSEEMS
	SEMILUNE		RELIEVOS	EEIMMSST	MISMEETS
EEILMNSY	MYELINES		VOLERIES	EEIMMSTU	SEMIMUTE
EEILMOPS	POLEMISE	EEILORSW	OWLERIES	EEIMNNOS	NOMINEES
EEILMOPZ	POLEMIZE	EEILORVV	OVERLIVE	EEIMNNRS	REINSMEN
EEILMORT	MOTELIER		OVERVEIL	EEIMNOPS	EPISEMON
EEILMOST	MESOLITE	EEILOSST	ESTOILES		SEMIOPEN
	MISLETOE	EEILOSSX	ISOLEXES	EEIMNORS	EMERSION
EEILMPST	IMPLETES	EEILOSTW	OWELTIES	EEIMNORT	TIMONEER
EEILMPSX	IMPLEXES	EEILOSTZ	ZEOLITES	EEIMNORV	OVERMINE
EEILMQTU	MIQUELET	EEILOSVW	VOWELISE		VOMERINE
EEILMRSS	RIMELESS	EEILOTTT	TOILETTE	EEIMNOST	MONETISE
EEILMRST	TERMLIES	EEILOVWZ	VOWELIZE		SEMITONE
EEILMRSV	VERMEILS	EEILPPSS	PIPELESS	EEIMNOTX	XENOTIME
EEILMSST	TIMELESS	EEILPPSY	EPILEPSY	EEIMNOTZ	MONETIZE
EEILMSTT	MELTIEST	EEILPRRS	REPLIERS		ZONETIME
EEILMSUV	EMULSIVE	EEILPRSS	SPIELERS	EEIMNPRS	SPERMINE
EEILNNOT	NONELITE	EEILPRST	EPISTLER	EEIMNPRU	PERINEUM
EEILNNST	LENIENTS		PELTRIES	EEIMNPRZ	PRIZEMEN
	SENTINEL		PERLITES	EEIMNPST	SEPIMENT
EEILNNSV	ENLIVENS		REPTILES	EEIMNQSU	MESQUINE
EEILNOPR	LEPORINE		SPIRELET	EEIMNRRT	TERMINER
EEILNORS	ELOINERS	EEILPRSU	SUPERLIE	EEIMNRRV	RIVERMEN
EEILNOST	NOSELITE	EEILPSSS	PELISSES	EEIMNRST	MISENTER
EEILNOSV	NOVELISE	EEILPSST	EPISTLES	EEIMNRSV	MINEVERS
EEILNOVV	LOVEVINE	EEILPSSU	EPULISES	EEIMNRTU	MUTINEER
EEILNOVZ	NOVELIZE	EEILPSSV	PELVISES	EEIMNRTV	VIREMENT
EEILNPPZ	ZEPPELIN	EEILPSTY	EPISTYLE	EEIMNSSS	MISSENSE
EEILNPRS	PILSENER	EEILQRSU	RELIQUES	EEIMNSSW	MISWEENS
EEILNPRU	PERILUNE	EEILRRSV	RELIVERS	EEIMNSTT	MINETTES
EEILNPRV	REPLEVIN		RESILVER	EEIMNSTV	MISEVENT
EEILNPST	PENLITES		REVILERS	EEIMOPRS	MOPERIES
	PLENTIES		SILVERER		PROMISEE
EEILNQUY	EQUINELY		SLIVERER		REIMPOSE
EEILNRSS	REINLESS	EEILRRTT	LITTERER	EEIMOPSS	EPISOMES
EEILNRST	ENLISTER	EEILRSST	LEISTERS	EEIMOPST	EPISTOME
	LISTENER		RITELESS		EPITOMES
	REENLIST		TIRELESS		EPSOMITE
	SILENTER	EEILRSSU	LEISURES	EEIMORSS	ISOMERES
EEILNRSV	LIVENERS	EEILRSSV	SERVILES	EEIMORST	TIRESOME
	SNIVELER	EEILRSSW	WIRELESS	EEIMORSZ	SIEROZEM
EEILNRTT	NETTLIER	EEILRSTT	RETITLES	EEIMORTV	OVERTIME
EEILNRTY	ENTIRELY	EEILRSVY	LIVEYERS	EEIMORTX	OXIMETER
	LIENTERY	EEILSSTW	WITELESS	EEIMOSSS	SEMIOSES
EEILNRUV	UNVEILER	EEILSSTX	EXITLESS	EEIMOSSW	SOMEWISE
EEILNSST	LITENESS		SEXTILES	EEIMOSSX	EXOMISES
	SETLINES	EEILSSVW	VIEWLESS	EEIMOTTT	TOTEMITE
EEILNSSV	EVILNESS	EEILSSVX	SILVEXES	EEIMPPRS	EPISPERM
	LIVENESS	EEILSTTX	TEXTILES	EEIMPPST	PIPESTEM

EEIMPRRS	PREMIERS	EEEINORST	ONERIEST	EEINRSUV	UNIVERSE
	REPRIMES		SEROTINE	EEINRSVX	VERNIXES
	SIMPERER	EEINORSV	EVERSION	EEINRSWW	NEWSWIRE
EEIMPRSS	EMPRISES	EEINORTT	TENORITE	EEINRTTY	ENTIRETY
	IMPRESES	EEINORTX	EXERTION		ETERNITY
	IMPRESSE	EEINOSSS	ENOSISES	EEINSSST	SESTINES
	MESPRISE		NOESISES	EEINSSSW	WISENESS
	PREMISES	EEINOSST	ESSONITE	EEINSSSX	SEXINESS
	SPIREMES	EEINOSTT	NOISETTE	EEINSSTW	NEWSIEST
EEIMPRST	EMPTIERS		TEOSINTE	EEINSSTX	SIXTEENS
EEIMPRSX	PREMIXES	EEINPPSS	PEPSINES	EEINSSTY	SYENITES
EEIMPRSZ	EMPRIZES	EEINPRRS	PRERINSE	EEINSSUX	UNISEXES
	MESPRIZE		REPINERS	EEINSTTT	NETTIEST
EEIMPSST	SEPTIMES		RIPENERS		TENTIEST
EEIMPSSY	EMPYESIS	EEINPRSS	EREPSINS	EEINSTTW	TENTWISE
EEIMPSTT	EMPTIEST		RIPENESS		TWENTIES
EEIMQRSU	REQUIEMS	EEINPRSU	PENURIES	EEINSTTX	EXISTENT
EEIMQSTU	MESQUITE		RESUPINE	EEIOPPRS	EPISPORE
EEIMQTUZ	MEZQUITE	EEINPRTU	PREUNITE		POPERIES
EEIMRRST	MERRIEST	EEINPRTX	INEXPERT	EEIOPPST	EPITOPES
	MITERERS	EEINPSST	PENTISES	EEIOPRRS	ROPERIES
	RIMESTER	EEINPSTT	INEPTEST	EEIOPRRT	PORTIERE
	TRIREMES		SPINETTE	EEIOPRRV	OVERRIPE
EEIMRRTT	REMITTER	EEINQRRU	ENQUIRER	EEIOPRST	POETISER
	TRIMETER	EEINQRSU	ENQUIRES		POETRIES
EEIMRSST	MEISTERS		INQUERES	EEIOPRTZ	POETIZER
	MISSTEER		SQUIREEN	EEIOPSST	POETISES
	TRISEMES	EEINQSTU	QUIETENS	EEIOPSTZ	POETIZES
EEIMRSTT	EMITTERS	EEINQSUY	QUEYNIES	EEIORRRS	ORRERIES
	TERMITES	EEINRRSS	RESINERS	EEIORRSS	ROSERIES
EEIMRSTU	EMERITUS	EEINRRST	INSERTER		ROSIERES
EEIMRTTY	TEMERITY		REINSERT	EEIORRTV	OVERTIRE
EEIMSSST	MESSIEST		REINTERS	EEIORRTW	TOWERIER
	METISSES		RENTIERS	EEIORRTX	EXTERIOR
EEINNNPS	PENNINES		TERRINES	EEIORRUV	OUVRIERE
EEINNOPS	PENSIONE	EEINRRSU	REINSURE	EEIORSST	EROTESIS
EEINNPTT	PENITENT	EEINRRSV	VERNIERS		EROTISES
EEINNRST	INTENSER	EEINRRTU	REUNITER	EEIORSSX	OREXISES
	INTERNES		UNRETIRE	EEIORSTZ	EROTIZES
EEINNRSU	NEURINES	EEINRRTV	INVERTER	EEIORSVW	OVERWISE
EEINNRSV	INNERVES	EEINRRTW	WINTERER	EEIORSVZ	OVERSIZE
	NERVINES	EEINRRTX	INTERREX	EEIORVVW	OVERVIEW
EEINNRTT	INTERNET	EEINRSST	INTERESS	EEIORVWW	WIREWOVE
	RENITENT		SENTRIES	EEIPPPRR	PREPPIER
EEINNRTV	INVENTER		TRENISES	EEIPPPRS	PREPPIES
	REINVENT	EEINRSSU	ENURESIS	EEIPPPST	PEPPIEST
EEINNRUX	XENURINE		ERINUSES	EEIPPQRU	EQUIPPER
EEINNSST	TENNISES	EEINRSSV	INVERSES	EEIPPRRS	PERSPIRE
EEINNSTT	SENTIENT		VERSINES	EEIPPRRT	PERIPTER
EEINNSTW	ENTWINES	EEINRSTT	INERTEST	EEIPPRST	PEPTISER
	WENNIEST		INSETTER	EEIPPRTY	PERIPETY
EEINNSTZ	NETIZENS		INTEREST	EEIPPRTZ	PEPTIZER
EEINOOPT	OPTIONEE		STERNITE	EEIPPSST	PEPTISES
EEINOPPR	PEPERINO		TRIENTES	EEIPPSTT	PIPETTES
	PEPERONI	EEINRSTU	ESURIENT	EEIPPSTZ	PEPTIZES
	RONEPIPE		NEURITES	EEIPQRSU	PERIQUES
EEINOPRS	ISOPRENE		RETINUES		REEQUIPS
	PEREIONS		REUNITES		REPIQUES
	PIONEERS	EEINRSTV	NERVIEST	EEIPQSTU	PEQUISTE
EEINOPTY	EYEPOINT		REINVEST	EEIPRRRS	PERRIERS
EEINORRR	ORNERIER		SERVIENT	EEIPRRSS	PRISERES
EEINORRT	ORIENTER		SIRVENTE		REPRISES
	REORIENT	EEINRSTX	INTERSEX		RESPIRES
EEINORSS	ESSOINER	EEINRSTY	SERENITY	EEIPRRSV	REPRIVES

EEIPRRSW	PREWIRES	EEIRTTVV	VETIVERT	EELLMRSV	VERMELLS
EEIPRRSX	EXPIRERS	EEISSSTV	VITESSES	EELLNNOV	NONLEVEL
EEIPRRSZ	REPRIZES	EEISSTTT	TESTIEST	EELLNORR	ENROLLER
EEIPRRTT	PRETERIT	EEISSTTU	SUETIEST		REENROLL
	PRETTIER	EEISSTTV	STIEVEST	EELLNORS	RELLENOS
EEIPRRTW	TWERPIER	EEISSTTW	STEWIEST	EELLNOUV	NOUVELLE
EEIPRSSS	PRESSIES	EEISSTTZ	ZESTIEST	EELLNPRU	PRUNELLE
EEIPRSST	RESPITES	EEISTTTX	TETTIXES	EELLNRSU	SULLENER
EEIPRSSV	PREVISES	EEISTUXZ	ZEUXITES	EELLNSSS	LENSLESS
EEIPRSTT	PRETTIES	EEJJLNUY	JEJUNELY	EELLNSST	SNELLEST
EEIPRSTX	PREEXIST	EEJKMOOS	JOKESOME	EELLNSSW	WELLNESS
EEIPRSTY	PERSEITY	EEJKNRTU	JUNKETER	EELLNSTU	ENTELLUS
	YPERITES	EEJKORST	JOKESTER	EELLNSUV	UNLEVELS
EEIPRSVW	PREVIEWS	EEJLLMSU	JUMELLES	EELLOPSS	ELLOPSES
EEIPRSZZ	PREZZIES	EEJLLORY	JOLLEYER		POLELESS
EEIPRTUV	ERUPTIVE	EEJLPSTU	PULSEJET	EELLORRR	REROLLER
EEIPSSSS	SPEISSES	EEJNOORS	REJONEOS	EELLORSS	ROSELLES
EEIPSSTT	PESTIEST	EEJNORSY	ENJOYERS	EELLORST	SOLLERET
EEIPSSTW	SPEWIEST		REENJOYS	EELLORSV	OVERSELL
	STEPWISE	EEJORSST	RESOJETS	EELLORSZ	ROZELLES
EEIPSTTT	PETTIEST	EEJPRRRU	PERJURER	EELLORTX	EXTOLLER
EEIQRRRU	REQUIRER	EEJPRRSU	PERJURES	EELLORVY	VOLLEYER
EEIQRRSU	QUERIERS	EEJPRSTU	SUPERJET	EELLORWY	YELLOWER
	REQUIRES	EEJQRRSU	JERQUERS	EELLOSSS	SOLELESS
EEIQRRTU	REQUITER	EEKKORWW	WORKWEEK	EELLOSSV	LOVELESS
EEIQRRUV	QUIVERER	EEKKOSTV	VETKOEKS	EELLOSUV	LEVULOSE
	VERQUIRE	EEKKRRST	TREKKERS	EELLPRSS	PRESELLS
EEIQRSSU	ESQUIRES	EEKLLNRY	KERNELLY		RESPELLS
EEIQRSTU	QUIETERS	EEKLLNSV	KNEVELLS		SPELLERS
	REQUITES	EEKLLSUU	UKULELES	EELLPRST	PRETELLS
EEIQRSTW	QWERTIES	EEKLMRSZ	KLEZMERS	EELLPSST	PELTLESS
EEIQRTUY	QUEERITY	EEKLNNNU	UNKENNEL	EELLQRSU	QUELLERS
EEIQSSSU	ESQUISSE	EEKLNOSS	KEELSONS	EELLRSSU	RULELESS
EEIQSTTU	QUIETEST	EEKLNOST	SKELETON	EELLRSSW	SWELLERS
EEIRRRST	RETIRERS	EEKLNOSV	VELSKOEN	EELLSSTU	TELLUSES
	TERRIERS	EEKLOSSU	LEUKOSES	EELLSSTW	SWELLEST
EEIRRRTW	REWRITER	EEKLOSSY	YOKELESS	EELLSTVY	SVELTELY
EEIRRSST	RESISTER	EEKLRSST	KESTRELS	EELMMPSU	EMPLUMES
	TRESSIER		SKELTERS	EELMMPUX	EXEMPLUM
EEIRRSSU	REISSUER	EEKNNSTT	KENNETTS	EELMNOOS	LONESOME
EEIRRSSV	REVERSIS	EEKNOPRS	RESPOKEN		OENOMELS
	REVISERS	EEKNORTY	KEYNOTER	EELMNORS	SOLEMNER
EEIRRSSW	WERRISES	EEKNOSTY	KEYNOTES	EELMNSUY	UNSEEMLY
EEIRRSTV	RESTRIVE		KEYSTONE	EELMNTTU	TEMULENT
	REVERIST	EEKNSSST	KNESSETS	EELMNTUY	UNMEETLY
	RIVERETS	EEKNSSSW	SKEWNESS	EELMOOSV	LOVESOME
	RIVETERS	EEKNSSTU	NETSUKES	EELMOPRS	PLEROMES
EEIRRSTW	REWRITES	EEKOOPPS	PEKEPOOS	EELMOPRY	EMPLOYER
EEIRRSVV	REVIVERS	EEKOORST	KREOSOTE		REEMPLOY
EEIRRTTT	TITTERER	EEKOPRTV	OVERKEPT	EELMOPST	LEPTOMES
EEIRSSSU	REISSUES	EEKOPSTU	OUTKEEPS	EELMOPSY	EMPLOYES
	SEISURES	EEKORRSV	REVOKERS		POLYSEME
EEIRSSSV	IVRESSES	EEKORSST	RESTOKES	EELMORST	MOLESTER
EEIRSSTT	RESTIEST	EEKORSTV	OVERKEST	EELMORSW	EELWORMS
EEIRSSTU	SURETIES		VOERTSEK	EELMORTV	OVERMELT
EEIRSSTV	SIEVERTS	EEKRRSUZ	KREUZERS	EELMORTY	MOTLEYER
	TREVISES	EEKRRTUZ	KREUTZER		REMOTELY
	VESTRIES	EEKRSSTY	KEYSTERS	EELMOSSV	MOVELESS
EEIRSSTW	SWEIREST	EELLLLMP	PELLMELL	EELMOTVW	TWELVEMO
EEIRSSUZ	SEIZURES	EELLMORS	MORELLES	EELMPPRU	EMPURPLE
EEIRSTTU	SUETTIER	EELLMORW	MELLOWER	EELMPSST	SEMPLEST
EEIRSTVV	VETIVERS	EELLMOSS	MOSELLES		STEMPELS
EEIRSTVY	SEVERITY	EELLMPTU	PLUMELET		STEMPLES
EEIRTTTZ	TERZETTI	EELLMRSS	SMELLERS	EELMPSTT	TEMPLETS

EELMRRTU	MURRELET	EELORRUV	OVERRULE	EEMMOSSU	MOUSMEES
EELMRSST	RESMELTS	EELORRVV	REVOLVER	EEMMRSST	STEMMERS
	SMELTERS	EELORSSS	ROSELESS	EEMMRSTY	STEMMERY
	TERMLESS	EELORSST	SOLERETS	EEMMRTUX	EXTREMUM
EELMRSTY	SMELTERY	EELORSSV	RESOLVES	EEMNNOPR	PRENOMEN
EELMRTUX	LUXMETER	EELORSTT	LORETTES	EEMNNOPW	PENWOMEN
EELMSSST	STEMLESS	EELORSTU	RESOLUTE	EEMNNOSV	ENVENOMS
EELMSSTT	STEMLETS	EELORSTV	OVERLETS	EEMNOOSS	SOMEONES
EELNNOSS	LONENESS	EELORSVV	EVOLVERS	EEMNOOSY	MOONEYES
EELNNRTU	TUNNELER		REVOLVES	EEMNOPRS	PROSEMEN
EELNNUVY	UNEVENLY	EELORTTU	ROULETTE	EEMNORRS	SERMONER
EELNOORS	LOOSENER	EELORTUV	REVOLUTE	EEMNORSS	MORENESS
EELNOPPU	UNPEOPLE		TRUELOVE	EEMNORST	SERMONET
EELNOPRT	PETRONEL	EELOSSST	OSSELETS		STOREMEN
EELNOPSV	ENVELOPS	EELOSSSU	SOLEUSES	EEMNORSU	MOUNSEER
EELNOPSY	POLYENES	EELOSSTT	TELEOSTS	EEMNORSV	OVERSMEN
EELNOPTY	POLYTENE	EELOSSTU	SETULOSE		VENOMERS
EELNOQTU	ELOQUENT	EELOSSTV	VETOLESS	EEMNORSY	MONEYERS
EELNORST	ENTRESOL		VOTELESS	EEMNORTU	ROUTEMEN
EELNORTT	TELETRON	EELOSTTX	SEXTOLET	EEMNPRSS	PRESSMEN
EELNORTV	OVERLENT	EELOSTUV	EVOLUTES	EEMNPRSU	SUPERMEN
EELNOSSS	NOSELESS		VELOUTES	EEMNPRTU	ERUMPENT
	SOLENESS	EELPPSSU	PEPLUSES		UNTEMPER
EELNOSST	NOTELESS	EELPPSTU	SEPTUPLE	EEMNRSTU	MUENSTER
	TONELESS	EELPQRSU	PREQUELS	EEMNRSTW	TREWSMEN
EELNOSSU	SELENOUS	EELPRRSU	REPULSER	EEMNSSTU	MUTENESS
EELNOSSY	ESLOYNES	EELPRSST	SPELTERS		TENESMUS
EELNOSSZ	ZONELESS	EELPRSSU	REPULSES	EEMNSTTV	VESTMENT
EELNOSTT	NOTELETS	EELPRSTY	PEYTRELS	EEMOOPRT	PROTEOME
EELNOSTU	TOLUENES	EELPRSTZ	PRETZELS	EEMOORRT	OROMETER
EELNOSUV	VENULOSE	EELPRSUX	PLEXURES	EEMOORRV	MOREOVER
EELNOTVV	EVOLVENT	EELPRTXY	EXPERTLY	EEMOORTT	ROOMETTE
EELNRSST	NESTLERS	EELPSSTZ	SPELTZES	EEMOOSSX	EXOSMOSE
	SLENTERS	EELPSSUX	EXPULSES	EEMOPRRS	EMPERORS
EELNRSTT	LETTERNS		PLEXUSES		PREMORSE
	NETTLERS		SUPLEXES	EEMOPRSV	PREMOVES
EELNRSUV	NERVULES	EELPSTUX	SEXTUPLE	EEMOPRSW	EMPOWERS
EELNSSSW	NEWSLESS	EELRRSTW	WRESTLER	EEMOQRSU	MORESQUE
EELNSSTT	TENTLESS	EELRSSST	RESTLESS	EEMOQTTU	MOQUETTE
EELNSSTU	TUNELESS		TRESSELS	EEMORRSS	REMORSES
	UNSTEELS	EELRSSTT	SETTLERS	EEMORRSU	UROMERES
EELNSSTV	VENTLESS		STERLETS	EEMORRSV	REMOVERS
EELNSSTY	ENSTYLES		TRESTLES	EEMORRTU	MOUTERER
EELNSSUV	UNSELVES	EELRSSTU	STREUSEL		OUTREMER
EELNSTTU	LUNETTES	EELRSSTV	SERVLETS	EEMORSST	SOMERSET
	UNSETTLE	EELRSSTW	SWELTERS	EEMORSTT	REMOTEST
EELOORVV	OVERLOVE		WRESTLES	EEMORSTU	TEMEROUS
EELOPPRS	PEOPLERS	EELRSSTY	RESTYLES	EEMOSSST	MESTESOS
EELOPPSS	PEPLOSES		TYRELESS	EEMOTTTU	TEETOTUM
	POPELESS	EELRSSTZ	SELTZERS	EEMOTTZZ	MOZZETTE
EELOPPST	ESTOPPEL	EELRSTWY	WESTERLY	EEMPPRST	PREEMPTS
EELOPPSZ	ZEPPOLES	EELSSSTV	VESTLESS	EEMPRRST	PRETERMS
EELOPRRX	EXPLORER	EELSSSTZ	ZESTLESS	EEMPRRSU	PRESUMER
EELOPRSV	PRESOLVE	EELSSTTV	SVELTEST		SUPREMER
EELOPRSX	EXPLORES	EELSSTTX	TEXTLESS	EEMPRSST	SEMPSTER
EELOPRTT	TELEPORT	EELSSTUY	EUSTYLES	EEMPRSSU	PRESUMES
EELOPSST	POETLESS	EEMMNNOY	MONEYMEN		SUPREMES
EELOPSTU	EELPOUTS	EEMMNOOP	MENOPOME	EEMPRSTT	TEMPTERS
	OUTSLEEP	EEMMNOST	MEMENTOS	EEMPRSTU	PERMUTES
	SLEEPOUT	EEMMNOTV	MOVEMENT	EEMPSSTT	TEMPESTS
EELOQRUY	REQUOYLE	EEMMNNRY	MERRYMEN	EEMPSSTY	EMPTYSES
EELORRSV	RESOLVER	EEMMOORS	MEROSOME	EEMRRSSU	RESUMERS
EELORRTV	REVOLTER	EEMMOOSS	MESOSOME	EEMRRSTU	MUSTERER
EELORRTW	TROWELER	EEMMOSST	MESTOMES	EEMRRSUU	EREMURUS

	REMUEURS	**EENQSSTU**	SEQUENTS	**EEORRSTV**	EVERTORS
EEMRRTTU	MUTTERER	**EENRRRTU**	RETURNER		RESTROVE
EEMSSTTU	MUSETTES	**EENRRSSU**	ENSURERS	**EEORRSTX**	EXTRORSE
EENNNOSS	NONSENSE	**EENRRSTV**	RENVERST	**EEORRSTY**	OYSTERER
EENNNOTV	NONEVENT	**EENRRSUV**	NERVURES	**EEORRSUV**	OVERSURE
EENNNPTY	TENPENNY	**EENRRTUV**	VENTURER	**EEORRTTT**	TOTTERER
EENNOORT	ROTENONE	**EENRSSSU**	SURENESS	**EEORRTTX**	EXTORTER
EENNOPSS	OPENNESS	**EENRSSTT**	STERNEST	**EEORRTUV**	OVERTURE
EENNOPTX	EXPONENT		TESTERNS		TROUVERE
EENNORRW	RENOWNER	**EENRSSTU**	TRUENESS	**EEORSSST**	OSSETERS
EENNORST	ENTERONS	**EENRSSTW**	WESTERNS	**EEORSSTT**	ROSETTES
	TENONERS	**EENRSSTY**	STYRENES	**EEORSSTV**	ESTOVERS
EENNORSU	NEURONES	**EENRSTUV**	VENTURES		OVERSETS
EENNOSTT	NONETTES	**EEOOPPRS**	REOPPOSE	**EEORSSUV**	OVERUSES
EENNQSUU	UNQUEENS	**EEOOPRST**	PROTEOSE	**EEORSSVW**	OVERSEWS
EENNRSUV	UNNERVES	**EEOOPRSX**	EXOSPORE	**EEORSTTU**	OUTSTEER
EENNSSSU	UNSENSES	**EEOOPRTZ**	ZOETROPE	**EEORSTUV**	OUTSERVE
EENNSSTX	NEXTNESS	**EEOORRVW**	OVERWORE	**EEORSTVW**	OVERWETS
EENOORST	OESTRONE	**EEOORTVV**	OVERVOTE	**EEORSTVX**	VORTEXES
	ROESTONE	**EEOOSSST**	OSTEOSES	**EEORTTTZ**	TERZETTO
EENOORTU	EURONOTE	**EEOPPRRR**	PROPERER	**EEOSSSVW**	VOWESSES
EENOORTV	OVERTONE	**EEOPPRSS**	PORPESSE	**EEOSSTTT**	SESTETTO
EENOPPRS	PREPONES		PREPOSES	**EEPPRRSS**	PREPRESS
	PROPENES	**EEOPPSTT**	POPETTES	**EEPPRSST**	STEPPERS
	PROPENSE	**EEOPPSTU**	OUTPEEPS	**EEPPRSTY**	PRETYPES
EENOPPST	PEPTONES	**EEOPRRRT**	REPORTER	**EEPPSSUW**	UPSWEEPS
EENOPRSS	RESPONSE	**EEOPRRRV**	REPROVER	**EEPQRRUU**	PERRUQUE
EENOPRST	PROTENSE	**EEOPRRSS**	REPOSERS	**EEPRRSSS**	PRESSERS
EENOPRTT	ENTREPOT	**EEOPRRST**	PRESTORE	**EEPRRSST**	PRESTERS
EENOPRTU	OUTPREEN	**EEOPRRSU**	REPOSURE	**EEPRRSSU**	PERUSERS
EENOPRXY	PYROXENE	**EEOPRRSV**	REPROVES		PRESSURE
EENOPSST	PENTOSES	**EEOPRRSW**	REPOWERS	**EEPRRSTV**	PERVERTS
	POSTEENS	**EEOPRRTT**	POTTERER	**EEPRRSUU**	REPURSUE
EENOPSTT	POSTTEEN	**EEOPRRTV**	OVERPERT	**EEPRRSVY**	REPRYVES
	POTTEENS	**EEOPRRTX**	EXPORTER	**EEPRRTTU**	PUTTERER
EENOPSTY	NEOTYPES		REEXPORT	**EEPRSSTT**	PRETESTS
EENORRSV	OVERRENS	**EEOPRSSS**	ESPRESSO	**EEPRSSTX**	SEXPERTS
EENORRTT	ROTTENER	**EEOPRSST**	PORTESSE	**EEPRSSUX**	SUPERSEX
EENORSSS	SORENESS	**EEOPRSSU**	ESPOUSER	**EEPRSTTU**	UPSETTER
EENORSST	ESTRONES		REPOUSSE	**EEPRSTTX**	PRETEXTS
EENORSSU	NEUROSES	**EEOPRSSX**	EXPOSERS	**EEPSSTTY**	TYPESETS
EENORSTT	ONSETTER		EXPRESSO	**EEQRSSTU**	QUESTERS
EENORSTV	OVERNETS	**EEOPRSTT**	PROETTES		REQUESTS
EENORSTX	EXTENSOR		TREETOPS	**EERRSSST**	RESTRESS
EENORSVW	OVERSEWN	**EEOPRSTU**	OUTPEERS	**EERRSSTU**	TRESSURE
EENORTVW	OVERWENT	**EEOPRSTV**	OVERSTEP	**EERRSSTW**	STREWERS
EENOSSST	STENOSES	**EEOPRSTY**	SEROTYPE		WRESTERS
EENOSSSY	ESSOYNES	**EEOPRSUX**	EXPOSURE	**EERRSSVW**	SWERVERS
EENOSTTT	TONETTES	**EEOPRTVY**	OVERTYPE	**EERRSTTU**	REUTTERS
EENOSTUV	VENTOUSE	**EEOPSSSU**	ESPOUSES		UTTERERS
EENPPRST	PERPENTS		POSEUSES	**EERRSTUV**	VESTURER
EENPRSST	PENSTERS	**EEOPSSTW**	SWEETSOP	**EERRSTVY**	REVESTRY
	PERTNESS	**EEOPSSTY**	EYESPOTS	**EERRSUVY**	RESURVEY
	PRESENTS	**EEOPSTUW**	OUTSWEEP	**EERSSSST**	STRESSES
	SERPENTS		OUTWEEPS	**EERSSSTU**	ESTRUSES
EENPRSSU	PURENESS	**EEOQRSTU**	REQUOTES	**EERSSSUY**	SEYSURES
EENPRSTT	STREPENT	**EEOQRTTU**	ROQUETTE	**EERSSTTU**	TRUSTEES
EENPRSTV	PREVENTS	**EEORRRST**	RESORTER	**EERSSTTY**	SYRETTES
EENPRTUX	UNEXPERT		RESTORER	**EERSSTUU**	UTERUSES
EENPSSSU	SUSPENSE		RETRORSE	**EERSSTUV**	VESTURES
EENPSSTY	STEPNEYS		RETORTER	**EERSTTTU**	UTTEREST
EENPSTTU	PETUNTSE	**EEORRSST**	RESTORES	**EERSTTUX**	TEXTURES
EENPTTUZ	PETUNTZE	**EEORRSSV**	REVERSOS	**EESSSTTT**	SESTETTS
		EEORRSTU	REROUTES	**EESSTTTX**	SEXTETTS

EFFFGINO	FEOFFING	**EFFLOSSU**	SOUFFLES
EFFFILRU	FLUFFIER	**EFFLRRSU**	RUFFLERS
EFFFINOS	INFEOFFS	**EFFLRSTU**	TRUFFLES
EFFFISTU	FUFFIEST	**EFFNRSSU**	SNUFFERS
EFFFLRSU	FLUFFERS	**EFFNSSTU**	FUNFESTS
EFFFOORS	FEOFFORS	**EFFOOORT**	FOREFOOT
EFFGILRU	GRIEFFUL	**EFFOORRS**	OFFERORS
EFFGINOR	OFFERING	**EFFOPRRS**	PROFFERS
EFFGINSU	EFFUSING	**EFFORRST**	TROFFERS
EFFGIRRU	GRUFFIER	**EFFORRUV**	OVERRUFF
EFFGRSTU	GRUFFEST	**EFFORSSW**	SWOFFERS
EFFHIILS	FILEFISH	**EFFRRSUU**	FURFURES
EFFHIIRW	WHIFFIER	**EFFRSSTU**	RESTUFFS
EFFHIISW	FISHWIFE		STUFFERS
EFFHIITT	FIFTIETH	**EFFSSSUU**	SUFFUSES
EFFHILRW	WHIFFLER	**EFGGGILN**	FLEGGING
EFFHILSW	WHIFFLES	**EFGGIINN**	FEIGNING
EFFHIRSS	SHERIFFS	**EFGGILOS**	SOLFEGGI
EFFHIRSW	WHIFFERS	**EFGGINRU**	REFUGING
EFFHISTU	HUFFIEST	**EFGGIORR**	FROGGIER
EFFHISTW	WHIFFETS	**EFGGIOST**	FOGGIEST
EFFHLLSU	SHELFFUL	**EFGGIRRS**	FRIGGERS
EFFHLRSU	SHUFFLER	**EFGGIRTU**	EGGFRUIT
EFFHLSSU	SHUFFLES	**EFGGISTU**	FUGGIEST
EFFHOOOR	FOREHOOF	**EFGGLORS**	FLOGGERS
EFFHOORS	OFFSHORE	**EFGGORRY**	FROGGERY
EFFIIMST	MIFFIEST	**EFGHHIIL**	HIGHLIFE
EFFIINRS	SNIFFIER	**EFGHIILS**	FLEISHIG
EFFIINSS	IFFINESS	**EFGHILNS**	FLESHING
EFFIINST	NIFFIEST		SHELFING
EFFIIPRS	SPIFFIER	**EFGHINRS**	FRESHING
EFFIIPSS	SPIFFIES	**EFGHINRT**	FRIGHTEN
EFFIISST	STIFFIES	**EFGHIOSY**	FOGEYISH
EFFIKLLO	FOLKLIFE	**EFGHIPRT**	PREFIGHT
EFFIKLRU	RUFFLIKE	**EFGHIRST**	FIGHTERS
EFFIKLSS	SKIFFLES		FREIGHTS
EFFILNRS	SNIFFLER		REFIGHTS
EFFILNSS	SNIFFLES	**EFGHNOTU**	FOUGHTEN
EFFILORT	FORELIFT	**EFGHORTU**	REFOUGHT
EFFILPRS	PIFFLERS	**EFGIIINS**	IGNIFIES
EFFILPRU	PLUFFIER	**EFGIILNR**	REFILING
EFFILRRS	RIFFLERS	**EFGIILNT**	FILETING
EFFILRRU	RUFFLIER	**EFGIILNU**	FIGULINE
EFFILRSU	SIFFLEUR	**EFGIILRU**	UGLIFIER
EFFINOSU	EFFUSION	**EFGIILSU**	UGLIFIES
EFFINRSS	SNIFFERS	**EFGIIMNS**	MISFEIGN
EFFINRSU	SNUFFIER	**EFGIINNR**	ENFIRING
EFFINSST	STIFFENS		INFRINGE
EFFIOPRS	PIFFEROS		REFINING
EFFIORST	FORFEITS	**EFGIINNT**	FEINTING
EFFIORSX	FOXFIRES	**EFGIINNX**	ENFIXING
EFFIOSTT	TOFFIEST	**EFGIINPR**	PRIEFING
EFFIPSTU	PUFFIEST	**EFGIINRR**	FRINGIER
EFFIQRSU	SQUIFFER		REFIRING
EFFIRSTT	TRIFFEST	**EFGIINRU**	FIGURINE
EFFIRSTU	STUFFIER	**EFGIINRX**	REFIXING
EFFISSTT	STIFFEST	**EFGIINRY**	REIFYING
EFFISSUX	SUFFIXES	**EFGIINRZ**	FRIEZING
EFFLLOSS	SELLOFFS	**EFGIITUV**	FUGITIVE
EFFLMNUU	UNMUFFLE	**EFGIKLLU**	GULFLIKE
EFFLMRSU	MUFFLERS	**EFGIKLOR**	FROGLIKE
EFFLNRSU	SNUFFLER	**EFGIKNOR**	FOREKING
EFFLNRUU	UNRUFFLE	**EFGILLNO**	LIFELONG
EFFLNSSU	SNUFFLES	**EFGILLNU**	FUELLING

EFGILLUU	GUILEFUL
EFGILMOR	FILMGOER
EFGILNNS	FLENSING
EFGILNOR	FLORIGEN
EFGILNRS	FLINGERS
EFGILNRU	FERULING
EFGILNRY	FERLYING
	REFLYING
EFGILNSS	SELFINGS
EFGILNST	FELTINGS
EFGILNTT	FETTLING
EFGILNTW	LEFTWING
EFGILPRU	FIREPLUG
EFGILSST	GIFTLESS
EFGILSTU	FUGLIEST
	GULFIEST
EFGIMNST	FIGMENTS
EFGIMOSY	FOGEYISM
EFGIMRUU	REFUGIUM
EFGINNNP	PFENNING
EFGINNPS	PFENNIGS
EFGINNRS	FERNINGS
EFGINORV	FORGIVEN
EFGINORW	FOREWING
EFGINPUY	PINGUEFY
EFGINRRY	FERRYING
	REFRYING
EFGINRSU	GUNFIRES
	REFUSING
EFGINRSW	SWERFING
EFGINRTT	FRETTING
EFGINRTU	FEUTRING
	REFUTING
EFGINRTY	GENTRIFY
EFGIOOST	GOOFIEST
EFGIOPTT	PETTIFOG
EFGIORRV	FORGIVER
EFGIORSV	FORGIVES
EFGIRRST	GRIFTERS
EFGIRRSU	FIGURERS
EFGLOOTY	FETOLOGY
EFGLOOVX	FOXGLOVE
EFGLORST	FROGLETS
EFGLRSUU	SURGEFUL
EFGLSSTU	SLUGFEST
EFGNOSST	SONGFEST
EFGNSSUU	FUNGUSES
EFGOORRS	FORGOERS
EFGORRSU	FERRUGOS
EFGORSTU	FOREGUTS
EFHHIRSS	FRESHISH
EFHIIKLS	FISHLIKE
	FLEISHIK
EFHIILLT	HELILIFT
EFHIILNS	FISHLINE
EFHIILRT	FILTHIER
EFHIILST	TILEFISH
EFHIIMSU	HUMIFIES
EFHIINRS	FINISHER
	REFINISH
EFHIINSS	FINISHES
EFHIIPPS	PIPEFISH
EFHIIPRS	FIRESHIP
EFHIIRST	SHIFTIER

EFHIISST	FISHIEST	**EFIILMST**	FILMIEST	**EFIKLRSU**	SURFLIKE
EFHIKLOO	HOOFLIKE	**EFIILNRT**	FLINTIER	**EFIKLRTU**	TURFLIKE
EFHILLSY	ELFISHLY	**EFIILNTY**	FELINITY	**EFIKLSTU**	FLUKIEST
	FLESHILY		FINITELY		LUTEFISK
EFHILOPS	FISHPOLE	**EFIILOQU**	FILIOQUE	**EFIKNNOS**	FINNESKO
EFHILRSU	FLUSHIER	**EFIILRRT**	FLIRTIER	**EFIKNORS**	FORESKIN
EFHILSSS	FISHLESS	**EFIILRST**	FILISTER	**EFIKNRSU**	REFUSNIK
EFHILTWY	WHITEFLY	**EFIILRSU**	FUSILIER	**EFIKNSTU**	FUNKIEST
EFHINNOT	FENTHION	**EFIILSTT**	FITLIEST	**EFIKORRW**	FIREWORK
EFHINSST	FISHNETS	**EFIILSTY**	FEISTILY	**EFIKORST**	FORKIEST
EFHIOOOR	FORHOOIE	**EFIIMMNS**	FEMINISM	**EFIKRRSS**	FRISKERS
EFHIOPRS	FORESHIP	**EFIIMNOS**	FISNOMIE	**EFIKRSST**	FRISKETS
EFHIORRT	FROTHIER		OMNIFIES	**EFILLLNU**	FLUELLIN
EFHIORSS	ROSEFISH	**EFIIMNRR**	INFIRMER	**EFILLMSS**	FILMLESS
EFHIORSV	OVERFISH	**EFIIMNRS**	MISINFER	**EFILLMSU**	SMILEFUL
EFHIORTT	FORTIETH	**EFIIMNST**	FEMINIST	**EFILLOOS**	FOLIOLES
EFHIPRSS	SERFSHIP	**EFIIMNSU**	MUNIFIES	**EFILLORV**	OVERFILL
EFHIPRSU	FURPHIES	**EFIIMNTY**	FEMINITY	**EFILLORW**	LOWLIFER
EFHIRRTU	THURIFER	**EFIIMRRS**	RIMFIRES	**EFILLOSW**	LOWLIFES
EFHIRSST	SHIFTERS	**EFIIMRSS**	MISFIRES	**EFILLPRS**	PREFILLS
EFHISSTU	SHUFTIES	**EFIINNOS**	SINFONIE	**EFILLRRS**	FRILLERS
EFHISSUW	HUSWIFES	**EFIINNST**	FINNIEST	**EFILLRUY**	IREFULLY
EFHKLNOU	FUNKHOLE	**EFIINORR**	INFERIOR	**EFILLSTY**	STELLIFY
EFHLLLSU	SHELLFUL	**EFIINORT**	NOTIFIER	**EFILLTUY**	FUTILELY
EFHLNORS	HORNFELS	**EFIINOST**	NOTIFIES	**EFILMNOS**	FOILSMEN
EFHLNOUY	HONEYFUL	**EFIINPSV**	FIVEPINS	**EFILMNSU**	FULMINES
EFHLOOSS	HOOFLESS	**EFIINPSX**	SPINIFEX	**EFILMOST**	FILEMOTS
EFHLOOSX	FOXHOLES	**EFIINRRT**	FERRITIN	**EFILMRSS**	FIRMLESS
EFHLOPST	FLESHPOT	**EFIINRST**	SNIFTIER	**EFILMSSS**	SELFISMS
EFHLOPSU	HOPEFULS	**EFIINRSU**	UNIFIERS	**EFILMSST**	FILMSETS
EFHLORSY	HORSEFLY	**EFIINRSY**	RESINIFY		LEFTISMS
EFHLORVY	HOVERFLY	**EFIINSTT**	NIFTIEST	**EFILMSUY**	EMULSIFY
EFHLOSSU	FLOUSHES	**EFIINSUV**	INFUSIVE	**EFILNNTU**	INFLUENT
EFHLOSUU	HOUSEFUL	**EFIIORSS**	OSSIFIER	**EFILNOOR**	ROOFLINE
EFHLOSUY	HOUSEFLY	**EFIIOSSS**	OSSIFIES	**EFILNORU**	FLUORINE
EFHLRSSU	FLUSHERS	**EFIIPRRU**	PURIFIER	**EFILNOSU**	NOISEFUL
EFHLSSTU	FLUSHEST	**EFIIPRST**	SPITFIRE	**EFILNOSX**	FLEXIONS
EFHLSTTW	TWELFTHS	**EFIIPRSU**	PURIFIES	**EFILNRTT**	FLITTERN
EFHNORST	FORHENTS	**EFIIPRTY**	TYPIFIER	**EFILNRYZ**	FRENZILY
EFHNOSUU	FUNHOUSE	**EFIIPSTY**	TYPIFIES	**EFILNSUX**	INFLUXES
EFHOORSW	FORESHOW	**EFIIRRST**	FIRRIEST	**EFILNUWY**	UNWIFELY
EFHORRST	FROTHERS	**EFIIRRTU**	FRUITIER	**EFILOOSS**	FLOOSIES
EFHORRTY	FROTHERY	**EFIIRRZZ**	FRIZZIER	**EFILOOSZ**	FLOOZIES
EFHRRSTU	FURTHERS	**EFIIRSTT**	RIFTIEST	**EFILOPPR**	FLOPPIER
EFHRSTTU	FURTHEST	**EFIIRSZZ**	FRIZZIES	**EFILOPPS**	FLOPPIES
EFIIILRV	VILIFIER	**EFIIRTUV**	FRUITIVE	**EFILOPRR**	PROFILER
EFIIILSV	VILIFIES	**EFIIRVVY**	REVIVIFY	**EFILOPRS**	PROFILES
EFIIIMNS	MINIFIES	**EFIISSTT**	FISTIEST	**EFILORRU**	FLOURIER
EFIIINNT	INFINITE	**EFIISSTW**	SWIFTIES	**EFILORRV**	FRIVOLER
EFIIINSV	VINIFIES	**EFIISTTW**	WIFTIEST	**EFILORSS**	FLOSSIER
EFIIIRVV	VIVIFIER	**EFIISTZZ**	FIZZIEST	**EFILORST**	FLORIEST
EFIIISTX	FIXITIES	**EFIJLORS**	FRIJOLES		TREFOILS
EFIIISVV	VIVIFIES	**EFIJLOST**	JETFOILS	**EFILORTU**	FLUORITE
EFIIKLLM	FILMLIKE	**EFIKKLLO**	FOLKLIKE	**EFILOSSS**	FLOSSIES
EFIIKLNT	FLINKITE	**EFIKKLOR**	FORKLIKE	**EFILOSSX**	SEXFOILS
EFIIKLRS	FLISKIER	**EFIKLLOT**	LOFTLIKE	**EFILOSTT**	LOFTIEST
EFIIKNPR	FIREPINK	**EFIKLLOW**	WOLFLIKE	**EFILOSTU**	OUTFLIES
EFIIKRRS	FRISKIER	**EFIKLMOR**	FOREMILK	**EFILPPRS**	FLIPPERS
EFIILLNT	TEFILLIN	**EFIKLNSU**	FLUNKIES	**EFILPPST**	FLIPPEST
EFIILLRR	FRILLIER	**EFIKLOOR**	ROOFLIKE	**EFILPPSU**	PIPEFULS
EFIILLRS	FRILLIES	**EFIKLOOT**	FOOTLIKE	**EFILPRTU**	UPLIFTER
EFIILMRS	FLIMSIER	**EFIKLORS**	FOLKSIER	**EFILPSTU**	SPITEFUL
EFIILMSS	FLIMSIES	**EFIKLORW**	LIFEWORK	**EFILRRST**	FLIRTERS
	MISFILES	**EFIKLOST**	FOLKIEST		TRIFLERS

EFILRRSU	FLURRIES	EFIORRWZ	FROWZIER	EFLLSUUY	USEFULLY
EFILRRZZ	FRIZZLER	EFIORSST	FOISTERS	EFLMMRUY	FLUMMERY
EFILRSST	RIFTLESS	EFIORSTU	FOUSTIER	EFLMNOOU	MONOFUEL
	STIFLERS		OUTFIRES	EFLMNOST	LOFTSMEN
EFILRSTT	FLITTERS	EFIORSTW	FROWIEST	EFLMNRUU	FRENULUM
EFILRSTW	FEWTRILS	EFIORTTU	REOUTFIT	EFLMORRY	FORMERLY
EFILRSTY	FLYTIERS	EFIPPRRS	FRIPPERS	EFLMORSS	FORMLESS
EFILRSVV	FLIVVERS	EFIPPRRY	FRIPPERY	EFLMORSU	FULSOMER
EFILRSZZ	FRIZZLES	EFIPPRST	FRIPPETS	EFLMOSTT	LEFTMOST
EFILRTTU	FRUITLET	EFIPRRUY	REPURIFY	EFLMPRSU	FRUMPLES
EFILSSST	SELFISTS	EFIPRSST	PRESIFTS	EFLNOOSU	FELONOUS
EFILSSTT	LEFTISTS	EFIPRSTU	SUPERFIT	EFLNORSU	FLEURONS
EFILSSTU	SULFITES	EFIPRSUX	SUPERFIX	EFLNORTT	FRONTLET
EFILSTTU	FLUTIEST	EFIPRTTY	PRETTIFY	EFLNORYZ	FROZENLY
	FUTILEST	EFIRRRSU	FURRIERS	EFLNOSSU	FOULNESS
EFILSTTW	SWIFTLET	EFIRRRUY	FURRIERY		SULFONES
EFIMMRSU	FERMIUMS	EFIRRSSU	FRISEURS	EFLNOSTT	FLETTONS
EFIMNORR	INFORMER		FRISURES		FONTLETS
	REINFORM	EFIRRSTT	FRITTERS	EFLNOSTY	STONEFLY
	RENIFORM	EFIRRSTU	FRITURES	EFLNSSTU	NESTFULS
EFIMNORS	ENSIFORM		FRUITERS	EFLNSSUY	SYNFUELS
	FERMIONS		FURRIEST	EFLNSTTU	TENTFULS
EFIMNRSS	FIRMNESS	EFIRRSZZ	FRIZZERS	EFLNSUUU	UNUSEFUL
EFIMNSTT	FITMENTS	EFIRRTUY	FRUITERY	EFLOOPRV	FLOPOVER
EFIMOORR	FIREROOM	EFIRSSSU	FISSURES	EFLOORRS	FLOORERS
EFIMORRT	RETIFORM	EFIRSSTU	SURFEITS	EFLOORSS	FORSLOES
EFIMORRW	FIREWORM		SURFIEST		ROOFLESS
EFIMORST	SETIFORM	EFIRSSTW	SWIFTERS	EFLOORST	FOOTLERS
EFIMOSST	SEMISOFT	EFIRSTTU	TURFIEST	EFLOORSW	FORESLOW
EFIMOSTT	OFTTIMES		TURFITES	EFLOORSZ	FOOZLERS
EFIMPRRU	FRUMPIER	EFIRSTUX	FIXTURES	EFLOORTU	FOOTRULE
EFIMRSTU	FREMITUS	EFIRSTUZ	FURZIEST	EFLOORUV	OVERFOUL
EFINNORS	INFERNOS	EFISSSTU	FUSSIEST	EFLOORVW	OVERFLOW
EFINNPSU	FINESPUN	EFISSTTU	FUSTIEST	EFLOOSST	FOOTLESS
EFINNRST	FERNINST	EFISSTTW	SWIFTEST	EFLOPPRS	FLOPPERS
EFINNSTU	FUNNIEST	EFISTTTU	TUFTIEST	EFLOPRUW	POWERFUL
EFINOPRS	FORPINES	EFISTUZZ	FUZZIEST	EFLOPRUX	FOURPLEX
EFINOPTX	PONTIFEX	EFKLLOOR	FOLKLORE	EFLORRUY	RYEFLOUR
EFINORRT	FRONTIER	EFKLMNOS	MENFOLKS	EFLORSSS	FLOSSERS
EFINORSU	REFUSION	EFKLMOOT	FOLKMOTE	EFLORSTT	FORTLETS
EFINORTY	RENOTIFY	EFKLMORS	MERFOLKS	EFLORSTU	FLOUTERS
EFINOSSX	FOXINESS	EFKLNRSU	FLUNKERS	EFLORSTW	FELWORTS
EFINOSSZ	FOZINESS	EFKLNSUY	FLUNKEYS	EFLORSUY	YOURSELF
EFINOSTT	FISTNOTE	EFKLOPSU	POKEFULS	EFLORSVY	FLYOVERS
EFINRRRU	FURRINER	EFKLORSS	FORKLESS	EFLOSUUX	FLEXUOUS
EFINRSST	SNIFTERS	EFKLORUW	FLUEWORK	EFLPRRSU	PURFLERS
EFINRSSU	INFUSERS	EFKLPSSU	SKEPFULS	EFLPRSSU	PRESSFUL
EFINRTTU	UNFITTER	EFKNOORW	FOREKNOW	EFLPRSUU	PURSEFUL
EFIOOPST	POOFIEST	EFKNRSTU	FUNKSTER	EFLRSSTU	FLUSTERS
EFIOORST	ROOFIEST	EFKOOPRS	FORSPOKE		TURFLESS
EFIOOSST	FOOTSIES	EFKORRTW	FRETWORK	EFLRSTTU	FLUTTERS
EFIOOSTT	FOOTIEST	EFLLLOOW	WOOLFELL	EFLRSTUU	FRUSTULE
EFIOOSTW	WOOFIEST	EFLLLOWY	FELLOWLY		SULFURET
EFIOPRRS	PORIFERS	EFLLLPSU	SPELLFUL	EFLRSTUY	FLUSTERY
EFIOPRRT	PORTFIRE	EFLLNSSU	FULLNESS	EFLRTTUY	FLUTTERY
	PROFITER	EFLLNTUY	FLUENTLY	EFMNNNUY	FUNNYMEN
EFIOPRST	FIREPOTS	EFLLOORW	FOLLOWER	EFMNNORT	FRONTMEN
	PIEFORTS	EFLLOOTW	FOOTWELL	EFMNORTY	FROMENTY
	POSTFIRE	EFLLORSU	FLORULES	EFMNRTUY	FRUMENTY
EFIORRST	FROSTIER	EFLLORUV	OVERFULL		FURMENTY
	ROTIFERS	EFLLORUW	WOFULLER	EFMOORST	FOREMOST
EFIORRSW	FROWSIER	EFLLOSST	LOFTLESS	EFMOORSU	FOURSOME
EFIORRTT	RETROFIT	EFLLOUWY	WOEFULLY	EFMOPRRS	PERFORMS
EFIORRUZ	FROUZIER	EFLLRUUY	RUEFULLY		PREFORMS

EFMOPRST	POMFRETS	EGGIIJLR	JIGGLIER	EGGIOSST	SOGGIEST
EFNNOOOR	FORENOON	EGGIIJST	JIGGIEST	EGGIPRRS	PRIGGERS
EFNNORST	FORNENST	EGGIILLN	GINGELLI		SPRIGGER
EFNNORSU	FENURONS	EGGIILNR	NIGGLIER	EGGIPRRY	PRIGGERY
EFNNORUZ	UNFROZEN	EGGIILNS	GINGELIS	EGGIPRSU	PUGGRIES
EFNOOOTT	FOOTNOTE	EGGIILRW	WIGGLIER	EGGIPSSU	SPUGGIES
EFNOOPRT	PENTROOF	EGGIINNN	ENGINING	EGGIPSTU	PUGGIEST
EFNOORRW	FOREWORN	EGGIINNR	GREINING	EGGIRRST	TRIGGERS
EFNOOSST	EFTSOONS		REIGNING	EGGIRSSW	SWIGGERS
	FESTOONS	EGGIINNS	SINGEING	EGGIRSTT	TRIGGEST
EFNOPRST	FORSPENT	EGGIINNT	TINGEING	EGGIRSTU	RUGGIEST
EFNORRST	REFRONTS	EGGIINNW	WINGEING		STUGGIER
	RENFORST	EGGIINRV	GRIEVING	EGGIRSTW	TWIGGERS
EFNORRSU	FORERUNS		REGIVING	EGGISTUV	VUGGIEST
EFNORRSW	FROWNERS	EGGIIPST	PIGGIEST	EGGJLORS	JOGGLERS
EFNORSTU	FORTUNES	EGGIIRTW	TWIGGIER	EGGJLRSU	JUGGLERS
EFNOSSST	SOFTNESS	EGGIISTW	WIGGIEST	EGGJLRUY	JUGGLERY
EFNOTUZZ	FUZZTONE	EGGIKLNO	GONGLIKE	EGGLMOOY	GEMOLOGY
EFNRSSTU	FUNSTERS	EGGIKLNS	KEGLINGS	EGGLMRSU	SMUGGLER
EFOOOPRT	FOOTROPE	EGGIKNOS	GINGKOES	EGGLMSSU	SMUGGLES
EFOOORST	FOOTSORE		GINKGOES	EGGLNSSU	SNUGGLES
EFOOPRRS	PROOFERS	EGGILLNY	GINGELLY	EGGLORSS	SLOGGERS
	REPROOFS	EGGILMNU	EMULGING	EGGLORST	TOGGLERS
EFOOPRSS	SPOOFERS	EGGILMSS	LEGGISMS	EGGLORUY	GURGOYLE
EFOOPRST	FORETOPS	EGGILNNO	LONGEING	EGGLPRSU	PLUGGERS
	POOFTERS	EGGILNNT	GENTLING	EGGLRSSU	SLUGGERS
EFOOPRSY	SPOOFERY		GLENTING	EGGLRSTU	GURGLETS
EFOOPRTW	WETPROOF	EGGILNNU	LUNGEING		STRUGGLE
EFOOPSTT	FOOTSTEP	EGGILNRS	NIGGLERS	EGGMNTUY	NUTMEGGY
EFOORRSW	FORSWORE		SNIGGLER	EGGMRSUY	SMUGGERY
EFOORSTT	FOOTREST	EGGILNRU	GRUELING	EGGMSSTU	SMUGGEST
EFOORSTV	OVERSOFT		REGLUING	EGGNOOST	GEOGNOST
EFOORSTW	WOOFTERS	EGGILNRY	GINGERLY	EGGNOOSY	GEOGNOSY
EFOOSTUX	OUTFOXES	EGGILNSS	SNIGGLES	EGGNORST	GONGSTER
EFOPRRSU	PROFUSER	EGGILNSU	LUGEINGS	EGGNRRSU	GRUNGERS
EFOPRSTU	POUFTERS	EGGILNSY	GLEYINGS	EGGNRSUY	SNUGGERY
EFORRRUW	FURROWER	EGGILOOS	GOOGLIES	EGGNSSTU	SNUGGEST
EFORRSST	FORTRESS	EGGILOST	LOGGIEST	EGGOORSU	GORGEOUS
EFORRSTW	FROWSTER	EGGILQSU	SQUIGGLE	EGGOPRRS	PROGGERS
EFORRSTY	FORESTRY	EGGILRRW	WRIGGLER	EGGSSSTU	SUGGESTS
EFORRSUV	FERVOURS	EGGILRSW	WIGGLERS	EGHHHIST	HEIGHTHS
EFORRTTU	FROTTEUR		WRIGGLES	EGHHIIMS	SEMIHIGH
EFORSSST	FOSTRESS	EGGIMNNU	EMUNGING	EGHHIIRS	HIGHRISE
EGGGIILR	GIGGLIER	EGGIMNRS	MERGINGS	EGHHILTY	EIGHTHLY
EGGGILNS	LEGGINGS	EGGIMORS	SMOGGIER	EGHHINSS	HIGHNESS
EGGGILOR	GOGGLIER	EGGIMSTU	MUGGIEST	EGHHIORV	OVERHIGH
EGGGILRS	GIGGLERS	EGGINNNR	GRENNING	EGHHORUW	ROUGHHEW
EGGGINPS	PEGGINGS	EGGINNOR	ENGORING	EGHHOSSW	SHOWGHES
EGGGIORR	GROGGIER	EGGINNSS	GINSENGS	EGHIIKLS	SIGHLIKE
EGGGLORS	GOGGLERS	EGGINORR	GORGERIN	EGHIILLS	GHILLIES
EGGGNNOR	RONGGENG		ROGERING	EGHIILNR	HIRELING
EGGGOOOS	GOOSEGOG	EGGINORU	ROGUEING	EGHIILNS	SHEILING
EGGGORRY	GROGGERY	EGGINOUV	VOGUEING		SHIELING
EGGHIINN	NEIGHING	EGGINRRU	GRUNGIER	EGHIIMRT	MIGHTIER
EGGHIINW	WEIGHING		REURGING	EGHIINNR	INHERING
EGGHIKSW	EGGWHISK	EGGINRSS	GRESSING	EGHIINRR	REHIRING
EGGHILRS	HIGGLERS		SERGINGS	EGHIINRT	THINGIER
EGGHINSS	GHESSING		SNIGGERS	EGHIINST	HEISTING
EGGHIRST	THIGGERS	EGGINRSY	GREYINGS		NIGHTIES
EGGHISSU	SHUGGIES	EGGINSSU	GUESSING		THINGIES
EGGHISTU	HUGGIEST		SNUGGIES	EGHIINSV	INVEIGHS
EGGHLORU	ROUGHLEG	EGGINSTT	GETTINGS	EGHIINTV	THIEVING
EGGHLOSS	SHOGGLES	EGGINSTU	GUESTING	EGHIIRST	RIGHTIES
EGGHRTUY	THUGGERY		GUNGIEST		TIGERISH

EGHIISTY	HYGIEIST	**EGHIOOSS**	SHOOGIES	RINGLIKE
EGHIKNRS	GHERKINS	**EGHIOPSS**	PISHOGES	**EGIIKLNW** WINGLIKE
EGHIKRSS	SKREIGHS	**EGHIOPSU**	PISHOGUE	**EGIIKLTW** TWIGLIKE
	SKRIEGHS	**EGHIORST**	GHOSTIER	**EGIIKNNR** REINKING
EGHILLNO	HELLOING	**EGHIORSU**	ROUGHIES	**EGIIKNNS** SKEINING
EGHILLNS	SHELLING	**EGHIOSTT**	GOTHITES	**EGIILMMN** IMMINGLE
EGHILMNW	WHELMING	**EGHIOSTU**	TOUGHIES	**EGIILMST** LEGITIMS
EGHILMOR	HOMEGIRL	**EGHIOSTV**	EIGHTVOS	**EGIILNNO** ELOINING
EGHILMPS	MEGILPHS	**EGHIOTUW**	OUTWEIGH	**EGIILNNR** RELINING
EGHILNNU	UNHELING	**EGHIQRTU**	REQUIGHT	**EGIILNNS** ENISLING
EGHILNOV	HOVELING	**EGHIRRST**	RIGHTERS	ENSILING
EGHILNPS	HELPINGS	**EGHIRRUY**	HIERURGY	**EGIILNNT** LENITING
EGHILNPT	PENLIGHT	**EGHIRSST**	RESIGHTS	**EGIILNNU** LINGUINE
EGHILNPW	WHELPING		SIGHTERS	**EGIILNNV** LIVENING
EGHILNRS	HERLINGS	**EGHIRSTT**	RIGHTEST	**EGIILNOR** LIGROINE
	SHINGLER		STREIGHT	RELIGION
EGHILNSS	SHINGLES	**EGHISSTU**	GUSHIEST	REOILING
EGHILNST	ENLIGHTS	**EGHISSTY**	HYGEISTS	**EGIILNPR** PERILING
	LIGHTENS	**EGHISTTT**	TIGHTEST	**EGIILNPS** SPEILING
EGHILNSV	SHELVING	**EGHISTUV**	VUGHIEST	SPIELING
EGHILNSW	WELSHING	**EGHKLNOU**	GUNKHOLE	**EGIILNRS** RESILING
EGHILNUW	GLUHWEIN	**EGHLLOPU**	PLUGHOLE	RIESLING
EGHILORT	REGOLITH	**EGHLLOSU**	LUGHOLES	**EGIILNRT** GIRTLINE
EGHILOSU	GHOULIES	**EGHLMNOP**	PHLEGMON	GLINTIER
	OUGHLIES	**EGHLNORS**	LEGHORNS	RETILING
EGHILPRT	PLIGHTER	**EGHLNPSU**	ENGULPHS	TINGLIER
EGHILPST	PIGHTLES	**EGHLNRUY**	HUNGERLY	TIRELING
EGHILRST	LIGHTERS	**EGHLOOOR**	HOROLOGE	**EGIILNRV** LIVERING
	RELIGHTS	**EGHLOORY**	RHEOLOGY	RELIVING
	SLIGHTER	**EGHLOOSS**	GOLOSHES	REVILING
EGHILSSS	SIGHLESS		SHOOGLES	**EGIILNST** LIGNITES
EGHILSST	SLEIGHTS	**EGHLOOST**	THEOLOGS	LINGIEST
EGHILSTT	LIGHTEST	**EGHLOOTY**	ETHOLOGY	**EGIILNSV** VEILINGS
EGHIMNNS	MENSHING		THEOLOGY	**EGIILNSW** WISELING
EGHIMNOR	HOMERING	**EGHLOPRU**	PLOUGHER	**EGIILRRS** GRISLIER
EGHIMNSS	MESHINGS	**EGHLOPRY**	HYPERGOL	**EGIILRSS** GRISLIES
EGHIMNUX	EXHUMING	**EGHMNOOY**	HOMOGENY	**EGIILRST** GIRLIEST
EGHIMPRU	GRUMPHIE	**EGHMNORS**	GEMSHORN	**EGIILRTU** GUILTIER
EGHIMSTT	MIGHTEST	**EGHMNOSU**	HUMOGENS	**EGIILRTZ** GLITZIER
EGHINNOY	HONEYING	**EGHMOPUY**	HYPOGEUM	**EGIIMMNO** MIMEOING
EGHINNSS	NIGHNESS	**EGHMOSSU**	GUMSHOES	**EGIIMMNW** IMMEWING
EGHINNST	SENNIGHT	**EGHNOOPT**	PHOTOGEN	**EGIIMMNU** INGENIUM
EGHINNSU	UNHINGES	**EGHNOOSS**	HOGNOSES	**EGIIMNOS** IGNOMIES
EGHINORT	THROEING	**EGHNOOTY**	THEOGONY	**EGIIMNPR** IMPINGER
EGHINORV	HOVERING	**EGHNORSU**	ENROUGHS	**EGIIMNPS** IMPINGES
EGHINOSS	SHOEINGS		ROUGHENS	**EGIIMNRS** REMISING
EGHINOST	HISTOGEN	**EGHNORUV**	HUNGOVER	**EGIIMNRT** MERITING
EGHINOSU	GINHOUSE		OVERHUNG	MITERING
EGHINOSY	HOSEYING	**EGHNOSTU**	TOUGHENS	RETIMING
EGHINPRS	SPHERING	**EGHNOSUU**	GUNHOUSE	**EGIIMNRX** REMIXING
EGHINPSS	SPHINGES	**EGHNRSTT**	STRENGTH	**EGIIMNST** MINGIEST
EGHINQTU	QUETHING	**EGHOOOSW**	HOOSEGOW	**EGIIMNSV** MISGIVEN
EGHINRRS	HERRINGS	**EGHORRSU**	ROUGHERS	**EGIIMNTT** EMITTING
EGHINRRU	HUNGRIER	**EGHORRTW**	REGROWTH	**EGIIMOPT** IMPETIGO
EGHINRRY	HERRYING	**EGHORSTU**	RESOUGHT	**EGIIMORR** GRIMOIRE
EGHINRST	RIGHTENS		ROUGHEST	**EGIIMPST** GIMPIEST
EGHINRSU	USHERING	**EGHOSTTU**	TOUGHEST	**EGIIMRST** GRIMIEST
EGHINRSW	SHREWING	**EGHPSSUU**	UPGUSHES	TIGERISM
	WHINGERS	**EGIIINSV**	VISIEING	**EGIIMSSV** MISGIVES
EGHINRTW	WRETHING	**EGIIJLNR**	JINGLIER	**EGIINNPR** REPINING
EGHINSTT	SHETTING	**EGIIKKLN**	KINGLIKE	RIPENING
	TIGHTENS	**EGIIKLLO**	KILLOGIE	**EGIINNRS** RESINING
EGHINTTW	WHETTING	**EGIIKLNN**	LIKENING	**EGIINNSS** SEININGS
EGHINTUW	UNWEIGHT	**EGIIKLNR**	KINGLIER	**EGIINNST** GINNIEST

	STEINING	EGIKLNOS	SONGLIKE	EGILNOPP	PEOPLING
EGIINNSV	VEININGS	EGIKLNPS	SKELPING		POPELING
EGIINNSW	SINEWING	EGIKLNRS	ERLKINGS	EGILNORS	RESOLING
EGIINNTU	UNTIEING	EGIKLNSS	KINGLESS	EGILNORW	LOWERING
EGIINNVW	VINEWING	EGIKLNST	KINGLETS		ROWELING
EGIINNWZ	WIZENING	EGIKMNPS	KEMPINGS	EGILNOSS	LIGNOSES
EGIINOPR	PEIGNOIR	EGIKMNRS	SMERKING		LOGINESS
EGIINORS	SEIGNIOR	EGIKNNNS	KENNINGS	EGILNOSU	LIGNEOUS
EGIINPPT	PIPETING		SKENNING	EGILNOSW	LONGWISE
EGIINPRS	SPEIRING	EGIKNNOT	TOKENING	EGILNOTW	TOWELING
	SPIERING	EGIKNNRS	KERNINGS	EGILNOVV	EVOLVING
EGIINPRV	PRIEVING	EGIKNNSY	ENSKYING	EGILNPRS	PINGLERS
EGIINPRX	EXPIRING	EGIKNORV	OVERKING		SPERLING
EGIINPSS	PIGSNIES		REVOKING		SPRINGLE
EGIINQTU	QUIETING	EGIKNPPS	SKEPPING	EGILNPRY	REPLYING
EGIINRRS	RERISING	EGIKNRRS	SKERRING	EGILNPSS	SPIGNELS
EGIINRRT	RETIRING	EGIKNRSU	RESKUING	EGILNPST	PELTINGS
EGIINRRW	REWIRING	EGIKNSTT	SKETTING		PESTLING
EGIINRST	GIRNIEST	EGIKNSTU	GUNKIEST	EGILNPSY	YELPINGS
	IGNITERS	EGILLMNS	SMELLING	EGILNPTT	PETTLING
	REISTING	EGILLNNO	LONGLINE	EGILNRRU	RULERING
	RESITING	EGILLNNS	SNELLING	EGILNRRY	ERRINGLY
	STINGIER	EGILLNOS	LOGLINES	EGILNRSS	RINGLESS
	STRIGINE	EGILLNOV	LIVELONG		SLINGERS
EGIINRSU	SIGNIEUR	EGILLNPS	SPELLING	EGILNRST	LINGSTER
EGIINRSV	REVISING	EGILLNQU	QUELLING		RINGLETS
EGIINRSW	RINGWISE	EGILLNST	GILLNETS		STERLING
	SWEIRING		STELLING		TINGLERS
	SWINGIER		TELLINGS		TRINGLES
EGIINRSZ	RESIZING	EGILLNSW	SWELLING	EGILNRSW	NEWSGIRL
EGIINRTU	INTRIGUE		WELLINGS	EGILNRUV	VELURING
EGIINRTV	RIVETING	EGILLNSY	YELLINGS	EGILNSSS	SIGNLESS
EGIINRTX	GENITRIX	EGILLNTU	GLUTELIN	EGILNSST	GLISTENS
EGIINRVV	REVIVING	EGILLOOR	GLORIOLE		SINGLETS
EGIINSSS	SEISINGS	EGILLORS	GIROLLES		SNIGLETS
EGIINSST	STINGIES	EGILLRRS	GRILLERS	EGILNSSU	GLUINESS
EGIINSSZ	SEIZINGS	EGILLRRY	GRILLERY		UGLINESS
EGIINSTW	WINGIEST	EGILMMNS	LEMMINGS	EGILNSSW	SWINGLES
EGIINSTX	EXISTING	EGILMMRS	GLIMMERS		WINGLESS
EGIINSTZ	ZINGIEST	EGILMMRY	GLIMMERY	EGILNSTT	LETTINGS
EGIINSVW	VIEWINGS	EGILMNNO	LEMONING		SETTLING
EGIIOPRS	PIROGIES	EGILMNNU	UNMINGLE	EGILNSTW	SWELTING
EGIIPPRR	GRIPPIER	EGILMNOT	LONGTIME		WELTINGS
EGIIPRST	GRIPIEST	EGILMNPU	IMPLUNGE		WINGLETS
EGIIPRSW	PERIWIGS	EGILMNRS	GREMLINS	EGILNSUV	EVULSING
EGIIPSST	PIGSTIES		MERLINGS	EGILNSUY	GUYLINES
EGIIRRTT	GRITTIER		MINGLERS	EGILNTUX	EXULTING
EGIITUXY	EXIGUITY	EGILMNRU	RELUMING	EGILNVXY	VEXINGLY
EGIJKNOS	JINGKOES	EGILMNST	MELTINGS	EGILOOOS	OOLOGIES
EGIJKNRS	JERKINGS		SMELTING	EGILOOPR	GLOOPIER
EGIJLLNY	JELLYING	EGILMNSU	GUMLINES	EGILOORR	GROOLIER
EGIJLNRS	JINGLERS		LEGUMINS	EGILOOSU	ISOLOGUE
EGIJLNRU	JUNGLIER		MULESING	EGILOOTY	ETIOLOGY
EGIJLNST	JINGLETS	EGILMOOR	GLOOMIER	EGILOPPR	GLOPPIER
EGIJMMNY	JEMMYING		OLIGOMER	EGILORRW	GROWLIER
EGIJNNOS	JONESING	EGILMORS	GOMERILS	EGILORSS	GLOSSIER
EGIJNNOY	ENJOYING	EGILMOSU	ELOGIUMS	EGILORTV	OVERGILT
EGIJNQRU	JERQUING	EGILMOUU	EULOGIUM	EGILORTY	GYROLITE
EGIJNSST	JESTINGS	EGILMPRS	GLIMPSER	EGILOSSS	GLOSSIES
EGIJNTTY	JETTYING	EGILMPRU	GLUMPIER	EGILOSST	ELOGISTS
EGIKKLNS	LEKKINGS	EGILMPSS	GLIMPSES	EGILOSTU	EULOGIST
EGIKKNRT	TREKKING	EGILNNST	NESTLING	EGILPPRS	GRIPPLES
EGIKLLNN	KNELLING	EGILNNTT	NETTLING	EGILPSTU	GULPIEST
EGIKLLNV	KVELLING	EGILNNTU	GLUTENIN	EGILRRZZ	GRIZZLER

EGILRSST	GLISTERS		**EGINNRSV**	NERVINGS	
	GRISTLES	**EGINNRTU**	RETUNING	
	GRITLESS		TENURING	
EGILRSTT	GLITTERS	**EGINNRTV**	VENTRING	
EGILRSTU	GURLIEST	**EGINNSSS**	SENSINGS	
EGILRSTY	GREYLIST	**EGINNSST**	NESTINGS	
EGILRSUV	VIRGULES	**EGINNSTT**	NETTINGS	
EGILRSZZ	GRIZZLES		STENTING	
EGILRTTY	GLITTERY		TENTINGS	
EGILSSTW	TWIGLESS	**EGINNSTV**	VENTINGS	
EGIMMNOV	EMMOVING	**EGINNSUW**	UNSEWING	
EGIMMNST	STEMMING	**EGINNSUX**	UNSEXING	
EGIMMRST	GRIMMEST	**EGINNSVY**	ENVYINGS	
EGIMMSTU	GUMMIEST	**EGINOORV**	INGROOVE	
	GUMMITES	**EGINOOSS**	ISOGONES	
EGIMNNNO	MIGNONNE	**EGINOOST**	GOONIEST	
EGIMNNOV	ENMOVING	**EGINOPRS**	PERIGONS	
	VENOMING		REPOSING	
EGIMNNSW	SWINGMEN		SPONGIER	
EGIMNNUW	UNMEWING	**EGINOPRW**	POWERING	
EGIMNOOR	GERONIMO	**EGINOPRY**	PIGEONRY	
EGIMNORS	NEGROISM	**EGINOPST**	PONGIEST	
EGIMNORV	REMOVING	**EGINOPSU**	EPIGONUS	
EGIMNOST	MITOGENS	**EGINOPSX**	EXPOSING	
EGIMNOSU	GEMINOUS	**EGINOPSY**	POESYING	
EGIMNOSY	MOSEYING	**EGINOPXY**	EPOXYING	
EGIMNPRS	IMPREGNS	**EGINORRS**	IGNORERS	
EGIMNPRU	IMPUGNER	**EGINORSS**	GORINESS	
EGIMNPST	EMPTINGS		SIGNORES	
	PIGMENTS	**EGINORST**	GENITORS	
EGIMNPTT	TEMPTING		ROSETING	
EGIMNPTY	EMPTYING	**EGINORSW**	RESOWING	
EGIMNRSS	GRIMNESS	**EGINORSY**	SEIGNORY	
EGIMNRSU	RESUMING	**EGINORTT**	OTTERING	
EGIMNRUY	ERYNGIUM	**EGINORTU**	OUTREIGN	
EGIMORSS	OGREISMS		ROUTEING	
EGIMORST	ERGOTISM	**EGINORTV**	REVOTING	
	GORMIEST	**EGINORTW**	TOWERING	
EGIMOSST	EGOTISMS	**EGINORTX**	OXTERING	
EGIMOSTW	TWIGSOME	**EGINORTZ**	ROZETING	
EGIMPRRU	GRUMPIER	**EGINORVW**	OVERWING	
EGIMSSSU	MISGUESS		WINGOVER	
EGINNNOT	TENONING	**EGINORXX**	XEROXING	
EGINNNOZ	ENZONING	**EGINOSTT**	TENTIGOS	
EGINNNRS	RENNINGS	**EGINOTUV**	OUTGIVEN	
EGINNNST	STENNING	**EGINPPPR**	PREPPING	
EGINNNUY	ENNUYING	**EGINPPRS**	REPPINGS	
EGINNOOR	RONEOING	**EGINPPST**	STEPPING	
EGINNOOS	IONOGENS	**EGINPRRS**	RESPRING	
EGINNOPR	REPONING		SPERRING	
EGINNOPS	OPENINGS		SPRINGER	
EGINNORS	NEGRONIS	**EGINPRRU**	REPURING	
EGINNORT	NITROGEN	**EGINPRSS**	PRESSING	
	RINGTONE		SPERSING	
EGINNORV	VIGNERON		SPRINGES	
EGINNORZ	REZONING	**EGINPRST**	PRESTING	
EGINNOSU	ENGINOUS	**EGINPRSU**	PERSUING	
EGINNPRT	PRENTING		PERUSING	
EGINNPSU	PENGUINS		SUPERING	
EGINNRRS	GRINNERS	**EGINPRTU**	ERUPTING	
EGINNRRU	UNERRING		REPUTING	
EGINNRST	RENTINGS	**EGINPRTY**	RETYPING	
	STERNING	**EGINPRUV**	PREVUING	
EGINNRSU	ENSURING	**EGINPRYY**	PERIGYNY	

EGINPSSY	PIGSNEYS
EGINPSTT	PETTINGS
	SPETTING
EGINQRUY	QUERYING
EGINQSTU	QUESTING
EGINQSUU	QUEUINGS
EGINRRST	RESTRING
	RINGSTER
	STRINGER
EGINRRSW	WRINGERS
EGINRRSY	SERRYING
EGINRRTY	RETRYING
EGINRSST	RESTINGS
	STINGERS
	TRESSING
	TRIGNESS
EGINRSSV	SERVINGS
	VERSINGS
EGINRSSW	SWINGERS
EGINRSSY	SYRINGES
EGINRSTT	GITTERNS
EGINRSTV	STERVING
EGINRSTW	STREWING
	WRESTING
EGINRSVW	SWERVING
EGINRTTU	UTTERING
EGINSSTT	SETTINGS
	TESTINGS
EGINSSTV	VESTINGS
EGINSSTW	STEWINGS
	WESTINGS
EGINSTTT	STETTING
EGINSTTW	WETTINGS
EGIOOPST	GOOPIEST
EGIOORRV	GROOVIER
EGIOOSST	GOOSIEST
EGIOPRSS	GOSSIPER
	SERPIGOS
EGIOPRSU	GROUPIES
	PIROGUES
EGIOPRTU	PORTIGUE
EGIORRTT	GROTTIER
EGIORRTU	GROUTIER
EGIORRTV	OVERGIRT
EGIORSST	GORSIEST
	STRIGOSE
EGIORSSU	GRISEOUS
EGIORSTU	GOUSTIER
EGIORSTV	VERTIGOS
EGIORSTY	OYSTRIGE
EGIORSTZ	ZORGITES
EGIORSUV	GRIEVOUS
EGIOSSTT	EGOTISTS
EGIOSTTU	GOUTIEST
EGIOSTUV	OUTGIVES
	VOGUIEST
EGIOSUUX	EXIGUOUS
EGIPPRRS	GRIPPERS
EGIPRSUU	GUIPURES
EGIRRRSU	GURRIERS
EGIRRSST	GRISTERS
EGIRRSTT	GRITTERS
EGIRRSTY	REGISTRY
EGIRSSTU	SURGIEST

EGIRSTTT	GRITTEST	EGLRSTTU	GUTTLERS	EGORSSST	GROSSEST
EGIRSTTU	TURGITES	EGLRSUZZ	GUZZLERS	EGORSSTU	GROUSEST
EGISSTTU	GUSTIEST	EGLSSSTU	GUSTLESS	EGOSSTUU	OUTGUESS
	GUTSIEST	EGLSSUUV	VULGUSES	EGPRSSTY	GYPSTERS
EGISSUWY	WISEGUYS	EGMMNOOR	MONOGERM	EGPRSSUU	UPSURGES
EGISSYYZ	SYZYGIES	EGMMORST	GROMMETS	EHHIIPRS	HEIRSHIP
EGISTTTU	GUTTIEST	EGMMOSSU	GUMMOSES	EHHIISTV	THIEVISH
EGJLNORU	JONGLEUR	EGMMRSTU	GRUMMEST	EHHIKSSS	SHIKSEHS
EGJLNOTU	JELUTONG		GRUMMETS	EHHILMNT	HELMINTH
EGJOSSTT	GJETOSTS	EGMNNOOY	MONOGENY	EHHILOPR	RHEOPHIL
EGKLORSW	LEGWORKS		NOMOGENY	EHHILOST	SHITHOLE
EGLLMORW	GROMWELL	EGMNNOSW	GOWNSMEN	EHHINOPT	THIOPHEN
EGLLOOPR	GOLLOPER	EGMNOOOS	GONOSOME	EHHIOPRS	HEROSHIP
EGLLOOPY	PELOLOGY		MONGOOSE	EHHIORTT	HITHERTO
EGLLOPSY	GOSPELLY	EGMNOORY	MEROGONY	EHHIPRSS	HERSHIPS
EGLLPSSU	PLUGLESS	EGMNOOSU	MUNGOOSE	EHHIPSST	PHTHISES
EGLMMSTU	GLUMMEST	EGMNORSU	MURGEONS	EHHIRSSW	SHREWISH
EGLMNOOS	ENGLOOMS	EGMNOSYZ	ZYMOGENS	EHHIRSTW	WHITHERS
	LONGSOME	EGMNRSSU	GRUMNESS	EHHISSTU	HUSHIEST
EGLMNOOY	MENOLOGY	EGMNSSSU	SMUGNESS	EHHLOOST	SHOTHOLE
EGLMNORS	MONGRELS	EGMOORRS	GROOMERS	EHHNOORS	SHOEHORN
EGLMNSSU	GLUMNESS		REGROOMS	EHHOOPST	THEOSOPH
EGLMOORS	LEGROOMS	EGMORSTU	GOURMETS	EHHOOSSW	WHOOSHES
EGLMOPRU	PROMULGE	EGNNOOTY	ONTOGENY	EHHOOSTU	HOTHOUSE
EGLMORSS	GORMLESS	EGNNORST	RONTGENS	EHHORSTU	SHOUTHER
EGLMOSSS	SMOGLESS	EGNNOSTU	GUNSTONE	EHHRSSSU	SHUSHERS
EGLNNOOR	LONGERON		NONGUEST	EHHRSSTU	THRUSHES
EGLNNOSS	LONGNESS	EGNNOTTU	UNGOTTEN	EHIIIKST	HEITIKIS
EGLNNTUY	UNGENTLY	EGNNSSSU	SNUGNESS	EHIIIPSX	PIXIEISH
EGLNOOOY	OENOLOGY	EGNNSTTU	TUNGSTEN	EHIIKLPT	PITHLIKE
EGLNOOPR	PROLONGE	EGNNSTUU	UNGUENTS	EHIIKLPW	WHIPLIKE
EGLNOOPY	PENOLOGY	EGNOOOPR	GONOPORE	EHIIKNST	HINKIEST
EGLNOORV	OVERLONG	EGNOOPRS	PROGNOSE	EHIIKSSW	WHISKIES
EGLNOOVY	VENOLOGY	EGNOORRV	GOVERNOR	EHIILLST	HILLIEST
EGLNOPYY	POLYGENY	EGNOOTUX	OXTONGUE	EHIILLSW	WHILLIES
EGLNORSU	LOUNGERS	EGNOPPRU	OPPUGNER	EHIILMOS	HOMILIES
EGLNORUU	LONGUEUR	EGNOPRSS	SPONGERS	EHIILNPS	HIPLINES
EGLNOSSS	SONGLESS	EGNOPRSY	PYROGENS	EHIILNRS	LINISHER
EGLNOSSY	LYSOGENS	EGNORRST	STRONGER	EHIILNSS	LINISHES
EGLNOSUV	UNGLOVES	EGNORRSW	WRONGERS	EHIILOSS	HELIOSIS
EGLNOSXY	LOXYGENS	EGNORSST	SONGSTER	EHIILPSU	HUIPILES
	XYLOGENS	EGNORSSU	SURGEONS	EHIILRRW	WHIRLIER
EGLNOSYY	LYSOGENY	EGNORSTT	TONGSTER	EHIILRSV	LIVERISH
EGLNPRSU	PLUNGERS	EGNORSTU	STURGEON	EHIILRSW	WHIRLIES
EGLNRSSU	RUNGLESS	EGNORSTW	WRONGEST	EHIILSTT	LITHITES
EGLNRSTU	GRUNTLES	EGNORSUY	YOUNGERS		THELITIS
EGLNRTUY	URGENTLY	EGNOSTUY	YOUNGEST	EHIIMMRW	WHIMMIER
EGLOOORY	OREOLOGY	EGNPRRSU	RESPRUNG	EHIIMMSS	SHIMMIES
EGLOOPRU	PROLOGUE	EGNPRSUU	SUPERGUN	EHIIMNNO	HOMININE
EGLOOPTY	LOGOTYPE	EGNRRSTU	GRUNTERS	EHIIMNOS	HOMINIES
EGLOORSS	REGOSOLS		RESTRUNG		HOMINISE
EGLOORSY	SEROLOGY	EGOOPRRU	PROROGUE	EHIIMNOZ	HOMINIZE
EGLOOSXY	SEXOLOGY	EGOORRSV	GROOVERS	EHIIMNSS	MINISHES
EGLOPRTU	GROUPLET	EGOORRVW	OVERGROW	EHIIMPST	MEPHITIS
EGLOPSTU	GLUEPOTS	EGOORSTT	GROTTOES	EHIIMRSW	WHIMSIER
EGLORRSW	GROWLERS	EGOORSTU	OUTGOERS	EHIIMSST	SMITHIES
EGLORRWY	GROWLERY	EGOPRRSS	PROGRESS	EHIIMSSW	WHIMSIES
EGLORSSS	GLOSSERS	EGOPRRSU	GROUPERS	EHIINNOS	INHESION
EGLORSSU	ROSESLUG		REGROUPS	EHIINNOT	THIONINE
EGLORSUU	RUGULOSE	EGOPSSUY	GYPSEOUS	EHIINNQU	HENIQUIN
EGLORSUY	RUGOSELY	EGORRSSS	GROSSERS	EHIINNRS	INSHRINE
EGLPRRSU	SPLURGER	EGORRSST	GROSERTS	EHIINNRW	WHINNIER
EGLPRSSU	SPLURGES	EGORRSSU	GROUSERS	EHIINNSS	SHINNIES
EGLPRSUY	GYPLURES	EGORRSTU	GROUTERS	EHIINNSW	WHINNIES

EHIINRRT	HIRRIENT	EHILLRRS	SHRILLER	EHILSSSU	SLUSHIES
EHIINRST	INHERITS	EHILLRRT	THRILLER	EHILSSSW	WISHLESS
EHIINRSZ	RHIZINES	EHILLRST	THILLERS	EHILSSTT	THISTLES
EHIINSST	SHINIEST	EHILLRTY	LITHERLY	EHILSSTU	LUSHIEST
	SHINTIES	EHILLSST	HILTLESS	EHILSSTW	WHISTLES
EHIINSTW	WHINIEST	EHILLSSW	SWELLISH	EHILSTTU	THULITES
EHIINSVX	VIXENISH	EHILLSTU	HULLIEST	EHILSTTW	WHITTLES
EHIIPPRW	WHIPPIER	EHILLSVY	ELVISHLY	EHIMMNUY	HYMENIUM
EHIIPPSS	SHIPPIES	EHILMNOS	LEMONISH	EHIMMRSS	SHIMMERS
EHIIPPST	HIPPIEST	EHILMOOR	HEIRLOOM	EHIMMRRY	SHIMMERY
EHIIPRSV	VIPERISH	EHILMOST	HELOTISM	EHIMMSSY	SHIMMEYS
EHIIPSTT	PITHIEST	EHILMPSW	WHIMPLES	EHIMNOPR	MORPHINE
EHIIRRST	SHIRTIER	EHILMPSY	SYMPHILE	EHIMNORT	THERMION
EHIIRRSW	WHIRRIES	EHILMQUU	UMQUHILE	EHIMNOSS	HOMINESS
EHIIRRTX	HERITRIX	EHILMSTT	MELTITHS		MONISHES
EHIIRSSU	HUISSIER	EHILNOOP	OENOPHIL	EHIMNOST	HOISTMEN
EHIIRSSW	SWISHIER	EHILNOPS	PINHOLES	EHIMNOSU	HEMIONUS
EHIIRSTT	SHITTIER	EHILNOPT	THOLEPIN	EHIMNOTT	MONTEITH
	THIRTIES	EHILNORU	UNHOLIER	EHIMNPRS	NEPHRISM
EHIIRWZZ	WHIZZIER	EHILNOSS	HOLINESS		PHRENISM
EHIISSST	HISSIEST	EHILNOST	HOLSTEIN	EHIMNPST	SHIPMENT
	STISHIES		HOTLINES	EHIMNRRU	MURRHINE
EHIISSTT	STITHIES		NEOLITHS	EHIMNRRY	MYRRHINE
EHIISTTW	WHITIEST	EHILNOSV	NOVELISH	EHIMNRSU	INHUMERS
	WITHIEST	EHILNOTX	XENOLITH		RHENIUMS
EHIISTTX	SIXTIETH	EHILNPSY	SYLPHINE	EHIMNSTY	THYMINES
EHIJNNOS	JOHNNIES	EHILNSTY	ETHINYLS	EHIMOOSS	HOMEOSIS
EHIKKLOO	HOOKLIKE	EHILNSWY	NEWISHLY	EHIMOOST	SMOOTHIE
EHIKKLSU	HUSKLIKE	EHILOOPZ	ZOOPHILE	EHIMOPRS	SOPHERIM
EHIKKRSS	SHIKKERS	EHILOOST	HOOLIEST	EHIMOPSS	PHIMOSES
EHIKLMNY	HYMNLIKE	EHILOPRS	POLISHER	EHIMORSS	HEROISMS
EHIKLMOT	MOTHLIKE		REPOLISH	EHIMORST	ISOTHERM
EHIKLMPU	HUMPLIKE	EHILOPRT	HELIPORT		MOITHERS
EHIKLNOR	HORNLIKE	EHILOPSS	POLISHES	EHIMORSZ	RHIZOMES
EHIKLNOS	SINKHOLE	EHILOPST	HELISTOP	EHIMORTU	MOUTHIER
EHIKLOOP	HOOPLIKE		HOPLITES	EHIMOSTT	MOTHIEST
EHIKLOSY	YOKELISH		ISOPLETH	EHIMOSTW	SHOWTIME
EHIKLOTY	LEKYTHOI	EHILOPXY	OXYPHILE	EHIMPPSS	PSEPHISM
EHIKLRSU	RUSHLIKE	EHILORSS	SLOSHIER	EHIMPRRS	SHRIMPER
EHIKLSTU	HULKIEST	EHILORSU	HOURLIES	EHIMPRSU	MURPHIES
EHIKMNST	METHINKS	EHILORTY	RHYOLITE	EHIMPRSW	WHIMPERS
EHIKNORS	SHONKIER	EHILOSST	HOSTILES	EHIMPSTU	HUMPIEST
EHIKNOSS	HOKINESS	EHILPRST	PHILTERS		HUMPTIES
EHIKNPSU	SHUNPIKE		PHILTRES		TUMPHIES
EHIKNRRS	SHRINKER	EHILPRSU	PLUSHIER	EHIMPSUU	EUPHUISM
EHIKNRST	RETHINKS	EHILPRSY	SYLPHIER	EHIMPTTU	UMPTIETH
	THINKERS	EHILPSSS	SHIPLESS	EHIMRRTY	HERMITRY
EHIKNSTU	HUNKIEST	EHILPSST	PITHLESS	EHIMRSST	SMITHERS
EHIKOOST	HOOKIEST		THLIPSES	EHIMRSSU	HEURISMS
EHIKOPRS	POKERISH	EHILPSSY	PHYLESIS	EHIMRSTT	THERMITS
EHIKRRSS	SHIRKERS	EHILPSTU	SULPHITE	EHIMRSTW	MISTHREW
EHIKRSSW	WHISKERS	EHILRRSW	WHIRLERS	EHIMRSTY	SMITHERY
EHIKRSWY	WHISKERY	EHILRSST	SLITHERS	EHIMRTUU	HUMITURE
EHIKSSTU	HUSKIEST		THRISSEL	EHIMSSTU	MUSHIEST
EHIKSSTW	WHISKETS	EHILRSSU	SLUSHIER		TUMSHIES
EHIKSSVY	WHISKEYS	EHILRSSV	SHRIVELS	EHIMSSTY	METHYSIS
EHILLLMO	MOLEHILL	EHILRSTT	THRISTLE		MYTHISES
EHILLMOP	PHILOMEL	EHILRSTU	LUTHIERS	EHIMSSWY	WHIMSEYS
EHILLMOY	HOMELILY	EHILRSTW	WHIRTLES	EHIMSTTY	MYTHIEST
EHILLNOS	HELLIONS		WHISTLER		THYMIEST
EHILLNSS	INSHELLS	EHILRSTY	SLITHERY	EHIMSTYZ	MYTHIZES
EHILLOOS	OILHOLES	EHILRTTW	WHITTLER	EHINNORT	INTHRONE
EHILLOPY	LYOPHILE	EHILRTTY	TRIETHYL	EHINNOTW	NONWHITE
EHILLPTY	PHYLLITE	EHILSSST	SHITLESS	EHINNRST	THINNERS

EHINNRSY	SHINNERY
EHINNSST	THINNESS
EHINNSSU	SUNSHINE
EHINNSSY	SHINNEYS
EHINNSTT	THINNEST
EHINOOPS	ISOPHONE
EHINOPPR	HORNPIPE
EHINOPRT	TRIPHONE
EHINOPST	PHONIEST
	SIPHONET
EHINOPSW	WINESHOP
EHINORRT	THORNIER
EHINORSS	HERISSON
EHINORST	HORNIEST
	ORNITHES
EHINORTV	OVERTHIN
EHINORZZ	HIZZONER
EHINOSST	HISTONES
EHINOSTU	OUTSHINE
EHINPPRU	UNHIPPER
EHINPPSS	SHIPPENS
EHINPRSU	PUNISHER
EHINPSSU	PUNISHES
EHINPSSX	SPHINXES
EHINRSSU	INRUSHES
EHINRSTZ	ZITHERNS
EHINSSST	THISNESS
EHINSSUW	UNWISHES
EHIOOPST	ISOPHOTE
EHIOOPSW	WHOOPIES
	WHOOPSIE
EHIOORTT	TOOTHIER
EHIOOSST	STOOSHIE
EHIOOSTT	HOOTIEST
EHIOPPPS	POPESHIP
EHIOPPRS	SHOPPIER
EHIOPPST	HOPPIEST
	POETSHIP
EHIOPPSU	EOHIPPUS
EHIOPRSS	POSERISH
	ROSEHIPS
	SPOSHIER
EHIOPRST	TROPHIES
EHIOPTTW	WHITEPOT
EHIORRST	HERITORS
EHIORRTU	ROUTHIER
EHIORRTW	WORTHIER
EHIORSST	HOISTERS
	HORSIEST
	HOSTRIES
	SHORTIES
EHIORSTT	THEORIST
	THORITES
EHIORSTU	OUTHIRES
	SHOUTIER
EHIORSTV	OVERHITS
EHIORSTW	WORTHIES
EHIORTUY	YOUTHIER
EHIORTWZ	HOWITZER
EHIOSSSW	WHOSISES
EHIOSSTT	TOSHIEST
EHIOSSTU	HOUSESIT
	HOUSIEST
	STOUSHIE

EHIOSSTW	SHOWIEST
EHIOSSTY	ISOHYETS
EHIOSTVY	YESHIVOT
EHIOTTUW	WHITEOUT
EHIPPRSS	PRESHIPS
	SHIPPERS
EHIPPRSW	WHIPPERS
EHIPPSSU	HIPPUSES
EHIPPSTW	WHIPPETS
EHIPQSUY	PHYSIQUE
EHIPRSST	HIPSTERS
	THRIPSES
EHIPRSSW	WHISPERS
EHIPRSTU	SUPERHIT
EHIPRSTW	WHIPSTER
EHIPRSWY	WHISPERY
EHIPSSTU	PUSHIEST
EHIPSTUU	EUPHUIST
EHIQSSSU	SQUISHES
EHIRRRSU	HURRIERS
EHIRRSSV	SHRIVERS
EHIRRSTT	THIRSTER
EHIRRSTV	THRIVERS
EHIRRSTW	WHERRITS
	WHIRRETS
	WRITHERS
EHIRRTTU	TRUTHIER
EHIRSSSW	SWISHERS
EHIRSSTU	RUSHIEST
EHIRSSTW	SWITHERS
EHIRSTTW	WHITRETS
	WHITSTER
	WHITTERS
EHIRSWZZ	WHIZZERS
EHIRTTTW	WHITTRET
EHISSSTU	STUSHIES
EHISSSTW	SWISHEST
EHISSTUW	THUSWISE
EHISSUVW	HUSWIVES
EHKLNOOT	KNOTHOLE
EHKLOOSS	HOOKLESS
EHKLOOST	HOOKLETS
EHKLOOSZ	KOLHOZES
EHKLOSTY	LEKYTHOS
EHKLSTUY	LEKYTHUS
EHKMOORW	HOMEWORK
EHKMOOSS	SMOKEHOS
EHKMORSU	HUMORESK
EHKMORSW	MESHWORK
EHKMOSSY	SKYHOMES
EHKNNRSU	SHRUNKEN
EHKNOOOS	HOOKNOSE
EHKNORSU	UNKOSHER
EHKOOSSS	SKOOSHES
EHKOPSSY	KYPHOSES
EHKRSSTU	TUSHKERS
EHLLMOPY	PHYLLOME
EHLLNSSU	UNSHELLS
EHLLNSTU	NUTSHELL
EHLLOOOP	LOOPHOLE
EHLLOORW	HOLLOWER
EHLMMOSW	WHOMMLES
EHLMMSUW	WHUMMLES
EHLMNOST	MENTHOLS

EHLMNOSY	HOMELYNS
EHLMNOTU	MOLEHUNT
EHLMNOUY	UNHOMELY
EHLMNSSY	HYMNLESS
EHLMOORW	WORMHOLE
EHLMOOST	LOTHSOME
EHLMOPSY	MESOPHYL
EHLMORTY	MOTHERLY
EHLMOTXY	METHOXYL
EHLMPSSU	HUMPLESS
EHLNNOPU	UNHOLPEN
EHLNOPSU	SULPHONE
EHLNORSS	HORNLESS
EHLNORST	HORNLETS
EHLNOSST	LOTHNESS
EHLNOSTY	HONESTLY
EHLNRSTU	LUTHERNS
EHLNSSSU	LUSHNESS
	SHUNLESS
EHLNSTYY	ETHYNYLS
EHLOOPRT	PORTHOLE
	POTHOLER
EHLOOPSS	HOOPLESS
EHLOOPST	POSTHOLE
	POTHOLES
EHLOOPTY	HOLOTYPE
EHLOORVY	OVERHOLY
EHLOOSSS	SLOOSHES
EHLOPPRS	HOPPLERS
EHLOPPRT	THROPPLE
EHLOPSSS	SPLOSHES
EHLOPSSY	SPYHOLES
EHLORSST	HOLSTERS
	HOSTLERS
EHLORSTT	THROSTLE
EHLORSTW	WHORTLES
EHLORSTY	HOSTELRY
EHLORSUV	OVERLUSH
EHLORTTT	THROTTLE
EHLOSSTT	SHOTTLES
EHLOSSTW	THOWLESS
EHLOSSTY	THYLOSES
EHLOSTXY	ETHOXYLS
EHLPSSTU	PLUSHEST
EHLRSSTU	HURTLESS
	HUSTLERS
	RUTHLESS
EHLRSTTU	SHUTTLER
EHLSSTTU	SHUTTLES
EHMMOOOR	HOMEROOM
EHMMOOSS	HOMMOSES
EHMMRRTU	THRUMMER
EHMMSSUU	HUMMUSES
EHMNNOTY	ETHNONYM
EHMNNSTU	HUNTSMEN
EHMNOOPR	NEOMORPH
EHMNOORS	HORMONES
	MOORHENS
EHMNOOST	SMOOTHEN
EHMNOOTW	HOMETOWN
	TOWNHOME
EHMNOOTY	THEONOMY
EHMNOPSU	HOMESPUN
EHMNPRYY	HYPERNYM

EHMNPSTY	NYMPHETS	EHOOPRTY	ORTHOEPY	EIIKLLLY	LILYLIKE
EHMNSTTU	HUTMENTS	EHOOPSTT	PHOTOSET	EIIKLLMN	LIMEKILN
EHMOOOTZ	ZOOTHOME	EHOOPSTU	HOUSETOP	EIIKLLNO	LIONLIKE
EHMOOPRT	HOMEPORT		POTHOUSE	EIIKLLRS	SKILLIER
EHMOOPTY	HOMOTYPE	EHOOPSTY	OOPHYTES	EIIKLLSS	SKILLIES
EHMOORRS	SHROOMER	EHOOPTYZ	ZOOPHYTE	EIIKLLST	SLITLIKE
EHMOORST	RESMOOTH	EHOORSST	ORTHOSES	EIIKLMRS	MISLIKER
	SMOOTHER		RESHOOTS	EIIKLMSS	MISLIKES
EHMOORTU	OUTHOMER		SHEROOTS	EIIKLMST	MILKIEST
EHMOOSSS	SHMOOSES		SHOOTERS	EIIKLNOR	IRONLIKE
	SMOOSHES		SOOTHERS	EIIKLNRS	SLINKIER
EHMOOSST	SMOOTHES	EHOORSTV	OVERSHOT	EIIKLNRT	TINKLIER
EHMOOSSZ	SHMOOZES	EHOOSSSW	SWOOSHES	EIIKLPSS	PLISKIES
EHMOPRSW	MORPHEWS	EHOOSSTT	SOOTHEST	EIIKLPSW	WISPLIKE
EHMORSST	SMOTHERS	EHOOSTUU	OUTHOUSE	EIIKLRTT	KITTLIER
EHMORSTU	MOUTHERS	EHOPPRSS	SHOPPERS	EIIKLSST	SILKIEST
EHMORSTY	SMOTHERY	EHOPPRST	PROPHETS	EIIKLSTU	SUITLIKE
EHMORTUV	VERMOUTH	EHOPPRSW	WHOPPERS	EIIKMPRS	SKIMPIER
EHMOSSUU	HOUMUSES	EHOPPRSY	PROPHESY	EIIKMRRS	SMIRKIER
EHMOTUZZ	MEZUZOTH	EHOPRRSY	ORPHREYS	EIIKMRST	MIRKIEST
EHMPRSTU	THUMPERS	EHOPRSST	HOTPRESS	EIIKNNOS	NOISENIK
EHMRRSTU	MURTHERS		STROPHES	EIIKNNRS	SKINNIER
EHMRSTUV	VERMUTHS	EHOPRSSW	PRESHOWS	EIIKNNSS	INKINESS
EHMRTUYY	EURYTHMY	EHOPRSTU	POUTHERS	EIIKNNST	KINETINS
EHMSSTUY	THYMUSES		SUPERHOT	EIIKNNSW	WINESKIN
EHNNOPRS	NEPHRONS	EHOPRSTY	TROPHESY	EIIKNRST	STINKIER
EHNNOPSY	HYPNONES	EHOPRSUV	PUSHOVER	EIIKNSST	SINKIEST
EHNNORRT	NORTHERN	EHOPRTUY	EUTROPHY	EIIKNSTW	TWINKIES
	THRONNER	EHOPSSTY	PHYTOSES	EIIKNSTZ	ZINKIEST
EHNNORTU	UNTHRONE	EHORRSTW	THROWERS	EIIKPPRS	SKIPPIER
EHNNOSTU	UNHONEST	EHORRSTY	HERSTORY	EIIKPSST	SPIKIEST
EHNNRSSU	SHUNNERS	EHORSSTT	SHORTEST	EIIKQRRU	QUIRKIER
EHNOOPTY	HONEYPOT	EHORSSTU	SHOUTERS	EIIKRSST	RISKIEST
EHNOORRS	HONORERS		SOUTHERS	EIIKSSTV	SKIVIEST
EHNOORRU	HONOURER	EHORSTUY	OUTHYRES	EIIKSSVV	SKIVVIES
EHNOORSS	SOREHONS	EHORTTUW	OUTTHREW	EIILLLVY	LIVELILY
EHNOORSW	WHORESON	EHOSSSTU	STOUSHES	EIILLMMR	MILLIREM
EHNOORTW	HONEWORT	EHPRSSSU	SPRUSHES	EIILLMMS	MILLIMES
EHNOOSSW	SNOWSHOE	EHPRSSUU	UPRUSHES	EIILLMNR	MILLINER
EHNOOSTU	OUTSHONE	EHPRSTTU	TURPETHS	EIILLMNS	MILLINES
EHNOPRSW	PRESHOWN	EHPSSTUY	TYPHUSES		SLIMLINE
EHNOPRSY	HYPERONS	EHQRSSUU	QURUSHES	EIILLMNU	ILLUMINE
EHNOPSSS	POSHNESS	EHQSSSUU	SQUUSHES	EIILLMRS	MILLIERS
EHNOPSSY	HYPNOSES	EHRRSTTU	THRUSTER	EIILLNST	NIELLIST
EHNORRRS	SHNORRER	EHRSSSTY	SHYSTERS	EIILLNSU	SUILLINE
EHNORRST	NORTHERS	EHRSSTTU	SHUTTERS	EIILLNSV	VILLEINS
EHNORRTY	ERYTHRON	EIIILMSS	SIMILISE	EIILLNTV	VITELLIN
EHNORSST	SHORTENS	EIIILMSZ	SIMILIZE	EIILLPSS	ELLIPSIS
EHNORSSU	ONRUSHES	EIIILNRV	INVIRILE	EIILLRST	STILLIER
	UNHORSES	EIIILPPR	LIRIPIPE	EIILLRVY	VIRILELY
EHNORSTT	THORNSET	EIIILRSV	VIRILISE	EIILLSST	SILLIEST
EHNORSTU	SOUTHERN	EIIILRVZ	VIRILIZE	EIILLSTT	LITTLIES
EHNORTUV	OVERHUNT	EIIIMMNS	MINIMISE		TILLIEST
EHNOSSUU	UNHOUSES	EIIIMMNZ	MINIMIZE		TILLITES
EHNOSTUU	NUTHOUSE	EIIIRRTV	TIRRIVIE	EIILLSTW	TWILLIES
EHNOSTUY	YOUTHENS	EIIIRSST	IRITISES	EIILLSUV	ILLUSIVE
EHNPSSXY	SPHYNXES	EIIJKNRT	JIRKINET	EIILMMOS	MILESIMO
EHNRSSTU	HUNTRESS	EIIJMPST	JIMPIEST	EIILMMOT	IMMOTILE
	SHUNTERS	EIIJNRSU	INJURIES	EIILMNNT	LINIMENT
EHNSSSTU	THUSNESS	EIIKKLLM	MILKLIKE	EIILMNOT	LIMONITE
EHOOPRRT	HOROPTER	EIIKKLLS	SILKLIKE	EIILMNSS	LIMINESS
EHOOPRST	HOOPSTER	EIIKKLLT	KILTLIKE	EIILMOPT	IMPOLITE
EHOOPRSW	WHOOPERS	EIIKKLNS	SKINLIKE	EIILMPPR	PIMPLIER
EHOOPRSX	HORSEPOX	EIIKKNST	KINKIEST	EIILMPRS	IMPERILS

	LIMPSIER	**EIILSSTU**	ULITISES	**EIINNOSU**	UNIONISE
EIILMPRT	PRELIMIT		UTILISES	**EIINNOSV**	ENVISION
EIILMPST	LIMEPITS	**EIILSTUY**	TUILYIES	**EIINNOUZ**	UNIONIZE
EIILMRSS	SLIMSIER	**EIILSTUZ**	TUILZIES	**EIINNPSS**	SPINNIES
EIILMRST	LIMITERS		UTILIZES	**EIINNQSU**	QUININES
	MIRLIEST	**EIIMMNNO**	MENOMINI	**EIINNRTV**	INVERTIN
EIILMRZZ	MIZZLIER	**EIIMMNNT**	IMMINENT	**EIINNSST**	TININESS
EIILMSSS	MISSILES		MINIMENT	**EIINNSSW**	INSINEWS
EIILMSST	ELITISMS	**EIIMMNSU**	IMMUNISE	**EIINNSTT**	TINNIEST
	SLIMIEST	**EIIMMNTU**	IMMINUTE	**EIINNSTW**	INTWINES
EIILMSSV	MISLIVES	**EIIMMNUZ**	IMMUNIZE	**EIINOPRS**	RIPIENOS
EIILMSTT	MILTIEST	**EIIMMPRU**	IMPERIUM	**EIINOPRT**	POINTIER
	MISTITLE	**EIIMMRSW**	SWIMMIER		POITRINE
EIILMSTY	MYELITIS	**EIIMMSSS**	SEISMISM	**EIINOPST**	SINOPITE
EIILNNOT	LENITION	**EIIMMSST**	MIMSIEST	**EIINOPTT**	PETITION
EIILNORS	LIONISER		MISTIMES	**EIINORRT**	INTERIOR
EIILNORT	TRIOLEIN	**EIIMNOPT**	PIMIENTO	**EIINORSS**	IONISERS
EIILNORZ	LIONIZER	**EIIMNOSS**	EMISSION		IRONISES
EIILNOSS	ELISIONS		SIMONIES		SIRONISE
	ISOLINES		SIMONISE	**EIINORST**	IRONIEST
	LIONISES	**EIIMNOSV**	VISNOMIE	**EIINORSV**	REVISION
	OILINESS	**EIIMNOSZ**	SIMONIZE		VISIONER
EIILNOST	ETIOLINS	**EIIMNOTV**	MONITIVE	**EIINORSZ**	IONIZERS
EIILNOSV	OLIVINES	**EIIMNPRS**	PRIMINES		IRONIZES
EIILNOSZ	LIONIZES	**EIIMNRSS**	MIRINESS		SIRONIZE
EIILNOTT	TOILINET		RIMINESS	**EIINOSST**	INOSITES
EIILNQTU	QUINTILE	**EIIMNRST**	INTERIMS		NOISIEST
EIILNRSS	RESILINS		MINISTER	**EIINOSTV**	NOVITIES
EIILNRST	NIRLIEST		MISINTER	**EIINPPRS**	SNIPPIER
	NITRILES	**EIIMNRSV**	MINIVERS	**EIINPPSS**	PIPINESS
EIILNSSW	WILINESS	**EIIMNRTT**	INTERMIT	**EIINPPST**	NIPPIEST
EIILNSTT	INTITLES	**EIIMNRTX**	INTERMIX	**EIINPRRS**	INSPIRER
	LINTIEST	**EIIMNSTT**	MINTIEST	**EIINPRSS**	INSPIRES
EIILNSTY	SENILITY	**EIIMNSTU**	MUTINIES	**EIINPRST**	PRISTINE
EIILNSVY	SYLVIINE	**EIIMNSTV**	MINIVETS	**EIINPSST**	SNIPIEST
EIILNTTU	INTITULE	**EIIMOPRX**	MIREPOIX		SPINIEST
EIILNTUV	VITULINE	**EIIMOPSS**	MISPOISE	**EIINPSSX**	PIXINESS
EIILOPPT	POPLITEI	**EIIMOPST**	OPTIMISE	**EIINPSTZ**	PINTSIZE
EIILOPRS	LIRIOPES	**EIIMOPSZ**	EPIZOISM	**EIINPTUV**	PUNITIVE
EIILOPST	PISOLITE	**EIIMOPTZ**	OPTIMIZE	**EIINQRRU**	INQUIRER
	POLITIES	**EIIMOSSS**	SEMIOSIS	**EIINQRSU**	INQUIRES
EIILORST	ROILIEST	**EIIMOSSV**	OMISSIVE	**EIINQSSU**	QUINSIES
EIILORTT	TROILITE	**EIIMOSTY**	MOYITIES		SQUINIES
EIILOSST	SOILIEST	**EIIMOSUX**	EXIMIOUS	**EIINQSTU**	INQUIETS
EIILOTVV	VOLITIVE	**EIIMOTVV**	VOMITIVE	**EIINQTUY**	EQUINITY
EIILPPRR	RIPPLIER	**EIIMPRRS**	PRIMSIER		INEQUITY
EIILPPRS	SLIPPIER	**EIIMPRSS**	MISPRISE	**EIINRRTW**	WINTRIER
EIILPPST	LIPPIEST		PISMIRES	**EIINRSST**	INSISTER
EIILPRST	TRIPLIES	**EIIMPRSZ**	MISPRIZE		SINISTER
EIILPRSU	PLURISIE	**EIIMPSST**	PIETISMS	**EIINRSSW**	WIRINESS
EIILPRTT	TRIPLITE	**EIIMPSTW**	WIMPIEST	**EIINRSTT**	NITRITES
EIILPSST	PITILESS	**EIIMQSTU**	QUIETISM		STINTIER
	SPILITES	**EIIMRRRS**	SMIRRIER	**EIINRSTU**	NEURITIS
EIILPSTY	PYELITIS	**EIIMRSTT**	METRITIS		UNITISER
EIILPSUZ	SPUILZIE	**EIIMRSTW**	MISWRITE	**EIINRSTV**	INVITERS
EIILQSSU	SILIQUES	**EIIMSSSS**	MISSISES		VINTRIES
EIILRRSW	SWIRLIER	**EIIMSSST**	MISSIEST		VITRINES
EIILRRTW	TWIRLIER	**EIIMSSSV**	MISSIVES	**EIINRTUZ**	UNITIZER
EIILRSTT	SLITTIER	**EIIMSSSZ**	SIZEISMS	**EIINRTVY**	INVERITY
	STILTIER	**EIIMSSTT**	MISTIEST	**EIINSSSZ**	SIZINESS
EIILRSTU	UTILISER		SEMITIST	**EIINSSTU**	UNITISES
EIILRTUZ	UTILIZER	**EIINNNPS**	NINEPINS	**EIINSTTT**	NITTIEST
EIILSSTT	ELITISTS	**EIINNOOR**	ONIONIER		TINTIEST
	SILTIEST	**EIINNOSS**	INOSINES	**EIINSTTW**	TWINIEST

EIINSTUZ	UNITIZES	EIJNPRSU	JUNIPERS	EIKLRSST	KLISTERS
EIIOPRRS	PRIORIES	EIJNRRSU	INJURERS	EIKLRTUZ	KLUTZIER
EIIOPSTV	POSITIVE	EIJNRRUY	REINJURY	EIKLSSTT	SKITTLES
EIIORRST	RIOTRIES	EIJNSTTW	TWINJETS	EIKLSSTU	SULKIEST
EIIORSST	RIOTISES	EIJRSTUY	JESUITRY	EIKLSTTT	KITTLEST
EIIORSTZ	RIOTIZES	EIJSSSUV	JUSSIVES	EIKMMRRS	KRIMMERS
EIIOSSTT	OSTEITIS	EIKKLNOO	NOOKLIKE	EIKMMRSS	SKIMMERS
	OTITISES	EIKKLNOT	KNOTLIKE	EIKMNNOO	MONOKINE
EIIOSSTZ	ZOISITES	EIKKLNRS	KLINKERS	EIKMNORS	MONIKERS
EIIOTTTV	TOTITIVE	EIKKLSTU	TUSKLIKE	EIKMNOST	TOKENISM
EIIPPPST	PIPPIEST	EIKKNRRS	SKINKERS	EIKMNOSU	MOUSEKIN
EIIPPQRU	QUIPPIER	EIKKNRSU	SKUNKIER	EIKMOPSS	MISSPOKE
EIIPPRRS	RIPPIERS	EIKKOOST	KOOKIEST	EIKMORTW	TIMEWORK
EIIPPRRT	TRIPPIER	EIKKSTUY	YUKKIEST	EIKMOSST	SMOKIEST
EIIPPSTT	TIPPIEST	EIKLLMOO	KILOMOLE	EIKMOSSU	KOUMISES
EIIPPSTZ	ZIPPIEST	EIKLLMPU	PLUMLIKE	EIKMOSSY	MISYOKES
EIIPRRSS	PRISSIER	EIKLLMSS	MILKLESS	EIKMPSSU	MUSPIKES
EIIPRRST	STRIPIER	EIKLLNSW	INKWELLS	EIKMRRSS	SMIRKERS
EIIPRRSU	SIRUPIER	EIKLLNUY	UNLIKELY	EIKMRSTU	MURKIEST
EIIPRRTW	TRIPWIRE	EIKLLNXY	LYNXLIKE	EIKMSSSU	KUMISSES
	TWIRPIER	EIKLLOOW	WOOLLIKE	EIKMSSTU	MUSKIEST
EIIPRSSS	PRISSIES	EIKLLORV	OVERKILL	EIKNNORS	EINKORNS
EIIPRSST	SPIRIEST	EIKLLOSS	SKOLLIES		NONSKIER
EIIPRSTT	RISPETTI	EIKLLOSU	SOULLIKE	EIKNNOST	INKSTONE
	TRIPIEST	EIKLLRSS	RESKILLS	EIKNNPSS	PINKNESS
EIIPRSTU	PURITIES	EIKLLSSS	SKILLESS	EIKNNRSS	SKINNERS
EIIPRSTV	PREVISIT	EIKLLSST	SKILLETS	EIKNOORS	ROOINEKS
	PRIVIEST	EIKLMNNS	LINKSMEN	EIKNOOST	NOOKIEST
EIIPRSTY	PYRITISE	EIKLMNOO	MOONLIKE	EIKNOPSS	POKINESS
EIIPRSVV	SPIVVIER	EIKLMNOS	MOLESKIN	EIKNORST	INSTROKE
EIIPRTYZ	PYRITIZE	EIKLMNRS	KREMLINS	EIKNORSV	INVOKERS
EIIPSSTT	PIETISTS	EIKLMORV	OVERMILK	EIKNORTT	KNOTTIER
	STIPITES	EIKLMORW	WORMLIKE	EIKNOSTW	WONKIEST
	TIPSIEST	EIKLMOSS	MOSSLIKE	EIKNPRRS	PRINKERS
EIIPSSTW	SWIPIEST	EIKLMPPU	PUMPLIKE	EIKNPRSU	SPUNKIER
	WISPIEST	EIKLNOOR	OERLIKON	EIKNPRTU	TURNPIKE
EIIPSTTT	PITTITES	EIKLNOPR	PLONKIER	EIKNPSSU	SPUNKIES
EIIPSTTU	PITUITES	EIKLNOSW	SNOWLIKE	EIKNPSTU	PUNKIEST
EIIQSTTU	QUIETIST	EIKLNPRS	PLINKERS	EIKNRRTU	RETURNIK
EIIRRSTW	WRISTIER		SPRINKLE	EIKNRSST	STINKERS
EIIRSSTV	REVISITS	EIKLNPRU	PLUNKIER	EIKNRSSW	SWINKERS
	VISITERS	EIKLNRRU	KNURLIER	EIKNRSTT	KNITTERS
EIIRSTTU	UTERITIS	EIKLNRSS	SLINKERS		TRINKETS
EIIRSTTW	TWISTIER	EIKLNRST	LINKSTER	EIKNSSSU	UNKISSES
EIIRSTTZ	RITZIEST		STRINKLE	EIKNSSTT	SKINTEST
EIISSSST	SISSIEST		TINKLERS	EIKNSTUZ	KUNZITES
EIISSSTZ	SIZEISTS	EIKLNRSW	WINKLERS	EIKOOPRS	SPOOKIER
EIISSTTV	STIVIEST		WRINKLES	EIKOORST	ROOKIEST
EIISTTTW	WITTIEST	EIKLNRTW	TWINKLER	EIKOOSST	STOOKIES
EIIJJNTUY	JEJUNITY	EIKLNSSS	SKINLESS	EIKOPPRS	PORKPIES
EIJKKSSU	JUKSKEIS	EIKLNSST	LENTISKS	EIKOPPRW	PIPEWORK
EIJKNOSS	JOKINESS	EIKLNSSY	SKYLINES	EIKOPRST	PORKIEST
EIJKNSTU	JUNKIEST	EIKLNSTT	KNITTLES	EIKOPRSV	OVERSKIP
EIJKORRS	SKIJORER	EIKLNSTW	TWINKLES	EIKORRWW	WIREWORK
EIJLLORS	JOLLIERS	EIKLOOPR	PLOOKIER	EIKPPRSS	SKIPPERS
EIJLLOST	JOLLIEST	EIKLOORT	ROOTLIKE	EIKPPSST	SKIPPETS
EIJLMTTU	MULTIJET	EIKLOPRU	PLOUKIER	EIKPRRSU	SPRUIKER
EIJLOSTT	JOLTIEST	EIKLOPRW	PILEWORK	EIKRRSST	SKIRRETS
EIJLOSTW	JOWLIEST	EIKLOPSU	SOUPLIKE		SKIRTERS
EIJMNPSS	JIMPNESS	EIKLORTY	KRYOLITE		STRIKERS
EIJMPSTU	JUMPIEST	EIKLOSSU	LEUKOSIS	EIKRRSSU	SKURRIES
EIJNORST	JOINTERS	EIKLOSTY	YOLKIEST	EIKRSSTT	SKITTERS
EIJNORTU	JOINTURE	EIKLPSSU	PUSSLIKE	EIKRSSTU	TURKISES
EIJNOSTT	JETTISON	EIKLRSSS	RISKLESS	EIKRSTTY	SKITTERY

EIKRSTWY	SKYWRITE
EIKSSTTU	TUSKIEST
EILLLNOY	LONELILY
EILLLOVY	LOVELILY
EILLLPUV	PULVILLE
EILLMNNO	MONELLIN
EILLMNOS	SEMILLON
EILLMNOU	LINOLEUM
EILLMNQU	QUILLMEN
EILLMNST	STILLMEN
EILLMNSU	MULLEINS
EILLMOPR	IMPELLOR
EILLMOPS	PLIMSOLE
EILLMOST	MELILOTS
EILLMPSS	MISSPELL
	PSELLISM
EILLMPTU	MULTIPLE
EILLMSST	MISTELLS
EILLMSTU	MULLITES
EILLMUVX	VEXILLUM
EILLNOPT	PLOTLINE
EILLNOPY	EPYLLION
EILLNOST	STELLION
EILLNOTU	LUTEOLIN
EILLNPSW	PINSWELL
EILLNPUU	LUPULINE
EILLNSST	LINTLESS
EILLNSTY	SILENTLY
	TINSELLY
EILLNSUV	LEVULINS
EILLNSVY	SNIVELLY
EILLNUVY	UNLIVELY
EILLOORW	WOOLLIER
EILLOOSW	WOOLLIES
EILLOPSS	SLIPSOLE
EILLOPTY	POLITELY
EILLORST	TRILLOES
	TROLLIES
EILLORSU	ROUILLES
EILLORSZ	ZORILLES
EILLORWW	WILLOWER
EILLOSSS	SOILLESS
EILLOSST	TOILLESS
EILLOSTW	LOWLIEST
EILLOSVW	LOWLIVES
EILLPRSS	SPILLERS
EILLPSSS	SLIPLESS
EILLQSTU	QUILLETS
EILLRRST	TRILLERS
EILLRSST	STILLERS
EILLRSSW	SWILLERS
EILLRSTT	TESTRILL
EILLRSVY	SILVERLY
EILLSSST	LISTLESS
	SLITLESS
EILLSSTT	STILLEST
EILLSTTT	LITTLEST
EILLSTUV	VITELLUS
EILMMNOS	MOLIMENS
EILMMPRU	PLUMMIER
EILMMRSS	SLIMMERS
EILMMRSU	SLUMMIER
EILMMSST	SLIMMEST
EILMMSTU	LUMMIEST
EILMNOOS	OINOMELS
	SIMOLEON
EILMNOPT	PILOTMEN
EILMNORS	MISENROL
EILMNOST	MOLINETS
EILMNOSU	EMULSION
EILMNOSV	NOVELISM
EILMNOTU	MOULINET
EILMNOTY	MYLONITE
EILMNPSS	LIMPNESS
	PLENISMS
EILMNPSU	SPLENIUM
EILMNPTU	TUMPLINE
EILMNRST	MINSTREL
EILMNSSS	SLIMNESS
EILMNSSU	EMULSINS
EILMNSTU	MUSLINET
EILMNTUY	MINUTELY
	UNTIMELY
EILMOOPS	LIPOSOME
EILMOORS	SLOOMIER
EILMOOST	TOILSOME
EILMOOSV	MOOLVIES
EILMOPRR	IMPLORER
EILMOPRS	IMPLORES
	PELORISM
EILMOPST	MILEPOST
	POLEMIST
EILMORRS	LORIMERS
EILMORSY	RIMOSELY
EILMOSTT	MOTLIEST
EILMOSTU	OUTSMILE
EILMOSUV	VOLUMISE
EILMOUVZ	VOLUMIZE
EILMPPRU	IMPURPLE
	PLUMPIER
EILMPRRU	RUMPLIER
EILMPRSS	SIMPLERS
EILMPRSU	SLUMPIER
EILMPRUY	IMPURELY
EILMPSST	MISSPELT
	SIMPLEST
EILMPSSU	IMPULSES
EILMPSTU	LUMPIEST
	PLUMIEST
EILMRSSU	MISRULES
EILMRSSY	REMISSLY
EILMRSTU	MURLIEST
EILMRSTY	LYMITERS
EILMSSTU	LITMUSES
EILMSSTY	MISSTYLE
EILMSTUU	MULTIUSE
EILMSUUV	ELUVIUMS
EILMTTUU	LUTETIUM
EILMTTUY	MULTEITY
EILNNORS	ONLINERS
EILNNOST	INSOLENT
EILNNOSV	NONLIVES
EILNNOSW	SNOWLINE
EILNNOTT	NONTITLE
EILNNOTV	VINOLENT
EILNNPSU	PINNULES
EILNNSSU	LUNINESS
EILNNSTU	UNSILENT
EILNNTTY	INTENTLY
EILNOOPP	EPIPLOON
EILNOOPS	POLONIES
	POLONISE
EILNOOPZ	POLONIZE
EILNOOST	LOONIEST
	OILSTONE
EILNOOSV	VIOLONES
EILNOPPS	PLENIPOS
EILNOPPY	POLYPINE
EILNOPRS	PLERIONS
	PROLINES
EILNOPRT	TERPINOL
	TOPLINER
EILNOPRU	NEUROPIL
EILNOPSS	EPSILONS
EILNOPST	POINTELS
	POTLINES
	TOPLINES
EILNOPTU	UNPOLITE
EILNOPTY	LINOTYPE
EILNORRS	LORINERS
EILNORRT	RITORNEL
EILNORSS	IRONLESS
EILNORST	RETINOLS
EILNORTT	TROTLINE
EILNORTU	OUTLINER
EILNORTW	TOWNLIER
EILNORVV	INVOLVER
EILNOSSU	ELUSIONS
EILNOSSW	LEWISSON
EILNOSTU	ELUTIONS
	OUTLINES
EILNOSTV	NOVELIST
	VIOLENTS
EILNOSTW	TOWLINES
EILNOSUV	EVULSION
EILNOSVV	INVOLVES
EILNOTUV	INVOLUTE
EILNOTXY	XYLONITE
EILNOTYZ	ZYLONITE
EILNPRSS	PILSNERS
EILNPRST	SPLINTER
EILNPRSU	PURLINES
EILNPRUY	UNRIPELY
EILNPSSS	SPINLESS
EILNPSST	PLENISTS
EILNPSSU	SPINULES
	SPLENIUS
EILNPSUY	SUPINELY
EILNQUUY	UNIQUELY
EILNRRUU	UNRULIER
EILNRSST	SLINTERS
	SNIRTLES
EILNRSTU	INSULTER
	LUSTRINE
EILNRSTY	TINSELRY
EILNRTUV	VIRULENT
EILNRTWY	WINTERLY
EILNSSTT	TINTLESS
EILNSSTU	UTENSILS
EILNSSTW	WESTLINS
EILNSSVY	SYLVINES
EILNSTTU	LUTENIST

EILNSUWY	UNWISELY		TIPPLERS	EIMMNORS	MISNOMER
EILOOPRR	POORLIER		TRIPPLES	EIMMOPRU	EMPORIUM
EILOOPST	LOOPIEST	EILPPRSU	PERIPLUS	EIMMOPST	METOPISM
EILOOPTZ	ZOPILOTE		SUPPLIER	EIMMOSSV	MISMOVES
EILOORST	OESTRIOL	EILPPRSY	SLIPPERY	EIMMOSTT	TOTEMISM
	TROOLIES	EILPPRTU	PULPITER	EIMMPRRS	PRIMMERS
EILOORTV	OVERTOIL	EILPPSST	STIPPLES	EIMMPRST	PRIMMEST
EILOOSST	OSTIOLES	EILPPSSU	SUPPLIES	EIMMPRSU	PREMIUMS
	STOOLIES	EILPPSSW	SWIPPLES	EIMMPSSU	PESSIMUM
EILOOSTW	WOOLIEST	EILPPSTU	PULPIEST	EIMMRRST	TRIMMERS
EILOOSTY	OTIOSELY	EILPRSST	RESPLITS	EIMMRSST	MISTERMS
EILOOSTZ	ZOOLITES		SPIRTLES	EIMMRSSW	SWIMMERS
EILOPPPR	POPPLIER	EILPRSTT	SPLITTER	EIMMRSTT	TRIMMEST
EILOPPRS	SLOPPIER		TRIPLETS	EIMMRSTU	RUMMIEST
EILOPPST	LOPPIEST	EILPRSTY	PRIESTLY	EIMMSSTU	MUMSIEST
EILOPPTY	POLYPITE		SPRITELY	EIMMSTUY	YUMMIEST
EILOPRRT	PORTLIER	EILPRSUU	PURLIEUS	EIMNNOOT	NOONTIME
EILOPRSS	SPOILERS	EILPRSUY	PLEURISY	EIMNNOPT	IMPONENT
EILOPRST	POITRELS	EILPRTTY	PRETTILY		PIMENTON
EILOPRSU	PERILOUS	EILPSSSU	PUSSLIES		POINTMEN
EILOPRSV	OVERSLIP	EILPSSTT	SPITTLES	EIMNNOST	MENTIONS
	SLIPOVER	EILPSSTU	STIPULES	EIMNNOTT	OINTMENT
EILOPRSY	PYROLISE	EILPSSUY	SPULYIES	EIMNNOUY	EUONYMIN
EILOPRTT	PLOTTIER	EILPSSUZ	SPULZIES	EIMNOOPS	EMPOISON
EILOPRTW	PILEWORT	EILQRRSU	SQUIRREL	EIMNOORS	IONOMERS
EILOPRYZ	PYROLIZE	EILQRSTU	QUILTERS		MOONRISE
EILOPSSS	PSILOSES	EILQRSUU	LIQUEURS	EIMNOORT	MOTIONER
EILOPSST	PISTOLES	EILQRSUY	SQUIRELY		REMOTION
	PTILOSES	EILQSTUU	LUSTIQUE	EIMNOORV	OMNIVORE
	SLOPIEST	EILRRSSU	SLURRIES	EIMNOOSS	ISONOMES
EILOPSSV	PLOSIVES	EILRRSTU	SULTRIER		MONOSIES
EILOPSTT	PISTOLET	EILRRSTW	TWIRLERS	EIMNOOST	EMOTIONS
	PLOTTIES	EILRRTWY	WRITERLY		MOONIEST
	POLITEST	EILRSSST	STIRLESS	EIMNOOSX	EXOMIONS
EILOPSTU	SOUTPIEL	EILRSSTT	SLITTERS	EIMNOPPU	PEPONIUM
EILOPSTX	EXPLOITS		STILTERS	EIMNOPRS	PROMINES
EILOPSUV	PLUVIOSE		TESTRILS	EIMNOPRT	ORPIMENT
EILORRTU	ULTERIOR	EILRSSTU	SURLIEST	EIMNOPSS	MOPINESS
EILORSSS	RISSOLES	EILRSSTV	LISTSERV		PEONISMS
EILORSST	ESTRIOLS	EILRSSTY	SISTERLY	EIMNOPST	EMPTIONS
EILORSSU	SOILURES		STYLISER		NEPOTISM
EILORSTT	TRIOLETS	EILRSSUV	SURVEILS		PIMENTOS
EILORSTU	LOURIEST	EILRSSZZ	SIZZLERS	EIMNOPTT	IMPOTENT
	OUTLIERS	EILRSTTU	SLUTTIER	EIMNOPTV	PIVOTMEN
EILORSUV	RIVULOSE		SURTITLE	EIMNORSS	MERSIONS
EILORSZZ	SOZZLIER	EILRSTTW	WRISTLET	EIMNORSU	INERMOUS
EILORTTY	TOILETRY	EILRSTTZ	STRELITZ		MONSIEUR
EILORTUV	OUTLIVER	EILRSTUV	RIVULETS	EIMNORSW	WINSOMER
EILORVWY	OVERWILY	EILRSTYZ	STYLIZER	EIMNORTW	TIMEWORN
EILOSSST	LOSSIEST	EILRSUUX	LUXURIES	EIMNORTY	ENORMITY
EILOSSTU	LOUSIEST	EILRSWZZ	SWIZZLER	EIMNOSST	MESTINOS
EILOSTTT	STILETTO	EILSSSTY	STYLISES		MOISTENS
EILOSTUV	OUTLIVES	EILSSTTU	LUSTIEST		SENTIMOS
	SOLUTIVE	EILSSTTY	STYLIEST	EIMNPRSS	PRIMNESS
EILOSTUW	OUTWILES		STYLITES	EIMNPSST	MISSPENT
EILOTVVY	VOTIVELY	EILSSTUU	LITUUSES	EIMNPSTU	NUMPTIES
EILPPPRY	PREPPILY	EILSSTVY	SYLVITES	EIMNRSST	ENTRISMS
EILPPRRS	RIPPLERS	EILSSTYZ	STYLIZES		MINSTERS
EILPPRRT	TRIPPLER	EILSSWZZ	SWIZZLES		TRIMNESS
EILPPRRU	PURPLIER	EILSTWZZ	TWIZZLES	EIMNRSSU	NEURISMS
EILPPRSS	SLIPPERS	EIMMMNOT	IMMOMENT	EIMNRSTU	MUNTRIES
EILPPRST	PRESPLIT	EIMMMORZ	MOMZERIM		TERMINUS
	RIPPLETS	EIMMNNOT	MONIMENT		UNMITERS
	STIPPLER	EIMMNNTU	MUNIMENT		UNMITRES

EIMNRSTY	ENTRYISM		STUMPIER	EINNSSTT	TENNISTS
	MISENTRY	EIMPSSST	MISSTEPS	EINNSSTU	SUNNIEST
EIMNSSSS	SENSISMS	EIMPSSTU	SPUMIEST	EINNSSUW	UNSINEWS
EIMNSSTU	MISTUNES		STUMPIES	EINNSSWY	SWINNEYS
EIMNSTTU	MINUTEST	EIMPSSTY	EMPTYSIS	EINNSTUW	UNTWINES
EIMNSUZZ	MUEZZINS		MISTYPES	EINOOPRS	POISONER
EIMOORST	MOORIEST	EIMPSTTU	TUMPIEST		SNOOPIER
	MOTORISE	EIMQRRSU	SQUIRMER		SPOONIER
	ROOMIEST	EIMQSSTU	MESQUITS	EINOOPSS	OPSONISE
EIMOORTZ	MOTORIZE	EIMQSTUY	MYSTIQUE		SPOONIES
EIMOOSST	OSTOMIES	EIMQSTUZ	MEZQUITS	EINOOPSZ	OPSONIZE
EIMOPPRR	IMPROPER	EIMRRRSU	SMURRIER	EINOORSS	EROSIONS
EIMOPPST	MOPPIEST	EIMRRSSU	SURMISER	EINOORST	SNOOTIER
EIMOPRRS	PRIMEROS	EIMRSSST	MISTRESS	EINOORSW	SWOONIER
	PRIMROSE	EIMRSSSU	MISUSERS	EINOORSZ	OZONISER
	PROMISER		SURMISES		SNOOZIER
EIMOPRRT	IMPORTER	EIMRSSTT	METRISTS	EINOORZZ	OZONIZER
	REIMPORT	EIMRSSTY	SMYTRIES	EINOOSST	ISOTONES
EIMOPRRV	IMPROVER	EIMRSSUU	MIURUSES	EINOOSSZ	OOZINESS
EIMOPRSS	IMPOSERS	EIMRSTTU	SMUTTIER		OZONISES
	PROMISES	EIMRSTUV	VITREUMS	EINOOSTW	TWOONIES
	SEMIPROS	EIMRSTUX	MIXTURES	EINOOSTZ	ZOONITES
EIMOPRST	IMPOSTER	EIMSSSSU	MISSUSES	EINOOSZZ	OZONIZES
EIMOPRSV	IMPROVES	EIMSSSTU	MUSSIEST	EINOOTXX	EXOTOXIN
EIMOPRSW	IMPOWERS	EIMSSTTU	MUSTIEST	EINOPPRS	POPERINS
EIMOPRUU	EUROPIUM	EIMSTUZZ	MUZZIEST	EINOPRRS	PRISONER
EIMOPSST	STOMPIES	EINNNORT	NONINERT	EINOPRSS	PORINESS
EIMOPSTY	PEYOTISM	EINNOOTX	NEOTOXIN		PRESSION
EIMOQSTU	MISQUOTE	EINNOPPT	PENPOINT		ROPINESS
EIMORRSS	MORRISES	EINNOPRU	PREUNION	EINOPRST	POINTERS
EIMORRST	MORTISER	EINNOPRY	PYRONINE		PORNIEST
	STORMIER	EINNOPSS	PENSIONS		PROTEINS
EIMORRTT	REMITTOR	EINNOQSU	QUINONES		REPOINTS
EIMORRTV	OVERTRIM	EINNORSS	IRONNESS		TROPINES
EIMORRWW	WIREWORM	EINNORST	INTONERS	EINOPRSU	PRUINOSE
EIMORSST	EROTISMS		NOINTERS	EINOPRSV	OVERSPIN
	MORTISES		TERNIONS		PROVINES
	TRISOMES	EINNORSU	REUNIONS	EINOPRTU	ERUPTION
EIMORSSV	VERISMOS	EINNORSV	ENVIRONS	EINOPSSW	WINESOPS
EIMORSTT	OMITTERS	EINNORTT	TONTINER	EINOPSTT	NEPOTIST
EIMORSTU	MISROUTE	EINNORTU	NEUTRINO	EINOPSTU	POUTINES
	MOISTURE	EINNORTV	INVENTOR	EINOPSWX	SWINEPOX
EIMORSTV	VOMITERS		NOVERINT	EINOQSTU	QUESTION
EIMORSTW	MISWROTE	EINNORWW	WINNOWER	EINOQTTU	QUOTIENT
	WORMIEST	EINNOSSS	NOSINESS	EINORRSS	ROSINERS
EIMORSTY	ISOMETRY	EINNOSST	TENSIONS	EINORRST	INTRORSE
EIMORSVW	OVERSWIM	EINNOSSU	NONISSUE		SNORTIER
EIMORTXY	OXIMETRY		UNSONSIE	EINORRTV	INVERTOR
EIMOSSST	MOSSIEST	EINNOSSV	VENISONS	EINORRTW	INTERROW
EIMOSSTT	MOISTEST	EINNOSTT	TINSTONE	EINORSSS	ROSINESS
EIMOSSTU	MOUSIEST		TONTINES	EINORSST	OESTRINS
EIMOSSTX	EXOTISMS	EINNOSTU	NOUNIEST		TERSIONS
EIMOSSTZ	MESTIZOS	EINNPRSS	SPINNERS	EINORSSU	NEUROSIS
EIMOSSYZ	ISOZYMES	EINNPRST	ENPRINTS		RESINOUS
EIMOSTTT	MOTTIEST	EINNPRSY	SPINNERY	EINORSSV	VERSIONS
	TOTEMIST	EINNPSST	SPINNETS	EINORSTT	SNOTTIER
EIMOSTTU	TIMEOUTS	EINNPSSU	PUNINESS		TENORIST
	TITMOUSE	EINNPSSY	SPINNEYS		TRITONES
EIMPRRST	PRETRIMS	EINNPSTU	PUNNIEST	EINORSTU	NITREOUS
EIMPRRSU	PRIMEURS	EINNPSXY	SIXPENNY		ROUTINES
EIMPRSST	IMPRESTS	EINNRSTU	RUNNIEST		SNOUTIER
EIMPRSSU	PRIMUSES		STURNINE	EINORSTV	INVESTOR
EIMPRSTU	IMPUREST	EINNRSTV	VINTNERS	EINORSTY	SEROTINY
	IMPUTERS	EINNRTTU	NUTRIENT		TYROSINE

EINORSTZ	TRIZONES
EINORSUV	SOUVENIR
EINORTTU	RITENUTO
EINOSSSS	SESSIONS
EINOSSST	SONSIEST
	STENOSIS
EINOSSTT	SNOTTIES
	STONIEST
EINOSSTW	SNOWIEST
EINOSTTT	TOTIENTS
EINOSTTW	NOWTIEST
	TOWNIEST
EINOSTUU	TENUIOUS
EINOSTVY	VENOSITY
EINPPRRT	PREPRINT
EINPPRSS	SNIPPERS
EINPPSST	SNIPPETS
EINPPSTY	SNIPPETY
EINPRRST	PRINTERS
	REPRINTS
	SPRINTER
EINPRRTU	PRURIENT
EINPRRTY	PRINTERY
EINPRSST	SPINSTER
EINPRSTU	REPUNITS
	UNPRIEST
	UNRIPEST
EINPRTTU	INPUTTER
EINPSTTX	SPINTEXT
EINPSTTY	TINTYPES
EINQRSTU	SQUINTER
EINQRTTU	QUITRENT
EINQSSTU	INQUESTS
EINQSTTU	QUINTETS
EINQSTUU	UNIQUEST
	UNQUIETS
EINQTTTU	QUINTETT
EINRRSSU	INSURERS
EINRSSST	INSTRESS
EINRSSSU	SUNRISES
EINRSSTT	ENTRISTS
	STINTERS
EINRSSXY	SYRINXES
EINRSTTU	RUNTIEST
EINRSTTW	TWINTERS
EINRSTTY	ENTRYIST
EINRSTUV	UNRIVETS
	VENTURIS
EINRSTUW	UNWRITES
EINRTUUV	UNVIRTUE
EINSSSST	SENSISTS
EINSSTTU	NUTSIEST
EINSSTTW	ENTWISTS
	TWINSETS
EINSSTUW	UNWISEST
EINSSTUX	UNSEXIST
EINSSTXY	SYNTEXIS
EINSTTTU	NUTTIEST
EINSTTTW	TWITTENS
EIOOPPRS	PORPOISE
EIOOPPST	OPPOSITE
EIOOPRST	PORTOISE
	ROOPIEST
EIOOPRSW	SWOOPIER
EIOOPSST	ISOTOPES
EIOOPSTV	POOVIEST
EIOOPTYZ	EPIZOOTY
EIOORRSS	SORORISE
EIOORRST	ROOTSIER
EIOORRSZ	SORORIZE
EIOORSTT	ROOTIEST
	TORTOISE
EIOOSSST	OSTEOSIS
EIOOSSTT	SOOTIEST
	TOOTSIES
EIOOSTTZ	ZOOTIEST
EIOOSTWZ	WOOZIEST
EIOPPPST	POPPIEST
EIOPPRTW	PIPEWORT
EIOPPSST	SOPPIEST
EIOPPTTY	TIPPYTOE
EIOPQRSU	PIROQUES
EIOPQSTU	POSTIQUE
EIOPRRSS	PRIORESS
EIOPRRST	PIERROTS
	SPORTIER
EIOPRRSU	SUPERIOR
EIOPRRSV	PREVISOR
EIOPRRTV	OVERTRIP
EIOPRSSS	PROSSIES
EIOPRSST	PERIOSTS
	PROSIEST
	PROSTIES
	REPOSITS
	RIPOSTES
	SPORTIES
	TRIPOSES
EIOPRSTT	PORTIEST
	RISPETTO
	SPOTTIER
EIOPRSTU	ROUPIEST
	SPOUTIER
EIOPRSTV	OVERTIPS
	PIVOTERS
	SORPTIVE
	SPORTIVE
EIOPRSUV	PERVIOUS
	PREVIOUS
	VIPEROUS
EIOPRTTT	TRIPTOTE
EIOPRTTY	PETITORY
EIOPRTUZ	OUTPRIZE
EIOPSSST	SEPIOSTS
EIOPSSSU	POUSSIES
EIOPSSTT	SPOTTIES
EIOPSSTU	PUTOISES
	SOUPIEST
EIOPSSTX	EXPOSITS
EIOPSSTY	ISOTYPES
EIOPSTTT	POTTIEST
EIOPSTTU	POUTIEST
EIOPSTTY	PEYOTIST
EIOPSTUW	WIPEOUTS
EIOQRSTU	QUOITERS
EIOQSTUX	QUIXOTES
EIORRRST	ERRORIST
	TERROIRS
EIORRRSW	WORRIERS
EIORRRTU	ROTURIER
EIORRSST	RESISTOR
	ROISTERS
	SORRIEST
EIORRSSV	REVISORS
EIORRSTT	RORTIEST
EIORRSTU	STOURIER
EIORRSTV	OVERSTIR
	SERVITOR
EIORRSUV	OUVRIERS
	REOVIRUS
EIORRSVV	REVIVORS
EIORRSVY	REVISORY
EIORRTTU	TROUTIER
EIORSSTT	STOITERS
EIORSSTY	SEROSITY
EIORSTTU	TOUSTIER
	TUTORISE
EIORSTTV	VIRETOTS
EIORSTTW	SWOTTIER
EIORSTUV	VIRTUOSE
	VITREOUS
	VOITURES
EIORTTUW	OUTWRITE
EIORTTUZ	TUTORIZE
EIOSSSTT	TOSSIEST
EIOSSTTT	STOTTIES
EIOSSTTU	TOUSIEST
EIOSSTTW	TOWSIEST
EIOSSTUZ	OUTSIZES
EIOSTTTT	TOTTIEST
EIOSTTTU	TOUTIEST
EIOSTTUZ	TOUZIEST
EIOSTTWZ	TOWZIEST
EIPPQRSU	QUIPPERS
EIPPRRST	STRIPPER
	TRIPPERS
EIPPRRSV	PERSPIRY
EIPPRRTY	TRIPPERY
EIPPRSTT	TRIPPETS
EIPQRSTU	QUIPSTER
EIPRRRSU	SPURRIER
EIPRRSST	STRIPERS
EIPRRSSU	SPURRIES
	SURPRISE
	UPRISERS
EIPRRSTZ	SPRITZER
EIPRRSUV	UPRIVERS
EIPRRSUY	SYRUPIER
EIPRRSUZ	SURPRIZE
EIPRSSST	PERSISTS
EIPRSSSU	SUSPIRES
EIPRSSTT	SPITTERS
	TIPSTERS
EIPRSSTU	PURSIEST
EIPRSSTZ	SPRITZES
EIPRSTTU	PURTIEST
	PUTTIERS
EIPRSUVW	PURVIEWS
EIPRSVVY	SPIVVERY
EIPSSSTU	PUSSIEST
EIQRRSTU	SQUIRTER
EIQRSSSU	SQUIRESS
EIQRSSTU	QUERISTS

EIQRSTTU	QUITTERS	EKLSSSTU	TUSKLESS	ELLNOSST	STOLLENS
EIQRSTUU	SEQUITUR	EKLSSTTU	SKUTTLES	ELLNOSSU	NOUSELLS
EIQRSUZZ	QUIZZERS	EKMMORSU	MURKSOME	ELLNOSVY	SLOVENLY
EIQRUYZZ	QUIZZERY	EKMMRSSU	SKUMMERS	ELLNOSXY	XYLENOLS
EIQSSUZZ	SQUIZZES	EKMNOSSU	MUSKONES	ELLNOUVY	UNLOVELY
EIRRRSST	STIRRERS	EKMNOSUX	MUSKOXEN	ELLNPSSU	UNSPELLS
EIRRSSTV	STRIVERS	EKMOOPRR	MOREPORK	ELLOORRV	ROLLOVER
EIRRSTTU	TRUSTIER	EKMOOPST	SMOKEPOT	ELLOOSST	TOOLLESS
EIRRSUVV	SURVIVER	EKMOORSW	WORKSOME	ELLOOSSW	WOOSELLS
EIRSSSTU	SUITRESS	EKMOOSSS	KOSMOSES	ELLOOSTU	TOLUOLES
	TSURISES	EKMOOSTU	OUTSMOKE	ELLOPRRS	PROLLERS
EIRSSTTU	RUSTIEST	EKMOSSUY	KOUMYSES	ELLOPRST	POLLSTER
	TRUSTIES	EKMRSTUY	MUSKETRY	ELLOPRTU	POLLUTER
EIRSSTTW	RETWISTS	EKNNOORT	KENOTRON	ELLOPRUV	PULLOVER
	TWISTERS	EKNNOPSU	UNSPOKEN	ELLOPSST	PLOTLESS
EIRSSTUV	REVUISTS	EKNOOPRW	OPENWORK	ELLOPSTU	OUTSPELL
	STUIVERS	EKNOORSS	SNOOKERS		POLLUTES
EIRSSUVV	SURVIVES	EKNOORST	STROOKEN	ELLORRST	STROLLER
EIRSSUVW	SURVIEWS	EKNOPPSU	UPSPOKEN		TROLLERS
EIRSTTTU	RUTTIEST	EKNOPSSY	PYKNOSES	ELLORSTY	TROLLEYS
EIRSTTTW	TWITTERS	EKNORSST	STONKERS	ELLOSSSS	LOSSLESS
EIRSTTUX	TUTRIXES	EKNORSTT	KNOTTERS	ELLOSSSU	SOULLESS
EIRTTTWY	TWITTERY	EKNORSTW	NETWORKS	ELLOSSTU	OUTSELLS
EIRTTUWZ	WURTZITE	EKNORSUY	YOUNKERS		SELLOUTS
EISSSSTU	TUSSISES	EKNRSTUY	TURNKEYS	ELLOSSYY	LYOLYSES
EISSSTUW	WUSSIEST	EKOOOPRT	POKEROOT	ELLOSTTU	OUTTELLS
EISSTTUW	WETSUITS	EKOOORTV	OVERTOOK	ELLOSTUW	OUTSWELL
EISTTTUV	VUTTIEST	EKOOPRRV	PROVOKER		OUTWELLS
EJLLORSY	JOLLYERS	EKOOPRRW	ROPEWORK	ELLOSTUY	OUTYELLS
EJLOPSTU	PULSOJET	EKOOPRSV	PROVOKES	ELLPPSSU	PULPLESS
EJLORSST	JOSTLERS	EKOOPRSY	SPOOKERY	ELLPPSUY	SUPPLELY
EJLRSSUY	JURYLESS	EKOOPSTU	OUTSPOKE	ELLPSSUW	UPSWELLS
EJMOPRUV	OVERJUMP	EKOORRVW	OVERWORK	ELLSSSTU	LUSTLESS
EJNORRSU	REJOURNS	EKOORSST	STOOKERS	ELMMNOTU	LOMENTUM
EJNORSUY	JOURNEYS		STROOKES	ELMMNOTY	MOMENTLY
EJNRSTUU	UNJUSTER	EKOORSTW	KOTOWERS	ELMMOPSU	PUMMELOS
EJNSSSTU	JUSTNESS	EKOORSUU	EUROKOUS	ELMMORST	TROMMELS
EJOORSVY	OVERJOYS	EKOORTWW	KOWTOWER	ELMMOSUX	LUMMOXES
EJOPPRST	PROPJETS	EKOPRRSW	PREWORKS	ELMMPSTU	PLUMMEST
EJOPRSTT	JETPORTS	EKOPRSTU	UPSTROKE		PLUMMETS
EJORSSTU	JOUSTERS	EKOPRSUY	KOUPREYS	ELMMRSSU	SLUMMERS
EJORSTUV	OVERJUST	EKORRSST	STROKERS	ELMMRSTU	STRUMMEL
EJOSSTTU	OUTJESTS	EKORRUVY	KURVEYOR		TUMMLERS
EKKLNPRU	KERPLUNK	EKORSSTU	KURTOSES	ELMMRSUY	SUMMERLY
EKKLOOSY	OLYKOEKS	EKORSTWY	SKYWROTE	ELMMSSTU	STUMMELS
EKKLOOSZ	KOLKOZES	EKPPSSUU	SEPPUKUS	ELMNNOSU	UNSOLEMN
EKKLRSSU	SKULKERS	ELLLMOWY	MELLOWLY	ELMNNOTU	UNMOLTEN
EKKMORSY	KROMESKY	ELLLNSUY	SULLENLY	ELMNOOOP	MONOPOLE
EKLLMSSU	SKELLUMS	ELLLORRS	LORRELLS	ELMNOOSS	MOONLESS
EKLLNORS	KNOLLERS	ELLLOWYY	YELLOWLY	ELMNOOST	MOONLETS
EKLLOSSY	KYLLOSES	ELLMNOOS	MOELLONS	ELMNOPSU	PULMONES
	YOLKLESS	ELLMNOSY	SOLEMNLY	ELMNORSS	NORMLESS
EKLLRRSU	KRULLERS	ELLMNOTY	MOLTENLY	ELMNOSTW	SNOWMELT
EKLNOOOR	ONLOOKER	ELLMNOUW	UNMELLOW	ELMNPPSU	PLUMPENS
EKLNOPRS	PLONKERS	ELLMNPUY	LUMPENLY	ELMNPSUU	UNPLUMES
EKLNORSS	SNORKELS	ELLMOORS	MORELLOS	ELMNUUZZ	UNMUZZLE
EKLNOSST	KNOTLESS	ELLMORRS	MORRELLS	ELMOOPPS	POMPELOS
EKLNPRSU	PLUNKERS	ELLMOSTU	OUTSMELL	ELMOOPSY	POLYSOME
EKLNPSSU	SPELUNKS	ELLMPSUU	PLUMULES	ELMOORST	TREMOLOS
EKLOOORV	LOOKOVER	ELLNNOST	TONNELLS	ELMOORSY	MOROSELY
	OVERLOOK	ELLNNSSU	NULLNESS	ELMOOSSY	LYSOSOME
EKLOOPSW	SLOWPOKE	ELLNOORV	LOVELORN	ELMOPRST	PREMOLTS
EKLORSSW	WORKLESS	ELLNOOSW	WOOLLENS	ELMOPRSY	POLYMERS
EKLOSSTV	STOKVELS	ELLNOPRU	PRUNELLO	ELMOPRTY	METOPRYL

ELMOPRYY	POLYMERY	ELOORSTT	ROOTLETS	ELRSTUUV	VULTURES
ELMOPSYY	POLYSEMY		TOOTLERS	ELSSSTUY	STYLUSES
ELMORSSU	EMULSORS	ELOORSTU	TORULOSE	ELSSSTYY	SYSTYLES
ELMORSTT	MOTTLERS	ELOORSUV	OVERSOUL	EMMMNOTU	MOMENTUM
ELMORSTU	MOULTERS	ELOORSVW	OVERSLOW	EMMMNOTU	MONUMENT
ELMORUUV	VERMOULU	ELOOSSST	SOOTLESS	EMMNOOOS	MONOSOME
ELMOSTTU	OUTSMELT	ELOOSSTT	TOOLSETS	EMMNOORS	MONOMERS
ELMOSTUU	TUMULOSE	ELOOSSTU	OUTSOLES	EMMNOORT	MOTORMEN
ELMOSYYZ	LYSOZYME	ELOOSSWY	WOOLSEYS	EMMNOOST	MOMENTOS
ELMPPRSU	PLUMPERS	ELOOSTUV	OUTLOVES	EMMNOOSY	MONOSEMY
ELMPPSSU	PUMPLESS	ELOOSVVX	VOLVOXES	EMMNORSU	RESUMMON
ELMPPSTU	PLUMPEST	ELOPPRRY	PROPERLY		SUMMONER
ELMPRSSU	RUMPLESS	ELOPPSST	STOPPLES	EMMNORSY	MERONYMS
ELMRRTUU	MULTURER	ELOPPTYY	POLYTYPE	EMMNORVY	MERONYMY
ELMRSTUU	MULTURES	ELOPRRSU	PROULERS	EMMNOSTU	OMENTUMS
ELMRSUZZ	MUZZLERS	ELOPRRSW	PROWLERS	EMMNOSTY	METONYMS
ELNNNOOV	NONNOVEL	ELOPRRSY	PYRROLES	EMMNOTTU	TOMENTUM
ELNNOOSU	UNLOOSEN	ELOPRRTY	PORTERLY	EMMNOTVY	METONYMY
ELNNOPSU	NONUPLES	ELOPRSSS	PLESSORS	EMMOOORS	ROOMSOME
ELNNOPTU	NONUPLET	ELOPRSST	PORTLESS	EMMOOSTY	MYOTOMES
ELNNORSS	LORNNESS	ELOPRSSU	SPORULES	EMMOPRRS	PROMMERS
ELNNOSSU	NOUNLESS	ELOPRSTT	PLOTTERS	EMMOPRSU	SUPERMOM
ELNNOSTY	NONSTYLE	ELOPRSTU	PLOUTERS	EMMOPTTY	POMMETTY
ELNNRSTU	TRUNNELS		POULTERS	EMMRRRUU	MURMURER
ELNOOPPR	PROPENOL	ELOPRSTW	PLOWTERS		REMURMUR
ELNOOPST	PELOTONS	ELOPRSTY	PROSTYLE	EMMRRSTU	STRUMMER
ELNOOSST	SOLONETS		PROTYLES	EMMRSTYY	SYMMETRY
ELNOOSSU	UNLOOSES	ELOPRSUV	OVERPLUS	EMNNNOOU	NOUMENON
ELNOOSSZ	SNOOZLES	ELOPRSYY	PYROLYSE	EMNNNOOY	NONMONEY
ELNOOSTZ	SOLONETZ	ELOPRXYY	PYROXYLE	EMNNOOOT	MONOTONE
ELNOPPRY	PROPENYL	ELOPRYYZ	PYROLYZE	EMNNOORT	NONMETRO
ELNOPRVY	PROVENLY	ELOPSSST	SPOTLESS	EMNNOPTY	NONEMPTY
ELNOPSTU	PLEUSTON		STOPLESS	EMNNOSTW	TOWNSMEN
ELNOPTTY	POTENTLY	ELOPSSSU	SOUPLESS	EMNNOSVY	SYNONYME
ELNOPTYY	POLYTENY	ELOPSSTY	STYLOPES	EMNNPSTU	PUNTSMEN
ELNORSSU	NOURSLES	ELOPSSUU	OPULUSES	EMNNSTTU	STUNTMEN
ELNORSTU	TURNSOLE	ELOPSTTU	OUTSLEPT	EMNOOPST	METOPONS
ELNORSVY	SLOVENRY		OUTSPELT	EMNOOPTY	MONOTYPE
ELNORTTY	ROTTENLY	ELOPSTUY	OUTYELPS	EMNOORST	MESOTRON
ELNOSSST	LOSTNESS	ELORSSTT	SETTLORS		MONTEROS
ELNOSSSW	SLOWNESS		SLOTTERS	EMNOORSU	ENORMOUS
	SNOWLESS	ELORSTUY	ELYTROUS		NEMOROUS
ELNOSSTV	SOLVENTS		SOUTERLY	EMNOORSW	NEWSROOM
ELNOSSTW	TOWNLESS		UROSTYLE	EMNOORTY	NOOMETRY
	WONTLESS	ELORTTTU	TROUTLET	EMNOOSST	MOONSETS
ELNOSTTW	TOWNLETS	ELOSSSTY	SYSTOLES		MOOTNESS
ELNOSTUZ	ZONULETS	ELOSSTUU	SETULOUS	EMNOOSUV	VENOMOUS
ELNOSUUV	VENULOUS	ELOSSWZZ	SWOZZLES	EMNOOTTY	TENOTOMY
ELNOSUVY	VENOUSLY	ELPPRSTU	PURPLEST	EMNOOTUV	OUTVENOM
ELNPPSUU	UNSUPPLE	ELPPRSUY	RESUPPLY	EMNOOTWY	TOYWOMEN
ELNPRTUU	PURULENT	ELPPSSTU	SUPPLEST	EMNOPSSU	SPUMONES
ELNPRUUY	UNPURELY	ELPRRSSU	SLURPERS	EMNORRSU	MOURNERS
ELNPUUZZ	UNPUZZLE	ELPRSSSU	SPURLESS	EMNORRTY	RETRONYM
ELNRSUUY	UNSURELY	ELPRSSTU	SPURTLES	EMNORSST	MONSTERS
ELNRSUZZ	NUZZLERS	ELPRSTTU	SPLUTTER	EMNORSTT	SORTMENT
ELNSSUZZ	SNUZZLES	ELPRSTUU	PULTURES		TORMENTS
ELOOPPRY	POLYPORE	ELPRSUZZ	PUZZLERS	EMNORSTU	MONTURES
ELOOPRSS	RESPOOLS	ELPSSSUY	PUSSLEYS		MOUNTERS
	SPOOLERS	ELPSSTUU	PUSTULES		REMOUNTS
ELOOPRSU	SUPERLOO	ELPSTUXY	SEXTUPLY	EMNORSUU	NUMEROUS
ELOOPRTV	OVERPLOT	ELRRSSTU	RUSTLERS	EMNOSSST	STEMSONS
ELOOPRUW	OWERLOUP	ELRRSTTU	TURTLERS	EMNOSUUY	EUONYMUS
ELOOPSSS	SESSPOOL	ELRSSSTU	RUSTLESS	EMNOSUVY	EVONYMUS
ELOORSST	ROOTLESS	ELRSTTUY	SLUTTERY	EMNRSSTU	MUNSTERS

	STERNUMS	ENOOOSSZ	ZOONOSES	EOOPPTTY	TOPOTYPE
EMOOPRRT	PROMOTER	ENOOPPRS	PROPONES	EOOPRRSS	SPOORERS
EMOOPRSS	OOSPERMS	ENOOPPST	POSTPONE	EOOPRRST	PROTORES
EMOOPRST	PROMOTES	ENOOPRSS	POORNESS		TROOPERS
EMOOPRSY	POMEROYS		SNOOPERS	EOOPRRTU	OUTROPER
	PYROSOME	ENOOPSSY	SPOONEYS		UPROOTER
EMOOPRSZ	ZOOSPERM	ENOOPSTT	POTSTONE	EOOPRSST	STOOPERS
EMOOPSSU	ESPUMOSO		TOPSTONE	EOOPRSSW	SWOOPERS
EMOORRST	RESTROOM	ENOORRVW	OVERWORN	EOOPRSTU	OUTROPES
EMOORSST	MOROSEST	ENOORSSW	SWOONERS		PORTEOUS
EMOORSSU	UROSOMES	ENOORSSZ	SNOOZERS	EOOPRSTV	OVERPOST
EMOORTYZ	ZOOMETRY	ENOORSTU	OUTSNORE		OVERTOPS
EMOOSSTW	TWOSOMES	ENOORSVW	OVERSOWN		STOPOVER
EMOOSSTY	MYOSOTES	ENOOSSTT	TESTOONS	EOOPRSTW	TOWROPES
EMOOSSXY	OXYSOMES	ENOOSTXY	OXYTONES	EOOPRTUW	OUTPOWER
EMOOSTUV	OUTMOVES	ENOPPRRU	UNPROPER	EOOPSTTV	STOVETOP
EMOPPRRT	PROMPTER	ENOPRRSU	PRONEURS	EOOPSTYZ	ZOOTYPES
EMOPPRUV	OVERPUMP	ENOPRSST	POSTERNS	EOOQTTUU	OUTQUOTE
EMOPPSTU	UPTEMPOS	ENOPRSTT	PORTENTS	EOORRRSW	SORROWER
EMOPRRSU	PROSUMER	ENOPRTUW	UPTOWNER	EOORRSST	ROOSTERS
EMOPRSST	STOMPERS	ENOPSSST	STEPSONS	EOORRSVW	ROWOVERS
EMOPRSSU	SPERMOUS	ENOPSSSY	SYNOPSES	EOORSSTU	OESTROUS
	SUPREMOS	ENOPSTTU	OUTSPENT	EOORSSVW	OVERSOWS
EMORRRUU	RUMOURER	ENOQSTUU	UNQUOTES	EOORSTUW	OUTSWORE
EMORRSST	STORMERS	ENORRSST	SNORTERS	EOORTTUV	OUTVOTER
EMORRSSU	MORSURES	ENORRSTT	TORRENTS	EOORTTUW	OUTTOWER
EMORSSSU	SMOUSERS	ENORRSUV	OVERRUNS		OUTWROTE
EMORSSTU	OESTRUMS		RUNOVERS	EOOSTTUV	OUTVOTES
	STRUMOSE	ENORRTUU	TOURNURE	EOPPRRSS	PROSPERS
EMORSUVW	OVERSWUM	ENORRTUV	OVERTURN	EOPPRRST	STROPPER
EMOSSSTT	MOSTESTS		TURNOVER	EOPPRRSU	SUPERPRO
EMOSSTTW	WESTMOST	ENORSSSU	SOURNESS	EOPPRRTY	PROPERTY
EMOSSTVZ	ZEMSTVOS	ENORSSTT	SNOTTERS	EOPPRSST	POPSTERS
EMOSTTTU	TETOTUMS		STENTORS		STOPPERS
EMPRRTUY	TRUMPERY	ENORSSTU	TONSURES	EOPPRSSU	PURPOSES
EMPRSSTU	RESTUMPS	ENORSTTU	STENTOUR		SUPPOSER
	STUMPERS	ENORSTTY	SNOTTERY	EOPPRSSW	SWOPPERS
	SUMPTERS	ENORSTUV	VENTROUS	EOPPSSSU	SUPPOSES
EMPRSSUU	RUMPUSES	ENORSTUY	TOURNEYS	EOPRRSST	PORTRESS
EMPRSTTU	STRUMPET	ENOSSSUU	SENSUOUS		PRESORTS
	TRUMPETS	ENOSSTTU	STOUTENS		SPORTERS
EMRRSSTU	STURMERS	ENPRRSSU	PRESSRUN	EOPRRSTU	POSTURER
ENNNOORW	NONOWNER		SPURNERS		RESPROUT
ENNNOOVW	NONWOVEN	ENPRSSSY	SPRYNESS		TROUPERS
ENNNORTY	NONENTRY	ENPRSSTU	PUNSTERS	EOPRRUVY	PURVEYOR
ENNOOORT	TENOROON	ENPRSSUU	PRUNUSES	EOPRSSTT	PROTESTS
ENNOOOTZ	ENTOZOON		UNPURSES		SPOTTERS
ENNOOPPT	OPPONENT	ENPRTTUY	UNPRETTY	EOPRSSTU	OUTPRESS
ENNOORST	NORTENOS	ENRRRTUU	NURTURER		POSTURES
ENNOORTV	NONVOTER	ENRRSTUU	NURTURES		SEPTUORS
ENNOOSTT	NONETTOS	ENRSSSTU	UNSTRESS		SPOUTERS
ENNOPRSU	UNPERSON	ENRSSTTU	ENTRUSTS	EOPRSSUU	POURSUES
ENNOPRUV	UNPROVEN	ENRSSTUU	UNSUREST		UPROUSES
ENNOPTWY	TWOPENNY	ENRSTTUU	UNTRUEST	EOPRSSUV	OVERSUPS
ENNORSST	STERNSON	EOOOPRSS	OOSPORES	EOPRSSUW	POURSEWS
ENNORSSU	NONUSERS		SOPOROSE	EOPSSSTU	UPTOSSES
ENNORSSW	WORNNESS	EOOOPRSZ	ZOOSPORE	EOPSSTTT	POSTTEST
ENNORSTU	NEUTRONS	EOOOPRTZ	ZOOTROPE	EOPSSTTU	OUTSTEPS
ENNORTTU	UNROTTEN	EOOORRST	ROSEROOT	EOPSSTTW	STEWPOTS
ENNOSSTU	NEUSTONS	EOOPPRRS	PROPOSER	EOPSTTUW	OUTSWEPT
	SUNSTONE	EOOPPRSS	OPPOSERS	EOQRRSTU	TORQUERS
ENNPPTUY	TUPPENNY		PROPOSES	EOQRSSTU	QUESTORS
ENNRSSTU	STUNNERS	EOOPPRSV	POPOVERS	EORRRTTU	TORTURER
ENOOORSV	OVERSOON	EOOPPSST	POSTPOSE	EORRSSST	STRESSOR

	TROSSERS				
EORRSSTT	STERTORS	FFGIKNOS	SKOFFING	FGGIINNR	FRINGING
EORRSSTU	ROUSTERS	FFGILMNU	MUFFLING	FGGIINRT	GRIFTING
	TRESSOUR	FFGILNPU	PLUFFING	FGGIINRU	FIGURING
	TROUSERS	FFGILNRU	RUFFLING	FGGIISZZ	FIZZGIGS
EORRSSTW	STROWERS	FFGILNSU	SLUFFING	FGGILNOR	FROGLING
	TROWSERS	FFGILRUY	GRUFFILY	FGGILNOS	GOLFINGS
EORRSSTY	ROYSTERS	FFGINNSU	SNUFFING	FGGINOOR	FORGOING
	STROYERS	FFGINOPU	POUFFING	FGGINORS	FORGINGS
EORRSTTT	TROTTERS	FFGINORS	GRIFFONS	FGHIIKNS	KINGFISH
EORRSTTU	TORTURES	FFGINOSW	SOWFFING	FGHIILNT	INFLIGHT
	TROUTERS		SWOFFING	FGHIINSS	FISHINGS
EORRSUVY	SURVEYOR	FFGINPSU	PUFFINGS	FGHIINST	INFIGHTS
EORRTUUV	TROUVEUR	FFGINSTU	STUFFING		SHIFTING
EORSSSTU	TUSSORES	FFGIORTU	FOGFRUIT	FGHILLTU	LIGHTFUL
EORSSTTT	STOTTERS	FFHIINSS	SNIFFISH	FGHILMTU	MIGHTFUL
	STRETTOS	FFHIISST	STIFFISH	FGHILNSU	FLUSHING
EORSSTTU	OUTSERTS	FFHIISTY	FIFTYISH		LUNGFISH
	TUTORESS	FFHIKNSU	HUFFKINS	FGHILRTU	RIGHTFUL
EORSSTTW	SWOTTERS	FFHILOOS	FOOLFISH	FGHINOOW	WHOOFING
EORSSTUX	SEXTUORS	FFHILOSW	WOLFFISH	FGHINORT	FROTHING
EORSTTUW	OUTWREST	FFHILOSY	OFFISHLY	FGHINOTU	INFOUGHT
EORSTTUY	TUTOYERS	FFHIOPSS	SPOFFISH	FGHINRSU	FRUSHING
EORSTUUV	VERTUOUS	FFHIRSSU	SURFFISH	FGHIOPST	GIFTSHOP
EOSSTTTU	STOUTEST	FFHOOOST	OFFSHOOT	FGHIOTTU	OUTFIGHT
EPPPRTUY	PUPPETRY	FFHOOSSW	SHOWOFFS	FGHLORUU	FURLOUGH
EPPRRSUU	PURPURES	FFHOSSTU	SHUTOFFS	FGHNOORS	FOGHORNS
EPPRSSSU	SUPPRESS	FFIILMOR	FILIFORM	FGHNOTUU	UNFOUGHT
EPPRSSUY	SUPERSPY	FFIILNSY	SNIFFILY	FGIIIKNN	FINIKING
EPRRRSSU	SPURRERS	FFIILNTY	FLINTIFY	FGIIINNX	INFIXING
EPRRSSTU	SPURTERS	FFIILPSY	SPIFFILY	FGIIKLNS	FLISKING
EPRRSSUU	PURSUERS	FFIINOOS	SOFFIONI	FGIIKNNS	KNIFINGS
	USURPERS	FFIKLORT	FORKLIFT	FGIIKNRS	FRISKING
EPRRSSUY	SPURREYS	FFIKLRSU	FRISKFUL	FGIILLNR	FRILLING
EPRRSTUU	RUPTURES	FFILLLSU	FULFILLS	FGIILLNS	FILLINGS
EPRSSTTU	SPUTTERS	FFILLOPP	FLIPFLOP	FGIILMNP	FLIMPING
EPRSTTUY	SPUTTERY	FFILLTUY	FITFULLY	FGIILNNT	FLINTING
EQRRTUUU	TRUQUEUR	FFILNSUY	SNUFFILY	FGIILNOO	FOLIOING
ERRSSSTU	TRUSSERS	FFILRTUU	FRUITFUL	FGIILNOS	FOILINGS
ERRSSTTU	TRUSTERS	FFILSSTU	FISTFULS	FGIILNPP	FLIPPING
ERRSSTTY	TRYSTERS	FFILSTUY	STUFFILY	FGIILNRS	RIFLINGS
ERRSTTTU	STRUTTER	FFIMORSU	FUSIFORM	FGIILNRT	FLIRTING
ERSSTTTU	STUTTERS	FFINOOST	FINFOOTS		TRIFLING
FFFGILNU	FLUFFING	FFINOPRT	OFFPRINT	FGIILNSS	FISSLING
FFFILLUY	FLUFFILY	FFINOPSS	SPINOFFS	FGIILNST	STIFLING
FFFILOST	LIFTOFFS	FFINOPST	PONTIFFS	FGIILNTT	FLITTING
FFFMOOTU	FOOTMUFF	FFJMOPSU	JUMPOFFS	FGIILNZZ	FIZZLING
FFGGIILN	GLIFFING	FFKLORSU	FORKFULS	FGIINNST	SNIFTING
FFGGINRU	GRUFFING		FORKSFUL	FGIINNSU	INFUSING
FFGHIINW	WHIFFING	FFLLOOSU	LOOFFULS	FGIINNUX	UNFIXING
FFGHINOU	HOUFFING	FFLMNOOU	MOUFFLON	FGIINNUY	UNIFYING
FFGHINOW	HOWFFING	FFLNOTUU	FOUNTFUL	FGIINOQU	QUOIFING
FFGHINSU	HUFFINGS	FFLORRUU	FURFUROL	FGIINOST	FOISTING
FFGHIORS	FROGFISH	FFNORSTU	TURNOFFS	FGIINRRS	FIRRINGS
FFGHIRSU	GRUFFISH	FFNSTUUY	UNSTUFFY	FGIINRST	FRISTING
FFGIIKNS	SKIFFING	FFOOPSST	STOPOFFS	FGIINRTT	FRITTING
FFGIILNP	PIFFLING	FFOORRUU	FROUFROU	FGIINRTU	FRUITING
FFGIILNR	RIFFLING	FGGGIINR	FRIGGING	FGIINRZZ	FRIZZING
FFGIILNS	SIFFLING	FGGGILNO	FLOGGING	FGIINSST	SIFTINGS
FFGIINNS	SNIFFING	FGGGINOR	FROGGING	FGIINSTT	FITTINGS
FFGIINPS	SPIFFING	FGGGINRU	FRUGGING	FGIINSTW	SWIFTING
FFGIINRS	GRIFFINS	FGGHIINT	FIGHTING	FGIINSZZ	FIZZINGS
FFGIINST	STIFFING	FGGHIISS	FISHGIGS	FGIIRSTU	FIGURIST
	TIFFINGS	FGGHINTU	GUNFIGHT	FGIKLNNU	FLUNKING
		FGGIILNN	FLINGING	FGILLNOW	WOLFLING

FGILLNOY	FOLLYING	FHIKLLLO	HILLFOLK	FIINOSSS	FISSIONS
FGILMNPU	FLUMPING	FHIKMNOS	MONKFISH	FIINTUXY	UNFIXITY
FGILMNUY	FUMINGLY	FHIKNORT	FORTHINK	FIIOPSST	POSITIFS
FGILNNTU	GUNFLINT	FHILLOOT	FOOTHILL	FIIQUYZZ	QUIZZIFY
FGILNOOR	FLOORING	FHILLORT	HILLFORT	FIKKLNOS	KINFOLKS
FGILNOOS	FOOLINGS	FHILMPSU	LUMPFISH		KINSFOLK
FGILNOOT	FOOTLING	FHILMRTU	MIRTHFUL	FIKLLLSU	SKILLFUL
FGILNOOZ	FOOZLING	FHILOPST	SHOPLIFT	FIKLLOSY	FOLKSILY
FGILNOPP	FLOPPING	FHILORSU	FLOURISH	FIKLNOSW	WOLFKINS
FGILNOPS	FOPLINGS	FHILORTY	FROTHILY		WOLFSKIN
FGILNORS	ROLFINGS	FHILPSSU	SHIPFULS	FIKLNSSU	SKINFULS
FGILNORU	FLOURING	FHIMNOOS	MOONFISH	FIKLSSTU	KISTFULS
FGILNOSS	FLOSSING	FHIMORSW	FISHWORM		LUTFISKS
FGILNOST	SOFTLING	FHIMPRSU	FRUMPISH	FIKNORSW	FORSWINK
FGILNOSU	FLOUSING	FHINOSSU	FUSHIONS	FIKNOSSX	FOXSKINS
	FOULINGS	FHINRTTU	UNTHRIFT	FIKRSSTU	TURFSKIS
FGILNOSW	FOWLINGS	FHINSSTU	UNSHIFTS	FILLLUWY	WILFULLY
	WOLFINGS	FHIOOPTT	PHOTOFIT	FILLNSUY	SINFULLY
FGILNOTU	FLOUTING	FHIOPSSX	FOXSHIPS		SULFINYL
	OUTFLING	FHIORSTY	FORTYISH	FILLNUUW	UNWILFUL
FGILNPRU	PURFLING	FHIPSSTU	UPSHIFTS	FILLOPPY	FLOPPILY
FGILNPSU	UPFLINGS	FHKORSTU	FUTHORKS	FILLOPSU	SPOILFUL
FGILNRRU	FLURRING	FHLLLOTU	LOTHFULL	FILLOSSY	FLOSSILY
FGILNSTU	FLUTINGS	FHLLOSTU	SLOTHFUL	FILMNOOS	MONOFILS
FGILNSTY	FLYTINGS	FHLMORUU	HUMORFUL	FILMOPRS	SLIPFORM
FGILNUZZ	FUZZLING	FHLMOTUU	MOUTHFUL	FILMORRY	LYRIFORM
FGIMNORS	FORMINGS	FHLNORSU	HORNFULS	FILMOSSU	MOFUSSIL
FGIMNPRU	FRUMPING	FHLOOSTU	SOOTHFUL	FILMOSTU	MOISTFUL
FGIMNRSU	SMURFING	FHLOOTTU	TOOTHFUL	FILMPRUY	FRUMPILY
FGIMORRU	GRUIFORM	FHLOPSSU	SHOPFULS	FILNNSUU	UNSINFUL
FGIMOSSY	FOGYISMS	FHLORTTU	TROTHFUL	FILNORSU	FLUORINS
FGINNORT	FRONTING	FHLORTUW	WORTHFUL	FILNOSUX	FLUXIONS
FGINNORW	FROWNING		WROTHFUL	FILOOOPR	OILPROOF
FGINOOPR	PROOFING	FHLORTUY	FOURTHLY	FILOOSTW	WITLOOFS
FGINOOPS	SPOOFING	FHLOSTUU	OUTFLUSH	FILORSST	FLORISTS
FGINOORS	ROOFINGS	FHLOTUUY	YOUTHFUL	FILORSTY	FROSTILY
FGINOOST	FOOTINGS	FHLRTTUU	TRUTHFUL	FILORUYZ	FROUZILY
FGINORST	FROSTING	FHNOSTUX	FOXHUNTS	FILORWYZ	FROWZILY
FGINORTU	FOUTRING	FHOOORST	FORSOOTH	FILRSTTU	TRISTFUL
FGINRRSU	FURRINGS		HOOFROTS	FILSSTTU	FLUTISTS
FGINRSSU	SURFINGS	FHOOOSTT	HOTFOOTS	FILSTTUY	STULTIFY
FGINRSTU	TURFINGS	FIIIMNST	FINITISM	FIMMNOOR	OMNIFORM
FGINSTTU	TUFTINGS	FIIINNOX	INFIXION	FIMMORRU	MURIFORM
FGIORSTW	FIGWORTS	FIIINNTY	INFINITY	FIMMORSS	MISFORMS
FGISSTUU	FUGUISTS	FIIKLRSY	FRISKILY	FIMNORSU	UNIFORMS
FGKLNOOS	FOLKSONG	FIILLMOP	PLIOFILM	FIMOORRT	ROTIFORM
FGLLMOOU	GLOOMFUL	FIILLMOS	MILFOILS	FIMOORSS	ISOFORMS
FGLLNSUU	LUNGFULS	FIILLMSY	FLIMSILY	FIMOPRRY	PYRIFORM
FGLNORSU	FURLONGS	FIILLMTU	MULTIFIL	FIMORRSU	URSIFORM
FGLNORUW	WRONGFUL	FIILLNTY	FLINTILY	FIMORTUY	FUMITORY
FGLOOOST	FOOTSLOG	FIILLSSU	FUSILLIS	FIMOSTUY	FUMOSITY
FGLORSUU	FULGOURS	FIILMNRY	INFIRMLY	FIMRSTUU	FUTURISM
FGLSSTUU	GUTSFULS	FIILMOPR	PILIFORM	FINOOPSY	OPSONIFY
FGNOORSU	FOURGONS	FIILMPSY	SIMPLIFY	FINOPRST	FROSTNIP
FGNOORTU	UNFORGOT	FIILNOST	TINFOILS	FINOPSSU	SOUPFINS
FHHIKOOS	FISHHOOK	FIILRTUY	FRUITILY	FINORSSS	FRISSONS
FHHOORST	SHOFROTH	FIILRYZZ	FRIZZILY	FINORSUY	INFUSORY
FHIKLLS	FISHKILL	FIILTTUY	FUTILITY	FIOORSSU	FURIOSOS
FHIIKLMS	MILKFISH	FIIMMNSU	INFIMUMS	FIORTTUY	FORTUITY
FHIIKNSS	FISHSKIN	FIIMOPRR	PIRIFORM	FIOSTTTU	TOFUTTIS
FHIILLTY	FILTHILY	FIIMOPRS	PISIFORM	FIRSTTUU	FUTURIST
FHIILNOS	LIONFISH	FIIMOSTY	MOISTIFY	FIRTTUUY	FUTURITY
FHIILRST	FLIRTISH	FIINNOSU	INFUSION	FJLLOUYY	JOYFULLY
FHIILSTY	SHIFTILY	FIINORTU	FRUITION	FJLNOUUY	UNJOYFUL

FKKLOORW	WORKFOLK	GGGIILNW	WIGGLING	GGIILMNY	GINGLYMI
FKKOORTW	KOFTWORK	GGGIINNS	SNIGGING	GGIILNNP	PINGLING
FKLMOOOT	FOLKMOOT	GGGIINPR	PRIGGING	GGIILNNS	SINGLING
FKLMOOST	FOLKMOTS	GGGIINPS	PIGGINGS		SLINGING
FKLNOOTW	TOWNFOLK	GGGIINRS	RIGGINGS	GGIILNNT	GLINTING
FKLNRTUU	TRUNKFUL	GGGIINRT	TRIGGING		TINGLING
FKLOORWW	WORKFLOW	GGGIINSW	SWIGGING	GGIILNPS	PIGLINGS
FKMOORRW	FORMWORK	GGGIINTW	TWIGGING	GGIILNRS	RIGLINGS
FKNORSUW	FORSWUNK	GGGIJLNO	JOGGLING	GGIILNTZ	GLITZING
FKOOORTW	FOOTWORK	GGGIJLNU	JUGGLING	GGIIMNOS	MISGOING
FKRSSSUY	SKYSURFS	GGGIJNOS	JOGGINGS	GGIIMNPU	GUIMPING
FLLNOSUY	SULFONYL	GGGIJNSU	JUGGINGS	GGIIMPRS	PRIGGISM
FLLOOPUW	FOLLOWUP	GGGIKNSU	SKUGGING	GGIINNNR	GRINNING
	UPFOLLOW	GGGILNOO	GOOGLING	GGIINNNS	GINNINGS
FLLRSUUY	SULFURYL	GGGILNOS	LOGGINGS	GGIINNOR	GROINING
FLMNOOSU	MOUFLONS		SLOGGING		IGNORING
FLMNORUU	MOURNFUL	GGGILNOT	TOGGLING	GGIINNOS	INGOINGS
FLMOOORW	MOORFOWL	GGGILNPU	PLUGGING	GGIINNOT	INGOTING
FLMOOOST	TOMFOOLS		PUGGLING	GGIINNOW	WONGIING
FLMOORSU	ROOMFULS	GGGILNRU	GURGLING	GGIINNRS	RINGINGS
FLMORSTU	STORMFUL	GGGILNSU	SLUGGING	GGIINNRW	WRINGING
FLNOOPSU	SPOONFUL	GGGILORY	GROGGILY	GGIINNSS	SIGNINGS
FLNOORRS	FORLORNS	GGGIMNSU	MUGGINGS		SINGINGS
FLNOOSTU	SNOOTFUL		SMUGGING	GGIINNST	STINGING
FLNOOTUW	OUTFLOWN	GGGINNOS	NOGGINGS	GGIINNSW	SWINGING
FLOOOPTT	POLTFOOT		SNOGGING	GGIINNTW	TWINGING
FLOOOSTU	OUTFOOLS	GGGINNSU	SNUGGING	GGIINNUV	UNGIVING
FLOOPTTY	TOPLOFTY	GGGINOPR	PROGGING	GGIINPPR	GRIPPING
FLOORSSW	FORSLOWS	GGGINORT	TROGGING	GGIINPSY	GIPSYING
FLOOSTUW	OUTFLOWS	GGGINOSS	SOGGINGS	GGIINRST	RINGGITS
FLOPRSTU	SPORTFUL	GGGINPSU	PUGGINGS	GGIINRTT	GRITTING
FLORTTUU	TROUTFUL	GGGINRSU	RUGGINGS	GGIINSSU	GUISINGS
FLRSTTUU	TRUSTFUL	GGGINSSU	SUGGINGS	GGIINSTU	GIUSTING
FMNOOOOR	MOONROOF	GGGINSTU	TUGGINGS	GGIIRRSS	GRISGRIS
FMOOPRST	POSTFORM	GGHHIINT	HIGHTING	GGIITTUU	GUITGUIT
FMRSSTUU	FRUSTUMS	GGHHINOU	HOUGHING	GGIKKNOR	GROKKING
FNNOOORT	FRONTOON	GGHHISTU	THUGGISH	GGILLNOY	GOLLYING
FNNOORST	FRONTONS	GGHIILNT	LIGHTING	GGILLNUW	GULLWING
FNOOORTW	FOOTWORN	GGHIINNO	HONGIING	GGILLNUY	GULLYING
FNOOPRSU	SUNPROOF	GGHIINNW	WHINGING	GGILLOOW	GOLLIWOG
FNOORRSW	FORSWORN	GGHIINPT	PIGHTING	GGILMMNO	GLOMMING
FNOORSSU	SUNROOFS	GGHIINRT	GIRTHING	GGILMNOO	GLOOMING
FNOORTUW	OUTFROWN		RIGHTING	GGILNNOP	PLONGING
FOOOPRST	ROOFTOPS	GGHIINST	SIGHTING	GGILNNOS	LONGINGS
FOOOPSTT	FOOTPOST	GGHIINTW	WIGHTING	GGILNNOU	LOUNGING
FOOORSTT	FOOTROTS	GGHIIPRS	PRIGGISH	GGILNNPU	PLUNGING
FOOOSTTU	OUTFOOTS	GGHILSSU	SLUGGISH		PUNGLING
FOORSTTX	FOXTROTS	GGHIMSTU	THUGGISM	GGILNNUU	UNGLUING
FOPSSSTU	FUSSPOTS	GGHINORU	ROUGHING	GGILNOOP	GLOOPING
GGGGIILN	GIGGLING	GGHINOST	GHOSTING	GGILNOPP	GLOPPING
GGGGIINR	GRIGGING	GGHINOSU	SOUGHING	GGILNORW	GROWLING
GGGGILNO	GOGGLING	GGHINOTU	OUGHTING	GGILNORY	GLORYING
GGGGILNU	GLUGGING		TOUGHING	GGILNOSS	GLOSSING
	GUGGLING	GGHINOTY	HOGTYING		GOSLINGS
GGGGINOR	GROGGING	GGHOOPRS	GROGSHOP	GGILNOSV	GLOVINGS
GGGHIILN	HIGGLING	GGIIILLN	GINGILLI	GGILNOSZ	GLOZINGS
GGGHIINT	THIGGING	GGIIILNS	GINGILIS	GGILNOTU	GLOUTING
GGGHIINW	WHIGGING	GGIIINNT	IGNITING	GGILNRUY	URGINGLY
GGGHINOS	HOGGINGS	GGIIJLNN	JINGLING	GGILNTTU	GLUTTING
	SHOGGING	GGIIKLNN	KINGLING		GUTTLING
GGGIIJLN	JIGGLING	GGIILLNR	GRILLING	GGILNUZZ	GUZZLING
GGGIIJNS	JIGGINGS	GGIILLNY	GILLYING	GGILQSUY	SQUIGGLY
GGGIILNN	NIGGLING	GGIILMNN	MINGLING	GGIMMNSU	GUMMINGS
GGGIILNS	LIGGINGS			GGIMNOOR	GROOMING

GGIMNOOS	SMOOGING	GHIILNST	TINGLISH	GHILNRSU	HURLINGS
GGIMNPRU	GRUMPING	GHIILNTW	WHITLING	GHILNRTU	HURTLING
GGINNNSU	GUNNINGS	GHIILOTT	OILTIGHT	GHILNRUY	HUNGRILY
GGINNOOS	ONGOINGS	GHIILTTW	TWILIGHT	GHILNSSU	SLUSHING
GGINNOPP	PINGPONG	GHIIMMNS	SHIMMING	GHILNSTU	HUSTLING
GGINNOPR	PRONGING	GHIIMMNW	WHIMMING		SUNLIGHT
GGINNOPS	SPONGING	GHIIMNNU	INHUMING	GHILOPRS	SHOPGIRL
GGINNORW	WRONGING	GHIIMNST	SMITHING	GHILORSW	SHOWGIRL
GGINNOSS	SINGSONG	GHIIMRST	RIGHTISM	GHILORSY	OGRISHLY
GGINNOTU	TONGUING	GHIINNNS	SHINNING	GHILPRTY	TRIGLYPH
GGINNRTU	GRUNTING	GHIINNNT	THINNING	GHILPSTU	UPLIGHTS
GGINNUVY	UNGYVING	GHIINNNY	HINNYING	GHIMMNSU	HUMMINGS
GGINOORV	GROOVING	GHIINNRS	SHRINING	GHIMNOPR	MORPHING
GGINOOST	STOOGING	GHIINNST	HINTINGS	GHIMNOPU	GUMPHION
GGINOOTU	OUTGOING		NITHINGS	GHIMNOPW	WHOMPING
GGINOPRS	PROGGINS	GHIINNSW	WHININGS	GHIMNORU	HUMORING
GGINOPRU	GROUPING	GHIINNUV	UNHIVING	GHIMNOSS	MOSHINGS
GGINOPSU	UPGOINGS	GHIINOST	HOISTING	GHIMNOTU	MOUTHING
GGINORSS	GROSSING	GHIINPPS	HIPPINGS	GHIMNPTU	THUMPING
GGINORSU	GROUSING		SHIPPING	GHIMNPUW	WHUMPING
GGINORSW	GROWINGS	GHIINPPW	WHIPPING	GHIMNSSU	SMUSHING
GGINORTU	GROUTING	GHIINRRS	SHIRRING	GHIMNSTU	GUNSMITH
GGINOSUV	VOGUINGS	GHIINRRW	WHIRRING	GHIMPRSU	GRUMPISH
GGINPRSU	PURGINGS	GHIINRST	SHIRTING	GHIMPSYY	PYGMYISH
GGINPSYY	GYPSYING	GHIINRSV	SHRIVING	GHIMRSSU	SIMURGHS
GGINRSSU	SURGINGS	GHIINRTT	TRITHING	GHINNNSU	SHUNNING
GGINSSUY	GUSSYING	GHIINRTV	THRIVING	GHINNOOR	HONORING
GGLLOOWY	GOLLYWOG	GHIINRTW	WRITHING	GHINNOPY	PHONYING
GGLLPUUY	PLUGUGLY	GHIINSSS	HISSINGS	GHINNORS	HORNINGS
GHHIILST	LIGHTISH	GHIINSST	INSIGHTS	GHINNORT	NORTHING
GHHIINPS	PHISHING	GHIINSSW	SWISHING		THORNING
GHHIINSW	WHISHING		WHISSING		THRONING
GHHIIRST	RIGHTISH		WISHINGS	GHINNOST	NOTHINGS
GHHIISTT	TIGHTISH	GHIINSTT	SHITTING	GHINNSSU	SNUSHING
GHHILOSU	GHOULISH		TITHINGS	GHINNSTU	HUNTINGS
GHHIMNPU	HUMPHING	GHIINSTW	WHISTING		SHUNTING
GHHIMOST	HIGHMOST		WHITINGS	GHINOOPT	PHOTOING
GHHINOOS	HOOSHING	GHIINSVV	SHIVVING	GHINOOPW	WHOOPING
GHHINSSU	SHUSHING	GHIINTTW	TWINIGHT	GHINOOST	SHOOTING
GHHIOPST	HIGHSPOT	GHIINWZZ	WHIZZING		SOOTHING
	HIGHTOPS	GHIIORSV	VIGORISH	GHINOOSW	WOOSHING
GHHIORSU	ROUGHISH	GHIIPSSY	GIPSYISH	GHINOOTT	TOOTHING
GHHIOSTU	TOUGHISH	GHIIRSTT	RIGHTIST	GHINOOTW	WHOOTING
GHHIRSST	SHRIGHTS	GHIKLNTY	KNIGHTLY	GHINOPPS	HOPPINGS
GHHOORTU	THOROUGH	GHIKLSTY	SKYLIGHT		SHOPPING
GHHOSTTU	THOUGHTS	GHIKNNTU	THUNKING	GHINOPPW	WHOPPING
GHIIIKNO	HIKOIING		UNKNIGHT	GHINOPSS	GINSHOPS
GHIIILNS	SHILINGI	GHIKNSSU	HUSKINGS	GHINORSS	HORSINGS
GHIIJNOS	JINGOISH	GHIKRSTU	TUGHRIKS		SHORINGS
GHIIKNNT	THINKING	GHILLNOO	HOLLOING	GHINORST	SHORTING
GHIIKNPS	KINGSHIP	GHILLNOU	HULLOING	GHINORSV	SHROVING
GHIIKNRS	SHIRKING	GHILLOTW	LOWLIGHT	GHINORSW	SHOWRING
	SHRIKING	GHILLSTY	SLIGHTLY		SHROWING
GHIIKNSW	WHISKING	GHILMNSU	MULSHING	GHINORTT	TROTHING
GHIILLNO	HILLOING	GHILMPSU	GLUMPISH	GHINORTW	INGROWTH
GHIILLNS	SHILLING	GHILNOOS	SHOOLING		THROWING
GHIILMST	MISLIGHT	GHILNOPP	HOPPLING		WORTHING
GHIILMTY	MIGHTILY	GHILNOPS	LONGSHIP	GHINOSST	HOSTINGS
GHIILNOT	LITHOING	GHILNOPY	HOPINGLY	GHINOSSU	HOUSINGS
GHIILNPR	HIRPLING	GHILNOSS	SLOSHING	GHINOSSV	SHOVINGS
GHIILNRS	HIRLINGS	GHILNOST	SLOTHING	GHINOSSW	SHOWINGS
	HIRSLING	GHILNOSU	HOUSLING	GHINOSTT	HOTTINGS
GHIILNRT	THIRLING	GHILNOSW	HOWLINGS		SHOTTING
GHIILNRW	WHIRLING	GHILNPSU	INGULPHS		TONIGHTS

GHINOSTU	HOUTINGS		JOISTING	GIILMNOS	SMOILING
	SHOUTING	GIIKKLNP	KINGKLIP	GIILMNPR	RIMPLING
	SOUTHING	GIIKKNNS	SKINKING	GIILMNPS	LIMPINGS
GHINOSTW	SOWTHING	GIIKKNRS	KIRKINGS		SIMPLING
GHINOSUY	YOUNGISH		SKRIKING	GIILMNPW	WIMPLING
GHINOTTU	OUTNIGHT	GIIKLLNS	KILLINGS	GIILMNPY	IMPLYING
GHINPPUW	WHUPPING		SKILLING	GIILMNSS	SMILINGS
GHINPSSU	GUNSHIPS	GIIKLMNS	MILKINGS	GIILMNST	MISTLING
GHINPTTU	PHUTTING	GIIKLNNP	PLINKING	GIILMNSY	MISLYING
GHINRRUY	HURRYING	GIIKLNNS	INKLINGS	GIILMNZZ	MIZZLING
GHINRSSU	RUSHINGS		SLINKING	GIILMPRS	PILGRIMS
GHINRSTU	UNGIRTHS	GIIKLNNT	TINKLING	GIILMPSU	PUGILISM
	UNRIGHTS	GIIKLNNW	WINKLING	GIILNNNU	UNLINING
GHINSSTU	HUSTINGS	GIIKLNRS	SKIRLING	GIILNNPP	NIPPLING
	UNSIGHTS	GIIKLNST	KILTINGS	GIILNNPS	SPLINING
GHINSTTU	HUTTINGS		KITLINGS	GIILNNPU	UNPILING
	SHUTTING	GIIKLNTT	KITTLING	GIILNNTU	UNTILING
GHIORTTU	OUTRIGHT	GIIKMMNS	SKIMMING	GIILNNTW	TWINLING
GHIOSTTU	OUTSIGHT	GIIKMNPS	SKIMPING		WINTLING
GHIPRSST	SPRIGHTS	GIIKMNRS	SMIRKING	GIILNNUV	UNLIVING
GHIPRSTU	UPRIGHTS	GIIKNNNS	SKINNING	GIILNOPS	PIGNOLIS
GHIPRSUU	GURUSHIP	GIIKNNOV	INVOKING		SPOILING
GHIPSSYY	GYPSYISH	GIIKNNPR	PRINKING	GIILNOPT	PILOTING
GHLMOOOS	HOMOLOGS	GIIKNNPS	KINGPINS	GIILNORS	LIGROINS
GHLMOOOY	HOMOLOGY		PINKINGS	GIILNOSS	SOILINGS
GHLNNOOR	LONGHORN	GIIKNNSS	SINKINGS	GIILNOST	TOILINGS
GHLNOORU	HOURLONG	GIIKNNST	STINKING	GIILNPPR	RIPPLING
GHLNOOYY	HOLOGYNY	GIIKNNSW	SWINKING	GIILNPPS	LIPPINGS
GHLNORSU	SLUGHORN		WINKINGS		SIPPLING
GHLOOORY	HOROLOGY	GIIKNNTT	KNITTING		SLIPPING
GHLORTUU	TURLOUGH	GIIKNNTW	TWINKING	GIILNPPT	TIPPLING
GHMNOOOY	HOMOGONY	GIIKNORS	SKIORING	GIILNPPU	UPPILING
GHMORSSU	SORGHUMS	GIIKNPPS	SKIPPING	GIILNPPY	PIPINGLY
GHMOSSTU	MUGSHOTS	GIIKNPSS	PIGSKINS	GIILNPRS	SPIRLING
GHMPSSUY	SPHYGMUS	GIIKNQRU	QUIRKING	GIILNPRT	TRIPLING
GHNNOOOZ	GOHONZON	GIIKNRRS	SKIRRING	GIILNPSS	LISPINGS
GHNOPRSY	GRYPHONS	GIIKNRSS	GRISKINS		SPILINGS
GHNOPYYY	HYPOGYNY	GIIKNRST	SKIRTING	GIILNQSU	QUISLING
GHNOSSTU	GUNSHOTS		STRIKING	GIILNQTU	QUILTING
	SHOTGUNS	GIIKNSSV	SKIVINGS	GIILNRSW	SWIRLING
GHNOSTUU	UNSOUGHT	GIILLMNS	MILLINGS	GIILNRTW	TWIRLING
GHNOSTUY	YOUNGTHS	GIILLMNU	ILLUMING	GIILNRVY	VIRGINLY
GHOOOSSW	HOOSGOWS	GIILLNOR	GRILLION	GIILNSST	LISTINGS
GHOORTUY	YOGHOURT	GIILLNOS	GILLIONS	GIILNSTT	SLITTING
GHOPRTUW	UPGROWTH	GIILLNPR	PRILLING		STILTING
GHORSTUY	YOGHURTS	GIILLNPS	PILLINGS		TILTINGS
GIIILMNT	LIMITING		SPILLING		TITLINGS
GIIILNNS	INISLING	GIILLNQU	QUILLING	GIILNSTU	LINGUIST
GIIILNNU	LINGUINI	GIILLNRT	TRILLING	GIILNSTW	WITLINGS
GIIILOTV	VITILIGO	GIILLNST	STILLING	GIILNSTY	STINGILY
GIIIMMNX	IMMIXING		TILLINGS	GIILNSZZ	SIZZLING
GIIINNOS	IONISING	GIILLNSW	SWILLING	GIILNTTT	TITTLING
GIIINNOT	IGNITION	GIILLNTT	LITTLING	GIILNTTU	TITULING
GIIINNOZ	IONIZING	GIILLNTW	TWILLING	GIILNTTV	VITTLING
GIIINNTV	INVITING	GIILLNVY	LIVINGLY	GIILNTTW	TWILTING
GIIINORS	SIGNIORI	GIILLNWY	WILLYING	GIILNZZZ	ZIZZLING
GIIINRSS	GRISSINI	GIILLOPW	POLLIWIG	GIILOSST	OLIGISTS
GIIINSTV	VISITING	GIILLPSW	PIGSWILL	GIILPSTU	PUGILIST
GIIJMMNY	JIMMYING	GIILLTUY	GUILTILY	GIILRSST	STRIGILS
GIIJMNOS	JINGOISM	GIILLTYZ	GLITZILY	GIILRTTY	GRITTILY
GIIJNNOS	JOININGS	GIILMNNP	PLIMMING	GIIMMNPR	PRIMMING
GIIJNNOT	JOINTING	GIILMMNS	SLIMMING	GIIMMNRS	RIMMINGS
GIIJNNRU	INJURING	GIILMNNU	LUMINING	GIIMMNRT	TRIMMING
GIIJNOST	JINGOIST		UNLIMING	GIIMMNRU	IMMURING

GIIMMNSW	SWIMMING		RIOTINGS	GIKMNPPU	PUMPKING
GIIMMNOP	IMPONING		ROISTING	GIKNNOOS	SNOOKING
GIIMMNNOR	MINORING		ROSITING	GIKNNOPR	PRONKING
GIIMMNNOY	IGNOMINY	GIIINORSV	VISORING	GIKNNOQU	QUONKING
GIIMMNNTU	MINUTING	GIIINORSY	SIGNIORY	GIKNNOST	STONKING
	MUNITING	GIIINORTZ	ROZITING	GIKNNOSW	KNOWINGS
	MUTINING	GIIINORVZ	VIZORING		SNOWKING
GIIMMNNUX	UNMIXING	GIIINOSTT	STOITING	GIKNNOTT	KNOTTING
GIIMMNOPS	IMPOSING	GIIINPPQU	QUIPPING	GIKNNOTU	KNOUTING
GIIMMNOST	MOISTING	GIIINPPRT	TRIPPING	GIKNNOUY	UNYOKING
GIIMMNOTT	OMITTING	GIIINPPST	TIPPINGS	GIKNNPSU	SPUNKING
GIIMMNOTV	MOTIVING	GIIINPRSS	PRISSING	GIKNNRTU	TRUNKING
	VOMITING		RISPINGS	GIKNOOPS	SPOOKING
GIIMMNPPR	PRIMPING	GIIINPRST	SPIRTING	GIKNOOST	STOOKING
GIIMMNPRS	PRIMINGS		STRIPING	GIKNOOTW	KOTOWING
GIIMMNPRU	UMPIRING	GIIINPRSU	SIRUPING	GIKNOPST	KINGPOST
GIIMMNPTU	IMPUTING		UPRISING	GIKNORRW	RINGWORK
GIIMMNRRS	SMIRRING	GIIINPSTT	PITTINGS	GIKNORST	STROKING
GIIMMNRST	SMIRTING		SPITTING	GIKNORSW	WORKINGS
GIIMMNSST	MISTINGS	GIIINPSTW	WINGTIPS	GIKNSSTU	TUSKINGS
GIIMMNSSU	MISUSING	GIIINPSUZ	UPSIZING	GILLMOOY	GLOOMILY
GIIMMNSSW	SWINGISM	GIIINPTTU	TITUPING	GILLMPUY	GLUMPILY
GIIMMNSTT	SMITTING	GIIINQRSU	SQUIRING	GILLNNSU	NULLINGS
GIIMMNSTU	MUISTING	GIIINQRTU	QUIRTING	GILLNOPR	PROLLING
GIIMMNSTY	STIMYING	GIIINQTTU	QUITTING	GILLNOPS	POLLINGS
GIIMMORRS	RIGORISM	GIIINQUZZ	QUIZZING	GILLNORS	ROLLINGS
GIIINNNOO	ONIONING	GIIINRRST	STIRRING	GILLNORT	TROLLING
GIIINNNOT	INTONING	GIIINRSTV	STRIVING	GILLNOST	TOLLINGS
	NOINTING	GIIINRSTW	WRITINGS	GILLNOSY	LOSINGLY
GIIINNNPS	PINNINGS	GIIINSSSW	SWISSING	GILLNOVY	LOVINGLY
	SPINNING	GIIINSSTT	SITTINGS	GILLNPUY	PULINGLY
GIIINNNRU	INURNING	GIIINSSTU	SUITINGS	GILLNPYY	PLYINGLY
GIIINNNST	TINNINGS		TISSUING	GILLNRUY	LURINGLY
GIIINNNSW	WINNINGS	GIIINSTTW	TWISTING	GILLNSUV	SULLYING
GIIINNNTW	TWINNING		WITTINGS	GILLOOPW	POLLIWOG
GIIINNOPR	PROINING	GIIINSTUW	WINGSUIT	GILLOPWY	POLLYWIG
GIIINNOPS	PIONINGS	GIIINSWZZ	SWIZZING	GILLORVV	GILLYVOR
GIIINNOPT	POINTING	GIIINTTTW	TWITTING	GILLOSSY	GLOSSILY
GIIINNOQU	QUOINING	GIIORRST	RIGORIST	GILMMNSU	SLUMMING
GIIINNORS	IRONINGS	GIIORSSV	ISOGRIVS	GILMMTUY	MULTIGYM
	NIGROSIN	GIIPRSTZ	SPRITZIG	GILMNOOS	SLOOMING
	ROSINING	GIJKLNOY	JOKINGLY	GILMNOPY	MOPINGLY
GIIINNORT	IGNITRON	GIJLLNOY	JOLLYING	GILMNORS	MORLINGS
GIIINNPPS	SNIPPING	GIJLNOST	JOSTLING		SLORMING
GIIINNPRT	PRINTING	GIJLNSTU	JUNGLIST	GILMNORT	MORTLING
GIIINNPSS	SNIPINGS		JUSTLING	GILMNOSS	MOSLINGS
GIIINNPSU	PINGUINS	GIJMNPSU	JUMPINGS	GILMNOSU	MOUSLING
GIIINNRSS	RINSINGS	GIJNOSTT	JOTTINGS	GILMNOSY	SMOYLING
GIIINNRSU	INSURING	GIJNOSTU	JOUSTING	GILMNOTT	MOTTLING
	RUININGS	GIJNTTUY	JUTTYING	GILMNOTU	MOULTING
GIIINNRTU	UNTIRING	GIKKLNSU	SKULKING	GILMNOUV	VOLUMING
GIIINNRUW	UNWIRING	GIKKNNSU	SKUNKING	GILMNOVY	MOVINGLY
GIIINNSSW	INSWINGS	GIKLLNNO	KNOLLING	GILMNPPU	PLUMPING
GIIINNSTT	STINTING	GIKLLNOS	SKOLLING	GILMNPRU	RUMPLING
	TINTINGS	GIKLLNSU	SKULLING	GILMNPSU	SLUMPING
GIIINNSTU	UNITINGS	GIKLNNOP	PLONKING	GILMNSUY	MUSINGLY
GIIINNSTW	TWININGS	GIKLNNPU	PLUNKING	GILMNUZZ	MUZZLING
GIIINNUVW	UNWIVING	GIKLNNRU	KNURLING	GILMOOSY	MISOLOGY
GIIINOPST	POSITING		RUNKLING	GILMOOXY	MIXOLOGY
	SOPITING	GIKLNNUY	UNKINGLY	GILMPRUY	GRUMPILY
GIIINOPTV	PIVOTING	GIKLNOPR	PORKLING	GILMPSSY	GYMSLIPS
GIIINOQTU	QUOITING	GIKLNRSU	LURKINGS	GILNNOOS	GLONOINS
GIIINORSS	SIGNIORS	GIKLORRW	WORKGIRL		LOONINGS
GIIINORST	IGNITORS	GIKMNOSS	SMOKINGS		SNOOLING

GILNNOSU	NOUSLING	GILOORSS	GIROSOLS	GINNNTUU	UNTUNING
GILNNOTU	NONGUILT	GILOORSU	GLORIOUS	GINNOOPS	SNOOPING
GILNNOTW	TOWNLING	GILOORVY	VIROLOGY		SPOONING
GILNNOUV	UNLOVING	GILOOSSS	ISOGLOSS	GINNOOST	SNOOTING
GILNNRSU	NURSLING	GILOOSST	OLOGISTS	GINNOOSW	SWOONING
GILNNSSU	UNSLINGS	GILOOSTW	TWIGLOOS	GINNOOSZ	SNOOZING
GILNNUZZ	NUZZLING	GILOOSTY	SITOLOGY	GINNOPPU	UNPOPING
GILNOOOY	OINOLOGY	GILORSTT	TRIGLOTS	GINNOPRU	UNROPING
GILNOOPS	LOOPINGS	GILOSSST	GLOSSIST	GINNOPSS	SPONGINS
	SPOOLING	GILOSTUY	GULOSITY		SPONSING
GILNOOPT	POOTLING	GIMMMNSU	MUMMINGS	GINNOPTU	GUNPOINT
GILNOORT	ROOTLING	GIMMMNUY	MUMMYING	GINNOPTY	POYNTING
GILNOOSS	LOOSINGS	GIMMNOTY	TOMMYING	GINNORSS	SNORINGS
GILNOOST	LOOTINGS	GIMMNSSU	SUMMINGS		SORNINGS
	STOOLING	GIMMNSTU	STUMMING	GINNORST	SNORTING
	TOOLINGS	GIMMOSSU	GUMMOSIS	GINNORSU	GRUNIONS
GILNOOSY	SINOLOGY	GIMMPSYY	PYGMYISM	GINNOSST	STONINGS
GILNOOTT	TOOTLING	GIMNNORS	MORNINGS	GINNOSTT	SNOTTING
GILNOOVY	VINOLOGY	GIMNNORU	MOURNING	GINNOSTU	SNOUTING
GILNOOWY	WOOINGLY	GIMNNOTU	MOUNTING		STOUNING
GILNOPPP	PLOPPING	GIMNNOUV	UNMOVING	GINNOSTY	STONYING
	POPPLING	GIMNNSTU	MUNTINGS	GINNOSUW	SWOUNING
GILNOPPS	LOPPINGS	GIMNOOOU	OOGONIUM	GINNPRSU	PRUNINGS
	SLOPPING	GIMNOOPR	PROMOING		SPURNING
GILNOPPT	TOPPLING	GIMNOOPS	SPOOMING	GINNRSSU	NURSINGS
GILNOPRU	PROULING	GIMNOORS	MOORINGS	GINNRSTU	TURNINGS
GILNOPRW	PROWLING		SMOORING		UNSTRING
GILNOPSU	SOUPLING	GIMNOORT	MOTORING	GINNSTTU	NUTTINGS
GILNOPSY	POSINGLY	GIMNOORV	VROOMING		STUNTING
	SPONGILY	GIMNOOSS	OSMOSING	GINNSTUY	UNTYINGS
GILNOPTT	PLOTTING	GIMNOOST	MOOTINGS	GINOOPPS	OPPOSING
GILNOPTZ	PLOTZING		SMOOTING		POGONIPS
GILNORSU	LOURINGS	GIMNOPRT	TROMPING	GINOOPRS	SPOORING
GILNORTU	TROULING	GIMNOPST	STOMPING	GINOOPRT	TROOPING
GILNORVY	ROVINGLY	GIMNOPTU	GUMPTION	GINOOPSS	SOOPINGS
GILNOSSW	SLOWINGS	GIMNORRU	RUMORING	GINOOPST	STOOPING
GILNOSTT	SLOTTING	GIMNORRW	RINGWORM	GINOOPSW	SWOOPING
GILNOSTU	TOUSLING	GIMNORST	STORMING		WOOPSING
GILNOSVW	WOLVINGS	GIMNORSU	ROUMINGS	GINOORST	ROOSTING
GILNOSWY	YOWLINGS	GIMNORSW	MISGROWN		ROOTINGS
GILNOSZZ	SOZZLING	GIMNOSST	GNOMISTS	GINOORTW	WROOTING
GILNOTUY	OUTLYING	GIMNOSSU	MOUSINGS	GINOOSTT	TOOTSING
GILNOTUZ	TOUZLING		MOUSSING	GINOPPPR	PROPPING
GILNPPRU	PURPLING		SMOUSING	GINOPPQU	QUOPPING
GILNPPSU	SUPPLING		SOUMINGS	GINOPPSS	SOPPINGS
GILNPRSU	PURLINGS	GIMNOSTU	MOUSTING	GINOPPST	STOPPING
	SLURPING		SMOUTING		TOPPINGS
	SPURLING	GIMNOSYY	MISOGYNY	GINOPPSW	SWOPPING
GILNPRYY	PRYINGLY	GIMNPRTU	TRUMPING	GINOPRSS	PROSINGS
GILNPSSU	PLUSSING	GIMNPSTU	STUMPING	GINOPRST	SPORTING
GILNPUZZ	PUZZLING	GIMNRRSU	SMURRING	GINOPRSU	INGROUPS
GILNRRSU	SLURRING	GIMNSTTU	SMUTTING		POURINGS
GILNRSTU	LUSTRING	GIMNSTYY	STYMYING	GINOPRSV	PROVINGS
	RUSTLING	GIMORSSW	MISGROWS	GINOPRTU	TROUPING
GILNRTTU	TURTLING	GIMPSSYY	GYPSYISM	GINOPSST	POSTINGS
GILNRTYY	TRYINGLY	GIMRSSUU	GURUISMS		SIGNPOST
GILNSSTU	SINGULTS	GINNNOOS	NOONINGS		STOPINGS
	TUSSLING	GINNNOST	STONNING	GINOPSSU	SPOUSING
GILNSSTY	STYLINGS	GINNNOSU	NONUSING	GINOPSTT	SPOTTING
GILNSTTU	SUTTLING	GINNNOSW	WONNINGS	GINOPSTU	POUTINGS
GILNTUUY	UNGUILTY	GINNNPSU	PUNNINGS		SPOUTING
GILNUWZZ	WUZZLING	GINNNRSU	RUNNINGS	GINOPTTY	TYPTOING
GILOOORS	ROSOGLIO	GINNNSTU	STUNNING	GINOQRTU	TORQUING
GILOOOST	OOLOGIST		TUNNINGS	GINORRWY	WORRYING

GINORSST	RINGTOSS	GLLLOORS	LOGROLLS	HHIINNST	THINNISH
	SORTINGS	GLLOOPTY	POLYGLOT	HHIIPSST	PHTHISIS
GINORSSU	SOURINGS	GLLOOPWY	POLLYWOG	HHILMOSS	SHLOSHIM
GINORSTU	OUTGRINS	GLLOOXYY	XYLOLOGY	HHILPSSY	SYLPHISH
	OUTRINGS	GLMMSSUU	SLUMGUMS	HHIMMOSS	MISHMOSH
	ROUSTING	GLMNOOOS	MONOLOGS	HHIMNPSY	NYMPHISH
	ROUTINGS	GLMNOOOT	MONOGLOT	HHIMPSSU	SUMPHISH
	TOURINGS	GLMNOOOY	MONOLOGY	HHINOOSW	NOHOWISH
GINORSTW	STROWING		NOMOLOGY	HHINOPPS	PHOSPHIN
	WORSTING	GLMNORUW	LUNGWORM	HHIORSST	SHORTISH
GINORSTY	ROYSTING	GLMNRTUU	NGULTRUM	HHKKSSUU	KHUSKHUS
	STORYING	GLMNSUUU	UMLUNGUS	HHMRSTUY	RHYTHMUS
	STROYING	GLMOOOPY	POMOLOGY	HHOOPPRS	PHOSPHOR
GINORTTT	TROTTING	GLMOOORS	MOORLOGS	HHOOSSTT	HOTSHOTS
GINORTTU	TROUTING	GLMOORWW	GLOWWORM	HIIILMNS	NIHILISM
	TUTORING	GLMOOVYZ	ZYMOLOGY	HIIILNST	NIHILIST
GINOSSSS	SOSSINGS	GLMORSUW	LUGWORMS	HIIILNTY	NIHILITY
GINOSSST	TOSSINGS	GLNNOORS	LORGNONS	HIIINRST	RHINITIS
GINOSSSU	SOUSINGS	GLNOOOSV	NOSOLOGY	HIIISSTV	SHIVITIS
GINOSSSW	SOWSSING	GLNOOOTY	ONTOLOGY	HIIKMNST	MISTHINK
GINOSSTT	SOTTINGS	GLNOOPRS	PROLONGS	HIIKMRSS	SKIRMISH
GINOSSTU	OUTSINGS	GLNOOPSY	POLYGONS	HIIKNNSS	SHINKINS
	TOUSINGS	GLNOOPYY	POLYGONY	HIIKNPSS	KINSHIPS
GINOSSTV	STOVINGS	GLNOPRSU	LONGSPUR	HIIKOPRS	PIROSHKI
GINOSSTW	STOWINGS	GLNOPVYY	POLYGYNY	HIIKOPRZ	PIROZHKI
GINOSTTT	STOTTING	GLNORSTY	STRONGLY	HIIKQRSU	QUIRKISH
	TOTTINGS		STRONGYL	HIIKSSTT	SKITTISH
GINOSTTW	SWOTTING	GLNORTUW	LUNGWORT	HIILLMMO	MILLIMHO
GINOSTUW	OUTSWING	GLNOSSUW	SUNGLOWS		MILLIOHM
	OUTWINGS	GLNOSTTU	GLUTTONS	HIILLSTT	LITTLISH
GINOTUVY	OUTVYING	GLNOTTUY	GLUTTONY	HIILMMSS	SLIMMISH
GINPPPUY	PUPPYING	GLOOOPSY	POSOLOGY	HIILMOST	HOMILIST
GINPPRSU	UPSPRING	GLOOOPTY	OPTOLOGY	HIILMPSU	SILPHIUM
GINPRRSU	PURRINGS		TOPOLOGY	HIILMPSY	IMPISHLY
	SPURRING	GLOOORUY	OUROLOGY	HIILMSTU	LITHIUMS
GINPRSTU	SPURTING	GLOOPRYY	PYROLOGY	HIILMSWY	WHIMSILY
GINPRSUU	PURSUING	GLOOPSSY	GOSSYPOL	HIILMTUY	HUMILITY
	USURPING	GLOOPTYY	LOGOTYPY	HIILOPST	PISOLITH
GINPRSUY	SYRUPING		TYPOLOGY	HIILPSST	THLIPSIS
GINPSSUW	UPSWINGS	GLOORSUU	ORGULOUS	HIILPSSY	SYPHILIS
GINPSTTU	PUTTINGS	GLOOSTUW	OUTGLOWS	HIILRSTT	TRILITHS
GINPTTUY	PUTTYING	GMMPSUUW	MUGWUMPS	HIILRSTY	SHIRTILY
GINRSSTU	RUSTINGS	GMNNOOOY	MONOGONY	HIILSSTT	SHITLIST
	TRUSSING	GMNNOOYY	MONOGYNY		STILTISH
GINRSTTU	RUTTINGS	GMNOORSU	GUNROOMS	HIILSTTY	SHITTILY
	STURTING	GMNOORSW	MORWONGS	HIIMNSTT	TINSMITH
	TRUSTING	GMORSTUW	MUGWORTS	HIIMOPSS	PHIMOSIS
GINRSTTY	TRYSTING	GNNOPRSU	UNSPRUNG	HIIMSSTT	SHITTIMS
GINRSTUU	SUTURING	GNNRSTUU	UNSTRUNG	HIINNNSY	NINNYISH
GINSTTTU	TUTTINGS	GNOOORSS	GORSOONS	HIINNOST	THIONINS
GIOOORSV	VIGOROSO	GNOOOSSS	GOSSOONS	HIINORST	HISTRION
GIOOPRRS	PORRIGOS	GNOORSUW	WRONGOUS	HIINPSTW	TWINSHIP
GIOORRSU	RIGOROUS	GNOORTUW	OUTGROWN	HIIOPRSW	POWHIRIS
GIOORSTU	GOITROUS	GNOPRSTU	GUNPORTS	HIIORSST	HISTRIOS
GIOORSUV	VIGOROUS	GNOPRSUW	GROWNUPS	HIIPPQSU	QUIPPISH
GIOPRRSU	PRURIGOS	GNOSTUUW	OUTSWUNG	HIIPRTTU	PUIRTITH
GIOPRSSY	GOSSIPRY	GNPPRSUU	UPSPRUNG	HIIQRSSU	SQUIRISH
GIOPRSTU	GROUPIST	GOOPRSST	GOSPORTS	HIISSSSY	SISSYISH
GIORSTUY	RUGOSITY	GOOPRTUU	OUTGROUP	HIISSTTT	TSITSITH
GIOSTYYZ	ZYGOSITY	GOORSSTU	OUTGROSS	HIISSTXY	SIXTYISH
GJLMNOPU	LONGJUMP	GOORSTUW	OUTGROWS	HIITTTZZ	TZITZITH
GJOORSTT	JOGTROTS	GOORTTUW	GOUTWORT	HIKKNSUU	INUKSHUK
GKKNOOSS	SONGKOKS	HHIIIOOP	PIHOIHOI	HIKLNOST	HOTLINKS
GKLOOOTY	TOKOLOGY	HHIILOPT	THIOPHIL	HIKLORTY	KRYOLITH

HIKMNSUU	MINSHUKU	**HIMOPSST**	MOSHPITS	**HLPRSUUY**	SULPHURY
HIKMOSTZ	SHKOTZIM		PHOTISMS	**HMMNOOSY**	HOMONYMS
HIKNNORS	INKHORNS	**HIMORSST**	RIMSHOTS	**HMMNOOYY**	HOMONYMY
HIKNNSTU	UNTHINKS	**HIMORSTU**	HUMORIST	**HMMOORSU**	MUSHROOM
HIKNOOSU	HOKONUIS		THORIUMS	**HMMRSTUU**	HUMSTRUM
HIKNOTTU	OUTTHINK	**HIMORSTW**	MISTHROW	**HMNOOOST**	MOONSHOT
HIKOOPRZ	PIROZHOK	**HIMOSTTV**	MITSVOTH	**HMNOOOTY**	HOMOTONY
HIKOOPSS	SPOOKISH	**HIMOTTVZ**	MITZVOTH	**HMNOORRW**	HORNWORM
HIKOPSSY	KYPHOSIS	**HIMPRSTU**	TRIUMPHS	**HMNOOSTU**	UNSMOOTH
HILLMSUY	MULISHLY	**HIMPSTUY**	PYTHIUMS	**HMNOPSYY**	HYPONYMS
HILLNOUY	UNHOLILY	**HIMRSSTY**	RHYMISTS		SYMPHONY
HILLOOPT	LOPOLITH	**HIMRSTTU**	MISTRUTH	**HMNOPYYY**	HYPONYMY
HILLOOST	LITHOSOL	**HIMSSTTY**	MYTHISTS	**HMOOOPRZ**	ZOOMORPH
HILLOPST	HILLTOPS	**HINNORST**	TINHORNS	**HMOOORSW**	SHOWROOM
HILLOSWY	OWLISHLY	**HINNPSSU**	NUNSHIPS	**HMOOPTYY**	HOMOTYPY
HILLPSUY	PLUSHILY	**HINNSSUY**	SUNSHINY	**HMOORSUU**	HUMOROUS
HILLSSUY	SLUSHILY	**HINOORST**	HORNITOS	**HMOORTUU**	OUTHUMOR
HILMMOSU	HOLMIUMS	**HINOORSZ**	HORIZONS	**HNNORTTU**	NONTRUTH
HILMNOOT	MONOLITH	**HINOPPSS**	SHIPPONS	**HNNOSSTY**	SYNTHONS
HILMOOPT	PHILOMOT	**HINOPSSS**	SONSHIPS	**HNOOOOPR**	OOPHORON
HILMOPSY	MOPISHLY	**HINOPSSY**	HYPNOSIS	**HNOOPPYY**	HYPOPYON
HILMOPYY	MYOPHILY	**HINOPSTW**	TOWNSHIP	**HNOOPRSW**	SHOPWORN
HILMOSSW	WHOLISMS	**HINORSST**	HORNISTS	**HNOOPRTU**	HORNPOUT
HILMOTUY	MOUTHILY	**HINORTXY**	THYROXIN	**HNOOPSTY**	TYPHOONS
HILMPPSU	PLUMPISH	**HINOSSTU**	SNOUTISH	**HNOORRTW**	HORNWORT
HILMPRTU	PHILTRUM	**HINPPSSU**	PUSHPINS	**HNOORSTU**	SOUTHRON
HILMPSYY	SYMPHILY	**HIOOOPRT**	HOROPITO	**HNOOSSTU**	UNSHOOTS
HILMSTUU	THULIUMS	**HIOOOPRZ**	ZOOPHORI	**HNOPRTUW**	UPTHROWN
HILNOPSU	UNPOLISH	**HIOOPRTT**	POORTITH	**HNORSTUW**	UNWORTHS
HILNORTY	THORNILY	**HIOORSST**	ORTHOSIS	**HNORTUWY**	UNWORTHY
HILNOSTY	THIONYLS	**HIOOSSTT**	SHOOTIST	**HNOSSTUU**	UNSHOUTS
	TONISHLY	**HIOPRSSW**	WORSHIPS	**HNOSTTUU**	OUTHUNTS
HILOOPYZ	ZOOPHILY	**HIOPRSUZ**	RHIZOPUS	**HNRSTTUU**	UNTRUTHS
HILOOSTT	OTOLITHS	**HIOPSSST**	SOPHISTS	**HOOOSTTU**	OUTSHOOT
HILOOSTZ	ZOOLITHS	**HIOPSSTU**	UPHOISTS		SHOOTOUT
HILOOTTY	TOOTHILY	**HIOPSSTY**	PHYTOSIS		
HILOPPSY	POPISHLY	**HIORRSSY**	SORRYISH	**HOOPPSST**	POTSHOPS
HILOPSXY	OXYPHILS	**HIOSSTTU**	STOUTISH	**HOOPPSTY**	PHOTOPSY
HILORSTU	UROLITHS	**HIOSTTUW**	WITHOUTS	**HOOPPRST**	PORTHORS
HILORSUU	URUSHIOL	**HIPPPSUY**	PUPPYISH	**HOOPSSTT**	HOTSPOTS
HILORTUW	OUTWHIRL	**HIPSUYZZ**	ZIZYPHUS		POTSHOTS
HILORTWY	WORTHILY	**HJNNOOSS**	JOHNSONS	**HOOPSSTU**	UPSHOOTS
HILOSSTW	WHOLISTS	**HKKLOOSY**	KOLKHOSY	**HOOPSSTW**	POSTSHOW
HILOSSTY	HYLOISTS	**HKKLOOYZ**	KOLKHOZY	**HOOPSSTY**	TOYSHOPS
	THYLOSIS	**HKKOOPYY**	HOKYPOKY	**HOOQSSUY**	SQUOOSHY
HILOSTWW	WHITLOWS	**HKKOOSSY**	SKYHOOKS	**HOORTTUW**	OUTTHROW
HILOSTYY	TOYISHLY	**HKMNORRU**	KRUMHORN		OUTWORTH
HILPPRSU	PURPLISH	**HKMOOORW**	HOOKWORM	**HOOSSTTU**	OUTSHOTS
HILPPSUY	UPPISHLY	**HKNNRSUU**	UNSHRUNK	**HOOSTTUU**	OUTSHOUT
HILPRSUW	UPWHIRLS	**HKNOORRW**	HORNWORK	**HOPPRRYY**	PORPHYRY
HILSSTTU	SLUTTISH	**HKNOOSWW**	KNOWHOWS	**HOPRRSUY**	PYRRHOUS
HIMMOPRU	PHORMIUM	**HKOOOPST**	POTHOOKS	**HOPRSSTU**	HOTSPURS
HIMMSSTY	MYTHISMS	**HKOOPRSW**	WORKSHOP	**HOPRSTUW**	UPTHROWS
HIMNOPRS	MORPHINS	**HKOORRUW**	WORKHOUR	**HOPSSTTU**	SHOTPUTS
HIMNOPRX	PHORMINX	**HKOOSVYZ**	SOVKHOZY	**HORRSTTU**	THRUSTOR
HIMNOPSY	PHISNOMY	**HLLLOOWY**	HOLLOWLY	**HOSSTTUU**	SHUTOUTS
HIMNOSTY	THYMOSIN	**HLLMNOOU**	MONOHULL	**HPRSTTUU**	THRUPUTS
HIMNSSTY	HYMNISTS	**HLLOPPRY**	PROPHYLL		UPTHRUST
HIMOOPRS	ISOMORPH	**HLMOOSTY**	SMOOTHLY	**IIIJJLNS**	JINJILIS
HIMOPRRT	TRIMORPH	**HLMORRSY**	MYRRHOLS	**IIIKLNPS**	SPILIKIN
HIMOPRSS	ORPHISMS	**HLNOOPPY**	POLYPHON	**IIIKMNNS**	MINIKINS
HIMOPRSW	SHIPWORM	**HLOOSTUW**	OUTHOWLS	**IIIKMNSS**	MINISKIS
HIMOPRWW	WHIPWORM	**HLOPRSTY**	PROTHYLS	**IIILLMMN**	MINIMILL
HIMOPSSS	SOPHISMS	**HLPRSSUU**	SULPHURS	**IIILLMNP**	MINIPILL

IIILLMNU	ILLINIUM	IILMRSSY	MISSILRY	IINNQSTU	QUINTINS
IIILLNOS	ILLISION	IILNNOOT	NOLITION	IINNSTTU	TINNITUS
IIILMRSV	VIRILISM	IILNNOQU	QUINOLIN	IINOOPST	POSITION
IIILMUVX	LIXIVIUM	IILNNOST	NITINOLS	IINOPSSS	ISOSPINS
IIILRTVY	VIRILITY	IILNNSSU	INSULINS	IINORSST	IRONISTS
IIIMMMNS	MINIMISM	IILNOOST	INOSITOL	IINORSTT	INTROITS
IIIMMNST	INTIMISM	IILNOOTV	VOLITION	IINOSTTU	TUITIONS
	MINIMIST	IILNOPST	PINITOLS	IINOSTVY	VINOSITY
IIIMMPRS	IMPRIMIS	IILNORSS	SIRLOINS	IINRTTUY	TRIUNITY
IIIMNSTT	INTIMIST	IILNPPSY	SNIPPILY	IINSSTTW	INTWISTS
IIIMNTTY	INTIMITY	IILNRTWY	WINTRILY	IIOOPSTV	OVIPOSIT
IIINORRS	IRRISION	IILOOPPR	LIRIPOOP	IIOORRRR	RIRORIRO
IIINPRST	INSPIRIT	IILOPRST	TRIPOLIS	IIOOSTTY	OTIOSITY
IIINQTUY	INIQUITY	IILOPSSS	PSILOSIS	IIOPRRTY	PRIORITY
IIINSSTU	SINUITIS	IILOPSST	PTILOSIS	IIOPRSSS	PISSOIRS
IIIOSTTU	OUISTITI	IILOPSTY	PILOSITY	IIORRRSY	IRRISORY
IIISSTTW	WISTITIS	IILORSTT	TROILIST	IIORSSTV	IVORISTS
IIJJSTUU	JIUJITSU	IILORSTV	VITRIOLS		VISITORS
IIJLLNOS	JILLIONS	IILOSSTV	VIOLISTS	IIORSTUV	VIRTUOSI
IIJMNOSS	MISJOINS	IILPRSSY	PRISSILY	IIOSSTTU	OUSTITIS
IIJNNOST	INJOINTS	IILRSSTU	SILURIST	IIPRSSTU	SPIRITUS
IIJNNSTU	NINJITSU	IILSSTTT	TITLISTS	IJJMSSUU	JUJUISMS
IIKKLNOS	KOLINSKI	IILSTUUV	UVULITIS	IJJSSTUU	JUJUISTS
IIKKMMUU	KUMIKUMI	IILSTUVV	VULVITIS		JUJUISTS
IIKKNPSS	KIPSKINS	IIMMMNSU	MINIMUMS	IJJSTUUU	JIUJUTSU
IIKLLNOS	SKILLION	IIMMNOOT	MINIMOTO	IJKLLOSY	KILLJOYS
IIKLLNSY	SLINKILY	IIMMNTUY	IMMUNITY	IJLNOQSU	JONQUILS
IIKLMNPS	LIMPKINS	IIMMOORR	MIROMIRO	IJMPSTUU	JUMPSUIT
IIKLMPSY	SKIMPILY	IIMMOPST	OPTIMISM	IJNNOSTU	UNJOINTS
IIKLMRSY	SMIRKILY	IIMMOPSU	OPIUMISM	IJNNSTUU	NINJUTSU
IIKLNOSS	OILSKINS	IIMMSTTU	MITTIMUS	IKKLNORW	LINKWORK
IIKLQRUY	QUIRKILY	IIMNNOOT	MONITION	IKKLNOSY	KOLINSKY
IIKMNNOO	MONOKINI	IIMNNOSU	MISUNION	IKKMNOSU	KIKUMONS
IIKMNORS	KIRIMONS		UNIONISM	IKKMOOOR	KOROMIKO
IIKMNPSS	SIMPKINS	IIMNNOTU	MUNITION	IKKNORST	KIRKTONS
IIKNOSTT	STOTINKI	IIMNOOSS	OMISSION	IKKORSSY	SIKORSKY
IILLLMUX	MILLILUX	IIMNOPRS	IMPRISON	IKLLMORW	MILLWORK
IILLLPTU	LILLIPUT	IIMNOPST	MISPOINT	IKLLOOTV	KILOVOLT
IILLLPUV	PULVILLI	IIMNORTT	INTROMIT	IKLLOSSY	KYLLOSIS
IILLMNOS	MILLIONS	IIMNORTY	MINORITY	IKLLOSTU	OUTKILLS
IILLMRTU	TRILLIUM	IIMNOSSS	MISSIONS	IKLLPSSU	UPSKILLS
IILLMUUV	ILLUVIUM	IIMNOSST	SIMONIST	IKLMNPSU	LUMPKINS
IILLNOOR	ORILLION	IIMNOSTX	MIXTIONS	IKLMOOSS	LOOKISMS
IILLNOPS	PILLIONS	IIMNPRST	IMPRINTS		LOOKSISM
IILLNORT	TRILLION		MISPRINT	IKLMOPSS	MILKSOPS
IILLNOST	STILLION	IIMNPTUY	IMPUNITY	IKLMORSW	SILKWORM
IILLNOSU	ILLUSION	IIMNRSTY	MINISTRY	IKLMORTW	MILKWORT
IILLNOSZ	ZILLIONS	IIMOPSTT	OPTIMIST	IKLMOSSY	SOYMILKS
IILLNSST	INSTILLS	IIMORSTY	RIMOSITY	IKLNOOST	KILOTONS
IILLNSTT	LITTLINS	IIMOSSTY	MYOSITIS	IKLNOOSW	WOOLSKIN
IILLOPQU	PIQUILLO	IIMOTTVY	MOTIVITY	IKLNOPST	SLIPKNOT
IILLOPUV	PULVILIO	IIMPRTUY	IMPURITY	IKLNOTTY	KNOTTILY
IILLPPSY	SLIPPILY	IIMRRTUV	TRIUMVIR	IKLNPSSU	SKULPINS
IILMMNSU	LUMINISM	IIMRSTTU	TRITIUMS	IKLNPSUY	SPUNKILY
IILMMPSS	SIMPLISM	IIMRSTUV	TRIVIUMS	IKLOOPSY	SPOOKILY
IILMMSUU	SIMULIUM	IIMSSSTU	MISSUITS	IKLOOSST	LOOKISTS
IILMMSWY	SWIMMILY	IIMSSTUW	SWIMSUIT	IKLOOSTT	TOOLKITS
IILMNORT	MIRLITON	IINNOOPS	OPINIONS	IKLOSSSU	SOUSLIKS
IILMNOSS	LIONISMS	IINNOPPT	PINPOINT	IKMNNOSW	MISKNOWN
IILMNSTU	LUMINIST	IINNOPTU	PUNITION	IKMNOOOS	OKIMONOS
IILMORSS	SIMILORS	IINNOSTU	INUSTION	IKMNOORS	OMIKRONS
IILMORST	TROILISM		UNIONIST	IKMNOOSS	MONOSKIS
IILMOTTY	MOTILITY		UNITIONS	IKMNOSSW	MISKNOWS
IILMPSST	SIMPLIST	IINNPSST	TINSNIPS	IKMNPPSU	PUMPKINS

IKMNRSTU	TRINKUMS	ILNNORSU	LINURONS	IMNOORTY	MONITORY
IKNNOPSY	PONYSKIN	ILNOOPRT	PLIOTRON		MORONITY
IKNNRSTU	TURNSKIN	ILNOOPSS	PLOSIONS	IMNOORVY	OMNIVORY
IKNOOPRT	PINKROOT	ILNOOPSV	VOLPINOS	IMNOOSUX	OXONIUMS
IKNOORRW	IRONWORK	ILNOOPSY	SNOOPILY	IMNOPPSU	PUMPIONS
IKNOOSST	ISOKONTS		SPOONILY	IMNOPRSW	PINWORMS
IKNOPRSW	PINWORKS	ILNOORSS	ROSINOLS	IMNOPSSU	SPUMONIS
IKNOPSST	INKSPOTS	ILNOORTW	TOILWORN	IMNORRSU	MURRIONS
IKNOPSSY	PYKNOSIS	ILNOOSST	SOLITONS	IMNORSTY	TRIONYMS
IKNOPSTT	STINKPOT	ILNOOSTU	SOLUTION	IMNOSTUU	MUTINOUS
IKNOPSTW	TOWNSKIP	ILNOOSTY	SNOOTILY	IMNRSTUU	UNTRUISM
IKNORSTW	TINWORKS	ILNOOTUV	VOLUTION	IMOOPRRS	PROMISOR
IKNPSSTU	SPUTNIKS	ILNOPRSU	PURLOINS	IMOOPRST	IMPOSTOR
IKORSSTU	KURTOSIS	ILNOPSSU	PULSIONS	IMOOPRSU	IMPOROUS
IKORSTTU	OUTSKIRT		UPSILONS	IMOOQSTU	MOSQUITO
ILLLMOPS	PLIMSOLL	ILNOPSSW	SNOWSLIP	IMOORRTT	TRIMOTOR
ILLLMPPU	PULPMILL	ILNOPSSY	YPSILONS	IMOORSTT	MOTORIST
ILLLOOPP	LOLLIPOP	ILNOPSTU	UNSPOILT	IMOORSTU	SUMOTORI
ILLLOOWY	WOOLLILY	ILNORSST	NOSTRILS		TIMOROUS
ILLLOPPY	POLYPILL	ILNORSSU	SURLOINS	IMOORSTY	MOROSITY
ILLLOPUV	PULVILLO	ILNORSTU	TORULINS	IMOORTVY	VOMITORY
ILLMNOSU	MULLIONS	ILNORSTY	NITROSYL	IMOOSSTY	MYOSOTIS
ILLMNRSU	MILLRUNS	ILNORTXY	NITROXYL	IMOOSTUV	VOMITOUS
ILLMOORS	MOORILLS	ILNOSSTW	STOWLINS	IMOPPRRU	PROPRIUM
ILLMOOST	TIMOLOLS	ILNOSSTY	TYLOSINS	IMOPRRSY	PRIMROSY
ILLMOPRW	PILLWORM	ILNOSTTY	SNOTTILY	IMOPRSST	TROPISMS
ILLMOPSS	PLIMSOLS	ILNOSTUV	VOLUTINS	IMOPRSTU	PROTIUMS
ILLMOSSY	LISSOMLY	ILNOSUVY	VINOUSLY	IMOPSSST	MISSTOPS
ILLMPSUY	PSYLLIUM	ILNPSUUV	PULVINUS	IMOPSSTU	UTOPISMS
ILLMPTUY	MULTIPLY	ILOOORSS	ROSOLIOS	IMORSSST	MISSORTS
ILLNOORT	TORNILLO	ILOOPPRS	PROPOLIS	IMORSSTU	TOURISMS
ILLNOQSU	QUILLONS	ILOOPSST	POLOISTS	IMORSTTU	MISTUTOR
ILLNORSU	RULLIONS		TOPSOILS		TUTORISM
ILLNPSUU	LUPULINS	ILOORSTU	RISOLUTO	IMOSSSTU	MISSOUTS
ILLOOPRW	POORWILL	ILOOSSST	SOLOISTS		SUMOISTS
ILLOORSZ	ZORILLOS	ILOPPSTU	POPULIST	IMOSSTUW	OUTSWIMS
ILLOORTT	ROTOTILL	ILOPPTUU	OUTPUPIL	IMPPPSUY	PUPPYISM
ILLOPPSS	SLIPSLOP	ILOPRSTY	SPORTILY	IMRSSSTU	SISTRUMS
ILLOPPSY	SLOPPILY	ILOPSSTU	SLIPOUTS	IMRSSTTU	MISTRUST
ILLOPRTW	PILLWORT	ILOPSTTY	SPOTTILY	IMRSSTTY	MISTRYST
ILLOPRXY	PROLIXLY	ILOPSUUV	PLUVIOUS	IMRSTTUY	YTTRIUMS
ILLOPSST	POLLISTS	ILOQRTUU	LOQUITUR	INNNNOOU	NONUNION
ILLORSTU	TROLLIUS	ILPPRTUY	PULPITRY	INNNOOPT	NONPOINT
ILLORSUY	ILLUSORY	ILRSTTUY	TRUSTILY	INNNOPRT	NONPRINT
ILLOSSYY	LYOLYSIS	ILRSTUUX	LUXURIST	INNNORSU	RUNNIONS
ILLOSTUW	OUTWILLS	ILSSSTTY	STYLISTS	INNNORTU	TRUNNION
ILLOSTXY	XYLITOLS	IMMNOORS	MORONISM	INNNOSTY	SYNTONIN
ILLOTTWY	WITTOLLY	IMMNOSSU	MUSIMONS	INNOOPRT	TROPONIN
ILLRSTUY	SULTRILY	IMMNOSUU	MUONIUMS	INNOOPRU	PROUNION
ILMMSSSU	SLUMISMS	IMMOORTU	MOTORIUM	INNOOPSS	OPSONINS
ILMNOOPS	POLONISM	IMMOPSTU	OPTIMUMS		SPONSION
ILMNOOPU	POLONIUM	IMMOSSTU	STOMIUMS	INNOOPSU	UNPOISON
ILMNOSUU	LUMINOUS	IMMRSTUY	SUMMITRY	INNOORST	NOTORNIS
ILMNOTTU	MULTITON	IMMSSSTU	SUMMISTS	INNOPRSU	UNPRISON
ILMOPPSU	POPULISM	IMNNNOSU	MUNNIONS	INNORTTU	NOTTURNI
ILMORSTU	TURMOILS	IMNNOORS	NORIMONS	INNOSSTU	NONSUITS
ILMORSTY	STORMILY	IMNNOOTT	MONOTINT	INOOOSSZ	ZOONOSIS
ILMOSTUV	VOLUMIST	IMNNOSUU	NUMINOUS	INOOOTXZ	ZOOTOXIN
ILMOSTUY	TIMOUSLY	IMNOOPPS	POMPIONS	INOOPRST	PORTIONS
ILMPPTUU	PULPITUM	IMNOOPST	TOMPIONS		POSITRON
ILMPSSTU	PLUMISTS	IMNOOPSU	OPSONIUM		SORPTION
ILMPSTUY	STUMPILY	IMNOORRS	MORRIONS	INOOPSSS	POISSONS
ILMSSTUU	STIMULUS	IMNOORST	MONITORS	INOOPSST	POSITONS
ILMSTTUY	SMUTTILY		TROMINOS	INOOPSTT	SPITTOON

Letters	Word(s)
INOOPTTU	OUTPOINT
INOORSST	ISOTRONS
	TORSIONS
INOORSSU	ROSINOUS
INOORSTT	TORTONIS
INOORSTY	SONORITY
INOOSTTV	STOTINOV
INOPPSST	TOPSPINS
INOPRTTU	PRINTOUT
INOPRTUY	PUNITORY
INOPSSSU	POUSSINS
INOPSSSY	SYNOPSIS
INOPSSTU	SPINOUTS
INORSSUV	UNVISORS
INOSSTUW	SNOWSUIT
INPPRRUU	PURPURIN
INPRRSTU	SURPRINT
INPRSSTU	UNSTRIPS
INPRSSTY	TRYPSINS
INPRSTTU	TURNSPIT
INRSSTTU	INTRUSTS
INRSTTUU	UNITRUST
INSSSTUU	SUNSUITS
INSSTTUW	UNTWISTS
IOOPRRSV	PROVISOR
IOOPRSSV	PROVISOS
IOOPRSSY	ISOSPORY
IOOPRSTT	POSTRIOT
IOOPRSTY	ISOTROPY
	POROSITY
IOORRSTY	SORORITY
IOORRTTT	TROTTOIR
IOORSSTT	RISOTTOS
IOORSSUV	VOUSSOIR
IOORSTTU	TORTIOUS
IOORSTTY	TOROSITY
IOORSTUV	VIRTUOSO
IOORSUUX	UXORIOUS
IOOSSTTU	STOTIOUS
IOPPPRST	PITPROPS
IOPPRSST	RIPSTOPS
IOPRRSUV	PROVIRUS
IOPRSSTT	PROTISTS
	TROPISTS
IOPRSSUU	SPURIOUS
IOPRSTTU	OUTSTRIP
IOPRSTUU	POURSUIT
IOPRSTUY	PYRITOUS
IOPRSUVX	POXVIRUS
IOPSSTTU	UTOPISTS
IOQRSTTU	QUITTORS
IOQRSTUU	TURQUOIS
IOQRTUXY	QUIXOTRY
IORRSSST	TSORRISS
IORRSUVV	SURVIVOR
IORSSTTU	TOURISTS
IORSSTTW	TWISTORS
IORSSUUU	USURIOUS
IORSTTUY	TOURISTY
	YTTRIOUS
IORSTUUV	VIRTUOUS
IPPTTTUY	TITTUPPY
IPRRSSTU	STIRRUPS
IPRRSTUU	PRURITUS
IPRSSTUU	PURSUITS
JJSSTUUU	JUJUTSUS
JLNSTUUY	UNJUSTLY
JLOOSUYY	JOYOUSLY
JMOPSTUU	OUTJUMPS
JNNOORRU	NONJUROR
JNOORSSU	SOJOURNS
JNOOSUYY	UNJOYOUS
KKMMOOOO	MOKOMOKO
KKNOORTW	KNOTWORK
KKOOOOTT	TOKOTOKO
KKOOSSUU	KOUSKOUS
KLLMNSUU	NUMSKULL
KLLMOSSU	MOLLUSKS
KLNORSTY	KLYSTRON
KLOOORWW	WOOLWORK
KLOOOSTU	LOOKOUTS
	OUTLOOKS
KLOOPRSW	SLOPWORK
KLOSSTUU	OUTSULKS
KMOOORRW	WORKROOM
KMOORSTU	MUSKROOT
KNNNOSUW	UNKNOWNS
KNOOPSTT	TOPKNOTS
KNOPPSTU	POSTPUNK
KNOPRSTY	KRYPTONS
KNORRSTY	KRYTRONS
KOOORSTV	VOORSKOT
KOOPRSTW	TOPWORKS
	WORKTOPS
KOORSTUW	OUTWORKS
	WORKOUTS
KORRSTWY	TRYWORKS
KORSTTUW	TUTWORKS
LLLMMSUU	MULMULLS
LLLOOPPY	LOLLYPOP
LLMOOPRS	ROLLMOPS
LLMOPRUU	PULLORUM
LLOOPRST	TROLLOPS
LLOOPRTY	TROLLOPY
LLOOPSTU	OUTPOLLS
LLOORSTU	OUTROLLS
	ROLLOUTS
LLOPSTUU	OUTPULLS
	PULLOUTS
LLOSUUVV	VOLVULUS
LMNOOOPY	MONOPOLY
LMNOOPYY	POLYONYM
LMOOOOPR	POOLROOM
LMOOOORT	TOOLROOM
LMOOPRTU	PULMOTOR
LMOOPSYY	POLYSOMY
LMOORSWW	SLOWWORM
LMOOSSSU	MOLOSSUS
LMOOTXYY	XYLOTOMY
LMOPPRTY	PROMPTLY
LMOSTUUU	TUMULOUS
LMRSSTUU	LUSTRUMS
LNOOOPRT	POLTROON
LNOOOPYZ	POLYZOON
LNOOPPRY	PROPYLON
LNOOPSSU	UNSPOOLS
LNOOPSTU	PULTOONS
LNOOPSWW	SNOWPLOW
LNRSTUUV	VULTURNS
LOOOORSS	OLOROSOS
LOOPPSUU	POPULOUS
LOOPPSUY	POLYPOUS
LOOPRSTT	STOLPORT
LOOPRSUY	POROUSLY
LOOPSTTU	OUTPLOTS
LORSSTUU	LUSTROUS
MMNNOOSY	MONONYMS
MMNOOOSY	MONOSOMY
MMOORTTY	TOMMYROT
MMOPSSTY	SYMPTOMS
MNNOOOSS	MONSOONS
MNNOOOTY	MONOTONY
MNNOORSU	MONURONS
MNNOPRTU	NONTRUMP
MNNOSSYY	SYNONYMS
MNNOSYYY	SYNONYMY
MNOOOPPS	POMPOONS
MNOOOPRT	MOONPORT
MNOOORTW	MOONWORT
MNOOORXY	OXYMORON
MNOOPRTU	PRONOTUM
MNOOPSTY	TOPONYMS
MNOOPTYY	TOPONYMY
MNOORSSU	SUNROOMS
MNOOSTTW	TOWMONTS
MNORSSTU	NOSTRUMS
MNORSTUU	SURMOUNT
MOOOPRRT	PROMOTOR
MOOORRTW	MOORWORT
	ROOTWORM
	TOMORROW
	WORMROOT
MOOPSSSU	OPOSSUMS
MOORRSUU	RUMOROUS
MOORSTUU	TUMOROUS
MOORSTUY	UROSTOMY
MOPRTTUU	OUTTRUMP
MORRSSTU	ROSTRUMS
MORSSTUU	STRUMOUS
MSSTTUUU	TSUTSUMU
NNOOOPST	PONTOONS
	SPONTOON
NNOOPRSU	PRONOUNS
NNOOPSSS	SPONSONS
NNOOPSST	NONSTOPS
NNOORSTY	NONSTORY
NNOORTTU	NOTTURNO
NOOOPPRS	PROSOPON
NOOORSSU	SONOROUS
NOOPRSSS	SPONSORS
NOORSSTU	UNROOSTS
NOORSTUW	OUTSWORN
NOPSSSTU	SUNSPOTS
NORSTTUU	OUTTURNS
	TURNOUTS
NOSTTTUU	OUTSTUNT
NRSSTTUU	UNTRUSTS
NRSTTUUY	UNTRUSTY
OOOOPRST	POTOROOS
OOOPRSSU	SOPOROUS
OOOPRSTU	OUTROOPS

OOORSTTU	OUTROOTS	OOPSSSTT	TOSSPOTS	OPRSSSUU	SOURPUSS
OOPRSSSU	SOURSOPS	OOPSSTTU	OUTPOSTS	ORRSSTTU	TRUSTORS
OOPRSSTV	PROVOSTS	OORSTTTU	OUTTROTS	ORSSTTUU	SURTOUTS
OOPRSTTU	OUTPORTS	OORSTTUU	TORTUOUS	RRSSSUUU	SUSURRUS
	OUTSPORT	OPPRRSTU	PURPORTS		
OOPRSTUU	OUTPOURS	OPPRSSTU	SUPPORTS		

Transposals

Some words consist of two elements which can be transposed to give a different word. These are some of the easiest anagrams to remember, and so we include a complete list here.

Transposals, A–Z

ABACAS	– CASABA	**CAPA**	– PACA	**EXUL**	– ULEX
ADDY	– DYAD	**CAPI**	– PICA	**FENI**	– NIFE
ALAN	– ANAL	**CEDI**	– DICE	**FERLIE**	– LIEFER
ALBA	– BAAL	**CHIN**	– INCH	**FESTER**	– TERFES
ALCO	– COAL	**CHIT**	– ITCH	**FOIN**	– INFO
ALME	– MEAL	**CHOREE**	– REECHO	**FRYPAN**	– PANFRY
ALOD	– ODAL	**CHOU**	– OUCH	**GAME**	– MEGA
ANKH	– KHAN	**COATTAIL**	– TAILCOAT	**GASMAN**	– MANGAS
ANNA	– NAAN	**CODE**	– DECO	**GAVE**	– VEGA
APSO	– SOAP	**COMEDOWN**	– DOWNCOME	**GAZY**	– ZYGA
ARCH	– CHAR	**COMEOVER**	– OVERCOME	**GEARHEAD**	– HEADGEAR
ARKS	– KSAR	**CONGAS**	– GASCON	**GERMAN**	– MANGER
ARLE	– LEAR	**COSE**	– SECO	**GERMIN**	– MINGER
ARSE	– SEAR	**CUTOFF**	– OFFCUT	**GESSED**	– SEDGES
ARTI	– TIAR	**DELO**	– LODE	**GORE**	– REGO
ARTS	– TSAR	**DEMO**	– MODE	**GOSSAN**	– SANGOS
ARVO	– VOAR	**DENI**	– NIDE	**GUTROT**	– ROTGUT
ATABAL	– BALATA	**DERE**	– REDE	**HANDOVER**	– OVERHAND
BABU	– BUBA	**DERO**	– RODE	**HANGOVER**	– OVERHANG
BACKFALL	– FALLBACK	**DESI**	– SIDE	**HAPU**	– PUHA
BACKFIRE	– FIREBACK	**DEVA**	– VADE	**HEADLONG**	– LONGHEAD
BACKLIFT	– LIFTBACK	**DIETED**	– TEDDIE	**HEADRAIL**	– RAILHEAD
BACKSEAT	– SEATBACK	**DIKA**	– KADI	**HERMIT**	– MITHER
BAJU	– JUBA	**DINO**	– NODI	**HILLSIDE**	– SIDEHILL
BALSAM	– SAMBAL	**DISA**	– SADI	**HOLDOVER**	– OVERHOLD
BARSTOOL	– TOOLBARS	**DISMAN**	– MANDIS	**HOMETOWN**	– TOWNHOME
BEDE	– DEBE	**DOOR**	– ORDO	**HOTSPOTS**	– POTSHOTS
BEDLAM	– LAMBED	**DORE**	– REDO	**HOWRES**	– RESHOW
BEMA	– MABE	**DOUN**	– UNDO	**HUNGOVER**	– OVERHUNG
BIRDCAGE	– CAGEBIRD	**DOUP**	– UPDO	**IDOL**	– OLID
BIRDSONG	– SONGBIRD	**DOVERING**	– RINGDOVE	**ILKA**	– KAIL
BITTUR	– TURBIT	**DOWNPLAY**	– PLAYDOWN	**INRO**	– ROIN
BOHO	– HOBO	**DOWNTURN**	– TURNDOWN	**INSOLE**	– OLEINS
BOILOVER	– OVERBOIL	**DYED**	– EDDY	**ISLE**	– LEIS
BOKO	– KOBO	**EDGE**	– GEED	**JAYVEE**	– VEEJAY
BOLO	– LOBO	**ELSE**	– SEEL	**JOMO**	– MOJO
BONEFISH	– FISHBONE	**EMIT**	– ITEM	**JOYPOP**	– POPJOY
BOOKCASE	– CASEBOOK	**ENAMEL**	– MELENA	**KATA**	– TAKA
BOOKWORK	– WORKBOOK	**EREV**	– EVER	**KATI**	– TIKA
BOOTJACK	– JACKBOOT	**ERGO**	– GOER	**KAWA**	– WAKA
BOZO	– ZOBO	**ERIC**	– ICER	**KEPI**	– PIKE
BUSHFIRE	– FIREBUSH	**ESKY**	– KYES	**KERMAS**	– MASKER
BUYOUT	– OUTBUY	**ESPY**	– PYES	**KERO**	– ROKE
CALO	– LOCA	**ESSE**	– SEES	**KETA**	– TAKE
CALPAS	– PASCAL	**ETAPES**	– PESETA	**KETO**	– TOKE

KOTO	– TOKO	METE	– TEME	PERVES	– VESPER
LAMA	– MALA	MISE	– SEMI	PITSAW	– SAWPIT
LAME	– MELA	MISSAL	– SALMIS	PORE	– REPO
LANA	– NALA	MOSH	– SHMO	PYRO	– ROPY
LARVAL	– VALLAR	NAVE	– VENA	RAGTAG	– TAGRAG
LATE	– TELA	NESTER	– TERNES	RASE	– SERA
LAVE	– VELA	NETE	– TENE	RASTER	– TERRAS
LAYOUT	– OUTLAY	NEVI	– VINE	RATA	– TARA
LENO	– NOLE	OAST	– STOA	RATO	– TORA
LEVA	– VALE	OFFPUT	– PUTOFF	RAVE	– VERA
LEVE	– VELE	OFFSET	– SETOFF	RITTER	– TERRIT
LEVO	– VOLE	ONTO	– TOON	ROADSIDE	– SIDEROAD
LIMA	– MALI	OPPO	– POOP	ROOTWORM	– WORMROOT
LINGSTER	– STERLING	OTTO	– TOOT	RORTER	– TERROR
LINTEL	– TELLIN	OUTPUT	– PUTOUT	ROTA	– TARO
LOCKPICK	– PICKLOCK	OUTRED	– REDOUT	ROTI	– TIRO
LOOKOVER	– OVERLOOK	OUTRIG	– RIGOUT	ROTO	– TORO
LYRE	– RELY	OUTRUN	– RUNOUT	RUTH	– THRU
MANE	– NEMA	OUTSET	– SETOUT	SALTUS	– TUSSAL
MANO	– NOMA	OVERPASS	– PASSOVER	SALVER	– VERSAL
MASA	– SAMA	OVERSLIP	– SLIPOVER	SELVES	– VESSEL
MASULA	– ULAMAS	OVERTAKE	– TAKEOVER	SERVER	– VERSER
MATESHIP	– SHIPMATE	OVERTURN	– TURNOVER	SHWA	– WASH
MEMO	– MOME	OVERWING	– WINGOVER	STYE	– YEST
MENO	– NOME	PANTRY	– TRYPAN	TACTIC	– TICTAC
MERI	– RIME	PARSEC	– SECPAR	TOUN	– UNTO
MESA	– SAME	PATE	– TEPA	WOODWORM	– WORMWOOD
MESE	– SEME	PEPO	– POPE		
META	– TAME	PERI	– RIPE